BIRTHDAY PERIOD OF FIRST PERSON

BIRTHDAY PERIOD OF SECOND PERSON

Second Person \ First Person	Sep 19–24	Sep 25–Oct 2	Oct 3–10	Oct 11–18	Oct 19–25	Oct 26–Nov 2	Nov 3–11	Nov 12–18	Nov 19–24	Nov 25–Dec 2	Dec 3–10	Dec 11–18	Dec 19–25	Dec 26–Jan 2	Jan 3–9	Jan 10–16	Jan 17–22	Jan 23–30	Jan 31–Feb 7	Feb 8–15	Feb 16–22	Feb 23–Mar 2	Mar 3–10	Mar 11–18
March 19–24	226	226	227	227	228	228	229	229	230	230	231	231	232	232	233	233	234	234	235	235	236	236	237	237
March 25–April 2	249	250	250	251	251	252	252	253	253	254	254	255	255	256	256	257	257	258	258	259	259	260	260	261
April 3–10	272	273	273	274	274	275	275	276	276	277	277	278	278	279	279	280	280	281	281	282	282	283	283	284
April 11–18	295	295	296	296	297	297	298	298	299	299	300	300	301	301	302	302	303	303	304	304	305	305	306	306
April 19–24	317	317	318	318	319	319	320	320	321	321	322	322	323	323	324	324	325	325	326	326	327	327	328	328
April 25–May 2	338	339	339	340	340	341	341	342	342	343	343	344	344	345	345	346	346	347	347	348	348	349	349	350
May 3–10	359	360	360	361	361	362	362	363	363	364	364	365	365	366	366	367	367	368	368	369	369	370	370	371
May 11–18	380	380	381	381	382	382	383	383	384	384	385	385	386	386	387	387	388	388	389	389	390	390	391	391
May 19–24	400	400	401	401	402	402	403	403	404	404	405	405	406	406	407	407	408	408	409	409	410	410	411	411
May 25–June 2	419	420	420	421	421	422	422	423	423	424	424	425	425	426	426	427	427	428	428	429	429	430	430	431
June 3–10	438	439	439	440	440	441	441	442	442	443	443	444	444	445	445	446	446	447	447	448	448	449	449	450
June 11–18	457	457	458	458	459	459	460	460	461	461	462	462	463	463	464	464	465	465	466	466	467	467	468	468
June 19–24	475	475	476	476	477	477	478	478	479	479	480	480	481	481	482	482	483	483	484	484	485	485	486	486
June 25–July 2	492	493	493	494	494	495	495	496	496	497	497	498	498	499	499	500	500	501	501	502	502	503	503	504
July 3–10	509	510	510	511	511	512	512	513	513	514	514	515	515	516	516	517	517	518	518	519	519	520	520	521
July 11–18	526	526	527	527	528	528	529	529	530	530	531	531	532	532	533	533	534	534	535	535	536	536	537	537
July 19–25	542	542	543	543	544	544	545	545	546	546	547	547	548	548	549	549	550	550	551	551	552	552	553	553
July 26–August 2	557	558	558	559	559	560	560	561	561	562	562	563	563	564	564	565	565	566	566	567	567	568	568	569
August 3–10	572	573	573	574	574	575	575	576	576	577	577	578	578	579	579	580	580	581	581	582	582	583	583	584
August 11–18	587	587	588	588	589	589	590	590	591	591	592	592	593	593	594	594	595	595	596	596	597	597	598	598
August 19–25	601	601	602	602	603	603	604	604	605	605	606	606	607	607	608	608	609	609	610	610	611	611	612	612
August 26–September 2	614	615	615	616	616	617	617	618	618	619	619	620	620	621	621	622	622	623	623	624	624	625	625	626
September 3–10	627	628	628	629	629	630	630	631	631	632	632	633	633	634	634	635	635	636	636	637	637	638	638	639
September 11–18	640	640	641	641	642	642	643	643	644	644	645	645	646	646	647	647	648	648	649	649	650	650	651	651
September 19–24	652	652	653	653	654	654	655	655	656	656	657	657	658	658	659	659	660	660	661	661	662	662	663	663
September 25–October 2	652	664	664	665	665	666	666	667	667	668	668	669	669	670	670	671	671	672	672	673	673	674	674	675
October 3–10	653	664	675	676	676	677	677	678	678	679	679	680	680	681	681	682	682	683	683	684	684	685	685	686
October 11–18	653	665	676	687	687	688	688	689	689	690	690	691	691	692	692	693	693	694	694	695	695	696	696	696
October 19–25	654	665	676	687	697	697	698	698	699	699	700	700	701	701	702	702	703	703	704	704	705	705	706	706
October 26–November 2	654	666	677	687	697	707	707	708	708	709	709	710	710	711	711	712	712	713	713	714	714	715	715	716
November 3–11	655	666	677	688	698	707	716	717	717	718	718	719	719	720	720	721	721	722	722	723	723	724	724	725
November 12–18	655	667	678	688	698	708	717	725	726	726	727	727	728	728	729	729	730	730	731	731	732	732	733	733
November 19–24	656	667	678	689	699	708	717	726	734	734	735	735	736	736	737	737	738	738	739	739	740	740	741	741
November 25–December 2	656	668	679	689	699	709	718	726	734	742	742	743	743	744	744	745	745	746	746	747	747	748	748	749
December 3–10	657	668	679	690	700	709	718	727	735	742	749	750	750	751	751	752	752	753	753	754	754	755	755	756
December 11–18	657	669	680	690	700	710	719	727	735	743	750	756	757	757	758	758	759	759	760	760	761	761	762	762
December 19–25	658	669	680	691	701	710	719	728	736	743	750	757	763	763	764	764	765	765	766	766	767	767	768	768
December 26–January 2	658	670	681	691	701	711	720	728	736	744	751	757	763	769	769	770	770	771	771	772	772	773	773	774
January 3–9	659	670	681	692	702	711	720	729	737	744	751	758	764	769	774	774	775	775	776	776	777	777	778	779
January 10–16	659	671	682	692	702	712	721	729	737	745	752	758	764	770	775	779	780	780	781	781	782	782	783	783
January 17–22	660	671	682	693	703	712	721	730	738	745	752	759	765	770	775	780	784	784	785	785	786	786	787	787
January 23–30	660	672	683	693	703	713	722	730	738	746	753	759	765	771	776	780	784	788	788	789	789	790	790	791
January 31–February 7	661	672	683	694	704	713	722	731	739	746	753	760	766	771	776	781	785	788	791	792	792	793	793	794
February 8–15	661	673	684	694	704	714	723	731	739	747	754	760	766	772	777	781	785	789	792	794	795	795	796	796
February 16–22	662	673	684	695	705	714	723	732	740	747	754	761	767	772	777	782	786	789	792	795	797	797	798	798
February 23–March 2	662	674	685	695	705	715	724	732	740	748	755	761	767	773	778	782	786	790	793	795	797	799	799	800
March 3–10	663	674	685	696	706	715	724	733	741	748	755	762	768	773	778	783	787	790	793	796	798	799	800	801
March 11–18	663	675	686	696	706	716	725	733	741	749	756	762	768	774	779	783	787	791	794	796	798	800	801	801

How to use this chart:

Locate the period of the first person's birthday across the top of the chart and the period of the second person's birthday along the side. The point where the two lines intersect is the page number where the relationship profile of this combination can be found.

Each individual birthday is contained within forty-eight periods of the year. Personology profiles of each period are located on pages 19 to page 211.

RELATIONSHIP LOCATION FINDER

THE SECRET LANGUAGE OF
RELATIONSHIPS

THE SECRET LANGUAGE OF
RELATIONSHIPS

YOUR COMPLETE PERSONOLOGY
GUIDE TO ANY RELATIONSHIP WITH ANYONE

GARY GOLDSCHNEIDER

A JOOST ELFFERS PRODUCTION

PENGUIN STUDIO

ACKNOWLEDGMENTS

Text: Gary Goldschneider

Editor: Marie Timell

Text Editor: David Frankel, with Barbara Ross

Photo Research: Alan A. Gottlieb
Photo Editor: Alan A.Gottlieb, with Susan Lusk and Mark Gabor

Photo Production Assistant: Jane Ramp
Couples Research: Susan Lusk, Mark Gabor
Caption Research: Susan Lusk
Photo Captions: Mark Gabor
Indexer: Louise B. Ketz

Design: Dianna Russo and Mary Tiegreen

Front and Back Cover Design and
Electronic Illustration: Mary Tiegreen and Dianna Russo

Layout Production: Susan Lusk
Symbol Design: Iwan Baan
Symbol Consultant: Shelly Eshkar

Creative Director: Joost Elffers
Project Manager: Eng San Kho

PENGUIN STUDIO
Published by the Penguin Group
Penguin Putnam Inc., 375 Hudson Street,
New York, New York 10014, U.S.A.
Penguin Books Ltd, 27 Wrights Lane,
London W8 5TZ, England
Penguin Books Australia Ltd, Ringwood,
Victoria, Australia
Penguin Books Canada Ltd, 10 Alcorn Avenue,
Toronto, Ontario, Canada M4V 3B2
Penguin Books (N.Z.) Ltd, 182–190 Wairau Road,
Auckland 10, New Zealand

Penguin Books Ltd, Registered Offices:
Harmondsworth, Middlesex, England

First published in 1997 by Penguin Studio,
a member of Penguin Putnam Inc.

1 3 5 7 9 10 8 6 4 2

Copyright © Gary Goldschneider and Joost Elffers, 1997
All rights reserved

Illustration credits appear on pages 817–819.

CIP data available
ISBN 0–670–87527–9

Printed in the United States of America

To Marie Timell
with many thanks for her
inspiration and guidance

How To Use This Book

METHOD ONE

A. Find the week or period during which your birthday falls along the side of the chart on the endpapers at the front or back of this book.

B. Then, along the top of the same chart, find the week or period during which the person who interests you is born. This can be anyone: friend, parent, child, lover, mate or co-worker.

C. Use one finger to point to your birth period and another to find the other person's birth period. Locate the point of intersection of the two. There you will find the page number of the relationship description for your combination.

D. Turn to the page indicated to learn about your relationship.

METHOD TWO

A. Go to the chart on page 12 to determine in which period your birthday falls. Next, find the period in which the person who interests you was born.

B. Consult the four pages dedicated to your birth period, found on pages 19 to 212. There you will find the chart of all your relationships with people born in the other forty-eight periods and the page location of the relationships description. You will also find a list of recommendations for best relationships.

C. Turn to the page indicated to learn about your relationship.

Contents

"THE DANCE OF THE ZODIAC"

Introduction

Aside from our entrance into this world and our exit from it, it is rarely our fate to be alone. In fact, the common wisdom is that creatures raised in isolation withdraw, go mad, can even wither and, ultimately, die. So, this need for others appears to be inescapable.

The inevitable other can be friend or foe, lover or mate, parent or child, employer or servant. Some would say that our lives consist of nothing more than a series of interactions with these and other people. These interactions, whether brief or long-lasting, are relationships. But such relationships in themselves may not satisfy our deepest longings. Most of us desire that one special person with whom we can share our joys and sorrows, our triumph and despair, the one with whom we can be most ourselves. For many of us, just one other person is enough, and the magic of meeting such a person, the shock of recognition, can be among the most heartfelt and thrilling of human experiences. Searching for this individual gives us a reason to go on, becomes of paramount importance. Without an appreciative partner with whom to share our lives, the glory of riches, of fame, of achievement fades to dust and ashes.

Most of our relationships are due to chance. Truly, few of our significant others are chosen by us. We do not pick our parents, siblings, children, co-workers, or neighbors. Even those who are closest to us, our lovers, mates or friends, have usually come to us through some fortunate twist of fate that placed them in our path. Rarely are our relations due to objective forethought. Love is indeed blind to conscious decision making. It is the most subjective of experiences.

Just who, exactly, are these others who populate our lives? What are their deepest longings, sorrows, triumphs and joys? Can any of us possibly understand them any more than we understand ourselves? In fact, interaction with others takes much of our energy and fills our waking hours with a myriad of emotions and thoughts, as we sail through our days and are forced to encounter those who are, essentially, strangers. And what about the firm rule of many psychological theories and spiritual teachings: the other is the self? That is, the being that we encounter in the other is really just an aspect of ourselves, positive or negative, and thus is nothing more than a mirror for who we are.

Looking into the eyes of another and seeing our own image leads us to wonder whether that other person is not really a reflection of our own psyche, a summoning up of our needs, our wants, our expectations. Further, if this is the case, is it because we attracted or are attracted to someone like ourselves, or because we are unable to perceive anything beyond our own experience? Whatever the case, the other may also serve a practical purpose—may be someone whom we need emotionally or physically and who provides great interest but also one on whom we come to depend symbiotically to fulfill the responsibilities of everyday life. Yet there are those who never look beyond the roles or needs that others fill, or reflect on the enigma of another's inner life.

But the mystery of a human being is surpassed by a still deeper paradox, and that is the nature of the relationship we form with the other. A person is real, at times all too real, and his or her existence can be affirmed at any moment by the senses of sight, touch and hearing. The Third entity, the relationship itself is just as real but more difficult to apprehend or define. Individual differences are somehow transcended in the process of its formation, and it can have an enormous influence on the individuals who comprise it, often altering them significantly for life.

A relationship is a rather mysterious and amazing third entity, one that can come to lead an existence independent of the will or desire of its two partners, once things get going. As a matter of fact, in certain cases a relationship can prove far stronger than either individual, leading us to believe that a certain kind of synergy is at work. The energy of the whole (the relationship) is often far greater than that of the sum of its parts (the two individuals who make it up).

In the *Tao Te Ching,* Lao Tzu wrote, "The Tao begot the one. The One begot two. Two begot three. And the three begot the ten thousand things." In this context, the third is the relationship, and it is through relating to others that many of us reach our most creative peaks, and achieve our greatest ends. Formed by the co-mingling of its partners' energies, if you will, or strengths, weaknesses, and personality quirks, this new third form, the relationship, has its own personality, its own strengths, its own weaknesses. It is a wise person who understands this. Moreover, is it possible that what attracts us to someone in many cases is less who the other is and more what the relationship is—what we may potentially create together. Is it possible that our subconscious minds are sufficiently sophisticated to know, on a very subtle level, what a relationship's potential is even as our eyes first meet at someone else's across a room?

Surely relating to others is the crucible through which most of us experience our greatest sorrows and most ecstatic joys. Often, it is the locus of our greatest personal lessons and growth. Our struggle with the other leads us always back to ourselves. Thus the circle closes.

As everyone knows, not all relationships are easy ones for any given individual. Many are fraught with difficulties, and some types are more complicated than others: for example, the employer-worker relationship will be different from the sibling one, carrying with it different expectations and sensitivities. Of course, the type of relationship that often engages most of our interest and energy is the intimate one. It is this much sought-after relationship, the romantic one, that is highly prized in our popular culture today.

Unfortunately, not all couples, by a long shot, are suited to be in love relationships with each other. Successful and long-lasting love affairs require a special chemistry that many long for but few attain, aside from, perhaps, at fleeting moments. So much of falling in love seems based on illusion, which, although pleasurable initially, can leave a swath of destruction in its wake. Both partners can be struck by a thunderbolt, swept away on the wings of desire, only to wake up one day a bit sadder and wiser. Friendships may be longer lasting, sometimes for a lifetime, but may also slowly disintegrate, wear out their usefulness, or suddenly collapse overnight. Some of the most powerful emotive states known to mankind carry with them little guarantee of success or permanence. Yet along with marriage, these are the very states in which most individuals are willing not only to invest everything they have but also to submerge or even sacrifice their own individuality.

Thus the topic of relationships is a key one in our lives, and our successes and failures go a long way toward determining our level of contentment. Building a good relationship is really less an act of construction than working with what exists. It seems to depend a great deal on maintaining a healthy balance between the individual ego and the group spirit, or between selfishness and surrender. Above all, building a good relationship depends on understanding each person's wants and needs, and the relationship's own positive and negative qualities, and then negotiating and crafting something that takes all of this into consideration. It is an act of creation based on a few givens.

Never before in the history of mankind have so many of us been so free to make our relationships into whatever we wish them to be. The stranglehold of proscribed social and political roles and even sexuality is lessening in many parts of the world. As the old structures are being torn down, will we be able to build new ones based on mutual respect and consideration? Simply by virtue of living in this time, many of us have been given the opportunity to create our relationships as we would like to have them. We do not need to have the same relationship that our neighbor has, that our parents have, that our children have. We can create, but the "we" in that sentence is all important, for, like most things in our lives, we must do it with someone else.

Perhaps relationships are ultimately more human than people themselves. After all, if we look at the human being anatomically or biochemically, we will find much in common with all living creatures here on earth, but what separates us from them, in many ways, is the great range and complexity of the way we relate to each other. In fact, it could be argued that aliens would find our relationships with each other infinitely more interesting and revealing than our individual bodies and psyches alone. To picture a person in isolation makes practically no sense—it contradicts what the human being is all about, namely, personal and social interaction.

The Book's Structure

In the pages that follow, this volume attempts to illuminate relationships as entities. Presented here are 1,176 descriptions of different relationships. These were arrived at using the personology theory outlined in this book's companion volume, *The Secret Language of Birthdays*. It is our hope that these relationship descriptions will be used as a jumping-off point for those interested in deepening their understanding of their relationships.

The Grand Cycle of Life

The theory of personology posits that astrology, history and psychology are related to the congruence of three cycles: the astrological zodiac, the earth's rotation around the sun as represented by the seasons of the year and the typical path of a human life. First presented in *The Secret Language of Birthdays,* "The Grand Cycle of Life" shows how the twelve signs of the zodiac, the seasons of the year and the stages of human life from childhood to old age unfold in a similar fashion. In personology, the twelve primary astrological signs as symbols of personality type are replaced by forty-eight periods—twelve cusps and thirty-six weeks. The result is a more detailed approach to personality characteristics.

The Secret Language of Relationships presents "The Grand Cycle of Life" on pages 9 through 17 in order to orient the reader to the personology system. This is followed by a greatly amplified description of the forty-eight periods that goes far beyond that presented in *The Secret Language of Birthdays*. These forty-eight sturdy pillars of the personology system are highly original representations of the middle ground between the more specific 366 personality types keyed to each birthday of the year, on the one hand, and the more general twelve zodiac signs, on the other.

The Personology Periods

The forty-eight personology periods, made up of twelve cusps and thirty-six weeks, are units between six and nine days in length. Personology predicts the personality characteris-

tics of anyone born within these dates. In other words, those born in the same period will share certain predictable character traits. While this may not completely represent every individual, it is sufficient to provide an understanding of his or her basic energies. Extrapolating from the personology periods, it is possible to predict the nature of the relationship between any two people. Thus *The Secret Language of Relationships* combines each period of the year with itself and every other period to predict the nature of the resulting relationship.

For example, a person born on March 31 falls into the Aries I period. This is the Week of the Child, which symbolizes the freshness and openness of early childhood and of the spring season (lasting from March 25 to April 2). People born during this time are characterized by a childlike, enthusiastic orientation. This in contrast to a person born on November 10, who would be a Scorpio II (encompassing November 3 to 11). Born in the fall, which is symbolically likened to middle age, this week takes Depth as its central symbol. Thus, it becomes possible to consider the theoretical implications of an Aries I–Scorpio II relationship.

It is recommended that readers get to know their own particular period as well as possible, and for this reason four pages are devoted to each of the forty-eight periods or weeks. In addition, when studying your relationship with another person, you should also review in some depth the description of his or her period. This will help you better understand your relationship profile. Try to apply this understanding in your daily life. The personology period descriptions appear on pages 19 to 212. Also included is a handy reference table to the location and name of each period's matchup with every other.

The Combinations or Profiles

Many astrology books have presented the signs in love, showing how Gemini and Virgo or Capricorn and Aquarius relate to each other, but, as discussed earlier, personology posits that there are five equally important types of Geminis. Each will behave differently, including in relationships. Thus in personology, much more specific relationships can be defined.

Using This Book

Using the book is extremely simple. First, consult the chart found on page 12 to determine in which period your birthday falls. Next, find the period in which the person who interests you is born. This can be anyone: friend, parent, child, lover, mate, co-worker. Finally, consulting the endpapers at the front and back of this book (next to the covers), point to your birth period with one finger and to the other person's birth period with another and find the point of intersection, as though you were using a road mileage map to find the distance between two cities. At that point you will find the page number to be consulted for your relationship. Or, if you would prefer, consult your birth period, found on pages 19 to 211. There you will find the chart of all your relationships with people born in the other forty-eight periods and their page locations.

The Secret Language of Relationships gives a description of the 1,176 combinations of the forty-eight personology periods with each other. If you are a Leo II, for example, you will be able to find all of your possible forty-eight combinations, including that with another Leo II. Each matchup is discussed in relation to five principal life areas: love, marriage, friendship, family and work. Of course, these may overlap, to a greater or lesser extent. Other types of relationships, such as teacher-student, adversarial or competitive, primarily sexual, acquaintanceships and partnerships, are also considered.

The possible number of different combinations of the forty-eight periods with each other is given by the formula n(n+1)/2 and calculates out to 1,176 possible matchups. Traditional sun-sign astrology describes only seventy-eight possible relationship types between the twelve signs. *The Secret Language of Relationships* offers about fifteen times as many combinations can as sun-sign astrology and thus can be much more specific.

The 1,176 matchups begin on page 213 and are presented in the following manner. Beginning with the first period, Pisces-

Aries cusp, all the forty-eight relationships of these people born between March 19 and March 24, including the relationship between Pisces-Aries cusp and Pisces-Aries cusp, are laid out, two to a page. Following these, the forty-seven new relationships of the following period, Aries I, are shown. Why only forty-seven? Because the relationship of Aries I with Pisces-Aries cusp (its preceding period) has already been discussed in the section on Pisces-Aries relationships. When Aries II's relationships are presented, there are now only forty-six, since two have already been discussed, one under Pisces-Aries and one under Aries I. Thus the number of possible relationships becomes 48,47,46,45. . . until the last relationship, Pisces III with Pisces III, is reached. The formula n(n+1)/2 , where n=48, is revealed as being equal to 1+2+3+4+5 . . . 48. As mentioned previously, your relationship can be found by using the charts on the inside of the cover at the front and back of the book, or by looking up your period on pages 19 to 211 to find the table of each period's matchup with every other period and the page number of your matchup with your partner.

A Brief Overview of Personology

Personology is like astrology in that it recognizes the original twelve heavenly constellations (and the signs derived from them) that form the band called the zodiac, which encircles our earth. However, personology goes further by concentrating on the overlapping area between two signs called the cusp. For example, four of the twelve cusps have immense importance for life as it is lived here on earth, since the spring equinox, the summer solstice, the fall equinox and the winter solstice mark the boundaries of the seasons themselves. Spring, summer, fall and winter succeed one another in an orderly rhythm, for the most part, and structure life on the planet along with the unvarying diurnal changes of day and night. In terms of the signs, these cusps are Pisces-Aries (spring equinox), Gemini-Cancer (summer solstice), Virgo-Libra (fall equinox) and Sagittarius-Capricorn (winter solstice), in the northern hemisphere. In personology the names of these cusps are The Primal Cusp, The Cusp of Magic, The Cusp of Beauty and The Cusp of Prophecy, respectively. In personology, those born during these and the other eight cusp periods of six to seven days will share certain characteristics, the descriptions or predictions of which are far broader than those of single sun signs as in astrology. In other words, there is such a thing as a distinct cusp personality.

Cusp people are different from others not only because they embody a blend of the sharply contrasting traits of two adjacent signs (such as Aries and Taurus, or Gemini and Cancer) but also because their individuality is not determined by a major sign of the zodiac but frequently by something more indefinable. They are earth-oriented, unpredictable, difficult, unconventional, perhaps. Often those born on cusps find each other extremely attractive, which may or may not bode well for their forming a permanent relationship.

Further, in those astrological periods of about a month between cusps, traditionally known as signs, we find different representations of personality based on where a week or period falls in the month. In personology, these months or signs are further divided into three weeks. For example, Libra I's are Libras in orientation but have certain traits that are unique and that differentiate them from Libra III's.

Looking at each of the astrological signs from a personological point of view, we find five principal types of each sign: on either side the two cusps that demarcate it and in its center the approximately week-long periods, three in number. For this reason, while a sun-sign astrologer speaks about an Aries, a Scorpio or a Capricorn, a personologist may refer to an Aries II, a Scorpio-Sagittarius, or a Capricorn III. Instead of there being a "Virgo" personality, as presented in the sun-sign astrology system, in personology there are five types of Virgos: Leo-Virgo cusp (August 19–25, The Cusp of Exposure), Virgo I (August 26–September 2, The Week of System Builders), Virgo II (September 3–10, The Week of the Enigma), Virgo III (September 11–18, The Week of the Literalist) and finally, Virgo-Libra cusp (The Cusp of Beauty, September 19–24). Of course, since cusps are shared by two signs, this last cusp becomes the first period of the five different kinds of Libras. In *The Secret Language of Birthdays*, these periods were further broken down into discrete personality characteristics for each day of the year.

Which Are the Best Combinations for You?

Conventional sun-sign astrology has maintained that in general the best signs for you are the ones that are trine to your sun sign (120° away from your sign in the zodiac). In fact, this means the signs that are of the same element as yours. In other words, if you are a Taurus (an earth sign), things should go well with Virgo and Capricorn, the other two earth signs. Similarly, the three water signs (Cancer, Scorpio, Pisces), the three air signs (Gemini, Libra, Aquarius) and the three fire signs (Aries, Leo, Sagittarius) are recommended to each other. Although this theory makes sense, it does not always work in practice, particularly when it comes to sustaining interest over a long period of time. In fact, it often seems that the best combinations are ones that sun-sign astrology rarely suggests: the two signs on either side of and the one opposite yours. For example, if you are a Taurus, it is not necessarily the other two earth signs but rather the sign before yours, Aries, the sign after yours, Gemini, and the sign opposite yours, Scorpio, that are a good bet and your favorites.

In *The Secret Language of Relationships* the situation is much more complex, since there are not only five types of each sign but also at least five different areas of life in which relationships can manifest themselves. Making any hard and fast rules is difficult. However, if you look at the four-page descriptions of your period you will find a list of the best periods for you to get involved with in each of the categories, a list that has been culled from the results found in your forty-eight matchups.

Once you begin to embrace personology and work with *The Secret Language of Relationships,* you may be interested to see which types of people you tend to be involved with. Observe your relationships past and present. You might find, as we did, that many of the people in your life are frequently born in the same weeks of the year. In other words, we are attracted to the same personality types and combinations, over and over again.

Recommendations for the best combinations by category for any one period are provided on a chart in each period description found on pages 19 to 211.

How the Relationships Were Revealed

Four primary but different tools were used to create the relationship profiles or combinations in this book. The first was to draw a bead on what the relationship between two people is all about, its main energies or focus. This was crafted based on a traditional astrological tool called the "composite chart," a fascinating method propounded and endorsed by astrologer Robert Hand, in his book *Planets in Composite.* It involves synthesis, in which a combination horoscope is made from the two originals. This composite chart is built up from a series of midpoints between the planets of the two individual charts. The composite or midpoint method creates a new chart for the relationship itself; it is viewed as a new entity, with it own character, strengths and weaknesses: a synergy, if you will, of each person's traits.

Also employed was another traditional astrological tool called synastry. This second method involves examining both partners' individual characteristics and comparing them point by point for compatibility. Thus we go from viewing the relationship as a discrete entity in itself to focusing on the individuals and their interaction.

The third method used was to create an imaginary psychodrama, in which hypothetical individuals from two periods were allowed to interact. For example, by placing a theoretical prototype of a Gemini II and Scorpio III in a variety of situations (domestic, professional, intimate, etc.), their interaction could be viewed and studied psychologically.

Finally, biographical as well as personal information about well-known couples and those personally known to the authors provided a reliable source of insight and most interesting observations.

Thus relationship profiles presenting their core energies and tendencies were created. However, these could be applied to many different kinds of relationships, so a decision was made to look at five of them.

The Five Relationship Categories
Love

Under this category are included intimate relationships ranging from platonic to sexual in nature. It should be noted that love means different things to different people. In addition, every type of relationship probably involves some sort of love, to a greater or lesser extent. Yet to call a mother-son relationship, a sibling matchup or a friendship a love relationship does not seem appropriate. Therefore, love is used as the name of this category, without implying in any way that it lays claim to that emotion exclusively.

Traditionally, a love affair is considered by psychologists as an entity limited in duration and more likely than not to eventually disintegrate, perhaps due to a lack of social commitment, involvement and support. These relationships tend to be characterized by an emotional intensity that may be difficult to sustain and an absence of reality-based thinking on the part of the partners. Many love relationships are kept hidden because of fear of disapproval or rejection, often familial in nature. The fact that such relationships tend not to have a realistic basis does not make them less likely to occur; on the contrary, it is often the incongruous and unimaginable that precipitates them taking place.

Sexual attraction is discussed in this category for the most part. Yet romantic feelings are not in any way restricted to the erotic, and some romance can manifest itself in many of the personology combinations that have little to do with physicality.

In most love relationships, psychological projection, replaying scripts from childhood, acting out, and a whole host of emotions including jealousy, anger, a desire to dominate and control, nurturing and protective impulses, violence, narcissism, idolatry and even worship struggle for the ascendancy. Maddening, exalting, thrilling and frustrating, the promise of love continues to drive human beings into these situations in their search for the perfect partner.

Marriage

In an age in which over half of marriages end in divorce, it is puzzling why so many people still get married. What is even more puzzling is why they take the oath to love each other exclusively in the light of statistics on infidelity. Yet marriage is a powerful social institution, and the raising of children within the conjugal family unit is still the widely accepted norm. *The Secret Language of Relationships* considers that the question of whether two people are suited for one another maritally is of vital importance, particularly if children are to be involved. Moreover, it cannot be assumed that love is always the main motivating factor in marriage or the one that holds such units together. The emphasis in this area is on pointing out matchup strengths having to do with shared values that are of a more practical, financial, social, intellectual or aesthetic nature.

Friendship

Deep friendship has elements of love and marriage built into it. Two friends can be extremely self-sufficient and not in need of much external input. Should such friends also be engaged in professional ventures with each other, they may in fact spend much more time together than lovers or spouses. If one makes a list of close friends, it is quite likely that their birthdays are not spread out equally around the year but are clumped into certain areas. *The Secret Language of Relationships* does its best to alert the reader to certain combinations that can prove highly beneficial in the sphere of friendship and others that, although attractive, had best not be developed.

Family

The family relationships most often discussed are parent-child and sibling combinations, although grandparents and more distant relatives are also mentioned occasionally. Here some of the most possessive and destructive drives of human beings come out, whereby many parents are all too prone to push their children to make up for their own failures and inadequacies. Parents and children are urged to build bonds of trust and acceptance, because sooner or later they will have to confront their problems and come to some sort of peace with each other.

Work

Most work relationships are fortuitous; two individuals are thrown together in an office or other work unit and have to make the best of it. However, it may be useful for personnel officers to check both *The Secret Language of Birthdays* and *The Secret Language of Relationships* for a quick hit on whether two people have compatible personalities. In the work category, *The Secret Language of Relationships* considers co-workers, boss-employee pairs, administrative colleagues, business partners, entrepreneurs and freelancers as categories worthy of special recommendation or warning. Also, certain work relationships are more likely to develop into productive friendships than others.

Three analogies may help to describe the nature of a relationship in terms of certain physical and metaphysical models:

1. Physical versus Chemical Reaction

In a physical reaction two substances are mixed or ground together without being transformed—that is, both can be recovered from such a mixture in their original state. A chemical reaction, on the other hand, produces an entirely new substance from the two reactants, one that is very different from either of the reactants and does not easily yield the original substances back again. A relationship is more like the resulting compound in a chemical reaction—it is a discrete third entity that is more than just a mixture of the other two, rather a new substance in itself.

2. Interface

When two objects touch each other, the edge or border at which they meet, the interface, has quite different properties from those of the original objects. Interfaces are not easy to define, and in some ways transcend the two objects themselves. When you slowly reach out to touch the image of yourself that you see in a mirror, the point of touching the glass can be as strange as disturbing your reflection in a pool of clear water or trying to shake free from your shadow. A relationship could be motivated by the desire on the part of one or both partners to break through the interface and interact with the person on the other side. Such interactions usually involve a mingling or merging of your being with theirs, often resulting in a miraculous transformation.

2. Ecstasy

The poet John Donne conceives of the process as one of soul-merger. In his poem *The Ecstasie*, he pictures two lovers lying on a grassy bank, staring into each other's eyes. Their souls, marching forth from their confinement in the body, proceed to advance toward each other along the "double string" of their eye connections until finally merging with each other. Although the lovers' bodies are physically entwined, more important is that their spiritual selves also become joined. The word "ecstasy" is from the Latin *ex stasis*, meaning to stand outside of oneself. In other words, it is the soul expressing itself beyond the bounds of the physical.

Keys to a Good and Lasting Relationship

When a relationship between individual A and individual B is discussed, do we mean the dynamic that goes on in private between these two individuals or the relationship unit AB, which interacts with the world around it? Of course, the relationship AB is present in public or private, but the degree to which A and B identify with it, and give up their individual identities to become it, is of utmost importance. There are no hard and fast rules for such surrender to the relationship. In some cases, or at certain times in the life of a relationship, it will be necessary for A or B to pull back and affirm his or her own individual identity once more, perhaps even to the point of setting out once again on his or her own path. However, peak experiences between two people are only really possible through surrender—that is, giving up a good measure of individual ego in service of the relationship, AB. Each person will get something back that is much more valuable. A few additional guidelines follow:

1. Listen to what your partner is saying.
2. Truly share. Solely giving or taking is not the answer, but only a combination of the two in equal measure.
3. Give unconditionally. To give while expecting a return or certain results is the same as paying for something.
4. Kindness, understanding, trust and consideration are worth more than all the selfish pleasure you can gain. If you are in it only for what you can get, forget about meaningful relationships.
5. Don't let anyone treat you abusively. Demand respect.
6. By refusing to make decisions, express disapproval or take a stand you may really be just avoiding taking responsibility for your own actions. Fear of rejection is usually behind such an agreeable facade.
7. Beware of possessiveness and claiming behavior. Your partner is his or her own person and should never be treated as an object or possession.
8. Refuse to allow others to push your buttons. One trick is to grow a whole new set of buttons that cannot be pushed so easily.
9. Much can be learned from self-observation. In the midst of an argument, try backing off and observing yourself. By being both the observer and observed, you will increase your awareness.
10. Control your aggressive and violent side. At the same time, seek outlets for your feelings and do not repress them. Working out differences through calm discussion is often the best way.
11. Learn to postpone your gratification through patience, trust and understanding.
12. Acceptance is important but does not imply agreement. Agree to disagree. Do not insist that you and your partner must see eye to eye.
13. Try to distinguish between needs and wants. What you seem to want most is not what you really need, in many cases.
14. Be sensitive to *kairos*, the right time for an action to take place. What will work well under one set of circumstances will be entirely wasted under another.
15. Respect your partner's space.

The Grand
Cycle of Life

The Grand Cycle of Life

All of life can be conceived symbolically as one grand cycle. By analogy, three important areas can be studied and compared within a circular framework: human life, nature, astrology. For humans, the circle may represents a lifetime, from birth to death; for nature, the inexorable succession of the seasons through a year; in astrology, the zodiac, depicting the signs and their positions. The circle on which these three worlds are based is divided by two axes: one horizontal, one vertical. To travel through a cycle, one need only begin at the left end-point of the horizontal axis and proceed in a counterclockwise direction until one arrives back at the beginning.

The four most important points on the circumference of the circle are where the two axes touch it (see Fig. 1 below).

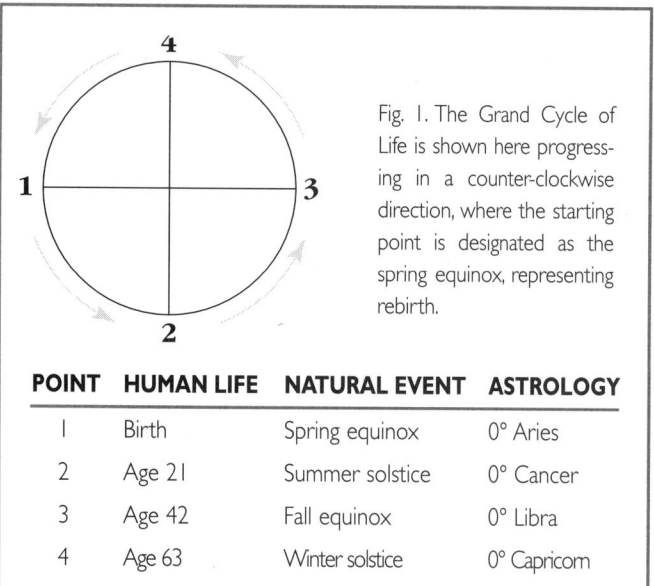

Fig. 1. The Grand Cycle of Life is shown here progressing in a counter-clockwise direction, where the starting point is designated as the spring equinox, representing rebirth.

POINT	HUMAN LIFE	NATURAL EVENT	ASTROLOGY
1	Birth	Spring equinox	0° Aries
2	Age 21	Summer solstice	0° Cancer
3	Age 42	Fall equinox	0° Libra
4	Age 63	Winter solstice	0° Capricorn

Upper and Lower Halves of the Circle

As shown in Fig. 2, the horizontal axis splits the circle into two halves. The lower half of the circle, or first half of the life cycle, represents objective, outward growth in human and natural terms (birth to age forty-two, spring to fall). During this period, dramatic physical growth takes place that transforms both individuals and the landscape. These objective changes in humans are paralleled by a deeply personal way of viewing the world. Thus, in astrological or psychological terms the lower

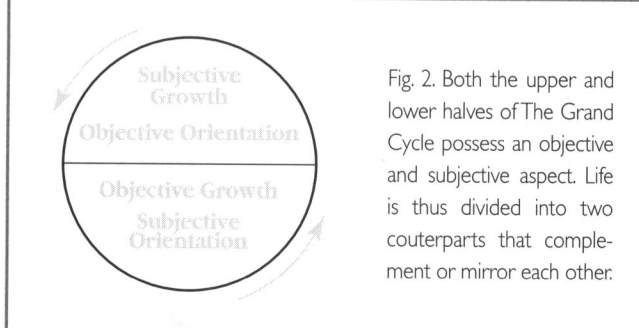

Fig. 2. Both the upper and lower halves of The Grand Cycle possess an objective and subjective aspect. Life is thus divided into two couterparts that complement or mirror each other.

half may be seen as subjective (more unconscious) and the first six signs, ruled by the "inner" planets (Mercury, Venus, Mars) and two luminaries (Sun, Moon) in our solar system, can be classified as "personal" signs. These five heavenly bodies are almost always viewed in terms of everyday feelings and emotions, familial and romantic relationships with others, and matters of the here and now, rather than more complex philosophical matters or universal concerns. The dominant faculties here are themselves more subjective—intuition and feeling. We may say, then, that the first half of life manifests objectively but is unconscious in its psychological orientation.

The upper half of the circle, or second half of the life cycle, represents subjective, inward growth in human and natural terms (age 42–84, fall to spring). During this period, both in nature and the human psyche, a deepening and maturation takes place beneath the surface of life. This "underground" activity is accompanied by an ever-increasing objectivity in the way human beings are able to view events around them, resulting in a wiser outlook and perhaps a more pragmatic view of things. Thus, in

Fig. 3. As the diagram clearly shows, aside from the summer and winter solstices, there is no time in the year that is not either waxing or waning. Thus, at any point on the circle, there is movement toward increasing light or darkness.

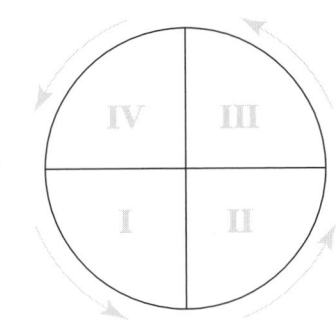

Fig. 4. The seasons of the year, the ideal duration of a human life (one Uranus cycle of eighty-four years) and the twelve signs of the zodiac are here equally divided in four.

QUAD	SEASON	AGE	SIGNS	CHANGE	MANIFESTATION	ORIENTATION
I	Spring	0–21	A,T,G	Waxing	Objective	Unconscious
II	Summer	21–42	C,L,V	Waning	Objective	Unconscious
III	Fall	42–63	L,S,S	Waning	Subjective	Conscious
IV	Winter	63–84	C,A,P	Waxing	Subjective	Conscious

astrological and psychological terms the upper half can be viewed as being objective (more conscious): signs 7–9 can be classified as "social" and signs 10–12 "universal." Except for Libra, these six signs are all ruled by the "outer," impersonal planets in our solar system (Jupiter, Saturn, Uranus, Neptune, Pluto). These massive and distant bodies carry more universal and philosophical associations. They symbolize larger social questions: fate, destiny, and the inexorable and eternal aspects of life. The dominant faculties here are more objective ones—sensation and thought. Thus, the second half of life is the reverse of the first, i.e., it manifests subjectively (inside, beneath the surface) but is more conscious in its psychological orientation.

Left and Right Halves of the Circle

By contrast, the vertical axis divides the circle into a right half and a left half (see Fig. 3, opposite page). The left hand side of the zodiac wheel (from Capricorn to Cancer) represents **waxing**—during the seasons winter and spring the days get progressively longer. The right hand side (from Cancer to Capricorn) represents **waning**—as we pass through the seasons summer and fall the days get ever shorter. Since the points of summer and winter solstices are at the ends of this vertical axis, they show the maximum polarity: long day–short night (June 21) and short day–long night (December 21). In the *I Ching* (The Book of Changes) these extremes or poles represent the most *yang* and *yin* points of the year, respectively. The equinoxes, on the other hand, mark points of maximum movement either toward (March 21) or away from (September 23) the sun, and demonstrate a perfect day-night balance.

The Quadrants

The two sets of hemispheres just presented (upper-lower, left-right) may be combined simply by superimposing them on each other. In this way, the three hundred and sixty degree circle of life is divided into four quadrants. In the human lifetime of eighty-four years, each of these quadrants represents a period of twenty-one years; in the yearly cycle of nature, a season; in astrology, a group of three signs (the order of which is invariably cardinal, fixed and mutable). This information is summarized in Fig. 4 above.

In addition, each of these quadrants may be associated with a mode of apprehending the world:

I Intuition   III Sensation
II Feeling   IV Thought

Each of the four quadrants then, whether representing a season, a twenty-one year period of life or a ninety-degree slice of the zodiac, can be assessed in terms of change, manifestation, orientation and a mode of apprehension.

Because personology is based on a distinctly earth-oriented system, the two equinoxes and solstices occupy a position of central importance in demarcating The Grand Cycle of Life. In this respect, the traditional heavenly-oriented astrological view is given a shift of emphasis to the here and now of our daily life—the eternal cyclical progression of the seasons and life periods, the rhythms of existence which we experience year after year on our home planet.

The 48 Periods and Cusps

Personology divides the year into forty-eight periods, each associated with distinct personality characteristics typical of people born during these periods. The essence of these traits is represented by the name of each period. Personology's forty-eight periods and their names are listed here.

PISCES–ARIES CUSP
MARCH 19–24
The Cusp of Rebirth

ARIES I
MARCH 25–APRIL 2
The Week of the Child

ARIES II
APRIL 3–10
The Week of the Star

ARIES III
APRIL 11–18
The Week of the Pioneer

ARIES–TAURUS CUSP
APRIL 19–24
The Cusp of Power

TAURUS I
APRIL 25–MAY 2
The Week of Manifestation

TAURUS II
MAY 3–10
The Week of the Teacher

TAURUS III
MAY 11–18
The Week of the Natural

TAURUS–GEMINI CUSP
MAY 19–24
The Cusp of Energy

GEMINI I
MAY 25–JUNE 2
The Week of Freedom

GEMINI II
JUNE 3–10
The Week of New Language

GEMINI III
JUNE 11–18
The Week of the Seeker

GEMINI–CANCER CUSP
JUNE 19–24
The Cusp of Magic

CANCER I
JUNE 25–JULY 2
The Week of the Empath

CANCER II
JULY 3–JULY 10
The Week of the Unconventional

CANCER III
JULY 11–18
The Week of the Persuader

CANCER–LEO CUSP
JULY 19–25
The Cusp of Oscillation

LEO I
JULY 26–AUGUST 2
The Week of Authority

LEO II
AUGUST 3–10
The Week of Balanced Strength

LEO III
AUGUST 11–18
The Week of Leadership

LEO–VIRGO CUSP
AUGUST 19–25
The Cusp of Exposure

VIRGO I
AUGUST 26–SEPTEMBER 2
The Week of System Builders

VIRGO II
SEPTEMBER 3–10
The Week of the Enigma

VIRGO III
SEPTEMBER 11–18
The Week of the Literalist

VIRGO–LIBRA CUSP
SEPTEMBER 19–24
The Cusp of Beauty

LIBRA I
SEPTEMBER 25–OCTOBER 2
The Week of the Perfectionist

LIBRA II
OCTOBER 3–10
The Week of Society

LIBRA III
OCTOBER 11–18
The Week of Theater

LIBRA–SCORPIO CUSP
OCTOBER 19–25
The Cusp of Drama and Criticism

SCORPIO I
OCTOBER 26–NOVEMBER 2
The Week of Intensity

SCORPIO II
NOVEMBER 3–11
The Week of Depth

SCORPIO III
NOVEMBER 12–18
The Week of Charm

SCORPIO–SAGITTARIUS CUSP
NOVEMBER 19–24
The Cusp of Revolution

SAGITTARIUS I
NOVEMBER 25–DECEMBER 2
The Week of Independence

SAGITTARIUS II
DECEMBER 3–10
The Week of the Originator

SAGITTARIUS III
DECEMBER 11–18
The Week of the Titan

SAGITTARIUS–CAPRICORN CUSP
DECEMBER 19–25
The Cusp of Prophecy

CAPRICORN I
DECEMBER 26–JANUARY 2
The Week of the Ruler

CAPRICORN II
JANUARY 3–9
The Week of Determination

CAPRICORN III
JANUARY 10–16
The Week of Dominance

CAPRICORN–AQUARIUS CUSP
JANUARY 17–22
The Cusp of Mystery and Imagination

AQUARIUS I
JANUARY 23–30
The Week of Genius

AQUARIUS II
JANUARY 31–FEBRUARY 7
The Week of Youth and Ease

AQUARIUS III
FEBRUARY 8–15
The Week of Acceptance

AQUARIUS—PISCES CUSP
FEBRUARY 16–22
The Cusp of Sensitivity

PISCES I
FEBRUARY 23–MARCH 2
The Week of Spirit

PISCES II
MARCH 3–10
The Week of the Loner

PISCES III
MARCH 11–18
The Week of Dancers and Dreamers

The Grand Cycle of Life

Spring
March 21–June 21

The beginning of the astrological year has been fixed as 0° Aries (March 21) by modern astrology. On this spring or vernal equinox, which symbolizes rebirth, days and nights are of equal length. Astrology has taken the northern hemisphere for its model (March 21 marks the beginning of spring in the northern hemisphere, but in the southern hemisphere spring begins around September 23). As spring wears on, the days grow longer and the nights shorter. Spring is the first quarter, or 90° segment, of the yearly cycle. It extends from the spring equinox to the summer solstice.

Springtime is traditionally the period of new growth. As the earth and air heat up, the fire of the sun melts the winter ice and snow. Spring rains coupled with swollen rivers bring water to the earth and new life bursts forth. Planting of crops and vegetables begins once the nights become shorter and all danger of freezing is past. Seeds germinate in the earth, plants sprout and quickly begin to grow. The first flowers blossom, and in combination with the birds and animals, perhaps newly-born, returned from migrations or awakened from hibernation, add beauty and liveliness to this quadrant of the year. Analagously, people spend more time outside and wear fewer but more colorful clothes as the days lengthen and the average temperature rises. More daylight means more time available for recreation and the enjoyment of natural surroundings.

The Signs and Life Periods

Spring comprises three astrological signs: the cardinal fire sign Aries, the fixed earth sign Taurus and the mutable air sign Gemini. In human terms, these three signs can be likened to the life of the individual from birth until age twenty-one. This active period of human development, which spans birth, infancy, childhood and adolescence, displays many of the same processes of growth, differentiation and development which occur in nature's springtime.

This first quadrant of The Grand Cycle of Life is governed by the faculty of intuition and can be seen as a waxing period which manifests objectively and has an unconscious orienta-

ZODIAC POSITION
0° Aries–0° Cancer

QUADRANT
First

HUMAN AGE
0–21

CUSP CONCEPTS
Rebirth, Power, Energy

SIGNS
Aries, Taurus, Gemini

RULERS
Mars, Venus, Mercury

SYMBOLS
The Ram, The Bull, The Twins

ELEMENTS
Fire, Earth, Air

MOTTOS
I Am, I Have, I Communicate

DOMINANT FACULTY
Intuition

tion. That is to say, although objective growth is taking place externally in nature and in the human being during this period, the internal state is highly subjective.

Astrologically, this has to do with the fact that the signs Aries, Taurus and Gemini are ruled by the planets Mars, Venus and Mercury, respectively, all of which can be classified as "inner" or "personal" planets. This means that they are relatively small and close to the earth and the sun.

The period of human development age 0–21 also shows a highly subjective or personal orientation. The developing child sees the world largely as an extension of him/herself. Its apprehension of life is colored by intuitions and by powerful unconscious drives. The power of the child to absorb and assimilate impressions from the outside world is astonishing. Sometimes the young person is at the mercy of such powerful forces, and does not act in the most rational or conscious manner.

The Springtime Personality

Generally speaking, those born in the springtime manifest an enthusiasm for life. Their energy is prodigious where initiating projects is concerned, and their ability to survive and/or adapt is noteworthy. Often more extroverted than introverted, springtime people tend to impact heavily on their environment. However, their capacity to dutifully or doggedly stick to one activity is not necessarily great.

Springtime people like to share what they think, create and produce, and they are, more than those born in other seasons, in need of fairly constant appreciation and approval for what they do. A desire to be free characterizes many born in this season, and they may not react well to having restrictions imposed on them. Springtime people need to grow, expand and make their mark on the world.

Those born in the spring often carry a childlike air about them their whole life long. Innocence, spontaneity, impulse— these are all characteristic of springtime people. Generally positive in their outlook, they may be put off by highly serious attitudes and have little patience for those with negative orientations.

Summer
June 21–September 23

The summer solstice usually occurs on June 21 in the northern hemisphere (this date marks the beginning of summer in the northern hemisphere, but in the southern hemisphere summer begins on December 21). At this magical time, days are longer and nights shorter than at any other time of the year. As summer wears on, however, the days shorten and the nights lengthen. Summer is the second quarter, or 90° degree segment, of the yearly cycle. It extends from the summer solstice to the fall equinox.

Summer is traditionally the period in which the new life of springtime grows to maturity. Temperatures are at their warmest during this period, and most of animal life experiences lazy afternoons when it is too hot for much movement. This is traditionally the time for vacations, for taking off from work to enjoy all kinds of outdoor activities. School is out, and more young people are thus active and about in the mornings. Colorful flowers and blossoms abound. All the fullness and abundance of nature is revealed. The rhythm of life in this quadrant is slower and more sensual, but diets tend to be lighter, and clothing freer. Life is in many respects easier in summer than at any other time of the year.

The Signs and Life Periods

Summer comprises three astrological signs: the cardinal water sign Cancer, the fixed fire sign Leo and the mutable earth sign Virgo. In human terms, these three signs can be likened to the life of the individual aged 21–42. This dynamic period of human development, which spans early adulthood to the mid-life period, displays many of the same processes of growth, flowering and producing which occur in nature's summertime.

This second quadrant of The Grand Cycle of Life is governed by the faculty of feeling and can be seen as a waning period which manifests objectively and has an unconscious orientation. That is to say, although objective growth is taking place externally in nature and in the human being during this period, such growth has already slowed down. Like childhood, the orientation remains primarily subjective.

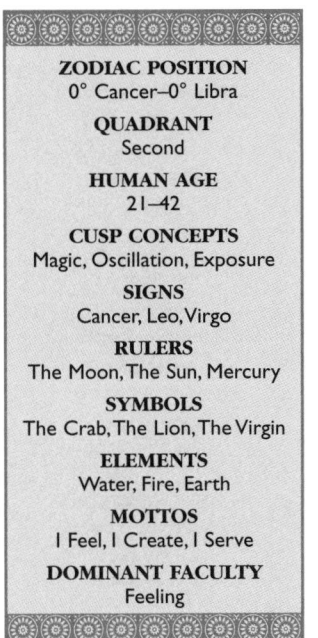

ZODIAC POSITION
0° Cancer–0° Libra

QUADRANT
Second

HUMAN AGE
21–42

CUSP CONCEPTS
Magic, Oscillation, Exposure

SIGNS
Cancer, Leo, Virgo

RULERS
The Moon, The Sun, Mercury

SYMBOLS
The Crab, The Lion, The Virgin

ELEMENTS
Water, Fire, Earth

MOTTOS
I Feel, I Create, I Serve

DOMINANT FACULTY
Feeling

Astrologically speaking, this has to do with the fact that the signs Cancer, Leo and Virgo are ruled by the heavenly bodies The Moon, The Sun and Mercury, all of which are said to be "inner" or "personal" in the solar system. This means that they are relatively close to the earth and take approx. one month (for the Moon) and one year (for the Sun and Mercury) to travel around the zodiac.

Like childood and adolescence, the period of human development age 21–42 is highly personal in outlook, but much objectivity and acquired wisdom has also manifested. The maturing adult is able to discriminate between his/her internal self and the outside world. Not everything is so highly colored by intuitions and powerful unconscious drives as before. Although the capacity to absorb and assimilate impressions is still great, many entryways to the personality and ego have already closed. The maturing adult is also far less at the mercy of the subjective self, and now acts in a more rational and conscious manner than before.

The Summertime Personality

Generally speaking, those born in the summertime have more measured responses than those born in the spring and, although enthusiastic, are more critical. Their energies are perhaps a bit less focused on initiating projects and more on bringing them to fruition. Summertime people tend to be a mixture of introvert and extrovert, but feelings now play a more important role in coloring their lives. Empathic urges to help and become involved with others are strong during this period. Summertime people often experience an emotional interaction not only with people but with their work and environment.

Summertime people may not display an overwhelming need to bring their contributions out in the world. Many hidden characteristics develop at this time, and being appreciated is not always the most important thing. Rather than placing their freedom and independence above all else, summertime people are prepared to serve others and also to invest time in them. Summertime people need to be needed.

Fall
September 23–December 21

The fall equinox usually occurs around September 23 in the northern hemisphere (though, of course, in the southern hemisphere fall begins on March 21). At this time of harvest, days and nights are again of equal length. As fall wears on, however, the days grow shorter and the nights longer. Fall is the third quarter, or 90° degree segment, of the yearly cycle. It extends from the fall equinox to the winter solstice.

Fall is traditionally the period at which time the final harvest of summer growth takes place—afterwards, much of the ground is covered by leaves or mulch for the winter. A decomposition of plant life now begins by which the earth is enriched. Most of the farmland lies fallow during this period but some winter crops can be planted. Temperatures begin to drop as the sun shares less of itself, and freezing nights are evinced by morning frost. Some animal life goes into hibernation or migrates to a warmer climate. Deciduous trees change color in riotous displays, and an autumn nip is in the air. The rhythm of life of this quadrant is quicker and more survival-oriented. High-energy or bulk diets are preferred here (both by animals and humans). The bounty of foodstuffs is waning, and life again becomes more difficult.

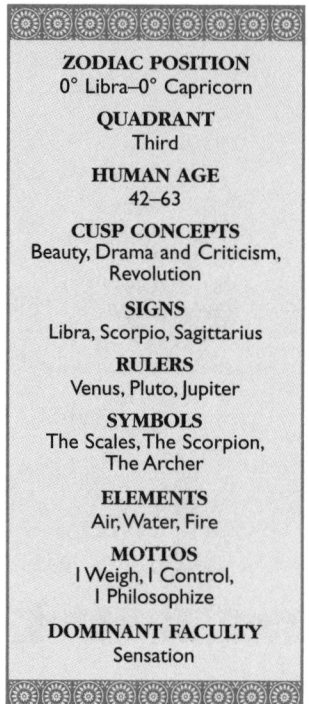

ZODIAC POSITION
0° Libra–0° Capricorn

QUADRANT
Third

HUMAN AGE
42–63

CUSP CONCEPTS
Beauty, Drama and Criticism, Revolution

SIGNS
Libra, Scorpio, Sagittarius

RULERS
Venus, Pluto, Jupiter

SYMBOLS
The Scales, The Scorpion, The Archer

ELEMENTS
Air, Water, Fire

MOTTOS
I Weigh, I Control, I Philosophize

DOMINANT FACULTY
Sensation

The Signs and Life Periods

Fall comprises three astrological signs: the cardinal air sign Libra, the fixed water sign Scorpio and the mutable fire sign Sagittarius. These three signs can be likened in human terms to the years 42–63 in the life of an individual. This powerful period of human development which spans the onset of the mid-life period to late middle age, evidences some of the same aspects of maturation, conservation of movement and energy, and added emphasis on survival, as does nature's autumn.

This third quadrant of The Grand Cycle of Life is governed by the faculty of sensation and can be seen as a waning period which manifests subjectively and has a conscious orientation. That is to say, subjective, underground, interior activity has replaced outward growth in both nature and the human being. But psychologically, a conscious and objective awareness of the process of aging are all too clear. Difficulty in accepting such changes, and often a need to control them, are also apparent.

Astrologically, this is related to the fact that the signs Libra, Scorpio and Sagittarius are ruled by the heavenly bodies Venus, Pluto and Jupiter, the last two of which are outer, "universal" planets. These outer planets are far from the earth and take approx. 12 years (for Jupiter) and 248 years (for Pluto) to travel around the zodiac. Venus, on the other hand, is a "personal" planet which lends strong social and sensuous influences.

Unlike the period from birth to the mid–life, the outlook of the adult at this time is more social than personal. Objectivity, criticism, conscious thought, and awareness characterize this intensely realistic period. A new seriousness and philosophical attitude appears. Intuition, feeling, and thought are all exercised, but sensation becomes a unifying theme, i.e., objective assessment of phenomena as well as a more conscious enjoyment of sensuous pleasures.

The Autumnal Personality

Generally speaking, those born in the fall demonstrate both a greater ability and need to control their external environment. Autumnal people are rarely as enthusiastic as those born in the spring and summer, being rather more selective and critical. Maintenance is the overriding consideration here rather than initiation or development of new projects. In some respects, autumnal people tend to be more introverted and thoughtful than springtime and summertime people. Feelings are kept under stricter control. Yet, social urges are more maturely and fully expressed here also—friendships, group and community activities, direct working contributions to society are important at this time. Autumnal people manifest a strong urge to share and take part in serious and fulfilling relationships.

Those born in the fall have a heightened awareness of what is going on around them, perhaps greater than that of any other seasonal group. Impulse and emotion may be lower key in autumnal people, but often more subtle and complex. Both self–understanding and self–control are given high priority.

Winter

December 21–March 21

The winter solstice usually occurs on December 21 in the northern hemisphere (this date marks the beginning of winter in the northern hemisphere, but in the southern hemisphere winter begins around June 21). At this time of stillness, nights are longer and days shorter than at any other time in the year. As winter advances through the bitter days and on to the hint of spring, the nights grow shorter and the days longer. Winter is the fourth and last quarter, or 90° degree segment, of the yearly cycle. This season extends from the winter solstice to the spring equinox.

Winter is traditionally the period at which the water in ponds and rivers freezes, snow falls, the sounds of nature are muted and the land lies sleeping under a white blanket. Trees stretch their bare arms into a gray sky only lit a few hours a day by a low rising sun. Although much of nature seems dead, this is only a surface view. Deep within the earth, powerful forces are engaged in a metamorphosis, the results of which will be evident to the eye in spring. Nothing really dies but is transformed into another state. There is a feeling of waiting, and of expectation. Life has moved inside and underground. Warmth is sought in caves and in houses from bitter, howling winds. Fire keeps humans warm and foods that have been stored for the winter are eaten by both people and animals.

The Signs and Life Periods

Winter comprises three astrological signs: the cardinal earth sign Capricorn, the fixed air sign Aquarius and the mutable water sign Pisces. These three signs can be likened in human terms to the life of the individual aged 63–84. This spiritual period of human development from late middle age to death, evidences many of the same aspects of stillness, interiorization of experience and a quieting of instinctual demands that characterize nature's winter.

This fourth quadrant of The Grand Cycle of Life is governed by the faculty of thought and can be seen as a waxing period which manifests subjectively and has a conscious orientation. Although subjective, underground, interior activity has completely replaced outward growth in both nature and the human being, objective changes are on the way. In the case of humans, consciousness may have become less concerned with the externals

---

ZODIAC POSITION
0° Capricorn–0° Aries

QUADRANT
Fourth

HUMAN AGE
63–84

CUSP CONCEPTS
Prophecy, Mystery and Imagination, Sensitivity

SIGNS
Capricorn, Aquarius, Pisces

RULERS
Saturn, Uranus, Neptune

SYMBOLS
The Goat, The Water Bearer, The Fish

ELEMENTS
Earth, Air, Water

MOTTOS
I Master, I Universalize, I Believe

DOMINANT FACULTY
Thought

---

and more with the worlds of thought, religion, philosophy, spirituality and other universal concerns.

Astrologically, this is related to the fact that the signs Capricorn, Aquarius and Pisces are ruled by the heavenly bodies Saturn, Uranus and Neptune, which are all heavy, "outer" planets. These bodies are big and far from the earth, taking approximately 28, 84 and 165 years, respectively, to travel around the zodiac.

The outlook of the adult at this time is more universal. Such concerns as competing in the marketplace, raising a family, reproducing, building a powerful exterior and striving to change the world of society are generally diminishing or even completely absent now. The elder must prepare psychologically for the coming of the end of a life cycle.

The Wintertime Personality

Generally speaking, wintertime people are more concerned with the larger picture. They can be dominant types who rule their space with assurance, but often also display a greater degree of flexibility, sensitivity, acceptance and spirituality than those born at other times of the year. Although those born in the winter are often quiet types, many manifest great excitement through their thoughts, ideals and work. They are particularly distinguished by an active imagination and fantasy life. The most successful of wintertime people can objectify these visions and perhaps make them a source of creativity rather than be victimized by them. The allegiance of wintertime people is not so much to society or to personal considerations as to the world of ideas.

Wintertime people are less concerned with the state of the world as it is now and more with how it could and should be. A real reforming spirit can show itself in this personality, and an interest in matters concerning political and economic justice is very common.

The Forty-eight
Periods

The Cusp of Rebirth

March 19–24

The Pisces-Aries cusp is an admixture of the last sign of the zodiac, Pisces, and the first sign of the zodiac, Aries. This cusp can be likened symbolically to the beginning of each human life on earth as well as literally being the beginning of the astrological new year. Thus the Pisces-Aries cusp may be said to represent rebirth. Many civilizations have viewed the onset of spring (approx. March 21 in the northern hemisphere) as marking the year's beginning. This is emphasized by the words for spring in various languages: Italian—primavera, French—printemps, Dutch—voorjaar. Wisdom can be seen in this older way of looking at the yearly cycle, and instead of arbitrarily naming January 1 as the first day of the year, astrologers and other more traditionally minded thinkers prefer to consider the spring equinox, March 21, as the first day.

The days that comprise the Pisces-Aries cusp reveal not only the uncomplicated, fiery forwardness expected of Aries but also watery Piscean traits of dreaminess, active fantasy, quietude and sensitivity.

Those born on the Pisces-Aries cusp are unusually direct in their approach to life, and their outspokenness can make them alternately admired or misunderstood. Born on this primal cusp, they are basic, elemental individuals. The puzzling thing about Pisces-Aries is that although they themselves think that they see things in a simple and unclouded way, those who know them well often describe them as unrealistic dreamers, unable to get a handle on the harsh realities of the world. These individuals outwardly present a dynamic directness that often belies a sensitive, emotionally complex, even troubled

ZODIAC POSITION
Approximately
27° Pisces–4° Aries

SEASONS
Late winter/Early spring
(equinox)

ELEMENTS
Water/Fire

RULERS
Neptune/Mars

SYMBOLS
The Fish/The Ram

MODES
Feeling/Intuition

inner life. Thus they are doers as well as dreamers and have a no-nonsense, "what you see is what you get" attitude that actually tells only part of the story.

Misunderstandings about them abound. Out of the purest motives possible, for example, a Pisces-Aries may make a generous offer, perhaps of time or money. Yet before you know it, he or she is being accused of acting holier-than-thou, or of behaving condescendingly when those on the receiving end feel resentment. Meanwhile, the Pisces-Aries feels bewildered and hurt. Such scenarios are not uncommon in the lives of those born on the Pisces-Aries cusp. As a matter of fact, the more simply and directly they behave, the more others misread their intentions.

This directness of Pisces-Aries people inevitably arouses antagonism. However, those who are unwise enough to oppose them directly will quickly regret it. In addition, because of their quickness in grasping concepts and, often, in implementing their intuitive hunches, Pisces-Aries people may encounter resistance from those who move more slowly. Such a response has little effect on them, only arousing their impatience. Thus, particularly in group endeavors they must learn to curb their impetuosity, to listen to the often helpful suggestions of others, to slow their tempo and come into synch with the group rhythm. Ultimately, they must learn to weigh alternatives carefully before speaking or acting. Once they accomplish this, their logic can be remarkably persuasive and their thoroughness compelling.

Although their effect on people should teach them that something about their own behavior is amiss, Pisces-Aries generally refuse to change. They cannot

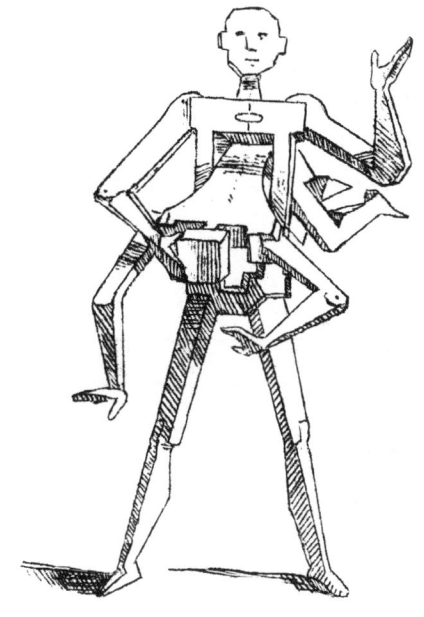

"REBIRTH"

really see any fault in what they do since, in their view, they are acting out of pure intentions. In the end, they often do get their way, whether by forging ahead without letup or by just sticking to their guns until the other party gives in.

Dealing with failure can be particularly difficult for those born on the Cusp of Rebirth. Since outright failure is not really in their vocabulary, when confronted with unavoidable defeat they are often baffled and bewildered. But their defense mechanisms in this respect are superb, and they are often spared defeat simply by their refusal to recognize it. They are not usually so unrealistic as to mistake losing for winning, but they do often view losing as just a partial setback on the way to a victory only temporarily postponed.

Others can learn, however, how to deal with Pisces-Aries successfully. One of the main rules is not to dig too deeply into their motives or to urge them to explain themselves. Another is not to try to analyze their personalities, or even to push them toward self-analysis. Yet those who use example rather than precept in encouraging them gently to be more objective about themselves can meet with success. This is not to say that Pisces-Aries can't learn from their own mistakes, simply that they must from time to time be encouraged to do so.

Another, even simpler route to getting along with Pisces-Aries is just to do what they say, at least for the time being. If you can come up with a better idea later, they will be pre-

pared to listen, but rarely if ever in their first burst of enthusiasm. It is important to recognize how important impulses, hunches, and first actions are to Pisces-Aries people. Blunting or negating their intuitions with advice and alternative suggestions can easily alienate them forever. Rarely, however, will anyone succeed in breaking their spirit or damping their forward movement for long.

In relationships, Pisces-Aries can be faithful partners, although their faithfulness may be more emotional than literal. They can love deeply and passionately, in other words, giving a great deal of attention to their love object, but at the same time they are not always monogamous; their intuitive, fiery side is always vulnerable to some exciting new prospect that suddenly appears. Their partner is generally the one expected to play the more stable, long-suffering role. Not that they themselves demand monogamy from their mate; actually, in many cases, a relationship that is more open on both sides suits them better, since it allays any guilt they might feel about their own indiscretions.

Pisces-Aries people generally function better as parents than they did as children, feeling more loyalty and responsibility to their offspring than they did to their elders when they were younger. Family can have surprisingly strong meaning for these highly independent souls, but family in the larger sense, including friends and associates as well as kin.

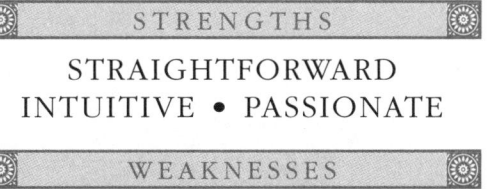

STRENGTHS

STRAIGHTFORWARD
INTUITIVE • PASSIONATE

WEAKNESSES

MISUNDERSTOOD • IMPATIENT
UNREALISTIC

ADVICE:

Learning patience is your most important task. Develop social skills through working alongside others. Try to curb your impetuous side—weigh alternatives and consider consequences before speaking or acting. Get to know yourself better.

PISCES-ARIES CUSP NOTABLES

How fitting that the spring equinox, the beginning of the astrological year, should be the birthday of **Johann Sebastian Bach**. Viewed by many as the ultimate source of classical music, Bach combined the many strands of earlier Renaissance and Baroque music

and also created new and highly original forms. The German Bach family included many professional musicians from the 16th to the 18th centuries. The family name means "brook" and symbolically suggests neverending movement, clear and flowing from a pure source. The deeply religious Piscean element and the

JOHANN
SEBASTIAN BACH

dynamic Aries drive are mixed in Bach's music, which is highly complex structurally yet simple in its appeal.

Achieving fame in the film *The Piano,* **Holly Hunter** conveys an image and presence far beyond her diminutive size. She typifies an indomitable spirit and refusal to be slowed down that are characteristic of those born on the Pisces-Aries cusp. Chameleonlike, she is able to play a wide variety of roles with apparent ease, emphasizing her Piscean side, and to uncompromisingly project her

HOLLY HUNTER

direct and piercing energies, an Aries trait. She can also portray a character who acts straightforward but is hard to read, typical traits of those born on the Cusp of Rebirth. Few birth images in film match that of Holly in *The Piano,* when she frees herself under water from her parlor grand and rises to the surface to be reborn.

Brooklynite **Spike Lee** burst onto the film scene after his graduation from NYU Film School. Like others born on the Pisces-Aries cusp, Lee has been both a dreamer and a doer, often misunderstood. He has done more than any other director to present the modern African-American experience in an uncompromising fashion. In *Do the Right Thing* and *Malcolm X,* Lee's unique mix of politics and history promoted a more aware spirit in American cinema. His films aim for clarity with sharp and uncompromising accents, revealing an underlying sensitivity, which are all characteristic of those born on the Cusp of Rebirth.

SPIKE LEE

More Pisces-Aries: Stephen Sondheim, Matthew Broderick, Pamela Harriman, Pat Riley, Gary Oldman, Glenn Close, Andrew Lloyd Webber, Joan Crawford, William Shatner, Bruce Willis, Ingrid Kristiansen, Akira Kurosawa, Chaka Khan, Moses Malone, William Jennings Bryan, Serge Diaghilev, Philip Roth, Ruth Page, George Benson, Ursula Andress, B.F. Skinner, Jesus Alou, Lynda Bird Johnson, Pat Bradley, Fanny Farmer, Wyatt Earp, Wernher von Braun, Steve McQueen, Clyde Barrow, Wilhelm Reich.

Relationship Guide for Pisces-Aries Cusp

BONNIE PARKER (LIBRA 1)
CLIVE BARROW (PISCES-ARIES CUSP)
PAGE 226

BEST RELATIONSHIPS

LOVE
Aries I
Cancer-Leo Cusp
Leo-Virgo Cusp
Virgo-Libra Cusp
Libra II
Scorpio III
Sagittarius-Capricorn Cusp
Capricorn-Aquarius Cusp
Aquarius-Pisces Cusp
Pisces III

MARRIAGE
Aries III
Gemini III
Virgo I
Capricorn II
Aquarius II

FRIENDSHIP
Aries-Taurus Cusp
Taurus II
Cancer II
Cancer III
Leo II
Virgo II
Libra I
Libra-Scorpio Cusp
Scorpio I
Scorpio II
Scorpio-Sagittarius Cusp
Sagittarius II
Sagittarius III
Aquarius III
Pisces I

FAMILY
Taurus III
Gemini II
Gemini-Cancer Cusp
Pisces-Aries Cusp

WORK
Pisces-Aries Cusp
Taurus II
Taurus-Gemini Cusp
Cancer I
Cancer II
Leo I

Page Locator for All Relationships

ARIES I
The Week of the Child

March 25–April 2

The Aries I period takes The Child as its central image, and, because it can be likened to the earliest portion of a human life, its characteristics are typically those of wonder, awe, simplicity, curiosity and primal energy.

The days that comprise Aries I symbolically reveal the first explorations of a new person contacting the fresh and curious world around it. Each Aries I day illustrates another facet of The Child's makeup and shows that, though this newly emerged being is filled with wonder and awed by a bewildering complexity of sensory experience, it is tough and strong enough to survive. Aries I reveals the human dichotomy of a child's being able to absorb impressions and become part of its environment while at the same time preserving its own individual selfhood.

Because Aries I's show the frank and open demeanor of the child, they are sometimes accused of having a naive or superficial view of life. But the so-called naiveté that they project is only one manifestation of the awe and wonder they experience in response to the world around them, which they are constantly rediscovering. An intense need to express this wonder, and to share their observations with others, is also characteristic. Like children, they not only exhibit spontaneity and liveliness themselves but also appreciate these qualities in others. In fact, many may not understand how deep their need for direct expression really is.

As children, Aries I's are faithful, on their own terms, but not particularly dutiful, particularly when it comes to fulfilling the expectations of parents who project their own dreams and wishes on them. Although born in the Week of

ZODIAC POSITION
Approximately 3–13° Aries
SEASON
Early spring
ELEMENT
Fire
RULER
Mars
SYMBOL
The Ram
MODE
Intuition

the Child, young Aries I's often give an impression of independence, as if they didn't need parents at all, but this conceals subtle emotional dependencies and needs that can manifest in small ways. Rarely will an Aries I child make a great show of feelings toward parents, preferring instead to express such emotion in the form of thoughtful everyday deeds. Parents of Aries I's quickly learn not to make the mistake of babying them, particularly as adolescents. Aries I's also dislike being reminded of their childlike demeanor when older, for it is vitally important to them that others regard them as mature and responsible.

The less outgoing Aries I's give the impression of being thoughtful, serious individuals, and even gregarious and talkative Aries I's tend to lead a highly private personal life. They have a quiet world to which they must retreat at frequent intervals, and it is inviolable. Often, an enclosed, even isolated existence has been forced on them in childhood through repeated criticism or misunderstanding, even that of parents who love and protect them. The danger of this is that as adolescents and mature adults they can fall into periods of brooding or depression, from which it may be difficult for them to work free. Moreover, Aries I people are slow to seek psychological help, preferring to handle their emotional difficulties by themselves.

Although Aries I's tend to spend long periods alone when away from work, their careers inevitably involve group or team endeavors. They have strong organizational energies, and others naturally come to depend on them. Rarely dictatorial, they even avoid being elected a group's leader, preferring instead to occupy an important role right in the center of things.

The morality of Aries I's is usually fixed and will not allow them to act in ways that they see as underhanded. This inflexibility, reflecting both their strong beliefs and their idealism, can cause problems at times; if their ethical belief in what they are doing is strong enough, in fact, they will not hesitate to go against the established order of things, even to the point of committing actions that may be illegal in their society's eyes.

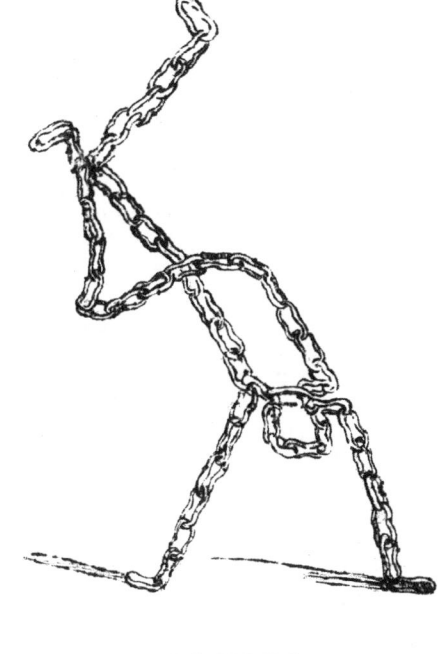

"CHILD"

things in perspective, and a life of his or her own. As far as friendships are concerned, Aries I's are dependable up to a point, that point usually arriving when they begin to feel that they are being taken advantage of. Again, those sensitive to their needs will protect the relationship's longevity by avoiding pushing them to that point. In any kind of relationship with Aries I's, knowing when to back off is essential. Confrontation should only be attempted with great care and sensitivity.

The behavior of Aries I's is usually a mixture of lively and highly measured responses. They are capable of swinging quickly from spontaneity to thoughtfulness, depending on the situation. Those involved with Aries I's must be sensitive to their moods or risk seeing them fly off the handle, usually as a result of feeling that they have been misread or misunderstood. Although some Aries I's can explode in anger, their more characteristic response is to turn heel and quickly leave the room. As those who are close to them will attest, however, Aries I's are usually agreeable to serious discussion of the problems of a given situation, as long as the conversation does not turn personal.

Generally speaking, a stable family life, including children, may not be the best prospect for Aries I's as young adults; they are better suited to this kind of life when they are older and have sown their wild oats. Their love relationships tend to the unusual, to say the least: they can be extremely unrealistic in their choice of partners, and their relationships may at times be suffused with a fairy-tale quality. Aries I's rarely respond to societal pressures to have a recognized love object, much preferring abstinence to maintaining pro forma relations with a spouse, lover or fiancé.

STRENGTHS

FRANK
SPONTANEOUS • DYNAMIC

WEAKNESSES

NAIVE • TRANSGRESSIVE
OVERIDEALISTIC

Extramarital affairs are not at all uncommon for Aries I's, who may not see such actions as transgressions. Such relationships underline their curiosity and their need for adventure, while at the same time announcing their refusal to be bound by society's conventional strictures. An unconventional Aries I relationship can easily be carried on for years. Oddly enough, it is precisely in these areas that the most noble, moral and loyal sentiments of an Aries I may be expressed.

Aries I's demand a lot of understanding from their mates and friends. Those best suited for intimate relationships with these energetic individuals are willing to leave them the freedom to act and to be themselves, without attempting to place restrictions on them. The person perhaps best suited for an Aries I is down to earth, and has a good sense of humor, the ability to put

ADVICE:

Cultivate your quiet side, yet do not neglect your aggressive urges or let them get bottled up inside. When you feel frustrated, try to understand the problem and then take the initiative. Acknowledge your need for affection and support. Do not hesitate to ask for help when you need it.

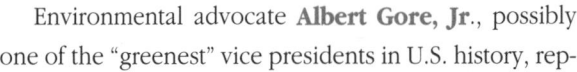

ARIES I NOTABLES

Actor-director **Leonard Nimoy** is best known as the pointy-eared character Spock in the *Star Trek* tv series and films. His appeal to young and old alike is unmistakable, but his youthful appeal to childhood fantasy is one of his most endearing traits. Nimoy conveys an openness and innocence characteristic of an Aries I, as in his role in *The Invasion of the Body Snatchers*, but also a

feeling that he hides a very private life both on and off the screen, typical of those born in this week. Those who attempt to probe the depths of the Aries I personality or seek ulterior motives may be in for a rude surprise, because with either Spock or Nimoy, what you see is what you get.

LEONARD NIMOY

Rock & roll's **Aretha Franklin**, mother of 4, has an exciting and direct singing style that betrays a certain childlike quality, perhaps because she has retained the openness and enthusiasm she manifested while growing up singing gospel music in her father's Detroit Baptist church. Few, if any, people have been strong enough to hold back the extremely independent Aretha for very long or so foolhardy to attempt to deprive her of her freedom. Her Grammy Legend Award and induction into the Rock and Roll Hall of Fame are indications of the determination and dynamism that characterize those born in the Week of the Child.

ARETHA FRANKLIN

Environmental advocate **Albert Gore, Jr.**, possibly one of the "greenest" vice presidents in U.S. history, represents the Clinton administration worldwide on a variety of crucial issues. Born and bred in Carthage, Tenn., Gore owns a small farm there, emphasizing the important link to childhood felt by many Aries I's. Gore's frank and open demeanor and his dislike of complica-

ALBERT GORE, JR.

tion and subterfuge and of being analyzed are also marks of one born in the Week of the Child. His youthfulness, along with that of the president, was instrumental in their 1992 election as the first post–WWII-born duo to head the nation. Gore spoke with obvious pride when presenting the very new and up-to-date Information Superhighway to the public.

More Aries I's: Diana Ross, Eric Clapton, Vincent van Gogh, Sandra Day O'Connor, Tennessee Williams, Sarah Vaughan, John Major, Gloria Swanson, Marvin Gaye, Warren Beatty, Mariah Carey, David Lean, Paul Verlaine, Quentin Tarantino, Francisco Goya, Casanova, Emile Zola, Hans Christian Andersen, Arturo Toscanini, Flannery O'Connor, Simone Signoret, Astrid Gilberto, René Descartes, Nikolai Gogol, Cesar Chavez, Rhea Perlman, Sergei Rachmaninoff, Alec Guinness, Camille Paglia, Joseph Campbell.

Relationship Guide for Aries I

Page Locator for All Relationships

GLORIA SWANSON (ARIES 1)
ERICH VON STROHEIM (VIRGO-LIBRA CUSP)
PAGE 249

BEST
RELATIONSHIPS

LOVE
Pisces-Aries Cusp
Gemini II
Gemini-Cancer Cusp
Cancer-Leo Cusp
Scorpio II
Scorpio-Sagittarius Cusp
Capricorn-Aquarius Cusp
Aquarius I

MARRIAGE
Taurus II
Cancer II
Leo II
Virgo II
Capricorn II
Capricorn III
Aquarius III

FRIENDSHIP
Aries I
Aries-Taurus Cusp
Taurus III
Gemini I
Gemini-Cancer Cusp
Leo-Virgo Cusp
Virgo III
Libra II
Libra III
Sagittarius I
Sagittarius II
Capricorn I
Aquarius-Pisces Cusp

FAMILY
Aries III
Leo I
Virgo-Libra Cusp
Libra II
Aquarius III
Pisces I

WORK
Taurus I
Taurus-Gemini Cusp
Gemini III
Cancer I
Cancer III
Virgo I
Libra I

ARIES II
The Week of the Star

April 3–10

The Aries II period takes The Star as its central image. It can be likened to the time when a child first emerges from its protected, nurturing environment—not only to become more aware of life around it but perhaps also to feel itself at the center of what is going on.

The days that comprise Aries II reveal a period characterized by experimental, initiatory and social concerns. In human terms, this "Star" of childhood is a shining enthusiastic entity busy with its first attempt at self-definition, around which other figures revolve. The child develops a concept of self (ego formation) and refers to itself, first using its own name and only later using the word and concept "I." Only by constant experimentation can its environment be probed and understood; this process involves a certain amount of daring and of necessity going too far or too fast at times. Indeed, the natural assertiveness of the child must be made manifest in order for normal development to take place.

Aries II people need to be at the center of things. They often feel lonely, even in the midst of a crowd, and consequently they rarely allow themselves to be alone. Born in the Week of the Star, they must have satellite planets revolving around them: admirers, supporters or co-workers. These individuals may seem self-centered, but even as they insist that their central position not be jeopardized or threatened, many are able to let go of their ego to a surprising degree by giving themselves fully to a project, cause, movement or religion. Aries II's can be swept away by their own vanity, and this can be unpleasant for those around them. Unfortunately, how-

ZODIAC POSITION
Approximately 12–21° Aries
SEASON
Early spring
ELEMENT
Fire
RULER
Mars
SYMBOL
The Ram
MODE
Intuition

ever, it is an ever-present pitfall for them that they fall in love with their own ideas, projects and even, in extreme cases, with themselves.

Those born during the Aries II period are highly goal oriented. Unfortunately, in order to get where they need to be, they may occasionally act amorally, and may neglect the feelings of others. This is probably not particularly painful for Aries II's themselves, since they don't generally rank high in empathy for or even in awareness of the emotions of others. Furthermore, their external striving can take the spotlight away from what should take center stage: their own inner being. Lack of introspection, simply not knowing themselves well, can hold these individuals back from spiritual growth. On the other hand, Aries II's who are challenged to realize that this inner peak is the one most worthy of being climbed are indeed fortunate people. Climbing it may well be the most important experience of their lives.

When it comes to a competitive, will-to-win kind of spirit, Aries II's have few equals. The upside of this driving energy is the ability to implement their often visionary and courageous ideals; the downside is an impatience with slower-moving minds and bodies, an irritability that can easily explode in destructive anger. Indeed, extreme behavior and a tendency to excess—basically not knowing when to stop—can land Aries II's in hot water again and again. This type of Aries must be particularly wary of letting their fire get out of control, and so must those who provoke them. Outright suppression or repression of their feelings is certainly not the answer, however, since this invariably results in frustration and depression, which can then initiate a new cycle.

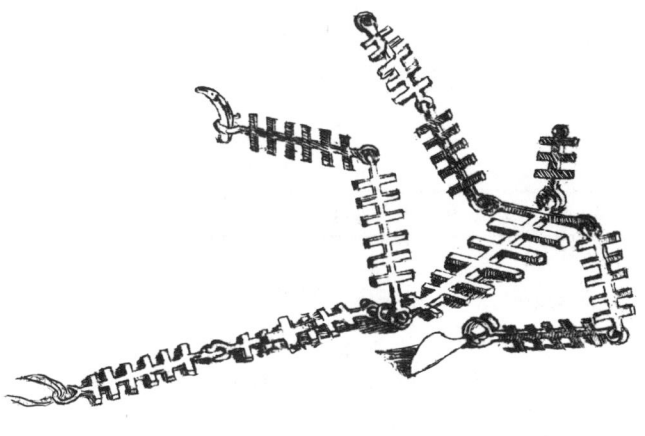

"STAR"

On the other hand, Aries II's who remain balanced and relaxed and who keep their energy freely flowing are certainly individuals to be admired.

Transforming their abundant energy into hard work is often the solution sought by Aries II's. Consequently, one real way to relate to them is to get right in there with them, to work side by side with them and share their frustrations and joys. Those who can keep up with them often make successful partners and mates for them, although the prodigious energy required passes beyond the usual bounds of friendship.

Aries II's often put themselves into indispensable positions; they are highly dependent on the feeling that others need them. This is ironic, since at heart they like nothing better than being free to act, to move, to decide, without the encumbrance of familial or societal responsibilities. A time comes in the lives of many Aries II's when they are rejected or ignored by their fans and are thrown back on themselves. When painful experiences like this make them finally face and overcome their need to be needed, they may be pushed into discovering their essential self. It is not at all unlikely for Aries II's to show their truly independent side much later in life, perhaps even in their sixties and seventies, when they may travel, exercise, explore creative activities or hobbies or in other ways strike out on their own.

Is it possible for Aries II's to find emotional fulfillment in a relationship? What about those who become involved with them—what can they expect? Certainly not many days off; being involved with an Aries II can be a full-time job. Yet those who relate to them most successfully are often put in the role of friend or advisor first, mate or lover second. The love relationships of Aries II's often burn out quickly, like shooting stars. Their selfish drives to conquer and dominate, unfortunately, come out in passionate relationships; quick to get involved, they can just as quickly get uninvolved.

Those who seek to touch an Aries II person on a direct emotional level may find themselves rebuffed. Aries II's have a real problem opening up at a deep level. They rarely let others into their inner world, and, indeed, it sometimes seems that they deny access to their emotional life even to themselves. Given their air of aloofness or detachment, emotional types often feel rejected by them. Nevertheless, they do have a need for a sympathetic and understanding mate or close friend who can help them understand themselves better. Those who are best for them are those who hang in there, not only exerting great patience and willpower but encouraging them to express and discuss their feelings. Finally, despite their aloofness, jealousy is not uncommon among Aries II's; to be replaced as the object of someone's affections is not at all what they have in mind for themselves.

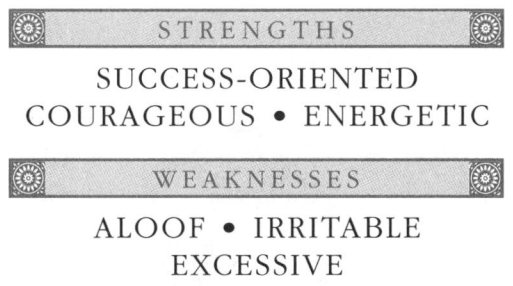

STRENGTHS

SUCCESS-ORIENTED
COURAGEOUS • ENERGETIC

WEAKNESSES

ALOOF • IRRITABLE
EXCESSIVE

ADVICE:

Resist overwhelming people with your energy. Act responsibly.
Try not to be too needy of attention and beware of leading others on.
Confirm your inner values and develop hidden talents.

ARIES II NOTABLES

Marlon Brando, whose star has blazed brightly across Hollywood's heavens, began as the quintessential

MARLON BRANDO

50s rebel. From *On the Waterfront* and *A Streetcar Named Desire* to *The Godfather, Last Tango in Paris,* and *Apocalypse Now,* Brando established his own acting style, with a bit of help from Lee Strasberg and method acting. Born in the Week of the Star, Brando has little choice but to be the center of attention and in the middle of whatever is going on. He has had his share of problems, but his tremendous willpower has largely been his to summon whenever it is needed. Characteristic of an Aries II is Brando's penchant for excess and his tendency to land in hot water when events get too far out of control.

Billie Holiday, one of the greatest of all jazz singers, was a prototype of the Aries II Star. Working with the finest musicians of her generation, notably the bands of Lester Young, Teddy Wilson, Count Basie and Artie Shaw, "Lady Day" was at her best singing with small groups in more intimate settings. Her personal life was in many ways a disaster, and she was worn down by alcohol and drugs. With a typical Aries II disinterest in self-analysis, she forced people to take her as she was. Compromise was not in Billie's vocabulary. Paradoxically, it is her older, more mature voice that many prefer today, even though it was diminished by her destructive lifestyle.

BILLIE HOLIDAY

Chairman of the Joint Chiefs of Staff **Gen. Colin Powell** was catapulted into the nation's political limelight in 1996, when some Republicans sought to make him the first African-American presidential candidate. Having shared honors with Gen. Norman Schwarzkopf for the victory in the Gulf War of 1991, Powell feels extremely comfortable at the center of command but is more of a team player who enjoys striving shoulder to shoulder with others and achieving concrete goals. His ability to balance his energies and hang loose in the saddle reflect the qualities of the most highly evolved Aries II's. Relaxed and

GEN. COLIN POWELL

confident, the modest and quiet Powell has become a beacon for the hopes and aspirations of many young African-Americans.

More Aries II's: Eddie Murphy, Jane Goodall, Helmut Kohl, Marguerite Duras, Maya Angelou, Francis Ford Coppola, Bette Davis, James Watson, Spencer Tracy, Charles Baudelaire, Gregory Peck, Betty Ford, Gil Hodges, Merle Haggard, Barry Levinson, Buster Douglas, Robert Downey, Jr., Mary Pickford, Max von Sydow, Marsha Mason, Omar Sharif, Paul Robeson, Andre Previn, Ravi Shankar, Jacques Brel, Carmen McRae, Michelle Phillips, Doris Day, Harry Houdini, Judith Resnik, Steven Seagal, James Mill.

Relationship Guide for Aries II

SPENCER TRACY (ARIES II)
KATHARINE HEPBURN (TAURUS III)
PAGE 264

BEST RELATIONSHIPS

LOVE
Gemini II
Gemini-Cancer Cusp
Sagittarius III
Capricorn II

MARRIAGE
Taurus I
Cancer II
Virgo I
Virgo III
Libra II
Sagittarius I
Capricorn II
Capricorn-Aquarius Cusp
Aquarius III
Pisces II

FRIENDSHIP
Leo II
Leo III
Scorpio I
Scorpio II
Scorpio III
Sagittarius II
Capricorn III
Aquarius I

FAMILY
Aries III
Taurus-Gemini Cusp
Cancer I
Virgo-Libra Cusp
Sagittarius-Capricorn Cusp
Aquarius II
Aquarius-Pisces Cusp

WORK
Aries II
Aries-Taurus Cusp
Gemini I
Gemini III
Leo-Virgo Cusp
Libra I
Libra-Scorpio Cusp
Pisces I

Page Locator for All Relationships

ARIES III
The Week of the Pioneer

April 11-18

The Aries III period takes The Pioneer as its central image. Symbolizing the further socialization of the child, it pictures a personality displaying humanity and taking an active interest in group activities. Along with cutting his/her first adult teeth, The Pioneer begins to come to grips with the vast repository of human culture through reading, writing and the media.

The days that comprise Aries III show a personality unfolding against the backdrop of social issues and activities. In The Grand Cycle of Life, the Aries III period occupies the time when a person demonstrates an interest in learning and begins the formal educational process. The spirit of exploration is strong here and accompanies the desire of the child to make its mark on its immediate environment and perhaps go beyond it. The Aries III period shows more group involvement than is traditional for the sign of Aries, anticipating the powerful social expression of the upcoming sign of Taurus.

Aries III's are quite uncharacteristic of the more self-centered, egoistic Aries types; much more social in nature, they must interact dynamically and regularly with their fellow humans, particularly with regard to bettering their living and working conditions. They are often true leaders, more concerned with doing good for their followers than with their own glory. Pioneers, they are often idealistic types who follow their visions fearlessly. Needless to say, they cannot exist side by side for long with another dominant personality, particularly one who challenges their authority. Such struggles may confuse or bewilder those born in this week, who believe that they are only acting for the good of all.

ZODIAC POSITION
Approximately
20–29° Aries

SEASON
Early spring

ELEMENT
Fire

RULER
Mars

SYMBOL
The Ram

MODE
Intuition

Aries III's sometimes fall victim to their own desire to help out. Because they often look to do good, and can be overly generous with their resources, these giving individuals can easily be taken advantage of. Guests invited to visit for a few days wind up staying for weeks, months or years. Small loans or donations to good causes may be granted with increasing frequency, turning into major financial support. A few minutes given each day to visit an invalid or to do volunteer work can lengthen to hours. Such largesse can put intolerable strain on the family of which the Aries III is a member.

Those born in the Week of the Pioneer may also choose the path of sacrifice, which their family or social group is usually expected to share. If their ideology calls for a certain type of health diet, say, or for a drastic reduction in the importance of food altogether, then so be it. Adult Aries III's can engender rebellious attitudes in their children or other young people under their sway, from whom they constantly demand sacrifice.

Both iconoclasts and traditionalists, Aries III's sometimes change roles when they move from one activity to another, or from one period of life to another. It is because they know the rules so well that they are able to break them. Their often high degree of creativity may express itself in the discovery, development or sale of useful products, particularly those that improve on methods used in the past.

Aries III's do not do well living alone, while going out into the world to work; yet neither can they give themselves easily to simple one-on-one conjugal relationships. They need to surround themselves daily with children, family and communal or social groups, which they

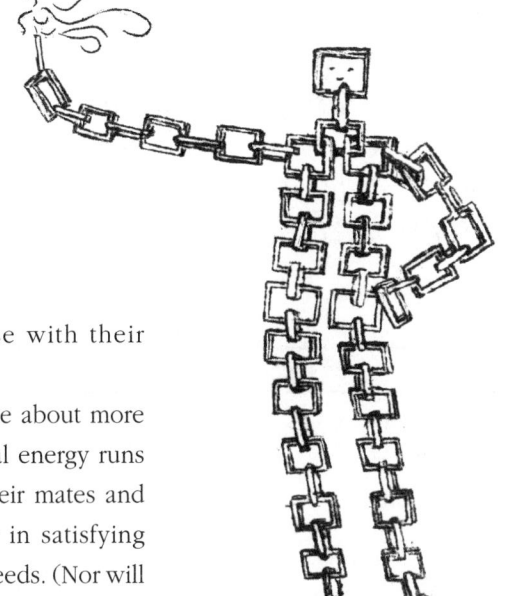

"PIONEER"

invariably seek to infuse with their dynamic idealism.

Aries III's are passionate about more than just their ideas: sexual energy runs high in this group, and their mates and lovers may be kept busy in satisfying them or living up to their needs. (Nor will an Aries III usually hesitate to find satisfaction elsewhere if it is denied at home.) They will sometimes see having children as a way of creating their own following, and this view of parenthood demands an agreeable, understanding and capable mate. Such a partner will inevitably be called upon to shoulder enormous responsibilities, and without complaint.

In relationships, Aries III's principal problem is the habit of forcing their ideas on others, putting abstractions ahead of personal considerations. Their children can have special problems in this regard; those born in this week sometimes hurt children's feelings, either by overlooking them or by refusing to recognize them. Such attitudes can apply also to Aries III's mates, who may be left at home feeling neglected while their partners are off challenging the world. Should Aries III males choose to apply their ideas to their living space, their wives or lovers may come to feel completely disenfranchised and lost.

The protectiveness of Aries III's toward their friends and family is generally valuable as long as it does not smother, or run out of hand. Better on defense than offense, those born in this week know how to disable an unreasonable opponent effectively with only a few words, or even a swift physical counterattack, though their proficiency in the fine art of diplomacy usually forestalls such out-and-out confrontations. Indeed, the classic Aries III will see the storm clouds gathering miles off, and will prepare for them well in advance of their arrival.

Another problem for the intimates of Aries III's is that, although these individuals are usually ready to listen, and are generous with their energy for fixing things, they may be unable to express true sympathy or to empathize. Due to their intensely positive attitude they have little time for nagging or complaining. Such "negative" expressions, however, can be highly useful in a relationship for blowing off steam and, if denied, can result in a buildup of frustration. In their lack of sympathy for complaints, Aries III's may only be postponing a problem that may one day bring their partner to a depression, or a volcanic explosion of anger, or even, eventually, may end in the breakup of the relationship.

The benefits of involvement with an Aries III, on the other hand, can be great. They have much to teach, and since they do so by example, they leave little doubt about their honesty—they put it on the line each time. They also convey a nobility and a depth of conscience and commitment that are highly admirable. Finally, they are not solemn moralists but truly fun-loving people who revel in activities like cookouts, summer vacations, outings and parties of all sorts.

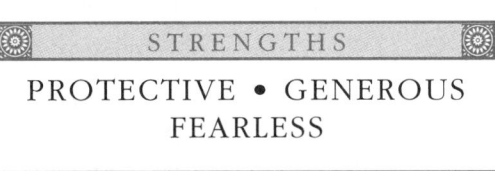

STRENGTHS

PROTECTIVE • GENEROUS
FEARLESS

WEAKNESSES

UNREALISTIC • UNYIELDING
SELF-SACRIFICING

ADVICE:

Tune in to what people are really saying. Beware of those who wish to monopolize your time and energy. Ideals and ideas can be worthy of devotion, but also destructive. Make sure that others want to be helped or led before you offer. Try to keep in touch with the actual state of things. Beware of being carried away by your own enthusiasm.

ARIES III NOTABLES

The quintessential Renaissance man, **Leonardo da Vinci** was an accomplished painter, poet, inventor and expert

LEONARDO DA VINCI

in the areas of geology, anatomy, botany, mechanics, aeronautics and many other fields. Few who have seen his *Mona Lisa* or beautifully elaborate and technically correct drawings have attempted to deny his absolute mastery of realistic painting and drawing. His study of the human body and his attempts to make life more pleasurable for those around him mark Leonardo as an Aries III, more socially than selfishly oriented. His breakthrough, hallmark discoveries and inquisitive mind mark him as a true Pioneer. Leading others with ideas rather than commands, this truly universal thinker blazed a path to the pinnacle of human achievement.

Loretta Lynn, known by her signature song as the *Coal Miner's Daughter*, grew up real fast in Butcher Hollow, Kentucky. She was married at 13, a mother of 4 at 17 and a grandmother with 6 children by the age of 31. Her pioneering spirit was clearly in evidence when she became the first woman to have a country music album go gold. An Aries III to the core, Lynn taught herself music and then proceeded to march to the very top of her profession. In 1988 she became a member of the Country Music Hall of Fame.

LORETTA LYNN

Ideas and ideals, plus an innate sense of humanity and nobility in the face of adversity, clearly mark **Charlie Chaplin** as an Aries III. Born in

CHARLIE CHAPLIN

wretchedly poor circumstances and forced to watch his father die from alcoholism and his mother go insane, Chaplin fought his way out of London's gutters onto the Hollywood movie screen and into the hearts of moviegoers the world over. As the lovable Tramp, his moustache, baggy trousers, hat and cane were personal trademarks, and his social attitudes in *Modern Times* and *The Great Dictator* reveal him clearly as a Pioneer. Both his formation of United Artists Studios and persecution as a communist in the early 50s illustrate Chaplin's inability to stay removed from business and social controversy.

More Aries III's: David Letterman, Thomas Jefferson, Evelyn Ashford, John Gielgud, Bessie Smith, Isak Dinesen, Joel Grey, Madalyn O'Hair, Garry Kasparov, Tama Janowitz, Nikita Khrushchev, Merce Cunningham, Ethel Kennedy, Buddha, Clarence Darrow, Anne M. Sullivan, Oleg Cassini, Henry James, Samuel Beckett, Dennis Banks, Pete Rose, Scott Turow, Ali Akbar Khan, Julie Christie, Harold Washington, Charles Evans Hughes, Kareem Abdul-Jabbar, Ellen Barkin, Harry Reasoner, J.P. Morgan, Mildred Bailey.

Relationship Guide for Aries III

HELEN KELLER (CANCER I)
ANNE SULLIVAN MACY (ARIES III)
PAGE 289

BEST RELATIONSHIPS

LOVE
Gemini II
Gemini-Cancer Cusp
Cancer III
Leo I
Virgo III
Scorpio I
Scorpio III
Scorpio-Sagittarius Cusp
Capricorn-Aquarius Cusp
Aquarius I

MARRIAGE
Pisces-Aries Cusp
Taurus II
Cancer II
Virgo II
Libra III
Sagittarius III
Capricorn II

FRIENDSHIP
Aries-Taurus Cusp
Taurus III
Taurus-Gemini Cusp
Virgo-Libra Cusp
Libra-Scorpio Cusp
Scorpio II
Sagittarius I
Capricorn I
Capricorn III
Aquarius II
Aquarius III
Pisces II

FAMILY
Aries I
Gemini III
Libra I

WORK
Aries III
Gemini I
Cancer I
Leo III
Virgo I
Libra II
Sagittarius-Capricorn Cusp
Aquarius-Pisces Cusp
Pisces III

Page Locator for All Relationships

ARIES-TAURUS CUSP
The Cusp of Power

April 19–24

The Aries-Taurus cusp is an admixture of the first sign of the zodiac, Aries, and the second sign of the zodiac, Taurus. This cusp can be symbolically likened to the period around seven years of age in the human life and falls at the beginning of mid-spring in the northern hemisphere. The Aries-Taurus cusp may be said to represent Power. During this period of the year the forces of nature are fully released with beautiful, sometimes terrifying, intensity. The onset of spring may be seen as heralding an idyllic, pastoral season but has also been the time of violent blood rituals both in primitive cultures and in the Christian Easter Jewish Passover celebrations. In spring, the melting snow of the mountains discharges torrents of water, rains come and colorful new life thrusts up through the earth seeking light and air. In humans, the age of seven usually marks the arrival of many of the second teeth, and the child passes over into a stage in which he/she begins to feel and express newfound powers. Ideally, identification with the parent of the same sex has occurred by now and the child seeks to assert his/her growing independence and autonomy.

The days that comprise the Aries-Taurus cusp reveal some of this manifestation of Power, not only in the fiery forwardness and willfulness expected of Aries, but also in earthy Taurus traits of practicality, endurance and nurturing.

Those born on the Aries-Taurus cusp strive for power in their daily lives, but their personalities temper and ground the fiery dynamism of Aries through the solidity and earthiness of Taurus. The undeniable trademark of

ZODIAC POSITION
Approximately
27° Aries–4° Taurus

SEASONS
Mid-spring

ELEMENTS
Fire/Earth

RULERS
Mars/Venus

SYMBOLS
The Ram/The Bull

MODES
Intuition/Sensation

those born in this week is a preoccupation with power. They see their birthright as nothing less than the very best that life has to offer. Yet they generally know how to pursue their goals without arousing antagonism in others. Powerfully persuasive, they make it easier and more advantageous to agree with them than to disagree. Whether it takes a long or a short time to achieve their ends matters little to Aries-Tauruses as long as they get there. Above all, they have a superb sense of timing, and of *kairos*—knowing the right time to act and not to act.

In first meetings, they often impress others as quiet and self-assured—as people who know how to watch and wait. Aries-Tauruses do not waste their time proving anything to anyone, preferring to hang back confidently and save their energy for when it counts. In this respect they make formidable enemies and capable co-workers. Their approach to work is highly professional, and those involved with them must understand that their career will always be at least as important to them as their relationships.

Those involved with Aries-Tauruses can benefit tremendously from their powerful presence and capabilities. They know the value of money, and also how to get it. Their goal, however, is usually not so much financial security as a steady cash flow that they derive from their work, and that permits them to spend freely. As they see it, financial dependency on someone else is a liability; they would just as soon do the supporting themselves, since they have little desire to give up their personal freedom. Learning to accept financial and other kinds of support from mates, family and friends may be difficult for them, but, like love, it will ultimately bring them a step forward in their personal development.

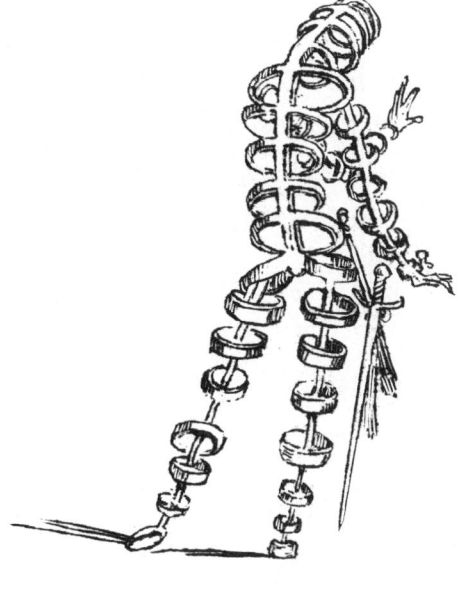

"POWER"

The unspoken secret of Aries-Taurus people is that what they secretly long for most is to give up the daily battles of the world and simply submit to fantasy, pleasure, perhaps to another individual, perhaps to sheer laziness. This is usually impossible for them to accomplish for very long, but in their hard-driving approach to daily life it is always a comforting thought, an idea that gets them through many a tough day. Certainly Aries-Tauruses do best when they can periodically empty themselves out (through sleep, for example, or leisure time, massage, meditation or vacations), allowing themselves to recharge.

In relationships, no matter how high or low their station, Aries-Tauruses make their presence felt in their interactions with others. They are big people, capable of prodigious mistakes as well as of glittering successes, and they leave little doubt about where they stand. They tend to choose rather than to be chosen. Once they have fixed their sights on someone the matter is settled. This is not to say that their judgment is perfect: they will quickly take credit when they have chosen well, but their inability to admit to a major mistake tends to make them very long-suffering. Aries-Tauruses hang in there not only because they are faithful but, more important, because to quit would be an admission of failure, and failure is very hard indeed for them to handle.

Those born on the Cusp of Power are extremely generous, but on their terms. They only give when it suits them, and they are equally capable of taking back not only their gifts but their affection—not out of capriciousness or malice, but because they feel that their gifts have gone unappreciated or were undeserved. Not infrequently, the degree of their giving can itself be intimidating, arousing insecurity in less robust souls. Such lavishness can create dependencies in both the giver and the recipient, and these may later be difficult or impossible to break.

An important lesson that Aries-Tauruses must learn is to give up a certain amount of their power, and to replace it with a degree of sharing, cooperation and acceptance. That they become more powerful, in a human sense, by doing so is a realization that will grow with the years. In this respect, a warm and giving mate or friend, and the mutual affection engendered through family life of some kind, are essential for their development.

A second lesson, related to the first, is that the greatest power may be the power of love. Whether sexual or affectionate, romantic, platonic or religious, love has an undeniable softening effect on those born on the Cusp of Power. Although they may take and discard lovers when it pleases them, they do best on a steady diet of love from one special person. They reach their zenith and shine most brightly when this love involves an unconditional giving on their part, which is perhaps the closest they can come to true selflessness.

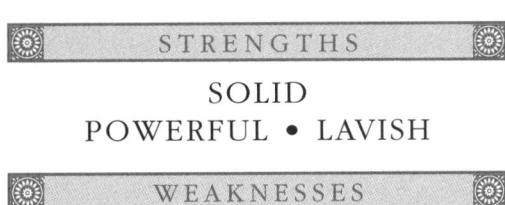

STRENGTHS

SOLID
POWERFUL • LAVISH

WEAKNESSES

BLUNT • MERCENARY
LAZY

ADVICE:

Try not to overpower others. Learn to back off and allow things to happen as they will. Although your hands may itch to do the job, give others a chance to do it their way, even if they make mistakes. Try to remain sensitive to the feelings of those around you.

ARIES-TAURUS CUSP NOTABLES

Leader of the Bolshevik Revolution in Russia, **Vladimir Ilyich Lenin** was a living embodiment of Power. Shipped from Germany in a sealed railway car, Lenin entered Russia's revolutionary bloodstream like a hidden virus, which then spread, multiplied and raged out of control. Lenin's mastery of the rules of power was soon evident, as his small political party gained and maintained control over the world's largest country. Lenin's

VLADIMIR
ILYICH LENIN

plans for world revolution did not materialize, however, and only 3 years after he established the Third International, he was paralyzed by his first stroke, dying 2 years later in 1922. Interestingly, his Sagittarius-Capricorn successor, Joseph Stalin, and Aries-Taurus Adolf Hitler were also fire-earth combinations. (Aries and Sagittarius are fire signs, Taurus and Capricorn earth.)

QUEEN ELIZABETH II

Thought to be the wealthiest woman in the world, **Queen Elizabeth II** of Great Britain has quietly and firmly ruled her country for almost half a century. Although opposed by not inconsiderable forces that wish to scrap the monarchy and plagued by divorce and scandal within her own family, Elizabeth has managed to maintain an iron grip on many affairs of state. Although supposedly only a figurehead, this powerful monarch continues to exert economic and political influence on those who guide the destiny of her country. While the British Empire is no more, the queen still occupies a unique place in the hearts and minds of the majority of her subjects.

Brooklyn-born film director, producer, singer-songwriter, actress and musical comedy star **Barbra Streisand** has parlayed her talents into success with her guts, willpower and genius. Immensely ambitious, Streisand succeeded where many have failed. Throughout her tempestuous life, she has reigned over Hollywood and the Broadway stage with a power and resolve equaled by few others in her generation. She owes a great deal to her many fans, who have supported her unceasingly through thick and thin. Thanks to the special

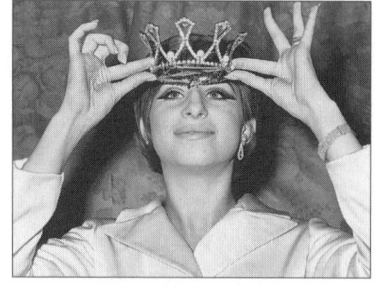

BARBRA STREISAND

rapport she establishes with her audiences, she is revered like a goddess, who grants a glimpse of the heavens through her grace and strange beauty.

More Aries-Tauruses: Catherine the Great, William Shakespeare, Willem de Kooning, Shirley MacLaine, Richard Daly, Jr., Shirley Temple Black, Jack Nicholson, Adolf Hitler, Joan Miró, Yehudi Menuhin, Patti LuPone, Jessica Lange, Daniel Day-Lewis, Luther Vandross, Paloma Picasso, Dudley Moore, Lionel Hampton, Ryan O'Neal, Don Mattingly, Al Unser, James Woods.

Relationship Guide for Aries-Taurus Cusp

QUEEN ELIZABETH II (ARIES-TAURUS CUSP)
PHILIP MOUNTBATTEN (GEMINI II)
PAGE 310

BEST RELATIONSHIPS

LOVE
Virgo II
Virgo-Libra Cusp
Libra II
Libra-Scorpio Cusp
Scorpio II
Scorpio III
Capricorn III
Aquarius III

MARRIAGE
Taurus-Gemini Cusp
Gemini-Cancer Cusp
Cancer III
Leo II
Aquarius I

FRIENDSHIP
Pisces-Aries Cusp
Aries I
Aries III
Aries-Taurus Cusp
Taurus III
Gemini II
Cancer II
Libra I
Libra III
Scorpio I
Scorpio III
Scorpio-Sagittarius Cusp
Capricorn II
Aquarius-Pisces Cusp
Pisces I

FAMILY
Taurus I
Taurus II
Cancer-Leo Cusp
Sagittarius-Capricorn Cusp
Pisces II

WORK
Aries II
Gemini I
Cancer I
Leo III
Virgo I
Virgo III
Sagittarius I
Capricorn-Aquarius Cusp

Page Locator for All Relationships

TAURUS I
The Week of Manifestation

April 25–May 2

The Taurus I period takes Manifestation as its central image. This period can be likened to the time in a child's life when real power can be exercised, often by giving concrete form to ideas and implementing them effectively. Learning to build physical structures and to set up workable systems is part of this manifestative process.

The days that comprise Taurus I symbolically reveal the elementary school-aged child developing an ever-evolving individual personality of his or her own within the larger structures of established institutions and society. Problems involving power struggles, diplomacy, autonomy, compromise, survival and defense arise on a daily basis and must be met. Out of this crucible character is formed.

Taurus I's are hard-headed pragmatists and those born in the Week of Manifestation are among the most dominant individuals of the year. When seized by an idea or plan, they will not let it rest until it is implemented. Rarely will this idea be one that has not already been proven, or does not show great promise; Taurus I's are convinced of most of their enterprises' success from the start.

Manifesting or giving shape to a concept might include setting up a home or family as well as a business or other organization. A feeling for structure, particularly of a hierarchical kind, comes naturally to Taurus I's. Technically oriented, they love to find out how and why things work, not hesitating to take them apart and put them back together again. This penchant for practical analysis applies to artistic and financial models as well as mechanical ones.

ZODIAC POSITION
Approximately
3°–13° Taurus

SEASONS
Mid-spring

ELEMENTS
Earth

RULERS
Venus

SYMBOLS
The Bull

MODES
Sensation

Although the leadership abilities of Taurus I's are undeniable, it is less the kick of leading others that drives them than the vision of personally implementing their ideas through group endeavors. Taurus I's prefer sitting and ruling the roost to vying with others for power or seeking new worlds to conquer. Among the most stubborn of all Tauruses, they are impossible to convince of the need for change, unless you can demonstrate that they will gain an unequivocal advantage by modifying their plans.

As bosses but also as co-workers, Taurus I's can be highly successful through their diplomacy and their understanding of their colleagues' needs. Their role at work often mirrors that at home: they are protectors and nurturers. The Taurus I boss stresses employees' need to get along with each other and to work as a team. Taurus I's are not always psychologically prepared for infighting, or for situations in which they are ignored, belittled or unappreciated. They are quite capable of getting rid of troublemakers but may also withdraw, or even fall into a depressive slump. In the same way, they become bewildered and confused when their generosity in personal relationships goes unappreciated. This works against their ability to implement their ideas. Learning not to take things personally, and particularly not to feel let down or betrayed when people disagree with them, will increase their effectiveness.

Taurus I's are intensely physical people; sex, food, comfort, and sports and recreation of all kinds are important to their mental and physical well-being. One way to get close to them is to share a daily regimen with them, perhaps jogging, swimming, squash or tennis. This kind of activity will help build a bond of mutual trust, allow-

"MANIFESTATION"

ing them to open their hearts and share their secrets. Taurus I's usually know when to stop in the area of physical endeavor, but overindulgence in sedentary pleasures can be damaging and dangerous to them. Often passionately interested in food, they can have major problems with overweight, alcohol, high cholesterol and related physical disorders.

Taurus I's can avoid many problems by adjusting their self-image to correspond more with reality. What they think they are (tough, no-nonsense, stable) and what they really are (sensitive, emotional, tending to exaggerate) are too often at variance. Unfooled by their cool, often gruff exterior, those who know them well know how emotionally vulnerable they are, and instinctively seek to protect them. In business and social affairs, Taurus I's can easily be knocked off-balance, particularly when they put on a big act for the benefit of others, who may perceive them as blowhards. Sticking to the issues, being themselves, and avoiding personal involvements are essential for their relations with fellow employees. Above all, Taurus I's should avoid trying to show how generous and big-hearted they are; they should learn to let their actions speak for themselves. Smugness and a know-it-all attitude only arouse resentments that can backfire later.

In relationships with Taurus I's, head-on confrontations should be avoided. A much more sensible method, particularly when they are your parents or mates, is to appeal to their need for affection and harmony. Emotional manipulation or appeal, particularly at moments of good feeling, is likely to work better than knock-down, drag-out argument. Since Taurus I's like to run the show, shouldering huge burdens all day at work, they may feel that the relief of the peaceful home environment is worth protecting at all costs.

Of course, this peace can have its downside: Taurus I's can be so happy with their living situation that they ignore its warning signs. Prone to procrastination, those born in this week often downplay matters needing attention, whether a squeaky door, a drafty window or the needs of a family member. The desire of Taurus I's for peace and quiet, and their resistance to change, can become oppressive, even stifling, to those who live with them.

In general, Taurus I's tend to preserve and hold on to what they've got. At some point in their lives, however, they may have to learn to walk away from a relationship instead of trying to hold it together or patch it up: if it falls apart, something better may emerge. Should they fail to learn this, their inability to let go may leave both them and their partners in limbo. Their conviction that problems may get better, or may go away, only makes painful issues harder to deal with. Such avoidance may lead both parties to feel trapped: unable to work things out yet unable to leave.

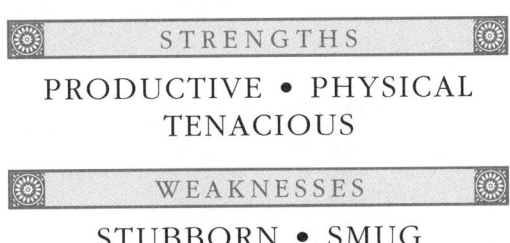

STRENGTHS

PRODUCTIVE • PHYSICAL
TENACIOUS

WEAKNESSES

STUBBORN • SMUG
EXAGGERATING

ADVICE:

Beware of taking on too much responsibility. Consciously work on changing yourself periodically. Beware of procrastinating in the name of prudence or good sense. Open up your horizons by exposing yourself to different disciplines and points of view.

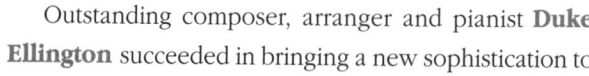

TAURUS I NOTABLES

Czech-Austrian industrialist and businessman **Oskar Schindler** saved over 1,000 Jews from the Nazi death camps. With the stubbornness and pragmatic viewpoint only a Taurus I could exhibit, Schindler refused to let "his Jews" be taken away from their jobs in his factory.

OSKAR SCHINDLER

Stubbornly arguing that they were aiding the war effort, Nazi Party member Schindler succeeded in tricking German officials, particularly when he courageously entered the concentration camps himself to get his workers back. Immortalized in Steven Spielberg's film *Schindler's List,* most people had never heard of the man before Spielberg brought him to prominence. Dedication to manifesting their ideas in cold, hard reality characterizes Taurus I's like Schindler.

Outstanding composer, arranger and pianist **Duke Ellington** succeeded in bringing a new sophistication to jazz. Associations with Igor Stravinsky and Billy Strayhorn showed Ellington as a master of the jazz ensemble. Highly individual in its approach, the Ellington band did not aim for the hard-swinging quality of Count Basie, the excitement of Benny Goodman or the commercialism of Glenn Miller, but

DUKE ELLINGTON

took the high ground in putting Ellington's artistic concepts to work, much to the delight of creatively oriented audiences the world over. The Duke was a master of Manifestation, with his band, compositions, arrangements, performances and recordings being proof of his ability to bring his ideas to fruition.

The stunning good looks of actress **Michelle Pfeiffer** are characteristic of the Taurus I kind of Venusian beauty. Pfeiffer has managed to bowl people over with her overwhelming goddesslike demeanor and acting skills. Choosing to adopt a baby girl and raise her as a single mother demonstrates Taurus I determination to carry through on an idea and assume responsibility for the welfare of another. Forty years old in 1997, Pfeiffer has never looked better and will undoubtedly continue to maintain her radiant appearance in typical Taurus I style.

MICHELLE PFEIFFER

More Taurus I's: Al Pacino, Talia Shire, Ella Fitzgerald, Andre Agassi, Joseph Heller, Bianca Jagger, Saddam Hussein, Jerry Seinfeld, Duke of Wellington, Coretta Scott King, Queen Juliana, Queen Mary II, Willie Nelson, Ulysses S. Grant, I.M. Pei, Bernard Malamud, Michel Fokine, David Hume, Rita Coolidge, Bobbie Ann Mason, Ollie Matson, Pierre Teilhard de Chardin, Terry Southern, Chuck Bednarik, Jill Clayburgh, Emperor Hirohito, James Monroe, Ann-Margret, Kate Smith, Casey Kasem, Sandy Dennis, Anouk Aimee.

Relationship Guide for Taurus I

Page Locator for All Relationships

MARTIN LUTHER KING, JR (CAPRICORN III)
CORETTA KING (TAURUS I)
PAGE 346

BEST RELATIONSHIPS

LOVE
Pisces-Aries Cusp
Taurus-Gemini Cusp
Gemini-Cancer Cusp
Leo-Virgo Cusp
Scorpio I
Capricorn-Aquarius Cusp
Pisces III

MARRIAGE
Aries II
Taurus III
Gemini II
Cancer III
Scorpio II
Sagittarius II
Capricorn I
Capricorn III
Aquarius II
Aquarius III

FRIENDSHIP
Cancer I
Leo I
Virgo II
Virgo III
Libra-Scorpio Cusp
Scorpio-Sagittarius Cusp
Sagittarius-Capricorn Cusp
Aquarius I
Pisces II

FAMILY
Aries-Taurus Cusp
Taurus I
Taurus II
Leo II
Virgo-Libra Cusp
Pisces I

WORK
Aries I
Taurus I
Gemini I
Gemini III
Cancer-Leo Cusp
Leo III
Virgo I
Scorpio III

TAURUS II
The Week of the Teacher

May 3–10

The Taurus II period takes The Teacher as its central image. This period can be likened to the time in a child's life when formal learning and education have taken a central role. Study becomes the basis for a future time in which the young adult will take his/her place in society.

The days that comprise Taurus II reveal the development of this formal learning process and stress the importance of the teacher as a role model. Devotion, awakening, moral development and independent action are all important elements here. Also, the child at this stage of life discovers how this personal orientation fits in with the larger scheme of things, particularly with regard to other subcultures and nationalities. Ultimately, the student develops the capability to teach or transmit what he/she has learned to others.

Those people born in the Week of the Teacher are mainly involved in the development of ideas and techniques. No matter what the vocation or avocation of a Taurus II, they have a message to share. Verbalizing their ideas and observations, generating discussion, and leading by example are all Taurus II's favorite activities. It can be said that they have.a calling for imparting information and, more importantly, presenting it in a manner that others can understand.

It is not surprising that Taurus II's have a strong need for teacher-student–type interactions. They intuitively sense that teacher and student are two sides of the same coin, and that this coin is one they wish to invest in their future. Taurus II's generally do well enough at school, but fare best as students or teachers in one-on-one learn-

ZODIAC POSITION
Approximately
12–21° Taurus

SEASON
Mid-spring

ELEMENT
Earth

RULER
Venus

SYMBOL
The Bull

MODE
Sensation

ing or small group situations such as in dance, music, sports and the visual arts. For a Taurus II, being a good student is the first step toward becoming a good teacher. Taurus II teachers also know the value of learning on one's own and, instead of binding students to them, will encourage them to teach themselves.

Those born in the Taurus II period are movers and shakers, and, since they rarely deal with flighty or superficial topics, they are capable of influencing others. Part of the key to this lies in the fact that Taurus II's live so much of their lives in the realm of ideas, of ideologies. Excellent entrepreneurs, they can set up both businesses and families without an excessive need to dominate or impose an inflexible structure on those with whom they live and work. They do, however, often establish lines that should not be crossed.

Taurus II's are very interested in the living conditions of those around them, and particularly in social groups that are foreign to them. How and where others live, work, play, eat, worship, vote and exercise has enormous fascination for Taurus II's, who also tend side with the underdog and to feel all forms of unfairness and discrimination keenly. Not surprisingly, interracial or cross-cultural relationships are common for Taurus II's. Similarly, older Taurus II's may be attracted to younger people and younger Taurus II's to those much older than themselves.

The moral stance of the Taurus II is usually strong, even unyielding. They have firm ideas about right and wrong, which they do not hesitate to express. Although you probably wouldn't call them straitlaced, they may exhibit prudish or even puritanical tendencies, particularly when young. And such early tendencies, even though outgrown,

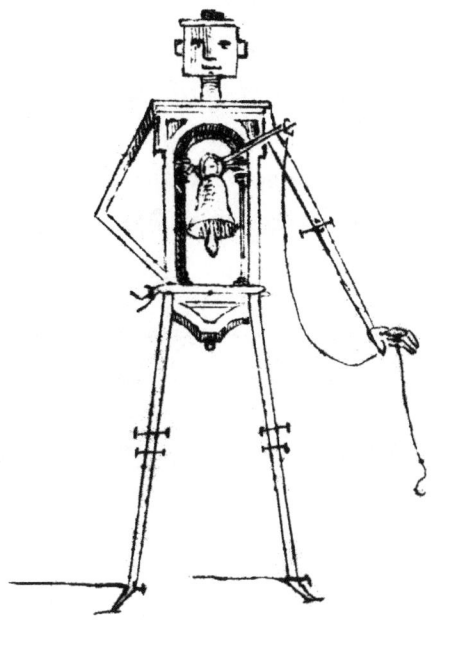

"TEACHER"

may surface in times of stress when they are adults, much to the surprise of those who know them as free-thinkers. The area in which the ethical orientation of Taurus II's is most unequivocal is their insistence on fairness. One might say, in fact, that they are obsessed with injustice, prejudice and discrimination in all forms. Their reaction to any form of racism is scathing, uncompromising and immediate. Actually, anger may erupt suddenly in almost any area of the lives of Taurus II's, and those born in this week must learn how to handle their feelings of upset healthily, while not suppressing them.

Physical activity, whether sports, dance, music, or fitness training, comes naturally to Taurus II's, yet they do not convey the impression of being earthy, sensuous types. They generally create a strong first impression, and make a heavy impact on their environment, but this may be due more to their mental qualities than to their physical ones. Even those of a small or average body type often project an image far greater than their actual size on first meeting.

Although excellent bosses, parents and teachers, Taurus II's are not always the easiest people to be involved with day-to-day as mate, lover or friend. Demanding and critical, those born in this week make their dislikes known sharply and incisively, often alienating or insulting those of a softer or more sensitive disposition. Their insistence that people be hard and tough, able to take the truth in a straight dose, is not everyone's cup of tea. When

Taurus II's become happier and more comfortable with themselves, and as they grow older, many of their critical characteristics will mellow or even disappear.

With their Venusian love of beauty and their great charm and personal magnetism, Taurus II's often have a host of admirers. They are not really comfortable with a great deal of attention, however, and do not like finding themselves imprisoned in a social circle of their own making. At such times those born in this period have little choice but to withdraw into a more isolated existence. More successful Taurus II's therefore learn to control their own attractive powers and to create fewer problems for themselves.

Those who relate best to Taurus II's in personal relationships are those who understand their need to be left alone rather than being fussed over or spoiled. Taurus II's prefer their mates to show their enthusiasm for the relationship simply by upholding their share of it rather than by displays of gratitude or affection. In intimate situations, Taurus II's can be extremely passionate, but in their everyday routine they insist on a certain distance. They prefer romance to sentimentality, but like a realistic and frank approach to love and sex even better. They do not generally react well to others' requests for attention or affection, even when those others are intimates; anything that looks like pleading or begging usually turns them off completely. Taurus II's like their partners to be strong and dignified above all.

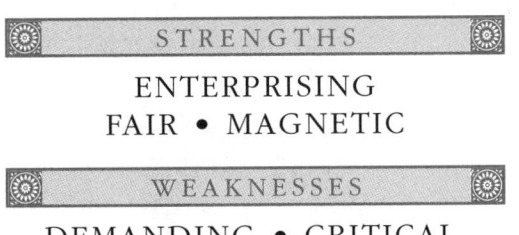

STRENGTHS

ENTERPRISING
FAIR • MAGNETIC

WEAKNESSES

DEMANDING • CRITICAL,
INFLEXIBLE

ADVICE:

Seek to be more affectionate and playful. Beware of strident, dogmatic or inflexible attitudes. Remember that others have gifts to teach also, and that the best teacher is often an eternal student. Set a good example by admitting your mistakes. Rework and revise your ideas periodically.

TAURUS II NOTABLES

The didactic quality of actor-director **Orson Welles** squarely marks him as a Teacher. The innovations in his first film, *Citizen Kane,* pointed the way for future filmmakers as no other film before. Whether he spoke as an actor, director or simply creative genius, Welles was a master of the telling observation and of witty repartee

ORSON WELLES

and sarcasm. Interested in ideas for their own sake, Welles was a true intellectual, but at the same time he had the contempt for second-rate ideas or phoniness that all experts possess. The problem with all this is that Welles was an amateur magician and conjurer himself, so that despite his brilliance people were not always prepared to believe him. Nevertheless, he displayed a mastery of language as evidenced by his storytelling on film.

The tumultuous life and times of **Eva Perón** are known to many, due to Andrew Lloyd Webber's musical *Evita* and the song *Don't Cry for Me, Argentina.* She was the illegitimate child of a mother who sought to control through men, and such a role model influenced Evita in choosing a string of lovers who could advance her career. As the wife of

EVA PERÓN

Argentine dictator Juan Perón, she became the heroine of the working class and, characteristic of many Taurus II's, the protector and champion of the poor and disadvantaged. Indeed, through Perón, she succeeded in making inroads in improving the living conditions of Argentina's workers. Uncompromising, she refused to give up her moral struggle when confronted by the military. Possessed of a characteristic Taurus II temper, she was said to be her own worst enemy when out of control.

Founder of psychoanalysis, and the first modern psychologist, **Sigmund Freud** is considered one of the pioneers of 20th-century thought. His written works and lectures mark him clearly as a Teacher, particularly in the areas of the unconscious, dream interpretation and clinical psychiatric treatment. But he is also characteristic of the rigidity and dogmatism of Taurus II's and their refusal to admit mistakes. Many of his original observations have been discredited because they were based on a relatively small group of patients, but the universal truth of his more important concepts, particularly his emphasis on parent-child interactions in the first years of life, have generally been upheld.

SIGMUND FREUD

More Taurus II's: Karl Marx, Greg Gumbel, Sugar Ray Robinson, Golda Meir, Audrey Hepburn, Roberto Rossellini, Dave Prater, Sid Vicious, Keith Haring, Tammy Wynette, Willie Mays, Rudolph Valentino, Glenda Jackson, Candice Bergen, Fred Astaire, Judith Jamison, Keith Jarrett, Randy Travis, Johannes Brahms, Peter Ilyich Tchaikovsky, Gary Cooper, Mary Lou Williams, Ariel Durant, Pancho Gonzalez, John Brown, Ricky Nelson.

Relationship Guide for Taurus II

EVITA PERON (TAURUS II)
JUAN PERON (LIBRA II)
PAGE 360

BEST RELATIONSHIPS

LOVE
Taurus III
Gemini III
Cancer II
Leo II
Leo III
Virgo II
Sagittarius II
Capricorn I

MARRIAGE
Aries I
Aries III
Taurus II
Gemini II
Cancer I
Cancer-Leo Cusp
Libra II
Scorpio-Sagittarius Cusp
Aquarius I
Pisces II

FRIENDSHIP
Pisces-Aries Cusp
Gemini-Cancer Cusp
Leo I
Leo-Virgo Cusp
Scorpio II
Capricorn II
Pisces I

FAMILY
Aries-Taurus Cusp
Virgo III
Scorpio I
Sagittarius I
Sagittarius-Capricorn Cusp
Aquarius-Pisces Cusp
Pisces III

WORK
Gemini I
Cancer III
Virgo I
Virgo-Libra Cusp
Libra III
Scorpio III
Sagittarius III

Page Locator for All Relationships

TAURUS III
The Week of the Natural

May 11–18

The Taurus III period takes The Natural as its central image. This period can be likened to the time when a fast-maturing child establishes a relationship with society but also wishes to be him/herself without undue societal demands. The onset of puberty means having to accept new sexual changes that are taking place and attempting to develop a more mature attitude, free of shame or stigma.

The days that comprise Taurus III reveal the tremendous release of energy that accompanies late childhood. These changes are not only physical but occur in the fantasy and unconscious world as well. Attraction, inhibition and lack of it, rebellion, mischievousness and acting out of unconscious wishes all play their part in this activity. Saying goodbye to childhood may indeed be a painful process, and many children feel the need to withdraw when they are so boldly thrust into the world by their natural drives and development. In the Taurus III period the normally more static nature of Taurus becomes increasingly dynamic, even impulsive, anticipating the energy of the upcoming sign of Gemini.

Taurus III's are highly sensitive individuals who need to be left free to express themselves as directly and naturally as they wish. Taurus III's do not react well when others try to correct, reform or change their basic habits. These spontaneous, fun-loving, zany individuals insist on being themselves: indeed, they seem to have no other choice. Yet society can put pressures on an individual to conform, and Taurus III's may consequently encounter serious frustrations and obstacles while growing up. Nervousness and neurotic behavior not infrequently result and, in more

ZODIAC POSITION
Approximately
20–29° Taurus

SEASON
Mid-spring

ELEMENT
Earth

RULER
Venus

SYMBOL
The Bull

MODE
Sensation

extreme cases, depressions and acutely repressed feelings.

A Taurus III child, like many Taurus III adults, is generally fun-loving and imaginative, full of fantastic thoughts and colorful behavior. These individuals are drawn throughout their lives to the natural world, in part due to the freedom it represents. In childhood, problems may arise when a parent, sibling, family member or teacher lacks sympathy for their "wayward" behavior and attempts to straighten it out. Those born in the Week of the Natural often lack the toughness to resist strong criticism, and they can be deeply hurt by a lack of understanding from those close to them. In the long run, however, they may also benefit from any resistance to them, becoming stronger and more capable of dealing with a hostile and critical environment. Leaving home and getting out on their own come early in the life of a Taurus III, and even those who seem docile and content often secretly yearn for the time when they can exert their independence. As they grow up, most Taurus III's succeed in finding friends who appreciate them, and rarely will Taurus III's carry hurtful or revengeful thoughts against childhood adversaries into adulthood. However, they may well retain some scars from childhood battles that, if repressed, can lead to sudden and baffling depressions or emotional outbursts.

It is hard for Taurus III's to keep a low profile. Craving action and excitement, and often unable to keep their strong opinions on those around them to themselves, they can easily get into hot water. Taurus III's can be very emotionally volatile, and easily bored, qualities that invariably lead to many changes of friends, lovers and generally of their entire scene. An eternal fascination

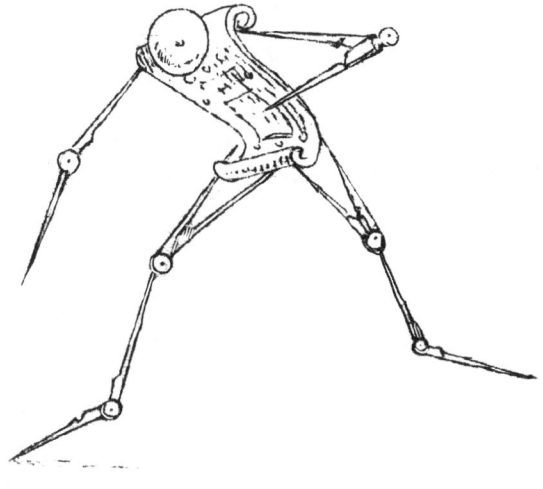

"NATURAL"

with the oddball, unusual aspects of life will always threaten to remove them from steadier and more stable situations and individuals. On the other hand, their instability can make them crave the grounding influence of people, places and professions, and for varying periods of time they may doggedly hold on, knowing that to let go could result in aimlessness and lack of direction.

This duality between a natural impulsiveness and a need for stability (often a result of a fear of their own unsettledness) can be the key factor in all of the adult relationships of Taurus III's. Although insecurities abound in their personalities, these can act as a powerful fuel for their drive to succeed in life, rise in their jobs and break through societal barriers. In this sense, paradoxically, their dynamism can itself become a stabilizing force, and their ambition both a rock they can hold to and a compass pointing the way. Thus many born in this week who might have been satisfied with an enjoyable, unstressed, easygoing life, and better suited to it as well, are driven upward by their own quest for security, frequently a goal involving financial independence. Taurus III's are, above all, people who create their own challenges.

Although one would imagine that adventure, sex, drugs and all forms of wild behavior would exert a powerful pull on Taurus III's (as they inevitably do at some point in these individuals' lives), those born in this week are not invariably prone to lifelong obsessions and addictions. They are supported not so much by their

good sense as by an understanding of the basic nature of these areas of behavior, and this kind of kinship or familiarity allows them to navigate perilous channels without foundering on the rocks.

In relationships, rebelliousness against authority can haunt Taurus III's their whole life long. Those who enter into relationships with them, moreover, particularly their mates and lovers, risk coming to symbolize for them the repressive forces that those born in the Week of the Natural cannot abide. It is essential, then, to be understanding of the battles being waged in the psyche of a Taurus III, while at the same time refusing to become a football or emotional punching bag. Difficulties may particularly surface when Taurus III's want others to take them seriously—their combination of fantastic ideas and unpredictable behavior is not always conducive to inspiring trust, and they may have to battle long and hard before their ideas are accepted. Still, as with their drive to financial success, fighting over issues like these can give them direction and security. Successful Taurus III's are those who are able to give form to their fantasy, to embody it in a product, service or artistic activity. Such individuals can strike deep responsive chords in the imaginations of their fellows, who may feel they live in a more humdrum world from which they secretly crave release. In the same way, Taurus III's may draw others to them as friends and lovers.

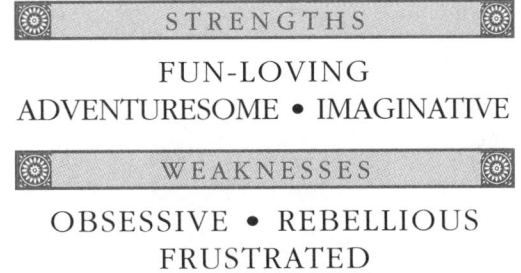

STRENGTHS

FUN-LOVING
ADVENTURESOME • IMAGINATIVE

WEAKNESSES

OBSESSIVE • REBELLIOUS
FRUSTRATED

ADVICE:

*Dig deeper and explore the depths of your personality. Try to take matters
a bit more seriously if you wish others to do the same in regard to you.
On the other hand, never give up your natural and instinctive approach to life.
Set your personal standards a bit higher and expect more of yourself.*

TAURUS III NOTABLES

Dennis Hopper has been called many things—pretentious, swaggering, wild man, madman—but rarely has anyone implied that Hopper is anything but himself. His antiestablishment and manic edge has kept moviegoers on the edge of their seats from his appearances in *Rebel Without A Cause* and *Easy Rider* (which he

DENNIS HOPPER

directed) to *Blue Velvet* and *Waterworld.* Always on the outside, Hopper has followed his fantasy like few others and has often succeeded in pulling audiences after him. Although his private life has been strung out at times, he has often straightened it out. Perhaps expanding our view of the natural to include the unnatural has been his single most constant preoccupation.

With Ruth St. Denis and Isadora Duncan, the "mothers" of modern dance in America, **Martha Graham** succeeded in creating a distinctly American choreography. Legendary for having danced into her 80s and 90s, Graham brought a new, natural approach to dance. Rather than draw from the stylized postures of the past, she reached into the world of nature for her inspiration and uncovered organic and timeless forms that she brought to light on the stage. Although dynamic, her static poses may be her most characteristic and memorable. Aaron Copland's *Appalachian Spring* was one of her greatest vehicles and clearly displayed her strong American roots.

Spanish artist **Salvador Dalí**, largely self-taught, was fascinated by the oddball and unusual. He became the supreme embodiment of those qualities himself and expressed his outrageousness in both his life and his art. Yet to imagine him as a wide-eyed dreamer is far from the truth. Dali was a technical genius in every sense of the term, shown in documentaries before the camera's watchful eye transforming the most simple materials into dazzling works of art

SALVADOR DALI

in only a few seconds or minutes. Dali was also a traditionalist, a student of the past who built his career on earlier discoveries. His irreverence for present-day authority, however, was undeniable, and his ability to be mischievous, play pranks or be outright offensive was unparalleled.

MARTHA GRAHAM

More Taurus III's: George Lucas, Lindsay Crouse, Joe Louis, David Cronenberg, Pope John Paul II, David Byrne, Jiddu Krishnamurti, Natasha Richardson, Henry Fonda, Jasper Johns, Katharine Hepburn, Harvey Keitel, Margot Fonteyn, Stevie Wonder, L. Frank Baum, Debra Winger, Brian Eno, Joseph Cotten, Frank Capra, Margaret Rutherford, Andre Gregory, Phil Silvers, George Carlin, Yogi Berra, Emilio Estevez, Daphne du Maurier, Olga Korbut, Eric Satie, Liberace, Bertrand Russell.

Relationship Guide for Taurus III

Page Locator for All Relationships

SALVADOR DALI (TAURUS III)
GALA (VIRGO II)
PAGE 379

BEST RELATIONSHIPS

LOVE
Taurus II
Gemini-Cancer Cusp
Leo I
Virgo II
Libra I
Scorpio-Sagittarius Cusp
Sagittarius I
Capricorn I
Aquarius-Pisces Cusp
Pisces II

MARRIAGE
Taurus I
Cancer II
Cancer-Leo Cusp
Leo II
Virgo III
Scorpio I
Capricorn III
Aquarius II
Pisces III

FRIENDSHIP
Aries I
Aries III
Aries-Taurus Cusp
Gemini I
Gemini III
Cancer III
Leo III
Virgo I
Capricorn-Aquarius Cusp

FAMILY
Taurus III
Cancer I
Leo-Virgo Cusp
Libra III
Capricorn II

WORK
Taurus-Gemini Cusp
Libra II
Scorpio II
Sagittarius II
Pisces I

TAURUS-GEMINI CUSP
The Cusp of Energy

May 19–24

The Taurus-Gemini cusp is an admixture of the second sign of the zodiac, Taurus, and the third sign of the zodiac, Gemini. This cusp may be symbolically likened to the period around fourteen years of age in the human life and falls at the beginning of late spring in the northern hemisphere. The Taurus-Gemini cusp may be said to represent Energy. During this period of the year the prolific growth of plant life is apparent. Days grow increasingly longer and the shorter nights warmer, both of which speed up the growth of vegetables, fruits and herbs. In human development, at the age of fourteen adolescence is usually under way and the young teenager bids farewell to childhood. This is a period in which Energy plays a key role—in terms not only of output but input. The appetite increases enormously as growth and maturation suddenly take off. This is generally not an easy time or a well-regulated one. Both psychologically and physically, early adolescence brings transformative changes that alter an individual irrevocably—sometimes creating what seems to be a whole new person.

Those born on the Taurus-Gemini cusp can easily see themselves more as a force than as a person. Not specialists in self-awareness, from an early age they forge a role in life that is active rather than passive, dynamic rather than static. Interested as children in everything around them, those born on the Cusp of Energy often fly every which way in their search for stimulation. Sometimes to the despair of their parents, who correctly accuse them of spreading themselves too thin and not sticking to any one activity, they want to do it all, to take

ZODIAC POSITION
Approximately
27° Taurus–4° Gemini

SEASONS
Late spring

ELEMENTS
Earth/Air

RULERS
Venus/Mercury

SYMBOLS
The Bull/The Twins

MODES
Sensation/Thought

on the world in a direct frontal assault. Some of those born on this cusp fail to form a strong ego early in life. Wanting to please, and fearful of rejection, Taurus-Gemini's may accept the wishes of others at the expense of their own. Self-assertion and building a powerful ego can become a lifelong occupation for them.

Taurus-Geminis' abundant energy, keen interest in the world around them and charm tend to draw innumerable friends and lovers. However, those involved with them are in constant fear of losing them. For some people this is both challenging and appealing. Others, however, may be turned off by Taurus-Geminis' reputation for untrustworthiness, and such preconceptions may hurt them, particularly in the areas of business and employment.

The brilliance of a Taurus-Gemini is not enough to guarantee success in a given field unless it is backed up by a string of undeniable accomplishments. Unfortunately, those born on the Cusp of Energy do not always manifest an endurance equal to their desires and impulses. While slower, more purposeful individuals just hang in there, Taurus-Geminis may find themselves being passed in life's race, as the hare was overtaken by a self-possessed and deliberate turtle. Drawing up a résumé can be a painful process for someone born in this week, since it may reveal an eclectic background lacking real depth, a short sojourn in each job and dubious accomplishments. Learning about the creation of structure and the value of limitations is essential to the growth of a Taurus-Gemini.

In relationships, Taurus-Geminis often come on too strong. Indeed the friends of Taurus-Geminis occasionally wonder why these people need to be the center of

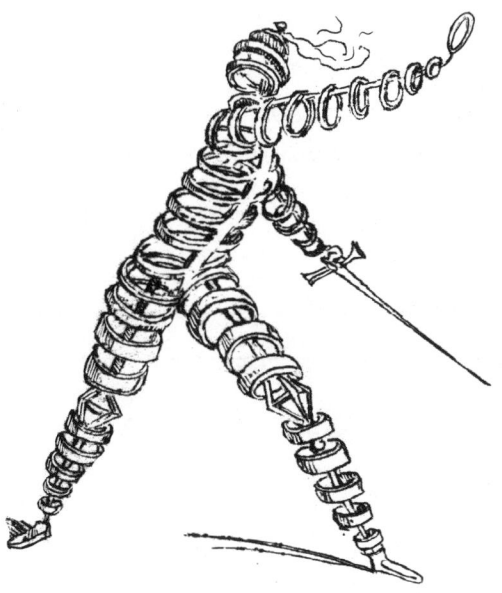

"ENERGY"

attention every minute of every day. They seem to find themselves fascinating, and to want to share that fascination with all around them. It may be necessary for them to cultivate a certain indifference to themselves if they are to improve the quality of their relationships, keeping their latest thought to themselves and making themselves more receptive and sympathetic to others. If friends, lovers or spouses come to feel that they are only there to watch or listen to the Taurus-Gemini, and are not really appreciated or needed for themselves, the days of the relationship may well be numbered.

As mates or partners, Taurus-Geminis may well spend their time heading off after the newest exciting prospect while their counterpart deals with the mundane tasks of home management, finance and general maintenance. This tendency may be worsened when it leads Taurus-Geminis to make unfavorable comparisons, picturing their partners as dull and uninteresting. Frictions and, ultimately, breakups can result. To participate in a successful ongoing relationship, Cusp of Energy people must sacrifice some of their "brilliance" to necessary everyday tasks, thereby asserting their interest in and commitment to the relationship as well as their respect for their partners' own needs for creative and quality time. In fairness to Taurus-Geminis, however, if their mate or partner can accept them as they are, they can prove loving and faithful.

Because Taurus-Geminis combine the earthy, sensuous traits of Taurus with the airy mental characteristics of

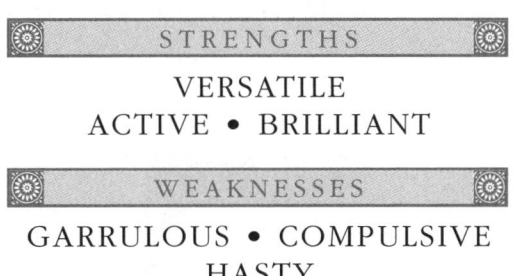

STRENGTHS

VERSATILE
ACTIVE • BRILLIANT

WEAKNESSES

GARRULOUS • COMPULSIVE
HASTY

Gemini, they can be both obsessively interested in physical matters and compulsive about checking things out. They may be characterized, in other words, by curiosity about the physical state of others, worry about their own bodies and a fascination with whether machines or equipment are generally working properly. The best partners for Taurus-Geminis are often those who are strong enough to maintain their own individuality, establishing boundaries that should not be violated or infringed upon while at the same time proving able to fulfill the Taurus-Gemini need to communicate. Sharing the interests of Taurus-Geminis is not nearly so important, however, as respecting and appreciating them.

Taurus-Geminis can make excellent parents, presenting a kaleidoscope of interests to their children. They should realistically ask themselves, however, whether their own needs do not preclude the kind of stability and empathy necessary to raise a family. Their periodic assessment of their own needs and desires, and their placement of strong limits on the scope of their activities, are in fact essential to their success in all areas of personal relationships. Before committing to a longer or deeper relationship, Taurus-Geminis need to get their priorities straight and to give deep consideration to the question of whether they are prepared to make the necessary sacrifices. Introspection, planning and soul searching do not come easily to a Taurus-Gemini but in the long run will save much pain and hardship for all concerned.

ADVICE:

Monitor the pace of your activities carefully. Seek to be more consistent and less casual in jettisoning people and ideas. Don't come on so strong. Turn off your mental motor from time to time. Confront your fears and insecurities.

TAURUS-GEMINI CUSP NOTABLES

Amazing variety has marked the career of **Grace Jones**, from model and movie actress (playing opposite

GRACE JONES

Conan the Destroyer and James Bond) to her performance videos *Slave to Rhythm* and *Warm Leatherette* and albums *Inside Story* and *Boomerang OMPST*. Refusing to be put in any category is typical of Taurus-Geminis, and Jones is no exception. Her remarkable looks and equally distinctive manner mark her as a true individual—one of a kind. Her explosive persona says "Handle with care," and her ferociously uncompromising stance is not recommended for the faint-hearted. Like others born on the Cusp of Energy, Jones has plenty of this commodity to spare for a wide-ranging multitude of projects.

Energetic and prolific, **Malcolm X** typifies the eclectic and highly original nature of those born on the Taurus-Gemini cusp. Black separatist and Black Muslim teacher, Malcolm spoke out fearlessly against the historical oppression of his people and demanded justice for them. In 1946 he began a 7-year jail sentence for armed robbery and while in prison converted to the Nation of Islam. Upon his release, he met with Islam leader Elijah Muhammad and began work for the organization, culminating in his appointment as first national minister, from which he resigned in 1964 to establish his own organiza-

MALCOLM X

tion. Feared by some Americans, Malcolm was also deeply loved by many who have continued to honor his memory since his assassination in 1965.

Wearing different hats comes naturally to Taurus-Geminis, and this is certainly true of the dynamic singer and actress **Cher**. A true entertainer, Cher appears equally at home in live performances and before TV and film cameras. Perhaps her most astonishing

CHER

feat was getting critics to take her seriously as an actress. Nominated for a Best Supporting Actress Academy Award for her work in *Silkwood*, Cher then won the Best Actress Award for her performance in *Moonstruck*. With film success, Cher's full and flamboyant expression of herself remains irrespressible. Her marriages to Sonny Bono and Gregg Allman and romantic links with Val Kilmer, Gene Simmons and Richie Sambora have been followed with great interest by her many fans.

More Taurus-Geminis: Bob Dylan, Arthur Conan Doyle, Mary Cassatt, Queen Victoria, Laurence Olivier, Andrei Sakharov, Nicole Brown Simpson, Richard Wagner, Henri Rousseau, Priscilla Presley, Marvin Hagler, Jean-Paul Marat, Socrates, Ho Chi Minh, Joan Collins, Jim Lehrer, Peter Townshend, Lorraine Hansberry, Jimmy Stewart, Albrecht Dürer, Armand Hammer, Fats Waller, George Washington Carver.

Relationship Guide for Taurus-Gemini Cusp

SIR LAWRENCE OLIVIER (TAURUS-GEMINI CUSP)
VIVIEN LEIGH (SCORPIO II)
PAGE 403

BEST RELATIONSHIPS

LOVE
Taurus I
Gemini III
Leo-Virgo Cusp
Libra II
Sagittarius-Capricorn Cusp
Aquarius II
Aquarius III

MARRIAGE
Aries-Taurus Cusp
Taurus-Gemini Cusp
Virgo I
Scorpio III
Capricorn-Aquarius Cusp

FRIENDSHIP
Aries III
Taurus II
Cancer I
Leo I
Virgo II
Libra-Scorpio Cusp
Scorpio II
Sagittarius I
Capricorn II
Pisces II
Pisces III

FAMILY
Aries II
Gemini I
Leo II
Virgo III
Libra III
Sagittarius II
Sagittarius III
Aquarius I

WORK
Pisces-Aries Cusp
Aries I
Taurus III
Cancer II
Cancer-Leo Cusp
Scorpio I
Capricorn I
Capricorn III
Aquarius-Pisces Cusp

Page Locator for All Relationships

The Week of Freedom

May 25–June 2

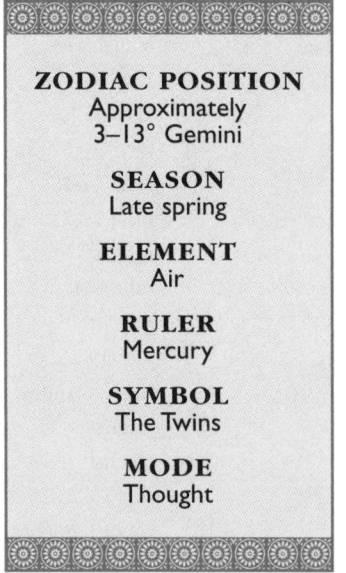

ZODIAC POSITION
Approximately
3–13° Gemini

SEASON
Late spring

ELEMENT
Air

RULER
Mercury

SYMBOL
The Twins

MODE
Thought

The Gemini I period takes Freedom as its central image. This period can be symbolically compared to a time in a young person's life when striving for independence and freedom of thought become very important. High rebelliousness is often part of this process; injustice is keenly felt and all forms of tyranny despised. However, by only defining a stance against certain established attitudes, some people at this age can be actually limiting their horizons rather than expanding them.

According to The Grand Cycle of Life, Gemini I falls approximately at the age when most teenagers are in the thick of high school. Consequently, the days that comprise Gemini I reveal an individual expressing individuality, enlarging on social and financial skills, cultivating the ability to assess the worth of things and dealing with problems of a personal and intellectual nature. Ideas and ideals come to have particular importance. This period of life can be especially painful for those who are unable to fit in with the crowd.

Gemini I's balk at restrictions and aim to maintain their freedom at all costs. Generally on the side of the individual, they hate oppression and exploitation, opposing them both in theory and in practice. Gemini I's will not usually back down from a fight. Naturally combative, they stick up for what they believe is right and will not hesitate to attack wrongdoing in any form, be it moral or practical, for Gemini I's believe there is a right way and a wrong way to do things, and that only the right way will yield uniformly positive results. One of their strongest weapons is laughter or ridicule, which

they do not hesitate to pull out of their formidable verbal arsenal. Still, Gemini I's are willing to give the other felow a second chance. Resilient, they will not quit valuable relationships easily; instead, they hang in there, letting go of resentments.

Bright, perky and alert, but also a tad abrasive, Gemini I's are high-speed players who get impatient with other people's slower responses. Often technically gifted, they can get annoyed when others are less skillful in performing a certain task. Given this low threshold of irritation, they may get stressed out easily, lashing out with irony or sarcasm. The aggression of Gemini I's is often a reaction to what they see as incompetence or stupidity, but it does not make them easy to live or work with.

Those born in the Week of Freedom have ultraquick impulses and fertile imaginations, sometimes overly so. They are constantly dreaming up new plans and schemes, perhaps at the expense of pressing matters that need attention (such as paying bills). In their lifetimes they may leave behind enough unfinished projects to occupy a dozen human beings. Gemini I's often lack the patience to implement their plans in a sensitive way. Further, they may make promises in good faith yet break them later due to new and pressing demands. Such actions undermine their own credibility.

Family life can have a grounding influence on their mercurial energies; likewise, clever mates and friends will put the quick wits and talents of Gemini I's to constructive uses, often by introducing them to interesting activities, jobs and businesses requiring close attention and maintenance. A relatively rootless Gemini I will often blossom when put to work in a structured position

"FREEDOM"

involving a lot of responsibility. If their work gives them the opportunity to innovate, Gemini I's may continue quite happily in the same position for years.

Those involved in relationships with Gemini I's, whether family, friends or lovers, won't need to do much guessing as to their state of mind. Those born in the Week of Freedom are both emotionally volatile and not at all shy about verbalizing any discontent they may have. In extreme cases, in fact, they can be constant complainers, though for the most part they just have a periodic need to get their dissatisfactions off their chest. Those close to them usually let them run on, picking out the core of the difficulty and letting the rest go in one ear and out the other. An emotional reaction to a Gemini I can escalate quickly into a full-scale fight. It is better to hear them out patiently, no matter how long it takes. Gemini I's have a habit of repeating themselves, so they cannot fairly accuse others of not listening to what they say.

Considering their emotional volatility and changeability, they are surprisingly loyal partners. They do tire of routine quickly, though, and may from time to time find it necessary to change the structures of their most intimate relationships to keep from being bored. Those best able to carry on with them will be able to accept their need for stimulation, variety and a regular change of scene.

Protective, Gemini I's are capable of putting their prodigious energies to use in rescuing others from trouble. Unfortunately, they sometimes wind up subjecting rescuees to their own brand of tyranny, in a benighted effort to make things turn out right. Their first impulses are often to relieve difficulties through prompt and rational action, yet the manner in which they proceed may somehow create more problems than it solves. A Gemini I may recognize the objective needs of a family member, for example, and may seek to satisfy him or her, yet may fail by not taking the relative's feelings into account. Gemini I's may give conditionally, using rewards as a means of control, and withdrawing rewards as a means of punishment.

Those born in the Week of Freedom are not at all above emotional manipulation. In fact, they rarely hesitate to turn on their considerable charm when they want to get their way. They are highly seductive, and few can resist their often considerable sex appeal. In time, however, their flirtatious and provocative allure may wear thin if not backed up by a reliably sympathetic stance.

As their mates and lovers will attest, Gemini I's can become unhinged with lightning speed; they are at their best when they keep their nerves under control. Accordingly, they should avoid all drugs and stimulants, particularly alcohol, that will alter their consciousness or cause them to be less present.

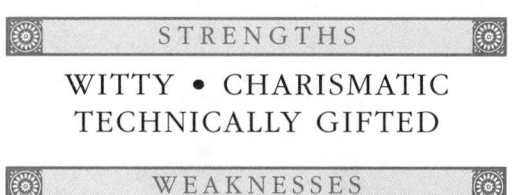

STRENGTHS

WITTY • CHARISMATIC
TECHNICALLY GIFTED

WEAKNESSES

TYRANNICAL • MANIPULATIVE
COMPLAINING

ADVICE:

Work to finish what you start. Develop the patience to interact fully with others.
Your ideals may have to be sacrificed at times for the sake of harmony.
Avoid escapism in its manifold guises. Keep busy and happy, but do not neglect
your inner emotional life.

GEMINI I NOTABLES

A symbol of sexual freedom for her generation, **Marilyn Monroe** exhibited the erratic behavior and tendency to get into trouble characteristic of Gemini I's.

MARILYN MONROE

Marilyn's emotional volatility and extreme need for change also characterize those born in the Week of Freedom. Marilyn's gift for comedy was discovered in Hollywood and gave her an important creative outlet. The flip side of her flamboyant exterior was deeply depressive, no doubt the effect of childhood poverty and sexual abuse. Perhaps Marilyn craved security and stability more than anything else, but, as with many Gemini I's, she found them impossible to achieve. Linked romantically with some of the most powerful men of her time and married to sports icon Joe DiMaggio and writer Arthur Miller, happiness was rarely her lot.

The mercurial nature of Gemini I's, moving quickly in thought and deed, is part of the astrological legacy of **John Fitzgerald Kennedy**. Bringing a new spirit of communication to the White House, Kennedy delighted in media contacts. More than any other single event, it was his tv debates with opponent Richard Nixon that resulted in his election. Kennedy symbolized a kind of political and personal freedom that inspired millions of Americans to adore their young president and increased the shock factor of the dark days after his assassination on Nov. 22,

JOHN FITZGERALD KENNEDY

1963. The day the lights went out in America was particularly horrifying because of the brightness with which they had blazed during his presidency.

Generally regarded as America's greatest poet, **Walt Whitman** lived a life in which freedom was the central symbol. A writer of free verse, a freethinker and one who urged others to express their freest impulses, Whitman was an archetypal Gemini I. Originally a Long Island schoolteacher

WALT WHITMAN

and editor of the *Brooklyn Eagle,* it was not until he was 36 that his poems were published in the single volume *Leaves of Grass.* Whitman was a pantheist who loved all humanity but also put his ideals on the line by working as a volunteer nurse during the Civil War. His homosexuality and controversial lifestyle led to church opposition to the naming of Philadelphia's Walt Whitman Bridge after him.

More Gemini I's: Isadora Duncan, Clint Eastwood, Henry Kissinger, Sally K. Ride, Jim Thorpe, Benny Goodman, John Wayne, Marquis de Sade, Tito, Hubert Humphrey, Miles Davis, Dashiell Hammett, Rachel Carson, Morgan Freeman, Charlie Watts, Sally Kellerman, Peggy Lee, Queen Mary, Ralph Waldo Emerson, Gene Tunney, Pam Grier, Herman Wouk, Brooke Shields, Wild Bill Hickok, Gale Sayers, Levon Helm, Julian Beck, Johnny Weissmuller.

Relationship Guide for Gemini I

ARTHUR MILLER (LIBRA III)
MARILYN MONROE (GEMINI I)
PAGE 421

BEST RELATIONSHIPS

LOVE
Cancer II
Leo II
Libra II
Libra-Scorpio Cusp
Sagittarius III
Capricorn III

MARRIAGE
Aries II
Gemini II
Gemini-Cancer Cusp
Leo I
Virgo II
Libra I
Sagittarius II
Capricorn I
Pisces I

FRIENDSHIP
Aries I
Taurus III
Gemini III
Cancer III
Leo-Virgo Cusp
Virgo III
Libra III
Scorpio III
Sagittarius I
Sagittarius-Capricorn Cusp
Capricorn II
Aquarius-Pisces Cusp
Pisces III

FAMILY
Taurus-Gemini Cusp
Scorpio-Sagittarius Cusp
Aquarius II

WORK
Aries III
Aries-Taurus Cusp
Taurus II
Cancer I
Cancer-Leo Cusp
Virgo I
Scorpio II
Capricorn-Aquarius Cusp
Pisces II

Page Locator for All Relationships

GEMINI II
The Week of New Language

June 3–10

ZODIAC POSITION
Approximately
12–20° Gemini

SEASON
Late spring

ELEMENT
Air

RULER
Mercury

SYMBOL
The Twins

MODE
Thought

The Gemini II period takes New Language as its central image. According to The Grand Cycle of Life, this period can be likened to the time when a young person is preparing to leave high school, either to enter the working world or to continue on to college. During this transition filled with uncertainty and promise, important career decisions must be made, planned out and verbalized.

The days that comprise Gemini II point to many of the areas that come into play at this juncture. Critical thinking and a concomitant ability to express ideas in written and verbal form become increasingly important. Accuracy and consistency are crucial, but so are imagination and vision. Finally, a strong sense of individuality must be cultivated, and with it a well-rounded character that recognizes both comic and tragic elements in life.

Gemini II's show a strong desire to communicate their thoughts and feelings verbally. They also need to be sure that others have understood their message and can see their point of view, even without agreeing with it. Yet the means of expression of Gemini II's are highly personal, to the point of the development of their own unique language. This may lead to all kinds of problems, tensions and frustrations, since they are frequently misunderstood. Moreover, when trying to put their point across, some Gemini II's use a barrage of words, relying on quantity over quality to win the day, or try different lines of argument all at once. In their intense desire to communicate, the meaning may get lost in the shuffle.

Entertaining and witty, Gemini II's know how to daz-zle, and how to hold the attention of their audience. Over the long haul required by committed relationships, however, this manner may lose its glow, being seen first as superficial, then as irritating. Also, a Gemini II's level of verbal and mental insistence may often be so high that others become fatigued or overwhelmed by the barrage. Sensing the urgency of a Gemini II's need for understanding, people may expediently pretend that they have understood when in fact they have not; their lack of comprehension may emerge later, in midstream, bringing blame and reproach on the Gemini II.

The spoken word is by no means the only mode of communication of Gemini II's. Their body language can be a powerful addition to their well-developed mental characteristics. Gemini II's have a great need for physical exercise and expression, particularly in their younger years but lasting on throughout their lives. Such activities provide the balance to their quick wits without which they might be deprived of sleep and appetite. In addition, healthy doses of affection provide an easy, nonverbal form of communication, making Gemini II's feel appreciated and loved, and reinforcing their need to share.

The competitive urges of those born in this week can easily get out of hand. Competition keeps Gemini II's sharp but may also make them contentious, and their rapier wit can leave deep scars. Unless they find a way to mute their impulse to criticize, Gemini II's may alienate even their closest friends. Gemini II's are equally hard on themselves. When this happens it is often a consequence of poor self-image, perhaps a result of parental accusations of irresponsibility, flakiness or incompetence. If this problem can be corrected

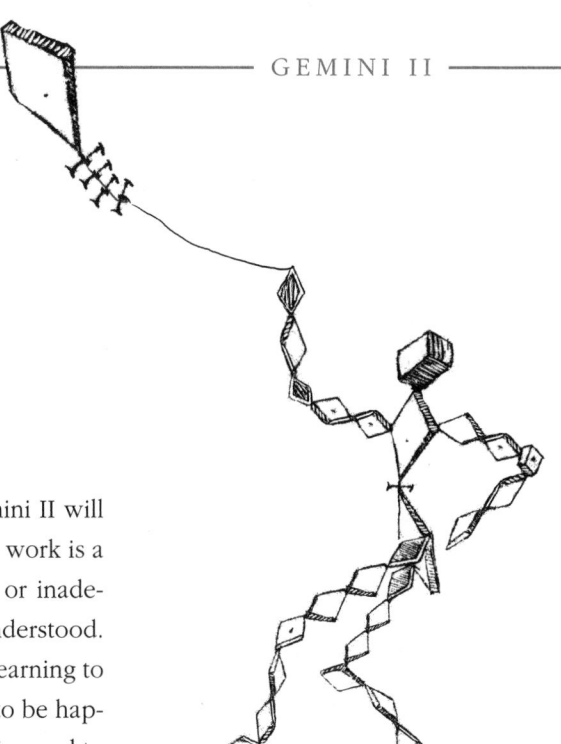

"NEW LANGUAGE"

the responses of the Gemini II will soften. Much of what is at work is a fear of appearing foolish or inadequate, or of being misunderstood. Rejecting old scripts and learning to be easier on themselves, to be happier and more self-accepting and to come to a rapprochement with their own dark side, they can arrive at more productive and fulfilling personal relationships.

In their choice of a mate, those born in this week are often carried away by their desires and only discover later that the person they have chosen to live with cares little about what they have to say and has no interest in devoting time to listening to it. Gemini II's can also be drawn to quiet, reserved people whose silence and need for privacy they may, unfortunately, end up interpreting as a rejection. Rarely, however, are other fluent communicators as attractive to those born in this week as the strong, silent types are. Not only do opposites attract, but Gemini II's are secretly fascinated by the dark side of life. Apparently extroverted and happy, they sometimes force their smiles and gaiety. Driven to repress their shadow personality by fear of rejection, Gemini II's frequently summon up such a dark side in the form of a lover or friend.

A more realistic approach to choosing a partner obviously aids Gemini II's. Tempted to choose people from radically different backgrounds, they often relate more successfully to those from the same city or neighbor-

hood, ethnic background or economic stratum. Shared associations and idioms often free the lines of static and make communication much easier for them. In time, such bonds of commonality can contribute more of lasting value to a Gemini II relationship than the passion of their dark-side attractions.

Gemini II's have a strong need for variety. Those involved with them are often called upon to provide new horizons and a change of scene, particularly when the Gemini II lacks the organizational talents to get such a project off the ground. Those born in this week match up well with practical types who can get the job done with little fuss or excitement. Such combinations meld over the long haul, with the Gemini II providing the innovative ideas and the partner the ability to ground, refine and implement them. Building a home base, raising a family and even working as a partner in a business or hobby are all possible results of such relationships.

When their needs are not met, Gemini II's will almost always seek out someone more understanding. If this person is able to maintain objectivity and fairness toward the Gemini II's primary lover, partner or mate, his or her sympathy may prove beneficial, even a lifesaver, to the primary relationship. Unfortunately, however, the third party is not always so scrupulous, and, consequently, breakups often occur. Gemini II's must be careful of attracting types who appear sympathetic but are actually pursuing selfish and destructive ends.

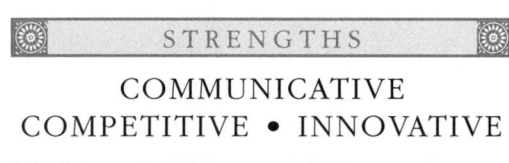

STRENGTHS

COMMUNICATIVE
COMPETITIVE • INNOVATIVE

WEAKNESSES

MISINTERPRETED • FLAKY
DISORGANIZED

ADVICE:

Try not to come on in a rush. Be clear in what you say but also diplomatic. Don't be inattentive to the impression you make or the idea others have of you. There is great value in silence. Take the time to develop deep friendships.

GEMINI II NOTABLES

The Wizard of Oz tapped America's mythic unconscious, but perhaps the film's impact would not have been as great without the presence of its young star, **Judy Garland**. In real life, Garland lived a tragic life filled with personal and drug problems, belying her innocent image of Dorothy in the film. Both as a singer

JUDY GARLAND

and actress, she specialized in developing a new form of communication in the entertainment industry, which lent her the stamp of someone born in the Week of New Language. Like many Gemini II's, Judy sought to deny and escape her shadow personality, but to no avail. Her death by suicide in 1969 at age 47 left her many fans grief stricken. Garland's daughter Liza Minnelli has carried on in her mother's grand tradition.

One of the leading poets of the Beat Generation, **Allen Ginsberg** was active in a wide range of protest activities, from the antiwar movement to gay rights. The "New Language" that he expressed in his mid-50s poem *Howl* was a wedding of prose and poetry, of statement and metaphor, of profanity and high-blown verse. Ginsberg, often bearded and sandaled, traveled widely to

ALLEN GINSBERG

deliver his message, accompanying himself on the harmonium and chanting his Zen-like messages. Obsessed with communication, Gemini II Ginsberg attended thousands of political meetings in order to make his unique

artistic contribution to fellow artists, students and the general public alike. Particularly in later years, his Jewish identity asserted itself strongly.

Credited with creating a new language in American architecture, **Frank Lloyd Wright** sought to express the organic and natural in his work, frequently adapting his creations to an already existing environment. First working in

FRANK LLOYD WRIGHT

the offices of Louis Sullivan designing houses, Wright broke away to establish his own personal style. Although his private life was filled with instability and many personal problems characteristic of a Gemini II, Wright designed 1,000 buildings, of which fewer than half were actually built. His controversial design methods for the Tokyo Imperial Hotel were vindicated when the structure survived the great earthquake of 1927. Wright wrote and lectured actively, had 7 children from 3 marriages and died 2 months short of his 90th birthday.

More Gemini II's: Paul Gauguin, Francis Crick, Barbara Bush, Cole Porter, Johnny Depp, Maurice Sendak, Richard Foreman, Prince Philip, (TAFKA) Prince, Rocky Graziano, Thomas Mann, Alexander Pushkin, Diego Velazquez, Billie Whitelaw, Laurie Anderson, Bjorn Borg, Federico Garcia Lorca, Bill Moyers, Judith Malina, Bruce Dern, Madame Chiang Kai-Shek, Josephine Baker, Spalding Gray.

Relationship Guide for Gemini II

BEST RELATIONSHIPS

LOVE
Aries I
Aries II
Cancer-Leo Cusp
Leo II
Leo-Virgo Cusp
Scorpio III
Sagittarius I
Capricorn I
Aquarius III
Pisces II
Pisces III

MARRIAGE
Taurus I
Taurus II
Gemini I
Gemini-Cancer Cusp
Virgo I
Virgo-Libra Cusp
Scorpio II
Capricorn II

FRIENDSHIP
Aries-Taurus Cusp
Gemini II
Cancer II
Virgo III
Sagittarius II
Capricorn-Aquarius Cusp
Aquarius I
Pisces I

FAMILY
Pisces-Aries Cusp
Cancer I
Libra I
Libra III
Scorpio I
Sagittarius-Capricorn Cusp

WORK
Taurus III
Gemini III
Cancer III
Leo I
Libra II
Sagittarius III
Capricorn III
Aquarius II

Page Locator for All Relationships

GEMINI III
The Week of the Seeker

June 11–18

T he Gemini III period takes The Seeker as its central image. This period can be compared to the time when a young person must say goodbye to the teenage years and actively prepare to find a place for him/herself in the adult world. Seeking a job, residence, friends, perhaps a mate, or searching for new ideas and horizons are activities that engage people of this age.

The days that comprise Gemini III point to issues that now emerge—being strong enough to confront and persuade, to seek adventure and roll back frontiers, and finally to invest in the future. The Seeker must be prepared to go as far as is necessary and to cut loose from self-imposed limitations and doubts that can only hold him/her back. This is a time of fearless exploration and of learning through life experience.

The primary drive of a Gemini III is to go beyond limitations imposed by society and nature. This may take the form of a drive toward success, or an overcoming of physical limitations. Gemini III's are never happier when they are on the move: probing, testing, tasting and exploring the most interesting things life has to offer. Not afraid to take chances, those born in this week are attracted by risk and danger. Adventurers in every sense of the word, Gemini III's are restless types. Their style is to remain unattached and thus free to progress as far as possible. Life is never dull with a Gemini III around. Those born in this period do not necessarily have to travel to far-off lands to explore and find challenge. For them all of life is an adventure. Thus Gemini III's keep others guessing as to their next move.

Those born in the Week of the Seeker are neither

ZODIAC POSITION
Approximately
19–28° Gemini

SEASON
Late spring

ELEMENT
Air

RULER
Mercury

SYMBOL
The Twins

MODE
Thought

teachers nor leaders. They may lack the patience and understanding to teach, and also the qualities necessary to lead: the dogged determination, ambition and desire to control others. Those who understand them will quickly realize their need to strike out on their own, and will not try to bind them to an executive or other responsible position in a business or family. Gemini III's are capable of taking the helm, particularly when they encounter incompetence or neglect; yet they may also show an indulgent, accepting side, proving content to drift and dream. Such self-satisfaction can prove a powerful deterrent to their progress in their careers.

Gemini III's often have a clouded self-image; they have difficulty seeing who they really are. This may have its beginnings in childhood with the idolization of a parent or family member, often of the opposite sex. Rejection, misunderstanding or abuse by such a person can be traumatic for them, giving them deep scars to carry into later life. Disillusionment in general can be a problem for Gemini III's; they tend to be extremely optimistic at the outset of an endeavor or relationship, often setting a person or activity up for a later fall from grace.

Gemini III's have an undeniable tendency to please others through charm, and many born in this week would rather stretch the truth a bit than be rejected for telling it as it is. Insightful about the needs of those around them, they can be powerfully controlling and persuasive in a subtle manner. They know how to get their way with people, and how to capture the hearts of their mates and friends. At the extreme end of the scale, those born in this week can tell tall tales, and may be suspected of being cons, flatterers or even liars.

"SEEKER"

Many Gemini III's are surprisingly good with money. They may not always give the appearance of financial practicality or foresight, but they can manage a family or a business quite well. They are also capable of latching on to a practical partner or someone else who can guarantee them the financial stability that they so sorely need. Money can come to symbolize freedom to Gemini III's, although they rarely have a desperate need to accumulate it for its own sake.

Those born in the Week of the Seeker often have a strong physical side yet choose to neglect it, seeking to transcend life's earthier pleasures. Thus they lack the grounded qualities of those who are capable of selfish and shameless indulgence. Metaphysical in the most basic sense of the word, those born in this week may see mastery of the tangible realities of life as only a first step toward higher attainment. Gemini III's must at times be wary of going too far, and of getting caught up in endless striving without achievement.

Love and affection are important to Gemini III's but are not usually given top priority. Those emotionally involved with those born in this week can find them sometimes warm and giving, in other moods quite cool and detached. Indeed, they are sometimes accused of blowing hot and cold, and with some justification. This is usually more the result of emotional sensitivity, however, than of a calculated desire to hurt.

Because of their intense need for change in relationships, Gemini III's may spend a period of their life moving from one partner to another. Even those who can establish a well-grounded primary relationship are constantly tempted away from it by a career, a hobby or another person. Gemini III's can be faithful, however, as long as their partner makes few demands on their fidelity and gives them room to breathe. Attempts to hold those born in this week to strict obligations and a formal routine are usually doomed to failure. On the other hand, these Seekers are quite capable of imposing stringent regimens and rules on themselves when they consider it necessary.

The seductive qualities of Gemini III's tend to land them in trouble. Their choice of a partner often shows remarkably good sense, but they may bind themselves to a friend or lover who can prove bothersome or destructive. Regretting such choices, Gemini III's may still find it hard to disentangle themselves from an emotionally messy situation. This may be partly due to an innate reluctance to reject or consciously hurt others, or to a feeling of helplessness and hesitancy in making the decision to cut ties. When a relationship must be ended, however, it is more often than not the Gemini III who either ends up doing the rejecting or allows or manipulates the other person to do so. Control of closure seems to be important to them, although they would prefer that relationships end as pleasantly as possible.

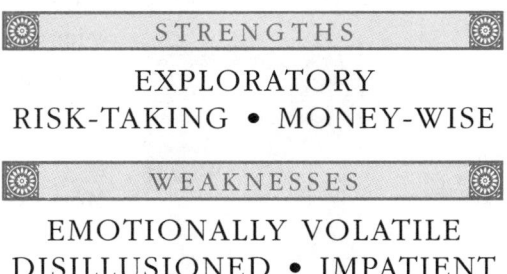

STRENGTHS

EXPLORATORY
RISK-TAKING • MONEY-WISE

WEAKNESSES

EMOTIONALLY VOLATILE
DISILLUSIONED • IMPATIENT

ADVICE:

Sometimes what is right in front of you is just as interesting as something risky or exotic. It may not be incumbent on you to influence the course of things. Allow yourself to express negativity when it is called for. Give yourself easy rewards, too.

GEMINI III NOTABLES

A Seeker in the true sense of the word, photographer **Margaret Bourke-White** was always ready to go that extra mile to get exactly the picture she wanted. One of

MARGARET BOURKE-WHITE

the first to shoot extensively from the air in civilian and military aircraft and balloons, fear did not stand in the way of this Gemini III's creative opportunities. The first female war correspondent, she survived shells and a torpedoing during WWII to bring her photos home to the American public. Her insistence on getting the right shot and capturing the moment, and her intensity in doing so, continued until the end of her career. A wide variety of her work was published in U.S. magazines and newspapers, as well as in illustrated books about her and in her own books.

The Nobel Prize-winning Irish poet **William Butler Yeats** sent his imagination out to distant lands, the farthest reaches of space and to other levels of reality to collect his images. Fantasy, imagination, history and the occult were all of tremendous interest to this Gemini III Seeker. Yeats was a curious blend of romantic and classicist, of traditionalist and modernist. In *Sailing to Byzantium* he speaks of "the young in one another's arms," while in *The Second Coming* he pictures the "rough beast [that] slouches toward Bethlehem to be born." A dreamer, admittedly, but a technical master and insightful observer as well,

WILLIAM BUTLER YEATS

Yeats' Gemini III coolness and detachment is probably best illustrated by his epitaph, written by himself: "Cast a cold eye on life, on death—Horseman, pass by."

Barbara McClintock won the Nobel Prize in physiology at age 81, an astonishing feat. She began her work as an American scientist in 1919 and forced a male-dominated profession to acknowledge her genius during a career that spanned over 60 years. McClintock was a true Seeker

BARBARA McCLINTOCK

who would not rest until she had made some of the most significant discoveries in the history of the biological sciences. Studying genetic phenomena in corn, McClintock was able to show the link between cellular structure and inherited traits long before the advent of advanced electronic microscopy and the discovery of DNA.

More Gemini III's: Anne Frank, Paul McCartney, Jacques Cousteau, Joe Montana, Steffi Graf, Igor Stravinsky, Isabella Rossellini, Vince Lombardi, Gene Wilder, Newt Gingrich, William Styron, Courtney Cox, James Brown, Waylon Jennings, Donald Trump, George Bush, Egon Schiele, Christo, Paavo Nurmi, Che Guevara, Jerzy Kosinski, Pierre Salinger, Borek Sipek, Xaviera Hollander, Erroll Garner, Edvard Grieg, Roberto Duran, Lamont Dozier, Adam Smith, Eddie Merckx, Peggy Seeger, Mario Cuomo, Jim Belushi.

Relationship Guide for Gemini III

JOHN LENNON (LIBRA II)
PAUL MCCARTNEY (GEMINI III)
PAGE 458

BEST RELATIONSHIPS

LOVE
Taurus II
Taurus-Gemini Cusp
Cancer I
Cancer III
Leo-Virgo Cusp
Virgo-Libra Cusp
Sagittarius-Capricorn Cusp
Pisces I

MARRIAGE
Pisces-Aries Cusp
Libra-Scorpio Cusp
Scorpio III
Sagittarius I
Capricorn-Aquarius Cusp
Pisces III

FRIENDSHIP
Taurus III
Gemini I
Cancer-Leo Cusp
Leo II
Leo III
Libra I
Scorpio II
Sagittarius III
Capricorn I
Aquarius I

FAMILY
Aries III
Gemini-Cancer Cusp
Libra II
Aquarius III
Aquarius-Pisces Cusp
Pisces II

WORK
Aries I
Gemini II
Gemini III
Leo I
Virgo III
Libra III
Scorpio I
Sagittarius II
Capricorn II
Aquarius II

Page Locator for All Relationships

GEMINI-CANCER CUSP
The Cusp of Magic

June 19–24

The Gemini-Cancer cusp is an admixture of the third sign of the zodiac, Gemini, and the fourth sign of the zodiac, Cancer. This cusp can be symbolically likened to the period around twenty-one years of age in the human life, and it marks the beginning of summer in the northern hemisphere. The Gemini-Cancer cusp may be said to represent Magic. During this period of the year many plants are coming into lush, full bloom. The day is longer and the night shorter than at any other point in the year. This is the time of traditionally magical "midsummer's eve," a warm, enchanted night, replete with bewitching smells and sounds, on which supernatural events take place. In human development, at the age of twenty-one, adolescence is over and adulthood is said to begin. Magic particularly plays a key role in terms of the magnetic power of love and the enchantment of romance. The young adult experiences an almost childlike wonder and awe at the beauty of the world and the horizons that have opened up.

Those born during the magical cusp of the summer solstice quickly fall under the spell of enchantment. Romantic and inspirational, Gemini-Cancers often put their talents and energies in service of a higher purpose, be it family, religion, philosophy, arts or political or social causes. Because they can wholeheartedly throw themselves into devotional activities, those born on this cusp often appear as mild, even self-effacing. For many of these individuals, anonymity is a goal in any career they follow. There are also more aggressive Gemini-Cancers, however, who become assertive as they mature and have few problems letting the world know who they are.

ZODIAC POSITION
Approximately
27° Gemini–4° Cancer

SEASONS
Late spring/Early summer
(solstice)

ELEMENTS
Air/Water

RULERS
Mercury/The Moon

SYMBOLS
The Twins/The Crab

MODES
Thought/Feeling

Easily seduced, Gemini-Cancers can also enchant others, whether consciously or unconsciously; these seductive individuals may have a sweetly innocent charm. They must be wary of being imposed upon, but they usually have good defensive instincts, and in the emotional sphere even mild Gemini-Cancers will gently lay down guidelines that should not be overstepped. The more aggressive Gemini-Cancers are often aware of their persuasive powers, which they may use without qualm to get their way, even when other individuals are hurt in the process.

Although possessed of charm and magnetism, Gemini-Cancers can be remarkably cool customers. They have a useful objectivity, and their reasoning powers make an effective foil to their deep emotions. Influenced by both Gemini and Cancer, they are in fact an interesting blend of logic and feeling. When those born on this cusp make an appeal to the emotions of others, they do so in a detached, thoughtful way. Not easily upset, they inspire confidence through their sympathy, concern and willingness to help. Summer-solstice people have a way of entering the hearts of those they love, and a reluctance to give up their position there, even when separations prove necessary.

Gemini-Cancers tend to be private people who will not easily grant access to their inner world. They frequently do best when they are able to work at home, and they often set up their home as a kind of retreat or sanctuary. To be allowed to share the living space of a Gemini-Cancer implies great trust and respect. An invitation to visit this highly personal world is more often felt as a true gift, or the reflection of a desire to share, than

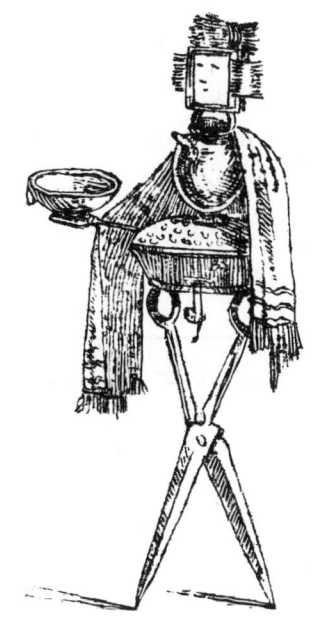

"MAGIC"

as a sign of ostentation or of a need for sociability.

Gemini-Cancers must beware of isolating themselves from the society around them and living in an unproductive dreamworld. Such detachment will hold them back in their personal and spiritual development, and toward the end of their lives they may view it as a sign of failure. Since staying in touch with reality is especially important for Gemini-Cancers, they may find friends and lovers who are more extroverted than they are an essential link to the world. They should also beware of a kind of passive selfishness, in which it seems to others that they think the world revolves around them and that they constantly demand attention, if without saying so. Their special needs and wants as sensitive individuals can impose heavy demands on their friends and intimates, who may at the same time find themselves denying their own emotional and physical requirements.

No area is more important to Gemini-Cancers than love. They see love as a primary reason to live, one that may get them through many a difficult period. Forced to choose between love, on the one hand, and wealth or power, on the other, those born in this week usually choose the former. Many Gemini-Cancers are quite able to love from afar; platonic love has a special meaning for them. Others see the possession of the love object as a necessary and blissful consummation, but they, too, are patient in the pursuit. Quiet persistence and a belief in their powers can guarantee them success.

Gemini-Cancers have a tremendous capacity for love but are equally capable of withholding it. No matter how deeply in love they fall, they are masters of their emotions and can consequently be very dangerous people to be involved with. You must listen to them carefully, for although they can give their hearts fully, the fact that they are spending their time with you is no guarantee that they have done so. Gemini-Cancers are capable of a wide range of personal interaction, from acquaintances and friendships to full-blown passion. Each relationship will have its own structure, including what is and is not allowed in the area of physical contact. Sensitivity to such laws is definitely a prerequisite for the relationship's future.

Gemini-Cancers can be nurturing parents, but many will think twice before they make the lifelong commitment of having children. This may be because, as children, they tend to enjoy the warmth of a close family; they can suffer terribly in conditions of marital strife or divorce. They have a tendency to idolize at least one of their parents, and to need to get along well with their parents once they are grown. It is not surprising, then, that once they decide they are truly in love (generally an important prerequisite to commitment for them), they can make faithful and devoted mates. Never take the romantic needs of one born on the Cusp of Magic for granted, however; candlelight dinners, vacations in glamorous locations, and the occasional spontaneous gift are all musts to keep the flame bright.

STRENGTHS

AFFECTIONATE
SEDUCTIVE • OBJECTIVE

WEAKNESSES

ISOLATED • SELFISH
DEMANDING

ADVICE:

Exercise your magical powers with care. You may need to be a bit tougher on yourself. Keep your eye on the goal and resist any tendency to drift. Do not lose yourself so readily in ecstatic experiences or you may have trouble finding yourself again. Beware of repressing your feelings or allowing destructive emotions to control you.

GEMINI-CANCER CUSP NOTABLES

The life of **Aung San Suu Kyi** reads a bit like a fairy tale and, although amazing is not always a pleasant one. The daughter of Aung San, formerly considered the father of his country, Burma, resided quietly in England until 1988, married to a British academic and raising their 2 children while continuing her studies. Almost overnight, during a visit to her mother in Burma in 1988, she became the leader of the country's prodemocracy movement, for which she was placed under house arrest between 1989 and 1995. In 1991 she was awarded the Nobel Peace Prize for her nonviolent struggle for democracy. The Magic of this slight, lovely woman who believes in the beauty of children and flowers is equal to the military might opposing her.

AUNG SAN SUU KYI

Master of the romantic adventure story, **H. Rider Haggard**, in over 40 thrilling novels, including *King Solomon's Mines* and *She,* laid the groundwork for the exotic exploits of later comic-book and film heroes such as *Tintin, Conan the Barbarian* and *Indiana Jones.* Filled with love, peril and wild fantasy, Haggard's books are often set in the African wilderness and involve lost civilizations and monumental, albeit primitive, battles. This Gemini-Cancer writer was able to give full rein to his inspiration and whisk his readers away on a magic carpet ride into unknown realms. Although his work is a bit dated today, it can still provide some gripping moments

H. RIDER HAGGARD

and transform a quiet evening alone into an exciting adventure through an undiscovered world.

This leading actress for both serious and romantic roles is both a Vassar and Yale Drama School graduate. **Meryl Streep** wowed audiences the world over in her performances in *The Deer Hunter, Kramer vs. Kramer, The French Lieutenant's Woman, Sophie's Choice* and

MERYL STREEP

The River Wild. Streep has the ability to portray a highly romantic image with much more than just good looks. The brand of Magic that this Gemini-Cancer works has more to do with voice and gesture than with just a beautiful face. Her years of experience in stage productions prepared her magnificently for the intimate moments she creates on screen.

More Gemini-Cancers: Benazir Bhutto, Jean-Paul Sartre, Nicole Kidman, Phylicia Rashad, Billy Wilder, Juliette Lewis, Errol Flynn, Josephine de Beauharnais, Martin Landau, Lillian Hellman, Prince William, Mike Todd, Lou Gehrig, Increase Mather, Jane Russell, Jeff Beck, Michelle Lee, Pier Angeli, Bob Fosse, Audie Murphy, Roy Disney, Terry Riley, Niels Bohr, Geena Rowlands, Kathleen Turner, Françoise Sagan, Howard Kaylan, Kris Kristofferson, Joseph Papp, John Dillinger, Klaus Maria Brandauer, Carl Hubbell, Bill Blass, Lindsay Wagner.

Relationship Guide for Gemini-Cancer Cusp

WALLIS SIMPSON (GEMINI-CANCER CUSP)
EDWARD VIII (GEMINI-CANCER CUSP)
PAGE 469

BEST RELATIONSHIPS

LOVE
Aries II
Aries III
Taurus I
Leo III
Libra III
Scorpio I
Scorpio III
Sagittarius III
Aquarius II
Aquarius III
Pisces III

MARRIAGE
Aries-Taurus Cusp
Gemini II
Gemini-Cancer Cusp
Cancer I
Virgo III
Scorpio II
Sagittarius-Capricorn
Aquarius I
Pisces I

FRIENDSHIP
Taurus II
Cancer II
Leo II
Virgo I
Libra II
Sagittarius I
Capricorn III
Aquarius-Pisces Cusp

FAMILY
Pisces-Aries Cusp
Gemini III
Cancer III
Sagittarius II

WORK
Cancer-Leo Cusp
Virgo II
Virgo-Libra Cusp
Libra I
Libra-Scorpio Cusp
Scorpio-Sagittarius Cusp
Capricorn-Aquarius Cusp
Pisces II

Page Locator for All Relationships

CANCER I
The Week of the Empath

June 25–July 2

The Cancer I period takes The Empath as its central image. This period can be compared to a time in the early adult life when the need to understand, feel and, to an extent, to identify with others comes to the fore. Such understanding may extend to the life history, feelings or personality of another person. It may also involve sympathy for another person's ideas or way of thinking. This process is not only important in developing basic humanity, but also because without some degree of empathy success in the world of society will be denied.

The days that comprise Cancer I symbolically reveal the young adult developing the capacity to open up and receive positive influences from the world but also to be more discriminating and resilient in defending against harmful energies. In addition, learning about how the emotional life works, how the unconscious functions and, in general, what motivates people to do what they do figure prominently.

Cancer I's are hard to figure out. Emotionally complex, they combine sharply contrasting qualities in their psychological makeup. They may give an entirely different impression than in another, according to their mood. A Cancer I may strike one person as outgoing, another as retiring, one as positive and expansive, another as negative and depressive, still others as easygoing, others as difficult. Only those who live with Cancer I's day in and day out are fully able to appreciate their depth and diversity.

Part of the reason for the variety of their emotional palette is their sensitivity. Empathic, Cancer I's quickly pick up on the feelings of others—so much so that they

ZODIAC POSITION
Approximately
3–11° Cancer

SEASON
Early summer

ELEMENT
Water

RULER
The Moon

SYMBOL
The Crab

MODE
Feeling

may mistake such feelings for their own. Those born in this week may find themselves replaying other people's scripts and hence playing a role in life's daily drama that is not really theirs. Developing their self-awareness, gaining an accurate view of their personal interactions and getting a grip on their emotions will be essential to them.

Because they are so at the mercy of the feelings of others as children, Cancer I's generally cry out for protection. Even when protection is granted, these Empaths may spend a lifetime seeking out people to mother and nurture them. But If those born in this week are instead exposed to tough and unsympathetic treatment by their families and, later, by the world, they are capable of surrounding themselves with a virtually impenetrable shell. Love can enable such Cancer I's to feel again, melting their outer defenses and allowing them to express their true emotions. A great deal of pent-up resentment and frustration may have to be voiced, however, before their hurt is eased and they are able to trust again.

One should not get the idea, however, that Cancer I's are wishy-washy characters out of touch with worldly realities. In fact, they are very clever in getting their way. Those born in this week generally give money a high priority, and they are often financially astute. Their investment sense can be excellent, and they can frequently make stocks and other holdings pay off. Also in the realm of technical skills, they show a good grasp of whatever material they make their own, and a good ability to implement their plans.

Aggression can play an ambiguous role in the lives of Cancer I's: they are naturally aggressive, and can have

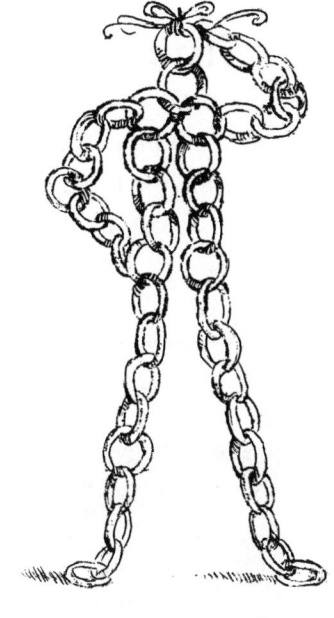

"EMPATH"

difficulty sublimating this instinct into positive expression, particularly in the sexual, verbal or athletic sphere. Too often they swing from angry outbursts to repression, which often leads them into melancholia, in extreme cases, their anger can be self-destructive. Finding a métier that allows them easy expression of their aggression is an important life task for them, and one that they often overlook.

Those born in this week are capable of withdrawing from the world for months or even years, doing battle with themselves in an attempt to come to grips with their problems. The challenge a Cancer I faces is to move from being a person helplessly adrift in a sea of feeling, just able to keep his or her head above water, into being one who can swim confidently in the swift currents of life. The most successful Cancer I's are those who can put their fantasy to work in a constructive way, and who can share their unique view of the world with others. First, of course, they must conquer their inner fears and liberate themselves from self- or parentally imposed behavioral stereotypes. Next they may have to overcome inflexibility and real or imagined handicaps. Through sheer guts and determination, they are often capable of overcoming these and other obstacles, and of putting their acute psychological perceptions to work in the service of those around them. Professionally they often do well when self-employed, operating from a home base that may be connected to their living space. Should they choose to have children, the caring and nurturing aspects of their personalities augur well for their abilities as parents.

For those who live with them, it may be difficult to stand by and watch as Cancer I's bottle up their feelings or enter into their self-imposed isolation. While it may look like self-torture, it is almost impossible, and in fact usually inadvisable, to get down in the soup with Cancer I's. A more beneficial stance is usually to back off and wait patiently until they surface and seek human interaction again. Patience is an obligatory virtue for those desiring a successful relationship with these individuals.

On the other hand, Cancer I's have a great deal to offer in a relationship: sympathy, technical proficiency, financial astuteness and a good managerial sense. Because of their need to spend time at home, they can be counted on to keep things in good working order and to provide comfort and security.

Cancer I's can be extremely persuasive, at times too much so. Their need to persuade can outstrip the advisability of their counsel, leaving them saddled with the guilt of having sent someone off in a wrong direction. Cancer I's pride themselves on doing their homework on given subjects, and when their research is thorough it will yield positive results. Good friends know, however, that emotional strain can cloud their thoughts, easily throwing them off track, so that they may offer confused judgments and advice with the same air of conviction and authority as cogent ones.

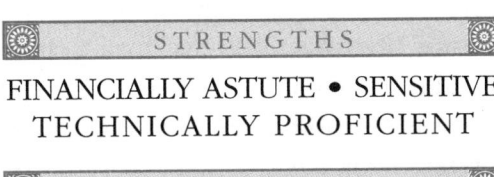

STRENGTHS

FINANCIALLY ASTUTE • SENSITIVE
TECHNICALLY PROFICIENT

WEAKNESSES

AGGRESSIVE • FEARFUL
NEEDY

ADVICE:

Don't armor yourself too heavily—on the other hand, remain discriminating.
Allow others the freedom to take risks. Though your salesmanship may be excellent,
it is not always appreciated. Don't only challenge your fears—overcome them
through self-liberation and action.

 CANCER I NOTABLES

Practically everyone knows the story of **Helen Keller**, the deaf, dumb and blind girl who overcame overwhelming odds in her struggle to read and speak. The primary obstacles in Keller's struggle, other than her disabilities, were her own aggression, anger and uncontrolled feelings, encountered in lesser degree by many Cancer I's. Perhaps the most significant event in her life was meeting her teacher, Annie Sullivan, and establishing a

HELEN KELLER

strong empathic bond with her. A true Empath, Keller was also able to feel the distress, despair and hope of the thousands of disadvantaged individuals she worked with during her lifetime. Dedicating herself to the cause of the blind and other physically disadvantaged people, she worked unceasingly to better their condition and give them the opportunity to learn as she had.

The German novelist and poet **Hermann Hesse** was less appreciated in his own time than in the 60s, when his works became immensely possible with a younger generation who saw him as an early explorer in the realms of imagination, drugs and higher states of reality and consciousness. Keyed into emotional expression, like many Cancer I's, Hesse explored the deep feelings of his unusual characters in such works as *Steppenwolf*, *Siddhartha* and *Narcissus and Goldmund*. The religious and spiritual elements of life inevitably played an important role in his work, but Hesse did not hes-

HERMANN HESSE

itate to show the anguish, humiliation, suffering and pain that are the basis of the human condition.

The former Princess of Wales, **Lady Diana Spencer** has garnered more front-page space for the past 10 years than many of the world's leaders. Although most of Britain's general public has viewed the royal family's shenanigans with a mixture of feigned horror and amusement, Lady Di has gained the respect of many around the world for emerging from her divorce from Prince Charles stronger and more self-assured. Her increasing dedication to philanthropic causes on her own and her ability to touch the hearts of those disadvantaged people whom she champions mark her as a Cancer I Empath. Her caring and nurturing aspects, both as a mom and as a social worker, are typical of those born in this week.

LADY DIANA SPENCER

More Cancer I's: Mike Tyson, Ross Perot, Babe Zaharias, George Orwell, George Sand, Carl Lewis, Jean Jacques Rousseau, Richard Rodgers, Ron Goldman, Jerry Hall, Gilda Radner, Dan Aykroyd, Emma Goldman, Lena Horne, Buddy Rich, Oriana Fallaci, John Cusack, Pamela Anderson, Nancy Lieberman, Jean Stafford, Mel Brooks, Patty Smyth, Meyer Lansky, Peter Lorre, George Michael, Sidney Lumet, Pearl Buck, Greg LeMond, Kathy Bates, Claudio Abbado, Dave Grusin.

Relationship Guide for Cancer I

JOHN BELUSHI (AQUARIUS I)
DAN AYKROYD (CANCER I)
PAGE 501

BEST RELATIONSHIPS

LOVE
Gemini III
Cancer-Leo Cusp
Scorpio I
Scorpio II
Sagittarius II
Capricorn III
Capricorn-Aquarius Cusp
Aquarius-Pisces Cusp
Pisces II

MARRIAGE
Taurus II
Gemini-Cancer Cusp
Cancer II
Leo III
Virgo I
Sagittarius III
Aquarius III
Pisces I
Pisces III

FRIENDSHIP
Taurus I
Taurus-Gemini Cusp
Cancer III
Leo I
Leo II
Virgo II
Virgo-Libra Cusp
Libra-Scorpio Cusp
Sagittarius-Capricorn

FAMILY
Aries II
Taurus III
Gemini II
Libra III
Scorpio-Sagittarius Cusp
Aquarius II

WORK
Pisces-Aries Cusp
Gemini I
Cancer I
Leo-Virgo Cusp
Virgo III
Scorpio III
Sagittarius I
Capricorn I

Page Locator for All Relationships

CANCER II
The Week of the Unconventional

July 3–10

The Cancer II period takes The Unconventional as its central image. This period can be likened to the time in a young adult's life when out-of-the-way activities and unusual people occupy interest. Moreover, the challenge to be personally unique may be a focus, not in an adolescent way but, rather, in the course of asserting individuality. No areas are considered too far out for consideration or study, and few if any activities are considered off limits. The value of privacy and of a private inner life are fully recognized at this time.

The days that comprise Cancer II deal with examining group values, revealing hidden secrets, expressing flamboyance, and calling up and exploring strange thoughts and fantasies. Destabilizing and self-destructive forces play their role here as well. In this fantasy-rich period of life, the thing most frowned upon is dullness or lack of imagination.

Cancer II's can appear quite normal, and may occupy ordinary positions in the working world, but they are irresistibly attracted to the unusual and the bizarre. Few colleagues and associates are ever granted access to their secret world; only their intimates come to realize, often after years of close association, how closely their fascination with all that is strange and curious mirrors their own inner self.

"Why can't you do things normally?" is a question too often reverberating in the heads of Cancer II's. Such questions, often reflecting internalized parental attitudes from childhood, may keep them at a desk job or other mundane task for years as they try to prove to the world

ZODIAC POSITION
Approximately
10–19° Cancer

SEASON
Early summer

ELEMENT
Water

RULER
The Moon

SYMBOL
The Crab

MODE
Feeling

that they are normal, or desperately attempt to escape their lonely inner world. An ordinary job can be a refuge, a secure hiding place for those born in this week. By burying their personality in an anonymous position with a firm or business, they may avoid scrutiny and allay their fears of being found out.

In their free time, however, they can allow their wacky, zany side a bit more freedom. Interactions with unusual friends allow them the opportunity to share their wilder side and to act out some of their unconscious fantasies. They may vacation in a far-off land, or dream of living there, or even actually do so for a time. Besides pursuing activities like these for their personal satisfaction, they sometimes achieve financial prosperity outside their day job, for they have imaginative ideas. Success in this area usually involves the auspices of a friend or partner of a more businesslike and practical bent; Cancer II's are rarely good at implementing their own vivid thoughts, and it takes others to see the commercial possibilities of their fantasy worlds. Once brought to light, however, these can strike a responsive chord in the community at large. Thus those born in this week are capable of achieving unexpected financial success far afield of their everyday work.

Those born in this week may be collectors, readers or movie watchers in their spare time, but only subjects filled with vivid fantasy will hold their attention for long. Particularly drawn to the dark side of human experience, Cancer II's are often fascinated by crime and colorful illicit activities. They often make friends with extreme types, and are capable of being so interested in such people that they wind up living with or marrying one.

Obsession may come to dominate the life of a Cancer II. It is hard for them to control their desires, particularly when they have become attached to a love object who is less than responsive. In fact a hopeless love can become the central sticking point of a Cancer II's life, and such individuals can ultimately manifest self-destructive tendencies. It is important, then, that they learn lessons of nonattachment, which usually means dealing effectively with their own compulsive needs. This kind of inner work is essential to the psychological health of those born in the Week of the Unconventional.

Unhappily, it can also happen that Cancer II's just get stuck in their own inner worlds. A profound fear of rejection, criticism or outright ridicule often makes them afraid to reveal their personal visions. The reality of the more introverted Cancer II's may come to be confined to the four walls of their home, from which they venture out seldom or never. Even those who take regular jobs are expert at hiding when they are away from their work, and many wish simply not to be disturbed.

Cancer II's share their lives best with others who also value privacy. Their homes can become museums, filled with objects both gorgeous and hideous often acquired through their collecting instincts or those of their unusual mate or partner. But Cancer II taste is itself highly personal, and is definitely not socially oriented the interior decorating of those born in this week can be quite shocking to the casual

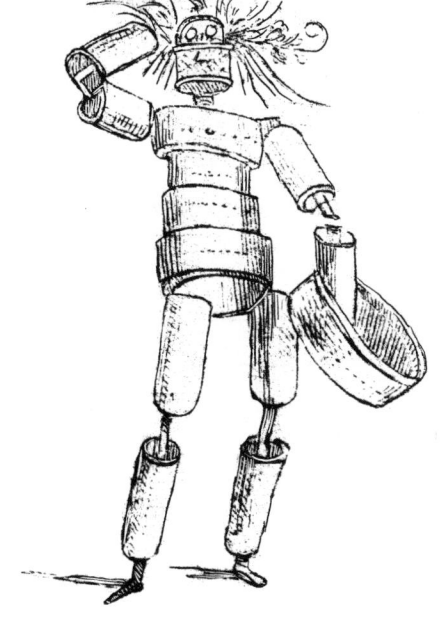

"UNCONVENTIONAL"

visitor. Cancer II's tend to be lavish in their expenditures, and will go to extraordinary lengths to make their living space vivid and flamboyant.

The more conservative, particularly parents and children of Cancer II's who have little choice but to live at least part of their lives with them, may have a difficult time getting those born in this week to act in a socially acceptable manner on all or even most occasions. Family members often find themselves simply holding their breath when it is time for a Cancer II relative to take center stage; there is really no telling what might come out of their mouths, or what moves it might strike their funny bone to make. Relatives may find it equally discomfiting, on the other hand, if the Cancer II simply withdraws and refuses to participate at all.

Many Cancer II's are actually mild individuals who ask little more than to be left alone. But they can be a great deal of fun for their close friends, who will find them sensitive, thoughtful and caring. Often the sensitivity of Cancer II's to the peculiarities of quite normal people, and their valuable psychological insights and support, especially in times of bereavement or of parental or marital difficulty, can earn them a valued position in the lives of others. By capturing their imaginations, they can achieve respect in their social circle or even in the commercial world. However, Cancer II's may suffer greatly if they fail to find an audience with which to share their thoughts.

STRENGTHS

FANTASY-RICH • FUN
PSYCHOLOGICALLY ASTUTE

WEAKNESSES

SELF-DESTRUCTIVE
OBSESSIVE • EMBARRASSING

ADVICE:

Make a real effort to get out in the world. Toughen your stance a bit and try not to be so sensitive. Develop your financial sense and cultivate your talent for maintenance and continuity. Keep contact with those who care about you. Put your active fantasy and imagination to productive use.

CANCER II NOTABLES

Winning back-to-back Oscars for *Philadelphia* and *Forrest Gump,* **Tom Hanks** displayed sensitive characterizations of two figures who, rejected by the world, demanded and received recognition and respect on their own terms. Hanks's fascination with the unusual and bizarre mark him as a Cancer II. Few would have

TOM HANKS

guessed 15 years ago that he would be regarded today as one of America's leading film stars, and, like many born in his week, his path has not been restricted to the straight and narrow. Hanks's deeply human qualities mark him as a compassionate individual who has known emotional pain and emerged from his experiences enriched on both a personal and a professional level.

The haunted, frightening world of **Franz Kafka** is filled with the kinds of extraordinarily imaginative visions that are typical of many Cancer II's. Like others born in this week, Kafka was not able to live a conventional life or express himself in conventional terms. In his story *The Metamorphosis,* the protagonist Gregor Samsa wakes up one morning to discover he has been changed into a gigantic insect and then is forced to live out his rejection at the hands of his family, who try to murder him and finally leave him to die out of sheer disgust for what he has become. In *The Trial,* an anonymous character called Joseph K. is arrested for no reason and hounded

FRANZ KAFKA

in and out of the courtroom until his execution. Dreamlike yet real, Kafka's images are unnerving and unsettling in the extreme.

The life of Mexican painter **Frida Kahlo** was filled with pain but also with artistic exaltation. Contracting polio at age 5 left her crippled, and at the age of 20, a collision damaged her spine, limbs and internal organs, necessitating over 30 operations. Yet her hunger for

FRIDA KAHLO

life and extraordinary artistic abilities sustained her, along with her passionate relationship with Diego Rivera, with whom she fell in love as a teenager and later married. Unconventional in almost every respect, Kahlo was typical of other Cancer II's in her obsessive refusal to give up on her marriage or career and her determination to share her highly unusual inner world with students and the public alike.

More Cancer II's: Gustav Mahler, Nikola Tesla, Elias Howe, Marc Chagall, Jean Cocteau, Tom Cruise, Anjelica Huston, Kevin Bacon, Abigail Van Buren, Ann Landers, O.J. Simpson, Geraldo Rivera, John D. Rockefeller, Philip Johnson, Tom Stoppard, Shirley Knight, the Dalai Lama, Sylvester Stallone, Elisabeth Kübler-Ross, Pierre Cardin, Giuseppe Garibaldi, Ringo Starr, Louis B. Mayer, P.T. Barnum, George M. Steinbrenner, Ron Kovic, Robbie Robertson, Bill Haley, Nancy Reagan, Janet Leigh, Robert Heinlein.

Relationship Guide for Cancer II

DIEGO RIVERA (SAGITTARIUS II)
FRIDA KAHLO (CANCER II)
PAGE 514

BEST RELATIONSHIPS

LOVE
Taurus II
Gemini I
Leo II
Virgo I
Virgo-Libra Cusp
Scorpio II
Scorpio III
Pisces II

MARRIAGE
Aries I
Aries II
Taurus III
Cancer I
Cancer III
Leo-Virgo Cusp
Libra I
Libra-Scorpio Cusp
Scorpio-Sagittarius Cusp
Sagittarius II
Capricorn II
Aquarius II
Aquarius-Pisces Cusp

FRIENDSHIP
Pisces-Aries Cusp
Gemini II
Cancer II
Cancer-Leo Cusp
Libra III
Sagittarius I
Capricorn I
Capricorn III
Aquarius I
Aquarius III
Pisces I
Pisces III

FAMILY
Virgo II
Virgo III
Sagittarius-Capricorn Cusp

WORK
Taurus-Gemini Cusp
Leo III
Scorpio I
Sagittarius III
Capricorn-Aquarius Cusp

Page Locator for All Relationships

CANCER III
The Week of the Persuader

July 11–18

The Cancer III period takes The Persuader as its central image. According to The Grand Cycle of Life, in human terms, this period relates to the years of one's mid- to late twenties, when persuasive powers can be applied both in business and personal relationships. This is a time when all avenues may be tried and opportunities exploited. Founding a business of one's own, finding a life partner, starting a family or seeking to widen opportunities are all typical of this period.

The days that comprise Cancer III symbolically illustrate the active interest of young adults to make something of themselves through investing in a career, taking advantage of situations, convincing and persuading others of their worth and using materials at hand to build a lasting and solid structure.

Cancer III people know how to convince others of their worth and get them to do their bidding. Powerful manipulators of their environment, Cancer III's often manifest great drive and determination. Even the shyest and most retiring Cancer III's nurse private ambitions; the more aggressive of those born in this week make little effort to conceal their desire to rise to the top of their profession. The underlying dynamic of their character, however, is that success, for them, is the best antidote for uncertainty. Yet they rarely fall victim to blind ambition, preferring to invest in themselves than indulge in materialism or ego-tripping.

Cancer III's know how to wait, watch and listen. Observant of what goes on around them, they are good at reading the signs of the times and knowing when to act. Persuaders, their ability to convince others is sup-

ZODIAC POSITION
Approximately
18–26° Cancer

SEASON
Early summer

ELEMENT
Water

RULER
The Moon

SYMBOL
The Crab

MODE
Feeling

ported by a solid bedrock of observation, and on having facts and results at their fingertips. Cancer III's, then, are comfortable dealing with the physical realities of life. In fact, they persuade others less by their words than by their presence alone. Strong personalities, those born in this period are not shy about quietly and effectively applying pressure.

Passionate people, Cancer III's are no strangers to the depths of human emotion. In the same way that insecurity can be viewed as the motor behind the ambition of Cancer III's, their passion for something can be viewed as the gasoline. And usually, their beliefs are something they are passionate about. By establishing contact with others of like mind, they are able to give solid support to their ideas. When they are convinced they are working for the highest good of an organization or group they are difficult to oppose and can usually obtain significant benefits for all concerned.

Whether at work or at home, they usually exert a powerful force behind the scenes, or as team members. Cancer III's make excellent managers and critics; they have a sixth sense for the weaknesses and inadequacies of others and can usually provide direction or guidance to remedy even the most extreme difficulties.

Part of the personal power of Cancer III's comes from their ability to control their own needs. In relationships, for example, they would sooner be alone than enter a dubious or unstable partnership. Knowing themselves well enough to recognize the limitations of their ability to commit to the responsibilities of everyday life, Cancer III's beginning a relationship will be honest with the other person from the outset, rarely pretending to be something they are not. In any case, living alone is not really a problem for those born in this week. They generally require few luxuries, and can efficiently order their lives, particularly financially, without interference from others. Cancer III's are well able to sublimate desire for social and romantic interaction into their career activities and to share common experiences with colleagues, friends and family.

The other side of the coin, however, is the sometimes prodigious tendency of Cancer III's to indulge in excess. Although they may deal with their needs well, their desires and wants can easily get out of hand. Those born in this week do not always know when to stop, when to back off, when to let go. Obsessive-compulsive behavior is not at all uncommon among Cancer III's, whether related to self-gratifying activities that provide direct pleasure or to neurotic ones that only yield frustration. For this reason, some form of spiritual training is often essential for their development.

Their most successful relationships are often with colleagues rather than in personal or romantic settings, where their directness may prove too threatening to others. It also happens that they can best handle their intensity in their work, for in their private lives their direct expressions of energy may boomerang and cause personal difficulty.

As friends and family members, those born in the Week of the Persuader can be giving, sharing and affectionate. Yet their drive to control is evident here, too. Cancer III's do not hesitate to advise and to judge. Their

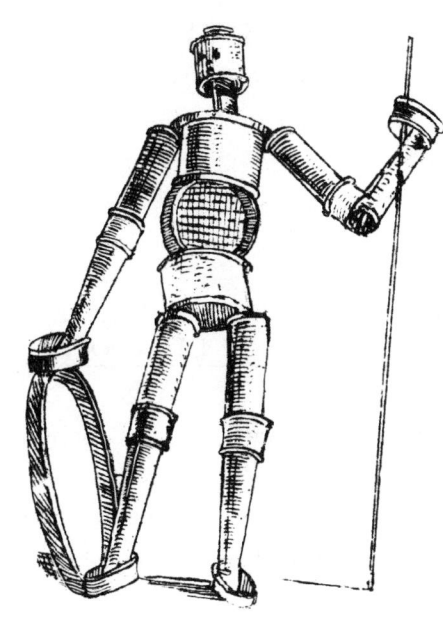

"PERSUADER"

instincts, fortunately, are often right on the mark, but by assuming a managerial role they often deny others the opportunity to guide their own destiny. In extreme cases, those born in this week can be insensitive and smothering, and their manipulations can wreak havoc on friends and intimates.

As spouses or lovers, Cancer III's often find it difficult to occupy anything but center stage. Not only must activities revolve around them, but they must take an active hand in shaping and forming whatever is going on. Conflicts often arise between these dominant individuals and those who question their authority. In such moments the most aggressive characteristics of Cancer III's are likely to emerge. Left alone to go ahead with their work and plans, however, which they usually see not as selfish but as intended for the good of the group, they are content, peaceful and even quiet in demeanor.

Is it possible or even desirable for Cancer III's to pursue long-standing, productive and satisfying love relationships? Yes, certainly, but their chances for success in such affairs are aided by good choices and sound judgment—which they too often allow to be impaired by the heat of their passions. In marriage or a permanent living situation, the answer is often a solid, practical partner, someone who lends structure and emotional stability.

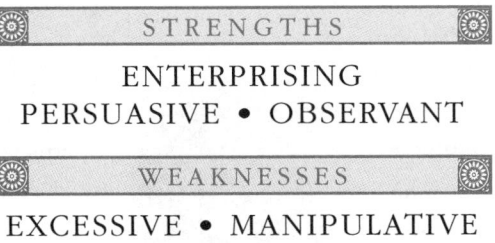

STRENGTHS

ENTERPRISING
PERSUASIVE • OBSERVANT

WEAKNESSES

EXCESSIVE • MANIPULATIVE
INSECURE

ADVICE:

Don't be too so sure you know what is right for people. Work to keep your own house in order. Allow others to express themselves freely. Perhaps no one doubts your good intentions, so it may not be necessary to justify them. Be confident of your abilities at a deep level.

CANCER III NOTABLES

A highly persuasive fellow, **Bill Cosby** talked his way from a North Philadelphia childhood to Temple University and onward, from standup comic to tv personality in *I Spy* and finally to *The Cosby Show*, becoming the highest-paid male entertainer in America—all with a twinkle in his eye, and a powerful twinkle at that! Typical of Cancer III's, Cosby is comfortable dealing with the physical realities of life and has proven to be quite a businessman. Moreover, the

BILL COSBY

intense Cancer III ambition in his case found laughter as its vehicle, and Cosby's ability to endear himself to his fans through both his feigned helplessness and his craftiness proved to be unbeatable. Few know the thoughts, hopes and dreams of the average person and the quirks of their individual personalities as well as Cosby.

From prisoner serving a life term to the presidency of his country, **Nelson Mandela** has never given up his intense love of his homeland. The smashing of apartheid by a strange alliance between F.W. de Klerk and Mandela (it was de Klerk who pardoned Mandela and released him from jail in 1990) signaled the entry of South Africa into the fold of democratic world powers. A master

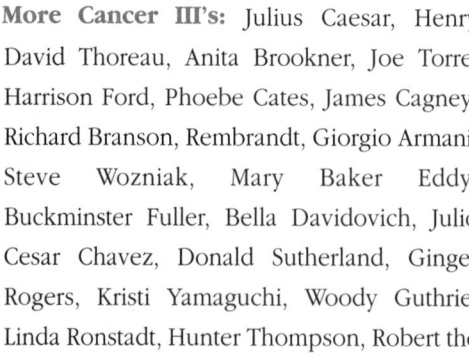
NELSON MANDELA

Persuader, Mandela never allowed himself to be talked out of his beliefs, even when he was offered his freedom if he did so.

Canonized by Pope Pius XII as the Heavenly Patroness of All Emigrants, **Saint Mother Cabrini** founded hospitals, schools, institutions and orphanages all over the world. Born in Italy, she was filled with the missionary spirit, and when she applied to Pope Leo XIII to work abroad, she was told that there was a great spiritual need on the part of Italian immigrants and others in the United States, to which she subsequently devoted herself. Four great hospitals were subsequently founded: two in Chicago, one in Seattle and the Columbia (Cabrini) Hospital in

SAINT MOTHER CABRINI

New York. A powerful Cancer III organizer and persuader, Mother Cabrini was able to put her ambition in the service of others.

More Cancer III's: Julius Caesar, Henry David Thoreau, Anita Brookner, Joe Torre, Harrison Ford, Phoebe Cates, James Cagney, Richard Branson, Rembrandt, Giorgio Armani, Steve Wozniak, Mary Baker Eddy, Buckminster Fuller, Bella Davidovich, Julio Cesar Chavez, Donald Sutherland, Ginger Rogers, Kristi Yamaguchi, Woody Guthrie, Linda Ronstadt, Hunter Thompson, Robert the Bruce, Leon Spinks, Marina Oswald, Yul Brynner, Christie McVie, Oscar Hammerstein II, Andrew Wyeth, Van Cliburn, John Dee.

Relationship Guide for Cancer III

HARRIET NELSON (CANCER III)
OZZIE NELSON (PISCES-ARIES CUSP)
PAGE 221

**BEST
RELATIONSHIPS**

LOVE
  Aries III
  Gemini III
  Sagittarius II
  Aquarius III

MARRIAGE
  Aries-Taurus Cusp
  Taurus I
  Cancer II
  Virgo I
  Virgo-Libra Cusp
  Scorpio I
  Sagittarius-Capricorn Cusp
  Capricorn II

FRIENDSHIP
  Taurus III
  Gemini I
  Cancer I
  Leo I
  Leo III
  Leo-Virgo Cusp
  Virgo II
  Libra II
  Libra-Scorpio Cusp
  Scorpio III
  Sagittarius I
  Sagittarius III
  Aquarius II
  Pisces I
  Pisces II

FAMILY
  Taurus-Gemini Cusp
  Gemini-Cancer Cusp
  Aquarius-Pisces Cusp

WORK
  Aries I
  Taurus II
  Gemini II
  Cancer III
  Cancer-Leo Cusp
  Leo II
  Virgo III
  Libra III
  Scorpio-Sagittarius Cusp
  Pisces III

Page Locator for All Relationships

CANCER-LEO CUSP
The Cusp of Oscillation

July 19–25

The Cancer-Leo cusp is an admixture of the fourth sign of the zodiac, Cancer, and the fifth sign of the zodiac, Leo. This cusp could be characterized as having an oscillating energy. The Cancer-Leo cusp can be symbolically likened to the period around twenty-eight years of age in the human life, and astrologically, this time marks the completion of one full cycle of the planet Saturn (which takes twenty-eight or twenty-nine years to return to the position in the zodiac it occupied at the time of one's birth). Both of these important planetary transits correspond to the point in human development when childhood, puberty, adolescence and young adulthood may be viewed for the first time in a historical context. Many people feel a need at this time to take stock of their lives—to evaluate them and to attempt to plan for the future. Often this is a time of identity crisis, and a time of change. Marriages, breakups, seeking new jobs, moving to another city or setting up a new house are often encountered here. The cyclic nature of the Cancer-Leo cusp underlines the oscillating energies found at this point in life, and the uncertainties and indecisions which manifest.

Those born on the Cancer-Leo Cusp show both the watery and receptive influences of the moon and the fiery, aggressive characteristics of the sun. Of all twelve cusps, this one most clearly shows the split influence of two adjacent signs almost opposite in their orientations: traditionally feminine (moon) and masculine (sun) orientations are combined equally in a single personality. This means that men born on this cusp are likely to have strong feminine sensibilities and women an accentuated

ZODIAC POSITION
Approximately
26° Cancer–3° Leo

SEASONS
Midsummer

ELEMENTS
Water/Fire

RULERS
The Moon/The Sun

SYMBOLS
The Crab/The Lion

MODES
Feeling/Intuition

masculine side. Integrated in a single individual in this way, contrasting characteristics can result in a highly balanced and healthy personality. When they vie for ascendancy, however, producing wide swings of mood, they can cause great psychic stress.

Dramatic changes of affect in those born on the Cusp of Oscillation can make it hard for others to know how to approach them. Those who understand them will often ease into conversations with them slowly, sitting quietly with them until their mood becomes apparent. It is generally difficult or impossible to push Cancer-Leos from one psychological state into another, for they are resistant to emotional manipulation. In their dealings with business partners and friends, they do best with people who are even in disposition and can promote a peaceful and constant environment in day-to-day relations. Steady jobs, steady relationships and a dependable mate are important in evening out their contrasting moods.

Cancer-Leos love being on the cutting edge of innovative projects and activities. Although they are not necessarily cut out to be leaders, their efficiency and their application to the task in front of them are admirable. They also know how to delegate authority and work with a team. Cancer-Leos usually prefer being in the thick of battle to sitting on the sidelines; those who can work with them, as true associates and partners, are often able to share such experiences with them, in this way penetrating deeply into their hearts and minds. It is essential to those born on the Cusp of Oscillation to work with people who are not only highly competent and can do their share of the work and more but who can understand them on a personal level.

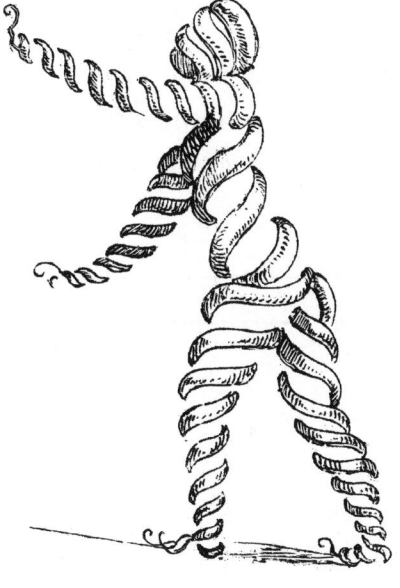

"OSCILLATION"

Cancer-Leos have a dynamic side that can put them in situations of risk-taking and danger. Those born on this cusp generally crave excitement; whether in business, romance or free time, they need to meet challenges dauntlessly. Their calm under fire, their moral courage and their decision-making potential usually stand them in good stead in crises and emergencies, but their drive toward challenge periodically gets out of control. At work this can manifest as megalomania, or the desire to take on the world. In their leisure time, primarily driven by an unconscious drive for near-death experience, they may seek out activities like hang-gliding, riverrafting or mountainclimbing. They may also sublimate these extreme impulses into a hyperactive fantasy life that can only be satiated through action movies, adventure novels or video games, often in excessive quantity.

However, Cancer-Leos also tend to get emotionally blocked from time to time. In this state they may describe an inability to feel, a removal from the sensitive, empathic parts of themselves. This experience, unusally manifesting as depression, can prove upsetting and frightening, particularly in adolescence and early adulthood. Obviously, those born on this cusp must walk a fine line to keep their psychological stability intact. On the one hand they need security in their surroundings and dependability in their relationships. Yet on the other hand they bore easily, and hanker for excitement, change and instability, which they often cannot handle, so that they go over the edge. Perhaps out of fear that their wildness will break out, they may impose restrictions on themselves that produce frustration and rigidity; yet too little self-discipline may result in excessive or addictive behavior and alarming mood swings. The most successful Cancer-Leos find the balance between security and uncertainty. Seeking the golden mean in all things may be the best solution for those born on this cusp. Professional counseling may also prove helpful.

In friendships, Cancer-Leos usually divide their energies equally between both sexes. And in their love relationships those born on the Cusp of Oscillation can express their desires over a wide variety of partner types. It is not that they are promiscuous, but that they have a wide palette of emotional and sexual expression. Many of them can be remarkably faithful to one or two mates, but if such relationships are to be successful, such partners must be able to hold their interest, in addition to being unusually accepting, open and understanding. Other Cancer-Leos may hang in there in stressful or marginally failed relationships with difficult and demanding individuals, meanwhile seeking pleasure and excitement elsewhere. In the end the best solution for Cancer-Leo is a close friend or understanding mate, one who is both psychologically perceptive and reassuring and who may be helpful during trying periods in getting Cancer-Leos through their difficulties.

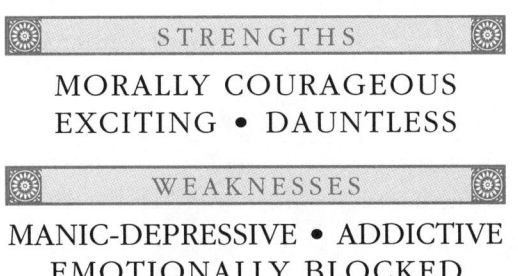

STRENGTHS
MORALLY COURAGEOUS
EXCITING • DAUNTLESS

WEAKNESSES
MANIC-DEPRESSIVE • ADDICTIVE
EMOTIONALLY BLOCKED

ADVICE:

Even out the highs and lows; the rewards of stability are great. Cultivate self-discipline but never lose your spontaneity. Build a calm center that bolsters your confidence and remains at the heart of your being. Concentrate more on living in the moment, free of past problems and future expectations. Pace yourself for the long haul.

CANCER-LEO CUSP NOTABLES

The risk-taking, uncertainty and excitement of those born on the Cusp of Oscillation characterizes the life of aviatrix **Amelia Earhart**. Her sudden disappearance on one of the final legs of a transglobal flight continues to arouse excited controversy and heated debate. Earhart not only flew airplanes, she knew a great deal about their

design and function and was an able mechanic. Although she also taught and wrote, it was the thrill of flying that drew her like a magnet. She established many aviation records, but the greatest lure of all was transoceanic flight. Only 7 years elapsed between her first transatlantic flight and her dis-

AMELIA EARHART

appearance over the Pacific, but in this short span she captured the world's attention with her daring exploits.

During the legendary and exciting life of **Ernest Hemingway**, he was his own best publicist, not being content just to write about exciting contemporary events but insisting on participating in them. Often his characters were loosely veiled embodiments of his own activities, real or imagined, and through him the American public was educated about war and revolution in Europe, where Hemingway lived as an expatriate. African adventures were

ERNEST HEMINGWAY

described in *The Snows of Kilimanjaro,* Caribbean ones in *To Have and Have Not* and, probably his finest work, *The Old Man and the Sea.* A typical Cancer-Leo, Hemingway suffered wide mood swings, oscillated between passivity and activity and exhibited both a strong masculine and feminine side.

Life was never dull for **Rose Fitzgerald Kennedy**. Married to a U.S. ambassador and self-made millionaire and mother to a U.S. president, attorney general and senator, life swirled around her, even in childhood. Coming from an extremely prominent Boston family, she married Joseph P. Kennedy and incurred the extreme dis-

ROSE FITZGERALD
KENNEDY

approval of her family. Her deep spirituality enabled her to live through the assassinations of two of her sons as the grand matriarch of the Kennedy clan. Hanging in there in a difficult but exciting marriage, keeping her equilibrium through huge crises and keeping calm under fire mark Rose Kennedy as a Cancer-Leo.

More Cancer-Leos: Simon Bolívar, Edmund Hillary, Woody Harrelson, Iman, Robin Williams, Natalie Wood, John Lovitz, Edgar Degas, Robert Graves, Diana Rigg, Bob Dole, Zelda Fitzgerald, Carlos Santana, Francesco Petrarch, Karl Malone, Hart Crane, Marshall McLuhan, Isaac Stern, Tom Robbins, Emil Jannings, Alexander Dumas, Sr., Omar Khayyam, Walter Payton, Florence Entwhistle, Billy Taylor, Don Drysdale, Leon Fleisher, Raymond Chandler, Danny Glover, Gregor Mendel, Edward Hopper, Kay Starr.

Relationship Guide for Cancer-Leo Cusp

F. Scott Fitzgerald (Virgo I)
Zelda Sayre (Cancer-Leo Cusp)
PAGE 540

BEST
RELATIONSHIPS

LOVE
Pisces-Aries Cusp
Aries I
Gemini II
Cancer I
Libra III
Sagittarius I
Capricorn II
Capricorn-Aquarius Cusp
Aquarius III

MARRIAGE
Taurus II
Taurus III
Leo I
Virgo II
Scorpio II
Aqarius-Pisces Cusp
Pisces II

FRIENDSHIP
Gemini III
Cancer II
Leo II
Virgo I
Libra I
Scorpio-Sagittarius Cusp
Sagittarius II
Sagittarius-Capricorn Cusp
Capricorn III
Aquarius I

FAMILY
Aries-Taurus Cusp
Libra II
Libra-Scorpio Cusp

WORK
Taurus I
Taurus-Gemini
Gemini I
Cancer III
Cancer-Leo Cusp
Leo-Virgo Cusp
Virgo III
Scorpio I
Scorpio III
Capricorn I
Aquarius II
Pisces III

Page Locator for All Relationships

LEO I
The Week of Authority

July 26–August 2

The Leo I period takes Authority as its central image. This period can be likened to the beginning of the mature adult life as an individual turns thirty. Confidence can run high at this point if the doubts and uncertainty of the first Saturn return (age twenty-eight or twenty-nine) have been resolved. Beginning the process of establishing oneself as an authority in a given field can be a focus at this time and an absorbing task. Some must assume the role of authority to their growing children, while others may look to an older, more experienced person who can serve as a teacher, a guide who can initiate them into a broader understanding of the world. Other Leo I's may strengthen their sense of confidence through what they learn from books, religious or spiritual teachings, philosophy, etc.

The days that comprise Leo I symbolically reveal the mature adult developing a truly original style, making important decisions for him/herself and the family or work group, and in general trying to be successful in life by making his/her name known and trusted.

Among the most powerfully authoritative of the year, Leo I's are intense, hard-driving individuals, dedicated primarily to their own personal activities, growth and development. Asserting themselves and being taken seriously is what appeals to them. Also, much of their energy is channeled inward rather than outward, toward developing their own strengths and abilities. Yet they do not view themselves as the be-all and end-all either—far from it. They believe in ultimate higher authorities, which they worship and serve: usually the abstract truths and principles embodied in the practice of their principal

ZODIAC POSITION
Approximately
2–11° Leo

SEASON
Midsummer

ELEMENT
Fire

RULER
The Sun

SYMBOL
The Lion

MODE
Intuition

endeavor, whether it lies in the arts, business, sports or philosophy. Although they have their heroes, it is usually to these principles rather than to people that they accord the highest value.

Many Leo I's can be highly competitive, and geared to coming out on top. Others don't really care that much for worldly success, being more interested in bettering their own personal best. It may be difficult for Leo I's to work for a boss, especially one they do not respect. Yet when they run their own company or business, they also encounter problems, since their capacity to dominate is often greater than their capacity to lead. They may work most easily with people who have been drawn to them as admirers, students or disciples; then the relationship is clear from the start. Another solution can be working on their own, perhaps as freelancers. Leo I's can best become team players with co-workers and associates when it is clear that they are all working together for a common, usually higher cause.

Leo I's are highly physical individuals, magnetically drawn to exciting and confrontational experiences. Those born in this week need to prove themselves repeatedly, whether in the sports arena, the wild world of nature, the jungle of corporate finance or the intimacy of the bedroom. So intense is this area of their personality that intimates and enemies alike may feel a bit ignored, for much of their striving is impersonal in nature, and basically an expression of the Leo I will to overcome. Even in more mundane, everyday activities, mates and lovers periodically feel the Leo I's detachment.

Being involved with such individuals is rarely an easy task. Their standards for themselves are extremely high,

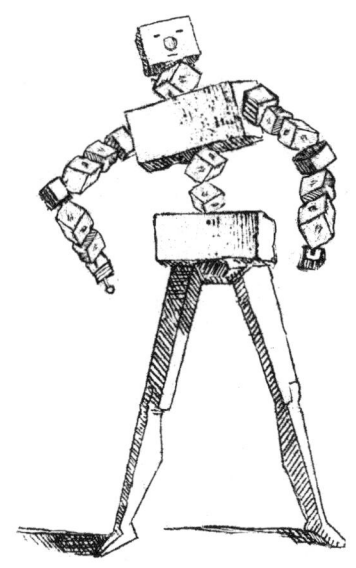

"AUTHORITY"

and they too often want others to show a similar intensity and devotion. In the end, however, they usually do expect more of themselves than of others, and do show an understanding of their colleagues' and intimates' limitations. Realistic Leo I's will not have disproportionately high expectations of co-workers and mates but will only expect the best of which they are capable. This in itself can be a heavy enough load for them to bear.

Leo I's can make loyal and faithful friends. It is usually only from such intimates that a Leo I can accept advice, particularly of a personal nature. Leo I's will not usually accept help from a colleague, professional counselor or stranger. Perhaps once in a lifetime, however, those born in the Week of Authority may put themselves in the hands of another person to whom they ascribe almost godlike status, often a kind of teacher or guru. Such trust is not given easily, and should it fail, tremendous disillusionment will surely follow.

Most of those born in the Week of Authority would do well to work on their treatment of their fellow human beings, particularly in the areas of kindness, patience and understanding. Those involved with these tough customers must themselves be prepared to show these three traits in abundance. When the high expectations of Leo I's are not met, they can become unusually frustrated and bitter. Also, they do not react well to negativity, nagging and constant criticism. Those who live and work most successfully with Leo I's, then,

are those whose attitudes are open, determined and optimistic.

Family life works out for some Leo I's; for others it is a great mistake. Rarely, however, does a Leo I deeply need it. Should they choose to be parents, they will have a lot to give; they have much to teach, are protective and inspire confidence. But their children and mates must quickly come to appreciate their need for their own space, and for time away from home. Trying to get the undivided attention of a Leo I can be a frustrating experience. Too often their idea of caring and attention may be limited to intense encounters, rather than steady displays of understanding and sympathy.

As lovers, Leo I's are usually passionate rather than sensuous. They may also exhibit a certain detachment, or a preoccupation elsewhere. Predictable and routine circumstances often dull sexual gratification for those born in this week. More often than not, their most pleasurable sexual experiences come not with their mates or partners but in casual, chance encounters, or in clandestine affairs of longer standing. Successful spouses of Leo I's know how to keep the romantic flame alive through a combination of variety, skill and imagination.

Leo I's must learn to relax and have fun or risk burnout. Those who can seduce them away from their work and their intense preoccupations will play important roles in their lives. Casual friends who can do this often experience the best that those born in this week have to offer.

STRENGTHS
TRUTH-LOVING
LOYAL • PASSIONATE

WEAKNESSES
FRUSTRATED • DEMANDING
EGOTISTICAL

ADVICE:

Learn to accept people as they are—both the positive and negative. It is probably useless to try to camouflage yourself, but do try to be more diplomatic and sensitive. Although you are good at making decisions for others, you may have overlooked making some crucial decisions for yourself. It doesn't make you less of a person to be a bit more easygoing.

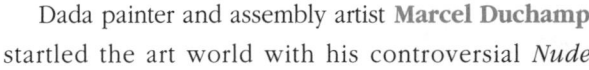

LEO I NOTABLES

Swiss psychoanalyst **Carl G. Jung** had an enormous influence on popular, esoteric and intellectual thought in the second half of the 20th century. Overshadowed by his more empirical and pragmatic colleague, Sigmund Freud, Jung broke with him in 1913 to develop his own school of psychiatry. Jung became the Authority in such

areas as the human personality and the study of symbols, partly by creating links between our dream world and the myths and icons found the world over in ancient and so-called primitive societies. From astrology to semiotics, from cultural anthropology to afterlife experience, Jung's theories have helped to

CARL G. JUNG

unravel hitherto unsolved metaphysical puzzles.

With the determination and drive of a true Leo I, **Jacqueline Kennedy Onassis** married one of the world's most powerful and then one of the world's richest men—John F. Kennedy and Aristotle Onassis, respectively. Quite successful careerwise, socially and financially both before and after she met both, Jackie never really depended on anyone to make her life a full one in worldly terms. One of the world's most photographed women, it was difficult for Jackie to take a step without a horde of photographers buzzing around her, and an already tough stance toward publicity only intensified over the years. Self-preservation is an instinct strongly at work in those born in the Week of Authority, and Jackie was no exception.

JACQUELINE KENNEDY ONASSIS

Dada painter and assembly artist **Marcel Duchamp** startled the art world with his controversial *Nude Descending a Staircase*. Greatly expanding the vocabulary of modern art, Duchamp moved from his Cubist and Futurist beginnings to explore more distant artistic horizons, particularly after founding the New York Dada movement. Painting, poetry, film and sculpture took on new mean-

MARCEL DUCHAMP

ing in his hands. His hard-driving approach to further his own personal development and his devotion to the highest principles of his art identify him as a Leo I. Tough and uncompromising, Duchamp was only able to work with others whose depth of commitment, technical mastery and understanding matched his own. His drive for perfection led him to largely give up art for chess in his later years.

More Leo I's: Stanley Kubrick, Emily Bronte, Primo Levi, Jerry Garcia, Henry Ford, Myrna Loy, Mick Jagger, Elizabeth Hanford Dole, Dag Hammarskjöld, Patti Scialfa, George Bernard Shaw, Pina Bausch, Leo Durocher, Casey Stengel, Geraldine Chaplin, Arnold Schwarzenegger, Beatrix Potter, Michael Spinks, Bobbie Gentry, Herman Melville, Bill Bradley, Vida Blue, Nick Bollettieri, Elizabeth Hardwick, Alexander Dumas, Jr., Clara Bow, Riccardo Muti, Mikis Theodorakis, Benito Mussolini, Peggy Fleming.

Relationship Guide for Leo I

MICK JAGGER (LEO I)
KEITH RICHARDS (SAGITTARIUS III)
PAGE 563

BEST RELATIONSHIPS

LOVE
Aries III
Taurus III
Leo-Virgo Cusp
Libra I
Libra II
Scorpio II
Sagittarius I
Aquarius II

MARRIAGE
Gemini I
Cancer-Leo Cusp
Scorpio III
Sagittarius III
Capricorn I
Capricorn-Aquarius Cusp
Aquarius-Pisces Cusp
Pisces III

FRIENDSHIP
Taurus I
Taurus-Gemini Cusp
Cancer I
Cancer III
Virgo-Libra Cusp
Libra III
Scorpio I
Aquarius III
Pisces I

FAMILY
Aries I
Leo III
Virgo II
Scorpio-Sagittarius Cusp
Sagittarius II
Aquarius I

WORK
Pisces-Aries Cusp
Gemini II
Leo II
Virgo I
Virgo III
Libra-Scorpio Cusp
Sagittarius-Capricorn Cusp
Capricorn II
Pisces II

Page Locator for All Relationships

LEO II
The Week of Balanced Strength

August 3–10

The Leo II period takes Balanced Strength as its central image. This period symbolizes a time in the adult life when the need to adopt a heroic, protective, or nurturing stance comes to the fore. Usually such feelings emerge in family situations or in work with social groups. Adopting and playing a role fully is important at this time and to that extent, taking life seriously. Showing the courage to stand up for one's convictions and not forsake one's ideals no matter what are characteristic of this period.

The days that comprise Leo II symbolically reveal the mature adult developing poise and composure, maximizing effectiveness, exerting both power and influence in a variety of social roles, and commanding respect. Assertiveness, honor, dignity and faithfulness are qualities stressed here.

Solid and tough, Leo II's do not back down from challenges; in fact, they thrive on them, and are often at their best when facing problems and difficulties. Although drawn toward experiences that hold an element of danger, they are usually not foolhardy enough to attempt the impossible. Realists, they are well aware of their limitations, which they may stretch to the limit if necessary but will rarely try to overleap. Fixed attitudes characterize those born in this week, so it will take a great deal of patience and persistence to get them to change their mind. Leo II's pride themselves on their ability to spot phoniness and nonsense, and are particularly critical of metaphysical ideas not strongly grounded in the here and now

Leo II's generally exercise tremendous powers of concentration, but through their fixation on their object

ZODIAC POSITION
Approximately
9–18° Leo

SEASON
Midsummer

ELEMENT
Fire

RULER
The Sun

SYMBOL
The Lion

MODE
Intuition

they may lose the peripheral vision necessary for keeping in touch with their surroundings. In a related problem, their reliance on logical reasoning can detract from what may well be their best suit— that is, their capacity for strong hunches and their intuitive strengths. These traits may lead them to get out of touch with reality while at the same time remaining convinced of their rightness—a dangerous combination.

Gifted with endurance and tenacity, Leo II's hang in there for the duration. The upside of this character trait is their intense loyalty and devotion; the downside is a streak of masochism—a tendency, for example, to suffer while trying to hold a romance, marriage or business together. Leo II's can continue in an unhappy or stressful relationship for years without undue complaint, patiently seeking ways to make it work. Although they would sometimes do better by quitting, they will usually refuse to take the easy way out, and they may have little respect for those who lack their level of commitment. When long-standing relationships that have proven unsatisfactory finally do collapse, perhaps due to a stroke of fate, or to the partner's unwillingness to continue, Leo II's have a tendency to sink into depression. Too often they blame themselves. A long period of grieving may be necessary before they are once again able to function well.

They can certainly be their own worst enemies. Those born in the Week of Balanced Strength exude power and self-confidence when their prodigious energies meld, but these same energies also get out of control and can threaten to tear them apart. At such times they make a piteous sight. Alcohol or drug binges and borderline or outright criminal activities can all be the

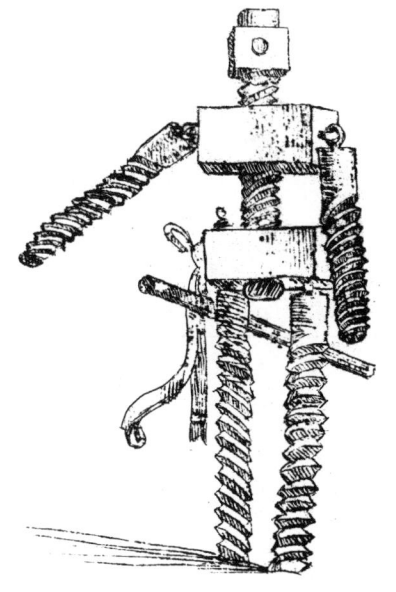

"BALANCED STRENGTH"

evidence of Leo II energies run amok. Keeping balanced is less an ideal for them to attain than an absolute condition for their healthy survival. The children and friends of Leo II's can be severely jolted if these normally reassuring presences disintegrate. Thus the Leo II desire to be a protector of the weak and a friend to the underdog can backfire.

Those born in the Week of Balanced Strength do well in highly structured situations of their own making, situations in which they are at the helm. They periodically feel an acute need to withdraw into a private place, however, and sometimes to a strictly isolated one. The problem here is an accompanying tendency to nurse hurts and slights, and in extreme cases to manifest paranoia. Developing an accepting attitude and working to diminish dogmatic and intolerant thought are essential to their mental health.

For the most part, Leo II's are extraordinarily faithful people. They see themselves as champions of the downtrodden and protectors of the weak. They despise exclusion and condescension and, for this reason, generally side with the common person rather than the privileged. It is not that they do not have an ability to mix well with a variety of social classes; rather, they dislike insincerity or pretension.

In their toughness, Leo II's are able to withstand many disappointments. They usually weather the storm and win out through knowing how to wait, "having the long breath." They like being independent, but nonetheless tend to build a well-defined life in which they exert maximum power with a minimum of fuss.

Those involved with Leo II's, whether as co-workers, employees, family, mates or friends, know that those born in this week must not be pushed or prodded when in a negative frame of mind but, rather, must be left alone to work things out for themselves. Leo II's are also sometimes accused of insensitivity. This is more often a result of their being preoccupied than of a lack of understanding on their part, for many born in this week are psychologically astute; yet although they can comprehend another person's emotional state, they may feel no need to sympathize with it. Leo II's are not especially empathic with those around them, and are capable of a stony detachment. Many born in this week find emotional matters simply too messy to get involved in, a response that is sometimes traceable to unpleasant childhood experience. When the parent, child or lover of a Leo II is of a more feeling type, conflict can result.

Being straightforward and unpretentious themselves, Leo II's dislike people who put on airs. Nothing excites their often uncontrollable temper more than insincerity, lying or disingenuousness. Leo II anger and hotheadedness can weaken the psychological balance on which their strength depends. Those closest to these intense individuals know how to use sensual persuasion and a fun-loving outlook to keep their partners happy .

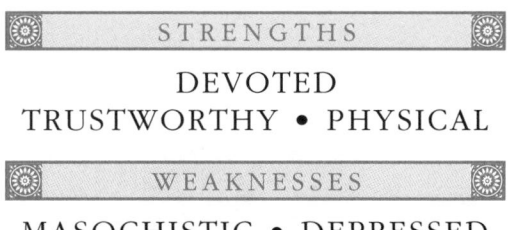

STRENGTHS

DEVOTED
TRUSTWORTHY • PHYSICAL

WEAKNESSES

MASOCHISTIC • DEPRESSED
GUILTY

ADVICE:

Watch your temper. Hotheadedness can throw you off balance and aid your opponent. Compromise and diplomacy are virtues to be cultivated, not weaknesses to be despised. Remain open and vulnerable to love. Don't be too hard on yourself, or too demanding. Ease up a bit on the expectations you place on others.

LEO II NOTABLES

Not even the Beatles were able to produce seven #1 hits in a row—but **Whitney Houston** did. The enormously successful and talented Houston specializes in firsts, such as being the first female recording artist to

WHITNEY HOUSTON

enter the charts with an album at #1 or having her first film, *The Bodyguard,* be a box office hit. Keeping her balance has not always been easy for Whitney, but as a Leo II she thrives on challenge, like keeping her marriage with unpredictable Bobby Brown afloat. However, in all areas of life,

suffering and a refusal to back down or admit defeat are also Leo II characteristics that Whitney will have to be careful do not turn into sheer masochism.

Thinking of basketball's New York Knicks without Leo II **Patrick Ewing** is like trying to imagine a peach without a pit. The durable and powerful center of the Knicks' attack personifies the Balanced Strength of the team. Quiet and controlled on court, Ewing does his job without a lot of fuss or bother in a sport more devoted each year to the cult of personality. To call him a workhorse is to state the obvious, but there are few players who give their all with more dignity.

Despite a long film history, director **John Huston** has never received the homage he deserved, largely due to the disappointing

PATRICK EWING

quality of many of his films and also because of a 20-year gap in his career between 1953 and 1973. But the man who directed *The Maltese Falcon* and then went on to do *The Treasure of the Sierra Madre, The African Queen* and *The Man Who Would Be King* can hardly be ignored in film history. Huston led an exciting and varied life in which the physical Leo II nature expressed

JOHN HUSTON

itself, whether he was working as a professional boxer or a lieutenant in the Mexican cavalry. Huston was also an actor, like his father, Walter, and like his daughter, Anjelica is.

More Leo II's: Andy Warhol, Percy Bysshe Shelley, Melanie Griffith, Dustin Hoffman, Mata Hari, Raoul Wallenberg, Anne Klein, Rosanna Arquette, Martin Sheen, Martha Stewart, Courtney Love, Tony Bennett, Maurice Richard, Isabel Allende, Neil Armstrong, Lucille Ball, David Robinson, Louis Leakey, Patti Austin, Alfred, Lord Tennyson, Roland Kirk, Nicholas Ray, Emil Nolde, Manitas de Plata, Alberto Salazar, Leonide Massine, Nigel Mansell, Esther Williams, Arthur J. Goldberg, Jean Piaget, Bob Cousy, Brett Hull.

Relationship Guide for Leo II

Page Locator for All Relationships

Mary Leakey (Aquarius II)
Louis B. Leakey (Leo II)
PAGE 581

BEST
RELATIONSHIPS

LOVE
Taurus II
Gemini I
Gemini II
Cancer II
Leo III
Virgo I
Scorpio II
Aquarius III
Aquarius-Pisces Cusp

MARRIAGE
Aries I
Aries-Taurus Cusp
Taurus III
Scorpio I
Sagittarius I
Sagittarius II
Aquarius I
Pisces I

FRIENDSHIP
Aries II
Gemini III
Cancer I
Leo II
Libra I
Libra-Scorpio Cusp
Scorpio III
Capricorn I
Pisces II

FAMILY
Taurus-Gemini Cusp
Virgo II
Virgo-Libra Cusp
Libra II
Scorpio-Sagittarius Cusp
Capricorn II

WORK
Cancer III
Leo I
Virgo III
Libra III
Sagittarius III
Capricorn III
Capricorn-Aquarius Cusp
Aquarius II

LEO III
The Week of Leadership

August 11–18

The Leo III period takes Leadership as its central image. This period can be likened to a time in the prime of one's life when the right combination of experience, enthusiasm, energy and knowledge can make one a strong candidate for positions of responsibility. Perhaps for the first time, taking over the reins of a business, club or family and leading it to new heights can seem natural and appropriate. Such a leadership role may be a proving ground for assuming even greater roles of this sort later in life—for example, when a manager becomes a partner or owner, or a parent becomes a patriarch or matriarch.

The days that comprise Leo III picture the adult validating his/her skills and experience, learning when to rely on conventional wisdom and when to take risks, and discovering the most effective way to galvanize a team and lead it effectively, inspirationally and tirelessly.

Leo III's often assume a commanding role in their family and social or work group. They have highly developed instincts to lead, but not necessarily to dominate or to rule; it is simply that action comes naturally to these dynamic individuals. They are also good planners, well capable of organizing an effective plan of attack and seeing it through. Building an effective team is essential to their continued success, and learning to delegate authority is key to stopping them from shouldering unrealistic burdens alone, which can result in burnout or breakdown.

Both men and women born in this week have a heroic view of themselves. Aggressive, Leo III's know what they want and how to get it. They may lack consideration

ZODIAC POSITION
Approximately
17–26° Leo

SEASON
Midsummer

ELEMENT
Fire

RULER
The Sun

SYMBOL
The Lion

MODE
Intuition

for the wishes of others, arousing antagonism and getting them in trouble, particularly since they are not, in fact, insensitive to what others are feeling but may choose to ignore what they know and follow their own desires. By occasionally riding roughshod over the emotions of those in their lives, they arouse resentment, fear and anger. But those born in this week may also inspire tremendous loyalty, respect and love in others, so much so that their acquaintances and friends often overlook the more selfish elements of the Leo III character.

Those born in the Week of Leadership have an overwhelming faith in their own abilities. In extreme cases they see themselves as infallible, and seek to project a godlike demeanor. Obvious problems may result from this egotistical stance, not the least of these being the loss of faith that can be engendered in their children, mates and co-workers when they get tripped up. The fall from grace that inevitably follows may result in deep disillusionment; this can impair the relationship permanently, but it can also lead to a more realistic view of the Leo III personality.

Careerwise, Leo III's specialize in breathing new life into an ailing business or social or family group. Their prodigious energy and single-mindedness may be just what is needed to get things back on track. Those born in this week must see their endeavors bear fruit. Watching their restructuring and its implementation bloom is enormously satisfying to them; conversely, seeing their efforts fail is usually intolerable. Because Leo III's are not easily approached on an emotional level, striving shoulder to shoulder with them in such endeavors may be an effective means of getting close to them.

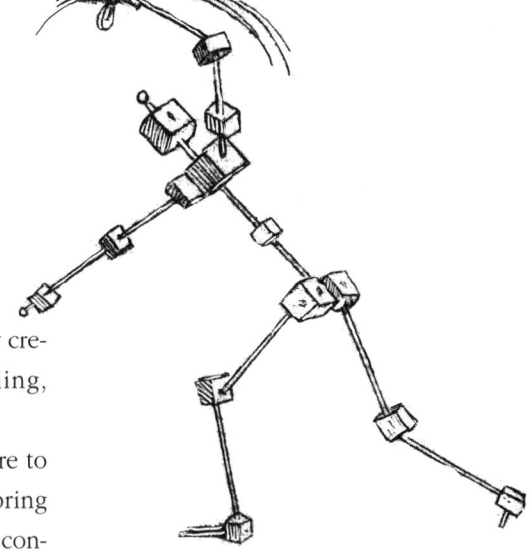

"LEADERSHIP"

Such working relationships may create deep ties of mutual feeling, which sometimes last a lifetime.

If those born in this week are to ground their self-image and bring themselves into closer everyday contact with others, it may be important for them to share quite menial tasks. In particular, they will earn greater respect from family members if they shoulder ordinary, everyday responsibilities at home on a daily basis. A refusal or inability to "lower" themselves to this human level may result in tensions, frustrations and arguments. More balanced Leo III's will avoid such needless difficulties by getting their chores done quickly and efficiently, with little fuss, thus freeing themselves up for what they view as more important endeavors.

The creativity of Leo III's often runs high. Although they are capable of selfishness and narrowness in their personal dealings, in their careers their imagination, philosophical perspective, and wide range of expression often result in artistic, financial and social creations of a very high order. Many of their friends, acquaintances and co-workers, in fact, are not really so much enamored of the Leo III's themselves as drawn to the aura surrounding them and the work they produce.

Other strong personalities inevitably clash with Leo III's, and relationships with those born in this week are likely to be stormy affairs unless the other party is willing to compromise or back down. But the more clever, and devious, partners and mates of Leo III's know exactly how to soothe the savage lion or lioness. Leo III's are not unaware of their charisma, and consequently come to value the constant love and appreciation of that very special person. In fact, they may not actually be at all aggressive toward those they love. As long as they are honored and respected, they will be generous and kind, even to a fault: they will often refuse to see anything wrong in the behavior of a favored family member, a trait that can make them quite unrealistic. Having a thoroughly spoiled mate or child is a Leo III trademark. In love, Leo III's are subject to sudden, explosive, violent and passionate displays of emotion. Their feelings are capable of smoldering under the surface for a long period only to break out unexpectedly and volcanically.

Those involved in love affairs with Leo III's may appreciate their searing intensity and almost total involvement, but at the same time may have difficulty with their often overbearing, combative and unforgiving attitudes. In personal relationships, although faithful up to a point, Leo III's are not particularly long-suffering, and will not hesitate to break things off if they are wounded or see little hope for the future. Coming to feel that they apply a double standard to their relationships, their partners, angry and disgusted, may rudely drop them, which can amaze the more unaware Leo III'— just when things were going so well! Indeed, Leo III's may show little interest in seeing things from the other person's point of view.

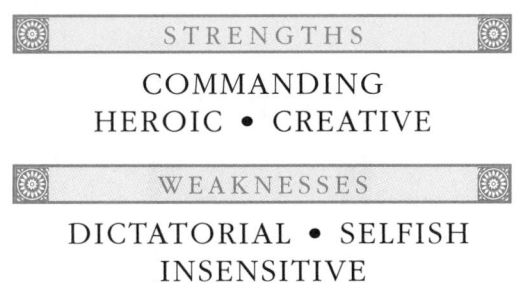

STRENGTHS

COMMANDING
HEROIC • CREATIVE

WEAKNESSES

DICTATORIAL • SELFISH
INSENSITIVE

ADVICE:

Try to tone down your demanding and commanding side. Hold the mirror up to yourself as well—examine your motivations carefully. Battle to keep the combatant in you more peaceful. Take some distance from yourself. Admitting weakness can also be a sign of strength.

LEO III NOTABLES

A giant of a leader, although of diminutive size, **Napoleon Bonaparte** was the prototype of the Leo III personality. Frequently riding roughshod over the feelings and wishes of others, he nonetheless inspired worship and extreme loyalty in his followers. Napoleon's faith in himself and his ability to get his Corsican family

and the French nation back on track further identify him as being born in the Week of Leadership. Known primarily for his military genius, Napoleon instituted social reforms that changed the face of France and of Europe in general, including a reworking of civil law, education, finance

NAPOLEON BONAPARTE

and administration. A revolutionary and true student of history, Napoleon is said to have created the beautiful, wide boulevards of Paris to make the erecting of barricades more difficult and, thus, his position more secure.

Superstar **Madonna** has captured the world's attention as much through her outrageous behavior as through her enormous talent. Dancer, model, singer, songwriter, actress, she has blazed a path across the entertainment firmament like few, if any, stars in recent years. Her challenge of social conventions, particularly those dealing with sex and the role of women, has made her a kind of unofficial social Leader for millions of fans and admirers worldwide. Typical of the Leo III personality, she has largely welcomed such a

MADONNA

commanding role. Her stormy marriage to Sean Penn (also a Leo III) and other intimate relationships fit the Leo III mold of being passionate and tempestuous.

MAGIC JOHNSON

NBA All-Star **Magic Johnson** has won the love and respect of the general public through his untiring efforts on behalf of the victims of AIDS. His life changed radically after he was diagnosed as HIV-positive, but he was able to translate his enormous leadership and team skills to the social arena as a spokesman for those with the disease. His achievements include being 3-time MVP and 9-time All NBA First Team, which attest to his fantastic playing ability and enormous popularity among players, fans and sportswriters alike. Magic's Leo III heroic and creative side, as well as his social commitment, are attested to by his Grammy–winning album *What You Can Do to Avoid AIDS*.

More Leo III's: T.E. Lawrence, Julia Child, Angela Bassett, Sean Penn, Alex Haley, Lina Wertmuller, Steve Martin, Gary Larson, Robert De Niro, Edna Ferber, Roman Polanski, David Henry Hwang, Helena Blavatsky, Shimon Peres, Alfred Hitchcock, Kathie Lee and Frank Gifford, William Goldman, Jim Courier, Pete Sampras, Fidel Castro, Annie Oakley, Philippe Petit, Kathleen Battle, Robert Redford, Rosalynn Carter, Malcolm-Jamal Warner, Robertson Davies, Ted Hughes.

Relationship Guide for Leo III

NAPOLEON BONAPARTE (LEO III)
JOSEPHINE DE BEAUHARNAIS
(GEMINI-CANCER CUSP)
PAGE 472

BEST RELATIONSHIPS

LOVE
Taurus II
Gemini-Cancer Cusp
Leo II
Virgo I
Libra II
Scorpio II
Sagittarius I
Sagittarius-Capricorn Cusp
Capricorn II
Aquarius I
Aquarius II

MARRIAGE
Cancer I
Leo III
Virgo-Libra Cusp
Libra I
Libra-Scorpio Cusp

FRIENDSHIP
Aries II
Taurus III
Gemini III
Cancer III
Virgo II
Libra III
Scorpio I
Scorpio-Sagittarius Cusp
Sagittarius II
Aquarius-Pisces Cusp

FAMILY
Leo I
Capricorn III
Pisces II

WORK
Aries III
Taurus I
Gemini II
Cancer II
Leo-Virgo Cusp
Virgo III
Scorpio III
Sagittarius III
Capricorn I
Capricorn-Aquarius Cusp
Pisces I
Pisces III

Page Locator for All Relationships

LEO-VIRGO CUSP
The Cusp of Exposure

♍♌

August 19–25

The Leo-Virgo cusp is an admixture of the fifth sign of the zodiac, Leo, and the sixth sign of the zodiac, Virgo. This cusp can be likened to the period around thirty-five years of age in the human life and also to the actual time of year at which it occurs—the winding down of summer in the northern hemisphere. During this period of the year, grass must be cut to make hay for the winter, some vegetables harvested and others prepared for harvesting. The days grow shorter and the nights longer, fall approaches and vacation time is almost over. In human development, at the age of thirty-five, adulthood is in full swing. This is a period in which the theme of Exposure figures prominently—particularly in terms of personal development, career and family life. At this time an individual may discover and perhaps reveal to others secret or undiscovered parts of his/her personality. In doing so, new sources of power may be accessed while a sense of identity is strengthened. Both sexes reevaluate their marriages or ongoing relationships, and wish to bring hidden matters out in the open for discussion. Unattached individuals may seek to define a more meaningful living situation for themselves.

Those born on the Leo-Virgo cusp are an interesting blend of introvert and extrovert. Leo-Virgo people combine the practical, earthy qualities of Virgo with more intuitive, fiery traits of Leo, producing quietly inspired individuals who keep their light within. Some Leo-Virgos give a muted, almost nondescript first impression while concealing more flamboyant tendencies; others come across as exhibitionistic but are actually sensitive, private types. They may hide certain personal qualities, or facts about

ZODIAC POSITION
Approximately
27° Leo–3° Virgo

SEASON
Late summer

ELEMENTS
Fire/Earth

RULERS
The Sun/Mercury

SYMBOLS
The Lion/The Virgin

MODES
Intuition/Sensation/
Thought

themselves, for years, but their inner flamboyance will break out periodically in even the most introverted of those born in this period when one day they reveal themselves to the world, in full awareness of what they are doing. Many of them will come to realize that self-concealment is futile the more they try to hide, the more the world seems to take notice of them. By aiming to be more transparent, letting others see what they really are instead of hiding, Leo-Virgos will even out some of their swings between introverted and extroverted behavior.

Leo-Virgos born in unremarkable surroundings, or at the bottom of the social ladder, can be late starters in the struggle to move up in the world. Even once they get going, it is only through tremendous tenacity and willpower that they can maintain their momentum. Indeed, many born in this week can succumb to their worst fear, a life of boredom and mediocrity. Their belief in themselves is often inversely proportionate to the world's belief in them; just when they are gaining self-confidence, in other words, others take less notice of them.

While applause is not crucial to Leo-Virgos, who do not need attention in the same way as many born in other periods of the year, no matter how quiet or self-contained Leo-Virgos may be, they have a burning sense of their own worth. It is characteristic of them not to reveal the truth about themselves or show their real inner feelings until they get to where they are headed, socially or professionally. In fact, this desire to divulge, to show, can be the fuel that powers their drive toward a goal. Those who do reach the top and have carried lifelong secrets are prone to be found out, but usually through their own statements and behavior. This tendency can be

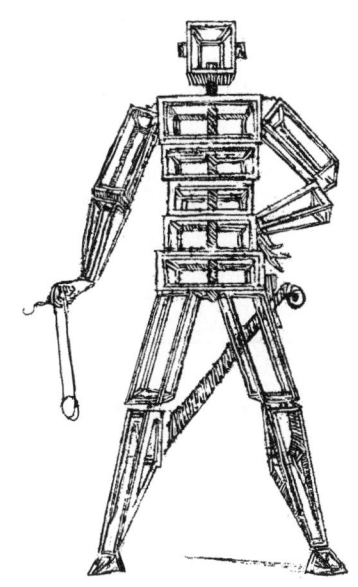

"EXPOSURE"

viewed as a strange blend of narcissism and masochism, of self-indulgence and punishment.

Those born on the Cusp of Exposure are often outstanding observers and judges of character. They know how to watch, silently, without drawing attention to themselves. Further, they are often good at recording their impressions in thought or word, and at expressing them later after long periods of rethinking. Their associates and co-workers will often come to depend on their memory, judgment and objectivity. When able to achieve emotional stability, Leo-Virgos can be dependable and reliable friends.

Leo-Virgos who use concealment and revelation alternately, as weapons or as ploys to get their way, must come to realize the childishness and nonproductivity of such games. Often the solution to such problems comes when they meet just one person, or a very few, who can accept them exactly as they are; through acceptance, love and trust, they can eliminate the need for hide-and-seek. Emotional immaturity may plague those born on this cusp until they fully accept the challenges of growing up.

People who like mysteries and detective work will like Leo-Virgos, and those who take the trouble to understand them will be richly rewarded. Although Leo-Virgos do not deeply need appreciation, kudos or flattery, they do cry out for understanding. This silent call

STRENGTHS
SELF-CONTAINED
OBSERVANT • FLAMBOYANT

WEAKNESSES
NARCISSISTIC • SECRETIVE
NONSHARING

is heard only by those sensitive enough to take notice, on a deep level, of those born on the Cusp of Exposure.

Trust is obviously a big issue for those born on the Cusp of Exposure: their friends must be trustworthy enough to keep their secrets, and their lovers must be trusted to be faithful. Those born in this week do not easily attach their passion and affection to someone. If betrayed by a friend or lover, a Leo-Virgo may suffer emotional collapse.

Characteristically, Leo-Virgos form long-lasting relationships with those who first penetrate their shield of mystery. Those who can accept the fully revealed Leo-Virgos, continuing to like them even after they show more of themselves, become their closest, lifelong friends and partners. Leo-Virgos may not make the best parents or the best children. Their private nature can make intergenerational sharing difficult or impossible. There may well be a family member, however, a cousin or sibling, to whom they periodically open their hearts and with whom they share their secret worlds. Such peers are valuable role models for possible mates later in life; indeed, Leo-Virgos may often cast their life partners in the role of brothers and sisters. Although usually far too self-centered, secretive and unattached to sacrifice themselves for family life, Leo-Virgos can be counted on to discharge their obligations in the daily living situation, as long as the demands placed on them are not excessive.

ADVICE:

Don't blame the world for not recognizing you if you hide yourself away. Be more transparent—let people see what you are really like. Beware of keeping secrets even from yourself. Allow others in, to share in both your joys and sorrows.

LEO-VIRGO CUSP NOTABLES

U.S. President **Bill Clinton** is not an easy personality to fathom. Characteristic of those born on the Cusp of Exposure, he chooses to hide or reveal just as much as suits him at the time. Although an intensely private person, he gives the impression of extreme sociability and openness but in fact may keep much to himself. An observer, Clinton has learned much in life from watching and waiting, rather than heedlessly plunging in headfirst. Thoughtful, he knows when to compromise and even how to baffle his opponents by adopting their own stance rather than opposing them. Even when neglected or overlooked in his youth, Clinton, like other Leo-Virgos, carried within him a burning sense of his own importance, which he knew one day he would impress on the world.

BILL CLINTON

When liberated woman **Gabrielle "Coco" Chanel** opened her first shop in Paris in 1914, she filled it with unisex clothes made from army-navy materials, an innovation that was at least 50 years ahead of its time. When she launched Chanel No. 5 perfume in 1921, she was again in the forefront. The point is that Chanel did manage to put sex appeal in a bottle and sell it—on her own terms and in her own way. Chanel never made a fashion statement just for the sake of making it or because she needed to. Patiently, she would wait until she had something significant to say—like many Leo-Virgos.

GABRIELLE "COCO" CHANEL

Chanel was never in any hurry to show her stuff and in fact lived to be 88 years old.

Before **Sean Connery** started as an actor, he had been a coffin-polisher, swimsuit model and bodybuilder, representing Scotland in the Mr. Universe contest (1950). His first acting job, in the chorus of the London production of *South Pacific*

SEAN CONNERY

(1951), led to small and medium parts in repertory, tv and film. But it wasn't until 1962 that Connery reached prominence as James Bond in *Dr. No.* His wit, charm and virility brought him instant stardom—and he went on to make six other Bond films. But over the years Connery wasn't satisfied with his constant identification as the sexy-spy Bond character. Characteristically a Leo-Virgo, he knew he had much more to offer as an actor. Using his superstar power, he carefully chose a wider range of roles—gradually establishing himself as a well-rounded performer in such films as *The Name of the Rose* (1986; British Film Academy award), *The Untouchables* (1987; Best Supporting Actor Oscar) and *The Hunt for Red October* (1990). Connery knew that eventually he'd be recognized as the versatile artist he truly is.

More Leo-Virgos: Orville Wright, Deng Xiaoping, Cal Ripkin, Jr., Leonard Bernstein, Lola Montez, Wilt Chamberlain, Elvis Costello, Shelley Long, Martin Amis, Gene Roddenberry, Jill St. John, Madame du Barry, Eero Saarinen, Connie Chung.

Relationship Guide for Leo-Virgo Cusp

HILLARY CLINTON (SCORPIO I)
BILL CLINTON (LEO-VIRGO CUSP)
PAGE 603

BEST RELATIONSHIPS

LOVE
Pisces-Aries Cusp
Taurus I
Taurus-Gemini Cusp
Gemini II
Gemini III
Leo I
Libra I
Libra II
Libra-Scorpio Cusp
Sagittarius II
Aquarius II

MARRIAGE
Cancer II
Libra III
Sagittarius I
Aquarius III
Pisces II

FRIENDSHIP
Aries III
Taurus II
Gemini I
Leo-Virgo Cusp
Virgo II
Scorpio III
Sagittarius-Capricorn Cusp
Pisces I
Pisces III

FAMILY
Aries-Taurus Cusp
Taurus III
Cancer III
Scorpio II
Scorpio-Sagittarius Cusp
Sagittarius III
Capricorn III

WORK
Aries II
Gemini-Cancer Cusp
Cancer I
Leo III
Virgo I
Virgo-Libra Cusp
Scorpio I
Capricorn II
Aquarius-Pisces Cusp

Page Locator for All Relationships

VIRGO I
The Week of System Builders

August 26–September 2

The Virgo I period takes System Builders as its central image. This period can be likened to the time in a person's life when the instinct to consolidate and solidify existing structures, marriages or partnerships, businesses, etc., asserts itself. Also, at this time, many individuals take part in service-oriented activities, whether in their family, professional or social life. The desire to be helpful and to constructively influence the course of events manifests here.

The days that comprise Virgo I symbolically reveal the mature adult beginning to apply his/her energies in the service of social ideals, perhaps working with and supporting a partner, building dependability and efficacy, and taking a more no-nonsense and businesslike attitude toward the world. This may indeed be a time when overly carefree or irresponsible individuals recognize it is time to clean up their act.

Structure is an important theme in the lives of Virgo I's, a kind of insurance policy they inevitably fall back on in times of stress. It underlies many of their attitudes toward the world. Mental insistence and concentration are often their greatest strengths, and consequently they suffer most when emotional pressures leave them unable to think clearly or manage their affairs well. They are particularly upset by chaos, so building an effective daily routine, a practical home, or an efficient work space is essential to their mental health. Inflexibility or rigidity is also a possible outcome of such structuring, however, and must be guarded against.

The careers of Virgo I's often involve service. In their family role, similarly, they often care for those who need

ZODIAC POSITION	Approximately 2–10° Virgo
SEASON	Late summer
ELEMENT	Earth
RULER	Mercury
SYMBOL	The Virgin
MODES	Sensation, Thought

help, or provide the bulwark of dependability in everyday life. Not all Virgo I's are well cast in such roles, however, and despite their tendencies and talents to help others, they can find themselves resenting heavy responsibilities loaded on their backs. Although those born in the Week of System Builders seem to do well living and working with people who know how to cooperate and to share the burdens of everyday life, it cannot be assumed that they want to be team players. Virgo I's need to spend a lot of time alone, and do best when their contributions to the well-being of a social or family group are made on their own terms.

Virgo I's are not usually cut out for solo leadership roles, but they can make excellent partners and co-workers. They like to sit back and watch, preferring to observe carefully before acting; this quality of objectivity, and the evaluations that result from it, can make them extremely valuable to a company or family. Writing reports, stating conclusions verbally, and chronicling in different media what they see around them are often some of their best-developed abilities.

Women born in this week can have a shy, demure appeal; male Virgo I's are often taken for strong, silent types. Rather than acting aggressively, Virgo I's typically prefer to be discovered by others. This behavior is powerfully ingrained, since they thereby avoid rejection and reinforce their power to choose. In fact, choice is crucial to Virgo I's if they are to feel empowered. Yet they are capable of making unfortunate choices in lovers and friends—in personal matters their decisions are sometimes disastrous. Their objectivity about the world does not involve a corresponding realism about and aware-

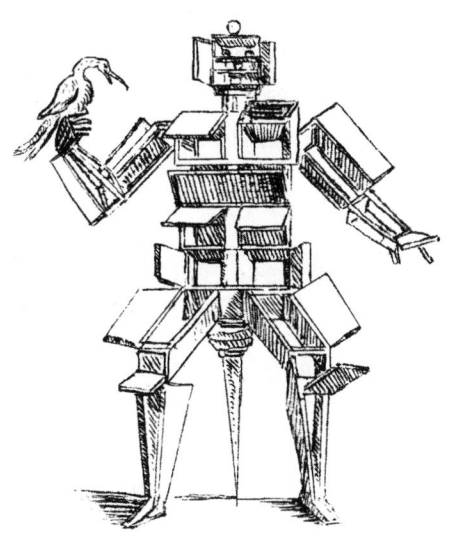

"SYSTEM BUILDERS"

ness of their own emotions. Consequently, Virgo I's can suffer from acute nervous instability and depression when they meet disappointment. Feelings of inadequacy or failure are prone to surface and can prove to be too much for them to handle.

Virgo I's tend to be fixed in their mental attitudes, and this is likely to arouse antagonism, particularly from those who prefer a more spontaneous, flexible or free-flowing lifestyle. As dominant family figures or parents, those born in this week may be prone to making excessive numbers of rules, and to enforcing them overdiligently. Should they believe that people must be free to choose and act according to their own dictates, on the other hand, they may implement such beliefs with equal zeal. Virgo I's may benefit from personal involvements or working relationships with more easygoing types, who just take things as they come without needing to rely on planning them out in advance.

Since learning to loosen up is essential for Virgo I's, their best relationships are often with those with whom they can just let go and have a good time. These relationships with fun-loving types can prove mutually advantageous, with the Virgo I's providing structure and dependability, the other party the unserious, relaxed attitude that those born in the Week of System Builders may lack. In love relationships, alas, Virgo I's may not prove so dependable, for if their emotional state is unsettled they can feel they have little to give. Seeking to withdraw, they become unable to cope with the other person's feelings.

Virgo I's themselves can encounter problems when their service-oriented stance and practical abilities attract dependent, needy types, who drain their energies and exhaust their capacity to give. Fostering such dependencies may be a subtle form of self-destructive behavior for them, for although the need to share and to solve problems may initially provide positive common bonds, relationships with insecure and needy individuals can ultimately bring out a corresponding negativity in those born in this week.

Since living through others may be a temptation for Virgo I's, they must learn to stand up for themselves and become less self-sacrificing. Building a truly independent lifestyle, one less dependent on the needs and wishes of others, whether parents, clients, friends or lovers, may be the greatest challenge they face. In the long run, then, close relationships with highly independent people, particularly those who can demonstrate how to set limits in human interactions, may prove the most productive and rewarding for them. Even if such personalities initially seem selfish or egotistical, they are especially beneficial to Virgo I's as role models. Those born in this week may need to free themselves from the constant demands of other people if they are to gain the space they need to develop their own expressive, creative and financially productive side.

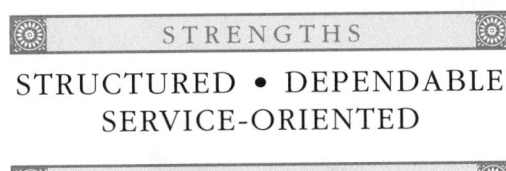

STRENGTHS

STRUCTURED • DEPENDABLE
SERVICE-ORIENTED

WEAKNESSES

RIGID • EMOTIONALLY UNAWARE
SELF-DESTRUCTIVE

ADVICE:

Soften your stance a bit—take things as they come and let them go as they will.
Try to keep your work and home life separate. Step out a bit and demand dependability
from others, too. Protect yourself from hangers-on and parasites.
Occasionally be more selfish and unashamedly demand benefits for yourself.

VIRGO I NOTABLES

The overwhelming beauty of **Ingrid Bergman** in no way overshadowed her intelligence and great mental strength. Characteristic of Virgo I's, she depended on structure and stability in her private life to be able to perform at her best, and, consequently, when as a married woman she fell in love with director Roberto Rossellini,

her career took a nosedive. She made 6 films and had 3 children with the Italian director, including actress Isabella Rossellini. During this time she was barred from making films in the U.S. for 7 years. In her most famous role, opposite Humphrey Bogart in *Casablanca,* she is caught between her love for her

INGRID BERGMAN

husband and her lover and becomes unhinged when her rational and emotional sides come into conflict.

The German poet **Johann Wolfgang von Goethe** has always been pictured as his country's Universal Man. As a scientist, linguist, lawyer, critic, philosopher, painter, poet, novelist and playwright of the 18th and 19th centuries, there were few areas that escaped Goethe's keen interest. Evident in all his work is the love of system and structure that identifies him as a Virgo I, especially in his scientific works, such as *The Metamorphosis of Plants.* Goethe was also very interested in the occult and in its complex hierarchies, which he put to artistic use in his greatest work, *Faust.* A strange blend of Classical, Gothic, Renaissance and Romantic, Goethe's literary

JOHANN WOLFGANG
VON GOETHE

work is regarded stylistically as some of the most beautiful and elegant ever written in the German language.

Possibly the single greatest domination of any sport by an individual was that of **Edwin Moses** over a 10-year span, in which he was undefeated as a hurdler in 122 races. To think of coming in first, second or third in several international events is in itself mind-

EDWIN MOSES

boggling, but to never be less than first through national, international and Olympic track events in over 100 starts against the best in the world, under every condition, is almost inconceivable. Always in top physical condition, Moses was also very disciplined mentally, like many Virgo I's. Analytical and articulate, with an almost professorial attitude toward his work, Moses studied the technique and physiology of hurdling in great detail.

More Virgo I's: Michael Jackson, Charlie Parker, Mark Harmon, Antonia Fraser, Lyndon Johnson, Mary Shelley, Rocky Marciano, Timothy Bottoms, Gloria Estefan, Yasir Arafat, Peggy Guggenheim, Georg Hegel, Maria Montessori, Frank Robinson, Lou Piniella, Geraldine Ferraro, Richard Gere, James Coburn, William Friedkin, Slobodan Milosevic, Alan Dershowitz, Jimmy Connors.

Relationship Guide for Virgo I

Roberto Rossellini (Taurus II)
Ingrid Bergman (Virgo I)
Page 358

BEST RELATIONSHIPS

LOVE
Cancer II
Leo II
Leo III
Virgo-Libra Cusp
Libra III
Sagittarius II
Capricorn II
Capricorn-Aquarius Cusp
Pisces I
Pisces II

MARRIAGE
Pisces-Aries Cusp
Aries II
Taurus I
Gemini II
Cancer I
Cancer III
Virgo II
Libra I
Scorpio I
Scorpio III
Sagittarius III
Capricorn I
Capricorn III

FRIENDSHIP
Taurus III
Gemini-Cancer Cusp
Cancer-Leo Cusp
Libra II
Scorpio II
Sagittarius I
Aquarius II

WORK
Aries III
Aries-Taurus Cusp
Taurus II
Gemini I
Leo I
Leo-Virgo Cusp
Virgo I
Libra-Scorpio Cusp
Sagittarius-Capricorn Cusp
Aquarius I
Pisces III

Page Locator for All Relationships

VIRGO II
The Week of the Enigma

September 3–10

The Virgo II period takes The Enigma as its central image. According to The Grand Cycle of Life, in human terms, this period falls at the close of one's thirties, when for many people there comes a serious realization that they are no longer young, and that it may be necessary to reevaluate their life. Thus many difficult and puzzling aspects of existence are symbolized by this period. The feeling that youth has flown brings to mind serious issues, usually of a personal nature, and a need to solve one's psychological problems or change one's ways may be felt. Ethics, morals and resolutions to better oneself all play their role here.

The days that comprise Virgo II symbolically reveal the mature adult breaking away from previous systems or modes of living in order to build imaginatively, seek greater success using intelligent means, and fathom the mysterious, enigmatic and problematical side of the self. The attainment of private goals now assumes a high priority.

Virgo II's are puzzling individuals, often proving difficult even for those closest to them to figure out. Their faces do not easily reveal what they are really thinking; indeed, showing emotion can be difficult for them. Behind their attractive or impressive exterior may lurk an unexpectedly guarded individual. Sphinx-like, Virgo II's are not above constructing devious defenses and cultivating an air of mystery about themselves and what they do. They sternly resist attempts to analyze them, and often make it clear that they are in no way interested in discussing their personal or family life. The reason for this is seldom insecurity, but showing vulnerability

ZODIAC POSITION
Approximately
9–18° Virgo

SEASON
Late summer

ELEMENT
Earth

RULER
Mercury

SYMBOL
The Virgin

MODES
Sensation, Thought

can be a problem for Virgo II's, and can keep other people from getting really close to them. So strong is the belief of Virgo II's in their own individuality that some of them will put themselves above accepted social codes. Such people can become isolated and lonely, appearing unapproachable. Those born in the Week of the Enigma are blessed with great inner strength. Many Virgo II's inspire confidence in others, and they may often be called upon to help out or take charge. Yet those born in this week can find it difficult to respond when high expectations are placed on them. Their natural tendency at such moments is to withdraw into their private, often secretive world.

Communication can be a top priority for Virgo II's, particularly in their career, and as a means of clarifying their own thoughts. But they may find it hard to share more personal experiences. This is due less to a lack of verbal ability than to a need to keep their inner struggles to themselves, and to undergo their trials alone. Many Virgo II's are kind, thoughtful, considerate people who see no need to bother those around them with their difficulties. Asking for help may be a real problem for them; they seem fated to work things out alone. Many of those born in this week are true believers in doing the right thing. For these highly ethical individuals, human beings gain in moral stature through individual effort.

Virgo II's have a zany side, and love humor in many forms. They can sometimes look foolish and naive, but they are usually able to see their faults, and to laugh at themselves. Carried too far, this attitude can result in a low self-image, but for the most part the ability of Virgo II's to joke about themselves is a sign of strength rather

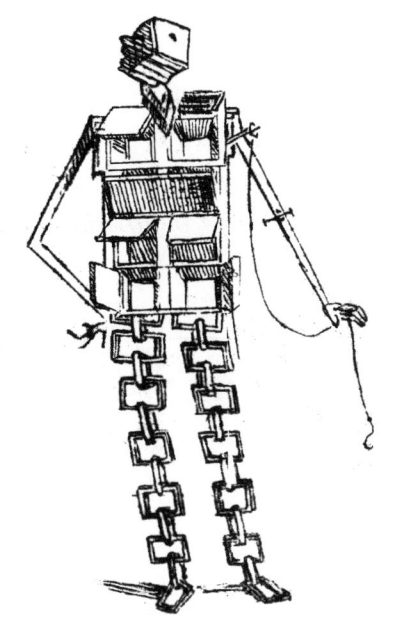

"ENIGMA"

than weakness. For all their practicality in everyday matters, those born in this week lead a rich fantasy life, which complements their comic sense. Even the most dour and serious of Virgo II's has a wry sense of humor, perhaps a bit bitter or sarcastic at times, but nevertheless funny.

Virgo II's are discriminating types who pride themselves on their good taste, in people as well as in intellectual matters. They have extremely high standards, which can lead them to reject other people as friends or to be rejected by them as overly picky. Their social circle consequently tends to be small. Critical but also honest, they invariably subject themselves to the same merciless criteria as they do others. Such attitudes certainly don't make them relaxed, and those born in this week can put themselves under enormous stress, which often leads to acute physical symptoms. More than with others in the year, organic illness in a Virgo II is often the result of psychic disturbance.

Behind their mask of confidence and their occasional bravado is an individual who needs love as much as we all do. Finding that special individual to whom they can open up (for Virgo II's, usually a friend rather than a lover) is often the first step toward unlocking their deepest sources of self-expression. For some, however, it will be a challenge to breach the defenses of Virgo II's, who may appreciate their efforts: lifelong friendships and even marriages can often result from such aggressive behavior. Those born in this week don't really mind others coming on to them, for they are quite confident of their ability to repulse any really undesirable attack. They also often enjoy being involved with active, outgoing types, who are a good foil to their thoughtful and at times withdrawn personalities.

The sexual expression of Virgo II's does not have to involve deep feeling. They have a curious way of throwing up invisible barriers between themselves and their lovers, and can detach themselves from the sexual act without being detected. Virgo II's often have a taste for the unusual in intimate relations. They may send out silent messages about this to their lovers, which, heeded, bring great satisfaction, but if ignored long enough can spell the end of the relationship. Blowing hot and cold, giving way to sudden, inexplicable fits of passion that quickly pass, is also a typical trait of those born in the Week of the Enigma.

Many Virgo II's have no real need to live with others, but if family life proves inviting they are capable of fitting in well, as long as they have enough time and space to themselves. As parents, their overexacting tendencies may have to be kept under control, and as mates their limited ability to accept the foibles of others will surely be put to the test. Through daily interactions with other people, at home and at work, those born in this week will deepen their own humanity. Being forced to strive with others to solve mutual problems will teach them about forgiveness, acceptance and sympathy.

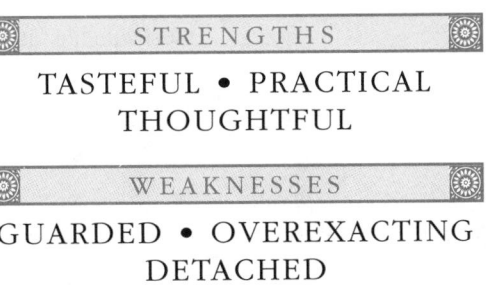

STRENGTHS

TASTEFUL • PRACTICAL
THOUGHTFUL

WEAKNESSES

GUARDED • OVEREXACTING
DETACHED

ADVICE:

Try to maintain flexibility and acceptance without compromising your high standards. Open your heart in love relationships. Be aware of your condemning and unforgiving side. Gentleness, kindness and diplomacy are traits worth developing. Beware of putting yourself above the law or outside society. Don't be afraid to show your vulnerability.

VIRGO II NOTABLES

A mother of 10 children who tended the farm and made potato chips, **Grandma Moses** began her painting career at age 78. She died at 101, and in the last 23 years of her life painted over 1,500 paintings. The subject of these naturalistic, primitive and childlike compositions were images and memories from her childhood and stories she had grown up with. An inexplicable phenomenon, like many Virgo II's, she was completely self-taught and was able to improve the quality of her work as the years went by. Seen the world over and highly prized by collectors, Grandma Moses was able to get only a few dollars for her paintings while she was alive. A puzzling exception in the world of art, Grandma Moses's artistic process has defied analysis.

GRANDMA MOSES

Master of dialects and accents, comedian and film actor **Peter Sellers** was also a master of disguise. In real life few penetrated his mask of secrecy, and even his family could not claim to really know him. Some felt that Sellers lacked any true identity, which explained why he could so easily impersonate others. In his many roles, from the president of the United States to a British lieutenant to an insane German scientist (all in one film, *Dr. Strangelove*), Sellers so identified himself with the character he portrayed that he merged with it. As with other Virgo II's, he was subject to short, unexplainable fits of passion, often manifested by falling in love with his lead-

PETER SELLERS

ing lady (as with Sophia Loren) and wanting to give up his life and family for her.

Tenor saxophonist **Sonny Rollins** is one of the leading exponents of technique on his horn after almost 50 years as a jazz musician. Rollins has recorded with every jazz great, including Charlie Parker, Thelonius Monk and Miles Davis, but perhaps was best

SONNY ROLLINS

when playing with his own group. His unaccompanied work in the 60s was often enigmatic and hard to follow, and like many Virgo II's, Sonny felt misunderstood. At one point he was overshadowed by the more popular John Coltrane. Effecting a kind of fusion between his more technical style and calypso and American dance music, Rollins later became much more popular with the general public.

More Virgo II's: Leo Tolstoy, Joseph P. Kennedy, Queen Elizabeth I, Louis H. Sullivan, Daniel H. Burnham, Louis XIV, John Cage, Otis Redding, Jean-Louis Barrault, Raquel Welch, Dweezil Zappa, Amy Irving, Charlie Sheen, Jane Curtin, Jane Addams, Buddy Holly, Paul Brown, Louise Suggs, Freddie Mercury, Richard I, Sid Caesar, Colonel Sanders, William Bligh, Margaret Trudeau, Karl Lagerfeld, Yma Sumac, Elvin Jones, Anton Dvorak, Grace Metalious, Patsy Cline, Anton Bruckner, Oskar Schlemmer.

Relationship Guide for Virgo II

ROSE KENNEDY (CANCER-LEO CUSP)
JOSEPH KENNEDY (VIRGO II)
PAGE 541

BEST RELATIONSHIPS

LOVE
Aries II
Aries-Taurus Cusp
Taurus II
Taurus III
Virgo III
Libra III
Scorpio I
Sagittarius II
Capricorn I

MARRIAGE
Aries III
Gemini I
Cancer-Leo Cusp
Virgo I
Libra II
Libra-Scorpio Cusp
Scorpio II
Aquarius II
Aquarius III
Pisces II
Pisces III

FRIENDSHIP
Pisces-Aries Cusp
Taurus I
Taurus-Gemini Cusp
Cancer III
Leo III
Leo-Virgo Cusp
Scorpio III
Sagittarius-Capricorn Cusp
Capricorn II
Aquarius I
Pisces I

FAMILY
Cancer II
Leo I
Virgo II
Virgo-Libra Cusp
Sagittarius I

WORK
Gemini-Cancer Cusp
Libra I
Scorpio-Sagittarius Cusp
Sagittarius III
Capricorn III

Page Locator for All Relationships

VIRGO III
The Week of the Literalist

September 11–18

The Virgo III period takes The Literalist as its central image. In The Grand Cycle of Life, Virgo III can be compared to the time when a person turns forty and approaches the midlife period. At this time the adult needs to grow ever more realistic and make hard choices—whether to opt for a big career change or continue in a long-standing position, realign relationships or make marital adjustments, and, for some women, to decide for the last time to have children or not.

The days that comprise Virgo III symbolically display the fully mature adult making vital decisions, developing a more fearless attitude and having the courage to go for what he/she really wants. Perhaps critical faculties and pragmatism are at their height during this time, but personal aspirations and needs should not be neglected, either. The days in this period stress the Virgo III's need to arrange things just as he/she sees fit, manipulating and ordering the environment to advantage.

The willful individuals born in the week of Virgo III generally persist until they get their way. Yet long periods may go by in which they refuse to take any sudden action. Their goals are so tangible to them, so real, that they may express their confidence in the final outcome through a kind of procrastination. Virgo III's know that a strong mental orientation can often have a decisive influence on the events unfolding around them.

Those born in the Week of the Literalist have a practical emphasis in their characters that can make them easily puzzled and even angered by irrationality. But since they usually control their feelings well beyond an immediate expression of irritation or disgust, it takes an especially annoying or upsetting stimulus to bring their true emotions to the surface. Even the more easily aroused Virgo III's usually mellow out with age. They feel emotion deeply, but may be stirred up only by the most personal encounters with lovers and mates. For the most part, those born in this week do not like emotional displays, particularly public ones, which they see as a sign of ostentation and a lack of self-control.

Virgo III's also dislike phoniness and pretension. Literalists, they like people to behave as they really are, and to be truthful to themselves, no matter how difficult this may be. On the other hand, Virgo III's do not like trouble or unpleasantness, and feel that a modicum of courtesy, consideration and gratefulness is demanded in almost any human situation. They are sometimes torn, then, between their love of truth and their need for harmony.

Virgo III's have a definite flair for the sensational. At times highly dramatic, those born in this week seek to uncover the truth and to reveal it to the world. Virgo III's can be fearless and courageous in confronting social mores, perhaps promoting ideals of free speech, free lifestyle and free love; revolutionary fervor often runs high in this group. They should not succumb, however, to the lure of sheer rebelliousness in their moral crusades. Otherwise calm, the passions of those born in this week ignite around a cause or an ideal more often than around a person.

Shrewd evaluative instincts are among the strongest suits of Virgo III's, but they must be careful not to let their acuteness in this area get out of hand.

ZODIAC POSITION
Approximately
17–26° Virgo

SEASON
Late summer

ELEMENT
Earth

RULER
Mercury

SYMBOL
The Virgin

MODES
Sensation/Thought

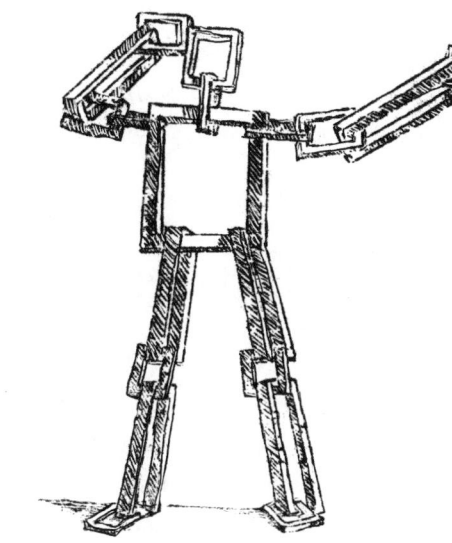

"LITERALIST"

Professionally, they may be put into executive positions in which they are called upon to judge their colleagues on a daily basis, and in doing so they must try to be sensitive to the feelings of others, in whom they can easily engender feelings of rejection and disappointment. Resentment of those born in the Week of the Literalist may build to a pitch of negative energy that can become destructive and debilitating. Few achievements arouse the admiration of those born in this week more than the mastery of craft. Role models are thus extremely important to Virgo III's, and may prove a direct inspiration and stimulus for their own success. These Literalists can make excellent partners in creative, business and practical endeavors of all sorts, particularly when their partners are capable of producing high-caliber work. Virgo III's are able to put up with a lot, both in their career and in personal relationships, if the quality of their work or love life is high enough.

In relationships, Virgo III's are highly demanding, expecting the very best for themselves. Their lovers and mates will have to get tough in order to handle the energies of those born in this week, who, however, are often affectionate and caring people, particularly in times of adversity. Virgo III's have strong nurturing and protective instincts, which emerge strongly when their loved one is suffering or under attack. Extremely capable, they can keep troubled or problematical relationships alive for years through their perseverance and dedication. Facing and overcoming obstacles, in fact,

can be a specialty of Virgo III's in all aspects of their lives. Their need for order and their striving for fulfillment usually find special satisfaction when a particularly challenging task or project is at last completed. Results are important to these pragmatic personalities, who are likely to lose interest or walk away when the fruits of their endeavors are regularly denied them. Virgo III's have an ethical feeling about what they are entitled to, and may suffer terribly under unfair treatment.

Those born in this week must be careful not to succumb to selfish and manipulative drives. Friends, co-workers and employers may at times find them ruthless in cutting off personal and work relationships that no longer suit them. In the mind of the Virgo III, this is usually justified as realistic and fair, but it can also indicate a blindness in seeing the other person's point of view. More successful Virgo III personalities will learn to bring relationships to a close more gracefully, without leaving a bad aftertaste.

The most positive human traits of Virgo III's often emerge in family life. They can make excellent parents and loving and dutiful children. For all of their independence and iconoclasm, Virgo III's are usually quite conventional in family matters, particularly enjoying holiday dinners and outings. Actually, those born in the Week of the Literalist have a great respect for authority, as long as it is honest, caring and just. All forms of favoritism, discrimination or unfairness in the treatment of children and parents are highly objectionable to Virgo III's.

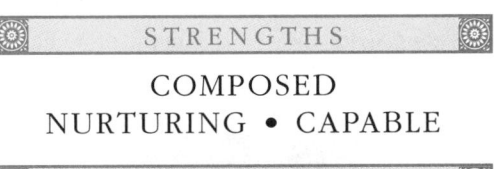

STRENGTHS

COMPOSED
NURTURING • CAPABLE

WEAKNESSES

SENSATIONALISTIC
JUDGMENTAL • RUTHLESS

ADVICE:

Try to be more sympathetic to the feelings of others. Not everyone is as strong-willed and directed as you. Don't get bottled up in your head; cultivating a love of food, sleep and sensuous activities is essential to the grounding of your energies. Do not hide behind or rely too heavily on those who would serve you.

VIRGO III NOTABLES

Critic and commentator on the American scene, **H.L. Mencken** was a true Literalist. Hopelessly devoted to the written and spoken word, Mencken wrote for the *Baltimore Sun* for much of his life but also published a

considerable number of books on various topics. Probably the leading authority on the American language, Mencken was one of its staunchest defenders, particularly against those who felt the British owned English. Like many Virgo III's, Mencken's shrewd evaluative instincts were his

H.L. MENCKEN

strongest suit, but this frequently meant his becoming overly judgmental when voicing opinions, which he had on practically any subject.

"I want to be alone, " said actress **Greta Garbo**, and one of the great careers in film ended. Although this famous line came from the film *Grand Hotel*, it was for many fans the only clue they could find for her permanent retirement from the screen at the age of 36. Garbo lived an incredible 49 years in self-imposed isolation while the world went its way and finally forgot her, although her image lived on. Her Virgo III coolness and objectivity are evident in most of her films, but when she lets herself go emotionally in *Anna Karenina* and *Ninotchka,* the screen explodes. Garbo's life illustrates how hardheaded Virgo III's can be when exercising their freedom of choice.

GRETA GARBO

One great inconsistency of **D.H. Lawrence** was that he tried to elevate the body and the soul in importance above the mind but in fact illustrates in almost every paragraph of his work what a cerebral Virgo III he really was. Born in the Week of the Literalist, Lawrence was never able to shake his strongly mental orientation, as much as he tried to drown it in torrents of feeling. In his third novel, *Sons*

D.H. LAWRENCE

and Lovers, he reveals the struggles that were to occupy him for a lifetime, particularly his family triangle with a brutal coal miner father and a sensitive but psychologically beaten mother, whom he adored. Lawrence gave himself over to the feminine in his writing and thus had difficulty dealing with his own male side, which bound him the more tightly to his father.

More Virgo III's: Agatha Christie, Jean Renoir, Lauren Bacall, Bruno Walter, Amy Madigan, Zoe Caldwell, O. Henry, Tom Landry, Jessica Mitford, Lola Falana, Brian De Palma, Clara Schumann, Oliver Stone, Tommy Lee Jones, Claudette Colbert, Leo Kottke, Jesse Owens, George Jones, Alfred A. Knopf, Jacqueline Bisset, Bela Karolyi, Jessye Norman, Roald Dahl, Margaret Sanger, Kate Millett, Henry V, B.B. King, Dennis Connor, Karen Horney, Hank Williams, Frederick Ashton.

Relationship Guide for Virgo III

D. H. LAWRENCE (VIRGO III)
FRIEDA WEEKLEY (LEO III)
PAGE 586

BEST RELATIONSHIPS

LOVE
Aries III
Virgo II
Libra II
Sagittarius I
Capricorn III
Aquarius-Pisces Cusp

MARRIAGE
Aries II
Taurus III
Gemini-Cancer Cusp
Leo I
Scorpio I
Scorpio III
Aquarius I
Aquarius III

FRIENDSHIP
Aries I
Gemini I
Gemini I
Virgo-Libra Cusp
Libra III
Sagittarius II
Capricorn II

FAMILY
Taurus II
Taurus-Gemini
Cancer II
Libra-Scorpio Cusp
Scorpio II
Capricorn-Aquarius Cusp
Aquarius II
Pisces II

WORK
Aries-Taurus Cusp
Taurus I
Cancer III
Cancer-Leo Cusp
Leo II
Leo-Virgo Cusp
Virgo III
Libra I
Scorpio-Sagittarius Cusp
Sagittarius III
Pisces III

Page Locator for All Relationships

The Cusp of Beauty

September 19–24

ZODIAC POSITION
Approximately
26° Virgo–2° Libra

SEASONS
Late summer/Early fall
(equinox)

ELEMENTS
Earth/Air

RULERS
Mercury/Venus

SYMBOLS
The Virgin/The Scales

MODES
Sensation/Thought

The Virgo-Libra cusp is an admixture of the sixth sign of the zodiac, Virgo, and the seventh sign of the zodiac, Libra. This cusp can be likened to the period around forty-two years of age in the human life. The time is marked by the fall equinox, when the length of days and nights is again equal. Astrologically, this time marks the completion of one and a half Saturn cycles. It has now come directly opposite its starting point. This Saturn transit is paralleled by Uranus having also moved to a position directly opposite that which it occupied at the time of birth. Because the human life is taken ideally to equal eighty-four years (one Uranus cycle), forty-two years of age may be regarded as the midpoint in the cycle. At this time in life, a crossroads is often encountered (referred to as the mid life point) where people can become taken up with the pursuit of an ideal. Some at this time grow concerned with their own appearance (perhaps involving themselves in health or cosmetic treatments), and others seek to identify or associate with those who possess youth or physical attractiveness. Still others are able to discover a new, more mature ideal that is both profound and enduring. Accordingly, the days that comprise the Virgo-Libra cusp exemplify a search for beauty.

Those born on the Virgo-Libra cusp are fatally taken up with the pursuit of an ideal. Attracted to physical, sensuous beauty, whether in art objects, nature or people, the lure of color, shape, form, texture and the intriguing sound of music or a voice pushes all their emotional buttons and brings them creative inspiration. Influenced by the planets Mercury (ruler of Virgo) and Venus (ruler of Libra), those born on the Virgo-Libra cusp are extremely sensitive to external stimuli. They react strongly to unusual tastes and smells, and are easily jarred by disturbing sights and sounds. Those born on the Cusp of Beauty, then, must create a highly aesthetic environment for both their living situations and their work.

Virgo-Librans pride themselves on being up-to-date and aware of the latest trends in fashion, design, art and technology. Others may see their interests in these areas as merely trendy, but there is no denying that the information and taste of those born on this cusp can be extremely valuable to the organizations with which they are affiliated. Often, Virgo-Libras also have excellent executive, marketing and management skills, in which their sixth sense for current developments in their field stands them in good stead.

Because of their interest in the outward appearances of the physical world, Virgo-Libras may be seen as superficial and glitzy. Sooner or later in their lives, these individuals will have to address spiritual matters, for they usually discover at some point that their love of externals is an inadequate preparation for the more unpleasant, yet inevitable, aspects of life—disease, accidents, suffering, death. Classically, those born on the Cusp of Beauty will encounter one of these areas unprepared and will feel bewildered and inadequate. As a result, they will be impelled to scratch a bit deeper beneath the surface of existence.

Virgo-Libras are fun to have as friends. Imaginative and free-spirited, they lend life to any gathering. Yet those born on this cusp also have an emotional dark side, which their friends and mates have to cope with. In times of financial stress or emotional turmoil, addictive tendencies

"BEAUTY"

may surface, for Virgo-Libras have a tendency to turn to drugs and alcohol rather than encounter and overcome the vicissitudes of life head-on. It is here, in particular, that their sensuous nature can be most self-destructive. Those born on this cusp must also beware lest the healthy expression of their sexuality be sublimated into neurotic and possessive drives, in an attempt to flee from reality.

The most successful Virgo-Libras do not lose the common touch or forget their origins, no matter how humble. Yet those born on this cusp have a tendency to isolate themselves in an ivory-tower situation in which they become increasingly out of touch with the more basic aspects of their fellow human beings. This can work at cross-purposes with their ability to keep abreast of public taste, and it can undermine their usefulness. In extreme cases they may become snobbish and elitist, only associating with individuals they feel are worthy of their attentions, or through whose influence they can advance socially.

Heralding the arrival of autumn, the fall equinox takes place on the Virgo-Libra cusp, symbolizing the harvest. Perhaps John Keats' poem "To Autumn" with its opening lines, "Season of mist and mellow fruitfulness, / Close bosom-friend of the maturing sun" best expresses the mood and images of this fecund period, The energy of those born on this cusp is indeed "mellow": they will avoid arguments, confrontations and unpleasantness in general whenever possible.

Lovers, co-workers and family members of Virgo-Libras know how sensitive they are to irritating or jarring elements in their immediate surroundings. Similarly, those born on the Cusp of Beauty usually require that the people with whom they choose intimate involvement are very good-looking. The one exception to this tendency occurs when Virgo-Librans themselves happen to be extremely attractive, in which case their partners can be of the most unusual physical types. Actually, those born on the Cusp of Beauty have an ambivalent attitude toward physical deformity in others, finding it both repugnant and fascinating.

Virgo-Libras may often make a connection with a stable and powerful figure as a mate or friend. Indeed, those born on this cusp may need to maintain a close partnership of some kind with such a dependable figure throughout their lives, if not in their personal lives then perhaps at work, with a co-worker or partner. However, these relationships are frequently affected by psychological projections of parents or family members.

Although Virgo-Librans periodically need to indulge their sense of touch, they may appear removed or untouchable themselves, and may only allow physical contact at special times. Many born on this cusp are content to admire beauty from a distance, seeing it as a quality to be adored or worshiped from afar, rather than one to approach or possess. Platonic relationships often have a special appeal for those born on the Cusp of Beauty.

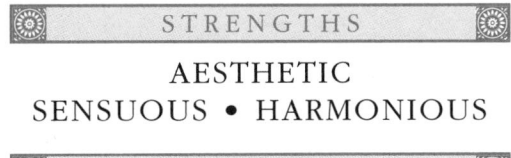

STRENGTHS

AESTHETIC
SENSUOUS • HARMONIOUS

WEAKNESSES

SNOBBISH • ADDICTIVE
UNSETTLED

ADVICE:

Don't be overly concerned with appearances. Keep alive in your search for beauty—avoid becoming jaded, trendy or compulsive. Beware of neglecting spiritual goals or falling prey to excessive materialism. Keep your nervous system under control.

VIRGO-LIBRA CUSP NOTABLES

Soul and rhythm-and-blues singer **Ray Charles** is still as much in love with music and performing as ever in his mid-60s. His highly sensuous approach to touch and sound marks him clearly as a Virgo-Libra cusp person. Blinded in his childhood by glaucoma, Charles is one of many musicians who have lived in a world where

RAY CHARLES

senses other than sight have been enhanced by loss of vision. Well known to the general public, Charles's career got a boost in 1980 when he made an appearance in the wild and wacky film *Blues Brothers*. His soaring and ecstatic style shows him totally surrendering to the electric flow of his music, particularly in songs like *What'd I Say*, which brought audiences to their feet dancing in the 50s and 60s.

Gorgeous **Sophia Loren** epitomizes the statuesque, earthy beauty symbolized by the Virgo-Libra cusp. Her highly sensuous qualities were apparent to producer Carlo Ponti, who picked her out of a beauty contest when she was 17 and launched her on her film career. Six years later Ponti (24 years her senior) married Sophia while his previous divorce was still being contested, setting off a furor in Italy and forcing the couple to move to France. The voluptuous Loren became an outstanding actress, her talent particularly evident in her roles opposite Italian star Marcello Mastroianni, and in 1961 she received an Oscar for best actress for her role in *Two Women*.

SOPHIA LOREN

Best-selling novelist, short-story writer and screenwriter **Stephen King** continues to top the charts year after year. King's ability to keep his finger on the public pulse, while taking a hand in defining taste through his works, characterize him as a Virgo-Libra cusp person. The darker side of King's character is also representative of those born on the Cusp of Beauty, but in his case, his works have provided a

STEPHEN KING

highly creative and lucrative outlet for his shadow. Although preferring relative isolation in his Maine home, King has never retreated to a snobbish ivory tower, a constant temptation for those born on this cusp. The gripping screenplays for *The Shining* and *Misery*, along with his successful serialization, *The Green Mile*, stand out as masterpieces.

More Virgo-Libras: John Coltrane, H.G. Wells, Ricki Lake, Bill Murray, Sister Elizabeth Kenny, William Golding, Leonard Cohen, F. Scott Fitzgerald, Bruce Springsteen, Gunnar Nelson, Linda McCartney, Jason Alexander, Romy Schneider, Joseph P. Kennedy, Fay Weldon, Tommy Lasorda, Joan Jett, Jim Henson, Stevie Smith, Larry Hagman, Cheryl Crawford, Red Auerbach, Cass Elliot, Guy Lafleur, Julio Iglesias, Donald A. Glaser, Brian Epstein, Twiggy, Shirley Conran, Erich von Stroheim, Mickey Rooney, Allen Lane.

Relationship Guide for Virgo-Libra Cusp

SOPHIA LOREN (VIRGO-LIBRA CUSP)
CARLO PONTI (SAGITTARIUS III)
PAGE 657

BEST RELATIONSHIPS

LOVE
Pisces-Aries Cusp
Aries-Taurus Cusp
Gemini III
Cancer II
Virgo I
Scorpio I
Sagittarius III
Pisces III

MARRIAGE
Gemini II
Cancer III
Leo III
Libra II
Scorpio III
Sagittarius I
Aquarius III
Aquarius-Pisces Cusp

FRIENDSHIP
Aries III
Cancer I
Leo I
Virgo III
Libra III
Scorpio II
Scorpio-Sagittarius Cusp
Capricorn-Aquarius Cusp
Aquarius II
Pisces I

FAMILY
Aries I
Aries II
Taurus I
Taurus III
Leo II
Virgo II
Libra-Scorpio Cusp

WORK
Taurus II
Gemini I
Gemini-Cancer Cusp
Cancer-Leo Cusp
Leo-Virgo Cusp
Virgo-Libra Cusp
Capricorn III
Aquarius I

Page Locator for All Relationships

LIBRA I
The Week of the Perfectionist

September 25–October 2

The Libra I period takes The Perfectionist as its central image. This period can be likened in human terms to the years just following the midlife point when a new determination to integrate, direct and perfect specific areas of one's life takes hold. The emphasis here is on self-improvement but also on the upgrading of one's lifestyle and social activities. Tending to problems, fixing things—in a word, maintenance—is particularly important at this time.

The days that comprise Libra I symbolically reveal the mature adult beginning to develop greater objectivity, verbal ability, application to his/her work, social skills and the patience needed to carry through on long-range projects. Ideally, the individual now faces challenges with steadfast determination and learns how to solve the technical and psychological problems of life more effectively.

Libra I's are often highly attractive personalities, yet they are not overly social ones. This can create problems for them, for although they have a great need to be in the limelight, they have a greater need to spend time alone. Many born in this week are not really cut out for public life at all, and some of them may give up a socially oriented career to spend more time on personal, private, anonymous enterprises. Indeed it is not at all uncommon for those born in this week to work a quite ordinary job, while devoting their real interest and energy to hobbies or other part-time endeavors.

Libra I's have perfectionist tendencies, which may infuse every area of their lives with a desire to find out

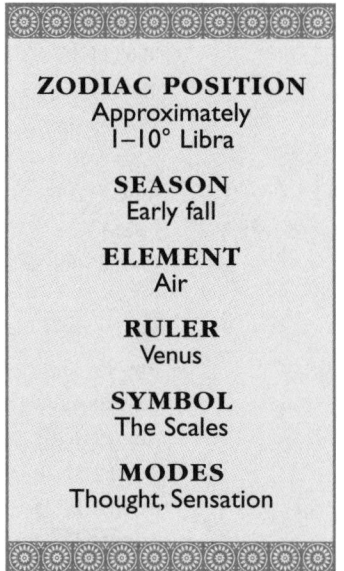

ZODIAC POSITION
Approximately
1–10° Libra

SEASON
Early fall

ELEMENT
Air

RULER
Venus

SYMBOL
The Scales

MODES
Thought, Sensation

what's wrong and to try to fix it. This theme of putting things right reflects their knowledge and technical know how, and also their conviction that they know what's best for those around them.

In their drive for perfection, Libra I's are prone to apply their often mercilessly high standards equally to themselves and to those around them. At the heart of their perfectionism may well lie a voice from their childhood constantly telling them that they aren't good enough. Their critical attitudes can certainly run out of hand, and this can make them extremely difficult to live with. In areas of their daily lives, from the workplace to the kitchen to the bedroom, Libra I's may have checklists that they apply exactly, leaving little room for failure or neglect on the part of the other person.

Do not be surprised if the hunger for perfection of Libra I's sometimes drives them to become obsessive and compulsive. In an attempt to master their material, they may adopt overly rigid routines. Those involved with Libra I's on a daily basis will appreciate their savvy but may come to resent their inability to leave things alone. "If it's not broken, don't fix it" is a lesson that all born in this week will have to learn sooner or later.

Insecurity drives those born in this week to be overachievers. They are extremely thorough in carrying out their plans, and in bringing their activities to a successful conclusion. Thus, while they are often seen as highly successful, those around them do not always appreciate how unsettled their inner life actually is. Their inflexibility in laying down rules for themselves, and their refusal

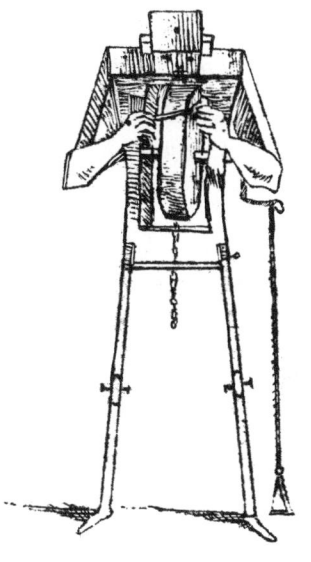

"PERFECTIONIST"

to compromise their ideals, puts them under tremendous pressure, which may drive them equally to success or to despair.

Libra I's are usually intense personalities, capable of great achievements. Yet they can be torn by indecision, even spending years trying to make up their minds what course to follow. At times they may put so much time and exertion into a nonproductive effort, perhaps a hobby or a relationship, that they leave themselves little time or energy for more positive endeavors. Highly challenged by problems, they may find it difficult to give up, fail or even admit that they have been wasting their time.

Libra I's are usually quite emotionally complex. They often give an impression of coolness that masks a maelstrom of inner emotions. They have a tendency not only to get bottled up inside but to resist the attempts of others to help them out. Mastery of their feelings is usually a high priority for them, the danger being that their conscious self-control may over time become unconscious repression, a difficult state to rectify. The challenge of penetrating to the emotional core of these fascinating and challenging individuals may keep their intimates busy for a lifetime.

The Libra I inability to share or discuss their feelings at a deep level, however, may ultimately prove debilitating to any relationship. Those personally involved with Libra I's would do best to keep feelings out in the open from the start, even to the point of insisting that those born in this week vent their emotions, whether positive and negative–not only happiness, joy and love but anger, jealousy, dislike and even hatred. Once both parties' feelings are made known, and the air has cleared, issues of vital concern to each person can be reasonably discussed rather than being avoided.

Swings between overinterest and disinterest may also have an adverse effect on the stability of Libra I relationships. Their lovers and mates may enjoy their sexual intensity but may ultimately need to withdraw a bit in order to establish a private space. On the other hand, those born in this week are just as capable of ignoring those they live with, particularly when absorbed in their own work, leaving their partners a tad frustrated.

Libra I's have a wry sense of humor and often a biting wit, which can express itself in many forms, but principally in irony and sarcasm. Their humor is not generally intended to hurt, however, or even to make others laugh, but to make them think. Libra I's can make scathing criticisms that may wound those close to them deeply, yet they probably don't fully realize the emotional effects of their statements. If they want to live harmoniously with those who care for them, they must become more tactful and gentle in expressing their dissatisfaction.

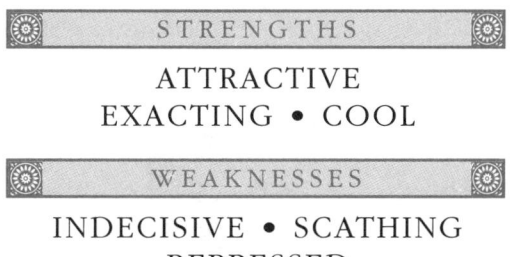

STRENGTHS

ATTRACTIVE
EXACTING • COOL

WEAKNESSES

INDECISIVE • SCATHING
REPRESSED

ADVICE:

Cultivate self-confidence. Beware of being too aggressive in your criticism of others—your bark can bite. Be consistent in your stance. Fight the impulse to procrastinate, but at the same resist interfering with things that work, even if they do not meet your expectations. Mistakes are just part of the game.

LIBRA I NOTABLES

Canadian pianist **Glenn Gould** once occasioned conductor George Szell to quip, "The nut's a genius!" A Perfectionist to the nth degree, Gould caused many recording executives, engineers and conductors to pull out their hair over the years and ultimately was at his best working alone. Gould's antics included arriving for recording sessions bundled in a fur coat and gloves in the heat of summer, insist-

GLENN GOULD

ing on playing seated on a beat-up chair his father made for him, singing and conducting himself as he played and, perhaps most unnerving for other musicians, not paying a whole lot of attention to them. His achievements include some of the finest renditions of Bach and pre-Bach music. Gould's legendary technique forced pedagogues to reexamine many of their assumptions about piano playing.

Like many Libra I's, sex goddess **Brigitte Bardot** had the intense need to be in the limelight. Eventually, she quit her film career to devote herself to animal-rights interests, which had previously been more of a hobby. Her pout and revealing clothes became a trademark in the 50s, when her first film, *And God Created Woman*, caused a furor over its sexually explicit material. Her first interviews in America show her fully living up to her movie image. In turning her social involvement to more personal and meaningful work, she is typical of many born in her week.

Leader of the zany Marx Brothers, **Groucho Marx** was the most outspoken, sharp and ironic of the three, as might be expected of a Libra I. His quick repartee and off-the-cuff quips became his trademark and continued after his film career, when he hosted the popular TV quiz show *You Bet Your Life*. Groucho's appeal was primarily verbal but he also duckwalked, lifted his eyebrows and wielded his cigar

GROUCHO MARX

with telling effect. Brothers Chico and Harpo, writers S.J. Perelman and George Kaufmann and Paramount Pictures all deserve credit, but in the final analysis, it was Groucho who was most important in the success of their films. The Marx Brothers had a tremendous impact on succeeding generations of comics, and their popularity continues unabated.

BRIGITTE BARDOT

More Libra I's: George Gershwin, Edith Abbott, William Faulkner, Sting, Heather Locklear, Bryant Gumbel, Anita Ekberg, Madeline Kahn, Mark Hamill, Gwyneth Paltrow, Scottie Pippen, Jimmy Carter, Donny Hathaway, Dmitri Shostakovich, Michael Douglas, Truman Capote, Mahatma Gandhi, Jane Smiley, Marcello Mastroianni, Christopher Reeve, Julie London, Annie Leibovitz, Lynn Anderson, Samuel Adams, Mike Schmidt, Heather Watts, Meat Loaf, Bud Powell, Caravaggio, Ed Sullivan, Jerry Lee Lewis.

Relationship Guide for Libra I

GEORGE GERSHWIN (LIBRA I)
IRA GERSHWIN (SAGITTARIUS II)
PAGE 668

BEST RELATIONSHIPS

LOVE
Taurus III
Leo I
Leo-Virgo Cusp
Virgo I
Virgo-Libra Cusp
Libra I
Libra-Scorpio Cusp
Capricorn III

MARRIAGE
Gemini I
Cancer II
Leo III
Virgo I
Libra III
Scorpio III
Capricorn I
Aquarius III
Pisces III

FRIENDSHIP
Pisces-Aries Cusp
Aries-Taurus Cusp
Gemini III
Cancer-Leo Cusp
Leo II
Sagittarius III
Capricorn II
Aquarius II
Pisces I

FAMILY
Aries III
Gemini II
Cancer I
Virgo III
Libra III
Sagittarius II
Sagittarius-Capricorn Cusp
Aquarius I

WORK
Cancer III
Leo II
Virgo II
Libra II
Scorpio II
Sagittarius I
Aquarius-Pisces Cusp

Page Locator for All Relationships

LIBRA II
The Week of Society

October 3–10

The Libra II period takes Society as its central image. In human terms, this period can be compared to a time in one's middle life when a more meaningful relationship with society, or an increase in time given to social entities (political causes, clubs, religious organizations, study groups, neighborhood or community associations, etc.), often takes place. During this period, deepening one's social ties can be central to life, not only with the institutions mentioned but also with lifelong friends and family members.

The days that comprise Libra II symbolically reveal certain aspects of middle age: taking the lead in defining social mores, making difficult judgments, acquiring objective wisdom about human psychology and learning to husband one's physical and financial resources.

The paradox about those born in this week is that although their social skills are highly developed, they may really be loners by nature. Their knowledge of current events, fashions and matters concerning lifestyle is impressive, and family and friends usually consult them as to the choice of materials or methods to get the job done in the most tasteful way possible. Constantly in demand, Libra II's often have difficulty finding time for themselves, and at some point must learn how to limit the time and energy they are prepared to give.

Generally well liked as people, Libra II's are also highly sought after as confidants and counselors. They inspire trust in those who are meeting them for the first time. Their nonthreatening approach makes other people quickly feel that they have nothing to fear from Libra

ZODIAC POSITION
Approximately
9–18° Libra

SEASON
Early fall

ELEMENT
Air

RULER
Venus

SYMBOL
The Scales

MODES
Thought, Sensation

II's, to whom they can open their hearts and unburden themselves. Indeed Libra II's rarely behave hurtfully or maliciously toward those who confide in them. Those who seek them out feel safe with them.

Although fair, just and agreeable in most situations, Libra II's can also be extremely sharp and critical. Because their insights are so often right on, their barbs can sting. Associates and employers who listen to them can probably learn something, but the fury of a Libra II attack often arouses too much negative emotion in the assaulted party to allow for clear listening. Only later will the truth of their criticisms begin to sink in.

Libra II children can be demanding of their parents, and Libra II parents can be strict with their children. When young, those born in this week may be extremely rebellious or at the very least troublesome to those in authority. Libra II's are guided by a sense of fairness but also by an extreme antipathy to stupid, harmful and needless regulations and laws. Too often young Libra II's may see the harm or waste being caused by a social or parental attitude yet feel helpless to do much about it. As they grow up, they may become crusaders or reformers, but they can just as easily turn into quiet observers who watch and listen but only offer their opinions and judgments when asked to do so.

Emotional instability may be the single biggest problem that Libra II's face. It can undermine their relationships, making them prone to jealousy, irritation, possessiveness and all sorts of negative emotions that they could really do without. Physical problems and even lifelong disabilities can result. Involvement in some form of

"SOCIETY"

spiritual, religious or physical training is often essential to Libra II's, to provide the stability and grounding that those born in this week require if they are to keep on an even keel.

There is too often a glaring discrepancy between what Libra II's think they want and what they truly need. Those born in this week may blunt their own desires by not taking them seriously. Thus, through their own insistence that they don't need something, they can stunt the development of their will. Any resulting confusion, unhappiness or despair may serve them well, if they can take advantage of it. Through depression, they can get in touch with themselves at a deep level and, stripped of externals, will find out what their deepest needs really are.

An ever-present danger for these imaginative individuals is that they will come to live too much in a fantasy world in which all things are possible. Through complacency, and narcissistic enjoyment, they can fail to take action. This lack of aggression may affect their professional life. Worldly ambition can be very healthy for Libra II's, since it can spur them on to be more assertive, and to demand from the world what they really want. The problems here are they aren't always sure what their true wishes are, and they are too often satisfied with what they have and indecisive in charting out a realistic course of action.

Libra II's are highly valued by their friends, not least for their light and fun-loving manner. They are often good conversationalists, and even the most shy Libra II blossoms in activities involving a small group of companions, such as parties, dinners or outings. Those born in this week are highly responsible in such surroundings, and may be depended upon to make a contribution. Yet as aware and realistic as they are about other people, to the same or a greater degree they can be unrealistic about themselves. It may be an unfortunate trait of Libra II's to pull the wool over their own eyes. Such self-deception can lead to disastrous choices of partner, and also to professional blunders. Simply put: without a clear view of themselves, Libra II's cannot make cogent personal choices, and are constantly landing themselves in trouble. Fortunately, they are highly resilient. Still, they must not take their ability to snap back from injury or defeat for granted, or rely on it unduly.

During rocky periods in their personal relationships, Libra II's tend to be more hurtful toward themselves than to the other person. This is a sign less of masochistic tendencies than of low self-esteem, and of a habit of putting the needs and wants of a lover or friend before their own. Their difficulty in expressing anger and aggression leads them to blame themselves when things go wrong. They may consequently sink into a quiet depression, tumbling into a well of loneliness from which it may be extremely difficult for them to climb out.

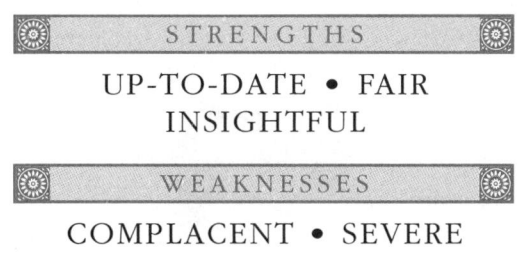

STRENGTHS

UP-TO-DATE • FAIR
INSIGHTFUL

WEAKNESSES

COMPLACENT • SEVERE
SELF-DECEIVING

ADVICE:

Try to find your true heart's desire. Once you have found it, remember to show you really care. Don't always give things away—hold on to what is most valuable in yourself. Learn to limit your explorations of interesting but distracting subjects that can sidetrack you from your main purpose. Make some hard choices, but preserve your dreams and visions.

LIBRA II NOTABLES

The involvement of **Rev. Jesse Jackson** in the civil rights movement dates back 35 years to his days as a college undergraduate. As a Libra II, most of his adult life has been taken up with social issues, such as helping to advance the cause of African Americans. Having marched with Dr. Martin Luther King in Selma, Ala., he then joined the Southern Christian Leadership Conference. In the 70s and 80s Jackson became active internationally and also worked to promote voter registration. A prominent voice at Democratic national conventions, Jackson has enormously developed people skills and a keen insight into social problems and the ability to express them with power and eloquence. His talent for working with groups was evident in his Operation Breadbasket and the Rainbow Coalition.

REV. JESSE JACKSON

Oscar-winning actress **Susan Sarandon** blew everyone away with her performance opposite Sean Penn in *Dead Man Walking*. Respected in the film world for her refusal to compromise herself in less demanding or more glitzy roles, Sarandon is an individualist who does what she wants but also what she feels is best. A devoted mother and companion, it seems her life off the screen is at least as important to her as that on it. Her good-natured sociability is characteristic of Libra II's, as are her vivacious feistiness and outspoken political views. Other virtuoso perfor-

SUSAN SARANDON

mances in films such as *Atlantic City* and *Thelma and Louise* mark her as one of the outstanding American film actresses of the 80s and 90s.

The most socially aware of the Beatles, **John Lennon** had insights into the workings of society that enabled him to become the spokesman for a whole generation of young people. In typical Libra II fashion, Lennon could be extremely cutting and critical of social

JOHN LENNON

conventions that stood in the way of personal development. Increasingly political, Lennon was largely responsible for the Beatles' anarchical ideologies but also embodied a certain idealism, as in his solo hit *Imagine*. With wife Yoko Ono at his side, Lennon's stature as a cultural icon grew and he matured as a person. While in a period of depressive withdrawal, Lennon was murdered outside his New York City apartment in 1980.

More Libra II's: Buster Keaton, Armand Asssante, Soon-Yi Previn, Vaclav Havel, Elizabeth Shue, Desmond Tutu, Helen MacInness, Amiri Baraka, June Allyson, Jackson Browne, Harold Pinter, Thelonius Monk, Britt Ekland, Ben Vereen, Helen Hayes, James Clavell, Giuseppe Verdi, Klaus Kinski, Janet Gaynor, Matt Biondi, Miguel de Cervantes, Sigourney Weaver, Juan Perón, Chevy Chase, Yo-Yo Ma, Jenny Lind, Carole Lombard, Bob Geldof, Terence Conran.

Relationship Guide for Libra II

SUSAN SARANDON (LIBRA II)
TIM ROBBINS (LIBRA III)
PAGE 676

BEST RELATIONSHIPS

LOVE
Pisces-Aries Cusp
Aries-Taurus Cusp
Gemini I
Leo I
Leo III
Virgo III
Scorpio II
Scorpio III
Scorpio-Sagittarius Cusp
Sagittarius II
Sagittarius-Capricorn Cusp
Aquarius II
Aquarius-Pisces Cusp
Pisces III

MARRIAGE
Aries II
Taurus II
Virgo II
Virgo-Libra Cusp
Libra-Scorpio Cusp
Capricorn III

FRIENDSHIP
Aries III
Gemini-Cancer Cusp
Cancer III
Virgo I
Libra II
Sagittarius III
Capricorn II
Aquarius III
Pisces II

FAMILY
Aries I
Gemini III
Cancer-Leo Cusp
Leo II
Libra III
Scorpio I
Aquarius I

WORK
Taurus-Gemini Cusp
Gemini II
Cancer I
Libra I

Page Locator for All Relationships

LIBRA III
The Week of Theater

October 11–18

The Libra III period takes Theater as its central image. This period can be likened in human terms to a person's late forties, by which time full social integration of the individual has usually been accomplished or attempted. The adoption of a given social role is generally well set by now. What remains is to play that role consummately on life's stage. Particularly important at this time are the development of expressive qualities and the bringing of one's powers to bear on building a great success in, one hopes a pleasing and judicious way.

The days that comprise Libra III symbolically reveal the confident adult in middle life striving to balance the many social demands made on him/her, exercising shrewd judgment and sound leadership, and, through sensing the rhythms of life, staying attuned to the large line all the while furthering the action.

If "all the world's a stage," as Shakespeare wrote, then Libra III's are some of the finest players upon it. Acting out the drama of their own lives in everyday affairs is a specialty of those born in this week. Libra III's know the value of image in their professional lives and spend a lot of time working on how they present themselves to the world. Their detachment, even coolness, may sometimes irritate or infuriate those around them, but it is misleading; if they seem to lack affect, this is usually a result of a studied and rigorous training they put themselves through. Libra III's are actually very emotional people.

Hardheaded, Libra III's may stick to the same course for years, whether it is right for them or wrong. Their drive to move ahead at any cost makes them mistrust silence and repose; they prefer doing to thinking. Their

ZODIAC POSITION
Approximately
16–25° Libra

SEASON
Early fall

ELEMENT
Air

RULER
Venus

SYMBOL
The Scales

MODES
Thought, Sensation

mistakes can consequently be big ones, since they may give themselves wholeheartedly and sometimes prematurely to an endeavor without either analyzing and planning it or tuning in to their intuitions about it beforehand. Accidents of all types may well result from this unheeding attitude.

Leadership qualities are often highly developed in Libra III's, who typically find themselves at the head of a social group or business. Once again, however, in leading a family or assuming an executive role they may act with a certain hubris or sense of infallibility, neglecting to gauge the effects of their actions on co-workers, employees or relatives. On top of this, if they are finally forced to face failure they may be confronting something they had hitherto considered an impossibility, and the shock can prove too much for them. Libra III's who can cultivate true humility with respect to their fellow humans will be much happier in the long run.

Libra III's who have faced great disappointment may become cynical. Such world-weary individuals can be revived through love and affection, but these are the very qualities they usually find most difficult to share. Opening their hearts to a trusted friend or family member is essential to their psychological well-being. Perhaps psychological help is the obvious solution, but most born in this week are resistant to it. In times of trouble, the loved ones of Libra III's must often assume a heavy load indeed, knowing that they and they alone are keeping their partners going.

Worldliness is perhaps the greatest strength of Libra III's; their knowhow, knowledge and experience give them the confidence they need to enjoy the challenges of

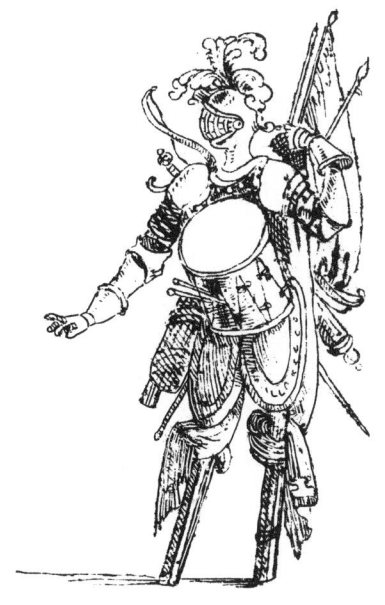

"THEATER"

their chosen field. Almost invariably specialists or experts of some kind, Libra III's are quite capable of dominating their professional field. They have a need to be well informed, and if they are ignorant in some area, they characteristically make this a challenge to learn. Although hardheaded, Libra III's will give consideration to any idea, no matter how far out, not out of a sense of fairness but because of the chance that it will contribute something to their knowledge. To them, knowledge is power.

Difficulties arise in the personal relationships of those born in this week when their lovers or mates feel neglected. In truth, Libra III's are not terribly interested in other people, or in their feelings, and although they suffer exceedingly when misunderstood, they seldom go out of their way to understand others. Those born in the Week of Theater are uncomfortable when heavy emotional expectations are put on them, and either withdraw or flee. They see themselves as serious, responsible and ethical, but they may relate more immediately to other people's ideas or values, and what these represent, than to who these people actually are.

The friend or mate of a Libra III may have to play a subordinate role, since those born in the Week of Theater usually take center stage. Yet they also have a needy side, and they often do best in relationships with strong, even dominant personalities whom they can lean on. When someone becomes partially or completely dependent on them, on the other hand, Libra III's can become uncomfortable and restless, longing to escape. They must feel able to assume and discharge responsibilities generously and of their own accord, rather than being forced to do so.

The masculine and the feminine come together strongly in Libra III's. They can be extremely intense in the bedroom, an area that permits their full range of emotional expression. Once released, however, these passions may well spill over in anger and upset, which they vent on their partner in the form of arguments replete with recrimination and blame. Libra III anger is violent but for the most part mercifully short-lived, for those born in this week are not inclined to bring strife into their daily lives.

Probably the best thing that can happen emotionally to a Libra III is to be or become an active member of a family group that can provide the affection, support and appreciation these hard-driving individualists need. The problem is, many Libra III's are not particularly interested in families—whether spouses, children or their own parents. As a substitute, they may seek to live, work or play with a group of long-standing friends whom they trust and respect. Even so, the workaholic tendencies of Libra III's will often prevent them from spending a great deal of time with whatever group or individual they choose to live with, and may in fact reflect their true preference—to live alone.

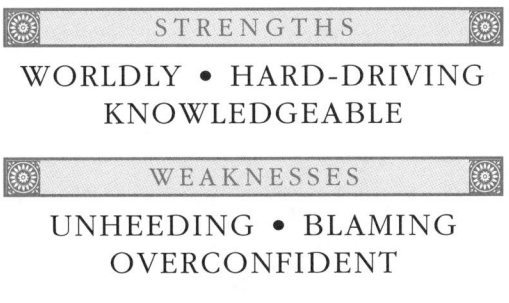

STRENGTHS

WORLDLY • HARD-DRIVING
KNOWLEDGEABLE

WEAKNESSES

UNHEEDING • BLAMING
OVERCONFIDENT

ADVICE:

Beware of making promises you can't keep. Consider carefully the possible repercussions of your actions. Sometimes it is necessary to play at a part but don't kid yourself in the process. Be more considerate of the feelings of others; devote sufficient time and patience to emotional matters.

LIBRA III NOTABLES

The Italian opera superstar **Luciano Pavarotti** has been seen by millions of people worldwide in his telecasts of the Three Tenors, with Jose Carreras and Placido Domingo, and it appears he loves every minute of it. A consummate showman, Pavarotti is master of the grand gesture and the theatrical. Like others born in the Week

LUCIANO PAVAROTTI

of Theater, Pavarotti seems more comfortable on the stage than off. Most at home singing in Italian, Pavarotti has capitalized on the popularity of opera in our time but also has done much to create a whole new audience for the art due to his infectious Libra III enjoyment of what he does.

Daughter of a greengrocer, "The Iron Lady" **Margaret Thatcher** ruled Great Britain as prime minister and head of the Conservative party from 1979 to 1990. Thatcher molded the country along the lines of her own thinking in the 80s, instituting a political philosophy known as "Thatcherism," which more or less tried to get rid of government supports and worked to put everyone on their own, for better or worse. Her strongly moral convictions led her to condemn South Africa, Argentina and Iraq. Thatcher brought a strong sense of Theater to the political arena. Also typical of Libra III's, Thatcher had highly developed leadership qualities but also an air of infallibility and a refusal to admit failure, which finally led to her being dumped by her party.

MARGARET THATCHER

With all his artistic inconsistencies and failures, **Eugene O'Neill** still remains the giant of American theater. The tragedies of his personal life are mirrored in the fact that out of 60 plays he wrote only one comedy. His father was an alcoholic, his mother a morphine addict, his oldest son committed suicide, and he refused to ever speak to his daughter Oona after she married Charlie Chaplin. But Theater was in his blood, and

EUGENE O'NEILL

he moved the Provincetown Players to New York to present his own works. The strange workings of fate powered the tragedy of O'Neill's plays, which were largely about relationships gone wrong. In some ways O'Neill came to represent the kind of Libra III who has become cynical through great disappointment, but his best dramas rose above such attitudes to become universal in scope.

More Libra III's: Eleanor Roosevelt, Arthur Miller, Dick Gregory, Lee Harvey Oswald, Oscar Wilde, Mario Puzo, Martina Navratilova, LaMonte Young, Sarah Ferguson, Art Blakey, Rita Hayworth, Melina Mercouri, Chuck Berry, Pam Dawber, Pierre Trudeau, George C. Scott, Roger Moore, Lenny Bruce, Nancy Kerrigan, Lotte Lenya, Margot Kidder, Montgomery Clift, Nathaniel West, David Ben-Gurion.

Relationship Guide for Libra III

ELEANOR ROOSEVELT (LIBRA III)
FRANKLIN ROOSEVELT (AQUARIUS I)
PAGE 693

BEST RELATIONSHIPS

LOVE
Gemini-Cancer Cusp
Cancer-Leo Cusp
Virgo I
Virgo II
Sagittarius I
Aquarius I
Aquarius III
Aquarius-Pisces Cusp

MARRIAGE
Aries III
Leo-Virgo Cusp
Libra I
Sagittarius II
Sagittarius-Capricorn Cusp
Capricorn I

FRIENDSHIP
Aries I
Aries-Taurus Cusp
Gemini I
Cancer I
Cancer II
Leo III
Virgo-Libra Cusp
Libra III
Scorpio I
Capricorn III
Aquarius II
Pisces II

FAMILY
Taurus III
Taurus-Gemini
Gemini II
Libra II
Sagittarius III
Pisces III

WORK
Taurus II
Gemini III
Cancer III
Leo II
Libra-Scorpio Cusp
Capricorn II
Capricorn-Aquarius Cusp
Pisces I

Page Locator for All Relationships

The Cusp of Drama and Criticism

October 19–25

The Libra-Scorpio cusp is an admixture of the seventh sign of the zodiac, Libra, and the eight sign of the zodiac, Scorpio, where the airy, social, theatrical Libra nature confronts the more serious, deeply feeling and critical nature of Scorpio. This cusp can be likened to the period around forty-nine years of age in the human life and comes in the middle of fall in the northern hemisphere. In human development, at the age of forty-nine, the midlife period is ending and middle age approaching. This is a period that can be characterized by the themes of Drama and Criticism. A heightened sense of the drama of life, both in a philosophical and personal sense, leads to an increased awareness of the dynamics of one's own existence, past and present; a highly critical attitude emerges that cuts away careless generalizations and sloppy thinking, and aims for the essence of truth. Such an attitude can lead to profound changes in personal relationships, how leisure time is spent and in general to a reevaluation of one's place in the world.

Big personalities, those born on the Libra-Scorpio cusp may prove too much for anyone to handle. Their influence can not only dominate their immediate circle but go far beyond it; that influence is surely personal, for these are charismatic individuals, but also often intellectual, since their ideas are well thought out and highly developed. Libra-Scorpios usually have something to say on almost any subject. Their penchant for preaching from the pulpit makes them well suited to be teachers, whether professionally or informally, and their students usually come to depend heavily on them for guidance.

ZODIAC POSITION
Approximately
26° Libra–3° Scorpio

SEASON
Mid-fall

ELEMENTS
Air/Water

RULERS
Venus/Pluto
& Mars

SYMBOLS
The Scales/The Scorpion

MODES
Thought, Sensation, Feeling

Those born on this cusp meld the airy (mental) nature of Libra and the watery (emotional) characteristics of Scorpio—not always an easy task. These two aspects of their personality are often at war, with the head guiding and the heart denying, or viceversa. Libra-Scorpios can get into a real mess with themselves when their intellectual and emotional natures clash. Periods of Libra indecision may be broken by outbursts of Scorpio aggression, and self-assured Scorpio determination and control may be undermined by Libra procrastination and love of repose. The tensions and disappointments of life can at times prove too much for them, such that they retreat into isolation. Thus Libra-Scorpios benefit from physical exercise, fitness training, sound diets and all activities that promote healthy contact with the world. and relationships and activities that lessen their tendency to isolate themselves from the world or will prove beneficial to them.

The mental orientation of those born on the Cusp of Drama and Criticism appears in their perceptiveness and sharp insightfulness. The twin dangers here are a sense of personal infallibility and a tendency to be overcritical; the disapproving or denigrating attitudes of Libra-Scorpios can hurt those close to them, undermining their confidence in subtle ways. The intimates of Libra-Scorpios may have to fight back against such negative expectations and predictions, not just to protect but to liberate themselves. Those born on this cusp should seriously think about the project of learning to back off, and of not only keeping their opinions to themselves but in many cases letting go of them completely.

Those born on this cusp have a decidedly modern

"DRAMA AND CRITICISM"

approach in most areas, but also shelter an undeniable sense of tradition. This is particularly clear in their devotion to parents and children, in whose lives they play a large role–sometimes too large. Not that Libra-Scorpios too easily accept their parents' values—far from it. Their attachment is more emotional. After a stormy and rebellious adolescence, those born on this cusp often return to an extremely close relationship with their parents in later life.

As responsible as many Libra-Scorpios seem in many areas of everyday life, they have an undeniably wild, unpredictable side. Dramatic and impulsive, they will unhesitatingly fly in the face of society's moral codes to assert their values or express themselves, which they can do both cogently and flamboyantly. Even the mildest of those born on this cusp have an exhibitionistic side, and want and need others to take notice of them. The private lives of Libra-Scorpios may include many love affairs, charting a path strewn with the broken hearts of those who have had relationships with them. Their particular brand of charisma, impulsiveness and mental power makes them formidable and sometimes even dangerous individuals to be involved with.

Sensuousness and passion are important themes in the lives of those born on the Cusp of Drama and Criticism. In their relationships with others, however, they may exhibit a split between these two areas, treat-

ing sexuality quite differently from sensuality, and basing a relationship squarely on either one or the other, and only rarely on both. Libra-Scorpios express their sensuousness in their love of the beautiful and tasteful objects with which they surround themselves, or in an appreciation of art, music and literature.

Those romantically involved with Libra-Scorpios must beware of addictive tendencies in such relationships. Unduly deep attachments that go beyond usual or even healthy limits may result in debilitating dependencies and painful partings and breakups, even in symptoms resembling drug withdrawal. The most successful type of Libra-Scorpio personality is able to structure relationships so that both parties have their own space and retain their identities; less successful individuals born on this cusp may be fated to experience a painful string of failed relationships. A combination of deep love and friendship in a marriage with a Libra-Scorpio is possible, however, and such a bond will overcome almost any difficulties that may arise.

With children, whether their own or those of other family members or friends, Libra-Scorpios take seriously the role of responsible adult guide, but can lose their objectivity and wind up getting too emotionally involved. Those born on this cusp must learn to be respectful of children, students and other young people, and to realize how damaging their feelings and desires, and perhaps their unrealistic expectations, may prove.

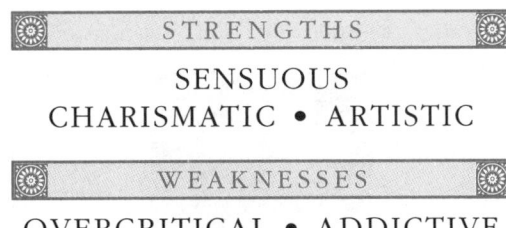

STRENGTHS

SENSUOUS
CHARISMATIC • ARTISTIC

WEAKNESSES

OVERCRITICAL • ADDICTIVE
RIGID

ADVICE:

Try to relax and have fun. Learn to be less picky. Do not cut yourself off from unusual experiences but maintain your poise and balance. Continue to battle with life and resist escapism or the throes of self-pity. Leave the past behind and embrace the future. Cynicism and sarcasm are poison to you.

LIBRA-SCORPIO CUSP NOTABLES

What was it about **Sarah Bernhardt** that made her a stage legend? Of slight build, with frizzy red hair and a pale face, she looked soulful but not overly impressive. That is, until she started to speak and move. Drama flowed from Bernhardt, from every pore, mesmerizing her audiences and sending them into other worlds. "The Divine Sarah" on stage was charismatic and hypnotic. However, like other Libra-Scorpios, she could be wild, unpredictable and fly in the face of authority. Not easy to get along with, Bernhardt was kinder to her audiences than to those with and for whom she worked. Finally, tired of being bound to other companies' whims, she established her own theater in Paris. Bernhardt could play a variety of parts and even performed the lead role in Shakespeare's *Hamlet*.

SARAH BERNHARDT

Heavyweight champion of the world **Evander Holyfield** was able to defeat Buster Douglas, Riddick Bowe and Mike Tyson to gain the title on three separate occasions. A serious underdog to Tyson, it was clear at fight's end that almost everyone had underestimated Holyfield's capabilities and determination. Drama has surrounded Holyfield during much of his life, but he is a humble man who is religious and unassuming. Although diagnosed with a heart problem that disqualified him for boxing, the condition miraculously cleared up, which allowed him to continue

EVANDER HOLYFIELD

his career. Like many Libra-Scorpios, Holyfield's determination to improve his physical condition brought him into closer touch with the world.

Considered by many to be the greatest artist of the 20th century, **Pablo Picasso** could pay for any meal by simply signing the napkin. Although sensuousness and passion characterized his affairs and

PABLO PICASSO

marriages, so did emotional problems, typical of many Libra-Scorpio relationships. Immensely critical of himself and others, Picasso mastered many styles of 20th-century painting. This can be readily observed by viewing a retrospective of his extremely varied work, which in some ways resembles a history of modern art. The Spanish master was also an accomplished sculptor, ceramicist and lithographer. Extremely prolific, Picasso worked almost continuously for 80 years and produced many thousands of artworks. Political views were uncompromising—his antifascist stance is embodied in his great masterpiece *Guernica*.

More Libra-Scorpios: Peter Tosh, Catherine Deneuve, Robert Rauschenberg, Annette Funicello, Pelé, Johnny Carson, Midori, Helen Reddy, Dizzy Gillespie, Ursula LeGuin, Carrie Fisher, Benjamin Netanyahu, Jelly Roll Morton, Arthur Rimbaud, Bobby Seale, Mickey Mantle.

Relationship Guide for Libra-Scorpio Cusp

CHARLIE PARKER (VIRGO I)
DIZZY GILLESPIE (LIBRA-SCORPIO CUSP)
PAGE 616

BEST RELATIONSHIPS

LOVE
Aries-Taurus Cusp
Gemini I
Leo-Virgo Cusp
Libra I
Scorpio II
Scorpio-Sagittarius Cusp
Capricorn-Aquarius Cusp
Pisces I

MARRIAGE
Gemini III
Cancer II
Leo III
Virgo II
Libra II
Sagittarius I
Sagittarius III
Capricorn I
Aquarius II

FRIENDSHIP
Aries III
Taurus I
Taurus-Gemini Cusp
Cancer III
Leo II
Libra-Scorpio Cusp
Scorpio III
Capricorn II
Aquarius-Pisces Cusp

FAMILY
Taurus III
Cancer-Leo Cusp
Virgo III
Virgo-Libra Cusp
Pisces III

WORK
Aries II
Leo I
Virgo I
Libra III
Scorpio I
Sagittarius-Capricorn Cusp
Capricorn III
Aquarius III
Pisces II

Page Locator for All Relationships

SCORPIO I
The Week of Intensity

October 26–November 2

The Scorpio I period takes Intensity as its central image. According to The Grand Cycle of Life, this period can be likened to the onset of middle age, when the power of an individual begins to fully emerge, to peak at some future point in the fifties or early sixties. In the Scorpio I period the ability to take control, to effectively husband and exert one's powers over the environment, to subdue wayward elements to one's will are manifested.

The days that comprise Scorpio I illustrate the underlying theme of Intensity, and the accompanying capacity to formulate, guide and finally transform unpolished materials creatively and efficiently into highly valuable and viable entities. Though biological drives may be lessened or eliminated by this time of life, sexual or romantic expression is not necessarily diminished in importance; many even report feelings of a greater intensity that are more measured and directed, and less diffuse or unstable.

Scorpio I's are demanding personalities, who have few equals in attention to detail and applying their powers of concentration to the task at hand. Those born in the Week of Intensity are extremely discriminating, possibly to the point of being judgmental. Particularly in matters of fairness and ethics, they are likely to evaluate people more for their motives than for their actions and sternly pass sentence on those they see as transgressing the bounds of morality. They can be equally strict themselves, however, and are highly prone to guilt over wayward thoughts and deeds. Thus their conscience is always powerfully at work. Getting the job done is important to them, but the way in which it is done has

ZODIAC POSITION
Approximately
1–11° Scorpio

SEASON
Mid-fall

ELEMENT
Water

RULER
Pluto (co-ruler: Mars)

SYMBOL
The Scorpion

MODE
Feeling

top priority. Even the mildest of those born in this week have more than a touch of the performer to them. Their virtuoso energies are often the outward manifestation of a needy side—a craving for approval and affection from their families and friends.

More than most people, Scorpio I's have a charged, polarized personality with two sides—one sunny, one dark. Their sunny side gives them a radiance and a seductive charm that can melt the hardest hearts; their dark side is destructive, and when out of control can inflict serious damage, not only on those around them but on themselves. It is this intensity that makes them unlikely to back down from confrontation, so that they often hang in until the bitter end. When they are troubled, their lack of confidence comes to the fore, and may manifest, for example, in a conviction that they cannot get anything right, or that those they care for dislike them. Accusing others of having negative emotions (such as anger, jealousy, or feelings of rejection) that they in fact are feeling and projecting themselves is too often the mechanism they use to ease their pain.

Those born in this week pride themselves on being aware of what they do, and on accepting responsibility for their actions. As a consequence, when another person commits an act against them they most often assume that it was done knowingly or willfully. This refusal to believe that the other person acted innocently or without premeditation can precipitate conflict. Further, Scorpio I's usually refuse to accept excuses for, say, lateness, or for missing an appointment altogether through forgetfulness. They too often view the claim of a memory lapse as a disguise for an intended hurt. Nor do Scorpio I's

"INTENSITY"

equally accept all the apologies other people make for their actions: they are more willing to forgive a false move than an impure motive.

It may be difficult for Scorpio I's to forgive, but it is almost impossible for them to forget slights, condescension and anything they see as an insult to their intelligence. They are thin-skinned when it comes to criticism, so those close to them will have to tread lightly to avoid arguments. Such conflicts can ultimately have a destructive influence on a relationship, and may lead to a breakup; but they can also have the positive effect of clearing the air, promoting honesty and in general bringing partners to work on improving relations. Excepting in certain moral areas, which remain closed, Scorpio I's most often prefer discussion to combat, but must beware of argument for argument's sake. If attacked directly, however, either verbally or physically, they will fight it out.

Still, the main thrust of Scorpio I judgments is not destructive per se—quite to the contrary. Those born in this week tend to feel that they wouldn't even be bothering with someone unless they cared enough about them to help improve their lot. Scorpio I's believe in the positive value of criticism and doubt that a bad situation will get better by itself. Yet their lovers and friends may grow tired of their often painfully sharp analyses, no matter how perceptive these judgments may eventually prove to be. A "blame, blame, guilt and shame" mantra may, unfortunately, be the only message

that either party remembers hearing.

Because Scorpio I's value quality far above quantity, they are suspicious of those who are overly versatile, or who make elaborate claims for the merit of all of the different parts of their work equally. Those born in this week think it better to do one thing really well than to do many things acceptably well. Their friends may be few, their contacts with their parents may be carefully planned and controlled, their relations with co-workers or business partners may be highly selective. Those picked as the friend or mate of such discerning, often knowledgeable individuals often feel honored. To have the undivided attention of a Scorpio I who is attractive, interesting and single-minded can be very gratifying, particularly to egos in need of bolstering.

Lovers will attest to the highs of intimate relations with those born in this week, and friends know the warmth and good feelings that they engender. Of particular note is their sense of humor—they can keep those around them rolling around on the floor. Scorpio I's are often excellent mimics, imitating accents, gestures and movements equally well. They are also terrible teasers, one moment mock serious, then exploding in derisive laughter. Once they have found your weak spot or funny bone, they will not give up in their tickling, even when your amusement begins to become uncomfortably like its opposite.

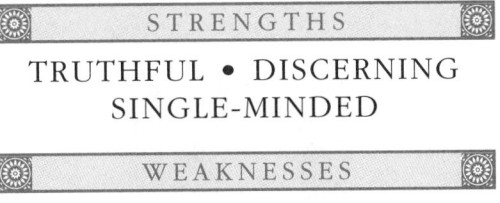

STRENGTHS
TRUTHFUL • DISCERNING SINGLE-MINDED

WEAKNESSES
HURTFUL • STERN SELF-DESTRUCTIVE

ADVICE:

Supply the same constancy you expect from others, but also be less hard on yourself when it comes to mistakes. If at all possible, try to both forgive and forget. Leave excess baggage behind—the injuries of the past can be too heavy for anyone to bear, even you.

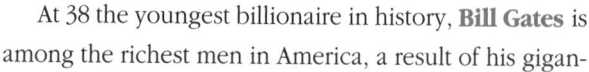

SCORPIO I NOTABLES

An extraordinarily gifted poet, **Dylan Thomas** led a tempestuous and tragic emotional life. Dead at 39 from acute alcohol poisoning, the Intensity he lavished on his poetic art had turned inward and destroyed him. Welshman Thomas published his first book of poems when he was only 20 and was immediately recognized as a literary genius. His plays *Under Milk Wood* and *A Child's Christmas in Wales* have

been heard and loved by audiences around the world on BBC radio, for whom Thomas was also a commentator. The number of Thomas's poems is small, emphasizing his Scorpio I attentiveness to detail and insistence on quality rather than quantity. Although many find his poetry difficult to understand, few can deny the beauty of his highly original language, rich sense of metaphor and rhetoric.

DYLAN THOMAS

At 38 the youngest billionaire in history, **Bill Gates** is among the richest men in America, a result of his gigantic Microsoft empire. Since most of the computers in the world run on Microsoft's software, it is not hard to realize why the company is worth over $25 billion and surpasses most car and aircraft companies in financial clout. Gates himself has been pictured as a nerd, often appearing sheepishly

BILL GATES

dressed in rumpled clothes. His startling vision, expressed in his book, *The Road Ahead*, combined with his achievements thus far, illustrate that the future belongs to those who create it. Characteristic of Scorpio I's, Gates does his homework and learns from his mistakes. Single-minded and discerning, he has little doubt where he is headed.

U.S. First Lady **Hillary Rodham Clinton** has always been a hardworking and dynamic individual. Her Intensity is unmistakable, as she turns her laser light on whatever issue is at hand. She has brought her attentiveness to many areas, as a brilliant student, lawyer, professor, chairperson, social program director and family member. Typical of Scorpio I's, Hillary Clinton is a highly charged and demanding personality who has assumed an extremely active role as First Lady. Her intelligence and courage under fire are particularly evident. Like a true Scorpio, she is often at her best when under attack.

HILLARY RODHAM
CLINTON

More Scorpio I's: Erasmus, Niccolo Paganini, Sylvia Plath, François Mitterrand, Julia Roberts, Kinky Friedman, Larry Flynt, Christopher Columbus, Jan Vermeer, John Cleese, Ruby Dee, John Keats, Lauren Holly, Grace Slick, Joanna Shimkus, Pat Sajak, Teddy Roosevelt, Maxine Hong Kingston, Edith Head, Francis Bacon, Jane Alexander, Burt Lancaster, John Candy, Daniel Boone, Shere Hite, Said Aouita, Marie Antoinette, Stephen Crane, Pat Buchanan, Umberto Agnelli, Gary Player.

Relationship Guide for Scorpio I

LOUIS XVI (LEO-VIRGO CUSP)
MARIE ANTOINETTE (SCORPIO I)
PAGE 603

BEST RELATIONSHIPS

LOVE
Aries III
Taurus I
Gemini-Cancer Cusp
Cancer I
Virgo II
Capricorn II
Aquarius II
Pisces II

MARRIAGE
Taurus III
Cancer III
Leo II
Virgo I
Virgo III
Scorpio I
Scorpio-Sagittarius Cusp
Pisces III

FRIENDSHIP
Pisces-Aries Cusp
Aries II
Aries-Taurus Cusp
Leo I
Leo III
Libra III
Sagittarius-Capricorn Cusp
Capricorn-Aquarius Cusp
Aquarius III
Pisces I

FAMILY
Taurus II
Libra II
Scorpio III
Sagittarius III
Aquarius I

WORK
Taurus-Gemini Cusp
Gemini III
Cancer II
Cancer-Leo Cusp
Leo-Virgo Cusp
Libra-Scorpio Cusp
Sagittarius II
Capricorn I
Aquarius-Pisces Cusp

Page Locator for All Relationships

SCORPIO II
The Week of Depth

♏

November 3–11

The Scorpio II period takes Depth as its central image. This period can be likened symbolically to the time in a middle-aged individual's life when deeper areas of the personality make their demands and a new, profound source of power may be uncovered. In the Scorpio II period, contact is made with unconscious and chthonic forces capable of effecting transformative changes in a person.

The days that comprise Scorpio II symbolically reveal the more serious side of human life, and the ability to go beyond ordinary experience through a revelation, metamorphosis and probing of the internal and external world. As when oil is struck and a geyser explodes, tremendous energies can be released from the deep layers of the unconscious. Such energies must, of course, be welldirected, or destruction could easily result. Ideally, powerful new insights may result at this time.

Profundity in all forms is an irresistible attraction to Scorpio II's. Shunning superficiality, those born in the Week of Depth take a measured and serious view of life, both at work and at home. This is not to say that they don't like to have fun—far to the contrary. In pursuing their hobbies, pastimes and lighter activities, however, they show the same full-bodied intensity and concentration that they do in the more purposeful parts of their lives.

Those born in the Week of Depth are highly competitive in their careers and leisure activities, but they seldom allow this impulse into their private lives. Jealousy and envy are naturally close to their passionate core, but Scorpio II's are generally able to understand and control such emotions to prevent them from running riot. In

ZODIAC POSITION
Approximately
10–20° Scorpio

SEASON
Mid-fall

ELEMENT
Water

RULER
Pluto (co-ruler: Mars)

SYMBOL
The Scorpion

MODE
Feeling

extreme cases, however, these feelings may emerge powerfully in the Scorpio II personality, threatening to engulf it entirely.

One area in which the position of Scorpio II's is firmly fixed is that of finance. They are well aware of the power of money in daily life, and rarely will they knowingly put themselves at an economic disadvantage. They may even worry unduly about financial matters, and although they are not miserly, they do tend to hold on to what they have. They can get very upset with mates and business partners who are too free with their spending or downright fiscally irresponsible. Yet they must beware of applying a double standard, for they, too, can go overboard, spending money on themselves shamelessly. To allay their own feelings of anxiety, Scorpio II's need to be good earners.

Scorpio II's can be empathic with the suffering of others, for they know what it is to suffer themselves. Those born in the Week of Depth don't generally seek out painful situations, but they know that a life without hardship and struggle has little meaning. They will feel, say, the death of a parent, friend, child or mate deeply—so deeply, in fact, that it can have an overwhelming or catastrophic effect on them; indeed, they may never recover from it. Scorpio II's may not ruminate on the subject of death, and usually try to put it out of their minds, but at a deeper level they are often obsessed with the subject. The need to sleep soundly for long periods yet the failure to remember their dreams can be characteristic of such personalities, who need a lot of time for unconscious expression and often cut off the content of such activities from daily awareness.

It can be difficult to get Scorpio II's to open up emo-

"DEPTH"

tionally and to talk about whatever may be bothering them. Even a trusted life partner or dear friend must pass all kinds of roadblocks before getting close to the inner feelings of those born in this week. To listen to what Scorpio II's are finally ready to say requires patience, understanding and nonclaiming love. Any deep bond formed with such an individual obviously cannot be taken lightly; not everyone is ready for such deep and heavy commitment.

Scorpio II's are fascinated by forms of escape. Physical or psychic retreat to a safe haven, and the ability to switch off their mental motor at will, allows those born in this week to deal with aspects of daily life that they would rather not face. Television, movies, music and books are healthy habits for them, but addiction, to drugs, alcohol, sex or violence, is always a real possibility, too. When such activity involves others, Scorpio II's are not necessarily the initiators; they often repress their shadow side. Instead, however, they may summon up possessive or violent behavior in their immediate environment, forcing their mates and lovers to act out their own repressed negativity. This may be directed against the Scorpio II, who then becomes his or her own victim.

Scorpio II's are not the best choice for victimization, for they are counter-punchers by nature and can be fierce in protecting themselves and their loved ones. Few who have experienced their anger will seek to arouse it a second time. It is typical of Scorpio II's, in fact, to be occasionally subject to volcanic outbursts of emotion, which, although rarely seen, are not easily forgotten.

Scorpio II's generally make steadfast friends and faithful lovers and mates. This is only partly a matter of morality; being overly flexible and changeable is really not possible for those born in this week, so turning from one partner to another, or adopting new methods and techniques in their work, is generally not an option for them. Being forced to make such switches by circumstances or fate can bring out their worst side.

Both lovers and friends can testify to the softer side of Scorpio II's. Although their presence is often formidable, they can be unusually kind, giving, and even quite sentimental. Those born in this week are generally kind to animals and small children, who awaken their protective and nurturing instincts. Scorpio II's can make excellent parents.

Those born in this week can be secretive and controlling—typical Scorpio traits. Their sexual needs and demands often also run high, but they can equally well go for long periods of time without wanting intimate contact. Scorpio II's are, generally speaking, very physical, enjoying the pleasures of table and bed. As long as they remain sensitive to their partners and capable of moderation, such drives and appetites can have a positive effect on their relationships. Indeed, Scorpio II's are often only able to overcome their strong attraction to fixed habitual behaviors by learning to share true affection and love.

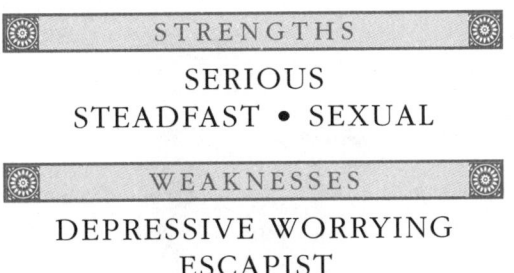

STRENGTHS

SERIOUS
STEADFAST • SEXUAL

WEAKNESSES

DEPRESSIVE WORRYING
ESCAPIST

ADVICE:

*Let the sun shine in and the light within you shine out. Don't take things so seriously.
Work on leveling out your moods and see how much happiness you can bring
to yourself and others. Put your singular insight to productive use.
Learn to laugh more at the illusions of the world and also at yourself.*

SCORPIO II NOTABLES

The only person to win Nobel Prizes in both physics and chemistry, Polish-born scientist **Marie Curie** was a

MARIE CURIE

genius of rare magnitude. Co-discoverer with her husband, Pierre, of two new elements, radium and polonium, Madame Curie studied the properties of X-rays and their ability to kill harmful cells. Discovering many hidden atomic secrets, Curie's probing into deep, plutonic realms of matter symbolize her Scorpio II orientation. Able to couple investigative instincts and the Scorpio II need to control, Curie was ideally suited to conduct her experiments. Her husband was killed in a tragic car accident, while she herself finally succumbed to the cumulative effects of the radiation she worked with most of her life in the form of leukemia.

Symbolizing the passionate sexual orientation of Scorpio II, Austrian actress **Hedy Lamarr** blew a few circuits with her first Hollywood film appearances. Having already aroused a storm of protest over her nude appearance in the Czech film *Ecstasy*, neither American film moguls nor Lamarr herself were oblivious to her stimulating effect on audiences.

HEDY LAMARR

The dark-haired Scorpionic beauty may not have been a great actress, but opposite Victor Mature in the film *Samson and Delilah*, she manifested a kind of earthly temptation that both Samson and the audience found irresistible. Her films include *Tortilla Flat, Her Highness and the Bellboy, White Cargo* and *Lady Without a Passport*.

Fyodor Dostoevski, Author of *Notes from the Underground*, was a writer of great Depth who sought to look into the innermost areas of the human soul. In his greatest works, *The Brothers Karamazov, The Idiot* and *Crime and Punishment,* Dostoevski explore psychologi-

FYODOR DOSTOEVSKI

cal torment and spiritual exaltation in a way never attempted before in the annals of literature. Redemption through suffering is a constant theme of Dostoevski, who was starkly existential in his insistence that life be lived to the fullest and on its own terms. His "Legend of the Grand Inquisitor" from *The Brothers Karamazov* shows Christ coming a second time, only to be sentenced to death by the very church established in his name. Dostoevski's philosophical discussion of bread versus freedom anticipates the dilemma of communism.

More Scorpio II's: Ennio Morricone, Yanni, Kate Capshaw, Robert Mapplethorpe, Bonnie Raitt, Sally Field, Erika Mann, Raymond Loewy, Tatum O'Neal, Ivan Turgenev, Roseanne Barr, Shah of Iran, Richard Burton, Will Rogers, William of Orange, Art Carney, Ida Minerva Tarbell, Ike Turner, Elke Sommer, Roy Rogers, Florence Sabin, John Philip Sousa, James Naismith, Robert Elder von Musil, Maria Shriver, Joan Sutherland, Angel Cordero, Jr., Rickie Lee Jones, Christie Hefner, Kazuo Ishiguro, Florence Chadwick, Mabel Normand, Mike Nichols.

Relationship Guide for Scorpio II

PIERRE CURIE (TAURUS III)
MARIE CURIE (SCORPIO II)
PAGE 383

BEST RELATIONSHIPS

LOVE
Aries I
Aries-Taurus Cusp
Cancer I
Leo II
Leo III
Libra II
Libra-Scorpio Cusp
Aquarius I
Aquarius III
Pisces III

MARRIAGE
Taurus I
Gemini II
Gemini-Cancer Cusp
Cancer-Leo Cusp
Virgo II
Scorpio III
Sagittarius I
Sagittarius III
Capricorn III
Aquarius II
Pisces II

FRIENDSHIP
Pisces-Aries Cusp
Aries II
Taurus II
Taurus-Gemini Cusp
Gemini III
Virgo I
Scorpio II
Sagittarius II
Capricorn I
Capricorn II
Capricorn-Aquarius Cusp

FAMILY
Leo-Virgo Cusp
Virgo III
Aquarius-Pisces Cusp

WORK
Taurus III
Gemini I
Cancer III
Libra I
Scorpio-Sagittarius Cusp
Sagittarius-Capricorn Cusp

Page Locator for All Relationships

SCORPIO III
The Week of Charm

November 12–18

The Scorpio III period takes Charm as its central image. This period can be compared in human terms to the time in a middle-aged person's life when the ability to influence others through magnetic and charismatic powers is heightened. In the Scorpio III period intense emotion may be used with telling effect to gain positive and constructive results, but equally well may be expended in furthering egotistical and narcissistic ends.

The days that comprise Scorpio III symbolically reveal the attractive powers of the middle-aged adult, and the ability to forward aims (but also gain satisfaction) through investigation, observation, seductive charm and a judicious use of leadership skills. Expressive emotions may be directed constructively as a powerful tool for inspiring others but should not be exercised as a controlling mechanism. Instead, by gaining the trust of co-workers, employees or clients, an emotional bond can be formed that promotes success for all concerned.

Realists first and foremost, Scorpio III's rarely overreach themselves. Because they have a realistic view not only of their own capabilities but of others' as well, their judgment is generally trustworthy and their assessments keen. Those born in this week do well in administrative positions or as leaders of a social group or working team, roles in which their evaluative, organizational and practical abilities can come to the fore.

Because Scorpio III's have a great deal together internally, many of them risk becoming complacent, or perhaps self-satisfied. This may be particularly clear in their careers, where they may reach an attainable point, then

---

ZODIAC POSITION
Approximately
19–27° Scorpio

SEASON
Mid-fall

ELEMENT
Water

RULER
Pluto (co-ruler: Mars)

SYMBOL
The Scorpion

MODE
Feeling

---

make no effort to rise higher. Unless those near and dear to Scorpio III's encourage them to take chances from time to time, they may stagnate and, eventually, come to regret lost opportunities. The Scorpio III's who prove the most successful in life, whether in their careers or in their personal and spiritual endeavors, are often those who have dared to strive toward realizing their most impossible dreams.

The passions of Scorpio III's are as strong as their control. Thus those born in this week may be subject to raging internal wars, which can even threaten to destroy them. The charming or inscrutable facade that Scorpio III's present to the world often hides tremendous inner conflicts. Those who are the objects of such passions, and the causes of such conflicts, may never realize how much emotion they are arousing, and therefore can hardly be expected to assume responsibility for it. Scorpio III's who are able to show or at least discuss a small part of their feeling for another person will be closer to realizing success in their personal relationships.

Those born in this week are not accustomed to putting themselves in a disadvantageous position, no matter how much they desire a job or person. Their dignity is important to them, and they will rarely compromise it. Should they reach one of those points in life where an attraction is so overwhelming that it does obstruct their good sense, Scorpio III's will only succumb after a tremendous inner struggle. Addictions of all sorts, whether to drugs, medicines, people or behavior patterns, they only break with difficulty, but such compulsions, once mastered, are rarely readopted.

Scorpio III's must be careful lest they dominate others through overprotective or controlling attitudes. Such

"CHARM"

influences may be quite subtle, since those born in this week rarely seem smothering or dictatorial on the surface: fair and understanding, they arouse loyalty not only at home but at work. People tend to follow their bidding willingly, since they would never ask anyone to do something they wouldn't do themselves. Yet those born in the Week of Charm often throw up an unapproachable or forbidding exterior. Those who relate best to them are usually not put off by such a stance, or just don't see it at all. These are the people who can penetrate Scorpio III defenses and win their hearts.

Those who want to make friends with Scorpio III's must keep in mind their aversion to anyone looking for a free ride. Those born in this week are often attracted to self-sufficient individuals with something unusual to offer. On the other hand, the more seductive Scorpio III's are sometimes quite vulnerable to the seductive skills of others. In particular, the Scorpio III's who choose to follow a more questionable or unscrupulous path are in danger of getting conned by those with superior powers of deception.

Striving to remain open, even vulnerable, is the best hope for Scorpio III's if they are to avoid loneliness, particularly as they grow older. In seeming to have so much together, they often fail to arouse sympathy in others, yet their deeper needs are as great as anyone else's. The ability to admit to their weaknesses and faults, and the courage to own up to their failures or to grieve openly over their losses, will be important for

them in forming deep and lasting love relationships. A life partner may only materialize for these capable individuals once they have truly begun to master—and ultimately, perhaps, to relinquish—their own controlling attitudes.

Scorpio III's rarely kid themselves about their romantic lives. No matter how much in love they seem to be, they are rarely found hanging on to relationships that have proved unproductive or detrimental; usually resourceful, self-possessed individuals, they know that there are always more fish in the sea. Yet they are faithful and sincere, and will give a relationship its best chance—but not more. Their sexual partners and mates learn soon enough not to take the attentions of Scorpio III's for granted, and to heed all warning signs—or find that what has been freely given can also be withheld, or withdrawn entirely.

Close friendships are important to Scorpio III's who have chosen to live alone, or who lack the support of a family group. Those born in the Week of Charm can build a complete world around good friends, who, at certain points, may take the place of siblings, parents, children, mates or lovers for them. They often spend time with people who are very different from themselves, making for friendships in which each member supplies what the other lacks. By forging a circle of friends, Scorpio III's may succeed in making up for all, or almost all, of their deficiencies.

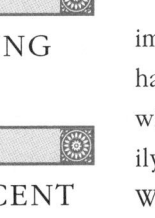

STRENGTHS
TOGETHER • CHARMING RESOURCEFUL

WEAKNESSES
DEFENSIVE • COMPLACENT CONTROLLING

ADVICE:

Keep a critical eye on yourself. Respond to the highest challenges and occasionally take meaningful risks. Be mindful of what is important in life, of what endures and has lasting value. Always aim high, and don't be afraid of failure.

SCORPIO III NOTABLES

It was a long trip for Philadelphia socialite **Grace Kelly** from the banks of the Schuylkill River to the Mediterranean kingdom of Monaco, where she ruled as Princess Grace. Epitomizing the alluring Charm of many Scorpio III's, Grace's modeling and stage acting attracted Hollywood's attention, and she became a movie star, first in *High Noon* opposite Gary Cooper and later in three Alfred Hitchcock films: *Dial M for Murder, Rear Window* and *To Catch a Thief.* She caught Prince Rainier's eye at the Cannes Film Festival, and the rest is history. Her fairy-tale story came to an abrupt end when her car hurtled off a cliff.

GRACE KELLY

Irrepressible actress and comedienne **Whoopi Goldberg** has gone from standup comic to Oscar winner and presenter but has not lost one ounce of her strong personality. A Scorpio III realist, her off-the-cuff remarks cause many to cringe, but to Whoopi the truth is the truth, even if it hurts. Few would make the mistake of taking her on in a frontal assault, and the image of her approaching actor Danny Glover with razor in hand in the film *The Color Purple* is still chilling in retrospect. Whether playing a reluctant clairvoyant (*Ghost*) or basketball coach (*Eddie*), the steel behind Whoopi's smile is quite evident. Thanks to her determination, she has succeeded in establishing herself as a Hollywood and Broadway fixture.

WHOOPI GOLDBERG

For a man who has been in the news so much for the past 30 years or so, not that much is known about the real person behind the image of His Majesty **Prince Charles**, Prince of Wales and heir to the British throne. A secretive Scorpio III, Charles has thrown out lots of false clues as to his identity—in his roles as sportsman, husband, dutiful child, lover, architectural theorist,

PRINCE CHARLES

etc.—but none of these really rings true. Perhaps the role in which he will best express himself is not currently available. Because those born in this week do so well in administrative positions and thrive on responsibility, it may be that until Charles becomes king, we may not find out what he is really like.

More Scorpio III's: Claude Monet, Jawaharlal Nehru, Neil Young, Sun Yat-Sen, Nadia Comaneci, Tonya Harding, Auguste Rodin, Brenda Vaccaro, Robert Louis Stevenson, Demi Moore, Charles Manson, Joseph McCarthy, Boutros Boutros-Ghali, Aaron Copland, Georgia O'Keeffe, Burgess Meredith, W.C. Handy, George S. Kaufman, Dwight Gooden, Buck Clayton, Danny De Vito, Martin Scorsese, Lauren Hutton, Wilma P. Mankiller, Linda Evans, Alan Shepard, Veronica Lake, Erwin Rommel, Yaphet Kotto, Peter Arnett, St. Augustine.

Relationship Guide for Scorpio III

Page Locator for All Relationships

PRINCE RAINIER (GEMINI I)
GRACE KELLY (SCORPIO III)
PAGE 423

BEST RELATIONSHIPS

LOVE
Pisces-Aries Cusp
Aries III
Aries-Taurus Cusp
Gemini II
Gemini-Cancer Cusp
Cancer II
Libra II
Sagittarius II

MARRIAGE
Taurus-Gemini Cusp
Gemini III
Leo I
Virgo III
Virgo-Libra Cusp
Libra I
Scorpio II
Sagittarius III
Sagittarius-Capricorn Cusp
Aquarius-Pisces Cusp

FRIENDSHIP
Aries II
Gemini I
Cancer III
Leo II
Leo-Virgo Cusp
Libra-Scorpio Cusp
Scorpio-Sagittarius Cusp
Capricorn I
Aquarius II
Pisces I
Pisces III

FAMILY
Taurus III
Scorpio I
Aquarius I

WORK
Taurus II
Cancer I
Leo III
Virgo II
Libra III
Sagittarius I
Capricorn II
Aquarius III
Pisces II

The Cusp of Revolution

November 19–24

The Scorpio-Sagittarius cusp is an admixture of the eighth sign of the zodiac, Scorpio, and the ninth sign of the zodiac, Sagittarius. The combined energies of the emotionally deep, serious and secretive Scorpio and the intuitive, outwardly directed, freedom-loving Sagittarius reflect the need first to understand oneself and then to act to institute change. The Scorpio-Sagittarius cusp may be said to represent Revolution. It is symbolic of the beginning of a new period of human life, around fifty-six years of age, when inescapable changes must take place: retirement may be coming up, marriages and other relationships may be forsaken, and physical limitations may have to be confronted. In addition, a greater empathy with one's fellow human beings and, with it, an interest in international or even universal concerns (religion or spirituality) may manifest now. Many people at this stage can feel resentment and rebelliousness at not having done what they really wanted to do in life and see this period as a "last chance" for them. The Revolutionary nature of this cusp can underline the need for total reorganization if crucial changes have not yet been made.

Not all revolutionaries are wide-eyed, bomb-throwing idealists; within the souls of many fighters for human rights lurk secret autocrats, who, once in power, may themselves be toppled by a further revolution. The revolt that engages those born on the Scorpio-Sagittarius cusp is often the fight against sloppiness, bad taste, ineffectualness, stupidity and old-fashioned, outworn attitudes. They are capable of exploding old myths, true, but they are equally capable of reviving and preserving myths that they view to be

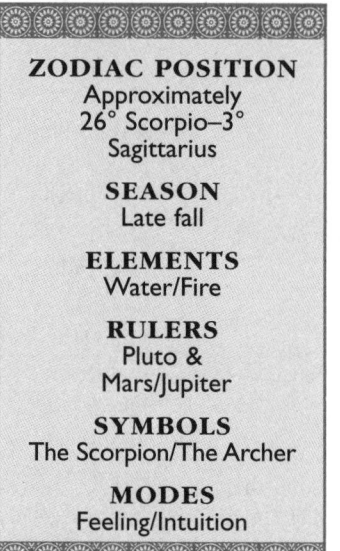

ZODIAC POSITION
Approximately
26° Scorpio–3°
Sagittarius

SEASON
Late fall

ELEMENTS
Water/Fire

RULERS
Pluto &
Mars/Jupiter

SYMBOLS
The Scorpion/The Archer

MODES
Feeling/Intuition

useful. Thus those born on this cusp can also be secret traditionalists at heart.

Characterized by a disdain for middle-of-the road policies and middle-class ethics, most Scorpio-Sagittarians would rather be very rich or very poor, an aristocrat or a working-class hero or heroine, than anything in between. This hankering after extremes leads many born on this cusp to indulge in excess, sometimes in more than one area of their lives.

Scorpio-Sagittarians are usually aware from an early age that they are different from other people. An unusual blend of opposites, those born on the Cusp of Revolution combine the watery sensitivity of Scorpio with the fiery, freedom-loving nature of Sagittarius. In their family, then, they may occupy a lonely position in relation to parents or siblings, and their assessment of their peculiar abilities and strong drive to succeed often dates from their childhood years. Making plans for the future, dreaming up elegant new schemes and guiding a decent percentage of them to fruition are all characteristic of Scorpio-Sagittarian imagination and determination. Goal- and result-oriented, those born on this cusp often show the same stubbornness in picking out a friend or life partner, whom they may pursue with unrelenting zeal.

Scorpio-Sagittarian laughter is a direct barometer of their mental health. If you don't hear it in the first few minutes of conversation with them, you can generally be pretty sure that something is wrong. Those born on the Cusp of Revolution can use cutting sarcasm and derision not only to make a laughingstock of their enemies but to give even their dearest friends a good poke in the ribs every now and then. In this respect they operate with a bit of a double standard, for they do

"REVOLUTION"

not take kindly to being talked down to or derided themselves, seeing such teasing as an attempt to humiliate them. They will not submit to this more than once from anybody.

Moral questions are important to those born on the Cusp of Revolution. They strive to be honest, but don't always manage it; they believe in being truthful, but often cannot measure up to their own standards. Finding it hard to be completely open and honest with those close to them, they may tell only a part of the truth, only to be embarrassed and regretful if they are found out later. Yet their undeniable charm, and their well-meaning, faithful and loyal attitudes, usually lead those who love them to forgive them.

Even the most serious critics of those born on the Cusp of Revolution admit that they have guts. Making it a specialty to say the unspeakable to the unapproachable, they not only seem to lack fear in dealing with authority figures without compromising, but demonstrate the power of such a stance. Yet they are, in fact, excellent at compromise, and know when to give ground and when to stand and fight. Their instinctive side is highly developed and will come to their aid when they believe enough in their own powers to trust it fully. Intuitive types, Scorpio-Sagittarians get muddled or confused when they try to depend too much on their rational abilities.

Those born on the Cusp of Revolution rarely forget either a slight or an act of true friendship. They are fully aware of the power of money but would rather not pursue an oppor-

tunity, even a lucrative one, if it means working with someone they do not respect. On the other hand, Scorpio-Sagittarians depend highly on their friends, of both sexes, and may be remarkably successful in doing business with those to whom they feel emotionally close, usually as partners or members of a team. They really see such associates as family.

Scorpio-Sagittarians are not the most stable of individuals in their romantic relationships. When they are young, their wildness and sense of adventure can lead them from one partner to another; meanwhile, of course, any commitment to a single deep relationship. Some Scorpio-Sagittarians may find a permanent mate necessary later in life, but this new setup may cause them to chafe at the bit, longing for the freedom they once knew. Others marry earlier but seek out a "modern" marriage, in which both spouses carry on their own lives more or less independently of each other. Spending a lot of time away from their partners guarantees Scorpio-Sagittarians the freedom they need with a minimum of jealousy and recrimination.

Lovers and mates of Scorpio-Sagittarians will testify to their highly sexual nature, which is not only passionate but also, to an extent, competitive and combative; those born on the Cusp of Revolution are confrontational in both work and play, and they do not leave this quality behind at the bedroom door. Scorpio-Sagittarians do have a sweet, affectionate side as well, but in their sexual contacts the carnal and ecstatic usually overshadow the soft and sensitive.

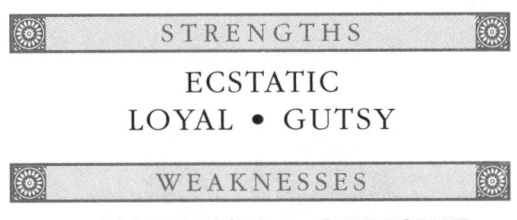

STRENGTHS

ECSTATIC
LOYAL • GUTSY

WEAKNESSES

AUTOCRATIC • DERISIVE
WILD

ADVICE:

Follow your vision of life but don't lose touch with where others are.
Keep your intentions honest and your motives pure. Develop the objectivity to stand back
and observe yourself living. Try to be more forgiving and less possessive.

SCORPIO-SAGITTARIUS CUSP NOTABLES

Robert Kennedy was only 35 years old when he took over the Justice Department as attorney general in 1961, appointed by his brother the president. Bobby quickly established himself as a force to be reckoned with. Somewhere between a working-class hero and an aristocrat in his sympathies and demeanor, Kennedy was

ROBERT KENNEDY

typical of many born on the Cusp of Revolution. In his political position, Bobby had a chance to make even more enemies than his brother John, both in the government and organized crime, but, like many Scorpio-Sagittarians, he thrived on conflict and challenge. Competitive, combative and uncompromising, Kennedy fought his way into the Democratic party leadership and the hearts of Americans as a feisty, intractable opponent of all that was unfair. Like his brother, he succumbed to an assassin's bullet.

Perhaps the most passionate and violent of Mexico's muralists, **Jose Orozco** expressed his feelings fearlessly. Like many born on the Cusp of Revolution, Orozco was not afraid to make his opinions known, and his mastery of the mural enabled him to make statements in a big way. Originally trained as an architect, Orozco changed direction and gave his life to painting, drawing, murals and printmaking. Scorpio-Sagittarians are feeling-intuitive types, and Orozco was no exception, giving very direct expression to his emo-

JOSE OROZCO

tional state. He played an extremely important role in the development of modern art in Mexico and through his dramatic murals was able to encourage its principles to be accepted by the general public.

NADINE GORDIMER

Winner of the Nobel Prize for literature in 1991, South African novelist **Nadine Gordimer** was witness and scribe of the events in her country under apartheid. She grew up in a South African mining town, the daughter of European Jewish immigrants. An important theme in her writing was the position of the European in Africa and how people like her own family were able to adjust to a totally new way of life. Born on the Cusp of Revolution, Gordimer sought to express her opposition to apartheid quietly, as an objective observer rather than an activist. Nonetheless, three of her novels were banned by the oppressive South African government. Her uncompromising stance in the face of authority marks her squarely as a Scorpio-Sagittarius.

More Scorpio-Sagittarians: Jodie Foster, Ahmad Rashad, Jamie Lee Curtis, Boris Becker, George Eliot, Charles DeGaulle, Veronica Hamel, Voltaire, Goldie Hawn, Ken Griffey, Jr., Harpo Marx, Andre Gide, Dr. John, Mariel Hemingway, Billy the Kid, Boris Karloff, Spinoza, Billie Jean King, Toulouse-Lautrec, Ted Turner, Marilyn French, Coleman Hawkins, Jeane Kirkpatrick.

Relationship Guide for Scorpio-Sagittarius Cusp

Ted Turner (Scorpio-Sagittarius Cusp)
Jane Fonda (Sagittarius-Capricorn Cusp)
Page 736

BEST RELATIONSHIPS

LOVE
Aries I
Aries III
Taurus III
Libra-Scorpio Cusp
Sagittarius-Capricorn Cusp
Capricorn III
Capricorn-Aquarius Cusp
Aquarius II

MARRIAGE
Taurus II
Cancer II
Scorpio I
Pisces II

FRIENDSHIP
Pisces-Aries Cusp
Aries-Taurus Cusp
Taurus I
Cancer-Leo Cusp
Leo III
Virgo II
Virgo-Libra Cusp
Scorpio III
Sagittarius I
Sagittarius II
Capricorn II
Aquarius III
Pisces I
Pisces III

FAMILY
Gemini I
Cancer I
Leo I
Leo-Virgo Cusp
Libra I

WORK
Gemini-Cancer Cusp
Cancer III
Virgo I
Virgo III
Libra II
Scorpio II
Sagittarius III
Capricorn I
Aquarius I

Page Locator for All Relationships

SAGITTARIUS I
The Week of Independence

November 25–December 2

The Sagittarius I period takes Independence as its central image. According to The Grand Cycle of Life, this period can be likened to the time, just following the second Saturn return at age fifty-six (see Scorpio-Sagittarius cusp), in which a desire for a new kind of independence manifests in the middle-aged adult. The emphasis here is on striking out on one's own, perhaps devoting more energy to oneself and a bit less to family or career. Joyfully embarking on a fresh path but building on areas of real interest from one's past is characteristic of this period.

The days that comprise Sagittarius I symbolically reveal a mature adult purposefully asserting an individualistic position, feeling renewed excitement in being alive, seeking more expansive horizons and perhaps relearning how to be alone (and enjoy it). All attempts to dampen or smother such impulses will be steadfastly resisted.

Sagittarius I's are hard to control. In many ways the most independent people of the year, those born in this week must feel free to act on their impulses and intuition. People who try to exercise power over them in personal relationships are in for a rough ride. When Sagittarius I's respect their spouse or living partner, they will cooperate, sharing their feelings and dividing the chores. When they feel that their respect has not been earned, though, or when it is lost, expect constant conflict and strife. Honor and trust are high on the Sagittarius I list of priorities; without these, they feel, life ceases to have meaning and reverts to the law of the jungle.

Sagittarius I's have a thing about fairness, expecting it

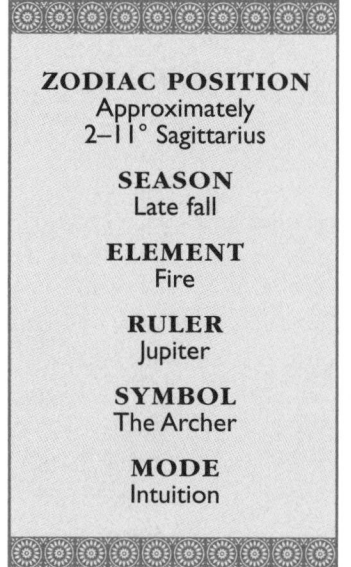

ZODIAC POSITION
Approximately
2–11° Sagittarius

SEASON
Late fall

ELEMENT
Fire

RULER
Jupiter

SYMBOL
The Archer

MODE
Intuition

not only of themselves but of others, too. Their nurturing side is particularly evident in their relations with animals, small children and the less fortunate members of society; they simply will not tolerate mistreatment of the dependent or helpless in their presence. They often act impulsively to protect the defenseless, without a thought for their own safety.

Those born in the Week of Independence try to project an air of self-assurance and confidence, but behind this facade there often lurks a sensitive and even insecure individual. This becomes quickly evident when they are put under stress, either through negative criticism or through some challenge to their character. In such situations Sagittarius I's can easily and instantaneously fly off the handle, drowning those around them with their anger. Those alert enough to see the storm clouds gathering will try to avoid unleashing the emotional thunderbolts of those born in this week.

Sagittarius I's have enormous willpower. The loyalty of Sagittarius I's is a matter not only of principle or of emotion but of stubbornness; sticking to their guns is a character trait. In fact, they very often get their way, simply because they allow no other possibility. Anyone deeply involved with a Sagittarius I is likely to know their highly competitive nature—winning is essential for those born in this week. Learning to submit, and to accept defeat graciously, is not usually possible for these dynamic individuals. Those few who do learn this lesson may have succeeded in meeting their greatest challenge, and thereby in gaining a high degree of maturity.

Sagittarius I's can be unreasonable, but they are usually open to discussion. Actually, these quick, witty individuals thoroughly enjoy verbal repartee and debate.

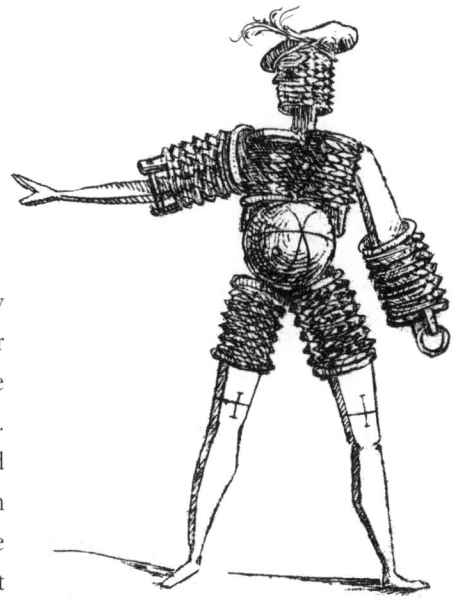

"INDEPENDENCE"

This can become a problem if they reach a subject that sticks in their craw, when they can easily become contentious and argumentative. Friends know what subjects to avoid and how to smooth over rough spots through playfulness, but those meeting Sagittarius I's for the first time are sometimes taken aback by their forthrightness and their at times outrageous observations and proposals.

Many born in the Week of Independence have a greater need to give than to receive. Their generosity is directly related to their feelings of self-worth and self-esteem, for they have a need to see themselves as caring rather than needy people. There are also Sagittarius I's who are not at all bashful about stating their demands, and who will not object to being served by others. Both character types, however, will often occupy an indispensable position in their family: shouldering substantial responsibilities, but on their own terms, is extremely important to them.

Sagittarius I's generally have only one or two people—whether friend, mate, co-worker or family member—with whom they feel close enough to share their innermost thoughts. The bond between Sagittarius I's and their parents or their children is extremely deep, and may be considered a true friendship. Such soulmates know those born in this week as highly ethical individuals who value integrity and character more than anything else, except, per-haps, their freedom. A Sagittarius I who feels betrayed by a family member or close friend can go through untold agonies of evaluation, judgment or rejection. In these struggles, assessing the intentions of the person in question is usually of great importance.

Those who want to spend time with Sagittarius I's usually have to be able to keep up with them: their friends and lovers must share the fast pace they set, whether in sports, travel, work or hobbies. A special person for a Sagittarius I, however, may also be someone who sticks close to home or place of business. Those born in this week have an acute need for stability; an individual who is always there to return to may prove to be the anchor in their lives. Although most Sagittarius I's would be capable of living alone, and in fact are well suited to it, they will generally make a firm decision to be a person's spouse or living partner and then continue in that role, even if they outgrow the need for it.

Sagittarius I's are ardent and unconstrained in their emotional expression, particularly in the sexual arena. They make the intensity of their energy fully apparent to their partners, who will remember vividly the full-bodied encounters in which these types engage. Sagittarius I's take pride in their sexual desirability or prowess, often exhibiting quiet confidence in their ability to satisfy their partners. They are extremely giving of their feelings but demand a great deal in return.

STRENGTHS

HONORABLE
INTUITIVE • RESPONSIBLE

WEAKNESSES

OVERCOMPETITIVE
IMPULSIVE • TEMPERAMENTAL

ADVICE:

Strive to keep your emotions on an even keel. Beware of allowing yourself an overly high-minded or high-handed attitude. Keep control over your expectations and try to be more forgiving. There is nothing wrong with compromise, or with occasionally losing. Watch your tendency to exaggerate.

SAGITTARIUS I NOTABLES

Actress, singer, comedienne and entertainer **Bette Midler** fits the Sagittarius I model perfectly, with her highly independent and outrageous nature. Although her first film, *The Rose*, in which she gave a virtuoso performance as a rock star, was a huge success, the failure of her second film, *Jinxed!*, almost finished off her career.

However, she came a long way from the early 80s with hits such as *Outrageous Fortune*, *Beaches*, and *The First Wives Club*. Born on the same day as Woody Allen (and thus both Sagittarius I's), she interacted hilariously, and uninterruptedly, with him in *Scenes from a Mall*.

BETTE MIDLER

From gag writer to comedian to actor, playwright and film director, **Woody Allen** has steadily evolved in an increasingly creative and authoritative direction. But he did it in his own way and always made one demand wherever he worked—that he be given as high a degree of Independence as possible. Although his Sagittarius I temperamental and impulsive nature has frequently worked against him, Allen's intuitions have been right on the mark enough times to guarantee his continuing success. His oscillations between serious and comic films have upset some viewers and critics who think he should stick to one or the other, but the level of his brilliance in his signature low-budget productions has given him a high degree of freedom to express his personal vision in a manner practically unparalleled in modern film.

Certainly the sexiest grandmother in the entertainment business, **Tina Turner** just doesn't slow down as the years go by. Tina suffered for many years on a personal level through an abusive marriage and, typical of many Sagittarius I's, through lack of a stable

TINA TURNER

force in her life. Since she turned to Buddhism in the 80s, she has established a rock-solid basis through chanting and meditation and a personal relationship that brings her a great deal of happiness. One of the most dynamic performers, Tina specializes in live concerts but won back-to-back Grammys 3 years in a row (1984-1986) for best Rock Vocal of the Year. In 1991 Turner was voted into the Rock and Roll Hall of Fame.

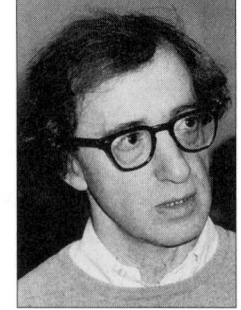

WOODY ALLEN

More Sagittarius I's: Winston Churchill, Maria Callas, Mark Twain, Mary Martin, Richard Pryor, Monica Seles, Jonathan Swift, Jimi Hendrix, Bruce Lee, Nikos Kazantzakis, William Blake, Randy Newman, Giovanna Fontana, Bruce Paltrow, David Mamet, Joe DiMaggio, Jacques Chirac, Adam Clayton Powell, Jr., Petra Kelly, Charles Ringling, Julie Harris, Clyfford Still, Dick Clark, Shirley Chisholm, Abbie Hoffman, Louisa May Alcott, Berry Gordy, C.S. Lewis, Friedrich Engels, Alexander Godunov, Caroline Kennedy, John F. Kennedy, Jr.

Relationship Guide for Sagittarius I

MARILYN MONROE (GEMINI I)
JOE DIMAGGIO (SAGITTARIUS I)
PAGE 424

BEST RELATIONSHIPS

LOVE
Taurus III
Gemini II
Cancer-Leo Cusp
Leo I
Leo III
Virgo III
Libra III
Sagittarius III
Aquarius II

MARRIAGE
Aries I
Aries II
Gemini III
Leo II
Leo-Virgo Cusp
Virgo-Libra Cusp
Libra-Scorpio Cusp
Scorpio II

FRIENDSHIP
Aries III
Taurus-Gemini Cusp
Gemini I
Gemini-Cancer Cusp
Cancer II
Virgo I
Libra I
Scorpio-Sagittarius Cusp
Capricorn-Aquarius Cusp
Pisces III

FAMILY
Taurus II
Virgo II
Sagittarius II
Sagittarius-Capricorn Cusp
Capricorn I
Aquarius I
Pisces II

WORK
Aries-Taurus Cusp
Cancer I
Scorpio III
Sagittarius I
Capricorn II
Aquarius III

Page Locator for All Relationships

SAGITTARIUS II
The Week of the Originator

December 3–10

The Sagittarius II period takes The Originator as its central image. This period can be compared in human terms to a time in middle age when independent impulses have paved the way for individual forms of expression. Ideally, at this juncture in life, a person can assert newfound feelings of newfound freedom in terms of inventive projects and original activities that reflect a truly unique and experienced outlook. The desire to let it all hang out reflects not only enthusiasm in being alive but also a lack of fearfulness regarding success or failure, winning or losing, even mortality.

The days that comprise Sagittarius II symbolically reveal a mature person having the courage to go for it in terms of simply being him/herself. A take-it-or-leave-it attitude, increased self-confidence and guts, and a minimum of self-consciousness and shame are typical of this period. Also, the courage to be transparent is characteristic here. Eccentricities and idiosyncrasies tend to manifest now which only intensify as old age approaches.

Sagittarius II's are different and are not afraid to show it. Among the more unusual people of the year, even the most apparently normal of them may come to seem a tad peculiar once you get to know them better. They rarely consider doing anything in any way but their own. It would be one thing if they were content with being different, but they usually expect others to understand them somehow. In consequence, Sagittarius I's commonly encounter rejection, which they must learn to handle without becoming frustrated or bitter. They usually become dependent on one or two close

ZODIAC POSITION
Approximately
10–19° Sagittarius

SEASON
Late fall

ELEMENT
Fire

RULER
Jupiter

SYMBOL
The Archer

MODE
Intuition

friends or family members for acceptance and emotional support.

Sagittarius II's need to realize that by taking the path of least resistance they will arouse the least opposition. Unusual occupations or co-workers will allow them to work in a way more suited to their idiosyncrasies. Many success-oriented Sagittarius II's will push to get ahead and rise to the top at any cost; this may be a result of their tremendous need to be accepted. Strangely enough, it is often only when the unpredictable individuals born in this week forget about success that they suddenly achieve it—as if by accident.

The most successful of those born in the Week of the Originator are those who can cash in on their own wacky way of seeing and doing things. True, some Sagittarius II's can get mired in frustration and self-pity, and may find their friends teasing them with jokes about their weirdness or strangeness; but for the most part they are proud of who they are, although perhaps unable to explain how they got that way. Even so, those born in this week have escapist tendencies, often feeling impelled to retreat or even flee from the problems and exigencies of everyday life. The danger that they will involve themselves in questionable activities or drug states is high, and an ever-present threat to their physical and mental health.

Those born in this week are often clever—good with their hands, quick with their minds, technically proficient in their principal pursuit. Whatever their eccentricities, success can be theirs for the asking. Their talents may lead them into overconfidence, however, and by overestimating their faculties and abilities they can slip and fall. They can be slow to learn this lesson. In fact

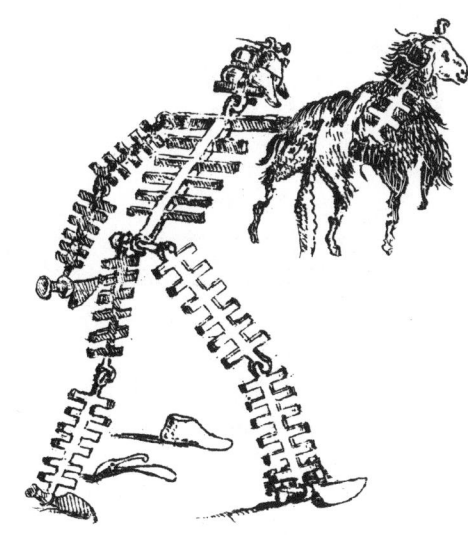

"ORIGINATOR"

becoming more realistic about themselves and the world around them is generally a struggle for Sagittarius II's, who often take on too many activities at once, and occasionally the wrong ones. A good working relationship as a member of a team, or perhaps the reliability of a practical business partner, may serve to ground and direct their energies, keeping them from becoming scattered.

This week sports its share of expressive and exhibitionistic individuals. Perhaps out of an inner drive to show people who they really are, Sagittarius II's can sometimes let aggression run riot, whether it be territorial, intellectual, sexual or emotional. Perhaps the greatest need of those born in this week is to turn some of their outwardly directed energy inward, and to develop their spiritual side. They will also benefit by seeking to understand others better, particularly by listening, and to expand their circle of friends and acquaintances. Engagement in humanitarian pursuits or community projects will help them to normalize their relations with their fellow human beings.

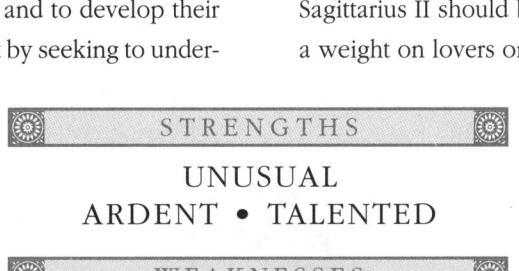

STRENGTHS

UNUSUAL
ARDENT • TALENTED

WEAKNESSES

PECULIAR • IRRESPONSIBLE
REJECTED

may experience more than average disappointment in romantic relationships; a common scenario involves idolizing someone who does not return their enthusiasm. A number of rejection notices from several different addresses may be necessary to make them more realistic about their feelings and choices. When they do meet someone who will love and understand them, their first response may be to push this person away, perhaps in disbelief. Once a bond of trust is formed, however, and particularly if that process has been long and difficult, Sagittarius II's may become emotionally fixated and clinging. Depending on the depth of the love felt, the other person can get nervous, and back off in fear. The Sagittarius II should be wary, then, of laying too heavy a weight on lovers or friends, and particularly of trying to convince them that they are the "only one who understands"—a burden that is almost certain to be counterproductive to the relationship.

Sagittarius II's have an intensely physical side that cries out for satisfaction. Because they tend to give themselves fully to their experiences, they make ardent lovers and appreciative mates and friends. Often extremely attractive, either in their person or their personality, those born in this week can be true heartbreakers. Yet their equally strong tendency to act irresponsibly or destructively may finally lead even the most patient of lovers to break up with them.

In general, Sagittarius II's will save themselves and others a great deal of agony by seeking out people who will appreciate their uniqueness and avoiding the effort to impress or be accepted by those who will not. This is true of both marriage and business partners. Those born in this week are liable to give their all for love, and sometimes to get hurt in the process. When young, they

ADVICE:

Try to get out a bit more and do what others do from time to time. Don't drive yourself into a corner by believing that no one can understand you. Make an effort to let others into your private world. Resist turning off to life: keep things fresh and renew your commitment.

SAGITTARIUS II NOTABLES

The art of cartoon animation in America is synonymous with the name **Walt Disney**. Although today Disney refers to a gigantic entertainment empire, it all began with Walt at the drawing board, as the Originator of Mickey Mouse, Donald Duck and friends. Disney created the first feature-length cartoon, *Snow White and the Seven Dwarfs*, which had flawless synchronized sound. *Pinocchio, Dumbo, Bambi, Lady and the Tramp* and many other animated features followed. Giving a whole new spin to the archetypes of the collective unconscious, the Disney characters provided material that filled the dreams of American kids. Perhaps Disney's greatest artistic success was *Fantasia*, which featured both abstract and story-line visual creations inspired by and synched to Leopold Stokowski's performances of Stravinsky and other classical composers.

WALT DISNEY

A recluse for many of her days, few in the village of Amherst, Mass., knew that **Emily Dickinson** wrote poetry. Regarded as the outstanding American woman poet, it is a bit shocking that almost all her poems were unpublished in her lifetime and completely unknown for years after her death. The peculiar nature and escapist tendencies of Sagittarius II's were magnified in Dickinson, but so was the unique creative expression that made her a true Originator. Preferring to live alone and never marry, Dickinson had secret relationships

EMILY DICKINSON

with three men in her life, the last of which, a Philadelphia clergyman named Charles Wadsworth, fanned the sleeping embers of her creativity to full flame.

Russian Expressionist painter, teacher and theorist **Wassily Kandinsky** characterized the kind of creative originality associated with the Sagittarius II period. Meeting the great challenge of those born in the Week of the Originator, Kandinsky was also able to turn much of his outwardly directed energy inward and develop his spiritual side, the fruits of which may be seen in his great work *On the Spiritual in Art*. A founding partner of the Blue Rider School with Franz Marc, Kandinsky was the leading spokesman for Expressionism for most of his life. In fact, some experts credit him as the most important figure in the formulation of nonfigurative, abstract and geometrical painting in modern art.

WASSILY KANDINSKY

More Sagittarius II's: Kenneth Branagh, Joan Didion, Jean-Luc Godard, Katarina Witt, Joseph Conrad, Sinead O'Connor, David Carradine, Kirk Douglas, John Malkovich, Jim Morrison, Redd Foxx, Joan Armatrading, T.V. Soong, Lillian Russell, Tom Waits, Little Richard, Francisco Franco, Larry Bird, Anton Webern, Fritz Lang, George Custer, Ira Gershwin, Dave Brubeck, Sammy Davis, Jr., John Cassavetes, Dorothy Lamour, James Galway, Kim Basinger, Willa Cather.

Relationship Guide for Sagittarius II

MAGIC JOHNSON (LEO III)
LARRY BIRD (SAGITTARIUS II)
PAGE 592

BEST RELATIONSHIPS

LOVE
Taurus II
Cancer I
Cancer III
Leo-Virgo Cusp
Virgo I
Virgo II
Libra II
Scorpio III
Aquarius III
Pisces I
Pisces III

MARRIAGE
Taurus I
Gemini I
Cancer II
Leo II
Libra III
Aquarius-Pisces Cusp
Pisces II

FRIENDSHIP
Pisces-Aries Cusp
Aries I
Aries II
Gemini II
Cancer-Leo Cusp
Leo III
Virgo III
Scorpio II
Scorpio-Sagittarius Cusp
Sagittarius III
Capricorn I

FAMILY
Gemini-Cancer Cusp
Leo I
Libra I
Sagittarius I
Sagittarius II
Capricorn III

WORK
Taurus III
Gemini III
Scorpio I
Capricorn II
Aquarius II

Page Locator for All Relationships

SAGITTARIUS III
The Week of the Titan

December 11–18

The Sagittarius III period takes The Titan as its central image. This period can be likened in human terms to the years of a person's early sixties, when, for many, retirement is just in sight (or already begun), and those who have asserted newfound freedoms seek to expand their horizons. At this time plans are often made for the coming years that reshape financial priorities, meet the challenge of filling in larger blocks of leisure time and allow the individual to follow highly imaginative and creative pursuits.

The days that comprise Sagittarius III symbolically reveal a mature person growing more attentive to physical considerations, and having time to perfect hobbies and avocational projects but also to soar imaginatively with all kinds of expansive thoughts and activities. For the first time since adolescence and young adulthood, many individuals feel free enough to make major choices that will shape their personal future.

Born in the Week of the Titan, Sagittarius III's think on a grand scale. Their minds are usually geared to big projects, whether planning a family get-together or mapping out a business strategy. Disliking pettiness in all forms, they see the total picture first, and generally avoid getting hung up on the details. Sagittarius III's are big-hearted, and give shamelessly, but are realistic enough to expect something in return.

Sagittarius III's reach for the stars, but they keep both feet solidly on the ground. Their ambitions and aspirations are firmly rooted in the here and now. Whether small or large of frame, they are physically imposing, and make their presence felt in any gathering. The persona

ZODIAC POSITION
Approximately
18–27° Sagittarius

SEASON
Late fall

ELEMENT
Fire

RULER
Jupiter

SYMBOL
The Archer

MODE
Intuition

they project is big, and hard to take in all at once. This feeling that they are difficult to walk around can also extend to the sense that they can't easily be gotten out of the way—can't be bamboozled by airy schemes or faulty reasoning. Those personally involved with these powerful individuals will inevitably have to reckon with playing a subordinate role.

It can be dangerous to come between Sagittarius III's and their goals, for once they have made up their mind they move with lightning speed. Their friends and family learn soon enough what a given mood foretells—quiet or action. The people who get along best with them try to read their emotional weather report at the beginning of the day, for it may well determine the outcome of any project at the day's end. The more disturbing aspects of Sagittarius III's may have to be overlooked or ignored in the cause of group harmony and effective action.

There are moody and disturbing elements to the Sagittarius III personality that may strain living and working relationships. If Week of the Titan people are depressed, they are hard to budge. They often internalize external pressures and may, in consequence, exhibit chronic (rather than acute) physical and mental symptoms. Those close to them will eventually have to try to cheer them up, or get them to take a more positive view of their lives, but often to no avail—for Sagittarius III's actually find these dark moods an essential way of withdrawing from the world to chew things over. Extremely thoughtful, they can ruminate over a problem or plan for weeks or months before finally coming up with a solution. In this activity they are best left alone.

Since the emotions of Sagittarius III's come from a

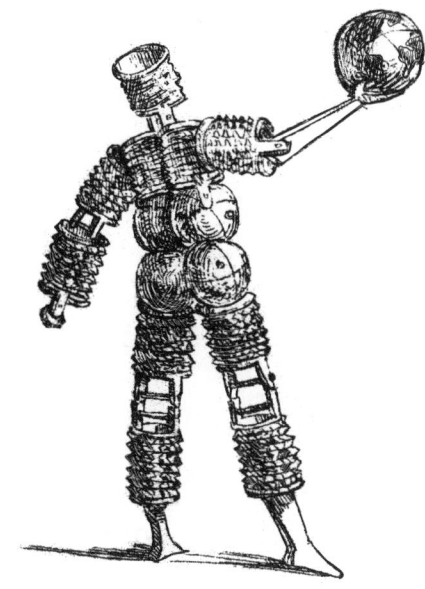

"TITAN"

very deep place, their eruptions of feeling can be nothing short of volcanic. It is extremely important, then, that they spend time with people who are sympathetic to them, and with whom they can periodically unburden themselves by discussing whatever is on their mind. Like a pressure cooker, smoldering crater or grinding tectonic plate, they need to let energy loose in small doses if they are to avoid being shaken apart by the "big one." Complaining is actually healthy for those born in this week, and those who understand them welcome their occasional fussing and grumbling; the alternative is a good deal worse.

Those born in this week are drawn to magical and ecstatic experiences, not only in their personal lives but also in their careers. What basically attracts them, after all, is the impossible challenge, and they love to pull off miracles both minor and major before their astonished colleagues' eyes. Yet these Titans cannot be called competitive, since there seems to be so little to fear from their fortified citadels that no real competition is possible. That outlook may seem egotistical, but it gives some idea of the self-confidence and assurance of Sagittarius III's.

And yet, behind the massive bulwark of their personality, somewhere in a remote back passage lurks insecurity. This is their greatest enemy. A wee voice still murmurs from time to time, Are you really as rock-solid as you seem? The answer, of course, is no, but the world is usually fooled until a crack appears in the Mount Rushmore–like facade. Everyone has some kind of insecurity, of course, so it should come as no surprise that Sagittarius III's do, too; what is important, however, is their inability to recognize or deal with it. This lack of self-awareness may be the high price they pay for their peace of mind.

The most successful lovers and mates of those born in the Week of the Titan are often those who can weave a magical spell around them, after first lulling them into letting their guard down. Sagittarius III's actually enjoy being enchanted by those very special individuals who can lighten their ponderous workload or their crushing personal responsibilities. The mates of Sagittarius III's will benefit from their protective and capable ways but can also come to feel imprisoned, and may chafe under the feeling that the full expression of their own talents and abilities is denied.

Sagittarius III's are so focused and single-minded by nature that there is usually little difficulty in distinguishing between their desires and their needs, which are in some cases identical. Those emotionally involved with them know what they demand, and usually face only one decision—comply or resist. Negotiation or compromise is not in the picture. Still, like the giant in a fairy tale, Sagittarius III's can be fooled, often without finding out about it until later.

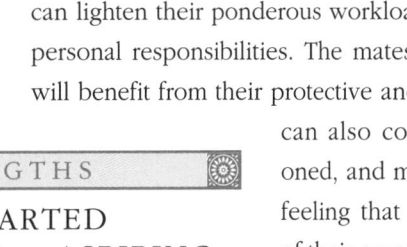

STRENGTHS

BIG-HEARTED
SELF-ASSURED • ASPIRING

WEAKNESSES

SELF-UNAWARE
SECRETLY INSECURE • FUSSY

ADVICE:

Learn to enjoy the little things, the simple pleasures of life. Try to be more understanding of others. Apply your ethical standards to yourself and concentrate more of your energies on personal growth. Find a way to blend in when necessary and avoid ruffling feathers.

SAGITTARIUS III NOTABLES

The giant of post–WWII Russian literature, **Alexander Solzhenitsyn** presents a titanic view of Soviet Russia and, in particular, of Stalin's brutal system of camps known as the Gulag, in which untold millions died. Imprisoned for years himself, Solzhenitsyn wrote directly from his own experience. After recovering from

ALEXANDER
SOLZHENITSYN

cancer, Solzhenitsyn wrote *Cancer Ward*, which brought him great literary acclaim, and he won the Nobel Prize for literature in 1970. His largest works are *August 1914* and the mammoth *Gulag Archipelago*, for which he was banished from the Soviet Union. After living on a farm in Vermont, he was allowed to return to his

homeland following the overthrow of communism.

Epic, blockbuster, gargantuan—all describe the nature of the mammoth film productions of **Steven Spielberg**. Seeing things in the expansive Sagittarian manner does not preclude an eye for detail, however Spielberg is also a meticulous craftsman. Although he is a master at manipulating his audiences into believing the unbelievable, Spielberg can also deal masterfully with factual and historical material, as in the black-and-white masterpiece *Schindler's List*, which won seven Oscars. Nonetheless, it is probably for his fantasy films *E.T.*, the *Indiana Jones* series, *Close Encounters of the Third Kind* and *Jurassic Park* that this highest- grossing

STEVEN SPIELBERG

director and producer of all time will be most fondly remembered. His latest commercial venture, DreamWorks, will no doubt serve as a vehicle for his ever-expanding vision.

LIV ULLMANN

Norwegian stage and film actress **Liv Ullmann** was brought to worldwide attention by Ingmar Bergman, who starred her in several of his most important films. She lived with Bergman, described in her book *Choices,* published after she liberated herself from his tyrannical control and emerged as an individual in her own right. Physically imposing on the screen, Ullmann's moods and deep emotions are characteristic of those born in the Week of the Titan. She is able to portray a variety of states, from deep meditative contemplation to frightening psychological imbalance. Born on the birthday of Beethoven, Ullmann shares his affinity for the long line and monumental effort.

More Sagittarius III's: Beethoven, Frank Sinatra, Helen Frankenthaler, Gustave Flaubert, Dick Van Dyke, Arthur C. Clarke, Margaret Mead, William Safire, Arthur Fiedler, Michael Ovitz, Teri Garr, Fiorello LaGuardia, Carlo Ponti, Dionne Warwick, Emerson Fittipaldi, Edward G. Robinson, J. Paul Getty, Noel Coward.

Relationship Guide for Sagittarius III

FRANK SINATRA (SAGITTARIUS III)
AVA GARDNER
(SAGITTARIUS-CAPRICORN CUSP)
PAGE 757

BEST
<u>RELATIONSHIPS</u>

LOVE
Aries II
Gemini I
Gemini-Cancer Cusp
Cancer-Leo Cusp
Virgo-Libra Cusp
Sagittarius I
Sagittarius-Capricorn Cusp
Capricorn II

MARRIAGE
Aries III
Cancer I
Leo I
Virgo I
Libra-Scorpio Cusp
Scorpio II
Scorpio III
Capricorn I
Aquarius I

FRIENDSHIP
Pisces-Aries Cusp
Gemini III
Cancer III
Libra I
Libra II
Sagittarius II
Aquarius III
Pisces II
Pisces III

FAMILY
Taurus-Gemini Cusp
Leo-Virgo Cusp
Libra III
Scorpio I
Pisces I

WORK
Taurus II
Gemini II
Cancer II
Leo III
Virgo III
Scorpio-Sagittarius Cusp
Sagittarius III
Capricorn III
Aquarius II

Page Locator for All Relationships

SAGITTARIUS-CAPRICORN CUSP
The Cusp of Prophecy

December 19–25

The Sagittarius-Capricorn cusp can be symbolically likened to the period around sixty-three years of age in the human life and also marks the beginning of winter in the northern hemisphere. During this period most of the land lies fallow, some animals go into hibernation, the winds blow cold, and on the winter solstice, the night is longer and the day shorter than at any other time in the year. This is the time at which druids at Stonehenge made astronomical observations and prophecies, and when fortunes were often cast. Indeed the Sagittarius-Capricorn cusp may be said to represent Prophecy.

In human development, at this juncture in life, middle age is drawing to a close and old age is about to begin. The emerging elder must face a time when traditionally his/her usefulness to the material world has lessened. However, the individual's usefulness in the spiritual sense may increase greatly, as a mentor and inspiration to others. The days that comprise this cusp exemplify some of the manifestations of Prophecy (using wisdom to look into the future), where the visionary, intuitive Sagittarius nature combines with the pragmatic, empirical nature of Capricorn.

Sagittarius-Capricorns are influenced by both the planet Jupiter (ruler of fiery Sagittarius) and Saturn (ruler of earthy Capricorn). The energies of these two planets are diametrically opposed: Jupiter stands for expansion, jollity and optimism, Saturn for contraction, seriousness and realism. A kind of push-pull effect is at work in the personalities of the unusual individuals born on this cusp—they may want to have fun, for example (Jupiter) but be too serious to do so (Saturn). Conversely, on another occasion, they may set out to buckle down to the job at hand

ZODIAC POSITION
Approximately
26° Sagittarius–
4° Capricorn

SEASONS
Late fall/Early winter
(solstice)

ELEMENTS
Fire/Earth

RULERS
Jupiter/Saturn

SYMBOLS
The Archer/The Goat

MODES
Intuition/Sensation

(Saturn) but be lured by a new horizon (Jupiter). The more successful Sagittarius-Capricorns are able to integrate both these influences in their personalities.

The fiery and earthy natures of Sagittarius-Capricorns speak of highly developed faculties of intuition and sensation, respectively, but do not necessarily point to either a strong mental or a strong emotional orientation. Those born on this cusp are consequently at their best when trusting their hunches and their five senses, particularly sight and hearing. Their articulation and expression of their thoughts and feelings may be more problematical. Ultimately, the development of extrasensory abilities, or even a single sixth sense, is often the most unique and remarkable quality that those born on the Cusp of Prophecy can offer to the world.

Masters of the art of silence, those born on the Sagittarius-Capricorn Cusp have no need for speech to get their point across. It is often hard for them to get what they have to say into writing, or express it over the phone, and they may consequently feel that they have to deliver their messages in person. Whether happy, seductive, threatening or punishing, Sagittarius-Capricorns make their moods known very unambiguously, leaving little if any doubt about how they feel.

Those born on this cusp are at their best when they are confident of their powers but at the same time kind and understanding to others. They are at their worst when they feel self-pity, usually a result of worldly failure or of personal rejection. In some Sagittarius-Capricorns, feelings of hurt or frustration about something they are convinced they can do nothing about are psychologically gratifying, relieving them of the responsibility of taking

"PROPHECY"

positive action. In others, a militant attitude may be engendered when suppressed feelings burst forth and cause trauma. Put to a positive use, however, such energies can achieve creative and remarkable results.

Cassandra-like, those born on the Cusp of Prophecy do not expect to be liked by other people, although it often happens that they are. Being independent of the approval of others gives Sagittarius-Capricorns a power and freedom that many lack. On the other side of the coin, they may themselves like few of the people they meet, and may thus be seen as antisocial. There is generally speaking only one requirement for being a close friend to a Sagittarius-Capricorn, besides the fact that you like them: you must accept them without reservation for what they really are. Those born on this cusp have their antennae out to detect when others are flattering them or simply being polite, which doesn't cut the cake. Consequently, only a few individuals manage to get close to most Sagittarius-Capricorns.

For some Sagittarius-Capricorns there is a danger in all this, namely that, like children, they will repeat the somewhat exaggerated words "No one likes me" and will set up this motto as a self-fulfilling prophecy. They can make it come true by neglecting their physical appearance or, as adolescents, by being unresponsive. Many teenagers born on the Cusp of Prophecy appear quite introverted, and those who are more extroverted may have a greater need for recognition and approval—or, perversely, for

rejection. Most often it is actions rather than words that are so outrageously expressed.

Those born on the Cusp of Prophecy may have rough childhoods due to conflicts with their parents, most often with the parent of the same sex. They themselves can make attentive and generous parents, but some run the risk, through identification, of making precisely the same mistakes their own parents did. Strong ties with siblings or other family members often carry over into adult life, however, and the success of these fraternal bonds may make those born in this week very comfortable relating to those younger than themselves as equals.

The deep, passionate natures and highly sexual orientation of those born on this cusp can bind others to them magnetically. Friends and lovers of certain Sagittarius-Capricorns understand their need to be alone, and often gain great satisfaction from sharing a private or secluded life with them. Partners of the more outgoing Sagittarius-Capricorns, on the other hand, often provide a link between them and the world, and bring them out of their shell. The joy gained in watching a Sagittarius-Capricorn bloom socially may be considerable. Only one warning: there is always a chance that, Pygmalion-like, the partner who goes to this effort may finally be rejected when the Sagittarius-Capricorn "fair lady" (or gentleman) comes down off her or his pedestal and says good-bye.

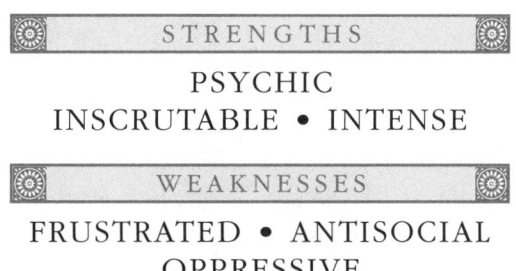

STRENGTHS

PSYCHIC
INSCRUTABLE • INTENSE

WEAKNESSES

FRUSTRATED • ANTISOCIAL
OPPRESSIVE

ADVICE:

*Learn to temper your intensity. By understanding yourself better,
you will be less at the mercy of your moods. Work on improving social relationships
and continue to befriend others. Beware of any tendencies to close yourself off.
Allow your warm and loving side full rein and keep your heart open.*

SAGITTARIUS-CAPRICORN CUSP NOTABLES

Like many born on the Sagittarius-Capricorn cusp, **Florence Griffith-Joyner** did not need speech to get her message across but did it in a convincing physical

manner. Winner of an incredible 3 gold and 1 silver medals at the 1988 Olympics, world record-holder Joyner impressed people as much with her beauty, grace and style as with her speed. Sharing the spotlight with her Olympic champion husband and sister-in-law, Al and Jackie Joyner-Kersee, has brought tremendous satisfaction to all concerned. The Florence Griffith-Joyner Youth Foundation has been set up to give disadvantaged young people opportunities denied to Florence when she was growing up in Los Angeles.

FLORENCE
GRIFFITH-JOYNER

The Israeli psychic **Uri Geller** is the first of his profession to teach some of his secrets to the public at large and to encourage them, particularly children, to develop their own psychic abilities. Born on the Cusp of Prophecy, Geller not only predicts and influences the future but believes that if children could be taught in school to trust their psychic intuitions more, the future could be very different from the present. Geller's widely publicized paranormal abilities include not only his legendary bending of spoons but also the undeniable gift to describe covered drawings at a distance and to move

URI GELLER

objects. A devoted family man, his Sagittarius-Capricorn qualities are a mixture of the fun-loving and the serious elements of life.

French songwriter and *chansonnier* **Edith Piaf** led a tragedy-filled life. Born in a bordello and blinded by meningitis as a child, brought a depth of expression to her art perhaps unsurpassed in French popular music. Her

EDITH PIAF

peculiar blend of an earthy and fiery nature identifies her as a typical Sagittarius-Capricorn. Sorrow seemed to be her lot in life, for aside from other disappointments in her personal life, she lost her lover, boxer Marcel Cerdan, in a plane crash. Although she first became famous for her nightclub performances, she later appeared on the international scene in films and recordings. Her most famous hit was *La vie en rose*, which became her trademark song.

More Sagittarius-Capricorns: Joseph Stalin, Cosima Liszt, Nostradamus, Sissy Spacek, Diane Sawyer, Ismael Merchant, Cicely Tyson, Kiefer Sutherland, Frank Zappa, Jane Fonda, Bobby Colomby, Lila Bell Wallace, Jean Genet, Edith Piaf, Richard Leakey, Lady Bird Johnson, Robert Bly, Joseph Smith, Leadbelly, Howard Hughes, Ava Gardner, Clara Barton, Rod Serling, Ricky Henderson, Larry Csonka, Annie Lennox, Helena Rubinstein, Anwar Sadat.

Relationship Guide for Sagittarius-Capricorn Cusp

JACKIE ROBINSON (AQUARIUS II)
BRANCH RICKEY
(SAGITTARIUS-CAPRICORN CUSP)
PAGE 766

BEST RELATIONSHIPS

LOVE
Pisces-Aries Cusp
Taurus-Gemini Cusp
Gemini III
Leo III
Libra II
Scorpio-Sagittarius Cusp
Sagittarius III
Capricorn III
Aquarius I
Aquarius III
Pisces III

MARRIAGE
Gemini-Cancer Cusp
Cancer III
Libra III
Scorpio III
Sagittarius I
Capricorn II
Aquarius II

FRIENDSHIP
Aries II
Taurus I
Gemini I
Cancer I
Cancer-Leo Cusp
Leo-Virgo Cusp
Virgo II
Scorpio I
Sagittarius-Capricorn Cusp
Pisces II

FAMILY
Aries-Taurus Cusp
Taurus II
Gemini II
Cancer II
Libra I

WORK
Aries III
Leo I
Leo II
Virgo I
Virgo-Libra Cusp
Libra-Scorpio Cusp
Scorpio II

Page Locator for All Relationships

CAPRICORN I
The Week of the Ruler

December 26–January 2

The Capricorn I period takes The Ruler as its central image. According to The Grand Cycle of Life, this period corresponds to the human age when most people prepare to retire from the working world. The emphasis here is on taking control of one's life, making decisions about one's day-to-day activities without career restraints. Those who choose to continue their careers may do so with a greater feeling of control and autonomy. As elders, those of this age may exert a kind of rulership in family matters, assuming a patriarchal or matriarchal role.

The days that comprise Capricorn I symbolically reveal the elder displaying survival toughness, taking command, finding new areas of service, and deepening aesthetic and spiritual interests.

Highly dependable, Capricorn I's are able to assume many of the responsibilities of daily life without complaint. Not necessarily leaders, they often assume the position of ruler by default, or take over because they can't bear to watch the way others are running things. Ruling their family, business, department or social organization is their forte, and they are excellent at delegating responsibility and seeing that things run smoothly, to the mutual advantage of all concerned.

To unseat a Capricorn I from any executive position is extremely difficult. Indeed, when those born in the Week of the Ruler give up their authority because of ill health, say, or are forced to step down due to allegations of mistakes, personality clashes or a need for younger blood, they take it pretty hard. Dealing with loss of face, status and power is generally the most difficult challenge they face.

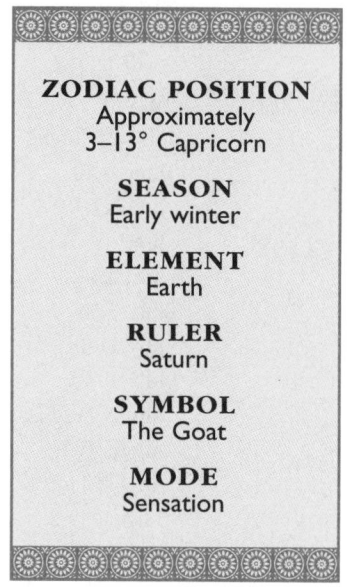

ZODIAC POSITION
Approximately
3–13° Capricorn

SEASON
Early winter

ELEMENT
Earth

RULER
Saturn

SYMBOL
The Goat

MODE
Sensation

When Capricorn I's speak, they expect others to listen. They are often authoritarian types, and their high opinions of themselves and of their ideas may, in extreme cases, approach a belief in their own infallibility. Even if their spouse is an accepting or submissive person, they may have problems with children and other family members who will not endure their strictness and dogma so readily. Indeed, conflicts and rebelliousness may rage out of hand in their families, with the Capricorn I's setting ironclad rules, issuing ultimatums, uttering threats and generally making daily life difficult for children or relatives who simply do not agree with them. Capricorn I's can make powerful weapons out of guilt and shame.

Many Capricorn I's, of course, are not tyrants at all, and exert highly positive influences on their families through their insistence on structure and on accepting personal responsibility. Even so, not all mates are willing to accept Capricorn I rule, and the best solutions are often those in which each partner has his or her own domain. The pragmatic side of those born in this week allows them to see the value of such a division of labor. In addition, the recurring power struggles that feature in some Capricorn I families are replaced in others by the stimulating exchanges of ideas that develop when each partner makes suggestions about the other's work. There is usually a limit, however, to the amount of debate a Capricorn I will tolerate, and they will not usually submit to criticism of their basic principles.

Ultimately, those born in the Week of the Ruler are even more attached to ideologies and ethics than to common sense. Thus they may occasionally lose touch with those around them. Even long-standing friendships

"RULER"

can collapse overnight if Capricorn I's feel their morals have been breached, or they confront financial irresponsibility or outright underhandedness. They also subject their love relationships to similarly rigorous standards of trust and honesty.

Money is generally very important to Capricorn I's, who know its power and how to put it to work. Shrewd calculators, they can have an instinct for turning a profit. These are the people you want to have around to analyze the deficiencies of a failed company, or to get a bankruptcy back in the black. Reorganizers, Capricorn I's have a special genius for improving the efficiency of any group, whether social or business. Yet their honesty and sense of fairness may undercut their own ambitions by hindering them from reaching the top of their profession. This might not be a problem if Capricorn I's weren't ambitious. They are, however, and consequently are often caught in a bind. Many born in this week find a comfortable career niche for themselves and stay there. Thus they too often settle for second best, much to the frustration of their family and friends, who know what their talents are.

Acceptance does not come easily to Capricorn I's. It is not that they are bigoted or prejudiced—quite the contrary. Capricorn I's are admirable in their willingness to oppose injustice fearlessly. Overall, they have a very healthy respect for tradition; they are more oriented toward making improvements in a given system than in tearing it down. Rarely will they reject a time-tested solu-

tion. Yet they also keep abreast of all the latest developments in society or their professional field.

Despite all this, the people born in the Week of the Ruler may have a hard time being open to the individuality of those close to them. Stern taskmasters, Capricorn I's may expect their mates and children to understand that there is only one way to be. Too often, that way is simply the Capricorn I way. In fairness, however, their viewpoint is seldom arbitrary; most often it reflects values of hard work and excellence of achievement. Capricorn I's have workaholic tendencies, and expect others to work at least as hard as they do. Goofing off, cowardice, low morals and laziness are the four sins that those born in this week would condemn most emphatically.

Emotional expression does not come easily to those born in this week; often creatures of deep feeling, they can get all wrapped up inside a cocoon of repressed emotion. Since love relationships are a direct means of liberating such feelings, their mates and lovers may be indispensable for their mental and physical health.

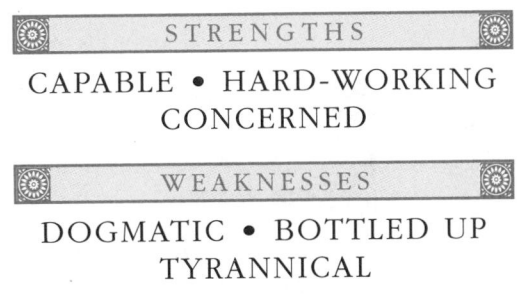

STRENGTHS

CAPABLE • HARD-WORKING
CONCERNED

WEAKNESSES

DOGMATIC • BOTTLED UP
TYRANNICAL

Capricorn I's are usually extremely faithful—they may be tempted to stray from their primary relationship, but they generally choose to stay. Although not overly sentimental, they can be quite affectionate, and they often sublimate more passionate drives into feelings of friendship for dear ones. Associates of those born in this week know them as caring, concerned and trustworthy individuals.

ADVICE:

Let others take the lead more often. You may be wise, but remember that wise men learn more from fools than fools from wise men. Work hard at trying to admit mistakes when you make them. There is no particular merit in holding on to an outworn creed or outdated idea.

CAPRICORN I NOTABLES

Impeccably trained at the drama school of Max Reinhardt and the Berlin Music School, German actress and singer **Marlene Dietrich** became an overnight international hit after her legendary film appearance in *The Blue Angel.* A seductive vamp, and a dangerous one, her role in the film draws on Dietrich's Capricorn I pow-

MARLENE DIETRICH

er and her imperious, strict and coldly-detached manner. Ironically, Dietrich, who had been offered a lot of money by Hitler to make Nazi films, wound up entertaining American troops during WWII, in a kind of hardheaded retaliation typical of one born in the Week of the Ruler. Sexy and highly intel-

ligent, Dietrich acted in American films for some of the greatest directors and opposite the leading actors of her day.

The life of American writer **Henry Miller** can be divided into three parts, according to where he lived—New York, Paris, California. In each of these settings Capricorn I Miller did not really change a lot from his normal dogmatic and crusty self, but his viewpoints about life and his writing did. For the early *Tropic of Cancer* and *Tropic of Capricorn* he was accused of being a degenerate, and in the later *Big Sur* and *Oranges of Hieronymus Bosch,* he sounds more like a flower child. In all his work his lust for life and strong command of the language are evident. Many of his works were banned for years as

HENRY MILLER

obscene and could only be obtained with some difficulty.

Born in the Week of the Ruler, **Mao Zedong** was chairman of the People's Republic of China from 1946, when he drove Chiang Kai-shek's armies from the mainland, until his death in 1976. As a young man of 18, Mao joined the revolution against the Manchu

MAO ZEDONG

Dynasty and in 1921 took part in forming the Chinese Communist party. His Capricorn I patience and toughness was evident in the 6,000-mile Long March to Shensi Province, where the Red Army could regroup against their enemies. For the last 30 years of his life, Mao strove to implement his social ideas, culminating in the Cultural Revolution, in which all opposition, real or imagined, was ruthlessly stamped out. The tenets of Maoism were distributed throughout the world in the form of the Little Red Book.

More Capricorn I's: Henri Matisse, Diane von Furstenberg, Louis Pasteur, Denzel Washington, Anthony Hopkins, Carlton Fisk, Mike Nesmith, Ted Danson, Madame de Pompadour, Tracey Ullman, Isaac Asimov, Patti Smith, Bo Diddley, Davy Jones, Ray Knight, Gelsey Kirkland, Peter Quaife, Paul Bowles, Lee Salk, Pablo Casals, Mary Tyler Moore, William H. Masters, Gerard Depardieu, Maggie Smith, Donna Summer, John Denver, Betsy Ross, Paul Revere.

Relationship Guide for Capricorn I

VIRGINIA JOHNSON (AQUARIUS III)
WILLIAM MASTERS (CAPRICORN I)
PAGE 772

BEST RELATIONSHIPS

LOVE
Taurus II
Taurus III
Gemini II
Virgo II
Scorpio III
Aquarius II

MARRIAGE
Taurus I
Gemini I
Leo I
Virgo I
Libra I
Libra III
Libra-Scorpio Cusp
Sagittarius III
Capricorn I
Aquarius I
Aquarius III

FRIENDSHIP
Aries I
Aries III
Gemini III
Cancer II
Leo II
Scorpio II
Sagittarius II
Capricorn III
Capricorn-Aquarius Cusp

FAMILY
Cancer-Leo Cusp
Virgo-Libra Cusp
Sagittarius I
Pisces I
Pisces III

WORK
Pisces-Aries Cusp
Taurus-Gemini Cusp
Cancer I
Cancer III
Leo III
Virgo III
Libra II
Scorpio I
Scorpio-Sagittarius Cusp
Capricorn II

Page Locator for All Relationships

CAPRICORN II
The Week of Determination

January 3–9

The Capricorn II period takes Determination as its central image. This period can be related in human terms to the time of life when an elder seeks to develop new interests and is, ideally, free to explore them. A greater universality and a deepening of outlook now manifest strongly. Illnesses may have to be overcome; the ability to come back from physical setbacks, and a positive outlook, which lends psychological resiliency that are crucial here.

The days that comprise Capricorn II symbolically reveal the elder engaged in new explorations, having the time to travel, formulating philosophical or religious points of view, substantiating gains already made, and manifesting ambition (perhaps for further wealth and power, perhaps for more personal and spiritual goals). During this time the individual seeks the very best for him/herself.

Those born in the Week of Determination often have the drive and ambition necessary to reach the top of their profession. Whether or not they succeed, no one can fault them for not trying. Capricorn II's are strivers, like the mountain goat who seeks out the highest crags. Once embarked on a course of action, they are extremely difficult to dissuade from their plans. No matter how great or modest their gifts, Capricorn II's make the most of their abilities and stretch their talents to the outer edge of the envelope.

Capricorns are generally pictured as hard-headed, down-to-earth thinkers, but those born in the Week of Determination are often interested in theoretical, even metaphysical, religious or spiritual subjects and practices. Nor are their ideas in these areas at all conserva-

ZODIAC POSITION
Approximately
11–20° Capricorn

SEASON
Early winter

ELEMENT
Earth

RULER
Saturn

SYMBOL
The Goat

MODE
Sensation

tive; they may, in fact, be rather radical. No idea is too strange or far out for Capricorn II's to at least consider, and they have an undeniable tendency to let their minds range over the broadest questions of cosmology and human existence. This philosophical bent, however, is usually based on fact and observation, for Capricorn II's have little time for idle or ill-founded speculation.

Capricorn II's often appear tough and aggressive, but most are highly sensitive, perhaps hypersensitive, underneath. They react strongly to criticism, often with denial. Although acutely aware of the disapproval of others, however, they usually have the strength to continue along their path if they believe in their heart that they are right. Of course, there are also immoral Capricorn II's who get away with as much as they can whether they can justify it or not, for they know something about power and how to wield it. They may be vulnerable to using slightly underhanded or unscrupulous methods. Even the more idealistic, who put their energies into serving a cause or organization, may wind up making questionable judgment calls. Classically, Capricorn II's often believe the end justifies the means.

They usually despise weakness in almost any form, and will not hesitate to use the deficiencies of those around them to their advantage. Such a person can only view personal failure as the ultimate humiliation. To say that Capricorn II's are unprepared for failure is an understatement: for many born in the Week of Determination, in fact, admitting failure is not really a possibility. In their philosophy, defeat is only a temporary setback, and the very weapons that destroyed their project must be used to rebuild it. Letting go of or giving up on something can be

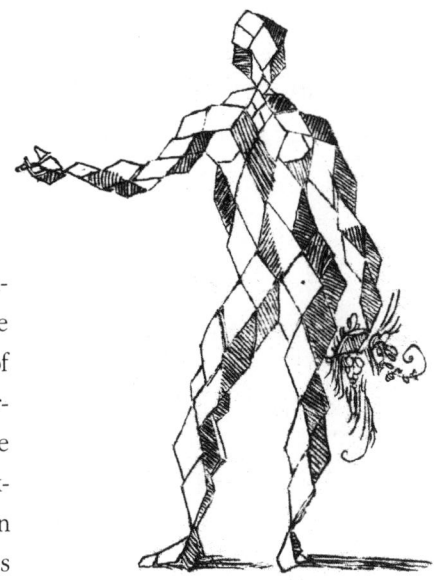

"DETERMINATION"

extremely difficult in these circumstances. It may be years, then, before Capricorn II's can free themselves of the baggage of the past that they carry on their able shoulders. On the other hand, they are capable of taking big chances at crucial points in their lives, in this way appearing as those prototypes of success who dare to fail.

In a strange way, Capricorn II's are masters of both reality and illusion, for many are so persuasive that they can convince others that an illusion is in fact reality. If those born in this week come to believe in their own illusions, however, they may become ineffectual in that they lose their credibility with those around them. Thus a single good friend who refuses to be conned and has the courage to report what he or she has seen, honestly and objectively, may be the most valuable resource a Capricorn II can have.

In their personal lives, Capricorn II's are happiest when they have a partner with whom to share the joys and sorrows of everyday life. They can live alone but most often choose not to do so. They may well insist, however, that their work is an inviolable area that they have no duty to share with their mate, who may get the idea that he or she occupies only second place in the Capricorn II's heart—that work comes first with these individuals. Consequently, those born in this week should consequently avoid involvements with dependent types who need attention and are unable to keep their nose out of their mate's business. It is not at all uncommon for Capricorn II's to marry a spouse whose work has little, if anything, in common with what they do themselves.

On the other hand, the friends of Capricorn II's are often colleagues, or at least work on similar pursuits. Extremely close relationships may develop with such individuals, and mates must accept this or face unhappiness, jealousy or feelings of rejection. Many Capricorn II's come to lead three quite separate and mutually exclusive lives: their work life, their social life and their intimate personal life. They may have no interest in integrating these areas, and, indeed, it is often unnecessary for them to do so.

Extremely resourceful, those born in this week are good at making the best of a bad situation. This and their loyalty enable them to hang in there for years trying to make a difficult or even somewhat undesirable relationships work out. What motivates them is less sympathy with or understanding of their partner than a refusal to admit failure. A Capricorn II can be extremely devoted not so much to a person as to the relationship itself, and to a belief in the concept of marriage or living together.

As realistic as they are, Capricorn II's are often seen as idealistic and even at times naive. Naiveté, in fact, can be considered their Achilles' heel, but also may be a reason for others to love or feel fondness or sympathy for them. Being vulnerable and admitting to weakness is essential to sharing love, and many born in this week handicap themselves by maintaining a strong facade.

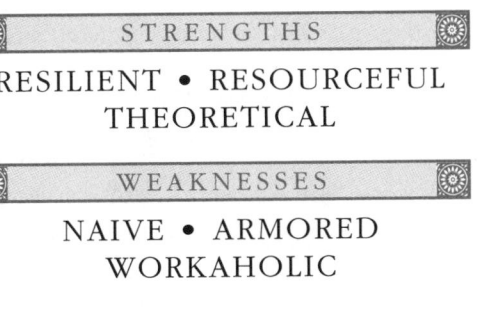

STRENGTHS

RESILIENT • RESOURCEFUL
THEORETICAL

WEAKNESSES

NAIVE • ARMORED
WORKAHOLIC

ADVICE:

Recognize your limitations—they do exist. Allow yourself to give in occasionally, even to fail and acknowledge it. Showing your more vulnerable side should not be threatening. Try to keep your ideals grounded and be sure your "reality" is not in fact an illusion.

CAPRICORN II NOTABLES

Republican President **Richard Nixon** was probably the most controversial individual to occupy the White House in this century. Typical of those born in the Week of Determination, Nixon took the talents he had been given and drove them mercilessly to the extreme in order to realize the high goals he had set for himself. In typical Capricorn II fashion, nothing was permitted to get in the way of Nixon's power drives or to thwart his ambition. Although credited with ending the Vietnam War and establishing U.S. relations with China, Nixon was never really trusted by a large percentage of the electorate. Finally brought down for his role in the Watergate scandal, he resembled a figure in Greek tragedy who destroyed himself through his own overweening pride and arrogance.

RICHARD NIXON

Leaders of the intellectual left and the existentialist movement in France, **Simone de Beauvoir** and Jean-Paul Sartre were lovers, colleagues and friends. De Beauvoir taught philosophy until 1943, when she turned to writing. Thereafter, she gave an accurate picture of the first half of the 20th century in autobiographical works. It was in her later nonfiction, however, that she achieved her greatest international fame, particularly *The Second Sex*, her analysis of the role of women in society. Another cause was that of the elderly, and her book *The Coming of Age* attacks social attitudes toward senior citizens.

SIMONE DE BEAUVOIR

A student of drama with Stella Adler and of dance with Martha Graham, **Alvin Ailey** formed his own dance company in 1958. One of Ailey's earliest and most successful works was *Revelations*, set to African-American spirituals. His most important solo piece, *Cry*, was choreographed for Judith Jamison and is dedicated to "all Black women everywhere—especially our mothers." Ailey had the tough exterior and hypersensitive interior of many Capricorn II's, accompanied by their interesting mix of realism and idealism. During his lifetime he created some 80 works, which were performed by many American dance companies, including the Joffrey Ballet and American Ballet Theater. Considered one of America's leading choreographers, Ailey was frequently praised for his belief in universal and multiracial brotherhood.

ALVIN AILEY

More Capricorn II's: Elvis Presley, Isaac Newton, Louis Braille, Steven Hawking, Diane Keaton, Mel Gibson, Dyan Cannon, Umberto Eco, Crystal Gayle, Chuck Noll, Carrie Chapman Catt, Jennie Churchill, Victoria Principal, George Reeves, Kathryn Walker, Carol Bayer Sager, Paramahansa Yogananda, Raisa Gorbachev, Carlos Saura, Maury Povitch, Jimmy Page, Earl Scruggs, Don Shula, Ray Milland, Steven Stills, Kahlil Gibran, Charles Addams, William Peter Blatty.

Relationship Guide for Capricorn II

PRISCILLA PRESLEY (TAURUS-GEMINI CUSP)
ELVIS PRESLEY (CAPRICORN II)
PAGE 407

BEST RELATIONSHIPS

LOVE
Aries II
Cancer-Leo Cusp
Leo III
Virgo I
Scorpio I
Sagittarius III
Capricorn-Aquarius Cusp
Aquarius III

MARRIAGE
Pisces-Aries Cusp
Aries I
Aries III
Gemini II
Cancer II
Cancer III
Sagittarius-Capricorn Cusp
Aquarius II
Pisces I

FRIENDSHIP
Aries-Taurus Cusp
Taurus II
Taurus-Gemini Cusp
Gemini I
Virgo II
Libra I
Libra-Scorpio Cusp
Scorpio II
Scorpio-Sagittarius Cusp
Capricorn III
Aquarius-Pisces Cusp
Pisces II

FAMILY
Taurus III
Leo II
Capricorn II

WORK
Taurus I
Gemini III
Leo I
Libra III
Scorpio III
Sagittarius I
Capricorn I
Aquarius I

Page Locator for All Relationships

CAPRICORN III
The Week of Dominance

January 10–16

The Capricorn III period takes Dominance as its central image. According to The Grand Cycle of Life, this period can be likened in human terms to a person's late sixties, when the wish to be dominant can manifest strongly. As long as such urges are expressed in technical areas, they are likely to bring positive results. However, in the personal sphere, the desire to rule the roost may cause strife with one's life partner, who may be thinking the same way. Not uncommonly, such conflicts can be the result of both people having too much time around the same house. Successful elders focus more of this powerful energy inward—particularly in acquiring greater control over wayward emotions, wasteful impulses and unrestrained fantasy. The days that comprise Capricorn III symbolize the energy of the elder seeking to order his/her environment by making realistic assessments and hard choices, while seeking greater comfort, happiness and fulfillment.

Many Capricorn III's find it unnecessary to rise to the top of their field, or even to lead, as long as they can express their dominance within the day-to-day dynamic of their family, work or social group. Although ambitious types may well be born in this week, Capricorn III's often reach a certain level in their particular circle and are content to stay there for the rest of their lives. They have tremendous diligence and dedication, which enable them to stick to the path they have set for themselves without being sidetracked.

Self-confidence is extremely important to the psychic well-being of Capricorn III's. As long as they are not beset by worry, do not probe too deeply into

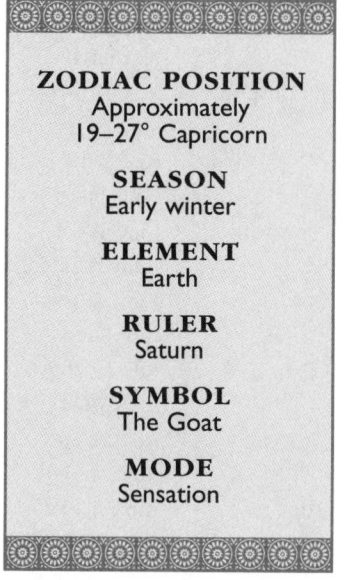

ZODIAC POSITION
Approximately
19–27° Capricorn

SEASON
Early winter

ELEMENT
Earth

RULER
Saturn

SYMBOL
The Goat

MODE
Sensation

their own motives or expect too much of themselves, they function well. A secret inferiority complex may plague them for years, however, until they can prove to themselves that they really are worthwhile people. Some born in this week may be unrealistic about their capabilities, overrating themselves—a desperate attempt to deny their deep feelings of inferiority, and one that can only set them up for failure. Those with a poor self-image often still suffer from the negative attitudes of a disapproving or overly demanding parent in childhood.

When young, Capricorn III's are prone to idolize an older figure of the same sex. As they grow more mature, they themselves are often cast in a heroic mold by others. Idolizing and idealizing can build up the expectations surrounding Capricorn III's to an unrealistic extent, again setting them up for the inevitable disappointment of a fall from grace. A strongly moral attitude, and a tendency to divide the world into good or evil, are characteristic of those born in this week; they need to learn not to judge others or be so extreme in their views. The happiest Capricorn III's are those who can take people as they are without rejecting them or laying on trips of guilt or shame.

Those born in the Week of Dominance are highly physical but not always sensuous or pleasure-loving. Some of them may make the overcoming of physical wants and needs their chief occupation, in fact, showing their dominance over their own feelings and bodies. Capricorn III's can be severe in dealing with themselves and with those close to them, notably their mates and families. Yet they can generally be counted on for hon-

"DOMINANCE"

est and straightforward opinions and advice. Rarely prone to unconscious self-deceit, they also have little interest in deceiving others; most often they mean what they say and say what they mean.

Capricorn III's value service highly. They are competent and thoroughly professional, but their giving attitudes may make them too self-sacrificing, or vulnerable to exploitation. Although they are capable of learning from such experiences how to say no to co-workers and acquaintances, they may still be unable or unwilling to deny the demands of their immediate family. Years of devotion to a needy family member can not only drain them of their energy and deprive them of time for themselves but also cause the buildup of tremendous frustrations, which, inevitably, produce unhappiness.

Capricorn III's are thoughtful people and can also be a great deal of fun. Their playful attitudes and scathing wit show their ability to put things in perspective and also to not take themselves too seriously. There is an undeniable streak of eccentricity in many born in this week. Although not overly social, they often like nothing better than an evening with friends, whether quiet or uproarious, depending on their mood. Capricorn III's enjoy being part of a group, sharing experiences and conversation with several individuals equally; they are less prone to have one single best friend. They are often attracted to team sports, hobbies

or clubs, and may contribute wholeheartedly to the planning and maintenance of such organizations.

In their careers, many Capricorn III's are hard workers. They often get their biggest kicks battling against high odds—for example, by struggling to overcome physical disabilities. Others born in this week are more realistic in the projects they take on but nonetheless show workaholic tendencies. A vivacious and interesting mate can be good medicine for those born in this week, taking their minds off career concerns and allowing them to relax and have fun. Capricorn III's often need someone at home who can lighten their mood when they walk in the door.

Although responsible, Capricorn III's are not dull by any means. Many born in this week have an arresting, even electric demeanor that can be highly charismatic, or at the very least can cause others to watch them in wide-eyed astonishment. Those born in this week rarely try to be outrageous, but they often wind up like that anyway. Capricorn III's are often unaware of the effects their statements and actions have on others, and basically may not care, either. They don't feel rejection keenly, partly because they know they aren't everyone's cup of tea, partly because they generally don't have a great need for the approval and acceptance of others. Self-contained, those born in this week must be careful not to keep too much under control, stifling their more expressive side.

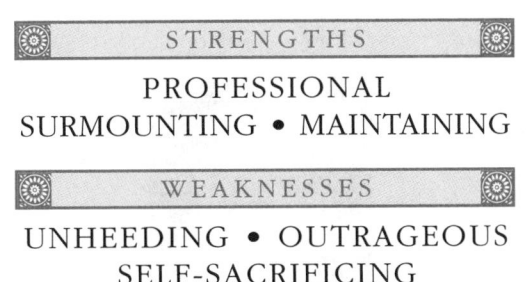

STRENGTHS

PROFESSIONAL
SURMOUNTING • MAINTAINING

WEAKNESSES

UNHEEDING • OUTRAGEOUS
SELF-SACRIFICING

ADVICE:

Don't be afraid to take chances. If you do not dare to fail you may not achieve your true heart's desire. Your insistence on security may be misplaced at times. Try to be more flexible where the feelings of others are concerned. Do not assume that your values have absolute or universal application.

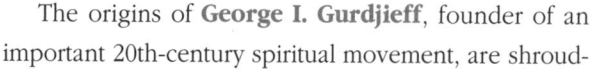

CAPRICORN III NOTABLES

In her best film performances, **Faye Dunaway** shows the kind of dominant attitudes and eccentricity that are characteristic of Capricorn III's. In roles opposite Warren Beatty in *Bonnie and Clyde* and Jack Nicholson in *Chinatown*, Dunaway displays not only her beauty and

fine acting but also her flair for the unusual. Such feeling for more bizarre roles is reflected in her incredible portrayal of actress Joan Crawford in *Mommie Dearest* and opposite Mickey Rourke in *Barfly*, where she plays a wealthy drunk. Dunaway has also been able to express her dominant side as a film producer, notably in 1990, with *Cold Sassy Tree*.

FAYE DUNAWAY

The legendary story has been told many times of how the young Greek immigrant **Aristotle Onassis** arrived in Argentina with only a few hundred dollars in his pocket. Showing the hard-working characteristics and single-mindedness of those born in the Week of Dominance, Onassis became a millionaire by the time he was 25, working first in the tobacco business and then using his profits to buy ships. By the time he met Jackie Kennedy,

ARISTOTLE ONASSIS

shipping magnate Onassis had amassed one of the largest fortunes in the world. Jackie and Onassis wed in 1968, and although many were bewildered by her choice, few could deny the power and self-assurance of her Capricorn III husband.

The origins of **George I. Gurdjieff**, founder of an important 20th-century spiritual movement, are shrouded in mystery. Having spent the first 40 years of his life in central Asia, Tibet, India and the Middle East studying the wisdom of several mystical and religious groups, Gurdjieff appeared in Russia and established his Institute for the Harmonious Development of Man with the help of his fol-

GEORGE I. GURDJIEFF

lowers. Forced by the Russian Revolution to relocate outside Paris, Gurdjieff's Institute was able to spread the master's ideas to a larger public. His books *Meetings with Remarkable Men* and *Tales of Beelzebub* attracted great interest over the years, although it was disciple P.D. Ouspensky's book *In Search of the Miraculous* that popularized Gurdjieff's ideas. Gurdjieff possessed the electrically dominant demeanor but also the fixed moral orientation that characterize many Capricorn III's.

More Capricorn III's: Martin Luther King, Jr., Albert Schweitzer, Alexander Hamilton, William James, Eva Le Gallienne, George Foreman, Joan of Arc, Howard Stern, Julia Louis-Dreyfus, Jack London, Kirstie Allie, Berthe Morisot, Ethel Merman, Trevor Nunn, Mary J. Blige, Gamal Abdel Nasser, Jason Bateman, Maharishi Mahesh Yogi, William James, Edward Teller, Chad Lowe, Alexander Hamilton, Max Roach, Dian Fossey, Gwen Verdon, Yukio Mishima.

Relationship Guide for Capricorn III

MARIA CALLAS (SAGITTARIUS I)
ARISTOTLE ONASSIS (CAPRICORN III)
PAGE 745

BEST RELATIONSHIPS

LOVE
Aries-Taurus Cusp
Gemini I
Cancer I
Leo-Virgo Cusp
Virgo III
Libra I
Scorpio-Sagittarius Cusp
Sagittarius-Capricorn Cusp
Capricorn III
Aquarius-Pisces Cusp

MARRIAGE
Pisces-Aries Cusp
Taurus I
Taurus III
Virgo I
Libra II
Scorpio II
Aquarius I
Pisces I

FRIENDSHIP
Aries I
Aries III
Gemini-Cancer Cusp
Cancer II
Cancer-Leo Cusp
Libra III
Capricorn I
Capricorn II

FAMILY
Cancer III
Leo III
Sagittarius II
Aquarius II

WORK
Taurus-Gemini Cusp
Gemini II
Leo II
Virgo II
Virgo-Libra Cusp
Libra-Scorpio Cusp
Sagittarius III
Capricorn-Aquarius Cusp
Aquarius III
Pisces III

Page Locator for All Relationships

CAPRICORN-AQUARIUS CUSP
The Cusp of Mystery and Imagination

January 17–22

The Capricorn-Aquarius cusp can be likened symbolically to the period around seventy years of age in the human life; it arrives at the time in winter when the days are lengthening but remain cold in the northern hemisphere. Indeed, nights are freezing and refuge must be sought inside. The Capricorn-Aquarius cusp may be said to represent Mystery and Imagination. In human development, at the age of seventy, one must certainly come to terms with one's own mortality. Preparations must be made to make one's remaining years comfortable but also productive and satisfying. Although external activities have usually slowed down considerably, ideally a corresponding increased tempo of the interior life—mental, emotional, spiritual—can manifest. The worlds of imagination, fantasy and dreams are active, and some feel and act in a childlike manner. The days that comprise the Capricorn-Aquarius cusp exemplify some of the manifestations of Mystery and Imagination where the practical, conservative Capricorn nature clashes with unpredictable, unconventional Aquarian impulses.

The vivid and expressive individuals born on the Capricorn-Aquarius cusp generate excitement wherever they go. Unable to keep out of the action for very long, they make their presence felt almost immediately on entering a room. Their viewpoints tend to be controversial, and whether conservative or radical are highly stimulating, often because of the dramatic way they are delivered. Capricorn-Aquarians' interest in the poor and downtrodden is more than theoretical: most of them will not hesitate to make direct contributions of time, money or energy to help anyone less fortunate than themselves.

ZODIAC POSITION
Approximately
26° Capricorn–
3° Aquarius

SEASON
Mid-winter

ELEMENTS
Earth/Air

RULERS
Saturn/Uranus

SYMBOLS
The Goat/The Water
Bearer

MODES
Sensation/Thought

At the same time, however, they have little sympathy for those they see as freeloaders or parasites, able to pull their own weight but refusing to do so.

The influence of the planet Saturn (ruler of Capricorn) lends structure and a feeling of responsibility to Capricorn-Aquarius personalities, but the unpredictable energy of Uranus (ruler of Aquarius) may tend to break this order apart at any moment. It is not uncommon for Capricorn-Aquarians to have wide mood swings; they can appear sensible and reasonable one moment, uncontrolled the next. Capricorn-Aquarians can get pretty wild, so it is not surprising that violence can feature in their lives, whether they attract it or enact it. Chaotic, out-of-control energies can produce tremendous unrest in the lives of those born on this cusp. Their regard for their personal safety is usually not high, a trait they may reinforce with a daredevil nature—a deadly or at least dangerous combination. A disregard for their health in general, and an insistent confidence that their prodigious energies will bail them out, time and time again, can wear them down over the years, or induce chronic physical conditions. Concerned mates and lovers may have a hard time, for example, weaning them away from heavy drinking and smoking.

Capricorn-Aquarians have a pronounced dark side. Not ones to keep anger inside for very long, they can explode in fits of temper that will send others scurrying. The image of a furious Capricorn-Aquarius hell-bent on punishment is at tremendous variance with the face they present when enjoying themselves and having fun. More than most, those born in this week can be at the mercy of their demons, so that their outbursts of temper are tru-

"MYSTERY
AND IMAGINATION"

ly spontaneous. Because they are rarely calculating, it is hard to blame them for their tremendous mood swings, which are usually forgiven, though not easily forgotten, by those closest to them.

Even the most settled and conventional of Capricorn-Aquarians will often have an active dream and fantasy life. They lead a kind of Walter Mitty existence, with few guessing the extent of their interior life or the degree of its inventiveness. Everyday situations can prove the springboard for bizarre mental gyrations, in which the Capricorn- Aquarian becomes the central character in an imaginary world. These flights of fancy rarely indicate pathological states–quite to the contrary, those born on this cusp show how important being in touch with one's fantasy life can be for mental health.

Capricorn-Aquarians love to tell and play jokes. Their mates, friends and family must not only understand but appreciate this need if those born in this week are to be kept happy. It isn't always easy, however, to keep up with Capricorn-Aquarians, who may one moment be dealing seriously with day-to-day problems, the next exploding in riotous laughter. They also have a conventional side that can make them extremely exacting: they generally expect all family members to do their duty and discharge their obligations to the fullest.

Those born on this cusp can only fully respect people who share daily chores and duties with them fairly.

Capricorn-Aquarians often seek hard-working, dependable mates rather than beautiful or intelligent ones. Outside their permanent or primary relationship, however, the impulsive Capricorn- Aquarius may be magnetically attracted to vivacious and exciting individuals, or to quieter but still passionate types. The sexual powers of those born on the Cusp of Mystery and Imagination are usually high, and their interest in sex is pronounced. When they stray, they suffer to an extent from guilt, but this can lend extra spice to their indiscretions. Although they may attach little importance to such flings, their partner may not be so understanding, and deep, long-lasting hurts may be inflicted. In their sexual and other escapades, Capricorn-Aquarians exhibit an immature side, like Peter Pan, who refused to grow up.

Youthfulness is, in fact, one of the most obvious Capricorn-Aquarius qualities. Those born on this cusp do not necessarily age well; many risk burnout in their tumultuous lifestyles, others deteriorate through neglect or abuse of their bodies. Haste and carelessness may not only wear them down physically but contribute to psychological instability. On the other hand, those Capricorn-Aquarians lucky enough to have a stable support group, whether in family, friends or, a mate, can have it all, establishing the many facets of their personalities. Capricorn-Aquarians who live alone may, in fact, build up great inner strength through dealing with the most difficult and elusive customer they have ever met—themselves.

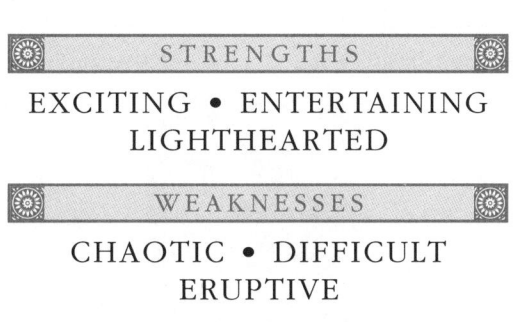

STRENGTHS

EXCITING • ENTERTAINING
LIGHTHEARTED

WEAKNESSES

CHAOTIC • DIFFICULT
ERUPTIVE

ADVICE:

You must find an outlet for your creative energy. Communicate what you experience. Try not to be discouraged by lack of understanding, ignorance or negative criticism. Don't go off the deep end, but, rather, find those who understand and appreciate you.

CAPRICORN-AQUARIUS CUSP NOTABLES

The former heavyweight boxing champion **Muhammad Ali** typified the vivid expressiveness and the activity and violence that frequently characterize those born on the Capricorn-Aquarius cusp. It was Ali's speed, dancing style and rope-a-dope techniques that set him apart from other heavyweights, but his ability to take a punch and hit hard were never seriously questioned. Ali has attracted as much attention out of the ring as in, particularly when he joined the Nation of Islam and later refused induction into the U.S. Army. Ali decisively defeated some of the toughest fighters of his day,

MUHAMMAD ALI

including Joe Frazier and George Foremen, winning the respect of fight fans the world over. His inimitable speech was frequently punctuated by "I am the greatest."

Janis Joplin characterized the vivacious, impulsive and wild nature of many born on the Cusp of Mystery and Imagination. Joplin lived the years of the 60s perhaps more intensely than any other major rock star. In large outdoor concerts she mesmerized thousands by her incredible intensity, which pushed her voice and body to the most painful limits. *Me and Bobby McGee* and *Lord, Won't You Buy Me a Mercedes Benz* were trademark songs, although it is unlikely the Almighty was moved by Janis's plea. Fronting Big Brother and the Holding Company and the Kozmic Blues Band, Janis conveyed her blues-oriented

JANIS JOPLIN

music with highly charged emotion. Her drug-related death in 1970 at 27 came, symbolically, as the 60s drew to a close.

Italian film director **Federico Fellini** began his work in the neorealistic cinema but could not resist the pull of fantasy and imagination felt so strongly by those born on the Capricorn-Aquarius cusp. His first masterpiece, *La Strada*,

FEDERICO FELLINI

which starred his wife, Giulietta Masina, shows how much the director's symbolic imagery had suffused his cinematic vision. In *La Dolce Vita* and *8 1/2*, strongly autobiographical and social elements were added, making the films highly personal commentaries on the times. In both films, Marcello Mastroianni is Fellini's persona, wandering through the maze of his own visions. *Juliet of the Spirits*, again starring his wife, along with *Satyricon* and *Amarcord* revel in the use of color, fantasy and exploration of images from childhood to create Fellini's surreal world.

More Capricorn-Aquarians: Benjamin Franklin, Edgar Allen Poe, Joe Frazier, Al Capone, Jill Eikenberry, Humphrey Bogart, William Harris, Moira Shearer, Geena Davis, Jean Moreau, Jim Carrey, Dolly Parton, Chita Rivera, Francis Picabia, Lord Byron, Sir Francis Bacon, D.W. Griffith, Sergei Eisenstein, John Hurt, Rasputin, Jerome Kern, August Strindberg, Placido Domingo, Stonewall Jackson, Ethan Allen, Jack Nicklaus.

Relationship Guide for Capricorn-Aquarius Cusp

JOE FRAZIER (CAPRICORN-AQUARIUS CUSP)
MUHAMMAD ALI
(CAPRICORN AQUARIUS CUSP)
PAGE 784

BEST RELATIONSHIPS

LOVE
Pisces-Aries Cusp
Aries I
Aries III
Taurus I
Cancer I
Cancer-Leo Cusp
Virgo I
Scorpio III
Scorpio-Sagittarius Cusp
Capricorn II
Aquarius III

MARRIAGE
Aries II
Taurus-Gemini Cusp
Gemini III
Leo I
Pisces III

FRIENDSHIP
Taurus III
Gemini II
Cancer III
Virgo-Libra Cusp
Libra II
Scorpio I
Sagittarius I
Capricorn I
Aquarius II
Pisces I

FAMILY
Leo-Virgo Cusp
Virgo III
Aquarius I
Aquarius-Pisces Cusp
Pisces II

WORK
Aries-Taurus Cusp
Gemini I
Gemini-Cancer Cusp
Cancer II
Leo III
Virgo II
Sagittarius III
Sagittarius-Capricorn Cusp
Capricorn-Aquarius Cusp

Page Locator for All Relationships

AQUARIUS I
The Week of Genius

January 23–30

The Aquarius I period takes Genius as its central image. According to The Grand Cycle of Life, this period can be symbolically likened to the years of a person's early seventies. At this time, a more universal understanding of nature, time and man has emerged. Having to impress others, struggling to accumulate money, striving for success, shouldering family responsibilities—for many, these are a thing of the past. Time can be spent reading and thinking, and perhaps considering philosophical matters or areas of social or international concern. Ideally, wisdom has crystallized, for the outlook of a person this age is now somewhat fixed. The days that comprise Aquarius I symbolically reveal the elder facing advanced age and coming to the hard realization that not so many years may be left. Concerns of character, withdrawal from the world, thoughts about human destiny, but also memories of high points in life, for oneself and others—extraordinary scientific, philosophical or physical achievements—may be mentally surveyed.

Although Aquarius I's may not necessarily be more intelligent than others in the year, they generally learn quickly and exhibit an alert, even high-strung demeanor. Like thoroughbreds, they are hot-blooded types, usually champing at the bit to get on with it. Patience is not one of their virtues, and Aquarius I's show a marked itchiness with those slower sorts who need time to express themselves and make decisions.

Aquarius I's often arouse other people's amazement, and also jealousy, due to the speed and ease with which they pick things up at the first go. When they are young,

ZODIAC POSITION Approximately 2–11° Aquarius
SEASON Midwinter
ELEMENT Air
RULER Uranus
SYMBOL The Water Bearer
MODE Thought

this ability may manifest as precocity, but parents and teachers who do not understand them may criticize them as superficial, and for lacking the stick-to-it-iveness to see a project through. But although it is true that Aquarius I's are easily bored, they are quite capable of perseverance when they feel it is warranted. Not everyone born in this week has the ability to learn so fast, but most value mental skills highly and try to develop them, whether born with them or not. They also prize education, but not always the kind found in school: Aquarius I's believe that experience is the best teacher and are often self-taught types. The lure of worldly excitement will often entice them away from the classroom, and travel to foreign lands can have a peculiar fascination for them.

In their careers, those born in this week want to have things their own way. They rarely do well in jobs where they are told what to do. Self-employment or independent positions suit them better, particularly if their work allows them the freedom to make choices, plan, change direction, follow their instincts and be true to what they believe. Although Aquarius I's can be excellent leaders, whether of families and social groups or in their professional environments, they have no essential need to either rule or dominate. Their greatest need in relation to other people may actually be just the need for attention, since every performer ultimately needs an audience.

It is extremely important for Aquarius I's to give every project they work on their own personal stamp. People who enjoy the individual expression of others are fond of those born in this week, but their often destabilizing and self-centered energies can affect group projects adversely. Aquarius I's often seem rebellious, but this is usually because of some attempt to tame or control them. Their impulsiveness can easily bring them into conflict with authority figures, or with those of a more conservative nature.

Once those born in this week accept their uniqueness and realize that their social needs and drives are less deep than they think, they will make great strides in their careers. More enlightened Aquarius I's may come to realize that they can use their strengths best by pursuing a career that does not necessarily involve social contact. There are many areas of science, music, art, publishing or economics that can fit the bill. Part of the problem Aquarius I's confront in working with others is that they tend to exhaust their talents and energies on those close to them, sometimes in a frustrated effort to fit in and feel that they really belong to a group.

On the negative side, the Aquarius I personality has a tendency to self-destructiveness. They are more hurtful to themselves than to others. They can be emotionally unstable, and at times can appear distracted, wired, self-absorbed, and can be easily upset. Their sensitivity to external stimuli may be pronounced in such moods, and they may have an acute need to withdraw to a quiet place, away from the bustle of the world. Easily stressed out, even prone to periodic breakdowns, Aquarius I's must learn to toughen themselves. If they can become less easily

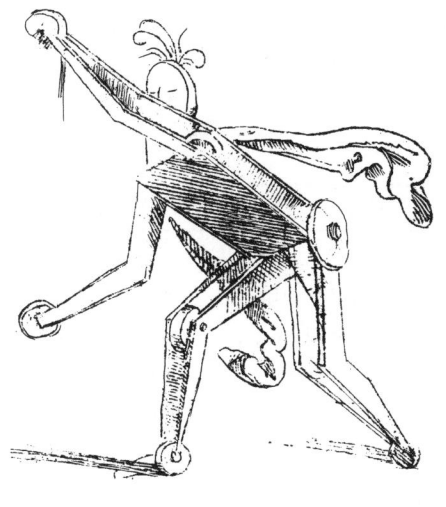

"GENIUS"

aroused, they will deal more effectively with the exigencies of everyday life.

In matters of love, Aquarius I's insist that their mates understand their need for freedom. They will not be tied down to fixed routines and schedules. Friends and lovers with more demanding expectations of them are in for a rude surprise; Aquarius I's will rarely accept restriction. Chafing at constraint, they may just try to find another free spirit to get involved with, a solution that may work in the short term but seldom provides the stability and permanence required for deeper commitment. Some Aquarius I's may indeed desire a permanent, faithful, giving and stable partner but may also seek the freedom to carry on all kinds of other relationships, sexual or otherwise, at the same time. By practicing this kind of double standard, these Aquarius I's seek to satisfy both their needs and their desires, but also show their disregard for others.

Those who choose family life will have to learn to direct their energies efficiently, share responsibilities, budget their time and, above all, conquer their need for attention. Their charismatic side often attracts the wrong kind of people, and this may keep their energy from those whom they love and who really need it, particularly family members. Restricting themselves to a well-chosen circle of close friends, and concentrating on those who have a stabilizing effect on them psychologically and are not needy people, will contribute greatly to their happiness.

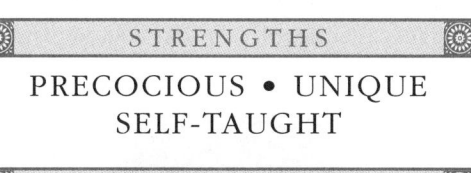

STRENGTHS

PRECOCIOUS • UNIQUE
SELF-TAUGHT

WEAKNESSES

RECKLESS • DISTRACTED
STRESSED-OUT

ADVICE:

Clarify a realistic picture of yourself in your mind's eye. A certain amount of undesirable personal interaction is always necessary; try to be a bit more thick-skinned and, if necessary, downright insensitive. Cultivate calm, patience and persistence rather than always going your own way. Learn to handle frustration and be tough enough to quietly demand the very best for yourself.

AQUARIUS I NOTABLES

Certainly the most precocious musical prodigy the world has ever known, Austrian composer **Wolfgang Amadeus Mozart** exemplifies the dazzlingly quick abilities of those born in the Week of Genius. Yet perhaps the greatest struggle for Mozart was taking his place in the adult world, where values like maturity, responsibility and hard work were stressed. That he was successful artistically in his struggle can be seen in works like the operas *Don Giovanni* and *The Magic Flute* and in his late symphonies and piano concertos, although his personal life remained somewhat chaotic. Dead at 35 under mysterious circumstances, leaving an unfinished commissioned requiem, which proved to be his own, the prolific Mozart had already written enough masterpieces for a dozen lifetimes.

WOLFGANG AMADEUS MOZART

TV and film star **Oprah Winfrey** fits the pattern of precocity frequently found in Aquarius I's, who tend to give public performances at an early age. Her first notable appearance was delivering the Easter sermon in church at age 2. Oprah majored in speech and drama in college, was voted Miss Tennessee and by the age of 19 was already a local CBS anchor. Reportedly the highest-earning woman in America for several years now, Oprah can attribute her tremendous success to the empathic bond she has formed with her audience, partly due to her honesty about her own childhood and personal life. Oprah reaches out and touches her audience not only figuratively but literally, making the human bond even stronger. Her role in the film *The Color Purple* demonstrates her extraordinary versatility.

OPRAH WINFREY

Elected U.S. president 4 times, **Franklin Delano Roosevelt** was possibly the most popular public figure in the 20th century. His New Deal reforms were credited with bringing America out of the Depression. As commander in chief, he guided the country in WWII and, more than anyone else, was responsible for winning the war. Although FDR fits the Aquarius I mold as impatient and itching to get on with implementing his latest schemes, he was also frivolous, reckless and overconfident when younger. Perhaps it was the polio that crippled and immobilized him in 1921 that was most responsible for allowing him to become more mature, thoughtful and compassionate.

FRANKLIN DELANO ROOSEVELT

More Aquarius I's: Lewis Carroll, Bridget Fonda, Paul Newman, Mikhail Baryshnikov, Nastassja Kinsky, Hadrian, John Belushi, Warren Zevon, Sharon Tate, Maria Tallchief, Virginia Woolf, Somerset Maugham, Etta James, Vanessa Redgrave, Gene Hackman, Barbara Tuchman, Greg Louganis, W.C. Fields, Germaine Greer, Ernie Banks.

Relationship Guide for Aquarius I

LAUREN BACALL (VIRGO III)
HUMPHREY BOGART (AQUARIUS I)
PAGE 648

BEST
RELATIONSHIPS

LOVE
Aries I
Aries III
Leo III
Libra III
Scorpio II
Sagittaarius-Capricorn Cusp
Aquarius III
Pisces I
Pisces III

MARRIAGE
Aries-Taurus Cusp
Taurus II
Gemini-Cancer Cusp
Leo II
Virgo III
Sagittarius III
Capricorn I
Capricorn III

FRIENDSHIP
Aries II
Taurus I
Taurus-Gemini Cusp
Gemini II
Gemini III
Cancer II
Cancer-Leo Cusp
Virgo II
Aquarius I

FAMILY
Leo I
Libra I
Scorpio III
Sagittarius I
Capricorn-Aquarius Cusp
Aquarius II

WORK
Cancer I
Cancer III
Virgo I
Virgo-Libra Cusp
Scorpio-Sagittarius Cusp
Pisces II

Page Locator for All Relationships

AQUARIUS II
The Week of Youth and Ease

January 31–February 7

The Aquarius II period takes Youth and Ease as its central image. Paradoxically, this period can be related in human terms to the years of a person's early to mid-seventies. In fact, a bond with children may spring up at this time (particularly one's own grandchildren), and thus the maturity and wisdom of old age can mesh with the open and wonder-filled world of the child. At this stage of life very youthful impulses can surface—indeed, some report a kind of "second childhood." Relaxing, taking it easy and in general having time on one's hands can be enjoyable now. The days that comprise Aquarius II symbolically reveal the elder dealing with old age and finding ways to fill his/her time with meaningful activity. Expressing a measure of eccentricity and willfulness, perhaps finding new friends of one's age, deepening relationships with children, universalizing one's thoughts, and maximizing one's comfort and happiness all manifest at this time.

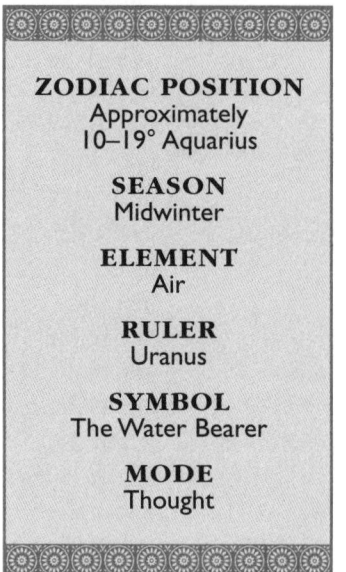

ZODIAC POSITION
Approximately
10–19° Aquarius

SEASON
Midwinter

ELEMENT
Air

RULER
Uranus

SYMBOL
The Water Bearer

MODE
Thought

"No hassles" could be the motto of most Aquarius II's. Listening to those born in this week, one would gather that they do not like trouble in any form and would do practically anything to avoid it. They value their happiness highly, both in the long term and in the short. Aquarius II's generally ask to be left alone to travel their own path with as little interference as possible. Not much interested in controlling others or meddling in their affairs, those born in this week are happy to accord the same treatment to other people that they demand for themselves.

Those born in this week have a tendency to virtuosity in their makeup: whether in the office, the laboratory, the building site or the kitchen, Aquarius II's display a mastery of their medium. Their craftsmanship is pronounced, and although they give the impression of performing their tasks effortlessly, years of hard work may well have gone into perfecting their technique. For many Aquarius II's, in fact, technique is not an end in itself but only a beginning, a means by which they can express their highest creativity.

Youthfulness of all kinds (physical, mental, emotional) is a characteristic of Aquarius II's. Not only do they often look far younger than their years, they may develop many of their full powers before the age of twenty, so that their abilities run throughout their lives rather than coming to them with age. In addition, children and childhood are often lifelong themes and preoccupations for them, whether they themselves become parents or not. They often hope to keep the natural qualities of the child—spontaneity, impulse, intuition and openness—alive in themselves to the end. Not surprisingly, those born in the Week of Youth and Ease are sometimes accused of emotional immaturity and superficiality. It's true that they are in some cases immature, but superficial they are not.

Aquarius II's tend to be so well-liked and admired that one might well wonder where their problems lie. But the popularity that is their strength can also be their undoing. For one thing, Aquarius II's can get hooked on other people's applause and, in particular, admiration of their free-and-easy approach. The consequence may be that they wind up spending most of their time pleasing others and fail to assert themselves for fear of losing their friends and fans. Other Aquarius II's may detach or even isolate themselves from those around them, for they find

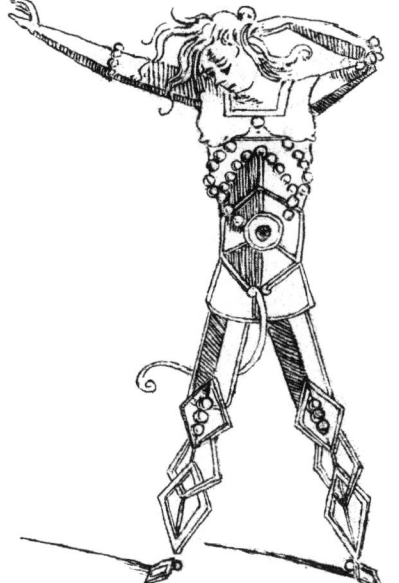

"YOUTH AND EASE"

it hard or undesirable to have to live up to others' expectations. Some of these individuals risk becoming haughty, dispassionate people, with little real sympathy for their fellow humans.

Given their high opinion of themselves, Aquarius II's may be prone to conceit. On the other hand, since this self-evaluation is generally based on their outward talents and abilities—and ultimately, that is, on other people's attitudes and responses to them—it does not come from a deep place within themselves and, therefore, may cover up grave insecurities and doubts. A great danger for Aquarius II's is the chance that they may adopt values not their own and live out their lives through the expectations of others, depriving themselves of a healthy ego that can function well in everyday life. The development of strong, heartfelt and fiercely defended beliefs, culled from their own internal struggles and life experience, can help them to come of age and function as mature individuals.

It would seem then, that those born in this week must work on acquiring a more realistic self-image. It may also be possible for them to strike a bal-

ance between the sunnier and the darker sides of their personalities by getting to know themselves better and coming to grips with their demons. We often don't really need to confront and slay the dragon in our innermost depths; we just have to get to know it better and, ultimately, perhaps, to make it our friend. By recognizing such a source of vitality and owning up to it, Aquarius II's

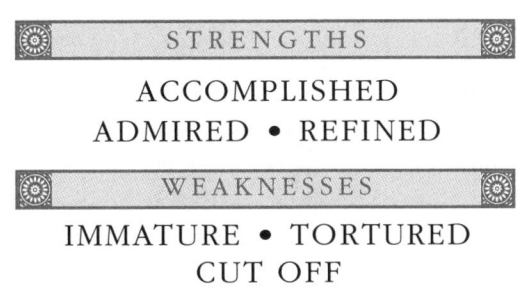

STRENGTHS

ACCOMPLISHED
ADMIRED • REFINED

WEAKNESSES

IMMATURE • TORTURED
CUT OFF

can actually empower themselves.

More out of choice than necessity, Aquarius II's may like to keep their relationships light, and to avoid serious or heavy involvements. But this should not be taken to mean that they cut themselves off from having their own families, long-standing love and marital relationships or steady friendships. Those closely involved with them will learn that if Aquarius II's insist on keeping a distance, it is to guarantee their own autonomy. They will rarely seek to merge their personality with that of the other person. Those born in this week know that by avoiding deep emotional entanglements they may well spare themselves some of the pain of future conflicts and separations.

Problems arise when Aquarius II's discover that they are often attracted to the very opposite kind of personality from what they think they want. Paradoxically, those born in the Week of Youth and Ease may be magnetically drawn to and need to be involved with deep, profound, even troubled people. This need may reflect a psychological dynamic in which they fall in love with a projection of their own shadow side, of which they are otherwise unaware. Emotionally complex personalities certainly fascinate Aquarius II's but at the same time frustrate them. Watching some of the agonies and mental torture of this type of Aquarius II relationship, one wonders if the happy-go-lucky image these individuals seek to convey is really as accurate as it appears.

ADVICE:

Try to get in touch with your own deeper feelings. Sometimes it is better to meet problems head on. A bit of pain now may prevent much more later. Don't be too dependent on others' opinion of you. Have the courage to be yourself and don't feel you have to please or entertain.

AQUARIUS II NOTABLES

When fastballer **Nolan Ryan** retired from baseball in 1993, he had 5,714 strikeouts, a lifetime ERA of 3.19 and a record of 324 wins and 292 losses in 27 years in the major leagues. Although he is the all-time record holder for strikeouts and no-hitters, Ryan never was the Cy Young winner or an MVP. Youthful Ryan fits the Aquarius II mold perfectly, still throwing strikeouts easily when he was over 40. In one incredible season, 1973, Ryan pitched 2 no-hitters and in the 2nd one struck out 17 batters. In his last start that season, he struck out 16 batters and broke Sandy Koufax's season record by one strikeout! Between the ages of 33 and 41, playing for the Houston Astros, Ryan had a record of 106-94 and an ERA of 3.14.

NOLAN RYAN

The name of Russian ballerina **Anna Pavlova** is synonymous with beauty, elegance and grace. Her legendary performances with the Ballet Russe in Paris established her as one of the world's greats. A typical Aquarius II, the Youth and Ease Pavlova had in abundance held audiences spellbound, as she exhibited her flawless technique with seeming nonchalance and detachment. Pavlova established her reputation with the classic roles of ballet literature, notably *Giselle* and *Chopiniana*. Her most famous role with the Ballet Russe, the *Dying Swan*, was created for her by the choreographer Michel Fokine.

ANNA PAVLOVA

The virtuosity and mastery of his medium but also a detached and slightly haughty attitude identify **Clark Gable** as an Aquarius II. Gable, as Rhett Butler in the film *Gone With the Wind*, infuriates Scarlet O'Hara with his conceit, and indeed this is the impression that Aquarius II Gable frequently gave. However, he was not called the "King of Hollywood" for nothing and personified the Hollywood leading man for 30 years. Ease characterized Gable's approach to most roles; difficulty, pain and suffering for his art were not really his *modus operandi*. His Aquarian inability to deal with his feelings was evident when he fell apart emotionally after his wife, Carole Lombard, died in a plane crash, and he escaped to the U.S. Air Force in WWII. He emerged as a real-life and highly decorated combat hero.

CLARK GABLE

More Aquarius II's: Franz Schubert, Bob Marley, Charles Dickens, James Joyce, Phil Collins, Betty Friedan, Babe Ruth, Mary Leakey, An Wang, Natalie Cole, Roberto Alomar, Blythe Danner, Philip Glass, Phil Collins, Jackie Robinson, Charlotte Rampling, Langston Hughes, John Ford, Ida Lupino, Jascha Heifetz, Chogyam Trungpa, Ronald Reagan, Laura Ingalls Wilder, William Burroughs, Adlai Stevenson, Arthur Ochs Sulzburger, Roger Staubach, Gertrude Stein, James Michener.

Relationship Guide for Aquarius II

ANNE MORROW LINDBERGH
(GEMINI-CANCER CUSP)
CHARLES LINDBERGH (AQUARIUS II)
PAGE 484

BEST RELATIONSHIPS

LOVE
Taurus-Gemini Cusp
Gemini-Cancer Cusp
Leo I
Leo-Virgo Cusp
Libra II
Scorpio I
Scorpio-Sagittarius Cusp
Sagittarius I
Capricorn I

MARRIAGE
Pisces-Aries Cusp
Taurus I
Taurus III
Cancer II
Virgo II
Libra-Scorpio Cusp
Scorpio II
Sagittarius-Capricorn Cusp
Capricorn II
Aquarius-Pisces Cusp

FRIENDSHIP
Aries III
Cancer III
Virgo I
Virgo-Libra Cusp
Libra I
Libra III
Scorpio III
Capricorn-Aquarius Cusp
Pisces II

FAMILY
Aries II
Gemini I
Cancer I
Virgo III
Capricorn III
Pisces I

WORK
Aries-Taurus Cusp
Gemini II
Cancer-Leo Cusp
Sagittarius II
Aquarius II
Pisces III

Page Locator for All Relationships

AQUARIUS III
The Week of Acceptance

3

February 8–15

The Aquarius III period takes Acceptance as its central image. This period can be symbolically likened to a time in a person's advanced age when a more accepting outlook has emerged. Many prejudices, preconceptions and judgmental attitudes have diminished in relevance and have perhaps been stripped away altogether. Although irritability and negativity can certainly rear their head at this late stage of life, many by this time have adopted a forgiving attitude toward themselves and the choices they have made, friends and loved ones—indeed, the world in general. For those who are religious, thoughts of the afterlife and a deepening sense of responsibility motivate charitable acts. Psychic powers, an enjoyment of the simple pleasures, humor and wisdom in thought and speech mark this time. Ideally, even those who may be struggling physically can manage to display a dignity and wholeness that is inspiring to younger people.

The theme of acceptance runs strong in the lives of Aquarius III's. Some of them are hardheaded and not particularly open to unusual ideas and people but become increasingly tolerant as the years go by. Others are overly accepting from an early age and allow themselves to be unduly manipulated or influenced by stronger, more selfish types. The challenge for Aquarius III's is to remain open to the world while at the same time retaining the ability to be selective in screening out harmful influences.

Having dealt with some of their own prejudices, Aquarius III's often become champions of the underdog. They despise intolerance and unfair treatment in any

ZODIAC POSITION
Approximately
18–27° Aquarius
SEASON
Midwinter
ELEMENT
Air
RULER
Uranus
SYMBOL
The Water Bearer
MODE
Thought

form. They also react instinctively against those who put on airs, or pretend to be something they are not. Poking holes in other people's balloons is often an Aquarius III specialty, and if they carry this tendency to an extreme, they can be extremely cutting and hurtful. The reasons for this behavior may be found in a low self-image, perhaps reflecting negative parental attitudes expressed toward them in childhood. Aquarius III anger is sudden and explosive but rarely lasts for long. Their friends and family usually realize that it is often better for all concerned if they can get their aggression and dissatisfaction out in one go rather than letting it simmer inside.

The resourceful individuals born in the Week of Acceptance are rarely at a loss for new ideas. Perhaps because they get themselves into difficult or challenging situations so often, Aquarius III's learn early on how to extricate themselves from dilemmas. That they often create and solve their own problems makes them like two mythological figures rolled into one: Daedalus, who created the labyrinth, and Ariadne, who showed Theseus how to get out of it. In a basic sense, Aquarius III's are their own worst enemy.

Rarely at rest for long, Aquarius III's love activity and movement. Their liveliness is an extremely positive trait as far as their friends are concerned, and they are often sought out for their attractiveness, unusual demeanor and colorful language. The downside of their character is more often felt by their families than by their associates, for it is in the daily task of living with others that their greatest problems often arise. Those born in this week may be constantly annoyed with family members, and because they do not rate high in self-awareness, they

"ACCEPTANCE"

may fail to see that it is actually they who are the annoying ones.

Those born in this week are easily affected by what others say and do. A bad remark or look can easily set them on the wrong foot for a few hours or even ruin their whole day. Aquarius III's are particularly vulnerable to personal attack. They can stand any amount of criticism of their unusual ideas and, in fact, defend themselves well but may fly apart when dealing with people who can push their emotional buttons. Learning to be less vulnerable to ad hominem arguments, and to laugh off the negativity of others, whether it is intentional or not, is important if they are to maintain their psychic balance.

Humor, irony and wit often appear in abundance in those born in this week. These are among the mechanisms by which they are able to survive in an often difficult and hostile world. Another method they may use is the making of silent promises to themselves not to make the same mistake again, or to better their lives through positive action. Making plans and resolutions of all sorts for the future enables them to get through trying times. Above all, they know that no matter how bad things get, tomorrow is another day. In this respect, they view the future as potentially positive and self-renewing.

In the present, on the other hand, Aquarius III's may get into a hopeless state in which they believe that everything has gone wrong. Friends stand by helpless while they complain about their own deficiencies, and about

the unfair treatment they receive from the world. If they have negative attitudes about themselves, these can involve feelings of shame that may be focused on their bodies or on mistakes they feel they have made. Such attitudes are empowered by guilt. Yet although Aquarius III's may blame themselves constantly, they can rarely hear reproach from others without a strong defensive reaction, perhaps involving a reciprocal attack on the accuser. Learning to listen to the suggestions of concerned family members may be almost impossible for them; it is easier for them to take advice from friends, or even strangers.

Week of Acceptance people may be extremely affectionate to others and may crave love themselves. Love is apparently hard for them to find, however, since they are constantly in search of it. Aquarius III's are rarely able to find the right person for themselves before the age of thirty, if at all. Their needs often demand a wide range of partners, associates, mates or friends. Aquarius III's are not easily satisfied and often bored. Their need for attention may run high, and the danger here is that they become the eternal butterfly, flitting from one delicious flower to the next. Their nonattachment is not in itself a negative trait—on the contrary, it is a lesson that all of us have to learn sooner or later. For Aquarius III's, however, the lessons that need to be learned are those of constancy, consistency, application and dedication.

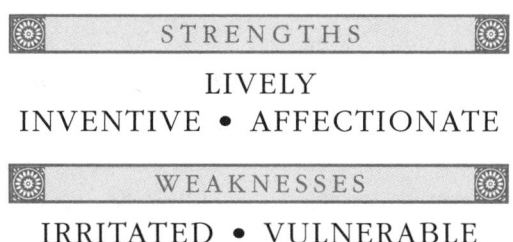

STRENGTHS

LIVELY
INVENTIVE • AFFECTIONATE

WEAKNESSES

IRRITATED • VULNERABLE
NEEDY

ADVICE:

Accept your need for other people and cultivate meaningful social interaction. Remain open and accepting, but demand that others accept you as you are, too. Your psychic abilities are valuable—use them constructively. Beware of allowing rejection to lower your self-esteem.

AQUARIUS III NOTABLES

Best known for her novel *The Color Purple*, for which she won the Pulitzer Prize, **Alice Walker** is also an essayist, poet and short-story writer. The film of the novel by Steven Spielberg brought Alice Walker to even greater public prominence. Born as the youngest child in a rural Georgia sharecropper's family, Walker was blinded in one eye as a child in an accident. Acceptance of her disability and recovering from her troubled adolescence marked her as a true Aquarius III. Working in the civil rights movement in Mississippi, she met and married lawyer Mel Leventhal, with whom she had a daughter, described in her novel *Meridian*. A more recent novel, *The Same River Twice*, reveals Alice Walker's struggles toward acceptance.

ALICE WALKER

On the basis of only three films—*Rebel Without a Cause*, *East of Eden* and *Giant*—and his death in a car crash at age 24, actor **James Dean** attracted a huge cult following. The three films were made in barely over a year, showing Dean as the quintessential rebel and an actor of enormous talent. Both in his life and films, typical Aquarius III problems, such as craving love, being easily bored, protecting the helpless, and having difficulty accepting advice (particularly when given by family members) all emerge strongly. Even Dean's own death at high speed in a sports car was due to his inability to accept limitations of time and space.

JAMES DEAN

Born in Hollywood, the daughter of actress Maureen O'Sullivan and director John Farrow, **Mia Farrow** was destined for stardom. She made her debut in one of her father's films, *John Paul Jones*, at age 14. Herself married to (or companion of) three famous men—Frank Sinatra, Andre Previn and Woody Allen—Farrow may have had to accept secondary positions in each relationship. Fittingly, in many of her screen roles she plays vulnerable characters with

MIA FARROW

adaptable egos who learn how to become tough. The elements of her life story include learning to stand up for herself, overcoming insecurities and becoming her own person. Mia Farrow is the biological or adoptive mother of 13 children.

More Aquarius III's: Abraham Lincoln, Galileo, Charles Darwin, Susan B. Anthony, Thomas Edison, Virginia E. Johnson, Jules Verne, Brendan Behan, Bertolt Brecht, Stella Adler, Charles Tiffany, Bill Russell, Paul Bocuse, Roberta Flack, Jack Lemmon, Greg Norman, Peter Gabriel, Claire Bloom, Carl Bernstein, Jack Benny, George Segal, Oliver Reed, Chuck Yeager, Georges Simenon, Leontyne Price.

Relationship Guide for Aquarius III

BILL RUSSELL (AQUARIUS III)
WILT CHAMBERLAIN (LEO-VIRGO CUSP)
PAGE 610

BEST RELATIONSHIPS

LOVE
Aries-Taurus Cusp
Taurus-Gemini Cusp
Gemini II
Cancer III
Leo II
Virgo-Libra Cusp
Libra III
Scorpio II
Sagittarius II
Capricorn II
Capricorn-Aquarius Cusp
Aquarius I
Pisces I

MARRIAGE
Aries I
Taurus I
Cancer I
Leo-Virgo Cusp
Virgo II
Libra I
Capricorn I
Aquarius III
Pisces III

FRIENDSHIP
Pisces-Aries Cusp
Aries III
Cancer II
Leo I
Libra II
Scorpio I
Scorpio-Sagittarius Cusp
Sagittarius III
Pisces II

FAMILY
Taurus III
Leo III
Aquarius II
Aquarius-Pisces Cusp

WORK
Taurus II
Virgo I
Scorpio III
Sagittarius I
Capricorn III

Page Locator for All Relationships

AQUARIUS-PISCES CUSP
The Cusp of Sensitivity

February 16–22

The Aquarius-Pisces cusp can be symbolically likened in human terms to the period around seventy-seven years of age, and comes amid the freezing, harsh weather of late winter in the northern hemisphere. However, winter will soon be over and spring on the way as the days lengthen.

In human development, at the age of seventy-seven, the close of the life cycle may be near. By this time the human being should have come to terms with his/her life and to peace with loved ones and friends. Breaking down any armor that remains and showing honest feelings are important now. Rarely will new projects be taken on at this time, but the explorations involved in ending life may come to represent a kind of ultimate peak experience for the highly philosophical. The days comprise the Aquarius-Pisces cusp exemplify some of the manifestations of Sensitivity (the central theme of this cusp), where the active, inventive and universal Aquarius impulses merge with watery, impressionable and dreamy Pisces qualities.

Those born on the Cusp of Sensitivity are often success-oriented individuals who give top priority to their career. They are usually fighters, an attitude sometimes based on underlying insecurity and the need to prove themselves. A chip-on-the-shoulder attitude in many Aquarius-Pisces makes them aggressive toward others and belligerent when attacked. A great personal challenge for Aquarius-Pisces, then, is to rediscover and acknowledge their inner makeup and to break down some of the barriers they have built up. The tough, even aggressive exterior of many born on the Aquarius-Pisces Cusp belies the sensitive personality inside. Extremely

ZODIAC POSITION
Approximately
26° Aquarius–4° Pisces

SEASONS
Late winter

ELEMENTS
Air/Water

RULERS
Uranus/Neptune

SYMBOLS
The Water Bearer/
The Fish

MODES
Thought/Feeling

vulnerable as children, Aquarius-Pisces react to criticism or abuse from others by building a wall around themselves. Carried with them into adulthood, this armor may give the impression of an inner self far different from the reality.

Since Aquarius is the most universal sign and Pisces one of the most intimate, it should not be surprising that many born on this cusp orient themselves to one of two extremes: either the most far-out, idealistic pursuits or the most inner, deep, profound ones. Combining such essentially unlike attitudes may be extremely difficult, and many Aquarius-Pisces swing from one to the other. In their work, for example, they may deal with abstract concerns, or with attempts to surpass objective limitations, while in their private lives they delve into the world of feelings, people and human affairs.

Important as it is for Aquarius-Pisces to reconcile these two extremes in their nature, they should also work to explore the middle ground between them—the social side of life. Being strung between the poles of the physical and the metaphysical often means neglecting interaction with other people.

Aquarius-Pisces may be closely bound to their families. Although parental disapproval and criticism will hurt them in childhood, strong emotional bonds tie them to mother, father, or both. (Usually the stronger and most influential relationship is with the parent of the opposite sex.) Breaking free of such attachments is essential if they are to emerge into adulthood as unique individuals—a truth, perhaps, for many of us, but adolescence may be particularly rebellious and stormy for Aquarius-Pisces. Those who do not succeed in breaking

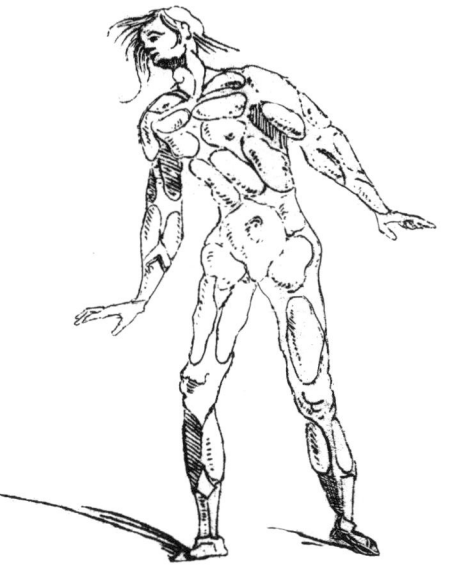

"SENSITIVITY"

away during this time may continue their struggle for the rest of their lives, even after the death of parents or other powerful family elders.

Particularly in matters of love, Aquarius-Pisces will have to struggle to be open, honest and accepting with their partner, and to allow themselves to be vulnerable, even at the risk of pain. Thus personal relationships may have the effect of putting Aquarius-Pisces back in touch with their essential self. Even Aquarius-Pisces who are forceful and hard-driving in their careers may be quite passive in their personal relationships. In addition, a tendency to display both masculine and feminine qualities in their love relationships, even to the point of bisexuality, can mark male Aquarius-Pisces as unusually sensitive and females as unusually aggressive. Such role reversals often favor their choosing a mate who is their opposite: a more sensitive Aquarius-Pisces male, for example, marrying a more aggressive female, and so on.

In relationships, fear of rejection figures prominently, for Aquarius-Pisces want to be liked but are often afraid of getting hurt, or don't know how to go about getting approval without compromising themselves. For some, a show of pessimism or dissatisfaction guards them against having to interact; others appear more pleasant or agreeable, but this, too, is a facade designed to preclude any deep involvement. Gaining the courage to struggle in their personal relationships as forcefully as in their careers, to risk rejection, stand up

for themselves and express their emotions powerfully, are challenges that those born on this cusp must eventually meet.

Friendship may be an important vehicle for bringing Aquarius-Pisces out into the world, enticing them to participate in club, community, philanthropic and school endeavors. The essential role that friends play for those born on this cusp goes beyond normal fellowship, companionship and personal sharing. Beyond having a small number of friends, Aquarius-Pisces gain by building bridges with colleagues, co-workers, acquaintances and more remote family members. By developing their people skills, they will widen their humanity and ease feelings of being isolated and misunderstood. Viewing the suffering of others first-hand can help those born on the Cusp of Sensitivity to realize that the unhappiness they have gone through themselves is in no way unique, allowing them the human points of identification that they desperately need.

Building their own family, including children, or living in a family situation is often a positive experience for Aquarius-Pisces, although their need to be alone and their difficulty in regular or intense interactions may make such relationships hard for them to maintain. Still, their nurturing qualities need to be expressed in some area of their lives—if not through family, perhaps through pets or career projects. Expressing their care, concern and sympathy is as necessary to Aquarius-Pisces as are love and passion.

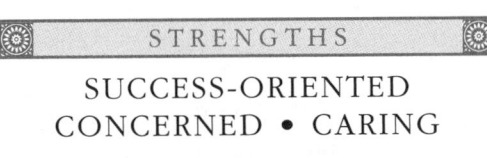

STRENGTHS

SUCCESS-ORIENTED
CONCERNED • CARING

WEAKNESSES

INSECURE • PESSIMISTIC
ISOLATED

ADVICE:

Don't give up on the world or retreat behind fences. If necessary tear obstructions down to rediscover your sensitive self. Learning to trust may mean ceasing to fear. Without denying your need to explore the depths and the heights, take the middle road more often.

AQUARIUS-PISCES CUSP NOTABLES

The most beloved of all writers of piano music, **Frederic Chopin** grew up in Warsaw, the son of a French father and Polish mother. At the astonishingly young age of 18, Chopin had already written the first of his études, nocturnes and piano concertos. Of an incredibly sensitive disposition, Chopin, personifies in his life and music, the qualities of those born on the Aquarius-Pisces cusp. He moved to Paris, where he met novelist George Sand. In their love affair Chopin showed the mixture of masculine and feminine traits and the passivity characteristic of many Aquarius-Pisces people. He made his living teaching piano and gave only a few public concerts, choosing to perform in private salons, occasionally with composer-pianist Franz Liszt.

FREDERIC CHOPIN

Born on the Cusp of Sensitivity, novelist and college professor **Toni Morrison** shows the unusually close family bonds in childhood and the orientation toward success that are characteristic of many an Aquarius-Pisces. Winner of the Pulitzer Prize and the Nobel Prize for Literature, the first African American to win the latter, she is author of the novels *The Bluest Eye, Sula, Song of Solomon, Tar Baby, Beloved* and *Jazz*. Morrison has also had a distinguished teaching career, beginning at Texas Southern and Howard universities and more recently at Harvard and Yale and as Robert F. Goheen Professor of

TONI MORRISON

Humanities at Princeton. Morrison worked in the publishing business as a senior editor at Random House.

In a sport where superstars abound, guard **Michael Jordan** has been called the greatest basketball player of all time. Jordan's extreme Sensitivity is well hidden behind a wall of self-assurance, characteristic of many born on the Aquarius-Pisces cusp. The public got a quick glimpse of his more personal feelings when Michael's father died. On the court, Jordan is unstoppable. His stats are overwhelming: 8-time All-NBA First Team, 8-time scoring leader, 10-time All-Star, 4-time MVP, as well as the highest scoring average in history, an amazing 32 points per game. In tv interviews, the impeccably dressed Jordan conveys a strong and articulate image but holds a lot of emotion quietly in reserve.

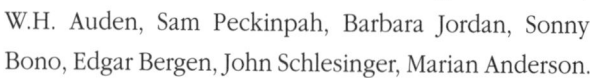

MICHAEL JORDAN

More Aquarius-Pisces: Yoko Ono, Amy Tan, Ansel Adams, Sidney Poitier, Charles Barkley, Margaux Hemingway, John Travolta, Ivana Trump, Matt Dillon, Milos Forman, Cybill Shepherd, Gloria Vanderbilt, Julius Erving, Helen Gurley Brown, John McEnroe, Giulietta Masina, Edward M. Kennedy, Anais Nin, W.H. Auden, Sam Peckinpah, Barbara Jordan, Sonny Bono, Edgar Bergen, John Schlesinger, Marian Anderson.

Relationship Guide for Aquarius-Pisces Cusp

Page Locator for All Relationships

YOKO ONO (AQUARIUS-PISCES CUSP)
JOHN LENNON (LIBRA III)
PAGE 695

BEST RELATIONSHIPS

LOVE
Pisces-Aries Cusp
Taurus III
Cancer I
Leo II
Virgo III
Libra II
Libra III
Capricorn I
Capricorn III
Pisces III

MARRIAGE
Cancer II
Cancer-Leo Cusp
Leo I
Virgo-Libra Cusp
Scorpio III
Sagittarius II
Aquarius II
Pisces I

FRIENDSHIP
Aries I
Aries-Taurus Cusp
Gemini I
Gemini-Cancer Cusp
Leo III
Libra-Scorpio Cusp
Sagittariius-Capricorn Cusp
Capricorn II
Aquarius-Pisces Cusp
Pisces II

FAMILY
Aries II
Taurus II
Gemini III
Cancer III
Capricorn-Aquarius Cusp
Aquarius III

WORK
Aries III
Taurus I
Gemini II
Leo-Virgo Cusp
Libra I
Scorpio I

PISCES I
The Week of Spirit

February 23–March 2

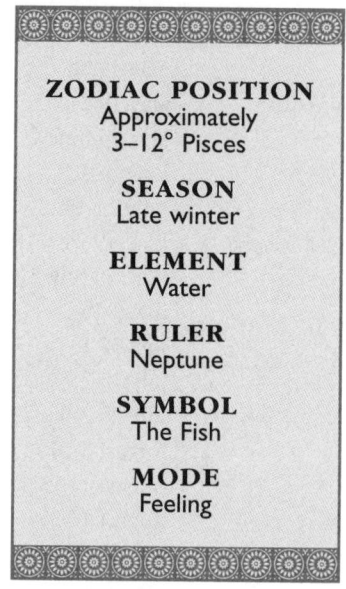

ZODIAC POSITION
Approximately
3–12° Pisces

SEASON
Late winter

ELEMENT
Water

RULER
Neptune

SYMBOL
The Fish

MODE
Feeling

The Pisces I period takes Spirit as its central image. This segment of the The Grand Cycle of Life can be likened in human terms to the years of a person's late seventies. At this time, in the twilight of life, many think of higher values and of spiritual goals. For some, religion plays an important role at this time, for others a cause that embodies their highest ideals. Realizing that they have already lived beyond the average lifespan gives many a feeling for the precious nature of life that they never had previously. Ideally, every week, month and year—ultimately, every day—becomes a special gift. However, others may have come to regard life as a burden and long for the release of the spirit from the body.

The days that comprise Pisces I symbolically reveal the elder embracing the present moment fully, either with joy or sorrow, but also pausing to contemplate the past and future more meaningfully than before. A higher consciousness of the meaning of life, sacrifice for a higher cause, belief in the afterlife or reincarnation, even a continued zest for living and a wish to remain ever young, are all possible at this time.

Those born in the Week of Spirit value the nonmaterial side of life. It's not that they lack either respect for money-making and business or abilities in these fields. It is simply that, whether engaged in the arts or in finance, in religion or in administration, Pisces I's generally approach their work devotionally, elevating it to an idealistic plane. Nor are they without strong physical drives, or a love of the pleasures of the table and the bed. A blend of a spiritual and a sensual approach is at the heart of their personalities. Many Pisces I's do not see spirituality as denoting an ascetic approach that would ask them to cut their bonds with the everyday world. On the contrary, since those born in this week seek the spirit in everything around them, they rarely feel the need to reject worldly considerations.

Spiritedness is also characteristic of Pisces I's, who are often lively and entertaining people. They have a youthful air that can belie their actual age. Not infrequently, those born in this week are also engaged in the personal pursuit of health or are advocates of it. It is important to them to lead a healthy life, so as to increase not only the longevity but the quality of their earthly existence. A desire to do good, in the sense of leaving one's immediate environment, or the world in general, a bit of a better place at the close of a career or a life, is characteristic of those born in the Week of Spirit. Watching environmental mistakes or catastrophes happen, then, may be particularly difficult for these involved, caring individuals.

The devotional and service-oriented side of Pisces I's urges them to give up their own wants, making them subservient to their need to give pleasure and benefit to others. As a consequence of this quality, they may easily become the target or prey of more selfish individuals, who see them as an easy touch, and a dependable source of sympathy, energy or money. Making big-hearted offers to others, and then coming to regret or resent these promises, may lead Pisces I's into arguments and emotional crises. Indeed, sending mixed signals is characteristic of those born in this week.

Pisces I's are prone to feeling hurt when others do not meet their high standards of friendship. In fact, they put such high expectations on their relationships that they set

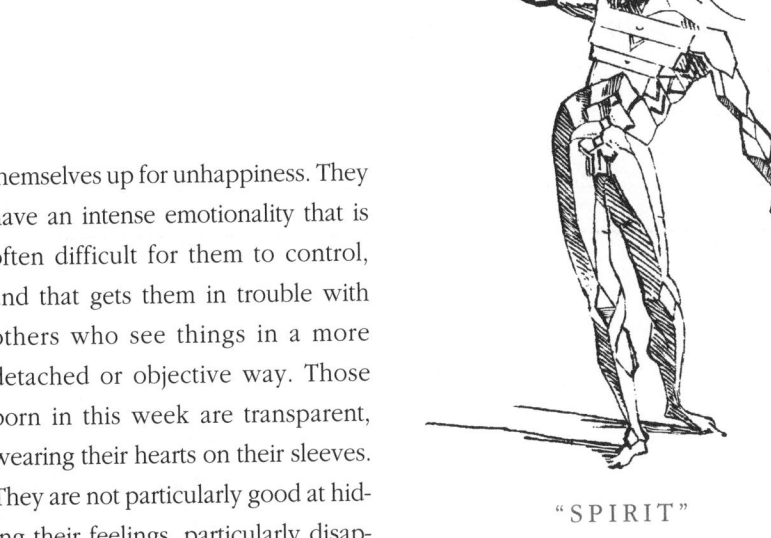

"SPIRIT"

themselves up for unhappiness. They have an intense emotionality that is often difficult for them to control, and that gets them in trouble with others who see things in a more detached or objective way. Those born in this week are transparent, wearing their hearts on their sleeves. They are not particularly good at hiding their feelings, particularly disappointment. In one relationship after another, they can refuse to learn how to protect themselves, or to keep their egos from merging with their love object, no matter how much they swear to do so.

For all their humanitarian and empathic qualities, Pisces I's may tend to imagine themselves on a higher plane than those around them, often without realizing it. This unconscious attitude may keep them from a deeper involvement with others, leading to a somewhat superficial involvement with life, or, worse, to negativity and bitter cynicism toward the world. The know-it-all attitude of some Pisces I's is difficult for others to deal with, and can lead to resentment and ultimately rejection in personal relationships. By admitting mistakes, and above all by being open to suggestions and criticism, the philosophical individuals born in this week will rise to an even higher personal level in their search for meaning in life.

Sharing at a deep level with family and friends is an essential need for Pisces I's—the knack for enjoying the pleasures of life alone is not usually part of their makeup. Unfortunately they are not always successful in their attempts to share, and this can be a source of continued frustration throughout their lives. In their love relationships Pisces I's often display an emotional instability. Changing partners can become a way of life for them. In fact, what they are really seeking is an ideal, and if they find it they will not hesitate to commit to it in a permanent relationship.

One of the biggest problems in their treatment of mates or spouses is backing off emotionally, though they remain loyal and devoted. In turn, they may make demands that others find suffocating; Pisces I's can be a lot to handle. And no matter how much they insist on their belief in mutual independence, or in an "open" marriage or relationship, they can be quite unrealistic in not recognizing their own possessive and jealous nature.

Rather than living in a world of expectations, concepts and ideas most of the time, Pisces I's would do well to accept the responsibility of simple everyday tasks and chores that will ground them in the here and now. The stability of their relationships will be enhanced if their mates and friends insist that they take on firm responsibilities, even performing mundane, repetitive tasks which are difficult to idealize. Partners who fail in this, perhaps just refusing to rely on the Pisces I and doing what needs to be done themselves, will simply reinforce their mate's bad habits: those born in this week are regretfully prone to walking forgetfully out of the kitchen before the dishes are collected and washed.

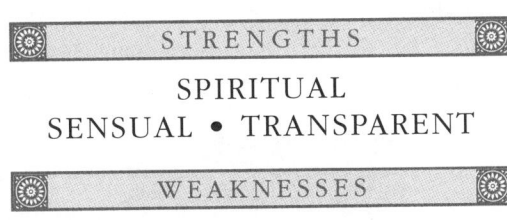

STRENGTHS

SPIRITUAL
SENSUAL • TRANSPARENT

WEAKNESSES

EMOTIONAL
IRRESPONSIBLE • CATASTROPHIC

ADVICE:

Sometimes you need to be more aggressive. Keep in touch with everyday matters and remain attentive to your needs and the needs of others. Beware of alienation through placing yourself on a higher plane. Seeking a higher state of consciousness need not mean avoiding shouldering the work of life.

PISCES I NOTABLES

Typical of those born in the Week of Spirit, film star **Elizabeth Taylor** has made many changes in her search for an ideal in love and has had difficulties protecting herself from her own feelings. In fact, Taylor has been

married 8 times, including twice to actor Richard Burton, opposite whom she won an Oscar for *Who's Afraid of Virginia Woolf?* Like many Pisces I's, Taylor blends high-spiritedness with intense physicality, traits that are evident both on and off the screen. She has been tireless in her work for the American Foundation for AIDS Research, of which

ELIZABETH TAYLOR

she was the founding chairperson. Her struggle with alcohol and painkiller dependency typical of Pisceans, has been widely publicized.

Embodying many traits of those born in the Week of Spirit, 2-time Nobel Prize–winning scientist **Linus Pauling** dedicated his life to making others more healthy and happy (he won a Nobel Prize for chemistry, and the Peace Prize). He was the leading authority on the use of vitamin C, which he urged most people to take at very high doses, usually up to several grams per day. Pauling refuted all reports of ill effects

LINUS PAULING

of megadoses of vitamin C and claimed its positive benefit in combating a host of illnesses and building resistance against disease, notably the common cold.

Founder of the Linus Pauling Institute of Science and Medicine in Palo Alto, Calif., he continued to be extremely active (and controversial) into his late 80s, which he attributed to a healthy lifestyle.

Political philosopher and the last Soviet president, **Mikhail Gorbachev** did more than any single figure to bring about the breakup of the Soviet Union and the emergence of democracy in Russia. He was

MIKHAIL GORBACHEV

notably the innovator of two major ideological concepts in his country: *perestroika* (restructuring) and *glasnost* (openness). Gorbachev was the only official in Soviet history to win the Nobel Peace Prize. In many ways a typical Pisces I, Gorbachev approached his work in a devotional manner and elevated his activities to an idealistic plane. Although extremely unpopular in the former Soviet Union today and blamed for the current economic woes there, Gorbachev is highly regarded internationally.

Pisces I's: W.E.B. Du Bois, Georg Friedrich Händel, Adelle Davis, Enrico Caruso, Tom Wolfe, John Irving, Peter Fonda, Lou Reed, David Sarnoff, Bernadette Peters, Vincente Minnelli, George Harrison, Joanne Woodward, Ralph Nader, John Steinbeck, Lawrence Durrell, Harry Belafonte, Dinah Shore, Dexter Gordon, Fats Domino, Jackie Gleason, Kasimir Malevich, James Farentino.

Relationship Guide for Pisces I

RICHARD BURTON (SCORPIO II)
ELIZABETH TAYLOR (PISCES I)
PAGE 724

BEST RELATIONSHIPS

LOVE
Gemini III
Virgo I
Libra-Scorpio Cusp
Sagittarius II
Aquarius I
Aquarius III
Pisces II

MARRIAGE
Gemini I
Gemini-Cancer Cusp
Cancer I
Leo II
Capricorn II
Capricorn III
Aquarius-Pisces Cusp

FRIENDSHIP
Aries I
Aries-Taurus Cusp
Taurus II
Gemini II
Cancer II
Cancer III
Leo I
Leo-Virgo Cusp
Virgo II
Virgo-Libra Cusp
Libra I
Scorpio I
Scorpio-Sagittarius Cusp
Capricorn-Aquarius Cusp

FAMILY
Taurus I
Virgo III
Sagittarius III
Capricorn I
Aquarius II

WORK
Aries II
Taurus III
Leo III
Libra II
Scorpio II
Sagittarius I
Pisces I
Pisces III

Page Locator for All Relationships

PISCES II
The Week of the Loner

March 3–10

The Pisces II period takes The Loner as its central image. According to The Grand Cycle of Life, in human terms this period relates to the time when a person reaches the majestic age of eighty. At this point, feelings of oneness with the nature of things but isolation from the world of man may arise. Many friends and perhaps a life partner have departed, leaving the octogenarian to carry on. This can be an extremely trying time both psychologically and physically—thus keeping positive about life may be difficult. Some now yearn for an easy end, but others may enjoy a final release from the responsibilities of this world and thus experience a sense of renewed freedom.

The days comprise Pisces II symbolically reveal a person very advanced in years turning inward and pursuing purely internal goals in relative isolation. Thinking creatively and imaginatively, contemplating rewards or punishments in the afterlife and apprehending a heightened sense of beauty in the nature of things are all typical of this period.

Pisces II's tend to live in a private world of their own. This is true not only internally but outwardly for their homes are often retreats from the world, places to which few are admitted. The healthier Pisces II's can give equal weight to their careers, on the one hand, and to their social and personal lives, on the other; less balanced individuals born in this week may choose to isolate themselves more than is good for them.

Pisces II's generally have an instinctive dislike of superficiality. They mistrust loud, aggressive or pushy individuals and find it hard to work with colleagues who

ZODIAC POSITION
Approximately
11–21° Pisces

SEASON
Late winter

ELEMENT
Water

RULER
Neptune

SYMBOL
The Fish

MODE
Feeling

lack sensitivity. This is not to imply that they lack force or ambition. For them, however, the way a thing is done is often more important than what that thing is, and the end therefore rarely justifies the means. Grace, honesty and an unassailable aesthetic and moral code prevent them from acting underhandedly or, in particular, hurtfully. On the other hand, Pisces II's may express their dislike of society's mores through blatantly antisocial deeds, acting, as it were, in defense of their own right to individual expression. A certain elegance and grace are evident in most things they do, and they are finely attuned to many kinds of physical expression, whether it be sports, dance or more sensual forms of movement. Those born in this week are great admirers of sensuous beauty, particularly in people and paintings, and their homes and surroundings generally show some kind of special touch.

Pisces II's have a strong soulful side, apparent in their love of music and in their empathy for all forms of human suffering. They generally believe that life is not just there to be enjoyed, and that one must in some way pay one's dues with a certain amount of suffering before obtaining any real benefit. Rarely will those born in this week escape at least one severe trauma in their lives, perhaps involving physical injury, disease or the untimely death of a parent or friend. They are often struck by such catastrophes without warning, but they are resilient and have an enormous capacity to bounce back from disaster. Like a cat, they are blessed with nine lives, at least a few of which they are sure to use up.

Pisces II's see a distinct difference between being lonely (which they rarely are) and being alone (which they are often). Their own best companion, they are capable of spending hours and days alone with a good book, or with their work, without needing to talk to anyone. Their friends will know when they want to be left alone and when they want company, and will learn not to intrude on their privacy. In the workplace they do well as freelancers, operating outside the office, but if employed by a company or business they will probably need a certain amount of time each day for working on their own.

Dangerous areas for the Pisces II personality include anything with a strong habituative or outright addictive quality—drugs, drink, sex. On the other hand, their ecstatic highs, spiritual insights and emotional joys can be incredibly intense and rewarding. Pisces II's often crave peak experiences, which are not bad things in themselves as long as those who seek them can handle them without undue attachment. If the Pisces II's remain free to move on, such experiences will leave them greatly enriched in their personal development. On the other hand, should they be unfortunate enough to get hooked on their own personal suffering or self-pity, they may wallow in such states for alarmingly long periods of time.

Generally speaking, Pisces II's ask only one thing from the world, and that is to be accepted as they really are. That the world often cannot grant their wish becomes the cross they bear. To comfort themselves, and to shield themselves from disappointment and rejection, they may surrender to the pur-

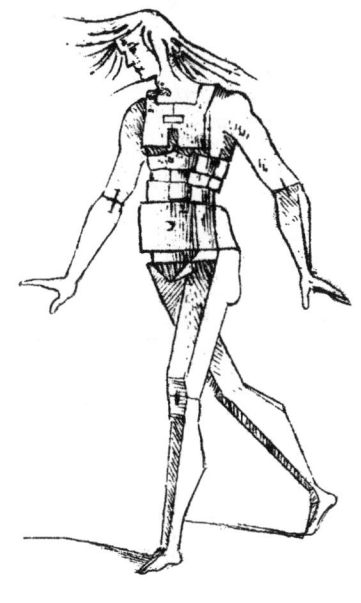

"LONER"

suit of money, or retreat to a fantasy-full interior life, often devoted to beauty and imagination. Whenever possible, Pisces II's should follow occupations that make solid and grounding demands on them without depriving them of creativity. This kind of work will help them to stay on an even keel.

Those born in the Week of the Loner usually have few friends, but those they have are often close and loyal. Many born in this week do not like large family gatherings or social events; intimacy is really their thing, and sharing intimacy with others, whether mates, friends, lovers or valued family members, is perhaps their most cherished activity. Highly personal interaction is their forte, and the sharing of joys and sorrows is essential to their happiness.

In love, perhaps because those born in this week have a greater ability to enjoy or appreciate such areas than others do, or perhaps their resistance to the lure of physical pleasure is lower; they are more prone than others to be snagged by a pretty face, sensuous voice or alluring body. Once attached to a person, their addiction to his or her company can be

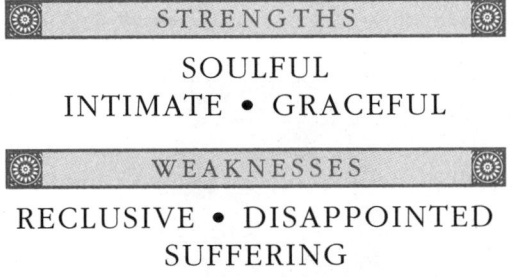

STRENGTHS

SOULFUL
INTIMATE • GRACEFUL

WEAKNESSES

RECLUSIVE • DISAPPOINTED
SUFFERING

even more severe than their attraction to physical substances. They will run the gamut of painful emotions, from jealousy to hatred, yet if they decide they want to get free of their love object they will feel powerful separation anxiety. Friends and mates of a practical nature tend to bring them down to earth. Meanwhile, children will help them share their sense of wonder and awe at the natural world.

ADVICE:

Try to remain realistic in your outlook. Resist the lure of escapes, in all their varied forms. On the other hand, leave a window open on the world. Continue to strive for trust and acceptance, but remember to stand up for yourself as well. Improving your social position may make certain things easier for you. Your suffering may neither be unique or, for that matter, necessary.

PISCES II NOTABLES

The name of **Tamara Karsavina** is not as well known in America as that of Pavlova and Nijinsky, but these three were undoubtedly the leading Russian ballet

TAMARA KARSAVINA

dancers of their time. She was a highly private Pisces II who lived very much in a world of her own. Nijinsky's partner, and his equal in classical technique, she lost him when he was hospitalized with schizophrenia at age 28. Diaghilev's prima ballerina at the Ballet Russe in Paris, Karsavina danced Stravinsky's ballet *Petrouchka* with Michel Fokine and also danced with Russian dancer-choreographer Léonide Massine. Karsavina was co-founder of the Royal Academy of Dancing in London and was known as a kind and understanding, albeit eccentric, teacher.

Although **Bobby Fischer** emerged as the world champion of chess after his historic match with Boris Spassky, he retreated in true Pisces II fashion and has made only one major public chess appearance since: in Montenegro in 1991 when he faced Spassky again. Very much a Loner, Fischer felt rejected by the chess world, particularly the Russians, whom he saw as a malignant influence on the game. Fischer proved himself not only an amazingly aggressive player but also a highly canny one who did not hesitate to use psychology against Spassky

BOBBY FISCHER

to undermine his confidence. To suggest that Fischer lost the 1st game to Spassky on purpose and deliberately forfeited the 2nd by not showing up seems inconceivable, but he may in fact have put himself at a 2-0 disadvantage intentionally to set his opponent up for his devastatingly destructive comeback.

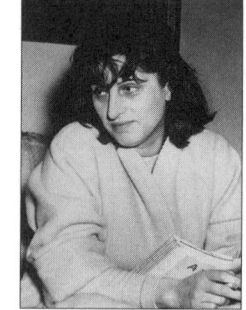

ANNA MAGNANI

Italian film actress **Anna Magnani** had the soulful, inner quality of a Pisces II woman. Her first early performance to gain international acclaim was in Roberto Rossellini's neorealistic film *Open City*. Although Magnani worked mostly in Italian cinema, she became known to the American public in 1955, when she made *The Rose Tattoo* with Burt Lancaster, for which she received an Oscar for best actress. Magnani had an earthy sexiness, but her unusual looks did not destine her to be a glamour queen. She did best in more serious and maternal roles. Thus Magnani impressed her audiences as an actress with deep feelings, characteristic of those born in the Week of the Loner.

Pisces II's: Alexander Graham Bell, Jackie Joyner-Kersee, Gabriel Garcia-Marquez, Michelangelo, Aidan Quinn, Piet Mondrian, Cyd Charisse, Ornette Coleman, Raul Julia, Lynn Redgrave, Franco Harris, Lynn Swann, Mickie Spillane, Harriet Tubman, David Rabe, Rosa Luxemburg, Oliver Wendell Holmes, Cyrano de Bergerac.

Relationship Guide for Pisces II

ELIZABETH BARRETT BROWNING (PISCES II)
ROBERT BROWNING (TAURUS II)
PAGE 370

BEST RELATIONSHIPS

LOVE
Taurus III
Gemini II
Cancer I
Cancer II
Virgo I
Scorpio I
Pisces I
Pisces II

MARRIAGE
Aries II
Taurus II
Cancer-Leo Cusp
Leo-Virgo Cusp
Virgo II
Scorpio II
Scorpio-Sagittarius Cusp
Sagittarius II

FRIENDSHIP
Aries III
Taurus I
Taurus-Gemini Cusp
Cancer III
Leo II
Libra I
Libra III
Sagittarius III
Sagittarius-Capricorn Cusp
Capricorn II
Aquarius II
Aquarius III
Aquarius-Pisces Cusp

FAMILY
Gemini III
Virgo III
Sagittarius I
Capricorn-Aquarius Cusp

WORK
Aries I
Gemini I
Leo I
Libra-Scorpio Cusp
Scorpio III
Capricorn III
Aquarius I

Page Locator for All Relationships

PISCES III
The Week of Dancers and Dreamers

March 11–18

The Pisces III period takes Dancers and Dreamers as its central image. Simply put, this period closes the Grand Cycle and represents the ending of this lifetime on earth. The great wheel has at last come full circle. Those about to leave this earthly plane feel the gravity of the earth's attraction more strongly than ever but also the inexorable pull of the world beyond. Even through pain and suffering, a range of emotions may be felt: from acceptance to expectation to excitement joy. A quickening sense of an experience far beyond what one has yet known or, in some cases, a glimmering recognition of such a state may be felt at this time. Both present and past are finally left behind in the body when the mind enters a dreamworld and the soul dances on. The days that comprise Pisces III symbolically reveal an individual embarking on the ultimate transition into the beyond. Exercising faculties of intuition and inspiration, encountering an inexorable fate (embracing it or struggling against it), rising to new spiritual heights and realizations and, finally, closing the life cycle that may lead again to rebirth are all part of this process.

Strongly philosophical, Pisces III's often spend time contemplating the intricacies of human thought and the wonders of the universe. Their minds roam freely over areas that many would find daunting or at least mysterious. They start wondering about the meaning of life early on, and often continue to puzzle over such questions for a lifetime—indeed, these issues can become the driving force behind their careers and lifestyles.

Although visionary in thought, Pisces III's have an intensely practical side and often well-developed techni-

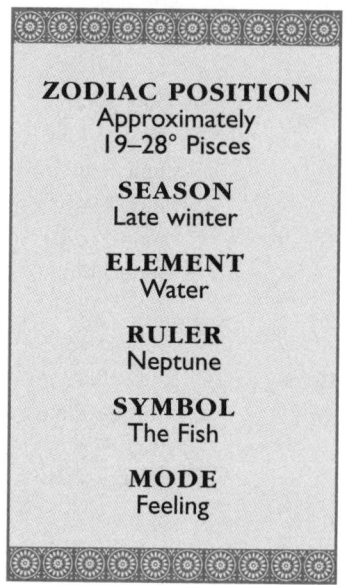

ZODIAC POSITION
Approximately
19–28° Pisces

SEASON
Late winter

ELEMENT
Water

RULER
Neptune

SYMBOL
The Fish

MODE
Feeling

cal or scientific skills. It is important to them to take an active hand in whatever is going on around them and to help other people solve their problems; they have a tremendous need to influence the lives of others and often manage to do so. Pisces III's may even become overinvolved, failing to recognize when to back off. Those around them may come to view their interest as meddling, mistrusting or resenting their good intentions.

One might accuse Pisces III's of being unrealistic if they didn't prove correct so much of the time. Making the unbelievable believable, or the impossible possible, is perhaps their greatest power. They may seem to be quite down-to-earth, pragmatic, even ordinary types, yet their achievements at times border on the miraculous. It is as if, although not actually believers in miracles, they were somehow able to realize or experience them. There is a marked tendency to the paranormal in the personalities of those born in the Week of Dancers and Dreamers, who can manifest clairvoyant or telepathic tendencies at an early age. If those around them downplay, scoff at or suppress their abilities, they may not feel secure enough to acknowledge and reveal these talents openly until later in life.

Pisces III's must beware of appearing too glib and learn when to speak on a given subject. Although much that they say is true, and of a high order of thinking, their omniscient manner can antagonize people. Developing humility and admitting mistakes will only add to their credibility—an important lesson, since they can become highly frustrated if their words fail to have the desired effect. They often see themselves as teachers, a role they aren't necessarily at all cut out for, and their disappointment over not having students, follow-

"DANCERS
AND DREAMERS"

ers or disciples can bring them a measure of unhappiness.

Those around Pisces III's may well find them strange or peculiar, a trait that can make them either more or less desirable, depending on whom they meet. Some Pisces III's have an air of self-importance, others radiate a kind of ineffectuality; both types may become complacent, however, figuring that wherever they are at that moment, whether in their career or in their living situation, is the best or at least the safest place for them to be. To an unusual degree, however, their lives are ruled by fate, and at a certain point, perhaps between the ages of twenty-eight and forty-two, a call will come to them in the form of a great challenge. Whether they respond to this unsolicited invitation from destiny may well determine the course of the rest of their lives. If they try to scale the heights, they have a better-than-average chance of succeeding, no matter how daunting the endeavor.

Comfort-loving, those born in this week know how to make life pleasant for themselves and for others; in furnishing their homes, for example, they are often tasteful and imaginative. Yet a curious wanderlust or impermanence in their lifestyles can make for frequent moves, in which they leave a string of well-furnished and improved dwellings behind them. Those who do manage to stay in one place for a time may periodically need to refurbish or renovate their living space, whether those who share it with them believe this to be necessary or not.

Although Pisces III's usually seem very independent, they often foster dependencies in others. They need to feel that they count, that they matter. This need to be needed may be one of their most vulnerable points: if their children, parents, colleagues or lovers assert a degree of independence, or cease to rely on them, they can fall apart. A family, whether biological or metaphorical, is usually essential for Pisces III's, and the degree of responsibility they assume in it may be quite impressive.

Those born in the Week of Dancers and Dreamers are finely attuned to the wants of others. Often highly empathic, they are good listeners and are quite able to relate to and make sense of other people's points of view. Pisces III's know well that the world is made up of many subjective viewpoints, each true for its author, and perhaps actually true also, in a relative sense. At the same time, however, Pisces III's tend to feel that behind these differing viewpoints stands an absolute that is not dependent on subjectivity at all but is objectively true in all situations and for all time. Thus the underlying philosophy of these individuals is a curious blend of subjectivity and objectivity, the relative and the absolute, the believer and the skeptic.

Pisces III's can be unstable and unrealistic in their romantic relationships and often get involved with the wrong partner. Yet if they make the commitment to a love that is positive and nurturing, they are quite capable of making loyal and devoted spouses.

STRENGTHS

PHILOSOPHICAL • HELPFUL
MIRACLE-WORKING

WEAKNESSES

INEFFECTUAL • IMPERMANENT
DEPENDENCY-FOSTERING

ADVICE:

Be more demanding of yourself in your personal development, and contribute actively to the life around you. Beware of neglecting to build a firm foundation. There is a limit to what you are capable of overcoming—make life easier for yourself, and be willing to compromise when necessary.

PISCES III NOTABLES

Born in Montgomery, Ala., **Nat King Cole** was the youngest son of a Baptist minister and sang solos in church as a child. When his three older brothers went into the music business, Nat followed them. In 1939 he formed his own jazz trio and was known for years as an influential jazz pianist. But like many Pisces III's, Cole was destined to follow his dreams, which in this case meant becoming a great pop singer. Astonishingly successful at his new profession, Cole wound up selling over 50 million records. His mellow voice and relaxed singing style captivated audiences around the world. Later in life he became the first African American to have his own tv show and had a role in the film *Cat Ballou* shortly before his death.

NAT KING COLE

It is hard to imagine that **Albert Einstein**, perhaps the greatest mind of the 20th century, was a late talker, did poorly in school, failed his college entrance exam and finally managed to land a job in the Swiss Patent Office. Fortunately, he had some time on his hands and was able to earn a doctorate from the University of Zurich before proceeding to revolutionize the study of physics with his startling theories. Einstein was a typical Pisces III who needed time to dream and would not be hurried in his thinking. In 1915 he published his *General Theory of Relativity*, which led to instant recognition and fame. His second great task was to unify the many physical forces under one theory, but he never succeeded in doing so.

ALBERT EINSTEIN

Actress, dancer, singer **Liza Minnelli** made her debut in film at age 2 playing opposite her mother, Judy Garland, in the film *In the Good Old Summertime*. Her father, Pisces Vincente Minnelli, was a director of Broadway musicals and Hollywood films. No wonder with such a background that Dancer and Dreamer Minnelli should have become a Broadway and Hollywood star with an Oscar for the film *Cabaret* and numerous other awards. Like many born in her week, Minnelli, has experienced disappointment in one with a number of failed relationships.

LIZA MINNELLI

Other Pisces III's: Grover Cleveland, F.W. de Klerk, Paul Ehrlich, Dorothy Schiff, Frank Borman, Ruth Bader Ginsburg, Jerry Lewis, Nijinsky, Kamal Atatürk, Quincy Jones, Rudolf Nureyev, Michael Caine, Diane Arbus, Bernardo Bertolucci, James Madison, Phil Lesh, Sylvia Beach, Billy Crystal, Charley Pride, Mercedes McCambridge, Kate Greenaway, Bonnie Blair, Wilson Pickett, Nicolai Rimsky-Korsakov, Irene Cara, Percival Lowell, L. Ron Hubbard, Walter H. Annenberg.

Relationship Guide for Pisces III

Page Locator for All Relationships

RALPH ABERNATHY (PISCES III)
MARTIN LUTHER KING, JR. (CAPRICORN III)
PAGE 783

BEST
RELATIONSHIPS

LOVE
Pisces-Aries Cusp
Taurus I
Gemini II
Gemini-Cancer Cusp
Virgo-Libra Cusp
Libra II
Scorpio II
Sagittarius II
Sagittarius-Capricorn Cusp
Aquarius I
Aquarius-Pisces Cusp

MARRIAGE
Taurus III
Gemini III
Cancer I
Leo I
Virgo II
Libra I
Scorpio I
Capricorn-Aquarius Cusp
Aquarius III

FRIENDSHIP
Gemini I
Cancer II
Leo-Virgo Cusp
Scorpio III
Sagittarius I

FAMILY
Taurus II
Libra III
Libra-Scorpio Cusp
Capricorn I

WORK
Aries III
Aries-Taurus Cusp
Taurus-Gemini Cusp
Cancer III
Cancer-Leo Cusp
Leo III
Virgo III
Scorpio-Sagittarius Cusp
Sagittarius III
Aquarius II
Pisces III

The Relationship
Profiles

STRENGTHS: ELEMENTAL, TRUTHFUL, UNCOMPROMISING

WEAKNESSES: CONTENTIOUS, UNPROTECTIVE, UNSYMPATHETIC

BEST: WORK

WORST: LOVE

ANDREW LLOYD WEBBER (3/22/48)
STEPHEN SONDHEIM (3/22/30)

These masters of musical theater, who share the same birthday, have created landmark works, among them Sondheim's *West Side Story, A Funny Thing Happened on the Way to the Forum* and *Into the Woods,* and Webber's *Jesus Christ Superstar, Cats* and *Evita.*

The Soulful Flame

This relationship is paradoxical: straightforward, simple, yet emotionally profound and complex. Each of these cosmic twins, both born on the Cusp of Rebirth, melds fire and water, an interaction generating a lot of steam—and symbolizing the tremendous pressure that simultaneously binds the relationship and threatens to burst it apart. The relationship is marked by an ethereal kind of passion, sometimes amorphous and other times flaming out of control. These qualities make it hard to define or grasp—except for each partner, who understands the coupling on a deep, almost subconscious level.

The relationship's primal nature is emphasized by its direct expression of emotions, usually of the black-and-white variety: love or hate, not affection; like or dislike, not sympathy; sex or abstinence, not sensuousness. Similarities and differences, attractions and repulsions—all avoid the gray, in-between areas. Fights between these two are intense, but periods of ease may be marked by remarkable camaraderie and good feeling. Both Pisces-Aries partners are at times bewildered by what is happening between them and at a loss to control it; like the weather, their relationship is truly elemental.

This combination is not recommended for stable love or marital relationships, but two Pisces-Aries can make good friends. They won't necessarily be close, however; there will always be a competitive element between them, no matter how deep their bond of understanding. Constant confrontation and criticism do not bode well for a day-to-day relationship but perhaps allow for one in which they see each other less often. Sexual encounters between individuals born on this cusp are likely to be brief and intense.

The directness of this relationship can also lead to mutual respect and, from there, to an unspoken decision not to compete or battle at all. It is possible for two such individuals to work cooperatively in the same company or even side by side, as long as the nature of their tasks, and the position they occupy in the group, are well defined and, ideally, do not overlap. Should they happen to be on the same side, their dynamism can sweep the field.

ADVICE: *Let up a bit in your intensity. Rethink your extreme position. Try to find a middle ground, even when it seems amorphous.*

STRENGTHS: ENTHUSIASTIC, IDEALISTIC, INNOVATIVE

WEAKNESSES: UNSTABLE, IMMATURE, BICKERING

BEST: LOVE

WORST: MARRIAGE

LEONARD NIMOY (3/26/31)
WILLIAM SHATNER (3/22/31)

The chemistry between Shatner as Captain Kirk and Nimoy as Mr. Spock helped make *Star Trek* tv's most popular adult sci-fi series. **Also: Matthew Broderick & Sarah Jessica Parker** (married; actors); **Bob & Ray** (radio team); **Steve McQueen & Ali McGraw** (married); **Kurasawa & Toshiro Mifune** (director/actor).

Passionate Innocence

The search for lost innocence that often plays a part in this relationship involves an impossible goal, true, yet also an ideal to strive for, in ways that may have a real effect on behavior. The unreachable image of perfect beauty that suffuses this bond gives its partners an air sometimes of detachment, if the ideal is not in sight, sometimes of intense involvement, if perfection appears at hand. The result is a relationship that features a kind of childlike wonder—or, on the other side of the coin, simple childishness. Whether objective, effective and conscious or subjective, diffuse and unaware, it is a relationship that puts myriad moods and feelings into play, calling up a broad spectrum of emotions from its partners. An ideal of perfection now seems attainable, now can only be hoped for; when it is not achieved, the partners may pick and snipe at each other.

Passionate love is possible between Pisces-Aries and Aries I's, with the former often assuming the active role, the latter the passive one. Aries I's frequently need to be involved with unconventional people in unusual relationships, and Pisces-Aries may fit the bill. Problems arise when Pisces-Aries prove too dominant and controlling, preventing Aries I's from feeling able to be themselves or what they need to be. On the other hand, Aries I's may not be dependable or trustworthy enough for Pisces-Aries, who may at first be charmed by their partner's childlike innocence but eventually find it threatening, or just a bit much to deal with.

Friendships and love relationships between these two can be very close but may also feature a lot of squabbling, bickering and temporary estrangements. When both parties act immaturely, there may be too little stability in the relationship to hold it together.

The relationship brings positive energy to the initiation of new endeavors. In the long run, however, and in day-to-day tasks of maintenance, its energy may flag and the partners' interests wane. What often signals the beginning of the end is a marked drop in enthusiasm on both sides. If the partnership is to survive, it will seek to move on to a new endeavor, perhaps one that grows organically out of a past success.

ADVICE: *Recognize the dark side, too. Don't smooth over pain and loss. Finish one project before going on to another. Work hard at maintenance.*

March 19–24

THE CUSP OF REBIRTH
PISCES-ARIES CUSP

April 3–10

THE WEEK OF THE STAR
ARIES II

The Seething Cauldron

Youthful energies vie for the ascendancy here; highly competitive, this relationship often resembles an all-out, no-holds-barred melee. The motivating factors, however, are rarely real hatred or destructive, violent feelings but, rather, jealousy and a desire to better or overcome. This makes the relationship a little easier, but not a lot. Contentious, it demands the very best that its partners have to offer and also asks that they perform at a high degree of excellence. Both will feel the strain but will also welcome the challenge. Attitudes will be honest and frank, leaving little doubt about where real feelings lie.

The emotionally complex Pisces-Aries craves understanding in this relationship, which may be precisely what Aries II is unable to give. Aries II's, for their part, probably won't appreciate Pisces-Aries' sharp outspokenness; sensitive to criticism, they need to be accepted unconditionally as they are. In addition, Pisces-Aries are very independent—probably too independent to satisfy the Aries II need to be needed. More likely, they will only deliver frustration, and to the wrong address.

Mutual respect in this relationship may only be possible after the dust has settled from a series of battles, perhaps over power or money, in which both participants have emerged somewhat the worse for wear. No matter where the relationship emerges—in work, love, friendship or family—and no matter how old its partners, it most resembles two youthful siblings slugging it out. Such fights can go on for years, and although mutual understanding may not readily emerge, both partners will undoubtedly benefit from the relationship's lessons in ego toughening and self-defense. There is really no reason why this combative stance cannot be softened over time, however, in favor of a negotiated armistice. Acceptance may well prove the key.

ADVICE: *Seek the calm in the eye of the hurricane. The hard way isn't always best. Your enemy may be a friend in disguise.*

RIC OCASEK (3/23/49)
PAULINA PORIZKOVA (4/9/65)

Ocasek was the leader of The Cars, a successful 80s new-wave band. Porizkova, a well-known Estée Lauder model, was once featured in a music video with him. The pair were wed in 1989. *Also:* **Joseph Pulitzer II & Joseph Pulitzer** (son/father; publishing empire); **Sergei Diaghilev & Pierre Monteux** (collaborators; ballet producer/conductor).

March 19–24

THE CUSP OF REBIRTH
PISCES-ARIES CUSP

April 11–18

THE WEEK OF THE PIONEER
ARIES III

Comic Relief

Laughter is used to lighten oppressive moods in this relationship. From slapstick to wordplay, from gentle cajoling to dark humor, comedy in many forms serves to clear the air and provides a common basis for communication. The sharpness of mind found in this relationship needs a reliable safety valve, and joking, whether sarcastic and ironic or more friendly, is usually effective.

Both partners are usually well served by the relationship and, in general, satisfied by it. The connection is often teacher-student or parent-child, with the Aries III adopting the more mature role. Fortunately, Aries III usually has the understanding and patience necessary to deal with Pisces-Aries complexity. When in torment, Pisces-Aries tend to lash out, but they will find Aries III's less reactive than most, more willing to listen and ready to communicate by poking fun. Aries III's are often limited in their capacity to give full-hearted sympathy, however, and in this respect Pisces-Aries needs may remain unsatisfied.

Whether romantic or platonic, the interaction between these two personalities is often physically oriented. They may be well suited for a sexual relationship, or for sharing sport, training or fitness programs, perhaps on the same team, or as opposing partners. Maintaining a healthy and attractive physical appearance is extremely, perhaps overly, important here. Competitiveness is unlikely to get out of hand and can yield positive results in gradually bettering each person's performance. This relationship is also strong in the mental sphere, where these two personalities may constantly be at work sharpening their wits on each other.

As co-workers and business partners, Pisces-Aries and Aries III's can work very well together, sharing tasks and supporting each other's efforts. As husband and wife, they can sustain both love and friendship over the long haul, as long as they both practice flexibility and tolerance.

ADVICE: *Share sorrows as well as joys. Remain empathic. Try to practice openness and understanding. Take care not to let jokes become weapons.*

CLARENCE DARROW (4/18/1857)
WILLIAM JENNINGS BRYAN (3/19/1860)

Lawyers Bryan and Darrow clashed in the celebrated 1925 Scopes trial, which pitted Darwin's theory of evolution against the teachings of the Bible. Darrow lost, but not before exposing evangelist Bryan's lack of biological and biblical knowledge. Bryan died a week after the trial ended.

RELATIONSHIPS

STRENGTHS: **POWERFUL, SUCCESSFUL, IRRESISTIBLE**

WEAKNESSES: **COMPETITIVE, WASTEFUL, NEEDY**

BEST: **FRIENDSHIP, BUSINESS**

WORST: **LOVE**

Contessa di Castiglione (3/22/1837)
Louis Napoleon III (4/20/1808)

A sexual liaison between Louis Napoleon III (Bonaparte's nephew) and the 19-year-old Sardinian adventuress succeeded in enlisting his aid in the struggle to unify Italy. ***Also:* Diaghilev & Prokofiev** (Ballet Russe founder/composer).

March 19–24
THE CUSP OF REBIRTH
PISCES-ARIES CUSP

April 19–24
THE CUSP OF POWER
ARIES-TAURUS CUSP

Star Wars

Power struggles may endanger, or at the very least seriously disturb, all projects undertaken in this relationship, as well as the well-being of anyone in its vicinity. The wheelhouse of this ship is too small to admit two captains; when both partners vie for the helm, the relationship is likely to go adrift or wind up on the rocks. If this duo is to succeed, the issue of who is boss will have to be settled, since competition for the star position will disrupt all other efforts. If power struggles can be kept at bay, however, the relationship will display a generosity to others that will win over many of those around it.

Synergistically yoked and pulling in the same direction, the strengths of Pisces-Aries and Aries-Taurus can be irresistible. This augurs well for business partnerships and joint operations with well-defined goals and adequate working capital. Generally speaking, however, speculative ventures between these two should be avoided in favor of projects in which the imaginative strengths of the Pisces-Aries and the conceptual power of the Aries-Taurus can be joined in a well-grounded, straightforward and no-nonsense way.

Since largesse is characteristic of this relationship in any sphere, serious financial problems can arise: carelessness with money and buying too much on credit are problems here. In the long run, the Aries-Taurus is much too realistic to meet the Pisces-Aries need for acceptance and sympathy. The rather thin-skinned Pisces-Aries, meanwhile, will often find the helpful suggestions and prodding of the Aries-Taurus intolerable.

A star war may rage over who is to be the center of attention. If so, Aries-Tauruses are a lot tougher than Pisces-Aries. Likewise, should the relationship be plagued by problems, and especially problems of insensitivity or neglect, Aries-Tauruses will hang in there and try to work things out, while Pisces-Aries tend to feel hurt and to flee. Ultimately no one will be the winner in battles for recognition, however, and the sooner these two make peace and fight on the same side, the more successful the relationship will be.

ADVICE: *Pay more attention to each other. Keep your sunny side up. Share adventuresome experiences. Try to be less needy of praise.*

RELATIONSHIPS

STRENGTHS: **SENSUOUS, SOCIAL, FUN**

WEAKNESSES: **EXPECTANT, TENSE, UNFULFILLED**

BEST: **SHARED LEISURE**

WORST: **MARRIAGE**

Gary Oldman (3/21/58)
Uma Thurman (4/29/70)

Oldman's first 2 screen roles were as doomed iconoclastic figures: punk performer Sid Vicious and irreverent gay playwright Joe Orton. Thurman's first noteworthy role was in *Dangerous Liaisons* (1988). Following their divorce, Oldman became engaged to Isabella Rossellini. ***Also:* Diaghilev & Fokine** (Ballet Russe founder/ choreographer); **Pamela Harriman & Edward R. Murrow** (affair).

March 19–24
THE CUSP OF REBIRTH
PISCES-ARIES CUSP

April 25–May 2
THE WEEK OF MANIFESTATION
TAURUS I

Good-Tasting Medicine

A healthy relationship in this combination does not involve deep bonding or emotional soul-searching but shared pleasures. Although it may lack a deep emotional tie, it has the virtue of being self-correcting: should the contrasting needs of its partners put it out of kilter, it will usually revert to a balanced state and be put right by a good, healthy dose of sensuous enjoyment. Thus the relationship can be likened to a physician who can cure people's ills simply by paying attention to them.

Here the voluptuous qualities of the Taurus I complement the subtle hedonism of the Pisces-Aries. The enjoyments of this matchup are more effective in casual relationships, however, than in those that demand a deeper commitment: being married or living together, for example, may prove problematic. Taurus I's are hard workers who need a quiet home environment, and Pisces-Aries are often too nervous and emotional to give them rest. Furthermore, Pisces-Aries may grow bored with the stolid approach of Taurus I's and may tend to roam, failing to live up to domestic responsibilities. Perhaps the relationship's main problem is that Pisces-Aries seek a deeper level of emotional involvement than Taurus I's are prepared or able to give.

In the family, a Taurus I parent may be unwilling to spend the necessary time trying to unravel the intricacies and subtleties of the Pisces-Aries child. Friendships between these two may not exhibit deep bonding if Taurus I's repress feelings and are unable to share emotionally. In general, the health of the relationship may suffer from conflicts in which Taurus I's are interested in results and Pisces-Aries in the motives behind people's actions, with blame and stricture being the results. A curative approach based on activities of pleasure and fun (food, travel, theatrical or musical performances, TV, a hobby or just plain doing nothing) may help the relationship to last, even if true passion has faded or was never there.

ADVICE: *Don't go too deep. Attend to bad feelings immediately. Concentrate on health. Social activities should be stressed. Remember that life is theater.*

May 3–10

THE WEEK OF THE TEACHER
TAURUS II

STRENGTHS: **APPRECIATIVE, EXCITING, GROUNDBREAKING**

WEAKNESSES: **UNREALISTIC, UNFOUNDED, IRRITATING**

BEST: **FRIENDSHIP, WORK**

WORST: **FAMILY**

Magical Mist

Mutual fascination, and a drive toward the unusual, strange, bizarre and theatrical sides of life, lie at the base of this relationship. Little time is given to introspection and thought. Always moving ahead with an eye on the attractive object, the relationship isn't able to see the path clearly; a haze of unreality gets in the way. A strong magnetic attraction may cause close bonds to form rather quickly, but these feelings can later evaporate just as fast. When danger signals begin to flash, the absence of established roots (since the relationship has developed too hurriedly) may seriously undermine any stability that has been attained.

Pisces-Aries and Taurus II can form a mutual-admiration society that leads them quite quickly into a love affair or marriage. The problem is that they may completely overlook their differences in the heat of the initial involvement, particularly if they share a strong physical attraction. Much later, when things begin to cool down, there will be stress. As time wears on, once-small irritations may develop into major antipathies. In the spheres of love and marriage, strong emotions may have been voiced; when these give way to the first expressions of dissatisfaction, major seismic waves will run through the relationship. Not naturally domineering, Taurus II's can accept their partners as they are and will encourage them to be themselves. Yet a Pisces-Aries is likely only to feel hurt by a Taurus II's first expression of what is intended as constructive criticism. This will bewilder the Taurus II, who was only trying to help.

The relationship may ultimately have to be restructured. If they back off in emotional areas and keep their contacts as objective as possible, partners can perhaps stay friends or, if they are co-workers, continue to collaborate on a common project. Feelings may deepen over the years if given time to develop a strong common basis. Pisces-Aries and Taurus II's are often able to help each other careerwise, since appreciation of each other's talents and enthusiasm is characteristic of this matchup.

HARRY S. TRUMAN (5/8/1884)
THOMAS E. DEWEY (3/24/02)

These 2 politicians faced off in the celebrated presidential election of 1948. Though Dewey lost by a slim margin to underdog Truman's "give-'em-hell" style, they maintained a mutual respect over the years.

ADVICE: *One step at a time. Excitement is stimulating, but its results are not always beneficial. Keep your vision focused. Criticism can be helpful.*

May 11–18

THE WEEK OF THE NATURAL
TAURUS III

STRENGTHS: **SPONTANEOUS, FANTASY-RICH, UNPRETENTIOUS**

WEAKNESSES: **REJECTED, MISUNDERSTOOD, ECCENTRIC**

BEST: **SIBLING**

WORST: **FRIENDSHIP**

Water Under the Bridge

This relationship is based on a spontaneous, honest and direct approach to experience. It reveals a lot of awe and wonder in respect to creation and the cosmos, since it synthesizes and elevates the childlike innocence of the Pisces-Aries and the love of nature and instinctual expression of the Taurus III. It is also characterized by unusual lifestyles and a shared interest in bizarre subjects. Behavior tending to the eccentric or outrageous can appear here and is not always conducive to stability.

Particularly in the realms of friendship, love and marriage, the relationship develops slowly. Pisces-Aries and Taurus III characteristically take little notice of each other at first; then one day they find themselves either strongly attracted or repelled, for no obvious reason. In fact, they have a bond of commonalty, but this will only become apparent after a lot of water has gone under the bridge.

The relationship, then, does not usually manifest as love at first sight. Initially, in fact, mutual dislike is more often the case. This allows each person an objective assessment of the other's strengths and weaknesses early on, an objectivity that may well prove a solid basis for further involvement; should the relationship continue, it will be characterized by realistic, down-to-earth attitudes curiously at variance with its often somewhat wild interests and behavior. Love and marriage are more common in this relationship than friendship, for the extremes of emotion aroused by friendship may have a strong physical side, which, whether positive or negative, may preclude the more controlled and straightforward attitudes one usually has toward friends and acquaintances. If this matchup manifests in the family sphere, especially when Pisces-Aries and Taurus III's are siblings, opposition to a judgmental parent or other oppressive family member may further unify this bond into a nurturing, caring and well-nigh unassailable entity.

OTTO KLEMPERER (5/14/1885)
WERNER KLEMPERER (3/22/20)

Otto Klemperer conducted the London Philharmonia Orchestra during the 60s. His actor son, Werner, was best known for his role as the inept Colonel Klink in the tv series *Hogan's Heroes*. **Also: Jesus & Felipe Alou** (baseball brothers); **William Morris & Dante Gabriel Rossetti** (collaborators; artist/poet).

ADVICE: *Tone down your outrageousness a bit—don't shove it in everyone's face. Accept normal behavior. Cultivate objectivity in all areas of life.*

STRENGTHS: **POWERFUL, WORK-ORIENTED, DISCERNING**

WEAKNESSES: **GUARDED, MISTRUSTFUL, PROUD**

BEST: **WORK**

WORST: **LOVE**

MALCOLM X (5/19/25)
SPIKE LEE (3/20/57)

Activist Spike Lee, one of America's foremost black filmmakers, directed the 1992 award-winning *Malcolm X*, 17 years after the assassination of the controversial religious and political figure. **Also: Dane Rudhyar & Alexander Ruperti** (modern astrologers).

March 19–24
THE CUSP OF REBIRTH
PISCES-ARIES CUSP

May 19–24
THE CUSP OF ENERGY
TAURUS-GEMINI CUSP

Power Play

A desire to work together lies at the forefront of this relationship, but underlying power plays create a curious difficulty in doing so. Open conflict is generally absent; instead, there is wariness and playful competition. As in the martial arts, no one lets down his or her guard, but such defensive postures prevent real intimacy. Also precluding openness, unconditional giving and sharing are ego and pride, which play strong roles here. Trust will have to be built up over many months and years; it cannot be expected to come easily. The realization that kindness, acceptance and love have their own kind of strength, which can only be tapped by relinquishing power games, must be a goal to strive for.

Pisces-Aries and Taurus-Geminis rarely get to feel completely comfortable with each other. Mutual respect is fought back at first; only later will appreciation of each other's talents and abilities emerge. Elemental differences prevail at the outset (Pisces-Aries combining water and fire, Taurus-Gemini earth and air), but as the relationship develops, fire and earth, symbolizing intuition and sensation, generally become dominant. If power games are put aside, then, the relationship may flourish in the area of physical activity, whether sports, sex or adventure. Business, too, can prosper.

At the start, Pisces-Aries are usually more attracted to Taurus-Geminis, with their flair and energy, than the other way around; at first, in fact, the emotional complexity of Pisces-Aries may even be a little daunting to Taurus-Geminis. Eventually, however, it proves too fascinating to resist. At this point the pendulum swings in the opposite direction and Taurus-Geminis may come on too strong, offending the sensibilities of Pisces-Aries or scaring them off. Given this to-and-fro tension, the relationship often finds its greatest success in the workplace, where these two may be forced to spend time together and get to know each other. Only after they are on the same wavelength will love and marital relations become possible.

ADVICE: *Rely more on your intuition. Use power to achieve mutual goals. Tune in to the power of love. To succeed, you must sometimes risk getting hurt.*

STRENGTHS: **QUICK, TECHNICAL, GROUNDING**

WEAKNESSES: **UNSTABLE, IMPULSIVE, CRITICAL**

BEST: **COMMON INTEREST**

WORST: **LOVE**

VIRGINIA RAPPE (5/29/1896)
FATTY ARBUCKLE (3/24/1887)

The career of silent-film comic Arbuckle ended in scandal when he was accused in the death of Rappe, a young actress-model who died from a ruptured bladder following an orgiastic drinking party. He was acquitted after 3 trials. **Also: Fatty Arbuckle & Dashiell Hammett** (Hammett was detective in Rappe case); **Pamela Harriman & Randolph Churchill** (married).

March 19–24
THE CUSP OF REBIRTH
PISCES-ARIES CUSP

May 25–June 2
THE WEEK OF FREEDOM
GEMINI I

Head-On Collision

This relationship will be strongly involved in the material world. Pisces-Aries is a water-fire mixture and Gemini I an air sign, so the relationship yokes these two together through earth, symbolizing not only sensuousness but also practicality, pragmatic attitudes and an appetite for both work and a materialistic approach to life. A mental orientation, symbolized by the exchange of ideas, usually predominates at the relationship's start, and in career and friendship there is often also a shared interest in technical matters. Self-understanding is not characteristic of this relationship, so energy is often wasted as the duo impulsively heads off in the wrong direction, particularly when things are going well. Only when breakdown or crisis forces a reorganization, whether of routines and habits or on the physical plane, will understanding and sensitivity have a chance to emerge. Unless both parties understand the relationship's practical nature (a difficult task at best for these two), no forward progress or development will be possible.

That Gemini I's have neither the time nor the interest to satisfy the Pisces-Aries need to be understood causes frustration in their partners in this combination, particularly in love affairs and marriages. But Gemini I's do have the mental objectivity that Pisces-Aries lack and can therefore be a great help to them, advising or guiding them in fiscal matters or planning their careers. Furthermore, hardheaded Gemini I's are difficult to convince, and if an imaginative Pisces-Aries needs to bounce an idea off someone, they can be crucial sounding-boards.

Both parties are extremely quick in grasping ideas and concepts, which augurs well for open channels of communication between them in the family. Gemini I's show particular fluency in dealing with technical matters or with issues of physical motion, and this can fascinate Pisces-Aries, who may seek to join in with such activities. They may also be satisfied to be appreciative bystanders, but if they do participate in Gemini I's interests, a common project may prove to be the physical manifestation that this matchup requires.

ADVICE: *Get the best out of the present before moving on to the future. Consolidate. Keep grounded. Build solidly on the physical plane.*

March 19–24

THE CUSP OF REBIRTH
PISCES-ARIES CUSP

June 3–10

THE WEEK OF NEW LANGUAGE
GEMINI II

STRENGTHS: **BENEFICIAL, FUN, SHARP-WITTED**

WEAKNESSES: **DISTRACTED, SUPERFICIAL, INCONSTANT**

BEST: **FAMILY**

WORST: **MARRIAGE**

Keeping It Light

This relationship thrives on free-and-easy contacts. Its trademark is an absence of heavy responsibilities or demands, which will only drag it down and make it oppressive. The principal problem here is how to keep the relationship intact while allowing maximum freedom and choice.

The relationship's greatest success may come when its partners are biologically related. Sibling pairs are particularly favored, but parent-child combinations can also prove close and understanding. In friendships, Pisces-Aries and Gemini II's often relate to each other as if they were siblings. Family activities that include such friends, whether outings, picnics, dinners or celebrations, usually go well.

Interestingly enough, the relationship often transcends a weakness common to both partners: Pisces-Aries and Gemini II's equally have an erratic streak, which can manifest in involvement with others as flightiness or extreme undependableness. In combination, however, these two will show a high degree of thoughtfulness and responsible, well-grounded behavior. This shared attitude may include an understanding that if either partner is absent or temporarily unable to hold up their end of the deal, the remaining one will be ready to do double work for a while to keep things going.

The relationship is likely to be lively and stimulating. Gemini II's are most entertaining, and Pisces-Aries can be enchanted or at the very least amused by them. Gemini II's also have the capacity to understand and appreciate the fascinating twists and turns of the Pisces-Aries mind. As long as physical and emotional contact between them is kept light and easy, this pair may carry on a successful relationship as friends, co-workers or business associates for years.

Should the relationship move a step or two farther, toward love or marriage, the greatest difficulty will be vulnerability to new attractions and involvements. Here, keeping the communication pipeline open can guarantee a frank assessment of needs and wants. Honesty is important above all.

ADVICE: *Don't take too much for granted. Keep in touch. Don't make heavy demands. Act responsibly. Keep the golden rule in mind.*

ROSIE STONE (3/21/45)
FREDDIE STONE (6/5/46)

Guitarist Freddie and sister, pianist Rosie, were original members of Sly and the Family Stone (all shown), formed in 1967. The multiracial band topped the charts in the late 60s with *Everyday People, Dance to the Music* and *Everybody Is a Star*— all upbeat, optimistic songs. In the 70s the group's music moved into more violent, militant imagery.

March 19–24

THE CUSP OF REBIRTH
PISCES-ARIES CUSP

June 11–18

THE WEEK OF THE SEEKER
GEMINI III

STRENGTHS: **HEALTHY, PATIENT, ENCOURAGING**

WEAKNESSES: **IMPULSIVE, SELFISH, TEMPTING**

BEST: **MARRIAGE**

WORST: **FAMILY**

Digging Deeper

This combination usually moves in a positive and mutually beneficial direction for its partners and can work out well over a broad spectrum of involvements—friendship, love, marriage. Moreover, it is characterized by the patience with which partners deal with each other's varying moods, and by their mutual encouragement in the direction of greater self-understanding. Health and stability, then, are usually important plusses in this relationship. The only question is how far it will develop, since selfishness may also be present here. In consequence, both love affairs and friendships in this combination may hinge on a delicate balance. The important issue is whether partners see real value in sustaining and deepening their bond, and in keeping their impulsiveness under control, or else give in to temptations that may ultimately prove destructive. Their attitudes toward their relationship, then, are crucial. Should they put their union first and their own individual interests second, the relationship will most likely survive. If not, it will be severely tested and, perhaps, broken.

On the positive side, Gemini III's have the energy to keep up with Pisces-Aries but also the understanding and patience to deal with their many moods. Pisces-Aries can take a lot from Gemini III's, including encouragement to get to know themselves better. Gemini III's are also good with money and can provide more impractical Pisces-Aries with the financial security they may never have had.

On the other hand, Gemini III's are extremely independent and will not tie themselves down until they are good and ready. Should they decide to marry or live with a Pisces-Aries mate, they may discover a whole new, domestic side to their personality. True, the Gemini III quest for meaning in life may leave a needy Pisces-Aries feeling neglected. But if the relationship itself can become a mutual quest, both partners' lives will be immeasurably deepened and enriched.

ADVICE: *Decide how far you want to go. Deepen your commitment by embarking on your quest and staying on your path. Beware of jealousy and dishonesty.*

JOSEF ALBERS (3/19/1888)
ANNI ALBERS (6/12/1899)

Josef Albers, abstract painter and writer, and wife Anni, an innovative textile designer, together explored design theory and application.

***Also:* Russ Meyer & Roger Ebert** (film collaborators); **Paul Reiser & Helen Hunt** (co-stars, *Mad About You*); **Gary Oldman & Isabella Rossellini** (engaged); **Diaghilev & Stravinsky** (ballet collaborators); **J.D. Rockefeller III & J.D. Rockefeller IV** (father/son).

AYRTON SENNA (3/21/60)
JUAN MANUEL FANGIO (6/24/11)

These South Americans were both the top Formula One drivers of their generation. Fangio won the world championship 5 times in the 50s; Senna, who idolized Fangio, won it 3 times. He was killed in a racing crash in 1994.

March 19–24

THE CUSP OF REBIRTH
PISCES-ARIES CUSP

June 19–24

THE CUSP OF MAGIC
GEMINI-CANCER CUSP

The Dangerous Apparition

This can be a perilous relationship but also an irresistibly magnetic one. Like a genie in a bottle, once it is released it may not be easy to control. The initial attractions here may be strong, as mesmerizing feelings weave their magic spell. Deep and dark powers far removed from everyday experience may bind the partners in a passionate embrace. Conjuring up such forces may have far-reaching consequences.

Both partners risk being swallowed up in this relationship. Their love can be profound, holding important life-lessons in store for them, but it may at the same time demand a degree of self-effacement and ego denial that cannot be healthy in the long run. Worshiping the relationship at the expense of their own selves, the partners may be called upon to sacrifice too much of their respective identities. They will have to develop toughness and practicality and to draw firm boundaries if they are to avoid a dissolution of personal responsibility and a loss of self-respect.

A casual relationship between Pisces-Aries and Gemini-Cancer is usually impossible, since they arouse such a storm of emotions in each other. They may well become adversaries or even enemies more easily than acquaintances or surface friends. Pisces-Aries are prone to being aggressively critical, but Gemini-Cancers have ways of fighting back, usually by just turning off, rejecting through silence. By withholding their enthusiasm, admiration, attention or love, Gemini-Cancers hit the Pisces-Aries ego where it really hurts.

As parents, Pisces-Aries may be extremely nurturing and protective of their Gemini-Cancer children but can also spoil them with excessive adoration. Gemini-Cancers, meanwhile, can accept and understand their Pisces-Aries children to a degree that will make them good parents overall, although they may also be upset by these children's rebelliousness. As siblings, Pisces-Aries and Gemini-Cancer will surely fight a lot but can be united by a deep bond of feeling and sympathy, which will most likely continue into adult life.

ADVICE: *Proceed with care. Don't get in over your head. Keep your self-respect. Too much pleasure can be a danger signal. Serve rather than sacrifice.*

CHARLES ROBB (6/26/39)
LYNDA BIRD JOHNSON (3/19/44)

One of President Lyndon Johnson's 2 daughters, Lynda Bird met the now Virginia senator "Chuck" Robb when he was a social aide in the Johnson administration. Successfully married, they are the parents of 3 daughters.

Also: Lynda Bird Johnson & Luci Baines Johnson (sisters); **Carl Reiner & Mel Brooks** (comedy collaborators).

March 19–24

THE CUSP OF REBIRTH
PISCES-ARIES CUSP

June 25–July 2

THE WEEK OF THE EMPATH
CANCER I

Lessons to Be Learned

Mutual protection, security and moneymaking figure strongly here. Despite these common goals and bonds of feeling, however, the relationship may also involve a lack of awareness that prevents it from attaining real emotional depth. If it is confronted by difficulties, whether from inside or outside, this lack of consciousness will leave it open to psychological trauma and strife and, ultimately, will most likely break it apart. Yet the level of awareness can be raised. This may not be easy, for considerable emotional complexities will be involved, but conscious and determined efforts must be made to bring it about. To guarantee the firm internal bonding sufficient to withstand adverse circumstances, a process of learning and understanding must be developed.

Many Cancer I's are aggressive types, who need to call the shots; but if they push in this direction, it is unlikely that Pisces-Aries will be able to assume a passive role for long. Friendships and love relationships in this combination are more apt to be possible if the Pisces-Aries takes the lead while the Cancer I hangs back, letting go of control. In that case, however, the outspoken, direct nature of Pisces-Aries may wound the sensitive Cancer I, driving a wedge between them. On the plus side, both Pisces-Aries and Cancer I share traits of deep emotion and sensitivity, which may enable them to perceive the lessons necessary for this relationship to deepen and grow.

This relationship may perhaps be most effective when put in service of a common cause in which Cancer I and Pisces-Aries are partners or colleagues. Through hard and committed work, the relationship will grow not just financially but spiritually, allowing both members to build the necessary bonds of trust and to learn the pragmatic lessons about each other (and about money) that will be crucial to continued success. Fortunately, Cancer I empaths will know immediately when Pisces-Aries are not feeling well and will know how to be receptive to their moods without coddling them. A Pisces-Aries will be impressed by a Cancer I's ability to generate ideas but will insist that the necessary concentration and devotion be exercised to bring these plans to fruition.

ADVICE: *Learn from your experiences. Analysis is the key to understanding. Face problems squarely. Strive to raise awareness. Work toward a common cause.*

March 19–24

THE CUSP OF REBIRTH
PISCES-ARIES CUSP

July 3–10

THE WEEK OF THE UNCONVENTIONAL
CANCER II

Unaffected Fascination

This naturally magnetic bond is characterized by a rich and full fantasy life. A soulful connection, the relationship features imaginative visions that can manifest on the everyday level as unusual interior decorating and design in the home, say, or through the hobby of collecting unusual objects. There may also be an attraction toward singular individuals and experiences, creating an ever-changing kaleidoscope of interests and activities.

Early on in the relationship, a choice can be made as to which of two directions to go in: ultraromantic, on the one hand, or platonic, on the other—that is, a friendship or business partnership that puts limits on personal involvement. Should the romantic plunge be taken, problems will probably arise involving attractions to third parties, and consequent jealousy, possessiveness and frustration: Pisces-Aries often have a roving eye. Cancer II's can be pretty inventive, however, in holding on to the one they love. They may be clever enough to allow Pisces-Aries the room they need and to let them think they are more free than they really are.

Rejection may be another issue should this combination turn romantic—Cancer II's who are turned down by Pisces-Aries may take it pretty hard. Becoming more convinced than ever of the need to love completely, they can sink into a pit of depression, refusing to recognize the hopelessness of their desire for the Pisces-Aries. Cancer II's must be very careful of giving up their self-esteem or their dignity in such a situation. They must not become addicted to unrequited love.

When this relationship goes well, on the other hand, whether it be romantic or platonic, the partners' mutual appreciation of each other's imaginative qualities will be more than enough to keep it going for years. Should it manifest in the work sphere as a career element in fields such as advertising, public relations, design or fashion, there is no limit to the success it can achieve, since this duo has a strong understanding of the

ADVICE: *Beware of sex and love addictions. In interpersonal dealings, stay objective. Claiming behavior can hold you back. Put your imagination and fantasy to work.*

 RELATIONSHIPS

STRENGTHS: **SOULFUL, MAGNETIC, PERCEPTIVE**

WEAKNESSES: **HURT, REJECTED, JEALOUS**

BEST: **FRIENDSHIP, BUSINESS**

WORST: **MARRIAGE**

SERGEI DIAGHILEV (3/19/1872)
JEAN COCTEAU (7/5/1889)

Cocteau—French poet, novelist, playwright, filmmaker, painter, and prominent figure in Paris' avant garde of the 20s and 30s—collaborated with Diaghilev, founder of the famed Ballet Russe in Paris, to create the scenario for the ballet *Parade*.

Also: **John D. Rockefeller III & John D. Rockefeller** (grandson/grandfather; businessmen-philanthropists).

March 19–24

THE CUSP OF REBIRTH
PISCES-ARIES CUSP

July 11–18

THE WEEK OF THE PERSUADER
CANCER III

Zealous Reform

This relationship carries the conviction that it knows what is right, not only for its own members but for the rest of the world, too. Not content to rest with this knowledge, the relationship seeks to implement its often revolutionary ideas, struggling to reform and reorganize other relationships, businesses, families and social groups. Free to give advice, this matchup can prove a potent force for change in its immediate social sphere. Advice is not always appreciated, of course, nor do groups easily change, so this duo must be ready for uphill battles in convincing others of the rightness of its views; but it is a pairing of great charisma. In argument, furthermore, it does not stick to cold, hard facts but works to persuade through displays of temperament as well as of charm. Nor is it easily dissuaded—opposition will usually only spur this combination on to increased effort.

Interesting interpersonal dynamics emerge within the relationship itself. As people, Cancer III's are probably tougher than Pisces-Aries usually like. Realists, they are unlikely to cut Pisces-Aries any slack and will force them to face up to their deficiencies. This may make for tensions, but it also means that Cancer III's can make good managers, and sometimes even spouses, for Pisces-Aries, whose best qualities they do recognize and appreciate, and whom they may be able to direct toward an attainable goal.

When Pisces-Aries take their usual direct approach with Cancer III's on an important issue, the latter may seem to agree with them at first, mainly to avoid argument, but will later work in a subtle way to reorient them. Pisces-Aries who figure this out may feel manipulated by it, creating resentments that may ultimately result in a direct challenge to Cancer III's authority. But Cancer III's may cannily allow Pisces-Aries to think they're in charge, thus avoiding friction while still maintaining control.

The stability and solidity needed in a marriage or other long-standing love relationship are usually absent here. There may well be an attraction, but chances are that any resulting sexual involvement will be brief, albeit intense. Greater understanding may emerge after an affair is over, when a more permanent friendship can well ensue.

ADVICE: *Tend to yourself, and let others be. Don't give advice so freely. Learn to back off. Allow things to happen of their own accord.*

 RELATIONSHIPS

STRENGTHS: **CRUSADING, PERSISTENT, INSIGHTFUL**

WEAKNESSES: **MEDDLING, MANIPULATIVE, UNWANTED**

BEST: **SEXUAL, FRIENDSHIP**

WORST: **MARRIAGE**

HARRIET NELSON (7/18/12)
OZZIE NELSON (3/20/06)

Ozzie and Harriet Nelson, together with their sons Ricky and David, were the real-life members of America's idyllic family tv sitcom, *Ozzie and Harriet* (1952–66).

Also: **Stephen Sondheim & Oscar Hammerstein II** (composer/mentor); **William Shatner & Patrick Stewart** (captains on 2 *Star Trek* series).

STRENGTHS: **COMMUNICATIVE, LOVING, EMPATHIC**

WEAKNESSES: **PROMISCUOUS, JEALOUS, IMPRACTICAL**

BEST: **LOVE**

WORST: **WORK**

PAT RILEY (3/20/45)
CHUCK DALY (7/20/30)

Basketball coaches Riley and Daly were rivals in the '88 and '89 NBA finals. In '88 Riley led the LA Lakers to victory in a close series; in '89 Daly's Detroit Pistons got even by winning the title in a 4-game sweep. *Also:* **Glenn Close & Woody Harrelson** (romance; actors); **Marcel Marceau & Etienne Decroux** (mime/teacher).

March 19–24
THE CUSP OF REBIRTH
PISCES-ARIES CUSP

July 19–25
THE CUSP OF OSCILLATION
CANCER-LEO CUSP

Tuned In

This can be an exciting and deeply personal relationship, focused on being oneself and expressing highly individual emotions. Both partners bring to it the gifts of intuition, passion and empathy, qualities associated with the relationship's dominant elements, fire (Aries and Leo) and water (Pisces and Cancer). In combination, these gifts reinforce each other, and the relationship further contributes to them with a high degree of mental and physical compatibility. The matchup, then, is marked by easy communication and sensuous enjoyment. It will never place undue demands on its partners, since there will always be a free and easy exchange between them. Neither will ever have to make excuses for their behavior or to suppress their basic instincts.

This combination's easygoing nature will make any type of relationship involving it likely to succeed, including work or business. On balance, though, it is best suited to love and friendship. Pisces-Aries–Cancer-Leo lovers generally feel good about their relationship and are for the most part satisfied. They have a silent enjoyment and understanding of each other—they are on the same wavelength. Here just a look tells the whole story. In such a relationship, love and affection may be expressed in an easy way, without overt displays of emotion or a need to impress others. Marriage can be successful, too, as long as a stable financial and emotional foundation is established. Providing this kind of security will take some work, and both partners may have to give up some individual freedom and set some limits on their impulsiveness. In the family, the empathy between these two favors both parent-child and sibling pairing.

Pisces-Aries and Cancer-Leos must be careful, however, not to give up too many of their individual prerogatives, particularly when it comes to other people. They have a need and a desire to share with each other, and they may well be open enough to share a circle of mutual friends. It is also possible, however, that jealousy and possessiveness may surface as undermining factors. Putting their relationship first while also keeping certain areas of their lives private and exclusive will provide the needed stability.

ADVICE: *Share, but don't give it all away. Sometimes you have to speak your mind. Don't take too much for granted. Respect the intimacy of others.*

STRENGTHS: **INTERDEPENDENT, DYNAMIC, SELF-ASSURED**

WEAKNESSES: **OMNISCIENT, REBELLIOUS, POLARIZED**

BEST: **WORK**

WORST: **LOVE**

WILLIAM MORRIS (3/24/1834)
GEORGE BERNARD SHAW (7/26/1856)

Both social reformers, Morris, the Victorian artist and poet who led the Arts and Crafts Movement, and fellow Englishman, playwright and critic Shaw shared an allegiance to Fabian Socialism. In 1887, they marched together in a celebrated socialist demonstration at Trafalgar Square in London.

March 19–24
THE CUSP OF REBIRTH
PISCES-ARIES CUSP

July 26–August 2
THE WEEK OF AUTHORITY
LEO I

Pulling Together

The central issue in this relationship is that of dominance and independence. No matter how strongly, or with what truth, the voice of authority speaks, rebellious impulses arise that cry out to be heard. Recognition is a big issue here: how can a small, intimate voice be recognized when the acknowledged authority has just asserted the facts of the case? What's left to say—perhaps a small joke, a slightly different spin, a new idea? And what if, just once, the mighty authority is wrong?

No relationship can be completely dominated by one of its partners—or if it can, it isn't really a relationship at all. In this one, Leo I dominance can be simply too much to handle for Pisces-Aries, who may just back off. Furthermore, since Leo I's spend so much time on their careers, it may be a struggle for them to give Pisces-Aries their true attention. Yet interaction is possible here, if not in the areas of love and friendship, then certainly in that of work, where Pisces-Aries can supply imaginative ideas that Leo I's can shape, form and then implement. Much can be learned in this relationship about both the value of having a strong ego and the problems such an ego can create in a person's interactions with the world. Pisces-Aries, for their part, struggling to hold their own in the relationship, may learn something about the dangers of going too far toward self-assertiveness. Insecurities can be aroused that will throw the relationship temporarily off balance but may also lead to an acknowledgment of vulnerability, an admission of mistakes, an openness. These are the lessons of being human. Moreover, the distracting elements in this relationship can be something other than an annoyance; they can lead to relaxation and fun.

The issue of dependency also appears in parent-child interaction. Authoritarian Leo I parents can provoke rebellion in Pisces-Aries children or cause them to withdraw, wounded. A greater danger, perhaps, is overdependence, with the Pisces-Aries child worshiping the apparently omniscient Leo I parent. A balance must be found that allows for a productive interdependency in which the relationship can grow without stultifying polarization.

ADVICE: *Allow vulnerability. Admit mistakes. Build on mutual experiences. Allow the small voice to be heard. Encourage interdependent efforts.*

March 19–24

THE CUSP OF REBIRTH
PISCES-ARIES CUSP

August 3–10

THE WEEK OF BALANCED STRENGTH
LEO II

High-Flying Eagles

RELATIONSHIPS

STRENGTHS: **HONEST, SERIOUS, FIERY**

WEAKNESSES: **PROBLEMATIC, UNCOMPROMISING, TRYING**

BEST: **FRIENDSHIP**

WORST: **MARRIAGE**

Simply put, this relationship focuses on freedom. Given that focus, it includes a lot of impatience and unwillingness to compromise—but also a real directness, and a dislike of subterfuge and dishonesty. The other side of that coin is that any deep psychological subtext may prove unfathomable to the parties and too trying to figure out. The time, inclination and ability to understand, and to express full-blown sympathy, may be wanting or even absent.

The relationship will probably be at its most successful in friendship—as long as individual freedom can be maintained. If it can, the partners should be able to live up to their responsibilities. Leo II's are among the most loyal people in the year, and Pisces-Aries will benefit from being able to count on them for help in times of crisis. The emotional ups and downs and occasional despair of Pisces-Aries can be difficult for Leo II's to deal with, but they will gain satisfaction from their ability to help out in an objective way and from seeing the positive results of their contributions. Both partners will value this friendship and will be serious about maintaining it.

The fiery elements of the Pisces-Aries–Leo II relationship may well find expression in a love affair, but Leo II's may be too demanding and controlling for Pisces-Aries in the physical realm. Although initially charmed by the more ephemeral qualities of Pisces-Aries, Leo II's can also lack a certain sensitivity, so that Pisces-Aries will ultimately be left feeling unappreciated and unfulfilled. Should a Leo II attempt an outright assault on the affections of a Pisces-Aries or be too aggressive in speech or action, the Pisces-Aries may get turned off and just quietly slip away, finding the whole affair not worth the trouble. This relationship will rarely achieve long life. Not only will it be undermined by problems, but that constant need for individual freedom will make a marriage or permanent living situation hard to maintain. On the other hand, however, an admission of outright failure will often be slow in coming, so that some relationships in this combination continue on stubbornly when they should really be abandoned. Long-suffering attitudes often accompany problem relationships. Pisces-Aries–Leo II is no different.

ADVICE: *Freedom may be important, but so is cooperation. Admitting failure can be a positive step—to give up can be to gain.*

FLO ZIEGFELD (3/21/1867)
BILLIE BURKE (8/7/1886)

Ziegfeld, the impresario who produced the lavish Broadway *Follies*, greatly influenced Hollywood musicals of the 30s. Under his aegis, Burke's musical comedy career soared to stardom. They were married until Ziegfeld's death in '32. ***Also:* Princess Eugenie & Queen Mother** (great-granddaughter/ great-grandmother); **Princess Eugenie & Princess Beatrice** (sisters; Fergie & Andrew's daughters).

March 19–24

THE CUSP OF REBIRTH
PISCES-ARIES CUSP

August 11–18

THE WEEK OF LEADERSHIP
LEO III

Taming the Tiger

RELATIONSHIPS

STRENGTHS: **MASTERFUL, CHALLENGING, INDEPENDENT**

WEAKNESSES: **TUMULTUOUS, INFALLIBLE, WAYWARD**

BEST: **SEXUAL**

WORST: **WORK**

There is a need in this relationship to take wayward energies in hand and to shape and direct them. Passions run high here, but any overbearing energies, whether within the relationship or outside it, will not be submitted to; those passions must be mastered, so long as this is achieved with dignity and choice. In the best-case scenario, the Pisces-Aries–Leo III combination can give a project direction or can bring together subtle feelings and define them. No attempt should be made to break this matchup's strongly independent spirit.

Since it will be extremely difficult for this relationship's partners to admit their mistakes, contention is likely to arise between them, with each person claiming something like infallibility. The end of a knock-down, drag-out argument may come in the form of exhaustion or uneasy truce but rarely of compromise or apology. Perhaps the most realistic approach is just to agree to disagree, or at least to agree not to argue. Unfortunately, this will do little to help solve the relationship's problems. Hard work will be required to keep the channels of communication open and to move toward building acceptance and understanding.

Both Pisces-Aries and Leo III's are emotionally deep individuals who live in a world of complex feelings. The passionate aspect of an erotic relationship between them may well become an outlet for each of them to express such feelings, whether positive or negative, and their relationship may accordingly prove highly satisfying and even long-lasting. The control of tumultuous energies being crucial in this combination, however, strong emotions that threaten the relationship's stability will probably lead to its breakup. Even so, it may reach an intensity that both partners will remember for a lifetime. Should some kind of balance or direction of the determined and willful energies present in this relationship be possible, much can be achieved.

Whether in friendships or love affairs, the key to deepening trust in this relationship may lie in the area of admitting mistakes and weaknesses. Any act of forgiveness here, any resistance to a tendency to blame or lay on guilt trips, may prove a major triumph. Ultimately, the taming of the tiger requires perseverance and respect.

ADVICE: *Master-slave will not work. Mutual respect is key. Mastery may be acquired with patience. Avoid blame. Balance wayward energies.*

JOHN DEREK (8/12/26)
URSULA ANDRESS (3/19/36)

Gorgeous Andress and handsome actor Derek were considered the perfect-looking couple until their divorce in '66. Derek later married much younger sex siren Bo Derek. ***Also:* Andrew Lloyd Webber & Sarah Brightman** (married; composer/socialite); **Lynda Bird Johnson & George Hamilton** (romance; president's daughter/actor).

March 19–24

THE CUSP OF REBIRTH
PISCES-ARIES CUSP

August 19–25

THE CUSP OF EXPOSURE
LEO-VIRGO CUSP

WILLIAM HURT (3/20/50)
MARLEE MATLIN (8/24/65)

Hurt was in a highly publicized relationship for several years with Marlee Matlin, the deaf actress and Oscar winner for *Children of a Lesser God* (1986), in which Hurt co-starred. **Also: Baroness Maria Vetsera & Archduke Rudolf** (ill-fated lovers); **Stephen Sondheim & Leonard Bernstein** (collaborators); **Spike Lee & Reggie Miller** (celebrity antagonists).

Hidden Language

Imbalance figures strongly in this relationship, but easy communication is likely to be a stabilizing factor. The Pisces-Aries–Leo-Virgo union likes to focus outside itself, sharing facts or gossip about others, or subjects that are off limits to others, and the secretive or private tone that often results from this preference may become a basis for friendship: essentially these two have their own, often whispered language. Care must be taken in such a relationship not to fall into patterns of isolation that cut the duo off from the world, so that it loses essential human contacts.

Despite its ability to put an "us against the world" face on things, the relationship suffers from an inherent instability, which demands significant adjustments from both parties to counter. The often precarious nature of the relationship creates excitement and unpredictability but provides little incentive to complete the ordinary tasks of everyday life. Leo-Virgos are often attracted to Pisces-Aries but may keep their feelings to themselves for a long time. If, when they finally open up, they find that the Pisces-Aries are similarly attracted, the results may be overpowering and tumultuous. Should their feelings not immediately prove mutual, on the other hand, Leo-Virgos may unhappily back off rather than hanging in there. Generally quite protective of their feelings, they will usually avoid or run from a situation in which they feel rejected, rather than masochistically seeking it out.

Although Pisces-Aries and Leo-Virgo share the common element of fire (Aries and Leo both being fire signs), watery Pisces is more concerned with feeling and earthy Virgo with practical matters and work. The fiery element can lend passion to any love relationship, and at least in the short term these two may climb to heights of sensuous experience. It is the element that is missing, however—air—and its strong mental orientation that can become the real reasons for the success of a Pisces-Aries–Leo-Virgo relationship. By clever and judicious planning, for example, this couple may secure a good financial basis for themselves. The development of common sense will prove a strong stabilizing factor that can always be counted on.

ADVICE: *Excitement is not the best goal. Use your common sense. Don't make your communication too exclusive. Beware of isolation.*

March 19–24

THE CUSP OF REBIRTH
PISCES-ARIES CUSP

August 26–September 2

THE WEEK OF SYSTEM BUILDERS
VIRGO I

WILLIAM MORRIS (3/24/1834)
EDWARD BURNE-JONES (8/28/1833)

Morris—artist, designer, poet and craftsman—met Burne-Jones, a leading painter and designer, at Oxford. Collaborators and lifelong friends, Burne-Jones was a prime illustrator for Morris' Kelmscott Press, founded in 1890.
Also: Lynda Bird Johnson & Lyndon Johnson (daughter/father).

Giant Steps

It is characteristic of this relationship to reach for the stars but keep its feet on the ground. Free, often chaotic and fantasy-rich thoughts and actions are typical of it, but it can effectively manage and ground them through the establishment of a few simple rules. Bringing order to the different areas of life, at home and in the workplace, will tend to counterbalance more scattered energies. Conversely, it is also true that this combination's acceptance of a little freedom of spirit will encourage its partners to step out of a more formal mode, so that their relationship will allow them to become more expressive and vibrant.

The relationship is usually more successful in friendship, work or marriage than in love, where unstable elements can surface that will quickly lead the partners to states of emotional upset. Unpredictable or impulsive feelings can be powerful agents here. In order to remain calm and make measured decisions, particularly financial ones, a ruthless ban of any disruptive energies may become necessary, no matter how enjoyable and attractive these may be. If the relationship is to survive, and particularly if it is a sexual one, practical considerations may demand a firm hand with self-destructive impulses.

Virgo I's often have the problem of getting involved with exactly the wrong people. Pisces-Aries may well fall into that number, particularly if they are needy types who will drain Virgo I energy. On the other hand, many Pisces-Aries are fun-loving enough to allow Virgo I's a respite from their own compulsiveness and workaholic tendencies. The principal problems between these two are that Virgo I's may have difficulty with that whirlwind Pisces-Aries energy and may have to withdraw into their own private world, while Pisces-Aries may be unable to stand the rule-making and prohibitive attitudes of Virgo I's, particularly around money.

Nonetheless, this relationship can sometimes assume gigantic proportions and, like an overly expansive and energetic plant, may need to be trimmed and cut back to size. Finding a proper sense of proportion, both within the relationship and in regard to the daily life around it, is perhaps the most pressing challenge of all.

ADVICE: *Cut back on activities. Don't be so dominant. Keep things in perspective. Strive for balance and proportion. Don't ignore pressing matters.*

March 19–24
THE CUSP OF REBIRTH
PISCES-ARIES CUSP

September 3–10
THE WEEK OF THE ENIGMA
VIRGO II

 RELATIONSHIPS

STRENGTHS: **THERAPEUTIC, STIMULATING, ADVENTURESOME**

WEAKNESSES: **MISUNDERSTOOD, HURT, ISOLATED**

BEST: **FRIENDSHIP**

WORST: **FAMILY**

Intrepid Exploration

It is not uncommon for a relationship to spring from a misunderstanding, but a Pisces-Aries–Virgo II meeting has a higher than average probability of resulting from such an event or from some other slightly unusual occurrence: both these parties have a tendency to be misunderstood or misread by others. On the plus side, this means that these two may find in each other a mutual point of empathy. Two negatives form a positive; similarly, the relationship that results from this synergistic combination can be far stronger than the individuals who constitute it. Fittingly, given the seeming misfit nature of the two parties, this relationship focuses on creating a private world, with time being given to inner exploration and recognition. Once bonds of trust and sharing are formed, cathartic and even ecstatic moments of mutual revelation may ensue. The duo may then be ready for further challenges, both in areas of psychological and spiritual growth and in the issues of the outer world—family, society, work.

It is possible for Pisces-Aries and Virgo II's to form a strong lifelong bond, whether as friends, lovers or spouses. Obstacles will arise, of course, but the mutual understanding between these two can be so great that they will be undaunted by personal problems and challenges, and may in fact be stimulated by them. One of the greatest difficulties of this relationship may lie in being tied to old scripts—negative parental or familial attitudes from childhood, for example. Role patterns like these can lead to acting out, in hurtful and denigrating ways. But these stances from the past can be recognized, acknowledged and released, or at the very least defused.

One great danger of this pairing is that it will develop into a kind of folie à deux, becoming restricted to a mutually supportive but highly private world in which the pair is confined by the belief that it marches to a different drummer. Actively building bridges to fellow human beings is essential, perhaps with the Virgo II making career contacts and the Pisces-Aries taking the lead socially. The relationship's flowering, and the mental health of both parties, may well depend on the success of such efforts.

ADVICE: *Beware of dependencies. Don't cut yourself off from the world. Engage in give-and-take with others. Keep pushing back your frontiers.*

SPIKE LEE (3/20/57)
ROSIE PEREZ (9/6/64)

After filmmaker Lee spotted dancer Perez performing at an LA club, he cast her in *Do the Right Thing*, his 1989 Oscar-nominated film. Perez went on to play dramatic parts in *Fearless* (1993) and *It Could Happen to You* (1994). **Also: J.S. Bach & J.C. Bach** (father/son; composers)

March 19–24
THE CUSP OF REBIRTH
PISCES-ARIES CUSP

September 11–18
THE WEEK OF THE LITERALIST
VIRGO III

 RELATIONSHIPS

STRENGTHS: **SUCCESSFUL, IMAGINATIVE, REALISTIC**

WEAKNESSES: **WARY, UNFORGIVING, STRESSED**

BEST: **BUSINESS ASSOCIATION**

WORST: **LOVE**

Well-Grounded Imagination

This relationship may well address itself to big projects born out of wide-ranging ideas and implemented with practiced expertise. The ambition of these projects may arouse expectations that are not always fulfilled, however, for strict maintenance is required even once the train is on the rails, and this relationship may not sustain such long-range efforts. Disappointments and setbacks may undermine the relationship's strength, particularly if heavy criticism and blame come to the surface.

This combination does not exhibit particularly great emotional strength and unity. Virgo III's tend to be extremely discriminating and careful in the expression of emotion; they have a good deal of control over their feelings and are apt to make deliberate decisions in any given situation as to how much or how little of themselves they want to reveal. Pisces-Aries are far less selective—in fact, they don't really choose to express emotion but do so naturally. It will be difficult, then, for Virgo III's to handle the more direct and unpremeditated feelings of Pisces-Aries. Moreover, Pisces-Aries are very sensitive to criticism of any kind—a Virgo III forte.

Unforgiving attitudes may dominate this relationship at times, and rarely is a second chance given when major mistakes are made. Once a promise is not kept, hopes held out in the future will be treated warily. Interpersonal bonds may not survive highly stressful emotional encounters.

Much can be learned in this relationship, and much accomplished, but not usually in the spheres of friendship, love or marriage. It is in acquaintanceship, work or in an advisory capacity that the matchup works best, particularly when there is not a lot of intimate contact. The combination's ingredients of fertile imagination and hardheaded realism may well interact to advance career success. And in the family sphere, where Virgo III's ground more diffuse Pisces-Aries energies, and Pisces-Aries stimulate Virgo III's to take action, a successful dynamic between two siblings or between parent and child may benefit all concerned.

ADVICE: *Stay objective. Don't let feelings get in the way. Avoid blame. Cultivate maintenance. Scale down unrealistic expectations.*

IRENE JOLIOT-CURIE (9/12/1897)
FREDERIC JOLIOT-CURIE (3/19/1900)

Frederic Joliot married Irene Curie, daughter of Marie and Pierre Curie (discoverers of radium). They won the 1935 Nobel Prize as the first to produce artificial radioactivity and were instrumental in neutron discovery and proving the phenomenon of fission. **Also: Adolf Butenandt & Leopold Ruzicka** (1939 Nobelists, chemistry).

OZZIE NELSON (3/20/06)
GUNNAR & MATTHEW NELSON (9/20/69)

Grandsons of the creator of tv's *Ozzie and Harriet* (1952–66), identical twins Gunnar and Matthew became rock stars during the late 80s/early 90s, following in the footsteps of their father, the late Ricky Nelson.

March 19–24
THE CUSP OF REBIRTH
PISCES-ARIES CUSP

September 19–24
THE CUSP OF BEAUTY
VIRGO-LIBRA CUSP

A Balancing Act

The cusps of Pisces-Aries and Virgo-Libra fall on the spring and the fall equinoxes, respectively; this rare and unusual matchup, then, is governed by the year's only equinoctial opposition, the only moment to carry the perfectly balanced energies of equal-length days and nights. As you might expect, the relationship between Pisces-Aries and Virgo-Libra is highly magnetic and magical, and is filled with mutual fascination, particularly in the area of physical or aesthetic sensuousness. (Should it manifest in the area of love, in fact, it may well evolve into a more permanent situation.) Pisces-Aries are emotion-and-intuition types (their elements being water and fire) and Virgo-Libras are sensation-and-thought types (their elements being earth and air); they share no common element in their makeup and have very different capabilities and outlooks. A relationship that joins them, however, combines all four elements equally and, although it may require some balancing and finesse of energies, is synergistically more powerful than the individuals who make it up.

Pisces-Aries are stronger in the subjective sphere, Virgo-Libras in the objective one. Pisces-Aries tend to be dreamers, following hunches and expressing themselves directly; Virgo-Libras often find it hard to express deep feelings and feel more comfortable dealing with down-to-earth, everyday concerns. As a working duo, whether of parents, co-workers, teammates or business partners, each can offer what the other lacks. Between them they cover the bases.

Problems arise between these two when Pisces-Aries grow impatient with a quality of Virgo-Libras that they see as superficiality or a concern with the surface phenomena of life. Virgo-Libras, on the other hand, may see Pisces-Aries as overly troubled or too involved with emotional matters that get them bogged down in inaction or indecision. They may also often feel that Pisces-Aries lack common sense and tend to fly off impulsively in the wrong direction. Accused of impracticality, Pisces-Aries may charge Virgo-Libras with being too materialistic. Despite the strong attraction in this relationship, it can begin to wane if the partners begin to lose respect for each other, with their manifest differences leading to serious animosity and conflict.

ADVICE: *Work together. Maintain respect. Accept differences; use them to your benefit. Recognize emotional needs. Be more accepting and less combative.*

BONNIE PARKER (10/1/11)
CLYDE BARROW (3/24/09)

Known to be deeply in love, Bonnie and Clyde were notorious robbers in the 1930s, killing 12 people before being ambushed and gunned down by police in 1934. **Also: Chico & Groucho Marx** (brothers; comedians); **Wernher von Braun & Willie Ley** (colleagues; rocketry); **William Hurt & Mary Beth Hurt** (married; actors).

March 19–24
THE CUSP OF REBIRTH
PISCES-ARIES CUSP

September 25–October 2
THE WEEK OF THE PERFECTIONIST
LIBRA I

Confrontational Honesty

This relationship involves a great deal of honesty and openness—perhaps too much; its success will depend, in fact, on its ability to cope with direct confrontations. These challenges may demand adjustments that are at odds with the basic nature of both personalities, and that they feel compromise their individuality. Giving in to the other partner's demands in a desperate effort to please, and to make the relationship work, may result in a loss of pride and self-esteem. Meaningful compromise is essential if the relationship is to work out in the long term, but giving ground may, unfortunately, be difficult or impossible. Battles between the partners will put tremendous strains on day-to-day living.

This is particularly true in sexual and financial matters, but in many other areas, too, the negative emotions created by the frank attitudes characteristic of this relationship are often too much to handle and arouse insecurity and unhappiness. The spotlight here often falls on the Pisces-Aries personality and what Libra I finds wrong with it. Should these two live together, as family members, mates or friends, Libra I's may see themselves as advisers to their Pisces-Aries partners, whose problems they will try to solve and whose needs they will tend. Pisces-Aries can, for their part, come to depend on this support and may even hold on to certain problems because they provide a way to gain attention. Libra I's, however, can easily swing from overinterest to disinterest, leaving Pisces-Aries baffled.

Pisces-Aries generally make few demands on Libra I's in terms of asking them to change, but one request they will certainly make is that the Libra I's open up and be sympathetic. Emotional honesty is so important to Pisces-Aries that if they cannot get it from their partner they will become depressed, unhappy and restless. To avoid these funks, they will keep pushing harder for honesty, even if this leads to unpleasantness. Real progress can be made in this relationship by open discussion, as long as fairness and justice keep such communication from degenerating into continual bickering.

ADVICE: *Try to be more responsive. Show sympathy and love openly. Demand emotional honesty. Don't be afraid to fight, but avoid bickering.*

March 19–24

THE CUSP OF REBIRTH
PISCES-ARIES CUSP

October 3–10

THE WEEK OF SOCIETY
LIBRA II

RELATIONSHIPS

STRENGTHS: **PLEASURABLE, ENTERTAINING, RELAXED**

WEAKNESSES: **EASYGOING, STAGNATING, REACTIONARY**

BEST: **LOVE**

WORST: **WORK**

Comfortable Enjoyment

Both the strength and the weakness of this relationship lie in its easygoing and pleasure-oriented nature. The partners' similar aesthetic tastes provide the basis for an enjoyable life built around the themes of comfort, sensuality and beauty, and the main attitude here is one of mutual support, in a wide variety of areas; this encourages not only career success but fun in social interactions. Yet unless the relationship is able to transcend its relaxed, satisfied quality and give its partners direction, it is likely to stagnate. Firm goals, rules, realistic deadlines and a bit of push now and then, even if these run counter to natural inclinations, will be needed if progress is to be made. Not only financial and other practical matters but also the natural love or friendship that these two feel for each other will benefit from a little toughening of attitudes. True spiritual growth may then be expected as well.

Libra II's tend to give a lot in love relationships and need to be needed. Should a Pisces-Aries accept their attention, affection and understanding, they may become dependent on satisfying this mate or lover and will suffer from an estrangement or breakup more than the Pisces-Aries will. Pisces-Aries can be quite selfish in satisfying their own needs and may ignore Libra II's for long periods of time, perhaps even getting involved with others. The long-suffering aspects of Libra II's, and their self-hurtful tendencies, may emerge during such times of trouble. Blaming themselves for what has happened often results in a serious loss of self-esteem.

Many Pisces-Aries have a crying need to know themselves on a deep level, and Libra II's can be very helpful in this respect, since they often make good counselors and are ready to lend a sympathetic ear. Pisces-Aries can be quite exasperating in falling back into old habits, however, and Libra II's will become increasingly impatient with such behavior over time.

BUSTER KEATON (10/4/1895)
FATTY ARBUCKLE (3/24/1887)

Keaton was once protégé to then-producer Arbuckle. The stone-faced comic started his own company in 1921 and became a giant of silent-film comedy. While Arbuckle's comedy took vengeance on the pompous, Keaton always searched for utopia.

ADVICE: *Don't dream your life away. Take action in order to improve. Push yourself a bit more. Raise expectations and goals. Be the best you can.*

March 19–24

THE CUSP OF REBIRTH
PISCES-ARIES CUSP

October 11–18

THE WEEK OF THEATER
LIBRA III

RELATIONSHIPS

STRENGTHS: **EXCITING, AMBITIOUS, FOCUSED**

WEAKNESSES: **OVERSERIOUS, ANGRY, REPRESSED**

BEST: **PROJECT PARTNERS**

WORST: **MARRIAGE**

Scaling the Heights

This relationship may appear rock solid and highly responsible, since success and scaling the heights of society's ladders are its consummate focus. Ambition, however, is not always enough, particularly when individual needs are neglected or suppressed, overrun by this duo's ambitious drives. The relationship can be flamboyant and exciting but may not be stable enough to survive the mundane demands of living together, particularly in marriage. Putting energies in the service of business or social groups will be highly stimulating and may result in new levels of achievement. Friendships or partnerships are particularly favored, especially when engaged in far-reaching projects. The ideal would find these two in businesses or occupations in which the relationship's charismatic and dynamic elements can find full expression in innovating new projects, establishing relations with clients or making sales.

A passionate love affair between a Pisces-Aries and a Libra III cannot by any means be ruled out, but the relationship's volatile nature may ensure a rough ride, with quite a few emotional ups and downs. Perhaps the biggest problem in such a romance is that Pisces-Aries may not be tough enough to cope with the tremendous self-confident career drive of Libra III's, which may leave them feeling abandoned or neglected for long periods of time. Bringing out their insecure, nervous side, such neglect may lead to recriminations, anger and resentment, which Libra III's will probably view with annoyance as an intrusion on their valuable time. The most immature aspects of Pisces-Aries may emerge in such moments, and Libra III's can come to feel they are dealing with a petulant child.

The breakdowns of communication and concomitant problems that surface at these times can be avoided if more honesty is practiced in the first place. Learning to be critical yet accepting, focused yet open, and practical yet emotional is key. Above all, these partners must not reject occasional lightheartedness, flamboyance or idiosyncrasy, which can only give the relationship character and individuality.

LEE HARVEY OSWALD (10/18/39)
JACK RUBY (3/23/11)

On the day after the assassination of President Kennedy, Oswald was shot and killed by Jack Ruby, a Dallas nightclub operator with reputed ties to the underworld. *Also:* **John Sirica & John Dean** (Watergate judge/defendant); **Andrew Mellon & Baron Joseph Duveen** (financier/art dealer); **Pamela Harriman & Leland Hayward** (married).

ADVICE: *Don't forget human considerations. You are not a machine. Allow for error and individuality. Do not suppress personal expression.*

STRENGTHS: **ECSTATIC, COLORFUL, UNCONVENTIONAL**

WEAKNESSES: **COMPETITIVE, JEALOUS, ADDICTIVE**

BEST: **FRIENDSHIP**

WORST: **SEX AND LOVE**

SERGEI DIAGHILEV (3/19/1872)
PABLO PICASSO (10/25/1881)

Diaghilev and Picasso became fast friends after Diagilev commissioned the artist in 1917 to design the sets and costumes for his ballet *Parade*. Picasso's curtain for the ballet featured a mural that was better received than the production itself.

March 19–24
THE CUSP OF REBIRTH
PISCES-ARIES CUSP

October 19–25
THE CUSP OF DRAMA & CRITICISM
LIBRA-SCORPIO CUSP

The Raging Heart

This relationship is likely to be an uncertain, unconventional and highly unpredictable one. In some cases it may develop an addiction to sex and love, in which both partners exert claims on each other and are unable to get free of their feelings. Such relationships can classically produce extremes of both pleasure and pain, with both peak experiences and depressions manifesting with some regularity, and this one is no exception. To avoid emotional, psychological or in extreme cases physical damage, limits may have to be placed on what is and is not allowed. Pisces-Aries and Libra-Scorpios share a common element, water (Pisces and Scorpio are both water signs), which represents the faculty of emotion in the human personality. Since Aries and Libra are fire and air signs, respectively, Pisces-Aries and Libra-Scorpios can make an explosive combination, particularly in the realm of feelings. Should theirs be a love relationship, it is likely to be a highly passionate one.

This pairing is not recommended for work or marital partnerships, since emotional conflicts are sooner or later likely to emerge and to become increasingly frequent, disrupting the work at hand. Should the relationship manifest as a friendship, it is likely to go well. Care must be taken to guard against jealousy, however, particularly when the partners share friends whose attention or affection they seek. When they are together with a group of their peers, Pisces-Aries and Libra-Scorpios can end up competing intensely with each other for the spotlight. On the other hand, each may well stimulate the other's more flamboyant side in social gatherings, making for a lively and at times contentious exchange that those around them may find highly entertaining, if it doesn't go too far. And this is perhaps the secret to harmony in this relationship—to tone down excess and learn to live at a more ordinary, albeit perhaps boring, level of experience.

ADVICE: *Avoid excess, but don't lose the spark. Keep on an even keel. Don't sacrifice intensity, but be reasonable. Beware of burnout.*

STRENGTHS: **AFFECTIONATE, ETHICAL, SERIOUS**

WEAKNESSES: **MISTRUSTING, REBELLIOUS, DECEPTIVE**

BEST: **FRIENDSHIP**

WORST: **FAMILY**

H.R. HALDEMAN (10/27/26)
JOHN ERLICHMAN (3/20/25)

Chief of staff Haldeman was Nixon's righthand man, wielding great power. Erlichman, the president's domestic affairs advisor and close aide, shared responsibilities with Haldeman. Both were deeply involved in the details of the Watergate break-in and subsequent cover-up and were forced to resign to face criminal charges.

March 19–24
THE CUSP OF REBIRTH
PISCES-ARIES CUSP

October 26–November 2
THE WEEK OF INTENSITY
SCORPIO I

Paying Dues

This relation usually begins in suspicion and distrust. Actions, not words, will be needed for each partner to convince the other and to engender mutual faith. If a bond is to be forged, the relationship's steel must go through the fire if it is to be tempered and dependable. But once the parties have paid their dues and endured the trials and tribulations that the relationship requires, openness and honesty can be achieved. Much will depend on the continued investment of time spent in serious talk and in the airing of different points of view. Only then may sympathy and understanding grow, and with them a deepening of the relationship and a measure of permanence.

Actions alone are not enough to convince Scorpio I's; ethical intent is vitally important to them. But Pisces-Aries often do things impulsively, without thinking. Even if their intention is pure enough in their own minds, they may consequently get into trouble with Scorpio I's, who tend to be suspicious of their apparent innocence and often harbor nagging suspicions about them, finding it hard to believe that they didn't have something deceptive or downright dishonest in mind after all.

Such suspicions may undercut this relationship, whether it appears in the realm of friendship, love or work. Furthermore, since neither of these types is particularly strong in self-understanding, deceptions of all types may actually abound. Pisces-Aries find their weaknesses and deficiencies harder to hide than Scorpio I's, who rarely if ever can be caught putting themselves at a disadvantage, particularly in any kind of argument. Soon learning that they can be hurt by Scorpio I's, since they are more vulnerable, Pisces-Aries may become less willing to open up, and more guarded. In the family sphere, this relationship may feature constant battles, particularly between siblings. A Scorpio I parent can place very heavy demands on a Pisces-Aries child, who may react with outright rebellion. Pisces-Aries cannot tolerate the Scorpio I need to control, so the outlook is often not good. Although increased affection and protectiveness may surface through struggle, marriages between Pisces-Aries and Scorpio I's are not particularly recommended.

ADVICE: *Don't always doubt intentions. Take things as they are. Faith is often more important than evaluation. Try to lighten up and have fun.*

March 19–24

THE CUSP OF REBIRTH
PISCES-ARIES CUSP

November 3–11

THE WEEK OF DEPTH
SCORPIO II

Dark Star

STRENGTHS: **INTIMATE, SYMPATHETIC, REWARDING**

WEAKNESSES: **RESTRICTIVE, INHIBITING, ANXIOUS**

BEST: **FRIENDSHIP**

WORST: **WORK**

A visual image representing this relationship might be that of a lonely solar system with a single dark star at its center—for this is an exclusive relationship, which may keep others away. Intimacy and complex interpersonal interactions are the keynotes here. The deep bonds of feelings and sympathy in the Dark Star relationship may be both mutually rewarding and long lasting. Because this duo shares thoughts and experiences so easily, other family members, spouses and friends will have to be understanding about their intimacy and control any envy or resentment.

Both parties generally feel favorable about this relationship, particularly if it is a long-lasting friendship. Yet Pisces-Aries need emotional change much more than Scorpio II's; they occasionally feel frustrated about being fixed in this orbit and may want to roam. If Scorpio II's in turn feel threatened by the other party's outside interests, they may cling to the relationship more tightly than ever.

Emotions are tricky in this matchup, particularly when it involves love and marriage. Here more depressive aspects may surface in the relationship, leading to worry and brooding. Part of the problem is an inability to maintain objectivity and boundaries, and a concomitant merging of personalities. Should drinking or other drugs be involved, shared addictions could prove extremely hard to conquer. Another possible form of addiction might involve sex and/or love, in which case separation would yield anxiety.

Should these two live or work together, Scorpio II's may become upset with Pisces-Aries over what they see as financial irresponsibility. Money is an important issue for Scorpio II's, representing control and power, whereas Pisces-Aries may view it much less seriously. Another area of conflict that can arise in day-to-day situations involves tempo: where Pisces-Aries are impulsive, Scorpio II's need to chew things over for long periods of time before acting. This may well result in friction, with Pisces-Aries always urging their slower-moving partner to hurry up, and Scorpio II's trying to get their more nervous partner to calm down.

ADVICE: *Take a break once in a while. Don't be so exclusive—include others in your plans. Brighten up. Worry and depression can drag you down.*

BRUCE WILLIS (3/19/55)
DEMI MOORE (11/11/62)

These superstar actors, married in 1987 by rock & roll singer-minister Little Richard, have 3 daughters. One of Hollywood's highest paid actresses, Moore posed nude on the cover of *Vanity Fair* while pregnant. **Also: Andrew Lloyd Webber & Tim Rice** (musical collaborators); **Fatty Arbuckle & Mabel Normand** (film team).

March 19–24

THE CUSP OF REBIRTH
PISCES-ARIES CUSP

November 12–18

THE WEEK OF CHARM
SCORPIO III

Captivating Charisma

STRENGTHS: **PERSUASIVE, SENSUOUS, SATISFYING**

WEAKNESSES: **DECEIVING, UNCOMMITTED, EXHAUSTING**

BEST: **LOVE**

WORST: **MARRIAGE**

Highly persuasive and convincing, this relationship exerts a magnetic influence on those around it, encouraging trust. (The flip side of the coin is that it can also encourage dependency in third parties who are drawn to it.) And yet, curiously, the power of Pisces-Aries and Scorpio III's to convince each other is far less than the power of the relationship as a unit—probably since each partner is too skilled in the arts of seduction and charm to fall for each other's tricks. Because of the relationship's ability to persuade, which usually derives from an ability to read the intentions of others quickly and clearly, there will of necessity be a fair amount of honesty and openness between the parties. Yet in certain crucial areas, facts or feelings may be deftly hidden and true emotions suppressed. Out of an instinctive fear of getting hurt, the other partner may choose to turn a blind eye to such secrets.

Relationships with Scorpio III's bring out the sensuous side of Pisces-Aries, allowing them to relax and to bring their nervousness under control. If there is a sexual attraction here, it is likely to result in a prolonged and complicated love affair. Marriage or a deep commitment to living together, however, is not particularly recommended for this matchup, since if serious problems arise, dreamier Pisces-Aries will tend to flee, while more realistic Scorpio III's will unilaterally modify or even break off the relationship. When things are good between these two, in other words, they can be very good, but when things turn sour, neither party may feel the relationship is worth the exhausting effort required to put it right.

As parents or bosses, Scorpio III's may prove much too authoritarian for Pisces-Aries. As business partners or equal colleagues, however, these two can be unbeatable, the persuasive character of their relationship working wonders on those they encounter. Pisces-Aries imagination and energy and strong Scorpio III money sense are underlying factors. The magnetism and charisma of this duo can woo others to buy any of its concepts, services or products, or to follow any cause.

ADVICE: *Be truthful. Persuasiveness may encourage others to be overdependent. Winning isn't everything. Examine motives carefully.*

PAMELA HARRIMAN (3/20/20)
AVERELL HARRIMAN (11/15/1891)

Averell was Pamela's 3rd husband. From the wealthy Harriman family, he was Russian ambassador (1943–46), NY State governor (1955–59) and ambassador at large (1965–68). After he died in '86, Pamela became a prominent contributor/fundraiser for the Democrats. In '93 President Clinton appointed her ambassador to France. She died in '97.
Also: Keith Reif & Chris Dreja (musicians, The Yardbirds).

SIRHAN SIRHAN (3/19/44)
ROBERT KENNEDY (11/20/25)

On the night of his 1968 California primary victory, moments after this photo (above right) was taken, Kennedy was fatally shot by Sirhan, a Jordanian immigrant who killed Kennedy for his pro-Israel views.
Also: **J.S. Bach & W.F. Bach**
(father/son; composers);

Wyatt Earp & Bat Masterson
(Dodge City gang).

March 19–24
THE CUSP OF REBIRTH
PISCES-ARIES CUSP

November 19–24
THE CUSP OF REVOLUTION
SCORPIO-SAGITTARIUS CUSP

The Slumbering Volcano

This relationship manifests primarily on the physical plane, with striving, fervent emotions struggling for supremacy. In fact, the synergy of this combination is less restful than fiercely passionate and even, occasionally, violent. This is because Pisces-Aries and Scorpio-Sagittarius are both water-fire combinations, each apprehending the world primarily through the faculties of feeling and intuition. So, while on the surface these two cusp people have a lot in common and should be able to understand each other quite well, in fact a relationship between them brings out their weakest elements: indecisiveness and a fiery temperament.

The great challenge facing this duo, then, is to maintain the dedication, conviction and mental concentration that will counteract the relationship's wildly veering nature and keep it on track. On the positive side, the determination to stick together is capable of becoming a transcendent goal that can hold the relationship intact. On the negative, this can discourage each partner from risking serious personal change independently of the other one. A kind of stubborn loyalty may develop here, one that neither Pisces-Aries nor Scorpio-Sagittarians may have felt so strongly for another person before.

Both of these types are extremely sensitive, and quite reactive and vulnerable to each other's actions and criticisms. Better suited to action than to reflection, each has a strong desire for success; as long as this drive can be limited to their careers, rather than spilling over into their own relationship as personal competition, harmony may be maintained. As friends or lovers, Pisces-Aries and Scorpio-Sagittarians will have a demanding, intense relationship, which they will want to live to the fullest. The dynamic of both business and marital partnerships will be complex, particularly over the question of who plays the dominant role. Either partner may choose to stay in the background for periods of time, letting the other take the lead; this good sense and diplomacy augurs well for the relationship's longevity. Wielding influence behind the scenes is the most effective means of control here—the outside world may know little of what goes on privately in this highly personal and mysterious relationship.

ADVICE: *Let go occasionally. Find time to relax. Follow natural and personal urges, too. You don't always have to hide. Be more transparent.*

JOHN SIRICA (3/19/04)
G. GORDON LIDDY (11/30/30)

Sirica, presiding judge at the 1973 Watergate trial, sent Liddy, one of the 7 original defendants, to prison. After his release, Liddy became something of a celebrity, lecturing on campuses, appearing in tv dramas, even hosting a talk show.

March 19–24
THE CUSP OF REBIRTH
PISCES-ARIES CUSP

November 25–December 2
THE WEEK OF INDEPENDENCE
SAGITTARIUS I

A Roller Coaster Ride

This relationship's emotional ups and downs make for instability. Outspoken and impulsive attitudes are prominent here, and peace and harmony are not the pairing's keywords. But the matchup isn't boring, either, and flying sparks can ignite passions that may lead to a tumultuous love affair. Both of these personalities will tell it like it is, demanding honesty from each other and refusing to hold back the truth themselves. Keeping things out in the open is the habit of Sagittarius I's more than of Pisces-Aries, however, and the latter may use more indirect, more manipulative methods to get their way.

Pisces-Aries and Sagittarius I's share their appreciation of nature and their delight in vigorous exercise or training. Whether as friends or partners in pursuits involving sports, fitness or adventure, they will feed off a reserve of mutual inspiration and excitement, in which challenge and competition figure prominently. A strong emotional bond can develop in such situations but does not have to and, in fact, may prove counterproductive to the activity at hand. Through bettering personal records and paying attention to technical matters, both of these highly subjective individuals will be able to cultivate the objectivity they so desperately need in their lives, personally and as a team.

In business and career matters, this relationship brings tremendous imaginative force and physical drive to its work, whether involving sales or services. Keeping its whirlwind energies under control may prove a problem, however; the matchup's fiery aspects may undercut the stability of its projects. Except in matters of fiscal planning and the handling of money, where the Sagittarius I is often the more capable, it will often be the task of the Pisces-Aries to make recommendations and plans that will put the talents of the Sagittarius I to best use. Unless both partners maintain a firm grip on reality and keep their contentiousness under control, they will repeatedly sabotage their best chances for success, particularly in the area of finances.

ADVICE: *Even out your mood swings. Maintain objectivity in money matters. Use your common sense more. Keep your physical impulses natural but under control.*

STRENGTHS: **QUIRKY, FUN, OPEN**

WEAKNESSES: **IMPRACTICAL, UNREALISTIC, CHAOTIC**

BEST: **FRIENDSHIP**

WORST: **WORK**

Inventive Entertainment

Idiosyncratic and quirky this is one of the more unusual relationships of the year. Enjoyment and fun are the hallmarks here, and also mutual understanding and support. This imaginative and stimulating matchup often finds itself at the center of a circle of friends, on which it usually has a positive influence. Comedy, play-acting and a love of games, even of gambling, may be some of the areas in which the relationship's particular chemistry works to lend liveliness to any gathering. Also important is the fact that this matchup allows its partners the opportunity to go their own ways, without negative criticism, blame or attempts at reform.

Both parties to this relationship are usually comfortable in it, since it offers a solution to the loneliness and asocial tendencies of which both are typically capable. As a team, Pisces-Aries and Sagittarius II's often lose a lot of their shyness and come out in the open. Living together may be difficult, however, since neither of them usually shows much interest in discharging domestic duties and tasks. Without some kind of formal agreement over the division of labor, this can lead to a fairly chaotic situation. Should Pisces-Aries and Sagittarius II's have children, one or another of their offspring may quite possibly have to assume responsibility for keeping the house in good running order. Not surprisingly, this combination is not particularly recommended for business relations and partnerships, since it may lack an important practical element.

Both of these personalities have an extroverted side, which may occasionally get out of hand in the case of Sagittarius II's, who often have problems getting to know themselves at a deep level. More sensitive, Pisces-Aries may be able to hold up the mirror to Sagittarius II emotions, helping in the process of self-discovery. As teachers, friends or guides, in fact, Pisces-Aries may well instigate or nurture spiritual awakenings in Sagittarius II's. In this case, however, Sagittarius II's must be careful not to become dependent on or to idolize Pisces-Aries, who may seem the only ones capable of understanding them, but are not.

ADVICE: *Try to be more serious occasionally. Daily chores matter. Don't leave the work to someone else.*

SAMMY DAVIS, JR. (12/8/25)
MAI BRITT (3/22/36)

Multitalented entertainer Sammy Davis, Jr., was also a member of the controversial "Rat Pack" that included Frank Sinatra, Dean Martin, Peter Lawford and Joey Bishop. Swedish actress Mai Britt was his wife from 1960–66.
Also: Chad & Jeremy (singing duo); **Joan Crawford & Douglas Fairbanks, Jr.** (married; actors).

STRENGTHS: **ENCHANTING, PROTECTIVE, VULNERABLE**

WEAKNESSES: **POWER-TRIPPING, SELFISH, UNFAITHFUL**

BEST: **FRIENDSHIP**

WORST: **LOVE**

Who's on First

The expression of a balanced sense of authority is the primary theme here. So long as both parties understand that it is the coupling itself that carries weight, things will run smoothly. This relationship works well when it is directed outward into the world, or, possibly, when it involves parenting. But neither member of this duo is happy playing second fiddle. It's not that struggle is the order of the day, but there often is a sense of discomfort over the role each party plays, with each one wishing to assert him- or herself as the authority figure. In consequence, subtle bids for power can undermine this combination, and long-term love or marital relationships are not particularly favored. What is most difficult here, however, is the obsessive inability to leave things alone, which makes an even, harmonious daily life hard to achieve.

The expansive manner of Sagittarius III's may be a bit intimidating or off-putting for Pisces-Aries, who do not think on quite so lofty or grand a scale. Sagittarius III's have a breezy and self-assured air, and recognize few limitations or barriers; Pisces-Aries need their privacy and resent intrusions on their space. The relationship may accordingly bring out Pisces-Aries' shy side, or even seriously erode their self-confidence, though they can also be capable of defending themselves assertively. On the other hand, Sagittarius III's may find themselves vulnerable to the fascination of Pisces-Aries, who know how to get their way through subtle forms of emotional manipulation. Pisces-Aries will not be above using the protective instincts of Sagittarius III's, or their need for admiration, to control them. Should a mutual attraction arise between these two types, a friendship may well ensue, with each enjoying the other's direct approach. In love, emotional differences prove a real stumbling block: Sagittarius III's tend to be passionate types, who give their all only in the most intimate moments, whereas Pisces-Aries are more sensuous, needing pleasure in regular doses throughout the day. The relationship probably works best as a business or, better, a creative partnership, particularly when both partners can act as the authority on their own topics or subject areas.

ADVICE: *Give up control. Work on give-and-take. Practice brainstorming and the sharing of ideas. Agree to be partners.*

AMANDA PLUMMER (3/23/57)
CHRISTOPHER PLUMMER (12/13/27)

Famous for his Shakespearean roles, actor Christopher Plummer was also Baron Von Trapp in the *Sound of Music* (1965). His daughter, Amanda, first gained stage recognition as the schizophrenic nun in *Agnes of God* (1982).

JESUS ALOU (3/24/42)
MATTY ALOU (12/22/38)

Born and raised in the Dominican Republic, Jesus and Matty, along with Felipe, were baseball's famous Alou brothers. Remarkably, each played a season of outfield for the Oakland A's in 3 successive seasons. **Also: Ruth Page & Robert Joffrey** (contemporary dancer-choreographers).

March 19–24
THE CUSP OF REBIRTH
PISCES-ARIES CUSP

December 19–25
THE CUSP OF PROPHECY
SAGITTARIUS-CAPRICORN CUSP

A Paradoxical Partnership

This relationship secretly yearns for ease of interchange and natural, childlike expression. At certain rare moments of mutual repose and comfort, this ideal can be reached; a strong intuitive sense allows each partner to know what the other wants. Perversely, however, individual willfulness and stubbornness can make each person refuse to satisfy the other's desires. Only strong determination and conviction will truly allow both parties to lower their guard and enjoy each other.

The main problem here is that Pisces-Aries and Sagittarius-Capricorns have very different approaches to everyday matters. Should they end up in a relationship, in fact, many people will probably wonder how they found each other. Strong clashes and stormy confrontations will usually epitomize their daily relations, and there will be periodic irritation and resentment. Both Pisces-Aries and Sagittarius-Capricorns have fiery sides to their natures, and they may have to establish a conscious truce to keep from upsetting harmony in the family or workplace. But although they may never fully accept each other's ways, true mutual understanding does exist at a deep level (albeit often with a certain accompanying sense of disapproval). And the relationship is characterized by honesty, no matter how painful. This is not one of those friendships that depend on flattery to keep up appearances and interests.

Both parties may somewhat resent this relationship yet be unable to do anything about it. Unfortunately, the solution they choose may be to express their resentment by making things even more difficult for each other. They may also procrastinate and hang back from expressing their feelings for long periods, then suddenly and unexpectedly break out in an emotional outburst. Both Pisces-Aries and Sagittarius-Capricorns have a tremendous need to share (whether opportunities, money, friends or other resources), but they also have problems in doing so. Marriages, friendships or business relationships between these two are not really recommended, then. Yet their love-hate relationships, however unstable or unpredictable, may go on for years.

ADVICE: *Let your guard down more. Try to be reasonable. Find the easy way. Don't set up roadblocks. Things can be more comfortable and enjoyable if you let them be.*

MILI BALAKIREV (1/2/1837)
MODEST MUSSORGSKY (3/21/1839)

Composer Mussorgsky and pianist-composer Balakirev were 2 of the 5 famed 1860s Russian musicians known as The Five. Balakirev led this group, which composed nationalistic music. Mussorgsky's works include *Boris Gudenov*, *Night on Bald Mountain* and *Pictures from an Exhibition*.

March 19–24
THE CUSP OF REBIRTH
PISCES-ARIES CUSP

December 26–January 2
THE WEEK OF THE RULER
CAPRICORN I

The Flagship

This matchup beautifully illustrates the synergistic merging of two very different personalities into a third entity, their relationship, which can be far more successful than either will be alone. Although Capricorn I's are strong people, their authoritarianism does not necessarily make them successful leaders; Pisces-Aries, meanwhile, have the imagination and fantasy to spark new ideas but are often too flaky and undisciplined to take them anywhere. Yet the relationship between these two, particularly if it appears in the commercial or social arenas, has leadership written all over it and may give dynamic direction, guidance and inspiration to a wide range of projects.

Domestic life, however, is a different story. Interpersonally, the authoritarian attitudes of Capricorn I's will be difficult for Pisces-Aries to accept should these two find themselves living together as mates or siblings. And Capricorn I's for their part will be critical of Pisces-Aries' imaginative schemes and at times lackadaisical attitudes. Thus a marriage between these two may have direction and energy yet still fail due to emotional conflicts. It can work out only if Pisces-Aries accept the need of Capricorn I's to call the shots, and if Capricorn I's accept the extreme individuality of the Pisces-Aries personality without attempting to suppress it. Marriage may also work better if the partners lead very separate lives, engaging in many mutually exclusive activities—yet even so, power struggles will inevitably arise at home. On the other hand, since Capricorn I's have such difficulty opening up emotionally, both as lovers and mates, Pisces-Aries energy can prove invaluable in allowing them to discover and express their deepest emotions—particularly those concerned with kindness, love and acceptance. In this sense the relationship may prove curative. And Capricorn I parents (born in the Week of the Ruler) and Pisces-Aries children (born on the Cusp of Rebirth) will find themselves in roles that resemble those of their basic personalities, so this, too, may be a comfortable fit. In the reverse-case scenario, the Capricorn I child may eventually come to assume a more mature and responsible role relative to a quite childlike Pisces-Aries parent.

ADVICE: *Share feelings openly. Minimize power struggles. Trust in your relationship's power. Work together efficiently. Keep the faith.*

March 19–24

THE CUSP OF REBIRTH
PISCES-ARIES CUSP

January 3–9

THE WEEK OF DETERMINATION
CAPRICORN II

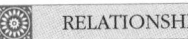 RELATIONSHIPS

STRENGTHS: **RELAXED,
APPRECIATIVE, ADMIRING**

WEAKNESSES: **DOMINANT,
COMPETITIVE, WORKAHOLIC**

BEST: **MARRIAGE**

WORST: **WORK**

Unspoken Admiration

The focus of this relationship is not just accepting differences but secretly admiring them: the combination's joint watchwords are independence and trust, implying both a tolerance for each partner's expressions of individuality and a loyalty to preserving common bonds. A need to share the joy of achievement and, further, to be appreciated are strong requirements here. A fascination with and openness to the offbeat and oddball side of life is often an underlying theme, perhaps a covert one; an orientation toward metaphysical, spiritual or religious subjects can bring shared experiences at many different levels. True, many Capricorn II's are pragmatic, no-nonsense types, but these hard-boiled characters will be remarkably tolerant of Pisces-Aries quirks and, in fact, may secretly be more interested in unusual subjects than they appear.

It may be difficult for ambitious Pisces-Aries and Capricorn II's to collaborate side by side as co-workers, since both have tendencies toward dominance. The competitive urges that are likely to arise in such a situation will be stimulating but ultimately counterproductive. Capricorn II's, however, tend to compartmentalize their lives into mutually exclusive areas, professional, social and personal, and Pisces-Aries may make fruitful appearances in either of the latter two spheres. They may even relish this kind of division, which may obligate them in one area but free them up in another, giving them the space they need. The combination can work well, then, as a friendship or marriage, and the more intimate the better. Pisces-Aries and Capricorn II's will enjoy relaxing together in the evening, after the trials and tribulations of career, domestic or social activities. They may swap stories or just silently share peace and good feeling—resting, emptying out and recharging before the next onslaught.

Workaholic tendencies in this relationship must not be allowed to get out of hand. These two will often match the week's demanding work with equally demanding play on weekends. There is a certain hardheadedness here, but the relationship does not usually degenerate into knock-down, drag-out fights.

ADVICE: *Slow down a bit at work. Keep your ambitions under control. Allow more time for relaxation. Don't be afraid to confront personal problems.*

JOHN ERLICHMAN (3/20/25)
RICHARD NIXON (1/9/13)

Domestic affairs advisor Erlichman, along with Bob Haldeman, formed Nixon's so-called palace guard, exercising immense authority in the president's name and filtering government information. Erlichman served 18 months in prison for his involvement in Watergate. Nixon resigned in 1974. **Also: Bill & Vera Allen Cleaver** (married; co-authors of children's books).

March 19–24

THE CUSP OF REBIRTH
PISCES-ARIES CUSP

January 10–16

THE WEEK OF DOMINANCE
CAPRICORN III

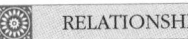 RELATIONSHIPS

STRENGTHS: **NURTURING,
EDUCATIONAL, TEAM-ORIENTED**

WEAKNESSES: **UNYIELDING,
LACKING INTIMACY, OVERSERIOUS**

BEST: **TEACHER-STUDENT**

WORST: **FRIENDSHIP**

Fostering Talents

This relationship works best when it reveals or nurtures the talents, energies and skills of its participants. Working toward this or a similar type of ideal or service is the best use of the combination's energies. The relationship is likely to grow out of some shared activity rather than through any magnetic attraction, and the pursuit of a common project or hobby can be its main role; acquaintanceship or partnership, then, possibly through group or team endeavors, is more likely than deep friendship. Since self-understanding and a grasp of the relationship's psychological underpinnings are unlikely, this matchup may not be the right one in which to try to resolve emotional problems—in fact, emotional honesty and the sharing of inner feelings may be difficult or impossible here. On the other hand, the combination can prove ideal for relationships such as teacher/student or mentor/acolyte, in which one partner fosters the talents and skills of the other and, in so doing, grows as an individual.

The more intimate kinds of relationships will prove problematic in this combination. Where Pisces-Aries usually hanker after intimacy, Capricorn III's may not need it so much and, on this ground, may find the relationship more comfortable than Pisces-Aries do. They may also find that a need that they do have—the need to be needed—will be rewarded when they lend stability to Pisces-Aries. The latter may be less happy, for in addition to feeling unsatisfied in their desire for intimacy, they may find Capricorn III's too overbearing, serious and severe for their tastes. And Pisces-Aries can be hard-driving and direct: should they find the Capricorn III in their way when they are ramming their way through to a goal, the outcome may be a bit like the irresistible force meeting the immovable object.

Despite their tremendous differences, Capricorn III's and Pisces-Aries can make good spouses if they are determined enough. Pisces-Aries will encourage Capricorn III's in their more imaginative side, making sure they relax and even get silly once in a while; Capricorn III's will adopt a supportive marital role, becoming the financial or practical rock on which Pisces-Aries can always depend. Should these two have children, they can offer a wide spectrum of abilities to their progeny and will also avoid the monolithic stance that so many young people dislike in parents.

ADVICE: *Develop more self-awareness. Sharpen psychological skills. Analysis and discussion often yield results. Don't give up.*

JOAN CRAWFORD (3/23/08)
FAYE DUNAWAY (1/14/41)

Posing a striking resemblance, Dunaway brilliantly portrayed the temperamental Crawford in the 1981 film *Mommy Dearest*, based on the best-selling biography in which Crawford's daughter, Christina, describes a cruel and manipulative mother.

STRENGTHS: **ECSTATIC, IMAGINATIVE, EASY**

WEAKNESSES: **RESTRICTIVE, RESENTFUL, DROWNING**

BEST: **LOVE**

WORST: **FAMILY**

WILLIAM SHATNER (3/22/31)
DEFOREST KELLEY (1/20/20)

DeForest Kelley was a relatively obscure 40s character actor until he got the part for Dr. Leonard "Bones" McCoy in *Star Trek* (1966-69), playing opposite Shatner, a.k.a. Captain Kirk.

Also: **Fatty Arbuckle & Mack Sennett** (actor/producer, silent films).

March 19–24

THE CUSP OF REBIRTH
PISCES-ARIES CUSP

January 17–22

THE CUSP OF MYSTERY & IMAGINATION
CAPRICORN-AQUARIUS CUSP

Lucid Dreaming

This relationship is characterized by a wide palette of emotions, featuring colorful imagination, vivid fantasy and an exciting outlook. There is certainly a sense of kindred spirits here, as if both partners were on the same wavelength. And there is also a strong sexual magnetism, so that the relationship may manifest as a stormy but ecstatic love affair. All in all, this can be a fascinating, albeit tempestuous, relationship—whether as friends, lovers, mates or family members—with rarely a dull moment.

As partners these two can clearly see each other's faults, but initially, at least, they are likely to overlook them, particularly if this is a love relationship. No doubt each partner sees him- or herself in the other, and this projection is not unreasonable, since their unconscious lives may be very similar. Yet the figures they see in each other are also highly idealized, representing the perfection they wish for in themselves. As zodiacal signs, Pisces-Aries combines water and fire, Capricorn-Aquarius earth and air, so that in their relationship with each other these two personalities unite all four elements. Together, this suggests, they can find the wholeness they lack as individuals. The most obvious problem, particularly in love relationships, is that in the urge to meld with each other they may neglect their own self-development, and if they eventually separate they may find themselves playing catch-up, having stopped evolving individually. This tendency toward self-loss in the relationship usually rules out long-standing marital or career partnerships, as one of the duo will eventually need to break away. Pisces-Aries are particularly likely to come to resent the relationship.

As family members, and despite their obvious sympathies and weaknesses for each other, these two can fight like crazy, particularly if they are parent-child pairs. In sibling relationships, however, feelings of rivalry may drop away over the years, allowing quite free and easy feelings to emerge and strong bonds of sympathy and understanding, actually present from the beginning, to come to the fore.

ADVICE: *Beware of emotional dependency. Don't idealize so much—you may be fooling yourself. Tone down emotions. Try not to overreact.*

STRENGTHS: **VERBAL, FUN, INVESTIGATIVE**

WEAKNESSES: **COMPETITIVE, IMMATURE, ARGUMENTATIVE**

BEST: **CONVERSATIONAL**

WORST: **LOVE**

DAVID LIVINGSTONE (3/19/1813)
HENRY MORTON STANLEY (1/28/1841)

Explorer Livingstone, feared lost after a 30-year African expedition, was found in 1871 by Stanley, a journalist-turned-explorer who purportedly uttered the famous line "Dr. Livingstone, I presume?" upon seeing him.

Also: **William Jennings Bryan & William McKinley** (presidential opponents in 1900); **Timothy Dalton & Vanessa Redgrave** (intimate companions; actors).

March 19–24

THE CUSP OF REBIRTH
PISCES-ARIES CUSP

January 23–30

THE WEEK OF GENIUS
AQUARIUS I

The Inquisitive Mind

A quick and perceptive mental orientation characterizes this relationship, and a fascination with intellectual roaming over the most varied areas of human experience. These two will have a great deal to discuss and dissect, whether in the area of sports, history, entertainment or the arts. A love of games, and of activities involving snap decisions and mental gymnastics, can also absorb a lot of the relationship's time; together, these partners may feel enormous relief over finally being free of the slower minds of those who place no value on such activities. Even in their first meeting, these two may engage in an animated conversation, the sheer enjoyment of which augurs well for further communication. Sooner or later, however, the downside of this strong connection will emerge: a tendency toward competitiveness that can lead to arguments and displays of one-upmanship and will ultimately have a destructive effect on the relationship's future.

Nor will such rivalry necessarily be limited to the relationship's internal attitudes and games. Pisces-Aries and Aquarius I's are liable to share friends for whose affection and attention they vie. A youthful marriage between this pair can often feature attractions to others in their social set, and even to marital indiscretions, with concomitant jealousies, possessiveness and displays of temperament. Stability may not be possible in such a relationship, and in fact these two may only be able to live together relatively peacefully in later life.

The desire to dig, reveal and gossip immaturely may further unsettle the relationship, be these two lovers or friends. (This combination is not particularly recommended for colleagues or co-workers, although investigative, scientific, computer or other technical fields—fields that involve the shared unraveling of puzzles—may be exceptions.) On the positive side, however, Pisces-Aries and Aquarius I's are both free spirits and are independent enough not to have to rely on each other for interaction, guidance or support. If one of them must take the lead in establishing guidelines or planning for the future, it will probably be best if that role falls to the Pisces-Aries, who can visualize goals and implement a course of action.

ADVICE: *Keep your nose out of other people's business. Try to be more mature. Get serious occasionally. Make more sensible plans for the future.*

March 19–24

THE CUSP OF REBIRTH
PISCES-ARIES CUSP

January 31–February 7

THE WEEK OF YOUTH & EASE
AQUARIUS II

 RELATIONSHIPS

STRENGTHS: **GENTLE,
SYMPATHETIC, EDUCATIONAL**

WEAKNESSES: **DENYING,
TROUBLED, UNREALISTIC**

BEST: **MARRIAGE**

WORST: **WORK**

Life Lessons

An interest in, even a yearning for, the life of ideas, music, art and dance will often appear in this relationship, which may also have a religious streak. Its view of life is often gentle, perhaps idealized, and its core emotional focus is more usually platonic than passionate or sexual. But sensuousness is also present here, in many different forms, with special emphasis on tactile and culinary pleasures. When the relationship is informed by understanding and sympathy, preferably along with some hedonism, the affectionate feelings that typify it may provide the basis for a long-standing marriage.

The relationship will often force both partners to confront certain issues they consider unpleasant. The presence and influence of Pisces-Aries, for instance, will lay bare the difference between what Aquarius II's want (no hassles) and what they need (to confront their dark side); Aquarius II's will probably dislike this aspect of the relationship but may realize that it is essential for their personal and spiritual development. And they, for their part, can help Pisces-Aries by encouraging them not only to recognize defeat but to admit when it has taken place, both in personal matters and at work. Pisces-Aries will not easily acknowledge failure, and their ability to accept this kind of help from Aquarius II's presupposes a great deal of trust.

These two will find it difficult to deal with the more troubled aspects of each other's personality. When reality sets in, or when they are pushed beyond their limit, they may acknowledge that they have made a mistake in partner choice. Thus the relationship may teach them important lessons, not only about closure but about future, more realistic partner choices and the need for openness and vulnerability in matters of love.

As friends, Pisces-Aries and Aquarius II's may share close, siblinglike ties, and their relationship may feature an air of relaxation and enjoyment. It is not usually as effective when they are co-workers or business partners, a context in which they may lack groundedness. On the other hand, their inspiration and motivation to bettering their social standing and job performance is undeniable.

ADVICE: *Trouble can be a teacher in disguise. Things can't be pleasant all the time. What you need may not be what you want. Learn how to admit defeat.*

JAMES JOYCE (2/2/1882)
NORA BARNACLE (3/21/1884)

Joyce met chambermaid Barnacle in 1904. He lived with Nora, who inspired his writing, and they had children but didn't marry until 1931. They left Ireland and settled down in Trieste, Italy. *Also:* **Robert & John Carradine** (son/father; actors); **Joan Crawford & Clark Gable** (affair); **Irving Wallace & David Wallechinsky** (father/son; co-authors); **John & Clark Gable** (son/father; actors).

March 19–24

THE CUSP OF REBIRTH
PISCES-ARIES CUSP

February 8–15

THE WEEK OF ACCEPTANCE
AQUARIUS III

RELATIONSHIPS

STRENGTHS: **CHAMPIONING,
CLOSE, SHARING**

WEAKNESSES: **RESENTFUL,
IRRITATED, REJECTING**

BEST: **FRIENDSHIP IN LATER LIFE**

WORST: **LOVE**

Beneath the Surface

Much more inscrutable than either of its partners may realize, this relationship demands introspection and self-understanding if it is to succeed. The enigmatic forces at work in it are difficult not just to fathom but to perceive at all. Rejection may figure prominently at first, whether it be rejection of each other or of other people or events, and the partners will find themselves bemused by its role in their relationship. Over the years, however, rejecting attitudes can change into approving and championing ones. Whether the relationship is a friendship, marriage or love affair, it will work best if both parties are older and more mature.

Aquarius III's may be entranced by Pisces-Aries, seeing them as the embodiment of the direct, purposeful and natural being whom they themselves secretly want to be. The danger here, especially when these two are romantically involved, is that less scrupulous or more selfish Pisces-Aries may take advantage of the vulnerability of Aquarius III's to their charms. With their sharp tongues and their talent for merciless criticism, they can cow less confident Aquarius III's, bending them to their will. Less selfish Pisces-Aries, on the other hand, may prove highly beneficial to unsure Aquarius III's who are looking for direction, and for whom Pisces-Aries can act as guides or teachers. In this respect Pisces-Aries parents can play important roles for their Aquarius III children.

Friendship between these two is favored when there is a basis for the relationship in an objective pursuit, perhaps a shared hobby or pastime. But any close emotional ties that develop out of such a friendship may be disrupted by mutual irritation, the cause of which is sometimes hard to understand. One source of irritation, particularly in marriage, is the attention that Aquarius III's may constantly need from Pisces-Aries—more attention than the Pisces-Aries can comfortably supply. Pisces-Aries need to be free and may come to see Aquarius III neediness as stifling. But should they seek an outlet in an extramarital affair, they may further damage Aquarius III self-esteem. Working relationships, whether as co-workers or partners, are not generally favored, since personal conflicts and resentments will tend to surface here.

ADVICE: *Things may not be what they seem. Try to dig deeper and to understand. Introspection will help you to see more clearly. Act fearlessly when sure.*

PHILIP ROTH (3/19/33)
CLAIRE BLOOM (2/15/31)

Novelist Roth is famous for *Portnoy's Complaint* (1969) and his Zuckerman quartet about a successful Jewish novelist. Actress Bloom reached prominence co-starring with Chaplin in *Limelight* (1952). Married in their late fifties, the pair had a troubled relationship. *Also:* **William Morris & John Ruskin** (Pre-Raphaelite collaborators).

STRENGTHS: INTIMATE, AESTHETIC, SECURE

WEAKNESSES: ISOLATED, OUT OF TOUCH, IMPRACTICAL

BEST: LOVE

WORST: MARRIAGE

CYBILL SHEPHERD (2/18/50)
BRUCE WILLIS (3/19/55)

Willis and Shepherd starred in the popular 80s tv series *Moonlighting*, a show about a former model who owns a detective agency managed by Willis. Full of double entendres, the show played off the chemistry between the 2 stars.

Also: **Irving Wallace & Sylvia Kahn Wallace** (married; authors).

March 19–24
THE CUSP OF REBIRTH
PISCES-ARIES CUSP

February 16–22
THE CUSP OF SENSITIVITY
AQUARIUS-PISCES CUSP

A Sheltered Cove

This relationship tends to serve as a haven of peace and security. Although it affords an intimacy that can be satisfying to both partners, however, it can also become a kind of lost world, one predicated on cutting vital ties with society. And should it turn into a buried inner sanctum in this way, it may stagnate, drift or fall apart, particularly if it lacks practical and pragmatic strengths. Building a more structured existence, particularly one firmly linked to the outside world, should be the overriding consideration here. Pisces-Aries is the more likely of the two partners to try to move in this direction, since the Aquarius-Pisces probably tends to fixate more on either abstract or personal concerns.

The matchup may be particularly successful in the area of friendship. Both Pisces-Aries and Aquarius-Pisces are hard-driving career people who need to relax, in close and enjoyable companionship, during their spare time, and a relationship between them may bring them to new heights in this area, since there is a synergy between their aesthetic and intellectual sensibilities. Emotional satisfaction is indicated here by the influence on both partners of watery Pisces, signifying feelings: each party is likely to have antennae out for the other's moods and unconscious wishes. Marriages and love affairs between these two are a bit more problematic and are not particularly recommended. They too can succeed, however, providing a degree of objectivity prevails and the relationship does not succumb to extremes of isolation. In love affairs, Aquarius-Pisces should be encouraged to lower their defenses and rediscover their emotional vulnerabilities; Pisces-Aries can be extremely helpful and understanding in this respect, though they will have to prove themselves in order to gain the trust of Aquarius-Pisces mates, who are likely to be very wary of letting down their guard. Should Pisces-Aries abuse this trust or show that they are unworthy of it, the relationship will most likely end then and there—no second chance will be granted. The knowledge that one big mistake might well be the relationship's last puts the Pisces-Aries partner in a rather precarious position.

ADVICE: *Keep windows open to the world. Don't get bogged down. Avoid the tendency to drift. Get a grip on yourself and develop motivation.*

STRENGTHS: DEVOTIONAL, ZEALOUS, FLEXIBLE

WEAKNESSES: FRAGILE, DEMANDING, SACRIFICIAL

BEST: FRIENDSHIP

WORST: WORK

JOAN CRAWFORD (3/23/08)
FRANCHOT TONE (2/27/05)

Tone was a stage and screen actor who co-starred in the mid-60s tv series *Ben Casey*. His first of 4 marriages (1935–39) was to Joan Crawford, whose own 4 tumultuous marriages punctuated her 50-year Hollywood career.

Also: **Martin Ross & Robert Conrad** (co-stars, *Wild, Wild West*).

March 19–24
THE CUSP OF REBIRTH
PISCES-ARIES CUSP

February 23–March 2
THE WEEK OF SPIRIT
PISCES I

Love's Altar

In whatever area the deepest sharing takes place in this relationship, spiritual or religious overtones may be apparent. The feelings involved in a love affair between these two can be pure and idealistic, suggesting that their relationship has become a kind of religion for them, in which their feelings for each other acquire the status of worship. Two dangers may surface here: first, that the partners will share a certain fanaticism; second, that the relationship may be too fragile to survive in a tough world. Cross-currents and complexities are common in this pairing. Fixed, long-term relationships, such as marriage or working together, are not particularly recommended, but friendships and love relationships may flourish if flexibility can be maintained. Particularly in the area of friendship, a loving, strong and deep bond may develop through mutual sympathy and understanding.

Pisces I's may be a tad threatened by direct Pisces-Aries energy, and if more aggressive may clash with it, if more passive may be overwhelmed and play a submissive role. (It is better for them to stand up and assert their prerogatives, since otherwise they risk submerging themselves in the service of the Pisces-Aries. It is even possible that the resulting loss of self-esteem may accelerate, leaving the Pisces-Aries fruitlessly trying to convince the Pisces I of their worth.) They may also find Pisces-Aries themselves overbearing and dictatorial. But they will admire Pisces-Aries' ability to deal with personal or worldly matters and act on them. For their part Pisces-Aries may be deeply touched by the quality of empathy they sense in Pisces I's, even though they may be unable to respond in kind.

The practical side of this matchup is by no means weak: Pisces-Aries have a strong pragmatic side, and Pisces I's may be surprisingly good with money. Yet these practical strengths will have to gel and blossom to be able to balance the relationship's natural fervor and zeal.

ADVICE: *Develop practical talents. Maintain individuality. Beware of getting lost. Cultivate enthusiasm for the material world. Stay flexible.*

March 19–24
THE CUSP OF REBIRTH
PISCES-ARIES CUSP

March 3–10
THE WEEK OF THE LONER
PISCES II

Playful Emulation

This relationship usually focuses on a light, unserious form of competition. Closeness is quite possible here, particularly in the area of friendship, as long as a natural tendency toward one-upmanship can from time to time be put aside, particularly when one of these two is demonstrating his or her artistic, spiritual, intellectual or political expertise. These partners may look as if they're fighting like cats and dogs, but their confrontations are usually playful—albeit still quite competitive. On an emotional level, there is often communication on a common wavelength in this relationship, which can usually encompass an agreement to disagree.

Pisces-Aries favor direct confrontation, but Pisces II's will generally choose not to tackle them head-on. More subtle means can be used to slow them down: Pisces II's who appear to be simply going about their business will often seem mysteriously inviting and will gain the attention and interest of Pisces-Aries on their own terms. Their idiosyncrasies and weirdnesses will be no problem for individualistic Pisces-Aries, who may, however, be troubled and weighed down by their dark, depressive and negative moods. For their part, Pisces II's will often resent having to speed up their normally slow pace in response to Pisces-Aries impatience. The more profound in thought and feeling of these two personalities, they may also complain about what they see as glibness or hastiness in a Pisces-Aries partner. Pisces-Aries, meanwhile, may well give Pisces II's the acceptance they need but, unfortunately, not the stability.

Although Pisces II's may dislike the direct, go-for-it approach of Pisces-Aries, while Pisces-Aries may criticize the directionlessness or laziness of Pisces II's, the unsettled nature of this relationship may work as a stimulating positive impulse. The chances that the relationship will flourish are good when it emerges in a domestic setting that allows meetings at a deep emotional level. Here differences may be put aside in favor of a harmony that will benefit all concerned. Parent-child relationships are favored over sibling pairings, which usually involve friction and competition.

ADVICE: *You don't know everything. Put disagreements aside. Search for the truth together. Include rather than exclude. Seek harmony and peace.*

ROB REINER (3/6/45)
CARL REINER (3/20/22)

Film and tv talents Carl and Rob Reiner are father and son. Comic actor and writer Carl starred on and wrote for Sid Caesar's *Your Show of Shows*, while Rob rose from the sitcom *All in the Family* to become a prominent film director. *Also:* **J.S. Bach & C.P.E. Bach** (father/son; composers).

March 19–24
THE CUSP OF REBIRTH
PISCES-ARIES CUSP

March 11–18
THE WEEK OF DANCERS & DREAMERS
PISCES III

Fantastic Experiences

This relationship may give a lot of attention to lifestyle and, indeed, to style in general. There is a strong orientation here toward life experience as opposed to book learning; each partner may have already demonstrated a tendency to live an experience rather than read about it, but together they take this characteristic to and beyond the limit. Pisces-Aries and Pisces III's not only recognize a kindred soul in each other but eventually realize that a common life path, particularly as friends or as lovers, will offer fantastic opportunities. The relationship is usually built less around psychological exploration than around shared activities, which represent its best chance for success.

This combination offers exciting romantic and sexual possibilities. Should deep emotions be stirred up, they may result in a passionate, heartfelt expression of feelings; sensual abandon may also be part of the fulfillment attainable here. If things don't work out, on the other hand, this is often particularly hard on the Pisces III, who generally adopts a more submissive role and may become dependent on the Pisces-Aries. If either partner ends up rejecting the other, usually the Pisces-Aries withdraws from the relationship, sometimes with little warning.

Marriage between these two can be a mistake, particularly if it is preceded by the kind of tumultuous love affair of which this combination is capable. When the fire has cooled down, Pisces-Aries may get restless, dissatisfied or bored with their Pisces III partner's complacency and self-satisfaction. It may be difficult for them to detach themselves from the Pisces III dream world, but they will have to if they are to continue on their own individual and dynamic path. The Pisces III, however, may be left bewildered and confused, and most likely in the grips of a deep depression.

Should a Pisces III and a Pisces-Aries decide to run a business together, join forces as co-workers or just share a mutual interest or hobby for fun, they may achieve a degree of success. The dangers that lie in wait may involve keeping the relationship superficial and being overly concerned with appearances.

ADVICE: *Realize that everything is not what it appears. Try to value psychological understanding. Beware of superficiality. Don't neglect your personal development.*

GEORGE BENSON (3/22/43)
QUINCY JONES (3/14/33)

Jones, pre-eminent pop-music arranger and producer, has worked with Michael Jackson, Ray Charles, Louis Armstrong, Aretha Franklin, Sinatra and others. Benson is an award-winning jazz guitarist and vocalist. Their first collaboration, *Give Me the Night* (1980), won 5 Grammys. **Also: Sergei Diaghilev & Vaslav Nijinsky** (ballet).

STRENGTHS: SPONTANEOUS, DYNAMIC, WELL-DEFINED

WEAKNESSES: REBELLIOUS, CONFLICTING, DISINTERESTED

BEST: FRIENDSHIP, WHEN YOUNG

WORST: LOVE

GLORIA SWANSON (3/27/1899)
WALLACE BEERY (4/1/1885)

The epitome of Hollywood glamour, silent-screen legend Swanson married major celebrity Beery, a screen "heavy," when she was 17. Together they made films for Mack Sennett's Keystone Company. They divorced after 3 years.

Youthful Denial

This relationship is characterized by a love of exploration and by a spontaneous, frank expression that can result in a kind of primal joy. But the impulsive and dynamic energy characteristic of this matchup can also carry both partners far from the stabilizing forces that are required in day-to-day life. The Aries I–Aries I relationship is more likely to manifest in childhood or early adulthood than in the friendships, love affairs, or marriages of maturity, since the kind of understanding that these partners need often becomes harder to achieve as their individual world views become more rigid with advancing age.

Aries I's are generally interested in unusual people who are quite different from themselves. Two Aries I's, then, will rarely choose each other as love partners. They will probably work together well enough, however, as long they don't need to engage in a lot of personal interaction, and as long as their jobs are straightforward ones in which the tasks they need to accomplish are specific and well-defined. Business partnerships or executive positions are not favored, and it's always better for Aries I's to work together as equals. Things will go more smoothly if both are asked to employ their own specialized expertise and nothing more. Only after years on the same job together will two Aries I's begin to develop anything approaching intimacy.

Family situations involving two Aries I's may work out all right, whether the relationship is of siblings or of parent and child, but not without conflict. Although this relationship manifests some of the strongest childlike energy of any in the year, it also features a stubborn refusal to be treated like a child, whether by partners or by parents. Two Aries I children in the same family may fight constantly if the older one adopts a parental role, treating the younger one in a patronizing or overly protective way. Rebelliousness is bound to surface in such a situation, or when a single Aries I child is coddled or babied by a dominant Aries I mother or father. Generally the greatest conflicts are with the parent of the same sex, the greatest emotional ties with the parent of the opposite sex.

ADVICE: *Don't demand too much. Allow time for feelings to grow. Denying immaturity invites suspicion. Let others help you.*

STRENGTHS: ORGANIZATIONAL, SOCIAL, ADVENTURESOME

WEAKNESSES: AGGRESSIVE, COMPETITIVE, NONNURTURING

BEST: TEAM PARTNERS

WORST: FRIENDSHIP

JACK WEBB (4/2/20)
HARRY MORGAN (4/10/15)

These actors turned their poker-faced cop characters on the famous crime show *Dragnet* into American icons. Webb originated the series, which ran from 1951–59. Morgan joined the show in its second incarnation in 1967. **Also: Sarah Jessica Parker & Robert Downey, Jr.** (romance; actors); **Kelly LeBrock & Steven Seagal** (married; actors); **Diana Ross & Billie Holiday** (film portrayal).

Playful Partnership

It is unlikely that the world of deep feelings will figure prominently in this very social relationship, whether its tone is cool or fiery. Love or close friendship may be ruled out here, then, but common bonds relating to a shared hobby, sports activity or other interest may create a certain amount of trust and permanence. The desire to explore nature, particularly if it is out-of-the-way and unusual, may find an outlet in adventuresome activities of all sorts, particularly those involving groups or clubs.

If Aries I and Aries II are siblings, they are likely to fight, since both guard their spaces and their prerogatives closely. Should their aggressive and competitive instincts get out of hand, particularly if they are siblings of the same sex, the family unit may be highly stressed, even torn apart. Relations between either combination of Aries I and Aries II parents and children may remain harmonious as long as the parent does not show tyrannical tendencies, which will invite rebellion. But the relationship does not usually show a well-developed nurturing side, or a love for the everyday chores of homemaking, housekeeping or child-rearing. Marriages are not particularly recommended here, then, unless the spouses can allow each other a good deal of independence to pursue separate careers and spend long periods of time apart.

As far as working together goes, the Aries II Star personality demands attention, and to be at the center of things. This may not sit well with Aries I's, and their egos are likely to clash; if so, the Aries I may withdraw, feeling hurt or neglected. If the relationship manifests at an executive level, however, where these two must share the planning, organization and general leadership of a business or company, they may be able to drive dynamically, shoulder to shoulder, toward common goals.

ADVICE: *Cultivate trust and openness. Seek out deeper feelings. Not everything has to be fun. Hard work will yield results.*

March 25–April 2
THE WEEK OF THE CHILD
ARIES I

April 11–18
THE WEEK OF THE PIONEER
ARIES III

In the Spotlight

Whether this relationship appears within a family or among a group of friends, it will have to occupy center stage. This suggests not only a need for attention but a desire to lead and give direction to the group's practices and activities. The Aries I–Aries III relationship is well skilled in dealing with people and is therefore usually prized by any group of which it is a part. If it is a family relationship or a friendship, it may be extended into a business endeavor, whether full- or part-time. At work, Aries I's will be willing to collaborate side by side with Aries III's, though it will usually be the Aries III who takes the lead. Friends and family members in this combination are also capable of living together as a domestic unit in everyday adult life.

Some, more-understanding Aries III's can make excellent parents for Aries I's, but others can get carried away with their ideologies, which they may impose rigorously on those around them. This may cause trouble, since Aries I's don't like to be told what to do or to be ruled by ironclad edicts. Other Aries III's, whether parents, friends or siblings, may come to play too great a role in the life of Aries I's, fostering dependencies in them that stunt their individual growth.

A love of physical movement and adventure characterizes this relationship and can lead to exciting projects, with little fear of scaling the heights or plumbing the depths of the natural world. Friendly competition may urge the relationship on to the very limits of physical prowess, and perhaps beyond. Both the romantic and the sexual intensity of a love affair in this combination can be high. Unfortunately, however, expressions of deep emotion or explorations of inner feeling are not usually forthcoming between these two, who may deal with each other mainly on a somewhat superficial level, albeit an exciting one.

ADVICE: *Internal exploration is exciting, too. Don't neglect feelings. Be responsible to the emotional needs of others. Meditation can help.*

RELATIONSHIPS

STRENGTHS: **EXCITING, ADVENTUROUS, COMMANDING**

WEAKNESSES: **SUPERFICIAL, EGOTISTICAL, NEEDY**

BEST: **FAMILY**

WORST: **LOVE**

HENRY II [FRANCE] (3/31/1519)
CATHERINE DE MEDICI (4/13/1519)

Henry II, whose rule bankrupted the Crown, had a dominating mistress (Diane de Poitiers) whom wife Catherine was obliged to tolerate. After his death Catherine ruled as queen mother. **Also: Jennifer Grey & Joel Grey** (daughter/father; actors); **Shirley Jones & David Cassidy** (co-stars, *Partridge Family*); **Warren Beatty & Julie Christie** (affair; actors); **Sydney Chaplin & Charlie Chaplin** (son/father; actors).

March 25–April 2
THE WEEK OF THE CHILD
ARIES I

April 19–24
THE CUSP OF POWER
ARIES-TAURUS CUSP

Limited Access

The basis of this matchup is the establishment of firm boundaries, whether between the two partners or, particularly, between the relationship itself and the outside world. The key here is privacy, both for the partners and the relationship; intrusions are resented. This makes it unlikely that emotional doors will be opened too often, so that, despite the presence of a good deal of mutual understanding, it can be hard to get a handle on what is happening within this relationship. Also, romantic rivalries are unwelcome, and jealousies over third parties may prove undermining. Since the pairing is most successful when personal interaction does not have to take place every day, friendships and work relationships usually go better than family, romantic or marital ones.

Diplomatic Aries I's will often defer to Aries-Taurus expertise in a given area but will still want to hold on to the real power in the relationship. The problem here is that Aries-Tauruses regard power as their inherent birthright and are usually unwilling to give it up easily. A truce will have to be reached and a spoken or unspoken agreement arrived at concerning what is permitted and what is not. Such an agreement need not involve bad feelings—it can often be built on mutual respect.

Love affairs between these two are not particularly suggested and, if they occur, are usually unsuccessful. Aries-Tauruses will often want deeper involvements than independent Aries I's are prepared to give. Marriages are even less favorable, since they usually involve too much personal interaction and a kind of sharing of space that neither partner may welcome. As members of the same family, these two may compete with each other for dominance, and often ultimately come to a stalemate in which they do their best to ignore each other.

As friends, particularly of the same sex, Aries I's and Aries-Tauruses may be extremely supportive of each other in times of need, whether financial or emotional. Although lengthy periods may elapse between their visits, appointments or phone calls, they rarely go long without thinking of each other. Such friendships may perfectly suit the needs of both partners, making few demands and leaving them the time they need to attend to their own affairs.

ADVICE: *Build personal bridges. Avoid power struggles. Seek common social activities. Beware of cutting yourself off. Open your heart more often.*

RELATIONSHIPS

STRENGTHS: **DEPENDABLE, RESPECTFUL, UNDERSTANDING**

WEAKNESSES: **SEPARATED, DETACHED, JEALOUS**

BEST: **FRIENDSHIP**

WORST: **MARRIAGE**

CATHERINE THE GREAT (4/21/1729)
CASANOVA (4/2/1725)

Catherine, empress at age 33, was also a beauty whose many love affairs are recorded in history. Among them was her liaison with the famed Casanova, who wrote extensively about his sexual exploits in his *History of My Life*. **Also: Warren Beatty & Shirley MacLaine** (siblings; actors).

STRENGTHS: **PIONEERING, DYNAMIC, IMPLEMENTATIVE**

WEAKNESSES: **INFLEXIBLE, DISRESPECTFUL, STUCK**

BEST: **WORK**

WORST: **PARENT-CHILD**

VINCENT VAN GOGH (3/30/1853)
THEO VAN GOGH (5/1/1857)

The brilliant but tormented Vincent was perhaps best appreciated in life by his brother, Theo, who supported the artist both financially and emotionally. Heartbroken, Theo died 6 months after his brother. They are buried side by side in Auvers, France. **Also: Eileen Ford & Wilhelmina** (rival model agency founders).

March 25–April 2
THE WEEK OF THE CHILD
ARIES I

April 25–May 2
THE WEEK OF MANIFESTATION
TAURUS I

An Achieving Spirit

This relationship has a strong pioneering spirit. Particularly when the two partners are engaged in a shared project, whether professional or social, their close association and common goals generally ensure success. The key here is careful planning followed by dynamic implementation. Taurus I's may feel threatened by the directness of Aries I energy, but as long as they stay in charge, and their dominant position goes unthreatened, the relationship can work out.

Problems often arise here, however, when Taurus I bosses or parents are confronted with what Aries I employees or children really think of them. They will not want to hear this, but because they are authoritative, and have a tendency to puff up their own importance, Aries I's may be unable to resist the temptation to puncture their balloon. In the family, where Taurus I parents need to be admired and respected unconditionally by their children, an open and honest Aries I child may raise acute problems. Similarly, an adoring Aries I husband or wife who idolizes his or her Taurus I spouse may be a rather rare specimen. The Aries I need to be free, and resentment of being treated like a child, may also prove difficult for overprotective Taurus I's.

Love relationships between these two may suffer from the fact that Taurus I's will not admit to problems in the relationship but will want to keep deriving pleasure from it for as long as possible. Aries I's can enjoy sex and sensuality with Taurus I's up to a point but may also have deep needs in other directions than the purely physical, which Taurus I's may be unable to meet.

Not particularly flexible, this relationship may still feature enough charm to melt the hardest heart, and to overcome stubborn and unyielding attitudes. Particularly if it emerges in the realm of friendship, it can grow strong when each partner's strengths grow and blossom around common interests, particularly those involving sports, adventure and other forms of physical challenge. An element of danger or risk only makes the attraction stronger and the bond deeper.

ADVICE: *Honesty is not always the most diplomatic solution. Be realistic about your capabilities. Recognize the need for freedom. Be flexible.*

STRENGTHS: **SENSUAL, CRITICAL, APPRECIATIVE**

WEAKNESSES: **FRUSTRATING, ADDICTIVE, STORMY**

BEST: **MARRIAGE**

WORST: **FRIENDSHIP**

ARISTIDE BRIAND (3/28/1862)
GUSTAV STRESEMANN (5/10/1878)

These prime ministers from France and Germany won the 1926 Nobel Peace Prize for their Locarno Pact, which stabilized relations between the countries of post-WWI Europe and brought Germany into the League of Nations.

March 25–April 2
THE WEEK OF THE CHILD
ARIES I

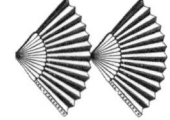

May 3–10
THE WEEK OF THE TEACHER
TAURUS II

Head and Heart

This relationship combines lively action and critical thought in quite a remarkable way. Potentially a deep and meaningful combination in both love and marriage, it often involves a strong sensual bond, but the attraction is by no means limited to the physical plane. The mental and emotional compatibilities that these two share may lead them to exert their energies over a wide range of activities, from businesses to hobbies to raising a family. Mutual understanding and, also, appreciation are indicated here, and the synergistic melding of the partners' direct and abundant energy, if it is well directed, points the way toward productive and successful endeavors.

Acquaintance-type friendships in this combination may be difficult to maintain, since the sexual pull is so strong here that it may become addictive. Platonic relationships can develop, however, if some bar to greater intimacy, such as one partner's commitment to another person, makes them necessary. If this pair's feelings for each other are unequal, frustrations may result but they can be surmounted through patience and understanding, usually emanating from the Taurus II. Aries I's are quite capable of transgressing the terms of an established relationship with a Taurus II, perhaps eventually leading to a breakup.

Both Aries I's and Taurus II's can be stubborn and unyielding, but this also means that they tend to hang in there and won't give up if the going gets rough. Their marriages, love affairs and business or other working relationships can consequently survive many a storm. Aries I's are generally receptive to Taurus II nurturing qualities but also have an extreme need for independence and an aversion to being babied, which Taurus II's must learn to accept. Yet Aries I's do have a great deal to learn from the Taurus II teacher, particularly in the area of philosophical detachment and emotional understanding. And Taurus II's, for their part, can become more playful, less fixed and repetitive in their behavior, under the influence of Aries I's.

ADVICE: *Continue to learn detachment. Keep your energy focused and directed. Work on your frustrations. Feelings need not be opposed to thoughts.*

March 25–April 2
THE WEEK OF THE CHILD
ARIES I

May 11–18
THE WEEK OF THE NATURAL
TAURUS III

Tug-of-War

L. MIES VAN DER ROHE (3/27/1886)
WALTER GROPIUS (5/18/1883)

The chemistry of this combination can be unsettling. Aries I's and Taurus III's have a lot in common—they share an open and natural approach to life—but together they may find stability hard to achieve; their relationship is often pushed and pulled in opposite directions. Power plays between them are not at all uncommon, lending their connection a competitive and at times combative cast.

The combination may not suit a love affair or marriage, then, but there is a mutual appreciation between these two that will allow for a close friendship. It may not be based on emotional sharing and mutual need or acceptance, but these partners will enjoy shared activities, particularly those of an adventuresome, challenging and even dangerous kind. (Aries I's and Taurus III's also make good opponents for each other, stimulating each other as competitors in team sports, or in fitness training.) Aries I's can be quite protective and sympathetic toward those Taurus III's whom others see as troublemakers, or who feel rejected by society in general or by their family in particular.

When these two are siblings, they may compete for parental attention. Aries I's are not submissive by any means, but they are more dutiful than Taurus III's, and jealousies may consequently arise in which Taurus III's view Aries I's as goody-goodies who curry favor to gain love, leaving themselves as bad guys or losers. If this combination manifests as a parent-child relationship, Aries I's will do better in the parental role; they are generally better suited for parenthood than Taurus III's, particularly later in life, when they have sowed some of their wild oats and acquired more self-confidence. Still, this relationship may be plagued by immature impulsiveness in adulthood, especially when anger or resentment unresolved and left over from childhood undercuts its stability and nurturing capabilities.

Gropius, a founder of the Bauhaus school of architecture, teamed up with Mies van der Rohe (and Le Corbusier) in 1933 to create the school of International Style. Both fled Germany, emigrating to America in the 30s. Gropius, who taught at Harvard, designed the school's graduate center; Mies van der Rohe's famous skyscrapers were most notable. The friends had a long, respectful association.

ADVICE: *Put the past behind you. Let go of old grudges and resentments. Power is not the answer. Try to be more accepting and kind. Pull together.*

March 25–April 2
THE WEEK OF THE CHILD
ARIES I

May 19–24
THE CUSP OF ENERGY
TAURUS-GEMINI CUSP

Psychological Motivation

BERNIE TAUPIN (5/22/50)
ELTON JOHN (3/25/47)

This relationship can be dramatic, yet it also tends to be introspective and analytical, with its partners discussing psychological issues in an objective way. Taurus-Geminis are more comfortable with this approach than Aries I's are, but it will in most cases be the self-awareness of the Aries I's that will blossom here, less through the direct influence or observations of their partner than through the spirit of openness that prevails in the relationship. Should psychological investigation become blocked, the tremendous energy and vision of this matchup can become scattered or bottled up inside. Tendencies to put things off, to deny the truth or to brood over past injustices must be dealt with and fought, for they will undermine more positive factors such as desire, ambition, self-esteem or hopefulness.

The psychological emphasis notwithstanding, close friendships, love affairs and marriages are unlikely with this relationship; these two often don't suit each other emotionally or sexually, nor is it easy for them to share interests. They can give each other good advice but are usually too independent and ornery to want to accommodate each other in personal relationships, and neither has a big talent for compromise. At work, on the other hand, Taurus-Geminis may prove inspiring and stimulating to Aries I's, particularly as colleagues on the same level. In fact, a relationship between these two is highly favored in the workplace, where Taurus-Gemini ideas and Aries I straightforwardness will usually combine effectively, Taurus-Gemini compulsiveness will usually have a positive effect on the Aries I tendency to procrastinate, and Aries I's will help to keep Taurus-Geminis attentive to the job at hand, preventing their interest from wandering.

There is, however, a major problem that will have to be solved if the relationship is to succeed at work, and also in the family: Aries I's have a need and talent for group involvement, while Taurus-Geminis have an aversion to it and usually prefer to work alone. The relationship may be able to overcome this roadblock through its psychological strengths, as the partners discuss this tension between them and gain insight into it.

Rivaling Lennon & McCartney, the creative and inspired working relationship of musician John and lyricist Taupin was formidable in the 1970s, yielding several #1 singles and 15 of their 19 albums going gold or platinum. ***Also:* Warren Beatty & Joan Collins** (affair; actors); **Elle MacPherson & Naomi Campbell** (restaurant partners; supermodels).

ADVICE: *Work on compromise. Cultivate social activities. Don't be so free with advice. Allow others their realizations. Show your emotions more openly.*

**STRENGTHS: UNITED,
PROTECTIVE, FAIR**

**WEAKNESSES: ANTISOCIAL,
REBELLIOUS, SUPERFICIAL**

BEST: FRIENDSHIP

WORST: WORK

ANNETTE BENING (5/29/58)
WARREN BEATTY (3/30/37)

Surprising the world, perennial bachelor Beatty married younger actress Bening in 1991, the year they co-starred in *Bugsy*. After their child was born, they appeared together again in the remake of the comedy classic *Love Affair*.

Also: Dana Carvey & Mike Myers (co-stars, *Wayne's World*); **Eugene McCarthy & Hubert Humphrey** (Democrat opponents).

March 25–April 2
THE WEEK OF THE CHILD
ARIES I

May 25–June 2
THE WEEK OF FREEDOM
GEMINI I

Guardians of the Downtrodden

The emphasis in this combination is on action. Excitement is essential if a slump in the relationship is to be avoided, and excitement will usually reawaken dormant interests and slumbering energies. Both of these partners usually need to escape into life experiences rather than away from them, and both need a "twin" with whom to share such experiences. The importance that the relationship gives to what may seem to be external issues, particularly in matters of technique and quality, may lead others to see it as superficial and not terribly serious. Such judgments may ignore the fact that worldly interests do not necessarily preclude soulfulness or spirituality.

Aries I's have the perfect blend of caution and courage to allow Gemini I's to have a good time and forget their troubles. In a Gemini I–Aries I friendship, no matter what the age difference, Aries I's find themselves treated as equals—a vitally important requirement for them. Gemini I's, for their part, cannot stand phoniness in any form and will find their Aries I partner unlikely to dissimulate.

Whether as friends, mates or lovers, Gemini I's and Aries I's in combination must be careful not to fall afoul of society or of the law. An extreme hankering for freedom and an uncompromising ethical stance may manifest as rebellion against any condition perceived as unjust or unfair. The result may be that outsiders view this couple as antisocial or even, in extreme cases, sociopathic, yet the relationship tends to work to protect the downtrodden and the weak. When spurred on to action by noble moral sentiments, this duo can have an awesome power.

ADVICE: *Don't be so moral or condemning. Come down off your white horse. Crusading isn't always appreciated. Cultivate spirituality. Meditate.*

**STRENGTHS: ROMANTIC,
FASCINATING, FULFILLING**

**WEAKNESSES: SUSPICIOUS,
UNCONSCIOUS, DISTRACTED**

BEST: LOVE

WORST: FAMILY

PAUL GAUGUIN (6/7/1848)
VINCENT VAN GOGH (3/30/1853)

These artists were staying together in Arles, France, when Van Gogh cut off part of his ear after one of their heated arguments. Police, finding Van Gogh unconscious, nearly arrested Gauguin, who subsequently left without a good-bye.

Also: Joseph Campbell & Bill Moyers (mythologist/journalist).

March 25–April 2
THE WEEK OF THE CHILD
ARIES I

June 3–10
THE WEEK OF NEW LANGUAGE
GEMINI II

The Reflecting Pool

This relationship, like a mirror, acts as a projection of deep and secret desires, particularly when it is romantic. While on the face of things it seems to be based on intense physical attraction, it is actually more about wish-fulfillment: through each other, these partners feel they can attain their most fervent desires, as if they stood by a magical lake in whose murky depths they could find all of their wishes, provided they chose to dive into its darkness. Though fascinating, then, this relationship also has a quality of blindness, like love itself. Even so, it may outlast many others in which reality has a more dominant, more irritating role.

Through falling in love with each other, both of these personalities can fulfill a secret wish. Aries I's, for example, often want to be brilliant conversationalists who can win others over with compelling arguments, Gemini II's to be action-oriented individuals who succeed by daring to fail; as partners, each of these two can be these things for the other. Areas outside romantic love, including marriage, are less suitable to this combination. Gemini II's have a tremendous need to be understood and may barrage a partner with a constant flow of words and ideas; this will only make Aries I's nervous and confused. Even if Gemini II's are articulate and skillful in expressing themselves, they will probably make Aries I's yearn for peace and quiet. In day-to-day living, then, this matchup may deprive Aries I's of one of their firmest requirements in any relationship—that they can withdraw to a quiet place when they need to be alone. Meanwhile, Gemini II's may view their attempts to pull back as rejection and may immediately feel judged and misunderstood. Situations where these two must see each other daily, then, including the family, marriage and work, often don't work out.

One characteristic of the relationship, in any area, is that debate, argument and discussion figure prominently in it, pleasing Gemini II's but frustrating Aries I's, who are generally more interested in doing than in talking. After an initial attraction, furthermore, friendship may not be possible here, since Aries I's will quickly enough begin to suspect that many Gemini II claims or ideas are a bit far-fetched.

ADVICE: *Be careful what you wish for. Beware of isolation. Keep your eyes open. Find out what's yours. Physical attraction isn't everything.*

March 25–April 2

THE WEEK OF THE CHILD
ARIES I

June 11–18

THE WEEK OF THE SEEKER
GEMINI III

 RELATIONSHIPS

STRENGTHS: **ASPIRING, EXCITING, PASSIONATE**

WEAKNESSES: **WARY, JARRING, HURTFUL**

BEST: **WORK**

WORST: **FRIENDSHIP**

Perilous Awakenings

There is a jarring, explosive quality in this relationship—a longing to reach for the stars can translate into a taste for daredevil exploits. The combination can consequently prove unsettling to any partner with conservative or pragmatic attitudes. Any romantic feelings that manifest here will be hard to control, making love affairs between these two extremely exciting and dangerous, particularly if one or both of the partners is already married or in an established relationship. Despite the upset this relationship can cause, it also has the capacity to teach its participants something of great value.

Exacerbating the relationship's radical nature is the fact that Aries I's have a particular tendency to be transgressive in matters of the heart, while Gemini III's can throw caution to the winds when prompted by their more tumultuous feelings. These two may enter into a torrid, perhaps destructive love affair, after which it is unlikely that they will form a permanent relationship. Unfortunately, it may in retrospect seem that one of the two has served mainly as the necessary vehicle or support to help the other bring a preexisting, established relationship to a close. As friends, Aries I's and Gemini III's risk the firestorm of emotions, positive or negative, into which their relationship can burst at any time. As a result, they never feel completely comfortable with each other, and lack the easy intimacy required for longevity. The relationship does best, then, in objective pursuits, with the partners being co-workers or colleagues who keep an eye on a common goal.

In families and marriages, the relationship characteristically oscillates in mood from highly constructive to highly destructive. Things may go well for weeks or months, then gradually start a downward slide, punctuated by emotional outbursts. Over the years, the combination's stormy side will bring the partners closer together in a mutual dependency after each healing takes place but will also make them increasingly wary of being open and trusting with each other. Both emotional honesty and a willingness to work on the relationship will be crucial to guaranteeing its continuation.

ADVICE: *Respect others' relationships. Justify openness and trust. Even out your emotions. Avoid mood swings. Beware of destructiveness.*

LAMONT DOZIER (6/16/41)
DIANA ROSS (3/26/44)

Ross began her singing career as a member of the Supremes, later pursuing individual stardom. Singer-songwriter Dozier belonged to Motown's successful composing team Holland-Dozier-Holland, whose songs took the Supremes to the top of the charts in the 60s.

Also: Dana Carvey & George Bush (*SNL* comic portrayal).

March 25–April 2

THE WEEK OF THE CHILD
ARIES I

June 19–24

THE CUSP OF MAGIC
GEMINI-CANCER CUSP

 RELATIONSHIPS

STRENGTHS: **CLOSE, TRUSTING, EDUCATIONAL**

WEAKNESSES: **UNFORGIVING, UNOBJECTIVE, INCESTUOUS**

BEST: **LOVE, FRIENDSHIP**

WORST: **FAMILY**

Trusting Tranquillity

The most crucial area in the pairing of Aries I and Gemini-Cancer is that of trust, for neither partner easily admits others to his or her private inner world. This trust, along with an ability to learn and develop together, may be slow to build, but if not harmed, will eventually emerge as the relationship's focus and, indeed, may prove the backbone of a long-standing friendship, marriage or love affair. And no matter how deep it runs, the connection between these two is vulnerable to being irreparably broken if infidelity or betrayal occurs on even one occasion. Forgiveness, then, is not characteristic of this relationship.

Gemini-Cancers often have a soothing effect on the Aries I personality. Aries I's have a stressed-out side and can push themselves too hard and too fast; a Gemini-Cancer energy waiting at home may allow them to relax in domestic tranquillity. This is not to say that these two always have a calming influence on each other, but in general the more intuitive side of Aries I's allows them to understand the sensitivity of Gemini-Cancers, while the emotional sensibility of Gemini-Cancers grants a sympathy with Aries I problems.

Should a friendship between these two emerge, a decision may have to be faced as to whether to allow it to go further. If limits are set (whether because one of the partners wants to avoid the uncharted waters of romantic or sexual involvement or because one partner already has a mate or lover whose jealousy must be appeased), they may take the form of simply restricting contact with each other. Most often such a decision will be hard to make: the understanding that can slowly develop between Aries I's and Gemini-Cancers is subtle and magical, and this relationship can only be scaled back with great difficulty and pain.

Much between these two remains unspoken, whether they are lovers or friends. As family members, Aries I's and Gemini-Cancers may be extremely close—so close, in fact, that their relationship may carry the danger of emotionally or, more rarely, physically incestuous overtones. In all connections between these two, objectivity may prove both a crying need and, alas, an impossible goal.

ADVICE: *Keep your head clear. Make every effort to open up. Try to be more forgiving and understanding. Clarifying the rules early may spare pain later.*

ST. TERESA OF AVILA (3/28/1515)
ST. JOHN OF THE CROSS (6/24/1542)

Longtime friends St. Teresa of Spain and St. John were both Carmelites and mystics. St. Teresa wrote great mystical literature classics; St. John was one of Spain's finest lyric poets. Together they founded the Discalced ("shoeless") order of Carmelites.

Also: Eric Clapton & Jeff Beck (early Yardbirds).

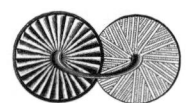

TOM MAGLIOZZI (6/28/37)
RAY MAGLIOZZI (3/30/49)

Dubbed the "Car Guys," brothers Tom and Ray host a popular PBS radio call-in show giving helpful auto advice. They are famous for their entertaining repartee with callers. ***Also:* Warren Beatty & Leslie Caron** (affair; actors); **William L. Bragg & William H. Bragg** (father/son Nobelists, physics); **Elton John & George Michael** (singers; friends).

March 25–April 2
THE WEEK OF THE CHILD
ARIES I

June 25–July 2
THE WEEK OF THE EMPATH
CANCER I

Feeling Natural

This relationship is characterized by simple, direct kinds of expression and gives emotions a high priority. This can be both good and bad: while the partners will be able to vent their feelings and be themselves comfortably and easily, too much directness can also cause an overstepping of boundaries, sometimes with calamitous results. Eventually this combination can lead to a respect for privacy, an increased sensitivity and the realization that some subjects are best left untouched. Once this happens, more extreme forms of individual expression can be accepted.

Aries I's and Cancer I's should feel comfortable with each other, since both favor direct expression. Cancer I's, however, tend to see feelings as their personal domain and can try to appropriate not only people but their emotions; Aries I's will not feel comfortable with such claims, which they may experience as threatening their need for privacy. And once Aries I's feel their freedom at risk, they're gone. Consequently, Cancer I's may wake up one morning to find that they have gone too far. This can prove a conflict in this relationship.

Interpersonal relations between these two, whether marriages, friendships or family connections, can only succeed if the Cancer I knows when to stop probing the heart and psyche of the Aries I. The Aries I may feel comfortable with the Cancer I's attention up to a point, but beyond that point will post more and more warning signs. Another part of the same problem appears when Aries I's, although they may feel great fondness for Cancer I's, become increasingly wary of expressing their feelings, fearing that they are flashing a green light. Cancer I's will find this very hard to deal with, since a relationship's emotional openness is very important to them.

Should strong natural feeling prevail, the dynamic aspects of Aries I's may be welcome in business ventures, and can meld well with the money sense and the protective and defensive instincts of Cancer I's. At work, an Aries I on offense and a Cancer I on defense together offer the basis of an effective all-around team. Enterprises can only succeed, however, if each party feels free enough in the relationship to express his or her individual point of view.

ADVICE: *Learn to be attentive without smothering. Back off and leave things alone. Retain your individuality—a relationship should not demand all.*

E. POWER BIGGS (3/29/06)
WANDA LANDOWSKA (7/5/1877)

Organist Biggs and harpsichordist Landowska each specialized in interpreting the works of J.S. Bach. Polish-born Landowska influenced today's performance of early music on period instruments; English-born Biggs is known for his complete organ works of Bach. ***Also:*** **Pearl Bailey & Louis Bellson** (married; singer/drummer); **Richard Chamberlain & Vince Edwards** (tv Drs. Kildare & Casey).

March 25–April 2
THE WEEK OF THE CHILD
ARIES I

July 3–10
THE WEEK OF THE UNCONVENTIONAL
CANCER II

Behind the Mask

The keynote to this relationship is an attraction to the unusual and the new—to quirks, peculiarities and revolutionary traits. That the relationship will be interested in somewhat rebellious or radical trends, whether in clothing, body ornament, interior decorating, dancing or music, is not particularly surprising: this couple itself has a certain charming quirkiness. It also has strength, and although it has a taste for the offbeat, it rests on a bedrock of stability. Sensing this, outsiders involved with the partners in this relationship will enjoy its unusualness all the more. In fact, this team is likely to be popular and in demand. As such, it can be a real force of change.

The lifestyle these two choose may well prove a basis for living together or marriage. Since many Aries I's are rather interesting and extreme types anyway, there is a reasonable chance that Cancer II's will find them intriguing, but the chemistry must be right, and the Aries I must be open to the kind of domestic security and nurturing qualities that the Cancer II can offer. Although extremely independent, Aries I's often need some kind of family life, and Cancer II's may be able to fill this need in a way that does not significantly limit their freedom.

Cancer II's, too, can be unusual, even bizarre personalities, but they often hide behind a facade of normality or take an everyday job. Similarly, Aries I's often present an outward persona (active, aggressive) that is at odds with their real inner state (quiet, even withdrawn). A relationship that allows these two to recognize each other as soulmates behind the masks they show the world may be well suited to both love affairs and marriages.

The problems that occur in this relationship usually arise in the area of misunderstanding: Cancer II's may mistakenly interpret Aries I independence as disinterest, and Aries I's may take the preoccupation of Cancer II's with their interior fantasy life as rejection. Sharing domestic responsibilities and having children, however, may cement the combination.

ADVICE: *Ordinary things can be interesting too. Don't make such a point of being different. Cultivate true individuality. Beware of trendiness.*

March 25–April 2

THE WEEK OF THE CHILD
ARIES I

July 11–18

THE WEEK OF THE PERSUADER
CANCER III

Conversational Interchange

	RELATIONSHIPS	

STRENGTHS: **COMMUNICATIVE, TEAM-ORIENTED, AMBITIOUS**

WEAKNESSES: **FRUSTRATED, TENSE, THREATENING**

BEST: **WORK**

WORST: **FAMILY**

Independence and boundaries are top priorities here. The relationship focuses on communication, but communication mainly through the spoken word: interactions often elude the physical and take place via telephone, fax or e-mail, with face-to-face meetings often restricted to certain convenient times and places. Generally speaking, this duo's choices are conscious and thought out, motivated more by intention and desire than by need. Even so, the relationship often features considerable emotional conflicts, which are likely to cause problems when it appears in the realms of family, love or marriage. Over the years, these frustrations and tensions may lead to greater understanding and ultimately to increased closeness, but the road to such acceptance may be long and rocky.

A romantic or sexual chemistry between these two is often missing, but Aries I's and Cancer III's may well be able to work together effectively, particularly as co-workers in a team involved in media endeavors. Both Cancer III's and Aries I's are ambitious, and together they may prove too aggressive in struggling to rise to the top; they must take care not to be threatening to other people or groups, who may be jealous or competitive and may work to counteract their aspirations. Power struggles within the relationship must also be monitored carefully, lest individual drives undermine the common cause.

Because of this matchup's strong mental orientation, more emotional Cancer III's and intuitive Aries I's will not always feel comfortable with each other. This relationship deemphasizes feelings and impulses. On the other hand, realistic and moneywise Cancer III's will make important contributions to the dependability and security of this duo, while Aries I's will often furnish drive and initiative. Although Cancer III's will have difficulty getting Aries I's to open up and be honest, and Aries I's will occasionally feel smothered or manipulated by Cancer III's, these two will find a working rhythm, no matter how strange or unconventional.

ADVICE: *Keep ambitions under control. Find ways to avoid frustration. Learn to relax and accept. Acknowledge unconscious drives and motivations.*

JACK JOHNSON (3/31/1878)
LUPE VELEZ (7/18/08)

The first black boxer to hold a world title, Johnson was flamboyant, outspoken, and the lover of many women, including Mata Hari. His affair with Velez, a volatile actress known as the "Mexican Spitfire," was intense but short-lived. ***Also:*** **Mariah Carey & Tommy Mottola** (married; singer/president CBS records).

March 25–April 2

THE WEEK OF THE CHILD
ARIES I

July 19–25

THE CUSP OF OSCILLATION
CANCER-LEO CUSP

Alleviating Distress

	RELATIONSHIPS	

STRENGTHS: **PROTECTIVE, SUPPORTIVE, EXCITING**

WEAKNESSES: **IMPULSIVE, UNSTABLE, DISTRESSING**

BEST: **LOVE**

WORST: **MARRIAGE**

There is a liberating quality to this relationship, a sense of being able to breathe, which can make this an ecstatic combination. Sympathy and protective instincts may blossom here, as well as moral fervor and passion. The relationship will find itself championing the oppressed and will not hesitate to fly in the face of tradition or custom in giving love and support to a needy partner in distress. It is not unusual, then, for it to emerge at a time when one or the other of the partners is involved in a troubled or failing love affair or marriage, and when it can provide the freedom and safety that both individuals seek. At such a time, this relationship can allow Aries I's to show the very best, heroic qualities they have to offer, even while they also extend understanding to the third party involved. For the Cancer-Leo, meanwhile, it is the covertness and the secret, unpredictable and exciting nature of such a liaison that usually provide the magic.

In love affairs not involving a third party, the attraction between these two may be less intense: Aries I openness often does not carry a highly charged enough emotional admixture to hold Cancer-Leo interest. Should Cancer-Leos fall in love with Aries I's, however, they may be challenged in holding on to them, since Aries I's can feel threatened and hemmed in by their aggressive stance. Cancer-Leos also demand a lot of understanding, which Aries I's may lack. In marital or other living situations, Aries I impulsiveness and Cancer-Leo instability do not bode well for permanence or longevity, particularly as their initial idealization of each other falls away.

The relationship's swirling energies can gel at work. These two don't usually stick to mundane activities but pursue projects involving adventure and travel, challenge and danger, often in the executive worlds of corporate finance, investment or advertising. Cancer-Leos' tendency to excess, and their penchant for wide mood swings, will need to be tempered and moderated by Aries I's, who may be gratified to be the more responsible and dependable ones.

ADVICE: *Try not to be so moral and judgmental. See the other person's point of view. Beware the destructiveness of covert activities. Stay balanced.*

DAVID EISENHOWER (4/1/48)
JULIE NIXON (7/25/48)

David, President Eisenhower's grandson, and Julie, Richard Nixon's daughter, spent their youth at the White House in the 50s when Nixon served as vice-president in Eisenhower's administration. They married during Nixon's presidency. **Also: Warren Beatty & Natalie Wood** (affair); **Rudolf Serkin & Peter Serkin** (father/son; pianists).

STRENGTHS: **ACHIEVING, FREE, LIKE-MINDEDNESS**

WEAKNESSES: **DESTRUCTIVE, COMBATIVE, CLAIMING**

BEST: **SIBLING**

WORST: **WORK**

JOSEPH CAMPBELL (3/26/04)
CARL JUNG (7/26/1875)

Jung's work in psychology, religion and myth was influenced by his mythological dreams and visions. Campbell's understanding of and fondness for Jung are measured by his many distinguished works on comparative mythology.

Also: **Eugene McCarthy & Myrna Loy** (actress active in presidential campaign).

March 25–April 2

THE WEEK OF THE CHILD
ARIES I

July 26–August 2

THE WEEK OF AUTHORITY
LEO I

Free-for-All

The underlying themes of this combination are likely to be freedom and independence of action. It is a relationship that constantly needs to move forward, change and grow—stagnation is a particular threat to this pairing. The partners will generally get along and understand each other well (because of their easy, trine relationship—120° apart in the zodiac—and because both Aries and Leo are fire signs), but the flame of their relationship will periodically flare up and burn out of control; instability and impermanence are a hallmark here. These conflicts don't actually reflect reality so much as the relationship's resistance to boredom. Even so, arguments can take on a life of their own, snowballing into destructiveness.

Passionate relationships between these two are likely to burn brightly but may quickly be extinguished once the fuel is used up. Furthermore, the emphasis on freedom of action here is likely to arouse jealousies and possessiveness, even should both partners really want to be free to get involved with others. Friendship is probably a better bet for Aries I's and Leo I's, as long as they can maintain objectivity and avoid conflict. The fact that they usually share a mutual understanding does not guarantee that they won't disagree, and over time this can grind down even the firmest bedrock of sympathy. In work, love and family matters, the relationship can become a battlefield of rivalries—for a job, for the affections of a third party, for the attentions of a parent. Winning is a high priority, but the Leo I usually has the upper hand; the Aries I may lack the necessary patience, or the love of tough infighting, that will be necessary to prevail here.

The relationship between a Leo I parent and an Aries I child may be particularly rocky, since it will fix both of them in roles surprisingly similar to the qualities of their individual characters, thus reinforcing dominant and childlike tendencies, respectively. Perhaps the best possibility for these two is as siblings, particularly of the opposite sex; here a sympathetic emotional bond can develop over the years. As brother and sister, this pair can replace competitive tendencies with mutual admiration and fondness, which will grow as the years go by.

ADVICE: *Don't pretend to be more free than you really are. Admit to dependencies. Beware of double standards. Avoid fixed role-patterns. Lessen conflicts.*

STRENGTHS: **NATURAL, UNPRETENTIOUS, ORIGINAL**

WEAKNESSES: **WACKY, FRUSTRATED, INEFFECTUAL**

BEST: **MARRIAGE**

WORST: **WORK**

DEBBIE REYNOLDS (4/1/32)
EDDIE FISHER (8/10/28)

"America's Sweetheart" and 50s film star, Reynolds married singer Fisher in 1955. Together they had daughter, actress Carrie Fisher. With their 1959 divorce only 3 hours old, Fisher married Elizabeth Taylor.

Also: **Rudolf Serkin & Adolf Busch** (son-in-law/father-in-law; pianist/violinist); **Jack Johnson & Mata Hari** (affair; boxer/spy).

March 25–April 2

THE WEEK OF THE CHILD
ARIES I

August 3–10

THE WEEK OF BALANCED STRENGTH
LEO II

One of a Kind

This relationship will often feature an original, even unique outlook on life. Ethics and idealism are the order of the day; this is a moral, courageous and loyal pair. Aries I's and Leo II's are well suited for domestic life, whether they are married or living together. They also share a great many positive qualities, which blend harmoniously in this relationship and can be taken to the limit. The matchup is also characterized by a need for privacy, with both partners demanding honesty from each other in their everyday interactions. Acting naturally, and being comfortable with assigned roles, these two mutually accept each other and, together, are at ease with themselves. There is an intense dislike in this matchup for pretension and disingenuousness.

On the other hand, the relationship may not be completely stable, depending on the ability of the Leo II to stay emotionally balanced. Leo II's have strong passions that can run out of hand, and career problems and failures can bring out a streak of masochism in them that can lead to serious depressions. Unfortunately, Aries I's may not be particularly good at bolstering a Leo II's sagging self-image. Neither Aries I's nor Leo II's are comfortable with strong expressions of feeling, and the relationship may consequently show signs of repression, particularly in times of stress. Periodic outbursts of anger may bring violent confrontations but, more characteristically, will result in expressions of bewilderment, frustration or helplessness.

In the family sphere, these two may for the most part be accepting and tolerant of each other, particularly as siblings. A natural amount of competitiveness will arise, of course, while they are growing up, but they can derive great satisfaction from shared activities involving hobbies, sports or pets.

Others may not like or understand the Aries I–Leo II relationship, particularly in its somewhat wild and wacky tastes and its idiosyncratic ideas or lifestyle. So relaxed are the attitudes here that the relationship may be ineffective in the workplace, lacking the push to advance a joint project.

ADVICE: *Beware of self-satisfaction and smugness. Try a bit harder. Don't be too moral or judgmental. Express feelings.*

March 25–April 2

THE WEEK OF THE CHILD
ARIES I

August 11–18

THE WEEK OF LEADERSHIP
LEO III

The Unknown Tongue

RELATIONSHIPS

STRENGTHS: **COMMUNICATIVE, ENERGETIC, SURMOUNTING**

WEAKNESSES: **COMBATIVE, OVERWHELMING, SELFISH**

BEST: **SEXUAL**

WORST: **FAMILY**

MADONNA (8/16/58)
WARREN BEATTY (3/30/37)

Prolific lover Beatty and the ever-adventurous Madonna were bound to cross paths. Amid rumors of marriage and possible pregnancy, they had a highly publicized, short-lived, passionate affair during their filming of *Dick Tracy* (1990), which he also directed.

***Also:* David Lean & Robert Bolt** (collaborators; director/writer).

In order for this relationship even to get off the ground, a common basis of communication will have to be created. But the relationship has a natural tendency to find a unique means of dialogue that will further understanding and help to transcend the conflicting personality elements of its two willful partners. The relationship can be put first, and more selfish or individualistic desires can be abandoned, if somewhat unusual avenues of communication are opened up, avenues that Aries I's and Leo III's may never have explored with earlier partners.

These two can share a powerfully effective working relationship, with the Leo III taking the lead and the Aries I applying prodigious energy to the job at hand. The Leo III is more likely to be found in an executive or managerial role, and the success of this partnership will depend on the Aries I's ability to accept him or her as an employer or boss. If intelligently directed toward a common goal, this duo's fused intuitive energies can sweep the field of opposition and surmount the most difficult technical or financial barriers. Should personal conflicts arise between these fiery types, however, communication breakdown may threaten an entire project's success.

For the most part, the relationship does not do well as a marriage, for destructive power struggles are likely to emerge when passions are aroused between these two. A love affair can bring the partners to heights of sexual excitement and fulfillment yet is unlikely to be long-lasting, since Leo III's, with their deep and often tumultuous feelings, will probably disturb the cool and detachment that Aries I's need if they are to stay on an even keel. In simple terms, Aries I's may ultimately find Leo III emotional energy too much to handle.

In the sibling or parent-child relationship, entrenched confrontational and combative stances are likely to be assumed, particularly if a Leo III parent or older sibling of the same sex sternly attempts to crush the spontaneity or individuality of an Aries I. A further danger appears when Aries I children idolize Leo III parents, becoming blind to their faults and unduly dependent on them.

ADVICE: *Always keep the lines of communication open. Beware of selfishness. Learn to sacrifice and to share. Minimize power struggles. Remember to be kind.*

March 25–April 2

THE WEEK OF THE CHILD
ARIES I

August 19–25

THE CUSP OF EXPOSURE
LEO-VIRGO CUSP

Confidential Projects

RELATIONSHIPS

STRENGTHS: **LARGE-THINKING, EXPANSIVE, CONSTRUCTIVE**

WEAKNESSES: **SECRETIVE, CLOSED, TRAPPED**

BEST: **FRIENDSHIP**

WORST: **LOVERS**

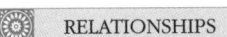

AL GORE (3/31/48)
TIPPER GORE (8/19/48)

Parents of 4 children, Vice-President Gore and wife Tipper are a highly visible political force in the promotion of family values; they annually moderate the Family Policy Conference in Nashville, Tennessee. ***Also:* Eric Clapton & Ginger Baker** (Cream); **Diane Cilento & Sean Connery** (married; actors); **Elle MacPherson & Claudia Schiffer** (restaurant partners; supermodels).

This relationship is characterized by an ability to originate large ideas or big projects, or at least to make expansive plans. But it tends to do so away from the watchful eyes of the world—this pair will often keep their plans to themselves, even as they slowly actualize their dreams. Their ability to think on a large scale is a real plus, but their need to keep their thinking secret can almost become pathological; this pairing is not served by the smoke screens it erects to maintain privacy.

Although Aries I's are much the more direct of this pair, their openness often belies a hidden side, not unlike Leo-Virgo secretiveness. And although Leo-Virgos usually share and reveal their secrets in the end, Aries I's rarely or perhaps never do so. Sharing their secrets with each other creates a bond of trust between these two personalities, and is often the way they begin to build a private life together, one in which they discuss their innermost dreams, goals and the other personal areas they tend to hide.

Aries I's who get involved with Leo-Virgos may have gotten in over their heads, particularly in emotional and romantic relationships. Leo-Virgos demand a lot of understanding, and Aries I's may not have the stamina or the interest to contend with their complex moods and feelings. Strong physical attraction may be unusual for this combination; sexuality is unlikely to be what draws these two to each other.

Despite the joys of working on a big family project together, a marriage between these two can undergo a severe crisis when fundamental personality differences emerge, perhaps months or even years after the wedding. Aries I's like their freedom and may feel trapped and hemmed in by emotional ties to Leo-Virgos, particularly as spouses. In the family sphere, particularly between siblings of the opposite sex, a close bond may develop in which Aries I dynamism and outgoing energy catalyzes Leo-Virgo thoughtfulness, to the benefit of all concerned.

ADVICE: *Recognize and acknowledge differences. Beware of cutting yourself off from the world. Remain transparent. Keep one foot on the ground.*

FREDERICK HENRY ROYCE (3/27/1863)
CHARLES STEWART ROLLS (8/27/1877)

Rolls and Royce, who founded the automotive company in 1903, established their distinctive style and quality reputation with the introduction of the "Silver Ghost" in 1906. Their partnership lasted until Royce's air-crash death in 1910. *Also:* **Max Ernst & Peggy Guggenheim** (married; artist/collector-patron); **Ed Begley & Martha Raye** (married; actor/comedienne).

March 25–April 2

THE WEEK OF THE CHILD
ARIES I

August 26–September 2

THE WEEK OF SYSTEM BUILDERS
VIRGO I

Seeking New Frontiers

This relationship will favor adventurous and challenging projects—anything that causes this pair to seek out a variety of experience, or the answers to a variety of questions. The differences between these two personalities, however, are such that the relationship may become wholly involved in seeking out a basis of understanding between them—an effort that may not receive much reward.

These partners have completely different approaches to life, with Aries I's acting on their intuition and Virgo I's tending to be more structured and logical. Faced with an upcoming event or challenge, Virgo I's tend to plan things out to the last detail, whereas Aries I's tend to fly by the seat of their pants. Yet these two can meld beautifully as co-workers, fighting the good fight or rolling back new frontiers, side by side. They often focus on objective pursuits of a technical, scientific or financial bent rather than on people-oriented projects.

In more intimate settings, the energies of Aries I's and Virgo I's can clash. Both love and marriage may be undermined by the Virgo I's emotional problems and by the Aries I's inability to deal with them. When a Virgo I sinks into a depression (perhaps caused by feeling rejected, unloved or ignored by an Aries I), there may be little that either party can constructively do. The nervous instability of a Virgo I can unsettle the positive, breezy attitudes of an Aries I, leaving both partners a bit unsteady and lacking the confidence to cope with any crisis that may arise. Similarly, friendships between these two are likely to demand an emotional investment that neither party may be prepared to make. The relationship usually lacks either sexual or financial reward.

As parents, Virgo I's can provide the kind of structure in everyday living that allows Aries I's to bloom and to express their most creative side. An Aries I parent may also benefit from having a Virgo I child who brings order to family life (although probably not the deep understanding needed in the emotional sphere, even as the child grows older).

ADVICE: *Keep seeking new challenges. Don't give up. Keep emotions under control. Don't worry so much. Beware of depressions. Try to relax.*

GLORIA SWANSON (3/27/1899)
JOSEPH KENNEDY (9/6/1888)

Kennedy—rich businessman, diplomat and father of JFK—was lover to silent-screen legend Swanson. He also financed her film productions, 2 of which won Oscar nominations, but her extravagance on von Stroheim's *Queen Kelly* hurt their relationship. *Also:* **Henry II (France) & Diane de Poitiers** (king/influential mistress).

March 25–April 2

THE WEEK OF THE CHILD
ARIES I

September 3–10

THE WEEK OF THE ENIGMA
VIRGO II

Take It or Leave It

Aries I's and Virgo II's may be extremely different, but they have at least three things in common: first, they both hate being analyzed; second, they believe they can work out their problems without anyone else's help; and third, they are fiercely individualistic. Their relationship synergistically drives these traits to an extreme. As a partnership, these two believe in making no excuses whatsoever for their thoughts, appearance or actions. Other people can simply take them or leave them.

Before meeting each other, both of these two may have had difficulty finding a partner they could live with, but together they often have a special chemistry. In fact, Aries I's and Virgo II's make excellent spouses, often marrying after an immediate physical attraction and an exciting love affair. All of the marital joys may be theirs, including home and children. Things don't always go easily for these high-strung individualists, and frequent disagreements and arguments dot the landscape of their relationship. Yet they have the ability to forgive and make up, and also to be there for each other in times of need.

Aries I's and Virgo II's get along less well as friends, when they often have an unsettling effect on each other. Competition over a mutual friend or lover may threaten or destroy the relationship. Virgo II moral attitudes can make Aries I's decidedly uncomfortable, particularly if directed against them in a disapproving and critical way. And Aries I's will sometimes appear impulsive or thoughtless to Virgo II's, who are usually much more discriminating and careful.

As co-workers or family members, these two can really get on each other's nerves. Their approaches to many problems are diametrically opposed and may generate frictions that are counterproductive to the efforts of the group. Although others may find the gyrations of this relationship entertaining, sooner or later the humor of the situation wears thin. One combination that can work out, however, is a boss-employee relationship with the Virgo II as the boss: Virgo II's generally know what they want, and Aries I's can usually deliver.

ADVICE: *Ease your moral stance a bit. Beware of impulsiveness. Don't push to the limit so much—forgiveness may not always be granted.*

March 25–April 2

THE WEEK OF THE CHILD
ARIES I

September 11–18

THE WEEK OF THE LITERALIST
VIRGO III

STRENGTHS: **COURAGEOUS, CONTROLLED, MAGICAL**

WEAKNESSES: **ADVERSARIAL, BICKERING, OVERDOMINANT**

BEST: **FRIENDSHIP**

WORST: **FAMILY**

Unacknowledged Magic

This is a relationship in which the partners' similarities are slow to be recognized: these two are very different, to the extent that they make a surprising pair. Yet even if it goes somewhat unnoticed, an ineffable magic surfaces periodically in their combination. An unspoken affection in the relationship betokens a personal loyalty that will surmount temporary disagreements or power struggles. Willfulness and courage manifest strongly here, accompanied by a love of truth and a dislike of phoniness and pretension. Keeping emotions under control is a strong requirement for this combination.

Aries I's often find Virgo III's unnecessarily theatrical, and also superior—with an Aries I, Virgo III's always seem to think they know best. For Virgo III's, meanwhile, Aries I's may appear uptight. But these attitudes may only be projections of each partner's frailties, or reactions when one of them feels threatened by the other. Family relationships are not favored for this combination, particularly brother-sister or father-daughter pairs. Both of these personalities can be pretty dominant types, the kinds of people who don't have to be loud to be heard, in almost any situation. Both are capable of hurling barbs with telling effect, and when these are directed at each other, they may escalate into an out-of-control conflict. And yet, again, a strange kind of magnetism between these two often wins out, and results in acceptance and increased respect. In friendships, these two are much too direct and outspoken about their likes and dislikes to allow their partner much rest. Their relationship may be characterized by a kind of kidding, bantering or bickering. With scarcely a dull moment, they will sharpen their wits on each other, often bringing out both the best and the worst in each other's characters. People meeting them for the first time may even take them as enemies or at least adversaries, but their insults are usually meant affectionately.

Sexual or romantic relations between these two will run the gamut between extremes of love and hate. Strong attractions and repulsions are characteristic of the pair, and should they be lucky or unlucky enough to have a brief fling and breakup, they will rarely come back for a second helping.

ADVICE: *Acknowledge what you have in common. Keep your bantering under control. Recognize magical moments. Stress the positive. Even out emotions.*

ED BEGLEY (3/25/01)
ED BEGLEY, JR. (9/16/49)

Ed Sr. was a gifted character actor of stage, screen. and tv during his long career (1931–70). In '62 he won an Oscar for *Sweet Bird of Youth*. Son Ed Jr. started as a tv actor and was nominated for 2 Emmys for his role in *St. Elsewhere* (1982–88). He has also made many films since '72.

March 25–April 2

THE WEEK OF THE CHILD
ARIES I

September 19–24

THE CUSP OF BEAUTY
VIRGO-LIBRA CUSP

STRENGTHS: **TASTEFUL, ARTISTIC, PROTECTIVE**

WEAKNESSES: **UNREALISTIC, COLD, SUPERFICIAL**

BEST: **FAMILY**

WORST: **MARRIAGE**

Aesthetic Mastery

This relationship may focus on a shared enthusiasm for art, design, music or literature, areas in which it will want to achieve mastery or technical proficiency. It may also achieve great success, since it has an ability to predict trends. Both Aries I's and Virgo-Libras are impressed with fine appearance and aesthetic taste, but their combination often drives such interests to the limit.

This relationship can be satisfying and mutually rewarding as long as feelings are kept on a more platonic, less intimate plane. Warning lights should go off, however, when Aries I's find themselves dazzled by Virgo-Libras. Should the feeling be mutual, the relationship may start off like a house on fire; but after passions have cooled down, problems will usually arise, particularly if an unpretentious Aries I suspects that he or she has become involved with a snob. Aries I's dislike pretense of any kind and may begin to withdraw if they think their partners are not what they seem to be on the surface, no matter how attractive that surface is. Virgo-Libras, on the other hand, are often irritated by Aries I moodiness, impetuosity and emotional problems. As far as marriage goes, then, the attraction these two initially feel for each other is unlikely to translate into the deep feelings necessary for a long-standing involvement. Should Aries I's and Virgo-Libras marry before they really know each other, the effects can be disastrous when they discover they really have little in common other than a shared aesthetic, and that even less holds them together. Financial obligations and property may be particularly painful issues at such times of crisis.

In sibling and parent-child pairs, this relationship can be highly empathic and supportive. Aries I's are protective of Virgo-Libra vulnerabilities, and Virgo-Libras can have a calming effect on the frenetic energies of Aries I's, particularly by making their domestic surroundings more comfortable and aesthetically satisfying.

ADVICE: *Dig a little deeper. Explore and understand emotions more fully. Attend to practical matters. Accept imperfection.*

GLORIA SWANSON (3/27/1899)
ERICH VON STROHEIM (9/22/1885)

Von Stroheim, most well-known for his screen portrayals of German officers, was also a brilliant, though extravagant, director. In 1928 he and lover Swanson made *Queen Kelly*—a financial fiasco that put an end to his directing career. They appeared together in *Sunset Boulevard* in 1950.

JIMMY CARTER (10/1/24)
BILLY CARTER (3/29/37)

Often characterized as a beer-toting, outspoken, down-home Georgia boy, younger brother Billy was a public-image problem for President Carter. They conflicted on many social and political issues. **Also: Jack Webb & Julie London** (married; actors); **Gloria Steinem & Clay Felker** (co-founders, *New York* magazine).

March 25–April 2
THE WEEK OF THE CHILD
ARIES I

September 25–October 2
THE WEEK OF THE PERFECTIONIST
LIBRA I

The Swirling Vortex

Aries I and Libra I are opposites in the zodiac, and their opposition can immediately translate into conflict, not only within the relationship but also outside it: together, these two can adopt an extremely aggressive stance toward the world. This tendency can best be harnessed if the relationship is geared to a cause; it can provide, for example, no small amount of success in business. Furthermore, as is often the case, conflict and passion are not far apart here, and this pairing can often include a magnetic physical attraction. In short, Aries I (fire) and Libra I (air) have a catalytic effect on each other. Such explosiveness does not usually augur well for marital and work relationships, where stability is so important over the long haul. A particular bone of contention will be the Aries I dislike of criticism; they are natural, spontaneous creatures who cannot handle constant scrutiny and judgment. Libra I's, meanwhile, often can't help being critical. They also try to keep their emotions under control at all costs, and will be disturbed by the honest emotional expressions and periodic spontaneous outbursts of an Aries I. In this respect they may be unconsciously reacting against traits that they secretly desire, since in some ways Aries I's are living models for what Libra I's most need to cultivate—the frank, open approach to the world that will allow them a release of their inner tensions and insecurities.

As the relationship develops and feelings emerge, Libra I's will be able to see what they view as Aries I problems more clearly, and will want to get in there and fix what they perceive as wrong. This Aries I's will not be able to abide. But Aries I's may make mistakes too, in passing moral judgment on what they see as incorrect behavior on the part of Libra I's. Thus the relationship will become a vortex of swirling feelings, both positive and negative. As siblings, these two may forever be fighting, particularly if they are of the same sex.

As friends, this duo craves action and excitement, and the relationship may be structured around sports, drama, adventure or social groups or clubs. The combination's saturation point for socializing is low, however—these two will often find it necessary to withdraw and find a quiet place.

ADVICE: *Allow for differences. Withhold undue criticism. Keep in contact with the world. Question your values. Don't assume you're infallible.*

HANS CHRISTIAN ANDERSEN (4/2/1805)
JENNY LIND (10/6/1820)

Famed fairy-tale writer Andersen adored singer Lind, known as the "Swedish Nightingale," showering her with gifts and poetry. A self-proclaimed virgin, he expressed only platonic feelings. **Also: Elton John & Sean Lennon** (godfather/godson; rock musicians); **Emile Zola & Alfred Dreyfus** (writer defended accused traitor); **L. Mies van der Rohe & Le Corbusier** (colleagues; Bauhaus architects).

March 25–April 2
THE WEEK OF THE CHILD
ARIES I

October 3–10
THE WEEK OF SOCIETY
LIBRA II

Empathic Comrades

This combination offers a good example of how a relationship can create synergies. When faced with problems or challenges, for example, Aries I's will act more from instinct, while more mental Libra II's will hang back a bit; yet this combination's greatest strengths are neither instinct nor thought but emotion, feeling and empathy. In the long run, the relationship will give each partner the sensitivity to know and understand the other's feelings.

Aries I outspokenness and Libra II reflectiveness may occasionally conflict, yet each has much to learn from the other. Often procrastinators, Libra II's may admire the ability of Aries I's to make up their mind and act without endless rumination; headstrong Aries I's, for their part, may learn from Libra II's how to be less rash and to use their common sense. Given the differences in each party's orientation, this combination would not traditionally be recommended for love affairs, but actually things can work out. The crucial factor will be how strong physical attraction is; that both parties to the relationship enjoy having fun is a big plus. Marriages, on the other hand, may work out very nicely even if sexual or sensuous considerations are downplayed. Comradeship, affection, acceptance—all of these grow stronger in Aries I–Libra II marriages as the years go by. A truly unselfish love is possible between these two, assuming that the Aries I is not overly egotistical and does not ignore Libra II needs. Libra II's, meanwhile, must respect the Aries I need for independence, yet without being masochistic and losing self-respect.

As family members, Aries I's can help protect Libra II's from being at the mercy of their dark side. Aries I's bring not only fun-loving qualities to the sibling or parent-child relationship but also understanding; they know what it is to be beset by moodiness themselves and can usually handle it better in others than deal with their own demons.

ADVICE: *Keep it light. Physical attraction is not the most important thing. Balance freedom and responsibility. Don't compare yourself to others.*

March 25–April 2

THE WEEK OF THE CHILD
ARIES I

October 11–18

THE WEEK OF THEATER
LIBRA III

RELATIONSHIPS

STRENGTHS: **FUN, AMBITIOUS, ACHIEVING**

WEAKNESSES: **POWER-TRIPPING, ANGRY, DISSENTING**

BEST: **FRIENDSHIP**

WORST: **WORK**

Determined Struggle

Hard-headed determination and a struggle for power provide the focus for this combination. As a long-standing relationship, particularly at work or as a marriage, it is often plagued by internal dissension, which can be damaging to colleagues or to children. If this relationship is to work out, responsibilities and authority must be carefully delineated, and a truce must be reached as to who is boss. It will also be necessary to work hard on developing mutually kind and understanding attitudes.

Love affairs in this combination can be complex and strongly unrealistic, particularly on the part of the Aries I, whose idealism and fixed ideas can get in the way of seeing things as they really are. This will often lead to an inability to let the relationship go, even once it has stagnated or moved downhill. Closure may also be impaired or prevented by Aries I loyalty and Libra III indecision. These two personalities can easily find themselves locked in an ongoing struggle, in which the Aries I will be overtly aggressive while the Libra III is more passive-aggressive.

There is a positive side: neither Aries I's nor Libra III's are particularly domestic types, and they will love to go out together and do fun things as friends. The theatrical side of an Aries I can blossom in the company of a Libra III. The friendship may also have a romantic quality, even if it lacks a physical or sexual component, which may in fact detract from it. Its alchemy involves a strange blend of realism and fantasy, in which even the most mundane topics and experiences can be exalted. All financial arrangements should be discussed and finalized before any action is taken.

The hard-driving, ambitious nature of this combination does not make parent-child or sibling combinations any easier. There is usually competition between these two if they are family members, with a possibility of angry or violent confrontations.

ADVICE: *Work on respect and kindness. The one giving the orders isn't always the one who's boss. Avoid power struggles. Have fun together. Define roles well.*

MARGARET THATCHER (10/13/25)
JOHN MAJOR (3/29/43)

Thatcher's successor as England's prime minister, Major was her protégé in a long-running hierarchical relationship, having been her appointee as chief treasury secretary, foreign secretary and chancellor of the exchequer.

Also: **Yves Montand & Simone Signoret** (married; actors).

March 25–April 2

THE WEEK OF THE CHILD
ARIES I

October 19–25

THE CUSP OF DRAMA & CRITICISM
LIBRA-SCORPIO CUSP

RELATIONSHIPS

STRENGTHS: **AESTHETIC, CARING, MARKETABLE**

WEAKNESSES: **STRESSED, UNSATISFYING, TROUBLED**

BEST: **WORK**

WORST: **MARRIAGE**

Unusual Tastes

This relationship may well feature an unconventional lifestyle but is nevertheless quite convincing to the world. The finely developed aesthetic taste of a Libra-Scorpio can meld well with the direct and dynamic energies of an Aries I, the result being a shared flair for interior decorating, architecture, design or fashion. These two can value their relationship with each other whether it is a family connection, a friendship or the basis of a business or professional endeavor. Aries I's are not known for their financial acumen, but Libra-Scorpios have a good eye for bargains and know how to cut costs, and the two can make a good team on the job, with a special talent for sales and marketing. "Pitching" unusual ideas is their forte.

On the down side, Libra-Scorpios are thinkers and commentators who can drive action-oriented Aries I's crazy by trying to analyze and correct their behavior. All kinds of arguments can result, particularly when Aries I's refuse to listen to Libra-Scorpios. Aries I's don't generally look for trouble, but in romantic relations with Libra-Scorpios they may well find it—love affairs and marriages are not recommended for this pair. Even as friends, they may hit it off better as companions and leisure-time partners who can share interests and have fun together than as intimates. Deep friendships often prove a bit stressful for this combination, and mutual benefits may not be satisfying enough for the partners to want to continue it.

Libra-Scorpio parents of Aries I children will generally be caring and protective but can be too insistent on laying down the rules. Some Aries I children, however, may feel more secure when sensible limits are placed on them, and when they are made to assume domestic responsibilities. Furthermore, the relationship may function to make the home a comfortable and aesthetic space. Aries I children often come to idolize Libra-Scorpio parents, and to bask in the warmth of their attention and care.

ADVICE: *Tone down arguments. Avoid using shock tactics just for the sake of being different. Discover practical skills. Work on concrete projects.*

DEBBIE REYNOLDS (4/1/32)
CARRIE FISHER (10/21/56)

The turbulent relationship between Fisher (Princess Leia of *Star Wars*) and Reynolds was dramatized in *Postcards from the Edge*—a 1990 film based on Fisher's autobiography, describing her drug addiction and living in her mother's shadow.

Also: **Paul Verlaine & Arthur Rimbaud** (famous liaison; poets); **Rostropovich & Vishnevskaya** (married; dissident soviet artists).

STRENGTHS: **CHALLENGING, ACHIEVING, DEPENDABLE**

WEAKNESSES: **UNSETTLING, DEMANDING, ESTRANGED**

BEST: **COMPETITION**

WORST: **LOVE**

ERIC IDLE (3/29/43)
JOHN CLEESE (10/27/39)

Brilliant improvisers Idle and Cleese were 2 of the groundbreaking 5-member British comedy troupe Monty Python's Flying Circus (1969–74). Now defunct, their unique satirical group enjoys cult status both in England and the US.

March 25–April 2
THE WEEK OF THE CHILD
ARIES I

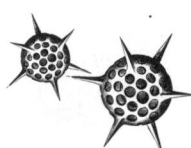

October 26–November 2
THE WEEK OF INTENSITY
SCORPIO I

A Rewarding Rivalry

The meeting of an Aries I and a Scorpio I holds an element of unpredictability, an uncertainty factor that may prove both exciting and unsettling. An adversarial role is common here, though not necessarily a hostile one—these two may do well as team-sport opponents, scientific or artistic rivals, or political or social contenders. With each party competing with the other's best efforts, the Aries I–Scorpio I matchup will often inspire new heights of achievement.

Should Aries I's and Scorpio I's be rivals for the affections of a lover, however, the intensity of their onslaught may ultimately prove too much for a single human to cope with. In love triangles, the gamut of passionate emotions may engulf all three parties, threatening to consume their relationships with each other. And as siblings, particularly when of the same sex, they may compete directly, perhaps for the attention of one or both of the parents. Yet in times of need and crisis, the pair may prove the bulwark of a family's fortunes, and the rock on which it may rebuild after an emotional or financial upset. Loss of a parent may bring the two back together after some years of estrangement and separation.

This relationship can provide an interesting but not necessarily stable marriage. In this form it will have many ups and downs, and will only hold together if internal resources of patience and understanding can be tapped. Certainly great courage will be required to deal with, say, the infidelity of one of the partners, including a decision to stand and fight rather than to give up in a hurtful, blaming or self-deprecatory stance. Children, pets, a home to be proud of, or hobbies and pastimes can all be steadying and rallying points of this relationship in times of unhappiness or turmoil.

ADVICE: *Don't carry competition too far. Learn to pull together. Keep in touch. Beware of love triangles. Keep the good of the group in mind.*

STRENGTHS: **SEXUAL, EXPRESSIVE, LOYAL**

WEAKNESSES: **INTENSE, OVERDEPENDENT, JEALOUS**

BEST: **LOVE**

WORST: **WORK**

WHITTAKER CHAMBERS (4/1/01)
ALGER HISS (11/11/04)

Time magazine editor Chambers accused Hiss of spying for the State Department in the 30s. Tried in '48, Hiss was found guilty of perjury and served jail time. He died at 92, still maintaining his innocence.

Also: Phil & Joe Niekro (baseball brothers).

March 25–April 2
THE WEEK OF THE CHILD
ARIES I

November 3–11
THE WEEK OF DEPTH
SCORPIO II

Twists and Turns

If the focus of this relationship is sexual, as it often is, the combination can be dynamite. Feelings of all kinds run high here as Scorpio II's bring out the most aggressive instincts of Aries I's and Aries I's challenge Scorpio II's to attain the complete expression of their emotional palette. Because of the depth of this relationship's involvement, Aries I's will have to deal with many elements of the human psyche that they would prefer to avoid: jealousy, possessiveness and rage, for example. The volcanic Scorpio II knows these emotions well and can be seen as the Aries I's teacher or guide in fathoming the deepest realms of human feeling.

The important point here is that where Scorpio II feels, Aries I often prefers not to. Many Aries I's think feelings get in the way of their performance, both at work and at play. Love affairs with Scorpio II's may put an end to their frivolity, at least for the time being, and make them confront the more serious aspects of life. Marriages between these two can work out, but sooner or later Aries I's may feel that the relationship's emotions have become too demanding, and may long to escape. Getting away from a Scorpio II may not be all that easy, however, and the struggle may only make bonds between the two tighter, whether they are positive or negative. Friendships in this combination may be meaningful and productive assuming that aggressive and competitive drives can be put away. Difficulties can arise with mutual friends, particularly if Scorpio II's mark out a domain and Aries I's challenge it. Unfortunately, such conflicts may escalate and, if so, they will eventually spell the end of the relationship.

Scorpio II's can be loyal and steadfast parents to Aries I children, often encouraging them to excel in sports. But there is often a danger that they will project their own frustrated ambitions on their offspring. Aries I parents, on the other hand, must learn to leave Scorpio II children alone to work out their moods and emotions. Aries I–Scorpio II siblings, particularly of the opposite sex, may form a mutually dependent bond that continues throughout life.

ADVICE: *Learn to give each other room. Avoid projection. Don't let destructive emotions snowball. Stay open and honest.*

March 25–April 2

THE WEEK OF THE CHILD
ARIES I

November 12–18

THE WEEK OF CHARM
SCORPIO III

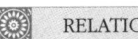

STRENGTHS: **VIVACIOUS, IMAGINATIVE, PRACTICAL**

WEAKNESSES: **IMPULSIVE, UNREALISTIC, CONTROLLING**

BEST: **BUSINESS, SOCIAL**

WORST: **LOVE**

Freewheeling Vivacity

The Aries I–Scorpio III combination can make for a dynamic and vivacious team, whether it engages in social or sports activities or in intellectual or business endeavors. The keynote here is vivid imagination, but also the practical skills to create from it, often in the visual arts. Others are often attracted to the relationship's flamboyance and eclectic excitement. The main problem here is a tendency toward impulsiveness, and perhaps toward taking on too much; with these leanings kept in check, it can do well as a business partnership. Scorpio III's know how to hold on to money and Aries I's how to spend it; if they can agree on their priorities, they can make a go of it as commercial partners.

In love relationships, Aries I's may disarm Scorpio III's with their childlike innocence, completely captivating them. Once Scorpio III defenses are up, they don't easily come down, particularly if built up through a number of failed relationships; yet Aries I may seem to be able simply to walk through Scorpio III walls as if they didn't exist. This relationship inspires positive feelings that can drag either partner out of a lethargic or depressive rut.

Even so, the relationship's challenges may prove too much in the long run. Although perhaps gratified by Scorpio III attentions, Aries I's will not easily share their deepest feelings, and after a short and enjoyable affair may take off for parts unknown—and without a lot of goodbyes, either. Too often this treatment will result in further Scorpio III withdrawal, and in yet another promise to themselves never to let it happen again.

In friendships, Aries I's may find Scorpio III's overly demanding and controlling. Not content with shared activities, Scorpio III's will seek to bring their conflicts and searing emotions to the Aries I door, only to find they have reached the wrong address. Aries I's are capable of giving a lot in a friendship, but only up to a point; make them feel taken advantage of and they're gone. The claiming, needy side of Scorpio III's may, unfortunately, bring them to that point.

ADVICE: *Limit your goals. Don't let your imagination carry you away. Focus on the practical. Allow for honesty. Act conservatively.*

RHEA PERLMAN (3/31/48)
DANNY DeVITO (11/17/44)

Comic actors Perlman and DeVito first met at a 1971 off-Broadway play, with DeVito as a demented stable boy. Their long live-in relationship and subsequent enduring marriage has seen them rise to independent stardom.

Also: Bart Conner & Nadia Comaneci (married; Olympic stars).

March 25–April 2

THE WEEK OF THE CHILD
ARIES I

November 19–24

THE CUSP OF REVOLUTION
SCORPIO-SAGITTARIUS CUSP

STRENGTHS: **INTUITIVE, INTENSE, CREATIVE**

WEAKNESSES: **UNREALISTIC, FLUCTUATING, UNDEPENDABLE**

BEST: **LOVE**

WORST: **MARRIAGE**

A Swinging Pendulum

Mood swings bordering on wildness, and contrasting ideas and feelings, are likely to dominate this relationship. Yet despite its bipolar nature, and the fact that both of these two have difficulty directing their energies constructively, the relationship allows them to adopt the role of authority figure together, perhaps as co-leaders of a project, and so to carve out a united path. With so many emotional ups and downs, honesty is an imperative; although both parties are strongly moral and do their best to be truthful, they are often unable to be honest about indiscretions or transgressions. An agonizing struggle for the truth is likely to surface here, then, often wasting prodigious creative energy that could be channeled more constructively.

Both Aries and Sagittarius are fire signs, and the fiery personality aspects that these two share will make them compatible with each other. Both tend to value their intuitive side and to follow their hunches. But the relationship points in the direction of emotions, and this can trouble Aries I's, who have little interest in getting bogged down in what they see as a swamp of muddled and contradictory feelings. Although able to relate to the more active side of Aries I's, whether inspirational or confrontational, Scorpio-Sagittarians may also see a coarse and superficial quality in the Aries I denial of subtler emotions. Aries I's may also not be tough enough to hang in there with Scorpio-Sagittarians, hard-headed realists who will probably have little patience for what they see as Aries I naiveté and childishness. Should these two meet as childhood friends or siblings, their relationship may be close and intense, but it will have difficulty surviving into maturity, particularly as Scorpio-Sagittarians become more sophisticated and view their previous ideas with disdain. Aries I's, for their part, may reject Scorpio-Sagittarians whom they see as snobbish and forgetful of their roots.

Neither marital nor business partnerships in this combination are recommended. Should these two fall in love, however, a high unreality factor may allow the relationship to continue for some time.

ADVICE: *Even out your moods. Set your sights on the goal. Morality is easier to talk about than to live up to. Face up to feelings. Relax and be consistent.*

ERIC IDLE (3/29/43)
TERRY GILLIAM (11/22/40)

These members of Monty Python's Flying Circus are famed for their satirical antics on British and American tv. Idle's specialty was portraying fatuous bores; Gilliam, the only American member of the troupe, contributed brilliant animation to the series and later went on to direct surrealistic feature films.

DIANA ROSS (3/26/44)
BERRY GORDY (11/29/29)

Gordy, founder of Motown Records, has been the guiding light in Ross' singing career, and over the years they have been romantically linked. In 1994, Gordy wrote of being the father of one of Ross' 3 daughters. **Also: Clementine Hozier & Winston Churchill** (married); **Marvin Gaye & Berry Gordy** (brothers-in-law; singer sister).

March 25–April 2

THE WEEK OF THE CHILD
ARIES I

November 25–December 2

THE WEEK OF INDEPENDENCE
SAGITTARIUS I

Unaffected Youthfulness

This classic trine relationship (120° apart in the zodiac) produces an easy compatibility and excellent prospects for longevity, particularly for marriage. Even more promising is the fact that the relationship's catalyst and focus usually lie in the area of thought, so that it produces an intelligence far surpassing that of its individual partners. Ideas about ethics and the raising of children, as well as far-reaching philosophical speculations, characterize this matchup. It is also marked by an unaffected youthfulness, most noticeable in the survival of a strong physical bond, despite advancing age.

The intensity of the passion in love affairs between Aries I's and Sagittarius I's may lead to early burnout. After ecstatic highs, particularly in the bedroom, the partners may experience a gradual falling off of intensity. Not infrequently, however, such a love relationship may settle into an easier friendship, with both parties making fewer demands. One even wonders if these two might not have been better off restricting their feelings to friendship in the first place, for they can make excellent friends, whether of the same or the opposite sex, and may share many gratifying and challenging experiences. They may also be able to open their secret hearts to each other in a way they cannot do with others.

Aries I–Sagittarius I siblings, particularly of the same sex, may be precociously competitive, with largely negative results: the Sagittarius I will to win is so strong that a younger Aries I brother or sister may suffer from it for years. As parents, both Sagittarius I's and Aries I's are often yet not always conscientious: they can be so devoted to their own endeavors that they don't always have the patience to unravel the complexities of their children's emotional states. Moreover, their encouragement of their offspring's independence may later open them to the charge of not having cared enough—of being insufficiently involved and committed. These two must also be careful not to be so one-sided in their views that they become rigid, refusing to bend before crises that demand flexibility, sympathy and understanding.

ADVICE: *Regulate the flame of your passions. Remember that fire consumes air and, if permitted, will leave you breathless. Be patient.*

LEON WILKESON (4/2/52)
GARY ROSSINGTON (12/4/51)

Bassist Wilkeson and guitarist Rossington belonged to Lynyrd Skynyrd, a popular hard-rock band. Though their collaboration ended after a plane crash killed 3 other members in 1977, the pair reunited in 1987 with a new incarnation of the band. **Also: Van Gogh & Kirk Douglas** (film portrayal).

March 25–April 2

THE WEEK OF THE CHILD
ARIES I

December 3–10

THE WEEK OF THE ORIGINATOR
SAGITTARIUS II

Seeing Clearly

This relationship usually hinges on the issue of trust versus rejection. Sagittarius II's often suffer from rejection in their lives, having a tendency to put all of their eggs in the wrong basket, so they may not be overly trusting of Aries I's; the tragedy is that in this respect they may be turning a blind eye to one of the few types in the year capable of understanding and accepting them. Viewed clearly, this relationship can be a source of strength, faithfulness and sustenance to both parties. Yet it can also be considerably passionate and romantic, which may further delude both parties into discounting it, failing to see its strong underlying foundation. Indeed, passionate relationships in this combination are likely to generate a kind of unrealistic haze, obscuring the vision of both parties.

In some cases, distrust between these two will produce the very events they fear. When this occurs, they must try to understand their own roles in creating the disaster. An Aries I who refuses to be put off by a partner's suspicion, aloofness or downright hostility may force a Sagittarius II to see the honesty of his or her intentions, and a satisfying, productive relationship, whether it be friendship or marriage, may result. On the other hand, although Aries I's are generally honorable enough not to degrade or humiliate their Sagittarius II partners, they may be bewildered or even frightened if Sagittarius II's get swept away by intense feelings, and may be put off by certain peculiarities inherent in the Sagittarius II personality. If so, they may withdraw from the Sagittarius II's advances and refuse to get further involved, sometimes by simply dropping out of sight and refusing to answer the phone. When these two work together, the Aries I desire just to get the job done may be frustrated by Sagittarius II idiosyncrasies. Accordingly, the combination is not recommended for most work situations. In the family, Aries I parents may be very understanding of the unusual nature of Sagittarius II children and patient with their need to do things their way. Sagittarius II parents, however, are not always accepting of the unidirectional, often unheeding stance of their Aries I children. Again, the key is trust.

ADVICE: *Keep your eyes open. Don't let your vision be clouded by preconceptions or by the past. Don't be discouraged by rejection. Seek higher guidance.*

March 25–April 2

THE WEEK OF THE CHILD
ARIES I

December 11–18

THE WEEK OF THE TITAN
SAGITTARIUS III

Tipping the Scales

Aries I's and Sagittarius III's make worthy opponents for each other, although the matchup between the Child and the Titan may at times resemble that between David and Goliath, or Alice and the Queen of Hearts. The key to a successful relationship here will be balancing the strengths of the parties involved and working toward common goals. A capacity to work on problems tenaciously is inherent in the relationship, although this ongoing work is hidden from the world. The ability to think things through and address issues is particularly helpful. Initial meetings, whether amorous or social, can have a confrontational edge, which may add spice and enhance the attractiveness of further involvement. Sagittarius III's rarely let their guard down, but Aries I's, through their innocence and spontaneity, may well be able to breach their defenses.

In marriage, one or the other of these two will dominate; there will rarely be an equal balance of power. A hard-driving, career-oriented Aries I may try to lay down the law, but this will only work for a while—sooner or later the assertive power of even the most suppressed Sagittarius III will emerge with a bang. Marriages in this combination will work best when Aries I's reconcile themselves to playing second fiddle to Sagittarius III's as long as their freedom to choose, to come and go, and to make up their own mind on important issues is not compromised or infringed upon. Such an arrangement is quite possible in this relationship.

When Aries I's and Sagittarius III's are lovers, power struggles will emerge between them sooner or later. The fact that only one of them can come out on top will mean that in the long run probably both will lose. Yet these decisive, unidirectional and fiery individuals are actually quite similar and compatible as long as their willfulness and confrontational tendencies stay under control. If one of the lovers makes a decision not to fight, the other will usually accept this kind of unilateral truce, and a harmonious balance can be achieved. At work, the struggle to be the boss threatens to disrupt shared projects; better results will be reached when one of the two is clearly in charge.

ADVICE: *Peace may be in your best interest. Take the high road. Try to listen and to compromise. Sometimes, agree on who's the boss.*

March 25–April 2

THE WEEK OF THE CHILD
ARIES I

December 19–25

THE CUSP OF PROPHECY
SAGITTARIUS-CAPRICORN CUSP

Don't Worry, Be Happy

The focus of a successful relationship here will be to seek acceptance, psychological understanding and the lightening of heavy moods. The combination supplies a good example of people being attracted to a relationship because it mirrors themselves; this, of course, accentuates not only the negative in each partner's personality, here a self-absorption and a moodiness bordering on the morose, but also the positive—charm, and the ability to work in the service of an ideal. If it chooses, this relationship can act as a guiding light for others.

Aries I's can be impatient with Sagittarius-Capricorns who have gotten stuck in some ideology or who are overly involved in their own emotional state. Sagittarius-Capricorns are usually much too deep and complex to express themselves directly (except in anger or aggression), and more often than not the more direct Aries I's may take their quietness or absence of affect personally. Yet Aries I's also demand a lot of understanding, which self-absorbed Sagittarius-Capricorns are always not ready to give. Friendships or marriages between these two may feature long periods of silence, with corresponding resentment or denial. Dependent on positive outlooks to relieve the inner pressure of their own dark side, Aries I's will find little respite from Sagittarius-Capricorns, whose own moods will tend to drive them further down into themselves. It is therefore essential for these two to work at having a positive outlook and a good time together, and to put their personal problems behind them. Aries I's may well be sexually attracted to the deep and passionate Sagittarius-Capricorn personality, but this is no guarantee that the relationship will succeed. The relationship's longevity is, unfortunately, no index of its quality, for these partners can easily get locked into a mutually dependent embrace that neither of them has the strength to break. Thus they may carry on a love affair that doesn't seem to be going anywhere, yet at the same time refuses to fall apart, for years.

It may be possible for Aries I's and Sagittarius-Capricorns to work together as business partners or coworkers. In this context dynamic Aries I energies and enduring Sagittarius-Capricorn strengths may meld.

ADVICE: *Don't hang on too long. Learn to let go. Have more fun. Try to enjoy life without worrying. Seek self-awareness.*

STRENGTHS: **AUTONOMOUS,
AUTHORITATIVE, PRODUCTIVE**

WEAKNESSES: **UNACCEPTING,
UNFEELING, INEFFECTUAL**

BEST: **FRIENDSHIP**

WORST: **LOVE**

EDWARD STEICHEN (3/27/1879)
ALFRED STIEGLITZ (1/1/1864)

In 1902, these giants of 20th-century American photography established the avant-garde Photo-Secession group that challenged contemporary photographic style. Stieglitz was also Steichen's right-hand man in the publication of *Camera World* (1903–17).

March 25–April 2
THE WEEK OF THE CHILD
ARIES I

December 26–January 2
THE WEEK OF THE RULER
CAPRICORN I

Autonomous Domains

The creativity of this relationship will lie in a dynamic in which the partners have the strength and wisdom to carve out their own unquestioned domains, in the form of physical locations, duties, functions or activities in which they are autonomous and the other party has virtually no say. This might seem selfish, but questions of leadership and acceptance are paramount in this relationship and are likely to require this drastic sort of solution.

Serious conflicts are bound to arise when Capricorn I's are in a position of authority over Aries I's—for example, in a parent-child or boss-employee relationship. In the early years of such a pairing, Capricorn I dominance may provide Aries I's with the security and structure they so badly need, but sooner or later their opposition and rebelliousness against all tyrannical tendencies will inevitably be aroused. Should the Aries I be the boss or parent, the more passive and dutiful tendencies of Capricorn I's may bring a degree of harmony and effectiveness, as long as Aries I's act responsibly and sensibly. If they prove ineffectual, however, Capricorn I's will usually be prepared to take over the decision-making functions of the company or family.

Marital and love relationships are not especially recommended for this combination, since Capricorn I's will usually seek to limit or modify the individuality and freedom of an Aries I partner, something most Aries I's will be unable to accept. In the emotional sphere, these two are unlikely to share any expression of deep feelings. Friendship is probably the best bet here, whether or not the partners are of the same sex. Capricorn I's will admire and be amused by Aries I directness, and Aries I's will find Capricorn I practicality helpful and reassuring. Dynamism and protectiveness may meld here, then, perhaps producing a partnership in which the establishment or administration of a club, team or other social unit becomes the linchpin of a long-lasting and productive relationship.

ADVICE: *Find your own niche and hold on to it. Don't let yourself be kicked around. Look for practical solutions that can benefit everyone.*

STRENGTHS: **ENTHUSIASTIC,
INDEPENDENT, NONCLAIMING**

WEAKNESSES: **MANIC,
WITHDRAWN, DISAPPROVING**

BEST: **MODERN MARRIAGE**

WORST: **LOVE**

CARL SANDBURG (1/6/1878)
ROBERT FROST (3/26/1874)

Contemporary poets Sandburg and Frost were archrivals in establishing their literary preeminence. Frost, known for his pastoral, traditional rhyming verse, strongly disapproved of Sandburg's non-rhyming style that changed the course of American poetry. ***Also:* Gloria Swanson & Pola Negri** (famous feud); **Edward Steichen & Carl Sandburg** (brothers-in-law).

March 25–April 2
THE WEEK OF THE CHILD
ARIES I

January 3–9
THE WEEK OF DETERMINATION
CAPRICORN II

A Modern Marriage

This relationship can exhibit highly introverted and extroverted tendencies, with great pains taken to hide certain issues, only to bring them unexpectedly and flamboyantly to light one day. Preoccupations with money and power may overshadow more personal matters, which are constantly relegated to second or even third place. A lack of empathy or insight may forestall the emotional understanding needed when moods dictate withdrawal from the world. To escape or even deny the realization that something is missing, quiet depression may alternate with outgoing enthusiasm. Both of these moods avoid the problem at hand, and also keep the world from finding out much about what is really going on in the relationship.

Capricorn II's will constantly be irritated by what they see as unrealistic choices in business associates or favored family members on the part of an Aries I friend or mate—this although they can be as naive as their partner, just in other areas of life. Aries I's, for their part, will see Capricorn II attitudes as oppressive, and will find little or no need to reform. Should Capricorn II ambition or Aries I extroversion get out of hand, each partner may view the other as immoral or selfish and may be strongly disapproving.

As spouses these partners may put their careers first and will discuss not having children, needy pets or demanding domestic responsibilities. The independent modern marriage that results can work out as long as the scrutiny, judgment or disapproval of neither partner becomes a factor, and as long as neither party needs constant emotional reinforcement or attention. If the Aries I–Capricorn III relationship is a friendship, it should perhaps be kept light, since the time, strength or interest in establishing a firm connection is not usually forthcoming. An exception may be the case of lifelong friends, who may need to see each other only once or twice a year to keep their bond viable.

ADVICE: *Deal with emotional problems directly. Don't try to escape the truth. Be more empathetic. Control ambition.*

March 25–April 2

THE WEEK OF THE CHILD
ARIES I

January 10–16

THE WEEK OF DOMINANCE
CAPRICORN III

 RELATIONSHIPS

STRENGTHS: **CONSCIOUSNESS-RAISING, FUN, SYMPATHETIC**

WEAKNESSES: **COMBATIVE, ISOLATED, OVERDOMINANT**

BEST: **FRIENDSHIP, MARRIAGE**

WORST: **PARENT-CHILD**

Peas in a Pod

This relationship will bring out unexpected sides in both its partners: together they will yearn to investigate universal ideas, and they will share a hunger for a variety of experiences that enhance and deepen consciousness. Neither of these tendencies could be considered typical of either Aries I or Capricorn III individually. Furthermore, because the relationship brings out each person's "higher side," conflicts one might expect to occur between them do not materialize. The synergy of this combination stresses sensitivity and mutual respect and can also allow for a great deal of fun.

Capricorn III's like a lively atmosphere, something many Aries I's can provide. Aries I's, in their turn, will benefit from the attention of Capricorn III's and will gain comfort from their often powerful physical presence. Strong attractions can appear, grow and be sustained by the sympathetic vibrations between the earthy Capricorn III and the fiery Aries I. Thus the combination may become the basis for an enduring, family-oriented marriage.

It will be unusual for these two to carry on a long-standing love affair, however—their relationship will tend to move either toward the permanence of marriage or toward a long-term friendship. Both Aries I's and Capricorn III's tend to be reserved a good deal of the time, yet together they have a flamboyant side that they will enjoy sharing with family and friends. The couple can function well within a social circle and will like to pursue sports, hobbies and club activities together. Yet the core of the friendship is highly private—to gain fulfillment, these two will want to spend long periods of time sitting, walking and dreaming together.

Capricorn III parents don't always do well with Aries I children: although protective and responsible, they tend to be overly dominant. Within a stressed or even dysfunctional family group, however, an Aries I–Capricorn III pair of siblings may be one of the few stabilizing forces, especially if the biological parents are absent or incapable of discharging their responsibilities. In more normal family groups, however, Aries I–Capricorn III siblings of the same sex may exhibit strong competitive and combative tendencies.

ADVICE: *Spend quality time together. Don't be afraid to discuss serious issues. Don't isolate yourself or become self-satisfied. Stay objective.*

SUNE KARL BERGSTROM (1/10/16)
JOHN R. VANE (3/29/27)

Vane and Bergstrom are 2 of the 3 biochemists who shared the 1982 Nobel Prize in medicine. They pooled their research acumen in the area of prostaglandins and, among other things, explained the effectiveness of the world's most widely used drug—aspirin.

March 25–April 2

THE WEEK OF THE CHILD
ARIES I

January 17–22

THE CUSP OF MYSTERY & IMAGINATION
CAPRICORN-AQUARIUS CUSP

 RELATIONSHIPS

STRENGTHS: **EXCITING, PROTECTIVE, SYMPATHETIC**

WEAKNESSES: **EXCESSIVE, ADDICTIVE, CHAOTIC**

BEST: **LOVE, FRIENDSHIP**

WORST: **WORK**

A Protective Cocoon

This relationship may manifest a secretiveness and sense of privacy that isolate its partners in a protective cocoon, keeping them a bit out of touch with the world yet safe from the glare of public scrutiny. Much time will be spent building a safe haven for the relationship, whether metaphorically or literally. The involvement here may be so total as to arouse jealousy in others, especially family members. Care must be taken, then, not to form a closed community but to leave energies open for involvement with others. When the relationship is a personal one, the danger, of course, is that the partners get so wrapped up in mutual fantasy that they forget about mundane but stabilizing everyday demands. Keeping at least one of their four feet on the ground may be an achievement for them.

Business partnerships and co-worker connections are not recommended for these two, since they may constantly distract each other from the job at hand, making objectivity difficult or impossible. In marriage they can have great times together but may be unable to fulfill domestic, financial and parental responsibilities, at times resulting in chaos. Indeed, the great challenge of the successful Aries I–Capricorn-Aquarius relationship is to bring structure and order to shared activities.

In the spheres of friendship and love, on the other hand, this can be an extremely exciting relationship. Capricorn-Aquarians bring out the most dynamic and outgoing tendencies in Aries I's, who shine in their presence. Although Capricorn-Aquarians have a powerfully dark and eruptive side, their more unstable and violent tendencies are soothed rather than aggravated by Aries I energy, for they find such innocent and childlike energies disarming. As lovers these two can reach the heights of passion, as friends they can attain the deepest levels of mutual understanding and sympathy. Care should be taken, however, not to fall prey to sex and love addictions. In this relationship it may be absolutely necessary to avoid drugs and alcohol, which will fan its already excessive flames still higher.

ADVICE: *Try to bring some order into life. Stay in contact with the world. Don't close the relationship off from others. Too much pleasure can be too much.*

MUHAMMAD ALI (1/17/42)
HOWARD COSELL (3/25/20)

Sportscaster Cosell, whose polysyllabic, abrasive style brought him notoriety in the 60s and 70s, had a long, dynamic friendship with protean heavyweight Ali and was the first to express outrage over Ali's stripped title in 1967.

Also: Emile Zola & Paul Cézanne (close friends; writer/painter).

STRENGTHS: **SPIRITUAL, ENTHUSIASTIC, COLORFUL**

WEAKNESSES: **UNSTABLE, FRENETIC, DISTURBING**

BEST: **LOVE**

WORST: **MARRIAGE**

TAMMY TERRELL (1/24/46)
MARVIN GAYE (4/2/39)

Very close friends, Terrell and Gaye are known for their immortal duets of the 60s, including *Ain't No Mountain High Enough*. Gaye was devastated following Terrell's death from a brain tumor. **Also: Haydn & Mozart** (close friends; composers); **David Lean & Ann Todd** (married; director/actress); **Otto von Bismarck & Kaiser Wilhelm II** (chancellor/emperor).

March 25–April 2
THE WEEK OF THE CHILD
ARIES I

January 23–30
THE WEEK OF GENIUS
AQUARIUS I

Free Spirits

This relationship is bound to be scintillating and colorful, emphasizing the spiritual plane above all others. It can be hard to understand, perhaps suggesting a "past-life" connection to its partners and undoubtedly confusing them. To feel fully comfortable in this relationship, both Aries I and Aquarius I will need a maturity that is unusual for them.

Aries I's and Aquarius I's may have a destabilizing effect on each other that does not bode well for them as co-workers or marriage partners. Both of them value their independence highly and are unlikely to want to give it up for the sake of their relationship with each other. Free spirits, Aries I's and Aquarius I's will certainly admire each other, and their mutual attraction may well lead to an intense but perhaps short-lived love affair, involving the physical, the mental and the intuitive planes. The relationship will tap and stir each partner's emotional depths to an unaccustomed degree. Friendships between these two can work out well, with mutual understanding and sharing. Neither will have much patience for the other's moods, however, or much interest in helping the other out of the doldrums; they are really fair-weather friends. Should one partner prove too needy, perhaps falling into a depression after the loss of a job or the breakup of a love affair or marriage, the other may be unwilling to take on the responsibility of dealing with such pain and suffering.

Aries I–Aquarius I siblings lend liveliness to everyday family life. The commotion they often arouse together, however, may be disturbing to quieter or more thoughtful types. Earth- and water-sign parents can have a calming effect on this duo's frenetic energies but may find it difficult to put a cap on their overbrimming enthusiasm. Close bonds may develop in Aries I–Aquarius I parent-child relationships, whichever of the two is the parent. But the adults might let the children go their own way in most situations, without placing many limits or restrictions on them, and this lack of structure may prove unsettling to both Aries I and Aquarius I children, who need a gentle but firm hand.

ADVICE: *Calm down. Try to accept what can't be defined. Give up some freedom. Spend time by yourselves to strengthen your bond. Cultivate patience.*

STRENGTHS: **VERBAL, DEEP, INTERACTIVE**

WEAKNESSES: **TROUBLED, IMMATURE, COMPETITIVE**

BEST: **COMPANIONSHIP**

WORST: **CO-WORKER**

GLORIA STEINEM (3/25/35)
BETTY FRIEDAN (2/4/21)

Bonded by political and social activism, these leading feminists have crusaded together in the women's movement. A prolific writer, Steinem co-founded *Ms.* magazine. Friedan co-founded National Organization for Women (NOW) and authored a best-seller, *The Feminine Mystique*.

March 25–April 2
THE WEEK OF THE CHILD
ARIES I

January 31–February 7
THE WEEK OF YOUTH & EASE
AQUARIUS II

Rocking the Boat

Because Aries I's and Aquarius II's both have a frank, open and spontaneous outlook, one would think they would be magnetically attracted to each other and form an immediate bond. Yet their relationship often shows a need to confront the dark or shadow side of life and may probe realms that are deeply emotional, even troubled. The combination is very communication oriented, so its explorations will usually occur in the form of long discussions or debates. The relationship also carries with it a hidden but rather rigid structure of mental rules and obligations that will tend to make both partners uncomfortable.

If the relationship can be kept light, Aries I's and Aquarius II's may make excellent acquaintances or friends, sharing many of life's pleasures. Problems arise if they get involved in love affairs or live together, because then their interactions will be more complex and, often, disturbing. Conflicts will surely arise for these two should they compete verbally for the attention of others. As siblings or co-workers, they usually find it difficult or impossible to function together on a daily basis; each will constantly seek to take the spotlight away from the other. Parents or bosses put in the position of siding with one against the other (in other words, of picking a favorite) may figure the task not worth the trouble and wind up ignoring or rejecting one partner or both.

Marriages between these two are unlikely to work well, since neither party is likely to want to assume a more mature role. Should they have children, there are likely to be role reversals in which their offspring (particularly if born under the earth signs, Taurus, Virgo and Capricorn) assume responsibilities at an early age through parental default. Aquarius II's don't look for problems, so they don't find relationships with Aries I's easy to deal with, filled as they are with contrasting moods and outspoken attitudes. In a love affair, for example, Aquarius II insistence on an easy sensuality may periodically be disrupted by Aries I dissatisfaction and frustration. Likewise, the more dynamic Aries I's may come to resent what they perceive as cloying and retarding Aquarius II influences in the career area.

ADVICE: *Lighten up a bit. Try not to be so competitive. Appreciate sensuous pleasures. Be frank and open. Don't get bogged down in debate.*

March 25–April 2

THE WEEK OF THE CHILD
ARIES I

February 8–15

THE WEEK OF ACCEPTANCE
AQUARIUS III

RELATIONSHIPS

Through the Facade

STRENGTHS: **INVESTIGATIVE, SENSITIVE, INTRIGUING**

WEAKNESSES: **MISLEADING, CLASHING, SECRETIVE**

BEST: **MARRIAGE, SIBLING**

WORST: **BUSINESS PARTNERS**

The keynote to this relationship is discovery—in particular, being able to see through any facade that hides secret or enigmatic desires. In its efforts in this direction, the relationship will tend to set itself apart, isolating itself so that the work of discovery can continue undisturbed. There are many secrets to be revealed here, both within each partner and in the outside world. The more outgoing and dynamic aspects of the Aries I, for example, often conceal a needy individual with subtle dependencies, despite an independent stance; Aquarius III's will be able to uncover and accept this, through a combination of sensitivity (a function of this relationship) and distance.

Although they make a great show to the contrary, both these personalities secretly love to be wooed. And as long as aggressive Aries I's do not intimidate or scare off softer and more accepting Aquarius III's, this relationship is conducive to courtship, and to matters of love and passion. At the same time, an Aries I–Aquarius III marriage or sibling pair may feature a realistic, tough and pragmatic attitude, the Aquarius III balancing the sometimes naive and idealistic Aries I. Marriages between these two can work, usually with the Aquarius III taking the lead. Aquarius III's have a way of unlocking the softer, secret side of Aries I's and allowing them to express sympathy, nurturing qualities, and even sentimentality. A brother-sister relationship between these two may be one of the most successful possible for this combination. Their mutual understanding will be deep from an early age, and when they grow older they usually try to live close to each other, or even to share space under the same roof. Parent-child relationships between these two, on the other hand, particularly when the Aries I is the parent, are usually not rewarding, for there is likely to be miscommunication and a clash of wills.

These two do not make good business partners or team members. Aquarius III's are often scientific and rational types, who, although quite emotional in their personal lives, can be objective and cool on the job; these strengths do not meld with the often impulsive, direct and highly intuitive approach of Aries I's.

ADVICE: *Find the real you. Don't waste time on building defenses. Be honest in acknowledging your needs. Appreciate the interest of others.*

CARL BERNSTEIN (2/14/44)
BOB WOODWARD (3/26/43)

These tenacious journalists gave new meaning to the term "investigative reporting." The symbiotic teamwork of "Woodstein," more than anything else, helped expose the Watergate scandal that undid the Nixon administration. Their work garnered a Pulitzer Prize for the *Washington Post* and led to their book and film, *All the President's Men*.

March 25–April 2

THE WEEK OF THE CHILD
ARIES I

February 16–22

THE CUSP OF SENSITIVITY
AQUARIUS-PISCES CUSP

RELATIONSHIPS

Disarming the Armor

STRENGTHS: **DISARMING, DISCOVERING, AFFIRMING**

WEAKNESSES: **THREATENING, CRITICAL, UNFULFILLED**

BEST: **FRIENDSHIP**

WORST: **PARENT-CHILD**

This relationship involves a refusal to be stopped by walls and defenses. It will break through barriers, especially internal or psychological ones, often through a verbal battering of many thrusts and parries. Needless to say, there lurks within this combination the unfortunate tendency to use criticism as a weapon—verbal exchanges can become very sharp here. If a degree of empathy and sensitivity can be maintained, however, a lot of trust can result from the relationship's emphasis on openness.

The relationship's chemistry allows Aries I's to break through the often heavy armor of Aquarius-Pisces, who will often be enabled, in this context, to express their deepest need: to acknowledge and affirm the sensitivity they had when young. For their part, while they can accept dynamic Aries I energies, they will also be able to encourage the emergence of buried sensitivities in their partner, often through a combination of aggressive, determined, but nonetheless sympathetic approaches. Childlike Aries I energy thus melds with the Aquarius-Pisces capacity for intimacy, and the two may have a rewarding friendship based on honesty and trust. Marriages between these two are also often happy, but difficulties can emerge over the years if the spouses' criticisms of each other become sustained. Aries I's can be tremendously assertive in demanding the attention of Aquarius-Pisces, who are apt to feel a bit inadequate or unfulfilled in this matchup.

Aries I parents are not ideal for Aquarius-Pisces children, who may throw up walls behind which to retreat from them. In many cases Aries I's are simply too direct for their sensitive children to handle. An Aries I sibling can act as a bridge between a brother or sister and the world, particularly through shared hobbies and sports or club activities, for Aquarius-Pisces tend to gravitate toward either the personal or the universal and thus to miss out on the joy of everyday events. The more ambitious elements of the relationship augur well for the success of entrepreneurial or artistic endeavors in which a highly personal and individualistic approach may sweep the field of serious opposition.

ADVICE: *Be honest but sensitive. Respect intimacies. Keep a hold on your **aggressions**. Know when to back off. Beware of fixed assumptions.*

JOHN TRAVOLTA (2/18/54)
GABE KAPLAN (3/31/45)

Before Travolta skyrocketed to stardom in *Saturday Night Fever*, he co-starred with Kaplan on the hit tv series *Welcome Back, Kotter*, where their off-camera friendship enriched their creative working relationship.

Also: Diana Ross & David Geffen (affair; singer/producer).

STRENGTHS: GENTLE, IDEALISTIC, UNPRETENTIOUS

WEAKNESSES: UNREALISTIC, IMMATURE, DEMANDING

BEST: FRIENDSHIP, SIBLING

WORST: MARRIAGE

GEORGE HARRISON (2/25/43)
ERIC CLAPTON (3/30/45)

Miraculously, the long friendship between these musical collaborators has endured, despite Clapton's love for Harrison's wife, Pattie Boyd. After the Harrisons' divorce, Clapton married Boyd, the inspiration for his hit song *Layla*.

March 25–April 2
THE WEEK OF THE CHILD
ARIES I

February 23–March 2
THE WEEK OF SPIRIT
PISCES I

An Imaginative World

This relationship will revolve around an imaginative world that emphasizes physical grace, vivid fantasy and gentle idealism. A kind of balancing act is emphasized here, as well as conflicting energies that must be addressed. The relationship is very much about coming to terms with the relative and the absolute, the objective and subjective, the pragmatic and ideal. Aries I's and Pisces I's feel a close kinship, for all their differences; this relationship carries their love of purity and lack of pretension to higher levels.

The sensitive world of feelings that Pisces I's inhabit is foreign to Aries I's, but attractive and strange. At the same time, the straightforward and direct spontaneity and intuitive strengths of Aries I's often challenge Pisces I's to action and spur them on to their best efforts. The combination is perhaps most beneficial for siblings or friends, as long as limits are put on their emotional interaction and their responsibilities for each other.

The matchup may prove difficult in marriage, work or love. The Pisces I need for attention can drive Aries I's crazy, stretching to the utmost their capacity to give it. And it won't just be attention that Pisces I's will demand; sooner or later, they will want a far deeper kind of emotional involvement than Aries I's are prepared for, whether as lovers or spouses. Working relationships between these two are not recommended on the executive level or as boss-employee, but should the two be involved in a project as co-workers, they will be able to work harmoniously side by side, as long as their functions are clearly delineated and don't overlap too much.

Love affairs between Aries I's and Pisces I's can blossom quickly, but will fade just as fast when reality sets in. In the best-case scenarios, Aries I protectiveness and Pisces I appreciation will remain after their passion has cooled down, and the two stand a good chance of continuing on as platonic friends—as long as practical matters such as money, residence and shared possessions have been fairly dealt with. The relationship does not handle resentment and frustration well, so wiping the slate clean of previous failures and starting anew is preferable to endlessly rehashing the past.

ADVICE: *Stay on your own side of the bed. Let others make their own decisions. Be the best you are capable of being. Dreams can become realities.*

STRENGTHS: APPRECIATIVE, AESTHETIC, ORGANIZED

WEAKNESSES: SACRIFICING, BIZARRE, IMPRACTICAL

BEST: WORK

WORST: LOVE

NATHANIEL CURRIER (3/27/1813)
JAMES IVES (3/5/1824)

Currier and Ives were trade lithographers whose colorful prints of sentimental scenes were popular in the 19th century. Great merchandisers, the 2 friends touted themselves as "Publishers of Cheap and Popular Pictures."

Also: **Elton John & Kiki Dee** (musical duet); **Shirley Jones & Jack Cassidy** (married; actors); **Diana Ross & Mary Wilson** (Supremes; bitter breakup).

March 25–April 2
THE WEEK OF THE CHILD
ARIES I

March 3–10
THE WEEK OF THE LONER
PISCES II

Concrete Beauty

The focus of this relationship is twofold: first, insisting on a more literal meaning in the patterns of thought and speech, and second, bringing a greater aesthetic appreciation to everyday life. Specifically, the relationship will force its partners to concretize their plans in any kind of endeavor, with little allowance for vagueness or drift. Moreover, the combination can itself create an atmosphere that sharpens one's perception of beauty.

Pisces II's let very few people share their private inner life and will rarely allow entry to an outgoing and dynamic Aries I. But this is not to say that they won't get along, or will be antagonists, for as acquaintances or casual friends they may well work out a viable relationship. Marriages between these two are not recommended, however, since the sacrifices that Aries I's would have to make in order to satisfy the Pisces II desire for privacy, and need to create their own world, are unlikely to be realistic ones. Friendships here are likely to be quite unusual, with meetings being severely limited in their frequency and occurring in quite out-of-the-way places.

A positive aspect of any relationship in this combination, whether social, familial or personal, is that it may bring Pisces II's into more meaningful contact with the world. Shared creative projects are especially favored, with Pisces II fantasy and imagination being brought to the attention of the public through Aries I dynamism. Furthermore, the imaginative, creative side of an Aries I will quite likely be deepened and developed by contact with a Pisces II partner. Business, financial or executive partnerships are not as favored here as free-lance work on original products that these two can design and market together. Should a company arise to manufacture and sell such products, it will have a good chance of success as long as legal and fiscal guidelines are followed.

ADVICE: *Seek reliable financial advice. Keep good records. Make the world a more beautiful place by starting at home.*

March 25–April 2

THE WEEK OF THE CHILD
ARIES I

March 11–18

THE WEEK OF DANCERS & DREAMERS
PISCES III

Inevitable Awakenings

The pattern in this relationship is for information or insight to come to light suddenly and sometimes shockingly. Neglected issues will often brew until they burst forth, either in a dramatic flash of realization or simply as a gradually emerging truth. A lack of awareness is typical here, so it is not uncommon for this pair to be buffeted by outside events. This can create growth in the relationship but can also endanger it. Attempts at greater consciousness could smooth out some of the shock waves.

Should an Aries I and a Pisces III fall in love, they can keep going for a long time before awakening to the contradictions in their relationship. Aries I's have an inextinguishable need for independence, and any binding of their energies to the needs and demands of a Pisces III will become increasingly strained as the months and years go by. Pisces III's, on the other hand (not known for making realistic partner choices), may fail to comprehend how dependent they have become on their Aries I partners; perhaps needing to be needed, they may undergo a psychological crisis when the Aries I's at last assert themselves. Aries I's who have gone this far in freeing themselves are unlikely to slip back into their old role pattern. Marriages, then, are not particularly recommended here. Friendships are possible between these two, but not openhearted ones characterized by a sharing of deep feelings. They are more likely to be companionships based on common activities, perhaps involving a love of adventure, collecting or performance. Pisces III's have a flamboyant side that can meld with Aries I energies, as long as competition for the attention of friends and family does not get out of hand. Conflicts between siblings, and also with parents of the opposite sex, may be colorful and at times even entertaining, but are ultimately debilitating to the family's stability. Pisces III's who take the lead in the familial, work, social or love partnership may have a tendency to preach and to impose their philosophical views on Aries I's, who are put in the position of student. This is extremely difficult for Aries I's to abide, since they are extremely sensitive to being talked down to or babied. It will usually be only a matter of time before they rebel.

ADVICE: *Be more aggressive in dealing with personal problems. Don't assume that all is well. Strive for equality and balance.*

PATTIE BOYD (3/17/45)
ERIC CLAPTON (3/30/45)

Though married to George Harrison, Boyd was the object of Clapton's love for many years, inspiring his 1971 plaintive hit *Layla*, reworked and released again as a '93 hit. After Harrison and Boyd divorced in '77, Clapton and Boyd were wed. They divorced in '89.

April 3–10

THE WEEK OF THE STAR
ARIES II

April 3–10

THE WEEK OF THE STAR
ARIES II

Stellar Twins

Two Stars—is there room for both in the same firmament? Probably, but under one roof it can get pretty chancy. Both parties in this relationship need to be at the center of things, which may be a simple impossibility. As siblings or as parents, these two are likely to slug it out for attention, with the stronger or more tenacious winning out. There are really no winners in such conflicts, and the two Stars are better off coming to a mutual decision not to fight, and to shine peacefully in their own spheres.

Love affairs between these two are likely to be tempestuous, adversarial, and mercifully short. Were they to run longer, both lights would risk burnout in a massive supernova. Rebound from such an intense relationship is likely to be attempted with a much more passive and less demanding type. After a torrid affair, two Aries II's are unlikely to continue as friends—there is usually little left in this kind of relationship after the passion has cooled.

Marriage between two Aries II's must only be attempted with great care and great courage. Ideally, it should also involve shared work or career. Power struggles and stress usually build up exponentially in this relationship, depriving both partners of rest. In all honesty, Aries II's are such extreme personalities that they usually do better with more normal, less remarkable types than with each other. Most Aries II's demand that a partner be something of an orbiting satellite around them; should that partner be another Star, this demand will obviously not be satisfied.

For the same reasons, the friendship of an Aries II has its limits, but if both partners have their own, mutually exclusive circles of friends, or sets of satellites, things may work out. The less these two share in the way of human resources the better, although at work they may be surprisingly good at sharing space, equipment and ideas, as long as limits are firmly set and drawn.

ADVICE: *Relinquish center stage. Power struggles take away from creative energy. Promote equality. Secure your own area. Work on common goals.*

HENRY LUCE (4/3/1898)
CLARE BOOTH LUCE (4/10/03)

American playwright and politician Clare Booth married Henry Luce, the powerful publisher who built the *Time*, *Life* and *Fortune* magazine empire. The couple shared a long, happy life together as celebrities in political and literary circles.

Also: **Roger Corman & Francis Ford Coppola** (director/protégé); **Leslie Howard & Ronald Howard** (father/son; actors).

STRENGTHS: **DARING, SOCIAL, OUTGOING**

WEAKNESSES: **OUTSPOKEN, SELFISH, SUPERFICIAL**

BEST: **BROTHER-SISTER**

WORST: **LOVE**

PETE ROSE (4/12/41)
A. BARTLETT GIAMATTI (4/4/38)

As commissioner of baseball in 1989, Giamatti, a former president of Yale, was forced to ban Rose from the sport for life because the Cincinnati superstar had been betting on the game, sometimes even on his own team. Rose, a record-breaking player, was later also banned from the Hall of Fame.

April 3–10
THE WEEK OF THE STAR
ARIES II

April 11–18
THE WEEK OF THE PIONEER
ARIES III

Social Savvy

This relationship focuses on acquiring social skills and coming into a more meaningful connection with the world. A stimulating and productive matchup, it is not afraid to take risks, but its energies, albeit entertaining and theatrical, must be given direction. Aries is not usually considered a sociable sign, but in combination these two will focus a lot of energy on socialization, figuring out the best ways to handle people and perhaps even to climb the ladder of their milieu's society. Both partners will learn valuable lessons in interpersonal dealings through this relationship. Even so, their social success is not guaranteed; mistakes are inevitable, since as a unit they can be brash and outspoken. Aries II's require a lot of patience and attention, but this is precisely what Aries III's may be prepared to give. They understand Aries II fire and spirit, and will rarely compromise or betray it, since they know that Aries II's, if properly led toward a goal, can be a real powerhouse.

One danger here is that Aries II's may find it hard to accept or understand an Aries III ideology, religious affiliation or philosophical stance, and become stubbornly resistant to it. Aries II–Aries III love affairs are not particularly recommended, since both parties can be selfish in their demands, and unprepared to share love or affection. Due to a lack of earthy feelings, deep emotions or both, only in rare cases will the sensual side of their relationship be highly developed. If primarily based around a common lifestyle or profession, marriages between these two may work well, but a meaningful social life, through quality friendships, clubs or organizations, is vital. As siblings, these two may support and mutually challenge each other, particularly if they are of the opposite sex. It is quite likely that each will become involved with the other's friends. But such brother-sister relationships can pose problems for less energetic parents, who may be unable to keep up with their children's prodigious energies, and may also be threatened or at the very least distracted by them. As the parents or bosses of an Aries II child or employee, Aries III's will be well qualified to guide and direct the Aries II's prodigious energies.

ADVICE: *Try to find out what makes people tick, and put what you discover to work. Learn from your social blunders. Don't forget to relate to each other sometimes, too.*

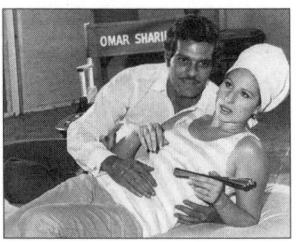
STRENGTHS: **PIONEERING, HARD-WORKING, EFFECTIVE**

WEAKNESSES: **SELFISH, UNSYMPATHETIC, OUT OF SYNCH**

BEST: **WORK OR SERVICE**

WORST: **FRIENDSHIP**

OMAR SHARIF (4/10/32)
BARBRA STREISAND (4/24/42)

Streisand's rise to stardom in the Broadway musical *Funny Girl* was furthered by the film version, where she played opposite Sharif. The romantic chemistry between them was electric, offending Streisand's then-husband, Elliott Gould.

Also: **Jerry Brown & Pat Brown** (son/father; CA governors);

Ravi Shankar & Yehudi Menuhin (musical collaborators).

April 3–10
THE WEEK OF THE STAR
ARIES II

April 19–24
THE CUSP OF POWER
ARIES-TAURUS CUSP

Forging Ahead

This relationship is usually without a strong emotional orientation, but business or labor-intensive projects can find great success, particularly those of a groundbreaking or pioneering nature. Hard work is characteristic of this matchup, although the partners' tempos are very different, and may clash. Even while focusing on their own goals, as a team these two rarely forget their fellow human beings. One can often find this duo forging ahead in areas with a large social purview, such as politics, even if only as a hobby or a form of service.

While Aries II's are go-for-it types who follow their instincts and react openly when stimulated, Aries-Tauruses are more controlled, and are masters of hanging back and waiting for the right moment to strike. They will often see Aries II's as impetuous and headstrong, and may in consequence be impatient or angry with them. Once the relationship gels, however, these two will usually be able to agree on the approach to and execution of a project, and can be most effective against strong competition in their field.

Interpersonally these two are unlikely to click. Aries II's need to be needed, while Aries-Tauruses pride themselves on needing no one—they hate to ask others for help, regarding this solution as a sign of weakness. There is usually little chance of love or sympathy arising between these two, particularly since both Aries II's and Aries-Tauruses resist others putting claims on them, and generally like to do the choosing when it comes to selecting a mate or friend. Should a powerful sexual attraction manifest here, tensions may build as the Aries-Taurus admires from a distance and makes plans to approach closer. An Aries-Taurus will never submit to being another admiring satellite revolving around the Aries II Star, but will usually wait for the latter to make the first move, or at least signal interest. Once Aries-Taurus does close in, however, it can be with frightening swiftness and power, and Aries II will either reciprocate or repulse the advance. Each partner can be equally selfish in demanding short-term gratification in this relationship, but although their parting may not be pleasant, they may at least have both gotten what they wanted.

ADVICE: *Build more for the future. Keep desires for immediate gratification under control. Don't be hasty—find the right time and rhythm for what you do.*

April 3–10

THE WEEK OF THE STAR
ARIES II

April 25–May 2

THE WEEK OF MANIFESTATION
TAURUS I

RELATIONSHIPS

STRENGTHS: **DEPENDABLE,
RESPECTFUL, INDOMITABLE**

WEAKNESSES: **DEPENDENT,
POWER-TRIPPING, SUPERFICIAL**

BEST: **MARRIAGE**

WORST: **FAMILY**

Power Partners

This combination can be a powerful one for partnerships of all kinds, especially in marriage or business. The focus here is mutual respect and an ability to delineate areas of dominance and expertise, as well as to hang in there and refuse to admit defeat—a trait that will hold this couple together through rough times. Rarely will these two reveal any problem or tension to the outside world; their relationship never forgets the importance of image, and always tries to make a good impression. It also favors group endeavors and is capable of powerful service to a cause, be it idealistic, commercial, artistic or familial.

The Aries II need to be surrounded by admirers will not necessarily annoy Taurus I's, who can be pretty thick-skinned, and also like to be needed—they will be happy to think an Aries II can't do without them. Indeed Taurus I's enjoy ownership, and may sometimes even come to think of an Aries II partner as another treasured possession. This will ultimately lead to rebellion from Aries II's, who in the end need freedom. They must be careful, however, to know how far they can go without arousing Taurus I anger, jealousy or revenge, which can be frighteningly destructive.

Love affairs between these two may last quite a long time, with the initial physical attraction even growing over the years. In fact Taurus I's and Aries II's can become quite mutually dependent, although neither will ever admit it. Should a power struggle arise over a particular person or issue, it will be only necessary for one partner to take a conciliatory stance to resolve things, at least temporarily.

These two have a good ability to handle issues within the relationship, but problems can arise if either of them sinks into a slump or depression, for the relationship is usually predicated on both of them being strong and dependable. If one shows weakness, the other may only be sympathetic up to a point. Similarly, chronic illness on the part of either the Aries II or the Taurus I can put an unbearable strain on the relationship.

ADVICE: *Quitting isn't always either the easiest or the worst alternative. Diplomacy and compromise are often required. Admit weaknesses. Release claims.*

VERNON CASTLE (5/2/1887)
IRENE CASTLE (4/7/1893)

A world-famous dance team, the Castles originated their own dances and popularized others. After Vernon died in a plane crash, the devoted Irene wrote her loving memoir, *My Husband*. **Also: Jos. Pulitzer & Wm. Randolph Hearst** (newspaper rivals); **Gerry Mulligan & Sandy Dennis** (married; saxophonist/actress); **Francis Ford Coppola & Talia Shire** (siblings).

April 3–10

THE WEEK OF THE STAR
ARIES II

May 3–10

THE WEEK OF THE TEACHER
TAURUS II

 RELATIONSHIPS

STRENGTHS: **SEXUAL, COOL,
OBJECTIVE**

WEAKNESSES: **UNCARING,
INHIBITING, ABRASIVE**

BEST: **SEXUAL**

WORST: **MARRIAGE**

Cool Detachment

This relationship often has a strongly mental and, furthermore, critical orientation, and is oddly lacking in emotional sensitivity. Even if sexual, it is cool rather than warm. This may prove a plus, however, since Aries II and Taurus II have a knack for getting on each other's nerves, so that the detachment inherent in the relationship can be its saving grace. Its talent for strategic thinking and the ability to know when to take action makes it well suited to a work situation; research in the social or physical sciences comes particularly to mind.

In love and marriage, on the other hand, tension is likely. Taurus II's have a strict moral stance that may lead them to question a great deal of Aries II behavior. And condemnation of what Aries II's see as perfectly natural may eventually eat away at their happiness and undermine their security. Taurus II's also like their mates to be strong and dignified above all, so that Aries II Stars will be barking up the wrong tree here in their constant need for compliments and attention. Moreover, the sharp and incisive way Taurus II's express themselves can get on the nerves of more balanced Aries II's and strongly upset more irritable ones. In the area of passion, the relationship may be more detached than soulful. Still, on a purely mechanical level sexual compatibility is high, and in erotic terms the relationship can be mutually fulfilling, featuring strong instinctual drives and perceptions. Aries II Stars must be free to shine and do their own thing, so they don't make particularly good students for Taurus II Teachers, and don't readily appreciate such a partner's didactic side. As co-workers, these two will inhibit each other, and frictions or blowups between them will slow down or stall their projects, unless they can maintain their detachment and their orientation toward a goal. If they are siblings, their competition for the attention of others can cause discomfort to all. Taurus II parents, however, can often be very encouraging of Aries II children's self-expression, and very understanding of their need to show their more outgoing and dramatic side, particularly if it makes other family members happy.

ADVICE: *Soften your stance a bit. Cultivate an easy sensuality. Learn to relax. Get emotionally involved. Don't be afraid to express your feelings.*

RUUD LUBBERS (5/7/39)
HELMUT KOHL (4/3/30)

Dutch minister-president Lubbers and German Chancellor Kohl were the political leaders of their countries during the 1980s. They worked closely together in the formation of a united Europe, the EEC (European Economic Community). Both men were also heads of their respective political parties (coincidentally with the same name), the Christian Democratic Party.

STRENGTHS: **EXUBERANT, STABILIZING, SATISFYING**

WEAKNESSES: **TROUBLED, UNCOMMITTED, ESCAPIST**

BEST: **COMPANIONSHIP**

WORST: **MARRIAGE**

April 3–10

THE WEEK OF THE STAR
ARIES II

May 11–18

THE WEEK OF THE NATURAL
TAURUS III

Stabilizing Companionship

This relationship can be highly energetic, filled with excitement, change and diversity. It has a wild streak, and strong attractions are typical here. The tendency is toward lack of inhibition, including a frankness of expression that can often come across as critical or hurtful. Often, however, the truth can be a blessing, since neither Aries I's nor Taurus III's are known for their self-awareness.

Since both the individuals involved are free spirits, difficulties may arise if their relationship requires them to give up any independence or accept any responsibilities. The fun-loving and zany side of Taurus III will appeal to the more extroverted type of Aries II, and they can have great times together as friends or lovers. But Aries II lovers are more realistic than Taurus III's, who tend to get carried away by their fantasies, and this may cause conflict. Mutually challenging activities, not the least of which may be satisfying each other, will keep these two from being bored and make them faithful, to an extent—both Aries II's and Taurus III's tend to have a roving eye. As friends of the same sex, Aries II's and Taurus III's may have a rewarding relationship of the kind that emphasizes companionship, and participation in a host of adventuresome or social activities, rather than the development of close emotional ties of sharing and trust. The lack of deep feeling here may actually be stabilizing, for the combination's tendency to outspokenness will cause less damage, and neither party will have to handle the other's shadow side, which can cause trouble if brought into the open. If Taurus III's direct their undeniable wild side toward drugs and similar obsessions, it will prove too much for Aries II's to handle. Aries II's may also be impelled to flee the relationship if sex and love addictions surface in the Taurus III; the level of pain may surpass the level of pleasure.

Marital and business partnerships between these two are usually unfavorable, since neither the ability nor the desire to endure suffering and work out problems, particularly of a personal nature, is high here. Better, then, to keep the relationship light, without too much responsibility, and to keep a back door open for escape if necessary.

ADVICE: *Have fun, but take responsibility for your actions. Try not to blurt out the first thing that comes to mind. Challenge helps growth.*

SPENCER TRACY (4/5/1900)
KATHARINE HEPBURN (5/12/07)

As an acting team in 9 films, Tracy and Hepburn were peerless, but their 27-year-long romance is legendary. Tracy never did divorce his Catholic wife, though they spent years apart. **Also: Michelle Phillips & Dennis Hopper** (briefly married; singer/actor); **Efram Zimbalist & Alma Gluck** (married; violinist/diva); **Francis Ford Coppola & George Lucas** (director/protégé).

STRENGTHS: **EXCITING, ENERGETIC, INTERESTING**

WEAKNESSES: **STUBBORN, RESISTANT, COMBATIVE**

BEST: **SIBLING**

WORST: **FRIENDSHIP**

April 3–10

THE WEEK OF THE STAR
ARIES II

May 19–24

THE CUSP OF ENERGY
TAURUS-GEMINI CUSP

Stubborn Refusal

The focus of this combination, unfortunately, is a stubborn refusal to give ground; also, both Aries II's and Taurus-Gemini's generally need to be the center of attention. As you can imagine, then, the relationship will rarely be suited for marriage, or for co-worker duos. It may even be difficult for these two to develop a friendship, since they may expect mutual friends to declare a primary allegiance to either one or the other. Adversarial competition and even combat may threaten here, but such conflict will rarely develop fully, since either or both parties will usually back off in dislike before the explosion, and will do their best to ignore animosities. Should these two put their power struggles aside, however, the relationship has an inherent capacity for building a home, team, company or other structure on a sound foundation.

Similarly, although Aries II's and Taurus-Geminis aren't usually attracted to each other physically, their high energy levels can guarantee some exciting moments. It is also possible for them to work out and even express their antagonisms in the sexual arena, so that their darker feelings and socially unacceptable impulses can lead them into some of the more interesting byways of love. In extreme cases, in fact, a kind of perversity can underlie this pairing. Taurus-Geminis want to please others, and will often sacrifice their egos in doing so; Aries II's, complementarily, have a tremendous need to be admired and served. On the surface, then, these two would seem to meld harmoniously, though perhaps unhealthily in certain cases, but for the fact that while Taurus-Geminis are happy to please others they are not prone to paying court to them. Taurus-Gemini parents may enjoy seeing their Aries II children shine and succeed in the world, particularly in the competitive sphere. Aries II parents, however, may be threatened by their Taurus-Gemini children, and may get into power struggles with them. Jealousy and antagonism between Aries II and Taurus-Gemini siblings is more rare—they can usually work out their conflicts through play, notably sports and games, and provide a good match for each other's boundless energies.

ADVICE: *Seek the high road whenever possible. Don't get bogged down in competition and combat. Not taking a stand at all is sometimes best.*

DOUGLAS FAIRBANKS (5/23/1883)
MARY PICKFORD (4/9/1893)

Dubbed the "king" of Hollywood royalty" and America's Sweetheart," these silent-film stars married in 1919. They entertained lavishly at their mansion, Pickfair. They founded United Artists with Charlie Chaplin and D.W. Griffith to take creative and financial control of their careers. Their famous marriage ended in 1935.

April 3–10

THE WEEK OF THE STAR
ARIES II

May 25–June 2

THE WEEK OF FREEDOM
GEMINI I

Solid Trust

GEORGE JESSEL (4/3/1898)
NORMA TALMADGE (5/26/1897)

Jessel, a vaudeville entertainer, was "America's Toastmaster General," famous for emceeing social and charity affairs. Although she was a popular silent-screen heroine, Talmadge failed to adjust to talkies. They married in '34 and divorced 5 years later.

Also: Albert Broccoli & Ian Fleming (film producer/author of James Bond novels).

The fire (Aries) and air (Gemini) of this combination form an explosive mixture, but the relationship's real focus is a bond of deep emotion, which can only be established through solid trust. As friends, lovers or mates, these two can only be successful together given near total independence for both parties; one of the few ways this can happen is through an open or free marriage or love relationship. If possessive attitudes are relinquished here, a remarkable acceptance and understanding can hold sway. Another scenario is that faithfulness or monogamy will rule the relationship, which is capable of fortifying parties who might otherwise be easily led astray. The prominence of humor here can lend a further strength to the relationship.

Aries II's and Gemini I's often have an unsettling effect on each other, however. Both are easily irritated and upset, and long periods apart may be necessary to calm things down. Yet such frictions can also be stimulating, and the relationship's moods and anger may quickly pass. In a day-to-day living situation, Aries II work capacity and energy combined with Gemini I quickness and technical expertise can guarantee the success of many domestic, creative or commercial endeavors. Indeed working relationships between these two can be splendidly productive, even though they may get on each other's nerves far more than is comfortable, experiencing a near-constant irritation and friction. Here humor helps a lot. And there are relationships that survive and even flourish on banter, bitter-sweet put-downs and even ridicule, whether well meant or not, and Aries II–Gemini I pairings may well be of this type.

Combative relationships between these two can be very destructive, and where possible should be avoided. Emerging in families, whether as parent-child or sibling pairs, they can be the despair of all around them, always rising to new levels of strife.

ADVICE: *Extend an open rein to each other. Others will often live up to your trust. Avoid adopting a double standard. Minimize bickering and strife.*

April 3–10

THE WEEK OF THE STAR
ARIES II

June 3–10

THE WEEK OF NEW LANGUAGE
GEMINI II

Problems As Lessons

L.A. REID (6/7/57)
BABYFACE (4/10/59)

One of R&B's most successful songwriting and production teams brilliantly together since '83, producing for such top vocalists as Paula Abdul, Bobby Brown and Whitney Houston. They formed the record company LaForce in 1989, but parted ways in 1993 due to creative differences.

Also: Maurice de Vlaminck & Raoul Dufy (Fauvist painters).

This is a relationship that can teach its partners a lot. Divisive problems are sure to emerge here, but seeing them as challenges to be worked on and solved, and as opportunities for growth, will offer a chance to achieve harmony and wholeness. These two will often want to share with other people what they have learned from their relationship with each other; they will also periodically need to distance themselves from the outside world in order to digest the lessons gleaned.

These partners may initially be attracted to each other: Aries II's will appreciate the vivacity of Gemini II's, finding them entertaining and funny, and Gemini II's will be attracted to the brighter side of Aries II's, admiring their robust approach to both work and play. Particularly on the physical level, this relationship can go like a house on fire at first. Unfortunately, though, it can burn out just as quickly. This is when the partners can start learning from each other. Aries II's, for example, have a shadow side that they often have a great deal of trouble getting to know and expressing; a Gemini II may well activate this shadow side, making it available to be explored. Working through difficult periods with a caring and attentive Gemini II may involve all kinds of emotional problems and depressions for an Aries II, but may also offer a real way of getting in touch with his or her deeper self. Married Gemini II's and Aries II's will share a love of entertaining friends, throwing parties, sharing sports and fitness activities, and going out in the evening. This extroverted streak will need to be balanced, however, by quiet and relaxed times together at home, something they may both have to work on. Here again there are important lessons to be learned, particularly if children are involved.

On the down side, Aries II's may be irritated by the flakier aspects of Gemini II's, and Gemini II's for their part may eventually become fed up with the excessive aspects of the Aries II personality. But it may not be possible for Aries II's to scale back their habits and activities, and if the Gemini II's impatience and the Aries II's dissatisfactions are not dealt with, the relationship may disintegrate.

ADVICE: *Keep impatience under control. When challenged, have faith in the power of love. Work actively on problems—the rewards can be great. Be sure to spend time alone.*

STRENGTHS: CHARMING, MAGNETIC, DEEP

WEAKNESSES: CLAIMING, UNREALISTIC, NEEDY

BEST: BUSINESS

WORST: LOVE, MARRIAGE

FANNY BURNEY (6/13/1752)
DR. CHARLES BURNEY (4/7/1726)

Dr. Burney was the foremost music historian of his time in England. His daughter, novelist and diarist Fanny Burney, wrote *Evangelina* in 1778, a landmark work in the novel-of-manners genre.

Also: **Colin Powell & George Bush** (general/commander-in-chief); **Francis Ford Coppola & Carmine Coppola** (son/father; director/composer); **Monteux & Stravinsky** (conductor/composer).

April 3–10
THE WEEK OF THE STAR
ARIES II

June 11–18
THE WEEK OF THE SEEKER
GEMINI III

A Magnetic Mirage

The initial phase of this relationship can be deep and magnetic, almost hypnotic, and is further augmented by an intriguing charm, pleasure orientation and overall sensuousness. The partners cannot help but be swayed by these influences, and once ensconced in the relationship they will find it difficult to emerge from it or leave it behind.

Neither Aries I or Gemini III is used to this kind of energy, and neither will know how to handle it. Gemini III's are likely to put Aries II's up on a pedestal; prone to hero- or heroine-worship when young, they are likely to repeat childhood patterns in their adult love relationships and friendships. If so, they will be casting the Aries II in the latter's favorite role, as star. The egotism of Aries II's may initially impress Gemini III's as strength and self-confidence until it becomes apparent how needy these personalities really are. Usually the more realistic of these two in their choice of mates, Gemini III's will probably realize early on that Aries II's are not for them. Even so, the relationship's magnetic attraction will prove difficult for them to get free of, attracted as they are to all that intrigues. In fact Gemini III's may find themselves morbidly fascinated by their own entrapment in the relationship, and by Aries II's seemingly fixed role as the centerpiece of an intricate web.

In the family, the Aries II–Gemini III relationship can be more rewarding, even outstandingly so, particularly with Gemini III's the parents to Aries II children, and as long as such parents don't release their own frustrations or disappointments by projecting their personal goals onto their children, forcing them to overachieve in challenging professions. These two can also make an effective combination as business partners, with Aries II's blazing the trail and Gemini III's attending to financial matters. Here the relationship's inherent charm can win over clients and win accounts. Both parties are risk-takers, but they will usually be cautious enough to make their calculated gambles pay off.

ADVICE: *Keep your distance. Maintain privacy. Don't be controlled by old scripts. Beware of fixed roles. Find your own real strengths.*

STRENGTHS: NATURAL, UNASSUMING, PASSIONATE

WEAKNESSES: CONFLICTING, UNSUITED, HURT

BEST: LOVE

WORST: BUSINESS

CHARLES FARRELL (6/19/02)
GALE STORM (4/5/21)

Farrell, one-time silent-film star, played opposite Storm in tv's *My Little Margie*, which featured 126 episodes that ran from 1952–55. The pair interacted well in their comic "womanizing widower" and "meddlesome daughter" roles.

Also: **James Garner & Mariette Hartley** (Polaroid commercials).

April 3–10
THE WEEK OF THE STAR
ARIES II

June 19–24
THE CUSP OF MAGIC
GEMINI-CANCER CUSP

Relaxed in Love

This relationship has a strong sense of the relaxed, natural and unpretentious, and a strong dislike of fuss and bother. Together these two exhibit a simple, even inspiring grace. Aries II's generally need to be surrounded by admirers, but may give all that up, preferring one unaffected glance, kiss or embrace from their Gemini-Cancer lover to all the starry-eyed attention of their fans. Since Gemini-Cancers give lavishly of their admiration and devotion if they are truly in love, this relationship can usually satisfy even the strongest Aries II needs. Aries II's may well respond with a passionate intensity that Gemini-Cancers will find sexually and emotionally rewarding. As marriage or living partners, these two may have a little difficulty in adjusting to each other, primarily because of the Gemini-Cancer need for privacy. Aries II's will be prepared to give up a lot for Gemini-Cancers, and can remain faithful, but their need for social contact may leave Gemini-Cancers sitting alone on many evenings, or, worse, trying to cope with a houseful of unwanted guests. Should the Aries II make it clear to others that their door is always open, the Gemini-Cancer may be forced to take steps to scale down the traffic, and conflicts are bound to result. In arguments, Aries II aggressiveness may prove too much for sensitive Gemini-Cancers, who may withdraw. Yet conflicts can be negotiated and tensions diffused, simply through the relaxation inherent in the relationship.

Robust Aries II career drives are unlikely to find favor with more low-key Gemini-Cancer ambition, and this relationship is not recommended in business and at work. Furthermore, Gemini-Cancers who truly desire worldly success must operate in their own, highly individual way, which will often limit their participation in group endeavors. Their tendency to take the lead will also reduce their ability to meld with an ambitious Aries II.

Gemini-Cancer parents can be understanding and sympathetic with their Aries II children, but Aries II parents of Gemini-Cancer children are less effective. Siblings in this combination can generally live and play naturally together, particularly when of the opposite sex.

ADVICE: *Try to compromise. Be diplomatic in making suggestions or demands. Be open to mutual social interaction. Beware of controlling attitudes.*

April 3–10

THE WEEK OF THE STAR
ARIES II

June 25–July 2

THE WEEK OF THE EMPATH
CANCER I

RELATIONSHIPS

STRENGTHS: **VISIONARY, BUSINESS-WISE, EXECUTIVE**

WEAKNESSES: **PAINFUL, ANTAGONISTIC, REBELLIOUS**

BEST: **COMPANIONSHIP**

WORST: **LOVE**

Not Too Close

The bond will be deep and the feelings intense, but combative and antagonistic drives rule this relationship. The deeper the feelings, in fact, the more rebellious the energies usually at work. Acquaintanceships and companionships, then, are more favorable with this combination than marriages, love affairs or friendships, and these two may function best of all as co-workers or business partners. As long as deeper personal contact is not required to any large degree, these two personalities' very different strengths may complement each other beautifully. The technical proficiency and sound money sense of many Cancer I's meld well with the ambition and drive of Aries II's. Together these two have an executive ability that can prove useful, and lucrative, in business.

Aries II's generally find Cancer I's much too strange to become deeply involved with, and Cancer I's in turn may be put off by Aries II aggression and need for attention. These two actually have a lot to teach each other, but their relationship is unlikely to overcome the emotional barriers between their fundamentally opposite natures. There may be a substantial sexual or romantic attraction between them, but it probably won't lead anywhere, and if it does, it may ultimately prove painful to both parties. As friends, these two are usually unsuited to deep emotional sharing, but their mutual strong need for physical expression can make them excellent sports or fitness partners, with Aries II's taking the lead.

Cancer I's can be very understanding parents but not particularly good role models for Aries II children, who will usually want a much more dynamic and self-confident choice than their Cancer I parent to emulate. Yet the emotional side of an Aries II, often repressed or ignored, can be deeply touched by a Cancer I parent, who may thus teach the Aries II the worth of emotions and of spiritual values early on in life. As parents, many Aries II's have neither the patience nor the understanding to deal with the difficulties and personal problems of Cancer I children.

ADVICE: *Keep it businesslike and objective. Develop respect and cultivate trust. Respect emotional differences.*

WILLIAM WYLER (7/1/02)
BETTE DAVIS (4/5/08)

This prodigious director and famous actress crossed romantic paths during the filming of *Jezebel* in 1937. The affair ended a year later, but they remained friends, with Wyler later directing Davis in *Little Foxes* (1941). In 1948 they attended the Oscar ceremonies together. ***Also:* Paul Robeson & Lena Horne** (friends; singers).

April 3–10

THE WEEK OF THE STAR
ARIES II

July 3–10

THE WEEK OF THE UNCONVENTIONAL
CANCER II

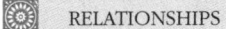
RELATIONSHIPS

STRENGTHS: **SELF-ACTUALIZING, PROLIFIC, ENERGETIC**

WEAKNESSES: **CONFLICTED, PROJECTING, OVERDEPENDENT**

BEST: **MARRIAGE**

WORST: **FAMILY**

Unlocking Energies

This combination tends to reveal to its partners sides of themselves that they never knew existed, or that they have always secretly wanted to know. It is a relationship, then, that sets both partners on a road to self-discovery. As such, it unlocks enormous energy, which usually becomes its focus: where is all that energy to be put? What does one do with the talents and skills that the relationship reveals? One puts them to use, of course, almost frantically. As a result, the relationship will be known for its frenetic pace, and its achievements.

Since Aries II and Cancer II birthdays are square to each other (90° apart in the zodiac), conventional astrology would predict that these two personalities would not get along or be a good match. They are indeed very different, and conflicts are indeed sure to arise, but a mutual fascination may result in a pleasurable love affair or an interesting and rewarding marriage. Once the relationship is established, the synergistic process of personal realization can begin. While Aries II's benefit from the much-needed self-discovery offered by this matchup, they can help Cancer II's step out into the world to realize some of their wishful fantasies. It may also happen that Cancer II's merely project their dreams and desires onto their partners, being satisfied to watch the Aries II act out their secret ambitions. A Cancer II parent who makes such projections on an Aries II adolescent may do no harm as long as both parties are aware of what is going on. Sensitive Cancer II's who engage in hero worship of an Aries II parent or authority figure, on the other hand, may find that the object of their admiration is busy with her or his own pursuits, and doesn't always have time for them.

In friendships, Cancer II's who show Aries II's their whole inner world of feeling can gain a deep and lasting relationship. The only danger of this very unusual matchup may be that the partners become too dependent on each other. The final test may come if one of the parties leaves, when it will become apparent whether or not they can function as well-rounded human beings without each other.

ADVICE: *Focus on individual strengths as you discover and follow your own path. Beware of mutual dependencies. Direct your energies wisely.*

MARSHA MASON (4/3/42)
NEIL SIMON (7/4/27)

Simon—brilliant playwright, film and tv writer, and librettist—is America's most popular comedy writer. In 1973 he married Mason, an accomplished stage and screen actress who appeared in 3 of his movies and won an Oscar nomination for *The Goodbye Girl.* Their marriage lasted until 1983. ***Also:* Walter Huston & Anjelica Huston** (grandfather/granddaughter; actors).

GERALD FORD (7/14/13)
BETTY FORD (4/8/18)

Former fashion model and dancer in Martha Graham's ensemble, Betty met the future president during a 1948 campaign. A forthright First Lady, she publicly discussed her mastectomy and, in her autobiography, revealed her alcohol and drug dependencies.
Also: Jerry Brown & Linda Ronstadt (affair; politician/singer).

April 3–10
THE WEEK OF THE STAR
ARIES II

July 11–18
THE WEEK OF THE PERSUADER
CANCER III

Chafing Against Restraint

Strikingly independent, this relationship chafes against almost any form of restraint. Together, this pair will overturn structure willy-nilly. The matchup's devil-may-care attitude toward the existing order will be very attractive and freeing, especially to Aries II's, but can ultimately prove dangerous. Sobriety will eventually set in as the two begin to revolt against each other. This relationship will cause others to want to follow its lead, so care must be taken to wield its power carefully.

Cancer III's are often persuasive people who could sell a salesman back his own product, but they may have little luck with Aries II's. For one thing, Aries II's are so busy striving toward their career goals that they usually have no time to stop and listen to Cancer III sales pitches. For another, Cancer III's may become so dazzled by the Aries II Star that they get tongue-tied and lose their chance. In any event, these two will usually lack both the shared traits and concerns that would hold their relationship together emotionally and the ability to handle the independence required here. Lasting love affairs or marriages in this combination are unlikely, then, but the matchup usually has better luck as a friendship—these two may enjoy good times together, as long as Cancer III's keep their judgmental, bossy side under control and Aries II's don't get carried away by selfishness or vanity.

As professionals working together, particularly in an entrepreneurial environment, Aries II's and Cancer III's may be able to achieve more than at any other time, and to advance their personal aspirations and standings. Their ambitions can meld well if they are partners on the same side, but if they are rivals their clashes can be terrifying. In out-and-out competition for, say, the lead position in an organization, each can be quite ruthless, or can unilaterally break off the relationship. Sibling relationships too may be competitive, even combative, and strife can emerge well into adulthood, perhaps on the death of a parent. Aries II children will often resent Cancer III parents as manipulating and controlling, and Aries II parents may bring out Cancer III children's insecurities, perhaps through hero worship combined with low self-esteem.

ADVICE: *Give up power struggles if you want to get closer. Put childhood conflicts behind you. Eliminate bossiness. Pull together.*

MARY WELSH HEMINGWAY (4/5/08)
ERNEST HEMINGWAY (7/21/1899)

As Hemingway's patient and forgiving 4th wife, Mary Welsh was made to order for this macho adventure novelist who dominated countless lovers and previous wives. The marriage lasted until his death in 1961.

April 3–10
THE WEEK OF THE STAR
ARIES II

July 19–25
THE CUSP OF OSCILLATION
CANCER-LEO CUSP

Exciting Activities

Outgoing and adventuresome, this combination values excitement and even danger; activities ranging from hang gliding to river rafting, scuba diving and snow-boarding are not unusual here. In this aspect the relationship can be a lot of fun, but psychological support and deep emotional understanding are seldom well developed here, so that friendships and marriages tend to stay at a relatively superficial level, and have little to fall back on in times of trouble or stress. This coupling works best when geared toward transcending physical or metaphysical limits.

With their hard-working natures and their desire to meet the everyday practical needs of others, Aries II's may nevertheless prove a great support to Cancer-Leos incapacitated by depression or moodiness. In fact the Aries II partner is often called upon to do double work until the next Cancer-Leo emotional upswing. Cancer-Leos also have a sensitive, emotion-oriented side, which can be sympathetic to the problems of Aries II's and may help them to discover and express themselves openly in more passionate relationships.

If these two are live-in lovers or mates, their biggest problem is likely to be that the security Cancer-Leos so desperately need is undercut rather than augmented by Aries II popularity. Watching their partner be surrounded by admirers, and being bombarded by the sounds of telephone, fax and front door bell, are unlikely to put Cancer-Leos in a settled frame of mind. As parents, Cancer-Leos may find this aspect of their relationship with an Aries II teenager almost unbearable at times.

Should the relationship manifest in the area of sports or business, it usually shows the kind of guts and drive that guarantees success; the challenging aspects of the matchup usually bring out the aggressive, ambitious sides of its partners. Even so, working relations may at times be unfulfilled, due to a lack of appreciation and understanding on a personal level.

ADVICE: *Seek emotional stability. Reflect on how you give support. Strive for deeper understanding. Express feelings honestly.*

April 3–10

THE WEEK OF THE STAR
ARIES II

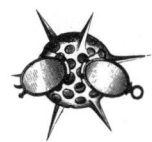

July 26–August 2

THE WEEK OF AUTHORITY
LEO I

Buffeting Competition

  RELATIONSHIPS

STRENGTHS: STIMULATING,
INDEPENDENT, UNIQUE

WEAKNESSES: OVERDRAMATIC,
UNCOMPROMISING, COMBATIVE

BEST: MUTUALLY CHALLENGING

WORST: FAMILY

Fortunately or unfortunately, the keynote of this relationship is often hard-fought competition or outright combat. The upside of this periodic open warfare is that it spurs the relationship on to new heights of achievement; the combination emphasizes independence and originality to an extreme degree. Both these personalities are self-assertive, and for good or ill, passions will run high here, while sympathy and understanding will be noticeably lacking. If the considerable ambitions of Aries II's and Leo I's are directed to the same goal, however, the relationship can be very successful.

If it reaches the stage of marriage, the Aries II–Leo I relationship can attain a modus vivendi, a sort of truce, including a tacit agreement not to fight. Should the partners disagree, and be unable to discuss their differences, they may choose to just ignore each other, or to walk away and leave things to sort themselves out. This approach, however, may lead to great frustration and eventually a breakup. When Leo I's set themselves up as unimpeachable experts on any subject, for example, their Aries II partner may well respond by turning a deaf ear, or may push their spouse's buttons by cleverly praising an established authority's contrasting point of view. On the other hand, the Leo I attachment to ideals and principles may lead more self-centered Aries II's feeling a bit left out in the cold.

Kindness, patience and understanding are unlikely to be passed on to the children of this relationship. In marriages and love affairs, this pair may experience ecstatic sexual highs between periods of hard work and independence, but may never reach deeper levels of human feeling, whether together or with others in the family.

Needless to say, in the work sphere this duo is extremely well matched, whether as adversaries or associates, since they are both extremely willful and usually know exactly what they want. Should they both desire the same object, person or job, open struggle is likely to surface. When working in smooth combination as team players, mates or co-workers, on the other hand, these two can be unbeatable.

GARY MERRILL (8/2/14)
BETTE DAVIS (4/5/08)

Merrill and the "First Lady of the American Screen" were married in 1950 while starring together in *All About Eve*. Merrill, who usually portrayed grim, humorless parts, lived in his famous wife's shadow. They divorced in 1960. **Also: Eddie Duchin & Peter Duchin** (father/son; pianists).

ADVICE: *Try to learn compromise. Tone down your more excessive drives. Keep lines of communication open. Be patient. Listen to suggestions and criticism.*

April 3–10

THE WEEK OF THE STAR
ARIES II

August 3–10

THE WEEK OF BALANCED STRENGTH
LEO II

Mutual Admiration Society

  RELATIONSHIPS

STRENGTHS: UNDERSTANDING,
ENERGETIC, COMMUNICATIVE

WEAKNESSES: OVERDEPENDENT,
UNREALISTIC, UNSTABLE

BEST: FRIENDSHIP

WORST: WORK

The trine relationship between Aries II's and Leo II's (approximately 120° apart in the zodiac) is traditionally thought to make their combination an easy, comfortable one, and indeed this matchup can work out well, particularly in the area of friendship. The relationship emphasizes communication, and will develop a personal and intimate common language—not necessarily a verbal one—that can be the basis for a great deal of intimacy. These two both work and relax well together, sharing humor throughout.

Marriages in this combination may be very successful. Aries II's must respect the Leo II need to be left alone, however, and must also resist depending too much on their spouse's habitual balance and stability: should the Leo II become unglued, the Aries II may go into a tailspin after years of dependency on his or her reliable mate. Nor should Leo II's glorify or idealize their partner too much—in fact this combination's tendency to form a mutual admiration society may undermine the relationship's stability by preventing it from confronting and working through problems. Aries II's tend to look up to Leo II's, and Leo II's are glad at last to meet someone who can match them in energy and intensity.

In love, Leo II loyalty will be important in holding the relationship together. This has its downside, however: if Aries II's are unhappy they will not hesitate to search around for solace or a change of scene, or perhaps will go on wild binges, leaving the Leo II doggedly hanging in there. Much pain may result for all concerned if the Leo II refuses to let the relationship fall apart even after it has outlived its healthy span.

As co-workers these two may have rough times. For all their strength and self-confidence, Leo II's can react badly when forced to confront failure. Aries II's are tougher, but the sight of them continuing blithely along after a crisis or setback may not be the easiest thing for Leo II's to accept.

JOHN HUSTON (8/5/06)
WALTER HUSTON (4/6/1884)

John directed unforgettable films, including *Treasure of the Sierra Madre*, for which father, Walter, and son both won Oscars. Hollywood rogues, Walter was a notorious womanizer, John a rowdy drinker. **Also: Hugh Hefner & Kimberly Conrad** (married); **Francis Ford Coppola & Martin Sheen** (director/actor; *Apocalypse Now*); **Mick Abrahams & Ian Anderson** (Jethro Tull).

ADVICE: *Keep in touch with the world. Acknowledge and solve problems. Don't put all your eggs in one basket. Cultivate diversity and flexibility.*

April 3–10
THE WEEK OF THE STAR
ARIES II

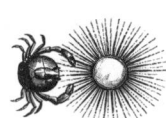

August 11–18
THE WEEK OF LEADERSHIP
LEO III

The Best and Worst

ROBIN WRIGHT (4/8/66)
SEAN PENN (8/17/60)

Known for his portrayals of rebels, outsiders and criminals, actor Penn now also directs. After a brief, tumultuous marriage to Madonna, he married Wright, Tom Hanks' love interest in *Forrest Gump*. The couple has 2 children. **Also: Francis Ford Coppola & Robert DeNiro** (restaurant partners; director/actor); **Mary Pickford & Buddy Rogers** (married; actors); **Rob't Downey, Jr. & Deborah Falconer** (married).

Looming large, this combination is one to be reckoned with: in any area, this pair won't hesitate to use whatever means are at their disposal, including unethical ones, to achieve their aims or to win. Depending on the goal, then, the matchup can bring out both the best and worst in its partners. Within the relationship, both personalities are unlikely to back down from a confrontation, making marital, business and other partnerships that require daily contact likely to be fraught with periodic conflict and crisis. The main issue will be over which partner dominates the other.

As a unit, the relationship has tremendous charisma, persuasiveness and power, and many will be attracted to it. If there is a love affair, it may well be a passionate one. Since each party has an intense need to dominate, ego-tripping and resentment are likely to abound. So great a challenge do these two represent for each other that the affair may go on for some time, particularly if it is a covert or illicit one.

Same-sex siblings are likely to fight for dominance as they enter adolescence, but opposite-sex siblings can form a close and enduring relationship. As parents and children, Aries II's and Leo III's are fated to work out dominant/rebellious drives, no matter which is the parent and which the child. Aries II–Leo III friendships can be very close, as long as competition is limited to some harmless and controlled arena, such as sports. Any other conflict, particularly over the affections of a third party, is likely to break up the team. The relationship must usually come first if it is to survive.

ADVICE: *Develop common ideals and try to live by them. Moderate ego and power drives. Beware of jealousy and relationship triangles.*

April 3–10
THE WEEK OF THE STAR
ARIES II

August 19–25
THE CUSP OF EXPOSURE
LEO-VIRGO CUSP

Acting Out

COUNT BASIE (8/21/04)
BILLIE HOLIDAY (4/7/15)

Intense, soul-wrenching blues singer Holiday toured the country with Basie, a pianist, composer and the leader of one of jazz history's greatest bands. They knew each other until Holiday's tragic death in 1959 from depression and drugs.

Also: Colin Powell & Norman Schwarzkopf, Jr. (Gulf War generals).

This relationship often involves psychological projection, since in many ways an Aries II is a Leo-Virgos revealed. Aries II's, in other words, with their forthright drive for success, act out the secret desires and the self-confidence that Leo-Virgos can keep inside for years; and when Leo-Virgos watch shining Aries II Stars in action, they may be viewing a living projection of their own suppressed self. Meanwhile, as Leo-Virgos seek in Aries II's their own ability to be the star, Aries II's will be learning from Leo-Virgos lessons about independence, self-sufficiency and the preservation of one's own inner privacy. What is the ultimate purpose, then, of this relationship? To seek and find in the other what has been lost, or never truly revealed, in oneself. Thus the relationship can serve an important function in each individual's quest for wholeness.

Leo-Virgos wait a long time before revealing themselves to the world. It is quite possible that they will initially disapprove of Aries II extroversion, which may strike them as impetuous and lacking in self-control. Yet a part of them may admire their Aries II friend's extroverted pose, since eventually they will want to experience this trait for themselves. It is unlikely, however, that they will ever fully join the Aries II fan club. To the same degree that Aries II's need other people to depend on them, Leo-Virgos are self-sufficient, and loathe depending on anyone. As lovers, Leo-Virgos are unlikely to give themselves completely to Aries II's, since they require a level of understanding and faithfulness that Aries II's just may not supply. The relationship is unlikely, then, to reach the heights or depths of love or passion. Similarly, an Aries II and a Leo-Virgo are unlikely to form the deepest of friendships, unless the former is really drawn irresistibly to investigate the mysterious turns and byways of the latter's character.

On the face of it, marriage may not be a good bet for these two. Should they marry, neither may be willing to make the commitment to having children or giving them the time and attention they need. Furthermore, the burden of domestic work and responsibility may tend to fall in the lap of the Aries II, who will become the central hub around which the family revolves.

ADVICE: *Remember that what you admire or dislike in others is usually a part of your own makeup. Find your own path and stay on it. Be more honest about your feelings.*

April 3–10

THE WEEK OF THE STAR
ARIES II

August 26–September 2

THE WEEK OF SYSTEM BUILDERS
VIRGO I

Getting the Job Done

RELATIONSHIPS

STRENGTHS: **HARD-WORKING,
RESPONSIBLE, ACHIEVING**

WEAKNESSES: **INSECURE,
CLAIMING, UNACCEPTING**

BEST: **MARRIAGE**

WORST: **ROMANCE**

Hard work will be of primary importance in this relationship; the focus will also be on dividing responsibility and roles to get the job done. The relationship may begin at work, on a leisure-time or professional project, and wind up as a fast friendship.

Aries II's have a deep need to share their work, and this may find fertile ground in the patience, devotion and discretion of the Virgo I personality. In fact Virgo I's may get closer to Aries II's than all of the latter's other admirers or flatterers, simply because they are willing to get in there alongside them to achieve the task at hand. Both these personalities are energetic workers, and their approaches, though different, do not clash. In the pursuit of their outward activities, Aries II's may actually be hiding from themselves, while the Virgo I work penchant has more to do with a need to serve, and also with a talent for taking structured action. Even though Aries II's may be unable to understand or relate to the more complex aspects of the Virgo I personality, these two may develop a sound marital or business partnership, with Virgo I's actually benefiting from the company of someone who does not take their moods or depressions too seriously, and who insists on either taking them out and having a good time or concentrating on objective pursuits.

Should the relationship involve romance, there is a danger that Aries II charisma will bring out Virgo I insecurities, particularly with the many admirers of the Aries II hanging around. Should Virgo I's feel rejected and suffer a loss of self-esteem, they may well back off and end the relationship. Ideally, this pair's ability to work hard at something will be applied to the relationship as well.

Siblings in this combination can benefit the family group greatly through their ability to satisfy the needs of others, as long as their efforts can be coordinated without too much conflict. In another family scenario, the spontaneity and excessiveness of Aries II children can be constructively guided by understanding Virgo I parents without robbing them of their individuality.

ADVICE: *Coordinate your efforts and structure your activities. Try to be more sympathetic. Work on psychological problems, especially insecurities. Escape is not the answer.*

CHRISTOPHER DARDEN (4/7/59)
MARCIA CLARK (8/31/53)

Darden and Clark, prosecutors in O.J. Simpson's trial, were rumored to be romantically involved. Afterwards, Darden stated they'd only become "close friends and confidants."

Also: **Michelle Phillips & John Phillips** (married; Mamas & Papas); **Hortense de Beauharnais & Louis Bonaparte** (married; Napoleon's stepdaughter/brother); **Billie Holiday & Lester Young** (friends; musical collaborators).

April 3–10

THE WEEK OF THE STAR
ARIES II

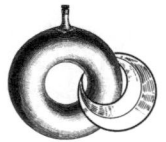

September 3–10

THE WEEK OF THE ENIGMA
VIRGO II

Uncommon Intimacy

RELATIONSHIPS

STRENGTHS: **IMAGINATIVE,
INTIMATE, CREATIVE**

WEAKNESSES: **BIZARRE,
INCOMPATIBLE, INEFFECTUAL**

BEST: **SEXUAL**

WORST: **WORK**

This relationship grows out of a strange combination, but it works in hidden ways that no outsider would suspect. Its essence is mysterious yet magical, and should love be permitted to bloom, it can be quite charming—much to everyone's surprise.

On the surface, Virgo II's are discriminating, even fussy individuals who would seem unlikely to be attracted to the raw energy characteristic of Aries II's. Yet they may be secretly attracted to Aries II charisma, even gaining vicarious satisfaction from the attention that others pay these Stars. Should they go so far as to feel that they possess or even just understand an Aries II, whether in fantasy or actuality, they may be proud of the fact that they can lay claim to such a sought-after item.

If sexual, the relationship may be close and even erotically adventurous, since both Aries II's and Virgo II's admire technical proficiency. If Virgo II's hanker after the kind of energy Aries II's can provide, things will be straightforward. If not, Aries II's are not about to change to fit the many complex and unusual requirements of Virgo II's, who may consequently be forced to use more subtly persuasive means to get what they need. Interesting and unexpected intimacies may emerge between these two, most of which will not be apparent to the outside world. Whether or not it gets physical, the relationship is marked by romantic fascination. These partners can truly admire each other from afar, being strangely attracted to what they view as their opposite—introverted Virgo II to a blazing extrovert, outgoing Aries II to a strange introvert. Like romances or affairs, friendship, family and business relationships in this combination can exhibit such an unusual bond as to confound those around them. No matter what the relationship's nature, neither partner is likely to want or be able to share profound emotional or spiritual levels of experience with each other. This will matter little, since the intimacies within the relationship will keep it on stable ground. In business, however, the relationship's chemistry may not be conducive to forwarding an enterprise's success.

ADVICE: *Pursue your fantasy, but be sensitive to conventional attitudes. Cultivate the spiritual side. Try to be more open. Don't exclude others.*

MIKLOS ESTERHAZY (4/8/1582)
PAUL ESTERHAZY (9/7/1635)

The Esterhazys, with a long family tradition of art patronage, also played a major role in Austrian and Hungarian history. Miklos rose to political prominence and wealth by loyalty to the Hapsburgs. In 1687 son Paul became imperial prince.

Also: **Charlotte Ford & Henry Ford II** (daughter/father; socialite author/Henry Ford's grandson).

KATHERYN MURRAY (9/15/06)
ARTHUR MURRAY (4/4/1895)

The Murrays taught social dancing to the nation from the 20s, later hosting a popular tv "dance party," and opening a dance studio chain. Inseparable, they symbolized ideal togetherness in both work and play.
Also: Washington Irving & James Fenimore Cooper (contemporary American writers);
James Garner & Lauren Bacall (romance; actors).

April 3–10
THE WEEK OF THE STAR
ARIES II

September 11–18
THE WEEK OF THE LITERALIST
VIRGO III

Stiff Resistance

As partners, these two are unlikely either to give ground to others or to be too flexible with each other. Their relationship is marked by battles to mark out territory and decide who will rule the roost. A forward, demanding attitude characterizes their combination; compromise or diplomacy are nearly impossible here. Unfortunately, each partner brings out the other's selfish aspects, so that marriages and friendships may travel a rocky road.

In marriage and at work, the relationship will benefit if common causes demand the attention of both partners. As long as they both benefit, these two can in fact get along and even cooperate. Should it become clear that one is being rewarded more than the other, however, almost any joint venture they are engaged in is likely to suffer. Virgo III's can be ruthless about walking away from living or working relationships with little explanation, but in Aries II's they may have met their match in the hot potato department—that is, in the ability to drop what they are doing with total abruptness if it turns troublesome.

These two are unlikely to form a lasting love relationship, even if they arouse each other's fire. Short and passionate romantic couplings are generally the order of the day. Aries II's and Virgo III's will rarely want to spend enough time together to become friends, but on the other hand they are not subject to the kind of mutually destructive drive that would make them enemies or rivals. The relationship often does best when its partners choose to keep a polite distance from each other, whether out of respect or out of lack of interest.

In the family the Aries II–Virgo III relationship is often willful and headstrong, and can catalyze tremendous battles, whether these two are siblings or parent and child. A lasting peace may be impossible here, but in times of stress the duo is capable of pulling together to salvage mutual interests.

ADVICE: *Try to be more flexible. Cultivate understanding and the ability to compromise. Tone down your combative stance. Take the time to explain.*

LINCOLN STEFFENS (4/6/1866)
WALTER LIPPMANN (9/23/1889)

An eminent journalist and political reformer, Steffens was the foremost muckraker of his time, exposing corruption in business and politics. He became a mentor to Lippmann, the brilliant editor, columnist and author whose writing influenced an entire nation of readers. Both were notably empathetic in their social and political causes.

April 3–10
THE WEEK OF THE STAR
ARIES II

September 19–24
THE CUSP OF BEAUTY
VIRGO-LIBRA CUSP

Deepen the Bond

The test of this relationship is whether the partners can empathize with each other. There is certainly no guarantee that they can, although their relationship can help make this happen. Since neither Aries II's nor Virgo-Libras are particularly concerned with the inner workings of either their relationships or themselves, in a way they are perfect for each other. Together they may try to understand the issues of their own connection. Not the least of these is the fact that this relationship wants to present itself to the outside world in the most refined light possible. Tinkering with its inner workings will be necessary to accomplish this aim. Almost inadvertently, this process will result in a deepening bond within the relationship—and in a deeper understanding.

Still, the relationship will initially be based on the superficial. Drawn to attractive people, Virgo-Libras can find much to admire in the appearance of Aries II's, and will find it gratifying that so many pay court to these Stars. Virgo-Libras can be extremely trendy, and will pride themselves on having a popular Aries II as a companion or lover. Aries II's for their part may be gratified to have been chosen by such discriminating and graceful individuals. If empathic feelings and the desire to look deeper do not eventually emerge, however, marriage or long-standing friendship is probably better not contemplated. Attractiveness and popularity fade, and so may Virgo-Libra desire for a no-longer-stunning Aries II partner. Unless Aries II's have a special interest in aesthetic matters, meanwhile, they may easily tire of Virgo-Libra interest in art objects, bric-a-brac and interior decorating or design. In the workplace, Virgo-Libras may both demand and fail to find a level of sophistication or chic in Aries II co-workers, who may conversely view Virgo-Libras as snobs. The Aries II desire to be at the center of every project may also run counter to Virgo-Libra taste and become a stumbling block to any joint effort. Perhaps the best combination for these two is as family members, where they will have a great deal to teach and share with each other, and will improve the image of their group.

ADVICE: *Beauty fades, character doesn't. Work on adopting less trendy values. Don't be swept away by glitz and glitter. Try to understand each other's feelings.*

April 3–10

THE WEEK OF THE STAR
ARIES II

September 25–October 2

THE WEEK OF THE PERFECTIONIST
LIBRA I

Career Goals

 RELATIONSHIPS

STRENGTHS: **WORLDLY,
DETERMINED, SUCCESSFUL**

WEAKNESSES: **MEDDLING,
COMPETITIVE, OVERINVOLVED**

BEST: **WORK, SEXUAL**

WORST: **MARRIAGE**

This relationship usually focuses on career. Aries II's and Libra I's characteristically share a drive toward success, and this becomes the core of their relationship. They may quite possibly meet as co-workers on a project and then decide to broaden their relationship when the job is done, or even while continuing to work together. They are both competitive people, and their ambition is often reflected in the intensity of their love or friendship. In such cases they must beware of burnout, for if they spend all their time working together, either their public or their private relationship is bound to suffer.

Libra I's may drive Aries II spouses crazy with their indecision and procrastination. Their efforts to present themselves as decisive will only make things worse, being quickly exposed as self-delusive by Aries II's whose expectations have not been met. Aries II's for their part will be stung by Libra I criticism and perfectionism. After all, they like being just what they are (and being admired for it), whereas Libra I's are born reformers who think they can improve anyone or anything. In objective pursuits, the Aries II motto is "If it works, don't fix it." Libra I's, on the other hand, usually can't keep their itchy hands from trying to making things run more smoothly.

These two are ardent lovers. Extremely attentive to their partner's romantic and sensual needs, Aries II's and Libra I's may carry on a long-standing sexual relationship. If their desires remained unspoken, things would probably work out fine, but Libra I's always want to talk about everything, particularly what they think needs improvement. Sooner or later, Libra I perfectionism will take its toll on Aries II's, who can't stand being constantly analyzed and corrected. Eventually the Libra I checklist of what they would like done for or to them in intimate situations will begin to bother Aries II's, who like to be themselves and to follow their intuition, avoiding fixed routines. The best outlet for this combination will always be career. If bent on the same goals, these two can accomplish more together than apart. Setting aside their differences in the name of achievement is possible and profitable for them.

ADVICE: *Try to identify clearly the goals you share, and put your focus there. Back off—your involvement is too heavy. Let things happen as they will.*

MARLON BRANDO (4/3/24)
ANNA KASHFI (9/30/34)

Brando divorced Kashfi, his first of 3 wives, in 1959 after a 2-year marriage. In 1964, she purportedly suffered a breakdown after forcibly taking their son, Christian, from Brando's home. *Also:* **Boss Tweed & Thomas Nast** (corrupt politician target of political cartoonist); **Dennis Quaid & Randy Quaid** (brothers; actors).

April 3–10

THE WEEK OF THE STAR
ARIES II

October 3–10

THE WEEK OF SOCIETY
LIBRA II

An Unconventional Education

RELATIONSHIPS

STRENGTHS: **EDUCATIONAL,
STIMULATING, SINGULAR**

WEAKNESSES: **STRANGE, DISHAR-
MONIOUS, DISAPPOINTING**

BEST: **MARRIAGE**

WORST: **CO-WORKERS**

This relationship's primary concern will be to analyze, chronicle and examine the workings of the people and the world around it. Since this is very much the forte of Libra II's, they will act as the teachers here and will probably enjoy the relationship more than Aries II's will. But Aries II's have much to learn in this regard, and in Libra II's they gain the perfect authority. More advanced Aries II's will engage in this relationship eagerly, knowing that it will be a real education for them. These two are exact opposites in the zodiac, positioned 180° apart. Their relationship, then, is highly unconventional, private and not easily understood by others.

There can be a strong attraction here, but Libra II's may ultimately have difficulty in handling the direct and uncompromising energy of Aries II's. In interpersonal relationships, an Aries II can approach a Libra II like a knife cutting butter. Libra II's will do their best to make the relationship more agreeable and less strange, but their penchant for compromise is usually a poor defense against Aries II willpower. Still, the ability to observe an Aries II at close range will often prove irresistible to them.

Libra II's know a great deal about the world and its inhabitants. They may be just the right people to take Aries II's under their wing, teaching them a great deal about how to dress, how to act, in fact how to present themselves generally in the most advantageous way. Always eager to be the center of attention, wiser Aries II Stars will lap this information up. As parents or mates, then, Libra II's can be excellent guides and helpers for Aries II's. Friendships between these two may be warm, with a strong bond of sympathy and appreciation.

As co-workers, on the other hand, these two may not gel. Busy as they are in observing the world and each other, it may be difficult for them to focus on getting ahead. The relationship will have its rewards, however: Libra II's tend to be indecisive and unsure of themselves, and in this area self-confident and driving Aries II's have their own lessons to teach Libra II's about becoming successful in the world. From Aries II's, Libra II's can learn how to promote themselves and to take more decisive action without waffling.

ADVICE: *Toughen up. Don't spurn more conventional solutions. Learn about the world through shared experience. Be understood. Try to speak each other's language.*

JULIAN LENNON (4/8/63)
JOHN LENNON (10/9/40)

Julian, Beatle John's son from a first marriage, spent most of his life in England, apart from his father, who lived with Yoko Ono in NY. Also a musician, Julian gained industry recognition with his successful first album, *Valotte*. *Also:* **Houdini & Buster Keaton** (godfather/godson); **Donald Barthelme & Frederick Barthelme** (brothers; writers).

April 3–10
THE WEEK OF THE STAR
ARIES II

October 11–18
THE WEEK OF THEATER
LIBRA III

Emotional Volatility

DARYL HALL (10/11/49)
JOHN OATES (4/7/48)

Hall and Oates teamed up in 1972 to become among the hottest rock & roll duets of the 70s and 80s. They separated in 1985 after their popularity waned. In 1988, they reunited without notable success.

Also: Lt. Charles Wilkes & John Wilkes (nephew/great-uncle; social reformer/explorer); **Paul Robeson & Eugene O'Neill** (collaborators; actor/playwright).

This relationship speaks of temperament, challenge and high passion. It has a tendency for dynamic confrontations, and puts a premium on grim determination and on the ability to persuade or convince. In all of these partners' struggles, the winner, or at least the least damaged party, is likely to be the one who can stay objective and not get carried away by a flood of emotion.

Aries II–Libra III love affairs are liable to be stormy, punctuated by breakups, play-acting, mock emotion and manipulation. For the most part, frustration, depression and repression are not issues here, since the relationship is so volatile as to leave little hidden. If these two can keep from tearing each other apart, however, they may find their challenging relationship pleasurable and fulfilling. Whether they are live-in lovers or spouses, their daily life can be highly rewarding, particularly for the Aries II, and as long as the extreme need of Libra III's for independence is respected—as long, that is, as there are no undue family or domestic responsibilities to cope with.

Either member of this duo is likely to bring out the other's extroverted side, and either can be the life of the party. One consequence of this is that competition and jealousy can recur between these two. The Libra III come-on, of course, is usually cooler and more detached than the fiery Aries II approach, but when these partners are on a collision course, Libra III's are capable of exploding in fury. Each of these personalities needs to be at center stage, and should they meet there, each will demand an equal share of the attention. Because of the relationship's competitive tendencies, its activities are sometimes better off confined to the gym or playing field than the bedroom or corporate boardroom. Rather than friendships, Aries II's and Libra III's are more likely to develop companionships in which they share dangerous adventures, or partnerships in a particular sport. Libra III's are not usually family oriented, but the one exception is a close bond with a sibling, usually of the opposite sex, when growing up, and Aries II's are a particularly good bet for this role.

ADVICE: *Try to give way to each other. Learn to share the spotlight. Develop more cooperation and communication. Cultivate emotional control.*

April 3–10
THE WEEK OF THE STAR
ARIES II

October 19–25
THE CUSP OF DRAMA & CRITICISM
LIBRA-SCORPIO CUSP

A Sword of Damocles

SAMUEL TAYLOR COLERIDGE (10/21/1772)
WILLIAM WORDSWORTH (4/7/1770)

These 2 major British Romantic poets together wrote the *Lyrical Ballads,* an important collection of poems. Powerfully entwined in life and work, intellectual Coleridge influenced the moody Wordsworth.

Also: Cornell Capa & Robert Capa (brothers; photographers); **Andre Previn & Dory Previn** (married; conductor-composer/singer); **Ram Dass & Timothy Leary** (friends; 60s hippie gurus).

Dominating others and each other will be an ever-present theme in this combination. Both Aries II and Libra-Scorpio tell it as they see it, leaving little room for niceties, an approach that can easily border on coercion in their relationship with each other. Should they be united in a common goal, however (unlikely though this may be), they can easily dominate others.

Aries II's who plunge in head over heels in love with Libra-Scorpios can expect some difficulty: like a child suddenly and ruthlessly exposed to the adult world, they will be practically defenseless against this controlling and critical partner's searching mind and emotional power. To put it simply, if the Libra-Scorpio is pleased, things will go well; if not, then Aries II's can expect endless frustration in trying to serve or please a dominant master who cannot or will not be satisfied. In many ways, this dissatisfaction is like a sword of Damocles that the Libra-Scorpio dangles precariously over the Aries II's head.

Marriage may be problematic for these two, as they have very different approaches to life, and both may seek to impose their own way on the relationship. Aries II's proceed more by intuition than by book learning, and often want to translate their ideas into immediate action; Libra-Scorpios, on the other hand, like to have time to mull things over, and may see Aries II energy as rash and impetuous, Aries II judgment as naive and untutored. A Libra-Scorpio parent may look on the energy of an Aries II child as raw material to be worked and molded into a more finished product. Unfortunately, this is usually not at all what the Aries II has in mind, and there may be endless argument and conflict. At work, the relationship has a better chance of success if the Libra-Scorpio is the company owner or executive and the Aries II is the employee. In this way Aries II energies can be directed and supervised, and if the job is a good one, few complaints or difficulties will arise.

ADVICE: *Strive for greater equality. Power struggles can be energy-depleting. Make a greater effort to share ideas and feelings. Cultivate patience.*

April 3–10

THE WEEK OF THE STAR
ARIES II

October 26–November 2

THE WEEK OF INTENSITY
SCORPIO I

A Mission Improbable

RELATIONSHIPS

STRENGTHS: **INTENSE, PLEASURABLE, FUN**

WEAKNESSES: **DEMANDING, POSSESSIVE, UNSTABLE**

BEST: **FRIENDSHIP, SIBLING**

WORST: **WORK**

This relationship is unstable, fluctuating and full of tension. At work, Scorpio I's may have little respect for the goal-oriented drives of Aries II's, which they can see as blind or even mindless. If principles stand between an Aries II and success, they will often go out the window, and this Scorpio I's cannot abide. Moreover, should an Aries II justify an action by pleading forgetfulness or claiming that he or she was misinformed, the Scorpio I demand for truthfulness will begin to glow red. It will be hard for Scorpio I's to believe that what they view as oversights, miscalculations or slights on the part of an Aries II were not deliberate, no matter how innocent or uncalculating these seem to others.

As a love affair, the relationship can be intense, but also painful and uncertain. Scorpio I's generally don't easily let go of those they love. Aries II's, on the other hand, must be free to do their thing, and won't hesitate to abandon a relationship if they feel it is counterproductive or unrealistic. Should their sexual involvement be deep enough, however, they may find themselves trapped and in certain situations at the mercy of a controlling Scorpio I, causing them great anguish and frustration. In such a situation an Aries II may have a need to serve the Scorpio II, yet may dread doing so, even while deriving great pleasure from the relationship.

As friends, these two may have fallings out over broken promises, missed appointments or unkept commitments, but the good humor and fun times they share can outweigh this downside of their relationship. Aries II's greatly enjoy Scorpio I's sense of humor, and can even stand to have it directed against them, as long as they know that their friend really cares about them. Scorpio I's will rarely betray the trust of Aries II's, but will make extremely exacting demands of them. As siblings, similarly, the pair can go through a lot together emotionally, and can maintain a close bond of mutual respect, despite tremendous rivalries and differences.

HUGH HEFNER (4/9/26)
LARRY FLYNT (11/1/42)

Although both are publishers of successful adult magazines, Hefner and Flynt despise each other and stand far apart: Hefner as arbiter of refined erotic taste and Flynt as First Amendment crusader and admitted disseminator of sleaze. **Also: David Frost & John Cleese** (Cleese wrote for *The Frost Report*).

ADVICE: *Understanding and forgiveness are closely related—develop both. Let go of claims. Beware of power struggles. Work on accepting differences.*

April 3–10

THE WEEK OF THE STAR
ARIES II

November 3–11

THE WEEK OF DEPTH
SCORPIO II

Stormy Weather

RELATIONSHIPS

STRENGTHS: **PASSIONATE, CHALLENGING, COLORFUL**

WEAKNESSES: **INSECURE, POSSESSIVE, VIOLENT**

BEST: **FRIENDSHIP**

WORST: **MARRIAGE**

This relationship tends to be highly problematic. While it offers quite a bit of magnetic fascination, hidden insecurities are likely to rise to the surface in this combination. As a result, the relationship is apt to swing back and forth between attraction and insecurity, in a frustrating kind of dance.

Both Aries II's and Scorpio II's are jealous types who demand to be the main object of their lover's or spouse's attention. They may arouse a storm of emotions in each other, particularly in the sexual sphere, and while their relationship may be swept by ecstatic passion, it may also involve possessiveness, dislike—even violence. A love affair between these two can be an emotional growth experience for Aries II's, putting them in touch with a welter of hitherto untouched or unknown sources of imagination and feeling. Unfortunately, a breakup of the relationship can be highly negative, resulting in hatred and vengeful behavior unless the partners make an effort to handle each other with respect and love.

Although Scorpio II's are highly controlling, they may have difficulty reining in the excessive aspects of the Aries II character. In the area of finances, for example, Scorpio II's may find Aries II's overlavish in their expenditures, even fiscally irresponsible. On the other hand, Scorpio II's themselves don't hesitate to spend money on themselves or on their interests, so Aries II's may feel victimized by a double standard. The fact that Scorpio II's are worriers and Aries II's are not only exacerbates this tension.

The relationship does best, perhaps, as a friendship, since a Scorpio II is better able to share an Aries II friend than an Aries II lover with others. Aries II's will enjoy the depth and intensity of Scorpio II's when the two of them share challenging physical activities. Scorpio II seriousness may at times weigh on the more happy-go-lucky Aries II, but will also lend purpose to Aries II efforts. Aries II–Scorpio II siblings, particularly of the same sex, will often have a colorful and volatile relationship that sometimes appears to be a true friendship. Such a relationship adds spice to family life, but can also disturb its tranquillity.

CHRISTIE HEFNER (11/8/52)
HUGH HEFNER (4/9/26)

Hefner's *Playboy* has been the top adult magazine since 1953. Because of its "wholesome" image of women, articles on the good life and contributions by major writers, "Hef" was able to successfully hand control over to daughter Christie. **Also: Leslie Howard & Vivien Leigh** (co-stars, *Gone With the Wind*); **Bette Davis & Gig Young** (affair).

ADVICE: *Emotional upset can be a learning experience, but don't take it too far. Act responsibly. Beware of double standards. Respond to challenges.*

STRENGTHS: PRIVATE, TRUSTING, SHARING

WEAKNESSES: MISLEADING, INSENSITIVE, MISUNDERSTOOD

BEST: FRIENDSHIP

WORST: WORK

ROCK HUDSON (11/17/25)
DORIS DAY (4/3/24)

This couple's screen chemistry is legendary. Starting with *Pillow Talk* (1959), they played in frothy 60s bedroom farces that featured Day as the innocent but spunky virgin and Hudson as the handsome "wolf." (Hudson's homosexuality was then unknown to the public.) *Also:* **Steven Seagal & Whoopi Goldberg** (restaurant partners; actors).

April 3–10
THE WEEK OF THE STAR
ARIES II

November 12–18
THE WEEK OF CHARM
SCORPIO III

Conscious Camouflage

This polarized relationship often presents a calm, unemotional, perhaps even gay and carefree face to the world, but hides a dark, volatile side. This act of camouflage and concealment is often quite studied and conscious; some very private goals are being assiduously worked on far from the public eye in this relationship. As a pair, these two want to be taken seriously. They are finely attuned to each other, which also means they can push each other's buttons at will, particularly in love relationships. Great trust and honesty will have to develop here if any kind of stability is to be achieved. Through this relationship, however, both partners can go far in developing their own strengths and abilities.

The desire of Aries II's to dominate and control comes to the fore in their personal relationships with Scorpio III's. Unfortunately for them, Scorpio III's are tough customers who cannot take orders blindly, and will not hesitate to give up a relationship that is unduly negative or unproductive. Thus Aries II's who cannot back off may be sowing the seeds of their own undoing. At the same time, though, a healthy amount of aggression is needed to penetrate Scorpio III defenses, and Aries II's may know exactly how far to go in disturbing Scorpio III composure on first meeting. Such encounters may lead these two to become acquaintances, companions and finally fast friends. Aries II's may be incapable of understanding Scorpio III's at a deep emotional level, but they have an intuitive understanding of Scorpio III needs, and know how to treat them in most situations. Because Scorpio III's may choose to live alone, giving up the benefits of life with a lover or family, they value friends highly, and perhaps none more so than Aries II's.

In a boss-employee relationship, Scorpio III's will generally make the better boss, but often also the better employee. The Aries II need to be the center of attention usually gels poorly with the purposeful, realistic and efficient work attitudes of Scorpio III's. In parent-child relationships, Scorpio III children may feel misunderstood, neglected or mistreated by Aries II parents, feelings that usually persist into adult life.

ADVICE: *Strive for openness and honesty. Learn when to back off. Keep aggressive impulses under control. Don't be afraid to show yourself.*

STRENGTHS: BRILLIANT, POWERFUL, FINANCIALLY ADEPT

WEAKNESSES: DISTURBING, SNOBBISH, FRUSTRATING

BEST: PARTNERSHIP

WORST: LOVE

MEG RYAN (11/19/61)
DENNIS QUAID (4/9/54)

Quaid and Ryan met while acting in Spielberg's *Inner Space* in 1987 and married soon after. While still his girlfriend, Ryan helped Quaid recover from drug addiction. The couple has a son. *Also:* **David Frost & Dick Cavett** (tv-host rivals); **Ken Griffey, Sr. & Ken Griffey, Jr.** (father/son; baseball stars).

April 3–10
THE WEEK OF THE STAR
ARIES II

November 19–24
THE CUSP OF REVOLUTION
SCORPIO-SAGITTARIUS CUSP

Controlled Evolution

This relationship often progresses from a brilliant and precocious beginning to a sense of boredom and a yearning for freedom from the rigors and exigencies of everyday life. It is a relationship that demands a great deal of inventiveness and free-spirited play if it is to last. Traditional concepts of commitment will not work here.

Aries II's and Scorpio-Sagittarians who form a solid friendship are better off not allowing their relationship to evolve in a more personal, physical or romantic direction, when it can turn combative. (The people who get closest to Aries II's are often advisors or friends rather than lovers or spouses.) Aries II's may lack the sensitivity to form a deep emotional bond with Scorpio-Sagittarians, who may become frustrated with Aries II selfishness and self-centeredness. But Scorpio-Sagittarians may also admire Aries II directedness, particularly in the professional sphere. In this respect Aries II's can help Scorpio-Sagittarians by teaching them, through example, how to further their careers. Aries II ambition often strikes a responsive chord in Scorpio-Sagittarians, and Aries II energy may be just the career catalyst a Scorpio-Sagittarius needs.

Marriages between these two are not strongly advised, because of the problem of boredom, but they can work out fine, particularly when built on a solid financial partnership. Both parties know something about power, and may enjoy sharing it in the form of money or property. There is more than a bit of the aristocrat in many Aries II's and Scorpio-Sagittarians, who are united by common admiration of a sophisticated lifestyle. Variety, and deliberate restraint of a tendency to tie each other down, are very much key here. Money can help, allowing travel and other pursuits that can give the marriage a sense of freedom. Business partnerships between these two can work out even better than marriages, as long as disturbing emotional elements are kept under control. The loyalty and protectiveness of Scorpio-Sagittarius parents may create a suitable environment for the development of an Aries II child, as long as their autocratic tendencies don't arouse rebellion.

ADVICE: *Knowing when to stop is a sign of wisdom. Be critical of plans to expand. Keep drives for power under control. Share openness and honesty.*

April 3–10

THE WEEK OF THE STAR
ARIES II

November 25–December 2

THE WEEK OF INDEPENDENCE
SAGITTARIUS I

Dynamic Balance

RELATIONSHIPS

STRENGTHS: **BALANCED, ENERGETIC, STIMULATING**

WEAKNESSES: **CONFLICTING, STRAINED, BURNED OUT**

BEST: **MARRIAGE**

WORST: **PARENT-CHILD**

This relationship must consciously strive to achieve a dynamic balance between high energy levels. Although well suited to each other in their mutual zest for life and need for independence, this duo will have important differences in outlook that can strain their relationship. Even so, this combination can be faithful, directed, upbeat, successful and, as lovers, romantic.

The relationship will do best if it emphasizes what the partners have in common (a general outlook) rather than their differences (in approach). For one thing, Aries II's are generally more ambitious than Sagittarius I's, whom they may find curiously passive at times in career matters. Conversely, Sagittarius I's have a strong ethical code, and can find serious fault with the Aries II desire to get ahead at any cost. Should Aries II's indulge in amoral or outright immoral behavior, Sagittarius I's may be disapproving or judgmental, and in extreme cases will abruptly end the relationship.

These personalities are highly compatible in marriage, but their love affairs run the risk of early burnout, so it's best for them to try to take things slowly—no easy task for these two! Friendships can develop easily here, and since same-sex Aries II's and Sagittarius I's make not only good partners for each other but also challenging adversaries, they may build a dynamic balance around sports or other competitive activities.

In the workplace and at home, this combination interacts intensely with co-workers and family members. But its need to be at the center of things and its competitive nature can lead to disturbing conflicts, regardless of how stimulating it may be in furthering group action. Sagittarius I's will generally make better bosses or parents for Aries II's than the other way around; an Aries II as boss will have an inflexible resolve to achieve concrete results, which may collide with the Sagittarius I requirement of fairness and independence. When young, these two can make excellent and stimulating playmates for each other, either within or outside a family setting.

ADVICE: *Friction can spark fire, but also just a lot of smoke. Direct your energies. Try to find the middle ground between results and ethics.*

MELVYN DOUGLAS (4/5/01)
HELEN GAHAGEN DOUGLAS (11/25/00)

This actress-turned-liberal-politician ran for senator against Nixon, who labeled her as a communist-friendly "pink lady." Douglas was a veteran screen actor. Extremely compatible, creatively and politically, they shared a long, close relationship.

Also: Efram Zimbalist & Efram Zimbalist, Jr. (father/son; violinist/actor).

April 3–10

THE WEEK OF THE STAR
ARIES II

December 3–10

THE WEEK OF THE ORIGINATOR
SAGITTARIUS II

Congenial Camaraderie

RELATIONSHIPS

STRENGTHS: **AMIABLE, FULFILLING, UNTROUBLED**

WEAKNESSES: **UNACCEPTING, COMPETITIVE, UNREALISTIC**

BEST: **FRIENDSHIP**

WORST: **SAME-SEX CO-WORKER**

This classic trine configuration (120° apart in the zodiac) augurs well for an amiable relationship, and indeed the focus of this combination can be an easy camaraderie, with few problems dotting the landscape. Although Aries II–Sagittarius II friendships may be as close and rewarding as any in the year, however, in the areas of love and marriage this relationship can encounter substantial problems, although in no way insurmountable ones. The main issue between these parties is that they both have their own way of doing things, and since neither of them is particularly accepting or understanding, conflicts result.

Both Aries II's and Sagittarius II's are often hard-driving, ambitious individuals, and this doesn't always make it easy for them to collaborate in the workplace, unless they are willing to subordinate their individuality to a higher cause. As siblings, co-workers or mates, they may be excessively competitive, threatening both the happiness they both desire and the stability of their work or family group. They operate most easily together if they are of the opposite sex, when a curious psychic chemistry may evolve between siblings or co-workers in this combination, making the relationship manifest as a single, dynamic and productive force.

Often physically attracted to each other, these two can enjoy a blossoming romance. Sagittarius II's are prone to hero worship, and it will please Aries II's to become the object of such adoration. Unfortunately, Sagittarius II's are often unrealistic in their partner choices, and run the risk of being hurt or rejected by Aries II's, who may not share their depth of passion and can be amoral or manipulative in pursuit of fleeting pleasures.

Although fulfilling marriages and friendships are often found in this combination, friendships are more likely to survive the heat generated by these fiery individuals. In marriage, conflicts over children, property and finances are likely to disturb domestic tranquillity. A free and easygoing camaraderie with few demands and lots of space for independent action is more congenial to both parties.

ADVICE: *Compromise when necessary. Try to see the larger picture. Don't let emotions get too heavy. Maintain independence. Keep it light and easy.*

KIM BASINGER (12/8/53)
ALEC BALDWIN (4/3/58)

This couple's marriage is romantic, durable and mutually fulfilling. Baldwin is a successful actor, as are brothers William, Stephen and Daniel. Basinger is a former Ford model. The couple co-starred in *The Marrying Man* (1991).

Also: Harry Houdini & Jean-Eugène Houdin (magician/"father of modern conjuring").

FRANCIS FORD COPPOLA (4/7/39)
STEVEN SPIELBERG (12/18/46)

These dynamic directors share a common ideal for movie-making centered on creating visionary new technologies. Coppola's effort, Zoetrope Studios, unfortunately failed, while DreamWorks, a Spielberg partnership, is thriving. ***Also:* Hugh Hefner & Bob Guccione** (rival men's magazine publishers).

April 3–10
THE WEEK OF THE STAR
ARIES II

December 11–18
THE WEEK OF THE TITAN
SAGITTARIUS III

Coming Out on Top

Power struggles are likely to emerge in this relationship over who is to be the leader. More than most combinations, the relationship will also need to star in its own personal drama, but it will be hard for either of these two to take a back seat, whether to the partnership or to each other. Aries II's have trouble subordinating themselves to a more powerful personality, but this is precisely what Sagittarius III's usually require. Yet Sagittarius III's can become so enchanted with Aries II's that they will sometimes let their guard down, virtually gaping open-mouthed in awe or admiration. Also, certain Aries II's may be able to assume a secondary position to Sagittarius III's, as long as their central, indispensable role in the family or company is not threatened or questioned.

Once the first blush of passion has passed in a love affair between these two, Sagittarius III's may begin to turn the screws in their need for control. They should realize that this can only end in disaster, and should try to be more sensitive to the Aries II need for independence of thought and action. On the other hand, Aries II's are capable of feigning submissiveness while actually keeping control through subtle manipulation. They are well acquainted with the brand of egotism that feeds off the attention of others, and can alternately give and withhold energy with their Sagittarius III partners to telling effect. Friendship between members of the same sex may not be possible in this combination, since both partners need to share the spotlight in their social circle. And should they try to restrict their friendship to themselves alone, one or the other of them may prove unwilling or unable to share or reciprocate. Marriages between these two may suffer for the same reason, although the pressure of daily responsibilities can force the recalcitrant partner to act responsibly.

Business or other working partnerships between these two are not always a good bet. Ambitious and goal-oriented impulses may sometimes unite them, sometimes divide them, but in either event fiscal irresponsibility and lack of patience for mundane details must be overcome.

ADVICE: *Give up the spotlight occasionally. Let others shine too. Anonymity has its benefits. Be responsible about money. Learn to share.*

GREGORY PECK (4/5/16)
AVA GARDNER (12/24/22)

Peck and Gardner are among Hollywood's most durable stars, appearing together most notably as screen lovers in *On the Beach* (1959), a grim tale about nuclear fallout destroying the planet's population. Their moving portrayals demonstrate the actors' superlative screen chemistry. ***Also:* Helmut Kohl & Helmut Schmidt** (successive German chancellors).

April 3–10
THE WEEK OF THE STAR
ARIES II

December 19–25
THE CUSP OF PROPHECY
SAGITTARIUS-CAPRICORN CUSP

Tongue and Groove

The crucial question here is whether the partners can accept each other without irritation or blame. Their differences are severe: Sagittarius-Capricorns are usually far too serious for Aries II's, who are exuberant and direct—qualities likely to get on the nerves of a secretive, emotionally complex partner. Sagittarius-Capricorns are sensitive to the profundity and significance of life's trials and tribulations, while the more carefree Aries II's would rather not confront or even think about them. Sagittarius-Capricorns may consequently see the Aries II lifestyle as trivializing all they hold dear. Luckily, this relationship holds something of value for both partners, including a built-in open-mindedness. The Sagittarius-Capricorn moral consciousness may just keep Aries II's in line, while Sagittarius-Capricorns for their part will be lighter than usual in this relationship, as its colorful, fun-loving orientation offsets their weightiness. The key may be the way each partner benefits from the strengths that the other provides.

Differences in tempo and tone can create tension when a deep Sagittarius-Capricorn and an impulsive Aries II are lovers or spouses. On the upside, the earthy qualities of Sagittarius-Capricorns can offer stability to the union, despite undermining influences from mutual fire. (Both Sagittarius and Aries are fire signs.) On the downside, the couple may periodically be swept away by destructive, albeit enthusiastic impulses, particularly in the financial sphere.

Aries II friends may be just what Sagittarius-Capricorns need to pull them out of their darker moods and spur them to action. Similarly, Aries II siblings or parents lend color and excitement to their surroundings, which can disturb Sagittarius-Capricorn concentration but can also make them more attentive to the present moment. Sagittarius-Capricorn parents tend to keep an eye on the future, a quality often sorely needed by impulsive Aries II children. In family situations, then, the relationship will provide compensation for each partner's deficiencies and allow their needs to be satisfied.

ADVICE: *Tend to money matters. Learn to be more practical. Minimize blame. Cultivate mutual ideals. Try to overlook differences.*

April 3–10

THE WEEK OF THE STAR
ARIES II

December 26–January 2

THE WEEK OF THE RULER
CAPRICORN I

Repressed Desires

The strong and silent face that this relationship may present to the world belies the burning sense of often frustrated ambition that it carries within. Hidden and repressed desires, and their exposure, are the keynotes here: each partner will nurture a concealed desire to be the leader, either within the relationship or in the world at large, yet each is likely to subsume this urge for the relationship's sake. Even so, whether at work or at home, the relationship can be complementary as well as inhibiting, with the Capricorn I bringing needed structure and planning to any undertaking, and the Aries II contributing drive and charisma.

An Aries II's ambition and drive can be suppressed in a matchup with a Capricorn I, who will usually be more insecure, and will more easily get stuck in a lesser position. If so, the relationship may not allow the Aries II, whether as a co-worker or a family member, to surpass his or her partner. In addition, Capricorn I's are likely to see Aries II lovers and mates as selfish, egotistical and unwilling to assume the responsibilities of everyday life in a practical or efficient enough way. Aries II's are actually quite capable of sacrificing their desires in service of a higher goal, whether it be a marriage, family or love, so it will annoy them to be accused of inefficiency or self-centeredness by a Capricorn I. The mixture of Capricorn earthiness and Aries fire may presage an ardent, at times even feverish love affair that offers little rest or tranquillity to either partner. Sex and love addictions must be guarded against; they can turn into a dark passion that is mutually consuming and destructive. Friendships between these two can be more stable and beneficial, although less exciting, and a business connection between equals may prove the best bet of all. At work, each partner can provide what the other lacks; as long as they keep personality clashes to a minimum, they can build a formula for success. Aries II bosses, however, may see the Capricorn I lack of initiative as evidence of lethargy or complacency. And Capricorn I bosses, or for that matter parents, may express their authoritative nature in ways that Aries II's will experience as highly oppressive. The intense Aries II need for freedom is likely to chafe under Capricorn I rules and restraints.

COLONEL WILLIAM DAWES (4/6/1745)
PAUL REVERE (1/1/1735)

Revere never completed his famous 1775 midnight ride to Concord, Mass,; he was captured enroute by the British. He also didn't ride alone. Co-patriots Dawes and Prescott set off from Lexington with him, with Dawes turning back and only Prescott making it to Concord.

ADVICE: *Differences can unite as well as divide. Minimize competition and jealousy. Allow personal expression. Beware of addictive tendencies.*

April 3–10

THE WEEK OF THE STAR
ARIES II

January 3–9

THE WEEK OF DETERMINATION
CAPRICORN II

Breaking Down Walls

Conventional astrology predicts a rocky road for those whose suns are square to each other (approximately 90° apart in the zodiac), which is the case with the Capricorn II–Aries II combination. Some believe such relationships should be avoided if possible, and many walls to intimacy will indeed have to be broken down, and personal defenses breached, if this relationship is to succeed. As a result, the relationship has an oddly prickly side, a sore spot, if you will, which, if pressed, can cause flare-ups of tension.

In love and marriage, striving rather than strife should be the keyword here. If both partners keep their respect for each other, they may spur each other on to new levels of sensitivity and awareness. Capricorn II's will enjoy having a highly independent partner, and Aries II fits the bill nicely. But independent though Aries II's are, they also need attention and to be needed, and this particular desire may not be filled by a Capricorn II, who may often be away from home, whether at work or socializing with friends.

At work, Capricorn II's certainly meet their match in Aries II's. These two can be excellent business partners, but by the same token they also make challenging competitors and formidable adversaries. Being co-workers at the same job level is not recommended for them, in fact, since each will tend to struggle to get ahead at the other's expense. When it comes to career, neither of these two is above taking unfair advantage of a situation to further their cause, and in a business dispute where there can only be one winner, neither will surrender without a fight.

In a marriage, this kind of contentiousness may actually advance the relationship's longevity, since both parties hate to admit failure. Even the most combative of marital relationships, then, may go on for years. As siblings or parent-child duos, Capricorn II's and Aries II's are likely to fall into predictable patterns of bickering, strife or in extreme cases all-out combat.

NICHOLAS CAGE (1/7/64)
PATRICIA ARQUETTE (4/8/68)

In 1987, Cage went on a "quest" to win Arquette's hand in marriage. After he returned with her chosen items, a black orchid and writer J.D. Salinger's signature, she turned him down. They finally married in 1995. ***Also: Gale Storm & ZaSu Pitts*** (co-stars, *Oh Suzannah!*); **Spencer Tracy & Loretta Young** (affair; actors).

ADVICE: *Why are your enemies hard to overcome? Perhaps the answer lies in yourself. Try to achieve the best in yourself. Uncover points of sensitivity.*

STRENGTHS: **GOAL-ORIENTED, NONTHREATENING, EVOLVING**

WEAKNESSES: **RIGID, IDOLIZING, LAWLESS**

BEST: **FRIENDSHIP**

WORST: **LOVE**

JANE GOODALL (4/3/34)
DIAN FOSSEY (1/16/32)

Both encouraged by famed anthropologist Dr. Louis Leakey, Goodall and Fossey did pioneering work in primatology. Goodall made long-term observations of chimpanzees in the wild, while Fossey studied the behavior of gorillas. Both bodies of research have led to an increased understanding of early humans.

April 3–10
THE WEEK OF THE STAR
ARIES II

January 10–16
THE WEEK OF DOMINANCE
CAPRICORN III

Flexible Structures

This relationship will be much concerned with uncovering or identifying the structures hidden within it, such as daily routines, rules of morality or unspoken agreements. It will work most easily when its activities and attitudes are flexibly structured, and love relationships may consequently prove difficult here, since moral expectations are likely to be rigid in this combination; if the tensions this causes can be survived, however, this kind of strictness can actually be a benefit to marital relationships. In any area, the Capricorn III tendency to dominate may meet with stiff resistance from Aries II's, who don't like being controlled and are bound to rebel against the structures this relationship throws up. On the other hand, Capricorn III's are prone to hero worship (usually a holdover from childhood), and if they come to idolize an Aries II Star, they may prove less rigid. An adored Aries II, meanwhile, may be willing to endure a few rules.

Friendships between these two can be magnificent. Sharing, mutual ego-support and an extroverted stance are characteristic of this nonthreatening relationship. Capricorn III's are highly physical, and an Aries II may prove the perfect companion for them in activities ranging from sport and fitness to adventure. Both parties like pushing limits, whether their own or the record book's. Such rolling back of existing structures gives the relationship both form and an outlet. The danger here may be a propensity to get into trouble, particularly with authority figures or the law.

Working together, whether as co-workers or a boss-employee pair, is not favored for these two, particularly if the Capricorn III is especially unyielding. An Aries II child will often have to struggle to get out from under an older Capricorn III sibling, especially one of the same sex, but if structural modifications in the relationship occur as a result, they will generally prove beneficial.

ADVICE: *Beware of the lure of danger. Breaking the law can become a bad habit. Push physical limits, not moral ones. Make rules flexible. Avoid rigidity of thought.*

STRENGTHS: **FUN-LOVING, SPIRITED, HARD-WORKING**

WEAKNESSES: **HOT-TEMPERED, ANTAGONISTIC, FRUSTRATED**

BEST: **MARRIAGE, CO-WORKER**

WORST: **FAMILY**

D.W. GRIFFITH (1/22/1895)
MARY PICKFORD (4/9/1893)

Griffith, the prodigious producer, director and screenwriter in early Hollywood, also developed talented actresses, notably Pickford, with whom he shared a long relationship. With Charlie Chaplin and Pickford's then-husband Douglas Fairbanks, they founded United Artists.

Also: **William & Catherine Booth** (married; Salvation Army founders);

Robert Sherwood & Alexander Woollcott (friends; writers-wits);

April 3–10
THE WEEK OF THE STAR
ARIES II

January 17–22
THE CUSP OF MYSTERY & IMAGINATION
CAPRICORN-AQUARIUS CUSP

Few Dull Moments

This relationship is likely to be lively and high spirited. The matchup works particularly well in marriage, promising an interesting and successful shared life. Neither party necessarily makes this stable a marriage with personalities of other weeks in the year, so that this is a somewhat unique relationship for these two, a niche of permanence and security. There is rarely a dull moment in an Aries II–Capricorn-Aquarius home. The latter's love of practical jokes will find an appreciative audience in Aries II's, even when they are the object of their spouse's lighthearted forays. Both these partners enjoy family get-togethers, parties and celebrations. Should they have children together, they are likely to furnish a warm and loving environment.

Even in the midst of such domestic tranquillity there will be a few problems, particularly involving excessive spending. Emotional upheavals arising from the cyclic mood swings of Capricorn-Aquarians can also be disruptive and disturbing. Fits of temper may prove even more upsetting in love affairs between this two, since both are hot tempered to begin with, and passionate or unstable feelings here can be like gasoline on a fire. Indeed, when an affair between these two goes wrong, particularly a hidden or illicit one, the whole relationship may go up dramatically in flames.

It will be difficult for these two to stay friends after a breakup. Friendships without a history of close personal or physical involvement may likewise not last, for they may involve a high frustration level, or a strain in maintaining objectivity. On the other hand, Aries II–Capricorn-Aquarius co-workers can build a solid relationship around mutual responsibility, respect and hard work. Working side by side, whether as spouses or career associates, is a fine way for these two to get to know each other and to build the trust necessary to sustain their relationship. As siblings, however, they may not get along at all, due to mutual irritations and antagonisms.

ADVICE: *Try to keep mood swings and high spirits under control. Build honesty and trust. Stick to a well-planned budget. Minimize irritations.*

April 3–10
THE WEEK OF THE STAR
ARIES II

January 23–30
THE WEEK OF GENIUS
AQUARIUS I

Burning Bridges

At the heart of this relationship lies a permissive attitude that not only allows but demands freedom, probably undermining any attempt to build on the kind of solid foundation that can bring longevity and happiness. Undercutting its own efforts, the relationship recalls the image of the man who burns his bridges behind him—often including, unfortunately, the very bridge he is standing on at the time. The question here is whether the combination's positive aspects (excitement, dynamism, impulsiveness) will fortify the relationship or run out of control. If the latter, the relationship will self-destruct. And even at best, positive and negative are so intimately related here that a wild and colorful relationship, without a whole lot of stability, is in the cards.

The relationship's highs are heavenly, its depths abysmal. Particularly in love affairs, ecstatic climaxes will do little to make either partner feel secure. This is one of those relationships motivated more by want than by need, and it will continue only as long as both parties desire each other. One unfavorable incident may be enough to discourage these fair-weather lovers. For the same reasons, marriages in this combination are unlikely to endure until death do them part, so that it may be wise for them to live together on a trial basis before naming a wedding day. In exceptional cases a free or open marriage may bring a measure of longevity to the relationship, but even so, this couple should think carefully before having children.

The levels of stress and impatience, and the lack of even moderate behavior in a pairing of these two personalities, rule out most working situations. As friends or family members, Aries II's and Aquarius I's combine their fiery and airy qualities in an explosive mixture that at once furthers the action and periodically disrupts its progress. As long as neither partner taps into the other's dark side, sibling and parent-child combinations may avoid violent confrontations, but triggering mechanisms and psychological projections guarantee that at any moment things may start teetering precariously on the edge of a new calamity.

ADVICE: *Pushing buttons is easy, keeping your hands off is not. Make things easier, not harder. Minimize stress. Cultivate stability. Moderation is key.*

M.W. NIRENBERG (4/10/1927)
ROBERT HOLLEY (1/28/22)

Nirenberg and Holley shared the 1968 Nobel Prize for medicine with fellow scientist H.G. Khorana. Their discovery of how genes determine cell function opened the way to breaking the genetic code, a major contribution to modern science. They were a dynamic and effective research team.

April 3–10
THE WEEK OF THE STAR
ARIES II

January 31–February 7
THE WEEK OF YOUTH & EASE
AQUARIUS II

Few Antipathies

This highly personal relationship stresses enjoyment unmarred by heavy or messy emotional entanglements. Interestingly, though, both of these personalities enjoy socializing within the relationship, so that they spend quite a bit of time alone together—so much so that the pairing can prove a little limiting, and they may end up bored.

Although objectively well suited to Aries II's as friends, lovers, mates or family members, Aquarius II's are often attracted to more troubled and, in their eyes, more exciting personalities, perhaps representing their own shadow side, so that they may not think an Aries II fits the bill at all. Consequently, although friendships and love between these two can be easy and fun, the magnetic attraction here may not be strong enough to keep Aquarius II's from detaching and moving on. Similarly, marriages between Aries II's and Aquarius II's don't usually involve deep sexual or romantic ties. On the other hand, a shared love of travel, entertainment, decorating or pets may far outlive either of these personality's passionate involvement with a person from another week of the year. An easy lifestyle, replete with the best that life has to offer, may be in store for this pair.

Since there is a trepidation here about deep romantic involvements, friendships involving shared social activities, perhaps involving clubs, or physical endeavors such as team sports, are perhaps the best bet. This is one of those rare combinations that can enjoy both working together and playing together regularly after work. In fact, remarkably few antipathies or points of irritation will generally surface in this relationship to drive its partners apart. Much more likely is a sense of loneliness when the partners are together that would cause them to look elsewhere for more meaningful connections. Aries II–Aquarius II siblings are often very close when growing up, and may room together while in school, or while working as young professionals. As long as financial matters and an equitable division of labor can be worked out, this combination may live together in harmony for many years, even as a parent-child relationship that lasts far beyond adolescence.

ADVICE: *Get tougher. Learn to take the bad with the good. Push a bit harder to achieve. Beware of complacency and dependency.*

BETTE DAVIS (4/5/08)
TALLULAH BANKHEAD (1/31/03)

These temperamental actresses had much in common. Onscreen, they excelled at playing sophisticated spitfires. Offscreen, they were stormy, demanding and rebellious. Their personalities melded in 1950 when Davis, whose career had been limping, bounced back in the role of a tempestuous Broadway star in *All About Eve*—a movie based on Bankhead's life.

MIA FARROW (2/9/45)
ANDRE PREVIN (4/6/29)

Actress Farrow and conductor Previn had twin sons in 1968. They married in 1970, adopted 3 girls and had another child. Their relationship was close and lasted nearly 10 years.

***Also:* Michelle Phillips & Chynna Phillips** (mother/daughter; singers); **Boss Tweed & Samuel Tilden** (corrupt politician/adversary); **E.Y. Harburg & Harold Arlen** (songwriter collaborators).

April 3–10
THE WEEK OF THE STAR
ARIES II

February 8–15
THE WEEK OF ACCEPTANCE
AQUARIUS III

A New Set of Buttons

The focus of this relationship can be a preoccupation with literal interpretations and a refusal to let go of troublesome details. This explosive combination of fire (Aries) and air (Aquarius) is prone to anger and irritation, but on a good day storm clouds will pass quickly and arguments or unfair remarks will soon be forgotten. Irritability is the most common problem in this pairing, so that if these two are to get along, either or both of them should toughen up, maybe growing a whole new set of buttons that can't be pushed so easily. Arguments that start over picky details can escalate to enormous proportions, threatening the very existence of a marriage, friendship or love relationship, so it is always best to stamp them out in their earliest stages.

Because Aquarius III's so value open and natural behavior, they may resent the attention that others pay to Aries II Stars. Such resentment can erode friendships and arouse acute jealousy in love relationships. Aquarius III insecurities may emerge if an Aries II partner or spouse is the object of too much attention from members of the opposite sex. Aquarius III's must learn to balance their emotions, be less reactive and perhaps be proud that so many see their mate as so desirable.

As children, Aquarius III's are often accepting and impressionable, so they may be influenced by or idolize an Aries II Star, particularly if there's one in the family. Such attachments often end in disillusion, since Aries II's will find it as hard as anyone else will to live up to Aquarius III expectations. Similar patterns can emerge when these two are adults, with Aries II's enjoying but also at times regretting Aquarius III attention. When the combination does not come about by choice, as in a family or work situation, bickering may get out of hand, and the pair would be better off separated.

ADVICE: *Be less reactive. Overlook small hurts. Try to see the big picture. Don't take things too literally. Not every remark is personal.*

MARLON BRANDO (4/3/24)
MOVITA CASTANEDA (2/17/14)

Brando married actress Castaneda while filming *Mutiny on the Bounty* (1960). He bought the tropical island near Tahiti, named Tetiaroa, on which the movie was shot. After filming was over, he went into exile there with his new wife, for a time escaping the realities and follies of Hollywood life. The marriage was annulled in 1967.

April 3–10
THE WEEK OF THE STAR
ARIES II

February 16–22
THE CUSP OF SENSITIVITY
AQUARIUS-PISCES CUSP

Bonds of Imagination

Rooted in fantasy and the spiritual, this relationship may be out of touch with everyday realities. It will be essential for its partners to work on objectivity, then, since romance or illusion may threaten to sweep them away.

A problem can materialize in love affairs when a sensitive Aquarius-Pisces, trying to express care and sympathy for an Aries II, encounters storms of passion and desire in return. This difference in style can cause mutual frustration. But the aggressiveness of an Aries II friend or lover may simply embody the other side of Aquarius-Pisces' sensitive and passive psyche, a more passionate side of which they only dreamed.

Marriages between these two, whether or not influenced by childhood role models, may be good and in certain cases magnificent. Both Pisces-Aquarians and Aries II's can have trouble opening up at a deep level, and the happy domestic situation they can achieve in this relationship may serve as the best therapy imaginable. An idyllic family life is possible here, with children and pets enriching and securing the adults' love. One warning: should either partner betray the other's trust, breaking the couple up, it may be a long time before the wronged party will be ready to reembark on the path of matrimony—if ever.

Siblings in this combination can be extremely close in childhood. An Aries II or Pisces-Aquarius brother or sister will often serve as a role model in the adult sibling's search for a spouse or living partner. As co-workers, Aries II's and Pisces-Aquarians may get along all too well, so that their strong bonds of imagination and emotion interfere with the work at hand. These two may have to struggle to stay on track and get their tasks done.

ADVICE: *Trust is at least as important as desire. Try to see things as they are. Seek your own path. Don't define yourself in terms of others.*

April 3–10

THE WEEK OF THE STAR
ARIES II

February 23–March 2

THE WEEK OF SPIRIT
PISCES I

Awakening

RELATIONSHIPS

STRENGTHS: **RENEWING,
COMPLEMENTING, VERSATILE**

WEAKNESSES: **RECALCITRANT,
IMPATIENT, CONFUSED**

BEST: **WORK**

WORST: **LOVE**

This relationship shows how very different individuals may have a positive effect on each other by bringing out dormant qualities that might otherwise go unexpressed. The central image here is that of rebirth: the relationship awakens long-forgotten individual characteristics and allows them creative expression. Aries II's, for example, tend to be more bound up with their sense of self than with the problems and concerns of others, but they have the capacity, often ignored, of giving themselves wholeheartedly to a cause. Pisces I's, on the other hand, are devotional types who often have difficulties with self-definition and tend to slip into the background around others. Together in a joint endeavor, they can lead the way in a cause involving service and social or spiritual reawakening.

A common goal can serve as the driving force behind this relationship, and the areas of common interest and emotional expression that it opens up can lead to friendship, love or marriage. The emotionality of Pisces I's may reawaken deep feelings in Aries II, while the driving ambition of Aries II's may serve as a model for Pisces I's who are a bit adrift or misdirected careerwise. There may be problems in love relationships between these two: Pisces I's can despair over the Aries II inability to express feelings or to show understanding and empathy, while Aries II's sometimes find Pisces I's needy and clinging. Since Aries II's must feel free to make their own decisions, this relationship is often short-lived.

Longevity is more likely in marriage here. Over the years, these two may compensate for each other's deficiencies, and can periodically breathe new life into their marriage. As family members, they may both want to improve the well-being of the domestic unit, particularly if it is a disadvantaged one, and may be united in this common interest.

GEORGE HARRISON (2/25/43)
RAVI SHANKAR (4/7/20)

Shankar popularized sitar music outside India, touring the US and Europe in the mid-50s. Harrison, the spiritual Beatle, studied with Shankar and went on to play the sitar in his music of the later 60s.

ADVICE: *Use differences to advantage. Beware of condemning attitudes. Develop patience and understanding. Every now and then, start all over again.*

April 3–10

THE WEEK OF THE STAR
ARIES II

March 3–10

THE WEEK OF THE LONER
PISCES II

A Love of Beauty

RELATIONSHIPS

STRENGTHS: **AESTHETIC,
APPRECIATIVE, ADMIRING**

WEAKNESSES: **MOODY,
STRANGE, SELF-CENTERED**

BEST: **MARRIAGE**

WORST: **WORK**

This relationship often centers around aesthetic experience, especially music, theater, art and design. Sharing likes and dislikes and exploring questions of taste together are among this combination's greatest joys. When these two are mates or friends, Aries II's may also crave the Pisces II gift of intimacy after a hard day of tilting at windmills. Outwardly directed, they rarely have the time or the talent to switch their minds off their principal activities, whether professional or domestic, and Pisces II's have the ability to lead them through intriguing byways of human experience, far removed from everyday concerns.

The relationship can manifest as a fruitful but unusual marriage. The world may be amazed that such unlike people can be successful together, but the Pisces II capacity for profound thought, planning and evaluation may prove a reassuring and directing influence on the spontaneous, dynamic energies of Aries II's. Also, when Pisces II's sink into depression, as they sometimes do, the positive outlook of Aries II's may prove indispensable. And both these partners will be able to learn to stand aside rather than intrude on the other's moods.

Nevertheless, many Pisces II's will not initially be attracted to Aries II's, whose loud, outgoing and egotistical nature will often turn them off. And Aries II's may find the inwardness of most Pisces II's, although intriguing, still far too strange to get involved with. Acquaintanceships or partnerships in activities involving aesthetic matters or physical grace may be the closest these two care to get to each other.

Pisces II's are rarely hard driving enough to keep up with Aries II's at work. Their moodiness may also be counterproductive to getting the job done on schedule, which ambitious Aries II's will not appreciate. As parents, these personalities reinforce each other's tendency to be too self-centered to give children the attention they need.

PIERRE MONTEUX (4/4/1875)
MAURICE RAVEL (3/7/1875)

One of 20th century's leading maestros, Monteux conducted exclusively for Diaghilev's Ballet Russe in Paris from 1911–14, during which he premiered Ravel's *Daphnis et Chloe*. It became a popular standard in the ballet company's repertory.

***Also:* Jan & Dean** (singing duo).

ADVICE: *Develop your love of beauty. Make time available to help others. Beware of self-centeredness. Fight a tendency to moodiness.*

STRENGTHS: **HELPFUL, UNDERSTANDING, SUCCESSFUL**

WEAKNESSES: **SEVERE, UNCOMPREHENDING, NEEDY**

BEST: **SOCIAL PARTNERSHIP**

WORST: **LOVE**

PHIL LESH (3/15/40)
BILL KREUTZMANN (4/7/46)

Drummer Kreutzmann and bassist Lesh are original members of the legendary Grateful Dead band and have performed together since the 60s. The band boasts legions of "Deadhead" fans who lovingly preserve its hippie values and styles.
Also: **Marilu Henner & Judd Hirsch** (co-stars, *Taxi*).

April 3–10
THE WEEK OF THE STAR
ARIES II

March 11–18
THE WEEK OF DANCERS & DREAMERS
PISCES III

Needing to Be Needed

This relationship will be oriented toward fulfilling individual needs and providing nurturing, help and understanding. Both of these individuals need to be needed, but in different ways; their ability to create a long-lasting relationship will depend on how capable each of them is of filling the other's needs, and how deep those needs go.

Aries II's usually like accomplishing tasks for others, thereby allowing themselves to feel indispensable. With a Pisces III partner, they are apt to emphasize their own necessity by pointing out how unrealistic, unambitious and impractical that partner is, though this is often not the case. This may wound the soulful and romantic Pisces III, who, though appreciating Aries II capability and decisiveness, will feel unacknowledged. Pisces III's need to be needed emotionally, something to which Aries II would never admit. These two must become more fully aware of their different ways of showing love, and to accept that not all their needs can be filled. It may be wise for them to realize that their differences here lie in style, not in intention.

When this pair are friends and colleagues, the philosophical side of the Pisces III is unlikely to be appreciated by the Aries II, who is likely to be geared more to action than to speculation. Unless they share a common activity or pursuit, then, they probably won't grow close. The Pisces III mind must roam over the broad arena of human existence, plumbing the depths of our theories and beliefs about ourselves. Aries II's are more concerned with the here and now. To them, and to their disappointment, their Pisces III companions often sell themselves short in terms of personal goals they could attain. Aries II parents, then, can be very hard on their Pisces III children, whom they may see as underachievers. These two may succeed, however, in heading up a business, social organization or work team, in which Pisces III does the planning and idea work and Aries II is concerned with implementation.

ADVICE: *Would you rather be alone? Appreciate what you have while you have it. Open lines of sympathy and empathy. Wants are as important as needs.*

STRENGTHS: **FAIR, GIVING, SOCIABLE**

WEAKNESSES: **DISAGREEING, FRUSTRATING, DOMINATING**

BEST: **CO-WORKER**

WORST: **MARRIAGE**

J.P. MORGAN, SR. (4/17/1837)
NIKITA KHRUSHCHEV (4/17/1896)

Though these men share the same birthday, they are at ideological extremes: J.P. Morgan, one of the world's leading capitalists and financiers, founded the Morgan Bank and US Steel; anti-capitalist Khrushchev headed Russia at its communist peak. A common concern, however, was railroads. Morgan reorganized them in the eastern US; Khrushchev directed construction of Moscow's.

April 11–18
THE WEEK OF THE PIONEER
ARIES III

April 11–18
THE WEEK OF THE PIONEER
ARIES III

Constant Struggle

The prevailing theme in this relationship may unfortunately be frustration, for in many areas of life this is not a realistic combination. Aries III's are usually engaged in doing things with and for other people—planning, organizing, executing, maintaining—but can rarely allow others to do anything for them. One can expect quite a bit of struggle in this relationship, then, over who will do what. On the upside, these two are sure to attract a constant stream of people coming and going, and this kind of activity may be enough to keep them both satisfied.

Two Aries III's living together or in a love affair may experience impossible difficulties in the long run. Usually guided by fixed ideas and ideologies, they may engage in a constant struggle for supremacy, unless they have exactly or at least close to the same viewpoint. They should really get involved with personalities other than their own, with people who have other needs for their strengths to fill. Things can be extremely difficult for children exposed to the conflict within an Aries III–Aries III marriage, and even worse for them in the "perfect" situation of both parents sharing the same beliefs, when they will be expected to measure up to a monolithic set of standards with no chance of appeal to another point of view.

Friendships and family relationships between Aries III's are likely to suffer from ideological conflicts, but if at least one of the partners is diplomatic, as these personalities are likely to be, there may be an equitable give-and-take of ideas and energies. Because Aries III's have well-developed social skills and need a lot of social interaction, they are likely to see eye-to-eye on the need to contribute to the welfare of others. Sharp disagreements can break out as to how and when such contributions are to be made, but these differences can be worked out if mutual goals are kept in sight. As co-workers, two Aries III's can get a tremendous amount done and achieve success in a wide variety of endeavors as long as they can keep their need to dominate under control. Their innate sense of fairness and their sensitivity to the good of the group will help to make this possible.

ADVICE: *Keep your ideas under control. Practice flexibility. Avoid a monolithic stance. Get enough rest. Hard work isn't always required.*

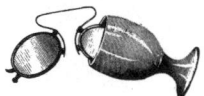

April 11–18
THE WEEK OF THE PIONEER
ARIES III

April 19–24
THE CUSP OF POWER
ARIES-TAURUS CUSP

A Stimulating Rivalry

This matchup is often highly dramatic and critical. Both Aries III's and Aries-Tauruses are willful, strong-minded individuals, and their relationship magnifies those characteristics to such a degree that they may argue about how almost anything is to be done. But the combination is a powerful one if unified and outwardly directed, so that its abilities both to attack and to defend may guarantee the safety and security of those around it, whether family members or co-workers. As individuals, Aries-Tauruses and Aries III's make fearsome rivals in matters of career and love, and since neither is quick to admit defeat, their sharp verbal combat can be prolonged and damaging.

Both these personalities are highly physical, and their love affairs are likely to be intense indeed, particularly sexually. Aries III's tend to deny their emotions, but with an Aries-Taurus they can exhibit rather theatrical expressions of feeling. And while Aries-Tauruses can be terrible procrastinators, this relationship's critical attitudes and dramatic displays may have the effect of goading these recalcitrant personalities into motion.

Friendships between these two are a good bet. Both parties are usually responsible in discharging their duties as friends. Extremely capable, they can both be counted on in joint activities—making travel arrangements, reservations, payments (perhaps a tad late, however), or seeing that a rented car is returned in at least as good shape as it was delivered. Aries III's have more of a need for physical activity, and the chemistry here can be catalytic for Aries-Tauruses: usually content to relax on the beach, they may instead be miraculously stimulated to scuba dive, hang-glide or mountain-climb. The relationship may also have the effect of encouraging Aries III's to be more openly affectionate and appreciative than usual.

ADVICE: *Being able to admit weakness may be a sign of strength. Don't question everything. Learn to relax. Empty out—so you can recharge.*

RELATIONSHIPS

STRENGTHS: **DARING, STIMULATING, RESPONSIBLE**

WEAKNESSES: **HYPERCRITICAL, WILLFUL, DAMAGING**

BEST: **FRIENDSHIP**

WORST: **WORK**

OLEG CASSINI (4/11/13)
JAYNE MANSFIELD (4/19/32)

This famed designer of Jackie O's wardrobe was known for his erotic fixation on women. His intense affair with Mansfield, sexpot of 50s and 60s Hollywood films, was highly publicized. Mansfield died in a car crash in 1967.
Also: Charlie Chaplin & Harold Lloyd (rival silent movie comics).

April 11–18
THE WEEK OF THE PIONEER
ARIES III

April 25–May 2
THE WEEK OF MANIFESTATION
TAURUS I

Eat-to-Live Versus Live-to-Eat

This relationship could furnish the material for a whole textbook on power. Although both Aries III's and Taurus I's are highly dominant types, they express this dominance very differently: Aries III's are turned on by the kick of leading others, and of moving out into the world, while Taurus I's can be quite content to sit at home or in the office as long as they know that other people are implementing their ideas. In both cases, however, ruling the roost is a firm requirement, which can make a marriage or other permanent living situation between these two difficult or impossible. They may avoid conflict if they can negotiate a strict separation of duties and spheres of influence within the family or group, but it will be difficult.

To cite one example: food. What Taurus I's eat is very important to them, and many of them have a great fondness for cooking. Aries III's, on the other hand, are liable to eat whatever is there, using food simply as fuel. It might be said that Aries III's eat to live while Taurus I's live to eat. Also important to Taurus I's are other kinds of creature comfort, particularly home furnishings, which may not matter much to adventuresome Aries III's. Serious power struggles arise when Aries III's insist that quality food and furnishings are items that those they live with can and should be able to do without.

Their physical stamina and their devotion to ideas aside, Aries III's and Taurus I's may have little to share in a love relationship or marriage. As friends, Taurus I's have a need to express sympathy and affection, while Aries III's may play it cooler and try to keep their emotions under control (though not without occasional flare-ups). Friendships between these two are often built around involvements with social, community and family institutions, for neither party likes to be alone for very long.

ADVICE: *Givers must learn to be takers. Accepting help doesn't make you weaker. Power tripping can be a waste of time and energy. Chill.*

RELATIONSHIPS

STRENGTHS: **PERSEVERING, IDEA-ORIENTED, SOCIAL**

WEAKNESSES: **DOMINATING, POWER-TRIPPING, CONFLICTING**

BEST: **COMMUNITY, SOCIAL WORK**

WORST: **LOVE**

DAVID LETTERMAN (4/12/47)
JAY LENO (4/28/50)

These stand-up comics became archrivals competing for retiring Johnny Carson's host spot on NBC's *Tonight Show.* Leno won, and a ratings war began between them. Letterman, angry with NBC, later moved his *Late Night Show* to CBS.

RELATIONSHIPS

STRENGTHS: **FAIR, TOLERANT, ETHICAL**

WEAKNESSES: **STRICT, HYPERMORAL, NEGLECTFUL**

BEST: **MARRIAGE**

WORST: **LOVE**

JOHN HODIAK (4/16/14)
ANNE BAXTER (5/7/23)

Hodiak, a popular actor of the 40s and 50s, married actress Baxter in 1946. Baxter, who was a grand-daughter of architect Frank Lloyd Wright, won an Oscar for *The Razor's Edge* (1946) and played the scheming young actress in *All About Eve* (1950). The couple divorced in 1953.

April 11–18
THE WEEK OF THE PIONEER
ARIES III

May 3–10
THE WEEK OF THE TEACHER
TAURUS II

Lofty Ideals

The basis of this relationship can be an intense interest in social equality, supported by firm ideals and high ethical standards. Both Aries III's and Taurus II's have strong feelings of responsibility toward their fellow human beings, and are fair and responsive in their daily relations with others. Both dislike discrimination in any form. Their relationship, then, will often assume a role as protector of the weak and poor. Philanthropic or socially concerned organizations will benefit from the efforts of this combination, which may also prove an excellent matchup for heading up a business or social group.

Friendships are likely to work well here, with relatively few problems. But it doesn't necessarily follow that romantic or sexual feelings between Aries III's and Taurus II's will develop into a love affair. Both of these personalities are most often passionately drawn to people far different from themselves—particularly people who are disadvantaged, unusual or exotic, or from widely divergent racial, social or national backgrounds.

The Aries III–Taurus II matchup can make for an excellent marriage as long as the partners don't feel that they are compromising their lofty ideals. They may well have children, who will grow up in an environment of tolerance and high standards, but both parents must be careful not to inflict their principles too strictly on their offspring, who may be frustrated and rebellious unless they feel free to make their own choices. In their concern for people outside the family, moreover, these two should take care not to neglect their own children's emotional needs.

Aries III–Taurus II siblings can contribute greatly to their family's stability and happiness. A parent-child relationship in this combination may be built on strong mutual respect, with an emphasis on trust and character that can continue well into adult life. The only danger here is excessive dependency or hero worship, which will bind children to parents and slow their growth and maturity.

ADVICE: *High moral standards are sometimes best suppressed to allow for individual expression. Avoid condemning attitudes. Don't neglect feelings.*

RELATIONSHIPS

STRENGTHS: **EXCITING, VIBRANT, FUN**

WEAKNESSES: **UNSTABLE, UNCOMMITTED, RESENTFUL**

BEST: **FRIENDSHIP**

WORST: **MARRIAGE**

MARTHA GRAHAM (5/11/1894)
MERCE CUNNINGHAM (4/16/19)

The "mother of modern dance," Graham, together with her soloist Cunningham, created "choreography by chance." Cunningham later became leader of the avant garde movement in contemporary dance. **Also: Charlie Chaplin & Oona O'Neill** (married; actor/playwright's daughter); **Catherine de Medici & Margaret of Valois** (daughter/ mother); **Peter Behrens & Walter Gropius** (Bauhaus architects).

April 11–18
THE WEEK OF THE PIONEER
ARIES III

May 11–18
THE WEEK OF THE NATURAL
TAURUS III

Establishing a Focus

A determining issue in this relationship is whether it can establish a basis of stability and focus. Although focused ambition is generally not a hallmark of either of these personalities individually, together they have an ability to make their dreams happen. To do so, however, they have to overcome the differences in their outlooks and agree. Not that they argue and fight; it's just that it's hard for them to find goals that are equally important to both of them. Once they do, it is surprisingly easy for them to achieve success.

As friends and lovers, Aries III's and Taurus III's can have great times. They both have a sense of humor and love group activities, and their relationship can be exciting, vibrant, and colorful. Aries III's must be careful, however, not to be put in the position of giving too much, sacrificing their own comfort to a more irresponsible Taurus III partner. An Aries III–Taurus III marriage can have trouble attaining stability; differences in values, goals and philosophy can prove divisive and prohibitive. One solution can be a free or open marriage in which each party pursues his or her own idiosyncratic lifestyle, committing to the form of marriage without accepting its limitations.

In the family sphere there may be problems. Taurus III children can tire of an Aries III parent's ideologies and strange ideas, for these natural individuals above all need to be themselves and to follow their spontaneous urges, no matter how outrageous. Likewise, Aries III children may not get the security and consistency they need from a Taurus III parent, whom they may see as flaky and unreliable.

As co-workers or business partners, Aries III's and Taurus III's have little in common. Stronger playing together than working together, as a team they lack professional seriousness and commitment to financial and organizational values. Still, they can work well as part of a group developing new concepts and ideas, particularly in design, fashion, advertising or other areas relating to the taste and interest of the general public.

ADVICE: *Hear the other party out. Take things a bit more seriously. Find a solid basis for your activities. Commit more deeply if you can.*

April 11–18

THE WEEK OF THE PIONEER
ARIES III

May 19–24

THE CUSP OF ENERGY
TAURUS-GEMINI CUSP

A Profound Education

RELATIONSHIPS

STRENGTHS: **EDUCATIONAL,
INTENSE, QUICK-WITTED**

WEAKNESSES: **HASTY, FICKLE,
UNCONSCIOUS**

BEST: **FRIENDSHIP**

WORST: **WORK**

This relationship specializes in the learning and teaching of deep lessons: both personalities make wonderful friends and advisors to each other. Aries III's tend to ground and direct energetic Taurus-Geminis, and to confront them with the needlessness of their fears, worries and obsessions; they also know how to tickle Taurus-Gemini funny bones, making them laugh not only at human foibles in general but at themselves, which helps them to lose their anxiety. In return, Taurus-Geminis often fascinate Aries III's, and inspire them to new creative heights. It is only fair to say, however, that Taurus-Geminis usually take more than they give in this combination.

Although the relationship is particularly good at analyzing deep emotions, it may not be so effective in their day-to-day expression. This combination may not be ideal for love or marriage, then, since passions can fly as electrically here as in a summer thunderstorm. An Aries III–Taurus-Gemini love affair will be unforgettable for both partners, usually not for its longevity or depth, however, but for its quick appearance and vanishing.

Patient and understanding, Aries III's can make excellent parents for Taurus-Geminis. The Aries III children of a Taurus-Gemini are less lucky: they will not appreciate their parent's obsessive worrying and intrusiveness. As siblings these two can exhaust other family members, who will look on amazed at their high-energy antics and their endless streams of thought and speech.

Scintillating, exciting, inspiring: the Aries III–Taurus-Gemini relationship can be all these things, but it isn't practical. Business ventures and social projects start off like a house on fire, with the best intentions and full of confidence, only to fizzle or just plain collapse. Chances are, however, that this duo may not even notice—most likely they've already moved on to the next project.

ANATOLY KARPOV (5/23/51)
GARRY KASPAROV (4/13/63)

These 2 Russian chess giants shared a creative and high-spirited rivalry. Karpov was world champion from 1975 until Kasparov defeated him at their first meeting in 1985. Karpov has since tried in vain to recapture his title. *Also:* **Charlie Chaplin & Douglas Fairbanks** (best friends; actors).

ADVICE: *Look for emotional honesty. Strive for self-knowledge. Pay attention to everyday practical concerns. Budget carefully.*

April 11–18

THE WEEK OF THE PIONEER
ARIES III

May 25–June 2

THE WEEK OF FREEDOM
GEMINI I

Grounding Influence

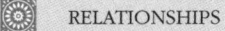

RELATIONSHIPS

STRENGTHS: **TECHNICAL,
STABILIZING, COMMUNICATIVE**

WEAKNESSES: **INHIBITING,
SARCASTIC, UNSYMPATHETIC**

BEST: **WORK**

WORST: **PARENT-CHILD**

Although Aries is a fire sign and Gemini air, this relationship has a grounding effect on both personalities, showing the influence of the earth element. Martian (Aries) and mercurial (Gemini) energies also coalesce around this duo's projects, and around the technical problems they're so skilled in solving; in fact they can accomplish a lot together, for their relationship can make them stay still long enough to focus. They should know, however, that the relationship's grounding influence will take time to be felt, and to help them learn and grow.

Aries III's in friendships with Gemini I's are usually quite understanding of their partners' need for constant change and will not try to confine them. And the absolute principles that Aries III's tend to believe in will stimulate the curiosity of Gemini's, who, however, may toss ironic or sarcastic barbs in the ensuing debates that can wound or annoy their Aries III partner. As lovers and mates, these two will initially have quite an exciting time, but the tempo will slow as they get to know each other. Gemini I's may also have difficulty remaining faithful to Aries III's, who are likely to show little sympathy for Gemini I gallivanting. Eventually, though, the relationship will settle down into something quite stable. Parent-child interactions may be less grounded than marriages: Aries III parents are likely to inhibit the Gemini I need for freedom, while Gemini I parents who don't really understand the lofty Aries III ideals and code of honor may become distant, cynical or tyrannical.

As partners in work projects, particularly of a conceptual nature, these two can communicate with lightning speed. Together they have an excellent feeling for the tastes of clients and the strategies of business adversaries. Gemini I attack melds well with Aries III defense, so that this duo can make a formidable commercial team.

TONY DOW (4/13/45)
JERRY MATHERS (6/2/48)

Dow and Mathers played the Cleaver brothers, Wally and young Theodore ("Beaver"), on the popular 50s tv sitcom *Leave It to Beaver.* The actors (shown here with tv mom) worked well with each other throughout the popular show's 6-year run.

Also: **Henry Kissinger & Nancy Kissinger** (married).

ADVICE: *Develop organizational strengths. Learn from each other. Without getting into conflict, deepen emotional bonds. Understand and accept.*

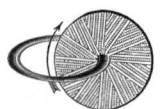

PAULETTE GODDARD (6/3/11)
CHARLIE CHAPLIN (4/16/1889)

Actress Goddard co-starred with Chaplin in the 1936 classic film *Modern Times,* marrying him that same year. Compared to his 2 previous marriages to 16-year-olds, this was a mature relationship in which the 2 actors enjoyed each other enormously.

Also: **Mary Healy & Peter Lind Hayes** (radio personalities).

April 11–18

THE WEEK OF THE PIONEER
ARIES III

June 3–10

THE WEEK OF NEW LANGUAGE
GEMINI II

Seductive Charms

This is a relationship of magnetic attraction and seductive charm, with each partner highly vulnerable to the other's sex appeal. But although physical attraction is a given here, emotional involvement is more of a struggle, since both of these partners try to keep their feelings under control, and to appear cool and composed. Even so, the relationship often brings them to depths of involvement that neither of them may have reached before. If so, they may find it difficult or impossible to detach.

Friendships between these two are often marred by mutual misunderstandings, which may lead to estrangements. Aries III's may find the highly personal language of Gemini II's hard to fathom. The fun-loving sides of both these partners will generally guarantee them a good time together at parties and other social events, but the Gemini II need to ventilate thoughts, often in a critical, biting or sarcastic way, may discomfit Aries III's, who like people to be quiet if they don't have something positive to say. This can put considerable strain on marital or family relationships. Nor will Aries III personal ideals be respected by Gemini II's, who will target the quality of inconsistency and unreality in their partner's beliefs with unmerciful accuracy.

Aries III's can make excellent role models and parents for young Gemini II's, who will look up to them and trust them. Gemini II parents, however, are prone to pry into Aries III children's lives and to worry about their unrealistic attitudes, which can only make them rebellious. Aries III–Gemini II siblings are likely to form strong bonds, but they will often challenge and combat each other both when young and in adult life, particularly in arguments over who performs mutual familial responsibilities.

ADVICE: *Find a balance between detachment and attachment. Strive for emotional honesty, but cultivate kindness and respect. Give enough.*

CLARENCE DARROW (4/18/1857)
RICHARD LOEB (6/11/05)

In his most famous trial, attorney Darrow defended Loeb, who confessed (along with accomplice Leopold) to a Chicago "thrill murder." Darrow managed to secure the pair life imprisonment rather than execution.

Also: **Charlie Chaplin & Stan Laurel** (Laurel started as Chaplin's understudy).

April 11–18

THE WEEK OF THE PIONEER
ARIES III

June 11–18

THE WEEK OF THE SEEKER
GEMINI III

Rolling Back Frontiers

This relationship can easily focus on the natural world—on exploring, for example, or preserving the environment. The combination can be excellent for a friendship or marriage based on challenge, travel, investigation and in general probing spatial and temporal limits, at home or abroad. Moreover, no matter where these two might roam, their relationship will make them feel physically and mentally comfortable, relaxed and natural.

In Gemini III's, Aries III's will meet their match in the areas of adventure, trailblazing and the tendency to spend hours in activities like wandering, climbing, swimming or flying. Gemini III's are usually unable to stick to one partner for long without looking around for new interests and horizons; but both these extremely independent personalities enjoy having a partner who is just as free, so that they can avoid the guilt, worry or concern they might feel with someone more dependent. These two may not plumb any great emotional depths together that would give them a history of sharing feelings, private struggles and personal problems to fall back on in times of stress or trouble. They would probably do well, then, to keep things light, avoiding quarrels or heavy confrontations.

Aries III–Gemini III siblings, particularly of the opposite sex, may make fine travel companions. This can also be an excellent parent-child relationship; irrespective of which of the two is the adult, the child will be guaranteed a varied palette of activities and interests, and his or her need for challenge will be understood. The mutual stimulation that is a trademark of this relationship can also manifest itself at work, where an Aries III and a Gemini III can comfortably share tasks as co-workers, or can head up an innovative and dynamic business together.

ADVICE: *Don't avoid problems. Dig deeper emotionally. Fight the good fight. Suffering is sometimes necessary. Acknowledge your needs.*

April 11–18
THE WEEK OF THE PIONEER
ARIES III

June 19–24
THE CUSP OF MAGIC
GEMINI-CANCER CUSP

Too Sweet?

RELATIONSHIPS	
STRENGTHS:	DEVOTED, PROTECTIVE, SYMPATHETIC
WEAKNESSES:	CLOYING, TERRITORIAL, REBELLIOUS
BEST:	LOVE
WORST:	WORK

This relationship can hold a seductive kind of charm for its participants while at the same time making them recklessly rebellious against its claiming and cloying attitudes. Its seductive power, in fact, can prove to be too much of a good thing.

Aries III's may begin with very protective feelings toward Gemini-Cancers, and once their sympathy is aroused, it is only a small step for them to fall head over heels in love. Seductive to the extreme, Gemini-Cancers may be unconsciously leading Aries III's on without realizing it. Actually, though, the Gemini-Cancer is more likely to become devoted than the Aries III, who may become uncomfortable with the extent of Gemini-Cancer feeling, and if so might feel forced to rebel. Otherwise, however, as a love affair this relationship can work out well.

Should marriage loom, on the other hand, Gemini-Cancers are much too private as people to be happy with the kind of entourage with which Aries III's surround themselves, especially at home. Territorial conflicts may also arise, since both of these two, and particularly Gemini-Cancers, must be able to call their home their own. If the marriage is to have a chance, both of them will have to learn to share, adjust and accommodate.

Within families, Gemini-Cancers may be able to give Aries III's the emotional understanding they need, but are unlikely to receive it in return. Whether as parents or siblings, Aries III's are likely to be overprotective and to stifle Gemini-Cancer development. Friendships between these two are likely to have a positive effect on Gemini-Cancers, bringing them more into touch with the social world around them. Aries III's too will benefit, getting a sympathetic shoulder to cry or lean on. As co-workers, these partners will distrust the charm of their relationship with each other, and one or both of them is likely to upset the apple cart.

SIRAMAVO BANDARANAIKE (4/17/16)
RANASINGHE PREMADASA (6/23/24)

Bandaranaike of Sri Lanka (Ceylon) was the world's first woman prime minister (1960–65, 1970–77). In '80 she was expelled from Parliament for political abuses. In her next bid for office, in '88, she lost to Premadasa, the first ever lower-caste president. Internal conflict led to his assassination in '93. **Also:** Nikolai Gumilev & Anna Akhmatova (married; Russian Acmeist poets).

ADVICE: *Agree on domestic matters. Cut down the traffic, but don't isolate yourself. Develop responsibility and trust.*

April 11–18
THE WEEK OF THE PIONEER
ARIES III

June 25–July 2
THE WEEK OF THE EMPATH
CANCER I

Fill 'Er Up

RELATIONSHIPS	
STRENGTHS:	TEAM-ORIENTED, GENEROUS, COOPERATIVE
WEAKNESSES:	ENERVATING, FRUSTRATING, UNAPPRECIATIVE
BEST:	BUSINESS PARTNER
WORST:	MARRIAGE

This relationship may revolve around energy, whether the issue is deciding what the best use and application of its energies might be, or figuring out what its energy requirements are and how are they being met. This will involve quite a bit of discussion and verbal exchange, which will themselves use a fair amount of energy. It is important for these two to verbalize their needs and to learn to focus—they can have plenty of fuel available to them but be ignorant of when and how to fill up the tank.

Aries III's often have energy to give, but don't understand Cancer I's well enough to know how to deliver it. And while they are unceasingly devoted, and always ready to help both humanity in general and individuals in particular, the deep, hard-to-satisfy needs of Cancer I's may still prove too much for them to handle. This is one reason why this relationship requires extraordinary and unceasing energy. Even an experienced, vital Aries III may be frustrated in trying to satisfy a Cancer I lover, friend or spouse. Cancer I's, on the other hand, will always understand Aries III needs, but usually lack the energy to keep up with them, let alone satisfy them.

Still, this duo can prove an excellent team in business. Cancer I's have a good feeling for money, and can often be wise investors; they will also be good at occupying home base and keep things functioning there while Aries III's are forging ahead elsewhere, lining up new accounts and clients, or selling a product. Initiative and the power to go for it are usually much higher in Aries III's, who may from time to time have to give Cancer I's a gentle push to get them moving. Unfortunately, unless Cancer I's are self-motivated in a given task or activity, they usually have difficulty achieving and sustaining forward momentum in this relationship.

HELEN KELLER (6/27/1880)
ANNE SULLIVAN MACY (4/14/1866)

Through sheer determination, in spite of the tantrums and hysteria of the frightened child Keller, teacher Macy helped her overcome blindness and deafness and learn to communicate. Keller went on to become a world-renowned author, lecturer and humanitarian with a profound influence on the lives of the handicapped.

ADVICE: *Work on being happy. Sometimes you don't know how lucky you are. Balance your energies. Learn to give and take. Be more understanding.*

"Baby Doc" Duvalier (7/3/51)
"Papa Doc" Duvalier (4/14/07)

From 1964 to 1971, Haiti's "Papa Doc" ran one of the world's most repressive governments. After his death, son "Baby Doc" inherited the post, but reneged on his reform promises. He was forced to leave Haiti in 1986. *Also:* **Ann Miller & Louis B. Mayer** (courtship; dancer-actress/studio mogul).

April 11–18
THE WEEK OF THE PIONEER
ARIES III

July 3–10
THE WEEK OF THE UNCONVENTIONAL
CANCER II

Independent—or Subordinate?

These very different personalities are diametric opposites in most of their respective psychologies—Aries III's oriented outward, toward the world, Cancer II's inward—yet both are very independent. The crucial issue in this relationship is whether they exercise their desire to be free or subordinate their individuality to being together. A Cancer II, for example, may join an Aries III partner in a drive toward success, or may decide that his or her own emotional life and inner development are more important priorities. In love and marriage, furthermore, Cancer II's are unlikely to allow Aries III's entrance to their private and often strange fantasy life. There are questions as to how deep or personal this relationship can become, then, from the outset. If these two do choose to be together, however, the synergy of their relationship may forge a bond that will surmount their individual differences.

Should these two marry they can achieve an uncommon unity of interest, with the Cancer II concentrating on the domestic and nurturing activities, the Aries III battling the world. Their differences can even complement and help each other, as Cancer II's put active Aries III's more in touch with their emotional center and Aries III's expose Cancer II's to social issues. Both parties are usually understanding enough of their mate to prevent themselves from precipitating arguments or reacting to differences in outlook with irritation or anger.

The Aries III need to communicate is likely to be frustrated when this relationship manifests in business, at work and in friendships, since Cancer II's find it difficult to share with a partner. They are often also too tied up with their own concerns to provide for all of the needs of an Aries III child. Aries III's, however, can prove remarkably understanding parents for Cancer II's, as long as they don't try to impose their ideas on them too heavily. From childhood through adolescence, Cancer II–Aries III siblings are likely to share a private world, concerned with collecting, fantasy or decorating their shared space.

ADVICE: *Without giving up your individuality, learn to share. Emphasize the qualities you have in common. Join in everyday tasks. Make up your mind about priorities.*

F.W. Woolworth (4/13/1852)
John Wanamaker (7/11/1838)

As 2 of America's most successful retailers, Wanamaker and Woolworth were tough economic competitors. Wanamaker's, a leading department store, opened in New York in 1896—the same year that Woolworth's opened its first NYC "5 & 10" store.

April 11–18
THE WEEK OF THE PIONEER
ARIES III

July 11–18
THE WEEK OF THE PERSUADER
CANCER III

Fighting for Freedom

The primary theme of this combination is the fight for personal freedom. The relationship will often involve power struggles, then, and is unlikely to be stable, especially since these two have trouble sticking to anything. There is a built-in desire here to be free of everything the relationship creates, whether it be a commitment or other structure, or simply a joint interest.

Aries III's and Cancer III's who become romantically involved will have an interesting, varied and intense relationship. Cancer III's usually have to have things their way, but their power to persuade and manipulate will be sorely tested by the resistance and willfulness of their Aries III partners in love and marriage. These two are better suited to each other as lovers than as spouses, since the combination's conflicts, tensions and searing passions go better with excitement, often sexual, than with stability and security. The Cancer III predilection to excess can be triggered if they find themselves playing second fiddle to more worldly Aries III's.

At work, Aries III's want only to be successful (though this is vital to them), while Cancer III's are driven to reach the top. For a Cancer III, a fight for personal freedom against the influence of a less ambitious partner is likely to be a theme of this matchup.

Friendships between these two are probably unusual, since career, social or economic competition is likely to take precedence over trust, sharing and just plain fun. Likewise, Aries III–Cancer III siblings are likely to engage in unproductive struggles that may disrupt family life. As parents these two are likely to be adversely influenced by each other to the point where they will engage in power struggles over children, particularly should the relationship break up. Cancer III parents will be frustrated by their inability to control or protect their independent Aries III child, who may see their influence as oppressive or smothering; Aries III parents are also likely to be challenged by a Cancer III child, particularly one of the same sex, and battles for supremacy within the family group may result, particularly if the other parent is the mutually desired object of their struggle.

ADVICE: *Struggle can make you strong, but also, alas, insensitive. Avoid unnecessary conflict. Respect the values of others. Seek stability.*

April 11–18

THE WEEK OF THE PIONEER
ARIES III

July 19–25

THE CUSP OF OSCILLATION
CANCER-LEO CUSP

A Peak Experience

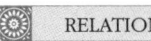
Dominated by the fiery aspects of both its partners, this relationship is striking for its intensity of feeling, sexuality or simply energy. Love between these two can be ardent and romantic, featuring trips to unusual places, physically challenging and dangerous endeavors, sexual or druglike highs and revelations abounding. Should such peak experiences or epiphanies materialize on just a few occasions, they may be enough to ensure the relationship's continuance. Should they be constantly sought for, however, they can grow addictive, the pure love once felt becoming muddied and dangerously unrealistic. A potentially painful and destructive separation may be necessary. To avoid this, Aries III's need to keep their self-sacrificial streak from getting out of control, and Cancer-Leos to beware of getting lost in possessiveness or overly needy demands.

Both Aries III's and Cancer-Leos are dauntless and courageous, making them good companions in challenging adventures and also protective parents and friends. Aries III's, however, generally have a high energy level, particularly when engaged in a project, while Cancer-Leos are prone to great fluctuations of energy and mood. If a Cancer-Leo goes into a depressive phase, this can create conflicts with an Aries III, who won't like hearing complaints and is likely to be worn down by excessive negativity. Should a Cancer-Leo fall into a downward spiral in the middle of a joint endeavor, an Aries III will likely grow impatient and frustrated, and may want to discontinue this working relationship. Aries III's who are married to Cancer-Leos tend to be more understanding of their moods, but even a deep love can be eroded away over time.

Cancer-Leo children are apt to find Aries III parents less than sympathetic to their emotional state. The Aries III will listen to, think about and discuss their problems, but may never really empathize. As a result, Cancer-Leo offspring often feel misunderstood by what they perceive as a godlike Aries III parent.

LYNDA CARTER (7/24/51)
LYLE WAGGONER (4/13/35)

Actor Waggoner began his career on the *Carol Burnett Show*, then co-starred with Carter on *Wonder Woman* (1977–79), which featured a comic-book romance between a curvaceous Nazi-fighting superhero and a handsome government agent.

ADVICE: *Go with the flow. Life has its ups and downs. Cultivate patience and understanding. Strive for empathy. Put matters of the heart first.*

April 11–18

THE WEEK OF THE PIONEER
ARIES III

July 26–August 2

THE WEEK OF AUTHORITY
LEO I

Bridging the Gap

This relationship has to find translation tools to bridge the gap between different modes of thought and communication. Misunderstanding is common here, since both partners consider themselves authorities on many subjects, and have their own, highly individual terminology. Nor is either likely to compromise in order to move toward understanding. Ideally, this relationship will evolve its own original language in which the duo can share their often contrasting ideas.

Aries III's have something to teach Leo I's about being more accepting of people, particularly those they disagree with. Leo I's, on the other hand, can help Aries III's learn how to direct their energies so as to strive for inward goals first before moving outward toward the world. Friendships in this combination, particularly when the partners are of the same sex, can be very close relationships featuring learning and sharing at a deep level.

In love, Aries III's and Leo I's tend to favor sexuality over sensuality. They are more likely to express warmth and affection in their friendships than in their love affairs. Leo I's demand variety and change in their sexual relationships, and hate being tied down to predictable patterns, and in this respect they will test Aries III's to the limit. But Leo I's also want a cheerful lover with whom they can have fun, and who will give them respite from their all-consuming work, and Aries III may fit both of these requirements well.

Family life of some sort is a must for Aries III's, whereas Leo I's can capably function alone, and have no crying need for an audience or a constituency. In marriages between these two, Aries III's must be prepared to shoulder the brunt of the responsibilities, since Leo I's are likely to be away a lot. The relationship has a great deal to teach its offspring, who, however, may not always be that eager to learn, and may come to see their parents' didactic attitudes as repressive of their own individual language.

RACHELE MUSSOLINI (4/11/1890)
BENITO MUSSOLINI (7/29/1883)

Mussolini, denied the daughter of his father's mistress, instead seduced and later married Rachele, the mistress' sister. She adored him but he was incurably promiscuous. The Italian dictator was executed in 1945 along with his mistress, not wife Rachele.

Also: **Thomas Jefferson & Polly Jefferson** (father/daughter; she died giving birth to his grandchild).

ADVICE: *Friendship and love need not be mutually exclusive. Beware of all-knowing attitudes. Be ready to listen and to learn. Play together.*

RELATIONSHIPS

STRENGTHS: **STIMULATING, GROUNDED, FAITHFUL**

WEAKNESSES: **UNSYMPATHETIC, INTIMIDATING, VIOLENT**

BEST: **OPPONENT, FRIENDSHIP**

WORST: **MARRIAGE**

CLARENCE DARROW (4/18/1857)
JOHN T. SCOPES (8/3/1900)

Criminal lawyer Darrow defended Scopes—accused of teaching Darwin's theory of evolution in Tennessee public schools—during the celebrated 1925 "Monkey Trial." Darrow skillfully debated fundamentalist prosecutor William Jennings Bryan over the biblical evidence against evolution. Scopes' guilty conviction was later overturned.

April 11–18
THE WEEK OF THE PIONEER
ARIES III

August 3–10
THE WEEK OF BALANCED STRENGTH
LEO II

A Titanic Battle

This relationship is often intensely confrontational, and its struggles can assume gigantic proportions. Neither party will show much willingness to back down. Marriages are not particularly recommended here, then, but may sometimes work out if a cease-fire and a suitable division of labor can be agreed upon, or if the partners unite together in a cause, or in a fight for something outside the relationship.

The central issue in this couple's love affairs will usually be love versus power. The level of the relationship's combativeness will often be directly related to its level of passion. Peace can come if both partners are willing to give up their struggles and commit themselves to unconditional love, but this often won't be possible, and the affair may bring great pain before it inevitably ends. Both of these partners are very physical types, so that bodily threat, which in more extreme cases may even be fulfilled, cannot be ruled out. These two are also capable of a great deal of emotional detachment, and neither should expect a great deal of sympathy from the other.

Because they are so evenly matched in their will to win, Aries III's and Leo II's make excellent opponents for each other in sport, business, love and other areas, including family, where they can exercise their competitive instincts in socially accepted ways. Outright enmity between them, though possible, is unlikely except in extreme cases, because of their mutual respect for each other's power and capabilities. Friendship often arise between Aries III's and Leo II's who were once opponents, then acquaintances, then companions, and finally friends, a process that allows a gradual but firm creation of bonds of trust. Forged in the crucible of experience, such relationships are likely to be able to withstand great stresses over the years, and these partners have the capacity to be extremely faithful to one another.

ADVICE: *To win, you sometimes have to surrender. Love can be stronger than power. When you give, give unconditionally. Keep antagonisms under control.*

RELATIONSHIPS

STRENGTHS: **ASPIRING, COMMANDING, INSPIRATIONAL**

WEAKNESSES: **EGO-INVOLVED, DIVIDED, JEALOUS**

BEST: **WORK**

WORST: **FAMILY**

DAVID JUSTICE (4/14/66)
HALLE BERRY (8/14/68)

A former beauty queen, Halle has appeared in 2 Spike Lee films and played opposite Kurt Russell in *Executive Decision* (1996). After a storybook romance, she married Atlanta Braves outfielder Justice, but was divorced soon after.

Also: **Nikita Khrushchev & Fidel Castro** (communist allies).

April 11–18
THE WEEK OF THE PIONEER
ARIES III

August 11–18
THE WEEK OF LEADERSHIP
LEO III

A Search for Common Goals

Aries III and Leo III occupy a position trine to each other (120° apart in the zodiac), so conventional astrology predicts an easy relationship between them. But this is rarely the case. These two strong individuals both want to involve themselves in the world, and the main theme of their relationship will always be the search to identify and achieve objectives. The search, moreover, will always be as important as the achievement, if not more so. The consequence is that these two arouse each other's competitive instincts like few other matchups in the year. Bringing out the worst in each other (as well as the best), they find it extremely hard to achieve a true sense of unity. Both are born leaders, and should they be able to function together in an executive capacity, they are capable of leading any group, company, social or sports endeavor to new heights, and of inspiring commitment and drive in those who work for them. It is equally possible, however, that their power struggles will tear their projects apart, and that their ego struggles will prevent them from focusing on the common good.

Leo III's are extremely difficult to get close to emotionally. In love and marriage they require extremely understanding partners and mates, and Aries III's don't always have the time or inclination (but often do have the psychological talent) to unravel the mysteries of their darker side. Still, in times of need and trouble, Aries III's may be among the few people Leo III's can turn to in order to relieve their pain and torment.

Children of this pair may not find either parent very empathic, but generally speaking, Aries III's make the more sympathetic parent of these two; Leo III's are prone to spoiling their favorite child, and can thus arouse antagonistic jealousy not only in their other children but in their mate as well. Family confrontations between Leo III's and Aries III's may be real knock-down, drag-out affairs that leave other relatives out of breath or exhausted. Such battles arise often, particularly over issues of power, with Aries III's proceeding more out of ideological motives and Leo III's more out of personal ones.

ADVICE: *Leaders should never forget their constituency. Listen to what others say about you. Don't be afraid to admit errors. Stay unified.*

April 11–18

THE WEEK OF THE PIONEER
ARIES III

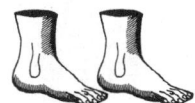

August 19–25

THE CUSP OF EXPOSURE
LEO-VIRGO CUSP

RELATIONSHIPS

STRENGTHS: **TRUSTING, EASYGOING, ADMIRING**

WEAKNESSES: **SECRETIVE, NEUROTIC, FRUSTRATING**

BEST: **FRIENDSHIP, WORK**

WORST: **LOVE**

A One-Way Street

This relationship is often a one-way street pointed in the direction of the Leo-Virgo, and mostly devoted to exposing their secret, hidden side. Moreover, this fact is usually itself only tacitly acknowledged, remaining an unspoken aspect of the combination—one that requires a strong basis in trust.

In love, marital and family relationships, Leo-Virgos demand to be understood by their partners. Aries III's who are expected to show this understanding may be capable of but not always interested in doing so. On the other hand, if their self-sacrificing side comes out, they just may roll up their sleeves and take on the task of unraveling a Leo-Virgo partner. Their success will not be guaranteed: Leo-Virgos usually have a few tricks up their sleeve, and at the very moment when Aries III's feel they are getting somewhere, Leo-Virgos are likely to take the wind out of their sails by revealing themselves in a thoroughly exhibitionistic display.

This may not be a passionate combination, and love affairs are probably best put aside in favor of acquaintanceships or easygoing friendships. Love is blind, however, and Leo-Virgos can develop secret passions for Aries III's. Whether or not they return this passion, Aries III's will be capable of discretion and deserving of trust, rarely revealing Leo-Virgo secrets at a later date.

Leo-Virgos and Aries III's can form firm friendships around a particular activity, usually one of a practical nature. They work well together, and are likely to combine a friendship with a shared career project; if so, this endeavor can often be successful and somewhat lucrative. Leo-Virgos can learn to express their ambition from Aries III role models, who are not at all shy about putting their best foot forward and forcing others to recognize their abilities. Mutual trust and admiration distinguish both working relationships and friendships between these two.

ADVICE: *Try to be honest. Don't play games. Self-centeredness is counterproductive. Hide-and-seek can be exhausting. Get to work.*

WILBUR WRIGHT (4/16/1867)
ORVILLE WRIGHT (8/19/1871)

These brothers first explored flight in 1896 by experimenting with kites and gliders. Working closely together, they built a light but powerful engine that enabled them to become the first to fly a self-propelled airplane.

Also: Kingsley Amis & Martin Amis (father/son; novelists).

April 11–18

THE WEEK OF THE PIONEER
ARIES III

August 26–September 2

THE WEEK OF SYSTEM BUILDERS
VIRGO I

RELATIONSHIPS

STRENGTHS: **MAGICAL, DEVOTIONAL, RESPONSIBLE**

WEAKNESSES: **NERVOUS, STRESSED, INSECURE**

BEST: **WORK**

WORST: **MARRIAGE**

Mysterious Mix

This relationship produces a powerful effect in one area in particular: career. The main point of departure between these two—Virgo I rationality in thought and planning versus Aries III intuition and spontaneity—may cause occasional flare-ups, but for the most part their respective strengths mysteriously complement each other when they work together. These service-oriented individuals can also bring out the more responsible side in each other, so that if their relationship focuses on the welfare of others, it can have a devotional streak. In those cases the combination can be of great benefit to humanity.

Virgo I's get nervous and stressed unless they keep their home and career lives separate. Aries III's find this kind of separation impossible, for they don't feel that their work in the world stops when they get home. This can put Virgo I–Aries III marriages under a lot of strain, particularly when the Aries III decides to invite over a bunch of friends, co-workers or disciples just when the Virgo I is snuggling into a warm, quiet domestic evening. It may be only a matter of time before the Aries III begins to look around for an escape. This too will make the Virgo I nervous, forcing him or her to hold on even tighter. Still, things can go well between these two, especially if the structure they set up in their living situation relieves Aries III's of responsibilities they would rather leave to a more orderly person anyway.

In the long run, Virgo I's may have a salutary, even magical effect on the energies of their Aries III children, who may not appreciate their parents at the time but will undoubtedly manifest more orderly personal habits and working methods later in life.

ADVICE: *Respect privacy. Try not bring your work home. Structure your living situation thoughtfully. Think of the greater good.*

LORETTA LYNN (4/14/35)
CONWAY TWITTY (9/1/33)

Following her best-selling rags-to-riches autobiography, country and western singer-songwriter Lynn was immortalized in the 1980 movie *Coalminer's Daughter*. Twitty, another very successful country-pop star, recorded several hit duets with Lynn and toured with her in 1970. Their concerts featured many hit songs that are now country classics.

STRENGTHS: **REFLECTIVE, OBJECTIVE, FORCEFUL**

WEAKNESSES: **UNEMOTIONAL, REJECTING, CRITICAL**

BEST: **MARRIAGE**

WORST: **FAMILY**

MERCE CUNNINGHAM (4/16/19)
JOHN CAGE (9/5/12)

Cunningham, acknowledged leader of the avant-garde dance movement, teamed up with experimental composer Cage, whose contribution to contemporary music included use of non-musical sounds. They have been collaborators and life partners since the 40s. **Also:**

J.P. Morgan & J.P. Morgan, Jr.
(father/son financiers).

April 11–18

THE WEEK OF THE PIONEER
ARIES III

September 3–10

THE WEEK OF THE ENIGMA
VIRGO II

Private Worlds

This relationship likes to investigate, unlock and gain mastery over more private and at times mysterious areas of experience. The matchup is interesting, since its theme of mastery manifests in two very separate, very different worlds: Virgo II's are taken up with very personal endeavors, Aries III's with very worldly ones. Though these two share a similar kind of drive, the spheres of influence in which they choose to express it are so wholly unrelated to each other that it would be hard for anyone to imagine a true union between them.

Virgo II's are seldom easily approached or understood, but they don't mind someone coming on to them forcefully (as Aries III's may), since they are confident of their ability to repulse attack. Often, in fact, they will secretly admire Aries III forcefulness and drive. As spouses they will appreciate the protectiveness of Aries III's, as lovers their ardent and dynamic nature. Virgo II's can live alone very well, so they may not jump at the opportunity to live with an Aries III, preferring their own space. And if they do decide to marry or live with an Aries III, the latter will have to adjust to their lifestyle, which demands privacy. If friction is to be avoided, Aries III's will have to give up some of their social life. But Virgo II's will go a long way to reach agreement in these matters if they are deeply enough in love.

Whether in marriage, love or family, the relationship does not favor deep emotion. Virgo II critical attitudes and Aries III drive and ideological preoccupations usually shift the spotlight away from the world of feelings, and the relationship can be rather cool and detached. This does not make for the most empathic parent-child or sibling relationship, but at least the partners will usually know where they stand with each other.

The caution and critical nature of Virgo II's can make it hard for more exuberant and positive Aries III's to work with them. Yet what Aries III's want and what they need are often quite different, and Virgo II's may actually ground and support their more dynamic and fanciful Aries III co-workers in a very positive way.

ADVICE: *Be ready to compromise. Find a balance between public and private. Emphasize trust and sharing. Distinguish between wants and needs.*

STRENGTHS: **DEPENDABLE, RESPONSIBLE, APPRECIATIVE**

WEAKNESSES: **UNSYMPATHETIC, UNSTABLE, OVERBEARING**

BEST: **LOVE, FRIENDSHIP**

WORST: **FAMILY**

LEOPOLD STOKOWSKI (4/18/1882)
GRETA GARBO (9/18/05)

Maestro Stokowski was the flamboyant conductor of the Philadelphia Orchestra from 1912–36. His glamorous image extended to a personal life highlighted by a long and notorious affair with the incomparable Garbo. For a time, the pair shared a romantic villa in Italy. **Also:** **Bill Irwin & David Shiner** (mime/comic collaborators).

April 11–18

THE WEEK OF THE PIONEER
ARIES III

September 11–18

THE WEEK OF THE LITERALIST
VIRGO III

Strict Requirements

Responsibility is usually the keynote of this relationship; each partner will live up to every requirement to be there for the other in a time of need or crisis. Although ordinarily the relationship often has its best chance in areas where dependability is more important than affection or sympathy, its staunchness may also create an unusual type of empathy.

A matchup between two such strong-willed individuals as these will certainly have its ups and downs. Virgo III's are extremely discriminating and selective in their choices; having passed rigorous tests, an Aries III will feel privileged to be the lover of a Virgo III. This couple's affairs can be intense, with Virgo III's tending to have the upper hand, since they usually know better than Aries III's do exactly what they want and don't want. Unless the relationship involves a strong bond of mutual respect, harmonious living or working situations may be impossible. If Aries III's find Virgo III's selfish, or Virgo III's see Aries III's as unrealistic or self-deceiving, the pairing may quickly become unstable or even confrontational. Aries III–Virgo III friendships can be extremely strong; the lack of romantic involvement will forestall many of the relationship's emotional problems, aiding its stability.

In marriage, the partners' strict demands and requirements for their living situation will not meld well. But once the devotion to duty inherent in this combination becomes apparent and living arrangements are worked out, this can prove a long-lasting, faithful union. Children of this pair will have to be tough if they are not to be dominated by their parents, both of whom can be devoted and understanding but also overbearing.

ADVICE: *Work on building respect. Don't be afraid to show affection. Beware of egotism and self-deception. Be as reasonable as possible.*

April 11–18

THE WEEK OF THE PIONEER
ARIES III

September 19–24

THE CUSP OF BEAUTY
VIRGO-LIBRA CUSP

RELATIONSHIPS

STRENGTHS: **EDUCATIONAL, SUPPORTIVE, UNDERSTANDING**

WEAKNESSES: **PROJECTING, RESTRICTIVE, QUARRELING**

BEST: **FRIENDSHIP**

WORST: **LOVE**

Possibilities for Personal Growth

This relationship may serve to open up both philosophical, social or aesthetic understanding and other, more worldly matters to its partners, who will use this understanding, however, more to advance their ambitions as a couple than as a spiritual resource. These two are generally pragmatic; unless they are strongly attracted to each other physically, which is unlikely, a passionate love affair is usually ruled out between them. Their rather unromantic striving for aesthetic or philosophic excellence may prove more important and gratifying to them if they are friends or spouses.

The relationship may require one of the partners to assume a parental or even paternal role, and that partner is likely to be the Aries III. Virgo-Libras need a strong and responsible mate or friend to support them, and Aries III's can play that part well. The heroic nature of the Aries III personality can also serve as the hook for a Virgo-Libra's psychological projections: having idolized or depended on a friend or family member when young, Virgo-Libras may unconsciously seek that person's qualities later in life, and may think they have found them in an Aries III. Seeing this happening, Aries III's may feel a certain resentment at being cast in this parental role; they will want to be loved and appreciated for who they are, not as a projection of someone else.

Even so, a marriage between these two can succeed. Aries III's are capable of a deep understanding of people, and will be able to see beyond the glitzy appearances with which Virgo-Libras often surround themselves, and to alert them to deeper possibilities for personal growth. There may be other difficulties, however, the most prominent of these being the fact that matters of taste and aesthetics are not of great interest to most Aries III's but are of utmost importance to Virgo-Libras. This couple may quarrel, then, over the importance of dress, furnishings, architectural design and decoration. But Aries III's can learn a great deal from Virgo-Libras about how to appreciate aesthetic beauty, and about its value and use in the world.

HENRY III (9/20/1551)
CATHERINE DE MEDICI (4/13/1519)

Catherine was wife to one king and mother of the last 3 Valois kings of France. She married Henry II in 1533. A believer in astrology, she was also a political realist. When King Henry III, her favorite son, was expelled by the Catholic League, which sought to control the crown, she negotiated with its leaders. Henry had them murdered; she was appalled and died shortly after.

ADVICE: *Learn through mutual appreciation. Explore spiritual and aesthetic areas. Beware of running old scripts. See people for who they are.*

April 11–18

THE WEEK OF THE PIONEER
ARIES III

September 25–October 2

THE WEEK OF THE PERFECTIONIST
LIBRA I

RELATIONSHIPS

STRENGTHS: **ADMIRING, SUCCESSFUL, EFFICIENT**

WEAKNESSES: **DESTRUCTIVE, OPPRESSIVE, MANIPULATIVE**

BEST: **FAMILY, CO-WORKER**

WORST: **MARRIAGE**

Unusual Glue

This relationship is an unusual, even rare pairing, and knows it. As such it may strive to be more conventional, or even just to be understood—generally to no avail. These two are very different, and the way their energies meld is hard to define. Nothing about the pairing or its behavior is typical.

Often completely unconscious of the subtleties of love and emotion, Aries III's may at first view a relationship with Libra I as the most perfect of all loves. Blinded by Libra I attractiveness, they may be totally unaware of how things really stand, and can find themselves chewed up and spat out without even realizing what's happening. In fact they may never find out how the Libra I really feels about them emotionally.

Libra I's for their part are rarely satisfied with themselves, let alone with anyone else. In the most meticulous way, they may succeed in destroying an Aries III's pride in winning them, thus depriving him or her of much-needed ego satisfaction. Their balloons popped, Aries III mates and lovers may have little choice but either to surrender utterly to the Libra I or simply to slink off and lick their wounds. Aries III's, however, have an iconoclastic streak, and may ultimately be pushed to tear apart a Libra I's perfectionistic and difficult facade. In the end, relieved to be understood, this may win the Libra I over. Each partner's shredding of the other will become the unconventional glue that binds them together.

It is probably better, however, if relationships between these two, particularly friendships and family and working pairings, are kept on the less personal, more unemotional side. A friendship between these two can work out well, with Libra I's earning kudos from Aries III's for their technical expertise and efficiency, and Aries III's being praised by Libra I's for their energy and drive. As co-workers, this team has a lot to offer a company or business, and in family situations both Libra I's and Aries III's will lend both dash and zest to the most boring gatherings.

DAVID CASSIDY (4/12/50)
SHAUN CASSIDY (9/27/58)

These teen-idol musicians are half-brothers through father Jack Cassidy. David played opposite stepmother Shirley Jones in *The Partridge Family*. Shaun starred in *The Hardy Boys Mysteries*. They also starred in Broadway's *Blood Brothers*.

Also: Thomas Jefferson & Martha Jefferson Randolph (father/daughter; president/acting First Lady).

ADVICE: *Romantic relationships are best avoided. Fight the tendency to dominate. Keep your self-esteem high. Appreciate your good points. Go your own way.*

STRENGTHS: ASTUTE, PERSUASIVE, ENTERPRISING

WEAKNESSES: INNERLY UNAWARE, OVERDEPENDENT, STUCK

BEST: WORK

WORST: LOVE

J.P. Morgan, Sr. (4/17/1837)
George Westinghouse (10/6/1846)

An inventor and very wealthy industrialist, Westinghouse founded Westinghouse Electric in 1886, but fought a bitter power struggle with banker and financier Morgan over the management of the company. *Also:* Peter Behrens & Le Corbusier (Bauhaus architects).

April 11–18
THE WEEK OF THE PIONEER
ARIES III

October 3–10
THE WEEK OF SOCIETY
LIBRA II

Knowing Thyself

More than most, this relationship will concern itself with the objective world and with ambition. If the pairing is to last, however, the key focus should be on understanding the subjective world of this couple's own relationship, and of their own and each other's inner lives. As a team, ironically, this duo may have a good understanding of the psychology of other human beings, and of society in general, but within the relationship, unreality is likely to be a big problem. Both Aries III's and Libra II's are prone to problematical love affairs, since both of them usually lack a clear idea of either themselves or their partner; in their relationship with each other, this trait is magnified.

Although unstable and rocky, Aries III–Libra II love affairs and marriages can nevertheless endure for long periods as the parties focus on their worldly goals. The relationship may unfortunately swallow up its partners' individuality, making separations and breakups extremely difficult and painful. On the plus side, Libra II's are fun to be with and can help take the minds of Aries III's off more serious matters; Aries III's can provide the security and confidence that Libra II's desire. Parent-child matchups in this combination, and in either possible version, can work out well, with mutual respect and love, as long as they are not dominated by competition and jealousy involving the other parent or another child. Libra II–Aries III sibling pairs have a great deal to offer, both to each other and to family life, particularly in the social sphere.

Aries III–Libra II friendships probably work best if they are career based. At work, business partnerships in this combination can be extremely persuasive and successful. An understanding of the collective makes success likely in fields such as advertising, public relations, health care, the arts, sales or marketing. Particularly telling is an awareness of what people need and want, so that dreaming up a product or service and getting it on the rails is a specialty here.

ADVICE: *Be there through good times and bad. Apply your insights to yourself. Clear away the haze. Have fun, but confront more serious matters too.*

STRENGTHS: HONEST, SEXUAL, AUTONOMOUS

WEAKNESSES: DOMINATING, ARGUMENTATIVE, COMBATIVE

BEST: MARRIAGE

WORST: FRIENDSHIP

Dwight Eisenhower (10/14/1890)
Nikita Khrushchev (4/17/1894)

In 1960, President Eisenhower denied charges of US espionage when Soviets shot down a U-2 spy plane. After Soviet leader Khrushchev produced the pilot, the president took responsibility. The pair feuded bitterly during a subsequent Paris conference.

April 11–18
THE WEEK OF THE PIONEER
ARIES III

October 11–18
THE WEEK OF THEATER
LIBRA III

Out Front

Prominent here are likely to be honesty and openness, but not necessarily closeness, since these two personalities are often competitive and even combative. (Aries III and Libra III are opposites, 180° apart in the zodiac.) Any covert or illicit activity will create problems, since both parties like to be up front about what they do. Concealment, and the fear, guilt and shame that for these two accompany hiding anything, do not suit the relationship. Since both parties are very sexual, and quite openly so, physical enjoyment will figure prominently in this pairing.

Both these parties are dominant and need to occupy center stage, but marriages between them can be quite successful. Although Libra III's can't stand other people to be emotionally dependent on them, they themselves occasionally need a strong figure to lean on, who can well be an Aries III. The relationship may require compromise, however, in the area of children: Aries III's love children and family in general, and Libra III's do not. Perhaps the number of children can be limited, or their care can be handled primarily by the Aries III, leaving the Libra III free to pursue a career.

Since both of these personalities need a lot of autonomy at work, they are an unlikely business team. Should each head up their own service, business or company division, they may form a relationship as equal allies, but are just as likely to battle it out as fierce competitors. Aries III's and Libra III's are dynamic, knowledgeable, ambitious and hard-driving individuals who will be more than a match for each other.

Two siblings of this combination are likely to be competitive and argumentative. Friendships will have the same qualities, and may be short-lived; tremendous conflicts can similarly arise in Aries III–Libra III parent-child relationships, threatening the family's very fabric. Curiously, both parent-child and sibling combinations may be more viable later in life, proving particularly capable and interested in dealing with financial and other practical problems.

ADVICE: *Compromise is often necessary. Work to get closer. Develop true sharing and acceptance. Tone down dominant tendencies.*

April 11–18
THE WEEK OF THE PIONEER
ARIES III

October 19–25
THE CUSP OF DRAMA & CRITICISM
LIBRA-SCORPIO CUSP

Persuasive Ideas

Ideas or ideologies will be the central focus of this relationship, which will be strongly concerned with persuading other people, or selling to them. In some cases, if the pair are united in a common outlook, the relationship can prove extremely charismatic and convincing in itself.

Both Aries III's and Libra-Scorpios are fascinated by ideas, but their approaches in this area are extremely different. Aries III's will enthusiastically support concepts that they believe provide a basis for their own actions; Libra-Scorpios are more intellectual and objective, rarely letting ideas control their lives. A certain level of conflict will ensue as these two try to balance their opposing views, and this may preclude a long-term love affair. A short, passionate involvement, however, especially a predominantly sexual one, may be possible.

Libra-Scorpios have intense and complex feelings, and Aries III straightforwardness may not be the most calming or effective way to approach them, particularly in an intimate relationship such as marriage. Aries III's are generally much too busy getting the job done to stop to argue with Libra-Scorpios, and are likely to consider what they see as negativity, or destructive criticism, from such a partner an annoyance or hindrance. Not being taken seriously is unbearable to Libra-Scorpios, and if this reaction becomes a pattern, it may end the relationship.

Friendships are often a better bet here, since they tend to be easier and lighter, and to favor the sharing of a variety of activities. Both Aries III's and Libra-Scorpios have a concern for their fellow human beings, and are drawn to group efforts; they may work well together in a social or service setting where the welfare of others is the primary concern. As a partnership, these two can be a powerful force for community good. The relationship will be less effective in family situations, where a host of personal irritations and emotional conflicts will cause unsettling oscillations of mood.

ADVICE: *It's sometimes a mistake to get emotional about ideas. Try to relativate. Keep the mood light. Reduce the irritation factor.*

RELATIONSHIPS

STRENGTHS: **IDEOLOGICAL, PERSUASIVE, VARIED**

WEAKNESSES: **IRRITATING, CONFLICTING, OSCILLATING**

BEST: **FRIENDSHIP**

WORST: **MARRIAGE**

JOHNNY CARSON (10/23/25)
DAVID LETTERMAN (4/12/47)

When Carson retired after 30 years on NBC's *Tonight Show* (1962–92), Letterman expected to replace him. But NBC selected Jay Leno for the spot, and Letterman was offended. By August '93 Letterman went to CBS with his own *Late Show*, competing directly with *The Tonight Show*, and the ratings war began.

***Also:* Thomas Jefferson & Martha Jefferson** (married).

April 11–18
THE WEEK OF THE PIONEER
ARIES III

October 26–November 2
THE WEEK OF INTENSITY
SCORPIO I

New Levels of Excitement

This relationship is likely to be vibrant and imaginative, though punctuated by occasional blowups. Its alchemy can be simultaneously mysterious and passionate. Both parties are often extremely sexual, and their love affairs with each other, often carried on in secret, can reach high peaks of desire and consummation. This comes, however, with no small level of emotional turmoil.

In love and marriage, Aries III's are likely to find themselves dominated by Scorpio I's. This relationship can stir up their deepest emotional layers, making it hard for them to work, and creating trouble in other areas of their lives—completely throwing them off balance. Scorpio I's are much more comfortable with this relationship's firestorms. They are no strangers to emotional turmoil, which is often a constant background for them in their creative or professional work. Controlling their own feelings while calling the shots in the powerful emotional world they share with another is a specialty of Scorpio I's, who will tend to control the inner workings of this relationship and many others as well.

Scorpio I's will tend to keep their Aries III spouses on a tight rein. They won't usually approve of Aries III largesse, or of the Aries III tendency to bring home the latest interesting person they have met. Good at making a little money go a long way, Scorpio I's will probably see Aries III spending as wasteful and counterproductive; where Aries III's see the big picture, Scorpio I's home in on the details. Although some of their attempts to make Aries III's more attentive and realistic will be helpful, they should be careful: too much blaming and criticism will have a negative effect. Despite their power as the spouse or mate of an Aries III, Scorpio I parents will have difficulty controlling their Aries III children, who must be free to do things their own way. Same-sex Aries III–Scorpio I siblings will usually compete with each other, their shared martian orientation (Mars rules Aries and co-rules Scorpio) leading to outbursts of anger and even perhaps violence. As friends, Aries III's and Scorpio I's can form a close bond, sharing exciting, challenging and somewhat dangerous experiences.

ADVICE: *Self-control can be liberating. Feelings don't have to be upsetting. Refine and broaden your emotional palette. Keep calm.*

RELATIONSHIPS

STRENGTHS: **SCINTILLATING, IMAGINATIVE, PASSIONATE**

WEAKNESSES: **ANGRY, BLAMING, VIOLENT**

BEST: **LOVE**

WORST: **FAMILY**

ERIC ROBERTS (4/18/56)
JULIA ROBERTS (10/28/67)

Though a quality actor, older brother Eric has mostly appeared in lukewarm films. In 1986, Julia debuted opposite him in *Red Blood*, but it was 1990's *Pretty Woman* that made her a superstar. Tabloids have rumored a rift between them.

***Also:* Bradford Dillman & Suzie Parker** (married; actor/50s model); **David Pirner & Winona Ryder** (romance; actors); **Thos. Jefferson & John Adams** (founding fathers).

ELIZABETH MONTGOMERY (4/15/33)
GIG YOUNG (11/4/13)

Montgomery, star of tv's *Bewitched*, was Young's 3rd wife from 1956–63. A debonair supporting actor, he won an Oscar for *They Shoot Horses, Don't They?* (1969). He killed his 5th wife and himself in 1978.

Also: **Dennis Banks & Russell Means** (Native American social reformers); **Charlie Chaplin & Mabel Normand** (affair; actors).

April 11–18
THE WEEK OF THE PIONEER
ARIES III

November 3–11
THE WEEK OF DEPTH
SCORPIO II

Differences in Tempo

This relationship will have to deal with uncertainty and instability, particularly in working situations. Since Scorpio II's are patient, long-suffering and watchful whereas Aries III's are generally impatient and in a hurry to move on to something new, differences in tempo, style and feeling will cause problems here. Furthermore, Scorpio II's can resent the leadership qualities of Aries III's, whom they may see as inflexible and dictatorial. A struggle may emerge over where the authority in the relationship lies.

Love between these two generally features storm and struggle. Because Scorpio II's tend to repress their emotions, they may work to make an Aries III partner manifest the repressed feelings of jealousy, anger or rage that they themselves have hammered down deep inside. Aries III's for their part may be taken aback by the emotionality they expose in this relationship, since they try to project a cool image, and avoid messy scenes.

On the positive side, pioneering Aries III's may learn from Scorpio II's that the greatest challenges they face may be internal, and that exploring their own selves may be the most daunting yet rewarding venture they could devise. In return, they can often waken Scorpio II's from their lethargy and inspire them to take part in the world around them. As friends or mates, then, Aries III's and Scorpio II's have much to teach each other.

In the family, serious struggles over authority may occur between these two, particularly when they are siblings of the same sex. Persisting into adult life, such encounters may involve finances, inheritances and dominance in the family group. In parent-child relationships, and particularly if the Scorpio II is the parent, the key to avoiding strife is the parent's ability to leave the child alone as much as possible.

ADVICE: *Learn when to care and when to back off. Avoid power struggles. Work on understanding. Accept common authority. Stay inspirational.*

OLEG CASSINI (4/11/13)
GRACE KELLY (11/12/29)

Before becoming Princess Grace of Monaco, the serenely beautiful Kelly had an exciting affair with Italian fashion designer and notorious lady's man Cassini.

Also: **Ed O'Neill & Katey Sagal** (co-stars, *Married with Children*); **Robert Delaunay & Sonia Turk** (married; artists); **F.W. Woolworth & Barbara Hutton** (mogul/socialite granddaughter).

April 11–18
THE WEEK OF THE PIONEER
ARIES III

November 12–18
THE WEEK OF CHARM
SCORPIO III

Wowie Zowie

Varied and exciting, this relationship may pursue many different areas of interest. It likes to be exposed to the unexpected, which can open up whole new worlds of expression. New and unusual ideologies may also open up new spiritual horizons.

Scorpio III's who are swept off their feet by Aries III's may have to give up their controlling attitudes. This can be good, since by keeping everything under control, Scorpio III's often miss out on some of life's most enjoyable and interesting experiences. In a relationship with an Aries III, a Scorpio III can enter a whole new world in which his or her deep emotional side can find full expression. And what do Aries III's get from Scorpio III's? A world of rich feelings that they may never have imagined. To gain a Scorpio III's love, of course, they'll have to give up something too, namely some of their focus on work or career: this relationship will demand a lot of attention. But if the result is that they take more care of their own emotional life, which they may have neglected for years, the relationship will have done them good.

Aries III–Scorpio III spouses may find that once their initial passions have cooled, an objectivity may arrive in which their attitudes to each other become more critical and unforgiving. Disagreement over domestic and financial management, child-rearing, vacations and a host of other subjects are likely, and can destabilize what once seemed an almost ideal matchup. On the upside, these two have a freshness of ideas that allows for a lot creative problem-solving.

Friendships and family relationships may be satisfactory but uninspiring. Attitudes about how friends or family members should act toward each other can be unyielding and sometimes morally overbearing. These two will have to try not to let their ideas on subjects ranging from group activities to social attitudes get rigid or dogmatic.

ADVICE: *Keep the relationship young. Don't get bogged down in disagreement. Fight overly dogmatic tendencies. Stay forgiving and flexible.*

April 11–18

THE WEEK OF THE PIONEER
ARIES III

November 19–24

THE CUSP OF REVOLUTION
SCORPIO-SAGITTARIUS CUSP

On the Mountain Top

This relationship will provide the ground for the deep social consciousness and ideological side that many Scorpio-Sagittarians and Aries III's have in common. Blooming in their relationship, this concern can prove deeply satisfying to both partners. Furthermore, the combination can create well-balanced marriages and friendships through the partners' shared ideas and feelings about the structure of society. It is not unusual for this duo to enjoy exploring new fields of thought together, perhaps even involving themselves in or leading a group dedicated to promoting social reforms or establishing new institutions. The partners themselves, family members or a group of friends or co-workers may serve as guinea pigs for such work.

Aries III's usually need to help those around them, but Scorpio-Sagittarians are stubbornly independent and cannot accept the kind of protection and aid that Aries III's have to offer. In some personal relationships, Scorpio-Sagittarians and Aries III's will reach a compromise in which Aries III's are free to inflict their help on one and all—except their Scorpio-Sagittarian partners.

In matters of love, Aries III's will have difficulty expressing their deeper feelings to Scorpio-Sagittarians. They in turn will find the complex inner world of Scorpio-Sagittarians hard to penetrate, assuming they are even interested in doing so. (Aries III friends of Scorpio-Sagittarians will have the same problem.) The relationship's shared ideological interests may be more of a focus than physical matters, so that regular sexual interaction is not usually required as the years go by. Strongly platonic feelings can well emerge over time, so that the relationship will evolve to a high, calm spiritual level, though it began like a house on fire.

Scorpio-Sagittarians will find the impetuosity and boundless energy of Aries III's hard to deal with, and may experience some frustration in trying to get them to sit down and think things out. On the other hand, sibling pairs in this combination are often on the same wavelength, and can appreciate and understand each other even in silence.

ADVICE: *Keep your ideas to yourself occasionally. Tend to everyday matters. Don't neglect finances. The body has to be fed too. Share feelings more.*

ROBERT KENNEDY (11/20/25)
ETHEL KENNEDY (4/11/28)

Though a career politician, Kennedy's personal life was family-oriented. Wife Ethel and he were close, despite his occasional straying. He was assassinated in 1968 after declaring his presidential candidacy, leaving behind 11 children. ***Also:*** **George Henry Lewes & George Eliot** (famous liaison; writers); **Oleg Cassini & Gene Tierney** (married; couturier/actress); **Hayley Mills & Juliet Mills** (siblings; actors).

April 11–18

THE WEEK OF THE PIONEER
ARIES III

November 25–December 2

THE WEEK OF INDEPENDENCE
SAGITTARIUS I

Enthusiasm Enough

A recurring theme in this relationship is an enthusiastic youthfulness that brings great joy and easy interaction. It is characterized by a quick-wittedness and a virtuosic ability to interact—in fact timing is always impeccable in this matchup. The key to the relationship, in whatever area of life it appears, is mutual self-respect. A strong belief in honor and fair play, for example, can form a solid basis for friendship.

Aries III's and Sagittarius I's are likely to become fast friends who will stick by each other through thick and thin. The appearance on the scene of a love object attractive to both of them, however, may spell great difficulties, with passion and ethics vying for ascendancy. Financial or professional competition is likely to pose less of a threat to this friendship than matters of the heart. Probably the most trying situation would be a love triangle in which one of the friends had fallen in love with the established mate or lover of the other.

Unlike Aries III's, Sagittarius I's have little need for company on a daily basis. Perfectly capable of living alone for long periods, they will rarely jump into a marriage, or into a permanent living situation with a lover. This combination is not the most likely one for marriage, then, although its love affairs can be deep, fulfilling and enduring.

As co-workers or business partners, these two can function extremely well, particularly in technical matters. An unrealistic financial outlook, however, may create problems. Enthusiasm there will be, but unless one of the partners (or someone outside the relationship) adopts a hard-headed, pragmatic approach and keeps a sharp eye on costs, these two may find themselves enjoying more fun than success.

Sagittarius I's often bond strongly to one parent, whom they tend to idolize; Aries III's are quite capable of handling the enormous responsibilities of this situation, and can make excellent parents in such a role. Sagittarius I's can also prove highly protective and stimulating parents for Aries III children.

ADVICE: *Overenthusiasm can be dangerous. Try to be realistic, and don't wear blinders. Beware of competition in love. Don't neglect money matters.*

WOODY ALLEN (12/1/35)
LOUISE LASSER (4/11/39)

Lasser, fetching pigtailed star of tv's quirky soap opera *Mary Hartman, Mary Hartman* (1976–77) was married to filmmaker Allen from 1966–70. Their relationship in work and play was positive, characterized by fun and mutual support. ***Also:*** **Charlie Chaplin & Mildred Harris** (married; actors); **David Letterman & Paul Shaffer** (tv host/bandleader).

April 11–18
THE WEEK OF THE PIONEER
ARIES III

December 3–10
THE WEEK OF THE ORIGINATOR
SAGITTARIUS II

KENNETH BRANAGH (12/10/60)
EMMA THOMPSON (4/14/59)

A brilliant British actor, director and screenwriter, Branagh has brought Shakespeare to contemporary audiences. Thompson, his talented peer and one-time wife, has appeared in virtually all of his film and theater projects, including the 1989 award-winning *Henry V.*

Effective Leadership

The success of this relationship will usually depend on whether effective leadership and direction can be established within it. Unfortunately, Sagittarius II's have an erratic and idiosyncratic side that will not suit Aries III's in areas that demand a lot of stability, such as marriage and work. There, Aries III's tend to have fixed moral ideas, and Sagittarius II's can find it difficult or impossible to live up to them. Hard-working and single-minded leaders capable of giving direction to any project, Aries III's will not always be understanding when Sagittarius II's decide they have had enough in midstream.

In love relationships between these two, passions will flare, with good and bad results. The partners' common fire energies (both Aries and Sagittarius are fire signs) will feed on each other and at times burn out of control, with Sagittarius II anger likely to run out of hand; Aries III's will tend to remain immovable in the face of such outbursts, refusing to give ground, particularly if their self-interest or the survival of the relationship itself is at stake. Sagittarius II's can be very demanding of their lovers, perhaps asking an Aries III to disassociate him- or herself from existing friends and admirers. If so, the Aries III may come to feel that the affair isn't really worth it. Marriages between these two may not last unless both partners continue to support the primacy of the relationship over their own needs for freedom and self-expression.

Siblings in this combination are likely to experience more than their share of combat and conflict, which is likely to upset the family group. Yet there is also a strange loyalty here, which will unite them against danger and threat. Even so, acquaintanceships and other casual relationships are likely to be the best bets for this pair, who otherwise tend to trigger each other emotionally. Their friendships are likely to be most successful if they don't demand deep feeling or daily interaction and contact.

ADVICE: *Take a stand, despite the risk. Don't change direction in midstream. Stay loyal through good times and bad. Beware of emotions running out of control.*

April 11–18
THE WEEK OF THE PIONEER
ARIES III

December 11–18
THE WEEK OF THE TITAN
SAGITTARIUS III

ALEXANDER SOLZHENITSYN (12/11/18)
NIKITA KHRUSHCHEV (4/17/1894)

Khrushchev, soviet premier from 1958–64, liberated millions of exiled prisoners from Stalin's overcrowded labor camps. Among them was writer Solzhenitsyn, who in 1962 sought to publish one of his novels. With Khrushchev's support, the book was published to international acclaim. *Also:* **Queen Frederika & King Paul** (married; Greek monarchs); **David Letterman & Teri Garr** (friends; actress/tv host).

The Challenge to Accept

This relationship's success will hinge on whether or not these two can accept each other. Aries III's and Sagittarius III's are trine to each other in the zodiac (120° apart), so they are supposed to have a relaxed, easy time of it together; but although they do understand each other intuitively, and may have solid friendships, they also tend to distrust each other's motives and energies, so that other relationships may have to be built brick by brick. This relationship will surely demand that each party work toward fuller acceptance of each other. In many areas, all-out struggles or confrontations may abound, and since neither of these fiery personalities (both Aries and Sagittarius are fire signs) will normally back down, one or both may get hurt in the process. These hurts are sometimes self-inflicted, since in competition either one of these two may try so hard to overcome the other that they go beyond sensible limits. Again, acceptance is the key if such struggles are to be avoided or at least minimized. Great reformers both, these two will undoubtedly struggle against all that they see as unacceptable in the world.

Aries III's and Sagittarius III's in love must acknowledge and accept absolute mutual equality, since neither of them can tolerate being dominated by the kinds of energies possessed by the other. Attraction, sexual and otherwise, can be strong between these two, and any negative feelings that emerge will be correspondingly deep. If emotional swings are to be avoided, the relationship will have to develop bonds of tenderness and sympathy, and egotism will have to be severely limited. Aries III–Sagittarius III marriages will benefit from the stability of home and family. They can be based on large projects that include children and relatives. When these two are co-workers or business partners, on the other hand, disagreements on the course of action to follow usually create friction. As siblings, particularly of the same sex, these two are a good match for each other. Few understand the Sagittarius III need to be left alone to figure things out as well as an Aries III brother or sister. Aries III parents may be less understanding of their Sagittarius III children and may make the mistake of either pressuring them into acquiescence or trying to work them out of a mood.

ADVICE: *Beware of dominance. Establish equality. Strive for unconditional acceptance and love. Agree to bury the hatchet. Work together.*

April 11–18

THE WEEK OF THE PIONEER
ARIES III

December 19–25

THE CUSP OF PROPHECY
SAGITTARIUS-CAPRICORN CUSP

A Beautiful Future

RELATIONSHIPS

STRENGTHS: **PROPHETIC, REVEALING, PURPOSEFUL**

WEAKNESSES: **MOODY, DREAMY, HURT**

BEST: **WORK**

WORST: **LOVE**

This relationship may revolve around the investigation of future scenarios and possibilities, including those of a more personal nature, with self-assurance and resolve. Keeping an eye to the future, and all types of prediction, will be important in this combination; both parties are interested in looking ahead, perhaps even in leading others there. They need, however, to avoid dreaminess and overoptimism, and to remember to focus on the practicalities of the here and now.

In a marriage or love relationship with a Sagittarius-Capricorn, Aries III's will often see great potential in their partner's more hidden personality, and will seek to draw it out or develop it. Great objectivity and care must be used here, since if Aries III's get carried away by their need to be needed by a Sagittarius-Capricorn, they may one day suffer a rude awakening when their beautiful creation comes down off its pedestal and, Pygmalion-like, walks away. Friendships between these two may not get very far, since Aries III's count on their friends for liveliness and enjoyment, and Sagittarius-Capricorn moods may be just too unpredictable. Sagittarius-Capricorns can actually be great fun, but when serious or withdrawn, they don't like to be disturbed. Furthermore, although Aries III's are capable of full commitment, they are put off by the sort of complaining and other forms of negativity of which Sagittarius-Capricorns are capable.

As parents, Aries III's are unlikely to be able to fathom the twists and turns of the Sagittarius-Capricorn personality, and may be simply too busy to supply the personal understanding such children need. But Sagittarius-Capricorn parents can have a strong physical bond with their Aries III children, encouraging them to excel in all sorts of strenuous activities and enthusiastically participating alongside them.

Sagittarius-Capricorns and Aries III's can work well together in projects that demand stamina and stick-to-it-iveness. Both have tremendous powers of concentration that enable them to work side by side with unflagging purpose. That determination might guarantee the success of a company or social organization.

ADVICE: *Respect privacy. Don't try to play god. Some areas are better left alone. Be helpful but not overbearing. Be encouraging but not intrusive.*

LILY PONS (4/12/04)
ANDRE KOSTELANETZ (12/22/01)

Married for 20 years, singer Pons and maestro Kostelanetz popularized classical music in the 20th century. Pons, known also for her many film appearances, was a leading soprano with the Metropolitan Opera from 1931–40. Kostelanetz was famous for his radio concerts and recordings. **Also: Loretta Lynn & Sissy Spacek** (singer/film portrayer).

April 11–18

THE WEEK OF THE PIONEER
ARIES III

December 26–January 2

THE WEEK OF THE RULER
CAPRICORN I

Little Fanfare

RELATIONSHIPS

STRENGTHS: **INVIGORATING, SUCCESSFUL, HARD-WORKING**

WEAKNESSES: **UNSYMPATHETIC, UNLOVING, POWER-TRIPPING**

BEST: **FRIENDSHIP, WORK**

WORST: **FAMILY**

The success of this relationship will depend on whether it contains or can develop sensitivity and responsiveness. Aries III's and Capricorn I's are objectively well suited to collaborating as equal co-workers, or of forming a business as partners, but their combination entails a danger of power struggles, animosities and lost tempers. Situations in which one partner is the boss and the other the employee should be avoided whenever possible. Most Capricorn I's are authoritarian in nature, and Aries III's, who are dominant themselves, are unlikely to find them easy to live with, whether as partner or mate. Furthermore, these two probably won't experience the kind of deep feeling of love that could lead to a close personal relationship. Through hard work and firm resolve, however, they are capable of developing enough sensitivity and empathy to make them exceptions to the rule.

These two can be quite close friends, since both of them value honor and a straight-ahead, up-front approach, with little fanfare accompanying it. In their dynamism and imaginativeness, Aries III's will inspire Capricorn I's, and will serve as excellent examples of how to move ahead in the world. In turn, they will benefit from Capricorn I reliability and practicality, a good foil for their own tendency to become unrealistic and to fall out of touch with some of life's harsher realities. As long as power is not an issue, and sexual jealousy or social envy don't rear their ugly heads, the friendship is likely to be stimulating, physically invigorating and productive.

This relationship is likely to strain family bonds, whether sibling or parent-child. Aries III's and Capricorn I's are likely to engage in ongoing and intense fights for dominance, with neither winning any permanent victory. Both, however, are likely to grow strong from such confrontations, and they may develop some sensitivity to each other's needs. Although they are unlikely to understand or sympathize with each other deeply, they will reach a mutual respect for the relationship's power over the years and will fully appreciate it later in life.

ADVICE: *Mastery often involves surrender. Develop sensitivity, empathy and understanding. Mute dominant drives. Learn to give and share.*

BETSY ROSS (1/1/1752)
THOMAS JEFFERSON (4/13/1743)

Jefferson and Ross were contemporary early American patriots. According to popular legend, Ross stitched the first American flag at George Washington's request. In 1777 the flag was officially adopted by the government. At the time, Jefferson was a congressman from Virginia.

STRENGTHS: **STRUCTURED, IMPROVING, TRUSTING**

WEAKNESSES: **CONFLICTING, UNREALISTIC, HARDHEADED**

BEST: **MARRIAGE**

WORST: **WORK**

LORETTA LYNN (4/14/35)
CRYSTAL GAYLE (1/9/51)

Gayle, a protégé of older sister Lynn, left country music for a mix of pop, blues and folk. Her career got started when Lynn took her on tour as a supporting performer. As Gayle developed her own style, she put professional space between herself and Lynn. *Also:* **Charlie Chaplin & Pola Negri** (affair; actors); **Sirimavo Bandaranaike & S.W.R.D. Bandaranaike** (married; Sri Lankan prime ministers).

April 11–18
THE WEEK OF THE PIONEER
ARIES III

January 3–9
THE WEEK OF DETERMINATION
CAPRICORN II

The Shape of Things

The keynote of this relationship is the establishment of firm guidelines and working operational structures. With this as a goal, a subtheme will be the exposure of weaknesses in the system, so that it may be repaired.

A Capricorn II who fixes on an Aries III for a partner will usually win out, no matter how unfortunate the choice. The question is really whether any structure or shape can be given to a relationship in which the Capricorn II basically just wants to tuck the Aries III away somewhere for his or her own private satisfaction—a cause of turmoil, for Aries III's are not very tuckable, and want to be socially in the eye of things. The best answer is usually to legalize the relationship, giving it a more palpable form. Marriages can succeed here, since both parties will usually be too busy with their own interests and careers to bother each other unduly. Children may not be recommended for these two unless they can decide beforehand who will take care of them.

This combination is less well suited for a career team, whether as business partners or co-workers. Conflicting ideas about organization and reorganization will abound, and attunement to reality will be low. Capricorn II's are prone to overestimate their capabilities and to be unable to deal with failure, which can be crippling to a project or business shared with an Aries III. Similarly, as family members, both partners will be too hardheaded to get along, but Aries III's can take the lead in being a bit more understanding and diplomatic.

Capricorn II's greatly need a special friend they can trust and with whom they can open up, and an honorable, protective and accepting Aries III may fit the bill nicely. Both of these friends like to work hard and play hard, so they are willing to invest time and effort in structuring a relationship in which they can sharpen their wits, by testing ideas on each other, and compete in challenging physical activities.

ADVICE: *Learning to listen is a good first step. You are not infallible. Set things up carefully. Allow enough space. Use time efficiently.*

STRENGTHS: **INSPIRATIONAL, SERVING, EFFECTIVE**

WEAKNESSES: **NEEDY, DOMINANT, CONTROLLING**

BEST: **FRIENDSHIP**

WORST: **FAMILY**

HENRY JAMES (4/15/1843)
WILLIAM JAMES (1/11/1842)

Wealthy intellectuals, these New York-born brothers spent much of their lives absorbing European culture. William, a philosopher and psychologist, wrote *The Varieties of Religious Experience*. Novelist Henry wrote dozens of classics, including *Daisy Miller* and *The Turn of the Screw*. *Also:* **Thomas Jefferson & Alexander Hamilton** (political adversaries).

April 11–18
THE WEEK OF THE PIONEER
ARIES III

January 10–16
THE WEEK OF DOMINANCE
CAPRICORN III

Furthering Mutual Interests

Strangely enough, although both Aries III's and Capricorn III's are dominant types, with each other they avoid power struggles in many areas. Sacrifice, service and flexibility are strong themes in this relationship, so that these two will go more than halfway to meet each other in most situations. Also, as long as both parties have their own areas of control, they don't need to rule the roost. Except when they are siblings or parent-child pairs, compromise between them is quite possible at home. When living together as lovers or spouses, this pair can make a powerfully effective team, joined in furthering both their individual and their mutual interests.

Friendships between these two are particularly favorable for Aries III's, who will benefit from the grounding and stable energies of Capricorn III's. But Capricorn III's will gain too, from exposure to Aries III ideas; they may even see their friend as their teacher. They must be careful not to idolize Aries III's unduly, however: in their weakness for hero worship, Capricorn III's tend to sell themselves short, making unfavorable comparisons between themselves and others. An understanding Aries III can help a Capricorn III come to grips with an inferiority complex that may be the result of harmful scripts learned in childhood. One difference between these two is that Capricorn III's, though hard on themselves, are not really needy of other people's approval, whereas Aries III's have a deep need to be told that they have made a difference. As lovers or family members, then, Capricorn III's will tend to be much more solitary than Aries III's.

When these two work alongside each other, issues of control and dominance can arise that will cause problems for the group. In acute cases it may be necessary to separate them. In many cases, however, Aries III's and Capricorn III's will inspire each other to new heights of achievement. Aries III's can have a good effect on Capricorn III's by encouraging them to take chances in advancing their careers rather than getting stuck in a boring or repetitive job.

ADVICE: *Giving can make one richer, not poorer. Stay flexible. Be open to new endeavors. Sacrifice selfishness to mutual gain.*

STRENGTHS: ROMANTIC, COLORFUL, PASSIONATE

WEAKNESSES: PUZZLING, UNSTABLE, ISOLATED

BEST: LOVE

WORST: MARRIAGE

Forbidden Love

This relationship can be a secret (for example if it is a love affair), and quite enigmatic and unknown to the outside world. As lovers, Aries III's and Capricorn-Aquarians are likely to reach new romantic heights, with vivid and colorful emotional expression being the order of the day. What the relationship lacks in stability it will make up for in excitement, and Aries III energies can be a stabilizing force at home. Marriage may not be recommended for these two, since it tends to dull their passions, and indeed they have little reason to commit to it, unless moral or ethical reasons demand it. In fact forbidden love affairs in this combination can be rich and rewarding, at least until the partners are forced back down to earth.

Aries III–Capricorn-Aquarius friendships can be trying, since both these personalities are capable of being hasty and careless, which can wear down the relationship. Furthermore, Capricorn-Aquarians can get carried away with bursts of enthusiasm for this or that person, and Aries III's, more faithful by nature, may grow tired of their friendship being neglected or taken for granted.

In the family, Aries III parents will find their Capricorn-Aquarius children hard to control. Because they are not always realistic, they may not realize that they are trying to hold down a Capricorn-Aquarian wildness that is in fact a projection of their own suppressed and hidden desires. Siblings in this combination can live in a private fantasy world together, in which imaginative beings and situations come to have more meaning than does everyday life. When Aries III's become more interested in social matters, however, and acquire new friends, their Capricorn-Aquarian brother or sister may experience this as a painful abandonment.

Only certain careers lend themselves to this matchup, particularly those that value imagination, new ideas, entertainment, vivid marketing schemes or promotional programs. Assuming the business doesn't go broke in the first year, the relationship's chemistry can appeal to other people, attracting them to the product or service offered.

ADVICE: *Take your time. Tone down your enthusiasm but don't lose the passion. Come out in the open a bit. Build a solid financial basis.*

CATHERINE DE MEDICI (4/13/1519)
FRANCIS II (1/19/1544)

At age 14, Catherine's oldest son, Francis II, King of France, married Mary Queen of Scots, whose Roman Catholic family wished to destroy the Hugenots. Catherine later opposed Francis and sought compromise between the factions.

Also: **Loretta Lynn & Dolly Parton** (country music superstars).

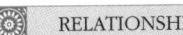

STRENGTHS: PERSONAL, PROTECTIVE, PLEASURABLE

WEAKNESSES: CHAOTIC, DIVIDED, IMPETUOUS

BEST: SEXUAL

WORST: WORK

Intimate Pleasures

This relationship often focuses on intimacy. These two are on a common wavelength, so that successful friendships, love relationships and marriages are all possible for them. Aries III's are often fascinated by the talents and abilities of Aquarius I's, for whom they may serve as a stable, protective force.

Aquarius I's are free spirits, and the sooner Aries III's find this out the better. Aries III's too can be impulsive or impetuous on occasion but are usually surpassed in these qualities by Aquarius I's, whose lightning-like minds and movements tend to amaze one and all. Working relationships between these two are not really recommended, then, since Aquarius I's will have trouble keeping to the single plans or systems that idealistic Aries III's like to set up. Aries III parents, similarly, will be understanding with their Aquarius I children and will fulfill their needs for security, but will have to make an extra effort to accept these children's need for variety, vibrancy and change.

Despite the intimacy here, conventional marriages between these two are unlikely, since their needs and wants are so different. Unwilling to hang around the house while Aries III's are busy working with other people, for example, Aquarius I's usually see nothing wrong with having several other close personal relationships, perhaps even lovers, away from home. Aries III's, on the other hand, tend to be monogamous, and will only find what they need in someone else's arms if they are unhappy. Aquarius I's are not really as social or in need of human contact as they think they are, and once they realize this, wide gaps may appear between them and an Aries III partner.

An Aries III who is unhappy at home with a spouse or mate may find an unconventional Aquarius I lover irresistible. Despite the intimate pleasures of such a relationship, emotional volatility may quickly lead it to a chaotic, albeit exciting, finale. In more committed love affairs, the relationship's high sexual energy can be explosive and fulfilling.

ADVICE: *Don't rush. Slowing down prolongs enjoyment. Don't shut out the world. Keep balanced. Understand the level of your commitment.*

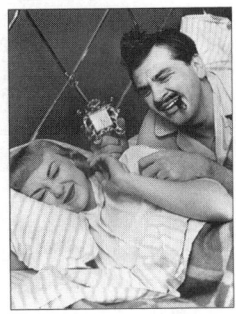

EDIE ADAMS (4/16/29)
ERNIE KOVACS (1/23/19)

With his oddball satirical shows, Kovacs pioneered early tv comedy. He had a strong, intimate marriage with singer Adams, who frequently appeared on his programs. Kovacs died in an auto crash in 1962.

Also: **Henry James & Edith Wharton** (novelist/protégé).

STRENGTHS: **INTEGRATED, ENTHUSIASTIC, RESPONSIBLE**

WEAKNESSES: **POLARIZED, JARRING, FLEETING**

BEST: **EASYGOING FRIENDSHIP**

WORST: **BUSINESS PARTNERSHIP**

THOMAS JEFFERSON (4/13/1743)
AARON BURR (2/6/1756)

Running against Burr, Jefferson barely won the presidency with a tie-breaking vote by the House of Representatives. In 1806 Jefferson had Burr arrested and brought to trial for allegedly conspiring to establish an independent republic. Burr was acquitted.
Also: Samuel Beckett & James Joyce (friends; Beckett was secretary to Joyce)

April 11–18

THE WEEK OF THE PIONEER
ARIES III

January 31–February 7

THE WEEK OF YOUTH & EASE
AQUARIUS II

Literal Integration

This relationship will not only call up starkly polarized character elements but, if it is to be successful, will demand their literal integration. Specifically, an Aries III relationship with an Aquarius II will have a double effect, albeit a contradictory one: first, it will sympathetically awaken either partner's slumbering child, and second, it will to bring to life their somewhat stern though understanding adult. This bewildering manifestation may initially pose psychological problems for the relationship, but these opposite characters can later be successfully integrated in daily life, powerfully melding enthusiasm and responsibility.

Simply speaking, Aries III's and Aquarius II's can get right down in the sandbox together and have a wonderfully uninhibited time. Whether they be siblings, friends, lovers or a parent-child combination, their relationship can be fun. Equally, though, when either partner feels sandbox time is over, he or she may blow the whistle on a somewhat startled companion, or furiously start ringing the dinner or bedtime bell. Unless the relationship, whether friendship or marriage, can absorb such abrupt changes of attitude, over the long run they may prove intolerable, and a breakdown of harmonious and easy attitudes will urge a breakup.

The relationship does not usually place much priority on self-examination; this pair like to keep things light. Even if they do take the time to explore deeper emotional levels together, their relationship, though it may avoid some kinds of problems, may still fail to create the solid basis that is so necessary for it to survive times of difficulty or outright disaster. Friendships here tend to be of the fair-weather variety, and love affairs may be pleasant enough, but not necessarily lasting.

As a co-worker or business partner, the hard-driving Aries III is not always suited to the seemingly more relaxed Aquarius II. Furthermore, Aquarius II's dislike trouble so much that they may not be tough enough to engage in sharp negotiating or competition, and this, coupled with the often unrealistic financial attitudes of Aries III's, can spell disaster for any joint commercial enterprise or relationship.

ADVICE: *Dig deeper. Investigate and integrate slowly and carefully. Don't forget to have fun, but clean up afterwards too. Difficulties demand resources.*

STRENGTHS: **SYMPATHETIC, SUPPORTIVE, FUN**

WEAKNESSES: **IRRITATING, NEGLECTFUL, DISINTERESTED**

BEST: **FRIENDSHIP, SIBLING**

WORST: **LOVE, PARENT-CHILD**

ROD STEIGER (4/14/25)
CLAIRE BLOOM (2/15/31)

Method actor Steiger's first movie was *On the Waterfront* (1954). English-born, classically trained Bloom played opposite Charlie Chaplin in *Limelight* (1952). Steiger and Bloom's marriage, from 1959–69, was thought to be an uncomfortable relationship.

April 11–18

THE WEEK OF THE PIONEER
ARIES III

February 8–15

THE WEEK OF ACCEPTANCE
AQUARIUS III

Soft, Fleecy Clouds

This relationship is often dreamy and gentle in tone, fostering sympathy, kindness and supportiveness. It can go a long way through the sharing of physical and emotional experiences that are very important to personal development, and it can also be a great deal of fun. Its understanding and accepting attitudes are more likely to lead to friendships than to sensuous love affairs or marriages; magnetic sexual or emotional attractions are more unusual here than empathy, warmth and sharing.

Aquarius III's can be very emotionally needy growing up and can require a lot of attention. Rather than to their parents, they may well turn to Aries III friends and siblings, who have a tremendous capacity to give, and may be quite devoted to them and attentive to their needs. They may easily re-create this relationship in adult life, but limits may have to be drawn: guilelessly but shamelessly, Aquarius III's can be quite dependent and even parasitic, draining Aries III energies.

Looking back, adult Aries III's sometimes accuse an Aquarius III parent of having neglected them in childhood, when actually the parent was simply giving his or her children the freedom these personalities need. Aries III parents may also have conflicts with their Aquarius III children, who often feel resentment over what they perceive as parental disinterest in their feelings. Such children can envy or even hate the ideas and organizations to which their Aries III parents devote so much time and energy.

In marriages and business partnerships, or when this pair are co-workers on the same project, Aquarius III depressions and dark moods may weigh heavily on Aries III's. Aquarius III's, in turn, are prone to find Aries III's irritating, not necessarily for any good reason: for all their understanding, Aries III's have a way of triggering Aquarius III anger and temperament, even though Aquarius III's pride themselves on being cool on the job.

ADVICE: *Express emotions, but don't let that mean losing your temper. Give and take, but don't take advantage. Develop emotional intelligence.*

April 11–18

THE WEEK OF THE PIONEER
ARIES III

February 16–22

THE CUSP OF SENSITIVITY
AQUARIUS-PISCES CUSP

STRENGTHS: **CARING, LIBERATING, RISK-TAKING**

WEAKNESSES: **MISTRUSTFUL, UNFEELING, OVERSUPPORTIVE**

BEST: **CO-WORKER, FRIENDSHIP**

WORST: **FAMILY**

Born Again

The main concern of this relationship is often rebirth, which can require breaking through barriers and defenses built up over many years. Specifically at stake here is the reemergence of Aquarius-Pisces sensitivities and feelings. Aries III's, for example, may see the social problems of Aquarius-Pisces friends quite clearly, understanding that these individuals' combination of pessimism and cheerfulness holds them back from deep interaction and involvement. The choice rests with the Aries III: accept Aquarius-Pisces as they are, or risk rejection or being accused of a breach of friendship and try to get deeply involved, pushing the Aquarius-Pisces to express their true feelings and discover who they really are. If successful, Aries III's who take the plunge into the Aquarius-Pisces personality may reap rewards far beyond those of their own giving attitudes, for Aquarius-Pisces love and affection, so won, may lead to a deep, lasting and fulfilling relationship.

In areas of love and marriage, the relationship can demonstrate great calm and understanding, particularly in times of need. Yet this calm may be an aspect of a curious lack of deep feeling. If so, Aquarius-Pisces barriers will not be breached, and an opportunity for them to regain their lost childhood sensitivities will be denied. Also, Aquarius-Pisces will rarely be called upon to do prolonged battle with Aries III partners, a kind of conflict that might be unpleasant but would also give them a chance to forge a strong ego for themselves. Thus the kindness and attentiveness of the relationship, although immensely supportive, in the long run may not necessarily advance personal development. Principally concerned with either abstract or personal concerns, Aquarius-Pisces can neglect the middle ground of human experience: their relationships with others. Relationships with Aries III's, who are particularly strong in this area, may help them to build bridges to their fellow human beings. Rarely, however, will they come to trust Aries III mates, lovers or close family members enough to fulfill this role. They are more comfortable with Aries III co-workers, acquaintances, colleagues or, when young, more remote family members, all of whom will be less threatening than those who are emotionally closer to them.

ADVICE: *Taking the plunge may be worth the risk. Dare to fail. Self-discovery carries rewards. Break through emotional barriers.*

LEOPOLD STOKOWSKI (4/18/1882)
GLORIA VANDERBILT (2/20/24)

Stokowski, who conducted baton-less, cut an aristocratic profile with his graceful hands and flowing hair. In 1945 he married the equally image-conscious Vanderbilt, a wealthy society woman and member of the fashionable elite. **Also: Hayley Mills & John Mills** (daughter/father; actors); **Charles Wilson Peale & Rembrandt Peale** (father/son; painters).

April 11–18

THE WEEK OF THE PIONEER
ARIES III

February 23–March 2

THE WEEK OF SPIRIT
PISCES I

STRENGTHS: **IDEALISTIC, AESTHETIC, PLATONIC**

WEAKNESSES: **STRAINED, POLARIZED, EXPLOITED**

BEST: **IDEALISTIC PURSUITS**

WORST: **COMMERCIAL ENDEAVORS**

Higher Ideals

The focus of this relationship is often aesthetic and idealistic. Aries III's and Pisces I's can make a wonderful team in service of higher ideals and beauty, particularly when they are both members of a social, spiritual or community group; both parties can be devotional types who need to put their energies into such projects, and the relationship can synergistically magnify their individual strengths severalfold.

Friendships between these two can develop out of one of these social groups. Although Aries III's tend to be more dynamic and aggressive and Pisces I's more relaxed and accepting, they initially appreciate each other's strong points. Both are self-sacrificing, and they should be aware that they can be taken advantage of by more selfish types.

Aries III's are passionate sorts who save their affections and their sexual urges for special intimate moments, while Pisces I's are more sensuous, needing to touch and taste the best that life has to offer in steady doses throughout the day. Because of these differences, love relationships and marriages may not be in the cards for these two. Platonic relationships in which sexuality is dormant or absent can be satisfying, lasting and, in the long run, quite satisfying for this combination, however.

Aries III–Pisces I siblings are likely to form strongly sympathetic and empathic bonds, particularly if they are of the opposite sex. But parent-child and other familial relations are likely to be strained, for these two employ quite different methods and tempos of working. Aries III's, for example, are the types who rise early and go straight to work, whereas Pisces I's may need a long time to wake up and get going. Then, at night, Aries III's may go early to bed, while Pisces I's tend to be night owls.

Because of its idealistic stance and its sometimes strong streak of unreality, this matchup is not recommended for business partnerships or other commercial projects. It can work well, however, in service, church, or other community-oriented endeavors.

ADVICE: *First build a strong ego, then get rid of it. Give, but don't be treated like a football. Wake up to reality. Be interested in everyday matters.*

A. PHILLIP RANDOLPH (4/15/1889)
W.E.B. DuBois (2/23/1868)

Randolph and DuBois crusaded for the civil rights of oppressed blacks. Randolph carried his people into the mainstream of the US labor movement; the more radical DuBois spoke and wrote of liberation through an educated black elite. **Also: Dean Acheson & John Foster Dulles** (successive secretaries of state).

April 11–18
THE WEEK OF THE PIONEER
ARIES III

March 3–10
THE WEEK OF THE LONER
PISCES II

DAVID CASSIDY (4/12/50)
JACK CASSIDY (3/5/27)

Stage-musical star Jack Cassidy and Evelyn Ward had son David, who became a pop singer and co-star of tv's *Partridge Family* (1970–74). Jack and David were close until Jack's tragic death at age 49 in a house fire.

Contact with the World

The main theme of this relationship is socialization. Pisces II's have an acute need for privacy and Aries III's need to surround themselves with people, so that their shared dealings with others will be a large issue. As a result, this combination is not generally a good one for marriage or living together. Yet should these two want to marry, each will have strong contributions to make (Pisces II's probably in the domestic sphere, Aries III's in the worldly or social sphere), as long as they can reach firm agreements as to how and when their living space is to be used by themselves and others.

Love relationships between these two may show abiding bonds of sympathy and affection but generally lack the searing emotion of full-blown love affairs. As friends, Aries III's will bring Pisces II's more into contact with the world, introducing them both to people and to potentially lucrative career opportunities. Aries III's have problems reaching their deeper feelings, and Pisces II's, masters at this, can help them to discover hidden and neglected areas of their psyches, just by insisting that they talk about how they feel. In this way Pisces II's can help Aries III friends live life much more deeply, making their relationships with others more meaningful and improving the quality of their social interactions. They can also give Aries III's the sympathy and emotional acceptance they need when they are misunderstood by their current spouse or lover. In return, Aries III friends can infuse Pisces II's with hope and inspiration when they feel bogged down in a stagnant or hopeless relationship.

These two can make an effective business team, with Pisces II's doing the inside work (planning, developing, producing) and their Aries III partner the outside work (PR, sales, marketing). As siblings, they can form a self-protective unit if exposed to unaccepting or abusive parents, teachers or other authority figures.

ADVICE: *Decide how you want to organize your life. Keep in contact with the world. Don't neglect self-exploration. Settle differences.*

April 11–18
THE WEEK OF THE PIONEER
ARIES III

March 11–18
THE WEEK OF DANCERS & DREAMERS
PISCES III

PAUL WANER (4/16/03)
LLOYD WANER (3/16/06)

Hall of Famers both, these brothers played outfield together with the Pittsburgh Pirates (Paul, 1926–40; Lloyd, 1927–40). Elder brother Paul, nicknamed "Big Poison," and Lloyd, "Little Poison," spent the '44 season with the Dodgers. *Also:* **Joel Grey & Liza Minnelli** (co-stars, *Cabaret*); **Charlie & Sydney Chaplin** (half-brothers; actor/manager).

The Emperor's New Clothes

This relationship is often a naive, even childlike one in which neither party really cares to understand the other at a deep level. Productive, lasting marriages and love affairs are rare in this combination, since these two often lack emotional, spiritual or physical maturity. They are often able to make objective and accurate psychological assessments, however, permitting them valuable insights. Like the child who saw the emperor naked in the fairy tale, they will maintain an atmosphere of honesty, although not always of comprehension or sympathy.

The Aries III ability to attract followers through teaching can arouse the jealousy of Pisces III's, who usually want nothing more than to affect their environment in this kind of way but have more difficulty doing so. Yet these two can form fast friendships, with admiration for each other's talent and ability playing an important role. In emotional areas, however, frustrations may emerge over an inability to share feelings at a deep level.

Although both parties have far-reaching ideas, Aries III's are more concerned with their fellow human beings and with society as a whole, Pisces III's with philosophical and universal concerns. In the family, an Aries III may see a Pisces III sibling as an unrealistic dreamer, taken up with cosmic, fantastic or New-Age pursuits, whereas a Pisces III may see an Aries III sibling as involved in messy interpersonal and idealistic endeavors that do not enhance personal growth. Aries III's may not have a great deal of respect for the Pisces III tendency to sink periodically into lethargy or self-pity and to be unable to advance their own cause.

At work, Pisces III technical skills and ability to make things happen can be of great value to Aries III associates. Aries III's have no end of ideas but are not always able to put them into practice; this is where Pisces III's can help. They often also have better financial judgment than their Aries III partners and will generally know where money is well spent and where it is wasted. It is at work that this relationship's objective and frank brand of honesty will be most valued.

ADVICE: *Retain a childlike openness, but deepen feelings. Develop mature relationships. Lessen unfavorable comparisons. Share and accept.*

RELATIONSHIPS

STRENGTHS: RESPECTFUL, RELAXING, HELPFUL

WEAKNESSES: CONFLICTING, CONFRONTING, POWER-TRIPPING

BEST: FRIENDSHIP

WORST: MARRIAGE

Lowering Your Guard

Since the ability to lower their guard when in the company of someone like themselves is a great relief to both of these powerhouses, this relationship is likely to be fairly relaxed and comfortable—to a point. Curiously enough, these two strong-minded individuals often get along quite well, since they mutually respect each other and know that outright combat between them would be folly. Yet they rarely get involved with each other as lovers or mates. And if they do get married (slowly, deliberately and carefully), they are likely to lack the ability or the desire to share domestic, financial and familial power. A love affair between two Aries-Tauruses can be comforting, since they know what to expect from each other, but those born on the Cusp of Power are more attracted to, and more satisfied by, partners very different from themselves.

Friendships here can work well as long as they don't demand daily contact. Shared activities, including just talking and updating each other on personal news, can be relaxing and fun for this pair. Two Aries-Tauruses can provide each other with mutual support and advice, but the relationship usually runs smoothest if they don't do the same work or share the same expertise. They are likewise ill-advised to work together; a co-worker or business-partner relationship is likely to arouse conflict and even confrontation. These two can make formidable opponents and enemies if working for rival organizations, or as direct financial or business competitors. Such confrontations usually have only one winner.

As family members, whether in sibling or parent-child relationships, Aries-Tauruses are likely to engage in ongoing power struggles with each other unless they can work out a modus vivendi involving mutual respect and acceptance.

SHIRLEY MacLAINE (4/24/34)
BARBRA STREISAND (4/24/42)

MacLaine—dancer, model, stage and screen actress, political activist, writer, and New Age spiritualist—shares a long friendship (and the same birthday) with Streisand, a superstar of stage, screen and music. They are also both active in liberal political causes.

ADVICE: *Build bonds of respect. Don't expect too much from each other. Enjoy fun activities. Keep it light. Avoid conflicts and confrontations.*

RELATIONSHIPS

STRENGTHS: REASSURING, PHYSICAL, SYMPATHETIC

WEAKNESSES: DULL, PREDICTABLE, IRRITATING

BEST: FAMILY

WORST: LOVE

A Safe Haven

A relationship between these two will tend to be intense, private and conflicted. The safest way for the matchup to work is by keeping focused on a base, such as a home, where Aries-Tauruses and Taurus I's will be capable of sharing a private, dependable and secure relationship.

Although truly comfortable, Aries-Taurus–Taurus I love affairs are usually fleeting, due to a lack of deep emotion coupled with occasional irritation and miscommunication. Yet marriages between these two can work; domestic harmony is quite possible in this combination. As spouses these two will have few surprises for each other and will find the security of knowing exactly what to expect quite comforting, albeit sometimes dull. At home, Taurus I's can be quite happy supervising the day-to-day running of things while leaving Aries-Tauruses the boss in making the larger, more strategic decisions, particularly of a financial nature, or in matters of design and taste. In this way both partners can be quite content. Their mutual capacity for stubbornness, however, can be divisive; they would both do well to learn to give in.

Aries-Taurus–Taurus I friendships can be dependable havens in times of need, not only for the partners themselves but for others. These two can share physical activities such as sports, hiking, swimming and other challenging outdoor projects with great satisfaction, whether as a team or as friendly opponents. Sibling and parent-child relationships in this combination can also work well, with each party providing mutual support and sympathy for the other. The reliability and dependability of such relationships often allow them to outlast the boundaries of childhood and adolescence and to persist well into adult life or old age.

Working relationships between Aries-Tauruses and Taurus I's can be quite satisfactory as long as roles are well defined and differentiated, and as long as power struggles don't surface, particularly involving career advancement. Since neither of these personalities will usually bite the hand that feeds them, they will rarely cause problems that affect the smooth running of their group or organization, which here serves effectively as the home base.

DANIEL DAY-LEWIS (4/20/57)
C. DAY-LEWIS (4/27/04)

Actor Daniel is the son of C. Day-Lewis, England's poet laureate (1968–72) and translator, professor and writer of detective fiction. Daniel has starred in several award-winning films, and won the Oscar for best actor as the crippled writer-painter in *My Left Foot* (1989).

ADVICE: *You can't move far when you keep both feet on the ground at the same time— don't be afraid to dare. Follow your heart. Allow spirited energy to emerge.*

STRENGTHS: **AESTHETIC, CULTURAL, SECURE**

WEAKNESSES: **CONDESCENDING, MERCENARY, UNINTERESTING**

BEST: **FAMILY**

WORST: **FRIENDSHIP**

KAI M. SIEGBAHN (4/20/18)
ARTHUR L. SCHAWLOW (5/5/21)

Swedish Siegbahn and American Schawlow won the 1981 Nobel Prize for physics (along with Nicolaas Bloembergen). Their contribution was the development of high-resolution electron spectrography, also known as laser microscopy. Siegbahn's father also won a Nobel Prize for physics (1924). **Also:**

Patti LuPone & Evita Peron
(Broadway portrayal).

April 19–24
THE CUSP OF POWER
ARIES-TAURUS CUSP

May 3–10
THE WEEK OF THE TEACHER
TAURUS II

Creature Comforts

Love affairs here feature a lot of sensuousness and physical attraction. But both Aries-Tauruses and Taurus II's are usually attracted to types far different from themselves, so that their earthy ties, although enjoyable, may not sustain their relationship in the long run. The relationship emphasizes accumulation: saving and investing are keynotes here, as are the collection, discussion and sharing of beautiful objects. What these things have in common, or what they represent or symbolize to both partners, is very simply security. For Aries-Tauruses, security is a form of power; for Taurus II's, it is the freedom to go into the world and give of themselves; for both it is a necessary foundation.

Marriages between these two can be highly successful, enhancing both parties' natural impulse to contribute. Their home will be a pleasant and stimulating place for one and all, full not only of the creature comforts that make life worth living but of culture—ideas, books, music, art. Parent-child relationships can also be rewarding and secure, but friendships may work less well. Taurus II's pick friends from all walks of life, including disadvantaged communities, while Aries-Tauruses have a tendency to be a little snobbish, preferring to hobnob with the powerful and successful. This will usually preclude these two from sharing a social group, and unless they have a common hobby—collecting antiques, for example—they may simply not move in the same circles.

The idealism of many Taurus II's may prevent them from working comfortably alongside Aries-Tauruses, who are usually interested in monetary return and career advancement. In fact, Taurus II's are often ambivalent about Aries-Tauruses, admiring their moneymaking skills yet at the same time resenting their mercenariness. Taurus II's may know well enough how to make and spend money, but they believe in unselfish service and may spend their time working for people or causes that Aries-Tauruses just don't find worth the effort.

ADVICE: *Money can't buy everything. Look for beauty everywhere. Don't be so selective in social relations. Break down rejecting attitudes.*

STRENGTHS: **FRANK, VARIED, EXCITING**

WEAKNESSES: **FRUSTRATING, JUDGMENTAL, REBELLIOUS**

BEST: **FRIENDSHIP**

WORST: **MARRIAGE**

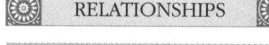

BOBBY DARIN (5/14/36)
SANDRA DEE (4/23/42)

This couple married shortly after their first film, *Come September* (1961), in which Darin debuted. Their movie careers waned after appearing in 2 additional films in the mid-60s. **Also: Richard Daley, Jr. & Richard Daley, Sr.** (son/father; mayors); **Aaron Spelling & Tori Spelling** (father/daughter; producer/ actress); **Erick Hawkins & Martha Graham** (married; dancers).

April 19–24
THE CUSP OF POWER
ARIES-TAURUS CUSP

May 11–18
THE WEEK OF THE NATURAL
TAURUS III

A Need for Honesty

The central need in this combination is honesty. Each of these personalities has an unerring sense of truth, and their relationship demands honesty from both of them on every level, especially those of the deepest emotion. Given honesty, the relationship will have a secure and stable foundation; without it, the partners are liable to feel frustrated and used. Powerful Aries-Tauruses, especially, are instinctively prone to seeing through any ruse.

Taurus III's may so badly want an objectively honest friend who can be depended on in times of stress that they look to Aries-Tauruses to fill needs far beyond the ordinary demands of friendship—the ability to share good times and pleasures. Aries-Tauruses, for their part, will value the natural, uninhibited responses of Taurus III's, which, although often unsettling, are also honest—Aries-Tauruses will like knowing where they stand. Not only are these two truthful with each other, they surround themselves with people who are straight-shooters.

An Aries-Taurus parent or mate can be a rock of security in an otherwise chaotic life, but Taurus III's hate to be told what to do or how to be, and should they think the Aries-Taurus too didactic, they may rebel. Aries-Tauruses, then, must be extremely understanding of their Taurus III lover's need to express themselves with others. If they see the Taurus III as fickle or unfaithful, and respond with blame or punishment, the Taurus III may see them as straitlaced and oppressive. Taurus III's are easily bored and are attracted to oddball situations, and if Aries-Tauruses refuse to accept their need for variety, and Taurus III's refuse to change their ways, marriage between these two may prove difficult to impossible. An open exchange of feelings and ideas can go a long way toward averting these kinds of problems. As parents, Aries-Tauruses can prove rather stern with Taurus III children, while a Taurus III parent may not provide the solid and constant support needed by an Aries-Taurus child. At work, similarly, Aries-Tauruses are usually most concerned with the good of the group or project and, therefore, may be judgmental about what they see as waywardness on the part of a Taurus III.

ADVICE: *Revealing the truth isn't always wise. Stay alert to the needs of others. Think, sometimes, before you react. You always pay the price.*

April 19–24

THE CUSP OF POWER
ARIES-TAURUS CUSP

May 19–24

THE CUSP OF ENERGY
TAURUS-GEMINI CUSP

Gaping in Amazement

This relationship offers many insights. It can teach valuable lessons to its partners, enhancing their consciousness. Family and friends may gape in amazement as two individuals whom they see as having little in common build a fulfilling life together. Moreover, these two will share what they have learned as a couple with others, often simply by example.

The combination is excellent for both marriage and friendship: Aries-Tauruses will provide the stability and dedication that Taurus-Geminis need, and Taurus-Geminis will contribute the interest and excitement required by Aries-Tauruses. Aries-Tauruses know what they want, and if what they want is a fascinating Taurus-Gemini, they will make the relationship happen through sheer force of will. Happily, Taurus-Geminis are often agreeable to being chosen, seeing many advantages in a permanent relationship with such a powerful and capable partner.

In love affairs (and sometimes, strong as the combination is in this area, in marriages), differences in style may require adjustments that will often be necessitated by a possibly painful lesson. Taurus-Geminis are usually too fickle to commit to a single love relationship, and Aries-Tauruses, with their strong instincts for self-protection and survival, are unlikely to be masochistic enough to humiliate themselves in order to hold onto their partner. Faced with an ultimatum to be faithful, Taurus-Geminis may try to comply, with partial success. They may also decide that closing their roving eye isn't really worth the effort. Working relationships in this combination may go well in certain specialized cases, namely when Taurus-Geminis are the innovators and Aries-Tauruses the shapers and redirectors of their efforts. Otherwise, the differences in tempo between these two (Aries-Taurus steady and sure, Taurus-Gemini flashing bolts of inspiration) could undermine the team or lead to accusation and recrimination. If these difficulties are overcome, however, this can be the model of a complementary partnership. As parents, Aries-Tauruses may prove too controlling for their Taurus-Gemini offspring, and Taurus-Geminis too weak to control their willful Aries-Taurus children.

ADVICE: *Get your priorities straight. Sacrifice and compromise will be necessary. Don't be so hardheaded. Learn to listen and profit by errors.*

RELATIONSHIPS

STRENGTHS: INSIGHTFUL,
FULFILLING, INTERESTING

WEAKNESSES: WILLFUL,
CONTROLLING, UNSTABLE

BEST: MARRIAGE, FRIENDSHIP

WORST: PARENT-CHILD

LAURENCE OLIVIER (5/22/07)
WILLIAM SHAKESPEARE (4/23/1564)

Olivier, stage and screen artist since the 1920s, has acted in and/or directed dozens of the Bard's plays in theater, movies and tv. He is, perhaps, the greatest Shakespearean interpreter of his time. *Also:* **Yehudi Menuhin & Hephzibah Menuhin** (siblings; co-performer musicians); **Lenin & Ho Chi Minh** (contemporary communist ideologues); **Lenin & Nicholas II** (revolutionary/czar).

April 19–24

THE CUSP OF POWER
ARIES-TAURUS CUSP

May 25–June 2

THE WEEK OF FREEDOM
GEMINI I

Reaping the Whirlwind

To say that this relationship can be problematical is an understatement. Aries-Taurus is ruled by fire and earth, Gemini I by air, but it is on the area of feelings (represented by the fourth element, water) that the relationship is focused. And it is precisely the emotional chemistry of the combination that goes periodically out of whack, often at points where things seem to be going well. When these two are mates, lovers or siblings, one unfortunate remark, omission or sign of neglect is enough to raise the temperature of the other partner to the boiling point.

This chemistry is exacerbated by the significant differences in the partners' personal style. Gemini I's think and move with amazing speed; Aries-Tauruses need time and refuse to be rushed. Thus Gemini I's can quickly grow frustrated with their partner's measured stance, which makes Aries-Tauruses just dig in their heels all the more. Aries-Tauruses, meanwhile, can grow nervous around Gemini I's, and if so, the bristly rejection they exhibit will just make things worse. In general, Aries-Tauruses tend to be long-suffering, while Gemini I's are more volatile and judgmental. A lack of tact and diplomacy on both sides can escalate existing animosities, particularly in marriage and family. Even though each party can have the best interests of the other at heart, when buttons are pushed, both tend to lash out, only regretting their behavior later—perhaps much later. As lovers, these two may have a whirlwind romance, replete with out-of-control passion, wide emotional swings, and highly expressive outbursts. Before too long, it will probably burn itself out.

Working relationships are often best for this pair, since the synergy of their powers of application to a given project and their concentration on getting it done can be considerable. But unless they agree from the start on their goals, and on what function each partner will play, their projects can founder and break up on the rocks.

RELATIONSHIPS

STRENGTHS: WELL-MEANING,
EXPRESSIVE, CONCENTRATED

WEAKNESSES: NERVOUS,
PROBLEMATICAL, VOLATILE

BEST: WORK

WORST: MARRIAGE

AL UNSER, JR. (4/19/62)
AL UNSER, SR. (5/29/39)

Among a family of Indy 500 champions that holds 9 titles, father Al holds the most remarkable record, with wins in '70, '71 and '78. He returned in '87 at age 48 to become the oldest champion ever. Al Jr. won the race in '92 and '94.

ADVICE: *Try to calm down. Learn emotional control. Don't allow your temper to be triggered so easily. Try to be objective. See the good side.*

PHILIP MOUNTBATTEN (6/10/21)
QUEEN ELIZABETH II (4/21/26)

Elizabeth and husband Philip, Duke of Edinburgh, married in 1947 and had 4 children—Prince Charles (b. '48), Princess Anne (b. '50), Prince Andrew (b. '60) and Prince Edward (b. '64). Their long, durable relationship is based on honoring the obligations of the monarchy.

April 19–24
THE CUSP OF POWER
ARIES-TAURUS CUSP

June 3–10
THE WEEK OF NEW LANGUAGE
GEMINI II

Natural Sympathies

This relationship is at its best when feelings can flow and experiences can be shared most naturally. It is characterized by appreciation and sympathy, particularly in times of need. Oddly comfortable with each other, these two could begin to suspect that they've known each other before, as though they'd been friends over many lifetimes. The relationship is at its most expressive when the partners spend time in nature, away from societal pressures—perhaps at a country home, on vacation or during a walk in the woods.

Sparkling Gemini II's may help to lift Aries-Tauruses' darker moods with entertainment and fun, and their vivaciousness and unique viewpoints will prove attractive to this partner. Quiet and serious, Aries-Tauruses may for their part intrigue Gemini II's as projections of their own shadow side. They can also be good counselors to Gemini II's, who can often benefit from business, social or marital partnerships with more practical and reliable types, such as Aries-Tauruses. In such relationships, Gemini II's may contribute new and original ideas that Aries-Tauruses implement through their command of the organizational skills necessary for a family, club or business. But the relationship is usually weighted in the Gemini II's favor, with the Aries-Taurus, unfortunately, doing most of the giving and the Gemini II most of the taking. Easy friendships are probably the best bet for these two; in love relationships and marriages, Gemini II superficiality may ultimately irritate or hurt Aries-Tauruses, and their endless stream of chatter can prove a turnoff romantically.

Aries-Taurus parents may have little understanding of their Gemini II children, whom they may see as flaky or irresponsible. Their domination in this relationship, particularly when the child is of the same sex, may create frustration: the child will need to identify with them as a role model, but will be unable to do so because of strong underlying differences in temperament.

ADVICE: *Try to understand your own frustrations. Minimize needs and demands. Keep it light. Retrench by periodically getting away from it all.*

NICOLA SACCO (4/22/1891)
BARTOLOMEO VANZETTI (6/11/1888)

These Italian-born anarchists, convicted of murder in 1920, were believed by many to be innocents prosecuted for their political views. After 6 years of appeals, they were electrocuted amid widespread demonstrations, some violent.

April 19–24
THE CUSP OF POWER
ARIES-TAURUS CUSP

June 11–18
THE WEEK OF THE SEEKER
GEMINI III

Revolutionary Charm

This quirkily charming combination can exert a magnetic influence over others. Not only is the relationship itself unusually seductive, it brings out the charisma in its participants. Influencing others is therefore a keynote here. In addition, hidden behind this couple's charming facade there may lurk a revolutionary zeal, which will often surprise its participants as they jointly embark on upsetting the apple cart.

Aries-Tauruses will value the way the relationship enhances their charm and thereby their personal power or magnetism. Gemini III's also enjoy motivating others, and though often the more charming of these two to begin with, they won't mind being part of a charismatic couple. Aries-Tauruses, on the other hand, will feel most uncomfortable with any kind of change within the relationship, but will happily become a provocateur or instigator if the goal is an increase in power. Gemini III's admire Aries-Tauruses' powerful approach to career matters and to the world in general, while Aries-Tauruses will enjoy hearing about a Gemini III partner's latest adventure or exploit. But Gemini III's, as children, have a tendency to idolize an authority figure who will inevitably let them down, and if, as adults, they project such feelings onto a capable Aries-Taurus spouse or lover, a complex emotional situation may arise.

If Aries-Tauruses prove unresponsive to Gemini III needs over the years of a long-lasting love affair or marriage, the Gemini III will often rebel by seeking solace and affection outside the primary relationship, even while staying committed to it. This can work all right as long as the liaisons are kept discreet and hidden from the Aries-Taurus partner, who would probably rather not know anyway. Particularly in marriages, Gemini III's may seem to be dependent on Aries-Taurus practicality, but in fact they are excellent with money and may subtly guide the family's financial fortunes. Because of their mutual appreciation of each other's strong points, companionships and friendships between these two can work out excellently.

ADVICE: *Analyze all the consequences before you act. Develop mutual values. Beware of psychological projection. If you can, be honest.*

April 19–24
THE CUSP OF POWER
ARIES-TAURUS CUSP

June 19–24
THE CUSP OF MAGIC
GEMINI-CANCER CUSP

Energy Flow

The keynote of this relationship is energy. Like many cusp people, both Aries-Tauruses and Gemini-Cancers tend to be extreme, all-or-nothing types; their energies, when well directed, can produce extraordinary results, and when misdirected bring chaos. The predominant energies in this relationship are two-fold: it highlights both the physical, with sensuousness becoming a form of communication, and the verbal, with lively conversation emphasized.

Marriages, love relationships and friendships between these two can work. Gemini-Cancers will bring out the more private side of Aries-Tauruses, and the duo will undoubtedly spend most of their time alone together, rather than socializing with friends or visiting with family. Shared intimacies can be very special in this relationship, which is strong in empathy, nurturing and protectiveness.

The energy within the relationship will always need to be channeled toward constructive aims, so the planning of activities and outlets can prove important. Also, differences in temperament will need to be kept in check. Gemini-Cancers, for example, are extremely picky about how they are approached, spoken to, touched and, of course, made love to. If Aries-Tauruses are insensitive to such matters, their love affairs with Gemini-Cancers are unlikely to last long. On the other hand, Aries-Taurus passion is of the more robust and literal sort, and the nuanced and ethereal treatment they get from Gemini-Cancers may not be solid or substantial enough to satisfy them.

Because of differences in value systems (Aries-Tauruses generally being interested in power and wealth, Gemini-Cancers in love and personal matters), this combination may not be recommended for working or business relationships; nor do sibling and parent-child relationships usually work out well. There is a certain guardedness and mistrust between these two: Gemini-Cancers may find Aries-Tauruses pushy and aggressive, while Aries-Tauruses may find Gemini-Cancers secretive and sneaky.

ADVICE: *Keep energies flowing smoothly. Work on blockages. Widen understanding of individual differences. Develop sympathetic and accepting attitudes.*

MEREDITH BAXTER (6/21/47)
DAVID BIRNEY (4/23/40)

Actors on the romantic series *Bridget Loves Bernie* (1972–73), this couple married in 1973. Baxter later starred in *Family Ties* and many other tv dramas. Birney played in dozens of tv movies and series. They divorced in the mid-80s.
Also: Elizabeth II & Prince William (grandmother/grandson).

April 19–24
THE CUSP OF POWER
ARIES-TAURUS CUSP

June 25–July 2
THE WEEK OF THE EMPATH
CANCER I

A Struggle for Independence

In the most favorable scenario, this relationship will involve a rebellion against domination, a process that can stimulate personal growth. Aries-Tauruses, for example, can be rather overbearing with more sensitive Cancer I's, who will accept such attitudes for a while and then will revolt, perhaps slowly gaining momentum in their struggle and then emerging as full-fledged and independent personalities. Thus a negative beginning may produce a positive result here.

In many love relationships and marriages, however, Cancer I's are far too sensitive and fearful to stand up to Aries-Taurus dominance. Initially, in fact, it may even be very difficult for them to figure out how to approach an Aries-Taurus, let alone actually do so. If Aries-Tauruses set romantic sights on Cancer I's, on the other hand, even only temporarily, Cancer I's will bask in the warmth of Aries-Taurus attention and affection, never allowing themselves to face the possibility that they are being played with or used, and that the next step may be the exit. As spouses, these two often make a bad combination, since Aries-Tauruses will grow impatient with the moods and what they perceive as the ineffectual or misguided actions of Cancer I's, while Cancer I's will eventually either resent or become too dependent on Aries-Tauruses' presence and support.

Close friendships in this combination are unlikely, due to personality clashes. But easy acquaintanceships, featuring the sharing of observations about common endeavors, may prove enlightening and stimulating. And working relationships between these two can be quite successful, being a synergetic product of Cancer I technical expertise and financial strengths and Aries-Taurus initiative and steadfastness. Both parties know well the value of money, with a constructive balance being struck between the Aries-Taurus urge to spend and the Cancer I need to save. Arguments will undoubtedly arise, since both may exhibit a know-it-all attitude, but if personal irritations, dislikes and animosities can be kept under control, the relationship is likely to survive.

ADVICE: *Stand up for yourself. Control domineering attitudes. Lessen small irritations. Give love unconditionally. Don't play with emotions.*

DANIEL DAY-LEWIS (4/20/57)
ISABEL ADJANI (6/27/55)

The intense Day-Lewis won an Oscar for *My Left Foot*. Adjani is currently France's top female stage and screen actress. Before breaking up, the couple was together for 5 years and had a child.
Also: Elizabeth II & Lady Diana (royal mother-/daughter-in-law); **Anthony Quinn & Katherine DeMille** (married; actors).

April 19–24

THE CUSP OF POWER
ARIES-TAURUS CUSP

July 3–10

THE WEEK OF THE UNCONVENTIONAL
CANCER II

ANJELICA HUSTON (7/8/51)
JACK NICHOLSON (4/22/37)

Lady's man Nicholson and former *Vogue* model Huston ended their 17-year romance when Nicholson revealed that his daughter's best friend, actress Rebecca Broussard, was carrying his child. The couple co-starred in *Prizzi's Honor*, directed by John Huston, Anjelica's father. **Also: Robert Penn Warren & Eleanor Clark** (married; writers).

A Relaxing Escape

At its best, this relationship can be an interesting respite from the world; these two may find freshness and joy in its stimulating conversation, shared activities or challenges, and ongoing movement. But the participants should be warned that commitment, structure and responsibility are not the norm here.

Cancer II's may not find much of interest in the more predictable, less subtle Aries-Taurus personality; they usually seek out far more unusual types. And when these two are lovers, Aries-Taurus conventionality and earthy passion are usually a bit boring to a Cancer II. Meanwhile, though Aries-Tauruses may be quite fascinated with Cancer II's, they are unlikely to choose such eccentricity for a deeper relationship. Nor are the kinkier and more bizarre characteristics of the Cancer II sexual makeup usually a stimulus to Aries-Tauruses. In some cases, however, more far-out Aries-Taurus tastes will integrate well with Cancer II's wide sexual palette.

Marriages between these two can work only as long as traditional expectations of the marriage contract are left at the door. Also, Aries-Tauruses must learn to tolerate the eccentric and often outlandish Cancer II preferences in interior decorating and lifestyle. Since Aries-Tauruses generally have balanced, Venusian tastes, demanding harmony and beauty (rather than outlandishness) in their surroundings, these two are unlikely to be able to live together comfortably.

Friendships in this combination are definitely possible. Aries-Tauruses will appreciate the vivid fantasy of their Cancer II friends, and will look forward to their time together as a relaxing escape from their all-too-predictable daily lives. Cancer II's, on the other hand, will benefit from Aries-Taurus worldliness, practical expertise and advice. An effective mutual support system may emerge here, as long as feelings of desire or envy do not manifest in one of the friends. This is generally true for siblings of this combination as well.

ADVICE: *Getting closer may involve giving up some freedom. Learn to share. Cultivate common endeavors. Look for more points of connection.*

April 19–24

THE CUSP OF POWER
ARIES-TAURUS CUSP

July 11–18

THE WEEK OF THE PERSUADER
CANCER III

JOHN PAUL JONES (7/17/1747)
CATHERINE THE GREAT (4/21/1729)

In 1788, Catherine appointed sailor-of-fortune Jones to the post of rear admiral in her Russian navy. Following a scandal linking Jones to a 10-year-old girl, Catherine dismissed the charges, but—possibly out of jealousy—forced him to leave Russia.

Sagacious Advice

Especially in marriage and work, this relationship can be original, creative and effective, emphasizing both independence and responsibility. Strength and power are prominent themes: both partners have an acute need for these qualities, and can supply them to each other in the form of support, wisdom and counsel. If common goals are defined, roles delineated and imaginative approaches agreed upon, this can be a hardworking, dedicated team. Together, however, these two must be careful not to exhibit smothering, bossy or overbearing attitudes toward children and employees.

Love relationships in this combination may be problematic. Although Cancer III's are persuasive, formidable and often attractive personalities, Aries-Tauruses will build up an immunity to their powers of seduction over the years. Highly passionate individuals, Cancer III's can lash out in fits of temper, anger or jealousy. This can be extremely unpleasant for Aries-Tauruses, who can take a great deal but only up to a point—that being, usually, the point where they feel their peace and well-being are threatened. On the other hand, the Aries-Taurus lack of emotional sensitivity can ultimately be a major problem for Cancer III's, who require a partner who understands their emotional nature. Should these two settle into a marriage, these issues may be overcome as common goals take precedence over them. Friendships and work relationships between Aries-Tauruses and Cancer III's can bring lasting value and mutual benefit over the years. Sharing personal matters and giving sagacious advice and sympathetic help, not only to each other but to family, friends and colleagues, are specialties here. Nor is this relationship a fair-weather one—it will survive both the best and the worst of times. Work partnerships here can be especially fruitful, as few have the business acumen of these two.

Should either of these partners be a parent to the other, he or she will be nurturing and caring, and the child will be appreciative. One danger, however, is that too close a parent-child bond could undermine the personal growth of both personalities.

ADVICE: *Allow for more individual expression. Accept others as they are. Back off and let it be. You are neither indispensable nor infallible.*

April 19–24

THE CUSP OF POWER
ARIES-TAURUS CUSP

July 19–25

THE CUSP OF OSCILLATION
CANCER-LEO CUSP

Keeping Lines Open

Aries-Taurus and Cancer-Leo cusps are square to each other (90° apart in the zodiac), and as such, in traditional astrology, are not expected to get along. Indeed conflict can be a hallmark of this relationship. The principal challenge here is that of open dialogue—whether there is enough communication to allow meaningful interaction to take place. It could be that these two will need to work out their own unique way of communicating. This requires time and energy, of course—harder investments for Cancer-Leo than for Aries-Taurus.

Cancer-Leos' hankering after instability and danger probably won't lead them into love affairs with Aries-Taurus partners, whom they may find much too sensible and practical. They instinctively find romance with unpredictable and impulsive types, who mirror their own manic side; a love relationship with a more stable Aries-Taurus may actually come much closer to what they really need, but will unfortunately fall short of what they think they want. Similarly, Cancer-Leos are likely to find Aries-Tauruses unsympathetic and uncommunicative as marriage partners. Aries-Tauruses can in turn grow impatient with their Cancer-Leo spouse's need for variety and excitement, and may even regard it as a personal affront. Both these partners may hang on to a relationship long after it has failed. The Cancer-Leo, however, is more likely to seek solace or distraction outside the marriage through involvements with more unstable types, further destabilizing the relationship.

In family settings, particularly as parents, Aries-Tauruses may prove a steadying influence on Cancer-Leos, although they can also be inhibiting and judgmental, or at least be perceived as such. Cancer-Leo children may find it difficult to be themselves here, since showing mood swings, or moving from more active to more passive roles and back again, can meet with parental displeasure. At work, Cancer-Leos have to interact with people who understand them, and are sympathetic while highly pragmatic. Aries-Tauruses usually have little time on the job to spend catering to other people's feelings.

ADVICE: *Admitting failure or defeat from time to time is positive. Be more sympathetic, but also more realistic. Be inventive in opening lines of communication.*

HERBERT MARCUSE (7/19/1898)
VLADIMIR LENIN (4/22/1870)

As founder of Bolshevism, Lenin espoused the Marxist philosophy in Russia. A generation later, philosopher-writer Marcuse advanced neo-Marxism in the US, updating Lenin's earlier thinking on Socialist reforms. Marcuse wrote *Eros and Civilization* (1955) and *One-Dimensional Man* (1964)—which made him a hero to 60s American radicals.

April 19–24

THE CUSP OF POWER
ARIES-TAURUS CUSP

July 26–August 2

THE WEEK OF AUTHORITY
LEO I

Fierce Struggles

This relationship is likely to be hard-driving and expansive. Both of these types are ambitious, but Leo I's can top even Aries-Tauruses in their drive for success. The easygoing side of Aries-Tauruses has to be satisfied from time to time, but this relationship will give them little rest. Because they can find Leo I demands annoying, the combination is unlikely to work out as a friendship. Moreover, the selfishness of each partner is augmented here, so that the easy give-and-take necessary in any friendship is likely to be absent.

As lovers, these two can have intense sexual encounters, but the relationship may not develop into a deep or lasting one. Each partner may try to control the other, and there are likely to be elements of combat and competition, up to and including displays of anger and jealousy. In Aries-Taurus–Leo I marriages these tendencies may become secondary as other areas of the relationship assume equal importance with sex—namely, prestige, social and financial status, and career advancement. Children of this combination may at times feel unappreciated for their own selves, sensing that they are being used or shown off as prestige objects. The marriage may be highly successful in the eyes of the world, and productive as far as the partners are concerned, but it will rarely contribute to their emotional or spiritual growth.

As young people, Aries-Tauruses need parental attention and input, but they are unlikely to get it from Leo I parents. Yet Leo I's are very loyal, and will seldom neglect their children financially. Siblings of this combination, particularly of the same sex, will engage in ferocious struggles while growing up, but later, as young adults, may pull together during tough times, making themselves the bulwark of the family group.

Aries-Tauruses and Leo I's are unlikely to collaborate well as co-workers, since each will be too concerned with personal advancement. Envy and outright sabotage cannot be ruled out in such a situation. If these two are the heads of rival businesses, or competitive freelancers, the relationship may be adversarial.

ADVICE: *Be more open and honest. Say what's on your mind. Beware of sneaky activities. Make reasonable demands. Expect participation and help.*

CHARLOTTE BRONTË (4/21/1816)
EMILY BRONTË (7/30/1818)

These novelist sisters shared a close childhood, with Charlotte assuming a maternal role upon their mother's early death. Emily was depressed after the disappointing reception of her *Wuthering Heights* (1847), especially after Charlotte's success with *Jane Eyre* the same year. Emily died in 1848.

RICHARD ANDERSON (8/8/26)
LEE MAJORS (4/23/40)

Majors starred in *The Six Million Dollar Man* (1973–78). His government agent "boss" in the series was played by Anderson, a popular supporting actor in 50s and 60s Hollywood movies. They were a memorable working team.

***Also:* Silvana Mangano & Dino DeLaurentiis** (married; Italian film star/producer).

April 19–24
THE CUSP OF POWER
ARIES-TAURUS CUSP

August 3–10
THE WEEK OF BALANCED STRENGTH
LEO II

Enterprising Explorers

Appearing in the areas of work or marriage, this relationship can flourish through a variety of challenging endeavors. Its keynote is the search for opportunity and growth, and then the use of them, in the most enterprising way. As a unit, these two can prove successful in any area that interests them. The combination is faithful and hard-working, and it avoids failure. But there is a downside to this, since an unwillingness to admit defeat can make the relationship go on longer than it sometimes should.

Aries-Tauruses and Leo II's are a match for each other in strength of character. These two measured individuals can go far in establishing a successful enterprise. Ego conflicts can be expected to arise here in love affairs and romances, but marriages can be extremely stable: each party has the ability to stick with it in difficult times, and the relationship itself provides enough variety, and enough concern for family, to make it all worthwhile. This combination will also make reassuring parents for young children, who will feel protected and cared for. As adolescents, though, the children of this marriage may provide firestorms if either parent proves unresponsive to their needs and wants.

Aries-Tauruses and Leo II's can make fast and faithful, tender and caring friends provided that they aren't distracted by some area of competition, ranging from a desired person to a job. Leo II's are usually more private in their friendships, and Aries-Tauruses more social, but if the Leo II demands more time away from crowds and mutual friends, the Aries-Taurus is likely to go along. Sharing sports activities, whether as participant or spectator, and going on vacations together are characteristic of this relationship, and satisfy its need for exploration and adventure.

Business partnerships or working combinations here are likely to be very successful; this matchup creates a team that will constantly be searching for ways to improve and expand its market.

ADVICE: *Rivalry is counterproductive. Line up on the same side. Follow your dreams. Pursue the search for excellence. Give up on unworkable tasks.*

QUEEN ELIZABETH II (4/21/26)
PRINCESS ANNE (8/15/50)

Princess Anne gave Elizabeth her first grandchild in 1977. While the modern role of the monarchy stressed family values, the personal lives of the royal family, increasingly exposed to public scrutiny, have contradicted such ideals.

April 19–24
THE CUSP OF POWER
ARIES-TAURUS CUSP

August 11–18
THE WEEK OF LEADERSHIP
LEO III

Dishing It Out

This relationship is likely to appear and feel immense to its partners—probably too much so for them to be comfortable in it. As a result, each person will erect defenses that will actually only contribute to the relationship's perceived magnitude. Interactions will be intense, with clashes the standard mode. Each partner is quite capable of dishing it out. One way of managing the scale of the relationship is to broaden its area of influence, giving it a wider theater; limiting it to a small domestic sphere is bound to result in a clash of titans.

Leo III's are tough to get close to emotionally, and Aries-Tauruses may have to win their hearts slowly, first gaining their trust and admiration. Their hot passions will flare often, but although they tend to discard old lovers as easily as banana peels, they may find it harder to get rid of an Aries-Taurus—a tough cookie who usually refuses to be treated badly or talked down to without a fight. In combat these two are a match for each other, each giving as good as they get. Fortunately, they will also give back what they get in the more positive aspect of mutual nurturing.

A powerful business or marital partnership between these two can be worked out in which there is a coalescence between the Leo III ability to further the action and the Aries-Taurus knack for handling the home base. When Leo III, the irresistible force, and Aries-Taurus, the immovable object, combine synergetically, the matchup may prove nearly invincible—unless it is rocked by internal dissention. Sexual, emotional and territorial considerations heighten the chances of such conflict arising in marriage. Business partnerships have a better chance of success.

Parent-child and sibling relationships in this combination, particularly between members of the same sex, are likely to be fraught with conflict and disagreement. These two will vie for nothing less than supremacy in the family unit.

ADVICE: *Take the easier way sometimes. Compromise and diplomacy can be a great relief. Surrender is often more pleasurable than battering.*

April 19–24

THE CUSP OF POWER
ARIES-TAURUS CUSP

August 19–25

THE CUSP OF EXPOSURE
LEO-VIRGO CUSP

A Retreat into Fantasy

This combination can prove profound and private. The relationship has a secret life that has very little to do with ordinary reality; imagination and fantasy figure prominently here. Yet both partners are quite pragmatic, so that over the long term one would expect the relationship to become uncomfortable for them. Leo-Virgos, however, will probably enjoy its secretive nature.

Both Aries-Tauruses and Leo-Virgos will generally apply hard work to difficult situations, but hard work is not the answer in this nebulous matchup. Leo-Virgos do not reveal themselves easily, moreover, and demand a lot of understanding; this Aries-Tauruses may be unwilling to supply, for they don't like secretive or misleading behavior, mistrust magic and miracles, and are apt to have little patience for what they see as Leo-Virgo game playing, illusion and ego massage. Love and marriage, then, are unlikely to be successful in this combination, despite the possibility of a romantic infatuation, uncharacteristic for both parties, at the relationship's start.

According to conventional astrology, Leo-Virgos and Aries-Tauruses are well suited to each other; their balance of fire and earth (Leo and Aries are fire signs, Virgo and Taurus earth signs) suggests that they have traits in common. It may be, however, that these very traits lead them into conflict. Both Virgos and Tauruses are materially oriented, for example, but Tauruses are more lavish and Virgos more selective, so that their financial orientation is very different. Still, in a friendship or companionship that permits a sharing of ideas and talents, these differences can be worked out, or can meld synergetically. In familial and working relationships, these two are likely to disagree over methodology. Where Leo-Virgos usually feel that the end justifies the means, Aries-Tauruses may be more severe in their ethics. Furthermore, Leo-Virgos are likely to hide their real intentions, or to retreat into fantasy, which can anger and frustrate Aries-Tauruses. This relationship will be most successful as a creative partnership emphasizing imagination, fantasy and role-playing.

ADVICE: *Investigating something before getting involved in it may be worth the time and trouble. Unify your financial orientation. Loosen up.*

MARIE TAGLIONI (4/23/1804)
AUGUST BOURNONVILLE (8/21/1805)

Bournonville—dancer/choreographer of romantic ballet and creator of the Danish ballet style—was ballerina Taglioni's favorite partner. They were internationally known celebrities of the 1830s and 40s. *Also:* **Elizabeth II & Princess Margaret** (royal sisters); **Hitler & Leni Riefenstahl** (Nazi dictator/ documentary cinematographer).

April 19–24

THE CUSP OF POWER
ARIES-TAURUS CUSP

August 26–September 2

THE WEEK OF SYSTEM BUILDERS
VIRGO I

A Catalytic Influence

Responsible, measured behavior, accompanied by a well-defined chain of command, is likely to be prominent in this relationship. The general tone here is one of weight and seriousness; anything even approaching frivolity will be unheard of.

Love affairs in this combination are likely to be less than inspiring, and Aries-Tauruses and Virgo I's who engage in them probably do so because they are looking for something they can rely on. Aries-Taurus–Virgo I marriages can indeed be very solid. They are characterized by hard work, with a good feeling for order and structure at home. The same goes for the matchup when it occurs in the workplace. The relationship may be rigid, however, in the application of principles and work methods, and this can have a stultifying effect on more creative energies, particularly in marriages. There is also a danger that others in the household, while benefiting from this combination's orderliness, may ultimately find its inflexible rules oppressive, and be forced to rebel against them.

Even so, Aries-Tauruses can be excellent role models for Virgo I's, particularly as friends or parents. Aries-Taurus strength, assurance and career success can have a catalytic influence on a Virgo I's approach to the world, which otherwise tends to be that of an observer rather than a participant. Although they rarely become as aggressive as Aries-Tauruses, Virgo I's can be inspired by this relationship to go for it.

Aries-Taurus–Virgo I working relationships can be highly satisfactory as long as Aries-Taurus is in the driver's seat, which is fine with Virgo I's, who are well able to work as part of a team and are unlikely to cause problems for an Aries-Taurus boss. Structure is a strong point with Virgo I's, and Aries-Tauruses will appreciate their ability to solve problems and straighten out inefficient or chaotic situations. A Virgo I who analyzes, writes reports and recommendations, and in general serves in an advisory capacity will be of tremendous value to any Aries-Taurus section leader, boss or executive.

ADVICE: *Try to stay flexible. Strictness can arouse opposition. Give energy to group efforts. Be understanding of the needs of others.*

ELLIOTT GOULD (8/29/38)
BARBRA STREISAND (4/24/42)

Streisand and Gould met during the production of *I Can Get It for You Wholesale,* a 1962 musical that launched Streisand's early success but did nothing for Gould's career. Married in 1963, they divorced in 1967. *Also:* **Dudley Moore & Tuesday Weld** (married; actors); **Lionel Hampton & Dinah Washington** (bandleader/singer).

STRENGTHS: **INTIMATE, RELAXED, SPICY**

WEAKNESSES: **IRRITATING, JUDGMENTAL, POWER-TRIPPING**

BEST: **LOVE, MARRIAGE**

WORST: **FAMILY, WORK**

WILLIAM SHAKESPEARE (4/23/1564)
QUEEN ELIZABETH I (9/7/1533)

These towering 16th-century figures epitomized perhaps the greatest cultural period in English history. Although there is no proof they ever met, Elizabeth was a leading patron of the arts, especially contemporary theater.

Also: Don Jose Echegaray & Frederic Mistral (1904 Nobelists, literature); **Jessica Lange & Patsy Cline** (film portrayal/singer).

April 19–24

THE CUSP OF POWER
ARIES-TAURUS CUSP

September 3–10

THE WEEK OF THE ENIGMA
VIRGO II

Domestic Tranquillity

This relationship tends to bring out the domestic side of both partners. Privacy is of prime importance here, and with it a quiet intimacy, removed from the unrelenting pressures of the world. Both partners welcome the relaxed atmosphere this relationship affords them when they walk in the door, with Aries-Tauruses particularly benefiting from a low-key attitude at home. Being able to leave workaday stresses behind can literally be a lifesaver for both parties.

As lovers, these two may have a deep physical bond. Should their passionate relationship work out, it is likely to move toward a more permanent living situation or marriage, since neither partner enjoys living alone. Aries-Taurus–Virgo II friendships can also go very deep. Indeed, lovers and spouses in this combination can usually continue to be friends even after an unfortunate breakup.

Aries-Tauruses are naturally attracted to unusual, enigmatic individuals like Virgo II's. Offbeat humor and an openness to sexual experimentation, even at times to the kinky, kooky or bizarre in relationships with other couples, lend spice and excitement to love affairs and marriages. Yet as siblings or other family members, Aries-Tauruses and Virgo II's can find each other irritating and stressful, and may rarely be able to agree without friction surfacing. Both partners will have to work hard on making their relationship less judgmental and condemnatory if the family is to have peace.

Because these two are extremely strong-minded, powerful individuals, a working relationship between them is unlikely to be easy. Power struggles inevitably arise here, but if boundaries and tasks are well defined, effective work for the good of the group is possible.

ADVICE: *Find a balance between tranquillity and excitement. Keep negative tendencies under control. Give others peace. Ease frictions a bit.*

STRENGTHS: **UP-FRONT, RESPECTFUL, DETERMINED**

WEAKNESSES: **SELFISH, UNSYMPATHETIC, COMBATIVE**

BEST: **WORK**

WORST: **MARRIAGE**

SHIRLEY MACLAINE (4/24/34)
HAL WALLIS (9/14/1899)

Wallis, who produced over 400 films in his lifetime, was in the audience during MacLaine's understudy performance in Broadway's *Pajama Game* in 1954. He immediately signed her to a movie contract.

Also: Yehudi Menuhin & Bruno Walter (violinist/conductor); **Queen Elizabeth II & Prince Henry** (grandmother/grandson).

April 19–24

THE CUSP OF POWER
ARIES-TAURUS CUSP

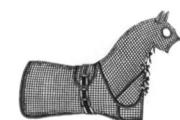

September 11–18

THE WEEK OF THE LITERALIST
VIRGO III

A Practical Modus Vivendi

This is a very determined relationship; knowing what is wanted and how to get it are high priorities here. It is a combination that is only interested in the material world and the practical aspects of life. Any sort of deeper feelings, sensitivity or emotion will be given short shrift here.

Both Aries-Tauruses and Virgo III's have a strongly selfish side, and their relationship only magnifies this tendency. After meeting a few times, each of these two will have little doubt that they have met a formidable opponent, one with at least as much will and survival instinct as they. Virgo III's are an interesting blend of conservative and iconoclast, and Aries-Tauruses, particularly in the early stages of the relationship, may bring out their rebelliousness: they are extremely sensitive about injustice and high-handedness in all forms, and can be disturbed by Aries-Taurus snobbism and other forms of social pretension. If necessary, however, these two will work out a highly practical modus vivendi, as soon as both realize that it is in their mutual interest to do so.

In friendships and love affairs, Aries-Tauruses will come to respect the critical powers and common sense of Virgo III's, who for their part will appreciate the sound judgment and effective actions of Aries-Tauruses. But when these two are lovers, power struggles between them—who will rule the roost?—may never lie far beneath the surface. Sharp anger and outright battling are more likely than continual bickering, since no time is wasted here on trivialities; instead, combative energies are saved for larger issues. Compromise is rare here, and a third party may sometimes be required to settle the relationship's disputes.

Although marriage can be attempted in this combination, the couple's inability to relate well on a day-to-day basis makes it unlikely to work out. These two may be sexually compatible, but the bonds of sympathy and feeling that might sustain the relationship are unlikely to develop.

In careers and at work, these two can be a formidable duo. Their relationship will be based on mutual trust and need, and they will rely on and consult each other on important matters.

ADVICE: *Respect born out of struggle is usually longer lasting. Put limits on selfishness. Work for the common good. Learn to compromise.*

April 19–24

THE CUSP OF POWER
ARIES-TAURUS CUSP

September 19–24

THE CUSP OF BEAUTY
VIRGO-LIBRA CUSP

A Conventional Facade

RELATIONSHIPS

STRENGTHS: **AESTHETIC, STYLISH, PRIVATE**

WEAKNESSES: **SUPERFICIAL, MISLEADING, ADDICTIVE**

BEST: **LOVE**

WORST: **FRIENDSHIP**

CATHERINE THE GREAT (4/21/1729)
GRIGORI POTEMKIN (9/24/1739)

The central focus of this relationship is often aesthetic, especially in its penchant for highly personal taste in surroundings, clothes, furnishings and manners. A highly private and perhaps unconventional home life may be hidden behind a more conventional facade. Both partners instinctively appreciate the good things of the material world and the value of money, a talent that the relationship will enhance. When these two are spouses, or partners in a business or other common enterprise, a strong bond may exist between them.

The relationship has a strong sensuous side, and can be deeply physical when these two are lovers—as long as it starts out with a strong attraction. Excessive attention and affection also indicate a darkly addictive tendency, probably hidden to the world; emotionally the relationship can have an unhealthy aspect. Despite these obstacles, and although breakups and separations will be painful for this duo, a love affair here will be truly unforgettable.

Marriages can be as promising as love affairs. These two will enjoy establishing a home together, decorating it somewhat unusually and making it a stylish and comfortable place in which to live. Both partners have refined tastes, making them likely to have friends who are educated and interesting, but alas not necessarily the most real or human in expressing their feelings. The children of such a marriage may feel as if they're walking on eggs most of the time to keep up appearances; they will never, for example, be allowed to mess up the neatness of the home. Accordingly they may become inhibited and frustrated if forbidden to express their own individuality. Friendships or working relationships between these two can be difficult, particularly if Virgo-Libras become obsessive about their partner. Aries-Tauruses don't like their friends to be clinging, and are uncomfortable when they feel that their relationships are ruled by the manipulative emotions of others, preferring more relaxed and easy comrades. If these partners are only acquaintances, or companions engaged in a common aesthetic pursuit, things could work out better for them.

One of her protégés and original supporters, Potemkin helped Catherine seize power in 1762. The affair between this 45-year-old empress and her 35-year-old "official favorite" lasted 2 years, after which they remained friends and Potemkin replaced himself with other "favorites."

Also: **Jill Ireland & David McCallum** (married; actors).

ADVICE: *Deal with the dark side. Painful choices may be necessary. Stiffen your resolve. Be more transparent. Open windows and let the sun shine in.*

April 19–24

THE CUSP OF POWER
ARIES-TAURUS CUSP

September 25–October 2

THE WEEK OF THE PERFECTIONIST
LIBRA I

A Need for Structure

RELATIONSHIPS

STRENGTHS: **FUN, HONEST, ENDURING**

WEAKNESSES: **UNSTABLE, ANGRY, FRUSTRATED**

BEST: **FRIENDSHIP**

WORST: **MARRIAGE**

J. ROBERT OPPENHEIMER (4/22/04)
ENRICO FERMI (9/29/01)

The question here is whether enough stability can be established to hold the relationship together. The combination's underlying theme is dominance, but the nature of its participants is such that they won't be able to dominate an area, subject, or group together; a structure must be created whereby they both have their own, separate sphere of influence. If this structure is already in place, so much the better. If not, whether or not it can be achieved will determine whether peace or chaos will prevail.

Although Libra I's and Aries-Tauruses seem well suited in many respects, the chemistry of their matchup is unstable, and they can drive each other crazy in a day-to-day living situation. Aries-Tauruses will admire Libra I technical skill and perfectionism, while Libra I's will value the Aries-Taurus habit of painstaking preparation and execution. The indecisiveness of Libra I's, however, will eventually push even the most patient Aries-Taurus to the brink.

If the heavy demands made by the Libra I personality are revealed to Aries-Tauruses during a love affair, they may feel compelled to leave—unless, that is, their sexual involvement with the intense Libra I has assumed addictive proportions. Should they fail to discover the difficult side of Libra I until after they marry, however, they are faithful and stubborn enough to hang in there until the bitter end. Marriages between these two are unlikely to be easy, for perfectionistic Libra I's tend to be nit-pickers and Aries-Tauruses need to be left alone. The Aries-Taurus insistence on emotional honesty will force Libra I's to express their real feelings, no matter how negative or destructive. This is exactly what Libra I's need to do, and a strong Aries-Taurus personality may well deepen and prolong a friendship or love affair with a Libra I by such confrontations.

Libra I's have a wild and wacky side that can lead to fun times in this relationship, whether it is a sibling or co-worker matchup or a friendship. Their sense of humor will be appreciated by Aries-Tauruses, whose heavier moods will be lightened by a Libra I presence.

Colleagues in the creation of the A-bomb, these physicists worked on the Manhattan Project, the government's code name for the research. Fermi built the first nuclear reactor. Oppenheimer, "father of the atomic bomb," designed the weapon.

Also: **Barbra Streisand & Donna Karan** (friends; actress/ fashion designer); **Prokofiev & Shostakovitch** (composers).

ADVICE: *Clearing the air may be the first step to understanding. Be open and honest. Bring more structure to your life. Lessen chaotic elements.*

RELATIONSHIPS

STRENGTHS: RELAXED, SOCIAL, PERSUASIVE

WEAKNESSES: OVERDEPENDENT, UNMOTIVATED, UNDERMINING

BEST: LOVE

WORST: BUSINESS PARTNERSHIP

TANYA TUCKER (10/10/58)
GLEN CAMPBELL (4/22/36)

Country singers Tucker and Campbell, who peaked in the 60s and 70s, still enjoy popularity today. Their highly publicized affair ended in 1981.

Also: **Hitler & Himmler** (chief Nazis); **J. Robert Oppenheimer & Niels Bohr** (Manhattan Project scientists).

April 19–24
THE CUSP OF POWER
ARIES-TAURUS CUSP

October 3–10
THE WEEK OF SOCIETY
LIBRA II

Congenial Persuasion

Interestingly, this relationship is primarily oriented toward persuading others, preferably a broader audience or society. Feelings run strong here, particularly with regard to whatever it is that this couple wants others to feel, think, understand or do. This is often quite an unconscious part of the pairing, which may be quite low-key in its overall intentions. Beware, however, should these partners become enemies, when all their combined persuasive power will be directed toward condemning each other.

In friendship, love or marriage, the relationship may be quite relaxed and accepting. Libra II's have the right mixture of peacefulness, charm and kookiness to interest an Aries-Taurus and assure his or her continued interest, and they in turn will benefit from being able to depend on a solid Aries-Taurus partner. Overdependence may become a problem here: Libra II's may be too self-sacrificing, and may suffer a loss of self-esteem, if they get too devoted to their Aries-Taurus mate, lover or friend.

Love may blossom between Aries-Tauruses and Libra II's after an introductory friendship. Both of them care about harmony and beauty, creating a synergy that will enhance each one's appreciation of art, music, literature, design, gardening and a host of aesthetic activities. Deciding to live together as lovers, they may feel no need to give their relationship the more solid stamp of marriage. But if they do marry, or even if they remain a long-standing couple, they will have a talent for dealing with people and social situations. They should take care, however, to take the time they need to be alone, and to limit the social element. Aries-Taurus–Libra II family relations can be characterized by good feeling and mutual understanding. As co-workers, these two may wind up enjoying each other so much that they forget about getting the job done. Although this scenario is somewhat extreme, since both are usually quite professional, their mutual appreciation of each other can lead to a loss of edge; this relationship is not the most hard-driving or self-sacrificing imaginable. Its energy, then, is better suited to easy partnerships than to highly ambitious or competitive ones.

ADVICE: *Harmony has its dangers too. Be a bit more ambitious. Think about who you are persuading, and why. Reflect on the nature of manipulation.*

RELATIONSHIPS

STRENGTHS: PROMOTING, EDUCATIONAL, COMMITTED

WEAKNESSES: CONTROLLING, STRESSED, UNCOMPREHENDING

BEST: FRIENDSHIP

WORST: MARRIAGE

DUDLEY MOORE (4/19/35)
SUSAN ANTON (10/12/50)

Singer, actress and former Miss America, Anton met Moore at a 1980 awards dinner. Though a seemingly improbable couple, the 5'2" actor-musician and the 6' Anton sustained a happy, long-term relationship.

Also: **Barbra Streisand & Ray Stark** (singer/producer); **Catherine the Great & Grigori Orlov** (lovers; co-conspirators).

April 19–24
THE CUSP OF POWER
ARIES-TAURUS CUSP

October 11–18
THE WEEK OF THEATER
LIBRA III

Few Demands

The success of this relationship depends on how it handles problems of dominance and subtle forms of manipulation. In fact, its attitudes may be much too inflexible and controlling to allow those who share it to live together in peace.

Despite strong initial attractions and mutually sensuous orientations, love affairs between these two are unlikely to reach the stratosphere. Actually, matters of the heart between these two are more likely to wind up where they should have started in the first place—as easygoing friendships, with few demands on either partner. Marriages too are unlikely to be very successful, particularly if they involve children or other relatives. Libra III's generally find it hard to give themselves to people in a family setting, preferring to save their energies for other areas, like career, social activities or favorite hobby or sport. Aries-Tauruses usually want to participate in the many aspects of family life when married, and this difference may cause irreconcilable problems.

The relationship can, however, be highly successful as a friendship. Both parties demand strength in their deepest friendships, and this one can be outstanding in promoting talent, ability and depth of commitment to life and work. Each partner will learn a great deal from this relationship, which also has much to teach to others. Shared evenings, occasional vacations and participation in cultural happenings are all possible here.

Aries-Tauruses are likely to make devoted parents of Libra III children, but will often understand them less and less as the years go by—a pity, since it is in adult life that Libra III's may be most needy of their parents. Libra III's will rarely make good parents for Aries-Tauruses, and as co-workers are often demanding and critical of them. In the workplace, in fact, the tensions in the relationship are counterproductive to achieving success. Aries-Tauruses like straightforwardness but also demand flexibility and compromise, which are anathema to Libra III's.

ADVICE: *Let things be. Back off. Allow events to unfold without influencing them. Have faith. Compromise is essential. Get priorities straight.*

April 19–24
THE CUSP OF POWER
ARIES-TAURUS CUSP

October 19–25
THE CUSP OF DRAMA & CRITICISM
LIBRA-SCORPIO CUSP

Oscillating Behavior

O pposites attract, and these two types, directly opposing each other in the zodiac, are indeed in many ways complementary. Aries-Taurus is a fire-earth combination, denoting an intuitive and sensuous type, and Libra-Scorpio an air-water coupling, indicating a yoking of thought and feeling. Between these two, then, they create the whole earth-air-fire-water spectrum, making this a strong combination for friendship and, possibly, love. Yet the synergy of the relationship, and the astrological opposition, also point to wide swings of feeling and behavior, so that the combination's hallmarks are instability, change, flux and oscillation. Ideally, challenges and goals need to be created for the relationship so that, rather than swinging to and fro, it can move forward.

Love affairs between these two can be quite spectacular when on and nothing short of disastrous when off. Libra-Scorpios are extremely charismatic types, and Aries-Tauruses smitten by their charms will be difficult to deter. Problems usually arise less at this stage, however, than after the goal, whether it be romantic or sexual, has been achieved. Libra-Scorpios can be a real handful emotionally, especially in this relationship, which brings out their dramatic and petulant side. In the sexual sphere, Libra-Scorpios tend to be more passionate than sensuous, while Aries-Tauruses are decidedly sensuous in all areas of life. Thus Aries-Tauruses may be upset by the relationship's coolness, while the Libra-Scorpios may miss a cataclysmic and intense sexual quality that they crave.

In friendships, familial and work situations, the relationship is complementary, but mutual willfulness and strong-mindedness will create problems in a daily setting. As parents and bosses, however, Aries-Tauruses will be strong enough to keep the energies of Libra-Scorpios on track, preventing their erratic side from getting out of control.

ADVICE: *Iron out mood swings. Appreciate the value of moderation. Try to be more consistent. Tend to practical matters. Work on challenges.*

RELATIONSHIPS

STRENGTHS: **SPECTACULAR, SEXUAL, INDEPENDENT**

WEAKNESSES: **DISASTROUS, OSCILLATING, DENYING**

BEST: **LOVE**

WORST: **FAMILY**

JOHN WATERS (4/22/46)
DIVINE (10/19/45)

Divine, a tranvestite performer, was a high-school friend of Waters, the audacious director who used Divine in many of his now-classic cult movies. The pair worked closely until Divine's death in 1989.

Also: **Napoleon III & Sarah Bernhardt** (affair; royalty/actress); **Mme. de Stael & Benjamin Constant** (affair; writers); **Lenin & John Reed** (revolutionary/journalist).

April 19–24
THE CUSP OF POWER
ARIES-TAURUS CUSP

October 26–November 2
THE WEEK OF INTENSITY
SCORPIO I

Testing the Mettle

I ssues of authority will be at the forefront in this relationship, in terms less of directing others (though this is part of the issue) than of inner resources and private goals. Poking deep into the relationship, one would expect to find an underlying insecurity linking this pair together. They will put a great deal of emphasis on helping each other achieve their main desire: upward mobility. The success of this endeavor will be the test of the relationship's mettle.

These two are often drawn to each other physically, and a desire-filled love affair may result. Scorpio I's can be difficult lovers for Aries-Tauruses, however, despite their ardor and passion, since they are extremely critical and exacting. They can also be quite cruel in extracting retribution when they feel rejected, and after a few bouts of what Aries-Tauruses may view as sadistic behavior on their partner's part, they may decide to call it quits.

Marriages here are not particularly advised, unless they are engaged upon purely for social aims. Even then, both partners must be ready to endure some wearing and painfully drawn-out episodes.

In friendships in this combination, the authority of each party must be equal. Status and power play a role in this relationship, and Scorpio I's in particular can feel resentful if a friend moves in more elevated social circles. This will also undercut their self-assurance. Conflicts may arise if high-placed Aries-Tauruses treat Scorpio I friends in what seems to be a condescending manner.

In the family and at work, Scorpio I's can be quite unforgiving when they believe those around them are operating out of impure or questionable motives. To perform the right action is not enough if it is done for the wrong reason, and since Aries-Tauruses are pragmatic in outlook, they may be quite bewildered when their Scorpio I partner criticizes them on this front. In working relationships the ethical stance of a Scorpio I can be quite bothersome to an Aries-Taurus, who will see it as unproductive, undermining efficiency and the job at hand.

ADVICE: *Beware of being snobbish. Cultivate kindness and consideration. Don't be cruel. Put away judgmental attitudes.*

RELATIONSHIPS

STRENGTHS: **PASSIONATE, EQUAL, UPWARDLY MOBILE**

WEAKNESSES: **JUDGMENTAL, EXACTING, PAINFUL**

BEST: **FRIENDSHIP**

WORST: **MARRIAGE**

CHRISTOPHER COLUMBUS (10/30/1451)
QUEEN ISABELLA (4/22/1451)

Columbus spent nearly 7 years in getting Isabella's support for his New World quest. Reluctantly, she agreed to finance his 1492 voyage. After his discoveries, she continued funding based on the prospect of a Spanish empire in the Americas.

Also: **Hitler & Goebbels** (Nazis); **Barbra Streisand & Fanny Brice** (portrayal in *Funny Girl*); **John Muir & Theodore Roosevelt** (early conservationists).

April 19–24
THE CUSP OF POWER
ARIES-TAURUS CUSP

November 3–11
THE WEEK OF DEPTH
SCORPIO II

Brilliant Challenge

JESSICA LANGE (4/20/49)
SAM SHEPARD (11/5/43)

Lange had 5 Oscar nominations, winning for *Blue Sky* (1994). Her long-term live-in relationship with NY playwright, screenwriter and actor Shepard produced 2 children. **Also: Elaine May & Mike Nichols** (comedy team); **Lenin & Trotsky** (communist leaders); **Ryan O'Neal & Tatum O'Neal** (father/daughter); **Jill Ireland & Charles Bronson** (married); **Michael O'Keefe & Bonnie Raitt** (married; actor/singer).

This combination can make for a highly unusual relationship, one of passion and brilliance. It will be most successful when the relationship's demands are not excessive and individual differences are respected. Freedom is a necessity here, yet given enough free rein, the relationship can endure, since neither party will ever find another partnership as powerful or unique. Both Aries-Taurus and Scorpio II are very powerful individuals, and a combination that outshines even them is quite a draw for them. In fact they may find themselves more attracted to the relationship than they are to each other.

A same-sex Aries-Taurus–Scorpio II friendship is often very comforting, and can also stimulate the careers of both partners. It will have a foundation of mutual respect, and each will generally admire the other party's achievement and power. Even more rewarding are this combination's love affairs, which can be deep, passionate and emotionally challenging for both partners. One issue between these two might be physical appearance: Aries-Tauruses are sensitive to comments on this subject, and Scorpio II's can be highly critical about such matters. Moreover, Scorpio II's tend to be controlling in all aspects of their love relationships, and this can create great difficulties for their Aries-Taurus partners, who will not be subdued or dominated. Conversely, Aries-Taurus toughness may leave Scorpio II's feeling hurt or misunderstood. These relationships can be incredible experiences both emotionally and sexually, but the partners must be able to arrive at a point of mutual acceptance, openness and sharing.

Overly demanding Scorpio II parents will engender rebellion in their Aries-Taurus children. Work relationships in this combination can be either highly productive or highly destructive, depending on the duo's orientation: these two can build an effective day-to-day work schedule if they keep personal matters in abeyance, but Scorpio II's are very careful with money, and there will surely be conflict over Aries-Tauruses' lavish tastes and free spending.

ADVICE: *Let up in your intensity. Be more forgiving and forgetting. Let the good times roll. Don't be uptight, it's only money. Power isn't everything.*

April 19–24
THE CUSP OF POWER
ARIES-TAURUS CUSP

November 12–18
THE WEEK OF CHARM
SCORPIO III

A Need to Be Faithful

PRINCE CHARLES (11/14/48)
QUEEN ELIZABETH II (4/21/26)

Charles, Elizabeth's oldest child and heir to the throne, was raised principally to become king. He lived at home until age 32. British media cast him as an emotionally deprived lad abandoned to nannies by his mother, later bullied into a marital charade. **Also: Elizabeth II & Prince Peter** (queen/first grandchild); **Dudley Moore & Peter Cooke** (comedy team); **Tony Danza & Danny DeVito** (co-stars *Taxi*).

If the issues of authority and of the balance of power that are so deeply embedded in this relationship are to be dealt with successfully, a concentration on developing faithfulness, trust and honesty will have to emerge. Both partners must feel free to speak their minds. Since both Aries-Tauruses and Scorpio III's are weighty individuals who are quite serious in outlook, the relationship's tendency to keep its partners upbeat and looking on the positive side is a definite plus.

Both Aries-Tauruses and Scorpio III's like people who have the inner resources to pull their own weight and pay their own way. When these two are companions and acquaintances, this mutual preference will manifest as the partners' healthy respect for each other in down-to-earth, everyday matters.

A love relationship here can be both attractive and quite romantic. But no matter how strong the sexual chemistry may be, deep involvement will not develop unless there is a solid bond of trust. Repressed storms of passion often rage within Scorpio III's, forcing their partner either to react with similar emotions or perhaps to turn off completely. Fortunately, Aries-Tauruses have a patient and understanding side, but they will still be troubled by the Scorpio III tendency toward possessiveness and jealousy. Such tendencies may have to be mastered or given up if the relationship is to move on to marriage or a more permanent living arrangement.

Whether or not these two can be friends depends on the Scorpio III's willingness and ability to open up to the Aries-Taurus in the personal sphere. This may be difficult if they find the Aries-Taurus too imposing, or if their feelings of inferiority are aroused. Scorpio III's have a strong need to be honest with another human being at a deep level, however, and if they can show their weaknesses and doubts to an Aries-Taurus (often a very understanding observer and listener) without feeling threatened, they may receive invaluable advice and guidance. Family members and co-workers in this combination may mutually distrust each other and never get very close. Despite their respect for each other, emotional honesty will be difficult between them.

ADVICE: *Admitting weakness can be a sign of strength. Accept honest attitudes. Cultivate faithfulness. Make it harder to push your buttons.*

April 19–24

THE CUSP OF POWER
ARIES-TAURUS CUSP

November 19–24

THE CUSP OF REVOLUTION
SCORPIO-SAGITTARIUS CUSP

Mutual Respect

This relationship can be a paradigm for easy and accepting attitudes. Aries-Taurus–Scorpio-Sagittarius is among the few combinations in the year where the partners can be both friends and lovers before, during and after their love affair. There is a deep understanding and loyalty in this relationship, and a mutual respect, especially on the mental plane. Yet as well as these two get along, it may not be in the cards for them to marry or even live together, since ease does not necessarily entail either emotional depth or the ability to commit.

Even if these two meet when either or both of them is involved with another steady partner or spouse, the seductive pull of a love affair between them will usually be so great that neither can resist. The results might be tragic, particularly for the third parties, but the maturity and control of which the Aries-Taurus–Scorpio-Sagittarius relationship is capable will have a strong tempering effect. So unshakable is the relationship's faith in itself, in fact, that it can show consideration for the feelings of others to a most unusual degree.

These two do not necessarily make a strong parent-child combination, principally because of the Scorpio-Sagittarians, who, as parents, can often be impatient with having children around and, as children, will probably be rebellious towards an overbearing or overprotective Aries-Taurus parent. A sibling relationship, however, particularly between opposite sexes, may be extremely close and affectionate, both in childhood and into more mature years.

In business, Scorpio-Sagittarians can exceed even Aries-Tauruses in their lavish tastes, so that this combination could eat up its profits. As co-workers they will get along well enough, but neither may be enthusiastic enough to put out their very best, either individually or together, within a company structure. Their optimal working combination may be as freelancers, consultants or advisors, a context that could free them to decide their courses of action and their work methods independently of each other, while at the same time being able to complement each other whenever there is mutual advantage in doing so.

ADVICE: *Have fun but stay respectful of others. Control selfish desires. Beware of elitist attitudes. Push yourself a bit more to scale the heights.*

ADOLF HITLER (4/20/1889)
CHARLES DEGAULLE (11/22/1890)

Hitler and DeGaulle were political and military enemies during WWII. After Hitler's *blitzkrieg* defeated the French armies in 1940, the French leader was instrumental in organizing anti-German activities in France, Algeria and England. He rose to world fame as the symbol of French resistance.

April 19–24

THE CUSP OF POWER
ARIES-TAURUS CUSP

November 25–December 2

THE WEEK OF INDEPENDENCE
SAGITTARIUS I

Cross Rhythms

The key to this relationship's success will be the ability to create balance and provide leadership and guidance in any project. An immediate problem is that of synchronization, for these two partners' rhythms may not gel with each other. Differences in style and tempo are substantial here: Aries-Tauruses are consolidators of energy and masters of the slow buildup, Sagittarius I's are more apt to explode in a fast break. Moreover, the internal motor of Sagittarius I's usually runs at a higher rate than that of Aries-Tauruses, who may still be warming up when the Sagittarius I is long gone.

Such differences in tempo may create difficulties in the emotional and sexual aspects of love relationships, but Sagittarius I intensity is usually sufficient to satisfy the most demanding of Aries-Tauruses. Highly charged emotional relationships can emerge between these two if one of them is already committed to a partner, creating a love triangle. Should all three be able to be friends, a positive outcome may be expected, but if either the Sagittarius I or the Aries-Taurus views the third person with hostility, a volatile situation is likely to arise.

In marriages and in business or other career settings, Sagittarius I's strongly benefit from having a stable, dependable partner who can hang back and be there for them without question. Aries-Tauruses may fit the bill perfectly. To have such a partner as advisor, manager, planner or director of their energies will be invaluable to Sagittarius I's, and to any team of which these two are a part. Executive qualities are highly effective here. For the same reasons, Aries-Tauruses can make understanding parents for Sagittarius I children—and also understanding children for Sagittarius I parents. Again, this duo will have a leadership role in the family. And should Aries-Taurus and Sagittarius I lovers decide to marry, they may be among the most nurturing combinations of the whole year, providing warmth, direction, safety and attention to their children. On the other hand, Aries-Tauruses and Sagittarius I's do not always make the best friends. Both of them are opinionated and strong-minded, and emotionally they may not always be on the same wavelength.

ADVICE: *Develop sensitivity to rhythms different from your own. Try to harness and coordinate energies. Seek effective leadership. Divide tasks fairly.*

HERVE VILLECHAIZE (4/23/43)
RICARDO MONTALBAN (11/25/20)

Suave and handsome Mexican-born Montalban was a screen actor of the 40s. He became a popular tv star on the series *Fantasy Island,* starring opposite the diminutive and comical Villechaize, who played his assistant.

STRENGTHS: **EXCITING, LOYAL, RELIABLE**

WEAKNESSES: **PROBLEMATICAL, IRRITATING, DISAPPROVING**

BEST: **SIBLING**

WORST: **MARRIAGE**

MANNE SIEGBAHN (12/3/1886)
KAI SIEGBAHN (4/20/1918)

Manne and his son Kai are both Nobelists in physics. Manne won the prize in 1924 for contributions to x-ray spectography. Kai won in 1981 for his development of a high-resolution spectrometer.

April 19–24

THE CUSP OF POWER
ARIES-TAURUS CUSP

December 3–10

THE WEEK OF THE ORIGINATOR
SAGITTARIUS II

Prepare to Compromise

Unless this relationship concerns itself primarily with the ability to accept, forgive and forget, the irritations and disapproving attitudes inherent here are likely to lead to difficulty, possibly even rejection or separation. Luckily this combination has a conscience, so that when infringements occur, awareness is not far behind. Matters will quickly be set right, allowing the relationship to move forward again.

Sagittarius II's have an unpredictable and impulsive nature that will often drive more responsible Aries-Taurus parents, bosses or mates to distraction. Typically sensitive, they will probably worry and wonder whether the Aries-Taurus accepts their more peculiar qualities. No matter how great the attraction between these two, a love affair between them is unlikely to last long; Aries-Tauruses will be worn down by its instabilities and petty conflicts. In certain rare cases, however, these partners may be able to focus on the relationship's more positive aspects, resulting in a more stable relationship (though never completely so). Marriages here can be highly problematic, and are not recommended unless the Sagittarius II is prepared to compromise and to tone down his or her personality, and the Aries-Taurus to be even more patient and accepting than usual.

At work, Sagittarius II's do best in occupations that allow them to express their unusual side, and Aries-Tauruses—generally pragmatic types who want the maximum progress for the minimum trouble—are unlikely to show a great deal of sympathy for such idiosyncratic behavior on the job. But friendships between these two can be very rewarding, the Sagittarius II contributing interest and excitement, the Aries-Taurus loyalty and reliability. As long as the pairing does not demand in-depth involvement in personal matters, it can prove highly satisfactory for companionship or social partnership. One danger may be, however, that Sagittarius II's can cast Aries-Tauruses in a parental role, projecting on them certain feelings from childhood.

An Aries-Taurus brother or sister—particularly an older one, perhaps one of the few constants in a Sagittarius II's childhood or adolescence—can provide a good grounding for Sagittarius II energy.

ADVICE: *Discuss differences openly. Work on compromise and acceptance. Don't give in to negativity or hopelessness. See things in a positive light.*

STRENGTHS: **CHALLENGING, FORMIDABLE, THOUGHT-PROVOKING**

WEAKNESSES: **MISTRUSTFUL, DOMINANT, ADVERSARIAL**

BEST: **COMPETITION**

WORST: **WORK**

DON JOHNSON (12/15/49)
BARBRA STREISAND (4/24/42)

Johnson, macho star of *Miami Vice*, had a short-lived affair with singer Streisand in 1988, soon after her break-up with ice-cream heir Richard Baskin. **Also: Elizabeth II & George VI** (daughter/father); **Queen Isabella & Catherine of Aragon** (mother/daughter; Spanish queen/first wife of British Henry VIII).

April 19–24

THE CUSP OF POWER
ARIES-TAURUS CUSP

December 11–18

THE WEEK OF THE TITAN
SAGITTARIUS III

Need to Be Boss

The question of leadership will be a sore spot in this pairing, which is likely to focus on conflicts over dominance. Furthermore, the relationship's underlying modus operandi is likely to involve each partner ripping open and exposing the other's weaknesses or dark side. This of course achieves nothing, and weakens the overall fabric of the relationship. The Aries-Taurus–Sagittarius III combination, then, is unlikely to be a good one for business or marital partnerships. Both personalities have a need to be the boss, and neither will give ground easily. Should these two head rival commercial, social or even family groups, they are likely to be formidable adversaries.

In love relationships the problem of dominance will also rear its ugly head. Sagittarius III's need to be adored, admired and praised, and Aries-Tauruses are not so easily impressed. Also, when another person gains at what they feel is their expense, Aries-Tauruses are likely to lose interest or back off. There may be a certain sexual intensity here, but it is likely to be an expression more of ego than of love, and to be motivated more by challenge than by desire. Sagittarius III's can have difficulty satisfying Aries-Tauruses' sensual side, and giving enough emotionally to their demanding partners.

At work, Sagittarius III's think big and are risk-takers who attempt the impossible, or at least the very difficult, while Aries-Tauruses tend to be skeptical, and are suspicious of grandiose schemes. Friendships can work better, featuring lively and thought-provoking philosophical discussions. And as companions in travel and challenging physical activities, Sagittarius III's can bring out Aries-Tauruses' more adventuresome side, although such a relationship may never manifest emotional closeness.

Aries-Taurus parents will do their best to instill a note of realism in what they may view as the idle views and runaway fantasies of their Sagittarius III offspring. On the other hand, an Aries-Taurus child may suffer disillusionment on seeing the puncturing of a Sagittarius III parent's perhaps inspired, perhaps inflated schemes.

ADVICE: *Try to give more emotionally. Tone down combative attitudes. Competition can be productive as long as it doesn't get out of hand.*

April 19–24
THE CUSP OF POWER
ARIES-TAURUS CUSP

December 19–25
THE CUSP OF PROPHECY
SAGITTARIUS-CAPRICORN CUSP

Silent Storms

Sensitivities run high in this relationship, which will involve a tendency to hide irritations and true feelings only to reveal them periodically in startling fashion. For good and bad, the relationship is characterized by strong emotions. This is partly because the combination's energy rarely focuses on the mundane, practical aspects of life. It is either directed completely outside the relationship (at the world at large) or at the relationship itself, which will inevitably begin to crack under the strain.

Aries-Tauruses will be disturbed by the relationship's silences and suppressive aspects, for they like up-front attitudes about thoughts and feelings. Sagittarius-Capricorns tend to hide their true personalities, and Aries-Taurus may see this as sneaky and manipulative, particularly when the two are of the same sex. Positive relations between these two, then, are usually unlikely or impossible; an adversarial role is much more common.

As far as love is concerned, deep sympathy or compassion is unlikely to appear here, yet there is often an attraction. Sexual relations of a passionate but often unfeeling nature may result, but unless variations or deviations are introduced, the relationship is likely to burn out fast. Often, however, the powerful sexuality of each of these partners is never called into play in the first place, for both of them think better than to get involved.

Marriages and business relations between these two are unlikely. Although Aries-Taurus and Sagittarius-Capricorn have qualities in common (they are both fire-earth combinations), they intuitively understand that involvement in any permanent situation could invite disaster. Aries-Tauruses will find Sagittarius-Capricorns' lack of business sense appalling, and Sagittarius-Capricorns may see Aries-Tauruses as cruel or unfeeling tyrants.

As family members, Sagittarius-Capricorns may look up to or admire an Aries-Taurus, but more often as a grandparent, aunt or uncle than as a parent. Likewise an Aries-Taurus child may find a Sagittarius-Capricorn intriguing and fascinating, and seek them out for advice, but also to learn about their experiences. Family relationships not of the parent-child variety are likely to be most productive and fulfilling.

ADVICE: *What is hidden is sometimes best left that way. Don't stir up trouble. Be honest, up to a point, and mind your manners. Be sympathetic.*

VLADIMIR LENIN (4/22/1870)
JOSEPH STALIN (12/21/1879)

These fellow revolutionaries first met in 1905. After gaining political prominence, Lenin appointed Stalin to various positions within the Bolshevik party. Lenin became wary of Stalin's overzealous nationalism and, before his death in 1924, tried to prevent Stalin's succession but failed. **Also:** Hitler & Stalin (WWII adversaries).

April 19–24
THE CUSP OF POWER
ARIES-TAURUS CUSP

December 26–January 2
THE WEEK OF THE RULER
CAPRICORN I

Breathing New Life

This relationship embraces correction and enhancement. It will be very involved in locating and revealing problems and weaknesses, enabling their repair. Making an object, person or system operate smoothly, healthily or efficiently is the ultimate goal. Should Aries-Taurus and Capricorn I share similar outlooks on how a company, club or family should run, they can make successful business or marital partners. The relationship will usually adopt a moderate or conservative stance, belying certain progressive or even radical tendencies on the part of these two personalities. It can be good with money—Aries-Taurus with making and spending it, Capricorn I with managing it. Although both of these partners are dominant types, power struggles are unlikely to arise often in their relationship, which will feature mutual respect and a realization that such struggles would be damaging to the group of which they are a part.

In love and family relationships, Aries-Tauruses will cry out for Capricorn I's to express their true and deeper feelings, and to show more sympathy and understanding. Conflicts may only be deepened if Aries-Tauruses grow frustrated with Capricorn I's and withdraw, or lash out periodically in anger. Small daily tensions, seemingly insignificant, can be blown out of all proportion, creating an unstable and counterproductive atmosphere. Generally speaking, enthusiastic romantic feelings will be difficult for these two to sustain, often being replaced by a more pragmatic attitude, particularly in sexual matters; it will be vital, then, for the relationship to renew itself periodically. As parents, both Capricorn I's and Aries-Tauruses will address the problems and provide the structure and support their children need, but their offspring do not always appreciate them, at times viewing their parents as tinkering with them. Friendships can succeed only if the relationship's high standards of approval are met. The partners must prove interesting to each other and continue to have something to offer each other. Bonds of friendship, painstakingly built, can be severely tested or broken by competition or jealousy. The loss of the friendship may prove demoralizing to either or both parties.

ADVICE: *A weakness for money does not imply power. Breathe new life into your activities. A sharp knife cuts better. Get in touch with your deeper feelings.*

YEHUDI MENUHIN (4/22/16)
NATHAN MILSTEIN (12/31/04)

Menuhin and Milstein, both born to Russian-Jewish parents, are among the greatest concert violinists of this century. New York-born Menuhin, a child prodigy, debuted internationally in the 20s. Russian-born Milstein decided to remain in the US after his debut in 1929. Both were very successful recording artists.

STRENGTHS: **PHILOSOPHICAL, SPIRITUAL, DOWN-TO-EARTH**

WEAKNESSES: **NEGLECTFUL, UNFORGIVING, UNEMOTIONAL**

BEST: **FRIENDSHIP**

WORST: **WORK**

VICTORIA FORDE (4/21/1897)
TOM MIX (1/6/1880)

Mix and minor actress Forde were married from 1918-30 and had a daughter, Thomasina. Their marriage lasted through the cowboy film star's busiest acting years. His contract called for 5 movies a year from 1917-28. Forde was his 3rd of 7 wives.

April 19–24
THE CUSP OF POWER
ARIES-TAURUS CUSP

January 3–9
THE WEEK OF DETERMINATION
CAPRICORN II

A Higher Plane

This relationship will be drawn over and over to matters of spirit, religion or philosophy. Materialistic or pragmatic concerns are not of primary importance here. True, Aries-Taurus–Capricorn II friendships have a practical, down-to-earth streak, especially in everyday matters; but beyond this their relationship will often evince a deep interest in aesthetics and philosophy, adding a whole new dimension to its partners' pragmatic natures. The relationship is characterized by an emotional warmth that is highly satisfying. Discussions of highly personal subjects generally stay objective, without the intrusion of undue emotion. The friendship makes space for vacations and other trips together, and financial responsibility is rarely an issue here.

Love and marriage will demand care, for Capricorn II's need to keep their private and career lives strictly separate. Aries-Tauruses are usually strong enough not to be overly demanding of their attention, and the relationship tends to feature a highly independent outlook in both career and social matters. But Aries-Tauruses generally need a lot more steady affection than Capricorn II's do, and although Capricorn II's can be sexually powerful, they are not known for exhibiting the day-to-day tenderness and sympathy that Aries-Tauruses require if they are to be happy and satisfied. Should power struggles arise, attitudes may become hurtful and unforgiving, yet a wise and realistic attitude will often prevail, allowing needs to be realized and resentments forgotten.

When these two are co-workers or business associates, Capricorn II ambition can prove a problem: in crucial situations, Aries-Tauruses may be suspicious of their partner's motives, particularly if they feel that the Capricorn II is putting his or her own interests ahead of the group's. Capricorn II's also have a workaholic side, whereas Aries-Tauruses need time off and would often prefer not to be working at all. Thus Capricorn II's may come to resent the fact that Aries-Tauruses are contributing less energy and commitment than they are.

ADVICE: *If you feel resentment you have a responsibility to express it. Tenderness is key to happiness. Emphasize the positive by embarking on a course of study together.*

STRENGTHS: **SENSUAL, SHARING, POWERFUL**

WEAKNESSES: **OVERDOMINANT, CRITICAL, INSECURE**

BEST: **LOVE**

WORST: **WORK**

HAROLD LLOYD (4/20/1893)
HAL ROACH (1/14/1892)

In 1917, producer-director Roach created Lloyd's famous persona— a perfectly average-looking man wearing oversized black horn-rimmed glasses (which became Lloyd's trademark). Until 1923 they collaborated successfully. Then Lloyd began producing his own films.

Also: Hitler & Goering (Nazis); **Eliot Ness & Robert Stack** (G-man/*Untouchables* portrayer).

April 19–24
THE CUSP OF POWER
ARIES-TAURUS CUSP

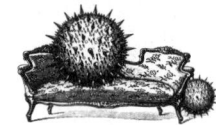

January 10–16
THE WEEK OF DOMINANCE
CAPRICORN III

Inscrutable Byways

This combination will tend to reveal its partners' hidden insecurities, making the relationship itself feel unstable. It often involves unfavorable comparisons, real or imagined; there will be a tendency to overachieve and overreach in an attempt to assert capability and expertise. Trying too hard, and displaying jealousy, only reveal the depth of such insecurities. The combination of admiration and jealousy can be both inspiring and inhibiting. The relationship, then, is likely to have elements of secrecy, enigma and complexity.

Capricorn III's may have a secret inferiority complex that a relationship with an Aries-Taurus can bring out. The relationship can also reveal Aries-Taurus insecurities. Both Aries-Tauruses and Capricorn III's need to dominate at home, and the house big enough to hold both of them, as spouses or live-in lovers, may not have been built yet. Children and others who live with them may witness power struggles of gigantic proportions, which can threaten to tear the family apart. In the worst-case scenario, the children are forced to take sides or, in a divorce struggle, are played off against the other parent. Should common sense prevail early on in a marriage, however, these spouses may be able to come to a common agreement about who rules what, avoiding conflict for all concerned. Their ability to agree on material possessions will be especially important.

As lovers, Aries-Tauruses and Capricorn III's may have a deeply sensual bond. The pleasures of table and bed attract both of them strongly, and should they find each other agreeable and desirable, their love affair may go on for some time. Such a love affair can be both preceded and followed by friendship. Should an Aries-Taurus–Capricorn III love affair end by mutual consent, without to-do or negativity, they may quite naturally want to continue seeing each other as friends, or to share a common activity from time to time.

This relationship is naturally work oriented, but the work arena, more than any other, is likely to cause tension and insecurity. Since both Aries-Tauruses and Capricorn III's need to dominate, they are probably best off not working together. If given no choice, they should structure clear and separate lines of responsibility.

ADVICE: *Beware of involving others in your power struggles. Diminish ego involvement. Avoid comparison. Be secure in who you are.*

324

Tidal Wave

Although Aries-Taurus and Capricorn-Aquarius are, respectively, fire-earth and earth-air combinations, the focus of their relationship will be in the area of the missing element, water, which symbolizes feelings. This is a highly emotional combination, one that can easily create an extremely private, isolated domain. These partners build walls of feeling that can threaten to overwhelm them. Only the hardiest of souls would venture to choose this hermetic, emotionally dangerous combination.

Aries-Tauruses may initially find Capricorn-Aquariuses unsettling, fascinating and attractive. Should they get involved, they can expect high passion and desire but also outbursts of anger and even violence. In love relationships, the relationship's synergy brings out its partners' best and their worst, since both know how to hit the raw nerves of the other's sensitivities. Such love affairs rarely develop into marriage or living together; although Aries-Tauruses have the kind of personality that will lend a measure of stability to the relationship, its emotional storms will make it impossible for them to control their own feelings to the necessary degree, and personal power and mastery are paramount for them.

Growing up in a family setting, Aries-Taurus and Capricorn-Aquarius siblings may fight constantly, particularly if they are of the same sex. Over the years, however, they may develop a close and mutually supportive bond, often starting to relate better to each other in early adulthood.

The relationship can work out well in the work sphere, as long as everyone sticks to the job at hand and resists getting sidetracked by personal differences and irritations. Aries-Tauruses will find Capricorn-Aquarian energies chaotic from time to time but will recognize that these personalities are hard workers as long as they know what is expected of them. Often an Aries-Taurus co-worker may exert a stabilizing force on Capricorn-Aquariuses, giving them the support and understanding they need if they are to continue in the team.

ADVICE: *Chaos is often something we attract rather than run into by chance. Understand your emotions better. Keep cool. Learn patience.*

AL CAPONE (1/17/1899)
ELIOT NESS (4/19/03)

Ness was hired by the Justice Dept. in 1929 to bring down Chicago gangster Capone. With his 9-man team of unbribable lawmen (hence the nickname "Untouchables") Ness' underworld infiltration produced evidence that nailed Capone for income-tax evasion.
Also: **William Shakespeare & Francis Bacon** (authorship controversy); **Charlotte Brontë & Anne Brontë** (sisters; writers).

Give and Take

This relationship has the potential to be satisfying and thoughtful, with an even-keeled level of feeling and a direct yet measured kind of communication. The relationship is inherently about boundaries—creating them and staying within them, to keep things functioning smoothly.

Aries-Tauruses and Aquarius I's are compatible in love affairs, partly because neither of them enjoys complex emotional interactions. Young Aries-Tauruses may be fascinated with the precocious energies of Aquarius I's, but when more mature they will have problems with the Aquarius I habit of practicing a double standard. Aquarius I's may lean heavily on Aries-Tauruses for support, gaining a measure of stability from their confidence and reliability. Should Aquarius I choose to roam, however, while expecting their partner to be faithful, an Aries-Taurus is likely either to lose interest or quietly to crack the whip.

Marriages in this combination can be successful and long lasting provided Aquarius I's pull their own weight and devote the necessary time and energy to family tasks, particularly those involving children. Although they give the impression of being free spirits who can and will not be tied down, Aquarius I's may need the stability of family if they are truly to blossom, and Aries-Taurus may be the perfect mate—appreciative, affectionate and, above all, able to get them moving. The chemistry here works both ways, for Aquarius I's will also get Aries-Tauruses out of the house more often, encourage them in their activities. Each can provide a kind of structure for the other. This combination is not particularly recommended for co-workers, associates or business partners, since Aries-Tauruses are likely to grow impatient with what they view as Aquarius I shortsightedness and impracticality. As family members, they may also grow dissatisfied and frustrated with having to clean up after Aquarius I siblings or children off having a good time. But Aries-Tauruses' condemnatory and judgmental attitudes to what they view as Aquarius I irresponsibility can in turn irritate and arouse the rebelliousness of Aquarius I family members.

ADVICE: *Follow the golden rule. Give and take equally. Service is one of the highest ends. Be sure your needs are satisfied.*

MIKHAIL BARYSHNIKOV (1/28/48)
JESSICA LANGE (4/20/49)

Actress Lange was a new star in 1976 (*King Kong*) when she began her affair with famous ballet star Baryshnikov. The couple had a love child, but Lange abruptly dropped Baryshnikov for Sam Shepard.
Also: **Valerie Bertinelli & Eddie Van Halen** (married; actress/rock star).

April 19–24

THE CUSP OF POWER
ARIES-TAURUS CUSP

ADOLF HITLER (4/20/1889)
EVA BRAUN (2/6/12)

Braun became Hitler's mistress in 1936 in a relationship believed more domestic than erotic. They married on April 29, 1945, as the Allies were closing in, and committed suicide the next day. **Also: Ryan O'Neal & Farrah Fawcett** (live-in parents); **Lee Majors & Farrah Fawcett** (married; actors); **Shakespeare & Marlowe** (Elizabethan playwrights).

Down in the Sandbox

This relationship focuses on creating the openness to follow imaginative impulses—or, more specifically, on fantasy and play. This freedom of enjoyment requires work, of course, primarily in finding the balance between conflicting points of view and energies, particularly in daily activities. Still, the relationship can be so playful that the partners will hardly know the work is being done. Aquarius II's tend to bring out the lighter side of Aries-Tauruses, who are serious and powerful people but also like to have fun. Generally speaking, the relationship will not go terribly deep, nor does it have to—as friends, these two will often find themselves having a good time.

In marriages and career partnerships, this can be an excellent pair. Aries-Tauruses will admire the accomplishments and talents of Aquarius II's; they themselves have to work much harder for what they get, but they are not jealous of people who can achieve a lot without undue effort. In marriages, however, problems may arise when things are going badly for Aquarius II's, who are prone to depression. Wrestling with their dark side is not easy either for them or for those they live with, and Aries-Taurus patience, particularly concerning infidelity, may be severely tried.

Aries-Taurus parents will be extremely proud of their Aquarius II children, even to the point of doting on them, yet they may be ineffective in teaching them sound and reasonable life principles. Aquarius II parents have a great deal to teach their Aries-Taurus children about sophisticated approaches to many areas of life, and will know how to keep the youthfulness they will need in this relationship: from time to time, it will be necessary for them to get down in the sandbox with these children. Love affairs of this combination are likely to be evanescent and unstable, on again and off again. Permanence and tradition are not usually in the cards for this relationship, no matter how attractive it may be to either or both parties at any one moment.

ADVICE: *Adults need play too. Find a balance between work and leisure. Everything is relative. Don't forget to attend to the practicalities.*

April 19–24

THE CUSP OF POWER
ARIES-TAURUS CUSP

February 8–15

THE WEEK OF ACCEPTANCE
AQUARIUS III

STEPHEN A. DOUGLAS (4/23/1813)
ABRAHAM LINCOLN (2/12/1809)

Lincoln lost the 1858 Illinois senatorial race to Douglas, his longtime foe. Their famed debates on the slavery question thrust Lincoln into national prominence. **Also: Tony Danza & Judith Light** (co-stars, *Who's the Boss*); **J.M.W. Turner & John Ruskin** (painter/art scholar-devotee).

House on Fire

Physical and sensuous, this relationship often also features an interest in current events and social doings. Romantically and sexually it can blaze like a house on fire, at least for a while; in fact, romance and a dreamlike quality give it a soft glow. There is a significant danger, however, that these partners will get caught up in seeking a perfect vision of a relationship rather than dealing with the realities of one.

Aries-Tauruses are fascinated by the colorful personalities of Aquarius III's, whom they may find romantically irresistible. Aquarius III's for their part can find the Aries-Taurus brand of sexuality extremely rich and rewarding. A problem in long-term relationships here is that the Aquarius III need for attention and affection is monumental. Since Aries-Tauruses usually have other things to do, they may find these demands tiring or wearing, particularly after a hard day's work. Marriages or permanent living situations, then, are often not meant to be.

One problem that these two run into as friends, mates and living partners is that Aquarius III's will tend to accuse Aries-Tauruses of things of which they themselves are guilty. Projection is a key word here. A lot of the time, Aquarius III's are exciting, bubbly and happy personalities, but when an Aries-Taurus sees the haze of unreality behind these positive attitudes, trouble is probably not far off. Masters of reality, Aries-Tauruses will probably be judgmental and critical of the optimism of Aquarius III's, who may feel that a damper is always being thrown over their enthusiasm. The resulting dark moods, anger and outbursts of Aquarius III's shadow side may fuel the fire.

Aries-Taurus parents have a great deal to teach their Aquarius III offspring but will generally find these children hard or impossible to control. (The children, in turn, often have trouble pleasing their Aries-Taurus parents, who seem to know better about almost everything.) Likewise, Aries-Taurus bosses and business partners may find irrepressible Aquarius III's difficult to manage or work with because of their insistence on doing things in their own highly individual and often peculiar way.

ADVICE: *Face yourself squarely in the mirror. Beware of illusions. Try to be more tolerant. Learn to compromise a bit. Try to limit dependency.*

April 19–24
THE CUSP OF POWER
ARIES-TAURUS CUSP

February 16–22
THE CUSP OF SENSITIVITY
AQUARIUS-PISCES CUSP

Nurturing Activities

This rather elemental combination is best accepted for what it is rather than analyzed for what it is not. At its best, it can symbolize the core aspect of creation—giving birth to the new and wholly unique. In fact, bringing new life into the world can stand as a symbol of this relationship. Marriages between these two are apt to include an urge to have children or, failing that, another kind of creative endeavor. Aquarius-Pisces will benefit from the stability and practicality that an Aries-Taurus mate has to offer, and Aries-Tauruses will find Aquarius-Pisces caring spouses. The more lonely or withdrawn type of Aquarius-Pisces personality may well bloom in a family setting that includes an Aries-Taurus. Nurturing activities, including sharing the responsibility of children (not necessarily their own), pets and a garden, are particularly suited to this relationship.

In love affairs, Aquarius-Pisces may lack the sexual intensity or romantic flair to keep their Aries-Taurus partners interested for long. Platonic friendships are more likely, since kindness and understanding are often more important to Aquarius-Pisces than physical contact is. This kind of relationship will allow Aries-Tauruses to express the more sympathetic elements of their personality, and their combative stance may soften when they have a nonthreatening partner.

Aquarius-Pisces have a chip-on-the-shoulder attitude that can well emerge around more threatening Aries-Taurus personalities, particularly colleagues or family members. But they can be aggressive themselves, as well as ambitious, and if they find themselves in direct competition with an Aries-Taurus they may become increasingly insecure. Except in directly confrontational situations, such as business, career or sibling rivalries, Aries-Tauruses may be baffled or bewildered by Aquarius-Pisces reactions, and with all best intentions will seek to make them less upset and more comfortable. As children, sensitive Aquarius-Pisces may feel misunderstood by an Aries-Taurus parent, and will seek to protect themselves by building a wall against what they perceive as criticism or aggression. Aries-Taurus children are likely to find Aquarius-Pisces parents caring and responsive.

ADVICE: *It's never too late for forgiveness and understanding. Don't be obsessed with your own problems. Brighten up. Listen to criticism.*

PHIL ESPOSITO (2/20/42)
TONY ESPOSITO (4/23/43)

These Canadian-born brothers are among pro-hockey's all-time greats. Boston center Phil was first to score more than 100 goals in a season, with 126 in 1968–69 and 152 in 1970–71. Goaltender Tony led his Chicago team to 423 wins, 3rd highest in NHL history.
***Also:* Harold Lloyd & Mildred Davis** (married; actors).

April 19–24
THE CUSP OF POWER
ARIES-TAURUS CUSP

February 23–March 2
THE WEEK OF SPIRIT
PISCES I

Sounding Board

This relationship is apt to focus on what its partners consider the finer things. Refined, aesthetic, perhaps even worldly in its energies, the combination loves beauty in any form, and beauty will bring these two together. A certain objective awareness and detachment, inherent here and necessary for the evaluation of any art form, precludes the formation of a deeper attachment.

Although psychological opposites in many respects, Aries-Tauruses and Pisces I's may like each other and enjoy spending time together, particularly when sharing joint interests. The emotional subtlety and deviousness of the Pisces I personality is likely to escape the more direct Aries-Taurus, who will soon tire of putting energy into being understanding of and catering to Pisces I feelings. Aries-Tauruses run the risk of being rejected by Pisces I's for being controlling, judgmental and mercenary. Love relationships and marriages between these two are generally ill-fated.

Friendships, on the other hand, can click. The pair will be understanding and sympathetic, particularly when Aries-Tauruses need to let off steam about whatever is bothering them at work and in their personal lives. The matchup can also provide ego support for Pisces I's by encouraging them to go for it and make the most of their talents. Pisces I's need a tremendous amount of acknowledgment, and this relationship can offer them an appreciative and enthusiastic sounding board, as well as a gratifying way for them to share their appreciation of art and music. The combination can also bring out its partners' physical side, encouraging them in activities ranging from long walks to one-on-one competitive sports. It does not recommend itself to business or other working relationships, however: Aries-Tauruses will have little time to satisfy Pisces I's emotional needs or to be attentive to their sensitivity in the heat of a project or negotiation.

As siblings these two can make a good pair, forming a highly synergistic unit—one more whole and integrated than either of the individuals who together make it up.

ADVICE: *Cultivate your love of beauty. Keep controlling tendencies in hand. Loosen perfectionistic attitudes. Work on intimacy.*

VLADIMIR LENIN (4/22/1870)
NADEZHDA KRUPSKAYA (2/26/1869)

Revolutionaries Krupskaya and Lenin met after his arrest around 1895, when she accompanied him into Siberian exile. They married in 1898. Aiding Lenin's Marxist crusade, she helped organize the Bolsheviks and held posts under him after the 1917 revolution.
***Also:* Clint Howard & Ron Howard** (brothers; actors).

April 19–24
THE CUSP OF POWER
ARIES-TAURUS CUSP

March 3–10
THE WEEK OF THE LONER
PISCES II

KING FERDINAND (3/10/1452)
QUEEN ISABELLA (4/22/1451)

Ferdinand's marriage to Isabella in 1469 was a political success that eventually unified Spain after Isabella was crowned Queen of Castile and Leon in 1474. The pair were known as the "Catholic kings."
Also: **Elizabeth II & Prince Edward** (mother/son).

A Threat to Peace and Quiet

Something about this relationship reminds one of the school yard. Its theme is a kind of tentative yet enthusiastic self-exploration, with sudden bouts of stubbornness and stormy altercations blowing over quickly against the backdrop of a welter of social activity. In short, this is a rather noisy, raucous kind of relationship, one that's unlikely to suit either of its partners for long.

The combination is unlikely to manifest as a passionate love affair. Pisces II's crave an unusual approach to love, often with an exotic or mysterious partner—a bill that solid Aries-Tauruses are unlikely to fit. Romantic, sensitive, poetic and creative, Pisces II's often get turned off by the direct Aries-Taurus approach, and must be wooed by subtler means. Both Aries-Tauruses and Pisces II's like a relationship to be less noisy, less busy, than this one. Marriages too are unusual, since the two great themes of marriage are social interaction and children, and Aries-Tauruses will rarely get either from a Pisces II spouse, who will probably prefer to lead a calm, isolated existence with few intrusions, even from children. And if marriage to a Pisces II means giving up on having children, an Aries-Taurus may back off. There are Pisces II's, however, who will want to take on the responsibility of a large family, and in such cases the relationship may succeed.

Parent-child relationships between these two are often close, and involve a steady interchange of affection and sympathy. Aries-Taurus parents will be attentive to the needs of Pisces II children, and Pisces II parents will be supportive and nurturing of Aries-Taurus children. But Pisces II's are likely to find an Aries-Taurus brother or sister aggressive, bossy and intolerant. These two are unlikely to work easily together in offices, work crews or business partnerships. Pisces II's resent power struggles, displays of ego and attempts to control, any of which may be exactly what this relationship is likely to serve up on their plate. Aries-Tauruses, on the other hand, may dislike a relationship in which they must accept a partner's easy attitudes and inability to stick to one line of thought, or to work solidly for long periods of time.

ADVICE: *To love fully, you have to be allowed to discover your own feelings. Don't push. Back off and allow it to happen. Be open to wonder and to miracles.*

April 19–24
THE CUSP OF POWER
ARIES-TAURUS CUSP

March 11–18
THE WEEK OF DANCERS & DREAMERS
PISCES III

BARBARA FELDON (3/12/41)
DON ADAMS (4/19/26)

Adams and Feldon co-starred for 5 years on the hit tv series *Get Smart.* Adams played an inept secret agent. Feldon (a real-life winner on *The $64,000 Question*) was his intelligent and resourceful sidekick. ***Also:***
Willem DeKooning & Elaine DeKooning (married; artists);
Max Planck & Albert Einstein (colleagues; physicists).

Outshining Each Other

This combination focuses on who will be the star, since the chemistry here promotes feelings of omniscience, and a tendency to vie for the attention of friends and family. The relationship features public disagreements and displays of know-it-all attitude; friendships are unlikely to develop unless such attitudes can be dropped. It is possible, however, for these two to adopt a healthily competitive stance, both in daily life and on the playing field, which may spur them on to better their own personal best.

Aries-Taurus–Pisces III love affairs can be intense on the physical level, with both partners giving their all. All too often, however, these affairs will involve power struggles, with each person struggling to dominate the other. Both, but particularly Aries-Taurus, must learn to give up control, and to realize the superior quality and power of unselfish giving and love. This also holds true for parent-child and sibling relationships.

In marriage, Pisces III's are likely to drive a practical Aries-Taurus spouse crazy with their idealism and philosophical detachment. Aries-Tauruses will often want more attention to the here and now from Pisces III's, who are more interested in far-out schemes and thoughts, and delight in convoluted peregrinations of the mind that may be too much for even the most patient Aries-Taurus to bear.

These two may develop a sound relationship as co-workers, since Pisces III technical expertise blends well with Aries-Taurus driving force. If they can put their competitive need for attention aside, they can form a potent combination capable of scaling the heights. Business partnerships, however, are unlikely to be successful, since these partners are unlikely to agree on ideas, strategies and implementation in any marketing drive.

ADVICE: *The will to overcome is best left at the bedroom door. Give love unconditionally. Allow for differences. Try to reach common ground.*

April 25–May 2
THE WEEK OF MANIFESTATION
TAURUS I

April 25–May 2
THE WEEK OF MANIFESTATION
TAURUS I

April 25–May 2
THE WEEK OF MANIFESTATION
TAURUS I

A Comfortable Nest

 RELATIONSHIPS

STRENGTHS: **SENSUOUS, EASY, DEPENDABLE**

WEAKNESSES: **STAGNANT, MONOLITHIC, DEPENDENT**

BEST: **FAMILY**

WORST: **LOVE**

The combination of two Taurus I's can be pictured as a secure and comfortable nest. It includes a love of repose in a home that is an inviolable haven of calm, far removed from the slings and arrows of everyday life. Taurus I lovers will have a sensuous life that is likely to be gratifying but predictable. The problem is that neither may be challenged enough by such a relationship to move forward in his or her personal development. A comfortable but stagnant situation may result. Should a more exciting or unstable third party come along, tempting one Taurus I to leave the other, both of them will inevitably suffer from guilt, remorse and repressed frustration. One of the greatest difficulties two Taurus I's face, whether in love or in marriage, is their inability to acknowledge a relationship's failure and to allow it to fall apart.

Taurus I friends generally form a tight bond, stressing fun through physical activities. If they grow up together they are likely to form an easy and rewarding relationship which will last them for life. Stubbornly tenacious and faithful (if sometimes more through an inability to admit failure than through true loyalty), the relationship is perhaps even better suited to career and family areas. Two Taurus I's, for example, would be good support for an aging parent or needy relative.

At work or at home, the relationship can form the bedrock of any group, lending it great stability. As parents, these two will have to beware of imposing too monolithic a set of rules or expectations on their children, making them either overly accepting or rebellious. The first of these is the more likely, a kind of tender-trap situation in which the children become too dependent on the parents and fail to develop independence and solid ego-formation. In business, this pair's strong, practical business acumen can produce success in any field. Mutually supportive, these partners usually understand each other well, and are particularly sympathetic when one of them feels let down or unappreciated by other people. They know how to share authority and delegate responsibility, skills necessary for any partnership to flourish.

JILL CLAYBURGH (4/30/44)
AL PACINO (4/25/40)

In contrast to college-bred Clayburgh's socially prominent, wealthy background, the brooding, volatile Pacino grew up in a rough NY neighborhood, holding menial jobs before he studied acting. They had a 5-year live-in relationship during the 70s. **Also: Henry Houghton & George Mifflin** (co-founding publishers).

ADVICE: *Comfort and ease aren't always the most stimulating conditions for growth. Seek challenges. Let go of attachments. Dare to fail.*

April 25–May 2
THE WEEK OF MANIFESTATION
TAURUS I

May 3–10
THE WEEK OF THE TEACHER
TAURUS II

Deep Feelings

 RELATIONSHIPS

STRENGTHS: **EMOTIONAL, ENJOYABLE, DEEP**

WEAKNESSES: **SUSPICIOUS, FRUSTRATED, OVERLY MORAL**

BEST: **PARENT-CHILD**

WORST: **FRIENDSHIP**

Although Taurus is an earth sign, orienting this personality toward the faculties of sensation and the material pleasures of life, the Taurus I–Taurus II relationship is highly charged. Any emotion that manifests will do so with intensity, so that upsets, hurt feelings and brooding are common. Together, these two are much concerned with the motives of others—they reinforce each other's ability to discover the truth, and the morality, in other people's actions. This is a duo that adopts a defensive posture against the rest of the world.

In living and work situations in this combination, emotional upsets will arise over what Taurus II's perceive as inflexibility or unfairness in Taurus I's. Taurus I's often picture themselves as being extremely, even overly fair and giving, a self-image that may impress Taurus II's as false and condescending. Feeling unappreciated and hurt by this judgment, Taurus I's may in turn withdraw their favors and retreat. This is a relationship in which suppressed feelings of frustration may one day build to a shattering climax.

Love affairs in this combination can prove quite passionate, in fact so passionate that their intensity of feeling will amount to a pressure against these two becoming life partners. Remaining uncommitted may also be preferable because the breakups or separations that are likely here will prove more painful when the couple are married, particularly in decisions over belongings, children and money. When difficulties arise in either love or marriage, Taurus II's are far more likely to see things realistically, albeit moralistically, and to insist on at least a trial separation, which Taurus I's may bitterly oppose. In friendships, the Taurus II's critical attitudes, and demands that the relationship move forward, are likely to disturb the Taurus I's enjoyment of things as they are. Relationships of this kind are unlikely to work out in the long run, despite many points of common interest and pleasure. As siblings, Taurus I's and II's are likely to clash in their stubbornness and their refusal to give ground. In parent-child relationships, either of these two is likely to supply the attention and reverence that will make them a good parent for the other.

ANOUK AIMÉE (4/27/32)
ALBERT FINNEY (5/9/36)

Better known in Europe than in the US for her acting, Aimée got an Oscar nomination for *A Man and a Woman* (1966). British stage and screen star Finney was married to her from 1970–78.
Also: Emperor Hirohito & Harry Truman (WWII enemies); **Wm. Randolph Hearst & Orson Welles** (publisher/portrayer in *Citizen Kane*).

ADVICE: *Judgments can be as unfair as the actions or attitudes they condemn. Be more accepting. Try to be honest about yourself. Preserve freedom.*

Delight and Teach

April 25–May 2
THE WEEK OF MANIFESTATION
TAURUS I

May 11–18
THE WEEK OF THE NATURAL
TAURUS III

STRENGTHS: IDEOLOGICAL, SECURE, EDUCATIONAL

WEAKNESSES: UNDERCUTTING, HOSTILE, PROJECTING

BEST: MARRIAGE

WORST: FAMILY

BERTRAND RUSSELL (5/18/1872)
LUDWIG WITTGENSTEIN (4/26/1889)

Viennese philosopher Wittgenstein began studying with British philosopher Russell in 1911 and advanced his teacher's thinking. Both guided postwar British philosophy in a more positivist direction.

This combination's energies are often geared toward the enthusiastic sharing of new or innovative ideas or techniques. As a unit, these two can find themselves considered unconventional—their message will be unique to them. Individually, each has a very different approach from the other, but together they create something new and fresh, and they want nothing better than a willing audience to be taught it.

Taurus III's often have a hard time sticking to something—simply dropping whatever is too difficult or doesn't work is their usual way to proceed. Taurus I's, on the other hand, cannot rest unless their or other people's ideas are implemented efficiently. Furthermore, Taurus I's need fun only occasionally, and only so long as it doesn't conflict with their need to work and produce, while Taurus III's are up for good times and adventure at almost any moment. Taurus I's may come to view Taurus III's as superficial or lazy, then, but Taurus III's naturalistic approach can be the very setting needed for a creative spark to emerge. In that case, a Taurus I will be the ideal person to nurture that spark into a full-blown idea, and to develop it into something useful.

Understandably enough, developing and sharing a common outlook is as important in love affairs between these two as is avoiding the adoption of strict roles. Taurus III's often project childhood models—especially repressive ones, parental or otherwise—onto their partners and spouses, and Taurus I's may become objects of their aggression, hostility or rebellion. Things can be going along fine between these two when an inexplicable bout of arguments or conflicts suddenly bursts on the scene with frightening intensity. It may be hard for Taurus I's to show the flexibility and understanding that will allow Taurus III's to express their volatile emotions without hostility emerging, often on both sides. Taurus III's need not only freedom but security, however, and this relationship, particularly if it ventures into marriage, may be especially good at satisfying the latter need. With some effort and lessons learned, these two can create an unusual form of marriage, one that provides a stable and loving home environment and promotes understanding, sympathy and learning.

ADVICE: *Be aware of psychological projection. Put past scripts away. Build a secure home base. Learning need not exclude having fun.*

Stirring the Embers

April 25–May 2
THE WEEK OF MANIFESTATION
TAURUS I

May 19–24
THE CUSP OF ENERGY
TAURUS-GEMINI CUSP

STRENGTHS: MAGNETIC, APPRECIATIVE, PHILOSOPHICAL

WEAKNESSES: UNSETTLING, UNFAITHFUL, VIOLENT

BEST: LOVE

WORST: FAMILY

ANITA LOOS (4/26/1893)
DOUGLAS FAIRBANKS (5/23/1883)

Loos' work as a screenwriter and playwright spanned 5 decades. From 1912–16 she created screenplays for D.W. Griffith. Her satirical scripts—and wisecracking titles—helped launch the silent-screen career of the irrepressible Fairbanks. ***Also:*** **Hedda Hopper & Jimmy Stewart** (columnist discovered actor).

This relationship is apt to stir up deep emotions, and magnetic attraction plays a strong role here. So strong is this attraction, in fact, that these two would be best off laying out some ground rules or a moral philosophy on which they can both agree. Otherwise the relationship's tendencies toward addiction or codependency could cause one or both of the partners to be hurt by their own unrealistic assessment of what is going on.

Taurus I's may be fascinated by their Taurus-Gemini lover's mind, Taurus-Geminis by Taurus I physical endowments and prowess. But Taurus-Gemini may prove too fickle a customer for Taurus I: infidelity, jealousy and outright competition can surface here, marring an otherwise fruitful relationship. If forgiving, understanding or permissive attitudes are developed, however, with the partners allowing each other free rein in spending time with other people (although probably drawing the line at outright sexual infidelity), the relationship might well stand the test of time in love and marriage.

Taurus-Geminis have much to learn from Taurus I's about hard work and sticking to the task at hand, while Taurus I's will benefit from a Taurus-Gemini example of flexibility and adaptability. Whether as co-workers, lovers or marriage partners, these two can work well side by side, filling in each other's deficiencies and appreciating each other's strengths. There is often a strong physical attraction between them, which can lead to intense sexual encounters; this intensity can also be sublimated into mutually rewarding competition, on the playing field or in the board room.

These two make good friends, particularly if they can freely and easily exchange ideas in the intellectual or philosophical sphere. Taurus-Geminis will not always meet the Taurus I expectation of fidelity and deep involvement, however, and the friendship may be irritated by missed appointments and other irresponsibilities. Taurus I parents' patience will be severely tested by energetic Taurus-Gemini children, and their need for peace and quiet at home after a hard day at work may be frustrated in this relationship.

ADVICE: *Develop tolerance. Minimize rules and condemning attitudes. Cultivate sports or exercise. Keep a handle on violent emotions. Meditate.*

April 25–May 2

THE WEEK OF MANIFESTATION
TAURUS I

May 25–June 2

THE WEEK OF FREEDOM
GEMINI I

RELATIONSHIPS

STRENGTHS: **NATURAL, FUN, STABLE**

WEAKNESSES: **SUPERFICIAL, UNPRODUCTIVE, IRRITATING**

BEST: **WORK**

WORST: **MARRIAGE**

Having Fun

This relationship is at its best when it is undemanding; having fun together and avoiding serious subjects are usually the best approaches here. Taurus I's and Gemini I's relate to each better as acquaintances or occasional companions than as close friends or spouses. Should they try to get closer, irritation, impatience and straightforward dislike may mar this pleasurable if somewhat superficial relationship.

Gemini I's often benefit from accepting a career position that is not too demanding but provides the stability they need; a Taurus I supervisor, colleague, owner or boss can serve them well in this respect. Marriages between these two may not work out so well, however, especially if Taurus I's make heavy demands on their Gemini I partners. Gemini I's must feel a sense of responsibility on their own, and act on it in their own good time and way, no matter how curious their methods seem. Taurus I's, however, often demand that their partner act responsibly and according to a fixed set of standards. This may be more than a Gemini I can bear.

In love affairs, sexual attraction is likely to be strong and playful. The relationship may not prove deep or all that productive, however. Sometimes, in fact, it is a covert affair, and particularly one in which either or both partners is already involved with or committed to someone very different from both themselves and the covert partner. Although such hidden liaisons are unlikely to be enduring, they may provide the psychological reinforcement and strength needed to make a decision—to continue the established relationship or leave it.

As parents, Taurus I's are likely to prove restrictive or smothering to their Gemini I children. Gemini I parents, on the other hand, are unlikely to provide their Taurus I children with the emotional stability they need. Siblings of this combination enjoy, understand and mutually support each other, despite their differences in temperament.

ADVICE: *Be more open and honest. Say what's on your mind. Beware of sneaky activities. Make reasonable demands. Expect participation and help.*

SHOSHANNA LONSTEIN (5/29/75)
JERRY SEINFELD (4/29/54)

In 1993 Seinfeld, stand-up comic and star of his own sitcom, created a media stir when he began dating Lonstein, a native New Yorker 19 years his junior. They broke up in '97.

Also: **Andre Agassi & Brooke Shields** (married); **Calamity Jane & Wild Bill Hickok** (unverified marriage); **Bing Crosby & Bob Hope** (friends; co-stars); **Anita Loos & John Emerson** (married; screenwriter/director-writer).

April 25–May 2

THE WEEK OF MANIFESTATION
TAURUS I

June 3–10

THE WEEK OF NEW LANGUAGE
GEMINI II

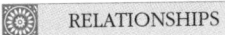

RELATIONSHIPS

STRENGTHS: **SENSUOUS, DOMESTIC, FULFILLING**

WEAKNESSES: **MISTRUSTFUL, HURT, TENSE**

BEST: **MARRIAGE**

WORST: **FRIENDSHIP**

A Love of Bed and Table

Characterized by a nearly all-absorbing sensuality, this relationship is likely to be quite unconventional. A certain rebelliousness is inherent in it, as the duo pursues the pleasures of food, love, wine and entertainment, no matter what the cost. Despite this tendency to indulge, or perhaps because of it, when they decide to get down to work, or set themselves a task or goal, they cannot be dissuaded until they achieve their aim.

In love, Gemini II's are often drawn to strong silent types, and Taurus I's may not have the dark and complex emotional side that can arouse and hold them. This pair may make better spouses than lovers, since the relationship's love of table, bed and steady, dependable physicality generally finds more fulfillment in a domestic setting than in a romantic one. Taurus I's will have to become good listeners, however, for Gemini II's need to be heard and understood. The strikingly new and original forms of verbal expression that are their trademark can prove attractive but also wearing to a Taurus I more interested in forceful action than in glib theorizing. If Gemini II's can back up their words with deeds, and be counted upon to assume daily tasks without complaint, Taurus I's may find themselves quite happy with this sparkling partner.

The sharing of sensual pleasures is unlikely to prove a sufficient basis for a friendship in this combination. In fact, these two are likely to be irritated by each other's know-it-all attitudes; neither will give the other full credit or sympathy. Relaxed and open sharing of intimate problems is not usually in the cards for this relationship, usually due to a lack of deep trust and also a certain amount of competitiveness.

Work and family relationships can initially be filled with difficulties and conflict. Gemini II's are usually much too idiosyncratic in their approach to everyday problems to satisfy the inflexible expectations of Taurus I's as to how things should be done. Furthermore, Gemini II's can be terribly critical of a Taurus I co-worker, parent or sibling, who may become first defensive, later aggressive under this barrage of blame, finally slinking off hurt, or withdrawing completely.

ADVICE: *Work on sharing. Minimize tension. Talking is not enough. Let what you do show what you think. Hang in for the duration.*

KARL FERDINAND BRAUN (6/6/1850)
GUGLIELMO MARCONI (4/25/1874)

Though Italian-born Marconi is generally credited as radio's inventor, German physicist Braun invented the rectifier, which increased the range of Marconi's transmitter and made radio practical for mass use. The pair shared the 1909 Nobel Prize for physics.

STRENGTHS: **CHALLENGING, DIVERSE, MONEY-SAVVY**

WEAKNESSES: **UNSHARING, ENVIOUS, SELF-DECEIVING**

BEST: **PARTNER, CO-WORKER**

WORST: **LOVE**

SADDAM HUSSEIN (4/28/37)
GEORGE BUSH (6/12/24)

Hussein was internationally condemned for his invasion of Kuwait in August 1990. When he refused to withdraw, Bush spearheaded a multinational coalition and engaged him in the Persian Gulf War, in which Hussein was swiftly defeated. *Also:* **Winthrop Rockefeller & David Rockefeller** (brothers; governor/banker).

April 25–May 2

THE WEEK OF MANIFESTATION
TAURUS I

June 11–18

THE WEEK OF THE SEEKER
GEMINI III

Kaleidoscopic Diversity

This relationship's great need for variety and change can undermine its stability but also contribute to keeping it alive. Even when responsibility and reliability are at their strongest here, there is usually also a yearning for new and challenging pursuits. Because the energy in the relationship is so restless, almost explosive, it requires a very narrow focus if it is to be successful. Moreover, its frenetic pace is generally too much for the domestic life.

Should marriage occur in this combination, change and diversity will have to be cultivated constantly. Otherwise, each party may create it by himself, perhaps in the form of a secret lover—or else maybe through a passion for independent travel, or for a hobby or sport that will dominate his thoughts and actions. Rarely will the partners risk damaging their relationship irreparably, but neither will they give up their often obsessive extracurricular (or extramarital) interests. Usually the most practical tack is to refuse to acknowledge the depth of the outside involvement, or even to reveal it. This approach can work out for years, since the relationship also has a penchant for self-deception, which acts as a protective shield.

Neither love nor friendship between these two is likely to be long-lasting, for there is a mutual lack of chemistry here, and few common points that could lead to a deep emotional attachment. This lack of commonalty, and a curious kind of personal envy, may undermine Taurus I–Gemini III family relationships, whether between parents and children or between siblings. Taurus I's may often envy the detachment shown by Gemini III's, who for their part may be jealous of Taurus I composure and patience, which they appear to despise but actually secretly long for in themselves. Taurus I bosses may find Gemini III employees hard or impossible to control, but as co-workers on an equal footing, these two will probably get along quite well. As business partners, similarly, Gemini III's bring surprising good sense and financial wisdom to deals inspired and directed by Taurus I's, as well as astute analytic and critical judgment.

ADVICE: *Don't tell all, but don't hide everything, either. Find points of commonalty. Fulfill responsibilities in an enjoyable way.*

STRENGTHS: **INTUITIVE, RESPECTFUL, PROTECTIVE**

WEAKNESSES: **MANIPULATIVE, DISAPPROVING, INCOMPATIBLE**

BEST: **LOVE**

WORST: **WORK**

RITA COOLIDGE (5/1/45)
KRIS KRISTOFFERSON (6/22/37)

Singer Coolidge and singer-actor Kristofferson met in 1971 and married 2 years later after acting together in *Pat Garrett and Billy the Kid*. They toured and recorded during the 70s, divorced in 1980. *Also:* **Ayatollah Khomeini & Salman Rushdie** (religious leader/condemned author).

April 25–May 2

THE WEEK OF MANIFESTATION
TAURUS I

June 19–24

THE CUSP OF MAGIC
GEMINI-CANCER CUSP

Sizzling Spell

For two such traditional people, this relationship holds a surprisingly fiery independence. Therein lies its considerable attraction. It makes its partners take risks and leaps of faith, and pushes them to base decisions on intuitive hunches, more than either ever would on his own. This can feel very freeing and, if the relationship is a romantic one, can make the flames of ardor burn more brightly.

Taurus I's and Gemini-Cancers can easily fall under the relationship's spell in matters of love. Hunches, spontaneity and first impulses are likely to be strengths here, given the relationship's focus on intuition. The ethereal nature of many Gemini-Cancers can thoroughly captivate earthy Taurus I's, and the harmony, repose or beauty of Taurus I's can prove irresistible to romantic Gemini-Cancers, but all spells eventually wear off, and only time will tell whether the relationship will endure. On the other hand, negativity, power struggles and loss of respect rarely surface in this couple's love affairs, making it possible for them to continue, whether developing into marriage or transforming into friendship, for many years. Burning with a steady flame, the relationship usually justifies the initially sizzling love attraction.

Friendships in this combination are rare unless preceded by a romantic or working relationship—these two rarely start out by being interested in each other as friends. Taurus I's will most likely find Gemini-Cancers a bit strange, and Gemini-Cancers will pull back from the direct approach of Taurus I's, resenting what they perceive as aggression and lack of sensitivity. Taurus I parents can be captivated by their refined Gemini-Cancer children, who will usually know how to manipulate through roundabout and seductive means. Gemini-Cancer parents can provide the warm and nurturing environment so important to Taurus I. At work, Gemini-Cancers will respect Taurus I dedication but may not approve of their ethics or attitude on the job, seeing them as exaggerated and self-satisfied. Taurus I's, on the other hand, may find Gemini-Cancers a bit too relaxed.

ADVICE: *Like wine, love should be enjoyed while it lasts. Keep friendships alive. Beware of being overly impulsive. Let intentions be judged by deeds.*

April 25–May 2
THE WEEK OF MANIFESTATION
TAURUS I

June 25–July 2
THE WEEK OF THE EMPATH
CANCER I

RELATIONSHIPS

STRENGTHS: **SELF-ACTUALIZING, UNDERSTANDING, SHARING**

WEAKNESSES: **DEPENDENT, FRUSTRATED, UNAWARE**

BEST: **FRIENDSHIP**

WORST: **FAMILY**

Proving Ground

LORENZ HART (5/2/1895)
RICHARD RODGERS (6/28/02)

Lyricist Hart and composer Rodgers became close friends and collaborated while students at Columbia University. After writing their first complete musical in 1925, they went on to create many other popular and successful shows, including *Pal Joey*.
Also: Queen Juliana & Prince Bernhard (Dutch queen/consort); **Bing Crosby & Garry Crosby** (father/son; singer/actor).

Standing up for oneself, or for what one believes in, is the core lesson in this relationship. A certain combativeness is inherent here, especially when the issue is personal freedom—which is likely to be the case. The upside is that participants in this relationship will learn how to take a stand, protecting themselves and their relationship against anyone who would have them be any other way.

The relationship's spotlight will fall on the Cancer I: will he or she be able to achieve freedom and independence here? An ultracapable Taurus I may provide the protection that Cancer I's so desperately need, but the price they pay for this security may be the inhibition of their personal growth. Cancer I's may already have encountered a Taurus I in childhood, as a parent, sibling, aunt, uncle or teacher, and their extreme empathy will make them eager to please a Taurus I by obeying this partner's commands and wishes faithfully, at the expense of their own self-expression. Eventually the Cancer I will have to find a way to be self-assertive, perhaps prompting an explosion of resentment and feeling.

Even without a Taurus I figure in their childhood, adult Cancer I's may unconsciously replay an old script with a Taurus I lover, mate or boss, much to this partner's bafflement. Taurus I's can also find themselves manipulated by charming yet unconscious Cancer-Geminis, but, in their usual fashion, they may refuse to take action. Eventually there will have to be a confrontation. Taurus I's and Cancer I's can often form successful love and even marital relationships when they meet later in life, after each has had time to develop more awareness. As a friendship, this combination may offer a ground for working out personal problems and for developing trust and understanding. It is a nurturing relationship that is generally rewarding, as long as it avoids undue dependency. At work, Cancer I's are better off operating by themselves, often at home, but they bring a financial astuteness to a working relationship with Taurus I, perhaps as a business partner or colleague. It is essential, however, that the balance between them be kept objective and equal.

ADVICE: *Work on self-understanding. Learn to give and take. Avoid dependencies. Stand on your own two feet. Free yourself from old scripts.*

April 25–May 2
THE WEEK OF MANIFESTATION
TAURUS I

July 3–10
THE WEEK OF THE UNCONVENTIONAL
CANCER II

RELATIONSHIPS

STRENGTHS: **ORIGINAL, UNUSUAL, CREATIVE**

WEAKNESSES: **WEIRD, UNATTRACTED, REJECTING**

BEST: **ACQUAINTANCESHIP**

WORST: **WORK**

A Unique Penchant

GUGLIELMO MARCONI (4/25/1874)
NIKOLA TESLA (7/9/1856)

Few know that Marconi utilized (some say stole) Tesla's radio patent and relied entirely on Tesla's research for his invention of radio. While Marconi received all the glory, Tesla died poor and bitter.
Also: Winthrop Rockefeller & Nelson Rockefeller (brothers; governors).

The challenge of this pairing is to accept originality. The relationship simply will not be governed by the usual social codes or rules of conduct; together, these two need to do things their own way. Being original has its advantages, however, and the duo's inventiveness can contribute to many fields of endeavor.

On the face of it, apparently impractical and overimaginative Cancer II's might seem much too strange for inherently conservative Taurus I's, yet they may often pique these personalities' curiosity and arouse their emotions. It is Cancer II's, in fact, who are unlikely to be interested in Taurus I's; inevitably attracted to more casual types, often with a dark side, they usually find Taurus I's dull and predictable. A Taurus I's desire for a Cancer II can often be hopeless, then, but should an atypical Taurus I have a quiet Venusian charm, and a hidden penchant for the unusual or bizarre, these two may be able to form a relationship, whether as lovers or as friends. If so, it will probably be highly original, especially in the sexual, aesthetic or social spheres. Taurus I's and Cancer II's could marry and lead an eventful life together. They might eventually lead separate lives, quite detached from each other, yet each will have a quiet admiration for his very different partner, which friends and family may never quite understand.

Taurus I parents will often demand from their children the one thing of which Cancer II's are incapable: being normal. This may engender feelings of hurt on both sides, unless the Taurus I's are willing to drop or amend their expectations. Cancer II parents are unlikely to provide the attention and security needed by their Taurus I children, who may be embarrassed by their attitudes and behavior in front of relatives and friends.

ADVICE: *Normalcy can be as strange to some as the bizarre is to others. Find common points. Build creatively. Don't be ashamed of being different.*

STRENGTHS: **COMMUNICATIVE, UNDERSTANDING, EXPRESSIVE**

WEAKNESSES: **BOSSY, CONTROLLING, COMPETITIVE**

BEST: **MARRIAGE**

WORST: **LOVE**

ALEXANDER BROOK (7/14/1898)
PEGGY BACON (5/2/1895)

Bacon was a noted printmaker, author, painter and book illustrator. Brook, a studio portraitist and painter in the romantic realist style, met Bacon while studying at the Art Students League in NY. They were married from 1920–40.

April 25–May 2
THE WEEK OF MANIFESTATION
TAURUS I

July 11–18
THE WEEK OF THE PERSUADER
CANCER III

Mutual Expression

This relationship concerns itself with all forms of expression. The channels of communication between these two must be open and direct, and other forms of expression, creative and otherwise, are also very important to them. The relationship is apt to be highly original, requiring more than just cooking up ideas. It has a deep need to manifest or actualize its creativity in the material world—whether through art, a business, or children, or simply as physical expression or body language.

Particularly important in this relationship is taking the time to understand not only thoughts but feelings. When this is done, marriages in this combination can be solid, effective, powerful units that will work even better if Cancer III's commit to them fully, and if they modify their need to be at center stage and to control. But the relationship often never gets off the ground, since many Cancer III's are attracted to a very different type, one more exciting and unreliable than Taurus I's—who may, however, be the ones best able to give them what they really need.

These two can build a successful working relationship as long as there is mutual respect. Without it, competitive drives and jealousies can get out of hand, particularly if either party sees the other as a threat to his or her present or future position within an organization or field. Should the Taurus I have the higher position, the Cancer III may be intimidated or made to feel insecure, and may become manipulative in trying to control and ultimately overcome the Taurus I's superiority. Should both personalities have their eye on the same position, Taurus I ruthlessness will meet its match in the Cancer III drive toward success, which will only become more pronounced when insecurities are aroused.

In the family, whether the relationship manifests as parent-child or sibling pairs, it can be protective and caring. But a Taurus I or Cancer III parent or older sibling can also prove bossy and even smothering of the younger family member, with a breakdown of relations or a total lack of communication being the final result.

ADVICE: *If flowers are to grow, the gardener sometimes has to back off. Don't play God. Reach compromises. Keep lines of communication open.*

STRENGTHS: **UNDERSTANDING, EXCITING, PASSIONATE**

WEAKNESSES: **UNSTABLE, STUCK, JUDGMENTAL**

BEST: **WORK**

WORST: **FAMILY**

WALTER PAYTON (7/25/54)
CHUCK BEDNARIK (5/1/25)

Bednarik and Payton were football heroes of their respective generations. Each had the high distinction of being voted All-Pro 7 times—Bednarik with the Philadelphia Eagles in the 50s and Payton with the Chicago Bears in the 70s and 80s.

April 25–May 2
THE WEEK OF MANIFESTATION
TAURUS I

July 19–25
THE CUSP OF OSCILLATION
CANCER-LEO CUSP

Off on Their Own

The challenge of this relationship is whether its need for variety and change can be satisfied without undermining its stability—which, fortunately, is quite strong and abiding. It has a tendency to hang in there, and when it appears in friendship, love or marriage, it resists quitting or admitting failure. With that kind of bedrock foundation, the partners can securely go their own way and pursue their own interests. The ideal, of course, would be for them to go through changes and seek interesting pursuits together, but Cancer-Leos in particular need to go off on their own—a trait that will demand understanding from their faithful Taurus I partner, who must not view it as implying rejection, disinterest or infidelity. Cancer-Leos themselves must realize that Taurus I's will not allow their interests to be compromised, no matter how accepting or understanding they are, and must learn when to curtail or halt some of their activities.

At work, this relationship can prove acceptable or even promising, providing that Cancer-Leos' need for risk-taking at certain moments does not upset more conservative Taurus I's. But for the most part, Cancer-Leos are cautious enough to meet Taurus I standards for security, and in fact the relationship often has the effect of increasing their self-discipline.

In the family, Taurus I relatives may view Cancer-Leos with despair, seeing them as unstable, self-destructive and poor role models for the young. Cancer-Leos may respond to these views with skepticism or laughter—they see themselves as quite responsible, and Taurus I's, often, as unimaginative, inhibiting and judgmental.

Cancer-Leos looking for a romantic fling are often attracted to highly physical Taurus I's, who will be happy to join in the fun but will also demand something more serious than Cancer-Leos have to offer. Such relationships generally have little stability and, although they may provide intense satisfaction, will probably dissolve fast.

ADVICE: *Even understanding has its limits. Don't push too hard. Preserve understanding and sensitivity. Beware of selfishness.*

April 25–May 2

THE WEEK OF MANIFESTATION
TAURUS I

July 26–August 2

THE WEEK OF AUTHORITY
LEO I

Monumental Scale

STRENGTHS: **EXPANSIVE, ASPIRING, LOYAL**

WEAKNESSES: **STUBBORN, FIXED, UNCOMPROMISING**

BEST: **FRIENDSHIP**

WORST: **MARRIAGE**

BIANCA JAGGER (5/2/45)
MICK JAGGER (7/26/43)

Bianca and Mick were international jet-set favorites during their marriage from 1971–79. Though Mick's humble beginnings contrasted with Bianca's wealthy background, their relationship was glamorous and larger-than-life.

Also: Andre Agassi & Nick Bollettieri (protégé; tennis coach).

Expansion is the theme of this pairing—the playing out of feelings, thoughts, actions and ideas on a monumental scale. The relationship tends to force its partners beyond themselves, indeed even beyond the ordinary limits of time and space, and it would come as no surprise to find this pair involved in the metaphysical. In any case, doing things in a big way comes naturally to them. The result is that the relationship makes them advance beyond the point where they would normally choose to go, since individually they have a tendency to dig in their heels and resist change. Loyalty, integrity and responsibility are the keywords of this relationship, and woe to the party that lets the other down in a pinch. In meetings between these two, the irresistible force (Leo I) meets the immovable object (Taurus I). Because Leo and Taurus are square (at 90°) to each other in the zodiac, one could expect conflict here. Sparks may indeed fly, but they can just as easily ignite the flames of passion, or stimulate a group endeavor, as they can unleash hostility and destructive forces.

As friends, these two make a strong duo, resistant to outside influences. A lifelong friendship may result after the dust has cleared from initial confrontations. Love and family relationships between these two are likely to be stormy and filled with conflict. Taurus I's are generally more sensuous and fond of repose, Leo I's more passionate and dynamic; these differences can prove divisive and lead to misunderstandings.

Given the stubborn nature of the participants, marriages in this combination can prove difficult, particularly since each party has a need to rule the roost. In rare circumstances, they may be able to share the dominant role in the family, but it more often happens that children and other family members find themselves the observers of periodic struggles for power. Should these two share a larger and loftier philosophical goal, they may set aside their differences in style for the greater good. Few compare to these two when it comes to conviction and commitment. At work, the relationship is characterized by an idealistic pragmatism.

ADVICE: *When sparks start to fly, anything nearby is likely to ignite. Keep destructive emotions under control. Bear the greater good in mind.*

April 25–May 2

THE WEEK OF MANIFESTATION
TAURUS I

August 3–10

THE WEEK OF BALANCED STRENGTH
LEO II

The Strong, Silent Type

STRENGTHS: **PRACTICAL, OBJECTIVE, STABLE**

WEAKNESSES: **DULL, COLD, UNROMANTIC**

BEST: **SIBLING, CO-WORKER**

WORST: **BUSINESS PARTNERSHIP**

HEDDA HOPPER (5/2/1885)
LOUELLA PARSONS (8/6/1881)

Actress-turned-gossip-columnist Hopper was Parsons' famous rival in the 40s and 50s. Though both were extremely influential in Hollywood, they constantly locked horns in their quest for power.

Also: Al Pacino & Martin Sheen (friends; actors).

The tone of this relationship is often strong and silent, with a knack for looking to the future. Sensuous expression is extremely strong, but feelings are usually kept under control, giving the relationship a quality of objectivity and cold detachment. Lines of defense are clearly drawn, and quarrels and differences are left unaddressed, in the hope that they will eventually subside. In hard times, the relationship will have a capacity to foresee upcoming problems and virtually to move mountains in order to restore equilibrium.

These two make an unlikely romantic pair, but once together they will tend to hang in there. If the romantic flame begins to fade, Taurus I's will see the need for change first but won't always be sure what direction to take. Leo II's, on the other hand, may exhibit masochistic tendencies in refusing to recognize a problem but will be able to create a plan for the future that can make the relationship more tolerable.

Marriages between these two are possible, since both are willing to commit. Characteristically, the visualization of a future state will aid or accompany the decision to marry; generally, in fact, a realistic attitude often prevails here, in which romance is not seen as a necessary ingredient. Instead, practical matters, especially financial planning. are pictured as taking up a great deal of time. The sexual side of the relationship may also be seen in pragmatic and nonidealized terms. Children of this combination will often find their parents devoted and at times enthusiastic about their progress, particularly in the areas of sports and academic achievement.

Working relationships here are unlikely to gel: as business partners or as a boss-employee pair, these two are apt to become embroiled in power struggles. But if both occupy an equal position as co-workers in an organization or firm, they can make a strong combination and prove extremely useful to the group. As siblings within a family structure, they may similarly provide a backbone of stability, as long as they don't clash with each other emotionally, especially through competition for parental attention or jealousy over material goods.

ADVICE: *Fires eventually die out if the embers aren't stirred occasionally. Acknowledge and empower the unexpected. Risk taking is important. Dare to fail.*

PETE SAMPRAS (8/12/71)
ANDRE AGASSI (4/29/70)

Old, close friends off court, these tennis champions are fierce competitors behind the net. In 1995, Agassi overtook the then seemingly unbeatable Sampras to become the world's top player. *Also:* **Ella Fitzgerald & Oscar Peterson** (collaborators); **Lionel Barrymore & Ethel Barrymore** (siblings; actors); **Baron von Richthofen & Frieda Lawrence** (siblings; WWI flier/Mrs. D.H. Lawrence).

April 25–May 2
THE WEEK OF MANIFESTATION
TAURUS I

August 11–18
THE WEEK OF LEADERSHIP
LEO III

Magical Success

The magical coalescence of strengths here can be especially successful in the area of career—but a certain romance and sensitivity are also at work. The combination bodes well, then, for virtually any endeavor. Together these two are inspired, seeming to be able to intuit what's necessary for success.

Both Taurus I and Leo III are dominant types, so work and business relationships between them might seem to be difficult or impossible. But there is a subtle difference in their dominance: Leo III's have to lead but not necessarily to control, whereas to Taurus I's, leadership is less important than ruling the roost. This is an unbeatable commercial combination, then, with Leo III's reorganizing, planning ever new conquests and leading the team into battle while Taurus I's guard home base and keeps things running smoothly. If trouble arises, it is usually when their duties and responsibilities overlap, but dedication and an awareness of what works best can minimize this pair's power struggles and ego conflicts, making the relationship truly formidable.

Love affairs, friendships and marriages between Leo III's and Taurus I's are rockier propositions, despite a certain inspired romantic glow. Taurus I's may be attracted to Leo III energy but will ultimately find it too unpredictable, disturbing or even violent; Leo III's, on the other hand, may bore easily with the soft sensuousness of their Taurus I partners. The biggest single difference, however, lies in the issue of harmony, which Leo III's mistrust (a boring or uneventful love or friendship, no matter how pleasurable, is usually intolerable for them) and Taurus I's need. Leo III's can also find Taurus I partners too fixed and unwilling to change. Even when it's obvious that things are not going well, Taurus I's may simply ignore suggestions of changes, or, if they are stated as demands, may stubbornly resist them. Marriage works best here when it also contains a business component—when the spouses also run some kind of commercial enterprise together. The kind of division of labor that is a prerequisite in business will spill over into the domestic scene, causing greater peace at home.

ADVICE: *Bring magic into your personal life. Balance predictability and unpredictability. Minimize needless conflicts. Be more romantic.*

PETER HORTON (8/20/53)
MICHELLE PFEIFFER (4/29/57)

Actor-director Horton is best known as Gary on the tv series *thirtysomething.* He married actress Pfeiffer in 1981, just as her career began soaring. They were divorced in 1988.

Also: **Bing Crosby & Bob Crosby** (brothers; singer-actor/bandleader).

April 25–May 2
THE WEEK OF MANIFESTATION
TAURUS I

August 19–25
THE CUSP OF EXPOSURE
LEO-VIRGO CUSP

Moment of Truth

This relationship's focus on knowledge may result in a kind of ongoing curiosity. The relationship particularly manifests a desire to find the answers to puzzles and mysteries. Their investment in knowing all can mean that these partners play emotional hide-and-seek, not only with each other but with others curious about what makes this strange duo click. Simultaneously wanting full knowledge and choosing not to reveal all of themselves, sooner or later they will usually be found out. This moment of truth can either end the relationship or prolong it, depending on whether or not they like what they see.

If the relationship is a friendship or a love affair, it can continue for years, with mutual benefit to both parties. These two can have fun with their complex games, puzzles, psychological investigations and physical exploration. The relationship can also lead them to career advancement, each introducing the other to people who have helpful connections or outright offers to make.

Marriage is a possibility for this combination, but Leo-Virgos are rarely too interested in raising children, which cause nurturing Taurus I's a certain frustration. They in turn will have to be understanding of the Leo-Virgo need to be alternately introverted and extroverted—whichever side is dominant at the time. In some cases, this relationship may have an unfavorable effect on the self-realization process of Leo-Virgos, who can fall into an apathetic or self-satisfied state from which their accepting Taurus I mates will not try to push them.

Leo-Virgos may share some of their deepest secrets with Taurus I parents or siblings, whom they will generally find trustworthy in respecting their confidences. At the same time, they themselves may be far too taken up with their own inner world and emotions to give Taurus I's the understanding and appreciation they need in return.

ADVICE: *Get more involved. Pry less. Make wholehearted commitments. Don't get caught up in idle pursuits. Try to play at a higher level.*

April 25–May 2

THE WEEK OF MANIFESTATION
TAURUS I

August 26–September 2

THE WEEK OF SYSTEM BUILDERS
VIRGO I

RELATIONSHIPS

STRENGTHS: **EMPATHIC, PRODUCTIVE, HAPPY**

WEAKNESSES: **UNINTERESTED, UNACKNOWLEDGED, FRUSTRATED**

BEST: **WORK**

WORST: **FRIENDSHIP**

A Good Dose of Happiness

A solid bond of empathy, respect and understanding is forged in this relationship, which usually has an easy camaraderie. These two know how to leave each other alone—their bond, often deepened over years, allows room for each partner's privacy. Happily, they can build a comfortable home together, and will always share a similar outlook on money and handle it well. This can be an excellent partnership for marriage or career.

In matters of love, the relationship may not be high in passion. Yet its ability to satisfy the partners' mutual needs can bring it longevity, and its accepting attitudes will provide them with a good measure of happiness. If problems arise, it will be Virgo I criticism, dissatisfaction and self-destructive tendencies that create them. Care should be taken to relieve the Virgo I's frustrations and issues, by acknowledging them and adjusting priorities accordingly. Taurus I's will enjoy playing the dominant role in this relationship, benefiting from the Virgo I desire to be helpful and to serve.

Since Virgo I's need to spend a great deal of time alone, and are often busy with family and work obligations, one would not expect them to form deep friendships with Taurus I's, who demand a healthy investment of time and energy. The strongest friendships between these two will most likely grow out of working relationships, or develop between more distant family members.

Taurus I bosses and Virgo I employees often work well together, as do Taurus I parents and Virgo I children. A productive and positive relationship here can mean a great deal to the continued existence of the companies and families of which they are a part.

AL PACINO (4/25/40)
TUESDAY WELD (8/27/43)

Pacino's affair with Weld wasn't highly publicized, but they were thought to be good for each other. Full of ups and downs, Weld's career and personal life made her a cult figure in the mid-60s.
Also: **Claire Clairmont & Mary Wollstonecraft Shelley** (stepsisters; literary friends).

ADVICE: *Empathy should not lead to apathy. Seek deeper challenges. Beware of self-sacrifice. Involve yourself more in the world.*

April 25–May 2

THE WEEK OF MANIFESTATION
TAURUS I

September 3–10

THE WEEK OF THE ENIGMA
VIRGO II

RELATIONSHIPS

STRENGTHS: **HUMOROUS, UNCONVENTIONAL, PROTECTIVE**

WEAKNESSES: **IMPATIENT, HAYWIRE, UNACCEPTING**

BEST: **FRIENDSHIP**

WORST: **WORK**

Uncharted Waters

This relationship can move in uncharted waters. A zany side in both partners will be magnified here, allowing them to externalize their fantasies and let it all hang out. Thus the relationship can become a marvelous arena for expressiveness, and for the release of hitherto suppressed desires. Humor too can play a prominent and delightful role. The question is: once Pandora's box is opened, can the spirits released be controlled or contained again? Should the relationship get out of control, it can threaten its partners' mental stability.

Interpersonal relationships based on choice—friendships, love and marriage—can be quite successful here. Taurus I protective and nurturing instincts are put to good use in cherishing Virgo II's who may have retreated into a private inner world; the relationship can strengthen their egos, as Taurus I's gently accompany and encourage them toward increased social contact. Virgo II's, on the other hand, allow Taurus I's to rediscover their playful side and to share imaginative visions in a noncondemning relationship. Friendships between these two may be involved in unusual hobbies or interests, and unconventional types of fun are the hallmark of all their activities.

Working matchups between these two are unlikely to work out: not only do they usually lack the emotional understanding granted in personal relations in this combination, but Taurus I pragmatic demands may be beyond a Virgo II's abilities to meet. Thus the co-worker situation can feature an impatience and frustration that hinder the effective completion of the job at hand.

In the family, siblings in this combination can influence each other positively, provided they can get along emotionally; parents, however, may feel that they overstimulate each other. Parent-child combinations, on the other hand, may have problems with communication, acceptance and mutual comprehension, unless united by an unusual or unconventional lifestyle.

I.M. PEI (4/26/17)
KENZO TANGE (9/4/13)

Both prominent 20th-century architects, Pei and Tange have each won the Pritzker Architecture Prize—the most prestigious honor in their field. Although influenced by Le Corbusier, Tange's work is more traditionally Japanese. Pei's structures are innovative, often controversial, such as the glass pyramid at the Louvre in Paris.

ADVICE: *Express fantasies, but keep in touch with reality. Even out emotions. Find a balance between introverted and extroverted drives.*

ALBERT KING (4/25/23)
B.B. KING (9/16/25)

Though they both hail from the same small town of Indianola, Mississippi, these Kings, remarkably, are not related. Among the most successful blues guitarists of all time, both had careers that peaked in the 60s and 70s. Albert played until he died in '92 and B.B., aspiring to be "ambassador of the blues," is still an active performer. **Also: Joyce DeWitt & John Ritter** (co-stars, *Three's Company*).

April 25–May 2

THE WEEK OF MANIFESTATION
TAURUS I

September 11–18

THE WEEK OF THE LITERALIST
VIRGO III

Profit Factor

A dogged determination to make things work, particularly in the career area, will feature strongly here. Both partners are pragmatic enough to know what is expected of them and can usually keep their temperature cool and their irritation threshold high. In whatever sphere the relationship manifestss, it will show a great interest in career matters, being especially concerned with job improvement and concomitant salary hikes. It will generally work out better if the Taurus I and Virgo III are co-workers rather than boss and employee. Often, the partners' determination is sparked or strengthened by the sucess-oriented stance of the relationship itself. Not surprisingly, it may achieve its greatest success as a business partnership, featuring the sharp management, production, marketing and sales skills needed to achieve high earnings.

Love and marital relationships are likely to be more vulnerable to dissension and discord. It is possible, however, for Taurus I pretension and snobbishness, and Virgo III selectivity and rigidity, to loosen. Virgo III's will tend to be more uncomfortable than Taurus I's with the combination's occasional instabilities. A love of table and bed appears often in this matchup, and if the partners' physical attraction is strong enough, they both may find this combination pleasurable and fulfilling. Virgo III's are likely to have difficulty with the fixed nature of the relationship, which will make them feel trapped; Taurus I's are more accepting of total commitment.

Friendships are unlikely to develop here, given the partners' differing interests and approaches, and their tendency to pick friends who are more fun than responsible. Parent-child relationships of either combination are likely to be stormy. As siblings, however, these two may form a tight bond to promote their mutual interests against the powerful pressures, whether social, financial or parental, that are arrayed against them.

ADVICE: *Let things happen. Don't feel you always have to hold it together. Give your willpower and stubbornness a rest occasionally. Lighten up.*

MARIE DE MEDICI (4/26/1573)
CARDINAL RICHELIEU (9/19/1585)

Richelieu was a peacemaker in the ongoing disputes between Marie and her son King Louis XIII. She regarded Richelieu as her protégé when he first entered the royal council in 1624, but he later proved to be her staunch political enemy. Soon after her unsuccessful efforts to have Richelieu dismissed, Louis banished her to Compiegne, but she fled instead to Brussels in the Spanish Netherlands.

April 25–May 2

THE WEEK OF MANIFESTATION
TAURUS I

September 19–24

THE CUSP OF BEAUTY
VIRGO-LIBRA CUSP

Artistic Dominance

A mbition, or the desire to dominate others in a particular field, is the prime mover here. This pair will often in some way be involved in the arts, where they may slowly but surely climb to the top. They will do whatever it takes to get there, insisting on their supremacy and developing quite a bit of resourcefulness along the way. This isn't to say that they lack refinement; in fact they have a great deal in common in terms of aesthetic appreciation, and they also share business acumen. Their biggest problem is that they want everyone around them to agree with them.

Love relationships here aim for a calm, grounded, measured approach, and are geared toward the outside world. But severe temperamental differences between these partners can lead to clashes: high-strung, unstable and nervous Virgo-Libras may annoy their more grounded Taurus I partners, who, however, are tough, and may be well suited to fulfilling the Virgo-Libra need for a stable, reliable figure. Should the couple decide to get married, things may go well during good times, but the relationship is not intrinsically resilient and resourceful in dealing with difficulties or outright disasters. Furthermore, there will often be an attitude of denying or ignoring problems that could be handled easily and efficiently if they were dealt with promptly, but will prove difficult if left too late. On the positive side, the creation of a beautiful home may be one of this pair's great joys and solid strengths, and an area where they may focus on something other than career.

Taurus I–Virgo-Libra friendships are likely to be fun, but not psychologically supportive or stable—they do not provide the insights or the orientation conducive to self-understanding or empathy. When the combination appears in the family, however, not only parents but, often, relatives such as aunts, uncles or grandparents of either sign are likely to form an effective relationship with children of the other sign, encouraging their growth and success. As ambitious as these two are together, working at the same company can bring out their competitiveness unless their roles are clearly defined. The same is true for business partners.

ADVICE: *Tend to small problems immediately. Don't get caught in a material web. Recognize that yours is not the only point of view. Cultivate an internal life.*

April 25–May 2
THE WEEK OF MANIFESTATION
TAURUS I

September 25–October 2
THE WEEK OF THE PERFECTIONIST
LIBRA I

A Chaotic Whirl

RELATIONSHIPS

STRENGTHS: **INTIMATE, SYMPATHETIC, REWARDING**

WEAKNESSES: **RESTRICTIVE, INHIBITING, ANXIOUS**

BEST: **FRIENDSHIP**

WORST: **WORK**

As a unit, this couple is powerfully persuasive in getting its way, but within the relationship itself manipulative attitudes may prove disturbing and disempowering, especially over the long haul. Both of these partners like things done a certain way, but not necessarily the same way. So the stage is set for argument, as each personality tries to persuade the other, usually through logic and reason, that their way of handling things is best. Should the two be united in their outlook, however, whether in a business, social or family setting, they can prove a potent reorganizing or reforming force.

The thrust of this relationship's need to persuade is usually practical rather than moral; it is based on common sense—at least as the persuader sees it. The "best" way of doing something, however, is often quite unrealistic here, as these two together tend to find not only exceedingly complex ways of accomplishing very simple things, but very simple solutions to potentially intricate problems. Marriages and friendships between these two are likely to be plagued by such contrasting methodologies, which can sometimes lend spice and humor but will ultimately get old and tiresome.

Love affairs here tend to be colorful but unrealistic. A relationship between Taurus I's and Libra I's exhibits some of the classic instability predicted by a quincunx aspect (150° apart in the zodiac), but since both Taurus and Libra are ruled by Venus, there is also a connection in matters of aesthetics and love. Still, love is truly blind here, as this relationship goes a long way to prove. When these two fall in love, ardor, foolishness, smugness, feigned emotion, posing, half-truths and manipulation all vie for the ascendancy. This chaotic whirl of feeling is not usually conducive to the relationship's long life or health.

Sibling pairings, particularly between members of the same sex, are likely to show dominant-submissive, extrovert-introvert and sadomasochistic overtones. The challenge is to find a balance in mood, and an equality that will allow each partner to develop on their own separate path.

ADVICE: *Let people make up their own minds. Work on making your outlook more realistic. Promote equality. Try to see more than one side of any situation.*

JERRY SEINFELD (4/29/54)
JASON ALEXANDER (9/26/55)

Alexander has risen to prominence as comedian Seinfeld's hapless, neurotic cohort on tv's hit series *Seinfeld.* The show's plot is based on a tightly knit group of friends. Both actors clearly enjoy their work and feed off each other's talent. *Also:* **Jack Paar & Ed Sullivan** (feud; tv hosts); **Lady Emma Hamilton & Lord Horatio Nelson** (married mistress/British admiral).

April 25–May 2
THE WEEK OF MANIFESTATION
TAURUS I

October 3–10
THE WEEK OF SOCIETY
LIBRA II

Giving Direction

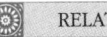 RELATIONSHIPS

STRENGTHS: **STRUCTURED, IMAGINATIVE, PLEASURABLE**

WEAKNESSES: **STAGNATING, FRUSTRATING, PROCRASTINATING**

BEST: **TEAM, CLUB MEMBERSHIP**

WORST: **FAMILY**

Focusing on boundaries, this relationship is strong in the areas of both structure and fantasy. Its principal challenge, then, may be to reconcile the two, or to apply rules and organization to imagination, creativity and play. Clearly this talent can allow the pair to work well as parents, as bosses, or as directors of, say, a club or team. They make an effective and understanding duo when it comes to acting in concert to give direction to a group.

Libra II's stand to benefit from marriages, love affairs and friendships with Taurus I's, who give them the solidity and dependability they so sorely need. Not only can they enchant and amuse the Taurus I in return, but, more important, they have the objectivity to encourage such a partner's personal development by supplying profound psychological insight into his or her own character. The relationship's outstanding weakness is that these two will tend to procrastinate, especially in decisions about the home, career, or financial obligations. Paralysis, avoidance and even breakdowns may sometimes set in when such decisions need to be made. But the couple will finally rally themselves and apply some organized thought to the situation at hand.

The hedonism in a Taurus I–Libra II friendship or marriage can become so pronounced that virtually all individual willpower is suspended. These partners may live in a pleasurable but notably unproductive vacuum. Libra II's will usually be more aggressive in trying to get things moving again, but in the face of formidable Taurus I resistance they may just give up, or take to sulking, nail-biting or other forms of escape or frustration.

Many types of work relationships between these two may not fly due to differences in style. Libra II's are generally unable to keep working away at something week after week, project after project, the way their Taurus I co-workers do—at least not without ill effects to their health. In families, similarly, Taurus I parents or siblings may grow frustrated with the inability or reluctance of Libra II's to give themselves wholeheartedly to domestic matters, leaving chores undone.

ADVICE: *Beware of drifting and dreaming. Set realistic goals and achieve them. Understand your capabilities. Fight the desire to postpone.*

BARON VON RICHTHOFEN (5/2/1892)
EDDIE RICKENBACKER (10/8/1890)

Forever linked as flying rivals, these 2 aces of early air combat were fearless and driven. German Richthofen shot down 80 Allied planes; Capt. Rickenbacker destroyed 26 enemy craft and became America's most decorated WWI pilot.

STRENGTHS: **AFFECTIONATE, GIVING, IRRESISTIBLE**
WEAKNESSES: **TRIGGERING, ASOCIAL, CONTROLLING**
BEST: **EXECUTIVE PARTNERSHIP**
WORST: **FRIENDSHIP**

TALIA SHIRE (4/25/46)
MARIO PUZO (10/15/20)

Actress Shire and novelist/screen-writer Puzo were both award winners for *The Godfather* movie series, directed by Francis Ford Coppola, Shire's older brother. She won the NY Film Critics Award for her role as Connie Corleone in *The Godfather, Part II* (1974). Puzo won screenplay Oscars for *The Godfather I* (1972) and *II*. **Also: Percy Heath & Art Blakey** (jazz bassist/drummer).

April 25–May 2
THE WEEK OF MANIFESTATION
TAURUS I

October 11–18
THE WEEK OF THEATER
LIBRA III

Conflicting Tendencies

The Taurus I–Libra III relationship will have its ins and outs and its ups and downs. The combination is bound to concern itself with trying to reconcile its partners' conflicting natures. A great deal of energy will need to be devoted to creating something settled between these two, thereby stunting the overall possibilities for the growth of the relationship or of its partners. The upshot is that certain areas are difficult or unlikely, particularly relationships such as marriage, involving children and a settled family life.

Taurus I's need to settle down, Libra III's resist it. Furthermore, a Taurus I's nurturing abilities will have no object in a Libra III, who probably won't want to be around a lot of the time. This will take most of the fun out of the relationship for the Taurus I. Group activities involving these two, whether social or business, are also problematic, given both the Taurus I's need to run the show and the Libra III's relative lack of interest in other people. The best roles for this duo would be as hard-driving executive partners in a business with well-defined roles.

More intimate relationships are likely to be unstable and stormy, especially if initial sexual energies run high. Taurus I's will not react well to a Libra III's alternate coolness and explosiveness in confrontations; their stubbornness will kick in and their placid side will be tested. Libra III's instinctively know how to push the buttons of Taurus I's, making them exasperated or desperate. To top it off, the Libra III will probably grow bored with the Taurus I in the end.

Friendships in this combination are likely to be unstable, and are not recommended. As sports opponents or team partners, however, this duo can be irresistible, sweeping the field before them. Family relations may be idealized, affectionate and giving, particularly between father and daughter, mother and son, and same-sex siblings. This tightly knit bond can prove the strongest axis in the family, but will also feature tremendous displays of temperament and furious confrontations, which relatives would be wise to stay out of.

ADVICE: *Try to keep on an even keel. Emotions should be put to constructive or pleasurable use. Get a bit tougher and don't let your buttons be pushed.*

STRENGTHS: **CONCEPTUAL, MONEY-SAVVY, AESTHETIC**
WEAKNESSES: **DAMAGING, DISRUPTIVE, OUT OF SYNCH**
BEST: **FRIENDSHIP**
WORST: **LOVE**

BRIAN AHERNE (5/2/02)
JOAN FONTAINE (10/22/17)

Aherne and Fontaine were married from 1939–45. English-born Aherne came to Hollywood in 1931 and played many romantic leads, often typecast as a tweedy, pipe-smoking Brit. Fontaine's career took off when she played the lead in 2 Hitchcock films, *Rebecca* (1940) and *Suspicion* (1941).

April 25–May 2
THE WEEK OF MANIFESTATION
TAURUS I

October 19–25
THE CUSP OF DRAMA & CRITICISM
LIBRA-SCORPIO CUSP

Conceptual Thought

This relationship is very much at home in the world of ideas and ideologies. Both parties bring to it a bias toward the kind of conceptual thought that is geared toward the pragmatic; this can be a powerful unifying force. Innovation and can be a positive offshoot of the relationship, making it a good combination for business or group endeavors. In personal relationships with each other, these two are apt to find the relationship somewhat hard to pin down or define.

The relationship may well feature a sharing of intellectual and aesthetic interests, and Taurus I's are likely to be in awe of Libra-Scorpio mental powers, and proud to be in a relationship that gives serious consideration to their own thoughts. But Libra-Scorpios are also likely to criticize or denigrate the ideas of Taurus I's, who will take such attacks personally. This can cause great upset. In the romantic or marital sphere, somewhat similarly, Libra-Scorpios may move in passionate and ecstatic realms that leave a Taurus I partner behind, on the plane of physical sensation. And their energies, sometimes erupting cataclysmically out of control in the form of scathing or sarcastic commentary, can hurt, bewilder or even frighten more stolid and calm Taurus I's, who may retreat in confusion, or simply be immobilized in a state of shock. On the positive side, however, such relationships are likely to provide strong economic security, featuring good investments, strong earning patterns and shrewd use of funds on a daily basis.

The most successful possibility for this combination may be friendship, where many of the pair's strengths can manifest without accompanying emotional turmoil. Since power struggles and sexual combat do not come into play here, the friendship may prove pleasurable, stable, psychologically supportive and intellectually interesting. In both the business and the family spheres, this duo can be a force for rationality and common sense. Its attitudes generally prove constructive and forward-looking. The relationship enhances the traditional side of both parties, who, particularly together, tend to promote values that have stood the test of time.

ADVICE: *Try to keep on an even keel. Promote financial endeavors. Cultivate group and organizational skills. Minimize power struggles.*

April 25–May 2

THE WEEK OF MANIFESTATION
TAURUS I

October 26–November 2

THE WEEK OF INTENSITY
SCORPIO I

Running the Gamut

RELATIONSHIPS

STRENGTHS: **EXPRESSIVE, TRUSTING, ECSTATIC**

WEAKNESSES: **CONTROLLING, DESTRUCTIVE, REBELLIOUS**

BEST: **LOVE**

WORST: **PARENT-CHILD**

AYATOLLAH KHOMEINI (5/1/1900)
SHAH OF IRAN (10/26/19)

Leader of a brutal, corrupt regime, the shah faced religious opposition from Khomeini supporters in 1978. His initial concessions failed to quell the mass demonstrations that led to his exile in 1979 and swept Khomeini into power.

Opposites attract—and how! Since Taurus I and Scorpio I are 180° apart in the zodiac, it is not surprising that a strong magnetic pull should be present here. And this initial attraction is nothing compared to the energies that can be generated, both for the good and the bad, once the relationship gets moving. Indeed this matchup runs the full gamut of expressiveness, from the most brilliant to the most passionate. Yet these are quintessentially fixed personalities, and their synergetic melding presents a solid and formidable exterior to the world. In short this can be an unbeatable combination, at work, on the playing field or in a family or social group.

Should these two fall deeply in love, they are likely to soar to the heights of physical sensation and sexual ecstasy, but they must beware of getting stuck there. Their passion can also be the prelude for spiritual forays, but they too often get mired in issues of possession and control, codependency and love addiction. Destructiveness can climb unacceptably here, with the relationship being rocked or torn apart by fierce battles for supremacy. Indeed the relationship's karma often seems to demand going this far before such conflicts can be finally resolved.

Taurus I–Scorpio I marriages don't usually do well if they grow from such love affairs. They have a better chance of success when they evolve out of friendships, where the bonds of trust, respect and tenderness that are so valuable in marriage can form in a less competitive context. Indeed friendships in this combination can be very close, approaching a true marriage of hearts and minds.

In the family, and especially in parent-child matchups, either possible arrangement of these two personalities will yield caring, protective and nurturing relationships, but also overprotective and controlling ones. Alas, the way out usually lies in the direction of rejection, rebellion or both.

ADVICE: *Know when to stop. Be aware of negative forces. Don't get stuck in destructive attitudes. Cultivate trust and tenderness.*

April 25–May 2

THE WEEK OF MANIFESTATION
TAURUS I

November 3–11

THE WEEK OF DEPTH
SCORPIO II

Take No Prisoners

RELATIONSHIPS

STRENGTHS: **DEPENDABLE, CHALLENGING, FINANCIAL**

WEAKNESSES: **INTOLERANT, DEPRESSING, COMBATIVE**

BEST: **MARRIAGE**

WORST: **SIBLING**

KING WILLIAM III (11/4/1650)
QUEEN MARY II (4/30/1662)

To protect political alliances, cousins William and Mary married in 1677. Although she was the legitimate heir to the English throne, Mary insisted they rule as joint sovereigns. Crowned together in 1689, Mary afterwards always deferred to William's wishes.

***Also:* Uma Thurman & Ethan Hawke** (romance; actors).

The challenge of this relationship will be to preserve a balance of power. Both partners consider themselves authorities on a variety of subjects, and may be extremely intolerant of other points of view. When they agree, their friends and family may face a solid wall of opposition or authority. When they disagree, the relationship can be rocked by the sounds of battle. "Take no prisoners" and "Give no quarter" are commands not conducive to harmony and tranquillity, but these two are each other's equals, and they may need confrontations like these to satisfy their need for combat, sharpen their argumentative skills and provide them with opportunities for the thrill of victory. Strife may be satisfying here, in other words, until the relationship acknowledges a greater kick: the substantial results that accrue from mutual cooperation and understanding.

Marriages in this combination are likely to have rather a heavy feel, but can be long-lasting, not to mention long-suffering. Successful in many respects, including financially and careerwise, they will feature day-to-day interactions in which wrestling for the reins of power, particularly in struggles over money, is never far away. Passions run high: joy, satisfaction, excitement, pain, suffering, depression. No matter what the partners' emotional or psychological state, they will inevitably return to the desire to acquire individual control and the need to give it up, whether through force or reason. Balance may eventually be achieved here, then, if only because of an inevitable averaging out of individual wins and losses, or, more positively, because of a realization that balance is essential for the relationship's health. The deep friendships that are possible here can be especially effective in promoting sports, family or social activities. They may become a bulwark of organizational dependability for a club or team, whether in fundraising, getting picnics or parties together or seeing to ordinary day-to-day problems. Familial relationships, on the other hand, particularly between siblings, are likely to be rocky. Particularly deadly may be struggles between two brothers or two sisters, where age differences will set up patterns of coercion and rebellion that may only be resolved later in life, if at all.

ADVICE: *Pull together for the common good. Try to minimize ego and power struggles. Lighten up and have fun. Acting silly isn't shameful. Let things happen.*

STRENGTHS: **EASY, UNDERSTANDING, PERCEPTIVE**

WEAKNESSES: **SPOILED, SUPERFICIAL, MANIPULATIVE**

BEST: **WORK**

WORST: **PARENT-CHILD**

EDWARD R. MURROW (4/25/08)
JOSEPH MCCARTHY (11/14/08)

Newsman Murrow was a torch for liberalism and integrity, while his ideological foe, Senator McCarthy, led a vicious anti-communist headhunt. Their conflict climaxed in 1954, when Murrow's tv program attacked McCarthy's investigative tactics.

April 25–May 2

THE WEEK OF MANIFESTATION
TAURUS I

November 12–18

THE WEEK OF CHARM
SCORPIO III

No Hassles

The slogan of this matchup could well be "No hassles." These two usually make well-defined demands, but their relationship, particularly in marriage, is remarkable for keeping their requirements of each other to a minimum, and for settling for what is rather than what could be. Taurus I's enjoy being able to walk through the door and relax after a tough day; Scorpio III's like being appreciated for what they have to give. The relationship satisfies important needs, then, but also encourages the easy give-and-take that makes living worthwhile.

Taurus I–Scorpio III love is for the most part likely to be magnetic, physical and sensuous, reaching new highs in torrid sexuality, much to the enjoyment of both partners. Very occasionally, it may also be volcanic, unleashing hostility along with desire and passion. In marriages, the home can become a reliable and comfortable haven from the world's pressures. Fighting can be kept to a minimum and peaceful evenings will unfold. This is not to suggest that these two are by any means turned off, but, rather, that the relationship's emotional intelligence is high. There is an understanding here of the value of compromise and understanding, and a realization that impatience and constant anger are counterproductive and undesirable.

Both friendships and working relationships in this combination are often relaxed and productive. In neither of them are the partners polarized, and equality can be assumed to be the norm. At work, whether the Taurus I is the boss and the Scorpio III the employee or vice versa, power will not be seen as threatening nor service as demeaning.

Should Taurus I and Scorpio III be a father-daughter or mother-son combination, there is the risk of the child being spoiled. Scorpio III children may know how to turn on the charm and get their way with a Taurus I parent who may otherwise seem remarkably resistant.

ADVICE: *Beware of lethargy. Seek stimulating activities. Don't fall into nonproductivity. Tension isn't always undesirable. Further the action.*

STRENGTHS: **IDEOLOGICAL, GENEROUS, LOYAL**

WEAKNESSES: **MISDIRECTED, ADRIFT, TEMPTED**

BEST: **FRIENDSHIP**

WORST: **WORK**

ELEANOR POWELL (11/21/12)
GLENN FORD (5/1/16)

Powell was a tap-dancing star in MGM's lavish musicals of the 30s and 40s. She retired from films after marrying screen actor Ford in 1943. Following their 1959 divorce, she enjoyed a successful nightclub comeback.
Also: Duke Ellington & Billy Strayhorn (musical collaborators); **Sheldon Harnick & Jerry Bock** (musical collaborators).

April 25–May 2

THE WEEK OF MANIFESTATION
TAURUS I

November 19–24

THE CUSP OF REVOLUTION
SCORPIO-SAGITTARIUS CUSP

Lavish Tastes

The central problem of this relationship, and its greatest challenge, is giving direction and leadership to its activities. Taurus I's and Scorpio-Sagittarians seem to reinforce each other's procrastinating, so getting things done is often a problem here. Furthermore, both partners are busy a lot of the time with ideas and plans, so that the relationship may be occasionally lacking in the sphere of implementation. Lavish and excessive qualities, especially in the physical realm, will be magnified here: often, too much of the relationship's time and money will be spent on eating, drinking and luxury items.

Loyalty plays an important role in friendships between these two, who are usually sensitive and understanding toward each other. Scorpio-Sagittarians will see through the tough exterior of Taurus I's, instinctively recognizing and responding to their sensitive, emotional side; Taurus I's meanwhile know when to leave Scorpio-Sagittarians alone to empty and recharge, and also to mull over their ideas in peace.

Love affairs, on the other hand, will put loyalty to the test. Scorpio-Sagittarians who are highly responsive to a Taurus I partner may still not make them the exclusive object of their affections. It is not so much that Taurus I's are incapable of satisfying them as that Scorpio-Sagittarians often get caught with their hand in more than one cookie jar. Their need for variety and change in sexual matters, and their difficulty in avoiding involvement with those they find attractive, prove a double problem in this relationship. Because Taurus I's are easily hurt, and feel rejected when Scorpio-Sagittarians roam, marriage in this combination is likely to be difficult.

Family and working relationships between these two may be problematic for two reasons. First, conflicts over methods, ideas and plans usually prove an insurmountable barrier. Second, both parties like to run the show, and to give direction to their projects. While they fight over the wheel, unfortunately, the ship may be heading toward the rocks.

ADVICE: *Try not to put things off. Keep on top of the situation. Give firm direction to projects. Agree on a course of action and stick to it.*

April 25–May 2
THE WEEK OF MANIFESTATION
TAURUS I

November 25–December 2
THE WEEK OF INDEPENDENCE
SAGITTARIUS I

Trials of Patience

RELATIONSHIPS
STRENGTHS: **HONEST, PHYSICAL, ACCEPTING**
WEAKNESSES: **FRUSTRATED, AGGRESSIVE, SELF-CENTERED**
BEST: **PARENT-CHILD**
WORST: **MARRIAGE**

The success of this relationship will be proportional to the degree to which the partners can patiently accept their individual differences for the sake of their mutual good. The relationship can cultivate objectivity and open-mindedness with some success if its partners are willing to give them a try. The final result may be that these two learn to accept and understand not only each other but those in their circle, friends, family, groups and others in general society. On the face of it, differences in approach may make it difficult for Taurus I's and Sagittarius I's to deal with each other effectively. Independent Sagittarius I's generally believe in education through the school of hard knocks, whereas more people-oriented Taurus I's live to implement ideas, which they often derive from either written or verbal models. Another difference is that move like greased lightning, while Taurus I's are steady and sure. Yet these contrasting attributes can enhance, deepen and enrich the Taurus I–Sagittarius I relationship, as long as acceptance is the central focus and patience prevails.

An emotional barrier in love and marriage may be the issue of give-and-take. Taurus I's have a strong nurturing side, which may be frustrated with Sagittarius I's, who are so independent that they will rarely accept help. Sagittarius I's do need to take, but often do so rather aggressively, in a way that makes them feel they have overcome or conquered something. Taurus I's have deep needs, but find it difficult to share feelings with self-centered and impatient Sagittarius I's.

Friendships and family relationships are more favorable. Parent-child combinations are likely to be mutually supportive and understanding. Of course, a Taurus I parent may be smothering and a Sagittarius I child wild and rebellious, but whichever personality falls into whichever role, the relationship is characterized by honesty and trustworthiness. Differences are accepted even in disagreements. Friendships are likely to be athletic or based on travel, even within a limited area. A love of nature and caring for pets can be shared and developed here, with particular emphasis on evolving a deeper understanding of biological and ecological matters.

ADVICE: *Build on your strengths and diversity. Learn to take what's given and to give when taking. Lower your defenses. Share feelings at a deeper level when possible.*

BING CROSBY (5/2/04)
KATHRYN GRANT (11/25/33)

Beauty queen Grant played leading roles in 50s films until she gave up her acting career in 1957 to become the 2nd wife of crooner Crosby. During the mid-70s she hosted a tv talk show in San Francisco. Their marriage lasted until Crosby's death in 1977.

April 25–May 2
THE WEEK OF MANIFESTATION
TAURUS I

December 3–10
THE WEEK OF THE ORIGINATOR
SAGITTARIUS II

Hidden Repository

RELATIONSHIPS
STRENGTHS: **CLOSE, SHARING, DEDICATED**
WEAKNESSES: **FRUSTRATED, OVERDEPENDENT, CONCEALING**
BEST: **MARRIAGE**
WORST: **WORK**

This complex relationship is governed by contrasting and often contradictory elements: acceptance versus rejection, rebellion versus a desire to please, the need to hide versus the need to reveal and share—all these impulses vie for the ascendancy. Of particular importance is knowing the time to conceal or expose aspects of oneself, or just information in general. Striking a balance between these two will often be a determining factor in how close the relationship will be. Sharing secrets is also a hallmark of the combination, and the relationship can become a repository of truths untold elsewhere. Sometimes its very existence will be based on the trust that its secrets will be kept—revealing what is private between these two could destroy it.

The relationship's intimacy will be predicated on whether and when its partners choose to expose themselves to each other. Sagittarius II's have definite problems with escapist tendencies, which, if revealed, will disturb Taurus I's, no matter how close or intense their love affair. The inability of Sagittarius II's to face responsibility, or perhaps their own addictions, can prove a problem; the Taurus I may accuse the Sagittarius II of failing to face up to reality, and the Sagittarius II will see this as a personal indictment. Taurus I's may secretly enjoy acting as protectors for Sagittarius II's, whom they perhaps view as flaky, while Sagittarius II's are apt to hide the fact that, deep down, they admire Taurus I solidity and orientation toward slow but sure achievement.

Marriages and friendships can be mutually supportive and understanding, albeit stressful. Because they have a low self-image, Sagittarius II's are initially suspicious of Taurus I advances, but in the end may become overly dependent on their highly capable partners. Taurus I's can feel good about the contributions they make to the relationship, but also frustrated at its inability to reach deeper levels of emotional interaction. And the deep need of Sagittarius II's for self-understanding and spiritual growth may similarly not be met in this relationship, so that they may have to be pursue this dimension outside of it. At work or in the family, the efforts of Taurus I's to build a team can be undercut by the extreme individualism of Sagittarius II's.

ADVICE: *Aim for openness. Examine your need to keep secrets. Past fears need to be confronted. Beware of cutting yourself off from the world.*

EDWARD IV (4/29/1442)
HENRY VI (12/6/1421)

Lancastrian king of England from 1422–61, Henry VI was an ineffectual ruler subject to bouts of insanity. In 1461, during the Wars of the Roses, Edward IV claimed the throne after defeating Henry's supporters. ***Also:*** **Carol Burnett & Carrie Hamilton** (mother/daughter; actresses); **Bing Crosby & Dorothy Lamour** (co-stars); **Al Pacino & Ellen Burstyn** (co-directors, Actors Studio).

STRENGTHS: **ATTUNED, SENSITIVE, TRUSTING**

WEAKNESSES: **TRIGGERING, BATTLING, UNBALANCED**

BEST: **WORK**

WORST: **FAMILY**

ANN-MARGRET (4/28/41)
ROGER SMITH (12/18/32)

Former 60s sex symbol Ann-Margret has withstood the test of time and is regarded as a versatile, multitalented actress. Her devoted husband and personal manager, tv-actor Smith, was instrumental in her 70s comeback.

April 25–May 2
THE WEEK OF MANIFESTATION
TAURUS I

December 11–18
THE WEEK OF THE TITAN
SAGITTARIUS III

Refined Sensibilities

At first glance, one would expect the major theme of this relationship to be simple: a power struggle between two determined individuals. Taurus is an earth sign, making for a pragmatic, stubborn nature, while the personality of Sagittarius, a fire sign, is more expansive and high-minded. But this interpretation ignores the deeper forces at work here, and the nature of the two individuals. Together they can bring out many heretofore unexpressed aspects in each other, including a spiritual side, greater emotional trust and awareness, and the ability to explore the larger issues and meanings.

In love, marriage and friendship, the successful Taurus I–Sagittarius III relationship will exhibit very refined sensibilities, both in dealing with the world outside itself and in allowing its own partners to reach deeper layers of sharing and trust. In such mutual explorations, rational faculties and common sense meld well with emotional openness. The downside of this heightened awareness is a tendency to overreact or to be knocked off balance. Indeed, the sensitivity of the relationship can become a problem, forcing these two to build a wall to protect themselves, so that they appear much tougher and more pragmatic than they really are. One glance or silent acknowledgment, however, is enough to attest to the relationship's continuing closeness.

In the family, these two may well engage in power struggles, with highly negative results for both themselves and the larger group. Parent-child and sibling relationships are likely to feature battles of mammoth proportions; an inability to back down or compromise is characteristic. Unfortunately, the sensitivity here triggers upset more often than it is used to reach deeper levels of understanding.

At work, Taurus I's and Sagittarius III's may prove a strong and well-integrated combination. Usually functioning better as partners heading up a business than as boss-employee or co-worker pairs, they show a mutual respect for each other's talents and strengths. And conflict may be spared within their organization because of an instinctive realization that energies are better spent opposing competitors than fighting each other.

ADVICE: *Stay open and trusting. Don't close off to feelings. Don't let your buttons be pushed so easily. Use sensitivity to reach deeper emotions.*

STRENGTHS: **ORGANIZED, NONTHREATENING, HONEST**

WEAKNESSES: **IRRATIONAL, STUBBORN, RECALCITRANT**

BEST: **FRIENDSHIP, WORK**

WORST: **LOVE**

EMPEROR HIROHITO (4/29/01)
EMPEROR AKIHITO (12/23/33)

The succession of Japanese emperors through the centuries has never strayed from the royal bloodline. Hirohito followed his father Yoshihito to the throne. His son Akihito succeeded Hirohito's 62-year reign after his death in 1989.

April 25–May 2
THE WEEK OF MANIFESTATION
TAURUS I

December 19–25
THE CUSP OF PROPHECY
SAGITTARIUS-CAPRICORN CUSP

Plans and Logistics

This relationship will emphasize structure and the implementation of plans and ideas. These are the core of the Taurus I nature, but when it comes to putting concepts to work, Sagittarius-Capricorns are no slouches either. Love relationships here are a bit problematic, since the complexities and difficulties of the Sagittarius-Capricorn personality may be too much for Taurus I's to handle. What appear to be reasonable agreements, plans or conversations about logistics can be swept aside by an outburst of great emotional intensity, perhaps resulting from pent-up resentment or frustration. Stubbornness and recalcitrance are also characteristic here, resulting in a refusal to express emotion or to agree to reasonable discussion.

In families, marriages and the workplace, this duo can shine in organizational matters. But it has an emotionally unstable and depressive side that can emerge when things don't go according to plan. An atmosphere of insecurity may arise for apparently no reason at all here, leaving lowered self-esteem and lack of confidence in its wake. The relationship may work out best in the area of friendship, which can provide a non-threatening atmosphere in which to express or discuss hidden needs. The degree of honesty that can be achieved here is impossible in relationships where the partners feel they have a lot to lose. The friendship will rarely prove competitive, unless a third party is involved who is the object of both partners' affections.

Work partnerships can be very rewarding for these two, who will feel comfortable as team members or equals. They complement each other well, since Sagittarius-Capricorns are excellent project initiators while Taurus I's enjoy maintenance. The relationship's energies are well geared to teamwork and working behind the scenes, and it is ideally oriented to service of any kind. Furthermore, the psychic abilities of Sagittarius-Capricorns often allow them to peer into the future and get an idea of what lies ahead. Taurus I's are much too practical to acknowledge these powers and perceptions, which they will probably write off as hunches or luck.

ADVICE: *Have confidence in yourself. When working, be objective and don't let feelings intrude. Show emotional intelligence. Make things easier.*

April 25–May 2

THE WEEK OF MANIFESTATION
TAURUS I

December 26–January 2

THE WEEK OF THE RULER
CAPRICORN I

From Matter to Spirit

The trine relationship (120° apart in the zodiac) between the earth signs of Taurus I and Capricorn I traditionally indicates an easygoingness, with a shared orientation toward work and sensuous pleasure. But this pair may aim at something more transcendent, beginning with the material but evolving toward the spiritual—not necessarily as a state in which they float through the world, at a distance from it, but as one in which they see the here and now in a more conscious and aware light. Since each personality brings a knowledge of and easy familiarity with material concerns to the relationship, together they can often take these things for granted, instead investigating aesthetic, religious, new-age and even psychic phenomena together.

Taurus I–Capricorn I love affairs emphasize an easy and highly pleasurable sensuality, although this is a sensuality of a kind conducive to reaching a kind of meditative or ecstatic peace in which matter is transcended and spirit liberated. Yet excesses in the area of food and drink, as well as sex and love addictions, are an ever-present danger here, and moderation must be observed or ill health can result.

Friendships and marriages between these two are strongly recommended. Practical matters will be handled efficiently and money will be well spent. For spouses, sharing the same activities enjoyed in love affairs—food, sex—may continue to be satisfying, but they will also enjoy creating a pleasant home together. One drawback of the combination may be a lack of push and drive, since the relationship is usually comfortable as it is, and may feel no need to strive toward difficult or impossible goals. On the one hand this makes it realistic, on the other it may also be a bit complacent and self-satisfied.

Parent-child relationships are often close and understanding, with nurturing playing a strong role, even when parents grow old and need the kind of attention they once gave their children. Care must be taken, however, that such relationships do not become too dependent or inhibit personal growth.

ADVICE: *Don't give up your individual path. Spur yourself on to greater achievement. Don't get stuck in a pleasure trap. Seek liberation.*

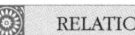

JACK PAAR (5/1/18)
STEVE ALLEN (12/26/21)

Allen and Paar were hosts of NBC's *Tonight Show* before the Carson dynasty. Allen hosted the program in 1954–57; his emphasis was on comedy and music, Allen himself being an accomplished pianist and composer. Paar hosted the show from 1957–62; more popular than Allen, Paar attracted a wider audience through conversation and controversy rather than humor.

April 25–May 2

THE WEEK OF MANIFESTATION
TAURUS I

January 3–9

THE WEEK OF DETERMINATION
CAPRICORN II

Made to Order

If this relationship is to endure it will need to build a successful organization, team or family tailored to satisfy personal needs, and particularly to tie its interests to those of the group. The structure of either the relationship or the organizations it fosters may not be especially well understood by those around it, who can view its methods as peculiar, its structure singular and its goals sometimes downright bizarre.

A Taurus I–Capricorn II team can be hard-driving and dynamic. One problem, however, is that Capricorn II's may be more interested in their own advancement or benefit than in that of the pair, so that they may jump ship at a crucial moment—and usually without any warning. Steady, devoted Taurus I's will find it harder to end the relationship, whether it manifests in the business, social or marital sphere.

Marriages, friendships and familial relationships in this combination may be quite ambitious in seeking social status in their community or circle. They highly prize money, prestige and power, considering them well worth whatever efforts are needed to attain them. Taurus I's may be a bit disturbed by the superaggressive, amoral approach of Capricorn II's, who in turn may see their Taurus I partner as a bit lazy or overly moral. A certain lack of emphasis on the human values of sympathy, kindness and affection may put the relationship in danger of becoming hard and unfeeling. Love affairs in this combination are often tough, sexually oriented confrontations in which the partners are not really prepared to give of themselves but tend to size each other up in terms of the profit they might gain from staying together.

If the relationship is a partnership in the business world, it will have to survive a lot of external criticism and lack of comprehension. It will have to develop good PR and emphasize its partners' unusual requirements. Should Taurus I's and Capricorn II's find these tasks fulfilling, they will go the extra mile to make their relationship capable of providing the top-notch goods or services that will satisfy the most demanding of customers.

ADVICE: *Examine your motives. The ends may not justify the means. Develop your caring and affectionate side. Take the time to know people. Share feelings.*

WM. RANDOLPH HEARST (4/29/1863)
MARION DAVIES (1/3/1897)

Despite his wife's refusal to divorce him, newspaper magnate Hearst's intense love affair with actress Davies lasted from 1917 to his death in 1951. Obsessed with her, he vowed to make Davies the world's greatest actress but failed.

***Also:** Al Pacino & Diane Keaton* (affair; actors); **Ann-Margret & Elvis Presley** (affair; actress/singer).

Alone in a Crowd

April 25–May 2
THE WEEK OF MANIFESTATION
TAURUS I

January 10–16
THE WEEK OF DOMINANCE
CAPRICORN III

MARTIN LUTHER KING, JR. (1/15/29)
CORETTA KING (4/27/27)

United in 1953 by Reverend King, Sr., the Kings had a profoundly devoted marriage that revolved around his career in civil-rights work. Coretta took care of children and home while fully supporting her husband's valiant crusade.

Also: Jerry Seinfeld & Julia Louis-Dreyfus (co-stars, *Seinfeld*).

Few individuals are as dominant as either of these two. One would not expect them even to form a friendship, then, let alone the most intimate of relationships. Yet the possibility exists in this combination for a true bond of the spirit, one that will set this relationship quite apart from others. These two can feel completely alone together in the middle of a crowded room. Perhaps some of the basis for their intimacy lies in the fact that these personalities, both highly ambitious, must actually understand each other quite well. So long as their spheres of influence don't clash, they may see in each other what each respects most, and this can become the basis for them to share their interior lives, which neither of them would do with someone they didn't admire. Furthermore, together they may find a more meaningful or socially responsible set of ideals to which to harness their ambition.

Even so, love affairs between these two can be quite difficult. Power struggles are likely to emerge constantly, particularly in purely sexual relationships. In a committed relationship or marriage, the partners should be sure to define their own unquestioned domains—otherwise their struggles may tear the relationship apart. But harmony will prevail if roles are well delineated and tasks defined, and the relationship's more positive aspects are more likely to unfold here, where there may exist a greater level of trust, empathy and understanding.

A family relationship will tie people together whether or not they choose it, so the question will become how these two can get along. Unfortunately they usually don't, and there is little to be done about it. Working on understanding, acceptance, thoughtfulness and ultimately love will be difficult when power plays are the order of the day, but if the relationship is to be productive rather than destructive, one partner will have to take the first step. A status quo, balance of power or truce is sometimes the best that can be hoped for, at least temporarily. At work, both individuals must control their immediate space, so it would make sense to place them in different departments.

ADVICE: *Declare an armistice. Find areas in which conflict is not an issue. Promote mutual cooperation to achieve common goals. Be kind.*

Solving the Puzzle

April 25–May 2
THE WEEK OF MANIFESTATION
TAURUS I

January 17–22
THE CUSP OF MYSTERY & IMAGINATION
CAPRICORN-AQUARIUS CUSP

ULYSSES S. GRANT (4/27/1822)
ROBERT E. LEE (1/19/1807)

In 1864, Union General Grant clashed with Confederate General Lee in a series of bloody Civil War battles. Though Lee held an early advantage, his Confederates were eventually worn down and forced to surrender at Appomatox, Virginia, in 1865.

Also: Claire Clairmont & Lord Byron (mistress/poet); **Judy Carne & Vidal Sassoon** (romance; actress/hair stylist).

These two have little in common. Their problem is how to reconcile manifestation and mystery, two very different concepts indeed. This pair's ongoing struggle will always be how to concretize the unfathomable and to spiritualize the concrete—in short, how to make sense of life while retaining one's awe of it; how to understand love in more than material terms yet express it in the real world; and how to approach abstract beauty closely enough to give it material form. These elusive goals can well keep this relationship together for quite some time, as each partner seeks what he or she lacks—rather like chasing butterflies.

The relationship will certainly be a safe haven for chaotic Capricorn-Aquarians to escape to, but it will also put them in touch with their dark side, either impelling them to understand it better or arousing worry and concern in both partners. Taurus I's, on the other hand, will be mesmerized by the relationship's more enigmatic aspects and will seek to unlock its puzzles. Thus the relationship will guide both partners toward inner psychological realms, the exploration of which will deepen their connection but also help them along their individual paths of self-realization.

In love, Taurus I's are likely to be attracted to the vibrancy of the Capricorn-Aquarius personality but will also gain satisfaction in being able to ground these exciting individuals in the physical plane, and to involve them in a relationship with a calming effect. Capricorn-Aquarians will appreciate the earthy sensuality of Taurus I's and will enjoy relaxing into a less frenetic relationship than they might ordinarily choose.

These two can prove an effective team as spouses or career partners, for both know how to work hard on a daily basis, and this relationship will bring out their more responsible side. They both have a strong tyrannical side, though, which can be magnified here, presenting grave problems for their children, employees or co-workers—and for each other.

ADVICE: *Try to even out emotions. Avoid worry and brooding. Seek healthy outlets for your energies. Use your insights constructively.*

April 25–May 2

THE WEEK OF MANIFESTATION
TAURUS I

January 23–30

THE WEEK OF GENIUS
AQUARIUS I

Universal Questions

RELATIONSHIPS

STRENGTHS: **THOUGHTFUL, IDEALISTIC, INSPIRATIONAL**

WEAKNESSES: **UNGROUNDED, REBELLIOUS, LOST**

BEST: **FRIENDSHIP**

WORST: **WORK**

EMPEROR HIROHITO (4/29/01)
FRANKLIN D. ROOSEVELT (1/30/1882)

In 1941 economic and diplomatic relations between Hirohito and Roosevelt fell apart. The US expected an eventual war with Japan but was totally surprised by the bombing of Pearl Harbor on Dec. 7—"a date which will live in infamy," said Roosevelt, then an avowed enemy of Hirohito.
Also: William Randolph Hearst & Julia Morgan (builder of Hearst Castle/architect).

This relationship can exhibit a high level of mental activity, much of it aspiring not only to answer universal questions but also to deal with emotions on a basic human level. These two will find themselves grappling with issues of how to balance the absolute and the relative, the subjective and the objective, the ideal and the pragmatic. Both parties will benefit from such explorations but must beware of getting carried away and forgetting about more practical considerations. Taurus I's usually have both feet on the ground, but may be seduced away from that stance by the relationship's magnetic pull, so that they occasionally find themselves a bit lost or bewildered. Aquarius I's are on more familiar ground and will enjoy leading their Taurus I partner through intricate realms of thought.

In love affairs, Aquarius I's are likely to be either a bit cool or a bit eccentric for Taurus I tastes. Similarly, although the earthy sensuality of Taurus I's may intrigue Aquarius I's for a short while, it may in the longer run seem predictable and unimaginative to them. These partners do share a love of higher ideals and principles, however, which may lead them to continue their relationship in the platonic sphere, without heavy physical involvement, and to enjoy sharing affection and sympathy.

Marriages and friendships in this combination are probably the best bet; they will allow idealistic and emotional areas to be thoroughly explored without damaging feelings being aroused, at least not too often. Practical and abstract matters gel well here, providing a good balance in daily life. The relationship will be especially well suited for interaction with other friends or with children, for whom it may be a source of inspiration.

Work and family relationships will have obvious problems if the boss or parent is the Taurus I and the child or employee the Aquarius I: in very basic respects, the Taurus I will invariably try to change the Aquarius I, who will not react well to being controlled or forced into a mold and is likely to rebel against Taurus I rules and expectations, particularly in the area of repetitive daily tasks.

ADVICE: *Don't get carried away. Tend to daily tasks. Keep your eye on the distant mountain but your feet on the ground. Balance your energies.*

April 25–May 2

THE WEEK OF MANIFESTATION
TAURUS I

January 31–February 7

THE WEEK OF YOUTH & EASE
AQUARIUS II

Languid Contentment

RELATIONSHIPS

STRENGTHS: **RELAXED, SENSUOUS, UNDEMANDING**

WEAKNESSES: **UNAWARE, COMPLACENT, ONE-TRACK**

BEST: **MARRIAGE**

WORST: **CO-WORKER**

GERTRUDE STEIN (2/3/1874)
ALICE B. TOKLAS (4/30/1877)

Toklas was writer Stein's secretary and lifelong companion from 1907 until Stein's death in 1946. This celebrated lesbian couple lived together in Paris for years and hosted prominent artists and writers in their famous salon.
Also: Mikhail Fokine & Anna Pavlova (choreographer/ballerina); **Queen Juliana & Queen Beatrix** (Dutch mother/daughter).

This relationship may well focus on a love of physical, sensuous beauty. The combination's hedonistic aspects are pronounced, most obviously in its partners' highly pleasurable interactions with each other and secondarily in a common love of the beautiful objects that bring joy to their lives. The danger here is that easy Aquarius II attitudes and the Taurus I love of repose may combine to give the relationship a somewhat lackadaisical, contented air, fostering laziness and procrastination. Indeed, the relationship may sometimes be so contented that it seems to lack any forward thrust and ambition.

In the work sphere, obviously, this can spell ruin, so this relationship is not recommended for co-workers or business partners. But friendships and love relationships in this combination can flourish and stand the test of time. Love affairs tend to be sensual rather than passionate, with the desire to please and be pleased being paramount. Drawbacks may include a lack of awareness or elevated consciousness, and a tendency to get mired down in the physical plane. Aquarius II's may pull back from the relationship for two reasons: one, a fear of getting too close to their Taurus I partner, and two, a need to be involved in more complex, troubled, even hurtful romantic pairings. Taurus I's may tend to back off when this side of their partner is revealed, but if they are deeply in love, or unduly attached to whatever the relationship gives them, pain is inevitable.

Taurus I–Aquarius II marriages can work out well, featuring a comfortable home life and an easy give-and-take in daily interactions. Children can benefit in this context, influenced by the prevailing harmony of their environment to develop the calmer side of their personalities. These marriages can last for life. If they are either or both spouses' second or third marriage, they may turn out to be the final one, and the happiest of all.

ADVICE: *Beware of laziness. Set firm goals and deadlines. Look beyond the physical realm. Don't look for trouble, but don't be afraid of it, either.*

STRENGTHS: **RENEWING, OPTIMISTIC, FULFILLING**
WEAKNESSES: **OVEREXPECTANT, UNREALISTIC, HYPERCRITICAL**
BEST: **LATE MARRIAGE**
WORST: **YOUNG LOVE**

JUDY CARNE (4/27/39)
BURT REYNOLDS (2/11/36)

Carne, the zany "sock-it-to-me" girl on tv's *Laugh-In* (1968–73), married the handsome actor in 1963. For Reynolds, it was one of many difficult relationships with women. Following their 1966 divorce, Carne claimed Reynolds had been an abusive husband.

April 25–May 2
THE WEEK OF MANIFESTATION
TAURUS I

February 8–15
THE WEEK OF ACCEPTANCE
AQUARIUS III

Catching a Butterfly

This rather puzzling combination defies easy definition. One senses something rather old and comfortable about it, yet it is also primarily concerned with all that is new and fresh, vulnerable and exciting. It is an action-oriented relationship—these two are likely to find themselves much on the move together. Exactly what they are moving toward will be the great question, since neither these personalities nor this relationship are comfortable with self-analysis: is all that movement a going-toward or a running-from?

Because the relationship is most at home in areas new, when these two are romantic partners one would expect them to have been involved in an earlier marriage, or in a string of exciting but ultimately unfulfilling love affairs, from which they approach each other with a feeling of "This is it." Whether that feeling is reasonable or advisable is open to question: too high an expectation of a love relationship is likely to backfire. Aquarius III's do not commit easily, and certainly not from the start, and their roving eye and, in early adulthood, their frequent inability to settle down will probably make their relationship with a Taurus I just one of many. Taurus I's, on the other hand, tend to commit and stay committed. Breakups are extremely difficult for them. Indeed a Taurus I holding onto an Aquarius III may refuse to let go—a futile exercise, like trying to catch a butterfly in a net with a hole in it.

Still, later in life, a Taurus I–Aquarius III marriage or close friendship can work out as a solution or compromise after earlier relationships have failed. Much water will have gone under the bridge by this time, and realistic choices are more likely. Aquarius III's will have learned to be more accepting and Taurus I's less easily upset, and less sensitive to disapproval. A boss-employee or parent-child relationship can be problematic in this combination. Taurus I's have a habit of putting on airs and pretending to be something they are not, and Aquarius III's need to poke holes in such balloons; Taurus I's also want to be well thought of, and the kind of derision that Aquarius III's can dish out will make them feel belittled and insecure, since they tend to react emotionally and are not as tough as they seem.

ADVICE: *Accept relationships for what they are—no more, no less. Seek new approaches but don't neglect old methods. Beware of old, perhaps hidden, patterns.*

STRENGTHS: **EFFICIENT, TECHNICAL, JOYFUL**
WEAKNESSES: **REPRESSED, PAINFUL, NEGLECTFUL**
BEST: **WORK**
WORST: **PARENT-CHILD**

WM. RANDOLPH HEARST (4/29/1863)
PATTY HEARST (2/20/54)

Granddaughter of the infamous newpaper mogul, Hearst heiress Patty shocked the world when, following her 1974 kidnapping by the Symbionese Liberation Army, she assisted her captors in a bank robbery. She later told the FBI she had been brainwashed.

April 25–May 2
THE WEEK OF MANIFESTATION
TAURUS I

February 16–22
THE CUSP OF SENSITIVITY
AQUARIUS-PISCES CUSP

The Merciless God of Perfection

This relationship is likely to want to sharpen skills and hone them to perfection. Its technical orientation in many ways complements the use of a strong outer persona or shell by both Taurus I's and Aquarius-Pisces to protect their inner sensitivity against the world. By emphasizing outward perfection, they can hide their emotional problems, but at the same time they run the risk of cutting themselves off from their deeper self. The danger in this relationship is that such attitudes will be mutually reinforcing, creating an environment that neglects or denies personal development and spiritual growth in the name of worldly success.

Love is one area where deeper emotions may be stirred. Because both parties tend to hide their feelings behind a wall, they may empathically share the sorrow of a lost childhood, and the grief of having sacrificed their hearts to the merciless god of perfection. The relationship carries the responsibility of reawakening such inner energies, a process that may be painful but can ultimately lead to joyful, even ecstatic expressions. Marriages too are favored in this combination, at least externally, for Taurus I–Aquarius-Pisces spouses will probably create an up-to-date household, full of modern conveniences and appliances to make work easier. Activities involving computers and the Internet, as well as other electronic equipment, are particularly emphasized. Unfortunately, personal emotions may be seen as messy in this technically advanced domestic sphere, and therefore may be suppressed.

Family members and friends in this combination generally share mutually satisfying interests or hobbies. Such relationships are not overly emotional, and may lack nurturing qualities, but may also be pervaded with gentle feeling and with sensitive consideration for personal matters. This relationship's coolness under fire can be especially beneficial to the groups of which it is a part.

Work relationships are highly favored here. Taurus I's and Aquarius-Pisces can make excellent co-workers or executive partners, leading their organization to heights of efficiency and effectiveness.

ADVICE: *Don't neglect emotion or spirituality. Perfection may not be worth the price. Making errors and admitting them is only human. Relax.*

April 25–May 2

THE WEEK OF MANIFESTATION
TAURUS I

February 23–March 2

THE WEEK OF SPIRIT
PISCES I

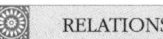
Young Blood

Focusing on childlike innocence and spontaneity, this combination features direct expression and openness. Both partners have a strong devotional streak that their relationship blesses and enhances, so that service to families, social and religious groups and business organizations comes quite naturally here. In providing such services, these two must be careful not to be taken advantage of, and should insist on getting something substantial in return. No matter what their situation, however, they will exude freshness, fun and charm—all of which is bound to make them an extremely popular pair.

Marriages and love here may take time to stabilize. Pisces I's may even push for open arrangements that leave them free to roam, or to relate to several partners, and the relationship may seem to be able to handle this; but Taurus I's need security, and in such an arrangement they may painfully realize how much they need their partner's exclusive attentions. On the upside, Pisces I's are sure to bring some zest and life to Taurus I's, who will return the favor with their protection and support. Hopefully, Taurus I's will be sufficiently charmed by Pisces I's so as to overlook their tendency to ignore the practicalities of life, and matters having to do with the material world.

The relationship's youthful qualities will find full expression in friendships and families. This pair's humor, fun and banter will lighten the mood of any group. It should be noted, however, that their energies may easily run out of hand, making them forget or ignore pressing responsibilities. Other friends and family members may look to these two when they want to have a good time, but ignore them when there is serious work to be done.

Obviously this combination can be well suited to sharing responsibilities on the job. The pair's childlike quality, however, can make them sometimes overly dutiful to authority, or even overawed by it, and other times too rebellious against it. The development of maturity will be crucial, and the team will come into its own after several years of seasoned experience and working together. As a partnership in freelance endeavors, it will be financially astute and responsive to clients' needs, but may lack assertiveness in demanding what it feels it is worth.

ADVICE: *Acknowledge mutual needs. Accept growing up as inevitable. Don't forget responsibilities. Force others to recognize your worth.*

JACK KLUGMAN (4/27/22)
TONY RANDALL (2/26/20)

The creative interdependency of these comic actors, who played personality-opposites Oscar Madison and Felix Unger, made *The Odd Couple* one of tv's most popular and durable shows.

***Also:* Rowland Evans, Jr. & Robert Novak** (journalist team).

April 25–May 2

THE WEEK OF MANIFESTATION
TAURUS I

March 3–10

THE WEEK OF THE LONER
PISCES II

Closer Social Contact

Pisces II's have a great deal to learn from this relationship, which focuses on social interaction and can bring them from an isolated position into closer contact with their fellow human beings. Taurus I's will also benefit here, deepening their social skills and understanding people better, rather than just using them to implement their ideas. As a team, this duo will have a mutually beneficial connection with clubs, organizations and other social groups.

Pisces II's and Taurus I's may get along well enough in love, friendships and marriages but will find greatest fulfillment in their interactions with others, usually friends. The relationship is likely to find itself at the center of one or more groups of friends, associates or onlookers who are anxious to be associated with it. Such magnetic powers speak well for the harmony between these partners, but even more for the synergy they generate. Arranging finances and logistics for dinners, parties, trips and visits to clubs or theaters are particular specialties.

In the family, the relationship may occasion jealousy and anger from others who see it as a mutual-admiration society taking energy away from the group, and demanding too much attention. If these two are siblings, the offended family member may be a parent, another sibling or an uncle, aunt or cousin who resents the Taurus I–Pisces II relationship for taking the spotlight away from them.

Working relationships between these two may be weaker on the technical and practical side and stronger on humor, information-gathering and communication. Often the life of an office party, this matchup also lightens the load and greases the wheels on the job. Of course things can get too pleasurable in the middle of a project—this pair may sometimes find themselves rebuked and ordered to get back to work so that production quotas or deadlines can be met.

ADVICE: *Don't neglect individual talents or self-expression. Concentrate more on self-improvement. Beware of arousing negative emotions.*

MARY WOLLSTONECRAFT (4/27/1759)
WILLIAM GODWIN (3/3/1756)

Godwin was a romantic philosopher and writer. Wollstonecraft, an early radical feminist, wrote *Vindication of the Rights of Women* (1792). Only months after their marriage in 1797, Wollstonecraft died in childbirth. Their daughter was Mary Shelley, author of *Frankenstein* and wife of poet Percy Bysshe Shelley.

***Also:* Jill Clayburgh & David Rabe** (married; actress/playwright).

BIANCA JAGGER (5/2/45)
MICHAEL CAINE (3/14/33)

Long after her celebrated marriage to Rolling Stones' Mick Jagger, Bianca had a well-publicized affair with British actor Caine, who led a swinging lifestyle before marrying a beauty queen and settling down. *Also:* **Jerome Leiber & Michael Stoller** (songwriting team).

April 25–May 2
THE WEEK OF MANIFESTATION
TAURUS I

March 11–18
THE WEEK OF DANCERS & DREAMERS
PISCES III

A Steady Diet of Kudos

Energies here will focus on who will be the star. No matter what the outcome, however, this charismatic couple is likely to cut quite a swath in any society and should be aware that attention will tend to follow them wherever they go. They must take care, then, as to what they let others see. Open conflict is not unlikely here, and needs to be kept in check. In some ways these two can even bring out the worst in each other, since any natural empathy or sympathy they have for others tends to fall by the wayside in their frolics.

Pisces III's are definitely drawn to the spotlight, and Taurus I's will not tolerate being shoved out of it for long themselves. As a result, their combination is apt to create a kind of unattractive competitiveness between them, which can lead to all sorts of conflicts if it runs out of control. Perhaps the key here is that the partners need to appreciate each other's talents, regularly supplying the kudos necessary to support each other's egos. Considering the feelings of other people should also be a priority. Another possible solution appears when the relationship itself attracts attention and is admired as an entity in itself, thus satisfying its partners' pride.

Marriage and love here will demand that the partners take an equal interest in each other: perhaps Pisces III's will admire Taurus I's for their practical abilities, Taurus I's Pisces III's for their imaginations. Being ignored or neglected is the worst punishment that can be dished out here, and unfortunately these two often use neglect as a weapon in their struggles with one another. Should the necessary attention be paid, however, nothing short of outright rejection or infidelity is likely to be powerful enough to split up the relationship.

In work and in friendship, Taurus I's and Pisces III's may form a mutual-admiration society. The danger here is that the partners may be so satisfied with the attention they receive from each other that they turn their back on both their own self-development and on other co-workers and friends. In family relationships, especially parent-child combinations, parents of either sign can project their own frustrated dreams and desires on their children, resulting in a big push to make them stars.

ADVICE: *Stop the competition. Work on self-development. Don't ignore others. Being admired isn't always productive. Eliminating ego needs leaves you freer.*

PHIL MAHRE (5/10/57)
STEVE MAHRE (5/10/57)

The Mahre twins are championship skiers who won the gold and silver medals in the men's slalom at the '84 Olympics. Phil also won 3 successive overall World Cup titles between 1981–83.

May 3–10
THE WEEK OF THE TEACHER
TAURUS II

May 3–10
THE WEEK OF THE TEACHER
TAURUS II

A Real Education

Frequent themes here, not surprisingly, will be learning and education. Since Taurus II's are not only good teachers but good students, this relationship may place one of the partners in the former role and the other in the latter. These roles may quickly reverse: Taurus II parents, aunts or uncles may see themselves as mentors to a Taurus II child until one day it becomes obvious that they are ones who are actually learning most in this relationship. These two can be expected to share an enthusiasm for physical activities as well as for mental ones.

Love relationships and friendships between these two may not be successful. Taurus II's are usually drawn to those unlike themselves, taking a special (but not exclusive) interest in anyone they consider disadvantaged; they are likely to be bored with someone resembling them, such as another Taurus II. Should they proceed to marry, the results can be quite productive: nurturing qualities are high here, favoring not only children but pets and gardening, and the marriage is also likely to include a deep interest in intellectual, aesthetic and creative activities (notably dance and music). But it is also likely to have a critical, at times irritating tone. Domestic responsibilities may have to be carefully shared and assigned, for Taurus II's are rarely much interested in housework. And although they are loving to their offspring, their highly moral side is accentuated here, resulting at times in overly strict rules and attitudes that may inadvertently inculcate guilt and shame in young ones. The frictions of a marriage like this one can escalate into open warfare, and once such conflicts erupt, their aftermath may trouble the landscape of the relationship for weeks or even months. There is, however, an arena in which these aggressive feelings can often be worked out: the bedroom. Both partners are equally frank and open in their approach to sex. Taurus II entrepreneurial and organizational skills can make this relationship indispensable to a business or family project. Once such a project is finished, however, it should not be assumed that these two efficient individuals can continue to work together harmoniously.

ADVICE: *Ease up in your criticism. Teaching and learning are two sides of the same coin. Don't point the blame. Be ethical and moral but not overly so. Lessen tensions.*

May 3–10

THE WEEK OF THE TEACHER
TAURUS II

May 11–18

THE WEEK OF THE NATURAL
TAURUS III

Crazy Love

RELATIONSHIPS

STRENGTHS: **SYMPATHETIC, EXCITING, FREE**

WEAKNESSES: **GUILTY, CRITICAL, HURT**

BEST: **LOVE**

WORST: **FAMILY**

These two partners carry strong earth energy (Taurus is an earth sign), signifying the world of sensation, practicality and groundedness. Yet their relationship is characterized by feelings. Together, they are apt to feel and express a depth and a range of emotion that may affect them profoundly. The gamut of feelings that can emerge here, in fact, may even confuse them, particularly when a more negative part of the spectrum, such as competitiveness or jealousy, is dominant. Luckily, this darker, more brooding aspect is offset by this pair's ability to have fun and to enjoy all forms of entertainment. Charm is never lacking here, and magnetism runs high.

The most successful friendships and family relationships (especially between siblings) in this combination are those in which mature attitudes prevail and thoughtfulness and consideration are not considered antithetical to pleasure. While these two are apt to have a great deal of fun together, they may invite guilt if they have come to feel they have escaped responsibilities by dumping them elsewhere.

In love affairs, the spontaneous and uninhibited aspects of the Taurus III character often bring out the similar, more natural side of Taurus II's, resulting in an often riotous or zany relationship that can be not only great fun but also emotionally meaningful, while it lasts. The extreme need of Taurus III's for freedom and independence is well matched by Taurus II's refusal to place heavy demands on them, while Taurus II's for their part will appreciate being left alone and not fussed over. Marriages may be less successful, due to a lack of stabilizing factors. Yet the combination is deeply sympathetic and compassionate, leaving its partners free to express deep emotion and discuss their differences openly, meeting acceptance rather than condemnation. Physically, this can be a satisfying, natural and sensuous partnership.

Working relationships between these two can work out well, particularly with a Taurus II boss who is comfortable when employees have a good time in the workplace, and who fulfills obligations because of a free wish to do so, rather than a requirement. Taurus III's are extremely comfortable with such attitudes.

ADVICE: *Try to balance enthusiastic and critical attitudes. Have fun, but take responsibility daily. Continue to explore emotional areas.*

RICHARD D'OYLY CARTE (5/3/1844)
ARTHUR S. SULLIVAN (5/13/1842)

D'Oyly Carte was the theatrical impresario who brought Gilbert and Sullivan's operettas to the English stage. He organized their opera company and in 1885 built the Savoy Theatre, which housed their productions exclusively. *Also:* **Randy Travis & George Strait** (country music rivals).

May 3–10

THE WEEK OF THE TEACHER
TAURUS II

May 19–24

THE CUSP OF ENERGY
TAURUS-GEMINI CUSP

Earning the Right to Express

RELATIONSHIPS

STRENGTHS: **APPRECIATIVE, ADMIRING, EASY GOING**

WEAKNESSES: **INSECURE, DISRUPTIVE, SUSPICIOUS**

BEST: **FRIENDSHIP**

WORST: **SIBLING**

Although this relationship focuses on being natural and relaxed, its underlying mood is less free and easy than one would expect. In fact, the right to express oneself openly in this pairing must be earned rather than taken for granted. Critical and demanding attitudes may prevail unless given a periodic airing, and irritations and resentments, if ignored or suppressed, can surface in unpleasant and unexpected ways. One partner's condemnation of the other's irresponsibility can be a frequent occurrence here. Similarly, a suspicion of ostentation and ego usually requires these two to be more muted in their behavior. It isn't necessarily that certain behavior invariably causes shame or blame, but rather that the relationship calls for a kind of dignity.

In love and marriage, Taurus-Geminis' high-strung and frenetic pace is unlikely to provide the sense of security that Taurus II's need. Particularly in marriage, the efforts of the Taurus II to bring stability to the relationship can be undercut by the Taurus-Gemini's inability to be tied down to a single partner. On the other hand, especially in love affairs, the frank and critical attitudes of Taurus II's can arouse quite a bit of insecurity in a Taurus-Gemini who may be hopelessly in love.

Friendships between these two are likely to be the best manifestation of this combination. A failed marriage or love affair may quite possibly settle into a friendship, perhaps suggesting that it would have been better this way from the start. An air of appreciation, admiration and mutual acceptance is likely to prevail here.

Family relationships, particularly father-daughter or mother-son, can be stormy but rewarding. The parent and child usually like each other, but find it difficult to get close; they even keep at a certain physical distance from each other, avoiding overt displays of affection, although affection is actually a strong need here, unfortunately often an elusive and frustrating one. Siblings with this matchup are likely to generate conflicting energies that will disrupt daily family life. Some types of work arrangement in this combination can work out well. Boss-employee relationships tend to be successful if Taurus II's are at the helm.

ADVICE: *Be more open about feelings. Needs can be discussed even if they are not expressed. Build respect and cultivate affection. Beware of double standards.*

JIMMY STEWART (5/20/08)
GARY COOPER (5/7/01)

Cooper's terminal cancer illness was accidentally revealed by close personal friend Stewart at the 1961 Academy Awards ceremonies, during which Cooper was presented with an honorary Oscar. *Also:* **George Clooney & Rosemary Clooney** (nephew/aunt; actor/singer); **Golda Meir & Moshe Dayan** (Israeli prime minister/defense minister); **Jean Henri Dunant & Frederic Passy** (first Nobel Peace Prize).

STRENGTHS: **MAGNETIC, PRODUCTIVE, EXCITING**

WEAKNESSES: **REBELLIOUS, JUDGMENTAL, DEMEANING**

BEST: **WORK**

WORST: **MARRIAGE**

DON AMECHE (5/31/08)
ALICE FAYE (5/5/15)

Ameche, whose career spanned 70 years, was often cast opposite actress Faye as the debonair leading man. Faye typically played the jilted woman who got her man—often Ameche—in the end. ***Also:* Wm. Henry Vanderbilt & Cornelius Vanderbilt** (son/father; railroad magnates, financiers).

May 3–10
THE WEEK OF THE TEACHER
TAURUS II

May 25–June 2
THE WEEK OF FREEDOM
GEMINI I

Push Me, Pull You

This volatile relationship is alternately magnetic and rebellious: its partners are drawn to each other yet repelled at the same time. Some form of wildness is unleashed as soon as they come too close, forcing a kind of distancing to achieve equilibrium again. Judgmental attitudes are often used to achieve this goal. As a result, true closeness is elusive here and may not exist at all except in brief moments.

When these two become involved, the didactic, even pedantic tone of Taurus II's often comes out, making Gemini I's recoil, rebel and flee. They can be attracted, though, by their similar views on justice and morality, and may do best together when fighting side by side for the same cause.

In love affairs, Gemini I free-spiritedness may at first be very attractive to a Taurus II but may eventually be perceived as wild ways that must be controlled or rejected. Taurus II's ultimately demand a devotion and a stability that Gemini I's are usually unable to give. Furthermore, although Gemini I's are often seductive and physically exciting individuals, when rejected by a Taurus II they may come unglued, indulging in undignified and in extreme cases pitiful behavior. Both marriages and friendships have the best chance of success when directed outward to shared activities. The biggest problem here is usually that Taurus II's will have little patience with Gemini I addictions, and will begin looking for the exit as soon as they first surface.

In family and working relationships (the latter being more productive), Taurus II parents and bosses are likely to be much more permissive toward Gemini I children and employees than vice versa. As parents, however, both of these personalities will periodically direct condemning moral attitudes at their children, which may cause bewilderment, since the overall approach is usually fairly easy. As for the offspring or employees, again of either of these weeks of the year, they are likely to break into rebellion at the first hint of tyrannical or unfair treatment, laying the responsibility on the authority figure to explain him- or herself and to avoid sending mixed signals, laying on guilt trips or indulging in other forms of ambivalent behavior.

ADVICE: *Never compromise your own or another's dignity. Examine your feelings. Be honest. Don't be afraid of rejection. Don't take too much for granted.*

STRENGTHS: **INVOLVED, INFLUENCING, ADAPTABLE**

WEAKNESSES: **MERGING, MESSY, CHAOTIC**

BEST: **MARRIAGE**

WORST: **WORK**

FRANK LLOYD WRIGHT (6/8/1867)
ANNE BAXTER (5/7/23)

Screen actress Baxter is the granddaughter of famed architect Wright. Raised in upscale Bronxville, NY, and privately educated before she began acting at age 13, she seems a direct contrast to Wright, whose life was marked by scandalous affairs. ***Also:* Archibald MacLeish & Bruce Dern** (uncle/nephew; poet-playwright/actor).

May 3–10
THE WEEK OF THE TEACHER
TAURUS II

June 3–10
THE WEEK OF NEW LANGUAGE
GEMINI II

Mountain Updrafts

This relationship can be active, versatile, many-sided and emotionally complex. Energy is the focus here, ebbing and flowing in fierce countercurrents and swirls of intensity. Earth and air energies, betokening sensation and thought, are dramatic, like mountain updrafts, with immediate reactions to external stimuli coalescing powerfully with the later, more objective examination of these reactions. These two individuals have marked effects on each other, influencing the most important areas of each other's lives—even without necessarily spending much clock time together, or even having that much to do with each other for long periods.

Even in the closest relationships in this combination, like love, friendship and marriage (which in some cases here overlap or are indistinguishable), these two sometimes spend more time with a third or fourth party known to both of them than they do with each other. The more destructive, dark-side attractions of Gemini II's and the Taurus II sympathy for the underdog and for the disadvantaged often play a complicating part here. Such triangles and quartets are likely to be as important and at least as strong as the Taurus II–Gemini II relationship itself. In situations like these, sharing thoughts and feelings, communicating honestly and building organizations (whether social, financial, artistic or athletic) are ever-present issues—as are dealing with jealousy, competitiveness, covetousness and resentment. The relationship will have to have the flexibility to adapt psychologically and physically to the larger group of which it forms a part. Marriages that go through such fire together and emerge intact often last for life.

Working relationships between these two are unlikely to gel, since both partners operate better on their own, with full freedom of movement and above all the right to make their own decisions. In the family, where members are bound together willy-nilly, many years will be needed for these two to adapt to each other. Gemini II intolerance and Taurus II stubbornness may be a constant source of grievances.

ADVICE: *Don't lose sight of what's most important. Keep your head together. Intense feeling is no guarantee of permanence—on the contrary.*

May 3–10

THE WEEK OF THE TEACHER
TAURUS II

A Truth Test

June 11–18

THE WEEK OF THE SEEKER
GEMINI III

RELATIONSHIPS	

STRENGTHS: **INDEPENDENT, ADVENTURESOME, NONCLAIMING**

WEAKNESSES: **IRRESPONSIBLE, ELUSIVE, UNFULFILLING**

BEST: **LOVE AFFAIR**

WORST: **FAMILY**

ROBERT LA FOLLETTE (6/14/1855)
PHILIP LA FOLLETTE (5/8/1897)

Philip, a 2-term Wisconsin governor, was responsible for the nation's first unemployment legislation. His father, Robert, led the progressive movement in the US and was a Wisconsin representative, senator and governor before running for president in 1924.

The focus of this relationship is independence, a need that Gemini III's must learn to express to a Taurus II partner and must teach and bring out in the Taurus II as well. Unfortunately, Taurus II's have a demanding side and may react to the Gemini III's need to seek out and follow other interests with an unprecedented degree of anger and possessiveness. The relationship may in fact become a good testing ground for the development of accepting and nonclaiming attitudes, a kind of truth test that both partners will eventually have to take.

In career, family and marriage, Gemini III's have problems binding themselves to a group. Taurus II's, who are seriously involved in such matters, will find it difficult to work with these elusive partners. An alternative, however, especially if children are not involved, is for the Taurus II to join the Gemini III in a relationship based on adventure, travel and other forms of investigation, exploration and learning. Here the theme of independence can refer to the relationship itself, rather than to its two members. Another possibility is for the Gemini III to function within a Taurus II–led company or organization as a financially astute free agent or adviser who has a lot of latitude in determining his or her schedule and deciding how responsibilities are to be fulfilled.

Love relationships here are likely to be exciting but ultimately unfulfilling, especially if of the conventional sort. But Gemini III's who have felt a need for variety in an already established relationship may seek out a more physical and attractive Taurus II with whom to have a fling, or even a long-standing affair. In secret relationships like these, Taurus II's may come to have quite protective feelings toward Gemini III's, convinced that they can give them the love, understanding and passion that they are denied in their primary relationship.

Highly independent friendships with few responsibilities can be successful here. The sharing of challenging activities can push the capabilities of both partners to the limit.

ADVICE: *Be as honest as you can. Commit to a single course of action occasionally. Be adventuresome but not foolhardy. Realize your common interest.*

May 3–10

THE WEEK OF THE TEACHER
TAURUS II

White Noise

June 19–24

THE CUSP OF MAGIC
GEMINI-CANCER CUSP

RELATIONSHIPS	

STRENGTHS: **FREE, OBJECTIVE, HONEST**

WEAKNESSES: **UNINVOLVED, UNSYMPATHETIC, UNCONNECTED**

BEST: **FRIENDSHIP**

WORST: **PARENT-CHILD**

MARY McCARTHY (6/21/12)
EDMUND WILSON (5/8/1895)

Wilson was a preeminent literary, political and social critic. After marrying book reviewer McCarthy, he encouraged her to apply her wit and analytic powers to fiction. She became a bestselling novelist.

***Also:* Gary Cooper & Lou Gehrig** (film portrayal of baseball star); **Alice Faye & Phil Harris** (married; performers); **Nancy & Beaumont Newhall** (married; photohistorian/photographer).

The emotional channels between these two are often clogged with static and missed connections. One can expect communication problems to abound between them. In fact they sometimes do better by not talking at all, abiding by each other in silence. A setup like this could well suit these two, both of whom hold privacy very dear. The inability to connect more meaningfully has an unfortunate side effect, however: the pair tend to leave a string of unfinished projects behind them.

Irritating elements abound in this relationship, especially in the area of romance. Taurus II's are much too matter-of-fact about physical matters to satisfy the Gemini-Cancer need for sensitivity and privacy. Furthermore, they are little interested in providing the kind of sympathy and gentle understanding that Gemini-Cancers require, regarding it not just as a nuisance but as a kind of soft coddling of which they don't really approve. Love affairs and marriages are likely to be problematic between these two. Friendships may succeed if they grant the maximum amount of freedom to each partner. But the question then becomes: is there anything binding these two together, anything to make a relationship possible or desirable at all? Chances are best if a shared pursuit can be found, one that is practical and down-to-earth yet that does not require daily attention (unlike gardening or caring for pets). Often an interest in art, movies, music or sports may fit the bill well.

Family relationships here are complex. Gemini-Cancer parents are capable of providing secure and loving homes for Taurus II children, who, however, may find this kind of context exactly what they dislike. Taurus II children are difficult to get close to emotionally, particularly when growing up. On the other hand, Taurus II parents of Gemini-Cancer children are likely to give them so much latitude (or, as the Taurus II's see it, so much responsibility) that they come to resent it, recalling it later in life as neglect or disinterest. As co-workers in a company or freelance project, these two may meet with a certain amount of success, but eventually their different emotional and ethical orientations may prove divisive.

ADVICE: *Find a common basis for sharing. Learn to compromise and to empathize. See the other person's point of view. Speak openly.*

STRENGTHS: **ORIGINAL, NURTURING, PROTECTIVE**

WEAKNESSES: **JEALOUS, UNCOMMUNICATIVE, REJECTING**

BEST: **MARRIAGE**

WORST: **WORK**

JEAN ACKER (6/27/1893)
RUDOLPH VALENTINO (5/6/1895)

Legendary lover and silent-screen star Valentino married actress Jean Acker in 1919. The first of his long string of relationships, the marriage was never consummated; on their wedding night, Acker locked him out of their bridal suite.

May 3–10
THE WEEK OF THE TEACHER
TAURUS II

June 25–July 2
THE WEEK OF THE EMPATH
CANCER I

Fertile Ground

Traditional rules of conduct will never govern this relationship, which will want to develop its own value system. In some ways this will give it a great deal of integrity. Indeed, the combination is likely to have an originality and an honorableness that both its partners value and even idealize, helping to make it quite long-lasting.

Both marriages and love affairs in this combination are apt to flourish. An appreciation is felt here for out-of-the-way people, places and things, resulting, for example, in unusual objects decorating the living space, and in friendships with other couples who elsewhere are not always appreciated or understood. The Taurus II need to nurture and protect those whom the world has treated badly surfaces in this relationship. The Cancer I, meanwhile, will enjoy trying to make the Taurus II's life more comfortable and secure, especially through the energy invested in the home base. Given this relationship's full palette of emotional expression, sympathy, kindness, love and understanding will probably find fertile ground here.

Good feelings are likely to dominate in friendships of this combination, and a common appreciation of hidden byways of life, whether in the realms of psychology, art and music, or nature, may become the basis for a strong bond. Care will have to be taken in the emotional sphere, however, for jealousy and feelings of rejection are likely to appear periodically, particularly where attentions to a third party are concerned. In the family, parents, grandparents, aunts and uncles of either sign tend to have highly protective relationships with children of the other sign. Should these close bonds overlap with a period of great stress and need in the lives of one of the partners, they will prove highly comforting. Working relationships here are less strongly recommended, since Taurus II's may need more independence than their more organizationally oriented Cancer I partners want to countenance. Furthermore, differing views on the handling of finances and the structuring of business, coupled with occasional arguments and breakdowns in communication, may make collaboration difficult.

ADVICE: *Try to discuss differences without arguing. Ordinary matters need your attention too. Don't reject conservative views out of hand. Stay open.*

STRENGTHS: **COMMUNICATIVE, PASSIONATE, EDUCATIONAL**

WEAKNESSES: **EXCLUSIVE, ENSLAVED, DESTRUCTIVE**

BEST: **LOVE**

WORST: **FAMILY**

JAKE LAMOTTA (7/10/21)
SUGAR RAY ROBINSON (5/3/21)

These boxers began their rivalry during 1942–43, when the classy Robinson beat street-brawler LaMotta in 2 out of 3 outings. Robinson officially beat LaMotta for the middleweight boxing crown in 1951.

Also: Pete Seeger & Ruth Crawford Seeger (son/mother; folksinger/composer).

May 3–10
THE WEEK OF THE TEACHER
TAURUS II

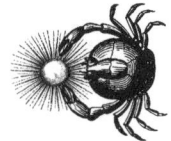

July 3–10
THE WEEK OF THE UNCONVENTIONAL
CANCER II

Mutual Fascination

The thrust of this relationship may be breaking through barriers to communication and opening up common avenues of expression. There may be an intense curiosity in uncovering hidden and perhaps unappreciated aspects of the other partner—in coming close, studying, learning, and above all understanding. Both of these people have an unusually strong need to express their points of view; here is a relationship geared specifically to just that. Taurus II's have much to teach Cancer II's, but also much to learn from them about how to be oneself without compromising one's individuality in the face of society's pressures, or enslaving oneself to the demands of work, school or family. Indeed pride in individuality may emerge as an important theme here.

Taurus II–Cancer II love affairs can be deep and passionate. Taurus II's have a deep weakness for unconventional Cancer II's and can give themselves here without reservation. They will encourage Cancer II's to reveal their more hidden or unconventional side within the safety of this relationship. Cancer II's may see Taurus II's as a bit staid or even dull in certain respects but will appreciate their enthusiasm for learning about unusual subjects and activities. They could well teach Taurus II's how to lighten up and laugh, especially by looking at the humor in the bizarre, and they will also enjoy Taurus II stability and security. In all these ways the relationship might be ideal for both partners.

Friendships between these two are likely to be exclusive affairs, oriented more inward, toward the partners themselves, than outward, as a unit interacting with others. Hours may be spent together in mutually fascinated discussion of each other's different ways of being, and of not only daily experiences but occasionally miraculous or even psychic ones. A danger exists here of becoming isolated and cut off from the world. For similar reasons, working and family relationships in this combination are likely to work against the good of the group; this pair's preoccupation with private matters will not be conducive to success.

ADVICE: *Beware of destructive and antisocial tendencies. Maintain objectivity. If swept away, remember you also have to come back. Follow both head and heart.*

May 3–10

THE WEEK OF THE TEACHER
TAURUS II

July 11–18

THE WEEK OF THE PERSUADER
CANCER III

Expansive Gestures

STRENGTHS: **MAGNANIMOUS, INITIATORY, OPTIMISTIC**

WEAKNESSES: **NAIVE, PUSHY, ONE-TRACK**

BEST: **WORK**

WORST: **LOVE**

GINGER ROGERS (7/16/11)
FRED ASTAIRE (5/10/1899)

Grand projects, far-reaching ideas and expansive gestures are the stuff of this relationship. Stinginess and pettiness are seen as downers here and are despised; the relationship galvanizes the more magnanimous side of both these personalities. With each other, they are more likely to give than to share, and as a unit relating to others they are likely to take the generous attitude that money given is a gift, while money paid back has been redefined as a loan. These two can be expected to be found working together toward a greater goal and in areas of social conscience.

Unconditional giving can have its drawbacks, however, particularly if it puts the pair at the mercy of spongers. As a marriage or friendship, in fact, this relationship will probably have to become a bit tougher in its dealing with the outside world if it is to avoid being taken advantage of, for even this giving couple will reach their limits sooner or later. There is also a pronounced tendency to bring other people into the relationship, a habit of openness to others that may often threaten the primary bond itself.

Taurus II–Cancer III love affairs may be passionate at first, but in romance Cancer III's are rarely able to follow their heart, since they have probably already given it to their cause or profession. Acute differences in needs and wants may also make this relationship difficult in the long term: Cancer III's may come to resent the didactic streak in Taurus II's, while Taurus II's may become critical of Cancer III ambition.

At work, these two make a powerful team, particularly as business partners or co-workers engaged in getting new projects off the ground. They are less successful as a boss-employee pair. Projects involving long-distance transportation, mammoth machinery (real, structural or on paper) or high-flying corporations are especially favored. In the family, this pair is likely to push too hard and too fast. Ambitious attitudes are likely to lead the family to overextend itself, especially in the financial sphere, with disastrous results.

Astaire and Rogers will always be remembered as the grandest dance team ever to grace the Hollywood screen. ***Also:*** **Oscar Hammerstein & Oscar Hammerstein II** (grandfather/grandson; impresario/composer); **Gary Cooper & Lupe Velez** (tragic affair; actors); **Pete Seeger & Woody Guthrie** (folksingers); **John Brown & Henry David Thoreau** (anti-slavery advocates).

ADVICE: *One step at a time. First things first. Some gifts imply expectations; love should not be one of them. Beware of parasites.*

May 3–10

THE WEEK OF THE TEACHER
TAURUS II

July 19–25

THE CUSP OF OSCILLATION
CANCER-LEO CUSP

Bettering Past Records

STRENGTHS: **ASPIRING, THOUGHTFUL, PRODUCTIVE**

WEAKNESSES: **UNSTABLE, UNREALISTIC, DISASTROUS**

BEST: **MARRIAGE**

WORST: **PARENT-CHILD**

ERNEST HEMINGWAY (7/21/1899)
GARY COOPER (5/7/01)

Although Taurus II's are governed by the earth element (Taurus is an earth sign) and Cancer-Leos by water and fire (Cancer is a water sign, Leo is fire), it is the fourth element, air (symbolizing thought), that rules this relationship. Seeking excitement and adventure, or perhaps trying to better past records or aspiring toward philosophical or spiritual goals, all come naturally here. Stability can be a problem, but financial success in several endeavors, if handled wisely over time, can often yield the necessary support.

Friendships and love relationships can thrive here so long as they not only guarantee their partners' freedom of thought and action but also direct the pair as an independent unit with shared aspirations. What is ultimately of greatest importance in the relationship is for Taurus II's its educational value, for Cancer-Leos the thrill of achievement. Planning endeavors, discussing their merits, making choices and, after the fact, evaluating and reorganizing for new onslaughts are specialties of this combination. The hard-headed, practical side of the Taurus II will coalesce with the intuitive and feeling sides of the Cancer-Leo, synergistically producing mental and communicative energy. Problems can arise, however, if too much intellectualization, ideation or fantasy about an experience supplants the experience itself.

Marriages in this combination can be highly successful, full of interesting and challenging activities. They thrive on problems, although care should be taken not to create unnecessary ones, or to fall into not completely involuntary patterns of cycles of disaster and salvation. These two may or may not include their children in their activities, but in either case may neglect a child's deep need for security.

Sibling relationships in this combination are apt to be competitive, but productively so, inspiring the partners to new achievements. Parent-child relationships, however, may suffer from conflicting energies and interests. The success of working relationships will depend on whether temperamental differences can be reconciled and negative emotions controlled or constructively redirected.

Tall, silent and intense, leading man Cooper played the archetypical Hemingway character in 2 of the novelist's movies, *A Farewell to Arms* (1932) and *For Whom the Bell Tolls* (1943). ***Also:*** **Sugar Ray Robinson & Gene Fullmer** (boxing rivals).

ADVICE: *Don't get carried away. Try to stay realistic. Stability will help you achieve your goals. Guard against negative expectations.*

CARL JUNG (7/26/1875)
SIGMUND FREUD (5/6/1856)

These psychoanalysts were close collaborators until they formally broke in 1912 from a sharp disagreement on theory. Jung, who emphasized symbolism, felt Freud relied too much on the sexual basis of neurosis. **Also: Gary Cooper & Clara Bow** (affair); **Alice Faye & Rudy Vallee** (chorus girl/singer in his band); **Thomas Huxley & Aldous Huxley** (grandfather/grandson; biologist/writer).

May 3–10
THE WEEK OF THE TEACHER
TAURUS II

July 26–August 2
THE WEEK OF AUTHORITY
LEO I

Told You So

This relationship often centers around using existing knowledge to look toward and predict the future. Even when these partners have strong hunches about how things will turn out, they inevitably look to some source to back up what they think. The relationship's conflicts and arguments, then, are likely to focus on who is right, who was right the last time, and who will be right in the future. Should both partners be able to agree on an unimpeachable source of authority, they are likely to wield it as a club against other individuals and couples.

Taurus II–Leo I marriages can grow out of friendships, love affairs, or both. The point is that moving toward marriage is often an evolutionary process for these two and can conceivably stop at any point along the way. Not infrequently, a school or other institution of learning is their first meeting ground—they may well be two students, two teachers, or a teacher-student pair. In this context, arguments and disagreements over knowledge and information are virtually inevitable between them, with one challenging the other to prove the reliability of a source or reference, say. The satisfaction of the I-told-you-so attitude will also appear more innocuously in playful or humorous bets over how an event will turn out.

As friends, Taurus II's and Leo I's are magnetically attracted to each other, especially when of the same sex. Friendships here are likely to be close. Yet there is also usually some big difference between these two, perhaps of stature, background or ideology, that belies or obscures their empathic bond, so that other people may mistakenly assume they are not at all intimate. A pet peeve here is when others make prejudicial assumptions and statements, particularly of a racist or sexist nature. When this button is pushed, the pair are likely to withdraw in distaste, or else go quickly into the attack mode. Family and working relationships in this combination often manifest a lot of friction, with fighting over who is right and condemnatory finger-pointing over who is wrong. Struggles over which person is to be the boss or authority figure are bound to be severe.

ADVICE: *Agree not to disagree too openly—others may not like watching you fight. Be tolerant and open to new ideas. Give up know-it-all attitudes.*

SYLVIA SIDNEY (8/8/10)
LUTHER ADLER (5/4/03)

As screen performers, Adler was powerful and versatile, while Sidney, with her trademark sad eyes and trembling lips, often played the downtrodden working-class girl. They were married from 1938–47. **Also: Admiral Peary & Matthew Henson** (North Pole explorers); **Keith Haring & Andy Warhol** (NY Pop Artists) **Bono Vox & Dave Evans** (bandmembers, U2).

May 3–10
THE WEEK OF THE TEACHER
TAURUS II

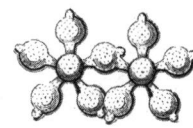

August 3–10
THE WEEK OF BALANCED STRENGTH
LEO II

Dedicated Devotion

Because these two are square to each other in the zodiac (90° apart), conventional astrology predicts frictions, problems and conflict between them, and indeed both of these fixed signs—Taurus, an earth sign, and Leo, a fire sign—are opinionated and stubborn. Actually, however, the Taurus II and Leo II personalities blend exceedingly well: both are no-nonsense individuals, with a heartfelt empathy for all less fortunate than they. Their relationship also reinforces this latter characteristic, emphasizing devotion and dedication, and softens the former one, allowing these two to be more inspirational and romantic than they usually are.

Magic is an important theme here: loves and friendships share a gentle, sensuous quality with a strong romantic overlay. These two may wander hand-in-hand through many an enchanted land, but both partners are responsible enough to live up to their part of the deal, and they don't see trustworthiness and reliability as antithetical to love—on the contrary, in fact, these qualities generate good feelings, actually contributing to romance. The relationship has a certain pride in itself, then, which appears to others as a kind of glow radiating in its partners' shy smiles.

Marriages are less strongly recommended, for much of the relationship's enchantment is dissipated in the sometimes humdrum continuity of everyday life. The partners may later express regret that they tried to solidify and give social meaning or structure to a combination once so natural and unassuming. Unfortunately, Taurus II's and Leo II's are usually unable to give a marriage the same kind of incandescence that characterized their love affair, no matter how hard they try.

Family relationships are likely to be affectionate and supportive, particularly between siblings of the same sex. Occasional explosions and stubborn confrontations may be inevitable, but they clear the air, and indicate the partners' honesty. A working relationship may be a bit mundane for these two unless it is devoted to a social cause, or to aiding the disenfranchised, in which case they would make an inspired and unusually successful team.

ADVICE: *Romance isn't always necessary. Learn how to work together effectively on an everyday basis. Explore imaginative endeavors.*

May 3–10

THE WEEK OF THE TEACHER
TAURUS II

August 11–18

THE WEEK OF LEADERSHIP
LEO III

A Difference in Attitude

 RELATIONSHIPS

STRENGTHS: **SUPPORTIVE,
WARM, INTENSE**

WEAKNESSES: **DISAPPOINTING,
UNFAIR, JUDGMENTAL**

BEST: **LOVE**

WORST: **WORK**

S truggles for power will tend to surface in this relationship. The reason behind many of these confrontations may be found in a difference in attitude: Leo III's are born leaders to whom achieving results and driving toward well-defined goals matter deeply, and although honor can be important to them, it is most often only as an expression of their inflated egos. Taurus II's, on the other hand, care about motives and ultimately about right and wrong. Thus Taurus II morality (how one gets somewhere counts) conflicts with Leo III aggressiveness (the fact that one gets somewhere counts). Particularly at work and in the family, these contradictory viewpoints can cause severe problems. Should these two be able to find a way to work together, however, they can have a considerable hand in shaping the future, perhaps becoming the authorities at the forefront of a field of endeavor.

Friendships and love affairs have a possibility of success—they are kinds of relationship in which this combination is likely to be able to avoid power struggles. Judgmental attitudes tend to be more relaxed, and combative levels lower or nonexistent a good deal of the time. Both partners take pride in the relationship's warmth of feeling, which, in the case of love affairs, may smolder for many years with unabated intensity.

Marital matchups encourage Taurus II dependence on Leo III's, who usually take the lead and like to give support to their mates and children. Should they fail to live up to their promises, however, or fall victim to their own hubris, Taurus II's are likely to take a dim view of them, especially if they also experience some kind of breakdown. Taurus II's require dignity above all in a mate, and a Leo III whose dignity is lost can be a pitiful sight.

Parental relationships are likely to be problematic here: in either parent-child combination, ethical Taurus II's are likely to judge Leo III actions rather harshly. And if Leo III's are the parents, they will have a tendency to spoil their children, a treatment Taurus II's actually tend to resent. At work, boss-employee pairs in either permutation of this combination often encounter power struggles over what the employee perceives as unfair treatment from the boss.

ADVICE: *Try to be more accepting and less judgmental. Enjoy yourself without reservations. Be more compassionate. Put yourself in the other's place.*

MADONNA (8/16/58)
EVITA PERON (5/7/19)

In her magnetic film portrayal of Evita, Madonna brought the part to life. They have much in common: humble backgrounds; ambitious social climbing, and both admiration and scorn from the public.

Also: Fred Astaire & Robyn Smith (married; dancer/jockey); **Lex Barker & Arlene Dahl** (married; actors); **Henry Brown Blackwell & Lucy Stone** (married; feminist advocates).

May 3–10

THE WEEK OF THE TEACHER
TAURUS II

August 19–25

THE CUSP OF EXPOSURE
LEO-VIRGO CUSP

A Sacred Trust

 RELATIONSHIPS

STRENGTHS: **SYMPATHETIC,
UNDERSTANDING, INTIMATE**

WEAKNESSES: **SUSPICIOUS,
THREATENING, CLOSED OFF**

BEST: **FRIENDSHIP**

WORST: **LOVE**

T he strongly sympathetic and understanding attitudes that appear in this relationship give it an atmosphere of trust. Private matters can be kept that way without threat of revelation. The downside of this is a heightened sensitivity to betrayals of confidence in any form, so that as trusting as it is, the relationship simultaneously contains a suspicious undertone; for the most part, however, confidences will be regarded as sacred and honored completely, and these two together will be trusted by others. This in turn allows them to persuade, teach and lead in whatever field suits them.

Whether or not Taurus II's and Leo-Virgos have interests in common at the start of their relationship, they will develop areas of sharing, pleasure and growth in their everyday life. In most respects this is a healthy bond, but certain tendencies will have to be monitored carefully, notably those leading to excessive privatization of feelings and consequent isolation from social interaction. Widening the circle of friendship to include others is essential here, not only to enrich the primary relationship itself but to learn the lesson of sharing in a wider social and universal sense. Friendships are particularly favored in this combination.

Love affairs, although understanding, may fail to ignite flames of passion or touch deeper layers of emotion. Marriages may not be that successful either, partly because Taurus II's need to nurture and Leo-Virgos have difficulties doing so. Having children is not recommended here, for Leo-Virgos tend to make their own needs paramount, and demand preponderant attention. Family relationships are likely to be close, replete with temperamental displays, especially with opposite-sex siblings. The profound emotions felt here may well continue into adulthood, even in some cases resulting in the siblings inhabiting contiguous living spaces.

Work relationships can succeed if the partners maintain a strict objectivity on the job at hand. They can be quite successful in any sales endeavor so long as it does not conflict with their personal ideals.

ADVICE: *Build bridges to the world. Secretiveness may arouse suspicions. Try to be more open. Remember your responsibilities to others.*

MEL FERRER (8/25/17)
AUDREY HEPBURN (5/4/29)

Hepburn and Ferrer had a close marriage (1954–68) and a fine working relationship. They co-starred in *War and Peace* (1956); he directed her in *Green Mansions* (1959); and he produced the film *Wait Until Dark* (1967), for which she received an Oscar nomination.

Also: Fred Astaire & Gene Kelly (film dance partners).

NICHOLAS ASHFORD (5/4/43)
VALERIE SIMPSON (8/26/48)

Ashford and Simpson began writing songs and performing together in the late 60s. Married in 1974, they are still a major force in the R&B music scene, touring and working as independent producers. *Also:* **Toni Tennille & Daryl Dragon** (married; The Captain & Tennille); **Roberto Rossellini & Ingrid Bergman** (scandalous affair, 1949).

May 3–10
THE WEEK OF THE TEACHER
TAURUS II

August 26–September 2
THE WEEK OF SYSTEM BUILDERS
VIRGO I

Serious Sacrifices

This relationship will push its partners to have the guts and determination to achieve well-defined and perhaps much-longed-for goals instead of sitting back and relaxing. The relationship's seriousness is reflected in the sacrifices that the partners are willing to make, often doing without for months and years so that ultimately they will get what they want and be where they want to be. This dedication implies tremendous unity of purpose. It also demands that channels of communication remain open so that counter-productive misunderstandings can be quickly rectified.

Virgo I's have a need for relatively unserious involvements that will let them loosen up and have fun. In love and marriage, then, their relationships with Taurus II's may be crippled by what they see as excessive rules, structures and moral imperatives that stand in the way of easy give-and-take. Tensions on both sides, then, may make enjoyment of the rewards of all the pair's hard work and dedication difficult or impossible. Although a Virgo I's choice of this particular mate may in many respects be realistic, the Taurus II may not respond with enough passion, and if this arouses the Virgo I's insecurities (feelings of being unattractive or unworthy, say), withdrawal and anxiety are likely to result.

This relationship is successful in the work sphere, and also in families in which a Taurus II–Virgo I parent-child combination runs a business or service together. Achieving short-term goals—perhaps arranging for loans, building new work space, getting clients, reorganizing bookkeeping, doing inventory and the like—will build the confidence these two need to keep moving toward their long-term objectives. Friendships here can also be an extremely positive career influence, inspiring each partner on in their respective fields. A professionally successful partner can serve as a role model for the other, especially when parental influences in childhood have been less than ideal or outright destructive.

ADVICE: *Relax enough to enjoy the fruits of your labor. Have fun. Aim for attainable short-range goals. Cultivate romantic settings.*

ADELE ASTAIRE (9/10/1898)
FRED ASTAIRE (5/10/1899)

Before Fred began his movie career in 1933, these siblings were vaudeville dance partners. They debuted on Broadway in 1917, becoming favorites of the 20s. Their partnership ended when Adele married sometime in 1932. *Also:* **Donovan & Ione Skye** (father/daughter; singer/actress).

May 3–10
THE WEEK OF THE TEACHER
TAURUS II

September 3–10
THE WEEK OF THE ENIGMA
VIRGO II

In the Face of Tradition

Unconventional is probably the best word to define this relationship, which tends to fly in the face of tradition and to oppose the expectations and wishes of friends and family members. To top it off, this duo will go one step farther by criticizing or harshly judging people with more traditional views. Born in the Week of the Enigma, Virgo II's are unusual, secretive individuals who are hard to get to know—exactly the kind of person to whom Taurus II's are often attracted. For their part, Taurus II's can breach Virgo II defenses with an irresistible combination of aggressiveness and charm.

Love affairs between these two are highly meaningful, often featuring a complex, pleasurable and non-traditional approach to love and lovemaking. The frank and honest Taurus II approach to sex, often eschewing sympathy and at times even romance, gels well with the Virgo II dislike of soppiness and sentimentality. When the relationship allows the carnal side of Taurus II's to predominate over the priggish, new heights of passion and inventiveness can be reached. This is not to say that the relationship necessarily stirs the inner depths of the Virgo II, or even reaches them, but continued intimate trust of a Taurus II love partner can introduce deeper levels of revelation and emotional involvement. Marriages are a distinct possibility, then, but one or both partners may have an aversion to tying the knot, preferring the freer atmosphere of living together.

Friendships can likewise be a first step toward closer sharing and trust, but these two don't always get that far. The trine aspect here (Taurus II and Virgo II are 120° apart in the zodiac) means that at least on a superficial level there is usually a comfortable rapport, so that co-worker acquaintanceships or companionships can emerge easily; but they may not lead to long-lasting friendships. As a work team, this pair can prove quite innovative, finding new ways to accomplish goals and achieve success. Family relationships usually feature a lack of understanding, with sharp critical attacks followed by withdrawal or silence.

ADVICE: *Keep bonds of trust intact. Work on emotional honesty to reach deeper levels of communication. Fighting conventional attitudes may be a waste of time and energy.*

May 3–10

THE WEEK OF THE TEACHER
TAURUS II

September 11–18

THE WEEK OF THE LITERALIST
VIRGO III

Determined to Succeed

RELATIONSHIPS

STRENGTHS: **HONEST, UNPRETENTIOUS, CARING**

WEAKNESSES: **STRUGGLING, ANTAGONISTIC, HARD-HEADED**

BEST: **FAMILY**

WORST: **FRIENDSHIP**

MAX MALLOWAN (5/6/04)
AGATHA CHRISTIE (9/15/1890)

Christie married noted British archeologist Mallowan in 1930. She was his assistant on his Middle East expeditions, which provided scientific background for several of her mystery novels. **Also: Tammy Wynette & George Jones** (married; country music stars); **Johannes Brahms & Clara Schumann** (close friends); **Peter Benchley & Robert Benchley** (son/father; writer/humorist).

The mutually hard-headed energies of Taurus II's and Virgo III's often collide in the form of struggles for dominance, but may also coalesce synergistically in a relationship that is dedicated and determined to succeed, whether in business or at home. The relationship may in fact become the linchpin, or at least an important bulwark, of a successful company or family. The determining factor here will often be whether these two like each other, pure and simple. They do share many qualities, such as a hatred of pretense and phoniness and an insistence on fairness, especially to the disadvantaged. This is no antidote, however, for their struggles for supremacy.

Personal relationships such as marriages, love affairs and friendships are likely to evidence the most conflict, alternating, however, with warm and caring expressions of emotion. Taurus II–Virgo III love affairs may prove highly pleasurable, but feelings tend to run deeper when one or both of the parties already has a primary relationship elsewhere. Generally speaking, opposing the tenets of society, and the dominance of the other partner, comes naturally to this relationship. These two will have no hesitation about flaunting their passions dramatically, feeling no need for secrecy or sneakiness.

Conflicts in marriages of this combination bring both positive and negative results. The relationship is often toughened and strengthened by honest discussion and even argument, the emotional element in these confrontations being quickly forgotten. Communication is a strength; the pair will be objective, hearing the other point of view clearly and responding logically, albeit with feeling. They are also responsible in their attitudes to domestic matters and children—as long as both partners keep up their end of the deal, without being forced to by destructive power struggles. Friendships here can be easy but a bit superficial. They are rarely of primary importance to their partners, who may not spend that much time together. Often respectful of each other's powers and talents, these two function best as siblings within a family, or as co-workers or partners on the job.

ADVICE: *Be aware of people's feelings. Don't succumb to power urges. Beware of ruthlessness. Never compromise the dignity or values of others.*

May 3–10

THE WEEK OF THE TEACHER
TAURUS II

September 19–24

THE CUSP OF BEAUTY
VIRGO-LIBRA CUSP

Influencing Tastes

RELATIONSHIPS

STRENGTHS: **HARMONIOUS, TASTEFUL, ATTRACTIVE**

WEAKNESSES: **MANIPULATIVE, AVOIDING, AMBIGUOUS**

BEST: **WORK**

WORST: **MARRIAGE**

F. SCOTT FITZGERALD (9/24/1896)
EDMUND WILSON (5/8/1895)

Wilson and Fitzgerald were close friends at Princeton. The erudite Wilson cultivated budding writer Fitzgerald's interest in literature. **Also: Billy Joel & Ray Charles** (collaborators; musicians); **Ricky Nelson & Gunnar Nelson** (father/son; rock & roll singers); **Orson Welles & John Houseman** (stage and film collaborators).

This relationship is likely to involve attempts to influence tastes and aesthetic views, not only those of the partners themselves but also those of others, be they individual or corporate. There are ambivalent feelings here, particularly in social issues and in matters of style. Part of the relationship's running commentary has to do with a split in the attitudes of Taurus II's: on the one hand, they are extremely interested in everything up-to-date, stylish and aesthetic; on the other, they hate snobbism, putting on airs and all forms of elitism, which of course abound in the worlds of fashion and art. Virgo-Libra attitudes, meanwhile, are for the most part unequivocally elitist, and the sensibility is highly refined.

Friendship and love between these two can be squarely based on physical attraction, and will feature seductive, often sensual forms of persuasion. In the interest of preserving harmony and good feeling, important issues that should actually be thrashed out may instead be avoided. Differences in fundamental value structures make Taurus II–Virgo-Libra marriages problematic: the Virgo-Libra's more superficial nature and social aspirations may prove unacceptable to the Taurus II, who will eventually come to judge his or her partner rather harshly.

Resentments and conflicts are less likely to surface in the office, or in freelance work. Should their business deal directly with matters of style or fashion, their unanimity may be total. Should the work be more personal, however, such as a restaurant, small store or other occupation in which one's public appearance can be freer or more casual, Taurus II's and Virgo-Libras will spend a lot of time debating this issue, each trying to persuade the other of their point of view. Should they come to an aesthetic agreement, they could generate enormous success by persuading others to follow their lead. Marketing is a forte here. In parent-child relationships in this combination, generational differences will lead to different approaches, but rather than arguing or attempting to intimidate, the partners will use more subtle forms of manipulation to convince each other.

ADVICE: *Let others make up their own minds. Try to find a solid basis for your life. Don't be blown about by the winds of change. Seek lasting values.*

BRYANT GUMBEL (9/29/48)
GREG GUMBEL (5/3/46)

Emmy-winning Greg is a tv sportscaster for NBC. He got his start through brother Bryant, who arranged Greg's first interview with the network. Magazine-show host Bryant has since moved to CBS with a very lucrative contract. He, too, has won several Emmys.
Also: Maxim Shostakovich & Dmitri Shostakovich (son/father; conductor/composer).

May 3–10
THE WEEK OF THE TEACHER
TAURUS II

September 25–October 2
THE WEEK OF THE PERFECTIONIST
LIBRA I

Balmy Midwinter's Day

Incisive thought is the primary theme here, leading to colorful and vibrant interactions and ideas. Critical and dominating aspects also feature strongly, so that stability is a little low: too often, worry and concern about doing the wrong thing will undermine the relationship's security, leading to judgmental or blaming attitudes that undercut any pleasure. One of those relationships that may not last long, like a balmy mid-winter's day, this pairing should nevertheless be thoroughly enjoyed without too much reflection.

Love affairs between these two can be highly satisfying, especially in the sexual sphere, where each partner will be excited by the other's physical attractiveness. Combining with the relationship's emphasis on the mental, this physical connection may give the relationship an obsessive quality, reducing conscious control and heightening the pain of any separation or breakup. The mental motor can be turned off, however, by total involvement in some absorbing but not necessarily intellectual area—work, domestic affairs, money-making or management activities.

Both Taurus II's and Libra I's are highly critical, and their business and marital partnerships tend to be somewhat unsettled and irregular. Things may go well for a while, but storm clouds will inevitably gather and lightning will flash. This duo risks running away from pressing problems, a habit that, particularly in marriage, may reflect a refusal to confront emotions and be honest about them (a notable trait of Libra I's). Taurus II partners may experience some frustration at being unable to reach Libra I's at a deep level, but with patience, over time, the relationship may become an effective tool for opening up closed doors in both partners and promoting sharing and trust.

The relationship's lack of emotional honesty can make friendships in this combination difficult, and there is also an inability to keep more extreme emotions under control. Family relationships, especially between siblings, are similarly likely to be stormy and at times violent.

ADVICE: *Don't succumb to escapism. Confront things as they are. Aim for emotional honesty and openness.*

JUAN PERON (10/8/1895)
EVITA PERON (5/7/19)

Evita (née Eva Duarte) was a radio and film actress before marrying Peron in 1945. After he won the Argentinean presidency in 1946, she became his right hand. Idolized by the masses, her 1952 death from cancer was a national tragedy.
Also: Daniel Berrigan & Philip Berrigan (brothers; 60s activists);
Mark David Chapman & John Lennon (assassin shot Beatle).

May 3–10
THE WEEK OF THE TEACHER
TAURUS II

October 3–10
THE WEEK OF SOCIETY
LIBRA II

Accentuate the Positive

Inherently volatile and uncertain, this combination can prove confusing. A continual forward push is needed here, for the tackling of challenges can help overcome the problem of being unable to define what's really going on.

Since this combination has a quincunx aspect (its two weeks being 150° apart in the zodiac), conventional astrology predicts some instability here and is, in this case, right on the mark. Both Taurus and Libra are ruled by Venus, suggesting harmony and a shared love of beauty, but more negative traits are also reinforced, such as procrastination, laziness and provocation. There may also be a refusal to leave things be, and a tendency to complain and to get hung up on details. Putting the accent on achievement can offset these traits.

Instability can prove exciting, particularly in love, and both partners may be stimulated by this relationship. Illicit and covert affairs have an allure here. Marriage is more challenging—perhaps the most challenging kind of relationship in this combination, in fact, and also the most potentially rewarding. Negative and positive traits coalesce synergistically here. The alliance is capable of generating sensual enjoyment, play, humor and comfort; the home of a Taurus II–Libra II couple may be richly decorated yet highly functional, with many areas of the living space thought out to the last detail. As one moves from room to room in such a dwelling, flair and color alternate rhythmically with sobriety and quietude. A remarkable tranquillity can rule the domestic scene in this marriage. Still, emotional mood swings are never absent for long.

At work, this pair may suffer from a periodic paralysis of the will, a slump or an inability to concentrate. Such breakdowns may prove unacceptably counterproductive, and a boss may separate these two by relocating them within the workplace. Family relationships, particularly parent-child, may suffer from regular bouts of mutual provocation, despite long periods of relative harmony and peace.

ADVICE: *Let up in your intensity. Be more forgiving and forgetting. Let the good times roll. Don't be uptight, it's only money. Power isn't everything.*

May 3–10

THE WEEK OF THE TEACHER
TAURUS II

October 11–18

THE WEEK OF THEATER
LIBRA III

A New Spin

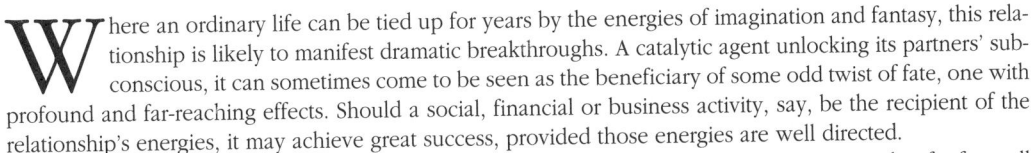

Where an ordinary life can be tied up for years by the energies of imagination and fantasy, this relationship is likely to manifest dramatic breakthroughs. A catalytic agent unlocking its partners' subconscious, it can sometimes come to be seen as the beneficiary of some odd twist of fate, one with profound and far-reaching effects. Should a social, financial or business activity, say, be the recipient of the relationship's energies, it may achieve great success, provided those energies are well directed.

Matchups in this combination can be close but trying. Libra III's need plenty of attention, but far from all the time; when they need it, though, they have to get it, no matter what. They do best with partners who don't put heavy demands on them, are quite independent and have strength of character. All of these requirements can be met quite handily by Taurus II's, who gain some benefit as well: usually this takes the form of learning social skills, using the Libra III's contacts and being entertained by them.

Marriages and love affairs may be bound up in a shroud of unreality. So strong is the projection of fantasy here that the relationship can seem to have been summoned genielike from Aladdin's lamp. The results can be illusory and destructive, but the principal problem in this combination will be conflict with the demands of everyday reality, social pressures and the perceptions of friends and family who don't share this pair's vision. Should these partners be able break with societal influences, instead believing totally in the personal reality of their relationship, they may make a success of it, for as long as it lasts.

In business, a partnership providing a service or product to the general public is most favored here. These two will usually find a hole in the market by coming up with something original, or giving a new spin to an old idea. Whether it's the delivery, packaging, advertising or personal approach involved in the product that is unusual, it has a good chance of attracting attention and making a significant impact on the market.

ADVICE: *Balance your personal and social life. Your fantasies may mean little to others. Take the time to explain yourself. Don't be self-centered.*

ORSON WELLES (5/6/15)
RITA HAYWORTH (10/17/18)

These self-absorbed stars married in 1948, the year Welles directed and co-starred with Hayworth in *The Lady from Shanghai*. She filed for divorce soon after the filming. **Also: Mike Wallace & Chris Wallace** (father/son; newsmen); **Robert Knievel & Evel Knievel** (son/father; stuntmen); **Dave Prater & Sam Moore** (Sam & Dave musical duo); **Dennis Thatcher & Margaret Thatcher** (married).

May 3–10

THE WEEK OF THE TEACHER
TAURUS II

October 19–25

THE CUSP OF DRAMA & CRITICISM
LIBRA-SCORPIO CUSP

Formidable Adversaries

These two have a great deal in common. Unfortunately, their common traits and talents tend not to coalesce and augment their relationship but rather to diminish it. The sticking point is generally the issue of authority: both partners have a strong need to be the authority figure or, more particularly, the teacher, and to have others listen to them. Student-teacher relationships are difficult or impossible here. Argument, criticism and disagreement are likely to keep this pair from moving in a positive direction.

When working for rival businesses, clubs or teams, these two make formidable opponents. Their true strengths often emerge in such relationships, where they can wield their intellectual skills in a display not unlike that found in swordplay or martial arts. Nor is the intention ever in doubt: to win, overcome, defeat. Working together in the same organization, they have a chance of success if they are equally situated in the hierarchy, have minimal personal contact and are engaged in objective or technical tasks, in, for example, the areas of science, computers, medicine or language.

Love affairs, friendships and marriages may be less dominating and combative but are usually just as competitive. All can prove difficult, but marriage is perhaps the best bet of the three, since these personalities' strong energies will be grounded there by shared daily tasks and responsibilities. In certain cases a lifelong truce is possible, with aggressive instincts being sublimated or directed outward, against other couples or individuals. Affairs tend to be either passionate or prosaic, with an emphasis on frankness and open physicality, and little likelihood of deeper feelings or sympathy. Family relationships, especially between equally matched siblings, can be as intense as any other in this combination. Parent-child relationships have little to recommend them: usually the parent, whether Taurus II or Libra-Scorpio, will dominate the child, at least until a rebellious adolescence is reached and interactions can be less one-sided.

ADVICE: *Try to bring out the best without undue conflict. Aim for positive goals. Minimize arguments, maximize understanding. Stick together.*

SIR GEORGE P. THOMSON (5/3/1892)
CLINTON J. DAVISSON (10/22/1881)

Thomson and Davisson shared the 1937 Nobel Prize in physics. Their combined research in electron diffraction proved that matter is both wavelike and particulate.

STRENGTHS: FAIR, INTELLIGENT, STIMULATING

WEAKNESSES: OVERZEALOUS, UNEMOTIVE, RESISTANT

BEST: FAMILY

WORST: LOVE

CANDICE BERGEN (5/8/46)
LOUIS MALLE (10/30/32)

In 1980—before her stardom as tv's *Murphy Brown*—Bergen married French director Malle, 14 years her senior. An accomplished photojournalist and playwright as well as an actress, Bergen supported his often controversial films, which explore eroticism, politics, subculture and social issues. Their marriage was a strong one. Malle died in 1995.

May 3–10

THE WEEK OF THE TEACHER
TAURUS II

October 26–November 2

THE WEEK OF INTENSITY
SCORPIO I

Crusading Spirit

The focus of this relationship is likely to be quick mental communication. Intelligence and the transmission of ideas are highly valued here, and there is also a shared interest in books, puzzles, games and feats of memory and reasoning. There will also be a concern with social and moral codes, issues of justice and injustice, and rather forward-thinking or visionary ideas. The connection between these two is often so close that each may know what the other is thinking without a word being spoken.

The determining factor in the success of both love and marriage in this combination is whether the couple's emotional communication is as good as the mental variety. Empathic bonds are somewhat rare here, since Taurus II's do not live on the more emotional levels, and usually resist the kind of intense psychological scrutiny that is the Scorpio I specialty. Even so, sympathy and understanding can become a trademark of this relationship as long as the couple are determined to make them so. Taurus II's will generally have an aversion to the Scorpio I dark side, but may also be fascinated by it. Luckily it is the sunnier Scorpio I aspects that the relationship tends to activate.

When these two are friends or business associates, their relationship will magnify their inherent involvement in the concept of fairness. It may well demonstrate a crusading spirit, making it socially and politically active, always on the side of the oppressed, disenfranchised or socially disadvantaged. A related concern with individuals who are seriously challenged, whether mentally or physically, can become the basis for a career of service.

In the family, Taurus II parents are well suited to Scorpio I children in terms both of what they can give them and what they can accept from them. Scorpio I parents tend to be stimulating, even inspiring, to their Taurus II children. In either combination, learning, helpfulness, understanding and, of course, fairness are likely to be prominent. Sibling matchups will probably be mutually supportive and giving, playful and mentally challenging, but temperamental, like the weather.

ADVICE: *Don't overemphasize logic. Acknowledge the value of feelings. Learn from each other. Develop paranormal abilities.*

STRENGTHS: ENTERTAINING, YOUTHFUL, RELAXED

WEAKNESSES: CLOSED OFF, MISDIRECTED, STUBBORN

BEST: FRIENDSHIP

WORST: LOVE

ARIEL DURANT (5/10/1898)
WILL DURANT (11/5/1885)

Married in 1913 when Ariel was just 15, the Durants popularized history for millions with their 11-book series, *The Story of Civilization* (1935–75). Inseparable to the end, they died a month apart in 1981.
Also: Mike Wallace & Morley Safer (co-hosts, *60 Minutes*).

May 3–10

THE WEEK OF THE TEACHER
TAURUS II

November 3–11

THE WEEK OF DEPTH
SCORPIO II

Second Childhood

This combination will encourage its participants to lighten up and have fun. Taurus II and Scorpio II lie opposite each other in the zodiac, making them apt to bring out each other's seriousness and wariness, yet their relationship also has a lighter side, sidestepping some of the weightiness in favor of a more playful or youthful outlook. Its aversion to power struggles and problems is such that its partners will want to maintain a healthy balance of power, carefully drawing lines of defense that they are equally careful not to transgress.

A friendship may be this duo's best chance to relax and enjoy life's more amusing side. As children, Taurus II's can make excellent playmates for Scorpio II's, and the pair's lightheartedness together may feel like a second childhood once they have grown up. Fostering humor and easy camaraderie, this relationship often works as a safety valve for the pressures and difficulties that its partners face in other areas of life.

Love and marriage, on the other hand, may involve problems with stress, emotional blockage and missed communication. Taurus II's can be very understanding, but a daily diet of Scorpio II depression and self-induced pain may push them beyond their tolerance threshold. And if aggression and resentment start flowing in their direction, they may back off or disappear altogether. Passions may run high here at first, but there is a danger that intensity and romance will lose their appeal over the years, and that deeper emotional areas will be closed off. At the same time, the relationship is likely to function quite well in more mundane areas, with daily responsibilities being faithfully discharged.

In group endeavors, whether at work or in the family, the relationship is likely to prove reliable and productive. Youthfulness can be an important theme in parent-child interactions, but the parent, of either week of the year, is sometimes apt to go overboard in trying to look young and to be hip, cool and up-to-date, while the child meanwhile strives to be more adult and mature. Such role reversals can produce interesting but at times ludicrous results.

ADVICE: *Stay youthful but be dignified. Accept maturity but don't be too serious. Loosen up and have fun. Don't close off or shut down.*

May 3–10

THE WEEK OF THE TEACHER
TAURUS II

November 12–18

THE WEEK OF CHARM
SCORPIO III

Balance of Power

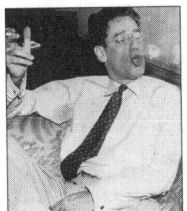

GEORGE S. KAUFMAN (11/16/1889)
MARY ASTOR (5/3/06)

RELATIONSHIPS

STRENGTHS: **BALANCED, UNSELFISH, MAGNETIC**

WEAKNESSES: **OVERWHELMING, UNFORGIVING, JEALOUS**

BEST: **WORK**

WORST: **FRIENDSHIP**

This relationship works on creating a balance of individual strengths so that they augment rather than fight one another, particularly in the service of a career or business endeavor. Power struggles rarely emerge here, and both partners can mute their ego drives in the pursuit of common goals, not only working together but learning from each other. Productive organizationally, the relationship also serves both partners' personal development.

A Taurus II–Scorpio III friendship can be vitally important to each of its participants, often more so than a love affair or marriage would be. Heavy expectations here can be counterproductive, however, and strict and unforgiving attitudes may make a free and easy exchange difficult or impossible. Taurus II–Scorpio III love affairs can be complex: passion, sexual attraction and jealousy can run high, with pain and suffering too inevitably close behind. A certain personal magnetism here may result in love triangles, which will have destructive results. The Scorpio III need for emotional honesty and full expression may be thwarted or wounded by Taurus II critical attitudes and frank assessments; also, Taurus II's like to be left alone a lot of the time, and the controlling or claiming stance of the classic Scorpio III is likely to annoy them.

Marriages between these two can be effective, especially when goals are well defined and the power structure is balanced. Enjoyable and fulfilling sexual interaction may continue right into old age. As parents, however, these two must be careful not to overwhelm their children, or to allow their respective, radically different approaches to raising them to cause confusion. Similarly, although Taurus II–Scorpio III family relationships may be quite favorable (particularly in times of need), the moral stance of a Taurus II parent and the controlling and protective attitudes of a Scorpio III elder can become disturbing or debilitating to a child of the other sign.

For actress Astor, her affair in the 30s with playwright Kaufman was euphoric; for him, it was just another sexual friendship. After her diary was publicized in 1936, Kaufman was dubbed "Public Lover Number One."

Also: **Tyrone Power & Linda Christian** (married); **John Wilkes Booth & Edwin Booth** (brothers; Shakespearean actors).

ADVICE: *Bring different points of view into balance. At home, work for the common good. Don't expect too much. Simplify love.*

May 3–10

THE WEEK OF THE TEACHER
TAURUS II

November 19–24

THE CUSP OF REVOLUTION
SCORPIO-SAGITTARIUS CUSP

Graduate School

MICHAEL PALIN (5/5/43)
TERRY GILLIAM (11/22/40)

RELATIONSHIPS

STRENGTHS: **ACCEPTING, DIVERSE, EXPRESSIVE**

WEAKNESSES: **DISHONEST, CONFLICTING, CHAOTIC**

BEST: **MARRIAGE**

WORST: **PARENT-CHILD**

Acceptance is the focus of this relationship, and the key to success in emotional, physical and spiritual matters as well as intellectual ones. The partners are likely to come from different social and religious backgrounds, and if they realize how rich in diversity, and therefore how valuable, such a relationship can be, they will work hard to protect these differences instead of insisting on meaningless uniformity. Taurus II's generally believe in the value of teaching, whether in an institution or one-on-one, while Scorpio-Sagittarians are often graduates of the school of hard knocks, and believe that life experience is the true teacher. Formed by such different sources, this relationship can gather knowledge from the broadest spectrum of wisdom, as long as it can make space for the acceptance of differences.

Love here is likely to be direct, intense and unpredictable. The more unstable sides of both partners will often meld in a wildly romantic affair, which sweeps everything before it. Carnally, each of these two will meet their match in the other, but they will need to check their combative instincts. Scorpio-Sagittarius "memory lapses" may be a problem, since Taurus II's are unlikely to be patient either with indiscretions and infidelities or with lying about them. Marriage is likely to dull the flame of romance, which feeds so richly here on uncertainty and secrecy. Yet this couple's stability may be enhanced by commitment, so that domestic matters benefit in the more permanent relationship. Taurus II's may be strong enough to hold on to Scorpio-Sagittarians, who combine a drive toward infidelity with an equal, but more hidden, need to be loyal. Family life may come to agree with this duo, sublimating their wildness to the steady energy needed for a whole spectrum of activities, from domestic projects to family businesses to travel.

Intimate friendships and sibling and business partnerships are likely between Taurus II's and Scorpio-Sagittarians of the same sex, but parent-child and boss-employee relationships may be destructive or counterproductive. In successful relationships here, trust, honor and, above all, acceptance receive high priority.

Palin and Gilliam are best known as members of *Monty Python's Flying Circus.* Oxford-educated Palin was an actor on the British comedy team; Gilliam, the only American member, created the brilliant animation on the BBC show.

Also: **Gerald Levin & Ted Turner** (media moguls).

ADVICE: *Keep differences alive. Condemning and repressive attitudes diminish your value. Be expressive but not chaotic. Ground yourself in daily life.*

RELATIONSHIPS

STRENGTHS: **DIRECTED,
CHALLENGING, HONORABLE**

WEAKNESSES: **STORMY,
SCANDALOUS, DISASTROUS**

BEST: **FAMILY**

WORST: **LOVE**

KARL MARX (5/5/1818)
FRIEDRICH ENGELS (11/28/1820)

Considered the "fathers of communism," Marx and Engels met in 1844. Sharing the same ideologies, they collaborated on the revolutionary *Communist Manifesto* (1848). They worked side by side for 40 years until Marx's death in 1883.
Also: Betty Comden & Adolph Green (musical writing team); **Pia Zadora & Meshulam Riklis** (married; actress/Fabergé perfumer).

May 3–10

THE WEEK OF THE TEACHER
TAURUS II

November 25–December 2

THE WEEK OF INDEPENDENCE
SAGITTARIUS I

Haven for the Dispossessed

This relationship may well involve a team that gives leadership and direction to new enterprises, whether businesses, social groups, families or marriages, that demand a knack for timing as an important part of their success. Both Taurus II's and Sagittarius I's are high-minded individuals, but their relationship may bring out a secretive aspect in them, possibly having to do with money. It can also provide an outlet for each partner's less stable or reliable side, possibly creating chaos or near disaster. Everything gets exposed here sooner or later, and covert activities may cause scandal when brought to light.

Love affairs are stormy here, to say the least, but highly exciting. It is a relationship in which sex does not by any means imply intimacy, for there may well be a lot of the former and far less of the latter, at least in the early stages. Later on, intimacy may take the place of passion, perhaps leading to friendship or marriage. Together, the partners may explore hidden emotional areas never before revealed to parents or the world (or else hidden since childhood or early adolescence).

Friendships in this combination are rarely static, and often evolve into business relations, marriages, social or sports partnerships, or challenging activities built around nature, camping or exploration. A conventional or comfortable relationship, exhibiting an easy give-and-take, is rarely possible here. Family relationships, whether sibling or parent-child, can demonstrate deep mutual understanding. Both Taurus II's and Sagittarius I's usually love animals, are great believers in truth and honor, and despise discrimination or injustice in any form. A family containing such a combination can become a haven for the dispossessed and a champion of the underdog, a class that may well include a reasonable percentage of neighborhood castoffs and strays. Partnerships and organizations in which these two work as boss and employee can flounder until financial weaknesses are pinpointed and addressed. Taurus II's will generally be the more realistic of the pair, while Sagittarius I's are often taken up with exciting new ideas that do not always pan out.

ADVICE: *Work on being more practical and less chaotic. Reconcile passion and intimacy. Don't get carried away by idealism. Not everything has to be revealed.*

RELATIONSHIPS

STRENGTHS: **SENSITIVE,
PERCEPTIVE, TOUGH**

WEAKNESSES: **RESENTFUL,
DISTRUSTING, REJECTING**

BEST: **LOVE**

WORST: **FAMILY**

SIGMUND FREUD (5/6/1856)
ANNA FREUD (12/3/1895)

Never married, Anna lived with her famous father, with whom she was very close. Following his psychoanalysis of her in 1918, she entered the field, becoming a renowned psychoanalyst herself. After his death in 1939, she focused on child analysis.

May 3–10

THE WEEK OF THE TEACHER
TAURUS II

December 3–10

THE WEEK OF THE ORIGINATOR
SAGITTARIUS II

An Invitation to Intimacy

This relationship can push its partners to explore deeper realms of feeling, spirituality, intimacy and other qualities. It is a pairing in which sensitivities must be handled with understanding and acceptance but also with toughness and resolution, so that sympathy does not lead to dishonesty or deviousness in confronting reality.

Sagittarius II's are notably hard to reach emotionally and tremendously demanding of understanding, especially in matters of love. They may find just the right partner in a Taurus II. These two astrological periods are quincunx to each other in the zodiac (150° apart), and in traditional astrology are therefore said to promote instability, but the excitement and interest generated by this relationship may well offset this disadvantage. Sagittarius II nervousness will get a Taurus II wound up as well, but Taurus II's have vast reserves of stability and understanding to ground the relationship and give it direction. Chances are that Sagittarius II's won't allow them to get too close emotionally at the outset, even when the two are physically intimate, but a solid trust may be built up over time. Psychologically astute Taurus II's have much to teach Sagittarius II's about themselves, and for their part will thoroughly enjoy this partner's original brand of thinking. On the downside, there is a risk that Sagittarius II's can become dependent on Taurus II's, and at times may sacrifice their dignity when asking for help (or even, in extreme cases where they sense rejection, when pleading for it). Taurus II's will find this intolerable; if the relationship is to succeed, dignity will have to be preserved.

Intimacy in love doesn't necessarily translate into intimacy in marriage, and a love affair here is usually better off without the effort to make it more permanent. Similarly, work and family relationships in this combination often run into difficulties precisely because they have the stamp of permanence. Long-lasting friendships may have the same problem. Little can be done about this when Taurus II–Sagittarius II spouses have children, but friends and co-workers may be better off as acquaintances and freelancers, seeking each other out only when they want or need to.

ADVICE: *Be honest. Confront yourself. Don't take sympathy for granted. Don't compromise your self-respect. Responsibility need not be a threat.*

May 3–10

THE WEEK OF THE TEACHER
TAURUS II

December 11–18

THE WEEK OF THE TITAN
SAGITTARIUS III

Tremendous Drive to Build

These two will build sound structures, whether ideological or physical. Their relationship is complementary: together they have the skills they need to create any system, no matter how large. This duo may be especially talented in matters of procedure and efficiency. Goals tend to be extremely well defined here. Taurus II's know that to come between Sagittarius III's and their intended destination is to court disaster. Also understanding enough to see that the same goes for Sagittarius III moods, they are not often stupid enough to attempt to rouse these Titans from the grand funks into which they periodically fall. Mature Sagittarius III's are likewise able to give Taurus II's the latitude they need, so that the relationship's tremendous drive to build something of lasting value—the major theme here—is rarely undercut or interrupted by emotional issues.

This combination is best suited for working situations and marriages, in which a business or family system needs to be set up, administered and maintained. Not only the literal structure of the office or house will benefit here but also the ideas, plans and strategies that bring success to career and domestic endeavors alike. In marriages, however, issues such as neglect, favoritism, insensitivity and rejection can become problematic and even explosive, whether expressed or repressed. Conflict here can bring things to a grinding halt. In love affairs, similarly, Taurus II's will not enjoy playing second fiddle to a Sagittarius III's career, or being dominated by this partner. These two may build friendships around shared activities, but the Sagittarius III need to be in control may make it difficult for the relationship to achieve easy camaraderie and equal participation. Family relationships, especially of the parent-child variety, are likely to arouse power struggles that can rattle the home's walls and its inhabitants' teeth; in this case, the relationship may weaken structure rather than reinforce it. As the children grow older, however, mutual respect may begin to grow between them and their parents, so that when they reach maturity much of the conflict will have been resolved.

ADVICE: *Lessen power struggles. Don't let emotions interfere with work. Increase understanding through mature attitudes. Promote equality.*

GREGORY BATESON (5/9/04)
MARGARET MEAD (12/16/01)

English-born Bateson, a psychological anthropologist, was 3rd husband to famed cultural anthropologist and popularizer Mead. Married from 1936–50, they championed the use of photography in anthropological studies. *Also:* **Wm. Henry Vanderbilt & Wm. Kissam Vanderbilt** (father/son; railroad moguls).

May 3–10

THE WEEK OF THE TEACHER
TAURUS II

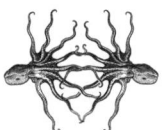

December 19–25

THE CUSP OF PROPHECY
SAGITTARIUS-CAPRICORN CUSP

Unspoken Communication

Despite each partner's preponderantly physical orientation in other matchups, this relationship is likely to concentrate on the more ethereal realms of the spirit. Together, Taurus II's and Sagittarius-Capricorns may enjoy the exploration or study of esoteric or metaphysical topics. Their strong psychic connection often transcends barriers of space. Unspoken understanding and communication are more characteristic of the relationship than sympathy and expressions of feeling; these two have a tendency to merge with each other, in fact, that if too pronounced can create boundary issues.

The success of love relationships in this combination generally depends on how far Taurus II's are willing to go in plumbing the hidden depths of the enigmatic Sagittarius-Capricorn personality. Often attracted to easier and more pleasurable relationships, they may be scared off by Sagittarius-Capricorn intensity, or may pull back at some negative interaction. Should the relationship continue, both parties must be ready for the gamut of emotions that tends to arise in their more intense exchanges, from the more disturbingly emotional areas of resentment, frustration and jealousy to exalted spiritual highs. Ultimately the partnership may become an ongoing flow of merger, separation, merger, separation, and so on.

Friendships and working relationships will exhibit a marked interest in spiritual and psychic matters, fostering interesting conversations and possible participation in new-age and other such leisure-time activities. These relationships are often better off remaining where they are than moving on to romance or marriage: should the Sagittarius-Capricorn be rejected in any way by the Taurus II, great suffering will probably result, and a breakup may mean losing the original relationship as well, or facing a level of damage that precludes beginning anew. Regret and grief over this kind of loss may be among the most difficult scenarios this relationship can face. Family relationships can be close here, especially parent-child combinations and those between siblings of the same sex.

ADVICE: *Even out highs and lows. Don't take communication for granted. Take time to explain yourself. Spend more time together. Share feelings.*

TONY MARTIN (12/25/13)
ALICE FAYE (5/5/15)

Musical actress Faye and actor-singer Martin were married from 1937–40. This first marriage for both lasted barely longer than their 3 musical film performances together: *Sing, Baby, Sing* (1936), *You Can't Have Everything* (1937) and *Sally, Irene and Mary* (1938). *Also:* **Ruth Prawar Jhabvala & Ismail Merchant** (collaborators; writer/producer).

NICCOLO MACHIAVELLI (5/3/1469)
LORENZO DE MEDICI (1/1/1449)

After Lorenzo (the Magnificent) lost control of his financial affairs, Machiavelli blamed foreign sources and advised him to restructure his business policies. Though Lorenzo failed and died with Florence in chaos, Machiavelli acquitted him of blame in an eloquent eulogy. ***Also:*** **Luther Adler & Jacob Adler** (son/father; actors); **Gary Cooper & Marlene Dietrich** (affair; actors).

May 3–10

THE WEEK OF THE TEACHER
TAURUS II

December 26–January 2

THE WEEK OF THE RULER
CAPRICORN I

Hard to Figure Out

To those who know Taurus II's and Capricorn I's as individuals, this relationship will probably be somewhat puzzling. Its raison d'être isn't always clear, even for its partners, should one ask them; they are often too busy giving structure to a family or business to be concerned with self-understanding. In fact, if the shared activity around which the relationship is built ends or falls apart, the partners may find little in the way of an emotional or spiritual bond to hold them together.

Intimate relationships here, especially love affairs and friendships, may be the hardest to figure out. Usually intensely private, they may not be deliberately hidden from the world, but they aren't actively exposed ,either. The partners may have been thrown together in the oddest and most unexpected circumstances, perhaps necessitated by the fact that they travel in such different circles, and have such mutually exclusive activities, that they might otherwise never have met. Yet they may have an immediate sympathy or fascination for each other, one that demands further interaction. The neglect of an existing relationship of some standing is often demanded here, increasing the level of tension, suspicion and mistrust all around. It may all be worth it, for this is seldom a quick fling; it is a serious, karmic relationship that must be thoroughly and laboriously worked through before it can be ended, with one lifetime perhaps not enough.

Taurus II–Capricorn I marriages will be enhanced by both partners' honesty and sense of tradition, but Taurus II's will find their mate's authoritarian attitudes oppressive, both to themselves and to their children or younger relatives. Wisely, Taurus II's will rarely try to oppose the Capricorn I need to take the lead, but in a subtle and diplomatic way will seek their own areas of concern and control within the relationship. Problems can arise if Capricorn I intolerance assumes a prejudicial tone, for discrimination, or even small jokes or assumptions about others, can have a very bad effect on Taurus II's. Parent-child relationships, especially when Capricorn I is the parent, may likewise feature battles over intolerant and unaccepting attitudes.

ADVICE: *Don't hide what you have. Respect other people's feelings, and put yourself in their place. Break down walls of mistrust.*

ALVIN AILEY (1/5/31)
JUDITH JAMISON (5/10/44)

America's foremost African-American dancer-choreographer, Ailey formed the Alvin Ailey American Dance Theater in 1958. Close friend and collaborator Jamison performed with the troupe from 1965–80, and was named director after his death in 1989. ***Also:*** **Rudolph Valentino & Pola Negri** (famous affair; silent-screen stars).

May 3–10

THE WEEK OF THE TEACHER
TAURUS II

January 3–9

THE WEEK OF DETERMINATION
CAPRICORN II

Withdrawal from Scrutiny

This relationship is likely to create a somewhat private domain, withdrawn from the scrutiny of the world—perhaps literally so, in an isolated, even secret location. Few are admitted to this close bond, whether as observers or third-party participants.

Love and friendship are intensely personal here. These partners view their relationship less as a social unit than as a haven, and when together they will rarely place themselves in the company of others. The fact that Taurus II and Capricorn II are trine to each other (120° apart in the zodiac) helps them to establish an easy and earthy familiarity. Given the relationship's introverted orientation, intimacy and the exploration of the inner life are priorities. Both partners may lead quite active and normal worldly lives by themselves, but when they are together their relationship has a way of shutting out external noise and distractions.

Marriages in this combination will value a getaway or vacation place in a beautiful natural setting, guaranteeing rest and relaxation for a period of time each year. One danger is that self-imposed isolation will have a somewhat harmful effect on children, particularly if this attitude also prevails at home. This couple's ability to allow others to share their joys and sorrows will be one indication of their relationship's security and health. Above all, incipient feelings of fear, xenophobia or, in extreme cases, paranoia should be nipped in the bud.

Family relationships, especially between single parents and their children, or between siblings of the opposite sex, can become too exclusive. Although such relationships can be rich, deep, rewarding and highly protective, they may become neurotically antisocial and not conducive to normal growth in childhood.

Co-workers of this combination in a company or organization can become lifelong friends. Breakups necessitated by sectional reorganizations or company relocations may prove painful, and a similar relationship may prove impossible to establish with others. As business partners, these two may enjoy each other's company and be too relaxed to achieve great commercial success, unless they are extremely well directed.

ADVICE: *Stay open to objective monitoring. Don't lose touch with reality. Pursue more outgoing activities. Intimacy need not isolate.*

May 3–10	January 10–16
THE WEEK OF THE TEACHER TAURUS II	THE WEEK OF DOMINANCE CAPRICORN III

Winning Out, Efficiently

RELATIONSHIPS

STRENGTHS: **EFFICIENT, COHESIVE, PLEASURABLE**

WEAKNESSES: **AGGRESSIVE, BEWILDERED, DEFEATED**

BEST: **BUSINESS PARTNERSHIP**

WORST: **MARRIAGE**

MIKE WALLACE (5/9/18)
ANDY ROONEY (1/14/19)

This often hard-driving and enthusiastic combination focuses powerfully on getting the job done in the most efficient and practical way possible. It is extremely adept at ferreting out all kinds of wasteful energies and redirecting them positively. Although this formidable duo can be a bit overbearing, it is usually impressive enough to inspire (or coerce) cooperation in the most difficult of individuals.

Love affairs here can be physically satisfying, to say the least. These relationships are not without combative elements, which, however, are not completely negative in effect; instead, they heighten intensity and raise the stakes—victory can be an important theme here. Strangely enough, although this kind of striving generally asserts a priority over kindness, love and consideration, it does not preclude them. Should the relationship break up as a consequence of one of these struggles, the partners may show true compassion for each other, and sadness rather than exultation is most often the dominant feeling.

Marriages and friendships are likely to lack the intensity of love affairs, but can certainly be more relaxed and pleasant. Taurus II's will suffer terrible bewilderment when power struggles do arise, since they haven't usually invested much time in building the tough, enduring and resilient attitudes of Capricorn III's. An unspoken truce should therefore periodically be put into effect at such times.

As the heads of commercial, social or sports organizations, or of families, these two are skillful at getting the best out of people. A decent showing is usually not enough for them; producing winning combinations is what this relationship is all about. The danger is that extreme differences of opinion within this relationship will tear the group as a whole into two camps, with sides being taken and internal conflict raging out of control. As long as this pair's individual egos are in the service of the group, or of a higher cause, harmony will usually prevail. The presence of a formidable enemy or rival can be useful in promoting internal cohesion.

Good friends Wallace and Rooney are veterans of tv's longest-running, top-rated prime-time program, *60 Minutes*. Wallace, a respected and provocative interviewer, joined at the show's start in 1968. In 1978 Rooney began contributing his satirical social commentaries.

ADVICE: *A win can also be a loss. True love has little to do with triumph. Cultivate kinder attitudes. Limit competitiveness. Play for fun.*

May 3–10	January 17–22
THE WEEK OF THE TEACHER TAURUS II	THE CUSP OF MYSTERY & IMAGINATION CAPRICORN-AQUARIUS CUSP

Dream World

RELATIONSHIPS

STRENGTHS: **IMAGINATIVE, EXCITING, COMMITTED**

WEAKNESSES: **EXPECTANT, UNREALISTIC, DISAPPOINTED**

BEST: **WORK**

WORST: **LOVE**

RUDOLPH VALENTINO (5/6/1895)
NATASHA RAMBOVA (1/19/1897)

This relationship often lacks a firm grounding in reality. Ideals, fantasies and dreams figure prominently here, which may be all well and good for creative work, but which makes it difficult for this pair to get their dreams off the ground. This will feel odd and undermining to them, since ordinarily they have a talent for laying out plans. Underlying the relationship is a lack of dependability, which in turn arouses insecurities and undercuts permanence.

Flashy Capricorn-Aquarians may be very appealing to Taurus II's, and earthy Taurus II sensuality and mental acuity are attractive to their exciting partners. Even so, this relationship is unlikely to go far. Fantasy and the desire to follow their dreams may pull Taurus II's away from their usual pragmatic and sensible stance, but the results will not always be what they had wished. The disappointment of failed expectations on both sides may prove to be the relationship's legacy, unless the effort is made to be more realistic and take things as they come.

It is in the areas of friendship and love that impractical expectations are likely to be most damaging. It is characteristic of these relationships for both parties to be swept away upon first meeting each other and subsequently sharing their dreams and visions. After spending time together (perhaps quite a bit of time), interacting with others as a couple and being forced to defend their relationship against criticism, they will probably have a slightly more realistic view of things. Finally, when disagreements surface and closeness fades, they may realize that much they had hoped for can never be. Accepting this can be difficult and sad, but alas is inevitable in most cases.

Marriages and family and work relationships have a better chance of permanence, partly because mutual commitment may come more easily here, and partly for logistical reasons: responsibility has a sobering effect on this relationship, and although somewhat detrimental to its romantic side, contributes powerfully to its longevity. Here the relationship becomes concerned less with the personalities and visions of its partners and more with effectiveness, efficiency and the attainment of tangible goals through group efforts.

Hollywood set designer Rambova, Valentino's 2nd wife, took charge of his career in the 20s and effeminized his screen image. Valentino was wholly dependent on her until his sudden death in 1926. *Also:* **Johnnie Taylor & Sam Cooke** (co-performers; musicians); **Gary Cooper & Patricia Neal** (affair; actors); **Audrey Hepburn & Danny Kaye** (UNICEF work).

ADVICE: *Keep your feet on the ground. Don't be too hopeful or expectant. Aim for short-term goals. Success can be achieved a step at a time.*

ALICE LIDDELL (5/4/1852)
LEWIS CARROLL (1/27/1832)

English writer Lewis Carroll (Charles Lutwidge Dodgson) was also a noted children's photographer. Liddell, his favorite model, was the inspiration for his classic work *Alice in Wonderland* (1865). *Also:* **Harry S. Truman & Douglas MacArthur** (president/fired general); **Alex Van Halen & Eddie Van Halen** (brothers; rock & roll musicians); **Truman & FDR** (vice-president/president).

May 3–10
THE WEEK OF THE TEACHER
TAURUS II

January 23–30
THE WEEK OF GENIUS
AQUARIUS I

Peeling Away Illusions

What a beautiful combination—the brilliant Taurus II Teacher and the Aquarius I Genius student! Or is it? Alas, geniuses are often maladjusted, teachers frustrated, and their personal interactions an emotional disaster. When these two get together, their high ideals fall away, and they find themselves focusing on the most literal, most mundane details—and, staking a position on these, engaging in wars of nit-picking and criticism. There is the possibility that Taurus II's and Aquarius I's will make a go of it as like admirers not so much of each other but of aesthetic beauty and creativity in art, music and literature. Lacking real depth of feeling and passion in their own relationship, they may choose to find it in the works of others. Besides enjoying the arts, they may also be drawn to physical and sensuous beauty in people or, less often, in nature.

Friendships and love affairs in this combination are often taken up with tangible realities, like ready cash, expensive gifts, new cars, exotic vacations and the like. They can be considered superficial, but exhibit a kind of creative thinking that allows them to reach a level that most can only dream of. They are also capable of moving on to more meaningful experiences, perhaps involving the abandonment of such worldly pursuits, once these desires have been fulfilled. Spirituality may for this pair be an end achieved only after pursuing, attaining and finally peeling away many levels of illusion.

Marriages in this combination may be quite sensible affairs, built on practical premises and seeking attainable goals. Much time may be given over to an immensely satisfying pursuit of beauty and pleasure, in a comfortable domestic setting. Family relationships—particularly between uncle or aunt and nephew or niece, or between grandparent and grandchild—are likely to feature mutual appreciation of entertainment, special family get-togethers and the joys of play, whether mild sports or games. If co-workers in this combination have fun with each other regularly away from work, the potential of their relationship will be more fully developed, producing positive effects in the workplace.

ADVICE: *Achieve material goals, then find more meaningful ones. Keep on searching. Stay on your path. Don't sell out to money.*

CHRISTIE BRINKLEY (2/2/54)
BILLY JOEL (5/9/49)

Singer-composer Joel's hit song *Uptown Girl* (1983) was inspired by supermodel Brinkley, whom he saw as unattainable for an average-looking Long Island musician. They were married from 1985–94. *Also:* **Amos 'n' Andy** (radio team); **Sid Vicious & Johnny Rotten** (Sex Pistols); **Stewart Granger & Jean Simmons** (married; actors).

May 3–10
THE WEEK OF THE TEACHER
TAURUS II

January 31–February 7
THE WEEK OF YOUTH & EASE
AQUARIUS II

New Life

The focus of this relationship is rejuvenation. Breathing new life into shared projects, the other partner or even oneself is the specialty here, particularly when one has suffered failed relationships in the past, or has become jaded toward life. Not only may Taurus II's and Aquarius II's themselves benefit from this effect, but their relationship can serve as a model for other individuals and couples, teaching by example rather than precept. Revived feelings and emotions, perhaps disavowed or buried, can spring to life here in a glorious new setting. Appreciation not only of the joys of human life generally but specifically of rebirth in nature, as in springtime revels, is characteristic.

In love affairs, Taurus II's may be more what Aquarius II's need than what they want. Taurus II's are likely to be the more serious and emotionally mature of the pair, and to see Aquarius II's as childish; yet Aquarius II's may also awaken childlike qualities in them, letting them have fun and relax. In marriage, Aquarius II's risk trying to please their Taurus II spouses too much; in trying to live up to their partner's expectations they may forsake their own identity and life path. Children are of course deeply appreciated in a relationship so squarely based on the theme of rebirth, and Taurus II–Aquarius II parents can truly cherish their offspring. This is no guarantee that they will be financially responsible or emotionally stable, but a caring and deeply interested attitude toward their children is usually characteristic of them.

The most comfortable family relationships in this combination usually come when a Taurus II is the parent, grandparent, uncle or aunt to an Aquarius II child. Friendships and working relationships in this combination are usually easygoing, but require constant renewal through a broad spectrum of at least mildly challenging experiences. The worst scenario in this kind of relationship is to get stuck in a rut of repetitiveness. Business relationships here are often formed around new endeavors. Starting up a business, or reviving a failed one, is preferred to taking over a functioning enterprise.

ADVICE: *Be more childlike, less childish. Renewal implies maintenance. Explore one thing thoroughly before moving on to another—but don't get stuck.*

May 3–10

THE WEEK OF THE TEACHER
TAURUS II

February 8–15

THE WEEK OF ACCEPTANCE
AQUARIUS III

RELATIONSHIPS

STRENGTHS: **EVOLVING, STRENGTHENING, LEARNING**

WEAKNESSES: **CRITICIZING, FIGHTING, COMPLAINING**

BEST: **WORK**

WORST: **PARENT-CHILD**

A Deeper Rapport

This relationship brings the critical natures of both partners to the fore. Irritations, arguments and complaints are common, but there is also the possibility of each partner learning from the other, and of a deeper emotional rapport. Despite strife and conflict, or actually through them, a fairly harmonious balance can often be reached. These two need to learn when to leave well enough alone, however; in this relationship they are prone to constant tinkering, not only with the relationship but with each other's characters.

A lot of this relationship is out in the open, so that it tends to avoid frustration and the kind of suppression of feelings that leads to depression. Love affairs in this combination bring out the more volatile and aggressive side of Taurus II's, and Aquarius III's will have to stretch their ability to accept such behavior to the limit. They may need more love and attention than Taurus II's can bear to provide. Rejections here are often temporary, however, leaving the door open to reconciliations in which the partners put negativity behind them and try to correct their problems and address their issues. The relationship is likely to be a maturing experience, in which a great deal is learned about living and, especially, about how two people get along together.

Marriages in this combination will test Taurus II patience, for Aquarius III's need constant variety and change and can act very irresponsibly on occasion. Taurus II's will positively influence them, however, to meet their everyday obligations. Should Taurus II moral attitudes, stubbornness and dominance come to the fore, however, recalcitrance and rebellion are likely to result from the Aquarius III, fracturing and disabling the relationship. At work and as friends, Taurus II's and Aquarius III's get along well unless the relationship's demands become too great. If either of these personalities are parents, the perfectionistic tendencies in the relationship may be hard on either Taurus II or Aquarius III children, who will find it hard to live with being constantly pushed to improve themselves.

ADVICE: *Be more patient. See conflict as a learning experience. Rejection should be temporary. Let go of resentments. Overlook imperfection.*

ABRAHAM LINCOLN (2/12/1809)
JOHN WILKES BOOTH (5/10/1838)

Booth, a Shakespearean actor, was also a Confederate secret agent. In 1865 he assassinated President Lincoln in a theater during a play. *Also:* **Harry & Bess Truman** (married); **Mary Astor & John Barrymore** (affair; actors); **Luther Adler & Stella Adler** (married; actor/acting teacher); **Tammy Wynette & Burt Reynolds** (affair; country singer/actor).

May 3–10

THE WEEK OF THE TEACHER
TAURUS II

February 16–22

THE CUSP OF SENSITIVITY
AQUARIUS-PISCES CUSP

RELATIONSHIPS

STRENGTHS: **ENLIGHTENING, YOUTHFUL, PSYCHOLOGICAL**

WEAKNESSES: **UNAWARE, DEPENDENT, PROJECTIVE**

BEST: **FAMILY**

WORST: **WORK**

Bringing Childhood Alive

This relationship often deals with childhood feelings and situations. The stirring up of childhood memories is a central issue in the lives of Aquarius-Pisces, and is seldom a pleasant experience, albeit therapeutically necessary in cases of near-total repression. Taurus II's are also likely to benefit from examining their early years, but their own experiences may be easier to deal with than those of an Aquarius-Pisces. The examination of one's childhood in a critical and constructive light is less a matter of intellectual history than of bringing the past alive in the present and dealing with it in a healthier way than one could at the time.

Much acting out of childhood role patterns may emerge in marriages, friendships and love affairs between Taurus II's and Aquarius-Pisces, especially when the former stands in the parental role and the latter in the child's. Should this dynamic go unrecognized, Taurus II's may be bewildered by the depth of feeling they arouse in their partners, until it starts to dawn on them that this welter of emotion is not meant for them but for someone else. This will inevitably lead to a certain amount of resentment, and will affront the Taurus II sense of fairness. These roles may also be reversed, which can be quite healthy for Aquarius-Pisces, who may at last have to confront and perhaps sympathize with the difficulty of being a parent when they are forced to play that part themselves.

Family relationships are likely to focus on the very youngest years, those of infancy. Themes of helplessness and dependency, but also of innocent love and life-giving support, are likely to emerge here. By caring for a newborn child, sibling, grandchild or niece or nephew, various combinations of Taurus II's and Aquarius-Pisces may relive positive and negative aspects of their own childhoods, consciously exploring how such elements hold over in the day-to-day running of their lives as adults.

ADVICE: *Psychological investigations can distract you from work. Be more aware of role patterns. Learn from your past, particularly your childhood.*

CANDICE BERGEN (5/8/46)
EDGAR BERGEN (2/16/03)

Candice had a close and stimulating relationship with her late father, Edgar Bergen, the famous radio and stage ventriloquist (with "Charlie McCarthy"). *Also:* **Patrick Ewing & Charles Barkley** (Dream Team); **Audrey Hepburn & Hubert de Givenchy** (friends; client/couturier); **Edmund Wilson & Edna St. Vincent Millay** (lovers; writers); **Harry S. Truman & Margaret Truman** (father/daughter).

NANCY SPUNGEN (2/27/58)
SID VICIOUS (5/10/57)

Vicious led the Sex Pistols, a 70s punk group that challenged the music establishment. In 1979, he stabbed girlfriend Spungen to death in NY's Chelsea Hotel. While out on bail, he died of a heroin overdose. *Also:* **David O. Selznick & Jennifer Jones** (married; producer/ actress).

May 3–10

THE WEEK OF THE TEACHER
TAURUS II

February 23–March 2

THE WEEK OF SPIRIT
PISCES I

Extra Traffic

The thrust of this relationship will probably be social. Although Taurus is an earth sign and Pisces water (respectively denoting sensation and feeling), together these two are likely to explore the realms of thought and communication, provinces of the element of air. Favored here are group activities within which the relationship can function as an integral unit. It would not be surprising to find this pair actively involved in charity work or other causes that would involve them with others.

Friendships and love affairs will depend heavily on social interaction. Indeed the relationship's quality is often defined by the nature of its behavior in social settings. Taurus II's and Pisces I's are often interested in music, dancing, film and other entertainments, and together they may prove the moving force in organizing a group of family and friends to share in such activities. Being with other people so much of the time moves personal problems out of the spotlight, and makes the pair more relaxed, but also deprives them of the ability to confront each other, work out issues and deepen their relationship. They are of course capable of enjoying intimacy, but it is the social dimension that provides the punch for these two.

Marriages can either benefit or suffer from all this socializing. Having friends constantly present may weaken or strengthen domestic bonds, and the extra traffic around the house may eventually prove nerve-racking. Furthermore, both of these individuals have a reclusive side that their relationship may suppress, almost certainly creating tension. Triangles are common here, often hiding behind a facade of friendship but capable of surfacing and shattering the fragile bonds of the primary relationship. Choices inevitably have to be made, and they may be hard and painful.

Family relationships, particularly sibling and parent-child matchups, can be close, sympathetic and supportive. In the workplace, the Taurus II–Pisces I relationship may be entertaining to the group but unable to hold up its end of things, especially when brute stamina, application and concentration are required.

ADVICE: *Spend enough time alone. Needing attention should not become addictive. Enjoy each other without distractions. Improve social skills.*

ROBERT BROWNING (5/7/1812)
ELIZABETH BARRETT (3/6/1806)

When these two met, Browning, unlike Barrett, was unknown. After a fervent courtship, they married in 1846 and settled in Florence. Barrett believed her husband's fame would surpass her own, but history proved otherwise. *Also:* **John Brown & Harriet Tubman** (abolitionists); **Audrey Hepburn & Rex Harrison** (co-stars, *My Fair Lady*); **Roberto Rossellini & Anna Magnani** (longtime friends).

May 3–10

THE WEEK OF THE TEACHER
TAURUS II

March 3–10

THE WEEK OF THE LONER
PISCES II

Eminently Qualified

There is a natural sympathy between these two, but also a competition over who will be the center of attention. This can be dealt with if each individual sacrifices ego needs for the good of the pair, concentrating on making the relationship itself shine in a circle of friends or family. Thus a divisive tendency can instead become a unifying theme, turning a weakness into a strength. Another example of positive metamorphosis here appears in the financial sphere, where Taurus II's and Pisces II's who tend to be spendthrifts, or who are unrealistic about long-range investments, can do a turnaround as a duo, together showing financial astuteness and good sense.

Love affairs are a notable area in which competition for attention can divide the partners and create open conflict. Needs and demands of this kind can get out of hand, and if the partners fail to receive attention from each other, they may be forced to seek it elsewhere. This can undermine the relationship's stability, and in worst-case scenarios can destroy it.

Friendships and marriages are probably the most likely setups in this combination to be successful in transforming egotistical drives. In these kinds of relationship, this pair may be eminently qualified to serve as a progressive force for change, a refuge for others in times of need and a dependable anchor in providing economic stability. This may also be true of Taurus II's and Pisces II's who go into business together, whether they are also spouses or friends or their connection is purely commercial. The Taurus II refusal to try to make rules governing the actions of those they live and work with can be helpful in avoiding conflict here, for this kind of attitude is essential for the happiness and productivity of Pisces II's.

In family relationships, particularly parent-child matchups of either combination, rebellion against strict authority is unlikely to be an issue. But the opposite attitude—excessive permissiveness and absence of guidance—may prove a problem if it encourages rebellious or sociopathic behavior in the outside world.

ADVICE: *Beware of being too permissive. Guidance is often a crying need. Don't let the need for attention get out of hand. Cultivate quiet confidence.*

May 3–10

THE WEEK OF THE TEACHER
TAURUS II

March 11–18

THE WEEK OF DANCERS & DREAMERS
PISCES III

Performance Arts

 RELATIONSHIPS

STRENGTHS: **EXTROVERTED, ARTISTIC, STIMULATING**

WEAKNESSES: **NOISY, BUSY, UNSYMPATHETIC**

BEST: **FAMILY**

WORST: **MARRIAGE**

This relationship stimulates extroversion, and indeed its focus may well be a fascination with performance, whether as participants or as audience. A melding of interests in music, dance, theater and design is often prominent here. The relationship may be known for its aesthetic orientation in its immediate environment, and can even reach a wider circle, perhaps by mounting stage productions or supervising activities of artistic interest.

In love affairs and marriages, a balance must be struck between intimacy, quiet, contemplation and extroversion. Passionate Taurus II's may at times be a bit threatening to mild Pisces III's, who, however, are quite capable of matching this partner's sensuousness on a regular basis. They may diverge when Taurus II's take a frank and uncompromising approach to the relationship, eschewing emotional sympathy and romance—essential qualities to many Pisces III's. Independent Taurus II's will also be unwilling or unable to satisfy the Pisces III need to be needed.

Within the family, this relationship may have a strong effect in promoting knowledge and enjoyment of performance arts. This influence can bring a great deal to the group's overall cultural awareness. A Taurus II–Pisces III friendship will similarly exert its influence on a social circle that enjoys going out to clubs and concerts.

It is essential to both Pisces III's and Taurus II's that both they and their co-workers (or, if they are bosses, their employees) be happy in the workplace and enjoy themselves at work-related social gatherings. In and of itself, work means little to them without this kind of emotional reward. And if they are business partners or executives, they are clever enough to realize that good will and happiness, as well as tangible signs of appreciation (perhaps in the form of gifts or bonuses), are powerful motivating factors in meeting deadlines and production quotas.

NICOLAAS BLOEMBERGEN (3/11/20)
ARTHUR L. SCHAWLOW (5/5/21)

Compatible co-workers, Schawlow and Bloembergen (along with Kai M. Siegbahn) shared the 1981 Nobel Prize for physics. Schawlow researched laser microscopy; Bloembergen, involved in the laser's early development, found enhancement techniques for spectroscopy.

ADVICE: *Develop your meditative side. Cultivate your inner space. Don't get carried away with social activities. Leave time for quiet intimacy.*

May 11–18

THE WEEK OF THE NATURAL
TAURUS III

May 11–18

THE WEEK OF THE NATURAL
TAURUS III

A Barrel of Monkeys

 RELATIONSHIPS

STRENGTHS: **UNINHIBITED, VIVACIOUS, ACCEPTING**

WEAKNESSES: **CHAOTIC, INSECURE, FICKLE**

BEST: **FAMILY**

WORST: **LOVE**

How natural can you get? Although this relationship has an undeniable tendency to let it all hang out, repressive and inhibiting tendencies may be at work as well, particularly if the partners' talents, interests and activities are divergent or mutually exclusive, with each disapproving of the other's approach. Yet if these two are able to respect such differences, as they usually can, the relationship's value will be enhanced rather than diminished. These two fun-loving individuals make an exuberant and joyous combination, albeit a chaotic one. On the downside, they may bring out each other's not inconsiderable insecurities, creating an underlying instability.

Two Taurus III's can be more fun than a barrel of monkeys. Enjoyment is of paramount importance here, and the only single rule is to be oneself. Love affairs and friendships are often affectionate and open rather than deep and passionate, and instability and infidelity can threaten the relationship's longevity, but sharing and acceptance often alleviate what for others could be insurmountable difficulties. Jealousy and claiming attitudes are seldom a problem here.

Marriages and work relationships in this combination can be highly productive, but vacations, entertainment and humor are essential to keep mates and co-workers in a positive frame of mind. Criticism from grandparents, bosses or other colleagues or family members on how children are raised or work is done can be an extremely sensitive point, often revealing underlying feelings of inferiority and producing anger and aggression; the relationship may impulsively switch into strong defense or attack modes.

Families with pairs of Taurus III parents, siblings, grandparents or aunts and uncles can be vivacious groups. These matchups will enliven the lives not only of family members but of those attached to them through bonds of friendship, love, work and marriage. But the energy level of these families can be chaotic at times, disturbing siblings or parents of a more serious or meditative nature.

ANDRE GREGORY (5/11/34)
RICHARD AVEDON (5/15/23)

Photographer Avedon and theater personality Gregory are close friends. Avedon has been voted one of the world's 10 greatest photographers, best known for his portraits. Gregory, a director-actor-producer, was star (and subject) of the quirky film *My Dinner with Andre* (1981). The friends appeared together in a 90s documentary.

Also: Henry Fonda & Margaret Sullavan (married; actors).

ADVICE: *Develop greater self-trust. Work on rooting out insecurities. Criticism need not be a threat. Stabilize your feelings. Seek moderation.*

STRENGTHS: **PERSONABLE, ENERGETIC, PRODUCTIVE**
WEAKNESSES: **REBELLIOUS, STUBBORN, OVEREMOTIONAL**
BEST: **WORK**
WORST: **LOVE**

MARCEL BREUER (5/21/02)
WALTER GROPIUS (5/18/1883)

From 1920–28 architect-designer Breuer worked with Gropius at the newly established Bauhaus, leaving Germany when the Nazis took power in 1933. They resumed collaboration in 1937 as professors at Harvard, working together closely until 1946. **Also: Henry Fonda & Jimmy Stewart** (early roommates; actors); **Frank Capra & Jimmy Stewart** (collaborators; director/actor).

May 11–18
THE WEEK OF THE NATURAL
TAURUS III

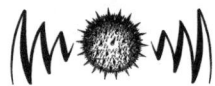

May 19–24
THE CUSP OF ENERGY
TAURUS-GEMINI CUSP

Hair-Trigger Responses

Although one would expect a melding of these two to produce "natural energy," the chemical equation here is not always straightforward or simple. True, the relationship is often positive and indeed charming, but rebelliousness and competitiveness can arise as well. A tendency for both partners to think they know best can undermine the relationship's solidity and its capacity to act effectively as a unit; these two often move in opposite directions from the start. Both Taurus III's and Taurus-Geminis have hair-trigger tempers when they receive what they see as unfair criticism, but their relationship with each other often magnifies such responses out of all proportion.

Although earth and air, elements of sensation and thought respectively, appear to dominate here (Taurus being an earth sign, Gemini air), feelings (water) tend to run high in this combination, and in fact are its greatest challenge. In love affairs and between friends, powerful emotions can be rewarding, destructive or both. Serious instabilities and mood swings can mar even the more blissful moments of such relationships, with the sudden surfacing of negative, even violently destructive feelings bewildering both partners.

The shared tasks of work and marriage often help stabilize this relationship. At work, intense productivity is possible if emotion can be kept out of the picture. The energy level here can be extremely high, but burnout and collapse are also constant dangers. Parents and bosses of either sign will have to show great sensitivity if they are not to arouse rebellious attitudes in their children and employees.

Parent-child and sibling relationships, although often warm and understanding, may also include serious difficulties with judgmental attitudes, rejection and lack of sympathy. Arguments often arise over the handling of domestic matters, with stubborn convictions being defended on both sides.

ADVICE: *Explore emotional areas with awareness. Understanding can alleviate rebelliousness. Conserve energies at work. Practice patience.*

STRENGTHS: **ECLECTIC, LIFE-SEEKING, COMMUNICATIVE**
WEAKNESSES: **NERVOUS, SPENDTHRIFT, UNFAITHFUL**
BEST: **FRIENDSHIP**
WORST: **LOVE**

JOHNNY WEISSMULLER (6/2/04)
MAUREEN O'SULLIVAN (5/17/11)

The brutish physique of Weissmuller, former Olympic gold-medal swimmer, and the petite charm of actress O'Sullivan gave this pair a unique screen presence as Hollywood's most famous Tarzan and Jane. They made 6 films together.

May 11–18
THE WEEK OF THE NATURAL
TAURUS III

May 25–June 2
THE WEEK OF FREEDOM
GEMINI I

An Eclectic Blend

Energy is the keyword of this combination, which manifests activity and movement, particularly of the kind that goes out into the world and gets what it wants. The relationship is characterized not so much by ambition, or a desire to control, as by a lust for life. Diverse in its interests, it manifests an eclectic blend of style, politics, philosophy, aesthetics and love of nature. The energy between the partners is palpable, virtually visible to the naked eye. These two affect each other profoundly, heightening each other's sensitivity to visual, auditory and olfactory stimuli but also making themselves nervous, impatient and irritable. The lines of communication between them are open, however, and they love conversation, often of the rapid, incessant variety that makes for scintillating exchanges (if also sometimes repetitive ones). This duo will often be invited to attend parties and other social gatherings where they can air their lively and up-to-date views on many subjects.

Love affairs in this combination may be problematic. Taurus III's will generally seek a deeper level of involvement than may be desired by Gemini I's, who may be disturbed by outlandish or erratic Taurus III behavior but can also back off because they often have difficulty making a total commitment. Taurus III's are sensitive to rejection, and are likely to read this behavior as one.

Once a commitment has been made, however, marriages in this combination can be quite solid. It's true that they can be plagued by ungrounded energies, particularly given both partners' tendency to roam—unfaithfulness here is no surprise. But over time, this can be reduced to an issue of no great importance. One of the joys of this relationship will be the development of unusual tastes in home decorating, clothing and music.

Taurus III–Gemini I business partnerships are often dynamic and successful. But the handling of finances can quickly run out of hand, featuring uncontrolled spending and concomitant personal debts and credit-card bills. Hiring good bookkeepers and accountants, and heeding their advice, may be a partial solution here.

ADVICE: *Cultivate calm and repose. Learn to relax. Turn off your motor mouth occasionally. Concentrate on one thing at a time. Control spending.*

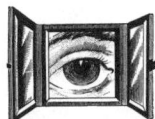

May 11–18

THE WEEK OF THE NATURAL
TAURUS III

June 3–10

THE WEEK OF NEW LANGUAGE
GEMINI II

A Creative Outlet

A wildness can manifest here, reinforcing these partners' freedom-loving, eccentric sides. Since the relationship focuses on independence, however, the resulting lack of stability or security is not necessarily bad for it. Furthermore, although the combination may encourage a desire to overthrow tradition, or to combat more sedate modes of thought or behavior, it isn't really as destabilizing as it can seem. These two are quite capable of settling down to work within the system if they want to, and the revolutionary temperament that they encourage in each other may be mainly a form of play or creativity that, if given an outlet, can leave them quite staid individuals.

Love and marriage will usually only work out if both parties can be independent in thought and action. Indeed, they may be happiest living separately, feeling no heavy responsibilities to each other, and above all getting together only when they want to. If one of them is needy, however, particularly a Gemini II in search of a strong, stable, dependable partner, he or she is likely to end up frustrated and resentful. Taurus III's tired of shouldering daily responsibilities may likewise begin to see Gemini II's as flaky and unreliable.

Undemanding friendships can work here, particularly since these two are likely to value innovative and unconventional attitudes, and in particular are likely to develop unusual forms of communication featuring creative uses of language. Both partners will probably be enthusiastic about this relationship as a creative outlet in their lives. Parent-child matchups may be less free than the relationship requires, leading to breakdowns in communication, but siblings are likely to admire each other's talents and abilities, which often coalesce effectively in sports, hobbies, clubs and other group endeavors. Perhaps the most successful relationships in this combination will be working ones, which may feature open channels of communication, a meeting of technical skills, and the provision of structure and stability—particularly when these two are co-workers at the same level in the hierarchy.

ADVICE: *Pursue common goals but retain your individuality. Don't expect too much. Give what is needed on a day-to-day basis. Learn from each other.*

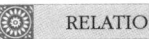

CZARINA ALEXANDRA (6/6/1872)
CZAR NICHOLAS II (5/18/1868)

Emerging as the dominant partner of this 1894 marriage, Alexandra's protectiveness over the insecure Nicholas, along with her social and political incompetence, seriously damaged the prestige of the Russian royal family. *Also:* **Natasha Richardson & Liam Neeson** (married; actors); **Salvador Dali & Federico Garcia Lorca** (artist/writer; Garcia Lorca's love for Dali was unrequited).

May 11–18

THE WEEK OF THE NATURAL
TAURUS III

June 11–18

THE WEEK OF THE SEEKER
GEMINI III

Absolute Freedom

In the best-case scenario, the extreme need for freedom here will apply to the relationship itself rather than to its partners. Together they may yearn to break through limitations of time and space, and even succeed in doing so. This pair will balk at all forms of constriction, definition, repression and dominance.

Absolute freedom is difficult to maintain within any love relationship, however, and this one is no exception. Thus friendships are more realistic here. The absence of sexual passion, jealousy and claiming attitudes will lessen internal conflict, while the duo will be able to act together dynamically in a variety of activities, whether in a social, outdoor or creative setting.

At work, Taurus III–Gemini III pairs may cause trouble to employers, bosses and executives, and may even have to be separated. If left to work on their own as a team, however, perhaps trouble-shooting or developing new projects, they can be of great value to an organization. Marriages between them may be less successful, especially if children are involved. The patience and domestic skills necessary to make close and stable family life feasible are not usually forthcoming in this relationship. If these two give themselves over to travel, on the other hand, periodically changing jobs, careers or residences—in short, constantly seeking new horizons, or believing they can if they want to—the marriage may be mutually satisfying. Gemini III financial skills and Taurus III social abilities will aid greatly in such innovative endeavors.

As siblings, Taurus III's and Gemini III's are likely to be rebellious against parental authority, and to seek autonomy at an early age. They will want to go where they want to, when they want to, without explanation or permission. If this freedom is granted, they may be quite affectionate and sympathetic to their parents, but if it is denied, expect the worst.

ADVICE: *Compromise occasionally. Learn the value of diplomacy. Others want their freedom, too. You can carry your home with you—inside.*

ROBERTO DURAN (6/16/51)
SUGAR RAY LEONARD (5/17/56)

In June, 1980, legendary Leonard lost his middleweight title to arch-rival Duran, the Panamanian with "fists of stone." Determined to regain it, he fought Duran again that year, forcing him to quit the fight with the words "no mas" ("no more"). *Also:* **Otto Frank & Anne Frank** (father/daughter; concentration-camp prisoners).

PAULA ABDUL (6/19/62)
EMILIO ESTEVEZ (5/12/62)

Besides acting, Estevez has also written, directed and produced movies. Equally versatile is pop singer Abdul, a dancer, choreographer and tv actress. The couple married in 1992 and divorced 2 years later.

May 11–18
THE WEEK OF THE NATURAL
TAURUS III

June 19–24
THE CUSP OF MAGIC
GEMINI-CANCER CUSP

Opening New Worlds

This relationship focuses on larger realms, foreign lands, and philosophical or religious systems, to which it needs to apply independent thinking. It expands the higher mind. The problems lie in its handling of the mundane: these partners are quite different in their needs, wants and styles, ebullient Taurus III extroversion and enchanting Gemini-Cancer introversion making them an unlikely pair. Still, although Taurus is an earth sign and Gemini-Cancer fuses air and water, their relationship emphasizes fire, the element of initiation and intuition. If they spend time originating projects and pursuing dreams, allowing themselves passion, excitement and challenge, their relationship will profit.

Love between these partners, particularly romantic love, will be charmed and seductive. Intimacy both at home (the Gemini-Cancer contribution) and in nature (a Taurus III specialty) will allow meaningful sharing. Psychologically, each partner may have a lifelong secret wish that can be satisfied only by someone almost their opposite; as in so many fairy tales, Gemini-Cancers and Taurus III's may fall in love with a projection of their own deepest, often unrecognized inner self. The differences between these two become more pronounced in marriages and friendships. Taurus III's will have to understand the Gemini-Cancer need for both privacy and intimacy, and to restrain themselves both from flooding the house with guests at all hours and from being away from home too much. Gemini-Cancers in turn may need to learn to be more sociable.

These two might do well as business partners marketing an exciting product or service, with Gemini-Cancer ideas being implemented by dynamic Taurus III energies. Gemini-Cancers could handle development, day-to-day operations and public relations while Taurus III's were out drumming up sales. But they would regularly have to consult financial advice, an area in which their relationship would lack natural strengths.

Misunderstandings are likely in the family, where exuberant Taurus III's will tread on tender Gemini-Cancer feelings. They will also be apt to read Gemini-Cancer introspection as rejection, making them prickly and nervous.

ADVICE: *Learn to compromise. Emulate each other's strengths. Work together when possible. Fulfill each other's dreams. Give many gifts.*

MARGARET SULLAVAN (5/16/1896)
WILLIAM WYLER (7/1/02)

Sullavan's stage and screen career peaked during the 30s and 40s. In 1934, she married director Wyler, her 2nd of 3 husbands. She appeared only once in his scores of films—*The Good Fairy* (1935). They divorced in 1936.

May 11–18
THE WEEK OF THE NATURAL
TAURUS III

June 25–July 2
THE WEEK OF THE EMPATH
CANCER I

Finding a Common Language

Problems of communication are central to this relationship. If these partners fail to learn to express their deeper and more complex needs, feelings and sensitivities, they may find little to hold them together and much to break them apart. Everything left unsaid builds until it explodes, aggressively and destructively. Not especially attracted to each other physically or romantically, Taurus III's and Cancer I's may have difficulty finding a common language, whether spoken or other. In certain family and work relationships, however, this lack of subjective response can actually support constructive communication.

Love and marriage will rarely prove fertile ground for this relationship. In exceptional cases, however, the Cancer I talent for empathy will gel with Taurus III human sympathy to create an atmosphere of emotional support and respect. Friendships are possible here, but they may be highly complex: when Cancer I's get bottled up inside, there is usually little anyone can do to help, and they may become envious of Taurus III extroversion and social skills. Taurus III's, meanwhile, may be brought down from their enthusiastic highs by Cancer I criticism, sarcasm and refusal to be motivated by their own natural energies. Taurus III's are subject to agonizing depressions, and it will be easy for them to blame such states on their Cancer I friends.

The obligatory day-to-day interactions and shared experiences of parent-child and sibling matchups may lead to improved communication, and there may also be hard-to-define genetic connections. Yet these two can still seem as different as night and day, and others will wonder how they became incarnate in the same family group. Working out such differences may be precisely the task that this lifetime holds for them, however, making their relationship a crucial learning process, with acceptance and understanding being the important lessons.

Work relationships here may be effective and efficient, especially if there is little personal contact. Objective skills, ranging from financial to technical, will make this pair a valuable asset to any company. Their differences may coalesce effectively in implementing projects, making their relationship much stronger than the sum of their strengths.

ADVICE: *Working out differences is the name of the game. Learn from each other. Cultivate understanding. Use objective strengths. Be sympathetic.*

STRENGTHS: **IMAGINATIVE,
EXPANSIVE, CREATIVE**

WEAKNESSES: **UNREALISTIC,
REJECTED, DISAPPOINTED**

BEST: **MARRIAGE**

WORST: **WORK**

Visionary Energy

This relationship can brew up some fantastic visions. Its grand, even gigantic ideas and plans represent a meeting of two separate, vivid fantasy worlds that can produce amazing results—if they are in synch. Alas, relatively few of these dreams come to fruition, and indeed most can be highly unrealistic. Yet their originality and imaginative content are memorable.

These two are capable of close friendships that can develop into love affairs and marriages. Quiet or hidden Cancer II's will often be fascinated by colorful, flamboyant Taurus III's, who perhaps mirror their own secret desire to be more extroverted. Cancer II's can become obsessed with the wishes of Taurus III's, who may in turn come to acknowledge them and help them to unlock their hidden visions. In the relationships formed in such cases, fantasy and dreams will blossom, encouraging intimate enjoyment and exciting projects in the shape of a full-blown romance.

Should the result be marriage or a permanent living situation, whether between friends or lovers, the most extraordinary domestic space can be created in which these two will be liberated to externalize their fantasies without fear of failure or rejection. Such a space can be a laboratory for social or artistic forays into the world, but also a sanctum to retreat to when an unappreciative public creates disappointments. Marriages can be rich and full, but Taurus III–Cancer II parents who are considered quirky or far out by their more practical children or family members must be careful themselves not to reject their family's views and feelings.

The visionary energy of siblings or co-workers in this combination will not be easy for a family or company to deal with on a daily basis. If these two undermine practical endeavors, they will be counterproductive to the best interests of the group. Occasionally, such a family or business may decide to follow the dreams and longings of the Taurus III–Cancer II pair, only to meet with disappointment. After such a failure, it will be difficult for them to make others take their ideas seriously again.

ADVICE: *Keep in touch with reality as well as with fantasy. Fewer expectations may produce fewer failures. Learn to handle disappointment. Stay strong.*

BILLY MARTIN (5/16/28)
GEORGE STEINBRENNER (7/4/30)

Despite winning 2 World Series together, Martin's hot temper as Yankees manager and owner Steinbrenner's meddling eroded their dreams for the team. Steinbrenner fired and re-hired Martin several times during their association.
***Also:* Henry Cabot Lodge & Henry Cabot Lodge, Jr.** (grandfather/grandson; Mass. senators); **Felipe Alou & Moises Alou** (father/son; baseball players).

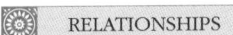

STRENGTHS: **STRIVING,
SPIRITUAL, SUCCESSFUL**

WEAKNESSES: **UNDERMINING,
NOISY, COUNTERPRODUCTIVE**

BEST: **FRIENDSHIP**

WORST: **MARRIAGE**

Fueling the Motor

This combination heightens its partners' ambition and aims to transcend all limitations, generally through the avenues of public life or career. These two want to go somewhere, and they want others to see them do it. Engaging in something bigger than you are can bring out feelings of inadequacy, however, which this relationship will magnify—both these personalities can overreact to insecurity. And unless they are shooting for the same goal, and are committed to being a team, their insecurities will pit them against each other: as soon as one person gets ahead, the other will be jealous, frustrated and angry.

Love and marriage here are problematic. Cancer III's are content alone, and if they do look for a partner, they will want someone stable and dependable. They may disapprove of or reject Taurus III wildness, and Taurus III financial irresponsibility can drive them up the wall. With Taurus III's requiring more freedom and Cancer III's more commitment, there may be a stalemate or breakdown here. And Cancer III's who feel insecure about their partners may respond by trying to manipulate or dominate them, Taurus III's by flooding them with charm; either of these reactions is likely to arouse further insecurity and resistance.

Friendships, particularly nondemanding ones, can be excellent here. A love of spiritual or environmental subjects may feature. These two will share without fear of censure; Taurus III's can stimulate Cancer III imagination, and Cancer III's can help teach Taurus III's about responsibility.

As colleagues, these two may be uncomfortably competitive. This will stimulate the quantity and quality of their work, but there is a danger that they will behave somewhat underhandedly or at least unhelpfully. Should they find themselves at the top of the heap, however, they may have to bury the hatchet, at least temporarily, to keep the business afloat. A solid partnership between them can achieve a lot. Antagonisms can also emerge in the family sphere, especially between opposite-sex pairs of siblings or cousins. But the ruckus these pairs raise usually sounds worse than it is, and their relationships may evolve into lasting and mature ones.

ADVICE: *Recognize insecurity and keep it in check. Don't let the tail wag the dog. Mute dissension. Preserve group tranquillity. Develop spiritually.*

LINCOLN ELLSWORTH (5/12/1880)
ROALD AMUNDSEN (7/16/1872)

Polar explorer and millionaire Ellsworth accompanied and financed Amundsen on the Polar Flying Expedition of 1925. In 1926, the pair (along with Umberto Nobile) completed the first transpolar dirigible flight.
***Also:* Thomas Wedgwood & Josiah Wedgwood** (son/father; photographic inventors).

May 11–18

THE WEEK OF THE NATURAL
TAURUS III

ARCHIBALD COX (5/17/12)
ELLIOT RICHARDSON (7/20/20)

During the 1973 Watergate cover-up scandal, special prosecutor Cox pressed Nixon to release his incriminating tapes of White House conversations. When Nixon ordered Attorney General Richardson to fire Cox, Richardson refused, then promptly resigned.

Shiva the Mascot

On-again-off-again, high-low, excess-lack—bipolar behavior is characteristic of this relationship, which is apt to have few dull moments. Indeed it may reinforce each personality's dark side, producing exciting and at times destructive behavior. Destruction, however, is very much part of the creative process, and in this respect Shiva, the Hindu god of creation and destruction, might be the relationship's mascot. Should Cancer-Leos want someone to provide a peaceful environment and to balance their contrasting moods, it is unlikely to be a Taurus III; these two are much more likely to bring out each other's wild sides and mood swings.

Love and family relationships will stir deep emotions, sudden passionate outbursts and expressions of undying love or hate. If hatred is in play, it may smolder quietly and go unnoticed for long periods before erupting, or be reflected by moods of disinterest or neglect masked by the appearance of toleration. Yet these two may be afraid of letting go, afraid of seeing everything fly apart. This fear often fixes such behavior, making suppressed anger difficult to dislodge.

Friendships and marriages may be much more satisfying. Busy with adventure, vigorous sports and other physically challenging activities, such relationships will have their emotional ups and downs, but these are usually subordinated to exciting confrontations that paradoxically provide a measure of stability—they let off steam. The positive attitudes and innovative approaches of Taurus III's will counter Cancer-Leos' tendency to get emotionally blocked, sweeping them out of their depressions. Taurus III's will benefit from being appreciated for such active stances. For these two to have children together will satisfy Shiva's lust for reproduction and stimulate creativity. When these two are co-workers or partners, they are only likely to achieve success if the Taurus III has the patience and interest to work unflaggingly side-by-side with the Cancer-Leo. But the Taurus III will probably lack the psychological understanding that Cancer-Leos need.

ADVICE: *Being bored is no crime. Cultivate more peaceful moments. Practice meditation or yoga. Center yourself in the here and now.*

May 11–18

THE WEEK OF THE NATURAL
TAURUS III

July 26–August 2

THE WEEK OF AUTHORITY
LEO I

LIBERACE (5/16/19)
GEORGE LIBERACE (7/31/11)

Liberace, the popular pianist known for his candelabras and flashy costumes, was America's highest-paid entertainer of the 60s and 70s. Brother George was his conservative straight man and business manager. *Also:* **Sian Phillips & Peter O'Toole** (married; actors); **Yogi Berra & Casey Stengel** (Yankee managers); **Oona O'Neill & Geraldine Chaplin** (mother/daughter).

A Private Enchantment

The Taurus III–Leo I mix can generate a strange sort of enchantment, even a kind of glitz, in which admiration of serious principles and sensuous enjoyment hedonistically combine. The serious side of Leo I's is likely to cast a shadow over the relationship, but this is by no means a one-sided matchup, for Taurus III energies provide a counterweight of enjoyment and fun. This unusual combination lets Leo I's relax and Taurus III's focus. Although both of its participants are ordinarily extroverted, its mystery is such that they are inclined to keep the magic between them private rather than place it on view. Yet its shine will be apparent to all.

Love affairs between these two are highly unconventional. As unattached lovers they rarely hit it off, but Leo I's who are already married or committed may quite possibly seek excitement, adventure and romance with a Taurus III outside their primary relationship. Taurus III's are unlikely to withdraw from such encounters out of fear; in fact their unconventionality and unrepressed natural instincts will often be stimulated by Leo I advances or availability. Such relationships can go on quite pleasurably for years without the world being much the wiser.

Friendships here are rarely of the sharing variety, and have a limited depth of contact. Partaking of this relationship's strange mixture of seriousness and pleasure, these two can share fun times together. They never sacrifice enough of their strong egos, however, to build a lasting and meaningful friendship.

Marriages, parent-child and working relationships are likely to be dominated by the clash of authoritarian and rebellious attitudes. Taurus III's will feel Leo I authority, no matter how muted or subtle, as a repressive force, and will want to be allowed to be what they are without criticism or censure. Although Leo I parents, bosses or spouses will reward Taurus III children, employees or mates fairly for jobs well done, they are unlikely to show any more kindness or understanding than that. Thus Taurus III's are likely to resent them, seeing their attitudes as inhuman and at times unnatural.

ADVICE: *Limit judgmental attitudes and rebelliousness. Share whenever possible. Sacrifice may be necessary. Beware of hurting others.*

May 11–18

THE WEEK OF THE NATURAL
TAURUS III

August 3–10

THE WEEK OF BALANCED STRENGTH
LEO II

Granting Guidance

RELATIONSHIPS

STRENGTHS: **STRUCTURED, SELECTIVE, FUN**

WEAKNESSES: **ADRIFT, COMBATIVE, CLOSED**

BEST: **MARRIAGE**

WORST: **LOVE**

The challenge of this relationship is adopting rules, or at the very least a recognizable structure, to provide guidance in everyday life. Once such a system is agreed upon (which may take weeks, months or even years), the relationship can move forward constructively. Until then, it is likely to drift according to whichever way the winds of desire are blowing, and is unlikely to drop anchor in a safe haven.

In love relationships Leo II's tend to be long-suffering. Also, where Taurus III's may be out the door in short order when things go wrong, Leo II's blame themselves. Love affairs between these two, then, may well end with a grieving Leo II and a damaged but quickly mending Taurus III on the loose. When things go well, on the other hand, the relationship can be highly rewarding in physical terms, and although sexual encounters tend to bring out power struggles, their pleasure is often proportional to their degree of conflict. And when passions have cooled, it may sometimes be possible for kindness, sympathy and true feelings of love to be expressed.

Leo II's need to lighten up and have fun, and in friendships and marriages Taurus III's can prove just right for them. This pair can recognize boundaries and still have a great time, whether in conversation or in some entertaining activity. Needing little group contact or large-scale social interaction, the relationship will admit only a very few friends or married couples to its circle, and if these drop out of the picture they are unlikely to be replaced easily, if at all.

Family and work relationships will benefit from structural hierarchies, where it is abundantly clear what is permitted and what is not. Whether as siblings or co-workers, Taurus III's and Leo II's have the capacity to pull together and make a dynamic team. But a Taurus III employee or child may find a Leo II boss or parent highly unsympathetic at times, and capable of a stony and forbidding silence.

EMILIO ESTEVEZ (5/12/62)
MARTIN SHEEN (8/3/40)

Sheen was born Ramon Estevez, after his Spanish father. Emilio chose his father's original surname when he began acting and has a close relationship with Sheen, who has helped guide his son's career. **Also: Ted Mann & Rhonda Fleming** (married; theater magnate/actress).

ADVICE: *Hang in there, but also know when to give up. Agree on common rules. Keep up your end of the bargain. Stay open to outside influences.*

May 11–18

THE WEEK OF THE NATURAL
TAURUS III

August 11–18

THE WEEK OF LEADERSHIP
LEO III

No Guarantees

RELATIONSHIPS

STRENGTHS: **EMPATHIC, LOYAL, RELIABLE**

WEAKNESSES: **SELFISH, UNSYMPATHIZING, RUTHLESS**

BEST: **FRIENDSHIP**

WORST: **WORK**

Conventional astrology correctly predicts a rough ride in this relationship because of a fixed and square orientation (these partners lie 90° apart in the zodiac; Leo and Taurus are fixed signs). The key concept here is empathy, but although the partners understand each other's feelings, there is no guarantee that they will be sympathetic to, honor or even pay attention to them; an aggression, even anger, is dormant in the relationship. This is, in fact, a curious combination of empathy and selfishness, so that the partners can be quite unfeeling and even ruthless toward each other, and also in dealing with other people.

Usually far more flexible than Leo III's, in this relationship Taurus III's are generally the ones most able to adapt and compromise. In love and family relationships, however, they may have no interest at all in doing so. When disputes arise between lovers, parents and children, or siblings in this combination, for example, Taurus III's are quite capable of soothing the savage Leo III lion or lioness, but will do so only when they want to, even though it is actually in their interest to do so. In addition, since Leo III's are not only normally leaders but tend to be very giving in relationships, virtually doting on those they love or are close to, this particular relationship may end up being directed—not necessarily very rationally—by the Taurus III, who will manipulate predictable Leo III attitudes.

In friendship, Leo III's are quite loyal but may not have enough interest in the Taurus III's activities to share them. These two are likely to be mutually supportive in times of distress, but not necessarily attentive to each other's needs during busy or successful periods. Their bonds will stay intact, however, and even when physically distant they will keep their lines of communication open through use of telephone, mail and fax.

At work, these two are often too reactive to each other's moods to make effective partners or co-workers. If they are friends or spouses, their careers are better kept separated.

DEBRA WINGER (5/16/55)
TIMOTHY HUTTON (8/16/60)

Winger and Hutton were married from 1986–90 and had a son. Their acting careers overlapped in *Made in Heaven* (1987), which starred Hutton and featured Winger in an uncredited role, playing the part of a goateed young man. **Also: Fürst von Metternich & Napoleon Bonaparte** (foreign minister/emperor).

ADVICE: *Try to be sympathetic as well as empathic. Show that you care. Be kinder and less selfish. Beware of insensitivity. Pay attention.*

STRENGTHS: **MOTIVATING, OPENING, DEEPENING**

WEAKNESSES: **TYRANNICAL, INSENSITIVE, DISEMPOWERING**

BEST: **FAMILY**

WORST: **CAREER**

PIERCE BROSNAN (5/16/52)
SEAN CONNERY (8/25/30)

Separated in age by 22 years, Connery and Brosnan have portrayed the oldest and newest 007s in the James Bond movies. Connery launched the series in '62 with *Dr. No*, and Brosnan gave us the latest addition in '95 with *Goldeneye*.

May 11–18
THE WEEK OF THE NATURAL
TAURUS III

August 19–25
THE CUSP OF EXPOSURE
LEO-VIRGO CUSP

A Demand for Openness

This combination asks its partners to keep their feelings and attitudes frank and open rather than hidden and suppressed. A relationship that makes natural and unaffected behavior its main requirement would seem pleasant enough, but this is precisely the area where most Leo-Virgos have problems, and they may sometimes see the relationship as tyrannical or insensitive to them. They are apt to retaliate by ferreting out the insecurities of the Taurus III, who will in turn find the relationship uncomfortable. In the long run, however, Leo-Virgos usually soften in their resentment as they lose their inhibitions, while Taurus III's enjoy the structure that the relationship imposes.

In love and at work, Leo-Virgos want the option of hiding or revealing. The pressure to be open all the time will make them frustrated, and they may envy the easier attitudes of the Taurus III. Likewise, when deprived of the ability to reveal themselves dramatically, whether physically, emotionally or spiritually, at moments of their own choosing, they feel disempowered and curiously deadened by the sameness of a boring (albeit natural) routine. The relationship's denial of choice is likely to make them rebellious and perverse.

The dominance of Taurus III's, or more correctly of their belief in the direct approach, will be strongly felt in their friendships and marriages with Leo-Virgos, who may, once again, come to feel insecure about their ability to meet the demand to be natural and open. They may also come to hate themselves for being closed and secretive. This conflict is not only harmful but unnecessary: in striving to be themselves (maybe against the current of the relationship), Leo-Virgos will become stronger, and will also influence their partners by demonstrating the value of intimacy. If a balance is reached between introversion and extroversion, a calmer, more balanced state may result. Sympathetic and lively Taurus III parents and siblings will have a healthy effect on moody Leo-Virgo children and brothers or sisters. Conversely, the twists and turns of the Leo-Virgo character will fascinate curious Taurus III's, waking them up to their own hidden fantasies and desires.

ADVICE: *Don't feel threatened. Open up. Reveal who you really are. Teach the value of intimacy. Privacy is important, too. Strike a balance.*

STRENGTHS: **UNUSUAL, SHARING, INSPIRING**

WEAKNESSES: **EXPECTANT, JUDGMENTAL, COERCIVE**

BEST: **FRIENDSHIP**

WORST: **PARENT-CHILD**

JANET JACKSON (5/16/66)
MICHAEL JACKSON (8/29/58)

Janet established herself as a preeminent pop-funk star in the late '80s. In 1995, she collaborated with her decades-long famous brother on the single (and video) *Scream*.
Also: Debra Winger & Gov. Bob Kerrey (romance; actress/politician); **Dante Gabriel Rossetti & Edward Burne-Jones** (collaborators; artists); **Walter Gropius & Alma Schindler** (married; architect/artist).

May 11–18
THE WEEK OF THE NATURAL
TAURUS III

August 26–September 2
THE WEEK OF SYSTEM BUILDERS
VIRGO I

Being Silly

At its best, this relationship is fun, expressing a certain zaniness and a great deal of humor, but this is not the kind of humor one would expect from these two. Together they have a pointedly observational approach to human interaction, and a dry and compassionate wit—they laugh with people, not at them. This can be very entertaining for them; their relationship takes them out of their ordinary selves. Taurus III's, while natural, are always a bit self-important, while Virgo I's are a little rigid. The greatest gift this relationship can give them is the ability to laugh at themselves and at each other.

These two are in many ways opposites—Taurus III more free-flowing, Virgo I demanding structure—but they can accommodate each other, often through unconventional solutions. The lives of Taurus III's have a kind of entropy, a natural tendency to disorder, which is precisely what Virgo I's need a bit of in their somewhat rigid lives. In fact Virgo I sternness and inflexibility may be a defense against unconscious fears of disorder. Through trust, understanding and perhaps love, a Taurus III can inspire a Virgo I to be a more complete person.

Service-oriented Virgo I's may benefit from love and family matchups with Taurus III's, who are independent and may give them something of a rest. Taurus III spontaneity will be somewhat exasperating for Virgo I's, but it will also perk them up, energizing them and pushing them out of depression. Friendship is probably the best relationship for this process. Here Virgo I's will appreciate Taurus III naturalness, and the pair will be able to relax and have fun. Little will be out of bounds here—to be silly, goofy or crazy for a while will be valued rather than criticized. More "serious" relationships—work pairings, marriages, love affairs—may involve expectations that make it difficult for either partner to be himself. Virgo I's are likely to be emotionally demanding yet unable to give, while Taurus III's will feel judged for their sloppy behavior. Parent-child and teacher-student relationships may also go in this direction.

ADVICE: *Beware of laying on expectations. Self-fulfilling prophecies do come true. Learn what others have to teach. Put energies to work efficiently. Laugh at yourselves.*

May 11–18

THE WEEK OF THE NATURAL
TAURUS III

September 3–10

THE WEEK OF THE ENIGMA
VIRGO II

The Best Person

Responsibility is the keyword of this combination, but it is of a rather uncustomary type. The emphasis here is on responsibility less to others than to oneself, and in particular to one's self-development, perhaps in a spiritual or moral sense. The relationship may have a single principal slogan, which is "Be the very best person you can be." In pursuing such a path of self-expansion, this pairing demands determination.

Friendships and love affairs can be extremely close here. They often begin with an aggressive or curious Taurus III hanging around and hoping to be noticed by an attractive but shy Virgo II—who, however, will almost always give a signal that some further advance would be appreciated. Once the pair have acknowledged their mutual interest, things can move quickly toward intimacy. Taurus III's have an interesting way of ignoring the defenses of Virgo II's and going right to the heart of their personalities. These two may share a sense of fantasy and of comedy, but the Virgo II tendency to withdraw emotionally will periodically frustrate Taurus III's, especially when it occurs during intimate moments. Taurus III's can go far, however, in convincing their partner of the need to be truly present and honestly involved.

In marriages and work relationships, the idea of self-development and personal achievement is extremely strong. Both partners will benefit from the relationship's self-actualizing orientation, but they will also be there for each other in times of need. Thus while both will be able to progress on their individual developmental and spiritual path, their partnership, relative to a family or company, will also evolve and grow in stature.

Family relationships here are more problematic. Responsibility in this context can have the meaning more of discharging duties and doing chores than of improving oneself. Parent-child or grandparent-child relationships of either combination as well as siblings relationships with a wide age-spread can tend to be bossy, demanding and critical.

ADVICE: *Continue on your path. Stress self-development but grow together as well. Lessen critical attitudes. Seek spiritual goals. Roll back frontiers.*

GALA DALI (9/7/1894)
SALVADOR DALI (5/11/04)

Gala met Surrealist artist Dali when he was at his most troubled psychological state, and it was she who saved him. They married and became inseparable, epitomizing one of the century's great love relationships. ***Also: Richie Valens & Buddy Holly*** (musicians; died in plane crash); **Mark Van Doren & Carl Van Doren** (brothers; educators); **Emilio Estevez & Charlie Sheen** (brothers; actors).

May 11–18

THE WEEK OF THE NATURAL
TAURUS III

September 11–18

THE WEEK OF THE LITERALIST
VIRGO III

The Fine Art of Persuasion

This relationship can elevate the art of persuasion to a high level indeed—but in attempting mastery of this ability, these two are usually more successful in convincing other people than each other. Each partner exerts extremely subtle forms of manipulation to nudge the other in the desired direction, yet both are usually quite aware of what's going on. Their manipulations may involve emotional blackmail ("I love you"), bribery ("That would make me love you") or disguised threats ("Maybe I don't love you"), in addition to devices like simply withdrawing affection or attention; rarely, however, will such behavior get out of hand or appear ugly or threatening, so skillfully is it employed. Taurus III's and Virgo III's are definitely individuals who know what they want, so the issue becomes perfecting the skill of getting it from each other.

Those on the outside of such a friendship, marriage or family tie may not even see what's going on, mistaking a dynamic process of give-and-take for harmony or agreement. This may be part of this pair's ability to be so influential with other people: by convincing them of the relationship's honesty, health and good feeling, they can effectively mesmerize them into cooperating. Taurus III–Virgo III friends, siblings and spouses may be sought out by others who are already prepared to be convinced when they come seeking ideas or advice.

Love relationships are notoriously manipulative endeavors, but the Taurus III–Virgo III relationship is curiously more honest than most. Once the relationship's romantic phase has settled into a more day-to-day pattern, persuasion and manipulation will no longer be so powerfully highlighted. Indeed the goal of a truly honest love relationship here will be to phase these behaviors out altogether, usually in a conscious and dedicated way.

In work relationships, such persuasiveness is only of limited value, even at the executive level. Sooner or later pragmatic results, such as sales, productivity, cost margins and simple bookkeeping, will reveal any unsavory truths that cannot be easily explained away.

ADVICE: *Let others make up their minds. Never manipulate a manipulator. Be less selfish and more giving. Convincing becomes unconvincing.*

ARCHIBALD COX (5/17/12)
SAM ERVIN (9/17/1896)

Cox and Ervin both spearheaded investigations of the Watergate scandal. Cox was appointed by Attorney General Richardson, who resigned rather than fire Cox on Nixon's orders. Ervin chaired the Senate's investigating committee, and is remembered for his wit and wisdom in chairing the hearings. ***Also: Margaret Rutherford & Agatha Christie*** (portrayer of Christie's Miss Marple).

STRENGTHS: **IMAGINATIVE, PLEASURABLE, AESTHETIC**

WEAKNESSES: **DEPENDENT, ADDICTIVE, ESCAPIST**

BEST: **PARENT-CHILD**

WORST: **LOVE**

TOMMY LASORDA (9/22/27)
BILLY MARTIN (5/16/28)

Archrival baseball managers Lasorda (LA Dodgers) and Martin (NY Yankees) met head-to-head in the '77 World Series—which the Yanks took 4–2. The 2 teams met again in the '78 series and the Yanks won—but Martin, replaced in mid-season, would not get to beat Lasorda twice. **Also: Julianne Phillips & Bruce Springsteen** (married; actress/rock star); **Archibald Cox & Leon Jaworski** (Watergate prosecutors).

May 11–18

THE WEEK OF THE NATURAL
TAURUS III

September 19–24

THE CUSP OF BEAUTY
VIRGO-LIBRA CUSP

A Desire to Surrender

This highly imaginative relationship is apt to be concerned with the pursuit of beauty and sensuousness. The danger is that living in a pleasurable and fantastic world will become intoxicating, making the parties submit to dominance from each other, or from anything—like drugs, sex or music—designed to prolong pleasure and fuel highs. Addictions here may get out of hand, and with them the ability to keep in touch with daily realities. Giving themselves over to their pursuits, these partners risk ignoring the feelings of others (including their parents, children, other friends, teachers and co-workers) in the all-consuming drive to satisfy ever-increasing needs.

Love relationships and friendships here are particularly prone to emotional dependencies and addictions. Craving only each other, these two may require more and more attention or love, ultimately becoming unable to do without them, and even suffering physical symptoms when they are withdrawn. The theme of beauty is characteristic here: the partners long for it, and want to surrender to it. Indeed the relationship requires that they sacrifice their egos on the altar of beauty, whether real or imagined, and whether belonging to the partners themselves or to some external source (painting, sound, taste or even drug-induced states of intoxication). The ultimate here is to merge with such beauty, and to leave the world's cares behind.

Such escapism is usually tempered in marriages and working relationships, which would otherwise be impossible to carry on. Even so, however, this kind of longing is likely to cause periodic breakdowns in these practical settings, with confusion, unhappiness and breakup often being the result.

Parent-child relationships are unlikely to go to the extremes of love affairs. Here imagination is often put to more positive ends, and the pair may show deep sympathy and understanding. Sibling relationships, especially of the opposite sex, can go too far in sharing intimate states based on fantasy, and may exhibit unrealistic or incestuous behavior.

ADVICE: *Get a handle on your desires. Beware of addictive behavior. Try to balance fantasy and reality in everyday life. Don't isolate yourself.*

STRENGTHS: **FRANK, SYMPATHETIC, SEXUAL**

WEAKNESSES: **PRESSURED, UNSTABLE, PROCRASTINATING**

BEST: **LOVE**

WORST: **FRIENDSHIP**

ETHEL ROSENBERG (9/28/15)
JULIUS ROSENBERG (5/12/18)

Despite public pleas for leniency, the Rosenbergs were the first US citizens executed for espionage after being convicted of supplying Russia with vital information on the atomic bomb. **Also: Joe Louis & Max Schmeling** (boxing foes); **Robert Morse & Truman Capote** (stage portrayal); **Burt Bacharach & Angie Dickinson** (married; composer/actor); **Harvey Keitel & Lorraine Bracco** (married; actors).

May 11–18

THE WEEK OF THE NATURAL
TAURUS III

September 25–October 2

THE WEEK OF THE PERFECTIONIST
LIBRA I

Stress Buildup

This relationship is unlikely to achieve much stability. Its critical attitudes and resentments are usually too intense to afford much rest. These two have extremely different attitudes to things, in particular in their approach to all matters physical, and one would expect them to have issues in that arena. Furthermore, Libra I's feel the need to improve their Taurus III partners, placing tremendous expectations on them which they are neither willing nor able to meet. Because Libra I's lack the ability to leave them alone, Taurus III's will in most cases either fight back, withdraw or break off the relationship.

Taurus III's have a lot to contribute to love affairs with Libra I's, especially in helping them to relax. The open Taurus III attitude to sex will teach appreciative Libra I's quite a lot, providing a stimulating and rewarding outlet to daily stress. Affection and sympathy can also be expressed in this relationship, deepening its levels of trust and acceptance.

In marriage, personal pressures will probably be too much to bear. Taurus III's usually return fire when criticized, and may accuse a Libra I of a drive for perfection that makes the relationship artificial, disconnecting it from natural feelings, thoughts and actions. The Libra I use of checklists to monitor the pair's activities, ranging from financial to sexual, is likely to become intolerable to Taurus III's.

Friendships can be still more problematic. Although these partners relate well enough, they may have little time to spend together, unless one special project captures their mutual imagination. Also, selfish attitudes are likely to deprive them of each other's help in times of need, and over the years they are likely just to drift apart. The same may happen in family ties. Working relationships in this combination may be quite satisfactory, as long as the partners' unit of co-workers or business associates is protected from too much stress or strict deadlines. These two have a tendency to be too relaxed at times, perhaps due to their shared venusian influence (Venus rules both Taurus and Libra), which promotes enjoyment and satisfaction with the status quo, and encourages procrastination.

ADVICE: *Tear up your checklist. Try to act more naturally, with fewer expectations. Be there in times of need. Strengthen family ties.*

May 11–18

THE WEEK OF THE NATURAL
TAURUS III

October 3–10

THE WEEK OF SOCIETY
LIBRA II

RELATIONSHIPS

STRENGTHS: **THOUGHTFUL, INVOLVED, IDEALISTIC**

WEAKNESSES: **UNAWARE, FLUCTUATING, SMUG**

BEST: **WORK**

WORST: **FAMILY**

Sparkling Thought

Stimulating ideas and strong feelings are likely to figure in this sparkling relationship, bringing this pair into action on the side of service groups and organizations. Areas of interest may be energy management, environmental concerns and society's response to them, and quality-of-life and freedom issues. The relationship has a strong orientation toward thought, especially of an idealistic or theoretical kind. Grounding such mental activity in the physical sphere will support the relationship, removing it from what could otherwise be idle fantasy and speculation.

Unless these two form strong bonds based on shared pursuits and interests, they are likely to blow hot and cold in love and marriage, and their relationships of this kind will often be subject to the instabilities of fluctuating emotions. Too often, fears and insecurities emerging in both Taurus III's and Libra II's will threaten the structure of the relationship. Neither party rates high in self-awareness in matters of love, and the relationship will often trigger Libra II irritation and depression and Taurus III volatility. Seeking stability in religious, psychological or spiritual pursuits, perhaps in the form of worship, workshops or therapy, can be helpful here.

Family relationships in this combination may exhibit a high degree of personal self-satisfaction, even smugness. The danger here is that an elitist, superior attitude will emerge, with the duo basking in its own supposed mental or social excellence. Parent-parent, parent-child or sibling matchups in this combination may foster such attitudes, resulting in stagnation and unrealistic outlooks.

Friendships and work combinations are favored here. They will usually emphasize projects and activities that demand a high degree of involvement. It is also possible that friends may engage in business or social endeavors and, vice versa, that co-workers and partners can form very close friendships. Perhaps the best combination here would be working in service of an environmentally aware company that is financially successful but pays strict attention to the needs and best interests of human society and of planet Earth.

ADVICE: *Cultivate personal as well as social awareness. Encourage spiritual activities. Beware of conceit. Don't get tied up in idle thoughts.*

LE CORBUSIER (10/6/1887)
WALTER GROPIUS (5/18/1883)

Swiss-French architect Le Corbusier worked in the Berlin studio of industrial designer Peter Behrens, where he met future Bauhaus leader Gropius (along with Mies van der Rohe). They shared architectural ideas and projects.

May 11–18

THE WEEK OF THE NATURAL
TAURUS III

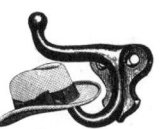

October 11–18

THE WEEK OF THEATER
LIBRA III

RELATIONSHIPS

STRENGTHS: **PASSIONATE, AMBITIOUS, FLAMBOYANT**

WEAKNESSES: **FRUSTRATED, NEGLECTFUL, CHAOTIC**

BEST: **FAMILY**

WORST: **MARRIAGE**

Wanted: A Boss

The most difficult issue to be addressed in this relationship, and the most essential, is who will shoulder what responsibility. These two must decide which of them will be the authority, and in what areas, and what standards are set. Without this focus, the relationship will probably fly apart, if it was ever much together in the first place. The problem is that neither of these two is very rocklike, despite the capable face they may present to the world. Undependability, disinterest, procrastination, neglect—all of these and more are likely to add to the problems here.

Passions may soar in love—and then just as quickly fade. A Taurus III looking for something deep may instead find a Libra III just out for a fling. Oh well, no matter. Taurus III's are resilient enough to bounce back from such disappointments, and to look again—or not.

Marriages are likely to be problematic unless an outlet can be found for their flamboyant and dramatic emotions. Should these be repressed, or go unrecognized, expect frustration and constant argument. Eventually a reliable source of authority will have to be set up, particularly if the couple has children. Libra III's have a finely honed sense of style, while Taurus III's are more natural and "let it all hang out"; in marriage, these two will need to agree upon the lifestyle they adopt.

Friendships may suffer from lack of focus and authority. One would not expect these two to become bosom buddies, neither of them being willing to give up much for the relationship. Perhaps acquaintanceships, sports or social partnerships, or career connections as colleagues are more desirable. Both of these partners are ambitious, and should they rise to an organization's upper levels, they may become friendly associates who occasionally see each other socially. This may also be true of co-workers within an office. In family relationships in this combination, a parent or grandparent will assert their authority. In most cases, this provision of structure and rules will not be harmful, and may in fact be required by more chaotic Taurus III's and Libra III's.

ADVICE: *Accepting authority is imperative. Insecurities will be eased by accepting rules. Acknowledge boundaries. Vent your feelings.*

JOSEPH ALSOP (10/11/10)
STEWART ALSOP (5/17/14)

These Ivy-League brothers and celebrated American journalists collaborated on the widely syndicated column "Matter of Fact" from 1945–58 and are best remembered for their doomsday articles about nuclear missiles. *Also:* **Margaret Sullavan & Leland Hayward** (married; actress/agent); **Katharine Hepburn & Leland Hayward** (once engaged; actress/agent).

May 11–18
THE WEEK OF THE NATURAL
TAURUS III

October 19–25
THE CUSP OF DRAMA & CRITICISM
LIBRA-SCORPIO CUSP

Realms of the Mind

STRENGTHS: **FUN-LOVING, EASY, THOUGHTFUL**

WEAKNESSES: **OVERRELAXED, SARCASTIC, SELF-SATISFIED**

BEST: **SIBLING, COUSIN**

WORST: **BUSINESS**

ROBERT RAUSCHENBERG (10/22/25)
JASPER JOHNS (5/15/30)

Longtime friends Rauschenberg and Johns belonged to the same circle of young NY artists in the 50s. Their innovative works challenged the precepts of abstract expressionism and laid the foundation for pop art in the 60s.
Also: Georges Braque & Pablo Picasso (friends; rival artists).

These two relate well to each other's youthful and wild side. In their relationship with each other, neither partner is looking for problems, although intellectual arguments are likely to arise. Quick-witted repartee may be prominent here, with irony, sarcasm and sharp humor abounding, but it is usually well meant and truly funny. Deeper and more passionate or serious relationships are generally not encouraged by this combination, which instead nurtures rather easygoing and pleasant ones.

Although friendships and love relationships are both favored here, marriages or more permanent living situations will often result from them. A friendship or love affair may in hindsight be seen as having been a proving ground from which a deeper commitment has evolved, but such relationships have great value in themselves, and are usually free of such expectations. Taurus III friends and lovers take great pride in the mental abilities of their Libra-Scorpio partners, who for their part admire the natural ease of Taurus III's. This relationship has much to teach its partners: Libra-Scorpios learn how to relax, Taurus III's how to focus their thoughts more effectively. Whatever the physical attractions here, the primary thrust of these relationships is not necessarily sexual or emotional but usually lies in the realms of the mind.

Marriages and business relationships both benefit and suffer from the combination's easy attitudes, which may undercut ambitions and dilute dynamic drives but can actually result in higher productivity and fewer losses due to argument and stress, especially in marriage. A common love of aesthetic matters may also serve to unite these two. Family relationships, particularly between siblings and cousins, can be great fun, and may evolve into the most important of all this pair's life attachments. From the earliest age, such relationships may demonstrate both precocity and easy interaction. Whether such siblings or cousins decide to run a business, share living space or just take occasional vacations together in adult life, their bonds are rarely broken and require little more than a call, letter or visit to keep them alive.

ADVICE: *Don't let sarcasm dominate. Don't let easy attitudes undercut your drive. Don't get bottled up in your head. Show you care, regularly.*

May 11–18
THE WEEK OF THE NATURAL
TAURUS III

October 26–November 2
THE WEEK OF INTENSITY
SCORPIO I

Strength in Difference

STRENGTHS: **COMPLEMENTARY, VARIED, ECSTATIC**

WEAKNESSES: **UNBALANCED, COMBATIVE, UNSETTLED**

BEST: **MARRIAGE**

WORST: **SIBLING**

DANIEL BAIRD WESSON (5/18/1825)
HORACE SMITH (10/28/1808)

Smith and Wesson were partners in gun invention and manufacture, working together for many years. They made important contributions to the development of handguns, including the invention of the cartridge-loading revolver.
Also: Louis Farrakhan & W.D. Muhammad (opposing factions of US Muslim movement).

This relationship aims to achieve a balance among the differing orientations and strengths of its partners, whom it encourages to find the middle ground, teaching them a lot about tempering their impulses. This, of course, does not come easily at first. Luckily, fidelity and patience are built into the relationship, which is quite long-sighted and provides the support for working out whatever may come along.

Taurus III's and Scorpio I's have much to learn from each other. Scorpio I's, for example, are naturally able to control their emotions, while Taurus III's are more gifted in expressing them; thus the challenge for more repressed Scorpio I's is to get their feelings out, whereas for more flamboyant Taurus III's it is to keep them under control. Intense Scorpio I's can also learn from the laid-back nature of Taurus III's, who for their part would do well to mirror some of Scorpio I's determination in the face of adversity. In these and other ways, the talents of one of these partners may closely correspond to the challenges and needs of the other.

Although Taurus III's are ruled by earth and Scorpio I's by water, connoting sensation and feelings, respectively, their relationship is governed by the element of fire, which is associated with intuition. Thus their love affairs tend to be exciting, passionate (sexual rather than sensual) and impulsive. As they lose themselves in ecstatic experiences that transcend both sensation and feeling, their love can soar to the heavens—but, like fire, it can also be consuming and dangerous. Balance is essential here if burnout, flare-ups of jealousy, and even hatred during or after an unpleasant breakup are to be avoided.

In friendship and marriage these two make a strong combination. They often like or even admire each other, and can learn a great deal from one another's approaches to life. Even when they come from different backgrounds and lifestyles, they see the merits—and also the deficiencies—of each other's attitudes. As friends and spouses they can make a good team, applying their complementary strengths to both business enterprises and artistic endeavors.

ADVICE: *Seek the moderate approach. Learn from each other's talents. Compromise is not a sign of weakness. Energies are not unlimited.*

Acceptance Without Reservation

May 11–18

THE WEEK OF THE NATURAL
TAURUS III

November 3–11

THE WEEK OF DEPTH
SCORPIO II

The deep, almost heavy emotions in this relationship can be lightened and even resolved, leading the partners away from the deeper wells of feeling to the airier realms of thought. The combination's objectivity and capacity for acceptance goes far in permitting the partners periodically to detach from one another and process whatever may be going on emotionally between them, no matter how profound or difficult. People often ignore the fun-loving side of Scorpio II's, emphasizing their sexual expressiveness, seriousness and need for control, but Taurus III's often provide the humor necessary to pry them from their darker moods. Taurus III's themselves are often conflicted, lacking the tools to sort through their feelings; proximity to the profound understanding of Scorpio II's will help them toward greater self-awareness.

Taurus III–Scorpio II love relationships magnify the physicality of both partners, and can be torrid and wrenchingly passionate. The need for detachment is acute here, and indeed these lovers are often able to objectify and discuss their problems. Although these affairs are often short-lived, they are memorable.

Marriages and friendships often begin more casually, growing out of chance meetings or quite ordinary circumstances. The pair may meet each other at social gatherings, at clubs or fitness centers, while traveling or through a mutual friend. (The connection rarely clicks, however, when effected through matchmakers or planned introductions at parties or dinners.) The partners' nurturing abilities meld well, making them sympathetic parents, or else effective caretakers of pets. Accepting each other without reservation becomes an important goal, which is tested through daily interaction. Scorpio II's can suffer deeply from the loss of a Taurus III family member, whether a parent, grandparent or sibling. They will see such an event as a tragedy, particularly since the Taurus III may have proved tremendously and perhaps uniquely sympathetic and understanding to them. When these two are co-workers and colleagues, Scorpio II faithfulness and dogged dedication can meld well with Taurus III physical energies.

ADVICE: *Develop nurturing attitudes. Have fun in all aspects of life. Understanding comes through acceptance. Hard work pays off.*

STRENGTHS: **HUMOROUS, NURTURING, DEPENDABLE**
WEAKNESSES: **UNACCEPTING, OVERATTACHED, EPHEMERAL**
BEST: **WORK**
WORST: **FAMILY**

PIERRE CURIE (5/15/1859)
MARIE CURIE (11/7/1867)

The Curies met in 1894 and got married a year later. Lifetime research partners, their work in radioactivity led them to the discovery of radium and polonium in 1898. They won the Nobel Prize in 1903. **Also: Mark Vonnegut & Kurt Vonnegut** (son/father; writers); **Emilio Estevez & Demi Moore** (once engaged; actors).

May 11–18

THE WEEK OF THE NATURAL
TAURUS III

November 12–18

THE WEEK OF CHARM
SCORPIO III

Taking the Lead

Issues swirl and dance in this volatile relationship, vying for ascendancy. But the overall themes are those of leadership and ego: these partners will surely fight over which of them will lead in what areas, and whose ego will receive the most stroking. A good rule of thumb is that whoever is least open about this goal wants it most, making this a difficult beast to fight. Tension and struggle, however, can lead to great lessons in release and acceptance.

The tension may also be resolved if the partners, as a couple, adopt a tone or role of leadership in relation to those around them. In fact their whole style can take on a royal demeanor—granting audiences and favors to friends, making dramatic entrances and exits, and generally encouraging a kind of glow or buzz around themselves. As they build up a mythology about their pairing, they can start to believe it themselves. Fortunately or unfortunately, the relationship's inner turmoil will bring them down to earth as some of their own more unsavory characteristics emerge, reminding them that they are mere mortals.

Adventuresome Taurus III's are likely to lead in friendships and love affairs. They have a great deal to teach more reclusive Scorpio III's. In marriage, however, these two operate differently, with Scorpio III's taking the lead in household matters and Taurus III's following and complementing.

Taurus III and Scorpio III are exactly opposite each other astrologically (180° apart in the zodiac), and both Taurus and Scorpio are fixed signs. Their relationship can feature great tension, then, but also great endurance and solidity. This polarity may appear most typically in parent-child relationships: Scorpio III's fit best in the parental role, and natural responses and feelings will predominate in Taurus III children. At work, Scorpio III bosses and Taurus III employees can combine effectively, Scorpio III's being directed, generous and considerate while Taurus III's are energetic and dedicated in fulfilling their assignments.

ADVICE: *Find a correct orientation. Play your role well. Don't upset the balance of power. Strong leadership does not imply servility.*

STRENGTHS: **WELL-DIRECTED, EDUCATIONAL, UNDERSTANDING**
WEAKNESSES: **EGOTISTIC, CHALLENGING, UPSETTING**
BEST: **PARENT-CHILD, WORK**
WORST: **ROMANCE**

SIR ARTHUR SULLIVAN (5/13/1842)
SIR WILLIAM GILBERT (11/18/1836)

The famous operatic collaboration of Gilbert and Sullivan between 1871–96 yielded 14 operettas still popular today. Though fruitful, their association was tempestuous, with librettist Gilbert, the creative leader, often being reined in by Sullivan. **Also: Irving Berlin & George S. Kaufman** (collaborators; composer/writer); **Martha Graham & Isamu Noguchi** (collaborators; choreographer/artist-set designer).

May 11–18

THE WEEK OF THE NATURAL
TAURUS III

November 19–24

THE CUSP OF REVOLUTION
SCORPIO-SAGITTARIUS CUSP

Elaborate Masquerade

OTIS CHANDLER (11/23/27)
HARRY CHANDLER (5/17/1864)

Harry joined the *LA Times* in 1885, increasing its circulation until his retirement in 1942. Grandson Otis continued the dynasty, following father Norman's retirement in 1960. Under Otis, the *LA Times* led American newspapers in advertising volume.

This relationship can bring out sides of both partners that are generally hidden from view, in particular the kind of unpredictable wildness or love of freedom that they share. The relationship puts great value on emotional honesty and openness, but while it encourages the partners to reveal themselves, they simultaneously fear rejection. A complex dynamic emerges, which ideally ends in acceptance—the best-case scenario for this relationship is when its partners feel free to be themselves, even to be wild, and are accepted for it. The worst situation imaginable for them is when they feel constantly forced to hide, for fear of being rejected or found out.

In love and marriage, of course, such issues surface regularly. The sticking points are often issues of truthfulness and fidelity raised by involvements with other people. Honesty can be difficult here, since the partners fear hurting each other, and also fear being either controlled or rejected. Yet they also tend to want to reveal their involvements, and although such revelation can lead to scenes and threats of breakup, in the long run it can also bring increased understanding and openness. Part of the secret to getting along here is to be honest in the small areas of daily life. A pattern of lying or deception in apparently trivial matters may become a nasty habit that pervades almost any part of the relationship, big or small.

Friendships in this combination are often less threatening and challenging. Being able to relax together, however, is no guarantee of more truthful or open attitudes. A great deal can be hidden here, and subtle forms of disingenuousness may manifest and undermine the relationship. When crises arise, or when one partner makes greater demands in a time of need, such friendships can collapse like a house of cards.

Working and family relationships are usually aggravated by negative emotions, especially mistrust and fear. Through a curious inability to be honest about responsibilities, personal efforts and goals, Taurus III's and Scorpio-Sagittarians may create doubt and anxiety in each other, and share in quite an elaborate masquerade.

ADVICE: *Promote honesty. Discover your mechanisms of self-deception. Allow privacy and foster trust. Drop game-playing. See through the mask.*

May 11–18

THE WEEK OF THE NATURAL
TAURUS III

November 25–December 2

THE WEEK OF INDEPENDENCE
SAGITTARIUS I

Devoted Friends

DAVID MAMET (11/30/47)
LINDSAY CROUSE (5/12/48)

Mamet—playwright, screenwriter and director—did most of his writing in a Vermont log cabin shared with wife, actress Crouse. Before their divorce, she appeared in 2 of his films, including the award-winning *House of Games* (1987).

The highlight of this combination is each partner's sensitivity to the other's needs. Responsive in nature, the relationship often demonstrates deeply understanding and giving attitudes. It is usually more extroverted than introverted, as a full slate of vigorous physical activities can attest. This combination encourages exploration and is characterized by a hunger for experience. Both Sagittarius I's and Taurus III's are fond of travel, particularly to settings of natural beauty.

These two make splendid friends. They often seem as close as brother and sister, gaining a family-like familiarity that has the added attraction of lacking the friction common between siblings. They do compete, but usually in positive pursuits such as sports and games. Trying to work together may be difficult due to a lack of objectivity about the job at hand.

Taurus III–Sagittarius I love relationships can be physically intense but also affectionate. Indeed, just as friends in this combination resemble siblings, lovers resemble devoted friends, and show the kind of inner understanding customarily reserved for family members. Natural behavior is valued highly, and all forms of snobbism or pretension are condemned. The danger does exist of forming an isolating mutual-admiration society, and if these partners cut their ties with friends, family and co-workers, a bewildering situation can arise if the love affair fails or founders, since neither partner will have a support group.

The relationship sometimes follows a natural evolution from friendship to love affair, from love affair to life partnership. The final seal of marriage may be especially fulfilling, not only because the spouse is a known quantity but because the relationship is already so rich. Both of these personalities are extremely independent, however, and they may postpone final commitments, preferring to keep their freedom rather than risk losing what they have.

This pair's spirited and freedom-loving nature makes them less-than-ideal co-workers. They will undoubtedly encourage each other to procrastinate, and in business, their loafing will prove a drain.

ADVICE: *Keep ties with family and friends intact. Beware of isolation. Don't be afraid of deeper commitments. Giving up some freedom may be worth it.*

May 11–18

THE WEEK OF THE NATURAL
TAURUS III

December 3–10

THE WEEK OF THE ORIGINATOR
SAGITTARIUS II

Mapping Uncharted Waters

The challenge here is to build an effective, even efficient relationship that can achieve worldly goals and interact meaningfully with others. Both partners are unconventional, and they may believe that worldly achievement is not their cup of tea. Actually, though, they need to own up to the fact that they want recognition, fulfillment and reward as much as the next person. Their relationship can help teach them how to work for these things.

One of the most gratifying things about this combination is that where others may attempt to correct and reform Taurus III's and Sagittarius II's, their relationship with each other usually shelters them from critical and judgmental attitudes. Each accepts the other's unusual, even bizarre side. Their relationship may be difficult for others to understand, but this will matter little to them, and may even prove a source of merriment.

The relationship activates the earth and fire elements in Taurus and Sagittarius respectively, and reinforces the corresponding faculties of sensation and intuition. Love and marriage can consequently be characterized by a passionate sensuality, with sex and sensuousness mingling pleasurably. A relationship that attains psychological and physical openness in a moderate and structured way, rather than a wild and chaotic one, will mitigate arguments, anger and other negative expressions. Friendships and family relationships, oddly enough, are not always so close. Although this relationship is protective of its partners' individuality, it must also make its way in a society more conservative and "straight" than it is itself; thus Taurus III's and Sagittarius II's friends and even siblings may spend relatively little time together.

In business pursuits, where some kind of structure is usually already made, Taurus III's and Sagittarius II's will do best in self-employment, perhaps as a duo or in a team that puts their unusual qualities to commercial use. Forced to learn bookkeeping, accounting and financial planning, the relationship will be forced to map uncharted waters and to eschew sloppiness in money matters.

ADVICE: *Be yourself in the world. Get to know all kinds of people. Don't always consider yourself so strange. Normality need not be an affliction.*

DANTE GABRIEL ROSSETTI (5/12/1828)
CHRISTINA ROSSETTI (12/5/1830)

Siblings Dante and Christina belonged to the pre-Raphaelite movement. A poet and painter, Dante became addicted to chloral, a sedative, following his wife's 1862 death. Christina, an outstanding Victorian poet, suffered permanent impairment from Graves' disease. **Also: Empress Maria Theresa & Francis I** (married; Austrian rulers).

May 11–18

THE WEEK OF THE NATURAL
TAURUS III

December 11–18

THE WEEK OF THE TITAN
SAGITTARIUS III

Tangible Goals of the Spirit

This relationship is often blessed with abundant energy and uplifting spirit. Its tendency is not only to soar into higher realms of thought but to plunge into profound depths of emotion. The emphasis is on the large line and the big picture, so that details often get overlooked. Believing in something is felt to be more important than thinking it is true; this sort of belief, however, is grounded in common sense and feelings.

As lovers, Taurus III's are strong enough to match this particular partner's desires. They tend to insist on deeply human values, however, while Sagittarius III's often get carried away with power and ego drives; as a consequence they are likely to feel unfulfilled and unsatisfied. For all the wrong reasons, Sagittarius III's may take this personally, and wind up feeling inadequate or unattractive. Marriages between these two are rarely recommended, for Taurus III's are likely to resent Sagittarius III attitudes, which most assuredly can arouse rebellion. Also, a quincunx position here (Sagittarius III and Taurus III are 150° apart in the zodiac) lends instability to this marital relationship, and augurs poorly for its future.

In friendships and family relationships, Sagittarius III's are again likely to dominate, usually in a protective way. Yet they may become quite dependent on Taurus III optimism and good spirits to keep them happy and free from depression, especially when these two are friends or siblings. These pairs can also become involved as equals in mutually uplifting spiritual pursuits in which they will relinquish their power struggles. The whole point of such activities, in fact, may be to teach this and other important lessons.

Working relationships between these two are likely to center around big projects of an artistic, social or religious and spiritual nature, often with Sagittarius III at the helm. As long as Taurus III's do not feel used or neglected, they can work well and enthusiastically as assistants to Sagittarius III's, moving toward tangible goals of the spirit. Their powers of persuasion meld well with forceful Sagittarius III leadership.

ADVICE: *Don't take things personally. Let go of overbearing attitudes. Strive for equality. Pursue goals of the spirit. Learn life's important lessons.*

BOBBY DARIN (5/14/36)
CONNIE FRANCIS (12/12/38)

Singer-songwriter Darin was popular in the 50s, winning 2 awards for million-seller *Mack the Knife*. From 1958–64, singer-actress Francis made 35 "Top 40" hits. Her 1984 autobiography revealed her secret romance with Darin. **Also: George Lucas & Steven Spielberg** (collaborators; directors); **Barbara Marx & Frank Sinatra** (married; Zeppo's widow/singer); **Margaret de Valois & Henry IV** (consort/king).

May 11–18

THE WEEK OF THE NATURAL
TAURUS III

December 19–25

THE CUSP OF PROPHECY
SAGITTARIUS-CAPRICORN CUSP

STRENGTHS: **FASCINATING,
SEDUCTIVE, APPRECIATING**

WEAKNESSES: **FRUSTRATING,
DEPRESSED, BEWILDERED**

BEST: **PARENT-CHILD**

WORST: **WORK**

Trapped in the Labyrinth

Things unseen seem to dominate this combination. Secrets, problems and fantasies are all felt as present here, yet the partners have no ability to get their hands on them or define them, much less deal with them. There is a kind of shroud hovering in the background, through which certain things can never be seen. This will obviously be a source of confusion, doubt and upset. If the pair can simply accept the mystery, however, without trying to analyze it, the relationship can be fairly fulfilling.

The more mysterious side of Sagittarius-Capricorns is activated by this relationship and threatens to dominate it. Taurus III's, often drawn to unusual individuals anyway, are strongly attracted to the passionate Sagittarius-Capricorn nature behind the inscrutable mask; they may be easily seduced by a Sagittarius-Capricorn, even away from a primary relationship, without realizing what they are getting into. Finally, trapped in a complex maze of emotions, they may find themselves at the mercy of their partner's powerful will.

This scenario is in no way inevitable in love affairs. Yet Taurus III's may indeed be at a loss to cope with a Sagittarius-Capricorn's emotions, particularly when these manifest in moods of stubbornness, frustration and depression. The positive Taurus III approach does not work with such partners, who must be left to work out their feelings without being prodded or pushed. The deepest desires are often stirred by these relationships, but idealistic Taurus III's must accept that their results are not necessarily positive. Marriages and friendships can center on appreciating and exploring nature. Gardening, domestic animals and pets may be interests here. If children are involved, nurturing activities often begin with the adults themselves, then extend to their progeny.

At work, misunderstandings within the relationship are likely to slow down or halt projects, resulting in counterproductive anger and frustration. Family relationships, especially parent-child ones, are deep and complex; these two can often understand each other far better than friends or lovers can. Mother-son and father-daughter relationships in this combination may be the determining factors in these individuals' lives.

ADVICE: *Don't get in over your head. Maintain objectivity. Keep feelings under control. Nurture, but don't be possessive. Be more understanding.*

HENRY FONDA (5/16/05)
JANE FONDA (12/21/37)

Jane was not close to father Henry as she grew up. He was not a particularly warm or demonstrative parent. In 1981, they were paired in the film *On Golden Pond*, depicting a strained father-daughter relationship parallel to their own. The film marked a symbolic reconciliation between them. ***Also:* Katharine Hepburn & Howard Hughes** (romance; actress/industrialist).

May 11–18

THE WEEK OF THE NATURAL
TAURUS III

December 26–January 2

THE WEEK OF THE RULER
CAPRICORN I

STRENGTHS: **DISCRETE,
INTIMATE, SUPPORTIVE**

WEAKNESSES: **CUT OFF,
DELUSIONAL, DESTRUCTIVE**

BEST: **LOVE**

WORST: **MARRIAGE**

Folie à Deux

This intimate relationship emphasizes privacy and discretion, isolating itself from the scrutiny of society. Its reclusiveness is not necessarily comfortable for either of its partners, both of whom need to be involved in the world; but the relationship can work if they are so outwardly directed outside the relationship that being alone together becomes a kind of peaceful retreat, a space for spirituality and renewal. After a hard day at the office, these two may seek each other out to share warmth and understanding.

Intimacy emerges most clearly in love, marriage and friendship. Taurus III–Capricorn I love affairs can be physically satisfying, sympathetic and supportive. Problems arise if Capricorn I's come to symbolize to Taurus III's the kinds of repressive forces that inevitably arouse their rebelliousness. Blaming and guilt trips may make things even more difficult. Capricorn I's need understanding, however, and their tendency to get bottled up inside may find relief in the arms of a nonjudgmental Taurus III. Should the latter finally decide to bail out, the Capricorn I will be left grieving over the loss of the relationship.

Intimacy may again be expected in marriage, but there is a danger that the couple's isolation will produce a folie à deux—a relationship based on delusional beliefs. Such a relationship can be destructive to its children, and also succeed in the family losing contact with friends, relatives and other social anchors.

Friendships in this combination can be split asunder by the insecurities of Taurus III's, which often spur them on to wild ambition. Capricorn I's, more content to find a niche and stay there, may be amazed at their antics and ultimately give up in despair.

Working and parent-child relationships between these two are seldom favorable. A Capricorn I boss's or parent's lack of sympathy for the spontaneity and naturalness of a Taurus III employee or child may produce dissatisfaction and rebellion. If the Taurus III is the boss or parent, he or she may prove too freewheeling, or too demanding of personal initiative, for structure-oriented Capricorn workers or offspring.

ADVICE: *Keep in touch with reality. Beware of cutting social ties. Be intimate but not isolated. Deal with guilt trips and rebelliousness.*

JEAN GABIN (5/17/04)
MARLENE DIETRICH (12/27/01)

A French star and international personality, Gabin had the rugged looks and strong, silent screen image that attracted Dietrich, who became his lover in 1942. Reputedly jealous over her bisexual escapades, however, he was known to beat her. ***Also:* Ellen Axson & Woodrow Wilson** (first wife of president).

May 11–18

THE WEEK OF THE NATURAL
TAURUS III

January 3–9

THE WEEK OF DETERMINATION
CAPRICORN II

RELATIONSHIPS

STRENGTHS: **INQUIRING, SYMPATHETIC, PLEASURABLE**

WEAKNESSES: **UNACCEPTING, CLAIMING, JUDGMENTAL**

BEST: **FAMILY**

WORST: **MARRIAGE**

Crying Out to Be Solved

This relationship concerns itself with puzzles crying out to be solved. The solutions can be achieved in two ways: first, by manifesting form out of chaos—that is, by pulling disparate elements into a coherent whole. Second, enigmatic phenomena can be subjected to logical and literal testing to solve a problem. Both Taurus III's and Capricorn II's have far-ranging interests, from the scientific to the paranormal, from computers to new-age topics, from art to music. Taurus III's are generally much more open to esoteric ideas, while Capricorn II's are more hardheaded, and often require physical proof. Conflicts may develop between their two viewpoints, but this determined couple will not stop until they find their answers.

In love affairs, Capricorn II's tend to hang in there no matter what, reluctant to admit defeat. Taurus III's are more interested in freedom, and will be involved in the relationship only as long as they want to be—Capricorn II attempts to control or hold them usually won't work. When the couple are getting along, however, their relationship may be physically quite pleasurable. The further step of marriage is not recommended, though, unless the Taurus III is prepared to make a serious commitment.

This combination can be close, sympathetic and productive in a parent-child or sibling matchup as long as the Capricorn II can back off occasionally and accept the Taurus III's different approach to life. Interest in games and puzzles abounds. The partners may have fewer disputes in friendships, where they may be united in their interest in and acceptance of not only metaphysical phenomena but also unusual friends and lovers who may join them in such interests. Emotional sharing is likely to be less important here than the areas under study and discussion.

At work, Taurus III's tend to forge ahead enthusiastically, particularly when new theories or products are being developed or tested. Capricorn II's tend to be more reserved and careful. Within the relationship, each partner is critical and often disapproving of the other's approach.

ADVICE: *Resolve conflicts between belief and logic. Accept differences in others. Claiming attitudes will not work. Never give up your freedom.*

BURT BACHARACH (5/12/29)
CAROL BAYER SAGER (1/8/47)

Fellow songwriters Bacharach and Sager were married for 10 years (1981–91). Sager is best known as the 1986 Grammy winner for *That's What Friends Are For.* Bacharach's top songs include *Walk on By* (1964) and *Arthur's Theme* (1981), from the movie *Arthur,* for which he won an Oscar.

Also: Dwayne Hickman & Bob Denver (co-stars, *Dobie Gillis*).

May 11–18

THE WEEK OF THE NATURAL
TAURUS III

January 10–16

THE WEEK OF DOMINANCE
CAPRICORN III

RELATIONSHIPS

STRENGTHS: **CONFIDENT, PHILOSOPHICAL, PLEASURABLE**

WEAKNESSES: **COMPLACENT, PROCRASTINATING, SELF-SATISFIED**

BEST: **MARRIAGE**

WORST: **BUSINESS**

Dreaming Up New Schemes

This combination is a classic. Since Taurus III and Capricorn III form an easy earth-sign trine (Taurus and Capricorn are earth signs 120° apart in the zodiac), astrology correctly predicts a positive, relatively trouble-free relationship here. The focus is emotional, with positive expectations playing a large part. The relationship may also be highly philosophical, at the same time that it contains a great deal of technical expertise. Dreaming up new ideas and schemes has no negative connotations here, and such seeds may often find themselves dropped in fertile ground.

In love, marriage and family relationships, Capricorn III dominant attitudes don't necessarily provoke rebellion in Taurus III's, as might be expected. Capricorn III's often admire the physical ease of Taurus III's, who are quick to sense their approval. The strongly sensuous bond that can exist here will afford much pleasure to both partners. In fact the relationship is often enjoyable and easygoing in its attitudes. One danger is that of complacency, since these two may feel little need to move forward when the status quo has already given them so much pleasure. This is one of the few relationships in which Taurus III's can see the benefit of giving up their wildness and ambition, perhaps because they feel secure for the first time. Marriages, then, can work out extremely well here.

Working relationships, like friendships, may tend to drift and lack focus. Although these two have few problems getting along as co-workers and colleagues, they may lack the spirit and drive to go beyond just getting the job done. Likewise, as business partners or executives, they may be carried away by idle schemes, or, confidently feeling that things are going well, can wait too long before making the necessary decisions. Procrastination and accompanying delays are ever-present dangers to the company or business influenced by this duo.

RAY BOLGER (1/10/04)
L. FRANK BAUM (5/15/1856)

Baum was the author of the book *The Wonderful Wizard of Oz,* first published in 1900. When it was adapted by Hollywood for the movie *The Wizard of Oz* (1939), song-and-dance man Bolger was chosen for the role of the floppy-legged scarecrow and gave a brilliant and indelible performance.

ADVICE: *The status quo may not be the best you are capable of. Push on. Test your limits. Ambition and aggression can be positive if they are well directed.*

LINCOLN ELLSWORTH (5/12/1880)
UMBERTO NOBILE (1/21/1885)

Ellsworth, a wealthy polar explorer, financed and organized the first dirigible flight over the North Pole. Accompanying him were Roald Amundsen and Italian aviator Nobile—the designer and owner of their airship, *Norge*.

Also: Frank Mankiewicz & Don Mankiewicz (brothers; journalist/screenwriter).

May 11–18
THE WEEK OF THE NATURAL
TAURUS III

January 17–22
THE CUSP OF MYSTERY & IMAGINATION
CAPRICORN-AQUARIUS CUSP

Garden of Earthly Delights

Since both these partners can be so lively, outgoing, uninhibited and natural, this would seem to be a wonderful matchup. The relationship strongly magnifies their earthy side and emphasizes their sensuousness. Indeed its focus is often sensuous beauty, whether in cooking fine meals, decorating a house sumptuously or indulging in the delights of massage, baths or lovemaking.

Both excitement and harmony are likely to emerge in love affairs; emotions of the tearing and wrenching variety rarely feature here. This in no way diminishes the relationship's passion; it simply makes things more enjoyable and less fractious. There is also likely to be an overemphasis on more superficial values, such as those connoted by good looks (which may openly acknowledge their debt to cosmetics), stylish clothes and trendy hairstyles. Even so, a natural image will be preferred.

Marriages here are likely to be happy and harmonious, for the most part. There may be too much interest in external appearances—the neatness of children, say, and matters of interior decorating, especially furniture. There is an undeniable urge to keep up with the neighbors, and a spiffy car or two parked in the driveway is usually a must.

The Taurus III–Capricorn-Aquarius matchup probably does best in the area of friendship. Sharing challenging activities (often involving travel), whether exploratory or sporting in nature, is par for the course. Such friendships often begin at work; co-workers and colleagues in this combination will not mind spending the day together in work-related activities and then going out together occasionally in the evening or on a weekend. They often share hobbies and interests of an aesthetic nature, involving, say, music, fashion or design.

In family settings this pair can enliven any special event, and will also provide good humor on an everyday basis. There are distinct problems in keeping it under control, however, for its ebullience can become quite turbulent, disturbing the concentration and sensibilities of other family members.

ADVICE: *Be aware of the values of others. Go a bit deeper in your approach to life. Enjoy beautiful things, but don't get hooked on them.*

NATASHA RICHARDSON (5/11/63)
VANESSA REDGRAVE (1/30/37)

Richardson began her career at age 4, acting opposite her mother, Redgrave. She once said, "I've spent half my life [getting] away from being Vanessa Redgrave's daughter, and now I've got to get away from being Liam Neeson's wife."

Also: Empress Maria Theresa & Frederick the Great (enemies); **Czar Nicholas II & Kaiser Wilhelm II** (cousins; heads of state).

May 11–18
THE WEEK OF THE NATURAL
TAURUS III

January 23–30
THE WEEK OF GENIUS
AQUARIUS I

At the Forefront

This combination is often busy with new ideas. Tremendously inventive, it puts little stock in worn-out traditions or empty ceremonies unless they can be revived in a meaningful way. Looking toward the future is the duo's real forte—whether working in new media, innovative art or technology, groundbreaking fashion or avant-garde art, they will want to be at the forefront. While these two may brim with ideas, separately their inertia in putting these in motion may be difficult to overcome; together, however, their relationship gives them a bit of a boost over initial obstacles.

Love affairs between these two are more scintillating than sizzling—their strengths lie in the realms of thought and intuition rather than that of feeling. Fun out of bed is usually just as important as fun in it, and visiting clubs, entertaining friends, taking walks, going out to dinner or shows, or enjoying tv, books and other media at home are essential.

Taurus III–Aquarius I marriages have much to recommend them, particularly if children are involved. These children need not be the couple's own—nieces and nephews, and the children of friends, may be constant visitors, and adoption or working with disadvantaged young people is always a possibility.

Taurus III–Aquarius I sibling relationships can be quite stormy but also very rewarding. They will often resemble close friendships—and friendships, meanwhile, will have the naturalness of sibling ties. Maintaining balance in such friendships may be difficult, however, for they will recognize few boundaries, and excessive involvement can wear both partners down. These two often exacerbate each other's nervous side, creating serious instabilities. Excellent career opportunities may open up for these two as freelancers or owners of a company. Employees are usually happy to work under such forward-looking bosses, who are not only motivated by efficiency and progress—they can be expected to provide the most up-to-date equipment to make jobs easier—but like the workplace to be fun and interesting.

ADVICE: *Tune in to other people's emotional states. Minimize frictions and irritations. Tradition has its value, too. Youth is no more valuable than age.*

May 11–18

THE WEEK OF THE NATURAL
TAURUS III

January 31–February 7

THE WEEK OF YOUTH & EASE
AQUARIUS II

Neglecting Deeper Areas

In many respects this relationship would seem perfect, and indeed it may involve an insistence that things run smoothly or even flawlessly. At least on the surface, Taurus III's and Aquarius II's both have a natural approach to life, and eschew hassles and problems. Furthermore, they are not the types who need to control each other, and in fact they insist on others being themselves. This approach, however, can neglect deeper problems, difficulties and also opportunities for growth.

Love relationships can go satisfactorily assuming that there is a physical attraction. If not, these two may form friendships that include platonic, but no less meaningful, feelings of love. Boundaries between love and friendship are often blurred here, allowing movement from one state to the other. This process may in fact be a way of handling uncomfortable situations and feelings when they arise, rather than confronting such disturbances head-on and trying to solve them. Drugs and other escapes can also pose problems. It is important for both partners to recognize their dark side, and to acknowledge that a relationship's problems are also challenges that can help it to grow and deepen. Marriages show the relationship in a different light. These spouses are more concerned with activities, albeit pleasurable ones, that challenge them mentally and physically. Designing a beautiful and functional home, making money, raising children, engaging in competitive sports or bettering their own personal best are all stimulating aspects in this area. As depth of commitment grows, these two may also indulge in psychological exploration and spiritual growth.

As co-workers these two have high standards of professionalism and technical expertise, which generally guarantee their success. If they are not appreciated, however, the quality of their work may fall off, and they may even quit.

Family members in this combination, especially parents (or grandparents) and children, are highly appreciative of each other. There is a tendency to spoil here, however, and neglect of structure can sometimes breed sloppiness and, ultimately, lack of respect.

ADVICE: *Dig a bit deeper. Easy attitudes are not always the most meaningful. Problems are opportunities. The exit door is rarely the answer.*

STAN GETZ (2/2/27)
WOODY HERMAN (5/16/13)

Saxophonist Getz was one of clarinetist Herman's top sidemen in the late 40s. Great jazz figures with superior techniques, they always maintained the highest professional standards.
Also: **Leo Stein & Gertrude Stein** (sibling writers); **Henry Fonda & John Ford** (collaborators; actor/director).

May 11–18

THE WEEK OF THE NATURAL
TAURUS III

February 8–15

THE WEEK OF ACCEPTANCE
AQUARIUS III

Creative Play

This relationship is often immature but highly vital and enthusiastic. Because Taurus III and Aquarius III are in a fixed and square aspect (90° apart in the zodiac, both fixed signs), conventional astrology predicts stubborn conflict. Yet although confrontations can be expected between these volatile personalities, the bond in this relationship is usually quite strong. Both partners' feelings are triggered easily by criticism or disapproval, and their fight to be themselves and resist such attacks may become the relationship's main theme.

In love affairs and marriages, the question of acceptance is paramount. Once these two have really accepted each other at a deep level, tremendous things are possible, but constant irritation may be present until then. They have so much in common to build a relationship on, yet may find it difficult or impossible to get along on a daily basis. What's worse, the more passionate their feelings become, the more instability manifests, creating a situation in which desire may ultimately threaten the relationship's very existence. Furthermore, these partners share a taste for sexual freedom and license with others, which often arouses undermining feelings of anger, jealousy and rejection. If any matchup can achieve an open marriage allowing true freedom of action, this would theoretically seem to be the one, but in practice it doesn't seem to work this way. Perhaps this indicates a lack of real trust.

In friendships in which responsibilities can be kept light, Taurus III's and Aquarius III's will enjoy seeing each other from time to time. Should they want to intensify their contact, however, they may only be asking for trouble. Acquaintanceships, colleague pairings and other contacts of a more casual nature usually work out better here, with the relationship's competitiveness egging its two partners on to greater and greater levels of accomplishment. Family matchups can work quite well, especially between siblings in childhood. These two will keep each other occupied for hours, playing creatively and having fun. When conflicts arise, wise parents will let them work things out between themselves, rather than coming down hard in blame or judgment.

ADVICE: *The key to success is acceptance. Try to be less irritable. Overlook small matters. Seek positive goals. Avoid blame. Keep it light.*

JIMMY HOFFA, JR. (5/15/41)
JIMMY HOFFA, SR. (2/14/13)

Jimmy Sr. is the Teamster union leader who was dogged by Bobby Kennedy for racketeering and who disappeared mysteriously in 1975. Son Jimmy Jr. is today an up-and-coming union official. *Also:* **Bertrand Russell & Alfred North Whitehead** (collaborators; philosopher-mathematicians); **Maureen O'Sullivan & Mia Farrow** (mother/daughter; actors).

May 11–18
THE WEEK OF THE NATURAL
TAURUS III

February 16–22
THE CUSP OF SENSITIVITY
AQUARIUS-PISCES CUSP

LOU DIAMOND PHILLIPS (2/17/62)
RICHIE VALENS (5/13/41)

Latin rock star Valens, who soared to the top with "La Bamba" in 1959, died in a plane crash (along with the Big Bopper and Buddy Holly) the same year. His life story inspired the hit movie *La Bamba* (1987), which starred Phillips. *Also:* **Lindsay Crouse & Russell Crouse** (daughter/father; actress/ musical dramatist); **Lowell Weicker & Barbara Jordan** (Senate Watergate investigation members).

Alleviating Insecurity

This relationship may well be built around social image and career. Both Taurus III's and Aquarius-Pisces carry a great deal of insecurity, which they often seek to alleviate through professional success and upward mobility. Childhood voices telling them they are inadequate or no good can only be stilled by a thundering ovation from the world, applauding their ambitious exploits. The relationship can also serve as an anodyne to distress or pain caused by Aquarius-Pisces negativity and Taurus III worry. It can prove therapeutic in helping both partners work out their insecurities in other ways than through ambition.

Aquarius-Pisces can learn social skills through understanding and stimulating friendships with Taurus III's, who are gifted in this area and will be gratified by being able to pass on these talents to their friends. The relationship itself may prove a sympathetic haven in times of need and distress. Through dealing constructively with the problems of others, as unofficial advisors or counselors, Taurus III's and Aquarius-Pisces can raise their own levels of confidence and self-esteem.

Love affairs may feature deeply empathic feelings. Both parties know what it is to be hurt, often having been so in childhood, and they can exhibit great sympathy to each other in sensitive psychological areas. Aquarius-Pisces may find themselves vaguely irritated by the optimistic attitudes of Taurus III's, who for their part can be annoyed by Aquarius-Pisces pessimism, but such polarities will soften over time as a middle ground is established. Indeed, learning to listen and compromise are important in this relationship, which has the potential for new levels of trust, fostering love, affection and ultimately passion. Marriages and working relationships here do not usually provide the stability such arrangements need. Family relationships are also tricky, since both these personalities, as children, are acutely sensitive to disapproval. Although a Taurus III or Aquarius-Pisces parent can be more understanding than most, inner pressures may force them to act out parental roles they knew in their own childhoods, and they may make the same mistakes.

ADVICE: *Don't follow old scripts. Break the disapproval cycle. Develop trust and understanding. Ambition only takes you so far. Seek underlying causes.*

May 11–18
THE WEEK OF THE NATURAL
TAURUS III

February 23–March 2
THE WEEK OF SPIRIT
PISCES I

DENNIS HOPPER (5/17/36)
PETER FONDA (2/23/39)

Hopper's and Fonda's work on the classic film *Easy Rider* went beyond acting. Hopper co-wrote the script with Fonda and directed, while Fonda produced. Both had reputations as being rebellious and sometimes immature. *Also:* **Barbara Marx & Zeppo Marx** (married); **Henry Fonda & Peter Fonda** (father/son; actors).

A Test of Maturity

The temptation for these partners is to engage in extremely subtle competition, each trying to outshine the other. The focus of a more enlightened Taurus III–Pisces I matchup will be overcoming such ego drives, first by becoming aware of them and then by working together to reinforce rather than divide the relationship. This may not be easy, however. Although these two are typically fairly understanding of each other, their relationship encourages neither empathy nor sympathy between them. They will have to do real work in order to learn to give each other the spotlight—but therein, of course, lies the opportunity for growth.

In love affairs in this combination, Taurus III's can be selfish without even being aware of it. Pisces I's tend to be more giving, even self-sacrificial, and must be careful not to be taken advantage of. Furthermore, they sometimes only give conditionally, holding on to resentment that they can unleash with fury on a Taurus III who has gone too far. Not only sharing but also unconditional giving (which expects no return) should be put into practice here.

Marriages can go along well enough during good times, but claiming attitudes will emerge after a falling-out. Children, house, car, cash, possessions—all or any of these may take over the spotlight. In many ways such items are only projections of the egotism of the relationship itself. Asking for equal treatment, but also refusing to indulge in destructive acts or speech, will be a true test of the relationship's maturity.

As friends these two can be free of material claims, but may be unbalanced by following an exclusive spiritual or philosophical path. They can be impressive and forward-looking in ideology, but may ignore the necessary responsibilities of everyday life.

Work situations can be therapeutic for these partners, forcing them to put group endeavors before their own needs. Here, all attempts to steal the spotlight may be counterproductive to the job at hand. Attention-seeking ploys will usually be dealt with sternly by bosses and even more so by angry co-workers.

ADVICE: *Try not to demand so much attention. Work for the good of the group. Demonstrate maturity by sharing. Attend to daily jobs that need doing.*

May 11–18

THE WEEK OF THE NATURAL
TAURUS III

March 3–10

THE WEEK OF THE LONER
PISCES II

Flaunt It!

Concerned with trends and styles, this relationship also has the potential to determine them. Whether as co-workers in an industry such as fashion or design or simply as a pair with an interesting approach to taste that is emulated by their friends, this duo can have a real impact on their environment. Never falling victim to the prevailing wisdom, they will always determine their own approach. As a unit they are very much in the public eye. If times or customs should go against them, they have the resilience and usually a close circle of intimates to help them weather the storm until their brilliant style is once again recognized—and until then they will flaunt it anyway. The relationship brings out the extroverted side of Pisces II's. The chemistry here makes for a pair who enjoy entertaining as well as entertainment, and in general being at the center of their circle. They are likely to be quite theatrical at times, dressing up both at home and abroad.

Love affairs here tend to the flamboyant. Pisces II's have a rich fantasy life that this relationship puts to work, and Taurus III's also generate excitement with particularly outlandish behavior. Little embarrassment is felt here. The relationship may arouse antagonism, even violence, in others who take such behavior as a personal affront.

Friendships have their own kind of intimacy. In the partners' wide-ranging discussions with other friends, the most outlandish views can be aired without fear of reprisal. Extroverted thoughts will find a counterweight in more moderate and peaceful settings. Marriages are usually less successful: somehow the kiss of respectability does not sit with the relationship's outrageous, even antisocial stance. A settled marriage is likely to be happy enough, but may slowly extinguish the fire that came when these two were lovers.

Working relationships here are not at all recommended unless they deal with fashion, design or a borderline or covert activity with romantic overtones. Family relationships are similarly unfavorable—these two may make each other nervous, and will fail to understand or sympathize with each other's often diametrically opposed views.

ADVICE: *Don't be too aggressive. Enjoy yourself, but don't always expect others to watch. Develop intimacy. Temper your views occasionally.*

May 11–18

THE WEEK OF THE NATURAL
TAURUS III

March 11–18

THE WEEK OF DANCERS & DREAMERS
PISCES III

Guaranteed Survival

As far as possible, this relationship looks forward. Often at the forefront of their social circle, family or student group, these two will want to go fearlessly where no one has gone before. They focus little on either past hurts or past achievements, but view yesterday as gone and tomorrow as all-important. This positive viewpoint can help them go far, but remembering today is not a bad idea for them. They may be the first of their friends to rent a vacation house, arrange a trip to an exotic island, or put themselves in debt for a spiffy renovation, but meanwhile they're missing appointments or forgetting to pay bills.

Taurus III–Pisces III spouses can be quite successful if they also work together. And whether they are in business together or not, supportive and advisory attitudes are prominent in their relationship. Taurus III's will listen to Pisces III advice because it is generally taken from life experience, and Pisces III's will admire the way Taurus III's interact easily with others and win their trust. Children may be a special joy for this couple if they can take time away from their many activities to look after them properly.

Love affairs here are often covert in nature. At least one of the partners is often already in an established relationship, making secrecy imperative. So good are these two at hiding their activities that others may not find out about them until years later, if at all.

The pioneering spirit is strong in Taurus III–Pisces III friendships; travel and adventure, especially at a danger level that would set other people's teeth on edge, are viewed as quite ordinary here. But the partners are quite prudent about observing the necessary safety rules, thus guaranteeing their survival for another exploit.

Taurus III–Pisces III sibling relationships can be very tight, particularly opposite-sex ones. Despite forthright vocal confrontations, brother-sister ties are often the closest in the family, and can stabilize the entire group. Such connections may continue into adult life, growing warmer and more understanding as the years go by.

ADVICE: *You may be endangering others. Try to be open and honest. Pay attention to those who need it. Don't take unnecessary risks. Be more reflective.*

May 19–24
THE CUSP OF ENERGY
TAURUS-GEMINI CUSP

May 19–24
THE CUSP OF ENERGY
TAURUS-GEMINI CUSP

LORD WALDORF (5/19/1879)
LADY NANCY ASTOR (5/19/1879)

This couple, married in 1906, has the exact same birthday. When Lord Waldorf succeeded his father and entered the House of Lords in 1919, Lady Astor won his open seat in the House of Commons, becoming the first woman member of Parliament.

Short Circuits

No lack of energy here! The question is, will lines of communication become frazzled? Will the relationship burn itself out? Whether energies are flowing in the right direction or not, short circuits may demand that these two take periodic breaks from each other while fuses are replaced. Luckily, blowouts due to power surges, which occur even in the most successful of this combination's scenarios, benefit from the relationship's built-in circuit breakers, safety valves that automatically spring into action when the juice gets too hot to handle. Such devices are, however, built up over many years, through experience, patience, trust and understanding.

Taurus-Geminis have difficulty remaining in each other's presence for too long. They may take a look, out of curiosity, and then leave in short order. Relationships involving firm commitment, like those in the marital and work spheres, are likely to work out better than friendships and love relationships, which tend to be ephemeral—simply because they can be. A love affair or friendship between Taurus-Geminis can be sweet but fleeting. A memory or two is about all that the partners can hope to carry away with them. Hurtful or resentful attitudes will rarely have time to develop.

When marriages between Taurus-Geminis are successful, they can be combined easily and well with working relationships. Here energies coalesce in a total involvement that keeps partners busy twenty-four hours a day tending to domestic and career matters. Curiously, this is a commitment not so much to each other as to common activities. Taurus-Geminis too often resemble people less than forces that get things done. This unusual couple, then, will have to make an effort to clear free time to explore personal realms together.

Should two Taurus-Gemini children be siblings, the family should prepare for the worst. Rarely will others be ready to handle this level of noise (both verbal and physical) and need for attention. Parent-child relationships between two Taurus-Geminis are likely to be filled with miscommunication, which, like static, will tend to annoy others.

ADVICE: *Try to limit your contacts. Understanding may take a long time. Don't give up. Structure your relationship around common activities.*

May 19–24
THE CUSP OF ENERGY
TAURUS-GEMINI CUSP

May 25–June 2
THE WEEK OF FREEDOM
GEMINI I

JOHN ROBERT SCHRIEFFER (5/31/31)
JOHN BARDEEN (5/23/08)

Close colleagues, Bardeen and Schrieffer (with Leon N. Cooper) shared the 1972 Nobel Prize for physics. They provided the first theoretical explanation of superconductivity. **Also: Bob Dylan & A.J. Weberman** (folk singer/ "Dylanologist"); **Susan Strasberg & Marilyn Monroe** (daughter of MM's acting teacher was close friend to actress).

Open Rivalry

This is not an easy relationship. Although these two share Gemini characteristics (mental agility, verbal ability, charm), what arise most often between them are challenge and combat. This is most often due to a rivalry for the attention or love of a third party, but can also be part of a battle of wits and wills to see who can win out. Competitiveness, and also a restlessly rebellious stance, are often at the heart of this relationship.

While it is possible for Taurus-Geminis and Gemini I's to get close, their relationship is more often apt to be based around a common activity or interest rather than on sharing emotions or trying to understand each other. If the common interest happens to be a person, however, disaster is probably looming. Envy, jealousy, even hatred can surface here, and the warfare can last for months or even years. Since these two are very equally matched, the relationship may resemble a battlefield littered with the dead and dying. Regrouping and fighting new battles can be the routine here, or, equally well, circumspectly avoiding direct confrontation, preferring to fight by other means. Colleagues and acquaintances often get along far better than closer friends. Being co-workers on a daily basis, or for that matter business partners, is not at all recommended.

Love relationships and marriages may be problematic: outright cheating, dishonesty and betrayal are likely to bring either of these relationships to a merciful conclusion. Marriages are the more tragic of the two, usually because of the time, money and expectations invested, or perhaps because of the presence of children.

Family relations—between cousins, or between aunts or uncles and nieces or nephews—tend to work better. Aunts and uncles of either personality type may become parent substitutes for the other, with inspiration, admiration and affection playing important roles. Cousins, too, may easily become closer than siblings, often strengthening or renewing ties between more emotionally distant family members.

ADVICE: *Beware of combativeness. Learn to be more diplomatic but honest. Put jealousies to rest. Open lines of communication. Confront more gently.*

May 19–24

THE CUSP OF ENERGY
TAURUS-GEMINI CUSP

June 3–10

THE WEEK OF NEW LANGUAGE
GEMINI II

Unacknowledged Fantasies

This relationship works in certain areas as long as both partners are free to pursue their own course. Projection often features here, with Gemini II's projecting their dark side on Taurus-Geminis and Taurus-Geminis projecting their deficiencies on Gemini II's, both at an unconscious level. Gemini II's will value communication with these particular partners, valuing their opinions highly and thriving on their attention. Taurus-Geminis, on the other hand, may just tolerate Gemini II garrulousness, or even criticize it, without realizing that they are equally talkative and are themselves open to rebuke.

In love affairs, Gemini II's are especially prone to the mechanism of projection, and Taurus-Geminis, ordinarily wilder and more unconventional than Gemini II's, may suddenly find themselves the object of this partner's uncontrollable passions. Such desires may smolder for years, often under the guise of friendship or harbored within a professional relationship, before suddenly bursting into flame. Frequently unrecognized or unacknowledged hidden dreams and sexual fantasies, in which Taurus-Geminis play the main role, are not uncommon with Gemini II's.

Marriage is not recommended between this pair, as they would be prone to fighting—if not sooner, then later. Critical and verbal abuse may follow bouts of lovemaking, and moods of all sorts wreak havoc on the relationship. Friendships are a better bet, but have a tendency either to dissolve or to evolve to another level. In many ways, teacher-student and boss-employee relationships are the best bet for these partners, but they work best when the Taurus-Gemini plays the dominant role.

Siblings of this combination are often good friends, particularly when of the opposite sex. Such brother-sister pairs exhibit empathy and understanding, while at the same time allowing tremendous freedom of action, thought and choice. Later in life, each of these two may seek out a relationship that mirrors this close family tie in childhood.

ADVICE: *Try to stay objective. Investigate yourself at a deeper level. Remember who you are. Don't give up your identity so easily.*

SIR JAMES YOUNG SIMPSON (6/7/1811)
QUEEN VICTORIA (5/24/1819)

Obstetrician Simpson's strong advocacy of ether use during childbirth was opposed by the clergy and other physicians, until the anesthetic was proven effective and safe. Victoria appointed him court physician in 1847 and made him a baronet in 1866. The queen had 9 children.

May 19–24

THE CUSP OF ENERGY
TAURUS-GEMINI CUSP

June 11–18

THE WEEK OF THE SEEKER
GEMINI III

Psychic Gifts

Unsatisfied with the mundane here and now, this relationship seeks to go beyond it and to achieve an original, even unique orientation. While both parties will insist on their independence, they may also find each other mutually fascinating, and so will feel the need to see each other more than occasionally. Such meetings are often highly private ones, in which what transpires is rarely public or even retold, except in the form of tantalizing gossip. The relationship's focus is fire, denoting intuition or warmth, creativity and joy.

Love affairs in particular may be covert. Far more than casual but also not necessarily deep, these relationships often express warmth, sympathy and admiration rather than searing emotion. Between Taurus-Geminis and Gemini III's, love and friendship may be very closely related. Psychic gifts and paranormal or synchronistic happenings may abound in this relationship; its strong mental orientation is often yoked to intuition.

Marriages between these two may not be really necessary, since it may have already taken place, in a sense, at least symbolically, in the couple's preceding friendship and love affair. As far as working together goes, despite the strong ties of understanding here, it is probably best if both partners pursue their own course, but touch base from time to time for consultations and evaluations of each other's work.

In the family, sibling relationships, especially between members of the opposite sex, may be strongly seductive. In both individuals, ego drives may be less strong than an overwhelming desire to please, and the two may become quite dependent on each other. Parent-child relationships may also exhibit covert or openly incestuous attitudes. Although loving, these bonds must eventually be broken or worked out in more mature relationships. If they are not, these childhood attitudes are likely to prove destructive in later life.

BRONSON PINCHOT (5/20/59)
MARK LINN-BAKER (6/17/54)

Pinchot and Linn-Baker co-starred in the tv sitcom *Perfect Strangers* from 1986–1993. Perfect foils for each other, Linn-Baker played a level-headed Chicagoan; Pinchot was his naïve immigrant cousin bewildered by American customs.

ADVICE: *Develop individuality. Avoid dependencies. Break immature bonds. Preserve your vision and originality. Develop paranormal abilities.*

May 19–24
THE CUSP OF ENERGY
TAURUS-GEMINI CUSP

June 19–24
THE CUSP OF MAGIC
GEMINI-CANCER CUSP

NICK CASSAVETES (5/21/59)
GENA ROWLANDS (6/19/34)

Cassavetes is the son of Rowlands and actor-director John Cassavetes. She is a distinguished actress of stage, screen and tv who appeared in most of her late husband's movies. Nick acted in several low-budget films in the 80s and early 90s. In '96 he wrote and directed *Unhook the Stars*, in which his mom is featured. *Also:* **William Gilbert & James I** (court physician/king).

Giving Counsel

This relationship focuses on communication, but not necessarily of a verbal kind. Its dominant mode can often be silence, and if the silence must be broken, this often happens in the most pleasing way possible, perhaps with music or a few murmured words. Written communication can often carry special meaning here, with perhaps an interest in books, manuscripts and their translations into different languages. Taurus-Geminis are a mixture of earth and air (Taurus is an earth sign, Gemini air) and Gemini-Cancers of air and water (Cancer is a water sign), so that the element they have in common is air, symbolizing thought.

One might expect love affairs to be of the more thoughtful variety, but the relationship's physical aspects, particularly those of touch, are also pronounced. Here the emphasis on silence and touch can lend romance, and the couple will need intimate and quiet spaces in which to meet. Intelligence and passion are in no way mutually exclusive here, and indeed work beautifully together. Covert love affairs between partners already involved with others may be particularly exciting, but may demand dishonest and ultimately hurtful behavior.

Marriages can work here, but, interestingly, may never materialize, due to circumstances or accidents of fate. Friendships may be possible, but seldom after the disappointing breakup of a love affair. Should these two meet first as friends, on the other hand, their relationship may either proceed farther, toward a love affair, or gradually dissolve away.

Professional and career relationships between these two, including student and teacher matchups, can be quite favorable. Not necessarily working together but advising and counseling each other, reviewing each other's work, and brainstorming new ideas are especially favored here. Gemini-Cancers are likely to admire the prodigious mental energies and eclectic knowledge of Taurus-Geminis, who for their part may learn a great deal from Gemini-Cancers' easy mastery of their field. Family relationships are favored in parent-child combinations. Parental Gemini-Cancer nurturing qualities are especially reassuring to unstable or nervous Gemini-Cancer offspring.

ADVICE: *Be careful of romantic involvement. Try to be open and honest. Don't be carried away by fantasy. Share ideas. Give counsel on a regular basis.*

May 19–24
THE CUSP OF ENERGY
TAURUS-GEMINI CUSP

June 25–July 2
THE WEEK OF THE EMPATH
CANCER I

RON GOLDMAN (7/2/68)
NICOLE BROWN SIMPSON (5/19/59)

Friends Goldman and Simpson's wife Brown were the murder victims in the infamous O.J. Simpson case. Prosecutor Christopher Darden described Goldman as a hero "who was killed trying to save [her] life." *Also:* **Jimmy Stewart & Olivia de Havilland** (almost engaged; actors); **Queen Victoria & Louis Mountbatten** (royal great-grandmother/great-grandson).

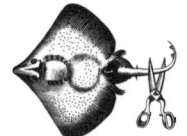

Tempering Enthusiasm

This relationship may focus on the worlds of both ideas and feelings, and in either area, its tendency is to push the boundaries back to their furthest limit. Big ideas and grand passions will be explored, either through discussion or actual experience. It is also possible for intellectual discussions to get carried away by the heat of argument and for feelings and experiences to be examined logically, thus blending areas of thought and emotion.

Expansive love affairs may carry desire to new heights, but frustrations arise through an inability to satisfy overblown expectations. Taurus-Geminis' frequent lack of self-understanding and the Cancer I tendency toward depression can prove a debilitating combination. In marriage, both parties need to be realistic, which means knowing when to scale back and when to encourage patterns of spending—whether of emotions, finances or life energy. Too often an imbalance here can lead to financial problems in which the relationship has few reserves to fall back on and little to give.

Friendships are likely to be difficult here between contemporaries, yet between old and young they may thrive, having a certain distance, perspective and objectivity that eliminate the anger or irritation felt with members of the same age group. Mutual respect is usually the antidote to such conflict. Work and family relationships are likely to bring out both partners' worst and best sides. Moderation is the key here, for emotions and unrealistic fantasy can quickly get out of control. Parent-child relationships are likely to demonstrate patterns of overvaluing or undervaluing, leading to feelings alternately of superiority or inferiority, conceit and self-esteem.

In all of the above relationships, it will be clear that temperance and balance are needed, but certainly not repression of enthusiastic attitudes. Sometimes a neutral third party or therapist may help move the awareness process along.

ADVICE: *Even out your moods. Beware of too high expectations. Take things as they come. Keep anger under control. Little is possible without respect.*

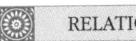

May 19–24

THE CUSP OF ENERGY
TAURUS-GEMINI CUSP

July 3–10

THE WEEK OF THE UNCONVENTIONAL
CANCER II

Excessive Interest

This can be an adventuresome and challenging matchup, given to searching for ever stranger and more out-of-the-way areas of experience. Assuming the partners agree on the areas they want to explore, they can share a great interest and involvement in subjects ranging from helping the disadvantaged to researching historical curiosities. Reading classified ads and visiting antique or junk stores, garage sales and auctions are all part of the picture. United by an interest in peculiar personal traits, the relationship may well find its own members the most interesting objects of study.

In love relationships and friendships, for example, these two can be excessively interested in each other's bodies and health. Anything abnormal or unusual is likely to fascinate. Taurus-Geminis have a propensity to check their immediate environment on a regular basis, and Cancer II's to become unduly attached to certain thoughts or fantasies; with tendencies like these, their relationship can easily become obsessive-compulsive, with Taurus-Geminis providing the compulsions and Cancer II's the obsessions. The result may be a total pre-occupation with physical processes, thoughts, responses and the most minute or seemingly insignificant actions. Such a relationship may not be completely healthy psychologically, but can prove absorbing and pleasurable.

Marriages in this combination are likely to be disturbed by obsessive-compulsive anxieties, worries and repetitive actions. Fear of almost anything, or almost everything, can drive these two, their children and everyone around them to distraction. Marriage is only recommended for them, then, as a means of facing and ultimately overcoming such fears. If this can be done, the couple can move from a therapeutic to a productive relationship.

Family relationships, especially parent-child matchups, can easily fall into neurotic patterns. Anxiety and guilt engendered in a Taurus-Gemini child by a Cancer II parent, or vice versa, can last a lifetime. Working relationships are probably this combination's most positive manifestations, particularly when the search to fulfill shared goals can be managed with a minimum of personal contact.

ADVICE: *Don't get hung up on details. Get rid of fears. Remember to forget occasionally. Checking everything constantly is a waste of energy.*

O.J. SIMPSON (7/9/47)
NICOLE BROWN SIMPSON (5/19/59)

At the time of her 1994 murder, Nicole was separated from her husband, O.J., with whom she had a tumultuous marriage. Although he was acquitted at his criminal trial, a civil-suit jury found him responsible for her death.

Also: Lillian Gilbreth & Frank Gilbreth (married; early efficiency engineers).

May 19–24

THE CUSP OF ENERGY
TAURUS-GEMINI CUSP

July 11–18

THE WEEK OF THE PERSUADER
CANCER III

Against All Odds

This powerful relationship often takes on big projects, and the intuitiveness of its assumptions, and of the way it implements them, may allow it to overcome and succeed against all odds. So intuitive is it, in fact, that it may find itself producing prophetic and predictive ideas about whether its endeavors will pan out and how rewarding they will be. Great care must be taken with prophecies, however, for fate has a strange way of making them true, but not always in the manner expected. A dark side manifests strongly in many areas of this relationship, raising the possibility of illicit, destructive and excessive forms of behavior.

Love affairs and marriages are likely to be tumultuous and unstable. Should Cancer III desires get out of hand, they may have to be capped, like a burning oil well. These personalities' wisdom, self-control and self-knowledge are usually great enough to prevent this from happening, but may lead to a different problem, resulting in a self-protectiveness that will prove a sexual challenge to more aggressive Taurus-Geminis, who long to break through such barriers. Although rebellious, Taurus-Geminis often back off in fear, and wind up depending instead on Cancer III protective, caring and nurturing qualities.

Friendships can work out well if the relationship's energies serve interests rather than end up wasted. The matchup's spiritual, paranormal and predictive tendencies favor activities ranging from self-actualization workshops to gambling at roulette or cards. In family settings this can be a strong relationship, especially when it offers Taurus-Gemini–Cancer III siblings protection against an unkind or abusive parent. In the case of absentee parents, brothers and sisters in this combination may play parental roles for other siblings and for each other.

Work pairings can be quite successful. Money-making is especially favored, but a spiritual approach may be of greater interest; these areas rarely coalesce, but when they do, the results can go beyond all expectations. Although this duo prides itself on being realistic, the partners will often be surprised, both pleasantly and unpleasantly, by events that contradict glib predictions.

ADVICE: *Know yourself better. Beware of excess. Repression will produce frustration. Find creative and spiritual outlets.*

BOB DYLAN (5/24/41)
WOODY GUTHRIE (7/14/12)

Guthrie's folksongs of the 30s and 40s laid the groundwork for Dylan's music. Dylan moved to New York in 1961 to be near his dying idol. He recorded a tribute to Guthrie with his first album, *Song to Woody*.

Also: Tommy Chong & Cheech Marin (comedy team); **Jimmy Stewart & Ginger Rogers** (romance; actors).

MARY CASSATT (5/22/1844)
EDGAR DEGAS (7/19/1834)

Cassatt's painting was strongly influenced by her close friend Degas. In 1874, he invited her to join the Impressionists and included her works in their exhibitions. They remained lifelong confidants. **Also: John Payne & Gloria DeHaven** (married; actors); **James Brown & Charles C. Little** (publishing partners).

May 19–24
THE CUSP OF ENERGY
TAURUS-GEMINI CUSP

July 19–25
THE CUSP OF OSCILLATION
CANCER-LEO CUSP

A Holistic Picture

Complete and well-balanced, this relationship also works magic. Taurus-Gemini is ruled by earth and air, Cancer-Leo by water and fire, a combination that in this case betokens a beautiful balance of all four elements. This holistic picture is appreciated by Taurus-Geminis and Cancer-Leos, two types who separately tend toward instability but together can bring it all together. The relationship itself is governed by two elements, air (thought) and water (feelings), which here means that logical planning in areas appealing to the emotions will often achieve success. Complementarity is the key to this relationship; these partners are able to fill in each other's gaps, making a synergistic whole far greater than the sum of its parts.

In love relationships, Taurus-Gemini talents and ideas can hold the interest of Cancer-Leos—an essential ability for them. Taurus-Geminis meanwhile can find adventure and excitement with this partner. Instability, at times through infidelity either real or imagined, will always be an issue here, but the duo's belief in itself, and in undying desire, will sustain it through rough times. The relationship's essential balance is usually restored after each tilt.

In work, family and marital relationships, the wedding of logic and emotion produces a kind of emotional intelligence that will carry these partners a long way. Rarely will irrationality tempt these partners to jeopardize their unity or work against their own interests. The magical element here gives them charisma, so that any products they are engaged in producing, and any children they have, will be irresistible or at least charming.

Friendships are more than possible—in fact the good feelings they are likely to include, and the desire to spend more time together, will often make them develop into work partnerships, marriages or love affairs. If so, however, the partners must be prepared to give up some of their freedom, and may later regret having gone farther. Sometimes the best answer for these friends is to stay that way, or even to back off and meet only on special occasions.

ADVICE: *Retain individuality. Groups are effective but only take you so far. Don't be overconfident. A good thing should not be taken for granted.*

JEAN PAUL MARAT (5/24/1743)
CHARLOTTE CORDAY (7/27/1768)

An avowed Girondist, Corday went to Paris in 1793 and, on the pretext of betraying Girondist dissidents, gained access to French Revolutionist Marat and stabbed him to death in his bath. She was guillotined 4 days later.

May 19–24
THE CUSP OF ENERGY
TAURUS-GEMINI CUSP

July 26–August 2
THE WEEK OF AUTHORITY
LEO I

Acute Differences of Temperament

The tone of this relationship is serious, perhaps a bit too serious for Taurus-Geminis, whose rebelliousness will be brought out by overbearing Leo I's, and whom these powerful partners may also reject as flaky or dilettantish. The standard of responsibility stressed here is often such that neither person feels able to live up to it. Yet scaling back and lowering expectations are not easily accomplished. There is also a need for a strong ruling force, which often, however, has to be outside the relationship—it cannot usually be embodied by either partner. Similarly, it can be a set of laws, but one that both partners can accept will be hard to formulate.

Problems of this type abound in marital, work and family relationships. For most Leo I's, uncertainty is unbearable, and they may be anything but reassured by their interactions with Taurus-Geminis, who are mercurial in the extreme and whose changing moods, desires and needs are likely to drive Leo I's up the wall. Should Leo I's try to yell or put their foot down, Taurus-Geminis are usually gone. Both of these partners do better as freelancers at work, as free agents in a marriage, and as independent family members, but unfortunately this kind of independence may weaken or dissolve the bonds that hold such relationships together. If Taurus-Gemini–Leo I marriages, work projects and parent-child relationships are to succeed, compromises will have to be worked out and firm agreements reached about responsibilities and rules. Until this is done, chaos may reign. Friendships here are much more desirable and easy. Same-sex matchups are especially favored, and can be among the more successful relationships between Geminis and Leos of any kind. Trust and honesty must be felt instinctively rather than imposed from without. This pair can discharge its weekly or monthly responsibilities easily as long as they are not too great, and in times of need the relationship will exhibit an open door and an open pocketbook. Taurus-Gemini–Leo I love affairs are infrequent and not recommended, chiefly because of acute differences of temperament.

ADVICE: *Compromise is necessary. Give up some of your independence. Pitch in and contribute. Rules are necessary, but don't forget to have fun.*

May 19–24
THE CUSP OF ENERGY
TAURUS-GEMINI CUSP

August 3–10
THE WEEK OF BALANCED STRENGTH
LEO II

Who's Feeling What?

These two are on the same wavelength. Understanding and sympathy are immediate and evident in this relationship, and feelings are empathic. The partners can identify with each other to a great degree, feeling each other's pain or joy. An interesting mechanism at work here, one often observed in empaths, is that if the Leo II feels an emotion, such as anger, but does not express it, the Taurus-Gemini may get angry without knowing why—actually taking on the other's affect, like a chameleon. So real are the emotions that partners often mistake the other person's feelings for their own.

Love and marriage may both be tempestuous—not surprising, given the level of feeling involved. Taurus-Gemini is ruled by air and earth, Leo II by fire, but the combination is governed by water, denoting emotion. This relationship tends to be passionate to the point of incandescence. Instability, anger, jealousy, violence—any or all of these may appear here. Although empathy manifests, too, swirling emotions and ego defenses often prevent it from manifesting in its pure form. It emerges more evidently and consistently in sibling matchups and friendships, siblings in particular being very close, almost like twins, or perhaps like Alexandre Dumas's Corsican brothers, who were able to sense each other's feelings miles apart. Friendships are also likely to be open and sharing.

Professional relationships between these two can be very successful. Both Taurus-Geminis and Leo II's are endowed with prodigious energy, and if they can make their energies work in tandem and in the right direction, much can be accomplished. Taurus-Geminis will supply the initial burst needed to get projects off the ground, while Leo II's will steadfastly and energetically push them to completion. When the pair are co-workers, competitive and personal feelings may get in the way, but boss-employee situations can work extremely well: despite rebellious tendencies in both these partners, each can accept the other as a boss when a hierarchical structure requires it, as long as they respect and even admire each other.

ADVICE: *Try to separate feelings. Take responsibility only for what is yours. Don't let your emotions get out of control. Encourage openness.*

ANDY WARHOL (8/6/28)
MARISOL (5/22/30)

Contemporary artist Marisol is best known for her large wooden sculptures, often combined with portraits of herself. In the 60s and 70s she was associated with the pop art crowd. Normally introverted, she often attended art openings and parties with her fame-obsessed friend Warhol.
Also: Roseanne Cash & Rodney Crowell (married; country-music stars).

May 19–24
THE CUSP OF ENERGY
TAURUS-GEMINI CUSP

August 11–18
THE WEEK OF LEADERSHIP
LEO III

Emotional Intelligence

Acknowledging personal emotions is the underlying theme of this relationship. The Taurus-Gemini and the Leo III must try to understand and accept not only their own and each other's feelings but those of people outside the relationship, and they must apply that understanding in social situations. This is the pairing's great challenge. The relationship can be successful only if each partner's feelings are mastered; emotional repression can only lead to frustration, anxiety and depression. Feelings must be dealt with maturely, and with patience, trust and understanding. These qualities don't come easy to either Taurus-Geminis or Leo III's, but they can be attained with work. The fact that this is not an unrealistic goal speaks well for this combination.

As individuals, Taurus-Geminis and Leo III's share three problems: a lack of deep self-understanding, a low threshold of patience, and a capacity for considerable self-involvement. Love and marriage between these two may worsen such tendencies to the point where it becomes doubtful that the relationship will last long enough to implement some of the emotional management it needs. Should a deep love emerge, however, it can be accompanied by a willingness to endure the necessary travail.

Family relationships in this combination, especially parent-child, need a lot of emotional intelligence. Taurus-Geminis are often anxious to please, and exhibit unformed egos; Leo III's have big egos and can ride roughshod over others. As parents, then, Leo III's are likely to crush or spoil their Taurus-Gemini children, while the Taurus-Gemini parent may be dominated by the powerful Leo III child.

At work, the relationship will demand understanding. If emotions aren't kept in check, the job will not get done. Deep emotional involvement is not favored, but as long as this is kept in mind, Taurus-Geminis and Leo III's who work together may do all right, particularly if they are colleagues or associates rather than bosses and employees. This relationship will allow them to build respect slowly, through cooperation, and to work out a healthy emotional balance.

ADVICE: *Keep trying. The result is worth the effort. Beware of selfishness and impatience. Get to know yourself better. Work out emotional problems.*

MALCOLM X (5/19/25)
ALEX HALEY (8/11/21)

Malcolm X, the radical advocate of Black Nationalism, shared a mutual respect with writer Haley, to whom he dictated *The Autobiography of Malcolm X*. It became a bestseller in 1965, the year of Malcolm's assassination.
Also: Sam Giancana & Fidel Castro (reputed mob hit plot).

The Hand of Fate

May 19–24
THE CUSP OF ENERGY
TAURUS-GEMINI CUSP

August 19–25
THE CUSP OF EXPOSURE
LEO-VIRGO CUSP

RICHARD WAGNER (5/22/1813)
LUDWIG II (8/25/1845)

"Mad King Ludwig," the Bavarian eccentric, was a great art patron who supported the final 20 years of composer Wagner's life, including the performance of his mature works and the construction of a concert hall of Wagner's design.
Also: Queen Victoria & William IV (niece succeeded uncle to English throne).

This combination may be unusual in many respects—how the partners meet, the speed with which their relationship develops, and the experiential byways that they explore together are seldom of the ordinary sort. The relationship's focus, too, is likely to be unconventional, and in a way not at all put on for the benefit of the other partner or for friends or family, but intrinsically so. Fate often plays a large role in bringing these two together, but when they meet it is as if they have known each other before, as if (or actually?) in another life. Thus the relationship is often permeated by a feeling of déjà vu, but in a good way—a way that heightens the excitement of its experiences by promoting a foreknowledge of whatever is going on.

Love affairs in this combination are apt to be highly expressive. Both partners often have the feeling that what's happening is right, or is meant to be, even when the relationship is covert or socially unacceptable in conventional terms. The affair draws these two like a magnet, and although it may be short and intense in length, after it is over the lovers may become friends. It may also be ended by the couple's marriage, but this step may prove unnecessary or premature, and should be considered carefully.

Friendships are likely to be enduring, whether the partners have been lovers or not. Quirky, even bizarre elements can emerge here. Each partner feels an admiration and sympathy for the intelligence and artistic sensitivity of the other, and an interest in the work the other does; thus friendships may evolve into working relationships, or vice versa. In whatever area, the matchup speaks of mutability, adaptability, and responsiveness to each other's needs. But problems arising from Leo-Virgo secretiveness and Taurus-Gemini megalomania can be severe, and may ultimately lead to a sudden breakup. In families, this unusual relationship is less likely to be successful between parents and children than between grandparents and grandchildren, uncles or aunts and nieces or nephews, or between cousins. Not only understanding but financial support is often forthcoming here, enabling the younger person to develop his or her skills.

ADVICE: *Don't surrender your free will. Not everything is written. What are you trying to prove? Find out your true wishes and desires. Think clearly.*

Success at Any Cost

May 19–24
THE CUSP OF ENERGY
TAURUS-GEMINI CUSP

August 26–September 2
THE WEEK OF SYSTEM BUILDERS
VIRGO I

QUEEN VICTORIA (5/24/1819)
PRINCE ALBERT (8/26/1819)

The marriage of these cousins was one-sided. Victoria had strong erotic interests, but Albert limited his attentions mostly to procreation. They had 9 children together.
Also: Priscilla Presley & Michael Jackson (mother-in-law/son-in-law; actress/rock star).

This couple will let nothing stand in their way—they are determined to succeed at any cost. Determination is the keyword here. Also emphasized is intelligence (evidenced by Mercury's rulership of both Gemini and Virgo), generally of a more practical than pedantic kind. In fact the practical ability here far exceeds that of these individuals by themselves. Planning is a prominent activity, and the relationship's shared visions and dreams are generally of a worldly, goal-oriented nature. By paying attention to detail and taking one step at a time, these two can ultimately achieve whatever aim they choose.

Love affairs are seldom successful here, even if the partners share a physical attraction. The Taurus-Gemini charm for other people makes Virgo I's insecure, and they are likely to withdraw, disappointed and hurt. Taurus-Geminis may feel guilty for inflicting pain, but this won't usually keep them from involvements elsewhere. Lacking a strong focus, the relationship is likely to drift and fall apart.

Business and marriage partnerships, and shared participation as volunteers in social activities, are more recommended. Especially favored are endeavors in which there is a great deal to lose and perhaps even more to gain, thus forcing the pair to be aspiring and watchful. The stress here can become enormous—perhaps too much for nervous Taurus-Geminis and Virgo I's to handle. It is usually self-induced, however, so readjusting conditions and work habits intelligently may alleviate (but rarely solve) the problem. Taurus-Gemini–Virgo I friendships are often built around a serious endeavor, whether mental or physical. Leisure-time interests as different as chess and football, or cards and fitness, illustrate the relationship's extremes. Taurus-Geminis will benefit from the structure that is usual here, while Virgo I's will refuel from Taurus-Geminis' abundant energy.

Brother-sister pairs in this combination may be symbiotically close, both while growing up and in adulthood. Their mental connection is strong not only in terms of reason and common sense but also, possibly, in the psychic sphere. Even so, the pair may consciously reject the idea that anything paranormal is at work.

ADVICE: *Don't get bottled up in your head. Learn to relax. Worry is poison. Turn off the big brain. Remember to forget. Avoid hurtful behavior.*

May 19–24
THE CUSP OF ENERGY
TAURUS-GEMINI CUSP

September 3–10
THE WEEK OF THE ENIGMA
VIRGO II

Point Counterpoint

This relationship is geared toward debate, argument and the detective work that results in a theory or answer for a question. Both partners will find themselves trying to convince the other of their viewpoint—and will surprise themselves by finding this so important. Each will be particularly concerned with trying to illuminate the meaning behind the other's actions. In conversation, for example, Taurus-Geminis, never known for tact, will analyze a Virgo II's enigmatic foibles, trying to make this partner understand what his or her own character is really about. But this is a tear-out-your-hair exercise, since Virgo II's rarely reveal all, and would never admit it if they did. Furthermore, they have often suffered in childhood from criticism by others, are thin-skinned, and may retaliate with their own refined critiques. Thus an open discussion can escalate into a battle of wills and words.

Love here is rarely out in the open. Falling short of a full-blown affair, it may encompass many stages of flirtation, courting and unnoticed come-ons, all piquing curiosity but only leading to frustration. Nor are marriages recommended: with Taurus-Gemini making demands and Virgo II refusing them, these partners will drive each other crazy. A folie à deux, fixed on a shared delusion, is only one of the nightmares perhaps awaiting this relationship.

Friendships, however, may work out well: although the partners' outside interests may eclipse their interest in each other, this only means that investigations of science, mathematics, aesthetics, philosophy and psychology may give their relationship a basis. A specialized interest in illicit activities, whether in mystery stories or in real life, may prove especially stimulating. Working and family relationships are only likely to be upset by the pair's almost obsessive activity. This team is not recommended for getting the job done: in the middle of a task, they are likely to be attracted by an interesting detail, causing an immediate detour and even the derailment of a project that only moments before was going nicely. Parent-child and boss-employee matchups in particular are liable to experience friction, worry and bother.

ADVICE: *Learn to back off. Voyeurism isn't always appreciated. Respect others' privacy. Try to keep on track. Living in interesting times can be a curse.*

WILLIAM GILBERT (5/24/1544)
QUEEN ELIZABETH I (9/7/1533)

Gilbert was the most distinguished man of science during Elizabeth's reign. Considered the "father of electrical studies," he focused his work on magnetism. In 1601 he became the queen's personal physician. **Also: Richard Wagner & Minna Planer** (composer's first wife).

May 19–24
THE CUSP OF ENERGY
TAURUS-GEMINI CUSP

September 11–18
THE WEEK OF THE LITERALIST
VIRGO III

Backbone of the Family

Excitement and imagination figure prominently in this bright and lively relationship, which is apt to focus on dramatic happenings in which change is the common denominator. Changes of residence, of mood, of financial status, of career—any and all of these, and more, may feature in the relationship's life. This mutability has a shadow side, in that its insecurity can lead to dominating or controlling tendencies. Virgo III's in particular, who like things to be clearly defined, will try to take matters in hand if they feel out of control.

Love affairs are likely to bring out the tempestuous side of both partners, and a tendency toward vociferous quarrels. Behind these arguments, however, lies a respect that endures no matter how strident the accusations. Blame and guilt trips are likely to emerge, but also ecstatic moments and long periods of good feeling. The mood here is unpredictable, a bit like the weather.

Marriages are not particularly recommended: they may feature a level of conflict and a lack of stability from which children can hardly benefit. Changing moods and attempts at control will not be conducive to either domestic tranquillity or mental health. Family relationships, on the other hand, especially with a parent and child of the opposite sex, and working matchups (co-workers, boss-employee, or professional colleagues) can be productive and understanding. Parent-child relationships can prove the backbone of the family, signaling an interesting combination of responsibility and changeableness. This duo can run a tight ship, using hope and good humor to roll with the storms of fate. Both at work and at home, the relationship eschews snobbishness, promotes fairness and equality and is on the side of the underdog. It usually views highly ambitious, pretentious or rich individuals with some suspicion.

Friendships between these two can be pleasant enough, but emotionally they rarely develop far. Gemini-Cancers and Virgo III's are usually too busy with their work, love and family relationships to devote a great deal of time to friendship with each other. The relationship may be counted upon, however, in times of need.

ADVICE: *Set aside quality time for relaxation. Reduce quarreling. Enjoy yourself. Don't get bogged down in work and responsibilities. Try to trust that all is well.*

ARTHUR CONAN DOYLE (5/22/1859)
AGATHA CHRISTIE (9/15/1890)

Doyle and Christie are England's preeminent mystery writers. Doyle's most famous character is the Victorian sleuth Sherlock Holmes, with his acute powers of deductive reasoning. Christie was more 20th-century, with her popular detective characters Hercule Poirot and Miss Marple. **Also: Richard Wagner & Clara Schumann** (rivals; composer/pianist).

May 19–24
THE CUSP OF ENERGY
TAURUS-GEMINI CUSP

September 19–24
THE CUSP OF BEAUTY
VIRGO-LIBRA CUSP

ANTHONY NEWLEY (9/24/31)
JOAN COLLINS (5/23/33)

Collins' career peaked on tv's *Dynasty* series (1981–89). Newley, a versatile actor, singer, composer and director, created Broadway's *Stop the World—I Want to Get Off.* They were married from 1963–70. **Also: Rosemary Clooney & Debby Boone** (mother-in-law/ daughter-in-law; singers).

Girl with the Curl

This relationship experiences wide fluctuations. Although their trine aspect (120° apart) in the zodiac is considered to promote ease, and the two partners share an earth-air orientation (Taurus and Virgo are earth signs, Gemini and Libra are air), the relationship is about water and fire, a combination producing changes in state (water extinguishes fire, fire turns water to steam). Such physical changes indicate an underlying instability and often sudden and unpredictable mood swings. Here we have a perfect example of the irony of relationships: two perfectly well-suited individuals together create the exact opposite of what each is looking for—peace and quiet—but in doing so they create a crucible for learning and growing.

In love affairs, marriages and family relationships, things may seem to be going well when upset manifests for no apparent reason. This is a real problem for this pair, neither of whom is particularly good at looking deeper into things. Moreover, Taurus-Geminis lack self-awareness and Virgo-Libras want peace and harmony, a combination disturbing to both when problems arise—Taurus-Geminis will become even more nervous than usual here. The obvious need is for a greater consciousness within the relationship, one that attempts to understand and address underlying problems and to avoid glossing over them by giving things a positive spin.

Friendships are less subject to outbursts and mood swings, but may not go very deep. More casual relationships, such as acquaintanceships or companionships centered around a common activity, often establish a calmer rapport, and may have an intellectual, philosophic or artistic orientation.

Working relationships tend to place excessive demands on both members, who will try to meet them but may ultimately fail. Taurus-Geminis will often urge Virgo-Libras to be more expressive, while Virgo-Libras will urge Taurus-Geminis to produce more beautiful or technically perfect work. Like the girl with the curl, this duo too often provides a product or service that is uncertain in quality—sometimes very good and sometimes, well, not horrid, but quite a bit below par.

ADVICE: *Try to even out your work. Aim for consistency. Promote self-understanding. Infections sometimes demand immediate attention.*

May 19–24
THE CUSP OF ENERGY
TAURUS-GEMINI CUSP

September 25–October 2
THE WEEK OF THE PERFECTIONIST
LIBRA I

RICHARD III (10/2/1452)
LAURENCE OLIVIER (5/22/07)

Olivier has been called the greatest actor of the 20th century, successful in modern works as well as the classics. One of his finest portrayals, on both stage and screen, was that of Shakespeare's *Richard III*, the power-crazed Duke of Gloucester who would stop at nothing to become king. In Olivier's performances of *Richard III*, actor and character merged into one.

Outwitting the Other

This relationship orients itself toward matters of the mind. Bringing perceptions to awareness, and drawing conclusions from them, are quick, sometimes almost immediate. An explosive streak threatens here, resembling summer storms, with their sudden intensity and heat lightning. Outbursts of this kind, however, may act as a warning, and rarely materialize in full-blown physical conflict. Because conclusions are arrived at so quickly, partners would do well to give themselves a cooling-off period before addressing issues, and then, having done so, to be sure to discuss everything. Should thoughts or feelings be suppressed here, anxiety, fear and jealousy may be sublimated into competitive drives. This relationship isn't always of the most trusting or stable sort. A polarity often emerges in which either the Taurus-Gemini or the Libra I becomes the teacher and their partner the student, either formally, in a school situation, or in relation to an activity, perhaps sport-related, musical or spiritual. The relationship can be based on a will to overcome, with attendant power struggles, friendly or not.

Love relationships may not last long in this combination, but their shortness may be merciful and they are fairly harmless. There is an undeniable sexual attraction, but both partners are wary of initiating action, preferring to joust with each other romantically until one of them senses an opening. It is not uncommon for these two to attach to each other when one or both of them is already in a troubled relationship.

In friendships, each partner's desire to outwit the other encourages feelings of competitiveness and envy. Familial and marital relations are more likely to be productive, as long as competition is positively oriented and attention to any third party can be kept under control. Physical contact is always tricky here, and will have to be treated with some sensitivity to avoid catastrophe. Mentally this pair may shine (especially siblings of the same sex), with the Taurus-Gemini providing the imagination and raw energy and the Libra I the technical expertise. Understandably, given the competitiveness here, working relationships between these two don't usually work out.

ADVICE: *Competitiveness should be mutually rewarding. Deal with negative feelings. Don't fool yourself. Winning out may mean losing.*

May 19–24

THE CUSP OF ENERGY
TAURUS-GEMINI CUSP

October 3–10

THE WEEK OF SOCIETY
LIBRA II

The Third Ear

RELATIONSHIPS

STRENGTHS: INTUITIVE, COMMUNICATIVE, SOULFUL

WEAKNESSES: UNREALISTIC, CONSUMING, SELF-EFFACING

BEST: LOVE

WORST: WORK

MALCOLM X (5/19/25)
ELIJAH MUHAMMAD (10/7/1897)

After converting to Islam while in prison in 1947, Malcolm X became spokesman and minister for Muhammad's Black Muslims. In March, 1964, he left the movement over an ideological rift with Muhammad. Malcolm was assassinated in April, 1965.
Also: Joan Collins & Jackie Collins (sisters; actress/writer); **Jimmy Stewart & Josh Logan** (classmates; actor/director).

This relationship often focuses on examining the written and spoken word. But although communication is important here, the matchup is actually more about intuitive knowing—listening with a third ear. These two are so much on the same wavelength that their mutual understanding is their most precious possession. They will enjoy their mental contact, gaining great satisfaction, for example, from discussions of business, aesthetic, spiritual and psychological matters. There is a need to keep things objective here, for these partners' intense emotions could easily sweep both of them away. But they do have the ability to retain their individual objectivity within this relationship, assuring its durability.

Still, love relationships can be somewhat dangerous here. This may make the attraction even stronger at times, for both partners can have an unrealistic streak in matters of the heart. But their intuitive wariness of each other with regard to sexual involvement usually betokens good sense, and makes them wait before becoming more deeply involved. Should this pair make a commitment, it will probably result in them getting married or living together. Taurus-Gemini–Libra II marriages can be solid but also soulful. Difficulties may arise due to Taurus-Gemini selfishness and Libra II low self-esteem, but love and understanding can often overcome these and other problems. Once their passions cool, these two will find that their relationship gives them a very positive outlook.

Friendships here may be close and warm, but, like love, will have to be kept under control. Family relationships may also have tempestuous tendencies. Meeting at appointed times, with a while between them, will aid the process of objectivity. Both partners must guard against losing themselves in the relationship.

Working relationships may succeed as long as argumentative tendencies are kept under control. Here the relationship's verbal and intuitive strengths find a constructive, possibly commercial outlet that can give direction to what might otherwise have become idle discussion, albeit an interesting one.

ADVICE: *Structure the relationship. Keep feelings under control. Find a creative outlet, possibly a financial one. Give counsel without getting involved.*

May 19–24

THE CUSP OF ENERGY
TAURUS-GEMINI CUSP

October 11–18

THE WEEK OF THEATER
LIBRA III

Forever Young

RELATIONSHIPS

STRENGTHS: EASY, JUST, FAIR

WEAKNESSES: UNCOMPROMISING, ARGUMENTATIVE, HYPERCRITICAL

BEST: FAMILY

WORST: WORK

LELAND HAYWARD (10/15/02)
JIMMY STEWART (5/20/08)

Hayward was a successful talent agent and producer who in 1952 negotiated a percentage-basis contract with Universal Pictures for his client Stewart. A financial bonanza for Stewart, it prompted other actors to follow suit.

This relationship is best when free and easy, with few responsibilities assumed by either partner. It may well focus on social and universal issues, and on not just discussing them but getting out of the house and doing something about the state of the world. This is not a crusading or visionary matchup, however, exerting its influence mainly within its immediate social, occupational or family circle. Nonetheless, it stands up for what it believes is right. Justice and fairness are strong values here, and although this partnership will explore all legal loopholes, rarely if ever will it take unfair advantage of people.

Love between these two is unlikely to be primarily romantic. If a love affair ends, it may not be entirely abandoned; this can be a platonic couple, developing strongly protective and supportive feelings about each other as passions decline. Critical attitudes are not suspended, however, and disagreements are to be expected. The strongly developed egos of many Libra III's may force Taurus-Geminis into playing a subordinate role, something they may not be ready to do.

In marriages and friendships, Libra III's will usually bring Taurus-Geminis into a more meaningful relationship with society in general and the professional world in particular. In this respect they become their partner's teachers. In one-on-one and family involvements, on the other hand, it is Taurus-Geminis who have much to show Libra III's.

Some family relationships can be excellent here. Youthful attitudes are encouraged, and parent-child combinations may succeed in keeping both parties forever young. Libra III's don't always realize how much they need to be part of a successful family group. Taurus-Geminis may succeed both in making Libra III's aware of these needs and in helping to satisfy them, perhaps as a step-parent, step-child or more distant relative. Taurus-Gemini–Libra III work relationships do not usually pan out, since both parties may be too hardheaded to compromise or agree.

ADVICE: *Keep it light. Be aware of deeper needs. Develop social and family contacts. It is never too late to start over. Clean up your act.*

RICHARD WAGNER (5/22/1813)
FRANZ LISZT (10/22/1811)

Wagner married Liszt's daughter Cosima in 1870 after her previous marriage was annulled. Liszt, disturbed over their earlier affair in 1867, had refused to attend the wedding, but he remained devoted to Wagner's music. **Also: Joshua Lederberg & George Wells Beadle** (1958 Nobelists, medicine); **Edmund Lynch & Charles Merrill** (co-founders of Merrill Lynch).

May 19–24
THE CUSP OF ENERGY
TAURUS-GEMINI CUSP

October 19–25
THE CUSP OF DRAMA & CRITICISM
LIBRA-SCORPIO CUSP

Mind Games

This combination's strength is its mind power. Both partners value mental functions, having a talent for reasoning and logic; yet their relationship generally focuses on intuition, or on active expression and will. What happens when these tendencies are combined? The appearance of a rather aggressive mental stance. Together these two may assume they are mentally superior to others, and may battle between themselves to prove who is smartest. The effects can be highly negative, featuring mind games and overintellectualizing. It is hard for the pair to avoid these battles of the brain completely, but if they can join forces and express themselves against the world, they can become leaders. Otherwise they will be pitted against each other.

In love affairs, Taurus-Geminis intent on pleasing this particular partner are in for a rude shock: their impatient earthiness will not gel with Libra-Scorpio ambivalence of feeling. Libra-Scorpios are often split between what they think they need and want emotionally and what they really do need and want. In the face of this lack of self-knowledge, Taurus-Geminis may go on a fruitless and frustrating wild-goose chase in trying to please them. Also, their own need to absorb punishment may dovetail with the Libra-Scorpio desire to dish it out, creating a nightmarish scenario. Marriage is not recommended here, but often occurs, banking on a kinship of thought that too often masks spiritual and emotional immaturity.

Friendships can be well balanced as long as emotional manipulation is kept out of the picture. The sharing of intellectual and artistic interests is a joy that may continue for a lifetime. This relationship may shine within a social circle that takes an affectionate pride in its achievements.

Work relationships may be productive, but power struggles and one-upmanship too often mar them unless a conscious effort is made at solidarity. In that case the pair's competitive stance can bring them far. Family relationships, particularly parent-child combinations, can be stormy, with the exception of brother-sister matchups, which come closest to friendships in achieving a sympathetic and dynamic balance.

ADVICE: *Tune in to your deepest self. Develop intuitive powers. Don't get sidetracked by ideas and discussion. Grasp what is most important.*

JOAN PLOWRIGHT (10/28/29)
SIR LAURENCE OLIVIER (5/22/07)

Olivier and character actress Plowright were happily married from 1961 until his death in 1989. She appeared with him in 2 films, *The Entertainer* (1960) and *The Three Sisters* (1970), also directed by Olivier. They raised a family and became mainstays of London's National Theatre.

May 19–24
THE CUSP OF ENERGY
TAURUS-GEMINI CUSP

October 26–November 2
THE WEEK OF INTENSITY
SCORPIO I

Unpredictable Petulance

This progressive, forward-looking and unpredictable relationship can go in any direction. Erratic impulses dot the landscape when it is on; when it is off, there is a deadly silence. The relationship's principal problem and challenge is acceptance. These two often get irritated with each other; each of them knows how to push the other's buttons. For one partner to stop doing this may solve only half of the problem, since the other partner also needs to make his or her buttons harder to push.

Love and marriage are difficult here. Scorpio I's are control freaks; Taurus-Geminis have to do things their own way, and despite their energy they are not tough enough to stand up to incessant Scorpio I demands. Interested in short-term gratification, Taurus-Geminis will probably be gone if Scorpio I's try to pin them down. Sometimes, however, a weary Taurus-Gemini will crave the control of a Scorpio I, finding it comforting to be unburdened of responsibility. This will usually occur later in life, after the Taurus-Gemini has sown every possible oat. Scorpio I's, meanwhile, may be better able to enjoy Taurus-Gemini energy and imagination once they too are older and their judgmental nature has mellowed.

Friendships and family relationships may be close, but can be upset or worse by what either partner perceives as a thoughtless act. Scorpio I's will condemn impure motives and Taurus-Geminis poor results, both laying on guilt and blame. The ability to forgive and accept (neither is likely to forget) will generally determine whether or not friends, parents and children, or siblings go on speaking to each other.

Working relationships may be both steadily productive and capable of epic feats. Scorpio I's are detail oriented and hate to be rushed, while Taurus-Geminis are impatient and may take shortcuts. The Taurus-Gemini drive to finish a task and move on will be countered by the dogged determination of Scorpio I's to stick to the task, even perhaps working it to death. This dynamic can produce wonderful results, however, as long as the co-workers do not drive each other crazy.

ADVICE: *Let go of the past. You are carrying heavy burdens. Lighten up. There may be an easier way to get work done. Control irritations. Accept.*

May 19–24

THE CUSP OF ENERGY
TAURUS-GEMINI CUSP

November 3–11

THE WEEK OF DEPTH
SCORPIO II

  RELATIONSHIPS

STRENGTHS: **DIRECTED,
EMPATHIC, INTUITIVE**

WEAKNESSES: **FOUNDERING,
DEPRESSED, DISAPPOINTED**

BEST: **FRIENDSHIP**

WORST: **MARRIAGE**

Follow the Leader

This relationship is characterized not by a struggle for power but by a serious attempt to give it direction. This cannot always be accomplished by unanimity of opinion, which too often leads to well-meaning decisions that are never implemented; one partner has to take the lead. This decision-making power, however, may change hands from one situation to another, reversing the roles of leader and follower. When areas of expertise are clearly defined, the choice of leader is obvious, but conflicts may arise in day-to-day situations as to how roles are played out, and it is here that the relationship's intuitive focus either succeeds or fails.

Love relationships usually favor Taurus-Geminis taking the lead. They are often highly passionate, but Scorpio II depression may emerge in direct proportion to sexual intensity. For a Taurus-Gemini who needs to be appreciated and expects joy to be the result of such lovemaking, this can be paralyzing. If neither partner is willing or able to take the lead and adopt a realistic hard line, marriages too may founder, tending to drift, lose direction and finally wind up on the rocks. Nervous or depressed parents preoccupied with their own problems rarely have time for children—an especially tragic result.

The best of all relationships in this combination is friendship. Here Taurus-Geminis and Scorpio II's, particularly of the same sex, may form an extremely close and empathic bond, and the lead will change hands effortlessly with little or no conflict. Resentments and annoyances will certainly surface, but can usually be expressed and released.

Co-workers and family members may be able to strike an equal balance, in which each holds up his or her end of the bargain. Mutual respect and a desire to work for the company's or family's good can guarantee success, but feelings of warmth are usually slow to develop. Building trust is essential before any meaningful emotional exchange is possible.

ADVICE: *Look on the bright side. Don't let yourself be dragged down. Give direction to your efforts. Take the lead whenever necessary.*

SIR LAURENCE OLIVIER (5/22/07)
VIVIEN LEIGH (11/5/13)

The couple met while filming *Fire Over England* (1937) and started a much publicized affair. Divorcing their spouses, in 1940 they began a tempestuous 20-year marriage. In 1960 Leigh divorced Olivier for adultery, naming Joan Plowright as participant.
Also: Richard Grant White & Stanford White (father/son; critic/architect); **Queen Victoria & Prince Albert** (mother/son).

May 19–24

THE CUSP OF ENERGY
TAURUS-GEMINI CUSP

November 12–18

THE WEEK OF CHARM
SCORPIO III

  RELATIONSHIPS

STRENGTHS: **PRECIOUS,
RESPECTFUL, SPIRITUAL**

WEAKNESSES: **ISOLATED,
CLAIMING, DEMANDING**

BEST: **MARRIAGE**

WORST: **LOVE AFFAIR**

Rare Crystal

Both parties treat this relationship with great care, knowing that its sensitivity renders it precious and fragile, like rare crystal. First meetings here are often warm but wary. A long and uninterrupted period is needed for trust and acceptance to begin to grow, and wise partners know not to push or try to accelerate this process. Respect generally emerges, not just the type that implies general human value, or that recognizes an undue level of dedication. It is the kind of respect generated when you realize that someone is capable of hurting you but chooses not to—and, also, a respect for the unique nature of a relationship that can see its partners through good times and bad.

Magnetic attractions, especially romantic or sexual ones, are not uncommon here. Often, however, they are hidden in nature, even to the partners themselves, except for occasional hints and glimpses. One day these passions may be revealed with terrifying force. The problem is that the partners may already have built a satisfying relationship in the spheres of work or friendship, relationships that may be sitting on a keg of dynamite. At the point when strong physical feelings are first sensed, work partners and friends have an obligation to bring them to light in order to avoid catastrophe later. But platonic friendships can be highly rewarding, particularly if they involve the sharing of artistic or spiritual pursuits. Likewise, in the most successful professional relationships, associates or boss-employee pairs sublimate primary drives into work projects.

In marriages and families, both Taurus-Geminis and Scorpio III's will benefit from group support and social influences. Such groups tend to mitigate this pair's tendency to isolate themselves, and by forcing them to interact socially on a daily basis, to both strengthen the relationship and make it more flexible. Scorpio III jealousy and claiming behavior, however, as well as Taurus-Gemini fickleness and game-playing, will have to be monitored and dealt with carefully. Whether the pair are siblings or spouses, demands are high. Neither party is unaware of the stakes involved.

ADVICE: *Keep feelings out in the open. Avoid ambiguities. Level with each other. Stay objective. Feelings are valuable but explosive. Give up claims.*

LEE STRASBERG (11/17/01)
SUSAN STRASBERG (5/22/38)

Lee founded the Actors Studio in NY in 1949. Daughter Susan never attended her father's prestigious Method Acting school, preferring to study other dramatic techniques.
Also: Todd Stottlemeyer & Mel Stottlemeyer (baseball father/son); **Malcolm X & Attallah Shabazz** (father/actress daughter).

STRENGTHS: **REVELATORY,
RESILIENT, TRUSTING**

WEAKNESSES: **REPRESSIVE,
SELF-SACRIFICING, RUTHLESS**

BEST: **PARTNERSHIP**

WORST: **MARRIAGE**

EVELYN KEYES (11/20/19)
ARTIE SHAW (5/23/10)

Actress Keyes was 8th wife to bandleader and clarinetist Shaw, following Lana Turner and Ava Gardner. Her revealing 1977 autobiography, *Scarlett O'Hara's Younger Sister*, focused on her Hollywood relationships, including her prior marriages to directors Charles Vidor and John Huston. **Also: Sam Giancana & Robert Kennedy** (alleged Mafia connection).

May 19–24
THE CUSP OF ENERGY
TAURUS-GEMINI CUSP

November 19–24
THE CUSP OF REVOLUTION
SCORPIO-SAGITTARIUS CUSP

A Conduit of Knowledge

Taurus-Gemini and Scorpio-Sagittarius lie opposite each other in the zodiac. Oppositions denote stress but also magnetic attraction, and in this case the latter is pronounced. The relationship's keynote is bringing hidden material to light, especially that of a spiritual, religious or ideological nature. Whether these secret concepts and ideas are revealed to a social circle or to the public at large, Taurus-Gemini–Scorpio-Sagittarius energies are powerful in transmitting them. The relationship is a conduit of knowledge.

Love and marriage between these two can work as long as they don't intrude on more important ground: both Taurus-Geminis and Scorpio-Sagittarians tend to put their work first. Romantic encounters must be carefully scheduled for special times and places. Problems will arise if domestic or relationship demands upset the rhythm of working. If unresolved Taurus-Gemini resentment, Scorpio-Sagittarius guilt or mutual emotional upsets are truly intrusive, they will often be dealt with ruthlessly, making it clear that personal feelings are of secondary importance to these two and must be eliminated if they prove a bother. In the long run, unfortunately, the refusal to deal with underlying personal problems will generally exacerbate tensions rather than alleviate them.

Friends or family members with this combination may succeed in working together—spouses and lovers will find it harder. Particularly between members of the same sex, it is possible and even necessary that close feelings of trust and affection prevail while the pair is working on a common project. Freelance or business partnerships, then, and the administration of social groups or organizations are especially favored here.

Given the priority of career over personal life, expectations of worldly success run high in the work sphere. Yet the true measure of the relationship's mettle will be its ability to survive failure and catastrophe and to come up fighting. Guts and determination often allow projects to take shape whether funding is present or not, so convinced are this pair of their worth. It will be a challenge for them to demand adequate recompense while the work is being done, rather than relying on confident expectations.

ADVICE: *Don't take personal matters for granted. Beware of excessive ambition. Demand recognition and reward. Build on the past, invest in the future.*

STRENGTHS: **CONSTRUCTIVE,
AWARE, ENERGETIC**

WEAKNESSES: **ESTRANGED,
RESENTFUL, ANGRY**

BEST: **FRIENDSHIP**

WORST: **LOVE**

JIMI HENDRIX (11/27/42)
JOE COCKER (5/20/44)

Soul singer Cocker and electric guitarist extraordinaire Hendrix are legendary musicians of the 60s. Both gave explosive performances at the Woodstock Festival in '69—Cocker with his arm-flailing rendition of *With a Little Help from My Friends* and Hendrix with his irreverent, ear-piercing *Star-Spangled Banner*. Both musicians had drug problems. Cocker overcame his; Hendrix died of an overdose in '70.

May 19–24
THE CUSP OF ENERGY
TAURUS-GEMINI CUSP

November 25–December 2
THE WEEK OF INDEPENDENCE
SAGITTARIUS I

Building Bridges

The challenge here will be twofold: first, to build understanding and acceptance between its partners; second, to use this understanding to create a viable structure for the relationship. Both of these personalities are independent types, and if it is truly a relationship they want, they will have to learn to accept the rules and boundaries that will keep them together, and the expressions of resentment and anger that will have to be vented occasionally. Examining past failures is of limited value here—what is needed more is putting some kind of mechanism in place for solving problems, getting on with the present situation and, ultimately, preparing for a more enlightened future. Repeating the mistakes of the past is seldom a problem in this relationship, which has a capacity to expose the causes of problems and to create solutions.

In love relationships these two may trigger each other's sensitivities. The relationship is apt to bring out their passionate side, and they must be careful not to let corresponding negative emotions get out of control. Demonstrating a lack of realism and awareness, the pairing can prove a classic "In bed it's heaven, outside it's hell" situation. If what is desired is a total relationship rather than a crippled and selfish one, many hours of work on introspection and self-understanding will have to be shared.

Marriages are not the best idea for this combination, since Taurus-Geminis get nervous and Sagittarius I's impatient around each other on a daily basis. If such irritations can be overcome, however, the couple will often provide an energetic, loving and nurturing home for their children or pets. Friendships and working relationships can be fun, cordial and productive, but deep emotional involvements should be discouraged. Neither party is usually stable enough to guarantee such relationships the grounded quality they require. Family matchups, particularly parent-child relationships, feature stormy adolescent flare-ups and periods of adult estrangement, but bonds of love and trust may be forged later in life. At work, Sagittarius I's may find Taurus-Geminis disingenuous and Taurus-Geminis may find Sagittarius I's inflexible and demanding.

ADVICE: *Forgive and forget. Move on. Go for the whole package. Don't hold back. You can have what you want, just be sure you know what it is.*

May 19–24

THE CUSP OF ENERGY
TAURUS-GEMINI CUSP

December 3–10

THE WEEK OF THE ORIGINATOR
SAGITTARIUS II

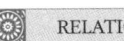 RELATIONSHIPS

STRENGTHS: **ENTHUSIASTIC,
IMAGINATIVE, SPIRITUAL**

WEAKNESSES: **PECULIAR,
UNAMBITIOUS, WITHDRAWN**

BEST: **SIBLING**

WORST: **WORK**

The Road Less Traveled

The focus of this relationship usually lies far from the world of ambition and success: these two unusual types, perhaps criticized and rejected a great deal over the course of their lives, choose to take a less-traveled road together. Although both may be considered extroverts by the world's standards, in this relationship the focus is more inward, imaginative and spiritual. This does not mean that these two are less than professional in their careers—far from it. Money and power, however, are not what their relationship is about.

Love affairs between often outrageous types such as these are surprisingly muted. Personal and affectionate, the relationship shows a fascination for the bizarre and out of the ordinary in love and romance, but keeps it quiet—few could guess what goes on behind the windows and doors of their rendezvous. One can only guess that sexual attitudes here rule out no interesting approach, and that the pair are open to experimentation.

Marriages or permanent living situations may be built around the spiritual, religious or artistic beliefs of one or both of the mates. Important social outlets generally emerge from such connections, providing relief from an often hectic personal and domestic life. At certain periods, communal living may be tried, usually with good but not necessarily lasting results.

As friends, Taurus-Geminis and Sagittarius II's may attack their common leisure-time interests and activities with as much relish and energy as they do their respective careers or love affairs. Thus the friendship represents a chance not to relax and be accepted but to forge ahead together in pursuit of common goals. Sports, fitness, travel, books or new media—any or all of these are likely to attract this couple.

The career connection here is less strong unless it is connected with a friendship or marriage, or else with an all-consuming interest. Family relationships, especially sibling matchups, tend to fill the house with excitement and good humor. Taurus-Gemini and Sagittarius III's will appreciate this relationship because of mutual enthusiasm for their more unusual qualities.

ADVICE: *Develop your social side. Bring a love of the spirit to others. Don't neglect career opportunities. Avoid getting too far out there.*

DOUGLAS FAIRBANKS, JR. (12/9/09)
DOUGLAS FAIRBANKS (5/23/1883)

As a father, the self-absorbed silent-screen star took little interest in his son's career. They became close only in the 30s, after Fairbanks Jr. married Joan Crawford in 1928 and began to rise as a star himself. **Also: Cher & Gregg Allman** (married; singer-actress/rock star).

May 19–24

THE CUSP OF ENERGY
TAURUS-GEMINI CUSP

December 11–18

THE WEEK OF THE TITAN
SAGITTARIUS III

 RELATIONSHIPS

STRENGTHS: **MYSTERIOUS,
COMPLEMENTARY, ADMIRING**

WEAKNESSES: **OVEREXPANSIVE,
MISUNDERSTOOD, EXTREME**

BEST: **FAMILY, WORK**

WORST: **LOVE**

A Strange Meld

Being misunderstood is characteristic of this combination. Others will often have difficulty understanding the attraction between two such different partners, and what keeps them together. They may feel the same way themselves—much in their relationship will be concerned with unearthing the truth about each other, and, in turn, with explaining themselves to the world. It's not that they don't want to understand each other, it's just that their energies and approaches are so different that it's hard for them even to begin. Sagittarius III's are weighty individuals, given to the contemplation of big issues, and are not particularly verbal; Taurus-Geminis, on the other hand, are chatty, suffer from foot-in-mouth syndrome and enjoy minutiae, details and nuance. But these opposites may meld and complement each other, forming a mysterious combination in which standards are rigorous, doing a job well is emphasized and expectations are firm.

Love affairs here are elusive. Powerful Sagittarius III's may be fascinated with a sparkling and optimistic Taurus-Gemini, who in turn may be attracted to this partner's stature and vision. But the Sagittarius III need to dominate in love may be resented by Taurus-Geminis, who need to remain free. Marriages similarly may be successful only if Taurus-Geminis are prepared to play a secondary role, which is hard for them. One positive aspect is that Sagittarius III depression and moodiness may be positively affected by bright and perky Taurus-Geminis, who know how to have a good time.

Friendships and family relationships can be extremely supportive. As friends or siblings, Taurus-Geminis and Sagittarius III's will be mutually protective, the former perhaps verbally and the latter physically. Furthermore, the relationship itself may prove a defender of the disadvantaged or impoverished, and helpful to weaker or shy family members. The pair's understanding of human nature may make others who likewise feel misunderstood by the world seek them out for advice. At work, Sagittarius III's may serve as excellent bosses or even managers for Taurus-Geminis.

ADVICE: *Take the time to explain yourself. Being misunderstood is not an advantage. Cooperate, yet never give up your individuality. Balance extremes.*

WILLIAM GEORGE FARGO (5/20/1818)
HENRY WELLS (12/12/1805)

In 1852, Fargo and Wells founded Wells Fargo & Co. which provided coast-to-coast mail and banking services. By 1866, Wells Fargo controlled all overland stagecoaching, providing a vital link between America's towns. **Also: Bob Dylan & John Hammond** (singer discovered by music critic).

QUEEN VICTORIA (5/24/1819)
BENJAMIN DISRAELI (12/21/1804)

Disraeli, Victoria's prime minister, became her confidant after Albert's death in 1861. Consoling and charming, he restored her interest in ruling by naming her empress of India in 1876. She made him an earl.
Also: Wagner & Cosima Liszt (married; composer/Liszt's daughter); **Wagner & Matilde Wesendonck** (composer in love with poet); **Artie Shaw & Ava Gardner** (married; bandleader/actress).

May 19–24
THE CUSP OF ENERGY
TAURUS-GEMINI CUSP

December 19–25
THE CUSP OF PROPHECY
SAGITTARIUS-CAPRICORN CUSP

The Private Eye

The focus of this relationship is likely to be a privacy that goes beyond ordinary bounds, even tending to the reclusive. Sagittarius-Capricorns are likely to allow Taurus-Geminis to see a bit of the darker side of their personalities, one that they show to few others in their lives. Natural detectives, Taurus-Geminis will be intrigued to investigate further, but the relationship is likely to require them to forsake certain outgoing aspects of their nature so as to be alone in an intimate or domestic setting with the more introverted Sagittarius-Capricorn. Astrologically, Taurus-Gemini is an earth-air combination and Sagittarius-Capricorn fire-earth. The missing element is precisely the one that governs the relationship: water, symbolizing feeling.

Love and marriage between these two are tender, personal and emotional in nature. The emphasis here is on giving, and although both partners can gain much from each other, it is the Sagittarius-Capricorn who is likely to rise in stature in the eyes of the Taurus-Gemini, and through their relationship, much like the statue in George Bernard Shaw's *Pygmalion* and like Eliza Doolittle in *My Fair Lady*. Unfortunately, when the statue becomes real and comes down off its pedestal, the sculptor gets left in the lurch when his beautiful creation walks out the door. Attachments and subsequent breakups here can be extremely painful.

Friendships in this combination also have the capacity to be deep. Mutual friends often become involved in love triangles or quartets with this duo, and may eventually supplant one of the primary partners. Jealousies, claiming attitudes and competitive urges may easily arise and grow to unhealthy proportions.

Work relationships are not recommended here unless they guarantee near autonomy to both partners, a difficult requirement. Family relationships, especially father-daughter or mother-son matchups, may prove extremely influential in the lives of both individuals, sometimes becoming a dominating force that inhibits personal growth.

ADVICE: *Beware of undue attachment. Don't turn your back on the world. Keep in touch. Danger lies in triangles. Remember who you are. Observe limits.*

J. EDGAR HOOVER (1/1/1895)
CLYDE TOLSON (5/22/1900)

Hoover was the director of the FBI for 48 years. In 1947 he appointed Tolson as associate director. Reputed to be homosexual lovers, their long and close association lasted until Hoover's death in 1972.
Also: Cher & Phil Spector (early collaboration; singer/record producer); **George Tabori & Viveca Lindfors** (married; writer-director/actress).

May 19–24
THE CUSP OF ENERGY
TAURUS-GEMINI CUSP

December 26–January 2
THE WEEK OF THE RULER
CAPRICORN I

Taking the Good with the Bad

The challenge of this combination is to be realistic. Although disappointment, conflict and difficulties of all sorts abound here, the relationship does tend to be open and honest, even blunt. Rarely will either party keep what is on his or her mind for long before airing their complaint. This doesn't mean that things can't go well here; many periods of good feeling and even ecstatic experiences manifest in Taurus-Gemini–Capricorn I relationships. Taking the good with the bad becomes a way of life here. There are two great threats to the relationship's health: breakdown of communication and loss of trust, the first more upsetting to the Taurus-Gemini and the latter to the Capricorn I.

Love affairs between these two can be deep but also unstable. If Capricorn I's get swept off their feet by an exciting and romantic Taurus-Gemini, it is usually only a matter of time before reality sets in and the relationship slows down or grinds to a halt. Should Taurus-Geminis stray from the relationship in its earlier stages and be found out, they may be surprised by the immediacy and severity of the Capricorn I response.

Marriages in this combination are painful to consider. Unless Capricorn I's are resigned to sitting at home and waiting into the wee hours for their busy Taurus-Gemini to come home, this one is best not attempted. Friendships and family relationships can be close and loving but also trying and difficult. This is particularly true of parent-child matchups. Being able to take the relationship for what it is, and to see it in a realistic light, stripped of illusions and symbolic projections, is a tough but worthwhile challenge for both partners.

In the professional sphere this relationship can work satisfactorily, with Taurus-Gemini personality and abundant energy gelling with Capricorn I practicality and good sense. These two generally do better working on the executive level or as business partners than as day-to-day co-workers, where conflicts are more likely to emerge.

ADVICE: *Beware of getting carried away by unreality. Try to see straight. Accept the best and worst. Keep trust and communication alive.*

May 19–24

THE CUSP OF ENERGY
TAURUS-GEMINI CUSP

January 3–9

THE WEEK OF DETERMINATION
CAPRICORN II

Coming Down to Earth

This relationship can explore the far reaches of thought and fantasy, but will also ground itself in the here and now. The metaphor of dance suggests itself—leaping, literally flying, then returning to the ground to gather energy. The relationship usually shows enough sense to build itself around a practical endeavor in which both partners feel fulfilled in their work. Without this basis, they are likely to drift, or sometimes to try to escape from the demands of daily life altogether. The relationship has an air of unreality.

Taurus-Geminis can be swept away by the combination's fancifulness. They are on the flighty side to begin with, and the illusions spun here may be too much for them. Capricorn II's, on the other hand, always serious and usually laden with responsibilities, will initially be liberated by the matchup's imaginativeness, but may later try to exert control. Taurus-Geminis will bear the brunt of the relationship's amorphousness.

Charming and piquant, as a love affair the relationship is at first blush the very essence of romance. Yet it is eventually likely to be secretive and to exhibit neurotic symptoms of anxiety and worry. Marriage is usually more favorable: domestic tasks, financial planning and building a family can be the grounding influences the relationship requires. The best bet of all is probably friendship, which will feature a never-ending stream of ideas for things to do, both intellectual and physical. Such friends may well travel, exercise and work together. Good feelings, affection and gift-giving are characteristic here.

Siblings in this combination will seem as different as night and day, but their personalities can dovetail well. The dangers here are overdependence and a lack of individual development. Differences of temperament in parent-child combinations (Capricorn II serious and demanding, Taurus-Gemini fun-loving and flexible) may establish a contentious but rarely boring family dynamic. Since the relationship does well grounding itself in daily activities, career matchups are favored. These two can work side by side for years and still maintain their individuality. They will constitute an effective unit for getting the job done efficiently and dependably.

ADVICE: *Keep in touch with daily demands. Be responsible but don't forget to dream. Master fear and anxiety. Don't suppress affection.*

PRISCILLA PRESLEY (5/24/45)
ELVIS PRESLEY (1/8/35)

They met when Priscilla was 14 and reputedly became intimate a year later. They married when she turned 21 and had daughter, Lisa Marie. Elvis's drinking, drug use and infidelities ended the marriage in 1973. **Also: Rosemary Clooney & Jose Ferrer** (married); **Bob Dylan & Joan Baez** (romance; friends-collaborators); **Richard Wagner & Hans von Bülow** (associates married same woman).

May 19–24

THE CUSP OF ENERGY
TAURUS-GEMINI CUSP

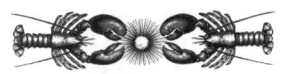

January 10–16

THE WEEK OF DOMINANCE
CAPRICORN III

Pure Lines

This couple can devote themselves to aesthetic appreciation, whether of art, music, literature or the grace of dance and sports. Their taste runs in the direction of clean pure lines and functional beauty. The relationship brings out the more practical side of Taurus-Geminis and the more artistic side of Capricorn III's. It can be a powerful one when figuring out the best way to get a project initiated or finished. The fusion of Taurus-Gemini swiftness and eclectic strengths with Capricorn III power and purposefulness can create an unstoppable combination.

Love relationships between these two will be strongly physical. Both sexual and sensuous activities will blossom. The couple's aesthetic appreciation of these activities should not be underestimated. Capricorn III's will initially find Taurus-Geminis fascinating and a real challenge to hold on to. Taurus-Geminis will benefit from Capricorn III solidity, practicality and dependability.

Marriage can work out, but many of the partners' more personal attributes will prove mutually irritating or disturbing. Although Taurus-Geminis can entertain serious Capricorn III's at the end of a long hard day, they may also prove too talkative and mentally frenetic. Capricorn III practical demands may also be too much for them to handle on a day-to-day basis.

Family relationships are extremely complex, especially between mother and son or father and daughter. Adoration, even worship in childhood may cause undue attachments that will be extremely difficult to break later in life, particularly at the beginning of young adulthood. Should both live long enough, they may make peace and grow close once again. Work relationships are most favored here. It is quite possible for Taurus-Gemini–Capricorn III friends to go into business together. Not only getting the job done, not matter how successfully, but the joys of sharing struggles and achievements with a close friend make this relationship special. Capricorn III dominance usually does not emerge as an issue here. Taurus-Gemini flexibility may be bewildering at times, but Capricorn III's will ultimately realize its benefits for their joint projects.

ADVICE: *Enjoy yourselves but get the job done. Don't get distracted from the work at hand. Keep feelings under control. Try to be more efficient.*

MARY CASSATT (5/22/1844)
BERTHE MORISOT (1/14/1841)

Cassatt, an American, and the French Morisot were the only women members of the 19th-century Impressionist group led by Degas. As such they are considered the most important female painters of their time. **Also: Sam Giancana & Judith Exner** (mobster/liaison with Kennedys).

STRENGTHS: **FUN, ZANY, FLAMBOYANT**

WEAKNESSES: **JEALOUS, UNREALISTIC, CRAZY**

BEST: **MARRIAGE**

WORST: **FRIENDSHIP**

ROBERT MACNEIL (1/19/31)
JIM LEHRER (5/19/34)

This compatible pair had extensive backgrounds in news before they joined up in 1976 to co-anchor the prestigious *MacNeil-Lehrer Newshour,* which ran on syndicated PBS stations until MacNeil's 1995 retirement.

May 19–24
THE CUSP OF ENERGY
TAURUS-GEMINI CUSP

January 17–22
THE CUSP OF MYSTERY & IMAGINATION
CAPRICORN-AQUARIUS CUSP

Going Over the Edge

This relationship is expected to be an easy one because of its trine aspect (120° apart in the zodiac), and these two may indeed have lots of fun together. The zaniest and wildest projects, plans or activities are likely to manifest here. The pair will appear highly extroverted in the eyes of the world, engaged in daring but at times crazy endeavors. This can be a danger, for the psychological stability of both partners is not innately high, and activities that are too demanding or unsafe could push one or both of them over the edge. Thus the relationship serves as a test of mature behavior and of the ability to balance excessive drives. The trick would be for both parties strictly to maintain their own individuality, and to bring to bear the personal strength they share—a highly developed and practical faculty for critical analysis.

Friendships and love affairs, although vivid and exciting, may suffer from often unconscious competitiveness. Both Taurus-Geminis and Capricorn-Aquarians love the spotlight and at times are unaware that they are jockeying for position. Because of their often colorful, flamboyant and charismatic natures, both of these partners are likely to attract many admirers; should such attractions prove too tempting, this can lead to jealousy and ultimately to grief. Yet possessiveness and claiming behavior are not necessarily characteristic here, and a tolerant or openly permissive attitude that allows moderate involvement with others, often in the name of enrichment or revitalization, can prove rewarding.

Marital, work and family relationships between Taurus-Geminis and Capricorn-Aquarians often benefit from a group's structure and support systems. Being around others may have a balancing effect, working to prevent wilder energies from getting out of hand. As spouses and parents, a Taurus-Gemini–Capricorn-Aquarius couple will have good times with their children, taking them on fine holidays and supporting activities outside their school syllabus. Parent-child relationships in this combination, however, may not be stable enough to work to either partner's benefit, and are often undermined by unrealistic expectations on both sides.

ADVICE: *Let up in your need for attention. Try to understand it. Put your many talents to use in the service of others. Share. Develop patience and understanding.*

STRENGTHS: **PERFECTIONIST, THRILLING, PSYCHIC**

WEAKNESSES: **FLAKY, CHAOTIC, BLIND**

BEST: **FAMILY**

WORST: **MARRIAGE**

DONNA REED (1/27/21)
JIMMY STEWART (5/20/08)

In perhaps his most memorable role, Stewart played opposite Reed in Frank Capra's 1946 romantic and sentimental movie classic, *It's a Wonderful Life.* **Also: Queen Victoria & Kaiser Wilhelm II** (grandmother/grandson; English queen/German king).

May 19–24
THE CUSP OF ENERGY
TAURUS-GEMINI CUSP

January 23–30
THE WEEK OF GENIUS
AQUARIUS I

Thrillingly Romantic

Air is the ruling element of this relationship, emphasizing thought, reasoning and connection. Reinforcing its partners' mental sides, the relationship tends toward perfectionism and is sensitive to the beauty in mathematics, logic and design. The problem is that it may apply these attitudes according to a double standard, being quite blind about its own lack of logic. Reserving critical scrutiny for others, in its enthusiasm and optimism the relationship may lose the ability to see itself and its goals clearly.

Love affairs are likely to be wild and unsettled. Neither Taurus-Gemini nor Aquarius I is known for stability in this area, and their coalescence here can get pretty chaotic. On the other hand, the relationship's excitement, sexual tension and energetic expression can sometimes be thrillingly romantic. Since freedom and infidelity are also magnified here, marriage is not especially recommended.

If these two are looking for a friendship with few responsibilities and a great capacity for fun, this is it. The sky's the limit for adventure and exploration of all types, and the strong mental connection points to board and video games, puzzles, Internet or computer involvement and possible interests in virtual reality or psychic phenomena. This can be a bit of a fair-weather friendship, however, lacking depth, and with the partners becoming less interested in each other during times of need. Financial responsibilities also tend to be a bit lax.

Family relationships can be close here, particularly between siblings of the same sex. Some kind of telepathic ability is not at all uncommon, and empathic connections are to be expected. Parent-child relationships tend toward the permissive, with both Aquarius I and Taurus-Gemini parents trying to encourage their child's freedom.

Working relationships that effectively utilize this pair's mind power can be highly successful. But employers may have to keep an eye on the Taurus-Gemini's financial irresponsibility and the Aquarius I's somewhat flaky judgments.

ADVICE: *Calm down. Beware of double standards. Be more self-critical. Even out your emotions. Enthusiasm can be deadly. Keep your eye on the ball.*

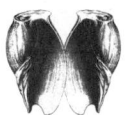

May 19–24
THE CUSP OF ENERGY
TAURUS-GEMINI CUSP

January 31–February 7
THE WEEK OF YOUTH & EASE
AQUARIUS II

STRENGTHS: **IMAGINATIVE, CHILDLIKE, INNOVATIVE**

WEAKNESSES: **OBLIVIOUS, CUT OFF, UNACKNOWLEDGED**

BEST: **LOVE**

WORST: **MARRIAGE**

RONNIE REAGAN (5/20/58)
RONALD REAGAN (2/6/11)
———
The son of former president Reagan, Ronnie remained in the background of his White House family. Trained in ballet, he danced with the Joffrey, then embarked on a tv career that lasted from 1986–92. **Also: Queen Victoria & Felix Mendelssohn** (queen's favorite composer).

Silver Bells and Cockle Shells

This relationship summons up images of a childhood kingdom in which young people play in paradisiacal surroundings. These partners may live in their own world, oblivious to everything but their own imaginations. Especially prominent is the living out of fantasies, which may assume a significance greater than society is prepared to acknowledge. In fact, others may see this couple as a bit bizarre and out of touch with reality. Should they work in an artistic, academic or business field, however, their efforts may be applauded.

Love relationships are often covert, and the feelings underlying them may themselves have been kept secret for years before the affair's start. These feelings may have manifested as fantasies, or may have been completely unconscious. The moment when these soulmates come together is exciting, of course, but not necessarily dramatic, seeming almost a fated inevitability. The Aquarius II will want to be certain the relationship is what the Taurus-Gemini really wants; the Taurus-Gemini may be taking a "Here's my chance" or "Now or never" attitude. These relationships can continue for years, even through changes of primary partners, living situations and family fortunes. Marriage seldom seems to be in the cards here; should it occur, however, it may succeed, although friends and family may never fully accept it.

As siblings or other family pairs, these two will seem extremely close. Their absolute refusal to stick to traditional family roles may confuse the rest of the family, or make them jealous. At work they can be strikingly successful, particularly in one of the more imaginative kinds of commercial enterprise. They do better as executive colleagues or business partners than as office or plant co-workers. Should the relationship emerge in a research and development group or in the marketing sector, it may develop innovative discoveries and methods. Teacher-student relationships can also be outstanding. As adult friends, these two may have as much fun as kids. Unself-conscious in the extreme, Taurus-Geminis and Aquarius II's can gain enormous pleasure from music, cuisine or the entertainment of a small group of family or intimates.

ADVICE: *Take a closer look at yourself. Beware of delusions and of hurting others. Find what is really of value. Think constructively.*

May 19–24
THE CUSP OF ENERGY
TAURUS-GEMINI CUSP

February 8–15
THE WEEK OF ACCEPTANCE
AQUARIUS III

STRENGTHS: **SUPPORTIVE, IMPROVING, AFFECTIONATE**

WEAKNESSES: **NERVOUS, OVERSENSITIVE, STRESSED**

BEST: **LOVE**

WORST: **WORK**

YELENA BONNER (2/15/23)
ANDREI SAKHAROV (5/21/21)
———
Sakharov got the 1975 Nobel Peace Prize for his nuclear disarmament and democracy crusade in Russia. Exiled from Moscow in 1984, he and activist wife Bonner were reprieved in 1986. **Also: Laurence Olivier & Claire Bloom** (affair); **Nora Ephron & Carl Bernstein** (married; writer/journalist); **Artie Shaw & Lana Turner** (married); **Sam Giancana & Phyllis McGuire** (affair; mobster/singer).

High-Strung Thoroughbred

This demanding relationship operates at a high level, but a stressful one. The perfection demanded here will improve the quality of daily life in general but may undermine it in any given instance, engendering nervousness and pressure. An attitude of merciless self-criticism may also be operative, with old scripts producing self-fulfilling prophecies ("You'll never be any good at that"). A positive attitude may be continually undercut.

The relationship's undeniable social drive favors friendships and marriages. Both Aquarius III's and Taurus-Geminis have a strongly gregarious side that must be expressed, and their matchup synergistically reinforces this tendency. In consequence, their relationship has to be defined willy-nilly in terms of others, whether family members, social groups, colleagues or friends. When social demands become too intrusive, however, resentment and resistance can arise between them, especially in Aquarius III's, who have a strong private side.

Love affairs between these two tend to be highly accepting and supportive. Although Aquarius III's are easily irritated, Taurus-Geminis have a way of lightening the mood and in general staying objective without overreacting. On the other hand, they also want to be the center of attention, a need that proud and self-occupied Aquarius III's may not satisfy, possibly causing frustration. Whether the relationship is passionate or platonic, it may be enduring and rewarding, but both partners will need to keep their nervous temperaments under control on a day-to-day basis.

Parent-child relationships here are complex. Taurus-Gemini parents tend to lay on guilt trips and in general to meddle too much in the lives of their Aquarius III children, who will react violently against such behavior. Aquarius III parents, on the other hand, tend to make their Taurus-Gemini children anxious and hysterical. Yet this relationship can be extremely affectionate, supportive and loving, with long periods of easy contact only occasionally being disrupted by an explosive reaction to a sharp remark, glance or critical observation. Working relationships are not recommended, since both parties have their own approaches.

ADVICE: *Cool down. Don't let your buttons be pushed. Voices from the past must be silenced. Learn to compromise. Aim for a balanced social life.*

SONNY BONO (2/16/35)
CHER (5/20/46)

Married in 1964, hippie duo Sonny and Cher's string of hits began with *I Got You Babe* in 1965. They also co-hosted a popular variety show and made 2 movies. Divorced in 1975, they have a daughter, Chastity.

May 19–24
THE CUSP OF ENERGY
TAURUS-GEMINI CUSP

February 16–22
THE CUSP OF SENSITIVITY
AQUARIUS-PISCES CUSP

Is the Spotlight Big Enough?

Conflict over who gets attention may mark this relationship. The partners are very different—one objective and extroverted, the other subjective and introverted—but both have a tremendous need for attention, both from each other and from friends and family. They are sure to come into conflict over who gets to be the star, particularly since their differing approaches will prevent them from understanding each other's desires—nor will they even see their own clearly. Should they work together on this issue they may make an effective team; by sharing the spotlight they can avoid conflict, particularly if they attribute their success to the relationship. If not, success can prove divisive, provoking envy and resentment. The square aspect of Taurus-Gemini and Aquarius-Pisces in the zodiac (they are 90° apart) in this case indicates tension and arguments, but also excitement, and encouragement to the partners to do better.

Love affairs are perhaps best kept that way: marriage may place excessive responsibility on these freedom-loving partners. Problems arise when neither Taurus-Geminis nor Aquarius-Pisces have formed a strong ego, for their desire to please each other may be repeatedly frustrated. In fact they may flounder together in a sea of unresolved and uncertain feelings, reacting somewhat purposelessly to the latest stimulus, with little long-range benefit.

Competitiveness may prevent these two from becoming close friends. But semicompetitive matchups—as sports partners or as game opponents—may express such rivalries productively, as long as each person can be the winner often enough.

Parent-child relationships may prove overwhelming, especially father-daughter and mother-son pairs. Rebellion often appears here, but there is also a great need to love. Sibling relationships of the same sex are bright, lively and entertaining (but also distracting) to other family members. These two can work well as colleagues or business partners. A product or service that combines their strengths can sweep the field. Breakups are especially debilitating here—the partners may need a great deal of time and effort to find their feet again.

ADVICE: *Know what you want and who you are. Beware of eagerness to please. Be less demanding of attention. Control competitive drives.*

PETE TOWNSHEND (5/19/45)
ROGER DALTREY (3/1/44)

Townshend and Daltrey rose from working-class backgrounds to form the legendary 4-man rock group The Who in 1964. Daltrey's stage-strutting and Townshend's windmilling guitar moves were trademarks.
Also: **Roseanne Cash & Johnny Cash** (father/daughter; singers); **Pete Townshend & Meher Baba** (musician/guru); **Jimmy Stewart & Glenn Miller** (film portrayal).

May 19–24
THE CUSP OF ENERGY
TAURUS-GEMINI CUSP

February 23–March 2
THE WEEK OF SPIRIT
PISCES I

Sparkling Exchanges

This undeniably flamboyant relationship may focus on social or intellectual issues or on an area of shared interest. These two make a scintillating combination, full of wit, good humor and spirit. Pisces I's have a tremendous need for the respect of Taurus-Geminis, who are similarly anxious to impress this partner with their achievements. Neither partner is likely to try to dominate the other, but an element of friendly competitiveness may be a constant.

More oriented toward thought than toward physicality, the matchup is not strongly suggested for love or marriage. Satisfactory platonic involvements are quite possible here, however, with sympathy and affection being openly expressed. Such relationships are characterized by interesting discussions and supportive attitudes.

Friendships have a bit more bite. Partners feel free to criticize each other and to indulge in amusing or insulting banter. Wit, irony, sarcasm and humor all vie for the ascendancy. These two may often be involved in an artistic endeavor, often featuring music, writing or design.

In family matchups, particular father-son and mother-daughter, close sharing breaks down boundaries but can also result in drift and lack of direction. The partners' involvement can become so total that both of them forget about practical matters like cooking dinner and paying the bills. Families will be enriched by this duo, but may tire of being forced to watch and listen to their sparkling exchanges.

Work relationships in this combination, particularly when the partners are executives or business partners, can work only if they acknowledge financial priorities and put their fiscal transactions firmly in the hands of the more capable member, usually Pisces I. Taurus-Gemini enthusiasm is sometimes likely to be highly unrealistic and damaging to any shared project, and it may be difficult for the Pisces I to explain the problem. On the other hand, Taurus-Geminis may grow tired of having to walk on eggs around sensitive Pisces I's, who are liable to turn on their heel and exit when treated insultingly or uninterestedly.

ADVICE: *Be aware of the existence of others. Talking is one thing, doing another. Keep your eye on the goal. Fight a tendency to drift. Hang tough.*

May 19–24
THE CUSP OF ENERGY
TAURUS-GEMINI CUSP

March 3–10
THE WEEK OF THE LONER
PISCES II

Untrodden Avenues

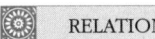
STRENGTHS: **INSIGHTFUL, EXPLORATORY, SUPPORTIVE**
WEAKNESSES: **IMPATIENT, IMPRACTICAL, CHAOTIC**
BEST: **FRIENDSHIP**
WORST: **WORK**

KAY KENDALL (5/21/26)
REX HARRISON (3/5/08)

Taurus-Geminis and Pisces II's can form extremely close bonds. Particularly in their personal relationships, they may seek to go beyond the bounds of convention, exploring untrodden avenues of the soul. Together they are pioneers of the human spirit, and recognize few barriers to emotional investigation. Taurus-Geminis are ruled by earth and air, Pisces II's by water, but their combination is governed by fire, symbolizing intuition, passion and perseverance. Thus the two partners and their relationship effect a balance of all four elements.

Relying on intuition, Taurus-Gemini–Pisces II friendships proceed on hunches. Although usually well informed on subjects of shared interest, these two prefer to fly by the seat of their pants, eschewing book learning and dry academic explanations. They want to find things out for themselves, testing their intuitions in the hot crucible of experience. These relationships very often grow so close that love and familial feeling are expressed quite naturally here.

Love affairs and marriages are less successful than might be expected. The couple's sexual needs and wants are not always compatible, and even when such relationships are at their most successful, they can reveal themselves as friendships in disguise. They also often ignore or neglect domestic responsibilities and daily routines in favor of more personal interactions, resulting in chaotic messes that eventually demand cleaning up.

Sibling relationships, especially of the same sex, can be extremely protective and supportive. This is particularly true when a parent or other adult lacks understanding or is abusive. Parent-child relationships in this combination, on the other hand, usually fail to supply the attention and patience necessary for the nurturing process to take place. Working relationships are very difficult if financial success is the primary goal. Neither party is usually efficient or businesslike enough to carry on the maintenance work needed here. On the personal level, moreover, a Taurus-Gemini may resent a Pisces II co-worker's dreaminess, while the Pisces II may dislike the Taurus-Gemini's outgoing and flamboyant persona.

ADVICE: *Don't neglect daily chores. Brilliance won't pay the bills. Keep emotions under control. Put hunches to practical use. Love should not grow old.*

Kendall's vivacious personality made her a popular screen comedienne in the 50s. She married Harrison in 1957, but died of leukemia 2 years later—a tragic loss for her deeply committed husband. **Also: Herbert Marshall & Edna Best** (married; actors); **Richard Benjamin & Paula Prentiss** (married; actors); **Lilli Palmer & Rex Harrison** (his first marriage; actors).

May 19–24
THE CUSP OF ENERGY
TAURUS-GEMINI CUSP

March 11–18
THE WEEK OF DANCERS & DREAMERS
PISCES III

The Realm of Ideas

STRENGTHS: **SYMPATHETIC, CONVIVIAL, IDEOLOGICAL**
WEAKNESSES: **OVERCONFIDENT, INFALLIBLE, OVERTHEATRICAL**
BEST: **FRIENDSHIP**
WORST: **LOVE**

JAMES MADISON (3/16/1751)
DOLLEY MADISON (5/20/1768)

This relationship often makes a specialty of ideas. The partners are sympathetic to each other, but emotion is not the keynote here; they are more absorbed by philosophical discussions, or simpler talks about the sociology of everyday life. Activities like taking regular walks or sitting at a café or coffee shop and discussing the week's events are accorded special importance. A major theme in this discourse is holding the tension between two opposites, finding the harmony in incongruence, living with ambiguity. This is no small task, but these two can talk and talk, and that is how they approach the job.

Taurus-Gemini–Pisces III friendships and marriages are apt to be convivial. Entertaining mutual friends at home—tastefully, but often with innovative touches—and engaging in hilarious or occasionally serious discussions over food and wine (real thought and time will have gone into the meal's selection and preparation) can become major social activities. Family gatherings on birthdays and holidays may also be counted on for fun and good feelings. More philosophical discussions are likely to be left until late at night, when the two are alone and can debate a subject fully without being bound by social constraints.

Love affairs between these two are somewhat uncommon. Both Taurus-Geminis and Pisces III's generally give themselves passionately to people very different from themselves, even barely known strangers. Their empathic feelings for each other often preclude such unbalanced yet exciting encounters. Family relationships favor sibling matchups, especially brother-sister pairs, which can exhibit telepathic abilities. At work these two can make a vital team. When both are graduates of the school of hard knocks—basically self-taught, or educated by their own experience more than by any formal schooling—between them they can cover a large range of expertise. The relationship exudes self-confidence, based firmly on the Taurus-Gemini's people skills and the Pisces III's practical and imaginative abilities. These coalesce well, especially in more dramatic and adventurous projects. Immodesty and feelings of infallibility will have to be guarded against, however.

ADVICE: *Never lose the good feeling, but be critical, too. Don't dream (or drink) your life away. Beware of self-satisfaction. Continue lively debate.*

James created a stir when he began courting the 17-years-younger Dolley, whom he married in 1794. As America's 4th president, he was puritanical and straightlaced, unlike Dolley, who adored the flamboyant French style. She became the country's leading hostess.

May 25–June 2

THE WEEK OF FREEDOM
GEMINI I

May 25–June 2

THE WEEK OF FREEDOM
GEMINI I

Anything Goes?

STRENGTHS: **INDIVIDUALISTIC, QUICK, TECHNICAL**

WEAKNESSES: **ARGUMENTATIVE, UNSYMPATHETIC**

BEST: **DISTANT RELATIVE**

WORST: **PARENT-CHILD**

MARILYN MONROE (6/1/26)
JOHN F. KENNEDY (5/29/17)

Monroe was linked to a secret romance with the president in the late 50s. At a 1962 fundraiser in NY's Madison Square Garden, she sang to him her famous *Happy Birthday Mr. President*. **Also: Clint Eastwood & Sondra Locke** (affair; actors); **R.W. Emerson & Walt Whitman** (friends; poets); **Todd Hundley & Randy Hundley** (son/father; baseball); **Sarah & John Churchill** (duchess/duke).

This lively relationship is unlikely to last long, if, indeed, it ever really gets started. These two can cooperate with and admire each other, but they also reinforce each other's need for freedom, and a relationship that focuses on opposition to restrictions may undercut its own chances of survival. Should freedom-loving Gemini I's be able to adopt an anything-goes outlook, they might have a chance to make their relationship work. Alas, this is often impossible—a secret tyrant dwells in many Gemini I breasts.

Gemini I love affairs are often intense and fleeting. Recognizing a kindred soul, the pair may make brief contacts whenever they have time, but not much more. Their marriages are hard to hold together, to the point where it is surprising to find them at all; live-in situations and long-term love affairs are more usual. These partners have a need to impose their ideas on each other, and in a situation of daily contact the disagreements can quickly become intolerable. Quick, strong-minded and willful, Gemini I spouses are unlikely to see each other's point of view or to express much sympathy for each other's feelings. Should they engage their fighting instinct on behalf of the relationship, however, they may be able to craft a situation that is open-ended enough to be workable for them.

Friendships have a good chance as long as their demands are not too heavy. They are not of the deepest sort, and may function best as partnerships in a particular project or activity, perhaps sporting or educational. Gemini I parent-child and sibling matchups are likely to be stormy, neither partner really giving the other the respect or stability they need. Relationships between somewhat distant relatives—grandparents and grandchildren, cousins, or aunts or uncles with nieces or nephews—are usually the most interesting, warm and exciting here.

Work relationships in this combination can work out, particularly if they demand technical expertise. Most Gemini I's are uncomfortable staying in the same job year after year, but as co-workers in this kind of position, they may offer each other ironic consolation.

ADVICE: *Quiet down. Pay more attention to feelings. Tune in to intuitions. Let go of your combative stance. Try to cooperate. Lessen friction.*

May 25–June 2

THE WEEK OF FREEDOM
GEMINI I

June 3–10

THE WEEK OF NEW LANGUAGE
GEMINI II

Chewing What You Bite

STRENGTHS: **ORIGINAL, INDEPENDENT, ACTIVE**

WEAKNESSES: **NOISY, UPSETTING, VULNERABLE**

BEST: **MARRIAGE**

WORST: **SIBLING**

JUDITH MALINA (6/4/26)
JULIAN BECK (5/31/25)

In 1947, this husband and wife formed the influential performing group The Living Theatre. In the 60s and 70s, they applied innovative theater techniques to themes of sexual, political and cultural revolution. **Also: James Arness & Dennis Weaver** (co-stars, *Gunsmoke*); **Tony Zale & Rocky Graziano** (middleweight rivals).

This relationship may make its participants pursue unusual experiences in order to further their own development. As a couple they are much more intuitive than they are individually. Mentally oriented, separately they operate in a quick-witted sort of way, often acting brashly on their first idea. Together, though, they can examine the issues, think things through and rationally envision the results of their actions—assuming that they sit still long enough to put their heads together rather than jumping into the deep end first. Since they favor large-scale endeavors, it is vital that they engage their synergistic capacity for seeing the bigger picture. Otherwise they may be biting off more than they can chew.

In love affairs, this couple may be objectively well suited in many ways. Despite their mercurial mutual strengths (speedy, communicative, clever), however, Gemini II's long for a quiet, deep, powerful partner—perhaps a projection of their own dark side. There is a conflict between what they may need (a Gemini I rather like themselves) and what they want (a shadow projection, their opposite). Gemini I's can become quite frustrated over this, especially since they know things should be going well here.

Marriages in this combination may be interesting, filled with activity, travel and interest. Surprisingly stable, they can last for years, brimming with vivacity, before the partners begin to tire of each other. Neither of these two is well grounded, but Gemini I's are usually the more practical of the two, and may grow impatient with Gemini II lack of focus. Still, the relationship's emotional instabilities can often be resolved through dedication to a large-scale project, such as raising children.

Gemini I–Gemini II friendships are original in their approach, but they may not be strong enough to unite these two in a bond that will overcome their individual flightiness. Work and family relationships may offer those around them little peace: whether the partners are getting along or not, the noise level may prove intolerable. The solution can be virtually locking them up and letting them work things out in private.

ADVICE: *Be considerate of others. Find a place to be alone. Beware of exhibitionistic tendencies. Quiet down. Meditate. Turn off the motor.*

May 25–June 2
THE WEEK OF FREEDOM
GEMINI I

June 11–18
THE WEEK OF THE SEEKER
GEMINI III

Verbal Bombardment

RELATIONSHIPS

STRENGTHS: **INNOVATIVE, PHYSICAL, INTUITIVE**

WEAKNESSES: **ARGUMENTATIVE, GARRULOUS, MISUNDERSTOOD**

BEST: **FRIENDSHIP**

WORST: **PARENT-CHILD**

WASHINGTON ROEBLING (5/26/1837)
JOHN ROEBLING (6/12/1806)

A father-and-son team, this pair of American engineers pioneered the development of suspension bridges. They designed and supervised the building of NY's Brooklyn Bridge, during which John was killed in a construction accident. **Also:** **Jessi Colter & Waylon Jennings** (married; country-music stars).

These personalities' tendency to talk at rather than with each other can make meaningful communication difficult in this combination. The relationship amplifies their garrulousness, allowing them little rest from a verbal bombardment that often precludes listening. Communication is so important here partly because both partners are Geminis—but they are Geminis of very different kinds. Gemini I's are quick-witted, jumping from thought to thought. This sorely irritates Gemini III's, who dislike channel-surfing, preferring to explore a subject deeply and then say a lot about it, often too much for a Gemini I's patience. Accordingly, one often sees these two blabbing away without real connection. Finding a way to communicate, whether verbally, emotionally or in writing, is the first step to understanding here.

The easiest language for Gemini I's and III's to understand may be the language of love: silent looks, tender caresses or outright flaming passion may all prove effective means of communication. These are rarely enough, however, to replace the need for verbal expression, and breakdowns are bound to occur.

Marital and work partnerships will have to convey information more literally, and here the partners may be able to evolve their own shorthand of idiosyncratic expressions and speech—in short, a language for the discussion of everyday matters. To the extent that this language may be highly original, it may be hard for other family members or colleagues to understand.

Friendships in this combination may work best if based on action, which usually tells its own story. Dangerous expeditions (real or imagined), fascinating investigations (in books or real life), and the more challenging side of life in general attracts this relationship like a magnet. In the family, this sibling pair, especially if of opposite sexes, often has an easy familiarity, each instinctively understanding the other's feelings. Gemini I–Gemini III parent-child combinations will have to work hard to correct misunderstandings. As coworkers, these two may lack the time to develop their own language. The result is a loss of efficiency.

ADVICE: *Listening is necessary for communication. Beware foolhardiness. Remember that others may find you confusing. Take the time to explain. Slow down.*

May 25–June 2
THE WEEK OF FREEDOM
GEMINI I

June 19–24
THE CUSP OF MAGIC
GEMINI-CANCER CUSP

Furthering Expansive Endeavors

RELATIONSHIPS

STRENGTHS: **EXPANSIVE, STRIVING, CHALLENGING**

WEAKNESSES: **ENERVATING, OVERCOMBATIVE, UNREALISTIC**

BEST: **MARRIAGE**

WORST: **LOVE**

JACK DEMPSEY (6/24/1895)
GENE TUNNEY (5/25/1898)

Heavyweights Tunney and Dempsey fought in 2 historically famous matches. In the first, Tunney unanimously beat champion Dempsey. Knocked down in the 2nd fight, Tunney was given the now famous "long count" of 13 seconds, after which he won the match. **Also: Dashiell Hammett & Lillian Hellman** (live-in relationship; author/playwright).

This fascinating relationship may feature participation in large-scale projects and a striving for monumental goals, though not always realistic ones. This pair attend to the world at large, and all that represents it—books, philosophies, political movements, theater. The partners sometimes need to take an adversarial stance to each other, for through conflict they can achieve results beyond the grasp of either of them alone. There are acute temperamental differences between the rawer energies of Gemini I's and the more sophisticated and refined approach of Gemini-Cancers.

Although Gemini I's may seem the more aggressive of these two, Gemini-Cancers are often more so, if subtly. They take this stance simply to get something other than cool rationality out of the Gemini I. In love affairs, such conflicts may lead to pleasurable resolutions, but Gemini I's will ultimately tire of the mental energy required to maintain the relationship. Only after the affair has ended will Gemini-Cancers fully appreciate their ex-lover's electric energies.

Gemini-Cancers can offer a peaceful home life to Gemini I spouses, who, however, will probably only upset this domestic tranquillity in return. But Gemini I's can bring worldly benefit to the marriage, particularly in terms of social contacts, an eye for bargains, and handy shortcuts in official matters. Their roving eye may prove a problem, but Gemini-Cancers may be sufficiently enchanted with this interesting partner to keep the relationship going, demonstrating a romanticism, devotion and refined emotional nature that may hold the Gemini I's attention far longer than usual. In friendships and at work, these two may be able to meld their different temperaments in the service of an idealistic common cause requiring vision and dedication. Along the way, combative tendencies may arise that can be very hard to sublimate into more constructive channels; the trick is to turn these impulses into the kind of striving that fuels shared causes and furthers expansive endeavors. Parent-child matchups are likely to work best with nurturing Gemini-Cancers in the parental role.

ADVICE: *Tone down combative stances. Put competitive drives to constructive use. Scale back your horizons a bit. Attend to daily tasks.*

STRENGTHS: **SEARCHING,
CRITICAL, COMFORTING**
WEAKNESSES: **NERVOUS,
UNHAPPY, DESPAIRING**
BEST: **WORK**
WORST: **FAMILY**

OTIS SKINNER (6/28/1858)
CORNELIA OTIS SKINNER (5/30/01)

A celebrated American actor, Otis toured with Edwin Booth's company before forming his own troupe in 1894. Daughter Cornelia was an actress who wrote verse, witty essays and stage monologues that she often performed herself.

May 25–June 2
THE WEEK OF FREEDOM
GEMINI I

June 25–July 2
THE WEEK OF THE EMPATH
CANCER I

A Mutual Search

Embedded within this relationship is a desire to seek the answers to broad questions, such as discovering the reasons for life's events, or trying to find one's place in the world—questions that in some way often relate back to the individual. This pair may engage in activities that generate either experience or educational opportunities. Interestingly, even though the quest is shared, the questions and therefore the answers will be different for each partner. Cancer I's will want to know the reasons for their feelings, Gemini I's will want to expand their awareness of how they think. The relationship's search may ultimately be for personal values that these two can share.

Love affairs can start off well, but may quickly nose-dive when independent Gemini I's fly off to their next adventure, leaving the Cancer I sitting at home, bored and unhappy. When the Gemini I finally calls, the Cancer I's reply will be full of guilt-inducing pain. Consolation, kissing and making up will work until the predictable cycle begins once again. Married Gemini I's are usually out in the world doing their thing, while Cancer I's ensure that the home is well kept, well repaired and in general a comfortable retreat. The combination can work out well, then, especially in the practical sphere, since Gemini I efficiency and Cancer I money sense are an effective combination. Building domestic situations together, or seeking value in a religious or spiritual pursuit or success in a mutual career endeavor, fulfills some of the relationship's needs. But emotionally the relationship can be a disaster, and all these wonderful plans may grind to a halt as Cancer I's fall into a pit of despair and Gemini I's stand by helplessly, nervous and acutely frustrated. Tensions rise, arguments and resentments fly and painful breakdowns result.

Friendships and family relationships usually polarize Gemini I–Cancer I differences rather than synergizing their strengths. Critical attitudes emerge that exercise mental faculties and encourage game-playing rather than yielding sympathy or relaxation. These relationships rarely bring harmony to a family or circle of friends.

ADVICE: *Beware of emotional manipulation. Deal with guilt and shame. Seek a more open and joyful approach to life. Don't get stuck.*

STRENGTHS: **INTERESTING,
CHALLENGING, DEEP**
WEAKNESSES: **ADDICTIVE,
DARK, PERVERSE**
BEST: **LOVE**
WORST: **FRIENDSHIP**

IRVING THALBERG (5/30/1899)
LOUIS B. MAYER (7/4/1885)

In 1923, Thalberg joined Mayer's small movie company, which merged into Metro-Goldwyn-Mayer studios in 1924. Under Mayer's management and Thalberg's artistic direction MGM became Hollywood's most glamorous film factory. **Also:**
Max Brod & Franz Kafka (friends; Brod published Kafka posthumously);
Connie Sellecca & John Tesh (tv co-hosts); **Levon Helm & Robbie Robertson** (The Band).

May 25–June 2
THE WEEK OF FREEDOM
GEMINI I

July 3–10
THE WEEK OF THE UNCONVENTIONAL
CANCER II

The Shadow Side

Gemini I's are rarely sensitive or sympathetic enough to give Cancer II's the kind of emotional understanding they need, and Cancer II's will rarely be amenable to the Gemini I desire to lay down the rules for living. Where, then, is this relationship's meeting ground? The answer lies in dark and hidden areas that these two might never approach in their relationships with others. The shadow side of human experience exerts a seductive pull here, uniting this duo in a search for the unusual. Whether through a Gemini I's fascination with an unconventional Cancer II, or through the Cancer II's amazement at the Gemini I's dormant awareness of his or her own shadow personality, the relationship seeks to explore the darker depths of experience. These two may show great interest in unusual happenings, circumstances and people, not just investigating them but seeking to become involved with hidden, perhaps prophetic or metaphysical powers.

In love and marriage the relationship is unlikely to ignore the mysterious aspects of sex, or to hold back from exploring this area in unusual ways—the tantra, for example. To Gemini I's who have been content to live at a more superficial level of existence, particularly in matters of love, such a relationship may prove a little threatening yet at the same time fascinating. Cancer II's may feel more at home here, even taking the lead, something to which Gemini I's may not be accustomed. Fishing in these deep emotional waters, however, is not without its dangers, especially when monsters of the psyche are roused from the depths.

In the family and at work, the anger, disapproval and aggression of Gemini I's and the hurt, withdrawal and claiming attitudes of Cancer II's must be resolved if the relationship is to prove productive. Addiction can sometimes be an issue in friendships, which may be enjoyable and fun but mask deep needs for affection and security. Alcohol, tobacco and mind-expanding or tranquilizing drugs may be involved. Unfortunately, the relationship may lack the self-control necessary to limit the use of such substances.

ADVICE: *Don't get in over your head. Beware of addictive tendencies. Apply what you learn to life. Increase human understanding. Share with others.*

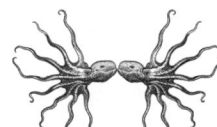

May 25–June 2

THE WEEK OF FREEDOM
GEMINI I

July 11–18

THE WEEK OF THE PERSUADER
CANCER III

Pleasurable Capitulation

RELATIONSHIPS

STRENGTHS: **CONVINCING, MAGNETIC, CAPABLE**

WEAKNESSES: **MANIPULATIVE, DESTRUCTIVE, MISLEADING**

BEST: **FRIENDSHIP, WORK**

WORST: **PARENT-CHILD**

RALPH WALDO EMERSON (5/25/1803)
HENRY DAVID THOREAU (7/12/1817)

Following his 1837 Harvard graduation, Thoreau became close to Emerson, who greatly influenced the younger writer, later taking him in when he was penniless. In 1845, he let Thoreau build his own cabin on the now famous Walden Pond. **Also: Johnny Weissmuller & Lupe Velez** (married; actors); **Nelson Riddle & Linda Ronstadt** (musical collaborators).

Highlighting its partners' charisma, this relationship can be magnetic and extremely persuasive in getting its way in the world. Creatively these two can accomplish a lot, since any artistic and even social endeavors they are engaged in usually have that extra-special something, that magic. This goes far in keeping them together. Manipulation and persuasion are their fortes as individuals, and their relationship magnifies these abilities, which is all well and good as long as they use them in pursuit of external goals. Games within the relationship, however, can prove destructive. Any battle that shapes up will pit a consummate Gemini I role-player against an emotionally savvy Cancer III. Ultimately, the Gemini I will prove no match for this partner's ability to get his or her way. Cancer III's will sometimes be irritated by the nervous chattiness of Gemini I's, who would do well to try to be more grounded.

Love affairs clearly reveal the ability of Cancer III's to determine the relationship's course: if attracted to a Gemini I, they will not be deterred. Gemini I's may shine and dazzle, but Cancer III's can zero in immediately on their insecurities and vulnerabilities, especially emotional ones. Should marriage be the Cancer III goal, the Gemini I, though ordinarily a hankerer after freedom, will probably recognize the benefits of domestic life with this capable partner and capitulate pleasurably. The relationship may ultimately prove lopsided: the Cancer III will rule the roost. Cancer III parents may view a gifted Gemini I child as excellent raw material to shape to their will. The child, however, may rebel against this controlling attitude. Gemini I parents generally occupy a magical position in the eyes of their Cancer III children, who may deceive themselves about these elusive individuals and ultimately face disappointment. Both partners will value friendships and working arrangements in this combination: melding their talents in social or business projects, these relationships can infuse a wide variety of endeavors with an extra pizzazz. Whether attracting others to their cause or lining up clients, these two specialize in convincing others of their ability to get the job done.

ADVICE: *Let others make up their own minds. Try not to be so pushy. Controlling and claiming attitudes can backfire. Establish more meaningful values.*

May 25–June 2

THE WEEK OF FREEDOM
GEMINI I

July 19–25

THE CUSP OF OSCILLATION
CANCER-LEO CUSP

Guiding the Boomerang

RELATIONSHIPS

STRENGTHS: **CHALLENGING, PASSIONATE, EXCITING**

WEAKNESSES: **UNSTABLE, INSECURE, DISRUPTIVE**

BEST: **WORK**

WORST: **SIBLING**

DASHIELL HAMMETT (5/27/1894)
RAYMOND CHANDLER (7/23/1888)

These writers first met in 1936 at a dinner for contributors to *Black Mask,* a detective magazine. Masters of the hard-boiled detective genre popularized in the 30s and 40s, both turned many of their novels into award-winning screenplays. **Also: Brooke Shields & Woody Harrelson** (romance; actors); **JFK & Rose Kennedy** (son/mother).

This relationship needs stability. Although these two have somewhat similar energies, tyrannical tendencies emerge here, as well as mutability and a sense of unsettledness. This makes each partner nervous, even when they are apart, and when they are together the discomfort and insecurity multiply unbearably. In an attempt to create order, one or the other of them will try to dominate, Gemini I's passively, by digging in their heels, and Cancer-Leos aggressively, by making demands. Cancer-Leos will generally be more irritated by Gemini I's than vice versa, for Gemini I's represent to them what they fear in themselves: their own qualities of distractedness or flakiness. It is Cancer-Leos who are apt to be the tyrants here, as their own insecurities boomerang.

Cancer-Leos are attracted to unpredictable individuals like Gemini I's, and insecurity only makes their love affairs burn brighter. Unless the relationship can galvanize practical energies, however, its passion may sweep it away. Cancer-Leos can never be sure of this particular lover's extracurricular activities, nor can Gemini I's predict a Cancer-Leo's moods. An exciting Gemini I may trigger a Cancer-Leo's psychological instability, sending him or her over the edge. Dedication will be needed on both sides to prevent early burnout or eventual catastrophe.

Working partnerships, marriages and friendships in this combination have difficulty over the question of responsibility. Whether in the workplace or at home, the partners are clever enough to see what is needed materially, and they are often technically gifted enough to set out to get it. But Gemini I's may tire of repetitive tasks and responsibility, and their longing to breathe free will make Cancer-Leos extremely nervous. Insecurities like this one may be the biggest problem these two face. Parent-child relationships in this combination may be highly positive and productive. Sibling matchups are often unstable and disruptive to family life; wise parents will give them joint responsibilities and accept no individual excuses. Being forced to hold up their end of the bargain collectively may induce cooperation and lessen strife.

ADVICE: *Be realistic in taking on responsibility. Work more efficiently. Don't let personal matters intrude. Balance emotional instabilities. Consider the role of projection.*

JOHN F. KENNEDY (5/29/17)
JACKIE KENNEDY (7/28/29)

The society event of 1953, the Kennedy wedding united very different personalities: a patrician and a tough politician. JFK expected Jackie to fit into his world, and as a classy First Lady she did, even amid rumors of his infidelities.

***Also:* Brooke Shields & Dean Cain** (romance; actors).

May 25–June 2
THE WEEK OF FREEDOM
GEMINI I

July 26–August 2
THE WEEK OF AUTHORITY
LEO I

Taken for Granted

The outside world views this relationship as sparkling and radiant. Gemini (an air sign) and Leo (a fire sign) combine in an explosive mix, especially in romantic and sexual interaction. There is also an ease of interaction here that promotes ease in others. Yet the relationship is governed by the element of water, associated with feeling, and its focus is empathic. This points to the relationship's more private side, which the world is not permitted to see.

Feeling and emotion often swirl in love relationships between these two, but are ultimately kept under control by their good sense and objectivity. Both of them tend to be detached and cool in personal matters; the relationship magnifies this trait, making it hard for them to admit to the depths of their feelings—which are capable of being extremely deep and passionate. Further, although empathy is high between them, they may ignore or even use it as a manipulative weapon to gain ascendancy. This can be the relationship's central tragedy, cutting off its best part for the sake of control and power.

The relationship's objectivity may speak better in marriage than in a transitory love affair. Both partners are more likely to hold fast to the former than to the latter, and can even come to depend on it as the anchor in their lives. The security of marriage, however, does not guarantee faithfulness or monogamy; both Gemini I's and Leo I's are likely to stray. Were their confidence in their relationship less great, they might remain more faithful, albeit frustrated. Although neither member is known for nurturing capabilities and devotion to children, their matchup synergistically boosts these tendencies—the pair can make excellent parents.

Friendships and work and sibling matchups are unlikely to be harmonious here. Leo I's usually demand more in such relationships than Gemini I's are prepared to give. Furthermore, the lion will give of its legendary steadfastness and faithfulness only up to a point, that point being the moment when he feels a less responsible person, possibly a Gemini I, is taking advantage.

ADVICE: *Be more honest about your feelings. Beware of control and power trips. Never take your relationship for granted. Discharge responsibilities.*

BENNETT CERF (5/25/1898)
SYLVIA SIDNEY (8/8/10)

While heading Random House from 1927–66, prominent book publisher Cerf was also a witty panelist on tv's popular *What's My Line* (1952–66). He and screen heroine Sidney were married briefly from 1935–36.

***Also:* Irving Thalberg & Norma Shearer** (married; producer/ actress); **Marilyn Monroe & Andy Warhol** (pop icon/pop artist).

May 25–June 2
THE WEEK OF FREEDOM
GEMINI I

August 3–10
THE WEEK OF BALANCED STRENGTH
LEO II

Hanging In There

The success of this relationship will depend on the Gemini I's ability to acknowledge the Leo II as the boss in appropriate situations. If this is impossible, a rocky road lies ahead for these two, assuming they wish to travel it. Both partners may be so determined to make this relationship work, however, that they will be willing to compromise. Thus Leo II's will be understanding of the Gemini I need for freedom, and of this partner's penchant for criticizing and making demands, while Gemini I's may give way to Leo II's when a leader is required, meanwhile keeping hold of the reins of power through planning and behind-the-scenes decision-making. These two may see eye-to-eye on fighting injustice or oppression. When united on this front, they can be unstoppable.

Romantic relationships here can be satisfying for both partners, particularly in the sexual sphere. Leo II's are demanding and will put Gemini I stamina to the test. Not at all understanding of infidelity, they will also keep a tight leash on Gemini I's, who will not enjoy facing their ultimatums. If anyone is guilty of a double standard, however, it may well be the Leo II: flexible Gemini I's are probably more compromising and forgiving.

In marriages and work partnerships Leo II's will hold up their end of the bargain and expect Gemini I's to do the same. This may or may not be wise, for too often a Gemini I will tend to lean on this powerful partner to get things done. Moreover, Leo II's can be long-suffering, and even if one day they realize they have made a bad choice in a frivolous or scattered Gemini I, they will often hang in there and continue to shoulder the relationship's responsibilities. Leo II's may actually prefer Gemini I's to be absent a lot of the time. Arguments over money are likely to plague this pairing.

Friendships and sibling relationships can work out well for these two, as long as Gemini I complaining or criticism does not push patient Leo II's beyond their limit.

ADVICE: *Try being more diplomatic. Compromise can make the impossible possible. Be aware of your limitations. Insist on equal participation.*

May 25–June 2

THE WEEK OF FREEDOM
GEMINI I

August 11–18

THE WEEK OF LEADERSHIP
LEO III

Former Enemies, Former Friends

RELATIONSHIPS

STRENGTHS: **COMPETITIVE, HONEST, REALISTIC**

WEAKNESSES: **DANGEROUS, UNCOMPROMISING, SUPPRESSIVE**

BEST: **COMPETITION**

WORST: **LOVE**

SAM SNEAD (5/27/1896)
BEN HOGAN (8/13/1896)

The world's dominant golfers during the 40s and 50s, "Slammin' Sammy" and Hogan were friendly rivals. Each won unprecedented numbers of championships and alternated as leading money winners of their time. **Also: Karl Buhler & Wilhelm Wundt** (rival psychologists); **Julia Ward Howe & Lucy Stone** (social reformers).

The aggressiveness of both these partners is likely to mask or supplant this relationship's more intimate aspects. Verbal and even physical encounters are likely, especially between young siblings and friends. Combative attitudes may be sublimated into healthy competition, or simply expressed in ironic and sarcastic banter. Put-downs of this kind can be dangerous if they result in a lowered self-image, which becomes more probable when parents or teachers utter them to their children or students. Both parties will need to be tough to survive in this relationship, but a realistic attitude urges those who can't stand the heat to get out of the kitchen.

Love affairs are likely to be scorchingly intense, even destructive. If the partners can get out of this relationship psychologically intact, they will go on to future liaisons wiser and more experienced. In marriage they are unlikely to be able to agree on who is boss, or to make the necessary compromises. Air-fire combinations like this one (Gemini being an air sign, Leo fire) can be dangerously explosive, with outbursts of anger common. But if the anger is suppressed, a Leo III depression may result, or the Gemini I may escape into drugs or drink. The use of sex as an outlet may work for a while, but will ultimately prove frustrating and futile. One solution is for each of the partners to establish an inviolable supremacy in their own important life areas, and to limit their shared activities to mundane ones that do not require strong leadership.

Friends and work colleagues may be former rivals or competitors whom mutual respect and changing fortunes have washed up on the same side. These relationships may also go in the other direction, however, with respect disappearing. No one would describe this relationship as "nice"—no love seems to be lost here. Yet it is honest and candid, and its partners wouldn't want it any other way. Their mutual dislike of pretense and phoniness underline this point.

ADVICE: *Translate combat into competition. Play by the rules. Your enemy may be a friend in disguise. Agree on areas of expertise. Minimize stress.*

May 25–June 2

THE WEEK OF FREEDOM
GEMINI I

August 19–25

THE CUSP OF EXPOSURE
LEO-VIRGO CUSP

Winning a Fair Fight

RELATIONSHIPS

STRENGTHS: **ASPIRING, DETERMINED, FAIR**

WEAKNESSES: **DESTRUCTIVE, UNTRUSTWORTHY, UNFOCUSED**

BEST: **FRIENDSHIP**

WORST: **SIBLING**

IAN FLEMING (5/28/08)
SEAN CONNERY (8/25/30)

Many of Fleming's 13 James Bond spy novels were made into films. Connery was chosen by a London newspaper poll to play James Bond in *Dr. No* (1962), which catapulted him to stardom. He starred in 5 other Bond films from 1963–71. **Also: Henry Kissinger & Jill St. John** (affair; dignitary/actress).

The focus of the relationship between these very different personalities can well be a drive toward success, whether as individuals or as a pair. Whatever ambition they have individually the relationship synergistically increases. It is most effective as a successful business partnership, or as an aspiring marriage or parent-child relationship. Although Gemini I's tend to be more direct and Leo-Virgos more secretive in accomplishing their ends, together they simply carry on, pragmatically and purposefully, neither demanding nor shunning the attention of others.

Gemini I–Leo-Virgo love affairs are unlikely to be effective, particularly if they lack this focus of ambition. Pure pleasure is rarely a lasting interest for this pair, and sexual encounters may often pan out as brief flings. Gemini I's are unlikely to understand or respect this partner's intense need for privacy, not realizing that a single Leo-Virgo confidence broken is likely to be the last one shared. In marriage, career and family, the relationship is ambitious but not necessarily ruthless. It shows a respect for others, and if winning is the goal, the fight will be a clean one. Victory will mean little for this pair if it is achieved through tricks or underhandedness. Instead, intelligent planning and tactics are given the highest priority.

Friendships in this combination may exist mainly on the mental plane, with an interest, perhaps, in games, puzzles and other activities of the mind. Gemini I friends are more trustworthy confidants than Gemini I lovers, and Leo-Virgos may come to depend on their often sage counsel, while also providing them with constructive criticism and advice about the furtherance of their careers.

Destructive conflicts over parental attention are likely to arise between Gemini I–Leo-Virgo siblings, especially of the same sex. Their struggles often spill out beyond the home, perhaps to school, the athletic field or social doings. Unfortunately, a bad habit of vying for the affections of a mutual friend or lover may continue into adolescence and adult life.

ADVICE: *Success isn't everything. Find meaning within. Don't get caught up in useless competition. Respect confidences. Seek constructive goals.*

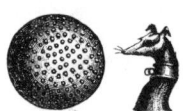

HUBERT H. HUMPHREY (5/27/11)
LYNDON JOHNSON (8/27/08)

Humphrey was Minnesota's gregarious senator from 1948–64 and Johnson's presidential running mate in '64. The close-working pair waged a low-key campaign, easily beating Barry Goldwater. Humphrey served 4 years as vice-president.

Also: John Hinckley & Jim Brady (would-be assassin/wounded victim).

May 25–June 2
THE WEEK OF FREEDOM
GEMINI I

August 26–September 2
THE WEEK OF SYSTEM BUILDERS
VIRGO I

Need for Change

This relationship's greatest achievement would be to harness its partners' skills to manipulate their environment and build something of lasting value. Their strengths can fuse synergistically in a powerful ability to persuade. Gemini I's have remarkable technical skills, yet rarely finish their projects. Should a Virgo I create a structure for them, these two could have a successful project, process or cause on their hands, together with an ability to convince others to buy, join, even believe. This area of strength, however, is also an area of conflict: Virgo I's need to preserve structure and Gemini I's to alter or eliminate it. The focus here can easily be the partners' struggle to convince each other of the need to either tighten or loosen a given structure (rules, the setup of home or workplace, schedules, budgets, etc.).

Emotional manipulation may play a role in love affairs. These two tend to bring out each other's nervous side, trying to influence each other by arousing fears and anxieties. The situation is unstable and offers little relaxation.

Persuasion plays an important role in marital, working and family relationships. Virgo I's usually feel more secure in an ordered situation that is only altered when a change will increase efficiency; Gemini I's prefer something looser, often changing things just because they enjoy it, and tire of stasis. But change itself isn't really the issue here, since ultimately both of these two can handle it comfortably. More to the point are the differences of opinion indicated by the square aspect (90° apart in the zodiac) between Gemini I and Virgo I. Their conflicts do provide the impetus for forward motion, but if harmony in the business or family group is to be preserved, they will have to be resolved.

Friendships can be relaxed, but here the partners' critical and analytical propensities (each sign is ruled by Mercury) come to the fore. If they can shift their mental emphasis into enjoyable activities involving thought (puzzles, games, books, the Internet, etc.), or apply it to cogent analyses of behavior—in other words, to self-insight—it can be extremely productive.

ADVICE: *Reduce stress and tension. Put anxieties to rest. Agree on structural changes. Only implement essential rules. Increase easy cooperation.*

JOHN F. KENNEDY (5/29/17)
JOSEPH KENNEDY (9/6/1888)

JFK's fiercely competitive nature was fueled by his demanding father, who, though never running for public office himself, had great political ambitions for his sons. He closely advised and financed his son's fateful rise to the presidency.

May 25–June 2
THE WEEK OF FREEDOM
GEMINI I

September 3–10
THE WEEK OF THE ENIGMA
VIRGO II

Creative Projects

This unusual relationship tends to bring out fantasy and imagination in its partners. Its creative projects may require a high degree of inventiveness, and technical skill and craft are highly favored here. Expect clashes, however, between traditional and newer, more radical approaches to whatever science, skill or artistic endeavor is afoot. Gemini I's and Virgo II's may create highly personalized domestic situations and explore the byways of pleasure. Gemini I's are initially intrigued by the mysterious calm and reserve of Virgo II's, who in turn are fascinated by the unfettered, will-o'-the-wisp persona of Gemini I's. Virgo II's tend to dominate in this relationship, which may be for the best, since they are the more practical and stable of the two. As career partners, the pair may run a common business or, if engaged in separate careers, be available to help out when needed.

Love affairs give both partners' sensuousness and imaginativeness full rein, while involving a less romantic, more frank approach to sex. Marriage is often the next step after an intriguing affair, but others may show concern over a union between two people they see as having little in common. In fact the couple tend to be no less misunderstood as the years go by—their stability and endurance may amaze friends and family alike.

Friendships between these two provide endless amusement for relatively somber, isolated Virgo II's and serve to introduce a more meaningful social element into their lives. At the same time, Virgo II mystery will prove an ever fascinating challenge to curious Gemini I's. Activities of all sorts, perhaps involving travel, research, business or investment, may gel here. A career partnership between Gemini I–Virgo II friends or spouses may often prove engrossing.

Gemini I–Virgo II opposite-sex siblings may live in an isolated fantasy world as children, sometimes acting out the adult roles that they will follow when they are older. This special relationship may exhibit jealousies and claiming attitudes in adult life.

ADVICE: *Beware of isolation. Fantasy should be grounded. Don't get stuck in unreality. Guard against claiming attitudes.*

May 25–June 2
THE WEEK OF FREEDOM
GEMINI I

September 11–18
THE WEEK OF THE LITERALIST
VIRGO III

RELATIONSHIPS

STRENGTHS: **VARIED, HONEST, COMMUNICATING**

WEAKNESSES: **OSCILLATING, IRRESPONSIBLE, HALF TRUE**

BEST: **FRIENDSHIP**

WORST: **MARRIAGE**

A Wave Function

Apparently unstable, this relationship, with its characteristic swings or oscillations, actually contains an innate regularity, a self-controlling mechanism. Like sound or radio waves, it has a periodicity of function, showing predictable highs and lows that appear at fixed intervals. It is not instability that typifies the relationship, then, so much as rhythmic change. Any kind of joint endeavor requiring the constant application of effort is not recommended here.

Both Virgo and Gemini are ruled by the speedy planet Mercury, which symbolizes change and communication. Thus Gemini I's and Virgo III's are on the same wavelength in matters of love, friendship and family. All of these relationships may resemble a roller-coaster ride, not unlike a literal graph of a wave function. Feelings in particular have marked peaks and troughs.

Marriages feature arguments about how things are to be done, and especially about who will do them. Gemini I's tend to take Virgo III practicality and capability for granted; annoyingly, they also tend to be absent just when a job needs doing. Such behavior can arouse resentment and anger in Virgo III's, resulting in bad looks and sharp commands. Friends and family may find such behavior overreactive or grouchy, but in fact it may be needed to keep wayward Gemini I's in line. The marriage is likely to feature battles over dominance and money.

Gemini I's and Virgo III's make excellent friends, but their friendships should be freed of the influence of romance or career. Neither partner should ever get the idea that the other has ulterior motives in mind. This relationship values natural and open behavior and has a hatred for pretentiousness or phoniness of any kind. Honesty is the yardstick for most of the pair's statements, so that Gemini I's are expected to curb their tendency to exaggerate while Virgo III's are urged to release hidden feelings. The half-truth may assume a curious role in such a relationship.

ADVICE: *If you expect honesty, don't bend the truth. Balance confrontation and avoidance. Even out emotional swings. Normalize daily behavior.*

CLAYTON MOORE (9/14/14)
JAY SILVERHEELS (5/26/22)

These actors complemented each other in early tv's *Lone Ranger* series (1949–57). Moore played the masked stalwart champion of justice opposite Silverheels, his faithful Indian companion, Tonto. ***Also:* Minnie Pearl & Roy Acuff** (co-stars, Grand Ole Opry); **Hank Williams, Jr. & Sr.** (son/father; country-music stars); **Vanessa Stephen & Clive Bell** (married; painter/art critic).

May 25–June 2
THE WEEK OF FREEDOM
GEMINI I

September 19–24
THE CUSP OF BEAUTY
VIRGO-LIBRA CUSP

RELATIONSHIPS

STRENGTHS: **ATTRACTIVE, MONEY-WISE, PERSUASIVE**

WEAKNESSES: **UNAWARE, UNGROUNDED, UNSTABLE**

BEST: **WORK**

WORST: **FRIENDSHIP**

Tenuous Connections

This relationship cries out for stability. Unfortunately, air, typical of fleeting and tenuous connections, is the predominant element here, making grounding unlikely. On the mental, thoughtful, logical or intellectual side, things can go extremely well, with eccentricity and imagination the hallmarks of mutual creativity. In more physical, emotional or instinctual matters, however, the relationship may demonstrate glaring deficiencies—not the least of them the inability to be there for each other in times of need.

Love relationships here will rarely go very deep. Good-looking Gemini I's to whom Virgo-Libras are attracted will feel appreciated, but may also sense that they are being treated more like beautiful objects than like worthwhile people. They may also find Virgo-Libra sensibilities snobbish, and think they are being treated patronizingly, something they will not tolerate. On the other hand, Virgo-Libras are not about to find the dependability they sorely need in Gemini I's. These affairs are perhaps better off if they do not lead to marriage.

Virgo-Libras and Gemini I's can make good acquaintances and occasional leisure-time companions. They seldom share deeply enough for real friendship to take place. The pity here is that these fair-weather friends may not take their casual but enjoyable bond for what it is, and may be disappointed when push comes to shove. Often this type of relationship will not survive such stress.

In family relationships, and particularly in parent-child matchups, it will be important to the partners to improve their image, surroundings, clothes, diet and education. Much of this drive will be the result of an unconscious need to keep up with the neighbors. Working relationships in this combination can be excellent, especially if they are built around fashion, design, music, investments, real estate or architecture. The relationship demonstrates a good eye for beauty and bargains, a solid appreciation of money and a good feeling for it, as well as a studied knowledge of the techniques of several fields of expertise. It also has the ability to convince customers.

ADVICE: *Try to develop spiritually and physically. Ground yourself in the here and now. Meditate. Examine your values. Seek soulfulness and character.*

JIM HENSON (9/24/36)
FRANK OZ (5/25/44)

This pair's collaboration as puppeteers and directors, along with Henson's production talent, resulted in tv's *Sesame Street* and *The Muppet Show*. Oz, who was also vice-president of the Henson organization, considered Henson his mentor. ***Also:* Pat Boone & Debby Boone** (father/daughter; singers); **Martha Vickers & Mickey Rooney** (married; actors).

STRENGTHS: **INTENSE, THOUGHTFUL, GRATIFYING**

WEAKNESSES: **DISTURBING, CONFLICTING, INTOLERANT**

BEST: **MARRIAGE**

WORST: **SIBLING**

ISADORA DUNCAN (5/27/1878)
SERGEI YESENIN (10/2/1895)

While visiting Russia in 1921, modern dance pioneer Duncan married Yesenin, a gifted young poet. They split up in 1923. A heavy drinker, he hanged himself in 1925, leaving behind a final poem written in his own blood.

Also: **JFK & Angie Dickinson** (affair; president/actress).

May 25–June 2

THE WEEK OF FREEDOM
GEMINI I

September 25–October 2

THE WEEK OF THE PERFECTIONIST
LIBRA I

Getting Along

These two individuals are not known for their social skills, a quality their relationship doesn't change. The primary challenge they face, then, will be to get along with each other on a daily basis. If they are to avoid argument, they will have to find sources of authority on which they can agree—neither of them is likely to take anything at face value. They are notoriously hard to convince, but together they may settle on a religious, political, philosophical, financial or artistic creed or set of beliefs that they can accept. (If they are co-workers, a company policy may do.) If this kind of common basis can be found, their arguments may become reasonable discussions, and the prediction of an easy relationship due to their trine position to each other (120° apart in the zodiac) will be partially fulfilled. They must take care, however, not to come off as bossy, authoritarian or supercilious toward others, at work or socially. Once they have formed a unit, they can easily adopt an "Us against the world" attitude.

Love between these two is likely to be intense—in fact, it must be moderated to avoid burnout. Even when their physical contact is gratifying, disagreements of all sorts may mar moods of contentment or exaltation. To know when to leave each other alone, they need to develop their intuition, and above all they must have faith in the relationship's abilities to heal wounds and promote understanding. Doubt, worry and control must be relinquished, leaving things to go as they will.

Marriages are most successful when the partners share a belief system. Coming from similar backgrounds can be a stabilizing factor. The danger is that intolerant or prejudicial points of view may influence children for the worse. Friendships and sibling relationships can be close, but if the pair hold opposing philosophies they can expect heated arguments. They typically get so involved in what they are doing that they are unaware of how disturbing they can be to others. Long after a Gemini I–Libra I confrontation has ended, observers may still be reeling from the fallout.

ADVICE: *Monitor your noise level. Others may be irritated. Establish common lines of agreement. Don't just believe what you see. Have faith.*

STRENGTHS: **LIGHT, EASY, FUN**

WEAKNESSES: **UNPREPARED, FAIR-WEATHER, SHALLOW**

BEST: **LOVE**

WORST: **MARRIAGE**

STEVIE NICKS (5/26/48)
LINDSEY BUCKINGHAM (10/3/47)

Members of Fleetwood Mac beginning in 1972, rockers Nicks and Buckingham were romantically linked in 1976 and split up soon after. They pursued separate careers, recording independently during the '80s, but performed together once more at Clinton's '93 inaugural party.

Also: **Marilyn Monroe & Bert Stern** (friends; star/photographer).

May 25–June 2

THE WEEK OF FREEDOM
GEMINI I

October 3–10

THE WEEK OF SOCIETY
LIBRA II

Laughing and Loving It

This relationship is generally just fun for both partners. It emphasizes enjoyment, whether in the personal, professional or family sphere. Not that the relationship can't get the job done; it can be extremely efficient and effective. But the partners believe that if something is worth doing it can be done the easy way or the hard way, and the easy way is obviously to be preferred. Loose and relaxed attitudes are valued highly here, and uptight, tense ones are eschewed.

Gemini I–Libra II love affairs and friendships are definitely pleasure oriented. Having a good time is given top priority. Those who view this relationship askance are likely to be thinking that it is shallow or superficial, but perhaps this is only jealousy; when two people can satisfy each other as easily and naturally as this pair, they must be doing something right. Particularly with friends, however, trouble may start just at the point where serious attitudes begin to emerge. Pollyannish relationships like this one are not really ready for trouble, and once it arises it may ruin the pair's good time. Should a major disaster or two appear—financial, academic, domestic or physical—this relationship may find itself on the brink of extinction.

Marriages usually have their share of woes and stress, and woes and stress are never the preferred mode for this couple. Unless they are prepared to take the bad with the good, ride through some heavy storms and even suffer unsolved problems for years, they had better not live together but remain friends or lovers.

Work relationships can be loads of fun, but can the work really get done? For the most part, yes—in fact Gemini I–Libra II co-workers can do a lot in addition to livening up the workplace. The social aspects of work are important, too, and the wit and ironic bite of this duo's sense of humor can serve to keep everyone on their toes—laughing, and loving it.

ADVICE: *Try getting serious once in a while—seriousness need not signal the end of enjoyment. At some point it may be necessary to grow up.*

May 25–June 2

THE WEEK OF FREEDOM
GEMINI I

October 11–18

THE WEEK OF THEATER
LIBRA III

Differences in Tempo

The challenge here will be to balance opposing energies. Tempo is a problem for these two: they can both be forceful, but Gemini I speed is disturbing to Libra III's, who are graceful and easy and prefer a measured approach. Perhaps seeing Gemini I's as interested more in getting what they want than in how they get it, Libra III's may feel rushed here. They in turn may annoy their partners through their consciousness of how others see them, a trait that Gemini I's may view as a despicably phony. The relationship must embrace compromise, tolerance and understanding if it is to have a chance of achieving balance. On the positive side, its innate persistence and ability to take on challenges can help these partners to find the middle way.

Love affairs may witness power struggles, with Gemini I's fruitlessly trying to control their partners. The Libra III need for a strong figure to depend on will not be met here, and the relationship's curve may describe a downward spiral. Marriages, though not enormously recommended, can work better because of their fixed and self-evident responsibilities. Their daily routines may ground Gemini I's, and physically maintaining a home may challenge their technical skills. Libra III's will appreciate these abilities, and by contributing their share to this job they may achieve a measure of balance. Gemini I's, however, may see themselves as having given up their most precious possession, freedom, and can feel cheated if career concerns keep their Libra III partner away a lot.

More balance may be achieved in friendships. These partners will seek each other out because they want to, not out of obligation. Their relationship can be dynamic and exciting, full of adventure and flamboyance, and is perhaps best when it offers a true escape from crushing responsibilities.

A lack of mutual respect and an inability to please each other make parent-child matchups difficult. Work relationships bound by fixed responsibilities may be more manageable, although differences in tempo can be annoying here, especially since, lacking intimacy, the partners may invest little energy in solving their personal problems.

ADVICE: *Take the time to understand. Don't be so hasty. Neglect is a form of abuse. Try to build respect. Use your powers of analysis to gain insight.*

MARILYN MONROE (6/1/26)
ARTHUR MILLER (10/17/15)

Monroe and Miller's 1956 marriage, though loving, suffered from cultural barriers. She divorced the playwright a week before *The Misfits*, a script written for her, opened in '61.

Also: Marilyn Monroe & Yves Montand (affair); **Ian Fleming & Roger Moore** (author/Bond portrayer); **Pamela Johnson & C.P. Snow** (married; authors); **JFK & Arthur Schlesinger, jr.** (president/special assistant).

May 25–June 2

THE WEEK OF FREEDOM
GEMINI I

October 19–25

THE CUSP OF DRAMA & CRITICISM
LIBRA-SCORPIO CUSP

A Fall from Grace

Love, affection and admiration may well be present in this difficult and complex relationship, yet these partners may ultimately find it difficult or impossible to accept each other. Part of the problem is the kind of adoration or worship that often occurs here: each partner's tendency to place the other on the pedestal offers the setup for a fall from grace. The relationship may continue for months or years in an almost paradisiacal state, but this only makes the inevitable departure from Eden all the more difficult. The greatest challenge here will be for the partners to see each other as they really are, minus the projections and expectations.

Love affairs are often ecstatic, intense and rewarding, but act as a smoke screen against reality. The gradual realization that the person one is in love with does not correspond to one's ideal image of a lover can be truly painful. As reality creeps in, the partners have at least a chance of accepting each other for what they are, but instead may lose interest in continuing the relationship. Alternatively they may be unable to let go, perhaps because of a sex and love addiction, and this may be the most painful experience of all.

Marriages and friendships will require great efforts at honesty. Strong differences must be faced. Libra-Scorpios may be rejecting, but may also feel neglected and misunderstood, while Gemini I's feel unappreciated and baffled. The power struggles here often develop from an individual's striving to grow, which may not be possible within the relationship as it is. Friendships are a bit more flexible and conducive to growth, but objectivity is difficult to maintain. Family relationships can be especially trying. Parent-child relationships of either combination demand parental understanding and acceptance of the child's true nature. Children should be encouraged to make their own choices and accept responsibilities. Both dependency and disapproval must be met and overcome. Unreality, lethargy and a tendency toward procrastination do not allow for the best business or work relationships, which are not recommended for this combination, the roles of business partners or executives being particularly discouraged.

ADVICE: *Cultivate acceptance and understanding. Suspend judgments. Make decisions and act on them. Don't let things drift. Learn to compromise.*

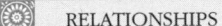

JACQUES-FRANÇOIS HALEVY (5/27/1799)
GEORGES BIZET (10/25/1838)

While studying under composer Halevy, Bizet married his daughter, Geneviève, in 1869. Bizet was to later complete Halevy's unfinished opera, *Noé*.

Also: Cornelia Otis Skinner & Emily Kimbrough (collaborators; writers).

STRENGTHS: **LOYAL, RESPONSIBLE, DETERMINED**

WEAKNESSES: **AGGRESSIVE, CONFLICTING, UNSTABLE**

BEST: **SIBLING**

WORST: **MARRIAGE**

MARIE ANTOINETTE (11/2/1755)
JOSEPH GUILLOTIN (5/28/1738)

Guillotin was a physician member of the National Assembly during the French Revolution. He designed the guillotine as a quick and painless form of execution. During the infamous Reign of Terror (1793–94), Marie Antoinette, found guilty of treason, was one of the blade's more notable victims. **Also:**

Miles Davis & Clifford Brown (contemporary jazz trumpeters).

May 25–June 2
THE WEEK OF FREEDOM
GEMINI I

October 26–November 2
THE WEEK OF INTENSITY
SCORPIO I

Alternating Currents

In the unlikely event that this pair comes together in any way, their relationship will be deep, emotionally complex and fired by volcanic and often dark energies. Once initiated, the combination is difficult to escape from; it becomes self-perpetuating, even to the point of creating a mythological or ritualistic aura around itself. As when the poles of two magnets can repel each other but can also switch their orientation, becoming strongly attracted, so it is with these partners. The relationship's focus will be on the question of who takes the leadership role. Both parties can be aggressive about asserting their priorities, so they may have to trade off dominant roles in different areas of their relationship—money matters, for example, being controlled by the Scorpio I, social interactions by the Gemini I.

Love affairs and marriages in this combination are likely to involve fierce power struggles, with emotional insecurities and outbursts dotting the landscape. At first these two often dislike each other intensely. A love affair will begin suddenly, startling everyone, including them. The Scorpio I suspicion of glibness and versatility may seriously undermine the Gemini I's confidence, while Gemini I sarcasm and innuendo will upset thin-skinned Scorpio I's.

As friends these partners will take equal responsibility for decision-making, but easy give-and-take is difficult here. Scorpio I's make strong demands on their friends and are especially severe in matters of intention and morality. Gemini I's are usually less concerned about the motives behind their actions, and are also likely to transcend conventional morality when it suits them, both of which may incur strong Scorpio I disapproval. Still, overall, the relationship is well suited to friendships. Family connections may be mutually protective. Scorpio I–Gemini I siblings often stay loyal to one parent over the other in cases of divorce; they will generally want to stick together in such situations, and in this case their intuitive allegiance to a common authority solves the leadership problem well. The same kind of loyalty, but this time to a company, can make these two effective co-workers.

ADVICE: *Give up power struggles. Try to talk without sarcasm or anger. Determine where talents lie. Take the lead only when necessary.*

STRENGTHS: **RESPONSIVE, VISIONARY, AWARE**

WEAKNESSES: **UNACCEPTING, COMPETITIVE, SELFISH**

BEST: **WORK**

WORST: **LOVE**

MARY TRAVERS (11/7/37)
PETER YARROW (5/31/38)

Travers and Yarrow, along with Paul Stookey (left), were members of Peter, Paul and Mary. Formed in 1961, they were the most popular acoustic folk group of the 60s. **Also:**

Peter Yarrow & Paul Stookey (Peter, Paul and Mary); **Julia Ward Howe & Samuel Howe** (married; social reformer/humanitarian).

May 25–June 2
THE WEEK OF FREEDOM
GEMINI I

November 3–11
THE WEEK OF DEPTH
SCORPIO II

Fine-Tuned Sensibilities

This relationship is apt to provide its partners with an opportunity to become more open-minded. If they are up to the task, it could open them to a whole new world, including the visionary or psychic. If this pair can get beyond their individual differences, they may enjoy an unusually colorful journey together.

In matters of love, rivalries may arise here over the affection of a common object of desire. Although both Gemini I's and Scorpio II's have an excellent sense of humor, together they may lack the ability to stay balanced. Competition between them can prove deadly serious. Marriage and love affairs in this combination, then, are not really recommended, since the prevailing mood can be one of mistrust. Harmony will be served if these partners can leave each other secure in their own value, resisting any impulse to try to tear down each other's character. They are likely to share a certain sensitivity, meaning both that they can be responsive to each other's needs and also, unfortunately, that they often get on each other's nerves. Should competition arise, the very insight into character that in other contexts has proved these personalities' strength can in this relationship become a weapon each of them uses to achieve selfish ends.

Should these two be friends, siblings or other relatives, the family or social group to which they belong can be rocked by rivalry. There are usually no winners here, and binding decisions are often difficult to agree upon or enforce. Unless parent-child or sibling combinations show great respect for and acceptance of each other, a mood of constant irritation may prevail. Gemini I's would do well to use their analytical powers and Scorpio II's their emotional understanding to lessen such tensions.

Unless these two are unbridgeably divided by age or cultural background, they can work well together, have a successful friendship, or even be friends who work together in the same career. Awareness of the other person's orientation, opinions and strengths is essential to success.

ADVICE: *Tone down rivalries and arguments. Agree to compromise. Deal with irritations promptly. Put sensitivity in the service of understanding.*

May 25–June 2

THE WEEK OF FREEDOM
GEMINI I

November 12–18

THE WEEK OF CHARM
SCORPIO III

A Parting of the Veil

Something makes these two keep secrets from the world: the inner workings of their relationship will always be private. Perhaps this is because they reveal sides of themselves to each other that they never show to anyone else, engendering a closeness that they may fiercely protect. Much energy will be tied up in how and when they confide in each other. Since they can't help but share their secrets, each of them ends up knowing a lot about the other one, and they may hold a kind of unspoken power or control over one another. One can't help but wonder what happens when the revelations run out: will the well of the relationship run dry, too?

Scorpio III's generally call the shots here, usually deciding how much of the relationship is revealed to the world, and when. Their self-sufficiency and stability inspire confidence in Gemini I children or employees, who may come to depend heavily on them as parents or bosses. Love affairs here are often covert, particularly if either partner is already involved in a primary relationship elsewhere. But Gemini I's have difficulty keeping secrets to themselves, and should they reveal Scorpio III confidences, or information about the affair itself, they will be sternly admonished and even threatened with rejection. In such situations Scorpio III's will rarely give them a second chance. The couple's passion is often directly proportional to how much of their relationship remains hidden.

Marriages between these two are extremely private, primarily through the influence of the Scorpio III. Freedom-loving Gemini I's may finally become fed up with this and seek solace elsewhere. Should they stray, they may be surprisingly good at hiding it from Scorpio III's, who may prefer not to know what's going on, or to suspect it but suffer in silence. Scorpio III's depend heavily on their friends, but Gemini I's must be careful not to take advantage of their good will. More independent Gemini I's will get along just fine in friendships with Scorpio III's, but more dependent ones will eventually be shown the door.

ADVICE: *Waste less energy on hiding. Develop freer attitudes. That much control isn't necessary. Let things unfold on their own.*

PRINCE RAINIER (5/31/23)
GRACE KELLY (11/12/29)

In a fairy-tale romance, Kelly left behind a successful screen career to marry Monaco's prince in 1956. At age 52 she died in a tragic car accident, leaving behind 3 children. **Also: DMC & Run** (rappers of Run-DMC); **William Pitt the Younger & William Pitt the Elder** (son/father; English prime ministers).

May 25–June 2

THE WEEK OF FREEDOM
GEMINI I

November 19–24

THE CUSP OF REVOLUTION
SCORPIO-SAGITTARIUS CUSP

A Spiritual Bond

The focus here is spiritual—this is a relationship in which the partners may explore deeper, more idealistic topics, or engage in quiet contemplation together. They may, in fact, believe they share a higher calling. This doesn't preclude a certain zest and love of life; indeed in all their areas of interest—the arts, music, dance, belief systems, politics—enjoyment and fun with the world of ideas are important to them. This pair is interested in anything that affects the human condition. The world may view their relationship as active and even frenetic, but in doing so may fail to observe its personal and intimate side.

Marriages and love affairs are tricky for this combination. Both have a tendency toward infidelity, which their relationship accentuates, so that if it is to survive it will have to be very open, with few rules and little guilt or blame. Children of these spouses may have a difficult time with their parents' attitudes, and when older may be highly disapproving, even condemning of them. Gemini I–Scorpio-Sagittarius love relationships are likely to include both high passion and deeply negative emotions, especially jealousy, which can be all-consuming.

Friendships and sibling relationships here are likely to be close, particularly when of the same sex. The relationship is characterized by a desire to defend the underdogs and the disadvantaged of this world, but it also has a curious respect for money and power. Care must be taken, in fact, that it does not succumb to this latter tendency, compromising its own spiritual strengths.

Working relationships between these two may well be highly successful. Generally speaking, however, the Gemini I–Scorpio-Sagittarius duo will work no harder than is necessary, and will often conserve its strength for extracurricular activities. An unusual feature of a business partnership may be a religious or spiritual orientation underlying its financial or social dealings, and supplying a basis of trust in money matters.

ADVICE: *Calm frenetic energies. Practice some form of meditation. Realize the value of silence, and of peace. Don't succumb to the lure of power.*

JODIE FOSTER (11/19/62)
JOHN HINCKLEY (5/29/55)

Hinckley's assassination attempt on President Reagan in 1981 was attributed to his delusional obsession with actress Foster, whom he wanted to impress. **Also: Marilyn Monroe & Robert Kennedy** (reputed affair; actress/JFK's brother).

STRENGTHS: **INDIVIDUALISTIC, EXPRESSIVE, MAGNETIC**
WEAKNESSES: **UNSETTLED, REBELLIOUS, SELF-CONSUMING**
BEST: **FRIENDSHIP**
WORST: **MARRIAGE**

JOE DIMAGGIO (11/25/14)
MARILYN MONROE (6/1/26)

This baseball hero and sex symbol seemed the perfect 50s match, but DiMaggio detested Hollywood's exploitation of Monroe and their marriage lasted less than a year. DiMaggio's love lives on in the daily placement of a flower on Monroe's grave. *Also:* **JFK & JFK, Jr.** (father/son); **JFK & Caroline Kennedy** (father/daughter); **R.W. Emerson & Louisa Alcott** (friends; writers).

May 25–June 2
THE WEEK OF FREEDOM
GEMINI I

November 25–December 2
THE WEEK OF INDEPENDENCE
SAGITTARIUS I

Rigid Independence

Two freedom-loving people like these don't build a relationship easily. Their focus together, then, and their greatest challenge, will be to find a structure within which they can function, whether they derive it from career or family or tailor it for the relationship's needs. Finding a modus vivendi for these highly individual characters, whose independent attitudes can metamorphose in each other's company into a kind of rigidity, will indeed be a test of the combination's mettle. Gemini I and Sagittarius I lie opposite each other in the zodiac, and their changeable, protean nature (both are mutable signs, Gemini an air sign, Sagittarius fire) is magnetically attractive, unsettling and explosive.

Love affairs between these two may start out like a house on fire, but will lack the stability and understanding to proceed further, and simply burn out. Neither partner will be especially adept at helping the other with their psychological problems, which their relationship may actually intensify. Each needs a stable partner, and since neither of them is likely to meet this need, marriages in this combination may be problematic. Although each partner enjoys the other's freedom-oriented temperament, responsible Sagittarius I's may resent the evasiveness of Gemini I's when it comes to hard work, while Gemini I's may find Sagittarius I's judgmental.

Friendships between these two can work out extremely well, particularly when built around sports, fitness training or other physical activities. But the fixed moral attitudes of Sagittarius I's may be hard for Gemini I's to accept, especially when directed against them. The more rigid structures of career and family relationships will inevitably awaken rebellious attitudes; close Gemini I–Sagittarius I co-workers or siblings can be a thorn in the side of an inflexible boss or parent. Their independent stance will in turn provoke even more repressive authoritarian attitudes, pushing them into further solidarity and resistance—a potentially explosive cycle. As a parent-child or business-partner combination, Gemini I's and Sagittarius I's are apt to find their interactions limited or constrained in some way, maybe needing, for example, to make appointments in order to see each other.

ADVICE: *Discharge tasks and obligations. Prove you are responsible. Create acceptable guidelines. Be more respectful of necessary rules.*

STRENGTHS: **CURIOUS, EXPLORING, ENDURING**
WEAKNESSES: **PROBLEMATIC, UNCOMPREHENDING, OBSESSIVE**
BEST: **MARRIAGE**
WORST: **FAMILY**

BOB HOPE (5/29/03)
DOROTHY LAMOUR (12/10/14)

Longtime friends Hope and Lamour (along with Bing Crosby) are memorable for their flirtatious performances in the 6 classic *Road to . . .* movies (1940–52), beginning with *The Road to Singapore.* Lamour also appeared on many of Hope's tv specials. *Also:* **John Gregory Dunne & Joan Didion** (married; bestselling authors).

May 25–June 2
THE WEEK OF FREEDOM
GEMINI I

December 3–10
THE WEEK OF THE ORIGINATOR
SAGITTARIUS II

Courtship Ritual

The need to understand others is crucial to this relationship. These two will be caught up in trying to figure out the morality of those around them, but perhaps their subconscious intention is to find a moral stance of their own, whether individually or together. Here we have a true meeting of equals, with mutual criticism and self-criticism playing roles in each partner's growth. The tone of the relationship is intellectual and rational, featuring analysis of each other's belief systems, or lack thereof. Sagittarius II complexity may intrigue Gemini I's, who, however, may ultimately be mystified by this partner's character; in fact, the Sagittarius II personality may become the pair's field of study. There may also be a fascination or obsession with the relationship itself, which demands understanding from its partners so that it can be nourished and grow.

Curiosity may be the force that brings Gemini I's and Sagittarius II's together. In friendships and love affairs, a growing mutual interest sparks investigation and a curious kind of courtship ritual, a dance through which they get to know each other. This organic process, proceeding in its own rhythm, will often be an indication of the relationship's health. At a certain point, it will either click or not. If it does, it may continue for years, changing and deepening; if it does not, it may simply fade away.

Marriages can work out here, often representing a positive evolution for their partners. They stand the test of time. These spouses will enjoy creating a living space together that reflects their unusual tastes. Particularly if children are involved, the marriage will be closely identified with its home base, and also with its neighborhood and social stratum. Sagittarius II's will feel accepted by Gemini I's, who in turn will be proud of their unusual mates, and inspired by their expressiveness and freethinking.

Gemini I–Sagittarius II co-workers will do better as freelancers, or perhaps as partners in a small business. Sibling and parent-child pairs are likely to be especially interested in solving the often considerable psychological problems raised by their own relationship.

ADVICE: *Don't be obsessed with yourself. Look to others for guidance. Don't anticipate or create problems. Keep curiosity in check.*

May 25–June 2

THE WEEK OF FREEDOM
GEMINI I

December 11–18

THE WEEK OF THE TITAN
SAGITTARIUS III

Unsettling Intimacy

RELATIONSHIPS

STRENGTHS: **PROTECTIVE, TRUSTING, EMPATHIC**
WEAKNESSES: **CONTRADICTORY, PUZZLING, COMPLAINING**
BEST: **LOVE**
WORST: **WORK**

This relationship is full of contradictions. Gemini I's and Sagittarius III's are often outgoing personalities, yet their relationship is earmarked to be intimate and sensitive. Further, Gemini I's are ruled by air, the element of thought, and Sagittarius III's by fire, that of intuition, yet their relationship is governed by feeling. Thus their relationship puts a wholly unexpected emphasis on their inner, emotional life. It is also changeable in nature, in a way that makes it unfathomable and in the long run unsettling to its partners.

Love and marriage in this combination may offer these gregarious individuals a protective retreat from the world, but one that is difficult for them to understand. Sagittarius III's may not be quite as confident and together here as they appear in other areas. Gemini I's sense insecurities in them almost immediately, empathizing with their hidden problems without even being told about them. Once the trust of Sagittarius III's is gained, they may come to rely on Gemini I's to discuss personal difficulties, or even just to listen to their complaints. Gemini I's can also be complainers, but Sagittarius III's may be less patient in furnishing their ear.

This pair's differences in outlook come to the fore in friendships and working relationships. Where Sagittarius III's tend to see the big picture, Gemini I's like to concentrate on the individual data of experience, one by one. Their relationship emphasizes this polarity. The more factual Gemini I and the more philosophical Sagittarius III often argue over what course to follow, but a rapprochement is not out of reach, and an integrated, versatile and productive relationship can result.

Differences in outlook are less important in family matchups. Siblings in this combination can form a soulful bond, giving intimacy and privacy the highest status. Sharing secrets and being sympathetic to each other's difficulties play prominent roles here.

DON JOHNSON (12/15/49)
PHILIP MICHAEL THOMAS (5/26/49)

Johnson and Thomas starred on tv's *Miami Vice* (1984–89), a hip detective show innovative in its use of atmosphere and music. Both were flashy dressers: Thomas' straight, clean-cut persona complemented Johnson's ultra-casual, European style.

Also: Marilyn Monroe & Frank Sinatra (affair; actress/singer).

ADVICE: *Reconcile differing points of view. Don't isolate yourselves. Develop intimacy but not dependency. Avoid giving the wrong impression.*

May 25–June 2

THE WEEK OF FREEDOM
GEMINI I

December 19–25

THE CUSP OF PROPHECY
SAGITTARIUS-CAPRICORN CUSP

Moth and Flame

RELATIONSHIPS

STRENGTHS: **EXPRESSIVE, DRAMATIC, LITERAL**
WEAKNESSES: **FROZEN, DISTANT, DISHONEST**
BEST: **FRIENDSHIP**
WORST: **LOVE**

Enigmatic in the extreme, this relationship brings out complex energies and swirling emotions quite at odds with its facade of detachment. The effort to keep up this front can make this pair become frozen, or else lock them in even more to the currents between them. When they are alone together, it is almost as though they have been sucked down to some cavernous place, womblike but without enough air.

Gemini I's are attracted to Sagittarius-Capricorns like moths to a flame. The flame is a dark one, but the flitting Gemini I nature cannot resist its smoldering intensity. The fire-earth combination in Sagittarius-Capricorns indicates a passionate nature that arouses Gemini I emotions and makes them feel alive. This is not necessarily a good feeling by any means, for a good deal of negativity can emerge here. Sagittarius-Capricorns frequently push this partner's buttons, often silently, for example, by refusing to react or respond, or by acting as if they don't understand. Gemini I's have a tendency to repeat themselves, which may be matched and perhaps stimulated by the Sagittarius-Capricorn ability to forget what they have said. Thus one could find literal Gemini I communication being constantly swallowed up or absorbed by a Sagittarius-Capricorn well of silence.

Love affairs, marriages and friendships can all involve a lot of play-acting, with each partner taking on different roles. These games are not of the healthiest sort, but they are only roles, after all, and do not represent what these two are really like. Furthermore, on the plus side, they do enable Gemini I's to vent deep feelings that they might otherwise simply ignore, and allow Sagittarius-Capricorns to come out of the shadows and into the spotlight, exhibiting a theatrical, expressive and vibrant energy.

Family and work relationships in this combination are apt to be confusing, particularly since without more intimate forms of communication, these two will probably have difficulty understanding each other.

MILES DAVIS (5/25/26)
CICELY TYSON (12/19/33)

Davis, an influential jazz trumpeter, was moody, reclusive and had a history of heroin addiction. Following a serious hip ailment in the late 70s, actress Tyson, his wife, encouraged him to make a new album, *Man with the Horn* (1981), and resume his concerts.

Also: Brigham Young & Joseph Smith (Mormon leaders).

ADVICE: *Drop the front occasionally. You don't have to act for the benefit of others. Strive for truth, not illusion. Be honest about your feelings.*

STRENGTHS: FUN, INTERESTING, CHALLENGING

WEAKNESSES: FRUSTRATING, IRRITATING, FUTILE

BEST: MARRIAGE

WORST: FAMILY

MARLENE DIETRICH (12/27/01)
JOSEF VON STERNBERG (5/29/1894)

Director von Sternberg discovered Dietrich in 1930 while looking for a lead for *The Blue Angel*. A 5-year relationship ensued, during which von Sternberg molded Dietrich's on- and off-screen *femme fatale* image. They were not thought to be romantically involved.

May 25–June 2
THE WEEK OF FREEDOM
GEMINI I

December 26–January 2
THE WEEK OF THE RULER
CAPRICORN I

Love Tango

Full of unrealities and impossibilities, this relationship has the quality of trying to catch air in a butterfly net, or drinking water out of a can with holes in it. On the surface, these two are a good match for each other: elusive, quick creatures who can evade responsibilities with maddening ease, Gemini I's might seem to be able to benefit from the company of Capricorn I's, who are masters of reality, setting boundaries and demanding observance of rules. But while they are effective in controlling their partner in other combinations, Capricorn I's simply can't get a handle on Gemini I's mercurial energies; the harder they try, the more slippery this partner becomes. Nor are Gemini I's attracted to traps, no matter how tender, so they are unlikely to let themselves be caught. They may temporarily pretend they have been caught, however, only to escape again when the careless Capricorn I gets overconfident and lax in vigilance.

In romantic relationships, the Gemini I–Capricorn I dance is a love tango in which the partners alternately catch each other and set each other free. As in a dream, realities shift quickly from the sensuous to the ethereal, from earthy to airy, from sexual to dispassionate. Emotions are as difficult to pin down as dancing partners in motion, and there are no guarantees of the outcome. In the end, however, the entire choreography is likely to resemble an exercise in frustration.

Marriages are quite uncertain, but this in itself is intriguing enough to keep freedom-loving Gemini I's and authoritative Capricorn I's from getting bored. On the outside the relationship might seem a futile search for stability, yet it can hang together mysteriously, year after year. Like an arch, the centerpiece is often held in place by gravity's downward pull on the other stones.

Friendships, family and work relationships are all both cursed and blessed by the unreality factor. Often the despair of others, the relationship is only understood by the partners involved—and then only on a good day.

ADVICE: *Hold a steady course. Try to understand each other. Are you suffering and pretending to have fun, or having fun while pretending to suffer?*

STRENGTHS: TOUGH, PRACTICAL, FRANK

WEAKNESSES: UNSYMPATHETIC, UNCOMPROMISING, ADVERSARIAL

BEST: FRIENDSHIP

WORST: LOVE

RICHARD NIXON (1/9/13)
HENRY KISSINGER (5/27/23)

Kissinger was Nixon's chief foreign-policy advisor and later secretary of state. Their professional association ran hot and cold, with Kissinger being either the man of the hour or pushed into the background. **Also: JFK & Nixon** (political rivals); **Kissinger & Terry Moore** (affair; dignitary/actress).

May 25–June 2
THE WEEK OF FREEDOM
GEMINI I

January 3–9
THE WEEK OF DETERMINATION
CAPRICORN II

A Hard Line

This relationship takes a hard line. Little need is felt here to cater to the niceties of etiquette or of polite society; formality is observed only when necessary, and no obligation is felt to be considerate of personal sensitivities or weaknesses. Indeed the relationship operates on the principle that experience is a toughening process, the ultimate education. Although the partners can feel warmly toward each other, particularly at the relationship's start, an adversarial stance may well emerge as they come to understand each other's outlooks, pulling them increasingly apart. If both partners are working toward a goal, however, as they are certainly capable of doing, the combination's toughness and practicality can achieve a lot.

Love affairs here are usually cool, no-nonsense and unemotional. Sex is dealt with frankly: the attraction is on or it is off; no attempt is made to compromise. Yet the relationship is not without romance, though a romance that may not be recognized as such by others, having a private meaning to the lovers themselves. Such relationships can develop into either marriages or friendships, but more often the partners slowly drift apart until their connection ends. Marriages between these two can be pragmatic. Capricorn II's contribute financial skills and domestic planning while Gemini I's lend a sharp eye for bargains and an aggressive instinct for furthering the family's interests. Although practicality is emphasized here, a love for beautiful objects and furnishings will lead this couple to spend time enhancing the ambiance of their home.

Friendships and work and family relationships will feature heated ideological or philosophical interchanges. The changeableness of Gemini I's will inevitably be confronted by the strong Capricorn II work ethic and stubbornness, while their finely honed critical faculties will pierce to the heart of any Capricorn II flaws. Mutual affection may offset the effects of insults and disparaging remarks. Boss-employee and parent-child relationships, in which the Capricorn II will probably play the dominant role, may exhibit pride in achievement but will rarely reach the kind of emotional understanding that allows easy exchanges to take place on a daily basis.

ADVICE: *Keep it light. Don't let yourself get too serious; don't stick stubbornly to your point of view. Break down barriers to understanding.*

May 25–June 2

THE WEEK OF FREEDOM
GEMINI I

January 10–16

THE WEEK OF DOMINANCE
CAPRICORN III

Going Through Labor

The challenge of this relationship is to promote psychological and spiritual growth. The problem is that both Gemini I's and Capricorn III's have an interest in antagonisms and struggles for power. Gemini I's are not really a match for this particular partner in this respect, but they are fighters, and their propensity not to give up may prolong any conflict. Capricorn III's are ultimately confident of their ability to dominate. Their need to be the boss is much greater than that of their partner in this combination, and if they appear to occupy a secondary position to a Gemini I boss, parent or even occasionally a spouse, this is only because they temporarily choose to do so. The relationship's struggles may seem to make mutual self-realization difficult or impossible, but conflict often serves to establish territory, to claim acknowledgment and respect for one's talents and to promote growth beyond individual differences. Between these two it may finally culminate in setting out on a more highly evolved path, either individually or as a pair.

Working through difficulties like these in love affairs, friendships and marriages is almost like going through labor in order to be born. The theme of rebirth often figures symbolically in such relationships, assuming that the two partners have enough interest and stamina to hang in there until the process is completed. Gemini I's sometimes opt out when the going gets rough, but their need for Capricorn III affection or sexual interaction can hold them magnetically. Capricorn III's are much less needy, but may find Gemini I's eminently entertaining to have around, and energetic and enthusiastic lovers.

Working and family relationships here are only favorable if they feature mutual respect. Otherwise, Capricorn III bosses or parents are unlikely to take Gemini I employees or children seriously, and vice versa. The more natural condition is for Capricorn III to play the dominant role, since Gemini I authority figures will probably find themselves at a loss trying to keep their Capricorn III subordinates in line. But roles that fit this pattern too closely may inhibit personal growth.

ADVICE: *Take each other seriously. Respect for ability is key. Work through difficulties to find your own path. Promote cooperation.*

WYNONNA JUDD (5/30/64)
NAOMI JUDD (1/11/46)

After years of hard work, this mother and daughter country-music duo rose to fame in the mid-80s. Together they won 5 Grammys. In 1991, Naomi retired, but Wynonna went on to even greater success.

Also: Isadora Duncan & Craig Gordon (affair; dancer/stage designer); **JFK & Judith Campbell** (affair; president/mistress).

May 25–June 2

THE WEEK OF FREEDOM
GEMINI I

January 17–22

THE CUSP OF MYSTERY & IMAGINATION
CAPRICORN-AQUARIUS CUSP

The Perfect Work of Art

This can be a wild and wacky combination. A thirst for excitement characterizes the relationship, but so does a longing to achieve something of lasting value. There is an affirmation and celebration of creativity here, whether in fine art, literature, music, film—in short, a cherishing of any great work that transcends its time. This love of the classic suggests that the relationship puts a high value on perfection. The perfect artwork would be an apt symbol for what it holds most dear, but it also values people, living situations and, of course, relationships, which it subjects to the same high standards of scrutiny with which it treats art. Unfortunately, this means that the Gemini I–Capricorn-Aquarius relationship itself is likely to fall victim to its own demands.

In love affairs, both partners may find it hard to live up to the demands of perfection and continuity. Both Gemini I's and Capricorn-Aquarians have an impulsive and freedom-loving side that detests being bound to set routines or expectations. They may find each other endlessly challenging and changing, however, and in their encounters discover a kind of lasting, albeit kaleidoscopic, ideal.

Marriages can also be fascinating. Should children enter the picture, a predictable danger, of course, is that they too will be forced to fit the perfection model. Prestige and social pressures are less of a problem here, since the relationship has its own strong value system, but friends and family may be needed as watchdogs to see that oppressive and stultifying influences do not get out of hand.

Friendships and work relationships, which may be combined, capitalize on this combination's high energy level and occasionally bizarre tastes. Interesting and even absorbing in the extreme, the pair will attract others both socially and financially, promoting their own interests without a great deal of effort. It will probably be necessary for them to learn to relax their standards of expectation a bit while at the same time intensifying their work efforts. In the family, sibling matchups tend to be wild and uncontrollable.

ADVICE: *Calm frenetic energies. Relax expectations. Perfection can be a tyranny. Take things as they are and as they come. The ordinary can be beautiful.*

DUNCAN GRANT (1/21/1885)
VANESSA STEPHEN BELL (5/30/1879)

Artists Grant and Bell were part of the Bloomsbury group in the early 1900s. Along with Bell's husband, critic Clive Bell, the 3 lived together. Grant, a homosexual, fathered Bell's daughter, Angelica (who was not told Grant was her father till she was 17). Vanessa was possessive of Grant, jealous of his male lovers.

Also: John Emerson & D.W. Griffith (director/producer).

RELATIONSHIPS

STRENGTHS: UNCOMPLICATED, QUICK, FUN

WEAKNESSES: UNSTABLE, IRRESPONSIBLE, STRESSED

BEST: COMPANIONSHIP

WORST: MARRIAGE

ELLEN DeGENERES (1/26/58)
ANNE HECHE (5/25/69)

In 1997 DeGeneres, star of tv's *Ellen*, announced via *Time* magazine and a Barbara Walters interview that she is a lesbian. Simultaneously, her character on *Ellen* "came out" to a prime-time audience of millions; she was romantically involved with fast-rising actress Heche, who appeared in the Al Pacino film *Donnie Brasco* (1997). **Also: Prince Rainier & Princess Caroline** (father/daughter; Monaco royalty).

May 25–June 2

THE WEEK OF FREEDOM
GEMINI I

January 23–30

THE WEEK OF GENIUS
AQUARIUS I

Soufflé, Olé!

Light, quick, uncomplicated—these are the watchwords of the Gemini I–Aquarius I relationship. Because these two positions are at a trine aspect to each other (120° apart) in the zodiac, traditional astrology predicts an easy relationship between them, and is in this case perfectly correct—but not entirely complete. For the relationship between these two air signs is itself ruled by fire, indicating how explosive and unstable the combination can become. Neither Gemini I's nor Aquarius I's are the most responsible people in the world, after all, a tendency magnified when they combine. They may have trouble paying bills on time, being punctual, feeding the kids or the dog and in general keeping daily life together. Furthermore, any desire for this relationship to reach a deeper emotional level will be unfulfilled.

Love and marriages are best kept as free of responsibilities as possible: these two may decide not to have children, not to own a house, not to get tied down to a strict schedule. Freedom is key here, which means that there may be little to hold the relationship together in times of intense need and stress. The couple's attitude is that such times are not what they came together for, and if things are going badly—well, it may be time to look for a new partner. Like a good contract, their relationship leaves a lot of open exit doors, so that they avoid the feeling of being trapped.

Deep friendships and family relationships are probably neither possible nor desired, but companionships and acquaintanceships built around pleasurable activities are probably a good bet. Shared activities are the hallmark here and will be quite enjoyable. These are sociable relationships, often widening to include other people—for example, other family members—in vacation or picnic plans. Working relationships similarly often involve shared friends, family members, and friends of friends and family members. Small-business and freelance enterprises that allow maximum freedom and minimum responsibility are favored—these two can easily get frazzled and stressed out.

ADVICE: *Dig a bit deeper. Taking on responsibilities will give you more stability. Plan a bit ahead. Face the fact that stress happens. Slow down a bit.*

RELATIONSHIPS

STRENGTHS: INVOLVED, SOCIAL, PROUD

WEAKNESSES: ISOLATED, DEPENDENT, STRESSED

BEST: FAMILY

WORST: WORK

QUEEN ANNE (2/6/1665)
SARAH CHURCHILL (5/29/1660)

When Anne became queen in 1702, she granted Sarah top court appointments, but Sarah's willfulness and political intrigues led to her dismissal in 1711. **Also: Charles II & Nell Gwynne** (king/mistress); **John Wayne & John Ford** (actor/director); **Lisa Hartman & Clint Black** (married; actress/country music star); **John Hinckley & Pres. Reagan** (attempted assassination).

May 25–June 2

THE WEEK OF FREEDOM
GEMINI I

January 31–February 7

THE WEEK OF YOUTH & EASE
AQUARIUS II

A Social Contract

Social interaction is this relationship's specialty. Directed out toward the world, and particularly concerned with establishing links between their own social or family group and a wider public, this pair can act as a kind of group representative, working to bring people and groups of people together and strengthen social ties. In short, these two are the ultimate networkers.

Even love relationships between Gemini I's and Aquarius II's are rarely isolated. Together they enjoy sharing with others the warmth and good feelings of their own relationship. This is not to imply a lack of intimacy—affection and love are prominent with this couple—but there is a need here, particularly on the part of the Aquarius II, to be appreciated by more than just their partner. The approval and appreciation of family and friends is quite important, then, and its absence may weaken the relationship.

Marriages in this combination are true social contracts. Family, friends, children, even co-workers are made welcome in the Gemini I–Aquarius II home. Feelings of fellowship and conviviality receive a high priority. But Gemini I's may need this kind of socializing a little less than their gracious partner, unfortunately, and may come to resent having to open their doors at all hours. Should this become a bone of contention between the two, somewhat crusty Gemini I's are likely to withdraw to their workroom, garage or bedroom and refuse to come out.

Friendships here are easy and of the no-hassle variety. The drawback is that they may be fair-weather choices, which may not survive even a moderately stressful period. By serving as a strong support group here, other friends and family may help preserve the relationship, providing the persistence that the combination itself does not. Gemini I–Aquarius II family and working relationships are often successful, but only within a firm social context. Should colleagues or co-workers become cut off or isolated from others, the relationship is likely to show tremendous strain and ultimately to break down.

ADVICE: *Don't depend so much on the presence of others. Learn to work alone. Approval isn't really so important. Find value within yourself.*

May 25–June 2

THE WEEK OF FREEDOM
GEMINI I

February 8–15

THE WEEK OF ACCEPTANCE
AQUARIUS III

RELATIONSHIPS

STRENGTHS: LOVING,
ACCEPTING, ACCOMMODATING
WEAKNESSES: NEEDY,
CRITICAL, REJECTING
BEST: PARTNERSHIP
WORST: LOVE

Taking Bows Together

Gemini I's and Aquarius III's tend to compete for attention. Although they are attracted to each other, their relationship can be torn apart if they both depend on the recognition of a third party. Should they totally accept and feel fully appreciated by each other, their competition may abate, but it will rarely disappear. Another scenario is that their relationship may become recognized as an important entity in itself, so that they occupy the spotlight and take their bows together, usually in business, sports or the arts.

In an affair, these partners are likely to be crazy in love at first, but may end up feeling rejected and dejected. It is not absolutely clear how the downward spiral begins, but it may start with the kind of picky criticisms of which Gemini I's are capable. If the more accepting Aquarius III is not strong enough to check it, this habit can reach the point of being intolerable. Aquarius III insecurities will begin to emerge, and trust will gradually be withdrawn. Meanwhile, Gemini I's may be quite unaware of the catastrophic effect they are having on the relationship.

Judgmental Gemini I attitudes are also likely to surface in marriages and friendships. They sometimes involve the need to be boss that Gemini I's often show in this combination—Aquarius III's frequently take a back seat, at least emotionally, to these vigorously assertive individuals. Aquarius III spouses and friends will go a long way to accommodate Gemini I partners, but sooner or later will reach the limits of patience and acceptance. It is sometimes only when they withdraw their affection, or transfer it to another, that Gemini I's begin to wake up and realize what they have lost.

In the family and at work, Aquarius III's and Gemini I's are quite capable of taking what they have for granted. They tend to see their relationship as something that has always been there and always will be, a deadly assumption. Needs and wants can change over the years; these partners must monitor their relationship to be sure that it is functioning effectively, and then adjust and compromise accordingly.

ADVICE: *Keep track of what is going on. Be sensitive to telltale signs. Don't take things for granted. Work to improve relations. Think constructively.*

JOAN MITCHELL (2/12/26)
BARNEY ROSSET (5/28/22)

Rosset was a pioneering publisher of key literary works from the 50s on. He founded Grove Press and *Evergreen Review*. In '47 he married noted American artist Mitchell, a member of the 2nd generation of abstract impressionists. They divorced in '52.
Also: Tom Mankiewicz & Joseph Mankiewicz (son/father; screenwriter-directors).

May 25–June 2

THE WEEK OF FREEDOM
GEMINI I

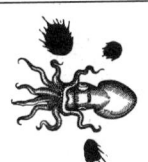

February 16–22

THE CUSP OF SENSITIVITY
AQUARIUS-PISCES CUSP

RELATIONSHIPS

STRENGTHS: IMAGINATIVE,
INNOVATIVE, STIMULATING
WEAKNESSES: MISUNDERSTOOD,
STRANGE, OVERAGGRESSIVE
BEST: FRIENDSHIP
WORST: CO-WORKER

Dramatic Impulses

This relationship brings out the flamboyant side of both personalities, especially when they are engaged together in furthering their joint ambitions. Success is important to them, but only if it can be achieved with a certain style. Image obviously matters to this pair; what is less obvious is the importance of quality work. They will struggle hard to achieve their standard of excellence, while making it look like they are doing is easy.

Aquarius-Pisces are sensitive but have a worldly side that Gemini I's stimulate, rousing them from their psychological or physical retreat and urging them outward. Gemini I–Aquarius-Pisces energy can be aggressive, operating effectively in business, sports or the creative arts. Meanwhile, in personal relationships, Aquarius-Pisces can also stimulate a Gemini I's sensitive side, encouraging introspection and meditation.

This latter influence is felt in love, friendship and marriage. Self-exploration is an important theme here: the couple may spend long periods in intimate settings, exploring private sides of their characters together. This is not easy for them, as they may not be really trusting of the other at a deep level, but they do usually try—in fact they work on the relationship as hard as they work on anything else. The main thrust here, however, is outward. Dramatic and theatrical impulses may characterize the pair's public appearances; the emotional sharing that precedes these vivid displays may give them a basis without which they might seem to be false or empty posturing. Friends and family will find this couple stimulating but a trifle strange.

Family relationships between these two are often protective but dynamic, especially with siblings of the same sex. Parent-child relationships are problematic, often featuring power struggles and misunderstandings; a relationship in this combination between a child and a different relative may be more accepting, and a stronger positive force in early years. At work these partners are often imaginative and innovative. If they are co-workers, these talents may disturb those around them, but at a company's executive level, or in a partnership, their full force will be manifested, and will often bring success.

ADVICE: *Be aware of disturbing others' feelings. Spend more time alone. Proceed on your path of self-discovery. Keep aggression under control.*

MARTHA WASHINGTON (6/2/1731)
GEORGE WASHINGTON (2/22/1732)

In 1789, Martha became America's first First Lady, a role she hated. While George reveled in the admiration of others, Martha reluctantly performed her social duties. **Also: Dixie Carter & Hal Holbrook** (married; actors); **Sharon Gless & Tyne Daly** (co-stars, *Cagney & Lacey*); **H.H. Humphrey & Muriel Humphrey** (married; politicians); **Al Unser & Bobby Unser** (brothers; auto racers).

RON HOWARD (3/1/54)
ANDY GRIFFITH (6/1/26)

Howard, the child actor who played cute little Opie on tv's popular *Andy Griffith Show* (1960–68), got an early start in acting playing opposite Griffith as his widowed dad, Andy Taylor, Mayberry's respected sheriff. ***Also: King George I & George Frideric Handel*** (patron/composer); **Giovanni Gentile & Benedetto Croce** (Italian fascist/anti-fascist).

May 25–June 2
THE WEEK OF FREEDOM
GEMINI I

February 23–March 2
THE WEEK OF SPIRIT
PISCES I

Personal Challenge

The main thrust of this relationship is likely to be toward self-development, particularly of the cultural and spiritual variety. Although traditional astrology predicts conflict for these two, given their square aspect in the zodiac (where they lie 90° apart), this kind of friction is often stimulating, and leads to a positive result. Gemini I's are not overly introspective, and in their frenetic world a relationship with a more sensitive Pisces I is likely to prove a calm and soothing retreat. Pisces I's are inevitably put in the position of teacher, not so much imparting information as gently showing Gemini I's by example how to develop the deepest parts of their personality constructively. The Pisces I will inevitably also grow through such a process, and the relationship itself tends to be self-actualizing.

In love affairs, these two usually exhibit great sensitivity to each other's needs. These relationships tend to be highly private—the inner growth they manifest is not for the world's scrutiny. Affection and pleasure are certainly part of such a relationship, but its principal value is educational, possibly of a spiritual kind, and especially for a Gemini I who has not previously been exposed to the influences or sensibilities typical of a Pisces I. Such relationships, however, may put great strain on Pisces I's, who may find their partner demanding and lacking in concentration, a trait that tends to make Pisces I's nervous.

Marriages here may affiliate themselves with a religious, spiritual or cultural group, which can become an important source of stability. Should this bond become too strong, however, and should it end in disillusionment, it may lead to extreme upset, often resulting in separation or divorce. Parents must beware of forcing religious or spiritual ideas or rituals on their children, ultimately encouraging rebellion.

Gemini I–Pisces I friendships and family and working relationships tend to be exclusive, often arousing animosity or jealousy in other people. The pair will have to develop their diplomatic skills if they are to avoid conflict.

ADVICE: *Don't close yourself off from people. Others may view your belief as conceit. Don't be self-satisfied. Strive for what is best in you.*

ALEXANDER GRAHAM BELL (3/3/1847)
DON AMECHE (5/31/08)

Known most recently for his 1985 Oscar performance in *Cocoon*, Ameche was a popular star in the 30s and 40s, best remembered for his entertaining lead-role interpretation in *The Story of Alexander Graham Bell* (1939). He died in 1993. ***Also: Peter Carl Fabergé & Czar Alexander III*** (czar commissioned jeweler to create famous Easter eggs for czarina).

May 25–June 2
THE WEEK OF FREEDOM
GEMINI I

March 3–10
THE WEEK OF THE LONER
PISCES II

A Thought/Feeling Split

This relationship would be expected to exhibit a polarization between emotion and logic. Pisces II's (ruled by the element water, which symbolizes feeling) and Gemini I's (ruled by air, which represents thought) are here brought together in a relationship in which such extremes rarely meld harmoniously, although things may go well for periods of time. The duo's real strength, and its greatest challenge, is the ability to combine their strengths so that they can meet crises with a compassionate yet commonsense point of view.

Love relationships here are rare. Their success depends on whether speedy Gemini I's can be sensitive and understanding enough of their slower Pisces I partners. The polarization of emotion and thought here can ultimately prove destructive to the relationship's chances for success. Marriages demand more unity, and domestic obligations will often both tie freedom-loving Gemini I's to fixed responsibilities and force Pisces II's to fulfill social roles sometimes that they would rather ignore. In the best-case scenario, although some inconvenience and even resentment may surface, compromise is possible.

Friends in this combination can be extremely understanding of the problems of other people, and their emotional intelligence as a pair often attracts others in need of psychological support or advice. In rare cases it is even possible for them to put this talent to professional use. Friendships do not arouse strong emotions, and the increased objectivity improves the matchup's atmosphere. Tendencies on the part of Gemini I's toward selfishness and of Pisces II's to self-pity will have to be dealt with, however, or they will undermine the relationship.

Working relationships on the job are not favored here, but freelance enterprises combining Pisces II imagination and Gemini I forcefulness can succeed. Family relationships, on the other hand, are difficult, especially parent-child matchups of the same sex. All kinds of conflicts emerge here, often due to extreme Pisces II sensitivity and need to be understood and Gemini I inability to do so. A rapprochement can be effected later in life, but Gemini I inconsiderateness and Pisces II resentment may remain insoluble problems.

ADVICE: *Have you really tried to understand? Look outside your own world. Pay attention to the needs of others. Calm your nerves and center yourself.*

May 25–June 2

THE WEEK OF FREEDOM
GEMINI I

March 11–18

THE WEEK OF DANCERS & DREAMERS
PISCES III

RELATIONSHIPS

STRENGTHS: **POWERFUL,
CONVINCING, EFFECTIVE**

WEAKNESSES: **UPSETTING,
ARGUMENTATIVE, OMNISCIENT**

BEST: **FRIENDSHIP**

WORST: **LOVE**

Displays of Temperament

If both partners are set on the same goal, this relationship is next to unstoppable. The secret is the pair's ability to think strategically, to plan and to wait for the perfect moment to act—so long, that is, as they are acting together. Separately, Gemini I's and Pisces III's lack these talents, and are actually somewhat out of touch with reality. The greatest challenge they face, however, will be their ability to get along on a daily basis. Irritation and dissatisfaction will often surface between them, and should the relationship develop into a power struggle, they are likely to tear it apart. Each partner's near-omniscient streak makes argument inevitable. If the relationship is characterized by a know-it-all attitude, it may become off-putting to friends and family, alienating those forced to listen to it.

Gemini I–Pisces III love affairs are not recommended. They tend to be contentious and exhibitionistic, and to include a range of emotional expression that is full but that leans to the negative variety. Outsiders sometimes get the idea that a fight is being staged for their benefit, and indeed this couple may secretly enjoy public displays of temperament. The power to upset each other and others is a constant temptation, and until the partners learn the value of moderation, passionate reconciliations are about the best they can expect.

When not arguing, Gemini I's and Pisces III's are remarkably well suited to each other as mates and friends, and can share many interests and activities. Should they have children, it will become essential for them to tone down their confrontations, which can induce nervous, neurotic and imitative behavior patterns in the young. What makes Gemini I–Pisces III work combinations so powerfully effective, despite their instabilities, is shrewd business sense and understanding of human nature. Running a business together or working as part of a project team takes the spotlight off personal conflicts and directs energies toward a common goal. Parent-child relationships here are stormy but also loving, particularly between fathers and daughters, mothers and sons. Brother-sister relationships can be especially close and understanding.

ADVICE: *Try to mute dissent. Turn arguments into conversations. Learn to compromise and back off. Relinquish omniscient attitudes.*

JAMES ARNESS (5/26/23)
PETER GRAVES (3/18/26)

Former screen actors, both brothers became stars of long-running tv series. Arness played the affable Marshal Dillon on *Gunsmoke* (1955–75). Graves headed the IMF team on *Mission: Impossible* (1966–73).

Also: **Bennett Cerf & Sylvia Beach** (pioneering publishers of Joyce's *Ulysses* in US & France).

June 3–10

THE WEEK OF NEW LANGUAGE
GEMINI II

June 3–10

THE WEEK OF NEW LANGUAGE
GEMINI II

RELATIONSHIPS

STRENGTHS: **VERBAL,
COMMUNICATIVE, FUN**

WEAKNESSES: **GARRULOUS,
MISUNDERSTOOD, BOTHERING**

BEST: **FRIENDSHIP**

WORST: **FAMILY**

Heavy Verbal Traffic

Verbal traffic is at an all-time high between these two communicators. Being together gives them the green light, and they are likely to shift into high gear fast. One danger is that the stream of words may eventually become no more than a hum or buzz. Another is that these motor mouths' mutual love of debating can take over the relationship, creating a win-at-all-costs attitude. The question is: Do they talk to each other or at each other? Listening is a challenge here, and listening is at least half of the communicative process. Furthermore, since both of these Gemini II's have their own, highly individual language, comprehension between them may not at first be high. Should the relationship gel, they may create their own private language, communicating with each other easily but having difficulty being understood by others.

If lovers in this combination want to deepen their relationship, they must try to put aside language in favor of physical, emotional and even spiritual communication. Nothing will more quickly put a damper on ecstatic sexual or romantic experiences than talking them to death, or analyzing them—either during or after. Marriages are likely to be hectic, even frenetic or, occasionally, hysterical. Gemini II's pay attention to details, and there are usually enough of these needing attention around the house to keep them busy for years. Should a mutual preoccupation with trivia prevail, the marriage may approach the obsessional and neurotic. Worry and anxiety are enemies here.

Friendships and work relationships may alleviate stress by objectifying emotions and putting the emphasis respectively on fun-filled activities and on getting the job done. But stress will increase enormously when problems arise or quotas and deadlines are not met, and the question is whether the relationship will have the resources to hang in there and cope with it. Gemini II verbal skills can sometimes be put to use solving this problem and planning for the future. Within the family, if the Gemini II stream of language is not well directed, endless debates, fights and misunderstandings are likely to occur.

ADVICE: *Practice listening. Find a quiet place inside, for example by practicing meditation. Learn to turn off the motor. Make a greater effort to be understood.*

CZARINA ALEXANDRA (6/6/1872)
DUCHESS TATIANA (6/10/1897)

Alexandra, granddaughter of Queen Victoria, was Nicholas II's wife and the mother of Tatiana. Alexandra meddled disastrously in politics, encouraging her husband's reactionary policies. In 1918 she and her family, including Nicholas, were imprisoned and then executed by Bolshevik revolutionaries.

Also: **Federico García Lorca & Dante Alighieri** (poets share same birthday).

STRENGTHS: **LIVELY, METICULOUS, EXPANSIVE**

WEAKNESSES: **UNSTABLE, JUDGMENTAL, UNCONTROLLED**

BEST: **WORK**

WORST: **FRIENDSHIP**

BARBARA BUSH (6/8/25)
GEORGE BUSH (6/12/24)

George was 20 and Barbara 19 when they married in 1944. Over the years Barbara has been the fulcrum of the family as well as an asset to her husband during his campaigns and presidency. The couple has 6 children. **Also:**

Judy Garland & David Rose (married; star/songwriter-conductor).

June 3–10
THE WEEK OF NEW LANGUAGE
GEMINI II

June 11–18
THE WEEK OF THE SEEKER
GEMINI III

The Details of the Big Picture

A lively and original relationship can spring up between these two. Their thinking begins with a love for details but steadily develops to encompass the larger line and the bigger picture. They may quite possibly engage in expansive entrepreneurial or social enterprises together, ambitiously plumbing uncharted waters. But if the relationship's feeling for adventure and excitement is not counterbalanced by a focus on security and dependability, the best-laid plans may dissolve into thin air.

Love affairs between these two are likely to be exciting but somewhat unstable. Sexual energy runs high, but romantic feelings alone are usually not enough to hold the relationship together for these two can be pretty cool customers who know what they want. Sharing activities of all sorts, but especially those involving communication, are essential if the affair is to proceed further. Should Gemini II's and Gemini III's marry, they will probably have precise plans for their home, children (if any), neighborhood, career, vacations and so forth.

Friendships can suffer a split in attitude—Gemini II's enjoy talking about things while Gemini III's prefer doing them. As a result, Gemini II's may see Gemini III's as a bit rash, uncontrolled and insufficiently thoughtful, and in return may find that their partner thinks of them as all talk, no action. Both work and family relationships will benefit from engagement in shared projects. These two travel well together, and can make an eloquent case for a company or family group. Presentation is a strong point with them, and they will pay close attention to image—clothing, personal hygiene, makeup, perfume, everything is covered down to the last detail. Parent-child and boss-employee relations may be particularly favorable, lacking resentment or rebellion, although healthy competition is to be expected among co-workers and siblings.

ADVICE: *Let up in judgmental attitudes. Not everything has to be under control. Let things take their course. Don't just talk—act!*

STRENGTHS: **INVESTIGATIVE, SUPPORTIVE, UNDERSTANDING**

WEAKNESSES: **CLAIMING, OVERPROTECTIVE, ISOLATED**

BEST: **MARRIAGE**

WORST: **WORK**

TRACY POLLAN (6/22/60)
MICHAEL J. FOX (6/9/61)

Fox rose to stardom in the tv sitcom *Family Ties* (1982–89). Pollan, who played his girlfriend, is Fox's real-life spouse. They share a farm in Vermont. **Also: Gordon Waller & Peter Asher** (singers Peter & Gordon); **Paulette Goddard & Erich Maria Remarque** (married; actress/writer); **Les Paul & Chet Atkins** (musical collaborators); **Charles & Maurice Saatchi** (brothers; ad agency partners).

June 3–10
THE WEEK OF NEW LANGUAGE
GEMINI II

June 19–24
THE CUSP OF MAGIC
GEMINI-CANCER CUSP

Richer Understanding

This relationship often involves a search for self. Questions about identity, fulfillment and the soul will predominate here, with the partners not only sharing their personal journeys but pondering their relationship as it deepens and grows. Although they may seek external goals, their relationship is more likely to try to deepen itself through inner exploration, plumbing psychological, emotional and perhaps spiritual realms. Gemini II's have a shadow side that longs for understanding; being good and sympathetic listeners, Gemini-Cancers are just the people to counter their fear of looking foolish and to help them to know themselves. The emphasis on inner growth here is also just the ticket for thoughtful and profound Gemini-Cancers, who will benefit from the enthusiasm of Gemini II's and from their ability to share ideas and information.

Love affairs are likely to center around both partners' need to be understood and accepted. Gemini-Cancers often know a good deal about themselves, but Gemini II's will often need a better understanding of themselves, especially their suppressed dark side, before the relationship really begins to develop. A complex process is often at work here: investigation of each partner's individual personality can broaden into a richer understanding not only of the relationship but of other people, even of life itself. Expressing love and intimacy is the reward of such a process. Marriages continue the evolution of these affairs. At first, Gemini II's are likely to back off from a long-term commitment—Cancer-Geminis will have to show patience and steadfastness here. Once the commitment is made, however, Gemini II's are devoted and dedicated spouses.

Gemini II–Gemini-Cancer friendships are more externally oriented. A love of nature may prompt this pair to explore beautiful countryside or simply to take walks in city parks. Peaceful relaxation together is also part of the picture. Work relationships are unlikely to be dynamic when they involve repetitive tasks and well-defined goals, but more inspirational endeavors may stimulate higher energy levels. Parent-child relationships can be accepting and nurturing, but overprotectiveness and dependency may inhibit growth.

ADVICE: *Deepen the process of understanding. Don't cut yourself off from the world. Stay physically active. Allow for individuality.*

June 3–10

THE WEEK OF NEW LANGUAGE
GEMINI II

June 25–July 2

THE WEEK OF THE EMPATH
CANCER I

  RELATIONSHIPS

STRENGTHS: **MAGNETIC,
COMMUNICATIVE, TECHNICAL**

WEAKNESSES: **UNFOCUSED,
FANCIFUL, JEALOUS**

BEST: **FAMILY**

WORST: **LOVE**

Drifting Off on a Cloud

Magnetic attractions can manifest between these highly different personalities. The focus here is often unrealistic, however, featuring grandiose schemes or plans and visions of idyllic futures. This pair could easily embark on the proverbial wild goose chase together. Part of the problem is a deep need to communicate, yet Gemini II's and Cancer I's have such different styles that the only time they seem to meet is when dreaming, predicting or prophesying. In fact, they could easily squander a lot of money running to mediums, channelers, tarot readers or other types of psychics.

Cancer I's are feeling types, but their mental faculties are often stimulated by a verbal and intelligent Gemini II. They may often be frustrated by Gemini II indirectness, but ultimately they are up to the task of learning this partner's language. Gemini II's for their part will benefit from this relationship's characteristic kind of communication, which occurs on a nonverbal, often emotional level. Sharing strengths is an important dynamic here.

Love affairs and marriages are not particularly recommended. Assuming there is a physical attraction, romantic feelings are likely to develop quickly, then just as quickly dissolve away. Relationships of these kinds usually lack a firm basis, sexual or otherwise. The couple are quite capable of drifting and dreaming together, and of enjoying an easily shared affection, but unless painful problems arise that challenge this relaxed stance, their relationship rarely goes deep. Friendships and family relationships are generally much more successful. A broad spectrum of emotions may be expressed here, and the pair's conversation and interaction will range from the most humorous to the most serious. Family members may be close friends, friends may assume the status of family. Work relationships too may be favorable, as long as subjective elements do not intrude. Both partners often have a knack for technical matters, allowing them to deal with serious problems as they arise. Well-defined daily tasks will give this duo structure and direction, while entrepreneurial endeavors may become fanciful and lose touch with financial realities.

ADVICE: *Try to stay grounded. Hard work helps to keep you in the present moment. Fight the tendency to focus too much on the future. Face problems and solve them.*

PRINCE PHILIP (6/10/21)
LADY DIANA (7/1/61)

When Prince Charles was courting Diana, Philip worried about his son's "dithering" and urged him to propose or end the relationship. Philip was delighted when Di agreed to marry Charles. Throughout the troubled marriage, Philip was sympathetic toward Diana, but during the separation and divorce he sided with his son. *Also:* **William Kunstler & Stokely Carmichael** (lawyer/defendant).

June 3–10

THE WEEK OF NEW LANGUAGE
GEMINI II

July 3–10

THE WEEK OF THE UNCONVENTIONAL
CANCER II

 RELATIONSHIPS

STRENGTHS: **IMAGINATIVE,
MAGICAL, PLAYFUL**

WEAKNESSES: **IMPRACTICAL,
UNSTABLE, BEWILDERED**

BEST: **FRIENDSHIP**

WORST: **MARRIAGE**

An Aura of Wonderment

This combination has a magical quality that can provide inspiration and light to each partner. Discussions will be lively, but an underlying emotional sensitivity can keep them from becoming combative or wounding—the relationship brings out caring attitudes. Its richness in fantasy can make it great fun but also unrealistic or unstable in the long run. Gemini II's should enjoy the lively imagination and sense of humor of Cancer II's but may not care to have financial dealings with them. Cancer II's will probably find elements of the Gemini II personality exciting but may ultimately judge this partner too critical and conventional. Both partners have a dark side that they rarely, if ever, share with others. Should they reveal themselves to each other, they might find a sense of wonder here.

Romantic relationships may manifest as a short fling, in which case vivid memories and perhaps some disappointment or bewilderment are the best and worst to be expected. If a Cancer II becomes obsessed with a Gemini II who is only interested in temporary pleasure, however, hurt will ensue. Gemini II's don't like being chased, and the Cancer II's unrequited love may become a frustrating, even humiliating experience.

Marriage and work combinations may not be advisable: these two are not a practical team. Both of them have an unrealistic side, which coalesces in their relationship and threatens to undermine most of their financial and technical endeavors. Although Gemini II–Cancer II homes are sometimes vividly decorated, the habit of paying for furniture and other household goods by stretching credit up to and beyond the limit does not bode well for family solvency. Friendships and family relationships can work out best in this combination. As friends or siblings, these two can build a magical world for themselves. The simplest activities can feel inspiring, being infused with innovative sparkle. Play in its most basic sense is brought to the level of a fine art here. Separately these two often lack the capacity to share with others; onlookers may not believe it when they see them playing together with such attention and abandon.

ADVICE: *Try to be objective. Don't overextend yourself financially. Take things as they come, without expectations. Keep your self-respect.*

TONY CURTIS (6/3/25)
JANET LEIGH (7/6/27)

Married from 1951–62, Curtis and Leigh became darlings of the print media and co-starred in 3 movies. Their daughter is actress Jamie Lee Curtis. *Also:* **Les Paul & Mary Ford** (married; guitarist/ singer); **Ruth Benedict & Franz Boas** (colleagues; anthropologists); **Happy & Nelson Rockefeller** (married); **Empress Carlota & Emperor Maximilian** (married; Mexican rulers).

STRENGTHS: **FORWARD-LOOKING, PRACTICAL, PRODUCTIVE**

WEAKNESSES: **AUTHORITARIAN, UNCOMMUNICATIVE, CRIPPLING**

BEST: **WORK**

WORST: **SIBLING**

HUME CRONYN (7/18/11)
JESSICA TANDY (6/7/09)

One of the closest and most durable couples in show business, Tandy and Cronyn were married from 1942 until Tandy's death in 1994. They appeared together in 4 Broadway plays as well as in the movies *Cocoon* (1985) and *Batteries Not Included* (1987).

June 3–10
THE WEEK OF NEW LANGUAGE
GEMINI II

July 11–18
THE WEEK OF THE PERSUADER
CANCER III

Back on Track

Life direction is a powerful theme for these partners, who seem to have an instinctive psychic link that enables each to understand exactly where the other is in his or her life's journey. Yet they are oddly detached—maintaining their boundaries, they keep a watchful eye on each other from a certain distance. Should one of them veer off course, the other will step in to help. Both have a practical side that their relationship brings out. Authoritarian attitudes should be guarded against here but are sometimes necessary in planning for the future. The pair may find themselves acting out their relationship in the public eye. If well directed and acting in consort, they are capable of steady progress together.

Love affairs and marriages may be affected by Cancer III attempts at dominance. Gemini II's will generally go along with beneficial ideas that lead to greater security, but they want their opinions to be taken into account and are adept at evading a Cancer III's grasp. The couple may have problems in communication: Cancer III's won't always understand a Gemini II's often far-out ideas. And if difficulties arise on the physical or sexual plane, as they may, it will be difficult for the couple to sit down and talk about them. Gemini II's have difficulty getting in touch with their feelings, and Cancer III's, although more sensitive in this area, may be reluctant to discuss private matters.

Work relationships can be excellent here, especially when the Cancer III is boss, giving direction to the highly original suggestions of a Gemini II employee. The pair will have a lot of respect for each other. As co-workers, however, they may have difficulty sustaining a demanding project, since both are likely to grow nervous as deadlines approach. Cancer III's can make caring and nurturing parents for their talented Gemini II children, both allowing them space and supporting them. Sibling relationships, particularly same-sex ones, can feature power struggles and argumentativeness, especially at family gatherings or other public affairs. Friendships in this combination are often forward-looking, egging their social circle on to new initiatives.

ADVICE: *Respect a need for direction and authority. Be more cooperative with the leader. Calm your nerves. Take the time to explain yourself.*

STRENGTHS: **EMPATHIC, ENERGETIC, INNOVATIVE**

WEAKNESSES: **OVERSENSITIVE, NERVOUS, UNSTABLE**

BEST: **LOVE**

WORST: **WORK**

ILIE NASTASE (7/19/46)
BJORN BORG (6/6/56)

Nastase and Borg were fierce tennis rivals in the early 70s, when the intense Swede was rising to dominance and the temperamental Romanian was ending his reign as #1 (1972–73). Their biggest match was at Wimbledon (1976), when Borg defeated Nastase on his way to the #1 spot (1978–80).

Also: Paul Gauguin & Edgar Degas (French Impressionists).

June 3–10
THE WEEK OF NEW LANGUAGE
GEMINI II

July 19–25
THE CUSP OF OSCILLATION
CANCER-LEO CUSP

Own Worst Enemy

The emotional side of this relationship is prominent—these partners have the ability to reach a deep level of understanding. "Empath" is the keyword here, signifying a kind of merger or blending of personalities, both for better and for worse. Both Gemini II and Cancer-Leo unfortunately have a nervous and unstable side that is reinforced in their combination, undermining interactions between them. There is usually no end to the energy, enthusiasm, innovation or salesmanship of this relationship, or to its ability to face challenges, no matter how dangerous, but it also generates such erratic, even frenzied energies that it becomes its own worst enemy.

Romance between these two can be passionate and exciting, carrying both partners away. When they return from the trip, however, they may see the relationship in an entirely different light. Travel, fashion, style, art and music are highly valued, and the ability to share in these areas is considerable. Creative or business activities between lovers are not unusual.

In marriage the matchup is likely to lose a lot of its spark. Predictable routines and responsible handling of tasks are not what this relationship is about at all. In a curious way, though, bad marriages may be more successful than good ones, since problems, imbalance and insecurity can fuel the relationship's motor. Marriages that have been falling apart for years, in other words, or that have experienced great stress, somehow continue to interest and unite these spouses. As friends sharing activities and interests, these two are quite emotionally reactive, so that conflicts are likely to erupt spontaneously between them with a certain regularity. Gemini II–Cancer III family relationships, particularly close ones, such as parent-child and sibling matchups are likely to be unstable. If the pair are to form business partnerships, or to work side by side for an organization, they must overcome their sensitivity to each other's feelings. Although helpful up to a point, this kind of empathy often subverts the practical and pragmatic attitudes needed to get the job done.

ADVICE: *Stabilize your activities. Find a quiet place within. Grow new buttons that can't so easily be pushed. Develop your practical side.*

June 3–10
THE WEEK OF NEW LANGUAGE
GEMINI II

July 26–August 2
THE WEEK OF AUTHORITY
LEO I

Regulating the Flame

This relationship can build character. Although a potentially explosive mix, the Gemini-air–Leo-fire combination burns with a bright flame that melts away any dross in the hot crucible of experience. Neither of these two is likely to hold back in their criticisms of each other, but if this testing of each other's personalities doesn't break them apart, it will strengthen their bond (assuming, that is, an equal amount of give-and-take on both sides). Should they form a team or partnership, their tremendous energy is likely to overcome even the most determined opposition. Should they fall out or, through the vagaries of fortune be set against one another as opponents, they are likely to give no quarter and make no concessions to their former relationship.

BARBARA BUSH (6/8/25)
MARILYN QUAYLE (7/29/49)

Bush and Quayle were First and Second Ladies during the Bush administration (1989–93). They were close friends and very active during their husbands' tenures. Mrs. Bush was particularly active in educational programs, establishing the Barbara Bush Foundation for Family Literacy.

Love affairs here are likely to be intense, perhaps too intense to last. If the relationship is to continue, the couple may just have to get married, a kind of relationship in which their energies are likely to be more balanced. Friendships between these two may turn to love, or vice versa, as long as their respect for each other remains intact. Platonic relationships in this combination are no less strong than passionate ones, and ultimately may prove more satisfying and enduring.

Gemini II–Leo I sibling or parent-child relationships can form a solid backbone for a family. Should problems or head-on confrontations occur, however, the group is likely to be shaken to its roots. Work projects are highly favored here: Leo I's will allow Gemini II's to lead, and vice versa, as long as mutual respect is maintained. Co-worker matchups are less in the cards for this duo than executive or entrepreneurial partnerships. The verbal and communicative strengths of a Gemini II meld powerfully with the wisdom and implementative abilities of a Leo I, the Gemini II more likely to set up or innovate, the Leo I to see the project through until the fruits of the pair's labor can be reaped.

ADVICE: *Relax. Regulate your flame to avoid burnout. Balance your energies, and make sure they are pointed in the right direction.*

June 3–10
THE WEEK OF NEW LANGUAGE
GEMINI II

August 3–10
THE WEEK OF BALANCED STRENGTH
LEO II

A Secret Irreverence

This relationship brings out the unusual side of both partners. Gemini II's and Leo II's respect tradition but do not worship it, agreeing that established conventions may simply be excuses for bad habits; what works, rather than what should work, is uppermost in their minds. In consequence, their relationship is markedly pragmatic in outlook. Unconventional attitudes prevail here, though the partners usually stay within the bounds of good sense. They also exhibit a good deal of humor. The result is a strange mix. Finding kindred spirits in each other, these two may enjoy a good joke at the expense of more traditional associates, or even a bit of gossip, both of these discreetly behind the scenes.

QUEEN MOTHER (8/4/1900)
PRINCE PHILIP (6/10/21)

Britain's Queen Mother is the mother of Queen Elizabeth and mother-in-law to Prince Philip. As royal consorts, Philip and the Queen Mother are required to serve Queen Elizabeth.

Gemini II–Leo II love affairs are likely to be honest but never fly in society's face. Publicly, in other words, they mute their relationship's uniqueness, sharing it mainly during more intimate moments. Both of them feel that what happens between two people is their business alone. In its physical aspect the relationship is likely to be frank, open and creative, with no holds barred. Kindness and consideration are certainly present here but are often of secondary importance. Marriages in this combination can be successful if the partners achieve a balance between their outlooks. Should they be able to effect a compromise between Gemini II criticality and independence and the Leo II drive toward dominance, lasting harmony can result. If not, expect the worst. Balance is harder to achieve in friendships and family relationships, where the frank and often cutting remarks of Gemini II's can wound and anger Leo II's, who are likely to reply with violent outbursts and then stony silences. Gemini II's are liable to feel misunderstood by Leo II's, who often don't seem to care much about them.

Working relationships in more traditional settings, such as corporations, are not recommended for this pair, given their unconventional attitudes. Their irreverence may well contribute to the success of an entrepreneurial endeavor, however, as long as adversarial tendencies are prevented from coming to the fore, making daily contact difficult and disturbing others in the workplace.

ADVICE: *Open lines of communication. Try to diminish conflict. Establish stronger ties with the world. Be aware of your effect on others.*

LEO G. GORCEY (6/3/15)
HUNTZ HALL (8/15/19)

Gorcey and Hall played gang members in film comedies of the 30s and 40s—first as the Dead End Kids, then the East Side Kids and finally the Bowery Boys. An outstanding team, Hall played the gang goofball opposite Gorcey's more serious punk persona. **Also:**

Sandra Bernhard & Madonna (friendship; comic/pop star).

June 3–10
THE WEEK OF NEW LANGUAGE
GEMINI II

August 11–18
THE WEEK OF LEADERSHIP
LEO III

Take No Prisoners

This relationship's indomitable facade conceals a bloody battle for supremacy. The overall attitude is "Take no prisoners." The major problem here is Leo III dominance and whether Gemini II's can accept it—not an impossible task for them, as long as they feel that their efforts are appreciated and rewarded. But their inability to keep quiet about whatever is bothering them will often lead to conflict, especially when they accurately accuse a Leo III of inefficiency or incompetence. The Gemini II way of bringing out a Leo III's insecurities may make it difficult or impossible for this pair to live or work together. Yet Leo III's do value Gemini II judgments and opinions and may even come to depend on them.

In their relationship with a Gemini II spouse and in the family hierarchy generally, Leo III's will want to be boss. Gemini II's, however, have a charm, cleverness and seductiveness that often enable them to get their way with Leo III's, who are tough but have an undeniable weakness here. A cycle may recur in which Leo III's try to control Gemini II's by spoiling them, showering them with gifts, and encouraging them to think they are actually in the superior position; should these favors later be withdrawn, Gemini II's are likely to feel helpless and defeated—and may respond by redoubling their manipulative efforts. Love affairs and friendships are not recommended here, since the level of conflict tends to be high, and honesty and depth of emotion will be difficult to achieve.

Work relationships, too, are complex. When Leo III's have to build a team, a sparkling Gemini II may be their single best lieutenant. There is a big problem here, however—not the efficiency of Gemini II's (they will have little problem understanding what Leo III's want and how to implement it) but their insubordination. Together, also, the pair will have an abrasive attitude toward co-workers. Leo III's and Gemini II's do not always work well together on an equal level, since vicious power struggles are likely to emerge between them.

ADVICE: *Try to be honest. Tone down abrasiveness. Minimize conflict. Be aware of manipulation. Develop your finest and most constructive qualities.*

RUBY KEELER (8/25/09)
AL JOLSON (6/7/1886)

Jolson married musical actress Keeler in 1928. Jolson's dispute with Warner Brothers in 1937 prompted Keeler to leave the studios as well, but it took a toll on their marriage and they divorced in 1940.
Also: Robert Cummings & Orville Wright (godson/godfather; actor/aviator).

June 3–10
THE WEEK OF NEW LANGUAGE
GEMINI II

August 19–25
THE CUSP OF EXPOSURE
LEO-VIRGO CUSP

Encouraging Self-Expression

The major theme of this combination is seduction—not in the sensual sense, but in that of lulling people into revealing themselves. It is a kind of seduction that encourages self-expression: each of these personalities, and particularly Leo-Virgo, has a dark or complicated side, but each is capable of advancing mutual understanding by persuading the other to reveal him- or herself. In this combination, Gemini II's can resemble salespeople trying to sell Leo-Virgos on the idea that they are worthwhile people who should emerge from their private world. In return, Gemini II's may be able to express themselves as never before: communication is the important thing for them, and Leo-Virgos are certainly acute enough to understand their unique language. Actually, in letting Gemini II's spend so much time persuading them, Leo-Virgos may have been just studying the Gemini II language style.

In love affairs these two can be explorers plumbing each other's emotions. Like Prince Charming and Sleeping Beauty, they can awaken each other's innermost feelings with a kiss. The breaching of both partners' defenses might also be difficult and dangerous, however, since Leo-Virgos seldom want help in choosing what to reveal, or when, and Gemini II's fear self-exposure as making them look foolish. Marriages can bring these tensions to a head: they may be full and rich, but Leo-Virgo resentment over the disruption of their privacy and autonomy can cause periodic outbursts and depressions, resulting in Gemini II frustration over being misunderstood. Gemini II–Leo-Virgo friends must learn to operate on an equal footing, which won't be easy. But if Leo-Virgos can share quiet times with Gemini I's, or join them in social forays—only of their own free will, and because they want to—the relationship has a chance of success. Gemini II bosses and parents can be nurturing and encouraging to Leo-Virgo employees and children. Any hint of patronization, however, will usually make Leo-Virgos go silent, and if more pronounced may damage their self-esteem. Great sensitivity must be shown here, then, and undue praise strictly avoided.

ADVICE: *Allow emotions to emerge spontaneously. Toughen your will and resolve. Be as concerned with wants as with needs. Find your heart's desire.*

June 3–10

THE WEEK OF NEW LANGUAGE
GEMINI II

August 26–September 2

THE WEEK OF SYSTEM BUILDERS
VIRGO I

Only a Finger's Breadth Away

This relationship reinforces air and earth qualities (associated with mental and pragmatic forces, respectively), but reconciling these forces won't always be easy or even possible: earthly drives to succeed, to enjoy and even to control others will vie here with more imaginative, impractical and unpredictable influences. In the best-case scenario, however, the result will be a coalescence in a pragmatic yet deeply imaginative combination. The common influence of Mercury (the ruling planet of both Gemini and Virgo) supplies an additional push toward logic and reasonableness.

Love affairs will feature a sensuous and stabilizing influence, encouraging back rubs, warm baths and cozy cuddling. But an equal, opposing and disturbing force can shatter repose in an instant, sending uncontrolled emotions flying, and it is never more than a finger's breadth away. Care must be taken that passions do not turn ugly and lead to violence, whether of word or of deed.

Marriages and work relationships between these two are often pragmatic and financially successful yet underlaid by instability. Both partners sometimes have a fatalistic feeling that their relationship could change in an instant, with favorable influences and expectations dissolving into thin air. This insecurity, however, may only push them to aim higher in their joint achievements, be these in the familial, domestic, financial or professional spheres. Spouses in this combination can often work together in exciting and imaginative career endeavors.

Friendships and family relationships can bring out the combination's nervous side. Anxiety and even paranoia can rear their ugly heads, making easy communication impossible. Parent-child relationships in particular are likely to bring out the worst, as the Gemini I propensity for relentless criticism and the Virgo I drive for order combine to drive everyone around them to distraction. It is when these two are most in agreement that they will be most trying for the rest of the family; when they disagree, other points of view will have a better chance of prevailing.

ADVICE: *Let the good times roll. Don't expect the roof to cave in all the time—one day it will! Follow your instincts and feelings more. Give others some rest.*

FREDERICK LOEWE (6/10/01)
ALAN JAY LERNER (8/31/18)

The brilliant collaboration between composer Loewe and lyricist Lerner, begun in 1947, yielded such musical masterpieces as *Brigadoon, Paint Your Wagon, My Fair Lady* and *Camelot*. *Also:* **Nancy Sinatra & Tommy Sands** (married; singers); **Bjorn Borg & Jimmy Connors** (tennis rivals); **Jessica Tandy & Jack Hawkins** (married; actors); **June Haver & Fred MacMurray** (married; actors).

June 3–10

THE WEEK OF NEW LANGUAGE
GEMINI II

September 3–10

THE WEEK OF THE ENIGMA
VIRGO II

Mixed Signals

Duality is the theme here, and synthesis in a coherent whole is likely to be the struggle. Each of these partners has two distinct (though not necessarily opposite) sides; thus four different couples can emerge in the relationship, causing much confusion. The combination also has a sibling- or twinlike style, making equality of talents its hallmark. Myths of twins such as Isis and Osiris, the married sibling gods of ancient Egypt, or Romulus and Remus, legendary builders of Rome, are invoked here. Such myths address the existence of a dark side in humanity, and this combination's ultimate goal is grappling with and integrating that dark side—into a creative endeavor of the self or of the relationship. Given the variety of personality aspects involved, and the size of the task, a lot of instability and mood swings are inherent here.

Love affairs, if they develop at all, often lack the tenacity to grapple with all this. Virgo II's are usually inaccessible to Gemini II's, who won't understand their mixed signals and puzzling responses. Although excellent at formulating verbal language, Gemini II's may have trouble translating the silent, highly personal language of Virgo II's. Marriages here face similar problems.

Gemini II–Virgo II friends are on the same mental wavelength but control their emotions tightly. Should Virgo II's withdraw into a depressive slump, Gemini II's usually know when to let them work things out by themselves and when to jump in and help. Work relationships can be productive, but mutual irritation can make everyday cooperation chancy, particularly with regular co-workers. As administrators or entrepreneurs, Gemini II's can provide the insights and Virgo II's the application to forge a unit that can be counted on for solving problems and drawing up agreements. The relationship can be especially strong in the legal sphere.

Family relationships, particularly parent-child and sibling matchups, are rocky. Sharp verbal exchanges are frequent, and should these two be left alone together for long, especially in late adolescence and early adulthood, an edgy feeling will emerge. Making peace, however, will become increasingly important in later life.

ADVICE: *Try to live less in your head. Rely on intuition more. Establish a firmer basis for your life. Let go of worries and anxieties.*

FRANK LLOYD WRIGHT (6/8/1867)
LOUIS SULLIVAN (9/3/1856)

A spokesman for organic architecture in the late 1890s, Sullivan was an immense influence in his day but died in obscurity and poverty. Wright, his most famous disciple, called him "lieber meister" as a young draftsman with Sullivan's firm. Wright published a tribute to him in 1949. *Also:* **Amanda Pays & Corbin Bernsen** (married; actors); **Elizabeth Hurley & Hugh Grant** (lovers; actors).

CLARA SCHUMANN (9/13/1819)
ROBERT SCHUMANN (6/8/1810)

In 1830, Robert moved into Clara's home to study piano under her father, who was also her teacher. Defying him, they married in 1840. In the midst of raising 8 children, Clara became a great concert pianist and Robert's composing matured. **Also: Prince Philip & Prince Henry** (grandfather/ grandson; royalty).

June 3–10

THE WEEK OF NEW LANGUAGE
GEMINI II

September 11–18

THE WEEK OF THE LITERALIST
VIRGO III

Opening to New Ideas

This relationship shines in the mental sphere. Its focus is likely to be intelligent conversation punctuated by good feeling. Although both partners can be hardheaded, in this matchup they communicate ideas well, exercise common sense and are adept at making plans for the future. They are also witty and funny. The relationship is likely to embrace team projects involving construction and creativity, perhaps in the areas of craft or design. Both partners are open to new ideas rather than bound by traditional ones.

Flexibility is a trademark of Gemini II–Virgo III love affairs. Nonattachment is generally cultivated here, with freedom of action not just a privilege but a requirement. These open attitudes actually encourage the partners to remain faithful to each other—strict rules might only make them break up. As long as they can breathe free, the relationship is likely to continue in relative harmony.

Marriages are a bit more problematic. Gemini II's are not always physically available, and the temperatures of Virgo III's are likely to rise if they get stuck with the brunt of the work. Arguments are likely not only over distribution of chores but over money and children. Both partners are verbal types, and their repartee can be highly stimulating but can also take a destructive turn toward irony and sarcasm. The dramatic side of both partners usually emerges at such times.

Gemini II–Virgo III family relationships and especially friendships can be outstanding. These two are often bound by strong bonds of loyalty and understanding. Should they become best friends, however, they must be careful not to shut others out. It is only to the extent that their relationship can become inclusive rather than exclusive that it guarantees its own longevity. Work relationships in this combination may shift into the areas of friendship and love, impairing their effectiveness.

ADVICE: *Don't shut others out or let humor turn hurtful. Don't neglect tradition. Avoid arguing about money. Be objective at work.*

MICKEY ROONEY (9/23/20)
JUDY GARLAND (6/10/22)

Early in their careers, Garland and Rooney appeared in 9 movies together, beginning in 1937 with *Thoroughbreds Don't Cry.* Rooney's energized comic presence complemented Garland's wide-eyed innocence. They became life-long friends. **Also: Jerry Stiller & Anne Meara** (married; comedy team).

June 3–10

THE WEEK OF NEW LANGUAGE
GEMINI II

September 19–24

THE CUSP OF BEAUTY
VIRGO-LIBRA CUSP

Needed: A Firm Basis

The challenge here is to find an underlying set of principles that will enhance both the relationship and its individual partners, providing a grounding influence. This source of authority could be financial, religious or aesthetic. Should this pair be interested in popular culture, especially music, film and design, they could easily base their lifestyle on appreciation of and participation in such areas. Because they are extremely caught up in being taken seriously by others and in appearing as "players," matters of style appeal strongly to them, and an up-to-date, modern outlook, together with a bit of snobbery, can be the basis of authority they need. Together they are capable of carving out a creative niche in whatever field interests them.

Gemini II's will enjoy telling Virgo-Libras about current happenings in the popular arts, and Virgo-Libras will like to investigate these areas for themselves. Love affairs, friendships and marriages in this combination, then, can be unashamedly based on activities that others consider superficial: watching films and television, listening to new CDs, reading books or fashionable magazines, cruising the Internet, developing a CD-rom library. For this couple, such subjects mean not only enjoyment but education, for they study them in depth and put the knowledge they gain to creative use. Should these two share a common domestic space, it often shows these influences graphically in its decor, art, etc.

Family matchups here are unlikely to arouse strong emotion. By getting along easily, however, Gemini II's and Virgo-Libras can develop strong bonds and a healthy outlook on life—they don't need anguish to bring them together. When crises arise, this calm affect can work positively on other family members, especially nervous or excitable ones. Should the relationship encompass an entrepreneurial enterprise, such as a shop or business, or should it include freelance work, great care will have to be paid to money matters. Although a career connection with a friend or mate may help to establish the common basis that the relationship requires, fiscal irresponsibility is a constant danger, and financial failure will throw the pair into turmoil.

ADVICE: *Adopt a set of principles and stick to them. Be aware of a tendency to act superior. Pay attention to your cash flow—you are probably relying too much on credit.*

June 3–10

THE WEEK OF NEW LANGUAGE
GEMINI II

September 25–October 2

THE WEEK OF THE PERFECTIONIST
LIBRA I

RELATIONSHIPS

STRENGTHS: **CONCEPTUAL, SHARING, UNDERSTANDING**

WEAKNESSES: **UNREALISTIC, UNDERMINING, FRUSTRATED**

BEST: **FAMILY**

WORST: **LOVE**

A True Meeting of the Minds

The strong mental connection between these two makes the sharing of ideas and concepts primary in their relationship. These ideas may be either intellectual or practical, depending on whether the pair share everyday responsibilities. The relationship can be extremely easygoing, and in fact may have to be—dealing with painful or disturbing subjects may not really be possible here. Outsiders sometimes view this matchup as near perfect, but of course they don't know what's going on at its heart. It is a relationship that emphasizes humor, intelligence and ease of interaction more than intensity or passion.

Frustrations can emerge in love and marriage. Gemini II's may be anxious to make contact with their Libra I partner at a deeper emotional level, and will feel defeated when such sharing is refused. Libra I's, on the other hand, may want Gemini II's to be less flaky and more organized. Actually, in both of these areas, the relationship often both demands and gets the best of which these two are capable. Indeed Gemini II–Libra I love affairs are pervaded by unrealistic and undermining attitudes—which can more or less disappear, however, once the marriage knot is tied. Expectation often plays too strong a role in marriage, setting the couple up for disappointment, but enough satisfaction is often gained to keep the relationship intact for years.

Friendships in this combination are comfortable and stimulating, but parent-child and sibling matchups are more apt to achieve true closeness. In fact, a father-daughter or mother-son relationship may resemble a friendship as much as or more than it does a family connection. In these meetings of the minds, mental and emotional sympathies diminish the chances of misunderstanding. A truly unselfish love is possible here.

Work relationships between these two are unlikely to be quite productive or innovative enough. Both of these individuals can sometimes be self-defeating in matters of career or work and should take great care to be conscious of their tendencies in this regard.

ADVICE: *Strive for unconditional giving. Selfish attitudes lead to separation. Be prepared to listen. Nothing human is perfect or eternal.*

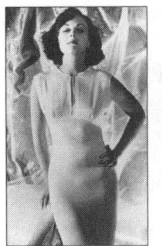 

PAULETTE GODDARD (6/3/11)
GEORGE GERSHWIN (9/26/1898)

Around 1936, Goddard and composer Gershwin had a serious romance while she was still married to Chaplin. Some biographers believe she was his greatest love, particularly since he implored her to leave Chaplin.

June 3–10

THE WEEK OF NEW LANGUAGE
GEMINI II

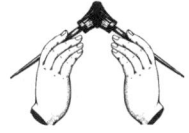

October 3–10

THE WEEK OF SOCIETY
LIBRA II

RELATIONSHIPS

STRENGTHS: **SUCCESSFUL, INTUITIVE, BALANCED**

WEAKNESSES: **UNFOCUSED, DRIFTING, SENSATIONALISTIC**

BEST: **WORK**

WORST: **LOVE**

Working Hunches

Rich in potential, this relationship has the capacity to achieve any goal as long as its partners choose to capitalize on its strengths: fidelity, patience and intuition. This pair would do well to proceed on hunches rather than on logic, and either to initiate projects or to point established ones in new directions. The challenge here, in fact, will be to develop a strong, trustworthy and reliable modus operandi for beginning and then maintaining new projects. The relationship promises peaceful coexistence, little friction and few problems, but tension is often the midwife of growth, and if these two want their pairing to be a dynamic one they will need to focus on goals outside themselves.

Love affairs, for example, may just drift and dream. They are pleasant enough, perhaps, but they lack strong conviction. These partners have a sensationalistic streak, and may be looking for the latest new thrill; if so, they are often hunting in opposite directions. If they instead get a bit more serious about the world in general and their relationship in particular, they will open up new worlds of mutual involvement. Discovering the joys of learning and self-discovery, whether through reading, research or life experience, will provide a positive focus.

Marriages here can be highly successful in the eyes of the world. In attending to domestic needs, however, these two may neglect to further their own development, both as a couple and as individuals. In this respect, even the happiest marriage may cheat Gemini II's and Libra II's of their inalienable birthright: personal growth. Friends, spouses and family members in this combination are quite likely to join together in career or business endeavors. These commercial relationships can be trusting and fun, and may go well—but with a bit more push they could do much better. This is the place where it is especially important for the partners to trust their intuition rather than logic or common sense, and quite simply go for it, rather than hanging back and weighing pros and cons.

ADVICE: *Develop more backbone. Give structure and directed energy to your work. Make more demands. Don't forget your own personal development.*

H. RAP BROWN (10/4/43)
WILLIAM KUNSTLER (6/7/19)

Kunstler was defense attorney to many radical black activists, including Brown, a proponent of "black power" in the 60s. Kunstler not only represented minority leaders, he often supported their causes.

COLLEEN DEWHURST (6/3/26)
GEORGE C. SCOTT (10/18/27)

A respected actress, Dewhurst is known for her work on the New York stage. Scott's distinguished career has been punctuated by 5 marriages—all to actresses. The couple was married and divorced twice (1960–65, 1967–72).

June 3–10
THE WEEK OF NEW LANGUAGE
GEMINI II

October 11–18
THE WEEK OF THEATER
LIBRA III

Tempting, Alluring, Maddening

An exciting relationship is likely to develop here. The crucial factor in whether it will endure is this pair's ability to accept each other, including all of their little imperfections and unpleasantries, once their initial interest in each other has faded. Resembling sometimes a football field, sometimes a battlefield, the relationship is tempting, alluring, maddening, unreasonable—kaleidoscopic in scope. Gemini II energy will attract Libra III's, who don't usually go out of their way to appear interested. Their coolness and objectivity will in turn appeal to Gemini II's and will often provoke their deeper feelings. Neither party is looking for trouble or problems in this relationship, but this is no guarantee of their absence.

Love affairs are likely to be particularly unstable. The emphasis here is on youthful energies and spontaneous displays of feeling. Sex tends to be unplanned and exciting, but there is the possibility that it will bring out some of both partners' more undesirable characteristics. Provocative or inflammatory scenes and downright meanness are quite likely here. Gemini II's may at times feel dominated by powerful Libra III's, but this can have its allure. Libra III's who get caught up in the frenetic energies of Gemini II's will find such loss of control uncomfortable.

Marriage may not be recommended as a next step in these tumultuous relationships. Nor is it often possible for cooled-down or failed love affairs to result in friendships. On the other hand, should Gemini II's and Libra III's meet first as friends, they are quite likely to be able to establish an easy give-and-take. Again, the relationship's solidity and depth will depend on its degree of acceptance.

Work relationships may be much too volatile too succeed. Libra III's have to be given free rein, and should Gemini II's become in any way dependent on them, rejection is inevitable. Parents and children in this combination are usually able to work out their differences over the years; quite loving attitudes may emerge from stormy childhoods, and reconciliations are possible in the maturity of adult life.

ADVICE: *Try to be more objective. Concentrate on love's positive aspects. Handle violent feelings with care. Work toward greater understanding.*

HARRY F. BYRD (6/10/1887)
RICHARD E. BYRD (10/25/1888)

Virginia-born brothers, Harry served as a governor (1926–30) and senator (1933–65), while Richard, an aviator and explorer, became a national hero after flying over the North Pole in 1926 and to the South Pole the same year. **Also: John Maynard Keynes & Lydia Lopokova** (married; economist/ballerina).

June 3–10
THE WEEK OF NEW LANGUAGE
GEMINI II

October 19–25
THE CUSP OF DRAMA & CRITICISM
LIBRA-SCORPIO CUSP

Impacting on the World

This combination could give forthright direction to a wide variety of projects: Gemini II's and Libra-Scorpios do well as a leadership team in clubs, schools and artistic or business enterprises. The emphasis of their relationship is generally less on their interactions with each other than on their joint impact on the world around them. These two have critical and verbal skills that meld, and working together they are likely to be able to achieve great success in publishing, journalism, teaching, work involving languages or translation, and perhaps politics or law. Given the relationship's leadership qualities, however, getting stuck together in a stuffy, boring or academic pursuit would be immensely frustrating. The Gemini II–Libra-Scorpio team must use their talents to convince, to stimulate and ultimately to lead others to high achievement, be it in more popular or more esoteric spheres. Another danger here is that the pair will lose their broad vision, feel unappreciated and retreat into a narrow circle of admirers, preaching to the converted. They do best together, in fact, when capable skeptics disagree with them and put up some real resistance, challenging them and provoking them to higher expression.

Friendships, love affairs and marriages are all possible between these two, but these relationships will almost always emphasize issues greater than the partners' personal feelings for each other. Should external outlets for their leadership energies be denied or unavailable, frustration will often result, and the relationship's energies will turn inward—potentially quite a destructive outcome.

Grandparents in this combination can set the tone for a family over two, three or perhaps more generations. Their forceful attitudes will bring forth feelings of pride and dedication in their children and grandchildren. A sibling duo, particularly of the same sex, may also be extremely influential in determining a family's social and financial direction. Care must be taken not to trample on the feelings of more sensitive and passive family members, for whom personal development has greater importance.

ADVICE: *Don't ignore personal feelings in yourself or others. Tone down your rhetoric. Allow others to decide for themselves. Hang back a bit.*

June 3–10

THE WEEK OF NEW LANGUAGE
GEMINI II

October 26–November 2

THE WEEK OF INTENSITY
SCORPIO I

An Emotional Pipeline

Sensitivities run high here—this pair can find themselves on the same emotional pipeline, both for better and for worse. On the plus side, they can give each other a lot of emotional sustenance and inspiration. Seeing each other daily, however, they easily get on each other's nerves. The challenge here will be getting along, diminishing points of conflict and irritation while capitalizing on the combination's ability to create color, intimacy and even joy. Exchanges between these two are likely to be lively and stimulating, but Gemini II's may find themselves on the receiving end of the strong Scorpio I moral side, which leads these personalities to condemn thoughts and actions that they consider even a tad questionable.

Love affairs here are likely to be intense but fleeting. Even if the partners struggle to accept each other's faults, their extreme temperamental differences, and their relationship's highly critical outlook, are apt to cause problems. The chemistry here tends toward the excitable, with lots of humor and good times but also a degree of instability. For this reason, marriages too may prove problematic.

Friendships are usually energetic but demanding of the partners' attention, at least if they are to endure. A Gemini II involved in a troubled or failing love relationship may turn to a Scorpio I friend for support; whether such friendships turn into love or not, the situation is potentially explosive, since Scorpio I's will be highly protective of their Gemini II friends and risk losing all objectivity in taking their side. The triangles that result can be highly destructive, especially for Gemini II's, who are liable to be the most vulnerable party.

Parent-child relationships in this combination can be empathic and understanding, particularly mother-son and father-daughter matchups. Gemini II parents tend to let their Scorpio I children go their own way, but Scorpio I parents must be careful not to try to control the lives of their Gemini II offspring. At work, these two must be careful not to get hung up on details, or to let critical attitudes slow down the job and promote divisiveness.

ADVICE: *Keep it light. Beware of claiming and condemning attitudes. Don't overreact to small problems. Try to keep things in perspective.*

RELATIONSHIPS

STRENGTHS: **EMPATHIC, ENERGETIC, UNDERSTANDING**

WEAKNESSES: **IRRITATED, CONTROLLING, DESTRUCTIVE**

BEST: **PARENT-CHILD**

WORST: **FRIENDSHIP**

CHIANG KAI-SHEK (10/31/1887)
MME. CHIANG KAI-SHEK (6/4/1899)

Mei-ling Soong, daughter of a wealthy, politically prominent family, married Chiang Kai-shek in 1927, a year before he became leader of the Nationalist Chinese and Taiwan government. Her sister married Sun Yat-Sen.

***Also:* Darci Kistler & Peter Martins** (married; ballet dancers); **Johnny Depp & Winona Ryder** (once engaged; actors).

June 3–10

THE WEEK OF NEW LANGUAGE
GEMINI II

November 3–11

THE WEEK OF DEPTH
SCORPIO II

Inside Out

This combination illuminates shadow qualities of the partners' psyches. That is, it draws out and brings to consciousness their darker, least-acknowledged tendencies. In some ways a Scorpio II is a Gemini II turned inside out: Scorpio II depth and emotional intensity actually lurk within Gemini II's, who, however, may not know it. Meanwhile the Gemini II qualities of eccentricity and unusualness exist within Scorpio II's but are rarely exposed for others to see. The focus of this relationship, then, is likely to be revealing hidden truths, especially emotional ones, about both partners. More often than not, the process is unconscious—the partners are not aware that it is happening.

Friends may find these two a strange pair altogether, since Gemini II's are often sparkling and outgoing, Scorpio II's quiet and brooding. Yet at heart they are less different than they seem. A major problem here is that if either of them lacks awareness, or is not striving for it, they will project their own shadow sides, both positive and negative, onto each other, accusing each other of the very behaviors or attitudes that they covertly harbor themselves. Gemini II–Scorpio II love affairs often last and even progress to marriage. For the most part these two are well suited to each other. If difficulties arise, they will come when Gemini II's get hyper or Scorpio II's depressive; Scorpio II verbal reticence can drive Gemini II's to distraction, and potentially to frustration and depression. Dealing with anger and projection are perhaps the hardest problems here. For the most part, however, shared activities, strong sympathy and understanding, emotional support and a powerful physical attraction typify this energetic and usually easygoing relationship.

Friendships are possible, but without an effort to be objective they risk occasional misunderstandings and emotional flare-ups. These two perhaps do better as acquaintances, companions, colleagues or business partners, relationships probably focusing on objective pursuits rather than personal issues. Sibling relationships can be stormy and parent-child matchups difficult; revelation and exposure figure strongly here.

ADVICE: *Take the time to understand. Try to be more honest about your own feelings. Trust must be earned. Secretiveness can be counterproductive.*

RELATIONSHIPS

STRENGTHS: **SUPPORTIVE, REVELATORY, ENDURING**

WEAKNESSES: **STORMY, PROJECTING, NERVOUS**

BEST: **MARRIAGE**

WORST: **FAMILY**

JOSEPHINE BAKER (6/3/06)
CROWN PRINCE ADOLF (11/11/1882)

Baker and Adolf (the future King Gustav VI of Sweden) had a passionate affair in 1929. After seeing the exotic dancer perform, the married royal invited her to his isolated summer palace. They spent an entire winter month together, after which they never met again.

441

June 3–10

THE WEEK OF NEW LANGUAGE
GEMINI II

November 12–18

THE WEEK OF CHARM
SCORPIO III

Freed Up

BURGESS MEREDITH (11/16/08)
PAULETTE GODDARD (6/3/11)

2 years after her divorce from Chaplin, Goddard married screen actor Meredith in 1944. They appeared together in several movies, notably Jean Renoir's *The Diary of a Chambermaid* (1946). They divorced in 1949.

This relationship is bound to be lively and pleasure oriented, without too much attachment. It is unlikely to focus on the material world. Scorpio III's, who often shoulder financial and real-world obligations, will feel some relief in this, although their sense of responsibility may remain high. Finding a less materialistic relationship more natural, Gemini II's may take the lead here, showing Scorpio III's how to free themselves of heavy obligations.

Letting go and nonattachment, both spiritual principles, are obviously important in this relationship. In love affairs, sexual ecstasy will serve a spiritual more than a carnal purpose. Romances of a more platonic nature may also develop easily here, with the physical element absent or quietly subdued. These partners may be excellent candidates for different forms of daily meditation or yoga (including tantric yoga, where enlightenment is achieved through sexuality). Gemini II's help Scorpio III's get started or moving, and Scorpio III's provide the security and stability that Gemini II's so desperately need.

Marriages will benefit from Scorpio III practicality but also from Gemini III astuteness and incisiveness. Parents in this combination are apt to be successful at raising children to be self-realized individuals, able to care for themselves. Family ties are important here, get-togethers with friends and relatives on holidays, birthdays and other special occasions being a particular joy. Parent-child relationships generally work best when the Scorpio III is the parent, usually exerting solid control without arousing a Gemini II child's antagonism. This is no guarantee, however, that subtle claiming attitudes will be absent. In the commercial sphere, a nonmaterially oriented Gemini II–Scorpio III relationship may occupy itself with serving others, community or church affairs, or any other spiritual, philosophic or religious orientation. The pair may find it especially easy—perhaps too easy—to handle money, which they will think of as a fluid energy medium rather than a commodity or possession. There is a risk that their lack of concern for money could bring on financial difficulties, even ruin.

ADVICE: *Beware of losing contact with the earth. Material and spiritual need not be opposed. Take money a bit more seriously. Carry out daily tasks.*

June 3–10

THE WEEK OF NEW LANGUAGE
GEMINI II

November 19–24

THE CUSP OF REVOLUTION
SCORPIO-SAGITTARIUS CUSP

A Refusal to Be Bound

BILLY THE KID (11/23/1859)
PAT GARRETT (6/5/1850)

Billy the Kid (William H. Bonney) was a notorious outlaw charged with 12 murders by the age of 18. In 1881, the West's legendary lawman, Sheriff Garrett, tracked down and shot the desperado after he escaped from jail and killed 2 more men.

***Also:* Tony Curtis & Jamie Lee Curtis** (father/daughter; actors).

The focus of this combination, and perhaps its greatest necessity, is to give structure to the sometimes wild and unpredictable actions of its partners. Gemini II's and Scorpio-Sagittarians share characteristics that their relationship may magnify, including a cutting, critical and sarcastic side that can lead to confrontation and conflict. A refusal to be bound by the laws of social behavior and conventional morality will constantly land them in hot water, not only with other people but with each other. Their independence and wildness become more pronounced when they are a couple, exposing them to the danger of social condemnation or ostracism.

Love affairs, marriages and friendships in this combination depend for their survival on the extent to which the partners can agree on simple commonsense principles or moral codes that will bring them at least a modicum of stability and support. Marriages have the best chance here, for they usually demand the hammering out of stronger commitments and tougher compromises. Simply setting up daily routines, paying bills and organizing meals and all the other little details of family life will provide both an important element of structure within the relationship and the basis for a more systematic approach to life in general. Alas, love affairs and friendships here are likely to blow with the wind. It is not that they cannot be enjoyable—in this sense they are often quite rewarding—but that they are likely to drift, rootlessly and to little purpose.

Workplaces and families again tend to impose some kind of structure. Here, however, Gemini II idiosyncrasy and Scorpio-Sagittarius rebellion are likely to arouse misunderstanding and anger. Co-workers and siblings in this combination will cling together in the face of company or parental fury. But if they can learn to compromise with authority figures and to begin to think of creative solutions, they will at last come of age, learning to coexist through a good mix of understanding and diplomacy.

ADVICE: *A refusal to compromise will only close doors. Try to be diplomatic. Let daily routines bring structure into your life. Put your house in order.*

June 3–10

THE WEEK OF NEW LANGUAGE
GEMINI II

November 25–December 2

THE WEEK OF INDEPENDENCE
SAGITTARIUS I

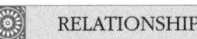
Early Retirement

This relationship is highly spirited, but the deep feelings that it also shelters, and the desire to withdraw from the hubbub of daily life, allow it to serve its partners as a true retreat from an often hostile and uncomprehending world. Those surprised that two such outgoing and extroverted individuals would seek a quiet life together are neglecting the more soulful side of both of these personalities—certainly the side that this combination brings out.

Love affairs here can be close. Having previously encountered rejection and misunderstanding in love, Gemini II's and Sagittarius I's in love will feel great relief at finally being understood and accepted. Their ties can go very deep, creating a loyalty that neither partner might easily permit anywhere else. Outsiders may be shocked to see these two free spirits committing to each other so deeply. Perhaps it is because they see themselves so clearly in each other that Gemini II's and Sagittarius I's can empathize in this way.

In marriage these two must be careful neither to close themselves off too much from the world nor to exhibit a bitter or defeated attitude, particularly if they have children. Any such children will have the capacity to play a positive role in keeping their parents interested in the world, and also in keeping them young. Nevertheless, Gemini II's and Sagittarius I's together have an undeniable tendency to "retire" from their multifarious but often unhappy social activities.

Friendships and sibling relationships in this combination are generally physical, being especially devoted to sports, fitness training and other forms of exercise. Enthusiastic and able to translate their intense concentration into a will to win, Gemini II–Sagittarius I partners are likely to galvanize the energies of any team or group of which they are a part. Similar energies will often characterize professional relationships between coworkers laboring for a common cause.

ADVICE: *Don't be cynical about the world. Concentrate on life's positive side. Develop your strengths. Be available to help.*

DIANE LADD (11/29/32)
BRUCE DERN (6/4/36)

Dern and Ladd married in the 60s and co-starred in *The Wild Angels* (1966). Both had famous literary relatives: Ladd was a cousin of Tennessee Williams and Dern a nephew of Archibald MacLeish. The couple, now divorced, are the parents of highly-praised actress Laura Dern.

June 3–10

THE WEEK OF NEW LANGUAGE
GEMINI II

December 3–10

THE WEEK OF THE ORIGINATOR
SAGITTARIUS II

Strange Tastes

This is a mysterious and puzzling relationship—even Gemini II's and Sagittarius II's themselves often don't understand how they ever came together. Sometimes they just drift into a relationship, perhaps after being introduced by a friend, meeting at a social event or being thrown together as part of a work team or community effort. Strangely, they can share a love affair for years before realizing how little they have in common and wondering how they could have been together for so long. Gemini II's and Sagittarius II's are directly opposite each other in the zodiac, which means they are polarized. One person's thoughts and actions go in one direction, the other's completely contrarily. The challenge they face is to synthesize their differences into a working whole. This will produce conflict and tension, but an awareness of the process at work will help the pair to achieve their goals, improve their understanding of the give-and-take of their relationship and lead to a great deal of joint creativity. Even then, however, they will have difficulty comprehending the nature of their relationship. It is as if they responded to each other without really knowing why, and found it hard to view the relationship objectively.

As friends and spouses, Gemini II's and Sagittarius II's often develop and indulge strange tastes indeed. Unusual habits are common, as well as singular interests in food, design, music, literature and film. These attitudes are not adopted to shock; the couple genuinely don't see anything offbeat in their actions and tastes—another example of the blind spot in their relationship. Similarly, those around them will think their family relationships border on the bizarre. Parent-child or sibling duos in this combination will pursue activities that have little or nothing to do with the rest of the family. In such pursuits they are best left to their own devices.

This kind of weirdness is rarely tolerated in the workplace, and it is usually best for these two not to make a daily team. If they do, their eccentricity could get them in hot water with authority figures.

ADVICE: *Sometimes try to be both the observer and the observed. Gain insight. Be patient with others. Recognize that your way is not the only way.*

[TAFKA] PRINCE (6/7/58)
KIM BASINGER (12/8/53)

Musician-performer [The Artist Formerly Known As] Prince created the soundtrack for *Batman* in 1989. During filming, he reputedly had a romance with its star, Basinger. She is now married to Alec Baldwin.

***Also: David Darius Brubeck
& Dave Brubeck*** (son/father; jazz musicians); **Madame Chiang Kai-shek & T.V. Soong** (siblings; Chinese statesmen).

FRANK SINATRA (12/12/15)
NANCY SINATRA (6/8/40)

Nancy made her singing debut on a 1960 tv special, appearing with her father and Elvis Presley. Though her song, *These Boots Are Made for Walkin'*, was a hit in 1966, her career eventually waned. In '85, she wrote her loving tribute, *Sinatra, My Father*.

June 3–10

THE WEEK OF NEW LANGUAGE
GEMINI II

December 11–18

THE WEEK OF THE TITAN
SAGITTARIUS III

Carrying Through on Commitments

These two are deeply involved in the idea of giving their word and holding to it. Truthfulness, honesty and carrying through on one's commitments are important ideas here. Yet because Gemini II's often have their own, highly individual language, and are likely to interpret what others say or write in an unusual way, it may not be easy to bind them to a simple agreement. Similarly, Sagittarius III's, who tend to see the larger line, may dismiss smaller details as petty or insignificant when in fact they have considerable meaning. Thus it may be extremely difficult for these two to come to an ordinary agreement, contractual or otherwise. Generally related to these issues is the fact that the written word will fascinate this pair—newspapers, magazines, novels and poetry will all hold a special place for them.

In marriages and work relationships, where matters of integrity are of basic and vital importance, problems won't necessarily arise immediately. Only when serious difficulties and even partial breakdowns surface does dispute over written or spoken intentions emerge. Gemini II's will try to hold Sagittarius III's to the minute details of any previous agreement, while Sagittarius III's will argue from a broad sense of the overall picture. These differences need not be irreconcilable as long as the partners can agree on how literally such statements should be taken.

Love affairs, family relationships and friendships are also likely to hinge on giving one's word, often in matters of emotional trust. In love and in parent-child matchups, promises made and broken may prove the sticking point—especially if the partner accused of breaking their word, sending mixed messages or leading their child to have false expectations is the Sagittarius III, usually the more dominant of the pair. A Gemini II lover, child or friend can be terribly wounded when a central fact that they have assumed to be true is suddenly called into question or revealed as an illusion. Misunderstandings among lovers, relatives and friends are likely to be much harder to deal with than those between spouses and co-workers.

ADVICE: *Try to stay flexible and open-minded. Literal interpretations often miss the nuances. Not everything is as simple as it seems.*

ISMAIL MERCHANT (12/25/35)
JAMES IVORY (6/7/28)

In their career-long partnership, Merchant has contributed his financial wherewithal and love of films to Ivory's acute directorial skills, resulting in numerous low-budget, high-quality cultural and literary films, including *Shakespeare Wallah* (1965) and *The Europeans* (1979).

June 3–10

THE WEEK OF NEW LANGUAGE
GEMINI II

December 19–25

THE CUSP OF PROPHECY
SAGITTARIUS-CAPRICORN CUSP

Drifting and Dreaming

These two can get out of touch with reality pretty easily. Both partners are likely to have illusions, about each other and about life in general, and since their relationship synergistically reinforces this trait, its outlook is often clouded. Predictions and attitudes that become self-fulfilling prophecies are common here; particularly hazardous are negative expectations based on past failures, which produce scenarios that are likely to be repeated again and again unless the partners can release them and move on. The challenge is to turn such expectations in a positive direction, and perhaps, ultimately, to drop them altogether, allowing a new emphasis on living in the moment and taking one day at a time. The opportunity that the relationship offers these two is to harness the power of their imaginations so that it will manifest for their good.

Love and marriage here are unlikely to ignite deep passion or to be pleasant and free of strife. Yet they have an imaginative quality that prolongs them: each partner encourages the other's illusions. There is a real danger of these two creating a dream world, becoming a folie à deux. An understanding, insightful, patient and dedicated third party may be able to reveal such illusions and, if the trust is great enough, make the relationship stronger and more whole than it was before.

Friendships and family relationships tend to be a bit more realistic. Even so, if these two limit their responsibilities or refuse to take them seriously, their relationship tends to drift. They can have wonderful times together, but a real focus or underlying meaning tends to be lacking. This deficiency will quickly grow clear in times of crisis, especially if drug use has figured in the equation.

Perhaps working relationships are the most difficult of all—business and financial expectations will be problematic for this pair. But if they can generate imaginative ideas and leave the practical nuts-and-bolts work to another associate or partner, they may prove valuable to a social or community organization.

ADVICE: *Periodically review your life story. Examine assumptions carefully. Pay attention to objective signs. Find a realistic basis for your thoughts.*

June 3–10

THE WEEK OF NEW LANGUAGE
GEMINI II

December 26–January 2

THE WEEK OF THE RULER
CAPRICORN I

STRENGTHS: **PHYSICAL, SENSUOUS, FULFILLING**

WEAKNESSES: **REJECTING, EXASPERATING, DICTATORIAL**

BEST: **LOVE**

WORST: **FRIENDSHIP**

Filled with Desire

This relationship usually focuses on physical beauty. The partners may be extremely attracted to each other, or may share a love of or interest in beautiful paintings, sculpture, crafts, design or music. The earthiness of Capricorn is felt here, but also the discerning eye of Gemini, and the coalescence of these qualities produces a relationship at once sensuous and filled with desire. The critical tendencies of both partners are invariably prominent, but their relationship usually applies them to aesthetic matters and makes them secondary to personal qualities.

Love affairs may be thrilling and fulfilling, particularly sexually. Gemini II's can be devoted lovers and Capricorn I's will appreciate their ardor. There is an underlying instability here, however, which may well lend excitement but may not augur well for permanence. The set of emotions these affairs unlock may recall Pandora's box: once opened, it may be difficult to shut.

Marriages are more successful. Capricorn I's are pragmatic in outlook, and Gemini II's may learn a great deal about practicality from them. They in turn will learn something about social grace and joie de vivre. Children will benefit from their parents' relationship, which both allows for fun and demands taking responsibility.

Friendships can be marred by communication difficulties. Gemini II's may feel that Capricorn I's only pretend to understand what they say and actually don't completely get it. If comprehension is indeed feigned, and the sham is uncovered at a later date, the Gemini II will be furious. Capricorn I's, meanwhile, may grow exasperated or even write the relationship off if Gemini II's continually miss appointments.

Conflicts may arise between Capricorn I parents or bosses and Gemini II children or employees, since in this combination the former tend to be dictatorial and the latter rebellious. Later in life these children may come to appreciate that their parents did their best, and these parents to accept their children for what they are. Making peace before an older parent dies will be essential for both partners' psychological well-being.

ADVICE: *Come to terms with each other. Don't be distracted by externals. Dig a bit deeper spiritually. Try harder to understand and accept.*

DR. SAMUEL SHEPPARD (12/29/23)
F. LEE BAILEY (6/10/33)

As a hungry, young criminal lawyer in '61, Bailey represented Sheppard in his 2nd trial for the '54 murder of his wife. Bailey succeeded in overturning Sheppard's conviction, claiming excessive press attention prejudiced the first trial. The case established Bailey's reputation as a no-holds-barred fighter for his clients.

June 3–10

THE WEEK OF NEW LANGUAGE
GEMINI II

January 3–9

THE WEEK OF DETERMINATION
CAPRICORN II

STRENGTHS: **HEALING, REVIVING, INITIATING**

WEAKNESSES: **IMPATIENT, PUSHING, CRISIS-PRONE**

BEST: **MARRIAGE**

WORST: **WORK**

Healing Wounds

This relationship's energy lies in rejuvenation and healing. The combination may have a reviving effect on its partners, then, after either has been wounded in a relationship elsewhere, or when they are trying to cope with a crisis in their relationship with each other. But while there is a great capacity here for healing wounds both old and new, there is also an inherent instability, since each person's approach to life is very different. This makes the relationship's final outcome uncertain; in some cases these two will come together just to heal, and then move on. Still, this matchup will promote longevity and growth so long as each person is willing to devote time and energy to it, and to let its inherent healing capacity be expressed.

If one of these partners is depressed, perhaps mourning the loss of a marriage or primary love, the other is likely to prove a tremendous comfort in helping him or her to cope. It is important not to expect too much in such situations, however, and to be patient. Gemini II's, impatient by nature, are less likely to play the support role. Should the Gemini II–Capricorn II love affair or marriage itself fail, it is not unusual for these partners to try again with each other after their emotions have cooled down and understanding and acceptance have begun to emerge. Encouraging a slow but steady healing, and refusing to let the flames of passion ignite too quickly, may lead to a successful reconciliation. Should the partners decide to put the relationship to rest, on the other hand, the healing capacity here can help them to move on.

Broken familial bonds, especially within parent-child and sibling pairs, may periodically need mending. Such wounds can take years to heal, but the process of reconciliation will often bring the partners even closer together. Damaged friendships and work relationships may be less open to healing. Keep in mind that such relationships are often formed to help one or both partners move past old wounds, and once this is accomplished, the friendship may not last.

ADVICE: *Don't give up. There may still be a chance. On the other hand, recognize when something has outlived its usefulness and learn to let go of attachments.*

NICHOLAS CAGE (1/7/64)
JOHNNY DEPP (6/9/63)

Cage is responsible for launching Depp's film career. When Depp first moved to LA, his ex-wife introduced to him to Cage, who suggested he try acting. After meeting with Cage's agent, Depp landed a role in *Nightmare on Elm Street.*

KATE MOSS (1/16/74)
JOHNNY DEPP (6/9/63)

Depp became a Hollywood film sensation following his role as the tragicomic lead in *Edward Scissorhands* (1990). Off-screen, he's attracted nearly as much attention with his romances, including one with English supermodel Kate Moss, which ended in '97.

***Also:* Parker Stevenson & Kirstie Alley** (married; actors).

June 3–10
THE WEEK OF NEW LANGUAGE
GEMINI II

January 10–16
THE WEEK OF DOMINANCE
CAPRICORN III

Meeting High Standards

These two make an attractive pair. Their relationship focuses on perfection, an idea that for them involves the idea of achievement: it is not an aesthetic ideal to be contemplated but a technical exactitude to measure up to, a moral integrity to live by. Capricorn III's play to win and have the steadfastness to do so. This attracts Gemini II's, who are also out to win but have less confidence in their ability and staying power. Still, Gemini II's usually accomplish their aims in their own way, and this affinity to the road less traveled appeals to Capricorn III's, who adhere more strictly to society's standards.

Few, however, could live up to the standards these two set themselves. Together they tend to view the world as terribly flawed, and to keep themselves impossibly aloof. Woe to the partner who fails to live up to the combination's standards: he or she will be damagingly self-punitive, suffering terribly even when the other partner casts no judgments at all. Usually it is the Capricorn III who plays the dominant role here and is better equipped to deal with the relationship's pressures—pressures that may make Gemini II's nervous and upset. It would make sense for these two to soften their perfectionist stance or to direct it to areas where productivity matters. In love, for example, this orientation can only prove harmful. A relationship that virtually hands out a checklist for appearance, sexual performance and emotional control will make the partners feel as if they were taking an exam. This can drive all spontaneity out of a love affair. In marriages and at work, on the other hand, high standards in domestic and professional tasks can be quite productive. Still, these two should drop firm expectations and investigate their relationship's real depth and potential. In doing so, they will also discover themselves as individuals.

Perfectionism rarely features strongly in most kinds of friendship, and the attempts of Gemini II–Capricorn III friends to achieve it are probably counterproductive. In the family, similarly, one family member demanding perfection may be bad enough, but two can be intolerable.

ADVICE: *Keep standards up, but beware of unrealistic expectations. Minimize stress. Encourage spontaneity and initiative. In love, the fewer the rules the better.*

DUNCAN GRANT (1/21/1885)
JOHN MAYNARD KEYNES (6/5/1883)

In early 20th-century London, Keynes, an economist, and Grant, a painter, were members of the elitist intellectual and cultural circle known as the Bloomsbury group. Although Keynes married and Grant had a long live-in relationship with Virginia Woolf's sister (and her husband), the friends reputedly had a homosexual relationship.

June 3–10
THE WEEK OF NEW LANGUAGE
GEMINI II

January 17–22
THE CUSP OF MYSTERY & IMAGINATION
CAPRICORN-AQUARIUS CUSP

Work and Play

This relationship emphasizes being oneself. At least for adults, its focus is rediscovering the child within, the truly natural part of oneself. Nietzsche once defined maturity as "reacquiring the seriousness one had as a child at play," and indeed so-called responsible adults can learn a great deal about dedication to a task from children. Gemini II's and Capricorn-Aquarians may have difficulties with concentration, since they are often so open to the newest exciting developments and diversions that come along. Their relationship can be a good teacher in this respect, and together, perhaps, they may learn how to give their undivided attention to a job, marriage or other life pursuit.

Gemini II's and Capricorn-Aquarians have rollicking times in love affairs, but also quietly intimate ones. In both cases they are usually able to forget themselves and be absorbed in the activities of the moment. True, introspection does not figure prominently here, but one can learn a lot about oneself from watching what one does, and thus the relationship may raise consciousness if the partners are aware enough to learn.

Marriages and work relationships will be grounds for learning how work and play can be related. An integrated connection between these two areas, or at least the partners' ability to achieve a unity or at least see a connection between them, is the key to success here. Success may be judged by productivity, but also by monitoring the levels alternately of stress and of happiness.

Friendships and sibling relationships are apt to be open to and sympathetic to childlike behavior and the spirit of play, both of which receive a high priority here. Not only is the discharging of responsibilities accomplished with the same verve with which the partners engage in play, but an imaginative spirit may be introduced in daily tasks to make them more palatable. Parent-child tensions are considerable and will periodically need to be resolved.

ADVICE: *Find the balance between childlike and adult behavior, and let each be a model for the other. Work need not be unpleasant nor play trivial.*

June 3–10

THE WEEK OF NEW LANGUAGE
GEMINI II

January 23–30

THE WEEK OF GENIUS
AQUARIUS I

Societal Expertise

Although this relationship is unlikely to be deeply emotional, it is strong socially. These well-suited partners make an excellent combination when interacting with others in clubs, family gatherings and community endeavors. Aquarius I quick wits and Gemini II communication skills coalesce to develop an effective and respected social expertise. The relationship is characterized less by empathy for others than by an objective savvy that guarantees the success of group endeavors. And since both partners are original thinkers, it would not be surprising to find them working quietly to bring new or innovative ideas or trends into a more visible social position. Although the relationship shines in certain areas, it is woefully deficient in others: the great challenge will be for it to confront itself, deepening and enriching itself interpersonally. Recognizing and grappling with problems, meeting painful situations head-on and coping with grief and loss will offer opportunities to make the relationship a less lopsided one.

In love, marriage and friendship, Gemini II's and Aquarius I's are usually less interested in their own development and interaction than in leaving the door open for friends and family to join them in social activities. Whether entertaining or just enjoying conversations, video, games, tv or the Internet, they often include a third or fourth party in the group. Going out is a big item, and among a circle of friends they often take the lead in organizing tickets for concerts, shows and films. They should not be seen as superficial by any means, for they often serve an important function in the group dynamic, lending a sympathetic ear to those in crisis and also, by example, helping others to acquire social skills.

Gemini II–Aquarius I pairs are well suited as co-workers and siblings, bringing liveliness to everyday activities. With these two around there is rarely a dull moment.

CZARINA ALEXANDRA (6/6/1872)
RASPUTIN (1/23/1871)

Rasputin (meaning "debaucher") appeared at the imperial court in 1907 and, with his hypnotic powers, became Alexandra's favorite. Through her, he greatly influenced Czar Nicholas, leading to the eventual collapse of the Romanov dynasty. ***Also:*** **Mme. Chiang Kai-shek & Mme. Sun Yat-Sen** (Soong sisters; wives of Chinese leaders); **Tony Richardson & Vanessa Redgrave** (married; director/actor).

ADVICE: *Dig deeper. Your relationship is as interesting and important as the rest of the world. Work on confronting problems, not escaping from them.*

June 3–10

THE WEEK OF NEW LANGUAGE
GEMINI II

January 31–February 7

THE WEEK OF YOUTH & EASE
AQUARIUS II

Blazing in the Firmament

Normally easygoing and independent, in combination these partners have a competitive side, particularly apparent in a desire to get the attention of others. Issues of needing and being needed figure prominently here. Both pretending not to need the other person at all and wanting the other person to need them more could be recurrent themes, as well as wanting to be needed by the world at large.

Gemini II and Aquarius II lie trine to each other in the zodiac (120° apart), so that traditional astrology predicts an easy time for this airy couple. Yet their relationship is ruled by fire, associated with intuition, and is therefore apt to involve struggle. By working through issues together, Gemini II's and Aquarius II's become uncharacteristically introspective and can truly examine themselves and their values.

The need to be needed is especially evident in love, family and marital relationships. Acute dependencies can arise here, accompanied by addictions to food, drink or drugs. The need to have a good time is sometimes made the most important value—a highly destructive move. Withdrawal symptoms will manifest if one partner decides he or she has had enough or is seduced away by a new prospect. These situations can spark explosive crises, replete with wide emotional swings but also tremendous opportunities for self-discovery and growth. Even anger and disillusionment may play constructive roles in demanding that feelings be faced.

Friendships are more likely to endure, especially if they practice objectivity and nonclaiming attitudes. The need to be the star will create competitiveness, but the pair are capable of becoming a true team, struggling together instead of against each other to gain attention. The overall process is no less egotistical, of course, but is more conducive to the relationship's longevity and worldly success.

Career matchups are perhaps the best for these two, being able to fulfill the relationship's aggressive and outgoing aspects and its need to blaze a trail in the firmament. As colleagues or business partners, Aquarius II's will often ease Gemini II tension while Gemini II's will encourage Aquarius II's to be more forthright and incisive.

JOAO GILBERTO (6/10/31)
STAN GETZ (2/2/27)

Gilberto was a Brazilian composer, guitarist and singer who made a great splash when he introduced the bossa nova and modern samba to America in the 60s. In 1962, Gilberto and Getz, an established tenor-saxist, recorded the album *Jazz Samba,* which won a Grammy.

ADVICE: *Don't lose the opportunity to grow. Beware of addictions. Try to see yourself clearly. Self-discovery is also a sign of success.*

JEFFERSON DAVIS (6/3/08)
ABRAHAM LINCOLN (2/12/1809)

Davis and Lincoln were concurrent presidents during the Civil War. Davis led the pro-slavery forces of the Confederacy, while Lincoln led the Union to victory, ending slavery and preserving a unified nation.

Also: Bruce Dern & Laura Dern (father/daughter;actors); **Judy Garland & Joseph Mankiewicz** (affair; star/director); **Robert McNamara & Dean Rusk** (60s pro-war cabinet members).

June 3–10

THE WEEK OF NEW LANGUAGE
GEMINI II

February 8–15

THE WEEK OF ACCEPTANCE
AQUARIUS III

Behind the Scenes

These two might bring out each other's nervous side. Unstable as the relationship can sometimes be, however, its essentially vital and flamboyant character is appreciated by both partners and by others in its neighborhood. Outright theatrical impulses can emerge here, and whether in a figurative or a real stage situation, Gemini II's and Aquarius III's are likely to put on a good show. Indeed, performance is likely to become the focus of this outgoing relationship.

Air, the element of thought, rules this relationship. Although love affairs may be filled with desire and passion, the mind is never omitted from the equation. Fantasy and quick communication characterize these affairs; the couple not only enjoy each other physically but heighten their pleasure through an acute consciousness and awareness of whatever is going on. The emphasis on the mental realm, however, with its constant analyzing and criticizing, can go too far at times, interfering with the unself-conscious or natural expression of feelings.

Marriages and friendships in this combination must be careful not to pull in negative energy. Such relationships are often magnetic, but the people they attract are just the wrong kind for them—disturbing or seductive influences who may prove divisive, threatening their survival. There is definitely a destructive element at work in these relationships, which have a dark side that may not be evident to the partners themselves but that may nevertheless have to satisfy their own deep needs. Should such shadow areas be ignored or pushed aside, uncontrollable impulses or monstrous problems may be summoned up, possibly involving children or mutual friends.

Parent-child combinations can be mutually devoted and on the same wavelength but can also be disturbing and demanding to daily family life. Favoritism within the relationship may be hurtful to other relatives, making them feel shut out and creating envy and resentment. In career matters, Gemini II's and Aquarius III's can go too far in creating drama and may display a disturbing lack of financial as well as of human understanding.

ADVICE: *Mute expressiveness a bit. Beware of creating jealousies. Tend to your dark side by confronting and dealing with self-destructive impulses.*

RELATIONSHIPS

STRENGTHS: **ENTERPRISING, GROUNDBREAKING, INDEPENDENT**

WEAKNESSES: **UNSYMPATHETIC, OVERAGGRESSIVE, UNAPPRECIATED**

BEST: **WORK**

WORST: **LOVE**

BJORN BORG (6/6/56)
JOHN McENROE (2/16/59)

Borg and McEnroe, 2 of tennis' most exciting rivals, competed in several US Opens and Wimbledon finals now considered some of the best matches in tennis history. **Also: F. Lee Bailey & Patty Hearst** (lawyer/client); **George III & George Washington** (enemies); **John Drew Barrymore & Drew Barrymore** (father/daughter); **Linda Evangelista & Kyle MacLachlan** (married; model/actor).

June 3–10

THE WEEK OF NEW LANGUAGE
GEMINI II

February 16–22

THE CUSP OF SENSITIVITY
AQUARIUS-PISCES CUSP

Groundbreaking Projects

These two may have problems living together day to day, but they are well suited to engaging in enterprising, even groundbreaking projects together. Overall, then, their relationship is likely to be connected with exploration and investigation. Aquarius-Pisces have an aggressive and success-seeking side that will probably meld well with Gemini II energies. They may, however, be too complex for Gemini II's to understand, and their need for silence and privacy may be disturbed by this partner's motor mouth.

Love affairs and friendships between these two are not highly recommended. The emotional depth and sensitivity of Aquarius-Pisces are unlikely to be acknowledged or even perceived by Gemini II's, who find it hard to handle strong feelings, and who may take this partner's silences as rejection. The fact that Gemini II's may well be attracted to such deep individuals does not make these two the best choices for each other.

Marriages may work out better, as long as the spouses have many joint activities to share and do not expect too much of each other emotionally. If this is not the case, they might have the kind of marriage in which they both go their own way, leading fairly independent lives and spending little, albeit quality, time together. Having children must be carefully considered here, however.

Conflict often manifests between these two in the family due to differences in temperament, but a parent-child or sibling pair can furnish the motivation for the family group to move forward in a search for something beyond the ordinary events of everyday life. Inspirational but also a bit kooky, the Gemini II–Aquarius-Pisces pair contributes diversity, daring, expectation and variety to the family of which they are a part.

Working relationships are likely to be excellent. Scientific and technical professions are particularly recommended, either as colleagues or co-workers. Teacher-student relationships may also shine in the areas of research, intellectual discussion and critical commentary.

ADVICE: *Try to be more sympathetic and understanding. Differences of temperament can be reconciled. Don't push too hard too fast.*

June 3–10

THE WEEK OF NEW LANGUAGE
GEMINI II

February 23–March 2

THE WEEK OF SPIRIT
PISCES I

Easily Punctured Balloons

RELATIONSHIPS

STRENGTHS: **LIVELY, PLAYFUL, MENTAL**

WEAKNESSES: **UNSTABLE, ILLUSORY, HYPERCRITICAL**

BEST: **FRIENDSHIP**

WORST: **MARRIAGE**

 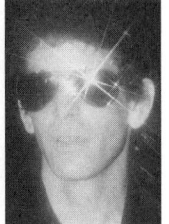

LAURIE ANDERSON (6/5/47)
LOU REED (3/2/42)

Through arts festivals and concerts, avant-garde performance artist Anderson successfully won over mainstream music audiences, especially in Europe. She and singer-songwriter Reed, "the godfather of punk," became romantically involved following his 1994 divorce. **Also: Judy Garland & Vincente Minnelli** (married; star/director).

This dramatic relationship is likely to emphasize critical thought and observation. Mental challenges of all kinds attract this pair, from puzzles to chess to computer games. There is often a friendly rivalry as to who knows best and who knows more. The frequent winner is an I-told-you-so. Vivid Pisces I imagination and Gemini II verbal skills coalesce to produce a lively combination. Pisces I's are pleased to indulge their mental capabilities here, for in many of their relationships it is their emotional side that is principally emphasized.

Love affairs may be unstable. The Gemini II–Pisces I chemistry tends to be volatile and expressive, with feelings flying every which way. Pisces I's may find Gemini II's irritating and undependable, Gemini II's may find Pisces I's dreamy and unincisive. Romantic illusions abound and, like balloons, are easily punctured. Marriages that evolve from such affairs require work on settling differences, becoming more realistic and building a foundation.

Gemini II–Pisces I friendships can be stimulating and fun. A mutual love of games will keep the pair busy, and as a unit they tend to have taste and discernment in matters of food, art and entertainment. Play for them is not just a way of passing time but an activity that they can raise to a high technical and artistic level. Competitiveness between these two is usually constructive, urging them on to better their personal and cumulative best. Nor does the relationship neglect intimacy, for Pisces I's usually have a great deal to teach their Gemini I friends about quiet and the sharing of meditative moments.

Family and work matchups in this combination tend to be busy and provocative in nature. Contention may swirl around this relationship, which seems fated to arouse competitive urges in those in the immediate vicinity. Like a catalyst, the Gemini II–Pisces I relationship may get things initiated or moving faster without really participating in the activity or process itself.

ADVICE: *Try to be more realistic in matters of love. Be aware of the difference between illusion and reality. Consider the outcomes of your words or actions on others.*

June 3–10

THE WEEK OF NEW LANGUAGE
GEMINI II

March 3–10

THE WEEK OF THE LONER
PISCES II

A Deep Inward Connection

RELATIONSHIPS

STRENGTHS: **EMOTIONAL, POWERFUL, SUCCESS-ORIENTED**

WEAKNESSES: **NERVOUS, INSECURE, UNCOMMUNICATIVE**

BEST: **LOVE**

WORST: **FRIENDSHIP**

MARY WILSON (3/6/44)
TOM JONES (6/7/40)

Singer-author Wilson is the best-known ex-Supreme after Diana Ross. She and Jones had a well-publicized affair enhancing his reputation as a sex symbol—even though he is a grandfather and still married to his first wife.

Unbeknownst to them, these two make a profound mark on their environment. Their relationship is about power, though not of the worldly kind that builds empires and conquers mountains; rather, it is something more personal that these two bring out in each other. This power becomes not only a symbol of but a reason for the deep inward connection here. With the relationship's support, these two can more courageously express who they are and who they want to be.

The quality of the Gemini II–Pisces II connection is often most apparent in their love affairs. This love is often more spiritual or platonic than physical, although sexual passion cannot be ruled out. Problems of communication arise, since Pisces II's may periodically go incommunicado, isolating themselves in their own world, removed from both the stresses of life and the anxious queries of their partner. They may also be made insecure by the Gemini II need to go outside the relationship periodically for comfort or affection, a step they tend to regard as an act of betrayal.

Marriages are emotionally rich and may work, though on the whole they lack the stability to hold together. Gemini II and Pisces II are square (90° apart) to each other in the zodiac, an omen of difficulty. Although that translates in this combination as nervousness, worry or depression rather than overt conflict, these passive states are actually much harder for Gemini II's to deal with than outright anger or aggression. Despite their difficulty in interacting, these spouses may have a hard time letting go of their marriage, which gives them so much in the way of growth and self-expression. Friendships may be a good bet, but can lack intensity and have a tendency to drift. Working partnerships, on the other hand, are powerful and success-oriented, although perhaps not overly ambitious. A realistic outlook based on the relationship's objective strengths and capabilities is likely to characterize these business connections. Parent-child relationships in this combination feature affection and sympathy, but also a tendency for quiet times to be interrupted by bickering and emotional upheavals.

ADVICE: *Don't be afraid to push a bit harder. Try to even out emotional moods. Keep lines of communication open. Beware of a compulsion to withdraw.*

LIZA MINNELLI (3/12/46)
JUDY GARLAND (6/10/22)

Liza was raised as an entertainer, appearing at age 2 in a film of her mom's and joining in her live performances while growing up. She began her own successful song and dance career in the 60s. They were great friends until Judy's tragic death in 1969.

June 3–10
THE WEEK OF NEW LANGUAGE
GEMINI II

March 11–18
THE WEEK OF DANCERS & DREAMERS
PISCES III

From Ecstasy to Catastrophe

Profound and intense, this relationship could prove too much for its partners, whose dynamic side it brings out. They may even come to resent it, since it takes so much time and energy, yet outside of it they may never feel so alive. Both of them believe that being unable to feel is probably the worst feeling of all, so that their relationship—painful possibly, boring never—may make them dissatisfied with other areas of their lives, which seem almost lifeless in comparison. Since together they attract a whirlwind of experiences, some joyful, others quite hard, it will seem from the outside that they are extremely lucky, cursed, or both.

Love affairs can range from the ecstatic to the catastrophic. Feelings of joy and sadness, happiness and despair, exaltation and depression may follow each other with bewildering intensity. Not knowing where they are headed or even sometimes where they came from, the couple are buffeted by storms of emotion. Yet their empathy is such that each can read the other's emotional language unerringly. For Gemini II's, whose strongest mode of communication is verbal, the Pisces III language of love can be an unforgettable experience.

Marriages and business relationships are discouraged here, since conflict is likely and intrusive emotional states may be debilitating. A company's smooth functioning can be brought to a halt here as quickly as if a monkey wrench had been dropped into a transmission. Family relationships are prone to breakdown when a sibling or parent-child combination suffers an emotional flare-up. It is best to avoid public scenes and work problems out behind closed doors. Friendships can work as long as lines of communication remain open and arguments and debates are limited. Pisces III's tend to hold forth on metaphysical subjects with almost religious intensity, while Gemini II's are likely to use reason and stick to the facts, often belittling matters of faith; if the pair of them can agree to disagree in a civilized way, and to fall back on activities and topics that are sympathetic to both, the relationship has a good chance of lasting.

ADVICE: *Tone down rhetoric without losing intensity. Love can often be fragile and is worth preserving. Show personal respect and consideration.*

CHRISTO (6/13/35)
JEANNE-CLAUDE (6/13/35)

Remarkably, this inseparable couple were born on the exact same day. They are environmental artists who pay for all their own projects. Their large-scale temporary works of art, at both urban and rural sites, include *Running Fence, Surrounded Islands* and wrapped *Reichstag*. They met in Paris in '58. Their son Cyril was born in '60.

June 11–18
THE WEEK OF THE SEEKER
GEMINI III

June 11–18
THE WEEK OF THE SEEKER
GEMINI III

Being Cool

This relationship is about encountering challenging situations on a daily basis. With this as a jumping-off point, these two might wind up emotionally close, but more probably will move in just the opposite direction: that of suppressing feelings and maintaining strict objectivity in the personal sphere. Free spirits, Gemini III's will tolerate very few rules, but if their relationship has a governing principle it could certainly be, "Be cool—don't get emotionally involved with each other." This is in fact the key to the combination's success. Indeed the survival not only of the relationship but also, in life-threatening situations, of the lives of one or both partners could depend on it.

Why would these independent and adventuresome people really need to live together? Conventional love and marriage may only be possible for unusual, less adventuresome Gemini III stay-at-homes. More typically their affairs and marriages have to allow them the greatest latitude to roam the world in search of adventure—probably alone, or with a non-Gemini III partner. It's true that a friendship or business based on travel, somewhat risky financial dealings, dangerous physical achievement or the like could lead them to spend a lot of time together, but stability, affection and coziness will rarely be the important values here—independence and freedom will remain paramount. One might ask why they would want this relationship at all, but what Gemini III's desire, they will have, and on their own terms.

In the family, more distant kinship ties, such as grandparent-grandchild pairs, tend to work better than parent-child or sibling matchups. Siblings will have great difficulty with the fact that simply growing up together will force them to relate to each other for years, and to face inevitable rules and responsibilities. Such a pair, even when they are twins, should be given as much as possible that is theirs alone and that they do not have to share. Nor should they be responsible for each other or perform the same chores.

ADVICE: *Have firm goals in mind. Don't get sidetracked by danger. Allow as much sharing as is possible or advisable. Be emotionally honest.*

June 11–18

THE WEEK OF THE SEEKER
GEMINI III

June 19–24

THE CUSP OF MAGIC
GEMINI-CANCER CUSP

Slaying Dragons

This relationship will devote its energy to trying to accomplish epic feats. Whether these attempts have a chance of success or will in retrospect be revealed as unrealistic will very much depend on the orientation here. "Epic feats" don't necessarily have to be on the scale of slaying dragons, or making a killing in the stock market; they can include bringing to fruition projects that might ordinarily be out of reach. The Gemini III aspiring outlook and the Gemini-Cancer ability to work magic can synergistically combine in a relationship with just such awesome powers.

Love and marriage between these two are likely to be secondary to their struggle to achieve their goals. Gemini-Cancers must be induced to be motivated here, for their basic tendency in such relationships is to give themselves to romance and the security of a home base. Gemini III's, then, must be able to prove to them what is at stake and how it can be achieved. Should the pair fail in their goals, Gemini-Cancers may grow to dislike and ultimately reject the relationship's values.

Friendships between these two are more apt to be easygoing, with fewer pressures. Gemini III's will usually go off and do their own thing here without trying to involve their Gemini-Cancer partner so much. The large-scale projects and expansive outlooks of friends in this combination may be more spectatorial or appreciative in kind—collecting the complete works of a rock band or author, say, or attending a season's worth of sporting events.

This relationship is likely to work best at work or in the family. Here the desire for epic feats can be put to the service of the group, and both Gemini III success drives and the Gemini-Cancer need for security can be satisfied.

ADVICE: *Don't always think so big. Be more realistic about the goals you can achieve. Don't forget to make your home base secure and happy.*

RELATIONSHIPS

STRENGTHS: **ASPIRING, EXPANSIVE, OPTIMISTIC**

WEAKNESSES: **UNREALISTIC, INSECURE, DISAPPOINTED**

BEST: **FAMILY**

WORST: **LOVE**

HENRY WARD BEECHER (6/24/1813)
HARRIET BEECHER STOWE (6/14/1811)

Novelist Stowe's *Uncle Tom's Cabin* (1852) brought her international renown. Her brother, Rev. Beecher, the notorious Christian orator, preached unorthodox sermons. His loyal followers supported him even during his 1875 adultery trial. *Also:* **Vic Damone & Pier Angeli** (married; singer/actress); **Jack Albertson & Freddie Prinze** (co-stars, *Chico & the Man*).

June 11–18

THE WEEK OF THE SEEKER
GEMINI III

June 25–July 2

THE WEEK OF THE EMPATH
CANCER I

Too Good to Be True

The Gemini III–Cancer I relationship has a magical quality that at times seems too good to be true. Rarely arousing envy, it instead seems to make many of those around it happy, perhaps because they are enchanted by its near-fairy-tale quality. One might expect a certain air of unreality here, but actually a realistic approach often substantiates the magic and gives it direction. Rather, a sense of rightness, a feeling that these two belong together, infects this couple and those who observe them. Such certainty is rare and should be treasured. Cancer I's will find themselves motivated by the electric dynamism of Gemini III's, who in turn will benefit from Cancer I empathic ability and skill in creating a cozy home base.

Romance can hit new highs here. Blissful states may be familiar to feeling-oriented Cancer I's; Gemini III's may have experienced glimmerings of such feelings in the adventuresome pursuit of external goals but now encounter them for the first time in a real live human being. Should such a relationship end, the partners will experience its loss as tragic and could have a hard time getting over it. This is especially true if one of the partners is called back from the affair to another, primary relationship, especially if this is a marriage involving children, career or social responsibilities.

Such a viable love relationship as this one can obviously evolve into marriage, but some of the magic may be lost in the process, resulting in disappointment or disillusion. The spouses may look back longingly to bygone rapture, wondering why pots and pans, bills and diaper-changing ever had to be added to the equation.

Siblings and friends of this combination are capable of a magical relationship. Cancer I's know intuitively when their Gemini III partner needs sympathy or consolation, and the seductive and cajoling manner of Gemini III's can help bring Cancer I's out of depressions. Working relationships generally demand a harder, more pragmatic approach than is possible in this combination.

ADVICE: *Don't get stuck. Try to keep a balance. Keep a philosophical outlook. Disappointment follows unrealistic expectations. Don't lose your way.*

RELATIONSHIPS

STRENGTHS: **MAGICAL, EMPATHIC, AMBITIOUS**

WEAKNESSES: **ATTACHED, DISILLUSIONED, GRIEVING**

BEST: **LOVE**

WORST: **WORK**

GILDA RADNER (6/28/46)
GENE WILDER (6/11/35)

Radner's brilliant, versatile comedy talent blended easily with that of screen comic actor Wilder. They had a close marriage from 1984 (Radner's 2nd) until her early death from cancer in 1989. *Also:* **Jeanette MacDonald & Nelson Eddy** ("singing sweethearts"); **George Bush & Ross Perot** (1992 presidential candidates).

DAVID ROCKEFELLER (6/12/15)
NELSON ROCKEFELLER (7/8/08)

These wealthy brothers were both prominent in their respective areas. David headed the Chase Manhattan Bank from 1962–81. Nelson was New York's governor for 4 terms (1959–73), then appointed as Ford's vice-president in 1974.

June 11–18
THE WEEK OF THE SEEKER
GEMINI III

July 3–10
THE WEEK OF THE UNCONVENTIONAL
CANCER II

Fantasy Versus Reality

The conflict in this relationship will be the struggle between fantasy and reality but also between the inner world and the outer. Compromise is not usually possible here. Gemini III's will want Cancer II's to leave their inner sanctum to join them in the outer world; Cancer II's will want Gemini III's to retire from a life of adventure and relax with them at home. Neither partner is really suited for the life of the other, yet it may be possible for each of them periodically to take the lead in their particular area and have their partner follow them for a time. In this way each can get to rule temporarily, and the need to find a common but watered-down meeting ground is circumvented.

The relationship is likely to stretch the limits of love and friendship. If these two vacation together, the Gemini III will want to go trekking in some God-forsaken outpost. There the Cancer II will take pictures to be gone through sentimentally at home, souvenirs of the trip; the Gemini III, meanwhile, will be off climbing. Later, the Gemini III will be forced to admire the Cancer II's photographs for the umpteenth time, all the while just itching to get away on a new adventure. Given this scenario, informal acquaintanceships or casual companionships are perhaps a better bet than close ties here.

Marriages too will have to demonstrate great understanding. The Cancer II will be the undisputed boss at home, but the Gemini III may not be around much to be bossed. Children will probably know their Cancer II parent better, but in fantasy and memory could elevate the Gemini III parent to a high place, and perhaps will want to join him or her on challenging projects and trips.

Successful work relationships between these two are unlikely. Business partnerships in particular suffer from a lack of practicality and financial acumen. In the family, endless disputes and conflicts are likely to surface between these contrasting personalities, except, strangely enough, when they are same-sex siblings, a matchup that enhances their compatibility.

ADVICE: *Work to find more in common. Follow the other's lead whenever possible. Compromise isn't really so bad. Try to be more diplomatic.*

DIAHANN CARROLL (7/17/35)
VIC DAMONE (6/12/28)

Damone was a popular crooner of both film and stage in the 50s. In 1989 he married singer-actress Carroll, the first black personality to star in a regular tv series, *Julia* (1968–71). ***Also:* Katharine Graham & Philip Graham** (married; publishers).

June 11–18
THE WEEK OF THE SEEKER
GEMINI III

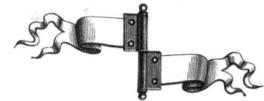

July 11–18
THE WEEK OF THE PERSUADER
CANCER III

Defying Society's Edicts

An empathic connection binds these two firmly. The partners sometimes feel related on a soul level; should they part, they may feel the relationship's loss for a lifetime. Other people will be confused by their apparent incompatibility—there are great differences between them, and they rarely understand or sympathize with each other's ideas and feelings. They usually come together, however, around a drive to control and ultimately conquer their environment. Cancer III's usually exert this drive in their careers, Gemini III's in their immediate surroundings, wherever in the world they happen to be. The relationship is challenge oriented and often hides underlying insecurities.

Cancer III–Gemini III love affairs will defy social edicts in their expression of passionate desire (assuming such desire is present). They demonstrate more than a hint of rebellion, showing little respect for stupid rules and outworn creeds. Both partners believe that what happens between two people is their business and theirs alone, yet curiously they make little effort to hide their affair from outside scrutiny. The exhibitionism and unprotectedness of this relationship may prove its downfall.

This couple is rarely interested in marriage, but a Cancer III who does want a Gemini III as a mate can be powerfully persuasive. Even so, free-spirited Gemini III's will ultimately only agree out of their own choice, and attempts to manipulate or control them may only put them off. Subtler Cancer III's will let Gemini III's think they have come up with the idea themselves, not realizing that it has been gently planted in them.

Gemini III–Cancer III friendships are not immediately suggested, but the relationship's empathic connection can take the pair a long way. A frequent theme in these situations will be talking about feelings. Although they may not see each other consistently, friends in this combination will be there for each other in times of need. Their selfishness in getting their own way often leaves little room for any third party in the equation. The same holds true for family and work relationships, but here, inconsistency of contact will prove much more problematic.

ADVICE: *Try to see things from the other person's point of view. Do what you need to do quietly. Don't be guided by rebelliousness—instead, follow your heart.*

June 11–18
THE WEEK OF THE SEEKER
GEMINI III

July 19–25
THE CUSP OF OSCILLATION
CANCER-LEO CUSP

Gritty Determination

This relationship has a gritty determination to succeed and to overcome all obstacles that stand in the way. Gemini III's activate the risk-taking urges of Cancer-Leos; their relationship is likely to center around exciting and challenging endeavors, whether in the world of nature or of finance. The problem here is that the relationship may put Cancer-Leos under excessive stress. They need a stable and supportive partner and a secure home base, and are less well suited to the risks and striving that this matchup encourages than their Gemini III partners. The wise course would be to make allowance for this, or else risk a breakdown in relations.

Love affairs in this combination can be highly romantic, but when they come down off cloud nine, Cancer-Leos may be made a little insecure by the Gemini III's desire to get on with the next challenge. The relationship will have to exhibit great flexibility to accommodate its partners' differing needs. Their marriages can be successful and enduring, however, with Cancer-Leos sometimes joining Gemini III's on their adventures, sometimes concentrating on the home base. Cancer-Leos may not be capable of handling parental, domestic, financial and nurturing activities completely on their own; some negotiation may be required as to the level of the Gemini III's involvement.

Gemini III–Cancer-Leo friendships are likely to work out well. They tend to include challenging activities, especially physical ones—sports, fitness, martial arts, travel. Business and sibling matchups in this combination are likely to have a destabilizing effect at work and in the family but also to provide a dynamic of encouraging enterprise and success through determination and risk-taking. At home these siblings can only function well if at least one of the parents can furnish stability and a pragmatic commonsense viewpoint. Otherwise there is likely to be periodic chaos.

ADVICE: *Don't attempt too much. Recognize your limitations. Build in a safety or security factor. Don't neglect your home base. Try to be realistic.*

CAROL KANE (6/18/52)
WOODY HARRELSON (7/23/61)

Kane won an Emmy for her notable role as Simka, playing opposite Andy Kaufman on tv's *Taxi* (1981–83). Harrelson, who gained popularity on *Cheers* (1985–93), has since become a major film actor. The pair were romantically involved.

June 11–18
THE WEEK OF THE SEEKER
GEMINI III

July 26–August 2
THE WEEK OF AUTHORITY
LEO I

A Force for Positive Change

This relationship may find itself involved in a social, moral, ethical or religious code or system of belief that champions equality and denounces exclusion or privilege. It might well be politically involved, its partners seeing themselves as champions of the downtrodden. If expansive Gemini III vision and motivating ability can meld with Leo I leadership skills, the relationship can be a force for positive change. Kindness, affection and sympathy are likely here; Gemini III's can often provide the patience and understanding that relationships with Leo I's require, and they also have a sound business sense that is likely to keep shared projects on the rails. The relationship is usually optimistic, but the partners must be careful neither to avoid self-criticism nor to dismiss the valuable suggestions of others as unwanted negativity.

Love affairs may click sexually, and should their romance fade, love of a less heated nature, leading to friendship or marriage, may take its place. These latter relationships often turn out to be more important than the original affair, which in retrospect may be seen simply as the means by which the pair was brought together. Elements of friendship and marriage can intermingle here, with the personal and human element in the forefront.

This duo is capable of highly unconventional work relationships, which they often put in the service of a cause. This endeavor may not be exclusively idealistic and noncommercial; innovative Gemini III's and Leo I's will find ways to make their idealism pay off, often developing a product or service that is a solid moneymaker. Even if profits fail to soar off the charts, the relationship will generally function well on a modest but reasonable cash return.

Parent-child relationships in this combination are tricky. Leo I parents can be powerful influences in the lives of their Gemini III children, but the crucial question is whether their influence is entirely beneficial— these powerful personalities are not invariably satisfactory role models. It is also questionable whether flighty Gemini III's can provide the unwavering attention and recognition a young Leo I needs.

ADVICE: *Listen to the suggestions of others. Be more self-critical. Beware of getting carried away by excessive idealism or conceit.*

GIORGIO VASARI (7/30/1511)
COSIMO DE MEDICI (6/12/1519)

The Medici dynasty comprised the greatest family of art patrons in Italian history. Cosimo is considered the true founder of this role. Vasari, a writer, painter and architect of the period, glorified the Medicis in a series of paintings in Florence's Palazzo Vecchio.

Also: Timothy Busfield & Ken Olin (co-stars, *thirtysomething*).

ERIK ERIKSON (6/15/02)
JEAN PIAGET (8/9/1896)

Danish-American Erikson and Swiss Piaget were contemporary psychologists and pioneers in the study of child development. Piaget is known for his research on children's cognitive and intellectual growth. Erikson focused on the influence of social, cultural and other environmental factors in the psychosexual stages of early development.

June 11–18

THE WEEK OF THE SEEKER
GEMINI III

August 3–10

THE WEEK OF BALANCED STRENGTH
LEO II

Fraught with Risk

This relationship exhibits a desire not just to achieve its goals but to achieve them totally. Whether the targets are shared or individual, results are what count here. These two are a good match for each other when it comes to exploring, adventure, risk-taking and in general performing feats that others would consider difficult or impossible. For Gemini III's and Leo II's, projects like these may be all in a day's work. Responsibility to each other is often crucial in this relationship, since both partners know that in hazardous situations one slip can be deadly.

Love affairs between these two can be fraught with risk, but Gemini III's are often drawn to danger. Leo II's are generally more stable and self-assured than Gemini III's, and will not hesitate to try to develop and protect the relationship, regardless of any social disapproval it incurs—for often one of the partners is already involved in a long-standing marriage or love partnership. Frowns from others just make Gemini III's rebellious. Rather than forming a triangle with the third person, this couple is likely to carry on in secret for a while, then one day just run off together. Should they themselves marry, this scenario might repeat again with someone else. If so, it is usually the Leo II spouse who remains faithful and is left behind.

Friendships and working partnerships often overlap, particularly in challenging and adventuresome projects. Spurred on by challenge, the pair are likely to achieve great success, whether fighting on the same side as executives in the board room or quietly planning and mapping out a strategy to counter powerful opposition. Unreliability here is viewed as a major breach of trust, and treachery is the worst possible crime. Breakups in such relationships are usually final and can result in animosity or hurt feelings for years thereafter.

Sibling matchups, especially those of the same sex, can be competitive in a positive way, spurring the partners on to better their own personal best.

ADVICE: *Ease up in your demands. Appreciate the delights of relaxation or even boredom. Mute competitive drives. Don't be too tempted by danger.*

FIDEL CASTRO (8/13/26)
CHE GUEVARA (6/14/28)

Guevara and Castro were co-plotters in the communist takeover of Cuba. After their successful 1959 revolution, they assumed power together. In 1965, Guevara was captured and executed in South America, where he was attempting to spread communist control.

Also: Jeanette MacDonald & **Gene Raymond** (married; singer/ actor).

June 11–18

THE WEEK OF THE SEEKER
GEMINI III

August 11–18

THE WEEK OF LEADERSHIP
LEO III

Achieving Consistency

This relationship is a study in complex emotions and power struggles. The central theme here is likely to be a mixture of persuasion and manipulation—it is often hard to say where one leaves off and the other begins. Within the relationship, Gemini III's are usually the masters in both of these activities, but Leo III's tend to take the lead in dealing with work, family or marital issues involving other people. In these situations the Leo III will treat the Gemini III as a right hand. Gemini III's are not averse to playing such a role, for in freeing them of responsibility and the obligation to fill the top spot, it allows them more liberty.

Although Gemini is an air sign and Leo fire, the Gemini III–Leo III relationship is governed by the element of water, associated with feeling. Many contrary emotions swirl around in this relationship's emotional mix, then, and a difficult blend of interest and apathy, desire and indifference, sympathy and hostility, is likely to dominate most relationships in this combination at any one time. Understanding and empathy are generally constant factors, however.

Love affairs between these two may continue for some time, or at least until either the Leo III or the Gemini III suddenly announces an interest in getting married—when they may as easily separate as proceed on together. In either sphere, sex is unlikely to be a crucial factor; these two enjoy each other's companionship in a wide variety of activities, and friendship is usually the underlying basis of all their personal relationships with each other. They might even be said to agree that without friendship they have little else together.

In work and family settings, Gemini III's and Leo III's may be emotionally close but are not always effective in getting the job done. Leo III's are obviously better in the role of parent or boss—Gemini III's in such roles may not be as effective in directing or parenting a Leo III employee or child.

ADVICE: *Aim for consistency and constancy. Solve power struggles by leaving them behind. Take responsibility for your actions. What are you afraid of?*

June 11–18
THE WEEK OF THE SEEKER
GEMINI III

August 19–25
THE CUSP OF EXPOSURE
LEO-VIRGO CUSP

Hide-and-Seek

This matchup might resemble a game of hide-and-seek, with the Gemini III the seeker and the Leo-Virgo the hider. But its focus is better defined as a mutual exploration into the fascinating worlds of mystery and imagination. Conflicts for domination of this realm are never far off. Leo-Virgos are often somewhat secretive and hidden personalities, just waiting for someone to find the key. Gemini III's are generally less interested in psychological exploration than in striving for success and recognition in the external world, but their relationships with Leo-Virgos usually have the effect of attracting them to emotional, spiritual, creative or even supernatural worlds worthy of their investigatory skills. Research into these areas may prove a strong and lasting bond for this pair.

Love affairs here are vivid and alive, but also quite intimate and private, possessing many meditative moments. This is one relationship in which Gemini III's can forget about their many tasks and lose themselves in a maze of feelings and sensations. Often they won't want to come out again. Getting lost together in the corridors of love may become a common experience for Gemini III–Leo-Virgo partners.

Marriages here tend to be more humdrum, losing the imaginative spark that the couple had as lovers. Friendships, on the other hand, although lacking a strong sexual or romantic component, can be intimate and creative. Leo-Virgos' sense of worth may get a big boost from more confident Gemini III's, who for their part will learn from this partner how to increase their personal power by keeping their thoughts and feelings private.

Sibling and parent-child matchups are unlikely to contribute much to family life, but these two may enjoy interactions outside the family setting. Parents must take care not to dominate children, especially when at play. At work, Leo-Virgos tend to be critical of the idiosyncratic methods of Gemini III's, even while they themselves tend to dwell in a private internal space where it is hard for this co-worker to communicate with them.

ADVICE: *Keep the flame alive. Try to understand yourself better. Meet problems head-on without running away. Work on communication.*

GEORGE BUSH (6/12/24)
BILL CLINTON (8/19/46)

In the 1992 presidential campaign, Clinton advocated new economic growth programs, healthcare and educational reform. Bush responded by attacking Clinton's character and record as Arkansas governor. Clinton won by a 43% to 38% margin.
Also: George Bush & General Norman Schwarzkopf (commander-in-chief/general).

June 11–18
THE WEEK OF THE SEEKER
GEMINI III

August 26–September 2
THE WEEK OF SYSTEM BUILDERS
VIRGO I

Need for Compromise

This relationship is likely to be unsettled, involving constant oscillations of mood. Much of the fluctuation is the result of changing or inconstant ideas or information within the relationship; a focus on practical matters will be necessary if that tendency is to be kept in check. This will always be an uphill battle, for Virgo I's are prone to unrealistic and even catastrophic partner choices, particularly in love and marriage, and a Gemini III might, unfortunately, represent just such a choice. Gemini III's are usually much too busy with their own activities to fit into the kind of structured life that Virgo I's require. They will rarely feel comfortable in a domestic situation marked by the kinds of rules and ordered physical setups that are the Virgo I trademark, and their inability to live by fixed schedules, or to compromise their freedom of movement in any way, will drive a Virgo I to distraction.

Friendships in this combination can work out much better. They will have their ups and downs, but the absence of rigid responsibilities, and the ability to express preferences without imposing them, create a greater chance of success. Virgo I's enjoy a relationship in which they are free to watch and even chronicle the activities of their unpredictable partner; Gemini III's like being able to relax periodically in an atmosphere where they know that everything is taken care of and under control. Differing attitudes do not conflict in these situations and are, in fact, appreciated.

At work and in the family, the kind of order imposed by Virgo I parents and bosses can be reassuring for Gemini III children or employees unless it is rigid and uncaring, when it will prove intolerable. Rebellion is often the consequence. Gemini III–Virgo I sibling or co-worker pairs usually get along well, often because of their differences rather than despite them. Brother-sister pairs are especially favored here, since their respective strengths can dovetail well in the family setting, and also because they often demonstrate empathy and understanding for each other.

ADVICE: *Learn the value of compromise. Beware of rigid attitudes. To insist on freedom is to be inflexible. Lighten up. Be kinder.*

KATHARINE GRAHAM (6/16/17)
BEN BRADLEE (8/26/21)

After her husband's 1963 suicide, Graham took over the *Washington Post* and *Newsweek*. During her 10 years at the *Post*, she appointed Bradlee as editor-in-chief.
Also: Paul McCartney & Michael Jackson (collaborators; Beatle/owner of Beatles song rights); **David Rose & Martha Raye** (married; bandleader/comedienne).

RELATIONSHIPS

STRENGTHS: **CONVERSATIONAL, INTELLIGENT, EDUCATIONAL**

WEAKNESSES: **ARGUMENTATIVE, IMPATIENT, NON EMOTIONAL**

BEST: **STUDENT**

WORST: **FRIENDSHIP**

NIGEL BRUCE (9/4/1895)
BASIL RATHBONE (6/13/1892)

Rathbone's aloof and suave qualities as a 30s Hollywood villain served him well as a convincing Sherlock Holmes a decade later. Bruce was the perfect foil as Dr. Watson—a stuttering, amazed witness to Holmes' revelations. They made 14 films together. *Also:* **Waylon Jennings & Buddy Holly** (rock & roll collaborators).

June 11–18
THE WEEK OF THE SEEKER
GEMINI III

September 3–10
THE WEEK OF THE ENIGMA
VIRGO II

The Eternal Student

The Gemini III–Virgo II relationship is likely to focus on the mental plane. Relationships between teachers and students, career colleagues and even more distant family relatives may be most successful here. Areas of study or interest in the humanities, perhaps in art, history, sociology or politics, are attractive to this pair. Whether their contacts take place in or out of school, discussion of written material can be stimulating and fulfilling to them. Gemini III's are intensely physical individuals, but they often try to overcome earthly limitations to find what lies beyond, and it is in this more metaphysical area that their relationship with Virgo II's may reach fruition. These two are unlikely to achieve deep union in the emotional and intuitive sphere, since neither will have enough patience or interest to delve deeply into the other's personality. It is in the more objective sphere, the world of thought and ideas, that they have the greatest chance to make contact.

This is not to imply that Gemini III's and Virgo II's should not become romantically involved. In their affairs and marriages, they usually keep their emotions tightly under control and in a secondary position to more intellectual activities; relationships that follow this pattern can easily be successful. Marriages can certainly be productive but are more likely to occur when the partners are older and have more appreciation for the matchup's mental orientation. Gemini III–Virgo II friends may lack the dedication and depth of understanding to make real contact and are usually better off as casual companions and acquaintances, perhaps as students or trainees in a learning or apprenticeship situation. Whatever the case, these two often have a catalytic effect on each other's ability to learn, and their relationship may be particularly well suited to supporting educational endeavors. Work relationships between these two can be excellent, especially in technically oriented fields. In close family relationships, however, particularly between siblings, Gemini III's and Virgo II's are likely to argue a lot and indulge in I-told-you-so or one-upmanship game-playing. Wise parents of such children will find more constructive outlets for their mental competitiveness.

ADVICE: *Balance mental and physical urges. Try to redirect game-playing. Deepen your emotional ties. Don't be afraid to show your feelings.*

RELATIONSHIPS

STRENGTHS: **FRANK, QUICK, PRINCIPLED**

WEAKNESSES: **HARD, UNSYMPATHETIC, NEGLECTFUL**

BEST: **BUSINESS PARTNERSHIP**

WORST: **PARENT-CHILD**

ALFRED KNOPF (9/12/1892)
ALFRED KNOPF, JR. (6/17/18)

In 1915 Knopf, Sr. started a book publishing company that held the industry's most prestigious literary titles. After training under his father, Knopf Jr. left in 1957 to form (with 2 partners) Atheneum Publishers, which quickly built its own distinguished list.

Also: **Courtney Cox & Brian DePalma** (actress discovered by director); **Joe Montana & Dan Marino** (rival quarterbacks).

June 11–18
THE WEEK OF THE SEEKER
GEMINI III

September 11–18
THE WEEK OF THE LITERALIST
VIRGO III

Hammering Out Basic Principles

Since these two lie 90° apart in the zodiac and thus form a square or hard aspect with each other, traditional astrology predicts struggle between them—and in fact one does find them vying for leadership. But although it is true that they are tough with each other, respect and understanding often emerge after several confrontations. The relationship's focus is likely to be finding an authority acknowledged by both partners. Should a basic set of principles be agree upon, perhaps hammered out on the hard anvil of experience, the relationship may become a firm and enduring bond.

Passion can certainly sweep both partners away in love affairs, but for the most part willpower and common sense master emotion. Mercury, ruler of both Gemini and Virgo, is especially strong in this particular combination of them, guaranteeing quick responses and giving the relationship a logical and discriminating outlook. Rarely will either of these partners allow their feelings to urge them into activities ultimately counterproductive to their best interests, either as individuals or as a duo.

Marriages can be based on pragmatic principles as long as both partners contribute equally. The constant difficulty is that Gemini III's may be gone a good deal of the time, or may skip out on work, leaving their Virgo III spouse to finish things up. These partners are capable of being excellent parents, both inspiring and educating. Setting up open channels with their children, and keeping these avenues open throughout their adolescent years, will be a great and rewarding challenge. Although capable of being good friends, Gemini III's and Virgo III's may not have either the time or the need to develop this kind of relationship. At work, on the other hand, these two can make excellent business partners, with Gemini III's contributing financial and worldly skills and Virgo III's the hard work, dedication and application needed to bring an enterprise success. Family relationships in this combination, particularly parent-child matchups, are fraught with emotional difficulties but are often more positive than either partner is prepared to admit.

ADVICE: *There is more to life than hard work. Take frequent, pleasurable and relaxing vacations. Try being a bit more sympathetic and affectionate.*

June 11–18

THE WEEK OF THE SEEKER
GEMINI III

September 19–24

THE CUSP OF BEAUTY
VIRGO-LIBRA CUSP

Serendipitous Occurrences

This easygoing relationship is likely to feature serendipitous occurrences that charm and delight. Just such an occurrence, in fact, probably brought these two together in the first place. Psychic or electric connections are likely to emerge between these partners, each of whom often knows what the other is thinking, and who can anticipate each other's actions before they happen. Seekers in search of beauty, Gemini III's can quickly turn their sights from that distant mountain to an attractive Virgo-Libra similarly occupied. Before you know it they have engaged in conversation, and a new relationship is born.

Romantic relationships have a feeling of destiny about them, as if they were meant to be. The upside here is that the relationship can run perfectly well by itself, without interference; the downside is a tendency to drift or stagnate, with neither partner having the willpower to do anything about it. This curious malaise may have to be cured by a good healthy kick in the pants from fate, often in the form of a somewhat threatening situation that demands prompt action. Such disturbing events occur with a certain frequency here, but their revival of a sleeping or dormant relationship is necessary from time to time.

Marriages can last for years, with both partners more or less devoted to each other. Their common love of beauty will be reflected in the furnishings and interior design of their home. Virgo-Libra possessiveness may lead to frustration and insecurity over what they see as an inability to get a firm grip on their independent Gemini III partner, who, meanwhile, may actually be perfectly happy with the love of their Virgo-Libra mate.

Friendships in this combination often demonstrate a love of both the natural and the artificial worlds, the former in most cases favored by Gemini III's, the latter by Virgo-Libras. Sharing and seeking to reconcile these interests can be highly fulfilling. In the family, parent-child combinations can show a special interest in aesthetic matters.

ADVICE: *Try to exert more willpower. Control claiming impulses. The lessons of fate usually prove beneficial. Bring your worlds together.*

PAUL McCARTNEY (6/18/42)
LINDA EASTMAN (9/24/42)

Former Beatle McCartney married American photographer Eastman in 1969. In 1971 they formed the popular rock group *Wings*, featuring Linda on keyboards and backup vocals. Honoring his musical achievements, Queen Elizabeth knighted McCartney in 1997.

June 11–18

THE WEEK OF THE SEEKER
GEMINI III

September 25–October 2

THE WEEK OF THE PERFECTIONIST
LIBRA I

Open to Scrutiny

Although this relationship is imbued with endurance and tenacity, it is challenged by the task of balancing its partners' energies so that they can keep their sights on their goals. Gemini and Libra are air signs, connected with thought, but the Gemini III–Libra I relationship is governed by fire, the element of drive and passion. This pair will be involved in leaping large hurdles. Separately neither of them has much staying power, but together they can outlast anyone.

Largely because of their ability to achieve, Gemini III–Libra I relationships can be powerfully influential to those around them. They often harbor a blind spot, however: the partners don't realize how open their private affairs are to the scrutiny of others. Their passionate impulses, for example, are visible to all. Moreover, these are fiery enough that they sometimes threaten to burn down structures—family, business or otherwise—that have taken years to build, probably terrifying the other people involved. The balance needed here will lie in agreements, whether verbal or unspoken, to act in a way that promotes harmony and minimizes upset for all concerned.

Perhaps the most challenging kind of relationship for this pair is marriage, or living together as adults. First, they will have to limit the frequency of their sexual contact to forestall a neurotic effect on other areas of life, and to avoid burnout. Second, they will have to be strictly honest with each other about their activities with other people, and about the time they spend away from home. Third and most important, they must establish an umbrella of mutual trust and respect that will reconcile Libra I critical tendencies and Gemini III vagueness and lack of commitment. Friendships in this combination can work well as long as extremes of feeling are avoided. Career matchups are rarely advisable, however, since the pair's high degree of subjective involvement is detrimental to the quality of their work. In family relationships, Libra I parents may feel they have everything running smoothly with regard to their Gemini III child, when the truth is just the opposite.

ADVICE: *Too much control is not the answer. Normalize relationships. Hiding the truth has unseen effects. Cultivate honesty, openness and trust.*

ERIC HEIDEN (6/14/58)
BETH HEIDEN (9/27/57)

These mutually supportive siblings were world-class speed skaters during the 70s and early 80s. In 1980, Eric became the first in history to win gold medals in all 5 speed skating events.
Also: Edward I & Henry III (son/father; English kings).

STRENGTHS: **ACCEPTING, EMPATHIC, MODERATE**

WEAKNESSES: **NOSY, SUPERFICIAL, ASEXUAL**

BEST: **SIBLING**

WORST: **MARRIAGE**

PAUL MCCARTNEY (6/18/42)
JOHN LENNON (10/9/40)

McCartney and Lennon were the originators of and creative force behind the Beatles. Their extraordinary teamwork was protected by a special agreement, that songs written by either of them would be credited to both. *Also: Keye Luke & Warner Oland* (son/ father portrayers in *Charlie Chan*).

June 11–18

THE WEEK OF THE SEEKER
GEMINI III

October 3–10

THE WEEK OF SOCIETY
LIBRA II

A Twinkle in the Eye

The keynotes of this relationship are a free-and-easy, relaxed overall approach, an emphasis on technical virtuosity and a kind of sensitivity or heightened awareness. What a mixture! With air the dominant element here, one can expect these partners to share a mental involvement with each other. Their verbal and technical agility is also enhanced by a kind of psychic connection. There are sensitivities here that can cause tension, but overall the combination is lively, humorous, relaxed and intimate.

Libra II's can have a softening effect on the often frenetic energies of Gemini III's, taking these personalities for what they are, with few reservations. Gemini III's are usually unprepared either to follow a Libra II's social lead or to escape with them in their periodic retreats from the world, but are willing to accept the Libra II personality in toto, on a take-it-or-leave-it basis. The relationship may provide a safe haven for both partners, especially when it emerges in the spheres of friendship and family. Marriages and love affairs, however, may lack that spark so necessary for Gemini III's; they are likely to be easy enough in many respects, but without that indefinable magic they may lack the bite or chemistry to get the partners involved at a deep level.

A tendency to live and let live allows friends, siblings and colleagues in this combination to communicate and empathize with each other despite their differences. Perhaps the greatest strength of these relationships is objectivity: the partners feel no need to influence each other's viewpoints or actions yet take great interest in observing each other's actions, sometimes dispassionately, sometimes enthusiastically, but always with a knowing twinkle in the eye. A lack of antagonism and competitiveness also lends relief here.

In general, the Gemini III–Libra II relationship is probably better off where it is than attempting to be something it is not. Although it can both scale the heights and plumb the depths of human experience, it also loses nothing by carrying on calmly and moderately. Other relationships could only wish for so much.

ADVICE: *Let your feelings loose occasionally. Don't be afraid of rejection. Resentments should be openly aired. What is your real interest?*

STRENGTHS: **ACTIVE, ENERGETIC, CREATIVE**

WEAKNESSES: **SELFISH, COMPETITIVE, POWER-TRIPPING**

BEST: **BUSINESS PARTNERSHIP**

WORST: **LOVE**

STEFFI GRAF (6/14/69)
MARTINA NAVRATILOVA (10/18/56)

Navratilova dominated women's tennis from 1982–86. Graf unseated her in the late 80s and has remained on top ever since. *Also: Prince Aly Khan & Rita Hayworth* (married; playboy/actress); **Joe Montana & Jerry Rice** (Superbowl teammates); **Harriet Beecher Stowe & Lyman Beecher** (daughter/father; abolitionists).

June 11–18

THE WEEK OF THE SEEKER
GEMINI III

October 11–18

THE WEEK OF THEATER
LIBRA III

On the Go

This outgoing and energetic relationship is characterized by a lot of dynamism and activity. These two are always on the go—but not always together. When they do find themselves in the same place at the same time, however, they will seek each other out to share their experiences. More importantly, if they join forces they will discover a new talent: together they have an ability to conceive and implement new, exciting and workable concepts. Traditional astrology accurately predicts an easy and pleasurable matchup here, due to a favorable trine aspect (Gemini III and Libra III being at an angle of 120° to each other in the zodiac). Passion lurks within the relationship, however, generating drive but also creating the risk of conflicts and emotional eruptions.

Libra III's are among the few people in the year who can keep up with the adventuresome pursuits of Gemini III's. This pair can make an unbeatable combination at the head of a company, small business, family or social group. An added plus here is that Gemini III money and investment sense together with Libra III social skills and flamboyance are an ideal combination in business. As long as the good of the group remains the highest goal, few problems will emerge, but if one of the partners turns selfish or greedy and tries to turn things to his or her own advantage, expect big trouble. The relationship is often unable to sustain such conflict and may break down or break up.

Gemini III–Libra III love affairs, friendships and marriages rarely remain in the purely intimate realm for long: each partner shows great interest in the other's work and career and is usually itching to get involved. This desire doesn't necessarily improve on the quality of the original relationship, however—in fact, it can create enormous problems where few existed before. Power struggles almost inevitably emerge over who is the leader and what direction should be followed. There is a danger, then, that the relationship's destructive side will emerge here, leaving little in its wake but smoking ruins.

ADVICE: *Keep your career and personal life separate. Mind your own business. Realize what you have to lose before starting new projects.*

June 11–18

THE WEEK OF THE SEEKER
GEMINI III

October 19–25

THE CUSP OF DRAMA & CRITICISM
LIBRA-SCORPIO CUSP

RELATIONSHIPS

STRENGTHS: **SENSITIVE, ACCEPTING, UNDERSTANDING**

WEAKNESSES: **IRRITABLE, MISLEADING, ESCAPIST**

BEST: **MARRIAGE**

WORST: **FAMILY**

The Joys of Anonymity

This couple will attract a good deal of attention, both as a duo and individually, but their relationship tends to be quite intimate and private—few others will know much about it. They share a hunger for experiences of all kinds, and the theme of exploration will figure prominently here, but they carry on their experience-gathering quietly, moving relatively unrecognized on the outskirts of life. Not that they hide intentionally or even consciously; most who view this couple, however, are blinded to the real nature of their relationship by its brilliantly extroverted side. Nor will they go out of their way to correct others' misconceptions about them, being quite content to preserve their privacy and their ability to be themselves when alone with each other. In such moments they taste the joys of anonymity.

Marriages, love affairs and friendships usually present a successful, vibrant and self-confident face to the world. In private, however, insecurities and frustrations emerge. These difficulties are seldom a result of the relationship itself but are personal and social in nature. Both Gemini III's and Libra-Scorpios tend to be somewhat irritable, nervous and angry a good deal of the time over their treatment by the world, and one of their principal functions for each other is to allow the expression of such negative feelings without fear of censure. In this dimension their connection with each other may become essential to their psychological well-being. Their personal feelings toward each other, sexual or otherwise, often take second place to this aspect of the relationship.

Family members and co-workers in this combination are often unusually sensitive to each other's quirks and foibles. Irritation can be a constant problem here, necessitating games and neurotic behavior to cope with unresolved annoyances. Work and family activities also become an avenue of escape. In whatever sphere the relationship manifests, the split between its private and its public personas may be essential for its well-being. Yet its partners should try to deal with their social and personal problems directly, rather than simply retreating to it as a protective or neutral space.

ADVICE: *Come to grips with your difficulties. Don't always look for the easy way out. Aim for greater social honesty. Minimize dependencies.*

WAYLON JENNINGS (6/15/37)
BIG BOPPER (10/24/30)

Jennings and the Big Bopper were both disc jockeys as well as musicians. In 1959, when Buddy Holly invited Big Bopper to join him on a Midwest tour, Jennings gave him his plane ticket. The plane crashed in a snowstorm, killing all on board, including the Big Bopper and Holly.

June 11–18

THE WEEK OF THE SEEKER
GEMINI III

October 26–November 2

THE WEEK OF INTENSITY
SCORPIO I

RELATIONSHIPS

STRENGTHS: **OPEN, SEXUAL, STRIVING**

WEAKNESSES: **MISLEADING, CONFESSIONAL, GUILT-RIDDEN**

BEST: **WORK**

WORST: **LOVE**

A Matter of Honesty

The theme here is determining when to reveal the truth and when to hide it. The issue is not dishonesty but timing: this pair usually has an excellent feel for the right moment to confront or duck an issue, as the case may be. They may not, however, be as much in control as they think, for outside forces too can force revelations. Even within the relationship, upsets or conflicts can lead to explosive outbursts of truth-telling before the time is right.

Whether complete honesty can be achieved here is an open question. Scorpio I's tend to be critical of Gemini III's who may actually be purely motivated, at least as far as they are aware, but perhaps are operating under the influence of unconscious forces. The tremendous Scorpio I sensitivity to such impulses allows them to perceive drives of which their partner is mostly unaware. Gemini III's may easily feel unfairly judged here, then. On the other hand, Scorpio I's sometimes knowingly commit and conceal indiscretions, sincerely believing that they are acting in the relationship's interests. Should the Gemini III find out later, however, the Scorpio I may be accused of applying a double standard.

Honesty is especially important in Gemini III–Scorpio I love affairs and marriages because sexual jealousy often features here. Suspicions can quickly lead to accusations, accusations to argument and open conflict. Putting less pressure on each other to be honest and letting go of possessive attitudes will be a start for these two. Usually under the guise of love, the relationship is prone to fostering a feeling that the partners own one another, a potentially quite destructive attitude. Family relationships and friendships, similarly, tend to overdo the need to get things out in the open. It should be remembered that trying to be honest, on the one hand, and being forced to confess, on the other, are extremely different things: the first emphasizes respect and responsibility, the second is motivated by guilt and blame. Work relationships may escape this problem somewhat, demanding dedication to the task at hand and taking trust and dependability for granted.

ADVICE: *Lay claim to yourself. Build a stronger ego. Don't be driven by fear and guilt. Blaming is easy to start but hard to stop. Draw boundaries.*

DONALD TRUMP (6/14/46)
MARLA MAPLES (10/27/63)

Billionaire Donald and ex-model Marla met in 1989 in the same church he had married first wife, Ivana. After a tumultuous courtship—and a 7.5-karat $250,000 engagement ring—they married in '93 at Trump's Plaza Hotel. They have a daughter, Tiffany. The marriage broke up amicably in '97.

Also: William Butler Yeats & Ezra Pound (friends; poets).

STRENGTHS: **INTIMATE,
PLEASURABLE, AUTONOMOUS**

WEAKNESSES: **ISOLATED, CUT
OFF, DISSATISFIED**

BEST: **FRIENDSHIP**

WORST: **LOVE**

GEORGE BUSH (6/12/24)
MICHAEL DUKAKIS (11/3/33)

In 1988, presidential candidate
Dukakis stressed competence over
ideology but ran a bland campaign.
Bush labeled Dukakis a soft liberal
and friend of unpatriotic marginal
groups. Reagan's popularity helped
Bush win by a very comfortable
54% to 46% margin.

June 11–18
THE WEEK OF THE SEEKER
GEMINI III

November 3–11
THE WEEK OF DEPTH
SCORPIO II

Self-Sufficiency

How deep will intimacy go? That is the question here. These two have different styles of closeness, and each will try to make the other conform to his or her own mode. The preference of Scorpio II's for removing the veils of their inner selves slowly won't fly with Gemini III's, who will want to jump into the fray of their activities and create closeness that way. By the very nature of the relationship, and through its involvement in the issue of intimacy, these two often become locked in together, making quite a tight pair. Gemini III's may find this a little uncomfortable. They are explorers from the word go, but should they set their sights on the undiscovered depths of the Scorpio II personality, they may find more than they bargained for there—and Scorpio II's are in any case rarely interested in being explored. They are, however, able to give themselves passionately in love, which may leave a Gemini III wanting to find out more.

Initially passionate, love affairs in this combination may soon prove unsatisfying. Scorpio II's will want to please their Gemini III lovers, but it may be months or years before they trust them enough to admit them to their private world. Generally wanting things to move faster, Gemini III's could feel rejected or unloved in this relationship, despite its sensual gratification.

These two can have a highly physical friendship centering around sports, fitness, food or adventure. Their relationship is quite self-sufficient, having little need to become part of a social or family circle. The danger here, and also in the couple's marriages, is that the relationship will cut itself off from normal social contact, becoming excessively isolated. During good times it may work fine, but in times of difficulty the presence of a support group will be sorely missed, particularly if children are involved.

Co-workers and siblings in this matchup can function effectively together at work and at play, needing little if any input from a boss or parent. In fact, an authoritarian presence is quite inhibiting to this pair.

ADVICE: *Take it slow, and savor deepening intimacy. Mysteries are better left alone. Keep your social and family contacts alive. Stay open to life.*

STRENGTHS: **STRUCTURED,
EXCITING, PERSUASIVE**

WEAKNESSES: **DECEIVING,
MANIPULATIVE, UNSTABLE**

BEST: **MARRIAGE**

WORST: **FRIENDSHIP**

MARTIN SCORSESE (11/17/42)
ISABELLA ROSSELLINI (6/18/52)

International actress and model
Rossellini is the daughter of Ingrid
Bergman and Roberto Rossellini.
Scorsese rose from New York's
tough Little Italy to become a
respected and original director.
They were married from 1979–83.
Also: **Dean Martin & "Dino"
Martin** (father/son).

June 11–18
THE WEEK OF THE SEEKER
GEMINI III

November 12–18
THE WEEK OF CHARM
SCORPIO III

Supporting or Eroding?

The primary challenge to this relationship will be to structure itself around stabilizing yet engrossing daily activities. Gemini is an air and Scorpio a water sign, but the relationship is ruled by earth, in this case standing for work and application. If their bond is weak, the partners will drift and dream uncertainly; the more grounded the relationship is, the stronger their ties. These two may play all kinds of mental and physical games with each other. Like con artists, they often try to persuade or manipulate each other in subtle ways, without revealing their true intent. In this respect they are an excellent match for each other. Perhaps firm ground rules should be laid, however, to keep this tendency from getting out of hand.

Because of their quincunx relationship (Gemini III's and Scorpio III's are 150° apart in the zodiac), instability often emerges here, making the need for structure all the more apparent. Scorpio III's can find love affairs with Gemini III's exciting and attractive, but should they decide that this partner is not good for them or is working destructively to undermine the relationship (whether consciously or not), they will not hesitate to move on. This can baffle Gemini III's, who will wonder what they have done to deserve such treatment. Marriages carry a high risk of breakup, but the seriousness and responsibility they involve can also help rather than hinder, tying the knot more securely.

The inherent structure of family and work groups guarantees the relationship more stability. The manipulative ploys of siblings in this combination, however, can undermine family structures and subtly erode parent-child bonds. Gemini III's are likely to fit into a company or organizational scheme less well than their partner here, for they tend to be rebellious and lack the superb Scorpio III organizational and directorial skills. Friendships between these two are likely to be short-lived, for Gemini III's need much more space and flexibility than Scorpio III's are prepared to allow.

ADVICE: *Don't expect too much from each other. Fulfill your daily responsibilities. Ground your activities. Take the time to care.*

June 11–18

THE WEEK OF THE SEEKER
GEMINI III

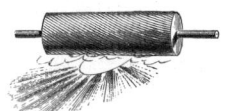

November 19–24

THE CUSP OF REVOLUTION
SCORPIO-SAGITTARIUS CUSP

RELATIONSHIPS	
STRENGTHS: **IDEALISTIC, INITIATING, MAINTAINING**	
WEAKNESSES: **SIDETRACKED, DISTRACTED, IRRESPONSIBLE**	
BEST: **PROJECT PARTNERSHIP**	
WORST: **MARRIAGE**	

NATHAN LEOPOLD, JR. (11/19/04)
RICHARD LOEB (6/11/05)

Tireless Dedication

At its heart, this relationship is directed inward. Though capable of being outgoing, its deepest concern is an unspoken spiritual bond ultimately aiming to help both partners become more fully realized individuals. Without the partners' mutual respect and tireless dedication to shared beliefs and principles, it will not work. The combination can gel effectively in the area of implementing ideas; in fact, getting projects off the ground may be its specialty, and keeping them running a constant preoccupation.

Probably the most successful relationships here are between colleagues engaged in social, religious, aesthetic or spiritual endeavors. Both Gemini III's and Scorpio-Sagittarians are usually quite capable of dealing with the financial side of such projects, but financial gain and money management are seldom the chief pursuits here—the relationship's thrust is idealistic. Even so, the duo's practical abilities are usually more than sufficient to guarantee success, unless they disagree on the direction the project should take.

Gemini III–Scorpio-Sagittarius friendships are likely to develop in connection with shared work. The feelings that surface are generally constructive and do not inhibit the work at hand. Care must be taken, however, to keep the relationship's focus in mind: having too much fun and getting sidetracked are constant dangers here. Love affairs in this combination are likely to be short and intense. They rarely develop into marriage, both partners usually being too independent to surrender to such a union, unless it can be structured in such a way as to leave them relatively free of responsibility. Having children may not be ideal for this pair.

Sibling relationships can seem competitive from the outside; few would suspect that behind the scenes they furnish a warm and loving bond of acceptance. In other family combinations, understanding Gemini III's are unlikely to arouse the rebellious streak in Scorpio-Sagittarians.

Wealthy and academically brilliant, Leopold and Loeb kidnapped and murdered a 14-year-old Chicago boy in 1924 for an "intellectual" thrill. Clarence Darrow's eloquent defense resulted in life sentences instead of the death penalty.
Also: Prince Aly Khan & Gene Tierney (affair; playboy/actress).

ADVICE: *Keep up your end of the bargain. Don't let differences of opinion interfere with the work. Learn to compromise. Keep your goal in mind.*

June 11–18

THE WEEK OF THE SEEKER
GEMINI III

November 25–December 2

THE WEEK OF INDEPENDENCE
SAGITTARIUS I

RELATIONSHIPS	
STRENGTHS: **CAPABLE, COMPLEX, INTERESTING**	
WEAKNESSES: **GAME-PLAYING, MISLEADING, MISUNDERSTOOD**	
BEST: **MARRIAGE**	
WORST: **WORK**	

BETTE MIDLER (12/1/45)
BARRY MANILOW (6/17/46)

A Cosmic Dance

No matter how successful this relationship seems, a hidden complexity in its emotional life perplexes and puzzles even the partners who constitute it. No matter how long these two have known each other, they are continually delighted, fascinated and exasperated by their own relationship, which, though rarely turbulent, has many twists and turns. The combination is such that it encourages the idiosyncrasy of its partners' already highly personal endeavors, exacerbating their tendencies in this direction. Building the foundation for a more committed or involved union becomes difficult and elusive under these circumstances. Initially attracted to each other by the number of interests they share, in this combination Gemini III's and Sagittarius I's will tend to become even more involved in their own activities, with the relationship suffering as a result.

Love affairs can be exciting at first and may well evolve into marriage or a permanent living situation. But even while ostensibly settling down to raise a family or share a life, Gemini III's and Sagittarius I's are actually engaged in a private cosmic dance. Observers might think they are leading completely separate lives when in fact they are engaged in a subtle personal interaction. The temptation exists for them to give their relationship over to game- and role-playing, spinning endless variations on this theme. Such activities, although fascinating, are not usually productive.

Gemini III–Sagittarius I friends, family members and mates should not be encouraged to share the same occupation. They are best off with a strict split between their work and private lives, and in careers of the most different sorts. People who know one partner professionally are often amazed when they meet the other. Sagittarius I family members and friends are likely to be exasperated with what they see as Gemini III flakiness, and tend to believe they are the more practical of the two. This is often true, but Gemini III money sense and ability to keep things running, albeit in their own unusual way, should not be underestimated.

Manilow met Midler when he filled in as a pianist at a NY gay club, the Continental Baths. Before launching his own successful singing career he was Midler's musical director and pianist. He arranged her 1972 Grammy-winning debut album and toured with her as a featured performer.
Also: Gene Wilder & Richard Pryor (film co-stars); **Steffi Graf & Monica Seles** (tennis rivals).

ADVICE: *Don't get caught up in your private dance. Seek deeper and more meaningful emotional interaction. Don't take too much for granted.*

TIMOTHY BUSFIELD (6/12/57)
PATRICIA WETTIG (12/4/51)

Busfield and Wettig played Elliot and Nancy Weston on the tv series *thirtysomething* (1987–91). The pair played their baby-boomer characters with strong psychological insight.

***Also:* Margaret Bourke-White & Alfred Eisenstaedt** (*Life* magazine's first photographers); **Paul McCartney & Little Richard** (Beatle influenced by early rock & roller).

June 11–18
THE WEEK OF THE SEEKER
GEMINI III

December 3–10
THE WEEK OF THE ORIGINATOR
SAGITTARIUS II

The Integration of Strengths

Empathy and emotional closeness run high in this combination—these partners share an unusual level of understanding and acceptance. This doesn't automatically mean that their relationship is stable, however, or even that it is good for them. In fact, it encourages escapism, entailing the risk that the partners, coming to idolize one another, will choose to live in their own private dream world, a place that will be fanciful, imaginative and creative but rarely grounded in reality. This is especially true if both partners feel misunderstood by the outside world.

Gemini III's usually look to the details while Sagittarius II's see the big picture, and their relationship can either integrate these strengths or be divided by them. Usually intent on survival, Gemini III's stress the importance of the bottom line—exactly what Sagittarius II's are prone to take for granted and overlook. Meanwhile, Sagittarius II's are likely to feel that Gemini III's are too focused on their immediate objective to see the larger context. Such differences are easily worked out in friendships but can prove divisive in marriages and families.

The area in which the partners' individual strengths can most successfully be integrated is that of work, especially when the pair are business partners or executives, positions requiring both attention to detail and a broader outlook. Yet here the relationship evinces a curious lack of leadership strength. In combination these two are better at coming up with ideas, and making plans as a unit than at heading up an aggressive business team.

Gemini III parents are likely to have misconceptions about their Sagittarius II children, although they love them dearly. Trying to protect them against the world is unnecessary and can even be harmful, for Sagittarius II's must learn about dealing with society's often disapproving and rejecting attitudes firsthand in order to toughen themselves and strengthen their resolve.

ADVICE: *Work to integrate differing points of view. Try to understand and to accept. Toughen yourself. Be more objective. Don't get carried away.*

ERSKINE CALDWELL (12/17/03)
MARGARET BOURKE-WHITE (6/14/06)

Bourke-White was among the original 4 photographers for *Life* magazine. Her husband, novelist Caldwell, wrote *Tobacco Road* (1932). During the 30s, they collaborated on pictorial documentaries of rural American life, particularly Southern poverty. ***Also:* Mario Cuomo & Ed Koch** (concurrent NY politicians); **Dean Martin & Frank Sinatra** ("Rat Pack" pals).

June 11–18
THE WEEK OF THE SEEKER
GEMINI III

December 11–18
THE WEEK OF THE TITAN
SAGITTARIUS III

Touching Base

This relationship has a lot to teach its partners about practical reality. Opposites in the zodiac, they can easily go soaring off on their most recent and expansive undertaking, but fortunately their relationship holds them fast and closer to the ground—probably saving them from a lot of near misses and dashed hopes. Here they learn the value of careful planning and caution, integration of skills, and the objective and literal consideration of any venture. For these two this is no small feat. The relationship constructively activates their energies, encouraging their vision yet adding a solid dose of groundedness, and laying the basis for the likely success of their projects or adventures. Gemini III's know the value of checking and rechecking the ropes before climbing, the tanks before diving, the facts before writing and, in general, of keeping an eye on the details. Sagittarius III's will have a great deal to learn in this respect, but in turn will teach their partner about power and how to wield it.

Sagittarius III's will usually play the dominant role in love affairs in this combination. Gemini III's are quite capable of enchanting them, however, and then of manipulating them, but may not choose to do so, instead confronting their partner head-on in potentially epic duels. Conflicts like this are often prevented in friendships and marriages, where the pair are better able to grant each other unquestioned areas of independent expertise and control. Gemini III–Sagittarius III sibling and parent-child combinations can be argumentative but are rarely destructive to the interests of the family group. Dynamic, stressful, exasperating and exhilarating, such relationships allow few dull moments. In office co-workers or colleagues, on the other hand, those energies might prove disruptive to a company or department; this pair is not recommended as a working team in daily contact. They can function well as a team in the field, however, for example as the managers of a project in which they both go their own way, occasionally touching base to keep track of each other and coordinate and analyze their efforts.

ADVICE: *Reduce stress levels. Drop expectations and let things happen. Lessen irritation by being accepting. Don't expect too much from each other.*

June 11–18

THE WEEK OF THE SEEKER
GEMINI III

December 19–25

THE CUSP OF PROPHECY
SAGITTARIUS-CAPRICORN CUSP

A Wake-Up Call

This relationship may involve revelatory, even transforming, experiences. After weeks, months or years of mutual involvement, the pair can undergo something like a Zen revelation in which a truth or realization comes in a flash, although usually only after long periods of struggle, and after they have given up expecting anything at all to happen. Since this kind of experience may be just what Gemini III's and Sagittarius-Capricorns have been searching for all their lives, their relationship, a lightning rod for this sort of thing, should be of great value to them. Yet they often only sense the chemistry between them in retrospect. Ironically, then, the content of the revelation they experience is sometimes just what the relationship means to them, a discovery they frequently make too late.

Love affairs and friendships here are mutually beneficial. Gemini III's bring Sagittarius-Capricorns out of their private world, encouraging a more positive and aggressive approach to life; Sagittarius-Capricorns help Gemini III's to become more thoughtful and quiet. A love affair usually puts both partners in touch with themselves at a level previously denied to them, giving them a chance to become more fully alive to each other.

Marital and working relationships can last for years, and it is here that the experience of revelation is most apt to occur. It may come in the middle of a predictable or boring task, but once grasped it may change the partners' outlook for good, ideally for the better. Should the pair experience an epiphany at the same instant, the relationship may lock in even a tighter bond. Such experiences should not be seen as illusory, harmful or isolating but as just the opposite: a reminder that these two are part of something much greater than themselves, something close to their fellow human beings and to Mother Earth.

Family members in this combination may well have psychic connections, first noticed when they sense each other's thoughts or perhaps both start talking about the same subject at once. Such connections often appear in parent-child matchups, and also in Gemini III–Sagittarius-Capricorn siblings.

ADVICE: *Peak experiences should foster self-realization. Aim for deeper levels of experience. Keep an eye out for synchronicities.*

WILLIAM BUTLER YEATS (6/13/1865)
MAUDE GONNE (12/20/1865)

In 1896, Yeats fell in love with Gonne, a zealous Irish nationalist, but she married another in 1903. After Gonne's husband was executed in 1916, Yeats proposed again, but she refused once more. ***Also:* Daphne Maxwell Reid & Tim Reid** (married; actors).

June 11–18

THE WEEK OF THE SEEKER
GEMINI III

December 26–January 2

THE WEEK OF THE RULER
CAPRICORN I

Lifelong Dreams

This relationship's attention is largely taken up by a search for an idealized form—a vision of an idyllic place to live, perhaps, or of a vacation paradise or a coveted aesthetic object. These dreams may be beyond the imaginings of either partner alone, but together the pair often long for a beauty that becomes a spur to their ambitions and efforts. In more reasonable or perhaps depressive moments, these longings can also become despairing, the visions being seen as illusions, impossible to achieve. The relationship can actually make the partners wonder what their idealized longings really represent, and what metaphysical source gave rise to them. Such questions might induce a focus on philosophical issues of expectation, openness, self-reward and visualization, an examination that will work to the partners' good.

Friendships and marriages are particularly suited to metaphysical searches. Gemini III's and Capricorn I's who have never dabbled in concepts like mind power, affirmation and visualization come to believe in them in this relationship. Extraordinary results can be achieved here. It can also be dangerous, of course, to make dreams come true, confirming the adage "Be careful what you wish for."

The relationship occasionally exhibits an inability to settle down in one place. To be always looking for the ideal setting or job can become a way of life for this pair. Even parents in this combination may adopt a nomadic existence, although their children will surely resent constantly changing schools and losing friends. Among the partners themselves, Capricorn I's will usually dig their heels in at some point and refuse to move. They may likewise fight to free themselves from the hopes that the relationship arouses, even coming to hate it at times. Gemini III's accept change more easily and may resent their partner's resistance to it. Such conflicts can tear the relationship apart though they may also make the couple sadder but wiser.

At work, other colleagues might see the pair's ideas and dreams as pie in the sky. Bringing their visions to work could lead these two to be viewed as flaky, not to be taken seriously.

ADVICE: *Be careful what you wish for. Examine your values carefully. Learn to be content with what you have. Don't insist on constant change.*

JACQUES COUSTEAU (6/11/10)
PHILLIPE COUSTEAU (12/30/40)

Pioneer marine explorer Jacques is the inventor of the aqualung and innovator in underwater photography. Author and award-winning filmmaker, he has given the world a better understanding of the marine environment. Son Phillipe has been diving since childhood and is employed by Jacques' research group, collaborating on projects and furthering his father's commitment to oceanography.

UTA HAGEN (6/12/19)
JOSE FERRER (1/8/12)

Hagen, a brilliant stage actress, was a prominent New York acting teacher and Ferrer's first wife, from 1938–48. Ferrer attained fame for his lead roles as *Cyrano de Bergerac* (1950) and as Toulouse-Lautrec in *Moulin Rouge* (1952).

Also: Paul McCartney & George Martin (Beatle/producer).

June 11–18
THE WEEK OF THE SEEKER
GEMINI III

January 3–9
THE WEEK OF DETERMINATION
CAPRICORN II

A Realistic Assessment

Together these two may hammer out a solid, hard-working relationship based on guts and a will to succeed. A perfectionist streak here places strong demands on both partners; unless care is taken to be sure that expectations are not unrealistically demanding, the stress may prove overwhelming and breakdowns will result. Whether directed inward, toward the partners, or outward, toward others, the relationship has a tendency to tinker with people—that is, to try to improve them, usually under the guise of helping them to grow or learn. Realistic assessments—of each other, of those around them and of the relationship itself—should be a priority for these two.

Marital and working relationships are most favored here. Gemini III's will bring vibrancy and flexibility to the matchup, Capricorn II's a practical hardheadedness. True, Capricorn II's may from time to time find Gemini III's silly and unrealistic, and Gemini III's might resent their partner's rigidity and stubbornness. For the most part, though, these partners' strengths coalesce effectively. In the financial sphere, although they will argue over how the money should be spent, both will be able to uphold their end of the deal. It is particularly important here that they do not try to change each other.

Gemini III–Capricorn II love affairs will often founder because constant harping criticism makes an easy give-and-take in intimate settings almost impossible. In family relationships, too, especially father-son and mother-daughter pairings, negative childhood scripts featuring a threat of rejection or abandonment can emerge, particularly when the Capricorn II is the parent. Friendships between these two should be kept light, and Capricorn II's will have to understand that demanding more responsible attitudes from their Gemini III friends will rarely work out. A better solution is for the pair to pursue a challenging project together, in which case the assumption of responsibilities will grow quite naturally out of the activities themselves rather than being imposed from without. Capricorn II's can easily match their Gemini III friends in daring and adventuresome situations, which may have the effect of making them more flexible.

ADVICE: *Remember to relax and have fun. Modify perfectionist attitudes. Beware of making unrealistic demands. Keep criticism positive.*

STAN LAUREL (6/16/1890)
HAL ROACH (1/14/1892)

In 1926, minor comedy actor Laurel signed a long-term contract with producer Roach as writer, gagman and director, but he soon returned to acting and enjoyed a long, propitious partnership with Oliver Hardy—resulting in some of Roach's most successful productions.

June 11–18
THE WEEK OF THE SEEKER
GEMINI III

January 10–16
THE WEEK OF DOMINANCE
CAPRICORN III

The Love of Obstacles

These two share a desire to win, even against overwhelming odds. Their relationship will always be involved in social or financial success, but also in working to better their own personal best, both as individuals and as a pair. Its outlook is surprisingly childlike, with enthusiasm and a positive outlook two of its chief qualities. In this, however, it misses the obvious, in that in most situations there is a path of least resistance that a more mature outlook is better able to discern. To a child, everything seems monumental, but this can become a self-fulfilling prophecy.

Gemini III's may simultaneously both resist and depend on the stable aspects of the Capricorn III personality. The relationship may make them assume more responsibility than they like; they sometimes resent this, but it can also give them the confidence they need to succeed. Capricorn III bosses or parents, then, may arouse very ambivalent feelings in their Gemini III employees or children.

Love affairs in this combination are likely to be quite unstable, as the quincunx position here indicates (Gemini III and Capricorn III are 150° apart in the zodiac). But it is an instability that can be exciting, especially in the bedroom. These passionate relationships rarely grow into lasting marriages or develop into friendships but tend to burn out or fizzle—unless, of course, the partners see marriage as an achievement, an "us against the world" view that they might adopt if their union is frowned upon socially or by their families. In such a case they will go all out to win. Gemini III–Capricorn III friends do best when they share physical activities, such as sports, dance, fitness or adventure; their philosophical aspects will also come to the fore here, and the relationship will thrive on investigations of social, technical or scientific subjects.

These partners sometimes assume an adversarial role with each other, particularly as competitors or opponents in challenging endeavors in which they spur each other on to new heights. Whether in commerce or in love, rivalry may bind these two more strongly than friendship, family or work relationships.

ADVICE: *Regulate your energy output. Rivalry can bring out the best but also the worst. Balance the physical and the philosophical. Develop maturity.*

June 11–18
THE WEEK OF THE SEEKER
GEMINI III

January 17–22
THE CUSP OF MYSTERY & IMAGINATION
CAPRICORN-AQUARIUS CUSP

A Marriage of True Minds

If anything, this relationship can be too exciting. Luckily, its many social interactions with friends and family are a stabilizing and calming influence. These two can get swept away with new projects and beckoning horizons, and their social contacts can provide them with an anchor. The relationship often tries to seek out and develop its roots, whether familial or geographic; these can offer a further source of stability. Should the partners be of different ethnic or racial backgrounds, the relationship will usually only benefit from such diversity.

Marriages and friendships are especially favored here. Indeed, spouses in this combination may resemble true friends, even seeking to include their children in this category. Both Gemini III's and Capricorn-Aquarians tend to have alert and quick minds, so it is no wonder that together they are attracted to anything mental. Their orientation is generally more intellectual than physical, more intuitive than emotional. As a result, Gemini III's and Capricorn-Aquarians would do well to develop and deepen their feelings for each other, whether in love affairs, friendships or marriages. Because they can easily reach a pleasant camaraderie in any of these areas, it may take a significant event of some kind to awaken them to the deeper value of their relationship, and to the necessity of pain and sorrow in order for spiritual growth to occur. Indeed, a principal weakness of this relationship may be its avoidance of everything unpleasant or disturbing.

In work and family settings, the Gemini III–Capricorn-Aquarius relationship lends spice to the daily routine. Bored easily, these two will always try to innovate, which may well lead them afoul of authority figures who are interested only in results. As co-workers or siblings, the pair may try to shake loose from the predictable job or family schedule and establish their own independently functioning unit.

ADVICE: *Life isn't always easy. Learn to confront difficulties. Running away is a temporary solution. Learn to calm yourself. Meditate daily.*

STAN LAUREL (6/16/1890)
OLIVER HARDY (1/18/1892)

These riotous buffoons pursued separate careers before teaming up in 1926. They made over 100 films together over the next 3 decades, their success attributable to their contrasting physical appearances and unique comic mannerisms. **Also: Carol Kane & Andy Kaufman** (co-stars, *Taxi*); **Isabella Rossellini & David Lynch** (romance; actress/director).

June 11–18
THE WEEK OF THE SEEKER
GEMINI III

January 23–30
THE WEEK OF GENIUS
AQUARIUS I

Hunger for Attention

This generally well-suited pair's relationship can easily find itself at the center of a family, social or professional group. A certain flamboyance points to a need for attention, but the partners will have to realize that preening is not enough—with the attention of other people comes responsibility. Yet leadership potential may be lacking here, and the pair may be incapable of doggedly and persistently supporting group endeavors. Their hunger for the spotlight may not be justified by the amount of work they are prepared to do. In addition, their need for attention is apt to be an issue within the relationship: discomfort or jealousy will be aroused if only one of the partners receives the recognition of other people. They may also be unhappy over the level or type of attention each gets from the other partner.

Gemini III–Aquarius I lovers usually demand a tremendous amount of attention from each other, a selfishness that can undermine the relationship. Its chances of survival are increased, however, by their willingness to work on building empathic bridges and to sacrifice their own preferences for their mutual good. Both partners may resent the relationship, Gemini III's because it restricts their need to explore, Aquarius I's because it restricts their impulsiveness. Such limitations, however, may ultimately prove beneficial to the individual character-building process. Marital and work relationships are not particularly recommended in this combination unless the pair are willing to make sacrifices. But a serious commitment can be made easier if compromises are worked out at every step of the way, with the partners trading off, say, periods of free time, and replacing individual priorities with joint duties and tasks. The rewards of enjoying time together after work or during vacations may help to provide the necessary motivation.

Gemini III–Aquarius I friends and family members will have to learn either to mute their need for attention or else to pursue that need with greater dedication. Their greatest challenge is giving up a measure of their freedom and individuality and acknowledging their responsibility to serve the group of which they are a part.

ADVICE: *Hang in there. Attention requires commitment. Justify your position. Compromise will be necessary. Be sympathetic and show that you care.*

GENE SISKEL (1/26/46)
ROGER EBERT (6/18/42)

Siskel and Ebert, film columnists from the *Chicago Sun-Times* and the *Chicago Tribune*, respectively, are famous for their "thumbs up/thumbs down" movie reviews. This engaging team seems to relish their differences of opinion. **Also: Jim Belushi & John Belushi** (brothers; comedians); **James Brown & Tammy Terrell** (romance; pop singers).

465

ROBERTO ALOMAR (2/5/68)
SANDY ALOMAR, JR. (6/18/66)

Baseball's Alomar brothers played together as San Diego Padres during the '88 and '89 seasons. Beyond that, it is Roberto's record that stands out: 5 Gold Gloves, 6-time All-Star and 1992 MVP. **Also: George Bush & Ronald Reagan** (vice-president/president); **George Bush & Dan Quayle** (president/vice-president); **Richard Strauss & Hugo von Hofmannsthal** (collaborators; composer/librettist).

June 11–18
THE WEEK OF THE SEEKER
GEMINI III

Party Time

January 31–February 7
THE WEEK OF YOUTH & EASE
AQUARIUS II

The extroverted tendencies of both partners are brought out by this relationship. Gemini III's and Aquarius II's like to socialize and have fun together, but these gratifying activities may not bring them far in advancing their individual or mutual cause. If they are low in ambition, they may continue in an unabated pursuit of pleasure for months or even years. This may lead them to a somewhat vacuous dead end, in which spiritual, emotional and self-realizing values are severely lacking or absent. One area these two could do well in, given sufficient ambition, is networking, building coalitions or uniting disparate groups of people. Here they can put their social skills and ability to glad-hand to work, ideally for a good cause.

The relationship's deficiencies will become blatantly obvious during times of need and stress, when its characteristic lack of moral reserves to fall back on will prove detrimental in a family, love or marital setting. Learning that pain and struggle are essential to psychological growth is a hard lesson, but an essential one for this pair to learn. It may be inevitable and necessary that their mutual tendency to drift and dream be startled by periodic jolts, shaking them into awareness.

Friendships in this combination tend to be self-protective, appearing successful but in fact being inhibiting. The most telling faults here can be an inability to face the truth and a mutual will toward self-deception. Since work situations tend to make realistic demands that have to be met on a daily basis, they may provide a context that, while perhaps less pleasurable for these partners, will ultimately be more conducive to their growth. On the other hand, bosses and employees in this combination can arouse powerful resentments in other workers who feel excluded from what seems to be a mutual-admiration society. Similarly, parent-child relationships may arouse the jealousy or resentment of other family members. The pair will have to become more aware of the needs of other people in their immediate environment.

ADVICE: *Strive to see the truth, however painful it may be. All pleasure eventually comes to an end. Build on a solid foundation. Seek more lasting values.*

KIM NOVAK (2/13/33)
PRINCE ALY KHAN (6/13/11)

India's Aly Khan was a notorious playboy to Hollywood actresses. His list of glamorous lovers included Novak, whose romances with Frank Sinatra and Cary Grant were widely publicized. Compared with Aly Khan, she reportedly found the others only "half-alive." **Also: Mark Van Doren & Charles Van Doren** (father/son; intellectual/quiz-show cheat).

June 11–18
THE WEEK OF THE SEEKER
GEMINI III

Being Whisked Away

February 8–15
THE WEEK OF ACCEPTANCE
AQUARIUS III

This relationship will stretch social and political limits. Already socially conscious, these partners will grow more so in combination, and activism will feel like a grand adventure to them. Of the two, Aquarius III's are the more committed to values; Gemini III's are usually just in it for the experience. For both of them, though, everything is relative, and they will favor one cause for a while, then fly off in another direction. The fun is being the first to adopt a certain position. The real hard work of activism is unheard of—for these two it's all in the romance. Aquarius III's enjoy running the delicious risk of being whisked away by their Gemini III partner on a magic-carpet ride, whether serving an organization or following adventure. Because of the trine position here (Gemini III and Aquarius III lie 120° apart in the zodiac), astrology predicts an easy relationship, and this is usually true, with lines of communication generally open.

Gemini III–Aquarius III friendships and love affairs will persist against social or familial disapproval—in fact, they thrive on it. If threatened, they simply become more discreet or covert. The partners must be careful that hiding does not become a bad habit, though, nor guilt a necessary ingredient for enjoyment.

Marital and working relationships can be productive here. The duo's pioneering spirit rolls back frontiers but at the same time leaves them open to unrealistic and unsettling influences. The courage to fail is a strength, but repeated failures are not at all desirable, and the partners must beware of a tendency to forget about the goal in emphasizing the joys of striving and tackling obstacles.

Gemini III–Aquarius III siblings, especially of the same sex, must be left free to roam and to dream up their imaginative projects. Learning from their mistakes is an essential preparation for their forays into adulthood. In all relationships in this combination, any attempt from a third party to suppress the enthusiasm and challenge-oriented stance of the Gemini III–Aquarius III pairing will usually be doomed to fail or else will inflict psychological damage.

ADVICE: *Avoid hiding things. Keep your goals in mind. Don't get sidetracked in unproductive struggle. Acknowledge realistic boundaries.*

June 11–18

THE WEEK OF THE SEEKER
GEMINI III

February 16–22

THE CUSP OF SENSITIVITY
AQUARIUS-PISCES CUSP

Style and Substance

This relationship's ideal is to carry a sense of style and image into all its activities. Charming and outgoing, it will be socially in demand. A work ethic is also pronounced here, with standards of quality being a definite priority. Interestingly, the need for style falls somewhat short in the area of communication, where the combination's piercing frankness may prove its undoing. If these two don't learn to criticize tactfully and sympathetically, they will come across as judgmental or blaming. Overall, however, their joint frankness helps them to grow and learn, so that the relationship affects them positively, bringing out their strengths and alleviating their weaknesses. First, it helps to bring Gemini III's to greater awareness of themselves and their feelings; second, it helps to push Aquarius-Pisces more out into the world to achieve their goals.

Love affairs in this combination encourage Aquarius-Pisces to be more open with their feelings and Gemini III's to dig a bit deeper into their own. This process must be allowed to unfold to its own rhythm rather than by applying homemade or textbook psychological methods. Counseling may prove helpful when roadblocks are encountered, but only with a special and perceptive third party. Serious love affairs may easily evolve into marriage, which, however, should only be attempted when personal and spiritual growth have already been demonstrated in the relationship. Friends and especially co-workers might overemphasize money. Business partnerships and executive pairings should place more stress on steady, solid growth and established financial principles of a more conservative nature, and less on high-risk speculative endeavors. Friendships should deemphasize money dealings and instead seek to develop both idealistic and practical goals of a noncommercial nature.

Family matchups in this combination, particularly between grandparents and grandchildren, or between aunts or uncles and nieces or nephews, can be empathic and rewarding, especially in childhood. They can also avoid the kinds of parental criticism and filial judgments apparent in Gemini III–Aquarius-Pisces parent-child matchups. A grandparent, aunt or uncle of the same sex as the child can often be a very satisfactory role model.

ADVICE: *Apply positive criticism respectfully. Don't psychologize. Allow processes to unfold. Try not to hurry or force things. Exercise patience.*

DONALD TRUMP (6/14/46)
IVANA TRUMP (2/20/49)

Billionaire real estate developer Trump (she dubbed him "The Donald") met his wife-to-be in 1975. She had been a Czech Olympic skier and fashion model before they married in '76, following an intense courtship. He made her executive VP in charge of design within his organization. They had their 3rd child in '84. They divorced in '90.

June 11–18

THE WEEK OF THE SEEKER
GEMINI III

February 23–March 2

THE WEEK OF SPIRIT
PISCES I

Turning Inward

Marked by a powerful sensitivity, this relationship has the potential to have a great impact on its environment or field of endeavor, since it greatly enhances its partners' individual power. This may partly be due to the combination's spiritual leanings, which encourage the values of nonattachment and calm; moods of meditation and contemplation are characteristic here and will prove a source of sustenance come what may. Usually directed toward external goals, Gemini III's may find themselves reoriented in this combination toward matters of the soul or a higher power. In this they are following the lead of Pisces I's, retiring types who, for their part, may find that some of the outgoing nature of Gemini III's will rub off on them.

In love affairs a whole new world may open up for these partners. Where the themes of their earlier relationships with others may have been romantic, sexual or emotional, the emphasis here lies on self-exploration, self-realization, empathy, understanding and psychological balance or health. The ability to love another person without flare-ups and disturbances may prove novel for both partners. A romance like this is an excellent foundation for marriage. Gemini III–Pisces I parents can provide admirable role models for their children, provided they can sustain the attitude toward love that they enjoyed before they wed.

In the family this pair, particularly when they are siblings, will urge the group in a spiritual direction but won't necessarily be appreciated for doing so. Tensions may only be increased by their preference for relaxation, peace and compromise, which winds up getting them branded as lazy or lackadaisical. Paradoxically, a relationship that actually abounds in spirit may be accused of lacking it. As a friendship this relationship may be aggressively targeted by other, less understanding friends, lovers or family members who are threatened by its contemplative stance or who feel jealous of it. Gemini III–Pisces I co-workers may not be aggressive or productive enough to suit their bosses. In a personnel department or one concerned with employees' well-being, however, they may prove a helpful and healthful influence.

ADVICE: *Don't ignore the reactions of others. Try to understand where they are coming from, but don't compromise your own beliefs.*

JOHNNY CASH (2/26/32)
WAYLON JENNINGS (6/15/37)

These country singers were close friends in the mid-60s and admittedly spent a drug-filled year and a half together in Nashville before going their separate ways. In 1985 they formed the Highwaymen (with Kris Kristofferson and Willie Nelson).

June 11–18

THE WEEK OF THE SEEKER
GEMINI III

March 3–10

THE WEEK OF THE LONER
PISCES II

Peak Experiences

On the surface of it, many problems could be in store for this couple. Pisces II's often dislike the aggressive attitude taken by Gemini III's, who, in turn, are sometimes less than sympathetic to what they view as the withdrawal or hypersensitivity of Pisces II's. The relationship's focus, then, could be mutual criticism—but these two also share a hunger for peak experiences, especially those that raise consciousness and forward the pursuit of lofty goals. Such endeavors may also feature an intensification of the pair's relationship with the natural world. If these two can learn the value of acceptance, a profound experience may await them.

The aim of raising consciousness is an admirable one, but if the means are questionable they may subvert and swallow up the goal itself. The critical attitude inherent in the relationship can be put to good use here, encouraging objectivity and exposing otherwise confused states of mind to the clear light of reason. One problem with Gemini III–Pisces II love affairs and marriages is the danger that drugs and artificial stimulants will be used to gain highs, thereby fostering addiction.

Family relationships (particularly sibling matchups of the opposite sex) and even friendships are capable of intense psychic connections. Peak experiences are likely between such close pairs; being hard to describe or share with others, these may limit the ability of these siblings or friends to get close to others in their lives, so that they sometimes form a closed and somewhat isolated unit. An interest in exploring the natural world often appears, whether during vacations, by living in the country or by keeping pets and reading about environmental issues in the city.

Many work situations are not favored by either this pair's overly critical or subjectively exploratory state of mind. The duo could, however, be involved together professionally in religion, psychology, teaching, or drug experimentation or rehabilitation, for example.

ADVICE: *Keep in contact with others. Follow your vision, but stay objective, too. Strive to communicate. Put your critical faculties to good use.*

June 11–18

THE WEEK OF THE SEEKER
GEMINI III

March 11–18

THE WEEK OF DANCERS & DREAMERS
PISCES III

A Surprising Result

This relationship has a surprising effect: though its partners are known individually as dreamers or seekers, together they become producers. Markedly practical and able to get results, the pair will surprise even themselves. They can provide others with a bedrock of harmony and cooperation as they seek their ends. Moreover, their creative and inspirational qualities will generate a never-ending supply of original ideas for them to put into action, manufacture, present, produce or sell. The only drawback in all this bounty is that while each separately is rather a flexible personality, together they are as immovable as a mountain.

The combination favors marital and working relationships, which will provide solid bases for any home or workplace. Gemini III adventurousness and Pisces III fantasy will be solidly grounded in either domestic or professional projects, which demand every ounce of their practical sense, daring and ingenuity. Because Gemini III and Pisces III form a square aspect (90° apart in the zodiac), astrology would predict friction and conflict between them. In this case, however, competitiveness and struggle are limited and, if present at all, are put to a practical use, particularly when the pair are co-workers striving for tangible goals.

Friendships here can feature a tendency toward arguments and rivalries over shared love objects. Yet any triangles that develop could be not only intense but loving—though also hurtful and destructive in the long run, especially to the person who ends up feeling excluded. Gemini III–Pisces III love affairs can easily make space for a third partner, usually a friend, but can also be maintained for years as long as mutually caring attitudes and a good degree of objectivity are put into practice.

Gemini III–Pisces III family relationships, particularly parent-child matchups, can parade uproarious and even riotous arguments before open-mouthed family members but can equally well give tangible support to the group structure.

ADVICE: *Don't only believe your senses. Minimize the pain of love triangles. Beware of exhibitionistic tendencies. Rivalry has a positive side.*

June 19–24
THE CUSP OF MAGIC
GEMINI-CANCER CUSP

June 19–24
THE CUSP OF MAGIC
GEMINI-CANCER CUSP

June 19–24
THE CUSP OF MAGIC
GEMINI-CANCER CUSP

STRENGTHS: **NURTURING, LOVING, PEACEFUL**

WEAKNESSES: **OVERPROTECTIVE, STAGNATING, INEFFECTIVE**

BEST: **MARRIAGE**

WORST: **WORK**

Brimming with Quietude

This relationship is peaceful and harmonious. These two generally have a calming effect on each other, and together their magic is muted to a personal, intimate level brimming with quietude. Interactions are sensitive verging on psychic. Rarely does a couple exhibit as much caring toward each other as these two. Whether they are married or live together as lovers, the couple establish an empathic world that will tolerate little disturbance. Silences can be shattered by outside intrusions but at the same time are powerful in setting a mood that only the most insensitive would dare to unsettle. The children of Gemini-Cancer parents may be surprisingly outgoing and boisterous, but at home they know exactly how far they can go. They will benefit from the nurturing qualities of their parents and from a home capable of furnishing many or all of their domestic needs. Gemini-Cancer lovers and spouses enjoy having good friends over from time to time, but for the most part they guard their privacy tenaciously and can go weeks or even months without much need for social contact. Obviously, they must beware of leading an isolated existence that will cut them off from the world.

Family relationships between these two, particularly parent-child and sibling matchups of the opposite sex, can be protective to the point of being debilitating. Loving each other a great deal and being extremely close, Gemini-Cancers can at the same time deprive each other of the individuality that both of them need if they are to be their own person. Detaching from the relationship in late adolescence or early adulthood may be a painful and difficult process.

Working matchups and friendships between these two will go easily enough but may prove ineffective in furthering career or social ambitions. Neither partner may have strong drives in this direction, and their relationship will do little to compensate. Should they settle into a relaxed and accepting mode, they run the danger of stagnating and losing the motivation necessary for professional and self-development.

ADVICE: *Promote individual action. Beware of stifling each other. Learn to back off. Disharmony and dissatisfaction have a part to play.*

WALLIS SIMPSON (6/19/1896)
EDWARD VIII (6/23/1894)

In one of the greatest romantic gestures of the century, Edward abdicated the British throne to marry Simpson after their long, secret affair was exposed to the public and Britain's political leaders. They moved to France and circulated in international high-society. **Also: Charles Lindbergh, Jr. & Anne Morrow Lindbergh** (kidnapped son/mother; same birthday).

June 19–24
THE CUSP OF MAGIC
GEMINI-CANCER CUSP

June 25–July 2
THE WEEK OF THE EMPATH
CANCER I

STRENGTHS: **DEEP, SENSITIVE, DEDICATED**

WEAKNESSES: **AGGRESSIVE, DISTURBING, DEMANDING**

BEST: **MARRIAGE**

WORST: **FAMILY**

Working Out Feelings

An emotionally complex situation can arise in this relationship. These two are linked psychically and in fact may share a prophetic vision that will bind them closely; their level of intimacy, however, may require the working out of deep personal feelings, a task that may require years of dedication. A lot is going on beneath the surface. It may never see the light of day in the short term, but it will have to be sorted out eventually. This will require the faith that the relationship is headed in the right direction, and also the patience to let time do its healing work. Assuming the interest is there for such subjective explorations, the relationship holds great promise. Gemini-Cancers are usually the cooler and more objective of the pair; Cancer I's tend to be more at the mercy of their feelings, and although they may pride themselves on their psychological astuteness relative to a Gemini-Cancer partner, they may be unable to see themselves clearly.

Love and marriage are likely to reach deep unconscious levels. Attending to practical matters and seeing that emotional stress is kept to a minimum, while getting to know each other calmly and building bonds of trust, are essential here. Cancer I's can handle money reassuringly skillfully but may have trouble building a career. This could disturb Gemini-Cancers intent on their own professional activities.

Sibling and parent-child pairs in this combination are likely to be overly sensitive to other family members and to demand undue attention from them. Gemini-Cancer–Cancer I co-workers can likewise be technically proficient, and dedicated enough to fulfill their obligations, yet contribute an emotional instability to the workplace. Not the least of the problems here is the pair's tendency to analyze and impose their subjective states on others.

Friendships are certainly possible between Gemini-Cancers and Cancer I's, but they will demand time and understanding. Cancer I aggressiveness may put Gemini-Cancers off from time to time but will also encourage them to be more forthright and assertive themselves.

ADVICE: *Increase your awareness. Don't lay your problems on others. Take responsibility for your feelings. Don't let your moods bog you down.*

JOSEPHINE DE BEAUHARNAIS (6/23/1763)
PAUL FRANÇOIS BARRAS (6/30/1775)

Before she married Napoleon, Josephine had a long affair with the powerful Barras. After tiring of his expensive mistress, he arranged for her to meet and marry Napoleon. **Also: Prince William & Lady Diana** (son/mother; royalty); **Errol Flynn & Olivia de Havilland** (screen partners); **Billy Wilder & I.A.L. Diamond** (collaborators; director/screenwriter).

NICOLE KIDMAN (6/21/67)
TOM CRUISE (7/3/62)

After Cruise first saw Kidman in *Dead Calm* (1989), he had her cast as his love interest in *Days of Thunder* (1990). They married that year, then co-starred in *Far and Away* (1992). The couple have 2 adopted children.

June 19–24
THE CUSP OF MAGIC
GEMINI-CANCER CUSP

July 3–10
THE WEEK OF THE UNCONVENTIONAL
CANCER II

Sharing and Trust

This relationship is strongly empathic. Its partners have an innate appreciation of and sensitivity to each other's dreams, likes and dislikes. Cancer II's will be able to pick up on and appreciate the tender-hearted romanticism of Gemini-Cancers, who in turn will accept the quirkier side of Cancer II's. Whether these two can fully satisfy each other's needs is another question, however: no matter how understanding they may seem toward each other, an essential dynamic spark may be missing here. In addition, the relationship tends to reinforce each partner's passive side, so that rousing each other from moods, or stimulating each other to take action, may not be easily accomplished.

Friendships and family relationships are more likely to prove rewarding than love and marriage. Passionate sexual feelings are rarely present in love affairs in this combination, which often eventually become platonic. These lovers are quite capable of evolving into friends, and it is also possible for a certain small percentage of them to marry. Whether as a marriage, friendship or romance, the relationship tends to feature sympathy and understanding more often than challenge, opposition and magnetically intuitive or emotional attractions.

Friendships and sibling pairings between members of the opposite sex have a certain chemistry here: friends in this combination will often resemble brother-sister pairs and vice versa. A respect for gender differences and a lack of aggressive intrusion are noticeable, but in fact subtle incestuous forces may well be at work. The trust and sharing in such relationships is particularly evident in matters of money, style, imagination and food. A love of cooking may be especially evident.

As far as working together goes, Gemini-Cancers and Cancer II's may well be able to operate a small business featuring a service such as catering, artist management, interior design or decorating. Sharp business sense is seldom one of their strong points, however, and they will have to hire a good business manager or accountant.

ADVICE: *Cultivate better business sense. Being agreeable may not always be helpful. Spur each other on to action. Raise your personal goals.*

PHYLICIA RASHAD (6/19/48)
BILL COSBY (7/12/37)

Rashad and Cosby co-starred on *The Cosby Show* (1984–92), one of tv's most popular sitcoms. Their portrayal as professional parents of an upper-middle-class Brooklyn family was both comic and realistic. **Also: Peter Asher & Linda Ronstadt** (manager/singer).

June 19–24
THE CUSP OF MAGIC
GEMINI-CANCER CUSP

July 11–18
THE WEEK OF THE PERSUADER
CANCER III

Crying Out for Direction

An unequal power structure may well emerge in this relationship, which often focuses on leadership and how it should be exercised. Cancer III's can overpower Gemini-Cancers. They are not always to blame in this, however, since this partner may be silently crying out for direction. The relationship's great challenge is to establish an equitable power structure in which decision-making is an open, honest and shared process, not some combination of absolutism and manipulation. It is as lovers, siblings and friends that these two have the greatest chance of establishing such a balance, through forthright discussion and debate. Verbalizing problems and differences of opinion are usually the first steps to take. Once a truce has been established, a positive relationship can ensue, with each partner being able to guide the other in some area.

In love and marriage, Gemini-Cancers may come to resent Cancer III absenteeism, seeing themselves as neglected by their career-hungry mates. Cancer III's, on the other hand, may have trouble with a relationship in which they are constantly called upon to motivate and make decisions for a partner whom they perceive as overly passive or apathetic. Should the relationship emerge in the work or family sphere, however, it may develop a significantly different power structure: here Gemini-Cancers often outdo their Cancer III partners in persuasiveness and manipulation, often using subtle methods that go totally undetected. Sexual and sensual innuendo or even outright favors may play a part here.

Parent-child and boss-employee relationships are prone to power struggles in which the Cancer III plays the role of top dog. In the family, an overbearing Cancer III parent may prove too strong an influence on a relatively docile Gemini-Cancer child. Rather than growing rebellious, Gemini-Cancers are likely to develop dependencies. They sometimes carry these old scripts into their adult lives, leading them to rerun the childhood relationship by finding a replacement for the dominant parent in the form of a boss, lover, spouse or friend.

ADVICE: *Keep lines of communication open. Build respect. Seek equality in all aspects of life. Beware of setting up inflexible power structures.*

June 19–24

THE CUSP OF MAGIC
GEMINI–CANCER CUSP

July 19–25

THE CUSP OF OSCILLATION
CANCER-LEO CUSP

A Bizarre Unit

This relationship is truly out of the ordinary. Magnifying the more unconventional aspects of both partners, it may prove quite remarkable to friends and family alike. Conventional friendships and marriages may not be possible for these two, who may replace them with unusual sorts of companionships, career connections or living situations. Tremendous differences in age, body type, background, diet or religion may be evidenced here, for example, representing not compromise but totally new, even bizarre combinations. Such a relationship must obviously grow strong and self-assured to withstand the criticism or ridicule of harsher, less sensitive souls.

Couples in this combination are more likely to flaunt their differences publicly than to try to hide them. Being the center of attention is not especially disturbing for this pair, who usually feel that others will have to adjust to them rather than vice versa. Color, style, movement, speech, humor—all of these may be extreme, sometimes to discordant or jarring effect, sometimes creating an overall impression that has been carefully calculated and designed. Show seems the obvious intent, but something quite unexpected may lurk behind the fanfare.

The motives for this pair's bizarre lifestyle are not so easy to uncover. Should the Gemini-Cancer–Cancer-Leo couple be family members, such as siblings or parent-child combinations, the psychology at work may involve feeling ostracized from the family group and seeking mutual solace as a form of defense. As business partners or co-workers in a small business (family members in this combination may well join together in some such professional endeavor), they might find a real commercial outlet for their impulses. At any rate, in society's eyes there is no clearer vindication of an unusual lifestyle than financial success. Money is rarely the most important thing for this couple, however, and success, if it comes, may arrive completely unwished for, by accident.

ADVICE: *Find meaningful forms of expression. Don't shock just for the sake of it. Share your fantasy with others. Don't compromise your individuality.*

STRENGTHS: **EXPRESSIVE, REMARKABLE, SUCCESSFUL**

WEAKNESSES: **DISCORDANT, JARRING, MEANINGLESS**

BEST: **BUSINESS PARTNERSHIP**

WORST: **FRIENDSHIP**

ERROL FLYNN (6/20/09)
LILI DAMITA (7/19/01)

Less than a year after arriving in Hollywood in 1935, handsome, roguish Flynn was an established star and married first wife, Damita, a minor actress. They had a son. They divorced after his 1942 acquittal on charges of raping 2 teenage girls on his yacht.

June 19–24

THE CUSP OF MAGIC
GEMINI–CANCER CUSP

July 26–August 2

THE WEEK OF AUTHORITY
LEO I

Yielding in Order to Overcome

This combination gives a new twist to an old theme by stressing passive rather than active dominance. Leo I's are used to playing the dominant role in their relationships, but seductive Gemini-Cancers are quite capable of soothing the savage lion. The relationship is governed by the element of earth, emphasizing the sensuous hold that Gemini-Cancers exert over their Leo I partners.

According to Lao-tzu, it is in yielding that things demonstrate the greatest strength, and so it is as softer Gemini-Cancers handle the fiery onslaught of Leo I's. All of the latter's belief in principles, ideals and authority may go out the window in the face of the magic in a Gemini-Cancer's eyes or voice. Particularly in the area of touch, tough Leo I lovers, who in other combinations find it hard to let other people near them, may melt purringly under a Gemini-Cancer caress. They may be surprised and pleased by their own vulnerability, but problems will arise if they are forced to acknowledge Gemini-Cancer superiority. Rejection at the hands of a Gemini-Cancer mate, lover or friend could prove devastating to the Leo I ego.

Work situations are not at all recommended here: Gemini-Cancers are rarely tough enough to work under Leo I bosses, and rarely decisive enough to serve as bosses to them. Even as co-workers on the same level, Leo I's may insist on a pace and dedication that are neither possible nor desirable for most Gemini-Cancers.

Leo I parents, especially in father-daughter and mother-son pairs, sometimes spoil their Gemini-Cancer children terribly. It is the children who will be the real losers here, since it may be impossible for them to gain respect for adult roles that they themselves will have to fill in later life.

ADVICE: *Pleasure isn't always the most important thing. Don't sell out your ideals. Be steadfast in your beliefs. Don't be lulled into false security.*

STRENGTHS: **PACIFYING, SENSUOUS, PLEASURABLE**

WEAKNESSES: **INDECISIVE, DOTING, REJECTING**

BEST: **SENSUAL**

WORST: **PARENT-CHILD**

CLARENCE THOMAS (6/23/48)
ANITA HILL (7/30/56)

Thomas was headed for an easy confirmation as Supreme Court justice until Hill, his former aide, accused him of sexual harassment, which he denied. After a tense televised hearing, he was cleared and confirmed. ***Also:* Pete Hamill & Jackie Onassis** (affair); **Jane Russell & Bob Waterfield** (married; actress/football star); **Benazir Bhutto & Asif Zardari** (ousted Pakistani leaders).

RELATIONSHIPS

STRENGTHS: **GUIDING, PROTECTIVE, PERSUASIVE**

WEAKNESSES: **MANIPULATIVE, DISENCHANTED, FRUSTRATED**

BEST: **CASUAL FRIENDSHIP**

WORST: **FAMILY**

SIR ALEXANDER FLEMING (8/6/1881)
ERNEST CHAIN (6/19/06)

Fleming and Chain (with H.W. Florey) won the 1945 Nobel Prize for medicine for their research leading to penicillin. Fleming is credited with the discovery, and Chain (with Florey) for purifying and testing the drug. They are responsible for ushering in the modern age of anitbiotics.

Also: Prince William & Queen Mother (great-grandson/great-grandmother; royalty).

June 19–24
THE CUSP OF MAGIC
GEMINI-CANCER CUSP

August 3–10
THE WEEK OF BALANCED STRENGTH
LEO II

Thawing Ice

These two have a tremendous effect on others, sometimes taking their social group to a whole new level. The ability of Gemini-Cancers to impart a sense of the magical, combined with the strength and fortitude of Leo II's, can create unforgettable experiences for those around them. When working for what they believe to be a good cause, which generally means for other people, the relationship is unstoppable. In their more private dealings, Gemini-Cancers sometimes try to control or dominate their Leo II partners; their aggressive side may emerge in this matchup. Leo II's are not known for passivity, but in their personal relationships with Gemini-Cancers they are capable of losing their emotional way and undermining their own self-assurance. They may initially adopt an overconfident stance with their Gemini-Cancer partner, then suffer tremendously when they are unable to live up to their own bluster. In such cases, Gemini-Cancers quietly win the upper hand, by default.

Romantic relationships between these two are complex. Leo II's can be cool and distant from time to time, but their Gemini-Cancer lovers will usually be able to thaw out these icy periods. Furthermore, Leo II's are not usually adept enough in the sphere of feelings to oppose Gemini-Cancers' emotional drives, which tend to assume the ascendancy. Overt or covert Gemini-Cancer manipulations usually keep Leo II partners in tow.

Marriages are not particularly recommended here. Leo II's are faithful, and hang in there; the masochistic side of their personality will not usually allow them to admit defeat, even when Gemini-Cancers fall out of love or become disenchanted with them, and shut down both physically and emotionally. The greatest difficulty Gemini-Cancers have with the Leo II personality is what they perceive as this partner's insensitivity.

Friendships are best kept casual, making as few demands as possible on the individual partners. Family matchups in this combination are rarely satisfying, and may in fact evidence great struggle and mutual misunderstanding. At work it is always best if these two work side by side on behalf of others.

ADVICE: *Maintain your self-esteem and confidence. Try to help each other grow. Beware of power struggles. Seek out what is best for both of you.*

RELATIONSHIPS

STRENGTHS: **ROMANTIC, SEXUAL, DEVOTIONAL**

WEAKNESSES: **DOMINATING, IMPATIENT, AGGRESSIVE**

BEST: **LOVE**

WORST: **WORK**

NAPOLEON BONAPARTE (8/15/1769)
JOSEPHINE DE BEAUHARNAIS (6/23/1763)

Josephine was passed on to Napoleon by former lover Count Barras, with (false) assurances that she was rich. Josephine expected to be Napoleon's mistress, not his wife. She claimed not to have loved him, but admitted to being overwhelmed by his compelling passion.

Also: Blaise Pascal & Pierre de Fermat (theory of probability).

June 19–24
THE CUSP OF MAGIC
GEMINI–CANCER CUSP

August 11–18
THE WEEK OF LEADERSHIP
LEO III

A Compelling Romance

This relationship can sweep both partners off their feet in a storm of passion. Its mood is romantic, intense and compelling. The focus here may well prove to be the realization of fantasies and imaginative impulses. Leo III's, who usually seek and demand admiration, may find themselves worshiping at the altar of Gemini-Cancers, who may not hesitate to exert dominant control over this partner once they feel they are in the driver's seat. Their influence is rarely destructive, however—in fact, the attitude of both partners toward their relationship tends toward the devotional.

Love affairs and marriages here are likely to be sexually exciting. Both partners are often stirred by their love to the very depths of their being, and these feelings tend to endure over time. Gemini-Cancers may find themselves responsible for maintaining the home base and providing a stable foundation for the relationship while their Leo III mates or lovers are out in the world overcoming obstacles and attaining success. On the domestic front, the Leo III will generally appear to be the boss but the Gemini-Cancer will be the real power behind the throne.

Friendships and sibling relationships between these two, particularly between members of the opposite sex, are likely to be understanding and supportive. Leo III's may be impatient from time to time with the more passive attitudes of Gemini-Cancers, who in turn may simultaneously resent and rely on Leo III aggression. Gemini-Cancer–Leo III parent-child relationships are often highly polarized, with traditional roles well defined and each partner quite attached to and emotionally dependent on the other.

Working relationships are not especially recommended here, since Gemini-Cancers may be forced to compromise too much of their self-esteem, integrity and individuality in following a dominant Leo III boss, colleague or partner.

ADVICE: *Exercise patience and care. Beware of burnout. Keep emotions on an even keel. Keep your wits about you in matters of feeling.*

June 19–24
THE CUSP OF MAGIC
GEMINI–CANCER CUSP

August 19–25
THE CUSP OF EXPOSURE
LEO-VIRGO CUSP

Evening Out

STRENGTHS: **STIMULATING, RESILIENT, FULFILLING**

WEAKNESSES: **UNBALANCED, WITHDRAWN, UNSETTLING**

BEST: **WORK**

WORST: **FRIENDSHIP**

SIR FRED HOYLE (6/24/15)
RAY BRADBURY (8/22/20)

Hoyle and Bradbury are contemporary science-fiction writers who approached their books from different perspectives. Hoyle is primarily an astronomer-cosmologist who believes life on Earth had extraterrestrial origins. Bradbury focuses on the dangerous power of the imagination in society, as depicted in his celebrated novel *Fahrenheit 451* (1953).

This relationship is likely to become unstable and blurred to understanding from time to time. Both partners can be tremendously secretive, a tendency synergistically magnified by their relationship. Together they can easily retreat from the world for long periods of time. Should such a period of withdrawal be prolonged, their worldly fortunes may hit a low, and a long and slow process may be necessary to rebuild their neglected careers. Gemini-Cancers are unlikely to provide the strong, solid support that Leo-Virgos require to keep their emotions on an even keel. As a matter of fact, the effect these two have on each other is likely to be unsettling, knocking both partners off balance.

Friendships, love affairs and marriages between Gemini-Cancers and Leo-Virgos are plagued by mood swings. Highs and lows alternate with frightful rapidity, leaving both partners breathless and exhausted. Although these relationships' highs are often wonderfully fulfilling, they offer little permanence or dependability. One highly positive aspect here, however, is resiliency, reflecting the combination's fundamentally healthy and healing orientation. No matter how unsettled things may appear at any one moment, both partners can count on the relationship's ability to encourage personal growth and development over the long run.

Family members in this combination tend to rely heavily on each other for emotional support. Leo-Virgo extroversion contrasts sharply with Gemini-Cancer introversion, but a good balance is often achieved. Either side of a parent-child matchup has the ability to work the other out of a low mood, creating a dynamic equilibrium that has a stimulating effect on the family group.

Successes may regularly be booked by Gemini-Cancer–Leo-Virgo business partners, co-workers and associates. Here the Gemini-Cancer generally provides imaginative and creative impulses, the Leo-Virgo compelling social strengths. Together they are likely to be effective in promoting a product or providing a community service, as long as they can keep their personal feelings objective and under control.

ADVICE: *Work on achieving balance. Even out mood swings. Maintain objectivity. Encourage healing aspects. Beware of isolation and neglect.*

June 19–24
THE CUSP OF MAGIC
GEMINI–CANCER CUSP

August 26–September 2
THE WEEK OF SYSTEM BUILDERS
VIRGO I

Everyday Serendipities

STRENGTHS: **EXCITING, PSYCHIC, CHALLENGING**

WEAKNESSES: **FOOLHARDY, POLARIZED, BIZARRE**

BEST: **FRIENDSHIP**

WORST: **FAMILY**

GOWER CHAMPION (6/22/21)
MARGE CHAMPION (9/2/23)

The Champions were married in 1947 and rose to fame as a dance team in 50s Hollywood musicals. Gower went on to tv and stage choreography as well as film direction. Marge pursued a career as an actress. The couple divorced in 1973. *Also:* **Mike Todd & Joan Blondell** (married; producer/actress).

The enchanting qualities of Gemini-Cancers and the logical, orderly Virgo I orientation make an unusual blend. The relationship that results has strong mental powers, not necessarily in mathematical or logical skills but in the psychic or paranormal realm. Synchronistic experiences and other observable phenomena for which there is no obvious explanation are common with these two. Virgo I's may have an inherent resistance to matters of metaphysics and spirituality, but the chemistry of their bond with Gemini-Cancers makes them increasingly open to such phenomena and mental states. Once convinced, both by their partner and by the irrefutable evidence of the occurrences that happen when they are together, they may take the lead in a newfound hunger for unusual experiences.

Love affairs and friendships between these two feature startling coincidences and juxtapositions that surprise and amuse both partners. Serendipity may prove such an everyday occurrence that after a while the partners come to expect it, their openness to it perhaps increasing its frequency. Virgo I's will rarely give up their critical, hardheaded stance completely, but Gemini-Cancers' distinctive blend of cajoling and good humor can certainly soften it. Relationships that remain love affairs and stubbornly refuse to move on to marriage are probably better off that way, since the viewpoints of Gemini-Cancers and Virgo I's are likely to become increasingly polarized as these mates get older and more set in their ways. At work, these two prefer challenging entrepreneurial or investment schemes to mundane or repetitive tasks. The relationship has a gambling instinct, being attracted to dangerous enterprises the outcome of which may rest on a single throw of the dice. Friendships too thrive on the kinds of challenges to the mind and body that expose the partners to real rather than imagined risk.

Family groups are likely to encourage the individual strengths of Virgo I's and Gemini-Cancers, appreciating their practical and their imaginative abilities respectively. Their penchant for danger will be discouraged in this context, and any paranormal abilities will be seen as contributing little to family life.

ADVICE: *Keep your tendency to gamble under control. Remember that others may be depending on you. Stay flexible. Let go of any fear of the inexplicable.*

STRENGTHS: **PHILOSOPHICAL, INSPIRATIONAL, AUTHORITATIVE**

WEAKNESSES: **REPRESSED, CONFLICTING, HIDDEN**

BEST: **WORK**

WORST: **MARRIAGE**

BRIAN WILSON (6/20/42)
AL JARDINE (9/3/42)

When guitarist-vocalist Jardine joined the original Beach Boys band, he was a friend of Wilson's—and was inspired by his songwriting through the years. Jardine has written several fine Beach Boys songs, including *Lady Lynda*, a tribute to his wife.

June 19–24
THE CUSP OF MAGIC
GEMINI-CANCER CUSP

September 3–10
THE WEEK OF THE ENIGMA
VIRGO II

Assertiveness Training

This relationship's great lesson is to teach its partners how to assert themselves and develop a sense of inner authority in order to be taken seriously in the world. It is important, however, that they train this assertiveness not on each other but outward. The pair are encouraged to use their joint intuitive strength to discover philosophical, religious, social or political ideas that may guide them on their way. The development of such systems or tactics will often be the driving force behind their daily interactions, helping two rather retiring personalities deal better with the world. The relationship serves as an inspirational motor to power their endeavors forward.

Gemini-Cancer–Virgo II love affairs can be highly secretive. Their covertness is important, however, to make the partners feel safe, and sometimes to avoid hurting others. Ideologies and beliefs are not of crucial importance in this intimate relationship, which is tied up with complex and at times repressed states of feeling. Parent-child and sibling relationships similarly have an almost confessional quality, sometimes keeping secrets from the larger family group for years, in absolute confidence. In both love and family, in fact, secrecy itself may prove the relationship's principal basis, providing a source of shared belief and authority.

Should these two meet first as friends, together they may find an occupation or profession that can sustain them physically while also feeding their spiritual and intellectual selves. Whether this activity is religious or social, personal or community oriented, Gemini-Cancers and Virgo II's will seek out the secret places in the hearts of others who can respond to their message. Perhaps only reaching a small percentage of the population of their city or town, they will sooner or later realize that their mission is meant for only the few prepared to listen to its unusual content. Spouses in this combination may also share a career, but given their emotional struggles and conflicts, the chances of things working out are slimmer.

ADVICE: *Try to lighten up a bit. Don't be so secretive. Learn to share emotions as well as ideas with others. Remember that assertion is not aggression.*

STRENGTHS: **PLEASURABLE, CARING, PROTECTIVE**

WEAKNESSES: **SACRIFICING, STAGNATING, ADRIFT**

BEST: **MARRIAGE**

WORST: **FAMILY**

MARTIN LANDAU (6/20/31)
BARBARA BAIN (9/13/32)

1994 Oscar-winner Landau co-starred on tv's *Mission: Impossible,* alongside wife Bain. While the show ran from 1966–73, the pair left it in '69 for monetary reasons.
***Also:* Lillian Hellman & Zoe Caldwell** (playwright/stage portrayal); **Alison Smithson & Peter Smithson** (married; architects); **Princes William & Henry** (royal brothers).

June 19–24
THE CUSP OF MAGIC
GEMINI-CANCER CUSP

September 11–18
THE WEEK OF THE LITERALIST
VIRGO III

Self-Nurturing

Neither of these two likes trouble in a relationship, and the watchwords of their matchup might be "No hassles." Easy attitudes are likely to prevail here. Healthy activities built around physical comfort and pleasure—working out, massage, aromatherapy, jacuzzi, sauna—may regularly prove attractive, and overindulgence in food is unlikely; in fact, a sensible approach to diet is likely to prevail. Such involvements are essentially self-nurturing, but these two apply themselves to them with inspired seriousness of purpose. They are also concerned for other people in these areas. A problem could be that this intense interest in health disguises an avoidance of the realm of feelings or of deeper psychological states. This can stunt the partners' own inner growth, and the growth of the relationship.

In love and marriage, the energies are apt to be more sensual than sexual. Both partners have a nurturing side that their relationship will synergistically reinforce, particularly when they are a married couple with children. The sensible attitudes and practical solutions of Virgo III's will be balanced by the imaginative and sensitive suggestions of Gemini-Cancers; the couple's children will probably benefit from both approaches. Should these spouses be without children, they may turn their protective natures to nieces and nephews, or, if they are in business together, to their own organization and employees. Watching human growth and development is a great joy for the Gemini-Cancer–Virgo III couple.

Parent-child combinations may lack decisiveness. Each partner may manifest a fierce desire to help the other at his or her own expense. Yet these sacrificial attitudes can easily be seen as selfish by other family members, who naturally feel cut out of the picture.

ADVICE: *Be honest about what you really want. Beware of self-sacrifice. Deprivation can breed resentment. Be cognizant of neglecting others.*

June 19–24

THE CUSP OF MAGIC
GEMINI-CANCER CUSP

September 19–24

THE CUSP OF BEAUTY
VIRGO-LIBRA CUSP

Appreciative Harmony

This relationship has a romantic quality that can suffuse its whole environment. Beauty and grace are paramount here. The relationship's strengths are its need and desire to remain in harmony with its surroundings, and to appreciate the wonder of life in all its aspects. Traditional astrology would predict strife in a square aspect like this one (two sun signs lie 90° apart in the zodiac here), but Gemini-Cancers and Virgo-Libras are typically a highly balanced pair. It is true, however, that when their relationship is thrown out of balance, they can suffer terribly, having come to depend on it as a source of power and inspiration. Believing the best about the relationship, then, is not always a good preparation for harder times. Gemini-Cancers and Virgo-Libras must learn not to blind themselves to their limitations and deficiencies as a pair, not only because this leaves them vulnerable but because it deprives them of the fighting spirit necessary to improve their situation. Friendships and love affairs are especially vulnerable in this respect.

Work relationships and marriages are less openly romantic than other relationships in this combination, because they present daily demands that have to be met, like it or not. A good dose of reality and responsibility will not hurt this pair, however, and is healthy insofar as it discourages their less realistic tendencies. But attendance only to the physical aspects of life, even if these have their aesthetic side, can cut off whole areas of experience—the emotional, religious and spiritual realms of life. A balanced Gemini-Cancer–Virgo-Libra relationship will really have to push itself to be motivated to investigate such areas. Self-satisfaction may be the greatest enemy here.

Smugness usually emerges most clearly between family members in this combination. The feeling that they and their family are superior to others, "the best" in their own circle, can be quite destructive to personal development and self-actualization.

ADVICE: *You are no better than anyone else. Beware of self-satisfaction. Push yourself to achieve the very best you can. Help to serve others.*

HENRY WARD BEECHER (6/24/1813)
VICTORIA WOODHULL (9/23/1838)

Beecher, a popular and influential orator and clergyman, attacked women's crusader Woodhull for her advocacy of free love. She retaliated in 1872 by instigating a sensational adultery scandal that linked Beecher to one of his parishioners. **Also: Ernest Chain & H.W. Florey** (1945 Nobelists, medicine).

June 19–24

THE CUSP OF MAGIC
GEMINI-CANCER CUSP

September 25–October 2

THE WEEK OF THE PERFECTIONIST
LIBRA I

Humorous Twist

Prone to worry and upset, this pair must struggle to relax and to view the world with humor. Self-induced tension is usually the biggest problem for Libra I's in any relationship, and relaxed Gemini-Cancer attitudes can have a paradoxically catalytic effect in this area, making them even more uptight than usual. Yet a Gemini-Cancer can also have a soothing effect on their nerves, calming them down. This curious ambiguity usually depends on their mood at the time. Often a small Gemini-Cancer remark, or a certain look, can provoke a reaction. Libra I's can be much too demanding for a sensitive Gemini-Cancer. The relationship's real challenge, in fact, may be whether or not they can relax and accept their partner.

Love affairs demand that both partners be extremely sensitive to each other's needs. Gemini-Cancers are easily wounded by Libra I criticism, Libra I's offended by Gemini-Cancer inattention. Sexually the relationship may at first go like a house on fire, then slowly fizzle. What is left once the thrill is gone will rarely be enough to form the basis for a lasting friendship. It is important that closure of such an affair be handled respectfully, otherwise resentments and frustrations may linger long after.

Marriages are not recommended here, since Libra I's generally lack both the patience to deal with Gemini-Cancers' emotional needs over the long haul and the ability to refrain from inflicting hurt when not satisfied. In family relationships, too, Libra I parents can be much too critical of their Gemini-Cancer children, who tend to be unduly influenced by them.

Casual friendships and relatively undemanding work relationships are probably the best bet for this combination. Here they can appreciate each other's talents and abilities, as long as their emotional involvement stays cool and objective attitudes prevail. Libra I technical skills and Gemini-Cancer imaginativeness may blend well in certain occupations, particularly those that involve creating a new and exciting product or service. The relationship generally lends a humorous twist to such endeavors.

ADVICE: *Tune in to each other's needs. Suspend criticism. Work on being more accepting. Appreciate small acts of kindness. Don't harbor grudges.*

JUNE CARTER (6/23/29)
CARLENE CARTER (9/26/55)

Member of a prominent country-music family, Carlene is June Carter Cash's daughter and Mother Maybelle Carter's granddaughter. As a child, she traveled on her mother's tours, then sang in the Carter Family Revue. She went solo in 1978.

STRENGTHS: **DIRECTED,**
INQUISITIVE, VERSATILE

WEAKNESSES: **SEDENTARY,**
VAGUE, OBSESSIONAL

BEST: **FRIENDSHIP**

WORST: **WORK**

AAGE NIELS BOHR (6/19/22)
NIELS BOHR (10/7/1885)

Niels and his son Aage were
Danish physicists who won Nobel
Prizes more than 50 years apart:
Niels in 1922 for his work in
atomic theory, and Aage in 1975
for discovering the asymmetry
of atomic nuclei.

June 19–24

THE CUSP OF MAGIC
GEMINI-CANCER CUSP

October 3–10

THE WEEK OF SOCIETY
LIBRA II

Finding Sense and Purpose

This relationship's great need, and inevitably the focus of its energies, is to find direction. Perhaps this pair needs to follow an ideology, person or group; perhaps they can find the strength to give sense and purpose to their activities within the relationship itself. These are the crucial questions here. Creating a self-motivating unit is of course the goal, but the relationship may have to find its way via a teacher of some sort, a person whose ideas are initially likely to prove dominant but may later be gradually set aside or even rejected. Given this tendency, it is not uncommon for Gemini-Cancers and Libra II's to meet for the first time in a school or other educational setting.

Love affairs and marriages between Gemini-Cancers and Libra II's often show a special interest in food, cooking, clothing and interior design. The greatest danger to this relationship is dietary, for a sedentary and easygoing lifestyle coupled with a love of eating can be a prescription for disaster. Here the issue of motivation enters again, since giving an outward drive to the relationship may help to save its members from overweight or clogged arteries. It is usually essential for these lovers and spouses to work out, swim or take long walks together.

Friendships between schoolmates or even siblings in this combination are classic. The relationship's chief characteristic is inquiry into hitherto unexplored and fascinating areas of thought and action. Libra II's are especially interested in people and Gemini-Cancers in aesthetics, but together they are likely to investigate a wide range of subjects, from history to music to sports.

In the professional sphere, working on mutual projects together is a good way for Gemini-Cancers and Libra II's to get to know each other. They must be careful, however, not to become so committed to what they are doing that their relationship enters the realms of workaholism and obsession.

ADVICE: *Find a balance between inertia and hyperactivity. Look within yourself for motivation and inspiration. Limit your interests a bit.*

STRENGTHS: **SENSITIVE,**
ACCEPTING, ORGANIC

WEAKNESSES: **IRRITATING,**
DEPENDENT, UNSHARING

BEST: **LOVE**

WORST: **FAMILY**

TERRY RILEY (6/24/35)
LAMONTE YOUNG (10/14/35)

Riley and Young are contemporaries
in avant-garde music and close
friends. In the 60s each experiment-
ed with basic sound elements to
establish themselves as the first
minimalist composers. In 1970, they
studied East Indian music with Pran
Nath. **Also: Rev. Henry Ward**
Beecher & Lyman Beecher
(son/father; orator/abolitionist).

June 19–24

THE CUSP OF MAGIC
GEMINI-CANCER CUSP

October 11–18

THE WEEK OF THEATER
LIBRA III

Doubly Dynamic

This relationship often enjoys a strong bond of understanding that does not demand daily interaction between its partners but guarantees a deep commitment and support whenever they are needed. These two have very different approaches to life, but their relationship is for the most part sensitive and accepting. The Gemini-Cancer world is, broadly speaking, private, the Libra III world generally more public, but Libra III's actually choose carefully when they want to be in other people's company, and may in fact spend most of their time alone. Action rather than contemplation is what appeals to them, and here they may spur their Gemini-Cancer partners on, doubling the relationship's dynamism. These two might easily dabble in the mystical, perhaps even bringing it to others in the form of a theatrical presentation or performance. Together they can prove quite inspiring. At bottom, too, their relationship is great fun.

In love and marriage, Libra III's may want a strong partner who can take the lead more effectively than they can, but they more often fall for dependent types who lean on them a bit—like Gemini-Cancers. In this particular case, however, the rewards for them are great: Libra III's may never before or after feel more loved and accepted than they do with devoted Gemini-Cancer partners.

As friends, these two often share a common activity that they pursue wholeheartedly. From stamp collecting to scuba diving, the range of possibilities is broad and unpredictable. The pair may well meet completely by chance, or be introduced by a third party; although interested, they don't usually attach themselves strongly to each other at the start, but over time their relationship will deepen organically, usually guaranteeing its longevity.

Work relationships between these two are not recommended, for both are usually better off doing their own thing and perhaps comparing notes at a later date. In family matchups, Gemini-Cancers and Libra III's may prove too sensitive to each other's foibles to forestall constant irritation.

ADVICE: *Don't permit yourself to be triggered so easily. Let others go their own way. Beware of being overly accepting. Show what you feel.*

June 19–24

THE CUSP OF MAGIC
GEMINI-CANCER CUSP

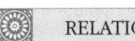

October 19–25

THE CUSP OF DRAMA & CRITICISM
LIBRA-SCORPIO CUSP

RELATIONSHIPS

STRENGTHS: REVELATORY,
FREEING, ANALYTICAL

WEAKNESSES: GAME-PLAYING,
TRIVIALIZING, CRIPPLING

BEST: BUSINESS PARTNERSHIP

WORST: CO-WORKER

Tough to Figure Out

The chemistry of this matchup favors revealing long-hidden secrets and freeing up private information. Once a bond of trust has been built, the pair will share much of a personal nature with each other. Should either of them fall into a more volatile emotional state, he or she may lose control and blurt out the secrets. Another common occurrence may be the surfacing of material that the relationship loosens in one partner's subconscious, for example through the recollection of dreams. Finally, a critical, interrogative Libra-Scorpio can simply drill away at a Gemini-Cancer until unconscious or repressed material comes to light. In whichever area this relationship manifests, the partners must beware of getting so absorbed in this game of hide-and-seek that they lose sight of personal growth and career development. Such wasted energies are likely to be the single most destructive element here, although the bringing of hidden material to light can have undeniably positive therapeutic effects.

Mental and emotional games may feature strongly in this relationship, particularly in its more intimate manifestations—for example, between lovers, family members and friends. Not only do both partners alternately hide and reveal secrets with each other, but together they have a habit of striking the same kind of covert stance in relation to other couples. Family members and other friends may view Gemini-Cancer–Libra-Scorpio marriages as secretive, puzzling, hard to figure. Much of this behavior is conscious, all part of a smoke screen designed to cover up whatever is really going on. More mature relationships between these partners will demonstrate less of a need for such activities.

Gemini-Cancer–Libra-Scorpio work relationships are best established on the entrepreneurial or executive level, where these partners can exert their different skills most effectively. By contrast, co-working on common projects as employees is not especially recommended.

AL HIRSCHFELD (6/21/03)
NINA HIRSCHFELD (10/20/45)

Al Hirschfeld is the pre-eminent caricaturist of Broadway personalities. After his daughter Nina's birth in 1945, he began hiding her name in various parts of his distinctive drawings. Millions of readers came to enjoy hunting for "Nina's" in his work. **Also: Meryl Streep & Carrie Fisher** (close friends; actresses).

ADVICE: *Be aware of destructive game-playing. Strive for greater transparency. Don't neglect personal growth and initiative. Beware of wasted energy.*

June 19–24

THE CUSP OF MAGIC
GEMINI-CANCER CUSP

October 26–November 2

THE WEEK OF INTENSITY
SCORPIO I

RELATIONSHIPS

STRENGTHS: SPIRITUAL,
SEXUAL, SENSUOUS

WEAKNESSES: OVERSENSITIVE,
GULLIBLE, IMPRACTICAL

BEST: LOVE

WORST: MARRIAGE

A Love of Silence

The deep and lasting bond of the spirit in this relationship will afford its partners great intimacy, and their understanding and trust will usually deepen over time. Interest in philosophical, religious or new-age thought is often prominent here, and the ideas derived from these schools are usually put into effect in practice. Even if the partners are not overtly involved in spiritual pursuits, however, their relationship manifests a love of silence, peace, meditation, contemplation and visualization, all of which points in the direction of true spirituality.

Love affairs are particularly favored in this combination. They are sometimes of short duration, but if both partners agree to persevere whatever the difficulties, the long-term prognosis is good. Sexual attraction can run high here. Although Gemini-Cancers express themselves more sensually and Scorpio I's more sexually, their relationship manifests a nice balance between the pleasurable and the erotic. Nor does it acknowledge a strict separation between the physical and the spiritual, viewing the pleasures of table and bed as only further evidence of the handiwork of God, or of a benevolent force in the universe. An openness to and interest in tantra, the Kama Sutra and oriental erotica in general are not uncommon here.

Marriage would seem the next step for this pair, but they often see it as unnecessary, usually for idealistic or ideological reasons. Friendships in this combination frequently develop as a result of the partners meeting at a workshop or during a community- or business-related activity. Such friendships can profitably be combined with a new career endeavor, especially in work dealing with the arts, self-development or health.

In the family, the emotional bond between parents and children in this combination, or between siblings, often sets the feeling tone for the rest of the family group. Thus, the relationship can often encourage a more spiritual orientation in those around it.

PRUNELLA SCALES (6/22/32)
JOHN CLEESE (10/27/39)

Scales and Cleese played ever-bickering husband-and-wife hotel owners in *Fawlty Towers*, the British sitcom that took PBS by storm in the 80s. As Sybil Fawlty, Scales was the bane of Cleese's pompously blundering character, Basil.

ADVICE: *Don't believe everything you hear. Maintain skepticism. Be respectful of the beliefs of others. Learn how to wait and persevere.*

STRENGTHS: **STRUCTURAL, ORGANIZATIONAL, INNOVATIVE**

WEAKNESSES: **FRUSTRATED, INSECURE, DEMANDING**

BEST: **MARRIAGE**

WORST: **WORK**

ROSEANNE BARR (11/3/52)
JOHN GOODMAN (6/20/52)

Goodman and Barr are the perfect match as working-class parents of 3 children in the top-rated tv sitcom *Roseanne* (1980–97), innovative in its frank and down-to-earth episodes.

Also: **Jean-Paul Sartre & Albert Camus** (existentialists); **Olympia Dukakis & Michael Dukakis** (cousins); **Bob Fosse & Ann Reinking** (romance; choreographer/ dancer); **Audie Murphy & Wanda Hendrix** (married; actors).

June 19–24

THE CUSP OF MAGIC
GEMINI-CANCER CUSP

November 3–11

THE WEEK OF DEPTH
SCORPIO II

Functional Aspects

This relationship is likely to emphasize building or organizing a structure, whether in a domestic space, at work or socially. Gemini-Cancer–Scorpio II emotional interactions are such that an efficient physical setup for their activities must be established before either of them will feel deeply secure. They usually have a good idea what they want and need here, but limitations of finances or space may demand compromise, flexibility and creative problem-solving. Once the structure is established, they can get down to the business of sharing themselves with each other and revealing who they are. Deeply private both, they almost seem to need these imaginary boundaries in order to feel safe.

Love, marriage and family relationships between these two will concentrate on furnishing and decoration, but also on functional issues, particularly with regard to practical areas such as cooking and career. It will usually be necessary for each partner to have his or her own private space, which may require quite a large house if children are involved. Not only is home entertainment important, a strong emphasis is also likely to be placed on studying or working at home. The couple will usually exercise care and forethought in planning the most efficient and effective use of the space. Gemini-Cancer–Scorpio II friendships are less concerned with physical structure but still function more smoothly in ordered situations—when schedules clearly indicate the time available for vacation, leisure, lunch and other possibilities for social interaction, for example. Most of their activities will be of a personal rather than a social kind, and they may well share a vocation. Co-workers in this combination will be frustrated if spatial limitations deny them the opportunity to organize their office or workspace in the manner best suited to their needs. They are usually better off working in a larger space, such as a good-sized store. The best possibility of all may be for the relationship to function on a managerial or executive level, where its decisions and visions can be implemented without a lot of red tape. Both technical and aesthetic strengths are usually demonstrated here.

ADVICE: *Don't be so demanding about physical space. Organize yourself internally so that you can function anywhere. Don't be afraid to show who you are.*

STRENGTHS: **CLOSE, INVOLVED, INTIMATE**

WEAKNESSES: **DEPENDENT, CLAIMING, ADDICTED**

BEST: **LOVE**

WORST: **FRIENDSHIP**

PRINCE WILLIAM (6/21/82)
PRINCE CHARLES (11/14/48)

Eldest of Charles and Diana's 2 sons, William is heir to his father's future throne. Owing to the royal breakup, William now ricochets between his parents' different worlds, while preparing for a future public role much like his father's.

Also: **Francoise Gauquelin & Michel Gauquelin** (married; statistician-astrologers).

June 19–24

THE CUSP OF MAGIC
GEMINI-CANCER CUSP

November 12–18

THE WEEK OF CHARM
SCORPIO III

Being Overly Involved

This highly personal relationship may find its partners spending long periods of time alone together. Concomitant to that, however, is a tendency for them to get too involved with each other, to the point where their ego boundaries blur and the relationship takes over. Individual partners may find themselves in open conflict with the relationship itself, which can sometimes prove demanding, involving and inescapable. Gemini-Cancers may feel especially oppressed by charming yet imposing Scorpio III's.

Love affairs, marriages and friendships must be carefully monitored for signs of undue dependency, which is often a warning that further involvement is inadvisable. Sex and love addictions are not at all uncommon here; drugs, too, prescription or otherwise, may pose a serious habitual problem. Magnetic sorts of desire figure prominently in the relationships of Gemini-Cancers and Scorpio III's generally, and their matchup with each other can synergistically intensify this trait to create an even higher kind of attachment. Breakups will be especially painful in these situations, and may press home the need to be wary of such all-absorbing involvements in the future.

It may be easier for these two to maintain their objectivity in their friendships than in their love affairs and marriages, but problems of dependency and jealousy usually still manifest. Work relationships may be the most objective of all, and as long as both co-workers have equal status, and are treated without favoritism by their superiors, they can be extremely productive. In the family, parent-child relationships may entail unusually close emotional bonds, particularly between fathers and daughters or mothers and sons. The pain of separation when the children reach adolescence will be acute in these cases of loving too much. Both partners should work on letting go of claiming attitudes as the years go by, allowing the relationship to grow in maturity and self-confidence.

ADVICE: *Beware of isolation. Keep contact with friends and family. Be careful around addictive substances. Learn the lessons of independence.*

June 19–24

THE CUSP OF MAGIC
GEMINI-CANCER CUSP

November 19–24

THE CUSP OF REVOLUTION
SCORPIO-SAGITTARIUS CUSP

An Air of Mystery

This interesting relationship is not an easy one to figure out, either for other people or for the partners themselves. Although both of them tend to be secretive types, this mysterious matchup will not only fascinate them but frustrate them. Both Gemini-Cancers and Scorpio-Sagittarians are more than capable of getting their way; indeed each is the other's match when it comes to persuasion and manipulation. The overall effect is one of shifting sands—of insecurity.

Physical attraction can be high between these two, but their love affairs tend to be unstable, as is suggested by the quincunx aspect here (Gemini-Cancer and Scorpio-Sagittarius are 150° apart in the zodiac). The cooler attitudes of Gemini-Cancers tend to put them in control, since emotional Scorpio-Sagittarians can find it hard to keep their feelings in check during confrontations, and lose their tempers more easily. Insecurities over the relationship run high on both sides, but the fallout is not completely negative: a blend of fear and excitement adds intensity to the couple's sexual interactions.

Trust is the most important consideration in marriages and friendships between these two. Since Gemini-Cancers tend to be faithful once their heart is given, they risk the greater hurt in these relationships. Scorpio-Sagittarius mates and friends rarely if ever tell all about their hidden activities, but perceptive Gemini-Cancers will usually sniff out their ability to juggle several relationships at one time. They may be quite loyal in their own way even as they are being unfaithful, however, and if the Gemini-Cancer can forgive them a minor indiscretion or two, the relationship is likely to endure.

Co-worker and business partnerships in this combination can prove effective, especially in the field of human services. When the partners see eye-to-eye, they can forge a potently persuasive force. Fortunately they are sensitive enough to allow others to decide for themselves. In family matchups, however, particularly between parent and child, they must be careful not to let manipulative drives get out of hand.

ADVICE: *Be sure to leave others enough space. Build bonds of trust. Work to understand yourself better. Strive for emotional honesty.*

AHMAD RASHAD (11/19/49)
PHYLICIA RASHAD (6/19/48)

TV actress Phylicia (*The Cosby Show*) is married to Ahmad, a retired football star and tv sportscaster. He proposed to his future wife while on the air during *NFL Live!* in 1985. **Also: Mike Todd & Evelyn Keyes** (live-in lovers; producer/actress); **Peter Pears & Benjamin Britten** (life-partners; singer/composer).

June 19–24

THE CUSP OF MAGIC
GEMINI-CANCER CUSP

November 25–December 2

THE WEEK OF INDEPENDENCE
SAGITTARIUS I

Common Dreams

The keynote here is the sharing of dreams and fantasies, and the degree to which such sharing can take place may well be the determining factor in the relationship's success. Sagittarius I's have a strongly private side, and it will be extremely rewarding for them to share their deepest feelings with Gemini-Cancers, who can be very understanding and accepting. Gemini-Cancers, however, are capable of withholding their most personal emotions from their partners at times, not wanting to annoy or bore them with what seem to be petty problems; in effect they sacrifice their own need for closeness. Sacrifice also figures in the many acts of unflinching service they tend to perform in work situations. Sooner or later this impulse will have to be addressed, or built-up frustrations will one day boil over in overwhelming anger.

Differences of pace make love affairs not immediately suggested here. They can certainly work out, though, as can marriages and friendships. These partners are temperamentally unlike: the Sagittarius I motor generally runs at a higher rpm than that of their Gemini-Cancer partner. That only means, however, that the Gemini-Cancer influence can be a calming one. Sagittarius I's often do well in a living situation with someone less assertive and argumentative than themselves, on whom they can depend for a measure of domestic tranquillity. Gemini-Cancers will also have a positive effect on their habits of orderliness on the home front.

Both friends and family members in this combination sometimes delve deeply into a shared fantasy life. Gemini-Cancer–Sagittarius I brothers and sisters can live in their own fascinating private world, replete with imaginative mythological figures. Childhood friends can be inseparable and can continue their relationship well into adulthood. A love of physical activity, particularly low-competition sports, dance and milder forms of adventure, will bind these two even closer.

ADVICE: *Give unconditionally or not at all. Aim for an easy give-and-take. Beware of cutting yourself off from daily realities. Don't be afraid to share.*

JOHN McVIE (11/26/45)
MICK FLEETWOOD (6/24/47)

Original members of the pop group Fleetwood Mac, the rhythm section of Fleetwood and McVie hasn't changed since its formation in 1967. Drummer Fleetwood and bassist McVie maintained the group's consistency through the years while other members frequently came and went. **Also: "Baby" Charles Lindbergh, Jr. & Bruno Hauptmann** (victim/kidnapper-killer).

GENA ROWLANDS (6/19/34)
JOHN CASSAVETES (12/9/29)

Actress Rowlands and actor-director-screenwriter Cassavetes were married from 1958 till his death in 1989. They were very close personally and professionally. She often appeared in his films, with *A Woman Under the Influence* (1974) earning her an Oscar nomination. **Also: Roy Disney & Walt Disney** (brothers; partners); **Robert Henri & Marjorie Organ** (married; artists).

June 19–24
THE CUSP OF MAGIC
GEMINI-CANCER CUSP

December 3–10
THE WEEK OF THE ORIGINATOR
SAGITTARIUS II

Tried and True

This relationship will prove a great challenge to both partners. Because it often demands literal and truthful attitudes from them, they may feel a bit restricted in the imaginative and flamboyant side that both of them like to display. Fact is more valuable than fiction in this relationship, a notion that will benefit both partners but that they will often find difficult to grasp. When either of them individually is faced with a problem, their first instinct is usually to think up a highly unusual solution. Here, though, they will be constrained to take the tried-and-true route that is certain to work.

In work and in the family, the Gemini-Cancer–Sagittarius II relationship will teach practicality and demand pragmatic points of view. Taking on serious responsibilities will often affect these free spirits for the better. Still, both of them will need plenty of free time for fooling around and having fun after they have discharged their work and family chores. Once they have met the demands of their respective circumstances, in fact, they may tend to go a little haywire when they are off on their own together. They will both need to learn to find a balance in their lives between boring responsibilities and fun irresponsibilities.

Love and marriage, especially of the more romantic kind, are not particularly recommended here, since they bring out the instabilities inherent in both partners. Their emotions rising and falling like the temperature in the desert, the couple will find little support or rest in such a relationship. Nothing is permanent here except change. Gemini-Cancers can get worn down and Sagittarius II's enervated by such extremes.

Friends in this combination try to do more than just enjoy themselves by any means. Social involvement with the physically or economically disadvantaged, and work with community-service groups, are likely to take up their time—that is, when they are not being challenged to help groups of friends and family with practical endeavors.

ADVICE: *Don't resent responsibility—learn and grow from it. By learning to be good at practical endeavors you will become more of a whole person.*

JULIETTE LEWIS (6/21/73)
BRAD PITT (12/18/63)

Lewis and Pitt first met in 1989 while filming the tv movie *Too Young to Die*. They fell in love and lived together for 4 years. **Also: Edward VIII & George VI** (brothers; kings); **Increase Mather & Cotton Mather** (father/son; colonial clergymen); **Errol Flynn & Patricia Wymore** (married; actors).

June 19–24
THE CUSP OF MAGIC
GEMINI-CANCER CUSP

December 11–18
THE WEEK OF THE TITAN
SAGITTARIUS III

New Hope

The focus of this relationship is new beginnings. Meeting after a previous relationship with each other has failed, these partners, older and wiser, may well decide to give it another try. They may equally meet in their younger years, when their relationship might represent a first serious attempt to explore a specific area, such as marriage or career. Whatever the case, both partners feel a sparkle, a vivacity, a new hope that the relationship will move in the right direction, justifying the expenditure of time and energy.

Assuming that the partners are strongly enough attracted to each other, the chances for love affairs and marriages in this combination are generally good. Gemini-Cancers are often wary of people like Sagittarius III's, who get and demand so much attention from others, but beneath that distrust may lurk a secret admiration. Sagittarius III's are often too busy to take the time to notice or get to know very private individuals, but the Gemini-Cancer enchantment may draw them like a magnet. With Sagittarius III's pursuing expansive goals and Gemini-Cancers grounding them in a happy and comforting domestic situation, the relationship may prove rewarding and successful. Care will have to be taken, however, that Sagittarius III's do not dominate their Gemini-Cancer partners, depriving them of the opportunity to develop on their own.

Sibling matchups and friendships are often highly protective, with the Sagittarius III Titan usually playing the nurturing and defensive role. Gemini-Cancers will often be happy with such an arrangement until they want to assert their own individuality, at which point Sagittarius III's must be able to let go if the relationship is to continue in harmony.

Work relationships are not particularly favored here, unless Gemini-Cancers are prepared to accept an assistant or secondary role to dominant Sagittarius III's. In rare cases, dynamic and powerful Gemini-Cancers may depend heavily on a Sagittarius III employee or co-worker, but the danger of confrontation and power struggles is never far away.

ADVICE: *Learn to let go of people and of the past. Be aware of the needs of others. Don't work so hard to convince yourself that things are better than they are.*

June 19–24

THE CUSP OF MAGIC
GEMINI-CANCER CUSP

December 19–25

THE CUSP OF PROPHECY
SAGITTARIUS-CAPRICORN CUSP

Beauty and Balance

RELATIONSHIPS

STRENGTHS: **ATTRACTING, AESTHETIC, INTIMATE**

WEAKNESSES: **REPELLING, POLARIZED, MISUNDERSTOOD**

BEST: **MARRIAGE**

WORST: **LOVE**

This is one of the most unusual relationships in the year. Gemini-Cancers and Sagittarius-Capricorns are born at the summer and winter solstices, respectively; the symbolic opposition between the longest day and the longest night can represent a conflict between the outward growth and unconscious orientation of summertime and youth, on the one hand, and the inward growth and conscious orientation of winter and adulthood, on the other. But the relationship these two form has its own character, too, and the dominant focus here may be a search for beauty and balance.

A complex dynamic is at work in this relationship, with its equally strong forces of attraction and repulsion. The partners differ temperamentally, but share a need for extreme privacy and intimacy; their relationship magnifies that need. Searching for beauty, they may look for it in each other or work together to find it in nature, art or humankind. They often overlook or forget their individual differences in this pursuit, accomplishing a fusion of extremely different personalities into a common whole. There is, of course, a danger here of a loss of individuality, but these personalities are generally strong enough to survive within the relationship.

Love affairs between these two will be difficult and trying. Emotional complexity and a curious inability to move the passionate relationship forward will underline the difficulties that these two have communicating with each other. Sagittarius-Capricorns will tend to turn silent and hurt, expecting their lover to understand them, while Gemini-Cancers may prefer to keep things cool, trying to avoid misunderstandings and problems altogether.

Gemini-Cancer–Sagittarius-Capricorn work relationships, marriages and parent-child matchups have a great deal to offer co-workers, children and other family members in terms of varying and contrasting points of view. The children of such parents, for example, will have a genuine choice about which parent to approach with any problem, and will not expect a monolithic response. The relationship's drive toward beauty and balance will usually exert a positive and harmonious influence on whatever group is a part of.

JANE RUSSELL (6/21/21)
HOWARD HUGHES (12/24/05)

Discovering her through a highly publicized national hunt for a buxom lead, multimillionaire Hughes cast Russell in his controversial and, at first, censored western *The Outlaw* (1943), which he produced and directed. Along the way, they had an affair.

ADVICE: *Keep your eye on the object. Don't get bogged down in feelings. Emphasize constructive activities. Appreciate your differences.*

June 19–24

THE CUSP OF MAGIC
GEMINI-CANCER CUSP

December 26–January 2

THE WEEK OF THE RULER
CAPRICORN I

High Tension

RELATIONSHIPS

STRENGTHS: **QUALITY-ORIENTED, DEMANDING,**

WEAKNESSES: **SARCASTIC, STRESSED, MISUNDERSTANDING**

BEST: **WORK**

WORST: **MARRIAGE**

This relationship is very demanding, especially if it manifests in the areas of family or business. Its perfectionist tone creates a lot of unfulfilled expectations and emotional complexities. Capricorn I's are as a rule rather demanding to begin with, both of themselves and of others; Gemini-Cancers may by their very nature be able to alleviate some of this, but they will not be able to ease the burdens of the relationship itself. In fact, this particular combination will put Capricorn I's under intense pressure and scrutiny. Tension may also spill over onto Gemini-Cancers, who will respond with self-criticism—as if it were in their power to do anything to better the situation. These two need to focus on learning to relax, worrying less and overlooking small problems.

Gemini-Cancer–Capricorn I love affairs are likely to reveal emotional difficulties. Capricorn I's can get quite emotional, but will rarely be able to discuss with their partner whatever is bothering them. Gemini-Cancers may doubt that Capricorn I's really understand or appreciate them. These two are often strongly attracted to each other physically, but this is unlikely to help much, and in fact may widen the gulf of misunderstanding.

Marriages in this combination are not recommended, since the relationship's perfectionist energy is apt to create the kinds of tension that prevent relaxation. Gemini-Cancers might come to resent the relationship for this reason, and Capricorn I's might dislike it for not living up to expectations.

As friends, this pair may be jointly critical of others rather than of each other. Drawn to irony and humor, they sometimes enjoy themselves by making fun of other people's foibles. The friendship will have to learn to laugh at itself, too, however, particularly when these energies boomerang back on it. In every area where it appears, whether career, family or personal, the Gemini-Cancer–Capricorn I relationship must maintain high standards but scale back the partners' persistent perfectionism in favor of a more accepting view.

BOB FOSSE (6/23/27)
JOAN MCCRACKEN (12/31/22)

Choreographer-director Fosse and musical-comedy star McCracken were married in the early 50s, divorced around '58. She was his 2nd wife and former dance partner. She starred in Broadway's *Billion Dollar Baby* (1945). Fosse was influential in stage and screen musicals. His fast-paced career was dramatized in *All That Jazz* (1979).

ADVICE: *Let up a bit in your expectations. Take things as they come. Lower tension, not quality. Improve personal relations. Practice kindness.*

STRENGTHS: **CHILDLIKE,
PLAYFUL, ENTERTAINING**

WEAKNESSES: **NAIVE,
DEPENDENT, NERVOUS**

BEST: **PARENT-CHILD**

WORST: **WORK**

SIMONE DE BEAUVOIR (1/9/08)
JEAN-PAUL SARTRE (6/21/05)

De Beauvoir was Sartre's disciple, companion and sometime lover during a 51-year relationship bonded by a common belief in existentialism. During their final 20 years together, they traveled constantly and cared tenderly for each other. **Also: Benazir Bhutto & Zulfikar Ali Bhutto** (daughter/father; Pakistani leaders).

June 19–24

THE CUSP OF MAGIC
GEMINI-CANCER CUSP

January 3–9

THE WEEK OF DETERMINATION
CAPRICORN II

Mitigating Seriousness

Rather mysteriously, this relationship exudes freshness and charm, infecting its partners and others with the most basic kind of enthusiasm possible. Together these two share a pure personal vision that demands to be expressed. They often have an almost childlike way of communing with each other—direct, simple and uncomplicated. The customary Capricorn II air of resoluteness is subverted by Gemini-Cancer playfulness. No matter how serious Capricorn II's get, their relationship with Gemini-Cancers will induce awe and wonder in their hearts, even at their most pragmatic. Beneath the hard-boiled Capricorn II exterior may rest a sensitive soul, which Gemini-Cancers know how to unearth and appreciate. One problem the relationship will encounter is that Gemini-Cancers can grow dependent on capable Capricorn II's, make them nervous.

Gemini-Cancer–Capricorn II love affairs and friendships will be warm and affectionate, as long as Capricorn II's devote enough time to them and are not distracted by their career involvements. Games, entertainment, dancing and other activities will be especially rewarding here, serving the dual purpose of encouraging the Gemini-Cancer social side and mitigating Capricorn II seriousness. The playfulness drawn out of Capricorn II's by this relationship may well encourage them to extend it into marriage and parenthood. Gemini-Cancers will generally exert a strong nurturing influence here, and will initiate their Capricorn II spouses into the joys of raising children. The couple will get right out on the playing field with their kids, and in doing so will keep their own childlike attitudes viable. Parent-child matchups in this combination often have rollicking times, and their high spirits can be infectious. Other family members will marvel at the chemistry here, for even the sternest Capricorn II parents can have their hearts melted in an instant by a loving Gemini-Cancer child. Gemini-Cancer parents are likely to provide the warmth and understanding that tough Capricorn II's secretly crave. A working relationship in this combination is not particularly favored, since its childlike naiveté is not always appreciated in an office, industrial or corporate setting.

ADVICE: *Never be ashamed of being childlike. Stay young by spending more time with children. Play is at least as important as work.*

STRENGTHS: **SOCIABLE,
GIVING, MOTIVATING**

WEAKNESSES: **OVERMORAL,
FEARFUL, SELF-SACRIFICING**

BEST: **FRIENDSHIP**

WORST: **LOVE**

BOB FOSSE (6/23/27)
GWEN VERDON (1/13/25)

Broadway dancer-singer Verdon was Fosse's 3rd wife and starred in the choreographer's directorial debut, *Redhead* (1959). After their divorce and a long stage absence, Verdon returned to Broadway in 1975 to star in *Chicago*, directed by Fosse. **Also: Phylicia Rashad & Debbie Allen** (sisters; actors); **Jeff Beck & Rod Stewart** (Jeff Beck Group); **Anna Akhmatova & Osip Mandelstam** (Russian acmeist poets).

June 19–24

THE CUSP OF MAGIC
GEMINI-CANCER CUSP

January 10–16

THE WEEK OF DOMINANCE
CAPRICORN III

Feeling Normal

The thrust of this relationship is a fellowship that opens out toward the world. Team activities come easily to these two, who will enter into group activities enthusiastically. This is especially significant since at bottom both of these characters feel a little bit like misfits. Together they have the courage to join in with gusto and to feel like they belong. The theme of sharing translates into their personal relationship, which exhibits an unusual degree of good will and give-and-take.

Love affairs in this combination are not as favorable, perhaps, as friendships, largely because of the strict moral attitudes of Capricorn III's and the fearfulness of Gemini-Cancers. Yet the Capricorn III tendency to dominate can be subverted by Gemini-Cancers into more tender attitudes, and sympathy and support are perfectly possible here. Marriages based mainly on social contact—for example, a marriage enabling its spouses to enter social realms otherwise closed to them—have quite a good chance of success.

Friendship and work are especially rewarding here. More often than not, the relationship will magnetically attract others to it, serving as the nucleus for other social groups, teams and business organizations. Capricorn III's will relish the opportunity that the relationship offers them to contribute mightily and to serve, while Gemini-Cancers will feel somewhat liberated from their isolation. Being able to feel normal yet at the same time be themselves will be a real bonus for both partners. Sooner or later, however, the pair will have to set limits on the time and energy they give to others.

Family relationships in this combination, particularly between aunts or uncles and their nieces or nephews, can be a strong motivating force behind family get-togethers. These matchups are especially good at healing old wounds, and at getting perennial adversaries to act decently, at least for a while.

ADVICE: *Don't sacrifice your individuality. Giving also implies being able to take. Feeling normal is not necessarily a self-realizing activity.*

June 19–24

THE CUSP OF MAGIC
GEMINI-CANCER CUSP

January 17–22

THE CUSP OF MYSTERY & IMAGINATION
CAPRICORN-AQUARIUS CUSP

STRENGTHS: **DEMANDING, SUCCESSFUL, DYNAMIC**

WEAKNESSES: **SUBVERTING, SELF-AGGRANDIZING, DISLOYAL**

BEST: **WORK**

WORST: **FAMILY**

A Central Position

KRIS KRISTOFFERSON (6/22/37)
JANIS JOPLIN (1/19/43)

Though ruled by fire, this relationship is emotionally quite cool. As a pair these two will be surprisingly inured to the feelings of others, focusing more on their own condition, jockeying for position and hoping that others are noticing them. This egocentric approach obviously leaves something to be desired interpersonally; it is surprising to find two magical individuals experiencing trouble relating to each other. Part of the explanation may be the fact that Gemini-Cancer and Capricorn-Aquarius lie at a quincunx aspect to each other (150° apart) in the zodiac. Also, while Gemini-Cancers generally don't seek the spotlight, in this relationship their competitive instincts are aroused, stimulating an urge to be noticed. Indeed one weapon in these partners' competitive arsenal is preventing themselves from showing too much interest in each other. And when the relationship attracts attention from outside, its unity can be shattered when one of the partners claims exclusive responsibility.

Loyalty is a big issue in all Gemini-Cancer–Capricorn-Aquarius relationships. The success or failure of marriages and love affairs may depend directly on the partners' ability to limit their prioritizing of their own needs. Even if these needs are satisfied, both partners (but Capricorn-Aquarians in particular) are capable of indulging a roving eye and suffering a loyalty lapse. Desires often outstrip needs here, and greed, demonstrated by a desire to have it all regardless of the other person's feelings, can occasionally run riot.

Friendships are less vulnerable to such subversion, particularly if they are kept casual and eschew deeper emotional involvement. Family matchups, especially between siblings, may be competitive, with both personalities vying to be the star. When competitiveness manifests in a parent-child relationship, perhaps over the affections of the other parent or another family member, the family will suffer great stress.

Work relationships between these two can be extremely successful, particularly when they are colleagues in fields such as PR, advertising and sales, either within a company or as freelancers or consultants. As long as the relationship is put first and the partners realize that recognition will benefit them both, things can go well.

Legendary blues-rock singer Joplin and singer-songwriter Kristofferson were lovers at some point in the 60s. Kristofferson wrote *Me and Bobby McGee*, which Joplin recorded on *Pearl*—the #1 album of 1971—prior to her drug-overdose death in 1970. *Also:* **James I & Francis Bacon** (king/minister).

ADVICE: *Think of the good of the group. You may be stronger as a pair than as individuals. Keep your desires in check. Think carefully before acting.*

June 19–24

THE CUSP OF MAGIC
GEMINI-CANCER CUSP

January 23–30

THE WEEK OF GENIUS
AQUARIUS I

STRENGTHS: **FLAMBOYANT, EMPATHIC, APPRECIATIVE**

WEAKNESSES: **CLOYING, INHIBITING, UNINTERESTED**

BEST: **MARRIAGE**

WORST: **SIBLING**

All the World's a Stage

ROMAIN ROLLAND (1/29/1867)
JEAN-PAUL SARTRE (6/21/05)

This relationship's energies are flamboyant, with theatrical influences and grand gestures predominating. It gives Gemini-Cancers the chance to come out of their shell, allowing them to enjoy expressing themselves in a social setting. Aquarius I's generally feel more at home in such situations, but will have to be careful not to offend or overwhelm their more reclusive partner. Sensitivity, patience and empathy will have to be practiced for this relationship to succeed—not an easy task, given that the overall tone here is one of detachment and objectivity.

Love affairs and marriages between these two will usually be stabilized on the domestic front by the Gemini-Cancer feeling for the home. Aquarius I's greatly need stability in their lives, and may well find it here. But Gemini-Cancers will have to be extremely understanding of their mate's need to be involved with others and to be away from home a lot of the time. Should Aquarius I's think that their partners are growing cloying and dependent, they may long to escape this exceedingly tender trap. Gemini-Cancers may feel depressed in this relationship because it woefully neglects their emotional side.

Co-worker relationships and business partnerships may develop into friendships and vice versa, and may be beneficial both financially and emotionally. Whether friends are professionally allied or not, they tend to allow each other the space they need to do their own thing—a tactic that further unites them. Both friendships and working relationships are attracted to vibrant settings that allow a wide range of expression. Jealousy and competitiveness may be aroused over the appreciation of common friends or co-workers.

In the family, relationships between siblings and cousins in particular will add vivacity and spice to family gatherings and special events. Brothers and sisters may find it hard to get along on a daily basis, and will be totally uninterested in each other's activities, especially if there is a large age difference. Parent-child combinations are often loving, appreciative and rewarding.

French writers Sartre and Rolland, Nobelists in 1964 and 1915, respectively, were both deeply committed to understanding the role of man in society. Rolland was a humanist whose best-known work is the 10-volume *Jean Christophe* (1904–12), an epic tale of a musician deeply involved in contemporary civilization. Existentialist Sartre's writings view the individual as an isolated being, adrift in a meaningless world.

ADVICE: *Limit competitiveness for others' feelings. Develop patience and understanding. Show more interest and you will receive more yourself.*

ANNE MORROW (6/22/06)
CHARLES LINDBERGH (2/4/02)

Morrow, a successful writer and daughter of the US ambassador to Mexico, married famed aviator Lindbergh 2 years after his 1927 solo transatlantic flight. Tragedy struck in 1932 when their son was kidnapped and murdered.
Also: **Lou Gehrig & Babe Ruth** (teammates; friends); **Ray Davies & Dave Davies** (The Kinks).

June 19–24
THE CUSP OF MAGIC
GEMINI-CANCER CUSP

January 31–February 7
THE WEEK OF YOUTH & EASE
AQUARIUS II

Facing Up to Challenge

These two can be very relaxed and comfortable together. Both of them are capable of enjoying themselves in an easy way for long periods of time, and their relationship magnifies this quality. Luckily, however, it is also able to motivate itself to move forward on the road of life and the path of self-actualization. The kind of self-satisfaction that can approach smugness is a prime difficulty here. Procrastination is also a problem, but these down times are possibly creative periods in which the seeds are planted for future adventure and dynamism.

Gemini-Cancer–Aquarius II love affairs can be extremely pleasurable and sensuous. Urging stoicism or heightened responsibility in the midst of such a garden of earthly delights would perhaps be puritanical as well as unnecessary, for the relationship's deepening physical and emotional involvement will usually lead to firm bonds of acceptance and trust. similarly, in family relationships this pair's relaxed attitudes should not be challenged, for they serve their highest purpose by lessening tensions and urging those around them to enjoy themselves more.

Friendships may be mainly concerned with having a good time and marriages with keeping their heads above water, but sooner or later both must face up to challenge, resistance, grief and pain if they are to deepen and mature. Any superficiality in the partners' attitudes will become immediately apparent during demanding and stressful periods. Deep reserves of emotional strength will have to be built up to avoid spiritual bankruptcy at such times.

Both as co-workers and business partners this pair is likely to let opportunities slip by and to hold on to the status quo. This attitude can be fatal in a competitive world, and for its own preservation the relationship will have to become more cognizant of such harsh realities.

ADVICE: *Learn when to relax and when to push. Certain situations demand that you be more dynamic. Never lose your capacity to enjoy yourself.*

JAMES DEAN (2/8/31)
PIER ANGELI (6/19/32)

Actress Angeli had an affair with the legendary Dean in the early 50s, but she upset him by marrying singer Vic Damone in 1954. Less than a year later, Dean died after crashing his new Porsche. *Also:*
Mary McCarthy & Kevin McCarthy (siblings; writer/actor);
Malcolm McDowell & Mary Steenburgen (married; actors);
Mary Livingstone & Jack Benny (married; comedians).

June 19–24
THE CUSP OF MAGIC
GEMINI-CANCER CUSP

February 8–15
THE WEEK OF ACCEPTANCE
AQUARIUS III

Parity Level

Both of these individuals are quite sensitive, and the critical faculty inherent in their relationship is apt to prick egos. There is a visionary capacity here, but its specialty is finding fault—with other people, morals, society, even just the world at large. Aquarius III's will take the lead here. In fact, they are likely to overpower Gemini-Cancers in the spheres of values and decision-making, and to be critical and bossy at times. Gemini-Cancers actually have a lot to teach—if only Aquarius III's were ready to listen. Matchups with Gemini-Cancers may confront them with the primary challenges in their lives: being open, dealing with their own irritations and being more understanding in general.

Love affairs bring these two to a level of parity. Through their quiet charm, in fact, Gemini-Cancers may even come to dominate some of the time. Aquarius III's have a lot to learn about themselves, and often have problems understanding themselves at a deep level. Gemini-Cancers can help them tremendously here. An affair in this combination is likely to prove warm, romantic and fulfilling, at least when it's on.

Marriages and friendships are usually dominated by Aquarius III critical attitudes. Gemini-Cancers' patience and calm will probably be stretched to the breaking point by their partner's needling and aggression, usually well meant but insensitive to the other person's needs. Frustrations are likely to emerge on both sides, in Aquarius III's over being unable to convince their partner, in Gemini-Cancers over feeling themselves constantly instructed. Similarly, in the family sphere Aquarius III parents will have to learn to stop pestering their Gemini-Cancer children. In school and at work, Aquarius III's may embarrass themselves with a know-it-all attitude when their Gemini-Cancer fellow students or workers actually have far more knowledge but keep quiet about it. As friends, Aquarius III's may push unsolicited opinions and advice on Gemini-Cancers, tending to dominate them. Their advice may in fact be quite sensible, but they will have to learn to back off and let their friends make up their own minds.

ADVICE: *Much can be learned if you listen. Back off at times. Frustration can be avoided if you are sensitive enough. Work on making things more equal.*

June 19–24
THE CUSP OF MAGIC
GEMINI-CANCER CUSP

February 16–22
THE CUSP OF SENSITIVITY
AQUARIUS-PISCES CUSP

Getting the Job Done

Both of these personalities have an ethereal quality that in other combinations sometimes makes them unassertive and capable of being taken advantage of. Yet they come together extraordinarily strongly. Anyone who knows them individually is liable to be shocked by their relationship: together they manifest raw energy and power. The reaction is nearly chemical, elevating strategic thought over emotional sensitivity, instinct over feeling, drive over indecision. This is an awesome combination. Although both of these partners mix air and water (Gemini and Aquarius are air signs, Cancer and Pisces water), their relationship is governed by fire and earth, associated with initiative and work. Its focus is passionate and powerful—the energy here builds to a tremendous intensity, both for the good and the bad. Such energies are best directed outward; infighting between these partners could tear them apart.

At work and in friendships and marriages, these two are a powerful force for getting projects on the rails in their immediate environment. Despite their often quiet and unassuming presentation, they can be called on to get the job done. Their power is not necessarily strongly physical, but may manifest psychologically or spiritually, often accomplishing wonders with little effort. The relationship is very good at teaching others by example, and their effects usually linger on after they both have departed. The success of these matchups will depend not only on their effectiveness but on their ability to relax together and be empathic.

In Gemini-Cancer–Aquarius-Pisces romantic relationships, liking is usually at least as important as loving. Affairs too often degenerate into power struggles, especially if the partners lose respect for each other and for themselves. Sexual manipulation may be used destructively here, and the threat to deprive each other of physical interaction, or to break off the relationship altogether, is not uncommon. Care will have to be taken that parent-child relationships in this combination do not indulge in struggle and combat. Usually, building quiet but firm bonds of trust and reliability will overcome such aggressive tendencies.

ADVICE: *Beware of power struggles. Affection is often more important than passion. Cultivate empathy. Point your energy in the right direction.*

JEAN-PAUL SARTRE (6/21/05)
ANDRÉ BRETON (2/19/1896)

Philosopher Sartre and poet Breton were ideological opponents. Breton dismissed Sartre's existentialism as "night school" and "academic quarrels." Sartre regarded Breton's surrealism as "a phenomenon … like the Charleston and the yo-yo." They met in 1945 and didn't like each other.

Also: Prince William & Prince Andrew (royal nephew/uncle).

June 19–24
THE CUSP OF MAGIC
GEMINI-CANCER CUSP

February 23–March 2
THE WEEK OF SPIRIT
PISCES I

Friendship to the End

No matter how different these two are temperamentally, their relationship will be close and intense. Yet although neither partner will hesitate to give the other a piece of his mind, what they tell each other is highly selective; they are capable of keeping secrets from each other for long periods of time. An inherent honesty is usually present, however—sooner or later they will tell all, but only when it suits them to do so.

In love affairs, Gemini-Cancer and Pisces I partners are capable of sharing a great deal with each other, but must work on being more independent. Mutually claiming attitudes may restrict their scope of expression. These attitudes will be laid bare if the relationship breaks up, when it may be difficult for the pair to pry themselves apart. More advanced types in this combination will have each other's interests at heart, however, and will be open to separations or splits if they feel that these are to their mutual benefit. These decisions are cool and rational—they do not mean that the partners love each other any less. These lovers will often remain friends, in fact, long after their affair has ended.

Should an affair evolve into marriage, it has a great chance of success, and having children will cement it through thick and thin. Both parents can be nurturing, complementing each other in many respects. A problem may arise if Gemini-Cancers and Pisces I's close their children off from the world, a protective gesture that actually deprives them of the rough knocks they need for normal development.

Family relationships in this combination, particularly parent-child matchups, are also likely to be mutually protective and rather closed in nature. Whether parent or child, the Gemini-Cancer is likely to defend and protect with unremitting zeal. Pisces I's are apt to be extremely empathic and sympathetic to Gemini-Cancers' feelings of pain and frustration. Business relationships are seldom financially astute enough to flourish.

ADVICE: *Overprotectiveness can hurt, too. Grant those dear to you their independence. Open up to the world, but cultivate inner strength.*

JUNE CARTER (6/23/29)
JOHNNY CASH (2/26/32)

In the mid-60s Carter helped Cash beat his long-term drug habit and convert to Christian fundamentalism. By the time they married in 1968, they were working together steadily and recorded many hit duets.

Also: Michelle Lee & James Farentino (married; actors); **Mike Todd & Elizabeth Taylor** (married; producer/star).

STRENGTHS: **GROUNDED, STRUCTURAL, THRIFTY**

WEAKNESSES: **MEDDLING, INTRUDING, AUTOCRATIC**

BEST: **BUSINESS PARTNERSHIP**

WORST: **FAMILY**

**WILLIAM HULL (6/24/1753)
ISAAC HULL (3/9/1773)**

William, governor of the Michigan Territory during the War of 1812, was sentenced to death (but later pardoned) for cowardice in 1812. That same year his nephew Isaac, a naval commander, became a hero after defeating a British ship in a decisive sea battle.

June 19–24
THE CUSP OF MAGIC
GEMINI-CANCER CUSP

March 3–10
THE WEEK OF THE LONER
PISCES II

A Grounding Influence

The intimacy between these two will often need material realization in the creation of a physical space to serve the relationship's needs. Whether domestic, professional or, in the case of friends in this combination, athletic or social, this space will occupy a good deal of the couple's time and energy, and in fact may become the focus of their relationship. Planning, setting up and maintaining it will have a grounding influence on both partners, who tend to live, both as individuals and as a duo, in the world of ideas and feelings.

As spouses and live-in lovers, Gemini-Cancers and Pisces II's will pay great attention to their living space, trying as much as possible to make its external reality correspond to their subjective inner state. The imaginative and fantasy-oriented side of both partners will be immediately apparent to anyone visiting them. Decorating is seen here not as a social activity, performed with visitors in mind, but as an almost entirely personal one, serving the private needs of the partners. Learning to be orderly and efficient in furnishing and decorating a space will mitigate this pair's tendency to be overly relaxed or even sloppy.

Co-workers in this combination may be frustrated working for a company where they have little say in how their workspace is set up. They do best as entrepreneurs in small businesses or executives or partners in larger ones where they have the final say about the physical structure of the workplace. The accompanying development of money sense and financial shrewdness is another gift that the relationship grants its partners.

In the family, relatives may not appreciate the need of the Gemini-Cancer–Pisces II relationship to reorganize, remodel or rethink the household's physical structure. Ideally, especially in the case of siblings in this combination, a compromise will be reached where the pair will be left free to do what they want with their own room or rooms (within reason) and leave shared living spaces alone.

ADVICE: *Let others make their own choices. Don't get obsessed with material needs and wants. Follow the spirit. Don't give up your freedom.*

STRENGTHS: **PERSONAL, DEEP, SEXUAL**

WEAKNESSES: **ISOLATED, WITHDRAWN, NARCISSISTIC**

BEST: **LOVE**

WORST: **MARRIAGE**

**BRIAN WILSON (6/20/42)
MIKE LOVE (3/15/41)**

Although they were original and collaborating members of the Beach Boys, first cousins Wilson and Love had a troubled relationship. In 1977 they had open personality differences. By '93 Love sued Wilson for defamation in his autobiography (settling out of court). In '95 Love sued again, over a royalty dispute, for which Wilson had to pay $3 million.

June 19–24
THE CUSP OF MAGIC
GEMINI-CANCER CUSP

March 11–18
THE WEEK OF DANCERS & DREAMERS
PISCES III

A Withdrawn Stance

This relationship needs to withdraw from the world periodically to build up its own personal strength and vision. It will sometimes go to great lengths to protect its partners by building barriers against all social intrusions. The danger of lasting isolation or withdrawal, and in extreme cases of sociopathic behavior, is obvious here. In whatever area of life the relationship emerges, its principal challenge is to prevent its drive toward intimacy from getting out of hand.

Gemini-Cancer–Pisces III marriages are prone to cutting themselves off from the world. Should children be involved, or if the family lives in a physically isolated situation in the country, conscious and vigorous steps will have to be taken to build a meaningful social life. Isolation will stimulate the imagination and fantasy of both partners, one of their best-developed psychic areas, but will have harmful effects as well.

In love affairs this pair can indulge their need for privacy and intimacy more fully. A deep sexual relationship can prove immensely satisfying to both partners, but can also stir up a host of feelings, including resentment and jealousy. These two tend to remain faithful to each other, but must be careful to forestall claiming attitudes and sex and love addictions. The use of drugs and alcohol may have an especially debilitating effect here.

Friends may become co-workers and vice versa. In this case the pair will carefully guard their leisure time together away from work, and their spouses and family members will have to be understanding of their need to spend so much time together. Jealous conflicts can emerge here.

Parent-child relationships in this combination, especially father-daughter and mother-son matchups, may alienate other family members through the partners' excessive need for each other. Great care will have to be taken that such exclusivity does not irreparably damage the family structure.

ADVICE: *Maintain objectivity. Use your common sense. Beware of addictive tendencies. Build a deep relationship but don't cut yourself off.*

STRENGTHS: **PERCEPTIVE, SENSITIVE, CARING**

WEAKNESSES: **CONFUSED, DEPRESSED, MOODY**

BEST: **WORK**

WORST: **MARRIAGE**

A Welter of Feelings

Cancer I ultrasensitivity will characterize this relationship. These two are unlikely to have an easy time of it together, particularly in more personal relationships. Cancer I's are very reactive to the feelings of others, and their boundaries are so fluid that their partners pick up on their moods without realizing it. Consider, then, the effect of two of them in combination: each magnifies the other's welter of feelings. The relationship becomes extremely complex emotionally. If it is to have a chance for success, the partners must use every ounce of their strength to maintain their objectivity and take responsibility for their feelings. For the most part, alas, they are neither willing nor able to make this effort, and the result is often a constant ricocheting of sensibilities, impressions and viewpoints.

Love affairs, friendships, marriages and family relationships will prove most problematic in this combination, becoming emotional minefields with explosions going off every other minute. It may be difficult for two Cancer I's to continue on with each other. They should approach these relationships with as much awareness as possible; working on their own individual evolutions will help immeasurably here.

Perhaps the areas of greatest benefit for this relationship have to do with work, study and other objective pursuits. As co-workers, especially in office work relating to publishing, design, manufacturing, computers and finance, Cancer I's can operate side by side faithfully over the long haul. Their attention to detail, concentration and easygoing nature might be highly prized by superiors and colleagues alike. They generally need to be given direction, however, and occasionally to be pushed to avoid complacency. Cancer I executive pairs are likely to be aggressive, and may antagonize people with their insistent and pushy attitudes. Motivation is often a prime difficulty for student and teacher-student pairs here. They can sometimes reach peaks of achievement, but the learning process is not always even or consistent—periods of inactivity, dreaminess or moodiness often prevail. Should the pair be engaged in sports, fitness or other athletic pursuits, they will have to fight off slumps and tendencies to go off track.

ADVICE: *Objectivity should be your rock. Beware of mirroring each other's feelings. Without repressing your emotions, keep them under control.*

ANNA MOFFO (6/27/34)
ROBERT SARNOFF (7/2/18)

Sarnoff is the son of David Sarnoff, founder of RCA and NBC. Robert became president of NBC in 1955 and was RCA chairman from 1970–75. He was married to opera star Moffo, who debuted with the Metropolitan Opera in NY in 1959 and had a distinguished international career.

STRENGTHS: **DETERMINED, INVESTIGATIVE, UNDERSTANDING**

WEAKNESSES: **NARCISSISTIC, DISAPPROVED OF, UNSUCCESSFUL**

BEST: **MARRIAGE**

WORST: **WORK**

Intriguing Mysteries

This relationship displays a remarkable determination to get to the bottom of things—to know, to probe, to understand. The areas of investigation are likely to be psychology or social science rather than, say, general science or math; people and their personalities usually exert the greatest attraction here. Perhaps the first difficult and fascinating area for these partners to explore will be their own relationship, since their own mysteries are every bit as interesting to them as those of others.

Cancer I Empaths are likely to understand their Unconventional Cancer II partners better than most. Instead of deterring them, Cancer II secretiveness interests them, and indeed this interest may provide the route by which this pair's love affairs and friendships initially begin. Home for a married couple in this combination is likely to be a very private place to which few gain admittance. Since this private hideaway shelters two people who both have strongly reclusive sides, they may spend hours here in safety and solitude, trying to understand the deepest levels of their relationship. Whether sharing feelings and thoughts, making love or expressing affection, busying themselves quietly with different activities or simply sharing a bond of silence, Cancer I's and II's will constantly enrich their understanding of each other and of the relationship itself.

Subjective preoccupations like these can be counterproductive in work situations, however, and unless the partners can concentrate on getting the job done rather than trying to analyze it or probe its meaning, they will not succeed together professionally. Nor will the daily life of a family group usually make space for such reflective or narcissistic forms of enjoyment, which may distract the pair from living up to their responsibilities. This might be unfortunate, for Cancer I and II siblings, particularly of the opposite sex, are likely to explore many life mysteries together as they grow. They generally carry this deep connection into their mature years.

ADVICE: *The world is not made up only of people. Show more interest in the natural world. Realize your thoughts through action. Simplify mysteries.*

GEORGE ABBOTT (6/25/1887)
GEORGE M. COHAN (7/3/1878)

Abbott and Cohan, playwrights, producers and directors, are legendary figures in Broadway musical theater. Cohan dominated American musical stage in the early 20th century, while Abbott was active from the 30s into the 80s. Abbott is most famous for *Pajama Game* (1954) and *Damn Yankees* (1955). Cohan is best remembered for his rousing songs *Over There* and *Give My Regards to Broadway*.

STRENGTHS: **UNUSUAL, CONFIDENT, LOYAL**

WEAKNESSES: **THREATENING, MISUNDERSTOOD, UNFULFILLED**

BEST: **FRIENDSHIP**

WORST: **MARRIAGE**

RICHARD RODGERS (6/28/02)
OSCAR HAMMERSTEIN II (7/12/1895)

Composer Rodgers and lyricist Hammerstein linked up fatefully in 1943 to create Broadway's most memorable musicals, including *Oklahoma!* (1953), *Carousel* (1945), and *South Pacific* (1949). Their work was central to the development of the musical as an American art form.

June 25–July 2
THE WEEK OF THE EMPATH
CANCER I

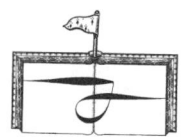

July 11–18
THE WEEK OF THE PERSUADER
CANCER III

Learning to Live and Let Live

A detached view of the world and of people will hold a lively interest for these two. Should those around this unusual relationship sense—and perhaps resent—an odd couple holding them up to an uncomfortable level of scrutiny, the pair may be somewhat beaten down by society, but it has the capacity to rise above this resistance, depending on how much the partners want to do so. Being antisocial has its pleasures here and may be the combination's raison d'être. Should the pair be sincerely interested in the relationship itself, however, rather than just enjoying a stance of "Me and you against the world," their belief could guarantee its survival. Cancer I's and III's can be quite determined when they put their mind to something and are extremely good on defense, protecting what they cherish. On the other hand, they should not shove the relationship in the face of those who find it difficult or offensive. These partners should develop a live-and-let-live attitude toward others.

In romances in this combination, Cancer III's should beware of a tendency to dominate. Cancer I's can stand up for themselves, but the arguments this demands are a waste of time and energy, and should be avoided. This couple's physical involvement can be extraordinary, featuring creativity and caring. It may benefit from an active fantasy life emanating from one or both of the partners. These relationships are sometimes better off if they do not proceed on to marriage, which may isolate the couple from other people.

Friendships here can be more relaxed. They often exude a quiet confidence that others respect. If the friends are youngsters, however, their parents may feel threatened by their relationship, exhibiting fear, worry or jealousy. It is here that this pair may prove most vulnerable to society's opinions. Steadfastness and loyalty usually win out, however. These two can prove a powerful professional combination, as long as Cancer I's are strongly motivated enough to let them play an active role. Their financial strengths can gel well with the persuasive Cancer III personality in many commercial endeavors, especially creative ones.

ADVICE: *Stand up for yourself, but beware of being offensive. Cultivate quiet confidence. Don't be so concerned about what others think.*

STRENGTHS: **SENSUOUS, CARING, MASTERING**

WEAKNESSES: **LABILE, MOODY, REPRESSED**

BEST: **LOVE**

WORST: **FAMILY**

JEAN-JACQUES ROUSSEAU (6/28/1712)
SIMON BOLIVAR (7/24/1783)

It was Rousseau's philosophy of the Enlightenment—whereby society had perverted natural man, a "noble savage"—that influenced Bolivar to liberate the countries of South America from Spanish rule. Bolivar was called the "Liberator."
Also: Dan Aykroyd & Donna Dixon (married; actors).

June 25–July 2
THE WEEK OF THE EMPATH
CANCER I

July 19–25
THE CUSP OF OSCILLATION
CANCER-LEO CUSP

Gaining Control

Together these two are unusually determined and will often succeed at the very least in carving out a niche for themselves. At best they might establish an empire. If they are to achieve their worldly goals, however, they will have to keep the relationship itself on an even keel, and this may be what requires their greatest stubbornness. Cancer-Leo mood swings combine with Cancer I emotional sensitivity to produce some emotional instability, and the relationship's challenge will be gaining control over emotions without unduly suppressing them. When threatened, both Cancer I's and Cancer-Leos too often tend to withdraw or shut down; here their relationship must strive for emotional expression, openness and acceptance. Cancer-Leos may be hard to reach, but healthier Cancer I's can use their empathic abilities and psychological skills to unblock this partner, especially in marriages and friendships. Should Cancer I's be the ones who are withdrawn or depressed, Cancer-Leos must be sensitive enough to know when to leave them alone and when to urge them gently toward more pleasurable activities.

Cancer-Leo–Cancer I love affairs emphasize sensuousness and physical pleasure. Saunas, massage, aromatherapy and other enjoyable activities are recommended, as well as summer vacations at spas or near lakes and rivers. Complex emotional states may arise here, but sheer will and guts, along with patience and understanding, will help these affairs to work out. Any tendency to procrastinate over problems or to escape through denial or drift can ultimately be overcome and mastered here. Marriages benefit from the pair's ability to establish an enterprise and keep it running. These two could found a dynasty.

In times of crisis, Cancer-Leo family members will benefit from the empathy of Cancer I's, who may be more in touch with Cancer-Leo feelings than Cancer-Leos are themselves. Cancer I's in turn can benefit from their partner's energy. Co-worker and sibling relationships benefit from Cancer-Leo drive and Cancer I sensitivity, qualities that they often magnify.

ADVICE: *Sense the right moment for action or stillness. Master emotions without blocking them. Show you care. Strengthen determination.*

June 25–July 2
THE WEEK OF THE EMPATH
CANCER I

July 26–August 2
THE WEEK OF AUTHORITY
LEO I

Luck and Success

RELATIONSHIPS

STRENGTHS: **PERSUASIVE, EFFECTIVE, SUCCESSFUL**

WEAKNESSES: **UNCONCERNED, MISUNDERSTOOD, NARCISSISTIC**

BEST: **FRIENDSHIP**

WORST: **LOVE**

JERRY HALL (7/2/56)
MICK JAGGER (7/26/43)

Moon-ruled Cancer I's and sun-ruled Leo I's are very different from each other, yet their relationship may evidence impressive synergistic strengths, particularly the ability to convince others and persuade them to their cause, be it commercial, social or spiritual. (Their persuasive talents don't usually work on each other, for both partners are convinced of their respective points of view and are highly resistant to manipulation.) Cancer I emotional perception and sensitivity coalesce with Leo I willpower and outgoing nature to produce a whole that is highly effective in personal and professional spheres.

Love affairs between these two are not especially favored. The inner life of Cancer I's may be much too complex for Leo I's to deal with or understand, assuming they are even interested. Cancer I's, for their part, may too tied up with their own emotional life to want to give Leo I's the devotion and even worship that these personalities require.

Friendships, working relationships and marriages in this combination are often at the center of their social or work groups. Internal conflicts flare from time to time, but these two usually have the saving grace of being able to work together successfully on another project. Cancer I's and Leo I's sometimes become convinced that their matchup has special powers, a feeling that can deprive them of the confidence to go it alone, or to move on to another partner or team. Any act of disloyalty or betrayal should not be undertaken lightly, since it could break the spell which brings these two luck and success. Although Cancer generally is considered a passive sign, Cancer I's can match Leo I's in aggression, and will not by any means be relegated to the kitchen or desk in this relationship. Although capable of working on their own for the betterment of their group, Cancer I's and Leo I's make their strongest impression when appearing together and can sometimes be irresistible in getting their way.

Supermodel Hall was Jagger's longtime lover before they finally got married in 1990. Jagger was considered the "catch" of the glitterati during this time, and Hall was at the top of her career. Sharing the high life seems to make this superstar couple work.

Also: George Orwell & Aldous Huxley (British futurist writers).

ADVICE: *Outward success is being overemphasized. Seek spiritual values and follow your heart. Be sure to honor and show interest in your partner's feelings.*

June 25–July 2
THE WEEK OF THE EMPATH
CANCER I

August 3–10
THE WEEK OF BALANCED STRENGTH
LEO II

Fits and Starts

RELATIONSHIPS

STRENGTHS: **EXCITING, COMMITTED, STIMULATING**

WEAKNESSES: **FRUSTRATED, ARGUMENTATIVE, DISTURBING**

BEST: **FRIENDSHIP**

WORST: **WORK**

OLIVIA DE HAVILLAND (7/1/16)
JOHN HUSTON (8/5/06)

Expression rarely manifests easily in this volatile relationship; these two may communicate only spasmodically, in fits and starts. Conflicts between Cancer I's and Leo II's can easily seem to appear out of nowhere. In fact they are really about feelings. Leo II's lack the empathic talents of Cancer I's, and are often insensitive to other people's emotions. The outbursts of anger and resentment that are likely to surface between these two may ostensibly occur over matters ranging from finances to aesthetics, but there is usually something personal behind these seemingly objective disagreements.

Cancer I–Leo II love affairs are likely to be vivid but somewhat unsettled. Any constancy of mood or evenness of tone may be difficult or impossible to achieve. Cancer I's will often feel that these partners are cold or unsympathetic, while Leo I's may be annoyed by what they consider emotional intrusions, which they would just as soon ignore. Marriage too will have its problems, but in some cases the partners will hang in there for years, out of loyalty or simply a refusal to give up. The relationship tends to be long-suffering, committed but troubled.

Friendships in this combination can be exciting and fun, emphasizing stimulating activities such as film, dance and music. These two will enjoy being part of a lively social scene only a small part of the time, however—they have a pronounced need for privacy. Most often the activities they enjoy are limited to the two of them alone.

At work, acute differences in temperament may lead to upset. As far as the family is concerned, parent-child relationships may feature a disturbing level of disagreement, at least from the point of view of other family members.

In 1945 Huston, just divorced from his 2nd wife, ardently courted de Havilland. According to the *Hollywood Reporter:* "The New Year kiss implanted on [her] by John Huston should have been photographed in Technicolor!" The sweethearts never married.

ADVICE: *Keep arguments to a minimum. Try to listen to what is being said. Even out your moods. Try to be more patient and understanding.*

STRENGTHS: **PROTECTIVE, AFFECTIONATE, HELPFUL**
WEAKNESSES: **UNSTABLE, EXTREME, PASSIVE-AGGRESSIVE**
BEST: **MARRIAGE**
WORST: **FRIENDSHIP**

PAUL FRANÇOIS BARRAS (6/30/1755)
NAPOLEON BONAPARTE (8/15/1769)

French National Convention member Barras ordered Napoleon in 1795 to defend the existing government against insurrectionists. When Napoleon succeeded he was rewarded with a post as commander of the army. A year later Napoleon married Josephine, Barras' former lover, whom Barras had introduced to the rising Napoleon.

June 25–July 2
THE WEEK OF THE EMPATH
CANCER I

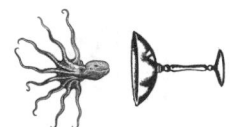

August 11–18
THE WEEK OF LEADERSHIP
LEO III

Likes and Dislikes

Trying to determine what each person wants or needs, and incorporating this into the relationship, is a strong theme here. Leo III's can bring out the aggressive side of Cancer I's, who likewise can bring out passivity in Leo III's. The relationship is likely to feature wide swings of mood, with the partners expressing what they like and dislike about each other with bewildering frequency.

Both somewhat aggressive, Cancer I's and Leo III's do not hesitate to pursue their desires—provided they can identify them. Their ability to help each other do this is their relationship's greatest strength. Complex Leo III's would seem capable of dominating Cancer I's, but, curiously, it is Cancer I's who often wind up being the bosses here, through their ability to sense, understand and either satisfy or frustrate the wants and needs of this particular partner. At the same time, the heroic qualities of Leo III's can be inspiring for Cancer I's when they are out in the world. Affectionate and loving feelings are often expressed in this relationship.

Constancy and moderation are hard to achieve in love affairs here, but are worthy goals. Leo III's need a calm and warm domestic environment in which to wind down from their high-energy work, and Cancer I's may be able to provide it. Cancer I empathy can also be put to use fathoming and soothing this partner's dark and volcanic side. Leo III's will provide the direction in marriages and love affairs, generally playing a sympathetic and protective role.

But for its instabilities, however, the Cancer I–Leo III relationship could be a true haven for both partners. It is to their advantage, then, to try to stabilize a marriage, work or family situation, eliminating upsetting influences as much as possible. Leo III bosses and parents can gain great satisfaction from providing for Cancer I employees and children, but it may in fact be Cancer I's who have more ability to grant psychological benefit to Leo III's—they certainly have this partner's best interests at heart. Thus the relationship can be an interesting blend of mutually helpful influences.

ADVICE: *Beware of power struggles. Work for the common good. Stabilize your relationship. Share duties and beware of sexist attitudes.*

STRENGTHS: **INTELLIGENT, COMMUNICATIVE, SUPPORTIVE**
WEAKNESSES: **SUPERFICIAL, ARGUMENTATIVE, IMPULSIVE**
BEST: **WORK**
WORST: **MARRIAGE**

BILL CLINTON (8/19/46)
ROSS PEROT (6/27/30)

Soon after Perot announced his presidential candidacy in March 1992, he surged ahead of both Clinton and Bush in national polls. Clinton benefited from Perot's later withdrawal, as many of Perot's grass-roots supporters turned to the Clinton camp. Perot reentered the race in October, but Clinton went on to win by a comfortable margin.

June 25–July 2
THE WEEK OF THE EMPATH
CANCER I

August 19–25
THE CUSP OF EXPOSURE
LEO-VIRGO CUSP

Intelligent Investigations

Cancer I's are ruled by water and Leo-Virgos by fire and earth, but their relationship is ruled by air, associated with thought. Their relationship's focus is likely to be invention and challenge, particularly in mental activities—games, puzzles, discussions and debates, the striving for academic excellence. Cancer I relationships too often bring out their emotional side, so that their brain power is neglected; their matchup with Leo-Virgos, however, will put their intelligence to the test. The relationship particularly emphasizes swift responses—if the partners are to avoid superficiality, they will have to remind themselves to give issues deeper consideration. Mutually critical attitudes are likely to cause argument but also to sharpen wits. Once Cancer I's and Leo-Virgos get their act together as a team, they will make formidable opponents for anyone who challenges them in the mental sphere.

In this relationship, an emphasis on mind power does not necessarily lessen sensual pleasures, and Cancer I–Leo-Virgo love is likely to include a robust physicality. Of course they will also want to talk about this side of their lives. Their keen interest in hedonistic pursuits will heighten their pleasure as long as their approach does not get too intellectual. Intelligent investigation, including reading, attending workshops and counseling, can have a positive effect on this matchup. Should the partners be tempted to move on to marriage or to a permanent living situation, they must take care not to rush in impulsively.

Sibling relationships and friendships, on the other hand, seem to be quite cool and objective. They usually subordinate feeling to thought, to the point where they risk blunting impulses and suppressing feelings. Yet these relationships will be mutually supportive. Their communication level is high—in fact, the partners have an almost telepathic link with each other. Should these two decide to go into business together, they might be highly successful in setting up a small company dealing with computer technology, software, Internet projects, advertising or consulting.

ADVICE: *Take your time and try to be more reflective when making decisions. Avoid unnecessary arguments. Beware of trying to appear too cool.*

June 25–July 2
THE WEEK OF THE EMPATH
CANCER I

August 26–September 2
THE WEEK OF SYSTEM BUILDERS
VIRGO I

Finding the Heart Center

This relationship has an outward authority that the world takes very seriously. Internally, however, it searches for matters of the heart. Ambition is prominent here, but only learning where they truly stand with each other will lead these two to success. Neither partner individually is likely to be able to guide the relationship to firm ground; they will have to investigate their ideas, feelings, beliefs and tastes in an organized way to learn what they share. This search is unlikely to be intellectual or even conscious; it will arise naturally through the pair's shared experiences. Piece by piece, things will fall into place, and the relationship's heart center will unfold. Once a true communion is established, the partners will taste success in many areas of their lives. Until then they may drift uncertainly.

Love affairs in this combination tend to be unstable but romantic. There is often a face-off here between Cancer I emotionality and Virgo I structure and logic. Virgo I's usually make demands that Cancer I's find hard to meet; they also refuse to recognize the importance of feelings to Cancer I's, and are resented for it. The time needed to find common ground is usually lacking here: a long-term commitment is unlikely unless the two are in a situation that forces them into regular contact, allowing the relationship to unfold.

The need for a solid underpinning will be evident in marriage, the family and at work. Procrastination and doubt can complicate even the simplest decisions. The directions taken are not always the best, and it can be months or years before mistakes are detected and corrected. Dramatic changes will be seen, however, if a solid foundation can be established. A rise in the partners' self-confidence will be especially noticeable since individually and in relationships with others they tend to lack either decisiveness or judgment.

As long as they are not dominated by mutual dependencies, friendships in this combination can tolerate differences. Direction may be gained here simply through common activities, perhaps physical or mildly competitive in nature, with both partners exerting their own particular strength.

ADVICE: *Persevere in your quest. Remain open to ideas and schools of thought. Dare to fail. Don't allow discouragement to get you down.*

 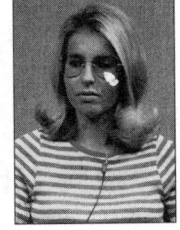

BEN BRADLEE (8/26/21)
SALLY QUINN (7/1/41)

Outspoken journalist-author Quinn was hired in 1969 by Bradlee, executive editor of the *Washington Post*, as a reporter for the Style section. Mutually supportive and politically aligned, they married in 1978. Quinn left the paper in '82 to have a baby and write novels. Bradlee left his post in '91 to become vice-president-at-large for the *Post*.

June 25–July 2
THE WEEK OF THE EMPATH
CANCER I

September 3–10
THE WEEK OF THE ENIGMA
VIRGO II

Lightening Moods

Two such hidden and secretive personalities as these would seem to reinforce each other's more withdrawn aspects. Yet the chemistry of their relationship acts to lighten their moods, and often to bring them more in touch with the world. Ease of interaction is the emphasis here, and will provide relief for partners who have probably met with tremendous obstacles and difficulties in their relationships with others in the past. The key here is a kind of unspoken communication and understanding. This can go a long way toward alleviating the conflict, discussion or negotiation prominent in other interactions.

In love affairs and marriages, these two have a strong ability to sense each other's desires, both intellectual and emotional. But they are not necessarily good at satisfying each other's physical needs, so that they may have to spend months or even years getting to know one another at this intimate level. Luckily, through discussion—the relationship's orientation is mental—understanding can prevail. Frustrations and hang-ups are best not taken too seriously; if it is possible simply to ignore them, they will fall away as the relationship grows.

Friendships are especially favored here. Emotional demands and financial responsibilities should be kept light, allowing the partners the time and space they need to come to a greater appreciation of each other. They will inevitably spend a lot of time alone, but as they grow more confident, their relationship will take its place as part of a larger social unit. Cancer I's will be fascinated by the twists and turns in the personalities of Virgo II's, who in return will find the depth and scope of Cancer I emotions a never-ending source of amazement.

As co-workers and family members, Cancer I's and Virgo II's may form a strongly empathic bond that will carry them through some difficult situations at work and home. As in other areas, the key is having a relaxed attitude and not making undue demands on each other, thereby reducing stress.

ADVICE: *Minimize demands. Let go of negativity. Alter pessimistic attitudes. Keep things unserious and relaxed. Open lines of communication.*

PETER LAWFORD (9/7/23)
PATRICIA KENNEDY (6/28/24)

Kennedy, sister of JFK, was married to actor Lawford (1954–66), making him JFK's brother-in-law and a member of the Kennedy clan. He was also a member of a less prestigious clan, the "Rat Pack," led by Frank Sinatra.

Also: **Henry VIII & Elizabeth I** (father/daughter); **Gilda Radner & Jane Curtin** (SNL comics); **Dan Rowan & Peter Lawford** (father-in-law/son-in-law, 1970s).

FERDINAND MARCOS (9/11/17)
IMELDA MARCOS (7/2/31))

After an 11-day courtship, this ruling Philippine couple were married. They had 3 children and lived luxuriously while most of their country suffered in poverty. They were ousted and exiled to the US in '86, and he died 3 years later.

Also: Carl Lewis & Jesse Owens (Olympic champions); **Mel Brooks & Anne Bancroft** (married; actors); **Medgar Evers & Charles Evers** (brothers; civil-rights activists).

June 25–July 2
THE WEEK OF THE EMPATH
CANCER I

September 11–18
THE WEEK OF THE LITERALIST
VIRGO III

Mind Versus Heart

This relationship is likely to involve a struggle to balance the often conflicting interests of heart and mind. Cancer I's are often controlled by their emotions, Virgo III's by their thoughts, and in their relationship these influences often polarize rather than coalesce. Both partners are no strangers to struggle, however, and if they are determined enough they will overcome the differences that divide them, at least enough to get along. Without this determination, the relationship will not have a favorable prognosis in the area of personal interactions.

Virgo III's usually keep their deeper feelings under control, but denying them an outlet can lead to frustration, depression and outbursts of anger. The problem is complicated by the fact that Cancer I's tend to pick up on the feelings of this partner and act them out themselves. Particularly in love affairs and marriages, they both must learn to own up to their own emotions and take responsibility for them. Both partners are prone to indulge in manipulation to get what they want. On the positive side, the combination gives its partners an unusual level of fidelity, steadfastness and endurance, helping them hang in there for the long haul.

Cancer I–Virgo III friendships and family relationships can be plagued by resentments, outbursts of anger and misunderstandings. Truth to tell, this negativity may emanate from the duo's relationship with a third party, perhaps a mutual friend, lover or parent, who often stirs up trouble without being aware of it. If problems are to be resolved, the development of psychological awareness will be the main task for all concerned.

Work possibilities can be excellent between these two. Here Cancer I's are capable of being objective enough, especially in the technical and financial spheres, to complement their practical Virgo III associates. Whether the pair are co-workers in a large organization or partners in an entrepreneurial effort, their relationship is likely to be a successful one that will survive and develop over the years.

ADVICE: *Persevere in getting to the root of problems. Discover your real strengths. Take responsibility for your feelings. Stay objective.*

HENRY VIII (6/28/1491)
ANNE OF CLEVES (9/22/1515)

Anne was the 4th wife of the English king. Their 1540 marriage was arranged to secure the allegiance between Henry and Anne's brother, a powerful German prince. Displeased with Anne's appearance, Henry had the marriage annulled after 6 months.

Also: Ilya Bolotowski & Esphyr Slobodkina (married; artists); **Patrice Lumumba & Kwame Nkrumah** (African leaders).

June 25–July 2
THE WEEK OF THE EMPATH
CANCER I

September 19–24
THE CUSP OF BEAUTY
VIRGO-LIBRA CUSP

Broadening Acceptance

This relationship may well be based on mutual admiration and characterized by humor, communication and color. The partners could find that they share a common vision. Furthermore, each can expose the other to new and exciting ideas, increasing each other's openness. Cancer I's will be drawn to the Virgo-Libra aesthetic side, secretly admiring this partner's up-to-date attitudes and ability to monitor the public pulse. Although Virgo-Libras will need to put extra effort into understanding the feelings of Cancer I's, they themselves will appreciate being understood psychologically, and accepted for who they are, by this perceptive partner. Generating broader and more accepting attitudes toward each other and, more important, to people outside the relationship may prove a principal focus here.

A keen interest in the arts—such as design, painting, sculpture and drawing—is characteristic. This interest is not only theoretical but practical, being reflected in their tastes in clothing and in their general lifestyle. It may be possible for them to form a business together based on such interests. In a friendship or professional relationship, they must be careful of becoming mutually exclusive, snobbish or intolerant.

A Cancer I–Virgo-Libra love affair, especially one hidden from a primary mate or lover, can be thrilling but also destructive. Should these two discover an ideal of beauty in each other, perhaps the classic recognition of an inner ideal, their affair could go on clandestinely for years, demonstrating addictive aspects. It is not generally advised for such a relationship to progress to marriage. It should be seen clearly for what it is, within a total picture that includes the third party in the love triangle. Family relationships, particularly parent-child matchups, will challenge the ability of Cancer I's and Virgo-Libras to accept their differences. Dark-side interactions here, especially featuring psychological projection and acting out, could disturb the family group. But the depth of the partners' interactions with each other might prove a godsend for them in discovering the truth about themselves, leading to greater health and self-confidence in the future.

ADVICE: *Strive for self-awareness. Beware of succumbing to trendiness. Don't blind yourself to faults. Act on your observations. Accept differences.*

June 25–July 2
THE WEEK OF THE EMPATH
CANCER I

September 25–October 2
THE WEEK OF THE PERFECTIONIST
LIBRA I

Sense of Purpose

Motivation is the crucial element in this relationship. Individually these two are tremendous self-starters, but their effect on each other can be likened to stalling out. Somehow their combination releases rather dark and complex forces, mucking up whatever they may be trying to achieve. This is compounded by the fact that neither of them is easy to get along with in the first place. The Cancer I–Libra I relationship is likely to stagnate if not given direction. A sense of leadership and purpose is the prime requirement here; since neither party is likely to lead with assurance, the task will be to find ways to create motivation or purpose within the relationship. Such willpower will require a tremendous effort from these partners, which can happen only if the desire and grit are there. Fortunately, awareness can lead to negotiation and compromise.

In love and marriage, a powerful motor for this pair can be their desire for each other. Passions can run hot and intense here. At one time or another, however, one of the partners is likely to serve notice on the other that if things don't start to move, they might as well quit. If the desire to continue (whether motivated by fear of loss, sexual attachment or love) is powerful enough, the relationship will usually find a way. Both partners must be prepared to compromise and to talk frankly and openly.

Friendships in this combination can drift apart, whether through neglect of the relationship or by taking it for granted. Warning signs, perhaps a long period of noncommunication, will alert the couple to the danger of losing their connection, spurring a resolve to do something about it and prevent it from happening again.

In family and work situations, often neither party is strong enough to play the role of boss or parent convincingly. Of the two, nurturing and caring Cancer I's generally do better in such roles than Libra I's. As siblings or co-workers, the pair often do better when an external source of leadership or authority is built in to the family or professional structure.

ADVICE: *Stiffen your resolve. Decide what you really want. Be prepared to compromise. Curb darker tendencies.*

BILLY DAVIS, JR. (6/26/40)
MARILYN McCOO (9/30/43)

Singers Davis and McCoo were members of the highly successful pop-soul group The Fifth Dimension from 1966–75. They were married in '69 and left the group in '75 to perform as a duo—but their marriage came apart, and by 1980 they had split up.
Also: **Patty Smyth & Richard Hell** (married rockers); **Gilda Radner & Barbara Walters** (*SNL* portrayal of "Baba Wawa").

June 25–July 2
THE WEEK OF THE EMPATH
CANCER I

October 3–10
THE WEEK OF SOCIETY
LIBRA II

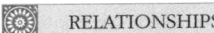
A Surfeit of Pleasure

The great strength of this relationship is the sensitivity and subtle communication between its members. As individuals they are quite aware and psychologically adept, and their relationship magnifies these qualities, synergistically producing an even higher level of understanding. These talents may be kept within the relationship, being used for the partners' benefit, or, if the pair are active in a social group, family or business, can be brought to bear on those around them, who will inevitably be attracted to them for advice and counsel. In any case, Cancer I–Libra II interactions will be closely observed by other people, who may view the relationship as a source of inspiration.

Marriages, love affairs and friendships are blessed with all these abilities. Yet they have problems with procrastination and indecision. A surfeit of pleasure or comfort is a factor here: the partners often feel no need to progress any further, either spiritually or financially, than they already have, so that the status quo assumes ascendancy. The enemy here is smugness and self-satisfaction, if only Cancer I's and Libra II's could see it. These two show so much awareness in the psychological and emotional realms; it is ironic that they often fail to see what is sapping the strength and growth of their own relationship.

Cancer I–Libra II co-worker matchups have an aptitude in the sphere of human services, whether social work, psychological counseling or community activities. Should these two enter into a business relationship, the task of making the partnership work financially will usually fall to Cancer I's. Libra II's may be stronger at interaction with customers, vendors or the public.

The strong bond between two family members in this combination will lend positive energy to the group as a whole. Other relatives will feel they can seek out this pair when they are misunderstood, and will have faith in its ability to turn weakness to advantage.

ADVICE: *Apply your advice to yourself. Be more aware of what you are not doing. Feeling good is not the only goal. Share your insights with others.*

H. RAP BROWN (10/4/43)
STOKELY CARMICHAEL (6/29/41)

Carmichael and Brown were successive chairmen of the radicalized SNCC from 1966, repudiating integration in favor of "black power"—a term introduced by Carmichael and carried forward by Brown. Due to its extremism and internal struggles, SNCC broke up in the early 70s. ***Also:***
Pamela Anderson & Tommy Lee (married; actress/rocker).

STRENGTHS: **ENCOURAGING, BALANCING, EDUCATIONAL**

WEAKNESSES: **UNHEEDING, FRUSTRATED, RESENTFUL**

BEST: **GRANDPARENT/-CHILD**

WORST: **WORK**

NANCY LIEBERMAN (7/1/58)
MARTINA NAVRATILOVA (10/18/56)

Basketball great Lieberman and tennis legend Navratilova began a 3-year association in 1981. Training together rigorously, Lieberman helped Navratilova reach her top form, both physically and mentally. They lived together during this period amid rumors of romance.

Also: John Cusack & Joan Cusack (siblings; actors); **Jean-Jacques Rousseau & Denis Diderot** (author-collaborators).

June 25–July 2
THE WEEK OF THE EMPATH
CANCER I

October 11–18
THE WEEK OF THEATER
LIBRA III

Becoming a Whole Person

Cancer I's and Libra III's have a catalytic effect on each other. There is an interesting psychological dynamic here, in which each partner incorporates some of the other's attitudes; this in turn leads them to discover or expose aspects of their own selves that have previously been concealed. Their combination urges Cancer I's to be more outgoing and to reveal more about their inner life, Libra III's to draw back a bit from their worldly involvements and to become more introspective. This relationship balances each partner's innate tendencies. In encouraging them in these directions, it creates a movement toward wholeness and psychological health. Even should it end, it will probably leave each partner more of a whole person, not only functioning better but having more to offer.

Libra III's often like a strong arm to lean on in their personal relationships, but with Cancer I's they will benefit from an anatomical part even more important to them—a sympathetic ear that knows how to listen. For their part, however, they may be unable or unwilling to give their Cancer I partners the attention they need, arousing frustration and some resentment toward their professional activities and associates. They are often uncomfortable with emotions, but their relationship with Cancer I's will teach them the hazards of a cool and unemotional facade. Learning to acknowledge and give vent to their feelings constructively will be an important lesson for Libra III's to learn. The dynamic of this combination almost seems to have a specific purpose in each individual's personal growth. Once that purpose is served, the pair may find that the relationship falls apart, having outlived its usefulness. Family members, particularly cousins and grandparent-grandchildren pairs, will respect each other's secrets. Yet they will also encourage each other to find the right time and place for such hidden material to be revealed, and perhaps along the way will help in working out attendant problems. Cancer I–Libra III co-workers are unlikely to be an effective team in daily desk, factory or service-related positions, or to function effectively as business partners.

ADVICE: *Build a well-rounded outlook. Acknowledge the importance of emotional expression. What can you offer? Be thankful for what you have.*

STRENGTHS: **HEARTFELT, SPIRITUAL, WELL MATCHED**

WEAKNESSES: **OVERSERIOUS, UNDIRECTED, EGO-DEFICIENT**

BEST: **FRIENDSHIP, COMPETITION**

WORST: **PARENT-CHILD**

OLIVIA DE HAVILLAND (7/1/16)
JOAN FONTAINE (10/22/17)

Sisters de Havilland and Fontaine were Hollywood leading ladies in the 30s and 40s. (Joan changed her name to Fontaine in '37.) They were both nominated for the best-actress Oscar in 1941. Fontaine won it for *Suspicion* (de Havilland lost for *Hold Back the Dawn*).

Also: George Sand & Franz Liszt (close friendship); **Mike Tyson & Evander Holyfield** (heavyweight boxing foes).

June 25–July 2
THE WEEK OF THE EMPATH
CANCER I

October 19–25
THE CUSP OF DRAMA & CRITICISM
LIBRA-SCORPIO CUSP

Acknowledging a Higher Power

This relationship is likely to be highly spiritual, no matter how physical it appears. These partners are often at one in their submission to and acknowledgment of a higher power. In this sense the relationship often has religious overtones, but not necessarily formal ones. In all of their activities together, Cancer I's and Libra-Scorpios will always give it their best shot, but they will ultimately leave the outcome up to fate, or a more personal deity. No matter what these two do, however, they will put their whole hearts into it.

These two will see their love affairs and marriages as blessed and consecrated. Neither of them is particularly selfish in this matchup; they are more interested in a precious kind of intimacy, which they know they must never take for granted or betray. These attitudes can make life difficult if the relationship breaks up—the partners are usually incapable of the sort of unserious, realistic or cynical stance that would make separating easier. A period of grieving is generally needed before new romantic connections with others can be undertaken.

Cancer I's and Libra III's are well matched, whether as friends, rivals or competitors. Fairness is usually an important issue here. Whether the partners are on the same side or not, they can admire each other's skills, and have few hard feelings about their confrontations. As business rivals competing for a contract or client, they will hold positive enough feelings about each other that they may later wind up working together for the same company.

Parent-child matchups in this combination are not always able to provide the kind of authority and direction required in child-rearing. Parents and children will too often relate as friends, a habit that can cause role-model problems later on, in adolescence and early adulthood.

ADVICE: *Take more personal responsibility for your actions. Gain a stronger sense of yourself. Play your role fully. Don't use fate as an excuse.*

June 25–July 2

THE WEEK OF THE EMPATH
CANCER I

October 26–November 2

THE WEEK OF INTENSITY
SCORPIO I

Setting Parameters

Although traditional astrology predicts an easy relationship here, because of a trine aspect (Cancer I and Scorpio I are 120° apart in the zodiac), this relationship is apt to be pretty complex emotionally. Its great challenge is to build bridges of verbal communication and to set parameters within which meaningful contact can take place. Cancer I's favor unplanned interactions, wanting as much breathing space as possible, while Scorpio I's push for rules and regulations that will guarantee them control. Power struggles are almost certain here, then, and will threaten the relationship's security if allowed to get out of hand. Patient diplomacy, compromise and discussion will be essential if this is to be forestalled.

Love affairs go deep here. Sexual bonds are likely to be passionate and long-lasting, and the partners' emotional encounters will stir them both profoundly. Negative as well as positive feelings will emerge. Before one of these affairs proceeds on to marriage, it would behoove the pair to outline the role and responsibilities expected of each partner, establishing general guidelines to guarantee the relationship a structural basis.

Cancer I–Scorpio I friendships can be close but are difficult to maintain. The partners are unlikely to see the necessity for creating guidelines for their interactions, let alone agreeing on them. Scorpio I's may also be suspicious of Cancer I motives (which they find dubious) and actions (which they see as sneaky). Cancer I's are likely to view Scorpio I's as overly moral control freaks. The result of all this is often a sort of on-again, off-again relationship.

In no area are Cancer I–Scorpio I relations as complex as in the parent-child sphere. No matter which party is the parent, the child may be bewildered by an interesting mix of spoiling and high expectation. Emotional manipulation, love, resentment, kindness and a host of other feelings are likely to intermingle and blur at the edges. Cancer I–Scorpio I co-workers can get along well when their tasks are well defined.

ADVICE: *Define roles more clearly. Agree on division of labor. Beware of hazy attitudes and expectations. Seek common principles for daily living.*

CHARLES LAUGHTON (7/1/1899)
ELSA LANCHESTER (10/28/02)

Actors Laughton and Lanchester married in 1929 before either was well known. They occasionally worked together in films, like *The Private Lives of Henry VIII* (1933), in which she played Anne of Cleves, and *Witness for the Prosecution* (1975), in which both played their parts with great comic teamwork. ***Also:* Patrice Lumumba & Mobutu Sese Seko** (Congo political foes).

June 25–July 2

THE WEEK OF THE EMPATH
CANCER I

November 3–11

THE WEEK OF DEPTH
SCORPIO II

Parallel Play

The primary force in this combination is its partners' tendency to merge with each other to the point where they shut out the world. The relationship can be reclusive, with the partners withdrawing from social contact with other people. Family and career ties will help them to stay in contact with the world. Their relationships sometimes build connections through religion, music, film or sports, which can bring an almost holy aspect to them, acting as bridges both between them and from them to other people. These two will periodically need to come up for air by withdrawing from each other for a time. This level of involvement borders on codependency, and is not ideal for the partners' individual growth.

Cancer I–Scorpio II love affairs can be highly sensuous, but they can equally well sublimate sexual pleasure into other spheres, such as food and physical comfort. The enjoyment here is rarely of the ecstatic, passionate sort, but rather is free-floating and diffuse. Sleep patterns can be especially important for this pair. The relationship may also evolve in a decidedly nonphysical direction, platonic feelings predominating and intensity being reserved for more spiritual pursuits. The lovers in such a relationship can continue as friends (and even sleep partners) long after their passions have cooled. Marriages and friendships in this combination can be counterproductive to mutual growth because of the partners' tendency to remove themselves from social life, spending all their time submerged in their own relationship. A situation can be set up not unlike that of parallel play among children, who can simultaneously sit next to each other and go about their own activities, seemingly unaware of each other's presence. Nonetheless, in a curious way, these Cancer I–Scorpio II relationships can work out, managing to serve the needs of both partners.

In the family and professional spheres, combative tendencies often arise between Cancer I's and Scorpio II's. Particularly between siblings, stepparents and stepchildren, and work colleagues, all sorts of competitive situations may bring out anger, upset and, often, jealousy and rivalry over the affections of a third party.

ADVICE: *Be sure to separate from each other sometimes. Let go of claiming attitudes. Limit combativeness. Strive for openness and understanding.*

BONNIE BRAMLETT (11/8/44)
DELANEY BRAMLETT (7/1/39)

Husband-and-wife duo Delaney & Bonnie were married a week after they met in 1967. Their musical successes are linked to their association with Eric Clapton, who recorded and toured with them. When Clapton moved on in the early 70s, their popularity waned. In '72, with the release of their final album *Together,* their marriage dissolved.

PRINCE CHARLES (11/14/48)
LADY DIANA (7/1/61)

After a fairy-tale wedding in 1981—watched by over 750 million people worldwide—and 2 children and a life of seemingly regal perfection, the royal couple came apart owing to marital infidelities, including Diana's public admission of adultery and Charles' ongoing affair with an old flame. Their marriage ended after 15 years.

June 25–July 2
THE WEEK OF THE EMPATH
CANCER I

November 12–18
THE WEEK OF CHARM
SCORPIO III

Can Honesty Prevail?

Too often the facade that this combination presents to friends, relatives and the public at large belies the true state of things. The relationship is enigmatic, then, and hard to grasp, even for the partners themselves. Although Cancer and Scorpio are both water signs (associated with feeling), the relationship's symbol is earth, giving it a pragmatic, grounded and physical side that emphasizes responsibility but can also be characterized as judgmental and prone to laying on guilt and blame.

In love affairs and marriages, Cancer I's are likely to resent Scorpio III controlling attitudes. They are usually on the receiving end of Scorpio III punishment, and the relationship may in fact have a slightly sadomasochistic character. Part of the problem is that Cancer I's have a desperate need to express their feelings while Scorpio III's build their entire ego structure around controlling theirs. Threatened by Cancer I displays of emotion, Scorpio III's will repress and dominate—when actually they would do well to learn a thing or two. Cancer I's, on the other hand, have an uncanny ability to needle Scorpio III's. And since neither partner will act especially long-suffering if they don't get what they want, they will not hesitate to seek satisfaction elsewhere if the relationship fails to provide it. Lest this picture look unduly gloomy, it should be said that they can also be happy together, but only if dedication, honesty, and accepting, nonjudgmental and affectionate attitudes prevail.

Friendships in this combination can be puzzling and are often misunderstood. The world tends mainly to see the couple's differences, and to view the relationship as somewhat vague and lacking in definition. Only when the relationship proves its efficacy and survives some hard knocks will family and friends at last acknowledge it and take it seriously.

In work and family matchups, Cancer I's and Scorpio III's will benefit from the protective umbrella of a group in which their roles, particularly as co-workers or siblings, are well defined. The duo does best when personal matters do not intrude, and when bosses and parents expect dedication and results from them .

ADVICE: *Be honest and open. Avoid double standards. Relinquish controlling attitudes. Don't let yourself be treated like a football.*

PAT BUCKLEY (7/1/26)
WILLIAM BUCKLEY (11/24/25)

Writer William is the founder of the politically conservative magazine *National Review*. He is a well-known syndicated columnist and frequent guest on tv talk shows, exhibiting keen intellectual sense and charming wit. His wife, author Pat, is a socially prominent figure who devotes much of her time to charity.

Also: George Abbott & Mary Sinclair (married; producer/painter).

June 25–July 2
THE WEEK OF THE EMPATH
CANCER I

November 19–24
THE CUSP OF REVOLUTION
SCORPIO-SAGITTARIUS CUSP

An Unreal World

This relationship will never follow the norm. Its partners find it difficult to define their interaction, which can be both positive and negative, depending on the point of view. Illusion figures prominently here, so pinning one's hopes and dreams on the relationship is usually a mistake. Cancer I's, the more traditional of the pair, will find the lack of focus more uncomfortable than freedom-loving Scorpio-Sagittarians do. Either way, the relationship is unlikely to be enduring. Cancer I's are prone to seeing something in this relationship that just isn't there. They are also rarely tough enough to stand up to Scorpio-Sagittarians, who can be slippery customers, and who, consciously or unconsciously, sometimes lead their partners on, making promises that they ultimately do not fulfill. Too often Scorpio-Sagittarians may get what they want, or think they want, out of this relationship and then move on, leaving a sadder and wiser Cancer I behind.

Romances can be mercifully short or unmercifully long. The short ones can be pleasurable for both partners, taking them into an unreal world from which, alas, they will eventually have to return. Longer-lasting matchups will encounter rejection, pain and blame that may sour memories of the relationship's auspicious start.

Friendships are only possible given some definite commitment. The choice ultimately rests with Scorpio-Sagittarians, whose missed appointments and forgotten phone calls too often let Cancer I's know that their friends care less than they do. Once they realize they have been taken advantage of, Cancer I's usually close the door. In fairness to Scorpio-Sagittarians, however, they may have been receiving mixed messages from this partner all along. Working relationships are probably the best bet here. Particularly recommended are imaginative efforts in which Scorpio-Sagittarius flair and taste can merge with Cancer I business sense and technical abilities. If the relationship can limit its tendency to drift and dream, it is capable of implementing its ideas in the commercial sector. Sibling and parent-child matchups are probably most successful when working to better the family situation, often by helping relatives to relax and enjoy themselves.

ADVICE: *Try to keep your feet on the ground and your eye on the goal. Don't delude yourself. Find your real strengths. Don't get off track.*

June 25–July 2
THE WEEK OF THE EMPATH
CANCER I

November 25–December 2
THE WEEK OF INDEPENDENCE
SAGITTARIUS I

Well-Grounded Pursuits

RELATIONSHIPS

STRENGTHS: **PLAYFUL, LITERAL, LIMITED**

WEAKNESSES: **UNGROUNDED, GARBLED, MISCOMMUNICATING**

BEST: **WORK**

WORST: **FAMILY**

This relationship grounds its partners and allows them clear objectives and priorities. But they need to be clear on exactly what they are talking about; if their communication isn't specific, misunderstandings can be common. They might also cultivate traits of discernment and selectivity—in fact, it is important that they do so. Cancer I's and Sagittarius I's will get along best when they have something specific to talk about or deal with. Should this basis be lacking, Cancer I vagueness and Sagittarius I philosophical flights of fancy may quickly send the relationship on a downward spiral.

Love affairs can become hopelessly lost or tangled up in miscommunication and garbled emotional language. Unless there is a solid physical attraction or some other definite reason for the two to get together, romance is unlikely to click. Marriage is often more likely to work out if the spouses share a good career relationship, or as a further evolution of a successful and objectively proven friendship.

Friendships are one sort of contact in which literal meaning may perhaps be less important. Here Cancer I's and Sagittarius I's can let it all hang out, relaxing, having fun and fooling around unseriously. Especially rewarding will be short summertime trips to the sea, lakes or rivers, as well as indoor activities like table tennis, pool and board games. It may be difficult for Cancer I–Sagittarius I relatives, especially parents or grandparents and children or grandchildren, to see eye to eye. Temperamental differences here may make mutual understanding difficult, creating emotional turmoil. In adolescence and young adulthood, such interactions go best when the scope of involvement is limited. Issues should always be well defined.

Cancer I–Sagittarius I work relationships are best off when they are built around self-employed or entrepreneurial activities that meld their separate skills effectively. Cancer I's are generally better at handling the home base and at designing, planning and budgeting, Sagittarius I's at being out in the field, traveling, doing hard physical work, solving problems and troubleshooting.

ADVICE: *Don't let your thoughts run away with you. Limit activities and direct them well. Develop your separate skills. Learn to cooperate.*

MIKE TYSON (6/30/66)
ROBIN GIVENS (11/27/64)

In a most improbable matchup, Givens, a highly educated and cultured African-American actress, married fighter Tyson, a street tough with a criminal record. Their marriage was stormy from the outset, with Tyson being accused of violence. Their divorce was inevitable. Givens' career, however, got a boost from the publicity.

June 25–July 2
THE WEEK OF THE EMPATH
CANCER I

December 3–10
THE WEEK OF THE ORIGINATOR
SAGITTARIUS II

Kindred Souls

RELATIONSHIPS

STRENGTHS: **INITIATING, ENTHUSIASTIC, FULFILLING**

WEAKNESSES: **CONFUSED, WEIRD, DISASTROUS**

BEST: **LOVE**

WORST: **FRIENDSHIP**

The Cancer I–Sagittarius II combination can be a fruitful one. There is a high and an enthusiasm in this relationship that the pair can use to initiate new endeavors, and that can do wonders in dispelling their negative moods. Both Cancer I's and Sagittarius II's have unusual qualities that in relationships with others will often mark them as strange and make them misunderstood, but with each other they may experience the fulfillment of meeting a kindred soul. Their acceptance and appreciation of each other's unconventional side often frees up the energy needed to initiate work projects together and to carry them through to completion.

Romantic relationships either click or don't. There are few gray areas or ambiguities here; Cancer I's and Sagittarius II's seldom beat around the bush, and are seldom indecisive about whether or not to continue together. In such all-or-nothing matchups, being able to be honest and direct about feelings will be a relief to both partners. Marriages between these two can work out wonderfully well or end in confused disaster. Before getting carried away with enthusiasm over how marvelous a marriage could be, or seeking to solve all their problems with a single throw of the dice, prospective Cancer I–Sagittarius II partners would do well to sit down and talk long and frankly about the advisability of such a step. Staying objective will be difficult but will save much pain in the long run.

Cancer I's and Sagittarius II's are unlikely to form deep friendships. Although they understand each other well, in this kind of relationship they may dislike many of each other's more unusual qualities. And without new projects to initiate, their relationship will probably lack strength and purpose. In the family, sibling and cousin pairs in this combination are likely to clash strongly and be unable to get along, unless they share a common hobby or artistic or athletic pursuit. Such interests can do a great deal to overcome temperamental differences.

ADVICE: *Enthusiasm can be deadly. Take your time and exercise good judgment in making decisions. Be prepared to follow through with what you begin.*

HENRY VIII (6/28/1491)
CATHERINE HOWARD (12/10/1520)

Howard was the 5th wife of Henry. They married in 1540, right after his annulment with Anne of Cleves. Howard was young, flirtatious, and indiscreet. She was accused of adultery in November 1541 and executed the following February.

Also: **Mike Tyson & Don King** (boxer/promoter).

STRENGTHS: **SHARING, APPRECIATIVE, AESTHETIC**

WEAKNESSES: **WITHDRAWN, POLARIZED, UNACKNOWLEDGED**

BEST: **MARRIAGE**

WORST: **FAMILY**

GEN. BENJAMIN DAVIS, JR. (12/18/12)
GEN. BENJAMIN DAVIS (7/1/1877)

Davis Sr. was the first black to become a general in the US Army. He was also a military-science teacher. Davis Jr., sharing his father's love of the military, served in the US Air Force and became a major general (1959) and lieutenant general (1965). **Also:**

Henry VIII & Catherine of Aragon (married; first wife);

Frank Loesser & Abe Burrows (Broadway musical collaborators).

June 25–July 2
THE WEEK OF THE EMPATH
CANCER I

December 11–18
THE WEEK OF THE TITAN
SAGITTARIUS III

A Gift of Sharing

The most successful Cancer I–Sagittarius III relationships share a system of values or a vision of beauty. These two must recognize and nurture the value of what they have—including the relationship itself. Cancer I's and Sagittarius III's may view the world somewhat superficially, but they always contribute something worthwhile, and usually on a grand scale. Sagittarius III's are often so concerned with career or personal goals that they have difficulty acknowledging how dependent they are on this relationship. Cancer I's, however, are usually sensitive enough to realize that Sagittarius III's are not ignoring or undervaluing the relationship, just failing to recognize it. Cancer I's would seem to be at a disadvantage in this combination, but the unconscious needs of less aware Sagittarius III's are an open book to them, and if they want to they can exercise a powerful psychological control here.

This seems to be a classic extrovert-introvert pair, but outsiders often don't see either the lower, withdrawn moods of Sagittarius III's or the active role Cancer I's can play in dealing with them. In love affairs and marriages, Cancer I's who are wise enough not to launch a frontal assault on Sagittarius III depression will show a valuable understanding and patience. Sagittarius III's usually adopt an aggressive, forceful attitude toward the world while Cancer I's pay attention to the domestic scene, but within the relationship such dichotomies are rarely so simple. By mutually worshiping a standard of beauty, perhaps in each other, their children, their home or common interests, these partners are granted the gift of sharing. In friendships Sagittarius III's often dominate, and Cancer I's may eventually need to break free of them. In family situations, too, a Sagittarius III parent may exert an overpowering influence on a Cancer I child, or a brother or sister on a sibling. Work relationships in this combination are challenged in co-worker or colleague matchups that demand equality. Less problematic will be simple boss-employee relationships in which the Sagittarius III is the "big picture" person and plays the primary role while the Cancer I manages the project's internal works.

ADVICE: *Openly acknowledge what you have. Strive for equality. Appreciate differences fully. Don't get locked into fixed roles. Stay flexible.*

STRENGTHS: **PLAYFUL, FANTASY-RICH, FUN**

WEAKNESSES: **IMMATURE, RECKLESS, UNREALISTIC**

BEST: **FRIENDSHIP**

WORST: **MARRIAGE**

WILLIAM THOMSON (6/26/1824)
JAMES PRESCOTT JOULE (12/24/1818)

Physicists Thomson [Baron Kelvin] and Joule are both known for their work in thermodynamics. They discovered the Joule-Thomson effect—the decrease in the temperature of a gas when it expands in a vacuum—which is the basis for all modern refrigeration and air-conditioning.

June 25–July 2
THE WEEK OF THE EMPATH
CANCER I

December 19–25
THE CUSP OF PROPHECY
SAGITTARIUS-CAPRICORN CUSP

Relief from the Shadow

The childlike nature of this relationship is usually apparent to both partners. Although their joint outlook may be somewhat naive at times, they have a chance to develop a playful and fantasy-rich connection. Needing privacy, they often keep their activities covert and hidden from the world, and it may take them quite a long time to begin to share their most intimate secrets with each other—behavior that the relationship will generally foster. Acceptance and trust will play a strong role here. The potential therapeutic value, for both partners, of their personal interactions should not be underestimated, since these two have a deep and depressive shadow side from which the relationship may at last offer them some relief.

Love affairs here may be immature and unrealistic, but romance is often high and infatuations can be pleasurably overwhelming. Both partners are likely to throw caution to the winds, but the flame that burns so brightly may also be quickly extinguished. Marriages are not recommended unless the partners are willing to adopt more mature attitudes and shoulder heavy responsibilities.

Cancer I–Sagittarius-Capricorn friendships and sibling matchups can be playful and close. The childlike element is given full rein here. Both partners are open to enjoying fun activities, whether in the areas of games, sports, media, music or adventure. Their matchups are generally closed to others, and a great challenge here is opening up the relationship to make such activities more inclusive.

The shadow side of the combination appears relatively little in friendships and sibling relationships. Solemn moments will occur here, but they are usually healthy ones, in which the partners feel able to share their problems and pain with each other. Work relationships in this combination may not be serious enough to succeed, but when Cancer I's and Sagittarius-Capricorns are co-workers and colleagues, they can brighten up the workplace with lighter, more frivolous attitudes.

ADVICE: *Preserve your youthfulness, but don't neglect your responsibilities. Be a wee bit more realistic. Look before you leap. Share with others.*

June 25–July 2
THE WEEK OF THE EMPATH
CANCER I

December 26–January 2
THE WEEK OF THE RULER
CAPRICORN I

Cost-Effectiveness

This relationship is generally rather severe and demanding; perfectionist drives make relaxation and easy interaction difficult here. Because Cancer I and Capricorn I lie opposite each other in the zodiac, astrology predicts difficulties, and in this case correctly so—the opposition translates into tension and pressure to produce a perfect result.

Cancer I's can be quite critical, and are likely to give Capricorn I's as good as they get. Should the relationship emerge in the family or at work, it may well demand more efficiency from others and exert pressure on relatives or colleagues to avoid wastefulness. Acumen and innate conservatism in money matters are characteristic enough that an insistence on cost-effective approaches is probable. Although Cancer is a water sign and Capricorn earth, the Cancer I–Capricorn I relationship is symbolized by the element of air, associated with thought, here suggesting planning, the implementation of ideas and also, unfortunately, a tendency to worry.

The cerebral attitudes found here are often counterproductive in the area of love. Checklists and evaluations should be left behind at the bedroom door, but often are not, putting both partners under pressure to perform properly and well. The strains engendered by these attitudes can lead to a lack of spontaneity and ultimately to inflexibility and even breakdown. The relationship's perfectionist slant may put married partners in this combination under unbearable stress, making them so worried about financial and domestic problems that they are unable to relax and enjoy themselves.

Friendships may circumvent such extreme attitudes, laying aside most of the matchup's usual unrealistic expectations. But a pickiness about details and a tacit expectation of a high level of quality can drive both partners to distraction. In the family, particularly when Capricorn I is the parent and Cancer I the child, dominating attitudes and the merciless application of rules will ultimately arouse resentment or, worse, produce an individual who cannot function without receiving strict orders.

ADVICE: *Ease up in your demands. Relax more. Allow other people their own approach and values. Beware of inflexibility.*

June 25–July 2
THE WEEK OF THE EMPATH
CANCER I

January 3–9
THE WEEK OF DETERMINATION
CAPRICORN II

A Need for Interaction

This matchup plays an important role for its partners by teaching them not only how to interact socially with others but, more crucial still, the value of the relationship itself. Both of these personalities can be single-minded about their own success; here they will learn to consider another person's needs and wants, to be more diplomatic and to negotiate, as well as the value of give-and-take. If they are adept students, this could be a successful combination.

The danger here is that the partners will instead choose to cut themselves off from other people and retreat to what they see as a safe space. It may not be as safe as they think. Away from the influence of friends and family, empathic Cancer I's may act out the frustrations, anger and other repressed feelings of their partner in this combination. They are prone to pick up unconsciously and very quickly on the feelings of Capricorn II's, expressing them as if they were their own. The personal problems of both partners also tend to become magnified the more time they spend alone together. For reasons of mental health, then, this pair should build bridges to the outside world.

Love affairs, marriage and friendships will have problems breaking through the partners' armor. In childhood, both of them have commonly suffered from the disapproving attitudes of parents, teachers and other authority figures, making them build a tough and resistant exterior. The task of all of these relationships is slowly to build bonds of commonality and trust that will dissolve these barriers. After making the effort to connect with the other partner, whether as lover, spouse or friend, these two may eventually begin to interact better with other friends and family members. In family relationships, especially parent-child, Cancer I's and Capricorn II's often try to break with old cycles and patterns that make them repeat past mistakes, and to act in less oppressive and more kindly and accepting ways. Boss-employee and teacher-student relationships should also be softened and brought down to a more human level involving openness and sharing.

ADVICE: *Let go of past baggage. You have been carrying too much on your shoulders. Beware of isolation. Establish social bonds.*

A.J. FOYT (1/16/35)
RICHARD PETTY (7/2/37)

Petty and Foyt were auto-racing competitors who each set significant records before their retirement in '92 and '93, respectively. Foyt, a 4-time Indy 500 winner, is the only driver in history to win the Indy 500, Daytona 500 and Le Mans. Petty, 7-time Daytona winner, is all-time NASCAR leader in races won.

June 25–July 2

THE WEEK OF THE EMPATH
CANCER I

January 10–16

THE WEEK OF DOMINANCE
CAPRICORN III

Humor Abounding

Competition for the spotlight is common in this combination, but it does not have to be serious. The relationship may feature a friendly rivalry abounding with good nature and humor. Perhaps out of embarrassment or not wanting to seem pushy, neither Cancer I's nor Capricorn III's are used to pushing for glory (although a fair share of them achieve it). In this relationship, then, they can have a great deal of fun teasing each other about trying to gain attention. In their personal interactions they may pretend to ignore their partner, or to be unimpressed by his or her achievements, as a kind of game-playing activity designed to push buttons and force a reaction.

Love affairs can be quite passionate here. Although Cancer is a water sign and Capricorn earth, the relationship is ruled by fire, in this case connoting the combustibility of a torrid love affair. Fire often introduces intuition, and in this area the relationship is strong. These partners will have good hunches about what is and is not allowed at any particular time. As lovers they often consider formal marriage unnecessary, preferring to live together, permanently or semipermanently.

Friends and siblings can have great times kidding each other and engaging in mock competitions and satirical debates. These battles sometimes turn serious, but any animosities that develop are quickly dispelled. One exception, which may prove deeply divisive, is when partners engage in rivalry for the attention of a common love object. The third party is often ultimately rejected and viewed quite coolly by both friends as not being worth losing the relationship over.

Cancer I–Capricorn III work relations can be outstanding, and co-workers who are separated when one partner moves on to a new position or changes jobs may preserve their relationship, at least for a time, as friends.

ADVICE: *Know when to be serious and when to let up. Don't let teasing get out of hand. Beware of third-party rivalries. Act with consideration to all.*

WILLIAM WYLER (7/1/02)
CARL LAEMMLE (1/17/1867)

When movie tycoon Laemmle opened his 230-acre Universal City in 1915, the gala was attended by thousands. When staffing his new company, "Uncle Carl," as he was known, thought first of his relatives—among them Wyler, a distant cousin of Laemmle's mother. This was the start of director Wyler's prodigious career.

June 25–July 2

THE WEEK OF THE EMPATH
CANCER I

January 17–22

THE CUSP OF MYSTERY & IMAGINATION
CAPRICORN-AQUARIUS CUSP

Dress-Up Time

Imagination, fantasy, flair—this relationship has all that and more. If Cancer I's and Capricorn-Aquarians have not discovered this aspect of their relationship, they don't know what they're missing. The self-image of Cancer I's could change drastically here, and almost overnight. Any vision they had of themselves as stick-in-the-mud stay-at-homes is liable to go right out the window, for their partner won't see them that way at all. Capricorn-Aquarians can feel very comfortable in this relationship, and will usually take the lead in showing some of the steps to their Cancer I partners.

Love affairs here tend to be romantic and flamboyant. Any Cancer I relationship is capable of intimacy, but the partners in this one figure that if you've got it—flaunt it! Letting it all hang out may be a whole new experience to Cancer I's, and one that they thoroughly enjoy. Just the relief over not feeling embarrassed or inhibited by public display is a reward in itself for these private personalities. Marriages are apt to be less exciting and more prosaic. The relationship does have a more thoughtful side that will emerge here, but ultimately it may not be in the cards for these two to take on more demanding responsibilities. Furthermore, the emotional depth needed for a longer-lasting commitment such as marriage is generally lacking here.

Cancer I–Capricorn-Aquarius friendships are likely to be no less outgoing than love affairs; public displays of affection between these friends should not be ruled out. Sibling matchups, especially between opposite sexes, may lift a few eyebrows when normal brother-sister inhibitions are thrown to the winds.

At work, this relationship is unlikely to flourish in a tedious or boring desk or factory job. Yet co-workers in such a situation may be pleased to make the money (even when not thrilled by the work), then go out after work hours and tie one on.

ADVICE: *Even eyebrows tire of being lifted. Don't overdo your effects. Keep something in reserve. Find the real you. Don't rule out thoughtfulness.*

June 25–July 2

THE WEEK OF THE EMPATH
CANCER I

January 23–30

THE WEEK OF GENIUS
AQUARIUS I

RELATIONSHIPS

STRENGTHS: APPRECIATIVE, INSPIRING, GROUNDBREAKING

WEAKNESSES: LONG-SUFFERING, OVERPROTECTIVE, UNSTABLE

BEST: WORK

WORST: FAMILY

Hatching New Ideas

This can be a brilliant combination for furthering projects and realizing goals. The relationship lets its partners know that they do well operating in a broad social context; together these two naturally take the lead in any endeavor, meanwhile sharing few tensions between themselves over dominance and control. They do, however, demand the highest quality both in others and in themselves. The relationship's quality of nurturing and understanding hatches new ideas the way a brooder hatches chicks. This team can often take the lead in their professional or social field, doing the pioneering work that others will follow. Although the relationship's focus is not necessarily practical, Cancer I's and Aquarius I's may well have the theoretical know-how and drive to succeed. Should Cancer I's be teachers, researchers or bosses and Aquarius I's their students, assistants or employees, these two are likely to spur each other to new heights of achievement.

In love affairs and marriages in this combination, Cancer I's are likely to be appreciative, nurturing and supportive of their partners. But they can be made very unhappy by Aquarius I instabilities and shenanigans, particularly flirting with others—even though they know that Aquarius I's need to be free, and are happiest when given the space they require. Aquarius I's demand constant appreciation, so much so that Cancer I's may be relieved sometimes to find themselves alone. Aquarius I's will generally enjoy the domestic comfort and security that Cancer I's can provide, assuming that they don't find it cloying or claiming.

In family matchups, Cancer I parents can be too protective and ambitious for their Aquarius I kids. They should certainly encourage these children, but must stop themselves from projecting their own frustrated wishes on them: the child's success should not be expected to make up for the parent's missed chances. Aquarius I parents may not be able to give their Cancer I children the protection and nurture they require. Friendships in this combination are likely to be mutually supportive but rarely go very deep, and eventually may just drift apart.

ADVICE: *Don't feel you have to push. Let things grow of their own accord. Beware of claiming attitudes. Share but observe boundaries.*

JOHN BELUSHI (1/24/49)
DAN AYKROYD (7/1/52)

These comics are best remembered together as the Blues Brothers, a 50s-style satirical duo that started as a pre-show warmup act for *Saturday Night Live* in 1977. They were so good, they soon had a hit record and a feature-length film.

Also: Peter Lorre & Humphrey Bogart (co-stars); Dan Rowan & Dick Martin (co-hosts, *Laugh-In*); Gilda Radner & John Belushi (co-stars, *SNL*).

June 25–July 2

THE WEEK OF THE EMPATH
CANCER I

January 31–February 7

THE WEEK OF YOUTH & EASE
AQUARIUS II

RELATIONSHIPS

STRENGTHS: INTELLIGENT, CRITICAL, IMPROVING

WEAKNESSES: NEGATIVE, UPTIGHT, DESTRUCTIVE

BEST: SIBLING

WORST: FRIENDSHIP

Intelligently Hedonistic

This relationship has a natural tendency to be analytical and to flex its mind power. The danger is that analysis can take the form of negative criticism—of nagging, complaining and other energy-draining activities that wear the partners down. Cancer I's are more prone to worrying and complaining than Aquarius II's, who are seldom tough enough to deal with this behavior and prefer a relationship with few if any hassles. If negative criticism reaches too high a level, Aquarius II's may figure the relationship is not worth the effort. Turning the mental orientation to positive purpose, then, is a worthy goal here.

Romantic impulses in this combination can be severely blunted by an overly mental orientation. Yet the relationship's mind power can also be put to work thinking up ever more delightful means of enjoyment. A host of new activities and improvements for old ones—more fulfilling vacations, more imaginative and pleasurable lovemaking, more delicious and well-planned menus—all of these and more can attest to an intelligently hedonistic attitude. Positive criticism, then, can bring enjoyment rather than dissatisfaction to both partners, while not denying the relationship's critical focus.

Marriages and friendships here must be careful not to be destructive toward others. Quite capable of bringing people down with their insightful and penetrating barbs, the Cancer I–Aquarius II relationship may be notorious in its social and family circles for puncturing overinflated egos. Although this behavior is sometimes necessary, overindulgence in it can intimidate other people and make them uptight. Cultivating diplomacy, kindness and consideration will allow others to accept their observations in a much more constructive spirit. At work and in the family, Cancer I–Aquarius II co-worker and sibling pairs may function as a reality test, being useful for telling the group when they have gone off course and how to get back on track again.

ADVICE: *Others should feel that your comments are well meant. Be diplomatic. Act out of consideration, not as a judge.*

HENRY VIII (6/28/1491)
SIR THOMAS MORE (2/7/1477)

In 1527 British Parliament member More refused to endorse Henry's divorce from Catherine of Aragon and was later imprisoned for refusing to acknowledge the king as supreme head of the Church of England. More was found guilty of treason and beheaded in 1535.

Also: Cheryl Ladd & David Ladd (married; actors).

LENNIE HAYTON (2/13/08)
LENA HORNE (6/30/17)

Blues/pop singer Horne's vibrant voice, beauty and sparkle took her to Hollywood in the 30s, where she became the first black to sign a long-term major studio contract. There she married Hayton, a noted composer and pianist-arranger and MGM musical director (1940–53). **Also: Dan Rowan & Phyllis McGuire** (romance; entertainers); **Henry VIII & Mary I** (father/daughter; British rulers).

June 25–July 2

THE WEEK OF THE EMPATH
CANCER I

February 8–15

THE WEEK OF ACCEPTANCE
AQUARIUS III

A Power Challenge

The focus of this relationship is power, whether the challenge is to seize it, exercise it or give it up. A spiritually evolutionary process may be implied in this, with the partners first striving for and grasping power, then learning more about themselves and their relationship, and finally relinquishing power in favor of higher ends. They may have to acknowledge their social or personal power, and live with it awhile, before they can give it up. Along the way, Cancer I's and Aquarius III's may come to realize that the greatest power of all is the power of love, which should be not given up but given away, and shared with others freely.

Love obviously has much to teach in this relationship. An affair may begin somewhat conventionally, with the partners being attracted to each other and falling in love, but after a time both will sense that they are fated to pursue a more spiritual course. This doesn't mean that they sacrifice physical contact, affection or sex, but that they reorient their priorities, making self-development along their common and individual paths the highest consideration of all. Marriages that can sustain such lofty goals and feelings may reach high levels of spirituality.

Friendships may have begun after the partners have once been professional or personal opponents or rivals. With this pair, admiration and respect can quickly displace combativeness and envy, and they rarely fall back into the earlier habit. The process also implies giving up competitive power and adopting more peaceful, open and accepting attitudes.

Parent-child relationships can be stormy, but often form the family's solid backbone. They can also share a lot of power, giving direction and force to all the family's activities. At work, Cancer I's and Aquarius III's must be careful not to fight over power nor to wield it unfairly over others. Instead, they should put it to the good of all.

ADVICE: *Try to be loving and accepting. Don't get carried away by power. Seek your own path. Simple acts of kindness can be very strong.*

GEORGE SAND (7/1/1804)
FREDERIC CHOPIN (2/22/1810)

Novelist Sand and composer Chopin had a 10-year affair, 1837–47. It is said she was the more masculine (dressed like a man, smoking cigars), while he was delicate, suffering from tuberculosis. When they parted she portrayed him in her writings as a weakling. **Also: Patty Smyth & John McEnroe** (affair; hard-rock singer/tennis star); **Sidney Lumet & Gloria Vanderbilt** (married; director/socialite).

June 25–July 2

THE WEEK OF THE EMPATH
CANCER I

February 16–22

THE CUSP OF SENSITIVITY
AQUARIUS-PISCES CUSP

A Unique Opportunity

This relationship is likely to reach a depth of empathy and sensitivity far beyond what either party is capable of alone or with other people. This special emotional intensity can work either beneficially or hurtfully, since it keys in to personal areas of great vulnerability. The relationship can develop a great deal of trust, for example, but if the results of this trust are negative, the partners may be forced to back off from each other, or even to break off the relationship. Both Cancer I's and Aquarius-Pisces may come into the relationship strongly armored or protected because of past hurts, yet be unable to close themselves off to each other due to the powerful chemistry between them.

Love and friendship in this combination offer unique opportunities for self-exploration, mutual growth and sharing. Cancer I's will generally be able to see deep into the inner lives of their Aquarius-Pisces lovers, who for their part may be made quite uptight by being so transparent; yet they in turn will have special powers in cases of Cancer I withdrawal and depression, leaving their partners feeling they have nowhere to hide. Both partners can benefit from their scrutiny of each other, then, yet both may have mixed feelings about it. Passions are likely to be intense here, hard to fathom and even harder to control. Particularly at the extremes of ecstatic and unhappy moments, lack of analytical skills and awareness may lead the partners to feel a bit helpless about what is happening to them, leaving them quite confused.

Marriages and work relationships often lack the solid commitment, practical abilities and technical skills necessary to get it together. Family business, too, may come grinding to a halt when Cancer I and Aquarius-Pisces interact. Not that Cancer I's and Aquarius-Pisces are completely lacking in these skills, but their relationship is so emotional that they may be handicapped in using them. If these relationships are to succeed, the partners must strive for objectivity, put feelings aside and keep their eye directly on what needs doing, without getting distracted.

ADVICE: *Gain insight into yourself. Try to be a bit analytical. Strive for objectivity. Remain open but more in control. Be aware of others.*

June 25–July 2
THE WEEK OF THE EMPATH
CANCER I

February 23–March 2
THE WEEK OF SPIRIT
PISCES I

The Long Haul

RELATIONSHIPS

STRENGTHS: **RELIABLE, SECURE, SPIRITUAL**

WEAKNESSES: **RESENTFUL, OVERDEMANDING, HEAVY**

BEST: **MARRIAGE**

WORST: **FRIENDSHIP**

Ruled by earth, this relationship brings solid and well-established values to bear. Its foundation is not flimsy or temporary—these two have the long haul in mind. Although their combination is governed by earth, both Cancer I and Pisces I are ruled by water; a trine relationship (120° apart in the zodiac) between water signs like theirs is classically one of the easiest and most compatible of the year. Their attitudes toward each other are accepting, but the demands they make on each other are considerable: their relationship promotes groundedness, pragmatism, responsibility and maturity, eschewing the kind of flakiness that both partners might be accused of individually. A kind of tenacity inherent here will help them over any bumps in the road.

The natural flow between Cancer I's and Pisces I's promotes relaxed attitudes in love affairs. These two are also grounded here in a sensuous appreciation of food, sex and comfortable surroundings. Marriages are encouraged as a further step in a life commitment to each other, as is having children. Financial security is essential to the well-being of all concerned.

In commercial, educational and social activities, these two give little value to ideas in themselves unless they are put into practice. The Cancer I–Pisces I relationship may be especially effective in seeing to the smooth running of an organization, work that will help keep these ordinarily private individuals in touch with the world. The partners will both appreciate the relationship and at times resent its heavy demands—which can, in fact, overwhelm friendships in this combination. Cancer I's and Pisces I's usually prefer just to have a good time when not working, and may back off from a relationship that is too heavy or laden with responsibility. In the family, parent-child relationships may have both the solidity and the flexibility necessary in everyday interactions, being both reliable and sensitive to the needs of others. Spiritual and religious values may be viewed as essential to giving meaning and direction to such a family unit.

ADVICE: *Keep it light. Don't get bogged down in responsibilities. Pursue spiritual values. Be realistic in your demands. Don't expect too much.*

ROBERT SARNOFF (7/2/18)
GEN. DAVID SARNOFF (2/27/1891)

Russian immigrant David rose to be head of RCA and founder of the NBC network. He was also a pioneer in tv technology. Following in his father's footsteps, Robert became president of NBC in '55 and introduced color tv. *Also:* **Meyer Lansky & Bugsy Siegel** (Murder Inc. gangsters); **Jean Stafford & Robert Lowell, Jr.** (married; writer/poet).

June 25–July 2
THE WEEK OF THE EMPATH
CANCER I

March 3–10
THE WEEK OF THE LONER
PISCES II

Deep Personal Involvement

RELATIONSHIPS

STRENGTHS: **DEEP, NURTURING, UNDERSTANDING**

WEAKNESSES: **CLAIMING, ISOLATED, ASHAMED**

BEST: **LOVE**

WORST: **HIDDEN AFFAIR**

Intense in feeling, this relationship can become a kind of womb, a place where the partners can feel nurtured and protected. In providing this safe harbor, the combination can catalyze self-transformation: it can teach the partners to give themselves over to and trust each other and the relationship itself. Neither Cancer I's nor Pisces II's form deep bonds easily, but they often know as soon as they meet that they have found someone they can trust. They may have been misunderstood in the past—by parents, lovers, even friends; here, suddenly, is someone who seems to accept them. Is this feeling to be believed? Is it just another setup for betrayal? How the pair respond will have a lot to do with how the relationship goes. Old wounds may make them distrustful and wary, setting up the conditions for disappointment. If they accept the bond with faith, however, it can be all that it promises.

Cancer I–Pisces II love affairs are generally more successful when visible than when concealed. These partners have to feel proud of each other; no matter how private their relationship, they gain satisfaction and confidence from appearing in public together without fear or shame. In marriage the partners must beware of jealousy. They should also take care that their individual developments and self-realizations are not inhibited by the closeness of their connection.

Friendships here may be possessive; it is important for the partners to learn to share friends, feel free to spend time with others and not be afraid to turn each other down. Both of them have an intense need to spend time alone, a trait that neither of them should view as a sign of the relationship's failure. On the contrary, they may come to resent their relationship if it deprives them of occasional solitude.

Family and career relationships can be healthy in making these two maintain contact with the world. Practical considerations and the need for caring, responsibility and nurture can provide the balance needed for their personal involvement.

ADVICE: *Beware of false expectations. Don't think too much—feel. Release worry and fear. Build personal bonds of trust and bridges to the world.*

HELEN KELLER (6/27/1880)
ALEXANDER GRAHAM BELL (3/3/1847)

Bell, inventor of the telephone, whose mother and wife were both deaf, was deeply concerned with the problems of this handicap. He was trained by his father to teach the deaf to speak. Keller, both blind and deaf, was his student and protégé. She became a celebrated lecturer and humanitarian. *Also:* **Carly Simon & Richard Leo Simon** (daughter/father; pop singer/publisher).

JAMES TAYLOR (3/12/48)
CARLY SIMON (6/25/45)

Singer-composers Simon and Taylor were married in 1972. They made several successful recordings together, most memorable their 1974 duet *Mockingbird*, from the album *Hotcakes*, which went gold. Happy at first, Simon and Taylor had 2 children, but their relationship came apart by 1981 and she divorced him in 1983.

June 25–July 2
THE WEEK OF THE EMPATH
CANCER I

March 11–18
THE WEEK OF DANCERS & DREAMERS
PISCES III

The Highway of Life

Many lessons can be learned from this relationship—indeed the themes of learning and teaching are important here. The combination encourages not only individual growth but the potential to grow as a pair. These two will always be involved with ideas and concepts—they may even believe they have a message to share. Cancer I and Pisces III partners are likely to join in a host of challenging activities, whether as students in formal classes or as partners on the highway of life. The relationship's focus is usually the acquisition of knowledge through experience. There are many ways of working out this theme, but since differences in age are no barrier here, teacher-student relationships are particularly favored.

In the sphere of love, neither romance nor pleasure is seen as the be-all and end-all. If these partners don't feel that their love is a learning experience for them, they quickly tire of it. If the affair is to be fulfilling, challenges must be met, barriers overcome and development visible. A certain amount of pain, suffering and difficulty is seen as in no way proof that the relationship is a failure—in fac,t it is understood as a challenge to grow. This positive attitude bodes well for marriages as well.

In the family, grandparent-grandchild matchups may be more profitable than parent-child ones. Sibling matchups and friendships are often played out against the backdrop of school. Social opportunities are every bit as important as educational ones here; in fact, they are viewed as an important part of the learning process. These partners must be careful of jealousies over mutual friends and competitive tendencies over position in the pecking order. It will be important for the relationship to present a united front, but also to avoid being a closed fraternity. Cancer I–Pisces III friends and family are quite likely to work together for a company or even to form their own business. It is important here that they are able to get away from each other when necessary to follow their own path of self-realization and development.

ADVICE: *Give each other enough space. Take things as they come. Let up a bit on your demands. Be patient. Beware of jealousy and competition.*

ABIGAIL VAN BUREN (7/4/18)
ANN LANDERS (7/4/18)

These personal-advice columnists are twins, neé Esther Pauline and Pauline Esther Friedman, respectively. Landers and (Dear Abby) Van Buren published their columns nationally for many years in syndicated newspapers for millions of readers. ***Also:*** **P.T. Barnum & James Bailey** (circus partners); **Walter Kerr & Jean Kerr** (married; drama critic/writer); **Ron Kovic & Tom Cruise** (film portrayal).

July 3–10
THE WEEK OF THE UNCONVENTIONAL
CANCER II

July 3–10
THE WEEK OF THE UNCONVENTIONAL
CANCER II

Off the Beaten Path

How unconventional can a relationship get? This matchup may not impress other people as being terribly out of the ordinary; many Cancer II's function well in regular jobs, and those around this pair may view them as quite normal. In private life, however, the truly unusual qualities of the Cancer II personality come to light, and this relationship only magnifies them. The fantasy world built up here can be vivid, highly imaginative and indeed extreme. The combination encourages an interest in the bizarre, whether in books, film, electronic media, design or dance. Cancer II couples may also enjoy elements of popular culture that appear quite ordinary to other people, but whatever catches their eye usually has an incongruous or peculiar aspect to it, and this is what strikes their fancy.

Romances and marriages demand a lot of privacy, in a space that is capable of sustaining or reflecting these partners' inner vision. Unusual designs, colors and shapes may be stimulating to this couple, but they may also play out their tastes against a neutral background, as if a projector were throwing colorful images onto a blank screen. This curious dichotomy is also reflected in the clothing of Cancer II combinations, some couples appearing outlandish, others unremarkable. In many other aspects of life, too, the relationship can either express its unusualness directly or it can mute, disguise or mask it.

Cancer II friends like to share secrets with each other, particularly concerning childhood traumas. Parental and societal disapproval often figure prominently here, and the relationship may be quite therapeutic for both partners in alleviating or erasing inferiority complexes and other old, outworn negative scripts. Acceptance is the keynote here, and with it an eagerness to leave the baggage of the past behind.

Cancer II–Cancer II family and work matchups are likely to be mutually sympathetic but unremarkable. Be they parent and child, siblings, co-workers, or boss and employee, both parties have a way of not drawing attention to themselves and, in fact, of deemphasizing their personal relationship in favor of their outward role.

ADVICE: *Don't be so defensive. Others may actually appreciate your more ordinary self. Share when trust is earned. Give more of yourself in everyday life.*

July 3–10

THE WEEK OF THE UNCONVENTIONAL
CANCER II

July 11–18

THE WEEK OF THE PERSUADER
CANCER III

Ebb and Flow

RELATIONSHIPS

STRENGTHS: **MONEY-WISE,
RELIABLE, RESPONSIBLE**

WEAKNESSES: **OVERAMBITIOUS,
SELFISH, MATERIALISTIC**

BEST: **MARRIAGE**

WORST: **LOVE**

ARLO GUTHRIE (7/10/47)
WOODY GUTHRIE (7/14/12)

Crusading social and political folk-singer Woody was father of Arlo, who followed in his dad's footsteps from the 60s on. Arlo is best known for his folk classic *Alice's Restaurant*. Woody is best remembered for *This Land Is Your Land*. **Also: Jamie Wyeth & Andrew Wyeth** (son/father; artists); **George Steinbrenner & Joe Torre** (NY Yankees baseball owner/manager).

This can be a surprisingly powerful combination, devoted to seeking success in the world. Cancers in general tend to be intimate and personal in character, but this relationship brings out their more worldly, hard-driving and ambitious side as well. Even when the pair's goals are unusual in some way, they will provide each other with a great deal of emotional and moral support in their individual efforts, exhibiting surprisingly little competitiveness or jealousy. They can also show incredible determination in getting what they want. Once their individual differences have been settled and a common course agreed upon, the pair can forge ahead in the world to attain its goals, whether these are lofty or intensely practical.

Love affairs and friendships in this combination can be conjoined with career endeavors but sometimes suffer in the comparison. Too often, emotional matters and personal responsibilities are put aside or even ignored because pressing professional matters are given priority. Cancer II–Cancer III lovers and friends do best when they can find a balance between personal and career needs. Married couples and family matchups usually display a strong interest in and talent for the organizational and structural elements of their group; they can be counted on to hold their own in contributing to special events, whether with logistical planning or, say, the preparation of food, and are especially capable in financial matters.

The relationship is favored in matters of work and career. Financial success is a real possibility here: this couple has a feeling for material things and for handling money, sensing the dynamics of give-and-take, buy-and-sell, ebb-and-flow. That the fluidity of the daily market is understood at the most basic level here is clear from the way impatience and the desire for a quick kill are wisely subordinated to watching, waiting and finally moving decisively at the right moment. Although the pair are usually fairly considerate of their associates and fellow employees, they also have an undeniably ruthless streak, and are quite capable of protecting their own interests.

ADVICE: *Don't neglect your personal life. Keep career drives under control. Balance ambition with self-development. Be kind to others.*

July 3–10

THE WEEK OF THE UNCONVENTIONAL
CANCER II

July 19–25

THE CUSP OF OSCILLATION
CANCER-LEO CUSP

Persuasive Leadership

RELATIONSHIPS

STRENGTHS: **CONVINCING,
SELF-ASSURED, COMMANDING**

WEAKNESSES: **MANIPULATIVE,
SENSATIONALISTIC, DISAPPOINTED**

BEST: **FRIENDSHIP**

WORST: **MARRIAGE**

LIONEL TRILLING (7/4/05)
DIANA TRILLING (7/21/05)

Lionel was an influential American literary critic whose work was infused with psychology, sociology and philosophy. He wrote many important books on the subject of mankind in the modern world. His wife Diana (married 1929) was also a critic and author. She wrote of their marriage in her book *The Beginning of the Journey.*

This relationship manifests an intense need to persuade others of the rightness of its cause and the appropriateness of its decision-making. Since these two are resistant to emotional manipulation from each other, their joint need to influence or manipulate another person's point of view is often expressed in relation to friends, family or the public at large. Cancer II's will benefit from their contacts with Cancer-Leos, who will encourage them to realize their fantasies. Their psychologically astute understanding will in turn help Cancer-Leos in their own process of self-discovery.

Love affairs here may have a taste for secrecy and risk-taking, a combination that can encourage extramarital and other covert relationships. A love of danger can really get out of hand, to the point where it becomes the main ingredient of the whole pleasure process. Cancer II–Cancer-Leo relationships are not recommended for marriage, since in reaching for stability and social approval they will probably lose their thrill.

Friendships are likely to feature adventure, often as part of a team that this pair will lead, giving it their direction and convincing it of their capability and strength. Together these two are persuasive leaders, able to face danger with equanimity. They usually keep the best interests of the team in mind—true, Cancer II fantasy will have to be scaled back from time to time, and Cancer-Leo mood swings ironed out, but the relationship will support and encourage these processes.

Family pairs, especially siblings, may make it their business to convince other family members of their point of view and persuade them to change their course. They often come to see themselves as the watchdogs who will alert the family to lurking and unperceived dangers. Cancer II–Cancer-Leo work relationships are most effective as partnerships or matchups between colleagues on the same level. Public relations, advertising, marketing and other areas that involve influencing retailers and the public are likely to be areas of strength.

ADVICE: *Avoid thinking that you are more important than anyone else. Others can do without you. Leave room for personal choice. Control your thirst for danger.*

ARNOLD SCHWARZENEGGER (7/30/47)
EUNICE KENNEDY SHRIVER (7/10/20)

Former bodybuilder and current superstar actor Schwarzenegger is the son-in-law of Eunice Shriver (by marriage to daughter Maria). Eunice is the founder (1963) and honorary chairman of the Special Olympics, to which she appointed Arnold international weight-training coach in 1979.

July 3–10
THE WEEK OF THE UNCONVENTIONAL
CANCER II

July 26–August 2
THE WEEK OF AUTHORITY
LEO I

Transcending Conflict

A classic confrontation emerges here: Leo I's base what they know and do on tradition, Cancer II's do things their own way and break with the past. The relationship's focus, then, is often a power struggle. This internal combat can be vivid and exciting to the partners, but they should be careful to prevent it from taking a violent turn. They are ultimately quite capable of carving out a relationship that finds a middle ground between conservative and radical impulses. If they manage this, they should discover quite a creative fertility and energy.

Love affairs and friendships accentuate a variation on this kind of confrontation: moon-ruled Cancer II's shine with reflected light, sun-ruled Leo I's blaze in their own fiery glory. Power struggles inevitably surface in such relationships, often over who will receive attention from others. Whether the partners are rivals or outright combatants, no quarter will be asked for or given in their struggles. Their interactions are often passionately intense, but the relationship has the potential to transcend their conflicts by integrating their contrasting energies at a higher level. These solid bonds will not be easy to forge. Once created, however, they will be hard to break. Marriages between Cancer II's and Leo I's are only possible if each has his or her own unquestioned turf or field of expertise. The alternative is constant conflict, making a relaxed and rewarding home life difficult or impossible for the spouses and their children. In family matchups, especially between parents and children, great understanding will have to be shown on both sides to avoid power struggles, which, however, are usually inevitable. Siblings may be rivals in their younger years but can grow closer as they mature into adulthood. Working relationships tend to be more successful or at least more comfortable at the executive level, where colleagues in different areas of specialty can complement each other. The most exciting and even productive relationships, however, may well be intense rivalries, which bring out both the best and the worst in Cancer II's and Leo I's, whether they work for the same organization or for competitors.

ADVICE: *Get the best out of your interactions. Play fair. Try to transcend differences. Avoid pettiness and minor irritations. Keep the big picture in mind.*

JOHN HUSTON (8/5/06)
ANJELICA HUSTON (7/8/51)

Daughter of pugnacious director John, Anjelica was raised in obscurity in Ireland. In 1969, at 17, she played in one of her father's lesser-known films. She rose to prominence in '85 in John's dark comedy *Prizzi's Honor*, for which she won the Oscar as best supporting actress. *Also:* **Janet Leigh & Norma Shearer** (actresses; Shearer discovered Leigh).

July 3–10
THE WEEK OF THE UNCONVENTIONAL
CANCER II

August 3–10
THE WEEK OF BALANCED STRENGTH
LEO II

Established Oppositions

This relationship has two distinct sides, and its energies oscillate between them—between light and dark, outer and inner, intuition and emotion. Little attempt is made to tone down contrasts or to arrive at compromise or synthesis. Understanding the wide swings imposed by the combination's pendulumlike nature, and learning to go with their flow, will go far toward creating peace here. Cancer II's will have an easier time of it; unconventional in nature, they may even enjoy the relationship's variety. Leo III's, on the other hand, have a strong need for balance. They will tense up in this combination, resisting its natural viability, and creating the potential for conflict.

Cancer II–Leo II love affairs are often romantic, involving deep emotional interaction and exciting and often risky activities, whether in career areas or out in the wild. Cancer II's feel most comfortable at home, but yearn for projects that will sweep them off their feet or whisk them away on a magic carpet. Leo II's may be just the opposite, spending their time breaking down barriers and reaching new heights of achievement but all the while dreaming of a warm fire and a comfortable bed. An ideal arrangement for these two would be to spend long periods first at home and then elsewhere, perhaps passing one part of the year in their own city or country and another part away or abroad. The more activities they can share, the better: both love affairs and marriages tend to be most successful when the partners are also engaged in a shared career endeavor. Lovers who also work together may not consider marriage a necessary step.

Cancer II–Leo II siblings will often complement each other productively, but more outside the family setting than within it. The relationship's swings and oscillations can generate domestic instability, but friends and schoolmates are more likely to bring excitement and variety of mood. Co-workers in this combination can generate upset in the workplace by keeping others from concentrating, but socially they may be the life of the party.

ADVICE: *Find your real needs and satisfy them. Don't settle for less than the best for yourself. Unify some of the different areas in your life. Let go and let it flow.*

July 3–10
THE WEEK OF THE UNCONVENTIONAL
CANCER II

August 11–18
THE WEEK OF LEADERSHIP
LEO III

Special Rapport

This unusual and powerful combination can achieve prominence through its outstanding mental talents. Its focus is a thoughtful approach capable of quickly assessing a problem at its roots and taking steps to solve it. The leadership qualities of Leo III's often coalesce with the uncanny ability of Cancer II's to anticipate their wishes, as well as problems or trends in the world at large. In this way these two can make an outstanding combination in many areas of achievement. The relationship reminds one a bit of the special rapport that is possible between a film or stage director (the Leo III) and an actor or actress (the Cancer II).

Lovers in this combination sometimes mirror and duplicate each other's moods, but the relationship offers them the psychological insight they need to figure out what is going on. Their comprehension is often immediate—they are capable of an almost instant awareness of the consequences of their actions and behavior together. This heightened consciousness allows for an interesting blend of physical and mental communication, and also obviates somewhat the need for bothersome discussions afterward. Marriages here can work out well, but care must be taken not to go too far in the mental direction, leaving important physical and emotional needs unmet.

Friends in this combination must beware of being too materialistic and of overvaluing logic at the expense of more spiritual considerations. Keeping in touch with the feelings the duo share is vitally important in sustaining such friendships. In family settings and at work, Leo III parents and bosses will find themselves easily understood and appreciated by Cancer II children and employees. The fact that Cancer II's are willing to work along with them and to match them in dedication and application means a great deal to them. They are also able to unburden themselves to these Cancer II's without fear of ridicule or rejection. In fact, the real power behind the regal Leo III throne may be an unusual and unassuming Cancer II.

ADVICE: *Don't ignore emotional and spiritual considerations. Try not to get too tied up in your thoughts. Promote equality. Keep in touch with others.*

SAM GOLDWYN (8/17/1882)
LOUIS B. MAYER (7/4/1885)

Despite the implicit partnership in "Metro-Goldwyn-Mayer," Goldwyn and Mayer had a hostile relationship. When MGM was formed in 1922, Goldwyn was edged out of the corporation, not part of the deal. He vowed never to have partners again—and never did.

***Also:* Steve Lawrence & Eydie Gormé** (married; singers); **Emp. Maximilian** [Mexico] **& Emp. Francis Joseph** [Austria] (brothers).

July 3–10
THE WEEK OF THE UNCONVENTIONAL
CANCER II

August 19–25
THE CUSP OF EXPOSURE
LEO-VIRGO CUSP

Finding the Connection

This combination has a crying need for a firm basis, whether ideological, financial or emotional, on which to ground itself. In times of need, these partners are likely to turn to their relationship to give them stability. The focus here often lies in hidden realms that have little meaning to anyone but the partners themselves. Cancer II's are magnetically drawn to unusual people, and the emotional world of Leo-Virgos may become an important point of interest for them. Leo-Virgos may likewise enjoy having the power to conceal or reveal as little or as much to their Cancer II mates as they wish. In all of this, however, the relationship must establish a solid connection between these psychological and personal explorations and the kind of basis described above.

Cancer II–Leo-Virgo lovers, friends and spouses may be able to unify and give structure to their lives through a common career, business, religion or spiritual path. This usually requires, however, that they spend most of their time together, and presupposes that they get along well enough to do so. Career or social activities will be grounding but will also benefit from the tremendous inner resources and strengths into which this combination can tap. Personal irritations may well arise here, and if so, it is important that anger and resentment as well as love and kindness be expressed without fear of rejection or censure. Guilt may be a big item between these two, particularly given the kind of secretiveness that the relationship fosters.

Cancer II and Leo-Virgo family members may experience conflict over living space, possessions and chores, which they may perceive as unfairly divided. Deep jealousies can injure closeness and arouse aggressiveness or betrayal. If such conflicts are to be resolved and laid to rest as children in this combination grow up, it will be crucial for them to find a common ideology or belief system.

ADVICE: *Build close bonds, but be able to find time away from each other as well. Develop common beliefs and projects. Beware of competition for the affections of others.*

KEVIN BACON (7/8/58)
KYRA SEDGWICK (8/19/65)

Actor Bacon has played many fine film roles since the 70s, including *Footloose* (1984) and *Murder in the First* (1995). He is married to Sedgwick, a stage, tv and screen actress best known for her roles in *Born on the Fourth of July* (1989) and *Something to Talk About* (1995). She produced his HBO directorial debut *Losing Chase* (1996).

GUSTAV MAHLER (7/7/1860)
ALMA SCHINDLER (8/31/1879)

In 1902, composer Mahler married Schindler, a talented musician herself, who moved in Vienna's artistic circles. Mahler's self-centered demands put great strain on Schindler, who, despite her emotional pain, stayed with him until his death in 1911.
Also: Ringo Starr & Barbara Bach (married; Beatle/actress); **Fred Gwynne & Yvonne DeCarlo** (co-stars, *The Munsters*).

July 3–10
THE WEEK OF THE UNCONVENTIONAL
CANCER II

August 26–September 2
THE WEEK OF SYSTEM BUILDERS
VIRGO I

Preoccupation with the Bizarre

This combination promotes eccentricity, and while both of its partners are normally very hard-working, together they occupy themselves mainly in the pursuit of pleasure and ease. Virgo I's can busily focus their attention on Cancer II's, perhaps even trying to construct a psychological system to define or contain their more unusual side. But the relationship promotes unconventionality, and the Cancer II is apt to slip out of the Virgo I's grasp. And the harder the Virgo I chases the Cancer II, the more bizarre his or her own behavior will begin to seem. The process can become addictive, and the couple may soon want nothing more than the freedom to pursue it.

Hiding from a third party, or from society's watchful eye, can become obsessive in Cancer II–Virgo I matchups, using up much too much energy. Love affairs and friendships do best when out in the open, then. Healthy affairs tend to evolve naturally toward temporary and then permanent living situations, and perhaps finally into marriage. The comfort and security afforded by a shared domestic space is one of the relationship's cornerstones; here the couple can indulge their preoccupation with the bizarre. They will naturally want to work together to enhance such a space, making it more aesthetically beautiful as well as more functional. The nurturing and service-oriented side of the relationship suggests having or adopting children, but parents in this combination must be careful to leave enough quality time for each other, and for themselves.

Work relationships are not recommended here, since they are seldom hard-driving enough to achieve success, and are likely to break with company policy. The emphasis is too often on relaxation and the kind of intimacy that can only be found after hours. Family matchups, especially between parents and children, can be respectful and affectionate, but sometimes also foster dependency and are emotionally debilitating. Encouraging independence and breaking with claiming attitudes may emerge as the challenges to be met if these two are to establish mature bonds later in life.

ADVICE: *Avoid secretiveness. Pay attention to how others see you. Beware of addictions.*

RICHARD ALDINGTON (7/8/1892)
HILDA DOOLITTLE (9/10/1886)

Doolittle, better known as "H.D.," married Aldington in 1911 in his native England. Both were poets of the Imagist movement who went on to write distinguished novels. He also wrote criticism and biographies; she wrote a tribute to Freud and an autobiography.
Also: Jean Cocteau & Elsa Schiaparelli (friends; artist/fashion designer); **Candy Barr & Mickey Cohen** (affair; stripper/gangster).

July 3–10
THE WEEK OF THE UNCONVENTIONAL
CANCER II

September 3–10
THE WEEK OF THE ENIGMA
VIRGO II

Finding Comfort

A surprisingly strong and balanced relationship can emerge from this matchup, which may focus on rejecting the judgmental attitudes of society and building a self-confident and constructive outlook. Cancer II's and Virgo II's could well find comfort in each other, for each will be sensitive to the extent to which the other has been misunderstood by the world. Some pairs in this combination may in fact adopt a vigorously defiant stance toward outsiders, and even in cases of a quieter and more humble posture, the partners will probably be strongly aware of what they are doing and will exert a determined effort to prove themselves, both personally and professionally.

The world is likely to see little of most Cancer II–Virgo II love affairs and friendships; they have a way of turning their backs on society, perhaps somewhat contemptuously. Past experience may have shown one or both partners how little the world can be trusted, so that they tend to put all of their social eggs in one basket, restricting their circle to a very few friends or even none at all. At least at first, this may enhance their relationship's chances of survival, but building a relationship on bitterness and disillusionment is a risky business, and once these two have formed a solid bond, they should begin, as a relationship, to open up to the world and create new ties. In the event of a breakup, both partners are likely to be more whole and healthy personalities than they were before.

Work and marital relationships are not so highly favored here: acknowledging the authority of a company, or, through the marriage contract, of society, is rarely to this relationship's taste. Even so, building their own entrepreneurial enterprise, with concrete goals and aimed at a specific target group, is something these two could handle. Cancer II–Virgo II sibling or parent-child relationships are unlikely to attract much attention within the family structure, yet are generally protected and understood there, and may wind up giving their stamp to the group itself.

ADVICE: *Don't try to build on negative feelings. Forgive and forget. Come to peace with your past. Fight antisocial tendencies. Make new friends.*

July 3–10

THE WEEK OF THE UNCONVENTIONAL
CANCER II

September 11–18

THE WEEK OF THE LITERALIST
VIRGO III

Learning Experience

Developing an open and relaxed attitude will be a learning experience for both of these partners, and is the key to their relationship's success. Virgo III's are unlikely to approve of Cancer II attitudes, but can come to accept them—an important step. Cancer II's will generally understand Virgo III's even when they don't agree with them, and will be content to let their ideas go without too much argument if afforded the same courtesy. But the judgmental side of Virgo III's is brought out here, and unconventional Cancer II's may find themselves accused, convicted and sentenced before they know they're on trial.

Love affairs and marriages are not recommended here without a considerable amount of tolerance. To start with, these two are rarely much attracted to each other. Should they be thrown together for any of a host of reasons, they will have to decide whether to make the best of it or just quit. Long-suffering attitudes are unlikely to produce good results. Sometimes both partners are better off just letting go.

Friendships are more apt to be productive, particularly when weighted in the direction of companionship in a particular area, perhaps sports or a hobby. But family and work matchups will try both partners' patience to the limit, especially where Virgo III is the parent or boss. Cancer II's are likely to feel misunderstood and unappreciated in this kind of relationship, Virgo II's unheeded and ignored. A big first step toward acceptance would be for the partners to see such situations as setups that little can be done about, and to work to make things more pleasant.

There are many partners in life who have not rushed to pick each other out. Those who believe in fate, predestination or reincarnation have ready answers for the existence of such couples, but however these relationships began, acceptance is usually the key to their endurance. By promoting positive thinking and constructive approaches, lessening irritations and disabling the mechanisms that trigger upset, this relationship could work as a training ground to make its partners more whole and mature as individuals.

ADVICE: *Life is a learning experience. Accept the inevitable. Take positive steps to improve the situation. Change your attitudes. Accept when possible.*

GRETA GARBO (9/18/05)
JOHN GILBERT (7/10/1897)

Gilbert and Garbo teamed up in the late 20s in 3 scorching screen romances. After each scene the smitten actor would rush to her dressing room. MGM publicized their romance with ads like "Garbo and Gilbert in *Love*" (the movie name). But Garbo tired of the impetuous Gilbert and ended their tryst, later totally denying the affair. *Also:* **George Sanders & Tom Conway** (brothers; actors).

July 3–10

THE WEEK OF THE UNCONVENTIONAL
CANCER II

September 19–24

THE CUSP OF BEAUTY
VIRGO-LIBRA CUSP

Taking Turns

Both of these partners have leadership qualities on which their relationship has a paradoxical effect. It may stimulate their heroicism, forcing them to try to work out a harmonious arrangement through which these drives can be recognized—by alternating the lead role on successive projects, for example. Power struggles would be the unwanted scenarios here. A more common problem, however, is the exact reverse: each partner is reluctant to take over command from the other. In this case the relationship is likely to drift until it gets an injection of willpower. These issues should be discussed and an effective plan worked out to forestall such indecision and breakdown. These two can achieve much if they apply their relationship to a worthy cause.

Cancer II–Virgo-Libra romantic relationships are quite rewarding. Virgo-Libras may find Cancer II's attractive and above all interesting, and Cancer II's will be flattered by their attention. Should these two engage in aesthetic pursuits together, Cancer II's will likely contribute a love of the bizarre and out-of-the-way to the couple's tastes, widening the horizons of more classically oriented Virgo-Libras. Often the relationship will open up a whole new world of beauty by acknowledging the aesthetic value of objects that both partners previously thought ugly or uninteresting.

Marriages in this combination will be a strain, since Virgo-Libras usually demand more social contact and Cancer II's less. Their contrasting attitudes can help Virgo-Libras to deepen their emotional self-awareness and Cancer II's the quality of their human interactions, but many compromises will have to be worked out along the way. Friendships will suffer from similar polarities, but again compromise is possible.

Siblings and co-workers in this combination will benefit from alternating the leadership role and promoting equality. All signs of permanent dominance and control on the part of either personality should be nipped in the bud, and a solution worked out to both partners' satisfaction.

ADVICE: *Take turns assuming command. Avoid dictatorial attitudes. Promote equality. Give direction to avoid drift. Widen aesthetic horizons.*

BURT WARD (7/6/46)
ADAM WEST (9/19/28)

Ward and West played Robin and Batman, respectively, on tv's *Batman* series (1966–68). Together, the Dynamic Duo helped the inept police force keep Gotham City's streets safe. Ward and West gave their roles a tongue-in-cheek campiness, in time gathering a considerable cult following. *Also:* **Gina Lollobrigida & Sophia Loren** (rival Italian sexpots).

STRENGTHS: **SENSITIVE, EMPATHIC, SPIRITUAL**

WEAKNESSES: **JUDGMENTAL, DOGMATIC, CODEPENDENT**

BEST: **MARRIAGE**

WORST: **WORK**

WILLIAM PALEY (9/28/01)
BABE PALEY (7/5/15)

William rose from his family's cigar business to create CBS. He built a small network of radio stations into a powerful force in tv entertainment programming for a mass audience. He was married to Barbara "Babe" Cushing, a socialite and great beauty who was regularly on the "best-dressed" lists.

July 3–10
THE WEEK OF THE UNCONVENTIONAL
CANCER II

September 25–October 2
THE WEEK OF THE PERFECTIONIST
LIBRA I

A Gossamer Fabric

As long as these two respect each other's space and refrain from judging each other, they can reach new heights of ethereal, ecstatic or spiritual experience together. Sensitivity and acceptance are enhanced here, and both partners could find themselves fully appreciated. But Libra I's tend to appreciate the matchup only for what they can gain from it. They are not always fully aware of what they have here, and fail to realize that critical, demanding and condemning attitudes can easily rend this vulnerable relationship's gossamer fabric.

Love, marriage and friendship can all represent evolutionary stages in the development of this relationship, or, at the highest level of the matchup, may even be combined in one. High ideals and challenging ideologies appeal to this pair, who are often consciously engaged in self-actualizing experiences either together or separately. New-age techniques, workshops and reading may be of special interest here. The ideas gleaned from such activities can be put into practice in the kitchen, work areas and sleeping quarters. Care must be taken that new ideas do not become rigid dogma, inhibiting the healthful impulses they are meant to foster.

Family members in this combination, especially parent-child and sibling pairs, are likely to be oversensitive to each other, certainly empathic and perhaps even telepathic. They will repeatedly have to redraw ego boundaries between them to distinguish their individual wants and needs. Although closeness in a relationship is generally a plus, in this particular one the partners risk losing their own personalities, and drowning as individual selves. At work, Cancer II–Libra I colleagues and co-workers may be unable to sustain the objectivity they will need if they are to fulfill their obligations to the organization that has hired them. Great control must be exerted to prevent small frictions and irritations from getting out of hand. Cancer II–Libra I partners in all walks of life will benefit from their great sensitivity to each other only if they give this attunement a positive spin.

ADVICE: *Be aware of benefits. Treat others with respect. Don't take anything for granted. Maintain boundaries. Strive for objectivity. Limit criticism.*

STRENGTHS: **SOCIALLY ADEPT, SENSUAL, HARBORING**

WEAKNESSES: **NONSHARING, DIFFICULT, MISCOMMUNICATING**

BEST: **COMPANIONSHIP**

WORST: **LOVE**

NIKOLA TESLA (7/9/1856)
GEORGE WESTINGHOUSE (10/6/1846)

Tesla was the inventor of the alternating-current (AC) motor. Westinghouse purchased the rights from Tesla and made it the basis for all Westinghouse products. In essence, this deal brought about the use of alternating current as the standard in American appliances.
Also: **P.T. Barnum & Jenny Lind** (promotor/"Swedish Nightingale").

July 3–10
THE WEEK OF THE UNCONVENTIONAL
CANCER II

October 3–10
THE WEEK OF SOCIETY
LIBRA II

A Respite from Society

The primary concern in this relationship is the degree to which it is ready to reveal itself to the outside world. The partners are preoccupied with how to relate more meaningfully, not only in social situations but to each other. At root here is a certain mistrust: in their own unique ways, each person has a pretty good understanding of human beings, and as a pair they don't much like exposing themselves to public scrutiny. In fact, they may not like other people much at all, viewing even the simplest invitation with suspicion. They really see their relationship as a retreat from the world.

In love and marriage, this couple's physicality is a heavy mixture of passion and sensuality, areas in which neither partner is entirely comfortable. The closer their relationship is to the platonic sphere of friendship, the more comfortable they may feel. Physical demands can easily be replaced here by more easygoing emotions and a happy-go-lucky feel. Since Cancer II and Libra II lie square to each other in the zodiac (90° apart), conventional astrology predicts a difficult matchup between them, but it is not beyond them to put these tensions to work in forwarding shared causes.

Companionships and undemanding acquaintanceships are perhaps the most realistic possibilities for these two. The social demands of these kinds of relationship will be easier for them to meet, and no blame or guilt need surface should they spend a long time apart. A more distant friendship will also be a safety valve when social demands elsewhere are heavy and the partners need an entertaining and nonjudgmental retreat from the world. In the family and at work, on the other hand, siblings and co-workers in this combination may find themselves forced together daily whether they like it or not, and they will often have to share the same living or work area. Conflicts will probably result, but may ultimately lead to an agreement on separation of duties, use of common space and even what topics are taboo. In this way the pair may be able to tolerate each other.

ADVICE: *Lessen demands. Leave each other as free as possible. Do what you have to in order to lower stress. Find creative solutions. Live and let live.*

July 3–10

THE WEEK OF THE UNCONVENTIONAL
CANCER II

October 11–18

THE WEEK OF THEATER
LIBRA III

An Outrageous Pose

RELATIONSHIPS

STRENGTHS: **HILARIOUS, UNATTACHED, SATIRICAL**

WEAKNESSES: **DISTRACTING, RESENTED, SUPERFICIAL**

BEST: **FRIENDSHIP**

WORST: **FAMILY**

Attuned to a common wavelength, these two make an excellent team in professional and social situations. Their relationship is able to change, chameleonlike and practically at will, assuming ever new shapes and orientations to fit its environment. Other people will be baffled at the ease with the relationship goes through these changes. In the end, too, they may despair over discovering the "real" Cancer II–Libra III pair behind the mask.

Spirit rather than matter is usually given the higher value in love affairs and marriages between these two. The partners will certainly enjoy food, sex and entertainment together well enough, but these appetites are usually stepping stones to more transcendental pursuits. This can be seen in their general refusal to be tied down or heavily dependent on any physical area—they prefer to stay free to explore and above all to play. Comedy, irony, satire and sarcasm come easily to this pair, who can be mercilessly and even destructively funny about individuals or couples who seem to them to have an inflexible or pretentious quality. Direct spiritual involvement is possible here, but a new-age orientation, featuring colorful, far-out and exciting activities, is more usual.

Friendships tend to the superficial but are great fun. These two will often strike an outrageous pose simply to push more conventional people's buttons, a trick they can usually manage in uproarious fashion. Their humor may also operate more subtly, however, sometimes being appreciated only by the partners themselves.

Role-playing and freedom-loving, the Cancer II–Libra III relationship does not always endear itself to bosses (in the case of co-workers) or parents (in the case of siblings). At work, these two can arouse hostility over their refusal to take the job seriously; at home, the same kind of levity may manifest as an avoidance of daily chores that other family members will consider irresponsible. Although often appreciated, Cancer II's and Libra III's will have to struggle if they are to win the respect of others.

ADVICE: *Take things a bit more seriously sometimes. By showing respect you gain respect from others. Dig a bit deeper. Consider stronger commitment.*

JERRY SIEGEL (10/17/14)
JOE SHUSTER (7/10/14)

Shuster and Siegel, originally teenage friends, conceived the comic book character Superman in 1933 and 5 years later sold the rights for $130 to their employer, National Periodicals. When *Superman* comics became a great commercial success, they received almost nothing. Siegel spent most of his life suing National. Shuster went into permanent seclusion.

July 3–10

THE WEEK OF THE UNCONVENTIONAL
CANCER II

October 19–25

THE CUSP OF DRAMA & CRITICISM
LIBRA-SCORPIO CUSP

Setting Up Schedules

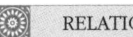

RELATIONSHIPS

STRENGTHS: **ECSTATIC, APPRECIATIVE, PLEASURABLE**

WEAKNESSES: **OBSESSIONAL, FRUSTRATING, FEARFUL**

BEST: **MARRIAGE**

WORST: **LOVE**

This emotionally complex combination can produce a mix of pleasure and pain. If the relationship is to grow, a structure will have to be agreed upon enforcing objectivity, individual expression, suspension of judgmental attitudes and above all an analytical insight capable of detecting and fending off hurtful remarks. Sensitive Cancer II's have a vulnerability to criticism that could allow them to be dominated by this partner: Libra-Scorpios pull no punches, and injured Cancer II feelings might become habitual. Cancer II's, too, have a knack for ferreting out a person's weak spot, and will use it when under attack. Both partners have a tendency to obsess, a habit that could become a dangerously pleasurable connection for them.

Love affairs here can go deep—so deep that there is a danger of a dependency on the relationship's emotional highs and ecstatic sexual experiences. The demand for increasing intensity and frequency of these experiences could stretch both partners' delicate nervous systems to the point of crash. Breakdowns induced by rejection, jealousy or fear of abandonment are ugly scenarios; schedules set up to moderate emotional contact can greatly reduce their likelihood. Such structures sometimes come more easily in marriage, which imposes a lot of objective daily routines that can have the effect of creating a sense of order and regulating feelings. The danger also exists, however, that a marriage will ultimately develop a rigid structure that will suppress deep feelings and heighten frustrations. In friendships, Libra-Scorpios will rarely reject Cancer II idiosyncrasies, making this unconventional partner feel appreciated. They may, on the other hand, be too free with their advice sometimes, which can have the effect of making Cancer II's either keep their distance or else become overly dependent on Libra-Scorpios for direction. The built-in structure of most jobs often allows co-workers in this combination the objectivity needed for a successful relationship. In the family, however, Cancer II–Libra-Scorpio relatives may feel unable to fit into the existing group structure. If so, a common reaction is to subvert parental or other authority with openly rebellious attitudes.

ADVICE: *Seek moderation. Provide a structure in which feelings can be expressed. Suspend judgments. Limit criticism. Promote individuality.*

JOHNNY CARSON (10/23/25)
DOC SEVERINSEN (7/7/27)

In 1967 trumpeter Severinsen joined Carson's *Tonight Show* as bandleader. His outlandish stage clothing became his trademark, inspiring many funny moments in Carson's monologues over the next 25 years. They retired from the show together in '92. **Also: Nancy Davis Reagan & Patti Ann Davis** (mother/daughter); **Jamie Wyeth & N.C. Wyeth** (grandson/grandfather; artists).

STRENGTHS: INTIMATE, EXCITING, POWERFUL

WEAKNESSES: DESTRUCTIVE, FEARFUL, SUFFERING

BEST: WORK

WORST: LOVE

FRANÇOIS MITTERRAND (10/26/16)
GEORGES POMPIDOU (7/5/11)

Pompidou was France's premier (1962–68) and president (1969–74) of the Fifth Republic. A strong supporter of DeGaulle's independent foreign policy, Pompidou also focused on domestic problems. When Mitterrand took over the presidency in '81, he turned many of Pompidou's policies around, leaning away from Gaullist conservatism.

July 3–10

THE WEEK OF THE UNCONVENTIONAL
CANCER II

October 26–November 2

THE WEEK OF INTENSITY
SCORPIO I

A Subterranean Plan

This relationship is likely to be highly secretive, virtually subterranean in its refusal to allow its goings-on to see the light of day. To carry through its covert plans without mishap, its partners must be dedicated, consistent and adept at deception. How unfortunate for the third party who is kept in the dark! Yet the thrill of an illicit or forbidden action is just too great to resist here. And hurting someone else is usually not part of the intention—in fact it is often either the Cancer II or the Scorpio I who suffers most in the end.

Love triangles are the classic scenarios here. Many subtle variations on this theme can play themselves out: usually the third party moves from being friends with both the Cancer II and the Scorpio I to being the lover of one and remaining a friend or becoming a rival to the other. In this case the relationship will center around the member of the triangle who is involved in two intimate relationships, often both sexual ones, at the same time.

Cancer II's and Scorpio I's can have happy marriages, but must beware of spending too much time alone together. Sharing friendships that do not carry the temptation or peril of ever new love triangles, but function simply and purely as friendships, will add stability. Both spouses tend to be good parents, providing their children with a good mix of nurture and inspiration, but they must take care that the child is not permitted to play one parent off against the other.

As friends or siblings, Cancer II–Scorpio I duos are good at keeping secrets and at concealing their true intentions from the watchful eyes of parents, teachers and other authority figures. Borderline or overtly illegal activities may exert a special attraction to them, and although money is often involved, it is primarily danger and power that supply the rush. Cancer II and Scorpio I can make excellent and financially successful business partners.

ADVICE: *Think a bit more about what you are doing. You may be playing with fire. Grow up a bit in your attitudes. Are you asking to get hurt?*

STRENGTHS: COMPELLING, MAGICAL, MYSTERIOUS

WEAKNESSES: DISSOLVING, OVERDEPENDENT, LOST

BEST: LOVE

WORST: PARENT-CHILD

KURT VONNEGUT, JR. (11/11/22)
GERALDO RIVERA (7/4/43)

Broadcast journalist Rivera became the son-in-law of novelist Vonnegut when he married the writer's daughter, Edith Bucket Vonnegut. Vonnegut expressed his disenchantment with modern society in his works. Ironically, Rivera hosts shows that often capitalize on society's losers. *Also:* **Eunice Kennedy & Sargent Shriver** (married; JFK's sister/first Peace Corps director).

July 3–10

THE WEEK OF THE UNCONVENTIONAL
CANCER II

November 3–11

THE WEEK OF DEPTH
SCORPIO II

Getting Lost

This is a mysterious one—the Cancer II–Scorpio II relationship is hard to fathom. These personalities are trine to each other in the zodiac (120° apart), and astrology predicts an easygoing and pleasurable relationship between them. Their involvement goes far beyond simple pleasure, however, being enigmatic even to the partners themselves. A deep magnetic pull often draws these two together, and once their relationship is formed it may be difficult to modify or to break apart. Feelings intertwine subtly and compellingly to create bonds of loyalty but also of dependency. The partners often mirror and act out each other's feelings without being aware of the process. Egos can dissolve here, then, boundaries can blur and individuality can fade.

Love affairs tend to be passionate and binding. The partners may not realize it, but they have often staked a claim to one another, and with that claim have taken on a huge responsibility. The mysteries of sex, love and relationships in general unfold here like an enchanted panorama that has these lovers under its spell. Even when trying for an analytic objectivity that would explain the process and plumb the depths of the mystery, the partners pull back from the shock of recognition, falling instead into the unconscious stream of forgetfulness and abandon. Marriage may suggest a more objective orientation, but getting lost together remains a constant activity here. Friendships and family and working relationships have a similar magnetism, but often replace the total involvement of love and marriage in this combination with a healthier empathy. (An exception is parent-child relationships, which are highly claiming.) Friends, siblings and co-workers maintain a certain objectivity and individuality, while still being closely attuned to each other's feelings. There is more awareness here; the relationship's mystery is better understood and to an extent consciously explored. Years will be required for this to take place, but the wonder never completely fades, nor is the enigmatic nature of the relationship ever fully exhausted. To the end, long periods of quite ordinary daily interaction are dotted with magical moments, unforgettable in their charm and illumination.

ADVICE: *Understanding isn't always possible. Love asks few questions and gives even fewer answers. Surrender is sometimes required.*

July 3–10

THE WEEK OF THE UNCONVENTIONAL
CANCER II

November 12–18

THE WEEK OF CHARM
SCORPIO III

STRENGTHS: **LOVING, MEDITATIVE, UPLIFTING**

WEAKNESSES: **LAZY, UNREALISTIC, WEAK**

BEST: **LOVE**

WORST: **WORK**

NANCY REAGAN (7/6/21)
HOWARD BAKER (11/15/25)

Rapt Attention

The delicious charm of forgetfulness periodically sweeps over this pair, and in its wake follow vividly beautiful dreams and visions. The relationship has a poetic and deeply spiritual quality. Peaceful meditation plays an important role; Cancer II–Scorpio III partners are capable of a connection that will provide peace and rest to both. No matter how stressful, mundane or prosaic the day has been, these two can seek each other out and find themselves at once in their own wonderful space together. These feelings are difficult to share directly with others, but the relationship has an energy that can prove infectious and uplifting to those around it. It exerts such a pull on its partners that breaking free may be extremely difficult.

Love affairs proceed from the physical to the metaphysical, using the sexual act to transport partners to other worlds and higher planes of experience. Lovemaking is a kind of cosmic dance, evocative and high, a true merging of spirit. These partners can also go for long periods without physical contact, touching only with a look or a kind word. Usually none of this magic will be at all apparent to the public eye; the children of such a couple, whether born in or out of wedlock, may even look on their parents with some amusement as sillies, hippies or freaks. Rarely, however, will they doubt their parents' abiding love for each other.

Cancer II–Scorpio III work relationships are not especially recommended, since these two seldom show much desire to win out over others and to succeed in the rough-and-tumble of the commercial sector. Partnerships between friends in this combination, however, can be highly successful in evoking shared dreams and visions in such a way that they strike a responsive chord in other people; despite the pair's seeming lack of aggression, financial success is quite possible here. Siblings and friends are likely to spend many quiet hours together in rapt attention, attuned to each other's thoughts and feelings. Parent-child pairs too can have a quality of friendship, creating unusually close, trusting and understanding bonds.

Influential First Lady Reagan pressed to get Baker appointed White House chief of staff during her husband's presidency in the 80s. She much preferred the agreeable Tennessee senator over the current chief of staff, Donald Regan, whom she detested and called a "leech."

ADVICE: *Spur yourself on to greater achievement. Others may be counting on you. Don't forget responsibilities. Keep awake to the needs of the moment.*

July 3–10

THE WEEK OF THE UNCONVENTIONAL
CANCER II

November 19–24

THE CUSP OF REVOLUTION
SCORPIO-SAGITTARIUS CUSP

STRENGTHS: **APPRECIATIVE, COMMERCIAL, FACTUAL**

WEAKNESSES: **VAGUE, CONTROLLING, EXPLOITATIVE**

BEST: **MARRIAGE**

WORST: **FAMILY**

JAMIE LEE CURTIS (11/22/58)
JANET LEIGH (7/6/27)

Current Realities

This relationship is likely to emphasize factual truth and dealing with reality. Scorpio-Sagittarius realism is likely to ground Cancer II fantasy, giving it a base. It's not that Scorpio-Sagittarians have no imagination themselves, or that they don't appreciate the unique and highly individual approach of Cancer II's. But they know where their bread is buttered and rarely do anything to compromise their worldly position. Should they take an interest in a Cancer II, then, they may bring his or her vision far along the road of social acceptance and commercial success.

Romantic relationships between Scorpio-Sagittarians and Cancer II's should be kept quite separate from the pair's commercial dealings and career concerns. Both partners must feel that they are loved for who they are, not for their financial or professional value. Also, when Scorpio-Sagittarians get behind the career plans of Cancer II's as advisers or managers, their autocratic side is likely to emerge, and Cancer II's may feel as if they are being controlled by their powerful partner. Professional connections are less of a problem in marriage, and in fact may form an important basis for such a relationship. The trick is to keep the romantic spark alive, for should it dim, the Scorpio-Sagittarian is likely to be attracted elsewhere.

Scorpio-Sagittarians enjoy working with their friends, and may build a close and long-lived career connection with a Cancer II. If the two are in business together as equal partners, rather than working together on occasional projects, they must draw up firm legal agreements to forestall problems later on and to finalize what may be only vague intentions. A crucial point, and one on which the relationship can founder, will be the continued honesty and openness of friends in both their personal and their business dealings with each other.

In the family, and especially in parent-child combinations, the relationship emphasizes sticking literally to one's word. Both partners will hold the other to what they have said, and will generally resist later attempts to revise and compromise.

Curtis is the daughter of actress Leigh, who was married to Tony Curtis (1951–62). Growing up with glamorous Hollywood parents, Jamie Lee understandably pursued an acting career—starting in 1978 in horror films, working up to more impressive dramatic roles. Leigh, an ingenue in 40s and 50s films, later took on more serious roles. **Also: Georges Pompidou & Charles DeGaulle** (French political allies).

ADVICE: *Be more diplomatic. Learn the value of compromise. Even facts are debatable. Beware of domination and submission. Maintain trust.*

GEORGES POMPIDOU (7/5/11)
JACQUES CHIRAC (11/29/32)

Pompidou was France's premier (1962–68) and president (1969–74). A close associate of DeGaulle's, he followed Gaullist policies throughout his tenure. Chirac was the leader of the Gaullist party and prime minister in 1974–76 and 1986–88. Throughout his career, he has been politically aligned with Pompidou.

July 3–10
THE WEEK OF THE UNCONVENTIONAL
CANCER II

November 25–December 2
THE WEEK OF INDEPENDENCE
SAGITTARIUS I

Naturally Playful

The central theme of this combination is often a search for natural attitudes and renewal. In fact, the relationship itself can be very uplifting to its partners—a place they go to recharge their batteries, and a kind of retreat or haven from the outside world. These two will feel very much at home in nature, taking walks, hiking, canoeing or camping. Sagittarius I's are likely to be protective of their Cancer II partners and to try to protect them against a hostile world; Cancer II's, meanwhile, are capable of putting Sagittarius I's back in touch with their childlike self and with their deeper world of feeling. There are simultaneous dangers here, then, of overprotectiveness and of living in an unrealistic dream world.

Cancer II–Sagittarius I love affairs can be tender and sympathetic. Affection is expressed easily here, and is often considered as important as sex. Warmth and understanding are usually more the norm in this relationship than wrenching emotion. Cancer II's can lead their excitable Sagittarius I partners to a deeper understanding of sensuality, and can in turn be introduced to new heights of passion. But although Sagittarius I's may appreciate the Cancer II brand of love for a while, they may eventually grow tired of it, feel trapped or controlled, and seek to escape.

Marriages and friendships value renewal, innovation and play. Entertainment, both personally invented and commercially provided, is thought to be an essential element of daily life for this pair. Avoiding boring or repetitive routines, Sagittarius I and Cancer II spouses and friends are drawn to vivid, exciting and fun experiences, both within the four walls of their home (or homes) and out in the world of clubs and restaurants. The emphasis is more often on domestic entertainment, though, with friends, family and children taking part.

Work relationships are perfectly satisfactory but tend to lack ambition and may fail to light the spark that leads to great success. In the family sphere, Cancer II–Sagittarius I siblings will compete for parental attention yet in other respects are mutually supportive.

ADVICE: *Beware of being overprotective. Don't run from responsibility. Push yourself a bit to achieve more. "Childlike" should not mean "immature."*

CHET HUNTLEY (12/10/11)
DAVID BRINKLEY (7/10/20)

These newscaster-commentators teamed up in 1956 for *The Huntley-Brinkley Report* on CBS-TV. Huntley's reserve coupled with Brinkley's acid wit made their coverage of politics outstanding in tv journalism. The show ran for 25 years before Huntley retired in '71.

***Also:* Ken Olin & Patricia Wettig** (married; co-stars, *thirtysomething*);

Frida Kahlo & Diego Rivera (married; artists).

July 3–10
THE WEEK OF THE UNCONVENTIONAL
CANCER II

December 3–10
THE WEEK OF THE ORIGINATOR
SAGITTARIUS II

Normally Outrageous

These two very different types are likely to find a point of meeting or balance, albeit precarious, in the area of aesthetics: style, fashion, popular design or art. Whatever each one does individually, it is in their feelings, thoughts and concerns about beauty that their relationship will find its basis and common expression. Conventional astrology predicts some instability in this combination, due to its quincunx aspect (Cancer II and Sagittarius II lie 150° apart in the zodiac), and indeed it does have an unstable side; both these personalities are eccentric, a quality the relationship magnifies, generating a very idiosyncratic tone. Nevertheless, these two are quite capable of achieving harmony through their shared loves.

Love affairs between these two are one of a kind. Unique all over, they take their cue from their partners' more bizarre characteristics, and may shock the sensibilities of friends and family. This relationship promotes the outrageous to the category of a normal daily event. The partners themselves probably consider what they are doing quite natural, and may be amazed at the consternation they cause. A desire to hurt, or to shock for the sake of it, is rarely their motivating factor. Marriages, too, generally favor unusual tastes in domestic decor, dress and lifestyle in general. Visitors may find the Cancer II–Sagittarius II home scene offbeat and eclectic, but will often admit that within a welter of jarring styles there is a strange kind of beauty and harmony. This decor can be taken as symbolic of the relationship itself.

As friends, Cancer II's and Sagittarius II's share interests and often bizarre tastes, which they sometimes take pleasure in flaunting. Siblings in this combination are likewise often more than a conservative family setting can handle; in this kind of relationship there is no guarantee that the pair will get along at all, so that parents and other relatives often have to cope not just with a strange relationship but with two distinct "weirdos." Two such co-workers may similarly be more than most work situations will comfortably tolerate.

ADVICE: *Don't compromise your tastes, but be aware of other people. Why create more difficulties than necessary? Don't just react against the norm.*

July 3–10

THE WEEK OF THE UNCONVENTIONAL
CANCER II

December 11–18

THE WEEK OF THE TITAN
SAGITTARIUS III

A Parent to Truculence

This combination has a tremendous energy, which, like that of the growing child, is difficult to contain and sensibly guide. The relationship will usually stand or fall with its ability to parent its often recalcitrant and truculent partners, and to provide the wisdom, security and direction that they so desperately require. In their imaginative scope and vision, Cancer II's can be a good match for Sagittarius III's. This also means, however, that these two can support and egg each other on in plans that pass the point of practicality. Dashed hopes may be the result. The strain this puts on the relationship is often more than it can handle, and wise partners will learn to back off and bring their ideas back down to earth.

Hidden love affairs here will not remain secret for long—as a rule, their energies will spill over into other areas of life. These hot streams of emotional lava are likely to leave devastation in their trail, not only for the Cancer II–Sagittarius III couple but for family, friends and spouses as well. Marriages are not particularly recommended here, unless the relationship can succeed in establishing guidelines, principles or structures that will forestall emotional eruptions and guarantee children the security they need. Breakups here can be particularly bitter and hurtful.

These two often combine friendship and work. They are capable of generating and implementing powerful ideas, but should make use of financial managers or consultants to guarantee their economic stability. The success of their endeavors will ultimately depend on their ability to remain objective and keep themselves from overreacting to each other on a personal level. Should their business plans fall apart, an incredible effort will usually be required of both Cancer II's and Sagittarius III's to put the pieces of their friendship back together and continue as before. Family matchups, especially parent-child, feature frequent confrontations and differences of opinion. These pairs should try to find a common ground, perhaps in a shared social or intellectual interest or a shared pleasure in sports.

ADVICE: *Be more supportive. Avoid stressful confrontations. Engage in common pursuits, but stay objective. Don't let energies get out of control.*

RELATIONSHIPS

STRENGTHS: **IMAGINATIVE, ENERGETIC, VISIONARY**

WEAKNESSES: **EXPLOSIVE, CONFRONTATIONAL, BITTER**

BEST: **WORK**

WORST: **LOVE**

GERTRUDE LAWRENCE (7/4/1898)
NOEL COWARD (12/16/1899)

Sparkling actress Lawrence was made in heaven for Coward's witty drawing-room comedies. She starred most memorably in his Broadway productions of *Private Lives* (1930) and *Blithe Spirit* (1941). They were also personal friends. *Also:*

Franz Boas & Margaret Mead (teacher/student; anthropologists);

Nancy Reagan & Frank Sinatra (close friends; First Lady/singer).

July 3–10

THE WEEK OF THE UNCONVENTIONAL
CANCER II

December 19–25

THE CUSP OF PROPHECY
SAGITTARIUS-CAPRICORN CUSP

Great Expectations

Neither partner in this relationship is much interested in the superficial level of life. Both value digging deeper and finding greater meaning, even if this involves suffering. The relationship's strong perfectionist tendency makes great demands on its partners. Mistakes are not easily explained away, nor are excuses readily accepted. This severity can create tension and in fact can make effective action more difficult, since neither partner does well when uptight. Learning to relax and accept life as it comes will be an important lesson for these two to learn.

In love affairs these partners can have difficulty living up to their own high expectations. Active Cancer II imagination and deep Sagittarius-Capricorn feelings make a potent mix, but one that is difficult to understand clearly, and is therefore somewhat unrealistic. Both partners could build up a false picture of what their relationship is really about, perhaps seeing it as a solution to all their personal problems. Using the relationship as an escape usually only makes things more difficult and can lead to an unhealthy situation. Marriages, too, may be based on false premises, and on an assumption of a kind of perfection that can never be realized in actuality.

Although Cancer is a water sign and Sagittarius-Capricorn a mixture of fire and earth, this relationship is ruled by air, associated with thought. In friendships and family matchups this can signify worry, excessive rumination and ultimately living too much in one's own head. It will be important for these friends and relatives to find physical outlets for their energies, whether in sports, exercise or play.

Working relationships benefit but also suffer from perfectionist drives. Stress thresholds will have to be established and not exceeded if breakdowns are to be avoided. It should be possible to keep quality at an acceptable and in fact high level without the partners getting stressed out.

ADVICE: *Don't expect too much. Go with the flow. Escapes are only temporary. Face things as they are. Thinking can become destructive.*

RELATIONSHIPS

STRENGTHS: **PROFOUND, INVOLVED, QUALITY-ORIENTED**

WEAKNESSES: **STRESSED, EXPECTANT, DEMANDING**

BEST: **FAMILY**

WORST: **WORK**

NICKY HILTON (7/6/26)
CONRAD N. HILTON (12/25/1887)

Conrad, father of Nicky (Conrad Jr.), started from a single family hotel and expanded it into one of the world's largest hotel chains, amassing a personal fortune along the way. His son Nicky was a celebrity playboy, married briefly to Elizabeth Taylor in 1950.

JESSICA HAHN (7/7/59)
JIM BAKKER (1/2/40)

Televangelist Bakker (along with his wife Tammy Faye) founded the PTL tv network in 1974, reaching millions in 50 countries. In the wake of a protracted scandal involving sexual encounters with Hahn around '80, Bakker was forced to resign in '87. Hahn emerged from the fracas with her own tv talk show. *Also:* **Barry Goldwater, Jr. & Barry Goldwater** (son/father; politicians).

July 3–10

THE WEEK OF THE UNCONVENTIONAL
CANCER II

December 26–January 2

THE WEEK OF THE RULER
CAPRICORN I

Starring Together

This pairing can be quite unequal, sometimes resembling a contentious parent-child relationship with the Capricorn I the parent. Part of the problem is that the matchup is distinctly success-oriented, with each partner wanting the other to be a star—which only makes them the more critical of each other. Capricorn I's are likely to be condescending toward Cancer II's, who, after a period of enjoying being taken care of by their partner, will ultimately rebel against this disempowerment. The situation is sometimes complicated by the fact that Capricorn I's can project thwarted ambitions on their Cancer II mates or children and can push them to overachieve in a field for which they may not be suited. In the short term these struggles may prove debilitating to the partners' self-esteem. In the long run, however, they can work positively, making Cancer II's more self-confident. And if the Cancer I truly earns this partner's respect, the Capricorn I will in turn be forced to be more accepting and less controlling.

Love and marriage here can certainly involve power struggles, with Capricorn I's fighting for control, Cancer II's for integrity and individuality. Fortunately, the relationship is usually quite private, and its seclusion from other people saves its partners some of the embarrassment their arguments might cause them in public. Their freedom to work things out on their own helps make it possible for the couple to gain in power and stature. Quite often these relationships improve over time, particularly in terms of increased understanding.

Although Cancer is a water sign and Capricorn earth, the Cancer II–Capricorn I relationship is ruled by fire, associated with intuition. Friends and family members in this combination do best when they trust their hunches and first impressions, and worst when they chew things over unnecessarily or get emotional about them. Equality can more often be reached in friendships and sibling matchups than in love affairs and marriages. Should they work together, such family members and friends can star in projects where Capricorn I practical and financial abilities coalesce with Cancer II imagination and flair.

ADVICE: *Trust your intuition. Be aware of dominating attitudes. Neither submission nor rebellion is the answer. Promote respect.*

P.T. BARNUM (7/5/1810)
TOM THUMB (1/4/1838)

Barnum, consummate showman and publicist, made a fortune with midget Thumb, whom he discovered in 1840. Thumb, who was 40 inches tall, performed as a cigar-smoking gentleman-general for audiences in the US and abroad. They were solid friends through their association. *Also:* **Dr. Watson & Sherlock Holmes** (colleagues; fictional detectives).

July 3–10

THE WEEK OF THE UNCONVENTIONAL
CANCER II

January 3–9

THE WEEK OF DETERMINATION
CAPRICORN II

Expressing Solidarity

Social success is important in this relationship. Although relating to others is problematic for these two as individuals, together their strengths coalesce, and they become much more adept at interacting with the world. Eventually, in fact, they may be much sought after by others. Cancer II's and Capricorn II's often begin on the outside of a social or family group, and show little interest in a closer bond with it. Over time, however, a hunger for social contact asserts itself, and the couple may well find themselves hoping to play an important part or even to assume the leadership role. This desire usually has a consolidating effect on their relationship.

Cancer II and Capricorn II lie opposite each in other in the zodiac. Conventional astrology accordingly predicts conflicts and difficulties between them, and in love affairs this may indeed be true. In this kind of relationship they have a tendency to isolate themselves, which can lead them astray, for it is precisely when cut off from contact with family and friends that insoluble problems can arise between them. Cancer II's are creatures of feeling, and need a good deal of emotional interaction and support; Capricorn II's are tougher, and have less need for other people's approval. It is easy, then, for Cancer II's to feel ignored and Capricorn II's somewhat besieged by each other.

Marriage can work, presuming the attraction is there and the circumstances propitious. Having children and building family ties usually have healthy effects on the relationship and give both partners a chance to express their service-oriented side. Care must be taken, however, that the partners get to spend enough quality time with each other. Friendships and family matchups can benefit from increased social contact. Parent-child and sibling pairs who work as a team, in club activities, say, or at family gatherings, will express solidarity and also acquire a reputation for being able to be counted on in times of need. Cancer II–Capricorn II work relationships, especially as colleagues and co-workers, are likely to be strained on the personal level.

ADVICE: *Give others a chance. Bridge the gaps with those around you. Take part in celebrations. Offer a helping hand, but leave time for yourself.*

July 3–10

THE WEEK OF THE UNCONVENTIONAL
CANCER II

January 10–16

THE WEEK OF DOMINANCE
CAPRICORN III

Eccentric Side

This relationship is likely to be extroverted, unserious and involved in the lighter aspects of life. A love of theater, film, dance and sports is characteristic here, and the partners themselves have a flair for the theatrical. They need not strike this pose professionally—it can emerge within a social or family group, or with mutual friends. Solid Capricorn III's do have an eccentric side, which melds well with the sometimes bizarre tastes of Cancer II's, lending more than a bit of quirkiness to this combination.

After a day of hard work, Capricorn III's look forward to being with their Cancer II friends and lovers to relax and have fun. Beyond that, moreover, their relationship can open up a whole new life for both partners, allowing them to express their most outrageous and uninhibited impulses. Capricorn III responsibility often gets them labeled conservative or stick-in-the-mud. Getting tired of this, they might welcome a relationship with a Cancer II, in which they can show just how vivacious they can be. Love affairs here can be exciting and colorful. Should they evolve into marriage, Capricorn III steadfastness and Cancer II domestic instincts can be a strongly grounding influence.

These partners can liven up the workplace considerably, but must be careful not to let things get out of hand. The Capricorn III is usually the anchor that pulls the relationship back to reality, assuring that deadlines be met and the job gets done. In the family, parent-child interactions in this combination can be quite emotional—but their expressions of feeling are sometimes put on for effect, with theater taking the place of real emotion. Relatives will eventually tire of such displays and demand a more serious and less distracting approach to daily activities.

ADVICE: *Be aware of your effects on others. Don't lose track of where you are. Keep a few more things to yourself. Repeated effects get old.*

JAMES McNEILL WHISTLER (7/10/1834)
JOHN SINGER SARGENT (1/12/1856)

Whistler and Sargent, contemporary 19th-century American painters, settled in London, where their careers were established. Both were technical virtuosos. Sargent is noted for dashing, flattering portraits of social celebrities. Whistler, a printmaker, watercolorist and painter, is known for superb draftsmanship. **Also: Dorothy Kilgallen & Johnny Ray** (close friends; columnist/singer).

July 3–10

THE WEEK OF THE UNCONVENTIONAL
CANCER II

January 17–22

THE CUSP OF MYSTERY & IMAGINATION
CAPRICORN-AQUARIUS CUSP

Trailblazing Stance

This relationship is likely to play a stimulating and directing role in any group or organization, often assuming a trailblazing stance. Part of this pair's power is a unique view of their fellow humans and what motivates them. Their faith in people, and their ability to inspire them, can be truly potent forces.

Although Cancer is a water sign and Capricorn-Aquarius a mix of earth and air, their relationship is fire-ruled, suggesting in this case an active and initiating tendency. Cancer II's can be stimulated to greater activity here, while Capricorn-Aquarians are provided with a positive outlet for their considerable energies. Both partners have active imaginations and must be careful to keep their fantasy from running away with them. Cultivating practical attitudes to money, and particularly to financial planning and cash flow, are vital to their success. Work relationships of the entrepreneurial or executive sort are favored between them, and friends or family members can well go into business together.

Love affairs between these two are fiery and tend to be unstable. Cancer II's have a need for security that is seldom met in this combination, and if the affair is illicit or secret, they may feel taken advantage of or used. Generally the more faithful and steadfast of these two, they are likely to be the ones who suffer most. Power struggles are rare in this pair's romances, which only means that Capricorn-Aquarians usually take the dominant role. Should the couple marry, Capricorn-Aquarians may have a tendency to stray; since Cancer II's are unlikely to tolerate such behavior, wedlock is not particularly favored here.

Cancer II–Capricorn-Aquarius parent-child matchups are generally more propitious when Cancer II's are the parents. They have nurturing qualities that are especially well-suited to the active Capricorn-Aquarian child. Capricorn-Aquarians provide exciting role models for Cancer II children, but often lack the patience and time to give them the emotional input and understanding they require.

ADVICE: *Direct your energy well. Others depend on you. Don't get carried away by ego concerns. Scale back your ambition. Emulate sound financial models.*

PAUL CÉZANNE (1/19/1839)
CAMILLE PISSARRO (7/10/1830)

Painters Cézanne and Pissarro were part of the famous *Salon Des Refusés* in Paris—Impressionists revolting against the tyranny of the official Academy. The 2 spent significant time together (1872–74) painting landscapes. Cézanne, 9 years younger, became Pissarro's protégé, greatly influenced by the Impressionist's skills and theories—notably to lighten his palette and do away with heavy earth colors.

NELSON ROCKEFELLER (7/8/08)
JOHN D. ROCKEFELLER, JR. (1/29/1874)

Nelson was the son of John Jr., billionaire businessman and philanthropist. Born into a life of privilege, Nelson became an art collector and patron, but is best known as the longtime governor of NY State (1958–73). *Also:* **Faye Emerson & Skitch Henderson** (married; actress/bandleader); **Tom Cruise & Mimi Rogers** (married; actors).

July 3–10

THE WEEK OF THE UNCONVENTIONAL
CANCER II

January 23–30

THE WEEK OF GENIUS
AQUARIUS I

A Lust for Learning

Since this relationship places such a premium on intelligence, its focus is likely to be education, which can become a passion for both partners but especially for Cancer II's who feel they have some catching up to do. The more emotional of these partners, Cancer II's are likely to admire mentally gifted Aquarius I's almost to the point of worship. Paradoxically, their Aquarius I mates may not encourage them toward formal schooling, since their mental gifts are often innate, or sharpened on the whetstone of experience. Be that as it may, Cancer II's often choose higher education as the means to satisfy their lust for learning.

Cancer II–Aquarius I love affairs are perhaps surprisingly passionate given the emphasis the relationship puts on brain power. But sex, too, is a nice subject for these two to ponder, although in this area they are likely to put aside their classwork in favor of hands-on research. Later on, when the temperature has cooled down, they are likely to be able to discuss these studies quite openly, and to offer objective and constructive criticism.

The problem about marriage in this combination is usually the ambivalence of Aquarius I's toward such a permanent relationship. On the one hand they enjoy the safety, security and comfort that Cancer II's can offer in a domestic setting. On the other hand they fly from it, straining to be free. Unfortunately they often try to have their cake and eat it too. Cancer II's may find themselves spending some lonely nights until they finally put their foot down, which they are quite capable of doing.

Cancer II's and Aquarius I's may meet and become friends through adult-education classes, advanced university courses or some kind of workshop. These friendships satisfy their love of learning and usually far outlast their actual school time together. In this case, learning does not stop when school is over, but continues to deepen and grow as life itself is acknowledged as the schoolmaster. Cancer II–Aquarius I work and family relationships are also likely to be looked on as learning experiences, especially in retrospect.

ADVICE: *Turn off your brain occasionally. University degrees don't guarantee intelligence. Dig deeper in the emotional realm. Try to be less critical.*

NANCY DAVIS (7/6/21)
RONALD REAGAN (2/6/11)

Actors Davis and Reagan met in 1951 in Hollywood and married the next year. They co-starred in her last movie, *Hellcats of the Navy* (1957). She took on the role of wife, mother and loyal supporter during Reagan's political rise and through his presidency. *Also:* **George Sanders & Zsa Zsa Gabor** (married; actors); **Noble Sissle & Eubie Blake** (musical collaborators).

July 3–10

THE WEEK OF THE UNCONVENTIONAL
CANCER II

January 31–February 7

THE WEEK OF YOUTH & EASE
AQUARIUS II

Alluring Quicksand

This relationship seems easygoing but conceals a tremendous thirst for power. Hidden beneath an amiable exterior is a core that no one who mistakes these two for an easy touch will quickly forget. Although Cancer is a water sign and Aquarius air, their relationship is ruled by earth and fire, here connoting smoldering desire and ambition. These volcanic seethings may cause tremendous frustration if not vented, but Cancer II–Aquarius II couples often have the patience and foresight to wait until they are called.

Part of this pair's power lies in their popularity. Lovers, friends and mates in this combination may be in high demand in their social circle. Their charisma, often of the charming and light variety, is a kind of hook with which they can snag the hearts of their admirers. The process need not be at all unpleasant, and in fact a good time is often had by all in the long run. The seductive power of the relationship itself is recognized and increasingly appreciated. Yet surprisingly little is usually known about the individuals themselves in the relationship, their dynamics, how they interact.

Siblings with this matchup are less likely to interact with others as a team than to play power games with each other. These activities are often more amusing than serious, and rarely cause harm. Parent-child relationships, however, can be quite damaging to both partners if they pursue the art of deception with real conviction.

Work relationships between these two can be ambitious, even ruthless. Cancer II–Aquarius II business partners will use every trick in the book to overcome their opponents. Those who attack them frontally often wind up charging futilely at thin air, dissolved by what seems to be good will. The easy come-on or inviting welcome may lure unwary adversaries into quicksand from which they may not easily emerge.

ADVICE: *You can't get away with it forever—or can you? You may become the victim of your own success. Cultivate simple human values. Be honest.*

July 3–10

THE WEEK OF THE UNCONVENTIONAL
CANCER II

February 8–15

THE WEEK OF ACCEPTANCE
AQUARIUS III

The Whole Package

This relationship combines an intensity of emotion with highly critical and rejecting attitudes. Neither partner should expect an easy time here. Cancer II's are easily fascinated by the more unusual or even bizarre aspects of Aquarius III's, and may be magnetically drawn to them. Problems arise when Aquarius III's are less than responsive, or perhaps impulsively respond, then just as quickly turn off. Cancer II's must be subtle in their approach to Aquarius III's, who will not be held down, and may be gone at the first signs of claiming attitudes.

Love affairs here are complex and difficult. True, Aquarius III's have a tremendous need for love, and should they find a Cancer II attractive they will be gratified by his or her attention. But Cancer II obsessiveness can drive Aquarius III's crazy, pushing all of their buttons. Even when things are going well, Aquarius III's tend to be irritated by little things about Cancer II's. If the relationship is to work, they will obviously have to learn to accept the whole package—they can't imagine they have the luxury just to choose the bits of the Cancer II personality they like. Marriage can be attempted here, but it will often magnify these problems, with constant bickering, missed communication and frustration as the results. Friendships between these two are usually built around shared and somewhat unusual activities. Furthermore, the partners don't approach their interests with moderation but with a certain extremity and intensity of emotion. Here, however, the mutual criticism that appears in other kinds of relationships in this combination is muted. A more relaxed attitude prevails, and friends are likely to find their relationship highly rewarding and pleasurable.

Parent-child relationships are usually stormy, featuring judgmental and often rejecting attitudes on both sides. Aquarius III parents may lack patience in dealing with their Cancer II children, and Cancer II parents can exert possessive and intrusive holds on Aquarius III progeny. At work, boss-employee relationships can have some of the same problems, but as co-workers these two are often able to reach an understanding.

ADVICE: *Soften your critical stance. Suspend judgments. Take things as they come. Don't let your buttons be pushed. Lessen possessiveness.*

JAMES WHISTLER (7/10/1834)
JOHN RUSKIN (2/8/1819)

Ruskin was a prominent 19th-century critic. In his book *Fors Clavigera*, he ferociously attacked Whistler's paintings, leading to an 1878 libel suit. The judgment was against Ruskin, whose public humiliation ruined his career. **Also: Hanns Eisler & Bertolt Brecht** (co-composers); **Merv Griffin & Eva Gabor** (romance; tv host/actress); **Nikola Tesla & Thomas Edison** (rival inventors).

July 3–10

THE WEEK OF THE UNCONVENTIONAL
CANCER II

February 16–22

THE CUSP OF SENSITIVITY
AQUARIUS-PISCES CUSP

A Miracle of Manifestation

These two may approach their relationship a bit like two lost souls who have had some disappointing experiences on the road of life, or just haven't yet met the right person. Their matchup is truly grounding, and the miracle of its manifestation may come as a tremendous relief and a source of joy to both of them. Crucial here is the element of trust, for the past may have taught both of these partners that other people should be kept at least at arm's length and not allowed inside their guard. Just being able to lower their defenses a bit, and to be relaxed with another person, can be a tremendous reward.

Once established, love affairs, marriages and friendships in this combination will usually grow steadily deeper and more dependable. Dangers of course exist: first, that the relationship will close itself off, making little if any contact with other people, and second, that if one of the partners passes away, the other will be left isolated, in despair. As to the first point, Cancer II's and Aquarius-Pisces must look on their meeting as a stepping stone to establishing trust with others, both individually and as a pair. Second, even if one partner is lost, the other will have wonderful memories and, after a period of grieving, will ideally begin again.

Work relationships, whether as business partners or as boss-employee or co-worker pairs, will do best setting up specific long-range projects and objectives and striving to implement them. Financial and organizational responsibilities will further ground this relationship. At home, siblings will benefit from being allowed to assume responsibility both for themselves and for the family; if coddled or spoiled by their parents, they may not form solid bonds with each other. Likewise, parents and children in this combination should make concrete demands on each other and meet them, establishing greater trust.

LUCIEN PISSARRO (2/20/1863)
CAMILLE PISSARRO (7/10/1830)

Father Camille was a better-known painter than son Lucien. Camille was famous for his Impressionist paintings, particularly city streets and country roads. Lucien, a minor pointillist painter, is noted as the most original book designer of his time.

ADVICE: *Establish trust at a deep level. Build bridges to the world. Open your heart. Be demanding. Stick up for yourself. Give-and-take matters.*

GEORGE HARRISON (2/25/43)
RINGO STARR (7/7/40)

Ringo, the last to join the Beatles, was "the best backbeat in the business," according to pal and fellow Beatle George. Shortly after the group broke up in 1970, George sponsored 2 benefit concerts for Bangladesh with Ringo appearing on drums. They have remained close friends through the years.

Also: Nicky Hilton & Elizabeth Taylor (married; playboy/actress).

July 3–10
THE WEEK OF THE UNCONVENTIONAL
CANCER II

February 23–March 2
THE WEEK OF SPIRIT
PISCES I

Loyalty to Ideas

This relationship can be a deep and absorbing one. Its energy is serious and its orientation philosophical, religious or even spiritual. This by no means implies an intellectualism here, but rather an orientation based on belief or faith. Cancer II's and Pisces I's are normally quite private people, and their relationship synergistically expands on this tendency, sometimes producing extremes of secretiveness. Most attempts to pry these two out of their shell will be met with resistance—they may just prefer spending time alone, either separately or together.

Love affairs are often more sexually than romantically oriented. Feelings are often kept inside in such matchups, rather than being expressed. If arguments and disputes are unusual, this is because the mood here can be a quiet one in which much is left unsaid. Communication often takes place on a nonverbal level—these partners usually know instantly how the other is feeling. But they should take care not to hammer down and repress their frustrations; they will need to create an atmosphere in which they can express criticism and disapproval without fear of upset or rejection.

Cancer II–Pisces I marriages are likely to be built around an ideology or outlook that becomes the basis of family life. The relationship will show great loyalty to such ideas, but must beware of becoming rigid about them. An emphasis is often put on spiritual matters, to the point where material goods and wealth may be seen as relatively unimportant. Such attitudes are not always easy for children of these parents to accept.

Friends and siblings in this combination are often passionately devoted to a lifestyle that involves wearing certain clothes, listening to certain music and associating with certain people. These couples may ultimately have to make a choice between the tastes of their own relationship and those of the social subculture to which they belong. At work, boss-employee and co-worker pairings often don't go so well.

ADVICE: *Don't get overly attached to your beliefs. Be somewhat skeptical from time to time. What do you have to hide? Try to be more open.*

LEONA HELMSLEY (7/4/20)
HARRY HELMSLEY (3/4/09)

Self-made real-estate multi-billionaire Harry married 2nd wife Leona in 1972. They basked in their wealth and power. The forceful Leona overshadowed Harry and they were eventually convicted for tax evasion. He was too old to stand trial; she went to jail.

Also: Jim Kerr & Patsy Kensit (married; singer/actor); **Doc Severinsen & Ed McMahon** (Carson's *Tonight Show* regulars).

July 3–10
THE WEEK OF THE UNCONVENTIONAL
CANCER II

March 3–10
THE WEEK OF THE LONER
PISCES II

Mining Gold

This combination is likely to emphasize what the partners can learn from it—the relationship itself becomes a teacher with much to impart. Since Cancer and Pisces lie trine to each other in the zodiac (120° apart), traditional astrology predicts an easy and enjoyable matchup here, and indeed these two water signs usually get along famously; in the case of Cancer II's and Pisces II's, however, a search for meaning becomes dominant, although this does not prevent the two from having fun. The objective lessons to be learned here are many, and include the skills of understanding others and acquiring conscious awareness, spiritual understanding, and patience and fortitude in the face of adversity.

In love affairs, Cancer II–Pisces II couples explore the realms of feeling and mine the gold in its subterranean depths. Insights, awareness and empathy are just a few of the valuables uncovered here, but the process is not without risks and effort; resentment, jealousy and a whole host of negative emotions are often encountered as well. Still, the partners are determined to do more than just enjoy themselves in their love, and generally persevere in their search for truth.

In marriages and friendships in this combination, the partners function as a unit to probe the mysteries of relating to others. Because of their serious psychological interests and emotional expertise, they are often sought out by family and friends in times of need, both personal and social. The children of such a matchup will generally find their parents sympathetic, understanding and capable of offering important advice.

Parent-child relationships in this combination may get a bit too close and exclusive, so that others in the family feel shut out or jealous. These pairs must try to share their good feelings with others and to light up the space around them. Working relationships between Cancer II's and Pisces II's may get a bit too relaxed, and will demand more effort and willpower if the job is to get done well and on time.

ADVICE: *Don't get lost in your search. Remember to have fun. Strengthen your resolve but beware of monomania. Share your insights with others.*

July 3–10

THE WEEK OF THE UNCONVENTIONAL
CANCER II

March 11–18

THE WEEK OF DANCERS & DREAMERS
PISCES III

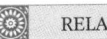
RELATIONSHIPS

STRENGTHS: **MAGNETIC, LONG-LASTING, PROFOUND**

WEAKNESSES: **DEPENDENT, SYBARITIC, ADDICTIVE**

BEST: **FRIENDSHIP**

WORST: **LOVE**

Succumbing to Pleasure

This relationship carries the danger of the unbridled pursuit of pleasure. It can easily be addictive, with the partners unable to get enough of each other or of the activities they pursue together in the world. Part of the problem is that the relationship goes so deep it has difficulty extricating itself. This high degree of attachment to a person, activity or substance may first be seen as merely habituating or obsessive and only later as outright addictive. Conscious awareness usually offers the only hope for stopping this process, but the partners too often ignore any telltale signs, or blind themselves to what is going on.

Sex and love addictions are not at all uncommon here; this couple's love affairs and marriages usually show at least some trace of such tendencies. Warnings are in order from the outset, then. Addictions may particularly be prompted by Cancer II low self-esteem or lack of confidence and by the Pisces III need to be important to the point of being idolized. The latter trait is especially dangerous, in that Pisces III's sometimes encourage other people to be overly dependent on them. Although sex is often highly rewarding between these two, it can become obsessive and claiming, and can stand directly in the way of a realistic and healthy approach to life.

Friendships are often magnetic and long-lasting, but here too there is a danger of shared drug use, whether the drugs are alcohol, tobacco or mind-expanding or pleasurable controlled substances. When friends and family confront such a couple with the truth, they often respond with denial. Although enjoyable, such friendships risk being exercises in self-deception, with the partners too readily succumbing to the lure of pleasure and good feelings. Work relationships can sometimes be workaholic and sometimes, alternatively, can be adversely affected by emotional or chemical dependencies. The pair may lack the willpower to get on track. In the family, emotional dependencies in parent-child relationships can lead to a stunting of psychological development and spiritual growth.

ADVICE: *Open your eyes to the truth. Beware of self-deception. Listen to the observations of others. Don't promote dependencies. Stay objective.*

OTTORINO RESPIGHI (7/9/1879)
NIKOLAI RIMSKY-KORSAKOV (3/18/1844)

Italian composer Respighi visited Russia twice (1900, 1902) and studied with famed composer Rimsky-Korsakov. Respighi is best known for his symphonic poems *Fountains of Rome* (1916) and *Pines of Rome* (1924). Rimsky-Korsakov had a great influence on the Italian's colorful orchestration.

July 11–18

THE WEEK OF THE PERSUADER
CANCER III

July 11–18

THE WEEK OF THE PERSUADER
CANCER III

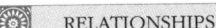
RELATIONSHIPS

STRENGTHS: **IRRESISTIBLE, LOYAL, FRANK**

WEAKNESSES: **COMBATIVE, INSECURE, POWER-TRIPPING**

BEST: **WORK**

WORST: **FAMILY**

Calling a Truce

The world will notice this powerful combination even when the partners aren't working to bring themselves to its attention. Aware that people are aware of them, however, they may subtly manipulate public perceptions of them, perhaps by making only very slight changes in dress, body language or presentation. Usually through a tacit agreement, these two will ensure that the world sees them as they want to be seen. Within the relationship, they usually trust and can be themselves with each other; but Cancer III's are quite comfortable being alone, and are unlikely to be forced into a pairing they think will be counterproductive. They may choose not to get involved with another Cancer III or, in fact, with anyone else at all.

Love affairs between two Cancer III's are more subject to power struggles than other relationships in this combination. Cancer III's are passionate people, and their insecurities can fly around like white-hot sparks. Both partners are likely to withdraw periodically when they find their emotional confrontations too threatening, leaving a deadly quiet battlefield. Marriages, on the other hand, can be highly successful and productive, with these spouses accomplishing much for their mutual good. An incredibly high level of capability can appear here, as well as a strong, loyal desire to stick together through thick and thin. Children of this matchup, however, are likely to be completely dominated by their parents. The worst part may be trying to find an alternative to one parent's point of view by appealing to another whose ideas turn out to be exactly the same.

These two do very well as friends or as co-workers in a professional setting. Here their emotions can be kept under control (with short, sharp and snappy lapses). When they funnel their energy into a commercial endeavor, few can withstand their momentum—once they get moving, they are like the waves of the mighty ocean or the irresistible pull of a river's current.

Family matchups can be true disasters, especially in the case of mother-daughter or father-son combinations.

ADVICE: *Find time for fun. Avoid trying to fix each other. Remember that opening up with each other can be good practice. Avoid power struggles.*

DAVE FLEISCHER (7/14/1894)
MAX FLEISCHER (7/17/1889)

Brothers Dave and Max were pioneers of animated cartoons. They invented the rotoscope (1917), a device for tracing live action into animated footage, which saved painstaking work. Their most famous cartoon creations are *Betty Boop* (1930) and *Popeye* (1933).

***Also:* Milton Berle & Bill Cosby** (comedians; same birthday).

STRENGTHS: **EFFECTIVE, PROFESSIONAL, SUCCESSFUL**

WEAKNESSES: **INCOMPATIBLE, OVERDOMINANT, BLUNT**

BEST: **WORK**

WORST: **LOVE**

BOB DOLE (7/22/23)
GERALD FORD (7/14/13)

Ford and Dole were running mates in the 1976 presidential race against Carter and Mondale. Ford, a moderate Republican, chose Dole for being a combative conservative. They ran a tough campaign, alluding to "Democrat wars," but were defeated by the opposition. **Also: Dr. Charles Menninger & Dr. Karl Menninger** (father/son; co-founders of Menninger Clinic).

July 11–18

THE WEEK OF THE PERSUADER
CANCER III

July 19–25

THE CUSP OF OSCILLATION
CANCER-LEO CUSP

Shoulder to Shoulder

Cancer III's and Cancer-Leos often heighten each other's practical abilities and are most effective when a job needs getting done. Their relationship is characterized, then, by responsibility and the shouldering of heavy duties. These partners may not be well suited to each other temperamentally, but their relationship patches up many of their personal differences, and generally melds their energies. As far as the world is concerned, the spotlight is often on the objectives and accomplishments of the duo itself, rather than on the individuals. Initial power struggles may well be smoothed over as the partners come to an agreement for purposes of unity, allowing the relationship to bring them both to a higher level of performance or expertise. Despite their practical orientation, these two can often be found dabbling in the indefinable and the mysterious.

Love affairs in this combination don't usually click—here Cancer III's and Cancer-Leos can be as incompatible as oil and water. Emotionally they may find each other a bit threatening, and will prefer to back off. But they can be very successful striving shoulder to shoulder together in a marriage (assuming they have some degree of physical attraction). Problems are bound to surface over dominance, but Cancer III's are often capable of diplomatically giving ground and establishing themselves as the power behind the Cancer-Leo throne.

Cancer III–Cancer-Leo friendships generally don't go very deep, and family relationships can manifest serious power struggles. Work relationships are perhaps most natural for these two: it is quite possible for former rivals, competitors or antagonists to get together in a new situation, smooth over differences and form an effective team. The key to this combination is the relationship's melding of Cancer III financial, managerial and theoretical expertise with Cancer-Leo leadership and team abilities, in particular the ability to delegate authority. What ultimately makes the relationship workable is the emotional understanding the partners have for each other. Honesty is an unwritten law between them; this frankness may ruffle feathers from time to time, but it rarely causes open conflict.

ADVICE: *Create plenty of space between you. Minimize power struggles. Realize what is in your best interest. Deepen understanding. Let your hair down occasionally.*

STRENGTHS: **FLEXIBLE, SHARING, TRUSTING**

WEAKNESSES: **RECALCITRANT, CHAOTIC, POWER-TRIPPING**

BEST: **FRIENDSHIP**

WORST: **WORK**

LEON SPINKS (7/11/53)
MICHAEL SPINKS (7/29/56)

The boxing Spinks brothers made history when they both won gold medals in the 1976 Olympics—Leon as a light heavyweight and Michael as a middleweight. Both went on to become professional heavyweight champions. **Also: Ginger Rogers & Rudy Vallee** (affair; actors); **Frances Lear & Norman Lear** (married; publisher/producer); **Brigitte Nielsen & Arnold Schwarzenegger** (affair).

July 11–18

THE WEEK OF THE PERSUADER
CANCER III

July 26–August 2

THE WEEK OF AUTHORITY
LEO I

Mutual Adjustment

This relationship is an ever-changing one that demands constant small adjustments. Yet because both partners are comfortable in this combination, these adaptations do not feel difficult, and they also provide opportunities for growth, calling on both personalities to evaluate their priorities and to make accommodations. The relationship often asks flexible Cancer III's to adjust to the fixed positions of Leo I's. By winning the respect and perhaps ultimately the love of this partner, Cancer III's can actually end up a powerfully controlling force in the relationship; it is simply that, ruled by the moon, they show many faces here, while sun-ruled Leo I's are fixed and blazing. Leo I's have little respect for those who don't stand up to them, so Cancer III's must know when to stand fast and when to give ground.

Love affairs emphasize give-and-take and flexibility. Leo I's will have to learn to bend a bit, but as they become more flexible they may begin to exhibit their more empathic side, coming to resemble their partner a little. Although Cancer III's are diplomatic, they are not about to knuckle under to their mates, and explosive scenes are possible here from time to time, even while the relationship usually keeps individual emotions well under control. Generally speaking, neither Cancer III's nor Leo I's have much need for marriage—which means that if they do decide to tie the knot, it will be because they have a genuine and conscious desire to do so.

Friendships here are apt to be more about help and support than about warmth and love. Trusting their Cancer III friends more than their colleagues, for example, Leo I's are likely to turn to them for financial advice, valuing it for its perspicacity and shrewdness. In the family, Leo I parents are usually adored by their Cancer III children, but are prone to spoiling them. A professional Cancer III–Leo I relationship can be problematic, whether it be boss-employee or co-worker. Power struggles here can cause chaotic fluctuations in the workplace.

ADVICE: *Be open to advice and influence. Maintain flexibility. Keep criticism positive. Beware of power struggles. Surrender the desire for control.*

RELATIONSHIPS	
STRENGTHS:	**THOUGHTFUL, STIMULATING, PRACTICAL**
WEAKNESSES:	**ADVERSARIAL, NOSY, UNCOOPERATIVE**
BEST:	**CO-WORKER**
WORST:	**SIBLING**

Practical Intelligence

The strengths of this relationship are active mental activity and a love of games and play. These partners are able to relax together and have fun, but can equally well apply themselves, and the clarity of thought that their relationship engenders, to any job at hand with good results. Although Cancer is a water sign and Leo fire, this relationship is ruled by air and earth, in this case signifying practical intelligence. Critical attitudes here are generally of the positive sort and will assure that the relationship's activities are pursued at the highest level possible.

Cancer III–Leo II love affairs are sensuous but rarely reach the wanton heights of abandon. These partners are always a bit wary of each other emotionally, and at times are suspicious of each other's motives. The relationship is rarely completely trusting. The partners may have difficulty committing themselves wholeheartedly to each other, and lengthy engagements may delay any plan to marry. Their doubts about carrying through, however, are often realistic, preventing later disappointments and catastrophes.

Friends in this combination usually enjoy board and video games, puzzles and all sorts of mysteries needing solutions. They may particularly enjoy mock-detective scenarios, playing out, say, Sherlock Holmes–and–Dr. Watson scripts. They will also take great pleasure in gossiping about the activities of others, to the point where their family and friends may see this pair as nosy or meddling, and will want to be left out of their investigations. Family matchups between siblings bring out the more extreme and antagonistic elements of both partners, leaving little room for cooperation and mutual achievement. Competition for parental affection is often highlighted here. Other family combinations, however, are generally more positive and fun. Boss-employee relationships in this combination usually function poorly, but co-worker matchups are often stimulating and productive. In certain cases, Cancer III–Leo II rivalries push both opponents to the limit. When they are working on the same team, Leo II's should think about leaving Cancer III's alone rather than pushing or ordering them around.

ADVICE: *Tone down competitive urges. Learn to be more cooperative. Others may not appreciate your interest. Switch some energy from head to heart.*

ROBERT TAYLOR (8/5/11)
BARBARA STANWYCK (7/16/07)

Handsome leading man Taylor was married to screen and tv actress Stanwyck (1939–51)—one of Hollywood's more durable pairings. She appeared with him in 2 films, *This Is My Affair* (1937) and *The Night Walker* (1965), her last film.

Also: Lucie Arnaz & Lucille Ball (daughter/mother); **Thomas Bulfinch & Charles Bulfinch** (son/father; author/architect).

RELATIONSHIPS	
STRENGTHS:	**PASSIONATE, AGREEABLE, POWERFUL**
WEAKNESSES:	**ERUPTIVE, FRUSTRATED, JEALOUS**
BEST:	**FRIENDSHIP**
WORST:	**LOVE**

On Whose Terms?

Whether consciously or unconsciously, this relationship makes its partners craft a set of rules for themselves. The likely questions are, Who will impose ideas and who will follow them? Though these two generally get along well, and have a lot of respect for each other, they have very different ideas as to what a relationship should be all about. Thus the focus here is the issue of what shared ideology will work for them. Power struggles need not emerge between these powerful individuals, since Cancer III's can readily accept the Leo III need to lead (but not to dominate or rule). As long as a shared outlook can be found, the relationship will probably be peaceful and agreeable.

Cancer III–Leo III love affairs can be sexually passionate but also combative and aggressive, both in and out of the bedroom. Cancer III's are every bit as strong emotionally and psychologically as Leo III's, and may frown on this partner's outbursts and volcanic explosions, preferring subtler forms of communication—communication on their own terms. Because Leo III egos need so much stroking, the devastating observations of which Cancer III's are capable will often be enough to lay low the powerful Lion; withholding approval will do it, too. Marriages can work here, but Leo III's will have to toe the mark in domestic matters and will be told what needs doing in no uncertain terms.

In parent-child relationships, Cancer III's generally function better in the parental role; they are severe with their Leo III offspring while also being protective and loving. Boss-employee relationships, on the other hand, often do better with Leo III's giving the orders. In both of these situations, domestic and professional, authority must generally be unquestioned and mutually agreed upon for things to work out. In friendships, however, authority is seldom a big issue, and the partners might adopt a rather free-and-easy attitude toward each other. Serious problems can arise, however, when friends are attracted to the same love object.

ADVICE: *Learn to compromise without resentment. Swallow your pride occasionally. Work for the common cause. Be more considerate.*

BILL COSBY (7/12/37)
ROBERT CULP (8/16/30)

Cosby and Culp were co-stars on tv's popular series *I Spy* (1965–68). They made an exciting, quick-witted duo, with Cosby (the first black to star in a non-comedy series) and Culp as spies posing as tennis professionals. They clicked beautifully together.

Also: Bill Cosby & Malcolm-Jamal Warner (*Cosby Show* father/son).

STRENGTHS: **FREE, EASY, THOUGHTFUL**

WEAKNESSES: **NONCOMMITTAL, COOL, PARANOID**

BEST: **FRIENDSHIP**

WORST: **LOVE**

MALCOLM FORBES (8/19/19)
STEVE FORBES (7/18/47)

High-profile Malcolm was owner/ publisher of his father's magazine, *Forbes*, from the mid-60s through the 80s. He died in '90. His son Steve, now editor-in-chief, is most famous for his try at the 1996 Republican nomination for the presidency—for which he spent millions from his personal fortune. ***Also:* Keith Godchaux & Donna Godchaux** (married; rock pianist/ vocalist with Grateful Dead).

July 11–18

THE WEEK OF THE PERSUADER
CANCER III

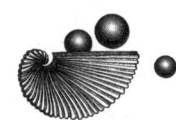

August 19–25

THE CUSP OF EXPOSURE
LEO-VIRGO CUSP

Uncorking the Bottle

The relaxed approach found in this combination lets the partners feel free to come and go at will, joining each other in moments of pleasure and play. Separately they both tend to set high standards, but although that emphasis carries through to their relationship, overall attitudes here are more relaxed. This ability to ease up a little without sacrificing quality is a benefit to these personalities, who both tend to be a bit intense. Moreover, they both have a very private side, which their relationship synergistically magnifies into a passion for having a space on which few if any others can intrude. Past experiences give Cancer III's and Leo-Virgos a certain sensitivity, and both are wary in relationships. In each other, however, they find someone they can trust. Instinctively accepted by Cancer III's, Leo-Virgos will feel comfortable opening up and revealing themselves. Their own discrimination, meanwhile, will allow them to view Cancer III's more objectively than most, and thus to provide the recognition these personalities crave.

Love affairs between these two are likely to suffer from an overemphasis on conscious mental activity. This can ultimately have a debilitating effect on spontaneous instinctual and emotional expression. Marriages and working relationships can work smoothly enough as long as neither partner is asked to bear more than his or her share of responsibility. Both partners here will grant their relationship itself the highest importance. Their self-confident kind of respect for each other makes it unnecessary for them to push or meddle. "If it works, don't fix it" is the motto of these marriages and affairs—when things are going well. Should stresses and emergencies arise, however, the relationship's mettle will truly be tested: insecurity, doubt and fear can easily become overwhelming, threatening to cause a kind of collapse. Thoughtfulness and patience may be lifesavers, coupled with the control that will forestall reacting too hastily.

Friendships and sibling matchups can be truly fun. An innocent, childlike and naive approach to life can be given full play here without fear of censure.

ADVICE: *Cultivate patience and let the truth come to you. Make firm plans once in a while. Relax privacy issues.*

STRENGTHS: **SOLID, STABLE, BALANCED**

WEAKNESSES: **MONOLITHIC, RIGID, FACELESS**

BEST: **MARRIAGE**

WORST: **LOVE**

PINCHAS ZUKERMAN (7/16/48)
TUESDAY WELD (8/27/43)

Zukerman is a prominent Israeli-American violinist whose recordings of Beethoven's sonatas and trios are ranked among the best. He is married to luminous actress Weld, whose screen roles and publicized offscreen life have made her a cult figure. ***Also:* Berenice Abbott & Man Ray** (photographer was early assistant to Dadaist); **Gustav Klimt & Alma Schindler** (married; artists).

July 11–18

THE WEEK OF THE PERSUADER
CANCER III

August 26–September 2

THE WEEK OF SYSTEM BUILDERS
VIRGO I

Nondescript Camouflage

This relationship can be a highly dependable one that nurtures mutual support, balance and harmony. Opposing forces come together here to create stability and an emphasis on honor, dignity and faithfulness. Both Cancer III's and Virgo I's are direct in their approach, and they are apt to communicate very easily with each other. Cancer III drive will also complement the Virgo I ability to systematize tasks, so that these two will do very well in realizing their goals.

Friendships and love affairs may be quiet and private, attracting little attention. It is quite possible for covert or illicit Cancer III–Virgo I affairs to continue for years, causing pleasure and pain alternately, but never either enough pain to break it off or enough pleasure to entice the partners into a permanent arrangement or marriage. It is not passion or desire that holds these lovers together but a kind of inertia, or even apathy.

Should they find themselves in a relationship built on strong commitment, however, such as marriages and work partnerships, Cancer III's and Virgo I's can make an impressive team. Temperamentally alike in many ways, they understand and accept each other. If they come from similar geographic or ethnic backgrounds, they may create a relationship that is monolithic in its outlook and more like both partners archetypally than even they themselves are as personality types. A kind of camouflage of nondescriptness hides this relationship from the world. Its character is quite recognizable to family and friends, but even when pushed, the partners themselves might be completely at a loss to describe it. Practical responsibilities are steadily and easily discharged here, and Cancer III–Virgo I business partners or parents will prove extremely reassuring to employees, co-workers or children. Both are strong in the area of financial acumen.

Parent-child combinations must overcome claiming and overprotective attitudes. They certainly lend stability to a family, but also an undeniable rigidity, as in a buttressed fortress that is not easily sapped or sacked. Here as elsewhere, structure has both advantages and disadvantages.

ADVICE: *Stability isn't always the best thing. Don't be afraid of change or of development. Taking a leap is sometimes necessary. Dare to fail.*

July 11–18
THE WEEK OF THE PERSUADER
CANCER III

September 3–10
THE WEEK OF THE ENIGMA
VIRGO II

RELATIONSHIPS

STRENGTHS: **CAPABLE, SHARING, INTENSE**

WEAKNESSES: **SECRETIVE, RESENTFUL, FRUSTRATED**

BEST: **FRIENDSHIP**

WORST: **LOVE**

Choice Rather Than Need

This relationship carries with it an unusual level of understanding. These two are generally quite comfortable with each other—Virgo II's surprisingly willing to open up, here more than elsewhere, and Cancer III's charmed by their easy manner. But the real question is whether the acceptance here is wholehearted or only conditional. Virgo II's can be quite flattered by the interest of Cancer III's, and will not object to this partner's aggressive approach, since they are confident of their ability to reject intrusions at any point. For all their panache, however, they are highly private individuals who are by no means crying out to be understood. They often want no more than to be left alone.

Love affairs between these two can be intense, but are not particularly sharing or revealing. For a Virgo II, having sex with a lover in no way implies emotional openness. Cancer III's may find this attitude highly frustrating; they have a great deal to teach about emotional honesty and empathy if only Virgo II's are prepared to listen. For their part, Cancer III's must learn to accept the Virgo II resistance to being analyzed.

Marriages will benefit from the Cancer III ability to take charge domestically. Care must be taken, however, lest Virgo II's feel their space is being invaded; they have their own set of ideas about how things should be done, and open conflict can easily emerge here. Both partners are quite capable of living alone. This may strengthen their marriage, however, for it is likely to be based more on choice than on emotional neediness.

Virgo II's often open up to special friends more easily than to lovers, and their friendships with Cancer III's are sometimes more emotionally satisfying than their love affairs in this combination. They can also take the initiative here in solving some Cancer III mysteries. Should these two accept each other, they will share many personal moments together, achieving an acceptance and trust that will allow them to reveal deep secrets that they have never discussed with anyone else.

ADVICE: *Work on conquering your fears. Open up and be more accepting. Share emotionally at a deep level. Give up some of your vaunted control.*

JOHN DEE (7/13/1527)
ELIZABETH I (9/7/1533)

Dee was a widely recognized 16th-century mathematician, magician and court astrologer for Elizabeth, whose favor he enjoyed. He named the propitious day for her coronation and tutored her on the mystical meaning of his writings.

July 11–18
THE WEEK OF THE PERSUADER
CANCER III

September 11–18
THE WEEK OF THE LITERALIST
VIRGO III

RELATIONSHIPS

STRENGTHS: **AMBITIOUS, WELL DIRECTED, SUCCESSFUL**

WEAKNESSES: **RESENTFUL, STRESSED, OVEREMOTIONAL**

BEST: **WORK**

WORST: **LOVE**

Ego Formation

This combination finds its partners working on issues of ego—which can be both good and bad. The question raised in this relationship will be "Who am I and what is my place here?" It is not surprising that even while these two are striving alongside each other, they will also be unduly sensitized to whatever each person has been able to carve out of life—who has the more interesting or successful career, the higher salary, the better partner, the larger home, the greater peace of mind, and so on.

Cancer III's who are attracted to Virgo III's will stretch their seductive and manipulative talents to the limit if their attentions are less than responsively returned. Even if both partners are interested from the start, the onus will still fall on Cancer III's to be convincing—Virgo III's are likely to prove recalcitrant, resenting the demands of both the partner and the relationship as a whole. It is important, then, to keep such demands reasonable. Virgo III's most often don't self-evidently take the lead in this matchup, preferring to be the silent partner, who may, however, quietly make many of the important decisions. In love and marriage, the relationship's emphasis on ego issues can prove divisive.

When Cancer III–Virgo III relatives and friends work together professionally, their leadership often has the force of family, tradition and experience behind it. The best-case scenario in this combination, in fact, is often for the pair to work together, consolidating their relationship around a career endeavor. These partnerships are especially productive in entrepreneurial endeavors such as restaurants or hotels, small stores, services and schools. In all such undertakings, however, the partners must be hardheaded enough to resist the lure of somewhat questionable or seemingly easy deals. Power struggles and individual exploitation should also be carefully avoided, and if business partners or co-workers who are also friends, mates or family members are to ensure mutual relaxation and enjoyment, they must be careful to draw a strict line between their work and their domestic or social life.

ADVICE: *Persuasion isn't always necessary. Maintain strong leadership. Understand your desires. Promote unity and set ego aside. Work for the common good.*

GRETA GARBO (9/18/05)
MAURITZ STILLER (7/17/1883)

Swedish director Stiller discovered Garbo at a Stockholm acting school in the early 20s. He soon became her teacher, mentor and close companion. In '24 he was approached by Louis B. Mayer to direct movies in Hollywood; Stiller made Garbo part of the deal. They arrived in '25 and, under Stiller's management, Garbo's career soared.

JULIUS CAESAR (7/12/100 BC)
AUGUSTUS [OCTAVIAN] (9/23/63 BC)

Octavian was 18 when his great-uncle Caesar was assassinated in 44 BC. In his will Caesar adopted Octavian, whose name later became Augustus, a title conferred on him by the Senate. Thanks to Caesar, Octavian rose to become emperor of Rome in 27 BC. **Also: Jules Mazarin & Anne of Austria** (prime minister/queen regent).

July 11–18

THE WEEK OF THE PERSUADER
CANCER III

September 19–24

THE CUSP OF BEAUTY
VIRGO-LIBRA CUSP

Accepting Irritation

This relationship manifests an unfortunate hypersensitivity. Usually unintentionally and even unconsciously, its partners have the talent of needling each other in their most tender spots. Cancer III's may appreciate the aesthetic sensibilities of Virgo-Libras, who in turn, if the Cancer III's are the more creative of the two, will see the possibilities in any joint work that can be brought to artistic and financial fruition. If both are artistically inclined to similar degrees, however, and in the same field (for example writing, painting or music), competition and jealousy are likely to mar their rapport, despite its level of understanding and sympathy. Perhaps the best possibility is for them to share their artistic appreciation as a hobby, particularly when it is far removed from their individual daily activities.

Empathy often features in love affairs, but desire isn't necessarily commensurate with it. The relationship may lack strong sexual and romantic feelings, in other words, even when it is kind and loving. Cancer III's may eventually tire of the relationship or even come to resent it, feeling it lacks the intensity that would make it worth their while, or that the Virgo-Libra is too involved with superficialities. In marriages, these spouses will appreciate a certain accepting ambiance in the relationship, as well as the opportunity to furnish a home beautifully. But inexplicable anxieties could arise for no apparent reason, and the thin skins that the relationship encourages could create a potentially overwrought emotional situation.

Co-workers and friends in this combination may occasionally prove oversensitive to each other and go through periods of irritation and estrangement. It will be important for them to be less reactive to each other and to develop the capacity to ignore or resist negative feelings. Family matchups, especially parent-child, can be appreciative and sympathetic but lacking in real warmth. Both partners must remember to express affection actively in daily life, and to show each other that they really care.

ADVICE: *Give more of yourself. Don't hold back so much. Develop a thicker skin. Be more aware of sensitive spots in each other.*

NELSON MANDELA (7/18/18)
WINNIE MANDELA (9/26/36)

Anti-apartheid activists, the Mandelas were drawn together by politics. Married in '58, they crusaded as a team until Nelson's imprisonment in '62. Winnie became a political hero. After his '90 release, they fell apart ideologically and divorced in '96. **Also: Eugenia Zukerman & Pinchas Zukerman** (married; concert soloists); **Richie Sambora & Heather Locklear** (married; Bon Jovi musician/actress).

July 11–18

THE WEEK OF THE PERSUADER
CANCER III

September 25–October 2

THE WEEK OF THE PERFECTIONIST
LIBRA I

Revealing Hidden Passions

Often outwardly directed, this relationship appears placid enough, and united in the face of common goals. A look at the relationship's inner workings, however, reveals something quite different: Cancer III's and Libra I's are unlikely to be temperamentally suited to one another. The things they have in common are their critical and demanding attitudes—not the qualities that will be conducive to peace and harmony. Although Cancer is a water sign and Libra air, this relationship is ruled by fire and earth, introducing volcanic and eruptive energies. Not surprisingly, an important theme of the relationship is bringing hidden passions to light, often in the glare of the public spotlight.

Love affairs here can be ecstatic, catastrophic or both. These partners need to express what is on their minds. The mental and physical combine uneasily here: it may be hard for these two to make up in bed after a serious argument, for conflict often erupts in the sexual sphere as well. In both love affairs and marriages, Cancer III's and Libra I's are likely to show the very best and worst of themselves, and their matchups in these areas are usually extreme in nature.

Cancer III's and Libra I's rarely seek each other out, so their friendships are unlikely to be emotionally based. Should they find themselves in a companionship or acquaintanceship based on common interests, however, perhaps having to do with money, politics or ideas, they may be absorbed and interested. And working relationships between these two can be outstanding as long as they are not too personal. Cancer III managerial and financial skills often gel well with Libra I precision and technical abilities.

In the family, each of these personalities is likely to be a disapproving and critical parent of the other. The child in such matchups will often feel misunderstood or even rejected, and in adulthood may get involved with similarly rejecting figures their whole life long.

ADVICE: *Try harder to get along. Overlook matters sure to cause conflict. Lessen critical attitudes. Even out emotional swings. Stay objective.*

July 11–18

THE WEEK OF THE PERSUADER
CANCER III

October 3–10

THE WEEK OF SOCIETY
LIBRA II

A Bond of the Spirit

This relationship can be quite close and understanding. It is often a bond of the spirit—loyal and true. Religion or spirituality are prominent here, and although these partners may have quite different orientations, each recognizes a kindred spirit in the other. Cancer III intensity may prove too demanding for Libra II's, who need to be free to fly, but who are also capable of being quite content in the relationship as long as they don't feel restricted. The ties between these two will be hard to break; the pair will share a lot, and having made this kind of investment in each other they will be loath to let go. Thus the beginning of the relationship can be fascinating, the middle productive and trusting, and the breakup extremely painful, if indeed such a relationship can ever really end.

Love affairs and friendships are often related here. These two are so natural with each other that they might be taken for siblings. Although physical, such relationships are more secure in the spiritual or intellectual realm, as meetings of minds and hearts. The combination has a quality of idealism—the type not read about or dreamed of but lived every day. These two may see no need to get married; in the most important way they are often already spouses, making the ceremony an empty formality.

In the family, Libra II's doing things with friends are likely to include Cancer III siblings, introducing them to people and bringing them out into more normal social activities. The Cancer III sibling, meanwhile, can teach the Libra II about how power and aggression work in the world. In either case the pair are likely to fight like cats and dogs, but through it all maintain an understanding and even spiritual bond.

Friends and lovers in this combination may try sharing occupational pursuits, but in the long run they are better off pursuing their separate professional interests. Should a Cancer III and Libra II find themselves working together as a boss-employee or co-worker pair, they will do well to keep their relationship light and filled with wit and good humor.

ADVICE: *Try to be a little more realistic. Beware of undue attachments. Make preparations for difficult times. Try to avoid overseriousness.*

July 11–18

THE WEEK OF THE PERSUADER
CANCER III

October 11–18

THE WEEK OF THEATER
LIBRA III

Harnessing Friction

These two can make a powerful combination. The emphasis here is on an objective, thoughtful, systematic approach to any idea, task or project; ideally engaged in establishing or running an organization, the Cancer III–Libra III relationship surmounts internal tensions and uses them as a driving force to achieve goals. Cancer III and Libra III form a square aspect to each other in the zodiac (90° apart), and traditional astrology would therefore view them as conflicting. That the relationship can harness such friction is characteristic of its ability to turn what seem to be disadvantages to its good. Ruled by earth, reflecting its grounded and stable orientation, this relationship brings out its partners' practical and ambitious sides.

Since neither of these partners puts love above ambition, romance is not particularly favored here. Although their affairs may be intense, especially sexually, there is usually no love lost between them, and they are more often in conflict than in harmony with each other. Marriages tend to be of the more practical and socially ambitious kind. Together, through determination and ambition, these two usually succeed in making a financial and social success of their collaboration.

Friendships are not particularly favored here because these two can rarely completely relax together and surrender to simple fun and entertainment. In the family, similarly, the ambition of parent-child relationships makes them likely to show marked stress. At work, on the other hand, this is a strong combination. Since the Cancer III–Libra III matchup is so strong organizationally, it does well heading up social, professional and commercial groups. Here personal differences are for the most part put aside in favor of bringing the group to the highest level of performance and success. Cancer III–Libra III leader teams must be careful to act considerately and humanely, however, toward those serving under them, for they have a tendency to overlook this responsibility in an often ruthless rush to the top. Their power drives tend to be overwhelming, and they are likely to push themselves and their associates or employees to the limit of their endurance.

ADVICE: *Call a truce in personal matters. Try to relax together occasionally. There is no shame in having fun. Be more considerate of others.*

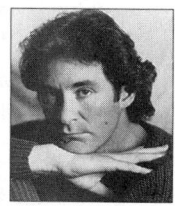

PHOEBE CATES (7/16/63)
KEVIN KLINE (10/24/47)

Versatile stage and screen actor Kline shined in *The Big Chill* (1983), *A Fish Called Wanda* (1988, supporting-actor Oscar) and *Dave* (1993). He married actress Cates, a dance prodigy, model and 80s-90s romantic lead in films. She took a 4-year break (1984–88) to focus on her new family. **Also: Andrew Wyeth & N.C. Wyeth** (son/father; artists); **Tab Hunter & Divine** (co-stars; John Waters movies).

July 11–18
THE WEEK OF THE PERSUADER
CANCER III

October 19–25
THE CUSP OF DRAMA & CRITICISM
LIBRA-SCORPIO CUSP

Swift Currents

This relationship is capable of touching its partners profoundly and being extremely complex emotionally, but it can also be isolated, even lonely. Together these two have great difficulty making meaningful connections with others, especially in the family and at work. The emphasis is usually on the dynamic between the partners themselves. Libra-Scorpios are notoriously hard to handle, so it will take every ounce of Cancer III persuasiveness to get through to them. Even so, these two can easily push each other's buttons, so that one of the relationship's real challenges is to maintain openness while simultaneously perhaps growing a whole new set of buttons that cannot be pushed so easily. Every bit of immaturity on both sides is bound to be expressed in conflict here sooner or later—but this can be a strength, for growing and working out a rapport can become a maturing process for both partners.

Assuming that these two are attracted to one another, their love affairs can be both difficult and intense. They will have trouble maintaining any sort of objectivity, since the relationship's emotional currents will run strong and conflict will always hover in the wings. Cancer III insecurities and the overly critical nature of Libra-Scorpios emerge in full bloom all too often. Furthermore, both partners have a penchant for excess, and should their involvement be deeply passionate, the relationship may have a problem with sex and love addictions—not to speak of struggles with alcohol or other drugs. In marriages as well as love affairs, such addictions often function as avenues of escape from the matchup's strong mental orientation, and from the nervousness that may accompany it. Cancer III–Libra-Scorpio friendships and work relationships are likely to be a bit more objective and stable. Jealousy and competition can arise over career issues or the sharing of friends, however, testing any bonds of understanding that have developed. Cancer III's generally have less need for attention than Libra-Scorpios, and may choose to back off when rivalries surface, being wise enough to try to find an alternative more in everyone's favor.

ADVICE: *Relaxation is key. Work on being less irritable and reactive. Beware of competition, however friendly. Moderate your excesses. Meditate.*

JOHN QUINCY ADAMS (7/11/1767)
JOHN ADAMS (10/30/1735)

John Adams, one of America's founding fathers and 2nd US president (1797–1801), was the father of John Quincy, who became the 6th president (1825–29). After educating his son in Europe, the senior Adams personally tutored him for 7 years, preparation for his major role in early foreign policy.

July 11–18
THE WEEK OF THE PERSUADER
CANCER III

October 26–November 2
THE WEEK OF INTENSITY
SCORPIO I

A Smoke Screen

Something about this combination will feel quite enigmatic to its partners, deeply perceptive individuals who are bound to feel frustrated by the fact that they can't quite seem to see or emotionally touch each other. It is as if the relationship were a smoke screen preventing full understanding. Even when Cancer III's and Scorpio I's work or live together or are close friends, a great deal between them is usually left unsaid, or actively concealed. There seems to be an inevitability in operation here, a fatal or karmic impulse that brings these two together willy-nilly, regardless of differences in background, training, race, religion or career interests, but that at the same time prevents a deeper union.

Romantic relationships in this combination have a strong sexual component. From flirtation to outright temptation and seduction, the pairing tends to produce the kind of provocative behavior that is likely to lead to some degree of sexual involvement. Both partners have a need to keep things hushed up, and they will usually be very discreet about when and where they meet. Should a third person be involved as the long-standing lover or mate of one of the pair, a breakup between two or even all three members of the triangle is often inevitable.

Cancer III–Scorpio I marriages have the potential to be more successful. The partners may still be unable to be honest with each other, however, resorting to manipulative ploys to get their way rather than expressing themselves directly. Scorpio I's often think their Cancer III mates use unethical tactics, and Cancer III's view Scorpio I spouses as selfish and controlling. Even so, these marriages can be enduring and productive.

In the family and at work, power struggles often emerge within parent-child and boss-employee pairs in this combination, but the family or company as a whole may benefit from the compromises and negotiations necessary to work out such problems. As long as the lines of communication are kept open and a certain amount of diplomacy is observed, Cancer III–Scorpio I pairs can develop a modus vivendi over time.

ADVICE: *Strive for honesty and openness. Let your guard down occasionally. Compromise can be beneficial. Face the consequences of your actions.*

July 11–18

THE WEEK OF THE PERSUADER
CANCER III

November 3–11

THE WEEK OF DEPTH
SCORPIO II

A Comfortable Niche

RELATIONSHIPS

STRENGTHS: **IMAGINATIVE, PLEASING, SECURE**

WEAKNESSES: **STAGNATING, DISCOURAGED, DELUDED**

BEST: **WORK**

WORST: **MARRIAGE**

ABIGAIL ADAMS (11/11/1744)
JOHN QUINCY ADAMS (7/11/1767)

John Quincy was the son of Abigail, wife of John Adams, then a little-known country lawyer. Abigail was thought to be brilliant and strong-willed, raising young John Quincy by the strictest standards of Puritanism, hard work and patriotism.

The theme of this relationship can be the realization of dreams and aspirations. The partners' motivation and willpower, however, may not be commensurate with their hopes and desires. Overcoming obstacles is a strong incentive here, and once embarked on a mission, these two will rarely give it up completely; yet even without severe opposition, subtle disappointments and setbacks, real or imagined, can undermine the relationship's positive thrust and wear down its determination. Too often these partners will settle for a comfortable niche in which they can keep dreaming about making a success of themselves one day. Meanwhile, on the other hand, there is a deep bond of feeling between Cancer III's and Scorpio II's, an empathic connection that can be counted on in times of trouble.

Both love affairs and marriages can be pleasant and relaxed—perhaps too much so. Easily satisfied together, these two rarely demand enough of each other to prompt them to evolve and grow. Physical comfort and security may play a disproportionately large role in such a relationship. Highly nurturing attitudes toward children are common here, along with a need to build a beautiful and safe home.

Siblings and friends in this combination usually share an active fantasy life. All kinds of imaginative schemes and dreams can occupy them, but may also rob them of the strength and resolve to carry projects through in real life. Neither party will necessarily acknowledge the importance of self-motivation, or even the need for it, especially if they are enjoying themselves.

At work, the most favorable situations for these two are probably as colleagues who have a hand in guiding the future of a company or other organization. Here the pair's imaginative vision can shine, as long as they have highly practical types around them to work with them to make their dreams come true. Questions can arise about the feasibility of Cancer III–Scorpio II schemes, but a few important successes will silence their most critical adversaries.

ADVICE: *Push yourself a bit. Be more self-critical and realistic. Dreams should not be a substitute for action. Use your imagination more actively.*

July 11–18

THE WEEK OF THE PERSUADER
CANCER III

November 12–18

THE WEEK OF CHARM
SCORPIO III

A Firm Foundation

RELATIONSHIPS

STRENGTHS: **PRACTICAL, RESPONSIBLE, SENSUOUS**

WEAKNESSES: **SELFISH, BOSSY, BORING**

BEST: **FRIENDSHIP**

WORST: **LOVE**

DANIEL BARENBOIM (11/15/42)
PINCHAS ZUKERMAN (7/16/48)

Pianist Barenboim and violinist Zukerman are friends and collaborators who have performed and recorded together frequently. Both musicians have devoted particular attention to Beethoven. Among their most celebrated collaborations are Beethoven's complete violin sonatas and, along with Jacqueline Du Pré (Barenboim's wife), Beethoven's piano trios.

This relationship will keep a code or set of rules that it will take quite seriously. Generally steadfast and traditional, it tends to discourage excessive emotion and to favor rationality. Given the passionate nature of the partners, this is quite a positive trend, and helps to establish the pairing on a firm foundation. Since Cancer III and Scorpio III are in trine aspect to each other (120° apart in the zodiac), traditional astrology predicts an easy and relatively trouble-free relationship between them. Although a fluid exchange of energy is possible and even likely between these two water signs, the relationship is quite practical. Once given, the partners' commitments and promises are likely to be taken literally.

Love affairs can be earthy and sensuous but may lack fiery passion. Since Cancer III's and Scorpio III's will rarely compromise themselves or undermine their own best interests, if either partner becomes dependent or needy the end may well be near. Marriages are a better use of the relationship's responsible and well-grounded orientation. Scorpio III's may well begin to relinquish their controlling attitudes around Cancer III's, who should enjoy letting these capable partners pull their own weight in the relationship.

Friendships in this combination can be terrific, having a tolerance and understanding that allow highly personal matters to be discussed and shared. Practicality being the relationship's strength, these friends could rely on each other strongly for advice. Cancer III–Scorpio III co-workers can function side by side for years in relative harmony; the emotional quality of their interactions will be understated, but in one way or another they will usually show respect and affection for each other. In the family, parent-child and sibling matchups are capable of being the foundation on which other family members can depend. Basic domestic matters, particularly those dealing with food and division of labor, will be well handled by a combination of Cancer III and Scorpio III managerial skills.

ADVICE: *Get out of the house a bit more. Share exciting experiences involving risk. Awaken sleeping passions. Others can serve you, too.*

REMBRANDT VAN RIJN (7/15/1606)
BARUCH SPINOZA (11/24/1632)

Artist Rembrandt and philosopher
Spinoza were both 17th-century
Dutchmen whose contributions
had a major cultural impact through
the years. They were productive
during Holland's Golden Age—
and lived and worked in the same
community in Amsterdam. Both
were deeply concerned with the
human condition, searching for
universals that would increase
our self-awareness.

The Uncertainty Principle

This relationship is often taken up with initiating new endeavors, and in fact its metaphorical trademark may be birth, or breathing new life into a traditional activity. The combination generally inspires confidence. These two rarely undertake a project with too high a risk of failure; they do not hesitate to stand up to authority together, and present a solid front when arguing for their principles. At the same time, the relationship also encourages the bit of the dreamer in both Cancer III's and Scorpio-Sagittarians, for these two do well with a bit of uncertainty—giving birth to new projects would be little fun if they knew of their success beforehand.

Love affairs here can be explosive getting started; feelings are likely to fly at first, but are quickly brought under control. Still, the relationship can bring out the excessive side of Cancer III's, making them feel they are getting in a bit over their head. Scorpio-Sagittarians will be attracted to Cancer III intensity, but if they tire of it they may have difficulty freeing themselves from this partner's emotional claims. On the other hand, they themselves have a tendency to fickleness, which, unfortunately, they may use somewhat manipulatively once they discover how vulnerable Cancer III's are to being wounded by it.

Marriages are more apt to be carried on dependably, and business contacts similarly will be completely professional. In both cases Cancer III insecurity and Scorpio-Sagittarius fear often lurk behind the facade, but these seemingly negative elements usually give the couple the kick they need to make their relationship successful. Cancer III–Scorpio-Sagittarius spouses make attentive parents, and as business partners these two are likely to treat their projects like their children, guiding them knowingly in the right direction. A Cancer III parent, however, is likely to arouse rebellion in a Scorpio-Sagittarius child, while a Scorpio-Sagittarius parent may lack the emotional stability that Cancer III children demand. Friendships are less common than rivalries here, for the matchup has a quality of intensity that often seems to demand expression through confrontation.

ADVICE: *Try to even out your feelings. Don't be afraid of rejection. Learn to trust and to share. Spend time together away from work or family.*

ABBIE HOFFMAN (11/30/36)
JERRY RUBIN (7/14/38)

Outspoken foes of bourgeois deca-
dence, Hoffman and Rubin spearheaded the 60s counterculture
movement. From the campus-based
SDS, these radical activists created
the Yippie movement, with its
satirical style of protest. Rubin and
Hoffman later parted ways.

Also: **George Eastman & John
Hyatt** (photo-process inventors);
Christine McVie & John McVie
(married; Fleetwood Mac members).

Rainbow Over Distant Mountain

A rare beauty characterizes this combination, like a rainbow spanning a distant mountain after a thunderstorm. These partners will hardly believe their good fortune: in all matters having to do with aesthetic taste and entertainment, they will be content in their dealings with each other, a quality that will spread into the rest of their relationship. Very different personalities, they would appear to have little in common: Cancer is a water sign and Sagittarius fire, and the Cancer III Persuader might seem to threaten the flame of Sagittarius I Independence. Yet the relationship is ruled by earth and air, so that a kind of completion occurs here—a balance of all four elements.

Cancer III–Sagittarius I love affairs are likely to be once-in-a-lifetime experiences—if they ever get off the ground. This is one of the less likely romantic combinations in the year, but these two may be able to discover in each other qualities that others have passed by, and if so, by a wondrous alchemy, these qualities can unite into a thing of beauty. Yet these relationships are often fleeting, and may leave the lovers wondering whether they were real or just a dream.

Marriages between these two can work out in theory, since both partners are serious and have strong nurturing abilities; oddly enough, though, this couple's love affairs rarely develop that far. Friendships, on the other hand, may be solid and fun for both partners. Cancer III's love fooling with their Sagittarius I friends, jokingly pressuring or tricking them into doing the most outrageous things. Sagittarius I's like to tease Cancer III's and ridicule their often overserious pose. Cancer III parents can provide Sagittarius I children with the authority, support and understanding they need, but must be extremely careful not to intrude on their private lives. Sagittarius I parents can be inspiring role models for Cancer III children, but may unknowingly hurt their feelings through hasty actions or decisions. Career matchups here can be excellent when the partners' projects demand vigilant application and hard work.

ADVICE: *Don't doubt what happens between you. Joking can be a form of affection. Take your time. Don't hold each other back. Value what you have a bit more.*

July 11–18

THE WEEK OF THE PERSUADER
CANCER III

December 3–10

THE WEEK OF THE ORIGINATOR
SAGITTARIUS II

High Demands

This combination is often a meeting of like minds. At its best it carries with it a demand for the perfection of ideas, techniques or outlooks, and Cancer III's and Sagittarius II's together have far more strength to stick to their principles than either of them could muster alone. They will feel entitled to believe in their relationship, then, but they may also grow dependent on it for backbone; this is particularly true of Sagittarius II's, who will respect the powerful directive and organizational thrust of Cancer III's, and will also feel that even the more unusual aspects of their own personalities are appreciated and understood by this partner.

As a love affair, the relationship can be highly demanding, not only sexually but in terms of social appearances. Cancer III's and Sagittarius II's are usually proud of each other and let others know it. At the same time, they will guard their privacy zealously, insisting on long periods of uninterrupted time alone.

Marriages in this combination are sometimes unrealistic. Both partners' satisfaction and happiness in the relationship can divert their attention from pressing problems, which will then be overlooked or ignored. Experience teaches this couple a strange lesson: whenever they feel euphoric, they can be sure that something is wrong or needs tending.

Friendships rarely remain only social or personal: Cancer III's and Sagittarius II's have a strong tendency to work together. This work can begin with a hobby, then evolve into a career. Technical expectations will be high here, and the pair's perfectionist bent will be clearly evident. Conversely, relationships that begin on the job, between colleagues or co-workers, often develop into friendships. In such cases it may be difficult for spouses, friends or family to relate to two people who are so wrapped up in their own thing—resentments and jealousies are often aroused this way.

ADVICE: *Let up in your technical demands. Pay more attention to everyday matters. Open up to others. Beware of undue dependency.*

RELATIONSHIPS

STRENGTHS: **INVOLVED, DEMANDING, HAPPY**

WEAKNESSES: **EXCLUSIVE, EUPHORIC, NEGLECTFUL**

BEST: **LOVE**

WORST: **FAMILY**

MILTON BERLE (7/12/08)
JOYCE MATTHEWS (12/5/19)

Comic Berle and showgirl Matthews were married twice (1941, 1949). Their reconciliations failed despite efforts to hold the marriage together by adopting a child. During this time, Matthews twice attempted suicide. **Also: Jane Welsh & Thos. Carlyle** (famous letters); **Ingmar Bergman & Sven Nykvist** (colleagues; director/cameraman); **Christine McVie & Dennis Wilson** (affair; rock stars).

July 11–18

THE WEEK OF THE PERSUADER
CANCER III

December 11–18

THE WEEK OF THE TITAN
SAGITTARIUS III

Interesting Byways

Fun-filled and imaginative, this relationship has a zest for pushing the envelope. Both partners are intensely curious, and they are unlikely to leave any interesting byways unexamined as they explore worlds of fantasy and adventure. Because Cancer III and Sagittarius III lie at a quincunx aspect to each other (150° apart in the zodiac), traditional astrology predicts some instability here. For these two, however, feelings of insecurity only tend to add to the excitement, spurring the relationship on to greater feats of daring.

Romantic relationships here will certainly include a strong element of fantasy and are likely to be brief but memorable. These two are seldom suited for the long haul—it's true that each can bring out the other's playful side, but they both have a depressive tendency as well, which will also be a factor between them. Still, although the partners might later see their affair as a mistake or even a disaster, they are likely to acknowledge its importance in their lives. Marriages are not particularly recommended, since Cancer III's and Sagittarius III's may both be much too busy with their careers to devote themselves to children and settled family life.

As family members, especially siblings of the opposite sex, this pair often becomes a lively focus of attention for parents and other relatives. They can be enchanting in their playfulness, creating many fairy-tale castles in the air. In the workplace, Cancer III's and Sagittarius III's are likely to argue for opposing plans and outlooks. Here the combination conflicts, and its tensions may be reflected in a rivalry within the company hierarchy.

Friendships are active and social. Here the partners will not be ashamed to act silly, although they may prove quite thin-skinned should others accuse them of childishness. As friends these two could have a positive effect in lowering the seriousness of any family or social group of which they are a part, encouraging others to get down in the sandbox with them.

ADVICE: *Try to hang in there a bit longer. Deepen your commitments. Beware of competitive career drives. A bit more seriousness wouldn't hurt.*

RELATIONSHIPS

STRENGTHS: **PLAYFUL, DARING, CHILDLIKE**

WEAKNESSES: **IRRESPONSIBLE, INSECURE, CHILDISH**

BEST: **FRIENDSHIP**

WORST: **MARRIAGE**

LIV ULLMANN (12/16/39)
INGMAR BERGMAN (7/14/18)

The intense professional relationship between director Bergman and actress Ullmann extended into their private lives. After divorcing their respective spouses, they lived together for 5 years and had a child. **Also: Bess Myerson & Ed Koch** (friends; NYC colleagues); **James Cagney & Edward G. Robinson** (movie gangsters).

531

STRENGTHS: ENCOURAGING, APPRECIATED, ADMIRED

WEAKNESSES: UNHAPPY, FRUSTRATED, PUSHY

BEST: MARRIAGE

WORST: LOVE

DONALD SUTHERLAND (7/17/34)
KIEFER SUTHERLAND (12/20/66)

Veteran actor Donald is the father of Kiefer, one of Hollywood's busiest young actors of the 80s and 90s. They appeared together in Kiefer's debut film, *Max Dugan Returns* (1983). *Also:* **Ginger Rogers & Howard Hughes** (affair; actress/industrialist); **Donald Sutherland & Jane Fonda** (friends; co-stars in *Klute*).

July 11–18
THE WEEK OF THE PERSUADER
CANCER III

December 19–25
THE CUSP OF PROPHECY
SAGITTARIUS-CAPRICORN CUSP

Bringing Out the Best

This relationship brings with it a striving for betterment. The partners usually encourage each other to improve, but they should take care that they are simply supporting each other's goals for growth, rather than imposing their opinions or judgments on each other. The tendency, unfortunately, is generally for them to have deep bonds but not necessarily happy ones. Cancer III's will try hard to bring out the positive side of Sagittarius-Capricorns, but their persuasive skills will truly be put to the test in trying to pressure these partners into being a bit more communicative, expressive and precise. Sagittarius-Capricorns may come to resent and even dislike a relationship that pushes them in such a direction, for they usually want to follow their own tempo, revealing themselves only when they are ready. Being themselves quite savvy, they for their part may try to encourage dowdier Cancer III's to be more with it.

A bit of the Cinderella complex emerges in love affairs in this combination: Sagittarius-Capricorns who lack self-confidence may refuse to admit that they have really been chosen by a Cancer III. All kinds of old scripts will run and rerun in their minds as they try to convince themselves that there's been some mistake and that they will eventually be unmasked as frauds. Granted, Cancer III's can enjoy the role of protector and savior, but they will gain much greater satisfaction out of a partner who can enjoy the relationship as his or her right.

The trick to making marriages and friendships work here is for the relationship itself to be seen as valuable and worthy of attention from outside—when the matchup succeeds in the eyes of relatives and friends. Appreciation and admiration of the pair as a unit is the heart of the matter, and achieving it is often the relationship's main focus. Cancer III parents tend to push their Sagittarius-Capricorn children out of their quiet world, and in return meet stubborn resistance. The partners are much more evenly matched in working relationships, but they can equally easily be powerful collaborators or powerful adversaries.

ADVICE: *Develop more self-confidence. Stop trying to prove yourself. Reach an equal level in daily life. Beware of overbearing and snobbish attitudes.*

STRENGTHS: FINANCIALLY ADEPT, MANAGERIAL, SENSIBLE

WEAKNESSES: MATERIALISTIC, WORKAHOLIC, DICTATORIAL

BEST: WORK

WORST: LOVE

JOE TORRE (7/18/40)
FRANK TORRE (12/30/31)

Yankee baseball manager Joe is the younger brother of retired ballplayer Frank, who once hit a World Series home run and held it over Joe. In '96 Joe led the Yankees to a World Series victory. Frank, still weak from heart surgery, called his brother to say, "Nice going, kid"—words that meant a great deal to Joe. *Also:* **Ginger Rogers & Lew Ayres** (married; actors).

July 11–18
THE WEEK OF THE PERSUADER
CANCER III

December 26–January 2
THE WEEK OF THE RULER
CAPRICORN I

United We Stand

The focus of this strong combination is likely to be operating as a unit in social or work groups. These two are apt to come together when they are feeling socially insecure; when each has attained a place in the larger group, the relationship may split. Achievement, ambition and career are emphasized here. The combination is not particularly comfort-loving, instead favoring work and achievement—perhaps too much so. Couples in this matchup have much to learn about social graces, and also about the nonmaterial side of life.

One would think that love affairs here would be sensible and practical, but this is rarely so. These partners are not invariably interested in each other, in which case, of course, they are unlikely to come together, but they are also capable of conceiving a strange passion for each other, in which case no amount of good sense will keep them apart. As a pair, they don't always handle emotions well, and can easily spin out of control. Perhaps two people who are so on the ball in other parts of their life occasionally need just to let it all out and run a bit amok in the fields of desire.

Friendships and marriages are more typical of the combination generally, tending to be extremely sensible. Here the partners' choices are likely to be deliberate and exact. Impulsiveness is repressed. Spouses in this combination are security oriented and extremely careful about how they spend their money. Neither is likely to be stingy, but expenses must be justified and money cannot be frittered away. As parents these two are likely to lay heavy trips on their children when it comes to assuming responsibility and working diligently.

The pair have considerable business strengths—in fact they may give economic considerations priority over all else. Any group they represent or manage will probably feel well looked after. Cancer III's and Capricorn I's can make excellent co-workers, and at the executive level they lend direction and good sense to corporate efforts. As boss-employee pairs, however, they are likely to resent each other's strictness.

ADVICE: *Realize that you can't control everything. Develop the flexibility to avoid freakout. Cultivate more spiritual values. Take care whom you value.*

July 11–18
THE WEEK OF THE PERSUADER
CANCER III

January 3–9
THE WEEK OF DETERMINATION
CAPRICORN II

Struggling to Overcome

This can be an unbeatable team, but as adversaries these partners will give each other the fight of their life. Both of them powerful and dominant individuals, Cancer III's and Capricorn II's don't always see eye to eye, especially when it comes to deciding who will call the shots. Even when they first meet, sparks sometimes fly, or else they just eye each other warily, showing little faith in each other. A lot of water usually has to flow under the bridge before this relationship is likely to show any sign of deeper trust. Once a bond is formed, however, the pair are usually attracted to the road less traveled; the tried and true has little interest for them.

Love affairs and friendships are not suggested here, for neither of these partners will go out of his or her way to take the first step to be kind, sympathetic or sharing. In marriages, working relationships or combinations of the two, however, a Cancer III and a Capricorn II can form a resolute unit. These latter pairings are seldom content with sitting on what they have, but are attracted to risky and even dangerous activities. Daring to fail is seen here as the given without which success is impossible. Indeed, the relationship is most comfortable when challenged, or even when beset by seemingly insurmountable odds. Marriages confronted by difficulties and hardships, and businesses suffering tremendous losses, are par for the course. Struggle becomes the watchword and rallying cry of such a relationship, helping it on its way to victory.

Family relationships, particularly parent-child matchups, are tricky here. Clashes of will abound in such relationships, and little is taken for granted. Cancer III's generally want Capricorn II's to talk about what is really bothering them, while Capricorn II's insist that Cancer III's make a deeper commitment to family life. These two often come closer together during times of crisis, when their relationship becomes the rock on which everything and everyone depends.

ADVICE: *Let up a bit in your intensity. Accept happiness if it comes your way. The easiest way is sometimes the best way. Don't summon up problems.*

RICHARD NIXON (1/9/13)
GERALD FORD (7/14/13)

President Nixon appointed Ford vice-president in 1973, when Spiro Agnew was forced to resign amid charges of bribery and tax violations. Ford became the 38th US president in 1974, following Nixon's resignation in the face of possible impeachment. As president, Ford, in a controversial move, pardoned Nixon for any crimes he may have committed.

July 11–18
THE WEEK OF THE PERSUADER
CANCER III

January 10–16
THE WEEK OF DOMINANCE
CAPRICORN III

Consummate Role-Players

This relationship seems to imagine life as a theater, and its partners as happy audience members commenting on the action. Yet these powerful individuals are quite capable of stepping onto the world stage themselves and taking part. Although these partners' opposition in the zodiac (where they lie 180° apart) leads traditional astrology to predict a rough ride for them, the friction they generate can also be warming. They don't take their infighting seriously, which is probably wise if their survival together is to be prolonged. They will also be sensible if they choose to operate in two different arenas, since neither likes the role of second fiddle.

Love affairs here are unlikely to develop beyond an initial encounter. Cancer III's may be threatened by the fearlessness of Capricorn III's, who for their part can be unsettled by this partner's sharp insights into their character. Marriages too are not as rewarding as they could be, and their consequences may be not just unproductive but destructive. Parent-child relationships, on the other hand, can be truly outstanding. Whichever of these two is the parent and which is the child, there is an understanding between Cancer III's and Capricorn III's that guarantees parental care and filial respect. Should a single parent be living with a single child in this combination, the two may play many different roles in the relationship's dramatic structure, so that they don't need a lot of input from outside their home base. The only drawback here is overprotectiveness and overattachment, which can be painful to deal with in early adulthood.

Cancer III's and Capricorn III's can quite possibly work together in a company, but usually do so best as equals on the same level. As soon as one occupies a higher position, annoying power conflicts may begin, although they rarely get completely out of hand. Cancer III–Capricorn III friendships can be vivid, exciting and a great deal of fun. They also have a slightly mocking and sarcastic quality: these two know how to express any antagonism through light and nonthreatening banter.

ADVICE: *How much is role-playing, how much is real? Be more objective about yourself. Strive for objectivity and understanding. Beware of isolation.*

LUISE RAINER (1/12/12)
CLIFFORD ODETS (7/18/06)

Playwright and screenwriter Odets rose to prominence in '31 with his first produced play, *Waiting for Lefty*. While working in Hollywood he met and married talented Oscar-winning actress Rainer in '37. When her career suddenly soured, many blamed it on bad advice from her husband. The couple divorced in '40.

DESI ARNAZ, JR. (1/19/53)
LUCIE ARNAZ (7/17/51)

Lucie and Desi Jr. are the children of Lucille Ball and Desi Arnaz. Lucie was born without fanfare, but by the time Desi came along the public was riveted: his photo graced the cover of *TV Guide*'s first issue. Both became tv/film performers.
Also: **Sidney Webb & Beatrice Webb** (married; Fabian Society); **Ginger Rogers & Cary Grant** (affair; actors); **Roald Amundsen & Umberto Nobile** (polar explorers).

July 11–18
THE WEEK OF THE PERSUADER
CANCER III

January 17–22
THE CUSP OF MYSTERY & IMAGINATION
CAPRICORN-AQUARIUS CUSP

Objectivity in Chaos

Instability is high in this relationship, and if it is to survive, a great deal of objectivity will have to be mustered to determine what it needs each time it runs into trouble. If it should fall off track, a supreme act of willpower might be necessary to right it. The relationship seesaws violently between emotional extremes, making any kind of settled life impossible. Cancer III's will generally engage in a lot of criticism, but unless these assessments are ultimately positive, they may only worsen the tension and lead to the relationship's demise. Capricorn-Aquarians do not react well to nagging, complaining or even positive suggestions, since they resent all limitations on their impulsiveness. Patient and mature Cancer III's, however, will often doggedly and determinedly exert every ounce of their persuasive power to put the relationship on a more even keel before admitting failure.

Love and marriage here are highly unpredictable. Since Cancer III's have much less need for attention than their partner, and since they generally prefer isolation to troublesome or messy involvements, it's hard to imagine them even entering such situations. If they do, they will periodically need to withdraw from the relationship's crazier aspects. These strategic retreats can actually promote objectivity; perhaps Capricorn-Aquarians would be wise to follow this example occasionally, too.

Friendships in this combination are best when limited in scope and kept from getting too deep emotionally. Cancer III and Capricorn-Aquarius friends do best when keeping things light. Sharing entertaining activities together, rather than solemn or stressful ones, is usually the best bet here.

Cancer III bosses or parents encountering impulsiveness and wildness in Capricorn-Aquarius employees or children are likely to be critical. At work and in families, attempts to objectify are not usually successful, since Capricorn-Aquarius rebelliousness and eccentricity and the Cancer III tendency to dominate often make a dangerously explosive mixture.

ADVICE: *Withdraw and observe. Analyze mistakes. Behave maturely. Even out feelings. Don't be controlled by your moods.*

LINDA RONSTADT (7/15/46)
AARON NEVILLE (1/24/41)

Singers Ronstadt and Neville were each successful in the 70s and 80s, but when they teamed up in '89 to record the chart-topping *Don't Know Much*, both careers soared to a new high. Neville's delicate falsetto, paired with Ronstadt's vocal robustness, led to many more successful recordings in the 90s.

July 11–18
THE WEEK OF THE PERSUADER
CANCER III

January 23–30
THE WEEK OF GENIUS
AQUARIUS I

A Hole in the Market

Here is an example of two people's strengths combining to form an even stronger and more powerful third entity. Although Cancer is a water sign and Aquarius air, this relationship is governed by fire and earth, in this case connoting passion and dedication. When Cancer III's and Aquarius I's set their sights on something, little will dissuade them from their aim. Especially knowing and intelligent in business, the relationship is quick in perceiving and filling holes in the market. In this and other areas of life, its intuitive strength allows its partners to follow their hunches and pull needed information seemingly out of nowhere, a helpful talent in times of crisis.

Love affairs here are often heavy and demand total involvement. The partners generally know when their lover is backing off emotionally, so faking responses is not a viable alternative—these relationships generally demand honesty. If a new involvement comes along, these partners will want to hear about it from each other, not from someone else. Marriages are most successful when power struggles can be put to rest from the start. The Cancer III will usually assume the dominant role, but the Aquarius I is capable of challenging this tendency. Once the power issue is resolved, the relationship may well find itself in a leadership position, at the center of its social or family group. Inventive in the extreme and capable of sharing whatever each partner has, no matter how little that is, friendships in this combination show marked improvisational talents. In the family, Cancer III–Aquarius I sibling pairs and parent-child combinations can be expected to disagree over the basic direction the family will take, particularly concerning matters of education, housing, and religion or ideology. In career matchups, these two are an excellent team, with Cancer III's contributing practical skills and hardheaded organizational abilities while Aquarius I's apply their quick intelligence to troubleshoot and solve problems. Aquarius I's have a penchant, however, for stretching their credit to the limit or simply spending more than they earn, and Cancer III's will have to keep a sharp eye on this habit.

ADVICE: *Settle power issues. Compromise on matters of ideology. Investigate the facts thoroughly. Don't assume you are headed in the right direction.*

July 11–18

THE WEEK OF THE PERSUADER
CANCER III

January 31–February 7

THE WEEK OF YOUTH & EASE
AQUARIUS II

A Fight for Honesty

This relationship has a hidden intensity that can break out suddenly like an unforeseen tidal wave, drowning everything in sight. On the surface, things appear harmonious enough, but resentments and frustrations often abound deeper down. For one thing, Cancer III's tend to be overdominant here. This makes Aquarius II's feel trapped and want to break free, which they often do—but covertly, without their partner suspecting. This may of course be because Cancer III's have blinded themselves to what is going on, but once they find out, their pain and anger can be volcanic. In a relationship with a facade that is as misleading as it is attractive, the core need is usually honesty .

No matter how nice friendships, love affairs and marriages in this combination seem, they often conceal tensions that may be ignored or even unsuspected by the partners themselves. It may be the people around this pair—the children of Cancer III–Aquarius II parents, say—who first begin acting out the repressed feelings and problems. Actually, this acting out by others may be the first sign that something is wrong with the relationship. And when the partners try to help the afflicted family member or friend, they may find themselves powerless, since it is really their own relationship that needs healing.

Aquarius II's too often operate on of a double standard. Cancer III's may go along with this either because they are overconfident, and don't feel threatened, or because they are hiding low self-esteem behind a mantle of bravado. Being honest enough to demand equal treatment, fostering communication and not taking things for granted are signs of health in a friendship between these two. In career and family matchups, too, the relationship must fight to demand honesty from its partners if it is to be successful.

ADVICE: *Dig a bit deeper. Don't kid yourself—you're probably overlooking a lot. Why let yourself be treated like a football? Maintain self-respect.*

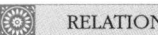

JAMES CAGNEY (7/17/1899)
RONALD REAGAN (2/6/11)

Cagney and Reagan were Hollywood actors whose friendship began in the 30s when they acted together in the comedy *Boy Meets Girl* (1938). With similar conservative political views, the friends remained close till Cagney's death in '89. Reagan delivered the eulogy at his funeral. **Also: Steve Wozniak & An Wang** (computer-industry entrepreneurs).

July 11–18

THE WEEK OF THE PERSUADER
CANCER III

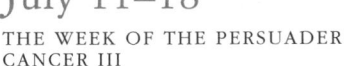

February 8–15

THE WEEK OF ACCEPTANCE
AQUARIUS III

Maddening Instability

This relationship is at its best and most easygoing when its activities are solid and well grounded. Trust is a big issue here: usually it's either present or it's not, and should these partners be unable to form a bond of trust, inherent instabilities will wreak havoc. In fact these partners have extremely different perspectives on life. Because Cancer III and Aquarius III lie in a quincunx aspect (150° apart) in the zodiac, astrology predicts a somewhat precarious relationship between them, and emotional instability can indeed run rampant here, driving them both to distraction. Unable to predict how the other person will respond in any given situation may be maddening. Interestingly, however, open conflict will be unusual here—unless one of the partners is driven right over the edge, in which case it will manifest in a big way.

Love affairs here can be extremely romantic and sensual, featuring all manner of seductive games and tricks. The relationship has a push-pull quality, with the lovers alternately drawn to each other at one moment and fleeing one another the next. Now they're afraid of losing each other, now that they'll be stuck with each other. Desire in this relationship is best accompanied by an escape route, then, which can always be held in reserve. Marriages may lend solidity to a faltering love affair but are in no way a guaranteed cure. Children, however, are often the cement that can help hold the relationship together.

Friendships in this combination should never be laden with too many responsibilities as a unit, nor should they expect too much from their own members. Free-and-easy interactions are best here. In family and work matchups, Aquarius III's may find themselves vulnerable to the fine Cancer III art of persuasion, but there is a limit to how far this partner can push them without making them angry. This particular tension will not easily disappear—it hangs around these relationships like an allergy, especially in parent-child and boss-employee matchups.

ADVICE: *Find common bonds in play and work. Strive for emotional consistency. Try to build strong bonds of trust. Always leave yourself a way out.*

YUL BRYNNER (7/11/15)
CLAIRE BLOOM (2/15/31)

Brynner and Bloom fell in love during the filming of *The Buccaneer* and *The Brothers Karamazov* (both 1958). The actors once had a rendezvous at Cecil B. DeMille's house in Paris. When their romance was over, Bloom said she had "immense, affectionate regard" for him. *Also:* **Gerald Ford & Sara Jane Moore** (attempted assassination).

STRENGTHS: CURIOUS, DEEP, CARING

WEAKNESSES: BIZARRE, OBSESSIVE, SECRETIVE

BEST: FAMILY

WORST: FRIENDSHIP

JAMES BROLIN (7/18/40)
ROBERT YOUNG (2/22/07)

Brolin and Young were co-stars in tv's long-running series *Marcus Welby, M.D.* (1969–79). Young played the kindly, paternal family doctor, while Brolin, his associate, played the next-generation counterpart. The actors worked together closely, creating a credible medical atmosphere.

July 11–18

THE WEEK OF THE PERSUADER
CANCER III

February 16–22

THE CUSP OF SENSITIVITY
AQUARIUS-PISCES CUSP

Twists and Turns

This relationship's core is deeply emotional. Its partners may find themselves engaged in a mutual exploration of the labyrinthine twists and turns of the human condition. The particular intricacies that engage them can certainly lie within the relationship itself, but as a pair these two are also interested in investigating other people's problems—including psychological ones—and perhaps helping to solve them. Cancer III's are among the few people who are likely to win the trust of Aquarius-Pisces (not an easy task), and to continue to justify that trust for many years.

This couple usually takes its love affairs and marriages very seriously. Both partners are quite aware of how important love and affection are in their relationship, and they tend to treat their bond with the greatest respect. If problems arise, in fact, it is sometimes because too much delicacy has been in play, with the partners virtually treading on eggs to avoid disturbing topics or activities. In being overprotective of their matchup and of each other, they may deny the confrontational and toughening experiences that move relationships forward in their spiritual and psychological growth. Cancer III's and Aquarius-Pisces should open up investigations of many more areas in their relationship beyond the few they find especially interesting.

As friends, Cancer III's and Aquarius-Pisces may show an interest in mystery and horror novels, gripping suspense thrillers and films, and other forms of art and popular culture that pique the imagination. Certain bizarre characteristics of their own relationship occasionally arise to excite their curiosity, which can even become obsessional at times. Secretive about such matters, these friends rarely reveal such interests to others.

As a professional team, Cancer III's and Aquarius-Pisces do best in freelance or service-oriented jobs, where they can express their interest in people and their desire to help them. Such caring attitudes are also likely to emerge in parent-child and grandparent-child matchups, which can come through powerfully in times of need.

ADVICE: *Lighten up a bit. Don't be so overprotective. Secrecy is less necessary than you think. When you are in need, you too can try expecting help from others.*

STRENGTHS: UNDERSTANDING, SENSITIVE, EDUCATIONAL

WEAKNESSES: UNCOMPROMISING, OVERMATERIALISTIC, SHOW-OFF

BEST: FRIENDSHIP

WORST: MARRIAGE

STEVEN JOBS (2/24/55)
STEVE WOZNIAK (7/11/51)

In the late 70s electronics engineer Wozniak and computer entrepreneur Jobs created a user-friendly PC that became the cornerstone for the Apple Computer Co. By the 80s they had started a revolution and an enormous new industry. *Also:* **Richie Sambora & Jon Bon Jovi** (Bon Jovi); **Lucie Arnaz & Desi Arnaz** (daughter/father; entertainers); **Milton Berle & Betty Hutton** (affair; comedian/actress).

July 11–18

THE WEEK OF THE PERSUADER
CANCER III

February 23–March 2

THE WEEK OF SPIRIT
PISCES I

A Message to Share

This relationship is often mainly concerned with the transmission of ideas, whether in financial, social or spiritual areas or as entertainment. The spotlight can be on the relationship itself or on what it is trying to say. Although Cancer and Pisces are both water signs, this relationship is ruled by earth, an element implying a thoroughly practical sensibility. Pisces I's are not known for their materialistic side, but in relationships with Cancer III's they can learn a great deal about the world and how it works, financially, politically and socially. They are less interested in money for its own sake and more in what can be done with it to improve the quality of life.

Love affairs between Cancer III's and Pisces I's can be highly sensuous but also sensitive and understanding. These partners will usually take the time to get to know each other, using their quiet time together to reach new levels of peace and contentment. But their relationship also has an outrageous and uninhibited side that it puts on for show. Humor can play a key role here, particularly when of the ironic and sarcastic sort. Marriages are not particularly recommended unless the partners are willing to undergo serious adjustments to each other's needs and to be willing to compromise and be flexible.

Cancer III–Pisces I friends may meet in their student years and continue such relationships until much later in life. Their bond is a hunger not necessarily for learning but for social maturation and development. Moving away from the role of student and into the role of teacher will be a highly satisfying experience, and is often the most positive direction the relationship can take as friends age.

Family matchups, especially sibling pairs of the same sex, can be close and understanding. But sensitivities are also very pronounced, so that these brother or sister pairs often clash emotionally. Working relationships between Cancer III's and Pisces I's may be improved if the co-workers take the time to get to know each other personally, perhaps in informal pursuits away from work.

ADVICE: *Be aware of your effects on others. Develop your spiritual side more fully. Flexibility and compromise are important. Be more accepting.*

July 11–18

THE WEEK OF THE PERSUADER
CANCER III

March 3–10

THE WEEK OF THE LONER
PISCES II

RELATIONSHIPS

STRENGTHS: **EMPATHIC, DEVOTED, RELAXED**

WEAKNESSES: **OVERDEPENDENT, OVERPROTECTIVE, ISOLATED**

BEST: **FRIENDSHIP**

WORST: **FAMILY**

Independently Dependent

The involvement between these two personalities is usually quite profound, plumbing to such a deep level that most of their interaction may occur on a subconscious or even psychic plane. Since much of what occurs here is nonverbal, the overall mood is rather comfortable. While both partners tend to spend a lot of time alone, their emotional understanding runs high, and they find it easy to be open with each other. There is a tendency for these two to become mutually dependent, then, in a rather independent way.

In romantic relationships, Cancer III's and Pisces II's rarely hold back with each other emotionally. Emotional interactions, sexual or otherwise, are prolonged and satisfying. These partners can be quite faithful to each other over the long haul, but an undeniable dependency manifests in this relationship, having both salutary and negative effects. The relationship functions very well when the partners can give their all to each other only when they choose to do so, each having their own space to which they can retreat, whether they live together or not. Although outright sex and love addictions are unusual here, Cancer III's and Pisces II's may bond to each other so strongly that they are unlikely to become deeply involved with another person even when the relationship is over. In both love affairs and marriage, the relationship should aim to be more open and partners to form meaningful friendships with others.

Cancer III–Pisces II friendships can be outstanding. Their tendency to isolate themselves is not so strong here. Cancer III's usually take the lead in bringing their Pisces II friends out in the world, encouraging them and furthering their career and social development. Pisces II's, meanwhile, furnish the sympathy and understanding that Cancer III's crave, particularly when their professional duties are put aside.

Parent-child and sibling relationships between Cancer III's and Pisces II's are usually empathic and accepting. Each values the other's opinion highly, and the pair share a great trust, which will cause deep pain if abused. Cancer III–Pisces II career matchups are often relaxed and financially productive.

ADVICE: *Form friendships with others. Widen social involvement. Justify trust. Stay objective. Beware of letting feelings dominate your life.*

YEVGENY YEVTUSHENKO (7/18/33)
IRINA RATUSHINSKAYA (3/4/54)

Yevtushenko and Ratushinskaya are among Russia's leading 20th-century poets. His poetry speaks out against social and religious injustice. He made several highly publicized tours of the US in the 60s. Ratushinskaya was a KGB prisoner (1983–86) and wrote hundreds of poems while in confinement, keeping them in her head until her prize-winning book was published in '88.

July 11–18

THE WEEK OF THE PERSUADER
CANCER III

March 11–18

THE WEEK OF DANCERS & DREAMERS
PISCES III

RELATIONSHIPS

STRENGTHS: **PEACEMAKING, NATURAL, SERVICE-ORIENTED**

WEAKNESSES: **SELF-DENYING, SACRIFICIAL, VULNERABLE**

BEST: **WORK**

WORST: **LOVE**

Natural Peacemakers

At heart this relationship is quite complex, but at the same time it is one of the most natural and comfortable matchups in the year. These two in many ways come at each other from different ends of the spectrum: Cancer III's are often practical types, taken up with worldly concerns and the structure of power, while Pisces III's are more idealistic about following their lifelong dreams. Yet because Cancer III and Pisces III form a classic water-sign trine (they lie 120° apart in the zodiac, and are both water signs), astrology predicts an easy relationship with an emphasis on feelings. Because of the natural sympathy between these two, they are capable of overcoming their differences, building acceptance and trust, and discovering what they have in common. The overall fit is relaxed.

The relationship is especially strong in the social sphere. Whether a friendship or a marriage, it can function magnificently to bring friends or family members together. It has a knack for reconciling hostile individuals or warring factions, and is naturally suited to play the role of mediator or peacemaker. Cancer III's are often realistic enough to recognize the essential truth of the Pisces III philosophical outlook, and can work hard to implement such ideas. One might say that belief is the bond between these two; belief not only in an ideal but in their relationship itself, which can accomplish so much in its concern for others.

Given the relationship's service-oriented stance, whether in the professional, family or interpersonal realm, Cancer III–Pisces III partners must be sure to leave enough time for themselves. One difficulty here is self-denial, with the partners often calling upon themselves to make the greatest sacrifice of all: neglecting their own relationship and denying it a certain amount of sustenance it needs for emotional and spiritual growth. They must be more selfish occasionally, deny the needs of others for a time so that they can deepen their own personal bond.

ADVICE: *Feed yourself as well as others. Don't put yourself last. Build a stronger ego. Let others contribute to you. Keep time free for personal matters.*

F.W. DE KLERK (3/18/36)
NELSON MANDELA (7/18/18)

De Klerk became president of South Africa in 1989. By '91 he had Mandela released from prison. Together they negotiated the repeal of apartheid legislation and worked to give blacks a national role in politics. In 1993 they shared the Nobel Peace Prize.

Also: **Berenice Abbott & Diane Arbus** (partners; photographers); **Bill Cosby & Bobby McFerrin** (entertainers; Cosby discovery).

July 19–25
THE CUSP OF OSCILLATION
CANCER-LEO CUSP

July 19–25
THE CUSP OF OSCILLATION
CANCER-LEO CUSP

ERIC HOFFER (7/25/02)
HERBERT MARCUSE (7/19/1898)

Hoffer and Marcuse were contemporary social philosophers of the mid-20th century. Marcuse was an academic radical advocating rejection of the existing social order. Hoffer was a self-educated longshoreman, critical of mass movements and causes, emphasizing a more individualistic approach. **Also: George McGovern & Bella Abzug** (political allies; 60s liberals).

Leveling Off

The Cancer-Leo personality is subject to wide swings of mood, which this relationship usually magnifies—sometimes to the point where they are intolerable. Yet a workable dynamic can also be achieved here, particularly if what the partners are doing together has to do with emotions, psychology, art and music, or the healing arts. In fact, pooled Cancer-Leo understanding of the creative process and the human psyche can be invaluable to any family, social or professional group.

Cancer-Leos often cry out for stability in their relationships, but they are unlikely to find it with each other. Emotions in this love affair can swing from sparkling and even wildly exciting to depressed and finally cold. Either a breakup or a breakdown is likely in short order. Should the couple try marriage, they will certainly need the steadiness that comes from a solid financial base, firm career commitments, a stable domestic situation and adequate pay and benefits, yet even should all these be present they will still have no guarantee of success unless they can achieve some kind of emotional balance.

As friends, Cancer-Leos will have to understand and adjust to the dynamic of their relationship, which can be difficult. Disaster looms when one of them is either too upbeat or too depressed, and a seesaw effect—whenever one is up, the other is down—can also be extremely frustrating. At home, a Cancer-Leo parent-child or sibling relationship will often keep things lively, but will also lend an air of instability and unpredictability to family life.

Work relationships between these two can be good as long the partners do not overreact to each other's mood swings. The engineering of a decrease in emotional interaction and an increase in objectivity is essential here. Enterprising and somewhat aggressive projects, in which challenge plays an important role, are especially favored. Another lesson that will have to be learned, perhaps the hard way, is holding back in situations where impulsiveness could be counterproductive, even deadly.

ADVICE: *Even things out. Strive for emotional control. Aim for objectivity. Fulfill basic requirements. Don't overreact or lash out blindly.*

BOB DOLE (7/22/23)
ELIZABETH DOLE (7/29/36)

Bob Dole, 1996 presidential candidate, has spent most of his career as an influential senator. He retired from office to run for the presidency. Wife Elizabeth, who is president of the American Red Cross, was a strong presence in his unsuccessful campaign. **Also: Albert Warner & Jack Warner** (brothers; co-founders Warner Bros.); **Alexandre Dumas père & Alexandre Dumas fils** (father/son; writers).

July 19–25
THE CUSP OF OSCILLATION
CANCER-LEO CUSP

July 26–August 2
THE WEEK OF AUTHORITY
LEO I

Getting to the Top

An electric energy manifests in this combination, which can lead both partners to great success. The relationship demonstrates a high level of intelligence, which it generally puts in the service of ambition: getting to the top is important for these two, who in fact usually rank the personal side of their relationship second in importance to its social, political or financial goals. Power drives must not be allowed to get out of hand here, however, for the relationship can run amok if not properly guided and controlled.

Love affairs here are rarely of outstanding depth or passion. They abound in energy, but don't always direct it well; sexual energy in particular may wind up sublimated into other activities. Marriages, on the other hand, can work out excellently, as long as both partners are given full independence and family responsibilities are kept to a minimum. As spouses these two may be very ambitious for each other, or may even team up in a career activity. They are quite capable of working out an arrangement crafted to suit them, managing to preserve whatever quality time together they need; for example, even when work demands prevent them from seeing a lot of each other. Their children, however, must not expect a great deal of fuss or attention from them.

In the family, both parent-child and sibling pairs can also be career oriented, either spurring each other on to new heights or actually working together professionally. These relationships can be inspiring, but they are not immune to competitiveness and even open combat. Friendships in this combination can begin at school and continue throughout life. They often find Cancer-Leos depending on rock-solid Leo I conviction and Leo I's depending on Cancer-Leos to help them recharge their batteries from time to time. If competitive feelings arise over a common love object, these friends often choose to stick together, ultimately rejecting the attractive intruder.

ADVICE: *Try to have more time for each other. Get a bit of distance on your career needs. Don't let ambition run out of control. Be sure you know what you need.*

July 19–25

THE CUSP OF OSCILLATION
CANCER-LEO CUSP

August 3–10

THE WEEK OF BALANCED STRENGTH
LEO II

RELATIONSHIPS

STRENGTHS: **SUPPORTED, STIMULATING, RELIABLE**

WEAKNESSES: **WITHDRAWN, REJECTED, UNSYMPATHETIC**

BEST: **FRIENDSHIP**

WORST: **WORK**

Woven in the Fabric

The Cancer-Leo–Leo II combination is quite goal oriented, but the goals are usually internal ones—that is, they are goals for the relationship itself. This is often a fairly private affair, then, with quite closeted aims. Yet oddly enough, as a couple these two will seem larger than life; it's just that no one will be able to see exactly what they hope to accomplish—until they see it themselves. While Cancer-Leos will bring verve and excitement to the pairing, they may also come to depend heavily on the steadfastness, constancy and balance that are the Leo II contribution. In fact, the inner stability of most Leo II's may be woven into the relationship's fabric, becoming its underlying strength. Problems will arise, then, should Leo II's go through a depression: if their self-confidence is undermined they can go into a slump and disintegrate before the horrified eyes of a dependent Cancer-Leo partner.

Love affairs here can be intense, full of exciting and romantic moments. This energy level will be hard to sustain: Cancer-Leos periodically need to withdraw into themselves, which can make Leo II's feel rejected, withdraw in turn, and show signs of hurt or even paranoia. The daily routine of married life will provide Cancer-Leos with a more objective base of stability and structure that will help keep them balanced. Leo II's are intensely loyal and devoted, further supporting the relationship's stability.

Sibling relationships between members of the same sex can be stimulating and supportive—friendships, too. But although these two are there for each other in times of need, their energies may clash when they are forced to interact on a daily basis. In addition, Leo II's may understand what is bothering Cancer-Leos but refuse to sympathize. Limiting contact, arranging for privacy and encouraging independence will often help to alleviate these problems. At work, Cancer-Leos are more team players and Leo II's rugged individualists who like to act on their own, so don't expect too much cooperation between them. Their goals will also be generally mysterious to their co-workers.

ADVICE: *Find other things to believe in besides each other. Establish a solid basis in practical activity. When working together, try to compromise.*

COURTNEY LOVE (8/9/64)
WOODY HARRELSON (7/23/61)

Harrelson and Love were co-stars in the Oscar-nominated film *The People vs. Larry Flynt* (1996). They gave convincing performances as the outrageous publisher of *Hustler* magazine and his drug-addicted wife, Althea. **Also: Ernest Hemingway & Mata Hari** (reputed affair; writer/femme fatale, spy).

July 19–25

THE CUSP OF OSCILLATION
CANCER-LEO CUSP

August 11–18

THE WEEK OF LEADERSHIP
LEO III

RELATIONSHIPS

STRENGTHS: **THOUGHTFUL, OBJECTIVE, FUNNY**

WEAKNESSES: **DISAPPOINTING, OVERBEARING, DISINTERESTED**

BEST: **ACQUAINTANCE**

WORST: **MARRIAGE**

Turning to Laughter

Problems can certainly arise in this relationship, but its quick-wittedness and its insistence on having fun and not taking things too seriously may be its saving graces. These two depend heavily on their mental strengths to get through emotional or physical bad times; turning to laughter to gain objectivity can be difficult for them as individuals. Together, though, they are able to smile at themselves and others, often indulging in ironic and satiric wordplay.

Love, marriage and family relationships are unlikely to be successful. Cancer-Leos have a sensitive side that craves understanding, and Leo III's are usually too busy with their own egos and projects to really pay attention. Leo III's for their part need to be adored, even worshiped, and this won't always sit well with Cancer-Leos, especially since they too want to be king of the jungle. Cancer-Leos are apt to turn a cold shoulder when their Leo III lovers, spouses or parents have just ignored them or accused them of something. Simply put, Cancer-Leos usually demand more emotional support than Leo III's are ready or able to give. It is a classic case of ego and neediness clashing, and all the humor this relationship has to offer will be needed to deal with it.

The success of a friendship between these two will generally depend on how much time and energy they are prepared to put into it. If they find themselves constantly disappointed by missed appointments and forgotten telephone calls, they might be better off rethinking the relationship and making it more of a fun acquaintanceship or companionship without any deep personal involvement. At work, Leo III bosses may expect a uniformly high result from Cancer-Leo employees and instead be confronted with erratic and unpredictable work. Likewise Cancer-Leos are likely to find their Leo III bosses overbearing and unsympathetic. Should these two be co-workers on the same level, they will encounter the same difficulties, but to a lesser extent, and good-natured teasing and kidding around will lighten the mood.

ADVICE: *Keep it light. Control judgmental attitudes. Accept lower expectations. Take life as it comes. Try to be more attentive.*

WILLIAM C. DeMILLE (7/25/1878)
CECIL B. DeMILLE (8/12/1881)

William, less known than his famous producer-director brother, was originally a NY playwright who went to Hollywood following his brother's initial success. William directed and produced on his own, doing moderately well—and also adapted his stage plays for others to direct, including brother Cecil.

STRENGTHS: **BALANCED,
EFFECTIVE, COMPOSED**

WEAKNESSES: **ANGRY,
SUPPRESSED, UNSTABLE**

BEST: **WORK**

WORST: **LOVE**

ALEXANDRE DUMAS *PÈRE* (7/24/1802)
LOLA MONTEZ (8/25/1818)

Dumas, author of *The Three Muske-teers* (1844), was the most prolific writer of the French Romantic school. He had a brief affair with provocative stage dancer Montez, the reigning sex symbol of her day. In 1870 Dumas died from syphilis, rumored to have been contracted from Montez. *Also:* **Bob Dole & Bill Clinton** (1996 political opponents).

July 19–25
THE CUSP OF OSCILLATION
CANCER-LEO CUSP

August 19–25
THE CUSP OF EXPOSURE
LEO-VIRGO CUSP

Finding Acceptable Compromises

The greatest challenge that this relationship faces is to create and maintain a sense of balance. Neither partner is known for emotional stability, and the relationship magnifies the problem of keeping emotions and particularly anger under control. In addition, ego issues are a hot button here. Whether these two work together, are rivals or both, they will need to maximize their control over their feelings, not only so that they can be seen in a better light but also to increase their effectiveness when doing battle in the realms of love, business, family or social life.

This combination may be too unsettled to last long in love and marriage. Trying to even out extremes will be a trying process, a battle under the fire of flying emotions. In the same way that the relationship amplifies instabilities, however, it may increase the chances of reconciling extremes and finding acceptable compromises. For better or worse, these relationships are challenging, ego-driven and highly emotional. They are also often rewarding.

In friendships, Cancer-Leos will be alternately pleased and appalled, depending on their mood, by the outrageous and extroverted side of Leo-Virgos. They may also find that when they are discouraged or depressed, Leo-Virgos who have their hands full coping with their own feelings may not have the time or the sympathy to cope with them. These friendships will benefit from social ties with other friends, couples and family members.

In the family and at work, the presence of a built-in social control and organizational structure will give this pair more stability. Personal animosities and small irritations should be kept under control or eliminated, at least in the presence of other people. If these partners suppress or bury their differences of opinion, however, anger and other destructive feelings will inevitably break out at a later date. Perhaps the best policy here is an objective honesty, where opinions are expressed politely and in private, without emotional overtones or innuendo.

ADVICE: *Find the middle ground. Control emotions without suppressing them. Guide feelings in a healthy direction. Try to be as honest as you can.*

STRENGTHS: **THOUGHTFUL,
CONSERVATIVE, ENDURING**

WEAKNESSES: **FEARFUL,
INHIBITING, DEPRESSED**

BEST: **FRIENDSHIP**

WORST: **MARRIAGE**

JIMMY CONNORS (9/2/52)
ILIE NASTASE (7/19/46)

Nastase and Connors were 2 of tennis' most crowd-pleasing players in the early 70s. They were also bad boys of the court, both hot-blooded and contentious with officials. They played each other often. In '72 and '73 Nastase was ranked #1, with Connors #3. From 1974–78 Connors was #1, while Nastase descended in the rankings.

July 19–25
THE CUSP OF OSCILLATION
CANCER-LEO CUSP

August 26–September 2
THE WEEK OF SYSTEM BUILDERS
VIRGO I

Delicate Duality

This relationship can fluctuate widely in mood, being now easygoing, now full of what can best be described as a kind of moral indignation. Both of these positions are limiting, since one of them represents too little judgment and the other too much. They also constitute a duality that imposes worry. These two would do well to realize that the truth is in the middle way, and to seek it there. Another problem here is that although Virgo I's may provide Cancer-Leos with needed stability, they also tend to be hard on themselves. Their depressions will cry out for attention. Instead, a dynamic sometimes emerges in which demanding and constantly moving Cancer-Leos push Virgo I's into a downward spiral, while themselves feeling pinned down by the Virgo I talent for systems. The relationship's challenge is to minimize dependencies while uncovering positive energies and fully expressing a sense of freedom. The most delicate balance may lie simply in acceptance.

In romantic relationships, Virgo I's may find the extremes of Cancer-Leo energy exciting but hard to accept, let alone control. Virgo I's can have a grounding effect here, but Cancer-Leos dislike and are bored by predictability, and may grow tired of this actually beneficial influence. Instead of complaining when things don't go as they wish, these partners will have to learn to accept the good with the bad.

Marriages and work relationships here tend to be either overcareful or overlax. There is sometimes an effort to compensate for imagined but expected difficulties while overlooking more concrete problem areas. This may produce a conservative, even fearful attitude, which blunts initiative and keeps the relationship from success, becoming a self-fulfilling prophecy. This problem does not undermine the relationship's stability, however, and can in fact guarantee its longevity. Friendships and family relationships are often intertwined, for siblings and their friends can form stable Cancer-Leo–Virgo I groups. Often arising during school years, such relationships can provide reliable and lasting enjoyment into late adulthood. Cancer I's and Leo-Virgos often go further toward accepting each other here than in other kinds of relationship.

ADVICE: *Try to accept the whole package. Self-fulfilling prophecies can ensure failure. Employ positive visualizations. Complaining can waste energy.*

July 19–25

THE CUSP OF OSCILLATION
CANCER-LEO CUSP

September 3–10

THE WEEK OF THE ENIGMA
VIRGO II

Feeding the Flame

Here is a fiery relationship, full of the passion and excitement that make life a romantic adventure. The great need here is for one of the partners, or even the relationship itself, to provide a firm direction that will take the pair to a higher level. Either partner is capable of assuming this role, but in many cases it is filled by the social, career or religious orientation of the relationship as a whole. Ambition is strong in this matchup. The partners are likely to sacrifice their personal needs to it, and indeed it may threaten the relationship itself.

Cancer-Leo–Virgo II love affairs may begin with powerfully romantic feelings, but do not easily penetrate to their partners' deeper emotions. As a result, the fuel that would feed the fire may be in limited supply, and the affair may quickly burn out. Marriages are a different story, for here one of the guiding orientations that the relationship itself can provide usually emerges to lay a solid foundation. Ambition in this case can be reflected in the high priority usually given to the career of one of the partners, probably the one most likely to achieve success. As parents these two must be extremely careful not to push their children unmercifully to overachieve in order to satisfy their own ambition.

Although family members often pursue their own careers, they will keep in close touch with each other in professional matters. The family itself may provide the strong basis and the leadership element on which its members depend. Cancer-Leos and Virgo II's often take great pride in their family's career achievements, and feel that they have to live up to its patterns of success. Cancer-Leo–Virgo II co-workers often have a family connection, and vice versa.

Friendships in this combination can be inspiring and competitive. Achieving a personal best often becomes the relationship's shared focus.

ADVICE: *You may be your own worst enemy. Beware of blind ambition. Power drives may boomerang. Make room for spirituality in your life.*

July 19–25

THE CUSP OF OSCILLATION
CANCER-LEO CUSP

September 11–18

THE WEEK OF THE LITERALIST
VIRGO III

Seeing the Other Point of View

The principal challenge in this relationship will be whether the partners can be sensitive enough to each other's needs. Insensitivity is likely to arouse tremendous conflict, and at times can threaten to tear the relationship apart. Critical and rejecting Virgo III attitudes are likely to arouse resentments and antagonisms in Cancer-Leos. Virgo III's in turn may be put off by Cancer-Leos' penchant for expressing their emotions publicly, and by their lack of sensitivity to their partner's need for privacy and discretion. Great care must be taken, then, to sense the other partner's point of view and to treat it with respect.

Love affairs here are likely to be on the cool side. As lovers these two rarely delude themselves about the nature of romance, which they may see as enjoyable but realistically perhaps an illusion in the end. The relationship rarely gives itself entirely in the emotional realm, then, tending to hold back and guard its vulnerabilities.

Marriages and working relationships can produce both practicality and flamboyance. Both Virgo III's and Cancer-Leos are no strangers to structure, and they work well within organizations. As team players they tend to preserve the good of the group, but only up to a point—they jealously guard their own interests. Idealism and faithfulness will only go so far with such a pair, and that boundary is usually reached when either individual feels taken advantage of or put in a compromising position. Power struggles are all too often the result.

In the family, Virgo III parents are not always sympathetic enough to their Cancer-Leo children's need for approval. They can also be brutally honest, letting their children know immediately when their behavior doesn't cut the cake. Even when very young, Virgo III's have standards of reasonable and constant behavior that Cancer-Leo parents may find unattainable. Cancer-Leo–Virgo III sibling pairs who are oversensitive to each other will strain the family patience with their bickering and sarcasm.

ADVICE: *Show greater sensitivity and respect. Don't hold back in love. Be aware of how you affect others. Too much realism can take the fun out of life.*

July 19–25
THE CUSP OF OSCILLATION
CANCER-LEO CUSP

September 19–24
THE CUSP OF BEAUTY
VIRGO-LIBRA CUSP

Meeting the Dark Side

The more these partners try to hide their relationship's less favorable side, the more it tends to come to light. Together they have a problem handling misfortune, pain and loss. As long as things are going well, the world is a rosy place; but when difficulties surface, they may be remarkably unprepared to handle them. There is a tendency here to ignore painful issues and to stuff them deep in a well of repression. The relationship's main challenge, and perhaps its chief focus, is to meet difficulties head-on, acknowledging that life indeed has a dark side that must be encountered, dealt with and integrated into the whole picture.

Cancer-Leo–Virgo-Libra love affairs can be exciting but extremely unstable. A hunger for sensation of all sorts drives them in the direction of ever new, ever more stimulating experience. When impossibly high thresholds of excitement can no longer be maintained, the relationship is likely to slip into deep depression. The partners must learn not to use the world of experience as an escape, and to get the most out of a situation before dashing off to the next attraction. Marriage is not recommended for this pair unless they can even out their life together by building a stable basis for the relationship and sticking to it. Increased responsibility, including children, may help in this process, but should not be undertaken lightly.

Sibling relationships and friendships in this combination are often oriented toward fun and exciting experiences. Such relationships may exhibit immaturity and irresponsibility from childhood right into early adulthood. Growing up is a real problem here—the reality factor is low. In business, Cancer-Leos and Libra-Virgos can be effective entrepreneurs together, particularly when Libra-Virgo taste and judgment are allowed to meld with Cancer-Leo leadership and innovativeness.

ADVICE: *Responsible actions can be fun, too. Life isn't always a bed of roses. Face your shadow and accept it. Pain is often necessary for progress.*

July 19–25
THE CUSP OF OSCILLATION
CANCER-LEO CUSP

September 25–October 2
THE WEEK OF THE PERFECTIONIST
LIBRA I

Never a Dull Moment

This relationship is definitely upbeat. Its focus is likely to be nonmaterial—perhaps an interest in new age or spiritual subjects—and as a result it will rarely feel grounded; these partners may just have to reconcile themselves to the idea that in this matchup stability and practicality were just never meant to be. The question is, can they handle the relationship without losing their grip. Neither of these personalities is the most firmly rooted. Both like excitement, and both are prone to becoming overwhelmed when faced with extreme emotion. Finally, Libra I criticism can have an unsettling effect on Cancer-Leos, and Cancer-Leo mood swings may prove too much for Libra I's.

Love affairs in this combination can be passionate but filled with turmoil. Libra I's will enjoy the intensity of emotion here, but will probably also find it interferes with their work. Cancer-Leos may discover all the romance they ever wanted, but will have trouble holding on to their attractive partners. Both partners will have ambivalent feelings toward this relationship, then. Marriages will not be dull, but are apt to bring out the depressive sides of both personalities, particularly when lack of interest and unresponsiveness rear their ugly heads.

As friends, Cancer-Leos and Libra I's often share a deep bond of the spirit that can help them to overcome any difficulties they encounter in other areas of their lives. Their openness with each other supports them in examining problems both in and beyond their relationship, and the advice they give each other for dealing with these issues is usually sound. In the family, too, parent-child relationships in this combination can be mutually accepting and caring.

At work, this couple can make an outstanding combination, especially at the executive level. Cancer-Leo leadership strengths and Libra I precision and technical abilities can be a highly effective combination. Both partners should find their own strengths rather than intruding on those of their partner. Both should also turn for financial advice to a third colleague, for Libra I's often have an unfounded confidence in their skills with money.

ADVICE: *Cultivate practical interests. Find a solid basis for your life. Acquire skill in money matters. Beware of thinking you know more than you do.*

Left sidebar (top)

RELATIONSHIPS

STRENGTHS: **FUN, EXCITING, CHALLENGING**

WEAKNESSES: **SUPERFICIAL, SENSATIONALISTIC, ESCAPIST**

BEST: **WORK**

WORST: **MARRIAGE**

F. SCOTT FITZGERALD (9/24/1896)
ZELDA SAYRE (7/24/1900)

Writer Sayre was overshadowed by Fitzgerald. Married in 1920, much of his life revolved around her, probably damaging his work. By the late 20s he was an alcoholic, while she was diagnosed as schizophrenic. The couple lived apart during the 30s. She was mentally ill; he turned to screenwriting till his death in 1940. *Also:* **George McGovern & Thomas Eagleton** (presidential running mates).

Left sidebar (bottom)

RELATIONSHIPS

STRENGTHS: **UPBEAT, CARING, NONMATERIAL**

WEAKNESSES: **UNGROUNDED, OVERCONFIDENT, DEPRESSIVE**

BEST: **FRIENDSHIP**

WORST: **LOVE**

 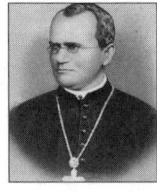

THOMAS HUNT MORGAN (9/25/1866)
GREGOR MENDEL (7/22/1822)

Mendel, an Austrian monk, discovered the laws of heredity and suggested the existence of genes. Later, American zoologist Morgan advanced Mendel's work in the field of genetics, for which he was awarded the 1933 Nobel Prize in physiology. *Also:* **Robin Williams & Christopher Reeve** (friends; actors).

July 19–25

THE CUSP OF OSCILLATION
CANCER-LEO CUSP

October 3–10

THE WEEK OF SOCIETY
LIBRA II

RELATIONSHIPS

STRENGTHS: **STRUCTURING, PRACTICAL, INSPIRATIONAL**

WEAKNESSES: **RIGID, UNSYMPATHETIC, DISSENTING**

BEST: **FAMILY**

WORST: **FRIENDSHIP**

Stabilizing Attitudes

This combination can achieve a curious kind of stability. It often focuses on building a workable structure that can give it definition and support, and this tendency will spread to other areas of the partners' lives, so that eventually they will find themselves running along quite smoothly. Care must be taken, though, not to stick too rigidly to the structures that are created. These two must also work on evaluation, and on learning to shed what isn't working. Cancer-Leos often lack a clear insight into themselves, and Libra II psychological skills can prove quite helpful here; conversely, Libra II's can benefit from the example of Cancer-Leo ambition, which can inspire them to further their own professional aspirations. These two have practical and stabilizing effects on each other.

In love and marriage, Cancer-Leos and Libra II's can suit each other well on the physical level, expressing affection easily. Yet true empathy may not emerge between them, and even if one of them understands what is bothering the other, there is no guarantee that he or she will feel sympathetic. Both partners have their own ideas about human behavior, and their relationship fosters a lot of individuality. When disagreements about lifestyle arise, as they inevitably do, Libra II's are usually the ones whose advice should be followed in social matters, while Cancer-Leos are more perceptive about careers. Marriages in this combination can attract needy individuals looking for direction and affection, motivations that may cause problems at times.

Friendships may have problems establishing constancy and building a sound connection. Operating systems may be unwelcome here, the partners preferring to be free and easy, and recognizing few guidelines or responsibilities. More casual ties are usually preferable to deep friendships. Family members in this combination often work to enhance the stability of their group, and especially to bring conflicts under control. More distant relatives rarely lose touch with each other entirely, and may tighten their bonds if they both wish it. Co-workers can function well as long as their roles are well defined and boundaries are not overstepped.

ADVICE: *Touch bases emotionally. Strive for empathy as well as understanding. See the big picture. Ignore minor irritations. Protect what you have.*

SUSAN SARANDON (10/4/46)
CHRIS SARANDON (7/24/42)

The Sarandons met when Chris was an aspiring actor and Susan an English major at college. She soon switched to drama. They married in 1969 and moved to NY. While accompanying him to an audition, she landed her first film role, in *Joe* (1970). Both careers took off in the 70s. They divorced in '79.

July 19–25

THE CUSP OF OSCILLATION
CANCER-LEO CUSP

October 11–18

THE WEEK OF THEATER
LIBRA III

RELATIONSHIPS

STRENGTHS: **FANCIFUL, INTROSPECTIVE, PRIVATE**

WEAKNESSES: **ISOLATED, MISUNDERSTOOD, ALIENATED**

BEST: **LOVE**

WORST: **WORK**

Introspective Investigations

This thoughtful relationship may encourage its partners to spend time alone together. Cancer-Leos and Libra III's feel very much at home in the spotlight, but their relationship enhances their more sensitive and reclusive side. Cancer-Leos will usually have made introspective investigation an important part of their lives much earlier on, but this may be the first chance Libra III's have had for a serious encounter with this part of themselves. Problems can arise if they come to resent the relationship for making them deal unduly with someone else's emotional problems up close. Cancer-Leos in turn are likely to feel rejected by Libra III lack of interest, and to get depressed; which will only make Libra III's feel misunderstood and isolated, engulfing both partners in a cycle of alienation. Much time and patience will have to be invested in this relationship to bring the partners closer together.

Both Cancer-Leos and Libra III's tend to have strongly balanced masculine and feminine sides. This not only makes many sorts of relationship possible between them but also becomes a trait of whatever relationship they end up with. A remarkable equilibrium is possible here. Friendships, marriages and love affairs seem surprisingly private in nature, considering the world's view of Cancer-Leos and Libra III's as extroverted people. Should these two live together, their space is likely to be a haven of security and a bastion against the intrusions of the outside world. Their relationship will guard its privacy jealously, and will not admit intrusion easily.

Cancer-Leo–Libra III family members, particularly siblings, are likely to live in their own little world, with dramas enacted daily and fantasy playing an important role. Such relationships, especially brother-sister combinations, often outlast childhood and may continue to be close throughout life. After work, colleagues in this combination may frequent favorite haunts where they can amuse themselves alone, and away from the watchful eye of a boss or supervisor.

ADVICE: *Probe deeply but remember to come up for air. Don't exclude others. Preserve privacy but beware of isolation. Keep feelings under control.*

ROBIN WILLIAMS (7/21/52)
PAM DAWBER (10/18/51)

Williams and Dawber were perfectly cast for tv's *Mork & Mindy* (1978–82). Comic Williams, playing an outcast alien from another planet, was a perfect foil to Dawber's all-American straightness. Eventually, the fictitious couple fell in love—made believable by their superior teamwork as actors.

***Also:* Charles Weidman & Doris Humphrey** (modern-dance partners).

JOSEPH ROISMAN (7/25/08)
ALEXANDER SCHNEIDER (10/21/08)

Roisman and Schneider were 1st and 2nd violinists of the Budapest String Quartet. Both gave up careers as soloists to join the Quartet and make it one of the greatest of all time, particularly for its Beethoven renditions. The violinists were beautifully compatible as a musical pair.

July 19–25
THE CUSP OF OSCILLATION
CANCER-LEO CUSP

October 19–25
THE CUSP OF DRAMA & CRITICISM
LIBRA-SCORPIO CUSP

Vulnerable to Temptation

Many surprising and mysterious elements emerge in this relationship. Often highly discriminating and sensual, it emphasizes craftsmanship or virtuosity. It is not without its tensions: each partner has a distinct and different viewpoint, and the relationship may magnify their habitual or addictive tendencies, reflecting a propensity for excesses and extremes of behavior. Because Cancer-Leo and Libra-Scorpio are in square aspect to each other in the zodiac (90° apart), astrology predicts friction and difficulty.

Escape can become a principal theme of love affairs, marriages and friendships. Albeit vivid and volatile, this is not the most stable combination, and the partners are prone to find security in sex and love addictions or in alcohol or other habit-forming drugs. Since excessive behavior comes naturally to this relationship, they are particularly vulnerable to such temptations. Emotional complexity and volatility are rife in daily interactions in all interpersonal relationships. Cancer-Leo mood swings and Libra-Scorpio emotional instabilities can be temporarily put to rest in the collapses that follow on binges, but are sure to surface again, necessitating a recurrence of the cycle. There is the danger here of a downward spiral, at the end of which both partners are left exhausted and the relationship in shambles.

The structure of a family or company is likely to aid siblings and co-workers in maintaining stability. Here one would expect these two to share their pleasure in fine wine, art, music, technical expertise and the like. In day-to-day situations, the presence of a parent or boss will keep the relationship's more extreme tendencies under control. Under the watchful eye of such an authority, siblings or co-workers often retreat into a secretive mode, engaging in highly personal forms of communication not readily understood by others. At their best, such duos can be hard-working and helpful to their group.

ADVICE: *Escape is not the answer. Confront your difficulties. Use your intelligence and willpower. Don't become your own victim.*

ERNEST HEMINGWAY (7/21/1899)
EZRA POUND (10/30/1885)

Hemingway went to France in 1921 and became part of a group of expatriate American writers, among them erudite poet Pound, who took an interest in Hemingway's writing. Pound encouraged him to cut out adjectives and adverbs.

Also: **Harry Cohn & Jack Cohn** (brothers; co-founded Columbia Pictures); **Woody Harrelson & Larry Flynt** (movie portrayal).

July 19–25
THE CUSP OF OSCILLATION
CANCER-LEO CUSP

October 26–November 2
THE WEEK OF INTENSITY
SCORPIO I

Ambivalent Feelings

This relationship will foster imagination and adventure. But although these two have a talent for dreaming up schemes together, they usually have different ways of implementing their ideas. After the initial, creative phase of a project, then, they could clash on the follow-up. Scorpio I's have a thirst for great deeds that is stimulated by Cancer-Leos, and they often admire the Cancer-Leo ability to put fears aside and just go for it. At the same time, though, they are cool and careful customers, and may find this partner a bit rash and hasty. Cancer-Leos will value Scorpio I control and meticulousness but may grow impatient with the time they usually take to plan their next move. Ambivalent feelings like these are common here; the partners are rarely completely comfortable with each other's ways of proceeding.

Love affairs accentuate this ambivalence. Scorpio I's can draw Cancer-Leos like a magnet, arousing passions that seek immediate fulfillment. They themselves, however, are much cooler, and prefer to wait until they are sure about their feelings. Then, once they do commit, they require an intensity in the relationship that Cancer-Leos are often unable to sustain over time. The acute differences in temperament here are exciting in the short run but undermine longevity.

Marriages and friendships can be built around travel and adventure. Scorpio I's will enjoy being swept away by a Cancer-Leo partner to exotic places and sites of natural beauty. Physical movement or exploration is central here, especially when it involves an element of danger. Scorpio I's may occasionally disapprove of Cancer-Leo motives and resent the relationship as somewhat superficial, but on the whole it benefits them by encouraging them to express themselves vividly. Work relationships in this combination can work out well if the pair are part of a larger team effort that directs their energies, demanding cooperation and limiting some of their emotional differences. As family members, particularly in parent-child combinations, Scorpio I parents will carefully guide the more wayward energies of their Cancer-Leo children and work to even out their mood swings.

ADVICE: *Exercise patience. Make plans with care, then execute them decisively and without reservation. Work with a team when possible. Reconcile differences.*

July 19–25

THE CUSP OF OSCILLATION
CANCER-LEO CUSP

November 3–11

THE WEEK OF DEPTH
SCORPIO II

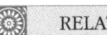

STRENGTHS: **PRACTICAL, LOYAL, RESPONSIBLE**

WEAKNESSES: **INFLEXIBLE, STRESSFUL, UNFORGIVING**

BEST: **MARRIAGE**

WORST: **FAMILY**

The Here and Now

This is a practical relationship in which the partners are expected to live up to well-defined obligations. Literal, firmly grounded in the here and now (this is largely the influence of the Scorpio II) and possessed of quite an air of self-confidence, it is a positive association for these two, both of whom have an introverted and insecure side. A word of caution: since everything is taken so literally here, the partners must be careful what they say. They are both very sensitive to slight, and may take the most casual comment the wrong way. The relationship's stability is beneficial to otherwise fluctuating Cancer-Leos, who will appreciate the opportunity available here to get work done and be productive. But if Scorpio II's feel worn down by the strain of keeping their partner on an even keel, they may come to resent the relationship as an energy drain.

In love affairs and marriages, both partners tend to be faithful and hang in there. If the relationship is going badly, it will probably be the Scorpio II who suffers most—Cancer-Leos are more likely to lead a double life and seek affection elsewhere. Children, financial entanglements and home ownership may pressure both partners to stay together no matter what. Mutual recriminations and arguments over money are characteristic in times of stress. If all possible solutions to the relationship's problems fail, the partners would do well to consider letting it go.

Friendships often obey a strict set of unwritten laws, transgression of which can alienate the pair from each other. There is an expectation here of honesty and fair treatment, not only between the partners: other people making promises to this duo will be expected to keep their word to the letter.

Sibling pairs here can be intensely rivalrous, especially when of the same sex. Scorpio II's can be vengeful and Cancer-Leos unforgiving. Cancer-Leo–Scorpio II co-workers do best with regular workloads and few surprises; as business partners and entrepreneurs they will often disagree over the direction their enterprises should take and how capital should be spent.

ADVICE: *Expectations may be too high. Loyalty is admirable, masochism is not. Give everything its best chance and no more. Lighten up!*

SARGENT SHRIVER (11/9/15)
GEORGE McGOVERN (7/19/22)

In the 1972 presidential campaign, McGovern was pressured into dropping his original choice for running mate, Sen. Thomas Eagleton. After reviewing his alternatives, McGovern selected Shriver— a Kennedy brother-in-law, Peace Corps director and traditional liberal Democrat—as the vice-presidential candidate. McGovern and Shriver hung in but lost the election to Nixon and Agnew.

July 19–25

THE CUSP OF OSCILLATION
CANCER-LEO CUSP

November 12–18

THE WEEK OF CHARM
SCORPIO III

STRENGTHS: **FASCINATING, INNOVATIVE, COMPLEMENTARY**

WEAKNESSES: **HASTY, EXTREME, DIFFERENT**

BEST: **WORK**

WORST: **LOVE**

Preserving Youthful Energies

The dynamic between Cancer-Leos and Scorpio III's is complex. Although very different temperamentally, these partners can form an effective working combination, particularly when innovating and developing new projects. Where Cancer-Leos are often risk-takers from the word go (or would like to be), Scorpio III's rarely take a chance that could threaten their security. These attitudes can complement each other in the workplace, giving Cancer-Leos the security they need and Scorpio III's a push to achieve. Such combinations of more radical and more conservative attitudes can coalesce to form a relationship that has ambition and drive but also knows when to hold back and wait. The downside can come when either impulse predominates, weakening the relationship by producing alternations between rashness and caution, or power struggles between the two directions.

Cancer-Leo–Scorpio III love affairs can start out like a house on fire, then quickly burn out. Should such relationships prematurely move on to marriage, there is the possibility of open combat between a more aggressive Cancer-Leo and a more defensive, but ultimately retaliating, Scorpio III. Friendships in this combination are exciting at the outset, the partners often being fascinated with each other's different approaches to life, and with each other generally. Later, after they have shared many experiences, they will also begin to realize that they actually have a lot in common. In all of these kinds of relationship, Cancer-Leos and Scorpio III's should never rush things in the beginning, and later on should work to preserve and nurture the innocent and youthful energy in which their tie was conceived.

In the family and at work, Scorpio III's make better parents and bosses for Cancer-Leos than the other way around. Although Cancer-Leos are team players who do well in group endeavors, as parents or bosses they may not be stable or strong enough to handle Scorpio III offspring or employees.

ADVICE: *Not so fast. Make love last. You may burn out like a shooting star. Appreciate your differences and let them enrich your life.*

ROBIN WILLIAMS (7/21/52)
WHOOPI GOLDBERG (11/13/49)

Fellow comedians and friends for many years, Williams and Goldberg link up annually as hosts (with Billy Crystal) of the HBO special *Comic Relief,* a yearly fundraising event for the homeless. They are both brilliant improvisers who interact with great energy.

Also: **Jason Robards, Jr. & Sam Robards** (father/son; actors).

ROBERT KENNEDY (11/20/25)
ROSE KENNEDY (7/22/1890)

Rose was the matriarch of the Kennedy family. She had high hopes for all of her children, and when JFK was assassinated in 1963, she (and husband Joseph) passed the political mantle on to Bobby, who was also assassinated (1968). This was part of a pattern of tragedy for the Kennedys.

July 19–25
THE CUSP OF OSCILLATION
CANCER-LEO CUSP

November 19–24
THE CUSP OF REVOLUTION
SCORPIO-SAGITTARIUS CUSP

A Reliable Formula

The focus of this relationship can be an appreciation of physical, sensuous beauty. Cancer-Leo and Scorpio-Sagittarius lie in a trine aspect to each other (120° apart in the zodiac), so that traditional astrology predicts an easygoing or harmonious time of it between them. Actually, conflicts and misunderstandings can easily arise here, but the relationship does have its own harmony—based more on what it values than on what it produces. The working dynamic here can be argumentative and even openly combative in daily life. But the dialectic of struggle between two opposing forces often results in a true synthesis, a beautiful creation—or even a relationship with a reliable formula for continued and gratifying success.

In matters of love, this couple's appreciation of sensuous beauty in the world of aesthetics may be carried over into the bedroom. Here Cancer-Leos and Scorpio-Sagittarians are likely to reach full agreement, although a challenging and competitive edge may still be present. Friends in this combination can enjoy each other fully without reservation or judgment. The highest value in these relationships is accorded to an appreciation of beauty, whether in the human form or in the worlds of art or nature.

In marital, family or working situations, Scorpio-Sagittarians are likely to be impatient with Cancer-Leo attitudes, viewing them as fearful and conservative. In this their opinions may differ from those of the rest of the world, which usually sees Cancer-Leos as forward-looking, risk-taking, even radical. Somehow Scorpio-Sagittarians end up damning Cancer-Leo thoughtfulness as insecurity, Cancer-Leo watchfulness as indolence and neglect. Often, however, Cancer-Leo judgment will be proven correct over time, eventually winning Scorpio-Sagittarians' respect. Cancer-Leos may not really understand the brilliance of Scorpio-Sagittarians, viewing them as somewhat eccentric know-it-alls.

ADVICE: *Try a bit harder to understand each other. Drop judgmental attitudes. Continue to share visions and successes. What are you afraid of?*

CAROLINE KENNEDY (11/27/57)
EDWIN SCHLOSSBERG (7/19/45)

Caroline, daughter of Jackie and JFK, met Schlossberg at NY's Museum of Modern Art. He was a cultural historian and she pursued tv projects. Their Catholic-Jewish marriage was approved by Jackie. They are the happy parents of 3 children.

Also: Rose Kennedy & Caroline Kennedy (grandmother/granddaughter).

July 19–25
THE CUSP OF OSCILLATION
CANCER-LEO CUSP

November 25–December 2
THE WEEK OF INDEPENDENCE
SAGITTARIUS I

Healing Wildness

This combination has a healing effect, bringing out the eternal child in its partners—the part in everyone that is able to overcome adversity and move forward in joy. The focus here is on spontaneity, intuition and trust. The relationship has a playful quality that will feel freeing to its partners and could make it a haven from sorrow. No matter what its circumstances, it will keep its partners youthful. Boredom is the enemy for these two, who like to indulge in all kinds of unusual or even risk-taking activities; just to keep things interesting, they will push each other right to the edge. There is the appearance here of a kind of wildness, then, but the relationship is not without control: these two have a good sense of how far they can properly go. Being a little bit out there is simply necessary to them—usually to relieve other pressures.

Cancer-Leo–Sagittarius I love affairs can be highly romantic, with the couple quite capable of throwing caution to the winds and flying in the face of society—even when one partner is already spoken for. These two can show remarkably little consideration for a third person, in fact, sometimes behaving thoroughly ruthlessly. Should they marry, a certain amount of latitude must be structured into the relationship, especially for the sake of Sagittarius I's.

Friends in this combination who meet as schoolmates are likely to dare each other on to ever greater risks. They are very interested in how things work, both practically and theoretically; curiosity is a prime element of their friendship. They may well integrate their careers, forming a strong professional association. The start-up phase of projects is particularly interesting to them—once things are running smoothly, they are apt to lose interest and move on.

As parent-child combinations, Cancer-Leos and Sagittarius I's can experience stormy, near-violent scenes. Rebelliousness and anger can break loose regardless of which personality is the parent and which the child. Controlling such explosiveness will be difficult at first, but will grow easier with maturity and advancing age.

ADVICE: *Make peace with yourself. You may be more effective when less emotional. Minimize violence. Show more consideration for others.*

July 19–25

THE CUSP OF OSCILLATION
CANCER-LEO CUSP

December 3–10

THE WEEK OF THE ORIGINATOR
SAGITTARIUS II

Control Through Mind Power

This is not an especially stable combination, since it magnifies each partner's volatile tendencies. In an effort to keep things under control, the relationship insists on everything being done without mistakes, to the highest possible level of quality. Thus the focus becomes a sort of perfectionism that imposes insistent and at times obsessive worry or thought. There is a danger that Cancer-Leos and Sagittarius II's will suppress their real intuitive strengths in an effort to control their impetuousness through mind power.

In matters of love, perfectionism in appearance, physicality or surroundings may drive both partners to distraction and unhappiness. In marriages, too, high standards will be maintained in domestic, financial and social areas. These drives toward quality can help to direct less stable tendencies, but should never be allowed to become rigid or compulsive. In both love and marriage, these partners should strive to hold on to the spontaneity and improvisational talents that are their birthright.

Both Cancer-Leos and Sagittarius II's must be themselves, and can suffer terribly when disapproved of, rejected or forced to play a role not their own. Parent-child and boss-employee pairs should be sensitive to each other's needs in this respect. Forcing each other to act the wrong part just to fulfill certain expectations or prophecies can cause friction and create unrest.

As friends, Cancer-Leos and Sagittarius II's tend to revel in sports, fitness training, exploring natural settings and travel. Their competitiveness with each other in these areas is healthy only up to a point; they would be better off turning this energy toward each partner bettering his or her own personal best. Perfectionist tendencies must be kept under control, however, to avoid mental and physical exhaustion.

JANINE TURNER (12/6/63)
ROB MORROW (7/21/62)

Morrow and Turner were co-stars in the offbeat tv comedy-drama *Northern Exposure* (1990–95). Morrow played a NYC physician assigned to a small Alaska town. Turner played a bush pilot who was his landlady and romantic interest. The characters got married during the program's 3rd year.

ADVICE: *Use mental powers sensibly. Beware of repressing what is best in you. Too much thinking makes headaches. Let up a bit in your expectations.*

July 19–25

THE CUSP OF OSCILLATION
CANCER-LEO CUSP

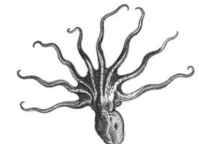

December 11–18

THE WEEK OF THE TITAN
SAGITTARIUS III

The Climb to the Top

This relationship tends to be extroverted and success-oriented. Although it will magnify the hidden insecurities of both partners, this only drives them on to ever-greater joint achievements. Whether in the social, family or professional spheres, this combination is determined to occupy the spotlight. Sagittarius III's tend to play the dominant role in most of their relationships, but Cancer-Leos are usually content to occupy a secondary position here, and to exercise their talent for being team players. The matchup's overall attitudes tend to be open, enthusiastic and optimistic, but also a tad naive and immature.

Should these two be attracted to each other, their love affairs can be intense and stormy: both are demanding, and Sagittarius III's will have little patience for Cancer-Leo mood swings. Passionate feelings can be expressed and enjoyed here, however. More needy Cancer-Leos may feel neglected or abandoned when a Sagittarius III partner shows little interest in acknowledging or supporting them through their depressions. Sagittarius III's are often much too busy with their careers to show Cancer-Leos the kind of personal attention they require.

Marriages and working relationships tend to be ambitious. Unfortunately, on their climb to the social or professional top, the pair may ignore or step on anyone in their way. Family members or friends who are slighted by Cancer-Leo–Sagittarius III couples may hold on to their resentment for years, later posing a threat to the duo at most unexpected and inopportune moments. For their own sake, then, Cancer-Leos and Sagittarius III's should pay more attention to the feelings of others and avoid arousing animosities.

As friends and family members, these two should take care to prevent their competitive drives and jealousies from running out of hand. Cancer-Leos and Sagittarius III's too often vie for the spotlight within social and family groups, undermining their own relationship. Reaching compromises and agreeing to scale back competition will prove a great relief to all concerned.

BELLA ABZUG (7/24/20)
ED KOCH (12/12/24)

In 1977 Abzug and Koch were opponents in the Democratic race for NYC mayor. Koch was conservative, while Abzug was a strong liberal and unabashed feminist. He won the nomination (also the election). She is remembered for her radical views and trademark wide-brimmed hats.

Also: **Gavrilo Princip &
Archduke Franz Ferdinand**
(assassin/royal; event started WWI).

ADVICE: *Be aware of your effect on others. Don't let blind ambition take over. Become more self-aware. Search for lasting spiritual values.*

EDITH PIAF (12/19/15)
MARCEL CERDAN (7/22/16)

Famous chanteuse Piaf's greatest love was Cerdan, an Arab-French boxer and middleweight champ in 1948. In 1949, while she was in NYC and he in Europe, she persuaded him to visit her and travel by air, rather than ship. He was killed when his plane crashed. She was devastated by the loss. **Also: Verdine White & Maurice White** (brothers; members of Earth, Wind & Fire).

July 19–25
THE CUSP OF OSCILLATION
CANCER-LEO CUSP

December 19–25
THE CUSP OF PROPHECY
SAGITTARIUS-CAPRICORN CUSP

More Social Activities

The thrust of this combination is primarily social. Separately these two loner types often have problems establishing group ties, but their relationship, whether personal, familial or professional, allows and encourages them to engage together in meaningful contact with others. Because Cancer-Leo and Sagittarius-Capricorn are in a quincunx aspect to each other in the zodiac (150° apart), traditional astrology predicts a need for significant adjustments between them. The emphasis here on social connections outside the relationship, however, can help bring them into balance. The matchup's light and playful approach is another real plus, since both partners have depressive sides. Sagittarius-Capricorns, with their antisocial tendencies or difficulties, will have ambivalent feelings about a relationship that encourages them toward human interaction. Cancer-Leos will usually take the lead here, but should be wary of Sagittarius-Capricorn resentment about going public. Care must be taken on both sides that the relationship allows itself enough quality time.

In love affairs, marriages and friendships, social interaction should be looked on as the principal means by which Cancer-Leos and Sagittarius-Capricorns find relief from the emotional claims and demands they make on each other in private. Both partners tend to be intense and prone to mood swings, qualities that their relationship augments. Taking part with friends, family and other couples in parties, vacations, sports, games and entertainment will tend to normalize psychological problems and even out passive-aggressive tendencies.

Working relationships between these two are difficult but will benefit from the presence of others, so that the partners do best as co-workers in a large firm demanding daily human contact. Parent-child matchups do best when their family unit is in steady touch with other relatives and friends, rather than being isolated for long periods of time. Cancer-Leo–Sagittarius-Capricorn sibling pairs do well when they can visit cousins and other contemporaries on a regular basis.

ADVICE: *Find the balance between public and private life. Work toward harmony and stability. Personal growth is essential. Develop social skills.*

SANDY KOUFAX (12/30/35)
DON DRYSDALE (7/23/36)

Dodgers Drysdale and Koufax were arguably baseball's greatest 60s pitchers. Both led their league in strikeouts for a total of 6 years. Drysdale won the Cy Young Award ('62) and once pitched 6 shutouts in a row ('68). Koufax won the Cy Young Award 3 times, was MVP ('63) and pitched 4 no-hitters. **Also: Jason Robards, Jr. & Jason Robards** (son/father; actors).

July 19–25
THE CUSP OF OSCILLATION
CANCER-LEO CUSP

December 26–January 2
THE WEEK OF THE RULER
CAPRICORN I

A Winning Combination

This relationship focuses on making itself a winning combination. Both partners have a need for dominance, but rather than frittering away their energy in useless battles with each other, they are smart enough to orient themselves to challenges outside the relationship, and to parlay their shared strengths into making themselves an unbeatable unit. Not only do they play to win, but, while they're doing it, they try to break new ground and overcome difficult or impossible hurdles. These efforts allow them to share in a great sense of satisfaction.

Love affairs between these two can be difficult, since both partners are often cut off from their emotions, and have difficulty with empathy. They may be unable to support each other in times of need. Marriages can work better, especially when the partners are united in the pursuit of shared social and financial goals; but these ambitions should be treated warily and perhaps scaled back, since the spouses often don't know what to do with their goals once they achieve them. This is a couple that fears success more than it does failure.

Friendships between Cancer-Leos and Capricorn I's do best when engaged in adventuresome forays into the world of nature. Exploring, climbing, diving, flying and a host of other challenging activities spur them on to higher achievement. Care must be taken, however, that fearlessness does not lead to carelessness and carelessness to self-destruction. Cancer-Leos will gain a responsible and structured approach from Capricorn I's, and in turn will infect Capricorn I's with their adventuresome spirit. In career matters, then, these two can make an excellent team, and may well find themselves at the executive level in any organization. Watchful Capricorn I parents know how to guide the energies of young Cancer-Leos in the right direction and to keep them on track; their children may resent their controlling stance early on in life, but can also come to depend on them utterly—a worse route to take. Cancer-Leo parents can be inspirational influences for their Capricorn I children, at least when they are in their more positive moods.

ADVICE: *Work on expressing your feelings. Understand yourself better psychologically. Let up a bit in your demands. Find time to relax.*

July 19–25

THE CUSP OF OSCILLATION
CANCER-LEO CUSP

January 3–9

THE WEEK OF DETERMINATION
CAPRICORN II

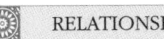
Putting On a Show

This relationship brings out its partners' more flamboyant and theatrical traits. Dressing up, partying and going out to clubs and to dinner are all given top priority. Cancer-Leos may be a little unhinged by such exciting activities, but Capricorn II dependability and responsibility can anchor them. The relationship, then, is potentially not only dramatic and vivid but directed and balanced. Capricorn II's are usually intrigued by Cancer-Leo energies and are well able to handle their mood swings and occasional depressions. The relationship is not possessed of great insight, but the partners do understand and are able to satisfy each other's needs.

Romantic relationships can be exciting for both of these two. Sexual expression is electric and powerful, intense and fulfilling. Both partners are liable to take the relationship seriously enough to contemplate marriage. That step should be considered carefully, however, since a subtle shift often takes place when the knot is tied: financial matters become more important, domestic and job pressures increase, and cracks can appear in a once rock-solid relationship. Capricorn II's are likely to voice their upset with silence, Cancer-Leos to be more emotionally volatile.

Work relationships in this combination often work out well, since both partners will respect each other for giving their all. In fact friendships and love affairs between these two often start at work. If the job is dull, co-workers will often party together after hours, or express their more flamboyant side at office parties and picnics. Cancer-Leo and Capricorn II family members and relatives might do well to form their own companies based on a service or product, where their stylish and polished manner can be expressed in PR and marketing, as well as in putting on a show for prospective clients.

ADVICE: *Dig a bit deeper. Find quiet time together. Monitor your energy output and beware of overload. Ease into new responsibilities.*

GEORGE MCGOVERN (7/19/22)
RICHARD NIXON (1/9/13)

When McGovern and Nixon battled for the presidency in '72, they couldn't have been further apart on the issues, particularly ending the Vietnam War. Nixon was for bombing the enemy into submission, while McGovern advocated a negotiated withdrawal. McGovern lost badly. **Also: Julie Nixon & Richard Nixon** (daughter/father); **Iman & David Bowie** (married; model/rock star).

July 19–25

THE CUSP OF OSCILLATION
CANCER-LEO CUSP

January 10–16

THE WEEK OF DOMINANCE
CAPRICORN III

Jolted into Awareness

Together these two usually make a strong combination, and indeed the focus of their relationship can be a thirst for power. The lessons of spirituality and selfless love (perhaps the greatest power of all) are often only learned after repeated successes and failures have jolted the pair into the awareness that there is more to life than ambition and ceaseless struggle. On the positive side, the energy manifest in this combination can be good for its partners. Solid Capricorn III's can give Cancer-Leos the firm support they require. Likewise, the more electrifying elements of the Cancer-Leo personality can recharge Capricorn III batteries and urge them on to greater heights, particularly if they have grown a tad complacent.

Love affairs and marriages between Cancer-Leos and Capricorn III's are too often dominated by power struggles in which each partner seeks to strengthen their position and selfishly demands more than their fair share. Money, social status and objects are often just pawns in the fight for dominance going on here. Capricorn III's are difficult to unseat in such struggles, and clever Cancer-Leos will often try to gain their ends through subtlety and indirectness. These relationships give both partners the opportunity to strengthen themselves, but also to evolve to a higher level and leave such struggles behind.

Family matchups, especially sibling pairs of the same sex and parent-child pairs of the opposite sex, may periodically drive relatives out of the house with their conflicts, furious power struggles that tend to spill over and engulf the entire domestic scene. With time, however, compromise and diplomacy may evolve, and later life could bring acceptance and understanding. Friendships in this combination can be highly stimulating, and if these two consolidate their strengths effectively they can accomplish a great deal in the service of a social group, team or club. Co-worker matchups tend to be destabilized by the fluctuating energies of Cancer-Leos, but as an executive pair these two can give firm direction to the organization or company they head.

ADVICE: *Don't be seduced by power. Learn to compromise. Giving should be unconditional. Cultivate kindness and consideration. Minimize conflict.*

NATALIE WOOD (7/20/38)
SAL MINEO (1/10/39)

Along with James Dean (shown center), actors Wood and Mineo co-starred in the powerful *Rebel Without a Cause* (1955). When Dean died shortly before the film's release, his distraught fans made him a martyr and latched on to the 2 actors who had worked with him in the cult classic. Ironically, Wood and Mineo also died prematurely: she drowned mysteriously (1981) and he was murdered (1976).

STRENGTHS: **PASSIONATE, DRAMATIC, STIMULATING**

WEAKNESSES: **UNSTABLE, SECRETIVE, ARGUMENTATIVE**

BEST: **LOVE**

WORST: **PARENT-CHILD**

DAVID BELASCO (7/25/1853)
RUTH ST. DENIS (1/20/1877)

St. Denis was an exotic pioneer of modern dance whose long career began in 1906. Through the years she was courted by many known figures, among them theatrical producer Belasco (who gave her the stage name St. Denis). Her devotion to career and her "strange aversion to what I thought sex to be" limited their relationship to a romantic fling.

July 19–25
THE CUSP OF OSCILLATION
CANCER-LEO CUSP

January 17–22
THE CUSP OF MYSTERY & IMAGINATION
CAPRICORN-AQUARIUS CUSP

Outrageous Behavior

Because both its partners are subject to wide mood swings and crave excitement, this relationship is unlikely to be stable. Conflicts between intellectual and emotional energies are apt to appear here, and to be resolved by a kind of blowing off of steam in the form of outrageous behavior. Cancer-Leo and Capricorn-Aquarius are opposite each other in the zodiac, so traditional astrology predicts tension and conflict between them, and their relationship is indeed dramatic, stressing dark and passionate feelings. It also has a strongly critical side, emerging when the couple try to use reason to deal with threatening outbreaks of uncontrollable emotion.

Cancer-Leo–Capricorn-Aquarius love affairs often involve secrecy. For one thing, these partners usually reserve their flamboyance for the bedroom, feeling a pressing need to reveal no trace of it to other people. Their relationships also show a tendency to become involved in love triangles, the third partner being the husband or wife of one or the other of them. Such covert or illicit love affairs may go on for some time undiscovered, and it is usually one of the partners themselves who ultimately reveals it, characteristically at a dramatic moment when the emotional or physical strain becomes unbearable. Instability and the likelihood of infidelity makes marriage in this combination unwise.

Friendships here can be highly public, even theatrical. The pair feel little need to suppress such impulses, and the most capricious sorts of social behavior may result—behavior in which they revel, gleefully pushing the buttons of all and sundry. As co-workers these two can have an outstanding relationship when following artistic pursuits, but lack the interest or application to succeed in business endeavors.

Parent-child relationships between Cancer-Leos and Capricorn-Aquarians can be vivid and stimulating to family life, but also highly disruptive. Overly critical attitudes within the relationship generally lead to the adoption of argumentative and rejecting stances.

ADVICE: *Work on staying balanced. Keep critical impulses in check. Use your emotional intelligence. Channel your passions more constructively.*

STRENGTHS: **ATTENTIVE, EVOLVING, INTENSE**

WEAKNESSES: **VOLATILE, NERVOUS, SUPERFICIAL**

BEST: **FRIENDSHIP**

WORST: **WORK**

JASON ROBARDS, JR. (7/22/22)
HUMPHREY BOGART (1/23/1899)

Actors Robards and Bogart were both married to beauty Lauren Bacall. Bogart died (1957) a hero in Bacall's heart. When she married Robards 4 years later, many saw the similarities—macho types, Scotch-drinking, strong actors. Robards had a hard time filling Bogey's mythic shoes—he got fed up with being referred to as "Mrs. Bogart's second husband."

July 19–25
THE CUSP OF OSCILLATION
CANCER-LEO CUSP

January 23–30
THE WEEK OF GENIUS
AQUARIUS I

Exasperatingly Unpredictable

Little rest will be found here—emotions fluctuate like a roller coaster ride in this intense relationship. Cancer-Leos can find Aquarius I's fascinating but exasperating. And Aquarius I's will be drawn into exciting experiences by Cancer-Leos, but they probably won't feel that comfortable about it. Both of these two do well with a stable partner on whom they can depend in times of need, but their relationship with each other seems only to undermine predictability, permanence and peace. Nervousness and argument often result, but at the same time the relationship fosters deep exchanges of feeling and allows the partners to discover a great deal about themselves. At its best, it may mark the start of a profound and thoughtful process in which these individuals really begin to grow.

This relationship is often unserious at the outset, particularly in the spheres of love and friendship, where both partners can start out just wanting to have a good time. As they get more deeply involved, however, it will become clear that there is potentially more to the matchup than a superficial hankering after excitement. Should they decide to continue, a difficult period will ensue in which more serious questions will emerge and the relationship will demand a more responsible attitude from its partners. Aquarius I's in particular may resent such demands and flee, but not necessarily irrevocably—they may ultimately find themselves hanging in there and going a bit deeper.

Marriages and working relationships may not survive the early stages of contact, which are stressful and demanding. Judgmental attitudes may get both partners so tense that they cannot function properly in the domestic or work environment. The prognosis here will be more favorable if both Cancer-Leos and Aquarius I's can learn to let small things go without constantly laying on guilt. In the family, sibling pairs in this combination, especially of the same sex, may be close but also highly competitive.

ADVICE: *Time and patience are needed for things to develop. Don't rush. Learn to calm yourself, perhaps through meditation. Self-realization is possible.*

July 19–25
THE CUSP OF OSCILLATION
CANCER-LEO CUSP

January 31–February 7
THE WEEK OF YOUTH & EASE
AQUARIUS II

STRENGTHS: **SOLID, PROBLEM-SOLVING, SENSUOUS**

WEAKNESSES: **FLAKY, BORED, STUBBORN**

BEST: **WORK**

WORST: **FRIENDSHIP**

Firm Resolve

This relationship is involved in bringing ideas and concepts into being and giving them a firm base in reality. The ideas in question will tend to revolve around issues of aesthetic taste, art and abstract concepts of creativity—yet this is a solid and practical matchup. In fact both partners, independently a bit flaky at times, will come to rely on the security it offers. Together these partners are more stubborn than they are normally, which could prove a divisive element. On the other hand, Aquarius II's dislike hassles and like easy and sensuous interactions, Cancer-Leos need liveliness and interesting challenges, and these desires are met here. All the imaginative dreaming in the world will meet little satisfaction in this relationship unless it is accompanied by a firm resolve to put ideas into practice; if this occurs, these two will meet with success.

Friendships and love affairs are likely to suffer unless they can find a practical outlet for their sparkling thoughts. Activities that ground these two in physical pursuits, such as sports, fitness training, jogging or daily walks or swims, are highly recommended. Affection and sensuousness characterize this matchup. In the family sphere, both siblings and spouses are likely to be interested in making domestic improvements. Cancer-Leos may get a bit upset with the Aquarius II insistence on comfort, while Aquarius II's may find Cancer-Leo energy a bit unsettling, but these two are generally able to live together in relative harmony.

Career connections between Cancer-Leos and Aquarius II's are especially favored. Should these two form a business partnership, serve as executive colleagues in a company or work side by side on the job on a daily basis, they stand a good chance of achieving success. Most effective when their ideas have a likelihood of being implemented, they can quickly grow bored with a position that demands only that they accomplish a predetermined task. Innovative in the extreme, these two make excellent problem-solvers, being capable of thinking up the most ingenious ways to get out of tight situations and come out on top.

ADVICE: *Come down off your cloud—you are at your best when implementing your ideas. Ground yourself in physical activity. Strengthen your resolve.*

PATRICK MACNEE (2/6/22)
DIANA RIGG (7/20/38)

Rigg and MacNee appeared together from 1965–68 in the tv action series *The Avengers*. MacNee played an urbane bon vivant, typically in a 3-piece suit and bowler, and Rigg played a liberated secret agent, often dressed in boots and leather. The actors brought a touch of class to 60s television.

Also: Ernest Hemingway & Gertrude Stein (literary friends).

July 19–25
THE CUSP OF OSCILLATION
CANCER-LEO CUSP

February 8–15
THE WEEK OF ACCEPTANCE
AQUARIUS III

STRENGTHS: **PROBING, COURAGEOUS, DEEP**

WEAKNESSES: **PROJECTING, PAINFUL, UNHAPPY**

BEST: **LOVE**

WORST: **MARRIAGE**

Lurking in the Background

The challenge of this combination may be to face up to problems lurking in the depths of both partners' personalities. The shadow side is powerful here, and if suppressed, ignored or misunderstood, it can threaten the entire relationship. Attention must be paid to deep feelings and psychological tendencies, particularly negative ones that seem too disturbing to handle. The inevitable necessity of facing up to such dark issues becomes apparent when problems arise that will not go away, and in fact get worse when neglected. When Cancer-Leo and Aquarius III partners decide to get to the bottom of their problems, their complex relationship may have to be unraveled by a professional, such as a psychologist or therapist. Through this kind of process of self-examination, however painful, Cancer-Leos and Aquarius III's will often grow closer and gain a renewed sense of commitment to each other.

Romantic but unrealistic relationships between Cancer-Leos and Aquarius III's are quite common. Love affairs may be deep, passionate but destructive. These partners tend to project their own negativity on each other and then to strike out against perceived moods and attitudes that are really their own. They may also force their mates to reenact the rejecting roles of people they knew in childhood, perhaps teachers or parents. Both partners must be encouraged to build up their own self-esteem before they can make progress as a couple. Marriages based on conflicting feelings may also tear themselves apart without a strong mutual will to heal individual problems.

In friendships, Aquarius III's can have difficulty accepting Cancer-Leos' direct and often overpowering attitudes and dealing with their emotional demands. The partners must make more of an effort to understand each other and open lines of communication. Parent-child relationships, too, can periodically break down unless both partners make an effort to talk about what is really on their minds. At work, the relationship's intensity may hamper the project of getting the job done; these two generally do better on their own.

ADVICE: *Face up to your problems. Promote self-understanding. Reject escapism. Honest discussion is a must. Deal with the dark side and don't ignore it.*

NATALIE WOOD (7/20/38)
ROBERT WAGNER (2/10/30)

Wood and Wagner were married twice, 1957–63 and 1972 to her death in '81. They were very close through most of their married years. During the filming of her last movie, she drowned mysteriously in an accident on their yacht.

Also: Harry Cohn & Kim Novak (producer discovered actress); **Rose Kennedy & John (Honey Fitz) Fitzgerald** (daughter/father).

RELATIONSHIPS

STRENGTHS: EDUCATIONAL, REWARDING, SELF-REALIZING

WEAKNESSES: JUDGMENTAL, DIDACTIC, RESENTFUL

BEST: MARRIAGE

WORST: FAMILY

JULIE NIXON (7/25/48)
TRICIA NIXON (2/21/46)

Julie and Tricia are the daughters of Richard and Pat Nixon. Tricia was born the same year her father launched his political career. The sisters grew up in a cramped duplex while Nixon was a congressman and moved into the more spacious White House during his presidency. Julie married David Eisenhower, grandson of President Dwight Eisenhower, and Tricia married attorney Edward Cox.

July 19–25
THE CUSP OF OSCILLATION
CANCER-LEO CUSP

February 16–22
THE CUSP OF SENSITIVITY
AQUARIUS-PISCES CUSP

Life Experience

These two have a great deal to teach each other. Both partners will learn more from their own interactions than from books, and their ability to gain knowledge from life experience bodes well for their relationship. Aquarius-Pisces will help Cancer-Leos find out more about themselves, Cancer-Leos will help Aquarius-Pisces to realize some of their secret dreams. Rediscovering lost or repressed feelings will be a positive effort here; should Cancer-Leos be unable to feel real emotion, Aquarius-Pisces may help them break through such frightening psychological blockages. Cancer-Leo and Aquarius-Pisces have a quincunx aspect to each other in the zodiac (they are 150° apart), suggesting a need for adjustment. In their day-to-day interactions, then, they will probably have to struggle to maintain balance.

If love affairs between these two are kept on an even keel, they can be immensely rewarding. Sensuality is prominent here, but the partners generally realize that it is in their interest to go beyond the purely physical and to emphasize self-realization. Growing and evolving together is quite possible under the aegis of this caring but psychologically ambitious relationship; love affairs in this combination may progress quite naturally to marriage, with renewed commitment to understanding and unconditional love. And marriages can evolve even further, becoming a source of inspiration to those around them, so that they teach by example.

Cancer-Leo–Aquarius-Pisces friendships and family matchups, on the other hand, run the risk of being overly didactic. A welter of unsolicited opinions can arouse resentment on both sides, and the partners can grow to resent a tyrannical relationship that deprives them of individual choice. More tolerance and openness can be achieved by lessening moral and judgmental assumptions and attitudes that foster guilt and shame. Cancer-Leos and Aquarius-Pisces can make an excellent co-worker team, especially well suited to teaching new employees the ropes and initiating them into the ways of the group or organization.

ADVICE: *Stay flexible. Learning should be open-ended. Avoid judgmental attitudes. Benefit from your experience. Teach by example.*

RELATIONSHIPS

STRENGTHS: SEDUCTIVE, ADMIRING, AFFECTIONATE

WEAKNESSES: INHIBITING, UNAWARE, DEPENDENT

BEST: PLATONIC LOVE

WORST: SIBLING

MICHAEL WILDING (7/23/12)
ELIZABETH TAYLOR (2/27/32)

Charming British leading man Wilding was Taylor's 2nd husband. They were introduced by his friend Montgomery Clift. Taylor pursued Wilding and they married in '52. They had 2 sons and ended their marriage amicably in '57 with a quick Mexican divorce. Next day, she married Mike Todd. ***Also:***

Michael Wilding & Margaret Leighton (married; actors).

July 19–25
THE CUSP OF OSCILLATION
CANCER-LEO CUSP

February 23–March 2
THE WEEK OF SPIRIT
PISCES I

Invisible Barriers

Although this combination will make its partners feel charmed or seduced, they may ultimately face disappointment here since there is usually a limit to the depth of their involvement. No matter how close they get, they eventually run up against an invisible barrier that keeps them from going further. Admiration and even passion figure strongly in this relationship, but even feelings like these cannot overcome the sense of distance that is also present. The pair's inability to merge into a unit may at some point make one or the other partner feel inferior; this is often the Pisces I, who, try as he or she may, can end up unable to please the Cancer-Leo and ultimately may face rejection.

Love affairs are sometimes better off staying platonic or limiting their degree of involvement. In fact, lovers might be better off if they were friends, since the deep differences of temperament and feeling between them may be too great to surmount. Affection and sympathy are often more naturally felt and expressed here than carnal desire; a selfless sort of giving, rather than a lustful hunger, is typical here. These partners may need long periods alone together to broaden and deepen their feelings for one another. Marriages can work out as long as the partners do not make heavy emotional demands on each other and leave room for freedom of choice and action. Dependency, jealousy and claiming attitudes often cause domestic pain.

Friendships and sibling matchups in this combination often exhibit a curious sort of rivalry, which is stimulating to both partners but ultimately blunts their efforts. Whether they are together or apart, an unwritten contract in the relationship seems to prevent them from surpassing each other in achievement. Masquerading as mutual admiration, this is actually a serious inhibition, and may betoken a psychological blind spot. The joint projects of Cancer-Leo–Pisces I friends or siblings often succeed at a lesser level than what either is capable of alone. In business dealings, care should be taken to remain objective and to prevent interpersonal dynamics from affecting the pair's endeavors adversely.

ADVICE: *Don't hold each other back. Loyalty has its limits. Be realistic about your feelings. Emotional honesty is a worthwhile goal.*

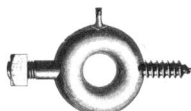

July 19–25

THE CUSP OF OSCILLATION
CANCER-LEO CUSP

March 3–10

THE WEEK OF THE LONER
PISCES II

Filling in the Gaps

RELATIONSHIPS

STRENGTHS: **COMPLEMENTING,
NATURAL, SUPPORTIVE**

WEAKNESSES: **DEPENDENT,
INEFFECTUAL, SUPERFICIAL**

BEST: **MARRIAGE**

WORST: **CO-WORKER**

TADEUS REICHSTEIN (7/20/1897)
EDWARD KENDALL (3/8/1886)

Swiss chemist Reichstein and
American biochemist Kendall won
the 1950 Nobel Prize for medicine
(along with Philip Hench) for
their research on hormones of
the adrenal cortex. This discovery
led to the use of cortisone as a
successful treatment for inflammatory diseases.

As different as these two are, their relationship proves relaxed, natural and easy. Each partner compensates for the other's weaknesses without stress or strain. Pisces II's are strong in introspection, and will influence Cancer-Leos to develop their more sensitive and spiritual side. Cancer-Leo social strengths will help Pisces II's come into more meaningful contact with their fellows. Thus the relationship will ameliorate the difficulties of both partners—the Cancer-Leo inability to get in touch with their feelings and the Pisces II tendency to isolate themselves. Actually, both partners risk becoming unduly dependent on each other and on the relationship. They should concentrate on assimilating what they learn into their character so that they can augment their personal growth as individuals and interact with others more effectively in the future.

In love affairs and marriages, each person is usually open to the other, psychologically and physically. Although Cancer-Leo is a water-fire combination and Pisces II is a water sign, the relationship is ruled by earth, an element here suggesting a sensuous connection. The relationship's practical, grounded outlook benefits both partners, particularly Pisces II's, who sometimes have difficulty discharging everyday responsibilities.

Friendships between these two are easy and comfortable. Neither partner tries to create problems, and both seek out their relationship as a relief from the stresses of other areas of life. In the family, matchups between siblings, parents and children, and other relatives are comparatively peaceful, but might be ineffectual in times of need unless an effort is made to deepen them. In the long run, though, it can be beneficial for these two to face problems and difficulties together, for this will create closer ties and foster understanding.

Cancer-Leo and Pisces II co-workers get along well personally but may make an ineffective team for getting the job done fast. Matchups at the executive level are often better able to meld these partners' individual skills and talents.

ADVICE: *Deepen your understanding of each other. Don't avoid difficulties. Beware of overdependence. Enrich and broaden your character.*

July 19–25

THE CUSP OF OSCILLATION
CANCER-LEO CUSP

March 11–18

THE WEEK OF DANCERS & DREAMERS
PISCES III

Agreeing to Disagree

RELATIONSHIPS

STRENGTHS: **STIMULATING,
RESPECTFUL, VISIONARY**

WEAKNESSES: **REBELLIOUS,
ARGUMENTATIVE, MANIPULATIVE**

BEST: **WORK**

WORST: **LOVE**

BARRY BONDS (7/24/64)
BOBBY BONDS (3/15/46)

Bobby and his son Barry have both
been baseball All-Stars. Bobby
played on 8 teams from 1968–81;
he stole 461 bases. Barry played in
the majors from '86 with Pittsburgh
and now plays for San Francisco.
He hit 33 home runs in '95. **Also:**
Robin Williams & Billy Crystal
(friends; actors); **Bella Abzug
& Daniel Moynihan** (NY Senate
race opponents, 1976).

This relationship will generally require an agreement to disagree. The energy here tends to be polite but guardedly confrontational—the partners often don't see eye to eye, but their acceptance of their differences of opinion implies respect and augurs well for the relationship's future. Although honesty is a high priority here, undeniably manipulative tendencies are clear in the partners' need to convince and influence each other. Their exchanges can appear witty, elegant and charming to bystanders, but may carry serious and powerful undertones for the partners themselves.

Seductive attitudes are prominent in love affairs and marriages, often being used to win or settle arguments. This kind of emotional manipulation is likely to cloud the original issue and blunt any impulse to seek out the truth. While these relationships may be pleasurable enough, then, they are also self-deceiving. Unless these partners can build strong beliefs and goals, they may fritter away their energies in game-playing activities that keep them amused but do nothing to help them develop and grow.

Parent-child relationships in this combination can be especially stormy, with constant argument testifying to an inability to agree. Maintaining respect and openness is extremely important here, for if these are lost, the level of combat may prove truly destructive both to the individuals and to the rest of the family. As friends, these two are often united in rebellion against what they see as outworn social creeds, stupid habits and bad taste. They would be wise to take care to build positive values, rather than always defining their stance negatively by saying what it is they oppose. Cancer-Leos and Pisces III's have imaginative strengths that can gel effectively in a wide variety of career endeavors, even when their opinions differ. As business partners or executives their far-ranging vision can bring a company or corporation far. But their maintenance skills may leave something to be desired, so that they will need other, more practical types to help with their organization's daily running, particularly in matters of personnel, structure and finance.

ADVICE: *Beware of manipulation. Give each other room to breathe. Winning arguments is not of primary importance.*

STRENGTHS: STRIVING, COMPETITIVE, POSITIVE

WEAKNESSES: INFALLIBLE, OVERCONFIDENT, OMNISCIENT

BEST: RIVALRY

WORST: LOVE

WILLIAM POWELL (7/29/1892)
MYRNA LOY (8/2/05)

Suave Powell and bubbly Loy became a movie team in the detective-comedy *The Thin Man* (1934), for which he received an Oscar nomination and she became Hollywood's #1 box-office actress. 6 more *Thin Man* sequels followed. Both witty and sophisticated, they had great chemistry on the screen. **Also:** **Casey Stengel & Leo Durocher** (rival baseball managers).

July 26–August 2
THE WEEK OF AUTHORITY
LEO I

July 26–August 2
THE WEEK OF AUTHORITY
LEO I

Magnificent Rivalry

Two Leo I's can make a great team but can also be magnificent rivals. How they match up is usually dependent on logistics. This pair can shine in a love affair or marriage, for example, but in a company, family or other organization there is often room for only one Leo I at the top. If both partners submit to an authority outside themselves, usually an ideology, they can strive shoulder to shoulder in support of their cause. But Leo I's who claim to be the living authority on a subject, or the head of a certain group, can expect their Leo I partner either to confront them directly or leave in search of their own group to head. The relationship's forceful, positive outlook will make it impossible to miss. Moreover, since being taken seriously is the key to this combination, it contains a large dose of desire for upward mobility and success.

In love and marriage there is always an element of competition between these two, no matter how wonderful their lovemaking or well directed their domestic life. Career competition, sexual competition, financial competition—you name it, they can't avoid it. Leo I's really enjoy battling it out with a worthy opponent. They are self-confident enough to be able to admire a good rival's skill and will to win, rather than fearing or envying them; and what better rival could they find than another Leo I? In a sense, then, Leo I's in romances or marriages together may really be seeking a better or at least equal version of themselves.

Friendships between Leo I's may be subtly intertwined with rivalries. They give a new spin to the saying "With friends like that, who needs enemies?" Sibling relationships are likely to prove both close and combative. At work, the most typical positions occupied by a pair of Leo I's are as heads of rival organizations. Here their relationship may spur both companies on to new heights of achievement.

ADVICE: *Competition may be less important than you think. Beware of conceit. Find authority within yourself. Seek more lasting values.*

STRENGTHS: THOUGHTFUL, DEDICATED, HARD-WORKING

WEAKNESSES: UNSYMPATHETIC, OVERCOMPETITIVE, OUT OF SYNCH

BEST: WORK

WORST: SIBLING

JOHN HUSTON (8/5/06)
HERMAN MELVILLE (8/1/1819)

Director Huston adapted Melville's great sea saga *Moby Dick* for the screen in 1956. Huston (shown on set) also co-scripted and produced the epic film. Melville's sense of scale was well matched in Huston's film version of the book. Both Huston and Melville were thrill-seeking adventurers in real life: Melville had been a whaler, once captured by cannibals; Huston was an obsessed African game hunter.

July 26–August 2
THE WEEK OF AUTHORITY
LEO I

August 3–10
THE WEEK OF BALANCED STRENGTH
LEO II

Gentility Versus Blood

Both of these partners tend to be hot-blooded, fiery types, but their relationship is ruled by something antithetical to fire—the element of air. The relationship is consequently much more reasonable, rational and intellectual than one would expect. It may not always be the most comfortable bond for this pair, who tend to overcompensate for the combination's mental aspect by trying too hard for relaxation and easygoing interaction. In reality, they'd rather be fighting it out, but a certain gentility prevents them from doing so.

Emotionally this relationship can be complex, in that the partners are not always in synch with each other's needs. Power struggles involving sex can disrupt the relationship, and although Leo II's are psychologically astute enough to understand their Leo I mates, they may nevertheless refuse to sympathize with them. Leo I's often require attention and support. They also like their partners to be optimistic and cheerful, and real problems can be raised by Leo II's periodic depressions. In marriage, the biggest problem is who will rule the roost, and in this case it may be the more intelligent partner of the two, not the strongest or most willful.

Friendships that arise during the school years sometimes reflect the value the relationship places on mind power: as friends, these two are apt to be interested in social and physical activities, but their highest value is reserved for learning and academic excellence. If they both have difficulties in this area, or if one partner has more natural ability or dedication than the other, frustration inevitably results. Leo I–Leo II siblings may compete for the attention of their parents by trying to outdo each other in their studies, a struggle later perpetuated by getting into better colleges and universities and securing higher-paid and higher-level career positions. Such sibling pairs should try to discover their own individual strengths and vie less fiercely for approval. On the job, co-workers in this combination often succeed through dedication and hard work.

ADVICE: *Discover your real strengths. Don't be ruled by the expectations of others. Try to be more thoughtful and attentive. Cultivate kindness and sympathy.*

July 26–August 2
THE WEEK OF AUTHORITY
LEO I

August 11–18
THE WEEK OF LEADERSHIP
LEO III

RELATIONSHIPS

STRENGTHS: **UNSWERVING, DEDICATED, LOYAL**

WEAKNESSES: **BOSSY, INSENSITIVE, DOMINATING**

BEST: **FAMILY**

WORST: **MARRIAGE**

Dauntless Self-Confidence

This relationship is outstanding for initiating and taking control of group projects and endeavors. Its focus is often a professional or social organization or activity that the partners head up. The striking attribute of the matchup is its ability to lend balance and harmony to a wide variety of endeavors. These two often achieve such balance through their physical presence, accompanied by solid intuition and dauntless self-confidence. Loyalty and unswerving dedication to a cause in the face of monumental obstacles are characteristic here.

Marital and love relationships are a bit tricky. In fact, the most intriguing and fulfilling of these may be hidden affairs, which arouse a wide spectrum of feeling and expression. Such clandestine relationships may go on for years, and can help both partners get through difficult times they are having with other people. Friendships allow emotions to be more openly expressed, without fear of censure; indeed, Leo I and Leo III friends usually display outstanding loyalty and devotion.

Families are usually fortunate to have a Leo I–Leo III pair to take control in times of emergency or loss. Such couples are also remarkably good at organizing celebrations and holidays but must beware of being bossy or insensitive. Age differences between these two in no way prohibit their adopting such roles together, and in fact can prove beneficial in bridging generation gaps.

Work and career connections between Leo I's and Leo III's are often idealistic in nature. A prevailing shared ideology will act as the motor, driving the couple's unflagging physical activity and granting them solace during periods of discouragement. Financial success is by no means ruled out, but the principal interest here is not usually monetary. Although both Leo I's and Leo III's are usually dominating personalities who like to wield power exclusively, they are remarkably compatible in a dual-leadership role. Sharing duties and responsibilities without strife or resentment is a special talent of this matchup.

ADVICE: *Stay open to the suggestions of others. Rest occasionally from your endeavors. Having fun is important too. Beware of hidden resentments.*

WILLIAM CLARK (8/1/1770)
MERIWETHER LEWIS (8/18/1774)

Lewis and Clark carried out a government-sponsored expedition to explore the territory between the Mississippi River and the Pacific Ocean, 1804–06. Brave and resourceful outdoorsmen, they were the first to reach the Pacific by an overland route.

Also: **Nick Bollettieri & Jim Courier** (tennis teacher/protégé).

July 26–August 2
THE WEEK OF AUTHORITY
LEO I

August 19–25
THE CUSP OF EXPOSURE
LEO-VIRGO CUSP

RELATIONSHIPS

STRENGTHS: **HEDONISTIC, EXTROVERTED, FUN**

WEAKNESSES: **OVERSERIOUS, WORKAHOLIC, STRESSED**

BEST: **LOVE**

WORST: **WORK**

Kicking Back

At its best, this relationship loves pleasure. But it can also be somewhat solemn when preoccupied with work, training or anything requiring practice to master, and keeping things light and conflict-free will not always be easy here. This goal should be pursued as diligently as more serious efforts. Assuming heavy responsibilities at work or in family matters leaves Leo I's and Leo-Virgos in need of kicking off and giving themselves over to fun experiences that can help them forget, at least temporarily, the demands placed on them by others. Others may criticize their relationship as superficial or hedonistic, but pleasure actually plays an important role in their mental health. Play acts as a tonic for these two.

In love affairs and friendships, these partners may turn to each other to take their minds off the stress of daily life. Leo I's tend to bring out Leo-Virgos' extroverted side; they themselves may be frustrated, though, by this partner's tendency to ignore them, since attention is something they need. On the whole, Leo-Virgos are stronger emotionally, since they really don't care a whole lot what others think of them. But they do crave understanding, which their Leo I partners are unlikely to provide.

A greater challenge awaits Leo I's and Leo-Virgos in the spheres of marriage, family and work, where pressures tend to pile up no matter how hard the pair work on making the daily mood lighter and more playful. Yet these pressures are often self-induced, for these two often overlook other people's willingness to do things for themselves. Together, in other words, Leo I's and Leo-Virgos tend to create difficulties for themselves, claiming to be mature and responsible but revealing underlying workaholic tendencies. Becoming more childlike and less "mature" is often the answer, if only these two could realize it.

ADVICE: *Learn from watching children play. Seriousness is not exclusive to adults. Learn to relax. Allow others to take care of their own needs.*

BILL CLINTON (8/19/46)
RON BROWN (8/1/41)

Brown was apponted secretary of commerce by President Clinton in 1993, following his chairmanship of the Democratic National Committee that helped get Clinton elected in '92. Because they were close friends, Brown's untimely death in a plane crash in '96 was a crushing blow for Clinton. Brown broke new ground in American politics by being the first African-American to chair a major political party.

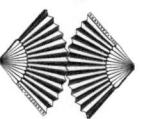

RELATIONSHIPS

STRENGTHS: WELL-DIRECTED, EFFICIENT, DEPENDABLE

WEAKNESSES: DISSATISFIED, NERVOUS, FRUSTRATED

BEST: WORK

WORST: LOVE

MARCEL DUCHAMP (7/28/1887)
PEGGY GUGGENHEIM (8/26/1898)

Artist Duchamp and wealthy heiress Guggenheim became close friends in 1938, when he helped her choose artworks for her London gallery, Guggenheim Jeune. It is said that her passion for modern art was exceeded only by her lust for modern artists. She and Duchamp reputedly had an affair.

Developing Joint Projects

This project-oriented relationship can be productive for both partners. One regularly finds Leo I's and Virgo I's developing ideas together, then coming up with a strategy to give them direction. Their projects are often humanitarian or charitable in nature. Leo I's can be admirable role models here, particularly in their extreme independence and self-sufficiency, which allow their partners in this combination to give of themselves and to put their energies in the service of joint efforts. Virgo I's are happy to function as co-workers or assistants, allowing Leo I's to take the lead; often, however, they are the real powers behind the regal Lion.

Interpersonally, things may not work out so well for this combination. Should objectivity wane in marriages, friendships and love affairs, the nervous and unstable side of Virgo I's and the disappointment, boredom and frustration into which Leo I's are capable of sinking can undermine the relationship. Leo I's crave a variety of experience (they hate predictability) that Virgo I's may be unable to supply. If they tire of the relationship, they may well hang in there faithfully but seek excitement and fulfillment elsewhere.

The most effective Leo I–Virgo I relationships are usually professional and familial. Leo I dynamism and creative force melds with Virgo I structure and efficiency, producing an effective pairing both for developing new and exciting projects and for keeping them running smoothly. As colleagues, business partners, co-workers or boss-employee combinations, Leo I's and Virgo I's can lift their organization to the highest level of performance and satisfy both financial and idealistic needs. On the domestic front, parent-child or grandparent-child combinations can keep the family on the right track while guaranteeing fair and equal treatment to all.

ADVICE: *Keep your eye on the object. Don't let personal considerations deter you at work. Try to be more understanding and sympathetic in love.*

RELATIONSHIPS

STRENGTHS: ACCEPTING, SENSITIVE, INTERESTING

WEAKNESSES: PECULIAR, UNEVEN, OUTSPOKEN

BEST: FAMILY

WORST: WORK

ALDOUS HUXLEY (7/26/1894)
DAME EDITH SITWELL (9/7/1887)

Huxley was one of England's most elegant and witty 20th-century novelists whose works focused on the pretentious intellectual circles of his day. Sitwell was a prominent poet of emotional depth who was known for her eccentric opinions and Elizabethan clothes. They were good friends.

Also: **Blake Edwards & Peter Sellers** (director/actor; *Pink Panther* movies).

Not Everyone's Cup of Tea

As partners these two will have the ability to accept each other's often peculiar personal characteristics and to be sensitive to each other's needs and wishes. Together they will also treat those outside the relationship the same way, usually giving every person or idea, no matter how strange, a fair chance without prejudgment. In fact, the relationship is particularly drawn to unusual and out-of-the-way experiences and people. Recognizing the odd and offbeat elements in everyday events is a specialty of this combination, and in their opinions they are likely to give a different spin to events and topics, throwing a whole new light on them. Their outspokenness, however, is not always appreciated—this combination may not be everyone's cup of tea.

A strong physical or sexual attraction is often missing between these two. Leo is a fire sign and Virgo earth, but their relationship is governed by a mixture of air and water, elements here implying lighter and less passionate or earthy feelings. The couple is often interested in intellectual, aesthetic or spiritual matters, then, and their love affairs and marriages, although highly empathic, are apt to be more platonic than sensuous. Virgo II's are often ambivalent about Leo I aggression, being alternately attracted to and repelled by it, and Leo I's find their Virgo II partners intriguing but ultimately a bit negative and critical.

Friendships here have their ups and downs. Both partners must feel free to go their separate ways, which generally means that Virgo II's have to be allowed to withdraw somewhat from the world and Leo I's to advance toward it. Parent-child relationships can demonstrate great sensitivity and understanding despite tremendous temperamental differences. No matter which of the two is the parent and which the child, they will respect each other's attitudes even when they don't sympathize with them. Working relationships, especially co-worker matchups, are ineffective unless the pair can settle their personal differences.

ADVICE: *Appreciate things as they are. Not everything has to be unusual. The bizarre is only one element of life. Try to pay attention to practical details.*

July 26–August 2
THE WEEK OF AUTHORITY
LEO I

September 11–18
THE WEEK OF THE LITERALIST
VIRGO III

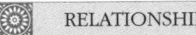
RELATIONSHIPS

STRENGTHS: **TRUTH-LOVING, CRUSADING, HONEST**

WEAKNESSES: **PRYING, SELFISH, UNCOMPROMISING**

BEST: **WORK**

WORST: **FAMILY**

Bringing Truth to Light

Both Leo I's and Virgo III's tend to be more concerned with principles and ideas than with people, and when they come together they often concentrate on bringing the truth to light—facts that have been hidden, or opinions that have been hushed up, in service of some less-than-ethical intent. Leo I–Virgo III couples are potential crusaders. Truth and honesty are more important to them than anything else, an uncompromising stance that sometimes prevents them from taking people's feelings into account, so that they can step on some sensitive toenails—particularly each other's. Both are strong-headed, and neither is at all shy about voicing his or her opinions. Things will run smoothly as long as they believe in the same ideas; expect clashes, however, should they disagree. Also, the truths they reveal often have more do with the underlying issues of their own relationship than with any abstract ideals.

Despite their concern for the truth, in their love affairs and friendships these partners may have little interest in uncovering disturbing facts about each other, especially when things are going well. During times of conflict, however, they are likely to dig deeper, revealing weaknesses and indiscretions in each other to be used as ammunition. Alternately ignoring and investigating the truth may become a typical pattern here. In marriage and career involvements, however, the avenging-angel side of the relationship is likely to emerge unequivocally. The partners will not rest until inequities are addressed and falsehoods exposed. Their particular dislike for pretension and privilege in the wealthy or powerful may lead them to try to humble the mighty. There is an undeniable Robin Hood–type feeling here, a sense of righting society's wrongs and defending the underdog.

Long-kept family secrets may hold a special fascination for Leo I–Virgo III relatives. Investigating such hidden areas is typical here, but so is having the good sense not to reveal them if their exposure could harm the family group. Even so, these two must beware of the temptation to use such facts to further their own selfish interests through subtle emotional blackmail.

ADVICE: *Don't always be sticking your nose in other people's business. Remember that curiosity killed the cat. Tend to your own problems. Cultivate kindness.*

VIDA BLUE (7/28/49)
GAYLORD PERRY (9/15/38)

Blue and Perry were 2 of baseball's finest pitchers in the 70s, both winners of the Cy Young Award (Blue in '71, Perry in '72). They were fierce rivals within the American League. Blue pitched a no-hitter ('70) and was MVP ('71). Perry retired in '83 with a stunning 314 wins and 3,534 strikeouts over 22 years.

July 26–August 2
THE WEEK OF AUTHORITY
LEO I

September 19–24
THE CUSP OF BEAUTY
VIRGO-LIBRA CUSP

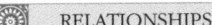
RELATIONSHIPS

STRENGTHS: **VISIONARY, IDEALISTIC, ROMANTIC**

WEAKNESSES: **DELUDED, DISILLUSIONED, DISAPPOINTED**

BEST: **FRIENDSHIP**

WORST: **PARENT-CHILD**

Yearning for the Beyond

At the heart of this relationship may lie stunning realizations and aesthetic visions. These imaginings can be heavenly or hellish in nature and can deal with either time future or time past; in either case, the relationship may be obsessed with science fiction, spirituality, quest—in short, a yearning for the beyond. These partners want to surpass the normal bounds of time and space. The urge to escape, but also to explore the possibilities of many planes of existence, is undeniable here. Both the Leo I adventuresome side and the Virgo-Libra need to seek ever newer and more aesthetic experiences are activated in this matchup. Leo I's may prove to be powerful figures for Virgo-Libras, being people on whom they can depend.

Love affairs between these two can be highly romantic, in ways that go well beyond carnal desire. Life can be a glorious adventure for this pair. Disillusion lurks just around the corner, however, for partners too carried away by idealism. Whether as friends, lovers, mates, parents or teachers, Leo I's and Virgo-Libras often put each other on pedestals, a tendency that may turn out to be a setup for disappointment when the godlike object of their worship turns out to be actually all too human, and fallible. A great challenge of this relationship is for the partners to see each other as they really are, stripped bare of psychological projections and expectations.

Working relationships between Leo I's and Virgo-Libras must be strongly grounded. Otherwise fantasy will lead to unreality, unreality to impracticality and unworkability, and unworkability to failure. One or both of the partners can often find the necessary objectivity and pragmatism within themselves, but if they are to be successful they must have the strength to back off from their exalted vision of their relationship and to view matters with a cold eye.

ADVICE: *Ground yourself in the here and now, but reach for the stars. Cultivate practical skills. Don't overlook what is right in front of you.*

PATTI SCIALFA (7/29/56)
BRUCE SPRINGSTEEN (9/23/49)

Vocalist Scialfa and Springsteen first got close when she joined his band in 1985. By '88 the tabloids had reported that they were having an affair. His wife, model-actress Julianne Phillips, sued for divorce. Scialfa and Springsteen married in '91 and now have 3 children. **Also:** **Francis Scott Key & F. Scott Fitzgerald** (blood relatives; composer/writer); **Carroll O'Connor & Larry Hagman** (friends; actors).

BLAKE EDWARDS (7/26/22)
JULIE ANDREWS (10/1/35)

Edwards is a highly respected film, stage and tv director, producer and screenwriter. He married Andrews in '69, during the filming of *Darling Lili*, in which she starred and which he directed. In recent years, she has worked almost exclusively on his projects. *Also:* **Polly Jefferson & Martha Jefferson Randolph** (Thos. Jefferson's daughters); **Benito Mussolini & Romano Mussolini** (father/son; dictator/jazz pianist).

July 26–August 2
THE WEEK OF AUTHORITY
LEO I

September 25–October 2
THE WEEK OF THE PERFECTIONIST
LIBRA I

Sensible Elegance

This relationship could prove a very comfortable fit for its partners, each enjoying different aspects of it for different reasons. Together this pair will take an orderly, reasoned and structured approach to just about everything. This will satisfy the Libra I need for attention to detail and will delight Leo I's, who always have to have a system to fall back on. In addition, the relationship grounds and gives form to the more excitable and aspiring aspects of both the Leo I and the Libra I characters.

No matter how romantic a love affair between a Leo I and a Libra I may be, it always has a strongly sensible streak running through it that will rarely allow it to be dominated by self-destructive or unrealistic impulses. The romanticism here is elegant, polished and highly nuanced. Perhaps a tad too self-conscious as a pair, Leo I–Libra I lovers and mates are always aware of their effect on other people. They will work carefully on polishing their style, dress, movement and speech before appearing together in public.

As friends, Leo I's and Libra I's can make strict demands on each other to keep their relationship on a high plane. Quality rather than quantity is important here. This may make it unnecessary for the partners to see each other that often: when they do, it really counts. Co-workers in this combination are similarly dedicated to producing quality work and will not hesitate to scrap efforts not up to their standards, no matter how much labor has gone into them. As business partners or company executives, these two may put each other and those working for them under excessive stress, since they rarely let up in their intense expectation of total involvement.

Parent-child relationships in this combination can be unmercifully demanding, but the two will also find time to relax and be proud of each other. It is quite possible for such pairs to work on artistic, commercial or playful pursuits together and to achieve results of high quality and interest.

ADVICE: *Without sacrificing quality, let up a bit in your demands. Be more natural and less self-conscious. Let things happen as they will.*

WILLIAM POWELL (7/29/1892)
CAROLE LOMBARD (10/6/09)

Powell and Lombard were married from 1931–33. Neither had reached their career peaks during the span of their marriage. It was in '34 that each rose to stardom—she in Howard Hawks' screwball comedy *Twentieth Century*, and he in *The Thin Man*.

July 26–August 2
THE WEEK OF AUTHORITY
LEO I

October 3–10
THE WEEK OF SOCIETY
LIBRA II

A Locus Within

This can be an inspiring combination in which the partners share a profound emotional contact. Their relationship encourages them to become more introspective, and they may in fact help each other to explore their own inner lives. The psychological astuteness of Libra II's, and their nonthreatening and understanding manner, may well show Leo I's how to slow down a bit in their external striving and to know themselves better and more deeply. Likewise, impressed by the willpower and determination of Leo I's, wiser Libra II's will seek a true locus of strength and determination within, knowing that simply trying to imitate the outwardly directed stance of Leo I's would do little good.

Love affairs in this combination can be highly emotional, yet seldom in an outwardly expressive way. When these partners are together, the magic chemistry of their relationship relieves them of their social and career responsibilities, allowing them to relax in the safety of mutual empathy. In short, these two feel comfortable, safe and trusting with each other. Such attitudes bode well for marriage. The only real problem here is whether the pair are willing to take on that responsibility, a question that may arouse indecision.

In work and family relationships this pair don't always see eye to eye. To Libra II employees or children, the attitudes of Leo I bosses or parents often seem didactic and rigid, while Leo I's are disturbed by Libra II indecision. Should Libra II's be in the driver's seat, they may have difficulty standing up to the powerful and often rebellious stance of a dissatisfied Leo I employee or child. Friendships between these two can be great fun but may also stir up feelings that unaccountably disturb both partners from time to time. This phenomenon may suggest a need to settle and resolve deeper issues.

ADVICE: *Search inside. Encounter your emotions and go beyond them. Find the path that is uniquely yours. Proceed fearlessly and with conviction.*

July 26–August 2
THE WEEK OF AUTHORITY
LEO I

October 11–18
THE WEEK OF THEATER
LIBRA III

RELATIONSHIPS

STRENGTHS: **DYNAMIC, LOYAL, SENSUAL**

WEAKNESSES: **SELF-UNAWARE, STUBBORN, MISUNDERSTOOD**

BEST: **FRIENDSHIP**

WORST: **MARRIAGE**

Extroversion Belied

These two strong-willed personalities will be more than a match for each other. The heart of their relationship is often hidden: apparently extroverted as individuals, they may actually be taken up in highly personal endeavors that they find difficult to communicate to anyone but each other. Possessed of a vision they cannot share, the pair may seem distracted to other people, who will often misunderstand their intentions and actions. Although Leo I's are highly dominant, they don't always feel comfortable as leaders, and the Libra III is more likely to run the relationship. This combination is explosive, combining the fiery nature of Leo with the airy makeup of Libra. Yet the relationship is ruled by earth, an element in this case connoting sensuousness, physical pleasure and also stubbornness.

Passions may run high in love affairs and marriages, which may also be strongly sensual. Yet they are seldom high in self-understanding and awareness. Neither of these partners is too interested in investing time or patience in recognizing their partner's nonsexual needs. Strangely enough, these two, who face so many challenges squarely, may be ill prepared to cope with the major issues of their own relationship.

As friends, Leo I's and Libra III's are well suited to each other. Since both are allergic to dependent types, they will appreciate each other's self-sufficiency. Power struggles are rare here. Libra III's may find in their Leo I partner a loyal figure they can depend on or even lean on in times of need. These friends often find themselves at the center of social, school or family groups, where they exert a grounding and directing influence. As co-workers, similarly, they can function as the dynamo driving a department.

Conflicts often abound in parent-child and sibling matchups in this combination. Here both partners' extroverted sides lead to flamboyant displays of temperament, which may point to a lack of self-awareness. The pair will benefit from staying calm and thinking through their problems together.

ADVICE: *Try to fathom your own mysteries. Pay attention to feelings. Take the time to understand. Find the calm at the eye of the tornado.*

LARAINE DAY (10/13/20)
LEO DUROCHER (7/27/05)

Durocher was a feisty and funny baseball manager for 24 years, winning 3 pennants, a World Series—and the heart of film actress Day. During their marriage (1947–60) she came to be called the "first lady of baseball." Her book *Day with Giants* (1952) is a memoir of their lives together. **Also: Geraldine Chaplin & Eugene O'Neill** (granddaughter/grandfather; actress/playwright).

July 26–August 2
THE WEEK OF AUTHORITY
LEO I

October 19–25
THE CUSP OF DRAMA & CRITICISM
LIBRA-SCORPIO CUSP

RELATIONSHIPS

STRENGTHS: **SUCCESSFUL, DEMANDING, GROUP-ORIENTED**

WEAKNESSES: **STRESSFUL, IMPERSONAL, UNREALISTIC**

BEST: **WORK**

WORST: **LOVE**

Sensitivity to Criticism

This relationship is often based in a profession or career, where it may be a winning combination. But it can leave a lot to be desired in the personal realm: it tends to make its partners hypersensitive, and since they are both already highly critical, their pairing can amount to a prescription for pain. Even outside this relationship, Leo I's are extremely sensitive to criticism, an Achilles' heel that Libra-Scorpios will target when challenged or hurt. Both partners tend to be demanding of each other, a trait that can be constructive at work or in marriage but will put a lot of stress on less structured kinds of comradeship.

In friendships, love affairs and sibling matchups, Leo I's and Libra-Scorpios often get lost in their own little world. As lovers they could give their sexuality too much importance in the relationship, generating problems rather than pleasure. Their marriages may well be powered by an idea, ideology or religious belief, areas that let them invest their emotions in some kind of group activity rather than reserving them for their personal lives. A tendency to go off the deep end is undeniable here. The couple must be careful not to lose sight of their domestic life together, particularly if they have children.

As friends these two will compete with each other, so that their relationship can help them try to better their own personal best. One can imagine that it might also cause them some hurt feelings if begun during adolescence. As siblings Leo I's and Libra-Scorpios often escape into fantasy, a protective mechanism against unkind or misunderstanding parental attitudes.

It is as colleagues that these two not only demand but usually get the best of which their relationship is capable. Both partners are open to investing all their energy in their projects, knowing beforehand that their endeavors will benefit all concerned. They are not one of those teams who need to operate on their own, as an entrepreneurial or business partnership; they can function very effectively within a group.

ADVICE: *Let up a bit in your demands. Be less critical of yourself and more critical of your ideas. Build emotional ties. Pay more attention to personal needs.*

PAUL ANKA (7/30/41)
ANNETTE FUNICELLO (10/22/42)

Singer-songwriter Anka was a 50s teen idol. Funicello was a pop singer and actress, known for her beach party films. She met and fell in love with Anka on Dick Clark's *American Bandstand.* Anka wrote 2 memorable hit songs dedicated to her, *Put Your Head on My Shoulder* (1959) and *Puppy Love* (1960). **Also: Clara Bow & Bela Lugosi** (affair; actors).

STRENGTHS: **TRUTHFUL, RESPECTFUL, SEXUAL**

WEAKNESSES: **CONFLICTING, UNFORGIVING, DEMANDING**

BEST: **FRIENDSHIP**

WORST: **PARENT-CHILD**

ALICE LEE ROOSEVELT (7/29/1861)
TEDDY ROOSEVELT (10/27/1858)

Alice Lee was the great love of young Teddy's life. They were married in 1880 and had 3 blissful years—until tragedy struck. On Valentine's Day 1884, only 2 days after the birth of a baby daughter, both Alice and Teddy's mother died of typhoid fever just hours apart. He wrote, "The light has just gone out of my life."

July 26–August 2
THE WEEK OF AUTHORITY
LEO I

October 26–November 2
THE WEEK OF INTENSITY
SCORPIO I

All or Not at All

Leo I's and Scorpio I's share a belief in being truthful no matter what. Their relationship synergistically increases this quality, which may well become its core focus. Things aren't too easy between these two, since both tend to be demanding and believe in giving their projects their all—or not at all. At the same time, they often see the truth as something relative, rather than an absolute written in stone. For the most part, however, both partners agree that honesty, integrity, ethical behavior and sticking to the facts as much as possible are of paramount importance.

Since Leo I and Scorpio I are square to each other in the zodiac (that is, at 90°), astrology predicts friction and conflict in their relationship. And given that these two are some of the most stubborn individuals of the year, friction is indeed a certainty. But friction can also mean passion. Although Leo is a fire sign and Scorpio water, the Leo I–Scorpio I relationship is governed by earth, an element here connoting a strong physical connection. Sexuality is usually important in this relationship. In love affairs, honesty continues to play its part, being combined with passionate and erotic intensity. Marriages may be no less passionate than love affairs but are certainly more demanding in terms of responsibilities.

Leo I–Scorpio I friendships can be very close. Despite disagreements and emotional upset, especially because of their honesty, these two usually have a great deal of respect for each other and can count on each other in times of trouble. As much as they hate to admit it, both partners will occasionally be forced to take personal or mitigating considerations into account and to allow for lapses in truthfulness, even in themselves.

Seemingly insurmountable difficulties may arise in parent-child and co-worker matchups, but these can also be challenges to break down or overcome barriers. Leo I pride and Scorpio I perfectionism may have to be sacrificed at times to hammer out compromises; but once an issue has been settled or agreed upon, partners will generally keep their word faithfully.

ADVICE: *Be more human in applying standards of truth. Forgive and forget. Cultivate empathy. Beware of rigidity. Bend with the wind.*

STRENGTHS: **DEVELOPMENTAL, TRANSFORMING, TORRID**

WEAKNESSES: **IRRITATING, PREDICTABLE, COMBATIVE**

BEST: **LOVE**

WORST: **CO-WORKER**

MARIA SHRIVER (11/6/55)
ARNOLD SCHWARZENEGGER (7/30/47)

The relationship between Shriver and Schwarzenegger is a media Cinderella story. The muscle-man champ of the world became a major movie star in the 80s. She is a glamorous journalist and niece of JFK. They married in '86, still vigorously pursuing their careers as a high-profile celebrity couple.

Also: **Henry Ford & Edsel Ford** (father/son); **Dom DeLuise & Peter DeLuise** (father/son; actors).

July 26–August 2
THE WEEK OF AUTHORITY
LEO I

November 3–11
THE WEEK OF DEPTH
SCORPIO II

Phoenix Rising

This relationship may be likened to the flame that consumes the phoenix and then summons it forth from the ashes. Metamorphosis, both of the partners and of the relationship itself, is characteristic here. This is especially true during those fateful periods in the lives of its partners when they reach a crossroads or dead end. At this point the magic of rebirth emerges, propelling both them and their relationship to a higher level. A spiritual or developmental transformation at the individual or personal level is implied here, but the rejuvenation of a company or family may also occur.

Leo I fire can really bring Scorpio II water to the boil in love affairs. The steam that results is blistering in its heat and can exert an irresistible pressure on both partners. Their already strong sexual drives are amplified by the relationship's synergy, raising their lovemaking to new heights. Still, unless they work to let the relationship grow and change, it may get old, and they may both tire of its predictability. Scorpio II's will have the greatest tendency to hang in there. Without periodic renewal, however, the relationship will not be what either partner really needs.

Sibling matchups are generally close and can act as the family's linchpin, or else as the force that propels it through periods of major change. In the course of such changes the sibling relationship may itself undergo a transformation or may act as a catalyst, advancing the chemical reaction in the family without being significantly changed itself. In the workplace, executives in this combination sometimes battle it out for the top spot, but collaborate later on with increased respect. Co-workers may not be able to spend long periods of time in each other's presence without getting itchy and irritable—they will have to work on establishing a modus vivendi. Adversarial relationships between these two can be frighteningly violent, with Leo I's generally initiating the conflict and Scorpio II's springing from a defensive posture into attack mode.

ADVICE: *Keep violent impulses under control, but blow off steam occasionally. In the emotional sphere, act wisely. Keep your love alive.*

July 26–August 2
THE WEEK OF AUTHORITY
LEO I

November 12–18
THE WEEK OF CHARM
SCORPIO III

Fitting and Proper

There is often a feeling of rightness about this relationship, a sense that it has achieved a certain balance and appropriateness. The partners generally have a feeling for *kairos* (the right time for action); they will seldom have to strain to achieve their goals but can ride the wave of inevitability and kismet. Such cosmic surfing shows the relationship's ability to "hook into the Force," whether of earthly, stellar or divine origin. Although Leo and Scorpio are fire and water signs, respectively, the Leo I–Scorpio III relationship is ruled by earth and air, the other two elements, here signifying an easy balance between the ethereal and physical poles of existence.

The relationship often fosters a need for justice and for righting wrongs. Whether it emerges at home, at work or in the social sphere, it will justify its own existence by working to bring everyone it encounters their just rewards or desserts, including the partners themselves. One result is that it can be seen as giving with one hand and chastising with the other, particularly when it is a marriage or a career or family matchup. If tendencies to be judgmental and to claim infallibility here are not kept under control, the relationship may wind up dispelling the atmosphere of fairness it sets out to create.

Friendships between Leo I's and Scorpio III's are less common than rivalries or outright enmities. If these two don't like each other, they will usually make no bones about it, even in the presence of others. They will also deal in short order with any group or individual who desecrates beauty or undermines harmony.

As enemies, these two will quite likely give no quarter and take no prisoners, whether in intellectual, emotional, physical or even spiritual or religious combat with each other. Such are the more uncompromising aspects of this relationship that it will face few problems with vagueness, indecision or miscommunication.

ADVICE: *Don't try to play god. Be more open and forgiving. Beware of succumbing to the dark side. Power may have to be relinquished. Foster kindness.*

ESTES KEFAUVER (7/26/03)
JOSEPH McCARTHY (11/14/08)

Congressman Kefauver and Sen. McCarthy are responsible for the first use of television in US civic affairs, starting in 1950. Kefauver headed a Senate subcommittee investigating organized crime, while McCarthy went head-hunting for communists in the State Dept. Their televised hearings brought issues into the homes of millions of Americans and set a media precedent.

July 26–August 2
THE WEEK OF AUTHORITY
LEO I

November 19–24
THE CUSP OF REVOLUTION
SCORPIO-SAGITTARIUS CUSP

Positive and Upbeat

These two are capable of evolving fresh and new ideas. Their relationship usually focuses on following its intuitions and hunches, especially in sniffing out what could be the sweet smell of success. Together they usually concentrate on the positive and upbeat side of life, and if success is not forthcoming, they waste little or no energy on detailed analyses of failure—in fact, they've probably already moved on to something new, provocative and exciting. Scorpio-Sagittarians are usually fairly realistic, but their relationships with Leo I's are generally optimistic. There is little room here for nagging or negative criticism.

Romantic and marital matchups between these two sometimes emphasize youthfulness by pairing partners of different generations. Rather than youth admiring old age here, the older partner, whether Leo I or Scorpio-Sagittarius, values the freshness and vitality of the younger one. The tragedy of such matchups is apparent when the older partner grows ill or incapacitated or the younger member becomes restive and wants to roam. All such relationships should stress the value of age and maturity equally with that of youth and innocence. Married couples in this combination may exhibit a special interest in children and small pets, whether their own or other people's. In the family, this is a natural combination for grandparents and grandchildren, or for older aunts or uncles and younger nieces or nephews. True intergenerational sharing is possible in such cases.

Friendships between Leo I's and Scorpio-Sagittarians can be lighthearted but will have an underlying air of purpose. These two rarely give themselves over to the pursuit of entertainment and pleasure only—they are likely to put their innovative talents in the service of some sort of larger group, such as a club or their own social circle. Working relationships between these two are seldom successful except at the highest executive levels, where innovation may be most appreciated.

ADVICE: *Encourage intergenerational understanding. Respect age differences. New wine is not always the best wine. Exercise a bit more patience.*

CHARLES VIDOR (7/27/1900)
EVELYN KEYES (11/20/19)

Hungarian-born director/screenwriter Vidor was married to actress Keyes from 1943–45. She appeared in 3 of his films, among them *The Desperadoes* (1943). But his most memorable films were *Gilda* (1946), which made Rita Hayworth a sex symbol, and *The Joker Is Wild* (1957). *Also:* **Nick Bollettieri & Boris Becker** (tennis teacher/tennis star); **Jackie Kennedy & Robert Kennedy** (in-laws; intimate friends).

STRENGTHS: **UNDERSTANDING, PASSIONATE, QUALITY-ORIENTED**

WEAKNESSES: **STRESSFUL, WILLFUL, UNPREDICTABLE**

BEST: **LOVE**

WORST: **FAMILY**

JACKIE KENNEDY ONASSIS (7/28/29)
MARIA CALLAS (12/2/23)

Callas had a long affair with Ari Onassis. In 1966 they talked of marrying, but he decided to court and wed Jackie Kennedy ('68). Callas was furious and felt that her rival was a gold digger. Shortly after his marriage to Jackie, Callas resumed her relationship with him. ***Also:* Jackie & John Kennedy, Jr.** (mother/son); **Jackie & Caroline Kennedy** (mother/daughter).

July 26–August 2
THE WEEK OF AUTHORITY
LEO I

November 25–December 2
THE WEEK OF INDEPENDENCE
SAGITTARIUS I

Molten Feelings

Communication between these two is usually swift and direct. Both for themselves and for others, their relationship can be extremely demanding, putting a particular stress on getting the job done as well as possible. Each partner brings out the other's perfectionist side. They are both normally impulsive, but here the relationship's wisdom kicks in, creating a feeling that things must be planned before being attempted. The slogan in this respect might well be a familiar rule of carpentry: "Measure twice, cut once." Both Leo and Sagittarius are fire signs, but the Leo I–Sagittarius I relationship is ruled by air, emphasizing mental concentration and willpower. Leo I and Sagittarius I are trine to each other (120° apart) in the zodiac, so that traditional astrology would predict a comfortable connection between them; but this fiery relationship can be fiercely competitive.

Passionate love affairs are not uncommon between these two. In bed things can get pretty wild, but such molten feelings can burn out over time. The hair-trigger temper of Sagittarius I's and the blockbuster energies of Leo I's can also collide and cause blowups. When things turn cold between these two, they may sometimes continue as friends at a lower emotional level. In marriage, Leo I and Sagittarius I honor and honesty stand them in good stead, but they can make excessive demands on their children and other family members. Learning to make fewer demands and lowering their perfectionist expectations will be essential if they are to maintain a modicum of domestic tranquillity. This can be a classic friendship. Warmth and understanding radiate between these two—at least when they are getting along. But competition over career matters, shared love objects, money or a host of other concerns can disrupt harmony at any point, turning the relationship into a clash of wills. Leo I parents are always fiercely protective of their children, but here this trait can manifest in expectations that are just too high, making Sagittarius I offspring rebel. Sibling and co-worker matchups are unpredictable; constancy in day-to-day interactions is difficult for this pair.

ADVICE: *Even out your feelings. Seek moderation in daily life. Beware of burnout and overload. Indulge your warm and hedonistic side. Relax.*

STRENGTHS: **ENERGETIC, SUPPORTIVE, IDEALISTIC**

WEAKNESSES: **REBELLIOUS, IMMATURE, ATTENTION-HUNGRY**

BEST: **SIBLING**

WORST: **MARRIAGE**

DEAN CAIN (7/31/66)
TERI HATCHER (12/8/64)

Cain and Hatcher are co-stars of *Lois & Clark: The New Adventures of Superman* (1993–). Cain as Clark Kent/Superman and Hatcher as Lois Lane had such good chemistry that the show's writers increasingly emphasized their romance. By the end of the 2nd season, the characters fell in love and Clark proposed to Lois. ***Also:* Benito Mussolini & Francisco Franco** (WWII allies; European dictators).

July 26–August 2
THE WEEK OF AUTHORITY
LEO I

December 3–10
THE WEEK OF THE ORIGINATOR
SAGITTARIUS II

Securing Success

Immature power-struggles may break out in this combination from time to time as these two compete for the spotlight. Since this problem can be eliminated when they work together to secure worldly success for themselves as a duo, partnerships of all types, including marital and professional, are often beneficial here. In personal relationships, Leo I's have a calming effect on the excessive aspects of the Sagittarius II personality, guiding this partner's energies in a more constructive direction. Sagittarius II's, for their part, may be inspiring for Leo I's.

Love affairs in this combination can be idealistic yet also selfish. The partners can become excessively hungry for attention from each other, in which case resentments inevitably arise over who is more (or less) interested in whom. It is not uncommon for childish rivalries to break out for the attention of a third person, often a mutual friend. Marriages are not particularly recommended here, not because the couple are incompatible but because they may be unable to achieve the maturity and balance necessary for them to create a peaceful domestic setting together, let alone raise children. Career connections can develop between spouses, however, providing an outlet that will direct attention away from problems at home.

Friendships between these two can be extremely supportive and understanding. Should they launch a concerted effort to make a go of it in a social, sport or business enterprise, they often succeed, but they are better at initiating a project than at running one day-to-day. Sibling relationships, especially of the same sex, are very close, despite the pair's differences: Leo I's usually value education through schooling, Sagittarius II's education through life experience. These matchups are usually important in inspiring the family and moving it forward. Leo I–Sagittarius II co-workers tend to rebel against unfair treatment and to push for the rights of their colleagues. They may set themselves up as the group representative in negotiations with management.

ADVICE: *Work at self-sufficiency. Don't be so needy of approval. Don't waste your energy on rivalry and rebellion. Seek constructive goals.*

July 26–August 2
THE WEEK OF AUTHORITY
LEO I

December 11–18
THE WEEK OF THE TITAN
SAGITTARIUS III

Doing the Dance

These two dominating personalities generally find themselves interacting most successfully in the kind of social setting that stresses knowing how to play the game. Whether they are partners or rivals, they will do their dance with each other according to well-established rules of conduct. Strategic thinking plays its part in this relationship, for both Leo I and Sagittarius III enjoy being able to bounce ideas about how to deal with others off a serious and knowledgeable partner. Sagittarius III's can get a bit serious sometimes, and their darker moods may weigh heavily on Leo I's. On the other hand, they themselves may sometimes find Leo I's a bit impetuous and premature in their judgments and actions.

Privacy is important in Leo I–Sagittarius III love affairs, which nevertheless tend to be quite involved with family and friends. Parties, outings and social gatherings of all types attract these two, who are likely to throw themselves into these events rather than be found standing on the sidelines. This kind of active social participation usually bodes well for the relationship's longevity, for if left alone too long, this couple may clash and fall into power struggles. Marriages specialize in advising other people and guiding them through difficult periods with compassion and understanding.

Parent-child relationships in this combination can be extremely problematic and trying. Leo I children often turn to authority figures other than their parents, who can be extremely intolerant of their children's need to think for themselves. When the relationship manifests among either friends and business partners or rivals and opponents, it will have its ups and downs, with friends sometimes acting hostile and competitors sometimes making friendly gestures. The pair respect each other, but more because they recognize each other's power than because they really acknowledge each other on a human level. Each of them knows well the other partner's ability to inflict pain.

ADVICE: *Reach agreement whenever possible. Don't waste time and energy in heavy disputes. Learn the art of compromise. Develop lasting values.*

MICK JAGGER (7/26/43)
KEITH RICHARDS (12/18/43)

Rolling Stones Jagger and Richards were both avid fans of American r&b. In '62 the Stones started up and the 2 performers began writing songs together. By '65 most Stones hits were co-written Jagger-Richards compositions.

Also: Clara Bow & Gilbert Roland (lovers; actors); **Jerry Van Dyke & Dick Van Dyke** (brothers; actors).

July 26–August 2
THE WEEK OF AUTHORITY
LEO I

December 19–25
THE CUSP OF PROPHECY
SAGITTARIUS-CAPRICORN CUSP

Dropping Bad Habits

The theme of this relationship has to do with moving from the past toward the future. Of course, development and evolution are implied here, but also both the passage from the old to the new and the continuance of tradition, both the dropping of bad habits and the streamlining of out-of-date approaches. As individuals, Leo I's and Sagittarius-Capricorns have both a strongly traditional side and modern thoughts that cry out to be recognized. They generally rely on intuition to know how much dead wood has to be cut away and what direction a family or business should take.

Love affairs in this combination may prove difficult. Sagittarius-Capricorns require their partners to have plenty of patience and an abiding interest in their problems and struggles, whereas Leo I's need an appreciative audience and freedom from heavy moods and negativity. The relationship rarely meets all these needs, often resulting in frustration and a desire to escape.

In marriages and career matchups, Leo I's and Sagittarius-Capricorns will want the benefits of both conventional and more forward-looking approaches. Together they will want to keep up with all the latest trends and even start some new ones, but they have the wisdom to build on past efforts, analyzing them in order to discover their weaknesses and their strengths. Leo I's will sometimes be put off by Sagittarius-Capricorn silence, often interpreting it as criticism or disapproval; Sagittarius-Capricorns will often find Leo I's overaggressive and will resent their claimed omniscience. But they will also appreciate the relationship's openness to their unusual ideas, and should these two overcome their personal differences, their relationship stands a good chance of succeeding. At its best, this is a pioneering duo capable of forwarding the aspirations of whatever group it represents. Friendships are likely to be difficult, polarizing Leo I extroversion and Sagittarius-Capricorn introversion. In parent-child relationships in this combination, the partners are likely to have problems communicating openly with each other and developing deep tolerance and understanding.

ADVICE: *Open up avenues of communication. Try to bridge gaps and overcome differences. Develop empathy. Increase personal understanding.*

CONSTANTINE I (8/2/1868)
GEORGE I (12/24/1845)

George succeeded to the Greek throne in 1863. During his reign the area of Greece was extended considerably. The last territories were won in the Balkan War, at the end of which he was assassinated. His son Constantine took the throne in 1913 and held it until he was forced to abdicate in 1922 after a military revolt.

July 26–August 2
THE WEEK OF AUTHORITY
LEO I

December 26–January 2
THE WEEK OF THE RULER
CAPRICORN I

An Escape from Reality

One might expect this combination of powerful personalities to be extremely heavy, but it is often the opposite, having a very theatrical quality—these partners act out their fantasies by projecting them onto each other. The relationship also has a tendency to flee from life's pressing realities, so that its partners may, for example, turn to drug use. Yet the matchup is not without ambition, and in fact both of these individuals have a great deal of drive. One finds a commitment to style in whatever they do. Combined with their desire to fulfill their fantasies, this produces a sometimes excessive flamboyance. This pair will probably ruffle quite a few feathers. Leo I and Capricorn I are in quincunx aspect to each other in the zodiac (lying 150° apart), which exerts a pressure to make them a somewhat unstable pair, underlining their tendency toward eccentricity.

Love affairs can be exciting but remarkably cool. A certain objectivity takes the place of deep passion and emotional exploration. The strong bursts of energy that usually emanate from Leo I and Capricorn I personalities somehow miss the mark in these relationships, which are almost ineffectual at times. Yet marriages can work here if the partners make themselves and each other uphold their mutual responsibilities. More often than not, they will be playful with each other, but they can be rather indolent when it comes to cleaning up or looking after the kids.

Working relationships are undermined by unserious attitudes and interpersonal instabilities. Pairs of friends and of siblings are likely to have a great old time, as long as not too much is expected of them—they will rarely develop deep bonds of understanding. Parent-child relationships generally bring out the heavier side of Leo I's and Capricorn I's, often resulting in a dictatorial parent and a rebellious child, especially when it is the Capricorn I who is the parent.

ADVICE: *Try facing up to the truth. Escaping can be pleasant but often unproductive. Build a firm basis for your life. Coordinate energies.*

MARIANNE FAITHFULL (12/29/46)
MICK JAGGER (7/26/43)

The early Rolling Stones hit *As Tears Go By* (1964), sung by Faithfull, was written for the angel-faced singer by Jagger. During their highly visible romance (1965–70), they co-starred in the movie *Ned Kelly* (1970), at which time she was hospitalized for drug overdose and had a miscarriage. **Also: Mussolini & Woodrow Wilson** (Italian invasion spelled failure for League of Nations).

July 26–August 2
THE WEEK OF AUTHORITY
LEO I

January 3–9
THE WEEK OF DETERMINATION
CAPRICORN II

Head to Head

Fortunately or unfortunately, there is no way around the power issues in this relationship. There seem to be only two alternatives for this pair: they either go head to head with each other or join forces in a drive to the top. Given that power is the focus here, Leo I's and Capricorn II's would seem to have little choice but to express the more ambitious and aggressive sides of their personalities. It is usually the Capricorn II's who win out, since these personalities generally don't even recognize defeat, let alone admit it. Leo I's, on the other hand, are often discouraged by a major setback or a series of smaller ones. This couple may ultimately need to learn the spiritual lesson that perhaps the greatest power lies in resisting ego drives and developing love, understanding, acceptance and kindness. Learning this lesson can be more rewarding than money, career success or triumphing over an opponent.

Love affairs here are too often more concerned with who has the upper hand than with real feeling. Leo I's and Capricorn II's may squander what love they have by transmuting it into a desire to control and dominate. Marriages are happiest when the partners share duties equally and leave each other alone much of the rest of the time.

Friendships may not work out at all for this matchup, not, at least, the kind based on sheer amicability and pleasure-loving pursuits. Terrible struggles can occur in parent-child relationships, whichever partner is the parent; both partners may eventually learn that at some point (usually before the parent simply leaves the room) it is in their own best interest to come to terms with each other. Career matchups are tricky, for Leo I's and Capricorn II's facing each other at the same level in a hierarchy may expend too much effort keeping each other down and not enough working together to make group efforts a success. Even when they do manage to push the company forward, they may do so for selfish reasons.

ADVICE: *Examine your values. Take time off and think about what you are doing. Cultivate spiritual values. Pay attention to the feelings of others.*

CARLOS SAURA (1/4/32)
GERALDINE CHAPLIN (7/31/44)

Chaplin and Saura have been constant companions since the mid-60s. Saura has been Spain's pre-eminent director and screenwriter since the late 50s. Chaplin, a delicate, serious-minded actress, has played the leads in some of Saura's films, doing her best acting under his direction. **Also: Thelma Todd & ZaSu Pitts** (co-stars, early Hal Roach film comedies).

July 26–August 2
THE WEEK OF AUTHORITY
LEO I

January 10–16
THE WEEK OF DOMINANCE
CAPRICORN III

Role Model

RELATIONSHIPS

STRENGTHS: **INSPIRATIONAL, CONSTRUCTIVELY CRITICAL**

WEAKNESSES: **UNBALANCED, DEPENDENCY-FOSTERING**

BEST: **TEACHER-STUDENT**

WORST: **LOVE**

These two share a frankness and a facility of the mind that will surely hold their relationship together—sometimes past the point of usefulness. Still, they will appreciate the combination's honesty, which will be of a kind they experience with few others. They are both strong and dominating people, and one would expect their matchup to be fraught with difficulty, but they are in fact quite capable of setting aside their power struggles in order to learn from each other. In this sense, each is the other's role model. Each one admires and learns from the other's strengths. They are happy to pit themselves as a unit against the world, using their relationship's strategizing skills to achieve their joint aims. Capricorn III's are prone to idealize someone they know, and Leo I's may well be the one they pick. Lacking a certain self-confidence, they may see a Leo I as the epitome of the successful and self-assured person they themselves would like to be some day.

Love between these two is exceedingly complex. Because Capricorn III's tend to idolize their Leo I lovers, they cede the upper hand in the relationship to them, at least temporarily. In doing so they may actually be unknowingly setting up the Leo I for a fall from grace in which he or she is totally rejected, having failed to live up to an image of perfection. Marriages are not particularly recommended unless they can strike a more equal balance of power, or unless the couple share specific worldly ambitions.

In teacher-student, boss-employee and parent-child relationships, Leo I's exert a marked influence on their partner but generally also understand how desperately Capricorn III's need to become their own person. A sensitive and understanding Leo I will guide a Capricorn III in the direction of ever-increasing responsibility. Care should be taken, however, to control the frankness that is typical of the relationship. Needless to say, an unaware or more brutal Leo I attitude can leave lifelong scars in the Capricorn III psyche.

ADVICE: *Scale back expectations. Even out the power structure. Beware of idolization and worship. Keep criticism from being unduly negative.*

ARISTOTLE ONASSIS (1/15/06)
JACKIE KENNEDY ONASSIS (7/28/29)

Jackie and Ari were married in 1968. Onassis offered the consolation of wealth to Jackie, who had been shattered both by JFK's death and that of Robert Kennedy. In return Jackie offered the companionship of one of the world's most glamorous women.

Also: **Henry Moore & Barbara Hepworth** (leading contemporary sculptors).

July 26–August 2
THE WEEK OF AUTHORITY
LEO I

January 17–22
THE CUSP OF MYSTERY & IMAGINATION
CAPRICORN-AQUARIUS CUSP

Extraordinary Chemistry

RELATIONSHIPS

STRENGTHS: **PRACTICAL, SENSUOUS, SUCCESSFUL**

WEAKNESSES: **DOMINATING, REPRESSIVE, DEBILITATING**

BEST: **MARRIAGE**

WORST: **PARENT-CHILD**

This relationship is one of the classics in the whole year for successful professional or marital partnerships. No matter how theoretical, idealistic or imaginative Leo I's and Capricorn-Aquarians may be as individuals, together they come down to earth with a bang. Their relationship brings out in them a practical and sensuous side of which neither may previously have been aware. In this respect the chemistry between them is quite extraordinary. Leo I's and Capricorn-Aquarians may fall in love at first sight or develop their relationship slowly and surely, but in either case their matchup has staying power over the years, and in retrospect may be viewed as a wonder that was simply meant to be.

Love, marital and professional pairings entail the danger that the partners, no matter how powerful individually, may submerge or lose their identities in the relationship. In this sense the matchup's very success may be its undoing. Should either person die, or be lost to the other through circumstance, extreme grief and feelings of deprivation or anger may prove debilitating—left alone, these partners may feel that their life is over, or that they cannot continue. While the relationship is at its height, then, great care should be taken to preserve individual prerogatives, so that the partners do not become totally wrapped up in the relationship's protective cloak.

Sibling matchups and friendships between Leo I's and Capricorn-Aquarians often stand a better chance of remaining objective. There may, in fact, be little interest on either side in elevating the relationship to a position of great importance. At the same time, it should not be taken for granted that easy and pleasurable attitudes will always prevail here. Assuming responsibility and bringing an element of hard work to the relationship will often ground it and lend it more permanence and satisfaction.

ADVICE: *Maintain individuality. Never take good feelings for granted. Hard work is necessary. Don't be self-sacrificing. Selfishness can be healthy, too.*

GRACIE ALLEN (7/26/06)
GEORGE BURNS (1/20/1896)

They met in 1925 and formed the Burns and Allen comedy team before they wed in '26. Her scatterbrained personality played against his cool, detached wit. He continued to worship her after her death in '64 until he died in '95. *Also:* **Yves Saint-Laurent & Christian Dior** (protégé/mentor; couturiers); **Duchamp & Picabia** (Dadaists); **Carroll O'Connor & Jean Stapleton** (co-stars, *All in the Family*).

STRENGTHS: CHALLENGING, ATTENTIVE, ADVENTURESOME

WEAKNESSES: IMPATIENT, RESENTFUL, OVERREACHING

BEST: SIBLING

WORST: LOVE

AUGUSTE PICCARD (1/28/1884)
JACQUES PICCARD (7/28/22)

In 1948 Auguste designed and built the first bathyscaphe, a propellered vehicle for deep-sea dives that could float underwater like a balloon. He and his son built a 2nd bathyscaphe in '53 and dived repeatedly to depths never before reached by scientists, gathering valuable data on the earth's deepest places.

July 26–August 2
THE WEEK OF AUTHORITY
LEO I

January 23–30
THE WEEK OF GENIUS
AQUARIUS I

An Inquiring Spirit

This relationship manifests a powerful attention to detail and to keeping wayward elements under control. Leo I and Aquarius I lie directly opposite each other in the zodiac, so that traditional astrology predicts difficulties and conflicts for this combination, but the intensity they generate can often be made to serve useful ends. Leo is a fire sign and Aquarius air, but the Leo I–Aquarius I relationship is ruled by water, an element that in this context asserts emotional and free-flowing energies. Leo I's are amazed at the natural intelligence of Aquarius I's and will occasionally feel some resentment that their partner has to work less hard than they do to acquire knowledge. Aquarius I's, on the other hand, may depend heavily on the steadfast strength of Leo I's, and on their ability to handle almost any situation that arises. Compensating for each other's weak spots is one of this relationship's greatest talents.

Love affairs between these two are not especially recommended. Aquarius I's can rarely supply the understanding and patience that Leo I's need, yet will expect Leo I's to be very attentive to them—a trait that may naturally arouse resentment. Marriages are more apt to be successful. Hard-working Leo I's will find the light, enthusiastic mood of Aquarius I's pleasant to come home to, and Aquarius I's will appreciate the capable and dependable shoulder that Leo I's always offer them to lean on.

Friendships and sibling relationships are challenge-oriented, ready for adventure at almost any moment. Spontaneous and lively, these companions will spur each other on to new heights of achievement. Career matchups can be especially outstanding: no subject is off limits to the relationship's insatiably inquiring spirit. Research and development projects are particularly suitable for them. Financial matters are best left to Leo I's, or to a good adviser, since this area is not a traditional Aquarius I strength.

ADVICE: *Spend time and energy on personal matters. Cultivate patience and understanding. Affection shows you care. Even you have limitations.*

STRENGTHS: DEEPENING, DIRECTING, FULFILLING

WEAKNESSES: CONFLICTING, MISCOMMUNICATING, HURTFUL

BEST: LOVE

WORST: PARENT-CHILD

MARILYN QUAYLE (7/29/49)
DAN QUAYLE (2/4/47)

In 1974–76 the Quayles shared a law practice. Their marriage was designed to look picture-perfect for his career as a politician. Once he was elected vice-president, she took on a relatively passive role as Second Lady. *Also:* **Carl Jung & Alfred Adler** (Freudian defectors); **Jackie Onassis & Ron Galella** (jetsetter/paparazzo).

July 26–August 2
THE WEEK OF AUTHORITY
LEO I

January 31–February 7
THE WEEK OF YOUTH & EASE
AQUARIUS II

Deepening Effect

To say that these two don't always see eye to eye would be an understatement. This relationship arouses deep feelings, and learning how to channel them in the right direction may be the overwhelming challenge here. Destructive and even hurtful tendencies emerge in the emotional realm, but at the same time the relationship can exhibit great pride in its partners' accomplishments. Leo I Authority does not always take a favorable view of Aquarius II Youth and Ease. Although Leo is a fire sign and Aquarius air, this relationship is governed by water, here betokening emotional expression and upset.

In friendships and love affairs, Leo I's can be enchanted by the easy energies of Aquarius II's, who will, in turn, be gratified to have aroused and satisfied this partner's drives, both sexual and other. The relationship's impulse toward deeper emotions and intensity comes into play in the likelihood that Leo I's will urge their partners to dig a bit further into themselves; Aquarius II's are in some circumstances capable of forsaking certain superficial attitudes of theirs and becoming more serious about emotional matters, and this may be one of those occasions. They will find the task hard at first, but ultimately rewarding. In Leo I–Aquarius II marriages, having fun has a high priority, but so does fulfilling family responsibilities.

Father-son and mother-daughter relationships in which the Leo I is the parent can fulfill the classic scenario for intergenerational conflict. These parents should not expect obedience and respect for their authority. If they are unwilling to accept their Aquarius II child as an independent, free-thinking individual, there will be room for little but strife. More understanding Leo I parents will let their children go their own way, and won't load them down with responsibilities that will be difficult or impossible for them to handle. The rewards for such wisdom can be felt when Aquarius II children, of their own free will, come to Leo I parents to ask advice. In the workplace, differences in approach and temperament probably doom the matchup to bickering and conflict.

ADVICE: *Allow emotional interaction to deepen. Learn to control outbursts. Be patient and act intelligently. Have fun, but realize the value of serious expression.*

July 26–August 2

THE WEEK OF AUTHORITY
LEO I

February 8–15

THE WEEK OF ACCEPTANCE
AQUARIUS III

RELATIONSHIPS

STRENGTHS: **SHARING, EXPERIENTIAL, LEARNING**

WEAKNESSES: **EXCESSIVE, EARTHBOUND, PROBLEMATIC**

BEST: **FRIENDSHIP**

WORST: **LOVE**

A Destiny of Experience

This relationship will put its partners through a series of formative or educational experiences that can have a determining effect on their lives. The relationship takes a practical approach, weighing all actions before making a decision. Its structure is solid. The partners' mutual enjoyment of food, wine, art and other sensuous pleasures is certainly a strength, but the relationship's challenge will be to strive for more metaphysical, spiritual or universal goals. Even so, the relationship can be great fun for both partners, and can feature extremely close bonds of understanding and sharing.

In matters of love, the relationship's physical side is likely to be more off than on—strong sexual attraction is not the rule here. Leo I's often come on too strong for the tastes of Aquarius III's, who may, for their part. impress their partner as erratic and emotionally volatile. Marriages can be settled and calm but rarely have a thirst for mutual experience (which is, however, a characteristic of friendships in this combination). Should either partner be a recognized teacher or other authority, the relationship is likely to succeed in moving in a more philosophical or spiritual direction.

As friends and schoolmates, Leo I's and Aquarius III's will seek to do as much as possible together, at times visiting each other so often that they practically live together. Telephone, e-mail, Internet chat—nothing will satisfy their desire for contact with each other. These close bonds will often continue into early adulthood before being loosened by other commitments or logistical realities. They also characterize siblings in this combination, so that they may often be taken for friends.

Leo I–Aquarius III co-workers function well as a team, generally trying to learn more about their profession and to advance together in the company hierarchy. More polarized matchups, such as boss-employee or parent-child, often arouse personal animosities that create problems for the organization or family of which they form a part.

ADVICE: *Look a bit beyond the here and now. Keep an eye on your physical condition. Beware of obsessions. Are you creating problems for others?*

BURT REYNOLDS (2/11/36)
DOM DeLUISE (8/1/33)

Offscreen personal friends, Reynolds and DeLuise worked hilariously together in several films. Reynolds was typically the rambunctious leading man and DeLuise the hapless clown. **Also: G.B. Shaw & Mrs. Patrick Campbell** (witty correspondents); **Cheryl Crane & Lana Turner** (daughter murdered mother's boyfriend); **Kate Bush & Peter Gabriel** (musical collaborators).

July 26–August 2

THE WEEK OF AUTHORITY
LEO I

February 16–22

THE CUSP OF SENSITIVITY
AQUARIUS-PISCES CUSP

RELATIONSHIPS

STRENGTHS: **SUPPORTIVE, CHARMING, PERCEPTIVE**

WEAKNESSES: **EXCESSIVE, ADDICTIVE, COOL**

BEST: **MARRIAGE**

WORST: **LOVE**

Palpable Magnetism

Together these two know how to charm the pants off people. Part of the reason their relationship is so magnetic is its deep understanding of what others want. But people are also just plain attracted to them because of the chemistry between them, which is magnetic itself, and palpable. Extremely up-to-date, they can sense coming trends and even help create them, whether working professionally or within a social or family circle. Among other things, this will make them, for example, infallible gift buyers—anyone getting a present from them will be proud to have received such a thing. With salesmanship like this, the pair can be successful at anything they do.

Leo I–Aquarius-Pisces love affairs can be deeply passionate, but the couple also risk becoming highly dependent on each other, or even falling into sex and love addictions. Should these habit-forming tendencies extend to drug use, they could prove deadly. Because magnetic desire plays such a powerful role here, both partners must be careful to stay somewhat objective and guard against excessive behavior.

Marriages and working relationships are especially favored here. At work, it is often Aquarius-Pisces who first attract the attention of superiors or potential clients, but this is in part because Leo I's have already lent them the emotional support they need to gain self-confidence. This support can also be financial and moral. Aquarius-Pisces, for their part, can help their Leo I mates and partners to discover their inner sensitivity, and to express their feelings more easily.

Friends and siblings in this combination can be real charmers as a duo, but generally see through each other's manipulative ploys well enough to view them with a cold eye. In fact, the reality factor here can be a bit too high, keeping the partners from expressing their true feelings for fear of playing the fool.

ADVICE: *You know what others want, but do you know what you need? Don't be afraid to show your feelings. Beware of all addictive drugs.*

DAVID BROWN (7/28/16)
HELEN GURLEY BROWN (2/18/22)

Hollywood film producer David is the husband of Helen, former high-powered *Cosmopolitan* editor and famed author of *Sex and the Single Girl* (1962). Before getting into the movie business in the 50s, David had been a managing editor of *Cosmo*. **Also: Rudy Vallee & Edgar Bergen** (radio co-stars); **Peter Bogdanovich & Cybill Shepherd** (married; director/actor).

STRENGTHS: **NATURAL, TRUSTING, SENSUOUS**

WEAKNESSES: **UNCERTAIN, INDOLENT, OVERLY ACCEPTING**

BEST: **FRIENDSHIP**

WORST: **WORK**

VIVIAN VANCE (7/26/12)
WILLIAM FRAWLEY (2/26/1893)

As Ethel & Fred Mertz, they played the neighbors and best friends of Ricky & Lucy Ricardo on tv's popular *I Love Lucy* (1951–57). Perfect foils for the stars, they always enhanced the show's hilarious predicaments.
Also: **G.B. Shaw & Ellen Terry** (affair; passionate correspondents); **Peter Bogdanovich & Dorothy Stratten** (lovers; director/actress); **Mussolini & Claretta Petacci** (dictator/mistress; hanged together).

July 26–August 2
THE WEEK OF AUTHORITY
LEO I

February 23–March 2
THE WEEK OF SPIRIT
PISCES I

Being Oneself

The hallmark of this relationship is unaffected and natural behavior. There is little need here to smooth over differences or even to reconcile opposing points of view, for the relationship fosters understanding and acceptance. Indeed, it usually only imposes a single demand and law: be yourself. Generally speaking, these two trust each other. Each knows where the other stands, and each respects the other for doing so. Leo I and Pisces I lie in quincunx aspect to each other in the zodiac (150° apart), a position susceptible to instability, but in this relationship any uncertainty often translates into excitement and the thrill of the unknown.

Love affairs and marriages between these two can be quite unusual. Leo I's habitually pursue internal rather than external goals, seeking to realize purely personal goals or to better their own best; Pisces I's are likely to assent and join them in this tendency. As a couple, then, they may give more priority to the interior creative life than to physical or sexual expression. Not that earthy elements are absent—in fact, the Leo I–Pisces I matchup is ruled by earth (even though Leo is a fire sign and Pisces water), and emphasizes a grounded and practical approach to life. But sensuous rather than sexual experience is usually stressed here, and the pleasures these two may well go for grow less out of physical contact than out of their mutual love of food, music, art and creature comforts.

Career relationships in this combination work out best when the pair's idealism and positive attitudes are given full rein. Routine, unimaginative or restrictive jobs are not recommended for these two. Parent-child and sibling matchups stress openness and, often, share a love of exploring or luxuriating in beautiful natural surroundings. Leo I–Pisces I friendships revel in the joys of life, but can show great compassion for suffering and may try to help the disadvantaged, perhaps through volunteer work in social, religious or community service.

ADVICE: *Be a bit tougher. Positive criticism can help. Push yourself a bit more. Even the most natural and comfortable behavior can be refined and better channeled.*

STRENGTHS: **CHARISMATIC, CREATIVE, COMMERCIAL**

WEAKNESSES: **OVEREXPOSED, REBELLIOUS, STORMY**

BEST: **WORK**

WORST: **MARRIAGE**

ROB REINER (3/6/45)
SALLY STRUTHERS (7/28/48)

Struthers and Reiner were the supporting actors on tv's *All in the Family* (1971–80). As the liberal daughter and son-in-law of redneck Archie Bunker, they were magnetic, both in harmony and discord.
Also: **William Powell & Jean Harlow** (engaged when she died); **Geoffrey Holder & Carmen DeLavallade** (close dancers); **Jackie Onassis & Lee Radziwill** (sisters; Ari was Lee's beau first).

July 26–August 2
THE WEEK OF AUTHORITY
LEO I

March 3–10
THE WEEK OF THE LONER
PISCES II

Attraction and Repulsion

This matchup has a peculiar effect on its partners: at first very seductive for them, it later somehow encourages a rebelliousness that could threaten its longevity. It can be highly charismatic to other people, attracting all sorts of admirers and hangers-on, but an overload of social and personal responsibility can prove debilitating to these partners, who are usually better off when they hide their light a bit and turn down the charm. Together they can make great strides on personal and spiritual levels, and it would be a true shame if they neglected such areas.

Love affairs in this combination can be stormy. Disagreements and clashes over responsibility, money and divided attention may periodically surface. Pisces II's are often the more faithful of the two and will suffer a great deal should their Leo I mate turn elsewhere for affection or solace. Marriages here are not especially recommended: the partners are unlikely to satisfy each other beyond a certain level and, in the long run, are unlikely to build a stable emotional life together.

Leo I–Pisces II friends and siblings have a strong rebellious side to express. Prone to trouble, they must be careful not to darken their name, gaining the kind of reputation that will make others cross to the other side of the street when they appear in public. These two should try to arrive at personal values that are not just defined in opposition to parental or societal moral codes. Other kinds of family relationship may be so close as to be smothering—the partners' rebellion here may be against each other.

At work, Leo I's and Pisces II's can do exceptionally well when engaged in artistic or creative pursuits together. If their creative impulses can be put in the service of a commercial enterprise, they can be professionally and financially successful. But they risk periodically losing sight of their business goals and getting lost in the creative or technical side of their work. Both partners must be able to pull themselves back to reality and tend to the practical and monetary side of things.

ADVICE: *Not everything you attract is desirable. Be more selective. Keep an objective eye on finances. Tone down the excitement factor.*

July 26–August 2
THE WEEK OF AUTHORITY
LEO I

March 11–18
THE WEEK OF DANCERS & DREAMERS
PISCES III

Sharing the Truth

Highly philosophical, this relationship seeks to share the truth with other people. Yet without its priority on communication, it would tend to isolate itself from the world and, in fact, will probably do so when its abilities to share beliefs and ideas are frustrated. Although Leo is a fire sign and Pisces water, their relationship is ruled by earth and air, here accentuating a mix of energies in the practical and ideological spheres.

Friendships and marriages are often built around spiritual, religious or intellectual ideas shared by the two partners. Perhaps it was these common beliefs that brought the pair together in the first place, although they may also have been fostered by the relationship itself while in progress. In either case, it is quite common for the pair to set up a structure for daily life based on such a system of belief, and to subordinate most of their activities to this higher authority. Any internal struggles within the relationship often result from irritations and frustrations caused by neglect of pressing emotional issues. Love affairs are possible, but here the tendency to embrace a structure of belief is less propitious. And should an affair develop, the couple are likely to see their romantic or sexual feelings elevated to an exalted plane—which only leads to disillusion if expectations are disappointed, as is often the case.

Leo I–Pisces III parent-child duos can suffer under the premature and rigorous influence of heavy ideologies. But should the family manage to establish a more tolerant and less serious setting, Pisces III's usually make the better parent in the matchup and can be extremely attentive, nurturing and understanding to their Leo I children. The emphasis on communication here is highly personal—parent and child must be careful not to cut themselves off from familial or societal interaction. Leo I–Pisces III commercial enterprises and work relationships are not usually favored.

ADVICE: *Try to see things on the human level. Don't neglect personal issues. Come down off your cloud sometimes. Promote flexibility.*

JERRY GARCIA (8/1/42)
PHIL LESH (3/15/40)

Guitarist-vocalist Garcia of the Grateful Dead (formed 1965) was also its principal composer and driving force. Lesh was the Dead's bass player-vocalist. They played together through ups and downs of drug-plagued decades. Garcia's 1995 death marked the end of an era. *Also:* **Alfonse D'Amato & Daniel Moynihan** (political foes; NY senators); **Maria Cole & Nat "King" Cole** (married; singers).

August 3–10
THE WEEK OF BALANCED STRENGTH
LEO II

August 3–10
THE WEEK OF BALANCED STRENGTH
LEO II

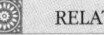
Standing Steadfast

Leo II's are often equally matched—if they are opponents or rivals they will give each other a run for their money. Whether this relationship is combative or supportive, it tends to allow its partners to express the best of which they are capable yet its energy will focus on supporting its own strengths rather than theirs as individuals. When one partner is depressed or hurt, for example, the other will often do double work for a time to keep the relationship's energy level constant. Leo II's tend to rely and depend on each other, however, and should one of this pair suffer a prolonged collapse the other may be unable to carry the weight for too long.

Love and marriage between two Leo II's can be either demanding or easy, depending on their reasons for choosing each other. The partner who loves less will generally have the upper hand in power struggles. Although Leo II's who love more are vulnerable, they generally wouldn't have it any other way, and will usually stand steadfast in times of trouble as long as they can keep on an even keel emotionally.

Should Leo II friends be romantically attracted to the same person, real problems will emerge. Their loyalty to their own relationship will be sorely tested, and if either of them deserts the other by following his or her desires as an individual, their friendship will probably disintegrate. Most often, however, Leo II's choose to remain loyal to each other in such situations, leaving the third party out in the cold. Leo II's generally befriend each other for life and can provide each other with tremendous mutual support and encouragement.

Sibling and co-worker matchups are strong, dependable and therefore of great value to the family or company of which they form a part. Occasional battles are inevitable between them, however, with Leo II fur flying in all directions. Little if any quarter is generally given in such combat; nor is it advisable to come between these adversaries—they must be left to settle things alone, whether physically or verbally.

ADVICE: *Minimize power struggles. Needs can be met through consideration and patience. Preserve emotional stability. Loyalty should be freely given.*

ANTONIO BANDERAS (8/10/60)
MELANIE GRIFFITH (8/9/57)

Griffith and Banderas fell in love during the filming of *Two Much* (1996). She became pregnant and proceeded to divorce husband Don Johnson. Griffith and Banderas then married. *Also:* **Eddie Fisher & Connie Stevens** (married; singers).

RELATIONSHIPS

STRENGTHS: **SELF-CONFIDENT, SENSUOUS, PROTECTIVE**

WEAKNESSES: **BLUNTING, OVERCONFIDENT, LAZY**

BEST: **LOVE**

WORST: **WORK**

DUSTIN HOFFMAN (8/8/37)
ROBERT REDFORD (8/18/37)

Using his own company, Wildwood Enterprises, Redford produced *All the President's Men* (1976), in which he co-starred with Hoffman. In the film they played Woodward and Bernstein, the *Washington Post* journalists responsible for exposing the Watergate scandal. As an acting team, they were brilliantly engaging. *Also:* **Paul Dirac & Erwin Schrödinger** (1933 Nobelists, physics).

August 3–10
THE WEEK OF BALANCED STRENGTH
LEO II

August 11–18
THE WEEK OF LEADERSHIP
LEO III

Radiant Warmth

This relationship is likely to be easygoing, with each partner enjoying the ability to bask in the steady radiance of the other's strength. These proud Leos are generally well suited, being relaxed and accepting with each other. The lack of open combat between them is surely a good thing, and even mandatory for the relationship's continuance, considering the alternative: these two have an enormous capacity to inflict mutual hurt. As it is, though, any threat against one of these lions, whether overt or insidious, will be considered an attack on the other, and each partner will come to the other's defense. This trait is so pronounced that it can almost be too protective, preventing the individual from handling their difficulties on their own.

Both friendships and love affairs can be warm and romantic. Sexual relations need not be as torrid as one might think—they lean more to gentleness and tenderness, which are the rule rather than the exception. The couple's preference for sensuous rather than highly sexual or erotic passions tends to emphasize passive rather than active attitudes, mentally as well as physically.

Leo II–Leo III business relationships and marriages share an aggressiveness and a will to succeed, blunted only by their easygoing self-confidence. This latter trait, however, can cause problems if the pair overlook present difficulties and refuse to acknowledge the seriousness of recurring problems until it is too late. Long before they themselves spot the warning lights, their employees or children may see danger ahead, but may have been taught by experience to stay quiet for fear of being accused of alarmism. Later on, though, their Leo II–Leo III bosses or parents may blame them for failing to report a warning, so that they're damned if they do, damned if they don't.

Leo II–Leo III sibling matchups, especially of the same sex, will be highly competitive in their early years. In time, however, they usually grow to be understanding, protective and accepting.

ADVICE: *Try to be more attentive. Heed warning signs. Don't just shrug off difficulties—do something about them. Listen to other people's opinions.*

RELATIONSHIPS

STRENGTHS: **WELL-DIRECTED, COMPROMISING, PROFITABLE**

WEAKNESSES: **SECRETIVE, STRUGGLE-ORIENTED, HURTFUL**

BEST: **WORK**

WORST: **MARRIAGE**

QUEEN MOTHER (8/4/1900)
PRINCESS MARGARET (8/21/30)

Queen Elizabeth II of England and Princess Margaret are the daughters of the strong-willed Queen Mother. She raised them with true royal spirit by keeping them in England during WWII, even when London was being bombed. Margaret was a precocious, irrepressible child and has grown up to be a popular royal celebrity. *Also:* **James Gamble & William Cooper Procter** (partners; Procter & Gamble Co.).

August 3–10
THE WEEK OF BALANCED STRENGTH
LEO II

August 19–25
THE CUSP OF EXPOSURE
LEO-VIRGO CUSP

The Driver's Seat

The focus of this relationship is the provision of effective leadership to attain specific goals, whether commercial, social or personal. A guide or authority figure is often necessary here—usually one of the two partners, but also sometimes the pair as equal partners leading other people. These two often find themselves involved in a higher cause or ideal to which they dedicate their relationship. By keeping the cause in mind, they may be able to avoid competition for leadership. Otherwise, Leo-Virgos of the more aggressive kind can run into problems with Leo II's over who will occupy the driver's seat. Leo-Virgos of the quieter type can be quite content to let Leo II's take control and to play a secondary role, perhaps as advisers. Sooner or later, however, they too will want an equal say.

Love between these two is likely to be secretive and passionate. Their affairs may well be illicit, with a Leo-Virgo unhappily married to an unresponsive spouse seeking appreciation and pleasure in the arms of a fiery Leo II. Marriages here easily grow stale with time, but both partners tend to hang in there, sharing leadership roles. As parents, Leo-Virgos are more dutiful than naturally attentive to their children and may depend on Leo II's to take up the slack.

In career matchups, Leo II's and Leo-Virgos can engage in fierce power struggles but are usually sensible enough to realize that these conflicts are a waste of time and energy and to apply themselves to the cause at hand. Often the most successful duos here are business partners, who recognize their individual strengths from the start and agree to compromise over who has the final say. Should Leo-Virgo analytical skills gel with Leo II steadying energies, career associations here are likely to be profitable. Because neither Leo-Virgos nor Leo II's are overly trusting, they may prefer to go into business together when they are already joined as friends, siblings or spouses.

ADVICE: *Settle power issues. Be aware of the effects of your actions. Develop deeper bonds of trust. Don't ignore those who need your attention.*

August 3–10

THE WEEK OF BALANCED STRENGTH
LEO II

August 26–September 2

THE WEEK OF SYSTEM BUILDERS
VIRGO I

RELATIONSHIPS

STRENGTHS: **EMPATHIC, SOULFUL, APPRECIATIVE**

WEAKNESSES: **REACTIVE, OVERSUBJECTIVE, ISOLATED**

BEST: **LOVE**

WORST: **FAMILY**

True Soulmates

These two may find themselves to be true soulmates. Difficulties seldom deter them from seeking each other out and establishing a relationship; as a matter of fact, social, racial or financial barriers will only spur them on. This combination is often highly personal, featuring mutual acceptance and sympathy. Strong empathic bonds assure close communication and sensitivity to each other's needs, not only in romances but in friendships and other social ties. It is a relationship that fosters both intellectual and emotional understanding.

Love affairs in this combination and the marriages that often result from them can be highly soulful. Virgo I's do not find emotional fulfillment easily and are subject to nervous instabilities, but relationships with Leo II's give them appreciation, support and the security to express their feelings constructively. Leo II's, for their part, benefit tremendously from Virgo I order and structure and appreciate the relationship's need for firm decision-making. Deep meditational states can appear here, but the relationship has a tendency to isolate itself and must beware of losing touch with worldly realities.

Friendships between these two tend to be idealistic yet to have a strong practical base. They are highly dependable and capable of shouldering heavy responsibilities, but their real focus is sharing philosophical or ideological concepts and putting them into practice in everyday life. Working matchups, on the other hand, may not be ideal, given the pair's vulnerability, subjectivity and sensitivity. In the family, similarly, sibling and parent-child pairs can be empathic to a fault—the partners overreact to each other's moods and have difficulty establishing stability.

MARY WOLLSTONECRAFT (8/30/1797)
PERCY BYSSHE SHELLEY (8/4/1792)

In 1814 Shelley and Wollstonecraft fell deeply in love and left England. After the suicide of his first wife (1816), they married and settled in Italy, a "paradise of exiles." They had 3 children; 2 died. After Shelley drowned in 1822, she kept his heart in a silk shroud and carried it with her for the rest of her life.

ADVICE: *Don't turn your back on the world. Keep in touch with everyday realities. Don't be guided by rebelliousness. Keep your ideals fresh and pure.*

August 3–10

THE WEEK OF BALANCED STRENGTH
LEO II

September 3–10

THE WEEK OF THE ENIGMA
VIRGO II

RELATIONSHIPS

STRENGTHS: **PRODUCTIVE, INTROSPECTIVE, TRUSTING**

WEAKNESSES: **REPRESSED, UNCOMPREHENDING, EXPLOSIVE**

BEST: **PARENT-CHILD**

WORST: **LOVE**

A Need for Introspection

The great challenge of this relationship is to uncover hidden feelings or psychological tendencies and allow them to be expressed. Both partners have a tendency to isolate themselves, which makes it difficult for them to become emotionally close to other people. Their relationship can magnify this leaning, creating emotional distance even between themselves. There is an acute need here, then, for greater awareness and self-examination. A conscious decision to be more open and trusting will help enormously. These two need to devote a lot of time to earnest discussion and personal exploration. Their forays into private and often repressed realms will require great willpower from them, but the rewards will be great.

Love here can be physically satisfying, even passionate, but usually in an objective sense rather than as a deep emotional involvement. These partners are often cool in such encounters, preferring detachment to merger. Marital and family relationships are often stormy battlegrounds of personal struggle, often with unconscious sources. Complex dynamics are at work here: feelings may run the gamut from adoration to resentment, from resentment to rejection. Periodic volcanic upheavals indicate the depth of feeling involved but also the shallowness of understanding. As spouses and as parent-child combinations, Leo II's and Virgo II's who take the time to tunnel deeply, in a patient, understanding way, will begin to fathom the nature of their problems. The many valuable realizations that can result will help to even out emotional expression and build bridges of understanding.

Friendships in this combination may focus on a given activity, such as a hobby, or may go deeper, exploring intensely personal realms. The choice is a tricky one, for a pleasurable association can be disturbed or even destroyed by curiosities that move too far too fast in trying to uncover well-kept secrets. Career involvements between Leo II's and Virgo II's can be productive and rewarding if personal differences can be settled.

MARTIN SHEEN (8/3/40)
CHARLIE SHEEN (9/3/65)

Intense actor Martin, well known for his role in *Apocalypse Now* (1979), is the father of 4 children, all actors. Most prominent is son Charlie, who made his debut at 9 in a tv movie starring his dad and had his adult career breakthrough in *Platoon* (1986). Father and son are known to have a strong relationship.

ADVICE: *Take time for inner exploration. Strengthen your will to understand, for understanding brings reward. Give whatever it takes.*

DUSTIN HOFFMAN (8/8/37)
ANNE BANCROFT (9/17/31)

One of the great comic pair-ups in movie history were Hoffman and Bancroft in their roles as naive college grad and middle-aged, wealthy seductress in *The Graduate* (1967). It was Hoffman's first major film. The actors brilliantly played off each other's stereotyped emotions. *Also:* **Queen Mother & Prince Henry** (great grandmother/great grandson).

August 3–10
THE WEEK OF BALANCED STRENGTH
LEO II

September 11–18
THE WEEK OF THE LITERALIST
VIRGO III

Emotional Challenges

This combination will prove quite a challenge for its partners, since it focuses on feeling and spirit—neither of them areas in which these two feel particularly comfortable. The relationship will certainly bring out previously repressed emotions. Its focus may be the difficulty Leo II's and Virgo III's generally have with feelings, which these tough individuals often see as messes they would rather avoid. In this combination that will be impossible. The relationship will confront them with an area of life that they need to explore further and, ultimately, to work out. Fortunately, the process will have a certain flow to it, so that the lessons it has to offer will occur before the partners even realize what's happening.

Love and marriage will have their problems. Virgo III's are oriented toward mental activity and practicality, and although Leo II's are attracted to intelligence, they actually do best when they rely on their intuition. In marriage, friendship and love, they are rarely strong enough to stand up to Virgo III criticism or relentless logic. Leo II anger and hot-headedness, meanwhile, will be difficult for Virgo III's. This couple's interactions often alternate from emotional outbursts to frustrated silences reflecting repressed anger.

Family matchups in this combination, especially between parents and children, are often confrontational. Virgo III children can be very critical of their Leo II parents, who are prone to being authoritarian. Should Virgo III's be the parents, they are likely to find their Leo II children wild and uncontrollable. Their attempts at discipline will rarely meet with success.

Career matchups may succeed in avoiding the sensitive subject of feelings, but the partners will still feel a certain emotional wariness around each other, which can make them tread a bit too lightly in each other's company. Otherwise, direct Leo II energy and Virgo III attentiveness can meld well. These two can be successful at a variety of tasks, preferably objective ones in which the job just needs to get done without fuss or bother.

ADVICE: *Learn how to handle your feelings, and beware of repressing them. Even out mood swings. The mind can only take you so far. Follow your heart.*

SIR ALEXANDER FLEMING (8/6/1881)
SIR HOWARD FLOREY (9/24/1898)

Fleming discovered the antibiotic penicillin in 1928. In 1939 Florey (working with Ernst Chain) purified penicillin and tested it successfully as a clinical drug. All 3 scientists were rewarded with the 1945 Nobel Prize in medicine.

August 3–10
THE WEEK OF BALANCED STRENGTH
LEO II

September 19–24
THE CUSP OF BEAUTY
VIRGO-LIBRA CUSP

Being Well Prepared

This relationship will focus on building a solid and dependable structure within a social, family or professional group. Overcoming technical obstacles and subduing tasks or problems to a smooth-running system are the forte in this combination, which makes for an excellent working arrangement, with the partners sharing leadership and occupying clearly defined roles. Creative problem-solving comes naturally here.

Virgo-Libras need a strong, reliable figure to depend on—a person quite like a Leo II. Co-worker, spouse and parent relationships are all favored here. But although Leo II's enjoy feeling appreciated, there is a danger that Virgo-Libra will view them as infallible. If they also represent a Virgo-Libra ideal of physical beauty, they may have difficulty extricating themselves from what may become an exceedingly tender trap. In another scenario, Leo II aggressiveness may not be entirely welcomed by Virgo-Libras, who are often extremely particular about how they are approached or touched.

Friendships, family ties and marriages in this combination tend to stress tradition, solidity and purpose within the context of their social circle. Leo II's will find it immensely rewarding to put their powers at the service of such a group, and Virgo-Libras will benefit from using their creativity and taste to make life more enjoyable and comfortable for those they care about. Power struggles rarely arise in this relationship, but unusually close attachments can blunt individual initiative, particularly in the case of Virgo-Libras. Should Virgo-Libras become unduly dependent on the relationship, Leo II's may get uncomfortable and back off.

As boss-employee pairs or co-workers in a team effort, Virgo-Libras are likely to give direction and purpose to projects that feature the near boundless energy of Leo II's. Efficiency and planning will figure prominently in such efforts, for these two tend to be well prepared when they go into battle.

ADVICE: *Keep things in perspective. Don't let needs and wants get out of hand. Ask what is in it for you. Don't refuse help when it is offered.*

August 3–10

THE WEEK OF BALANCED STRENGTH
LEO II

September 25–October 2

THE WEEK OF THE PERFECTIONIST
LIBRA I

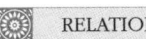 RELATIONSHIPS

STRENGTHS: **PHILOSOPHICAL, REALISTIC, FUNNY**

WEAKNESSES: **UNCARING, SAD, SARCASTIC**

BEST: **FRIENDSHIP**

WORST: **MARRIAGE**

Life's Passing Scene

The liveliness of this relationship is unmistakable, yet it is often accompanied by an underlying tinge of sadness. Leo II's and Libra I's certainly enjoy excitement, and can make rather a volatile combination, yet at the same time they are realists about the passing scene, and recognize life's transitory nature. Philosophical reflection is important to them and can become the focus of their relationship. Away from the bustle of the world, where they are viewed as extroverted and even exhibitionistic, the relationship offers them the quiet haven they need to explore spiritual and ideological issues.

Love affairs between these two can be emotionally volatile. Both partners tend to have strong sexual drives, but deep feeling is unlikely to develop between them, and there may be little to hold their relationship together. Marriages are not recommended for this pair, since neither partner is likely to be too interested in assuming domestic responsibilities or raising a family.

The combination's philosophical bent emerges strongly in friendships. Highly valued here are irony and humor, especially black humor, emphasizing life's grim side. Over the years, however, a quite negative and critical view of the world may progress to a more hopeful and spiritual one. The intellectual penchant of Libra I's and the intuitive strengths of Leo II's can both find expression in this matchup, but both partners often neglect the importance of feelings. They need to recognize that emotion plays a more decisive role in life than they are prepared to admit.

At work and in the family, Libra I bosses and parents can be hypercritical of their Leo II children or employees, who are often under the sway of their mental power. Leo II's are more geared for action, and often express themselves with an immediacy that Libra I superiors can find alarming. This relationship encourages Libra I's to be a bit more fearless and Leo II's a bit more thoughtful.

ADVICE: *Take life a bit more seriously. Don't just observe the passing parade—try to make a difference. Serving others can benefit you greatly.*

ANNE KLEIN (8/7/23)
DONNA KARAN (10/2/48)

Fashion designer Klein defined the American sportswear style. Upon her death in '74, Karan, once her trainee, continued co-designing the label until she founded her own very successful company in '84. ***Also:*** **Alfalfa & Spanky** (co-stars, *Little Rascals*); **Ruth Carter Stapleton & Jimmy Carter** (siblings; evangelist/president); **Norma Shearer & George Raft** (affair; actors).

August 3–10

THE WEEK OF BALANCED STRENGTH
LEO II

October 3–10

THE WEEK OF SOCIETY
LIBRA II

 RELATIONSHIPS

STRENGTHS: **FUN, INSIGHTFUL, EFFECTIVE**

WEAKNESSES: **PUZZLING, NERVOUS, DEPRESSIVE**

BEST: **SIBLING**

WORST: **LOVE**

Psychological Barriers

This relationship is more complex than one would think. Although the pair usually get along well, there are emotional and psychological barriers between them, which are most obvious in the role played in the relationship by approval and disapproval: each partner will use these judgments as a tool to try to get beyond the other's psychological boundaries—not a very healthy strategy. Differences in temperament between these two can bring out their nervous sides, yet despite their areas of conflict, the entertaining and sparkling side of Libra II's can lift the spirits of Leo II's. By example, Leo II's can, in turn, teach Libra II's how to be more assertive and to act decisively.

Deep psychological barriers may have to be overcome in love affairs. Libra II's can be extremely helpful in encouraging Leo II's to be introspective and gain insights into both themselves and the relationship. Too often, however, Libra II's themselves may resent the relationship (no matter how much they are in love) for putting these psychological demands on them. Their ambivalent feelings could well lead only to further indecision. Too often this affair is left hanging in a void. In marriages, too, positive attitudes and immense willpower will be needed to avoid judgmental attitudes and to encourage accepting ones if depression and uncertainty are to be beaten. Sibling relationships and friendships are likely to be mutually protective, with the powerful physical presence of Leo II's and the social expertise of Libra II's melding. Both partners will be able to call upon each other occasionally in time of need; even more important, they can regularly have great times together. Although Leo is a fire sign and Libra air, the Leo II–Libra II relationship is ruled by earth, an element here signifying practical abilities and the ability to work together. If they can put their personality differences aside, these two can serve well as co-workers, getting the job done effectively. In business partnerships and other entrepreneurial endeavors, however, the personal side of the relationship can prove unsettling, so that these arrangements are not recommended.

ADVICE: *Keep it light. Don't let moods get you down. Strengthen your determination to move forward. Keep positive goals in mind.*

RAOUL WALLENBERG (8/4/12)
HEINRICH HIMMLER (10/7/1900)

Himmler was considered the most ruthless of Nazi leaders, responsible for the concentration camp deaths of millions. Wallenberg, a Swedish envoy to Budapest in 1944, is credited with rescuing tens of thousands of Hungarian Jews by supplying them with Swedish passports before their deportation to death camps. It is reputed that he paid Himmler money for the release of many of these prisoners.

RAY BROWN (10/13/26)
HERB ELLIS (8/4/21)

Double-bassist Brown and guitarist Ellis were members of jazz's elegant Oscar Peterson Trio, which started up in 1951. They made many distinguished recordings—notably *The Oscar Peterson Trio at the Stratford Shakespearean Festival* (1956)—and performed widely on the jazz club circuit. Ellis and Brown were sympatico musicians who played off each other with great sensitivity.

August 3–10

THE WEEK OF BALANCED STRENGTH
LEO II

October 11–18

THE WEEK OF THEATER
LIBRA III

Two Captains at the Helm

The visionary or dreamlike quality in this combination can be unsettling. There is a choice—harness this trait's creativity or be unnerved by its fluctuations—but these two dominant personalities will find the energies at work in their relationship difficult to grasp. Feeling threatened, both are likely to dig in their heels. Power struggles and conflict may be inevitable, but if they can overcome their insecurities, the more aspiring elements of their personalities can meld, so that visionary projects can sometimes be launched and realized.

A big problem here is the flamboyant and dramatic nature of Libra III's, which Leo II's may see as highly artificial. Meanwhile, Libra III's might view the Leo II approach as too direct and unnuanced. But the first question that will have to be settled is, Who's the boss? The only solution may lie in compromise, with the partners sharing the helm. This will almost certainly be difficult, however.

Love affairs are likely to be stormy and short-lived, but working relationships and marriages have a good chance of success if duties are well defined. The relationship should set up clear boundaries, deciding clearly which areas are the province of each partner. It is when these two are constantly looking over each other's shoulder that troubles start, for each is extremely sensitive to the other's criticism and disapproval. These relationships often work best when other people take care of practical matters (such as bookkeeping, cleaning, taking messages, etc.) and the Leo II–Libra III pair is left free to follow the promptings of their joint imagination.

Siblings in this combination sometimes get lost in their own adventuresome world of fantasy, especially in childhood. Going through adolescence together may be painful for them—they will have to give up the wonderful times they had together earlier on and assume more responsible roles. Friendships are most successful when responsibilities are kept to a minimum. Dynamic and physical activities involving risk and danger are especially attractive to this pair.

ADVICE: *Try to hammer out agreements. Be diplomatic. Compromise is not a dirty word. Try to be more sensitive to each other's needs.*

BOBBY BROWN (10/25/69)
WHITNEY HOUSTON (8/9/63)

Wholesome pop singer Houston has won numerous Grammys. Brown, an r&b singer, also has a number of chart-toppers. Their marriage in '92 prompted cynics to suggest it was merely an effort to recast his bad-boy image. **Also: Eddie Fisher & Carrie Fisher** (father/daughter; singer/actress-author).

August 3–10

THE WEEK OF BALANCED STRENGTH
LEO II

October 19–25

THE CUSP OF DRAMA & CRITICISM
LIBRA-SCORPIO CUSP

Unspoken Agreement

The Leo II–Libra-Scorpio relationship is usually firmly grounded in the here and now. It often focuses on cold, hard facts and demands that the literal truth be told. Honesty in both work and personal matters is obligatory here, and woe to the partner who breaks this unspoken agreement. Although Leo is a fire sign and Libra an air sign, the Leo II–Libra-Scorpio relationship is governed by earth, an element here suggesting strong practical thinking but also sensuousness and seductiveness.

Love and marriage can be painful for these two if they do not see eye to eye, or if their physical relationship turns sour. Passion has a way of leading to provocation and provocation to combat, all in very short order. Formidable as Leo II's appear, in a knock-down, drag-out psychological confrontation they are usually no match for Libra-Scorpios, who will know exactly how to hurt them, wounding their pride and undermining their self-confidence. Should a stormy love affair lead to a difficult marriage, Leo II's tend to hang in there far beyond the point when it would be better for everyone if they quit.

Parent-child relationships in this combination can be loving but disillusioned, particularly if a Leo II parent falls from grace in the eyes of a Libra-Scorpio child. Both parents and children expect the promises they make to each other to be kept, and hold each other strictly to their word. Sibling matchups are no less unforgiving, although brothers and sisters can be much more objective about each other, and more respectful of each other's strengths and weaknesses.

Friendships and work relationships between Leo II's and Libra-Scorpios can generate tremendous energy. Getting projects and productions moving, whether commercial or social, is a forte in this combination. High-quality work is to be expected of such matchups, along with an equal demand for tasteful and unostentatious presentation.

ADVICE: *Forgive and forget. Don't allow expectations to build up. Try being a bit more flexible. Take things more figuratively and less literally.*

August 3–10

THE WEEK OF BALANCED STRENGTH
LEO II

October 26–November 2

THE WEEK OF INTENSITY
SCORPIO I

Experiencing Rebirth

RELATIONSHIPS

STRENGTHS: **ASPIRING, NURTURING, INNOVATIVE**

WEAKNESSES: **STUBBORN, OVERSERIOUS, COMBATIVE**

BEST: **MARRIAGE**

WORST: **SIBLING**

This combination is protective and nurturing but also generative. Creative forces are strong here—so strong, in fact, that together these partners may experience a sort of rebirth. Their relationship gives them a chance to move to a higher personal and spiritual level. Their respective fortes, Balanced Strength and Intensity, are well matched, complementing each other in career, educational and social undertakings that allow Leo II equanimity and Scorpio I drive to coalesce. Both Leo and Scorpio are fixed signs, so that neither of these personalities is likely to give ground in an all-out argument. By working side by side in a variety of endeavors, however, they can win each other's trust.

In love these two are seldom content to sit back and simply enjoy life's pleasures, sexual or otherwise: They have a drive to move forward. This will often move them in the direction of marriage. Having children and owning their own home can also be important parts of the scenario. They should be aware, however, that progressing in this way need not make them steadily more serious and inflexible, losing the spontaneity and fun that characterized their relationship in its beginnings.

Friendships and sibling relationships between Leo II's and Scorpio I's can be intense and competitive, especially on the physical plane. Whether rivaling each other as opponents or trying to beat their personal or mutual best, these two will sometimes compete unmercifully for victory. They should be careful not to hurt themselves by going too far in this direction.

In professional relationships, Leo II's and Scorpio I's are happiest when able to bring new ideas into the workplace. As an equal team, they are capable of working hard, but only when they choose. Motivation is an important consideration here, for they will give generously of their talents and energies if they believe in the products and goals of the organization they serve.

ADVICE: *Keep young at heart. Don't take on more responsibility than you can handle. Stay flexible and open in your outlook. Leave time for play.*

LARRY FLYNT (11/1/42)
RUTH CARTER STAPLETON (8/7/29)

In real life, as in the 1996 film *The People vs. Larry Flynt*, Stapleton, the evangelist sister of President Jimmy Carter, sought out Flynt in hopes of offering the publisher of *Hustler* magazine spiritual salvation. For a while, Flynt made religion part of his business. **Also: Sara Teasdale & Margaret Conklin** (friends; poet/actress).

August 3–10

THE WEEK OF BALANCED STRENGTH
LEO II

November 3–11

THE WEEK OF DEPTH
SCORPIO II

Heavy Energies

RELATIONSHIPS

STRENGTHS: **PLEASURABLE, SENSUOUS, AFFECTIONATE**

WEAKNESSES: **OBSESSIVE, FRUSTRATED, EXCESSIVE**

BEST: **LOVE**

WORST: **WORK**

This combination channels serious energies. As fixed signs, Leo and Scorpio tend to be stubborn and inflexible, so that Leo II's and Scorpio II's don't change easily and are not readily open to compromise. Furthermore, since these two are square to each other (90° apart) in the zodiac, traditional astrology predicts tension and problems for their relationship. Yet feelings run very deep between them. If they can only handle each other, their matchup will be richly rewarding emotionally. Fortunately, there is a uniting theme in their relationship—an appreciation for and enjoyment of physical, sensuous beauty. The whole question is how sensuousness, sensuality, sexuality and pleasure in general are to be approached here.

In love and marriage, these partners are sometimes more successful in a joint involvement in art, nature, fashion, music or film than they are in their interactions with each other. When they can objectively express sensuous desire or appreciation toward an object they both admire, they can experience a great deal of mutual satisfaction. Yet when sensual desire moves these same personalities toward each other, they can get bogged down in a maelstrom of conflicting thoughts and feelings. Sexual interactions between these two may be very powerful but can also be extremely upsetting if they are not handled well psychologically. Simple sensuous expressions—a touch, a look, an affectionate gesture—are rarely a problem, but overt sensuality can become quite problematical, especially if drug, food or love dependencies arise. It is in the sphere of friendship that outright addictions can prove most damaging, although highly pleasurable in the short term.

Leo II–Scorpio II family relationships, particularly parent-child matchups of the opposite sex, are deeply loving, but there is often some blockage in that love's expression. Mother-son and father-daughter pairs may be close but frustrating, and the closer they are the worse their problems may become. Learning to lighten the mood, to have fun together, and to share feelings with other family members can help. Working relationships between Leo II's and Scorpio II's are not recommended unless the partners can be strictly objective.

ADVICE: *Enjoy your mutual appreciation of beauty. Beware of addiction to physical pleasures. Cultivate true affection and kindness. Lighten up a bit.*

VACHEL LINDSAY (11/10/1879)
SARA TEASDALE (8/8/1884)

Poet Teasdale rejected poet Lindsay as a longtime suitor and married someone else in 1914. In 1929, 2 years after Teasdale's divorce, Lindsay committed suicide by drinking poison. She moved to NYC, where she lived in seclusion until her own suicide in '33. **Also: Courtney Love & Althea Flynt** (film portrayal); **Dustin Hoffman & Mike Nichols** (actor discovered by director).

PRINCE CHARLES (11/14/48)
QUEEN MOTHER (8/4/1900)

The Queen Mother is Charles' grandmother. He grew up in her presence and has inherited, through Queen Elizabeth, his grandmother's lifelong commitment to the responsibilities of the royal family. He moves about with the same dignity, humor and charm as his grandmother.

August 3–10

THE WEEK OF BALANCED STRENGTH
LEO II

November 12–18

THE WEEK OF CHARM
SCORPIO III

Good Humor

The partners in this highly entertaining matchup will really appreciate each other for who and what they are. Good humor often prevails when they are together, no matter how little time they may have available to spend with each other. Their relationship stays fresh and new over the years. It is also often somewhat unrealistic and naive about the world. Leo II's and Scorpio III's do learn important lessons from their experience, but they can be unusually willing to put any feelings of having been wronged behind them—in other words, to forgive and forget. This is because of the security they feel in their relationship, and the good feelings it engenders.

This security through good feelings is especially evident in love affairs, friendships and marriages. Although neither Leo II's nor Scorpio III's are too trusting in their relationships with other people, together they can open up emotionally to an astonishing degree. Conviviality is a big item here; this pair will enjoy few things more than sitting around a table with friends, indulging in good food and drink and, of course, conversation. Leo II's tend to seek excitement and challenge in many areas of life, but with Scorpio III's they can relax and be themselves. Scorpio III's, too, will enjoy letting their hair and defenses down, and also not having to play the boss, organizer or director.

Career matchups are less favorable here, since the kinds of relaxed attitudes that are typical between these two rarely bring people forward in the professional and business worlds. Leo II–Scorpio III partners interested in making a success of their endeavors will have to push themselves a bit more. In family settings, parent-child and grandparent-grandchild matchups in this combination can be rewarding and communicative, but also claiming, spoiling and overprotective.

ADVICE: *Enjoy yourself but don't forget your responsibilities. Good feelings are not the whole story. Trust might have to be earned. Protect your interests.*

JOHN HUSTON (8/5/06)
EVELYN KEYES (11/20/19)

Comely leading lady Keyes was most popular in the 40s and 50s. She was married to director Huston from 1946–50. Huston was a restless but persistent husband. He married Keyes after divorcing his first wife and ardently courting Olivia de Havilland. The day after divorcing Keyes, he married his 4th wife.

August 3–10

THE WEEK OF BALANCED STRENGTH
LEO II

November 19–24

THE CUSP OF REVOLUTION
SCORPIO-SAGITTARIUS CUSP

Doing One's Best

Great pressures can build up in this relationship through its insistence on getting everything just right. Extremely demanding of itself and others, it places perhaps too much emphasis on mental concentration. Since Leo II's are often more at home when they follow their hunches and Scorpio-Sagittarians when they deal with their feelings, both partners may be uncomfortable with the uncompromising focus on logical thought that emerges when they are together, cutting them off from their real strengths. For all their drive and intensity, both Leo II's and Scorpio-Sagittarians do best in relaxed circumstances where they can work at their own tempo. The relationship's insistence on perfection may undercut its effectiveness, then, and arouse frustration.

Both these personalities are full-blooded in their sexuality, yet this strength does not always emerge in the love affairs they have with each other. They can have a strangely inhibiting effect on each other's carnal side, as if they were expecting criticism or reproach. In marriages, too, high expectations can prevent good results. Interactions here are seldom free and easy. Leo II's tend to hang in until the bitter end, but the relationship's strains and pressures may make Scorpio-Sagittarians seek comfort and pleasure elsewhere.

In the family, on the other hand, this combination can be strengthening and stabilizing, particularly when it emerges between siblings of the same sex. These two can easily run the household when elders are away. Friends in this combination often share a common area of interest or activity, which they pursue with zeal. Their family members, spouses and other friends will have to be understanding of their time-consuming and often single-minded involvement with each other.

Work relationships between Leo II's and Scorpio-Sagittarians may have to loosen up a bit, leaving the partners free to operate in their own ways. As long as they touch base with each other from time to time, and refrain from being overly critical, things can go smoothly enough. Leo II directness and Scorpio-Sagittarius elegance and nuance don't always gel, but can complement each other if these guidelines are observed.

ADVICE: *Ease up a bit on your demands. Beware of high expectations. Don't neglect your real strengths. Work more in the service of others.*

August 3–10

THE WEEK OF BALANCED STRENGTH
LEO II

November 25–December 2

THE WEEK OF INDEPENDENCE
SAGITTARIUS I

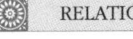 RELATIONSHIPS

STRENGTHS: **ENTHUSIASTIC,
YOUTHFUL, PHYSICAL**

WEAKNESSES: **DISILLUSIONING,
REJECTING, UNGROUNDED**

BEST: **MARRIAGE**

WORST: **WORK**

Falling in Love with Love

This enthusiastic, upbeat relationship is all fire. Extroverted and flamboyant, it lends verve to any gathering and also inspires the partners themselves. Youthful and childlike qualities are usually apparent here, energy is abundant and positive thoughts prevail, at least when things are on between these two. During down periods, however, the couple may lack the inner resources to deal with problems, especially emotional and psychological ones. Problems can also arise over who is getting the most attention. Leo II's and Sagittarius I's should be more aware of their own needs and learn how to deal with them without making demands on others.

The combination can be extremely romantic. For Leo II's and Sagittarius I's in love, all other aspects of life tend to pale in comparison with the bright flame between the two of them. Too often, however, falling in love is illusory for them, and has the hidden purpose of taking their minds off their own problems. The relief at apparently not having to deal with unhappiness any more, or at finally having found the right person (even although the partners may have felt similarly before, and ultimately been disappointed), never fails to raise spirits and renew self-confidence. Unfortunately, the opposite may also be the case: should one of the two suffer rejection or frustration, disillusion and depression can be severe. Marriages are usually more stable and lasting, especially when time is taken to allow a deep commitment to form before the actual wedding takes place. The couple should make an effort to keep their romance alive, balancing it with domestic and financial responsibilities in a healthy mix. Since overenthusiasm can be deadly in business pursuits, the matchup is not recommended for partnerships or executive pairs. And co-worker positions in a company hierarchy may bore this vibrant duo. Family matchups, on the other hand, particularly parent-child, can be mutually stimulating, and will tend to keep elders young at heart. Friendships between Leo II's and Sagittarius I's generally need a strong physical outlet, perhaps sports, fitness or other forms of training.

ADVICE: *Have fun, but take time to face the truth. Falling in love rarely solves all problems in the long run. Keep an eye on your feelings.*

PERCY BYSSHE SHELLEY (8/4/1792)
WILLIAM BLAKE (11/28/1757)

Shelley and Blake were both English Romantic poets. Blake came from an earlier generation (with Wordsworth and Coleridge) and Shelley from a later group (with Keats and Byron). Blake's work reflected a religious and mystical outlook while Shelley's was more liberal and freewheeling. **Also: John Huston & James Agee** (director/novelist-screenwriter); **Melanie Griffith & Steve Bauer** (married; actors).

August 3–10

THE WEEK OF BALANCED STRENGTH
LEO II

December 3–10

THE WEEK OF THE ORIGINATOR
SAGITTARIUS II

 RELATIONSHIPS

STRENGTHS: **SPONTANEOUS,
UNDERSTANDING, SOCIAL**

WEAKNESSES: **UNSYMPATHETIC.
VOLATILE, MISUNDERSTOOD**

BEST: **MARRIAGE**

WORST: **SIBLING**

Feeling Normal

This matchup is often oriented toward human interactions, whether in school, religious or social organizations or more informally within a group of friends. Both Leo II's and Sagittarius II's have a character trait of periodically feeling misunderstood, even abnormal. Together, however, they can make their way in the world without feeling strange about themselves. Thus the focus of their relationship is often social development, as the partners learn more about people, institutions and how they work. Since Leo II and Sagittarius II form a trine aspect (lying 120° apart in the zodiac), traditional astrology predicts an easy relationship here, for the most part correctly. Difficulties can arise, however, when each partner's fiery nature begins to flare.

As a romance this relationship can be spontaneous, impulsive, passionate and highly sexual. Emotional maturity is usually absent, however, and the landscape may be dotted with outbursts of feeling, both positive and negative. Leo II's are definitely the longer-suffering of these two: if Sagittarius II's feel rejected or frustrated they are liable to take their leave, and with little warning.

Marriages and friendships between these two can certainly be intense at times but are for the most part easygoing and pleasurable. That there is usually a great deal of understanding between Leo II's and Sagittarius II's doesn't mean there is always total sympathy. The partners are quite independent. A lot of the time they spend together may include the presence of other people, and since in a social setting they tend to be treated rather as if they were a single person, these situations will bring them closer together.

Sibling rivalries are highly challenging, especially between two sisters or two brothers. Matters come to a head quickly between such pairs, but once the storm has broken things quiet down pretty quickly. It is usually better if friends and family don't try to work together, but Leo II and Sagittarius II co-worker pairs often become fast friends. Sarcastic verbal jabs are signs of affection in such relationships.

ADVICE: *Show emotional intelligence. Develop patience and self-control. Give others more of a chance. Let go of the past. Don't hold grudges.*

GILLIAN ANDERSON (12/9/68)
DAVID DUCHOVNY (8/7/61)

Duchovny and Anderson are co-stars of the hip tv series about paranormal phenomena, *The X-Files* (1993–). He plays an Oxford-educated psychologist who believes his sister was abducted by aliens, while she plays an ex-medical student who approaches their cases more scientifically. In real life, Anderson believes in UFOs and ESP.

Also: Paul Claudel & Camille Claudel (siblings; dramatist/artist).

DON JOHNSON (12/15/49)
MELANIE GRIFFITH (8/9/57)

Actors Griffith and Johnson were married and divorced twice. She first moved in with him when she was 14 and he 22. They married in '76 and divorced a year later. In '88, on her way to a rehab clinic, she called him and renewed their love; they remarried in '89.

Also: Dino DeLaurentiis & Carlo Ponti (filmmaker partners); **Whitney Houston & Dionne Warwick** (cousins; pop singers).

August 3–10
THE WEEK OF BALANCED STRENGTH
LEO II

December 11–18
THE WEEK OF THE TITAN
SAGITTARIUS III

Unanimity of Purpose

The main thrust of this relationship is to play a pioneering role in the commercial, family or social organization to which the pair belong. Any cart pulled by two such powerful horses as Leo II and Sagittarius III is sure to get to its destination—as long as they are both pulling in the same direction: capable of giving leadership and direction to any endeavor, these two can also stalemate a project if they have a strong difference of opinion. An important challenge here, then, is to preserve unanimity of purpose. Leo II's will sometimes take a back seat to Sagittarius III's when a project obviously won't function with more than one boss, but more often a judicious division of responsibilities may be necessary, allowing the pair to codirect a project without too much fur flying.

Work and family relationships in this combination tend to be more effective when kept impersonal and goal-oriented. If personal feelings are not kept out of the workplace or home, aggression can explode, or quieter irritations can become the slow friction that finally brings a project screeching to a halt. It is important to both Leo II's and Sagittarius III's to find a human level on which to relate, however, so that the area of sharing thoughts and feelings is almost certain to create challenges for the relationship to face.

Love affairs and marriages between these two can experience tremendous power struggles over who will be top dog. For one partner to have a higher salary or career position than the other is likely to become an issue between them. Yet competitive social and economic drives can actually unify the relationship, not only by stressing common values but by underlining the necessity of hard and productive work to strengthen the bond. Both partners must take care that affection, tenderness, love and kindness do not get left out in the rush toward success. Friendships between Leo II's and Sagittarius III's must reckon with the fact that both personalities go through moods; at such times it's best for them to be left alone.

ADVICE: *Don't put all of your eggs in one basket. Seek spiritual and emotional values. Worldly success is not the only thing. Give up power struggles.*

LOUIS B. LEAKEY (8/7/03)
RICHARD LEAKEY (12/19/44)

Louis, wife Mary and son Richard are all dedicated anthropologists. Louis' research focused on primitive toolmaking, explaining how prehistoric hunter-gatherers acquired their food. After his death in '72, Richard and his mother continued their field research in Africa.

Also: James Randi & Uri Geller (conjurer critical of psychic).

August 3–10
THE WEEK OF BALANCED STRENGTH
LEO II

December 19–25
THE CUSP OF PROPHECY
SAGITTARIUS-CAPRICORN CUSP

Pulling the Strings

These two may find themselves acting out a drama over which they have no control. Their relationship has a peculiarly fated quality to it, with each partner taking on defined roles, as if someone were pulling the strings. Well directed and strong minded, the relationship knows where it is going and what it is supposed to do, but the question is: do its partners? As a unit, Leo II's and Sagittarius-Capricorns are unified by a single-minded purpose that can transcend many limitations and barriers. This relationship is governed by the element of air, granting it a great capacity for strategic thinking and deep powers of concentration.

Love affairs between Leo II's and Sagittarius-Capricorns can be deep and passionate. They will also show a high degree of curiosity: both of these individuals have a secretive side that few can penetrate, giving them ample room to flex their investigative muscles when they come together. Should they touch on a hidden nerve, however, or dig a bit too deep, quite theatrical displays of feeling are likely to result. Marriages in this combination can bring great joy to both partners but also deeply felt sorrow. In fact, the pair are likely to run the gamut of human emotion before they are finished with each other.

As friends or siblings, Leo II's and Sagittarius-Capricorns are likely to be quite extroverted, engaging in challenging and exciting activities. Danger often draws them like a magnet. Although comfortable in taking risks, the pair will have to recognize limitations and draw up boundaries that they must not overstep. Competition here is generally positive in nature, impelling mutual efforts forward.

In the professional sphere, Leo II's and Sagittarius-Capricorns can often work side by side for years on end. Their common purpose and feeling for the large line and the dramatic gesture are balanced by strict attention to detail. An important challenge for them will be allowing both partners their own individuality without compromising the interests of the group.

ADVICE: *You could be wrong. Be open to contrary points of view. Don't wear blinders. Keep your peripheral vision active. Answers create questions.*

August 3–10

THE WEEK OF BALANCED STRENGTH
LEO II

December 26–January 2

THE WEEK OF THE RULER
CAPRICORN I

 RELATIONSHIPS

STRENGTHS: **ASPIRING,
POWERFUL, AFFLUENT**

WEAKNESSES: **MONOLITHIC,
BLAMING, FRUSTRATED**

BEST: **FRIENDSHIP**

WORST: **LOVE**

A Monolithic Stance

Too often, this combination elevates power to a position of primary importance, ignoring more human considerations. And should the drive for power be internalized within the relationship, the couple are likely to slug it out, and in not too pretty a fashion. Strong conflicts will probably emerge between these two. Yet Leo II's and Capricorn I's also share many values, and may even at times adopt a monolithic stance that can be somewhat unfeeling to their colleagues, friends or children.

Power struggles can push love affairs onto the rocks if they are combative enough. The couple's inability to open their hearts to each other will signal the end, even if their sexual expression is still going strong. Capricorn I–Leo II marriages are likely to be ambitious, seeking the very best that life has to offer in terms of material wealth and possessions. Failure to accomplish these ends can deal a major blow to the relationship's confidence in itself, spawning anger, resentment and blame.

In friendships, extremely close bonds can develop, but they are not always of the most positive sort: Leo II's and Capricorn I's may offer each other a bitter sort of consolation for shared feelings of rejection or inadequacy. Shrugging off such attitudes and renewing the will to try again, and this time to succeed, may give the relationship the strength it needs to serve as an inspirational force in the lives of its partners.

In work and family matchups, Capricorn I's can be extremely critical of the methods of Leo II employees or children, who often adopt a straightforward attitude and just go for it. This offends the moral sensibilities of Capricorn I's, who like to insist on a particular way of doing things. Capricorn I's typically like to set up rules, Leo II's to break them.

PHIL SPECTOR (12/26/40)
RONNIE SPECTOR (8/10/43)

Influential music producer Phil met lead singer Ronnie of The Ronettes in '63. They married in '66. According to her autobiography, he held her prisoner in their LA mansion. They divorced in '74. **Also: Rosanna Arquette & Charley Weaver** (granddaughter/grandfather; actors); **Dustin Hoffman & Jon Voight** (co-stars, *Midnight Cowboy*); **Kristoffer Tabori & Viveca Lindfors** (son/mother; actors).

ADVICE: *Seek deeply human values. Limit your desire for power. Find constructive outlets for your energy. Accept what happens.*

August 3–10

THE WEEK OF BALANCED STRENGTH
LEO II

January 3–9

THE WEEK OF DETERMINATION
CAPRICORN II

  RELATIONSHIPS

STRENGTHS: **PHYSICAL,
CRITICAL, VICTORIOUS**

WEAKNESSES: **IMPERSONAL,
SELFISH, UNSYMPATHETIC**

BEST: **FAMILY**

WORST: **LOVE**

Predatory Pleasures

These two make a forceful and piercingly direct pair. Their strength of purpose is unmatched, and their relationship promises them an exhilarating ride of facing challenges and then conquering them. Not only is this combination physically strong, it has fine-honed taste and a perceptive eye—a predator's eye, even. Leo II and Capricorn II lie quincunx to each other in the zodiac (150° apart), so that traditional astrology predicts some instability in their matchup, but between these two instability can translate into excitement and impulsive spontaneity. As individuals, both of these personalities are likely to give their all for their profession or for a cause, and their relationship synergistically magnifies this trait. The result can be an almost monomaniacal drive to overcome and to win.

Strongly sexual feelings may come to dominate love and marriage. Without the attainment of deeper levels of understanding, kindness, acceptance and sharing, these relationships are liable to burn out, revealing selfishness as their true basis. But although both Leo II's and Capricorn II's are tough realists, romantic feelings can add something to their relationship, ultimately leading to the expression of more sympathy. Conscious efforts to expand the scope of the relationship beyond the physical plane will generally bring it longer life. All Leo II–Capricorn II relationships, including friendships, will benefit from a deliberate emphasis on kindness and consideration. Instabilities can be lessened considerably by finding lighter activities to share and enjoy outside the relationship's principal endeavor. Work and family relationships can be interrelated with these two. In both cases, the energies of the group are often aimed squarely at achievement and little else. The goals may be financial or professional but generally demand the pursuit of excellence at the highest level. The kick of these endeavors inevitably lies in competition, and in overcoming adversaries of worthy mettle. Highly analytic abilities are granted to this pair, whether boss and employee, parent and child, siblings or co-workers. Thus weaknesses are mercilessly exposed and improvements constantly made in order to ensure future success.

BRETT HULL (8/9/64)
BOBBY HULL (1/3/39)

Son Brett and father Bobby are in the elite class of hockey players. In what would seem like an impossible act to follow, Brett has achieved a great deal in the wake of his superstar father. Both have received MVP (Hart) awards and Lady Byng (sportsmanship) and all-star game trophies. **Also: Esther Williams & Fernando Lamas** (married; actors).

ADVICE: *Kick back after work. Learn to have fun. Losing graciously is an art. Respect your opponents. Give other people an even break.*

STRENGTHS: **PRACTICAL, LOYAL, ESTABLISHED**

WEAKNESSES: **STUBBORN, INFLEXIBLE, STUCK**

BEST: **WORK, MARRIAGE**

WORST: **FRIENDSHIP**

LOUIS B. LEAKEY (8/7/03)
DIAN FOSSEY (1/16/32)

Famous anthropologist Leakey was responsible for initiating the work of social scientist Fossey. As a pioneer in primate research, Leakey encouraged her to study gorillas. They both felt that such studies would increase our understanding of human behavior.

August 3–10

THE WEEK OF BALANCED STRENGTH
LEO II

January 10–16

THE WEEK OF DOMINANCE
CAPRICORN III

Giving One's All

This relationship confers on its partners a need to give or do, and to see the tangible results of their efforts. One is apt to see them actively involved in establishing, running and maintaining an organization or service. Leo II's are generally the more ambitious of these two: Capricorn III's are easily contented by reaching a certain level and staying there, but Leo II's are always seeking greater challenges, and this can be a source of tension in their relationship. Yet if Leo II's often serve as models of inspiration for Capricorn III's, whom they may succeed in launching on their way, Capricorn III's will be quite capable of continuing on without further help. The Leo II–Capricorn III relationship is solid, service-oriented and generally able to accept a niche that is challenging but not necessarily top level.

Love affairs and marriages between these two can be enduring, faithful, fulfilling and productive. Not overly given to imaginative or romantic impulses, they tend to be simply stable. The responsibilities of having children and running a household will come naturally to this pair. Physical sensation and pleasure have a primary importance here; comfort and security are usually top priorities for the Leo II–Capricorn III couple.

The practical abilities that tend to emerge in this combination make it ideal for business and career pursuits. Capricorn III's can teach Leo II's a great deal about handling money and can themselves be pushed to succeed by their partner's unflagging energy and ambition. Both personalities will give their all to their relationship while it produces good results. Even in the event of breakdown or failure, both partners will give resuscitation their best shot and will experience tremendous struggles between loyalty and good sense in figuring out when to call it quits.

Parent-child bonds in this combination can be strong and mutually supportive, whichever personality is the parent. Friendships may experience conflicts over the choice of activities, with both partners often showing great stubbornness and refusing to compromise.

ADVICE: *Learn to let go. How much security do you need? Take a few chances now and then. Accept failure. Learn to move on. Don't get stuck.*

STRENGTHS: **STIMULATING, INTENSE, RISK-TAKING**

WEAKNESSES: **STRESSFUL, UNFORGIVING, BURNED-OUT**

BEST: **WORK**

WORST: **SIBLING**

BUZZ ALDRIN (1/20/30)
NEIL ARMSTRONG (8/5/30)

Armstrong and Aldrin, the 1st and 2nd men to set foot on the moon, trained side by side to achieve the highest levels of skill for their famous 1969 Apollo 11 voyage. Armstrong said: "That's one small step for a man, one giant step for mankind."

Also: Melanie Griffith & Tippi Hedrin (daughter/mother; actors); Percy Shelley & Lord Byron (close friends; poets); Lucille Ball & Desi Arnaz, Jr. (mother/son; actors).

August 3–10

THE WEEK OF BALANCED STRENGTH
LEO II

January 17–22

THE CUSP OF MYSTERY & IMAGINATION
CAPRICORN-AQUARIUS CUSP

Laserlike Intensity

Together these two are capable of great achievements. Their relationship can be a dynamic one in which they stimulate each other to lift both their performance and their consciousness to a higher level. They must be sure, however, not to burn holes in themselves, or in other people, through the intensity of their connection. Exciting exploits can be this relationship's food, but the diet may be a tiring one, eventually leading to exhaustion. Drawing up guidelines, establishing structures and agreeing on boundaries and limitations will all be wise steps to take if the relationship's healthy survival and effectiveness are to be preserved.

Love affairs between these two can provide enjoyment, especially sexually, but usually only for the duration of a brief fling. If these partners are serious about each other they must be willing to invest time in patiently getting to know each other. Should they marry, Leo II calmness under fire will generally ground Capricorn-Aquarians' more excitable temperament, while Capricorn-Aquarians may at times bring a touch of humor to their overserious partner.

At work these two can be terribly demanding of each other. Unspoken agreements allow few if any excuses to be accepted for forgetfulness or inattention. Leo III's and Capricorn-Aquarians are geared to perform at the highest level of stress, and also of excellence. Hanging out together after work may bring out a whole new side of the relationship, one in which relaxation and pleasure can be pursued as avidly as professional goals are during the day. These two tend to work hard and play hard. Without this kind of work or leisure-time focus, friendships may lack intensity.

Parent-child relationships can be difficult, particularly during adolescence. All types of conflict will be magnified. Elsewhere in the family, sibling matchups, especially of the same sex, can lead to a search for adventure that could involve risk-taking activities bordering on the illegal.

ADVICE: *Seek moderation and calm. Lower your stress level. Direct your energies intelligently. Get to know each other better at a deep level.*

August 3–10

THE WEEK OF BALANCED STRENGTH
LEO II

January 23–30

THE WEEK OF GENIUS
AQUARIUS I

Trial and Error

Experience is the best teacher, at least according to this relationship. It is not uncommon for these two to team up on a project even when neither of them has had any formal training or experience related to it. They usually achieve surprising and original results. Although this is a potentially inflammable combination (Leo is ruled by fire, Aquarius I by air), it can also bestow a great deal of practicality and common sense. Through a judicious mixture of their natural talents and life experience, these two can put together results that are cogent and almost immediately understandable.

It is a simple fact that some people can learn from each other and others cannot. In this case, it is the relationship that is the true teacher, for it gives its partners the space, the impetus and above all the opportunity to innovate and experiment. In love and marriage these two proceed by trial and error, gaining in depth and understanding as they go forward. Together they tend to learn a great deal about each other and about themselves. Through experience they find out how to treat each other and how to get the most out of their time together. Although impatience, frustration and anger may often surface between this volatile pair, good sense usually prevails.

Boss-employee and parent-child relationships here can be highly productive, often achieving the kind of true equality one finds in co-worker relationships and friendships. Each partner usually has the good sense to know that extremes of authority and rebellion rarely bring projects forward, and that compromise is to be preferred to combat. At times a dangerous edginess can be sensed in this relationship, but it generally serves to further the action. Friendships between these two may concentrate on leisure and entertainment, never reaching deeper emotional levels. Having fun and relaxing together rather than raising consciousness are what these two usually have in mind.

ADVICE: *Keep on learning. Try to go deeper spiritually. Beware of volatile emotions. Don't neglect your personal development. Be patient.*

SAM ELLIOTT (8/9/44)
KATHERINE ROSS (1/29/42)

Actors Elliott and Ross appeared in 2 films together, *Butch Cassidy and the Sundance Kid* (1969) and *The Legacy* (1979), then married in '84. Ross got an Oscar nomination as Dustin Hoffman's heartthrob in *The Graduate* (1967). Elliott was her 5th husband. **Also: John Huston & Humphrey Bogart** (great working relationship; director/actor).

August 3–10

THE WEEK OF BALANCED STRENGTH
LEO II

January 31–February 7

THE WEEK OF YOUTH & EASE
AQUARIUS II

Attractive Opposition

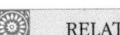

This is a highly magnetic relationship. No matter what difficulties these two encounter, the strength of their bond is usually enough for them to overcome problems that would stop others in their tracks. In fact, solving problems can become a way of life for this pair. Although Leo II and Aquarius II stand directly opposite each other in the zodiac, so that astrology might predict difficulties for this couple, the saying "Opposites attract" was never truer than here.

In love affairs, Aquarius II's will be amazed at the depth of feeling aroused in them by Leo II's—indeed, they may not always feel adequate to handle it. Leo II's are comfortable with the relationship's sexually passionate nature, but they, too, feel a little intimidated and puzzled by the complexity of their own emotions in this combination. The matchup challenges both partners in the area of feelings—traditionally an undeveloped area of their personalities, and one that they often prefer to neglect or ignore. In grappling with such issues, Aquarius II's and Leo II's may progress immeasurably in their personal development.

Work relationships and marriages, which these two have a tendency to combine, are usually of a very high order. Aquarius II–Leo II partnerships may do even better professionally than personally, being characterized by an ease of communication and strength of common purpose. Conflicts can arise between more relaxed Aquarius II and more aggressive Leo II spouses, but the relationship can also be characterized by soothing and stimulating attitudes that do both partners good.

As friends, Leo II's and Aquarius II's are likely to get in over their heads. A depth and complexity of emotion can easily emerge between them that they will be unable to handle. It is often better for them to back off a bit, and to meet at a more enjoyable level, albeit also a more superficial one, where they can be a bit more objective about each other, perhaps as occasional companions. In parent-child relationships of either possible arrangement, real opposition in temperament may lead to stormy conflict.

ADVICE: *Find your real strengths. Make differences work. Try to understand your emotions. Opposition can be beneficial. Be more accepting.*

KEITH CARRADINE (8/8/50)
JOHN CARRADINE (2/5/06)

John, one of Hollywood's most prolific character actors, appeared in over 220 films. Singer-actor Keith (2nd of John's 3 actor sons) has starred on Broadway and in films. In 1991 he played the title role in *The Will Rogers Follies*. **Also: Tommie Aaron & Hank Aaron** (baseball brothers); **Rosanna Arquette & Peter Gabriel** (romance; actress/musician); **Louis Leakey & Mary Leakey** (married; anthropologists).

LONI ANDERSON (8/5/46)
BURT REYNOLDS (2/11/36)

In 1988, lady-killer Reynolds married tv actress Anderson (*WKRP in Cincinnati*). They seemed to have a strong relationship for 5 years, until the marriage broke up in '93. There followed one of the ugliest Hollywood divorces of the 90s. ***Also:*** **Martha Stewart & Andy Stewart** (married; home designer/publisher); **Thomas Scopes & Charles Darwin** (teacher put on trial for teaching Darwinism).

August 3–10

THE WEEK OF BALANCED STRENGTH
LEO II

February 8–15

THE WEEK OF ACCEPTANCE
AQUARIUS III

A Sea of Good Feeling

Personality appeal and pizzazz rate high in this relationship. Often upbeat, the matchup is filled with a charm and a romantic appeal that are simply irresistible. Of course, both Leo II's and Aquarius III's have a darker side, which they may both be fleeing, but as escapes go, this is a pretty good one. Both of these personalities hate people who put on airs, and are likely to find the naturalness of their own relationship comforting. They have a way of lifting each other's moods. Even so, there is a danger here of deep depression. If both partners crash simultaneously, their effect on each other could work to hold them down and make it extremely hard to recover. It is in the relationship's best interest, then, that at least one of the partners be happy at any given time.

Love affairs here can be sparkling and fun. Entertainment figures high on the list of these partners' essentials, and if they are unable to keep each other amused, they are liable to seek pleasure elsewhere. They should be extremely careful around all addictive substances, from alcohol to painkillers to so-called mind-expanding drugs, for in their hedonistic wanderings they tend to go overboard. Marriages are not recommended unless these habit-forming tendencies, which may also include sex and love addictions, can be brought under control.

Leo II–Aquarius III friendships are likely to swim in a sea of good feeling, at least when all is going well. It may not be exactly accurate to call these two fair-weather friends, but they are not known for giving selflessly in times of need. Recognizing the dark side and not bailing out when the going gets rough are real challenges for the relationship.

Working matchups may not always have the persistence necessary for long-range projects. In the family, Leo II and Aquarius III family members rarely see eye to eye on most issues but can be extremely frank and honest with each other, and hence make trustworthy critics.

ADVICE: *Be there in good times and bad. Beware of dark-side takeovers. Escapism and addictions could lead to ruin. Learn the value of silence.*

COURTNEY LOVE (8/9/64)
KURT COBAIN (2/20/67)

Love and Cobain will be forever linked through rock & roll and his tragic suicide. Stars of their own rock groups (Hole and Nirvana), they were married in '92 and had a child they had to fight to keep because of their drug habits. Depressed, Cobain killed himself with a shotgun in '94. ***Also:*** **Jane Wyatt & Robert Young** (co-stars, *Father Knows Best*).

August 3–10

THE WEEK OF BALANCED STRENGTH
LEO II

February 16–22

THE CUSP OF SENSITIVITY
AQUARIUS-PISCES CUSP

Comfortable Openness

This relationship can be extremely honest, in the sense not of obeying moral imperatives but simply of being relaxed enough to allow for openness. Both Leo II's and Aquarius-Pisces are often guarded individuals who do not easily grant admittance to their private emotional world; yet their relationship has an ambiance in which they can share feelings comfortably. At the same time, it also augments both partners' tendency to indulge in flamboyant activities that hide the sensitive and perhaps wounded individual within. One problem here, then, is that the partners may get stuck together in a well of loneliness, depression or addiction from which it may be difficult or impossible for them to extricate themselves.

Love affairs, when on, can be highly sensuous and enjoyable. Although Leo is a fire sign and Aquarius-Pisces an air-water combination, the Leo II–Aquarius-Pisces relationship is ruled by earth, here producing a relaxed orientation on the physical plane. But the relationship can easily get out of balance, and some effort may have to be exerted to maintain its psychological stability, which is crucial for its success. Marriage is not recommended for this pair until they have known each other long enough to be sure of an acceptable level of mental health together.

Working relationships between Leo II's and Aquarius-Pisces are best when entrepreneurial, freelance or executive in nature, for as co-workers in a large organization the duo may be frustrated at being stuck at an unacceptably low level in the hierarchy. As a team these two may well prove quite ambitious, for they have an intense need to prove themselves. As siblings, Leo II's and Aquarius-Pisces must be able to make their collective voice felt in family business. If ignored or not taken seriously, they may respond rebelliously and disruptively. Friendships in this combination can be mutually protective and understanding.

ADVICE: *Work on maintaining stability. Even out moods. Don't be afraid to show who you really are. Aggression isn't necessarily productive.*

August 3–10

THE WEEK OF BALANCED STRENGTH
LEO II

February 23–March 2

THE WEEK OF SPIRIT
PISCES I

Ineffable Delights

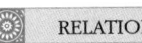 RELATIONSHIPS

STRENGTHS: **ROMANTIC, PRACTICAL, SUCCESSFUL**

WEAKNESSES: **REBELLIOUS, SELFISH, UNAWARE**

BEST: **MARRIAGE**

WORST: **LOVE**

Romance and charm are undeniable in this relationship, but so too may be the rebellion of one or both of its partners. Pisces I's will try to lead their partners in this combination into a captivating world of feeling and romance, but hardheaded Leo II's will only be led so far, and may reject what they perceive as overly claiming attitudes. Ultimately, Pisces I's are likely to get hurt, but the memory of the relationship's ineffable delights may haunt Leo II's for a lifetime.

In love, this relationship tends to whisk both partners away on a magic carpet ride. Unfortunately for Pisces I's, however, the direction the ride takes is often sternly dictated by the Leo II captain. Pisces I's tend to be the more narcissistic of the pair, and realistic Leo II's may see them as in the long run more caught up by their own self-love than by anything the Leo II can offer. Feeling captured but not really appreciated, the Leo II may silently stray off in another direction, barely even aware of having left a somewhat bewildered Pisces I behind. Breakups often occur when hurt Pisces I's close off to a Leo II lover.

Marriages have the potential to be long-lasting, and business or career matchups can also be successful, but both partners should have a clear idea of what they want. The goals of money and power usually come second to personal involvement here at first, but in the long run may surpass it. Pisces I's will rarely be able to stand up to Leo II's, who have the stamina to dominate the relationship and get what they want. On the other hand, they can also be extremely faithful and loving—when it suits their purpose.

Friendships and sibling relationships in this combination can be magnetic, emphasizing sensitivity and a practical sort of spirituality. Interests such as meditation, yoga, martial arts and a variety of artistic pursuits (particularly music) that can find expression in their daily lives will have special appeal for this pair.

ADVICE: *Be more aware of needs and wants. Keep lines of communication open. Don't be afraid to talk about problems. Romance can hold you back.*

LUCILLE BALL (8/6/11)
DESI ARNAZ (3/2/17)

Ball and Arnaz married in 1940, the year of his film debut in *Too Many Girls*. Over the years they reaped a fortune from *I Love Lucy* and many other tv shows. Following their 1960 divorce, she bought out his share in Desilu Productions, and he became an independent producer. *Also:* **Eddie Fisher & Elizabeth Taylor** (married; singer/actress).

August 3–10

THE WEEK OF BALANCED STRENGTH
LEO II

March 3–10

THE WEEK OF THE LONER
PISCES II

Endless Corridors

RELATIONSHIPS

STRENGTHS: **ENERGY-GIVING, SENSITIZING, MOTIVATIONAL**

WEAKNESSES: **EXHAUSTING, DEPENDENCY-FOSTERING, BIPOLAR**

BEST: **FRIENDSHIP**

WORST: **PARENT-CHILD**

This relationship generates a lot of energy, but its great challenge is putting that energy toward mutually beneficial ends and endeavors. The major problem here is that Pisces II's tend to sap the energy of their partner in this combination: Leo II's readily adopt a protective attitude to them, seeing them as a great personal treasure to cherish, yet rarely being able to thread the corridors of their emotional labyrinth without feeling exhausted and frustrated. Pisces II's rarely ask for such attention consciously but cry out for it on the unconscious level, to which Leo II's are finely tuned.

One difficulty romantic relationships and marriages will have to contend with is instability, underlined by the quincunx aspect between Leo II and Pisces II (which lie 150° apart in the zodiac). Their energies, however sexually fulfilling or pleasurable, too often go flying off in extreme directions that ultimately undermine their everyday balance. Putting together a few days, weeks or months of consistent behavior can be a real achievement here. Moments of ecstasy and deep depression often succeed each other with frightening rapidity. Boredom or innocuous behavior may be seen as signs of health in such a relationship.

Friendships between these two can make Leo II's more sensitive and Pisces II's more motivated. They often favor objective activities, usually more technical than social in nature, and may even make a success of limited business endeavors—projects on which they embark without financial gain in mind, but that then prove commercial despite themselves. Parent-child and boss-employee relationships can see Leo II's being overpowering even when relatively dormant. Pisces II children and employees may be steamrolled by their energy but may ultimately turn things around, using that energy to power their own motors. Curious and debilitating dependencies may result.

ADVICE: *Put energies to practical use. Ground activities in the here and now. Damping excitement may limit depression. Follow business plans.*

WILLIAM GODWIN (3/3/1756)
PERCY BYSSHE SHELLEY (8/4/1792)

Social philosopher Godwin was a revolutionary and libertarian. He greatly influenced the young poet Shelley when they met in 1812. Shelley supported Godwin financially until 1820, and his intellectual life continued to broaden through their association. Shelley married Godwin's daughter in 1816.

NEIL ARMSTRONG (8/5/30)
FRANK BORMAN (3/14/28)

Astronauts Armstrong and Borman were in NASA's manned space program from 1962–70. Though they were never on a flight together, they worked side by side on the ground. Both were command pilots on Gemini and Apollo missions. Borman was commander of the first lunar orbit (1968); Armstrong was first to set foot on the moon (1969).

August 3–10

THE WEEK OF BALANCED STRENGTH
LEO II

March 11–18

THE WEEK OF DANCERS & DREAMERS
PISCES III

Seeking to Surpass

Since this relationship has the effect of stimulating each partner's drive for independence, it is questionable whether they will be able to form and sustain a lasting relationship with each other. Leo II's and Pisces III's rarely have a settling or calming effect on each other and may feel little need to share with each other to any great degree. It is possible, however, for them to evolve a rivalry that in a strange way can bring them closer together, in space and time if not in emotions, than any friendship or love affair could.

Leo II's can be fascinated by the philosophical and independent thinking of Pisces III's, who can be equally thrilled by the commanding social and professional stance of Leo II's. Between friends and siblings such admiration often leads to competition, with each partner benefiting by emulating and even seeking to outdo the other's strengths. Both must be careful to prevent a tendency to try to win at all costs from getting out of hand. In commercial and other career matchups, Leo II's can vie with Pisces III's in a company, usually having the effect of forwarding the action rather than slowing it down. When these two compete directly with each other in rival organizations, Pisces III's will cleverly seek to undermine Leo II's strengths and turn them against them.

The question in love affairs and marriages will be how much time and effort the couple are willing to put into their relationship. No matter how much in love they are, their relationship encourages them to value their independence more than their desire to share or even take from each other. Underlying this mania to be free may be a secret fear of getting too deeply involved with each other on the part of both partners. If this fear can be overcome, renewed involvement and commitment, and less insistence on freedom at any cost, will result.

ADVICE: *Put your competitive drives to their best use. Fear may be holding you back from deeper involvement. Independence isn't always necessary.*

SEAN PENN (8/17/60)
MADONNA (8/16/58)

Penn and Madonna had a passionate but troubled marriage (1986–89). At times he was so volatile she needed the police. She claims he was drunk during most of their marriage, yet she considered him her most important love. **Also:**

Kathie Lee & Frank Gifford (married; tv co-host/sportscaster);

Ross McWhirter & Norris McWhirter (twins; *Guinness Book of Records* compilers).

August 11–18

THE WEEK OF LEADERSHIP
LEO III

August 11–18

THE WEEK OF LEADERSHIP
LEO III

The Greatest Power of All

Can one group have two leaders? Two commanding Leo III's can actually get along well in a family or marital situation, since neither wants to dominate or rule so much as to lead. If they can both establish their own, separate areas of influence in which they are the unquestioned authority, it is not impossible for their interactions to be quite peaceful. In career matchups, however, they are likely to be competitors or rivals, even if they serve on the same side. Needless to say, the extreme hardheadedness and power orientation of Leo III's can often lead to combat, although a few confrontations may convince both partners of the inadvisability of frontal assaults in the future. Strangely enough, this matchup may succeed in developing the more subtle side of Leo III's, if only as each tries to figure out a way to persuade or manipulate the other more effectively.

Love affairs between Leo III's, no matter how romantic, will always include some form of power struggle. Even in the most intimate areas, competition for supremacy may rear its ugly head. Perhaps the most important lesson such a couple can learn is that the greatest power of all is unconditional and unselfish love, and that the cultivation of kindness, understanding and consideration can be far more challenging and rewarding than winning.

Leo III spouses do best when they both have their own career. Although they may show interest in each other's projects, and even help each other out periodically, as professionals they are best off maintaining a strict separation. At work, it may be hard for two Leo III's to serve together in the same department, but as executives, advisors or heads of their own divisions they can get along quite well.

In parent-child and other family matchups, the key to avoiding combat is building strong bonds of trust and respect. Over time, and with great patience on either side, such links can be forged. Once they are broken, however, truly frightening scenarios can arise in which combat threatens to break the family asunder.

ADVICE: *Lessen power struggles. Develop patience and understanding. Simple acts of kindness carry great strength. Give more, be selfish less.*

August 11–18
THE WEEK OF LEADERSHIP
LEO III

August 19–25
THE CUSP OF EXPOSURE
LEO-VIRGO CUSP

Secret Aspirations

The bond in this relationship is highly empathic, encouraging openness, acceptance and sensitivity between its partners. But this doesn't necessarily translate to the outside world. Both of these personalities have a hidden side that can be dark, even volcanic; sensing and understanding this in each other takes them a long way in establishing a relationship unique to them. They can easily adopt an "us against the world" stance, which may simultaneously isolate them and support them in their individual aspirations. Leo III's and Leo-Virgos may play complementary roles, especially when Leo III's sit in the driver's seat with Leo-Virgos right behind them pushing them along. In the long run, Leo III's may become dependent on Leo-Virgos, not only for backing them up but also for believing in them.

In love and other close relationships, mutual dependency may continue unbroken throughout life, with each partner secretly needing the other's approval. Breaking such ties will be extremely painful but will sometimes be necessary if the partners are to develop and grow. In marriage, a Leo-Virgo spouse may unmercifully push a Leo III mate to achieve wealth and power, whether by moving up the corporate ladder or by some other means.

Friendships and sibling relationships in this combination may cripple the ability of Leo-Virgos to make it on their own. They will probably have had to play a subordinate role to the Leo III from an early age, which may make them secretive and repressed. Often frustrated in their own ambitions, and carrying the weight of a lifetime of longing for fame or wealth and of resentment over not having achieved it, Leo-Virgo parents can pin their hopes and dreams on Leo III children, who will unknowingly be programmed to be superachievers.

At work, Leo III's and Leo-Virgos are best off as equals in jobs where their strengths can meld profitably for the group without the emergence of invidious comparisons or competition.

ADVICE: *Define yourselves as individuals. Recognize what is yours. Be aware of what the relationship means to you personally. Promote equality.*

REGIS PHILBIN (8/25/34)
KATHIE LEE GIFFORD (8/16/53)

Philbin and Gifford are the co-hosts of *Live with Regis and Kathie Lee* (1989–), a weekday tv talk show. A winning combination, they are playful together, Gifford being the straight foil to Philbin's comic antics. **Also: Napoleon Bonaparte & Letizia Bonaparte** (son/mother); **Princesses Anne & Margaret** (niece/aunt; royalty); **George IV & William IV** (brothers; British kings).

August 11–18
THE WEEK OF LEADERSHIP
LEO III

August 26–September 2
THE WEEK OF SYSTEM BUILDERS
VIRGO I

An Inherent Transparency

This combination has a certain inherent transparency: it tends to reveal its partners, both to themselves and to other people, for what they really are. It is a completely straightforward relationship in which any secrets will be thrown up for the world to see. These two actually interact quite well with each other, experiencing few conflicts. Contributing to this, their relationship grants them an excellent sense of timing—they know when to act and to speak. Virgo I's are at least somewhat capable of working with or for Leo III's: they generally don't mind playing a secondary role to this dynamic, somewhat imperious partner. But in the long run Leo III energies will often prove too much for them to handle. Even so, they often have a deep understanding of the Leo III personality, and can lend them valuable support. Leo III's, for their part, may come to depend on having a Virgo I there for them, and in doing so may take this valuable association for granted.

In love affairs it is hard for these two to keep secrets from each other. Where Leo III's are happily dramatic, Virgo I's tend to be quiet and retiring observers; but that doesn't mean they escape the kind of scrutiny that is so common here. When they cannot handle this, nervous Virgo I's will often try to withdraw into their more private, structured world, which will make Leo III's feel rejected. These relationships can be passionate but also highly critical. If the partners can only take advantage of the opportunities they offer, they will be extremely beneficial to personal growth and development. Marriages in this combination are prone to be more judgmental—here Virgo I's will view Leo III's with a cold eye, being unimpressed by their histrionics.

Friendships and sibling relationships can be outstanding but are highly temperamental. In letting it all hang out, these duos show often collide powerfully in the emotional realm.

ADVICE: *Even out emotions. Stay open. Take advantage of your chance to develop. Work on eliminating self-consciousness. Let it flow.*

SUNNY VON BULOW (9/1/32)
CLAUS VON BULOW (8/11/26)

Aristocratic Claus was convicted in 1982 of trying to murder his socialite wife Sunny with an insulin injection. She fell into an irreversible coma. Claus was later cleared of the charges. The sensational case was the subject of the film *Reversal of Fortune* (1990). **Also: Shelley Winters & Vittorio Gassman** (married; actors); **Janice Rule & Ben Gazzara** (married; actors).

SUSAN SAINT JAMES (8/14/46)
JANE CURTIN (9/6/47)

Saint James and Curtin were the co-stars of the tv sitcom *Kate & Allie* (1984–89). They played a pair of divorced women with children, sharing an apartment in NYC's Greenwich Village. As actors, their teamwork and comic chemistry made the show highly popular. *Also:* **Sam Goldwyn & Sam Goldwyn, Jr.** (father/son; heads of Universal Pictures).

August 11–18
THE WEEK OF LEADERSHIP
LEO III

September 3–10
THE WEEK OF THE ENIGMA
VIRGO II

Spurred On

This relationship can be spirited and confrontational. Lively interchanges are probable between these very different individuals, and as working colleagues they usually respect each other's strengths, even if they don't care much for each other personally. Virgo II's may attack flamboyant Leo III's for insensitivity and egotism, and may be criticized in return for being uptight and judgmental. These two are extremely sensitive to disapproval, but there is a willingness to listen here, with the partners' ideas about each other often having a positive effect by spurring them on to better their best efforts.

If Leo III–Virgo II love affairs form at all, they are likely to be very direct, and short on emotional nuance. Underlying the couple's no-nonsense attitudes, however, may lie a welter of emotions that cannot be easily expressed. Suppressed feelings of anger, envy or even lust often dictate how these two treat each other in everyday life. The domestic responsibilities of marriages make them more likely to work out.

Friendships between these two can run extremely well. Close ties of belief, perhaps aesthetic, perhaps religious or spiritual, can open up new worlds, proving not just interesting but comforting. The matchup's need to share allows the partners to overcome their more selfish impulses and their fearfulness of being ignored or forgotten.

Career rivalries are not uncommon here, particularly when both partners have carved out their own niche. These two don't really deign to compete with each other, but they do keep a very close eye on each other's activities. Should Leo III's and Virgo II's work for the same organization, they are best off operating in different departments and having only occasional contact. Leo III–Virgo II sibling pairs may be extremely sensitive to each other's needs, but they can also be very irritable with each other—it is important that they both have their own private space.

ADVICE: *Join forces occasionally. Overlook differences and leave the past behind. Be a little tougher. Promote openness and understanding.*

AGNES DEMILLE (9/18/09)
CECIL B. DEMILLE (8/12/1881)

Choreographer Agnes, the niece of producer-director Cecil, was a major force in American ballet and musicals. Of her many triumphs, the choreography for Broadway's *Oklahoma!* (1943) may be her crowning achievement. *Also:* **Frieda Weekley & D.H. Lawrence** (married; cousin of Baron von Richthofen/writer); **Cecil DeMille & Jesse Lasky** (co-producers); **Sam Goldwyn & Jesse Lasky** (brothers-in-law; producers).

August 11–18
THE WEEK OF LEADERSHIP
LEO III

September 11–18
THE WEEK OF THE LITERALIST
VIRGO III

An Effective Working Combination

The strengths of this relationship are organizational and structural, so it is not surprising that the focus here can be reorganizing family, social or business groups or initiating new projects. Yoking the directional strengths and drive of Leo III's with the rationality and pragmatism of Virgo III's, these two can form an effective working combination. Virgo III's may not always approve of the showy manner of Leo III's, but they do not deny this personality's effectiveness in getting people's attention and holding it. When these two work together it is usually best for Virgo III's to do the early inside work (planning, writing proposals, doing research) and then send their well-prepared partner out into the world to make the case. When Leo III's return to report results, Virgo III's can close the circle by analyzing the data, beginning the cycle again.

In love affairs, both partners will usually be extremely guarded emotionally. Their sexual interactions can be quite thrilling, but this is no guarantee that the couple will reach any really deep level of feeling. They can both be quite selfish about getting what they want out of these relationships. As spouses they may cooperate and interact more easily, and will probably be very effective in setting up an efficient and workable family structure for daily domestic life, but they may also engage in power struggles. Although they both have nurturing tendencies, they would be advised to talk seriously about their ideas on child-rearing before committing themselves in this area.

Virgo III–Leo III parent-child relationships can be demanding and stressful, whichever partner is the parent. Even so, they will probably be the backbone of the family. Friendships in this combination, however, are likely to drift directionless if they lack a specific project to work on. Although both Virgo III's and Leo III's can stand sorely in need of relaxation, this relationship won't necessarily give it to them.

ADVICE: *Build greater bonds of trust. Try to have more fun. Share as much as possible, and in all areas of your life. Open your heart if you can.*

August 11–18
THE WEEK OF LEADERSHIP
LEO III

September 19–24
THE CUSP OF BEAUTY
VIRGO-LIBRA CUSP

Far from the Madding Crowd

More than most, this relationship is taken up with the personal side of its partners' lives. Its focus may be their mutual exploration of hidden areas of their characters—areas perhaps quite unknown to them, for both Leo III's and Virgo-Libras tend to lean heavily on social involvements, especially in their careers. This combination introduces them to a world of deep feeling. Perhaps just because they relate so well socially, they can feel relaxed enough with each other to begin exploring this private world, far from the madding crowd.

In love affairs, friendships and marriages these two often put social interests aside. Having gotten enough company during the workday, they tend to hang out with each other privately in the evenings or on weekends. They are not opposed to socializing occasionally with friends or family, and will add color to any gathering, but they often can't wait to get away to be alone together again. Should their relationship become an active pursuit of intimate pleasures, all well and good, but such pursuits are rarely enough in themselves: the relationship demands the kind of serious attitudes that lead to understanding and personal growth, and the partners will generally have little choice but to obey if they want to feel satisfied and fulfilled.

Career matchups between these two often don't work out, just because they cannot provide the intimacy that the relationship requires. At work, the deeper analyses of motives, plans and hunches into which these two naturally fall tend to make them self-conscious, and are most often counterproductive to the job at hand. Leo III's and Virgo-Libras bring flair and style to their family group, but their need to be alone together, particularly when they are siblings, may lead to their shutting out everyone else.

ADVICE: *Find a balance between social life and private life. Let go of claiming attitudes. Follow the evolutionary path. Don't shut others out.*

PRINCESS ANNE (8/15/50)
CAPTAIN MARK PHILLIPS (9/22/48)

Anne and Mark knew each other first as horse-riding enthusiasts. They married in 1973 with traditional royal fanfare and had 2 children. They gradually drifted apart amid rumors of Mark's affairs and a paternity suit. The couple separated in '89 and divorced in '92.

Also: Napoleon Bonaparte & Maria Borghese (brother/sister).

August 11–18
THE WEEK OF LEADERSHIP
LEO III

September 25–October 2
THE WEEK OF THE PERFECTIONIST
LIBRA I

The Perfect Facade?

The intensity of this very interesting combination can strike sparks, but these two can equally well seem to get along in an easygoing and comfortable way day-to-day. The face their relationship presents to the world can be a tad misleading, then. For one thing, the nagging question keeps arising as to what is on view here: something completely at ease, or a perfect facade? In fact, there is a lot more mystery here then anyone would care to admit. Although the relationship radiates self-assurance, insecurity lurks behind its doors.

Leo III–Libra I love affairs keep many secrets that not only never see the light of day but are never even suspected from outside. It's not that the couple has any great desire to conceal or hide things, it simply knows how to keep things to itself without arousing suspicion, an art indeed. Marriages, too, can develop a deep intimacy that precludes the need to talk about it to other people, even the closest family members. The same is true in friendships, which can adhere to pacts of loyalty that are both unbreakable and unspoken, never having been discussed or openly agreed upon.

Family secrets and the like are also characteristic of parent-child and grandparent-grandchild relationships. Leo III parents may exercise a strange and puzzling power over their Libra I children, and vice versa, as if each partner were always on the point of revealing something damaging about the other, especially in the area of broken promises. A love of humorous games, riddles and paradoxes is also characteristic of this relationship, which can keep both relatives busy and amused for hours.

In the professional world, business partners in this combination can be highly persuasive in selling a product, usually because they have an inspiringly natural and unassuming manner. Calculation will be quietly at work, however, particularly when there is the possibility of a good cash return. These two are rarely swindlers or cheaters—they believe in what they are selling, but not always as much as the buyer does.

ADVICE: *Are you being completely honest with each other? Something doesn't make sense. Have you solved your own mystery? Open up some doors.*

MISS LILLIAN CARTER (8/15/1898)
JIMMY CARTER (10/1/24)

Miss Lillian and son Jimmy, the former US president, were always very close. She commented, "Jimmy is sensitive and compassionate—painfully so. Once, when he was a little boy, his daddy shot a bird, and he cried. But he learned to fish and hunt. He's a learner."

Also: Steve Martin & Victoria Tennant (married; actors); **Rosalynn Carter & Jimmy Carter** (married).

STRENGTHS: SYMPATHETIC, PROTECTIVE, PLEASURABLE
WEAKNESSES: UNREALISTIC, DAMPENING, DOTING
BEST: LOVE
WORST: WORK

RICHARD, DUKE OF YORK (8/17/1473)
EDWARD V (10/6/1470)

Richard and Edward were the 2 child-princes lodged in the Tower of London in 1483 by order of their uncle, the scheming Duke of Gloucester (later Richard III). Upon their father's death, young Edward was king. But their parents' marriage was hastily declared invalid and the brothers illegitimate. Gloucester thus cleared the path to the throne, was proclaimed king, and the princes were murdered shortly after.

August 11–18
THE WEEK OF LEADERSHIP
LEO III

October 3–10
THE WEEK OF SOCIETY
LIBRA II

Brightening Up

This relationship can be extremely sensitive, sympathetic and understanding, especially in times of trouble. Libra II's have a way of lightening and brightening the day of a Leo III. Their psychological acumen can help Leo III's to work on emotional problems, teaching them how to deal with the demons that beset them. The relationship can also prove tremendously beneficial to Libra II's, strengthening their resolve and steadfastness. Leo III's may be protective of these partners to a fault, shielding them from worldly intrusions and taking a strong stand by their side when the going gets rough.

Love affairs between Leo III's and Libra II's can be sensual and pleasurable for both partners. Although Leo is a fire sign and Libra air, the Leo III–Libra II relationship is ruled by water, an element here producing free-flowing emotion and deep sympathy. Marriage can be recommended for this couple but will also test them: the hard realities of daily life may dampen their ecstatic moments and deaden their spontaneity and romantic impulses. They will either succeed magnificently or fail to cope with the exigencies of finance, child-rearing and other domestic responsibilities. Also, in both marriage and friendship, Libra II's may come to feel totally dominated by Leo III's, who only mean the best but can actually make their partners' personal development difficult or impossible. In cases such as this, Libra II's may learn invaluable lessons in standing up for themselves.

Fantasy may play too large a role in the relationship between Leo III's and Libra III's for them to make good business partners or co-workers. Siblings and parent-child combinations, however, can take their imaginative flights to the limit without causing much harm to other relatives. Leo III parents are prone to spoil their Libra II children and to dote on them.

ADVICE: *Back off a bit. Your concern may not be helping. Tend to practical matters. Learn to see the miraculous in the ordinary. Stay grounded.*

STRENGTHS: IDEA-ORIENTED, STIMULATING, RELAXED
WEAKNESSES: COMBATIVE, STORMY, DESTRUCTIVE
BEST: FRIENDSHIP
WORST: SIBLING

JIM SEALS (10/17/42)
DASH CROFTS (8/14/38)

Seals & Crofts were a popular, successful soft-rock duo in the 70s. Their vocalized harmonies captured the romantic spirit of the times in albums like *Summer Breeze* ('72) and *Diamond Girl* ('74). They were close friends and followers of the Baha'i faith. **Also: Shimon Peres & David Ben-Gurion** (protégé/ elder statesman; Israeli leaders); **Sam Goldwyn & Edgar Selwyn** (partners; movie pioneers).

August 11–18
THE WEEK OF LEADERSHIP
LEO III

October 11–18
THE WEEK OF THEATER
LIBRA III

All or Nothing

The emphasis in this combination is on practicalities—on fortifying intentions, clarifying issues, bringing projects to fruition. Yet intense rivalries can also emerge here. This is actually not at all surprising when one considers both partners' intense need to assume the leadership role, a need that can precipitate a break between them when they meet within an organization; they may both emerge at the head of separate and often competing groups. Ideology is a tremendously important issue in this matchup. It is usually ideas that unite or divide these two even more than personal likes or dislikes. Their relationship stresses philosophical orientation, facts and the given word. Relationships between these two can range from the relaxed to the stormy but are usually dynamic. They tend to be all or nothing—the partners are either absolutely united or bitterly opposed to each other. Even when they fight, though, there is often a common bond behind their struggle that ultimately makes them less enemies and more rivals, often over control of a common cause.

In love and sibling matchups, Leo III's and Libra III's may compete for the affections of a third party who might be enchanted by their attention but appalled at the level of combat involved. Their love affairs can be sexually satisfying and show real affection but are often marred by serious power struggles. Ideology is usually less important in marriages, but the spouses often have very different ideas about how to run the family. In the domestic and financial spheres particularly, tensions and friction will be the rule until binding agreements are reached.

Friendships here can be extremely close, with considerable mutual respect. They often grow out of professional associations, although they can also arise from them. Working together will bring out all of competition and strife of which the combination is capable, but if the partners hang in there and are willing to negotiate differences over and over again, the result could be an enormous success.

ADVICE: *Keep the good of the group in mind. Don't let struggles run out of hand. Keep an eye on other people who are not involved. Beware of ego drives.*

August 11–18
THE WEEK OF LEADERSHIP
LEO III

October 19–25
THE CUSP OF DRAMA & CRITICISM
LIBRA-SCORPIO CUSP

Closing the Circle

Although this relationship can feature a lot of conflicts and differences of opinion, it is often beneficial to both partners, and usually deals with carrying on the traditions and realizing the aspirations of the group to which they belong. Libra-Scorpios often have a greater feeling for tradition than Leo III's, who can, however, motivate them and encourage them in their worldly efforts. It is extremely important that a diplomatic balance be maintained here, for if the relationship fails in diplomacy it could be disastrously split by fierce confrontations and arguments from within.

In love affairs and friendships, compromise is very important. The partners must come to realize that it is in their own best interest to give their relationship their wholehearted support. Too often, Libra-Scorpios will go too far in their lacerating criticisms of Leo III's, assuming that these faithful Lions will stick around to take whatever they can dish out. Leo III's, for their part, may be overconfident, and may assume that their willpower can keep Libra-Scorpios in line. Keeping a realistic view and being more diplomatic will help in most areas.

In marital and business partnerships, the relationship will usually devote itself to practices that promote growth and development but will mainly use conventional methods that have worked in the past. In this way it winds up supporting and perpetuating the traditional systems on which those methods are based. A great challenge to the relationship will be thinking creatively without getting carried away by the kinds of urges to which both partners can be prone as individuals. True innovation will be difficult for this couple, but will also be necessary for their continued success.

In the family, parent-child relationships in this combination can be inspiring but also disillusioning. Mutually adoring but extremely possessive attitudes are common here. Again, a more realistic view is essential if disappointments and letdowns are to be avoided later on.

ADVICE: *Learn the value of compromise. Work for the common good. Give up possessive attitudes. Be as realistic as possible. Maintain stability.*

SHELLEY WINTERS (8/18/22)
TONY FRANCIOSA (10/25/28)

Actors Winters and Franciosa were married from 1957–60. Although Winters was first publicized for her earthy sexuality, she established herself as a quality actress from the 50s on. Franciosa moved from stage to screen to tv, where he starred in several series, most notably *The Name of the Game* (1968-71). Their marriage was her 3rd and his 2nd.

August 11–18
THE WEEK OF LEADERSHIP
LEO III

October 26–November 2
THE WEEK OF INTENSITY
SCORPIO I

An Underground Labyrinth

This extremely complex relationship is united by a common aesthetic—a love of beauty and harmony, and a shared creative vision—but may have a dark and labyrinthine emotional underground that few who view its shining exterior would suspect. Outwardly sunny, Scorpio I's deal with demonic intensities in their private lives, and Leo III's can trigger these in many hidden ways. Because neither partner rates especially high in self-understanding, the relationship risks being at the mercy of its own destructive forces.

Love affairs and marriages in this combination are often taken up with creating a happy home environment filled with design and art objects, color and light. In some ways this is an attempt to block out emotional disturbances that may be raging beneath the surface and threatening to break out. Scorpio I's may be conscious of a certain mastery over their Leo III lovers or mates, yet may simultaneously suffer from intense feelings of inferiority and despair. Leo III's are often unaware of their superior attitudes and uncaring of the suffering that Scorpio I's are going through. In arguments, when Leo III's go on a blazing attack, Scorpio I's usually retreat into their shell and then retaliate by lashing out defensively later on.

Friendships between Leo III's and Scorpio I's can be fruitful as long as they avoid deeper emotions. Patiently building trust and understanding can result in a relationship that is rock solid, reliable and trustworthy. At work, Leo III's and Scorpio I's can do well in creating attractive products and services that bring joy into the lives of others.

Parent-child relationships here are tricky and problematical. Leo III parents can dominate Scorpio I children, suppressing their more expressive side. Yet these children may come close to worshiping their Leo III parents, which will limit their personal development in ways that could prove highly debilitating in adult life. When Scorpio I's are the parents, Leo III children will probably rebel against overly controlling or claiming attitudes, in a desperate attempt to free themselves.

ADVICE: *Bring the light into your personal life. Beware of building such beautiful defenses. Put your intensity to work for you. Balance inner and outer.*

JERRY FALWELL (8/11/33)
LARRY FLYNT (11/1/42)

Baptist minister Falwell is a leader of religious-political conservatism in the US. Flynt is the infamous publisher of raunchy sex magazines. They clashed in a sensational libel suit (which Flynt won). The conflict was dramatized in the film *The People vs. Larry Flynt* (1996).

Also: Edith Kermit Carow & Theodore Roosevelt (married, his 2nd wife); **Ted Hughes & Sylvia Plath** (married; poets).

RELATIONSHIPS

STRENGTHS: IRREPRESSIBLE, POWERFUL, PLAYFUL

WEAKNESSES: AGGRESSIVE, INVULNERABLE, CRUSHING

BEST: LOVE

WORST: FRIENDSHIP

JELLYBEAN BENITEZ (11/7/57)
MADONNA (8/16/58)

Jellybean is a record producer and music remixer who became known through his disc jockeying. He met Madonna during one of his club dates, and she hired him to remix her first dance hit, *Holiday* (1983), after which they were romantically linked. They broke up right after the release of *Like a Virgin* (1984).
Also: **Menachem Begin & Yitzhak Shamir** (Israeli leaders).

August 11–18
THE WEEK OF LEADERSHIP
LEO III

November 3–11
THE WEEK OF DEPTH
SCORPIO II

Pretty Tough Customers

This combination can generate a great deal of fresh new energy. Direct in orientation and explosive in power, the Leo III–Scorpio II relationship can be unstoppable, or at the very least irrepressible. These two individuals are known to others as pretty tough customers, a quality that their matchup can magnify, but within the relationship they often show each other a sweeter side. Affection and sympathy are one thing, however, vulnerability is another, and neither partner is likely to show weaknesses or leave him- or herself exposed for long.

Love affairs between these two can be torrid but at the same time highly playful. A curious mix of childlike innocence and full-bodied maturity often characterizes the matchup. Direct confrontations here are not a pretty sight—Leo III's who are used to steamrolling their opponents may be in for a nasty surprise should they try this with a Scorpio II. Marriages are not recommended here unless the two are prepared to share domestic burdens and responsibilities. Should the relationship sour, Scorpio II's will tend to hang in there, but Leo III spouses who find the marriage oppressive are quite likely to seek solace or pleasure elsewhere, or, if the going gets rough, simply to quit.

A Leo III–Scorpio II working relationship is most effective when its prodigious energies can be put to work getting new projects on the rails, often ones that have never been attempted before. Work methods tend toward the unconventional here; the relationship rarely follows the textbook. Power-oriented, this team will not hesitate to crush any opposition. They should be aware, however, that this behavior could arouse powerful animosities, and if they really have the best interests of their organization at heart they will have to learn to temper their aggression. Leo III–Scorpio II friendships and sibling relationships are powerful but often unforgiving.

ADVICE: *Treat your enemies with a bit more respect. Direct your energies well. Victory is not the most important thing. Take time to relax.*

RELATIONSHIPS

STRENGTHS: FASCINATING, SOPHISTICATED, SUPPORTIVE

WEAKNESSES: STRESSED, SNOBBISH, CONTROLLING

BEST: WORK

WORST: FAMILY

ROBERT DeNIRO (8/17/43)
MARTIN SCORSESE (11/17/42)

Actor DeNiro and future friend director Scorsese grew up blocks apart in NYC's Little Italy. Scorsese used DeNiro for major roles in 9 films, often cast as the embodiment of urban society's neuroses. ***Also:*** **Malcolm-Jamal Warner & Lisa Bonet** (co-stars, *Cosby Show*); **John Derek & Linda Evans** (married; actors); **Hitchcock & Grace Kelly** (director/star); **Edna Ferber & George S. Kaufman** (co-authors).

August 11–18
THE WEEK OF LEADERSHIP
LEO III

November 12–18
THE WEEK OF CHARM
SCORPIO III

Dynamo-Gyroscope

This combination can be a very fruitful one. It often functions at a high level, with the partners spurring each other on to their best efforts. Should it appear at the center of a business, school or other organization, it can act as a dynamo in generating energy but also like a gyroscope, having a built-in capacity for stability. When it is a more personal kind of relationship, Leo III's will usually be fascinated with their charming Scorpio III partners and will not hesitate to enjoy fully what they have to offer. Scorpio III's will tend to lean on the powerful shoulders of Leo III's, particularly when they are friends or family, and will gain great comfort knowing that this partner's strength is available to them in time of need. Leo III and Scorpio III form a fixed square aspect in the zodiac (they are 90° apart, and Leo and Scorpio are fixed signs), which astrologically betokens unavoidable stress. In this case, however, there is also mutual stimulation, usually toward excellence in achievement. The pair has a perfectionist bent.

For love and marriage to be successful here, Leo III's and Scorpio III's must have a good mental and social connection as well as a physical or spiritual one. This is underlined by the fact that their relationship (a fire-water combination) is ruled by the element of air, here suggesting an aspiring and communicative nature. Leo III energies can unlock deep wells of Scorpio III desire, which will draw the Leo III like a magnet. Sensual feelings are likely to continue over the years, which augurs well for a permanent connection. Having children may be a great joy in this relationship.

Professional matchups between these two are often sophisticated in the extreme. They will not allow much personal involvement—objectivity plays a large role in their commercial success. These partners will not hesitate to put themselves under tremendous pressure in order to produce the highest quality work possible. Gaining each other's respect will help these two to work effectively together.

ADVICE: *Avoid overdependence. You can handle responsibility, but there is a limit. The end does not always justify the means. Respect other people.*

August 11–18

THE WEEK OF LEADERSHIP
LEO III

November 19–24

THE CUSP OF REVOLUTION
SCORPIO-SAGITTARIUS CUSP

Making a Splash

JOHN DEREK (8/12/26)
BO DEREK (11/20/56)

This combination is bound to be highly competitive. Even though these two understand each other on a deep level and have the potential to get along quite well, the nature of their relationship is such that this only raises the stakes—and the machinations. As individuals, Leo III's are usually more needy of attention than Scorpio-Sagittarians, but in this relationship both partners vie equally for the spotlight. Should Leo III's win their natural place as the star of the duo, or actually defeat their partner in business, love or sports, the humiliated Scorpio-Sagittarius will chafe and plot revenge. Fortunately, serious hatred is unlikely to emerge in the relationship, since both partners see their competition as ultimately an exhilarating game—in fact, they may grow to be close friends.

In love affairs and marriages, Leo III's tend to make the bigger splash in front of friends and family, but Scorpio-Sagittarians will usually hang back and wait for their opportunity to arise. It often takes just one well-aimed dart to burst the Leo III bubble. Leo III's who try to eclipse Scorpio-Sagittarians, or talk down to them, in their domestic life together may find themselves facing full rebellion and then all-out war. More sensitive Leo III's will generally avoid such confrontations—at least after the first one. Friendships between these two are competitive, seriously enough that both partners will give their all to win. Nothing could be more humiliating in these relationships than a victory that turns out to have been a gift from the opponent. The overall tone, however, is amicable. Sibling rivalries, on the other hand, may reach alarming proportions. An older child who is surpassed by a younger one in almost any area is apt to consider this indignity a wrong that must immediately be redressed. Nothing could be more embarrassing than competition between parents and children for the spotlight, but most Leo III–Scorpio-Sagittarius relationships of this kind are giving and supportive. In career matchups, co-worker pairs in this combination must be careful to avoid ego struggles that are counterproductive to the job at hand.

John and Bo married in 1974, whereupon he took control of her life and career. He spotlighted her in several mediocre movies for which he was director and cameraman. Many believe his guidance was detrimental to her career and that he turned her into a mannequin. He made money distributing photographs of her exquisite features.

ADVICE: *Give up childish struggles. Show some maturity. Have fun, but not at someone else's expense. Put your energy to a more positive use.*

August 11–18

THE WEEK OF LEADERSHIP
LEO III

November 25–December 2

THE WEEK OF INDEPENDENCE
SAGITTARIUS I

Cultivating Patience

ANGELA BASSETT (8/16/58)
TINA TURNER (11/25/38)

The focus of this relationship, and its greatest challenge, is coming into more meaningful contact with society. Both of these personalities have a rebellious or antisocial side that comes out in response to being told what to do by those in authority. Both Leo III's and Sagittarius I's have an innate sense of fairness and honesty that also often lands them in hot water. One of the important tasks for this relationship, then, is learning to be less outspoken and more diplomatic, not only toward other people but between the partners. This task will certainly include the cultivation of patience, for together these two tend to overreact.

In love affairs and marriages, each partner must quickly learn not to let the other push his or her buttons so easily. Learning to be more detached may be part of the solution; another part will be for both partners to be understanding enough to imagine themselves in the other's place. Passions often run high in this relationship, but natural affection and love will usually overcome other difficulties in the long run. Acquiring social skills as a couple interacting with others will often help maintain harmony, since it will include the attainment of politeness, diplomacy and tact.

Friendships in this combination have a chance of succeeding, but problems may arise over the strong Sagittarius I sense of right and wrong. Certain attitudes and activities of Leo III's, including their tendency to talk down to people they consider beneath them, may appear quite questionable to Sagittarius I's, who will also frown on their ability to overlook small daily tasks that they feel are just not worth their effort. Both career and family relationships will benefit from increased social contact. Sagittarius I's like to work without a lot of fuss or human interaction, and Leo III's can teach them something about the need to establish strong bonds with the people they deal with commercially. Parent-child relationships will similarly benefit from working together, and from bringing relatives together for celebrations and annual events.

Bassett turned in a powerful performance in her portrayal of rock star Turner in the 1993 film *What's Love Got to Do With It.* In preparation for the part, Bassett got to know Turner personally. Bassett's first leading role earned her an Oscar nomination.

ADVICE: *Cultivate social skills. Learn diplomacy and tact. Keep control of your emotions. Work on lessening your irritability. Be more open with others.*

STRENGTHS: ENTERPRISING, GENEROUS, PHYSICAL

WEAKNESSES: SELFISH, ARGUMENTATIVE, EXCESSIVE

BEST: FRIENDSHIP

WORST: MARRIAGE

DIAMOND JIM BRADY (8/12/1856)
LILLIAN RUSSELL (12/4/1861)

Wealthy businessman Brady and stage star Russell had a unique friendship based largely on such excesses as spending big money and overeating. He proposed to her often, once spilling $1 million into her lap. She declined, not willing to imperil a beautiful friendship.

Also: Gerty Cori & Carl Cori (married; Nobelists in medicine); **Magic Johnson & Larry Bird** (friendly basketball rivals).

August 11–18
THE WEEK OF LEADERSHIP
LEO III

December 3–10
THE WEEK OF THE ORIGINATOR
SAGITTARIUS II

Easy Outrageousness

This extremely enterprising matchup is full of life and energy. Whether these two are associates or opponents, their relationship fills the air with sparks and the night with shooting stars. This duo is not one to hang back when an especially demanding job needs getting done—they will generally be in the vanguard of any effort. So much enthusiasm and get-up-and-go can be a problem occasionally, causing the partners to overshoot the mark. Indeed, their excessive behavior can arouse the resentment and hostility of others, who may in fact be envious of their easy outrageousness.

Largesse is typical of social, professional and leisure-time activities here. These two will not hesitate to give of their time and money to assure that those they care about have what they need. Leo III's and Sagittarius II's are particularly tuned in to the socially disadvantaged, whose admiration they may awaken and whom they may inspire to better their condition. The more selfish aspects of the matchup often pop up in love affairs; especially in bed, both partners may be out for what they can get and may simply take their pleasure and run. Marriages are not recommended here without a radical reorientation of values.

Friendships between Leo III's and Sagittarius II's are often outstanding. Competitive sports and fitness activities are particularly recommended for them, helping them to engage their competitive drives and work off their frustrations. They will almost certainly have a tendency to argue, but their love of banter and light ridicule will often clear the air, allowing aggression to be expressed harmlessly. In the family, relationships between siblings of the opposite sex can be close and supportive; between siblings of the same sex, however, direct competition, of the kind that can end only in clear-cut victory or defeat, is usually the rule. Parent-child relationships may show a noticeable lack of understanding, sympathy and patience, whichever personality is cast in whichever part.

ADVICE: *Temper your stance a bit. Beware of excessive behavior, which can arouse hostility. Drives to overcome should be properly channeled.*

STRENGTHS: AMBITIOUS, HARD-WORKING, THEATRICAL

WEAKNESSES: UNREALISTIC, OVERCONFIDENT, UNFORGIVING

BEST: WORK

WORST: FAMILY

NAPOLEON BONAPARTE (8/15/1769)
MARIE LOUISE (12/12/1791)

When Josephine proved unable to give Napoleon an heir, he selected Austrian Marie Louise, an 18-year-old virgin whose prolific ancestry afforded him "the kind of womb I want to marry." True to her breeding, she presented him with a son shortly after their 1810 marriage.

Also: Rose Marie & Morey Amsterdam (co-stars, *Dick Van Dyke Show*).

August 11–18
THE WEEK OF LEADERSHIP
LEO III

December 11–18
THE WEEK OF THE TITAN
SAGITTARIUS III

The World Stage

This relationship is usually directed outward toward the world, the stage on which these partners enjoy playing their roles to the full. Whether in the fields of communication, politics, high finance or entertainment, they can work together effectively on big projects. Confrontation would seem inevitable between these two superstrong personalities, and it is true that neither of them likes to back down or give ground—but they can have tremendous respect for each other's abilities. Although clashes are inevitable in friendships in this combination, in marriages and love affairs these two can make a great combination, especially if they are dedicated to a common cause.

Marriages are usually a better bet than friendships or family matchup which are too often torn apart by struggles to see who will come out on top. Bringing their marriage to a high social, financial, cultural or intellectual level can often unite Leo III's and Sagittarius III's and overcome personal differences or combativeness.

When taking on opponents or putting together their own team, these two are tremendously aware of their image. As partners in business enterprises or professional productions, they instinctively know that their success depends on the message they convey to others, especially as concerns their own self-confidence and credibility. Allowing for human error on the part of their employees may be a problem for the pair, who can be severe and unforgiving—to their victims, their explosions of anger may feel like getting hit by a lightning bolt. Although able to inspire great confidence in their staff, Leo III's and Sagittarius III's should realize the importance of admitting failure and giving adequate and honest praise or acknowledgment to others, including opponents. Underestimating the enemy is one of this matchup's most glaring weaknesses and can lead to its downfall.

ADVICE: *Give credit to your opponents. Don't think yourself infallible or unbeatable. Assess your strengths realistically. Be more kind.*

August 11–18

THE WEEK OF LEADERSHIP
LEO III

December 19–25

THE CUSP OF PROPHECY
SAGITTARIUS-CAPRICORN CUSP

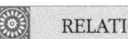
STRENGTHS: **POWERFUL, PASSIONATE, MAGNETIC**

WEAKNESSES: **DESTRUCTIVE, SUFFERING, RESTRICTIVE**

BEST: **LOVE**

WORST: **FRIENDSHIP**

Activating the Core

This matchup certainly has a core of power—the principal questions are how that power will be handled, and to what purposes it will be put. Radiant Leo III energies can penetrate to the darkest core of the Sagittarius-Capricorn personality, activating deep emotions, both positive and negative. Sagittarius-Capricorn emotional magnetism can likewise touch off smoldering Leo III energies, making them erupt volcanically. This combination of powerful forces in the relationship makes it a dangerous one, to be approached with great care. Fortunately, these partners rarely rush into involvements with each other; they characteristically hang back a little warily, assessing the territory with an experienced eye.

Love affairs between these two are often kept hidden from the prying eyes of the world. Neither partner is interested in exhibiting the relationship publicly—their energies are usually turned inward. They may find great sexual satisfaction here, but also emotional suffering and perhaps, on a regular basis, depression. Leo III's will be frustrated when Sagittarius-Capricorns clam up, and Sagittarius-Capricorns will find Leo III's bossy and restrictive, yet both may also experience all-time highs of passion with each other. They should try to understand their psychological states more fully and to even out their moods if they are to achieve lasting happiness in love or marriage.

At work and in friendships and sibling ties, Leo III's and Sagittarius-Capricorns can move between being on-again, off-again allies and being enemies at various stages of their lives together. It is not that their relationship is an on-again-off-again scenario, but rather that it is a real love-hate situation, in which extreme feelings are almost always present. If the power that the relationship generates can be turned outward to mutually rewarding projects, the pair will get along tolerably well. If it is turned inward on the partners, however, the results can be highly destructive. While the choice would seem to rest with the partners themselves, in reality it often lies with external circumstances and the subtle workings of fate.

ADVICE: *Lighten up. Try having fun with others in a social setting. Avoid extremes of feeling. Direct your energy toward a constructive goal.*

MENACHEM BEGIN (8/15/13)
ANWAR SADAT (12/25/18)

Following a costly war, Egyptian President Sadat decided in 1977 to initiate talks with Israeli Prime Minister Begin, culminating in the historic Camp David Accords. For this achievement both received the 1978 Nobel Peace Prize. **Also: Emperor Franz Joseph & Empress Elizabeth** (married; Austrian royalty).

August 11–18

THE WEEK OF LEADERSHIP
LEO III

December 26–January 2

THE WEEK OF THE RULER
CAPRICORN I

STRENGTHS: **INCISIVE, UNITED, QUALITY-ORIENTED**

WEAKNESSES: **CUTTING, MONOLITHIC, DEMANDING**

BEST: **WORK**

WORST: **LOVE**

Few Excuses

This pair's domination of any situation will be so complete that anyone in their vicinity will prefer getting out of their way to grappling with their monolithic relationship on any level. Their attitudes are highly critical, but they are as demanding of themselves as they are of others, accepting few excuses for shoddy or substandard work or results. When these two team up, their co-workers, employees or children may have a really tough time.

Love affairs between Leo III's and Capricorn I's can initially be quite dramatic, but over the years will become more conservative, even grave or humorless. Serious efforts should be made either to breathe new life into such relationships or else to let go of them and move on. Marriages may bleed over into career areas, with both spouses playing effective roles in business and professional endeavors. Capricorn I's want to rule, and may do well managing, organizing and administering affairs in the office or home, while Leo III's like to lead, and will take the initiative in the world, or inspirationally direct personnel in their endeavors. At home these two get along well enough as long as the division of labor is equitable and they both have their own unquestioned domain. Children should be given choices whenever they approach these parents for something, however, and their individuality should be encouraged.

Friendships in this combination can feature ironic and sarcastic attitudes that are also extremely funny. These two love a good joke and don't mind laughing at their own foibles, or at those of their relationship. Incongruities of all sorts attract their attention, and they are telling in their comments and cutting in their criticism.

In parent-child relationships of either possible combination, parents can be terribly demanding of their children, who tend to be obedient and respectful but also fearful. Unless avenues of communication are opened and empathy is deepened, the relationship can become increasingly silent and forbidding as the years go by.

ADVICE: *Maintain your individuality. Allow room for choice. Beware of repressive tendencies. Lessen inhibitions.*

LEW FIELDS (1/1/1867)
JOE WEBER (8/11/1867)

Weber & Fields were considered one of the great comic duos in vaudeville history. They debuted at age 10 and within 5 years had established themselves as the #1 roughhouse comedy act in the country. Typically, the skinny Fields tried to con the rotund Weber into doing something he didn't understand at all.

593

STRENGTHS: **RESPONSIBLE, PERSEVERING, DISCIPLINED**

WEAKNESSES: **DENYING, MISTRUSTFUL, OVERSERIOUS**

BEST: **LOVE**

WORST: **PARENT-CHILD**

FERNANDO LAMAS (1/9/20)
ARLENE DAHL (8/11/28)

Lamas and Dahl, for the 6 years of their marriage (1954–60), were the epitome of the Hollywood glamour couple. She was a ravishing redhead and he a slick-haired Latin lover. They appeared on screen together once, in *The Diamond Queen* (1953). Their son Lorenzo is a tv/film actor. **Also: Sam Goldwyn & Adolf Zukor** (movie moguls).

August 11–18

THE WEEK OF LEADERSHIP
LEO III

January 3–9

THE WEEK OF DETERMINATION
CAPRICORN II

Practical Dreams

This relationship is most fulfilled when ideas are brought down from loftier realms and grounded as realities. These two are specialists at achieving their dreams, and their highly practical intelligence prejudices results in their favor and guarantees success. They are capable of giving up a lot in order to get where they want to go. By learning to do without and subjecting themselves to strict discipline, they slowly build willpower and self-confidence. The road to success for this relationship is made up of many tiny steps, but the march toward the goal is unrelenting.

Love affairs between Leo III's and Capricorn II's take time to develop. Their passion is not immediately overwhelming, but grows as the relationship deepens and bonds of trust are formed. It is important to this couple that their love be recognized and taken seriously by family and friends. Whether or not they are married is less important than their mutual commitment—in fact, marriage is unlikely to change their relationship much. Taking absolute responsibility for one's actions is a given in this matchup.

It is usually best for lovers, mates and friends in this combination to have separate careers. They can help each other out from time to time, but they should have their own primary professional interest. If they do become co-workers or business partners, Leo III's and Capricorn II's do best when they avoid the personal realm, so that they can give all their energy to the job at hand.

Leo III's are usually attentive and caring parents to Capricorn II children but tend to dominate their lives. Adolescence generally brings the usual separation between parent and child, but this may take the form of Capricorn II kids firmly bidding their Leo III parents farewell and going off on their own, rather than growing rebellious.

ADVICE: *Be silly together occasionally. Be a bit more forgiving. Spoil yourself from time to time. Spartan attitudes are not necessarily fulfilling.*

STRENGTHS: **PHYSICAL, INTENSE, CHALLENGING**

WEAKNESSES: **UNPREDICTABLE, WARY, VIOLENT**

BEST: **SIBLING**

WORST: **WORK**

FIDEL CASTRO (8/13/26)
FULGENCIO BATISTA (1/16/01)

Castro was a 50s revolutionary who led a determined campaign to overthrow Cuban dictator Batista. He first organized his guerrilla movement in 1956. It took 3 years to depose Batista, who fled to Spain in '59 and died there in '73. **Also: Daffy Dean & Dizzy Dean** (baseball brothers); **J.P. Warburg & Felix Warburg** (nephew/uncle; financiers).

August 11–18

THE WEEK OF LEADERSHIP
LEO III

January 10–16

THE WEEK OF DOMINANCE
CAPRICORN III

Guarded Respect

This relationship is likely to be extremely intense. Leo III and Capricorn III lie quincunx to each other in the zodiac (150° apart), so astrology predicts some instability between them. In addition, they are both very stubborn and are unlikely to back down in any confrontation, so that their tempers can quickly flare and get out of hand. Anger, aggression and violence can emerge in this relationship, and special care will have to be devoted to handling them. It would be a mistake to suppress them, or to see them as unacceptable; a healthier approach would be to sublimate them into healthy competition, perhaps in sports but also in challenging card and board games like bridge and chess.

Love affairs between these two may not develop at all, since each has a certain wariness of the other's power to hurt them. But should they become fascinated with each other, they are likely to struggle to occupy the dominant role. Marriages are only recommended for highly evolved Leo III's and Capricorn III's who have fully thought out the implications of their heavy confrontations in a daily living situation. Should these spouses have children, they must be aware of being overprotective of them, smothering their independence and individuality.

Friendships are less likely in this combination than rivalries and outright hostilities. Where Leo III's tend to be lightning swift in their movements, Capricorn III's hang in there, providing effective resistance. Both partners are liable to cast themselves in heroic roles, depending on others to respond to their often charismatic leadership qualities.

Leo III–Capricorn III sibling relationships can be remarkable, particularly when of the same sex. Although the pair will inevitably argue and act unpredictably in childhood, later on they are likely to become an effective team in some field or another, possibly in the financial, political or physical realm. Business relationships and partnerships are not recommended in this combination.

ADVICE: *Get your differences out in the open. Confrontation may be necessary. Limit emotional involvement. Channel energies constructively.*

August 11–18

THE WEEK OF LEADERSHIP
LEO III

January 17–22

THE CUSP OF MYSTERY & IMAGINATION
CAPRICORN-AQUARIUS CUSP

Learning Endeavors

This combination suggests a teacher-student relationship. Even in the absence of a formal school situation, these two are likely to be united in a learning endeavor, often more practical than theoretical in nature. Should Capricorn-Aquarians be cast in the role of teacher, they will guide the abundant energies of Leo III's with unerring instinct. Leo III's may prove a bit dictatorial in their treatment of Capricorn-Aquarians, initially arousing their rebellion, but will ultimately earn their respect.

In love affairs and friendships the relationship's energy tends to go into deepening its ties of intimacy and sensuousness. There is often a secretive quality here. Although these two are emotionally flammable, their combination can be remarkably well grounded. They often prefer spending time alone together to social contacts, and should beware of becoming too isolated or mutually dependent.

Marital and family relationships between Leo III's and Capricorn-Aquarians can provide just the right balance between personal and social interaction. Parent-child relationships are often outstanding and especially educational, so long as the child is given room for self-expression and experiment. Whether as spouses or as other combinations of relatives, Leo III's and Capricorn-Aquarians are best together when they avoid a strictly didactic approach: the partner in the student role should be taught to teach him- or herself, gradually permitting the teacher to disengage from the whole learning process.

Career connections between these two can be terrific. Usually one partner has more experience and shows the other the ropes. Competitive urges seldom surface, for Leo III's and Capricorn-Aquarians generally concentrate on what they can learn from each other rather than getting involved in power struggles. The relationship emphasizes creative endeavors of all sorts, with connections relating to the arts being particularly favored.

ADVICE: *Take time out from your studies to have fun. Don't get too tied up in each other's thoughts. Maintain individuality. Personalize expression.*

SUZANNE FARRELL (8/16/45)
GEORGE BALANCHINE (1/22/04)

Ballerina Farrell trained at the American School of Ballet, where she was discovered by Balanchine. From 1948 to his death in '83, Balanchine devoted himself to the NYC Ballet, which Farrell joined in '61, rising to principal dancer in '65. After a 10-year absence, Farrell rejoined Balanchine's company in '75. **Also: Alfred Hitchcock & Tippi Hedrin** (director in love with star).

August 11–18

THE WEEK OF LEADERSHIP
LEO III

January 23–30

THE WEEK OF GENIUS
AQUARIUS I

Heavy Karma

This relationship can be deeply symbiotic. While not always mutually beneficial, the Leo III–Aquarius I matchup is extremely close, and in some cases the pair are inseparable. These two are especially conjoined in the realm of feelings, but this doesn't mean their connection will necessarily be loving or even sympathetic. One gets the impression, however, that the relationship has a heavy karma—that it was fated or meant to be.

Like other relationships in this combination, romantic ties here will have an air of inevitability. The way Leo III and Aquarius I lovers meet will almost always have a hint of the serendipitous. Nor do chance happenings end with early meetings: the unexpected is usually a part of the relationship's very fabric. Making schedules, dates or checklists is often considered undesirable here, for the spontaneous expression of feelings is a high priority.

In marriage, Leo III dominance usually emerges and, in fact, may be needed to get more flaky Aquarius I mates on track. Aquarius I's will benefit from this kind of pressure, usually becoming stronger and more responsible through the relationship's influence. And if things are going well with their Aquarius I partners, Leo III's may be able to give up their need to control and direct.

At work, Aquarius I mental creativity may arouse the envy and resentment of Leo III's, making them look as if they were moving in slow motion—even though they themselves are no slouches in creative agility. Yet the combination these two make together can be even more inventive and productive than either of them alone, assuming, of course, that they permit their respective strengths to coalesce. As in certain chemical reactions, a catalyst may have to be present to start the whole process off: perhaps a person, a place, even a certain kind of day. Sibling relationships and friendships can also be inseparable, but care must be taken not to arouse the jealousy of other friends and relatives.

ADVICE: *A little structure doesn't hurt. Don't overdo your reliance on spontaneity and chance. Be aware of the needs of others.*

AMADEUS MOZART (1/27/1756)
ANTONIO SALIERI (8/18/1750)

Although the film *Amadeus* (1984) portrays Salieri as a mediocre composer insanely jealous of Mozart's genius, in fact he was a celebrated operatic composer in his own right who admired Mozart. They were both considered gifted in their time. **Also: Mae West & W.C. Fields** (movie co-stars); **Roman Polanski & Sharon Tate** (married; director/actress); **Robert Redford & Paul Newman** (friends; co-stars).

STRENGTHS: **DIPLOMATIC, NATURAL, ENJOYABLE**

WEAKNESSES: **MANIPULATIVE, COERCIVE, SELFISH**

BEST: **LOVE**

WORST: **SIBLING**

NAPOLEON BONAPARTE (8/15/1769)
TALLEYRAND-PÉRIGORD (2/2/1754)

Talleyrand participated in the coup that helped Napoleon rise to power as emperor (1804). Napoleon rewarded him with property and titles. But after 1805, Talleyrand grew apart from the emperor, whose ambitions he regarded as excessive. He resigned in 1807 and began scheming with Napoleon's foreign enemies.

August 11–18
THE WEEK OF LEADERSHIP
LEO III

January 31–February 7
THE WEEK OF YOUTH & EASE
AQUARIUS II

The Path of Least Resistance

These two will invariably take the path of least resistance in whatever ventures and directions on which they embark. Their ability to identify and teach themselves the simpler and more direct route to any problem's solution will make them seem quite brilliant. Their relationship makes them nonconformists, unafraid to choose the road less traveled. It is usually the Aquarius II who shows the Leo III how to do things the easier way. Leo III Leaders tend to barge through any obstacles they face, whereas Aquarius II's usually find another way around any difficulties without confronting them directly.

In love affairs, Leo III intensity is tempered by the more relaxed attitudes of Aquarius II's, producing a matchup at once exciting and enjoyable. Both partners often grow to love their relationship as much as or more than they like each other. Thus the affair treads the middle ground, partaking of the best each partner has to offer. Its sensuous tendency is underlined by the fact that Leo III and Aquarius II, ruled by fire and air, respectively, form a relationship governed by the element of earth, here emphasizing carnal delights. Marriages between these two may not be taken completely seriously by other people but can work out well as long as Leo III's don't get too bossy and Aquarius II's too irresponsible.

Sibling matchups and friendships in this combination are not always harmonious, since each partner is all too aware when he or she is being coerced or manipulated by the other. The fist-in-the-velvet-glove routine works well on other people but is all too transparent when employed within the relationship itself. Career matchups, on the other hand, can go extremely well, usually with Leo III's taking the lead and Aquarius II's acting as their right hand, advisor and confessor. Hanging loose in the saddle is not a Leo III specialty, but this relationship's natural quality eases tensions all around. Leo III's lend dynamism to Aquarius II's, who, in turn, can make their partner's directives more palatable to other people.

ADVICE: *You can't have things your own way all the time—sometimes you have to conform. Take but also give. Be both more and less serious.*

STRENGTHS: **MAGNETIC, IDEALISTIC, MAGICAL**

WEAKNESSES: **SMUG, DISILLUSIONED, SHUNNED**

BEST: **PLATONIC LOVE**

WORST: **WORK**

MENACHEM BEGIN (8/15/13)
KING FAROUK (2/11/20)

It was Egypt's King Farouk whose ambitious nationalist foreign policy in the 40s brought about conflict with Britain and the disastrous Arab-Israeli war of 1948. Begin, then a military hero who led the guerrilla movement against the British, became an avowed enemy of Farouk.

August 11–18
THE WEEK OF LEADERSHIP
LEO III

February 8–15
THE WEEK OF ACCEPTANCE
AQUARIUS III

Bringing Ideals to Others

A study in polarity, and standing 180° apart in the zodiac, these two exert a tremendous pull on each other. Their relationship often has a magnetic attraction, irresistible in its charm. Working through synergy, it can reconcile and integrate its partners' extreme differences in attitude and lifestyle. Aquarius III's can be every bit as strong as Leo III's, but in a different way: they have a visionary power, which is often pitted against Leo III physical power but in the best-case scenario coalesces with it, so that the pair work together to bring higher ideals and beliefs to their immediate circle, or to the public at large.

The human condition is an important concern for these two, who will want to live life on a higher plane. The love they express for each other tends to be of the platonic variety, and abjures selfish advantage or pleasure. Leo III's discover a whole new side of themselves in this relationship, but must be careful of succumbing to the lure of exerting psychological power or attempting manipulation once they let go of their preoccupation with physical power. These two often view their marriages with a reverent and even religious awe. Disillusionment and rejection are often the fruits of such unrealistic visions and expectations.

At work and in the family, Leo III's and Aquarius III's must be careful not to get carried away by their ideas, particularly should they be tempted to try to convert their co-workers or relatives to their belief system. Proselytizing or better-than-thou attitudes on this pair's part may lead to their being shunned by others in their group. When they are friends, their shared idealistic impulses may involve them in each other's beliefs and goals, but should not so divest them of their egos that they no longer fully acknowledge their own individuality. Following a path of service, perhaps by taking on quite menial responsibilities and grounding itself in the here and now, will help this relationship keep its feet on the ground.

ADVICE: *Don't elevate yourself above others. Speak in simple language. Don't convince others against their will. Remember who you really are.*

August 11–18

THE WEEK OF LEADERSHIP
LEO III

February 16–22

THE CUSP OF SENSITIVITY
AQUARIUS-PISCES CUSP

RELATIONSHIPS

STRENGTHS: **AMBITIOUS, TRADITION-LOVING, RADICAL**

WEAKNESSES: **UNSYMPATHETIC, REPRESSED, OVERCOMPETITIVE**

BEST: **FRIENDSHIP**

WORST: **FAMILY**

Battering Down the Gates

The focus of this combination is an interesting blend of conservative and radical viewpoints. It is a relationship that simultaneously values traditions of all kinds and espouses modern, forward-looking ideas. Some might term it new age or consider it esoteric. Aquarius-Pisces are tough on the outside but hypersensitive on the inside, whereas Leo III's can be tough all the way through. While these two are very similar in their drive toward worldly success, then, they are quite different when it comes to their inner lives and their approach to their relationship.

In love affairs and friendships, Aquarius-Pisces have much to teach Leo III's about emotion, but first they usually have to unlock their own repressed feelings. The unique chemistry of their relationship with Leo III's can often accomplish exactly this, since they will have encountered a partner who will not take no for an answer if a deeper involvement with an Aquarius-Pisces is the goal. By hammering down their defenses, Leo III's often succeed in reaching that deep and invaluable emotional stratum in which Aquarius-Pisces have so much to offer.

Marriages and family relationships may suffer when Aquarius-Pisces end up having to shoulder crushing domestic burdens. True, their need to nurture must be met, but an unsympathetic Leo III should not be allowed to take advantage in this area. It is extremely important in these matchups for Leo III's to work side by side with Aquarius-Pisces in sharing mundane daily tasks, not only for their own personal development but to strengthen the relationship and show they really care.

At work, these two could well go to the top, whether as business partners or freelancers. The product they sell or the service they offer often has a claim to better existing alternatives through its mix of the traditional and the radical. Fiercely competitive against rivals, the relationship is usually united internally. Should its energy wane or its vision blur, however, squabbles and rifts will inevitably surface.

ADVICE: *Don't just steamroll your opponents. Show sympathy and understanding toward each other. Dig deep for emotional treasure.*

MICHAEL JORDAN (2/17/63)
MAGIC JOHNSON (8/14/59)

Jordan and Johnson, onetime basketball rivals, became teammates in 1992, when they were members of America's sensational Dream Team at the Olympics. They led the US team to a gold medal. On and off the court they are good personal friends.

Also: Princess Anne & Prince Andrew (sibling royalty).

August 11–18

THE WEEK OF LEADERSHIP
LEO III

February 23–March 2

THE WEEK OF SPIRIT
PISCES I

RELATIONSHIPS

STRENGTHS: **VERSATILE, COMMUNICATIVE, ENERGETIC**

WEAKNESSES: **UNFOCUSED, SELF-DEFEATING, CHAOTIC**

BEST: **WORK**

WORST: **MARRIAGE**

Overly Open

This relationship is all about communication and versatility, encouraging its partners to be more open and to branch out in their interests. Its energies will have to be controlled and directed, however, for they can easily get out of control. And although researching new areas is characteristic of the relationship, these two should be careful not to waver in their attention to the job at hand or to spread themselves too thin. Self-defeating in certain respects, the Leo III–Pisces I relationship needs to keep its feet on the ground and its eye on the prize.

Love affairs may suffer through an overly open outlook, with commitment seldom considered, let alone discussed. These partners often don't oppose each other's attractions to other people, and even encourage them, a trait that may undermine the relationship. And when they really need to spend a good deal of time together, slowly building their intimacy, they tend to be busily flying off in all sorts of other directions. The couple should not attempt marriage unless these tendencies can be kept under control and commitment can be worked solidly into the equation.

Professional relationships between these two can be excellent. Social and financial partnerships often succeed through their mix of Pisces I technical expertise, sensitivity and experience with Leo III aggression, leadership and drive. The relationship will be effective in a wide variety of endeavors, but will generally attain its greatest success in one area in which it should invest the bulk of its energy. Friends and family members are not advised to work together in business.

Parent-child relationships between Leo III's and Pisces I's are likely to be somewhat stormy. Leo III parents may dominate their younger Pisces I children, then face extreme discontent and rebellion when those children reach adolescence. Pisces I parents are unlikely to understand their Leo III children or to provide the kind of strong guidance they require.

ADVICE: *Try doing one thing at a time. Don't get sidetracked so easily. Keep your energies well directed. Be realistic about what commitment means to you.*

ANNIE OAKLEY (8/13/1860)
BUFFALO BILL CODY (2/26/1846)

In 1883 military scout Buffalo Bill organized a wild west show featuring sharpshooter Oakley from 1885–1902. For years they worked together on the show's dramatized presentations of stage robberies, Indian fights and buffalo hunts, touring the US and Europe.

Also: Shimon Peres & Yitzhak Rabin (Israeli leaders); **Steve Martin & Bernadette Peters** (affair; film co-stars).

KARL LIEBKNECHT (8/13/1871)
ROSA LUXEMBURG (3/5/1871)

Opposing German participation in WWI, Liebknecht and Luxemburg formed the radical Spartacus League (1916), a precursor of the German Communist party. In 1919 they attempted an uprising and failed. They were promptly arrested and executed by German troops.

August 11–18

THE WEEK OF LEADERSHIP
LEO III

March 3–10

THE WEEK OF THE LONER
PISCES II

Breathing Space

This relationship does best when its partners have a great deal of independence from each other in daily life. It's not that they aren't close—on the contrary; it's just that the Leo III–Pisces II relationship is usually at its most healthy when both partners have enough breathing space and don't feel crowded. Although Pisces II's are generally the more introverted of these two, they have an extroverted side that the relationship can activate. They will also be sensitive to the needs of their partner in this combination, which Leo III's will appreciate, although this does not mean that Pisces II's will ultimately be able to satisfy them—or even be interested in doing so.

In the bedroom, Leo III's may prove too demanding for Pisces II's, who often prefer to keep it light. Should Pisces II's get deeply involved emotionally, on the other hand—a very big "if"—they may have trouble letting go of their powerful leonine mates, and in extreme cases may manifest a sex-and-love addiction. The problem for Pisces II's is that Leo III's can give a great deal of intensity to a love affair without being really involved at a deep emotional level. The extreme independence of thought and action that is the byproduct of this matchup may make marriage difficult or impossible.

Friends and siblings in this combination are likely to relate very well, especially if they don't have to see each other that often. They may depend on each other quite heavily for advice in times of stress. Here the relationship stresses mutual support and represents a font of understanding for its partners.

Working relationships between Leo III's and Pisces II's are best formed in situations where they are not closely cooperating co-workers but are independent of each other and able to make their own decisions, perhaps consulting with each other from time to time. As business partners they must be sure to have a good bookkeeper, accountant and financial adviser, for their skills in this area are not always the best.

ADVICE: *Get your emotions sorted out. Decide how deeply you want to get involved. Walk your own path. Give unconditionally and fully.*

LEE SCHUBERT (3/14/1875)
JACOB SCHUBERT (8/15/1880)

Lee and Jacob were 2 of the 3 brothers (the other, Sam) who built a powerful theater syndicate. By the late 20s they owned more than 100, notably the Schubert, Booth, Broadhurst and Barrymore theaters in NYC's Times Square area. The Schubert dynasty continues to the present day, with 16 Broadway theaters in its ownership.

Also: FDR, Jr. & John Roosevelt (brothers; FDR's sons).

August 11–18

THE WEEK OF LEADERSHIP
LEO III

March 11–18

THE WEEK OF DANCERS & DREAMERS
PISCES III

Speaking with a Glance

The level of communication in this relationship is extremely high—thought ranges freely. Both of these individuals are interested in ideas, and their matchup is particularly characterized by intellectual concentration and attention to detail. Little escapes the relationship's attention. This means that it can be mercilessly critical, of both itself and other people; and all that mental energy can create nervousness and worry. To avoid headaches and other symptoms of stress, Leo III's and Pisces III's will have to learn to indulge their more playful, nonserious side, even trying consciously to emphasize the physical realm more.

In love affairs, these two feel free enough to express themselves without fear of rejection. Yet their relationship can be extremely unstable emotionally. Leo III and Pisces III lie quincunx to each other in the zodiac (150° apart), a situation of instability that tends to raise the level of sexual desire and excitement but does not do much for the relationship's longevity. Marriage should only be attempted after a long-standing love affair has developed deep bonds of understanding and trust.

The advantages of open lines of communication can be observed clearly in this pair's working relationships and friendships. Leo III's tend to be more direct, Pisces III's more subtle, but this is a combination in which everything can be said with only a quick glance or gesture, particularly in crisis situations. The partners certainly know how to meet deadlines and produce under pressure, an ability that is often their trademark.

Siblings, especially of the same sex, may suffer together under parental restriction and long to break free. The relationship will usually let them cover for each other, providing an umbrella of protection against punishment meted out from above. It is not uncommon for these siblings to break out of the home situation together, and even to share living space in their early adult life.

ADVICE: *Don't play as hard as you work—learn to relax. Empty so you can recharge. Deadlines can be postponed. Turn off your mental motor.*

August 19–25
THE CUSP OF EXPOSURE
LEO-VIRGO CUSP

August 19–25
THE CUSP OF EXPOSURE
LEO-VIRGO CUSP

August 19–25
THE CUSP OF EXPOSURE
LEO-VIRGO CUSP

Playing Peekaboo

Is there room in there for both of you? These two are capable of stuffing their secrets in a cupboard, then crawling inside themselves. Hide-and-seek is a favorite Leo-Virgo pastime, and secrecy can be twice as much fun for two Leo-Virgos as it is for one. This combination may focus on the game of hiding the truth, then suddenly revealing it—an amusing and involving pastime but not necessarily a productive one. The relationship's emotional quality can be lighthearted or serious, helpful or obstructive, friendly or vicious, but in all cases it tends to be unpredictable.

Love affairs here are complex, confusing and seldom emotionally or physically satisfying. They seem to augment this personality's need to play emotional games, so that the lovers in this on-again, off-again relationship will rarely know where they stand with each other. Marriages, too, tend to lack stability, and are not particularly recommended.

Friendships between Leo-Virgos can be a lot of fun but also somewhat frustrating. The partners are somewhat unwilling to show their hands and have trouble being fully open with each other. Their pleasure in alternate concealment and revelation may prevent them from establishing trust. It's not that they outright lie to each other, but stretching or hiding the truth is commonplace here.

Some Leo-Virgo parent-child and sibling pairs compete directly with each other, others support and benefit from each other. In either case, they usually take notice of each other, although not necessarily openly: in fact, it may be hard for them to get each other's full attention, since Leo-Virgos are often wrapped up in their own world. In family matters they should recognize their shared interests and put their preoccupation with their private games on hold. At work, Leo-Virgos make good partners only if they make an effort to be objective and to keep two sets of eyes on the store. Unfortunately, mistrust may make them so vigilant about watching each other that they don't realize the cash register is being rifled by someone else.

ADVICE: *Straighten out the confusion or nothing will get done. Be more honest. Spend less time playing games. Try to be more consistent and reliable.*

RELATIONSHIPS

STRENGTHS: REVELATORY, FUN, INVOLVING

WEAKNESSES: MISTRUSTFUL, DISHONEST, CONFUSING

BEST: FRIENDSHIP

WORST: MARRIAGE

KING LUDWIG I (8/25/1786)
LOLA MONTEZ (8/25/1818)

Montez was a beautiful Spanish dancer who became the Bavarian king's mistress. When he made her a countess, she exerted great influence over political affairs—for which she was considered a cause of the 1848 revolution. She was banished and eventually died (1861) in poverty in the US.
Also: Eliel Saarinen & Eero Saarinen (father/son; architects).

August 19–25
THE CUSP OF EXPOSURE
LEO-VIRGO CUSP

August 26–September 2
THE WEEK OF SYSTEM BUILDERS
VIRGO I

The Chance for Metamorphosis

Emotional instability is the bugaboo of both Leo-Virgos and Virgo I's. The synergy of their relationship magnifies this weakness, which means that it magnifies nervousness, sensitivity and insecurity. Because these personalities can have an unsettling effect on each other, they must work hard to maintain a modicum of stability between them. On the other hand, the sensitivity and the feelings of many sorts that are likely to emerge in any type of relationship in this combination are, in an odd way, an achievement for these two, who, as individuals, tend to repress and hide their problems. Their combination encourages their interest in any and all spiritual or psychological disciplines that may help in the journey.

The challenges of love and marriage are multiple for this pair. Faced with unfamiliar emotions that they may be feeling deeply for the first time, their relationship at first tends to have to struggle to find itself. Once the partners become more comfortable with each other's feelings, they will begin to build bonds of understanding and trust. If they can hang in there through what are likely to be many setbacks, changes of direction and minor successes, the relationship will come into its own, often becoming increasingly spiritual. Over years of personal development, then, a basically practical couple may undergo a complete metamorphosis.

Friendships do best when grounded in physical activity. Competition is good for these two, since it brings out their forceful side and encourages them to develop willpower and concentration. In business pursuits and other professional enterprises, the establishment of concrete goals will bring out Leo-Virgo–Virgo I aspiration and fighting spirit. The building of self-confidence can be tremendously furthered by the prior achievement of a string of small successes. In the family, parent-child pairs in this combination may be somewhat dull, failing to inspire each other.

ADVICE: *Discover feelings but keep stable. Stay practical but aim for the stars. Don't be discouraged. Develop self-confidence. Believe.*

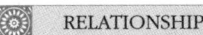

RELATIONSHIPS

STRENGTHS: DEVELOPING, TRANSFORMATIVE, FEELING

WEAKNESSES: UNSTABLE, NERVOUS, UNREMARKABLE

BEST: WORK

WORST: PARENT-CHILD

BERNARD BARUCH (8/19/1870)
PEGGY GUGGENHEIM (8/26/1898)

Baruch, an economic adviser and financier, was a close friend of art patron and collector Guggenheim, heiress to a family fortune. Baruch was a financial representative for the Guggenheims, developing investments and making profitable deals. **Also: William Rutherford Mead & Charles Follen McKim** (partners; architects).

STRENGTHS: **STRUCTURED, THEORETICAL, SYSTEMATIC**
WEAKNESSES: **OVERREACHING, HEAD-ORIENTED, UNFEELING**
BEST: **FRIENDSHIP**
WORST: **LOVE**

VALERIE HARPER (8/22/40)
JULIE KAVNER (9/7/51)

Following her popularity on *The Mary Tyler Moore Show*, Harper became the star of her own tv series, *Rhoda* (1974–78). One of the fine comic talents in the cast was Kavner, playing Rhoda's younger sister, Brenda. The players were excellent as down-to-earth New Yorkers. *Also:* **Louis Teicher & Arthur Ferrante** (piano duo).

August 19–25
THE CUSP OF EXPOSURE
LEO-VIRGO CUSP

September 3–10
THE WEEK OF THE ENIGMA
VIRGO II

Shifting Toward the Attainable

This relationship can get caught up in analyzing and creating all kinds of theoretical constructs. Becoming too reliant on a system of thought can be a problem here; a shift of emphasis toward the practical and objective is often desirable for these two. Their relationship has an inherent need for philosophical systems or structures, even a dependence on them, but it is important that these structures be periodically reevaluated or simply redirected. Leo-Virgos and Virgo II's may enjoy attempting the impossible together, but they are actually better off reaching for whatever is within their grasp. The problem is that backing a sure thing may prove a bit dull for them, taking the edge off the relationship's initiative and impulse.

Love and marriage between these two often don't gel. The more puzzling and inaccessible elements of their character somehow predominate here, preventing close contact. Sexual interactions can be exciting but without deep feeling.

Family relationships, especially between siblings, are sometimes extremely secretive. Keeping quiet about their shared activities is the categorical imperative for these two, with any infringements being severely punished. Parents of siblings in this combination may find it a tough nut to crack. As friends, Leo-Virgos and Virgo II's are similarly tight and often intensely physical, reveling in competitive sports and exercise. They also love games of strategy and humor, not excluding sarcasm, irony and even ridicule, and their own relationship has the ability not to take itself too seriously, pointing the finger as often at itself as at other people. This sign of health bodes well for these friendships, which have a mental power and an ability to interrelate that may help them to outlive many more "serious" matchups.

Working relationships here can be effective and efficient. These two are good at sniffing out wastefulness and inefficiency in other people's work, so that they can function well as managers, analysts and consultants. One drawback is that as a team they may overemphasize reason at the expense of intuition.

ADVICE: *Don't give up your spontaneity. Too much planning deadens creativity. Trust your heart more, your head less. Loosen up.*

STRENGTHS: **EDUCATIONAL, PERSONAL, EMOTIONAL**
WEAKNESSES: **EXCLUSIVE, PROJECTIVE, JUDGMENTAL**
BEST: **WORK**
WORST: **PARENT-CHILD**

DAVID COPPERFIELD (9/16/56)
CLAUDIA SCHIFFER (8/25/70)

Copperfield, master illusionist, has astounded audiences with his magic since 1977. He and his fiancée, supermodel Schiffer, live in NYC, where Schiffer opened the Fashion Cafe in 1995. *Also:* **Lili Boulanger & Nadia Boulanger** (sisters; composers); **Durward Kirby & Alan Funt** (co-stars, *Candid Camera*).

August 19–25
THE CUSP OF EXPOSURE
LEO-VIRGO CUSP

September 11–18
THE WEEK OF THE LITERALIST
VIRGO III

Freedom from Words

The partners in this highly personal relationship appreciate not only each other's abilities and talents but also their mutual chemistry. As individuals they are both cool customers, tending to be quite detached and objective, yet despite their strong mental connection the underlying foundation of their relationship is likely to be emotional. Leo-Virgos often see Virgo III's as role models or judges of their work, so that some kind of teacher-student relationship is common here, transmuting into the roles of guide or source of inspiration and follower or even worshiper. The relationship frequently appears in situations where the Virgo III is recognized as the established authority and the Leo-Virgo is cast as the young upstart on the scene.

Love affairs, friendships and marriages here can become isolated and exclusive, with neither partner having much time for anyone else but each other. Spiritual bonds may be as strong as physical ones here, but the heart of the relationship will be emotional. Both Leo-Virgos and Virgo III's sometimes have a strongly language-oriented, verbal side, which they enjoy sharing with each other. At the same time, they are both happy to establish a strong connection through unspoken feelings, taking pleasure in freeing themselves from the responsibility of expressing themselves with words. Indeed, their emotional interactions are often unspoken, which opens up whole new personal areas for mutual exploration.

Virgo III parents and bosses will fill a natural role with respect to Leo-Virgo children and employees, and will demonstrate great empathy and understanding. They will also have critical and judgmental opinions and attitudes to express, however, which should prove rewarding for Leo-Virgos, but if delivered too harshly could wound them deeply. Should Leo-Virgos idolize Virgo III's unduly, they may put these literal-minded realists in a very difficult position. They will have to shrug off these projections if they are to be themselves.

ADVICE: *Don't get so caught up with each other. Establish individual values. Open up to others. Beware of isolation. Balance the mental and the emotional.*

August 19–25
THE CUSP OF EXPOSURE
LEO-VIRGO CUSP

September 19–24
THE CUSP OF BEAUTY
VIRGO-LIBRA CUSP

Form Over Substance

This relationship skims along life's surface, preferring not to venture too deeply into motivations and feelings. Its emphasis is on outward beauty of form: although these two would certainly never accept something that was beautiful on the outside but rotten underneath, they probably wouldn't question its inner workings as long as it was functioning properly. This detached sort of objectivity does not bode well for deeper relationships. Leo-Virgos are drawn toward the worldliness and charm of Virgo-Libras, but are a bit appalled by their lack of interest in the deeper and more troubled elements in their own characters. Virgo-Libras may be highly attracted by the outward appearance of Leo-Virgos, but will have trouble understanding their preoccupation with the personal side of life. The pair may try to escape into an inviting pleasure labyrinth together, or may pursue the more exciting elements of social life and entertainment.

Love affairs in this combination are unlikely to be stable or deep. Sexual and sensuous fulfillment can soar, but the relationship does not foster deep understanding or trust. Despite their initial fascination, these two are basically uninterested in getting to know each other better. Nor are marriages much recommended: they can be a practical and sociable solution to problems the partners may have individually—loneliness, for example—but tend to be emotionally immature. Spouses in this combination will not want to rush into having children.

As family members, Leo-Virgos and Virgo-Libras may have trouble understanding each other. Breakdowns of communication will be common. As friends, however, they will have a lot of interests to share, perhaps as collectors or entertainment or sports fans. Games, too, can be absorbing and even obsessive for them. Working relationships may be more favorable still, with ambitious Leo-Virgos benefiting from the taste and the managerial and social expertise of Virgo-Libras, and more content Virgo-Libras getting the push they need from Leo-Virgo drive and willpower. Here the relationship shows great cleverness and adaptability, especially in finance. Leo-Virgos and Virgo-Libras are likely to be successful partners in freelance and business enterprises.

ADVICE: *Get to know yourself and each other better. Try to look deeper. Grow up emotionally. Puzzles can be solved, even human ones.*

BARBARA EDEN (8/23/34)
LARRY HAGMAN (9/21/31)

Eden and Hagman were the co-stars of the popular family sitcom *I Dream of Jeannie* (1965–70). In their roles as an Air Force officer who discovers a genie (Eden) in a bottle, they had a special chemistry during the show's run. At one point, the characters' platonic relationship grew into a tv marriage.

August 19–25
THE CUSP OF EXPOSURE
LEO-VIRGO CUSP

September 25–October 2
THE WEEK OF THE PERFECTIONIST
LIBRA I

Disinterest in Reality

This matchup shows a marked lack of interest in dealing with reality. Although both partners are more than capable of technical and practical accomplishment (in fact, as individuals they often place too much emphasis there), as a pair they are likely to give themselves over to the enjoyable pursuit of fantasy and imagination. By loosening the grip of their perfectionism, their relationship frees its partners and gives them a greater awareness of the sacred. Leo-Virgos consider themselves tougher and stronger than Libra I's, but here they will be more than willing to explore spiritual matters.

Love affairs in this combination can be an engaging blend of sensual and intellectual stimulation. It is not in the least unusual for the couple to discuss their sexual interaction even while in the midst of it. Both partners are open to experiment, and to giving their imaginations free rein. Seldom boring, Leo-Virgo–Libra I interactions may lack something in mystery, but they more than make up for it in excitement. Marriages may dull the intensity of love affairs, and the more intuitive Leo-Virgo and Libra I lovers may never seriously consider it.

Friendships and sibling relationships between these two are competitive but also mutually supportive and defensive. It may be unrealistic for the pair to take on heavy responsibilities—if they do, this could ultimately split them apart—but at the same time, meeting reasonable daily demands and deadlines will make them more responsible. Learning to share and abandoning selfish impulses will probably be the greatest challenge for this matchup. Animosities and rivalries often emerge between Leo-Virgo and Libra I business colleagues and co-workers. Secret envy may also play an important but undeclared role in their relationship. Outright competition and combat are quite possible between these two, especially when they serve rival organizations, and the insecurities that often come to the fore in such confrontations can bring out some of their very worst personal traits, particularly in terms of nastiness and aggression. It is also possible, however, for these situations to bring out their very best performances.

ADVICE: *Stop your worst side from coming out in argument. Take care of practical matters. Don't let responsibilities slide. Beware of taking on too much.*

GLENN GOULD (9/25/32)
LEONARD BERNSTEIN (8/25/18)

As a conductor, Bernstein performed and recorded together with pianist Gould. A child prodigy, Gould was noted for his unorthodox interpretations of Bach's music. While the music establishment often frowned on Gould's idiosyncratic renderings, the Canadian had a sizable public following. Bernstein more than once disavowed any connection with Gould's musical interpretations.

KEITH MOON (8/23/47)
JOHN ENTWHISTLE (10/9/44)

Moon and Entwhistle were original members of the great rock band The Who. Moon was known for his intense, hyperenergetic drumming style and Entwhistle for his agile, thundering bass lines. They played together from 1964 until Moon's death from a sedative overdose in '78. **Also: Harry F. Guggenheim & Robert Goddard** (financier of "father of rocketry").

August 19–25

THE CUSP OF EXPOSURE
LEO-VIRGO CUSP

October 3–10

THE WEEK OF SOCIETY
LIBRA II

Insatiable Interest

This combination manifests a considerable concern with its own needs, and with arranging life so that those needs are met and satisfied. It always handles these issues very practically, first analyzing a problem, then crafting a solution. If the partners are a tight-knit pair, this approach can go far in prolonging the relationship, but it can also happen that they are more concerned with their own needs than with their needs as a couple. An interesting dynamic can operate here when socially skilled Libra II's try to help the more personal side of Leo-Virgos—their inner life, ideas and thoughts—come to public light. As Libra II's discover this partner, they may want to get more involved. Leo-Virgos usually value their privacy, and will repel sheer inquisitiveness, but if they are interested in a Libra II's advances they could be surprisingly open to this partner's overtures.

Love affairs, marriages and friendships can all be sparked by the interest a Libra II takes in a Leo-Virgo. The more mysterious and inscrutable the Leo-Virgo is, the more interested the Libra II will often be. Should these two fall in love, the Leo-Virgo will often become even more completely the object of the Libra II's interest, but the relationship may grow more balanced over time. Together these partners will manifest an interest in all sorts of subjects, from science to film to psychology, and will seek to increase their knowledge through both study and experience. In marriages and friendships these pursuits may near the obsessive, and could eventually lead to a career path.

When these two work together the Leo-Virgo does best as the creative force, the Libra II as the producer, manager or promoter of the Leo-Virgo's work. A kind of hard practicality that sometimes emerges here goes a long way toward bringing success. The partners must be careful to prevent power drives from getting out of control—this combination can have a ruthless cast, through its driven desire to succeed. Libra II parents are unfortunately capable of exploiting a Leo-Virgo child.

ADVICE: *Try to be more moderate in your desires and interests. Monomania reduces peripheral vision. Value the privacy of those who interest you.*

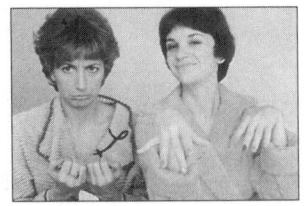

PENNY MARSHALL (10/15/42)
CINDY WILLIAMS (8/22/47)

Marshall and Williams were the co-stars of the popular sitcom *Laverne and Shirley* (1976–83), a spin-off from *Happy Days*. As Shirley, Williams was the perfect foil for the more dynamic comic persona of Laverne, played by Marshall, who also directed some of the 178 episodes produced. **Also: Renee Richards & Martina Navratilova** (transsexual coach/tennis star); **Aubrey Beardsley & Oscar Wilde** (illustrator/writer).

August 19–25

THE CUSP OF EXPOSURE
LEO-VIRGO CUSP

October 11–18

THE WEEK OF THEATER
LIBRA III

A Relaxed Collaboration

These two are likely to collaborate on projects that bring something new and exciting into the lives of other people. Whether their relationship emerges in the professional or the private side of their lives, it gives them an opportunity to kick ideas around in an environment of easy camaraderie. Libra III's can be powerfully dominant personalities, but their aggression is generally less apparent in this relationship. Leo-Virgos for their part may feel free enough with Libra III's to express their creativity, knowing they are appreciated and understood. The relationship may mark a high point in the lives of both partners, working to renew their good feelings about themselves and to reaffirm their self-confidence.

The condition these two could be in when coming out of a failed relationship or marriage might help a love affair between them take root. Their self-esteem will usually be low at this point. Such relationships generally start slowly, but move with a knowing purposefulness. Building trust is not always easy, but each small step increases confidence, establishing the idea that love might once more be a possibility. Leo-Virgos will appreciate not being hurried or pushed, and Libra III's will value simply being given a second chance to get it right.

Friendships in this combination may fall victim to temperamental differences, unless the pair are involved together in a hobby or social activity. Libra III parents tend to be bossy and a bit insensitive to the special needs of their Leo-Virgo children; Leo-Virgo parents can adore their Libra III children, but may feel inadequate to handle their often tumultuous energies.

In the professional sphere, this can be a truly special meeting of the minds, and its success can be tremendous. But as working teams Leo-Virgos and Libra III's often come together only for a single project; they rarely form lifelong partnerships. Even if their collaboration fades after the first endeavor, however, it may well mark a milestone in both partners' careers, and could launch them confidently in a whole new direction.

ADVICE: *Enjoy it while it lasts. Try to be more sensitive to each other's wishes. Build your self-confidence. Don't be unduly influenced by your past.*

August 19–25
THE CUSP OF EXPOSURE
LEO-VIRGO CUSP

October 19–25
THE CUSP OF DRAMA & CRITICISM
LIBRA-SCORPIO CUSP

An Imposing Front

This relationship puts a strong emphasis on outward appearance. Both partners here will be critical of each other's speech, looks, dress and manner, since they will assume that they will be hampered in their social aspirations if either of them appears looking dowdy or uncouth. Too much preparation before going out in public, however, may destroy the natural and unpremeditated air that can help put others at ease, so that a rigid insistence on turning an imposing face to the world may work against itself. Similarly, if this pair judges other people on how they look or act, it may miss out on the real person behind the mask. Bringing the inner and outer self into balance will be an important challenge for this relationship.

Love affairs here can be highly passionate, but the emphasis on superficial things bodes ill for deeper commitments. For these two, sexual enjoyment may actually depend on the other partner passing the objective tests of good looks and keeping fit. Since increasing age can obviously erode this ideal, relatively short-lived love affairs are more common than marriage between Leo-Virgos and Libra-Scorpios. Digging deep enough to appreciate the inner qualities of one's lover or mate is sorely needed in this combination.

Friendships and sibling relationships, too, may be powerfully affected by aesthetic likes and dislikes. Style and fashion often figure prominently, and not being "cool" enough in one's appearance or mien can be considered a grave sin indeed. Distressing situations can arise when one sibling or friend feels forced to reject the other for failing to meet the stern criteria of a social clique or individual. Looking back on such actions later in life, the partners may see their younger selves as immature, disloyal and unfeeling.

Leo-Virgos in the workplace are sometimes wary of Libra-Scorpio disapproval and a little distrustful of them. Libra-Scorpios meanwhile may be bothered by Leo-Virgo secretiveness. Forming a business or being executives in a company will be difficult for this pair, but they can be co-workers if their job is simple and well defined.

ADVICE: *Relax a bit about your appearance. Take the time to know the inner person. Ease up in judgments and criticism.*

FRANZ LISZT (10/22/1811)
LOLA MONTEZ (8/25/1818)

Liszt had an affair with the hot-blooded Spanish dancer, former courtesan of Bavaria's Mad King Ludwig. When Liszt got bored with their fling, he walked out on her one night as she slept in a hotel room, leaving money for the furniture he was sure she'd destroy in her outrage.

Also: Josef Strauss & Johann Strauss, Jr. (brothers; composers).

August 19–25
THE CUSP OF EXPOSURE
LEO-VIRGO CUSP

October 26–November 2
THE WEEK OF INTENSITY
SCORPIO I

Well Camouflaged

These two often convey a youthful impression and present an innocent and childlike exterior. The appearance of innocence has little to do with either the Leo-Virgo or the Scorpio I character; it is a product of their relationship. Both of these partners are actually objective, discerning people by nature, yet their relationship disguises their realism, presenting a facade that in many ways serves as a defense or smoke screen. Both of them are also highly secretive, and they make their convincingly sunny image a camouflage for whatever they are hiding. As Freud discovered, behind the open and trusting exterior that a child presents to the world lurks a dark side that can be chillingly selfish, ruthless and aggressive.

In love affairs and friendships the true nature of both partners can be revealed quite starkly, at least in private, where the childlike mask will be dropped whenever these two strong wills clash in combat. But few will see this side of the couple, who in public will be much less candid about their disagreements. And the relationship will still have a youthful quality—meaning that the partners' repartee will range from the playful, comic and good-natured to the immature, self-centered and petulant. When struggling with each other for dominance, these two often look like two children fighting over a toy.

Most marriages are necessarily more social in nature, and here the spouses don the child mask in confronting the world. This can pose problems for their children, who are sometimes robbed of their childhood by parents who don't yet seem to have become adults. Role reversals are common here, with the children having to act as the parents in some situations—as mediators in their parents' stormy relationship, for example.

Boss-employee and parent-child relationships between Leo-Virgos and Scorpio I's, of whichever combination, can have an objective and realistic outlook that doesn't kid itself about niceties and accepts a Machiavellian view of the world. Here the childlike may be openly eschewed in favor of a somewhat forced maturity and an attempt at the appearance of omniscience.

ADVICE: *Why hide? Let other people see what you are really like. Cultivate honesty and transparency. Give up power struggles. Your energy can be better spent.*

HILLARY CLINTON (10/26/47)
BILL CLINTON (8/19/46)

America's president and First Lady came to Washington from Arkansas, where he was governor until 1992. Despite allegations about his extra-marital activities and her questionable business practices, both remain staunchly loyal to each other. **Also: Louis XVI & Marie Antoinette** (married); **Giuseppe Guarneri & Niccolo Paganini** (violin maker/violin virtuoso); **Connie Chung & Dan Rather** (tv co-anchors).

STRENGTHS: **PERFECTIONIST, PRODUCTIVE, PROUD**

WEAKNESSES: **UNSYMPATHETIC, UNFORGIVING, STRESSFUL**

BEST: **PARENT-CHILD**

WORST: **FRIENDSHIP**

STANFORD WHITE (11/9/1853)
WM. RUTHERFORD MEAD (8/20/1846)

Architects Mead and White (with Charles F. McKim) were the founders of the influential firm McKim, Mead & White in 1880. White, in collaboration with his partners, designed numerous institutional, religious and public structures—many of them in the lavish Italian Renaissance style. A prime example is NYC's Washington Arch (1889).

August 19–25

THE CUSP OF EXPOSURE
LEO-VIRGO CUSP

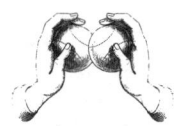

November 3–11

THE WEEK OF DEPTH
SCORPIO II

Pride in Achievement

This relationship demands the highest level of performance its partners are capable of. Giving less than one's best is considered an egregious sin in this matchup. Even the relationship itself, be it personal or professional, has to be near perfect—not that mistakes are completely unacceptable, but it must be obvious that they have arisen out of unavoidable or unforeseen circumstances rather than from human error. Great pride is taken in achievement here, but affection, sympathy and kindness are too often trampled in the rush toward the stunning victory or conquest. Recognition is important to these partners, but not really necessary; they are usually well aware of their own excellence, and don't need much in the way of kudos.

Love affairs here are curiously unconcerned with the outside world but no less devoted to excellence. Checklists and evaluations can pop up in the strangest places in these relationships, not least in more intimate areas such as the bedroom. Not only can the demand for an objectively high degree of performance put the partners under some strain, it can result in a loss of feeling. Unfortunately, the Leo-Virgo–Scorpio II couple often mistakes sympathy or forgiveness for a sign of weakness or sloppiness. Marriages may be overly concerned with status, money, possessions and other trappings of power. When these two get romantic, they have sometimes fallen in love with matter rather than spirit.

Co-workers in this combination can form an outstanding team, capable of predictably high achievement. This attribute is less useful in friendships, which are often dominated by the values of achievement and success rather than trust and intimacy. As friends these partners may never reach deep levels of understanding. Parent and child in this combination demand the best from and for each other, but although each partner may well be able to produce the results that the other requires, children may feel more exploited than loved. Reevaluations and reversals are possible here, however, and these two can reach a healthy compromise in which the pursuit of excellence is balanced by empathy and kindness.

ADVICE: *Don't forsake human values. Excellence isn't everything. Allow for mistakes—they are part of life. Learn from your errors. Be forgiving.*

STRENGTHS: **FLAMBOYANT, EXPRESSIVE, EMOTIONAL**

WEAKNESSES: **JEALOUS, ANGRY, EGOTISTICAL**

BEST: **FRIENDSHIP**

WORST: **MARRIAGE**

GEORGE S. KAUFMAN (11/16/1889)
DOROTHY PARKER (8/22/1893)

Critic and satirical writer Parker is linked with Broadway playwright-director Kaufman as prominent members of the elite Round Table at NY's Algonquin Hotel in the 20s and 30s. Both known for their wicked verbal exchanges, Parker and Kaufman sat regularly with the era's most brilliant wits. **Also: Queen Noor & King Hussein** (married; Jordanian rulers).

August 19–25

THE CUSP OF EXPOSURE
LEO-VIRGO CUSP

November 12–18

THE WEEK OF CHARM
SCORPIO III

Forces Beyond Its Control

This relationship can bring out the more flamboyant side of its partners. The chemistry here is intense, and may arouse feelings of all kinds, both positive and negative. These two hold back little in their confrontations, whether in the boardroom or the bedroom. The relationship often focuses on one of the partner's careers, or on the pair's popularity, no matter how humble its scope. Both partners can be cautious and mistrustful about exposing their deeper feelings, so that they may not really share their inner lives, no matter how passionate their interaction appears. The relationship is often driven by forces beyond its control, whether karmic, personal or social.

Love affairs can be sudden and torrid, but can also burn out just as quickly. Sympathy, kindness and consideration rarely play important roles here; in fact, both partners may be feeding off jealousy or anger toward a third person who completes their love triangle, often an individual who has ignored or badly treated one of them in the past. It does not usually occur to this couple to make a conscious decision about marriage one way or the other, and if it does occur to them, this may come about through either the pressure of circumstances or a lack of real concern.

Family matchups, especially between fathers and daughters or mothers and sons, are characterized by competition for attention. The partners may adore each other, but each of them often tries to highlight their own difficulties and struggles. Friendships are more equally balanced but can still be emotionally volatile. Either the Leo-Virgo or the Scorpio III may initially have begun the friendship out of a need to be associated with a better-known personality.

As co-workers, Leo-Virgos and Scorpio III's will often be sensitive about who gets the main credit for a job well done. Some time, even years, may have to pass before they are able to view their relationship itself as the entity to be acclaimed or blamed. Only then can they give themselves really selflessly to it.

ADVICE: *Be more aware of yourself. Realize your common interest. Be more kind and sympathetic. Don't monopolize other people's attention.*

August 19–25

THE CUSP OF EXPOSURE
LEO-VIRGO CUSP

November 19–24

THE CUSP OF REVOLUTION
SCORPIO-SAGITTARIUS CUSP

Rolling Up Sleeves

This relationship is primarily social. The partners do well together in projects that involve other people, particularly when they themselves form an important part of the team. Their interest is not just managerial or theoretical but intensely practical, for they don't mind rolling up their sleeves, getting in there and getting their hands dirty. Both Leo-Virgos and Scorpio-Sagittarians have a strong work ethic to draw on here.

Romantic involvements between these two are rarely in the cards, for their relationships as friends, associates or social partners are easily upset by physical intimacy. For these two, friendships and even marriages are better-functioning relationships than love affairs: as friends or spouses they will love entertaining, giving dinners or parties, decorating and planning celebrations. Leo-Virgo flair and Scorpio-Sagittarius charm complement each other, producing results that are pleasing and fun.

At work and in family life, colleagues and relatives in this combination are often found at the forefront in representing their group, or putting on productions and presentations. Here they have a tendency toward conflict, especially when it comes to determining what direction future endeavors should take. Leo-Virgo and Scorpio-Sagittarius are square to each other in the zodiac (they lie 90° apart), which makes traditional astrology predict friction and all kinds of emotional manifesting between them. These qualities may appear, however, as push, drive and the impetus to get things done. More often than not, the partners will work together on one or two big projects, or hook up occasionally from time to time, rather than working together steadily and without interruption. Particularly good at collaborating under pressure, they can be called on in times of emergency or stress to meet deadlines and accomplish what others might find difficult or impossible.

ADVICE: *Try for more consistency of action. Stress should not be the primary motivation. Ask others to help out, too. Don't be afraid to admit your weaknesses.*

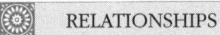
RELATIONSHIPS

STRENGTHS: **SOCIAL, PRACTICAL, HARD-WORKING**

WEAKNESSES: **TENSE, INTERMITTENT, CONFLICTING**

BEST: **FAMILY**

WORST: **LOVE**

INDIRA GANDHI (11/19/17)
RAJIV GANDHI (8/20/44)

Rajiv was the oldest son of Indira, who was India's prime minister for nearly 20 years. Daughter of India's first prime minister, Nehru, she was assassinated in 1984. Groomed for public life, Rajiv succeeded her but was himself assassinated in '89. **Also: Marion Seldes & Garson Kanin** (married; actress/writer).

August 19–25

THE CUSP OF EXPOSURE
LEO-VIRGO CUSP

November 25–December 2

THE WEEK OF INDEPENDENCE
SAGITTARIUS I

A Need for Attention

Temperamental to the point of occasional explosiveness, this relationship brings out Leo-Virgos' fiery side. Anger constantly gets in the way of this pair, who would objectively be capable of blazing new trails, especially professionally, were it not for their emotional differences. Part of their difficulty is the competitive nature of both the individuals and the matchup. These two fight for the attention of their group, or of a third party near and dear to both. Should they be able to put their need for attention behind them, they are capable of great things, but until then they are likely to fritter away their time hurling barbs at each other.

In love affairs, aggression can be sublimated into sex, with quite satisfying results. But it is in marriage that the combination's greatest successes often occur, particularly when important domestic, financial or career projects occupy the partners and make them work shoulder to shoulder. Lasting respect can be built over time here, but unavoidable conflicts can equally well emerge, eventually leading to a breakup. In either case, honesty will usually prevail. These relationships rarely drift without direction.

Friendships and sibling matchups do better when the partners don't spend a lot of time together with little to do. Unfortunately, Leo-Virgos and Sagittarius I's have a way of getting severely on each other's nerves. They sometimes annoy each other purposely, as if for kicks. Yet when, as friends, they let loose with their mutual appreciation of culture, sports or technical matters, or when they work on a pet hobby, their problems seem to disappear like magic.

Parent-child pairs in this combination are prone to compete for the other parent's affection. Although all-out war threatens to break out periodically, most of the time emotions are kept on a slow boil. In very subtle ways, the partners engage in countless games and intrigues, which have the effect, for better or worse, of binding the relationship closer rather than breaking it apart.

ADVICE: *Put your differences behind you. Compromise. Personal disagreements are holding you back. Put arguments to rest. Concentrate on your work.*

RELATIONSHIPS

STRENGTHS: **CAPABLE, GROUNDBREAKING, INVOLVED**

WEAKNESSES: **COMPETITIVE, MANIPULATIVE, ENVIOUS**

BEST: **MARRIAGE**

WORST: **PARENT-CHILD**

MARK TWAIN (11/30/1835)
BRET HARTE (8/25/1836)

Twain and Harte were American contemporary writers. Harte was known best for his picturesque short stories of the Old West, Twain for his satirical writings and *The Adventures of Huckleberry Finn* (1884). The 2 were friends but also rivals. At one point Harte, who envied Twain's greater notoriety, borrowed money from him. Later, Twain tried to discredit Harte's literary influence.

STRENGTHS: **OUTGOING, VIBRANT, COMMUNICATIVE**

WEAKNESSES: **UNAWARE, DEPENDENT, ESCAPIST**

BEST: **LOVE**

WORST: **WORK**

LYNN FONTANNE (12/6/1887)
ALFRED LUNT (8/19/1892)

Lunt and Fontanne, married in 1922, were considered the best acting couple of the American stage during their 40-year career together. They were noted for their wit and sophistication in plays by Shaw, Noël Coward, Shakespeare et al. Onstage they were magical entertainers.

August 19–25
THE CUSP OF EXPOSURE
LEO-VIRGO CUSP

December 3–10
THE WEEK OF THE ORIGINATOR
SAGITTARIUS II

Craving Entertainment

Outgoing tendencies prevail here. This matchup is characterized by a love of vibrant experience, which can take the form both of a craving for all sorts of entertainment (but principally dance, music, film and design) and of generating such work itself. These two have a knack for putting new twists to old themes, and can inspire each other to new heights of creativity. The life of any party, they are often socially popular. Unfortunately their extroversion sometimes serves as an escape from problems within the relationship that need attention. Leo-Virgos are usually more likely to be aware of these problems, but may be diverted from them by strong pressure from their partners; In quiet moments of reflection, however, they are capable of bringing Sagittarius II's face to face with a problem and encouraging them to talk about it rather than ignoring it. Such moments may mark the start of a sorely needed process of self-examination and personal growth.

Love affairs can open lines of communication and trust between these partners. If Sagittarius II's feel truly accepted by Leo-Virgos, they are likely to begin to trust them, and will not run so fast from any sign of psychological or emotional difficulty. Leo-Virgos must beware of a tendency on the part of their Sagittarius II partners to become unduly attached, apply undue pressure or become demanding. Sagittarius II's will often be heard saying, "You're the only one who understands." Marriages are a bit more subdued, especially with the arrival of children, whose presence can induce more self-awareness and feelings of responsibility in both parents.

Friendships and sibling matchups in this combination usually see the more theatrical side of the relationship emerging, and a seemingly inexhaustible desire to have fun with other people, punctuated by comedy, impersonations, virtuoso displays of feeling and a wide variety of dramatic devices. Since these tendencies also appear in work relationships, more traditional or corporate environments may not be particularly favored for this pair; creative fields of endeavor are more likely to be profitable.

ADVICE: *Enjoy being theatrical, but take a break sometimes. Learn more about yourself. Strengthen your identity. Learn to trust yourself more.*

STRENGTHS: **TRADITIONAL, FAMILIAL, LINEAL**

WEAKNESSES: **DOUBTFUL, COERCIVE, MISUNDERSTANDING**

BEST: **FAMILY**

WORST: **LOVE**

CAL RIPKEN, JR. (8/24/60)
CAL RIPKEN, SR. (12/17/35)

Baltimore Orioles baseball player Cal Jr. is best known for his 1995 "Iron Man" record of 2,153 consecutive games—formerly held by Lou Gehrig. Cal Sr. managed the team, with his son playing on it, during the '87 and '88 seasons.
Also: **Houari Boumedienne & Ahmed ben Bella** (Algerian political foes); **Gene Kelly & Betsy Blair** (married; actors).

August 19–25
THE CUSP OF EXPOSURE
LEO-VIRGO CUSP

December 11–18
THE WEEK OF THE TITAN
SAGITTARIUS III

Passing the Baton

This relationship is often concerned with the themes of succession and power—with whether the baton of authority, when it is passed from a Leo-Virgo to a Sagittarius III or vice versa, is handed on or taken by force. Such processes usually take place within the structure of a family, professional or social unit, although they may also involve a more personal passing of the mantle outside this kind of group context. Most often it is the Sagittarius III who is in the position of power and the Leo-Virgo who is given or takes control. The circumstances and feelings involved can be quite ambiguous, and are never as simple as they seem. Perhaps both partners appear to be on the same side when in fact they are rivals or even enemies; perhaps they seem to be combatants when in fact their lineages and even their very existences are interdependent. In the same way, the act of succession itself may seem voluntary to some observers, an act of coercion to others.

The theme of succession is not usually apparent per se in love affairs and marriages, but it is echoed in the issue of power. No matter how sensually rewarding the relationship is, Leo-Virgos will often feel misunderstood and unappreciated by their dominant Sagittarius III mates. Their self-esteem is likely to sink, to the point where the Sagittarius III's may have to deal with their depressions.

Succession is a more obvious issue between parents and children, or in an organization with a boss and a partner or subordinate. In more subtle forms, it can also appear in friendships. A family business often faces the seemingly inevitable process of succession as parents age and children grow into maturity: problems can arise when the children have doubts, or are not really interested in heading in a direction predetermined by the parent, forcing the business to be sold or passed out of the family altogether. Sagittarius III's are likely to be stubborn and unyielding in these situations. Leo-Virgos are more adaptable, but often because they are insecure and hungry.

ADVICE: *Be sensitive to needs and wants. Show more interest. Don't assume that group priorities are more important than individual ones.*

August 19–25

THE CUSP OF EXPOSURE
LEO-VIRGO CUSP

December 19–25

THE CUSP OF PROPHECY
SAGITTARIUS-CAPRICORN CUSP

The Third Person

 RELATIONSHIPS

STRENGTHS: **SYMPATHETIC,
INVESTIGATIVE, PRIVATE**

WEAKNESSES: **HURT,
MISUNDERSTOOD, DETACHED**

BEST: **FRIENDSHIP**

WORST: **MARRIAGE**

This combination has a powerful social awareness that is at once penetrating and detached. The partners are able to step back and evaluate the machinations at work in any situation—even their own, as if they were a third invisible person in their own relationship. These two have a lot in common. They both tend to be private individuals hiding a secret or two, and they don't readily trust people. They also have the same elemental makeup (both are fire-earth combinations), and their signs lie in a pleasing trine aspect (at 120° to each other) in the zodiac. In other words they interact well. Together they love observing other people, and they share a curiosity about riddles and mysteries, including their own, which they solve by applying both reason and intuition, like private detectives.

Love affairs and marriages between these two are not as common as one would think; they both have a need to hide themselves away somewhat, so that it will take someone really magnetic to draw them out. If they are brought together by a third person, however, they may opt for the safety of their similarity, rather than risking the possibility of further hurt or misunderstanding in a new relationship.

Friendships are usually the most fruitful relationships in this combination. They often include a shared interest—perhaps an area of study, an appreciation of the arts or some form of physical exercise. If Leo-Virgos and Sagittarius-Capricorns meet in their student days, they usually keep track of each other over the years, although their relationship may not continue to be close. They may share an involvement with a third person, whether romantically or as a friend, and this can give them overlapping knowledge and experience. Professional and business relationships can work well if the partners have a common interest, perhaps best applied in the area of research and development rather than in the executive sphere. In the family, Leo-Virgo and Sagittarius-Capricorn cousins may offer each other the affection and understanding that parents or other relatives are unable to provide.

ADVICE: *Take a firmer stand. Strengthen your will to succeed. Raise your self-esteem. Avoid self-pity like poison. Be more open with other people.*

PETER CRISS (12/20/47)
GENE SIMMONS (8/25/49)

Drummer Criss and bassist Simmons are original members of the theatrical hard-rock band Kiss, formed in '72. Wearing ghoulish face make-up and outlandish costumes, Kiss performances are highlighted by Simmons wild stage antics, including fire-breathing and blood-spewing.

August 19–25

THE CUSP OF EXPOSURE
LEO-VIRGO CUSP

December 26–January 2

THE WEEK OF THE RULER
CAPRICORN I

Hard Pragmatism

RELATIONSHIPS

STRENGTHS: **FINANCIALLY
ASTUTE, PRAGMATIC, DEMANDING**

WEAKNESSES: **SELFISH,
STUBBORN, HARD**

BEST: **WORK**

WORST: **PARENT-CHILD**

This matchup is stubborn and recalcitrant in the face of authority and all forms of domination, whether these stem from the other partner or whether the partners bond together against the outside world. The relationship often puts time and money into establishing an enterprise, which may well prove financially profitable; together these two have a hard kind of pragmatism, so that if success fails to arrive within a reasonable period, they will waste no more energy on the project. Capricorn I's are generally responsible enough to be trusted, but this is no guarantee that Leo-Virgos will let them into their lives.

Love affairs are not particularly recommended here: personal conflicts, and the partners' inability to open up to each other at even a reasonable level, will undercut the value of their physical involvement. Should they marry, buying a house and setting up their domestic infrastructure will be a primary concern for them. Leo-Virgos will appreciate the security this marriage will afford them, but overdominant Capricorn I's will seize the chance to exercise their talent for ruling the roost, and this will almost certainly lead to a head-on clash of energies. Leo-Virgos may serve in a secondary role for a while, even for years, but they will eventually have enough, rebel, try to express themselves more fully and demand more from the relationship. Parent-child matchups with Capricorn I's in the parental role may follow a similar pattern as Leo-Virgo children grow more assertive.

Work relationships benefit from Leo-Virgo analytic and observational skills and Capricorn I financial talent. Personal interaction is usually kept to a minimum here, at least if harmony is the goal. Friendships do best when they do not include business dealings, although volunteer work or community service can work out well as long as both friends have an equal say in the direction their association takes.

ADVICE: *Give each other a break. Drop judgmental attitudes. Be more sympathetic and sharing. Play and have fun together.*

MAO ZEDONG (12/26/1893)
DENG XIAOPING (8/24/04)

After being purged in 1976 from a top political job, China's Deng returned to a senior position following Mao's death. The older leader had been more isolationist than Deng, who in 1979 visited the US to seek closer economic ties.

***Also:* Shelley Long & Ted Danson** (co-stars, *Cheers*).

MAURY POVICH (1/7/39)
CONNIE CHUNG (8/20/46)

Povich and Chung are married tv personalities with separate careers. NBC's Povich has a daytime talk show. Chung was a CBS news anchor who has also had several newsmagazine shows. At one point she asked for time off so that they could try to have a baby.

Also: **Robert Plant & Jimmy Page** (Led Zeppelin musicians); **George Wallace & Richard Nixon** (1968 presidential race).

August 19–25
THE CUSP OF EXPOSURE
LEO-VIRGO CUSP

January 3–9
THE WEEK OF DETERMINATION
CAPRICORN II

A Controlled Emotional Response

Strong feelings are one hallmark of this relationship; a controlled emotional response to them is another. Privacy and secrecy often have a priority here, alongside a demand for a solid front against the intrusions of the world. Neither partner is especially interested in letting other people in on their thoughts and feelings, a tendency their relationship magnifies. Conflicts are inevitable between these two, and they are private enough people that deep rifts may form in the structure of the relationship without either of them being the wiser.

The power struggles in play here may revolve around ideology. In marriages and love affairs, these two seldom fully see eye to eye in their beliefs, which causes friction on an almost daily basis. Unless compromises are reached or truces agreed upon, these conflicts can wear the relationship down until they impair its ability to heal itself. The partners may have to learn to be diplomatic and to put their irritation with each other to rest. Emotional control is often used as a weapon here, with both partners maintaining silence for long periods, concealing their true feelings and withholding their approval.

The key to successful family matchups is mutual respect. Until this is accomplished, the relationship may be stormy, filled with recrimination and blame. Friendships are often able to channel the intensity here more constructively, particularly in pursuits that allow for a full expenditure of energy, whether physical or mental.

Work relationships can be outstanding, for both of these partners are capable of being absolutely determined that their projects will be successful, and their ambitions generally complement each other. Leo-Virgos and Capricorn II's know instinctively that giving up their individual ego prerogatives and putting their energies to the service of their common good can bring them both far.

ADVICE: *Learn to compromise. Put conflicts to rest. Building mutual respect is key. Don't be afraid to admit you were wrong; don't be afraid to show weakness.*

JILL ST. JOHN (8/19/40)
JACK JONES (1/14/38)

St. John was a vivacious redheaded star of Hollywood films of the 60s. One of her 4 marriages was to handsome nightclub singer Jones, 1967–69. *Also:* **Sean Connery & Jason Connery** (father/son; actors); **Melvin Van Peebles & Mario Van Peebles** (father/son; writer-director/actor); **Dorothy Parker & Martin Luther King, Jr.** (writer left civil-rights leader her estate).

August 19–25
THE CUSP OF EXPOSURE
LEO-VIRGO CUSP

January 10–16
THE WEEK OF DOMINANCE
CAPRICORN III

A Sacred Trust

The transmission of ideas is of paramount importance in this relationship; these two have a great deal to talk about and share. A one-on-one learning situation often works well here. The partners may be involved with a body of theoretical knowledge, possibly religious, technical, scientific or philosophical, which provides a common ground of study. This learning project can be serious, but doesn't have to be—it is often tremendously challenging, but it can also be fun. Nor does the emphasis on study mean that the physical side of life is absent, for the pair may well be involved in competitive sports and exercise. Whatever the area of study, Leo-Virgo–Capricorn III relationships usually settle on one topic and concentrate on it, rather than seeking diversity.

In matters of the heart, Leo-Virgos and Capricorn III's tend to give their all, and their love may reach for the stars in its soaring bliss. It will rarely fail to be grounded in the here and now, however. Although both partners can be stubborn and unyielding in arguments, they will usually make up their differences when locked in each other's embrace. Marriages may tend toward the prosaic, but the partners will rarely feel let down, for they will feel instinctively that these relationships involve a whole different set of parameters from a love affair, and that they constitute a sacred trust.

Friendships and family matchups usually include a central activity of study. Formal schooling, private lessons and workshops are all possible activities to be shared by Leo-Virgo and Capricorn III siblings or friends. Especially at the college or university level, where the mentor-protégé variety of relationship is quite likely, it also often happens that teacher-student relationships evolve into friendships and in rare cases into love affairs and even marriages. Should involvement in a particular area of interest become deep enough, Leo-Virgos and Capricorn III's might form a business partnership built around a school or other learning center. Devoting themselves to the development of young people can become a specialty for these two.

ADVICE: *Don't take advantage of your power. Respect the space and opinions of others. Study is only one way. Don't ignore the value of life experience.*

August 19–25

THE CUSP OF EXPOSURE
LEO-VIRGO CUSP

January 17–22

THE CUSP OF MYSTERY & IMAGINATION
CAPRICORN-AQUARIUS CUSP

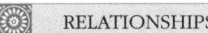
RELATIONSHIPS

STRENGTHS: **PROFOUND, REWARDING, EMPATHIC**

WEAKNESSES: **VOYEURISTIC, SELFISH, ENVIOUS**

BEST: **PARENT-CHILD**

WORST: **FRIENDSHIP**

A Personal Brand of Expression

This relationship generally cares little about what other people think, and will rarely let society's expectations get in the way of its own highly personal brand of expression. Leo-Virgos are stimulated by Capricorn-Aquarius verve, and Capricorn-Aquarians are fascinated by half-hidden Leo-Virgo energies. The synergy of their relationship often magnifies the more flamboyant side of both partners, creating quite an outrageous mutual stance. Deeply rewarding for both partners, this combination allows them a depth of feeling and a sense of freedom that are hard for them to come by elsewhere.

Leo-Virgo–Capricorn-Aquarius love affairs can be wild and wacky. Their tendency to let it all hang out often hides a more private, serious side to their relationship, which is actually quite deeply committed and loyal. Both partners may have a roving eye, but they can be surprisingly faithful to one another. Sexual currents run deep here, but are predicated on Leo-Virgos' complete trust, which Capricorn-Aquarians should never betray. Marriage can also work out well, with both partners giving generously of their energies to make the matchup a success.

Instabilities may arise in friendships through envy, covetousness or pride. Leo-Virgos and Capricorn-Aquarians must beware of undermining these relationships through excessive selfishness and holding back from true sharing. Learning to give unconditionally will be an important lesson for them both to learn. In boss-employee and parent-child relationships in this combination, the partners may be mutually fascinated with each other's world. The empathy of Capricorn-Aquarius bosses or parents for Leo-Virgos is often so profound that they can form a very clear picture of their employees' or children's minds, penetrating to deep, hidden worlds where the secrets of the heart can be read.

ADVICE: *Don't be so eager to shock. Be more confident of yourself. Beware of selfishness. Have more respect for privacy. Tend to yourself.*

CHRISTOPHER ROBIN MILNE (8/21/20)
A.A. MILNE (1/18/1882)

Christopher is the son of *Winnie-the-Pooh* author A.A. Milne. The book *When We Were Very Young* features young Christopher Robin as its leading character. Fame from the book left Christopher with a lifelong identity crisis and led to strained relations with his father.

***Also:* Dorothy Parker & Alexander Woollcott** (Algonquin Round Table literati).

August 19–25

THE CUSP OF EXPOSURE
LEO-VIRGO CUSP

January 23–30

THE WEEK OF GENIUS
AQUARIUS I

RELATIONSHIPS

STRENGTHS: **SENSUOUS, NATURAL, APPRECIATIVE**

WEAKNESSES: **LABILE, VOLATILE, INDISCREET**

BEST: **SIBLING**

WORST: **LOVE**

Easy Interchanges

A completely natural expression of feelings appears in this relationship, which does well with easy exchanges and less well when bogged down in heavy emotions. The relationship has a sensuous air—a love of food, say, and of physical pleasure in general. Both partners will enjoy good conversation, and will pick each other's brains over the minutiae of interesting topics. Quick-witted Aquarius I's will find Leo-Virgos a good match when it comes to following the latest scientific discoveries or appreciating current trends in the arts and entertainment. Should their conversations involve conflict, however, or grow heated, these two will begin to feel completely out of synch.

Leo-Virgos in love with Aquarius I's will have a difficult time if they expect this partner to be faithful. Aquarius I's have to be free, and do best with lovers, mates and friends who understand this. Because the relationship is natural in its focus, favoring honesty, openness and being oneself, the spectacle of infidelity might be openly paraded before the eyes of Leo-Virgos, making them feel let down or even betrayed. In some ways it would be better for Aquarius I's to be a bit more secretive or at least discreet about what they're doing when they're away. Part of the problem is that Leo-Virgos are unlikely to supply Aquarius I's with the emotional stability they crave in a partner, so that the relationship may exhibit great volatility.

Work relationships between these partners can work out in the short term, but will rarely succeed in establishing a lasting financial or ideological basis. Enterprises involving media, public relations, publishing and the arts are particularly favored here. In the long run, Aquarius I business partners may demand too much attention for Leo-Virgo taste, and may have too little psychological understanding of their colleague to keep him or her happy. Siblings in this combination often have great times together, enjoying the outdoors and seeking excitement, risk and adventure.

ADVICE: *Try to show more discretion. Keep it light. Demand less attention. Work on being more practical and responsible.*

GEORGE WALLACE (8/25/19)
CORNELIA WALLACE (1/28/39)

In his 2nd marriage, Alabama governor George Wallace wed the niece of a colleague in 1971. He was attracted to her youth and sensual beauty. In '72 he was shot and partially paralyzed. She moved out of the governor's mansion in '77 and they divorced in '78.

August 19–25

THE CUSP OF EXPOSURE
LEO-VIRGO CUSP

January 31–February 7

THE WEEK OF YOUTH & EASE
AQUARIUS II

Keeping Up Appearances

A combination symbolically governed by the element of water, this relationship is likely to involve a free flow of feelings. In fact these two may be magnetically drawn to each other, not only respecting each other at the most basic level but conceiving a deep mutual passion. Other people may see them as something of an odd couple, and they are indeed usually quite different as individuals, but their relationship itself has a unique charm for them—they are more attracted by their combination than they are by each other. We may find this pair trying to keep up an appearance of normalcy when in fact their relationship is quite unusual.

Love affairs can be sexually rewarding and can reach deep levels emotionally. Aquarius II's may occasionally find themselves out of their depth here, but they will be fascinated by the complexity of the Leo-Virgo personality and gratified to be involved with it. Leo-Virgos will enjoy the relative simplicity of their interactions with Aquarius II partners. These love affairs may well evolve toward marriage, which can work surprisingly well: Leo-Virgos can exercise a subtle hold on Aquarius II spouses that will keep them from looking elsewhere for gratification.

Complex dependency issues can arise between Leo-Virgo parents and Aquarius II children. Their efforts to please each other often go awry, signaling a basic problem of communication. Aquarius II parents, meanwhile, cannot always fathom the complexity of their Leo-Virgo children. Yet there is generally enough love and concern in these relationships to guarantee some reward in both combinations. Leo-Virgo–Aquarius II friendships have their ups and downs, but are unusually devoted and committed. In the career realm, Leo-Virgo's and Aquarius II's both have abundant mental abilities that are quite capable of coalescing. Their relationships can bring solid successes. Planning new projects and analyzing the drawbacks and defects of earlier ones are especially noteworthy skills here. But Leo-Virgos should make conscious efforts to keep their personal problems out of the workplace, for Aquarius II's will not allow such issues to intrude on their work.

ADVICE: *Don't take too much for granted. Hard work will be required. Be more accepting and less demanding. Time is the great healer.*

August 19–25

THE CUSP OF EXPOSURE
LEO-VIRGO CUSP

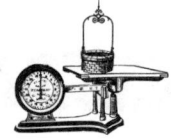

February 8–15

THE WEEK OF ACCEPTANCE
AQUARIUS III

Greater Than the Sum of Its Parts

These two can give as good as they get. The energy of their relationship is often extremely high—far greater than the sum of their energies as individuals. This synergistic chemistry is also effective when they are competitors battling it out in the financial, social, political or sporting arenas. One is impressed by the balance here, although Leo-Virgos often seem more inspirational to Aquarius II's than the other way around.

Love affairs here are spurred not so much by passion as by mutual interests and affection. It is more a matter of liking than of loving, which can augur well for the relationship's longevity. Empathy allows for understanding and understanding for trust. These love affairs often prove ideal candidates for marriages. Such is the closeness here that should one of the partners fall in love with a third person who is also a mutual friend, the relationship may continue along relatively successfully as a ménage à trois, formally or informally.

In the professional world it makes little difference whether Leo-Virgos and Aquarius II's are colleagues or rivals, since sooner or later they may wind up working for the same organization anyway. Their tremendous respect for each other takes them far beyond any shallow desire for conquest or victory. The equality of sibling matchups between these two, particularly when they are of the opposite sex, is reflected in similarly respectful and supportive attitudes. These relationships may continue to be active well into young adulthood and beyond.

In friendships, on the other hand, Leo-Virgos and Aquarius II's must be careful to keep their competitive drives from getting out of hand. Their overconfidence about their unbeatability as a team can eventually lead to disillusionment, internal strife and breakup. Scaling back their ambitions and saving their prodigious energies for other areas will allow them to relax and enjoy what could be a fun-filled association.

ADVICE: *Don't let competitive drives get out of hand. You might also work on enjoying yourself. Beware of expectations. Take things as they come.*

August 19–25

THE CUSP OF EXPOSURE
LEO-VIRGO CUSP

February 16–22

THE CUSP OF SENSITIVITY
AQUARIUS-PISCES CUSP

Resistance to Incursions

These two have a lot in common in their similar desire to hide their real selves from the world and to defend their cherished self-protective position. Reinforced when they come together, this attitude becomes an almost revolutionary zeal for being left in peace. But whereas Leo-Virgos sometimes tend to conceal, sometimes to reveal themselves in relation to the world, Aquarius-Pisces tend to build a wall around themselves so that no one can get in, ever. Lying opposite each other in the zodiac, these two form a polar relationship that can be very resistant to incursions into its private space. They can be aggressive with people who don't understand them, especially with authority figures such as parents or bosses—it's like them or leave them alone. But rebellious as they are when younger, they risk being overly dogmatic themselves once they rise to their own positions of power or authority. At this point, too, cracks can appear within the relationship itself, with major power struggles occurring between two previously oppressed individuals.

Lovers and spouses in this combination will simply turn their back on those who don't understand them, quickly tiring of family members who don't accept them and lashing out in anger, sarcasm or scorn. These periodic outbursts are extremely important, not only for dealing with pent-up aggressions but also for making the statement that the couple will no longer be treated like a doormat. The Leo-Virgo–Aquarius-Pisces relationship is highly protective; these partners will spring to each other's defense.

On the job, Leo-Virgo and Aquarius-Pisces co-workers form a solid bond against unfair treatment from superiors, never hesitating to stick up for and if necessary to represent other members of their group. A distaste for unfairness may lead them to get involved in union activities or less formal work groups. Friendships are similarly united, and sibling pairs in this combination form a solid bulwark against parental mistreatment or abuse. Indeed, they must be careful not to be too rebellious, causing major family rifts and possibly inviting severe countermeasures.

ADVICE: *Be more patient sometimes. Stand up for yourself but don't overreact. Beware of becoming intolerant. Keep your anger under control.*

RELATIONSHIPS

STRENGTHS: **PROTECTIVE, ASSERTIVE, FAIR**

WEAKNESSES: **DOGMATIC, OVERREBELLIOUS, INFLEXIBLE**

BEST: **WORK**

WORST: **FAMILY**

WILT CHAMBERLAIN (8/21/36)
JULIUS ERVING (2/22/50)

"Wilt the Stilt" and "Dr. J" played basketball for the Philadelphia '76ers in different years. Both are Hall of Famers, and both were MVPs during their careers. On the list of all-time career points, Chamberlain is #2 with 31,419 and Erving #3 with 30,026.

August 19–25

THE CUSP OF EXPOSURE
LEO-VIRGO CUSP

February 23–March 2

THE WEEK OF SPIRIT
PISCES I

Independence of Action

These two can be extremely close, but they have to be able to maintain their independence from one another at all costs. Pisces I's can play inspirational roles in the lives of Leo-Virgos, coming to represent a certain ideal of integrity and faithful commitment. Leo-Virgos, for their part, often bring an admirably critical outlook and a spark of excitement to the daily lives of Pisces I's. The pair can complement each other beautifully, particularly since their relationship functions well in both social and personal settings. The intimacy here is more soulful than physical—these partners treat one another with understanding and respect.

The challenge of friendships and love affairs is to bring the partners' moods into synch, so that the partners feel comfortable with and accepted by each other. Leo-Virgos can sometimes intrude on the more reflective side of Pisces I's when in the grip of a sudden impulse. But they will admire the altruistic Pisces I need to share and to serve, even though it will make them feel guilty or unworthy at times. The signal that things are going well in this relationship is an easy give-and-take on the part of both partners. Marriage may be impossible for these two, who tend to have a strong fear of losing their autonomy. Although both of them can handle giving up a certain amount of freedom by working in an organization, they will stubbornly resist losing independence in their private lives.

Careerwise these two are best off working as freelancers or as entrepreneurs, maintaining as much independence from each other as possible. The communication between them is often so good that they only occasionally need to touch base, being generally confident and aware of each other's thoughts and actions. Parent-child relationships of either combination must beware of arousing rebellion due to overly strict or judgmental attitudes, and of becoming too involved in each other's lives.

ADVICE: *Fear of losing independence may actually be fear of getting close. Be as honest as possible. Don't take too much for granted. Try harder not to hang on too tight.*

RELATIONSHIPS

STRENGTHS: **COMPLEMENTARY, SOULFUL, INSPIRATIONAL**

WEAKNESSES: **INTRUSIVE, GUILT-PROVOKING, FEARFUL**

BEST: **FRIENDSHIP**

WORST: **MARRIAGE**

CHELSEA CLINTON (2/27/80)
BILL CLINTON (8/19/46)

Chelsea is remarkably unaffected by her father's status as president of the United States. Through thoughtful parenting she has a clear sense of herself, with no trace of conceit or class consciousness. He is close and attentive to her, protecting her from the glare of his high office.

***Also:* Malcolm Forbes & Elizabeth Taylor** (good friends; millionaire publisher/movie star).

August 19–25
THE CUSP OF EXPOSURE
LEO-VIRGO CUSP

March 3–10
THE WEEK OF THE LONER
PISCES II

PRINCESS MARGARET (8/21/30)
ANTHONY ARMSTRONG-JONES (3/7/30)

Margaret and Armstrong-Jones (Earl of Snowdon) were married from 1960–78. Their marriage was filled with discreet affairs with various other partners. They had 2 children. **Also: Ring Lardner, Jr. & Ring Lardner, Sr.** (son/father; writers); **Claude Debussy & Maurice Ravel** (Impressionist composers); **Gene Kelly & Cyd Charisse** (dance partners in films).

Taking a Stand

This relationship seeks to free itself from restrictions. The emphasis here is on the relationship as a unit and on its liberty to act on its own, without restraint, and to exercise its own good judgment about what it thinks best. Especially resistant to the blandishments of society and to the limitations imposed by tradition, these two can be trailblazers in opening up new forms of expression. Leo-Virgos tend to be the more intuitive and original of the pair, Pisces II's the more sensitive and perfectionist, but their creative energies coalesce synergistically to produce results that may not be everyone's cup of tea but can exert a long-range effect.

Part of the challenge here will be to keep the momentum going, since these two can be extremely sensitive to criticism and at times will feel like giving up, particularly when they are married or work together. Their need to be free implies a certain willpower to resist, and if necessary to carry on a protracted struggle, but this kind of stamina can actually be lacking here. Still, although they may tend to give up when the going gets really rough, without real opposition the relationship can be long-lived, since these spouses and co-workers are usually well suited.

Although Leo-Virgo is a fire-earth combination and Pisces is ruled by water, the Leo-Virgo–Pisces II relationship is governed by air, an element here inducing a refusal to be tied down. Yet in matters of love and friendship these two are sometimes unable to see things realistically or to act decisively—rather than taking a stand in emotional matters, they have a tendency to drift and avoid confrontation, hoping or assuming that problems will go away. In short, they don't always show the best sense. Parent-child relationships here are too likely to assume unconventional attitudes that set other relatives' teeth on edge. The animosities engendered this way can ultimately prove detrimental to the family as a whole.

ADVICE: *Strengthen your will to resist and to go the distance. Don't just give lip service to freedom—live it. Taking a stand now will save you problems later on.*

August 19–25
THE CUSP OF EXPOSURE
LEO-VIRGO CUSP

March 11–18
THE WEEK OF DANCERS & DREAMERS
PISCES III

JOEY BUTTAFUOCO (3/11/56)
AMY FISHER (8/21/74)

16-year-old Fisher and married Buttafuoco had an illegal affair, for which he was convicted of statutory rape and sent to jail for 6 months. Fisher, the "Long Island Lolita," shot his wife in the head and is serving 5–15 years. **Also: Josef Strauss & Johann Strauss** (son/father; composers); **Claude Debussy & Stéphane Mallarmé** (composer inspired by poet).

Finding Common Ground

The driving force behind this combination is usually the partners' need to feel unique or special, or to be doing something unusual or thrilling. Whether for good or ill, they are likely to share an unequaled relationship, far different than any they have previously experienced. They tend to have developed along different lines: whereas Leo-Virgos are usually caught up with personal issues, Pisces III's are more geared toward universal, philosophical, social or even romantic concerns. As a consequence their relationship is sometimes out of synch, featuring broad splits and differences of opinion. It isn't always possible for it to become a long-lasting tie.

Stability is difficult to attain in love affairs. Leo-Virgos can be irritated by the dreamier character aspects of Pisces III's, who for their part may grow tired of Leo-Virgos' inability to learn from experience. They often take to marriage and can be highly nurturing, but they may not find the support and permanence they require in a Leo-Virgo spouse. As a couple they will tend to travel and move a lot rather than establishing their home in one place.

Friendships can be relatively long-lasting but will not necessarily involve the pair seeing each other more often. The relationship's penchant for originality can lead to some unusual meetings, associations or hobbies, in which Leo-Virgos and Pisces III's will often find deep fulfillment. Not infrequently, the more sensitive and inward side of each partner is activated here, and they may come to rely on each other's help in mutual introspection. When they meet as rivals or opponents, on the other hand, they may, in their clash, unwittingly touch deep emotional areas and activate each other's most basic beliefs. It may be possible for family members in this combination to work together in a business, religious or social activity. The relationship often combines practicality and idealism in a strange blend that will be interesting to those of a more down-to-earth philosophical bent. Dealing creatively with everyday matters is a specialty of this matchup.

ADVICE: *Take a stand. Running away from problems rarely helps. Face up to differences and work out solutions. Find common ground.*

To the Last Detail

Two Virgo I's can make an excellent match, but whether they will choose each other is another story—they most often pick people very different from themselves for their involvements. Service-oriented to the extreme, they can work well together in a variety of different settings. Because they both can function as assistants or co-workers, there should be little conflict between them over who takes the leadership role, unless a strong executive is not available and the group is in need of direction.

In love affairs and marriages Virgo I's tend to become involved either with strong figures, for whom they can assume the role of helpmate, or with needy people in whose company they can satisfy their need to serve. These choices sometimes turn out to be mistakes, but they do arouse Virgo I feelings, and this polarity is absent in their relationships with other Virgo I's. It is unlikely, then, that sparks of passion will fly here, even though the pair may have quite a satisfying physical relationship. Romance is also apt to be lacking in Virgo I marriages, although practical considerations and the day-to-day running of a household will usually take up much of the partners' energies and keep them fairly happy.

Friendships, family relationships and career matchups between Virgo I's may overlap. Should they meet for the first time on the job, they will usually be able to work together effectively as long as their duties and goals are well defined. Not always interested in really imaginative projects, they tend to put their efforts into practical endeavors that are well grounded and yield solid results. Virgo I friends can count on each other in times of need. As family members they have a feeling for tradition and for doing things in a structured, pre-ordained way, and are quite likely to go into business together, or to cooperate in heading up a sports, religious, political or community group. Communication tends to be close here—most rules and values are tacitly understood without being spoken.

ADVICE: *Sometimes you don't know what you've got until you lose it. Make the most of a good thing. Don't be sidetracked by self-defeating diversions.*

Workaholic Tendencies

Both of these partners have a strong tendency to withdraw regularly from the world and to lead highly private personal lives. The synergy of their relationship magnifies this trait, making isolation almost a prerequisite for them at times. It's not that they can't be forceful and reliable in their professional worlds—far from it. It is simply that there is a split between their public and their private lives that must be rigorously observed. Their friends, for example, often come from their own professional strata, but their meetings with these people are usually subject to social rules that determine when and how often they can appropriately see each other outside work.

Love affairs and marriages between Virgo I's and Virgo II's can be quietly emotional relationships in which feelings are expressed without a lot of fuss. Virgo I's may be a little unprepared for Virgo II sexual tastes, but once they catch on the relationship can prove mutually satisfying. The couple tends to stay together through thick and thin. If breakups do occur they can be extremely painful. Friendships and sibling matchups may suffer from hypersensitivity, nervousness and instability, since these partners do not have a stabilizing effect on each other emotionally.

Workaholic tendencies seem inevitable in the Virgo I–Virgo II professional relationship, but hard work is not the only norm here: these two usually get involved in projects they find interesting and absorbing in the extreme. Their relationship elevates their work to a position of primary importance, and their concentration on it is total. Virgo I's often have a somewhat rigid insistence on doing things the proper way, and this can bother Virgo II's, who enjoy doing things in their own strange manner. In truth, though, the irritation here is mutual, for this Virgo II trait can upset Virgo I's no end—they will see it as unnecessary and wasteful. Yet both partners are careful, and together they can exert a beneficial braking influence on more impulsive types in a group or organization.

ADVICE: *Try to relax a bit. Forget about work occasionally. Make some new friends who know how to have fun. Be more flexible and open.*

August 26–September 2
THE WEEK OF SYSTEM BUILDERS
VIRGO I

September 11–18
THE WEEK OF THE LITERALIST
VIRGO III

STRENGTHS: **INSTRUCTIVE, CUSTOMIZED, EXPERIENTIAL**

WEAKNESSES: **UNFORGIVING, ROUGH, UNCOMPROMISING**

BEST: **TEACHER-STUDENT**

WORST: **LOVE**

H.L. MENCKEN (9/12/1880)
THEODORE DREISER (8/27/1871)

Novelist Dreiser (*An American Tragedy*, 1925) and journalist-author Mencken were on-and-off friends who often argued about literature. Dreiser got Mencken his first job as a literary critic. They also collaborated on a magazine, *The Bohemian*. They had an active correspondence through the years in which Mencken supported Dreiser's fight against the literary establishment.

No Holding Back

You wouldn't predict this relationship—it comes out of nowhere, often taking friends and family by surprise. Yet besides being unusual it is highly symbiotic. Virgo III's often find themselves directing the physical energy of Virgo I's. They may also be cast in the role of parent, boss, teacher or manager, while the Virgo I becomes the child, employee, student or performer. Virgo III's are often the older and more experienced of the two, and quite likely have already played the performing role in an earlier setting. Virgo I's can fairly easily accept the advice and guidance of these older Virgo III's, who are powerfully perceptive and analytic and will encourage their native ability. Quite often, they go on to take the managerial role themselves later in life.

Strongest in the classroom, the sports field or on the hard road of life, this relationship is often a solid bond based on trust and mutual understanding. Yet it is not an easy pairing, emotionally, physically or spiritually. Both of these two can be extremely rough and uncompromising with each other. In reprimanding a missed signal or other error, they are unlikely to hold back, teaching a lesson that the other partner will remember for a long time. Relationships in this combination, and their methods of teaching and learning, are generally speaking quite different from each other, since each matchup will be tailored to its partners' specific needs and talents. This is not to say that they won't pass on established wisdom and existing methods in the most exacting way but only that they recognize that exceptions to the rule, and direct experience, are as important as the rules themselves.

Virgo I–Virgo III work relationships can be as rewarding for the boss as for the employee, and mutually beneficial to both, especially when the team's work is reviewed by superiors. Lovers, friends and mates in this combination are usually less successful in the emotional and sensual realms than when they team up on social, financial or educational projects.

ADVICE: *Don't take every mistake so seriously. When something stops being fun, maybe it's time to quit. Put more time into exploring thoughts and feelings.*

August 26–September 2
THE WEEK OF SYSTEM BUILDERS
VIRGO I

September 19–24
THE CUSP OF BEAUTY
VIRGO-LIBRA CUSP

STRENGTHS: **BELIEVING, SPELLBINDING, ECSTATIC**

WEAKNESSES: **OUT OF TOUCH, UNCONTROLLED, DISILLUSIONED**

BEST: **LOVE**

WORST: **FRIENDSHIP**

JOHN COLTRANE (9/23/26)
ALICE COLTRANE (8/27/37)

John Coltrane was one of jazz's most brilliant saxophone improvisers. His albums of the 50s and 60s are a testament to his virtuosity. Prominent in a later group was his pianist, wife Alice. After he died in '67, she helped organize a movement that sought to deify her late husband. ***Also:*** **Mark Harmon & Gunnar Nelson** (uncle/nephew; actor/rock musician); **Duke of Buckingham & Anne of Austria** (romance).

The Chain of Miracles

This relationship often focuses on its awe in the face of something bigger than itself, whether a belief, a vision of a strange world or a magnificent work of art. The beauty or aestheticism of Virgo-Libras can awaken deep emotion in even the most prosaic Virgo I's, who, spellbound by what this partner offers them, may quickly scrap their usual common sense, gladly trading it in for just a few moments of additional pleasure. Indeed the relationship can have a devastating effect on their whole outlook on life. At the same time it will show Virgo-Libras, who often see only surface beauty, how to look for deeper levels of meaning in life.

When love affairs are on, they may trash the Virgo I taste for preparation and planning in all things: they emphasize spontaneity and the manifold surprises of coincidence and accident. Virgo-Libras of the more conservative kind may also be amazed at the things that can happen once they give up control. Ecstatic peak experiences can emerge unpredictably here, dazzling both partners. Marriage need not dull this richness unless the spouses feel too much need to structure their activities, perhaps fearing that they are acting irresponsibly.

Career matchups are best off when the pair can share their sense of wonder with other people—perhaps in some spiritual field, which, however, can overlap with commercial possibilities. In fact wealth will seem to come of its own accord to these two, who will not view it as antithetical to enlightenment. They may well view money as just one more link in the amazing chain of miracles that seems to permeate their lives

Siblings of the opposite sex will have a magical relationship from an early age, imaginatively filled with genies, dragons, cyborgs and other fantastic creatures. Encouraged to leave these pursuits behind with childhood, Virgo I's and Virgo-Libras may rebel, refusing to give up their special fantasy bond. Friends who grow up together are more likely to drift apart, saying goodbye, with some sadness, to a relationship without which their imaginative creations may quickly fade away.

ADVICE: *Keep hold of awe and wonder but also of reality. Find beauty in the common things of life. Everyday things have their own magic.*

August 26–September 2
THE WEEK OF SYSTEM BUILDERS
VIRGO I

September 25–October 2
THE WEEK OF THE PERFECTIONIST
LIBRA I

What Lies Beyond?

This down-to-earth, no-nonsense matchup can view life extremely pragmatically. Results count more than intentions here; the Virgo I tendency toward structure and organization is complemented by the Libra I drive to get things right. Two problems arise here, one moral, the other practical. First off, the feeling that the ends justify the means can often be selfish or worse—uncaring or hurtful. Second, although a pragmatic attitude would seem quite workable, it can end up making for a relationship so rigid and stuck that its abilities are severely impaired. If this relationship is to be truly successful, it must temper its stance and moderate its drives.

The literal attitude to life here can drive the poetry and the romance from love affairs. In their pragmatic approach to pleasure, sex and love, couples in this combination must be careful not to lose their spark. Marriage might represent a practical goal for them, but if so they risk letting true feeling slip through their fingers. Trying to hold on is not the answer here: better to relinquish control, and to accept faults and mistakes as an essential thread woven into the warp and woof of life's tapestry.

When these two are friends, no matter how wonderful they feel their connection is, their relationship is unlikely to deepen unless feelings of acceptance and understanding are allowed to prevail. Parent-child relationships may be rather harsh and unforgiving, recalling Shylock in *The Merchant of Venice;* taking words literally and insisting on sticking to facts can have a supremely negative effect here. Learning to broaden meaning rather than restrict it, and above all to fathom the true meaning behind the other partner's words, will be an important lesson.

Virgo I's and Libra I's can form an effective working team, but can also stress themselves out, leaving the relationship exhausted. Rather than depleting their energies constantly, they should learn to be more economic with them, both husbanding their strengths and encouraging them to grow.

ADVICE: *Look at the whole picture. Don't take things so literally. All the world is a symbol. Try to peek into what lies beyond. Keep an open mind and heart.*

MARK HARMON (9/2/51)
TOM HARMON (9/28/19)

Actor Mark is the son of Tom, a legendary football hero of the 40s, recipient of the Heisman Trophy. Mark followed in his father's footsteps in college by becoming an All-American quarterback. After graduating in '74, he turned to tv and film acting. **Also: Elizabeth Ashley & George Peppard** (married; actors).

August 26–September 2
THE WEEK OF SYSTEM BUILDERS
VIRGO I

October 3–10
THE WEEK OF SOCIETY
LIBRA II

Broader Vision

It is not unusual for these two to find each other at exactly the right moment, usually when each of them is poised on the brink of something new yet unsure whether or not to jump. Their relationship often helps them to climb out of a well of loneliness and make a new start—a new life. Each partner here has the talents and skills to enable the other to see more clearly and with broader vision. Better able to scan the horizon, they will be able to make better choices. Libra II's have a light and fun-loving side that is just the tonic for cheering up Virgo I's. They also have an ability to assess other people and to act sociably, an invaluable support for more retiring and socially awkward Virgo I's. For their part, meanwhile, Virgo I's can show Libra II's how better to organize their lives, helping them to develop the analytic skills that will allow them to make clearer decisions.

Love affairs and friendships between these two are often workshops for accepting, resolving or working out personal problems. Libra II's have a lot of psychological understanding, making them well suited to helping Virgo I's begin to fathom their own personalities, a necessary step if they are to become more self-sufficient and less needy. Marriage will often deepen this pair's commitment to their relationship and increase the effectiveness of their mutual quest for self-actualization.

The pair can make an effective working team, with Virgo I's handling the books or administering the home base while their socially adept Libra II partners line up new clients and make deals. Close communication will be required here, for Virgo I's can be too wrapped up in technical matters and Libra II's can get carried away with human ones. Forming new companies and breathing life into old ones is a specialty of this duo. Siblings in this combination can play a similarly reconstructive role but can also be prone to apathy and laziness.

ADVICE: *Strengthen your willpower. Learn how to work yourself out of depressions. Build self-esteem. Let your heart guide you.*

HAROLD PINTER (10/10/30)
ANTONIA FRASER (8/27/32)

Historical novelist Fraser married playwright Pinter in 1980, immediately after his divorce from actress Vivien Merchant. Fraser is royalty, daughter of an earl. She had 3 sons and 3 daughters by her previous marriage, which ended in divorce in 1977. **Also: Michael Jackson & Sean Lennon** (good friends; singers).

JOHN L. SULLIVAN (10/15/1858)
"GENTLEMAN JIM" CORBETT (9/1/1866)

Sullivan was the last bare-knuckles heavyweight champion boxer (1882–92). Fighting under the new Marquis of Queensberry rules, he lost his title to Corbett, who proudly held the crown from 1892–97.

Also: **Branford Marsalis & Wynton Marsalis** (brothers; jazz musicians); **Mark Harmon & Pam Dawber** (married; actors).

August 26–September 2
THE WEEK OF SYSTEM BUILDERS
VIRGO I

October 11–18
THE WEEK OF THEATER
LIBRA III

Proud of Itself

This relationship will be a mutual-admiration society. It can even be quite narcissistic, for these partners are usually well aware of the value of what they have, and can be quite self-satisfied and proud of themselves. They should be careful of arousing the animosity and envy of other people, who might actually be no less happy or fortunate but could be annoyed by what they see—usually correctly—as conceit. Still, just a little bit of consciousness goes a long way here, and the fact that the couple value what they have is a huge plus for them, contributing to their relationship's longevity. Power struggles rarely surface between these two, since the Libra III's need to take the lead will be complemented by the Virgo I's contentment to serve as a helpmate.

Love affairs between these two are not so much passionate as sensuous. Fine food, massage, softly seductive music and a comfortable ambiance can all be part of the picture. This couple knows no greater pleasure than an intimate evening alone in quiet surroundings. In marriages there is a danger of polarization: Virgo I's can do all the giving and Libra III's all the taking, so that Virgo I's will have to be unduly dedicated and may end up resentful. No one would consider this combination the most intimate of relationships, but a lot of people might think it an ideal.

These two can do well as colleagues working on producing an attractive product, perhaps in publishing, film, fashion or design. In friendships, Libra III's may get the idea that Virgo I's are becoming too dependent on them, and whether or not this is true they will back off. Virgo I's can make excellent parents for Libra III's in that they will provide them with all their physical needs, but they may also unintentionally withhold the warmth and understanding these children need most.

ADVICE: *Be more aware of others. A smug attitude antagonizes those around you. Discover your true needs. Even out responsibilities and benefits.*

CHARLIE PARKER (8/29/20)
DIZZY GILLESPIE (10/21/17)

Gifted alto saxophonist Parker, a legend even before his untimely death at 35, got his first recognition in 1945 playing alongside Gillespie, whose trumpeting was on the same virtuosic level. Their recordings together defined the bebop style. Parker was plagued by a drug problem, however. While Gillespie went on to become a star, Parker fell apart.

August 26–September 2
THE WEEK OF SYSTEM BUILDERS
VIRGO I

October 19–25
THE CUSP OF DRAMA & CRITICISM
LIBRA-SCORPIO CUSP

Blistering Criticism

This relationship is prone to passionate outbursts and to intellectual expressions that often take the form of blistering criticism. The pair can be completely inept socially but also highly gifted creatively if their energy is channeled in the right direction. These two are some of the most perfectionist individuals of the year, and the creativity they generate together can bring them to heights of achievement and stimulation. Virgo I's have a good effect on Libra-Scorpios, taming their wilder impulses and limiting their occasional waywardness. Libra-Scorpios meanwhile lend verve and sophistication to Virgo I endeavors, often spurring them on to the best they are capable of.

Love affairs in this combination can upset the balance and composure of Virgo I's, bringing out their nervous side. They may be flattered by their partner's passion but unequal to his or her ardor, even when the Libra-Scorpio seems satisfied and happy. Virgo I's are prone to moods that prevent them from believing they are really pleasing to another person. This can be frustrating for Libra-Scorpios, but here more than anywhere it is important for them to temper critical outbursts. For as long as it lasts, this is generally an exciting relationship. Marriages are another kettle of fish: Virgo I's may feel more comfortable here, less nervous and more self-assured, but Libra-Scorpios are often much too complex to be happy in a long-range relationship with this relatively predictable partner.

Work relationships and friendships between these two sometimes overlap, and will benefit from both partners' critical attitudes and high standards. Exacting in its requirements, the pairing will put them under some strain, but as long as the partners are sensible enough to pace themselves and don't take on too much work at one time, they can keep on producing excellent results. Virgo I–Libra-Scorpio sibling and cousin pairs can be a strong force for tradition in the family (if they are appreciated) or a very rebellious one (if they are not). Their ties are usually close in times of trouble, but differences are likely to surface during calmer periods.

ADVICE: *Don't take on too much at once. Keep your intensity but learn to relax. Give others a chance to appreciate you. Direct criticism wisely.*

August 26–September 2
THE WEEK OF SYSTEM BUILDERS
VIRGO I

October 26–November 2
THE WEEK OF INTENSITY
SCORPIO I

RELATIONSHIPS

STRENGTHS: **ATTENTIVE, CONCENTRATED, TECHNICAL**

WEAKNESSES: **CONTROLLING, OVERCAREFUL, UNFORGIVING**

BEST: **MARRIAGE**

WORST: **BOSS-EMPLOYEE**

Attention to Detail

This talented and attractive pair focuses heavily on technical drive, a code of honor and generally sticking to the rules. Their greatest pleasure is finding solutions to problems, something the melding of their individual strengths makes them very good at. Virgo I's and Scorpio I's differ temperamentally, but they have one thing in common, which is often the basis of their relationship: attention to detail. They usually also have the ability to concentrate totally on the subject at hand. Not surprisingly, they may have a special interest in and talent for technical, scientific and other research areas. This interest may be put to use professionally, but can also emerge in hobbies such as bridge, chess, puzzles and other challenging board and also video games, all of which hold a special fascination for these two.

When Virgo I's and Scorpio I's fall into a romantic mood, they sometimes put these interests aside, but they may also pursue their amatory activities in the same avid and dedicated way. Care, control and attentiveness tend to characterize their love affairs. Always concerned with how the other person is feeling, both Virgo I's and Scorpio I's usually put the relationship's priorities before their own. They may make a kind of religion out of their love, with sacrifice playing an important role. Learning to give up and surrender to the moment may be a lesson that these two controlled personalities can study together. This combination can be an excellent one for marriage.

Trust is the primary element in this pair's friendships. Scorpio I's can be highly demanding and moral, but as long as the bond of trust remains intact they will forgive Virgo I's their occasional unconscious lapses in order to preserve the relationship. Should that bond be broken, however, they will rarely give their Virgo I friends a second chance. This relationship can be quite unforgiving. Scorpio I's and Virgo I's do better as co-workers or siblings than when cast in the roles of boss-employee or parent-child. Equality is crucial here—that and an absence of condescension, power plays, guilt trips and blame.

ADVICE: *Give in occasionally. Learn to submit. Try to be less unforgiving. Allow for mistakes. Don't use trust as a weapon. Let go.*

DR. ALBERT SABIN (8/26/06)
DR. JONAS SALK (10/28/14)

Sabin and Salk are both microbiologists who developed polio vaccines. Salk was first in 1953 with an inactivated-virus injection that was widely used until Sabin came up with his live-virus oral vaccine in 1960. Both are responsible for the dramatic reduction of polio worldwide.

August 26–September 2
THE WEEK OF SYSTEM BUILDERS
VIRGO I

November 3–11
THE WEEK OF DEPTH
SCORPIO II

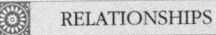

RELATIONSHIPS

STRENGTHS: **TRUSTWORTHY, RESPECTFUL, AUTONOMOUS**

WEAKNESSES: **NON-SHARING, SECRETIVE, OVERCOMPETITIVE**

BEST: **FRIENDSHIP**

WORST: **LOVE**

Autonomous Partners

Equality and balance count in this relationship. The focus here is achievement, but never at the expense of either partner; nor is it the relationship itself that the partners seek to further, but each of the two as an individual. The pairing depends, in fact, on their equal status. It is one of those unusual situations in which the self-actualization of both partners is given the same importance. This attitude prevails in both the personal and the professional realms.

The earthy qualities of Virgo I's and the deep emotions of Scorpio II's meld well in the areas of sexuality and feeling. Neither partner will hold back physically in their love affairs, but it may take time for them to reveal and share the more secretive areas of their personalities. Because they both tend to be trustworthy, the relationship often has great longevity and can be well suited to marriage. Should a romantic triangle form in which both Virgo I's and Scorpio II's are involved with the same third person, they are usually able—amazingly enough—to wish each other well rather than acting out of jealousy or vengefulness. Although war between them is rare, they could make excellent opponents, since they can give their all while still maintaining respect and even trust, each knowing that the other will abide by the fair rules of combat.

At work, the attitude here is "Either we both make it or neither of us does." Many professional teams have this attitude, of course, but what is unusual here is the emphasis on each person's autonomy. There is none of the clinging, dependency or false loyalty that characterizes many career efforts ("friends to the end … and this is the end").

Sibling and parent-child pairs in this combination, especially of the same sex, are often attracted to sports and other competitive and especially physical endeavors. Here the relationship acts as an incentive and inspiration for each partner to better their own personal best.

ADVICE: *Don't take your relationship for granted. Sacrifice for it occasionally. Spend more time on mutual efforts. Try to share.*

HUEY P. LONG (8/30/1893)
RUSSELL LONG (11/3/18)

For nearly 60 years the Long family dominated Louisiana politics. Huey, known as the "Kingfish," was governor from 1928–32 and senator from 1932 until his assassination in '35. His son Russell was senator from 1948–87. **Also: Charles F. McKim & Stanford White** (partners; architects); **Prince Albert & Edward VII** (father/son); **Goethe & Schiller** (literary friendship).

JOAN BLONDELL (8/30/09)
DICK POWELL (11/14/04)

Hollywood's vivacious, lovable Blondell was featured in many comedies and musicals in the 30s and 40s. She appeared with Powell in 10 films. He was a cherubic crooner in the 30s who later went on to dramatic roles. They were married from 1936–44. **Also: Harold Ross & William Shawn** (successive *New Yorker* editors).

August 26–September 2
THE WEEK OF SYSTEM BUILDERS
VIRGO I

November 12–18
THE WEEK OF CHARM
SCORPIO III

A Small Circle of Friends

This combination often revolves around a close circle of friends or family, which serves not only to satisfy the pair's strong social urge but to provide a support group that they can call on in time of need. They can acquire stability from this group, but they also contribute to it—this relationship will usually give at least as much to any group as it takes from it. Virgo I's will benefit from the self-possession and independence of Scorpio III's, Scorpio III's from the reliability and orderliness of Virgo I's. The relationship need not be romantic or physical; this pair can be quite fulfilled as friends, family members or co-workers.

There is no guarantee that Scorpio III's and Virgo I's will be attracted to each other, and any love affair they become involved in together is likely to lack the true spark of high passion. Marriages can be based more on practical and realistic grounds than on romantic ones, so that they can prove highly reliable and responsible, particularly when children are involved. In friendships these two will pursue many activities with other friends, probably involving travel and entertainment; within the group they may take the lead in planning, scheduling and coordinating these activities. As the years pass, this small circle of friends will suffer attrition from advancing age, and one or both partners may find themselves increasingly isolated unless they make a determined effort to broaden their circle.

Virgo I and Scorpio III family members often work in related fields or in the same business or organization. Such relationships are trustworthy and reliable, but if the co-workers restrict their social contacts to their immediate family group, the relationship may be somewhat closed, with narrow horizons and a limited capacity for personal or spiritual development.

ADVICE: *Widen your horizons. Don't restrict your circle out of fear. Try to develop all your potentials as fully as possible. Believe in yourself.*

BORIS BECKER (11/22/67)
JIMMY CONNORS (9/2/52)

Connors' and Becker's tennis careers overlapped in the mid-80s, when Connors was an "aging" veteran at 33 and Becker was an 18-year-old comer. In their many matches, Connors' experience and grit were pitted against Becker's strength and diving athletics. Their world rankings showed Connors ahead of Becker in '85, behind in '86, ahead in '87 and behind again in '88.

August 26–September 2
THE WEEK OF SYSTEM BUILDERS
VIRGO I

November 19–24
THE CUSP OF REVOLUTION
SCORPIO-SAGITTARIUS CUSP

Innovative and Visionary

These two are almost certain to demonstrate a pioneering zeal in any endeavor they engage in. They may have problems relating to each other interpersonally, however: Scorpio-Sagittarians sometimes see Virgo I's as formal and old-fashioned, while Virgo I's see Scorpio-Sagittarians as trendy and less innovative than they claim to be. And whether the pair are closely involved or not, Virgo I's may disapprove of the Scorpio-Sagittarian tendency toward inconstancy. Yet despite their differences, others may see these two as being in the forefront of their field, social group or family. Any rivalry here often appears less between the Virgo I's and Scorpio-Sagittarians themselves than between their respective supporters.

Romantic relationships are unusual between these two; Virgo I's can be much too emotionally demanding for Scorpio-Sagittarians, making them feel trapped. Nor are marriages much recommended, unless the partners work shoulder to shoulder in commercial or social endeavors. Easy friendships are perhaps more rewarding, although even here the partners are unlikely to see eye to eye. Scorpio-Sagittarius condescension to Virgo I's could spell the end of the relationship.

Virgo I parents can supply the physical necessities and often the financial resources that young Scorpio-Sagittarians want, but rarely the emotional understanding that these children need. In fact, they will often see their offspring as too wild and uncontrolled for their own good. At work, this combination can be impressive at getting results. Often innovative and visionary, it will give Virgo I's the chance to leave their somewhat conservative image behind and strike out for new and challenging terrain, often on the cutting edge. Scorpio-Sagittarians will appreciate the solid support this relationship affords them. Being backed up by someone so dependable will often enable them to do some of their best work. These partners should stop themselves from trying to get too close emotionally, however, for if they lose their objectivity they risk losing the whole thing.

ADVICE: *Stick to the work at hand. Sharing secrets may be like opening a can of worms. Ease up in your demands, go with the flow, and try to lighten up.*

August 26–September 2

THE WEEK OF SYSTEM BUILDERS
VIRGO I

November 25–December 2

THE WEEK OF INDEPENDENCE
SAGITTARIUS I

RELATIONSHIPS

STRENGTHS: **CHALLENGING, FLAMBOYANT, EXCITING**

WEAKNESSES: **ADVERSARIAL, ARGUMENTATIVE, TENSE**

BEST: **FRIENDSHIP/RIVALRY**

WORST: **WORK**

Friends or Enemies?

This hard-headed and success-oriented matchup is characterized by persistence and consummate role-playing. In commercial endeavors this pair can work to win—the cool, relaxed and objective face they present to the world is bound to infuriate competitors into making mistakes. The relationship is by no means perfect; in fact, it can produce extreme tension, so much so that it is discouraged for intimate pairings. Conflict will inevitably emerge between these two, the question being whether the purpose it is put to is constructive or destructive. Because Virgo I and Sagittarius I lie square to each other in the zodiac (90° apart), traditional astrology predicts friction between them. Yet they are also mutable signs, so that the relationship can go through a lot of changes, watching friendships turn into enmities and vice versa, for example.

As a romance this relationship is likely to strike sparks—sexual tensions run high here. The couple will often be openly critical of each other, Virgo I's seeing Sagittarius I's as unsettled and unrealistic, Sagittarius I's seeing Virgo I's as picky and difficult. Differences like these may make marriages ill-advised, but if these two become spouses they will never complain that their relationship is dull.

Friendships and rivalries are often intertwined here. Even the closest of friends in this combination will enjoy pitting themselves against each other in various activities, usually physical but inevitably one on one. The competition between them will be highly challenging, for they are often well matched. Virgo I–Sagittarius I friendships are sometimes split apart by jealousies, career conflicts or financial disagreements, but if so, the former friends often suffer pain and remorse over their breakup, and do not make enthusiastic adversaries. Meanwhile, former rivals and combatants can form solid friendships, sometimes laughing about their hostile past in good-natured banter. Siblings and co-workers can go through rough periods together, with tempers flaring and disagreements abounding. Yet through it all they have an understanding that holds them together. The most consistent element of their relationship can be an agreement to disagree.

ADVICE: *Keep the combat level reasonable. Learn the value of diplomacy and compromise. Winning is only part of the story. Never lose respect.*

EDGAR RICE BURROUGHS (9/1/1875)
BURNE HOGARTH (11/25/11)

Burroughs is the author of 24 Tarzan books based on his original novel, *Tarzan of the Apes* (1912). Hogarth is the cartoon artist who gave Tarzan a whole new life in newspaper comic strips from 1937–47, when he quit to found NY's prestigious School of Visual Arts. In '72 Hogarth began illustrating other books based on Burroughs' creations. **Also: Michael Jackson & Berry Gordy** (pop star/record producer).

August 26–September 2

THE WEEK OF SYSTEM BUILDERS
VIRGO I

December 3–10

THE WEEK OF THE ORIGINATOR
SAGITTARIUS II

RELATIONSHIPS

STRENGTHS: **UNASSUMING, DISCOVERING, POWERFUL**

WEAKNESSES: **INDECISIVE, PASSIVE, REMOVED**

BEST: **LOVE**

WORST: **FAMILY**

Unlocking Dormant Power

One theme of this relationship is unlocking the inner power lying dormant in individuals, groups or materials. Often of a technical, scientific or theoretical bent, these two make a highly curious and investigative pairing, being magnetically drawn to revealing the secrets of whatever it is they study. The systematicness of Virgo I's is fully realized here, giving structure and form to ideas that may have lain dormant for some time. This quality is unusually well complemented by the originality of Sagittarius II's, who have a strong ability to provide a new twist or unusual view on old ideas.

Virgo I's and Sagittarius II's in love affairs can unlock powers in each other that had previously lain undiscovered. The relationship's chemistry, and its interest in revelation, are useful for two individuals such as these, who tend to keep their thoughts and feelings to themselves, and who prefer being explored to exposing themselves by being more outgoing and aggressive. Both partners may have experienced their share of rejection and misunderstanding, and may come to the relationship badly bruised emotionally. A low-key relationship in which they are accepted, and have few expectations placed on them, may be what they both have in mind. Happily, it usually comes as a wonderful surprise to them when their relationship blossoms. These love affairs can be ideally suited to proceed on to marriage.

In the family and in friendships, Virgo I's and Sagittarius II's tend to be highly private, favoring quiet intimacy. In career matchups they can cooperate well on a daily basis, but they often do better working on their own and keeping in close touch by telephone, e-mail or fax. Since they live very much in the world of ideas, their physical presence in the same room is seldom really necessary, and they may brainstorm best when they think out their ideas on their own, then bounce them off each other in their fully formed state. These two can be successful in any of a variety of fields ranging from finance to science.

ADVICE: *Be more assertive now and then. Don't shut others out of your world. Take emotional risks. Don't be ruled by past failures.*

BEN GAZZARA (8/28/30)
JOHN CASSAVETES (12/9/29)

Actor Gazzara and actor-director Cassavetes were famous Hollywood friends and collaborators. Gazzara appeared in 3 of Cassavetes' films, most notably the highly respected *Husbands* (1970), for which Cassavetes was producer, director and co-star. Cassavetes' drinking problem is said to have contributed to his death in 1989. Gazzara's acting continued prodigiously into the 90s.

August 26–September 2

THE WEEK OF SYSTEM BUILDERS
VIRGO I

December 11–18

THE WEEK OF THE TITAN
SAGITTARIUS III

Bound to Clash

LEE DE FOREST (8/26/1873)
EDWIN ARMSTRONG (12/18/1890)

De Forest and Armstrong were both inventors in the field of radio who clashed over the years in a series of lengthy patent suits (1925–33). Most notably, De Forest challenged Armstrong's claim as inventor of FM radio. Armstrong, in poor health and out of money, committed suicide in 1954.

This combination is highly critical, with debates, arguments and outright battles likely to surface at any time. These two often find it hard to accept each other. After all, they have serious differences in temperament: Virgo I's tend to be highly suspicious of the domineering attitudes of Sagittarius III's, who in turn make things no easier when they brush off Virgo I's as nit-pickers. At times this seems to be a case of people who can't see the forest for the trees (Virgo I's) fighting it out with people who can't see the trees for the forest (Sagittarius III's). The Virgo I preoccupation with order and detail cramps the style of high-flying, expansive Sagittarius III's. Fundamentally opposed in their outlooks, these two are bound to clash.

This combination rarely reaches magical heights of romance or passion in love and marriage, but a strong physical bond can hold the couple together for a long time. The relationship tends to be faithful, and is supportive in time of need, but too often the partners ignore each other, stubbornly maintaining their own points of view. In the family and in friendships, Virgo I's will criticize what they see as Sagittarius III neglect and sloppiness. This can grow unbearable for their partner. Sagittarius III parents rarely have enough time for their Virgo I children, who usually give up trying to get their parent's attention after a while.

As executives or department co-workers, Virgo I's and Sagittarius III's can be overly sensitive to each other's progress, particularly if their achievements overlap. Battles over who gets the raise, promotion or credit after a job well done are especially common. But should the pair be able to put the good of the group before their own private interests, they could become a valued and trusted team.

ADVICE: *Try to be more diplomatic. Don't be so vocal. Listen to criticism occasionally. Put more effort into sharing.*

August 26–September 2

THE WEEK OF SYSTEM BUILDERS
VIRGO I

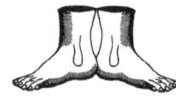

December 19–25

THE CUSP OF PROPHECY
SAGITTARIUS-CAPRICORN CUSP

A United and Unyielding Front

LADY BIRD JOHNSON (12/22/12)
LYNDON JOHNSON (8/27/08)

Lyndon and Lady Bird met when he was a congressional secretary in Texas. After a whirlwind courtship, they were married in 1934. They had 2 daughters, Lynda Bird and Luci Baines. All through Lyndon's rise to the presidency, Lady Bird was a great asset to his career—warm, intelligent, ambitious and active on the campaign trail.

This combination may be stubbornly opposed to change, both in its environment and within its own structure—unless, that is, the change is initiated by the partners themselves. Often monolithic in their outlook, the pair tend to move and think as one. They are drawn to the pursuit of power, and they know that if they present a united front and drive toward a common goal, their relationship can be unstoppable. Together they have a ruthless streak, but they generally behave kindly and thoughtfully enough to win the trust of their family and social milieu. Extremely capable and hard-working, Virgo I's and Sagittarius-Capricorns have a way of getting what they want, then digging in their heels and refusing to budge.

Intimate relationships between these two are less romantic and more realistic. Love and power may be inextricably combined here. At its heart, the relationship emphasizes the secret, more ambitious sides of its partners, and socially and financially this can propel it forward. Feelings of inadequacy in both partners tend to combine in a determination to prove themselves, and to succeed in their endeavors as a couple. They are usually better suited to marriage than to a love affair; as spouses, they tend to make their home a castle, their children princes and princesses. In their careers they try to build an empire, no matter how modest. In the family, they do best when working in the interests of the group, and worst when they try to oppose or take advantage of their relatives for their own private benefit. In all of these relationships, Virgo I's and Sagittarius-Capricorns would do well to make their outlook a bit wider and more flexible, and to modify their stance of power in favor of a little more empathy and understanding.

Work relationships and friendships are usually very socially conscious. The partners can depend on each other in seeking advancement and recognition. "United we stand, divided we fall" could be the pairing's watchword.

ADVICE: *Develop spiritual pursuits. Beware the lure of power. Be more empathic in your personal relationships. Acts of kindness will be rewarded.*

August 26–September 2
THE WEEK OF SYSTEM BUILDERS
VIRGO I

December 26–January 2
THE WEEK OF THE RULER
CAPRICORN I

RELATIONSHIPS	
STRENGTHS: **SERIOUS, THRIFTY, INTENSE**	
WEAKNESSES: **STINGY, STRESSFUL, RIGID**	
BEST: **MARRIAGE**	
WORST: **FRIENDSHIP**	

Tectonic Plates

Both Virgo I's and Capricorn I's have very definite ideas on how things are done. If their ideas coincide they are likely to get along quite well, but if not there can be the devil to pay. Virgo I's will not be interested in playing a secondary role to Capricorn I's in this relationship; things usually work best here when the partners share the power between them, with each having their own area of expertise. In certain departments, however, in particular the financial one, neither is likely to give ground very easily. Traditional astrology predicts an easy time between Virgo I and Capricorn I because of their trine aspect in the zodiac (they lie 120° apart), but their relationship is actually quite intense. Both earth signs, they can collide with the force of two tectonic plates.

Love affairs between these two can be sensuous, even passionate, but an element of control is always present—control of emotions, control of power, control of choice. No matter how gratifying the physical side of the relationship is, strains and stresses will eventually surface, undermining the pleasure factor. Power is even more of an issue in marriages, but here the couple can work out compromises and even outright deals. The marriage may in fact prove enduring, being virtually impervious to the buffeting of external factors that could penetrate a less unified front.

As friends, Virgo I's and Capricorn I's can get along well, but they usually keep a wary eye on each other. Their stinginess, or at the very least their somewhat tight attitude to finances, will assure that they get value for money, whether in consumer goods or entertainment. Parent-child relationships of whichever variation also put money first—the very worst sin in these matchups might be financial imprudence or overgenerosity. At work these two can achieve steady successes and even solid financial gains, but their fearfulness about taking risks can hold them back.

ADVICE: *Loosen up. Don't take money so seriously. What good is it if you can't enjoy it? Sharing and compromise are necessary.*

LYNDON JOHNSON (8/27/08)
BARRY GOLDWATER (1/1/09)

Johnson and Goldwater were political opponents in the 1964 presidential race. Goldwater saw Johnson as a grandiose, overbearing manipulator who would do anything to win a political battle. Johnson characterized Goldwater as an "extreme reactionary" and a hawk on the Vietnam issue. Johnson won by a landslide.

August 26–September 2
THE WEEK OF SYSTEM BUILDERS
VIRGO I

January 3–9
THE WEEK OF DETERMINATION
CAPRICORN II

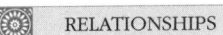

RELATIONSHIPS	
STRENGTHS: **RELAXED, COOPERATIVE, INSTRUCTIVE**	
WEAKNESSES: **LAZY, LACKING DRIVE, INEFFICIENT**	
BEST: **LOVE**	
WORST: **WORK**	

Setting an Example

These two can make excellent helpmates. In working together so successfully they often set a good example or model for family and friends, demonstrating the power of positive interactions and good feelings. It is often Capricorn II's who take the lead while Virgo I's serve in a lesser capacity, but whichever the case, power and control are seldom issues here. What is most obvious in this relationship is that the partners are enjoying themselves. This gives them a lot of satisfaction, and indeed they both would argue that without this mutual pleasure the value of even the most stunning accomplishments would be greatly diminished.

Love affairs and marriages here can be highly fulfilling. An easy sensuousness usually permeates the couple's daily life, the only downside being that things may not always get done in the quickest or most efficient manner. But the relationship is certainly responsible enough to guarantee that all concerned, including children, will be well looked after. Physical comfort is highly valued in these pairings, which, however, are also capable of going without for long periods of time, and of living on the warmth that comes from within. At its least successful, the relationship is merely satisfying, but should it have an element of spirituality and a desire for personal development, these two can reach new levels of self-actualization.

Working teams in this combination are sometimes a bit too relaxed and accepting, lacking the drive to succeed at the highest professional level. Parent-child relationships, too, whichever partner is the parent, may put too little emphasis on personal development and success, although they more than counterbalance this problem through their easygoing, sympathetic attitudes in everyday domestic life. Virgo I–Capricorn II friendships can be mutually instructive. These two sometimes meet as students and study an area of common interest together, but for the most part their relationship learns from experience.

ADVICE: *Don't get too relaxed. Push yourself a bit. Enjoyment and success need not conflict. Be aware that others are watching you.*

GERALDINE FERRARO (8/26/35)
WALTER MONDALE (1/5/28)

By running together as Democratic candidates in the 1984 presidential election, Mondale and former congresswoman Ferraro lowered a historic barrier against women at the highest levels of government. **Also: Tuesday Weld & Elvis Presley** (romance; actress/singer); **Michael Jackson & Elvis Presley** (posthumously son-/father-in-law; singers); **J.M. & J.E. Montgolfier** (brothers; invented hot-air balloon).

STRENGTHS: **SOLID, FINANCIALLY ASTUTE, RELIABLE**

WEAKNESSES: **OPPRESSIVE, OVERMATERIALISTIC, STUCK**

BEST: **MARRIAGE**

WORST: **FAMILY**

K-CI (9/2/69)
MARY J. BLIGE (1/11/71)

K-Ci is the lead member of the Jodeci neo-doo-wop musical group. Blige is considered the queen of hip-hop soul (the "Aretha Franklin of Generation X"). She appeals to older fans with her blend of soul sensibility and hip-hop savvy. These top performers are engaged to be married.

August 26–September 2

THE WEEK OF SYSTEM BUILDERS
VIRGO I

January 10–16

THE WEEK OF DOMINANCE
CAPRICORN III

Not Easily Overlooked

The weight of this relationship is palpable. In whatever sphere of life it manifests, it is a combination of moment, and it demands attention. Not that these two are particularly needy individually; they both can go for years of work without demanding to be singled out for praise. Their relationship, however, is hard to overlook. Even if it is taken for granted for a while, its impact on its surroundings will be felt later on—sometimes when it is no longer on the scene.

As lovers and spouses these partners expect each other to toe the line and do their share. Their relationship takes little for granted when it comes to fulfilling responsibilities; indeed, it can be extremely unforgiving. Sexual expression here is usually direct, and perhaps somewhat unnuanced. Should the flame cool down, sensuality can be sublimated into other areas, particularly those having to do with food or athletic or fitness training. Children usually grow up seeing their parents as reliable and active.

Parent-child relationships, no matter which personality is the parent, are often characterized by affectionate physical contact and by attentiveness to each other's material needs. Friendships and other types of family relationships have an undeniable tendency to be overly materialistic, which can slow down personal development. Capricorn III's will usually take the lead when the couple feels stuck or bogged down, often encouraging the relationship to move in more philosophical, religious or spiritual directions.

As co-workers or business partners, Virgo I's and Capricorn III's are usually sensible about production, sales and financial management. The relationship is comfortable about handling money, and when possible will make lots of it, but will also be satisfied with modest gains, as long as they are steady. Attentive to the needs of others, Virgo I's and Capricorn III's will rarely forget those who work with or for them.

ADVICE: *Don't forget to market yourself. Don't be so serious. Others can take care of their own needs. Pay more attention to your own self-development.*

STRENGTHS: **UNAFFECTED, SPONTANEOUS, BASIC**

WEAKNESSES: **NONSENSICAL, IRRELEVANT, DISTURBING**

BEST: **LOVE**

WORST: **MARRIAGE**

SYLVIA FINE (8/29/13)
DANNY KAYE (1/18/13)

Fine and Kaye were married from 1940 until his death in '87. Kaye, a versatile actor-singer-dancer-comedian, was one of America's most loved all-around entertainers. During their long marriage much of his comedy material and many of his songs were written by her. *Also:* **Man Ray & Francis Picabia** (Dadaist innovators).

August 26–September 2

THE WEEK OF SYSTEM BUILDERS
VIRGO I

January 17–22

THE CUSP OF MYSTERY & IMAGINATION
CAPRICORN-AQUARIUS CUSP

Clearing the Air

This relationship emphasizes the sharing and transmission of ideas and observations. Both partners naturally appreciate each other's thinking, so that even if they disagree over details, they invariably agree on the large line or the big picture. The relationship shuns both the false trappings of sentimentality and the phoniness of snobbism, and tries to express itself at a rather basic level. One problem with this approach is that those around it may consider it nonsensical, particularly if they are bound to more tightly traditional approaches. The relationship will have to be steadfast in its beliefs if it is to stand up to what could become overwhelming criticism.

Love affairs and friendships may attract attention through their unaffected and spontaneous behavior. Virgo I's will appreciate these relationships, which do not force them into a conservative mold, or insist that they repress their more outgoing side. Here they have the freedom they are often denied elsewhere. Capricorn-Aquarians feel at home here, and will rarely burden Virgo I's with duties or inhibit them by encouraging their desire to serve. Feelings are expressed openly and without censure in these relationships.

Marriages and work relationships between these two may not function so well in a standard social or career setting, since both Virgo I's and Capricorn-Aquarians demand something more out of life than just the ordinary. They will often reject the idea of marriage, doubting that it is really necessary or appropriate for them. In the professional sphere, these two do better if they are self-employed, or are entrepreneurs in a small-business or creative venture.

Virgo I and Capricorn-Aquarian family relatives often seek each other out. Despite any differences in age or social position, they are on the same wavelength, and will outrage more conservative family members with their unusual behavior and thought. This relationship often clears the air within its circle, but also stirs up animosity and resentment in those who refuse to take it seriously.

ADVICE: *Walk a bit more softly—be aware that you arouse antagonism. Do your own thing, but allow others the space to do theirs. Neither compromise nor provoke.*

August 26–September 2
THE WEEK OF SYSTEM BUILDERS
VIRGO I

January 23–30
THE WEEK OF GENIUS
AQUARIUS I

 RELATIONSHIPS

STRENGTHS: **AFFABLE, CHARMING, SOCIAL**

WEAKNESSES: **TROUBLED, UNSTABLE, HYSTERICAL**

BEST: **WORK**

WORST: **FAMILY**

Magnetic Appeal

This combination is likely to radiate attractiveness and charm. As a couple, these two enjoy spoiling each other and themselves, and their relationship emphasizes sensuality. This is not to suggest a pairing without problems—these partners won't necessarily have an easy time of it interpersonally. Astrologically Virgo I and Aquarius I lie quincunx to each other (150° apart) in the zodiac, and their relationship can consequently be expected to be somewhat unsettled and to require adjustment. This is epitomized by the fact that the partners may not be wholly comfortable with their own relationship's emphasis on pleasure. In some ways they are antithetical to each other, and to the relationship itself: Virgo I's tend to be more conservative, solid and predictable, Aquarius I's more cerebral, flighty and spontaneous. If together they generate a magnetic appeal, drawing others to them, they also hide a lot of frustration and dark, claiming qualities beneath the surface.

Shadow elements often emerge in love affairs between these two. Virgo I's have difficulty with their deeper emotions (both in dealing with them and in expressing them) while Aquarius I's have no need to confront their own inner life. The synergy of the relationship also magnifies the more nervous, worried and at times self-destructive side of both partners. The tensions in the combination can result in exciting sexual interactions, but unfortunately can also produce emotional outbursts and rejecting attitudes. In many ways, and quite unlike their characters in other combinations, these partners have difficulty staying objective about each other. Given the considerable level of instability here, marriages may not be recommended for them. Friendships and family matchups are usually undermined over the long haul by a Virgo I–Aquarius I chemistry that seems to bring out overemotional, even hysterical tendencies and differences in temperaments and values. Yet in the professional or commercial sector the partners can convey a tremendous affability and allure that transcend any personal differences they have. Curiously, conflicting energies can be transformed into magnetic ones here. The social side of this relationship is often successful in convincing others and inspiring belief in its powers.

ADVICE: *Don't deliberately give the wrong impression. Work on resolving personal differences. Learn balance, objectivity—and to listen.*

HUMPHREY BOGART (1/23/1899)
INGRID BERGMAN (8/28/16)

Bergman and Bogart will be linked forever for their roles in the 1942 classic film *Casablanca*. This was Bogart's first romantic part since he achieved stardom as a tough guy. Their screen magnetism was and still is unforgettable. **Also: Antonia Fraser & Hugh Fraser** (married; novelist/British MP); **Huey Long & FDR** (political enemies); **William Friedkin & Jeanne Moreau** (married; director/actress).

August 26–September 2
THE WEEK OF SYSTEM BUILDERS
VIRGO I

January 31–February 7
THE WEEK OF YOUTH & EASE
AQUARIUS II

 RELATIONSHIPS

STRENGTHS: **VERSATILE, ENERGETIC, IRREPRESSIBLE**

WEAKNESSES: **MIXED UP, ARROGANT, FAILURE-PRONE**

BEST: **FRIENDSHIP**

WORST: **PARENT-CHILD**

Shifting Roles

This relationship often centers around promoting a cause, one powered by tremendous, almost inexhaustible energies. Yet fun and structure are also built into its endeavors if one looks closely enough. Aquarius II's certainly have something to show Virgo I's about learning to let go, kick back and have fun, and Virgo I's can show Aquarius II's a great deal about how to order their lives more efficiently. When they come together their respective playfulness and organizational talents can be combined, enabling them to enjoy their work and structure their play. Luckily for them, both work and play are usually imbued with an irrepressible energy. Tireless though they may seem, though, they may need to watch out for the early-warning signals of burnout.

Friendships, love affairs and marriages in this combination simply will not be denied. Whether or not they work out in the long run, they have tremendous drive and spirit, surmounting social disapproval and scattering critics left and right. Admittedly this can sometimes seem a peculiar choice of partners, even to the partners themselves, but they acknowledge no laws but their own, which gives them a chance to overcome personal differences and difficulties. Their relationship can often move easily between friendships, marriages and love affairs, as if they didn't recognize that for other people rather well-drawn boundaries generally exist between these states. The emotional versatility with which they shift roles gives them a chance to stay in each other's lives for years. Passive and active, masculine and feminine, extrovert and introvert stances can quickly be switched as well.

Parent-child matchups in this combination often feature a mix-up of identity in which the child is the more mature of the two. At work, Virgo I's and Aquarius II's can carry through social or business projects with unstoppable force. If they fail, it is because of an alienating tendency toward overconfidence and arrogance. Being more realistic and controlled will help this couple achieve their goals.

ADVICE: *Keep your goals realistic. Learn to reorient your views intelligently. Don't be blinded by emotion. Beware of overrating your capabilities.*

LISA MARIE PRESLEY (2/1/68)
MICHAEL JACKSON (8/29/58)

It made world headlines when superstar Jackson wed Elvis' daughter. Married only 20 months, she filed for divorce, citing "irreconcilable differences." **Also: Isabel Sanford & Sherman Hemsley** (co-stars, *The Jeffersons*); **Jim & Sarah Brady** (married; gun-control lobbyists); **Eldridge Cleaver & Huey Newton** (black activists); **Peggy & Solomon R. Guggenheim** (niece/uncle; art collectors).

JOHN PHILLIPS (8/30/35)
CHYNNA PHILLIPS (2/12/68)

Chynna is the daughter of 2 of the original members of the great 60s folk-pop group The Mamas and the Papas. Chynna was born to John (and Michelle) Phillips and grew up in a musical environment. In '89 she joined with the 2 daughters of Brian Wilson (the Beach Boys' creative force) to form the pop-rock group Wilson Phillips. *Also:* **G.W. Pabst & Bertolt Brecht** (film director/composer; *Threepenny Opera*).

August 26–September 2

THE WEEK OF SYSTEM BUILDERS
VIRGO I

February 8–15

THE WEEK OF ACCEPTANCE
AQUARIUS III

Protecting the Downtrodden

This relationship is interpersonally tense and rebellious but has its rewards. These partners will contend not only against each other but as a duo against the outside world. They will ignore any differences between them if the chance comes to stand up for others—indeed, their protective instinct has a knee-jerk quality, and may emerge at any moment. The pair can get on each other's nerves, but they also serve real needs in each other. Aquarius III's can generate chaos around them, which upsets Virgo I's, yet they are also able to roll up their sleeves and get to work bringing order into the relationship. The Virgo I need to have everything planned out beforehand, however, will not sit well with them, since they are spontaneous folk for whom half the fun is playing things by ear. Should the pair be attacked while fighting out a disagreement of their own, they will usually unite against an outside threat.

As lovers these partners often direct the relationship's inherent rebelliousness at each other, especially if one of them tries to exert too much power or control. But these confrontations usually work out all right, since neither of them is likely to play the tyrant for long. The biggest problem in marriage will be Virgo I resentment over having to clean up after Aquarius III's, who are often quite negligent domestically. Their freedom-loving nature may in the long run make it difficult for them to meet Virgo I demands of fidelity and marital responsibility. In the family and at work, Virgo I parents and bosses often arouse Aquarius III rebelliousness, but at the same time bring a much-needed structure to the lives of these somewhat erratic personalities.

Both Virgo I's and Aquarius III's have a strong sense of fairness, which, when offended, leads them into contention. Their friendships are particularly reactive against authority or outright despotism, whether it comes from teachers, bosses or parents. The protection of the disadvantaged and downtrodden is common in these relationships, and can even become a career or way of life for them.

ADVICE: *Don't overreact. Still your rebellion and save your energy for the big struggles. Know who your friends are. Discuss what is bothering you.*

RICHARD GERE (8/31/49)
CINDY CRAWFORD (2/20/66)

Sexy leading man Gere was married to supermodel Crawford from 1992–95 amid international rumors of alleged homosexuality (of both) while maintaining the marriage just for appearances. In '94 the couple placed an ad in the *London Times* vigorously denying the rumors. *Also:* **Christopher Isherwood & W.H. Auden** (lifelong friends; writers); **Hegel & Schopenhauer** (philosophical opponents).

August 26–September 2

THE WEEK OF SYSTEM BUILDERS
VIRGO I

February 16–22

THE CUSP OF SENSITIVITY
AQUARIUS-PISCES CUSP

A Free-Thinking Struggle

Freedom of each partner's distinctive way of thought is this relationship's imperative but also its most likely source of conflict. Virgo I's may reinforce and abet Aquarius-Pisces striving toward success, or they may discourage it; when they support it, a close friendship or working relationship may result, but when they oppose it, Aquarius-Pisces may be forced to battle them openly or may retreat somewhat but prepare for further struggle. Virgo I's, on the other hand, will find themselves defending what Aquarius-Pisces term their rigidity—of thought, habits and patterns. Actually both of these partners have a tightly wound side, which this pairing often springs, producing resistance and fighting spirit. The relationship can go from friendship to rivalry depending on a whole host of variables, not the least of them being circumstance.

Love affairs here have their ups and downs, but are often extremely close and affectionate. The couple's freedom of thought and action tends both to unite and to divide them at various points in their relationship's development. Virgo I hardheadedness and Aquarius-Pisces sensitivity may well clash, but can also meld beautifully, especially in the sexual sphere. Ideology and belief play a considerable role in marriages in this combination, with disagreement or agreement in these areas sometimes determining the entire course of the relationship.

Career connections, friendships and family matchups are more likely to find Virgo I's and Aquarius-Pisces as rivals than as partners. Even when they serve on the same business or professional team their disagreements are likely to be vehement. A fundamental difference in thought, or a personal dislike, may lie at the heart of their animosity, but it also often involves the Aquarius-Pisces' need to challenge the Virgo I's supremacy and threateningly rocklike presence. Yet the pair may subtly and often unconsciously recognize each other's insecurity, and work to make their relationship more self-assured, even if it is always at least somewhat contentious.

ADVICE: *Play fair. You can disagree without engaging in character assassination. Competition can bring out the best and the worst.*

August 26–September 2

THE WEEK OF SYSTEM BUILDERS
VIRGO I

February 23–March 2

THE WEEK OF SPIRIT
PISCES I

STRENGTHS: **FULFILLING,
INDEPENDENT, DIFFERENT**

WEAKNESSES: **DISUNITED,
UNSOCIAL, CONFLICTING**

BEST: **LOVE**

WORST: **CO-WORKERS**

Outside Organizational Limits

Virgo I and Pisces I lie exactly opposite each other in the zodiac, yet when these opposing forces combine, the relationship that results is often highly autonomous and independent, a coherent single entity. These partners do best when acting on their own, free from the influence of others and outside the limitations imposed by organizations and other group endeavors. A further dynamic here involves the Virgo I tendency to bring diffuse, cosmic Pisces I energy down to earth. In return for this grounding influence, Virgo I's themselves receive a tremendous infusion of spiritual energy, like radio receivers, satellite dishes or lightning rods pulling energy out of the atmosphere.

As lovers these two can be overwhelmingly attracted to each other, like oppositely charged particles. It is precisely their polarity that makes their love affair whole and fulfilling. Although their marked differences of opinion and of temperament will sometimes lead to conflict, they show an underlying understanding and acceptance, and their relationship rarely pressures either of them into being something they are not. Their views of each other are realistic and accurate, and neither of them expects any more or less from their partner than he or she is able to give. Marriages in this combination can work out well, and offer a broad spectrum of difference to their children, who will know instinctively which parent to approach in which situation.

Virgo I–Pisces I professional relationships may be less effective if the pair work on the same project or material, when their differing approaches may come between them and the result desired. If, on the other hand, they work as freelancers, business partners or executives with separate departments or areas of expertise, the independent action they exercise will usually pay off. Sibling relationships and friendships between these two, particularly when of the opposite sex, can be extremely close, particularly in childhood and early adolescence but sometimes also throughout adult life.

ADVICE: *Try to improve your social skills. Even out differences and resolve internal conflicts. Independence may be less necessary than you think.*

ELIZABETH TAYLOR (2/27/32)
MICHAEL JACKSON (8/29/58)

Jackson and Taylor have been close friends and confidants for many years. In '91, when she married Larry Fortensky (her 8th), Jackson gave her away on the grounds of his ranch in a lavish ceremony. *Also:* **Yasir Arafat & Yitzhak Rabin** (enemies; PLO leader/Israeli leader); **George Montgomery & Dinah Shore** (married; actor/singer); **Elizabeth Ashley & James Farentino** (married; actors).

August 26–September 2

THE WEEK OF SYSTEM BUILDERS
VIRGO I

March 3–10

THE WEEK OF THE LONER
PISCES II

STRENGTHS: **SUPPORTIVE,
UNIQUE, INFLUENTIAL**

WEAKNESSES: **GUILTY,
CONDEMNING, PECULIAR**

BEST: **LOVE**

WORST: **PARENT-CHILD**

A Taste for the Peculiar

Independence of thought can be considered the higher power in this relationship. These two are apt to craft their matchup into something wholly unique, and will seek to touch the sublime, whether physically or mentally. Creative and original energies run high here, with the partners rarely doing anything in any way other than their own. Other people will often see them as peculiar oddballs. Their independence is such that they may not get along well in situations that are forced on them rather than chosen—as family members, say, or in working teams—but in interpersonal relationships that they do choose they often appreciate each other quite fully. Friendships or creative activities, love affairs and marriages can all do well here.

The relationship is ruled by fire, implying passion and intuition, especially in close personal matchups. Virgo I's admire the grace and emotional honesty of Pisces II's, Pisces II's the physicality and forthrightness of Virgo I's. Pisces II's can have problems with what they perceive as this partner's cynicism, which is really, however, the refusal of Virgo I's to bow down before models they see as irrational. For their part Virgo I's approach life with mocking wit, and may find Pisces II's much too fervent and serious. Yet these partners do have the ability to learn from each other, and to incorporate some of each other's strengths into themselves. The nature of the relationship is such that any attempt to fit it into more traditional forms may bring its end, but after it is over the partners may carry on stronger and better equipped than before.

As mates and as friends, these two will be faithful to each other in times of need. They will rarely forsake each other at such times, or hold back in what they are prepared to give, morally, spiritually or financially. This giving is usually unconditional, but later on may bring out feelings of guilt in the partner on the receiving end, who has not felt worthy of such attention.

ADVICE: *Don't always expect agreement. Differences are what make the world go around. Stay objective in career matters. Make peace with parents.*

EMILIO ESTEFAN (3/4/53)
GLORIA ESTEFAN (9/1/57)

Gloria and Emilio were original members of the disco-pop and salsa band Miami Sound Machine (1975). They married in '78. As the band grew in popularity, so did she—becoming a major force in the pop world. He turned from performing to managing. They have a son. *Also:* **Oliver Wendell Holmes & Oliver Wendell Holmes, Jr.** (father/son; writer/Supreme Court justice).

STRENGTHS: **INNOVATIVE, COMMUNICATIVE, TECHNICAL**

WEAKNESSES: **REJECTING, MISUNDERSTOOD, FRUSTRATING**

BEST: **WORK**

WORST: **FAMILY**

QUINCY JONES (3/14/33)
PEGGY LIPTON (8/30/47)

One of pop music's most prodigious figures, Jones is a musician, composer, arranger and producer who has won a long string of Grammys. In the late 60s he married Lipton, star of tv's *The Mod Squad* (1968–73). The couple later divorced. **Also: William Friedkin & Lesley-Ann Down** (married; director/actress).

August 26–September 2
THE WEEK OF SYSTEM BUILDERS
VIRGO I

March 11–18
THE WEEK OF DANCERS & DREAMERS
PISCES III

Honing Concepts

This combination is often concerned with the development and communication of new ideas. In fact, the mental connection here can be so acute that it makes the relationship irresistible. More pragmatic Virgo I's may be mostly concerned with what is being said, imaginative Pisces III's with how it is being said, or with what is being symbolized. Virgo I's will help Pisces III's to hone their concepts to a fine edge, while Pisces III's will impart a vivid spark to Virgo I thoughts, making them more attractive to others.

The communication in love affairs and marriages between these two may be of a more personal sort, with lovers and spouses developing a private language not fully understood by other people. Their understanding of each other is high, but they must be careful not to become isolated from or misunderstood by family members and friends. In friendships the partners often show a lot of interest in technical innovations of all kinds, but particularly in those concerned with new computer software, video games and Internet developments. In pursuing these interests they sometimes overload on each other's company, creating problems in their contact with intimates outside their own relationship. Their lovers and spouses will feel rejected and resentful. When the Virgo I–Pisces III combination emerges within a family, other relatives can feel similarly excluded, and sibling pairs in this combination are often criticized by parents at their wits' end in trying to establish some minimal degree of contact with them.

Work relationships can be contentious—Virgo I and Pisces III co-workers seldom see eye to eye. Yet their discussions and arguments will often have the effect of sharpening their perceptions and increasing the cogency and logic of their thinking. Communication skills, then, can be improved tremendously within these relationships, especially when other people lend input of their own. Whether or not these partners are right in their arguments will be proved by the results they get, but whether they succeed or fail they will contribute immeasurably to raising the level of communication within their group.

ADVICE: *Don't assume that others understand what you are saying. Remember, there are other ways to communicate than just the verbal. Less is sometimes more.*

STRENGTHS: **FUNNY, UNIQUE, TECHNICAL**

WEAKNESSES: **MISLEADING, MISUNDERSTOOD, MIXED-UP**

BEST: **FAMILY**

WORST: **LOVE**

DWEEZIL ZAPPA (9/5/69)
JOHN CAGE (9/5/12)

While not personally connected, Cage and Zappa are contemporary musical artists who share the same birthday. Dweezil is Frank Zappa's son. He was a solo artist in the 80s and formed the group Shampoo-horn with his brother in the 90s. Cage is the famed avant-garde composer who redefined music in the 20th century.

September 3–10
THE WEEK OF THE ENIGMA
VIRGO II

September 3–10
THE WEEK OF THE ENIGMA
VIRGO II

Unfathomable

The partners in this combination will find it extremely hard to share on a personal level. How lucky, then, that their need to share may not be so great to begin with—but they can still make life extraordinarily difficult for each other if that's what they want to do. Virgo II's react poorly when a lot of demands are made on them, but they are quite demanding with each other. They can have a great time together, particularly since they both love to laugh, but even here they might curb their tendency to make fun of each other, which can send their self-esteem into a nose dive. Paradoxical and hard to figure though they can be, these complex individuals may not be half as difficult to fathom as their relationship with each other is.

The textbook analysis of this relationship could be encyclopedic in length and depth. The combination's rarity is easily understandable: Virgo II's might be found in the same field, the same company, the same family, but they seldom remain under the same roof. It isn't so much that they are incapable of doing so as that, if given the choice, they prefer not to do so. In some ways Virgo II's are well suited to each other, since they both maintain rigorous standards that few but themselves will be able to live up to. They are also likely to share a high level of intellectual interaction and an interest in anything requiring a lot of expertise.

Virgo II couples have a way of being misunderstood that defies analysis. There is something so enigmatic in their relationship that even in the simplest, most common daily tasks a kind of mystery clouds their motives, their actions, their goals. One reason misinterpretations abound, perhaps, is that Virgo II's specialize in sending mixed signals. Their love affairs, marriages and friendships can be as confusing to the partners themselves as to other people, since they are unable to view each other or their relationship objectively. These two do best when focusing on anything standing concretely outside their relationship.

ADVICE: *Don't take yourself too seriously. Try to enjoy rather than analyze. Beware of sending mixed messages. A bit less mystery would help.*

September 3–10

THE WEEK OF THE ENIGMA
VIRGO II

September 11–18

THE WEEK OF THE LITERALIST
VIRGO III

STRENGTHS: FANTASY-RICH, GOOD-HUMORED, PRIVATE

WEAKNESSES: WITHDRAWN, EXCLUDING, PROCRASTINATING

BEST: LOVE

WORST: WORK

Hard to Pin Down

This relationship is likely to be private, somewhat isolated and quite idiosyncratic. Since an important element here will be the realm of feelings, an area where both partners traditionally have problems, their matchup may be highly beneficial to them in allowing them to express themselves more fully. At the same time, however, the partners' difficulties with all that is not concrete may produce a kind of struggle. As individuals they will often feel uncomfortable with their combination's interest in spiritualism, religion or the arts—in things that are amorphous or hard to pin down. Another tension here may stem from the conflict between the Virgo III effort to make Virgo II's toe the line, and keep to their word, and the Virgo II tendency to bring out the procrastinating side of the Virgo III personality, encouraging them to kick back a bit. The winner of this particular battle will vary from situation to situation, but in general it is the more easygoing Virgo II influence that proves the stronger.

Sparks seldom fly in love affairs, but the partners do have an understanding of each other, and what they lose in excitement they can gain in stability. At their best, these affairs are fairly open and accepting and allow a moderate expression of feeling. In marriages and at work, the burden usually falls on Virgo III's to bring the more isolating and fantasy-oriented qualities of the relationship into line; by insisting on more social and commercial involvement with the world, they guarantee at least a modicum of healthy interaction with other people. Marriages will require great patience on both sides but can work out. Co-worker or employee positions in a company, on the other hand, are best avoided, since both partners usually do best in their own sphere.

Friends and siblings in this combination usually have quite private relationships that tend to shut others out. The pair's private jokes and humor tend to keep them in a good mood.

ADVICE: *Push yourself to achieve a bit more. Don't retreat too far from the world. Share your sense of humor with others. Allow yourself greater self-expression.*

ROBERT A. TAFT (9/8/1889)
WILLIAM HOWARD TAFT (9/15/1857)

Robert is the son of William, 27th US president. William ran against Teddy Roosevelt in 1912, splitting the Republican vote and enabling Democrat Woodrow Wilson to win the election. Robert was a US senator for 3 terms (1939–53) and became known as "Mr. Republican." *Also:* **Jean Foucault & Hippolyte Louis Fizeau** (collaborators; early photo process innovators).

September 3–10

THE WEEK OF THE ENIGMA
VIRGO II

September 19–24

THE CUSP OF BEAUTY
VIRGO-LIBRA CUSP

STRENGTHS: TRADITIONAL, HARMONIOUS, RESPONSIVE

WEAKNESSES: PREDICTABLE, OVERSTRUCTURED, STRESSED

BEST: FAMILY

WORST: LOVE

Traditional Guidelines

This relationship is governed by rules, spoken or unspoken, that should never be transgressed. If any of these prove ambiguous or open to interpretation, or if they aren't completely known or understood, problems will arise, but the partners often do understand them clearly, so that harmony reigns in the relationship a lot of the time. Together these two will work out effective working methods that will guarantee results. The relationship is often traditional in its approach, no matter how unusual the partners' individual predilections may be. In careers, perhaps in a family business, these two usually do things according to tried-and-true methods that have worked in the past. They should be careful to keep excessively rigid adherence to rules from destroying their spontaneity, resulting in a somewhat predictable way of life.

Love affairs are a bit complicated and chancy. Virgo-Libras are often intrigued by the mysteriousness of Virgo II's, but when mystery shades over into emotional complexity they may find it hard to fathom. Since Virgo II's do not depend on other people for praise or support, they may think that Virgo-Libras weaken themselves by giving in to such needs. Should the relationship gel on the physical plane (which isn't overly likely), the couple might contemplate marriage, but as orderly as they are, marital and domestic responsibilities may impose too much structure and responsibility for them to handle.

In friendships Virgo II's are more likely to value their private life, Virgo-Libras their public life. But differences like this are in no way insurmountable, and in fact may help to provide variety within the relationship. Further complementarity can be seen in the way Virgo-Libras give expression to Virgo II fantasy, often being able to translate this partner's wishes into vivid and original representations, whether in matters of style, design, decorations or furnishings.

Virgo II–Virgo-Libra parent-child, sibling and co-worker pairs can be the bulwarks of the families or organizations of which they are a part.

ADVICE: *Keep your flame pure. Don't compromise away your beliefs. Beware of the rigidity that results from too many rules. Assumptions can be dangerous.*

ANNE OF AUSTRIA (9/22/1601)
LOUIS XIV (9/5/1638)

Louis, son of Anne, succeeded his father to the throne at age 4. While Anne was regent during his boyhood, a revolt was undertaken by the *parlement*, resulting in the French royal family being twice driven out of Paris. At one point, Louis and Anne were held prisoner in the royal palace. *Also:* **Isaac K. Funk & Adam W. Wagnalls** (publishing partners).

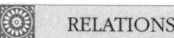
STRENGTHS: **ANALYTIC, REORGANIZING, PHYSICAL**

WEAKNESSES: **EGOISTIC, HYPERCRITICAL, COOL**

BEST: **WORK**

WORST: **MARRIAGE**

RICHARD I (9/8/1157)
ELEANOR OF AQUITAINE (9/28/1122)

Richard the Lionhearted was the son of Eleanor. During his reign (1189–1204) she was a dominant figure in English politics. In addition, she was a great beauty who was queen to 2 kings and mother of 2 others during her lifetime. Richard was known as a great crusader, spending much of his reign abroad. *Also:* **Dweezil Zappa & Moon Unit Zappa** (siblings; musicians).

September 3–10
THE WEEK OF THE ENIGMA
VIRGO II

September 25–October 2
THE WEEK OF THE PERFECTIONIST
LIBRA I

Rigorous Scrutiny

This relationship tends to hypervigilance in its attention to detail, especially in the partners' approach to each other. Their unending scrutiny of each other can be annoying and destructive. At the same time, the relationship's analytical approach is often its greatest strength, increasing the efficiency and productivity of, say, a work team through judicious and well-thought-out criticism. Both Virgo II's and Libra I's have an exacting side that leads them to subject whatever they come across to a rigorous once-over. They can be of great value to a work or family group, testing hypotheses, evaluating performances and reorganizing existing structures. Quite often they will come up with a new plan that may be much more effective than the one employed in the past.

Love affairs are often strongest in the sexual sphere. The partners are frank with each other on this subject, and neither of them has a whole lot of energy for romanticism or sentiment, or much interest in them, either. In satisfying mutual physical needs and wants, the relationship can be highly gratifying. Unfortunately, emotional conflicts can arise between the lovers from their criticism of each other's appearance or performance, inevitably puncturing ego balloons. Should they decide to begin a new life together as spouses, their enthusiasm may be considerable, certainly enough to carry them through their early years of marriage. As parents, however, they have a tendency to be too demanding of their children. Friendships in this combination generate fun times and provide an ambiance within which games, puzzles and other forms of challenging mental entertainment can be enjoyed. At work, the pair can perform well as consultants, analysts and even as ordinary employees. Superiors and top executives will rely on them for their frank and objective appraisals; in fact, they will be invaluable to management, since they will know their area well and are in touch with the needs of fellow workers. In the family, parents might often consult Virgo II–Libra I sibling pairs for advice during periods of stress and change. The siblings themselves, however, are apt to tease each other unmercifully.

ADVICE: *Loosen up a bit. Don't be so critical all the time. Nursing a bruised ego can become a bad habit. Be less demanding with close relatives.*

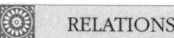
STRENGTHS: **HARMONIOUS, BALANCED, TRANSPARENT**

WEAKNESSES: **UNAMBITIOUS, UNEMPATHIC, DIVIDED**

BEST: **MARRIAGE**

WORST: **WORK**

PETER SELLERS (9/8/25)
BRITT EKLAND (10/6/42)

Swedish-born Ekland was a leading lady in international films in the 60s and 70s, following her brief career as a model. She married actor Sellers in '63, the year he began his film series as the bumbling Inspector Clouseau. They were divorced in '68. *Also:* **Giuseppina Strepponi & Giuseppe Verdi** (married; prima donna/composer).

September 3–10
THE WEEK OF THE ENIGMA
VIRGO II

October 3–10
THE WEEK OF SOCIETY
LIBRA II

A Transparent Interface

This can be an easygoing relationship in which the partners learn from each other and benefit from their respective strengths. It is like a window between two people, one looking out (Virgo II), the other looking in (Libra II). What they both see appears through the window as an object of great beauty: the more private Virgo II, for example, admires the social world of the Libra II, and vice versa. The relationship rarely melds these contrasting views but does allow the preservation of its partners' individuality. Their polarity poses no threat to their unity.

Admiration and affection may lead to love between these two. The partners have the ability to express true tenderness for each other, even when empathy isn't really an option. Their differences in temperament often create an atmosphere of romantic fascination and awaken strong protective feelings. As spouses Virgo II's and Libra II's will be extremely proud of one another, and happy to be living with someone so different from themselves. The window effect between them separates them but allows a transparency, so that hiding secrets from each other will difficult or impossible and sharing will be encouraged. Having children is recommended for this couple, since their polarity is essentially healthy, and gives their offspring a clear choice when in need of consultation or advice.

Since the harmony and balance between Virgo II's and Libra II's can limit the striving and aggression that are necessary in the business world, commercial matchups in this combination may lack the will and push to succeed. Harmony and balance will be more appreciated in the family, where other members of the group may see this pair as peacemakers, not through coercion but by example. Friendships here are generally relaxed and enjoyable. Here the partners sometimes don't share deep feelings or strongly emotional interactions, but they may reap rewards in an area too often overlooked in our stressful times: happiness.

ADVICE: *Try to feel what others are feeling. Put yourself in their place. Perhaps you need to try a bit harder. When you see something you want, go for it.*

September 3–10

THE WEEK OF THE ENIGMA
VIRGO II

October 11–18

THE WEEK OF THEATER
LIBRA III

 RELATIONSHIPS

STRENGTHS: **ENTHUSIASTIC, YOUTHFUL, GROUNDING**

WEAKNESSES: **RASH, UNRELIABLE, IMMATURE**

BEST: **LOVE**

WORST: **FRIENDSHIP**

An Excellent Foil

This couple usually creates an enthusiastic, youthful impression, putting others at ease. Their relationship has the kind of verve and dash that will make it effective in helping Libra III's fulfill their career ambitions. They will find a Virgo II an excellent foil for their outgoing personalities, and valuable when serving as their assistant, in an advisory capacity or simply as a capable helpmate. The problem here will be staying relaxed, for Virgo II's have a nervous side and may be unable to handle the pressures to which Libra III's expose them. Should they withdraw, or show signs of stress, the relationship's aspirations may be in danger. Libra III's may feel helpless to do anything about their partner's state.

Love affairs between these two can sweep both partners off their feet. Impetuosity can prove a problem here, but even if things don't work out in the long run, the memory of a natural and uninhibited love affair will remain. The relationship's youthfulness is often carried over into marriage. Children of such a union will enjoy their parents' positive outlook but must not be made to feel that they are sacrificing their own youthfulness to it. Interestingly, the detachment that both partners sometimes exhibit in relationships in any combination is understood and completely at home here.

Friendships here can suffer from irresponsibility, not only as a pair toward the outside world but between the partners as well. The most distressing part of this is usually the relationship's inability to come through in times of need. Family matchups, particularly between parents and children, may suffer from arguments that again reveal a certain immaturity. In work situations Virgo II's can ground the flightiness of Libra III's and can help resolve their periodic indecision. The relationship can also supply the stimulus and inspiration for many worthwhile projects and entrepreneurial endeavors.

ADVICE: *Don't get carried away so easily. Exercise more prudence and care. Be there in times of need. Take responsibility for your actions.*

PIERRE TRUDEAU (10/18/19)
MARGARET TRUDEAU (9/10/48)

Margaret, socialite and author (*Beyond Reason*, 1979), was the wife of Pierre, Canada's prime minister (1968–84). He promoted Canada's economic independence and quelled the secessionist movement in Quebec. The couple were popular with the international jet set and were known for their partying lifestyle. They eventually divorced.

September 3–10

THE WEEK OF THE ENIGMA
VIRGO II

October 19–25

THE CUSP OF DRAMA & CRITICISM
LIBRA-SCORPIO CUSP

 RELATIONSHIPS

STRENGTHS: **ASPIRING, EXCELLING, HARD-DRIVING**

WEAKNESSES: **STRESSED, UNREALISTIC, ADDICTIVE**

BEST: **MARRIAGE**

WORST: **LOVE**

Pressures to Succeed

This combination brings out the more demanding side of both partners. Together they are likely to produce work of high quality, and to have high expectations of each other in their personal interactions. The pressures to succeed and excel in this relationship are self-induced rather than dependent on social or parental input. Ultimately, however, the rarefied air at the top may not really suit either partner, and a rejection of or rebellion against their relationship's values may spell the end. If the relationship is to succeed, it will have to acquire a more realistic sense of its partners' capabilities.

Recognizing limits and assuming a more moderate stance can prove difficult in love affairs and friendships in this combination. The tendency here is to go overboard and indulge in all sorts of excesses. The pair sometimes revel in binges, the direct results of their self-inflicted stresses and perfectionist drives. Seeking relief from the unbearable tensions of their own demands and expectations, they may turn to escapist activities for release. Should Virgo II's and Libra-Scorpios form a hard-driving business partnership or other professional relationship, they may similarly reward themselves with wild bouts of spending and drinking.

Marriages between Virgo II's and Libra-Scorpios can show great ambition, with the relationship pushing the spouses and their children to ever higher rungs on the social ladder. Finding more substantial personal values and feelings of inner worth can prove a rewarding challenge for them. The need for balance and moderation here is obvious, and perhaps the place for them to start is by letting up a bit in their expectations. A related problem can appear in parent-child relationships of either variation: the parents will seek to project their own frustrated ambitions onto their children, who may be ill suited to the careers for which they are being groomed.

ADVICE: *Make realistic assessments of your capabilities. Don't push too hard or too fast. Allow time for events to unfold. Escapes are not the answer.*

MICKEY MANTLE (10/20/31)
ROGER MARIS (9/10/34)

Maris and Mantle were the NY Yankees' greatest high-powered hitting duo, setting many records. While great pals, they both vied in '61 to break Ruth's 60-home-run record. Maris succeeded. ***Also:*** **Buddy Holly & Big Bopper** (rock & roll singers; died in same plane crash); **Kitty Carlisle & Moss Hart** (married; actress/playwright); **Alan Ladd & Alan Ladd, Jr.** (father/son; actor/producer).

RELATIONSHIPS

STRENGTHS: COMICAL, COMPETENT, TOUGHENING

WEAKNESSES: AVOIDING, DISRUPTIVE, DIFFICULT

BEST: LOVE

WORST: FAMILY

FANNY BRICE (10/29/1891)
BILLY ROSE (9/6/1899)

Brice was the first Yiddish comic to work in mainstream musical comedy and radio ("Baby Snooks"). In 1927 she moved into a NYC apartment with theater impresario and producer-songwriter Rose. They married in '29. She starred in several of his musical revues in the 30s.
Also: Hilda Doolittle & Ezra Pound (close poets); **Capt. Bligh & Capt. Cook** (Bligh was sailing master on Cook's last voyage).

Mock Aggression

Humor in many forms, but particularly irony and sarcasm, is prominent in this playfully competitive relationship. Virgo II's love to kid their Scorpio I partners, who, although usually more serious, may tease them unmercifully in return. These provocations are usually light in tone, and can be quite amusing, but underlying them there is sometimes something darker, which cannot be expressed directly. One-upmanship can be the order of the day here: the partners often try to outdo themselves and each other, lifting the relationship into ever higher spheres of joking yet simultaneously earnest banter.

The problems that arise in love affairs and marriages in this combination can often be resolved in these conversational and often energetic exchanges. Mock aggression can be a useful way of working out resentments and frustrations. A point may come, however, where difficulties grow more severe and have to be confronted directly, and here trouble can be expected, precisely because the partners have no tradition of real discussion. But this is not to say that Scorpio I's and Virgo II's never have wonderful, even ecstatic times together—they often do.

Friendships and work relationships can overlap and can be more complex and serious than other relationships in this combination. Their level of competence is usually high, they discharge their responsibilities fully and they can rely on each other, particularly in times of crisis and need. Competitive impulses can arise, however, and at times will run out of hand. Seeking to outdo the other partner's technique, making a fool of the other partner (albeit subtly) or working to surpass the other partner's achievements are all likely tactics here. Competition between Virgo II and Scorpio I siblings can disrupt the family scene but have a toughening effect on the individuals themselves. Knowing when to stop is often the stumbling block, since these two are not always aware of the effects their shenanigans are having on other people.

ADVICE: *Find quiet time to open serious discussions. Explore underlying motives. Cultivate honesty. Don't lose your comic sense, but know when to stop.*

RELATIONSHIPS

STRENGTHS: PASSIONATE, ALLEVIATING, SOCIAL

WEAKNESSES: IMPRACTICAL, DEPRESSED, UNWORKABLE

BEST: MARRIAGE

WORST: WORK

EDSEL FORD (11/6/1893)
HENRY FORD II (9/4/17)

Edsel, son of the original Henry Ford (1863–1947), was president of Ford Motor Co. from 1919 to his death in '43. The now-classic Edsel automobile was named for him. His son, Henry Ford II (a.k.a. "Hank the Deuce") is credited with the revival and modernization of the company during the 40s. He was chairman and CEO from 1960–80. **Also: Max Reinhardt & Hedy Lamarr** (director discovered actress).

Unexpected Socialization

Both of these partners have a withdrawn, private side, so that they would often just as soon spend their time alone. The chemistry of their matchup is surprising in that it activates their impulse for social interaction with other people. This is a relationship that tries to turn its partners away from their preoccupation with the personal, giving them the chance to balance that side of themselves with family, community, club and team-sports interests. Virgo II mystery and Scorpio II silence will never be completely erased, but this relationship gives its partners an opportunity to combine their more introverted sides with other aspects of life that they might well have neglected.

Virgo II–Scorpio II love affairs can be dark, passionate, even stormy. They activate deep areas of their partners' psyches, creating a smoldering intensity. At the same time, the relationship has a social drive that prevents these lovers from wallowing in the moods and depressions to which they are prone, motivating them to seek out the company of others. Marriages between these two can be highly successful, even if the partners sometimes need a little relief from each other—which they are likely to find in parties, entertainment, vacations, games and other lighthearted activities involving friends or family.

The combination brings out a light, unserious side of both partners in friendships and sibling pairs, lending them both some relief from their own problems and a more carefree approach to life. Work relationships between Virgo II's and Scorpio II's are capable of success but will more likely bring out the partners' negativity, reinforcing whatever it was that gave them both a lowered self-confidence in the first place. Raising their self-esteem, perhaps by changing their attitude toward work, can make their pairing more effective, but their bond may ultimately have to be examined objectively and, if recognized as unworkable, to be modified or terminated.

ADVICE: *Follow your more social instincts. Don't assume you have to be alone to be understood. Share hopes and dreams with others. Lighten up.*

September 3–10

THE WEEK OF THE ENIGMA
VIRGO II

November 12–18

THE WEEK OF CHARM
SCORPIO III

The Best Foot Forward

The surprising thing about this couple is that they know how to put their best foot forward and achieve worldly success. This is in part because their relationship is ruled by fire, here signifying dynamism and initiative, and making for a highly adventuresome matchup that does not hesitate to step out and take the lead. Magically, it mobilizes the most extroverted side of Virgo II's, which it melds with Scorpio III managerial abilities to make a winning pair. The relationship's intelligence is high, although it is more intuitive than mental. The partners know instinctively how to get people's attention and hold it. Furthermore, the Scorpio III ability to convince works more easily and naturally when based in the Virgo II–Scorpio III relationship, which avoids controlling or claiming attitudes. Other people enjoy this relationship and rarely resent its persuasions.

It is in career connections and friendships that the combination's complex chemistry operates best to propel the pair forward. Unfortunately, Virgo II's and Scorpio III's may not be quite as successful living together as lovers, mates or family members. In day-to-day emotional interactions in which they themselves are the central focus, the difficulties seem to climb. On the surface, this would seem unlikely to be a very long-lasting relationship: Virgo II's prefer to work things out alone and are usually resistant to being pushed, manipulated or charmed; Scorpio III's traditionally motivate or manipulate their partners seductively but quickly grow tired if they themselves feel unappreciated. Also, although Virgo II's are quite independent, Scorpio III's may see them as having to be pushed or, worse yet, supported, something Scorpio III's are loath to do. If the relationship lacks an external focus, it tends to devour itself in dissension or fritter away its energies.

ADVICE: *Work on interpersonal understanding. Get to know each other better. Be more accepting. Beware of making assumptions. Exercise patience.*

SID CAESAR (9/8/22)
IMOGENE COCA (11/18/08)

Caesar and Coca were co-stars of *Your Show of Shows* (1950–54), early tv's greatest variety program that riveted the American public. Perfect foils for each other, they had a comedic magnetism that kept viewers in stitches for 90 minutes every Saturday night. . **Also: Jane Curtin & Lorne Michaels** (*SNL* comic/producer).

September 3–10

THE WEEK OF THE ENIGMA
VIRGO II

November 19–24

THE CUSP OF REVOLUTION
SCORPIO-SAGITTARIUS CUSP

Exaggerative Statements

As a pair, these two know full well that all the world's a stage, and that their own personal drama is only one of many being acted out. They take great interest in the events unfolding around them, and try to find where their own personal relationship fits in. In fact, making social sense out of the personal is perhaps the main focus of this relationship. Rather than engaging in power struggles with each other, these two are more caught up in the nature of society—in watching and understanding the flow of power in the broader world.

Romantic relationships, marriages and even family matchups in this combination can have a certain objectivity and detachment about them that facilitates understanding others—their motivations, their foibles, their frustrations. The partners may pursue interests in areas such as psychology, being fascinated by the study of emotions like jealousy, hatred, love, and so on. At the same time, they are not particularly prone to sensing these emotions in their pure form in their relationship. Paradoxically, the Virgo II–Scorpio-Sagittarius relationship may be strangely unable to cope with its own problems, or in many cases even to realize that they exist. Its detachment and lack of awareness can severely detract from its level of intimacy.

Friendships and rivalries here are usually highly spirited. Volatile in the extreme, the relationship is not conducive to keeping either positive or negative feelings inside for very long. Given to the grand gesture and the exaggerated statement, the matchup is likely to call up dramatic response from other people, matching its own.

Professional pairings may be concerned with the conditions under which people work. Their basic creature comforts, and the conditions that will make them happiest and therefore most productive, are of primary importance. Discussions of how work can be intelligently scheduled, and attention to the special significance of holiday parties, special observances and company or group traditions, underline the pair's social interests. Similarly, parent-child combinations treasure family festivities of all types.

ADVICE: *Drop the play-acting occasionally. Try to get down to the nitty-gritty. Don't neglect self-understanding. Open your heart more.*

JAMES GARFIELD (11/19/1831)
CHARLES GUITEAU (9/8/1841)

Guiteau was President Garfield's assassin. Garfield's political party declined Guiteau's offers of help in the 1880 campaign and later refused to find him a job in the president's administration. In 1881, as Garfield was leaving for a family trip from the railroad station in Washington, DC, the disgruntled Guiteau shot him. He was hanged.

ROBERT GOULET (11/26/33)
CAROL LAWRENCE (9/5/32)

Goulet, the singer-actor who debuted to stardom in Broadway's *Camelot* (1960), was married to musical actress Lawrence, best remembered for her stage role as Maria in *West Side Story* (1957). Both went on to pursue successful careers on stage and tv.

Also: **Merna Kennedy & Busby Berkeley** (married; actress/choreographer).

September 3–10
THE WEEK OF THE ENIGMA
VIRGO II

November 25–December 2
THE WEEK OF INDEPENDENCE
SAGITTARIUS I

Strong Direction

These two tend to bring out each other's outgoing side. Together they can make a powerful team—in fact, their relationship often focuses on the exercise of power, whether in the family, in business or in society generally. It works less to dominate and control, however, than to act as a catalyst for dynamic forces and unusual ideas. Although Virgo II–Sagittarius I pairs have a highly private side to their lives that few know about, as individuals they also have powerfully aggressive personas that have to find their way in the world, a quality the synergy of their relationship magnifies. Each partner here is especially open to the influence of the other: Sagittarius I's have something to teach Virgo II's about trusting their intuitions, and Virgo II's can show their Sagittarius partners a lot about matters of taste, encouraging them to be a bit more patient.

Love affairs, marriages and friendships in this combination can be romantic, affectionate and rewarding, but the partners must beware of getting caught up in ego struggles. Sagittarius I's have a moral and unforgiving side that may make them critical of the less-than-perfect ethical stance of Virgo II's, who have a tendency to justify the means by the ends, and a certain ruthlessness in getting their way. Sagittarius I's are no less insistent on what they want but will try to be fair—and will say so. This can irritate Virgo II's, leading them to criticize their partners as holier-than-thou. Meanwhile, Virgo II selectivity may rub Sagittarius I's the wrong way, provoking charges of elitism, pickiness and snobbism.

In business partnerships and creative or research endeavors, this pair's vision can give strong direction to any working group. They are rarely split by a struggle for power, and can exercise leadership jointly if this is what is needed. Parent-child combinations are prone to some of the same frictions that appear in other interpersonal relationships but can still prove inspiring to family members and other relatives.

ADVICE: *Minimize internal strife. Discuss differences openly. Don't let arguments destroy love. Try to be more openhearted and forgiving.*

ELI WALLACH (12/7/15)
ANNE JACKSON (9/3/26)

These NY actors have had a happy and durable marriage since 1948. Jackson, principally a stage actress, and Wallach, mainly a screen actor, have often shared the limelight.

Also: **Cliff Robertson & Dina Merrill** (married; actors); **Donnie & Bobby Allison** (brothers; auto racers); **Elizabeth I & Mary, Queen of Scots** (royal enemies); **Billy Rose & Joyce Matthews** (married twice; bandleader/actress).

September 3–10
THE WEEK OF THE ENIGMA
VIRGO II

December 3–10
THE WEEK OF THE ORIGINATOR
SAGITTARIUS II

Out of the Ordinary

When two of the most unusual types in the year get together, almost anything can happen. Both partners here have an idiosyncratic view of the world, ranging from the out of the ordinary to the peculiar to the downright weird. This tendency is intensified by their relationship, which is therefore quite open to be misinterpreted and misunderstood by other people. Whether these two turn out to be friends or enemies, they usually have great insight into each other, to the point where each of them may feel that the other one is the only person who really understands them.

Virgo II's and Sagittarius II's are quite aware of their own values—they know what they want. Yet because they often lack insight into themselves, they don't always know what they need or how to get it. Their love affairs and friendships are highly complex emotionally, then, but the understanding present in the relationship can help them to gain self-awareness. This will inevitably involve struggle and pain but will also be highly meaningful. Through the depth and psychological insight that this relationship affords, the partners may finally come to terms with rejections and misunderstandings they have suffered in the past. Their bond can grow strong in the process, but they should beware of becoming too dependent on their relationship. Divorces here can be particularly traumatic, but the partners may be able to form better later relationships through the lessons they take away from this one.

Since Virgo II and Sagittarius II lie in square aspect (90° apart) in the zodiac, astrology predicts friction between them. Sparks can certainly fly if they are rivals or enemies, but if they are allies their family and business groups can benefit from the constructively critical attitude that their relationship offers. In all of their relationships, the Virgo II–Sagittarius II couple must walk a fine line between offending others with their unusual stance and compromising their beliefs. They should try to find a middle way between a nonconformist and therefore isolating stance and one that craves and seeks social acceptance.

ADVICE: *Be yourself, but also be prepared to compromise. Take the time to review your past. Work on self-improvement. Make yourself clear.*

September 3–10

THE WEEK OF THE ENIGMA
VIRGO II

December 11–18

THE WEEK OF THE TITAN
SAGITTARIUS III

Empire Building

The extension of personal power is a prime theme in this combination; the partners often come together because they perceive their ability to expand their capacities together. Sometimes, however, their interactions degenerate into power struggles over the most mundane things. The relationship can effectively run a business, family or social organization, but may also view its province as its own personal empire, whether it is contained within the partners' home or office or extends farther afield. Virgo II's see all the tiny details, and are fact-oriented, while Sagittarius III's see the big picture and are caught up with ideas. At their best, then, they have all the bases covered, but if they fight, their different orientations will bring endless argument.

Virgo II's sometimes feel neglected in love and marriage with Sagittarius III's. Emotionally complex, they require a degree of effort, patience and understanding that Sagittarius III's may be unprepared to provide. Sagittarius III's, too, can feel ignored by Virgo II mates or friends, who may be less interested in their latest plans and more in the work at hand. Even so, love affairs here can be thrilling, both in and out of the bedroom, with strong romantic feelings on both sides. Whether these feelings can be maintained over the long haul of marriage is another story.

Parent-child matchups between these two, whichever of them is the parent, tend to emphasize tradition, succession and passing the mantle of family finances, business or property from generation to generation. Problems arise when the next in line has no interest in such traditions or behaves irresponsibly. In the commercial sphere, Virgo II's usually know where to go for financial counsel when they can't answer all the questions themselves. Sagittarius III's can have a feeling for making money but could use Virgo II advice as to what to do with their earnings, for they are sometimes penny wise but pound foolish. They will usually take the lead in career and social endeavors, but Virgo II's are no slouches when it comes to power, so that problems may arise if Sagittarius III leadership falters or fails.

ADVICE: *Be more patient and understanding. Show more interest, if possible. Don't assume that what you are doing is more important.*

AMY IRVING (9/10/53)
STEVEN SPIELBERG (12/18/46)

Producer-director Spielberg married stage, screen and tv actress Irving in 1985. Her career in the late 80s was overshadowed by the marriage and her role as mother of their son Max. They went through an especially rough divorce, ending the marriage in '89. ***Also: Darryl Zanuck & Richard Zanuck*** (father/son; producers); **Peter Lawford & Frank Sinatra** (Rat Pack pals; actor/actor-singer).

September 3–10

THE WEEK OF THE ENIGMA
VIRGO II

December 19–25

THE CUSP OF PROPHECY
SAGITTARIUS-CAPRICORN CUSP

Us Against the World

This combination could encourage its partners' less savory tendencies by allowing them to indulge each other's self-pity. In this sense their relationship has a supportive function, but also a tendency toward an us-against-the-world stance that can be dangerously isolating. Both Virgo II's and Sagittarius-Capricorns have a private, introverted side that the chemistry of their relationship heightens. They have often suffered some frustration and unhappiness at the hands of the world, and find some compensatory sympathy in each other—they may make each other feel that they have met a kindred spirit who understands what it is to have suffered life's slings and arrows.

Love affairs between these two are capable of deep passions. Extremely private, the lovers may resent any intrusions, and will consider the betrayal of a confidence the worst of sins. The relationship is deeply empathic but can include blame, guilt and shame trips that are often echoes of or scripts left over from unhappy childhood experiences. The partners must be careful to let each other know when they begin to act like disapproving parents. And should they become parents themselves, Virgo II's and Sagittarius-Capricorns should foster the intention of breaking with old patterns rather than repeating the mistakes of the past.

In friendships and working relationships, Virgo II's can inspire the creativity of Sagittarius-Capricorns and serve as their models in successful business and social endeavors. As a co-worker team, these two may be able to discharge their duties within a company or organization year after year, quietly and efficiently, steadily and without complaint. They are faithful to each other, rarely breaking their bond in order to gain advancement or remuneration. Unfortunately, this means they run the risk of getting stuck.

Siblings or cousins in this combination, especially of the opposite sex, may have a secret society going on within the family structure that few know about or even suspect. Their communication may be unspoken, but nevertheless rings loud and clear to them.

ADVICE: *Support each other but don't pull each other down. Leave room for individual growth. Be more forgiving and less fearful. Open up to other people.*

DAVE STEWART (9/9/52)
ANNIE LENNOX (12/25/54)

Stewart and Lennox are the principal members of the powerful pop group the Eurythmics. When they met in the late 70s they immediately began a romantic as well as musical relationship. By the time they started the Eurythmics in '80, their affair had ended. ***Also: Dweezil Zappa & Frank Zappa*** (son/father; rock musicians).

ANTON DVORAK (9/8/1841)
PABLO CASALS (12/29/1876)

Composer Dvorak, popularly known for his *New World Symphony* (1893), wrote one cello concerto. Casals, greatest cellist of the 20th century, gave famous performances of Dvorak's concerto and made what is considered the definitive recording of the work. **Also: Pierre Troisgros & Alain Chapel** (nouvelle cuisine innovators).

September 3–10
THE WEEK OF THE ENIGMA
VIRGO II

December 26–January 2
THE WEEK OF THE RULER
CAPRICORN I

Parallel Evolution

This relationship emphasizes learning, experimentation and personal development through experience. Virgo II's and Capricorn I's usually have enough respect and trust for each other to be able to rely on each other's observations and input. Even without living and working together, in many ways they will parallel each other in their evolution, needing only to contact each other from time to time in order to touch base. In fact, it may be difficult for these two to establish their relationship in the same physical space, for they tend to be territorial and possessive, and find it hard to share what they see as their own.

Struggles usually emerge in marriages over space and ownership. The extent of these controlling attitudes can become all too apparent should the spouses break up—divorces can feature vehement fighting over property and children. Love affairs are less troubled. Here Virgo II's and Capricorn I's may place a much higher value on ideals, affection and consideration—in short, intangibles. Their matchup is also quite sensual; in fact gustatory, tactile and sexual areas draw this couple like a magnet and may prove a solid basis of their relationship. Still, avoiding the common ownership of possessions is a good idea in these romances.

Work and career relationships show a striking ability to digest and disseminate information. Sharing their discoveries is perhaps the greatest single joy of the Virgo II–Capricorn I professional relationship; commercial motives such as the fear that secrets will be stolen will rarely make this team repress its desire to learn, share and assimilate. Education also has a priority in the spheres of family and friendship. The conviction that learning should be valued above all else does not always have a beneficial effect, however, since this relationship is capable of exerting an unwelcome and unconstructive pressure on people who are not really suited to study.

ADVICE: *Don't impose your will on others. Respect differing opinions. Give people time to make up their minds. Drop possessive attitudes.*

RICHARD NIXON (1/9/13)
JOHN MITCHELL (9/5/13)

Mitchell was Nixon's attorney general from 1969–72. In '72 Nixon appointed him chairman of the Committee to Re-elect the President. However, Mitchell's involvement in the ensuing Watergate scandal resulted in his conviction (1975) for perjury and other charges. He was sent to prison for 4 years. Mitchell, who died in '88, remained loyal to Nixon right to the end.

September 3–10
THE WEEK OF THE ENIGMA
VIRGO II

January 3–9
THE WEEK OF DETERMINATION
CAPRICORN II

Peas in a Pod

In some ways these two go together like peas in a pod. Lying 120° apart in the zodiac, Virgo II and Capricorn II have a trine aspect between them, which astrology views as favorable and easygoing. And the relationship is quite comfy—until problems arise. The matchup goes much deeper, however, than superficial liking or acceptance, particularly in emotional realms, and its depth only becomes more apparent in times of crisis and chaos. The bonds that tie Virgo II's and Capricorn II's together have an almost fatalistic or karmic cast to them. One gets the feeling that these two deserve or were made for each other, for better or for worse.

Love affairs here are often highly physical and sexually fulfilling. But worry, and fear of rejection, can plague the couple, and if their relationship is to retain a measure of balance it must become more aware, more self-confident (but not arrogant) and, above all, a bit lighter. Learning to have fun and to take itself less seriously may become a requirement for its health and, ultimately, its survival. Marriage and work are often interconnected, again raising stress levels and increasing workaholic tendencies. Parent-child relationships of either variety should struggle to get hidden material out in the open, where it can be dealt with and then, perhaps, forgotten.

Friendships and work relationships look to the rest of the world like the tip of the iceberg: a lot is hidden below the surface here. Extremely secretive, the partners make their own rules and do what they have to do, paying little attention to the consequences. In some cases ruthless, in others merely preoccupied or unconcerned, they patiently support and protect each other, knowing that their fortunes are inextricably tied. Yet they lack deep moral or empathic commitment. Should one of them fail in business, social or financial dealings, threatening to take them or their organization under, the other will show coolly pragmatic survival instincts.

ADVICE: *Lighten up. What good is it if you can't enjoy yourself? Be more honest. Acknowledge personal responsibilities. Lower stress levels.*

September 3–10

THE WEEK OF THE ENIGMA
VIRGO II

January 10–16

THE WEEK OF DOMINANCE
CAPRICORN III

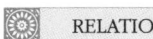
Assimilating Experience

This solid, tough relationship can stand a lot of knocks. At the same time, it is characterized by an ease in assimilating experience and by a natural feeling between the partners. It shows imagination, vision and an orientation toward the future. Sometimes the only thing needed to bring out someone's creativity is a relaxed and open approach, and Capricorn III's will particularly appreciate this relationship for allowing their creative side to be activated, a side too often neglected by people who lean on their strong shoulder for support. Virgo II's, too, will be happy that their unusual ideas and personalities are finding an understanding audience. True, challenging experiences are bound to confront these two, but the more roadblocks they face, the more determined they will be to break through, and the more they can hope to learn.

Virgo II's and Capricorn III's are an excellent match in love affairs, although these affairs may not be strongly romantic. Both partners have a natural attitude to sex and can express affection easily. Their marriages might also click, but in a different way: here responsibilities, and the opportunity to build an effective family unit, usually gain ascendancy. Many disagreements and arguments over day-to-day details can emerge, for as spouses these two don't necessarily see eye to eye on practical matters, and both will regard themselves as specialists in these areas. Building, restoring or refurbishing a home can be especially stressful in this relationship.

At work these partners make an outstanding combination. Virgo II's are especially good at tending to financial and business matters, while Capricorn III's contribute powerful skills in planning and administering projects. Friendships and family relationships (parent-child or sibling) in this combination may experience power struggles in which each individual strives to impose his or her own direction on the other. In order for such relationships to remain intact, some understanding, tolerance and compromise will have to be established. All-out conflict is a scenario best avoided here, at almost any cost.

ADVICE: *Give each other enough space. Place limits on your disagreement. Work for the good of the group. Put personal power struggles behind you.*

JESSE JAMES (9/4/1847)
FRANK JAMES (1/10/1843)

The James brothers (shown here with mom) formed an outlaw gang following the Civil War. They robbed banks, stagecoaches and trains—and built a Robin Hood reputation in the process. In 1882 Jesse was killed by a fellow outlaw for the reward. Frank later surrendered to authorities and was acquitted. *Also:* **Daniel Hudson Burnham & John Wellborn Root** (architects of first skyscrapers).

September 3–10

THE WEEK OF THE ENIGMA
VIRGO II

January 17–22

THE CUSP OF MYSTERY & IMAGINATION
CAPRICORN-AQUARIUS CUSP

Compelling Coalescence

This relationship often sees Virgo II practicality and Capricorn-Aquarius inventiveness coalescing in a compelling way. It has the ability to convince others, not only through ideas but through charm, and exerts a magnetic influence on its environment. Its internal dynamics are not always the most settled, but frictions and differences of opinion often have the effect of generating dynamic power. Virgo II's and Capricorn-Aquarians sometimes engage in outright enmities, but they are more likely to demonstrate competitive impulses that are ultimately positive in effect, pushing both partners to better their own personal best and to improve the quality of their work.

In love affairs, temperamental differences between Virgo II's and Capricorn-Aquarians usually keep them from forming a lasting or emotionally deep relationship. Both partners are likely to avoid being honest about their feelings and to find it hard to empathize. Even a strong sexual bond is not usually enough to sustain this relationship for very long. Marriages, too, are not much recommended here.

Competitive and even combative tendencies may threaten to destroy friendships, even if they are exciting. Prone to jealousy and possessiveness, friends in this combination are likely to become rivals when they share an object of their affections. They will ultimately have to choose, which may be painful. Work relationships between these two are best kept objective and should not involve family members, spouses or friends. Virgo II's may grow exasperated with impractical Capricorn-Aquarians, particularly in the financial sphere, but at the same time will be dependent on their creative input. Capricorn-Aquarians can resent Virgo II criticism and bossiness but need their pragmatic guidance. These partners' talents and needs are usually complementary and may lead to career success. Parent-child relationships, especially with the Virgo II as the parent, may prove stressful and experience periodic breakdowns in communication.

ADVICE: *Try to be more honest and sympathetic. Put yourself in the other person's place. Keep lines of communication open. Take time to care.*

ARNOLD PALMER (9/10/29)
JACK NICKLAUS (1/21/40)

Palmer and Nicklaus are among the greatest and most popular golfers in the history of the sport. Nicklaus had his first major victory in the 1962 US Open in a playoff against Palmer, becoming one of the youngest golfers ever to win that title. These pros are longtime friends. *Also:* **Matthew Boulton & James Watt** (steam engine manufacturing partners).

STRENGTHS: **OBJECTIVE, AMICABLE, ADVISORY**

WEAKNESSES: **GUARDED, ENVIOUS, BLOCKED**

BEST: **FRIENDSHIP**

WORST: **LOVE**

FRANKLIN ROOSEVELT (1/30/1882)
ALF LANDON (9/9/1887)

Landon was favored in the 1936 presidential race against Roosevelt. In fact, Roosevelt won by a landslide. Confidence in Landon came from the fact that he was the only Republican to hold onto his governorship in the '32 elections. Following his loss to Roosevelt, he retired from national politics.
Also: Stefano Casiraghi & Princess Caroline of Monaco (married).

September 3–10
THE WEEK OF THE ENIGMA
VIRGO II

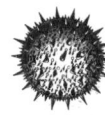

January 23–30
THE WEEK OF GENIUS
AQUARIUS I

Amicability and Animosity

This mix of amicability and animosity keeps both individuals on their toes. The guardedness that results between them causes a kind of energy blockage that can hamper both the relationship's results and its development. These two have much to offer one another, but their respective strengths are unlikely to merge, coalesce or complement each other, for this would demand exactly the free flow of energy that this combination lacks. The customs here, especially in business combinations and friendships, are distance and blockage. Furthermore, the relationship may include a certain enviousness—Virgo II's toward Aquarius I's for their quick perceptions and creativity, Aquarius I's toward Virgo II's for their practicality and money sense. Aquarius I's tend to overshadow their partner in this combination, but Virgo II's exert their own subtle influence and can function as the Aquarius I's most valuable critic, adviser or even teacher. Aquarius I's will be attracted by Virgo II complexity and secretiveness, perhaps trying to unravel this intriguing personality's mystery. Observation is a hallmark here, but usually to no avail, as inherent blockages keep the combination from progressing.

Love affairs bring out the nervous sides of both of these partners. Insecurities abound here, and the couple tend to worry a lot about whether they are pursuing the right path or were really meant to be involved with each other in the first place. The domestic responsibility of marriages will benefit the relationship a bit, but too often Virgo II's will be left doing the work while their Aquarius I partners are off having a good time. The resentments that Virgo II's may consequently feel they often just hammer down inside, resulting in depression and withdrawal.

Virgo II's are likely to be proud parents of Aquarius I's, and can also provide the kind of reliable home environment that these children require. Yet they may fall short in their ability to understand young Aquarius I's, and to supply them with what they need emotionally. Much of the guardedness in Virgo II–Aquarius I friendships can be alleviated when both partners are given lots of time and space of their own.

ADVICE: *Free yourself from unnecessary worry. Accentuate the positive. Share responsibilities equally. Beware of invidious comparisons.*

STRENGTHS: **LOVING, IDEALISTIC, SYMPATHETIC**

WEAKNESSES: **DISAPPROVING, DISEMPOWERING, REBELLIOUS**

BEST: **MARRIAGE**

WORST: **FRIENDSHIP**

QUEEN BEATRIX (1/31/38)
PRINCE CLAUS VON AMSBERG (9/6/26)

Beatrix ascended to the Dutch throne in 1980 on the abdication of her mother. Her earlier marriage (1966) to German diplomat von Amsberg raised some initial opposition due to his background and to Dutch anti-royalist sentiment. They have 3 sons. **Also: Elinor Wylie & William Rose Benet** (married; poet/*Saturday Review* founder).

September 3–10
THE WEEK OF THE ENIGMA
VIRGO II

January 31–February 7
THE WEEK OF YOUTH & EASE
AQUARIUS II

Unfavorable Judgments

This can be a loving relationship, with a marked idealism, but it has its difficulties. Inherent differences in character can draw a lot of criticism out of these partners: each has a tendency to attack the other. Astrologically, Virgo II and Aquarius II lie in a quincunx aspect to each other in the zodiac (150° apart), which usually indicates some instability. Aquarius II's like problem-free lives, which means that they have to feel free to go their own way; Virgo II's may have other ideas, but every time they raise an objection or express a disagreement, they are made to feel that they are rocking the boat. After a while they could just give up, while holding on to their resentment and frustration. The point is that many Virgo II's are not really built psychologically for just going with the flow—they thrive on challenge, problems and difficulties. If Aquarius II's disapprove of this approach, Virgo II's will feel disempowered.

Warmth and sympathy are apparent in love affairs, and the partners present a solid and mutually supportive front. Aquarius II's are often the aggressive ones in initiating a romantic relationship, and Virgo II's have no objection to being so sought after. This is no guarantee, however, that they will open up to Aquarius II's once they are caught. One immediate problem arises when friends and family members make comparisons between these partners; it is usually the Virgo II who is found lacking. Once these personalities' pride is wounded, it may be difficult or impossible for Aquarius II's to get through to them again.

Marriages and business partnerships in this combination can work out well, with Virgo II taste, wit and discrimination offsetting the more youthful and enthusiastic approach of Aquarius II's. A mutual coolness emerges as one of the relationship's chief characteristics, and this may later grow into a deep reserve. The couple often presents a polished and serene face to the world that belies all sorts of underlying psychological problems. Virgo II–Aquarius II friendships and sibling relationships may exhibit youthful rebelliousness against parents, teachers and other authority figures.

ADVICE: *Don't take to heart what other people say. Continue along your own path. Be more transparent. Scale back disapproving attitudes. Feed your love.*

September 3–10

THE WEEK OF THE ENIGMA
VIRGO II

February 8–15

THE WEEK OF ACCEPTANCE
AQUARIUS III

Freedom from Negativity

This relationship faces two major challenges around the issue of freedom. The first is to help free the partners from their own negative thought patterns and low self-esteem. The second, assuming that the first can be tackled, is the preservation and celebration of the partners' individual freedom while honoring the relationship. Although these two seem quite different from the outside (Virgo II's more reserved, Aquarius III's vivacious), they actually have a lot in common. They are both sensitive to criticism, yet do not hesitate to voice their own critical dissatisfaction with the world. They also tend to play the victim—listening to them, one would think they had had a bad time of it, but there is an element of dramatic self-pity, and an inability to let go of the past, in most of their stories. Together these two can work at releasing their negative thoughts and habits— their simultaneous negativity seems to be so unbearable that the dam bursts and they mend their ways. They both (not just Aquarius III's) may have problems with acceptance and they both (not just Virgo II's) may be hard to figure out.

The closer these two get in romantic relationships, the more insecurity they may feel. Each is usually afraid of being rejected or abandoned by the other partner, usually in favor of a competitor who is better looking, more intelligent, more capable, etc. This relationship can heal their low self-esteem, but not miraculously— both partners must work on their own problems, occasionally touching base. In marriages the emphasis is more on the careful allowance of individual freedom of action, style, even taste.

Parent-child relationships find Virgo II parents somewhat severe and demanding, Aquarius III children stubborn and rebellious. Aquarius III parents, on the other hand, can be quite neglectful of their Virgo II children, leaving them pretty much to their own devices. Friendships and work matchups in this combination can reinforce both negative attitudes and the partners' feeling that the world is hostile and uncaring. At work this tendency will have an unfortunate effect on the team's projects.

ADVICE: *Respect your differences, and don't try to gloss over or eliminate them. Solve your own problems. Try to emancipate yourself from old scripts.*

ELIZABETH I (9/7/1533)
MARY I (2/8/1516)

Catholic Queen Mary was England's monarch from 1553 to her death in 1558. During her reign, Elizabeth, her Protestant half-sister, lived quietly, waiting to take the throne. She reigned from 1558–1603.
Also: **Carl & Charles Van Doren** (uncle/nephew; writer/game-show cheat); **Elsa Schiaparelli & Marisa Berenson** (grandmother/-daughter; designer/actress); **Vince & Dom DiMaggio** (baseball brothers).

September 3–10

THE WEEK OF THE ENIGMA
VIRGO II

February 16–22

THE CUSP OF SENSITIVITY
AQUARIUS-PISCES CUSP

Working Both Ways

Although both of these partners have an undeniably independent streak, Virgo II's often assume the role of guide to Aquarius-Pisces, who, although quite tough and aggressive enough to make it in the world, benefit tremendously from their analytic powers and objectivity. Virgo II's, for their part, not only get tremendous satisfaction out of seeing their Aquarius-Pisces protégés succeed, but may also gain renown and financial reward themselves in the process. Within any family or social group, Virgo II's and Aquarius-Pisces will be strongly independent figures but at the same time will depend on their relationship with each other for counsel and inspiration.

In love affairs and marriages, Virgo II's show great empathy with Aquarius-Pisces' walled-off sensitivities, and vice versa. Both know when to be there with a willing ear and a sympathetic shoulder, and when to back off. The great trust that can emerge in such a relationship, however, may not be fixable once broken. This relationship is ruled by fire, here signifying passion, willfulness and instinct. With this level of sensitivity and passion, it is no wonder that these relationships can be very fulfilling, at least as long as mutual respect is maintained.

Parent-child relationships are strongest when Virgo II's are the parents. There is a danger, however, that Aquarius-Pisces children may worship them unduly and then be disillusioned when the truth is revealed. And although Virgo II's can be excellent role models for their Aquarius-Pisces children, they may also teach them a few bad habits, including secretiveness and arrogance. As indicated, Virgo II–Aquarius-Pisces friendships and social and career relationships can be outstanding. Whether in or out of the classroom, teacher-student relationships with Virgo II's as mentors flow in both directions: education here will be a mutually experiential process rather than a mere imparting of knowledge.

ADVICE: *Never betray a sacred trust. Beware of arrogance. Respect is fragile and easily broken. Elevating someone can be a prelude to their fall.*

EDWARD KENNEDY (2/22/32)
JOSEPH KENNEDY (9/6/1888)

Rich diplomat Joseph's youngest son is Edward ("Teddy"), a US senator from 1962 to the present. Joseph's great ambitions for his sons were thwarted when the oldest was killed in WWII combat and 2 others were murdered by political assassins. Joseph died in '69.

STRENGTHS: **INTELLIGENT, GIVING, SHARING**

WEAKNESSES: **LABILE, UNHAPPY, INDECISIVE**

BEST: **FRIENDSHIP**

WORST: **LOVE**

RALPH ELLISON (3/1/14)
RICHARD WRIGHT (9/4/08)

Wright and Ellison were contemporary African-American novelists whose work furthered the cause of blacks in the US. In 1936 Ellison met Wright and became associated with the Federal Writers Project, during which time Ellison was inspired by Wright. **Also:**

Louis XIV & Charles Le Brun (king/court artist).

September 3–10
THE WEEK OF THE ENIGMA
VIRGO II

February 23–March 2
THE WEEK OF SPIRIT
PISCES I

Mapping Out the Future

This relationship is likely to focus on thought, intelligence, inspiration and the sharing of ideas. Personal difficulties may mar this outstanding mental connection, however. The saving grace will be the Virgo II ability to provide a stabilizing force in the up-and-down lives of Pisces I's, who tend to be quite uncertain and indecisive. Virgo II's will have a lot to put up with, and should they feel rejected or neglected, they will probably become unhappy and depressed. But if they have the patience to hang in there, their Pisces I partner may well come back after wandering off, or take a stand after a bout of confusion.

One of the biggest problems in love affairs is the emotional instability of Pisces I's, who may, however, find the cool, relatively detached Virgo II approach reassuring. Both partners are service oriented and they can generally be counted on to make their contribution to the relationship. In marriages, too, they are likely to give a great deal to each other and to their children. Pisces I's do sometimes forget or ignore their daily tasks, and Virgo II's can be helpful in keeping them in line. Domestic duties like cleaning and washing up will help ground Pisces I flightiness.

Friendships between these two can be outstanding. A Pisces I may well be that special friend with whom a Virgo II can open up and share, feeling unthreatened and interested and instinctively knowing that there is nothing to fear. It is in career and family matchups that the relationship's ability to generate ideas and discuss concepts is especially apparent. Engaged in shared research and development projects, mapping out the future course of a family, cultural or business organization, or providing a needed service together, Virgo II's and Pisces I's make an effective team and see eye to eye in most things.

ADVICE: *Seek greater stability. Keep on sharing, but don't overemphasize problems. Tend to everyday matters. Push yourself a bit more.*

STRENGTHS: **HELPFUL, CREATIVE, VOLUNTEERING**

WEAKNESSES: **UNREALISTIC, WEAK, LOST**

BEST: **MARRIAGE**

WORST: **FAMILY**

SALT (3/8/64)
PEPA (9/9/69)

Female rap group Salt-n-Pepa, formed in 1985, was one of the first to cross over to the pop charts. Salt (Cheryl James) and Pepa (Sandy Denton) first met when they were employees at Sears Roebuck. They've been on the rise ever since. **Also: Dweezil Zappa & Sharon Stone** (romance; singer/actress); **August Wilhelm von Schlegel & Friedrich von Schlegel** (brothers; Romantic writers).

September 3–10
THE WEEK OF THE ENIGMA
VIRGO II

March 3–10
THE WEEK OF THE LONER
PISCES II

Maintaining Objectivity

This relationship generates tremendous creative energy, being capable of expansive thinking, innovation and reaching for lofty goals. It is an energy that arises out of opposition: Virgo II and Pisces II lie across from each other in the zodiac (they are 180° apart). Capable of constituting a strong bond that can work to stabilize any group or organization, the relationship is also quite capable of standing on its own, so that business partnerships and close professional associations are especially favored here. Virgo II's will tend to deal with planning, finances and management while Pisces II's supply the imagination and often the theoretical or technical know-how.

In personal relationships these two tend to get lost in each other. There are so many mysteries in their hidden personalities that they can become obsessed with personal exploration, losing contact with everyday realities. Love affairs between Virgo II's and Pisces II's can be deep and emotional. There is a real danger of the partners losing their personal identities and merging in an all-absorbing relationship that takes every bit of their energy.

Friendships and marriages are likely to be more objective, and conducive to individual personal growth. The Virgo II–Pisces II relationship can be an extremely active social unit within its circle of friends and beyond; it is not uncommon for the pair to assume an important role in the development of community, church or athletic organizations, where their service-oriented side can be fully expressed. This work is usually done on a volunteer basis, and seeks little if any remuneration.

Virgo II and Pisces II relatives can give direction to the family group as long as they can stay objective in their feelings for each other. Unfortunately, they sometimes lack the toughness or willpower to withstand disappointment. The danger here is that they may disappear into their own cocoon and turn away from their responsibilities, particularly if they feel hurt or rejected.

ADVICE: *Pull yourself together. Toughen your resolve. Don't let yourself dissolve away. Keep your focus on the creative.*

September 3–10

THE WEEK OF THE ENIGMA
VIRGO II

March 11–18

THE WEEK OF DANCERS & DREAMERS
PISCES III

The Miraculous and Unexpected

Secret dreams, often dormant in these individuals for years, can blossom in this relationship, and when they are revealed the partners may be amazed at their correspondences and parallels of thought. The miraculous and the unexpected figure prominently here. The relationship focuses on aspirations and visionary thinking, both as a journey and as a destination.

Through marriages and love affairs, Virgo II's can be introduced by Pisces III's to a whole world of family relationships in which they were previously uninterested or else that they felt inadequate to become involved with. On the other hand, both of these individuals require a lot of emotional understanding, which for some reason it is difficult for them to give each other. Perhaps it is because the focus here is more on outward than on inward shared goals. Marriages will often give both partners the opportunity to work out childhood hang-ups, especially those concerned with the disapproval of authority figures. These two can be particularly successful in planning or building a new house together, or in fixing up an old one. Domestic pursuits like these can come to occupy most of the relationship's time and effort.

As friends, Virgo II's and Pisces III's make excellent traveling companions. Their expansiveness of thought as a pair is evident in the way they plan long vacations, or even expeditions into relatively remote parts of the world. Unfortunately, many of these projects never get off the drawing board, but the one or two that do are usually exciting and fulfilling. Although Virgo is an earth sign and Pisces a water sign, the Virgo II–Pisces III matchup is ruled by fire, here signifying a longing for dynamic endeavors.

Career connections may prove somewhat unrealistic. Dreams and aspirations often outstrip pragmatic realities here, leaving them far behind. In financial, business or entrepreneurial endeavors, Virgo II–Pisces III partners may fail to reach their objectives, and although they are capable of booking moderate successes they may ultimately give up out of sheer disappointment.

ADVICE: *Form a more realistic picture of yourself. Examine your plans carefully. Don't be content with fantasies. Proceed methodically, step by step.*

PETER SELLERS (9/8/25)
LIZA MINNELLI (3/12/46)

In the 70s Minnelli's career was frantic, with a nearly impossible performing and recording schedule. During this period her 1973 romance with actor Sellers turned into a heartbreaker under the strain of her other commitments. She soon needed treatment for alcohol abuse (1984–86). *Also:* **Dr. Michael DeBakey & Jerry Lewis** (physician/patient; dr. assisted actor with pill addiction).

September 11–18

THE WEEK OF THE LITERALIST
VIRGO III

September 11–18

THE WEEK OF THE LITERALIST
VIRGO III

Undiluted Doses

These two are unlikely to try to kid each other a whole lot; Virgo III's are brutally honest, and a pair of them will expect the truth in undiluted doses. It's not that their relationship is overserious—banter and light humor actually figure prominently here. Behind every humorous statement, though, is a knowing quality, an assumption that the listener knows what's going on in the world. Virgo III's, in fact, assume a great deal about each other, and when their partner fails to live up to their expectations, derision may be their only recourse.

Virgo III–Virgo III love affairs are usually frank and down to earth, more sexual than romantic. The partners know what they want and usually think they can get it. A principal problem in relationships of this kind is selfishness, both of the physical and the psychological varieties. Although the partners are very much alike, it rarely occurs to either of them to try to put themselves in the other's place and see how it feels. Marriages between Virgo III's are often practical and pragmatic. Should they prove fractious, the couples will hang in there for what they consider a reasonable time, but then won't hesitate to call it quits.

Two Virgo III's in one family can be a problem for other family members, since these personalities tend to inflict their critical attitudes, strong wills and demanding natures on those around them. Autonomy is usually so important to them that Virgo III siblings will battle it out to protect their prerogatives. Conflicting choices may be a special problem for them. Parent-child relationships in this combination will expect absolute adherence to the written and spoken word; their promises are written in stone, and they will expect the same of others. Virgo III friends and business partners can get on splendidly as long as they don't expect too much attention from each other. These relationships should be kept as objective as possible—emotionally charged areas will be difficult here.

ADVICE: *Forgive and forget. Try to be more flexible. Let some things go without comment. Put yourself in your partner's place. Don't expect too much.*

AGATHA CHRISTIE (9/15/1890)
JAMES FENIMORE COOPER (9/15/1789)

Christie and Cooper, both world-famous fiction writers, share the same birthday. Cooper's best-known novels are American frontier tales full of adventure and historical atmosphere. Christie wrote over 75 books, mostly detective fiction, and introduced millions of readers to characters Hercule Poirot and Miss Jane Marple.

MARGARET SANGER (9/14/1883)
H.G. WELLS (9/21/1866)

Sanger was an early pioneer in the crusade for birth control. Among her many lovers was the celebrated English writer H.G. Wells. He was known as a notorious womanizer. Their passionate affair began in 1921 and continued on and off for many years. *Also:* **Theodore Roosevelt, Jr. & Elliot Roosevelt** (cousins; both D-Day generals); **Jesse Lasky & Jesse Lasky, Jr.** (father/son; producer/screenwriter).

September 11–18

THE WEEK OF THE LITERALIST
VIRGO III

September 19–24

THE CUSP OF BEAUTY
VIRGO-LIBRA CUSP

Launching New Projects

This relationship is likely to create new outlooks and orientations, which might result in the realization of new projects, or more simply but more basically, in new ways of thinking—as long, that is, as the partners let things gel between them. If these two rub each other the wrong way (always a possibility), they will deny the relationship the chance to work its effects. Virgo III's can offer Virgo-Libras a commonsense, down-to-earth, practical approach, and Virgo-Libras can teach Virgo III's something about sensuous pleasure, enjoyment and relaxation. Thus both partners can have a grounding effect on each other. Once this quality begins to enter their relationship, Virgo III's and Virgo-Libras may decide to take off on a new undertaking, most likely an ambitious one. That this imaginative new effort should arise spontaneously may come as a surprise to both of them.

In love affairs, the somewhat stern Virgo III attitude to anything they consider immoral may soften under Virgo-Libras' persistently sensual tutelage. At any rate, it should, and if it doesn't, Virgo-Libras may start to chafe under their partner's severity of judgment. Virgo III's would do well to learn to relax and enjoy the spontaneous affection that this relationship offers. In marriage too, the Virgo III expectation that his or her spouse will toe the line can arouse resentment and bewilderment unless they learn to temper it.

Friendships and work relationships often overlap, and might be based in the exploration of far-out theoretical areas. They have a good chance of being commercially successful. Virgo III common sense and Virgo-Libra taste can be an excellent combination, but the pair should guard against the Virgo III tendency to be overly critical and Virgo-Libra trendiness. Siblings in this combination may vie for attention, especially when they are of the same sex. Their selfish, possessive and controlling drives may lead to conflict and argument that upset the family. They will absolutely need their own unquestioned space, possessions and priorities. It is usually a big mistake for parents to push or require them to share.

ADVICE: *Try to avoid being irritated by each other. Focus on whatever is mutually relaxing and enjoyable. Learn the gift of giving. Working together requires patience.*

WILLIAM FAULKNER (9/25/1897)
SHERWOOD ANDERSON (9/13/1876)

Writers Faulkner and Anderson were close friends who first met in New Orleans and shared an apartment. After Faulkner wrote an unsuccessful book of poetry, Anderson persuaded him to write his first novel, *Soldier's Pay* (1926), which Anderson also helped publish.

September 11–18

THE WEEK OF THE LITERALIST
VIRGO III

September 25–October 2

THE WEEK OF THE PERFECTIONIST
LIBRA I

A Search for Harmony

This combination is often involved in a search for harmony, both within the relationship itself and in its surrounding environment, both in the partners' own joint projects and in the creative output and endeavors in which they are involved with other people. Harmony within the relationship may or may not be achieved, but in terms of creating beauty of form, these two have no match. Their standards are usually very high. Perfectionist Libra I's meet their match in Virgo III's, and both partners have first-rate critical minds. Despite the possibility of personal conflict, these two can work well together when their ideals of high-quality work mesh. Without mutual respect and admiration, however, emotional irritations and clashes can drive them apart. The synergy here will magnify not only perfectionist and critical drives but a tendency to procrastinate; for Virgo III's this has something to do with overconfidence, for Libra I's with indecision.

Love affairs and friendships may be difficult for these two, since they are temperamentally so different. The direct intensity of Libra I's often puts off more subtle and discriminating Virgo III's, who, for their part, are likely to be threatening to Libra I's through the quality of their intelligence—an area where Libra I's need to dominate. Marriages can be much more successful, particularly when the partners can ground their abilities and visions in concrete daily tasks. The acid test here will be whether caustic disagreements can be avoided when setting up the domestic space.

Work relationships between Virgo III's and Libra I's work out best when the two personalities have an equal say in their projects, whether they are co-workers, business partners or executives. Their personal contact should be limited and their attitudes kept objective. Their insistence on high standards can make them respected but also feared by their fellow workers and employees. Parent-child relationships in this combination can be unsettling: patience will be a rare commodity here, and explosive disagreements can break out at almost any time.

ADVICE: *Scale back disagreements. Try to be more relaxed and less critical. Don't let important matters go for too long. Stay as objective as possible.*

September 11–18

THE WEEK OF THE LITERALIST
VIRGO III

October 3–10

THE WEEK OF SOCIETY
LIBRA II

Dropping One's Guard

This relationship can be trusting, open, even innocent. As such it has the capacity to breathe fresh life into the viewpoints of two often jaded individuals. Virgo III's and Libra II's are tough nuts when it comes to the rest of humanity, and sensing the ability to let down their guard in this relationship can give them a whole new energy level and a new lease on life. They may find that they are able to tackle projects that would otherwise have daunted them. In fact, the relaxation here may foster a whole new level of creativity for them.

Romances in this combination can be highly rewarding. A mixture of personal understanding and sensuousness guarantees a warm and loving relationship. These partners could continue close for years—they might feel no need to marry, but might eventually make a decision to live together. When they do get married, Virgo III's sometimes feel they have to assume too large a share of the couple's daily responsibilities, which they resent.

As friends and siblings these two usually have a positive effect on other friends and family members. Their attitude is generally constructive, and they enjoy playing a low-key but significant role in the activities of the larger group. Occasionally Virgo III–Libra II "innocence" can irritate people who see it as a ploy to avoid work or responsibility. Generally speaking, in fact, this relationship may need to adopt more mature attitudes if it is to escape the accusation of acting childishly or irresponsibly and to gain the respect of others. The success of Virgo III–Libra II working relationships in particular may depend on the pair's ability to toughen up a bit and be more realistic. Although the matchup will usually bring good feelings to the workplace, it may also reinforce indolent and indecisive tendencies in others. Superiors would do well to push these two, who are capable of high-quality work if encouraged in the right way.

ADVICE: *Be a bit harder on yourself. Prove that you are mature enough to handle responsibility. Seek out sources of inspiration and motivation.*

MICHAEL KORDA (10/8/33)
SIR ALEXANDER KORDA (9/16/1893)

Producer-director Alexander was a major figure in British and American movies for 25 years, turning out such memorable films as *The Four Feathers* (1939) and *The Third Man* (1949). His nephew Michael is an American publisher and writer (*Charmed Lives*, 1979) who holds a top position at Simon & Schuster. *Also:* **Greta Garbo & Rouben Mamoulian** (romance; actress/director).

September 11–18

THE WEEK OF THE LITERALIST
VIRGO III

October 11–18

THE WEEK OF THEATER
LIBRA III

The Highest Values

Social feelings generally predominate in this combination, which focuses on making daily interactions more pleasurable and rewarding. It makes for a relaxed relationship that aims for peace and harmony. It is by no means dull, and it has a demanding side that asks its partners to do their best at all times, but the basic setup here rarely allows those demands to become unreasonable or stressful. In fact, the relationship's highest values seem to be consideration and kindness.

The relationship is at its most demanding in marriage. Usually powered by the insistence of Virgo III's and the large presence of Libra III's, this couple is a force to be reckoned with in any social or family context. Their children will get attention and respect from both of them, although Libra III's can seldom supply as much nurturing energy as their Virgo III partners. As parents these two may also err in having too high expectations of their children.

Friendships and love affairs in this combination are more relaxed. Humor is important here, but it tends to be directed toward other people; the relationship takes itself a wee bit seriously at times. Activities of all types attract this pair, but they are particularly interested in entertainment and self-improvement. A tendency to extreme, even fanatical involvements in programs of weight loss, fitness training and health should be watched and avoided.

Perfectionism emerges most prominently in the family and at work, which are also less easygoing manifestations of the relationship. Both Virgo III and Libra III parents can be extremely critical of their children of the other sign; the same goes for bosses and employees. Even though rebelliousness is rarely an issue here, these parents should be extremely careful not to alienate the affections of their children, who, again whether they are Virgo III's or Libra III's, may carry psychological complexes into maturity that will make it difficult or impossible for them to relate normally to authority figures.

ADVICE: *Try to laugh at yourself occasionally. Seek the middle way. Hedonism isn't always best for you. Be a bit more skeptical of extreme behavior.*

DICK HAYMES (9/13/16)
RITA HAYWORTH (10/17/18)

Crooner and romantic film actor Haymes was a major celebrity in the 40s. Glamorous Hayworth was the 4th of his 6 wives. After they wed in '53 she proved to be a serious drain on his finances, leading to their breakup in '55. *Also:* **John Ritter & Suzanne Somers** (co-stars, *Three's Company*); **Milton Eisenhower & D.D. Eisenhower** (brothers; educator/president)

ANNETTE FUNICELLO (10/22/42)
FRANKIE AVALON (9/18/40)

Singer-actors Funicello and Avalon became symbols of 60s teen culture when they teamed up for 5 beach-party films between 1963 and 1965. After a long hiatus, they re-joined for a nostalgic beach-party reprise, *Back to the Beach* (1985), during which Annette discovered early symptoms of multiple sclerosis. They toured the US together in '88.

September 11–18
THE WEEK OF THE LITERALIST
VIRGO III

October 19–25
THE CUSP OF DRAMA & CRITICISM
LIBRA-SCORPIO CUSP

Youthful Sparkle

The childlike exuberance in this combination is such that the world is bound to notice it—these two have a certain capacity for fame. Fortune, however, may escape them. Youthful sparkle dominates here and can overcome the partners' respective personality traits, which in both cases tend toward the severe. Their relationship also encourages them to show initiative, although to realize this drive they will both have to overcome a desire for overly careful planning. If they can add the insightful commentary and capable management that are common in this matchup to the other traits they share, they can achieve a lot. On the down side, tempers can flare here as well.

In love and family pairings, a third person often figures in the Virgo III–Libra-Scorpio relationship, a person who occupies the spotlight and around whom the partners revolve, whether as a complementary or a warring pair. Jealousies and competitiveness can figure strongly in such triangles. Ideally, Virgo III's and Libra-Scorpios will eventually recognize the inner logic of the situation (which may be fated to continue for years) and work out a kind of truce. But one problem here is that both Virgo III's and Libra-Scorpios are usually much better geared to social pursuits and physical activities than to matters of human psychology and emotional understanding. They may have problems coming to deeper realizations about the dynamics of their relationship, particularly with respect to others. Marriages and working relationships in this combination are apt to generate a lot of attention from others. One would expect success here, given both partners' high degree of competence, but the matchup is unfortunately seldom enduring. The partners are often much too opinionated, and too attached to their own approach, to work together for very long or even to live under the same roof. Friendships can work out better, especially when both partners share an interest or pursuit, often involving the arts, travel or collecting. As long as this activity takes the spotlight, competition for attention between Virgo III and Libra-Scorpio friends will not generally mar their relationship.

ADVICE: *Try to see yourself as others sometimes see you. Don't compromise yourself too much. Recognize the importance of diplomacy.*

SAMUEL JOHNSON (9/18/1709)
JAMES BOSWELL (10/29/1740)

English writer and wit Johnson met Scottish diarist Boswell in 1763. Boswell joined Johnson's literary crowd, forming a lasting friendship. In 1773 the pair journeyed through Scotland, a trip Boswell chronicled in a biography, *The Life of Samuel Johnson*, a literary masterpiece.
Also: Theodore Roosevelt, Jr. & Theodore Roosevelt (son/father; writer-politician/US president).

September 11–18
THE WEEK OF THE LITERALIST
VIRGO III

October 26–November 2
THE WEEK OF INTENSITY
SCORPIO I

A Form-Fitting Dynamic

This relationship demonstrates a kind of self-consciousness over how it fits into the family, career or group hierarchy of which it is a part, so that its thrust is social in nature. An interesting molding dynamic is at work here, more so than in other relationships: Virgo III's and Scorpio I's have the ability to adapt themselves in serious ways to each other and to their environment without compromising their essential individuality. They achieve this through the taste for quiet reflection and thoughtfulness that their relationship engenders. This pair will periodically need to withdraw in order to assess the situation in which they find themselves. Having done so, they will reemerge more malleable, fitting either into some new form or more comfortably into an old one.

Friendships and sibling matchups often cast Scorpio I's as observers, a role to which they are suited. Their natural attentiveness may lead them to obsessive examinations of their Virgo III partner, who may be flattered by this at first but will ultimately be made quite uncomfortable by it. Virgo III's are very stable in this combination, which can make Scorpio I's quite dependent—they must be careful not to let the matchup assume too much importance in their life. Both partners will eventually come to resent the relationship if it binds them too tightly. Love affairs and marriages between Virgo III's and Scorpio I's are highly social. Rather than burying themselves in secretive and hidden activities (which both of these personalities might do in other combinations), they thrive on interactions with other people, perhaps during parties, dinners, outdoor events or vacations. It is usually through their social contact with outsiders to their relationship that they really get to know and appreciate each other. These partners must be careful to foster intimacy between them and to give it time to develop. Working relationships between them can be excellent as long as they maintain respect and preserve some semblance of equality. The tendency of Virgo III's to dominate their Scorpio I partners must be watched carefully, for it can lead to resentment and even rejection.

ADVICE: *Leave enough time for personal matters. Be less concerned with your image. Beware of obsessive tendencies. Promote equality.*

September 11–18

THE WEEK OF THE LITERALIST
VIRGO III

November 3–11

THE WEEK OF DEPTH
SCORPIO II

Tight Team

This powerfully persuasive matchup tends to ignore society's rules, setting its own standards and doing pretty much as it pleases. The relationship's focus is likely to be an important activity or project in which the two partners function as a tight team. Virgo III's may resent Scorpio II dominance, and Scorpio II's can find Virgo III's manipulative, but all in all they both are willing to pull together in a common effort. Scorpio II's will enjoy the mental stimulation offered by the relationship, and Virgo III's its intense emotional involvement.

As lovers these two can initially be swept away by passion, but Virgo III's will begin to back off if they feel claimed or controlled. If the relationship is sexually rewarding, this distancing will be a difficult and painful process. Scorpio II's may retaliate, but if they choose to fight, they will find the Virgo III tongue sharp and may have to suffer in silence. Repression often sets up a vicious circle in which the blocked energies of Scorpio II's repeatedly summon up attacks from Virgo III's. Marriage can work out better; both partners have nurturing tendencies that the synergy of their relationship intensifies, so that they will probably provide both their offspring and each other with a protective, caring environment. Virgo III and Scorpio II parents can make an effective business team or can successfully share a creative hobby or sport.

Virgo III and Scorpio II friends may decide to work together as freelancers or to run a small business together. But problems over money can arise if Scorpio II tastes prove too expensive for thrifty Virgo III's, and working relationships between these two may eventually break up if they cannot reach or stick to firm financial agreements. In the family, Virgo III–Scorpio II parent-child relationships of either kind can be excellent, but their success will ultimately depend on whether or not the parent can prove an acceptable role model to the child, particularly if the two are of the same sex.

ADVICE: *Give vent to feelings. Think constructively. Take account of wishes and needs. Balance your cash flow but don't be stingy or spendthrift.*

MARILYN BERGMAN (11/10/29)
ALAN BERGMAN (9/11/25)

Alan and Marilyn are movie songwriters and lyricists. They are among the most successful husband-and-wife movie-score teams, winning several Oscars for their work from the 60s to the 80s. Among their films credits are *The Way We Were* (1973), *A Star Is Born* (1976), *Tootsie* (1982) and *Big* (1988). *Also:* **D.H. Lawrence & Dorothy Brett** (affair).

September 11–18

THE WEEK OF THE LITERALIST
VIRGO III

November 12–18

THE WEEK OF CHARM
SCORPIO III

Scintillating Presentations

The focus of this matchup is likely to involve being the moving force behind commercial presentations, family celebrations and cultural manifestations. Although as individuals these partners tend to lead controlled and muted personal lives, their relationship allows them an extroversion that could be called scintillating, most obviously in any projects they share. The relationship is highly successful in directing energies to where they really count, rather than frittering them away on emotional displays. Although Virgo is an earth sign and Scorpio water, the Virgo III–Scorpio III relationship is ruled by air, an element in this case signifying thought and entertainment. Realists first and foremost, Virgo III's and Scorpio III's will not kid themselves about their relationship.

In love affairs these two rarely get carried away by romantic drives. The relationship can be somewhat dangerous for them, since neither of them will hesitate to withdraw or break it off should it run counter to their interests or wishes. Yet it can be highly satisfying and even sometimes thrilling, especially sexually. Marriages in this combination can work out well, for the partners usually take their domestic and parental duties seriously and will rarely compromise the family unit by untoward behavior.

As friends, these two can depend heavily on their relationship for support and advice. But Scorpio III's may find Virgo III's a bit selfish while Virgo III's think Scorpio III's are sometimes too concerned with their social image. Parent-child relationships of either variation feature rather strict parental attitudes and dutiful filial ones.

At work this pair has a keen eye out for success. Aware of what others want, the partners know how to provide it in an exciting and attractive manner without unduly compromising their own standards. Honesty is extremely important to them, and they will rarely pretend to be something they are not in order to achieve financial or career advancement.

ADVICE: *Loosen up emotionally. Don't be afraid of feelings. Try to be more kind and understanding. Consideration of others is of utmost importance.*

BELA KAROLYI (9/13/42)
NADIA COMANECI (11/12/61)

Romanian-born gymnast Comaneci wowed the world at the 1980 Olympics by winning 2 gold and 2 silver medals under the guidance of Karolyi. He discovered her in '67 at age 6. He became coach of the Romanian team for the 1980 games. *Also:* **Harold Clurman & Lee Strasberg** (co-founders of Group Theater); **Nadia Boulanger & Aaron Copeland** (music teacher/student-composer).

RELATIONSHIPS

STRENGTHS: **TOUGH,
NEGOTIATING, COMMERCIAL**

WEAKNESSES: **CLASHING,
JUDGMENTAL, MISTRUSTFUL**

BEST: **WORK**

WORST: **PARENT-CHILD**

JOHN FIELD (11/22/21)
SIR FREDERICK ASHTON (9/17/06)

Field and Ashton were prominent figures with London's Royal Ballet. A former dancer, Ashton was one of its founder-choreographers (1933–70) and was named co-director (1963–70). Field worked closely with Ashton as assistant director (1957–70) and co-director from 1970. Both men served in the RAF during WWII.

September 11–18
THE WEEK OF THE LITERALIST
VIRGO III

November 19–24
THE CUSP OF REVOLUTION
SCORPIO-SAGITTARIUS CUSP

Pragmatic Discussions

P ower struggles are likely to be the theme here, and the relationship's success tends to rise or fall depending on whether the partners gain and keep each other's respect. It is crucial that they negotiate with each other fairly; they will rarely see eye to eye without extensive, open and pragmatic discussion. Both partners appreciate free and easy communication, which, however, is never more valuable to the relationship than negotiation. Tough agreements will usually have to be hammered out here, whether the relationship emerges in the domestic, commercial or family sphere.

The sticking points in love and marriage will be Scorpio-Sagittarians' need to roam, or generally to maintain their independence, and the ability of Virgo III's to accept and allow such behavior. Their stern judgments will drive Scorpio-Sagittarians up the wall, eventually alienating them completely. There may be a strong physical attraction here, but it is usually insufficient to override or mitigate these problems. On the other hand, power struggles in these relationships are not always divisive, since the partners are a good match for each other and are quite capable of gaining satisfaction from their interactions.

Friendships can be marred by stubborn confrontations between these sometimes willful and headstrong personalities. And confrontation is even more likely in the family, particularly in parent-child bonds in which Virgo III's are the parents. The strictures they impose will produce only rebellion and wildness in Scorpio-Sagittarius children, inevitably resulting in serial clashes.

Virgo III's and Scorpio-Sagittarians can work excellently together as long as they respect and trust each other. This last item is important, since Virgo III's may find Scorpio-Sagittarians slippery customers and may not always be certain of them or of their motives when they are out of sight. Scorpio-Sagittarians, on the other hand, sometimes find Virgo III's a bit conservative and inflexible. If a workable dynamic is achieved, however, commercial and artistic success is within the partners' grasp.

ADVICE: *Suspend judgments when possible. Try to be more accepting. Don't get carried away with power struggles. Stay flexible and open.*

RELATIONSHIPS

STRENGTHS: **PEACEMAKING,
DISCRIMINATING, FORGIVING**

WEAKNESSES: **OVERCRITICAL,
SELF-CONSCIOUS, EXPLOSIVE**

BEST: **LOVE**

WORST: **WORK**

ED HARRIS (11/28/50)
AMY MADIGAN (9/11/50)

Actor Harris has appeared in a wide variety of movies, most notably as astronaut John Glenn in *The Right Stuff* (1983). In '83 he married versatile stage, screen and tv actress Madigan. They've made 2 movies together, *Places in the Heart* (1984) and *Alamo Bay* (1985). *Also:* **Jacqueline Bisset & Alexander Godunov** (romance; actress/dancer).

September 11–18
THE WEEK OF THE LITERALIST
VIRGO III

November 25–December 2
THE WEEK OF INDEPENDENCE
SAGITTARIUS I

A Discriminating Approach

N aturally lively and affectionate, this pair is apt to be attractive to other people, even as they stand back somewhat detachedly and secretly analyze and criticize the very people who are drawn to them. Their relationship puts a high value on honor and integrity, but its true focus is likely to be a discriminating and critical approach toward the material world, and especially toward people. Virgo III's are attracted to the naturally expressive qualities of Sagittarius I's, Sagittarius I's to Virgo III grace and cool elegance. Although Virgo III's are more at home in this world, Sagittarius I's will appreciate being able to express their more selective side and to share high standards with their partner. Another of the relationship's themes is the generation of excitement, and here Sagittarius I's usually take the lead.

Love affairs here can be highly romantic. Passion often manifests strongly, and physical involvement can reach a fever pitch. Yet discriminating and critical qualities are not left behind at the bedroom door. Both partners are very much aware of their ability to please and be pleased by their demanding mate, especially sexually. The strong feelings between these two are unlikely to fade with marriage; in fact, they usually deepen. Such marriages are temperamental, featuring bouts of explosive anger but also a tendency to kiss and make up.

Siblings in this combination are often extremely close. They have a deep understanding and acceptance of each other, particularly when they are of opposite sexes, and their ability to think through problems and come up with workable solutions can be very valuable to the family of which they are a part. They will often be thought of as compromisers and peacemakers, a role that Sagittarius I's especially will enjoy, since in other relationships they more often play the part of activist or rebel.

In their friendships and work relationships, mental Virgo III's may have conflicts with their intuitive partner. Their critical qualities may also unnerve Sagittarius I's, who will often be unable to explain how they feel about a given problem to the satisfaction of Virgo III's.

ADVICE: *Evaluate others less—life isn't a contest. Work on keeping your opinions to yourself. Take the time to understand.*

September 11–18

THE WEEK OF THE LITERALIST
VIRGO III

December 3–10

THE WEEK OF THE ORIGINATOR
SAGITTARIUS II

Reconciling Different Outlooks

The focus of this relationship, and also its challenge, is to set up a business, family or system to achieve mutual goals. Many difficulties can be expected, not the least of them the problem Virgo III's will have accepting the more unusual aspects of their partner's personality. They may not see themselves as straitlaced, but more far-out Sagittarius II's will quite likely make them feel uptight and conservative. The difficulties here will emerge not just in getting along on a daily basis but in reconciling differing outlooks and attitudes.

Virgo III parents can be a bit severe with their Sagittarius II children, whom they probably see as wayward and needing discipline. Young Sagittarius II's may withdraw or try to escape when a parent does not understand them; they may also start to prefer the other parent, a choice that will likely only cause more tension. Friendships here can succeed wonderfully, on the other hand, arriving at unanimity of opinion while thriving on diversity and difference. Since it is precisely for their little peculiarities that these two are so fond of each other as friends, their relationship exerts little or no pressure on them to be anything but themselves.

It is probably marriages and live-in love affairs that suffer most from the partners' differences in temperament and from the power struggles inherent in this combination. As spouses these two could find their greatest fulfillment in buying a house or in building or redesigning one; Sagittarius II's have a practical energy that can go to work here extremely effectively. The only danger is that they may have problems sustaining their efforts, so Virgo II's will have to be patient. In matters of business and education, Sagittarius II's are apt to depend heavily on their partner in this combination for support and help. As a result, Virgo III's may find themselves tending to most of the practical details of life while their imaginative partners are more absorbed with their creative work. Resentments and frustrations may consequently build up here, as well as blame and recrimination centering on Sagittarius II unreliability or eccentricity.

ADVICE: *Reconcile differences whenever possible. Try to be more accepting and understanding. Find a balance between having fun and being responsible.*

PETER FALK (9/16/27)
JOHN CASSAVETES (12/9/29)

Falk and Cassavetes were longtime personal friends. Falk, famous as tv's Colombo, acted with Cassavetes in several films and was directed by him in 2 others, notably *A Woman Under the Influence* (1974), which they also financed and distributed. *Also:* **Ben Shahn & Diego Rivera** (WPA muralists); **Greta Garbo & Paul Bern** (actress/production executive); **Henry V & Charles VI** (warring English & French kings).

September 11–18

THE WEEK OF THE LITERALIST
VIRGO III

December 11–18

THE WEEK OF THE TITAN
SAGITTARIUS III

Stimulating Tensions

This relationship is supportive and understanding but intense. It demands that its partners work to win each other's respect, and the road to this goal can be rough indeed. The difficulty is underlined by the fact that Virgo III and Sagittarius III lie square to each other in the zodiac (90° apart), so that astrology would predict problems between them. The tension between them, however, has the positive effect of stimulating them both to ever higher levels of achievement.

As lovers these two can reach emotional levels untouched in their prior relationships. Powerfully intense, their sexual interaction can sweep them away emotionally. Although it may not be possible for either partner to stay objective at such times, later on Virgo III's will be able assess the state of the relationship. They may keep their findings to themselves, however, realizing that Sagittarius III's will have no interest in their analysis. Marriages between these two tend to suffer from power conflicts; Sagittarius III's might try to force Virgo III's into a subservient role that they will find difficult to accept.

Friendships and sibling matchups in this combination are likely to be extremely close, particularly when of the same sex. As friends Virgo III's and Sagittarius III's might be taken as pairs of brothers or of sisters. Competition and even combat are to be expected between them, but over the years their bond will deepen. They can invariably count on each other for help in times of crisis or emergency.

At work, especially at the professional level, Virgo III's and Sagittarius III's will recognize each other's talents, whether they are co-workers or rivals. Assessment is the key concept here; these two tend to be each other's own best critics. Should they work for the same company or organization, their relationship will be recognized as a powerful force in reorganization, market analysis or the kind of research and development that produces startling innovations and inventions.

ADVICE: *Control combativeness. Find common agreement. Put tensions to positive use. Stay positive in outlook. Relax whenever possible.*

ROBERT BENCHLEY (9/15/1889)
MARC CONNELLY (12/13/1890)

Benchley and Connelly were both members of the famous Round Table—a group of witty literati who met and drank regularly in NY's Algonquin Hotel during the 20s and 30s. Benchley was a drama critic and humor writer. Connelly was a playwright whose work includes the Pulitzer Prize-winning *The Green Pastures* (1930).

BOBBY COLOMBY (12/20/44)
DAVID CLAYTON-THOMAS (9/13/41)

Vocalist Clayton-Thomas and drummer Colomby were 2 early members of the jazz-rock group Blood, Sweat and Tears (1967). Clayton-Thomas left in '72 for an unrewarding solo career, then returned in '74. Colomby stopped performing in '76 and produced the group's album *Brand New Day*. He then joined with Clayton-Thomas as co-owner of the band's name and catalog.

September 11–18

THE WEEK OF THE LITERALIST
VIRGO III

December 19–25

THE CUSP OF PROPHECY
SAGITTARIUS-CAPRICORN CUSP

Blown by the Winds of Chance

To the extent that these partners are able to work together, their relationship will be enriched by opposing talents and points of view and may even focus on what they can learn from each other. Yet it is doubtful that they will be able to live in harmony for long. This is not an easy relationship: Sagittarius-Capricorns are too frequently off on a starry-eyed trip or are too involved with their latest project to take much notice of their Virgo III partner. When they are in one of their deep, silent moods, they are also likely to feel the down-to-earth common-sense statements of Virgo III's as a threat (or at the very least as a criticism). The dynamic here is a kind of tug-of-war in which Sagittarius-Capricorn abstraction struggles with Virgo III pragmatism.

Love affairs and marriages are likely to suffer from a lack of understanding. Yet these two will usually learn a great deal about themselves from the relationship, if only by becoming aware of their dislikes and other negative feelings. Conflicting ideologies and points of view can be particularly disruptive.

Co-worker and teacher-student relationships between Virgo III's and Sagittarius-Capricorns can work well when their activities are limited to a specialized area. Indeed, specialization may become the relationship's saving grace, for it encourages a kind of objectivity not otherwise possible for these two in personal areas. Analysis and discussion of technical subjects can be especially fruitful.

Parent-child relationships can see a reversal of roles in which the child proves the parent's teacher and even, in later life, a role model. In actuality the child may be acting out the healthiest parts of the adult's repressed wishes, which will make their unspoken bond extremely strong. Virgo III–Sagittarius-Capricorn friendships and enmities can alternate within the relationship, fluctuating with circumstance and blown by the winds of chance.

ADVICE: *Take a stand. Don't leave things to chance. Be honest about your feelings. Accept differences. Stay objective and keep cool.*

GRETA GARBO (9/18/05)
MARLENE DIETRICH (12/27/01)

Rivals Garbo and Dietrich were Hollywood imports whose European charms caught America's attention. It was rumored that Swedish Garbo listened to Dietrich's records to see how close the German's accent came to her own. In reviewing Dietrich's first American film, *Morocco* (1930), *Variety* mused "whether she's another Garbo." **Also:** **Taft & Wilson** (1912 presidential opponents).

September 11–18

THE WEEK OF THE LITERALIST
VIRGO III

December 26–January 2

THE WEEK OF THE RULER
CAPRICORN I

Butting Heads

These two hardheaded individuals inevitably butt up against each other, particularly in family settings. Neither of them is likely to be too flexible or understanding in this relationship, although they often gain each other's respect—at least enough to know that neither will allow the other to aggress on their territory. Circumstances usually determine whether or not Virgo III's and Capricorn I's will be found on the same side of the fence. If they are allies, their relationship can become the solid backbone of any organization; if they are opponents, they will usually fight to the last. Although Virgo and Capricorn are both earth signs, the Virgo III–Capricorn I relationship is ruled by water, an element here signifying emotional depth and seriousness of purpose—a seriousness that can determine the relationship's tone.

Love affairs are unlikely to be taken lightly. These partners demand a serious commitment from each other and are sensitive to each other's lapses in conduct or breaches of ethics. This often proves a strain for Virgo III's, who find Capricorn I inflexibility too much to bear. Capricorn I's, on the other hand, can feel threatened by the freethinking and questioning style of Virgo III's. Marriages between these two can be effective in many practical areas but lack the spark necessary to sustain active feelings over the years.

Friendships and working relationships between Virgo III's and Capricorn I's are usually solid, dependable and responsible. Neither partner is likely to have many illusions about the other as far as either their capabilities or their personality is concerned. Financial dealings are bound to be pretty sharp—although these partners can be generous on a personal level, they will usually expect to be paid what is owed them to the last penny. Should Virgo III's and Capricorn I's work in the same department or as executives concerned with finances, they must beware of a tendency to hold back in their cash outlays, usually out of conservatism or a fear of incurring losses. If the relationship is to book significant commercial successes, its greatest challenge will be to dare to fail sometimes.

ADVICE: *Try to stay open and flexible. Taking chances yields greater success. Be diplomatic and seek compromise. Keep the flame of desire aglow.*

September 11–18

THE WEEK OF THE LITERALIST
VIRGO III

January 3–9

THE WEEK OF DETERMINATION
CAPRICORN II

STRENGTHS: **PLAYFUL, SENSUOUS, FAITHFUL**

WEAKNESSES: **PREOCCUPIED, OVERWORKED, EXCESSIVE**

BEST: **FRIENDSHIP**

WORST: **LOVE**

Having a Good Time

Earthy qualities coalesce in this combination. Not only are both partners pleased with a relationship that lets them agree, for the most part, on practical matters, but also the synergy between them intensifies their sensuous tendencies, resulting in a love of food, comfort and physical pleasure. The pair will be galvanized into action by Capricorn II ambition and will benefit from the practical common sense of Virgo III's. These two generally know how to have fun together—in fact, their relationship may focus on having a good time. Lest the combination sound superficial, it should be pointed out that these partners know how to work as hard as they play.

Love affairs here can be highly sensual, yet each partner's commitment to work may preclude their spending enough quality time together. Even in the most intimate settings, Virgo III's and Capricorn II's have trouble forgetting about worrisome career matters and may be unable to give themselves to each other 100 percent. Their marriages, on the other hand, have a good prognosis for healthy survival. Jealousy and infidelity are rarely a problem here.

As friends and mates, Virgo III's and Capricorn II's may find it opportune to share a career or at the very least to serve each other in an advisory capacity or as helpers. Should they be unacquainted when they first meet as co-workers or associates, they stand a good chance of forming a fast friendship, which will continue after hours. Both of them value the relationship's natural approach, which lets them be themselves without fear of criticism or judgment.

Virgo III parents will usually have more time for their Capricorn II children than Capricorn II parents for Virgo III children. But the latter are independent, will not be overdemanding of their parents and may even appreciate being left on their own a lot of the time.

ADVICE: *Try to scale back on your work activities a bit. Beware of going overboard or bingeing. Use your analytic faculties to help maintain moderation.*

EARL SCRUGGS (1/6/24)
BILL MONROE (9/13/11)

Monroe is considered the "father of bluegrass." His legendary group, the Blue Grass Boys, formed in 1945, included Scruggs (banjo). Their sound combined blues, gospel, jazz, country and folk to create bluegrass. In '48 Scruggs left the group to form the Foggy Mountain Boys. **Also: Dan Marino & Don Shula** (Miami Dolphins quarterback/coach); **Jesse Lasky & Adolph Zukor** (partners; early film moguls).

September 11–18

THE WEEK OF THE LITERALIST
VIRGO III

January 10–16

THE WEEK OF DOMINANCE
CAPRICORN III

RELATIONSHIPS

STRENGTHS: **EASY, MAGNETIC, NONTHREATENING**

WEAKNESSES: **OBSESSIVE, OVERDEPENDENT, ISOLATING**

BEST: **LOVE**

WORST: **BOSS-EMPLOYEE**

Muted but Direct

This relationship works surprisingly easily in many areas of life; the trine relationship between Virgo III and Capricorn III (they lie 120° apart in the zodiac) predicts as much. The emphasis here is on an easy emotional give-and-take. An immediate understanding often emerges between these two, accompanied by a muted but direct sort of communication. Capricorn III's tend to have a secret inferiority complex, but it somehow is not activated in this combination, although they do admire Virgo III intelligence and achievements. Virgo III's, on the other hand, often come to depend on their powerful partner for protection and financial advice. At times their rationality will have problems with the more religious, spiritual or metaphysical interests of Capricorn III's, but it also happens that these qualities prove inspirational to them.

Love affairs in this combination are magnetic and nonthreatening. They can occasionally prove exclusive and even in certain cases physically obsessive, so the partners must beware of a tendency to cut themselves off unduly from society. The undeniable self-sufficiency that manifests here may thus become the relationship's simultaneous strength and weakness. The couple has a tendency to serve others, and should they marry, this trait will be magnified, auguring well for raising children, keeping pets or caring for each other, particularly in advancing years.

Childhood friendships and sibling relationships of the same sex are close and fruitful. The partners are extremely close in their formative years, and when they get older they will have to make an effort to establish separate lives while at the same time keeping their bond intact. Career matchups between these two are most successful in business areas, where Virgo III watchfulness and boundless Capricorn III energy can gel to create the nucleus of an effective group effort. Capricorn III bosses are likely to arouse rebellious instincts in Virgo III employees with whom they interact on a daily basis, and this situation should be avoided.

ADVICE: *Preserve equality as much as possible. Stay open to the world. Give unconditionally, without resentment, or not at all. Be patient.*

TEX RITTER (1/12/06)
JOHN RITTER (9/17/48)

John, co-star in tv's *Three's Company* (1977–84), is the son of Tex, a country singer and songwriter. Tex's career peaked in the 30s and 40s as he established the stereotype of the "singing cowboy." His most popular song was *Do Not Forsake Me*, which he sang in the film *High Noon* (1952). **Also: Greta Garbo & Cecil Beaton** (romance; actress/photographer).

STRENGTHS: **PLAYFUL,
ENERGETIC, COMMUNICATIVE**

WEAKNESSES: **OFF-PUTTING,
OVERWHELMING, CRISIS-PRONE**

BEST: **FAMILY**

WORST: **WORK**

PATRICIA NEAL (1/20/26)
ROALD DAHL (9/13/16)

British writer Dahl married actress
Neal in 1953. After a severe stroke
in '65, she battled back to resume
her career. Her bravery and his devotion were the subject of an '81
tv film. His affair with a close friend
of hers caused their divorce 2
years later. **Also: Hans Arp
& Sophie Taeuber** (married;
Dadaists); **Betsy Drake & Cary
Grant** (married; actors).

September 11–18

THE WEEK OF THE LITERALIST
VIRGO III

January 17–22

THE CUSP OF MYSTERY & IMAGINATION
CAPRICORN-AQUARIUS CUSP

Few Deep Conflicts

These two create a naturally energetic combination, but Virgo III's must be careful that the relationship's considerable electricity does not short out their circuits. Although the partners are temperamentally different, they find their relationship highly satisfying and experience few deep conflicts. They may have difficulty dealing with the darker areas of life, however, and during times of trouble they experience stress that can be great enough to be overwhelming. Capricorn-Aquarians tend to rely on their Virgo III partners for stability and common-sense know-how, while Virgo III's are entertained by Capricorn-Aquarian humor and fantasy.

Love affairs here can be challenging and sensual. Capricorn-Aquarians may be a bit baffled by Virgo III coolness and reserve but will be intrigued by the mysterious aspects of this partner's personality. Virgo III's will be flattered by Capricorn-Aquarian attention but put off by a stance that in this combination can be overly aggressive, even violent. Marriages between these two can be highly problematic, since Capricorn-Aquarians may find it difficult to live up to the expectations of Virgo III's or to listen to their continual criticism.

Family relationships in this combination tend to be open and communicative, especially when there is a wide age gap between the pair, eliminating competitiveness and allowing affection and playfulness. Friendships are particularly close when the pair share a common area of endeavor, often in sports, entertainment or media; they are more often observers than participants, but in developing these interests together they may become more actively involved in these areas, whether at an amateur or a professional level. In work relationships, conflicts between the wide-open Capricorn-Aquarius style and Virgo III carefulness can quickly escalate to alarming proportions. The judgmental attitudes of Virgo III's can quickly puncture Capricorn-Aquarians' balloons, arouse their insecurities and dampen their enthusiasm. In the long run, however, the influence of this partner will prove positive (albeit discouraging) for them.

ADVICE: *Even your energy has its limits—try to budget it. Pay attention to and use each other's strengths. Keep criticism to a minimum.*

STRENGTHS: **INDOMITABLE,
OUTSPOKEN, FAIR**

WEAKNESSES: **REBELLIOUS,
SUBVERTING, VOLATILE**

BEST: **MARRIAGE**

WORST: **CO-WORKER**

LAUREN BACALL (9/16/24)
HUMPHREY BOGART (1/23/1899)

Bogie and Bacall fell in love while
filming *To Have and Have Not*. After
their 1944 wedding, the romance
continued onscreen and off. Bogart
had been a legendary drinker and
carouser before settling down with
Bacall. His death from cancer in
1957 left her devastated.

Also: **Friedrich von Steuben &
Frederick the Great** (Prussian
officer/ruler).

September 11–18

THE WEEK OF THE LITERALIST
VIRGO III

January 23–30

THE WEEK OF GENIUS
AQUARIUS I

Feisty Intractables

Sparks can fly when these two get together. This feisty relationship does not believe in knuckling under to any form of coercion and will stubbornly maintain its integrity at all costs. Virgo III's and Aquarius I's value their individuality highly. As a matter of fact, what binds them together most tightly may be their joint rebelliousness against external authority, which can even become the relationship's focus. Virgo III's have an interesting and undeniable tendency to subordinate themselves to their Aquarius I partner. This is rarely because of power struggles between them but because of the greater need of Aquarius I's to be the center of attention.

Love affairs here can be dynamite—unstable and explosive. Although Virgo is an earth sign and Aquarius air, the Virgo III–Aquarius I relationship is ruled by fire and water, which together suggest the pressure that builds up when this couple's emotions come to the boil. The only predictable element in the relationship may be its unpredictability. Marriages may not necessarily add stability to the matchup or elicit more responsible behavior, but they are important as a social statement and, even more so, as an expression of the partners' belief in the relationship's rightness.

Co-workers in this combination can cause problems for any commercial organization of which they are a part, for they will not hesitate to speak their minds in any situation that they feel involves unfair treatment. Should the matchup find itself at the top of the corporate ladder or engaged in a business partnership, it is likely to be considerate but demanding of those who work under it and will often gain their respect. Sibling pairs here can be extremely rebellious during their teenage years, but the battles they fight can make them mutually loyal; they will have enough on their hands without fighting each other. Although friendships between these two can be close, they may be periodically tested by serious disagreements, which pit Virgo III strong will against Aquarius I rapierlike wit.

ADVICE: *Don't give too much energy to feather-ruffling. Find constructive outlets for your energies. Avoid disagreeing just for its own sake.*

September 11–18

THE WEEK OF THE LITERALIST
VIRGO III

January 31–February 7

THE WEEK OF YOUTH & EASE
AQUARIUS II

STRENGTHS: **TELEPATHIC, FREE, INTELLIGENT**

WEAKNESSES: **UNEMOTIONAL, UNCOMMUNICATIVE, SEPARATED**

BEST: **FAMILY**

WORST: **LOVE**

Made in Heaven?

This seems to be one of those natural combinations, a matchup made in heaven. Yet it is often hard to imagine how two such fiercely independent individuals ever got together in the first place—and sometimes they don't! It's not that Virgo III's and Aquarius II's are really any more independent than any other types in the year, but their relationship certainly brings out this quality in abundance. Capable either of teaming up closely or seeing each other rarely, adopting the same ideology or battling out opposing points of view, being scarily on the same wavelength or totally incommunicado, Virgo III's and Aquarius II's will not bind each other to strict rules or established patterns. Theirs is the kind of relationship in which the partners might not see each other for years and then take up exactly where they left off, virtually in mid-sentence.

Personal relationships in this combination—whether friendships, love affairs or marriages—are not particularly oriented toward emotional expression. Their emphasis is more on thought, wit, intelligence and speech than on anything else. Not that emotion is by any means ruled out, but it is secondary to matters of the mind—although it can in fact be enhanced by them. Whether a relationship is concerned with love or friendship also matters less than what and how it communicates. Virgo III's and Aquarius II's meeting for the first time quite commonly feel closer—or perhaps angrier and more upset with each other—than they have ever felt with anyone in their lives. Past life or karma is inevitably suggested by such meetings, which may also involve feelings of déjà vu.

When two such individuals grow up together as family members, they almost inevitably become involved in sharing the theory or practice of a given area, whether artistic, athletic, scientific or game-oriented. Such "hobbies" often lead to career connections, especially in areas where mental coordination and interaction figure prominently. Should Virgo III's and Aquarius II's meet at work, their job may later be seen as only fate's pretext for bringing them together.

ADVICE: *Try being more consistent. Sacrificing some of your freedom may be worth it. Don't be afraid to share feelings. You have the right to ask.*

ARTHUR HAYS SULZBERGER (9/12/1891)
ARTHUR OCHS SULZBERGER (2/5/26)

Arthur Hays Sulzberger became publisher of the *NY Times* in 1935, following the death of Adolph Ochs, his boss, mentor and father-in-law. After many years of improvements, his son, Arthur Ochs Sulzberger, took over, continuing to introduce changes in format and content. **Also: Charlie Byrd & Stan Getz** (jazz collaborators); **Margaret Sanger & Havelock Ellis** (affair; social reformer/psychologist).

September 11–18

THE WEEK OF THE LITERALIST
VIRGO III

February 8–15

THE WEEK OF ACCEPTANCE
AQUARIUS III

STRENGTHS: **DEVELOPMENTAL, SELF-ACTUALIZING, LIBERATING**

WEAKNESSES: **STRUGGLING, OVERDEPENDENT, COMPARING**

BEST: **MARRIAGE**

WORST: **LOVE**

Freedom from Dependency

A curious dynamic emerges here: a need to be supported and nurtured conflicts with an equal need for independence. Overall, however, the relationship's energy is beneficial to both partners. Aquarius III's often derive inspiration and strength from Virgo III's, who will sometimes have preceded them down the road they are traveling; but the benefits they receive from the relationship may become habituating, and their reliance on their partner can become a bad case of overdependency. Somewhat paradoxically, they will be able to turn to Virgo III wisdom to help them in their struggle for autonomy within the relationship. Virgo III's, too, have much to learn here, though their lessons will be more absorbed than struggled over. In their own way, they can be quite rigid, and they could learn something from Aquarius III's about the freedom they might find by accepting things as they are and moving on.

Virgo III patience will be necessary in love affairs if Aquarius III's become starry-eyed over them. Because Virgo III and Aquarius III lie quincunx to each other in the zodiac (150° apart), astrology correctly predicts instability in their relationship. Maintaining a kind of dynamic equilibrium of feeling will be a principal challenge here. In marriages, too, Aquarius III's will need to come into their own as equal partners. The relationship usually gives them the chance to do so.

Siblings and friends in this combination, especially when of the same sex, will have a rough time of it in childhood through their habit of unfavorable mutual comparisons. Angry arguments, including physical confrontations, will not be unusual in these cases and in fact may be expected. As the two mature, however, they grow much closer and can achieve mutual respect as they free themselves from childhood roles. Career connections require sensitivity from both partners if they are to avoid power struggles and promote equality. Since Aquarius III's are prone to seeing Virgo III's as role models, they must beware of falling too much under their influence. As a result, boss-employee relationships are less recommended here than co-worker or colleague matchups.

ADVICE: *Stand up for yourself. Inspiration is healthy, domination is not. Avoid unfavorable comparisons like the plague. Promote consideration.*

EDDIE ANDERSON (9/18/05)
JACK BENNY (2/14/1894)

Benny was one of the few radio stars to make a successful transition to tv. *The Jack Benny Program* (1950–65) featured his supporting players from radio, among them "Rochester," his gravelly-voiced valet and wisecracking comic foil. **Also: Zoe Caldwell & Stella Adler** (stage portrayal); **H.L. Mencken & George Nathan** (friends; writers); **Dolores Costello & John Barrymore** (married; actors).

STRENGTHS: **INDIVIDUALISTIC, STRIKING, CREATIVE**

WEAKNESSES: **UPSETTING, PROVOKING, REBELLIOUS**

BEST: **LOVE**

WORST: **MARRIAGE**

BOBBY SHORT (9/15/26)
GLORIA VANDERBILT (2/20/24)

Short, a classy supper-club singer-pianist, had a long relationship with wealthy socialite Vanderbilt, who had successful careers as an actress, painter, writer and fashion designer. *Also:* Phil Jackson & Michael Jordan (basketball coach/star player); Alexander Korda & Merle Oberon (married; director/actress); Nathan Mayer Rothschild & Mayer Amschel Rothschild (son/father; financiers).

September 11–18

THE WEEK OF THE LITERALIST
VIRGO III

February 16–22

THE CUSP OF SENSITIVITY
AQUARIUS-PISCES CUSP

Shock Treatment

This relationship tends to explore new horizons and fearlessly confront the mores of an organization, family or social group with its own individualistic vision. Its innovations sometimes have to do with ideas, speech or appearance, sometimes with personal ethics or feelings, but in either case the combination often focuses on forcing other people to accept it for what it is. No excuses whatsoever are made here. Criticism and challenge are welcome in the relationship, but the partners must beware of getting overstressed or of living their lives in permanent rebellion against the attitudes of others.

Love affairs between Virgo III's and Aquarius-Pisces can be deep and passionate but also undeniably theatrical. These two often try to shock or upset more conventional souls. Maintaining privacy, quiet and calm will be hard for them; try as they may, they inevitably stand out in the public eye, no matter how small their social or family circle. Friendships here are often difficult for others to understand or penetrate, having a highly personal form of communication that only the partners can fully understand.

Marriages and work pairings between Virgo III's and Aquarius-Pisces are often interwoven. Virgo III good sense and Aquarius-Pisces ambition gel effectively, but a certain ruthless tendency sometimes manifests here, so that the partners must be careful not to arouse the animosity of those around them. They really create their own difficulties, which they could in many cases avoid by being more tactful and kind. By the same token, they could also avoid personal problems by being careful to schedule enough time away from each other. Parent-child combinations are often close but must beware of arousing jealousies through the exclusiveness of the relationship. In the long run, including rather than shutting out other people will be much more expedient in forwarding the family's interests.

ADVICE: *Don't go out of your way to shock or provoke. Go about your work quietly. Strive for balance and calm in your personal life.*

STRENGTHS: **GIVING, NURTURING, ORIGINAL**

WEAKNESSES: **IRRITATING, IMPATIENT, INSOLVENT**

BEST: **SIBLING**

WORST: **WORK**

RUDOLF STEINER (2/27/1861)
BRUNO WALTER (9/15/1876)

Austrian philosopher-scientist-artist Steiner and German conductor Walter shared a belief in "anthroposophy," a doctrine originated by Steiner asserting that humans possess the faculty of spiritual cognition, or pure thought, separate from the rest of our senses.

September 11–18

THE WEEK OF THE LITERALIST
VIRGO III

February 23–March 2

THE WEEK OF SPIRIT
PISCES I

Strikingly Different

The accent here is on giving, and the relationship generally asks for little in return, aside from warmth and affection. These two are as different as night and day, but their matchup is proof of how differences can be transformed through the magic of a relationship. Pisces I energy is as diffuse as it comes while Virgo III's are practical and grounded, yet their combination partakes of both elements and comes up with a result that is strikingly different and above all generous. Their relationship is certainly original but also decidedly service oriented, usually working for a cause, a family or an ideology.

Love affairs in this combination are seldom as successful as friendships are. As lovers Virgo III's and Pisces I's arouse each other's impatience and irritation in proportion to their desire, creating what is often an unbearable situation. They do better as friends, particularly if they have few responsibilities or worries on their hands and have lots of time to hang out together.

Marriages can be successful as long as they draw on every ounce of the relationship's creativity and originality. Virgo III's may be driven crazy by Pisces I financial irresponsibility, and if they are required to be the main breadwinner and/or the watchdog of the finances, they will resent it. Sometimes this matchup does better when living on less, perhaps in the relationship's initial stages. Should the spouses eventually succeed in evolving an unusual way of making money linked to their equally personal lifestyle, their relationship can prove quite happy and fulfilling.

This is seldom a good combination for business, rarely being tough, selfish or aggressive enough to succeed in the hard commercial world. Within a family, however, its capability and nurturing qualities will be appreciated by close and distant relatives alike. As sibling pairs of opposite sexes, Pisces I's and Virgo III's often bond for life, and, even if separated by continents, will still feel each other's spiritual presence.

ADVICE: *Be a bit more practical. You deserve to be served also. Demand to be adequately compensated for your work. Work on being more patient.*

September 11–18

THE WEEK OF THE LITERALIST
VIRGO III

March 3–10

THE WEEK OF THE LONER
PISCES II

RELATIONSHIPS

STRENGTHS: **CHALLENGING, INSPIRATIONAL, OVERCOMING**

WEAKNESSES: **IMPRUDENT, UNCONTROLLED, SUFFERING**

BEST: **FAMILY**

WORST: **LOVE**

Calculated Gambles

The innate sympathy between these two, combined with their open kind of communication, can lead to the pursuit of challenging goals and far-reaching thoughts and ideas. As a pair, they enjoy exploring areas beyond ordinary limitations and in fact have a tendency to get carried away. Virgo III's will have to exert every ounce of self-control they have to keep the relationship grounded. Highly inspirational, this matchup can overcome substantial odds in its battle against daunting forces.

As lovers, Virgo III's will generally be sensitive to the Pisces II need to spend time alone. They will certainly want attention at some point, having needs of their own, but periodic expressions of love and sympathy from Pisces II's will go a long way toward satisfying them. In marriage, the relationship may encounter a chronic health problem in one of the spouses, which will demand extreme loyalty, patience and understanding from the other. Should this difficulty be overcome, it will often deepen and broaden the bond.

At work, ordinary desk or factory jobs are seldom what this relationship has in mind. These two demand challenge, and in daring to fail they may achieve high goals that few others could reach. Their particular forte is taking calculated risks, but knowing where to stop will be important, since they are sometimes tempted to gamble everything they have earned on a single throw of the dice. In the family, relatives in this combination usually seek each other out, regardless of age difference, and may embark on exciting financial, educational or spiritual endeavors together. Friends in this combination like adventure and are likely to travel together to distant lands or to seek out somewhat dangerous activities that spur them to give their all.

HERSCHEL WALKER (3/3/62)
TOM LANDRY (9/11/24)

Walker joined Landry's Dallas Cowboys football team when the USFL folded in 1985. Under Landry's leadership (1960–88), Dallas became one of football's top teams. In '88, Landry's final year, Walker led the NFL in rushing.

ADVICE: *Keep something in reserve. Try to act more prudently. Moderation is not a dirty word. Don't always choose the most difficult path.*

September 11–18

THE WEEK OF THE LITERALIST
VIRGO III

March 11–18

THE WEEK OF DANCERS & DREAMERS
PISCES III

RELATIONSHIPS

STRENGTHS: **LEARNING, ENERGETIC, CONSCIOUSNESS-RAISING**

WEAKNESSES: **UNREALISTIC, MEGALOMANIAC, PROJECTING**

BEST: **MUNDANE WORK**

WORST: **FAMILY**

Megalomania

This combination tends not to bother itself with anything but epic projects. The problem is that it is usually completely unprepared for activities of such scale and would do much better cutting back on its goals. Virgo III and Pisces III lie directly opposite each other in the zodiac, and this polarity often energizes their relationship and pushes it to go beyond reasonable limits. Although Virgo is an earth sign and Pisces water, the Virgo III–Pisces III matchup is ruled by fire, here emphasizing the danger of getting swept up by inflammatory desires.

In love affairs and friendships, feelings may go far beyond realistic boundaries. The partners have a penchant for thinking that their relationship is the best, the most romantic, the most sensual, etc. Learning to be a bit more realistic about what they have may be impossible for them, and in fact they may only learn how far off their perceptions were through hindsight. It is not so much the relationship itself that is lacking here than an objective assessment of it.

Particularly when Pisces III's are cast in the parental role, parent-child relationships in this combination must fight a tendency for the child to be exploited by having to act out the parent's hidden ambitions. Grandparent-grandchild matchups are likely to err just as strongly in this direction; spoiling grandchildren may give them very unrealistic ideas about themselves, setting up for a very rude awakening.

Thinking big and fantasizing about wealth and power can severely cripple working relationships in this combination. These matchups would do much better to try small steps first, establishing a firm career base before taking off for the moon. Although Virgo III's and Pisces III's may find mundane jobs quite boring, hanging in there promotes psychological stability. In the long run, modest positions can contribute more to the relationship's self-esteem than more ambitious ones. In marriage, too, dwellings are best kept small-scale and manageable.

HAL WALLIS (9/14/1899)
JERRY LEWIS (3/16/26)

In '49 producer Wallis signed comedian Lewis (and partner Dean Martin) to appear as supporting cast in a minor comedy, *My Friend Irma*. Their comic antics led to movie stardom and 16 more Wallis films before the team split up in '56. ***Also: Arthur Hays Sulzberger & Adolph Ochs*** (father-in-law/ son-in-law; *NY Times* publishers).

ADVICE: *Take one step at a time. Get control of your fantasy life. Remember that having a thought is in itself a powerful and influential act.*

STRENGTHS: TREND-SETTING, OBJECTIVE, COOL

WEAKNESSES: SUPERFICIAL, AVOIDING, UNEMOTIONAL

BEST: WORK

WORST: LOVE

GUNNAR NELSON (9/20/69)
MATTHEW NELSON (9/20/69)

Gunnar and Matthew are identical-twin sons of the late rock star Rick Nelson, who died tragically in a plane crash in 1985. With waist-length blond hair and videogenic looks, the twins were pop-rock naturals. They grew up in a hip Hollywood environment—a far cry from the lifestyle portrayed by their grandparents, Ozzie and Harriet Nelson, American icons of the 50s.

September 19–24

THE CUSP OF BEAUTY
VIRGO-LIBRA CUSP

September 19–24

THE CUSP OF BEAUTY
VIRGO-LIBRA CUSP

Skin Deep

The ideal relationship for two Virgo-Libras is a platonic one in which they are able to appreciate art, or the beauty of the natural world, without passion or possessiveness getting in the way. A cool objectivity or detachment is likely to characterize this relationship, which can achieve an almost perfect balance, given the absence of messier human concerns. Although such a duo can be enormously popular within their own social and family circles, they are not really interested in compromise—in a lowering of standards or sacrifice of ideals—in order to widen their sphere of influence. Actually, these individuals see no contradiction between commercial success and artistic integrity, so sure are they of the quality of their work. Should it be appreciated, fine; if not, so be it.

Nonetheless, setting trends, or at the very least recognizing them, seems to be the fate of this couple. Thus two Virgo-Libras can be of great use to an organization as independent consultants or as permanent members of an executive team. It is not only that they have their fingers on the public pulse; they know how to make that pulse rate quicken or slow at will. In this regard, however, one might say that they act more like experimental psychologists, testing their themes in the antiseptic environment of the lab, than like therapists who interact with clients on a one-to-one basis—their understanding of human nature is not that great.

Love relationships between two Virgo-Libras can stretch narcissism to its limit. Each partner tends to be a mirror for the other—preening, making up, putting on the best face possible. True empathy and depth of feeling are not given top priority. In marital relationships, full emphasis is given to social considerations, which does not exclude putting on a show for the neighbors. Such matchups must beware of passing along false or superficial values to their progeny. Friendships and family relationships between two Virgo-Libras may show a marked aversion to darker feelings, which are frequently repressed. Escaping problems through drugs is a Virgo-Libra tendency that can, unfortunately, be synergized by this relationship.

ADVICE: *Pay more attention to human feelings. Don't be so concerned about what others think. Find deeper meaning in your life. Beauty may be only skin deep.*

STRENGTHS: TRUSTING, OPEN, PLAYFUL

WEAKNESSES: GULLIBLE, EXPLOITED, UNREALISTIC

BEST: PARENT-CHILD

WORST: MARRIAGE

MARCELLO MASTROIANNI (9/28/24)
SOPHIA LOREN (9/20/34)

Loren and Mastroianni were 2 of Italy's pre-eminent film personalities from the 50s through the 70s. From their first film together in '55 to their last in '94 (*Ready to Wear*), the 2 international stars exuded the essence of Italian sex appeal and emotionality.

Also: **Cardinal Richelieu & Louis XIII** (statesman/king); **Anne of Austria & Louis XIII** (queen/king).

September 19–24

THE CUSP OF BEAUTY
VIRGO-LIBRA CUSP

September 25–October 2

THE WEEK OF THE PERFECTIONIST
LIBRA I

Melting Hardened Hearts

This relationship can be a highly enjoyable one, in which an unassuming attitude and natural behavior figure prominently. The Virgo-Libra–Libra I combination also fosters trust and understanding, allowing the partners to lower their guards significantly. Playfulness is a frequent attribute here—one especially appreciated by intense Libra I's, who often find it hard to relax. Thus the relationship is likely to have a childlike aspect, an aura of innocence that is likely to melt the more hardened hearts that the partners encounter on life's path—including their own. The biggest problem for this duo is their own naïveté, which may leave them vulnerable to victimization.

Love affairs between Virgo-Libras and Libra I's are often preoccupied with the pursuit of fun, in private and in public. Carefree and social to the extreme, these two are ill prepared for serious problems when they do arise; barring catastrophe, however, they are likely to proceed undeterred. The relationship is less well suited to marriage, where the lack of insight on the part of Virgo-Libras, combined with the tendency of Libra I's to worry, may create a perilous situation.

Friendships and working relationships between these two can be interrelated, with co-workers developing friendships on the job or friends deciding to go into business together. One of the real strengths of such relationships is the partners' ability to give each other sound advice; that both critical Libra I's and tasteful Virgo-Libras are able to take such advice is a tribute to the relationship's openness. Both are difficult to please, and their working relationship is a demanding one, with excellence the goal. In the family sphere, parent-child combinations are generally oriented toward more youthful values. Childhood games, holiday trips and other forms of recreation and amusement are likely to have a salutary effect on the relationship by drawing parents and children close together through the bond of mutual enjoyment.

ADVICE: *Be trusting, but not completely so. Try to be a bit more realistic. Growing up need not mean leaving amusements behind.*

September 19–24

THE CUSP OF BEAUTY
VIRGO-LIBRA CUSP

Little Rest

October 3–10

THE WEEK OF SOCIETY
LIBRA II

RELATIONSHIPS

STRENGTHS: **MODERN,
DOMESTIC, AFFECTIONATE**

WEAKNESSES: **JEALOUS,
ELITIST, IRRITATING**

BEST: **MARRIAGE**

WORST: **FRIENDSHIP**

JOHN LENNON (10/9/40)
BRIAN EPSTEIN (9/19/34)

The determination of both Virgo-Libras and Libra II's to be always at their best is magnified by their relationship, which therefore grants them little rest. Being thoroughly up-to-date on the latest issues and trends is important to these two. Newspapers, magazines, television, the Internet—all are used to feed their incessant hunger for new information. Not only quantity is important here, but quality as well; indeed, the focus of the Virgo-Libra–Libra II relationship may be a relentless search for the perfect style, the perfect house—in short, the ideal situation. Learning patience and becoming attuned to *kairos* (the right time to attempt something) will be important here. One danger of the relationship is an undeniably elitist attitude that can arouse the antagonism and envy of others if not held in check.

Libra II's value their privacy highly and need to insist on being left completely alone from time to time, which can irritate their less understanding Virgo-Libra lovers and friends. Love affairs between these two are usually more affectionate than erotic, but there is often a corresponding lack of tension and annoyance as well. Cooking, shopping and decorating are special interests for the couple, whether they live together or not. Success in these and other domestic activities augurs well for marriages or permanent living situations. Since Libra II's and Virgo-Libras are not particularly self-aware, their relationship may at times be plagued by unaccountable depressions that can cause anxiety and bewilderment.

Should Virgo-Libras and Libra II's work together, they will do best if self-employed or involved in small-business partnerships, where responsibilities are lighter and there is greater freedom of choice. Virgo-Libras are generally quite astute in assessing the capabilities of their Libra II partners and putting them to best use. Sibling matchups of the opposite sex are mildly antagonistic, but such pairs are usually able to work out their difficulties within the context of shared social involvements. Jealous rivalries over a favorite parent or friend are common here—a tendency that should be watched.

ADVICE: *Be aware of your effect on others. Do not exhaust yourself in pursuit of the latest trend. Seek traditional values.*

Epstein first discovered the Beatles in 1961 at a Liverpool club. Within 2 months he became their manager, cleaning up the act by replacing their black leather jackets, tight jeans and pompadours with Pierre Cardin suits and more androgynous hairstyles. Early on, Lennon complained about Epstein, saying that "he was doing nothing and we were doing all the work."

September 19–24

THE CUSP OF BEAUTY
VIRGO-LIBRA CUSP

Solar Flares

October 11–18

THE WEEK OF THEATER
LIBRA III

RELATIONSHIPS

STRENGTHS: **SHARING,
INSPIRING, RADIANT**

WEAKNESSES: **ABRUPT,
LIMITED, EGOTISTICAL**

BEST: **FRIENDSHIP**

WORST: **MARRIAGE**

SARA ROOSEVELT (9/21/1855)
ELEANOR ROOSEVELT (10/11/1884)

Virgo-Libras and Libra III's are stars in the same firmament. Although the relationship is oriented outward, and is at times quite extroverted, it derives its power and energy from a very deep place indeed: each partner's need to find the perfect outer representation of his or her own inner vision and to make it shine. Equality between the partners in such relationships is essential, but it is more often Libra III's who are the more exciting. Not infrequently, Libra III's spur Virgo-Libras to outstrip themselves—to strive for the very best of which they are capable. The most common scenario here is that these two individuals spend a certain amount of time together and then go their separate ways, each enriched by their contact with the other. Thus the relationship may be fleeting, or it may last for a number of years, but in either case it must be phased out once it has outlived its usefulness.

Love affairs and marriages can be profound but rarely last long. The contact is often viewed, in retrospect, as having been necessary and valuable to both individuals' personal development. Friendships and sibling relationships can be mutually supportive and stabilizing. Although competition inevitably arises, especially between partners of the same sex, such activities have a toughening effect and rarely result in serious animosities. Virgo-Libras and Libra III's both need to be in the spotlight a good deal of the time, but eventually will have to seek their own arena in which to perform, which usually means terminating, or at least severely limiting, their relationship.

Work or career connections, no matter how brief, generally allow for an unusually high degree of inspiration and collaboration. Rarely will either partner hold back from giving the other the best he or she has to offer professionally. In all of the above relationships, friends and family alike will marvel at the partners' abilities to exchange spiritual and creative gifts with one another, considering how much attention they both require. There is an apparently innate understanding that whatever benefits one benefits both.

ADVICE: *Don't exploit each other unduly. Develop your caring side—sharing is not enough. Express your emotions. Keep things simple.*

Sara was the mother of President Roosevelt, who married Eleanor in 1905. Eleanor became famous as the "First Lady of the World" for her many national/international humanitarian accomplishments. Her mother-in-law Sara was the 2nd wife of wealthy scion James Roosevelt. Sara raised Franklin in their elegant estate at Hyde Park, NY, where the entire family spent much time together.

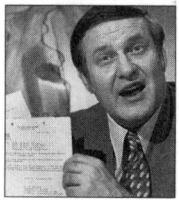 

JACK ANDERSON (10/19/22)
THOMAS EAGLETON (9/24/29)

Sen. Eagleton—George McGovern's Democratic vice-presidential running mate in 1972—was forced to withdraw when Republican newspaper columnist Anderson revealed Eagleton's history of nervous disorders. Anderson drew harsh criticism for his treatment of Eagleton—who was later reelected to the Senate. **Also: Gunnar Nelson & Tracy Nelson** (brother/sister; musician/actress).

September 19–24
THE CUSP OF BEAUTY
VIRGO-LIBRA CUSP

October 19–25
THE CUSP OF DRAMA & CRITICISM
LIBRA-SCORPIO CUSP

A Curious Split

This relationship may experience a curious split between its social and its personal aspects. Combining Virgo-Libra taste and Libra-Scorpio I initiative, it is extremely interested in both aesthetic and group affairs—possession, of either objects or people, is not an unusual theme here. These two may vie with each other for dominance of social groups. Both are willing to go to the ends of the earth to find collectibles of good value, or simply to have a one-time glimpse of an exquisite art object. Such love of beauty may belie the tremendous psychological problems that can mar this relationship. Certain dark tendencies, carefully hidden from the view of concerned friends and family members, may reach obsessive or even addictive proportions. Too often, Virgo-Libras and Libra-Scorpios are unaware of the subtle connections among their love of beauty, desire for social position, and negative thoughts about themselves.

Love affairs and marriages between these two may be controlled by dark forces beyond their ken. Erotic rather than affectionate impulses predominate here, and the partners may be tightly bound to each other not only by passion but by desperation and fear. All of this may go on behind a brilliant social facade. Unless one partner has marked analytic skills, it is unlikely that the relationship will furnish an environment in which self-understanding can flourish.

Friendships, family relationships and career connections are likely to overlap. These two know a great deal about the world, particularly the latest styles and fashions. If involved with the arts, architecture, fashion, music or design, then, they are likely to be highly successful. In all the foregoing areas, the Virgo-Libra–Libra-Scorpio relationship would do well to spend even a fraction of the energy it devotes to outside concerns on its own internal problems. Building self-confidence, accompanied by a thorough psychological housecleaning in which old scripts and tapes are swept out the door, is most important here.

ADVICE: *Put your house in order, and illuminate dark corners. What attracts you may reflect negatively on yourself. Move forward with self-confidence.*

LEON JAWORSKI (9/19/05)
BOB HALDEMAN (10/27/26)

Jaworski was special prosecutor in the 1973 Watergate investigation. He presented evidence to a federal grand jury that led to the indictment of the key players in the scandal, among them Haldeman, Nixon's powerful White House chief of staff. Haldeman was given a 4-year prison sentence. **Also: John Dankworth & Cleo Laine** (married; jazz performers).

September 19–24
THE CUSP OF BEAUTY
VIRGO-LIBRA CUSP

October 26–November 2
THE WEEK OF INTENSITY
SCORPIO I

A Contentious Dynamic

This combination is likely to be an unsettled and suspicious one, but also one in which a persistently contentious dynamic forwards the action on life's stage. Thus the relationship is characterized by impulse and aggression. Things will not go well between these two if Scorpio I's feel that Virgo-Libras, as arbiters of taste, are treating them in a condescending way. They may easily see Virgo-Libras as snobs, and the Virgo-Libra approach as elitist. Feeling personally attacked on such a level will only cause the partners to take countermeasures.

No matter how gratifying a love affair here might be in the sensual sphere, Virgo-Libras may eventually give up on this partner if they feel they have been made the objects of unrelenting scrutiny or criticism. Nor will they enjoy periodic blowups with their Scorpio I lovers, which tend to knock them off balance. Marriages, too, are unlikely to click here, principally because Virgo-Libra social tastes may be irreconcilable with Scorpio I wishes in this area. Most often a Virgo-Libra will make friends out of people who are likely to enhance their social and career opportunities. This will be unbearable to Scorpio I's, who keep their few friends for highly personal reasons, often involving trust and honor.

Career connections are often of the more ambitious sort. Neither will shy away from using the other's talents to advance his or her own purpose, but when push comes to shove, real appreciation and loyalty may be sadly lacking. Most upsetting will be the justifications they may give for breaking off their connection, which purport to be ethical but in fact ring hollow. Ambition will also play an important role between parents and children. Both partners are likely to push each other at various points to further their careers, supposedly for the benefit of the group. Attempts to engage in a family business can be emotionally catastrophic, and should be avoided unless strict objectivity can be maintained.

ADVICE: *Keep things a bit lighter. A deep involvement may not be a good idea. Beware of making promises you can't keep. Tone down your morality.*

September 19–24

THE CUSP OF BEAUTY
VIRGO-LIBRA CUSP

November 3–11

THE WEEK OF DEPTH
SCORPIO II

Boisterous Variety

This pair can enjoy a variety of social activities together, often complementing each other and filling in the gaps. Of particular note is their sense of humor, which is often boisterous. The satire and parody exhibited here are not directed solely against other people, however; the partners' ability to laugh at themselves is a prime indicator of their compatibility.

These two would seem to be diametrically opposite in orientation—Virgo-Libras are more concerned with social matters and externals, Scorpio II's with personal issues and their complex inner lives. Yet the extroverted side of Scorpio II's is revealed here, especially in the sphere of friendship; being able to indulge in theatrical displays without risk of disapproval can be a liberating experience for them. Furthermore, the deep concentration of which Scorpio II's are capable is an excellent tool for directing Virgo-Libra attention to the matters at hand.

In love affairs, Scorpio II's may be a bit too much for their partner in this combination to handle. Their moods can be oppressive, leaving Virgo-Libras feeling helpless and overwhelmed. Virgo-Libras who like to keep it light may back away when they get their first glimpse of the subterranean levels to which Scorpio II's can descend. Marriages between these two can thrive on social interaction, which often helps to brighten the darker side of the relationship.

Virgo-Libra parents admire the energy of their Scorpio II children but may be hard put to keep up with them. Should Scorpio II's be cast in the parental role, they will generally enjoy sharing light, entertaining activities with their amicable Virgo-Libra offspring, on whom they can exert an overwhelming influence. Their children of the opposite sex particularly may be influenced by them in choosing friends or partners later in life. At work, Virgo-Libras and Scorpio II's had best avoid fixed situations. If they pursue any career at all together, it should only be one that allows them flexibility and mutual independence.

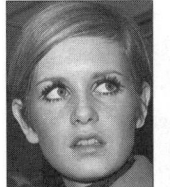

TWIGGY (9/19/49)
JEAN SHRIMPTON (11/6/42)

Britishers Twiggy and Shrimpton were 2 of the world's most popular and successful models during the 60s. Shrimpton was cast in the classic high-fashion mold, while Twiggy, with her 92-pound, 5'6" frame, was the epitome of the spare, offbeat, mod style unique to the 60s.

ADVICE: *Be aware of your influence on each other; bring energies into balance. Laughter is the best medicine, but be serious when it really counts.*

September 19–24

THE CUSP OF BEAUTY
VIRGO-LIBRA CUSP

November 12–18

THE WEEK OF CHARM
SCORPIO III

Going for the Goodies

The hunger for beauty in all its forms that these individuals share is transmuted by the chemistry of their relationship into a bid for all the material, and immaterial, rewards that money and influence can bring. This is an extremely dangerous combination, since its partners' combined will to power is potentially strong enough to demand that they sacrifice affection, love, kindness—practically all the fundamental human values—to their ambition. Their relative positions in the relationship are usually fixed, and they are not particularly susceptible to internal power struggles—the overriding focus here is outside conquest.

Love affairs, friendships and sibling matchups between these two are likely to manifest strong competitive urges, which can best be kept positive if sublimated into healthy physical interaction or game-playing. Should such impulses turn negative, however, they may cause untold harm, not only to the partners themselves but to the social and family units of which they are a part. Marriages are often defined by a desire for upward social mobility. If this impetus can be controlled and better directed, however, these relationships have an excellent chance for success in the sphere of personal development.

In work and family settings, power is often transferred from one generation to the next. Great sacrifices can be required in such groups; ironically, although luxury and ease may seem to be the ultimate goals, the demands of hard work and a Spartan lifestyle leave little time or energy for enjoying the fruits of their labors—the means become ends in themselves. Cultivating a balance between business and pleasure is important here, since the Virgo-Libra–Scorpio III relationship is capable of going to the opposite extreme, and of periodically giving itself over to the fanatical pursuit of pleasure—a work-hard, play-hard ethic that ultimately leads to both psychological and physical problems.

TIBERIUS (11/16/42 BC)
AUGUSTUS (9/23/63 BC)

Augustus tried to arrange for his successor during his lifetime. Since he had no sons, he tried to align first his daughter's 2 husbands, then her 2 sons—but all died prematurely. Ultimately, he was forced to adopt his daughter's 3rd husband, Tiberius, whom he disliked, as his successor.

Also: **Bill Murray & Lorne Michaels** (SNL actor/producer).

ADVICE: *Find a balance between work and play; know when to quit. Enjoy the fruits of your labors. Share with others outside your group.*

STRENGTHS: **TASTEFUL, EXCITING, BALANCED**

WEAKNESSES: **ELITIST, FRUSTRATED, ALIENATING**

BEST: **FRIENDSHIP**

WORST: **FAMILY**

DAVID McCALLUM (9/19/33)
ROBERT VAUGHN (11/22/32)

McCallum and Vaughn made a high-energy action team in tv's *The Man from UNCLE* (1964–68). Vaughn played secret agent Napoleon Solo (a name borrowed from Ian Fleming's *Goldfinger*), and McCallum played his partner, Ilya Kuryakin. *Also:* **Suzanne Valadon & Toulouse-Lautrec** (lovers; circus performer, also artist Utrillo's mother/artist); **Jos. Patrick Kennedy III & RFK** (son/father; congressman/senator).

September 19–24
THE CUSP OF BEAUTY
VIRGO-LIBRA CUSP

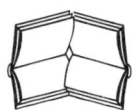

November 19–24
THE CUSP OF REVOLUTION
SCORPIO-SAGITTARIUS CUSP

What Never Was–Could Never Be

This highly exciting matchup has a tremendous capacity for initiating and maintaining projects. But critical tendencies are also abundant here, with each partner censuring the other for the very strengths he or she brings to the relationship. This judgment is viewed as unfair, of course, and is met with opposition. A potential instability is mitigated by the presence in this relationship of all four elements—earth (Virgo), air (Libra), fire (Sagittarius) and water (Scorpio). Although activity here is often at fever pitch, the energy of the matchup is rarely wasted, and is ultimately used constructively.

Sensuality manifests in this relationship toward food, sex and in particular art. Love affairs and marriages are often marked by frustration: since neither partner can be happy with what they have, things rarely seem quite right. It is not so much finicky attitudes (although these certainly do exist) as a vague dissatisfaction, involving unfavorable comparisons to past or idealized loves, that keep them apart. Paradoxically, they readily share in their appreciation of art and the pleasures of the table. The relationship may eventually become a platonic one, its partners de facto friends and companions rather than lovers and mates.

Friendships are perhaps the most balanced of the Virgo-Libra–Scorpio-Sagittarius relationships. There are many areas here that afford mutual enjoyment and development, free of attendant emotional problems. Such a relationship can become central to the lives of both partners for years, and intense feelings of loss may be experienced by either individual on the departure or death of the other.

Work relationships between married couples or friends are suggested here, especially in publishing, television and other areas of mass communication. The relationship does run the danger of becoming elitist and snobbish, however, which can alienate other people. Family matchups, particularly those of parent and child, also reiterate a theme of incompleteness or regret, as if both partners were separated at times by an impassable barrier.

ADVICE: *Examine what's holding you back. Try to abandon impossible ideals. Let go of the past—appreciate what you have in the present.*

STRENGTHS: **ESTABLISHED, FREE-THINKING, ENERGETIC**

WEAKNESSES: **DEPRIVED, GREEDY, JEALOUS**

BEST: **MARRIAGE**

WORST: **LOVE**

JOEL COEN (11/29/54)
ETHAN COEN (9/21/58)

Before 1997 the screenwriting Coen brothers were recognized in the movie business for their flamboyance and eccentricity in films like *Raising Arizona* (1987) and *Barton Fink* (1991). In '96, however, they stunned the world with their brilliant *Fargo*, which earned them an Oscar for best screenplay. *Also:* **Larry Hagman & Mary Martin** (son/mother; actors).

September 19–24
THE CUSP OF BEAUTY
VIRGO-LIBRA CUSP

November 25–December 2
THE WEEK OF INDEPENDENCE
SAGITTARIUS I

Building Brick by Brick

This pair may be found designing, decorating or even building physical structures, which themselves lend shape to the family, social or professional groups that occupy the partners. The relationship allows for the merger of Virgo-Libra taste and Sagittarius I initiative, and its strength lies in its capacity for giving material form to its beliefs—a bit of the empire builder characterizes the matchup. Although neither of its partners is especially patient, it confers the stamina and the ability to build something slowly, brick by brick. Moreover, it is highly symbiotic: its partners are undeniably dependent upon each other. Rarely will either partner advance his or her own interests at the other's expense, for both instinctively realize that what's best for the relationship is best for the individual.

Sagittarius I's will enjoy this relationship because it grants them a solid foundation for their lives without compromising their conspicuous need to be free; Virgo-Libras will appreciate having the relationship's considerable energies to draw on to institute their artistic and technical vision. In love affairs and marriages, despite an orientation toward security, neither partner feels particularly bound by conventional notions of fidelity. Without compromising their loyalty to each other, Virgo-Libras and Sagittarius I's often feel free to carry on full-blown love affairs with other people. This can strain the relationship socially, but family and friends soon realize that these two can, for the most, part handle such tricky situations in a mature way. The real difficulty arises only when one partner feels relegated to second-best, or feels a negative shift in the relationship's energy. Virgo-Libra–Sagittarius I mates, family members and friends can work together as business partners or in allied professional fields. Their plans are often far-reaching, for the relationship is rarely satisfied with only moderate success: Virgo-Libras and Sagittarius I's will always aim for the top. Learning to have more realistic expectations—to be content with having reached a respectable level of success, and to have a gritty determination to stay there—is an important lesson for this pair.

ADVICE: *Don't ignore conventional wisdom. Cultivate humility. Curb your ambition—learn to be satisfied with what you have.*

September 19–24

THE CUSP OF BEAUTY
VIRGO-LIBRA CUSP

December 3–10

THE WEEK OF THE ORIGINATOR
SAGITTARIUS II

Beauty and the Beast

This relationship is usually a very straightforward one, emphasizing intensity of emotion and an appreciation of beauty—passions run high here. At its simplest the combination is about the Sagittarius II being attracted to and inspired by Virgo-Libra beauty and charm, engendering a desire to become involved with the Virgo-Libra in mutually rewarding or pleasurable activities. Sagittarius II's usually take the initiative here, but Virgo-Libras are just as often attracted to Sagittarius II's for their innovative thinking and vision. Not infrequently, career and personal involvements are interconnected with these two, making it difficult for professional relations to be maintained after the breakup of a friendship, love affair or marriage. Thus it is usually best if a choice is made at the outset as to whether the relationship should concentrate on personal issues or career matters; it should not deal with both.

Love affairs between these two sometimes experience a split between Virgo-Libra physical beauty and Sagittarius II intellectual strength, but this division will also bring the partners together—it is the classic attraction of beauty to brains and brains to beauty. Should the age difference between them be extreme, the couple will have to develop a sense of humor if they are to cope with other people's snide comments about "beauty and the beast" or "age before beauty." Marriages may suffer from an implied power structure based on whose prime attributes—beauty, age or intelligence, for example—are valued more by society. Maintaining equality while at the same time acknowledging differences will be the principal challenge here.

Teacher-student relationships, usually with Sagittarius II's in the dominant role, may involve the process of discovering Virgo-Libra talents and abilities for the first time. Tremendously flattered by such attention, Virgo-Libras may respond either by working harder or, conversely, by taking it easy, secure in their ability to manipulate their admiring instructor at will. Parent-child and boss-employee relationships in this combination may follow a similar pattern.

ADVICE: *Separate work and play. Be aware of critics, but stick to your guns. What happens between two adults is ultimately their own business.*

STRENGTHS: **INTENSE,
INSPIRATIONAL, ACCEPTING**
WEAKNESSES: **MANIPULATIVE,
POLARIZED, RIDICULED**
BEST: **TEACHER-STUDENT**
WORST: **MARRIAGE**

LOUISE NEVELSON (9/23/1899)
DIEGO RIVERA (12/8/1886)

Sculptor Nevelson is famous for her black-box sculptures made from furniture parts and other wooden objects. Before she had her first show, in 1941, she worked as an assistant to Mexican muralist Rivera, whose dramatic work concentrated on social and political themes. *Also:* **Anna Karina & Jean-Luc Goddard** (married; actress/director).

September 19–24

THE CUSP OF BEAUTY
VIRGO-LIBRA CUSP

December 11–18

THE WEEK OF THE TITAN
SAGITTARIUS III

Finding Out for Themselves

The great mutual respect that is common in this relationship promotes easy interaction on a daily basis, and precludes feelings of condescension and struggles for power. The Virgo-Libra–Sagittarius III matchup, whether it is a solid family bond, a friendship or a sensual love affair or marriage, has a strongly physical quality. Virgo-Libras rarely mind playing a secondary role here; usually being able to enchant Sagittarius III's, they seldom have trouble getting their own way. Virgo-Libras and Sagittarius III's are often able to learn a great deal from each other but can learn even more from the relationship itself.

Love affairs are usually quite romantic and feature a kind of adoration. Each partner has a lasting idealized image of the other that generally goes far beyond mere physical appearance. Marriages can be successful as long as Virgo-Libras do not require too much attention from their hard-working Sagittarius III mates and Sagittarius III's do not impose their heavy moods on Virgo-Libra spouses.

Friendships and sibling matchups emphasize mutual growth and development, but at various stages Sagittarius III's may need to push a little bit to get things going. Virgo-Libras won't resent such encouragement now and then but will want to feel included in the making and implementation of decisions. Such matchups often rebel against parents and teachers who wax didactic, not from a particular dislike of authority, but rather because this duo would rather find things out for themselves.

Work relationships between these two can be outstanding. Sagittarius III vision and Virgo-Libra taste meld exquisitely and give the stamp of success to many of their endeavors. But financial matters will require expert advice from an accountant or business manager—this combination is not the most astute when it comes to money.

ADVICE: *Don't close your ears to other people's advice, or make unreasonable demands on yourself—when you need help, ask for it. Allow for mistakes.*

STRENGTHS: **EXPERIENTIAL,
IDEALISTIC, SENSUOUS**
WEAKNESSES: **MOODY,
RECALCITRANT, UNBALANCED**
BEST: **LOVE**
WORST: **SIBLING**

SOPHIA LOREN (9/20/34)
CARLO PONTI (12/11/10)

Statuesque Loren and diminutive Ponti, 24 years her senior, first met in 1949 when she was a beauty contestant at 15. He groomed her as an actress and they married in '57. They have a son, Carlo Jr. *Also:* **Bruce Springsteen & John Hammond** (rock star discovered by critic-producer); **Charles Parker & George Parker** (brothers; founded board game company).

AVA GARDNER (12/24/22)
MICKEY ROONEY (9/23/20)

Rooney, the pint-sized dynamo whose screen career spanned 8 decades, was married 8 times, typically to tall, well-endowed mates. His first wife was Gardner, the seductive, husky-voiced star of the 40s and 50s. When she married Rooney in '42 her career got a boost from all the publicity.
Also: H.G. Wells & Rebecca West (affair; writers).

September 19–24
THE CUSP OF BEAUTY
VIRGO-LIBRA CUSP

December 19–25
THE CUSP OF PROPHECY
SAGITTARIUS-CAPRICORN CUSP

In Over Their Heads?

Powerful and magnetic, this relationship is also apt to be highly contentious. Strongly unconventional and asocial tendencies may be aroused here, underlined by the couple's striking need for privacy and penchant for secrecy. The Virgo-Libra cusp coincides with the fall equinox and the Sagittarius-Capricorn cusp with the winter solstice, two of the four power points of the year. Lying square to each other in the zodiac (90° apart), Virgo-Libra and Sagittarius-Capricorn produce strongly contrasting personalities for whom astrology would predict friction and difficulty. Becoming involved with someone as spirited as themselves may prove irresistible to this pair, however. Once the two are involved, they may both end up feeling that some dark force or fate has them in its grip.

Virgo-Libras will often be confronted by a projection of their own dark side in love affairs and marriages in this combination. Sagittarius-Capricorns may function as animus or anima figures for Virgo-Libras, becoming the irresistible object of their secret desires. Falling in love here can have grave repercussions for both partners, who may be getting in way over their heads—caught up in a maelstrom of feelings, they can be drawn to levels of emotion deeper than any they have yet approached. Siblings in this combination can be extremely close, with the older sibling often serving as a parent substitute or role model in adolescence or young adulthood. Virgo-Libra–Sagittarius-Capricorn friendships may also fulfill a need insofar as they compensate for the absence of satisfactory family relationships. Such matchups can be extremely close, but possessiveness, overdependency and inhibition of personal development in the name of loyalty to the relationship must all be carefully monitored.

Ideas and ideals are extremely important to Virgo-Libras and Sagittarius-Capricorns in their professional relationship. As members of a business or social organization they are likely to have the best interest of others at heart, and to be untiring in their capacity to give of themselves. Often champions of the dispossessed or downtrodden, they will fight the good fight together to guarantee fair treatment for all concerned.

ADVICE: *Keep an eye on yourself, and on your own best interests—don't be swept away. Remember to give each other room to breathe.*

MAURICE UTRILLO (12/26/1883)
SUZANNE VALADON (9/23/1865)

Valadon, mother of artist Utrillo, was herself a versatile painter who had previously been a seamstress, circus performer and artists' model. She inspired her son to become a painter. He is best known for his interpretation of Paris street scenes, often painting the tawdry, dismal atmosphere of the Montmartre quarter.

September 19–24
THE CUSP OF BEAUTY
VIRGO-LIBRA CUSP

December 26–January 2
THE WEEK OF THE RULER
CAPRICORN I

A Search for Meaning

Natural feelings and attitudes predominate in this free and easy relationship. In many ways liberating, the Virgo-Libra–Capricorn I matchup can powerfully influence both partners in their search for meaning in life, and also in their self-development. Thus Virgo-Libras learn a great deal from their Capricorn I partners, who, in turn, benefit tremendously from the aesthetic influences of Virgo-Libras, which can open up whole new worlds for them.

Romance is possible between these two; it will seldom be of the wilder sort, yet it will be more uninhibited than either partner is used to. Capricorn I's will be enchanted by their Virgo-Libra partners but, unfortunately, will also regard them as possessions. Virgo-Libras can only be flattered to a point, and will back off if they feel claimed or controlled. In marriage, they benefit from Capricorn I practicality and common sense. They will not be dissatisfied with playing a supporting role, but must beware that their own personalities are not swallowed up by the relationship.

As friends, these two enjoy taking courses together that lead to mutual self-improvement, whether commercial, physical or artistic. A common hobby often emerges that unites the pair and becomes the basis of the relationship. Virgo-Libras should not be surprised at Capricorn I thriftiness but should edge the relationship away from a stingy attitude that can limit its possibilities and inhibit creativity.

Parent-child relationships can be extremely favorable, with both partners sharing, learning and growing together. Artistic and spiritual bonds may be formed here that continue into adult life. In the work sphere, Capricorn I's tend to think they are omniscient, a trait that, if encountered on a daily basis, will grate on the nerves of Virgo-Libras. These two relate best as independent colleagues or freelancers who touch base occasionally to share their thoughts and observations.

ADVICE: *Learn from each other, but maintain your independence—beware of claiming attitudes. Cultivate artistic and spiritual pursuits.*

September 19–24

THE CUSP OF BEAUTY
VIRGO-LIBRA CUSP

January 3–9

THE WEEK OF DETERMINATION
CAPRICORN II

Fateful Resolution

Constructive outlets must be found for the emotional and often physical intensity of this relationship. The partners are magnetically, even fatally, attracted to each other, but the interactions that result are not necessarily pleasant. An undeniably antagonistic or violent energy pervades the relationship. The partners are better off not making excuses for this, since they will usually need direct confrontation to resolve any conflict. Should such confrontations be avoided, the relationship is likely to suffer from frustration and to stagnate and remain unfulfilled.

Love affairs exhibit a great deal of sensuality and mutual attraction; the emphasis here is on a deeply satisfying physical and emotional involvement. Sexual striving might seem to indicate conflict but, in fact, leads primarily to greater pleasure. Marriages should aim for harmony and stability, or perhaps should not be initiated in the first place, since the outcome of marital disputes and eventual breakups here is not a pretty one. Should mates become adversaries, the situation is likely to turn into all-out warfare as the partners struggle to settle disputes over possessions, money and children.

Friendships and sibling relationships in this combination may be either amicable or adversarial, or may fluctuate between the two. Ambivalence and ambiguity will sometimes cloud the real nature of the relationship, since love and hate are so closely intertwined here. Often, many years will pass before the true meaning and focus of this relationship are revealed to its partners. Professional matchups between these two best exemplify these observations. Realistic in the extreme, both partners know exactly where they stand in the relationship; in fact, for either of them even momentarily to abandon realism for sentimentality could prove a fatal mistake. Although adversarial roles often manifest here, the dance in which this couple indulges is so well synchronized that opponents appear, even in battle, to be harmoniously linked. A lack of underhanded behavior indicates the willingness of both partners to abide by the rules and to eschew personal gain in favor of fair play.

ADVICE: *Limit confrontations if possible, but do not avoid them—resolve your difficulties. Accentuate the positive.*

FLOYD PATTERSON (1/4/35)
INGEMAR JOHANSSON (9/22/32)

Swedish Johansson took the heavyweight boxing title from American Patterson in 1959 in a stunning upset. Patterson won it back in '60, making him the first ever to regain the crown. Patterson beat Johansson once more in '61. Their 3 fights are legendary. They became great and deeply respectful friends. *Also:* **Brian Epstein & George Martin** (Beatles manager/producer).

September 19–24

THE CUSP OF BEAUTY
VIRGO-LIBRA CUSP

January 10–16

THE WEEK OF DOMINANCE
CAPRICORN III

Thick and Thin

This energetic relationship is capable of getting new projects on the rails and of enhancing communication within the groups to which it belongs. Capricorn III admiration for Virgo-Libra physical attractiveness is only thinly disguised here, and Virgo-Libras may learn a great deal about forcefulness, self-confidence and willpower from Capricorn III's. Such qualities complement each other well in a relationship focused on establishing and maintaining its position through thick and thin.

Subtle conflicts may arise in love affairs and marriages between these two, since Capricorn III's are anxious to control and even deny their physical needs and Virgo-Libras are all too willing to indulge them. One problem is that Capricorn III's are by nature pleasure-loving, yet are intent on withstanding their hedonistic impulses; as such, they can be very susceptible to Virgo-Libra influence, which they may later regret. Thus Capricorn III's are likely to resent the temptations this relationship places in their paths, and Virgo-Libras to wind up feeling frustrated when blamed or excluded.

Parent-child relationships in both possible arrangements are characterized by a mutual admiration that can at times approach worship. Difficulties must be expected during adolescence, when painful separations may prove necessary to enhance individuality. Once the partners have spent enough time apart, they may reunite, having achieved a new level of trust and respect. Virgo-Libra–Capricorn III friendships usually interest themselves in a wide variety of activities, and dislike getting stuck in one particular area of endeavor. This relationship must beware of nervousness and overexcitement resulting from spreading itself too thin.

In career matchups, these two will work themselves into a solid position but will often be content to stay there rather than going for the top. Thus Virgo-Libras and Capricorn III's make excellent co-workers within a department of a large corporation, where over the years they may continue to impress others with both the quality of their work and their facility for promoting cooperation.

ADVICE: *Take things as they come. Don't be too adoring. Give each other enough space—separation may be necessary at times.*

JOHN MARSHALL (9/24/1755)
ALEXANDER HAMILTON (1/11/1755)

Marshall and Hamilton were leading Federalists instrumental in the creation and structure of American government. Hamilton, whose essays published in *The Federalist* did much to get the Constitution ratified, influenced Chief Justice Marshall, who established basic principles of constitutional law, most notably judicial review—the power of the Supreme Court to rule on acts of the other branches of government.

GAIL RUSSELL (9/23/24)
GUY MADISON (1/19/22)

Handsome, all-American-type Madison starred in 50s action films and 60s low-grade European movies. He was married to Russell (1949–54), a beautiful Hollywood leading lady of the 40s and 50s. She was an insecure introvert who suffered from stage fright and was driven to alcoholism.

September 19–24

THE CUSP OF BEAUTY
VIRGO-LIBRA CUSP

January 17–22

THE CUSP OF MYSTERY & IMAGINATION
CAPRICORN-AQUARIUS CUSP

Reactive Rebellion

This relationship is a strange blend of accord and dissension. Although a trine aspect here augurs well for an easygoing relationship (Virgo-Libra and Capricorn-Aquarius lie 120° apart in the zodiac), this only tells part of the story. At ease with each other one moment, these two can suddenly explode, in a spontaneous eruption that leaves others breathless in its wake. Like so many cusp combinations, this one contains elements that are singularly unpredictable. Should either partner attempt an overt power play, the result will surely be a full-scale revolution. Indeed, rebelliousness can be the focus of such a relationship, especially in family and work settings.

Although Virgo-Libra and Capricorn-Aquarius are both earth-air combinations, their relationship is ruled by water and fire and may all too quickly boil over. In marriages and love affairs, the rule is often excitement and sensuality but, equally, psychological and emotional instability—something neither of these individuals is temperamentally equipped to handle. Virgo-Libras, attracted to their mate's imaginativeness, may keep their cool for long periods, but if Capricorn-Aquarians push them too far they can spring into attack mode.

Friendships between these two, particularly in their school years, will be unlikely to allow perceived insults by teachers or fellow students to pass without challenge. Both may acquire reputations as spoilers or troublemakers, when in fact they are simply refusing to be pushed around. Parent-child and boss-employee relationships are often fiery, especially when Capricorn-Aquarians are in the dominant position. These personalities have an authoritarian streak; they can give effective direction to the family or work group but can also sometimes needle good-natured and peace-loving Virgo-Libras, even ridiculing them publicly on occasion. All this Virgo-Libras can bear good-naturedly, until Capricorn-Aquarians pick on weaker colleagues or family members and finally arouse Virgo-Libra opposition. Such confrontations may actually be necessary for reinforcing the self-esteem and confidence of Virgo-Libras, particularly if they are able to triumph over their formidable adversaries.

ADVICE: *Keep your cool, but don't let others manipulate you. Maintain self-respect while giving others their due. Be consistent.*

RICHARD OLDENBERG (9/21/33)
CLAES OLDENBERG (1/28/29)

The Oldenberg brothers are both major figures in the art world. Claes became a leading pop artist in the 60s, known for his oversized replicas of ordinary objects such as gadgets, food and clothing. Richard was director of the Museum of Modern Art in NY from 1972–94. **Also: Octavian & Livia Drusilla** (married; Roman rulers); **Mickey Rooney & Carolyn Mitchell** (married; actors).

September 19–24

THE CUSP OF BEAUTY
VIRGO-LIBRA CUSP

January 23–30

THE WEEK OF GENIUS
AQUARIUS I

Intricate Workings

The focus here is to be found in the intricate and labyrinthine workings of the human mind. Not at all easy to figure out, even for the partners themselves, the combination is a devious one, and rarely follows the straight and narrow path. This couple tends to be arrogant, and to assume that they are a law unto themselves. Stressing freedom for themselves, they sometimes apply a double standard, demanding that others toe the line. This relationship suggests the classic pairing of beauty and brains, and to get others to do its bidding, it often makes use of both an attractive exterior and clever arguments. Not surprisingly, honesty is not a strong suit here.

Serious power struggles emerge in love affairs and marriages, especially if one partner feels trapped or oppressed by the other, but by no means are these interactions predicated on such a scenario. Usually one of the partners likes to come out on top, at least from the standpoint of providing direction or giving orders. Mind games are likely to be used in surprising variety, again indicating the degree to which each partner will manipulate the other to get his or her own way.

Friendships are unlikely to be very intimate or deep between Virgo-Libras and Aquarius I's and usually occur only when shared work or property is at stake. For the most part, individual interests undercut the possibility for sharing in such a relationship. Siblings in this combination are likely to defend their own interests aggressively. Indeed, the family unit of which they are a part may founder in a sea of dissension unless they recognize the extent to which they are weakening it.

Career connections between these two can be highly effective, even brilliant, but also a tad ruthless or dishonest. The reckless drive to succeed is a sign not only of ambition but of how little this couple may be aware of the feelings of others. This pair will dream up complex plans to further their own interests, then will efficiently put these plans into effect.

ADVICE: *Take feelings into account. Beware of ruthless tendencies. Power is less important than love. Double standards arouse resentments.*

September 19–24

THE CUSP OF BEAUTY
VIRGO-LIBRA CUSP

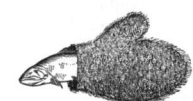

January 31–February 7

THE WEEK OF YOUTH & EASE
AQUARIUS II

RELATIONSHIPS

STRENGTHS: **FUNNY,
INDEPENDENT, BRILLIANT**

WEAKNESSES: **SARCASTIC,
HURTFUL, DARK**

BEST: **FRIENDSHIP**

WORST: **LOVE**

The Gift of Laughter

This relationship carries with it the gift of laughter. The pair will enjoy having a good time as much as any other matchup in the year and will not care a bit whether they are having it at someone else's expense. Independence of thought and action features strongly here, and as a unit these two can be guided unerringly to lock onto a target and fire at will. Having humor as its focus could open the relationship to charges of superficiality, were it not for the fact that its barbs sting and, in doing so, wake people up and make them think. Often hiding a more serious message behind a ribald or outrageous facade, this duo can succeed where parents, teachers and philosophers may fail.

In love affairs and marriages, this couple, who can be outrageously funny around others, may suffer from depression when alone. In fact, there is a fair amount of hopelessness or despair at the center of the relationship, thinly disguised as sarcasm and dark jokes. The source of this unhappiness usually has to do with a certain soullessness or lack of true intimacy, which the partners feel as a vague dissatisfaction, since neither of them usually has the psychological insight needed to pinpoint what is wrong. Private confrontations between these two can be anything but funny and, in fact, may be excruciatingly painful, since resolutions are unlikely.

Friendships of this type are unambiguously, unashamedly and unconditionally dedicated to having fun. Some sensitivity will have to be shown to the feelings of others if this matchup is not to become something from which others instinctively turn away in fear or disgust. In the family sphere and at work, Virgo-Libras and Aquarius II's can be counted on to lighten the mood. Should they be attacked or reproved for their irreverence, however, they are quite capable of launching scathing attacks that may send their critics running for shelter. One such incident is usually enough to teach others to avoid this pair's wrath as they would a swarm of bees.

DUKE SNIDER (9/19/26)
JACKIE ROBINSON (1/31/19)

Snider and Robinson were Brooklyn Dodgers teammates from 1947–56. Both had outstanding records. In '56, The Duke led his league in home runs; in '55 he led in RBIs. Robinson was Rookie of the Year in '47, MVP in '49 and had a 10-year batting average of .310. Both players are Hall of Famers.

ADVICE: *In making jokes at someone else's expense, you may be harming yourself. Try to react less violently; be more diplomatic. Work on intimacy.*

September 19–24

THE CUSP OF BEAUTY
VIRGO-LIBRA CUSP

February 8–15

THE WEEK OF ACCEPTANCE
AQUARIUS III

RELATIONSHIPS

STRENGTHS: **COMMUNICATIVE,
OPEN, UNDERSTANDING**

WEAKNESSES: **SELFISH,
NERVOUS, EXCLUSIVE**

BEST: **MARRIAGE**

WORST: **FRIENDSHIP**

A Psychic Link

The reason for the success of this relationship can often be traced to the very personal kind of communication that exists between the two partners. Because this communication rarely takes the form of a system of thought or an actual language, it will be difficult to let others in on the process. This unknown tongue may lead to misunderstandings with those outside the relationship, and even to envy and resentment. Defining this pair's channel of communication is not easy, but the elements involved are openness, respect, acceptance and understanding, in addition to a special psychic or intuitive link.

In love affairs, both partners will derive pleasure from not having to work to explain themselves, something neither likes doing. Very much tuned in to each other's wishes, Virgo-Libras and Aquarius III's will immediately know how to please each other—but of course won't always choose to do so. Thus in arguments they are more apt to charge each other with willful neglect rather than offer the excuse that either one of them is simply unaware.

Marriages and working relationships between Virgo-Libras and Aquarius III's are, for the most part, solid. These matchups thrive on having an interest to protect, be it financial, domestic or perhaps even their own reputations. The partners will rarely forsake their best interests or sell them to the highest bidder, knowing instinctively that giving up such permanence would subject the relationship to tidal drift and, eventually, to breakup. Friendships can be extremely close, but also somewhat unstable. A nervous quality pervades this matchup, as does a tendency to blow with the latest wind, which leads to occasional acts of selfishness and inconsiderateness.

In the family sphere, the open channels of communication within a parent-child pair in this combination can be a blessing to the family unit of which it is a part but also a thorn in the side of family members who feel excluded from it. Including others whenever possible will be in the best interest of all concerned.

RED AUERBACH (9/20/17)
BILL RUSSELL (2/12/34)

Basketball's legendary Auerbach was Boston Celtics coach from 1950–66, winning 9 NBA titles, a record 8 of them in a row. During Auerbach's reign, Russell was the Celtic's defensive center, perhaps the best in basketball history with over 21,000 rebounds. He was an NBA All-Star 11 times, MVP 5 times.

Also: Twiggy & Mary Quant
(mod model/mod fashion designer).

ADVICE: *Hold on to what you've got, but don't shut others out. Beware of selfishness. Acting in a superior fashion arouses resentment.*

RELATIONSHIPS

STRENGTHS: **UNUSUAL, AESTHETIC, FIERY**

WEAKNESSES: **UNGROUNDED, PECULIAR, RASH**

BEST: **MARRIAGE**

WORST: **LOVE**

SINEAD CUSACK (2/18/48)
JEREMY IRONS (9/19/48)

Brilliant stage and screen actor Irons first emerged in *The French Lieutenant's Woman* (1981). Since then he has enjoyed great success, most notably as Claus Von Bulow in *Reversal of Fortune* (1990), for which he won an Oscar. In '78 he married Irish-born actress Cusack, daughter of poet Cyril Cusack.
Also: **Jim Henson & Edgar Bergen** (puppeteer inspired by ventriloquist).

September 19–24
THE CUSP OF BEAUTY
VIRGO-LIBRA CUSP

February 16–22
THE CUSP OF SENSITIVITY
AQUARIUS-PISCES CUSP

Singular Vision

This matchup is a highly unusual and not necessarily stable one. In fact, the partners may have to work consciously toward being more grounded and practical in their outlook and actions if they are to preserve their relationship. There is a tendency here for instability to increase in proportion to idiosyncrasy. These two share visionary ideas with each other; it is a relationship more dreamlike than either individual is accustomed to, and can be a loving and caring one. Aquarius-Pisces have the sensitivity, and the drive, that Virgo-Libras need, and Virgo-Libras are able to share their aesthetic interests with their Aquarius-Pisces partners. These two may surround themselves with beautiful objects, and spend as much time as possible in unspoiled nature. It will be very important for the pair to be engaged in projects that will allow them fully to share the relationship's singular vision. Because of a quincunx aspect between Virgo-Libra and Aquarius-Pisces (which lie 150° apart in the zodiac), astrology predicts imbalance in the relationship, and the partners may have to work hard to keep themselves on an even keel emotionally.

Marriage and work relationships are particularly rewarding, since many opportunities emerge here to implement a world view or lifestyle that is to the liking of both partners. Travel may also be important, providing new sources of inspiration for the couple's principal endeavors. Care must be taken to manage the partnership's tendencies toward impulsive behavior and risk-taking. Especially in friendships, love affairs and marriages, the partners should work to ground themselves in daily responsibilities, which can keep their relationship afloat and on an even keel.

Problems arise in sibling relationships and friendships when conflicting wishes clash. The need of both partners for companionship may be well satisfied by their relationship, yet their individual desires—notably those of Virgo-Libras for material goods and of Aquarius-Pisces for more philosophical pursuits—may be at odds.

ADVICE: *Value traditions—they've survived for a reason. Pay attention to finances. Take on a greater share of responsibility.*

RELATIONSHIPS

STRENGTHS: **COMMITTED, HONORABLE, SEARCHING**

WEAKNESSES: **POLARIZED, CONFLICTING, INDOLENT**

BEST: **FRIENDSHIP**

WORST: **MARRIAGE**

BRIAN EPSTEIN (9/19/34)
GEORGE HARRISON (2/25/43)

Beatles manager Epstein shaped their image as a group and worked hard to get them their first record contract. Even when companies turned the group down, Epstein remained optimistic. Harrison, recalling his lack of confidence in Epstein's efforts, said, "But we still used to send up the idea of getting to the top."

September 19–24
THE CUSP OF BEAUTY
VIRGO-LIBRA CUSP

February 23–March 2
THE WEEK OF SPIRIT
PISCES I

Reconciling the Material and the Spiritual

In many ways, this combination seeks to reconcile and unite the superficial and spiritual elements of existence, an approach in which both comfort and contemplation figure prominently. The pair seeks the meaning behind all beauty—the essence that empowers it. Not satisfied with material existence alone, these two will always yearn for something else; in their relationship, financial success can be viewed as an aspect of spiritual reward. Conflicts are bound to arise between more materialistic Virgo-Libras and more spiritually oriented Pisces I's. Yet the relationship is not one to avoid challenge, and if both partners are willing to go beyond themselves, they may be united in a common search, and gain as a result.

Love affairs between Virgo-Libras and Pisces I's will often succeed or fail depending on the degree of commitment present. Surrender is an important theme here, whether to this couple's own love or to a higher source—perhaps a teacher, a philosophy or a religion. Should one partner be wholly committed to the relationship and the other only partly so, discussions, arguments and even battles may become the rule, hastening the relationship's demise. Marriages between these two should not be attempted until ideological differences have been settled.

Friendships here may be squarely based on a search for truth and knowledge. Profoundly idealistic, the Virgo-Libra–Pisces I matchup is likely to set high standards for honor and trust, which, once violated, are not easily reestablished. This relationship is generally easygoing, as long as the partners are in fundamental agreement on issues of morality and decency. Such friends can have wonderful times together, while also indulging their more serious sides. Quietude occupies a special place here. In the family and vocational spheres, Virgo-Libras and Pisces I's can be of great help to one another in getting the daily work done. Although the partners may not be of the most ambitious or hard-working sort, their relationship is generally able to discharge responsibilities in a relaxed fashion, which can lower the stress level of the organizations of which they are a part.

ADVICE: *Sort out your priorities and find common points of agreement. Beware of indolence. Try to be more forgiving and less judgmental.*

September 19–24

THE CUSP OF BEAUTY
VIRGO-LIBRA CUSP

March 3–10

THE WEEK OF THE LONER
PISCES II

A Rarefied Atmosphere

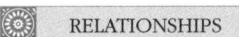

RELATIONSHIPS

STRENGTHS: ARTISTIC, SACRIFICING, APPRECIATIVE

WEAKNESSES: IMPRACTICAL, UNREALISTIC, ALIENATED

BEST: CREATIVE WORK

WORST: MARRIAGE

The expansiveness of this relationship is likely to carry it to the farthest reaches of the stratosphere. In this rarefied atmosphere, the Virgo-Libra–Pisces II pair is preoccupied with a kind of abstractness of thought that others will not easily understand. This pair will have to reconcile itself to the fact that only a select group of family, friends or co-workers may ever really understand them on anything more than a superficial level. Somewhat mysterious, though not really by design, Virgo-Libras and Pisces II's may simply decide to go their own way, grateful for each other, and let everyone else try to sort it all out.

Love affairs and friendships between these two are often based on an appreciation of dance, music or film, as art forms rather than sources of entertainment. This sensibility is carried over into their everyday life as well, where grace of movement, immaculate taste and highly selective attitudes toward people are emphasized. Carried to an extreme, such an approach may result in elitism or snobbism, pushing the relationship toward alienation or isolation.

Virgo-Libra–Pisces II marital and family relationships often benefit from the presence of a single appreciative relative, perhaps a child or parent. Such an individual may have a strong grounding influence on this duo, or at the very least supply them with a companion on their flights of fancy. The belief of just one such individual in the relationship can lend it the credibility that it requires to maintain its pride and self-respect.

Work relationships in this combination are rarely interested in making a quick killing but can be content with earning enough to break even. More interested in the quality of the product or service and less in filling the cash register, Virgo-Libras and Pisces II's are usually happiest when they can devote themselves to what they truly believe in. These two will sacrifice a great deal on the material level to be allowed to go on with their work, even under adverse circumstances.

ADVICE: *Don't be too extreme; maintain contact with others. Cultivating a bit of practicality won't hurt. Beware of sacrificing your own best interests.*

REX HARRISON (3/5/08)
RACHEL ROBERTS (9/20/27)

Debonair British star Harrison is best remembered for his role as Professor Henry Higgins in *My Fair Lady* (stage and film). He was married to actress Roberts (the 2nd of 6 wives) from 1962–71. She was an Oscar nominee for *The Sporting Life* (1963) and went on to tv in the 70s. **Also: John Coltrane & Jimmy Garrison** (jazz quartet musicians).

September 19–24

THE CUSP OF BEAUTY
VIRGO-LIBRA CUSP

March 11–18

THE WEEK OF DANCERS & DREAMERS
PISCES III

Colorful Dreamworld

RELATIONSHIPS

STRENGTHS: IMAGINATIVE, COLORFUL, ROMANTIC

WEAKNESSES: UNCERTAIN, AMBIGUOUS, UNSUITABLE

BEST: LOVE

WORST: WORK

A romantic and emotional matchup, Virgo-Libras and Pisces III's are likely to live in their own colorful dreamworld, mesmerized by each other's charms. Highly imaginative, this relationship may seek out experiences where uncertainty, ambiguity and magic all play important roles. The couple generally eschews rigid schedules and predetermined directions, preferring to allow things to happen rather than making them happen. In fact, the partners may firmly believe that making things happen is not really possible, and that most of life is really a matter of fate or chance.

As lovers or friends, Virgo-Libras and Pisces III's often meet in a way that substantiates this belief. In retrospect, the odds against their even encountering each other seem prodigious, giving their meeting a kind of miraculous air. Their conviction that the relationship was meant to be may give it tremendous momentum, sustaining it over many a difficult period. Marriages may wear thin over time, however, with only such miraculous claims to sustain them. In fact, the partners may discover that they are not really suited to each other at all, or simply grow apart as the years spin by.

Parent-child relationships in this combination may be complex emotionally. Pisces III parents tend to adore and spoil their Virgo-Libra children. Virgo-Libra parents, on the other hand, may be impatient with their Pisces III offspring and may make demands—for neatness, efficiency or common sense—that the children find difficult or impossible to meet. In both cases, having fewer preconceived ideas and accepting children as they are will be of the utmost importance if psychological problems are to be avoided here.

Virgo-Libra–Pisces III working relationships may not be at all well suited for full-time positions in companies or organizations. Should these two form their own business, they must be extremely careful not to be carried away by their fantasies and risk losing everything financially.

ADVICE: *Keep your eyes open. Make more of an effort to see things as they are, not as you want them to be.*

SHEILA MACRAE (9/24/24)
GORDON MACRAE (3/12/21)

Sheila and musical star Gordon were married from 1941–67. Best remembered for his screen roles in *Oklahoma!* (1955) and *Carousel* (1956), he later performed in nightclubs with Sheila. She went on to a tv career, for a while playing Alice Kramden on *The Jackie Gleason Show* (1966), then hosting her own talk show (1971). **Also: Ray Charles & Quincy Jones** (musicians had early band together).

RELATIONSHIPS

STRENGTHS: INSIGHTFUL, CONCISE, BRILLIANT

WEAKNESSES: NEGATIVE, HYPERCRITICAL, DEVASTATING

BEST: LOVE

WORST: BOSS-EMPLOYEE

JULIE ANDREWS (10/1/35)
STANLEY HOLLOWAY (10/1/1890)

Andrews and Holloway not only shared the stage in the Broadway production of *My Fair Lady* (1956) but also share the same birthday. She played Eliza Doolittle, daughter of Alfred Doolittle, portrayed by Holloway. Like everything else in the successful musical, these actors were stage magic together. *Also:* **Vittorio Mussolini & Romano Mussolini** (brothers; sons of Italian dictator; jazz critic/jazz pianist).

A Mocking Edge

The principal energy of this relationship is likely to go into wordplay. Like fencers, these two are masters of the riposte. It would be difficult for a third party to tell when either of them is voicing sincere sentiments, since there is often a mocking edge to their words or in the tone with which they are delivered that could indicate irony, sarcasm or a double meaning. Nor are Libra I's above using either body language—hand movements, a frozen facial expression, even a simple shrug—or silence to get their message across. Skilled in ambiguity and subtlety, each Libra I will usually get the point the other is making, even if it goes over the head of other listeners.

Love affairs and marriages between these two can be highly romantic yet at the same time not entirely serious. Thus there is a kind of healthy self-consciousness at work here that alerts the relationship to its own pretense. Both partners are realistic enough not to kid each other, but occasionally they get carried away with their own histrionics. One partner, seeing the other shed crocodile tears, may have trouble controlling his or her laughter. In fact, laughing at each other gently or scornfully, if carried to excess, can be one of the worst habits of this relationship.

Libra I–Libra I friends demand a quality to their experiences, whether entertainment, sport or adventure. They will rarely pretend to have had a good time when they have not, and when united in their criticism of a person or an event they can be quite devastating. Such friends must be careful not to succumb to the lure of negativity, that is, steadfastly ignoring the better parts of whatever is under discussion in order to cut it skillfully to the bone.

Work and family relationships can be extremely difficult because of continual strife within boss-employee and parent-child pairs of Libra I's. Since both partners are likely to insist on having the last word, verbal sparring may go on endlessly.

ADVICE: *Do you know when you are serious? Keep your negativity under control—look for the best in things. Enjoy without critical examination or comment.*

RELATIONSHIPS

STRENGTHS: AMBITIOUS, DETERMINED, CLOSE

WEAKNESSES: BITTER, COMPETITIVE, DEPENDENT

BEST: WORK

WORST: LOVE

TOMMY LEE (10/3/62)
HEATHER LOCKLEAR (9/25/61)

Actress Locklear has starred in tv's *Dynasty, T.J. Hooker* and *Melrose Place* (whose audience jumped 50 percent when she joined the show). She was married to Mötley Crüe drummer Lee from 1986–94. He has since married tv actress Pamela Anderson. *Also:* **Sebastian Coe & Steve Ovett** (rival milers).

Worthy Opponents

Competitive urges often arise between these two and can become the focus of this relationship. They are of two types—the first, in which they vie for the spotlight within their family, social or professional group, and the second, in which they compete to surpass a stated objective or to outstrip each other. In either case, this adversarial relationship does not necessarily have to involve animosity and can be quite a friendly one. Libra I's have the drive and critical intensity, Libra II's the charm and deep insight, to be worthy opponents.

An interesting mix of ease and demand is operative in love affairs. At times Libra I's and Libra II's are content to loll and laze, but at others they can imbue the relationship with the fury of a hurricane. Such unpredictable swings of mood will have to be evened out if a modicum of psychological stability is to be achieved. In both love and marriage, competition for the attention of mutual friends may temporarily drive these two apart.

It is in the professional sphere that the most productive sorts of competition arise between Libra I's and II's. Here one gets the idea that they actually need each other to achieve the best of which they are capable, especially when they are bitter rivals. If they serve on the same team within a company, this competitive edge is no less present, but here it can be put to good use by a clever boss or superior to benefit the organization as a whole. Libra I's and II's often treat each other with such cordiality that a visitor might remark on how well they get along.

Friendships and sibling matchups often evidence not only a desire to win in sports, games and play but also a struggle for the attention of other friends and family members. Nevertheless, this relationship can be an extremely close one. In fact, a kind of affection, and in certain cases even love, is predicated on the very conflict that at times seems to indicate hostile conflict.

ADVICE: *Beware of unproductive competition. You may not be as far apart as you seem. Strive for greater understanding. Sometimes winning is losing.*

September 25–October 2

THE WEEK OF THE PERFECTIONIST
LIBRA I

October 11–18

THE WEEK OF THEATER
LIBRA III

A Social Whirl

The thrust of this relationship is usually social in nature. As a pair, these two are interested in putting their best foot forward, whether in a family setting or among a circle of friends. Being badly thought of will be terribly wounding to such a relationship, and thus partners are usually careful to observe the proper codes of behavior. The problem is, it is not always so easy for such individuals as these to behave in a conventional manner. Libra I's are too iconoclastic and Libra III's too flamboyant to be able to conform fully, and this may put enormous strains on the relationship.

In love affairs and marriages, Libra I's and Libra III's would be content to relax with each other and maintain a rather private lifestyle, but their relationship dictates otherwise. Somehow another meeting, appointment or responsibility looms just around the corner and too often requires the attention, if not the presence, of both partners. In desperation, these two may seek to absent themselves from social responsibilities by taking frequent vacations, yet on their return they seem to have ten times more to attend to than before.

The Libra I–Libra III pair may be far more successful in meeting the social demands of friendship. Here the problem could be the opposite one, namely, that the partners enjoy social interaction so much that their relationship is weakened by their inability—or, eventually, by their lack of desire—to spend much time alone together. Likewise, parents and children in this combination may busy themselves with a spate of school, extracurricular, family and other activities that may give them little time to build a strong personal bond. This deficiency may become apparent in later life when crises of a life-or-death nature arise.

Business partnerships and other commercial dealings will benefit from the extensive contacts the relationship engenders and also from a canny approach to money matters. But Libra III fiscal conservatism can clash with the wilder, more speculative approach of Libra I's.

ADVICE: *Fight for time alone together. Don't be so concerned with your social image—other people will have to understand. Cancel appointments if you must.*

CHRISTOPHER REEVE (9/25/52)
MARGOT KIDDER (10/17/48)

In all 4 Superman movies ('78, '80, '83, '87), there was no greater screen chemistry than that between Reeve and Kidder. Their Clark Kent/ Superman and Lois Lane characters were brought to life with charm, humor, irony and romance as portrayed by these fine actors. **Also: Tom Bosley & Angela Lansbury** (co-stars, *Murder, She Wrote*).

September 25–October 2

THE WEEK OF THE PERFECTIONIST
LIBRA I

October 19–25

THE CUSP OF DRAMA & CRITICISM
LIBRA-SCORPIO CUSP

Romantic Fulfillment

This can be one of those ultraromantic relationships that many people yearn for, a relationship of passion, excitement and daring. This pair will share their innermost desires and dreams with each other; they are secure enough to reveal their most sensitive sides without fear of reprisal. Their relationship has few problems of a mundane and practical sort.

In love, this pair will let itself be swept away on a romantic wave. Libra I's and Libra-Scorpios have so much under control in other areas that they have tremendous self-confidence as a couple. Thus they have no fear of losing all in a headlong rush of passion. The relationship generally proclaims what it is openly, and if it is somewhat unconventional, it is prepared to take the flak that society may aim in its direction. Some love affairs may be of the more outrageous sort, not because the partners are intent on flaunting their connection but simply because they do not believe in tempering their affection for each other, privately or publicly. Libra I's and Libra-Scorpios are tremendously critical people, however, and this tendency is synergized by their relationship, making it an extremely demanding and at times stressful one. Miraculously, in love (but less often in marriage) these two usually succeed in meeting each other's high standards, whether physical, financial or social. There may not, however, be a correspondingly deep emotional bond here, which can indicate a lack of self-awareness and an unwillingness to confront feelings directly.

Friends and family members in this combination will also share deeply, perhaps exchanging tales of romance and faraway lands. Those who seek to work together, possibly forming a small business, will do particularly well as consultants, troubleshooters or technical problem solvers. Libra I's and Libra-Scorpios can make a powerful team, helping both individuals and organizations get back on track. Should co-worker pairs first meet on the job, they may continue their relationship after hours, first as companions, later as fast friends.

ADVICE: *Don't be afraid to examine your feelings critically. Dig a bit deeper emotionally. Give the opinions of others serious consideration.*

MARK HAMILL (9/25/51)
CARRIE FISHER (10/21/56)

Hamill and Fisher were unknowns until they appeared in the *Star Wars* trilogy ('77, '80, '83) as Luke Skywalker and Princess Leia. Hamill's identification with Luke blocked his subsequent efforts to find new movie roles. Fisher's early success led to emotional and drug problems. **Also: Marcello Mastroianni & Catherine Deneuve** (longtime lovers; actors); **Jimmy Carter & Amy Carter** (father/daughter).

STRENGTHS: DRAMATIC, FLAMBOYANT, EXCITING

WEAKNESSES: FRENZIED, ADDICTIVE, UNSTABLE

BEST: PARENT-CHILD

WORST: WORK

T.S. ELIOT (9/26/1888)
EZRA POUND (10/30/1885)

Poets Eliot and Pound had a long-standing association that began in 1914, when they first met at Pound's flat in London. Eliot's commitment to write poetry was encouraged by Pound, who helped get Eliot's *Love Song of J. Alfred Prufrock* published (1915). **Also: Bryant Gumbel & Jane Pauley** (tv co-hosts, *Today Show*); **Samuel Adams & John Adams** (2nd cousins; revolutionary patriot/US president).

September 25–October 2

THE WEEK OF THE PERFECTIONIST
LIBRA I

October 26–November 2

THE WEEK OF INTENSITY
SCORPIO I

Kicking Off from Excitement

The exciting chemistry between these two often encourages dramatic events to swirl around them. Even if their life together is fairly conventional, this pair may have difficulty achieving stability, and indeed may have little interest in doing so. Involvements in film, theater and other entertainment fields may become an effective means of compartmentalizing and objectifying this need for excitement. Dissatisfaction or boredom will continue to be the principal problem here, generating a need for ever-more-interesting experiences. Unfortunately, the pursuit of excitement can be addictive, causing these two to pack more and more events into their available time, leading ultimately to nervous exhaustion and even breakdown.

In love affairs it may be important to learn that the paramount goal is not excitement but rather the kind of satisfaction that comes from acceptance of both the self and the other. Likewise, in marriages and friendships that indulge in a frenzied search for gratification there is probably something dreadfully wrong at home. People should find each other interesting enough to want to be alone together rather than run out all the time. Moreover, constantly comparing their relationship with those of others is destructive.

In familial relationships, as in the ones already discussed, a reexamination of values—perhaps even a total rethinking and restructuring of daily life—is probably in order to ensure greater stability. Kicking the addiction to stimulation can be accomplished in a parent-child relationship, but it requires self-awareness, which initially will have to come from the parent and only later from the child. Libra I–Scorpio I professional matchups will find ordinary work unsatisfying, but if the relationship emerges in more flamboyant sorts of careers, these two may grapple with a high level of criticism of each other.

ADVICE: *Calm down a bit. Be objective about what you are doing. Find more fulfilling activities. Furnish your own entertainment and creativity.*

STRENGTHS: REALISTIC, SELF-CONFIDENT, SEXUAL

WEAKNESSES: PROVOCATIVE, ARGUMENTATIVE, BURNT-OUT

BEST: WORK

WORST: LOVE

JACQUES CHARRIER (11/6/36)
BRIGITTE BARDOT (9/28/34)

French actor Charrier made headlines when he married sex kitten Bardot while co-starring with her in *Babette Goes to War* (1959). Their bumpy marriage was marked by his nervous breakdowns and suicide attempts, leading to divorce in '60. **Also: Gene Autry & Roy Rogers** (50s singing cowboys); **Brigitte Bardot & Alain Delon** (lovers); **Groucho Marx & George Fenneman** (co-stars, *You Bet Your Life*).

September 25–October 2

THE WEEK OF THE PERFECTIONIST
LIBRA I

November 3–11

THE WEEK OF DEPTH
SCORPIO II

The Hard Facts of Existence

This is an intense combination that won't flinch when confronted with the truth. The Libra I–Scorpio II pair has a much greater respect for the cold hard facts of life than for all the theories in the world about what things are supposed to be like. Power struggles within the relationship are generally kept to a minimum out of mutual respect but also from both personalities' desire to advance their own cause. Thus the relationship usually has the approval and solid backing of its partners, who are confident in their ability to withstand almost any onslaught through a united defense.

Business partnerships and colleague matchups are particularly favored here. Realistic and tough, this pair is not without its personal charm as well. The relationship has a strong sense of how power works in the corporate and business worlds and does not hesitate to wield it authoritatively. Likewise, in the family sphere, Libra I and Scorpio II relatives are well able to defend family interests and to make wayward relatives fall into line. Such combinations must be careful not to arouse the ire or resentment of other strong-minded family members.

Love affairs and marriages are a bit tricky. Power struggles are likely to emerge here, particularly in the sexual arena. Scorpio II's need to dominate physically, Libra I's mentally, and the intensity of these encounters can reach seismic levels. Unfortunately, arguments and emotional conflicts of equal intensity often precede or follow such interactions. Some balance or compromise will have to be reached if this relationship is to avoid burnout. Moreover, the heavy emphasis here on cold reality and the nature of power leaves a lot to be desired in the way of warmth, sensitivity and kindness. Ultimately, even these two tough customers may find that passion isn't enough. Friendships here are at their best when the partners are able to spend their time together relaxing, perhaps indulging in easy conversation, sharing a meal or just hanging out.

ADVICE: *Reach important agreements. Moderation and compromise are essential. Don't get carried away with power. Sex can be a dangerous weapon.*

September 25–October 2

THE WEEK OF THE PERFECTIONIST
LIBRA I

November 12–18

THE WEEK OF CHARM
SCORPIO III

Closed Ranks

A split in character type is likely to be emphasized in this relationship. Libra I's adhere to the more tried-and-true way of doing things and believe in maintaining the highest possible standards and codes of conduct. Scorpio III's, on the other hand, seek to be modern and up-to-date and are more than willing to cut corners. Should the pair be attacked or opposed, however, it will usually stand firm against a common threat, making this a relationship that generally shows less unanimity when unpressured. Libra I perfectionist tendencies generally make a strong impression on Scorpio III's, who will try to emulate them with more or less success. In return, Scorpio III charisma can often be used to convince exacting Libra I's of the need for compromise—to their benefit. Luckily, the partners' positive attributes and their ability to mitigate their negative tendencies helps this pair to arrive at a happy balance.

Love affairs and marriages can be highly passionate but also warm and affectionate. Dramatic displays of emotion are unavoidable, since the relationship brings out the more temperamental aspects of both partners. Libra I's are highly demanding of their mates in the physical sphere, but Scorpio III's are usually more than a match for their intensity and stamina, and in fact may even surpass them on occasion. The sexual relationship does not usually display bipolar or frustrating tendencies but is able to create an energy flow that is for the most part constant and sustaining. Parent-child combinations are most favorable with Scorpio III in the parental role, guiding and nurturing their precocious Libra I offspring. Likewise, in working relationships Scorpio III's make the better bosses and Libra I's the better employees, as long as duties are well defined from the outset. In friendships this pair is able to merge contrasting energies and points of view into a cohesive unit. Such combinations often feel almost euphoric, and at such moments the partners may believe they can take on the world. In their social, business and family circles they can be inspirational, but they also suffer from extremely low periods when their energy or self-confidence wanes. Too much time spent together without purpose or direction can lead to internal squabbles, indecision and torpor.

ADVICE: *Reconcile opposing points of view. Learn to motivate from within. Fight lethargy and indecision. Maintain self-confidence.*

JAWAHARLAL NEHRU (11/14/1889)
MAHATMA GANDHI (10/2/1869)

Indian political and spiritual leader Gandhi met politician Nehru in 1916. Gandhi, a leading figure in the struggle for India's independence, was Nehru's mentor over the years. Nehru, India's first prime minister, was the more westernized, and his international views often clashed with Gandhi's narrower Indian focus. **Also: Michael Douglas & Brenda Vaccaro** (live-in lovers; actors).

September 25–October 2

THE WEEK OF THE PERFECTIONIST
LIBRA I

November 19–24

THE CUSP OF REVOLUTION
SCORPIO-SAGITTARIUS CUSP

Manifesting the Lighter Side

This combination makes a definite impression on its surroundings and tends to leave something memorable behind after its passing. The matchup is characterized by grit, determination and staying power. Despite its rather heavy and palpable effects on its environment, this combination is particularly marked by its lighter side. Libra I's tend to bring out more of the Scorpio-Sagittarian wit and sense of ease, particularly noticeable when these two start kidding around. Scorpio-Sagittarian irreverence toward authority stimulates and supports the strongly individualistic stance of Libra I's. The focus of this relationship is likely to involve breaking with established traditions and attempting to set up an independent structure within a family, social or professional setting.

In their love and marital relationships, these two can share many carnal delights. While Scorpio-Sagittarians tend to be more sensuous, however, enjoying food and comfort as much as sex, Libra I's are often more-passionate types, reserving and funneling most of their sensual energy directly into sex. Furthermore, Libra I ideas and ideals may keep them from participating physically at certain times, making Scorpio-Sagittarians frustrated and unhappy. Marriages can be both practical and fun but ultimately won't adhere to tradition.

In friendships and work relationships these two are likely to brighten up their environs through their humorous exchanges. Given the chance, however, they would rather structure and manage their own organization. The problem here is that this pair is actually better able to work for others and in fact may lack the administrative and practical financial skills to succeed on its own. In the family sphere, both sibling and parent-child combinations can successfully impose structure on daily activities, and galvanize other relatives toward involvement in team efforts.

ADVICE: *Don't take on more than you can handle—be realistic about your capabilities. Be careful not to arouse the wrath of authority figures.*

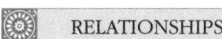

HARPO MARX (11/23/1893)
GROUCHO MARX (10/2/1890)

Groucho and Harpo were 2 of the 4 Marx Brothers (along with Chico and Zeppo). They made more than a dozen movies together and established themselves as a major force in American comedy. Quick-witted Groucho was master of the ad lib, while Harpo, playing mute, was a brilliant pantomimist. **Also: Christopher Buckley & William Buckley** (son/father; writers).

STRENGTHS: **PERSUASIVE, PROTECTIVE, SUPPORTIVE**

WEAKNESSES: **UNAWARE, PROCRASTINATING, DENYING**

BEST: **WORK**

WORST: **MARRIAGE**

LECH WALESA (9/29/43)
ZBIGNIEW BUJAK (11/29/54)

In 1981 Walesa and Bujak crusaded side by side for Solidarity in Poland, working against the repressive communist government. Bujak, in hiding, called on soldiers and police to resist martial law. Walesa was arrested, then released in '82 by a nervous Polish military fearing a major uprising. He received the Nobel Peace Prize in '83. **Also: Gwyneth Paltrow & Bruce Paltrow** (daughter/father; actress/tv producer).

September 25–October 2

THE WEEK OF THE PERFECTIONIST
LIBRA I

November 25–December 2

THE WEEK OF INDEPENDENCE
SAGITTARIUS I

Twisting Arms

This dynamic matchup will not back down from a fight. It is explosive in its mixture of elements: Libra is an air sign, Sagittarius is fire, and the relationship is also ruled by water, here signifying deep emotion. Powerfully persuasive, this relationship knows when and how to twist arms to get its way. The partners most often feel best when protecting or representing the best interests of others, even more so than when pushing their own relationship. Libra I critical instincts and considerable ambition may bother Sagittarius I's, whose ideas and morality will in turn grate occasionally on Libra I nerves, but these two make it their business to get along, often for the sake of fellow employees, children or other family members.

This pair's love affairs will be exciting, but they are also likely to be highly unstable. A deluge of feeling threatens to overwhelm this couple, which seems ill-prepared to cope. Emotional awareness is not at its highest in this relationship, and unconscious elements will often prevail over conscious ones. Marriage is not highly recommended here unless the partners make a concerted effort to get to know themselves and each other better at a deep level.

As friends, Libra I's and Sagittarius I's need specific activities to be involved in, often of a technical nature. Such matchups can suffer from emotional difficulties, but problems are often simply ignored or put off until a later date. So close is this relationship that real sharing is possible in most areas but is rarely or never discussed. An unspoken code is often silently agreed upon; breaking it can cripple or even destroy the relationship.

In family and work relationships, the Libra I–Sagittarius I duo can be both a strong force for change and a solid support in times of need and crisis. Social and political awareness are usually strong here, lending a highly realistic outlook to any group of which the relationship forms a part. Libra I charisma and Sagittarius I energy gel effectively enough for this matchup to assume a leadership role in such areas.

ADVICE: *You need to discuss things more openly—beware of silent condemnation. Fight the good fight. Guard against selfishness, and don't neglect personal matters.*

STRENGTHS: **ARTISTIC, FINANCIAL, INSTRUCTIVE**

WEAKNESSES: **OPPOSING, SELFISH, STUBBORN**

BEST: **FAMILY**

WORST: **LOVE**

GEORGE GERSHWIN (9/26/1898)
IRA GERSHWIN (12/06/1896)

Composer George and lyricist Ira first collaborated on *Lady Be Good!* (1924), after which Ira wrote most of the lyrics for his brother's music until George's death in '37. Together they wrote more than a dozen Broadway musicals and many hit songs for films. **Also: Michael Douglas & Kirk Douglas** (son/ father; actors).

September 25–October 2

THE WEEK OF THE PERFECTIONIST
LIBRA I

December 3–10

THE WEEK OF THE ORIGINATOR
SAGITTARIUS II

Whetstone Sharp

The Libra I–Sagittarius II combination is one-of-a-kind. Although there is an undeniable tendency for one partner to assume the role of mentor in this relationship, the focus here is to acquire experience and knowledge within a certain area that can then be put to specific social, financial or artistic use. It is not uncommon to find teacher-student interactions here, but the roles are regularly reversed. Moreover, although autonomy is important to both Libra I's and Sagittarius II's, there is no denying the benefits of their working together in equal partnership. For either partner to act in a selfish or self-aggrandizing fashion runs counter to their own self-interest, since the real benefits of this relationship accrue from the interactions between these two. Love affairs and marriages between Libra I's and Sagittarius II's can be quite stressful. The perfectionist tendencies of Libra I's may lead them to evaluate their lover or mate in this combination as a trifle sloppy or negligent, while Sagittarius II's may consider Libra I's overly tense. When the level of physical satisfaction is high enough here, such annoyances are quickly forgotten; but the partners should take the time to discuss problems and possible solutions rather than bounce back and forth between periods of stress and more pleasurable times. Friendships and rivalries are extremely challenging and often fulfilling. A competitive edge is rarely lacking here, and the relationship often acts as a whetstone to keep its partners sharp.

The stubbornness, even defiance, of the Libra I–Sagittarius II pair may prevent family members from getting together for some time. Competition unavoidably surfaces here, particularly between relatives of the same sex, but experientially both partners gain from such encounters, no matter how unpleasant they may seem at the time. The mental quickness of Libra I's and the high degree of creativity that characterizes Sagittarius II's gel at times and at others collide, but obstinacy leads both partners to continue on rather than abandon the relationship. Both parent-child and sibling matchups often have marketable qualities, which they can explore either in terms of a family business or as freelancers providing a service or craft.

ADVICE: *Keep antagonisms under control. Act in the best interests of all. Two heads are often better than one. Discover hidden possibilities.*

September 25–October 2

THE WEEK OF THE PERFECTIONIST
LIBRA I

December 11–18

THE WEEK OF THE TITAN
SAGITTARIUS III

RELATIONSHIPS

STRENGTHS: **SEXUAL, SERIOUS, EMOTIONAL**

WEAKNESSES: **FRUSTRATING, UNFULFILLED, INCOMPATIBLE**

BEST: **FRIENDSHIP**

WORST: **FAMILY**

Secret Love

This is a profound matchup overall, one that brings out deep feelings in its partners—not always comfortably. These two are not known for their emotionalism; in fact, both of them have a knack for detachment and objectivity. Yet emotions here are intense and sometimes inexplicable, often manifesting in an explosive and frightening manner. The relationship often carries with it a secret known only to its partners, one perhaps rarely discussed. That secret may contribute to the depth of the relationship.

Even so, Libra I–Sagittarius III couples will not necessarily achieve a blissful consummation. Frustration is as likely to predominate here as satisfaction, since the operative emotions are often confused. Thus in love affairs one partner's feelings, desires and hopes may feed off those of the other, yet without permitting any lasting happiness or fulfillment. Although tremendous sexual satisfaction may be achieved for a period of time by one or both partners, it is rarely sustainable. In marriage, Sagittarius III's may have highly unrealistic expectations that cannot ultimately be met, while Libra I's can be baffled by their inability fully to satisfy their partner. Instead of looking for such ultimate experience or for consistently high levels of pleasure, the Libra I–Sagittarius III couple would do well to be content with their emotional bond, which is often considerable.

Family pairs in this combination are prone to emotional upsets and rejection scenarios that may play out over years. Unresolved feelings are usually at the root of such difficulties—feelings that must be brought out into the open and discussed, perhaps under professional guidance. Libra I–Sagittarius III friendships can be serious and committed, yet may not have a capacity for the enjoyment of great times. Complex emotions are usually less of a problem here, except when personal or career drives arouse jealousy or the need to compete. As co-workers, Libra I's and Sagittarius III's may experience conflicts arising from the former's drive for technical perfection and the latter's grand plans for success or overly optimistic view.

ADVICE: *Lower your expectations. Take things as they come. Happiness may be closer than you think. Examine what lies behind your dissatisfaction.*

BRAD PITT (12/18/63)
GWYNETH PALTROW (9/28/73)

Paltrow, the daughter of actress Blythe Danner and producer Bruce Paltrow, co-starred in *Seven* (1995) with her then love, 90s sex symbol Pitt. Pitt's first important role was as the devious hitchhiker in *Thelma & Louise* (1991). ***Also:*** **Juliet Prowse & Frank Sinatra** (affair; dancer/actor-singer); **Olivia Newton-John & Max Born** (granddaughter/grandfather; singer/Nobel physicist).

September 25–October 2

THE WEEK OF THE PERFECTIONIST
LIBRA I

December 19–25

THE CUSP OF PROPHECY
SAGITTARIUS-CAPRICORN CUSP

RELATIONSHIPS

STRENGTHS: **LOYAL, NATURAL, SYMPATHETIC**

WEAKNESSES: **REPRESSIVE, NEGLECTFUL, ANGRY**

BEST: **FAMILY**

WORST: **WORK**

A Study in Contrasts

These two are very well suited to each other in certain respects and not well at all in others, which creates a study in contrasts. Sagittarius-Capricorns enjoy the lighthearted, conversational side of Libra I's at the outset of their relationship, but continual exposure reveals a certain shallowness that the more profound Sagittarius-Capricorn disdains. Similarly, Sagittarius-Capricorn quietude and silence may be unnerving for Libra I's, who depend on the responsiveness and, ultimately, the appreciation of their partners. Both of these personalities value simplicity and a lack of artificiality; they may share a love of organic foods, soft fabrics, muted colors and, in general, a natural lifestyle. Living in pleasant surroundings with at least a touch of greenery is also conducive to a feeling of well-being here.

Love affairs are curious in that the partners can feel very close to each other and be extremely affectionate in their sexual interactions, yet cold and distant in daily life. Repressed anger on the part of Sagittarius-Capricorns and a hypercritical, bossy Libra I approach are the determining factors here. A breakdown in communication is signaled by a deadly quiet that casts its pall over everything. In marital situations, Libra I's and Sagittarius-Capricorns tend to suffer from Libra I involvement in outside hobbies or social affairs that leave Sagittarius-Capricorns sitting at home feeling neglected or abandoned.

In many ways Libra I's and Sagittarius-Capricorns are better suited for friendship and family relationships than for love. Partners here are able to exhibit loyalty and compassion toward each other. Such relationships often serve as a haven for two individuals who feel ignored by the world, and can afford both partners much-needed sympathy and understanding. Working relationships here seldom function well on either the executive/entrepreneurial or the co-worker level; Libra I's will be impatient with Sagittarius-Capricorns' slower pace and need to do things their own way.

ADVICE: *Talk openly about what's on your mind. Allow for disagreement without anger. Show more patience. Accept differences. Don't condemn.*

MOON UNIT ZAPPA (9/28/68)
FRANK ZAPPA (12/21/40)

Outrageous jazz-rock musician Frank first used his daughter Moon Unit in a recording that satirized success, *Valley Girl* (1982). The song parodied spoiled daughters of the California entertainment world and featured 14-year-old Moon Unit making an inspired mimicry of valley-girl talk. ***Also:*** **Shostakovich & Stalin** (composer under communist tyrant's rule).

JAYNE MEADOWS (9/27/26)
STEVE ALLEN (12/26/21)

Meadows and Allen are among the most durable couples in show business—married in 1954 and never divorced. *The Steve Allen Show* started in '50 and went on for 26 years in various incarnations. TV actress-personality Meadows was a frequent guest on his shows. **Also: François Boucher & Mme. de Pompadour** (artist sponsored by king's mistress); **Mahatma Gandhi & Ben Kingsley** (film portrayal).

September 25–October 2

THE WEEK OF THE PERFECTIONIST
LIBRA I

December 26–January 2

THE WEEK OF THE RULER
CAPRICORN I

Agreeably Uncompromising

These two could have a thoroughly agreeable and charming relationship. Conventional astrology predicts a difficult time here, since Libra I and Capricorn I form a square aspect in the zodiac (lying 90° apart), but this can also indicate an honest, realistic and often uncompromising attitude. Thus neither partner lets much go by without making comment, but this can often be done in a light, easy and, above all, considerate manner that is unlikely to arouse anger. There exists within this relationship the kind of diplomacy that can guarantee the possibility of harmony on a daily basis. Nonetheless, an edge is almost always present, and partners must never forget that a full-blown argument could easily erupt should courtesy and respect be neglected even for a second.

Love affairs and marriages are particularly favored between Libra I's and Capricorn I's, who can be stern, demanding and unforgiving in their relationships with others but exhibit a certain softness when together. This is because both partners respect and trust each other enough to let down their guard, allowing each to see the other's more vulnerable, human side. Friendships in this combination can founder when brutally honest attitudes offend one of the partners, usually the thinner-skinned Libra I. Similarly, parent-child relationships can suffer from real or perceived insults. In both sectors, Libra I and Capricorn I friends and parent-child pairs must learn to be more diplomatic as well as more forgiving.

Libra I–Capricorn I work relationships can be excellent, with the practical and financial skills of Capricorn I's complementing the Libra I drive to get things right. But unless an effort is made to keep personal and business matters strictly separate, emotional conflict is inevitable. Although Capricorn I's usually need to be the boss in other relationships, they have no problem taking orders from Libra I's if these are given in a respectful manner.

ADVICE: *Be as diplomatic as possible—keep your temper under control. Retain respect and openness. Don't be afraid to show your vulnerability.*

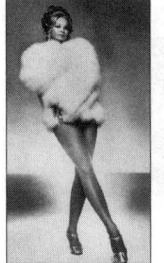

JULIET PROWSE (9/25/36)
ELVIS PRESLEY (1/8/35)

Prowse is the South African-born long-limbed actress of stage, tv and films. She made several movies in the 60s and starred in her own tv series, *Mona McClusky* (1965–66). She had a reputed affair with Elvis. **Also: Christopher Reeve & George Reeves** (film Superman/tv Superman); **Carter & Mondale** (president/vice-president).

September 25–October 2

THE WEEK OF THE PERFECTIONIST
LIBRA I

January 3–9

THE WEEK OF DETERMINATION
CAPRICORN II

Thriving on Success

This couple likes to take things as they come, with few expectations or pieces of textbook advice determining their actions. Tremendously energetic, the Libra I–Capricorn II pair can marshal its forces and direct them in a highly effective manner. Achieving specific objectives is often the strong point of this relationship but can become a sticking point when such achievement is difficult or perhaps impossible; an evident setback will usually serve to lower the confidence and self-esteem of its partners. This is a combination that thrives on success but is not particularly well prepared to handle failure.

Love affairs between these two can be highly sensual and exciting. Libra I's are attracted by the earthiness of Capricorn II's and the stability they afford, while Capricorn II's are turned on by the intellectual brilliance of Libra I's. Although of extremely different temperaments, their energies can dovetail beautifully, coalescing into mutual appreciation and cooperation. Unfortunately, some of their romantic spark is often lost when they marry; as they settle down into a more humdrum existence, they may find themselves at loggerheads.

Friendships wear better over the years, and here Libra I–Capricorn II differences are likely to keep the relationship vital. Stimulating disagreements and discussions, mild competition in sports-related activities, and playful rivalries for the affections of others are all characteristically part of the game. Sibling relationships, on the other hand, are more likely to erupt into open conflict, and the pair will have to learn to compromise and share if they are to get along at all. Libra I's and Capricorn II's can have an efficient and productive relationship as co-workers in a large firm or as executives guiding the destiny of such an organization. If extraordinary success is to be achieved, however, the pair will have to become tougher, more flexible and resilient.

ADVICE: *Don't be so easily discouraged—stiffen your resolve. Stay confident. Don't remain tied to past mistakes.*

September 25–October 2

THE WEEK OF THE PERFECTIONIST
LIBRA I

January 10–16

THE WEEK OF DOMINANCE
CAPRICORN III

RELATIONSHIPS

STRENGTHS: **SOPHISTICATED, ELEGANT, PERSISTENT**

WEAKNESSES: **INCONSISTENT, IRREVERENT, UNAWARE**

BEST: **LOVE**

WORST: **PARENT-CHILD**

Resolution Without Fuss

This is a relationship that thrives on difficulty yet does not expend a lot of energy solving problems. Its style, rather, is to go with the flow and attempt to resolve issues quietly, with little fuss. Actually, the Libra I–Capricorn III pair finds public displays a bit distasteful and much prefers to go its own way without attracting a lot of attention. Capricorn III's can provide stability for Libra I's while at the same time often becoming enchanted with Libra I charm. These two individuals can form a relationship that is quite sophisticated and refined, yet also one strong enough to maintain its integrity in the face of internal conflict or outside pressure.

Love affairs between Libra I's and Capricorn III's are likely to be highly private in nature. Few outsiders are allowed to see the relationship's inner workings, and, truth to tell, its mysteries may be beyond the ken of the partners themselves. The contrast between heavier Capricorn III and lighter Libra I energies is marked—family and friends often find the success of this relationship puzzling. The secret, of course, is that without too much fuss, each partner receives what he or she needs from the other. What Libra I's need is a broadening of themselves; what Capricorn III's need is deeper emotional understanding. Such love affairs may progress to marriage, maturing and becoming wiser through the years.

Friendships between Capricorn III's and Libra I's that form in childhood, perhaps at school, show a tendency toward rebellion against unjust treatment from teachers and other authority figures. They also often fall under the influence of a powerful older figure, one who may dominate the partner's early intellectual and spiritual lives. As parents, Capricorn III's can be alternately lenient and severe with their Libra I children, which can create confusion. Libra I parents often demand far too much of their Capricorn III offspring. In the workplace, too, Libra I bosses may drive their Capricorn III employees excessively, and come to put too much responsibility on their broad shoulders.

ADVICE: *Be a bit more realistic in your expectations. Sometimes it's necessary to take a stand. Learn from those more experienced than you.*

FAYE DUNAWAY (1/14/41)
MARCELLO MASTROIANNI (9/28/24)

Glamorous, gifted actress Dunaway and Italian movie idol Mastroianni fell in love during the filming of the poorly received romantic movie *A Place for Lovers* (1969). They had a well-publicized 2-year romance that broke up in '71. *Also:* **Julia Louis-Dreyfus & Jason Alexander** (co-stars, *Seinfeld*).

September 25–October 2

THE WEEK OF THE PERFECTIONIST
LIBRA I

January 17–22

THE CUSP OF MYSTERY & IMAGINATION
CAPRICORN-AQUARIUS CUSP

RELATIONSHIPS

STRENGTHS: **FREE, HAPPY, CONTENT**

WEAKNESSES: **UNREALISTIC, RESTIVE, POSSESSIVE**

BEST: **WORK**

WORST: **SIBLING**

Freedom to Act

This combination allows both partners to be themselves. If the relationship's focus is to ensure the freedom of its partners, how is it possible for it to hang together at all? Why is it even necessary? Herein lies the mystery of the relationship. Paradoxically, these two are fully committed to each other when together and are at no risk of losing their individuality. At the same time, their absolute trust that neither partner will compromise the relationship frees them to act as they choose when they are apart. Libra I's tend to be as demanding as Capricorn-Aquarians but are not always as energetic or imaginative. Capricorn-Aquarians are likely to prove the more unpredictable of the pair, Libra I's the more moderate and reasonable.

Love affairs and marriages between these two rise and fall on the partners' ability to leave each other free to interact with others. Such matchups outside the primary relationship need not be threatening or sexual. As accepting of each other's activities as these two seem, however, they are only human; jealousy, anger and the need to possess may lie just a scratch beneath the surface. Either such open attitudes work or they don't, but certainly the most important indication of the relationship's success is the high degree of happiness within it, which should be carefully monitored by both partners.

Work relationships may be a trifle tricky, since here each partner tends to want exclusive rights to the other, and both may grow restive when a third party tries to entice one of them away. In fact, their professional reputations can be so strongly linked within an organization or as freelancers that one of them is seldom thought of without the other. Thus their marketplace value as individuals is often less than that of their partnership. Friendships and sibling relationships are most effective when requirements and claims are few and far between.

ADVICE: *Let each other know you care. If you need something, say so. Don't assume you can do it all. Scale back desires—increase commitment.*

MARCELLO MASTROIANNI (9/28/24)
FEDERICO FELLINI (1/20/20)

Italian actor Mastroianni gained international acclaim as the morally vacuous, world-weary lead character in director-screenwriter Fellini's *La Dolce Vita* (1960). The actor continued to function as Fellini's main protagonist and alter ego in several films from 1963–87, among them *8½* and *Intervista*.

STRENGTHS: FREETHINKING, LIBERATING, FORWARD-LOOKING

WEAKNESSES: UNSTABLE, NERVOUS, OVERSOCIAL

BEST: FAMILY

WORST: LOVE

ROGER VADIM (1/26/28)
BRIGITTE BARDOT (9/28/34)

In '56 Vadim made his directorial debut with *And God Created Woman*, a boldly erotic film featuring his wife Bardot in the nude. While he pursued erotic themes in his subsequent films, she became Europe's greatest sex symbol.

Also: Julie Andrews & Maria von Trapp (film portrayal, *Sound of Music*); **Samuel Adams & John Hancock** (revolutionary leaders).

September 25–October 2
THE WEEK OF THE PERFECTIONIST
LIBRA I

January 23–30
THE WEEK OF GENIUS
AQUARIUS I

Undermining Authority

The Libra I–Aquarius I couple is likely to have a liberating effect on those with whom it comes into contact. The emphasis in this relationship is not so much on the independence of each partner but on their combined power to undermine authority and loosen the bonds of tradition—in general, to promote a freethinking and forward-looking ideology or lifestyle. Libra I and Aquarius I lie in trine aspect to each other in the zodiac (they are 120° apart), suggesting an ease between them. Here, however, this ease translates into a relaxed attitude or air of negligence that can subvert more conservative approaches.

Live-in love affairs and marriages are largely concerned with personal matters but can still find expression in conjunction with social groups seeking redress for unfair treatment. Libra I's and Aquarius I's tend to have a fairly social lifestyle together but should not neglect the need for intimacy and for time alone. The steady stream of traffic through the domestic space that is typical for this relationship can cause instability and nervousness in both partners, ultimately weakening their relationship. These matchups enjoy the constant interaction and activity, the holidays and special celebrations, inherent in family life.

In friendships and working relationships, Libra I's and Aquarius I's are likely to be quite outspoken against teachers or bosses who attempt to impose their will on their students or employees. These two are often active in student organizations or labor unions, working to see to it that their fellows are treated in a fair and just manner. Nor will promises and good intentions succeed in placating such drives, for partners want results immediately, in writing and in deed. Although Libra and Aquarius are air signs, the Libra I–Aquarius I relationship is ruled by fire, an element here indicating a passionate commitment to their cause that encourages spontaneous acts of defiance.

ADVICE: *Reserve enough quality time for yourself. Beware of spreading yourself too thin. Posit constructive alternatives for what you oppose.*

STRENGTHS: FUNNY, PLEASURE-LOVING, UP-TO-DATE

WEAKNESSES: IRRITATING, AWKWARD, LUDICROUS

BEST: FRIENDSHIP

WORST: MARRIAGE

JIMMY CARTER (10/1/24)
RONALD REAGAN (2/6/11)

In the 1980 presidential election, challenger Reagan attacked incumbent Carter on issues ranging from the evils of liberalism to fears of US military weakness. Carter tried to exploit Reagan's age (near 70) and right-wing conservatism. But Reagan's style prevailed and he won easily.

Also: Gwyneth Paltrow & Blythe Danner (daughter/mother; actors); **Groucho Marx & S.J. Perelman** (collaborators; comic/screenwriter).

September 25–October 2
THE WEEK OF THE PERFECTIONIST
LIBRA I

January 31–February 7
THE WEEK OF YOUTH & EASE
AQUARIUS II

In Need of Roots

This relationship is not well suited to high seriousness. Its principal focus is on keeping the mood light and safely on the surface; humor and quick-wittedness are characteristic here. Perhaps fated to a degree of superficiality, the Libra I–Aquarius II combination is often geared toward having a good time, employing the full roster of entertaining activities, from games to parties to films and television. Religious, philosophical or spiritual reflection is rarely found at the core of such a relationship but may be sorely needed by a matchup that lacks a firm ideological foundation. The relationship may, however, attempt to substitute more transitory values of a social, political or artistic nature to help fulfill this need.

In love affairs, neither partner seems interested in causing problems for the other. Yet this is precisely what Libra I's will do: their overly critical and at times fastidious manner can make their more relaxed Aquarius II partner uptight. Furthermore, the somewhat lackadaisical Aquarian approach may madden Libra I partners in search of a more clearly defined philosophy. Sexually, Libra I sexual intensity may prove threatening to the more sensual Aquarius II. Marriages between these two are not particularly recommended.

Friendships involving this pair may be given over entirely to the pursuit of pleasure, in which sarcasm and wordplay assume prominent roles. Personal hang-ups and thin-skinnedness, however, are likely to cause sudden explosions of temper. Libra I–Aquarius II relatives are apt to get on each other's nerves but may act out melodramatic scenarios that other family members find quite amusing. In the professional sphere, co-workers may intentionally or unintentionally become the butt of jokes, for their relationship will have an oblivious and awkward side.

ADVICE: *Be a bit more aware of what others are thinking. Commit to serious ideas or beliefs. Work on tempering irritation.*

September 25–October 2

THE WEEK OF THE PERFECTIONIST
LIBRA I

February 8–15

THE WEEK OF ACCEPTANCE
AQUARIUS III

Channeling Irrepressible Energies

This relationship is ruled by fire, here symbolizing a wellspring of energy that can be either used constructively or simply left to flood out of control. Thus this matchup may be characterized as a continual struggle on the part of Libra I's to harness the irrepressible energies of Aquarius III's. If they are successful, and the necessary discipline is imposed, this pair can be highly effective in bringing Aquarius III energy to a wider public; in the best-case scenario, the result is a merger of Libra I technical know-how and Aquarius III creativity. If they are unsuccessful, battles between the two will rage, with neither side prepared to compromise.

In love affairs there is a hint of the kind of idiosyncrasy of which this pair is capable. Unusual, even peculiar practices may well emerge here, which partners are likely to accept as normal but which society, if made aware of them, would frown on as kinky or bizarre. No matter how far Libra I's and Aquarius III's are apt to explore less-traveled roads, however, they rarely cause any serious harm, either to themselves or to others. Their pursuits are not restricted to the physical plane by any means but may well emerge in intellectual or even spiritual practices. Marriages are often based squarely on one such field of practice, which may involve an ideology or a social or political group to which this relationship devotes its energies.

Parent-child or boss-employee relationships in which Libra I's play the commanding role will hinge on the tractability of the Aquarius III child or employee. Ultimately, Aquarius III's will demand to be treated equally, and the resulting combination may prove more effective than before. Libra I–Aquarius III friendships often flaunt an unusual style, whether in looks, clothing, musical tastes or sexual preference.

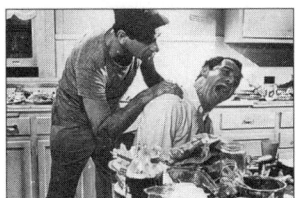

WALTER MATTHAU (10/1/20)
JACK LEMMON (2/8/25)

Matthau and Lemmon have made 9 movies together. From *The Fortune Cookie* (1966) to *Out to Sea* (1997), all but one (*JFK*, 1991) are side-splitting comedies, showing their superb acting skills and natural rapport together.
***Also:* Fran Drescher & Charles Shaughnessy** (co-stars, *The Nanny*); **Donny Hathaway & Roberta Flack** (duets); **Barbara Walters & Hugh Downs** (tv co-hosts, *20/20*).

ADVICE: *Listen carefully to each other. Maintain equality whenever possible. Keep wilder energies under control. Flaunt who you are, but respect other people's preferences.*

September 25–October 2

THE WEEK OF THE PERFECTIONIST
LIBRA I

February 16–22

THE CUSP OF SENSITIVITY
AQUARIUS-PISCES CUSP

A Prelude to Adventure

This relationship is on the move, forever in search of new horizons. Libra I dynamism combines with Aquarius-Pisces ambition to produce a hard-driving and uncompromising relationship that makes few excuses for its actions and none for its intentions. Tending toward the idealistic, these partners generally proceed from a strongly ethical or moral standpoint and thus feel justified in what they do. Although the focus of the relationship may well be on worldly adventures and challenges, its greatest need is for introspection and self-understanding.

In love affairs, friendships and marriages it is essential for the partners to spend time getting to know each other well. If other activities have to be postponed or meetings canceled for this to be accomplished, so be it. Aquarius-Pisces may lead the way in this endeavor, although they are often loath to open up areas in themselves that they have successfully sealed off. The trick here is for both partners to begin not with self-analysis but with discussions of the relationship itself. These can be the prelude to a highly exciting adventure of a different sort. The realization that self-discovery is a worthy challenge will lead the pair to explore this new territory more fully.

Work relationships between Libra I's and Aquarius-Pisces can be highly productive. This duo is particularly interested in the most current happenings, whether in politics, finance or entertainment. The information gleaned will be processed and put to work for the relationship's benefit but may become the basis for a professional endeavor in and of itself. Family members in this combination are likely to see eye to eye on many issues, but temperaments can clash. Remaining cool and controlling emotional outbursts, trying to be more accepting of each other and finding common areas of interest—all will be important in keeping the peace.

BARBARA WALTERS (9/25/31)
JOHN WILLIAM WARNER (2/18/27)

Walters worked her way up from tv reporter to one of the top-paid magazine-show co-hosts (*20/20*) and special interviewers. Warner is one of the US Senate's most prominent and active committee members. Walters and Warner are said to have been romantically involved. ***Also:* Edward Cox & Tricia Nixon** (married; lawyer/president's daughter).

ADVICE: *Seek deeper emotional and spiritual values. Understand yourself better. Take periodic rests from worldly activities—find a quiet place within.*

September 25–October 2

THE WEEK OF THE PERFECTIONIST
LIBRA I

February 23–March 2

THE WEEK OF SPIRIT
PISCES I

Far-Reaching Thoughts

Libra I's and Pisces I's together are often entranced by lofty ideals. When the pair can reach agreement, their relationship is capable of great things in the realm of abstract thought; when they are not, it is likely to be torn apart by internal struggle. In the zodiac, Libra I and Pisces I lie at a quincunx aspect to each other (150° apart), a position that often indicates an unstable partnership. Libra I's and Pisces I's are highly subjective, and fierce arguments over abstract concepts, the nature of justice being a favorite, may become the order of the day. Libra I's pride themselves on their precision and may look on Pisces I thinking as a bit wild or sloppy. Pisces I's, on the other hand, will often feel that Libra I's have missed the point completely or failed to grasp the essence of whatever is under discussion.

Love affairs and marriages tend toward the highly romantic, albeit changeable; both partners must make an effort to ground themselves in the here and now or risk losing contact with reality. Moreover, they are often unsettled by ideological, religious or spiritual differences. Since objectivity is lacking here, it may be necessary for them to back away from such topics if they are to achieve any stability. There is a shared tendency to become emotionally overwrought, leading to irritations, quarrels and endless misunderstandings.

Friendships, too, are best when kept light and entertaining, with few fixed responsibilities. Although they can be lasting, rivalries and adversarial relationships are perhaps equally common. Work relationships between these two are not recommended, except within the confines of a spiritual or religious organization with which they are in sympathy. In the family sphere, serious ideological and emotional differences will spark confrontations between Libra I's and Pisces I's, upsetting other relatives.

ADVICE: *Ground yourself in practical activities. Be realistic. Don't get carried away by romantic ideas or ideals.*

September 25–October 2

THE WEEK OF THE PERFECTIONIST
LIBRA I

March 3–10

THE WEEK OF THE LONER
PISCES II

Comical Charm

An unusual mix results from the precise and direct Libra I energies and the more sensitive, diffuse ones of Pisces II's. When these react in the formation of their relationship, the result is magical and can exert a strange enchantment over those it touches. Pisces II's have a social side that balances their primary need for isolation, Libra I's a strong need for isolation to balance their tendency to be in the public eye. Thus each partner has strengths that attract the other and lay a firm foundation for sharing within the relationship. Difficulties arise when Libra I's put too much emphasis on spoken communication and Pisces II's on unspoken, but given time and the will to get along, partners can usually work out these differences amicably.

In love affairs, temperamental differences are pronounced but still reconcilable. Libra I's may prove overdemanding at times for Pisces II's, who wish to be left in peace. On the other hand, the inability of Pisces II's to articulate their thoughts can prove exasperating to Libra I's. Libra I–Pisces II marriages often suffer from indecision and procrastination; these relationships have a certain comical charm for family and friends but can ultimately prove highly debilitating.

Libra I–Pisces II friendships are often surprisingly relaxed in attitude. Humorous situations of all sorts attract these two, more often as observers than as participants. With their special psychological awareness of human frailties, the pair can gather funny material that will endlessly delight friends, family and colleagues.

Parent-child and boss-employee relationships usually feature Libra I's issuing the orders and Pisces II's trying to follow them. The problem here is that things seldom go right, either through Pisces II misinterpretation of Libra I directives or through Libra I rigidity and unreasonable expectations. Libra I parents are usually aware of the extreme sensitivity of their Pisces II offspring and are most successful when they remain patient, understanding and not overly demanding.

ADVICE: *Be sensitive to each other's needs. Flexibility and extreme patience are needed. Find a balance between your public and private lives.*

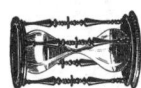

September 25–October 2
THE WEEK OF THE PERFECTIONIST
LIBRA I

March 11–18
THE WEEK OF DANCERS & DREAMERS
PISCES III

Miraculous Powers

This relationship is apt to involve itself heavily in a detailed examination of all aspects of life, focusing on the operations of chance, synchronicity, prophecy and extrasensory perception. In some ways the matchup could be described as a duel between an arch-skeptic and an arch-believer. Although this characterization is a bit extreme, there is a grain of truth to it. Libra I's often depend solely on their rational faculties and deny what they cannot apprehend through their senses. Pisces III's, on the other hand, happily put their faith in what cannot be seen, which has just as much reality to them; they also view everyday objects and events as being imbued with supernatural powers or significance and point up the inability, or unwillingness, of others to recognize the miraculous in the everyday.

In love affairs and marriages, Libra I's and Pisces III's can show great interest in discussing how they met and all the coincidences that led to their establishing a close bond. Not surprisingly, both partners value the unexpected, unpremeditated and spontaneous in their interactions, particularly in the sexual sphere. Family relationships and friendships often focus on exploring the unknown, perhaps through an interest in science fiction, perhaps through personal exploration. Libra I's may well be skeptical about indulging in this sort of activity at the outset, but in their relationships with Pisces III's their reluctant curiosity becomes an avidity for finding out more. The greater their initial resistance to such studies, the deeper their immersion in them later on (generally speaking), much to the delight of Pisces III's.

In work relationships, these two will take a special interest in letting things go as they will, without forcing them to happen—the elements of play, risk and fate enter powerfully into Libra I–Pisces III business transactions. They may not fully admit to it, but as fellow employees or colleagues these two are also interested in the psychological aspects of business, with special emphasis on the telepathic.

ADVICE: *Be realistic, but don't compromise your beliefs. Trust your senses and your judgment. Follow both your heart and your head.*

RELATIONSHIPS

STRENGTHS: **INVESTIGATIVE, SPONTANEOUS, BELIEVING**

WEAKNESSES: **GULLIBLE, ONE-TRACK, DELUDED**

BEST: **MARRIAGE**

WORST: **WORK**

EDGAR CAYCE (3/18/1877)
J.B. RHINE (9/29/1895)

Cayce and Rhine were both major figures in the scientific study of parapsychology, investigating psychic phenomena. Working at Duke University, Rhine concentrated on ESP and psychokinesis (mental influence on physical objects). Cayce, considered a leading psychic of his day, conducted his own independent research. Both have contributed to our understanding of the paranormal.

October 3–10
THE WEEK OF SOCIETY
LIBRA II

October 3–10
THE WEEK OF SOCIETY
LIBRA II

The Vantage Point

Although Libra II's devote a great deal of their time to family and professional groups, when paired they are apt to shut out as much of the world as possible and enjoy some relative isolation together. From this vantage point, their interest in other people is no less keen—they simply are absolved from any responsibility to interact. Nor do they feel any less need to share their observations of others' psychologies; indeed, this kind of interest can become the focus of their relationship. Friends and acquaintances may seek out this pair, either individually or as a unit, to confide in—an involvement that eventually may acquire a professional aura.

Love affairs between Libra II's tend to be romantic but, alas, also unrealistic. Perhaps not well suited to each other at all, Libra II's may be swept away on a magic carpet of euphoria that, unfortunately, may come back down to earth all too quickly. Basically, this can occur because both partners pursue what they want without giving much thought to what they need. They could well share in professional activities in the social-service area. It is most likely that family members will regularly consult these two for advice and insight. The Libra II tendency to be overstrict with their children may in fact be mitigated by their matchup, since they are often quite critical of each other's attitudes in this regard.

Friendships involving this combination can be a lot of fun if kept light. Partners should avoid depending heavily on each other for emotional support or demanding an inordinate amount of attention. Such relationships can certainly be the life of the party, but afterward this pair likely will provide the most insightful commentary during the postmortem.

Forming a business, or working for one, that deals with human services is quite possible for a pair of Libra II's. Making it work financially is another matter, however—this duo will be more successful as part of a team, the other members of which can supply the practical skills they lack.

ADVICE: *Don't just stand back and watch—get personally involved with others. Try to be more realistic in matters of love. Insist on what you need.*

RELATIONSHIPS

STRENGTHS: **OBSERVANT, INSIGHTFUL, ADVISING**

WEAKNESSES: **UNREALISTIC, OVERROMANTIC, EUPHORIC**

BEST: **FRIENDSHIP**

WORST: **LOVE**

SEAN LENNON (10/9/75)
JOHN LENNON (10/9/40)

Sean was born on Beatle John's 35th birthday. For the next 5 years John devoted himself exclusively to the care of Sean, living at home as a self-proclaimed "house-husband" while wife Yoko took care of their business affairs. John returned to recording in early 1980.

***Also:* Camille Saint-Saëns & John Lennon** (composers share same birthday).

STRENGTHS: **ENTERTAINING, APPRECIATED, POLITICAL**

WEAKNESSES: **IGNORING, OVERCOMPETITIVE, DESPERATE**

BEST: **FAMILY**

WORST: **LOVE**

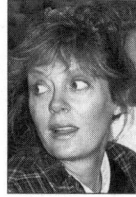

TIM ROBBINS (10/16/58)
SUSAN SARANDON (10/4/46)

Robbins and Sarandon have a longstanding live-in relationship. They met during the filming of *Bull Durham* (1988) and have worked together several times since. 12 years his senior, Sarandon has had 3 children, 2 of them with Robbins. He is best known for his lead role in Robert Altman's *The Player* (1992). She won the best actress Oscar for *Dead Man Walking* (1995).

October 3–10
THE WEEK OF SOCIETY
LIBRA II

October 11–18
THE WEEK OF THEATER
LIBRA III

Zealous Attention-Seeking

Libra II's and Libra III's seek to gain the attention of those around them. How they go about this, and for what purpose, is open to question. These two could easily compete with one another to be the star of the show; if clever, though, they will realize that their relationship can be the real headliner, if only they give up their own selfish desires and pitch in together. In fact, the combination of Libra II psychological insight and Libra III style and motivation make these two formidable when it comes to stealing the spotlight from others. But why do they need the focus to be on themselves? More highly evolved Libra II's and III's may see themselves acting in a larger social context, and choose to use their high visibility as a tool for pioneering efforts on behalf of others. With their fiery zeal for bettering the human condition and an ability to foster consensus, it is possible to find this pair involved in politics. In fact, the real gift of this relationship just may be its social consciousness, providing individuals already quite socially oriented on their own with a greater mission.

In love affairs and marriages there is the danger that partners will compete for one another's attention. Perversely, they may use their mutual need for attention as a weapon in internal conflicts, each ignoring the other in hopes of winning out. But there are no winners in this game. Ultimately the partners may have to seek out more attentive mates, usually signaling an end to the relationship.

In the family or work sphere, sibling or co-worker pairs may build up tremendous rivalries, which, curiously enough, do not tend to disrupt the home or workplace. Such competitive matchups prove interesting to those around them and, in fact, can benefit the group by raising the standard of the contribution made by this pair. The Libra II–Libra III relationship may count itself successful when its members are recognized for their joint contributions and achievements. Friends in this combination love entertaining and being entertained and will go out of their way to put on a show or take one in.

ADVICE: *Don't waste energy playing games. Try to grow up a bit. Seeking attention only weakens you. Use your power constructively.*

STRENGTHS: **AWARE, THEATRICAL, OBJECTIVE**

WEAKNESSES: **CYNICAL, MOCKING, TRIVIALIZING**

BEST: **MARRIAGE**

WORST: **ROMANTIC LOVE**

AUGUSTE LUMIÈRE (10/19/1862)
LOUIS LUMIÈRE (10/5/1864)

The brothers Lumière in 1894 developed the Cinématographe, a combination camera and projector. A year later they projected some films for the first time to a paying public in Paris—thereby marking the historical beginning of world cinema. *Also:* **Eleanor Duse & Sarah Bernhardt** (rival stage actresses); **Camille Saint-Saëns & Franz Liszt** (friends; composers).

October 3–10
THE WEEK OF SOCIETY
LIBRA II

October 19–25
THE CUSP OF DRAMA & CRITICISM
LIBRA-SCORPIO CUSP

Play-Acting

This is one of the most theatrical combinations of the whole year. Play-acting is usually the focus of this relationship, whether one takes the partners as a couple or individually. Although few make it to the stage, television or film, Libra II's and Libra-Scorpios are caught up in playing the roles of everyday life, and playing them well. The awareness that "all the world's a stage" is what really sets this relationship apart, allowing it fully to embrace the various opportunities for role-playing that life has to offer. With their particular interest in the illusory aspects of existence, these two nevertheless manage to keep a firm grip on reality, and view the shenanigans in which others indulge with the clear eye of insiders who know what it is to fake it.

Such realists can enjoy romance together, but by no means fully, since both understand how much is put on and how little deeply felt. Such a relationship will rarely fall in love with love, but, rather, will acknowledge the comedy inherent in many romantic attitudes. Laughing at themselves is perhaps healthy—but should the partners carry this attitude too far, they may become cynical, losing all innocence and the capacity for awe. Marriages between these two are likely to be highly practical in nature. For these couples, parties, family affairs and quiet dinners with friends are enjoyable opportunities for the study of the many feints and twists of dressed-up human nature.

Professionally, this relationship could well represent the partners' own or another's products or services as sales representatives, executives or consultants. Particularly adept at meetings and presentations, this duo will know how to impress both physically and verbally. As friends and siblings, Libra II's and Libra-Scorpios love to play games of all types but must beware not to live life only on the surface and thereby trivialize its more serious aspects.

ADVICE: *Jaded, cynical attitudes can be deadening. Stay alive in the moment—lose yourself occasionally in what you are doing. Drop the mask.*

October 3–10

THE WEEK OF SOCIETY
LIBRA II

October 26–November 2

THE WEEK OF INTENSITY
SCORPIO I

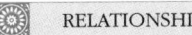 RELATIONSHIPS

STRENGTHS: **ENERGETIC, AMBITIOUS, IDEOLOGICAL**

WEAKNESSES: **STRESSED, POWER-OBSESSED, INHUMAN**

BEST: **FAMILY**

WORST: **LOVE**

Power's Fatal Attraction

This relationship is fatally attracted to power. Its greatest challenge may be to put its considerable energies toward productive and favorable ends and to be critical of its own power drives—to learn how to limit them and perhaps eventually even to give them up. The struggle for power thus becomes the struggle to understand power, to be its master rather than its slave. Libra II's and Scorpio I's must never succumb to the lure of power for power's sake, for this is the greatest danger they will face. One of the most significant tasks for this relationship is to serve human values that emphasize fairness, kindness and, above all, love for one's fellows. Despite the people skills of Libra II's, they are clearly out of their depth here—often, power doesn't really interest them. In this game Scorpio I's hold all the cards.

Love and marital relationships will often be marred by the partners' ruthless ambition: loving interaction is difficult here, since more tender human emotions are considered expendable in the drive toward a specific social or financial goal. It is possible for friendships between Libra II's and Scorpio I's to be highly rewarding in terms of person development, and a great deal of fun, but such friendships will face hard decisions in moments of crisis, when the partners are forced to choose between loyalty to the relationship and their interests as individuals.

In business and family matters, this relationship naturally seeks to exert its control over others and to occupy a prominent position in the hierarchy of the group. Usually working in its own best interest, the Libra II–Scorpio I pair may sacrifice its own comforts and personal needs to give its all. But placing itself under stress and strain is exactly what this relationship should not do. In fact, being more self-indulgent may be good for these two, since possessions and a bit of luxury will ground them more in the physical plane.

ADVICE: *Limit power drives. Try to be loving and kind. Beware of being swept away by ideologies and beliefs. Ground yourself in the here and now.*

ELIJAH MUHAMMAD (10/7/1897)
WALLACE D. MUHAMMAD (10/30/33)

Elijah, calling himself "the messenger of Allah," was leader of the Nation of Islam (Black Muslims) from 1934 to his death in '75. He was succeeded by son, Wallace, who lifted his father's restrictions on political activity and military service, while moving the sect closer to orthodox Islam. **Also: Heinrich Himmler & Paul Joseph Goebbels** (Nazi high command).

October 3–10

THE WEEK OF SOCIETY
LIBRA II

November 3–11

THE WEEK OF DEPTH
SCORPIO II

 RELATIONSHIPS

STRENGTHS: **ADVISING, GUIDING, DIRECTING**

WEAKNESSES: **OMNISCIENT, BOSSY, SNOOPING**

BEST: **LOVE**

WORST: **FAMILY**

The Detached Observer

Taking everyday events and turning them into bits of drama is the specialty of this relationship. Thus the rising action, climax and inevitable denouement of life as lived by ordinary people is the partners' chief interest, but principally as observers and commentators rather than as participants. By putting themselves outside the sphere of human action, they sometimes accord themselves a kind of godlike status. They may also be tempted from time to time to influence the action around them, but usually by advising, motivating or even ordering others to act in a certain way. Here they resemble directors rather than actors in the drama of life.

One area in which these two do not hesitate to get involved, however, is in their own love affairs, marriages and friendships. Though dramatic, such relationships have little pretense—they are spontaneous, honest, and impassioned. Libra II's and Scorpio II's throw themselves into matters of the heart with little reservation but often lack the insight to fully comprehend what is happening to them. Too often, reality is overturned, as they follow an excessive, obsessive and perilous course.

Within business and family circles, the Libra II–Scorpio II duo works best when personal interactions between them are kept to a minimum. Here, observing and furthering life's action is essential to the success of their professional and familial involvements. In the latter sphere, they are sometimes seen as busybodies who should keep their noses out of other people's business, but in business their advice and motivation are usually appreciated and even commercially sought after.

ADVICE: *Be more objective about yourself and less critical of others. Keep your opinions to yourself occasionally—not everyone needs your advice.*

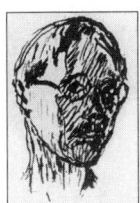 

PIERRE BONNARD (10/3/1867)
EDOUARD VUILLARD (11/11/1868)

Artists Bonnard and Vuillard shared a studio. Both rejected academic painting after coming under the influence of Gauguin and established a new style of decoration that led to the development of Art Nouveau in the late 1890s. **Also: Helen Hayes & Charles Gordon MacArthur** (married; actress/playwright); **Edward Davis Jones & Charles Henry Dow** (financial journalists; Dow-Jones).

A Dependable Unit

The Libra II–Scorpio III combination can be strong both professionally and interpersonally, because it imparts stability to both partners. Libra II's are usually able to take orders from Scorpio III's, and Scorpio III's to give effective leadership and direction to the relationship. This arrangement usually obviates the problem of Libra II indecision, although Scorpio III's must be careful not to become too overbearing, for Libra II's also have a rebellious streak. The important thing here is that decisions be fair and equitable, and that the best interests of the relationship be served.

Romantic and marital interactions are likely to coalesce around an easygoing, relaxed outlook that encourages a stable mixture of independence and responsibility. In such an environment love and affection can flow easily. Should things get a bit too pleasant and relaxed, however, such relationships may become a means of escaping harsher realities. Partners have to beware of a tendency to isolate themselves and to be overly protective.

In parent-child and boss-employee matchups, Scorpio III's do far better in the dominant role. The only danger here is that they will wield too much influence and as a consequence dominate the lives of more passive and agreeable Libra II's, ultimately provoking resentment. As friends these two are quite capable of being a dependable unit within a larger social group, or possibly even the one that takes the lead in setting up and running organized activities. However, should Libra I and Scorpio III friends be interested only in themselves and perhaps a small social or family group, they can be quite happy and self-sufficient.

ADVICE: *Beware of running away from problems. Keep in touch with what is going on. Preserve equality as much as possible. Stick to the plan.*

DICK POWELL (11/14/04)
JUNE ALLYSON (10/7/17)

Powell and Allyson had one of Hollywood's more durable marriages. They were wed from 1945 until his death from cancer in '63. Both were extremely popular in their day, making scores of films from the 30s through the 50s. **Also:**
Joan Helpern & David Helpern (married; shoe designers).

COLEMAN HAWKINS (11/21/04)
HARRY "SWEETS" EDISON (10/10/15)

Edison was a prominent jazz trumpeter with Count Basie's band from 1938–50 and was a soloist for Frank Sinatra from '52 to '78. Tenor saxophonist Hawkins played in top bands, including his own, from 1921–67. Both toured on and off with "Jazz at the Philharmonic" from 1950–67. **Also: Pierre Bonnard & Toulouse-Lautrec** (French Impressionist painters).

Mood Reinforcement

These individuals have their own turf to defend, and their first meeting may be somewhat confrontational. In addition, both have dark tendencies that their relationship may trigger, for better or for worse. They are apt to put considerable energy into working out certain deep feelings in an intense, highly charged manner. If one partner is on a high and the other depressed, the polarity is likely to increase, for it is difficult for a Libra II to pull a Scorpio-Sagittarius out of the depths—and vice versa. Yet both can fly high together or commiserate when blue, providing emotional reinforcement without exerting any pressure to change. When the partners' dark moods overlap, both of them can gain tremendous insights.

Love affairs between Libra II's and Scorpio-Sagittarians can be highly satisfying sexually and will continue to be pleasurable as long as few demands are made. The partners are capable of enjoying each other's company tremendously and love to be enchanted and entertained by each other. Extramarital involvements between Libra II's and Scorpio-Sagittarians, whether with each other or outside the relationship, are especially tempting to both partners. Marriages will generally prove too much for this combination, however, since the practical burdens of everyday life do not really suit their preference for the easy pursuit of pleasure.

Friendships and sibling matchups between pairs of the same sex are likely to be mutually respectful for the most part, but not without occasional flare-ups caused by overactive egos. Territorial needs and pride in their own work usually keep this pair from getting too close. In the professional sphere, the refined tastes of both partners can coalesce, producing a working partnership that may be successful in the areas of design, decoration, illustration or publishing. Financial acumen is not a strong suit here, however, and spendthrift tendencies will have to be carefully watched. Libra II's and Scorpio-Sagittarians usually work best as part of a team within a larger organization.

ADVICE: *Learn from your depressions. Don't run from emotional confrontations. Being naughty seems harmless but can cause great pain for all.*

October 3–10

THE WEEK OF SOCIETY
LIBRA II

November 25–December 2

THE WEEK OF INDEPENDENCE
SAGITTARIUS I

Handle with Care

Inspiration and education are the themes that run through this relationship. Sagittarius I's often assume such roles in the lives of Libra II's, but Libra II's are no less an inspiration to their Sagittarius I partners. What is suggested here is an asexual or platonic relationship, such as those of teacher-student, close friends or intergenerational relatives. In light of the importance that such a relationship could assume in their lives, it is extremely important that the partners remain objective, in part because there exists here an easy physicality that could become sensual if boundaries are crossed. Obviously, this means that the combination may sometimes be fraught with psychological peril—"Handle with care" may well be the warning implicit here.

In platonic love affairs and friendships, the ideal that each partner symbolizes for the other can be extremely fragile, easily destroyed by even the hint of physical involvement. As long as emotions are kept in check, Libra II's and Sagittarius I's can maintain these ideals and learn a great deal about and from each other. Marriages between Libra II's and Sagittarius I's may be a bit lopsided, with Sagittarius I's more often adopting the master role and Libra II's appearing more as the student or the obedient one. This matchup will generally have to be brought into greater balance if hostility and resentment are to be avoided.

Overt teacher-student relationships can work out well here, with either Libra II's or Sagittarius I's in the instructor's role. Communication is free and easy, with the relationship itself often becoming something of a model or providing a valuable lesson to others. Family matchups are tricky and unavoidably flirtatious; truly affectionate feelings between close relatives may actually cause problems within the family. The whole question of trust is paramount here, and acting in an honorable and respectful way, particularly when age differences are pronounced, will be vitally important for psychological well-being.

ADVICE: *Stay as objective as possible. Honor your commitments. Be conscious of the role you are playing, and act with sensitivity and awareness.*

SOON-YI PREVIN (10/8/71)
WOODY ALLEN (12/1/35)

During the highly publicized breakup between Allen and Mia Farrow, it was revealed he had been having an affair with Soon-Yi, Farrow's oldest adopted daughter. Allen maintained there was nothing morally wrong in their having the relationship. **Also: Stephanie Zimbalist & Efram Zimbalist, Jr.** (daughter/father; actors); **Janet Gaynor & Mary Martin** (actress-friends in car accident; Gaynor died of injuries).

October 3–10

THE WEEK OF SOCIETY
LIBRA II

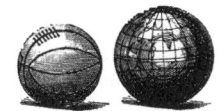

December 3–10

THE WEEK OF THE ORIGINATOR
SAGITTARIUS II

Well-Rounded

These two are likely to establish a deep emotional bond. The Libra II–Sagittarius II relationship is often highly intimate, and conducive to personal expression. It is often well rounded, with each partner offering something of great benefit to the other. Libra II's can be influential in bringing their Sagittarius II partners into a more meaningful relationship with society, and Sagittarius II's can encourage Libra II's to express their own individuality and to feel less compelled to please others. Their complementary strengths and intense rapport make this an unusually healthy and vibrant matchup. Proceeding from this basis, these two are able to place the relationship in a meaningful social context without compromising their fundamental beliefs.

No matter how perfunctory the introduction or how superficial the initial involvement, love affairs here can be very meaningful. This relationship continues to broaden and deepen, and to encourage self-actualization for both partners; these two evolve together, creating a bond that is difficult to break. It can be quite natural for marriage to be a further step for these lovers, but it should not be taken for granted that personal development will continue at such a steady pace after the knot is tied.

Family matchups and friendships between Libra II's and Sagittarius II's can be extremely close, marked by deep empathy and affection. But claiming attitudes may also surface here, with accompanying jealousies and dependencies. The challenge in such relationships is to maintain an open atmosphere that allows for individual expression, since Sagittarius II's, if denied this, will lose their most essential character trait and eventually become deeply frustrated.

Professional relationships between Libra II's and Sagittarius II's work best if confined to freelance and entrepreneurial endeavors where maximum independence is assured. Although obligations must be met, each partner should have well-defined areas of responsibility that will not be encroached upon by the other.

ADVICE: *Maintain your individuality, and beware of claiming attitudes. Compromise just enough. Remember to encourage each other's personal and spiritual growth.*

JACKSON BROWNE (10/9/48)
DARRYL HANNAH (12/3/61)

Soulful singer-songwriter Browne has been influential in pop music since his first album, *Asylum* (1972). His 90s romance with Hannah was declared abusive by the actress, and their breakup generated a lot of negative publicity for the singer. **Also: Gore Vidal & Thomas P. Vidal** (grandson/grandfather; writer/senator).

STRENGTHS: **ENRICHING, NATURAL, PRODUCTIVE**

WEAKNESSES: **DISCONTINUOUS, ERRATIC, UNCOMMITTED**

BEST: **FRIENDSHIP**

WORST: **MARRIAGE**

MICHAEL ANDRETTI (10/5/62)
EMERSON FITTIPALDI (12/12/46)

Andretti and Fittipaldi are both auto racers with special records in the Indy 500 race. Andretti (son of Indy winner Mario, '69) won Rookie of the Year honors in '84. Fittipaldi won the Indy race twice, '89 and '93. Both drivers are fierce competitors.

Also: Tommy Lee & Bob Guccione (lawsuit; musician/*Penthouse* publisher).

October 3–10
THE WEEK OF SOCIETY
LIBRA II

December 11–18
THE WEEK OF THE TITAN
SAGITTARIUS III

Grounded Skill and Feeling

This relationship focuses on balancing technical proficiency with an instinctive approach to creative endeavors. One of the more important decisions these two will make is whether to be competitors or to join forces in a common enterprise. While Libra II's can furnish the psychological awareness and attention to detail that Sagittarius III's lack, the Libra II tendency to procrastinate is countered by Sagittarius III ambition, drive and intuition. Generally these two do best when they sacrifice personal gain to the good of the relationship, joining forces to create something of lasting value. The Libra II–Sagittarius III relationship will rarely continue uninterrupted but will follow a more erratic off-again, on-again pattern.

Love affairs involving these two are usually more successful than marriages—unconditional commitment is seldom in the cards here. Both partners have a tendency to become involved romantically, emotionally or sexually with third parties, which can have the effect, briefly, of enriching their primary relationship with each other. At the same time, however, such involvements, unfortunately, do not enhance the longevity of the relationship. Friendships usually depend on the amount of time the partners are willing to invest, for their individual schedules tend to be hectic. Characteristically, these two will find small blocks of time when they can be alone and share thoughts and feelings without being interrupted. In the family sphere, Libra II–Sagittarius III sibling matchups can be quite volatile and competitive. Parent-child relationships can bring out the stricter and more detached side of both the Libra II and the Sagittarius III parent, fostering a judgmental and critical attitude toward their offspring. The principal challenge here will be encouraging feelings of acceptance and open channels of communication. Work relationships are best if somewhat detached, with each partner fulfilling his or her work quota and not asking for too much help from the other. Although such co-workers may display natural and relaxed attitudes toward each other, they should perhaps avoid too much personal contact. Much depends on whether these two are involved in the actual production of something or not.

ADVICE: *Make some lasting decisions, pro or con; commitment is more important than you think. Don't miss an opportunity to join forces.*

STRENGTHS: **EMPATHIC, DEEP, PASSIONATE**

WEAKNESSES: **UNSTABLE, OSCILLATING, UNCLEAR**

BEST: **LOVE**

WORST: **WORK**

GIUSEPPE VERDI (10/10/1813)
GIACOMO PUCCINI (12/22/1858)

Verdi and Puccini were both famed operatic composers. The younger Puccini was inspired by Verdi's work, particularly *Aida*. When Puccini's *Tosca* (1900) and *Madame Butterfly* (1904) were presented to the public, the composer was hailed as the successor to Verdi—the highest acclaim he could have achieved.

Also: Thomas Wolfe & Aline Bernstein (affair; novelist/stage designer).

October 3–10
THE WEEK OF SOCIETY
LIBRA II

December 19–25
THE CUSP OF PROPHECY
SAGITTARIUS-CAPRICORN CUSP

Fever Pitch

This is a passionate and emotionally complex matchup. The partners' dark sides are activated here, bringing feelings to a fever pitch. Although there is a marked empathy between these two, the relationship can become a battleground, with conflicts arising from unacknowledged erotic fantasies or desires. Should this be a relationship that does not permit the expression of such intense feelings, frustration and animosity are the inevitable results. In this case it's best for these two to avoid each other. This is especially true for Libra II's, who are unused to this kind of scenario. Seeing the darker aspects of their natures at work could prove too great a shock.

Deep and lasting friendships, love affairs or marriages—perhaps even all three—can be in the cards for the Libra II–Sagittarius-Capricorn relationship. Psychological projections are so intense here that the boundaries of the partners' personalities are often blurred, making it impossible for either individual to form a clear idea of him- or herself without the other. Although each ultimately has the other's best interests in mind, this is no guarantee that they will act fairly or sensibly. For periods of time, a more platonic arrangement can work, giving partners a rest and a grain of objectivity. Their frustrations and fantasies may run out of hand, however, in the end plunging them back into a sexual relationship. The most difficult task for these two interpersonally will be establishing and observing their own boundaries. If this isn't possible, separation may be the only possible solution that guarantees the self-preservation of both.

The feeling of being unable to live either with or without each other comes to the fore in family matchups. Love-hate or, at the very least, like-dislike polarities are common here, creating an emotional seesaw that affects partners and relatives alike. Work relationships between Libra II's and Sagittarius-Capricorns are unlikely to achieve the stability necessary for building a career together.

ADVICE: *Strive for objectivity, and consider your own survival—ask yourself if you're happy with things as they are. Meditate deeply, make a decision, then act.*

October 3–10

THE WEEK OF SOCIETY
LIBRA II

December 26–January 2

THE WEEK OF THE RULER
CAPRICORN I

Getting Off the Ground

The greatest challenge for this couple is to overcome a tendency to be uncommunicative. Should this block be great enough, it's unlikely the relationship will get off the ground. Assuming that it does, however, considerable energy will have to be expended to keep lines of communication open and operable. At heart, Capricorn I's may not really approve of Libra II's, seeing them as social and thus superficial creatures—not people to be taken seriously. Moreover, since Libra II's are likely to do what feels good and are not particularly bound by society's standards for moral behavior, their Capricorn I partners may condemn them as eccentric—Libra II's will not enjoy many aspects of a relationship that is uptight and judgmental.

Should this pair be physically attracted to one another, their relationship may still not go far beyond the early stages for the reasons above. Marriage can result only if Capricorn I's can be convinced of the seriousness of Libra II intentions. In reality, they might benefit substantially from the social savvy that Libra II's have to offer, while Libra II's could profit from Capricorn I financial and practical acumen. The relationship may supply both partners with a great deal of what they need, even if it's not exactly what they want.

Family relationships in this combination usually suffer from mutually disapproving attitudes. Both individuals will have to work very hard to accept one another as they are and to withhold judgment of their behavior. Friendships tend to be more understanding, with differences a source of interest and delight rather than condemnation.

At work, things proceed most smoothly when Libra II taste and psychological insight meld with Capricorn I leadership capabilities and hard-headed pragmatism. Energetic enterprises in which Libra II's handle design, buying, marketing or public relations while Capricorn I's deal with production, sales or money management can be highly successful.

ADVICE: *What you need can prove more valuable than what you want. Work toward greater acceptance and a lessening of judgmental attitudes. Utilize differences.*

 RELATIONSHIPS

STRENGTHS: **BENEFITING, MELDING, ENERGETIC**

WEAKNESSES: **UNACCEPTING, UNCOMMUNICATIVE, JUDGMENTAL**

BEST: **WORK**

WORST: **LOVE**

GRANT HILL (10/5/72)
CALVIN HILL (1/2/47)

Calvin is a 14-year veteran of football's NFL whose career was boosted when he won Rookie of the Year in 1969. Basketball's Grant Hill is following in his dad's athletic footsteps, having been voted 1995 Rookie of the Year. They are very close. **Also: Eliza McCardle Johnson & Andrew Johnson** (First Lady/US president).

October 3–10

THE WEEK OF SOCIETY
LIBRA II

January 3–9

THE WEEK OF DETERMINATION
CAPRICORN II

A Decided Edge

Capricorn II's often occupy the dominant role in this combination. Libra II's may appreciate the relationship or not, but it may well arouse their rebelliousness. Astrologically, Libra II and Capricorn II lie in square aspect to each other (90° apart in the zodiac), and as such they are expected to disagree—these two will experience quite a bit of tension and friction. There is often a choice here: either the partners can fritter away such contentious energy in endless squabbling, or they can use it constructively, to move the relationship forward, possibly in social, creative, technical or commercial spheres.

Love affairs between these two have a decided edge to them. Sexual tension may be a prominent feature here, and can lead to either frustration or fulfillment. Outright emotional warfare is possible at times; the danger here is that an ever-expanding spiral of excitement will be necessary to the partners' satisfaction. Marriages tend to be highly ambitious, with both partners striving together for greater social prestige or recognition—a use of the tensions inherent in the combination to the partners' mutual advantage. Care must be taken to avoid applying this edge to child-rearing, however. Capricorn II's and Libra II's may become good friends, even if their relationship originated as a competitive or adversarial one. The relationship can find itself engaged in adventure and risk-taking activities—these two are magnetically drawn toward outright danger. In parent-child relationships where Capricorn II's have the dominant role, Libra II's will often be aroused to rebellion, but such situations do not inevitably escalate into open warfare. With understanding and, often, the intervention of a third family member, both partners can come to see the advantages of their getting along, and thus be able to settle differences rationally. In the professional sphere, the Libra II–Capricorn II combination will often aim for the top within its chosen field, achieving the highest levels of expertise and success. Personal disagreements and incompatibilities don't usually enter the picture, being put aside in favor of harmonious cooperation. When slowdowns and breakdowns occur, patience often wears thin, and the tensions underlying the relationship can be dramatically revealed.

ADVICE: *Put tension and edginess to the best use possible. Limit the scope of arguments; don't reject the advice of a peacemaker. Take necessary precautions.*

RELATIONSHIPS

STRENGTHS: **FORWARD-LOOKING, AMBITIOUS, FULFILLING**

WEAKNESSES: **SQUABBLING, IMPATIENT, INCOMPATIBLE**

BEST: **FRIENDSHIP**

WORST: **PARENTS**

DYAN CANNON (1/4/37)
ARMAND ASSANTE (10/4/49)

Actors Cannon and Assante started their romance in the late 70s. In '78 the short-fused Assante punched a paparazzo at JFK airport for taking their picture. The next year the macho actor asserted, "She is the demonstration of my manhood, just as I am of her womanhood. It is *va-r-ro-o-o-o-m.*" (*People* magazine). **Also: John Lennon & George Martin** (musician/record producer).

October 3–10
THE WEEK OF SOCIETY
LIBRA II

January 10–16
THE WEEK OF DOMINANCE
CAPRICORN III

The Other Side of the Fence

This relationship is imbued with contrasts—its energy can shift from the known to the unknown, from the potential to the kinetic and, often, from the acceptable to the questionable. Harnessing such energy can make the relationship a powerful force for change in whatever social, family or professional context it finds itself. The Capricorn III tendency to dominate comes to the fore here, but only if Libra II's give their partners the chance to exercise it. Libra II's are quick on their feet, and their often radical stance can pose a real threat to more solid, sure and slower-thinking Capricorn III's. Yet the danger Capricorn III's face here is more subtly subversive than powerfully confrontational, since Libra II's may be influential in eroding their more conservative position, thereby freeing them to act.

Libra II's are likely to lead their Capricorn III partners through the labyrinths of love, introducing them to many earthly delights and physical pleasures. In this respect, Capricorn III's usually prove to be eager, enthusiastic students. Marriages between these two can be surprisingly stable, but also very broad-minded.

Libra II and Capricorn III relatives can have violent arguments over politics and social issues when their respective radical and conservative viewpoints clash. Such resistance to each other's ideas may continue for years, and will be viewed warily, but with some humor, by other family members. Libra II–Capricorn III friendships are less common than friendly rivalries or even serious enmities, since too often these individuals find themselves on different sides of the fence.

In the commercial sector, the Libra II–Capricorn III business partnership or co-worker matchup can be highly dynamic. But Capricorn III's may eventually resent having to shoulder the brunt of the hard work, since Libra II's are slippery customers when it comes to meeting fixed responsibilities and work quotas.

MARTIN LUTHER KING, JR. (1/15/29)
JESSE JACKSON (10/8/41)

Religious leaders King and Jackson were committed to the crusade against social injustice for African-Americans. When King spearheaded the civil rights protest movement of the 60s, Jackson was one of his key lieutenants and was with him when King was assassinated. **Also: Britt Ekland & Rod Stewart** (palimony suit; actress/rock star).

ADVICE: *Equalize the work load. Present your views objectively, and respect the beliefs of others. Subversion can be positive but is a dangerous tool.*

October 3–10
THE WEEK OF SOCIETY
LIBRA II

January 17–22
THE CUSP OF MYSTERY & IMAGINATION
CAPRICORN-AQUARIUS CUSP

A Hornet's Nest

This lively matchup is likely to lend its sparkling energy to any group of which it is a part. Because of its highly independent nature, however, the relationship may not be able to fulfill fixed responsibilities or meet rigid schedules, and does best in organizations where it is free to determine its own working schedule—within acceptable limits. These two can become extremely cantankerous and rebellious if treated unkindly or unfairly, or if they see an innocent third party receiving harsh treatment. There is a bit of the champion and protector of the downtrodden and disenfranchised here, for nothing will arouse these partners to fury more quickly than seeing someone deprived of his or her rights.

Love affairs between Libra II's and Capricorn-Aquarians develop as fast as a summer thunderstorm and may pass just as quickly. Quick, sharp responses betray the combination's emotional sensitivity. Generally, fiery sexual interactions lessen considerably in their intensity in marriages or longer-term commitments, which, in fact, may do a great deal to help stabilize this relationship.

In the family sphere, parent-child relationships of either variation will have to develop patience, especially because of a shared tendency to fly off the handle when faced with small irritations. Learning not to let the partners push each other's emotional buttons so easily is paramount to maintaining a modicum of peace and harmony. Friendships in this combination are often devoted to having fun and keeping it light. This duo generally steers away from causing problems for each other, but, if criticized or attacked by outsiders, like a disturbed hornet's nest they will give their opponents more than they bargained for.

Libra II–Capricorn-Aquarius work relationships are perhaps most successful when partners are self-employed and engaged in service-oriented endeavors, or even in the social services. Troubleshooting and consulting are specialties of this team, since they are especially quick in isolating problems and solving them.

WARNER OLAND (10/3/1880)
AUGUST STRINDBERG (1/22/1849)

Swedish dramatist and novelist Strindberg had in Oland the most unlikely English translator of his work. Oland was born in Sweden and arrived in the US at age 10. He became a film actor at 32, appearing as Oriental detective Charlie Chan in 7 movies (1931–38).

Also: Allen Ludden & Betty White (married; tv personalities); **Andy Devine & Guy Madison** (co-stars, *Wild Bill Hickok*).

ADVICE: *Quiet down a bit—find a space for meditation and reflection. Don't react so quickly; develop objectivity and patience. Discharge responsibilities.*

October 3–10
THE WEEK OF SOCIETY
LIBRA II

January 23–30
THE WEEK OF GENIUS
AQUARIUS I

RELATIONSHIPS

STRENGTHS: **TUNED-IN, LIBERATED, AFFECTIONATE**

WEAKNESSES: **NOISY, HAMPERING, OPPRESSIVE**

BEST: **PARENT-CHILD**

WORST: **MARRIAGE**

The Same Wavelength

There is an ease of communication that approaches the telepathic in this relationship. These partners are on the same wavelength; they are so closely aligned that the principal problem here may be their shared tendency to make unwarranted assumptions when anticipating each other's wishes. Furthermore, each may have the attitude that he or she knows what is best for the other in any given situation. Thus the relationship is an interesting combination of freedom and oppression, liberation and manipulation. Overall, the situation could be vastly improved if the partners were more firmly grounded and less engaged in mental gymnastics.

In love affairs, Libra II's and Aquarius I's often find each other highly desirable, and their passions are likely to run high. Possessiveness and jealousy are to be expected here, making noisy rows all too common. This usually proves to be healthy behavior, however—by clearing the air, the partners can for the most part avoid frustration. Both of these attractive individuals will be tempted to stray and will also be favored by more predatory types interested in a quick fling. When married, Libra II–Aquarius I couples are likely to attract a needy third party, often a friend, who will seek to instigate a love triangle. This may have disastrous effects on the primary relationship. Friendships in this combination are sometimes too close. If they are to remain healthy, the partners will have to take regular breaks from one another, so that they can further their development as individuals and also interact with others. Relationships that can observe moderation and pace themselves will avoid burnout and may remain intact for many years. Parent-child relationships in this combination can be outstanding, with affection, admiration, empathy and acceptance all in abundance. Two such volatile individuals may fight like cats and dogs, of course, either on occasion or regularly, but such confrontations largely serve to sharpen wits and will ultimately bring partners closer together. In the professional sphere, co-worker pairs work well together but must beware of being split over demands for individual recognition and advancement. These two will also generate a profusion of ideas, but few of them will be realized.

ADVICE: *Give each other enough space. Beware of predators. You may not be as free as you think. Use your communicative gifts prudently.*

DAVID LEE ROTH (10/10/55)
EDDIE VAN HALEN (1/26/55)

David and Eddie were members of the Van Halen band, formed in 1974. David's showy good looks and media magnetism contrasted with Eddie's reticence. They were considered one of rock's oddest couples. Just after the release of David's *Crazy from the Heat* (1985), he left the group.

Also: **Klaus Kinsky & Nastassja Kinsky** (father/daughter; actors).

October 3–10
THE WEEK OF SOCIETY
LIBRA II

January 31–February 7
THE WEEK OF YOUTH & EASE
AQUARIUS II

RELATIONSHIPS

STRENGTHS: **VIVACIOUS, ORIGINAL, CREATIVE**

WEAKNESSES: **STRESSED, UNPREDICTABLE, CONTENTIOUS**

BEST: **LOVE**

WORST: **WORK**

A Merry Chase

These two are likely to lead each other on a merry chase. Free spirits not easily caught, each makes a worthy quarry for the other. This does not mean that an adversarial relationship is the theme here. Libra II's and Aquarius II's garner satisfaction from their unusual dance, which will often be a verbal one. Since Libra II and Aquarius II form a trine aspect to each other in the zodiac (lying 120° apart), their relationship is a pleasant and easy one. It is also highly original and versatile. Aquarius II's are especially elusive, and it is never easy for Libra II's to get them firmly in hand. Returning a sense of freedom to each other in the midst of a relationship will bring out the best in this duo.

Love affairs and marriages here are extremely complex matchups indeed. It will usually be impossible for the empathic Libra II–Aquarius II couple to lead a conventional life together, since their highly original personalities demand unusual alternatives. Distributing household chores, organizing working patterns, keeping financial records—all of these may be handled in an out-of-the-ordinary and somewhat unpredictable way. Generally these two follow their impulses, doing things on the spur of the moment. Children of such a couple may well prove the most responsible members of the family. In the social and work spheres, Libra II's and Aquarius II's may be friends and co-workers, but their ability to stay in each other's presence for very long may be limited. If the partners are required to be constant in their attitudes and feelings, these relationships will inevitably feel the strain. Libra II–Aquarius II sibling or parent-child combinations lend fun and life to any family gathering. Ultraconservative and dour relatives can be made unbelievably uptight by this duo, which delights in provoking and ridiculing intolerant attitudes.

ADVICE: *Strive for consistency. Stick to your plans—spontaneity is not always a desirable trait. Keep combative urges under control.*

CLARK GABLE (2/1/01)
CAROLE LOMBARD (10/6/08)

"Hollywood's happiest couple," Gable and Lombard were married in 1939. Gable, usually reserved, was attracted instantly to the zaniness and risque humor of the petite blond actress. But tragedy struck in 1942 when Lombard died in a plane crash on a war-bonds selling tour.

Also: **Gore Vidal & Norman Mailer** (bitter foes; writers).

FELICIA FARR (10/4/32)
JACK LEMMON (2/8/25)

Farr, Lemmon's 2nd wife, was a leading lady in about a dozen Hollywood films between '55 and '92. They married in '60. He directed her in his film *Kotch* (1971), and they acted together memorably in Blake Edwards' *That's Life!* (1986). **Also: Soon-Yi Previn & Mia Farrow** (adopted daughter of actress).

October 3–10

THE WEEK OF SOCIETY
LIBRA II

February 8–15

THE WEEK OF ACCEPTANCE
AQUARIUS III

Learning to Be

This relationship is actively involved in a search for happiness—not an easy contentment, but an active and dynamic striving that is in itself fulfilling. The danger here is that a kind of nervous exhaustion may set in; for this determined pair, the means can become an end in itself. Libra II's can prove to be an inspirational force in the lives of Aquarius III's, helping to bring their unconscious desires more fully into the open and aiding them in the process of maturation. Aquarius III's are grateful for such a relationship, which acknowledges their worth as individuals and recognizes the significance of their efforts at growth. With all this striving, however, these two would do well to learn how to relax, to turn off all that mental clatter and simply be in the moment.

Love affairs in this combination are somewhat adoring. Both Libra II's and Aquarius III's regard their matchup as bordering on the sacred, and in their reverence for it they may fail to recognize problems when they arise. Should they be completely blind to the relationship's failings, they may experience a rude shock should it one day prove nonfunctional. Marriages between these two are more soberingly realistic, and less susceptible to profound disillusionment.

Family relationships and friendships here are chatty, and partners appreciate a good bit of gossip every now and then. This is a forgivable failing, however, when one considers how considerable their work load may be, at least for short periods of time—neither of them has the will to sustain a combined effort over the long haul. Workwise, Libra II and Aquarius III colleagues and business partners are likely to need a tremendous amount of variety; both bore easily and regularly change direction. A lack of intuition too often results in such a relationship wasting its energies in an effort to reach a goal it never aspired to in the first place. Consequently, more emphasis on practicalities, thorough planning and perseverance are needed if this duo is ever to achieve its stated objectives.

ADVICE: *Stay on the path—don't be so easily sidetracked. Scale back your work efforts to a moderate level. Keep to your initial resolve if possible.*

JOHN LENNON (10/9/40)
YOKO ONO (2/18/33)

John and Yoko met in a London gallery in 1966. They were soon collaborating on projects. Married in '69, their honeymoon was a much-publicized "Bed-In for Peace." In '80 John was murdered by a deranged fan. Yoko maintains her commitment to the Lennon legacy.

Also: Sean Lennon & Yoko Ono (son/mother); **Elizabeth Shue & Andrew Shue** (sibling actors).

October 3–10

THE WEEK OF SOCIETY
LIBRA II

February 16–22

THE CUSP OF SENSITIVITY
AQUARIUS-PISCES CUSP

Reaching for the Stars

This is a relationship that reaches for the stars—perhaps an appropriate image for a matchup that begins in the physical realm and strives for the metaphysical. Highly ebullient, the Libra II–Aquarius-Pisces matchup is expansive in both plans and outlook and is rarely willing to compromise on even a single point. As long as the partners share the same perspective, things go well enough between them, even if worldly success isn't quickly forthcoming. But when cracks begin to appear in the relationship's ideological foundations, trouble can be expected. Recriminations, anger and resentment are all likely to rear their ugly heads.

Love affairs in this combination are highly idealistic, but also frank and sensual. Usually of great benefit to each other psychologically, the partners are often able to work through childhood problems and hang-ups through conscious role-playing, using each other to represent authority figures and others who caused difficulty in the past. As long as this process is undertaken with full awareness, the likelihood of healing is great. Marriage is generally the next step for a relationship as solid and unswerving in its commitment as this one.

Although Libra is an air sign and Aquarius-Pisces an air-water combination, the Libra II–Aquarius-Pisces relationship is ruled by fire, here symbolizing intuition and initiative. In work efforts these matchups do well when initiating projects and setting up new organizations; the partners are not always equally adept at maintaining them, however, and may leave others in charge while they go on to the next thing. Familial relationships in this combination often grow impatient and angry with other relatives who seek to restrict their efforts or rein in their idealism. As friends, Libra II's and Aquarius-Pisces are extremely optimistic, and as a result may not see trouble when it is coming their way.

ADVICE: *Don't blind yourself to the truth. While following your dream, keep your feet on the ground. Be more patient and less intractable.*

October 3–10
THE WEEK OF SOCIETY
LIBRA II

February 23–March 2
THE WEEK OF SPIRIT
PISCES I

RELATIONSHIPS

STRENGTHS: **LUCKY, IN-TUNE, AWARE**

WEAKNESSES: **WEAK-WILLED, PASSIVE, PROCRASTINATING**

BEST: **WORK**

WORST: **MARRIAGE**

The Right Time

This can be one of those relationships where everything the partners touch seems to turn to gold. Working its own special brand of magic, this combination is especially adept at turning disadvantage into advantage, leaving observers with their mouths gaping in astonishment. Turning the miraculous into an everyday occurrence is possible here, but, as with any sleight-of-hand, the explanation may be surprisingly simple. These two are simply in tune with the workings of chance and are often fully open to things turning their way without being overly expectant or anxious about them doing so. This relationship has a feeling for *kairos*—that is, the right time to attempt something—and for the workings of synchronicity.

Such luck is no indication that these two will necessarily achieve easy success interpersonally. A lot of hard work is often required for Libra II's and Pisces I's to come to a deep understanding and acceptance of each other. Fortunately, they have a great deal in common, particularly their aesthetic sense, love of harmony and need for affection on a daily basis. In marriages they may not be demanding enough—as spouses they may be content to remain at the same social, financial and developmental level for years on end. Learning how to be more forceful in demanding the best for themselves will involve not only developing willpower but also learning to break the habit of procrastination.

It is in the professional sphere that this relationship may achieve its greatest success. The Libra II–Pisces I business matchup has a real talent for sensing the mood of the times and knowing what others want and need. Because of their nonthreatening approach, they are often able to inspire trust in others, who tend to believe what they say. Family relationships and friendships are sharing and partners are sympathetic to each others' needs.

MICHAEL ANDRETTI (10/5/62)
MARIO ANDRETTI (2/28/40)

Mario is the patriarch of an auto racing family—sons Michael and Jeff and nephew John. Michael has had 29 career wins and was 1984 Indy 500 Rookie of the Year. Father Mario won the same honor in '65, then became the only driver to win the Daytona 500 ('67), Indy 500 ('69) and Formula One world title ('78). Father and son are very close.

ADVICE: *Don't be satisfied merely with what comes your way. Work on building initiative and willpower—visualize what you want and go for it.*

October 3–10
THE WEEK OF SOCIETY
LIBRA II

March 3–10
THE WEEK OF THE LONER
PISCES II

RELATIONSHIPS

STRENGTHS: **PREDICTIVE, CURIOUS, SENSUAL**

WEAKNESSES: **NERVOUS, UNSTABLE, INSECURE**

BEST: **FRIENDSHIP**

WORST: **FAMILY**

Eyeing the Future

This combination has a sixth sense when it comes to a knowledge of what might be lurking just around the corner. The relationship is especially interested in the future and usually very good at predicting it. An interest in science fiction, fantasy literature and utopian ideas is often present here. Libra II's add their knowledge of human behavior to the Pisces II store of technical, artistic and philosophical information, filling the relationship's data banks to the bursting point.

Lest this relationship be categorized as an exclusively intellectual one, it should be noted that it shows no less interest in the pleasures of the table and the bed, adding a strong element of sensuality to the matchup. Love affairs and marriages are highly satisfying, and the partners try to balance their theoretical and practical interests. Reading books on food is usually a prelude to cooking and eating, those on sex to lovemaking. Because Libra II and Pisces II form a quincunx aspect in the zodiac (they lie 150° apart), astrology forecasts some instability here. A heightened nervousness, worry or emotional insecurity is to be expected, but this often increases the partners' excitement, and the corresponding reward.

Libra II and Pisces II friends may quite possibly work together, but do not need to, since they are quite capable of amusing themselves in a wide variety of endeavors. These two can rely on each other in a pinch. Family members in this combination may experience problems getting chores done, and often ignore domestic problems that need attention.

In the professional sphere, this pair can form an outstanding working relationship. Although the partners' interests may already run in the same direction, the matchup is enhanced by their ability to get along, and to serve side by side on a daily basis. These two will do well in positions that require trend-spotting and forecasting skills, as well as in the area of researching and developing new products or techniques.

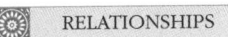

NIELS BOHR (10/7/1885)
GEORGE GAMOW (3/4/04)

Danish-born Bohr and Russian-born Gamow were theoretical physicists who worked together as scientists in Europe c. 1930. They went on to distinguish themselves separately in their fields. Gamow was an early proponent of the big bang theory of the universe; Bohr combined quantum theory with his own concept of atomic structure.

ADVICE: *Pay attention to the here and know—don't trip over your shoelaces while eyeing the distant mountain. Keep calm.*

October 3–10
THE WEEK OF SOCIETY
LIBRA II

March 11–18
THE WEEK OF DANCERS & DREAMERS
PISCES III

Down the Corridors of Time

The repercussions of the relationship between Libra II's and Pisces III's can echo down the corridors of time. Romantic and inspired to the extreme, this relationship also has intensely pragmatic aspects that allow for a certain magic in professional and other ties as well. But the partners can get carried away with each other, so that they neglect societal criticism and opposition. Overconfidence and in some cases a certain arrogance typifies this pair's attitude toward life, which may cause nagging problems in the long run, even though things seem to be going well for the present. The Libra II–Pisces III relationship can arouse jealousies and animosities, although it has many admirers.

Love affairs between Libra II's and Pisces III's can be ultraromantic. Giving their all for love, the partners seldom hold back emotionally or sexually. Such passionate relationships don't often lead to marriage, however, for they invariably lose that special spark, and either break off or continue on a more ordinary plane. As the partners age, they inevitably look back on their more active years with a mixture of nostalgia and regret.

Libra II and Pisces III friends and lovers are able to work together, often putting some of their inspirational energy into mutual business, artistic or social activities. Such efforts need not be big moneymakers, for the idealism of the matchup dictates working on projects that both partners truly believe in, heart and soul. Often impractical, this pair's schemes sound good at the outset but don't often come to fruition, and in retrospect seem almost too good for this world.

In the family sphere, parent-child matchups of either combination tend to be affectionate and empathic. Sensitivity to each other's moods and wishes can be a problem, since each feels the other's pain or distress so deeply. Both will have to strive for more objectivity, and in adolescence should work to develop their individuality, so that both of them may proceed along their respective paths without encumbrance.

ADVICE: *Give each other enough breathing room—don't stunt individual growth and development. Don't be oversensitive to each other's feelings.*

October 11–18
THE WEEK OF THEATER
LIBRA III

October 11–18
THE WEEK OF THEATER
LIBRA III

Ceaseless Repartee

This relationship is marked by a kind of instant recognition—Libra III's will know that they have met someone of like mind, with whom they can communicate openly and honestly. Yet most Libra III couples project a cool image, without much display of their feelings or talk about what is bothering them. This is often because they themselves do not know what is on their own minds, and in fact this relationship does not rate high in self-awareness. Libra III's are geared for action, so if the relationship is becalmed by the malaise of indecision it can truly suffer. Dealing with anxieties and depressions will be very difficult for this duo, since neither is likely to be able to drag the other out of a well of loneliness or despair.

Libra III lovers will have a difficult time of it, since their feelings will not always gel in the romantic and sexual spheres. Often out-of-synch, their interaction can suffer from misunderstandings, misplaced energies and mixed signals. If both partners accept the increased and fixed responsibilities of marriage, however, the relationship will benefit. These two can also make conscientious and dedicated parents.

Friendships here can be truly outstanding, as long as the level of responsibility and expectation is not unduly high. The ability of these two to have fun together is practically unlimited, and their quick minds and agile tongues engage easily in almost ceaseless repartee. Arguments will rarely get out of hand here, particularly if each party respects the other's viewpoint.

Family is not really Libra III's thing. Two relatives born in this week can liven up any gathering—too often, unfortunately, by not seeing eye to eye; their arguments and blowups can be extremely disruptive. In the workplace too, their dramatic shows of affect may not help get a project completed, proving more counterproductive than entertaining.

ADVICE: *Be more contemplative. Get to know yourself better. Don't be afraid to show your true feelings. Your image is not so important.*

October 11–18

THE WEEK OF THEATER
LIBRA III

October 19–25

THE CUSP OF DRAMA & CRITICISM
LIBRA-SCORPIO CUSP

RELATIONSHIPS

STRENGTHS: **POWERFUL,
AMBITIOUS, STRIVING**

WEAKNESSES: **REPRESSIVE,
FEARFUL, FRUSTRATING**

BEST: **WORK**

WORST: **PARENT-CHILD**

A Quest for Power

The partners in this relationship must be careful about getting carried away by ambition and the quest for power; their combination often sacrifices sympathy, kindness and love for striving, domination and control. Since neither of them is willing to admit to vulnerability or weakness, their relationship is often characterized by a certain coolness, an avoidance of open emotion. Both partners are extremely aware of the outward impression they convey and are intent on having their relationship play a proper role in its social milieu. Ultimately, the thirst for power or control could become the partners' undoing.

Critical Libra-Scorpios may directly confront more dominant Libra III's, trying to bring them down a peg. Whether as lovers, friends or mates, these two will often engage in one-upmanship, trying to prove their verbal, intellectual or physical superiority. Battles may rage between them, but not vindictively; each wants more to surpass than to defeat or humiliate the other. Basically, in fact, each really just wants to be respected by the other, the goal being not to rule but simply to be treated as an equal. These two may feel great affection for each other at certain points in their relationship, but they may be afraid to show it, considering it a sign of weakness. Letting each other know that they care, then, is the challenge here. Partners who can show how they feel are displaying more self-confidence and assurance than partners who cannot.

Libra III–Libra-Scorpio parent-child matchups of either possible variation often do not work out because of excessive expectations. Both parents and children can try to push their partners beyond their potential, causing frustration and, eventually, the relationship's breakdown.

Work relationships may be obsessed with overcoming the opposition and rising to the top of the heap. These stressful efforts are fraught with perils for the pair, not the least danger being the blame and rejection that lie in store for the weaker and less successful partner. The preservation of true equality between partners, however, can contribute greatly to mutual advancement.

ADVICE: *Mute your power drives. Cultivate sympathy and understanding. Let things go as they may. Give up childish urges to win at any cost.*

OSCAR WILDE (10/15/1854)
LORD ALFRED DOUGLAS (10/22/1870)

Wilde, the notorious Irish poet, playwright and wit, fell for "Bosie," a rich, handsome young poet in 1891. The affair provoked Douglas' father, the Marquis of Queensbury, to accuse Wilde of sodomy. Wilde sued for libel, lost, and was charged with homosexual criminal behavior. The sensational trial about "love that dare not speak its name" resulted in a 2-year jail sentence. **Also: Paul Simon & Carrie Fisher** (married).

October 11–18

THE WEEK OF THEATER
LIBRA III

October 26–November 2

THE WEEK OF INTENSITY
SCORPIO I

RELATIONSHIPS

STRENGTHS: **TASTEFUL,
DISCRIMINATING, SPECIALIZED**

WEAKNESSES: **SNOBBISH,
CONTEMPTUOUS, SELFISH**

BEST: **FRIENDSHIP**

WORST: **LOVE**

The Elitist Position

Partaking equally of the Libra element of air (indicating thought) and the Scorpio element of water (indicating feelings), this pair tries to find a balance between intellectual and emotional expression but is usually weighted more toward the intellectual. Since Libra III's and Scorpio I's are often united by a discriminating and critical view of the world, their relationship may also focus on good taste, at least as they see it; part and parcel of this attitude may be a derisive or contemptuous attitude toward those with more common preferences. Thus this relationship risks leading its partners toward isolating themselves in an elitist position.

In love affairs, partners are unlikely to take each other to the deeper levels of desire. Although their sexual interaction can be intense, it is characteristically unemotional and a bit selfish, with both partners out for what they can get. Romance does not usually figure prominently either here or in marriage, which is often remarkably objective in its outlook.

Friendships are usually better off going their own way than striving to be at the center of a social group. These partners' highly individual, strong-willed attitudes succeed best when concentrating on specific areas of expertise in which Libra III feeling for the big picture and Scorpio I attentiveness to detail can dovetail.

Parent-child matchups in this combination can be quite stressful and demanding. Rejecting attitudes are likely to be prominent, and it may be many years before these two can really accept each other as they are. Interestingly, though, they don't much approve of anyone else, either, so in the end they favor each other by default. If they fail to put limits on their conflicts and disagreements, the relationship may reach a point of no return beyond which any reconciliation may be difficult or impossible. Similarly, boss-employee relationships in this combination are likely to be difficult; co-worker relationships are more successful, though the partners must beware of belittling their fellow employees, and of unduly asserting their superiority.

ADVICE: *See things from another point of view. Don't raise yourself up too high above other people. Cultivate a few common tastes. Simple feelings will take you a long way.*

RAY STARK (10/13/17)
FANNY BRICE (10/29/1891)

Stark, the son-in-law of Yiddish comedienne Brice, produced her screen biography, *Funny Girl* (1968), starring Barbra Streisand. It was one of his greatest successes.

***Also:* Empress Farah Pahlevi & Shah of Iran** (married); **Eleanor Roosevelt & Teddy Roosevelt** (niece/uncle); **Jerome Robbins & Peter Martins** (co-ballet masters, NYC Ballet); **e.e. cummings & Ezra Pound** (lifelong friends; poets).

STRENGTHS: CHARISMATIC, UNITED, UNCOMPROMISING

WEAKNESSES: SQUABBLING, INCOMPATIBLE, UNRESOLVED

BEST: SIBLING, WORK

WORST: MARRIAGE

PAUL SIMON (10/13/41)
ART GARFUNKEL (11/5/41)

Simon and Garfunkel started harmonizing in the 6th grade, c.1953. By 1990 they were in the Rock & Roll Hall of Fame. In between, they sold over 20 million albums in the US alone. As the years went on, they grew further apart because of creative differences.

Also: Lillie Langtry & Edward VII (actress-mistress/monarch); **Dwight Eisenhower & George Patton** (WWII US generals).

October 11–18
THE WEEK OF THEATER
LIBRA III

November 3–11
THE WEEK OF DEPTH
SCORPIO II

For Better and for Worse

This relationship contains a powerful chemistry for establishing an uncompromising position—it often focuses on taking a stand, which it will fearlessly defend. It also has the capacity to win the hearts and minds of other people and is likely to find itself at the center of a social, family or professional group. The Libra III–Scorpio II relationship is unlikely to back down from any challenge from outside; these two will present a united front. Internally, however, the matchup may be bedeviled by disagreements and dissenting opinions from the start. Often such contrasts give it an intense dynamism, but they may also periodically threaten to break it asunder.

In matters of love, the outgoing qualities of Libra III's and the introverted tendencies of Scorpio II's can come into direct conflict. At first the relationship can thrive on such differences, but over time, this temperamental incompatibility may prove insurmountable. The Scorpio II may find the Libra III superficial and self-aggrandizing, while the Libra III may be unable to cope with the Scorpio II's moods and depressions. Marriage is a big step for this relationship and should be considered seriously before being attempted. Should such a marriage wind up on the rocks, the partners must be prepared for a painful breakup marked by agonizing on-again, off-again oscillations rather than any real finality. Friendships and same-sex sibling relationships in this combination can be very strong, both competitive and supportive. Against a common enemy, these two are a model of solidarity. When such a threat is absent, however, unity is likely to disappear in a flurry of squabbling. Rather than relying on parents or other friends to settle their disagreements, Libra III's and Scorpio II's generally insist on taking care of things themselves. These two can be an unbeatable professional team. Commercial endeavors bring out their best side—their differences fade, and the relationship assumes primary importance. Career recognition generally enhances rather than undermines unity, but at a certain point working partners may make a rational decision to go off on their own and try something new.

ADVICE: *Assess your position objectively. Agree to disagree. Limit your responsibilities. Preserve unity in good times as well as bad.*

STRENGTHS: FORMIDABLE, INTENSE, ENDURING

WEAKNESSES: OBSESSIVE, COMBATIVE, ESCAPIST

BEST: WORK

WORST: LOVE

NANCY KERRIGAN (10/13/69)
TONYA HARDING (11/12/70)

In a bizarre 1994 incident between these world-class figure skaters, Harding plotted to injure her rival, Kerrigan, to keep her out of Olympic competition. Kerrigan, however, won the silver medal; Harding came in 8th and was stripped of her US title.

Also: Penny Marshall & Garry Marshall (siblings; actress-director/producer); **Dwight & Mamie Eisenhower** (married).

October 11–18
THE WEEK OF THEATER
LIBRA III

November 12–18
THE WEEK OF CHARM
SCORPIO III

Declaring a Truce

This matchup can be very deceptive: many will have the impression that Libra III's and Scorpio III's get along well, since their public persona is usually so positive. But this is often a facade. Their relationship is actually likely to be intense, conflicted and competitive. Although rarely shown in public, the degree of struggle here can be considerable, with each partner seeking to best the other, emotionally, mentally or physically. These two may be obsessively caught up with each other, so that their relationship sometimes threatens to engulf all other aspects of their lives. They may consequently need to spend long periods of time apart. When together, moreover, they may need to declare a formal truce.

Love affairs between Libra III's and Scorpio III's can be exciting but emotionally wrenching. When the tension becomes too great, these partners, whether separately or as a couple, have a tendency to seek solace in drink or drugs. Should the relationship itself become addictive, many years may be needed to work out the problems engendered. But it also happens that marriages between Libra III's and Scorpio III's reach a status quo, which, although neither inspiring nor even satisfactory from a psychological point of view, may have remarkable longevity.

Libra III's and Scorpio III's are more likely to become rivals than friends. Even when they are on the same side, outright hostility can flare up between them and may seriously impair any group effort of which they are a part. Sibling rivalries between these two are also common, with Libra III dominating tendencies meeting their match in the powerfully controlling streak of Scorpio III's. If compromise is not reached, the family's stability may be eroded. Perhaps the trickiest area for Libra III–Scorpio III interactions is the career sector. When pulling together, these two make a formidable combination, but should competitive urges arise, they can be split asunder in an instant. There is generally little loyalty or love between these two, but when they realize that it is in their best interest to cooperate, they may be able to get along.

ADVICE: *Consider the good of the group, yet be honest about your feelings. Continuing at any cost isn't always the best thing. If possible, call a truce.*

October 11–18
THE WEEK OF THEATER
LIBRA III

November 19–24
THE CUSP OF REVOLUTION
SCORPIO-SAGITTARIUS CUSP

STRENGTHS: EDUCATING, SHARING, ENRICHING

WEAKNESSES: IMITATIVE, OPPORTUNIST, VOYEURISTIC

BEST: TEACHER-STUDENT

WORST: MARRIAGE

Eye on Each Other

The focus of this relationship is often learning one's craft as well as possible. Although competitive energies are part and parcel of the relationship, they are rarely destructive or out of control. In fact they usually serve to spur partners on to learn from each other and share what they know. Whether they serve together in the same organization or simply acknowledge each other as colleagues or relatives, these two will always keep an eye on each other, watching carefully for indications that may have personal meaning for themselves. This relationship is rarely the most important factor in the life of either partner, but it can bring about a sort of mutual education.

Love affairs between these two are often free and nonbinding. The tie will probably be temporary or passing; it will rarely get heavy or possessive. If it does lead to marriage, however, its relaxed nature may help it to establish itself firmly. Libra III–Scorpio-Sagittarius marriages often feature a considerable age difference between the partners. The older of the two may play the role of teacher, the younger that of apt and avid student. Some pain and grief is inevitable if the older member passes away, or if the younger finds it necessary to throw off the elder's influence and go off on his or her own.

Teacher-student relationships, in fact, whether in a one-on-one life encounter or formalized in a school or college, are strong in this combination. More often cast in the teacher's role, Scorpio-Sagittarians are able to pass on a great deal of philosophical, technical and professional wisdom to their Libra III students. In other career settings, Libra III's and Scorpio-Sagittarians are capable of working steadily side by side for years in the same organization. In friendships and sibling pairs, they are enriched by common experiences in which life is the teacher and the Libra III–Scorpio-Sagittarius relationship is the student. The meaningful bonds formed in this way usually continue intact through the years.

ADVICE: *Beware of being too easily influenced. Maintain your individuality. Share as much as possible, and avoid competition. Remain sympathetic.*

CALVIN KLEIN (11/19/42)
RALPH LAUREN (10/14/39)

Fashion competitors Klein and Lauren have many parallels. They both come from Bronx, NY, families and grew up in the same neighborhood. They started their own businesses in 1968 and went on to expand their clothes fashions to other lines, such as eyeglasses and fragrances. Both have received several Coty awards. **Also: Martina Navratilova & Billie Jean King** (friends; tennis doubles partners).

October 11–18
THE WEEK OF THEATER
LIBRA III

November 25–December 2
THE WEEK OF INDEPENDENCE
SAGITTARIUS I

STRENGTHS: UNDERSTANDING, EMOTIONAL, COMMITTED

WEAKNESSES: IMPATIENT, SELFISH, CONDEMNATORY

BEST: LOVE

WORST: WORK

Beneficial Dependencies

This relationship is often a serious one, and, if so, neither partner will deny its importance, particularly if it occurs during the mature years, when it can be fully appreciated. The combination almost always involves some dependency, yet is in no way debilitating or addictive; in fact, it is strengthening, since each partner is likely to have a total (but objective) involvement with the other's needs in any time of crisis. Furthermore, when that demanding time has passed, the partners will feel free to engage in matters unrelated to each other's lives, although they will remain involved.

Love affairs between Libra III's and Sagittarius I's can be rewarding both physically and emotionally. Libra III indecision and Sagittarius I temper can create difficulties, and impatience may break out when the relationship is under stress, but the understanding and commitment found in this pair will generally overcome such problems. Clashes between these strong-willed individuals are inevitable, but often result in a renewed sense of purpose. The greatest challenge for love affairs and marriages often lies in the spiritual realm, since the relationship may involve a certain gap or lack that can only be filled by selfless service and belief in a higher power.

Marriages and work relationships are favored here. Libra III and Sagittarius I usually share moral beliefs, and thus proceed with a common underlying sense of what behavior is correct and what is not. Ignoring or neglecting this mutually understood code will not be tolerated, and the penalties meted out will usually be severe, even running to the termination of the relationship itself. When attacked from outside, on the other hand, the relationship will not only defend itself admirably but will often mete out severe punishment to the aggressor. Work and family matchups in this combination are often money- and career-oriented to the exclusion of all else. Although they can be commercially profitable, it is vitally important for the partners to develop human values, particularly by cultivating kindness and consideration.

ADVICE: *Lower your stress level. Find time to meditate and relax. Quiet your busy mind. Acknowledge a higher power. Develop more patience.*

RITA MAE BROWN (11/28/44)
MARTINA NAVRATILOVA (10/18/56)

Tennis star Navratilova and novelist Brown met in 1978 and had a love relationship until '81. Brown, a radical feminist and active in lesbian issues, was a strong intellectual influence on Navratilova. They bought a house together in Virginia and lived there when Navratilova was not on tour. **Also: Dwight Eisenhower & Winston Churchill** (WWII allies; president/prime minister).

RELATIONSHIPS

STRENGTHS: **EXPRESSIVE, NATURAL, ENERGETIC**

WEAKNESSES: **HYPERCRITICAL, UNAWARE, MISGUIDED**

BEST: **MARRIAGE**

WORST: **FRIENDSHIP**

MARIE OSMOND (10/13/59)
DONNY OSMOND (12/9/57)

Following a decade with the singing Osmond Brothers, Donny teamed up with Marie for the tv show *Donny and Marie* (1976–79). Through the years sister and brother scored one success after another, singly and as a duo. In '78 they co-starred in the film *Goin' Coconuts*. In the 80s they continued to record hit songs. **Also: Demond Wilson & Redd Foxx** (co-stars, *Sanford & Son*).

October 11–18

THE WEEK OF THEATER
LIBRA III

December 3–10

THE WEEK OF THE ORIGINATOR
SAGITTARIUS II

Letting It All Hang Out

The Libra III–Sagittarius II matchup tends to indulge in flamboyant gestures and colorful language, whether negative or positive in attitude—it lets it all hang out. Critical of snobbism and pseudosophistication, this pair can pour scorn and abuse on those who demand exclusive treatment. Yet it may itself be an example of what it condemns, since it often has little sympathy with the needs of the common man, and in fact can be quite selfish and standoffish. Hypocrisy in this and in other areas can be a problem for the relationship, which involves a certain lack of self-awareness.

Love affairs and marriages between these two can be exuberant and fun. Able to get physical without shame or guilt, Libra III's and Sagittarius II's can give themselves wholeheartedly to each other. On the other hand, their unserious attitudes may eventually take them down a trail that leads nowhere, resulting in bewilderment and disillusionment. If this relationship wants to survive, it is essential that it question itself a little, examining its motives and making firm resolves about its behavior.

In family relationships and friendships, both Libra III's and Sagittarius II's may too easily get involved in other people's business. Quick to condemn, as a pair they may be self-righteous, winding up overaggressive and hasty in their judgments. On the other hand, the relationship's tremendous energy and positive spirit can invigorate many projects that have gotten stuck and would otherwise proceed no further.

Work relationships in this combination may find the Libra III impatient with the Sagittarius II's unusual ways of doing things. Furthermore, Sagittarius II's may find Libra III's much too bossy. Unless both partners have their own undisputed areas of business, then, so that they only occasionally have to interact, career matchups are not recommended.

ADVICE: *Don't be so quick to condemn. Get to know yourself better. Make firm decisions and stick to them. Give your life more direction and better purpose.*

RELATIONSHIPS

STRENGTHS: **DESIRING, PASSIONATE, COMFORTING**

WEAKNESSES: **DOMINATING, UNCOMPROMISING, EXCESSIVE**

BEST: **FAMILY**

WORST: **FRIENDSHIP**

MELINA MERCOURI (10/18/23)
JULES DASSIN (12/18/11)

Actress Mercouri and director Dassin fell in love during the filming of *Never on Sunday* (1960), for which she received an Oscar nomination. They married in '66 and had a close relationship till her death in '94. In the 70s she pursued a political career in Greece; he continued making movies. **Also: Chuck Berry & Keith Richards** (early rock & roller/disciple, a Rolling Stone).

October 11–18

THE WEEK OF THEATER
LIBRA III

December 11–18

THE WEEK OF THE TITAN
SAGITTARIUS III

Hearts on Their Sleeves

Attraction and desire play strong roles in this relationship; both partners tend to wear their hearts on their sleeves, and make no bones about liking each other. Still, the question remains as to how deeply these powerful individuals want to get involved, since both are equally unlikely to let themselves be swept away by a passion that will dominate their lives (or at least so they think). In consequence, the relationship may focus on keeping feelings under control, particularly in front of other people. Although the partners may express their emotions in private, in company they will maintain a cooler facade, shrinking from the public acknowledgment of the relationship's meaning that would help to seal its permanence. Commitment, clearly, is an important issue here. Perhaps just because both Libra III's and Sagittarius III's can generally be taken at their word, solemnly dedicating themselves to each other doesn't come easily.

Love affairs here can be tumultuous. This may cause problems: if the partners cannot strictly compartmentalize their strong feelings for each other, their professional, family and social lives will be profoundly affected. They can also expect to experience the full gamut of emotions, which, however, may not always survive their bouts of feeling intact. After a time, in fact, the relationship is likely to show unmistakable signs of wear and tear. Should they marry, this couple must learn moderation and compromise.

Friendships may be more settled, yet also less understanding and flexible. Each partner has high expectations of the other, and disappointment can be severe. Parent-child and sibling matchups in this combination are often empathic, particularly when the partners are of the opposite sex. Protective and understanding, these two may turn to their relationship for solace from life's difficulties.

Two powerhouses like these will rarely see eye to eye in the workplace. Both demand a lot of attention, and both seek to dominate any organization of which they are a part. Perhaps the best that can be done with these two in a work group is to keep them apart; separately, both will have skills to contribute.

ADVICE: *Try to relax. Don't take things so seriously. Back off a bit from the leadership stance. Give others a chance. Even out emotions.*

October 11–18

THE WEEK OF THEATER
LIBRA III

December 19–25

THE CUSP OF PROPHECY
SAGITTARIUS-CAPRICORN CUSP

RELATIONSHIPS

STRENGTHS: **STEADY,
UNFAILING, EFFORTLESS**

WEAKNESSES: **ROCKY, STORMY,
FEARFUL**

BEST: **MARRIAGE**

WORST: **PARENT-CHILD**

Blast Off!

This relationship is united by a bond of energy, steady in its intensity, unfailing in its production. Like a turbine running on a river's dammed-up power, it can be counted upon to deliver without letup. The chemistry here is interesting: the relationship often forms when Sagittarius-Capricorns pick out their most reliable ally, formidable adversary or apt student as the target of their formidably laserlike powers of concentration. When the Libra III catches fire, the entire relationship ignites, taking off for its destination like a rocket ship. Certain things are clear from the outset: first of all, the correct flight path must be keyed in to the guidance system right at the start. Second, the relationship must be tough enough to stand the enormous gravitational stress it will encounter.

To follow this analogy a little longer: love affairs between these two are most stressful upon takeoff and landing—that is, when beginning and ending. During flight, they need only an occasional thrust of power to continue effortlessly on course. Sagittarius-Capricorns will like the fact that once the relationship is launched, it only needs low-maintenance energy from them to keep it going. Libra III's too will be happy not having to make decisions, solve problems or alleviate emergencies. In this way, marriages in this combination can enjoy many pleasant years, although they may have stormy beginnings before their patterns are established. The fear of the relationship's ending, however, can be considerable, and the actual rumblings of breakup can be terrifying. At such points, the partners will tend to hang on, refusing to believe that the trip is over.

Friendships, family relationships and career matchups follow a similar route. Parent-child combinations may have a rough time of it in childhood, then suddenly gel in late adolescence and early adulthood. Friendships and working relationships must likewise get over initial dislikes and irritations before continuing on course.

ADVICE: *Get over the rough spots. Conquer your fear of failure. Don't expect too much—take it as it comes. Meet emergencies intelligently.*

YVES MONTAND (10/13/21)
EDITH PIAF (12/19/15)

Piaf was France's pre-eminent chanteuse from the 30s to the 50s. Montand, originally a music hall singer, was discovered by Piaf while performing at the Moulin Rouge in Paris. She guided his career and gave him his first film role in one of her movies, *Star Without Light* (1946). *Also:* **George C. Scott & Ava Gardner** (romance; actors); **Martina Navratilova & Chris Evert** (tennis rivals).

October 11–18

THE WEEK OF THEATER
LIBRA III

December 26–January 2

THE WEEK OF THE RULER
CAPRICORN I

 RELATIONSHIPS

STRENGTHS: **ASSERTIVE,
PROGRESSIVE, UNUSUAL**

WEAKNESSES: **PUGNACIOUS,
TROUBLEMAKING, RESENTED**

BEST: **MARRIAGE**

WORST: **WORK**

Discarding the Outworn

This relationship has an unusual way of doing things; its partners will often be found reacting against outworn styles, ideologies or beliefs, and trying to substitute something more meaningful in their place. Within its circle of friends or family, this pair is likely to be a force for change. Although Capricorn I's tend toward the conservative, they will appreciate the relationship for giving them the space to voice some of their more far-out thoughts. Libra III's, for their part, will enjoy having a strong partner on whom to lean occasionally, as well as the grand drama created by the relationship's rebelliousness.

Love affairs and marriages between Libra III's and Capricorn I's are usually of the responsible sort. Yet these partners will not hesitate to fly in the face of tradition rather than compromise their belief in their relationship, or knuckle under to society's demands. If the relationship is a love affair, then, it can easily be a secret or illicit one, although both partners will usually treat any third party involved with as much consideration as possible. Should the lovers marry, they are apt to work out their own special arrangement, which, although not always easily comprehensible to the outside world, works well enough for them. Such marriages generally work for the common good rather than following their own selfish interests.

As co-workers, this pair may fail to achieve its maximum impact if it spends too much of its energy on fighting bosses and opposing the status quo. Companies and other organizations may finally give up on a team in this combination as more trouble than it's worth. Libra III–Capricorn I siblings tend to rebel against parents and other family figures, usually for reasons more ideological than personal. As friends, pairs in this combination have no problem standing up for themselves against authority. Should either party feel dominated or controlled by the other, however, they may fall into frequent disagreements with each other.

ADVICE: *Try to make less trouble for others. Learn the value of diplomacy and compromise. Try to hear what other people are saying to you.*

WOODROW WILSON (12/28/1856)
EDITH BOLLING GALT (10/15/1872)

Galt was the 2nd wife of President Wilson (1913–21). In 1919 he suffered a stroke and was seriously incapacitated. For nearly 2 years the gravity of his condition was hidden from the public while she, in effect, ran the country until his term ended. *Also:* **James II & Charles Edward Stuart** (grandfather/grandson; British king/Bonnie Prince Charlie).

DWIGHT EISENHOWER (10/14/1890)
RICHARD NIXON (1/9/13)

Nixon was Eisenhower's vice-president from 1953–61. Though Nixon often represented the president at home and abroad, they were never personally close. In '55, when Eisenhower suffered a heart attack, Nixon effectively filled in until the president could resume his duties. **Also: John Dean & Richard Nixon** (key Watergate witness implicated president).

October 11–18
THE WEEK OF THEATER
LIBRA III

January 3–9
THE WEEK OF DETERMINATION
CAPRICORN II

A Tad Misleading

This relationship may perhaps mislead its partners a bit in giving them the feeling of having a lot more freedom than they really do or should. Both partners may be guilty of overweening pride, and thus be at times a trifle arrogant; keeping an eye on reality, and refusing to get carried away by self-importance, are therefore crucial for them. Both Libra III's and Capricorn II's can be strong, self-confident and ambitious individuals, and when they pair up, the relationship that results may synergistically intensify these tendencies and blow their egos all out of proportion. Particularly important to this pair, then, will be an awareness of other people's feelings, and an understanding of the boundaries and limitations that they should not overstep. On the other side of the coin, they will be strongly united by common bonds.

In love affairs, friendships and marriages, neither Libra III's nor Capricorn II's are always able to tolerate the other partner's need to go off alone for a spell. Neither is overly hungry for attention, but there is a limit to the degree to which they can take their relationship for granted—a time will come when they will have to give it some serious input. Both of them must make the effort to break their busy schedules and make time for shared vacations, hobbies and entertainment. Showing care through a thoughtful gift, flowers or a candlelight dinner will do wonders to blow new life into this relationship.

As co-workers, Libra III's and Capricorn II's are capable of sustained effort and high-quality work. There is a tendency, however, for both partners to go their own way—they don't always listen to each other. When one of these two works for the other, whichever of the two is the boss must be careful to treat the employee with respect, never compromising his or her dignity. Likewise, in parent-child relationships in this combination, serious problems can arise if the child is either babied or treated too much like an adult. Kindness works better than sternness here.

ADVICE: *Don't kid yourself. Give your partner the proper time and effort. Keep the channels of communication open. Put your ambition on a tight rein.*

E.E. CUMMINGS (10/14/1894)
JOHN DOS PASSOS (1/14/1896)

Poet cummings and novelist Dos Passos were school chums when they attended Harvard (1912–16). They continued their friendship in Paris in the 20s as part of the international literary group that settled there, which included Hemingway and Fitzgerald. During this period cummings and Dos Passos traveled extensively together. **Also: Doris Humphrey & Jose Limon** (dance company partners).

October 11–18
THE WEEK OF THEATER
LIBRA III

January 10–16
THE WEEK OF DOMINANCE
CAPRICORN III

Keeping Their Own Individuality

The focus of this relationship may well be independence of thought, manner and speech. Keenly interested in the average person, this pair sometimes sees itself as a staunch protector of the disenfranchised—an image that can, in fact, be true, particularly when the partners are young, a period when their relationship is often marked by quite radical philosophical viewpoints. With advancing ing age, however, they will forsake or modify many of their ideals in a more conservative direction, a tendency particularly noticeable in Capricorn III's. As the years go by, moreover, they may begin to close off to the world, even while remaining just as open with each other.

Although Capricorn III's generally need to be the boss in most relationships, here that overpowering drive is muted a bit. Nor do powerful Libra III's need to take the helm, as long as they aren't prevented from forwarding their ideas and translating them into action. Capricorn III and Libra III form a square aspect in the zodiac (where they lie 90° apart), a position that can sometimes cause friction and stress, but in this case such irritants most often give the relationship a forward push. The Capricorn III–Libra III combination has a tendency toward procrastination, but its slight impatience can periodically give it a shove, ideally in the right direction.

Love affairs and marriages in this combination are not always completely stable. They may from time to time be rocked by dissension, with the partners stubbornly refusing to give in on most issues. Although these two do have the ability to express love and sympathy, their greater need seems to be keeping their own individuality, so that they will often make a point of not compromising, or will make up only after the argument has subsided. That both partners can be brutally honest may make things better in the long run but is extremely trying in the short term.

Friends and siblings of the same sex are particularly close. Work relationships in this combination do best when the two parties are co-workers rather than business partners or boss-employee pairs.

ADVICE: *Soften your stance. Learn the value of diplomacy and compromise. Don't abandon your ideals. Minimize stress whenever possible.*

October 11–18
THE WEEK OF THEATER
LIBRA III

January 17–22
THE CUSP OF MYSTERY & IMAGINATION
CAPRICORN-AQUARIUS CUSP

STRENGTHS: **IMAGINATIVE, IMPLEMENTATIVE, ENTERTAINING**

WEAKNESSES: **FAIR-WEATHER, OVERSTIMULATED, FRAZZLED**

BEST: **WORK**

WORST: **FRIENDSHIP**

A Stimulus Requirement

This couple is attracted to innovative ideas and endeavors. Wordplay and witty or caustic repartee are typical here, but this constant verbal or mental activity can strain the relationship. Capricorn-Aquarians love to dream up novel projects, which Libra III's wait in the wings to implement; yet the relationship can be stymied by Capricorn-Aquarius temper, which can stupefy Libra III's, rendering them inactive. They, for their part, may detract from the relationship by simply refusing to see the Capricorn-Aquarius point of view. Given the relationship's emphasis on the mental rather than the physical or emotional, it may not be strong enough to sustain such dynamic interaction.

Romances and marriages in this combination search endlessly for change. Both Libra III's and Capricorn-Aquarians bore easily and require a lot of stimulus—which isn't always for the best, for overstimulation can bring frazzled nerves and, eventually, collapse. Learning to avoid excess, and to be content with moderate activity and interest, is vital to the relationship's health.

Friendships in this combination easily form a mutual-admiration society and often don't run deep. In fact, although these two will enjoy each other's company during good times, they may be unavailable to each other in times of stress or illness. Capricorn-Aquarius parents will probably find their Libra III children highly entertaining but can also be hard on them, seeing them as not really serious about making something of themselves. Libra III parents, on the other hand, can be protective and supportive of their imaginative Capricorn-Aquarian children. In the professional world, this matchup has enough charisma for an army—it can talk anyone into anything. It could do well in public relations, sales or marketing, whether in a freelance or a corporate setting. It could also prosper running a small, aggressive enterprise, but Libra III's and Capricorn-Aquarians should watch the books: they can both be good at making money but are even better at spending it freely, which can make a hash of financial planning.

ADVICE: *Find the middle way. Avoid extremes. Scale back your need for stimulation. Find a quiet place within. Seek spiritual values.*

JEROME ROBBINS (10/11/18)
GEORGE BALANCHINE (1/22/04)

Robbins and Balanchine are among the 20th century's most distinguished figures in the ballet world. In the 70s and 80s they shared positions as ballet masters of the NYC Ballet, each creating prodigious choreography combining American and European dance traditions. *Also:* **Tex McCrary & Jinx Falkenberg** (married; radio co-stars); **Lillian Gish & D.W. Griffith** (actress protégé/director).

October 11–18
THE WEEK OF THEATER
LIBRA III

January 23–30
THE WEEK OF GENIUS
AQUARIUS I

STRENGTHS: **UNIQUE, CREATIVE, PROTECTIVE**

WEAKNESSES: **ISOLATED, STRANGE, OVERDEPENDENT**

BEST: **LOVE**

WORST: **WORK**

Atmospheric Electricity

This one-of-a-kind relationship impresses by its uniqueness. Although it can be enormously original and productive, however, it can equally well be quirky and difficult to reach. Whether it takes a positive tack or immerses itself in its own peculiarities depends not so much on the partners' talents and abilities as on their attitude, and also on when they meet. Should they get together after an experience of rejection and disappointment, for example, they may adopt a to-hell-with-it attitude and escape into a mutually protective relationship. But if they meet when young and unspoiled, they may try to set the world on fire with their own brand of idealism.

In love affairs, Libra III's can be fascinated by their free-spirited Aquarius I partners, who, for their part, may rely heavily on Libra III's for support and direction. Passions can run high here, since the relationship brings out the temperamental aspects of both partners, guaranteeing an electric atmosphere for a good deal of the time. For Libra III's, the relationship will bring out their enjoyment of the full range of their own mental powers; for Aquarius I's, it will emphasize their more sensual side. Marriages are unlikely to have much permanence in the conventional sense but may offer interesting possibilities if the partners are open to them.

In friendships and sibling relationships, creativity appears less in what this relationship produces than in what it embodies. The partners are likely to put all their energy into the relationship itself, which becomes their creative focus. Where others would work on a house, car or educational program, these two may invest time, energy and money in building something solid between them that can survive over the long haul. Disillusionment can hit such idealism like a sledgehammer. Work and business relationships between Libra III's and Aquarius I's can be highly successful artistically but may go bust unless built on a firm financial foundation. These two often want to form their own business but find they need the security that only a larger organization can offer.

ADVICE: *Back off a bit—you may be trying too hard. Seek the creative solutions that will be your legacy. Beware of setting yourself up for disappointment.*

FRANKLIN ROOSEVELT (1/30/1882)
ELEANOR ROOSEVELT (10/11/1884)

Franklin and Eleanor met at a dance in 1899 when she was 15. After a long courtship, the distant cousins were married in 1905. Through the years they complemented one another, each becoming a historic national figure with strong influence on the other's socioeconomic view. *Also:* **Charles Sumner Greene & Henry Mather Greene** (brothers; architects); **Rita Hayworth & Victor Mature** (engaged; actors).

STRENGTHS: **TRUSTING,
FLEXIBLE, DARING**

WEAKNESSES: **OVERAMBITIOUS,
CARELESS, GULLIBLE**

BEST: **FRIENDSHIP**

WORST: **FAMILY**

JIMMY BRESLIN (10/17/30)
NORMAN MAILER (1/31/23)

Breslin and Mailer are both writers known for their fearless, if not arrogant, stances against the establishment. In an effort to effect change, they ran for office in the 1969 NYC mayoral race. They lost. **Also:**

Dwight Eisenhower & Adlai Stevenson (1952, 1956 presidential opponents); **McLean Stevenson & Adlai Stevenson** (son/father; actor/politician); **Ziggy Marley & Bob Marley** (son/father; musicians).

October 11–18
THE WEEK OF THEATER
LIBRA III

January 31–February 7
THE WEEK OF YOUTH & EASE
AQUARIUS II

Casting Fate to the Wind

This highly ambitious combination may go for the top, whether or not the partners' expectations are realistic. The devil-may-care attitude that may prevail here will seem irresponsible to some people but may just show a lot of trust in the workings of chance or destiny. The relationship may encourage its partners to feel they have little to lose and a great deal to gain by casting their fate to the wind. It will allow Libra III's to relax, which they sorely need to do, and will give Aquarius II's the opportunity to get their teeth into substantial projects with the potential to advance their interests. Both partners will want to give their all to a relationship that shows such promise.

Friendships, love affairs and marriages are generally concerned with something greater than pleasure or physical satisfaction: they usually have some sense of purpose, even if the goal is not immediately clear. Over the years, they will eventually reveal their true meaning, which can come as a surprise to the partners but may fulfill a vague feeling they have had all along. Other Libra III and Aquarius II friends and lovers will be quite content with what they have, and have no idea of attaining anything else—yet even here, sudden changes probably lie in wait.

Whether they be competitors or colleagues, rivals or allies, as a professional pair Libra III's and Aquarius II's are a study in contrasts, with Aquarius II's usually proving the more unpredictable of the two. Usually well suited to each other, this pair makes a fascinating study for fellow co-workers. If it appears at the executive level of a company or social organization, progressive change is to be expected. In the family, Libra III–Aquarius II siblings of the same sex can be overdemanding, expecting more from parents and relatives than they can give.

ADVICE: *Don't ask more from others than you are prepared to give yourself. Leaving everything up to fate may be taking the easy way out.*

STRENGTHS: **HONEST, OPEN,
GENEROUS**

WEAKNESSES: **NAIVE,
UNREALISTIC, UNCOMMITTED**

BEST: **LOVE**

WORST: **FRIENDSHIP**

BENITA HUME (10/14/06)
RONALD COLMAN (2/9/1891)

Hume was a London stage actress who made her movie debut in 1925. She played dignified roles in a number of British and Hollywood films until she married romantic lead actor Colman in 1938, when she retired from the screen. **Also:**

Lotte Lenya & Bertolt Brecht (collaborators; actress/playwright); **Wendy Wilson & Chynna Phillips** (celebrity children formed Wilson Phillips rock group).

October 11–18
THE WEEK OF THEATER
LIBRA III

February 8–15
THE WEEK OF ACCEPTANCE
AQUARIUS III

An Open-Door Policy

This relationship carries with it a unique brand of generosity, whether of feelings or of finances, and an inherent optimism. Committed to honesty and openness, Libra III's and Aquarius III's will find it difficult to hide things from each other, not so much out of a need to reveal the truth, or a moral imperative, but simply because they prefer it that way. This is partly because their relationship doesn't fixate on details but tries to understand the larger picture, so that any one detail, or secret, may not have that much importance. Although both Libra and Aquarius are air signs, the relationship between them is ruled by fire, which, in this case, indicates following intuition and not holding back.

Generous and spontaneous though the relationship may ultimately be, love, marriage and sibling matchups will put these attitudes to the test. The partners being only human, they may feel jealousy, competition and possessiveness in relation to each other, but they will strive to overcome and let go of such responses, and are usually successful. The feelings between them are seldom of the heavy sort that lead to depressions or power struggles, and should the relationship be a love affair, this can be a great relief for both partners after quite different experiences with other people. They will enjoy this matchup, then. Even so, they may be unwilling to invest what it takes to make a long-lasting relationship possible.

Friendships in this combination are usually less successful than acquaintanceships or other, more casual kinds of companionships. There is an easy trine aspect between Libra III and Aquarius III, which lie 120° apart in the zodiac; in general, then, this duo prefers the casual approach. As co-workers in professional relationships, Libra III's and Aquarius III's may get into trouble when they expect their colleagues or rivals to be as up front as they are. A certain naïveté in the relationship can be counterproductive or worse in the business world.

ADVICE: *Let up in your intensity. Be more forgiving and forgetting. Let the good times roll. Don't be uptight, it's only money. Power isn't everything.*

October 11–18
THE WEEK OF THEATER
LIBRA III

February 16–22
THE CUSP OF SENSITIVITY
AQUARIUS-PISCES CUSP

 RELATIONSHIPS

STRENGTHS: **ROMANTIC, UNDERSTANDING, INEVITABLE**

WEAKNESSES: **UNPREPARED, DISILLUSIONED, FRUSTRATED**

BEST: **LOVE**

WORST: **PARENT-CHILD**

Across Space and Time

This highly romantic relationship will often go like a house on fire at the start. Few would predict these two would even like each other, but subtle magnetic feelings draw them together irresistibly. It is one of those relationships in which the partners seem to call out to each other silently across the boundaries of space and time. They may be fated to meet, and once they are in each other's company there seems to be no force in the universe strong enough to keep them apart.

Although fully committed, however, such relationships don't always have staying power. Disappointment and disillusionment will follow any separation or breakup, for which no preparation is generally possible: to this starry-eyed duo, the future stretches out unendingly, replete with all the joys life has to offer. External resistance may be easy for such a pair to handle in the early stages, but the relationship may be worn down over time by a dedicated, purposeful opponent.

As friends, this pair can be mutually protective and extremely understanding of each other's needs. Even so, the requirements of their careers and family life are usually so great that the relationship will show signs of strain over the lack of time being available for it. In the family, Libra III parents may be too demanding and critical of their ultrasensitive Aquarius-Pisces offspring, in whose lives they may occupy an overly dominant role that can continue on into adulthood. Liberation from such attitudes will be difficult.

In the work sphere, co-worker and boss-employee relationships in this combination are not usually destined to succeed, at least not without a struggle. Libra III's are likely to appear overdominant to Aquarius-Pisces, who have their own brand of ambition to express; meanwhile, Aquarius-Pisces may be much too defensive and secretive for Libra III tastes.

PRINCE ANDREW (2/19/60)
SARAH FERGUSON (10/15/59)

Ferguson ("Fergie") and Andrew were marred in 1986 in what was thought to be the perfect match between a fun-loving worldly lass and happy-go-lucky hedonist. But her extramarital gaffes led to their separation in '92. Now divorced, the royal pair are good friends and are rumored to have an ongoing affair. *Also:* **Kelly Preston & John Travolta** (married; actors).

ADVICE: *Hang in there. Try to see things as they are. Get tough or risk going under. Don't turn a blind eye toward aggressors. Kindness has limits.*

October 11–18
THE WEEK OF THEATER
LIBRA III

February 23–March 2
THE WEEK OF SPIRIT
PISCES I

RELATIONSHIPS

STRENGTHS: **UNIFIED, WISE, FORESIGHTFUL**

WEAKNESSES: **SELFISH, UNPREDICTABLE, IMPATIENT**

BEST: **WORK**

WORST: **LOVE**

Inherent Wisdom

The Libra III–Pisces I relationship has a certain inherent wisdom about it—it often seems to sense where its best interests lie. These two can touch each other's lives at a deep level, and often assume some sort of responsibility for each other. At its best, then, the relationship can be faithful and unified, with the partners sooner or later realizing that their greatest advantage lies in staying together and working for the common good. Unfortunately, this realization may not be forthcoming: one of the partners may break off the relationship in a fit of impatience, or after meeting another person with whom he or she is more totally absorbed.

Love affairs here are somewhat unpredictable, since these two are often preoccupied with their own interests, which can call them away at any moment. When together, though, they have a passionate, sensual time of it. Libra III–Pisces I lovers should seriously consider the further step of marriage, which could well lend greater unity and permanence to their relationship. When meeting a new and interesting person, the partners should share this friendship, introducing the new figure into their social and family circle.

As friends, Libra III's and Pisces I's may be fascinated by gambling, playing the stock market, figuring out odds—by activities, in other words that depend not only on predicting the future but also on backing up one's beliefs with action. Work relationships in this combination can be highly imaginative and productive. Whether collaborating on business, artistic or social projects, both partners will use their strengths—Libra III's to lead, Pisces I's to give spiritual inspiration. Sibling combinations, particularly of the opposite sex, may silently resolve to further the family's interests when young and preserve them when older.

LOTTE LENYA (10/18/1898)
KURT WEILL (3/2/1900)

Actress-singer Lenya married composer Weill in 1926. He is best known for his collaboration with Bertolt Brecht on *The Threepenny Opera* (1928) and she for her role as Jenny in the same musical work. *Also:* **Robert Walker & Jennifer Jones** (married; actors); **Arthur M. Schlesinger, Jr. & Arthur M. Schlesinger** (son/father; historians); **Richard & Karen Carpenter** (brother/sister; singing duo).

ADVICE: *Put your relationship first. Learn to share what is most valuable to you. Develop patience. Curb your impulses. Think things over carefully.*

**PENNY MARSHALL (10/15/43)
ROB REINER (3/6/45)**

When Marshall and Reiner were married (1971–79), they were rising tv actors—she in *The Odd Couple* and he in *All in the Family*. Since then both have gone on to become major film directors and producers. *Also:* **Margot Kidder & John Heard** (married; actors); **George C. Scott & Trish Van Devere** (married; actors); **Paul Simon & Edie Brickell** (married; singer-composers).

October 11–18

THE WEEK OF THEATER
LIBRA III

Years of Work

March 3–10

THE WEEK OF THE LONER
PISCES II

This combination often focuses on forging a strong bond of empathy. Emotional understanding is not immediately forthcoming between Libra III's and Pisces II's, and their relationship usually needs many years of work to build trust and acceptance. It is also troubled by a tendency to take the easy way out—to withdraw or even give up during times of crisis. Although the relationship can be extremely productive and successful, dealing with personal problems is not really its forte.

In love affairs, Pisces II's can become inaccessible just when Libra III's need them most. (In sex particularly, Libra III's can make demands that are too heavy for Pisces II's to meet.) In turn, Libra III's may be unable to handle the emotional needs of Pisces II's or to give them the attention they require. Despite such ups and downs, however, Libra III's and Pisces II's do have a certain magic that could enable them to get along remarkably well. If they can work out certain compromises and adjust to each other in these and other areas, they could even attempt marriage. If not, they had better forget about it.

In parent-child relationships where the Libra III is the parent, there are often tremendous gaps between what the Pisces II child needs and what the Libra III is prepared to provide. A Pisces II in a relationship with a more distant Libra III relative, who can give more freely on a less regular basis, may do much better, with fewer disappointments and frustrated expectations.

Libra III's and Pisces II's often combine friendship with work. As a matter of fact, it may be necessary for them to have a close personal relationship in order to work together well. This can mean spending a lot of time together, perhaps even living and working under the same roof. Between uninterrupted work sessions, it is best for these couples to schedule periods of time apart.

ADVICE: *Scale back needs and demands. Don't expect too much. Compromise is crucial to continuing. Don't lose patience; the goal is worthwhile.*

**LILLIAN GISH (10/14/1896)
DOROTHY GISH (3/11/1898)**

The Gish sisters were early Hollywood beauties whose entire lives revolved around movies. Lillian, the "First Lady of the Silent Screen," was a great dramatic actress, while Dorothy excelled in pantomime and light comedy. Both were popular in their time and shared the screen in several movies. In 1920 Lillian directed her sister in *Remodeling Her Husband*.

October 11–18

THE WEEK OF THEATER
LIBRA III

Answering the Question

March 11–18

THE WEEK OF DANCERS & DREAMERS
PISCES III

Who is the boss here? The question touches many areas of this relationship. It isn't that there are invariably power struggles between these two, however, but only that the question must be answered. Determining who plays the dominant role at certain times or in certain circumstances is important, since both of these partners will usually respect and follow whichever of them takes the lead. As a matter of fact, the best situation possible is often when this pair itself assumes a commanding role in a group or organization, demanding that Libra III's and Pisces III's share the reins of power equally.

In the zodiac, Libra III and Pisces III lie quincunx to each other (150° apart), which can reinforce a tendency to instability in their love affairs and marriages. And in fact indecision may plague the relationship, with both partners unable to make up their minds on the direction in which they want the relationship to continue, or whether it is to end. In friendships, it can happen that neither party is interested in taking the lead or exerting real power over the other, and this can deprive the relationship of direction, so that it drifts. To get it back on track, either one of its partners may have to make some firm decisions, and carry them through.

Professional and family matchups are often very successful. Giving direction to the group may be a specialty of this pair, whether as executives or siblings. Boss-employee and parent-child matchups in this combination can also be successful if the employees and children, again whether Libra III or Pisces III, are agreeable to their boss or parent's approach. The danger may be that the authority figure exerts an undue influence on those dependent on them for direction, and thus comes to dominate their lives and stunt their individual initiative. The principal challenge for the boss or parent, again of either sign, may be to encourage their employees or children to take more initiative and think for themselves.

ADVICE: *Don't be afraid to take the lead. Direction is needed—you may have to supply it. Strengthen your will to avoid indecision.*

October 19–25

THE CUSP OF DRAMA & CRITICISM
LIBRA-SCORPIO CUSP

October 19–25

THE CUSP OF DRAMA & CRITICISM
LIBRA-SCORPIO CUSP

Letting Go

Libra-Scorpios are not easy people to get along with, and when two of them get together, an extremely complex relationship can result. Demanding and particular, they will find it difficult to live together. If this relationship is to succeed, then, it must feature agreements on matters of, for example, taste—furnishing, design, color. Domestic questions like these can become a whole world of controversy. Add to them others like what diet to follow, where to settle or how to set up financial or tax structures, and this relationship may demand hours, days, even years in endless pro-and-con discussions before any subject is settled.

Some topics can be much easier to deal with. Being open to social gatherings and regular visits from friends is seldom a problem; nor is an endless variety of intellectual discussion and debate. In the latter respect, Libra-Scorpios can be a wonderful match for each other—stimulating, engrossing and perhaps more strongly driven by either purely conscious or purely unconscious impulses than most.

Love affairs, marriages and friendships between Libra-Scorpios will often feature the same head-heart split that these two grapple with as individuals. Two Libra-Scorpios on the same mental or emotional wavelength have a chance to reach the heights together, but when the feelings of one butt up against the thoughts of the other, consternation and chaos will reign. Arguments can be severe and constant but will rarely result in the kind of irreparable damage that will lead to separation or breakup, since most fights and cross words will be taken with a grain of salt. The other side of Libra-Scorpio intensity is an extreme kind of relaxation and conviviality, in which all is forgotten. Although Libra-Scorpio pairs often are not faithful in the conventional sense, they can be extremely loyal to each other, devoting themselves to each other completely. Sibling and co-worker combinations can be very close and understanding of each other and can get along well on a daily basis.

ADVICE: *Let things be boring sometimes. Learn to relax. Try to find the middle ground between your head and your heart. Let things go without discussion.*

October 19–25

THE CUSP OF DRAMA & CRITICISM
LIBRA-SCORPIO CUSP

October 26–November 2

THE WEEK OF INTENSITY
SCORPIO I

Hot Debate

This can be a productive matchup, replete with good feeling, or it can fritter its time away in debates and arguments. Part of the problem here is deciding who will take control or make the major decisions; it is often impossible for these two to come to a mutual agreement, and if any situation is to be resolved, one partner must take a leadership role. It is at this point that power struggles usually surface, sometimes resulting in a no-win situation where things just wind up staying the way they are. Actually, both partners may prefer it that way, since they secretly enjoy the debate and stimulation that would be eliminated by agreement or strong leadership. This relationship is often paradoxical: it seems to involve strong-minded individuals who know what they want, yet they are beset by indecision, and by fuzzy, even irrational thinking. Beneath their daily interactions lies a streak of perversity that sometimes threatens to subvert all their constructive efforts. This self-destructive tendency undercuts many Libra-Scorpio–Scorpio I endeavors. If, however, the pair can devise a way of reaching agreement, such as giving up their power struggles, they may find they get along quite well.

Love affairs and marriages in this combination can be lively, even hectic and stressful. Sexual interaction goes either like a house on fire or not at all—an extreme reflected elsewhere as well. Sympathy and understanding, for example, can alternate with coldness and incomprehension, leaving both partners uncertain, frustrated and bewildered.

Friendships and parent-child relationships in this combination can be very affectionate—these two often seem to have eyes only for each other. In fact, they can sometimes make others in the vicinity feel left out, a problem of which they themselves may be blissfully unaware. This is rather unusual behavior for two individuals who value attentiveness and conscious awareness. At work, Libra-Scorpios and Scorpio I's can make an excellent combination. Objectivity triumphs and personal differences are prevented from interfering, as both partners concentrate on the materials at hand and the goals to be achieved.

ADVICE: *Stand back and take a look at yourself. Be aware of the forces driving you. Decide to end self-destructive behavior. Strengthen your willpower.*

 RELATIONSHIPS

STRENGTHS: **STIMULATING, CONVIVIAL, COMMITTED**

WEAKNESSES: **CONTENTIOUS, CHAOTIC, UNFAITHFUL**

BEST: **FRIENDSHIP**

WORST: **LOVE**

RICHARD BYRD (10/25/1888)
FLOYD BENNETT (10/25/1890)

Besides sharing the same birthday, Byrd and Bennett won medals of honor for being the first to fly over the North Pole (1926). Byrd was an aviator and explorer, Bennett an aviator and ace mechanic. On the celebrated trip, Byrd served as Bennett's navigator. **Also: Rose Dolly & Jenny Dolly** (sisters; vaudeville stars).

RELATIONSHIPS

STRENGTHS: **PRODUCTIVE, ATTENTIVE, AFFECTIONATE**

WEAKNESSES: **UNAWARE, MISUNDERSTANDING, STRESSED**

BEST: **WORK**

WORST: **MARRIAGE**

TIMOTHY LEARY (10/22/20)
WINONA RYDER (10/29/71)

Utopian guru Leary was the godfather of intense Hollywood actress Ryder. (Her father was Leary's archivist.) In the 60s, Leary was ejected from Harvard for sharing LSD with undergraduates and soon became an icon for the hippie generation. Ryder spent part of her childhood in a hippie commune in California. **Also: Jean Dausset & Baruj Benacerraf** (1980 Nobelists, genetics).

STRENGTHS: **TRUSTWORTHY, HONORABLE, TALENTED**

WEAKNESSES: **UNFORGIVING, INCOMPATIBLE, FRUSTRATED**

BEST: **SEXUAL**

WORST: **FRIENDSHIP**

ART CARNEY (11/4/18)
JOYCE RANDOLF (10/21/25)

Randolf and Carney co-starred on Jackie Gleason's *The Honeymooners* (1952–70), one of early tv's most popular series, which enjoyed reruns through the 90s. Carney was Ed Norton, a city sewer-worker who was at once dimwitted and graceful; Randolf played his doting wife Trixie. *Also:* **Will Rogers, Jr. & Will Rogers** (son/father; actor/humorist); **Sarah Bernhardt & Edward VII** (affair; actress/royal).

October 19–25
THE CUSP OF DRAMA & CRITICISM
LIBRA-SCORPIO CUSP

November 3–11
THE WEEK OF DEPTH
SCORPIO II

Buildup of Intensity

The Libra-Scorpio–Scorpio II relationship features a gradual buildup of intensity that is both its strength and its weakness. The relationship can focus on developing deeply nurturing bonds of trust and honor, but once these begin to materialize, the stakes go up—the partners expect more, judge more and forgive less, so that the relationship doesn't always last long enough for such bonds to emerge fully. Although they can have great times together, these two can eventually get on each other's nerves or become frustrated with each other, necessitating time apart now and then. Bitterness and vituperation can be the unhappy accompaniment of breakups here.

Love affairs often include strong sexual expression that can continue unabated throughout marriages of quite long standing. The difficulties likely to drive these two apart are usually not physical but emotional: what begins as a simple argument or disagreement can build to a terrifying crescendo. Too many of these scenes finally end in mutual rejection. The partners should be extremely careful to nip them in the bud and never, under any circumstances, ignore their importance or let them get out of control.

In friendships, Scorpio II's often make demands that Libra-Scorpios find hard to meet. Libra-Scorpios, for their part, have a talent for biting disapproval that may be more than Scorpio II's can handle; stung to the quick, Scorpio II's are likely to withdraw their affection, retreating into a world of hurt and self-pity. Sibling relationships in this combination, particularly when the two are of the same sex, have an unrelenting intensity about them that makes it difficult for the partners to relax and have fun in an easy way. The relationship too often involves guilt and blame, particularly if parental disagreements turn up the tension. Objectively, Libra-Scorpios and Scorpio II's can be well suited to each other, with shared talents and interests. Emotional incompatibilities, however, usually prevent work relationships between these two from becoming successful.

ADVICE: *Let up the pressure a bit. Beware of feeling sorry for yourself. Try to be a little more emotionally understanding.*

STRENGTHS: **INSTRUCTIVE, INTERESTED, MATURING**

WEAKNESSES: **OBSESSIVE, STAGNATING, CONTROLLING**

BEST: **FRIENDSHIP**

WORST: **PARENT-CHILD**

MOSS HART (10/24/04)
GEORGE S. KAUFMAN (11/16/1889)

Hart and Kaufman were brilliant dramatists and directors who collaborated as playwrights on some of America's funniest and most successful stage comedies, among them *Once in a Lifetime* (1930), the Pulitzer Prize-winning *You Can't Take It with You* (1936), and *The Man Who Came to Dinner* (1939)—all 3 made into movies.

October 19–25
THE CUSP OF DRAMA & CRITICISM
LIBRA-SCORPIO CUSP

November 12–18
THE WEEK OF CHARM
SCORPIO III

Pruning and Cultivating

This combination, like wine, often gets better over time. There is a limit, however, to how long its maturation will go on if it gets too little attention—the relationship has a tendency to stagnate, and then to start fraying around the edges. It needs care and hard work to keep moving in the right direction. These two have an innate talent for tending to their relationships, but unfortunately, in this case, they can be blindsided and may just leave this one alone. To survive, then, the relationship needs good diagnosticians, and, indeed, the matchup's focus is often the understanding of its own mechanics.

Love affairs and marriages usually find the partners taking an all-consuming interest in each other. This is not the same thing, of course, as paying attention to the relationship itself, which may be sorely in need. Partners can get obsessive about each other, perhaps even jealous and controlling, without realizing that this behavior itself may loosen the relationship's bonds rather than strengthen them. Learning to back off, give each other space and work objectively on improving the relationship, much as one would prune and cultivate a plant, will produce noticeable drops in tension and forestall problems.

Parent-child and boss-employee relationships generally work out better when it is the Scorpio III in the role of parent or boss. In both the family and the commercial spheres, however, sibling and co-worker matchups are usually more successful, since these partners do better on a more equal footing. As friends, Libra-Scorpios can give excellent advice to their Scorpio III companions, who, in turn, can supply important lessons in how to build willpower and consistency. Should the two meet as students, they will probably be absorbed and united more by a common interest, as the years pass, than by their personal feelings for each other.

ADVICE: *Don't take things for granted. Regular maintenance is needed. Things won't get better by themselves. Be your own best diagnostician.*

October 19–25
THE CUSP OF DRAMA & CRITICISM
LIBRA-SCORPIO CUSP

November 19–24
THE CUSP OF REVOLUTION
SCORPIO-SAGITTARIUS CUSP

A Fragile Balance

STRENGTHS: **FULFILLING, FASCINATING, DEEP**

WEAKNESSES: **COMPETITIVE, ENVIOUS, IMMATURE**

BEST: **LOVE**

WORST: **SIBLING**

BELA LUGOSI (10/20/1882)
BORIS KARLOFF (11/23/1887)

This relationship can be unexpectedly emotional for both partners. These characters view themselves, and each other, as pretty cool customers, so they may be amazed at the feelings engendered in them by the other person's presence. Another surprise element here is the shadow qualities or dark side of the partners' psyches that are likely to emerge. Grappling with these could prove emotionally tumultuous. Indeed, emotion may become the focus of this sensitive and complex relationship. The partners will find themselves unconsciously fascinated by the depth of their feelings for each other and may seek to restrict other relationships and even their careers in order to spend more time alone together. Libra-Scorpios will be attracted to Scorpio-Sagittarius incisiveness, taste and feeling for power, while Scorpio-Sagittarians will admire Libra-Scorpio mental ability and, often, physical appearance.

Love affairs here can be long-lived and fulfilling. The sexual relationship usually develops more fully over time, and blends well with feelings of friendliness and respect. Animosity and competition are usually minimal here, and lovemaking is usually complementary rather than competitive or dominating. This can prove a great relief to both partners, who are often engaged in power struggles in other areas of their lives. Marriage, however, is not always a good idea here, since fixed commitments and heavy responsibilities may disturb the fragile balance of emotions between these lovers. Friends and siblings in this combination find their relationship more supportive as the years go by. As schoolmates, they may be competitive, trying to dominate each other academically, socially or in sports, despite any age difference. Fighting for the attention of shared friends is especially common. The combination requires the maturity of adulthood to bring the partners into a more meaningful and productive relationship.

This matchup can make an effective team of co-workers or business partners, the Libra-Scorpio often providing the imagination and fantasy and the Scorpio-Sagittarius the shrewd insight necessary for success.

ADVICE: *You may be neglecting certain responsibilities. Mute competitive drives. Seek peace and harmony. Don't disturb what is going well.*

Lugosi and Karloff have never been surpassed as horror-film actors. Karloff got his big break as the monster in *Frankenstein* (1931), a role that Lugosi turned down while filming *Dracula* (1931). They later appeared together in many movies, forming the most macabre and awesome duo in film. Karloff was considered the better actor, Lugosi the stronger screen personality.

October 19–25
THE CUSP OF DRAMA & CRITICISM
LIBRA-SCORPIO CUSP

November 25–December 2
THE WEEK OF INDEPENDENCE
SAGITTARIUS I

Fits of Temper

STRENGTHS: **CONCERNED, UNAFFECTED, SPONTANEOUS**

WEAKNESSES: **UNSTABLE, TEMPESTUOUS, EXPLOSIVE**

BEST: **MARRIAGE**

WORST: **WORK**

PABLO PICASSO (10/25/1881)
FRANÇOISE GILOT (11/26/21)

Little is held back in this relationship. It sweeps its partners away in a whirlwind of exciting confrontations, both physical and verbal, that allow little room for objective thought or detachment. The relationship values natural behavior and honesty highly, yet it may not be very sharing—these partners are capable of living at quite close quarters together without having a whole lot to do with each other. Tensions will be eased if each has his or her own inviolable space, completely beyond the jurisdiction or watchful eye of the other partner. The problem here is that both Libra-Scorpios and Sagittarius I's have a lot to say about each other's habits. It may sometimes be hard for them to back off, or to mute their criticism or concern.

In matters of love, this relationship is often unstable and incendiary. Fits of temper or passion are likely to burst loose at almost any moment; harmony and emotional balance are hard to maintain. Furthermore, although Libra-Scorpios will be relieved to be able to be honest with their Sagittarius I partner (who, in turn, will benefit from—without always enjoying—Libra-Scorpio powers of observation), this may also mean that these two may not really be interested in keeping things artificially cool or polite. Marriage may help to channel the relationship's wild energies in the right direction. Having children can also bring it a bit more calm, although those children will often feel seismic tremors threatening to break loose beneath the surface of their parents' relationship.

Parent-child relationships, in fact, can have their own intensity, and can feature serious and long-lasting struggles, with like and dislike, love and hate, respect and disrespect alternating with bewildering speed. The bond is a deep one, however. Friendship between these two can also be characterized by volatility, but shared activities may provide at least a modicum of stability. Work relationships between Libra-Scorpios and Sagittarius I's are not recommended—extreme differences in temperament often emerge.

ADVICE: *Work hard on controlling your emotions. Be honest but diplomatic. Be aware when the temperature starts to rise. Mind your own business.*

Three times her age, Picasso married Gilot just after WWII. She modeled for him, was intelligent, beautiful and independent—and a painter of some promise, in his mind. Art bridged their age gap, as did their 2 children, Claude and Paloma. *Also:* **Sonny Terry & Brownie McGhee** (blues duet); **Mickey Mantle & Joe DiMaggio** (NY Yankees baseball sluggers).

DON KING (12/6/32)
EVANDER HOLYFIELD (10/19/62)

King is considered boxing's most aggressive and controversial promoter. Heavyweight champ Holyfield had never been receptive to King's earlier offers, but in order to secure his 1996 title fight with Mike Tyson, he was forced to let King promote the match. Holyfield won.

Also: **Pablo Picasso & Wassily Kandinsky** (modernists; opposing esthetics); **Albert Boni & Horace Liveright** (NY publishers).

October 19–25

THE CUSP OF DRAMA & CRITICISM
LIBRA-SCORPIO CUSP

December 3–10

THE WEEK OF THE ORIGINATOR
SAGITTARIUS II

Capturing Hearts

This relationship is often competitive, sometimes in each partner's desire for the attention of a mutual friend, lover or family member. Both individuals here exert all their charm to capture the heart of this third party. In a very subtle way, it is not the other person they are especially interested in, but each other; this vying for affection is a subtle mechanism that they use to work out certain problems of which they are usually quite unaware. It behooves both partners, then, to concentrate more on their own relationship and try to come to grips with it.

Love affairs and marriages in this combination can be both affectionate and passionate but are too often caught up in emotional triangles. The third person is often a friend who spends a great deal of time with one partner or the other. In psychological terms, this person may in fact represent a figure from the relevant partner's childhood—a person who withheld approval and love. Libra-Scorpios and Sagittarius II's will go to great lengths to gain the affection of such a figure but will rarely go so far as to endanger their own relationship.

Friends and siblings in this combination will likewise be very competitive, seeking the attention of other friends or of parents. Sagittarius II's will have a tendency to retreat into their own private world and nurse slights and hurts, their Libra-Scorpio partners meanwhile showing little concern for their feelings. In the professional sphere, Sagittarius II talent and imagination can meld with Libra-Scorpio purposefulness, but too often both partners prefer to go their own way and develop their own approach. Their working relationship does best, then, when they can consult and advise each other as colleagues and are not placed in a fixed position as co-workers.

ADVICE: *Deepen your understanding. Eliminate competition whenever possible. Try to be honest about your feelings. Games can hurt others.*

GILBERT ROLAND (12/11/05)
CONSTANCE BENNETT (10/22/04)

Actress Bennett made her screen debut at 17 and grew into a popular leading lady of the silent screen and, later, talkies. She was married 5 times. One of her husbands (1941–45) was dashing Latin lover Roland , who had a long career in both leading and supporting roles. His first film was in 1925 and his last was made in 1982.

October 19–25

THE CUSP OF DRAMA & CRITICISM
LIBRA-SCORPIO CUSP

December 11–18

THE WEEK OF THE TITAN
SAGITTARIUS III

A Penchant for Excess

The combination of these strong-willed individuals is likely to involve clashes; they usually have enough respect for each other's strength, however, to avoid direct confrontations. Furthermore, their relationship may well allow them to put their prodigious energies in the service of a common cause, and this can alleviate their personal difficulties. Libra-Scorpios have a way of bringing out the insecurities of seemingly impervious Sagittarius III's, who may come to depend on Libra-Scorpio intellect and insight to tell them what needs to be done, on both the personal and the professional front. Sagittarius III's, who are more than a little prone to self-deception, may also come to value Libra-Scorpio honesty highly in the long run.

Marriages and career partnerships can be one and the same for Libra-Scorpios and Sagittarius III's; the combination is exceptionally strong in putting ideas into practice and realizing goals that others would find unattainable. Neither partner is likely to be awed by difficulty—in fact, this highly energetic relationship thrives on problems, which often draw the partners closer together emotionally. Love affairs between Libra-Scorpios and Sagittarius III's are usually brief and subject to burnout, since a penchant for excess here is difficult to control.

Sagittarius III's may not have enough time to spend with their Libra-Scorpio friends but will rarely forget them. This is fortunate, since Libra-Scorpios can sometimes have a strong need for their Sagittarius III friends' moral support and financial help. Nevertheless, this relationship does best when not tied down to fixed commitments or responsibilities.

Parent-child matchups in this combination find Libra-Scorpios proud of their Sagittarius III offspring but unable to control or perhaps even to guide them. Sagittarius III's may be inspiring role models for Libra-Scorpio children but are often too occupied with career questions to give them enough attention.

ADVICE: *Take more time out to have fun together. Acknowledge specific needs for one another. Moderate your energies a bit. Prolong pleasure.*

October 19–25

THE CUSP OF DRAMA & CRITICISM
LIBRA-SCORPIO CUSP

December 19–25

THE CUSP OF PROPHECY
SAGITTARIUS-CAPRICORN CUSP

STRENGTHS: **COMPLEMENTARY, EFFECTIVE, SUCCESSFUL**

WEAKNESSES: **UNPLEASANT, DESPERATE, CONFRONTATIONAL**

BEST: **WORK**

WORST: **FAMILY**

Resistance to Outdated Concepts

In some ways this is a matchup between the conscious and the unconscious: Libra-Scorpios are particularly strong in the conscious sphere, rating high in everything to do with logic, critical awareness, thought and speech, while Sagittarius-Capricorns are masters of the hidden realms that have to do with intuition and the deep, unconscious worlds of sleep, silence and the imagination. At first these two may not be attracted to each other or get along, but they may ultimately meld their talents into a complementary whole, far greater than the sum of its parts. Libra-Scorpios are ruled by the elements of air and water (symbolizing thought and feeling), while Sagittarius-Capricorns are a fire-earth combination (representing intuition and sensation). Together, then, they encompass all four elements—a powerful union. Inherent in this matchup, however, is a resistance to old-fashioned or outdated concepts, fueling the desire to overturn tradition, staid concepts of form and any type of formal structure.

Working relationships are perhaps best for these two, Libra-Scorpios contributing their intense concentration and language skills, Sagittarius-Capricorns lending powerfully persuasive and magnetic energies. This duo could run a company well, or cooperate as heads of its different departments. The connection is not tension free, quick and incisive Libra-Scorpio energies often being pitted against the slower-moving but deeper energies of Sagittarius-Capricorn—which usually triumph in the long run, through resolve and sheer stubbornness. Libra-Scorpios and Sagittarius-Capricorns are seldom well suited for friendships, love affairs and marriages—their temperamental differences generally prove too great. Sagittarius-Capricorns can certainly be physically attractive to Libra-Scorpios, but Libra-Scorpios are nevertheless likely to wound their Sagittarius-Capricorn partners through their fickle tastes and their inability to remain faithful—they demand a kind of freedom that Sagittarius-Capricorns are not prepared to give them. Family members in this combination are likely to confront each other directly and not so pleasantly. They can make daily life difficult, and so may need the option of privacy from each other.

ADVICE: *Reconcile your differences. Realize the strength of your combination and work actively to support it. Minimize confrontation. Make peace.*

COSIMA LISZT (12/24/1837)
FRANZ LISZT (10/22/1811)

Cosima was one of composer Liszt's 3 children from his long liaison with Countess Marie d'Agoult (1835–45). Cosima was raised mainly by her grandmother (Liszt's mother). Their relationship was remote—he wrote but did not see her often. He was focused on his own life and work. Her 2nd marriage, to composer Richard Wagner, enraged him.

Also: Jean Dausset & George Snell (1980 Nobelists, genetics).

October 19–25

THE CUSP OF DRAMA & CRITICISM
LIBRA-SCORPIO CUSP

December 26–January 2

THE WEEK OF THE RULER
CAPRICORN I

STRENGTHS: **COMMITTED, RESPONSIBLE, PROTECTIVE**

WEAKNESSES: **FRUSTRATING, CONFINING, DULL**

BEST: **MARRIAGE**

WORST: **LOVE**

Unattainable Ideal

For different reasons, this pair may erroneously see each other as the force of change that will bring them freedom from something or someone. The consequences of this idea are usually disastrous. First, of course, as a basic principle it can never be true, since people can only free themselves. Second, this pair is usually looking for freedom as an ideal, which, as such, is bound to be unattainable. This is how the relationship starts out. It generally ends up as an all-consuming battle consisting of many skirmishes revolving around the theme of freedom. Libra-Scorpios are apt to desire Capricorn I's in the belief that their solidity will be beneficial; unconsciously they are hoping to be freed from their own dark side, which is something they are none too comfortable with. Capricorn I's, meanwhile, are looking for the exotic—that combination of passion and refinement that Libra-Scorpios manifest but are hardly aware they possess—to free them from their structured, traditional lives. This combination carries its share of frustration. Capricorn I's may feel out of control in their relationships with Libra-Scorpios, who seem to run through their fingers like water; and Libra-Scorpios, in turn, may tire of fixed Capricorn I attitudes, which they can find confining and, ultimately, dull. The best scenario here is for the Capricorn I to become the fixed point around which the Libra-Scorpio revolves, free, to an extent, but still bound within certain limits.

Love affairs between these two can become an exercise in futility. Marriages work out better, since Libra-Scorpios often enjoy busying themselves with tasteful domestic pursuits while Capricorn I's handle practical matters. Friendships and sibling relationships in this combination are likely to suffer from endless strife, especially if Capricorn I's try to dominate their Libra-Scorpio partners. The other side of the coin, however, is protection, which Capricorn I's can offer in abundance and which Libra-Scorpios may welcome, despite their independent stance. In business, the Libra-Scorpio–Capricorn I matchup will usually function best if the two are co-workers in a large organization.

ADVICE: *Appreciate what you have. Don't ask for the impossible. Respect boundaries of privacy. Think carefully before making a commitment.*

DAVID BAILEY (1/2/36)
CATHERINE DENEUVE (10/22/43)

French actress Deneuve, who had a child with director Roger Vadim (1963) and another with actor Marcello Mastroianni (1972), was married only once—to British photographer Bailey—prior to her other liaisons. He is best known for his provocative fashion pictures. The Antonioni film *Blow-Up* (1966) was based loosely on Bailey's life. *Also:* **Franz Liszt & Countess Marie d'Agoult** (composer/mistress).

HANS VON BÜLOW (1/8/1830)
FRANZ LISZT (10/22/1811)

Conductor-pianist von Bülow studied piano with Liszt from 1851; they became close friends. In 1857 von Bülow married Liszt's daughter. When she left von Bülow 12 years later—for Richard Wagner—Liszt strongly disapproved. The friends continued their association through the years.

October 19–25

THE CUSP OF DRAMA & CRITICISM
LIBRA-SCORPIO CUSP

January 3–9

THE WEEK OF DETERMINATION
CAPRICORN II

Uncompromising Sovereignty

Since this matchup is likely to be volatile, having an explosive quality and a focus on independent action, it needs a great deal of care and diplomacy. Capricorn II's are extremely sensitive to criticism, so Libra-Scorpios need to tread carefully if the relationship is to survive. Unfortunately, this combination is not always completely realistic in its viewpoint, and it may bring itself down through a refusal to recognize its own weaknesses and limitations. Wise partners realize the difficulties facing a relationship that entails so much unwillingness to compromise sovereignty, and usually join forces in making the relationship itself a strongly independent one. In this way they are sometimes able to achieve more unrestricted expression together than either of them would be able to achieve alone.

Libra-Scorpios and Capricorn II's do particularly well in a work setup that combines partnership and friendship. A hard-driving and dynamic team, they may rebel against restrictions that they see as repressive to the human spirit. Making money is usually less important to them than fighting for ideals and freedom of thought; in consequence, they will do best in social, political or religious endeavors in which they truly believe and to which they can give themselves wholeheartedly.

Love affairs and marriages may likewise be built around idealistic pursuits in which mutual admiration and personal honor play an important role. Neither Libra-Scorpios nor Capricorn II's care much about what others think of their relationship. Self-sustaining and loyal, both partners tend to hang in for the duration.

In the family sphere, Libra-Scorpio–Capricorn II pairs may find themselves at odds with other relatives. Well aware of tradition but not always in agreement with it, they have their own ideas on how things should be done. The partners in this relationship often believe that those who are not their allies must be their enemies—to them, failing to share their enthusiasm is as great a sin as opposing them.

ADVICE: *Develop diplomacy and a spirit of compromise. Don't shut others out just because they don't agree. Take the time to explain yourself.*

HAROLD NICHOLAS (1/11/21)
FAYARD NICHOLAS (10/20/14)

The Nicholas brothers were a very popular tap-dance duo during the 30s and 40s. They performed for years at Harlem's Cotton Club, appeared in Broadway musicals and made films from '32 on. Self-taught, their act kept growing through the years. By '40 they were renowned for their acrobatic jumps, backflips and splits. Their most memorable movie was *Stormy Weather* (1943).

October 19–25

THE CUSP OF DRAMA & CRITICISM
LIBRA-SCORPIO CUSP

January 10–16

THE WEEK OF DOMINANCE
CAPRICORN III

A Bewildering Turnaround

Many difficulties arise in this often tortuous relationship. These two seem locked in a struggle to be honest with each other and to relate in a meaningful way, but at certain points in their lives their relationship can suffer breakdowns in communication that cannot be remedied, even if communication is what they want. Time is generally required before channels can be opened again, but when and how this will happen is usually dictated by circumstances outside the partners' control.

Successful love affairs are rare for this combination. Libra-Scorpios don't usually like the Capricorn III brand of control, nor do Capricorn III's always appreciate Libra-Scorpio sarcasm and biting wit. In marriages, outright power struggles can emerge, with each partner, sadly, trying to best the other. When children are involved, this pair can act in a most undignified way. It can also happen, however, that their offspring challenge them to behave more maturely.

When family members share this combination, and particularly when they are of the same sex, competition and antagonism may rule from childhood on. After a stormy adolescence, however, Libra-Scorpio–Capricorn III pairs who have been pitted against each other earlier on may slowly drift back together again. Friendships in this combination can be on again and off again, at times even manifesting antagonisms that border on real hostility. Yet sudden reversals are possible in which the partners find themselves friends again, in a bewildering turnaround.

Work relationships between Libra-Scorpios and Capricorn III's are prone to develop special, extremely personal modes of communication that are difficult for a third party to decipher. Whether using facial expressions, speech inflections or even silence to signal their approval or disapproval, they may communicate on their own wavelength. Such communication is often the real secret behind the success of their work together.

ADVICE: *Try to see the big picture. Don't give up your struggle to be more open and sharing. Give the other person a break. Forgive and forget.*

October 19–25  January 17–22

THE CUSP OF DRAMA & CRITICISM
LIBRA-SCORPIO CUSP

THE CUSP OF MYSTERY & IMAGINATION
CAPRICORN-AQUARIUS CUSP

STRENGTHS: **SEXUAL, ORIGINAL, COLORFUL**

WEAKNESSES: **ARGUMENTATIVE, BOSSY, UNCONTROLLED**

BEST: **SEXUAL**

WORST: **PARENT-CHILD**

Sure to Ignite

Sparks fly in this matchup, and something is sure to ignite—these two cusp people have a highly stimulating effect on each other. If their energies are well directed, their relationship can go to the heights. But the tension of these energies can also be so great that anything can happen—a stimulating situation, but one that could prove difficult as an ongoing state of being. Libra-Scorpio and Capricorn-Aquarius lie square to each other in the zodiac (they are 90° apart), usually a stressful position, but this particular relationship can benefit from friction, which manifests here as impulse and excitement. Highly original, it sees things differently from most others and is usually not afraid to let everyone know it.

This matchup is ruled by the element of fire, which can make its sexual relationships torrid, even scorchingly intense. But love affairs will inevitably have their share of arguments, which it is important to limit in scope—a psychological sprinkler-system designed to quench the flames is a vitally important self-regulatory mechanism. Should the relationship move on to marriage, it may cool down a bit but may also acquire a little more maturity and wisdom. The partners must be careful to take regular breaks from each other and not to let their careers wreak havoc on their personal lives.

Friendships in this combination are likely to incorporate unusual, even bizarre activities. Here the critical attitudes of Libra-Scorpios may clash with and inhibit the more natural approach of Capricorn-Aquarians. Even so, there is a synergy between the dramatic tendencies of both partners, bringing forth a vivid, colorful energy that friends and family alike will find arresting.

In general, both Libra-Scorpios and Capricorn-Aquarians do well when given the chance to be on an equal footing—they do not expect to take orders from each other. In the family and work spheres, then, sibling and co-worker matchups are usually more successful than parent-child or boss-employee duos.

ADVICE: *Learn to regulate your passions. Beware of violent impulses. Cultivate kind and loving attitudes. Direct energies constructively.*

TED SHAWN (10/21/1891)
RUTH ST. DENIS (1/20/1877)

Denishawn was the name of the dance company and network of schools founded by St. Denis and Shawn in 1915, laying the foundation for modern dance. Married in 1914, they developed their school for the next 18 years , which spawned such notables as Doris Humphrey and Martha Graham. Their marriage (and school) broke up in '32. *Also:* **Jeff Goldblum & Geena Davis** (married; actors).

October 19–25  January 23–30

THE CUSP OF DRAMA & CRITICISM
LIBRA-SCORPIO CUSP

THE WEEK OF GENIUS
AQUARIUS I

STRENGTHS: **ACTIVE, CHANGEABLE, FUN**

WEAKNESSES: **FICKLE, SUPERFICIAL, TRIVIALIZING**

BEST: **COMPANIONSHIP**

WORST: **MARRIAGE**

Temptations Along the Way

This relationship does best when kept light and easy. Its orientation is primarily mental, which does not, however, rule out a satisfactory and pleasurable physical side. The element of change plays an important role in this matchup and, although necessary, may undercut its stability. Aquarius I's are at the very least worthy opponents for Libra-Scorpio wit and wordplay, but the energy of this relationship is rarely used up in idle chatter; for this active combination, life would have little meaning without new challenges.

Love affairs and marriages are often devoted to sports, travel and culture. It is in these and other areas that this duo is likely to find the kinds of complexities and difficulties it must grapple with and, eventually, overcome. The combination tends to be high-strung, and the many temptations that offer themselves to each individual along the way can increase its natural nervousness and upset its balance and harmony. Infidelity is not the only danger area; almost any interesting byway can prove temporarily debilitating to these two. As parents, they tend to get much too involved with their children, and must concentrate on maintaining distance, objectivity and wisdom.

As friends, Libra-Scorpios and Aquarius I's don't always have the seriousness and commitment necessary to form a deep relationship. As occasional companions and acquaintances, however, or as sports partners, they can pass the time pleasantly enough, with little conflict. Co-workers in this combination can serve a company long and well. At one time or another it will certainly occur to this pair to start their own company together, but the relationship usually lacks the grit and determination necessary to stick it out over the long haul. Parent-child matchups of either combination can be great fun, but too often the element of maturity is lacking here. This is particularly clear when the partners vie with each other to give a more youthful impression.

ADVICE: *Develop perseverance. Resist the lure of ever-changing horizons. Devote time to getting over the bad spots before giving up.*

ROGER VADIM (1/26/28)
CATHERINE DENEUVE (10/22/43)

Gorgeous French actress Deneuve and erotic director-screenwriter Vadim had a famous liaison in the 60s, producing a son, Christian. In '87 Vadim published his book *My Life with the Three Most Beautiful Women in the World,* describing his love relationships with Deneuve, Brigitte Bardot and Jane Fonda. He directed son Christian in *Surprise Party* (1983).

STRENGTHS: **FAR-REACHING, INVOLVED, ARTISTIC**

WEAKNESSES: **REPETITIVE, OBSESSIVE, POSSESSIVE**

BEST: **MARRIAGE**

WORST: **FRIENDSHIP**

PETER TOSH (10/19/44)
BOB MARLEY (2/6/45)

Tosh and Marley formed the reggae group Bob Marley and the Wailers in 1963, singing of rebellion, determination and faith to audiences around the world. Tragically, both died young: Marley of cancer in '82; Tosh was murdered in Jamaica in '87. **Also: Adlai Stevenson & Adlai Stevenson II** (grandfather/grandson; vice-president/presidential candidate) **Sandy Alomar, Sr. & Roberto Alomar** (father/son; baseball stars).

October 19–25

THE CUSP OF DRAMA & CRITICISM
LIBRA-SCORPIO CUSP

January 31–February 7

THE WEEK OF YOUTH & EASE
AQUARIUS II

Serial Duplication

The focus of this relationship is often a desire to engage in a series of far-reaching projects. Once this couple gets a taste of success in a given area, they will usually try to duplicate it again and again. Finding a working formula is crucial to their plans, then, and if one is not forthcoming they may appear a bit rootless or lost. In a strange way, it doesn't really matter what activity they pursue in these types of projects. What is important is the replication of one good project.

Marriages, love affairs and friendships can become the basis for successful commercial or artistic enterprises. The kind of total involvement required by such activities may permeate every area of the partners' lives, so that they run the risk of becoming obsessively possessive of each other. Because they may be convinced that they cannot do without each other, they sometimes become desperate over their partner's absence, or extremely jealous should the partner direct any attention elsewhere. If tension, stress or pressures from their projects build to an intensity that threatens their relationship, they should have the good sense to back off, slow down or perhaps give up these projects altogether; such a decision may enable them to develop the more personal side of their relationship and to get to know each other better.

Sibling pairs here often engage in club, school or sports activities together, structuring their relationship around shared weekly or monthly activities that they both enjoy. Likewise, co-workers in this combination enjoy corporate work rhythms—the schedules and quotas that must be met, or the large and successive projects of which they can be a meaningful part.

ADVICE: *Don't try to do too much. The personal side of your life may be getting lost in the rush. Give up possessiveness. Keep it legal.*

STRENGTHS: **ROMANTIC, MAGICAL, COMFORTABLE**

WEAKNESSES: **UNREALISTIC, OVERIDEALIZED, ADDICTIVE**

BEST: **WORK**

WORST: **PARENT-CHILD**

JEFF GOLDBLUM (10/22/52)
LAURA DERN (2/10/67)

Actor Goldblum got his boost to celebrity with his role in the film *The Big Chill* (1983). Dern has risen through small roles to become one of Hollywood's gifted actresses. She and Goldblum co-starred in *Jurassic Park* (1993) and began a long romance in the 90s. **Also: Robert Reed & Florence Henderson** (co-stars, *The Brady Bunch*); **John Profumo & Harold Macmillan** (cabinet sex scandal threat to PM).

October 19–25

THE CUSP OF DRAMA & CRITICISM
LIBRA-SCORPIO CUSP

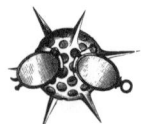

February 8–15

THE WEEK OF ACCEPTANCE
AQUARIUS III

Fantasy Needs

This combination is likely to get out of touch with reality pretty easily. Illusions of all sorts fascinate the relationship, particularly when they fulfill its partners' own fantasy needs. Such a couple must take care not to see only what they want to see and hear only what they want to hear. Although they may enjoy themselves together a good deal of the time, incorporating romance, play and creativity into their activities, they risk forming unhealthy habits or dependencies involving drink, drugs or sex and love. One might say that the couple's susceptibility to such activities is greater than most because of the particular nature of the combination's psychological makeup.

Libra-Scorpio–Aquarius III love affairs are often highly romantic and feature many magical moments. Falling in love with love is always a possibility here, but these partners generally feel compatible and comfortable with each other, and their solid mutual liking and appreciation for each other combats any dreamy fantasies. Should they fall out of love, they are capable of becoming fast friends in a relationship that has its own sort of romance, usually platonic in nature. Whether lovers or friends, this pair may admire each other to the point of worship. They are usually unaware that their attachment to the other person is simply a psychological projection of their own wishes for themselves—of their own idealized self. Such projections may imply a low self-image on the part of one or both partners.

Marriages and work relationships between these two may force a greater sense of reality on them, which is good in some ways and bad in others: the need to deal with daily responsibilities will lessen the magic but also the illusions of the matchup. Greater psychological health may be found in marriage, then, than in other Libra-Scorpio–Aquarius III relationships. Parent-child matchups in this combination may see Libra-Scorpio parents being overly demanding of their Aquarius III children, who may, for their part, be too easily dominated by their Libra-Scorpio parents.

ADVICE: *Be aware of your weakness for illusions. Try to keep a hold on reality. Attaining psychological health does not mean enjoying yourself less.*

October 19–25

THE CUSP OF DRAMA & CRITICISM
LIBRA-SCORPIO CUSP

February 16–22

THE CUSP OF SENSITIVITY
AQUARIUS-PISCES CUSP

A Good Fit

These two can fit together as easily as hand and glove. Libra-Scorpio and Aquarius-Pisces are usually quite different from each other, but they are in trine aspect in the zodiac (120° apart), a position usually implying natural and free-flowing energies. As easy as the relationship may be, though, it often engages in difficult or even impossible tasks. Interestingly, this is an example of a relationship that gives its partners something they lack individually—in this case, vision and the pragmatism to realize it. Having a goal or objective is inevitable here, with the partners often constituting a formidable combination that can arouse not only wonder but antagonisms and jealousies in the outside world. Not one to compromise, this matchup does things on its own terms. It is often able to touch the deepest emotional areas in other people, who instinctively realize that even if they are opposed to it, it represents the wave of the future.

Without a cause to devote themselves to, love affairs and marriages can show wide differences of opinion, which may lead to struggle, despite the ease with which these two communicate. Although the sensuality between them can be pronounced, Libra-Scorpios may get on the nerves of more sensitive Aquarius-Pisces, who, in turn, may try to force Libra-Scorpios to mute their outgoing side. As a result, frustrations can build up on both sides. The key to success here is for the partners to show more interest in the relationship itself, approaching it with the same fervor they would grant more idealistic or objective pursuits. In the family sphere, sibling pairs, particularly of the same sex, are usually competitive but also mutually supportive.

Friendships and work relationships can be outstanding, and often overlap. When placed in the service of a cause, whether social, commercial or artistic, the relationship can be rebellious against outworn tastes and ideals. An element of the prophetic accompanies this attitude; the matchup has a pretty good idea what it plans to substitute for the status quo.

ADVICE: *Don't take your relationship for granted. Don't get carried away by ideals. Keep your feet on the ground. Learn to inspire others without arousing envy.*

October 19–25

THE CUSP OF DRAMA & CRITICISM
LIBRA-SCORPIO CUSP

February 23–March 2

THE WEEK OF SPIRIT
PISCES I

Mutual Appreciation

An unusually close relationship can develop here, in which empathic feelings predominate. Although the partners are very different temperamentally, with Libra-Scorpio more head oriented and Pisces I's more heart oriented, they can usually forge their strengths into an effective operating unit. The key to the relationship, and often its focus, is the partners' ability to appreciate each other's talents and skills. Should emotional disappointment surface here, both partners are likely to be deeply hurt, but Pisces I's will usually be affected on a deeper level.

Friendships and love affairs in this combination are warm and sympathetic. Most often these two pose no threat to each other, either physically or psychically. Yet small problems can arise when Pisces I's feel rushed or pushed by their energetic Libra-Scorpio partners. The chemistry here is often less passionate than understanding and affectionate. Libra-Scorpios may sometimes end a love affair with a Pisces I because they tire of it, finding it not dynamic enough for them; it can also be the Pisces I's who withdraw, out of fear of deeper involvement with their Libra-Scorpio partner. Friendships that turn into love affairs often have a better prognosis, since the partners will have fewer illusions about what they are getting into.

Marriages here are usually sensuous and relaxed. Libra-Scorpios, particularly, will appreciate this, as a foil to their often hectic professional schedules. The emphasis is on domestic tranquillity, which neither partner will usually want to disturb or upset.

Sibling and co-worker matchups in this combination can be mutually supportive and understanding, assuming that Libra-Scorpios don't get too bossy. Should Pisces I's feel hurt or rejected, they can retreat behind a wall of silent frustration, rather than coming out and telling their partner what they really think. Rarely will such combinations be particularly dynamic or ambitious in their orientation.

ADVICE: *Push yourself a bit. Express the very best you have to offer. Beware of sinking into a rut. Keep awake to the present moment.*

STRENGTHS: **CHALLENGING, SELF-ACTUALIZING, FUN**

WEAKNESSES: **INEFFECTUAL, POLARIZED, SADOMASOCHISTIC**

BEST: **WORK**

WORST: **MARRIAGE**

ED MCMAHON (3/6/23)
JOHNNY CARSON (10/23/25)

Carson and McMahon originally worked together on the tv game show *Who Do You Trust?* (1957-62). When Carson took over *The Tonight Show* from Jack Paar in '62, he brought along his sidekick and they remained together for the next 30 years—the longest partnership in tv history. The pair will always be linked by McMahon's intro, "Heeere's … Johnny!"

October 19–25

THE CUSP OF DRAMA & CRITICISM
LIBRA-SCORPIO CUSP

March 3–10

THE WEEK OF THE LONER
PISCES II

Evident Inequalities

This combination emphasizes rulership and can seem abrasive to those who come in contact with it—a problem attributable to the Libra-Scorpio, who usually assumes the dominant role. If the relationship is not tempered by the sensitivity, understanding and more mild-mannered, unassuming air of Pisces II, in fact, it may not be viable. This important role of the Pisces II should be recognized but, unfortunately, more often goes unappreciated, leaving this partner feeling mistreated from time to time by the Libra-Scorpio. In extreme cases the relationship can have a sadomasochistic flavor. Both partners must be careful, then, not to settle into fixed roles in which the Pisces II's suffer at the hands of their more aggressive partners.

Inequalities like these may occur in marriage, work and family relationships but are not always obvious. The determining factors, surprisingly enough, are usually the attitudes not of the dominant Libra-Scorpios but of the quieter Pisces II's: should these personalities suffer from low self-esteem, or regressively replay old tapes from childhood, they may end up pushing their partner to act more aggressively, for their psychological expectations will cast the Libra-Scorpio as an oppressive authority figure from the Pisces II's youth. If the couple can go without such expectations, however, it is likely to work out a satisfactory and healthy relationship, in which Pisces II sensitivity has a salutary effect on Libra-Scorpios, tending to bring them into closer contact with their own emotions.

The success of love affairs in this combination, on the other hand, depends more on the Libra-Scorpios, and on their willingness to dive to the depths of feeling with their Pisces II partners. Should they hold back, or aim for more superficial sorts of satisfaction, Pisces II's will grow restive and dissatisfied. Friendships may be quite satisfied with less involvement, both partners being content to enjoy having fun together. But the relationship may be relatively ineffectual at handling heavy depressions, should these arise.

ADVICE: *Drop expectations. Stay flexible and open. Try to go emotionally deeper. Encourage health through self-understanding.*

STRENGTHS: **COHESIVE, RELAXED, UNCONVENTIONAL**

WEAKNESSES: **PECULIAR, PROVOCATIVE, SHOCKING**

BEST: **PARENT-CHILD**

WORST: **FRIENDSHIP**

JACK HALEY, JR. (10/25/33)
LIZA MINNELLI (3/12/46)

Haley and Minnelli were married from 1974–79. He is a producer-director who scripted MGM's compilation *That's Entertainment* (1974) and the son of actor Jack Haley, who played the Tin Man in *The Wizard of Oz* (1939). Singer Minnelli is the daughter of Judy Garland, who starred as Dorothy in the same film classic. **Also: Johann Strauss, Jr. & Johann Strauss** (son/father; waltz composers).

October 19–25

THE CUSP OF DRAMA & CRITICISM
LIBRA-SCORPIO CUSP

March 11–18

THE WEEK OF DANCERS & DREAMERS
PISCES III

Not by the Straight and Narrow

This can be a successful relationship right across the board, with the partners integrating their talents and abilities into a coherent and cohesive unit. This is not to imply, however, that they proceed by the straight and narrow: the Libra-Scorpio–Pisces III combination is unconventional and has its own peculiar methods of maintaining stability. The emotional level is exalted here, and this pair shares a deep understanding of it, not only to the benefit of their relationship but also to charm other people. Their expressions of feeling may seem strange, but they come from a very deep place and prompt an unusual degree of acceptance from others. The Pisces III tends to be the relationship's star, with the Libra-Scorpio partner serving as advisor, student, co-worker, assistant or just plain admirer. Although these charismatic Pisces III's are quite capable of standing on their own, they benefit tremendously from the support of their keenly perceptive Libra-Scorpio partners.

In love affairs and marriages, intimacy between these two can be very rewarding, both physically and emotionally. Libra-Scorpios enjoy this relationship because it lets them relax, Pisces III's because they like the attention of their intense, mentally challenging partners. Since both individuals have a strong need to develop their own clan, having children together may be the cement that holds the relationship together over the years. Libra-Scorpio–Pisces III friendships may have an outlandish side, with the partners flaunting the relationship's unusual aspects and obviously enjoying the shock they engender in others.

Family and work relationships usually function most naturally as parent-child and boss-employee matchups with the Pisces III in the top spot. These personalities can be sympathetic and understanding toward their Libra-Scorpio offspring or employees, without being in any way condescending.

ADVICE: *If others find you too aggressive, you will engender resistance. Tone down your image. Deepen your spiritual bond. Be less self-conscious.*

Compromises for Sanity

This intense matchup cries out for relief—how can these two possibly live under the same roof or work side by side? The key to the relationship's success may be a concerted effort by the partners to manage their defining characteristic: their intensity. They will periodically have to call a truce or give some priority to relaxation. In certain areas at certain times, their unstoppable energies will meld efficiently. At other times the partners can easily work to their own detriment, even careening out of control. They both occasionally need to let up in their attentiveness to detail and to try to see the larger picture. A recurring problem here is a tendency to fixate on an unpleasant event in the past, an absorbing one in the present or a dreaded one in the future, and to be unable to let go of it.

Sexually the relationship can be obsessive. Sometimes more concerned with performance and technical criteria than with enjoyment and pleasure, Scorpio I couples can plague each other with checklists. "Did you?" "Didn't you?" These are the kinds of questions that the lovers might ask, or at least think about, each time. Each of them can take it as their responsibility alone to bring satisfaction to the other, and when this doesn't happen they can assume it is their fault. Guilty, frustrated feelings often result. Marriages are likely to be no less demanding sexually. A tight ship is similarly the rule in domestic areas and finance, but here certain compromises can be worked out for the sake of sanity.

Friendships in this combination are likely to have an aggressiveness best worked out in sports, competitive games, fitness training or martial arts. In the family, a Scorpio I parent can be competitive with a Scorpio I child, whether for the attention of another family member or simply to gain physical or mental ascendancy. It can be a bad idea for two Scorpio I's to work in the same office or small group, since the tension of their energy can easily spread to other co-workers.

ADVICE: *Take a break from other people's demands. Empty your mind. Let yourself be bored occasionally. Work on accepting what fate dishes out.*

LYLE LOVETT (11/1/57)
JULIA ROBERTS (10/28/67)

Willowy beauty Roberts (sister of actor Eric) had a meteoric rise in the late 80s and was nominated for an Oscar in '90 for *Pretty Woman*. She surprised the public in '93 with her sudden marriage to Lovett, a mostly country singer with an eraser-head pompadour. They were divorced in '95. **Also: Shah of Iran & Riza Cyrus Pahlevi** (father/son).

Wary Circling

These two are often magnetically attracted physically. Although Scorpio is a water sign, their relationship is ruled by earth, here representing grounded, practical, sensuous energies. Encounters between these two indicate their belief that it can be fatal to underestimate one's opponent: warily circling each other, they are usually highly suspicious of each other on first meeting. Yet although they will never forget their first encounter, they may later become fast friends or lovers. From the outside this matchup can seem light and breezy; few would suspect its true nature—heavy and momentous. Scorpio I's and II's can actually have a lot to learn from each other, a mutual education they acquire through the experiences they go through together.

This learning experience is nowhere more evident than in the realms of sex and money. In these fields, whether as lovers or business partners, even the most naive Scorpio I's and II's will follow a crash course together, receiving a full education and probably even a graduate degree in record time. The chemistry here is such that without reading books, or even a whole lot of prior experience, the partners quickly develop an extraordinary appreciation of power and how it works. Their marriages must have a rock-solid material base for them to be truly satisfied and fulfilled. Once that foundation has been laid, the couple must be dedicated to maintaining it—something they are usually capable of doing—if their relationship is to grow and prosper.

Friendships manifest less interest in power than other relationships in this combination, and in fact these two may give up their concern with the material realm in favor of more spiritual goals. If this process involves a renunciation of practical values, it can be extremely painful for both parties. In the family, Scorpio I and Scorpio II relatives can get locked in titanic struggles over inheritances, property and cash, arguments that ultimately symbolize a thirst for parental or sibling love that has been withheld.

ADVICE: *Don't neglect the spiritual side of life. Acquisition can be the first lesson but nonattachment will be the final one. Don't be too stubborn to listen.*

DALE EVANS (10/31/12)
ROY ROGERS (11/5/12)

Evans and Rogers, married in 1947, had the quintessential cowboy/cowgirl romance. They made many movies together, starred in their own tv series, *The Roy Rogers Show* (1951–57), and got very wealthy through wise business ventures. **Also: Larry Flynt & Althea Flynt** (married; *Hustler* publishers); **John Adams & Abigail Adams** (president/First Lady); **Warren Harding & Nan Britton** (president/mistress).

STRENGTHS: **FATED, DEEP, COMMITTED**

WEAKNESSES: **REPRESSIVE, AGONIZING, MISTRUSTFUL**

BEST: **FAMILY**

WORST: **LOVE**

SUN YAT-SEN (11/12/1866)
CHIANG KAI-SHEK (10/31/1887)

Sun and Chiang were close allies during China's transition toward communism in the 20s. Chiang became politically prominent after Sun's death (1925) and was leader of the Nationalist government from 1928. Chiang and Sun were also brothers-in-law, married to sisters of the prominent Soong family.

Also: John Cleese & Peter Cook (co-performers, Cambridge Circus).

October 26–November 2
THE WEEK OF INTENSITY
SCORPIO I

November 12–18
THE WEEK OF CHARM
SCORPIO III

Ancient Roots

The roots of this relationship go deep. Whether these two are involved socially, emotionally or financially, one feels that their ties are inevitable, fated. Like and dislike are not the important motives here; free choice isn't really involved. Usually thrown together in serendipitous situations, the partners slowly come to realize that their fortunes are inextricably linked. Oddly enough, mutual understanding is often difficult for them, as if they had come from different planets. Over the years, however, they usually discover their common origins, and this process of self-discovery can become the focus of their relationship.

Love affairs are slow to develop—it can take years for these two to get together and more for them to begin to know each other. But exploring the meaning of their relationship together will lead each of them further on their own path of self-realization. In marriage, similarly, agonizing or at the very least painstaking processes must be undergone before the partners finally agree to tie the knot, but once they do so they rarely look back. Absolute commitment is the keynote here. Infidelities or even flirtations will not be tolerated.

Family relationships and friendships can become the basis for career connections, and vice versa. The point is that neither of these two trusts easily, so that they may need a firm commitment in one area of life before they can set up a relationship in another. They can be extremely close mouthed about what they do and will view any disclosure of inside information as a betrayal. Their strong moral codes may come to govern almost every area of their lives—yet they are not incapable of acting for amoral ends or staging power plays. They must at some point decide whether their relationship has achieved a choke hold over them against which they need to rebel, for the sake of preserving their individuality.

ADVICE: *Encourage freedom of choice whenever possible. Don't tie yourself down to repressive commitments. Follow your intuitions and your heart.*

STRENGTHS: **NATURAL, SEXUAL, NO-NONSENSE**

WEAKNESSES: **DANGEROUS, SECRETIVE, OBLITERATING**

BEST: **MARRIAGE**

WORST: **ADVERSARIAL**

GARSON KANIN (11/24/12)
RUTH GORDON (10/30/1896)

As well as an actress, Gordon was a successful playwright and screenwriter. She often collaborated with 2nd husband Kanin (married 1942), who was a screenwriter, director and author. They shared Oscar nominations for 3 Cukor films, *A Double Life* (1947), *Adam's Rib* (1949) and *Pat and Mike* (1952).

October 26–November 2
THE WEEK OF INTENSITY
SCORPIO I

November 19–24
THE CUSP OF REVOLUTION
SCORPIO-SAGITTARIUS CUSP

Throwing a Switch

This formidable combination can boast a tremendously natural ease and openness when it's on. When it's off—well, a deadly silence reigns. This stark polarity makes the pairing quite a dangerous one, fraught with perils that neither partner is likely to grasp fully until, quite suddenly, the switch turns to the off position. When this happens, family and friends can be truly shocked by the finality of the process; bringing the relationship back to life is difficult, sometimes impossible. Yet when these two meet they are apt to be overjoyed to find a kindred spirit. Both are deep, somewhat eccentric individuals who usually choose the road less traveled. Both can also be intense, wary and critical. There is no middle ground between them.

Love affairs between Scorpio I's and Scorpio-Sagittarians are characterized by an intensity of feeling combined with a tough, no-nonsense orientation. Romantic feelings seldom prevail here, nor are they particularly desired. Having a realistic view of their relationship, the partners have little difficulty voicing their opinions, desires and dissatisfactions. They may need time to take the step of marriage, but once the decision is made, things proceed quite naturally and successfully. Should problems emerge, though, the warning signs will probably be clear to both partners. Both of them are secretive in nature, and they may keep their own plans to themselves; then, quite suddenly, the switch is thrown and the relationship is over.

Not only in romances and marriages but also in rivalries and friendships, Scorpio I's tend either to be loose cannons or to set the parameters, while Scorpio-Sagittarians adjust as best they can. Ultimately, however, it is often the Scorpio-Sagittarius who turns off and out, deciding to make a change. Straightforward enmities and rivalries in this combination can go on for years, bringing out the best and worst in both partners. Sometimes, though rarely, these relationships survive a period of blackout, inaction or hibernation and then start up again with unbridled intensity. Co-worker and sibling relationships can also be quite natural, warm and supportive, then can suddenly subside with little warning.

ADVICE: *Give each other a fair chance. Beware of ultimatums. Finality may be irreversible. Be as honest as possible. Be sure of your intentions.*

October 26–November 2

THE WEEK OF INTENSITY
SCORPIO I

November 25–December 2

THE WEEK OF INDEPENDENCE
SAGITTARIUS I

Wheeling and Parrying

Scorpio I's and Sagittarius I's often need each other more than they will admit. Their relationship presents a magnetic, even charismatic exterior that can make them the center of attention in their social or family group. Strongly protective, their matchup will present a united front against the world when threatened. When they are alone, however, these two rarely see eye to eye and may seek to best each other at every turn. Highly competitive in the verbal, physical and mental spheres, the relationship is a classic study in attack and defense, with Sagittarius I's deftly wheeling and delivering lightning strokes and Scorpio I's astutely parrying them and going on the counterattack.

Love affairs and marriages in this combination are a bit enigmatic, although the partners can make charming hosts and welcoming friends once they have their own thing together. It is rather obvious to others when it is time to leave them alone, for the degree of confrontation and combat between them is usually all too apparent. Getting things out in the open is a remarkably healthy trait in this relationship, but the pair must put limits on their emotional outbursts, which can turn ugly and destructive.

Friends and siblings of the same sex have complex, paradoxical relationships. It is sometimes difficult to tell whether they are close or distant, sympathetic or cold, allies or enemies. Perhaps it is their very confidence in their unity that permits them to have such sharp disagreements, since they both know in their hearts that their relationship is ultimately unassailable and will withstand practically anything. Battering each other becomes a way of toughening and strengthening the relationship. These two can express genuine affection in a variety of subtle ways, including sarcasm, irony and downright insult, which makes the relationship difficult for others to read. Work relationships here are not at all recommended; the partners' disagreements over how to do things will too often prove paralyzing.

ADVICE: *There are limits to your strength. Don't be so sure of survival. Tone down the rhetoric. Mute competitiveness. Control outbursts.*

FRANÇOISE GILOT (11/26/21)
JONAS SALK (10/28/14)

Salk developed the first universal polio vaccine in 1953 and was director of the Salk Institute for Biological Studies, 1963–75. In '70 he married Gilot, a painter and former wife of Picasso. *Also:* **Kinky Friedman & Abbie Hoffmann** (singer-writer harbored fugitive radical); **Edmund Halley & Mark Twain** (astronomer/writer; Twain born/died on comet's passing).

October 26–November 2

THE WEEK OF INTENSITY
SCORPIO I

December 3–10

THE WEEK OF THE ORIGINATOR
SAGITTARIUS II

Plugged In

When these two plug in to each other their energy can be overwhelming. It is usually the Sagittarius II who serves as the theoretical brain behind their endeavors, the Scorpio I as the force of implementation. The matchup feels natural to both partners, and indeed a melding of biological, social and economic connections between them is not uncommon. But the highly individualistic methods of Sagittarius II's can arouse the disapproval of Scorpio I's, who for their part have a habit of a picky attention to detail that may get on their partner's nerves. Life is not a bed of roses between these two, then; there is an underlying tension between the expansive, optimistic view of Sagittarius II's and the more concentrated and critical approach of Scorpio I's.

Romantic involvements do not immediately suggest themselves here—the chemistry is usually wrong in the sexual sphere, so that love affairs are unlikely to go deep. But marriages and family and business or career matchups can be engrossing and highly productive. They also often overlap. Power is usually the cement that holds these relationships together, providing an explanation for why business partners may become relatives and vice versa: although both partners could continue on their way independent of each other, they seem to sense or to believe that their matchup is much more powerful than their own individual efforts could ever be. In this they are generally correct. These two can embark on projects of mammoth proportions, usually following a regular progression from one stepping stone to the next. Their relationship has a real feeling for the long line, and its vision is likely to sustain it over many years, sometimes a whole lifetime.

Friendships, on the other hand, are a bit complex and problematic. Contrasting tastes and temperaments prove stimulating, and indeed these two can have great times together, but their differences may ultimately prove too divisive or alienating.

ADVICE: *Keep things a bit more low-key. Settle differences quickly whenever possible. Be more diplomatic. Show patience with those who don't understand.*

STEPHEN CRANE (11/1/1871)
JOSEPH CONRAD (12/3/1857)

Crane, noted American author, poet and journalist, moved to England in 1898 with his mistress, a former brothel proprietor. Living lavishly, they entertained literary figures, among them Conrad, a close friend. *Also:* **Chiang Kai-shek & T.V. Soong** (brothers-in-law); **Mobutu & Don King** (dictator/promoter '74 Zaire Ali-Foreman fight); **C.W. Post & Dina Merrill** (grandfather/granddaughter; cereal maker/actress).

RELATIONSHIPS

STRENGTHS: **AFFECTIONATE, EMPATHIC, FUNNY**

WEAKNESSES: **OBNOXIOUS, REBELLIOUS, HAYWIRE**

BEST: **FAMILY**

WORST: **WORK**

OSSIE DAVIS (12/18/17)
RUBY DEE (10/27/24)

Dee and Davis have been happily married since 1948. Both have had stellar stage, screen and tv careers since the 50s. They have also been active in civil rights and humanitarian causes. He heads Third World Cinema, a movie company formed in the 70s to encourage talented blacks and Puerto Ricans. **Also:**
Jackie Coogan & Betty Grable (married; actors).

October 26–November 2
THE WEEK OF INTENSITY
SCORPIO I

December 11–18
THE WEEK OF THE TITAN
SAGITTARIUS III

Lively Debunking

Whatever these two do together in public, they are likely to do with a twinkle in their eye. Vivacious, provocative and oriented toward critical thinking, as a couple they specialize in stripping away false facades and telling it like it is. They can usually get away with their debunking without arousing too much antagonism, chiefly through their ability to let other people laugh at them. But they always risk causing serious problems with people who are not at all amused by what they do. They are feisty and will rarely back down from a challenge, but they should be aware when the challenge is actually emanating from them.

In love affairs, marriages and friendships, light banter is usually the order of the day. Care should be taken that this does not escalate into open warfare and to remember the importance of quiet displays of affection. The relationship may appear alternately thorny and cuddly, empathic and incompatible, depending on the partners' moods and circumstances. Irritations quickly surface when one partner rubs the other the wrong way. These relationships can go on for years, whether they are predominantly positive or negative, since like two old flintstones this lively pair just go on striking sparks.

In family matchups, particularly parent-child combinations, these two are more often than not the motor that powers the group and spurs it to action. Although they may not get along that well, their contentious energies keep the family on its toes and guard against dullness and complacency. At work, colleagues in this combination can bring projects toward a grinding halt when their emotions go haywire. In all of these areas the relationship has a tendency to rebelliousness. This will wear thin as the partners age and, one hopes, mature, a process that will sooner or later demand some softening of their attitudes (except in the most hardcore cases). Finally getting the point that they are just plain making things more difficult for themselves, these two might decide to kick back and mellow out.

ADVICE: *Chill out. Keep it light. Growing up is inevitable. Maturity demands more common sense. Don't make things more difficult than they already are.*

RELATIONSHIPS

STRENGTHS: **THOUGHTFUL, SERIOUS, FREEDOM-SEEKING**

WEAKNESSES: **EMOTIONALLY BLOCKED, UNCOMMUNICATIVE**

BEST: **FRIENDSHIP**

WORST: **LOVE**

FRANK SHORTER (10/31/47)
BILL RODGERS (12/23/47)

Shorter and Rodgers were world-class marathoners during the 70s. Shorter won the gold medal at the 1972 Olympics, the first American to win in 64 years. Rodgers won the NYC and Boston marathons 4 times each (1975–80).
Also: Julia Roberts & Kiefer Sutherland (once engaged; actors);
Ellsworth Statler & Conrad Hilton (competing hoteliers).

October 26–November 2
THE WEEK OF INTENSITY
SCORPIO I

December 19–25
THE CUSP OF PROPHECY
SAGITTARIUS-CAPRICORN CUSP

Room to Breathe

This relationship emphasizes matters of the mind—critical thinking, verbal agility, conversation. This is lucky because on their own these two are quite weighty, perhaps even depressive; their ability to bring out each other's lighter side is a blessing. This is not to say that the relationship is easy. Using their intellects to solve emotional problems is a formidable task for this pair, but it sometimes seems the only way open to them. They may both be interested in clearing the air, but their good intentions are not always enough. They will have to work hard and tackle complex emotional confrontations before they can breathe free. These two can often spend hours trying to figure out solutions to the relationship's problems. Unfortunately, concomitant worry and anxiety may play roles as well. If freedom is to be attained here, it will not be without a struggle.

In love affairs and marriages, the partners' belief in their ability to think problems through often runs up against a brick wall, creating considerable frustration. The relationship's theme of freeing itself from problems may mean that the partners will eventually free themselves of each other. As friends, Scorpio I's and Sagittarius-Capricorns can be loyal to each other and available in times of need. A lighter mood may periodically appear in the relationship, but it should not be forced. Parent-child relationships of either possible variation will usually find Scorpio I's trying to establish a direct emotional connection and Sagittarius-Capricorns backing off. To open avenues of communication (probably the crying need of this relationship in any sector), the partners will have to exercise great sensitivity and understanding, as well as a willingness to try different approaches. Creating a relaxed atmosphere through mutual cooperation is of course best.

At work, as long as both partners can agree on a protocol or method and stick to it, and as long as they are spared too much verbal interaction, the job will get done. Reasonable or even routine projects of short duration are probably the best choices for them, at least until they establish a working rhythm.

ADVICE: *Trying hard can sometimes be counterproductive. Let go of tensions and negative expectations. Avoid laying on guilt or shame.*

October 26–November 2

THE WEEK OF INTENSITY
SCORPIO I

December 26–January 2

THE WEEK OF THE RULER
CAPRICORN I

 RELATIONSHIPS

STRENGTHS: **INDEPENDENT, ASPIRING, RESPONSIBLE**

WEAKNESSES: **INTOLERANT, HURTFUL, INFLEXIBLE**

BEST: **WORK**

WORST: **FAMILY**

Cultivating Openness

This combination focuses on cultivating flexibility and openness. The partners will learn how to air significant differences of opinion without harming their relationship. When things are going well between them, they can go very well indeed, but this may presuppose a need on the part of one or both personalities, so that one partner gives in to the other's wishes. Should either partner feel the urge to exert their individuality, the matchup can be rocked to its foundations, since these two often have extremely different attitudes. The good times or mutual reassurance they can share is no guarantee of the relationship's underlying stability or health. Providing the freedom within the relationship for differences in individual style is the key to success.

Whether frustrating or satisfying—they can be both—love affairs usually show a high level of emotional involvement, sometimes torturously so. They are seldom taken up with power struggles, since for the most part these lovers are both doing their best and have no interest in controlling or injuring their partner. Yet injury often occurs, and it is sometimes best for the lovers to back off, give up their physical contact and try to be good friends. In marriages and work relationships, serious, responsible but also optimistic attitudes are usually the rule, with both partners giving their all for the common cause. With a modicum of effort, these can be excellent unions. Parent-child matchups often manifest serious power struggles when children begin to think for themselves, whether the child is Scorpio I or Capricorn I. Both personalities are extremely stubborn in either role, and adolescent conflicts are likely to resound around the neighborhood, the impact perhaps reminding listeners of the crash produced when an irresistible force meets an immovable object.

Friendships are quite possible between these two, but so are enmities. Should the pair find themselves on opposite sides of the ideological or social fence, or be engaged in business, love or sport competitions, neither can expect that the other will either give quarter or offer to capitulate.

ADVICE: *Create an open forum. Try to sense the needs of the moment. Don't create artificial barriers. Encourage individual expression.*

JONAS SALK (10/28/14)
LEE SALK (12/27/26)

Scientist-physician Jonas is famed for his development of the first polio vaccine (1953). Younger brother Lee is a distinguished psychologist, family columnist with *McCall's* magazine and author of *Familyhood: Nurturing the Values That Matter* (1992). ***Also:*** **Chiang Kai-shek & Mao Zedong** (rival Chinese leaders).

October 26–November 2

THE WEEK OF INTENSITY
SCORPIO I

January 3–9

THE WEEK OF DETERMINATION
CAPRICORN II

RELATIONSHIPS

STRENGTHS: **SUPPORTIVE, COMMUNICATIVE, PROFESSIONAL**

WEAKNESSES: **STRESSED, ARGUMENTATIVE, JEALOUS**

BEST: **LOVE**

WORST: **SIBLING**

Seeing Eye to Eye

The communication level in this relationship is extremely high—the partners work out their own shorthand. This unfortunately doesn't always mean they understand each other. One thing they usually have going for them is their admiration for each other's skills and talents; one thing they usually have going against them is their difficulty in seeing eye to eye on almost any subject. Disagreements, arguments, even pitched battles, can flare with the suddenness of spontaneous combustion. Yet the partners often have little difficulty understanding each other, and what they have to communicate comes through loud and clear. These two strong-willed people are not necessarily meant to get along. If they are determined to work out their differences, however, they can build a stable and supportive relationship.

Love affairs between Scorpio I's and Capricorn II's are often strong in the sexual sphere. Perhaps both partners have a secret hankering for romance, although they might not want to admit it—they generally present a tough, no-nonsense persona, repressing all signs of weakness in each other's company. Neither partner may see the need for marriage, and indeed their relationship is usually quite complete without it. Ambition, both in the social and the professional sense, is something they share, and in pursuing it they are likely to spend quite some time apart. Although they may both have their own field of professional expertise, they are quite sensitive about which of them receives the greater acknowledgment from other people or is viewed as more successful, especially when they are together socially. Work relationships in this combination are likely to be professional, demanding and unforgiving. Should either partner produce shoddy work or slow down some, they are likely to hear about it immediately. Although somewhat tense at work, they are quite capable of tying one on during their free time, but working hard and playing hard without some letup can eventually lead to breakdown. Siblings in this combination, particularly of opposite sexes, sometimes measure their achievements against each other, and if so they are capable of competing at the cost of all else.

ADVICE: *Find enough time to relax. Let up a bit in your demands. Competition doesn't help your personal life. Don't be afraid of vulnerability.*

EDMUND HALLEY (10/29/1656)
ISAAC NEWTON (1/4/1642)

Astronomer Halley and mathematician Newton were colleagues. Using Newton's method of tracking comet orbits, Halley computed that the orbits of 3 different comets were actually those of a single comet, whose return in 1758 he accurately predicted and which has been known ever since as Halley's comet. ***Also:*** **Robyn Moore & Mel Gibson** (married).

STRENGTHS: **CHALLENGING, POWERFUL, UNUSUAL**
WEAKNESSES: **DESTRUCTIVE, NEGATIVE, UNFULFILLING**
BEST: **WORK RIVALRY**
WORST: **MARRIAGE**

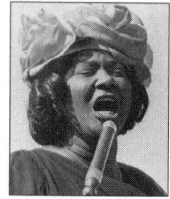

MARTIN LUTHER KING, JR. (1/15/29)
MAHALIA JACKSON (10/26/11)

Gospel-music great Jackson was a good personal friend of King's and shared in his spiritual crusade for black equality in America. She urged him to make the now-famous March on Washington in 1963, at which he gave the immortal speech "I Have a Dream." **Also: Paul Goebbels & Herman Goering** (Nazi high command); **John Adams & Alexander Hamilton** (early American political rivals).

October 26–November 2
THE WEEK OF INTENSITY
SCORPIO I

January 10–16
THE WEEK OF DOMINANCE
CAPRICORN III

Continuous Vigilance

The energy of this highly original relationship is spirited and all-consuming, but strong antagonisms are likely to emerge here. The strongest feelings between Scorpio I's and Capricorn III's often emerge in confrontations in which each partner tries to damage the other's reputation or to challenge the other's position within a family or professional or social group. Yet the relationship can lose its adversarial quality if both partners belong to the same group, and mutual defense against a common threat can become the important issue. Even at their best, however, the partners tend to be very wary of each other, as is clear from the kind of continuous vigilance they maintain on each other.

Love affairs in this combination can be torrid in their emotional intensity but will also feature power struggles and will rarely bring deep fulfillment. The inevitable emergence of negative feelings also augurs poorly for marriage, unless the spouses show a special willingness to cooperate and work out differences. Friendships will have their own strange values and may or may not involve conflicts. They sometimes also manifest as rather tame and disappointing, as though confrontation were an ever-present fear.

At work and in the family, conflicts will inevitably emerge in boss-employee and parent-child matchups of either possible variety, but responsible behavior will engender respect on both sides. The strong point about these relationships is that they are without ambiguity—both partners know full well where the other stands and what to expect if rules are broken or limits exceeded. Professional matchups and rivalries here may emerge as battles between Scorpio I quick intelligence and Capricorn III willpower. Capricorn III's will resist being unseated from their dominant position, but Scorpio I's are capable of applying many subtle pressures to get their way, knowing that a full-scale frontal assault might succeed only in arousing greater resistance.

ADVICE: *Seek mutual benefits. Keep destructive impulses from getting out of control; repair may be difficult later on. Use your good sense.*

STRENGTHS: **ADVENTURESOME, FUNNY, ENGROSSING**
WEAKNESSES: **UNSTABLE, INCONSISTENT, VIOLENT**
BEST: **FRIENDSHIP**
WORST: **SIBLING**

JIM CARREY (1/17/62)
LAUREN HOLLY (10/28/63)

Actress Holly and super-comic Carrey first got close on the set of *Dumb and Dumber* (1993). They were quietly married in 1996. Their plans were announced a month earlier in a press release by Carrey: "I am striving to live a loving and honorable life. Lauren is my proof and my reward."

Also: Ray Walston & Bill Bixby (co-stars, *My Favorite Martian*).

October 26–November 2
THE WEEK OF INTENSITY
SCORPIO I

January 17–22
THE CUSP OF MYSTERY & IMAGINATION
CAPRICORN-AQUARIUS CUSP

Riotous Ridicule

The focus of this relationship can be a search for the strange, bizarre, out-of-the-way or oddball elements of experience. Each partner has a terrific sense of humor, and these can gel well, while also providing a devastatingly effective weapon against adversaries. This pair is particularly good at using ridicule to the discomfiture of others, but shows its health in being able to laugh at itself as well. If the relationship fosters extroverted and riotous behavior, the other side of the coin is its activation of the partners' dark sides. They can be violent on occasion, not just verbally but physically, and this can later arouse mutual regret or guilt.

Love affairs and marriages in this combination are quite lively and rarely dull. Both partners give full rein to dramatic displays of feeling. (Too often, however, they are just putting on a show.) The deepest expressions of emotion can emerge in the sexual sphere, which is inventive and puts few activities off limits. There is a crying need here for stability and consistency, since the relationship is quite capable of going completely off track, or at the very least off the deep end.

Amusing, entertaining and adventuresome, friendships here can be outstanding. Here the partners are rarely interested in pursuing the sure thing; their attitude is that there is little to lose and lots to gain by such behavior. It is also possible for them to engage in business endeavors together, or to become involved in social, religious or educational pursuits. They will have to take care that these involvements do not become engrossing to the point where they exclude other important aspects of life. Sibling pairs in this combination may be continuously getting into trouble and mischief. This behavior is usually restricted to childhood or adolescence, but there is always the danger that it will lay the groundwork for asocial or even sociopathic behavior in adulthood.

ADVICE: *Know when to stop. Setting limits beforehand may be a good idea. Be more considerate of the feelings of others. Keep violence in check.*

October 26–November 2

THE WEEK OF INTENSITY
SCORPIO I

January 23–30

THE WEEK OF GENIUS
AQUARIUS I

Wider Horizons

This relationship often searches out wider horizons and larger-scale venues for its activities. The vision of its partners together is far broader than that of either alone; a big-picture approach is the hallmark of this matchup. There is usually a dynamic chemistry between these two, since Aquarius I and Scorpio I form a square aspect to each other in the zodiac (they are 90° apart), which provides tremendous energy and forward momentum, though also some friction and stress. Stability is seldom a problem here unless psychological strain or breakdowns in communication produce anxiety. It is usually Aquarius I's who take the lead, showing their partners another way of approaching life. Once Scorpio I's get the idea, however, they are more than able to hold up their end of the relationship.

In love affairs, Scorpio I's may show a penchant for influencing the relationship too strongly for their freedom-loving Aquarius I mates, who, no matter how strong the physical attraction or how compelling the emotional involvement, may back off in the face of controlling and claiming behavior. The Scorpio I need for the deeper side of life could remain unsatisfied if Aquarius I's insist on holding back or refuse to acknowledge the extent of their own emotions. Neither partner is likely to be too open or vulnerable with the other, and the relationship may suffer from a lack of sharing. If so, marriages are not especially recommended.

Pairs of friends and of siblings in this combination often indulge their physical side in sports and fitness activities, preferring high-speed, high-energy workouts. One-on-one as opposed to team endeavors are more likely to spur them to better their own personal best. Work relationships between Scorpio I's and Aquarius I's can be large or even mammoth in ambition and achievement. They tend to have an element of idealism, but the partners are usually realistic enough to know beforehand whether or not their plans have a chance of success. Frankness and forthrightness contribute significantly to clearing the air and preventing the buildup of resentments through misunderstanding.

ADVICE: *Promote sharing. Holding back can hurt you in the long run. Don't neglect smaller projects or daily chores. Be honest about your emotions.*

LEE KRASNER (10/27/08)
JACKSON POLLOCK (1/28/12)

Artists Krasner and Pollock were married from 1945 until his death in '56. They were both abstract expressionists who, in their last years together, lived and worked in East Hampton, NY. He is famous for his rhythmic, paint-dripped canvases and energized painting style. **Also: Grace Slick & Marty Balin** (rivalry; Jefferson Airplane members).

October 26–November 2

THE WEEK OF INTENSITY
SCORPIO I

January 31–February 7

THE WEEK OF YOUTH & EASE
AQUARIUS II

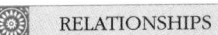
A Broad Spectrum of Admirers

This extremely charismatic relationship can be magnetic in attracting a broad spectrum of admirers, followers and hangers-on. There is in fact something extreme about the matchup, in terms of what it brings out not only in its partners but in their admirers. The danger here is that because these two attract a kind of edgy adulation, they start to believe it themselves, which induces all kinds of inappropriate behavior in them. Getting rid of an entourage can be harder than it seems, which the couple should perhaps think about before encouraging one in the first place. Within the relationship itself, these partners sometimes find themselves needing their partner's attention and approval, with Scorpio I's tending to be slightly the more dependent of the two. Aquarius II's have a relaxed approach that seems to yield great rewards in exchange for little effort. They are not big on suffering and generally figure the easiest way is the best. A little wary of this, Scorpio I's usually take the more difficult path, which has more meaning for them.

In love affairs, friendships and marriages, Scorpio I's may resent what they view as superficiality on their partner's part. To Aquarius II's, however, Scorpio I's seem no more profound than they are, just a bit more dedicated to cultivating pain. The relationship may not furnish the kind of understanding that Scorpio I's so desperately require but can often provide the kind of relaxation that they equally need. Passions seldom run high here, but both partners enjoy the relationship's steady sensuousness. Should these pleasures turn cloying, they may well seek temporary escape from each other in a more exciting and less certain direction.

Strong differences of opinion are common in career and family pairings. Generally speaking, Scorpio I's tend to be the more idealistic and egalitarian of the pair, Aquarius II's the more pragmatic and elitist. Excesses and extremes of thought and behavior are likely to polarize these two and also to set them in competition for the attention of colleagues or relatives.

ADVICE: *Exert more willpower. Direction is needed. Attention is not everything. Learn to do without. Build up your moral strength and decisiveness.*

JAMES JOYCE (2/2/1882)
EZRA POUND (10/30/1885)

In 1920 prose writer Joyce moved to Paris at the urging of poet Pound, who proceeded to launch Joyce's career, editing texts and arranging financial assistance. It was Pound who first serialized Joyce's *Portrait of the Artist as a Young Man* and then promoted its publication in the US as a book. **Also: François Mitterrand & Valéry Giscard d'Estaing** (French political rivals).

713

October 26–November 2

THE WEEK OF INTENSITY
SCORPIO I

February 8–15

THE WEEK OF ACCEPTANCE
AQUARIUS III

STRENGTHS: **CONFRONTING,
SELF-ACTUALIZING, PROFOUND**

WEAKNESSES: **DISTURBING,
DECEIVING, TURBULENT**

BEST: **FRIENDSHIP**

WORST: **LOVE**

A.J. Ayer (10/29/10)
Alfred North Whitehead (2/15/1861)

Ayer and Whitehead, both notable 20th-century philosophers, were ideological opponents. Whitehead's metaphysical *Principia Mathematica* (1910-13) is a landmark study of pure logic. Ayer's antimetaphysical *Language, Truth, and Logic* (1936) expounded the doctrine of logical positivism based on observation and experimentation.

Exploring the Shadow Side

The often turbulent chemistry in this relationship can force both partners to explore their shadow side. The confrontation with this shadow is the relationship's principal challenge and focus; it is often painful and difficult, but if the partners have the guts to hang in there, they have the potential to make excellent progress in their own personal development. The impetus for this self-exploration usually comes from Aquarius III's. They might appear to be dominated by their Scorpio I partners, and they are indeed at the very least wary of them, being afraid of their criticism and their aggression. Yet it is only the overt decision-making that Aquarius III's leave up to Scorpio I's, preferring to call the shots in a subtle way. This is demonstrated by the fact that Scorpio I's will rarely make a move without consulting their partner and asking for advice.

Love affairs are apt to be highly stressful. In order for them to last, Aquarius III's will have to show great patience with their Scorpio I partners. Both partners will enjoy the relationship's physicality, since this is one area where their dark side can be granted freer expression without accompanying disruption. They will learn a great deal from their emotional interactions, but it may still be necessary for the Aquarius III to continue to pretend that the Scorpio I is the boss. This attitude can continue into marriage. Here, however, Aquarius III's will usually take the lead openly, at least as far as dealing with children is concerned.

In friendships and in sibling and working relationships, Scorpio I's and Aquarius III's usually become not more dependent on but more independent of each other. The health of these relationships becomes apparent when their members move on to create new matchups with other people, carrying with them the valuable knowledge they have gained of themselves with each other. Self-actualizing, such relationships raise their partners to new levels of awareness and performance.

ADVICE: *Hang in there. Minimize turbulence. Awareness is of mutual benefit. The dark side is not to be feared. Make friends with internal enemies.*

October 26–November 2

THE WEEK OF INTENSITY
SCORPIO I

February 16–22

THE CUSP OF SENSITIVITY
AQUARIUS-PISCES CUSP

STRENGTHS: **COOPERATIVE,
COMMUNICATIVE, EMPATHIC**

WEAKNESSES: **CONTENT,
BORING, STAGNATING**

BEST: **WORK**

WORST: **LOVE**

Pat Sajak (10/26/46)
Vanna White (2/18/57)

In 1982 Sajak and White took over as co-hosts of *Wheel of Fortune* (1975–), which soon became the highest-rated game show in tv history. Sajak's easygoing, boyish personality combined with White's muted sex appeal continue to make the show a hit. *Also:* **Joanna Shimkus & Sidney Poitier** (married; actors); **John Adams & George Washington** (first US vice-president/president).

The Trustworthy Mirror

This relationship manifests as a bedrock of trust and understanding, a place the partners can turn to for thoughtful advice, empathy and support. Here they are called upon to be trustworthy mirrors of each other's feelings, reflecting them back to be viewed. With great gentleness, Scorpio I's will strive to bring Aquarius-Pisces' feelings out into the open and to help dissolve the defenses they have built up over the years. Aquarius-Pisces, meanwhile, are among the few individuals with the patience and insight to help Scorpio I's dig deeper into themselves. This personal dynamic would seem to have little connection with the efficient team these two can make in their careers, yet even worldly pursuits depend on a core of understanding at their base. These two often have an instinctual knowledge of how things work in their common field, and their joint mastery of technique can put many a successful enterprise on its feet.

In friendship, love and marriage, this combination can involve a strong empathic bond that provides mutual protection and support. Although love and understanding are usually present, passion may be curiously absent. As rewarding as these relationships can be, Scorpio I's may grow bored and long for greater intensity. Should they look elsewhere, or actually stray, Aquarius-Pisces could retreat behind their protective wall, resolving never to give away their heart so readily again. In the family, parent-child relationships in this combination can be sensitive and deeply empathic.

Work relationships between these two can be productive. It matters little which person is the boss and which the assistant, or even which has the higher position as co-workers within a hierarchy; this relationship is not about the exercise of power. It is rather about each partner's acute sensitivity to what the other is feeling—this is what makes their close cooperation and instant communication possible. There is no guarantee, however, that they will have the desire to develop their capabilities fully and dare to fail, for too often they are content to reach a reasonable position and stay there.

ADVICE: *Empathy may not be enough. Push yourself a bit more to achieve the very best you are capable of, in all areas. Strive for peak experiences.*

October 26–November 2

THE WEEK OF INTENSITY
SCORPIO I

February 23–March 2

THE WEEK OF SPIRIT
PISCES I

The Rules

This pair is united by a search for the underlying rules that govern human behavior and natural phenomena. Their relationship brings out their philosophical and serious sides, but this does not mean they are incapable of having fun together. The focus here is on a respect for tradition, a concomitant desire to do things properly and a solid pragmatism that lends support to any project. Scorpio I's appear the more practical, scientific and factual of the pair, Pisces I's more theoretical, metaphysical and dreamy. Whether they actually work together or not, Scorpio I's and Pisces I's often eventually come to respect each other's ideas.

The physical attraction between these two can be pronounced, and highly sensual interactions usually result. Since Pisces I and Scorpio I lie in trine aspect to each other (120° apart in the zodiac), astrology predicts an easy, pleasurable interaction between them, and as lovers these two may indeed give themselves over to the unbridled pursuit of pleasure. The need here is for self-understanding. If the partners are unable to gain psychological awareness, they are likely to feel helpless when struck by depression, anxiety or grief. Their relationship can be prone to obsession or addiction, both of which seem to serve the dual purpose of providing pleasure and preventing pain, but eventually lead to breakdowns. Serious thought should be given to such matters before taking the step of marriage.

It is in the sphere of career and friendship that the philosophical aspects of the relationship are most clearly revealed. Responsibility of thought, rather than of action, is crucial here, for each partner will follow high intellectual and moral principles in their activities, whether as professional or leisure-time partners. Family matchups, too, make serious demands and require great understanding and trust if natural jealousies and differences of opinion are to be surmounted.

ADVICE: *Connect emotion and intellect. Look for thoughtfulness in love. Be open to other points of view. Jealousy can prove divisive.*

October 26–November 2

THE WEEK OF INTENSITY
SCORPIO I

March 3–10

THE WEEK OF THE LONER
PISCES II

Ambiguous Fog

This is by no means an ordinary matchup—in fact, it is a highly complex relationship, at times extraordinarily close, at others barely viable. The reason for this is the depth of the partners' emotional involvement, which is usually pronounced, so that if either of them takes offense or feels neglected or unfairly treated by the other, communication breakdowns and withdrawals are to be expected. The relationship shows such enormous sensitivity that day-to-day interactions are more likely to be governed by feelings and moods than by reason.

Objectivity is difficult to achieve in the areas of love and friendship, which are apt to be intertwined. Since each of these personalities is extremely private and secretive, their ability to share at a deep level in this relationship raises serious issues of trust. Any breach of the relationship's personal code could be viewed as a serious betrayal. Furthermore, Scorpio I's and Pisces II's usually become overdependent on each other emotionally, which they realize only when they are deprived of each other's company, through separation or breakup. Together they inevitably face the problem of how to maintain their individuality and keep themselves from getting lost in an amorphous and ambiguous emotional fog.

The competitive aspects of the combination emerge in family, career and marital settings. It is particularly important that each partner's individual worth be recognized, no matter how successful they may be as a pair. Difficulties arise when Pisces II's feel that Scorpio I's are being aggressive and controlling, or when Scorpio I's find their Pisces II partners vague, misleading or uncommunicative. Working and living together on a daily basis may be difficult for these two given their emotional volatility and temperamental differences. If they can concentrate on the job at hand, they can complete small projects of limited scope, but they should think carefully before taking on a project of larger scale.

ADVICE: *Strive for objectivity. Don't be so unforgiving. As close as you are, you may still not truly understand each other. Try to give greater definition to your feelings.*

PAUL KANTNER (3/12/41)
GRACE SLICK (10/30/39)

Jefferson Airplane's Kantner and Slick had their daughter China in '71. During the pregnancy the band recorded their great *Blows Against the Empire* album. In '71 baby China was cover girl for the Slick and Kantner album *Sunfighter.* By '75 the romance was ending. Slick married the band's 24-year-old lighting director. **Also: Eddie Holland & Brian Holland** (brothers; Motown songwriting team).

October 26–November 2
THE WEEK OF INTENSITY
SCORPIO I

March 11–18
THE WEEK OF DANCERS & DREAMERS
PISCES III

Several Metamorphoses

Once the partners in this relationship set their minds on achieving something, they are unlikely to give up until they reach their goal. But making up their minds in the first place can be a problem. Scorpio I's can be hard to please, and their elaborate precision is likely to drive Pisces III's crazy. They obsess on details that Pisces III's are more than willing to overlook, being more interested in getting the show on the road. Although Scorpio and Pisces are water signs, their relationship is ruled by earth, which means that it emphasizes solidity, purpose and responsibility.

Scorpio I–Pisces III love affairs can be sexually intense but also claiming. Their involvements are hard for them to get any distance from, or, if necessary, to dissolve, without intense pain. These relationships can last for years but can also go through a number of metamorphoses, including a more platonic phase that resembles a close friendship. They could also survive a long period spent geographically apart. Marriages in this combination usually last for life, since the couple's emotional, financial and social involvements are characteristically too binding to be easily broken. These relationships can prove mutually advantageous, since both partners take an equal share in work efforts and in reaping their rewards.

Family and work involvements can overlap, so that they favor businesses and occupations in which the partners' family has a history dating back a few generations. It is not uncommon for Scorpio I parents and Pisces III children to learn a great deal from each other professionally and to share all decisions of a business nature. When these two are friends, on the other hand, they are best off keeping their personal relationship apart from their business and family involvements. These friendships tend to be private in nature and are deliberately kept that way to avoid both prying eyes (looking in) and alluring prospects (looking out)—for they tend to isolate themselves unduly from the world or else to occupy an elitist or exclusive social position.

ADVICE: *Don't get hung up on details. Keep the big picture in mind. Be open to the influence of others. If changes are necessary, don't oppose them.*

MARIA SHRIVER (11/6/55)
SARGENT SHRIVER (11/9/15)

Maria, Sargent's daughter, is a tv reporter-at-large, covering many special events. He is best known as the first director of the Peace Corps (1961–66). He was also ambassador to France (1968–70) and vice-presidential running mate with George McGovern in '72. Both are active in the Special Olympics, headed by Eunice Kennedy, his wife, her mother.

November 3–11
THE WEEK OF DEPTH
SCORPIO II

November 3–11
THE WEEK OF DEPTH
SCORPIO II

Well-Nigh Unassailable

This would appear to be an unavoidably heavy matchup but does not have to be. Although both of these partners may play a commanding role in their relationships with other people, in their own relationship they can be surprisingly undemanding. This is because they respect each other's power and feel little need to impress someone they consider at least as powerful—and as dangerous—as themselves with an aggressive or threatening stance. Their relationship, then, is often stable, self-assured and, at least as far as attacks from outside are concerned, well-nigh unassailable.

True, in times of emotional frustration these two can sink to all-time depressive lows together, and it will be hard for them to drag each other out of their mutual funk. Love affairs and marriages thus afflicted can experience great pain and suffering. The partners are no strangers to such phenomena, however, and will often manage to live with these difficulties for years, hanging in there without quitting and sometimes even overcoming or simply outlasting their problems. Third parties who make the mistake of trying to intrude, perhaps feeling that they can make one of the lovers happier, may get a double sting from this Scorpionic duo before they depart wiser.

Scorpio II's may be a bit too wary and suspicious of each other to make good business partners. Not so much conflict as a kind of quiet paranoia may keep them from trusting each other enough to allow the kind of freedom either of them will need to conclude business deals and work on developing products or marketing strategies. As siblings and friends, they will serve to toughen each other up and will also often protect each other from outside threat, for example from parents. Jealousy and competitiveness may be a problem for them, however, in relation to a common lover, parent or friend. Still, Scorpio II's know how to put such considerations aside in favor of preserving their own relationship.

ADVICE: *Nip depressions in the bud when possible. Beware of competition and jealousies. Loyalty can also be repressive. Don't hold on to your pain.*

November 3–11
THE WEEK OF DEPTH
SCORPIO II

November 12–18
THE WEEK OF CHARM
SCORPIO III

A Materialistic Haze

This relationship can be remarkably easygoing and natural. Its freedom from conflict and stress, however, can become a problem if the partners slip into a self-satisfied and materialistic haze in which they neither attain nor, sometimes, even desire any kind of personal or spiritual development. Scorpio II's may want the relationship to offer a fuller emotional palette and can show signs of impatience or frustration if it does not. Scorpio III's may prefer to be left alone and not reminded of whatever is lacking from the relationship, since they may be quite satisfied with things as they are.

Both love affairs and marriages between these two can be quite satisfying and long-lasting. The partners are generally thoughtful and considerate, loyal and hardworking. Love affairs usually acquire greater meaning when they develop into permanent living situations or marriages, and children can be a special blessing. Both partners can make attentive and nurturing parents, but they should be careful not to be overprotective, stifling their children's more creative or spiritual side. And when these children reach adolescence, they may put their Scorpio II–Scorpio III parents through the ordeal of facing a rebellion against the materialistic aspects of family life, depending on their individual makeup.

Members of the same sex may find themselves either friends or enemies, or, in the case of career connections, either colleagues or competitors. In all cases, the pairing has a certain ease about it, and rivalries can be carried on without resort to underhanded methods or cruelty; but this is not to say that the combat is any less fierce, since for both these personalities victory is the only possibility. Colleagues, co-workers and business partners in this combination must prevent their power drives as a pair from making them turn ruthless or unfairly take advantage of a situation that holds out the promise of advancement or profit. In family settings, relatives in this combination may be polite enough but often harbor secret animosities and grudges toward each other.

ADVICE: *Work harder on self-actualization. Don't neglect the spiritual side of life. Victory is less important than you think. Bring feelings out into the open.*

RELATIONSHIPS

STRENGTHS: **SATISFYING, NURTURING, EASYGOING**

WEAKNESSES: **MATERIALISTIC, STUNTED, RUTHLESS**

BEST: **MARRIAGE**

WORST: **FRIENDSHIP**

YANNI (11/4/54)
LINDA EVANS (11/18/42)

Actress Evans is best known for her role as Krystle on the tv series *Dynasty* (1981–89). She has also been the publicist-promoter for Yanni, an arranger-pianist who performs interpretive music for large audiences and sporting events. They are romantically linked. *Also:* **George Patton & Erwin Rommel** (WWII foes; generals); **Alger Hiss & Joseph McCarthy** (alleged spy/senate investigator).

November 3–11
THE WEEK OF DEPTH
SCORPIO II

November 19–24
THE CUSP OF REVOLUTION
SCORPIO-SAGITTARIUS CUSP

Style Over Substance

This relationship generally puts more emphasis on the way something is done than on what it is that is done—in short, it ranks style over substance. Manners, etiquette, convention and protocol are all necessary issues here. Some would argue that a relationship like this one is false, superficial or based on illusory values, but it is truer to say that it is concerned with style and with doing things in an elegant way. Conversations between Scorpio II's and Scorpio-Sagittarians can be so beguiling and seductive that it is difficult to remember afterward what was said. There is certainly an element of game-playing in all this, but it usually doesn't hurt anyone and the partners rarely kid themselves about what is really going on.

Love affairs and marriages are not especially recommended here. These partners have trouble expressing their real feelings, and when they do manage it, open warfare often results. Friendships in this combination are potentially a lot more successful, and in fact spouses and lovers who give up their physical relationship and become friends sometimes experience a marked relief from tension and can eventually enjoy and develop themselves much more productively. As a pair, these friends are likely to occupy a central position within a group; those around them are likely to rely on them for their strength and dependability.

In business and other professional endeavors in which both partners have an interest, they can work out contracts and deals with little pain and great profit on both sides—as long as they are happy to benefit mutually. Since both of them are capable of a lot of trickery between the lines, however, reading the fine print, at the very least, is strongly advised. Boss-employee relationships of either combination can work out satisfactorily with little blame or guilt. Likewise, parent-child relationships can be mutually respectful and relatively free of conflict.

ADVICE: *Your style is great—beef up your substance. Don't get carried away by illusion. Stick to your word. Remember that others depend on you.*

RELATIONSHIPS

STRENGTHS: **BEGUILING, RESPECTFUL, PRODUCTIVE**

WEAKNESSES: **REPRESSIVE, STILTED, TRICKY**

BEST: **WORK**

WORST: **MARRIAGE**

WILEY POST (11/22/1899)
WILL ROGERS (11/4/1879)

Post was a famous American aviator who made the first solo around-the-world flight (1933). Humorist Rogers, the celebrated entertainer, homespun philosopher and political commentator, was at the peak of his career in 1935 when he went flying with Post. Their plane crashed in Alaska and both were killed. *Also:* **Billy Graham & Billy Sunday** (revival-style evangelists).

TINA TURNER (11/25/38)
IKE TURNER (11/5/31)

Ike and Tina married in 1962 and, despite their success as a major soul act in the 60s and 70s, had a tumultuous—sometimes violent—relationship. She left him in '76 and became a solo superstar.

Also: Edward VII & Queen Alexandra (married royalty); **Walker Evans & James Agee** (collaborators; photographer/writer); **Mary Travers & Paul Stookey** (singers of Peter, Paul and Mary).

November 3–11
THE WEEK OF DEPTH
SCORPIO II

November 25–December 2
THE WEEK OF INDEPENDENCE
SAGITTARIUS I

An Exothermic Reaction

The air of calculation in this relationship indicates forethought and purpose. With each other, both of these partners are able to be sure of what they want and are willing to make the necessary sacrifices to get it. The result is the potential for great achievement. Scorpio II's and Sagittarius I's can be strongly attracted to each other; some type of partnership between them is quite common. Yet their chemistry is exothermic, meaning that the heat of their reaction isn't always put to good use. Unless they can focus some of this energy on goals of a higher, more spiritual nature, they risk a damaging kind of implosion. Sagittarius I's can awaken the sleeping energies of Scorpio II's, who in turn can ground the wilder and more flighty tendencies of Sagittarius I's.

Love affairs here are usually intense at the start, but feelings can sharply and quickly fall off. Like a lightning rod, Scorpio II's pull Sagittarius I fire from the sky. That energy is easily lost, but if it can be contained it will provide a driving current. This is a matchup that can rarely survive on romance or sexuality alone—it needs concrete goals. The project of building a family, career or lifestyle may well be what these personalities want, and marriage will often supply it. Their relationship can drive them both on willy-nilly, and in the process both of them might undergo a metamorphosis, or at the very least a significant change in their personalities.

Career, family ties and friendships are often related in this matchup. A Scorpio II can be a strongly controlling force whose guidance Sagittarius I's may be open to accepting. In business, Scorpio II's often handle the finances while Sagittarius I's give the partnership its dynamic public persona. Problems arise in these areas when too much is demanded of either partner, for versatility is seldom a strength here. Stricter separation of business and pleasure, career and home, and social and personal aspects of life may have to be maintained for the sake of sanity and stability.

ADVICE: *Don't expect too much. Make solid contributions that really count. Beware of using each other selfishly. Keep your eye on the object.*

BILL WALTON (11/5/52)
LARRY BIRD (12/7/56)

Basketball's Walton and Bird were MVPs. While Walton's career peaked in the 70s and Bird's in the 80s, these 2 great players were fierce competitors on the court. Walton led his Portland team to the NBA title in '77, and Bird led Boston to 3 titles ('81, '84, '86). They became Celtics teammates in the late 80s.

November 3–11
THE WEEK OF DEPTH
SCORPIO II

December 3–10
THE WEEK OF THE ORIGINATOR
SAGITTARIUS II

Expressing Disapproval

This can be an agreeable enough relationship, but it isn't necessarily a reliable one. It often focuses on expressing its disapproval of established mores, and it can even outright rebel. As a pair, these two are unable to accept the status quo. Their matchup is always trying to implement new values and ideas in place of old but is not invariably successful, since its internal cohesion is somewhat weak. When the partners are not facing any kind of external threat, for example, they tend to turn on each other, engaging in fierce disagreements or simply drifting apart. Furthermore, Scorpio II's have controlling impulses while Sagittarius II's need freedom and sometimes find their partner in this combination downright repressive. In extreme cases they will be forced to revolt against Scorpio II authority.

In love affairs and marriages these two will usually do things their own way, despite the disapproval of their family and friends. These relationships are rarely conventional, but the couple's antisocial attitudes can boomerang on them and also on any children they might have. Learning diplomacy and compromise will be extremely important for them, since their tendency to arouse antagonism in others can become a serious problem.

In friendships, Scorpio II's will encourage the introspective side of Sagittarius II's, so that the relationship may become an exercise in self-realization. It will also be quite physically active—this pair can be strongly oriented toward sports or exercise, a beneficial direction for relatively sedentary Scorpio II's. Siblings in this combination can affect each other favorably but must take care not to let their competitive and combative urges run out of hand. The matchup may not work out so well in the commercial sphere, since financially prudent Scorpio II's will probably disapprove of the loose Sagittarius II approach to money, and conflict is likely to result.

ADVICE: *Calm your rebellious urges. Be more patient and accepting. Innovation can be implemented quietly. Encourage personal and spiritual growth.*

November 3–11

THE WEEK OF DEPTH
SCORPIO II

December 11–18

THE WEEK OF THE TITAN
SAGITTARIUS III

RELATIONSHIPS

STRENGTHS: **STRUCTURED,
COMMUNICATIVE, FREE**

WEAKNESSES: **ALIENATING,
TEMPERAMENTAL, RESENTFUL**

BEST: **MARRIAGE**

WORST: **PARENT-CHILD**

Structuring Freedom

These two generate so much energy that there is no way their relationship can contain it. Energy like this is stimulating, exciting and a source of creative fuel, but it also demands the freedom to follow as many avenues of advance as possible. The relationship, then, should focus on creating freedom and latitude between its partners. It should be structured freely enough to allow them the space they need; if it is not, power struggles can easily emerge between them. These two may have a tendency to poke themselves into each other's affairs and in general to breathe down each other's necks. Paradoxically, in order to guarantee the maximum freedom to them both, they may have to agree upon and observe a set of fixed rules.

Open lines of communication are essential here; love affairs will certainly suffer without them, no matter how gratifying these affairs might be physically. Sagittarius III's will find smoldering Scorpio II passion highly pleasurable but may not enjoy the periodic depressions and resentments that accompany it. Scorpio II's sometimes feel neglected in this relationship but are usually self-sufficient enough to handle it. Marriages can be successful as long as the spouses agree on rules that they can observe strictly. They will not tolerate being dependent on each other financially, so the best situation will be for both of them to have their own income, or, if they do hold money in common, for those sums to be well enough budgeted that they can be spent without either partner having to ask the other's permission.

In the family, the Sagittarius III child's need for freedom may not be at all what controlling Scorpio II parents have in mind, and the relationship can be stormy. Scorpio II children may have to seek other role-models if their Sagittarius III parent is gone too much of the time. Friendships and co-worker matchups in this combination can work only if they focus on responsibility to a common activity or project, rather than on a mutual emotional need. Too often, temperamental differences eventually lead to alienation.

ADVICE: *Take the time for comprehensive discussion and planning. Freedom will not materialize by itself. Lighten up whenever possible, and relax.*

STEVEN SPIELBERG (12/18/46)
KATE CAPSHAW (11/3/53)

A former model and tv soap-opera star, Capshaw made her film debut in 1982 but was not well known until 1984, when she appeared as Harrison Ford's sidekick in *Indiana Jones and the Temple of Doom*, directed by blockbuster-maker Spielberg. Capshaw and Spielberg were later married, after his divorce (1989) from actress Amy Irving.

November 3–11

THE WEEK OF DEPTH
SCORPIO II

December 19–25

THE CUSP OF PROPHECY
SAGITTARIUS-CAPRICORN CUSP

RELATIONSHIPS

STRENGTHS: **LIGHTHEARTED,
LIVELY, PASSIONATE**

WEAKNESSES: **CONFLICTED,
DISAPPROVING, TENSE**

BEST: **MARRIAGE**

WORST: **WORK**

Lively Interchange

This matchup provides its partners with that elusive commodity: freedom from themselves. Weighty, perhaps even overserious individually, these personalities enjoy lighter, freer and more interesting times when they are together, yet do so without sacrificing their awareness of the deeper side of life. The energy here encourages self-reliance, but the partners can also share ideal, even ecstatic experiences and tend to learn quite a bit as well. For such profound individuals as Scorpio II's and Sagittarius-Capricorns, this pairing could be a once-in-a-lifetime experience, no matter what type of relationship it governs.

Love affairs and marriages here are likely to be quite passionate but lighthearted as well. Strongly sexual, the pair are also sometimes quite playful, which helps them on many levels. Nor are they lacking socially; they will delight in social occasions of all kinds, even while preferring those that are mentally broadening. Together they will love to observe the foibles of others but not in a mean-spirited way—they have a strong compassionate streak. The sense of freedom that is important to both of these personalities will not prevent their love affairs from becoming marriages as long as these affairs are structured properly. If they are not, the partners might still part as friends; in fact, the relationship's strengths—its wit, its relaxing quality, its orientation toward philosophical pursuits in the arts and sciences—mean that continuing a friendship after a love affair is very likely. The partners will be unwilling to give up what the relationship has to offer.

Conflict can be expected in the areas of work and family. Both of these individuals are prone to be dominant in their field. They are unlikely to share power comfortably, and neither is apt to give in to the other's wishes. The same strengths that appear in love affairs will cut the tension at crucial moments, but it is always best if each of these partners has his or her own clear sphere of influence. They value character and integrity and will rarely use underhanded methods to achieve their aims.

ADVICE: *Be sure not to become a circle of two. Focus on the need for freedom; don't assume it exists, and make allowances for it. Limit domineering tendencies.*

MIKE NICHOLS (11/6/31)
DIANE SAWYER (12/22/45)

Brilliant producer-director Nichols and tv co-anchor Sawyer (*Prime Time Live*) have been happily married since 1988. They live in NYC, pursuing busy, creative careers. Both have won many awards for the high quality of their work. *Also:* **Lulu & Maurice Gibb** (married; singers); **Trotsky & Stalin** (communist rivals); **Clifford Irving & Howard Hughes** (fraudulent biographer/industrialist-millionaire subject).

STRENGTHS: **VIGOROUS, DETERMINED, INNOVATING**

WEAKNESSES: **ABRUPT, UNFEELING, POWER-OBSESSED**

BEST: **FRIENDSHIP**

WORST: **FAMILY**

PATTI SMITH (12/30/46)
ROBERT MAPPLETHORPE (11/4/46)

Rock singer-poet Smith and homo-erotic photographer Mapplethorpe were good friends who roomed together when he attended NY's Pratt Institute in the 60s. Famous for his "X Portfolio" of S&M scenes which set off a furor in '89, he died of AIDS that year. Smith dedicated a performance to his memory in '93.

Also: Michael Dukakis & Kitty Dukakis (married; Mass. governor-presidential candidate/wife).

November 3–11
THE WEEK OF DEPTH
SCORPIO II

December 26–January 2
THE WEEK OF THE RULER
CAPRICORN I

Dropping the Hot Potato

This relationship emphasizes conversation, mental agility and innovative thought. As long as Scorpio II's and Capricorn I's can get along (something that is in no way guaranteed), they can come up with surprisingly original ideas. But all the theorizing in the world is of little interest to these pragmatic thinkers unless it can be put into practice—and ultimately unless it can succeed. Scorpio II's and Capricorn I's will not hesitate to drop ideas, or for that matter people, like a hot potato if they are not working out. In fact, the relationship generally tends to be a bit hard, abrupt and cold. It will be important for this pair to develop a more human, kind and accepting face.

Love affairs and friendships allow normally conservative partners to give vent to a wilder and more flexible side of their makeup. They will not be at all threatened by each other in these relationships and are likely to let it all hang out, not only in the sense of being emotionally expressive but also of being honest. Scorpio II's and Capricorn I's together will see flattery as poison. It is vitally important for them, whether as lovers or as friends, to share their objective evaluations with each other so that they can achieve quantifiable improvement.

Family matchups in this combination are often damaged by serious power struggles. As spouses Scorpio II's and Capricorn I's pursue their social and financial goals with unrelenting purpose and vigor, and as business partners and work colleagues they have a similarly tough, no-nonsense approach. Strong in the spheres of money and power, they make it their business to be successful and will not take no for an answer. Indeed, their relationship has a coercive quality, often using the fist-in-the-velvet-glove approach and making it quite clear what is in store for people who do not agree to their "reasonable" offers. Personal differences will rarely be allowed to intrude in professional matters here.

ADVICE: *Work on getting along. Don't be ashamed to show sympathy. Lacking kindness is nothing to be proud of. Develop more human qualities.*

STRENGTHS: **PROTECTIVE, UNUSUAL, DEDICATED**

WEAKNESSES: **ARROGANT, PECULIAR, SELF-DESTRUCTIVE**

BEST: **FRIENDSHIP**

WORST: **MARRIAGE**

JUNE HAVOC (11/8/16)
GYPSY ROSE LEE (1/9/14)

Havoc was the younger sister of Lee. Both actresses were driven by an ambitious stage mother. As young children they played the vaudeville circuit as "Madame Rose's Dancing Daughters." Havoc later became a dramatic stage and screen actress, while Lee became the most famous burlesque stripper of her day.

Also: Spiro Agnew & Richard Nixon (vice-president/president).

November 3–11
THE WEEK OF DEPTH
SCORPIO II

January 3–9
THE WEEK OF DETERMINATION
CAPRICORN II

Lending Credence to Normalcy

These two can get so obsessed with doing things in an unusual way that they often only make things hard for themselves. Their relationship can handicap itself, then, through its own idiosyncrasies. Not that these personalities really want to be different; on the contrary, as individuals they are often quite conservative and struggle to embody ideals that would lend credence to the idea of their normalcy. Try as they may, though, they are unlikely to shake off the peculiarities that their relationship engenders, and that will often come to govern their lives.

Fate can play a deciding role in this relationship. Whether tragically or comically, seriously or ridiculously, carefully or chaotically, the partners pursue a course that in retrospect seems predetermined yet that is very much directed by the vagaries of chance. No matter how much they seem to be in control of their destiny, the opposite is usually the case. Whether in their careers or in their love lives, the outcome of any project in which they are involved will most often be unexpected. Their work relationships and marriages are usually ambitious in nature, and success seems to be the only alternative they consider. Yet by not even admitting the possibility of failure and refusing to see any warning signs, the relationship may foster the very outcome it fears the most.

Friendships between these two are often protective and close. In fact, building a private kingdom to which few are granted admittance may become a way of life for them. Both exclusive and secretive, these friendships create their own highly original rules, which may be somewhat at variance with the rules of society but work well enough within this personal context. In family relationships, negative self-fulfilling prophecies are more often the rule than the exception; the partners' statements can reflect deep fears and insecurities, all hiding under a cloak of bravado. Both parents and children may be prone to such pronouncements about themselves or each other.

ADVICE: *Be more realistic about yourself. Beware of negative expectations. Slowly build a solid base of self-confidence. Accept your fate.*

November 3–11

THE WEEK OF DEPTH
SCORPIO II

January 10–16

THE WEEK OF DOMINANCE
CAPRICORN III

Relieving Bottlenecks

This powerfully confrontational matchup expends a considerable amount of mental energy on finding the best way to reconcile its differences. When these efforts are successful, they can result in greater understanding; when they are not, instability and disorder threaten. The relationship, then, will try to bring Scorpio II's and Capricorn III's closer and to open avenues of communication between them. Both partners can be recalcitrant when a third party attempts to mediate between them; they seem to need to work out their problems by themselves, under the relationship's umbrella. They will both feel enormous satisfaction when they hammer out an agreement but also disappointment and sadness if they break off their negotiations in anger—an outcome that always looms.

Love affairs between Scorpio II's and Capricorn III's can be physically passionate but often have difficulty reaching a deeper emotional understanding. Both of them tend to keep their true feelings to themselves, and their relationship will encounter bottlenecks of repression. Working through these roadblocks to a freer and easier sort of expression is often the crying need here. Sometimes neither partner is fully aware of this, however, and it may take the advice of a friend, or, in some cases, psychological counseling, to alert them to the problem. Even so, marriages between these two can be enduring. Both partners are likely to be faithful and devoted spouses. As friends and as rivals, Scorpio II's and Capricorn III's sit on a pendulum that can swing in either direction. Their negative and their positive feelings for each other are often equal in these relationships, so that they may alternately like and dislike each other, in cycles of a certain regularity. They should try, however, to limit the scope of any arguments they might have, for these are liable to escalate rapidly to a point of no return. An equally harmful alternative is for them to hammer down their negative feelings inside, which can produce frustration and depression. Parent-child and boss-employee matchups in this combination can often successfully reach a level of increased respect and understanding as the years go by.

ADVICE: *Don't give up on your quest for understanding. Put limits on disagreement. Beware of repression. Open avenues of communication.*

DOROTHY DANDRIDGE (11/9/23)
HAROLD NICHOLAS (1/11/21)

Musical actress Dandridge was among the first black performers to achieve star status in movies—*Carmen Jones* (1954), *Porgy and Bess* (1959). She married and divorced Nicholas of the famed Nicholas Brothers dance duo. After losing all her money in an oil scam, she was found dead from a drug overdose (1965). *Also:* **Stanford White & Henry K. Thaw** (architect murdered by jealous husband).

November 3–11

THE WEEK OF DEPTH
SCORPIO II

January 17–22

THE CUSP OF MYSTERY & IMAGINATION
CAPRICORN-AQUARIUS CUSP

Kiss and Make Up

This relationship causes its partners to look at the big picture but also to be optimistic. They can even get carried away by their waves of expectation. Not only can Scorpio II's and Capricorn-Aquarians have great times together, they can bring large-scale projects to fruition—as long as emotional flare-ups between them don't sabotage all their efforts and leave their projects in smoking ruin. This is emphasized by the fact that the relationship is governed by fire, an element indicating creativity and positive energy but also, lest we forget, capable of raging out of control and causing great destruction.

Love and family relationships can be especially volatile. Lovers and even parent-child pairs in this combination might love each other deeply but can still have trouble maintaining consistency and stability in their daily life together. Particularly when Capricorn-Aquarians are in the dominant role, Scorpio II's have a way of triggering their anger and setting off explosions of feeling, which often lead to unhappiness and bitterness. The partners may well be able to kiss and make up; in fact, they often do. But while Scorpio II's might be able to forgive what has happened, they will never really forget it and will be much more on their guard in the future.

Marriages and work relationships in this combination have their ups and downs. True, some projects reach a satisfactory conclusion, but many more never get off the ground. In the end, coming out with new ideas may become a tiring and even agonizing process for this pair as they develop a record of past disappointments. Having fewer expectations, trying to limit ideas and pursue only the workable ones, and muting optimism will help the relationship to be more realistic and perhaps more successful.

Friendships are best kept separate from business and social endeavors; as friends these two are capable of having such great times together that it seems a shame to spoil things by taking on increased responsibilities or developing more serious intentions.

ADVICE: *Overenthusiasm can be deadly. Keep your feet on the ground and work on being realistic. Be willing to forgive and forget.*

JOHN RAITT (1/19/17)
BONNIE RAITT (11/8/49)

Singer-songwriter Bonnie is the daughter of Broadway vocalist John, star of *Pajama Game, Carousel* and many other major musicals from the 40s to the 60s. Bonnie's career peaked with her 1989 chart-topping album *Nick of Time*, which sold 4 million copies and won the Album-of-the-Year Grammy. *Also:* **Stanford White & Ruth St. Denis** (affair; architect/dancer).

STRENGTHS: **MIRACULOUS, PRODUCTIVE, EXPLORATORY**

WEAKNESSES: **FRIGHTENING, SUSPICIOUS, UNCOMPREHENDING**

BEST: **LOVE**

WORST: **MARRIAGE**

EUGENE V. DEBS (11/5/1855)
WILLIAM McKINLEY (1/29/1843)

Debs founded several Socialist-party organizations before he chose to run against McKinley in 1900 as America's first socialist presidential candidate. Debs was a strong orator, famous for his statement, "I am for socialism because I am for humanity." Although he lost to McKinley, Debs established the Socialist party in America.

November 3–11
THE WEEK OF DEPTH
SCORPIO II

January 23–30
THE WEEK OF GENIUS
AQUARIUS I

Nothing Short of Amazing

When these two combine their energies the results can be nothing short of miraculous. Indeed, the chemistry here is somewhat unfathomable, for the partners themselves have difficulty figuring out how two such completely different approaches can yield such wonderful results. Aquarius I's don't always understand Scorpio II's that well, seeing them as people who always do things the hard way. Meanwhile, Scorpio II's are usually amazed when an Aquarius I does something in half the time it would have taken them, but they remain a little suspicious of their partner's methods. These two should not delve too deeply into such mysteries, since things often work best when their underlying mechanisms stay hidden.

Love affairs here can be highly romantic. Scorpio II's are usually solidly in control of these relationships, but since they generally find their Aquarius I lovers thoroughly captivating and charming, they can easily be manipulated, and their dominance is not oppressive. Should the romance lead to marriage, Scorpio II's may find their spouse troublingly flighty and unable to share their own serious approach to things. But few personalities in the year can take their minds off their career worries when they get home after a hard day's work as easily as fun-loving Aquarius I's. In fact, if Aquarius I's tire of Scorpio II's heaviness and seek excitement elsewhere, their depressions could reach all-time lows.

Youthful friendships and sibling relationships are drawn toward the supernatural—they love horror stories, science fiction and fantasy. Exploring the dark side of human experience, both on screen and off, is common here. The partners must beware of indulging in activities that can be harmful or frightening to other people, particularly those much younger or much older than they. Scorpio II's and Aquarius I's can produce fantastic results in the professional sphere but are too often divided by ideological differences. Keeping their opinions to themselves may be a prerequisite to getting the job done.

ADVICE: *Get back to the real world occasionally. Be careful of your effects on others. Don't succumb to the dark side. Use your energies constructively.*

STRENGTHS: **KNOWING, SEDUCTIVE, LASTING**

WEAKNESSES: **COMPETITIVE, JEALOUS, INSULTING**

BEST: **MARRIAGE**

WORST: **WORK**

CLARK GABLE (2/1/01)
VIVIEN LEIGH (11/5/13)

Gable and Leigh are forever linked as Rhett Butler and Scarlett O'Hara in *Gone with the Wind* (1939). Leigh had been chosen from among scores of aspirants for the part, many of them Hollywood's biggest stars. Ironically, Gable was reluctant to take the part that was to be his greatest screen role. *Also:* **Sally Field & Jock Mahoney** (actress-stepdaughter of stuntman).

November 3–11
THE WEEK OF DEPTH
SCORPIO II

January 31–February 7
THE WEEK OF YOUTH & EASE
AQUARIUS II

The Eternal Flame

The great temperamental differences between these two personalities will often arouse friction within the relationship. These tensions, however, are highly provocative, producing a dynamic at once challenging and seductive. Scorpio II and Aquarius II lie square to each other in the zodiac (they are 90° apart), which can cause all sorts of difficulties, but it also ensures that dull moments will be few. Aquarius II's will be pleased to have their emotions stirred so deeply but are also apt to be disturbed by their partner's intrusions. Scorpio II's will love the relationship's passion, even though they won't always take this partner too seriously. Actually the matchup as a whole is best taken with a grain of salt and a twinkle in the eye, a healthy way to avoid its otherwise inevitable tension and frustration.

In love affairs, smoldering desires can stir up all sorts of passionate feelings. If this fiery matchup ever dies down, its embers can quickly be rekindled to white heat. Marriages, too, tend to hold something in reserve—something to keep them from burning out. Even after spending long periods apart, when these two are together again they will feel an almost immediate warmth, as if lit by an eternal flame.

Friendships in this combination tend to engage in banter bordering on outright insult—the partners often have great fun trying to one-up each other or have the last word. Actually, serious competition and jealousy sometimes emerge here, but the partners are usually well aware of how quickly such feelings can be aroused and rarely let their relationship turn hostile.

In domestic and professional settings, Aquarius II's have a relaxed approach that will often captivate Scorpio II's, who, however, can nevertheless be extremely demanding and critical, disapproving of the very attitudes that attracted them in the first place. Aquarius II children and employees may consequently see their Scorpio II parents and bosses as having a dark, brooding intensity that serves no useful purpose.

ADVICE: *Beware of playing with fire. Your jokes may be taken seriously. Take the time to be clear about what you mean. Let up, relax.*

November 3–11

THE WEEK OF DEPTH
SCORPIO II

February 8–15

THE WEEK OF ACCEPTANCE
AQUARIUS III

RELATIONSHIPS

STRENGTHS: **PASSIONATE,
CONFRONTING, SOCIAL**

WEAKNESSES: **ESCAPIST,
JEALOUS, DIVIDED**

BEST: **LOVE**

WORST: **FRIENDSHIP**

Sharing Emotional Experiences

Empathic feelings provide the predominant energy in this relationship. But although sharing deep emotional experiences may ultimately be a positive experience for these two, in the short run they will run into a lot of rough spots, since neither of them much cares for exposing themselves. A pattern of closeness followed by distancing would be no surprise here. Still, Aquarius III's are quite capable of giving Scorpio II's the kind of understanding they crave, and indeed the relationship draws out not only the more accepting qualities of Aquarius III's but also their curiosity about their emotionally complex partners. It's true that Scorpio II's are also likely to activate the dark side of Aquarius III's, but this can ultimately lead them into passionate involvements and a good dose of self-analysis and confrontation.

Love affairs and marriages between these partners are often rewarding and pleasurable. Scorpio II's will be roused to new heights of passion by provocative and unreserved Aquarius III sensuality. Aquarius III's are deeply touched by their partner's total commitment; they tend to tire easily in love and marriage, but their Scorpio II partner will provide them with an almost inexhaustible palette of sensuous delights to pick from. As parents these two can make a dedicated couple. Having quite different points of view, they also provide their children with a real choice when it comes to voicing complaints and airing worries.

Co-workers and siblings in this combination rarely isolate themselves from their fellow employees and family members; they enjoy establishing social ties. This means that their relationship can become the central focus of their group and that they often act as advisors and mediators for other people. As friends, they can find many exciting activities to be involved in while rarely if ever losing sight of or taking for granted their own empathic bond. Tragic scenes may result, however, if both of them are romantically drawn to a third person and ultimately have to make an impossible decision against their own friendship.

ADVICE: *Beware of dangerous escapes. Confrontation is important here—don't run out on it. Don't throw away what is most valuable to you.*

BURT REYNOLDS (2/11/36)
SALLY FIELD (11/6/46)

In the late 70s Field and Reynolds began a long romance, working together in a number of undistinguished but commercial films. By '79 Field dropped her "Burt Reynolds' girlfriend" image and moved on to more dramatic parts, breaking up with him in the process. **Also: Herman Mankiewicz & Joseph Mankiewicz** (brothers; screenwriter/director); **Richard Burton & Claire Bloom** (affair; actors).

November 3–11

THE WEEK OF DEPTH
SCORPIO II

February 16–22

THE CUSP OF SENSITIVITY
AQUARIUS-PISCES CUSP

RELATIONSHIPS

STRENGTHS: **SERIOUS,
PRAGMATIC, SOCIAL**

WEAKNESSES: **CONFLICTING,
PROSELYTIZING, COERCIVE**

BEST: **SIBLING**

WORST: **LOVE**

Serious Ethical Issues

The question of which or whose rules to play by is addressed with great seriousness in this relationship, which is likely to be taken up with ethical problems or with putting ideals into practice. The greatest source of conflict here will be the issue of whose moral code to follow. Scorpio II's usually have the more refined sense of right and wrong, but they don't always articulate it consciously, and their moral indignation can manifest in destructive ways. They are usually right, but other people rarely admit it. Aquarius-Pisces, meanwhile, have a looser sense of honor, and the role of fantasy in their makeup should never be underestimated. It is crucial for this pair to agree on the structure their relationship is to follow. This will be a difficult task at best, since as individuals both of these personalities are prone to living on the very edge of the subconscious most of the time. The tyrannical quality in their relationship, in fact, is a result of this internal projection.

Love affairs and friendships seek to satisfy the more social side of these partners. Aquarius-Pisces secretly long for a strong figure to take the lead and draw them out socially. Once they are out in public, in fact, it may be hard for more reclusive Scorpio II's to get them to go home again, resulting in strange conflicts over the balance between social and personal interaction. Aquarius-Pisces must learn to be sensitive to the darker moods of Scorpio II's and to know when to back off and leave them alone. In marriages the stress will be on proper behavior and following the rules of good conduct. These rules should be explicitly stated if misunderstandings, accusations and conflicts are to be avoided and the marriage is not to be stormy. Sibling relationships in this combination, prone as they are to following the rules of the larger family unit, can be close and sympathetic.

In the professional sphere, these two seek a fulfillment beyond mere financial gain. To feel comfortable with their very likely success, they need a strong moral purpose.

ADVICE: *Don't expect others to sympathize with your views. Beware of turning others off with your fervor. Don't be so strict.*

JOHN McENROE (2/16/59)
TATUM O'NEAL (11/5/63)

Actress O'Neal married tennis great McEnroe in 1986. She made her movie debut in *Paper Moon* (1973), for which she won, at age 10, an Oscar for best supporting actress. Through the 70s and 80s she continued to act but slacked off during the marriage to care for their children. They split up in '93. **Also: Erika Mann & W.H. Auden** (Thomas Mann's daughter married gay poet to flee Nazi Germany).

RELATIONSHIPS

STRENGTHS: **SUCCESSFUL,
UNCONVENTIONAL, HEAVENLY**
WEAKNESSES: **PROBLEMATIC,
ESCAPIST, HELLISH**
BEST: **WORK**
WORST: **MARRIAGE**

RICHARD BURTON (11/10/25)
ELIZABETH TAYLOR (2/27/32)

Welsh actor Burton and superstar love goddess Taylor began their lavish but tempestuous relationship on the set of *Cleopatra* (1963). They worked together in several more films, most memorably *Who's Afraid of Virginia Woolf?* They were married twice, 1964–74 and 1975–76.

Also: **Tommy Dorsey & Jimmy Dorsey** (brothers; bandleaders); **Art Carney & Jackie Gleason** (co-stars, *The Honeymooners*).

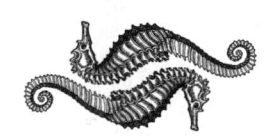

November 3–11
THE WEEK OF DEPTH
SCORPIO II

February 23–March 2
THE WEEK OF SPIRIT
PISCES I

Heaven or Hell?

This classic matchup seems to have been made in heaven—or perhaps in hell. In either case it is irresistible and often unconventional. The pair can achieve considerable professional success, but this is certainly no guarantee of the consistency or stability of their personal relationship. Scorpio II's are notoriously hard to reach, especially in their darker moods, and although Pisces I's understand them as well as anyone, their needs and demands will often prove too much for their partner in this combination to handle. Aggressive as they are, they will not find Pisces I's pushovers by any means; this couple's battles will be long and hard fought. Based squarely on feeling, the relationship will usually have a dual focus: working out emotional problems and putting the tremendous energy that the relationship releases in the service of a professional endeavor, whether in business or the arts.

Scorpio II's and Pisces I's in love can get too close. Swallowed up by their relationship, they may have to struggle to maintain their own identities; their private world is likely to be exclusive, shutting out everyone else. It is tempting to think they have been involved in previous lifetimes, so familiar and complex is their interaction. Emotional problems between these two often seem insoluble, yet they will rarely give up on them and can in fact make a lot of progress in working them out. Drugs and sex, however, are likely to be all-too-ready escapes in this exhausting process. Marriages are not recommended here unless the spouses are willing to commit themselves to a lot of serious psychological investigation.

Professionally this matchup can be one of the most successful in the entire year. Family members, friends and spouses or lovers often have interrelated careers or actually become business partners or co-workers. The crucial issue is how they will relate to each other personally. The decision may have to be made to limit their contact on the job, since their chaotic energies could prove disruptive to the project and to those around them.

ADVICE: *Take a break from each other occasionally. Follow the constructive path. Don't get sidetracked from your real purpose in life.*

RELATIONSHIPS

STRENGTHS: **RESPONSIBLE,
FLUID, GOAL-ORIENTED**
WEAKNESSES: **DISTRACTING,
SECRETIVE, PROCRASTINATING**
BEST: **MARRIAGE**
WORST: **FAMILY**

STANFORD WHITE (11/9/1853)
EVELYN NESBIT (3/8/1885)

Architect White and chorus girl Nesbit, married to rich businessman Harry K. Thaw, were carrying on an affair. In 1906, on the roof garden of NY's Madison Square Garden (which White designed), Thaw shot and killed White in a jealous rage.

Also: **Roseanne Barr & Tom Arnold** (married; actors); **Ole Olson & Chic Johnson** (vaudeville-movie comedy team).

November 3–11
THE WEEK OF DEPTH
SCORPIO II

March 3–10
THE WEEK OF THE LONER
PISCES II

The Coveted Goal

This is a highly seductive combination, and not just physically. Attraction and desire play a large role here, but the relationship's magnetism works not only between the partners themselves but between them as a pair and a goal they covet, whether social, financial or family oriented. The relationship brings out its partners' most determined sides, enabling them to achieve together what they might not achieve alone. Usually, though, this is more to the benefit of the Pisces II. Scorpio II and Pisces II are positioned trine to each other in the zodiac (120° apart), which here suggests an easy, sensuous orientation. Relationships in this combination can be very tightly knit. In some ways, in fact, they are indissoluble, since their watery nature is already so fluid. Yet they have another side as well, an earthy one, which is intensely practical and responsible. At times conflicts can arise between these two sides, with one pulling toward relaxation and procrastination, the other toward action and effort.

Love affairs here can be highly secretive. Family members and friends may think they know what goes on in private between Scorpio II's and Pisces II's, but they are usually wrong. Much of the relationship's psychological import is often hidden from the lovers themselves, who may not be terribly interested in self-analysis. Marriages might prove more successful than love affairs, since they would satisfy the need of both partners to take on responsibilities. Strong business or career ties could be the cement holding the whole thing together.

In the family, Scorpio II–Pisces II relatives can be highly controlling, claiming and demanding of attention. Friendships work out best when grounded by a common interest. Hobbies, sports and fitness activities, entertainment and adventure can lure these two away from other pressing duties and become the dominant focus in their lives. Co-workers in this combination often work side by side for years in relative harmony, with a steady output and little fuss.

ADVICE: *Decide where your priorities lie. Make up your mind and act. Find an outlet for your responsible side. Don't get muddled or mired down.*

November 3–11

THE WEEK OF DEPTH
SCORPIO II

March 11–18

THE WEEK OF DANCERS & DREAMERS
PISCES III

RELATIONSHIPS

STRENGTHS: PERSUASIVE, SOULFUL, MEDITATIVE

WEAKNESSES: EXAGGERATIVE, PAINFUL, REGRETFUL

BEST: LOVE

WORST: MARRIAGE

Powers of Persuasion

O nce these partners make up their minds about something, they are likely to get their way. Powers of persuasion are enormous in this relationship, so much so that people are liable to believe almost anything these two say. The result is that they have a tremendous moral responsibility not to betray the trust of those who follow them. Of course, it may not be so easy for Scorpio II's and Pisces III's to reach agreement or even to meet in the first place. Should they encounter each other later in life, they may deeply regret not having met sooner.

Love affairs are likely to be more soulful than romantic. An element of sorrow or pain may pervade these relationships, for they carry with them an awareness of the travails of life. Happiness here has a slightly bittersweet quality, being suffused with the belief that although life is not a bed of roses, things most often turn out for the best. In marriages, a spirit of resignation will carry the spouses through some pretty rough spots.

Professional and career matchups in this combination can be very successful and will rely heavily on the couple's persuasiveness. It is of crucial importance that the products or services they offer be sound and reliable, and even then they may have trouble living up to their reputation. Truth to tell, it is often not the Scorpio II's and Pisces III's who are blowing their trumpet but their consumers and clients, who in their enthusiasm often exaggerate things out of all proportion.

As siblings and friends these two may prefer to keep to themselves rather than play a strongly social role. Increased reflectiveness and spirituality often manifest here with age and maturity; after a stormy adolescence, the pair may slowly begin to develop meditative powers and to ponder the meaning of life.

EDWARD ALBEE (3/12/28)
SAM SHEPARD (11/5/43)

Albee and Shepard are contemporary American dramatists influenced by France's theater of the absurd during the 60s. Shepard, then a budding avant-garde playwright, went on to screenwriting and film acting. Albee also started in the avant-garde. His greatest success was *Who's Afraid of Virginia Woolf?* (1962). **Also: Ennio Morricone & Bernardo Bertolucci** (collaborators; film-score composer/director).

ADVICE: *Watch what you say. Don't give other people the wrong idea. Your persuasiveness can backfire. Don't exaggerate. Let your actions speak for themselves.*

November 12–18

THE WEEK OF CHARM
SCORPIO III

November 12–18

THE WEEK OF CHARM
SCORPIO III

RELATIONSHIPS

STRENGTHS: STIMULATING, CHALLENGING, ADMIRING

WEAKNESSES: SELFISH, INACTIVE, FEARFUL

BEST: ADVERSARIAL

WORST: LOVE

Giving Ground

A lthough Scorpio III's tend to be strong individuals, this relationship may be somewhat ineffective, for both of them want to be boss. As a result, they can easily find themselves pitted against each other, as competitors, rivals or enemies. The solution is for one of them to give ground, leaving the top spot to the other, or else for them both to compromise, de-escalating their power struggles and perhaps agreeing to a lower but equal footing within their group. This will be hard for them to do, for their relationship tends to bring out their aggression and fighting spirit. But the alternative is to wind up doing nothing or to settle fearfully for less than the best, since any initiative seems to arouse resistance.

Love affairs and marriages between these two are not unheard of but rarely work out. The Scorpio III tendency toward secrecy—these personalities like to hide their emotions behind smoke screens—is amplified here. In the absence of having any clue as to what the other person is thinking or feeling, the partners will have to try to interpret each other's behavior and will usually end up inferring devious motives and duplicity. The lack of empathy and the level of suspicion here bodes ill. Should one or both partners be only out for what they can get, the days of the relationship will be numbered, since a Scorpio III will rarely tolerate being treated this way (even when they are acting this way themselves).

Friendships in this combination have similar auspices—they are possible but not that common—and parent-child combinations rarely work well, since Scorpio III's will insist on both giving orders and refusing to obey them. On the other hand, competition and challenge often bring out the best in Scorpio III's who find themselves on different sides of the fence. Their rivalry seldom involves personal dislike or hatred; in fact, they may have the greatest respect and in some cases admiration for each other. Rarely, however, do they voluntarily come to work for the same company or successfully start a business together.

BERNARD MONTGOMERY (11/17/1887)
ERWIN ROMMEL (11/15/1891)

Britain's Montgomery and Germany's Rommel, both field commanders in Africa during WWII, were arch enemies. Montgomery's greatest moment was in 1942 when he decisively defeated Rommel's tank corps at the Battle of El Alamein in Egypt—regarded as the turning point in the Allied war effort.

ADVICE: *Try compromising a bit. Limit combative tendencies. If your rival demands respect, show it. Don't be afraid of success.*

STRENGTHS: **REWARDING, ENERGETIC, ASPIRING**

WEAKNESSES: **PROVOCATIVE, UNFORGIVING, SUBMISSIVE**

BEST: **FRIENDSHIP**

WORST: **PARENT-CHILD**

JAWAHARLAL NEHRU (11/14/1889)
INDIRA GANDHI (11/19/17)

Gandhi was the daughter of India's Prime Minister Nehru (1947–64) and went on to hold the same post from 1966–77 and 1980–84, when she was assassinated. She was considered more realistic than her father about Indian society and became quite popular among the working classes. **Also: Joseph McCarthy & Robert Kennedy** (senator/subcommittee counsel).

November 12–18
THE WEEK OF CHARM
SCORPIO III

November 19–24
THE CUSP OF REVOLUTION
SCORPIO-SAGITTARIUS CUSP

Sidestepping Clashes

Scorpio III dominance and Scorpio-Sagittarius rebellion would appear to be headed for a clash, but in fact the chemistry of this combination is most often highly auspicious and can be beneficial for both partners, emphasizing solidity, stability and open avenues of communication. As partners these two are able to harness their considerable energies in the service of a cause or organization, and the dynamic of their matchup is often much greater than the sum of their forces as individuals. On the other hand, the effects of their union, although favorable for the partners themselves, can have unfavorable consequences for others, so that the pair must be prepared to encounter animosity and stiff resistance.

Love affairs between Scorpio III's and Scorpio-Sagittarians can be hard to resist, even if one of the partners is already involved in a perhaps happy primary relationship. Great care must be taken in starting up such affairs, however, for self-destructive tendencies of which neither partner is at all aware may be at work here. The pleasure of the pairing can be great, but so can the pain, and in fact quite an agonizing scenario can emerge for everyone involved. Marriages usually involve a cast-iron commitment; these spouses will deal with any infidelity in an extremely unforgiving way.

Parent-child relationships in either possible variation may be power-oriented, with parents projecting their own wishes and desires onto their offspring. Rebellion is less the problem here than its opposite, that is, submission and even worship of the parent, particularly when the Scorpio III is the parent and the Scorpio-Sagittarius the child. This can usually be worked out only when children achieve recognition in their own right, and on their own terms, as adults. Friendships and working relationships in this combination are usually highly rewarding on the personal level, but if they lack adequate interest and challenge, frustration is sure to result.

ADVICE: *Try to listen to other people. Beware of arousing animosities. Cultivate flexibility and openness. You may be sabotaging yourself. Be watchful.*

STRENGTHS: **CREATIVE, FORMIDABLE, REFORMING**

WEAKNESSES: **SUSPICIOUS, STORMY, REBELLIOUS**

BEST: **WORK**

WORST: **LOVE**

ROBERT R. LIVINGSTON (11/27/1746)
ROBERT FULTON (11/14/1765)

Statesman-diplomat Livingston commissioned inventor-engineer Fulton in 1802 to design and build a steamboat that would operate on NY's Hudson River. Fulton's first steamboat was tested in France (1803). He returned to the US in 1806, and the next year his steamboat was launched in NY harbor. Called the *Clermont,* the boat proved to be commercially feasible.

November 12–18
THE WEEK OF CHARM
SCORPIO III

November 25–December 2
THE WEEK OF INDEPENDENCE
SAGITTARIUS I

A Combined Assault

There are two distinct possibilities in this relationship: the first is that the partners will waste their time in rebelliousness (usually a scenario that sees Scorpio III's trying vainly to boss Sagittarius I's around); the second, more meaningfully, has them combining their talents in an all-out joint assault on closed minds and reactionary attitudes. The latter alternative, of course, will give them a constructive outlet for their considerable creativity and will also bring them closer on a personal level. But they may have to deal with the first possibility first, since the early days or months of their relationship may be extremely stormy. Scorpio III's and Sagittarius I's sometimes take an instant dislike to each other, but it is usually more likely for them to eye each other suspiciously and wait until they know each other better before getting involved.

In both love affairs and parent-child matchups, Scorpio III's will often try to control their partner in this combination, usually to little avail. Their attempts, however, are bound to raise the temperature of Sagittarius I's, with the result that they either flee or fight. Scorpio III's can be tough customers in battle, and Sagittarius I's for their part usually refuse to admit defeat. There can be love between these two, but it is seldom of the completely unconditional sort; both partners will usually hold back from giving their all, even when they seem to have given their hearts away. Subtle permutations on this theme may have the effect, however, of binding the partners ever tighter.

Marriages and working relationships often witness the pair going on the attack. This is a fearful prospect indeed, and any who arouse their ire will be unlikely to make the mistake a second time. In both marriage and work, the relationship usually represents the family or organization's best interests and tries to advance itself economically and socially. If greater opportunity would accrue were a marriage to unite the interests of business partners, both partners might actively pursue such a bond.

ADVICE: *Find a creative outlet for your aggression. Beware of being ruled by blind ambition. Tend to matters of feeling. Give love unconditionally.*

November 12–18
THE WEEK OF CHARM
SCORPIO III

December 3–10
THE WEEK OF THE ORIGINATOR
SAGITTARIUS II

Immediate Activation

These two have the effect of freeing up each other's latent energies. The relationship is a liberating one, then, providing its partners with an atmosphere in which their creativity can bloom and flourish. Yet by emphasizing freedom of thought and action, the relationship sometimes allows these two to get bogged down in periods of frustration or despair in their lives and activities, periods when they feel as though, despite the options available to them, they can proceed no further. At these times they can feel horribly unappreciated and misunderstood. Should one of these funks mark the occasion of their serendipitous first meeting, however, they will often reactivate each other's energies immediately and be swept away by their newly formed relationship.

Love affairs in this combination can be extremely exciting. The partners sometimes meet at a point in their lives when they have just about given up hope of ever meeting that right person. The joy of their encounters can be intense, but if the partners let it blind them to reality, they might ultimately wind up adding their new relationship to a list of past failures. Proceeding on to marriage is recommended only if much soul-searching has been done. Allowing time to pass before tying the knot will let the partners grow closer while also putting their relationship to the test.

Sibling relationships and friendships in this combination can work out, but acute differences of temperament will often send feelings on a roller-coaster ride—stability is not the strong point here. Still, the relationship can often lift its partners' expressiveness to new heights. At work, this pair makes a good collaborative combination, with Scorpio III handling money and practical matters and Sagittarius II dealing with public relations and generating new ideas. Problems can arise if Scorpio III's find Sagittarius II proposals too wild, or if Sagittarius II's grow impatient with what they view as their partner's stick-in-the-mud attitudes.

ADVICE: *Look before you leap. Relief can fog your vision. Take the time to test your first impressions. Even out emotional highs and lows.*

AUGUSTE RODIN (11/12/1840)
CAMILLE CLAUDEL (12/8/1864)

Claudel, perhaps the most significant of Rodin's many mistresses, met him c. 1883 and was his model when they started their tumultuous affair. He, already a master, would not acknowledge her talent as a gifted sculptress—even though they collaborated on some of his works. He would neither marry her nor let her go, which led her into self-destructiveness, depression and eventual madness.

November 12–18
THE WEEK OF CHARM
SCORPIO III

December 11–18
THE WEEK OF THE TITAN
SAGITTARIUS III

Integrity's Stance

Integrity and its nature—what constitutes it, what causes it—will likely be the areas of focus in this combination. These questions arise with respect both to personal interactions between these two and to their interactions as a pair with the outside world. They will often attack each other's integrity, be it artistic, political, moral or philosophical. In part this is simply because their basic attitudes differ drastically. Scorpio III's have a selfish side and are not above using other people for their own gain. But when push comes to shove, they have a strange kind of integrity all their own and are not without compassion. Their Sagittarius III partners, meanwhile, talk big and think high-mindedly but don't necessarily live what they say. These strong individuals would do well to concentrate on preserving the integrity of their relationship rather than critiquing each other's moral stands or those of other people.

As lovers these two are unlikely to give their all for romance—they are much too sensible. They will allow themselves the pleasure of falling in love but not the illusion of believing in it. By always keeping one foot on the ground, they can guarantee their relationship's stability without seriously compromising its passion. Marriages can work well here, although their harmony is constantly threatened by power struggles. Spouses should not make social appointments without consulting each other first.

Friendships usually work best when Scorpio II's and Sagittarius III's see each other only occasionally. They are usually far too busy with their own lives to sacrifice much for their relationship—yet they can always count on each other in times of need. Parent-child relationships in this combination can be well balanced, with both partners respecting each other's power. When serious differences of opinion arise, especially in adolescence and young adulthood, either the parent or the child must have the sense to limit the scope of their arguments, since irreparable damage can occur between these two when their passions spiral out of hand. As co-workers, Scorpio III's and Sagittarius III's do best when they have equal say and status.

ADVICE: *Give enough to make things worthwhile. Avoid power struggles by promoting equality. Develop your social side. Let go occasionally.*

MARC CONNELLY (12/13/1890)
GEORGE S. KAUFMAN (11/16/1889)

Connelly and Kaufman collaborated to write some of Broadway's wittiest plays of the 1920s, among them *Dulcy* (1921), written for Lynn Fontanne; *To the Ladies* (1922), written for Helen Hayes; *Beggar on Horseback* (1924), and the musical *Be Yourself* (1924). They were both prominent members of the Algonquin Hotel's famous Round Table group of literary intellectuals.

DeWitt Wallace (11/12/1889)
Lila Bell Wallace (12/25/1889)

DeWitt and Lila Bell were the founders of *Reader's Digest*. They married in 1921, just after he put together a sample of the magazine to show to publishers. No one was interested, so they published it themselves in '22, distributing copies out of a basement beneath a Greenwich Village speakeasy. The magazine's circulation grew from 1,500 in '22 to 200,000 in '29 to 30 million in the 90s.

November 12–18
THE WEEK OF CHARM
SCORPIO III

December 19–25
THE CUSP OF PROPHECY
SAGITTARIUS-CAPRICORN CUSP

Perpetual Innovation

This relationship focuses not only on dreaming up new ideas and methods of communication but on how best to disseminate such ideas. As a pair, Scorpio III's and Sagittarius-Capricorns are never happier than when starting up new endeavors. This is not to imply that they are poor at sticking to their projects; in fact, their maintenance skills can also be outstanding. Perhaps, however, this is because they often look on maintenance as an opportunity not only to keep things running smoothly but also to start up countless new projects, perhaps spin-offs of the original. Once they begin a project together, it can become self-perpetuating and practically never-ending.

Marriage and career are often interwoven in this relationship. Since both of these personalities totally involve themselves in anything they do, they are comfortable with a relationship that gives them the opportunity to spend most of their time together, or working on related projects. The condition of their home is likely to reflect their business attitude and vice versa, so that by examining the state of either, one can make a good guess about the other. The relationship is often dominated by drives toward power, status and money. Care should be taken to balance such drives with an ethical, religious or spiritual orientation. The children of such a marriage should not be brought up to believe they are any better than anyone else.

Love affairs between Scorpio III's and Sagittarius-Capricorns can be intense, but if they lack the focus of a common goal, they are likely to burn out quickly or simply fade away due to lack of interest. Friendships and sibling matchups in this combination can be a bit dark-sided—the pair are likely to enjoy horror films and books, tales of the supernatural and science fiction. Obsessive interest in such subjects could have a deleterious effect on the partners' psychological stability and could also isolate them from people around them who simply do not understand.

ADVICE: *Beware of obsessive tendencies. Take a break occasionally. Find a quiet place within. Reexamine your values. Beware of dark-sided attractions.*

Alfred Stieglitz (1/1/1864)
Georgia O'Keeffe (11/15/1887)

In 1917 painter O'Keeffe's work was exhibited in a one-woman show by photographer Stieglitz at his NY gallery. They married in '24. His serial portraits of her are considered his most intimate photographic expressions. **Also: Aaron Copland & Roger Sessions** (concert series collaborators; composers); **Whoopi Goldberg & Ted Danson** (romance; actors); **Whoopi Goldberg & Frank Langella** (romance; actors).

November 12–18
THE WEEK OF CHARM
SCORPIO III

December 26–January 2
THE WEEK OF THE RULER
CAPRICORN I

The Art of Living

This is one of the most creative matchups in the year. Inspiration is its keynote: these two tend to inspire each other and can often share a unique vision, be it artistic, social or humanistic. Scorpio III's and Capricorn I's are dedicated and serious people, but as a pair they are able to indulge their lighter side and have great fun together. Problems can arise as to who is the star, but for the most part both partners take pride in each other's work and feel no need to struggle with each other for the limelight. Not only are joint endeavors favored here, but both partners can be spurred on to greater achievement in their own projects or fields. As individuals their activities are often quite different, even opposite, in nature, and a goal they work toward together is likely to be in no way a simple mixture of their strengths and interests but something utterly itself.

Some couples in this combination put all their effort into their lifestyle, rather than into a specific creative pursuit. The art of living is the highest end for them. Love affairs, marriages and friendships with such an outlook can be highly original in respect to domicile, decoration, dress, travel and entertainment. Sexual intensity or sensuousness might well be strong here, but the relationship's energy can equally be expressed in other areas. All of life may be a passionate experience for these couples, one to which they will be almost completely dedicated. Unfortunately, such attitudes can meet with resistance, resentment and, often, incomprehension from other people. Work relationships between Scorpio III's and Capricorn I's are best kept informal and spontaneous. That way both partners can tend to their own work, joining forces only when inspired to do so. Fixed co-worker positions or boss-employee matchups are not recommended here. Family matchups are something of an exception to the rule in this combination, being usually too fixed in their orientation to allow much freedom of expression or thought. Relatives will have to work hard to drop stereotypes or expectations that inhibit spontaneous expression.

ADVICE: *Avoid making rules. Restrictions will hamper your expression. If other people don't understand you, that's their problem. Don't compromise your beliefs.*

November 12–18

THE WEEK OF CHARM
SCORPIO III

January 3–9

THE WEEK OF DETERMINATION
CAPRICORN II

STRENGTHS: **ACTIVE, DARING, CHALLENGING**

WEAKNESSES: **NEGLECTFUL, TACTLESS, AGGRESSIVE**

BEST: **WORK**

WORST: **MARRIAGE**

Uncompromising Crusaders

This outspoken relationship will not hesitate to give its all for a cause, regardless of the consequences. Yet Scorpio III's and Capricorn II's are rarely a foolhardy pair and are unlikely to incur risk unless it is absolutely unavoidable. Their attitude is that the job will get done, either the hard way or the easy way—the choice is up to their opponents. In most cases the real threat to this relationship comes not from within but from without. Through the uncompromising nature of their beliefs, and their refusal to let up in their demands, the couple can arouse enmities and even lifelong hatreds. These crusaders are generally motivated by feelings of fairness and equality and stand on the side of the disadvantaged and dispossessed.

In love affairs, friendships and marriages, the partners' personal lives may suffer from their commitment to other activities. They will have to learn to say no and to be really more selfish with their time if love is to develop or survive between them. Devoting their time elsewhere, they may not even realize their relationship is foundering. At a certain point, however, a turnaround may occur, as lovers, friends and spouses realize that their relationship has challenging horizons of its own and that personal discovery can be as exciting and rewarding as large-scale group endeavors.

Work and professional relationships are most effective when they emerge in the fields of human services, communications or teaching. Scorpio III administrative ability gels well with driving Capricorn II ambition; these partners can lend any organization structure and purpose, respectively. In the family, pairs of relatives in this combination sometimes work no less hard for the good of the group, but their presence is often less than welcome at family gatherings, and the emotions they arouse can prove highly disturbing. They will have to learn something about tact and diplomacy if they are to make constructive contributions.

ADVICE: *Keep some time for yourself. Inward challenges are at least as exciting as outward ones. Love and personal respect are also worth fighting for.*

ELIZABETH CADY STANTON (11/12/1815)
LUCRETIA COFFIN MOTT (1/3/1793)

Stanton and Mott were early crusaders for women's rights. In 1848 they organized the Seneca Falls Convention (NY) to draft a Declaration of Sentiments, listing 16 forms of discrimination against women, including denial of suffrage and control over their wages, persons and children. The convention established the women's rights cause as an organized movement.

November 12–18

THE WEEK OF CHARM
SCORPIO III

January 10–16

THE WEEK OF DOMINANCE
CAPRICORN III

STRENGTHS: **POWERFUL, FEARLESS, INDOMITABLE**

WEAKNESSES: **THREATENING, OVERESTIMATING, EMBARRASSING**

BEST: **COMBAT**

WORST: **PARENT-CHILD**

No Holds Barred

This relationship can shape up as a battle of the giants, complete with titan-sized egos and tempers that flare out of control. Whether physically large or small, both Scorpio III's and Capricorn III's are big personalities who just have to be the boss in most situations, which makes them likely to clash resoundingly—nor is either of them likely to back off. Scorpio III's use very subtle methods to achieve victory, while Capricorn III's are more likely just to refuse to get out of the way. It will obviously be necessary for this relationship to establish boundaries and guidelines in its behavior and to find a way to avoid direct confrontation.

Love affairs and friendships of this type, however, are sometimes unusually passive. It is almost as if the two partners' energies canceled each other out. Thus we may find them giving up the idea of dominance altogether and behaving curiously meekly with each other. The problem here will be self-motivation, particularly when it comes to the effort to forward personal and spiritual development. Should lovers marry, they may overestimate themselves and fail to live each other's promises and expectations.

Parent-child combinations will usually engage in full-force power struggles. The sad fact is that these two usually have no choice but to battle it out, sometimes for years, until one partner emerges the clear victor. A strong realization that there can be no winner here can eventually bring such conflicts to a halt. In the professional world, Scorpio III's and Capricorn III's working for rival groups or organizations may engage in outright war, with no holds barred. If they serve on the same team or run a business together, these two must be careful not to let their aggressive energies run out of control and stampede the opposition—if they do, clients and customers will often run, too. Attending to smaller projects one at a time and not getting carried away with unrealistic, large-scale projects that overestimate the pair's capabilities may help to avoid embarrassing failures.

ADVICE: *Bury the hatchet. Look for subtler ways to advance your cause. Find common advantages. Get to know yourself a bit better.*

KING HUSSEIN I (11/14/35)
GAMAL ABDEL NASSER (1/15/18)

In the 1967 Six-Day War, Jordan's King Hussein and Egypt's President Nasser, as allies, invaded Israel and suffered humiliating defeats. Hussein lost West Jordan, which led to a domestic civil war; when Hussein put down the uprising, he achieved greater control of his country. Nasser's defeat by Israel did not affect his already strong political control over Egypt.

CARY GRANT (1/18/04)
BARBARA HUTTON (11/14/12)

Hutton and Grant were married (his 2nd of 4, her 2nd of 7) from 1942–45. Hutton was a wealthy socialite, granddaughter of F.W. Woolworth and heir to the family fortune. Grant was her only husband to earn his keep. She became a recluse in her later years, plagued by ill health and depression. **Also: Lee Strasberg & Konstantin Stanislavsky** (method-acting teachers).

November 12–18

THE WEEK OF CHARM
SCORPIO III

January 17–22

THE CUSP OF MYSTERY & IMAGINATION
CAPRICORN-AQUARIUS CUSP

Overoptimism

This matchup can carry both partners away on a flight of romance, yet has the ability to raise the red flag when there are problems. Electric Capricorn-Aquarius energy and Scorpio III seductiveness coalesce in an exciting and pleasurable relationship. These two will exhibit an eclectic and airy style. As a pair, they will be interested in many different intellectual pursuits, always maintaining a hopeful, optimistic and even enthusiastic outlook. For two such serious individuals this is really something. There is the danger, however, that in their optimism they might ignore deeper problems, which will accordingly fester and grow larger, perhaps even becoming irreparable. A typical issue is that while Scorpio III's are usually the more realistic, practical and financially sensible of the two, and are more than willing to shoulder responsibility, they may be angered by Capricorn-Aquarian's refusal to do a fair share of the work. Capricorn-Aquarians in turn can grow tired of Scorpio III nagging. They might consent to be more dedicated, if somewhat resentfully, or they might just turn off, becoming even more lax in their attitudes.

Love affairs can peak quickly in the bedroom, then fall off in their intensity over a period of months. When the thrill is gone, the relationship may have little left to sustain it emotionally. The partners sometimes marry for other-than-romantic reasons, particularly money, power or social prestige. These marriages are likely to be quite complex, and their unraveling, should it occur, will take longer than that of more ephemeral love affairs.

Friendships in this combination are usually dedicated to the pursuit of fun. Weighty Scorpio III's will appreciate the relationship for offering them diversions from other, more demanding areas of their lives but may ultimately tire of its superficiality. Capricorn-Aquarians will enjoy Scorpio III reliability but in the long run could find this partner a bit repetitive and dull. Work relationships in this combination are seldom successful when they serve large companies but do a bit better when they are freelance or entrepreneurial in nature. Both partners do best when they take things as they come.

ADVICE: *Be more realistic, but not calculating. There is more to life than money. Cultivate your cultural and spiritual interests. Self-development is key.*

DANIEL BARENBOIM (11/15/42)
JACQUELINE DU PRÉ (1/26/45)

Israeli pianist-conductor Barenboim and English cellist Du Pré married in 1967. Over the years he has made more than 100 recordings as pianist and/or conductor. Du Pré, who often concertized with Barenboim, was considered Britain's greatest string player until her career was sadly cut short by multiple sclerosis in 1972. **Also: Sun Yat-sen & Soong Ch'ing-ling** (married; revolutionary leader/secretary).

November 12–18

THE WEEK OF CHARM
SCORPIO III

January 23–30

THE WEEK OF GENIUS
AQUARIUS I

Trying to Comprehend

This relationship is fateful, perhaps karmic. The partners may sometimes get the strange feeling that they are being driven by forces beyond their control. Trying to understand the deeper aspects of their relationship is crucial for them if they are to have some measure of control over the events spinning wildly about them. The contrast between the more-serious energies of Scorpio III's and the lighter ones of Aquarius I's is marked, and the relationship has a decidedly dark-sided character. Together these two may find themselves forced to confront the more unpleasant aspects of life—particularly pain and loss.

Romantic relationships tend to be serious. Sexual intensity is seldom the focus here; as lovers Scorpio III's and Aquarius I's are more preoccupied, even obsessed, with the more elusive elements of each other's personalities. The reasons for these feelings are difficult to pinpoint and may ultimately have to be acknowledged, like so many other elements of the relationship, as an unfathomable mystery. Marriages are often inevitable between these two once they have joined in a strong love affair. Again one gets the feeling that as spouses the pair will demand not only a particularly deep commitment but also the necessary time for working out complex issues.

Easygoing friendship may be impossible between Scorpio III's and Aquarius I's, even when that is what both partners want. Frustrations over being unable to enjoy the relationship fully without grave problems emerging may lead to its early demise. Work relationships, especially lifelong career associations working for the same company, can be more permanent in nature. Although these two may not always be able to work with each other side-by-side, they seem fated to interact regularly over many years, particularly when involved in projects demanding their quite different skills and approaches. In the family sphere, relatives here are often interested enough in their connection to explore common cultural ties and genealogies.

ADVICE: *Your real fate may be to try to understand yourself. Take a more active role in assuming responsibility for your actions. Promote positive energies.*

November 12–18

THE WEEK OF CHARM
SCORPIO III

January 31–February 7

THE WEEK OF YOUTH & EASE
AQUARIUS II

STRENGTHS: **SYMPATHETIC, EMOTIONAL, SUPPORTIVE**

WEAKNESSES: **HYPERSENSITIVE, PROJECTING, IMMATURE**

BEST: **FRIENDSHIP**

WORST: **LOVE**

Sympathetic Vibration

This is a close relationship emotionally. Speech and thought are rarely the focus here; these partners are far more likely to concentrate on feelings, empathy and sympathy. They may even have psychic connections to each other, which they sometimes openly discuss, more often simply experience. The relationship's goals, often realized, are likely to be emotional openness and honesty. Its sensitivity can also extend to the projects that Scorpio III's and Aquarius II's develop together and that often bear their stamp: the results of these undertakings are apt to be refined and creative in nature. When the partners are working on such a project, the close psychic touch between them usually allows them to complete their work, even when they are separated in space and time, for they can act with full assurance that their partner would approve of their decisions.

Although sympathetic, love affairs here can be somewhat difficult and intense. Their unusual degree of sensitivity is certainly a strength, yet it can also manifest as irritation and emotional overreaction. The Aquarius II psyche often summons up projections of its own shadow side and falls in love with them, so that Scorpio III's may willy-nilly find themselves playing out an unconscious role for their partner. Of course the attention is gratifying, but Scorpio III's will want to be loved for themselves, rather than for the image they unwittingly supply of someone or something else. A commitment to psychological investigation will usually allow this couple to begin unraveling the complexities of their relationship. Marriage may let them mature even more—here they can really begin to self-actualize.

Family ties in this combination are usually empathic, supportive and understanding, and friendships and career matchups can show the same qualities in an even more positive light. This may be because they do not involve overwhelming emotion and passion but rather an easy flow of sympathetic vibrations. Scorpio III's are powerful in giving direction and Aquarius II's can provide a relaxed and easy atmosphere in which to work. As friends these two may well go into business together, usually with few regrets.

ADVICE: *Direct emotions constructively. Don't let your buttons be pushed so easily. Toughen up. Strive for self-understanding. Use reason as well.*

PRINCESS STEPHANIE (2/1/65)
PRINCESS GRACE (11/12/29)

Princess Grace of Monaco, the former actress Grace Kelly, was the mother of Stephanie. They were both in the car that crashed and tragically killed Grace in 1982. As a survivor, Stephanie has had to endure the vivid circumstances of her mother's death. It is speculated that Grace had a stroke while driving.

Also: **Omobono Stradivari & Francesco Stradivari** (brothers; violin makers).

November 12–18

THE WEEK OF CHARM
SCORPIO III

February 8–15

THE WEEK OF ACCEPTANCE
AQUARIUS III

STRENGTHS: **GROUNDED, DYNAMIC, DEVOTED**

WEAKNESSES: **CONDEMNING, NERVOUS, INTOLERANT**

BEST: **WORK**

WORST: **LOVE**

Hard Decisions

These two can do well as partners in a variety of endeavors. Their activities are usually well grounded in the here and now and have particular relevance to the times in which they live. Not especially attracted by either the future or the past, these partners want to affect the family, social or commercial environment around them in a meaningful way and to change things for the better. Because Scorpio III and Aquarius III form a square aspect to each other in the zodiac (they lie 90° apart), traditional astrology predicts friction and stress in their relationship, but also dynamism. This can certainly be the case—there will be few dull moments in this relationship.

Love affairs and friendships in this combination are usually intense and committed. Affairs can be highly passionate, friendships devoted, but if in addition to the personal there is also a social aspect to the relationship, and in particular a cause to which both partners are dedicated, they may to some extent neglect the private life they have together. They will often be faced with a hard decision: which should they devote more energy to, the social or the personal? In the best-case scenario, however, there is room for both in equal measure.

Scorpio III's and Aquarius III's often combine their marriages and their working relationships, with relatively good success. Their relationship gives them an unusually high capacity for commitment, as well as tough pragmatic attitudes and the ability to see things through. To understand how strong these pairings are, one has to look at them over the long run, since they can be expected to feature a lot of ups and downs. Scorpio III's will probably view wilder Aquarius III energies more than somewhat askance and may demonstrate a condemning side that will be intolerable to their partner—Aquarius III's tend to be nervous anyway. As parents, Scorpio III's are likely to impose strict rules and firm boundaries, usually fair ones, in an attempt to keep wayward Aquarius III energies in line.

ADVICE: *Be as open as you expect others to be. Ride over the rough spots. Get your priorities straight. Don't take your relationship for granted.*

MARIANNE MOORE (11/15/1887)
ELIZABETH BISHOP (2/8/11)

Moore, a celebrated American poet, wrote the oft-quoted definition of poetry: "imaginary gardens with real toads in them." Bishop's poetry, characterized by fastidious attention to detail, has often been compared to Moore's, whose verse is meticulous, witty and ironic.

Also: **Elizabeth Cady Stanton & Susan B. Anthony** (feminist co-authors); **Johnny Mercer & Harold Arlen** (music collaborators).

STRENGTHS: **UNUSUAL, INDIVIDUALISTIC, IMAGINATIVE**

WEAKNESSES: **MEDDLING, ALIENATING, INCONSIDERATE**

BEST: **MARRIAGE**

WORST: **WORK**

JOSEPH McCARTHY (11/14/08)
ROY COHN (2/20/27)

Attorney Cohn worked for Senator McCarthy, helping to create the anti-communist hysteria of the early 1950s. Cohn did most of McCarthy's dirty work, digging up suspicious liberal prey for the senator to attack in televised public hearings. Both men reveled in the publicity, loving the hunt for its own sake.

November 12–18

THE WEEK OF CHARM
SCORPIO III

February 16–22

THE CUSP OF SENSITIVITY
AQUARIUS-PISCES CUSP

A Vehicle for Projection

An undeniably bizarre quality suffuses this relationship; it is the odd and unusual aspects of Scorpio III's and Aquarius-Pisces that are activated here. And the oddest thing about this pair is that odd as they are themselves, together they can become obsessed with the unconventional behavior of others, yet exhibit no empathy for it. Perhaps chronicling, dissecting and ultimately passing judgment on the foibles of their peers is simply a rather knee-jerk reaction to their own fears and neuroses. In any case, the relationship is difficult to fathom. The fact that it is nothing but a huge and sometimes rather monstrous vehicle for projection may not at first be evident. That these partners are usually rather unconcerned with their public image allows them to be even more unruly and obnoxious. Friends and family are apt to feel increasingly alienated from them. Should serious problems threaten or break up the relationship, they could find they have no support group left.

Bored with the ordinary and conventional, this couple may have no interest at all in marriage, and should they take the big step their relationship is unlikely to follow the rules, beginning with the wedding ceremony and proceeding right on down the line from there. It is not uncommon for partners of very different backgrounds—racial, national, cultural, economic—to tie the knot, flying in the face of their families' traditions.

Friendships and sibling relationships between Scorpio III's and Aquarius-Pisces are usually private and exclusive. Isolation from social control can breed interesting fantasies, which are sometimes kept hidden in the personal sphere but can also be let loose on others in the immediate environment, with predictably unsettling effects. As youngsters these two are apt to be bullied. In career matchups, Scorpio III's and Aquarius-Pisces often share power drives, making their relationship potentially an ambitious and even ruthless one. In extreme cases this duo can even profit from making others uncomfortable or taking advantage of them.

ADVICE: *Take the feelings of others into account and don't profit from their misfortunes. Keep your friends. Cultivate kindness.*

STRENGTHS: **FAITHFUL, STEADFAST, CONSIDERATE**

WEAKNESSES: **MANIPULATIVE, STUBBORN, DISHONEST**

BEST: **FRIENDSHIP**

WORST: **FAMILY**

ELIZABETH TAYLOR (2/27/32)
ROCK HUDSON (11/17/25)

Actor Hudson's revelation of his homosexuality in 1985 came as a blow to his friends and worldwide fans. Just 10 weeks later, Hudson died of AIDS. At that point, his dear friend Taylor, in a powerful gesture of support, became the founding chair of the American Foundation for AIDS Research (AMFAR).

***Also:* Sir Frederick Banting & Charles Best** (discoverers of insulin).

November 12–18

THE WEEK OF CHARM
SCORPIO III

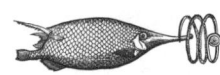

February 23–March 2

THE WEEK OF SPIRIT
PISCES I

A Sensitive Core

This relationship often focuses on fidelity, loyalty and a determination never to give up, no matter what. Although Scorpio and Pisces are water signs and are fluid in their orientation, the Scorpio III–Pisces I relationship is ruled by earth, an element emphasizing groundedness. The more these two are pressured or attacked, the more they resist, so that their matchup, for better and worse, is generally characterized by stubbornness. The relationship has a certain sensitivity, which it usually reserves, however, for interactions between the partners themselves. Thus its tough exterior can hide a sensitive and emotional core.

This is especially clear in love affairs and friendships, which can allow empathy and deep feeling. Scorpio III's and Pisces I's are capable of loving each other deeply, but this need not imply sensual or sexual activity or even romance; respect and understanding are more likely to determine these relationships' tone. Still more strong will be a realistic, even pragmatic, common-sense orientation. Should these lovers or friends decide to marry, they may make a go of it and have a good chance for a long life together, since they have few illusions about each other from the start. Problems can arise through hidden activities and a certain amount of dishonesty, intentional or not. But when Scorpio III's and Pisces I's do conceal painful information, it is often out of consideration for each other's feelings.

Co-workers and family members in this combination can play a protective and nurturing role in their respective business and family groups. But they can also be highly manipulative and controlling, eventually arousing the resentment of fellow workers and relatives. Over time, this process can erode their position in the group hierarchy, severely limiting their effectiveness. Learning to keep out of other people's business, or even to draw strict boundaries between what is theirs and what is the group's, may be critically important in assuring their credibility or status.

ADVICE: *Dishonesty only saves pain in the short run. Don't crowd people—back off. Try to listen to what is being said. Insist on what is yours.*

November 12–18

THE WEEK OF CHARM
SCORPIO III

March 3–10

THE WEEK OF THE LONER
PISCES II

Absorbing Trade-Offs

This relationship is an interesting mix of give and take, with affection, attention and absorption in each other's lives and work all playing a part. Since both partners are very private and need to be alone a good deal of the time, respecting each other's space is a requirement they can usually meet. On the other hand, they both are prone to escapes of different kinds, and should they fall into a habituating or outright addictive form of escape together, their bond could easily become unhealthy. This can be an emotionally complex matchup. Scorpio III's do not like anyone to be too dependent on them, and some Pisces II's can be extremely needy people. The other side of the coin is the Scorpio III need to control their partner, which Pisces II's usually meet with little resistance.

Emotional manipulation can be quite common in love affairs and marriages in this combination. The fine art of persuasion can reach a high level of sophistication here, often manifesting as a series of compromises, trade-offs, mildly coercive acts and other clever stratagems, which guarantee that each partner will get their way a sufficient part of the time. These maneuverings are not necessarily serious and may even be quite playful in character. Withholding sexual favors or limiting them in certain respects are also possibilities. These two are likely to stick together over the years. If they do break up, the separation will be extremely painful.

Career relationships between Scorpio III's and Pisces II's can be outstanding. Often distinguishing themselves in technical, scientific or research areas, this pair can fully concentrate on the job at hand while also sustaining the vision to attain far-reaching goals. The pair can work best side by side as co-workers, either as part of a team or independently. Scorpio III–Pisces II family members and friends can also have a strong career connection, which becomes the bedrock of their relationship.

ADVICE: *Beware of pleasurable escapes. Hold up your end of the deal. Don't foster undue dependencies. Face emotional problems squarely.*

JOSEPH NIEPCE (3/7/1765)
LOUIS JACQUES DAGUERRE (11/18/1787)

In 1826 Daguerre, who had been experimenting with early concepts of photography, heard of Niepce's similar research and in 1829 joined him in a partnership. They worked together until Niepce's death in 1833. The first true photographs—daguerreotypes—were made 4 years later. **Also: Sir William Herschel & Sir John Herschel** (father/son; astronomers).

November 12–18

THE WEEK OF CHARM
SCORPIO III

March 11–18

THE WEEK OF DANCERS & DREAMERS
PISCES III

Emotional Polemics

This relationship can be taken up with a struggle for dominance, not necessarily in the personal sphere but having more to do with ideas, methods, outlook and concept. Scorpio III's are generally attentive to detail and want to control the events unfolding around them, while Pisces III's are much more accepting and diffuse, rolling with the punches and being flexible when confronted by the blows of fate. Differences like these may lead these two into polemical attacks on each other in almost any area of daily life, causing endless discussions and confrontations. They also give the relationship an edge, however, a stimulus without which things could get pretty dull. Scorpio III and Pisces III lie in trine aspect to each other in the zodiac (they are 120° apart), encouraging sensuous, easy and relaxed feelings. Thus the relationship is characterized by a contrast between a sharply divided mental orientation and a unified and comfortable emotional state.

Scorpio III's bring out the more realistic side of Pisces III's, and their love affairs, although romantic, will always be fairly well grounded. Their sexual contacts tend to be more sensual than passionate, more pleasurable and long-lasting than agonizing and tumultuous. Empathic feelings generally guarantee respect and understanding between the partners. This augurs well for marriage, but the partners are careful about taking this step, perhaps because they are quite aware of the differences in their outlooks and will usually take the time for a serious consideration of the pros and cons.

Work relationships between Scorpio III's and Pisces III's can be remarkably well grounded, for their matchup is ruled by earth, an element here indicating practicality and a pragmatic outlook. With such a solid base, Scorpio III's, with their attention to detail, and Pisces III's, with their imagination, can coalesce well (despite acute differences of opinion), and whether they are business partners or co-workers on a project they can produce commercial successes. Friendships and parent-child relationships in this combination are usually warm, and although the partners often disagree, they accept each other's viewpoints.

ADVICE: *Limit the scope of your disagreements. Put individual strengths to work. Learn to accept opposing points of view. Cultivate kindness.*

LIZA MINNELLI (3/12/46)
MARTIN SCORSESE (11/17/42)

Minnelli starred in Scorsese's *New York, New York* (1977), a glitzy tribute to Hollywood musicals of the 40s. Around the time of the film they had a romance, ending in heartbreak for Minnelli due to the strain of her fast-paced career. Eventually, she went to the Betty Ford Center for treatment of alcohol abuse. **Also: Danny DeVito & Judd Hirsch** (co-stars, *Taxi*).

MAXWELL CAULFIELD (11/23/59)
JULIET MILLS (11/21/41)

English-born Mills started as a child actor and later played romantic leads in films and on tv. She married tv heartthrob Caulfield from *The Colbys* (1985–87). Mills' famous relatives include her mother, the novelist-playwright Mary Hayley Bell, actors father John and sister Hayley, and godfather Noel Coward.
***Also:* Larry King & Ted Turner** (same birthday; tv talk-show host works on media mogul's CNN).

November 19–24
THE CUSP OF REVOLUTION
SCORPIO-SAGITTARIUS CUSP

November 19–24
THE CUSP OF REVOLUTION
SCORPIO-SAGITTARIUS CUSP

Hard-Driving Intensity

Two Scorpio-Sagittarians could well work as part of the same team, but would rarely be able to live peacefully under the same roof. Hard-driving, uncompromising and insistent, these two will get the job done in their own way, refusing to be ordered or coerced. On the other hand, if suggestions are made to them in the right way, Scorpio-Sagittarius couples can be very open to new ideas, rarely rejecting any such proposal out of hand. Should two Scorpio-Sagittarians live together, for whatever reason, they will have to work out some kind of truce, in which the more aggressive side of their natures can be given a break. Open conflict or warfare between these two is unthinkable, and would make living together almost impossible.

Scorpio-Sagittarians are sexually intense as a rule, but this does not reveal much about their love matchups with each other. Here they may be much more wary, particularly in the initial stages of their relationship. Sensing a powerful adversary, whom they may not be able to dominate or humble so easily, makes both of them keep their distance or even back off. Once they are involved, it remains to be seen whether they can offer each other the freedom they require, for two Scorpio-Sagittarians can be surprisingly claiming of each other's attentions and affections. Their need for sexual freedom, and their use of a double standard vis-à-vis their mates, could make a successful marriage between them difficult or impossible.

Leaving each other alone will thus be crucial to the success of parent-child and sibling matchups. Friendships in this combination are sharp, quick and highly insightful, but partners are not always able to find a firm emotional basis for the relationship. In the professional sphere, two Scorpio-Sagittarians can work well together, but usually not in the same office, or even in the same department. They tend to work best on their own, advising each other only occasionally, and thus avoiding the rigors of day-to-day interaction.

ADVICE: *Grant each other the same rights. Beware of one-upmanship. Competition is best put to rest. Be more open to compromise.*

CHARLES I (11/19/1600)
HENRIETTA MARIA (11/25/1609)

In 1625 England's Charles married Henrietta, sister of France's Louis XIII. At first a marriage of royal accommodation, by 1630 she won his heart—and the future Charles II was born. In the next years Charles I was beset with political problems and in 1648 was convicted of treason. His last words before execution were about his loyalty as a sovereign and a loving father.

November 19–24
THE CUSP OF REVOLUTION
SCORPIO-SAGITTARIUS CUSP

November 25–December 2
THE WEEK OF INDEPENDENCE
SAGITTARIUS I

Opting for Conviviality

This relationship does best when the partners are with each other by choice rather than necessity, and both must be able to carry on their own lives as they will. The fact that they often freely choose to be with each other on a daily basis, and for long periods of time, attests to their essential compatibility. They will rarely choose to be tied down to overwhelming responsibilities as a couple, but, gypsylike, prefer to just get up and go when the urge seizes them. This does not imply any irresponsibility in their professional lives, for they can work diligently for years as individuals, each upholding their end of the deal financially. Yet, given their druthers, they would enjoy not working at all, and could easily dedicate themselves to a life of amusement, travel, socializing and spiritual study.

In love and friendship, often closely related here, the highest value is placed on conviviality—sitting down with friends for a meal, a few drinks and endless rounds of light, humorous conversation. Parties and games attract them as well, not excluding gambling in the least. A special interest in food and cooking is often found here, since this can involve a perfect blend of sensual delight and socializing. As far as marriage is concerned, these two free spirits may decide just to keep it the way it is, and to avoid the finality of a formal ceremony. Having children is rarely a priority here.

Working together at a regular job is not usually in the stars for these two, particularly as co-workers in a large organization. As family members, particularly siblings or cousins, Scorpio-Sagittarians and Sagittarius I's can have riotous times together, and are particularly prone to getting into trouble. An element of risk or danger is an important incentive for getting involved in certain activities, indicating a daredevil urge that must be satisfied.

ADVICE: *Don't party your life away. Find deepening and abiding interests, perhaps spiritual or religious ones. Beware of falling into a rut.*

November 19–24

THE CUSP OF REVOLUTION
SCORPIO-SAGITTARIUS CUSP

December 3–10

THE WEEK OF THE ORIGINATOR
SAGITTARIUS II

Ensnaring Honesty

The focus of this relationship may be a struggle to break free from the restrictions that it imposes on its partners, who want to act independently. One may then ask, Why did this pair become involved? No matter what the case, there is something about this relationship that ensnares them both. Perhaps it is the high level of truthfulness and integrity that neither is apt to find elsewhere. Despite this (or perhaps because of it), the relationship can well generate mutual disapproval between its partners. In most cases, Sagittarius II's occupy the dominant position, simply because they see things in their own peculiar manner and are unable to let go of, or even modify, their expectations. Scorpio-Sagittarians may first try to please, then later rebel against such attitudes, but in the end they must define their own values, free of any attempt to adapt to or rebel against the relationship's often idealistic stance.

In love affairs, Sagittarius II's may exert power over Scorpio-Sagittarians, threatening to or actually withholding their love. In such situations, Scorpio-Sagittarians are likely to give their all, but ultimately wind up frustrated and unhappy. Marriages between these two are unlikely to be very successful unless Sagittarius II's can limit their power games and act with more sympathy and kindness. In parent-child relationships, too, Sagittarius II parents can leave deep scars on their Scorpio-Sagittarius children through their disapproval or rejection.

Friendships here are likely to be more balanced. Both partners are able to maintain their independence from the relationship and yet contribute positively to it. This is often made possible by their recognition of, and respect for, each other's abilities, without any insistence on conforming to rules of social behavior. Extreme differences in approach mean work relationships rarely pan out. Sagittarius II eccentricity and need to be the center of attention can also pose problems when Scorpio-Sagittarius charm wins over colleagues.

ADVICE: *Work toward mutual acceptance through greater understanding. Examine your disapproval. Open your heart.*

GREGG ALLMAN (12/8/47)
DUANE ALLMAN (11/20/46)

The Allman Brothers Band was formed in 1968 and has proved to be one of the more durable rock & roll groups through the years, although beset with untimely tragedies. In '71, at the peak of their early success, guitarist Duane was killed in a motorcycle accident. Led by Gregg, the group played at his funeral and decided to continue without a new guitar player.

November 19–24

THE CUSP OF REVOLUTION
SCORPIO-SAGITTARIUS CUSP

December 11–18

THE WEEK OF THE TITAN
SAGITTARIUS III

The Negotiating Table

Although these two may become involved in acute power struggles, they are nonetheless generally successful in communicating with one another rationally. Experiencing few barriers in understanding allows each of them at least to know where the other stands. Working out compromises may be the focus of this relationship, since channels of communication are usually open, and experience teaches the Scorpio-Sagittarius–Sagittarius III pair that open conflict rarely results in anything more than bad feeling and loss of time. It may take a few knock-down, drag-out battles to wake the partners up to this fact.

Close friendships may not work so well for these two, nor will more casual companionships. Neither party may really have either the time or the interest to spend with the other on a regular basis—in fact, things usually work out better that way. Scorpio-Sagittarius parents will have great difficulty controlling their Sagittarius III children, and should they resort to serious punitive measures may risk losing them altogether. Sagittarius III parents may be adored by their Scorpio-Sagittarius children, who may in fact be overattached to them to the point of becoming emotionally crippled unless their own individuality is encouraged to develop.

In work relationships, these two are able to function well together only as business partners or co-workers after they have settled their power issues. Neither can usually accept the other as boss; in consequence, power must be shared or at least delegated in such a way that both partners are satisfied. The relationship itself may serve as a peacemaker in this respect, providing a space that resembles a negotiating table more than a battlefield. Witnessing commercial triumphs that are the fruits of the partners' labors will help consolidate this relationship; failures, on the other hand, will too often result in blame and renewed hostility—which in itself may serve as a strong incentive for success. Love affairs and marriages may lack the understanding to ride over rough spots and survive crises, whether financial, sexual or romantic. Despite the ease with which these two talk to each other, emotional feelings do not run very deep here. Partners may, however, be content with a workable companionship.

ADVICE: *Be loyal through thick and thin—only determination can weather the storm. Dig a bit deeper to build a firm base. Seek peaceful solutions.*

JOHN V. LINDSAY (11/24/21)
ED KOCH (12/12/24)

Lindsay and Koch were both popular mayors of New York City—Lindsay from 1965–73, Koch from 1977–89. Their styles were quite different: Lindsay as a liberal Yale glamour boy, and Koch as an ethnic, down-to-earth native NYer, epitomized by his favorite public utterance, "How'm I doing?"
**Also: Rodney Dangerfield &
Joan Dangerfield** (married).

TED TURNER (11/19/38)
JANE FONDA (12/21/37)

Media mogul Turner and actress Fonda married in 1984, following her breakup with politician (and former radical) Tom Hayden. Fonda has given up her acting career since she wed Turner, though both can often be seen performing the "tomahawk chop" at Atlanta Braves baseball games (he owns the team).
Also: Marlo Thomas & Phil Donahue (married; actress/talk-show host).

November 19–24
THE CUSP OF REVOLUTION
SCORPIO-SAGITTARIUS CUSP

December 19–25
THE CUSP OF PROPHECY
SAGITTARIUS-CAPRICORN CUSP

A Maverick Stand

This is a very solid relationship, but one in which the partners can only do things their own way—a way that resounds to the dismay of family, friends and employers. Remarkably resistant to hints or outright coercion, this couple takes a maverick stand from the start and then keeps going. As individuals, Scorpio-Sagittarians and Sagittarius-Capricorns may not be all that stable emotionally, and have certainly faced their fair share of travail and rejection; yet their relationship is a remarkably settled one, probably because of an almost organic coalescence of complementary attributes. Both partners here take refuge in a relationship that is at once protective and nurturing.

Love affairs and marriages often provide the partners with a safe haven. Both of them seem convinced that as long as they stick with each other, they will be protected, but should they part, the wild world, with all of its uncertainties and dangers, will encroach upon them. Fear does not bode well for personal development, so the partners should dedicate themselves to activities oriented toward increasing their self-understanding, taking each of them farther along the path toward self-actualization. The relationship itself will also develop more meaningfully if the partners embrace it less out of need and more from pure desire.

In friendships, these two should not use their relationship as a source of support but should work actively to develop ever newer and more productive activities, broadening its interactive base. Socialization is an important process here, and particularly building a social circle in which the relationship can take its rightful place. In the family, relatives who have felt rejected or left out may seek each other out to share hurt feelings and to commiserate. Positive results can be expected only if self-pity is ruthlessly excised from the relationship. As far as working matchups are concerned, this duo is usually not well suited as a team in the hard commercial world, unless it is running the show and issuing the orders.

ADVICE: *Deep-seated fears may be holding you back. Get to know yourself better. Develop your social side, but beware of your weakness for flattery.*

J. EDGAR HOOVER (1/1/1895)
ROBERT KENNEDY (11/20/25)

Technically, Attorney General Kennedy was Hoover's boss, and the FBI director wasn't happy about it. In their political infighting, Kennedy was after Hoover for harassing liberal activists. Hoover held his arch-enemy at bay by threatening to expose President Kennedy's liaisons with Marilyn Monroe and others.
Also: Voltaire & Madame de Pompadour (writer/royal patron).

November 19–24
THE CUSP OF REVOLUTION
SCORPIO-SAGITTARIUS CUSP

December 26–January 2
THE WEEK OF THE RULER
CAPRICORN I

Political Issues

This relationship has an undeniably political cast but does not necessarily imply a formal involvement in politics. The partners may work out such activities in the family, business or social sphere. Even if they are not active to any great extent, social and political issues will generally interest them and provide a basis for their relationship. Conversation and debate on a broad range of topics are apt to be hallmarks here. There isn't a nook or cranny of information that these two will overlook—particularly if it has to do with their favorite topic, politics and its machinations.

Love affairs and marriages can begin with a heavy emphasis on the physical (although this is by no means usually the case), but sensual feelings often fade if not deepen through emotional understanding and intellectual challenge. Because Capricorn I's need to dominate and Scorpio-Sagittarians to rebel against authority, such relationships do not have a rosy future, unless they succeed in transmuting these opposing characteristics into more compatible ones. A complete, harmonious metamorphosis is possible here, but unlikely. Friendships between Capricorn I's and Scorpio-Sagittarians can run very deep—trusting, dependable, affectionate. In such relationships as these, honor and a strong sense of morality are noteworthy. Career and family relationships in this combination may be particularly auspicious, yet because of acute temperamental differences, the more personal aspects of these relationships are best kept to a minimum. Thus it is as associates or not-so-close relatives respectively that most work and family matchups of this kind are successful, rather than as boss-employee or parent-child pairs. The great strength of the relationship is its partners' ability to view things objectively and to engage in dispassionate debate. Should they be able to reach agreement, such pairs may be ready to implement their plans, which often involve some form of reorganization within their group or place of employment. If they are on opposite sides of the fence, however, Capricorn I's and Scorpio-Sagittarians can battle to the death if necessary—when their relationship is adversarial, there is no love lost between these two.

ADVICE: *Keep combative urges under control, and learn to compromise. Let political issues be the gateway toward philosophical ones. Deepen your bond.*

November 19–24

THE CUSP OF REVOLUTION
SCORPIO-SAGITTARIUS CUSP

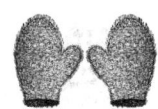

January 3–9

THE WEEK OF DETERMINATION
CAPRICORN II

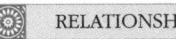
Never-Never Land

This relationship is unlikely to recognize ordinary limitations of time and space. Peak experiences of all types attract these two like magnets. Extremely expansive, Scorpio-Sagittarians and Capricorn II's seek out unusual, even bizarre concepts that ideally they will be able to incorporate into their lives and work. The greatest danger here is that the partners' psychological stability can be undermined, and they may come to live in a never-never land of unchecked fantasy.

Artistic, philosophical, religious and spiritual areas are particularly fertile fields of investigation for this couple. Whether lovers or friends, mates or co-workers, the relationship will inevitably be drawn in these directions, sometimes to the point where personal considerations are overlooked, forgotten or sacrificed. The romance of love affairs and friendships in particular is enhanced by such special interests—a spark that can be fanned into a flame of high intensity. Marriages are more pragmatic, particularly when children are involved, and in the day-to-day running of such relationships, escapist fantasies must not be allowed to run riot. Children of such a marriage may be forced into accepting heavy responsibilities at an early age in order to fill the gap left by their parents' far-flung involvements.

Fortunate indeed are the working pairs (who not infrequently are friends and family members) that can make their active imaginations pay off for them commercially. Not so much having peak experiences as marketing them can become the emphasis here, possibly leading to great financial success. In the best-case scenario, the couple will simply be paid to share their experiences—though of course their merciless exploitation of such events may leave them less and less time to enjoy them. Furthermore, bringing peak experiences down to earth will tend to flatten them out, eventually leaving the partners a bit bored.

RENÉ MAGRITTE (11/21/1898)
ANDRÉ MASSON (1/4/1896)

Magritte and Masson were contemporary artists whose Surrealism took different forms. Magritte developed dreamlike, hallucinatory imagery that was startlingly realistic. Masson's works were invested with emotional qualities arising from his exploration of the unconscious. *Also:* **Toulouse-Lautrec & Jose Ferrer** (film portrayal).

ADVICE: *Maintain contact with those around you. Use your imagination intelligently—beware of unbridled fantasy. Don't dull your experience.*

November 19–24

THE CUSP OF REVOLUTION
SCORPIO-SAGITTARIUS CUSP

January 10–16

THE WEEK OF DOMINANCE
CAPRICORN III

Beginning with Respect

This relationship often begins with the partners' respect or even admiration for one another's abilities. As it develops and deepens, they are likely to become attracted to each other personally, and may even ultimately fall in love. Because of the slow development here, such relationships often survive any snuffing of the romantic spark, and can continue on as friendships. An air of enchantment often suffuses this relationship, but it is not mere infatuation, for the magic worked between these two is usually long-lasting. Great care should be taken to avoid letting arguments escalate out of control, since hair-trigger tempers on both sides can lead to regrettable scenes.

In love affairs the partners are unlikely to sweep each other off their feet. For the most part, good sense and discretion are exercised here, particularly if one of the partners is already deeply involved with someone else. It is often the relationship itself that the partners find most interesting, despite the fact that they generally have many outside interests in common. Should marriage mean being forced to give up individual freedoms, it will rarely work. Capricorn III's are much too sure of what they want and Scorpio-Sagittarians of what they need to fool themselves or cast their fates to the wind.

Professional rivalries and personal enmities between Scorpio-Sagittarians and Capricorn III's are awful to contemplate. Scorpio-Sagittarius coolness under fire and refusal to back down are powerfully countered by the formidable presence and willpower of Capricorn III's. Such battles are seldom confined to verbal swordplay, but translate quickly into action. Friends and sibling pairs must beware letting their aggressive energies get out of hand when facing other people. Extremely protective, either partner could well fly off the handle if he or she feels the other is being threatened or attacked. Strong bonds of interdependence may develop here that are not easily broken.

AHMAD RASHAD (11/19/49)
DEBBIE ALLEN (1/16/50)

Rashad and Allen are brother- and sister-in-law via his marriage to her sister Phylicia Ayers-Allen (now Phylicia Rashad of *The Cosby Show*). Allen is a gifted actress-dancer-choreographer who performed in *Fame*, the 1980 film and subsequent tv series, winning 2 Emmys. Rashad is a retired football star, now a tv sportscaster.

ADVICE: *Beware of leaping too quickly to defend. Don't be so sure you know what you want and need—many surprises are waiting ahead. Give it time.*

STRENGTHS: **BALANCED, SENSUAL, ADVENTURESOME**

WEAKNESSES: **NERVOUS, STRESSFUL, EXPLOSIVE**

BEST: **LOVE**

WORST: **MARRIAGE**

JIM GARRISON (11/20/21)
KEVIN COSTNER (1/18/55)

Actor Costner portrayed New Orleans district attorney Garrison in Oliver Stone's controversial film *JFK* (1991). (The real Garrison had a small part in the film.) Garrison was the troubleshooting attorney who became obsessed with the idea that Kennedy was killed as the result of a conspiracy rather than by a single person. Costner played the role with convincing realism.

November 19–24
THE CUSP OF REVOLUTION
SCORPIO-SAGITTARIUS CUSP

January 17–22
THE CUSP OF MYSTERY & IMAGINATION
CAPRICORN-AQUARIUS CUSP

The Quiet Center

For all its excitement, this relationship is remarkably well balanced—a balance underscored by the fact that Scorpio-Sagittarius is a water-fire and Capricorn-Aquarius an earth-air combination. This combination contains all four elements, then, but it is ruled by fire and earth, here indicating passionate sensuality. These relationships go very deep, and are often serious in nature. Yet the partners often share an excellent sense of humor, one that is not merely comic but also sensitive to the ironies and bizarre coincidences that life so often serves up. Both loyal to the extreme, despite their wild and somewhat unstable natures, these two may find their relationship a silent and quiet center, a place in which to find respite from their own, often chaotic lives.

Love affairs between Scorpio-Sagittarians and Capricorn-Aquarians can be torrid, yet they are often quite calm emotionally, without undue argument or confrontation. Both partners are extremely temperamental, and there are few dull moments here, but contentment and harmony generally prevail. Marriages between these two can work out, but there is no guarantee of their longevity or stability, since financial and social stresses as well as the strains of child-rearing usually bring out the more nervous and excitable aspects of both partners.

In the family sphere, parent-child relationships of either possible variation can be warm and loving, albeit with a tendency to nervousness. Friendships in this combination are geared up for action on all fronts, being always on the lookout for adventure and excitement in both conventional and (more likely) out-of-the-way places. Business matchups are generally unfavorable. Removed from a domestic environment and exposed to the rigors of the commercial world, the Scorpio-Sagittarius–Capricorn-Aquarius relationship, although stable, may be tainted by the exigencies of survival.

ADVICE: *Find the quiet center. Be more cautious and patient in your worldly contacts. Minimize stress, and keep your nervousness under control.*

STRENGTHS: **UNDERSTANDING, SYMPATHETIC, AMUSING**

WEAKNESSES: **UPSETTING, NASTY, HUMILIATING**

BEST: **WORK**

WORST: **LOVE**

VOLTAIRE (11/21/1694)
FREDERICK THE GREAT (1/24/1712)

In 1749 French philosopher-writer Voltaire was at a low point, having lost his beloved and influential friend, Mme. du Châtelet. Prussia's Frederick, a longtime correspondent with Voltaire, invited him to stay at his court. Voltaire worked on several writing projects there until 1753, when differences between them compelled him to leave. **Also:**

Charles DeGaulle & Franklin Roosevelt (WWII allies).

November 19–24
THE CUSP OF REVOLUTION
SCORPIO-SAGITTARIUS CUSP

January 23–30
THE WEEK OF GENIUS
AQUARIUS I

Unmerciful Teasing

These two would seem to have a good understanding of each other, but this does not necessarily imply that they get along, for each knows well enough how to push the other's buttons. Whether or not the relationship is peaceful is largely up to the partners themselves, for it is in their power to be sympathetic and kind to each other or, just as easily, to be provocative and nasty. It is precisely because they are on the same emotional wavelength that it's so easy for them to upset each other. Scorpio-Sagittarians certainly appreciate the quick intelligence of Aquarius I's, who in turn can be in awe of Scorpio-Sagittarians' sense of purpose and driving ambition. As a work team, these two can be highly successful, as long as they remain objective and keep feelings from getting out of control.

In love affairs, marriages and sibling matchups, these two may tease each other unmercifully—whether as a form of humor or of sadism is not altogether clear. But both partners do get extraordinary pleasure from riling and then laughing at each other. They may often come equipped with a wild story or an exaggerated claim, encourage their partners to believe it and even to bruit it about—just to watch their final embarrassment and humiliation. Yet throughout such seemingly cruel behavior runs a streak of affection confirming that these two really do like each other. Strong sensual feelings seldom form the basis of love affairs here, nor is intimacy given high priority in marriages. Sibling relationships are surprisingly physical, but this is usually expressed in childhood games, mock fights and sports.

Friendships of this type rarely achieve constancy of mood. Up and down, on and off, low-key and aggressive, such relationships bring out the more unstable side of both partners. They can end badly when insults fly out of control, ending with the partners never meeting or speaking again.

ADVICE: *Don't take unfair advantage. Try to maintain consistency. Accentuate the positive. Don't assume that you will always be forgiven.*

November 19–24
THE CUSP OF REVOLUTION
SCORPIO-SAGITTARIUS CUSP

January 31–February 7
THE WEEK OF YOUTH & EASE
AQUARIUS II

Authoritative Power

The Scorpio-Sagittarius–Aquarius II relationship carries with it a healthy respect for and pride in tradition, an insistence on stability and considerable strength of purpose. It has the potential to provide a firm foundation for any endeavor. As a unit, this duo is quite powerful in a quiet, rather authoritative way. The likelihood, however, is that Scorpio-Sagittarians may consider themselves the real source of power in the relationship, viewing Aquarius II's as mere lightweights. In truth, however, it is the combination that carries the load here.

This romantic and sensual relationship is physically gratifying to both partners. Love affairs and marriages pit two willful and impulsive partners against each other; these two are loving and passionate—to be sure, loving—but often rebellious nonetheless. Aquarius II's like things nice and easy but are not about to knuckle under to authority, while Scorpio-Sagittarians don't like being bound by rules, unless these are of their own making. Setting up the relationship itself as the ultimate authority and methodically establishing firm guidelines are essential, and something that both partners may actually enjoy doing as long as both have an equal say. Agreeing on who will be the unquestioned boss in their own special areas of interest may also be a possible solution.

Friendships in this combination can be more difficult and emotionally complex. Aquarius II's may experience frustrations with Scorpio-Sagittarius tension, and Scorpio-Aquarians often want deeper involvement with, and greater commitment from, their more carefree Aquarius II partners.

Boss-employee and parent-child relationships in this combination can be full of strife if the top dog has little compassion for his or her dependent partner. Lack of respect on both sides usually spells doom for such a relationship. On the other hand, as co-workers or siblings, Scorpio-Sagittarians and Aquarius II's can have a highly rewarding association, one in which career and family connections may overlap.

ADVICE: *Take time for thorough discussion. Patience will be rewarded. Structure interactions with care and sensitivity—efforts now may preclude conflicts later.*

DICK SMOTHERS (11/20/38)
TOM SMOTHERS (2/2/37)

The Smothers Brothers , a comedy duo with several brilliant but short tv runs from 1967–75, used controversial political issues in their material, often prompting network censorship. Tom, playing an inarticulate bumbler, was really the more active, innovative force of the pair. **Also: Geraldine Page & Rip Torn** (married; actors); **Jamie Lee Curtis & Christopher Guest** (married; actors).

November 19–24
THE CUSP OF REVOLUTION
SCORPIO-SAGITTARIUS CUSP

February 8–15
THE WEEK OF ACCEPTANCE
AQUARIUS III

Above the Rules

This unusual relationship often places itself above society's rules, whether legally codified or socially customary. The partners' feelings may be amicable or hostile, but they are usually out in the open—a certain honesty prevails. On the other hand, they have a tendency to hide their most important dealings with each other from family, friends and colleagues, since in their eyes what happens between them at the most personal level is no one's business but their own. Actual meetings between these two may be infrequent or daily, depending on the relationship. Mercifully, serious confrontations are usually few and far between. The energies here arouse deep emotion, which, however, is often concealed behind a cool, even impersonal facade.

Hidden love affairs are common between Scorpio-Sagittarians and Aquarius III's. They are so well camouflaged that even when they appear at a party or other social gathering, few would guess that they were intimately involved. Thus the relationship can be deceptive, not only to other people but also to the partners themselves, who think they have it all figured out but in fact do not. Fate often takes a hand in such matchups, producing completely unexpected results. Marriages between these two can be topsy-turvy in nature. Such confusion can be stimulating, even fun, but must eventually be sorted out, particularly when children are involved.

Scorpio-Sagittarius–Aquarius III sibling relationships and friendships work best when they don't involve a lot of responsibility. The partners must feel free to go their own ways at will, pairing up only when it suits them to do so. Career matchups may be highly competitive and antagonistic, especially when they involve bitterly contested prizes, hierarchical or financial. Such struggles most often continue until there is a clear winner; even then, however, the loser may either refuse to give up or seek revenge. The battling here is often carried out less by the individuals themselves than by their dark sides, and this has a powerful influence on each partner's larger personality.

ADVICE: *Try to attain a deeper level of understanding. Bury the hatchet. Don't take on too much. Get your act together. Don't waste so much time on concealment.*

ROBERT KENNEDY (11/20/25)
JIMMY HOFFA (2/14/13)

As counsel for the Senate Rackets Committee (1957–59), Kennedy was responsible for exposing the underworld connections of Teamsters union boss Hoffa. Their enmity was made famous in the media. Kennedy wasn't satisfied until Hoffa was sent to prison in '67 for jury tampering and embezzling union funds. Out of prison, Hoffa disappeared in '75, presumably executed by mobsters.

STRENGTHS: **PRAGMATIC, MOTIVATED, PLEASURE-SEEKING**

WEAKNESSES: **RUTHLESS, MATERIALISTIC, LAZY**

BEST: **SIBLING**

WORST: **MARRIAGE**

MARGAUX HEMINGWAY (2/19/55)
MARIEL HEMINGWAY (11/21/61)

Ernest Hemingway's granddaughter Margaux took her own life in 1996, and gifted actress Mariel lost a close sister who seemed to have everything: beauty, glamour, fame. But Margaux was plagued with epilepsy, alcoholism, bulimia, debts, 2 failed marriages–and a sister who had eclipsed her creatively. **Also: Juliet & John Mills** (daughter/father; actors); **Rodo & Lucien Pissarro** (brothers; Impressionist artists).

November 19–24
THE CUSP OF REVOLUTION
SCORPIO-SAGITTARIUS CUSP

February 16–22
THE CUSP OF SENSITIVITY
AQUARIUS-PISCES CUSP

Ambition or Complacency?

Although both partners here are highly imaginative and creative, their relationship tends to be a responsible one that specializes in looking after practical matters. Thus artistic leanings do not by any means contradict or rule out running an efficient home or office. Furthermore, the duo can be quite ambitious—neither is content to sit and dream about what might be or could have been. Their plans for the future are likely to materialize, since they usually discard unworkable schemes along the way. Yet relaxed attitudes generally prevail here, owing to the easy and open communication between the partners—Aquarius-Pisces and Scorpio-Sagittarius are trine to each other in the zodiac (120° apart), so that these personalities get along well, with little tension. If taken too far, however, such attitudes can lead to complacency, undercutting the partners' ambitious drives. At work and at home, these two may oscillate between periods of high motivation and laziness. Thus the relationship tends to fall into a repetitive pattern of tension followed by relaxation.

Scorpio-Sagittarius–Aquarius-Pisces spouses are often social climbers, and can be quite ruthless in reaching their goals. Any feelings of inferiority that they harbor—and there may be quite a few—are translated into action and the raw determination to impress others. When the partners are friends, however, such desires are curiously absent. Here their more artistic sides are brought out, and they share a commitment of considerable energy to creative and perhaps spiritual endeavors. Love affairs in this combination are even more low-key and pleasure-seeking. More often than not, hedonism is the order of the day, and a lot of attention will be given to matters of sex, food and the home. Sibling relationships are often noteworthy here.

Work matchups can be very expressive venues for the partners' creativity. Down times allow dreaming and planning, while periods of greater determination see projects initiated and then up and running. These two obviously work best in project-oriented situations.

ADVICE: *Find a balance between ambition and complacency. Put money to use instead of sitting on it. Be kinder to others. Beware of snobbism.*

STRENGTHS: **CHARMING, PERSUASIVE, REALISTIC**

WEAKNESSES: **CONCEITED, PSEUDOARISTOCRATIC**

BEST: **FRIENDSHIP**

WORST: **FAMILY**

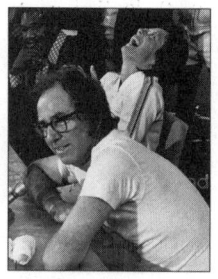

BOBBY RIGGS (2/25/18)
BILLIE JEAN KING (11/22/43)

King was one of the great female tennis stars in the 60s and 70s, winning many Grand Slam titles. In '73 Riggs, 1939 Wimbledon winner and self-proclaimed male chauvinist, challenged the 30-year-old King to a "battle of the sexes." She beat him soundly in 3 straight sets before the largest crowd ever to attend a tennis match (30,472).

November 19–24
THE CUSP OF REVOLUTION
SCORPIO-SAGITTARIUS CUSP

February 23–March 2
THE WEEK OF SPIRIT
PISCES I

The Right People

The partners in this relationship are often taken up with convincing others of their point of view—basically, with selling themselves or their product. Powerfully persuasive, these two know how to charm the pants off practically anyone. But they also know each other's methods of persuasion pretty well, so it may be a bit more difficult for them to work similar magic within their own relationship. One prerequisite for a dedicated salesperson is that they really know and believe in the service or product they're promoting. Thus Scorpio-Sagittarians and Pisces I's are likely to devote considerable time and energy to painstakingly putting their sales plans together. Luckily, this combination carries with it both managerial ability and a penchant for the careful preparation so crucial to success.

Snobbism and elitism often manifest in matchups of this type, and the partners risk coming across as conceited (which can undercut their efforts) but rarely overconfident (which strengthens them). A solid streak of pessimism and disbelief runs through their relationship, which also makes them difficult to convince. Realists, such partners rarely kid themselves; consequently, they know exactly what they can get away with.

In friendship and love, these two are apt to value their relationship highly, and are prepared to overlook slights or insults. Furthermore, both of them are usually willing to sacrifice individual gain for the sake of the relationship. Work matchups and marriages are generally effective in convincing others of their reliability and desirability, whether for financial or for social advancement. There should be little doubt that these are the right people to be involved with if you want to move onward and upward. The Scorpio-Sagittarius–Pisces I pair usually relies heavily on their track record, for no matter how good their spiel, other people are more likely to believe in the merits of their past success. In fact neither of these two impresses as money-hungry; the way something is done is actually at least as important to them as the result. The relationship affirms that style and finesse are often worth more than tangible goods, and that who you know is more important than what you know.

ADVICE: *Diamonds can be found in the oddest places—with your nose in the air, you may be missing something right at your feet. Keep your pride under control.*

November 19–24

THE CUSP OF REVOLUTION
SCORPIO-SAGITTARIUS CUSP

March 3–10

THE WEEK OF THE LONER
PISCES II

Environmental Control

No matter what sorts of difficulties this relationship encounters, the intense loyalty that characterizes it will see it through. Because the focus here is usually building a stable life together, every element of the partners' environment is brought under tight control. Particularly sensitive in the aesthetic sphere, Scorpio-Sagittarians and Pisces II's have excellent taste, which in this relationship means that designing, decorating, gardening and furnishing are all given top priority, along with other domestic concerns.

Love affairs, friendships and marriages may be closely related for couples in this combination. Sex is rarely the most important element in an interpersonal relationship between these two; rather, the focus is establishing bonds of friendship that pervade all areas of the couple's life together. Knowledge of affairs outside the marriage or primary love affair may at first be greeted with shock, but will be followed by deep understanding and acceptance. While empathic bonds are strong, emotion may be less easily expressed, and much is kept beneath the surface in everyday interactions.

Scorpio-Sagittarius parents, although sympathetic to their Pisces II children, sometimes lack sufficient time or interest to invest in them. Pisces II parents are nurturing toward their Scorpio-Sagittarius children, but can also be manipulative and controlling. More distant relatives, such as uncles, aunts, cousins or grandparents of either sign, may be much more suitable for fulfilling parental or sibling roles, and such relationships can be more satisfying, productive and supportive of the child's personal development.

Business partnerships and co-worker combinations are not always tough enough to survive in a dog-eat-dog world. The fierce competitive spark is often lacking in this matchup, along with any real desire to work hard for an organization on a daily basis. Freelance associations, involving fewer outside deadlines, are much more favorable for these two.

ADVICE: *Back off a bit and let things happen—accept what fate offers up without trying to control it. Appreciate the comic aspects of everyday life.*

VERONICA HAMEL (11/20/45)
DANIEL TRAVANTI (3/7/40)

Hamel and Travanti co-starred in the intense tv police series *Hill Street Blues* (1981–87). Hamel played a cool, professional public defender and Travanti a dedicated, responsible police commander. They were typically on opposite sides of issues but were also in love (and briefly married). The actors made a dynamic couple together.

Also: Sir Harold Nicolson & Vita Sackville-West (married; writers).

November 19–24

THE CUSP OF REVOLUTION
SCORPIO-SAGITTARIUS CUSP

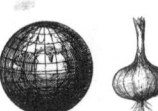

March 11–18

THE WEEK OF DANCERS & DREAMERS
PISCES III

Life on Earth

This relationship is not the most stable one, but the partners can usually count on each other for a good time. More serious Pisces III's get a chance to let it all hang out and Scorpio-Sagittarians to give vent to their wild side. Few topics are off limits to these two, nor are they afraid to put it on the line when it comes to challenging adventures. In order to maintain balance, it may be necessary to lower the level of excitement here, and for both partners to resist the lure of alcohol or other destabilizing drugs. Coming back down to earth can be a painful experience after a dramatic flight of fancy, but sooner or later the partners will realize that escapes, no matter how pleasurable or exciting, often only take the relationship away from the real work that needs to be done.

In love affairs, seeking ever more ecstatic highs may eventually prove enervating. Learning to balance mood swings or, in extreme cases, bipolar disorders that may manifest here is of prime importance. Professional help may have to be sought if this relationship lacks the resources to handle acute problems itself. Marriages between these two are often devoted to the pursuit of pleasure, but this search will rarely take the partners far on the road to self-realization.

Family members will have to be extremely understanding of this duo's need to spend time together—resentments and jealousies may be aroused on both sides. Scorpio-Sagittarius and Pisces III siblings, particularly of the same sex, can create a private fantasy world that satisfies both partners' emotional needs right up into adolescence. Growing out of such relationships in early adulthood can be extremely painful for both partners. Co-workers in this combination could develop close friendships; likewise, friends will often seek employment together. Such relationships can be extremely absorbing and protective, with the partners spending most of their time together.

ADVICE: *Even out your behavior. Don't be so quick to run away from yourself. Face problems squarely. Experience the joys of self-development.*

GOLDIE HAWN (11/21/45)
KURT RUSSELL (3/17/51)

Actors Hawn and Russell, while not married, have been living together and sharing a home life since 1986. They have a child, in addition to Hawn's 2 others by a previous marriage. Outside of Hollywood, they have a house in Aspen.

Also: Ted Turner & Rupert Murdoch (media-mogul adversaries).

THE WEEK OF INDEPENDENCE
SAGITTARIUS I

THE WEEK OF INDEPENDENCE
SAGITTARIUS I

Kinetic Energy

MARY MARTIN (12/1/13)
CYRIL RITCHARD (12/1/1897)

Martin and Ritchard, who share the same birthday, are linked for their roles in the Broadway musical *Peter Pan* (1954), she as Peter, he as Capt. Hook. They revived their magic in the extraordinarily popular 1955 tv production. ***Also:*** **Amos Bronson Alcott & Louisa May Alcott** (father/daughter; same birthday; philosopher/author); **Caroline Kennedy & JFK, Jr.** (siblings).

This can be a terrific matchup, in which Sagittarius I's finally encounter a partner not interested in controlling them, a kindred free spirit. Of course this is no guarantee that things will go smoothly, or even that the partners will get along on a daily basis—but when things are on between these two, the energy output can be enormous. Few in the year can generate the kind of electric excitement that Sagittarius I's can, and the synergy of these individuals together often sends indicators flying off the scale; but directing such energy and keeping it under control are other matters entirely. For the most part, however, two Sagittarius I's are able to handle each other's energies, whereas others might short-circuit.

Love affairs can be intense but brief. With nothing else to sustain or occupy Sagittarius I lovers except unrestrained romantic feelings, they are liable to burn out in a matter of months, or even weeks. As far as marriage is concerned, taking on individual responsibilities and working together on domestic projects can lend stability to the matchup and guarantee its survival for longer periods. Children of Sagittarius I parents will usually appreciate their energy and their level of interest and nurturing, but may find them a bit overprotective and sternly ethical.

Sagittarius I siblings can fight like cats and dogs, and compete unremittingly, but when the chips are down, they will stand up for each other courageously. As friends, Sagittarius I's may fill in the gaps where parental, love or marital relationships have failed. In fact, this can become an all-encompassing relationship, one that supplies full emotional support and understanding, but it may also promote overdependency and close individual partners off from worldly challenge.

Sagittarius I co-worker pairs can often get the job done in half the time, and do it well to boot. Although Sagittarius I's don't generally like taking orders, they welcome all forms of input if it is of benefit to them and conveyed in a respectful way, and thus Sagittarius I boss-employee relationships can work out if these criteria are met.

ADVICE: *Regulate energy output. Take on fixed responsibilities. Soften your disapproval. Don't allow competitiveness to spin out of control.*

THE WEEK OF INDEPENDENCE
SAGITTARIUS I

THE WEEK OF THE ORIGINATOR
SAGITTARIUS II

By Chance, Not Choice

DARRYL HANNAH (12/3/61)
JOHN KENNEDY, JR. (11/25/60)

Prior to his marriage to Carolyn Bessette in 1996, Kennedy was ranked America's most eligible bachelor. Hannah was one of his well-known, longer romances. Amid rumors of an engagement, it is said that his mother, Jackie Onassis, made it clear to her son that she didn't want him marrying an actress. ***Also:*** **Paul Desmond & Dave Brubeck** (saxophonist/pianist; Dave Brubeck Quartet).

These two seldom become involved by choice, but sometimes do by chance. A bit too alike in their more negative aspects really to get along, Sagittarius I's and II's are wary around each other. Any relationship that does develop here is characterized by a tremendous need for freedom and independence, which may, depending on the circumstances, make any really deep involvement difficult or impossible. Furthermore, the relationship is often extremely extroverted and lacking stability, since it is most often taken up with change and variety. If seriously interested in strengthening their bond, this duo will have to dig deeper and develop stronger emotional and spiritual ties. One plus this relationship has going for it is communication, for Sagittarius I's and II's generally have little trouble understanding each other or getting their points across.

Friendships and love affairs of this type can be particularly unstable. The best of them are more romantic in nature, eschewing any kind of settled domesticity for truly adventuresome pursuits, often involving travel and exploration. Marriage lends a bit more stability here, but neither of these two is quick to commit, and taking the big step impulsively, without serious consideration of the difficulties involved, is not at all recommended. In marriages consummated quickly, the spouses too often pay the price later for their rash actions.

Sibling matchups and parent-child connections between Sagittarius I's and II's can be warm, close and supportive. Strong physical and emotional bonds are characteristic of such relationships, and guarantee the presence of close ties throughout adult life. At work, executives and business partners of this type may experience many differences of opinion, some irreconcilable. But competition can also bring out the very best in both associates, ultimately tending to advance the cause of the group or organization they both serve.

ADVICE: *Take the time for personal exploration. Deepen emotional ties. Make a commitment if you are really serious.*

November 25–December 2

THE WEEK OF INDEPENDENCE
SAGITTARIUS I

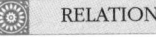

December 11–18

THE WEEK OF THE TITAN
SAGITTARIUS III

Unrelenting Crossfire

If these two were guns trained on each other, it would be best not to get caught in the crossfire, since they make an excellent match, whether as allies or opponents. Commanding presences that they are, Sagittarius III's are unlikely to withdraw from the fray; but Sagittarius I's are equally determined, and can attack with measured tempo or unrelenting fury if necessary. It is hard for these two highly individual personalities to serve on the same side, but should their energies gel, the resulting force is well-nigh irresistible. Whether amicable or adversarial, the relationship is extremely unusual, and its mutable qualities make flexibility under fire one of its strongest attributes.

Because this relationship is intensely physical, lovers, mates and friends in this combination will want to engage in sports and fitness activities, or at the very least to take long walks or go for swims. Lovers here will enjoy a frank and open attitude toward sex, but should be careful that built-in antagonisms do not result in power trips or insensitive, even violent behavior. The marked independence of spouses can mean that their children will have to look after themselves a good deal of the time.

Competitiveness usually cannot be avoided in Sagittarius I–Sagittarius III friendships, but should best be restricted to board or video games, or to the playing field. Should an attractive third party appear, this person should be shared equally as a friend, for if love enters the picture, ties of friendship can be strained to the limit.

Battling is apt to be the order of the day with sibling pairs, sometimes throughout their childhood and adolescence. Even when anxious parents or the partners themselves call truces, there is always a potentially explosive undercurrent. In professional matters, co-workers and colleagues in this combination can be valuable to any company, as long as they are getting along. If working for rival companies, their respect for each other's power will not keep them from tangling memorably.

ADVICE: *Keep violent urges under control. Try to see what is to your mutual advantage. Find constructive outlets for physical needs.*

DICK CLARK (11/30/29)
CONNIE FRANCIS (12/12/38)

Clark was the clean-cut emcee of the longest-lived music tv show, *American Bandstand* (1957–88). He presented every important pop act of its time, including the remarkable Francis, who, between '58 and '64, had 35 top-40 hits. They became close friends. **Also: Monica Seles & Arantxa Sanchez Vicario** (tennis rivals); **Robin Givens & Brad Pitt** (romance; actors).

November 25–December 2

THE WEEK OF INDEPENDENCE
SAGITTARIUS I

December 19–25

THE CUSP OF PROPHECY
SAGITTARIUS-CAPRICORN CUSP

The Grim Alternative

These two are constantly searching for ways to work out issues and improve their relationship. This search is based on the acknowledgment that problems exist, and on the premise that they need to be solved in order to proceed in a more productive and less antagonistic fashion. All of this sounds very logical, but in fact Sagittarius I's and Sagittarius-Capricorns are looking out for their own interests as well. It is the tension between what they can get and what they will have to give up as individuals that provides the dynamic here. At some moments, these two resemble politicians hammering out an agreement, at others a buyer and seller haggling over the price of merchandise.

Temperamentally, Sagittarius I's and Sagittarius-Capricorns couldn't be more different—the former lightning quick and overreactive, the latter more measured and difficult to arouse. Friendships between these two are generally more successful than love affairs. Because such affairs gyrate between passionate conflict and indifference, they are rarely reliable enough to hang together for long. In friendships, these partners generally surmount their differences, not least by fully respecting and even appreciating them. Such friends may pool their strengths when working on domestic or outside amateur projects together.

It is in marriage and family relationships that the true focus of this combination emerges most clearly, as problems are recognized and solved almost every day of the week. Perhaps this results from the fact that family pressures and practical considerations dictate the necessity of this process, and that in some sense survival is at stake. Having little choice but to cooperate, the partners can put their differences aside or work them out, for they know full well that the grim alternative may be the end of their relationship, or even of the group of which they are a part. Professional working relationships here don't always turn out that well. Sagittarius I's can get impatient with the slower pace of Sagittarius-Capricorns, who in turn can be irritated by Sagittarius I jumpiness and refusal to listen.

ADVICE: *Consider the needs of those around you. Stand up for yourself but be ready to compromise. Keep lines of communication open. Listen.*

JOSEPH STALIN (12/21/1879)
WINSTON CHURCHILL (11/30/1874)

Churchill and Stalin were allies during the final phases of WWII. In return for Soviet entry into the Pacific war, Churchill (and FDR) promised Stalin a number of economic and territorial concessions in Europe, despite Churchill's aversion to communism. His pact with Stalin prompted much criticism during the cold war era.

RELATIONSHIPS

STRENGTHS: **PHILOSOPHICAL, PLAYFUL, DEBATING**

WEAKNESSES: **AGGRESSIVE, ADVERSARIAL, NONEMPATHIC**

BEST: **FAMILY**

WORST: **FRIENDSHIP**

MARIA CALLAS (12/2/23)
RENATA TEBALDI (1/2/22)

Callas and Tebaldi, contemporary opera stars, were considered the leading sopranos of their generation. Inevitably, they were also rivals. Callas is best remembered for her bel canto roles during the 40s and 50s. Tebaldi performed in all the leading opera houses during the same period. Both retired in the mid-70s. **Also: Eugene Istomin & Pablo Casals** (pianist/cellist; co-performers).

November 25–December 2
THE WEEK OF INDEPENDENCE
SAGITTARIUS I

December 26–January 2
THE WEEK OF THE RULER
CAPRICORN I

Reveling in Debate

This combination is seldom taken up with small details; issues of the broadest scope come naturally under discussion. Philosophical, the relationship revels in debate and discussion of the most abstract concepts. Its physical side is also well developed, which can lead to confrontations that are variously playful and seriously aggressive. Should Sagittarius I's and Capricorn I's come to symbolize two very different points of view within a circle of family, friends or colleagues, their followers are likely to line up behind them and expect them to be their spokespersons or representatives. Willy-nilly, these two can find themselves at the center of very heated controversies that they might not have really looked for.

Although Sagittarius I's and Capricorn I's are very different temperamentally, marriages between them can work out as long as they can come to an agreement on important points. The inherent stability of Sagittarius I's and the good money sense of Capricorn I's will be effectively balanced by the latter's dynamism and liveliness. When faced with defeat or disappointment, this couple can take it hard, and may lack the resilience or self-understanding to cope. Love affairs in this combination rarely arouse strong sensual desires or empathy. For some reason, friendships are unlikely to develop past the stage of mere acquaintance, and in fact the more involved these two become, the more the relationship takes on an adversarial tone.

Professional and family encounters can be particularly intense. Generally speaking, Sagittarius I's will take the more radical point of view, while Capricorn I's are apt to defend the status quo. Even when liberal in viewpoint, Capricorn I's will defend the more traditional way of doing things, whereas Sagittarius I's will call into question any normally accepted view that doesn't make sense to them. Furthermore, the style of Capricorn I's is often relatively objective and dispassionate, whereas Sagittarius I's tend to be more individualistic and emotional.

ADVICE: *Keep some time for yourself. Don't avoid personal issues. Deepen understanding and acceptance. Closeness should not imply dissent.*

RELATIONSHIPS

STRENGTHS: **FASCINATING, HARDWORKING, CHARMING**

WEAKNESSES: **OVERSERIOUS, DEPRESSIVE, ARGUMENTATIVE**

BEST: **WORK**

WORST: **FRIENDSHIP**

JOHN KENNEDY, JR. (11/25/60)
CAROLYN BESSETTE (1/7/66)

The world sighed romantically as America's crown prince, Kennedy, married the lady of his dreams, Bessette, in 1996. The lawyer-cum-publisher and the former Calvin Klein publicist were quietly wed on an isolated Georgia island, then flew off for a Turkish honeymoon. **Also: Woody Allen & Diane Keaton** (romance); **Winston Churchill & Jennie Churchill** (British prime minister, son/American mother).

November 25–December 2
THE WEEK OF INDEPENDENCE
SAGITTARIUS I

January 3–9
THE WEEK OF DETERMINATION
CAPRICORN II

Misleading Lightness

The social image that this relationship conveys can be quite different from its personal realities. These two can work a magic on other people, so that even when arguments threaten to split them apart, onlookers continue to gape in fascination. The relationship can in some ways be characterized as being light, even flaky, emotionally. It is this very lightness that can be so misleading, for in fact the relationship can be a highly serious one. Neither of these two take either their careers or lives lightly, or expect that they will be easy. Thus struggle and hard work are no strangers to the relationship, which takes little for granted.

In private, heaviness or seriousness of purpose is apparent in love affairs and marriages. If this affect comes to dominate, it can at times lead the partners into depressions, but it is precisely during these episodes that great progress in personal development can take place for both partners, and particularly for Capricorn II's. Self-actualizing, the relationship can benefit in many subtle ways by solving emotional difficulties, and the harder the partners struggle, the more they may learn. Even if such relationships do not work out over the long term, the partners may nonetheless have benefited greatly by having gone through a metamorphosis, emerging as quite different individuals.

Sibling combinations may be particularly interested in art, film, video or Internet productions, not only as onlookers but also as active participants. Deep family ties can develop between Sagittarius I and Capricorn II relatives, despite competitiveness and acute differences of opinion. Sagittarius I–Capricorn II friendships are not particularly memorable, often because of an inability to share.

In the professional sphere this pair can work extremely well together, integrating Sagittarius I dynamism and the idiosyncratic, even nutty qualities of Capricorn II's. It is in this area that the more magical aspects of such relationships emerge, for these two specialize in mesmerizing an audience at business presentations, demonstrations or sales conferences.

ADVICE: *Bring your public and private selves more into focus. Work on emotional honesty—aim for greater transparency. Try to be more tolerant.*

November 25–December 2

THE WEEK OF INDEPENDENCE
SAGITTARIUS I

January 10–16

THE WEEK OF DOMINANCE
CAPRICORN III

An Impenetrable Center

The feelings in this relationship run deep and passionate. Although on the surface it would seem that clashes are inevitable between independent Sagittarius I's and dominant Capricorn III's, this combination does not have to involve conflict; in fac,t it is precisely its partners' differences that make it so strong and dynamic, for as a unit it can display great versatility in its interaction with other people. Extreme differences of temperament may dictate that the partners see each other only from time to time, rather than on an everyday basis. Since the relationship can be characterized as the Sagittarius I irresistible force meeting the Capricorn III immovable object, much is hidden here that neither partner wishes to have revealed to family, friends or society in general. The dark center of such a relationship may remain forever mysterious and impenetrable.

In love affairs, tensions are inevitable, and are particularly pronounced in the sexual sphere. Lovers must beware of power plays here—of becoming obsessed with controlling the other or winning out. Marriages are usually less favorable than love affairs, for here the materialistic aspects of the relationship often predominate. Breakups and divorces can be painful, not only emotionally but financially.

Friendships and sibling relationships certainly have their ups and downs. Neither party usually succeeds in controlling the other—but not for lack of trying. Rivalries, jealousies and competition, in sports and love, are all likely to characterize this matchup. Parent-child relationships in this combination will inevitably see the Capricorn III need to dominate challenged by rebellious Sagittarius I children, or a Capricorn III child's stubborn and recalcitrant side aroused by a Sagittarius I parent. In career matchups, this can be a strong combination, with boundless Sagittarius I energy and optimism melding well with the common sense, good money management and responsible attitudes of Capricorn III's. Classic differences of opinion arise over the Sagittarius I need to spend and the Capricorn III need to save, but the relationship could be the beneficiary of a sensible approach to cash management that would be the result of finding the middle way between these extremes.

ADVICE: *Don't try to reconcile your differences—put them to work for you. Try to understand yourself better. Learn the joys of total relaxation.*

RELATIONSHIPS

STRENGTHS: **DYNAMIC, VERSATILE, MYSTERIOUS**

WEAKNESSES: **CONTROLLING, TENSE, OVERMATERIALISTIC**

BEST: **SEXUAL**

WORST: **PARENT-CHILD**

ALBERT MAYSLES (11/26/26)
DAVID MAYSLES (1/10/32)

The Maysles brothers are noted documentary filmmakers who began collaborating in 1957 and produced a number of successful movies, among them *Salesman* (1969), *Gimme Shelter* (1970), *Grey Gardens* (1975) and the Emmy-winning short *Christo's Valley Curtain* (1972). **Also: Maria Callas & Aristotle Onassis** (longtime affair, before and after Jackie O).

November 25–December 2

THE WEEK OF INDEPENDENCE
SAGITTARIUS I

January 17–22

THE CUSP OF MYSTERY & IMAGINATION
CAPRICORN-AQUARIUS CUSP

Shooting Stars

This could be one of the most exciting and explosive matchups of the entire year. Unfortunately, little stability is guaranteed in such a relationship, so that these two are likely to blaze their way into darkness like shooting stars in the night sky. The partners are apt to be very attracted to how easily they can express their feelings with one another. The compassion and empathy between them betoken an instinctual understanding of each other that will help them overcome many difficulties.

Love affairs and friendships bring out the more sensitive side of each partner. Despite their popularity within their circle of friends or family, both Sagittarius I's and Capricorn-Aquarians are likely to feel misunderstood much of the time, and therefore in their relationship with each other may seek a variety of escapes—from drugs to sex and love to physical isolation—in an attempt to soothe hurt feelings and protect themselves from the slings and arrows of a hurtful world. To the extent that the relationship serves as a shelter in the storm, it may have both positive and negative effects on the personal development of its partners.

Marriages and work relationships between these two will have to accept the somewhat tedious social responsibilities incumbent on such roles. Although the world may view these two often outrageous and outgoing individuals as quite extroverted, in fact they have a highly private side, one that is clearly revealed by their relationship with each other. Moreover, when they do make public appearances, they may have something more exciting in mind than parent-teacher meetings and office parties. In the family sphere, siblings and cousins in this combination will liven up the atmosphere of gatherings, but will also render them a bit chaotic. Keeping the Sagittarius I–Capricorn-Aquarius relationship under control may be more than anyone is prepared to handle.

ADVICE: *Realize what you are getting into. Keep your impulsiveness under control. Conserve energy. Act sensibly, without sacrificing expression.*

RELATIONSHIPS

STRENGTHS: **EXCITING, SENSITIVE, EMPATHIC**

WEAKNESSES: **BORED, STIFLING, CHAOTIC**

BEST: **FRIENDSHIP**

WORST: **MARRIAGE**

JIMI HENDRIX (11/27/42)
JANIS JOPLIN (1/19/43)

Apart from having been lovers, rock superstars Hendrix and Joplin had other things in common: both gave explosive virtuoso performances at the 1967 Monterey Pop Festival; both had highly sexual stage personas; their music influenced the course of rock music; both died very young of drug overdoses. **Also: Bette Midler & Janis Joplin** (film portrayal, *The Rose*).

VIRGINIA WOOLF (1/25/1882)
LEONARD WOOLF (11/25/1880)

Writers Virginia and Leonard, core of the notorious Bloomsbury group, met in 1907 and married 5 years later. Together they founded and ran Hogarth Press, a small, prestigious publishing house. Though probably asexual due to her frigidity, their marriage was a long and devoted one. **Also: Benigno Aquino & Corazon Aquino** (married; Philippine leaders); **Churchill & Franklin Roosevelt** (WWII allies).

November 25–December 2
THE WEEK OF INDEPENDENCE
SAGITTARIUS I

January 23–30
THE WEEK OF GENIUS
AQUARIUS I

The Given Word

This relationship is a dignified one, in which personal worth and honor are given the highest consideration. Responsibility is the keynote here, and with it a guarantee of high-quality work. Written agreements are rarely necessary between these two, since the given word is law; to bring them to this point of agreement, however, is not necessarily easy. Although they may respect each other enormously, Sagittarius I's and Aquarius I's may not be prepared to entrust their future to such a relationship, nor to commit themselves to it with full force. Sagittarius I's may be suspicious of Aquarius I motives, while Aquarius I's are wary of Sagittarius I aggressiveness.

Love affairs and marriages are not especially suggested between these two—when passions emerge between them, so do acute instability and nervousness. Such relationships carry few guarantees that they will last, a fact underlined by their frenetic pace and, at times, lack of good sense. Family matchups, on the other hand, can be highly rewarding personally. They may also have professional or career aspects: not necessarily business people, relatives in this combination may pool their talents in social, artistic, health or sports-oriented activities, and as long as they decide to hire a good accountant and business manager, they are quite capable of achieving considerable commercial success.

In work relationships and friendships, admiration and affection between these two guarantee a high level of fulfillment. Often sharing the same or similar values, Sagittarius I's and Aquarius I's have little difficulty communicating with each other, although they may disagree on how to implement their plans. Once they agree on a course of action, they will follow through with steadfastness and determination. Quarrels can arise over one issue, however, and that is who will be the boss. More intelligent matchups choose to let the ultimate authority reside in the relationship itself, and to make all decisions with an eye to its longevity and welfare.

ADVICE: *Work toward greater trust and less suspicion—what are you afraid of? Use common sense to help you make decisions.*

BRUCE LEE (11/27/40)
BRANDON LEE (2/1/65)

Martial-arts movie star Bruce was an international cult figure even before his sudden death at 32 from a brain edema. Son Brandon, a rising star, was following in Bruce's footsteps when he was accidentally killed while filming *The Crow* (1994). **Also: Bruno Hauptmann & Charles Lindbergh** (kidnapper/ father of victim); **Bruce Paltrow & Blythe Danner** (married; producer/actress).

November 25–December 2
THE WEEK OF INDEPENDENCE
SAGITTARIUS I

January 31–February 7
THE WEEK OF YOUTH & EASE
AQUARIUS II

Getting Lost

This relationship seldom concerns itself with the ordinary way of doing things. It will seek out environments and activities that activate its fantasies, but should these two live in rather dull or conventional surroundings, they will generate imaginative projects within the walls of their own domestic space. The relationship is ruled by water, an element here emphasizing the world of dreams, visions and colorful feelings. Aquarius II's bring out the more unconventional side of Sagittarius I's, who often view them as far out and seek to get close to them by entertaining the prospect of unusual lifestyles or strange activities. Aquarius II's, on the other hand, appreciate the raw energy of Sagittarius I's, as well as their naturally inquisitive nature.

Romantic relationships in this combination may transport the partners to far-flung worlds of the mind, where they live on a plane at a distant remove from that of their friends, family and co-workers. Other people may view them askance, at times with a mixture of bewilderment and envy. Unfortunately, should their bubble burst, these lovers may have little of a substantive nature to hold on to. Marriages are not at all recommended here, unless a solid footing can be established in which to ground such ephemeral energies.

Friendships can be highly successful as long as demands are not too great. Both partners must feel free enough to go their own way, yet must not neglect to be there for each other in times of need. In the spheres of family and work, Sagittarius I's and Aquarius II's will be bound to fixed responsibilities, but this is no guarantee in itself that they will get along. Both partners must learn to concentrate on the job at hand and to keep their emotions from getting involved. Since the relationship is oriented towards feelings, this will not be an easy task, and these partners may find themselves constantly getting on each other's nerves.

ADVICE: *Don't get completely lost—pay attention to what's going on. If other people don't understand, take the time to explain. Be patient, and listen.*

November 25–December 2

THE WEEK OF INDEPENDENCE
SAGITTARIUS I

February 8–15

THE WEEK OF ACCEPTANCE
AQUARIUS III

Just a Memory

The key to holding this relationship together is the partners' ability to work together, whether in a domestic or a professional setting. Given the individual natures of Sagittarius I's and Aquarius III's, one probably wouldn't predict much stability for the relationship, but their combined chemistry can have a strongly stabilizing effect—at least as long as emotions aren't allowed to go haywire. Aquarius III's appreciate the attention given them by Sagittarius I's, whom they admire, and things go well when they are at the center of what is going on. Should Sagittarius I's occupy the dominant position, though, the relationship will be far less cohesive—the partners' changeability will carry it from pillar to post. Should honesty pervade the relationship, things have a chance of going well, but duplicity, deceit or outright cheating will often bring it crashing down around the partners' ears.

Love affairs are not so much romantic as practical. With few or no responsibilities, such an affair is likely to fade away to just a memory. Yet such relationships often do well when they progress to marriage, particularly when children are involved. The most crucial point here is discharging responsibilities easily and without resentment, and having a respect for children's individuality that approaches that of a sacred trust.

Friends may try to work together, but although things can seem very rosy at the outset, these relationships may not work out to anyone's advantage financially. The danger here is that the friendship may be adversely affected in the process, and after a business setback or failure may never be the same again. And if the partners do achieve success, this will bring difficulties of its own, since it will put the partners on a different footing. In the family sphere, Aquarius III parents may find coping with the energy of their Sagittarius I children exhausting. The task here is for them to learn patience and understanding, and to respect points of view far different from their own.

ADVICE: *Recognize boundaries and limitations. Don't take on too much. Ground yourself in practical endeavors. Remember who and what you are.*

MIA FARROW (2/9/45)
WOODY ALLEN (12/1/35)

Allen and Farrow had a long and close relationship although living apart. They adopted 2 children and had a biological son. In 1992, when she discovered Allen having an affair with Soon-Yi Previn, Farrow's earlier adopted daughter, a bitter, highly publicized breakup ensued.
***Also:* Joe DiMaggio & Dom DiMaggio** (baseball brothers); **Winston Churchill & Lord Randolph Churchill** (son/father).

November 25–December 2

THE WEEK OF INDEPENDENCE
SAGITTARIUS I

February 16–22

THE CUSP OF SENSITIVITY
AQUARIUS-PISCES CUSP

Impersonation

The lives of these two are fatefully intertwined, in a complex and not always obvious way. The focus of their relationship is often a kind of imitation, in which each seeks to emulate the other, going so far in some cases as to mimic his or her style or personal characteristics. Thus a principal theme in this matchup is interpretation, for its partners often go about copying each other in their own highly personal manner. Of course it's tempting to ask why they pick each other as models in the first place, but the answer invariably lies at a fairly deep psychological level. One suggestion is that the impersonator is roused by some important element in the life or character of the figure they are imitating, and wishes to be like that person. This is quite ironic, since in most cases the individual in question already carries, though unconsciously, the characteristics he or she perceives in the other.

Such personal and complex interchanges can make love affairs and friendships involved and difficult to fathom. Projection is often at work here, with Sagittarius I's becoming the focus of Aquarius-Pisces' secret wishes or fantasies, and vice versa. Animus-anima attractions—that is, falling in love with a projection of one's own idealized inner man or woman—are also evident. Marriages to a figure reminiscent of one's mother or father, or a dominant sibling, are common between Sagittarius I's and Aquarius-Pisces. Relationships like this may allow someone either to work out childhood difficulties or just to reenact them, but in either case it can be quite bewildering and frustrating for the other partner consistently to be treated as if he or she were someone else.

With psychological forces like this at work, career matchups in this combination can create unnecessary difficulties, which get in the way of doing the job. Family relationships confront the whole question of imitation much more squarely, particularly in parent-child matchups, where acceptable parental role models can be crucial to a child's development.

ADVICE: *Know who you are. Examine what attracts you to that special person Solve your own mystery. Don't lose yourself in someone else's drama.*

MARK TWAIN (11/30/1835)
HAL HOLBROOK (2/17/25)

Holbrook is a respected character actor celebrated for his portrayal of humorist Twain in the one-man, off-Broadway show *Mark Twain Tonight!* Through the years Holbrook has been acclaimed as Twain in over 2,000 international performances.
***Also:* John Kennedy, Jr. & Ted Kennedy** (nephew/uncle); **Cyril Cusack & Sinead Cusack** (father/daughter; poet/actress).

GAETANO DONIZETTI (11/29/1797)
GIOACCHINO ROSSINI (2/29/1792)

Donizetti and Rossini were contemporary 19th-century Italian opera composers. Rossini was the dominant figure during the early part of the century, creating over 40 operas in 2 decades, among them his comic masterpiece *The Barber of Seville* (1816). Donizetti emerged toward mid-century with such famous operas as *Don Pasquale* (1843) and *Lucia di Lammermoor* (1835).

November 25–December 2

THE WEEK OF INDEPENDENCE
SAGITTARIUS I

February 23–March 2

THE WEEK OF SPIRIT
PISCES I

Personal Responsibility

These free thinkers are usually united on one point: Death to the Tyrant! The whole question of dominance and authority is central to their thought. The problem they must solve is how to diminish the needs of those around them for an overriding authority by encouraging these individuals (who may be family, friends or co-workers) to take increasing personal responsibility for their actions. This point reveals the fact that this combination's orientation is not revolutionary or anarchistic per se, since it continues to seek order and structure simply by using other means.

In love affairs and marriages, the couple goes through many changes, from sexual to platonic, from physical to spiritual. Since Sagittarius I and Pisces I are square to each other in the zodiac (90° apart), conventional astrology predicts friction and stress between them, but also the dynamic energy to address problems. In friendships and family settings, the partners can seek to oppose and undermine authoritarian attitudes by encouraging free thought and open discussion. Their particular target in a family group is inevitably the patriarch, the matriarch or any adult figure who rules with an iron hand. Thus as siblings, for example, their stance may be seen or branded as rebellious, and they must be prepared for the worst in terms of punishment. As friends, they will make their influence felt widely in the social groups and gatherings of which they are a part.

Interpersonally, Sagittarius I's and Pisces I's may have problems getting along. Although resentment and jealousy are common between them, however, such considerations are usually overlooked in favor of the unity required by their common mission. This is dramatically demonstrated if they are attacked while in the middle of an argument, for each will immediately spring to the other's defense, going on the offensive with blinding speed. This trait is emphasized in career matchups, where these two can effectively serve an organization by working side by side. Union activities representing workers' rights are a natural setting for their efforts.

ADVICE: *Don't assume you know what's best. Keep your own house in order. Cultivate diplomacy—arousing opposition can cripple your efforts.*

MABEL HUBBARD (11/25/1857)
ALEXANDER GRAHAM BELL (3/3/1847)

Hubbard, deaf from childhood, was engaged to Bell on Thanksgiving Day 1875, her 18th birthday. Bell, whose mother was also deaf, had learned to teach and work with the hearing-impaired long before inventing the telephone in 1876. Hubbard's father financed Bell's commercial development of the telephone. ***Also:***

Samuel Reshevsky & Bobby Fisher (chess grand masters).

November 25–December 2

THE WEEK OF INDEPENDENCE
SAGITTARIUS I

March 3–10

THE WEEK OF THE LONER
PISCES II

On Again, Off Again

The Sagittarius I–Pisces II relationship careens through life like a roller coaster. On-again-off-again, it can exasperate those who must painfully watch or deal with it. Although the partners may swear their loyalty to each other and proclaim their undying love, the cold facts would seem to argue otherwise. Thus unreality is the principal problem this relationship must face, since the partners are often unaware of the games they are playing with each other. Things would not be so difficult were the level of feeling less high here, but emotions seem destined to prevail over reason again and again. Worse still, Sagittarius I's and Pisces II's are convinced that they are being rational, but in fact may be misled by faulty reasoning.

Love affairs can be passionate and rewarding. Yet just because this is so, Sagittarius I's and Pisces II's are all too prone to overlook serious problems that need their attention until it is too late. With little or no warning, one partner will often simply leave and never return—potentially a devastating experience for the other person, despite all his or her statements to the contrary. Marriages in this combination will have to face the disagreement between the extreme Sagittarius I need for independence and the need of Pisces II's for security, drives that can often clash. Each spouse is also likely to have close friends outside the relationship who may not get along well with the other partner.

Work relationships between these two tend to be chaotic, since each has a different idea about how things should be done. It is in the spheres of friendship and family that things perhaps go best for the Sagittarius I–Pisces II couple. Here self-deception is not so obviously at work, and the partners can be mutually supportive without kidding themselves about the true state of things. Empathy between siblings and in parent-child combinations is marked. And Sagittarius I and Pisces II friends are likely to bring each other into the bosoms of their own families, where they often meet with acceptance and respect.

ADVICE: *Open your eyes. Examine your need to convince yourself. Back off a bit emotionally—try to remain objective. Seek the advice of family and friends.*

November 25–December 2

THE WEEK OF INDEPENDENCE
SAGITTARIUS I

March 11–18

THE WEEK OF DANCERS & DREAMERS
PISCES III

 RELATIONSHIPS

STRENGTHS: **IMAGINATIVE,
ACTIVE, AFFECTIONATE**

WEAKNESSES: **NEGLECTFUL,
PROCRASTINATING, LAZY**

BEST: **FRIENDSHIP**

WORST: **LOVE**

Fantasy Realized in Action

This combination wants to go where the action is. It isn't enough for this pair to have imagination—they will eventually want their dreams to be translated into reality. The word "eventually" is crucial, though, for it can take months or years before fantasy is realized in action. But since these partners bring out each other's practical side, making plans for such endeavors, down to the last detail, can be highly satisfying for both of them. The theme of travel usually figures here in one way or another, for this couple takes great pleasure in regularly moving from place to place.

Love affairs and marriages between Sagittarius I's and Pisces III's favor long-distance trips, and if a period of time goes by without any mention of such travel, both partners may get itchy feet. Travel provides the perfect escape from the relationship's problems, but also acts as a safety valve, allowing the partners to let off emotional steam built up by frustration or neglect. Expressing anger is often a major problem for these two, in that it can be hard for them to find a socially acceptable way to let loose, or to avoid abusiveness or violence in such confrontations, whether physical or verbal.

Both professional relationships and friendships can be outstanding between these two, and they may also be interrelated, with particular emphasis on manual, technical or artistic skills. Although Sagittarius I jumpiness and Pisces III flakiness can be problems at times, when it comes to meeting deadlines and quotas these two can be counted on to come through. However, when a lot of time is available and demands are not high, both are very capable of goofing off together. In many situations, then, the Sagittarius I–Pisces III matchup will work no harder than it has to. In the family sphere, neither combination of the parent-child relationship is likely to be highly demanding or authoritative. Attitudes here are generally pretty free and easy, with a great deal of affection on both sides.

ADVICE: *Putting things off can become a bad habit. Be relaxed, but not too much. Find a sensible way to express your aggression. Meet challenges directly.*

KARL BENZ (11/25/1844)
GOTTLIEB DAIMLER (3/17/1834)

Benz and Daimler were German automotive pioneers who developed the first internal-combustion engines and automobiles. In 1886 Benz obtained a patent for a vehicle built in 1885 using a 4-cylinder engine—considered the world's first practical automobile. Daimler is credited with inventing the first high-speed engine (1885). In 1890 he founded the Daimler Motor Company, which later (1926) became Daimler-Benz.

December 3–10

THE WEEK OF THE ORIGINATOR
SAGITTARIUS II

December 3–10

THE WEEK OF THE ORIGINATOR
SAGITTARIUS II

 RELATIONSHIPS

STRENGTHS: **CONFRONTING,
VERSATILE, INDIVIDUALISTIC**

WEAKNESSES: **CONFLICTING,
DIFFICULT, INCOMPATIBLE**

BEST: **FAMILY**

WORST: **LOVE**

Longing for Someone Normal

The chances of two such idiosyncratic and highly individualistic people as these getting along together on a daily basis is alas not great. Both have their own ways of doing things, which are not only unlikely to gel but are actually prone to conflict. The fact that both partners tend to focus on the unique does not necessarily make it easier for them to sympathize with each other—indeed, both partners may long to be with someone more normal (as long as they can remain their own difficult selves, of course). One of the problems in getting such a relationship on the rails is that these partners need a while to adjust to each other's foibles, but may not be prepared to hang in there that long. In fact, family relationships between two Sagittarius II's can be the more successful ones, simply because, having grown up together over the years, they are used to each other's odd ways.

Love affairs and friendships between these two, to the extent that they are possible, tend to do best when the partners see each only occasionally. A hunger for more contact will often merely hasten the matchup's ultimate demise. Marriages can work out only if the partners have the necessary space that they can confidently call their own, without any interference or judgment. Children of such parents will not have an easy time of it, since their parental role models leave something to be desired. In fact, it may be that the children themselves become the stabilizing force in the relationship.

Sibling and parent-child relationships between Sagittarius II's are not easy ones to maintain, either, but a repetitive process of confrontation and resolution can help to some degree. Familial relationships between members of the opposite sex usually have a better chance for success. In the professional sphere, these two will be happiest as self-employed freelancers or as business partners, where the varied talents of both can be put to best use, but they will have to seek strong financial advice and management.

ADVICE: *Give things a chance to work out. Hang in there, but don't keep beating your head against a wall. Beware of double standards.*

BEAU BRIDGES (12/9/41)
JEFF BRIDGES (12/4/49)

Actor-brothers Beau and Jeff are the sons of veteran Hollywood and tv actor Lloyd Bridges. Starting their careers in child parts, Jeff's acting has stood out more in the eyes of critics. He has been nominated for 3 Oscars, notably for *Starman* (1984). They appeared together brilliantly in *The Fabulous Baker Boys* (1989). **Also: Mary, Queen of Scots & Lord Darnley** (married; queen/consort).

SAMMY DAVIS, JR. (12/8/25)
FRANK SINATRA (12/12/15)

Davis and Sinatra were members of Hollywood's "Rat Pack." More than that, they were great longtime friends and frequent co-performers on both stage and screen. In the late 80s they embarked on an enormously successful concert tour of the world (with Liza Minnelli). **Also: Walt Disney & Steven Spielberg** (fantasy-makers for kids).

December 3–10

THE WEEK OF THE ORIGINATOR
SAGITTARIUS II

December 11–18

THE WEEK OF THE TITAN
SAGITTARIUS III

An Arrow to the Future

With lots of energy to spare, this duo is up for new and exciting experiences, and also for rolling back boundaries. These partners may already be highly original individually, but the synergy of their combination magnifies this quality, making their relationship a potent force for change. Whether they work together directly or not, their presence in a family or social group, or as part of a work team, will give such organizations a tremendous impetus to move forward. Like an arrow pointed toward the future, this duo will lead the way.

Love affairs between Sagittarius II's and III's can be passionate, but they are also highly unstable and may not go very deep emotionally. A curious inability to express sympathy or kindness, which in no way implies that these emotions are not felt, may make such a relationship hard and uncompromising, albeit intense. Learning to slow down a bit and to place greater emphasis on understanding and acceptance are crucial to this relationship's survival. Marriage should not be considered unless these points are addressed.

Friendships are often of the more challenging sort. Outdoing each other in any field of endeavor can become the basis for such a relationship. Sagittarius II's may find their niche and stay there, while Sagittarius III's are seldom content until they have pushed their talents to the limit; the determination and stick-to-it-iveness of the former may find its match in the desire of the latter to overcome and emerge victorious. Confrontations are not at all necessary here, however, and this duo can be remarkably accepting of each other.

Sibling pairs, particularly of the same sex, may engage in constant competition and dialogue, but this usually has a salutary effect, acting to sharpen their individual skills. Work and career connections will rarely be possible between two such dynamic personalities, however, for they generally do best when working on their own, or on a team where they alone call the shots.

ADVICE: *Explore emotional realms carefully, but work on expressing feelings at a deeper level. Seek out compromises. Conserve energies in order to make them last.*

PRINCE PETER KROPOTKIN (12/9/1842)
JOSEPH STALIN (12/21/1879)

Though born of nobility, Kropotkin was an anarchist and early revolutionary. He was imprisoned 1874–76 for political activities, then fled Russia until the February Revolution (1917). After Stalin led the Bolshevik takeover in October, Kropotkin, then 75, retired from politics, disillusioned with the authoritarian Bolshevik regime.

December 3–10

THE WEEK OF THE ORIGINATOR
SAGITTARIUS II

December 19–25

THE CUSP OF PROPHECY
SAGITTARIUS-CAPRICORN CUSP

The Resolve to Prevail

This relationship often focuses on large-scale, even mammoth projects. Whether planning family vacations, social events or career coups together, the couple enjoy being in the thick of the fray, fighting either as a unit or against each other, for large stakes. They are often found at the head of respective organizations, but when they are colleagues they do not have to occupy a dominant role in their group; just being part of what is going on is usually enough for them. The thrill of confrontation is also an element here, and although defeat is not really a possibility they consider, they can accept it if they know in their hearts that they've given their all. Furthermore, their resolve to prevail in the next encounter is usually tremendous.

In sibling relationships and career matchups, the competitive aspects of this combination can be powerful, particularly when the partners are of the same sex. Generally, Sagittarius-Capricorns may have the advantage here, because they are so psychologically perceptive, but sheer energy may allow Sagittarius II's to win out. The most satisfying connections between these two may center on the theme of construction, whether of physical structures or more abstract ones. Bosses and parents may come to depend heavily on the support and dedication of co-worker and sibling pairs of this type.

In love affairs and marriages, Sagittarius II's can be attracted to the smoldering passion of Sagittarius-Capricorns, who in turn may be drawn to Sagittarius II drive and charisma. This can be an intense matchup, accessing deep emotional areas. Unfortunately, undermining and self-destructive feelings are as likely to emerge as healthy and constructive ones. The partners' intentions are very important here, and if the relationship believes in itself and wants to succeed, the results they get can directly reflect their attitudes. Friendships or enmities tend to be forged in the white heat of experience. There is usually little concerning their purpose in getting involved with each other that they leave to the imagination.

ADVICE: *Winning is not the only important thing. Learn from your mistakes. Maintain a positive attitude. Don't undercut your own efforts.*

December 3–10
THE WEEK OF THE ORIGINATOR
SAGITTARIUS II

December 26–January 2
THE WEEK OF THE RULER
CAPRICORN I

| RELATIONSHIPS |

STRENGTHS: ADMIRING, MAGNETIC, DIVERSE

WEAKNESSES: DISAPPROVING, OVERCONTROLLING, MISTRUSTFUL

BEST: FRIENDSHIP

WORST: MARRIAGE

Rarely Neutral

Should these two be able to get together, they may temporarily work a kind of magic as a pair, but in the long run their temperamental and ideological differences may prove too great a barrier to their relationship. Capricorn I's are likely to view Sagittarius II's with a wary eye—mistrust and an occasional twinge of jealousy must be overcome if the relationship is to move forward. No matter how far out, or even revolutionary, Capricorn I's are, at bottom they are rock-solid traditionalists who often disapprove of highly unusual and individualistic expressions such as those that emanate from Sagittarius II's.

Love affairs and marriages between these two do not have an outstanding prognosis. Capricorn I's have an earthy sensuality that may hold the interest of Sagittarius II's for a time, but they also show authoritarian tendencies that will ultimately leave Sagittarius II's longing to break free and looking elsewhere for what they need. Their own curiosity will probably be piqued by Sagittarius II originality, at least at first, but they will later come to view this quality as flaky and irresponsible, and will grow irritated and impatient with it.

Capricorn I parents can give their Sagittarius II children the stability and support they desperately need, but may ultimately prove too controlling. Friendships are a study in contrasts. Other people may find it hard to understand how such different people can remain close friends over the years, but this very special bond is often sustained through mutual need and admiration. Common interests invariably prove to be the cement that holds such a relationship together.

In career matters, this relationship can be either positive or negative, but will rarely be neutral in character. Should these two be rivals, they are likely to entice each other with dubious promises, and to try to catch each other off guard in their attempts to overcome. As colleagues or co-workers, they may succeed in generating a magnetism that can draw clients and bosses alike to their cause.

ADVICE: *Try to see the other person's point of view. Give things time to unfold and to change. Mute your disapproval. Find what is to your mutual advantage.*

MARLENE DIETRICH (12/27/01)
DOUGLAS FAIRBANKS, JR. (12/9/09)

In 1936, at the same time CBS head William Paley was courting her, Dietrich began having an affair with Fairbanks. This went on during the filming of her movie *Knight Without Armor* (1937) and his *The Prisoner of Zenda* (1937). **Also: T.V. Soong & Mao Zedong** (Chinese political foes; capitalist/communist).

December 3–10
THE WEEK OF THE ORIGINATOR
SAGITTARIUS II

January 3–9
THE WEEK OF DETERMINATION
CAPRICORN II

| RELATIONSHIPS |

STRENGTHS: IMAGINATIVE, TREND-SETTING, LUCRATIVE

WEAKNESSES: UPSETTING, BIZARRE, SELFISH

BEST: WORK

WORST: MARRIAGE

Nothing Permanent Except Change

This is the couple to watch if you are interested in keeping abreast of the times. They are particularly good at setting trends, or, at the very least, at recognizing and following them. This does not mean that the relationship is without its ups and downs. In fact, it is knowing how to surf the waves of chance that guarantees the combination's success, implying a wisdom capable of recognizing that nothing is permanent except change. Capricorn II's are highly ambitious, a quality that can be lacking in their partner in this combination, but they can certainly be attracted to out-of-the-way phenomena, and so may be captivated by the unusual attributes and concepts of Sagittarius II's. Furthermore, they are sensible enough to realize that today's weird notions may be tomorrow's realities, so that the relationship's vision often proves accurate, and even lucrative.

In love affairs, Sagittarius II's and Capricorn II's may be carried away on the wings of fantasy, but their idealistic interactions may in fact have surprising longevity. Marriages between these imaginative Sagittarius II–Capricorn II couples may not fare so well when confronted with the humdrum routine of domestic life. Friendships and sibling matchups in this combination often show an interest in fantasy, science fiction, horror films and the like. The friends and parents of such a couple may despair of ever dragging them back to the real world, but these pairs are well aware of the differences between what is real and what imagined.

Business relationships and career connections between these two can get on like a house on fire. They most often do best when free of the restrictions of a hierarchical or bureaucratic organization, but they may actually meet while in the employ of such a company and formulate ideas to go off on their own. Another common scenario is for Sagittarius II's and Capricorn II's to meet as freelancers or small-business people and to pool their efforts, often inspired by a totally new concept or idea.

ADVICE: *Acknowledge the existence of others. Respect more traditional attitudes. Tend to daily tasks. The unusual often resides in the ordinary.*

GYPSY ROSE LEE (1/9/14)
OTTO PREMINGER (12/5/06)

In 1971, just after Lee's death, director Preminger revealed to the public that he was the father of the stripper-actress' 26-year-old son, then casting director Erik Kirkland. He adopted Kirkland, who changed his name to Eric Lee Preminger.

Also: Francisco Franco & Juan Carlos (dictator/monarch successor); **Richard Sears & Alvah Roebuck** (mail-order moguls); **Jim Messina & Kenny Loggins** (musical duo).

DEANNA DURBIN (12/4/21)
ROBERT STACK (1/13/19)

Hollywood's Durbin was a major child star and leading lady in 30s and 40s romantic comedies. Stack's film career was launched at 20 with a burst of publicity as "the first boy to kiss Deanna Durbin on the screen," in *First Love* (1939). **Also: Beau Bridges & Lloyd Bridges** (son/father; actors); **Maximilian Schell & Maria Schell** (sibling actors); **Don King & George Foreman** (promoter/fighter).

December 3–10
THE WEEK OF THE ORIGINATOR
SAGITTARIUS II

January 10–16
THE WEEK OF DOMINANCE
CAPRICORN III

An Empathic Morass

There is an innate sympathy and depth of feeling between these two that can help the partners overcome many difficulties. Their relationship can be an extremely close one, providing shelter and protection against the misunderstanding or narrow minds of other people. Although Capricorn III's seem to be the more protective of the two, Sagittarius II's also offer solace in times of psychological need, serving to raise their partners' spirits when they are teetering on the brink of depression. Sagittarius II liveliness and sparkling imagination is not generally disturbing to Capricorn III's, nor is the Capricorn III tendency to dominate resented by Sagittarius II's, who may come to rely on this partner's stability and strength.

Love affairs and marriages between these two may create a bond of mutual dependency that is difficult to break. While things are going well, there may be few problems, but if personal development is neglected, neither Sagittarius II's nor Capricorn III's may be equipped to function confidently on their own. The strong empathy between these two can be seen both as a blessing and as a force that weakens individual egos, since it reduces the need to rise to challenges. Such relationships are pleasant enough, but may sink into an apathetic morass that generates little energy.

Family relationships, on the other hand, can be very dynamic, not only between siblings but also between parents and children in this combination. Capricorn III's are often role models for Sagittarius II's, their achievements acting as a stimulus to their partners, who want to be taken seriously and therefore must prove themselves. Relatives here are also capable of teaming up on joint efforts, to the benefit of their relationship. Friendships may result from working relationships, or vice versa, but feelings often get in the way here, and keep the relationship from functioning objectively. It is usually best for such pairs to decide whether friendship or work is the most important priority and to stick to such decisions, no matter how difficult that may be.

ADVICE: *Try to maintain objectivity. Stand up for yourself—a relationship can only do so much for you. Empathy has its good and bad effects.*

DON KING (12/6/32)
MUHAMMAD ALI (1/17/42)

One of fight promoter King's early grand-scale title bouts was between his pride and joy, Ali, and heavyweight champ George Foreman in Zaire, 1974. A magnetic Ali attracted all the publicity the promoter could have wished for. Ali won the title. The bout was the subject of the 1996 Oscar-winning documentary *When We Were Kings*.

Also: Bruce Nauman & Susan Rothenberg (married; artists).

December 3–10
THE WEEK OF THE ORIGINATOR
SAGITTARIUS II

January 17–22
THE CUSP OF MYSTERY & IMAGINATION
CAPRICORN-AQUARIUS CUSP

Auspicious Circumstances

On the surface of it, this combination would have all the ingredients for instability. Yet the natural flamboyance and extroverted qualities shared by these partners can be constructively channeled into highly grounded pursuits. Taking on concrete responsibilities, meeting deadlines and having to be concerned with the welfare of others all work to the benefit of this duo. True, they are equally capable of flying off the track and dissipating their energies in debilitating, albeit pleasurable pursuits, but at least the choice is there. In addition, fate usually takes a hand, serving up some auspicious circumstance that enables this pair to get back on the right path.

Learning to read the signs of the times is of crucial importance to the stability of this relationship. Thus it may be a combination of free will and serendipity that determines whether love affairs and friendships will work out or not. The circumstances under which these two meet are often as important as how they react to each other. Should one of them already be involved in a permanent relationship, the whole course of the matchup will be determined by whether the partners show patience and care, or rush right into an emotional involvement without giving it much thought. Here more than elsewhere, acting responsibly will help create an outcome more favorable for all concerned.

In the areas of family and career, parent-child and boss-employee relationships of either combination tend to be nervous and somewhat unstable. Parents usually find it difficult to keep their anger under control, and can become easily exasperated by their children. In co-worker combinations, particularly those having an outlet for imagination and personal initiative, this pair can be successful. Friendships between them tend to drift apart unless imbued with a strong sense of purpose. Engaging in community activities, common interests and even in small-business pursuits may be required to keep the friendship on an even keel.

ADVICE: *Don't try to escape your destiny. Surrender is important, but so is individual choice. Find activities that will give you direction.*

December 3–10

THE WEEK OF THE ORIGINATOR
SAGITTARIUS II

January 23–30

THE WEEK OF GENIUS
AQUARIUS I

Vying for Attention

RELATIONSHIPS

STRENGTHS: **LIGHT, PLAYFUL, CASUAL**

WEAKNESSES: **COMPETITIVE, TEMPERAMENTAL, EXPLOSIVE**

BEST: **ACQUAINTANCESHIP**

WORST: **SIBLING**

The uniqueness of character that these two possess can work against their establishing a strong relationship, since their combination only emphasizes their unconventional aspects, and also adds a dose of overemotionalism. Since this pair normally chooses to invest far more in themselves as individuals than they are willing to give a relationship, a relationship between them doesn't stand much of a chance. Spending a lot of time together may not be in the cards for these two, so that more casual relationships are favored. Emotions are often out-of-synch here as well, as is evident in the impatience and irritation that these two often feel with each other.

In love affairs and marriages, both partners seek attention; if they fail, they will often try to annoy each other or deliberately create a problem that cannot be ignored. Such couples will often vie for attention in gatherings of friends and family by showing off their talents and abilities, or by being obnoxious. Should these two be thrown together in a work situation, they will have to exert great discipline not to allow their emotions to be aroused and to keep their anger under control. In the sphere of friendship, these two often do best as occasional companions or acquaintances. Limiting emotional contacts can allow common interests to be the focus and playful feelings to emerge.

Examining families where these two grow up together can lend insight into their relationship. Both partners tend to be very self-centered, yet they can often establish bonds through childhood games and other forms of play. As long as they are involved in what they are doing, things can go quite well, but the appearance of an adult can spark competition for attention. Failing to gain it, one of the pair may throw a tantrum, start a fight or withdraw. Such sibling pairs have very different emotional requirements, and parents who find it easier to adopt one attitude toward both will inevitably arouse discontent. It is quite possible for these patterns to be replayed in the workplace.

ADVICE: *Make an effort to get along—put the relationship first. Promote harmony through sharing. Be the first to give attention and the last to demand it.*

DALTON TRUMBO (12/9/05)
HUMPHREY BOGART (1/23/1899)

Screenwriter Trumbo (*Thirty Seconds Over Tokyo*, 1944; *Exodus*, 1960) and actor Bogart were investigated in the 50s as suspected communists by Sen. Joseph McCarthy's witch-hunting committee. When called in to testify, Trumbo was broken by McCarthy and later sent to jail and blacklisted. Bogart stood up to McCarthy, refusing to name other suspects.

December 3–10

THE WEEK OF THE ORIGINATOR
SAGITTARIUS II

January 31–February 7

THE WEEK OF YOUTH & EASE
AQUARIUS II

Reaching the Top

RELATIONSHIPS

STRENGTHS: **AMBITIOUS, DETERMINED, PROUD**

WEAKNESSES: **CONCEITED, OVERAGGRESSIVE, DELUDED**

BEST: **WORK**

WORST: **LOVE**

There is an undeniably ambitious element in this relationship, and with these two the desire to reach the top in any given field is not necessarily selfish or even self-seeking; rather, it is the expression of what they feel is their path in life, their destiny, their fate. These partners often feel that together they are able to serve a cause more efficaciously and to forward not only their own dreams and aspirations but those of the group to which they belong. Such feelings of inevitability and justification make this relationship a very difficult one to oppose in the professional and business worlds. The partners must be careful, however, that they do not act unfairly or hurt others' feelings through an overaggressive or elitist attitude.

These ambitious attitudes often manifest in the family and the marital sphere, where the couple can come to be a kind of group representative. Even when the partners express their drive in different areas, and have little to do with financial interests, other relatives express great pride in their achievements. But jealousies over the couple's good fortunes can also be aroused in those who feel left out or perhaps insulted by such "uppityness," or through unfavorable comparisons.

As lovers, these couples may find it necessary to convince themselves and others that they have the best relationship possible, often through displays of romantic affection. Such demonstrations may really be a cover-up for problems that cannot be faced or even acknowledged. Friends in this combination find it less necessary to put on a show, but still may need to believe that their relationship is absolutely tops. This may well be the case, but they will eventually learn that these attitudes can also be harmful, since calling someone "best friend," or lauding one's own relationship to the skies, can actually become a setup for a later powerful letdown or betrayal.

ADVICE: *Don't blow your own horn. Conceit can undercut your efforts. Go about your work quietly and modestly—results speak for themselves.*

GUNNAR MYRDAL (12/6/1898)
ALVA MYRDAL (1/31/02)

Swedish husband and wife won separate Nobel Prizes for their accomplishments: Gunnar in 1974 in economics for his theory of money, and Alva in 1982 with the Peace Prize for her work on disarmament. **Also: David Carradine & John Carradine** (son/father; actors); **Bo Belinsky & Mamie Van Doren** (affair; baseball star/sexpot actress); **Jean-Luc Godard & François Truffaut** (New Wave directors).

STRENGTHS: **SHARING,
SOULFUL, RISK-TAKING**
WEAKNESSES: **WARY, PAINFUL,
FOOLHARDY**
BEST: **LOVE**
WORST: **WORK**

MARY LAMB (12/3/1764)
CHARLES LAMB (2/10/1775)

The Lambs were sister and brother writers who collaborated on children's books. He is best known for his charming, whimsical essays written under the pseudonym Elia. His mentally unstable sister, during a fit of insanity in 1786, murdered their mother. **Also: Sammy Davis, Jr. & Kim Novak** (black entertainer received death threats for dating white actress).

December 3–10

THE WEEK OF THE ORIGINATOR
SAGITTARIUS II

February 8–15

THE WEEK OF ACCEPTANCE
AQUARIUS III

Forceful Persuasion

Because of their unusual natures and special requirements, these two may recognize each other as soulmates. Furthermore, they are both quite likely to have suffered more than their share of rejection and misunderstanding before meeting each other. Sagittarius II's tend to be wary of the acceptance accorded them by Aquarius III's, and may initially back off. Later, however, they can become unduly dependent on this partner, once their trust has grown. Aquarius III's show their enthusiasm more openly, and are often mesmerized by the energies this relationship unlocks, yet they may still hold back. Thus the relationship's focus may well be the forceful persuasion that the partners exert on each other to open up and fully accept one another in their hurry to consummate what promises to be a wholly unique relationship for both of them.

In love affairs and marriages, these partners are capable of sharing at a deep emotional level. Once convinced that their secrets are safe with one another, they may open their hearts and discuss the most intimate and painful matters. They are both well aware that such trust could backfire, and that they risk betrayal, but they are usually willing to take the chance. Needless to say, should the relationship fail or suffer the loss of one partner, it could be years before such trust could again be established with another, if ever.

Friends and siblings in this combination usually indulge in physical activities ranging from sports to fitness to daring activities such as bungee-jumping or hang-gliding. These two bring out one another's extroverted side, particularly in areas involving challenge and danger. Sharing mutual friends may be a problem here because of the possessive feelings and petty jealousies that often arise. As co-workers, these two may find it hard to agree on what approach they should take in their projects. Likewise, as business partners or entrepreneurs, their differences in outlook may provoke dissension and ultimately precipitate a breakup.

ADVICE: *Overcome suspicions and open your heart. Don't be afraid to share. Possessiveness must be relinquished. Learn to work together.*

STRENGTHS: **OVERCOMING,
GROUNDING, RESOLVING**
WEAKNESSES: **STRESSED-OUT,
UNBALANCED, THREATENED**
BEST: **MARRIAGE**
WORST: **FAMILY**

LARRY BIRD (12/7/56)
MICHAEL JORDAN (2/17/63)

Friendly rivals Bird and Jordan are 2 of basketball's all-time greats. Bird led his team to 3 NBA titles, while Jordan led his to 4. Bird earned 3 MVP awards to Jordan's 5. Both players joined hands when they were members of America's '92 Olympic Dream Team (shown here). **Also: Tyra Banks & Seal** (romance; model/pop singer).

December 3–10

THE WEEK OF THE ORIGINATOR
SAGITTARIUS II

February 16–22

THE CUSP OF SENSITIVITY
AQUARIUS-PISCES CUSP

Grounding Wayward Energies

This pair tends to bring out each other's insecurities. Thus the struggle to overcome emotional imbalances is likely to become the relationship's focus, at least insofar as it seeks to perpetuate itself through healthy behavior. The domination of impulsive and self-destructive urges is of prime importance here. Sagittarius II's may find their partners in this combination very attractive, but could be frustrated in their attempts to penetrate Aquarius-Pisces' elaborate defenses. Aquarius-Pisces in turn will find it hard to adjust to the alternately aggressive and passive moods of Sagittarius II's. Establishing consistency in the relationship is a top priority; assuming responsibilities and grounding wayward energies in the regular activities of daily life may be at least a partial solution.

All activities of a physical or sensual nature—such as food, sex, exercise and sleep—should all be deeply explored. Love affairs and marriages are liable to show stress and nervousness when these areas are avoided or neglected. At times, the insecurities in such relationships seem to resemble chemical imbalances or deficiencies, since they can often be rectified when the right antidote is found. More often than not, love, affection and kindness turn out to be necessary supplements.

Working out their differences can be a lifetime task for relatives. As friends, Sagittarius II's and Aquarius-Pisces have their ups and downs. They often do best when in crisis or mutual need, exhibiting sympathy and warmth, but they can be surprisingly cold and offhand with each other when such times of trouble have passed.

Professional relationships between these two can do well when fixed requirements demand a steady, unwavering approach, but Sagittarius II's will eventually tire of inflexible and boring assignments, and long for change. Aquarius-Pisces often feel threatened, and even betrayed, by such feelings. In the family sphere, relatives in this combination may have difficulty getting along, creating dissension within the group.

ADVICE: *Promote calm and balance, and avoid extremes of behavior. Ground yourself in the here and now. Problems are challenges.*

December 3–10

THE WEEK OF THE ORIGINATOR
SAGITTARIUS II

February 23–March 2

THE WEEK OF SPIRIT
PISCES I

Varying Frequencies

The harmony between these two is in the nature of a sympathetic vibration. Like strings tuned to the same frequency, Sagittarius II's and Pisces I's are highly responsive to each other, such that the slightest upset or change of feeling in one will cause discord in the relationship. Because of the extreme sensitivity here, oscillations of mood are common, and it may be difficult to attain constancy or permanence. Yet this challenge can become the focus of the Sagittarius II–Pisces I relationship, as its partners seek to be ever more aware of their emotions and try to stay in tune with each other. Sooner or later, they will learn not to react so quickly to upset, and realize that being out of tune must also be accepted as a natural phenomenon that needs to occur from time to time.

In love affairs, the partners can enjoyably spend long periods of time with each other. But although they are good companions as well as lovers, they do best when each has his or her own space to which to retreat to be alone. Emotional interactions are complex here, since it is difficult for either the partners or an objective onlooker to know where feelings are coming from, so conjoined are they. Feeling the other person's emotions and taking them as one's own is quite a common phenomenon here. The difficulty that Pisces I's find in making commitments, and the problems that Sagittarius I's have in trusting at a deep level, may keep these two from getting married. Should they tie the knot, however, their union may prove highly successful.

Working together is only possible if the partners' innate sensitivity to each other's moods can be put aside for the sake of the project or the good of the group. Similarly, relatives in this combination cannot expect others to sit around and wait until they have smoothed over their differences. Sagittarius II–Pisces I friendships may be too close, stifling the individuality of both partners.

ADVICE: *Too frequent tuning takes away from the playing time. Let things go as they will. Worry less about what's wrong, and don't ask.*

CASIMIR MALEVICH (2/23/1878)
WASSILY KANDINSKY (12/4/1866)

Malevich and Kandinsky were the 2 giants of 20th-century Russian painting. They knew each other well and worked together to found Russia's abstract school, also known as suprematism. In the early 1900s Kandinsky traveled to Paris, where he joined other famous artists of his time. Malevich remained in Russia in relative obscurity. **Also: Nicolo Amati & Girolamo Amati** (son/father; master violinmakers).

December 3–10

THE WEEK OF THE ORIGINATOR
SAGITTARIUS II

March 3–10

THE WEEK OF THE LONER
PISCES II

Putting Patience to the Test

This relationship can turn out to be a highly provocative and lively one—not much boredom will ever manifest here. The partners must be extremely careful, however, to moderate their energies and avoid taking on too much. Both physical activity and highly imaginative endeavors are characteristic of this pair. Pisces II's often bring out the more introverted aspects of their Sagittarius II partners, and in their own private world these two can give vent to unlimited flights of fantasy. Kaleidoscopic, the relationship's everchanging thought patterns roam over vast areas of human endeavor.

Love affairs and friendships tend to the strange, even to the peculiar. Seldom interested in the straight and narrow, this relationship will go far afield to find what really stimulates and satisfies it, and it will rarely be content with middle-class values. If the partners deny or ridicule each other's needs for comfort and security, however—and these needs can be significant—they may be undercutting the relationship's longevity. In marriage, the drive for security may well emerge even more strongly, often bringing about a marked change in the values in a young Sagittarius II–Pisces II couple. Should these spouses have children, they will undoubtedly appreciate the value of a settled domestic life still more. Achieving financial stability is an important challenge for this marriage to face.

Working relationships between Sagittarius II's and Pisces II's are often successful in technical and practical areas, perhaps dealing with computers or finance. Although neither individual may be very practical on his or her own, the relationship can surmount such difficulties to create a sensible and well-ordered work space. Siblings in this combination may find it hard to maintain stability in their relationship, since they demand variety. In general, these pairs put the patience of parents and older relatives to the test.

ADVICE: *What you ridicule may be what you most need. Be aware of your effect on other people and respect their space. Get your financial act together.*

PAUL BERN (12/3/1889)
JEAN HARLOW (3/3/11)

Bern became a major force in movies during the 1920s. He was a production executive, director and screenwriter. In 1932 he married Hollywood's first great sex symbol, Harlow. A slight man, nearly twice her age, Bern apparently was impotent with her. He committed suicide 2 months after they married. **Also: Louis Prima & Keely Smith** (married; bandleader/singer).

December 3–10

THE WEEK OF THE ORIGINATOR
SAGITTARIUS II

March 11–18

THE WEEK OF DANCERS & DREAMERS
PISCES III

RELATIONSHIPS

STRENGTHS: PHILOSOPHICAL,
EXPLORING, SUBMITTING
WEAKNESSES: RESISTANT,
EGOTISTICAL, CLOSED
BEST: LOVE
WORST: FRIENDSHIP

JOHN MALKOVICH (12/9/53)
GLENNE HEADLY (3/13/55)

Malkovich and Headly were married from 1982–90. Headly, an accomplished actress, appeared in many 80s and 90s movies, notably as Tess Trueheart in *Dick Tracy* (1990). Malkovich is an unconventional leading man with many strong stage and screen roles, memorably as the seducer in *Dangerous Liaisons* (1988). **Also: Dina Merrill & Marjorie Merriweather Post** (daughter/mother; actress/heiress).

Following the Left-Hand Path

It may sometimes seem that this pair has come together for one purpose only—to help each of them on the road to self-realization and to find their individual creative cores. Once they are set solidly on the left-hand path of inner growth, their relationship may no longer be necessary. The success of this work may depend on the ability of Sagittarius II's to keep their ego drives under control and submit to a higher authority, whether moral, religious or spiritual. Pisces III's may be a strong influence on them in this respect, and may act as their spiritual guides in these relationships, gently encouraging them to temper their egotism and follow the path of true inner work. In turn, Sagittarius II's can share in the courageous and creative Pisces III approach to this process.

Love affairs will be passionate, but are no less in need of philosophical direction. Sufficiently pleasurable experiences may be had by both partners, but if they take the time to explore the depths of their own feelings, and to contemplate the many mysteries of life, they will add whole new dimensions to their interactions. Furthermore, such investigations tend to increase the likelihood of their staying together. Marriages may come to be squarely based on a particular ideology, whether a formal one or a more subjective one worked out by the partners themselves. Should this be the case, the couples must remember to be open to criticism and evaluation, and never to cut themselves off from the world's input.

As friends, Sagittarius II's and Pisces III's are liable to drift without direction unless they find a point to set their compass toward. As family members, particularly parent-child pairs, Pisces III's are more successful in the parental role, and must insist on their authority being respected. Sagittarius II–Pisces III co-worker pairs often do well putting their energies in the service of a company or organization. Inspirational aspects are extremely important here, and this professional duo does particularly well in activities demanding imagination and flair.

ADVICE: *Learn the lesson of surrender. Don't put yourself above the universe. Find your true self. Listen carefully to the suggestions of other people.*

RELATIONSHIPS

STRENGTHS: POSITIVE,
BELIEVING, IDEALISTIC
WEAKNESSES: INATTENTIVE,
OVEROPTIMISTIC, OUT OF TOUCH
BEST: WORK
WORST: MARRIAGE

ED KOCH (12/12/24)
FIORELLO LAGUARDIA (12/11/1882)

LaGuardia and Koch were both 3-term NYC mayors—LaGuardia from 1934–45, Koch from 1977–89. LaGuardia (a.k.a. "Little Flower") would read the Sunday "funnies" to a devoted radio audience. Koch was fond of asking his public, "How'm I doing?" **Also: Steven Biko & Es'kia Mphahele** (South African activist/writer); **Billy Ripken & Cal Ripken, Sr.** (son/father; baseball player/manager).

December 11–18

THE WEEK OF THE TITAN
SAGITTARIUS III

December 11–18

THE WEEK OF THE TITAN
SAGITTARIUS III

Sailing Off into the Great Beyond

Because of a shared tendency to think big, these two are likely to overlook some important details that may be staring them right in the face. Often so intent on the forest that they miss the trees, they allow idealistic visions to get in the way of their performance of necessary daily tasks. Thus the partners here may be dependent on others to clean up after them, and since such services rarely come for free, a good bookkeeper, accountant, domestic helper and yard worker, for a start, may be necessary. Partners who don't see what they don't want to see may ignore all kinds of warning signals until it is too late. They could perhaps rely on a partner of a different combination to serve this function, one who would also encourage them to kick off their high-energy projects. But alas, the relationship between two Sagittarius III's does not grant these and other benefits.

Love affairs, marriages and friendships are highly optimistic here, at times too much so. The partners' inability to see that their relationship doesn't warrant such confidence can guarantee bewilderment and despair for both if things fall apart. As siblings, Sagittarius III's may be dependent on parents who will take care of practical matters, allowing them to go sailing off into the great beyond.

Work relationships between Sagittarius III's are perhaps the most successful of all. When engaged in mammoth projects together, whether of a professional, social or familial nature, the partners will usually see them through to the bitter end—not because they are exceptionally responsible or even persevering, but because there is usually no other choice. Furthermore, projects that seem overly ambitious to some may be viewed as quite manageable by Sagittarius III's, and therefore easily accomplished. In career matters, the biggest problem for these two is that they sometimes don't know how to restrict their highly speculative enterprises. The belief that growth is inevitable, and unlimited, can create an extremely risky outlook, and in business it can prove fatal.

ADVICE: *Even you have limitations—recognize them. Deal with what is in front of you. Try to focus on the details once in a while.*

December 19–25

THE CUSP OF PROPHECY
SAGITTARIUS-CAPRICORN CUSP

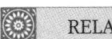

STRENGTHS: **FASCINATING, TENACIOUS, UNDERSTANDING**
WEAKNESSES: **PROVOCATIVE, CHAOTIC, CONFRONTATIONAL**
BEST: **LOVE**
WORST: **PARENT-CHILD**

Thriving on Struggle

This relationship certainly has its stormy side. The magnetism between these two is compelling—they fascinate one another, and in retrospect it may seem that their meeting and subsequent interactions were meant to be. Although high seriousness is often characteristic of both Sagittarius III's and Sagittarius-Capricorns, their relationship is a strange blend of clearly articulated thought and raw feeling. These two are unquestionably on the same wavelength, and whether or not they like each other, they usually have a deep understanding of each other's needs.

Whether positive or negative, love affairs and marriages are extremely close, with the partners well aware of where they stand with each other. Erotic desire is very much in evidence here, yet it does not necessarily emerge as the most important aspect of such relationships, particularly as they progress. Both partners are ultimately more concerned with establishing emotional bonds, and with keeping the romantic flame burning bright. Unfortunately, the turbulent nature of the feelings involved here can run counter to the development of empathy.

Sagittarius III's and Sagittarius-Capricorns are as likely to be enemies as friends. When they find themselves in opposition to each other, their struggles can be epic—incapable of being resolved by a single confrontation, these battles often continue throughout their lives. As friends, these two are extremely interested in one another's activities, and may attempt projects together of an artistic, social or political nature. Parent-child relationships are usually unfavorable; here these personalities will tend to trigger each other's emotions. Too often, Sagittarius-Capricorn silence and Sagittarius III anger conspire to undercut any real chance of communication. Colleagues and co-workers in this combination can make a powerful and effective working team, which thrives on opposition and struggle and often succeeds through sheer tenacity.

ADVICE: *Try to keep feelings under control. Work to develop empathy—keep lines of communication open. Don't be distracted in your search for values.*

FRANK SINATRA (12/12/15)
AVA GARDNER (12/24/22)

Sinatra and Gardner met in the late 40s, following her divorce from musician Artie Shaw. They had a much publicized stormy courtship before tying the knot in '51. However, their marriage wasn't much better. They separated in '54 and divorced in '57. It was the 2nd marriage for each. *Also:* **Tom Hayden & Jane Fonda** (married; politician/actress).

December 26–January 2

THE WEEK OF THE RULER
CAPRICORN I

STRENGTHS: **INTEGRATED, NATURAL, SUCCESSFUL**
WEAKNESSES: **DARK-SIDED, DESTRUCTIVE, VIOLENT**
BEST: **MARRIAGE**
WORST: **LOVE**

Encompassing a World

These two are poles apart, which means they can encompass a whole world between them. Sagittarius III's are by nature optimistic and effusive, Capricorn I's more realistic and selective. Though a potentially volatile mix, these two more often form a powerful union, with the qualities of one synergistically intensified by those of the other; whether they are rivals or serve on the same team, they complement each other perfectly. So natural and efficacious is this bond that the partners often fulfill more than one role in each other's lives, and reason correctly that success in one area could indicate a similar superiority in another. One disturbing element of this matchup is that the partners often activate each other's dark side, and must be sure to keep destructive tendencies from getting out of hand.

Friendships and marriages between Sagittarius III's and Capricorn I's may develop into career associations, and vice versa. Couples with as close emotional ties as these two have can be remarkably successful in business or sports, or in scientific or artistic pursuits. But financial disagreements, arising from the tension between Sagittarius III liberal spending and Capricorn I thriftiness, may be unavoidable. A friendly rivalry between the partners stimulates them both to higher levels of performance—a positive form of competitiveness on which their relationship seems to thrive. They are exceptionally willing to learn from each other; in certain areas, each may prove the other's best teacher. Love affairs can be perilous, however; darker desires may be aroused here that can lead just as easily to instability and violence as to sexual gratification.

In the family, Sagittarius III and Capricorn I relatives may be fated to battle it out, since each may come to represent a contrasting point of view within the group. Unfortunately, fixed familial roles and behavioral patterns may prevent these two from interacting personally and thus having a chance to work out their differences.

ADVICE: *Learn from your differences—don't compromise them away. Keep an eye on your dark side. Reach financial agreement. Avoid labels.*

DICK VAN DYKE (12/13/25)
MARY TYLER MOORE (12/29/37)

Van Dyke and Moore co-starred in the popular tv sitcom *The Dick Van Dyke Show* (1961–66). They had Emmy-winning chemistry as a typical American suburban couple. **Also: Tycho Brahe & Johannes Kepler** (astronomer-mathematicians); **Doc Blanchard & Glenn Davis** (football running-mates); **Abbe Lane & Xavier Cugat** (married; singer/bandleader); **Robert Koch & Louis Pasteur** (rival scientists).

December 11–18

THE WEEK OF THE TITAN
SAGITTARIUS III

January 3–9

THE WEEK OF DETERMINATION
CAPRICORN II

WILLIAM SAFIRE (12/17/29)
RICHARD NIXON (1/9/13)

Columnist Safire volunteered his services for Nixon's presidential campaign in 1968. Following Nixon's victory, Safire became the president's speechwriter and special assistant. They maintained their friendship through Nixon's post-presidential years. Safire writes political commentary and a popular *NY Times* column, "On Language."

Knowing What Is Best

As power oriented as this relationship seems, sympathy and understanding are woven into its fabric, and its focus is the strong emotional bond that exists between its partners. Sagittarius III's understand well the Capricorn II need for achievement and power. One could say, "It takes one to know one," for Sagittarius III's are no slouches themselves when it comes to ambition. A collision may be inevitable in this relationship, unless one or the other partner gives way. There are two possibilities here: first, the partners may not be headed for the same goal, or even interested in competing for it; second, one partner may be subordinated to the other, at least for the time being, as a helpmate or assistant. Generally speaking, outright combat, or even fierce competition, is uncharacteristic of this relationship, since the partners usually have enough good sense to know it is not in their common interest.

Because of their mutual understanding, Sagittarius III–Capricorn II pairs—whether mates, friends or co-workers—may be invaluable to each other as advisors. Being able both to comprehend one another's thoughts and to empathize with one another's personal feelings is a rare combination, and something this pair would not care to live without. Sagittarius III's can often tell what's best for Capricorn II's before Capricorn II's do themselves, and vice versa. In some ways, though, this makes the relationship weakening as well as strengthening, since neither partner here may want to make a move without knowing the other's opinion of it—and, ideally, getting his or her assent.

These two can impress other people as real tough cookies, but in their love affairs with each other they are surprisingly vulnerable. Allowing each other to see sides of themselves that they rarely show anyone else indicates tremendous trust, as well as a belief in the relationship's permanence. Parent-child relationships of either combination can also exhibit loving and trusting attitudes.

ADVICE: *Don't be so concerned with pleasing each other. Be honest about what you want, even if you risk rejection. Asking advice isn't always best.*

December 11–18

THE WEEK OF THE TITAN
SAGITTARIUS III

January 10–16

THE WEEK OF DOMINANCE
CAPRICORN III

CHRISTINA ONASSIS (12/11/50)
ARISTOTLE ONASSIS (1/15/06)

Christina was the daughter of shipping magnate Ari, who gained the world's attention when he married Jackie Kennedy (1968). Christina was, reputedly, not fond of Jackie. After Ari died in '75, Christina inherited all of his business interests. When she died in 1988 of an apparent heart attack, her daughter Athena became sole heir.

***Also:* Frank Sinatra & Frank Sinatra, Jr.** (father/son; singers).

A Battle for Supremacy

A battle for supremacy may be unavoidable in this relationship. Since Capricorn III's can be content with what they have, however, and are very service oriented, conflicts can be avoided if Sagittarius III's are smart enough not to question their partner's need to dominate in certain important areas. As a matter of fact, as long as this need is recognized, Capricorn III's might be quite content to let Sagittarius III's take the lead. Still, two personalities as big as these have to expect to bump into each other every once in a while. For a successful relationship in this combination, the focus should be on how the power structure between them can be set up in the most efficient and agreeable way, for neither partner should be overly interested in provoking arguments and fights.

Love affairs and friendships, sad to say, may be more taken up with power than with love or affection. Urges to dominate can be very difficult to keep under control, and struggles will sometimes rage out of hand. Both partners will have to relax occasionally, and to realize that, in love and friendship, a crushing victory may actually signal defeat.

As marriage partners and family members, Sagittarius III's and Capricorn III's tend to be extremely bossy around their children and other relatives. Rarely able to sit on the sidelines, these two often need to dominate a large family group, and will seek to control both its finances and its outlook. The arousal of resentment and resistance may be expected, along with endless conflict, unless the pair is more sensitive to the wishes of others.

In career matters, the Sagittarius III–Capricorn III pair is highly dominant, and usually has to rule the heap. They function best as business partners at the head of their own company, or as executives with real decision-making power. Should they be cast as lower-level co-workers in a large organization, they will invariably show frustration and dissatisfaction if unable to rise on their merits.

ADVICE: *Take a break. Listen to others. Lessen your need to control—delegate responsibility. Love is perhaps the greatest power of all.*

December 11–18

THE WEEK OF THE TITAN
SAGITTARIUS III

January 17–22

THE CUSP OF MYSTERY & IMAGINATION
CAPRICORN-AQUARIUS CUSP

RELATIONSHIPS

STRENGTHS: **OUTRAGEOUS, EXPRESSIVE, FLAMBOYANT**

WEAKNESSES: **FEARFUL, OBSEQUIOUS, GUILTY**

BEST: **WORK**

WORST: **LOVE**

A Round Peg in a Square Hole

The dynamics of this relationship work best, perhaps, when the partners accept their own idiosyncrasies and put them to work for them, without excuses or holding back. Many of their problems will clear up once they stop trying to act conventionally or to be accepted by those whose respect they crave—after all, once these two begin helping each other, they have quite a bit going for them careerwise. Lively and imaginative Capricorn-Aquarians are good at helping serious Sagittarius III's relax after work. Capricorn-Aquarians, for their part, are not always able to realize their fantastic schemes, and here Sagittarius III's can be of great help. Nonetheless, the road is not an easy one for these two interpersonally; although they can be a joy to each other in many respects, they can also get on each other's nerves—with dire results. Capricorn-Aquarians tend to vent their anger in a single, explosive reaction followed by a series of smaller aftershocks, whereas Sagittarius III anger simmers away, and inevitably turns to depression if not released.

In love affairs and marriages, this pair can be torn between a desire for a quiet and conventional life and a real need to be outrageous and flamboyant. Such conflicts between wants and needs make the relationship look like a round peg being forced into a square hole. Generally at the root of the problem are certain childhood scripts or parental expectations that continue to hold one or both partners in a viselike grip. Learning to be firm and bidding a fond farewell to parental guilt trips will be difficult, but is necessary if self-development is to continue.

Friendships and sibling relationships in this combination, particularly of the same sex, revel in upsetting adults. Playing pranks is more the pair's style than outright rebellion. Mischievous to the extreme, they are never happier than when they are pushing someone's buttons. The onset of maturity is often clearly marked by the cessation of such activities.

ADVICE: *Put your flamboyance to work—your lack of convention can help you succeed financially. Don't be guilty about your childhood shenanigans.*

MARC CONNELLY (12/13/1890)
ALEXANDER WOOLLCOTT (1/19/1887)

Writers Connelly and Woollcott were colleagues and drinking buddies at NY's Algonquin Hotel during the 20s and 30s. They shared in the literary repartee that characterized the famed Round Table clique of sophisticated editors and writers of the time. There they also bantered with George S. Kaufman, with whom each collaborated on separate Broadway plays.

December 11–18

THE WEEK OF THE TITAN
SAGITTARIUS III

January 23–30

THE WEEK OF GENIUS
AQUARIUS I

RELATIONSHIPS

STRENGTHS: **TALENTED, EXCITING, DETERMINED**

WEAKNESSES: **INSECURE, UNDERMINING, SUPERFICIAL**

BEST: **MARRIAGE**

WORST: **FRIENDSHIP**

Unbeatable on Paper

Careerwise this can be a match made in heaven. If the partners are able to integrate their energies, the sky is the limit; yet insecurity often undermines their determination. The combination looks unbeatable on paper, or if one simply examines their combined raw talent. Somewhere, however, there is a nagging voice that persistently raises doubts, lowers self-esteem and threatens to sabotage the whole enterprise. Furthermore, the kind of creativity this duo exudes is likely to arouse envy and insecurity in other people. So, in the end, only a rock-hard determination to succeed, accompanied by the ruthless extirpation of negative programming, will move these two forward in their work. If this kind of resolve is lacking, they are likely to languish in a less than optimal setting, despite all their ability.

Relationships between Sagittarius III's and Aquarius I's are quite exciting, but unless there is a firm commitment to building a deeper emotional bond, the matchup is likely to remain superficial, albeit enjoyable. When in need of the kind of help that demands sacrifice over a period of time, the partner in distress is, alas, all too likely to be left alone. Love affairs may be highly passionate initially, but can quickly fizzle. They are attractions that rarely involve a realistic possibility of marriage. Yet sheer guts and determination may result in the kind of success no one would have predicted for the relationship, and in the development of connections and new areas of interest previously unimagined by these two as individuals.

Parent-child relationships of either possible variation may see a concerted effort on the part of the parent to make the best of, or to exploit, the child's talents. Sagittarius III or Aquarius I hindsight may later indicate that such energy would have been better spent gently encouraging the attainment of more realistic goals.

ADVICE: *Dig in your heels. Don't depend on your talent or take success for granted—hard work is needed. Sheer guts can win the day.*

HELEN FRANKENTHALER (12/12/28)
ROBERT MOTHERWELL (1/24/15)

Frankenthaler and Motherwell are American Abstract Expressionists who, although once married (1958), belonged to different generations of painters. They lived/worked in NYC.

Also: **Christopher Plummer & Tammy Grimes** (married; actors); **Art Neville & Aaron Neville** (Neville Brothers; singers); **Beethoven & Mozart** pupil/teacher); **Helen Menken & Humphrey Bogart** (married; actress-producer/actor).

LUDWIG VAN BEETHOVEN (12/16/1770)
JOHANN ALBRECHTSBERGER (2/3/1736)

In 1794 in Vienna, Beethoven studied with Albrechtsberger, the chapel master at St. Stephen's Church. Albrechtsberger was a master of counterpoint and of the organ; he taught Beethoven a fusion of strict contrapuntal form with the gallant style characteristic of the period.

December 11–18

THE WEEK OF THE TITAN
SAGITTARIUS III

January 31–February 7

THE WEEK OF YOUTH & EASE
AQUARIUS II

Avoiding Trouble?

Management seems to be the hallmark of this relationship, and the primary tool the partners use in dealing with each other. It is actually a rather effective tool, since management implies both understanding and good will here, rather than manipulation. Sagittarius III's, for all their strength, may be helpless before the charm of Aquarius II's, who tend to sense their inner lack of self-confidence. In return they can provide stability to their restless partners, as well as build a firm professional and financial foundation for the relationship. Aquarius II's, for their part, will rarely oppose their powerful partners directly, and their persuasiveness can act as a subtle but effective guide. Although they claim to like it nice and easy, avoiding trouble like the plague, it is often to difficult personalities (like Sagittarius III's) that they end up being drawn.

Love affairs can work out all right, but are complex. Sagittarius III's and Aquarius II's will find self-examination an extremely painful process, but unless they attempt it, their relationship is unlikely to develop fully. These two can have great times together, at least until Sagittarius III seriousness or depression looms. The passion of Aquarius II's for their dark-sided partner may cool, and at this point they may want out of the relationship. Marriages between Sagittarius III's and Aquarius II's are not recommended unless both partners are committed to developing deeper ties of understanding and trust.

In the family, Aquarius II children may adore their Sagittarius III parents, but are often dominated by them, reinforcing these children's tendency to relax and let themselves be taken care of. Friendships are best when devoted to the pursuit of pleasure and entertainment; they will rarely go very deep, nor is there any particular need for them to do so. Career partnerships in this combination can be extremely persuasive and influential within their working sphere. Conflicts often arise, however, between more hardworking Sagittarius III's and easygoing Aquarius II's, and resentments can build.

ADVICE: *Develop self-understanding. Stick together through thick and thin. Letting yourself be spoiled weakens willpower and character.*

MARY TODD (12/13/1818)
ABRAHAM LINCOLN (2/12/1809)

Todd and Lincoln met in 1838 and had a bumpy courtship. They were engaged c. 1840 and broke it off in 1841 because she thought he loved another. Finally, they married in 1842. He was assassinated in 1865; she died in 1882, still wearing his ring. **Also: Steven Spielberg & John Williams** (director/composer of film scores); **Frank Sinatra & Mia Farrow** (married; singer/actor).

December 11–18

THE WEEK OF THE TITAN
SAGITTARIUS III

February 8–15

THE WEEK OF ACCEPTANCE
AQUARIUS III

Calling the Shots

The focus of this relationship may be well hidden behind the scenes, but it usually involves a struggle for power. The Sagittarius III–Aquarius III pair tries to show a happy and positive face to the world, but it is difficult for them to cover up their differences of opinion. Strong-minded, both partners know what they think and what they want, but too often the relationship demands the subservience of one to the other. No matter which partner is calling the shots, the other will feel resentment and anger at being dominated, and will sooner or later lash out. These partners would do better to work consciously and steadily on making their matchup more equal, taking the power from either individual and putting it in the hands of the relationship, where it really belongs.

Love affairs are best when they are more playful than serious in nature. Marriages between these two may strike the world as master-slave in type, which is usually not far from the truth. The partners' temperaments are such that they very naturally fit into these roles, with Sagittarius III's dominating and Aquarius III's accepting it. Such relationships, although seemingly undesirable, can last if at least a small percentage of the partners' needs are being met.

Family members in this combination often feel appreciated by each other, but in the long run they may be unable to share because of what they view as their partner's selfishness. Friendships between these two often see Sagittarius III's governing emotionally and Aquarius III's intellectually. Such relationships can work out well if the partners learn from each other and work to achieve balance.

In career matters, Sagittarius III's and Aquarius III's usually have few illusions about each other. Able to work effectively in the short term, they may nonetheless experience a break over differences of opinion concerning how their work should be done.

ADVICE: *Put power where it belongs. Foster dignity and respect. Even things out— neither partner should benefit at the other's expense. Wrongs don't go away.*

December 11–18

THE WEEK OF THE TITAN
SAGITTARIUS III

February 16–22

THE CUSP OF SENSITIVITY
AQUARIUS-PISCES CUSP

RELATIONSHIPS

STRENGTHS: **PATIENT,
CHANGING, ACCEPTING**

WEAKNESSES: **LONG-SUFFERING,
OVERINFLUENTIAL, INCONSTANT**

BEST: **BUSINESS PARTNERSHIP**

WORST: **SIBLING**

This Too Shall Pass

This relationship has the wisdom to recognize the transitory nature of all things. That viewpoint pervades all of their interactions, not only with each other but with others as well. The Aquarius-Pisces sensitivity to the daily fluctuations of life dovetails with the Sagittarius III ability to see the big picture, so that the relationship shows an awareness of constant change within the context of the overall scheme of things. Two immediate characteristics emerge: first, the ability to be aware of small changes but not to overreact to them or take them too seriously; and second, the patience and wisdom to wait to examine major trends before making decisions. These two can be highly effective as a business, social or political combination, or as friends, family members or a married couple who know how to invest their money wisely.

The longevity of friendships, love affairs and marriages between these two is enhanced by their philosophical outlook. The partners rarely choose to separate or break up unless every avenue of compromise and reconciliation has been explored, over a period of years. The disadvantage of all this is that the partners also tend to suffer silently, harboring the secret hope that things will work out and that their troubles, like everything else, will pass.

In parent-child relationships in this combination, Aquarius-Pisces may be unduly influenced by their Sagittarius III parent, particularly one of the opposite sex. Such attachments will have to be worked through in adolescence and early adulthood. Ups and downs between sibling pairs, where favorable periods alternate with horrible ones, can drive the family to distraction.

In business, the partners will usually create a product or service for which there is a demand but not a lot of competition, discovering a so-called "hole in the market." This pair is good not only at initiating ventures but at maintaining them, particularly in the area of reinvesting their profits.

ADVICE: *Tend to what needs fixing—don't leave it all up to fate. Make decisions and act on them decisively.*

STEVEN SPIELBERG (12/18/46)
DAVID GEFFEN (2/21/43)

In 1994 producer-director Spielberg and producer Geffen joined with entertainment executive Jeffrey Katzenberg to form DreamWorks SKG—the first completely new movie studio in 50 years. It is designed to generate creative, hi-tech movies of the 90s and beyond. *Also:* **Erasmus Darwin & Sir Francis Galton** (grandfather/grandson; doctor-poet/scientist).

December 11–18

THE WEEK OF THE TITAN
SAGITTARIUS III

February 23–March 2

THE WEEK OF SPIRIT
PISCES I

RELATIONSHIPS

STRENGTHS: **INSPIRATIONAL,
IDEALISTIC, SERVICE-ORIENTED**

WEAKNESSES: **STRESSED,
OVEROPTIMISTIC, MISLED**

BEST: **FAMILY**

WORST: **MARRIAGE**

Pragmatic Idealism

Good feelings and mutual admiration are at the center of this relationship, yet this should not imply that Sagittarius III's and Pisces I's have a relaxed time of it. This inspirational matchup can generate tremendous energy, which, if properly directed, can improve the lives of all those around it. This couple is often on the cutting edge of whatever is going on, and in many ways points the way toward the future. Let's call them pragmatic idealists: highly imaginative, they are interested in the kind of change that makes a difference in people's lives, and are not willing merely to wait for it to happen, either.

Love affairs here can be passionate and absorbing. Pisces I's have a lot to teach their partners, not only about sensuality but about spirituality, too, and Sagittarius III's can be apt pupils in this respect. In marriage, these two can make loyal and devoted spouses, although Pisces I nervousness can be a bit of a problem. Sagittarius III energy may not always have a calming effect, and Pisces I's often feel pushed beyond their limit.

As friends and family members, Sagittarius III's and Pisces I's find fulfillment in giving their energy to a cause, whether social, political or artistic. Their desire to serve is strong, so that they can make a valuable contribution to any group of which they are a part. Their optimism is not always rewarded, however, and they must be careful not to be taken advantage of by other people who are more selfish than they are. The best scenario for co-workers is to be able to make a living by working to further their ideals—not an easy situation to find. Compromises may have to be made, perhaps by working for a school, governmental department or community organization that may not be exactly in tune with their ideas but that provides the opportunity to get some constructive work done.

ADVICE: *Respect the ideals of others, and learn to compromise. Temper your optimism. Relaxation is important. Only give so much away.*

ALEXANDER SOLZHENITSYN (12/11/18)
MIKHAIL GORBACHEV (3/2/31)

Writer Solzhenitsyn was exiled from the Soviet Union in 1974 and his dissident writings banned. When Gorbachev came to power in '85, old-style controls over Soviet literature were abandoned through the new policy of *glasnost* (freedom of expression). As a result, censorship was abolished and the banned works of Solzhenitsyn were finally published in Russia.

STRENGTHS: DEDICATED, COMMITTED, INTERESTING

WEAKNESSES: MISTRUSTFUL, ENERVATING, UNCOMPROMISING

BEST: FRIENDSHIP

WORST: LOVE

MICHAEL OVITZ (12/14/46)
MICHAEL EISNER (3/7/42)

Ovitz was the founder of Creative Artists Agency and one of Hollywood's most powerful talent executives. In 1994 Disney head Eisner hired Ovitz, promising a partnership. Ovitz, unable to find a satisfactory role with Disney, left with a $90-million consolation prize. *Also:* **Chu Teh & Chou En-lai** (Chinese Red Army military leaders); **Catherine of Aragon & King Ferdinand** (daughter/father).

December 11–18

THE WEEK OF THE TITAN
SAGITTARIUS III

March 3–10

THE WEEK OF THE LONER
PISCES II

Moral Fervor

The moral fervor of this matchup is pronounced, and often becomes the basis for a deep interpersonal relationship. Sagittarius III's and Pisces II's may well find themselves on the same side of a cause, fighting for what they believe is right. They might meet at school, or at a demonstration or rally, and after several interesting discussions find that they want to get to know each other better. If brought together through a commonly held ideology or belief, or through a course of study, this philosophy or activity often continues at least through the early months and years of their relationship, and will remain a cohesive force. But it may in the end be replaced by the relationship itself, which then becomes the chief inspiration for this dedicated couple.

Love affairs and marriages of this type often demand most of their partners' energies. Although Pisces II's may find this situation satisfactory, Sagittarius III's are resistant to giving up their other interests, and may feel resentful at being forced to do so. Yet they have a great deal to learn from Pisces II's about depth of human feeling and meaningful action—assuming they are prepared to learn. And if Pisces II's are not really convinced of their partners' commitment, they may pull back. As family members, Sagittarius III's are generally much more demanding of attention than Pisces II's, who may feel neglected or cut out. Having common responsibilities will often help these two get on a more equal footing. Working relationships between them are possible if both of them believe in what they are doing, and here Sagittarius III's are more willing to blunt their ego drives in service of a common cause. Should Sagittarius III and Pisces II friends decide to put their relationship first, they could form a strong and lasting bond. If, however, their separate interests, or a lack of trust, keep them apart, they may be better off dropping the relationship altogether. Like other relationships between these two, such friendships seem to be of an all-or-nothing type.

ADVICE: *Be less rigid in your beliefs—cultivate flexibility and openness, and learn to accept other people as they are. Pursue practical, everyday activities.*

STRENGTHS: INTELLIGENT, LOGICAL, TECHNICAL

WEAKNESSES: ARGUMENTATIVE, INCOMPREHENSIBLE, INHUMAN

BEST: FRIENDSHIP

WORST: LOVE

HARRY JAMES (3/15/16)
BETTY GRABLE (12/18/16)

Wholesome actress Grable's claim to fame was her shapely "million-dollar legs." Her WWII image helped originate the term "pin-up." Trumpeter James had a highly successful big band in the 30s and 40s, selling records by the millions. The couple was married from 1943–65, one of Hollywood's better-known and more durable partnerships. *Also:* **Max Born & Albert Einstein** (friends; physicists).

December 11–18

THE WEEK OF THE TITAN
SAGITTARIUS III

March 11–18

THE WEEK OF DANCERS & DREAMERS
PISCES III

Brain-Buster

If either of these partners has even a bit of intellectual curiosity, this relationship is likely to bring it out, and if both partners are intelligent or idea-oriented to begin with, their matchup can be a real brain-buster. From cards, chess and word games to computers and technical or scientific research, these two are interested in sharpening their wits on each other. Although Sagittarius is a fire sign and Pisces water, the Sagittarius III–Pisces III relationship is ruled by air, here indicating the power of reason.

An obvious drawback of love affairs here is that they may neglect the physical and emotional side in favor of mind games and clever sorts of manipulation. Since Sagittarius III and Pisces III form a square aspect in the zodiac (where they lie 90° apart), astrology suggests stress and strife here—a prediction that is born out by a frequent tendency to argue. Such confrontations may actually be not about feelings at all but, rather, a kind of one-upmanship in which each partner strives to assert his or her mental superiority. Marriages between these two can go on for years, with the partners arguing all the way—they may even be held together by such battles.

Friendships and work relationships in this combination often overlap. Most likely of a technical nature, the work they produce may be important and engrossing, but also incomprehensible to all save a few who understand the complex jargon that is the relationship's specialty. The partners will have to come down from their ivory tower occasionally and speak ordinary language—if they don't, they face the possibility of arousing resentment or charges of elitism. It may be necessary for them to be their own public-relations team, getting to know others in a simple and straightforward way before proceeding further. In the family, cousins and siblings in this combination may have great fun in their youth playing board and video games and working out all sorts of puzzles.

ADVICE: *Take the time to explain yourself, using ordinary language. Don't neglect the human aspects of life. Not everything has to be so complex—simplify.*

RELATIONSHIPS

STRENGTHS: **INTIMATE, SYMPATHETIC, REWARDING**
WEAKNESSES: **RESTRICTIVE, INHIBITING, ANXIOUS**
BEST: **FRIENDSHIP**
WORST: **LOVE**

All-Consuming

This relationship may be too heavy even for these profound individuals to bear. To give themselves a rest from their own seriousness, Sagittarius-Capricorns usually seek out those who have lighter and more upbeat personalities; when they are with other people, they like to have fun. Unfortunately, two quiet Sagittarius-Capricorns getting together may simply reinforce each other's moods. If they are already in the depths of a depression, they may become immobilized by hopelessness.

Love affairs between Sagittarius-Capricorns could be intense physically, but somehow such matchups seldom arise, probably because these two are wary of this sort of deep involvement, intuiting that it might be all-consuming and ultimately painful. Children with Sagittarius-Capricorn pairs as parents may have a very difficult time communicating with them, and might long for relief from an oppressive domestic atmosphere. Siblings or cousins, on the other hand, sometimes form a strong bond, and support each other emotionally through all kinds of difficulties and crises. Here the partners share a deep kind of understanding that does not require a lot of conversation to sustain or develop it further. Two Sagittarius-Capricorns can make excellent friends. Psychic abilities are often brought out in such relationships, with each partner having some ability to read the other's mind. Although these friends rarely have an overt or professional interest in predicting the future, they can be remarkably good at it, and may even be consulted informally by family and friends. The relationship can be a refuge for both of them against a world that too often cannot accept them. However, their tendencies toward self-pity and the depression that accompanies it must be mercilessly rooted out, through sheer willpower, and prevented from taking over. If these two are thrown together in a professional capacity, two Sagittarius-Capricorns can make a powerful team, particularly in implementing the company philosophy. Any resentment and dissatisfaction they feel they often suppress, however, which can facilitate getting the job done but does not lead to a healthy psychological framework.

ADVICE: *Maintain some distance. Don't give in to oppressive moods—lighten up. Beware of repressing your true feelings. Build solid self-esteem.*

MAURICE GIBB (12/22/49)
ROBIN GIBB (12/22/49)

Maurice and Robin (along with Barry) are the twin brothers who formed the Bee Gees (1958). They gradually grew in popularity over the years until gaining world prominence in 1977 when they made the soundtrack for the film *Saturday Night Fever,* selling over 30 million albums. Bee Gees recordings continue to sell through the 90s.
Also: Sissy Spacek & Jack Fisk (married; actress/movie art director).

RELATIONSHIPS

STRENGTHS: **RESPECTFUL, EMPATHIC, PRAGMATIC**
WEAKNESSES: **CONFLICTING, COMBATIVE, UNLOVING**
BEST: **CO-WORKERS**
WORST: **PARENT-CHILD**

Strengthening Emotional Ties

At least these two know where each of them stands. Such hardheaded and tough-minded individuals are not always in agreement, but they do respect each other's practical side, and their joint ability to rally their forces in support of their positions. Neither of them usually has much success in trying to control the other, and in fact they rarely try to do so, perhaps knowing in advance that it would be a waste of time. Yet a strange kind of empathy operating between these partners enables them to sense, with great sensitivity and accuracy, the precise nature of each other's emotional state at any moment.

Love affairs between these two are uncommon, but although the romantic spark rarely ignites here, affection is possible to a limited extent. Highly pragmatic and ambitious marriages can manifest, but love is seldom the prime consideration for such connections. Nonetheless, these mates know one another's needs and wishes quite well, and can be highly attuned to each other's feelings.

Parent-child relationships in this combination can be highly, even brutally, combative. Sagittarius-Capricorn children are often extremely rebellious against dictatorial Capricorn I parents, and the worst is to be expected in their confrontations. Sagittarius-Capricorn parents are likely to be more giving and understanding toward their Capricorn I offspring, but also to be both aloof and highly demanding of them as they grow older.

Although boss-employee relationships in this combination seldom work well, co-workers and colleagues are more successful in their interactions. In the long run, however, personal problems may impair the efficiency of such a duo and finally lead them to call it quits. As friends, these two do best when united in a common activity, whether a hobby or semiprofessional interest, often of a highly physical nature, such as sports, fitness, dance or martial arts.

ADVICE: *Use empathic feelings to strengthen emotional ties. Open your heart a bit. Share your concerns and problems. Don't be afraid to be vulnerable.*

BENJAMIN DISRAELI (12/21/1804)
WILLIAM GLADSTONE (12/29/1809)

Disraeli and Gladstone had a long, acrimonious political rivalry in Queen Victoria's government from 1852 till Disraeli's death in 1881. Gladstone challenged most of Disraeli's proposals in the House of Commons. Disraeli was prime minister from 1874–80; Gladstone held the post 4 times between 1868 and 1894. Gladstone was never popular with the queen, while the flattering Disraeli was one of her favorites.

STRENGTHS: **POWERFUL, AMBITIOUS, CONTROLLING**

WEAKNESSES: **INSENSITIVE, RUTHLESS, MANIPULATIVE**

BEST: **MARRIAGE**

WORST: **FRIENDSHIP**

HOWARD HUGHES (12/24/05)
TERRY MOORE (1/7/29)

In 1983 Moore won a long court battle with the Hughes estate (he died in '76), by which she was declared his legal widow. According to Moore, they had been secretly married on his yacht in '49, and she bore him a stillborn baby girl in '52. They never divorced. *Also:* **Cosima Liszt & Hans von Bulow** (married; composer's daughter/pianist-conductor).

December 19–25
THE CUSP OF PROPHECY
SAGITTARIUS-CAPRICORN CUSP

January 3–9
THE WEEK OF DETERMINATION
CAPRICORN II

Battling for Ascendancy

It may be very difficult for these two to reach a point of compromise. Each arouses the other's ambitious side, so that their relationship is taken up with a lust for power, money or control. Such desires are often purely selfish, but they can be highly effective in helping this pair to achieve goals that are beneficial to them both, and to the groups to which they may belong, particularly familial ones. This relationship is very shrewd, able to judge when opportunities are ripe and when it is wiser to wait. Points of contention between Sagittarius-Capricorns and Capricorn II's may be numerous, but they are usually related to what can be a frightening struggle for power. The relationship is often lopsided to begin with, as a powerful Sagittarius-Capricorn or Capricorn II takes the lead and scoops up his or her less highly advantaged partner from a lower social or economic stratum. Capricorn II's, however, derive great strength from the relationship, and are soon able to challenge their partner for the dominant position. The outcome is difficult to predict, but one thing is sure: in a struggle like this one, no one gives up easily.

Love affairs, alas, may also be largely about power. Favors in intimacy can be awarded or withheld at will, and quite ruthless emotional manipulation may be practiced in order to exercise control. Marriages between Sagittarius-Capricorns and Capricorn II's tend to be highly ambitious and to try to climb as high as possible in their social sphere, accumulating money and power on the way. Such relationships can be enduring, cohesive and purposeful, although lacking in the development of human or spiritual qualities.

Friends in this combination are too often prone to using each other for their own ends. Selfish in the extreme, neither of these individuals is likely to stick around when sacrifice is demanded. Professional matchups between these two may be highly successful, particularly in the financial sphere, marred only occasionally by Sagittarius-Capricorn flakiness and Capricorn II overreaching.

ADVICE: *Develop your human side. Practice kindness and charity. Don't be eaten up by your lust for power. You have a need for spiritual development.*

STRENGTHS: **UNUSUAL, SUCCESSFUL, SINCERE**

WEAKNESSES: **COMPETITIVE, UNAPPRECIATED, TRENDY**

BEST: **LOVE**

WORST: **SIBLING**

FRANK ZAPPA (12/21/40)
CAPTAIN BEEFHEART (1/15/41)

Zappa and Beefheart (Don Van Vliet) first met c. 1954, and Zappa allegedly christened him Captain Beefheart. They had a falling out after working on Beefheart's album *Trout Mask Replica* (1970), when he accused Zappa of marketing him like "a freak." They reunited in '75 and collaborated successfully on Zappa's album *Bongo Fury. Also:* **Anwar Sadat & Gamal Abdel Nasser** (Egyptian presidents).

December 19–25
THE CUSP OF PROPHECY
SAGITTARIUS-CAPRICORN CUSP

January 10–16
THE WEEK OF DOMINANCE
CAPRICORN III

Marketing Unusual Aspects

This combination figures out a way to make its unconventional stance pay off. Whether active in groups favoring alternative cultures and lifestyles or attracting attention from the establishment, these partners may be outrageous but they are certainly not crazy. Clever enough to market their more unusual aspects, they can be highly successful financially—or else they can make just enough to get by. The point here is that both will try not to compromise their standards appreciably. Not only does the relationship convey an uncommon view of things, but its partners are quite able to share their more personal feelings as well. That they can do this speaks well for their depth of involvement, and for their sincerity.

Love affairs between these two can feature sharing at a deep emotional level, allowing a degree of self-expression that benefits both partners. Neither trusts others easily, and both may experience great relief at finally being able to reveal themselves to another person without fear of censure or ridicule. In marriage, partners are often able to find a balance between more conventional and far-out elements of style, color and design in their domestic setting.

Sagittarius-Capricorn–Capricorn III siblings of the same sex will often try to outdo each other in being more cool or modern in clothing styles, speech and action, but such attitudes usually fade after adolescence, in some cases to be replaced by more substantial lifestyle commitments. Friendships and career relationships are often interrelated, and in these areas this pair gives full expression to their flamboyance. Problems can arise if Capricorn III's prove dominating or insensitive, or if Sagittarius-Capricorns feel unappreciated, but for the most part things go well. Differences of opinion can arise about how commercial, or how successful, to become, for Sagittarius-Capricorns may feel that the relationship is forcing them to sacrifice too much of their artistic integrity for financial gain.

ADVICE: *Keep your flame pure, but remember that commercialism isn't necessarily a contradiction. Find a balance. Don't get caught up in trivialities.*

December 19–25

THE CUSP OF PROPHECY
SAGITTARIUS-CAPRICORN CUSP

January 17–22

THE CUSP OF MYSTERY & IMAGINATION
CAPRICORN-AQUARIUS CUSP

STRENGTHS: **IMAGINATIVE,
DETERMINED, FULFILLING**

WEAKNESSES: **VOLATILE,
UNSTABLE, IMPATIENT**

BEST: **WORK**

WORST: **LOVE**

Seeing It Through

This highly determined matchup has the imagination to conceive incredible ideas and the tenacity to see them through. These two are not content with idle speculation; their relationship will have meaning for them only if it can manifest substantial achievement, in the family, social or, perhaps, commercial sphere—although money is rarely the driving force here. As individuals, these two can be very self-centered, but as a pair they are service oriented. They may eventually resent the relationship for taking them away from their own personal pursuits; if they are successful, however, they will realize satisfaction and tremendous fulfillment from knowing that they have been able to help other people.

In love affairs these two may be an unstable combination. Unless they find activities to ground them, their volatile emotions may toss them from pillar to post. Marriages are more effective in providing stability, particularly when the partners are involved in organizing new and exciting activities to be enjoyed with their children—often vacation trips and special celebrations. In the family, relatives in this combination may be a potent force for reorganization. Seeing the needs of family members, coming up with imaginative solutions and making them work is their specialty. Of course, not all their relatives will appreciate either their interest or the methods they use—they must be prepared to encounter resistance. Parent-child combinations, particularly of the opposite sex, are very close, but have difficulty remaining objective about the issues at hand, particularly when the darker emotions of Sagittarius-Capricorns invite Capricorn-Aquarius violence.

As co-workers and friends, these two do well in social activities, but more in those involving organizational, service and production skills rather than human services. The relationship rarely has the patience to remain dispassionate when dealing with other people, and does best when challenged by the implementation of new ideas. Friends of this type can enjoy wonderful times together, but tremendous fights can break out periodically. These quickly blow over, however, preventing resentments and frustrations from building up.

ADVICE: *Try to remain objective—too often your emotions cloud the issue. Be sensitive to the wishes of others, and be aware that your ideas are unwanted.*

FLORENCE GRIFFITH JOYNER (12/21/59)
AL JOYNER (1/19/60)

Florence and Al are married track stars who have both won Olympic gold medals for the US. In '84 (Los Angeles) he won the triple jump. In '88 (Seoul) she won the 100 and 200 meters and 4x100 meters relay. **Also: Kit Carson & John Charles Frémont** (trail guide/explorer).

December 19–25

THE CUSP OF PROPHECY
SAGITTARIUS-CAPRICORN CUSP

January 23–30

THE WEEK OF GENIUS
AQUARIUS I

STRENGTHS: **CONVINCING,
VERSATILE, AFFECTIONATE**

WEAKNESSES: **IRRESPONSIBLE,
IGNORING, INSECURE**

BEST: **LOVE**

WORST: **MARRIAGE**

Speaks for Itself

These two would seem to have little in common. Slower, more profound and volcanic Sagittarius-Capricorn energies contrast markedly with the quick, light and easy approach of Aquarius I's. Yet there is a mutual fascination at work here, one that proves highly persuasive in overcoming the most marked socioeconomic, racial or temperamental differences. Apart, these two may not be known for their psychological stability; their union, however, can be surprisingly secure. Partners are often tremendously appreciative and proud of their counterpart's talents, and can rely on each other in many different areas of life, playing various roles.

Love affairs bring out either highly sensual or more platonic feelings; in either case, affection figures prominently here. Sagittarius-Capricorn and Aquarius I lovers are often also good friends, and, as such, truly have each other's best interests at heart. These feelings would seem to augur well for marriages, but just the thought of tying the knot may arouse insecurities in more free-thinking partners who are threatened by the finality of such a step. Sagittarius-Capricorn–Aquarius I sibling relationships, particularly of the opposite sex, are often extremely close, supportive and understanding. The good feelings engendered by such a relationship can give quiet support to the entire family, but can as easily arouse antagonism from relatives who feel ignored or slighted. In friendships, this combination is mutually rewarding. True, Sagittarius-Capricorns may not always be able to count on their more ephemeral Aquarius I partners, who, however, usually do try to make up for their occasional unreliability with sparkling wit. Sagittarius-Capricorn profundity and Aquarius I brilliance can gel in commercial endeavors in which these two are partners, particularly when they need to persuade others of the value of their service or product. They will rarely need to resort to any kind of underhanded manipulation, since the attitude in this relationship is an open one, proclaiming that what this duo produces speaks for itself. Clients and public are drawn to the clean emotional energy of this relationship.

ADVICE: *Go easy with those more conservative than you. Live up to your end of the bargain. Never be superior or condescending.*

ROGER VADIM (1/26/28)
JANE FONDA (12/21/37)

Actress Fonda and French director Vadim were married in 1965. During the 60s she made several French-American films with Vadim, who tried to mold her into another Brigitte Bardot (his former wife). His efforts culminated in *Barbarella*, a futuristic comic-book erotic film with Fonda as a hot, stripteasing sex goddess.

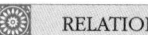
STRENGTHS: **TEMPERING, INSTRUCTIVE, ASSERTIVE**

WEAKNESSES: **ANTAGONIZING, OVERDEPENDENT, DRIVEN**

BEST: **MARRIAGE**

WORST: **FAMILY**

JACKIE ROBINSON (1/31/19)
BRANCH RICKEY (12/20/1881)

While Rickey was managing the Brooklyn Dodgers (1942–50), he broke the color barrier in baseball by signing up Robinson, who became the first black to play in the major leagues. Both were later inducted into the Hall of Fame. *Also:* **Sissy Spacek & Rip Torn** (cousins; actors); **Howard Hughes & Ida Lupino** (affair; producer/actress); **Conrad Hilton & Zsa Zsa Gabor** (married; hotelier/actress).

December 19–25
THE CUSP OF PROPHECY
SAGITTARIUS-CAPRICORN CUSP

January 31–February 7
THE WEEK OF YOUTH & EASE
AQUARIUS II

A Spruced-Up Image

The focus of this relationship is often a process of socialization, in which the dominant side of Sagittarius-Capricorns is tempered by the easy approach of Aquarius II's. Because Aquarius II's are often immediately liked by others, they have a great deal to teach harder-to-know Sagittarius-Capricorns about how to spruce up their image. Furthermore, although Sagittarius-Capricorns usually assume the superior role in this relationship, they are heavily dependent on the very likable and entertaining personas of Aquarius II's to help them take a break from their problems and worries. One might ask what the attraction is for Aquarius II's, but these types often fall in love with deep, serious individuals who are a projection of their own dark side—and Sagittarius-Capricorns fit the bill perfectly.

Love affairs between these two usually begin with the acute need of Sagittarius-Capricorns to assume the power role, but often end up with them eating out of the hand of charming Aquarius II's. In marriage, sex may not be of the greatest importance. More often, the focus here is the working out of a social role for the relationship within a small circle of friends, colleagues and family.

Family relationships between these two can be quite complex, particularly parent-child relationships where a serious Sagittarius-Capricorn parent tries to channel, in a constructive way, the energies of a talented but often wayward Aquarius II child. Friendships in this combination will overcome many obstacles that stand in their way, and may be driven to occupy a dominant position in their immediate environment. Such friends should be careful not to arouse serious enmities and antagonisms that can boomerang on them when they least expect it.

In career matters, these two are often highly dependent on each other. They can make good business partners, with Sagittarius-Capricorns planning, developing and reorganizing while Aquarius II's contact clients and work on public relations and sales.

ADVICE: *Strive for self-awareness—find out more about what is motivating you. Beware of arousing animosities. Understand how others see you.*

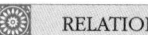
STRENGTHS: **DIVERSE, PSYCHIC, ARTISTIC**

WEAKNESSES: **UNSTABLE, IMPRACTICAL, POLARIZED**

BEST: **LOVE**

WORST: **FRIENDSHIP**

BURT REYNOLDS (2/11/36)
CHRIS EVERT (12/21/54)

Actor Reynolds, known to have had many affairs through the years, was romantically linked to tennis great Evert during the heyday of her career. While he was the #1 ladies' man, she was the #1 tennis player in the world 5 times, winning at least one Grand Slam title every year from 1974–86.

December 19–25
THE CUSP OF PROPHECY
SAGITTARIUS-CAPRICORN CUSP

February 8–15
THE WEEK OF ACCEPTANCE
AQUARIUS III

A Supernatural Connection

Although this relationship has a very close connection as its hallmark, it also shows wide swings of mood and affect. Often polarized, its partners inevitably clash in points of view, since neither is willing to give ground or compromise. Yet the positive aspects of the relationship are also prominent, particularly since Sagittarius-Capricorns and Aquarius III's sometimes share an amazing psychic connection, and are especially tuned in to the unexpected and the supernatural. The backgrounds of nonfamily partners in this combination are often extremely diverse, yet the relationship is able to bridge seemingly impossible gaps of time and space.

Love affairs here may feature acute ethnic, religious or cultural differences. Although the couple may give the impression of not being influenced by such considerations, they may in fact be making a point of them by always emphasizing how unimportant they are. The children of Sagittarius-Capricorn–Aquarius III spouses will ultimately benefit from the cultural diversity afforded them by their parents. Friendships between these two will be up and down in nature, one moment wildly enthusiastic and positive, another pessimistic and hurt or depressed. When the partners consciously work on balancing such moods and not taking them too seriously, real progress can be made.

Family members, particularly siblings and parent-child combinations, often manifest signs of telepathy and clairvoyance, which can be accepted as normal on most occasions but can prove frightening on others. Highly unusual experiences of this kind do not always help the stability of such relationships, but can make such connections special, even unique, within the larger family structure.

Career matchups may well be of an artistic nature or involve some form of communications, either in publishing or other media. The creative imagination of this duo is usually extremely high, but this does not guarantee financial success, since the relationship may not be geared toward the practical.

ADVICE: *Don't get attached to your moods. Avoid extremes of emotion when possible. Put your psychic abilities to work for you.*

December 19–25

THE CUSP OF PROPHECY
SAGITTARIUS-CAPRICORN CUSP

February 16–22

THE CUSP OF SENSITIVITY
AQUARIUS-PISCES CUSP

RELATIONSHIPS

STRENGTHS: **IMAGINATIVE,
COMPASSIONATE, REASSURING**

WEAKNESSES: **FEARFUL,
OVERDEPENDENT, PARANOID**

BEST: **FRIENDSHIP**

WORST: **MARRIAGE**

Things That Go Bump in the Night

This pair seems to attract unusual, occasionally frightening experiences to itself. It is almost as though the energy of these two is synergistically combined into a kind of lightning rod for the bizarre. The power of the imagination is also activated here, sometimes causing an abnormal level of fear or paranoia. Both of these individuals have often suffered some childhood trauma, which makes them attracted to each other. Luckily, the relationship shows deep compassion when it comes to being scared of things that go bump in the night. Dealing with the fantasies of childhood and frightening experiences, real or imagined, can become the focus here. The act of sharing such personal material from the past can create mutual dependencies, which, although reassuring, are not always of the healthiest sort.

On first meeting, Sagittarius-Capricorns and Aquarius-Pisces are not about to reveal themselves, but they do often sense in each other a kindred spirit, a person who has suffered and turned inward. As love affairs and friendships develop, these two may slowly begin to trust each other and to share their amazingly similar experiences. Particularly when violence has figured in the lives of one or both partners, the assurance that they have nothing to fear from each other can be of the greatest comfort. Children of these marriages may never know how much their parents' ability to love them openly, and to afford them protection, means to this couple. The greatest difficulty here can be overprotectiveness, with its accompanying parental fears, which may be absorbed by their children.

Siblings in this combination often inhabit a world of mystery and imagination, in which horror and fantasy films and books may play a central role. These siblings should not be allowed to spend too much time alone, but should be gently encouraged to develop their social side. In the professional sphere, co-worker pairs may succeed in a very low-key manner in getting the job done efficiently, without fuss or bother. Imaginative elements are seldom prominent here, and indeed are ordinarily best left out of business matters.

ADVICE: *Let go of the past. Beware of being overprotective and fearful. Develop a detached approach, but don't be afraid to love.*

ALEKSEI KOSYGIN (2/21/04)
LEONID BREZHNEV (12/19/06)

Brezhnev and Kosygin ruled the Soviet Union in tandem, following Nikita Khrushchev's downfall in 1964. Brezhnev succeeded the ousted leader as first party secretary, and Kosygin took over as premier. Together they dismantled many of their predecessor's reforms and introduced a more consistent and sophisticated foreign policy.

December 19–25

THE CUSP OF PROPHECY
SAGITTARIUS-CAPRICORN CUSP

February 23–March 2

THE WEEK OF SPIRIT
PISCES I

RELATIONSHIPS

STRENGTHS: **CURIOUS,
CREATIVE, PHILOSOPHICAL**

WEAKNESSES: **IMPRACTICAL,
FLIGHTY, SILLY**

BEST: **PARENT-CHILD**

WORST: **FRIENDSHIP**

A Law Unto Themselves

The focus of this relationship, and usually its biggest problem, is finding a point of reference or standard of behavior that both partners can recognize. Often split in their belief systems, this pair may have great difficulty reaching agreement on most major issues. In the personal realm, probably the greatest difference between them is that Pisces I's are in need of attention and approval while Sagittarius-Capricorns do not expect approval and would often prefer to do without it. This makes Sagittarius-Capricorns much the stronger partner in many ways, and they are usually able to win out in personal struggles between these two. This comparison, however, also indicates that Pisces I's operate by socially accepted norms of behavior more easily than do Sagittarius-Capricorns, who tend, through their isolation, to become a law unto themselves. Thus the struggle inherent in this relationship centers on whether it should orient itself toward others (easier for Pisces I's) or more or less isolate itself and seek its own values (easier for Sagittarius-Capricorns).

In love affairs, Sagittarius-Capricorns are not aware of hurting the feelings of their Pisces I partners, or of alienating them with their uncompromising stance. On the other hand they will find it difficult to handle the flightiness of Pisces I's, who have an intense need for variety. These love affairs may be quite passionate, but the partners' unwillingness to make fundamental changes in their personalities does not augur well for marriage.

Friendships in this combination may fail to find a middle ground of agreement, and as a consequence could spend most of their time flitting from one new interest to another. It will be difficult for others to take this relationship seriously if the partners allow it to be associated with impractical, even silly ideas. At work, these two usually lack the drive to compete in the marketplace, and are better off engaging in freelance, creative or educational pursuits. Parent-child relationships of the opposite sex can be extremely close in the early years, but will have to work hard to develop ties in other areas later on.

ADVICE: *Seek common interests and develop them—don't allow yourselves to drift apart. Make decisions and stick to them. Decide what you believe.*

ZERO MOSTEL (2/28/15)
JOSH MOSTEL (12/21/46)

Josh, character actor of stage, screen and tv, is the son of comic performer Zero—whose stage and screen career was shattered in the 50s, when he was blacklisted as a communist by HUAC, despite his denials. But he bounced back in the 60s with one of Broadway's greatest portrayals—Tevye in *Fiddler on the Roof* (1964).

Also: Joseph Stalin & Svetlana Stalin (father/daughter).

December 19–25

THE CUSP OF PROPHECY
SAGITTARIUS-CAPRICORN CUSP

March 3–10

THE WEEK OF THE LONER
PISCES II

Gossip and Chatting

STRENGTHS: **INSIGHTFUL,
CONVERSATIONAL, INTELLIGENT**
WEAKNESSES: **MEDDLING,
CATTY, INEFFECTUAL**
BEST: **FRIENDSHIP**
WORST: **FAMILY**

TONY MARTIN (12/25/13)
CYD CHARISSE (3/8/23)

Martin and Charisse married in 1948 and had a close relationship through the years, often appearing together in nightclub acts. He sang in film musicals, 30s to 50s. She was a dance partner of Fred Astaire and Gene Kelly. In '76 they published their memoirs, *The Two of Us.* **Also: Maurice Gibb & Andy Gibb** (brothers; Bee Gees); **Howard Hughes & Jean Harlow** (romance; industrialist-producer/actress).

This combination likes nothing better than being left alone to engage in its favorite form of entertainment—conversation, from the philosophical to plain old gossip. Both partners have a strongly reclusive side that their relationship enhances, and that may develop into a kind of obsession. Not interested in being seen together in public, these two often prefer to meet in either one's cozy kitchen and enjoy the conviviality of chatting while sitting at a table and drinking coffee or perhaps a glass of wine. These are often successful matchups, for the partners do not demand a lot from each other or use their relationship as a stopgap in times of need, but simply enjoy their regular, if not overly frequent, contact with each other.

Friendships are particularly noteworthy here. The couple's quick perceptions and telling observations may concern their own relationship or those of other people, but it is people that they are mainly interested in studying, in an intelligent and insightful manner. Such sessions are usually private in nature, and if a third person enters the scene, the mood may evaporate, and business may be postponed to a later date. This is not a comfortable pairing for love affairs, since there is a curious lack of passion here, but it can be well suited for companionships that ultimately lead to marriage.

Relatives in this combination make it their business to know exactly what is going on with the rest of the family. These two run the risk of being branded as busybodies, in fact, sticking their noses into everybody's business far too often. In the professional sphere, it will be quite possible for the partners to function side by side as co-workers for years on end. The job, however, is usually secondary to the conversation, so that this is not a particularly dynamic combination.

ADVICE: *Don't be so newsy. Learn to be more open and truly sharing. Your interest is not always appreciated. Beware of excessive isolation.*

December 19–25

THE CUSP OF PROPHECY
SAGITTARIUS-CAPRICORN CUSP

March 11–18

THE WEEK OF DANCERS & DREAMERS
PISCES III

Visualization

STRENGTHS: **CREATIVE,
BALANCED, SUMMONING**
WEAKNESSES: **OVERRELAXED,
UNDERVALUED, SELF-FULFILLING**
BEST: **LOVE**
WORST: **WORK**

MILEVA MARIC (12/19/1875)
ALBERT EINSTEIN (3/14/1879)

In 1903 Einstein married fellow student Maric in Zurich. Their marriage suffered because he felt she interfered with his work. In 1914 he moved to Berlin, leaving Maric (and their 2 sons). By 1916 he decided never to see her again and in 1919 they were divorced. He gave her the proceeds of his 1921 Nobel Prize. **Also: Diane Sawyer & Sam Donaldson** (co-anchors, *Prime Time Live*).

The Sagittarius-Capricorn–Pisces III combination is often able to bring things into being just by thinking about them. They have a balanced strength, which is unlikely to lead to big surprises or disasters. The matchup can be extremely effective in guiding the destiny of a particular group, whether social, familial or professional, simply by forming a clear picture of what is needed and miraculously realizing it. Some would say that little magic is involved here, just a kind of receptivity to pragmatic solutions. Extremely dependable, such a matchup could induce even skeptics to reconsider their denial of paranormal phenomena.

Love affairs and marriages between these two can be highly successful. The emphasis is more on the metaphysical than the physical, but warm and loving feelings also abound. Arguments are rare, but the relationship can be a bit too relaxed at times, lacking real snap and fire. In times of distress or depression, the partners must be careful of the power of their self-fulfilling prophecies, since their negative pronouncements are all too likely to come true.

Friends in this combination can be called on in times of need—their relationship is an unusually supportive one. During better times, they are likely to see each other only occasionally, when they meet to check up on each other's progress and have a pleasurable night out. In the family, relatives in this combination who live together may dominate their space, dictating what others can and cannot do there. These duos are powerfully united, and will be difficult to oppose. In professional matters, it is probably best if Sagittarius-Capricorns and Pisces III's consult with and advise each other rather than work together on a daily basis. And when they are business partners, although their schemes may well come to fruition in one form or another, they rarely carry much financial reward.

ADVICE: *Don't try to control too much territory—leave space for others to make decisions. Deepen emotional bonds and seek greater self-understanding.*

December 26–January 2

THE WEEK OF THE RULER
CAPRICORN I

RELATIONSHIPS

STRENGTHS: **DEPENDABLE, UNDERSTANDING, SENSUOUS**

WEAKNESSES: **DULL, SELFISH, STORMY**

BEST: **MARRIAGE**

WORST: **PARENT-CHILD**

Alternatives to Struggle

Despite their assertions to the contrary, Capricorn I's usually understand each other well—which is to imply not so much empathy between them as a very fundamental comprehension. It is quite possible, then, for them to work out a satisfactory agreement as to which of them will guide the destiny of their relationship, or that of any small group to which it belongs. There is a tendency here to conflict and open power struggles, but there are several ways these can be avoided, of which perhaps the best are sharing power as copartners and compartmentalizing the relationship so that each has his or her own unquestioned areas of dominance. Either of these alternatives can work well, depending on the circumstances and individual preferences. Should two Capricorn I's be unwilling or unable to reach agreement over who will rule, constant strife, argument and, ultimately, separation can be expected.

Capricorn I's are attracted to each other's earthy side, but their love affairs tend to be sensual rather than sexual. Lacking a certain amount of excitement and spark may enhance the longevity, but not the interest, of such matchups. Marriages here can be successful as long as the power issue can be settled satisfactorily. Practical in the extreme, such relationships are rarely divided by differing points of view over money, responsibilities and family structure. As friends, Capricorn I pairs are loyal and dependable. Should they lack shared interests, however, they are unlikely to develop the strong emotional bonds that would hold the relationship together. Capricorn I parent-child relationships can be stormy and punishing, particularly if either partner deviates from the behavior expected from them. As siblings, Capricorn I's of the same sex must each have space of their own, since their abilities to share with each other may be quite limited. But Capricorn I co-worker pairs can work together successfully for years on end, discharging their responsibilities with little fuss. Problems arise only if both have ambitions to rise higher within the company or organization, since they are likely to be quite selfish and ruthless toward each other when in competition.

ADVICE: *Work out agreements carefully. Try to be more flexible and less severe. Work toward greater emotional honesty. Settle power conflicts.*

MIKE NESMITH (12/30/42)
DAVY JONES (12/30/45)

Nesmith and Jones, original members of The Monkees, share the same birthday. The group was a prefabrication for *The Monkees* tv comedy series (1966–68), conceived to take advantage of the Beatlemania of the 60s. Nesmith had worked as a musician before; British-born Jones had been a stage actor and racehorse jockey. **Also: Barry Goldwater & J. Edgar Hoover** (right-wingers; same birthday).

RELATIONSHIPS

STRENGTHS: **TACTFUL, UNUSUAL, PROTECTIVE**

WEAKNESSES: **DISAPPROVING, UNFORGIVING, PUNITIVE**

BEST: **WORK**

WORST: **LOVE**

Masterfully Diplomatic

This relationship tends to look after its own best interests, and will encourage its partners to get along. For all of their power drives, Capricorn I's and II's can be united in dealing with important matters, since they are quick to figure out what might be of mutual advantage to them. Onlookers may be surprised by the forming of a bond between two people whose points of view and general characters seem to be irreconcilable, and their relationship may indeed be a highly unconventional, even bizarre matchup from certain standpoints. Yet these incongruities are not the primary issues on the minds of partners themselves, since they are usually far more interested in dealing with whatever matter is at hand. This practical relationship has little danger of falling into idle speculation.

Marriages are usually stronger here than love affairs, since the Capricorn I–Capricorn II relationship shows a marked tendency toward domesticity. Home may be the uppermost consideration for this couple—making it safe, secure, comfortable and functional as a place both to relax and to work. Children of such a marriage will probably be well looked after, although expected to toe the line. Disapproval and punishment must be kept within bounds, for the relationship can be excessive in both respects.

Friendships and sibling relationships in this combination are often supportive but also highly competitive, particularly in sports, school and love. This pair may compete may for the attention or affection of adults or, more likely, for peers. Should such strife get out of hand, alienation and an inability to forgive can be expected. At work, on the other hand, Capricorn I's and II's are usually able to mute their power struggles when they are members of the same organization, since they usually give the best interests of the group their top priority. Even when working for rival organizations, they can be masterfully diplomatic, seeking to find mutually beneficial solutions and to avoid open conflict.

ADVICE: *Continue to find mutually beneficial solutions, but don't neglect individual needs. Be more forgiving—open your heart a bit wider.*

NANCY LOPEZ (1/6/57)
RAY KNIGHT (12/28/52)

Knight and Lopez are a notable married sports couple. He is a former NY Met ('86 World Series), later manager of the Cincinnati Reds. She is a golf great—4-time Player of the Year, 3-time LPGA champion and a Hall of Famer by age 30. **Also: Mao Zedong & Richard Nixon** (world leaders; reestablished China-US relations); **Glenn Davis & Terry Moore** (married; football star/actress).

STRENGTHS: **DETERMINED, SELF-ASSURED, LOYAL**

WEAKNESSES: **KNOW-IT-ALL, INFLEXIBLE, FRUSTRATING**

BEST: **FRIENDSHIP**

WORST: **WORK**

KIRSTIE ALLEY (1/12/55)
TED DANSON (12/29/47)

Alley and Danson co-starred in the long-running tv sitcom *Cheers* (1982–93) from '87, when she joined the show. Danson played Sam, the womanizing bartender who futilely pursued Alley's character, Rebecca, the hapless bar manager. *Also:* **Xavier Cugat & Charo** (married; bandleader/singer); **Mary Tyler Moore & Grant Tinker** (married; actress/producer).

December 26–January 2
THE WEEK OF THE RULER
CAPRICORN I

January 10–16
THE WEEK OF DOMINANCE
CAPRICORN III

Outright Infallible

Both Capricorn I's and III's can be pretty determined individuals, and their relationship may synergistically harden this quality into a steely firmness. A lack of flexibility and sensitivity, in fact, is among the relationship's weakest points. As partners these two make up their minds immediately on most of the major issues, which, on the positive side, saves them from doubt and hesitation but may also imply that they sometimes rush to judgment. Results both good and bad may accrue from such uncompromising characteristics. The partners can gain advantage, for example, by getting in promptly on the ground floor of a new project, but they may also end up being saddled with involvements that they later regret. Since this matchup can rarely admit that it is wrong, its partners may be forced to suffer in silence, experiencing great frustration when things don't work out as planned.

Characteristically, love affairs and marriages in this combination exhibit periodic dissension and can be highly argumentative in private, but rarely show anything but a strong front publicly or in the partners' attitudes toward other people. These two understand each other very well and are apt to have the same goals. There is little room in their relationship for feelings, however, which can create major problems for a child of theirs who, having failed to find sympathy from one parent, seeks it from the other, only to run into a stone wall of unanimity. In extreme cases, also, the child may be asked to take sides with one parent against the other, with harmful results. Sibling relationships in this combination, particularly those of the opposite sex, tend to fight like cats and dogs, making life trying for other family members. Friendships of this type are generally loyal and enduring, but can suffer from an air of smug assurance or of outright infallibility that others can find difficult to deal with. Capricorn I's and III's are better off not engaging in professional or entrepreneurial pursuits together, since they have difficulty keeping their emotions out of business matters, and tend to trigger each other at the most inopportune moments.

ADVICE: *Learn to admit your mistakes. Drop your omniscient air when dealing with other people. Develop flexibility, and don't be threatened by change.*

STRENGTHS: **CHARMING, CONVINCING, AMUSING**

WEAKNESSES: **MANIPULATIVE, DISHONEST, UNTRUSTWORTHY**

BEST: **FRIENDSHIP**

WORST: **MARRIAGE**

TIGER WOODS (12/30/75)
JACK NICKLAUS (1/21/40)

Nicklaus is generally considered the greatest all-time golfer. He won 17 major championships, setting many world records. The young Woods, already a world-famous golfer, turned pro in '96, then won his first Masters ('97) easily, in what promises to be a brilliant career. Authorities believe it's just a matter of time before he eclipses Nicklaus' many records. *Also:* **Country Joe MacDonald & Janis Joplin** (affair; singers).

December 26–January 2
THE WEEK OF THE RULER
CAPRICORN I

January 17–22
THE CUSP OF MYSTERY & IMAGINATION
CAPRICORN-AQUARIUS CUSP

Wily Seduction

This can be a dramatic and exciting relationship. Confrontational in nature, it fosters an atmosphere in which both Capricorn I's and Capricorn-Aquarians will often attempt to use their wily powers of seduction to get from each other exactly what they're after. In highly manipulative interactions such as these, cleverness, perceptiveness and experience are all part of the relationship's arsenal. In general, Capricorn I's rely on quiet insistence, while Capricorn-Aquarians tend to be more emotionally overwhelming. As a team these two can be extremely persuasive and charming, but since their knowledge is deep, and they usually prepare their arguments thoroughly in advance, they do not need to rely on the force of their personalities alone.

Love affairs of this type are beguiling, enchanting—and filled with illusion. Beneath the romantic facade, some pretty heavy emotional manipulation may be going on, often out of fear that affections will be discontinued or misplaced. Marriage is not recommended, but if it is being seriously considered, both partners should work hard on building honesty and trust, rather than reverting to immature and childish feelings.

Parent-child relationships in this combination are also sometimes involved in the kind of game-playing that can be amusing to an extent but may eventually undermine belief and trust, and that may also cause other family members not to take the pair so seriously as a unit. Peak experiences are often the goal in Capricorn I–Capricorn-Aquarius friendships, whether through physically challenging endeavors or, perhaps, through drug-induced states. Moderating such drives and keeping in touch with reality are the main challenges here.

In the professional sphere, these partners can be very convincing, yet also a tad misleading. Should others get the idea that they are being conned or manipulated, word may get around that this couple cannot be trusted, and they may find that in seeking temporary gain they have cut their own throats.

ADVICE: *Beware of getting what you want—you may be fooling yourself. Examine what's spurring you on. Consider the ethical implications of your actions.*

December 26–January 2

THE WEEK OF THE RULER
CAPRICORN I

January 23–30

THE WEEK OF GENIUS
AQUARIUS I

Beyond Desire

The focus of the Capricorn I–Aquarius I relationship, and its principal goal, is often the kind of control that only unrelenting technical training can achieve. No matter in what area such effort is spent, this relationship sees control—whether of its partners' bodies, an appetite, an environment, an activity or the mind itself—as paramount. Such an uncompromising attitude implies some form of deprivation, and the ability to deny oneself what is most natural to a human being—if chastity were the goal for this couple, for example, they would be able to overcome their sexual urges; if they wanted to impose a special diet, their appetite for certain foods could be denied. On the other hand, the possession of such control can be a form of gratification in and of itself.

If love affairs are geared toward technical proficiency or mastery, their object may be exquisite sorts of sensual pleasure. The danger is that this sort of emphasis may lead the relationship in a very different direction, denying the need for the kindness, affection and sympathy that many lovers crave. Marriages in this combination may show a mania for domestic perfection, dictating that the partners spend most of their time renovating a home and making it beautiful. Carried to an extreme, such desires could lead this couple to fix up and sell several houses in succession, expending significant amounts of energy in bringing each one from a wretched to a glorious state.

Capricorn I–Aquarius I friends and siblings may be taken up with diet, technical projects, exercise and sport, or with artistic endeavors that demand a high degree of control, skill and an eye toward perfection. Unfortunately, human feelings often get lost in the shuffle. Work relationships between these two benefit from Capricorn I pragmatism and Aquarius I quickness and inventiveness of mind. But technical perfection can sometimes be counterproductive in business, for the costs of achieving it may be much higher than it's worth.

ADVICE: *Perhaps you are being a bit puritanical. Beware of enslaving yourself to your ideas. Let your hair down occasionally—relax and have fun.*

GELSEY KIRKLAND (12/29/52)
MIKHAIL BARYSHNIKOV (1/28/48)

Kirkland and Baryshnikov are ballet stars who have been romantically linked. Performing with the NY City Ballet (1968–74) and the American Ballet Theatre (1974–84), she is known for the technical purity of her dancing. Russian-born Baryshnikov, who defected to the US in '74, is considered simply the greatest male classical dancer of his generation. **Also: Steve Allen & Skitch Henderson** (tv host/bandleader).

December 26–January 2

THE WEEK OF THE RULER
CAPRICORN I

January 31–February 7

THE WEEK OF YOUTH & EASE
AQUARIUS II

The Middle Ground

This relationship may be a seesaw affair, oscillating between conforming to the partners' attitudes and trying to find a balance or middle ground between them. Capricorn I's, who are used to struggle, may somewhat resent Aquarius II's, who prefer to be spared the pain of work and are known to ridicule those who view it as their reason for living. These two are apt to expend considerable amounts of energy trying to convince each other of their individual points of view. As their relationship develops, its partners may discover that they can live a life in which they alternate between work and relaxation in quite a pleasant way, and avoid the excesses or either state.

Love affairs here should be viewed not as either frenzied or hyperrelaxed work projects in themselves but as moderate, and highly enjoyable, activities in their own right. Mature Capricorn I and Aquarius II lovers, furthermore, will learn from each other—Capricorn I's to be a bit less serious, Aquarius II's to be a bit more so. Marriages between these two can witness a splendid melding of work and love, supplying a steady flow of energy to both these aspects of the spouses' lives. Capricorn I's have a judgmental streak, however, and Aquarius II's a taste for silliness, and collisions of irritation are likely to occur between these two moods.

Parents and children in this combination, particularly with Capricorn I's in the parental role, will have to learn to take each other seriously without forgetting about having good times together. The best type of friendship between these two is also able to divide its time intelligently between serious and more lighthearted activities. As co-workers, the more successful Capricorn I–Aquarius II combinations will learn not only to relax but to study after work hours are over, even while approaching their jobs in a sensible, nonfanatical way and programming in regular breaks.

ADVICE: *Forget your differences. Achieving a middle ground is possible—there is much you can learn from each other. Avoid extremes and excesses.*

PETER QUAIFE (12/31/43)
DAVE DAVIES (2/3/47)

Quaife and Davies are original members of the British rock group The Kinks (formed 1963). Bassist Quaife endured the antagonism—sometimes onstage—between Davies and older brother Ray, the group's leader. Quaife remained a solid member of the band, while Davies followed solo pursuits, coming out with 2 moderately successful albums in the early 80s.

WILLIAM MASTERS (12/27/15)
VIRGINIA JOHNSON (2/11/25)

Sexologists Masters and Johnson were married from 1976–91. They published pioneering reports on human sexual responses in hetero- and homosexual relationships and trained thousands of sex therapists. *Also:* **Jacob Adler & Stella Adler** (father/daughter; Yiddish actor/acting teacher); **Ted Danson & Mary Steenburgen** (married; actors); **Madame de Pompadour & Louis XV** (influential mistress/king).

December 26–January 2
THE WEEK OF THE RULER
CAPRICORN I

February 8–15
THE WEEK OF ACCEPTANCE
AQUARIUS III

Neither Dull nor Unstable

This relationship derives its greatest satisfaction from putting wonderfully imaginative ideas into practice and recommending them to others, usually after trying them out in private. The trick here is a judicious blend of the theoretical and the pragmatic, for the partners in this relationship usually enjoy both qualities equally. Capricorn I's tend to be more responsible and Aquarius III's more explosive, but this doesn't seem to keep them apart. A really successful relationship here is neither dull nor unstable, since each partner's strong points mitigate the other's weak ones. Less successful or failed relationships between these two find Capricorn I's highly critical of what they perceive as Aquarius III irresponsibility and flakiness, and Aquarius III's growing bored and depressed by Capricorn I heaviness.

Whether or not these two feel a strong physical attraction for each other, they will usually appreciate each other's wisdom, making them as likely to be confidants as lovers. Forced to choose between love and friendship, many couples wisely choose the latter. Marriages between Capricorn I's and Aquarius III's can work out as long as sex does not become an issue. If nonjudgmental and accepting attitudes do not prevail, and physical fulfillment is not viewed as the sole responsibility of either partner, these couples can share warmth and affection, and can prove emotionally supportive.

In the family, relatives in this combination are likely to eye each other with a certain suspicion. The more conservative viewpoints of Capricorn I's often clash with the more radical or outspoken attitudes of Aquarius III's. Friendships in this combination, on the other hand, tend to thrive on their internal differences, providing an endlessly amusing study in contrasts for both the partners and those around them. Taking personal issues less seriously can be a big plus here. As co-workers, these pairs will often experience stress when Capricorn I's resent feeling that they have been left with the bulk of the work, or when Aquarius III's feel pushed beyond their limit.

ADVICE: *Try to be more understanding and helpful; it's too easy to find fault. Treat others as you wish to be treated yourself. Turn disadvantage to advantage.*

HENRY MILLER (12/26/1891)
ANAÏS NIN (2/21/03)

Miller and Nin became lifelong friends following publication of her book *D.H. Lawrence: An Unprofessional Study* (1932). Her famous erotic correspondence with Miller, published in '65, sparked new interest in her earlier work. Miller is best known for his erotic novels. *Also:* **Paul Bowles & Jane Auer Bowles** (married; writers); **Betsy Ross & George Washington** (flagmaker commissioned by president).

December 26–January 2
THE WEEK OF THE RULER
CAPRICORN I

February 16–22
THE CUSP OF SENSITIVITY
AQUARIUS-PISCES CUSP

Experiential Schooling

This relationship will be educational for both Capricorn I's and Aquarius-Pisces, and can be viewed as a kind of experiential school where both partners, locked in an ever-changing embrace, learn their lessons and do their homework. Although these two can be very close emotionally, they may have to battle it out to see who comes out on top. This can be a very liberating process for Aquarius-Pisces, who need to learn how to stand up and defend themselves in order to continue on their path of self-development. Such struggles may occur in the boardroom or in the bedroom, but if Capricorn I's are overconfident, they may be in for a big surprise, since Aquarius-Pisces will figure out how to get to them emotionally. The result could be, however, that Capricorn I's will learn something about their own feelings through such encounters.

In love affairs, exploration, experimentation and realization usually play an ultimately rewarding though sometimes painful, even destructive role. This combination often manifests passion in extreme forms. It is not merely the pleasures of sex per se that these two are concerned with, however; both of them view it within a broader context, and use their sexual relationship as a means of liberating the self. This process is less likely to surface in marital relationships; it often takes the instability of a love affair to allow such emotions to emerge in their purest form.

Sibling pairs in this combination can lessen conflict by acknowledging the unquestioned authority of their parents. In friendships, such problems of authority play a far less significant part, but these relationships nevertheless do best when dedicated to a common hobby or social activity. In the professional sphere, if these two can agree on certain underlying principles or on an overall philosophy, they may not need to compete for the superior position.

ADVICE: *Don't hold back from experience—life is a school you can learn in. Be more assertive. Kindness and sympathy should not be ruled out.*

December 26–January 2

THE WEEK OF THE RULER
CAPRICORN I

February 23–March 2

THE WEEK OF SPIRIT
PISCES I

A Philosophical Quest

Although this relationship shapes up as a confrontation between the practical and the spiritual, the emphasis here is on the power of the mind to seek out and find the answers to such philosophical questions. Inevitably, communicating such findings to other people is also important here. Thus the individual strengths of Capricorn I's and Pisces I's will be called upon, and their unique and profound understanding of the worlds of matter and spirit respectively will stand them in good stead. It is precisely in trying to iron out their marked differences that this pair will stumble upon more universal truths.

Love and marital relationships between Capricorn I's and Pisces I's are seldom particularly noteworthy, yet neither are they particularly negative. Friendships in this combination are more remarkable, particularly when partners can benefit from their own radically different outlooks. It is no surprise for such friends to challenge each other mentally and to engage in heated debates, which should be kept objective and prevented from flaring into emotional battles. As family members, these pairs are often able to bring their mental powers to bear with laserlike intensity on the problem at hand, whether emotional or financial. In parent-child relationships, Capricorn I's are likely to be overdominant if in the parental role, and face the possibility of stifling the creative spark of the Pisces I child.

In the professional sphere, this combination does best in occupations where thought and communication play important roles, for example in publishing, education or the arts. Although Capricorn is an earth sign and Pisces water, the Capricorn I–Pisces I relationship is ruled by the element of air, which underlines the matchup's mental orientation. No matter how lucrative their business relationship may be (and it can be highly successful in new-age endeavors), it will be viewed as ultimately unrewarding if it does not challenge the thought processes of both partners.

ADVICE: *Don't play God. Be more humble about your own ideas—others may disagree. Encourage free thought and mental initiative. Beware of followers.*

RELATIONSHIPS

STRENGTHS: **COMMUNICATIVE, THOUGHTFUL, PROBLEM-SOLVING**

WEAKNESSES: **STIFLING, DOGMATIC, OVEREMOTIONAL**

BEST: **FAMILY**

WORST: **LOVE**

JOHNNY WINTER (2/23/44)
EDGAR WINTER (12/28/46)

Brothers Edgar and Johnny are major figures in modern R&B and blues music. Johnny is regarded as the pre-eminent white bluesman of his generation. Edgar started with his older brother in the 60s, then left to pursue a solo rock-oriented career. While working separately, the brothers still recorded together on several albums. **Also: Phil Spector & George Harrison** (producer of his post-Beatles solo albums).

December 26–January 2

THE WEEK OF THE RULER
CAPRICORN I

March 3–10

THE WEEK OF THE LONER
PISCES II

Emotional Balance

The focus of this relationship is finding contentment by seeking out a peaceful orientation and a balanced state. The matchup has a good chance of being harmonious as long as the partners' more extreme feelings are kept under control. In the domestic sphere, these two can be quite content with running an efficient household, one in which everything is kept in its place. In most areas of life, in fact, Pisces II's appreciate Capricorn I orderliness and management skills. Capricorn I's meanwhile prize the sensitivity and consideration of Pisces II's, but can become short-tempered with their occasional blasé vagueness about important matters. Here a Capricorn I outburst will usually send Pisces II's scurrying for cover.

In love affairs and marriages, Pisces II's must step out and assume a role equal to that of their mate in this combination. There is inherently nothing wrong with the Capricorn I being the boss, however, as long as the views of the Pisces II are aired and respected. Pisces II's have a warm and loving side that will do a great deal to help Capricorn I's open up and express affection more easily. But when they get really upset, Capricorn I's may find themselves unable to help, and be forced to stand aside.

Pisces II parents are often nurturing and attentive to their Capricorn I children, as long as they themselves are not suffering from unhappiness or depression. In friendships, the worrisome dynamic of Capricorn I anger and Pisces II hurt is best dealt with through both partners' commitment to maintaining emotional balance as much as possible—alas, not always with notable success. In professional areas, co-worker pairs are capable of close daily contact with relatively few problems, as long as their tasks are well defined. As business partners, though, Capricorn I's may become dissatisfied with Pisces II disinterest or lack of resolve in pushing ahead.

ADVICE: *Don't expect too much. Exercise willpower—be resolute. Toughen up a bit emotionally, and don't let your buttons be pushed so easily.*

RELATIONSHIPS

STRENGTHS: **AFFECTIONATE, BALANCED, NURTURING**

WEAKNESSES: **REACTIVE, ANGRY, WOUNDED**

BEST: **CO-WORKER**

WORST: **FRIENDSHIP**

TAMMY FAYE BAKKER (3/7/42)
JIM BAKKER (1/2/40)

Televangelists Jim and Tammy Faye came to prominence in the 70s with their PTL Club. Cherubic Jim and heavily made-up Tammy Faye did fine until he was exposed in an extramarital sex scandal and later convicted of fraud/conspiracy and sent to jail. She soon remarried. **Also: Mao Zedong & Chou En-lai** (Chinese communist leaders); **Carole Landis & Rex Harrison** (affair; actors).

YURI GRIGOROVICH (1/2/27)
RUDOLF NUREYEV (3/17/38)

Grigorovich and Nureyev are major figures in 20th-century ballet. In 1946 Grigorovich joined the Kirov Ballet as a choreographer (and was later ballet master at the Bolshoi). Nureyev, the most celebrated male ballet dancer since Nijinsky, joined the Kirov in '58 as a soloist and worked with Grigorovich until Nureyev's '61 defection to the West.

December 26–January 2
THE WEEK OF THE RULER
CAPRICORN I

March 11–18
THE WEEK OF DANCERS & DREAMERS
PISCES III

Turning on the Charm

The focus of this relationship, and the barometer of its success, is the degree to which it can achieve relaxation, fun and ultimately contentment. The Capricorn I–Pisces III combination may suffer from conflict, since Pisces III's are often free spirits who must do things in their own inimitable way, and who might feel inhibited by the Capricorn I insistence on doing things their way. The answer is keeping things light, which can be possible if Pisces III's turn on the charm and seduce Capricorn I's into relaxing and letting down their guard.

In love affairs, more enlightened Capricorn I's will realize that their ability to enjoy themselves and have fun is directly related to how fully they accept themselves and how positive their self-image is. Pisces III's have a great deal to teach Capricorn I's in this respect, but themselves usually have the opposite problem—namely, that they are too content with themselves, and often lack the instinct for self-criticism. The danger here is that the partners will turn away from the relationship, thinking that whatever it offers may not be worth the effort it requires. This issue must be addressed before these two try marriage, which, for these partners, can be even more demanding than a love affair.

Friendships here may be more successful in achieving a relaxed and enjoyable state, but may sacrifice depth in order to do so. These two run the risk of being fair-weather friends who are not really there for each other in times of need. Only in sibling relationships, particularly those of the opposite sex, may it be possible for the combination to achieve balance between commitment and enjoyment, partly as a result of biological factors and partly because of enforced proximity to one another. Working relationships do best in low-stress jobs where the partners know what is required of them and there are few surprises.

ADVICE: *Make up your mind about what you want. More commitment may bring greater pleasure. Exercise patience in getting to know yourself better.*

GYPSY ROSE LEE (1/9/14)
CARRIE CHAPMAN CATT (1/9/1859)

Catt and Lee share the same birthday as 2 strong women who carved their independent lives in very distinct ways. Catt was a pioneering suffragist who organized the League of Women Voters and worked for the peace movement. Lee, a burlesque queen, wrote novels and plays. Her autobiography was turned into the Broadway hit *Gypsy* (1959), with 2 subsequent film versions (1962, 1993).

January 3–9
THE WEEK OF DETERMINATION
CAPRICORN II

January 3–9
THE WEEK OF DETERMINATION
CAPRICORN II

An Inexorable March

The combination of a pair of Capricorn II's does not presuppose that they spend a lot of time together. Extremely independent, Capricorn II's are allergic to hangers-on, flatterers and parasitic types, and so are able to have a frank and honest relationship with each other. That relationship, however, may be predicated on each partner being able to go his or her own way, although it will also make strict demands about responsibilities that must be unflinchingly discharged, both financially and domestically. Tough in the extreme, the relationship may be virtually closed to outside influences, which has advantages (not being bothered) as well as disadvantages (getting out of touch).

Love affairs, friendships and marriages between these two are likely to be built less on passion and more on mutual advantage. The biggest problem here is selfishness, for both partners are acutely aware of what they are getting or not getting, and neither will suffer in silence if they feel left out of the picture. Finding quiet times alone to express affection and share intimacies are important to the relationship's spiritual growth but not essential to its longevity. Topics of interest to Capricorn II's often have to do with new-age, psychic, spiritual and religious subjects, and by pursuing these areas the partners may be able to repair the split between their work and their personal lives. Capricorn II parent-and-child pairs are often able to see eye to eye on issues involving rules, power and responsibility.

In career matchups, Capricorn II's must be careful not to work themselves to death. Few checks on output will exist here, and in the process of clawing its way to the top, the combination can run out of gas unless it pursues its goals patiently. Also, powerful animosities can be engendered in those who are rudely pushed out of the way or simply crushed underfoot. Thus these two may have to remind themselves not to sacrifice their humanity to an inexorable march toward success.

ADVICE: *Moderate your power drives. Be more considerate of others. Learn the value of compromise. Kindness and sympathy are worth more than gold.*

January 3–9
THE WEEK OF DETERMINATION
CAPRICORN II

January 10–16
THE WEEK OF DOMINANCE
CAPRICORN III

Calling Their Bluff

MOLIÈRE (1/15/1622)
MADELEINE BÉJART (1/8/1618)

If these two want something from you, you might just have to give in. Very difficult to oppose, these two have a not so subtle way of convincing others: the implied or overt threat of force, which is usually persuasive enough to guarantee that the relationship will have its way. Several problems are likely to arise here. In the first scenario, other people will give in, but unwillingly and with resentment, which later will boomerang on the pair. In the second, Capricorn II's and III's will arouse the ire of other powerful figures, who will call their bluff and precipitate all-out conflict—something these two, for the most part, would actually rather avoid.

These partners will rarely get physical with each other when they disagree; rather, they will seek to persuade each other by more subtle emotional means. Capricorn III's often have deep-seated feelings of inferiority, which Capricorn II's can manipulate by alternately giving and withholding their approval. On the other hand, Capricorn II's are bound to certain illusions that Capricorn III's are good at either sharing or unmasking, and can control their partner that way. In such ways, love affairs, marriages and career matchups may be seen as manipulative in nature, and primarily interested in securing power and control.

Parent-child relationships of either combination, but particularly of the same sex, may exhibit great struggles, often including strong competition for the attention and affection of the other parent. In friendships between Capricorn II's and III's, energies are best directed into physical activity, but in team sports rather than one-on-one endeavors. Should both friends fall in love with the same person, their relationship will be put to the ultimate test, but most often the result will be that they stay loyal to each other in the long term. A difficult triangle like this one may sometimes split up the friendship, but it is usually the third party who winds up getting hurt the most.

Béjart was the lead actress in French playwright Molière's company, the Illustre Théâtre. Around 1640 she became his mistress. She had either a daughter or sister (unclear to historians) named Armande, whom Molière later married (1662). He and Armande had one daughter, born 1665. Historians are uncertain whether Molière was Armande's father. If so, it would mean he fathered his own granddaughter.

ADVICE: *Tend to your own business. Be careful not to arouse the wrath or resentment of other people. Don't be seduced by the allure of power.*

January 3–9
THE WEEK OF DETERMINATION
CAPRICORN II

January 17–22
THE CUSP OF MYSTERY & IMAGINATION
CAPRICORN-AQUARIUS CUSP

The Strings of Fate

CARY GRANT (1/18/04)
DYAN CANNON (1/4/37)

The synergy of this relationship tends to intensify the fantasy-oriented side of both its partners, particularly in the area of dealing with the more unbelievable aspects of life. Everything to do with imagining the impossible fascinates this couple, and indeed the focus of their relationship tends to be the domination of their waking thought by the supernatural elements that often arise from their unconscious. That personalities like these value their sleep and dream time highly is not surprising, but they may not be aware that this is the storehouse they are tapping for their waking visions. Whether they give in to their domination by the unconscious or choose to fight it is immaterial in the long run, for they will at best be able only to put limits on their desire, never to control it.

The presence of the unconscious is felt in everything this couple does, but in no area more than that of love. Here their fantasy is given full rein, and the romance inherent in these relationships is of the most fantastic, even mythic, sort. Consciously or unconsciously, these partners assume roles that are usually reserved for storybooks and films, and do it with apparent ease. Unfortunately, these relationships are not autonomous; in fact, they are moved too often by the vagaries of fate. Marriages usually begin with such romantic dawnings, but may become quite ordinary under the deadening pressures of everyday life.

Friendships and sibling relationships often revel in the world of fantasy, horror, violence and black comedy. Here unconscious drives can push both partners into antisocial or, in extreme cases, even sociopathic behavior. In the professional sphere, more fortunate pairs of this type will be able to put a small part of their imagination to work for them, but if they are dominated or obsessed by such drives they will turn out to be at best an entertaining nuisance in the workplace, at worst an agent of chaos there.

Actors Cannon and Grant were wed in 1965. She temporarily retired from show business to have his only child, a girl. He was past 60 at the time. Their marriage was known to be stormy and they divorced in '68, after which she resumed her career, notably as the uptight Alice in *Bob & Carol & Ted & Alice* (1969).

ADVICE: *Get a handle on your unconscious. Put your fantasy to constructive use. Choose your illusions well, and shape them intelligently.*

STRENGTHS: **CURIOUS,
INVESTIGATIVE, CHALLENGING**

WEAKNESSES: **UNSTABLE,
STORMY, UNHEEDING**

BEST: **WORK-FRIENDSHIP**

WORST: **LOVE**

CONSTANZE WEBER (1/4/1762)
WOLFGANG A. MOZART (1/27/1756)

Weber and Mozart were married in 1781. They were genuinely happy but lived beyond their means. A visitor once found the couple dancing around the living room in each other's arms to keep warm—they had no money for wood. She was shattered when he died in poverty at 35.

Also: **Har Gobind Khorana & Robert Holley** (1968 Nobelists, medicine).

January 3–9
THE WEEK OF DETERMINATION
CAPRICORN II

January 23–30
THE WEEK OF GENIUS
AQUARIUS I

Consuming Curiosity

The focus of this relationship is often an insatiable curiosity about almost everything that goes on around it. The Capricorn II–Aquarius I couple can generally play out its desire to investigate and to explore in a search for technical, scientific, artistic or historical truth. Engaged in such a search, these two may grow extremely close but will also suffer some instability in the emotional sphere. They are united by their need to uncover the truth, but temperamentally they are otherwise very different—slow, steady and unswerving Capricorn II's contrasts markedly with quick, fitful and easily distracted Aquarius I's.

Emotionally this combination is somewhat unstable—it has a certain fieriness that makes outbursts and spats pretty likely. This is reflected in the love affairs and marriages of Capricorn II's and Aquarius I's, which can be extremely stormy. Temperamental incompatibilities are not helped by the fact that Aquarius I's have a roving eye and find it difficult, if not impossible, to meet the demands of fidelity that Capricorn II's place on them.

Capricorn II's and Aquarius I's who are engaged side by side in an area of professional investigation or research are often also close friends. Capricorn II's have a need to compartmentalize, so that they often seal off this area of friendship and work from their marriages or family lives, and this can arouse jealousy from other people around them that may be directed against them or their Aquarius I partners. Yet the couple's achievements, even in the most jaundiced view, usually justify their spending so much time together. Few subjects are off limits to this intensely inquisitive pair. As family members, Capricorn II's and Aquarius I's often seek out adventure, which sings them a siren song that often makes them turn their backs on family responsibilities and the needs of relatives—a source of considerable resentment.

ADVICE: *Be more aware of the feelings of others. Don't neglect your responsibilities; this will lessen resistance and make things easier.*

STRENGTHS: **ENJOYABLE,
IMAGINATIVE, FUNNY**

WEAKNESSES: **AVOIDING,
NEGLECTFUL, OVERDEPENDENT**

BEST: **MARRIAGE**

WORST: **FRIENDSHIP**

ELVIS PRESLEY (1/8/35)
LISA MARIE PRESLEY (2/1/68)

Lisa is the daughter of Priscilla and Elvis. Though he was often on tour, they had a loving relationship. Once, when she said she'd never seen snow, he flew her to Utah. Lisa's inheritance on her 30th birthday amounts to about $150 million.

Also: **Loretta Young & Clark Gable** (reputed affair; actors); **Jane Wyman & Ronald Reagan** (married; actors).

January 3–9
THE WEEK OF DETERMINATION
CAPRICORN II

January 31–February 7
THE WEEK OF YOUTH & EASE
AQUARIUS II

Burning Brightly

Excitement and plenty of it is the keynote of this relationship. There is never a dull moment here—indeed, these two are likely to wear each other out, as well as those around them, if they don't moderate their drives a bit. Prone to overstressing themselves, Aquarius II's must be careful to keep the relationship from pushing them beyond their limits. Capricorn II's are usually tough enough to stay the pace but may come to resent the relationship's tendency to seduce them away from their work. The attraction toward ever more imaginative endeavors, however, is difficult to resist for these two, and they may wind up sacrificing whole areas of their lives to keeping its insatiable flame burning brightly.

Love affairs and friendships in this combination may be seriously dedicated to having as much fun as possible. Laughter plays an important role here, not only as an indicator of good times and close feelings but as an escape from more serious matters, often ones that desperately need attention. These relationships are characterized by a tendency to avoid the unpleasant, whether feelings, duties or deep psychological problems. They are capable of being enjoyable for years on end but may one day come crashing down under the accumulated weight of years of their partners' inattention to their problems.

Marriages and work relationships between these two seek to maximize pleasure while minimizing effort. Here the Aquarius II energy predominates, at times baffling workaholic Capricorn II's, but also seducing them to do what they most need to do: take it easy. Although capable of feeling guilty, Capricorn II's usually get in the swing of things, and learn through their matchup with Aquarius II's to stay loose in the saddle.

Difficulties arise in parent-child relationships that find Capricorn II's in the parental role, since their Aquarius II children may feel pressured and hemmed in by their rules and regulations. But Capricorn II's do offer safety and security, so that their Aquarius II offspring can alternatively become quite dependent on such responsible parents.

ADVICE: *Try to be more serious. Laughter and fun are great, but they may be used as avoidance tactics. Solve problems as they arise and don't let them accumulate.*

January 3–9

THE WEEK OF DETERMINATION
CAPRICORN II

February 8–15

THE WEEK OF ACCEPTANCE
AQUARIUS III

Aggressive Urges

 RELATIONSHIPS

STRENGTHS: **DYNAMIC,
PHYSICAL, AUTHORITATIVE**

WEAKNESSES: **ALIENATING,
ANGRY, AGGRESSIVE**

BEST: **LOVE**

WORST: **FAMILY**

The principal factor in this relationship is its own belligerence, and its focus is how best to cope with it. These partners have a will to combat that certainly makes them dynamic, but they must direct it carefully and prevent it from spinning out of control. Trying to suppress the relationship's aggressiveness seldom really works, for it pushes the partners' energies to burrow deep inside, causing frustration and, eventually, paralyzing depressions. Finding an orderly and constructive way of harnessing energy usually implies submitting to a law or plan, a kind of higher authority that sets the guidelines within which expenditures of energy are most effective.

Love affairs can be intense between these two, but not usually in a wild or chaotic sense. Here the relationship's energies are forceful and direct, but can be well modulated. Aquarius III hot-bloodedness and Capricorn II tough sensuality can make an odd but compelling sexual combination. In marriage, Capricorn II's have much to teach Aquarius III's about balancing their energies, and Aquarius III's can help Capricorn II's to become more open-minded and accepting. If children come into the picture, both parents must learn the wisdom of dispassionate judgment, and should beware of allowing anger to dictate unfair punishments.

Friends and relatives in this combination often have strong moral views that they impose on those in their social or family circle. Living up to these partners' expectations may be simply too much for anyone to bear, and this may have the effect of alienating other people from their cause. In youth, aggressions are best worked out on the playing field or gym floor, where energies may be expressed within strict boundaries, without involving resentment or rebellion. At work, this duo may exert powerful authority within a company or organization, or as equal partners in their own business.

JENNIE CHURCHILL (1/9/1854)
LORD RANDOLPH CHURCHILL (2/13/1849)

Parents to Winston Churchill, Jennie and Lord Randolph married in 1874, the year he entered Parliament. She was an American from a prestigious NY family. His promising career was cut short by a premature death in 1895. **Also: Fernando Lamas & Lana Turner** (romance; actors); **Carrie Chapman Catt & Susan B. Anthony** (suffragists); **Isaac Newton & Galileo** (Newton's theories based on Galileo's).

ADVICE: *Sticking to the rules is good; creating them is even better. Don't repress your aggressions, but direct them as constructively as you can.*

January 3–9

THE WEEK OF DETERMINATION
CAPRICORN II

February 16–22

THE CUSP OF SENSITIVITY
AQUARIUS-PISCES CUSP

A Font of Honesty

 RELATIONSHIPS

STRENGTHS: **RELIABLE,
PERCEPTIVE, LOYAL**

WEAKNESSES: **INFALLIBLE,
OVERCONFIDENT, COLD**

BEST: **FRIENDSHIP**

WORST: **WORK**

This relationship often serves a specific purpose—to be a font of honesty and mental clarity for its partners. Both of these individuals are all too aware of others trying to manipulate or influence them, and they long for someone who will gently but firmly tell it like it is. Their relationship fulfills that need for both of its partners, and continues to prove reliable over the years. Yet the matchup also involves a certain aloofness and objectivity. Although empathy is possible, wild passion or romantic fervor is usually denied this couple, since it would introduce a highly unreliable, subjective element.

Friendships are usually the most desirable type of relationship here. True counselors to each other, these two can turn to one another in times of decision or need for sound, practical advice, without fear of flattery or betrayal. Their advice may not always be accurate in matters of the heart, however, since neither of these two has a deep understanding of the many twists and turns of human relationships and their emotional and psychological bases. On the whole, love relationships here often do best when restricted to the platonic sphere. But if marriage does result, partners who are wise enough to stay with each other and resist the temptation of a younger face or figure will reap many benefits while growing old together.

Capricorn II parents of the opposite sex can play too great a role in the lives of their Aquarius-Pisces children, who tend to be unduly sensitive to their adult criticism and judgment, and may have to battle long and hard over the years to get free of it. Career matchups in this combination can get carried away on the wings of ambition. Both Capricorn II's and Aquarius-Pisces have a lot to prove, a quality amplified by their relationship. This could be a highly successful pairing as long as overconfidence and a belief in its own infallibility do not gain control, in which case disaster is all too likely.

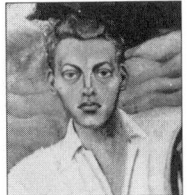

W.H. AUDEN (2/21/07)
CHESTER KALLMAN (1/7/21)

Poet Auden and poet-librettist Kallman were close friends and collaborators. They wrote several librettos together, including the text for Stravinsky's *The Rake's Progress* (1951). They also collaborated on a number of libretto translations. Auden was considered one of the greatest poets of his time. **Also: Richard Nixon & Tricia Nixon** (father/daughter).

ADVICE: *Be more modest and realistic about your abilities—you don't know everything. Open your heart a bit. Back off. Don't be so controlling.*

STRENGTHS: **LOYAL, SHARING, AFFECTIONATE**

WEAKNESSES: **SELF-EFFACING, SELF-SACRIFICING, FATALISTIC**

BEST: **MARRIAGE**

WORST: **FRIENDSHIP**

MIKHAIL GORBACHEV (3/2/31)
RAISA GORBACHEV (1/5/32)

As USSR president, Mikhail brought about the end of the cold war, fostering friendly relations with the West. In the process, he and wife Raisa became popular international visitors to Western countries. She was a distinctly modern woman, known for her liveliness and style. *Also:* **Jakob Grimm & Wilhelm Grimm** (brothers; folklorists); **Gerald Durrell & Lawrence Durrell** (brothers; writers).

January 3–9
THE WEEK OF DETERMINATION
CAPRICORN II

February 23–March 2
THE WEEK OF SPIRIT
PISCES I

Calm Under Fire

This can be an outstanding relationship in several areas of life. Showing great loyalty and respect, this pair will meet even the most acute crises with equanimity. Thus the relationship's focus, and perhaps its most admirable characteristic, is maintaining balance and staying calm under fire. In the course of their matchup, Capricorn II's give their Pisces I partners solid support, while Pisces I's contribute imagination and sensitivity. On the negative side, this duo can be perhaps a bit fatalistic at times, meaning that they lack the fighting spirit.

Sensuality may be present in this couple's love affairs to a generous degree, and it usually gives way or at least accords equal status to softer expressions of affection and sympathy. This ultimately bodes well for marriage, which for these two can be filled with love and understanding. Although a bit self-sacrificing and at times self-effacing, the relationship usually allows its partners the space they need to attend to their individual needs. Friendships in this combination may have a neutral quality, indicating an avoidance of extremes but also, perhaps, attitudes that are a bit complacent and unstimulating.

Although Pisces is a water sign and Capricorn earth, the Capricorn II–Pisces I relationship is ruled by fire, here signifying a tendency to follow intuitions. In business and family matters, these two instinctively know which course to pursue, usually to their advantage. Those in their immediate environment can benefit from their knowing and reassuring presence. Should family members decide to form business partnerships, they are usually able to work side by side and share the financial return from such ventures with employees and family members alike. Such sharing is not only an acknowledgment of work well done, and a gesture of generosity, but a solid investment in good will.

ADVICE: *Be tougher. Take what is rightfully yours. Don't let yourself be treated like a football. Generosity isn't always appreciated.*

STRENGTHS: **PLEASURABLE, EASY, NURTURING**

WEAKNESSES: **SUPERFICIAL, OVERRELAXED, DULL**

BEST: **FRIENDSHIP**

WORST: **MARRIAGE**

GEORGE REEVES (1/5/14)
PHYLLIS COATES (3/10/21)

Actors Reeves and Coates originated the roles of Superman/Clark Kent and Lois Lane on the *Superman* tv series (1951–57). They also performed together in the 1951 feature-length film *Superman and the Mole Men*. *Also:* **Jose Ferrer & Cyrano de Bergerac** (film portrayal); **Bob Denver & Alan Hale, Jr.** (co-stars, *Gilligan's Island*).

January 3–9
THE WEEK OF DETERMINATION
CAPRICORN II

March 3–10
THE WEEK OF THE LONER
PISCES II

No Problem!

This relationship does well when it is carried on casually, with few demands being made. It may not have a strong focus, or deal with deep emotions, but it can certainly be satisfactory enough, with relaxed and easygoing attitudes and good communication between its partners. Capricorn II's appreciate the unusual aspects of the Pisces II personality, and Pisces II's sense that Capricorn II's have a feeling for far-out experiences. Actually, one of the absorbing interests of this couple may be discussing fortuitous or out-of-the-way occurrences of an amusing or entertaining nature. Some may criticize the relationship for its appearance of superficiality, but such judgments rarely have much effect on the partners themselves.

Not taking things too seriously can actually help in love affairs and friendships between these two. After all, they are well aware that avoiding arguments gives them a lot more time to spend in pleasurable activities. The only drawback here is that serious problems may not be attended to until too late, but the partners could aptly point out that half of most people's problems lie in the fact that they are so convinced they have them. It often happens that as lovers these two have little interest in getting married; they prefer having the freedom to interact only when they want to, and not being bound to fixed responsibilities.

Parent-child matchups of either combination tend to be protective and nurturing, but rarely very stimulating or inspirational. In the professional sphere, these partners can get along with each other for years as co-workers in positions that are not terribly demanding, but the matchup is rarely well suited to boss-employee or executive relationships.

ADVICE: *Push yourself a bit more. Recognize that not everyone wants to be as relaxed as you do. Don't ignore too much; take some things seriously.*

January 3–9
THE WEEK OF DETERMINATION
CAPRICORN II

March 11–18
THE WEEK OF DANCERS & DREAMERS
PISCES III

True Teamwork

No matter which of these two assumes a leadership role, whether within the relationship or outside of it, the other is likely to respond with wholehearted support. The combination is extremely well suited to finding itself in a leading role within a family, or in a social or commercial organization as a boss-assistant pair, but Capricorn II's and Pisces III's rarely function well as co-rulers or co-workers. Serving in boss-assistant roles does not in any way imply subjugation, for neither partner would stand to be treated with condescension or humiliated by the other. Here the assistant role is viewed as essential help without which the boss would be unable to function. These two are a true team, working closely and conscientiously together to assure the success of any project, no matter how small.

The Capricorn III–Pisces III relationship will take a passionate approach to anything its partners are involved in. These two don't do things half-heartedly or simply by the book but with verve and enthusiasm. Their love affairs are likely to be highly romantic, the type that sweeps them off their feet, allowing them little time to think. Such relationships are rarely light in nature, but they are not heavy, either—they have a purposeful and serious air about them but are also characterized by good humor. Marriages between these two also have a good-natured attitude, in which blame, shame and guilt trips are rarely laid on, and quarrels are soon forgotten.

Capricorn II's and Pisces III's make good friends, but their friendships demand an equality that usually precludes the kind of boss-assistant working relationship in which they cooperate so well. On the other hand, these relationships are not usually practical in nature anyway, being concentrated on just having fun. In the family, parent-child relationships can work out extremely well in either variation. Such duos will also work well together in stress situations that demand dedication and sacrifice.

ADVICE: *Put your abilities to their most effective use. Beware of subjugating others to your will. Keep the best interests of the group in mind.*

RICHARD NIXON (1/9/13)
PAT NIXON (3/16/12)

Richard and Pat first met in 1938. It was love at first sight—for him. She agreed to date provided there was no talk of love or marriage. But she eventually came around, and they were wed in 1940. Their often strained marriage was poignantly depicted in the 1995 film *Nixon*.

Also: Kathryn Walker & James Taylor (married; actress/singer).

January 10–16
THE WEEK OF DOMINANCE
CAPRICORN III

January 10–16
THE WEEK OF DOMINANCE
CAPRICORN III

Hero Worship

Capricorn III's are a bit prone to idolize each other. No matter where in life their relationship emerges, they are bound to elevate their partner to a high position, but of course they are also likely to be raised to a corresponding position themselves. Their relationship, then, is not only highly complementary (and complimentary) but also in many respects quite unrealistic. Being set up for a fall is all too common here—one partner will come crashing down in the other's eyes through failure, misplaced trust or just the strain of not being able to live up to expectations. Only by exercising strong willpower, and by constantly reminding each other that they are ordinary human beings like anyone else, will this duo be capable of keeping a realistic eye on their relationship. Perhaps the greatest danger is according the relationship itself an unrealistically high order of merit, and developing a blind faith in its ability to accomplish miracles.

A love affair between two Capricorn III's is likely to be a sensuous, earthy relationship. By calling it the best they've every had, however, the partners might keep it from deepening spiritually and emotionally. In marriages too, smugness or oversatisfaction can inhibit personal growth. Too often these partners are liable to live in a bubble of happiness that may one day burst, finding both of them unprepared for a sudden inrush of problems and difficulties that they really haven't faced before.

As business partners or executives, Capricorn III's can work very well together, but may overestimate each other's capabilities. They usually have a great deal of loyalty to their firm or company, and their ability to make personal sacrifices seems unlimited. But, of course, they are only human, and if they sacrifice too much their resentments will steadily build, particularly if commensurate reward is not forthcoming. Parent-child combinations, too, are likely to be overattached to their family group; their unselfishness may allow them to be taken advantage of by more self-seeking family members. Two Capricorn III friends are extremely loyal but must beware of forming a closed mutual-admiration society.

ADVICE: *Try to be a bit more realistic. Don't have such high expectations. Belief in your infallibility can be deadly. You are no better than anyone else.*

MARTIN LUTHER KING, JR. (1/15/29)
JOAN OF ARC (1/15/1412)

Interestingly, these 2 political and spiritual martyrs share the same birthday. They both crusaded for major social causes of their time. While she prophesied the future, he had "a dream" of the future. Ironically, as a woman she pursued military battle; as a man he was totally committed to nonviolence.

MUHAMMAD ALI (1/17/42)
GEORGE FOREMAN (1/10/48)

Heavyweight champ Foreman lost his title to Ali in a stunning upset in their memorable, highly publicized bout in Zaire, 1974. This fight, and the surrounding conditions, were brilliantly depicted in the 1996 Oscar-winning documentary *When We Were Kings*. **Also: George Foreman & Joe Frazier** (boxers; Foreman won title from Frazier, '73); **Hal Roach & Mack Sennett** (rival film producers).

January 10–16
THE WEEK OF DOMINANCE
CAPRICORN III

January 17–22
THE CUSP OF MYSTERY & IMAGINATION
CAPRICORN-AQUARIUS CUSP

Treading on Toes

This is a touch-and-go combination. All too often, the antagonistic feelings that are likely to arise here lead the partners into confrontation. Because of their relationship's instability and unpredictability, these two will have to take great care not to tread on each other's toes or arouse animosity. They may also experience great excitement and challenge in the relationship, but a competitive element will often surface in the middle of a mutual project and set them at each other's throats. Keeping impulsiveness and deeper feelings under control, without dangerously suppressing them, and being able to work out differences of opinion will be essential to the well-being of this volatile pairing.

Love affairs in this combination can be passionate but transitory. The relationship will sometimes strike both partners with overwhelming intensity, then pass as suddenly as it appeared, like a summer thunderstorm. Such beginnings augur poorly for marriage, but should these two meet as friends rather than lovers, they may be able to develop a solid basis of trust and understanding. Energized by the constant emotional edge between them, however, their marriage will not allow them much relaxation.

Friendships and enmities between these two may be as close as the proverbial love and hate. Struggles over mutually desired goals, whether of a commercial or human sort, can both bring Capricorn III's and Capricorn-Aquarians together and drive them apart, depending on the circumstances. What is most important is that antagonistic, even violent impulses be kept under strict control, and consideration for all concerned be exercised to as great a degree as possible. In the professional sphere, the individuals in this pairing often find themselves on opposite sides of the fence, most obviously when they represent rival outfits but even when they work for the same organization. Their rivalries may be stimulating but can also bring out the very best and worst in them. In family matters, relatives in this combination must be careful to prevent open combat from emerging between them, precipitating an adversarial situation in which others are forced to take sides.

ADVICE: *Figure out what is to your mutual advantage. Don't let dissension get out of control. Be aware of your effect on others. Promote stability.*

WAYNE GRETZKY (1/26/61)
JANET JONES (1/10/62)

Performer Jones is the wife of hockey star Gretzky, known as the "Great One." He was the youngest player ever voted an MVP. Jones calls her biggest achievement "A healthy and happy marriage with children." **Also: Katy Jurado & Ernest Borgnine** (married; actors); **Berthe Morisot & Edouard Manet** (close friends; Impressionist painters); **Ethel Merman & Ernest Borgnine** (married; actors).

January 10–16
THE WEEK OF DOMINANCE
CAPRICORN III

January 23–30
THE WEEK OF GENIUS
AQUARIUS I

Adjusting the Pace

These two personalities are very different temperamentally, and at first they may have difficulty in adjusting their pace to each other. But they are capable of generating a lot of energy and enthusiasm, and of dreaming up schemes that they can later realize as real-life projects. Their relationship is a study in contrasts. Capricorn III's, with their slow and serious side, may have problems with the lightning-quick Aquarius I approach, yet they have a great deal to teach Aquarius I's about the control and accurate direction of their energies. In arguments and personality struggles, Capricorn III's have the advantage of being able to hang in there steadily and push their point with unwavering perseverance, but Aquarius I's will sometimes explode with a force that will be difficult or impossible to resist.

In love affairs and marriages, dominant Capricorn III's may clash severely, even violently, with Aquarius I's who refuse to be controlled or ordered around. These relationships usually face acute emotional conflict sooner or later, although they can be quite exciting, too. It will be essential to lay down firm guidelines as to what is and is not considered acceptable behavior, both at home and in social contexts. Furthermore, both partners should know what is expected of them domestically, especially since discharging fixed responsibilities can have a calming and salutary effect on this matchup. Friendships and sibling relationships will demand constant stimulation in terms of entertainment and adventure. These two are up for practically anything, and will seek out danger and challenge wherever they can find it.

The key to this relationship's success is being able to minimize personal differences while making the very different strengths of its partners work to advantage. In career areas, such as boss-employee relationships, a Capricorn III at the helm will find an Aquarius I worker extremely difficult to control and, often, to understand. Should these two be paired equally as co-workers, they will often have problems agreeing on a common course of action, but once they settle in they can get the job done, efficiently and in short order.

ADVICE: *Set strict limits. Attend to your daily tasks. Take care in roles sensitive to domination and rebellion. Get into synch.*

Self-Evaluation

This couple often lacks a clear picture of itself and of what it does—it needs help in self-evaluation. The focus here, then, is often a mutual search for a standard or objective criterion against which it can measure or evaluate its achievements. Should debilitating arguments arise, both partners may need to consult a counselor or mutual friend who can serve as a mediator. In interpersonal relationships, hard-working Capricorn III's often enjoy the free and easy attitudes of Aquarius II's, which can help them take their mind off their work and responsibilities. When Capricorn III's relax, they can be great fun, so that these two may thoroughly enjoy their leisure together. On the other hand, Aquarius II's will also get on the nerves of Capricorn III's who are in a serious mood or are busy with a project. Capricorn III's sometimes find Aquarius II's extremely irritating and distracting.

Love affairs rarely develop between these two, since Capricorn III dominance is usually more than easygoing Aquarius II's can handle. In marriage too, Capricorn III's are likely to set themselves up as absolute authorities—a stance not acceptable to Aquarius II's, and unworkable within the relationship. These two partners tend to define their likes and dislikes extremely clearly with each other, so that the issues in their friendships and rivalries are usually all out in the open. Friendships generally bring out the best, and enmities the worst, in this combination.

Career matchups will feature strife and competition until both parties can agree on certain key points. Should Capricorn III's and Aquarius II's be co-workers, a perceptive boss will usually be able to keep peace between them, but the strain they put on the group may at times prove overwhelming. As cousins or siblings, they can relate splendidly, preferring to spend their time as far from adult supervision as possible. These partners make their own rules for themselves and consider social and even legal strictures not really applicable to them.

ADVICE: *Try harder to work things out. Don't let your buttons be pushed so easily. Enjoy goofing off together. Don't take things too seriously.*

ALEXANDER HAMILTON (1/11/1755)
AARON BURR (2/6/1756)

Hamilton and Burr were bitter political enemies. After Hamilton criticized Burr at a dinner party, Burr challenged him to a gun duel. Although Hamilton had an aversion to dueling, he was honor-bound to accept Burr's challenge. Reportedly shooting into the air, Hamilton was then shot and killed by Burr. *Also:* **Cole Younger & Belle Starr** (lovers; Wild West outlaws).

Planning Campaigns

The traits that Capricorn III's have in abundance—constancy, consistency, application, etc.—are precisely those that Aquarius III's need to develop. And Aquarius III's also have a great deal to offer their partners in this combination in the way of initiative and invention. Between them they may build a highly creative relationship that can succeed brilliantly in impressing its talents, and even occasionally its genius, on other people. Humor is often present in this relationship, figuring prominently in the form of irony and wit. Capricorn III's too often emphasize their serious side in their interactions with other people, so they appreciate their relationship with Aquarius III's for letting them give vent to their playful, even silly moods.

Love affairs of this type can be complex, since although there is usually a base of good will, the partners arouse emotions in each other at a deep level, often touching dangerous shadow areas best left alone. Volcanic upheavals and truly wild expressions of feeling may periodically disrupt what is otherwise a remarkably peaceful relationship. Marriages are a bit more even, but as spouses these two tend to feel neglected, slighted and taken advantage of, and they usually only make their displeasure known after long periods of brooding. As friends, Capricorn III's and Aquarius III's are really good at cheering each other up. Should both of them fall into a serious depression at the same time, however, neither one may be strong enough to emerge from the pit alone, and these moods will have to run their course.

In career matters, Capricorn III's and Aquarius III's work extremely well together, meeting few emotional difficulties. True, their feelings seldom enter into the picture anyway, since the thoughtful and often intellectual content of what they do is of primary importance here. Particularly good at planning out projects and campaigns, they also have the tenacity to see their plans through. In the family, similarly, Capricorn III and Aquarius III relatives often team up when celebrations or other festivities need organizing.

ADVICE: *Treat unconscious material with care. Make sure to get enough dream time. Don't let signs of depression go unattended. Give your mind a rest.*

MATHEW BRADY (1/15/1823)
ABRAHAM LINCOLN (2/12/1809)

Brady has been described as "Mr. Lincoln's cameraman" for his being first on the scene to photograph and document the Civil War (1861–65). Brady's ambitions included his desire to photograph all the notable people of his day. His portraits of Lincoln are his most celebrated examples. *Also:* **Gamal Abdel Nasser & King Farouk** (Egyptian president/deposed king).

JUSTINE BATEMAN (2/19/66)
JASON BATEMAN (1/14/69)

Jason and his sister Justine are well-known tv actors. He played David on *It's Your Move* (1984–85), a show that was created for him. He went on to greater prominence in *The Hogan Family* (1986–91). Justine co-starred in *Family Ties* (1982–89), playing the unscholastic teen Mallory, sister of Alex (Michael J. Fox). **Also: Joan of Arc & Charles VII** (French soldier-saint/sovereign).

January 10–16

THE WEEK OF DOMINANCE
CAPRICORN III

February 16–22

THE CUSP OF SENSITIVITY
AQUARIUS-PISCES CUSP

Inner Strength

As individuals, these partners often give the impression of being tougher than they really are. Whether through physical or psychological armoring, their exterior may seem unassailable; they seem to be walking evidence for the idea that strength is an external manifestation. Actually, though, they probably believe just the opposite, and their relationship with each other may be beneficial to them in that it will allow them more fully to discover the nature of inner strength. In some cases, in fact, the relationship can become an introduction to spirituality. In this way the couple's combination can have the effect of transforming their forbidding exterior, making it softer and less threatening, since they no longer have the need to impress anyone with muscular development or aggression.

Love and family relationships in this combination are often led to many sorts of spiritual discovery through the development of inner balance and strength. Such couples can find yoga, tai chi, kung fu and other Eastern disciplines extremely instructive in this respect. Capricorn III's and Aquarius-Pisces are no strangers to self-denial, being perhaps more prepared for disciplines that demand it than most initiates, but their relationship magnifies their readiness. Learning and practicing the true differences between mind and body can create greater strength in both areas.

Marriages and working relationships may see their principal endeavor as only a small part of life, and will want to give it greater meaning by connecting it with other areas, or with life as a whole. Aware and philosophical viewpoints like these, which are fundamentally spiritual in nature, lend greater meaning to the pair's marital and professional endeavors, although in work situations they may make them less commercially productive. For friends in this combination, various forms of entertainment and excitement often begin to lose their glow with time, and to exert less of a pull. Such friends may eventually find silent meditation and thoughtful discussion much more stimulating and strengthening because they come from within rather than without.

ADVICE: *Keep in touch with reality. Inner balance is important, but so is your social life. Don't turn your back on others. Make the connection.*

MAHARISHI MAHESH YOGI (1/12/11)
GEORGE HARRISON (2/25/43)

Harrison (along with the other Beatles) went to Wales in 1967 and had a 6-month involvement with transcendental meditation under the guidance of the Maharishi. This led them to India for 2 months the following year. Harrison was one of the first 60s musicians to take an interest in Indian culture.

January 10–16

THE WEEK OF DOMINANCE
CAPRICORN III

February 23–March 2

THE WEEK OF SPIRIT
PISCES I

Belief as Fabric

This relationship is easygoing and pleasurable. Both Capricorn III's and Pisces I's know the nature of struggle, but in their relationship with each other they are able to put aside painful problems and difficulties, let their guard down and relax. An eternal youthfulness characterizes this matchup, and its childlike nature and openness protect its partners more thoroughly than any thick-walled defenses ever could. Defenses like that, of course, invite attack, whereas these two silently believe that true innocence is unassailable. Although other people may find their belief naive, they themselves feel they can make it work in daily life. In fact, it can become part of the relationship's inner fabric. This is not necessarily a religious combination but features a kind of easy self-confidence and trust in each other's love and in the relationship itself.

Marriages between these two can be outstanding. Both partners make excellent parents—nurturing, patient and supportive in the extreme. Love affairs and friendships, on the other hand, can be unstable and transitory; here Pisces I's are less focused, Capricorn III's less devoted. These relationships are unlikely to withstand emotional upset, and if either partner has any immaturity (particularly probable with Pisces I's), they may actually turn out to be quite selfish and self-absorbed.

Capricorn III parents can be very severe with their Pisces I children, yet also overprotective. Pisces I parents may try to coddle their Capricorn III children but rarely succeed in doing so. Sibling pairs of the opposite sex in this combination usually have difficulty growing up. The bond they form in childhood can last throughout their lives but often interferes with their ability to form mature adult relationships with other people. Breaking such a bond may prove impossibly painful.

Both of these individuals do best when they have their own particular area of expertise. They do not make an outstanding combination, then, as business partners, company executives or co-workers.

ADVICE: *Not everyone deserves your trust. Keep your individuality alive. Let go of claiming bonds. In certain respects you may be kidding yourself.*

January 10–16

THE WEEK OF DOMINANCE
CAPRICORN III

March 3–10

THE WEEK OF THE LONER
PISCES II

Not as Simple as It Appears

RELATIONSHIPS

STRENGTHS: **THEORETICAL, REORGANIZING, RELIABLE**

WEAKNESSES: **UNCONTROLLED, MISDIRECTED, DESTRUCTIVE**

BEST: **WORK**

WORST: **MARRIAGE**

HARRY K. THAW (1/12/1872)
EVELYN NESBIT (3/8/1885)

Showgirl Nesbit was having an affair with architect Stanford White when she married Thaw, described as a "psychotic millionaire." Intensely possessive of his young wife, Thaw shot and killed White in 1906 at NY's Madison Square Garden. *Also:* **William James & Oliver Wendell Holmes** (philosopher/jurist; members of "Metaphysical Club"); **Edward Teller & George Gamow** (Big Bang theorists).

This relationship usually centers around providing effective leadership. Capricorn III's would seem to be the bosses here, since Pisces II's are rarely capable of or even interested in dominating their powerful partner. But things are not as simple as they appear in this respect: although they cannot govern Capricorn III's, Pisces II's generally demand to be on an equal footing with them in terms of power and control. It is often the relationship itself that assumes a leadership role in its immediate social, professional or family environment. Since this relationship carries the possibility of passionate involvement, ironing out these issues may prove far from easy.

In love affairs, passions are likely to be uncontrolled unless the relationship has some direction and purpose. Pisces II's can be highly unconventional, and balk against social restrictions, while Capricorn III's may insist on following the rules. Marriages between these two are not recommended unless agreement can be reached on social and financial matters. And when they founder, they are likely to generate extremely painful and destructive energies.

Friends in this combination find great joy in discussing the latest ideas and trends, from fashion to politics. They often show great empathy for each other, and can call upon each other in times of need. As family members these two often take the lead in planning the group's activities, and they are also able to represent the family when social obligations must be fulfilled.

In professional matters, this relationship can prove extremely valuable and rewarding for all concerned. Of a decidedly philosophical bent, it does best in areas where planning, theorizing, reorganization and preparation play a primary role. Although able to work as part of a larger team, these two probably do best on their own as independent freelancers, researchers or consultants.

ADVICE: *Don't lose emotional control. Lead others wisely—beware of abusing power. Don't get lost in theorizing. Keep your feet on the ground.*

January 10–16

THE WEEK OF DOMINANCE
CAPRICORN III

March 11–18

THE WEEK OF DANCERS & DREAMERS
PISCES III

Thinking the Best of Others

RELATIONSHIPS

STRENGTHS: **FAIR, HONEST, TOLERANT**

WEAKNESSES: **GULLIBLE, IMPRACTICAL, HYPERMORAL**

BEST: **WORK**

WORST: **FRIENDSHIP**

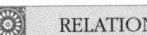

CHAD LOWE (1/15/68)
ROB LOWE (3/17/64)

TV actor Chad is Rob's younger brother. Chad starred in *Spencer* (1984–85), co-starred in *Life Goes On* (1989–93). Movie actor Rob, a member of Hollywood's "Brat Pack," had his career briefly threatened when he was sued for having videotaped sex with a teenage girl. *Also:* **Martin Luther King, Jr. & Ralph Abernathy** (civil-rights leaders); **Hamilton & Madison** (co-authors, *The Federalist*).

Great humanity is exhibited by this relationship, and a concomitant desire to better the lives of others both in the pair's immediate environment and beyond. Capricorn III's are ruggedly fair and honest in their accepting attitudes toward all, and Pisces III's are universal enough in their thinking to eschew any selfish striving after money or power. Idealistic in the extreme, these partners must remind themselves that guarantees, deadlines and legal agreements also have their place in the scheme of things. They are sometimes a bit naive to the abuses of power and must remind themselves to be tough and demanding, and to insist that guarantees will be backed up with rock-solid commitment.

In love affairs, Capricorn III's too often sit at home waiting for their elusive Pisces III partners to return. Pisces III's are masters of the excuse, but they will find their partner in this combination somewhat hard to convince, and remarkably unforgiving. After several punishing sessions, Pisces III's will either learn to toe the line or find another partner.

Friendships and marriages here tend to be a bit gullible. The partners too easily accept the word of others, putting their own finances and reputations at risk. Thinking the best of others until proven wrong is an admirable but not always practical quality, particularly when it comes to gray areas involving close relatives or friends who are less than reliable. Trust and acceptance can also be big issues between the partners themselves. In this area Capricorn III's tend to be severe, unyielding and moral, Pisces III's flexible, accepting and difficult to pin down.

A Capricorn III parent will often spoil a charming Pisces III child quite shamelessly but will also exercise absolute control. In the professional sphere, this matchup can be a powerful force for tolerance and opportunity. Employees of social and commercial organizations will benefit from having such a duo as their representatives.

ADVICE: *Your accepting attitudes hide a condemning side. Don't allow yourself to be manipulated. Demand firm guarantees, even from those you love.*

RELATIONSHIPS

STRENGTHS: GENEROUS, VIVACIOUS, ARTISTIC

WEAKNESSES: VIOLENT, EXCESSIVE, SELF-CONSUMING

BEST: WORK

WORST: LOVE

JOE FRAZIER (1/17/44)
MUHAMMAD ALI (1/17/42)

These heavyweight foes who share the same birthday fought 3 times, emerging as lifelong friends. Frazier won the first bout, Ali the 2nd—each by unanimous decisions. But their greatest bout was the "thrilla in Manila," which Ali won decisively with a 12th-round TKO.

Also: **Robert E. Lee & Stonewall Jackson** (Confederate generals); **Mack Sennett & D.W. Griffith** (early movie director-producers).

A Roaring Inferno

These two may not be the best combination for each other. True, they appreciate each other's liveliness and vivacity, but their matchup has two major drawbacks: first, that its synergy magnifies not just their talents but their instabilities, making them dangerously unpredictable; and second, that each of them is often more attracted to quiet, passive types. Because of their ability to trigger each other's shadow side, violent outbursts are to be expected in this relationship, which can be terribly destructive both psychologically and physically.

Interpersonal relationships like friendships, marriages and love affairs are particularly susceptible to this kind of triggering. Furthermore, since both partners are fascinated with imaginative and dangerous pursuits, they may lack some kind of checking or limiting mechanism to keep them from being caught up in various types of excessive behavior, perhaps involving drugs, violence, sex or fantasy. Each partner merely feeds the other's flame until the relationship is fanned to white heat. A roaring inferno or eruptive volcano of emotion can sweep away everything in its path, including the relationship itself. As relatives, Capricorn-Aquarians have a quick, almost telepathic bond that allows them to act as one, a quality particularly helpful in emergency situations that demand lightning-quick reflexes. Nurturing instincts are also well developed here, but the pair must be careful about their violent reactions to people they consider intruders in the family space.

Substantial controlling mechanisms do appear, on the other hand, within the professional and the familial spheres. Capricorn-Aquarius combinations can make excellent partners in business, industrial and artistic pursuits. Hard-working and responsible attitudes emerge here, and with them a firm commitment to achieving success. The couple's human qualities are also strongly marked, so that these two will rarely take advantage of others. In fact, their matchup can be generous, and is highly considerate to the feelings of other people, particularly socially disadvantaged ones.

ADVICE: *Shooting first and asking questions later is not advised. Keep your temper under control. Seek moderation in all things, if possible.*

RELATIONSHIPS

STRENGTHS: ENERGETIC, STIMULATING, SUPPORTIVE

WEAKNESSES: UNSTABLE, UNRELIABLE, IRRITATING

BEST: SIBLING

WORST: MARRIAGE

GEORGE BALANCHINE (1/22/04)
MARIA TALLCHIEF (1/24/25)

Ballet master Balanchine and prima ballerina Tallchief were married from 1946–52. She was the featured dancer of the NY City Ballet (which he co-founded) during its early years, 1947–65. They often worked together, Tallchief creating many important parts in his choreography.

Also: **Konstantin Stanislavsky & Anton Chekhov** (director/playwright); **Cary Grant & Randolph Scott** (close friends; actors).

Enforcing Agreements

Although these two may understand each other well and have abundant energy to put in the service of their shared projects and of their relationship itself, things will not usually work out between them unless they can see eye to eye on certain issues. Once they reach agreement on financial, philosophical and cultural matters, they can proceed further, but they must be diligent about preventing periodic lapses in what has been agreed upon. The problem here is emotional instability and uncertainty of purpose. Impetuosity will too often gain ascendancy in this relationship, destroying weeks, months or even years of hard work. The relationship is built on a delicate, even precarious balance, and since it is not known for toughness or resiliency, disruption can lead to disaster in very short order.

Love affairs can develop quickly, perhaps too much so, since this may keep them from having the time to put down solid roots. Furthermore, both Capricorn-Aquarians and Aquarius I's have a roving eye, and unless they can work out an agreement to have a free or open relationship, jealousies, blame and recrimination may result. Marriages should obviously not be attempted between these two unless such agreements are reached first and, just as important, there is a resolute attitude toward enforcing these agreements.

Friendships here are best kept unserious, for Capricorn-Aquarians have a temper that can rage out of hand if they find their Aquarius I friend unfaithful or unreliable. In the family, Capricorn-Aquarian parents can be very intolerant toward young Aquarius I's; they may acknowledge these children's talent and intelligence yet insist that they perform quite menial tasks, just like anyone else. Sibling relationships, on the other hand, can be highly stimulating and mutually supportive. As business partners and co-workers, Capricorn-Aquarians and Aquarius I's are capable of great things, but they must learn to overcome small irritations in their daily interactions.

ADVICE: *Make rules and stick to them. Try to curb your impetuosity. Think of the good of the group. Don't demand the impossible of each other.*

January 17–22

THE CUSP OF MYSTERY & IMAGINATION
CAPRICORN-AQUARIUS CUSP

January 31–February 7

THE WEEK OF YOUTH & EASE
AQUARIUS II

RELATIONSHIPS

STRENGTHS: **ENTHUSIASTIC,
ENJOYABLE, RELAXED**

WEAKNESSES: **CHAOTIC,
SUPERFICIAL, REGRETTABLE**

BEST: **FRIENDSHIP**

WORST: **LOVE**

Satisfaction or Dissatisfaction?

This relationship features quick communication, but not always of the positive sort. This volatile pair easily voices both satisfaction and dissatisfaction; the partners rarely leave each other in any doubt where they stand. Although Aquarius II's are attracted to the deeper, shadow areas of the Capricorn-Aquarius personality, they may not always appreciate the problems attendant upon relationships with these wonderful but maddening individuals. Both of these personalities have an extremely youthful quality, but Capricorn-Aquarians, with their often hectic lifestyles, are unlikely to age as well as Aquarius II's. The relationship is generally a positive one, but its enthusiasm must not be allowed to get out of control and obliterate good sense.

Love affairs can be exciting but emotionally unpredictable. Aquarius II's often have trouble handling tumultuous Capricorn-Aquarians, and although they may crave what these individuals' deep and passionate nature seems to promise, they ultimately cannot handle its intensity. Capricorn-Aquarians, for their part, may enjoy the attention of Aquarius II's but may ultimately tire of what they could come to view as an increasingly superficial involvement.

In marriages and working relationships, Capricorn-Aquarians can be sensible and practical in technical areas (traits that are welcome to Aquarius II's) but also chaotic emotionally and financially (traits that are not). Aquarius II's will often throw up their hands in despair at their partner's latest shenanigans, and will bemoan the fact that they ever chose this relationship. Capricorn-Aquarians, however, are eminently forgivable, particularly by Aquarius II's, who are quite relaxed once they calm down.

As friends, these two can have a great time of it, whether visiting clubs together, going on vacations and to films or just plain hanging out. Capricorn-Aquarians in this kind of relationship with an Aquarius II will feel completely comfortable, and able to relax, kick back and enjoy their time together fully. Siblings in this combination also make excellent companions for each other, particularly when they are of the opposite sex.

ADVICE: *Can you handle it? Remember that wishes come true. Get a hold on your emotions. Predictable need not mean dull. Deepen your commitment.*

MICHAEL TUCKER (2/6/44)
JILL EIKENBERRY (1/21/47)

Eikenberry and Tucker had featured roles in the successful tv drama series *LA Law* (1986–94). On the program they fell in love and got married; in real life they were already married. **Also: Phil Everly & Don Everly** (brothers; pop duo); **Ray Anthony & Mamie Van Doren** (married; musician/actress); **Jack Abbott & Norman Mailer** (convict-writer sponsored by author).

January 17–22

THE CUSP OF MYSTERY & IMAGINATION
CAPRICORN-AQUARIUS CUSP

February 8–15

THE WEEK OF ACCEPTANCE
AQUARIUS III

RELATIONSHIPS

STRENGTHS: **MODERATING,
PROFESSIONAL, LOYAL**

WEAKNESSES: **STORMY, SELF-
DEFEATING, TENSE**

BEST: **LOVE**

WORST: **PARENT-CHILD**

Cool Under Heat

These two bring out each other's wild side. The biggest problem their relationship has, and often its principal focus, is whether it can succeed in moderating its drives and putting them to work in a more balanced way. The nature of the involvement here is tempestuous, to say the least. The question is, will the fire rage out of control or be contained? For the most part it is contained, for this pair can often advance their cause and further their interests in a professional manner that belies the intensity of their pairing. Keeping cool under fire is characteristic of them—they know how to go about their business without attracting or creating much commotion, if they so wish.

Love affairs, friendships and marriages in this combination can be extremely devoted and loyal. Aquarius III's are basically able to accept the whole Capricorn-Aquarius package without reservation, even if they may not fully agree with it. Capricorn-Aquarians are often charmed by their Aquarius III companions, and are strongly attracted to them physically. Although these relationships can all be stormy at times, they tend to hold together over the years, confounding critics who predicted that their instability would lead to an early demise. Parent-child relationships in either possible variation struggle for balance and may finally achieve it later in life.

In business dealings, work projects and other career endeavors, these two can make an effective combination. Getting the job done according to plan emphasizes the fact that things are often worked out meticulously before any sort of presentation or confrontation is allowed to take place. But emotional tensions and disagreements can surface at the most inopportune moments, throwing a monkey wrench into the works. Self-sabotage is too often the result of this pair's endeavors, for they are less apt to be tripped up by others than by themselves.

ADVICE: *Don't let the fire get out of control. Achieve balance and maintain it. Beware of undercutting your own best efforts. Keep an eye on yourself.*

EMILY HARRIS (2/11/47)
WILLIAM HARRIS (1/22/45)

William and Emily were a married couple in the Symbionese Liberation Army, a political terrorist group that kidnapped newspaper heiress Patti Hearst in 1974. After a police shootout, the Harrises and Hearst—by then compatriots—remained at large, crisscrossing the US until they were captured by the FBI in '75.

Also: David Lynch & Laura Dern (colleagues; director/actress).

RELATIONSHIPS

STRENGTHS: NATURAL, IMAGINATIVE, ENCHANTED

WEAKNESSES: UNREALISTIC, IMPROVIDENT, RIDICULOUS

BEST: FAMILY

WORST: MARRIAGE

FEDERICO FELLINI (1/20/20)
GIULIETTA MASINA (2/22/21)

Fellini and Masina met as students in 1942 and were married a year later. She appeared in his directorial debut, *Variety Lights* (1951), but will be forever remembered as the simple-hearted, docile gamine in his early masterpiece *La Strada* (1954). To Fellini she was more than an actress—she was the muse who gave new dimension to his art.

January 17–22
THE CUSP OF MYSTERY & IMAGINATION
CAPRICORN-AQUARIUS CUSP

February 16–22
THE CUSP OF SENSITIVITY
AQUARIUS-PISCES CUSP

Fairy Tales

This very natural combination specializes in the easy expression of imaginative thoughts and ideas. Both partners lead a large inner life, but even if one of them is content with merely having fantasies, the other is sure to draw him or her out, usually simply through curiosity. Then, acting out these fantasies can become the couple's specialty. They often love to dress up for parties and other events, or even to perform theater within the privacy of their own home. This is not really exhibitionism, and certainly not a manifestation of asocial tendencies, but rather the pure expression of a delight in play-acting, theater and make-believe. Living in an easy and youthful world of enchantment, much as children do when caught up in fairy tales, can become the trademark of this couple.

Love affairs are usually more romantic than physical, more fantastic than earthy. These lovers come to live on another plane, one that they share only with each other. Confiding the most intimate childhood secrets, and playing games that many adults would be ashamed of, often become commonplace activities here. The couple may have little interest in TV or the movies, for they usually furnish their own entertainment. Should they marry, their unions don't always get much understanding from other people, including their own children. Growing old together in a family environment while persisting in youthful and imaginative activities may cause some amusement, or even serious worries that the couple has gone round the bend.

As friends these two may decide to put their fantasies to work for them in commercial activities. Making money with the subject matter of daydreams can be very pleasurable indeed, but the help of a shrewd business manager and a dependable accountant may be all that stands between this couple and financial ruin. Cousins and siblings in this combination will delight in playing for hours, needing few props but for some household articles and a few old clothes.

ADVICE: *Be a bit more aware of your image. Don't send other people the wrong messages. Pay more attention to financial realities.*

RELATIONSHIPS

STRENGTHS: WELL-DIRECTED, ADMIRING, AFFECTIONATE

WEAKNESSES: MANIPULATIVE, DOMINATING, FEARFUL

BEST: FRIENDSHIP

WORST: PARENT-CHILD

MICK TAYLOR (1/17/48)
BRIAN JONES (2/28/42)

Taylor is the guitarist who replaced the Rolling Stones' Jones in June 1969. Jones left the band because he could "no longer see eye-to-eye with the others" on their recordings. A month later he was found dead in his swimming pool, the apparent victim of depression and drug abuse. **Also: Duncan Grant & Lytton Strachey** (cousins, lovers; painter/ biographer); **Larry Fortensky & Elizabeth Taylor** (married).

January 17–22
THE CUSP OF MYSTERY & IMAGINATION
CAPRICORN-AQUARIUS CUSP

February 23–March 2
THE WEEK OF SPIRIT
PISCES I

Discovering a Proper Rhythm

The success of this relationship usually depends on its discovery of the proper rhythm—something usually, and literally, just a matter of time. Success is also dependent on finding the right activities to be involved in. If Pisces I's feel a personal connection with what they are doing, they will give their all. Capricorn-Aquarians often have the wisdom to realize this and will fight the Pisces I tendency to drift and dream. One of these partners, after all, must be the more practical of the two, and must take the lead if anything is to get done. This is a role that Capricorn-Aquarians can enjoy, up to a point; and although they can begin to feel a tad frustrated should their dynamism fail to strike sparks in their Pisces I partner, they usually don't give up.

Love affairs and friendships between these two can be understanding and affectionate. Pisces I's sometimes feel that their Capricorn-Aquarius partner is coming on too strong, but they will appreciate the attention and secretly admire the forceful approach they are receiving. Insensitivity from Capricorn-Aquarians, however, will grate on them, often to the point where they retreat or flee. Meanwhile Capricorn-Aquarians in these relationships may feel rejected and unappreciated, which usually results in suppressed feelings of anger and depression. Capricorn-Aquarians will usually take the lead in marriages, seeking to convince their milder Pisces I partner that the relationship is in their best interest. In parent-child relationships, Capricorn-Aquarius parents may play a tyrannical or dominating role in their Pisces I children's lives. Breaking free of these influences will be difficult for the children, who can suffer for years from a mixture of worship and fear of such a parental figure. Successful business partnerships and other working relationships are possible between these two when Capricorn-Aquarians invite Pisces I's to join them in undertakings of mutual interest. Pisces I's will benefit greatly from the commercial contacts to which tougher Capricorn-Aquarians can introduce them, and will learn much from this partner about how to survive in a dog-eat-dog world.

ADVICE: *Stay sensitive to each other's needs. Increase understanding. Try to share leadership roles. Allow time for initiative to develop.*

January 17–22

THE CUSP OF MYSTERY & IMAGINATION
CAPRICORN-AQUARIUS CUSP

March 3–10

THE WEEK OF THE LONER
PISCES II

A Working-Out Process

RELATIONSHIPS

STRENGTHS: **PERSISTENT, TRUSTING, EMPATHIC**

WEAKNESSES: **BATTLING, SELFISH, CONTROLLING**

BEST: **FAMILY**

WORST: **FRIENDSHIP**

This relationship has an empathic connection, but its greatest challenge and focus is often mutual acceptance. The key here is building trust, which can require some patience, for these partners are very different temperamentally and may not get along at all for long periods of time. Learning to relate, however, can turn into a marvelous process of self-discovery for them, one that will help them realize the true value of their relationship with each other. There is a strange chemistry at work here, in which competition can ultimately foster admiration, irritation can lead to acceptance and selfishness can become sharing. It is often through a common activity or interest that this working-out process takes place.

Love affairs between these two hinge on Capricorn-Aquarians' ability to accept not only the need of Pisces II's for privacy but also their choices in friends. Capricorn-Aquarians can be very demanding of Pisces II attention and must feel that they are number one in their partner's affections. In friendships too, being dubbed the "best friend" of a Pisces II is perhaps of overly great importance to Capricorn-Aquarians, perhaps indicating in both situations a somewhat immature and egocentric attitude. Marriages have a chance for success if the Capricorn-Aquarius learns to back off rather than being possessive and controlling of the Pisces II spouse. Pisces II's themselves may have to relinquish claiming attitudes and to give their Capricorn-Aquarius mate more freedom.

In work and family relationships, competitive challenge often becomes a major issue. These partners may be competing for the attention of a boss or parent, for a higher rung in the pecking order or for objective superiority through achievement, but in most cases their struggles can have an ultimately positive result. At the time, however, co-workers and relatives will have to exercise great patience in standing aside and letting Capricorn-Aquarians and Pisces II's work, or battle, things out.

ADVICE: *Exercise greater patience. The road to acceptance is not an easy one. Demonstrate your willingness to compromise. Cultivate diplomacy.*

AL JOYNER (1/19/60)
JACKIE JOYNER-KERSEE (3/3/62)

Brother and sister, Al and Jackie became US track stars in the 80s. He won Olympic gold for the triple jump in '84. She won gold for the heptathlon and long jump in the '87 world championships and '88 Olympics. She repeated her heptathlon performance in the '92 Olympics. In '86 she received the Sullivan Award as the nation's best amateur athlete.

January 17–22

THE CUSP OF MYSTERY & IMAGINATION
CAPRICORN-AQUARIUS CUSP

March 11–18

THE WEEK OF DANCERS & DREAMERS
PISCES III

Private Archives

RELATIONSHIPS

STRENGTHS: **CHRONICLING, THERAPEUTIC, TRUSTWORTHY**

WEAKNESSES: **GOSSIPY, SENSATIONALISTIC, INDISCREET**

BEST: **MARRIAGE**

WORST: **WORK**

This relationship brings out the secretive side of its partners. Their matchup is likely to become, among other things, a repository for all sorts of hidden information, not only about themselves but about others. Not surprisingly, they show a special interest in gossip, reading the paper and watching the news, since much of what they see throws added light on their private archives, and perhaps enriches them. Should the relationship discreetly keep such information to themselves, their preoccupation with collecting such material could be viewed as just a harmless hobby, but in fact this information is often revealed at certain opportune or inopportune moments, with overwhelming effect.

The challenge of the love affair or marriage in this combination is to deal with material from each personality's own past—sensitively and with understanding. Both partners are likely to have buried many painful memories, which the relationship is capable of dealing with in a therapeutic fashion. Through openness and mutual discussion, much of this material can be worked through, and old scripts can be dealt with and discarded. A great deal of trust is necessary, of course, with the consequence that for one of the partners to break off the relationship could arouse devastating anxiety.

Family members in this combination are likely to be chroniclers of past events who share many but not all of their files with other relatives. They often keep hidden material kept back to serve their own advantage one day. As friends, these two are especially interested in the goings-on of their social set. Co-workers in this combination sometimes accumulate damaging information about their company, which they are usually sensible enough to keep to themselves. Should they be dismissed from their jobs, however, it will be dangerously tempting for them to go public with this information or even, in extreme cases, to offer it to the highest bidder.

ADVICE: *Don't get on a big power trip. Beware of emotional blackmail. You may be playing a dangerous game. Let up a bit from your preoccupations.*

RENNY HARLIN (3/15/59)
GEENA DAVIS (1/21/57)

Davis won supporting actress Oscar for *The Accidental Tourist* (1988) but may be better remembered for her role as the fugitive housewife in *Thelma & Louise* (1991). Following her 1990 divorce from *The Fly* co-star Jeff Goldblum, she married action-director Harlin (*Cliffhanger*, 1993). **Also: Telly Savalas & Kevin Dobson** (co-stars, *Kojak*); **Desi Arnaz, Jr. & Liza Minnelli** (romance; actor/entertainer).

RELATIONSHIPS

STRENGTHS: **COMMUNICATIVE, LUCID, PSYCHIC**

WEAKNESSES: **UNPREDICTABLE, UNRELIABLE, UNSTABLE**

BEST: **FRIENDSHIP**

WORST: **FAMILY**

The Speed of Light

These two can rarely provide each other with the stability they need. Although Aquarius I's can be more fun than a barrel of monkeys, they are not necessarily able to contribute much more than entertainment and sparkling wit to a relationship, and their matchups usually depend on the other partner to supply heavy doses of responsibility, seriousness and stick-to-it-iveness to keep them viable—a more likely contribution from other personalities than from each other. Aquarius I's can be loving and kind to each other, or equally well cool and cynical, depending on their mood. Their unpredictability is magnified by their relationship—probably no one will know what they are likely to serve up next. Quick and accurate communication is a plus in this relationship; messages sometimes seem to flash back and forth with the speed of light. In fact, it is not uncommon for telepathy to play a role here, either with or without the partners' awareness of it.

Love affairs between two Aquarius I's tend to be brief but memorable. Extremely unstable, they bloom suddenly and dramatically, like certain tropical plants, then fade just as quickly. Marriages between Aquarius I's can be surprisingly enduring once the spouses understand that they must grant each other the same freedom they demand for themselves. Fixed qualities will emerge in domestic and financial matters in these relationships.

At work, Aquarius I's collaborate well together, but only in their own strange way. An inspirational team, they often do well when they don't have much contact but are able to touch base with each other when necessary for consultation and advice. In the family, Aquarius I relatives will not always agree on important issues (and, in fact, can be quite argumentative), but at the very least are able to comprehend each other's point of view. When Aquarius I siblings are in agreement, they can make their case very cogently indeed. As friends, Aquarius I's make marvelous companions in a wide variety of endeavors. Once these two put their mind to something, it is likely to yield the most astonishing results.

ADVICE: *Try to be more consistent. Keep your impetuosity under control. Explore emotions more deeply. Don't be guilty of applying a double standard.*

JEAN PICCARD (1/28/1884)
AUGUSTE PICCARD (1/28/1884)

The Piccard twin brothers were 19th-century pioneers in ballooning and ocean dives. In 1932 physicist Auguste ballooned to an altitude of 55,000 feet. After 1946 he made ocean dives in a bathyscaphe he designed. Chemical engineer Jean accompanied his brother on many ascents, both researching cosmic rays. *Also:* **Pierre Beaumarchais & Wolfgang Mozart** (playwright inspired composer's *Figaro*).

RELATIONSHIPS

STRENGTHS: **OPEN, EASY, INDEPENDENT**

WEAKNESSES: **AVOIDING, DENYING, IMMATURE**

BEST: **PARENT-CHILD**

WORST: **WORK**

Paying the Bill

This relationship aims to be as trouble-free as possible. These partners' mutual allergy to problems for the most part tends to give their relationship a happy-go-lucky air. The price they pay for this balance, however, can be heavy, since by avoiding difficulties whenever possible, the relationship may wind up causing more of them in the long run. Although Aquarius II's will enjoy giving their dark side a rest in this relationship, that is no guarantee that peacefulness will result, since the inner shadow does not take well to being ignored and may well demand attention. The relationship can nevertheless be extremely enjoyable for both partners, at least while it is still functional.

Love affairs and friendships can be especially enthusiastic but may lack longevity because of both partners' difficulties in making a lasting commitment. Easy interchanges and few responsibilities are the keywords here. A childlike air suffuses the relationship but, unfortunately, a childish and immature one, too. These two may at times resemble kids who never grew up—and never wanted to, either.

Relationships that demand more of a fixed commitment, such as career matchups and marriages, are not particularly favored by this combination. The degree of independence the partners require, and their inability to submit to controlling and claiming authority, is usually prohibitive in both cases. Conditions can be ameliorated by keeping the power equally divided between them, whether at home or at work, and preventing authoritarian or holier-than-thou stances.

In the family, parent-child matchups in either possible variation may be free and permissive. The partners' attitude is actually that freedom is not something you are given but something you take. In some ways, children come to be more responsible through being accountable for their own actions than they might be in a more authoritarian setting.

ADVICE: *Sooner or later the bill will have to be paid. Avoidance may only create greater difficulties. Take care of things now. Own up to your responsibilities.*

ALAN ALDA (1/28/36)
MIKE FARRELL (2/6/39)

Alda and Farrell co-starred on one of tv's most popular and durable comedy series, *M*A*S*H* (1972–83), as army surgeons in the Korean War. Alda, the witty Hawkeye, and Farrell (who joined the show in its 3rd season), as his prankish partner B.J., had great natural chemistry together. *Also:* **John Ireland & Joanne Dru** (married; actors); **Troy Donahue & Suzanne Pleshette** (married; actors).

January 23–30

THE WEEK OF GENIUS
AQUARIUS I

February 8–15

THE WEEK OF ACCEPTANCE
AQUARIUS III

As Pleasant as Possible

As far as possible, this duo chooses the path of least resistance. Both of the partners know that there are two ways to do things: a hard way and, preferably, an easy way. It isn't that they in any way avoid responsibilities and problems, for as a pair they are more than aware of the dangers of this approach. It's more that their relationship is quite fatalistic about accepting what has to be done, and will try to do it in as pleasant a way as possible. Furthermore, the decisions these two make can be self-assured, swift and decisive, since they know that by getting the inevitable out of the way now they will have more time for fun later.

Love affairs between these two are often more sensuous than sexual. Pleasure-loving to the extreme, they often enjoy food, massage, art, music and other such earthly delights, all equally. Married couples in this combination will give great attention to the layout of their home and, especially, to the colors and fabrics they use to decorate it. Designing the dwelling can be a delight for them, although they can expect a lot of heated disagreements along the way due to their differing tastes.

As friends and siblings, these two can be extremely close in their formative years, and will have great times together. Some rebelliousness and impatience with authority are inevitable here, but the pair will often work out a better way of doing things, and in doing so will ultimately prove how reliable they are. It is possible but not always advisable for Aquarius I's and III's to work together. The playful side of life, after all, is the area where their relationship does best, and a boring or repetitive occupation can deaden feelings between them. On the other hand, if they are business partners or co-workers in a field that challenges their imagination and gives them enough variety, they can work side by side quite contentedly and productively.

FRANKLIN ROOSEVELT (1/30/1882)
LEO SZILARD (2/11/1898)

Hungarian-born physicist Szilard was one of several scientists who, in 1939, prevailed upon Einstein to urge Roosevelt to develop an atomic bomb before the Germans did. Szilard helped draft the letter that Einstein sent to the president, resulting in Roosevelt's ordering the US effort.

ADVICE: *You don't have all the answers. Follow other people's advice occasionally. Pleasure isn't always the most important thing.*

January 23–30

THE WEEK OF GENIUS
AQUARIUS I

February 16–22

THE CUSP OF SENSITIVITY
AQUARIUS-PISCES CUSP

Standing Outside

The partners in this relationship may discover that they are without deep social needs and that they prefer to stand outside ordinary human interactions, as observers rather than participants. They will rarely feel isolated, however, although they will have to be careful not to neglect their responsibilities to family and friends. Should Aquarius I's take the lead in the relationship, Aquarius-Pisces may feel a bit frustrated at being left out of the decision-making, so it is usually wise for power to be shared as equally as possible. Aquarius-Pisces also tend to be a bit defensive around Aquarius I's, standing somewhat in awe of their mental powers and leadership abilities. Yet Aquarius-Pisces actually tend to have a deeper emotional understanding of things than Aquarius I's do, and therefore have much to teach their gifted partners.

In romance this combination manifests as volatile and somewhat impulsive, perhaps even rash. This is particularly true in love affairs, which can be entered upon hastily, only to leave both partners with a sense of regret that they did not exercise greater patience and forethought. Should the lovers contemplate marriage, they should give themselves plenty of time to get to know each other first. Of particular interest will be how they will divide responsibilities ranging from money-making to domestic management.

Friendships between Aquarius I's and Aquarius-Pisces can be very sensitive about success—the partners will probably compete with each other to achieve greater recognition and higher status or salaries. Although their competition can be playful, it also has a serious edge, which they should discuss and phase out as much as possible. Boss-employee and parent-child matchups in this combination will rely on firm leadership. Too often, the employee or child will be angered by a lack of direction emanating from the top and will ascribe it to weakness or indecision on the part of boss or parent, thus engendering loss of respect. Co-worker and sibling relationships are often more successful, since here equality is more likely between the partners.

JOHN TRAVOLTA (2/18/54)
DIANA HYLAND (1/25/36)

Hyland was a gifted and promising tv actress (*Eight Is Enough*) who in 1977 died of cancer at 41. Although 18 years Travolta's senior, she was his first serious love. They were lovers for 9 months before she died in the 22-year-old Travolta's arms.
Also: FDR & Wendell Willkie (1940 presidential opponents).

ADVICE: *Discover and exercise your true social self. Find a meaningful connection with other people. Status is less important than involvement.*

RELATIONSHIPS

STRENGTHS: **SPIRITUALIZED, ACCEPTING, VERSATILE**

WEAKNESSES: **POLARIZED, UNDERMINING, UNRECONCILED**

BEST: **LOVE**

WORST: **FAMILY**

PAUL NEWMAN (1/26/25)
JOANNE WOODWARD (2/27/30)

Newman and Woodward met in 1953 and married in '58, sharing one of Hollywood's most durable and successful relationships. Outside of their stellar acting careers, they are highly visible political activists, committed to many charities and social causes. *Also:* **Alan Alda & Robert Alda** (son/father; actors); **Bridget Fonda & Peter Fonda** (daughter/father; actors).

January 23–30
THE WEEK OF GENIUS
AQUARIUS I

February 23–March 2
THE WEEK OF SPIRIT
PISCES I

Spiritualized Thought

This combination symbolically represents a blending of the mind (Aquarius I) and the soul (Pisces I). Of course, the distinctions between these areas are not always black and white, but for the most part it is Aquarius I mental characteristics and Pisces I spirituality that will react within the crucible of the relationship. The outcome of this fusion directly depends on the degree of the partners' acceptance of one another, for if this is incomplete, their respective qualities will remain partially opposed and unreconciled. Should acceptance be total or near it, however, a whole new entity can arise, eradicating any polarity and replacing it with a heightened awareness, a kind of spiritualized thought. This highly unusual entity will sometimes function autonomously of partners themselves, usually serving as a higher mind, a guide for their every action.

The degree of love in romances and marriages is in itself proof that a fusion of mind and spirit has taken place. Sexual expression, sympathy and affection are by no means contraindicated here, and indeed are usually all present. From acceptance follows understanding and, ultimately, empathy, indicating a true commonalty of feeling. Tremendous differences can exist within the relationship, for as individuals these partners rarely even begin to resemble each other or to think and act alike. This diversity, however, speaks well for the matchup's psychological health.

As friends and siblings, Aquarius I's and Pisces I's are capable of reaching levels of awareness as high as lovers and spouses do. More often, however, these friendships and familial pairings progress a good deal less far, and in fact might remain polarized throughout the partners' lives. Seldom able to accept each other completely, these two can share many activities harmoniously without feeling any real soul connection.

Work relationships are best kept separate from interpersonal interactions. The very different business and technical approaches of Aquarius I's and Pisces I's offer versatility but can also act to undermine the unanimity of opinion that can be vital in commercial dealings.

ADVICE: *Don't hold back. Give yourself to the experience. Great things are possible once you accept each other fully. Listen to your guides.*

RELATIONSHIPS

STRENGTHS: **CLEVER, SELECTIVE, SOPHISTICATED**

WEAKNESSES: **MISLEADING, CHEATING, ILLUSIONARY**

BEST: **WORK**

WORST: **SIBLING**

STEDMAN GRAHAM (3/6/51)
OPRAH WINFREY (1/29/54)

Multi-Emmy-winning talk-show host Winfrey has had a longtime relationship with her handsome friend and companion Stedman. After being officially engaged for 4 years, Oprah declared, "I have the right not to get married." *Also:* **Boris Spassky & Bobby Fischer** (chess foes); **Virginia Woolf & Vita Sackville-West** (lovers; writers); **Vanessa & Lynn Redgrave** (sisters; actors).

January 23–30
THE WEEK OF GENIUS
AQUARIUS I

March 3–10
THE WEEK OF THE LONER
PISCES II

Throwing Others Off the Track

This combination will have difficulty trying to hide itself away, and is often controversial, yet it is also extremely private. The partners' friends and family might be led to the conclusion that they must really be exhibitionists, since they inevitably wind up in the spotlight, yet nothing would seem further from the truth: the really intense moments in the relationship are highly personal, whether or not the partners are physically alone. Even in the midst of uproar and hubbub, they can drop their curtain and isolate themselves in the throng. Part of the relationship's secret is that it carries with it a unique and deep understanding of the dynamics of private and public behavior, an understanding it can use to advantage.

Love affairs in this combination might be controversial if the partners chose to reveal the particulars of their intimacy, but few may even guess that romance could exist between some of these couples—it is surprising enough that they are together in the first place. Marriages lay down another sort of smoke screen, that of respectability; the appearance of conventionality may be misleading here, being totally at odds with the truth. In both love and marriage, Pisces II's can play the role of the introvert and Aquarius I the extrovert, when the truth is just the opposite.

Friendships and sibling relationships can hide many secrets. These two often get a kick out of shocking others, often by a surprising revelation that throws people off the track. As a matter of fact, the pair may hide themselves not by concealing their real activities but by revealing a string of phony ones that just serve as a diversion. Teasing parents with their peek-a-boo stance is one of the chief delights of Aquarius I–Pisces II siblings.

In business and career matters, these two may find themselves in a fixed position relative to each other, but their behavior in broad daylight can be so sophisticated that few will really understand what is going on. Even if they see it, they may not believe the direct evidence of their senses.

ADVICE: *Be more honest. Who are you trying to fool? Deception can grow tiring. Once others see what you are doing, they may never believe you again.*

January 23–30
THE WEEK OF GENIUS
AQUARIUS I

March 11–18
THE WEEK OF DANCERS & DREAMERS
PISCES III

Theoretical Realms

RELATIONSHIPS

STRENGTHS: **THEORETICAL, SENSITIVE, SPECULATIVE**

WEAKNESSES: **INTRUSIVE, PAINFUL, MIRRORING**

BEST: **LOVE**

WORST: **FAMILY**

This relationship is likely to focus on theoretical realms not easily approached or understood by other people. Philosophical speculation comes naturally to these two as individuals, a trait that the synergy of their relationship magnifies. Aquarius I's and Pisces III's have antennae out for each other. They are extremely sensitive to each other's wishes and moods, often anticipating them in a highly gratifying way, which reinforces the relationship's psychic solidarity. Although Aquarius I's are more mentally and Pisces III more emotionally oriented in everyday matters, such differences are more likely to complement than to disturb their relationship.

Love affairs between these two can be magical, ephemeral and hard to pin down. They are extremely empathic; each partner's sensitivity to what the other is feeling may cause them real pain. They gladly share each other's problems, but at times may have trouble distinguishing their own difficulties from those of their lover—for ego boundaries blur here, and identities merge. In marriage, resolute willpower will have to be employed to retain each person's individuality, a quality that children often have a need for in their parents. Too often here a monolithic front signals a breakdown of autonomous personalities.

Family members and friends in this combination can be extremely sensitive to one another, which means that they can at one moment be thoughtful and considerate toward each other, the next get on each other's nerves. Finely tuned, these two must learn to blank their screens when they are together and, in loosening the connection, preserve their own stream of inner meditation. Work combinations can be found in all walks of life, but even the most mundane and ordinary occupations may feature highly sophisticated conversation over lunch and after hours. When these two engage in scientific research, teaching, gambling, game-playing or financial speculation, they may be able to indulge both their love of the theoretical and their fascination with chance to the full. Trying to uncover the laws behind daily reality can become a lifelong search here.

ADVICE: *Find a balance between empathy and individuality. Share, but also lay claim to what is yours. Try not to dump your problems on others.*

MIKHAIL BARYSHNIKOV (1/28/48)
RUDOLF NUREYEV (3/17/38)

Russians Baryshnikov and Nureyev are considered the 2 greatest male ballet dancers of the 20th century. Both were lead performers with Leningrad's Kirov Ballet when, at different times, they defected to the West. They both sought the greater freedom in choreography and lifestyle that the West had to offer.
Also: FDR & Albert Einstein (president/science adviser).

January 31–February 7
THE WEEK OF YOUTH & EASE
AQUARIUS II

January 31–February 7
THE WEEK OF YOUTH & EASE
AQUARIUS II

Attracting Problems

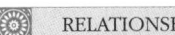

RELATIONSHIPS

STRENGTHS: **POPULAR, RELAXED, SOUGHT-AFTER**

WEAKNESSES: **ELITIST, CONCEITED, HUNTED**

BEST: **WORK**

WORST: **MARRIAGE**

For people who like things nice and easy, these two surely attract their share of problems. Part of the explanation for this is the tendency of Aquarius II's to summon up elements of their own shadow side in their surroundings—a tendency that this relationship amplifies. The couple's difficulties are related to their need to attract attention, for along with that attention their relationship is likely to pull in all kinds of potentially debilitating energies. It usually favors two alternatives: first, to carry on with its impulse to stay in the limelight; second, to withdraw to a safer position, a choice that sometimes even demands that the partners split up and go their separate ways, like fugitives in the night. In either case the relationship is being driven by its need for attention within its social, family or professional worlds. Were this desire scaled back to a reasonable level, the alternatives faced in the relationship would be less problematic.

Friends, lovers and family members in this combination are all too likely to attract hangers-on who want to get emotionally involved with them. Arousing these parasitic tendencies in others can become a real problem for Aquarius II's, and in extreme cases can weaken or even destroy their bond. Should the relationship survive this subtle onslaught, on the other hand, it will emerge chastened, wiser and certainly better able to cope with these problems—often self-induced—in the future.

In professional settings these two are most comfortable with a low-key approach. By not taking on too many responsibilities, they can discharge those they do shoulder in a relaxed and efficient way, and can also implement their often brilliant ideas without arousing undue animosity or resistance. On the other hand, marriages of Aquarius II's are quite likely to arouse jealousies and dislikes in other people because of their often elitist and high-flown manner. These couples' superior attitudes, and their transparent efforts to rise to the top of the social ladder, will make life difficult for them and for their children.

ADVICE: *Scale back your need for attention. Be more prudent about whom you associate with. Don't be tripped up by your own conceit.*

RONALD REAGAN (2/6/11)
SARAH BRADY (2/6/42)

Sarah is the wife of Jim Brady, Reagan's press secretary who in 1981 was seriously wounded by a gunshot in an assassination attempt on the president's life. Subsequently, Sarah, with Reagan's support, championed the passage of the "Brady Bill," restricting the sale of firearms to the public. It was signed into law by President Clinton in '93. Her birthday, coincidentally, is the same as President Reagan's.

EVA GABOR (2/11/21)
ZSA ZSA GABOR (2/6/19)

The glamorous Hungarian Gabor sisters arrived in Hollywood around 1940. Eva did more acting while Zsa Zsa tended to pursue rich husbands and lovers rather than film roles. Zsa Zsa is best known as a sharp-tongued tv talk-show personality. **Also: Jennifer Jason Leigh & Vic Morrow** (daughter/father; actors); **Phil Collins & Peter Gabriel** (Genesis); **Andreas & Georgios Papandreou** (son/father; Greek PMs).

January 31–February 7
THE WEEK OF YOUTH & EASE
AQUARIUS II

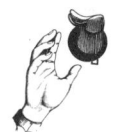

February 8–15
THE WEEK OF ACCEPTANCE
AQUARIUS III

A Car with No Driver

Which of these two personalities will wind up in the driver's seat? On the surface of it, neither of them may be much interested in dominating or taking the lead, but circumstances often force such roles on them in their professional lives. And in their personal relationships with each other there may be even more compelling reasons for one of them to take the lead, for without such leadership the pair may drift without direction. Yet the relationship may feature a marked resistance to assertive behavior from one partner, which is unfortunate, since in their desire to leave things as they are these two may be spoiling their own best chance for personal, social and even financial success.

Love affairs and friendships might seem less in need of real leadership than other personal relationships in this combination. In friendships, however, leadership could take the form of encouraging self-development, spiritual growth and emotional enrichment, and if the relationship lacks this kind of impulse it may be necessary for one of the partners to push it a bit in this direction. Love affairs may suffer from complacency, friendships from disinterest, but someone will have to take up the slack if progress is to be made. Marriages as a rule tend to need financial direction, and if this cannot be found within the relationship itself, professional advice will have to be sought. In some cases, an astute child may fill some gaps in later life.

Companies and families suffer acutely from lack of leadership, and here the pair might be pushed into a position of responsibility out of default. Should incompetent or ineffective leadership already exist, the partners may be faced with the unpleasant but necessary task of unseating it, which might win them animosity and even hatred. Boss-employee and parent-child relationships in this combination often witness a passing of power from the older generation to the younger, not without some friction and difficulty, but usually with near full agreement from both partners, along with that of co-workers and family.

ADVICE: *Do something with your life. Don't just hang around. You may be needed to take the lead. Motivation is crucial. Beware of complacency.*

BETTY FRIEDAN (2/4/21)
HELEN GURLEY BROWN (2/18/22)

Friedan, author of *The Feminine Mystique* (1963), is considered the founder of modern feminism in the US. Her ideological opponent is former *Cosmopolitan* chief editor Brown, author of *Sex and the Single Girl* (1962), whose different sense of feminism encouraged women to use traditional female wiles to get ahead in the world—the "Cosmo Girl" image.

January 31–February 7
THE WEEK OF YOUTH & EASE
AQUARIUS II

February 16–22
THE CUSP OF SENSITIVITY
AQUARIUS-PISCES CUSP

Who Are You?

At the very heart of this combination lies an acute need for self-acceptance—for the relationship to accept itself as a unit, and for the partners to accept themselves as individuals. Both Aquarius II's and Aquarius-Pisces have a dark side at the center of their personalities that they would just as soon forget about. They have both built sunnier personae for themselves, often at great psychological cost, and they simply don't want to be bothered with upsetting subjects. Yet in doing all this they may have denied an important part of themselves, which will plague them later on until they finally recognize and accept it. Their relationship amplifies and echoes this need for self-realization.

Love affairs here can thrive once disturbing elements are acknowledged and shared. Sexual interactions are often intense but also marked by a lack of consciousness of the forces involved. There is a certain fear that once the partners understand the true basis of their relationship, their passions will dissipate, but this is not the case. In marriage, too, increased understanding, acceptance and trust can unlock hidden areas and trigger a whole renaissance of sensuality.

As family members, especially in parent-child and grandparent-child combinations, Aquarius II's and Aquarius-Pisces can struggle to accept each other but may have to come to terms with their own self-acceptance first. Friendships here are best kept light and unserious. As friends these two often use the relationship to fill in gaps in their own personalities, which means that they can postpone the necessity of really dealing with their own deficiencies. In the commercial sphere, these matchups have no need to touch the partners' hidden personal areas to achieve success and, indeed, are better off leaving well enough alone. Aquarius-Pisces ambition is infectious here, and often inspires Aquarius II's to push themselves a bit. Meanwhile, Aquarius II' can teach Aquarius-Pisces something about hanging loose.

ADVICE: *Find out who you really are, and accept this person. What else can you do? Then build your relationship on a solid foundation.*

January 31–February 7

THE WEEK OF YOUTH & EASE
AQUARIUS II

February 23–March 2

THE WEEK OF SPIRIT
PISCES I

Moderate Behavior

These two enjoy a relaxed relationship in which they can let it all hang out. There is little need for concealment or exhibitionism between them, since they feel natural with each other, so that moderate rather than extreme behavior is the rule here. Pisces I's, however, have a much greater need for solitude than Aquarius II's, and may resent the relationship's tendency to be gregarious. They are also moody and changeable in nature, and this, combined with Aquarius II fickleness, can create instabilities within their relationship. They will try to be as honest with each other as they can but will inevitably keep a lot of their feelings to themselves, even when they are being quite up front about their actions.

Aquarius II's and Pisces I's don't always succeed in being faithful to each other in their love affairs, even though they do their best to be loyal. Their combination is fired by emotionally complex, even volcanic energies that run deep and dark. Conscious awareness is not at a premium here, so that even though the relationship is predominantly relaxed, there will also be some frustration in these kinds of relationships, with desires being aroused but not satisfied. Marriages between Aquarius II's and Pisces I's are not recommended unless such problems of loyalty and sexuality can be worked out.

Friendships in this combination can work out better, particularly when they are relatively free of responsibility and both partners can give themselves unhesitatingly to the pursuit of entertainment and pleasure. Sharing troubles, working out problems and coming to each other in times of need will usually be impossible, however, and may not even be desired. Family members in this combination, especially parent-child pairs, should be able to form a sympathetic bond and to experience few problems with dominance or rebellion. At work, these two are able to work side by side quite pleasantly for long periods of time at quite ordinary jobs, as long as demands are not too great.

ADVICE: *Make reliable social contacts. Work on being more helpful in times of crisis. Take on a few added responsibilities of an undemanding nature.*

STRENGTHS: **RELAXED, NATURAL, HONEST**

WEAKNESSES: **UNFAITHFUL, UNRELIABLE, UNSTABLE**

BEST: **FAMILY**

WORST: **MARRIAGE**

STEVEN JOBS (2/24/55)
AN WANG (2/7/20)

Wang and Jobs were both successful computer entrepreneurs. Studying pre-microchip technology at Harvard (1948), Wang started his own office computer company in '51, which became one of the biggest hi-tech operations of the 70s. Jobs designed and built a user-friendly PC that became the cornerstone of Apple, Inc., the company he co-founded. **Also: Norton Simon & Jennifer Jones** (married; industrialist/actress).

January 31–February 7

THE WEEK OF YOUTH & EASE
AQUARIUS II

March 3–10

THE WEEK OF THE LONER
PISCES II

A Bland Mixture

The focus of this relationship is the partners' responsiveness to each other's needs. But although these two may be quite aware of what each of them needs, they are not always sure of what they want. The result is that they have difficulty making strong, sensible decisions and definite choices. This problem may be related to a certain lack of desire in the relationship. Neither partner has a lot of objections to most of their shared activities, but neither has much yearning for them either. Thus they can live or work together in quite a satisfied state for years without ever really making strong demands on each other, or on their relationship. Although happiness should not be sneered at, in this case one often gets the feeling that something vital is missing.

Love affairs can be affectionate in some respects, quite cool in others but they are rarely passionate. Whether overt or covert, they can last for years without having to face a serious crisis. Marriages, too, can be mutually satisfying, and also somewhat uneventful. The spouses' children will benefit from the relationship's stability but might find it a bit uninspiring.

Within the family, a service-oriented approach is seen in relatives in this combination, who tend to make their energies as a pair available to any family member in need of assistance. Aquarius II–Pisces II friendships can succeed in satisfying mutual needs and providing warm and caring attitudes. The partners will be extremely comforting in times of need, and nurturing to friends and even strangers who need a sympathetic ear or psychological counsel.

Professional matchups of this type may go well enough but will rarely have the drive or ambition to achieve great success. In the sphere of human or social services, however, both partners show great sympathy for the needs of others and may be highly effective in giving professional help.

ADVICE: *What is it you really want? Dig deep to find your heart's desire. Be more demanding, less easily satisfied. Liven up your life a bit.*

STRENGTHS: **HELPFUL, SYMPATHETIC, RELIABLE**

WEAKNESSES: **BLAND, OVERACCEPTING, UNINSPIRING**

BEST: **FRIENDSHIP**

WORST: **WORK**

FRAN TARKENTON (2/3/40)
FRANCO HARRIS (3/7/50)

Minnesota quarterback Tarkenton and Pittsburgh running back Harris were on opposing sides in the 1975 Super Bowl. Although Tarkenton was one of the best all-time Super Bowl passers, Harris' superior rushing frustrated the Minnesota team. As the #1 all-time Super Bowl rusher, Harris singlehandedly negated Tarkenton's efforts.

STRENGTHS: **GROUNDED, ORGANIZED, IMAGINATIVE**

WEAKNESSES: **EXCESSIVE, ADDICTED, GLUTTONOUS**

BEST: **WORK**

WORST: **LOVE**

NATALIE COLE (2/6/49)
NAT "KING" COLE (3/17/19)

Nat, popular 1930s–50s singer-pianist, whose hits included *The Christmas Song* (1946) and *Mona Lisa* (1950), died when daughter Natalie was 15. In '91 she had a Grammy-winning album, on which—with technical wizardry—she sang a posthumous duet with her father, *Unforgettable*. It was the #1 song of the year.

Also: James Joyce & Sylvia Beach (writer/bookdealer first to publish *Ulysses*).

January 31–February 7
THE WEEK OF YOUTH & EASE
AQUARIUS II

March 11–18
THE WEEK OF DANCERS & DREAMERS
PISCES III

Boosting Confidence

These two have the potential to build something of substance together, and their relationship is often a solid one, emphasizing structure but also understanding. The partners are extremely encouraging of each other's talents, and the mutual appreciation in their pairing gives both of them a noticeable boost in self-confidence. Drawing out each other's more creative side and grounding it in substantial and tangible forms is a specialty for the two of them.

In love affairs, problems often arise in the area of sensual excess. Addictions are common here. A kind of fantasy or unreal situation may arise that could threaten to overwhelm the couple's good sense and practicality. Marriages in this combination usually put a lot of energy into realizing creative visions in the domestic sphere. Aquarius II's and Pisces III's are not always able to agree on matters of color, style, design, etc., since they have very different ideas on such subjects, but once they reach a compromise they can institute their decisions swiftly.

Friendships too have a weakness for excess, but it is mainly contained in the areas of entertainment and of simple, nonharmful pleasures. Family members in this combination tend to work hard on their shared projects but also to reward themselves a bit extravagantly; these relatives will have to take care that their love of food, drink, and spending money does not run out of hand. Business matchups specialize in moving far-out schemes and products along to the point where they become credible—the relationship has a record of bringing the most imaginative projects to fruition. Making fantasy pay off commercially through flawless planning and execution is a specialty here.

ADVICE: *Keep your passions under control. Don't get carried away by excess. Beware of addictions. Seek compromise. Lessen unreal states.*

STRENGTHS: **ENERGETIC, FUN-LOVING, SENSUAL**

WEAKNESSES: **DISTRACTED, NERVOUS, AGGRAVATED**

BEST: **MARRIAGE**

WORST: **WORK**

CHARLES DARWIN (2/12/1809)
ABRAHAM LINCOLN (2/12/1809)

Darwin and Lincoln were born on precisely the same day. Both had powerful impacts in their respective spheres during their lifetimes. Lincoln preserved the Union through the Civil War and abolished slavery. Darwin offered a scientific solution to the mystery of the origin of mankind through his theory of evolution. Both made great contributions to the advancement of modern society.

February 8–15
THE WEEK OF ACCEPTANCE
AQUARIUS III

February 8–15
THE WEEK OF ACCEPTANCE
AQUARIUS III

Glint of the Mirror

These two may have acute problems getting along on a daily basis. The irritation that they usually experience with other people is heightened in their relationship, and they are likely to develop a habit of mutual accusations, charging each other with annoyances of which they are actually more guilty themselves. Antagonistic battles can rage between two Aquarius III's who are mirroring each other's emotions. Blinded by the glint of the mirror they hold up to one another, they are unable to see either themselves or their partner clearly. On the other hand, there is a terrific potential for energy in the relationship if it can be properly tapped and directed. And precisely because it is so confrontational and uncompromising, the matchup can bring both partners far in their personal development, if only they have the patience to hang in there and the toughness to survive.

Love affairs and friendships in this combination are likely to be ephemeral. Explosive and reactive, two Aquarius III's will have a stormy time of it in these personal kinds of interaction, and the relationship will give them little cushioning against each other's assaults. In marriage, on the other hand, the more stable and responsible elements of the Aquarius III personality are likely to emerge. A love of food and cooking, physical exercise, sex or travel will provide the cement in the relationship, whether or not there are children. A free or unconventional lifestyle is common here, but the partners will have to learn to grant each other the same freedom they demand for themselves.

As co-workers, business partners or executive pairs, Aquarius III's will love the challenge of business or brainstorming activities but will often lack the stability to carry through on their endeavors. Easily detoured, they are likely to be off doing something else when they are most needed. In the family, Aquarius III relatives lend liveliness to any gathering—perhaps too much so; although they are helpful, their presence is not always conducive to stability or to the completion of repetitive tasks.

ADVICE: *Finish one thing before going on to the next. Organize your life. Be aware when you generate chaos. Look at yourself squarely.*

February 8–15

THE WEEK OF ACCEPTANCE
AQUARIUS III

February 16–22

THE CUSP OF SENSITIVITY
AQUARIUS-PISCES CUSP

STRENGTHS: **PRODUCTIVE,
WELL-DIRECTED, DYNASTIC**

WEAKNESSES: **UNSTABLE, OVER-
INTENSE, BURNT-OUT**

BEST: **FAMILY**

WORST: **FRIENDSHIP**

Unrelenting Zeal

An extremely productive relationship can result from this combination, one that will make major contributions to the lives of those around it. It is difficult or impossible for these two to hide their light or energy under a bushel—indeed, any attempt they make to do so will likely result in the bushel catching fire and attracting attention anyway. Aquarius III's may not have a whole lot of ideas about what to do with their energy, but Aquarius-Pisces will often point the way. Bursting with talent, this relationship succeeds best when restricting itself to one area of endeavor that it can pursue with unrelenting zeal.

Romances in this combination are likely to be torrid. This is underlined by the fact that the relationship is characterized by fire and earth, elements here indicating earthy passion. The partners must be careful, however, to keep the relationship from burning out too quickly. Marriages in this combination often aim for the dynastic, with children playing an important role and money matters arranged with succession in mind. Achieving social status is important here, but the relationship's elitist tendencies will rarely sit well with egalitarian Aquarius III's.

As family members too, Aquarius III's and Aquarius-Pisces are prone to building dynasties, so that they work well together. In certain cases business partners will move into the family sphere through marriage. Power struggles can emerge here, but more often an instinct for mutual benefit prevails. Friendships can lack the stability afforded by a group, and here the partners do best when they don't spend too much time alone but, if possible, take their place in a social circle of close friends.

Professional connections can be highly profitable and emotionally rewarding for both partners. Highly inventive, this duo can work for long periods in private together before emerging with a new discovery.

LOUIS TIFFANY (2/18/1848)
CHARLES TIFFANY (2/15/1812)

Charles founded the prestigious NYC store that bears his name. Starting with a simple stationery shop, he built it up to be a trendsetter for silverware and fine jewelry. Louis, uninterested in his father's firm, became the most notable American craftsman in the art nouveau style.

Also: Charles Darwin & Francis Galton (cousins; naturalist/eugenicist); **Chynna Phillips & William Baldwin** (romance; singer/actor).

ADVICE: *Seek group stability. Cement family connections. Focus your energies on a single endeavor. Don't try to hide your talent—it won't work.*

February 8–15

THE WEEK OF ACCEPTANCE
AQUARIUS III

February 23–March 2

THE WEEK OF SPIRIT
PISCES I

STRENGTHS: **OPEN, UPBEAT,
SENSITIVE**

WEAKNESSES: **DEMANDING,
PECULIAR, OBNOXIOUS**

BEST: **LOVE**

WORST: **WORK**

Getting Goofy

These two have a great deal of understanding and appreciation for one another. Because of the extreme sensitivity their relationship involves, they have the potential to overcome tremendous cultural, age and personality differences. The relationship takes little account of conventional barriers and in many ways gives the impression of making a statement about tolerance or lack of prejudice. Actually, the partners are just acting naturally toward one another, without any preconceptions or doctrines in mind. A main focus in this relationship is humor. Laughter, or the lack of it, is an immediate barometer of the partners' prevailing mood.

Love affairs and friendships are often lively, flirtatious and infectiously funny. The mood here is decidedly unserious and upbeat. Aquarius III's contribute irrepressible energies and Pisces I's vivid emotional expression to what others may view as a zany and idiosyncratic relationship. This pair can really get crazy or goofy together and on occasion may even convince other people that they have totally lost it. The more serious or conservative can certainly find them offensive, and may come away from encounters with them feeling insulted.

Work relationships and marriages here are often highly unconventional, yet these matchups make the sometimes severe demand of themselves that they function well. They may insist on certain types of food, furniture, workspaces, colors and a whole host of peculiarities that allow them to feel comfortable but that often get others in the neighborhood quite uptight. Learning to compromise just a bit will help tremendously in allowing everyone to get along without constant friction. Siblings in this combination are likely to liven up almost any family gathering. The only problem—which, however, invariably arises—is how to get these two to stop once they have really gotten wound up.

JACKIE GLEASON (2/26/16)
AUDREY MEADOWS (2/8/24)

Meadows and Gleason are forever linked as the Kramdens on tv's eternally popular *The Honeymooners* (1952–70). Short-fused Ralph, whose wacky schemes always backfired, adored his weary wife Alice, even through all their tribulations—"Baby, you're the greatest!"

Also: Burt Reynolds & Dinah Shore (romance; actor/singer); **Bertolt Brecht & Kurt Weill** (collaborators; playwright/composer).

ADVICE: *Make sure other people are enjoying themselves, too. Don't monopolize the space. Tone down your act a bit. Don't be so demanding and needy.*

PENN JILLETTE (3/5/55)
TELLER (2/14/48)

Penn & Teller, eccentric illusionist-performers since 1975, have a show that has been a long-running hit on and off Broadway. They are frequent guests on tv talk shows and have won Emmys for their specials. They have also appeared in movies and written best-selling books. *Also:* **John Barrymore & Evelyn Nesbit** (affair; actor/showgirl); **Alan Hale, Sr. & Alan Hale, Jr.** (father/son; actors).

February 8–15

THE WEEK OF ACCEPTANCE
AQUARIUS III

March 3–10

THE WEEK OF THE LONER
PISCES II

Daily Routine

The biggest problem this relationship faces is being able to find or build a structure in daily life within which it can function adequately. Luckily, it provides itself with the impetus to do so. Aquarius III's and Pisces II's are not exactly on the orderly side; unless they give serious consideration to schedules and fixed duties, the result is likely to be projects or activities that are at best ineffective, at worst chaotic. Such relationships must submit to the establishment of daily routines, standard operating procedures and mechanized systems, or they risk failing to discharge their responsibilities.

Love affairs between these two are highly private and secretive matters. Hidden from the scrutiny of the world, they occupy a very special place in the hearts of their partners; although they are often ephemeral in nature, they will be hard to forget. Marriages are not recommended unless both partners can guarantee a firm commitment to take care of practical matters.

As family members and co-workers, Aquarius III's and Pisces II's do best when they are not required to work closely as a team. If they do have to collaborate closely, they will benefit from strict regulations of the amount of time they spend on their duties, the quality of work required and the quotas they have to meet. It is not to be expected that they will have enough self-discipline to function effectively on their own as freelancers. Friendships in this combination can be extremely pleasant, as long as expectations are not too high or responsibilities too heavy. Games, sports and other forms of play attract this duo, especially those including mysteries and puzzles, since accepting the rules built into the structure of these activities is not a problem for the partners and, in fact, enhances their enjoyment.

ADVICE: *Try to get your act together. Put a little more energy into organizing your day. Making fixed commitments will help. Work as part of a group.*

PETER ALLEN (2/10/44)
LIZA MINNELLI (3/12/46)

Minnelli and singer-songwriter Allen were engaged in 1964 and married in '67. In '70 they separated on the same day he broke up with his performance partner Chris Bell. Allen and Minnelli divorced in '73 but remained good friends until his death in '92. *Also:* **Amy Lowell & Percival Lowell** (sister/brother; poet/astronomer).

February 8–15

THE WEEK OF ACCEPTANCE
AQUARIUS III

March 11–18

THE WEEK OF DANCERS & DREAMERS
PISCES III

United by Differences

This relationship is characterized by a very close emotional or spiritual bond. This pair's differences of temperament seldom divide them but rather unite them, for there is a mutual fascination at work here. Intellectually they are a good match for each other, usually being able to understand each other's intention and line of thought, even if relatively unfamiliar with the subject matter. This kind of unfamiliarity is often a stimulus to learning; both partners often show great interest in acquiring more knowledge about their partner's area of expertise, although such areas rarely overlap. Consideration and sympathy are of the highest importance here. Should Aquarius III's grow impatient with Pisces III's, or should Pisces III's feel Aquarius III's are pushing them too hard, the relationship will suffer not so much from stress than from having to acknowledge a lack of understanding. This is a very loyal pairing, dedicated to helping out in times of crisis.

Love affairs here are often empathic, accepting and affectionate rather than highly sensual or passionate. They can go on for years, and if they have evolved from friendships, the couple may ultimately return to that role. Should lovers try marriage, their chances of success are excellent, since they are capable of showing so much consideration for each other. Should one of the partners fall in love with a third party, however, the primary relationship may be swept by storms of passion, and some hard choices will be necessary.

Friendships and sibling relationships between Aquarius III's and Pisces III's can be outstanding. The partners must be careful, however, not to isolate themselves from friends or family. Taking up fixed responsibilities in social or family groups, if possible, usually serves as a tonic to the relationship's health and the partners' well-being. In professional areas, these two make good business partners, or executive teams working in the service of a large organization, but do less well as lower-level co-workers.

ADVICE: *Back off and give each other enough space. No one is the property of anyone else. Remember where your best interests lie. Seek challenge.*

February 16–22
THE CUSP OF SENSITIVITY
AQUARIUS-PISCES CUSP

February 16–22
THE CUSP OF SENSITIVITY
AQUARIUS-PISCES CUSP

Role Reversals

The greatest danger in this relationship is that these two will link up their defenses and retreat behind them in an attitude of supportive self-pity. Extreme sympathy to each other's plight may prove a deadly poison indeed, since it will encourage withdrawal from the very types of confrontation that the relationship desperately needs. But Aquarius-Pisces are tough, and if these two are determined to bring down the walls of their self-imposed isolation, they may make quite a triumphant entry into the world. The great challenge to this relationship, and often its primary focus, is building bridges to society, making friends and setting up a rich and varied social life.

Love affairs and marriages between Aquarius-Pisces can be extremely interesting psychologically. Since both masculine and feminine character traits may be prominent in each partner, these two have many possibilities for interaction: they can easily reverse or modify the roles they play, opening up endless opportunities for change and variety. Yet what this relationship really cries out for may well be stability, and sooner or later this couple will have to come to a silent understanding in this respect. Such frequent change may also cause great confusion for children born into such a marriage. As friends, two Aquarius-Pisces magnify their individual tendency either to isolate themselves in a personal cocoon or to busy themselves with universal issues, ignoring the middle ground or the social side of life. Building new friendships, together and separately, is often the focus of their relationship, which strives for self-actualization and individual personal development. The partners may sometimes give too much emphasis to this direction, at the expense of the primary relationship, but some kind of swing in this direction may be necessary, and balance will usually be established over time.

Boss-employee and parent-child relationships in this combination can be highly ambitious, seeking the full expression of talents and the realization of dreams. These pairs must remain sensitive to both their own and other people's feeling, and should not be too tough or ruthless in their approach.

ADVICE: *Make firm decisions and stick to them. Build a meaningful social life. Sympathy can be harmful. Don't protect each other from the world.*

W.H. AUDEN (2/21/07)
ANAIS NIN (2/21/03)

Auden and Nin share the same birthday. Both were significant contemporary writers whose work often focused on amorous themes. She is best known for her 6-volume *Journals* (1966-76), recording her erotic and artistic development. A number of Auden's poems reveal his homosexual interests.

February 16–22
THE CUSP OF SENSITIVITY
AQUARIUS-PISCES CUSP

February 23–March 2
THE WEEK OF SPIRIT
PISCES I

Hardheaded Attitudes

These two would seem to be sensitive individuals, very much taken up with aesthetic pursuits, but their combination is in fact a highly practical one. Both partners have a side that is good with money, and that their relationship magnifies, so that strong financial management, sensible tax structures and sensible insurance coverage are all part of the package. Pragmatic, hardheaded attitudes are the order of the day here. Aquarius-Pisces ambition is somewhat softened or diverted, however, by the Pisces I need for emotional contact and sympathy, which throws the emphasis somewhat on interpersonal rather than commercial interactions.

In marriage these two often try to combine the professional and the personal sides of their lives and to help each other out with their careers. They do also sometimes insist on a fairly strict separation of work and private life, but in either case heartfelt feelings, sympathies and support are never far away. Both partners may come to depend heavily on their relationship for psychological support and can suffer terrible letdowns in times of a crisis or separation between the two of them. Love affairs between these two are usually emotionally unstable and unable to sustain themselves for any period of time.

Family relationships can often be very helpful in handling the finances for older or incapacitated family members, as well as looking after the best investment interests of the family group. Although they are sensitive to the feelings of others, these two rarely let their good sense be swayed by emotional considerations. In this respect they may occasionally seem hardhearted in other people's eyes. Friendships in this combination may take part in organized activities such as clubs, teams and educational groups, but must be careful not to give up too much of their free time, or to let themselves be manipulated by more self-seeking individuals.

ADVICE: *Be careful not to get too involved in other people's business. Don't always assume that you know best. What can other people do for you?*

HARRY BELAFONTE (3/1/27)
SIDNEY POITIER (2/20/24)

Actor Poitier and singer-actor Belafonte are distinguished African Americans who paved the way for other black performers to enter the mainstream of commercial entertainment. They are also close personal friends, both active in social and political causes. ***Also:*** **Merle Oberon & David Niven** (once engaged, actors); **John Warner & Elizabeth Taylor** (married; senator/actress).

SONNY BONO (2/16/35)
CHASTITY BONO (3/4/69)

Chastity is daughter to Sonny and Cher, singing duo of the 60s and 70s. She was named from the film *Chastity* (1969), starring Cher, written by Sonny. After their divorce, Cher became an actress and Sonny a politician. In '91 he wrote a book, *And the Beat Goes On*, alleging that Cher, a cold, calculating careerist, neglected their daughter, now a gay rights activist. *Also:* **Prince Andrew & Prince Edward** (royal brothers).

February 16–22

THE CUSP OF SENSITIVITY
AQUARIUS-PISCES CUSP

March 3–10

THE WEEK OF THE LONER
PISCES II

Other Ways Around

Lots of energy here! The focus of this relationship is a kind of steady stream of emotional expression, which seems inexhaustible. The partners can go on producing or contributing for years on end without getting tired or running themselves into the ground. Rather than feeling stressed, or pushing obstacles aside, they seem to be able to plug into some kind of universal energy source that carries them along with little effort. Both partners also have a natural feeling for *kairos*, the right time for an action to take place, so that they will usually have the patience to wait and to sense the best moment to make their move. They will rarely discuss or even verbalize these concepts but, rather, will live them, quite instinctively.

Friendships and sibling relationships are particularly favored here. Involvement or interest in artistic pursuits, especially music, dance and the performing arts, is characteristic. The couple's creativity is high and is not of the kind that imitates other people's; instead it tends to strike out on its own. Working to establish its unique vision within a given field of endeavor, and aiming for recognition and financial reward, are typical with this combination. If, in their formative years, they are faced with opposition from adults, they will tend to find other ways forward rather than turning rebellious or stubborn.

The success of work relationships is usually dependent on the partners' ability to get along emotionally. Pisces II's will sometimes want to be left to their own devices, and this can make being their co-worker extremely difficult for Aquarius-Pisces, who are often left with extra work, and resent it.

Love affairs and marriages here are rarely calm, since in these kinds of relationship the partners both provoke and overreact to each other. These responses are hardly positive ones, and in order to begin to diminish them each person may have to concentrate hard on becoming less oversensitive, making their buttons more difficult to push or growing a whole new set.

ADVICE: *Stand outside the action and observe. Don't let others control you by making you irritated. It is also necessary to stand up and be counted.*

ANN SHERIDAN (2/21/15)
GEORGE BRENT (3/15/04)

Prolific film actors Sheridan and Brent were married from 1942–43 following their romance while making *Honeymoon for Three* (1941). Known as the perky "Oomph Girl" in the 30s, the former beauty queen proved in *King's Row* (1942) that she could act. Brent's career, like Sheridan's, peaked in the 30s–40s. He played romantic lead opposite Hollywood's top stars; among his credits are 11 successive films with Bette Davis.

February 16–22

THE CUSP OF SENSITIVITY
AQUARIUS-PISCES CUSP

March 11–18

THE WEEK OF DANCERS & DREAMERS
PISCES III

Steps to the Underworld

This can be a very mysterious relationship—not a lot of people know much about it. But it reaches deep emotional levels, and at its core it offers ever more complexity and challenge for the partners to penetrate. It is a relationship in which adventure, danger and risk are conceived not in external but in internal terms. Aquarius-Pisces and Pisces III's realize that the great adventures in life are to be found within, and that the enormous risks (and rewards) in the inner search are not to be taken lightly. After all, they reason, a person can get lost, even die, in a wilderness, but to get permanently lost in the maze of one's own mind can become a more horrible living death. Nonetheless, this pair accepts the challenge gladly, and takes the first steps into the underworld with confidence.

Love affairs and friendships in this combination can occasionally be frightening, because of the monsters revealed to each partner in the mirror of the other's eyes. These two see themselves for what they are, stripped of any role-playing or pretense. Facing up to the more unpleasant aspects of their own personality is daunting indeed, but it is necessary if they are to attempt further personal or spiritual development. It is not the pleasure or satisfaction offered by these relationships that is so valuable to this couple, but rather the opportunity to take the first steps toward self-actualization.

Marriages and work relationships can either bring out the more practical side of both partners or else reveal its lack, in which case the relationship will founder and ultimately fall apart. The relationship is a test, then, that is either passed or failed. Family matchups are highly secretive, so much so that other relatives rarely realize that they go so deep. Their real strength, however, only emerges if they can be acknowledged and seen clearly by others in the light of day.

ADVICE: *Don't be afraid to dig deeper—you will be protected. Don't slay monsters—make friends with them. You don't have to hide.*

February 23–March 2

THE WEEK OF SPIRIT
PISCES I

February 23–March 2

THE WEEK OF SPIRIT
PISCES I

 RELATIONSHIPS

STRENGTHS: **PHILOSOPHICAL, SERVICE ORIENTED, REORGANIZING**

WEAKNESSES: **CHAOTIC, CYNICAL, ADRIFT**

BEST: **WORK**

WORST: **MARRIAGE**

Finishing Up

This can be a slightly chaotic relationship if the partners do not fulfill their domestic responsibilities. Both have a tendency to walk away before the job is finished, not because they are shirkers but because they have simply lost interest. On the other hand, Pisces I's tend to live on a high philosophical plane, and to engage in activities that can be of great benefit to those around them. Service in its purest form, and in abundance, is something they have to offer their family or their social or work group. But the relationship's focus may be blurred, particularly in defining and articulating its real wants. The partners may be constantly giving up on what they really want to do as individuals in order to serve each other's needs, and their relationship can lack direction.

Love affairs between two Pisces I's are not very common, and when they do emerge they are highly complex emotionally. Needs and wants may become confused to the point where the partners don't really recognize the difference any more. It is not usually recommended that Pisces I's attempt marriage, for their mutable qualities are so pronounced that they usually have difficulty sustaining a constant level of feeling for very long, and are quickly lured away by new prospects.

Friendships and family relationships in this combination may suffer from being alternately overoptimistic and cynical, at one moment lost in the clouds, the next having a firm grip on things. When not balancing each other in this respect, the partners are susceptible both to getting carried away by a new trend and to sinking into a seemingly bottomless well of depression. In the professional sphere, two Pisces I's are of tremendous value to their work group. Service-oriented to the extreme, they can pull off minor miracles with a minimum of effort, and will rarely arouse antagonisms or jealousies by doing so. They do, however, have an undeniable air of infallibility, which can get other people uptight. A Pisces I duo has outstanding organizational abilities, seeing very quickly what needs to be done and offering constructive suggestions.

ADVICE: *Distinguish between your desires and your needs. Form a clearer idea of what you want. Maintain emotional consistency. Don't be a know-it-all.*

DINAH SHORE (2/29/16)
JIMMY DORSEY (2/29/04)

Bandleader Dorsey and singer Shore were musical entertainers who share the same leap-year birthday. Their careers both started and rose during the 1930s. She hosted a popular tv variety show (1951–61), and he joined his trombonist brother Tommy in '53 to re-form their 1930s big band, The Dorsey Brothers.

February 23–March 2

THE WEEK OF SPIRIT
PISCES I

March 3–10

THE WEEK OF THE LONER
PISCES II

 RELATIONSHIPS

STRENGTHS: **DEEP, INSIGHTFUL, EASYGOING**

WEAKNESSES: **NERVOUS, UNCRITICAL, SELF-DESTRUCTIVE**

BEST: **LOVE**

WORST: **FAMILY**

Unraveling Secrets

Puzzling to others, this highly personal relationship does not easily reveal itself to the world. A jealous guarding of its private life grants it an air of mystery—which only makes other people want to try to unravel its secrets. The depth of emotional profundity here can be extreme, with silence playing an important role. Partners are strong in the feeling realm but also in that of thought. Pisces I–Pisces II relationships can show great interest in historical, critical and technical matters and can share a lot of insights. The partners' social life is ordinarily restricted to only a few friends or family members. Most often, all this relationship really asks for is to be left alone.

Romantic tendencies can be marked in love affairs of this type, which are often highly affectionate. Sensuousness rather than passion is usual here, with the partners showing an interest in touching, tasting and, in general, experiencing the best that life has to offer. Yet another side can also surface here, a side that is self-destructive and uncritical, and that can move the relationship into dangerous waters without the lovers realizing it. Marriages can last for years, with few problems surfacing but many being hidden away.

Insecurity can be a problem in family relationships, particularly those between parents and children, where mixed signals and a high degree of empathy can obliterate individual boundaries and enhance mutual dependencies. Friendships do best when easygoing, but may not hang together for very long without some common interest or focus. Work relationships in this combination are seldom successful, for they can be lacking in vigor and initiative. Pisces I's and II's bring out each other's less ambitious side, but they can also make each other nervous when they have fixed deadlines to meet.

ADVICE: *Strive a bit harder to reach your goals. Be clear about your feelings. Beware of isolation and secretiveness. What are you afraid of?*

MAX LINCOLN SCHUSTER (3/2/1897)
RICHARD LEO SIMON (3/6/1899)

Simon and Schuster joined together in 1924 to form the book publishing company of the same name, working from a 3-room office in NYC. Their first title was a best-selling crossword puzzle book. Over the years, they published a prodigious list of distinguished fiction and nonfiction. **Also: George Frideric Handel & C.P.E. Bach** (composers; Handel influenced J.S. Bach's son).

Pulling Back

These two can be extremely close yet still not get along well on a day-to-day basis. There is a marked tendency in the relationship for the partners to pull back from each other and retreat into their own private world. They can gain great satisfaction from being together yet at the same time can experience great loneliness when their needs are not being met. Part of the problem is that both of them have a deep need for each other's attention, which they simply take for granted most of the time, not noticing how much they count on it until it is withdrawn. They are extremely sensitive to each other's disapproval, which in certain cases can be wielded as a powerful weapon to gain the ascendancy.

Love affairs and family matchups, particularly parent-child pairs of the opposite sex, are emotionally complex. The partners in these relationships can be tremendously irritated by each other but may also show deep vulnerabilities, leading to pain and hurt. Extremely loyal, these two are proud of each other's achievements and steadfast in their support for each other. Interconnections and mutual dependencies often guarantee that they will stay together, although not necessarily in the greatest harmony or psychological health.

In the marital and professional spheres, Pisces I's and III's can be extremely effective in setting up and running a business, a family or both. As a couple they have strong nurturing qualities, with accompanying domestic and maintenance skills contributing to a stable and efficient home base. On another side of their relationship, however, their accepting and overly generous qualities can lead them into being taken advantage of by freeloading types.

Friendships in this combination are often pleasure-seeking, relaxed but also devoted to spiritualized, religious or new-age pursuits. Such relationships do best when the partners are free to withdraw from them for periods of time, without fearing accusations and without arousing feelings of rejection.

ADVICE: *Be more selective about who you invite in. Give each other the breathing space you need. Beware of using disapproval as a weapon.*

STRENGTHS: SENSITIVE, NURTURING, SPIRITUAL

WEAKNESSES: ARGUMENTATIVE, IRRITATED, REJECTING

BEST: WORK

WORST: LOVE

GEORGE HARRISON (2/25/43)
PATTIE BOYD (3/17/45)

Harrison and Boyd, a model, first met in early 1964, while filming the Beatles' *A Hard Day's Night*, in which she had a bit part. They wed in '66, but the marriage began coming apart within a few years. They separated but didn't divorce until '77. She later married George's friend, guitarist Eric Clapton.
Also: Shakira Baksh & Michael Caine (married; actors).

Think Twice

Pisces II's are among the most difficult and unusual personalities in the year, and the chances that one of these two will be a demanding person is quite high. This, then, would seem to be a relationship with a greater chance for trouble than other Pisces II matchups. On the other hand, Pisces II's have an exceptional capacity for acceptance and understanding, which can have the effect of counterbalancing this tendency. Whatever the case, this can be an unusual, even extraordinary relationship—if it ever develops at all. When two Pisces II's meet, they may recognize a kindred soul, but not necessarily one they want to get involved with. Another scenario is that along with the shock of recognition comes a decision to put off further contact until a later, less hectic time. In the family and at work, where choice is not involved, two Pisces II's can often make the best of the situation, despite their powerful disagreements and contrasting points of view.

Love affairs and friendships between Pisces II's can be passionate and claiming but also fun, whether they last for days, months or years. Turbulent emotions are likely to be aroused here, which knock the partners off balance and sometimes threaten to sweep them away. There is a strong feeling of having finally met a true soul mate, which, however, might later be recognized as somewhat illusory. Marriages based on such unstable ground are unlikely to work out unless the spouses are dedicated to discharging their domestic tasks and responsibilities, which can well be the case. A tendency to encapsulate the relationship in an isolated cocoon is perhaps unavoidable.

Professional relationships involving creative business endeavors or artistic pursuits can work out well between two Pisces II's. But co-worker or boss-employee combinations, carrying fixed and repetitive responsibilities, are not recommended. As family members, particularly sibling pairs of the opposite sex, dramatic and exhibitionistic confrontations are likely to alternate with withdrawal and depression.

ADVICE: *Think twice before getting involved—it may not be the right time. Do your best to get along. Maintain objectivity. Beware of illusion.*

STRENGTHS: UNDERSTANDING, FUN, PASSIONATE

WEAKNESSES: PROBLEMATICAL, CLAIMING, ILLUSORY

BEST: LOVE

WORST: MARRIAGE

LYNN SWANN (3/7/52)
FRANCO HARRIS (3/7/50)

In addition to having the same birthday, football players Harris and Swann were 2 of the winningest offensive teammates in Super Bowl history. In the 70s they brought the Pittsburgh Steelers to the Super Bowl 4 times. Harris is the #1 Super Bowl rusher, Swann a top receiver; they were back-to-back Super Bowl MVPs (1975–76). **Also: Craig Reid & Charlie Reid** (twins; musicians, The Proclaimers).

March 3–10
THE WEEK OF THE LONER
PISCES II

March 11–18
THE WEEK OF DANCERS & DREAMERS
PISCES III

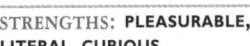 RELATIONSHIPS

STRENGTHS: **PLEASURABLE, LITERAL, CURIOUS**

WEAKNESSES: **IRRITATING, EXCESSIVE, MISUNDERSTANDING**

BEST: **HOBBY-ORIENTED**

WORST: **FAMILY**

Just for Fun

This relationship can prove extremely interesting and rewarding for both partners and often involves a shared pursuit of a highly factual, technical, artistic or even scientific nature, whether this is a hobby or a professional endeavor. Pisces II's and III's are likely to see eye to eye on many subjects. A Pisces III may tend to become something of a teacher or role model for Pisces II's, helping them to shape their ideas into a commercially salable form, and showing them how to bring these concepts to the attention of the world. The relationship may focus on mutual appreciation, and with it a desire to be of help whenever possible. This may unfortunately make other people feel excluded—there is a real danger that they will see the matchup as a closed society and feel envious and resentful.

As lovers Pisces II's and Pisces III's might have a warm and affectionate relationship, which could go on for years without experiencing many problems. Less passionate than sensuous, they will revel in the delights of table and bed, as well as a whole host of possible activities such as massage and mild drug use. Marriages between these two can easily become a mutual-admiration society, with unreal states prevailing.

Friendships in this combination are often filled with good feeling and the unmitigated pursuit of entertainment and pleasure. Excess can prove a real problem here, and in the end the partners will have to adopt some moderating influences. Professional matchups are often less successful than more casual ones when it comes to expressing interest in a given subject. Deadening routines may injure Pisces II–Pisces III relationships—these two suffer from fixed expectations and are usually more productive when sharing leisure time, working together just for fun, with few or no demands made. In this way the spirit of true investigation can flourish. Family matchups can be empathic and mutually enjoyable, but also irritating and continually fostering misunderstandings.

ADVICE: *Keep it light. Seek the middle ground. Curb excesses. Beware of arousing the resentment of others. Remain open to human contact.*

C.P.E. BACH (3/8/1714)
GEORG PHILIPP TELEMANN (3/14/1681)

During his lifetime composer-organist Telemann was regarded as one of Germany's greatest musicians. He was a good friend of J.S. Bach and godfather to his son, C.P.E. Bach. Telemann was musical director of the 5 largest churches in Hamburg. Upon his death in 1767, C.P.E. Bach was appointed to replace him.

March 11–18
THE WEEK OF DANCERS & DREAMERS
PISCES III

March 11–18
THE WEEK OF DANCERS & DREAMERS
PISCES III

 RELATIONSHIPS

STRENGTHS: **MONEY-WISE, IMAGINATIVE, SPECULATIVE**

WEAKNESSES: **DEPENDENCY-FOSTERING, CONCEITED, GREEDY**

BEST: **WORK**

WORST: **LOVE**

Fusing Thought and Action

This relationship can fuse thought and action at a very high level. Often extremely successful in commercial endeavors, two Pisces III's know how to make their ideas pay off; they usually see philosophical and financial speculation as not at all contradictory, considering the creative use of money a highly artistic activity. They must be careful, however, not to get carried away by their endeavors, which they tend to imbue with an unimpeachable status. It can also happen, on the other hand, that they may suddenly abandon a successful endeavor, or one heading in that direction, having tired of it over time, or even having entered a fit of boredom with it. Leaving a string of unfinished business, social or intellectual projects behind them can be characteristic of this combination. They must also fight a tendency to appear infallible or godlike, an image not always of their own fashioning. They should be very careful, in fact, not to attract a whole army of hangers-on, believers and dependents.

Friendships between Pisces III's often evolve into something else, whether a love affair, marriage or business endeavor. Trust and understanding are the crucial factors here, as well as a very special chemistry, which indefinably brings these two farther than most of their other relationships. It is possible for Pisces III's friends to spend hours, days and weeks in each other's company with few irritations or difficulties arising. Their bond is so close that they may sometimes be mistaken for siblings.

Romances between Pisces III's often have a strong aura of unreality, as hindsight may prove. Adoration, worship and unearned trust are the danger signals to be heeded. Actually these partners usually fall in love with their relationship itself, rather than with each other, and at a certain point they can find that they are intimately involved with a stranger. Marriages, too, they may estimate at an unreasonably high value that bears little resemblance to reality.

ADVICE: *Don't get stuck on yourself. Beware of flattery and followers. Keep your flame pure. Follow your path. Illusion can lead you astray.*

BEN COHEN (3/18/51)
JERRY GREENFIELD (3/14/51)

Ben & Jerry, friends from childhood, started their popular ice cream company in 1978 out of a renovated Vermont gas station. Their initial investment of $12,000 (one-third borrowed) has become a booming business, known for its many innovative ice cream flavors. The partners are dedicated to social activism and community affairs.

Also: Neil Sedaka & Howard Greenfield (top songwriting team).

Index
of Notables

Index

Boldface numbers indicate pages with illustrations.
T = top paragraph.
B = bottom paragraph.

C

O'Sullivan, Maureen, **372,** 389
Oswald, Lee Harvey, **227, 527**
Oswald, Marina, **527**
O'Toole, Peter, 376
Ouspensky, P. D., 178
Ovett, Steve, 664
Ovitz, Michael, **762**
Owens, Jesse, 492
Oz, Frank, **419**

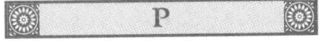

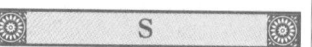

S

Picture Credits

Agence France Presse/Corbis-Bettmann: 174B, 357TL, 382T, 524TR, 569B, 600B, 770BL.

AP/Wide World Photos: 360TR, 394BL, 397TR, 465B, 626BL, 669BL, 762TL.

Archive Photos: *Chris Felver,* 759BL.

Courtesy Blue Moon Books: 429T.

Gilles Boyer/ Courtesy LaMonte Young: 476B.

Bridgeman/Art Resource, NY: 588T.

Corbis: 704TL; *M. Gerber,* 669T; *Lynn Goldsmith,* 704TR; *Chuck Jackson,* 265B; *Ira Margolin,* 664B; *Time Mosenfelder,* 622TL; *Daniel Storace,* 624TL; *Tom Zuback,* 624TR.

Corbis-Bettmann: 22L, 26L, 27, 30B, 31, 34L, 34R, 35, 39, 46B, 46R, 47, 50L, 50R, 58R, 67, 74L, 74T, 78B, 78R, 83, 90L, 98L, 99L, 99R, 106L, 106B, 111, 114B, 114R, 118B, 122L, 134L, 138L, 138R, 139L, 139R, 142L, 142B, 142R, 143, 150B, 158R, 170L, 186L, 187, 190B, 198L, 202L, 206L, 206R, 207L, 207R, 214B, 216T, 217TL, 220TR, 221T, 221B, 222BL, 223TL, 224B, 225B, 227T, 228T, 231B, 232B, 233BL, 234TL, 234B, 235BL, 236T, 238TR, 238BL, 239T, 239B, 241TR, 242B, 243B, 244BL, 245T, 249B, 250BL, 255B, 256BL, 258TR, 260BL, 260BR, 264B, 266TR, 266TL, 271BL, 271BR, 272BL, 274BR, 274BL, 276T, 280BR, 280BL, 281BL, 281BR, 282BL, 283BR, 284BL, 285TL, 289B, 290BR, 291BL, 291BR, 292TR, 293T, 294BL, 295BL, 295TL, 296TL, 296TR, 299T, 301BL, 301TR, 301BR, 302B, 303TL, 303TR, 304TL, 304TR, 304B, 305TR, 306TL, 306TR, 308B, 309TR, 309TL, 313TR, 313BL, 313BR, 315TL, 316TL, 316TR, 317TL, 317TR, 317BL, 317BR, 319B, 320T, 321TR, 323BL, 323BR, 324BL, 326BL, 326BR, 328T, 328B, 330TL, 330BR, 331BR, 333BL, 333BR, 336BL, 338BL, 338BR, 339BL, 339BR, 341B, 343BL, 343BR, 344T, 345B, 347B, 348BL, 349BL, 349BR, 352TR, 352BR, 353TL, 353BR, 353BL, 354TR, 355T, 355BL, 356TR, 356TL, 356BR, 356BL, 357TR, 359BR, 363TR, 364T, 364BL, 364BR, 366TL, 366TR, 367B, 368TL, 368TR, 369T, 370BL, 370BR, 372TR, 373T, 380B, 381T, 383T, 383B, 383BR, 385T, 386BL, 386BR, 387BR, 389TR, 391T, 393TR, 393TL, 393B, 396TR, 396BL, 396BR, 398TL, 398TR, 398B, 399TL, 399TR, 400BL, 402TL, 402TR, 405BL, 405BR, 406T, 407BR, 408TR, 408TL, 408B, 411BR, 411BL, 413TL, 413TR, 414TL, 415TL, 415TR, 415BR, 420T, 421T, 421BL, 421BR, 422TL, 422TR, 425T, 428BR, 428BL, 429B, 430BR, 430BL, 431TR, 431TL, 431BL, 431BR, 436T, 436B, 437BR, 438TR, 438TL, 439TL, 440BL, 440BR, 441T, 441BL, 442BL, 442BR, 446BR, 447TL, 447TR, 448TL, 448TR, 449TR, 451T, 453BR, 453BL, 454TR, 454BL, 460T, 462T, 465T, 469T, 469BL, 469BR, 472TR, 472BR, 472BL, 473B, 474B, 475TL, 475TR, 478T, 480T, 483BL, 484T, 485TL, 485TR, 486TL, 486TR, 488BL, 488BR, 490TL, 490TR, 491B, 492BL, 492BR, 497BL, 497BR, 498BL, 498BR, 499TL, 499TR, 501BL, 501BR, 502BL, 502BR, 503TL, 505BL, 507B, 508TL, 508BR, 510BL, 510BR, 515T, 527TL, 517TR, 517BL, 519TL, 521TL, 521TR, 523B, 525TL, 525TR, 526TL, 526TR, 527TL, 527TR, 528BL, 528BR, 529TL, 529TR, 530TL, 530TR, 535TR, 535BL, 536T, 537TR, 540TL, 540TR, 541T, 541B, 542T, 542BR, 542BL, 544T, 544BR, 550BR, 553TL, 553TR, 554T, 554BR, 555TL, 555TR, 556BR, 558B, 560TL, 570T, 571TR, 571TL, 572BL, 572BR, 573BR, 575BL, 577TL, 577TR, 580TL, 581BR, 583BR, 583BL, 586BR, 592TL, 592TR, 592B, 593B, 595BL, 595BR, 596TL, 596TR, 597BL, 597BR, 598TL, 599T, 599BL, 600T, 601TL, 601TR, 601BL, 601BR, 603TL, 603TR, 604BL, 605BL, 607B, 610TL, 614T, 616T, 617BL, 617BR, 620TR, 627BR, 628TL, 628TR, 631B, 634TL, 635T, 636TR, 637TL, 637TR, 638TR, 639BR, 640BL, 642B, 645TL, 645B, 646BL, 646BR, 647BR, 647BL, 649B, 655BR, 655BL, 657BL, 658BR, 659BL, 659BR, 671TR, 674B, 676B, 678T, 680BL, 680BR, 682BL, 682BR, 683B, 685BL, 686TL, 686BL, 687BR, 692BR, 695B, 696B, 698TL, 698BL, 698BR, 699TL, 699TR, 699B, 700BL, 700BR, 702TR, 702TL, 703T, 708TR, 708B, 709BL, 709BR, 711BL, 711BR, 713BR, 714TR, 715BL, 715BR, 717BL, 722TR, 724BR, 726BR, 726BL, 727BR, 728B, 729TL, 729TR, 733T, 734B, 738B, 739T, 743TL, 744TL, 744TR, 746TL, 747BL, 747BR, 748TL, 748TR, 749TL, 749TR, 750BL, 751BR, 751BL, 754T, 755TR, 757B, 759TR, 760TL, 760TR, 760BL, 760BR, 762B, 763BR, 768T, 774BL, 774BR, 775TL, 776TL, 776TR, 777TL, 777TR, 777BL, 779BR, 781T, 781BL, 781BR, 784BL, 794BL, 794BR, 797TL, 799TR, 799B, 801TL, 801TR; *Ruth Chin,* 656B; *Frank Driggs,* 135, 270BR, 474T, 616B, 668B, 678BL; *Peter C. Jones/ Alex Gotfryd,* 118R, 397BR; *Malcolm Lubliner,* 182B, 294TR, 382TL, 382TR, 569TR, 626BR, 660BR, 662BR, 664TR, 666TR, 764BL; *MacFadden,* 523T; *Ernest Paniccoli,* 622TR, 638B; *Gordon Reims,* 87; *Amalie Rothschild,* 395BL, 404BL, 718T, 735T, 745BL, 745BR; *Roberto Thoni,* 705BL.

Frank Driggs Collection: 614BR; *Joe Alper,* 614BL; *Dunc Butler,* 678BR; *Paul J. Hoeffler,* 574T.

Courtesy Al Hirschfeld: 477T.

©1980, The Estate of Robert Mapplethorpe/A+C Anthology: 720TR.

Michael Ochs Archives, Venice, Ca.: 258TL, 495B, 588B, 764BR; *©Ray Avery,* :579T; *Joel Axelrod,* 404BR.

509T, 509B, 510T, 511T, 511BR, 511BL, 512TR, 512BR, 512BL, 513TL, 513TR, 513B, 514TL, 514B, 515BL, 515BR, 516TL, 516TR, 516B, 518T, 518B, 519TR, 520T, 520B, 522T, 522BL, 522BR, 524TL, 525B, 527BL, 527BR, 529BR, 530B, 531T, 531B, 532TL, 532B, 533T, 533B, 534T, 534BL, 536B, 538TL, 538TR, 538B, 539B, 540B, 543TR, 543TL, 543B, 544BL, 545T, 546B, 547BL, 547BR, 548TR, 548TL, 548B, 549TL, 549TR, 550TL, 550TR, 550BL, 551T, 551B, 552T, 552B, 553BR, 556TL, 556TR, 556BL, 557TL, 557TR, 558T, 559T, 559BR, 560TR, 560B, 561TL, 561TR, 561B, 562TL, 562TR, 563T, 563BL, 563BR, 564T, 564B, 565T, 565B, 566T, 566B, 567TR, 567TL, 567B, 568T, 568B, 569TL, 570B, 571B, 573TL, 573BL, 575TR, 575T, 575BR, 576T, 576B, 578BL, 578BR, 579BR, 580BL, 580BR, 581TL, 582T, 583T, 584TL, 584T, 584B, 585BR, 585BL, 586BL, 587T, 587B, 589T, 589BL, 589BR, 590TR, 590B, 591T, 591BR, 593T, 594BL, 594BR, 595TL, 595TR, 596BL, 596BR, 598TR, 598BL, 598BR, 599BR, 602TL, 603B, 604TL, 604BR, 605T, 605BR, 606T, 606B, 607T, 608B, 609T, 609B, 610TR, 610B, 611TL, 611TR, 612T, 613TR, 613B, 614TL, 615T, 615B, 617TL, 617TR, 618T, 618B, 619TL, 619TR, 619BL, 619BR, 620TL, 620B, 621TL, 621TR, 621B, 622B, 625B, 626TR, 626TL, 627TL, 627TR, 627BL, 628B, 629T, 629B, 630TR, 630TL, 630B, 631T, 632T, 632B, 633T, 633B, 634TR, 634B, 635B, 636TL, 636B, 637B, 638TL, 639T, 639BL, 640TL, 640TR, 640BR, 641TR, 641B, 642T, 643T, 643BL, 643BR, 644TL, 644TR, 645TR, 645B, 646T, 647T, 647TL, 648T, 648B, 649TL, 649TR, 650TL, 650BR, 651T, 651BL, 651BR, 652T, 653T, 653B, 654TR, 654TL, 654BL, 654BR, 655TL, 655TR, 657TL, 657B, 658BL, 659T, 660T, 660BL, 661TR, 661TL, 661B, 662T, 662BL, 663T, 663B, 664TL, 666TL, 666B, 667T, 668TR, 670T, 670BL, 670BR, 672T, 672BL, 672BR, 673BR, 674TL, 675TR, 675TL, 675BR, 675BL, 676TR, 676TL, 677TL, 677TR, 679BL, 680TL, 681TR, 681BL, 682TR, 682TL, 684B, 685T, 685BR, 686TR, 687BL, 688T, 689TL, 689BR, 689BL, 690T, 690B, 691TL, 691TR, 691B, 692T, 692BL, 693TL, 693TR, 693B, 694T, 694B, 696T, 697T, 697BL, 700TR, 701T, 701B, 703B, 705TL, 705TR, 706T, 706B, 707B, 708TL, 709T, 710T, 710B, 711TL, 711TR, 712TL, 713T, 713BL, 716T, 716BR, 717TL, 717TR, 717BR, 718BL, 718BR, 720TL, 720B, 721TL, 721TR, 721B, 722TL, 723B, 724T, 724BL, 725TL, 725TR, 725BL, 725BR, 726T, 727BL, 728T, 729B, 730T, 730B, 731T, 731BL, 731BR, 732T, 732BR, 733B, 734T, 735BL, 735BR, 736B, 737BL, 737BR, 738TL, 739B, 740T, 740B, 741T, 742T, 743B, 745T, 746BL, 747T, 750T, 750BR, 751T, 752B, 753TL, 753TR, 753BL, 753BR, 755B, 756TR, 756BL, 756BR, 757T, 758TL, 758TR, 758BL, 758BR, 759TL, 758BR, 761BL, 762R, 763T, 763BL, 764TR, 765B, 766T, 766BL, 766BR, 767T, 767BL, 769TL, 769TR, 769B, 770T, 770BR, 771T, 771B, 772T, 772BL, 772BR, 773B, 774TR, 775B, 776B, 778T, 779T, 779BL, 780T, 782BL, 782BR, 783TL, 783TR, 784T, 785B, 786T, 786BR, 787TL, 787TR, 788T, 788B, 789TL, 789TR, 789BL, 789BR, 790T, 790B, 791T, 791BL, 792T, 792BL, 792BR, 793TL, 793TR, 793BL, 793BR, 794T. 796T, 796B, 797TR, 797B, 798T, 798B, 799TL, 800T, 800BL, 800BR.

Wolfgang Volz/Courtesy Christo and Jean Claude: 450B.

Name	Birthday	Relationship Name	Page

Name	Birthday	Relationship Name	Page

Name	Birthday	Relationship Name	Page

Name	Birthday	Relationship Name	Page

RELATIONSHIP LOCATION FINDER

How to use this chart:

Locate the period of the first person's birthday across the top of the chart and the period of the second person's birthday along the side. The point where the two lines intersect is the page number where the relationship profile of this combination can be found.

Each individual birthday is contained within forty-eight periods of the year. Personology profiles of each period are located on pages 19 to page 211.

BIRTHDAY PERIOD OF FIRST PERSON

BIRTHDAY PERIOD OF SECOND PERSON	March 19–24	March 25–April 2	April 3–10	April 11–18	April 19–24	April 25–May 2	May 3–10	May 11–18	May 19–24	May 25–June 2	June 3–10	June 11–18	June 19–24	June 25–July 2	July 3–10	July 11–18	July 19–25	July 26–August 2	August 3–10	August 11–18	August 19–25	August 26–September 2	September 3–10	September 11–18
March 19 – 24	214	214	215	215	216	216	217	217	218	218	219	219	220	220	221	221	222	222	223	223	224	224	225	225
March 25 – April 2	214	238	238	239	239	240	240	241	241	242	242	243	243	244	244	245	245	246	246	247	247	248	248	249
April 3 – 10	215	238	261	262	262	263	263	264	264	265	265	266	266	267	267	268	268	269	269	270	270	271	271	272
April 11 – 18	215	239	262	284	285	285	286	286	287	287	288	288	289	289	290	290	291	291	292	292	293	293	294	294
April 19 – 24	216	239	262	285	307	307	308	308	309	309	310	310	311	311	312	312	313	313	314	314	315	315	316	316
April 25 – May 2	216	240	263	285	307	329	329	330	330	331	331	332	332	333	333	334	334	335	335	336	336	337	337	338
May 3 – 10	217	240	263	286	308	329	350	351	351	352	352	353	353	354	354	355	355	356	356	357	357	358	358	359
May 11 – 18	217	241	264	286	308	330	351	371	372	372	373	373	374	374	375	375	376	376	377	377	378	378	379	379
May 19 – 24	218	241	264	287	309	330	351	372	392	392	393	393	394	394	395	395	396	396	397	397	398	398	399	399
May 25 – June 2	218	242	265	287	309	331	352	372	392	412	412	413	413	414	414	415	415	416	416	417	417	418	418	419
June 3 – 10	219	242	265	288	310	331	352	373	393	412	431	432	432	433	433	434	434	435	435	436	436	437	437	438
June 11 – 18	219	243	266	288	310	332	353	373	393	413	432	450	451	451	452	452	453	453	454	454	455	455	456	456
June 19 – 24	220	243	266	289	311	332	353	374	394	413	432	451	469	469	470	470	471	471	472	472	473	473	474	474
June 25 – July 2	220	244	267	289	311	333	354	374	394	414	433	451	469	487	487	488	488	489	489	490	490	491	491	492
July 3 – 10	221	244	267	290	312	333	354	375	395	414	433	452	470	487	504	505	505	506	506	507	507	508	508	509
July 11 – 18	221	245	268	290	312	334	355	375	395	415	434	452	470	488	505	521	522	522	523	523	524	524	525	525
July 19 – 25	222	245	268	291	313	334	355	376	396	415	434	453	471	488	505	522	538	538	539	539	540	540	541	541
July 26 – August 2	222	246	269	291	313	335	356	376	396	416	435	453	471	489	506	522	538	554	554	555	555	556	556	557
August 3 – 10	223	246	269	292	314	335	356	377	397	416	435	454	472	489	506	523	539	554	569	570	570	571	571	572
August 11 – 18	223	247	270	292	314	336	357	377	397	417	436	454	472	490	507	523	539	555	570	584	585	585	586	586
August 19 – 25	224	247	270	293	315	336	357	378	398	417	436	455	473	490	507	524	540	555	570	585	599	599	600	600
August 26 – September 2	224	248	271	293	315	337	358	378	398	418	437	455	473	491	508	524	540	556	571	585	599	613	613	614
September 3 – 10	225	248	271	294	316	337	358	379	399	418	437	456	474	491	508	525	541	556	571	586	600	613	626	627
September 11 – 18	225	249	272	294	316	338	359	379	399	419	438	456	474	492	509	525	541	557	572	586	600	614	627	639
September 19 – 24	226	249	272	295	317	338	359	380	400	419	438	457	475	492	509	526	542	557	572	587	601	614	627	640
September 25 – October 2	226	250	273	295	317	339	360	380	400	420	439	457	475	493	510	526	542	558	573	587	601	615	628	640
October 3 – 10	227	250	273	296	318	339	360	381	401	420	439	458	476	493	510	527	543	558	573	588	602	615	628	641
October 11 – 18	227	251	274	296	318	340	361	381	401	421	440	458	476	494	511	527	543	559	574	588	602	616	629	641
October 19 – 25	228	251	274	297	319	340	361	382	402	421	440	459	477	494	511	528	544	559	574	589	603	616	629	642
October 26 – November 2	228	252	275	297	319	341	362	382	402	422	441	459	477	495	512	528	544	560	575	589	603	617	630	642
November 3 – 11	229	252	275	298	320	341	362	383	403	422	441	460	478	495	512	529	545	560	575	590	604	617	630	643
November 12 – 18	229	253	276	298	320	342	363	383	403	423	442	460	478	496	513	529	545	561	576	590	604	618	631	643
November 19 – 24	230	253	276	299	321	342	363	384	404	423	442	461	479	496	513	530	546	561	576	591	605	618	631	644
November 25 – December 2	230	254	277	299	321	343	364	384	404	424	443	461	479	497	514	530	546	562	577	591	605	619	632	644
December 3 – 10	231	254	277	300	322	343	364	385	405	424	443	462	480	497	514	531	547	562	577	592	606	619	632	645
December 11 – 18	231	255	278	300	322	344	365	385	405	425	444	462	480	498	515	531	547	563	578	592	606	620	633	645
December 19 – 25	232	255	278	301	323	344	365	386	406	425	444	463	481	498	515	532	548	563	578	593	607	620	633	646
December 26 – January 2	232	256	279	301	323	345	366	386	406	426	445	463	481	499	516	532	548	564	579	593	607	621	634	646
January 3 – 9	233	256	279	302	324	345	366	387	407	426	445	464	482	499	516	533	549	564	579	594	608	621	634	647
January 10 – 16	233	257	280	302	324	346	367	387	407	427	446	464	482	500	517	533	549	565	580	594	608	622	635	647
January 17 – 22	234	257	280	303	325	346	367	388	408	427	446	465	483	500	517	534	550	565	580	595	609	622	635	648
January 23 – 30	234	258	281	303	325	347	368	388	408	428	447	465	483	501	518	534	550	566	581	595	609	623	636	648
January 31 – February 7	235	258	281	304	326	347	368	389	409	428	447	466	484	501	518	535	551	566	581	596	610	623	636	649
February 8 – 15	235	259	282	304	326	348	369	389	409	429	448	466	484	502	519	535	551	567	582	596	610	624	637	649
February 16 – 22	236	259	282	305	327	348	369	390	410	429	448	467	485	502	519	536	552	567	582	597	611	624	637	650
February 23 – March 2	236	260	283	305	327	349	370	390	410	430	449	467	485	503	520	536	552	568	583	597	611	625	638	650
March 3 – 10	237	260	283	306	328	349	370	391	411	430	449	468	486	503	520	537	553	568	583	598	612	625	638	651
March 11 – 18	237	261	284	306	328	350	371	391	411	431	450	468	486	504	521	537	553	569	584	598	612	626	639	651